Daniel Barron Brightwell

A concordance to the entire works of Alfred Tennyson

Daniel Barron Brightwell

A concordance to the entire works of Alfred Tennyson

ISBN/EAN: 9783337120597

Printed in Europe, USA, Canada, Australia, Japan

Cover: Foto ©Thomas Meinert / pixelio.de

More available books at **www.hansebooks.com**

" For deeds doe die, how ever noblie donne,
  And thoughts of men do as themselves decay :
  But wise wordes taught in numbers for to runne,
  Recorded by the Muses, live for ay ;
  Ne may with storming showers be washt away,
  Ne bitter-breathing windes with harmfull blast,
  Nor age, nor envie shall them ever wast."
—*Spenser.*

CO[...]CE

AL[...]SON,

E. MOXON[...]EET, W.

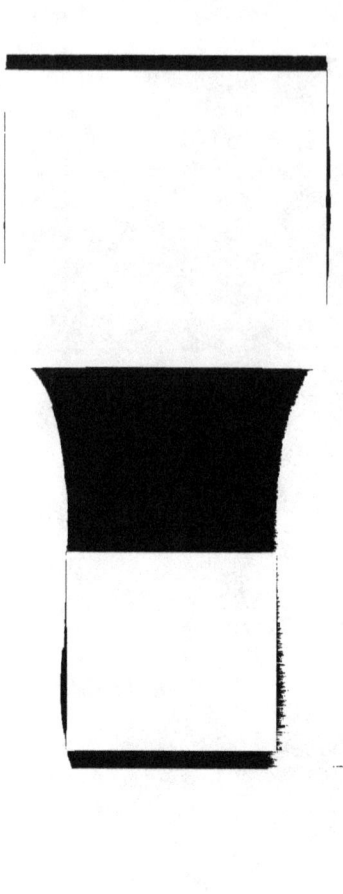

PREFACE.

THE qualifications essential for the production of such a work as that which is here offered to the admirers of our Laureate are of no very high order. Prominently stand patience, accuracy, and a certain knack of arrangement. To the first of these requisites, I think I may lay some claim. I have full confidence that the public will decide with justice how far I may be credited with the others.

It is, perhaps, advisable to say one or two words as to the principle which has been adopted. Probably it would not be easy to find half-a-dozen persons, who would arrive at precisely the same conclusion as to the words which should be included in a Concordance, but it is tolerably safe to predicate that there are few who consult such a volume in vain, without a feeling of irritation, and even a sense of personal wrong. I judged, therefore, that the error of including too much would be more venial than that of including too little, and that the increase of bulk consequent upon the admission of a few words of doubtful importance would be a less serious defect than the omission of any key-word necessary for verifying a quotation. Under the influence of this impression, I originally designed to omit only the particles, and had made considerable advance towards the completion of this scheme, when it became evident that some condensation would be necessary. To accomplish this without impairing the utility of the book, a selection had to be made of those words least likely to occur to the mind without their context. Adjectives and adverbs, in immediate contact with the words they modify, have been thus rejected, but they will be found quoted in all cases where they form part of a predicate, or where, by the structure of the sentence, they are divorced from their respective better-halves. Compound forms of the adjective and derivatives from proper names have been uniformly retained. The titles *King, Queen, Prince, Princess, Earl, Lord, Lady, Sir, Aunt,* etc., when used simply as affixes; some verbs of very frequent occurrence such as *make, made, seem,* etc., in passages otherwise and sufficiently repre-

sented; *answered, asked, said, replied,* etc., when introducing a direct quotation; the nouns *hand, times, haste,* etc., in the phrases *at hand, at times, in haste,* etc., and some other words—have been omitted. When all deductions have been made, however, if that, at which I aimed, has been accomplished, it should be found that there is no clause in Tennyson's Works to which reference is not given under one or more of its prominent words.

It appeared desirable, if possible, to adopt some plan of reference which should be uniform, and at the same time applicable to all editions. To attain this end there seemed no way better than that of giving the poem and line, and although this makes the reference to some of the longer poems apparently awkward, I trust that the Tables which have been prefixed will obviate any serious difficulty, and render the use of the volume easy to those in whose ears there yet lasts the echo of those measured strains which, for the last quarter of a century, have enjoyed so unprecedented a share of popular favour.

A few poems have no distinct titles; several are addressed, "To ——;" and the heading, "Song," is common to one or two others. To avoid confusion, these are referred to in the following pages by the first word or two of each poem.

A plan of the work was first submitted to Messrs Moxon in the spring of 1868, and received from them the most prompt and courteous consideration. A specimen which had been prepared met with their approval, and I was requested by them to undertake the completion of the scheme. This date, which under ordinary circumstances would have been a matter of trivial importance, may possibly, in the light of more recent events, possess a certain interest.

The execution of my project has been to me a labour of love, and without professing indifference to those "possibilities" which, as that acute observer, Sir Hugh Evans, has justly remarked, "is good gifts," no other fruit that my undertaking may yield will be so grateful to me as the approval, should I be so fortunate as to win it, of those to whom "lucky rhymes" are

"scrip and share,
And mellow metres more than cent for cent."

D. BARRON BRIGHTWELL.

5 GOWER STREET, BEDFORD SQUARE.

I.

A COMPLETE INDEX

OF

TENNYSON'S WORKS.

A

POEM.	VOLUME.	PAGE.
Adeline	. Poems	. 33
Alexandra, Welcome to	Enoch Arden, etc.	164
Amphion	. Poems	. 326
Arabian Nights	. "	. 19
"A spirit haunts," etc.	"	. 31
Audley Court	. "	. 221
Aylmer's Field	. Enoch Arden, etc.	51

B

Beggar Maid, The	. Poems	. 365
Blackbird, The	. "	. 166
Boädicea	. Enoch Arden, etc.	169
"Break, break," etc.	Poems	. 378

C

Captain, The	. Selections	. 37
Cauteretz, In the Valley of	. Enoch Arden, etc.	151
Character, A	. Poems	. 36
Circumstance	. "	. 57
Claribel	. "	. 3
"Clear-headed friend," etc.	"	. 13
"Come not when I am dead," etc.	. "	. 376
Coquette, Sonnets to a	Selections	. 196

D

Daisy, The	{ Maud, and other Poems }	. 153
Day-Dream, The	. Poems	. 312
Death of the Old Year, The	. "	. 168
Dedication, A	. Enoch Arden, etc.	166
Dedication (Idylls)	. Idylls of the King, iii.	
Deserted House, The	Poems	. 45
Dirge, A	. "	. 49
Dora	. "	. 214
Dream of Fair Women, A	"	. 150
Dying Swan, The	. "	. 47

E

POEM.	VOLUME.	PAGE.
Eagle, The	. Poems	. 376
Edward Gray	. "	. 337
Edwin Morris; or, the Lake	. "	. 230
1865–1866	. Good Words, ix.	144
Elaine	. Idylls of the King	147
Eleänore	. Poems	. 78
Enid	. Idylls of the King	1
Enoch Arden	. Enoch Arden, etc.	1
Epic, The	. Poems	. 189

F

Farewell, A	. Poems	. 364
Fatima	. "	. 96
Flower, The	. Enoch Arden, etc.	152

G

Gardener's Daughter, The	. Poems	. 203
Godiva	. "	. 285
Golden Year, The	. "	. 262
Goose, The	. "	. 184
Grandmother, The	. Enoch Arden, etc.	114
Guinevere	. Idylls of the King	225

H

"Home they brought him slain," etc.	. Selections	. 207
Hendecasyllabics	. Enoch Arden, etc.	175

I

Iliad, Specimen of a Translation of the	. Enoch Arden, etc.	177
In Memoriam	. In Memoriam	. 1
Isabel	. Poems	. 7
Islet, The	. Enoch Arden, etc.	157

L

| Lady Clara Vere de Vere | Poems | . 126 |

INDEX

POEM.	VOLUME.	PAGE.
Lady Clare	Poems	354
"Lady, let the rolling drums," etc.	Selections	207
Lady of Shalott, The	Poems	65
Letters, The	Maud, and other Poems	131
Light Brigade, The Charge of the	"	167
Lilian	Poems	5
Locksley Hall	"	268
Lord of Burleigh, The	"	358
Lotos-Eaters, The	"	142
Love and Death	"	52
Love and Duty	"	258
"Love thou thy land," etc.	"	179
Lucretius	Macmillan's Mag. xviii.	1

M

Madeline	Poems	15
Margaret	"	163
Mariana	"	9
Mariana in the South	"	73
Maud	Maud, and other Poems	1
May Queen, The	Poems	130
Mermaid, The	"	60
Merman, The	"	58
Miller's Daughter, The	"	85
Milton	Enoch Arden, etc.	174
Morte d'Arthur	Poems	191
Mourner, On a	Selections	220
"Move Eastward," etc.	Poems	377
"My life is full," etc.	Selections	191

N

Northern Farmer, The	Enoch Arden, etc.	128

O

Ode on the Duke of Wellington	Maud, and other Poems	137
Ode to Memory	Poems	26
Œnone	"	98
"Of old sat Freedom," etc.	"	177
Oriana, The Ballad of	"	53
Owl, The, I.	"	17
Owl, The, II.	"	18

P

Palace of Art, The	Poems	112
Poet, The	"	38
Poet's Mind, The	"	41
Poet's Song, The	"	379
Princess, The	The Princess	1

R

POEM.	VOLUME.	PAGE.
Requiescat	Enoch Arden, etc.	154
Ringlet, The	"	160

S

Sailor Boy, The	Enoch Arden, etc.	155
St Agnes' Eve	Poems	331
St Simeon Stylites	"	236
Sea Dreams	Enoch Arden, etc.	96
Sea-Fairies, The	Poems	43
Sir Galahad	"	333
Sir Launcelot and Queen Guinevere	"	362
Sisters, The	"	109
Spiteful Letter, On a	Once-a-Week, N.S.,i.	13

T

Talking Oak, The	Poems	245
Tithonus	Enoch Arden, etc.	139
To E. L.	Poems	352
To J. M. K.	"	62
To J. S.	"	171
To Rev. F. D. Maurice	Maud, and other Poems	161
To the Queen	Poems	v.
To —— (with the Palace of Art)	"	111
Two Voices, The	"	289

U

Ulysses	Poems	265

V

Victim, The	Good Words, ix.	17
Vision of Sin, The	Poems	366
Vivien	Idylls of the King	101
Voyage, The	Enoch Arden, etc.	144

W

Wages	Macmillan's Mag. xvii.	271
Walking to the Mail	Poems	225
Will	Maud, and other Poems	165
Will Waterproof's Monologue	Poems	339
Window, The	(Privately printed.)	

Y

"You ask me why," etc.	Poems	175
"You might have won," etc.	"	350

II.

DATES OF PUBLICATION.

Poems	.	.	1830	Maud . . July 25th	1855
" 2 vols.	.	.	1842	Idylls of the King . July 11th	1859
Princess	September 23d	1847	Address to Alexandra March 11th	1863
In Memoriam	June 1st	1850	Enoch Arden, etc. . August 1st	1864
Ode to the Queen	March	1852	Selections . . January 24th	1865

III.

TABLE OF LINES AND PAGES OF THE LONGER POEMS.

POEM.	LINES.	PAGE	VOLUME.	POEM.	LINES.	PAGE	VOLUME.
Aylmer's Field	1 to 12	51	Enoch Arden, &c.	Aylmer's Field	808— 826	93	Enoch Arden, etc.
"	13— 31	52	"	"	827— 846	94	"
"	32— 50	53	"	"	847— 853	95	"
"	51— 69	54	"	Brook, The	1— 11	117	Maud, and other Poems.
"	70— 89	55	"				
"	90— 109	56	"	"	12— 30	118	"
"	110— 129	57	"	"	31— 50	119	"
"	130— 147	58	"	"	51— 69	120	"
"	148— 167	59	"	"	70— 88	121	"
"	168— 187	60	"	"	89— 105	122	"
"	188— 206	61	"	"	106— 123	123	"
"	207— 225	62	"	"	124— 142	124	"
"	226— 244	63	"	"	143— 161	125	"
"	245— 263	64	"	"	162— 181	126	"
"	264— 282	65	"	"	182— 200	127	"
"	283— 301	66	"	"	201— 216	128	"
"	302— 321	67	"	"	217— 228	129	"
"	322— 340	68	"	Elaine	1— 13	147	Idylls of the King.
"	341— 360	69	"				
"	361— 379	70	"	"	14— 32	148	"
"	380— 399	71	"	"	33— 51	149	"
"	400— 418	72	"	"	52— 70	150	"
"	419— 437	73	"	"	71— 88	151	"
"	438— 457	74	"	"	89— 107	152	"
"	458— 477	75	"	"	108— 126	153	"
"	478— 496	76	"	"	127— 145	154	"
"	497— 516	77	"	"	145— 163	155	"
"	517— 535	78	"	"	164— 183	156	"
"	536— 555	79	"	"	184— 201	157	"
"	556— 575	80	"	"	202— 220	158	"
"	576— 594	81	"	"	221— 239	159	"
"	595— 613	82	"	"	240— 258	160	"
"	614— 632	83	"	"	259— 277	161	"
"	633— 650	84	"	"	278— 296	162	"
"	651— 670	85	"	"	297— 316	163	"
"	671— 690	86	"	"	317— 335	164	"
"	691— 710	87	"	"	336— 355	165	"
"	711— 729	88	"	"	356— 375	166	"
"	730— 748	89	"	"	376— 395	167	"
"	749— 768	90	"	"	396— 413	168	"
"	769— 788	91	"	"	414— 432	169	"
"	789— 807	92	"	"	433— 452	170	"

TABLE OF LINES.

POEM.	LINES.	PAGE	VOLUME.	POEMS.	LINES.	PAGE	VOLUME.
Elaine	453— 471	171	Idylls of the King	Enid	150— 169	9	Idylls of the King.
"	472— 489	172	"	"	170— 188	10	"
"	490— 508	173	"	"	189— 208	11	"
"	509— 527	174	"	"	209— 226	12	"
"	528— 547	175	"	"	227— 245	13	"
"	548— 566	176	"	"	246— 264	14	"
"	567— 586	177	"	"	265— 284	15	"
"	586— 604	178	"	"	285— 303	16	"
"	605— 623	179	"	"	304— 322	17	"
"	624— 643	180	"	"	323— 341	18	"
"	644— 663	181	"	"	342— 355	19	"
"	664— 683	182	"	"	356— 374	20	"
"	684— 701	183	"	"	375— 393	21	"
"	702— 719	184	"	"	394— 412	22	"
"	720— 739	185	"	"	413— 431	23	"
"	740— 758	186	"	"	432— 451	24	"
"	759— 777	187	"	"	452— 471	25	"
"	778— 797	188	"	"	472— 489	26	"
"	798— 817	189	"	"	490— 507	27	"
"	818— 837	190	"	"	508— 526	28	"
"	838— 856	191	"	"	527— 545	29	"
"	857— 875	192	"	"	546— 565	30	"
"	876— 895	193	"	"	566— 585	31	"
"	896— 914	194	"	"	586— 604	32	"
"	915— 934	195	"	"	605— 623	33	"
"	935— 954	196	"	"	624— 642	34	"
"	955— 971	197	"	"	643— 662	35	"
"	972— 990	198	"	"	663— 681	36	"
"	991—1006	199	"	"	682— 700	37	"
"	1007—1023	200	"	"	701— 720	38	"
"	1024—1043	201	"	"	721— 738	39	"
"	1044—1061	202	"	"	739— 757	40	"
"	1062—1078	203	"	"	758— 777	41	"
"	1079—1097	204	"	"	778— 796	42	"
"	1098—1117	205	"	"	797— 816	43	"
"	1118—1135	206	"	"	817— 834	44	"
"	1136—1155	207	"	"	835— 851	45	"
"	1156—1174	208	"	"	852— 870	46	"
"	1175—1193	209	"	"	871— 890	47	"
"	1194—1212	210	"	"	891— 909	48	"
"	1213—1230	211	"	"	910— 926	49	"
"	1231—1249	212	"	"	927— 945	50	"
"	1250—1267	213	"	"	946— 964	51	"
"	1268—1285	214	"	"	965— 983	52	"
"	1286—1304	215	"	"	984—1000	53	"
"	1304—1321	216	"	"	1001—1019	54	"
"	1322—1341	217	"	"	1020—1037	55	"
"	1342—1360	218	"	"	1038—1056	56	"
"	1361—1377	219	"	"	1057—1076	57	"
"	1378—1397	220	"	"	1077—1093	58	"
"	1398—1417	221	"	"	1094—1113	59	"
"	1418—1419	222	"	"	1114—1132	60	"
Enid	1— 13	1	"	"	1133—1151	61	"
"	14— 33	2	"	"	1152—1170	62	"
"	34— 53	3	"	"	1171—1190	63	"
"	54— 72	4	"	"	1191—1207	64	"
"	73— 91	5	"	"	1208—1226	65	"
"	92— 110	6	"	"	1227—1246	66	"
"	111— 130	7	"	"	1247—1266	67	"
"	131— 149	8	"	"	1267—1284	68	"

TABLE OF LINES.

POEM.	LINES.	PAGE	VOLUME.	POEM.	LINES.	PAGE	VOLUME.
Enid	1285—1304	69	Idylls of the King.	Enoch Arden, etc.	555— 572	31	Enoch Arden, etc.
"	1305—1324	70	"	"	573— 592	32	"
"	1325—1343	71	"	"	593— 611	33	"
"	1344—1361	72	"	"	612— 629	34	"
"	1362—1380	73	"	"	630— 649	35	"
"	1381—1398	74	"	"	650— 668	36	"
"	1399—1417	75	"	"	669— 687	37	"
"	1418—1436	76	"	"	688— 705	38	"
"	1437—1455	77	"	"	706— 724	39	"
"	1456—1475	78	"	"	725— 742	40	"
"	1476—1493	79	"	"	743— 761	41	"
"	1494—1510	80	"	"	762— 779	42	"
"	1511—1528	81	"	"	780— 797	43	"
"	1529—1545	82	"	"	798— 816	44	"
"	1546—1564	83	"	"	817— 835	45	"
"	1565—1582	84	"	"	836— 855	46	"
"	1583—1601	85	"	"	856— 874	47	"
"	1602—1620	86	"	"	875— 894	48	"
"	1621—1640	87	"	"	895— 910	49	"
"	1641—1659	88	"	"	911— 916	50	"
"	1660—1678	89	"	Gardener's Daughter,			
"	1679—1698	90	"		1— 15	203	Poems
"	1699—1718	91	"	"	16— 43	204	"
"	1719—1736	92	"	"	44— 70	205	"
"	1737—1756	93	"	"	71— 98	206	"
"	1757—1775	94	"	"	99— 126	207	"
"	1776—1793	95	"	"	127— 152	208	"
"	1794—1813	96	"	"	153— 179	209	"
"	1814—1818	97	"	"	180— 206	210	"
Enoch Arden, etc.	1— 11	1	Enoch Arden, etc.	"	207— 234	211	"
"	12— 30	2	"	"	235— 262	212	"
"	31— 49	3	"	"	263— 273	213	"
"	50— 68	4	"	Guinevere	1— 13	225	Idylls of the King.
"	69— 87	5	"	"			
"	88— 106	6	"	"	14— 32	226	"
"	107— 126	7	"	"	33— 52	227	"
"	127— 145	8	"	"	53— 71	228	"
"	146— 163	9	"	"	72— 91	229	"
"	164— 181	10	"	"	92— 111	230	"
"	182— 200	11	"	"	112— 131	231	"
"	201— 217	12	"	"	132— 149	232	"
"	218— 235	13	"	"	150— 168	233	"
"	236— 253	14	"	"	169— 184	234	"
"	254— 271	15	"	"	185— 204	235	"
"	272— 289	16	"	"	205— 221	236	"
"	290— 309	17	"	"	222— 240	237	"
"	310— 324	18	"	"	241— 260	238	"
"	325— 342	19	"	"	261— 278	239	"
"	343— 361	20	"	"	279— 298	240	"
"	362— 380	21	"	"	299— 317	241	"
"	381— 399	22	"	"	318— 335	242	"
"	400— 418	23	"	"	336— 352	243	"
"	419— 437	24	"	"	353— 372	244	"
"	438— 456	25	"	"	373— 391	245	"
"	457— 475	26	"	"	392— 410	246	"
"	476— 493	27	"	"	411— 429	247	"
"	494— 512	28	"	"	430— 449	248	"
"	513— 531	29	"	"	450— 469	249	"
"	532— 554	30	"	"	470— 489	250	"
				"	490— 509	251	"

POEM.	LINES.	PAGE	VOLUME.	POEM.	LINES.	PAGE	VOLUME.
Sea Dreams	264— 278	111	Enoch Arden, etc.	Vivien	547— 563	130	Idylls of the King
"	279— 296	112	"	"	564— 581	131	"
"	297— 304	113	"	"	582— 600	132	"
			Idylls of the King.	"	601— 618	133	"
Vivien	1— 12	101	"	"	619— 636	134	"
"	13— 32	102	"	"	637— 654	135	"
"	33— 52	103	"	"	655— 674	136	"
"	53— 71	104	"	"	675— 693	137	"
"	72— 91	105	"	"	694— 712	138	"
"	92— 111	106	"	"	713— 731	139	"
"	112— 130	107	"	"	732— 750	140	"
"	131— 149	108	"	"	751— 769	141	"
"	150— 168	109	"	"	770— 788	142	"
"	169— 188	110	"	"	789— 808	143	"
"	189— 207	111	"	"	809— 823	144	"
"	208— 226	112	"	Wellington, Ode on the Duke of,			Maud, and other Poems.
"	227— 243	113	"
"	244— 259	114	"	"	1— 7	137	"
"	260— 279	115	"	"	8— 20	138	"
"	280— 297	116	"	"	21— 39	139	"
"	298— 316	117	"	"	40— 56	140	"
"	317— 335	118	"	"	57— 76	141	"
"	336— 355	119	"	"	77— 92	142	"
"	356— 375	120	"	"	93— 112	143	"
"	376— 394	121	"	"	113— 132	144	"
"	395— 413	122	"	"	133— 150	145	"
"	414— 433	123	"	"	151— 168	146	"
"	434— 452	124	"	"	169— 188	147	"
"	453— 470	125	"	"	189— 205	148	"
"	471— 490	126	"	"	206— 225	149	"
"	491— 509	127	"	"	226— 242	150	"
"	510— 527	128	"	"	243— 262	151	"
"	528— 546	129	"	"	263— 281	152	"

A CONCORDANCE

TO THE

WORKS OF ALFRED TENNYSON.

A

	POEM.	LINE.
a.		
Mouthing out his hollow oes and *aes*	*The Epic*	50
'aäporth.		
Joänes, as 'ant a *'a* o' sense	*N. Farmer*	49
'aäste.		
summun said it in *'a*	*N. Farmer*	27
Abaddon.		
A and Asmodeus caught at me	*St S. Stylites*	169
abase.		
A those eyes that ever loved	*Princess,* ii.	405
abashed.		
all *a* she knew not why	*Enid*	765
A Lavaine, whose instant reverence	*Elaine*	417
so forlorn As I am!' half *a* him	*En. Arden*	287
abate.		
A the stride, which speaks of man	*Princess,* ii.	407
Abbess.		
Our simple-seeming *A* and her nuns	*Guinevere*	307
till in time their *A* died	"	684
Was chosen *A*, there, an *A* lived	"	688
and there, an *A*, past	"	689
Abbey.		
'Come out,' he said, 'To the *A*	*Princess,Pro.*	51
But we went back to the *A*	" *Con.*	106
Abbey-rain.		
Carved stones of the *A-r*	*Princess,Pro.*	14
Abbey-wall.		
I see the moulder'd *A-w's*	*Talking O.*	3
Abbot.		
An *a* on an ambling pad	*L.of Shalott,*ii.	20
Abdiel.		
Titan angels, Gabriel, *A*	*Milton*	5
abear.		
I couldn *a* to see it	*N. Farmer*	64
a-begging.		
never came *a* for myself	*Dora*	138
abeyance.		
winters of *a* all worn out	*Princess,* iv.	420
abhor.		
I hate, *a*, spit, sicken at him	*Lucretius*	196
abhorr'd.		
fell and made the glen *a*	*Elaine*	43
abhorrent.		
A of a calculation crost	*En. Arden*	470

	POEM.	LINE.
abide.		
Trust me, in bliss I shall *a*	*Pal. of Art.*	18
Tho' much is taken, much *a's*	*Ulysses*	65
In whose least act *a's* the nameless charm	*Princess,* v.	67
you failing, I *a* What end soever	"	395
A: thy wealth is garner'd in	*In Mem.* li.	15
A a little longer here	" lvii.	11
bid her *a* by her word?	*Maud,* I. xvi.	25
shalt *a* her judgment on it	*Enid*	584
will *a* the coming of my lord	"	980
the wife Whom he knows false *a*	*Guinevere*	511
hate me not, but *a* your lot	*Spiteful Let.*	11
abidest.		
a lame and poor, Calling thyself	*Two Voices*	197
abiding.		
A with me till I sail	*In Mem.*cxxiv.	13
able-bodied.		
Grew plump and *a-b*	*The Goose*	18
abler.		
A quarter-sessions chairman,*a* none;	*Princess,Con.*	90
abode.		
at the farm *a* William and Dora	*Dora*	1
those four *a* Within one house	"	164
Wherein the younger Charles *a*	*Talking O.*	297
a his coming, and said to him	*Enid*	988
stately Queen *a* For many a week	*Guinevere*	144
mightiest of my knights, *a* with me	"	427
Clave to him, and *a* in his own land	"	437
abodest.		
while thou *a* in the bud	*Two Voices*	158
abolish.		
Caught at the hilt, as to *a* him	*Enid*	210
abominable.		
The *A*, that uninvited came	*Œnone*	220
shatter it, hold it *a*	*Boädicea*	65
shapes of lust, unspeakable, *A*	*Lucretius*	158
abruptly.		
broke the sentence in his heart *A*	*Enid*	891
absence.		
mourn'd his *a* as his grave	*En. Arden*	246
absolution.		
A sort of *a* in the sound	*Sea Dreams*	61
absorb.		
in its onward current it *a's*	*Isabel*	31
abstraction.		
They do so that affect a here	*Princess,* ii.	338

A

	POEM.	LINE.
abuse (s.)		
lest from the *a* of war	*Princess*, v.	120
bore without *a* The grand old name	*In Mem.* cx.	21
abuse (verb.)		
wayward grief *a* The genial hour	*In Mem.* civ.	9
abused.		
God's great gift of speech *a*	*A Dirge*	44
abyss.		
the waste wide Of that *a*	*Two Voices*	120
to sound the *a* Of science	*Princess*, ii.	159
lighten thro' The secular *a* to come	*In Mem.* lxxv.	6
from the distance of the *a*	" xcii.	11
acacia.		
Was lispt about the *a's*	*Princess*, vii.	235
The slender *a* would not shake	*Maud*, I. xxii.	45
Academe.		
The softer Adams of your *A*	*Princess*, ii.	180
this your *A* Whichever side be victor	"	212
acanthus-wreath.		
many a wov'n *a-w* divine	*Lotos-E's.*	142
accent.		
an *a* very low In blandishment	*Isabel*	19
She replies in *a's* fainter	*L. of Burleigh*	5
With nearing chair and lower'd *a*	*Aylmer's F.*	267
accept.		
do *a* my madness and would die	*Maud*, I. xviii.	44
God *a* him, Christ receive him.	*Odeon Well.*	281
acceptance.		
Blithe would her brother's *a* be	*Maud*, I. x.	27
access.		
closed her *a* to the wealthier farms	*Aylmer's F.*	503
acclaim.		
the tumult of their *a* is roll'd	*Dying Swan*	33
And follow'd with *a's*	*Will Water.*	138
wrought with tumult of *a*	*In Mem.* lxxiv.	20
let a people's voice In full *a*	*Odeon Well.*	143
accompanied.		
oft *a* by Averill	*Aylmer's F.*	137
accompanying.		
brethren slowly with bent brows *A*	*Elaine*	1133
accomplice.		
The *a* of your madness unforgiven	*Princess*, vi.	259
accomplish.		
Which did *a* their desire	*Two Voices*	217
A thou my manhood and thyself	*Princess*, vii.	344
accomplished.		
Who thro' their own desire *a*	*Aylmer's F.*	776
accomplishment.		
win all eyes with all *a*	*Coquette*, ii.	4
accorded.		
A with his wonted courtesy	*Elaine*	635
according.		
mind and soul, *a* well	*In Mem.Pro.*	27
account (s.)		
of the crowd you took no more *a*	*Elaine*	106
dodged me with a long and loose *a*	*Sea Dreams*	145
a hard friend in his loose *a's*	"	158
account (verb.)		
Eat and be glad, for I *a* you mine	*Enid*	1495
accounted.		
Is thy white blamelessness *a* blame	*Vivien*	648
accoutrement.		
Among piled arms and rough *a's*	*Princess*, v.	52
accrue.		
Delight a hundredfold *a*	*In Mem.* cxvi.	8
accurate.		
your fine epithet Is *a* too	*Vivien*	383
accurst.		
Thro' you, my life will be accurst	*The Letters*	36
accusation.		
Like bitter *a* ev'n to death	*Love and Duty*	79
people's talk And *a* of uxoriousness	*Enid*	83

	POEM.	LINE.
breathe but *a* vast and vague	*Vivien*	551
accuse.		
sent for Blanche to *a* her	*Princess*, iv.	220
A her of the least immodesty	*Enid*	960
ache (s.)		
In coughs, *a's*, stitches,	*St S. Stylites*	13
ache (verb.)		
would not let your little finger *a*	*Godiva*	22
achievable.		
if our end were less *a*	*Princess*, iii.	266
achieving.		
some have striven, *A* calm,	*Two Voices*	209
Achilles.		
see the great *A*, whom we knew	*Ulysses*	64
acknowledge.		
in my heart of hearts I did *a* nobler	*Elaine*	1205
acorn.		
An *a* in her breast	*Talking O.*	228
nor yet Thine *a* in the land	"	260
acorn-ball.		
wear Alternate leaf and *a-b*	*Talking O.*	287
acre.		
dinner To the men of many *a's*	*Maud*, I. xx.	32
acreage.		
No coarse and blockish God of *a*	*Aylmer's F.*	651
acrimony.		
flowed in shallower *acrimonies*	*Aylmer's F.*	563
act (s.)		
saying hard to shape in a 'Love thou thy land' etc.	*M. d'Arthur*	49
swift mind In *a* to throw	"	61
king demand An *a* unprofitable	"	96
In *a* to render thanks	*Gardener's D.*	159
which I clothed in *a*	*Princess*, i.	192
a tiger cat In *a* to spring	" ii.	267
by single *a* Of immolation	" iii.	267
all creation is one *a* at once	"	308
One *a* a phantom of succession	"	312
makes Such head from *a* to *a*	" iv.	432
least *a* abides the nameless charm	" v.	67
creatures native unto gracious *a*	" vii.	12
How much of *a* at human hands	*In Mem.*lxxxiv.	38
dream she could be guilty of foul *a*	*Enid*	120
hearts who sees but *a's* of wrong	"	438
So splendid in his *a's* and his attire	"	620
act (verb.)		
up and *a*, nor shrink For fear	*Princess*, iii.	248
For who can always *a*?	*In Mem.* cx.	9
be born and think, And *a* and love	" Con.	127
acted.		
If more and *a* on, what follows	*Princess*, ii.	211
weaker grows thro' *a* crime	*Will.*	12
after madness *a* question asked	*Enid*	1661
acting.		
A the law we live by without fear	*Œnone*	146
action.		
in all *a* is the end of all	*Œnone*	120
until endurance grow sinew'd with *a*	"	162
enough of *a*, and of motion we	*Lotos-E's.*	150
I myself must mix with *a*	*Locksley H.*	98
A life of civic *a* warm	*In Mem.* cxii.	9
shape His *a* like the greater ape	" cxix.	11
Adair (v. Ellen A.)		
Adam.		
when *A* first embraced his Eve	*Day-Dm.*	253
The softer *A's* of your Academe	*Princess*, ii.	180
Since *A* left his garden yet	*In Mem.* xxiv.	8
add.		
a A crimson to the quaint Macaw	*Day-Dm.*	15
Nor *a* and alter many times	*Will Water.*	9
a my diamonds to her pearls	*Elaine*	1218
months will *a* themselves	*Guinevere*	618
added.		
set the words and *a* names I knew	*Audley Ct.*	60

	POEM.	LINE.		POEM.	LINE.
Had surely *a* praise to praise	*In Mem.* xxxi.	8	*advantage.*		
weight is *a* only grain by grain	*Enid*	526	He took *a* of his strength	*Princess*, ii.	136
a of her wit A border fantasy	*Elaine*	10	Forbore his own *a* (rep.)	*Guinevere*	329
a wound to wound And ridd'n away	"	566	*advent.*		
Were *a* mouths that gaped	"	1242	Wink at our *a:* help my prince	*Princess*, iii.	144
a to the griefs the great must bear	*Guinevere*	203	dividing clove An *a* to the throne	" iv.	265
address.			Expecting still his *a* home	*In Mem.* vi.	21
Began to *a* us, and was moving on	*Princess*, ii.	167	*adventure.*		
address'd—addrest.			battle, bold *a*, dungeon, wreck	*Aylmer's F.*	98
faces toward us and *a* Their motion	*Princess*, iv.	529	*adversary.*		
now *a* to speak—Who spoke few words	" Con.	93	robbers mock at a barbarous *a*	*Boädicea*	18
suddenly *a* the hoary Earl	*Enid*	402	hearing her tumultuous *adversaries*	"	78
Adeline.			*advice.*		
Faintly smiling *A*	*Adeline*	2	he wouldn't take my *a*	*Grandmother*	4
Shadowy, dreaming, *A* (rep.)	"	10	*a-dying.*		
Spiritual *A* (rep.)	"	22	the old year lies *a*.	*D. of the O. Year*	5
Who talketh with thee, *A*?	"	24	*Æolian.*		
Thou faint smiler, *A*	"	48	Æ harp that wakes No certain air	*Two Voices*	436
Than your twin-sister *A*	*Margaret*	48	*Æon.*		
adieu.			the great Æ sinks in blood	*In Mem.* cxxvi.	16
uttered it And bade *a* for ever	*Love and Duty*	81	*Æonian.*		
'*A, a*' for evermore	*In Mem.* lvi.	16	Draw down Æ hills	*In Mem.* xxxv.	11
the' my lips may breathe *a*	" cxxii.	11	Æ music measuring out The steps	" xciv.	41
What more? we took our last *a*	*The Daisy*	85	*aërially.*		
adit.			less *a* blue	*Margaret*	51
yourself and yours shall have Free *a*	*Princess*, vi.	283	a murmur heard *a*	*Boädicea*	24
adjust.			*affair.*		
a My vapid vegetable loves	*Talking O.*	182	I never whisper'd a private *a*	*Maud*, II. v.	47
admire.			kinsman travelling on his own *a*	*Vivien*	567
a Joints of cunning workmanship	*Vision of Sin*	185	*affect.*		
not to desire or *a*, if a man	*Maud*, I. iv.	41	They do so that *a* abstraction	*Princess* ii.	338
admired.			*affection.*		
when now *a* By Edith	*Aylmer's F.*	231	The still *a* of the heart	*Miller's D.*	225
admiring.			Thus he spoke, Part banter, part *a*	*Princess, Pro.*	166
sat beside the couch, *A* him	*Enid*	80	old and strange *a* of the house	" i.	13
the two Were turning and *a* it	"	637	cared not for the *a* of the house	"	26
admission.			like a flash the wierd *a* came	" v.	466
beat *a* in in a thousand years	*Princess*, iii.	139	wing'd *a*'s clipt with crime	" vii.	297
admit.			My old *a* of the tomb (rep.)	*In Mem.* lxxxiv.	75
No other thought her mind *a*'s	*In Mem.* xxxii.	2	With what divine *a*'s bold	" xciii.	1
The time *a*'s not flowers or leaves	" cvi.	5	a mood Of overstrained *a*	*Vivien*	372
ado.			Stabb'd through the heart's *a*'s	"	717
why make we such *a*?	*May Queen*, iii.	56	with full *a* flung One arm	*Elaine*	1345
adoration.			*affiance.*		
Meet *a* to my household gods	*Ulysses*	42	dwelt upon your old *a*	*Princess*, iii.	123
shaken voice And flutter'd *a*	*Vivien*	14	in whom I have Most love and most *a*	*Elaine*	1348
adore.			*affianced.*		
How may measured words *a*	*Eleänore*	45	*a* years ago to the Lady Ida	*Princess*, ii.	197
To stand apart, and to *a*	"	79	*A*, Sir? love whispers may not	"	203
on the meadow grass and *a*	*Maud*, I. v.	26	with Melissa Florian, I With mine *a*	" iii.	338
the power that all men *a*	" x.	14	*affirm.*		
adored.			*A*'s your Psyche thieved her theories	*Princess*, iii.	76
A her, as the stateliest	*Enid*	20	*affirmed.*		
was *a*; He, loved for her	*Aylmer's F.*	178	she *a* not, or denied	*Princess*, iv.	215
a-drooping.			*affirming.*		
locks *a* twined Round thy neck	*Adeline*	57	*A* that his father left him gold	*Enid*	451
adulation.			*A* each his own philosophy	*Lucretius*	213
golden eloquence And amorous *a*	*Elaine*	647	*affright.*		
adultery.			nothing there her maiden grace *a!*	*Maud*, I. xviii.	71
mother of the foul *adulteries*	*Aylmer's F.*	376	*affrighted.*		
advance (s.)			Round *a* Lisbon drew	*Ode on Well.*	103
these are the days of *a*	*Maud*, I. l.	25	*after-beauty.*		
advance (verb.)			that *a-b* makes Such head	*Princess*, iv.	431
The years with change *a*	*Two Voices*	52	*after-days.*		
Let all my aeonial spirits *a*	*In Mem. Con.*	77	It grows to guerdon *a-d* 'Love thou thy land' etc.		27
gain in life, as life *a*'s	*To F. D. Maurice*	39	*after-dinner.*		
A and take as fairest of the fair	*Enid*	553	It seems in *a-d* talk	*Miller's D.*	31
A and take your prize The diamond	*Elaine*	502	'Twas but an *a-d*'s nap	*Day-Dm.*	156
advanced.			*after-hands.*		
Something far *a* in State	*Ode on Well.*	275	whence *a-h* May move the world	*Princess*, iii.	246
who *a* Each growling like a dog	*Enid*	1406			
the King himself *A* to greet them	"	1727			

		POEM.	LINE.
	after-heat.		
might have drawn from *a-h*	.	*In Mem.* lxxx.	12
	after-life.		
she will pass me by in *a-l*	.	*Princess,* v.	88
my dead face would vex her *a-l*	.	*En. Arden.*	892
	after-love.		
A-l's of maids and men	.	*The Window*	130
	aftermath.		
meadow smooth from *a*	.	*Audley Ct.*	13
	after-morn.		
left my *a-m* content	.	*In Mem.* cii.	4
	afternoon.		
In the *a* they came unto a land	.	*Lotus E's.*	3
it seemed always *a*	.	"	4
That *a* the Princess rode	.	*Princess,* iii.	153
all That *a* a sound arose	.	" vi.	358
in the all-golden *a* A guest	.	*In Mem.* lxxxviii.	25
in the falling *a* returned	.	*Enid*	1439
made the laughter of an *a*	.	*Vivien*	19
brief repast or *a* repose	.	*Guinevere*	392
Bright was that *a*, Sunny but chill	*En. Arden.*	670
Half-sickening of his pensioned *a*	.	*Aylmer's F.*	461
	after-time.		
sung or told In *a*	.	*M. d'Arthur*	35
relic of my lord Should be to *a*	.	"	99
some old man speak in the *a*	.	"	107
a And that full voice which circles	*Princess,* ii.	30
men we shall prize in the *a*	.	" v.	402
	agape.		
A rabbit mouth that is ever *a*	.	*Maud,* I. x.	31
	agaric.		
learned names of *a*, moss and fern	*Ed. Morris*	17
	agate.		
Turkis and *a* and almondine	.	*The Merman*	32
bottom *a's* seen to wave and float	.	*Princess,* ii.	306
	Agavè.		
One tall *A* above the lake	.	*The Daisy*	84
	age.		
makes me talk too much in *a*	.	*Miller's D.*	194
the great *a's* onward roll	.	*To J. S.*	72
most blessed memory of mine *a*	.	*Gardener's D.*	273
thrifty too beyond her *a*	.	*Dora*	14
until he grows Of *a* to help us	.	"	125
old sore breaks out from *a* to *a*	.	*Walkg. to the M.*	71
Of different *a's,* like twin sisters	.	*Ed. Morris*	32
suffer'd long For *a's* and for *a's*	.	*St S. Stylites*	98
float about the threshold of an *a*	.	*Golden Year*	16
an *a,* when every hour Must sweat	.	"	67
Old *a* hath yet his honour	.	*Ulysses*	50
thro' the *a's* one increasing purpose	*Locksley H.*	137
I the heir of all the *a's*	.	"	178
know that *a* to *a* succeeds	.	*Two Voices*	205
As all were order'd, *a's* since	.	*Day-Dm.*	74
'Tis vain! in such a brassy *a*	.	*Amphion*	65
found My spirits in the golden *a*	.	*To E. L.*	12
every clime and *a* Jumbled together	*Princess,* Pro.	16
'The climax of his *a!*	.	" ii.	36
emblematic of a nobler *a*	.	"	111
Some *a's* had been lost	.	"	137
second-sight of some Astræan *a*	.	"	420
reasons drawn from *a* and state	.	" v.	347
got a friend of your own *a*	.	" vi.	234
left for human deeds In endless *a?*	*In Mem.* lxxii.	12
take the print Of the golden *a*	.	*Maud,* I. i.	30
many a million of *a's* have gone	.	" iv.	35
Wretchedest *a,* since Time began	.	" II. v.	21
A tonsured head in middle *a*	.	*The Brook*	200
To such a name for *a's* long	.	*Ode on Well.*	76
For many and many an *a* proclaim	"	226
tho' the Giant *A's* heave the hill	.	"	259
suffering thus he made Minutes an *a*	*Enid.*	964
his own wish in *a* for love	.	*Vivien*	41
Who paced it, *a's* back	.	"	403
more fitly yours, not thrice your *a*	*Elaine*	949
when *this* Aylmer came of *a*	.	*Aylmer's F.*	407
huge cathedral fronts of e ery *a*	.	*Sea Dreams*	211

		POEM.	LINE.
at your *a,* Annie, I could have wept (rep.)	.	*Grandmother*	20
a is a time of peace	.	"	97
Immortal *a* beside immortal youth	*Tithonus*	22
Milton, a name to resound for *a's.*	*Milton*	4
I hear the roll of the *a's*	.	*Spiteful Let.*	8
palsy, death-in-life, And wretched *a*	*Lucretius*	155
to-morrow, And that's an *a* away	.	*The Window*	175
	agent.		
Thro' many *a's* making strong { 'Love thou thy land,' etc.		39
	aghast.		
a The women stared at these	.	*Princess,* vi.	341
not a word!' and Enid was *a*	.	*Enid*	867
men and women staring and *a*	.	"	1652
a the maiden rose, White as her veil	*Guinevere*	360
	Agincourt.		
'this,' he said, 'was Hugh's at *A*	.	*Princess,* Pro.	25
	agitated.		
around the royal chariot *a*	.	*Boädicea*	73
	Aglaïa.		
a double April old, *A* slept	.	*Princess,* ii.	96
my sweet *A,* my one child	.	" v.	98
Came Psyche, sorrowing for *A*	.	" vi.	13
	Agned Cathregonian.		
And up in *A C* too	.	*Elaine*	300
	agoän.		
whoy, Doctor's abeän an' *a*	.	*N. Farmer*	2
	agony.		
melody Of an inward *a*	.	*Claribel*	7
an *a* Of lamentation, like a wind	.	*M. d'Arthur*	200
killed with some luxurious *a*	.	*Vision of Sin*	43
With *agonies,* with energies	.	*In Mem.* cxii.	18
into wastes and solitudes For *a*	.	*Elaine*	253
up the side, sweating with *a.*	.	"	493
Brain-feverous in his heat and *a*	.	"	850
modest bosom prest In *a*	.	*Aylmer's F.*	417
as cried Christ ere His *a*	.	"	793
wail of women and children, multitudinous *agonies*	.	*Boädicea*	26
Roman slaughter, multitudinous *agonies*	.	"	84
	a-gooin'.		
beänt *a* to breäk my rule	.	*N. Farmer*	4
	agreed.		
so it was *a* when first they came	.	*Princess,* iii.	20
A to, this, the day fled on	.	"	160
his wish, whereto the Queen *a*	.	*Elaine*	1163
then they were *a* upon a night	.	*Guinevere*	96
a That much allowance must be	.	*Aylmer's F.*	409
	agrin.		
visage all *a* as at a wake	.	*Princess,* v.	510
	Agrippina.		
the Roman brows Of *A*	.	*Princess,* ii.	71
	aid (s.)		
for lack of gentle maiden's *a*	.	*Elaine*	761
	aid (verb.)		
O Lord, *A* all this foolish people	*St S. Stylites*	219
a me Heaven when at mine	.	*Enid*	502
a me, give me strength Not to tell her	*En. Arden.*	786
	aiding.		
serve them both in *a* her	.	*Princess,* vii.	252
	aidless.		
leave thee thus, *A,* alone	.	*M. d'Arthur*	41
	ail.		
mother thought, What *a's* the boy?	*Miller's D.*	93
What *a's* us, who are sound,	*Walkg. to the M.*	95
	ail'd.		
told his gentle wife What *a* him	.	*Enid*	1353
What *a* her then, that ere she enter'd	*En. Arden.*	514
	aileth.		
What *a* thee? whom waitest thou	*Adeline*	45
	aim (s.)		
Embrace our *a's: work out your freedom*	.	*Princess,* ii.	75

	POEM.	LINE.
fear our solid *a* be dissipated	*Princess*, iii.	249
works Without a conscience or on *a*	*In Mem*.xxxiv.	8
so I wake to the higher *a*'s	*Maud*,III.vi.	38
kept his mind on one sole *a*	*Vivien*	476
a's Were sharpen'd by strong hate	*Guinevere*	20

aim (verb.)
one would *a* an arrow fair	*In.Mem*.lxxxvi.	25

aim'd.
A at the helm, his lance err'd	*Enid*	1006
fairy arrows *a* All at one mark	*Aylmer's F.*	94
Nay, but she *a* not at glory	*Wages*	4

aiming.
near storm, and *a* at his head	*Aylmer's F.*	727

air (atmosphere.)
living *a*'s of middle night	*Arabian N's.*	69
a is damp, and hush'd and close	'*A spirit haunts*,' etc.	13
when little *a*'s arise How the merry	*Adeline*	33
With melodious *a*'s lovelorn	"	55
Life in dead stones, or spirit in *a*	*A Character*	9
Wide, wild and open to the *a*	*Dying Swan*	1
reveal'd themselves to English *a*	*Eleänore*	2
a Sleepeth over all the heaven	"	38
The very *a* about the door	*Miller's D.*	103
earth and *a* seem only burning fire	*Œnone*	264
the summer *a*'s blow cool	*May Queen*, ii.	27
the languid *a* did swoon	*Lotos-E's.*	5
Falls and floats adown the *a*	"	76
warm *a*'s lull us, blowing lowly	"	134
no motion in the dumb dead *a*	*D.of F. Wom.*	65
sea and *a* are dark	{'*Love thou thy land*,' etc.	63
made the *a* Of Life delicious	*Gardener's D.*	68
murmur broke the stillness of that *a*	"	146
Felt earth as *a* beneath me	"	207
deep *a* listened round her	*Godiva*	54
soften'd *a*'s that blowing steal	*Two Voices*	406
yearn to breathe the *a*'s of heaven	*Sir Galahad*	63
touch'd, are turn'd to finest *a*	"	72
clouds are highest up in *a*	*Lady Clare*	5
green From draughts of balmy *a*	*Sir L.and Q.G.*	9
sweet as English *a* could make her	*Princess*,Pro.	154
each light *a* On our mail'd heads	" v.	234
for this wild wreath of *a*	"	308
went The enamour'd *a* sighing	" vi.	63
with a tender foot, light as on *a*	"	72
shake To the same sweet *a*	" vii.	54
like a broken purpose waste in *a*	"	199
In that fine *a* I tremble	"	333
no ruder *a* perplex Thy sliding keel	*In Mem*. ix.	9
deep peace in this wide *a*	" xi.	13
circle moaning in the *a*	" xii.	15
Was as the whisper of an *a*	" xvii.	3
light as carrier-birds in *a*	" xxv.	6
seem to have reached a purer *a*	" xxxiii.	2
Sweet after showers, ambrosial *a*	" lxxxv.	1
shook to all the liberal *a*	" lxxxviii.	7
drink the cooler *a*, and mark	"	15
The memory like a cloudless *a*	" xciii.	11
With summer spice the humming *a*	" c.	8
the stirring *a*, The life re-orient	" cxv.	5
ruin'd woodlands drove thro' the *a*	*Maud*, I. i.	12
essences turn'd the live *a* sick	" xiii.	11
fed With honey'd rain and delicate *a*	" xviii.	21
sweet half-English Neilgherry *a*	*The Brook*	17
breath Of tender *a* made tremble	"	202
black yew gloom'd the stagnant *a*	*The Letters*	2
thro' the long-tormented *a*	*Ode on Well.*	128
snowy dells in a golden *a*	*The Daisy*	68
Flash'd as they turned in *a*	*Lt. Brigade*	28
for God's love, a little *a* I	*Elaine*	504
spouting from a cliff Fails in mid *a*	*Guinevere*	603
could not breathe in that fine *a*	"	638
a touch of light, an *a* of heaven	*Aylmer's F.*	5
rush of the *a* in the prone swing	"	86
flush his blood with *a*,	"	459
Drank the large *a*, and saw	*Sea Dreams*	34
A soft *a* fans the cloud apart	*Tithonus*	32
Like Fancy made of golden *a*	*The Voyage*	66

	POEM.	LINE.
Clash, ye bells, in the merry March *a*	*W. to Alexan.*	18
All the *a* was torn in sunder	*The Captain*	43
Bird in *a*, and fishes turn'd	*The Victim*	19
towering o'er him in serenest *a*	*Lucretius*	178
flushing the guiltless *a*, Spout	"	236
soul flies out and dies in the *a*	"	270
cloud in my heart, and a storm in the *a*	*The Window*	40

air (strain of music.)
Æolian harp that wakes No certain *a*	*Two Voices*	437
With the *a* of the trumpet round him	*Princess*, v.	155
slightest *a* of song shall breathe	*In Mem*.xlviii.	7
singing an *a* that is known to me	*Maud*, I. v.	3
while I past he was humming an *a*	" xiii.	17
hum An *a* the nuns had taught her	*Guinevere*	161

air'd.
into the world, And *a* him there	*Aylmer's F.*	408

airing.
A a snowy hand and signet gem	*Princess*, i.	120

aisle.
ambrosial *a*'s of lofty lime	*Princess*, Pro.	87
'Dark porch,' I said, 'and silent *a*	*The Letters*	47
sombre, old, colonnaded *a*'s	*The Daisy*	56
in the middle a Reel'd *a*	*Aylmer's F.*	818

Ajalon.
like Joshua's moon in *A*	*Locksley H.*	180

akin.
Maud to him is nothing *a*	*Maud*, I. xiii.	38
lawful and lawless war Are scarcely even *a*	" II. v.	95

Akrokeraunian.
The vast *A* walls	*To E. L.*	4

a-laäid.
fun un theer *a* on 'is faäce	*N. Farmer*	33

alarm.
when fresh from war's *a*'s	*D.of F. Wom.*	149
I shook her breast with vague *a*'s	*The Letters*	38

Albert.
with him *A* came on his	*Talking O*	105
Hereafter, thro' all times, *A* the Good	*Idylls, Ded.*	42

alder.
blowing over Meadowy holms and *a*	*Ed. Morris*	96
Came wet-shot *a* from the wave	*Amphion*	41
here will sigh thine *a* tree	*A Farewell*	9

ale.
mellow'd all his heart with *a*	*The Brook*	155
A mockery to the yeomen over *a*	*Aylmer's F.*	497

a-leaning.
Truth *a* on her crutch	'*Clear-headed friend*,' etc.	18

ale-house.
Jack on his *a-h* bench	*Maud*, I. iv.	9

Alexandra.
Sea-king's daughter from over the sea, *A*	*W. to Alexan.*	2
Danes in our welcome of thee, *A*	"	5
all Dane in our welcome of thee, *A*	"	34

Alfred.
was our England's *A* named	*Ode on Well.*	188

Alice.
My own sweet *A*, we must die	*Miller's D.*	18
Pray, *A*, pray my darling wife	"	23
A, what an hour was that	"	57
Sweet *A*, if I told her all	"	120
Go fetch your *A* here	"	143
But, *A*, you were ill at ease	"	146
song, I gave you, *A*, on the day	"	162
none so fair as little *A*	*May Queen*, i.	7
In there came old *A* the nurse	*Lady Clare*	13
said *A* the nurse	" 17 *et pass.*	

alighted.
Francis just *a* from the boat	*Audley Ct.*	6

alive.
Joying to feel herself alive	*Pal. of Art.*	178
pass away before, and yet *a* I am	*May Queen*,iii.	1

	POEM.	LINE.
palace-front *A* with fluttering scarfs	*Princess,* v.	498
strive To keep so sweet a thing *a*	*In Mem.* xxxv.	7
Dark bulks that tumble half *a*	" lxix.	11
at fifty Should Nature keep me *a*.	*Maud,* I. vi.	32
not always certain if they be *a*	*Grandmother*	84
there's none of them left *a*	"	85

all-accomplish'd.
| How modest, kindly, 'a-a, wise | *Idylls, Ded.* | 17 |

all-amorous.
| Brushing his instep, bow'd the *a-a* Earl | *Enid.* | 1209 |

Allan.
With farmer *A* at the farm	*Dora*	1
a day When *A* call'd his son	"	9
bells were ringing, *A* call'd His niece	"	39
said *A*, 'did I not Forbid you	"	89
A said, 'I see it is a trick	"	93
seal that hung From *A's* watch	"	133
A set him down, and Mary said	"	136

all-armed.
| *A-a* I ride, whate'er betide | *Sir Galahad* | 83 |

all-assuming.
| The *a-a* months and years | *InMem.* lxxxiv. | 67 |

all-comprehensive.
| might express *A-c* tenderness | *InMem.* lxxxiv. | 47 |

allegiance.
| from all neighbour crowns Alliance and *a* | *Œnone* | 123 |

allegory.
| send you here a sort of *a* | *To——. With Pal. of Art.* | 1 |

Allen.
| At Francis *A's* on the Christmas-eve | *The Epic* | 1 |

alley.
From the long *a's* latticed shade	*Arabian N's.*	112
plaited *a's* of the trailing rose	*Ode to Mem.*	106
a's falling down to twilight grots	"	107
every hollow cave and *a* lone	*Lotos-E's.*	148
And *a's*, faded places	*Amphion*	86
firefly-like in copse And linden *a*	*Princess,* i.	206

all-fragrant.
| slip at once *a-f* into one | *Princess,* vii. | 55 |

all-generating.
| *a-g* powers and genial heat Of Nature | *Lucretius* | 97 |

all-golden.
| in the *a-g* afternoon A guest | *InMem.* lxxxviii. | 25 |

all-graceful.
| *A-g* head, so richly curl'd | *Day-Dm.* | 250 |

alliance.
| from all neighbour crowns *A* | *Œnone* | 123 |

allied.
| However she came to be so *a* | *Maud,* I. xiii. | 36 |

all-in-all.
with that mood or this Is *a-i-a* to all	*Will Water.*	108
take them *a-i-a*, Were we ourselves	*Princess,* v.	192
trust me not at all or *a-i-a* (rep.)	*Vivien*	234
Philip was her children's *a-i-a*	*En. Arden*	345
her good Philip was her *a-i-a*	"	521

all-kindled.
| *A-k* by a still and sacred fire, | *En. Arden* | 71 |

allot.
| The sphere thy fate *a's* | *Will. Water.* | 218 |

allotted (part.)
| show'd an empty tent *a* her | *Enid.* | 1733 |
| quit the post *A* by the Gods | *Lucretius* | 149 |

allow.
To one of less desert *a's* This laurel	*To the Queen*	6
our true king Will then *a* your pretext	*Elaine*	153
answer for a noble knight? *A* him	"	202
Will well allow my pretext	"	585

allowance.
| To make *a* for us all | *In Mem.* l. | 16 |

	POEM.	LINE.
much *a* must be made for men	*Aylmer's F.*	410
more and more *a* for his talk	*Sea-Dreams*	75

allow'd.
leave To see the hunt, *a* it easily	*Enid*	155
loyal worship is *a* Of all men	*Elaine*	111
Lightly, her suit *a*, she slipt away	"	774
Scorn was *a* as part of his defect	*Guinevere*	44
thro' his cowardice *a* Her station	"	512

allowing.
| *A* it, the Prince and Enid rode | *Enid* | 43 |

all-perfect.
| *A-p*, finish'd to the finger-nail | *Ed. Morris* | 22 |

all-puissant.
| noble breast and *a-p* arms | *Enid* | 86 |

all-seeing.
| Delius, or of older use *A-s* Hyperion | *Lucretius* | 126 |

all-shamed.
| thence I rode *a-s*, hating the life | *Enid* | 1700 |

all-silent.
| Sigh fully, or *a-s* gaze upon him | *Vivien* | 38 |

all-subtilising.
| *A-s* intellect | *InMem.* lxxxiv. | 48 |

all-too-full.
| *a-t-f* in bud For puritanic stays | *Talking O.* | 59 |

allure.
| beacon-blaze *a's* The bird of passage | *En. Arden.* | 729 |

allured.
| *A* him, as the beacon-blaze allures | *En. Arden.* | 729 |

allusion.
| phrases of the hearth, And far *a* | *Princess,* ii. | 295 |

all-weary.
| pensive tendance in the *a-w* noons | *Princess,* vii. | 87 |

ally (verb.)
| *a* Your fortunes, justlier balanced | *Princess,* ii. | 51 |

Almesbury.
in the holy house at *A*	*Guinevere*	2
she to *A* Fled all night long	"	126
when she came to *A* she spake	"	137
even here they talk at *A*	"	206

Almighty.
| O God *A*, blessed Saviour, Thou | *En. Arden.* | 783 |
| Sir Aylmer Aylmer that *a* man | *Aylmer's F.* | 13 |

almond-blossom.
| The sun-lit *a-b* shakes | *To the Queen* | 16 |

almondine.
| Turkis and agate and *a* | *The Merman* | 32 |

alms.
| set himself, Scorning an *a*, to work | *En. Arden.* | 813 |
| free of *a* her hand—The hand that | *Aylmer's F.* | 697 |

almsdeed.
| wear out in *a* and in prayer | *Guinevere* | 679 |

aloe.
| Of olive, *a*, maize and vine | *The Daisy* | 4 |

alone.
A and warming his fine wits (rep.)	*The Owl*	6
sure thou art not all *a*	*Adeline*	25
Death, walking all *a* beneath a yew	*Love and Death*	5
A I wander to and fro	*Oriana*	8
'Ah,' she sang, ' to be all *a* (rep.)	*Mariana in the S.*	11
She thought 'My spirit is here *a*	"	47
So be *a* for evermore	"	68
thou shalt be *a* no more	"	76
I shall cease to be all *a*	"	95
you and I were all *a*	*Miller's D.*	136
Came up from reedy Simois all *a*	*Œnone*	51
from that time to this I am *a*	"	189
And all *a* in crime	*Pal. of Art.*	272
Let us *a*. Time driveth onward	*Lotos-E's.*	88
Let us *a*. What is it that will last?	"	90
leave thee thus, Aidless, *a*	*M. d'Arthur*	41
I might be more *a* with thee	*St S. Stylites*	84
In which we sat together and *a*	*Love and Duty*	54
both with those That loved me, and *a*	*Ulysses*	9

	POEM.	LINE.
About the hall, among his dogs, a	Godiva	17
Ah, let the rusty theme a l	Will. Water.	177
A, 'I said, 'from earlier than I know	Princess, vii.	292
A, a, to where he sits	In Mem. xxiii.	3
When I contemplate all a	" lxxxiii.	1
light Went out, and I was all a	" xciv.	20
she will let me a	Maud, I. i.	74
am I not, am I not here a	" vi.	65
I am here at the gate a	" xxii.	4
ill and weary, a and cold	The Daisy	96
endured Strange chances here a	Enid	1658
I was all a upon the flood	Elaine	1040
shaped, it seems, By God for thee a	"	1358
who speaks with Him, seem all a.	En. Arden.	621

Alpine.

gazing up an A height	Two Voices	362
an A harebell hung with tears	Princess, vii.	100

Alps.

Sun-smitten A before me lay	The Daisy	62

Alraschid.

good Haroun A (rep.)	Arabian N's.	11

altar.

Leads her to the village a	L. of Burleigh	11
at the a the poor bride Gives	Princess, v.	367
saw the a cold and bare	The Letters	4
Cold a, Heaven and earth shall meet	"	8
fire, That burn'd as on an a	En. Arden.	72
Burnt and broke the grove and a.	Boädicea	2
priest in horror about his a	The Victim	7

altar-cloth.

Fair gleams the snowy a-c	Sir Galahad	33

altar-fire.

mounts the heavenward a-f	In Mem. xl.	3

altar-flame.

made my life a perfum'd a-f.	Maud, I.xviii.	24

altar-stairs.

Upon the great world's a-s	In Mem. liv.	15

altar-stone.

To the a-s she sprang alone	The Victim	72

alter.

Sequel of guerdon could not a me	Œnone	151
Nor add and a, many times	Will. Water.	15
as the fiery Sirius a's hue	Princess, v.	252
Persuasion, no, nor death could a her	Aylmer's F.	418

alter'd (part. and verb.)

For I was a and began	Miller's D.	94
tho' you have grown You scarce have a	Princess,ii.	286

alum.

chalk and a and plaster are sold	Maud, I. i.	39

amaracus.

Violet, a, and asphodel	Œnone	95

amaranth.

propt on beds of a and moly	Lotos-E's.	133

amaryllis.

A milky-bell'd a blew	The Daisy	16

a-maying.

Had been, their wont, a	Guinevere	24

amaze.

the hush'd a of hand and eye	Princess, iii.	122
In much a he stared On eyes	The Brook	205
Suddenly honest, answer'd in a	Enid	1259

amazed.

A he fled away Thro' the dark land	Princess, v.	46
A am I to hear Your Highness	" vi.	304
a They glared upon the woman	"	340
Enid asked a 'If Enid errs	Enid	131
the armourer turning all a	"	283
plover's human whistle a Her heart	"	898
when he found all empty, was a	"	1065
A am I, Beholding how you butt	"	1524
more a Than if seven men had set	Elaine	349
the Queen a 'Was he not with you?	"	571
He a, 'Torre and Elaine I why here?	"	791
A and melted all who listen'd	En. Arden.	650

	POEM.	LINE.
Averill solaced as he might, a:	Aylmer's F.	343
half a half frighted all his flock	"	631

amazement.

stood Stock-still for sheer a	Will Water.	136

Amazon.

Glanc'd at the legendary A	Princess, ii.	110

ambassador.

My father sent a's with furs	Princess, i.	41
Sir Lancelot went a, at first	Vivien	624
A, to lead her to his lord	Guinevere	380

ambassadress.

are yon a'es From him to me?	Princess, iii.	187

amber (adj.)

lights, rose, a, emerald, blue	Pal. of Art.	169

amber (s.)

fans Of sandal, a, ancient rosaries	Princess, Pro.	19

ambition.

Down with a, avarice, pride	Maud, I. x.	47
the lawless perch Of wing'd a's	Idylls, Ded.	22
No madness of a, avarice, none	Lucretius	209

ambrosia.

Hebes are they to hand a	Princess, iii.	97

ambrosial.

oak tree sigheth, Thick leav'd, a	Claribel	5
her deep hair A, golden	Œnone	174

ambrosially.

fruit of pure Hesperian gold, That smelt a	Œnone	66

ambuscade.

In every wavering brake an a	Enid	900

ambush.

Lances in a set	D. of F. Wom.	28

Amen.

yet I take it with A	Elaine	1217

amend.

might a it by the grace of heaven	Enid	902

amends.

She made me divine a	Maud, I. vi.	13
A hereafter by some gaudy day	Enid	818
Can thy love, Thy beauty, make a	Tithonus	24

amiss.

somewhat in this world a	Miller's D.	19
kind to Maud? That were not a	Maud, I. xix.	82
pray you check me if I ask a	Guinevere	322
my doubts and fears were all a	The Ringlet	19

amity.

idioted By the rough a of the other	Aylmer's F.	591

Ammon.

Hew'd A, hip and thigh	D. of F. Wom.	238

Ammonite.

Huge A's, and the first bones of Time	Princess,Pro.	15

amoighty.

The a's a taäkin 'o you to 'issén (rep.)	N. Farmer.	10

amorous.

with argent-lidded eyes A	Arabian N's.	135
Of temper a, as the first of May	Princess, i.	2
High nature a of the good	In Mem. cviii.	9

amorously.

kiss Thy taper fingers a	Madeline	44
shall we dandle it a?	Boädicea	33

Amphion.

In days of old A	Amphion	10

amulet.

What a drew her down	Aylmer's F.	507

Amy.

I said 'My cousin A, speak	Locksley H.	23
O my A, mine no more	"	39

amygdaloid.

trap and tuff, A and trachyte	Princess, iii.	34

ana.

Ere days, that deal in a	Will Water.	179

8   CONCORDANCE TO

anadem.
	POEM.	LINE.
Lit light in wreaths and *a's*	Pal. of Art.	186

Anahim.
I felt the thews of A	In Mem. cii.	31

Anathema.
Thunder ' A,' friend, at you	To F. D. Maurice	8

anatomic.
not found among them all One *a*	Princess, iii.	290

ancestor.
those fixt eyes of painted *a's*	Aylmer's F.	832

anchor (s.)
With silver *a* left afloat	Arabian N's.	93
there was no *a*, none,	The Epic	20
lay At *a* in the flood below	In Mem. cii.	20
A's of rusty fluke, and boats	En. Arden.	18
your cares on God; that *a* holds	"	222
Nor *a* dropt at eve or morn	The Voyage	82

anchor (verb.)
To *a* by one gloomy thought	Two Voices	459

anchor'd.
Tho' *a* to the bottom, such is he	Princess, iv.	238
A tawny pirate *a* in his port	Vivien	408

Ancients (s.)
we are *A's* of the earth	Day-Dm.	231

ancle.
From head to *a* fine	Talking O.	224
One praised her *a's*, one her eyes	Beggar Maid	12
hook'd my *a* in a vine	Princess, iv.	249
Behind his *a* twined her hollow feet	Vivien	89

anemone.
burn'd The red *a*	D. of F. Wom.	72
Crocus, *a*, violet	To F. D. Maurice	44

'ang'd (hanged.)
Noäks wur '*a* for it oop at 'soize	N. Farmer	36

angel (adj.)
So sweet a face, such *a* grace	Beggar Maid	13
With books, with flowers, with A offices	Princess, vii.	11
a dearer being, all dipt In A instincts	"	302
Rings to the roar of an *a* onset	Milton	8

angel (s.)
strange *a* which of old	'Clear-headed friend,' etc.	24
temper'd with the tears of *a's*	To ——. With Pal. of Art	19
An *a* look'd at her	Pal. of Art	100
a's rising and descending met	"	143
I heard the *a's* call	May Queen, iii.	25
saw An *a* stand and watch me	St S. Stylites	34
Is that the *a* there	"	200
thyself a little lower Than *a's*	Two Voices	199
Three *a's* bear the holy Grail	Sir Galahad	42
stricken by an *a's* hand	"	69
lest some classic A speak In scorn	Princess, iii.	54
the woman's A guards you	" v.	400
No A, but a dearer being	" vii.	301
My guardian *a* will speak out	In Mem. xliii.	15
I found an *a* of the night	" lxviii.	14
An *a* watching an urn Wept	Maud, I. viii.	5
pray him send a sudden A down	Elaine	1414
face Which then was as an *a's*	Guinevere	590
been as God's good a in our house	En. Arden.	420
Fair as the A that said 'hail'	Aylmer's F.	681
himself Were that great *a*	Sea Dreams	27
devil in man, there is an *a* too	"	267
His *a* broke his heart	"	269
whose Titan *a's*, Gabriel, Abdiel	Milton	5

anger (s.)
Delicious spites, and darling *a's*	Madeline	6
Then wax'd her *a* stronger	The Goose	30
his *a* reddens in the heavens	Princess, iii.	367
The bitter springs of *a* and fear	Maud, I. x.	49
I with as fierce an *a* spoke	" II. i.	17
vassals of wine and *a* and lust	"	43
their ravening eagle rose In *a*	Ode on Well.	120
ruth began to work Against his *a*	Enid	951
hot, God's curse, with *a*	"	1509

anger (verb.)
As some wild turn of *a*	Vivien	371
turn of *a* born Of your misfaith	"	381
Vivien frowning in true *a*	"	541
breaths of *a* puff'd Her fairy nostril	"	697
his *a* slowly died Within him	"	740
too faint and sick am I For *a*	Elaine	1081
storm of *a* brake From Guinevere	Guinevere	359
as with a kind of *a* in him	En. Arden.	389
troubled, as if with *a* or pain	Grandmother	65
all their *a* in miraculous utterances	Boädicea	23
an *a*, not by blood to be satiated	"	52

anger (verb.)
A's thee most, or *a's* thee at all	Lucretius	75

anger-charm'd.
Sat *a-c* from sorrow	Aylmer's F.	728

anger'd (adj.)
The flush of *a* shame	Madeline	32
dragon eyes of *a* Eleanor	D. of F. Wom.	255

anger'd (verb.)
Jealousies Which *a* her. Who *a* James?	The Brook	100

angerly.
Again thou blushest *a*	Madeline	45

angle (s.)
We rub each other's *a's* down	In Mem. lxxxviii.	40

angled.
a in the higher pool	Miller's D.	64
a with them for her pupil's loye	Princess, iii.	77

angrier.
I never ate with *a* appetite	Enid	1082

angry.
Hungry for honour, *a* for his king	Princess v.	304
Hortensia, pleading: *a* was her face	" vii.	117
it makes me *a* now	Grandmother	44

anguish.
Life, *a*, death, immortal love	Arabian N's.	73
down in hell Suffer endless *a*	Lotos-E's.	169
Beauty and *a* walking hand in hand	D. of F. Wom.	15
loveth her own *a* deep	To J. S.	42
Thine *a* will not let thee sleep	Two Voices	49
that this *a* fleeting hence	"	235
My deeper *a* also falls	In Mem. xix.	15
My *a* hangs like shame	Maud, II. iv.	74
in her *a* found The casement	Guinevere	580
Shall I heed them in their *a*?	Boädicea	9

animal (adj.)
a heat and dire insanity	Lucretius	163

animal (s.)
The single pure and perfect *a*	Princess, vii.	288

animalism.
Hetairai, curious in their art, Hired *a's*	Lucretius	53

ankle (v. ancle.)

ankle-bells.
To make her smile, her golden *a-b*	Vivien	429

ankle-bones.
feet unmortised from their *a-b*	Vivien	402

ankle-deep.
brushing *a-d* in flowers	In Mem. lxxxviii.	49

ankle-wing.
as it were with Mercury's *a-w*	Lucretius	198

annals.
Holding the folded *a* of my youth	Gardener's D.	239
with a day Blanch'd in our *a*	Princess, vi.	47
Told him, with other *a* of the port	En. Arden.	703

Anne.
is gone, you say, little A?	Grandmother	1
I had not wept, little A,	"	63

Annie.
A Lee, the prettiest little damsel	En. Arden	11
While A still was mistress	"	26
make a home For A	"	48
a home For A, neat and nest-like	"	59
Enoch and A, sitting hand in hand	"	69
set A forth in trade	"	138

	POEM.	LINE.
moving homeward, came on *A* pale	*En. Arden*	149
break his purposes To *A*	"	156
A fought against his will	"	158
Bought *A* goods and stores	"	169
A seem'd to hear her own	"	174
work for *A* to the last	"	180
A's fears Save as his *A*'s	"	183
When *A* would have raised him	"	231
A from her baby's forehead clipt	"	234
same week when *A* buried it	"	270
A, seated with her grief	"	279
A with her brows against the wall	"	313
for *A*'s sake, Fearing the lazy gossip	"	331
Philip did not fathom *A*'s mind	"	341
one evening *A*'s children long'd	"	359
A would go with them	"	361
For was not *A* with them	"	368
fearing night and chill for *A*	"	440
At *A*'s door he paused	"	444
A weeping answer'd, 'I am bound	"	448
A could have wept for pity	"	464
chanced That *A* could not sleep	"	486
never merrily beat *A*'s heart	"	509
The babes, their babble, *A*	"	607
Where *A* lived and loved him	"	686
later but a loftier *A* Lee	"	749
His gazing in on *A*	"	864
my daughter, *A*, whom I saw	"	883
my *A* who left me at two	*Grandmother*	77
my own little *A*, an *A* like you	"	78

annihilate.

eagle's beak and talon *a* us	*Boädicea*	11

annulet.

into many a listless *a*	*Enid*	1107

announced.

A the coming doom, and fulminated	*Sea Dreams*	22

answer (s.)

Not rendering true *a*	*M. d'Arthur*	74
some sweet *a*, tho' no *a* came	*Gardener's D.*	156
have an *a* to my wish	*Dora*	28
The sullen *a* slid betwixt	*Two Voices*	226
must be *a* to his doubt	"	309
I spoke, but *a* came there none	"	425
an *a* peal'd from that high land	*Vision of S.*	221
therewithal an *a* vague as wind	*Princess* i.	44
this report, this *a* of a king	"	69
Her *a* was, 'Leave me to deal	" iii.	133
a which, half-muffled in his beard	" v.	224
oozed All o'er with honey'd *a*	"	232
lagg'd in a loth to render up	"	289
shall have her *a* by the word	"	317
Last, Ida's *a*, in a royal hand	"	361
what *a* should I give?	" vi.	369
doubts and *a*'s here proposed	*InMem.*xlvii.	3
What hope of *a*, or redress	" lv.	27
Death returns an *a* sweet	" lxxx.	9
A faithful *a* from the breast	" lxxxiv.	14
win An *a* from my lips	" cii.	50
Make *a*, Maud, my bliss	*Maud,* I. xviii.	57
Made *a* sharply that she should not	*Enid*	196
moving without *a* to her rest	"	530
he flung a wrathful *a* back	"	995
Made *a*, either eyelid wet	*Vivien*	229
an *a* for a noble knight?	*Elaine*	201
when she drew No *a*, by and by	*Guinevere*	160
a mournful *a* made the Queen	"	339
Rejoicing at that *a* to his prayer	*En. Arden*	127
such a voluble a promising all	"	903
hush'd itself at last, Hopeless of *a*	*Aylmer's F.*	543
before thine *a* given Departest	*Tithonus*	44
Bark an *a*, Britain's raven!	*Boädicea*	13
it seemed that an *a* came	*The Victim*	24

answer (verb.)

will she *a* if I call?	*Miller's D.*	118
you dare to *a* thus!	*Dora*	24
To that man My work shall *a*	*Love and Duty*	28
He will *a* to the purpose	*Lockley H.*	55

	POEM.	LINE.
a should one press his hands?	*Two Voices*	243
He *a*'s not, nor understands	"	246
thou canst *a* not again	"	310
thou wilt *a* but in vain	"	312
Scarce *a* to my whistle	*Amphion*	68
in gentle murmur When they *a*	*L. of Burleigh*	50
to *a*, Madam, all those hard things	*Princess* ii.	324
you should *a*, *we* would ask	"	332
told me she would *a* us to-day	" iii.	150
a echoes, dying, dying, dying	"	353
A each other in the mist	*In Mem.*xxviii.	4
whatever is as ask'd her, *a*'s 'Death'	*Maud* I. i.	4
wilt thou not *a* this?	" xviii.	59
it shall *a* for me	*Vivien*	236
a, darling, *a* no	"	247
could *a* him, If questioned	*En. Arden*	654
shall know Thy voice and *a*	*'My Life is full,' etc.*	10
(*A*, O *a*) We give you his life	*The Victim*	15
Is *he* your dearest? (*A*, O *a*)	"	55
what use to *a* now?	"	59

answered.

in that time and place she *a* me	*Gardener's D.*	226
a me; And well his words	*Ed. Morris*	24
plagiarised a heart And *a*	*Talking O.*	20
She *a* to my call	*Will Water.*	106
Echo *a* in her sleep	*Princess Pro.*	66
a sharply that I talked astray	" iii.	124
a nothing, doubtful in myself	"	255
when have I *a* thee?	" vi.	367
The "wilt thou" *a*	*In Mem. Con.*	54
ask'd it of him, Who *a* as before	*Enid*	205
a with such craft as women use	"	1201
Enid *a*, harder to be moved	"	1542
truest eyes that ever *a* heaven	"	1690
I am *a*, and henceforth	*Vivien*	728
well and readily *a* he	*Elaine*	269
Lancelot spoke And *a* him at full	"	286
a not, Or short and coldly	"	882
whom she *a* with all calm	"	991
Lancelot *a* nothing, but he went	"	1378
was a softly by the King	*Guinevere*	45
should have *a* his farewell	"	608
A all queries touching those	*Aylmer's F.*	465
Doubt ye not the Gods have *a*	*Boädicea*	22
Gods have *a*; We give them the wife	*The Victim*	83

answering.

a under crescent brows	*Princess,* ii.	406
a not one word, she led the way	*Enid*	1345

antagonism.

in the teeth of clench'd *a*'s	*Princess,* iv.	445
toppling over all *a*	*Enid*	491, 1688

anthem.

a sung, is charmed and tied	*D. of F. Wom.*	193
sound of the sorrowing *a* roll'd	*Ode on Well.*	60

anther.

With *a*'s and with dust	*Talking O.*	184

Antibabylonianism.

loud-lung'd *A*'s	*Sea Dreams*	244

antiquity.

front of timber-crost *a*	*En. Arden*	693

Antony.

friend, Where is Mark *A*?	*D. of F. Wom.*	140
My Hercules, my Roman *A.*	"	150

anvil.

silver hammers falling On silver *a*'s	*Princess,* v.	213
a bang'd With hammers	" v.	493

anything.

Behold, we know not *a*	*In Mem.* liii.	13
can see elsewhere, *a* so fair	*Enid*	499
in all the world at *a*	"	1498
never meant us *a* but good	*En. Arden*	888

apartment.

died Of fright in far *a*'s	*Princess,* vi.	351

ape (s.)

In bed like monstrous *a*'s	*St. S. Stylites*	171

CONCORDANCE TO

	POEM.	LINE.
let the *a* and tiger die	*In Mem.*cxvii.	28
action like the greater *a*	" cxix.	11
ape (verb.)		
should *a* Those monstrous males	*Princess*, iii.	292
as far As I could *a* their treble	" iv.	74
Aphrodite.		
Here comes to-day, Pallas and *A*	*Œnone*	84
Idalian *A* beautiful	"	170
Apocalyptic.		
as if he held The *A* millstone	*Sea Dreams*	26
Apollo.		
strange song I heard *A* sing	*Tithonus*	62
another of our Gods, the Sun, *A*	*Lucretius*	125
apology.		
ended with *a* so sweet	*Enid*	1243
appall'd.		
a them, and they said	*Elaine*	1246
apparel.		
in her hand A suit of bright *a*	*Enid*	678
store of rich *a*, sumptuous fare	"	709
a as might well beseem His princess	"	758
clothed her in *a* like the day	"	1796
appeal (s.)		
She the *a* Brook'd not	*Princess*, vi.	123
makest thine *a* to me	*In Mem.* lv.	5
tho' it spake and made *a*	" xci.	4
lifted up A face of sad *a*	*Vivien*	83
appeal'd.		
a To one that stood beside	*D. of F. Wom.*	99
with a larger faith *a*	*Talking O*	15
appealing.		
A to the bolts of Heaven	*Princess*, iv.	353
appear.		
Shadows of the world *a*	*L.of Shalott.*ii.	12
made *a* Still-lighted	*M. in the S.*	17
marble bright in dark *a*'s	*In Mem.* lxvi.	5
makes *a* the songs I made	" *Con.*	21
Shall I *a*, O Queen, at Camelot	*Elaine*	143
let *a* the brand of John	*Aylmer's F.*	509
a the work of mighty Gods	*Lucretius*	102
appear'd.		
blew and blew, but none *a*	*Princess*, v.	326
very graves *a* to smile	*The Letters*	45
work To both a so costly	*Enid*	638
now that shadow of mischance *a*	*En. Arden*	128
appearing.		
A ere the times were ripe	*In. Mem.Con.*	139
appeased.		
Gods, they must be *a*	*The Victim*	49
Appertain.		
a's to noble maintenance	*Enid*	712
appetite.		
never ate with angrier *a*	*Enid*	1082
applauded.		
mildly, that all hearts *A*	*Enid*	1806
applause.		
might reap the *a* of Great	*Princess*, iii.	245
he for whose *a* I strove	*In Mem.* l. .	5
and his comrades to *a*	*Enid*	1145
apple.		
full-juiced *a*, waxing over-mellow	*Lotos-E's.*	78
swung an *a* of the purest gold	*Enid*	170
apple-arbiter.		
beardless *a-a* Decided fairest	*Lucretius*	91
apple-blossom.		
Fresh *a-b*, blushing for a boon	*The Brook*	90
apple-cheek'd.		
bevy of Eroses *a-c*	*The Islet*	11
application.		
liberal *a*'s lie In Art	*Day-Dm.*	209
appraised.		
A the Lycian custom	*Princess*, ii.	112
A his weight, and fondled	*En. Arden*	154

	POEM.	LINE.
apprehend.		
thro' thick veils to *a*	*Two Voices*	296
approach (s.)		
less achievable By slow *a*'es	*Princess*, iii.	267
Preserve a broad *a* of fame	*Ode on Well.*	78
approach (verb.)		
let him presently *A*	*St.S.Stylites*	213
A and fear not	*Princess*, vii.	332
a To save the life despair'd of	*En. Arden*	831
approach'd.		
a Melissa, tinged with wan	*Princess*, iii.	8
as the great knight *A* them	*Elaine*	180
A him, and with full affection	"	1345
approaching.		
A, press'd you heart to heart	*Miller's D.*	160
A thro' the darkness, call'd	*Elaine*	994
approve.		
wishes me to *a* him	*Maud* I. xix.	71
approv'd.		
A him, bowing at their own deserts	*The Brook*	128
She wore the colours I *a*	*The Letters*	16
approven.		
by miracle was *a* king	*Guinevere*	294
approvingly.		
often talked of him *A*	*Aylmer's F.*	474
April (adj.)		
A nights began to blow	*Miller's D.*	106
A hopes, the fools of chance	*Vision of Sin*	164
clad her like an *A* daffodilly	*Princess*, ii.	39
trouble live with *A* days	*In Mem.*lxxxii.	7
all the years of *A* blood	" cviii.	12
regret Becomes an *A* violet	" cxiv.	19
For all an *A* morning	*Elaine*	893
April (s.)		
('Twas *A* then) I came and sat	*Miller's D.*	59
A's crescent glimmer'd cold	"	107
babe, a double *A* old	*Princess*, ii.	95
To rain an *A* of ovation	" vi.	50
From *A* on to *A* went	*In Mem.* xxii.	7
Make *A* of her tender eyes	" xxxix.	8
keenlier in sweet *A* wakes	" cxv.	2
May or *A*, he forgot, The last of *A*	*The Brook*	151
in *A* mournfully Breaks	*Enid*	338
balmier than half-opening buds of *A*	*Tithonus*	60
apt.		
supple, sinew-corded, *a* at arms	*Princess*,v.	524
a at arms and big of bone	*Enid*	489
Arab.		
delicate *A* arch of her feet	*Maud* I. xvi.	15
Arabian.		
nodding together In some *a* night	*Maud* I. vii.	12
Arac.		
Not ev'n her brother *A*	*Princess*, i.	152
rumour of Prince *A* hard at hand	" v.	108
speak with *A*: *A*'s word is thrice	"	217
midmost and the highest Was *A*	"	247
genial giant, *A*, roll'd himself	"	264
whereas I know Your prowess, *A*	"	394
those two bulks at *A*'s side	"	488
From *A*'s arm, from a giant's flail	"	489
but *A* rode him down	"	521
A, satiate with his victory	" vii.	75
Arbaces.		
A, and Phenomenon, and the rest	*The Brook*	162
arbour.		
read in *a*'s clipt and cut	*Amphion*	85
arbutus.		
there? yon a Totters	*Lucretius*	184
Arc v. Joan of *A*.		
arc (part of circle.)		
thro' a little *a* Of heaven	*To J. S.*	26
Bear had wheel'd Thro' a great *a*	*Princess*, iv.	195
sine and *a*, spheroïd and azimuth	" vi.	239
Run out your measured *a*'s	*In Mem.* civ.	27

	POEM.	LINE.		POEM.	LINE.
Arcady.			*a* in *a*, we went along	*Miller's D.*	163
To many a flute of *A*	*In Mem.* xxiii.	24	true heart thine *a's* entwine	"	216
arch (s.)			The kiss, The woven *a's*	"	232
Thro' little crystal *a'es* low	*Arabian N's.*	49	Puts forth an *a*, and creeps	*Œnone*	4
grots of *a'es* interlaced	*Pal of Art.*	51	Paris had raised his *a*	"	185
Many an *a* high up did lift	"	142	that my *a's* Were wound about thee	"	193
whirl'd in an *a*, Shot	*M. d'Arthur*	138	Sat smiling, babe in *a*	*Pal. of Art.*	96
to three *a'es* of a bridge	*Gardener's D.*	43	my *a* was lifted to hew down	*D. of F. Wom.*	45
Yet all experience is an *a*	*Ulysses*	19	humid *a's* festooning tree to tree	"	70
then we past an *a*	*Princess*, i.	206	mailed Bacchus leapt into my *a's*	"	151
under *a'es* of the marble bridge	" ii.	434	with one *a* about her king	"	270
delicate Arab *a* of her feet	*Maud* I. xvi.	15	held a goose upon his *a*	*The Goose.*	5
bloom profuse and cedar *a'es*	*Milton*	11	took the goose upon his *a*	"	41
archive.			one summer noon, an *a* Rose up	*M. d'Arthur*	29
of crimeful record all My mortal *a'es*	*St S. Stylites*	157	an *a* Clothed in white samite	"	143, 158
archway.			with pain, reclining on his *a*	"	168
Gleam thro' the Gothic *a's*	*Godiva*	64	One *a* aloft—Gown'd in pure white	*Gardener's D.*	124
shatter'd a plum'd with fern	*Enid*	316	in the circle of his *a's* Enwound us	"	211
Arden.			thrust him in the hollows of his *a*	*Dora*	129
Enoch *A*, a rough sailor's lad	*En. Arden.*	14	Francis, with a basket on his *a*	*Audley Ct.*	5
know Enoch *A* of this town?	"	846	folded in thy sister's *a*	"	62
You *A*, you! nay—sure	"	855	haply dream her *a* is mine	"	63
Proclaiming Enoch *A* and his woes	"	869	folded in Emilia's *a*	"	64
Eh, let me fetch 'em, *A*	"	872	in my weak lean *a's* I lift	*St S. Stylites*	116
argent (s.)			leg and *a* with love-knots gay	*Talking O.*	65
polish'd *a* of her breast	*D. of F. Wom.*	158	sank her head upon her *a*	"	207
argent-lidded.			close and dark my *a's* I spread	"	225
Serene with *a-l* eyes	*Arabian N's.*	135	Roll'd in one another's arms	*Locksley H.*	58
Argive.			each softly-shadow'd *a*	*Day-Dm.*	89
On *A* heights divinely sung	*In Mem.* xxiii.	22	on her lover's *a* she leant	"	165
argosy.			*a's* across her breast she laid	*Beggar Maid*	1
argosies of magic sails	*Locksley H.*	121	her *a* lifted, eyes on fire	*Princess, Pro.*	41
arguing.			long *a's* and hands Reach'd out	" i.	28
seem As *a* love of knowledge	*Princess*, ii.	43	lapt In the *a's* of leisure	" ii.	152
A boundless forbearance	*Aylmer's F.*	317	holding out her lily *a's*	"	283
argument.			Herself and Lady Psyche the two *a's*	" iii.	19
Half buried in some weightier *a*	*Lucretius*	9	Oaring one *a*, and bearing in my left	" iv.	165
arise.			drew My burthen from my *a's*	"	174
Come forth I charge thee, *a*	*Ode to Mem.*	46	A Niobëan daughter, one *a* out	"	352
when little airs *a*	*Adeline*	33	stretch'd her *a's* and call'd	"	475
feel the tears of blood *a*	*Oriana*	77	Arac's *a*, as from a giant's flail	" v.	489
Many suns *a* and set	*Miller's D.*	205	With Psyche's babe in *a*	" vi.	15
A, and let us wander forth	"	239	on every side A thousand *a's*	"	21
I will *a* and slay thee	*M. d'Arthur*	132	axe was broken in their *a's*	"	35
mighty wind *a's*, roaring seaward	*Locksley H.*	194	*a's* were shatter'd to the shoulder-		
when a fountain should *a*	*Vision of Sin*	8	blade	"	36
The thoughts that *a* in me	*'Break,' etc.*	4	with the babe yet in her *a's*	"	58
pillars of the hearth *A* to thee	*Princess*, vii.	202	reach its failing innocent *a's*	"	122
A, and get thee forth and seek	*In Mem.* lxxxiv.	79	in your own *a's* To hold your own	"	161
A and fly The reeling Faun	" cxvii.	25	*a* that dandled you	"	165
Morning *a's* stormy and pale	*Maud* I. vi.	1	from mine *a's* she rose Glowing	" vii.	144
ah for a man to *a* in me	" x.	67	moves his doubtful *a's*	*In Mem.* xiii.	3
A, my God, and strike	" II. i.	45	Science reaches forth her *a's*	" xxi.	18
war would *a* in defence of the right	" III. vi.	19	dark *a's* about the field	" xciv. 16,	52
dreary phantom *a* and fly	"	36	mix in one another's arms	" ci.	23
lord *a* and look upon me	*Enid*	1498	watch'd her on her nurse's *a*	*Concl.*	46
yonder man upon the bier *a*	"	1505	find the *a's* of my true love	*Maud.* II. iv.	3
my dear lord *a* and bid me do it	"	1513	rush'd into each other's *a's*	*The Letters*	63
himself *a* a living man	"	1554	dear a life your *a's* enfold	*The Daisy*	93
yearning for thy yoke, *a*	*Tithonus*	40	*a's* on which the standing muscle	*Enid*	76
arisen.			breast and all-puissant *a's*	"	86
mountains have *a* since	*Vivien*	525	folded more in these dear *a's*	"	99
arising.			gray walls with hairy-fibred *a's*	"	323
at Bible meetings, o'er the rest *A*	*Sea-Dreams*	191	by the length of lance and *a*	"	1312
aristocrat.			woven paces, and with waving *a's*	*Vivien*	56
what care I, *A*, democrat	*Maud*, I. x.	65	curved an *a* about his neck	"	90
ark.			lithe *a* round his neck Tighten	"	464
sought'st to wreck my mortal *a*	*Two Voices*	389	wizard cast a shielding *a*	"	757
leave this mortal *a* behind	*In Mem.* xii.	6	Her *a's* upon her breast across	"	759
arm.			to make *A's* for his chair	*Elaine*	437
with a sweeping of the *a*	*A Character*	16	battle-writhen *a's* and mighty hands	"	808
her right *a* whirl'd	*The Poet*	54	innocently extending her white *a's*	"	928
sweet faces, rounded *a's*	*Sea Fairies*	3	armlet for the roundest *a* on earth	"	1177
Fold thine *a's*, turn to thy rest	*A Dirge*	3	an *a* to which the Queen's Is haggard	"	1220
A glowing *a*, a gleaming neck	*Miller's D.*	78	flung One *a* about his neck	"	1346
			often in her *a's* She bare me	"	1400
			milk-white *a's* and shadowy hair	*Guinevere*	413
			Sir Lancelot, my right *a*	"	426
			Then she stretch'd out her *a's*	"	620
			laid the feeble infant in his *a's*	*En. Arden.*	152

	POEM.	LINE.
strong *a's* about his drooping wife	En. Arden	227
rear'd his creasy *a's*	"	752
he spread his *a's* abroad	"	911
grove-like, each huge *a* a tree	Aylmer's F.	510
a's stretch'd as to grasp a flyer	"	588
sideways up he swung his *a's*	Sea-Dreams	24
waved my *a* to warn them	"	128
rais'd your *a*, you tumbled down	"	137
soft *a*, which, like the pliant bough	"	278
Jenny hung on his *a*	Grandmother	42
turn'd and claspt me in his *a's*	"	55
I wither slowly in thine *a's*	Tithonus	6
Mute with folded *a's* they waited	The Captain	39
cast her *a's* about the child	The Victim	33
stay'd his *a's* upon his knee	"	58
roll thy tender *a's* Round him	Lucretius	82

arm-chair.

father left his good *a-c*	Talking O.	103
small goodman Shrinks in his *a-c*	Princess, v.	444
When asleep in this *a-c*	Maud, I. vii.	4

armed.

a Her own fair head	Princess, Pro.	32
Sleep must lie down *a*	Maud, I. i.	41
wholly *a*, behind a rock	Enid	906
horsemen waiting, wholly *a*	"	970
each of them is wholly *a*	"	992
issuing *a* he found the host	"	1256
two stood *a*, and kept the door	Elaine	1240

armlet.

a for the roundest arm on earth	Elaine	1177
a for an arm to which the Queen's	"	1220

armour.

as he rode his *a* rung	L. of Shalott, iii.	17
mortal *a* that I wear	Sir Galahad	70
forefathers' arms and *a* hung	Princess, Pro.	24
Your very *a* hallow'd	" v.	403
When *a* clash'd or jingled	" vi.	343
who scour'd His master's *a*	Enid	258
will have his horse And *a*	"	912
possess your horse And *a*	"	924
three gay suits of *a*	" 944,	1030
suits Of *a* on their horses	"	946
heap'd The pieces of his *a*	"	1223
glimmer'd on his *a* in the room	"	1235
Five horses and their *a's*	"	1258
heart enough To bear his *a*	"	1339
Bled underneath his *a*	"	1351

armourer.

riding further past an *a's*	Enid	266
the *a* turning all amazed	"	283

armoury.

| from Jehovah's gorgeous *armouries* | Milton | 6 |

arms (weapons.)

a or power of brain, or birth	To the Queen	3
show it at a joust of *a*	M. d'Arthur	102
broke a close with force and *a*	Ed. Morris	131
forefathers' *a* and armour hung	Princess, Pro.	24
clash'd in *a*, By glimmering lanes	" v.	5
piled *a* and rough accoutrements	"	52
they clash'd their *a*	"	240
armies and the noise Of *a*	"	336
none to trust Since our *a* fail'd	"	417
sinew-corded, apt at *a*	"	524
whose *a* Championed our cause	" vi.	45
Roll of cannon and clash of *a*	Ode on Well.	116
a On loan, or else for pledge	Enid	219
a, *a*, *a* to fight my enemy?	"	282
A? truth! I know not	"	289
thought to find *A* in your town	"	418
know Where I can light on *a*	"	422
heard me praise Your feats of *a*	"	435
true heart,' replied Geraint, 'but *a*	"	474
A, indeed, but old And rusty	"	477
apt at *a* and big of bone	"	489
rusted *A* Were on his princely person	"	543
fight my way with gilded *a*	"	870
three goodly suits of *a*	"	973

	POEM.	LINE.
laden with jingling *a*	Enid	1037
A horse and *a* for guerdon	"	1067
a to guard his head and yours	"	1276
paid with horses and with *a*	"	1335
loosed the fastenings of his *a*	"	1360
grow In use of *a* and manhood	Elaine	65
while she watch'd their *a* far off	"	394
a low thunder of *a*	"	459
glittering in enamelled *a*	"	616

arms (ensigns armorial.)

painting on it fancied *a*	Vivien	324
guess'd a hidden meaning in his *a*	Elaine	17

arm's-length.

| costly fruit Out at *a-l* | Œnone | 134 |

army.

there was an army in the land	Princess, iv.	463
compassed by two *armies*	" v.	335
preach our poor little *a* down	Maud, I. x.	38
Charging an *a*, while	Lt. Brigade	30
councils thinn'd, And armies waned	Vivien	423

Arno.

| unfamiliar *A*, and the dome | The Brook | 189 |

Arnon.

| from Aroer On *A* unto Minneth | D. of F. Wom. | 239 |

Aroer.

| from *A* On Arnon unto Minneth | D. of F. Wom. | 238 |

arose.

a wind *a* And overhead	Œnone	96
a, and I releas'd The casement	Two Voices	403
rain had fallen, the Poet *a*	Poet's Song	1
wind *a* and rush'd upon the South	Princess, i.	96
a Once more thro' all her height	" vi.	143
sound of hoof And chariot	"	358
Star after star, *a* and fell	" vii.	35
on one side *a* The women up	"	107
four sweet years *a* and fell	In Mem. xxii.	3
at the last *a* the man	" cxvii.	12
could bear it no more, But *a*	Maud, I. iii.	10
Nor ever *a* from below	" II. ii.	36
not to die a listener, I *a*	The Brook	163
a, and raised Her mother too	Enid '.	535
a The cry of children	"	1812
with smiling face *a*	Elaine	551
a Eager to bring them down	En. Arden	872
a the labourers' homes	Aylmer's F.	147
footstool from before him, and *a*	"	327
thorpe and byre *a* in fire	The Victim	3

aroused.

So sleeping, so *a* from sleep	Day-Dm.	233
a Lancelot, who rushing outward	Guinevere	105
A the black republic on his elms	Aylmer's F.	529

arrange.

A the board and brim the glass	In Mem. cvi.	16
Dispute the claims, *a* the chances	To F. D. Maurice	31

arranged.

men and maids *A* a countrydance	Princess, Pro.	84
A the favor, and assumed the Prince	" iv.	579
a Her garden, sow'd her name	Aylmer's F.	87

arras (adj.)

| In Arthur's *a* hall at Camelot | Vivien | 99 |

arras (s.)

| hung with *a* green and blue | Pal. of Art. | 61 |

array (s.)

| of men that in battle *a* | Maud, I. v. | 8 |

array'd.

with her own white hands *A*	Enid	17
a herself therein	" 139,	849
Queen *a* me like the Sun	"	1549

arraying.

| morn by morn, *a* her sweet self | Elaine | 902 |

arrival.

| will harangue The fresh *a's* | Princess, ii. | 82 |

arrive.

| *A* at last the blessed goal | In Mem. lxxxiii. | 41 |

	POEM.	LINE.
arrived.		
A, and found the sun of sweet content	The Brook	168
arriving.		
A all confused among the rest	Princess, iv.	205
arrow.		
The viewless *a*'s of his thoughts	The Poet	11
bitter *a* went aside, (rep.)	Oriana	37
damned *a* glanced aside,	"	41
Within thy heart my *a* lies,	"	80
into the dark *A*'s of lightnings.	To J. M. K.	14
A random *a* from the brain.	Two Voices	345
Fly twanging headless *a*'s	Princess, ii.	380
one would aim an *a* fair,	In Mem. lxxxvi.	25
into silver *a*'s break	" c.	15
Before an ever-fancied *a*,	Enid	1380
look'd a flight of fairy *a*'s	Aylmer's F.	94
arrow-seed.		
a-s's of the field flower,	The Poet	19
arrow-slain.		
loss of half his people *a-s;*	Vivien	415
arrow-wounded.		
your *a-w* fawn Came flying	Princess, ii.	251
arsenic.		
A, a, sure, would do it,	Maud, II. v.	62
art.		
discovery And newness of thine *a*	Ode to Mem.	88
knowledge of his *a* Held me	D. of F. Wom.	9
words, tho' cull'd with choicest *a*,	"	285
I and he, Brothers in *A*;	Gardener's D.	4
will you climb the top of *A*.	"	165
liberal applications lie In *A*.	Day-Dm.	210
in clubs, of *a*, of politics	Princess, Pro.	160
in *a*'s of government Elizabeth	" ii.	145
a's of war The peasant Joan.	"	146
a's of grace Sappho	"	147
inmost terms Of *a* and science:	"	424
A And Science, Caryatids	" iv.	182
owning but a little *a*	In Mem. xxxvii.	14
From *a*, from nature, from the schools	" xlviii.	1
on mind and *a*, And labour	" lxxxvi.	22
The graceful tact, the Christian *a*;	" cix.	16
all, as in some piece of *a*	" cxxvii.	6
dear to Science, dear to *A*	Idylls, Ded.	39
knew the range of all their *a*'s,	Vivien	23
seem the Master of all *A*,	"	318
Her *a*, her hand, her counsel	Aylmer's F.	151
piece of inmost Horticultural *a*,	Hendecasyllabics	20
Hetairai, curious in their *a*,	Lucretius	52
Artemesia.		
Carian *A* strong in war,	Princess, ii.	67
Arthur.		
burnt His Epic, his King *A*.	The Epic	28
King *A*'s table, man by man	M. d'Arthur	3
about their Lord, King *A*.	"	5
'King *A*'s sword, Excalibur	"	103
King *A* panted hard	"	176
that *A* who, with lance in rest	"	222
my Lord *A*, whither shall I go?	"	227
sail with *A* under looming shores,	" Ep.	17
King *A*, like a modern gentleman	"	22
cried '*A* is come again:	"	24
my lost *A*'s loved remains,	In Mem. ix.	3
My *A*, whom I shall not see	"	17
holy Death ere *A* died .	" lxxix.	1
My *A* found your shadows fair	" lxxxviii.	6
To show Sir *A*'s deer	The Brook	133
Geraint, a knight of *A*'s court	Enid	1
some gay knight in *A*'s hall	"	118
A on the Whitsuntide before	"	145
Cavall, King *A*'s hound	"	186
eat in *A*'s hall at Camelot	"	432
Shalt ride to *A*'s court,	"	582
rising up, he rode to *A*'s court	"	591
Of Modred, *A*'s nephew	"	595
A knight of *A*'s court	"	1623
knight of *A*'s Table Round	"	1641

	POEM.	LINE.
will not go to *A* Then will *A* come	Enid	1663
With *A* to Caerleon upon Usk	"	1794
Vivien stole from *A*'s court	Vivien	6
A walking all alone, Vext	"	9
leaving *A*'s court he gain'd	"	46
In *A*'s arras hall at Camelot	"	99
rose and fled from *A*'s court	"	146
complexities of *A*'s palace	"	583
the royal rose In *A*'s casement	"	590
A, blameless King and stainless man?'	"	628
jousts, Which *A* had ordain'd	Elaine	32
A, when none knew from whence	"	34
A came, and labouring up the pass	"	48
A, holding then his court	"	75
Has *A* spoken aught?	"	118
A, my lord, *A*, the faultless King	"	122
I am yours Not *A*'s	"	136
who eat in *A*'s halls	"	184
Known am I, and of *A*'s hall	"	188
our good *A* broke The Pagan	"	279
having been With *A* in the fight	"	287
where he sat At *A*'s right	"	551
A to the banquet, dark in mood	"	563
'our true *A*, when he learns	"	584
A's wars were render'd mystically	"	797
A's palace toward the stream	"	1172
as *A*'s queen I move and rule	"	1215
some do hold our *A* cannot die	"	1251
A bad the meek Sir Percivale	"	1257
A spied the letter in her hand	"	1263
My lord liege *A*, and all ye	"	1282
A answer'd 'O my knight	"	1316
A leading, slowly went The marshall'd	"	1321
Then *A* spake among them	"	1329
A, who beheld his cloudy brows	"	1344
Alas for *A*'s greatest knight	"	1409
a man Not after *A*'s heart	"	1410
in the Table Round Of *A*	Guinevere	19
knight of *A*'s noblest dealt in scorn	"	41
Which good King *A* founded	"	219
the bard Sang *A*'s glorious wars	"	284
And that was *A*	"	293
lead her to his lord, *A*	"	381
The silk pavilions of King *A*	"	391
think How sad it were for *A*	"	492
'Oh *A* !' there her voice brake	"	601
artist.		
hast thou done, great *a* Memory	Ode to Mem.	80
A more ideal *A* he than all	Gardener's D.	25, 169
golden moods Of sovereign *a*	Princess, v.	187
an unknown *a*'s orphan child	Sea Dreams	2
Artist-like.		
A-l, Ever retiring thou dost gaze	Ode to Mem.	92
Ascalon.		
was old Sir Ralph's at *A*:	Princess, Pro.	26
ascend.		
Take wings of fancy, and *a*	In Mem. lxxv.	1
ascending.		
with the dawn *a* lets the day	Enid	1540
A tired, heavily slept till morn	En. Arden.	181
ascension.		
spheroid and azimuth, And right *a*	Princess, vi.	239
ash (tree).		
Young *a*'es pirouetted down	Amphion	27
Delaying as the tender *a* delays	Princess, iv.	88
hoary knoll of *a* and haw	In Mem. xcix.	9
ashamed.		
believe him *a* to be seen?	Maud, I. xiii.	25
A am I that I should tell it thee	Enid	577
ashbud.		
a's in the front of March.'	Gardener's D.	28
ashen-gray.		
seems But an *a-g* delight.	Maud, I. vi.	22
ashes.		
heap their *a* on the head 'Love thou thy land,' etc.		70
will not let his *a* rest! 'You might have won,' etc.		28

	POEM.	LINE.
from his *a* may be made	In Mem. xviii.	3
dust and *a* all that is	" xxxiv.	4
who knows? We are *a* and dust	Maud, I. i.	32
A to *a*, dust to dust;	Ode on Well.	270
youth gone out Had left in a	Vivien	95
Slipt into *a* and was found no more	Alymer's F.	6
And all I was, in *a*	Tithonus	23

ashy.

quivering brine With *a* rains	The Voyage	43

ask.

a her if she love me	Lilian	3
a thou not my name	D. of F. Wom.	93
a me, why, tho' ill at ease 'You ask me why,' etc.		1
has a mint of reasons; *a*	The Epic	33
A's what thou lackest	Two Voices	98
Sheba came to *a* of Solomon.'	Princess, ii.	325
you should answer, we would *a*	"	332
'O *a* me nothing,' I said	" iii.	43
a for him Of your great head	" vi.	293
A me no more (rep.)	"	364
would but *a* you to fulfil yourself.	" vii.	131
I *a* you nothing, only if a dream	"	133
a a thousand things of home	In Mem. xiv.	12
a me how it came to pass	Maud, I. xviii.	49
one should *a* me whether	" xx.	17
I will not *a* thee why (rep.)	" II. iii.	2
to *a* her, 'take me, sweet	" iv.	87
I charge you, *a* not but obey	Enid	133
'Then will I *a* it of himself	"	197
will not *a* your meaning in it	"	1591
silent then And *a* no kiss	Vivien	103
a your boon, for boon I owe you	"	155
wherefore *a*; And take this boon.	"	158
never *a* some other boon?	"	225
feels no heart to *a* another boon	"	232
has tript a little; *a* yourself.	"	452
never could undo it; *a* no more	"	536
I *a* you, is it clamour'd	"	621
for the diamond, *a* me not	Elaine	191
a you not to see the shield	"	650
should *a* some goodly gift of him	"	908
yield me sanctuary, nor *a*	Guinevere	140
they spared To *a* it	"	144
pray you check me if I *a* amiss	"	322
came to *a* a favour of you.'	En. Ard.	284
favour that I came to *a*	"	312
what is it that you *a*?	"	424
then to *a* her of my shares	Sea Dreams	111
A her to marry me by and by?	The Window	91

asked.

I *a* him, and he said	Dora	142
once I *a* him of his early life	Ed. Morris	23
I *a* him half-sardonically	"	59
her we *a* of that and this	Princess i.	228
when I *a* her 'how'	" iii.	13
mutual pardon *a* and given	" v.	44
a but space and fairplay	"	272
again The 'wilt thou' *a*	In Mem. Con.	55
whatever is *a* her, answers	Maud, I. i.	4
a If James were coming	The Brook	105
what the price he *a*	"	142
to the dwarf, and *a* it of him	Enid	199
after madness acted question *a*	"	1661
a her not a word, But went apart.	"	1728
a this very boon, Now *a* again	Vivien	172
died Thrice than have *a* it once	"	768
proof of trust—so often *a* in vain	"	769
a of court and Table Round.	Elaine	268
would if *a* deny it.	En. Arden	44
her strength, and *a* her of it.	Sea Dreams	109
a; but not a word	"	112
a That which I *a* the woman	"	142
if *a* to her face, Might say no	The Window	96

askew.

all his conscience and one eye *a* (rep.)	Sea Dreams	176

asking.

therefore at your *a*, yours	Enid	479

	POEM.	LINE.
not so strange as my long *a* it	Vivien	161
braved *a* riotous heart in *a* for it	Elaine	358
Not *a* overmuch and taking less	En. Arden	251
grant mine *a* with a smile	Tithonus	16

asleep.

smiling *a*, Slowly awaken'd	Eleänore	84
I fall *a* at morn	May Queen ii.	50
Falling *a* in a half-dream!	Lotos-E's	101
that dear soul hath fall'n *a*	To. J S.	34
fall *a* with all one's friends	Day-Dm.	216
when faith had fall'n *a*	In Mem. cxxiii.	9
When *a* in this arm chair?	Maud, I. vii.	4
come to her waking, find her *a*	" II. ii.	81
half *a* she made comparison	Enid	651
fell *a* again; And dreamt herself	"	653
fell *a*, and Enid had no heart	"	1228
not seem as dead But fast *a*	Elaine	1155

Asmodeus.

Abaddon and A caught at me	St S. Stylites	169

Aspasia.

not for all A's cleverness	Princess, ii.	323

aspect.

pensive thought and *a* pale	Margaret	6
More bounteous *a*'s on me beam	Sir Galahad	21

aspen.

Willows whiten, *a*'s quiver	L. of Shalott, i.	10
here thine *a* shiver	A Farewell	10

aspen-tree.

in the meadows tremulous *a-t*'s	Elaine	409
showers, And ever-tremulous *a-t*'s	"	523

asphodel.

Violet, amaracus, and *a*	Œnone	95
weary limbs at last on beds of *a*	Lotos-E's	170

aspick.

Showing the *a*'s bite	D. of F. Wom.	160

ass.

whisper'd 'A*es*' ears' among the sedge	Princess, ii.	98

assail.

a this gray preëminence of man!	Princess, iii.	218

assail'd.

They that *a*, and they that held	Elaine	454

assassin.

earls, and caitiff knights, A's	Enid	36

assay.

A it on some one of the Table Round	Vivien	539

Assaye.

Against the myriads of A	Ode on Well.	99

assemble.

plans And phantom hopes *a*	Will Water.	30

assembled.

in to where they sat *a*	Vision of Sin	16

assent.

I gave *a*: Yet how to bind	Princess, Con.	7

assented.

Enoch all at once *a* to it	En. Arden	126

assert.

a None lordlier than themselves	Princess, ii.	127
a's his claim In that dread sound	Ode on Well.	70

assigned.

purpose of God and the doom *a*	Maud, III. vi.	59
quest A to her not worthy of it	Elaine	822
kiss the child That does the task *a*,	"	825

association.

A fresh *a* blow	In Mem. c.	18

assume.

lose the child, *a* The woman	Princess, ii.	135

assumed.

Arrang'd the favour and *a* the Prince	Princess, iv.	584
A from thence a half consent	" vii.	67
A that she had thank'd him	Enid	1496

	POEM.	LINE.
assumption.		
heart In its *a's* up to heaven	*In Mem.* lxii.	4
assurance.		
A only breeds resolve.'	*Two Voices*	315
assure.		
may now *a* you mine	*Vivien*	399
Assyrian.		
oil'd and curl'd *A* Bull	*Maud,* I. vi.	44
Astolat (see *Lord of A, Maid of A.*)		
Ran to the castle of *A*	*Elaine*	167
Came at last, tho' late, to *A*	"	615
far away the maid in *A*	"	741
To *A* returning rode the three	"	901
that day there was dole in *A*	"	1130
Astræan.		
second-sight of some *A* age	*Princess,* ii.	420
astrology.		
brought to understand A sad *a*	*Maud,* xviii.	36
a-taäkin'.		
what a's doing *a* o' meä?	*N. Farmer*	45
ate.		
let the horses graze, and *a*	*Enid*	1060
Geraint *A* all the mowers' victual	"	1064
never *a* with angrier appetite	"	1082
a with tumult in the naked hall	"	1453
ever among ladies *a* in Hall	*Elaine*	255
athlete.		
Until she be an *a* bold '*Clear-headed friend,*' etc.	21	
an *a*, strong to break or bind	*Pal. of Art*	153
Athos.		
Tomohrit, *A*, all things fair	*To E. L.*	5
Atlantic.		
wish they were a whole *A* broad.'	*Princess, Con.*	71
atmosphere.		
Floating thro' an evening *a*	*Eleänore*	100
love possess'd the *a*	*Miller's D.*	91
Cold in that *a* of Death	*In Mem.* xx.	14
atom.		
If all be *a's*, how then should the Gods	*Lucretius*	114
Vanishing *a* and void, *a* and void	"	254
atomic.		
Being *a* not be dissoluble	*Lucretius*	115
atom-stream.		
I saw the flaring *a-s's*	*Lucretius*	38
atonement.		
shine So rich in *a* as this	*Maud,* I. xix.	6
attain.		
A the wise indifference of the wise	*A Dedication*	8
attain'd.		
have *a* Rest in a happy place	*Œnone*	128
attempt.		
Vivien should *a* the blameless King	*Vivien*	20
attend.		
each ear was prick'd to *a*	*Princess,* vi.	263
in his presence I *a*	*In Mem.* cxxv.	2
attendance.		
make her dance *a*	*Amphion*	62
with no *a*, page or maid	*Enid*	1171
attended.		
So she goes by him *a*	*L. of Burleigh*	25
attest.		
A their great commander's claim	*Ode on Well.*	148
attic.		
round the *a's* rumbled	*The Goose*	46
attire.		
in her poor *a* was seen	*Beggar Maid*	10
splendid in his acts and his *a*	*Enid*	620
attired.		
women who *a* her head	*Enid*	62
Geraint to greet her thus *a*	"	772

	POEM.	LINE.
attribute.		
crown'd with *a's* of woe	*In Mem.* cxvii.	18
all the gentle *a's* Of his lost child	*Aylmer's F.*	730
Aubrey.		
Ellen *A*, sleep, and dream of me	*Audley Ct.*	61
Ellen *A*, love, and dream of me	"	72
audibly.		
Half inwardly, half *a* she spoke	*Enid*	109
audience.		
at the palace craved *A* of Guinevere	*Elaine*	1157
Audley.		
picnic there At *A* Court.'	*Audley Ct.*	3
A feast Humm'd like a hive	"	3
auger.		
hammer and axe, *A* and saw	*En. Arden*	174
aught.		
I would not *a* of false	*Princess,* v.	392
Unfaith in *a* is want of faith in all	*Vivien*	239
augur-hole.		
Boring a little *a-h* in fear	*Godiva*	68
augury.		
light upon *auguries* happier?	*Boädicea*	45
aunt.		
maiden *A* Took this fair day	*Princess, Pro.*	107
the maiden *A* (A little sense of wrong	"	212
A showery glance upon her *a*	" Con.	33
Aurelian.		
the Palmyrene That fought *A*	*Princess,* ii.	70
Ausonian.		
stay'd the *A* king to hear	*Pal. of Art*	111
austerely.		
took Small notice, or *a*	*Lucretius*	8
Australasian.		
the long wash of *A* seas	*The Brook*	194
authority.		
A forgets a dying king	*M. d'Arthur*	121
some one with *a* Be near her	*Princess,* vi.	219
All people said she had *a*	"	221
autocrat.		
Aristocrat, democrat, *a*	*Maud,* I. x.	65
autumn (s.)		
A, in a bower Grape-thicken'd	*Eleänore*	35
A brought an hour For Eustace	*Gardener's D.*	202
A, dropping fruits of power;	*Princess,* vi.	39
A, with a noise of rooks	*In Mem.* lxxxiv.	71
A, laying here and there *A* fiery	" xcviii.	11
a into *a* flash'd again	*En. Arden*	453
with the traveller's-joy In *A*	*Aylmer's F.*	154
A's smock sunshine of the faded woods	"	610
after *A* past—if left to pass His *a*	*A Dedication*	9
autumn-fields.		
looking on the happy *A-f*	*Princess,* iv.	24
autumn-sheaf.		
Than of the garner'd *A-s*	*Two Voices*	114
avail (s.)		
I count it of no more *a*	*Enid*	1563
avail (verb.)		
Let this *a*, just, dreadful	*St S. Stylites*	9
branding summer suns *a*	*In Mem.* ii.	11
Avalon.		
dozing in the vale of *A*	*Pal of Art*	107
avarice.		
Down with ambition, *a*, pride	*Maud,* I. x.	47
evil tyrannies, all her pitiless *a*	*Boädicea*	80
No madness of ambition, *a*	*Lucretius*	209
Ave.		
'*A* Mary' made her moan (rep.)	*Mariana in the S.*	9
'*A, A, A*,' said, 'Adieu, adieu'	*In Mem.* lvi.	15

avenge.

Peace! there are those to *a* us . *Princess*, iv. 480
will *a* this insult, noble Queen . *Enid* . . 215

avenged.

crime Of sense *a* by sense . . *Vision of Sin* 214

avenging.

learn his name, A this great insult *Enid* . . 425

avenue.

ever-echoing *a's* of song . . *Ode on Well.* 79
city glitter'd, Thro' cypress *a's* . *The Daisy* . 48
at the far end of an *a* . . *En. Arden* . 355

aver.

a That all thy motions . . *In Mem.* xv. 9
clasping brother-hands, *a* . . " lxxxiv. 102

Averill.

A, A at the Rectory Thrice over . *Aylmer's F.* 37
might not A, had he will'd it so . " . 46
'Some other race of *A's*' . . " . 54
his brother, living oft With A . " . 58
A was a decad and a half His elder " . 82
He wasted hours with A . . " . 109
oft accompanied By A . . " . 138
let that handsome fellow A walk . " . 269
his heart at *A's* ear: Whom A solaced " . 342
A seeing How low his brother's mood " . 403
Forbad her first the house of A . " . 502
A wrote And bad him with good heart " . 543
A went and gazed upon his death " . 599
Long o'er his bent brows linger'd A " . 625

averring.

A it was clear against all rules . *Princess*, i. . 176

averse.

with sick and scornful looks *a* . *D. of F. Wom.* 101

Avilion.

To the island-valley of A . . *M. d'Arthur* 259

await.

strength *a's* Completion '*Love thou thy land*,' etc. 57
draught of Lethe might *a* . . *Two Voices* 350
for all the vales A thee . . *Princess*, vii. 201
happier hours A them . . *In Mem. Con.* 66
Yea, let all good things *a* . *Ode on Well.* 198

awaiting.

Beheld her first in field, *a* him . *Enid* . . 540

awake (adj.)

All night I lie *a* . . . *May Queen*, ii. 50
lying broad *a* I thought of you . " iii. 29
deep-asleep he seem'd, yet all *a* . *Lotos-E's.* . 58
might kiss those eyes *a*! . *Day-Dm.* . 240
I have walked *a* with Truth . *Maud*, I. xix. 4
rose was *a* all night for your sake . " xxii. 49
lilies and roses were all *a* . . " . 51
watch'd *a* A cypress . . *The Daisy* 81
shook his drowsy squire *a* . *Enid* . . 125
grasping her To get her well *a* . " . 677
Held her *a* : or if she slept . *Guinevere* . 75

awake (verb.)

bee Is lily-cradled: I alone *a* . *Œnone* . 29
a her with the gleam . . *Elaine* . 6

awaked.

myself have *a*, as it seems . *Maud*, III. vi. 56

awakened.

Slowly *a*, grow so full and deep . *Eleänore* . 85

award.

would seem to *a* it thine . *Œnone* . 71

aware.

was *a* of three tall knights . *Enid* . . 905
she by tact of love was well *a* . *Elaine* . 978
a lingering—ere she was *a* . . *En. Arden* 267

awe.

hold a fretful realm in *a* . . *Locksley H.* 129
springs of life, the depths of *a* . *Two Voices* 140
beat thick with passion and with *a*. *Princess*, iii. 174

feel once more, in placid *a* . *In Mem.* cxxi. 5
all in *a* For twenty strokes . *Elaine* . 715
kiss'd her feet For loyal *a* . " 1167

aweary.

She said 'I am *a* (rep.) . . *Mariana* . 11
I am all *a* of my life . . *Œnone* . 32

awed.

a and promise-bounden she forbore *En. Arden* 870
Still It *a* me.' . . . *Sea Dreams* 200
And my dream *a* me :— . . " 239

awe-stricken.

hold *A*-s breath, at a work divine . *Maud*, I. x. 17

awful.

all she is and does is *a* . . *Princess*, i. 139

awning.

ample *a's* gay Betwixt the pillars . *Princess*, ii. 11

awoke.

with these the king *a* . . *Day-Dm.* . 149
a in the heart of the child . *Maud*, I. xix. 48
a him, and by great mischance . *Enid* . . 112
Refused her to him, then his pride *a* " . 448
strongly striking out her limbs *a* . " . 1230
flickering in my eyes A me.' . *Sea Dreams* 101

axe.

ere the falling *a* did part . *Margaret* . 38
lift His *a* to slay my kin . *Talking O.* 236
Nor wielded *a* disjoint . . " . 262
The woodmen with their *a's* . *Princess*, vi. 28
The glittering *a* was broken . " . 35
by *a* and eagle sat . . " vii. 113
hammer and *a*, Auger and saw . *En. Arden* 173

axelike.

That *a* edge unturnable . . *Princess*, ii. 186

Aylmer.

So Lawrence A, seated on a style *The Brook* . 197
Sir A A that almighty man . *Aylmer's F.* 13
A followed A at the Hall . . " . 36
like an A in his Aylmerism . . " . 123
Sir A half forgot his lazy smile . " . 197
Sir A past And neither loved . " . 249
did A know The great pock-pitten " . 256
had Sir A heard—Nay but he must " . 261
did Sir A (deferentially . . " . 266
Sir A A slowly stiffening spoke . " . 273
parted, and Sir A A watched . " . 277
Things in an A deem'd impossible " . 305
Sir A reddening from the storm within " . 322
To shame these mouldy *A's*. . " . 396
when *this* A came of age— . . " . 407
Sir A watch'd them all . . " . 552
with her the race of A, past . . " . 577

Aylmer-Averill.

There was an A-A marriage once *Aylmer's F.* 49

Aylmerism.

like an Aylmer in his A . *Aylmer's F.* 123

azimuth.

sine and arc, spheroïd and *a* . *Princess*, vi. 239

azure.

Her eyes a bashful *a* . . *The Brook* . 71
stared On eyes a bashful *a* . " . 206
A, an Eagle rising or . . *Vivien* . 325

B

Baäl.

honour thy brute B . . *Aylmer's F.* 644
came a Lord in no wise like to B . " . 647

babble (s.)

b of the stream Fell . *Mariana in the S.* 51
night goes In *b* and revel and wine *Maud*, I. xxii. 28
But babble, merely for *b* . . II. v. 46
The babes, their *b*, Annie . *En. Arden.* 607

babble (verb.)

Howe'er you *b*, great deeds cannot *Princess*, iii. 237

	POEM.	LINE.
brook shall *b* down the plain .	*In Mem.* c.	10
b, merely for babble .	*Maud*, II. v.	46
I *b* on the pebbles .	*The Brook*	42
scoff and jeer and *b* of him	*Enid*	58
you dream they *b* of you	*Vivien*	540

babbled.

b for the golden seal	*Dora*	132
b for you, as babies for the moon	*Princess*, iv.	408
b 'Uncle' on my knee	*In Mem.* lxxxii.	13
moving homeward *b* to his men	*Enid*	1211
While thus they *b* of the King	*Elaine*	1253

babbler.

garrulously given, A *b* in the land.	*Talking Oak*	24
like many another *b*, hurt	*Guinevere*	352

babbling.

runlets *b* down the glen	*Mariana in the S.*	44
his wheat-suburb, *b* as he went	*The Brook*	123

babe.

Sat smiling, *b* in arm	*Pal. of Art*	96
maiden *b*, a double April old	*Princess*, ii.	95
come to his *b* in the nest	"	468
vassals to be beat, nor petty *b's*	" iv.	128
my *b*, my blossom, ah my child	" v.	79
My *b*, my sweet Aglaïa	"	98
With Psyche's *b*, was Ida watching	"	501
With Psyche's *b* in arm	" vi.	15
with the *b* yet in her arms	"	58
b that by us, Half-lapt in glowing	"	117
burst The laces toward her *b*	"	133
soft *b* in his hard-mailed hands	"	191
built upon the *b* restored	" vii.	60
bring her *b*, and make thy boast	*In Mem.*, xxxix.	26
youth and *b* and hoary hairs	" lxviii.	10
kills her *b* for a burial fee	*Maud*, I. i.	45
red man's *b* Leap, beyond the sea	" xvii.	19
poison our *b's*, poor souls !	" II. v.	63
As clean as blood of *b's*	*Vivien*	194
his wife And two fair *b's*	"	557
seven months' *b* had been a truer gift	"	561
With his first *b's* first cry	*En. Arden*	85
a blessing on his wife and *b's*	"	188
be comforted, Look to the *b's*	"	219
give his *b's* a better bringing up	"	298
know his *b's* were running wild	"	303
gilded dragon, also, for the *b's*	"	536
The *b's*, their babble, Annie	"	607
lived and loved him, and his *b's*	"	686
rosy, with his *b* across his knees .	"	747
a ring To tempt the *b* .	"	752
glancing often toward her *b* .	"	755
the *b* Hers, yet not his .	"	760
shall see him, My *b* in bliss .	"	899
The *b* shall lead the lion	*Aylmer's F.*	648
the *b* Too ragged to be fondled	"	685
One *b* was theirs, a Margaret	*Sea Dreams*	3
the *b*, Their Margaret cradled near	"	56
a leg for a *b* of a week!'	*Grandmother*	11
b had fought for his life .	"	64
little *b's* about thy knee	'Lady, let the rolling,' etc.	6

babe-faced.

| He came with the *b-f* lord | *Maud*, II. i. | 13 |

Babel.

| let be Their cancell'd *B's* . | *Princess*, iv. | 59 |
| As of a new-world *B* | " | 466 |

baby (s.)

in her bosom bore the *b* Sleep	*Gardener's D.*	263
ruthless as a *b* with a worm .	*Walk. to the M.*	98
babies roll'd about Like tumbled fruit	*Princess, Pro.*	83
babbled for you, as babies for the moon	" iv.	408
The *b* new to earth and sky .	*In Mem.*, xlv.	1
lightly rocking *b's* cradle	*En. Arden*	194
from her *b's* forehead clipt	"	234
Her *b's* death, her growing poverty	"	706
What does little *b* say 'rep.)	*Sea Dreams*	289
knew them all as babies	*Grandmother*	88

baby-germ.

| gambol'd on the greens A *b-g* | *Talking O.* | 73 |

	POEM.	LINE.
b's, and dear diminutives .	*Aylmer's F.*	539

Babylon.

| *B* be cast into the sea . | *Sea Dreams* | 28 |

Babylonian.

| foundress of the *B* wall . | *Princess*, ii. | 66 |

baby-oak.

| magnetise The *b-o* within . | *Talking O.* | 256 |

baby-rose.

| dimple The *b-r's* in her cheeks . | *Lilian* | 17 |

baby-sole.

| tender pink five-beaded *b-s's* . | *Aylmer's F.* | 186 |

Bacchus.

| mailed *B* leapt into my arms . | *D. of F. Wom.* | 151 |

back (s.)

undress'd goatskin on my *b* .	*St S. Stylites*	114
How she mouths behind my *b*	*Vision of Sin*	110
my father's clamour at our *b's*	*Princess*, i.	104
Her *b* against a pillar .	" iii.	164
daily burden for the *b* .	*In Mem.* xxv.	4
b turn'd, and bow'd above his work	*Enid*	267
the brutes of mountain *b*	*Vivien*	426
long *b's* of the bushless downs	*Elaine*	399, 785
rascal in the motions of his *b*	*Sea Dreams*	163

backbiter.

| Face-flatterers and *b's* are the same | *Vivien* | 673 |

bad (adj.)

fear to slide from *b* to worse .	*Two Voices*	231
O base and *b* ! what comfort ?	*Princess*, v.	75
My dreams are *b* .	*Maud*, I. i.	73
here beneath it is all as *b*	" II. v.	14
She wur a *b* un, she is	*N. Farmer*	22

bad (pret. of bid.)

do the thing I *b* thee	*M. d'Arthur*	81
b you guard the sacred coasts	*Ode on Well.*	172
b the host Call in what men .	*Enid*	1134
Prince *b* him a loud good-night	"	1210
Nor waved his hand, Nor *b* farewell	*Elaine*	981
b a thousand farewells to me .	"	1051
coldly went nor *b* me one	"	1051
Arthur *b* the meek Sir Percivale	"	1257
left her and I *b* her no farewell	"	1296
b him with good heart sustain	*Aylmer's F.*	544

bade (pret. of bid.)

I made a feast: I *b* him come	*The Sisters*	13
utter'd it, And *b* adieu for ever	*Love and Duty*	81
b him cry, with sound of trumpet	*Godiva*	36
Thro' which he *b* her lead .	*Enid*	878
gown he *b* me clothe myself .	"	1550

Badon.

| yet once more on *B* hill . | *Elaine* | 280 |
| on the mount Of *B* . | " | 303 |

baffling.

| Then *b*, a long course of them | *En. Arden* | 542 |
| blown by *b* winds . | " | 629 |

bag.

| not dip His hand into the *b* . | *Golden Year* | 71 |
| With *b* and sack and basket . | *En. Arden* | 63 |

Bagdat.

| By *B's* shrines of fretted gold | *Arabian N's.* | 7 |
| domes aloof In inmost *B* . | " | 123 |

bailiff.

his *b* brought A Chartist pike	*Walk. to the M.*	62
how he sent the *b* to the farm	*The Brook*	141
b swore that he was mad .	"	143
met the *b* at the Golden Fleece	"	146
found the *b* riding by the farm	"	153

bairn.

| See your *b's* before you go ! . | *En. Arden* | 871 |

bait.

| the *b's* Of gold and beauty . | *Aylmer's F.* | 486 |
| Christ the *b* to trap his dupe . | *Sea Dreams* | 187 |

B

CONCORDANCE TO

bake.
	POEM.	LINE.
whose brain the sunshine *b's*	St S. Stylites	161

Bala.
| south-west that blowing *B* lake | Enid | 1777 |

balance (equipoise.)
| As the wind-hover hangs in *b* | Aylmer's F. | 321 |

balance (verb.)
| would cast and *b* at a desk | Audley Ct. | 43 |
| souls that *b* joy and pain | Sir L. and Q. G. | 1 |

balanced.
| Your fortunes, justlier *b* | Princess, ii. | 52 |
| Well, she *b* this a little | " iii. | 149 |

balcony.
| Under tower and *b* | L. of Shalott, iv. | 37 |
| lean'd upon the *b* | Mariana in the S. | 88 |

baldness.
| wag their *b* up and down | Princess, v. | 18 |

baldric.
| from his blazon'd *b* slung | L. of Shalott, iii. | 15 |

bale.
| dropping down with costly *b's* | Locksley H. | 122 |
| tho' they brought but merchants' *b's* | In Mem. xiii. | 19 |

balk'd.
| with a worm I *b* his fame | D. of F. Wom. | 155 |

ball.
No compound of this earthly *b*	Two Voices	35
Is to be the *b* of time	Vision of Sin	105
whereon the gilded *b* Danced	Princess, Pro.	63
Flung A *b* to the brightening moon	" ii.	230
tost a *b* Above the fountain-jets	"	436
Quoit, tennis, *b*—no games?	" ii.	199
him who grasps a golden *b*	In Mem. cx.	3
The day comes, a dull red *b*	Maud, II. iv.	65
like a *b* The russet-bearded head	Enid	1576
tost his *b* and flown his kite	Aylmer's F.	84

ballad.
From time to time, some *b*	Princess, Pro.	234
something in the *b's* which they sang	" Con.	14
flung A *b* to the brightening moon	In Mem. lxxxviii.	28
A passionate *b* gallant and gay	Maud, I. v.	4
To the *b* that she sings	" II. iv.	43
carolling as he went A true-love *b*	Elaine	701

ballad-burthen.
| Like *b-b* music, kept | The Daisy | 77 |

balm.
steep our brows in slumber's holy *b*	Lotos-E's	66
desires, like fitful blasts of *b*	Gardener's D.	67
spikenard, and *b*, and frankincense	St. S Stylites	208
caress The ringlet's waving *b*	Talking O.	178
Beat balm upon our eyelids	Princess, iii.	107

balm-cricket.
| The *b-c* carols clear | A Dirge | 47 |

balm-dew.
| drop *B-d's* to bathe thy feet! | Talking O. | 268 |

balmier.
| kisses *b* than half-opening buds | Tithonus | 59 |
| *B* and nobler from her bath of storm | Lucretius | 175 |

Baltic.
| side of the Black and the *B* deep | Maud, III. vi. | 51 |
| shaker of the *B* and the Nile | Ode on Well. | 137 |

baluster.
| leaning there on those *b's* | Princess, iii. | 103 |

balustrade.
| Ran up with golden *b* | Arabian N's. | 118 |

band (s. a tie.)
single *b* of gold about her hair	Princess, v.	502
No spirit ever brake the *b*	In Mem. xcii.	2
A *b* of pain across my brow	The Letters	6
bound her in her rosy *b*	Coquette, i.	6

band (a company.)
| held debate, a *b* Of youthful friends | In Mem. lxxxvi. | 21 |

bandage.
	POEM.	LINE.
in a dream from a *b* of the blest	Maud, III. vi.	10
we will have him of our *b*	Enid	1402

bandage.
| raised the blinding *b* from his eyes | Princess, i. | 240 |

bandied.
| *B* by the hands of fools | Vision of Sin | 106 |

bandit.
I saw three *b's* by the rock	Enid	921
thro' the bulky *b's* corselet	"	1008
now so long By *b's* groom'd	"	1042
half a *b* in my lawless hour	"	1643
the *b* scatter'd in the field	"	1666
redden'd with no *b's* blood	Aylmer's F.	597

bandit-haunted.
| past The marches, and by *b-h* holds | Enid | 879 |

bane.
| courtesies of household life Became her *b* | Guinevere | 87 |
| mockery of my people, and their *b* | " | 522 |

bang'd.
| palace *b*, and buzz'd and clackt | Day-Dm. | 146 |
| iron-clanging anvil *b* With hammers | Princess, v. | 494 |

bank.
cool soft turf upon the *b*	Arabian N's.	96
wave-worn horns of the echoing *b*	Dying Swan	39
From the *b* and from the river	L. of Shalott, iii.	33
broad stream in his *b's* complaining	" iv.	3
Shadow forth the *b's* at will	Eleänore	110
The little life of *b* and brier	{ 'You might have won,' etc.	30
group'd In the hollow *b*	Princess, iv.	173
shadowing bluff that made the *b's*	In Mem. cii.	22
Behind a purple-frosty *b*	" cvi.	2
Full to the *b's*, close on the	Maud, I. xviii.	6
With many a curve my *b's* I fret	The Brook	43
Parts from a *b* of snow	Enid	735
happily down on a *b* of grass	"	1356

banner.
droops the *b* on the tower	Day-Dm.	33
hedge broke in, the *b* blew	"	141
the maiden *b* of our rights	Princess, iv.	482
undulated The *b*	" v.	244
March with *b* and bugle and fife	Maud, I. v.	10
to the *b* of battle unroll'd!	" III. vi.	42
With *b* and with music	Ode on Well.	81

banquet.
baron at the *b* sleeps	Day-Dm.	57
with this our *b's* rang	Princess, i.	131
b in the distant woods	In Mem. lxxxviii.	32
flowers or leaves To deck the *b*	"	cvi. 6
Spice his fair *b*, with the dust	Maud, I. xviii.	56
made him leave The *b*	Elaine	561
Arthur to the *b*, dark in mood	"	563
knights at *b* twice or thrice	"	732
against the floor Beneath the *b*	"	739
from a binn reserved For *b's*	Aylmer's F.	406
distant blaze of those dull *b's*	"	489

banquet-hall.
| Into the fair Pelcian *b-h* | Œnone | 221 |

banter (s.)
| he spoke Part *b*, part affection | Princess, Pro. | 166 |
| hated *b*, wished for something real | " Con. | 18 |

banter (verb.)
| did Eustace *b* me | Gardener's D. | 164 |

banter'd.
| I *b* him, and swore They said | Golden Year | 8 |
| we *b* little Lilia first | Princess, Con. | 12 |

bantling.
| let the *b* scald at home | Princess, v. | 448 |
| Lo their precious Roman *b* | Boädicea | 31 |

bar (obstruction.)
| lock'd in with *b's* of sand | Pal. of Art | 249 |
| looking thro' his prison *b's*? | Margaret | 35 |

	POEM.	LINE.
stream'd thro' many a golden *b*	Day-Dm.	179
spirit beats her mortal *b's*	Sir Galahad	46
squeezed himself betwixt the *b's*	Princess, Pro.	112
breaks his birth's invidious *b*	In Mem. lxiii.	5
The *b* of Michael Angelo	" lxxxvi.	40
Unlov'd, by many a sandy *b*	"	c. 9
I linger by my shingly *b's*	The Brook	180
Low breezes fann'd the belfry *b's*	The Letters	43
yet had laid No *b* between them	Aylmer's F.	118
nor conscious of a *b* Between them	"	134

bar (tribunal.)

himself The prisoner at the *b*	Sea Dreams	172

bar (body of barristers.)

year or two before Call'd to the *b*	Aylmer's F.	59

bar (division of music.)

a random *b* of Bonny Doon	The Brook	82

bar (verb.)

b The secret bridal chambers	Gardener's D.	243
block and *b* Your heart with system	Princess, iv.	442

barbarian.

gray *b* lower than the Christian child	Locksley H.	174
such wild *b's*? Girls?	Princess, iii.	26
B's, grosser than your native bears	" iv.	516

barbarous.

These women were too *b*	Princess, ii.	278

bard.

b has honour'd beech or lime	Talking O.	291
B, and knew the starry heavens	Vivien	25
her *b*, her silver star of eve	"	803
many a *b*, without offence	Elaine	112
Yea, one, a *b*; of whom	Guinevere	275
the *b* sang Arthur's glorious wars	"	283
O foolish *b*, is your lot so hard	Spiteful Let.	5

bare (adj.)

plain was grassy, wild and *b*.	Dying Swan	1
God, before whom ever lie *b*	Pal. of Art.	222
breast to sight Laid *b*	D. of F. Wom.	159
walks were stript as *b* as brooms	Princess, Pro.	182
strip a hundred hollows *b* of Spring	" vi.	49
B of the body, might it last	In Mem. xlii.	6
breathing *b* The round of space	" lxxxv.	4
saw the altar cold and *b*	The Letters	4
Flash'd all their sabres *b*	Lt. Brigade	27
wound *B* to the sun	Enid	322
love and reverence left them bare?	Aylmer's F.	785

bare (pret. of bear.)

hoofs *b* on the ridge of spears	Princess, v.	478
b Straight to the doors	" vi.	328
b The use of virtue out of earth	In Mem. lxxxi.	9
upon him *b* the bandit three	Enid	933
he, she dreaded most, *b* down	"	1005
B victual for the mowers	"	1031
b her by main violence to the board	"	1502
guilty love *b* the Queen	Elaine	245
the love he *b* his lord	"	246
all together down upon him *B*	"	481
came the hermit out and *b* him in	"	518
often in her arms She *b* me	"	1401
creatures took and *b* him off.	Guinevere	108
first that ever I *b* was dead	Grandmother	59

bare (to lay open.)

Falsehood shall *b* her plaited brow	'Clear-headed friend,' etc.	11
b the eternal Heavens again	In Mem. cxxi.	4

bared (verb.)

tho' it spake and *b* to view	In Mem. xci.	9
b the knotted column of his throat	Enid	74
b her forehead to the blistering sun	"	1364
rites prepared, the victim *b*	The Victim	70

bare-footed.

B-f came the beggar maid	Beggar Maid	3

bar-grinning.

the *b-g* skeleton of death!	Vivien	696

bare-headed.

	POEM.	LINE.
Some cowled, and some *b-h*	Princess, vi.	61

bareness.

make old *b* picturesque	In Mem. cxxvii.	19

bargain.

May rue the *b* made	Princess, i.	73
closed a *b*, hand in hand	The Brook	156

barge.

Slide the heavy *b's* trailed	L. of Shalott, i.	20
there hove a dusky *b*	M. d'Arthur	193
'in the *b*, And to the *b* they came	"	204
answer'd Arthur from the *b*	"	239
b with oar and sail Moved	"	265
a *b* Be ready on the river	Elaine	1116
that stream whereon the *b*	"	1135
slowly past the *b*	"	1234
the *b*, On to the palace-doorway	"	1238
b that brought her moving down	"	1382

barge-laden.

creeps on, *B-l*, to three arches	Gardener's D.	43

bark (vessel.)

a *b* that, blowing forward, bore	M. d'Arthur, Ep.	21
I find a magic *b*	Sir Galahad	38
sit within a helmless *b*	In Mem. iv.	3
unhappy *b* That strikes by night	" xvi.	12
spare thee, sacred *b*	" xvii.	14
b had plunder'd twenty nameless isles	Vivien	409
Down on a *b*, and overbears the *b*	Elaine	484
lading and unlading the tall *b's*	En. Arden.	817
this frail *b* of ours, when sorely tried	Aylmer's F.	715
swiftly stream'd ye by the *b!*	The Voyage	50

bark (of a tree.)

silver-green with gnarled *b*	Mariana	42
Could slip its *b* and walk	Talking O.	188

bark (verb.)

B an answer, Britain's raven! (rep.)	Boädicea	13

barking.

b for the thrones of kings	Ode on Well.	121

barley.

Long fields of *b* and of rye	L. of Shalott, i.	2
In among the bearded *b*	"	29
raked in golden *b*	Will Water.	128

barley-sheaves.

rode between the *b-s*	L. of Shalott, iii.	2

barmaid.

Bitter *b*, waning fast!	Vision of Sin	67

barn (bairn.)

Bessy Marris's *b* (rep.)	N. Farmer	14

baron.

Each *b* at the banquet sleeps	Day-Dm.	57
b's swore, with many words	"	155
gaunt old *B* with his beetle brow	Princess, ii.	222
bush-bearded *B's* heaved and blew	" v.	20
Heard from the *B* that, ten years	Elaine	272
Count, *b*—whom he smote, he overthrew	"	464

baronet.

No little lily-handed *B* he	Princess, Con.	84
hoar hair of the *B* bristle up	Aylmer's F.	42
B yet had laid No bar	"	117

barred.

All *b* with long white cloud	Pal. of Art	83
Every door is *b* with gold	Locksley H.	100
door shut, and window *b*	Godiva	41
But now fast *b*	Princess, v.	357
entering *b* her door	Elaine	15
home-circle of the poor They *b* her	Aylmer's F.	505

barren.

it is wild and *b*	Amphion	2
The soil, left *b*, scarce had grown	In Mem., lii.	7

barren-beaten.

left the *b-b* thoroughfare	Elaine	161

barricade.
	POEM.	LINE.
pile her *b*'s with dead	In Mem. cxxxvi.	8

barrier.
trumpet blared At the *b*	Princess, v.	475
burst All *b*'s in her onward race	In Mem. cxiii.	14
Back to the *b*; then the heralds	Elaine	499

barring out.
graver than a schoolboys' *b o*	Princess, Con.	66

barrow.
gray down With Danish *b*'s	En. Arden	7
Pass from the Danish *b* overhead	"	439
grassy *b*'s of the happier dead	Tithonus	71

barter.
not being bred To *b*	En. Arden	249

base (adj.)
him that uttered nothing *b*	To the Queen	8
O *b* and bad! what comfort?	Princess, v.	75
is he not too *b*?	Maud, I. iv.	36
myself so languid and *b*	" v.	18
therefore splenetic, personal, *b*	" x.	33
know I whether I be very *b*	Enid	468
to keep down the *b* in man	Guinevere	476
Ungenerous, dishonourable, *b*	Aylmer's F.	292
nothing that she meets with *b*	On a Mourner	4

base (s.)
Upon the hidden *b*'s of the hills'	M. d'Arthur	106
hum About the column's *b*	St S. Stylites	38
in dense cloud from *b* to cope	Two Voices	186
the *b*'s lost In laurel	Princess, i.	227
has a solid *b* of temperament	" iv.	235
roots of earth and *b* of all	" v.	436
move the stony *b*'s of the world	" vi.	42
breaks the Pharos from his *b*	"	319
great the crush was, and each *b*	"	333
drown The *b*'s of my life in tears	In Mem. xlviii.	16
at the *b* with slanting storm	Vivien	485
gathering at the *b* Re-makes itself	Guinevere	603
The broken *b* of a black tower	Aylmer's F.	511
sees itself from thatch to *b*	Requiescat	3

based.
b His feet on juts of slippery crag	M. d'Arthur	188

basement.
brought His creatures to the *b*	Guinevere	103

baseness.
knows a *b* in his blood	Two Voices	301
equal *b* lived in sleeker times	Princess, v.	375
no *b* we would hide?	In Mem. l.	3
finds the *b* of her lot	" lix.	6
To leave an equal *b*	Vivien	679

basest.
Altho' I be the *b* of mankind	St S. Stylites	1
The *b*, far into that council-hall	Lucretius	171

bashfulness.
His *b* and tenderness at war	En. Arden	288

basis.
All but the *b* of the soul 'Love thou thy land,' etc.		44

bask.
to *b* in a summer sky	Wages	9

basked.
b and batten'd in the woods	In Mem. xxxv.	24

basket.
Francis, with a *b* on his arm	Audley Ct.	5
set down His *b*, and dismounting	Enid	1059
Clung but to crate and *b*	Vivien	475
holiday With bag and sack and *b*	En. Arden	63

basking.
city Of little Monaco, *b*, glow'd	The Daisy	8

Bassa.
by the shore Of Duglas: that on B	Elaine	290

bassoon.
liquid treble of that *b*	Princess, ii.	404
heard The flute, violin, *b*	Maud, I. xxii.	14

bastion.
	POEM.	LINE.
looming *b* fringed with fire	In Mem. xv.	20

bastion'd.
from the *b* walls Like threaded spiders	Princess, i.	106

bat.
After the flitting of the *b*'s	Mariana	17
laid up like winter *b*'s	Princess, iv.	126
b's wheel'd, and owls whoop'd	" Con.	110
b's went round in fragrant skies	In Mem. xciv.	9
the black *b*, night, has flown	Maud, I. xxii.	2

bath.
the *b*'s Of all the western stars	Ulysses	60
dipt in *b*'s of hissing tears	In Mem. cxvii.	23
a faded beauty of the *B*'s	Aylmer's F.	27
nobler from her *b* of storm	Lucretius	175

bathe.
Balm-dews to *b* thy feet!	Talking O.	268
Soft lustre *b*'s the range of urns	Day-Dm.	29
she *B*'s the Saviour's feet	In Mem. xxxii.	11
Coldly thy rosy shadows *b* me	Tithonus	66

bathed.
lying *b* In the green gleam	Princess, i.	92
b your feet before her own	Vivien	133

battened.
bask'd and *b* in the woods	In Mem. xxxv.	24

battenest.
b by the greasy gleam	Will Water.	221

batter.
b at the dovecote-doors	Princess, iv.	151

batter'd.
flints *b* with clanging hoofs	D. of F. Wom.	21
He *b* at the doors	Princess, v.	327
Cyril, *b* as he was, Trail'd himself	" vi.	138
b with the shocks of doom	In Mem. cxvii.	24

battering.
B the gates of heaven	St S. Stylites	7

battery-smoke.
Plunged in the *b-s*	Lt. Brigade	32

battle (s.)
heard the steeds to *b* going	Oriana	15
b deepen'd in its place	"	51
the noise of *b* roll'd	M. d'Arthur	1
drunk delight of *b* with my peers	Ulysses	16
distant *b* flash'd and rung	Two Voices	126
beat to *b* where he stands	Princess, iv.	555
gives the *b* to his hands	"	557
prove Your knight and fight your *b*	"	572
Breathing and sounding beauteous *b*	" v.	154
doing *b* with forgotten ghosts	"	469
have fought Your *b*	" vi.	208
War with a thousand *b*'s	Maud, I. i.	48
rumour of *b* grew	" III. vi.	29
Far into the North, and *b*,	"	37
to the banner of *b* unroll'd!	"	42
talk of *b*'s loud and vain	Ode on Well.	247
Some ship of *b* slowly creep	To F. D. Maurice	26
ride with him to *b* and stand by	Enid	94
'Do *b* for it then'	"	561
great *b* fighting for the king	"	596
wont to hear His voice in *b*	"	1024
In *b*, fighting for the blameless King	"	1818
after furious *b* turfs the slain	Vivien	507
In *b* with the love he bare	Elaine	246
four wild *b*'s by the shore	"	289
hast been in *b* by my side	"	1349
In open *b* or the tilting-field (rep.)	Guinevere	328
In twelve great *b*'s ruining	"	429
that great *b* in the west	"	567
ere he goes to the great *B*	"	645
boyish histories Of *b*, bold adventure	Aylmer's F.	98

battle (verb.)
For them I *b* till the end,	Sir Galahad	15

battle-axe.
Bloodily, bloodily fall the *b-a*	Boädicea	56

	POEM.	LINE.
battle-bolt.		
b-b sang from the three-decker	*Maud*, I. i.	50
battle-club.		
b-c's From the isles of palm;	*Princess, Pro.*	21
battled (adj.)		
glow Beneath the *b* tower	*D. of F. Wom.*	220
battled (verb.)		
b for the True, the Just,	*In Mem.* lv.	18
battle-field.		
Be shot for sixpence in a *b-f*,	*Audley Ct.*	40
battle-flag.		
and the *b-f's* were furl'd	*Locksley H.*	127
battle-song.		
hear again The chivalrous *b-s*	*Maud*, I. x.	54
battle-thunder.		
thine the *b-t* of God.'	*Boädicea*	44
battle-writhen.		
b-w arms and mighty hands	*Elaine*	808
bawl.		
b for civil rights: No woman named, *Princess*, v.		377
bay (arm of the sea.)		
spangle dances in bight and *b*	*Sea Fairies*	24
glassy *b's* among her tallest towers.'	*Œnone*	117
b runs up its latest horn	*Audley Ct.*	10
farmer's son, who lived across the *b*	"	74
The *b* was oily calm	"	85
sings in his boat on the *b*!	*'Break, break,' etc.*	8
long waves that roll in yonder *b*?	*Maud*, I. xviii.	63
bubble into eddying *b's*	*The Brook*	41
b's, the peacock's neck in hue ;	*The Daisy*	14
caves about the dreary *b*	*Sailor Boy*	10
bay (barking.)		
Where he greatly stood at *b*.	*Ode on Well.*	106
heard The noble heart at *b*	*Enid*	233
bay (verb.)		
tho' dogs of Faction *b*,	*'Love thou thy land,' etc.*	85
baying.		
chiefly for the *b* of Cavall	*Enid*	185
bay-window.		
from some *b-w* shake the night	*Princess*, i.	105
beach.		
crisping ripples on the *b*	*Lotos-E's.*	106
rounded by the stillness of the *b*	*Audley Ct.*	9
Here about the *b* I wander'd	*Locksley H.*	11
breaker breaking on the *b*	*In Mem.* lxx.	16
the scream of a madden'd *b*	*Maud*, I. iii.	12
here and there, on sandy *b'es*	*The Daisy*	15
shore-cliff's windy walls to the *b*	*Enid*	1013
leaving Arthur's court he gain'd the *b*	*Vivien*	46
tremulously as foam upon the *b*	*Guinevere*	362
on this *b* a hundred years ago	*En. Arden.*	10
beacon (s.)		
like a *b* guards thee home	*In Mem.* xvii.	12
beacon (verb.)		
Not in vain the distance *b's*.	*Locksley H.*	181
beacon-blaze.		
b-b allures The bird of passage	*En. Arden.*	729
beacon-star.		
with a *b-s* upon his head,	*Guinevere*	239
beacon-tower.		
like a *b-t* above the waves	*Princess*, iv.	472
bead.		
number'd *b*, and shrift	*Talking O.*	46
beaded.		
woolly breasts and *b* eyes ;	*In Mem.* xciv.	12
beak.		
stood with the down on his *b*,	*Poet's Song.*	11
swoops The vulture, *b* and talon	*Princess*, v.	373
ever ravening eagle's *b* and talon	*Boädicea*	11

	POEM.	LINE.
beaker.		
b brimm'd with noble wine	*Day-Dm.*	56
beam (ray.)		
gird their orbs with *b's*	*The Poet*	29
Into two burning rings All *b's* of Love	*D. of F. Wom.*	175
deep-blue gloom with *b's* divine	"	186
the white dawn's creeping *b's*	"	261
fresh *b* of the springing east ;	*M. d'Arthur*	214
lane of *b's* athwart the sea	*Golden Year*	50
will one *b* be less intense	*Two Voices*	40
b's, that thro' the Oriel shine	*Day-Dm.*	54
spaces cloth'd in living *b's*	*Sir Galahad*	66
a *b* Had slanted forward	*Princess*, ii.	122
first *b* glittering on a sail	" iv.	26
b Of the East, that play'd upon them	" v.	248
A *b* in darkness: let it grow.	*In Mem. Pro.*	24
A chequer-work of *b* and shade	" lxxi.	15
golden *b* of an eyelash	*Maud*, I. iii.	3
Like a *b* of the seventh Heaven	" xiv.	21
smitten by the dusty sloping *b*	*Enid*	262
b of Heaven Dawn'd sometime	*Aylmer's F.*	684
the first *b* of my latest day ?	*Lucretius*	59
beam (timber.)		
shape it plank and *b*	*Princess*, vi.	30
beam (verb.)		
More bounteous aspects on me *b*	*Sir Galahad*	21
beam'd.		
Love's white star *B*	*Gardener's D.*	162
ghostly grace *B* on his fancy	*Elaine*	882
b, Beneath a manelike mass	*Aylmer's F.*	67
beän (s. bean.)		
'ere a *b* an' yonder a pea	*N. Farmer.*	46
bear (s.)		
grosser than your native *b's*—	*Princess*, iv.	516
Bear (Constellation.)		
B had wheel'd Thro' a great arc	*Princess*, iv.	194
bear (verb.)		
canst thou *b* my weight?	*Œnone*	233
proud to *b* your name	*L. C. V. de Vere*	12
whatever sky *B* seed of men	*'Love thou thy land,' etc.*	20
b blossoms of the dead	"	94
I will not *b* it longer.'	*The Goose*	32
b me to the margin ;	*M. d'Arthur*	165
Less burthen, by ten-hundred-fold, to *b*	*St S. Stylites*	24
B witness, if I could have found	"	54
(thou wilt *b* witness here)	"	127
that which *b's* but bitter fruit ?	*Locksley H.*	65
he *b's* a laden breast	"	143
b's relation to the mind	*Two Voices*	177
sons grow up that *b* his name	"	256
Three angels *b* the holy Grail	*Sir Galahad*	42
b's a season'd brain about	*Will Water.*	85
b me with thee, smoothly borne	*'Move eastward,' etc.*	9
The king would *b* him out ;	*Princess*, i.	180
Earth Should *b* a double growth	" ii.	163
b that heart within my breast	"	313
much I *b* with her	" iii.	65
I *b*, Tho' man, yet human	" iv.	404
if thou needs must *b* the yoke	" vi.	188
help thy foolish ones to *b*	*In Mem. Pro.*	31
thy vain worlds to *b* thy light	"	32
b thro' Heaven a tale of woe	" xii.	2
pure hands and *b* the head	" xviii.	9
loved the weight I had to *b*	" xxv.	7
life that *B's* immortal fruit	" xxxix.	18
that ideal which he *b's*?	" li.	10
often brings but one to *b*	" liv.	12
b's the burthen of the weeks.	" lxxix.	11
growing, till I could *b* it no more	*Maud*, I. iii.	9
heart enough To *b* his armour?	*Enid*	1339
b him hence out of this cruel sun	"	1393
b him to our hall	"	1401
b's, with all its stormy crests	*Elaine*	482
Then will I *b* it gladly ;'	"	1100
I myself must *b* it.'	"	1102

	POEM.	LINE.
seize me by the hair and *b* me far	*Elaine*	1415
added to the griefs the great must *b*	*Guinevere*	203
B with me for the last time	"	451
beseech you by the love you *b* Him	*En. Arden.*	306
'Too hard to *b*! why did they	"	782
boat that *B*'s the hope of life	"	831
b it with me to my grave	"	897
B's about A silent court of justice	*Sea Dreams*	169
skater on the ice that hardly *b*'s him	*Hendecasyllabics*	6
jam the doors, and *b* The keepers down	*Lucretius*	169
who *b*'s one name with her	"	232

beard.

b Was tagged with icy fringes	*St S. Stylites*	30
His *b* a foot before him	*Godiva*	18
'By holy rood, a royal *b*!	*Day-Dm.*	152
b has grown into my lap	"	154
paw'd his *b*, and muttered 'catalepsy'	*Princess*, i.	20
answer which, half-muffled in his *b*	" v.	224
father's face and reverend *b*	" vi.	87
under-fringe of russet *b*	*Enid*	1386
took his russet *b* between his teeth	"	1561
part The lists of such a *b*	*Vivien*	94
shaggy mantle of his *b*	"	105
no more sign of reverence than a *b*	"	128

beard-blown.

b-b goat Hang on the shaft	*Princess*, iv.	60

bearded.

In among the *b* barley	*L. of Shalott*, i.	29
b meteor, trailing light	" iii.	26
the *b* grass Is dry and dewless	*Miller's D.*	245

beardless.

b apple-arbiter Decided fairest	*Lucretius*	91

bearer.

Save under pall with *b*'s	*Aylmer's F.*	827

bearest.

love thou *b* The first-born	*Ode to Mem.*	91

bearing (part.)

b on My shallop	*Arabian N's*	35
Oaring one arm, and *b* in my left	*Princess*, iv.	165
not openly *b* the sword	*Maud*, I. i.	28
sent him to the Queen *B* his wish	*Elaine*	1163
B a lifelong hunger in his heart	*En. Arden.*	79
b hardly more Than his own shadow	*Aylmer's F.*	29
b in myself the shame	"	355

bearing (bringing forth) s.

b and the training of a child	*Princess*, v.	455

bearing (mien.)

thro' these Princelike his *b* shone	*Enid*	545

bearing (armorial.)

gateway she discerns With armorial *b*'s	*L. of Burleigh*	43

bearing (force.)

To change the *b* of a word	*In Mem.* cxxvii.	16

beast.

people here, a *b* of burden	*Pal. of Art.*	149
deep cry Of great wild *B*'s	"	263
I a *b* To take them as I did?	*Ed. Morris*	71
even *B*'s have stalls	*St S. Stylites*	107
Like a *b* with lower pleasures	*Locksley H.*	176
but a little more Than *b*'s	*Two Voices*	197
many-headed *b* should know.' { 'You might have won,' etc.		20
laws to scare the *b* of prey	*Princess*, v.	383
b that takes His license	*In Mem.* xxvii.	5
Move upward, working out the *b*	" cxvii.	27
not in vain, Like Paul with *b*'s	" cxix.	4
skins the wild *b* after slaying	*Enid*	942
as sullen as a *b* new-caged	"	1704
beauteous *b* Scared by the noise	*Vivien*	271
weak *b* seeking to help herself	"	348
b's themselves would worship	"	425
like a subtle *b* Lay couchant	*Guinevere*	11
subtle *b*, Would track her guilt	"	59
like a *b* hard-ridden	*Aylmer's F.*	291
surely lives in man and *b*	*Sea Dreams*	68

	POEM.	LINE.
What *b* has heart to do it?	*Lucretius*	230
b or bird or fish, or opulent flower	"	245

beastlier.

B than any phantom	*Lucretius*	193

beast-like.

b as I find myself	*Lucretius*	228

beat.

B time to nothing in my head	*Miller's D.*	67
heart would *b* against me	"	177
should know if it *b* right	"	179
howl, mother, or the death-watch *b*	*May Queen*, iii.	21
wind, that *B*'s the mountain	*To J. S.*	1
heart of existence *b* for ever	*Locksley H.*	140
where my life began to *b*	"	154
winter rains that *b* his grave	*Two Voices*	261
frozen heart began to *b*	"	422
Music in his heart *B*'s quick	*Day-Dm.*	127
spirit *b*'s her mortal bars	*Sir Galahad*	46
b her foes with slaughter	*Princess, Pro.*	34
convention *b*'s them down	" "	128
B balm upon our eyelids	" iii.	107
b admission in a thousand years	" "	139
heart *b* thick with passion	" "	174
vassals to be *b*, nor petty babes	" iv.	128
b to battle where he stands	" "	555
they will *b* my girl	" v.	85
clash'd their arms; the drum *B*	" "	241
One pulse that *b*'s true woman	" vi.	164
greater than all knowledge, *b* her down	" vii.	223
faith in womankind *B*'s with his blood	" "	310
dance with death, to *b* the ground	*In Mem.*	ii. 12
B's out the little lives of men	"	ii. 8
makes me *b* so low?	"	iv. 8
life that *b* from thee	"	vi. 12
my heart was used to *b*	"	vii. 3
flower *b* with rain and wind	"	viii. 15
darken'd heart that *b* no more	"	xix. 2
hearts that *b* from day to day	"	lvii. 6
plays with threads, her *b*'s his chair	"	lxv. 13
pulses therefore *b* again	"	lxxxiv. 57
b's within a lonely place	"	cx. 110
seeks to do in time with one	"	cxv. 115
crash'd the glass and *b* the floor	"	lxxxvi. 20
he *B* his brother down	"	xcv. 10
hearts of old have *b* in tune	"	xcvi. 10
let no footstep *b* the floor	"	civ. 17
heart was used to *b* So quickly	"	cxviii. 1
heart *b* stronger And thicker	*Maud*, I. viii.	8
B to the noiseless music	"	xviii. 77
B, happy stars, timing with things	"	81
B with my heart more blest	"	82
heart would hear her and *b* (rep.)	" xxii.	69
Is it gone? my pulses *b*—	" II. i.	36
broad light glares and *b*'s	"	iv. 69
hoofs of the horses *b*, *b* (rep.)	"	v. 8
heart of a people *b* with one desire	" III. vi.	49
fierce light which *b*'s upon a throne	*Idylls, Ded.*	26
B thro' the blindless casement	*Enid*	71
Invaded Britain, 'but we *b* him back	"	746
Not *b* him back, but welcom'd	"	748
B, till she woke the sleepers	"	1253
sun yet *b* a dewy blade	"	1295
never merrily *b* Annie's heart	*En Arden.*	509
B's out his weary life	"	731
b a pathway out to wealth	*Aylmer's F.*	439
her heart had *b* remorselessly	"	799
b me down and marred	*Tithonus*	19
b the twilight into flakes of fire	"	42
b with rapid unanimous hand	*Boädicea*	79
B upon his father's 'Home they brought him,' etc.		9
b quicker, for the time Is pleasant	*On a Mourner*	12
B breast, tore hair, cried out	*Lucretius*	273

beaten.

B with some great passion	*Princess*, iv.	369
no bolder than a *b* hound	*Enid*	910
a way which, *b* broad	"	1285
b back, and *b* back Settles	*Vivien*	221
weeping like a *b* child	"	704
dint a sword had *b* in it	*Elaine*	19

	POEM	LINE
beating.		
b hearts of salient springs	Adeline	26
his *b* heart did make	Lotos-E's.	36
heard with *b* heart The Sweet-Gale	Ed. Morris.	109
The two-cell'd heart *b*	Princess, vii.	289
B from the wasted vines	Ode on Well.	109
B it in upon his weary brain	En. Arden.	797
b up thro' all the bitter world	"	803
bosom *b* with a heart renewed	Tithonus	36
beauteous.		
reflex of a *b* form	Miller's D.	77
Breathing and sounding *b* battle	Princess, v.	154
whispers of the *b* world	In Mem. lxxviii.	12
b in thine after form	" xc.	15
the *b* beast Scared by the noise	Vivien	271
when the *b* hateful isle Returned	En. Arden.	618
heart so near the *b* breast	Coquette, ii.	7
beautiful.		
spirit-thrilling eyes so keen and *b*	Ode to Mem.	39
said the earth was *b*	A Character	12
Her *b* bold brow	The Poet	38
B Paris, evil-hearted Paris	Œnone	49
Idalian Aphrodite *b*	"	170
How *b* a thing it was to die	D. of F. Wom.	231
Twin-sisters differently *b*	Ed. Morris.	33
'She is more *b* than day'	Beggar Maid	8
made His darkness *b* with thee	In Mem. lxxiii.	12
Perfectly *b*; let it be granted	Maud, I. ii.	4
flash'd over her *b* face	" iv.	16
Silence, *b* voice!	" v.	19
O *b* creature, what am I	" xvi.	10
Not *b* now, not even kind	" II. v.	66
not dream'd she was so *b*	Elaine	352
his own children tall and *b*	En. Arden.	763
ever thus thou growest *b*	Tithonus	43
stars about the moon Look *b*	Spec. of Iliad	12
beautiful-brow'd.		
B-b Œnone, my own soul	Œnone	69
beautifully.		
So lightly, *b* built	Pal. of Art	294
dress her *b*, and keep her true'—	Enid	889
beauty should go *b* (rep.)	"	1529
beauty.		
spake of *b*: that the dull	A Character	7
now thy *b* flows away	Mariana in the S.	67
thy *b* gradually unfold	Eleänore	70
loved his *b* passing well	The Sisters	23
love *B* only *B* seen In all To—	With Pal of Art	6
Knowledge for its *b*	"	8
Good only for its *b*	"	9
B, Good and Knowledge are three	"	10
B and anguish walking hand in hand	D. of F. Wom.	15
I had great *b*: ask thou not	"	93
B such a mistress of the world	Gardener's D.	57
Her *b* grew; till Autumn brought	"	202
many a group Of beauties	Talking O.	62
murmurs of her *b* from the South	Princess, i.	35
All *b* compassed in a female form	" ii.	20
beauties every shade of brown and fair	"	414
underneath the crag, Full of all *b*	" iii.	319
moon of *b* in the South	" iv.	95
Another kind of *b* in detail	"	428
for the *b* of their skins	" v.	149
became Her former *b* treble	" vii.	10
orb of flame, Fantastic *b*;	In Mem. xxxiv.	6
rail Against her *b!*	" cxiii.	2
the singular *b* of Maud	Maud, I. i.	67
Done but in thought to your *b*	" iii.	6
O child, you wrong your *b*	" iv.	17
B fair in her flower	"	25
dream of her *b* with tender dread	" xvi.	14
know her *b* might half undo it	"	19
The *b* would be the same	" II. ii.	12
Remembering all the *b* of that star	Idylls, Ded.	45
make her *b* vary day by day	Enid	
prize of *b* for the fairest	"	485
seen all beauties of our time	"	498
won it for thee, The prize of *b*.'	"	555
b is no *b* to him now	"	1179

	POEM.	LINE.
put your *b* to this flout and scorn	Enid	1523
b should go beautifully (rep.)	"	1529
Guinevere, The pearl of *b*	Elaine	115
Your *b* is your *b*, and I sin	"	1180
her *b*, grace and power Wrought	Guinevere	142
b such as never woman wore	"	545
wife a faded *b* of the Baths	Aylmer's F.	27
whose pensive *b*, perfect else	"	70
the baits Of gold and *b*	"	467
Willy, my *b*, my eldest-born	Grandmother	9
So Willy has gone, my *b*	"	101
glorious in his *b* and thy choice	Tithonus	12
thy love, Thy *b*, make amends	"	24
renew thy *b* morn by morn	"	74
Light Hope at *B's* call	Coquette, i.	3
live with *B* less and less	"	9
b still with his years increased	The Victim	25
shamed At all that *b*	Lucretius	14
became.		
Therefore revenge *b* me well	The Sisters	5
well his words *b* him	Ed. Morris	25
b Her former beauty treble	Princess, vii.	9
Lancelot, as *b* noble knight	Guinevere	326
beck (brook.)		
the dark and dimpled *b*	Miller's D.	80
beck (call.)		
move, my friend, At no man's *b*	Princess, iii.	211
beckon'd.		
She ended here, and *b* us	Princess, ii.	165
beckoning.		
b unto those they know	In Mem. xiv.	8
become.		
b's no man to nurse despair	Princess, iv.	444
bed.		
Upon her *b*, across her brow	Mariana	56
wilt not turn upon thy *b*	A Dirge	15
after supper, on a *b*	The Sisters	16
as he knelt beside my *b*	May Queen iii.	16
sit beside my *b*, mother,	"	23
I listened in my *b*	"	33
propt on *b's* of amaranth and moly	Lotos-E's.	133
limbs at last on *b's* of asphodel	"	170
feels a nightmare on his *b*	M. d'Arthur	177
so to *b*: where yet in sleep	" Ep.	16
packs up his *b's* and chairs	Walk. to the M.	31
pack'd the things among the *b's*	"	36
to the college tower From her warm *b*	"	82
In *b* like monstrous apes	St. S. Stylites	171
See that sheets are on my *b*	Vision of Sin	68
then to *b*, where half in doze	Princess, i.	242
glitter'd like a *b* of flowers	" ii.	416
as if caught at once from *b*	" iv.	266
for an hour in mine own *b*	" v.	424
on my *b* the moonlight falls	In Mem. lxvi.	1
From off my *b* the moonlight dies	"	10
tends upon *b* and bower	Maud, I. xiv.	1
Hung over her dying *b*—	" xix.	36
On a *b* of daffodil sky	" xxii.	1
Were it earth in an earthy *b*.	"	70
By the curtains of my *b*	" II. iv.	54
flush'd the *b* Of silent torrents	The Daisy	33
hurl'd his huge limbs out of *b*	Enid	114
o'er a shingly *b* Brawling	"	243
now get you hence to *b*	Elaine	387
lowly by the corners of his *b*.	"	822
the little *b* on which I died	"	1111
on the black decks laid him in her *b*	"	1141
Started from *b*, and struck	En. Arden.	490
yet a *b* for wandering men	"	(9)
the house, his chair, and last his *b*	"	827
then homeward and to *b*	Sea Dreams	40
In her *b* at peep of day?	"	290
they hover about my *b*—	Grandmother	83
a sittin 'ere o' my *b*	N. Farmer.	9
along the valley, down thy rocky *b*	V. of Cauteretz	7
bedded.		
With all its casements *b*	Audley Ct.	17

Bedivere.

	POEM.	LINE.
bold Sir *B* uplifted him	*M. d'Arthur*	6
Sir *B*, the last of all his knights	"	7
went Sir *B* the second time	"	82
quickly rose Sir *B* and ran	"	133
Sir *B* Remorsefully regarded	"	170
loudly cried the bold Sir *B*	"	226
stood Sir *B*, Revolving many memories	"	269

bedridden.

infancy Or old *b* palsy	*Aylmer's F.*	178

bee.

the wild *b* hummeth	*Claribel*	11
Chaunteth not the brooding *b*	*A Dirge*	16
or the yellow banded *b's*	*Eleänore*	22
the hum of swarming *b's*	"	29
golden *b* Is lily-cradled	*Œnone*	28
the *b* would range her cells	*Two Voices*	70
With all her *b's* behind her	*Amphion*	36
here by thee will hum the *b*	*A Farewell*	11
stopt as he hunted the *b*	*Poet's Song*	9
Made noise with *b's* and breeze	*Princess*, Pro.	88
swarm as *b's* about their queen	" i.	39
murmuring of innumerable *b's.'*	" vii.	207
shake off the *b* that buzzes at us	*Elaine*	781
like the working *b* in blossom-dust	*En. Arden*	363
b's are still'd and the flies are kill'd	*The Window*	52

beech.

Moving in the leavy *b*	*Margaret*	61
like a purple *b* among the greens	*Ed. Morris*	84
wish'd myself the fair young *b*	*Talking O.*	141
bard has honour'd *b* or lime	"	291
Coquetting with young *b'es*	*Amphion*	28
the winds were in the *b*	*In Mem.* xxx.	7
the *b* will gather brown	" c.	3
seated on a serpent-rooted *b*	*The Brook*	135
b and lime Put forth and feel	*On a Mourner*	14

bee-like.

b-l instinct hiveward	*Princess*, iv.	181

beeswing.

richest *b* from a binn reserved	*Aylmer's F.*	405

beetle (adj.)

gaunt old Baron with his *b* brow	*Princess*, ii.	222

beetle (s.)

At eve the *b* boometh	*Claribel*	9

beetling.

b crag to which he clung	*Aylmer's F.*	229

beeves.

whole hogs and quarter *b*	*Enid*	1450

befall.

Shame might *b* Melissa	*Princess*, iii.	131
I hold it true, whate'er *b*	*In Mem.* xxvii.	13
aught of things that here *b*	*Ode on Well.*	138

befit.

tale for summer as *b's* the time	*Princess*, Pro.	205
As *b's* a solemn fane	*Ode on Well.*	250

befooled.

being much *b* and idioted	*Aylmer's F.*	590

before.

Or see (in Him is no *b*)	*In Mem.* xxvi.	10

beg.

b of him to take thee back	*Dora*	121
steal or plunder, no nor *b*	*Enid*	1336

began.

when my passion first *b*	*Talking O.*	9
'When first the world *b*	*Two Voices*	16
fares it since the years *b*	*Will Water.*	169
He *b*, the rest would follow	*Princess*, Pro.	196
So I *b*, And the rest followed	"	235
b A blind and babbling laughter	" vi.	121
seem'd my worth since I *b*	*In Mem.* Pro.	34
total world since life *b*	" xlii.	12
Whose life in low estate *b*	" lxiii.	3
In tracts of fluent heat *b*	" cxvii.	9

	POEM.	LINE.
Wretchedest age, since Time *b*	*Maud*, II. v.	21
greatest sailor since our world *b*	*Ode on Well.*	86

beget.

Many a chance the years *b*	*Miller's D.*	206

begetters.

worldly-wise *b's*, plagued themselves	*Aylmer's F.*	482

beggar maid.

Bare-footed came the *b m*	*Beggar Maid*	3
'This *b m* shall be my queen!'	"	16

beggar (s.)

no *b's* at your gate	*L. C. V. de Vere*	67
a *b* born,' she said (rep.)	*Lady Clare*	37
tho' she were a *b* from the hedge	*Enid*	230
her, he loved, a *b*	*En. Arden*	117

beggar-woman.

silken rag, the *b-w's* weed	*Enid*	1528

begged.

At last she *b* a boon	*Princess*, i.	145
then they *b* For Father Philip	*En. Arden*	361

begin.

to *b* implies to end	*Two Voices*	339
B's the scandal and the cry	{ *'You might have won,' etc.*	16
noise of life *b's* again	*In Mem.* vii.	10
whence clear memory may *b*	" xliv.	10
overhead *B's* the clash and clang	" Con.	61
made a selfish war *b*	*To F. D. Maurice*	30

beginning (part.)

world's great work is heard *B*	*In Mem.* cxx.	11
B to faint in the light that she loves	*Maud*, I. xxii.	9

beginning (s.)

end and the *b* vex His reason	*Two Voices*	298
The low *b's* of content	*In Mem.* lxxxiii.	48
be the fair *b* of a time	*Guinevere*	463
blind *b's* that have made me man	*Lucretius*	242

begone.

'You must *b*,' said Death	*Love and Death*	7
B; we will not look upon you	*Princess*, iv.	526

beguile.

To *b* her melancholy	*Maud*, I. xx.	3

beguiled.

well, well, well, I may be *b*	*Maud*, I. vi.	89

begun.

help me as when life *b*	*Locksley H.*	185

beheld.

b great Herè's angry eyes	*Œnone*	186
Since I *b* young Laurence dead.	*L. C. V. de Vere*	28
ere a star can wink, *b* her	*Gardener's D.*	121
b her ere she knew my heart	"	270
when the boy *b* His mother	*Dora*	134
I *b* her, when she rose	*Princess*, v.	167
what I am *b* again,	*In Mem.* cxxiii.	21
b The death-white curtain	*Maud*, I. xiv.	33
B the long street of a little town	*Enid*	242
Geraint *B* her first in field,	"	540
Turn'd, and *b* the four	"	558
b A little town with towe.s,	"	1045
never yet *b* a thing so pale	"	1463
b a lily like yourself	"	1468
B the man you loved	"	1795
b the King Charge at the head	*Elaine*	303
Arthur who *b* his cloudy brows	"	1344
three spirits mad with joy	*Guinevere*	250
B at noon in some delicious dale	"	390
glancing up *b* the holy nuns	"	658
B the dead flame of the fallen day	*En. Arden*	438
b His wife his wife no more,	"	759
b the Powers of the House	*Aylmer's F.*	287

behest.

not to disobey her lord's *b*	*Enid*	1299

behold.

B this fruit, whose gleaming rind	*Œnone*	70

	POEM.	LINE.
Mayst well *b* them unbeheld,	Œnone	87
B her there, As I beheld her	Gardener's D.	269
Who is this? *b* thy bride,'	Love and Duty	49
in me *b* the Prince	Princess, ii.	196
B your father's letter.'	" iv.	448
B the man that loved and lost	In Mem., i.	15
B me, for I cannot sleep	" vii.	6
B a man raised up by Christ!	" xxxi.	13
An inner trouble I *b*	" xl.	18
O happy hour, *b* the bride,	Con.	69
reverent people *b* The towering car	Ode on Well.	54
did Enid, keeping watch, *b*	Enid	967
B me overturn and trample on him	"	1691
b me come To cleanse this	"	1742
I *b* him in my dreams	Elaine	759
dost thou *b* thy God	Aylmer's F.	657

beholden.

| being so *b* to the Prince | Enid | 623 |
| Prince To whom we are *b* | " | 727 |

beholding.

B one so bright in dark estate	Enid	787
B how you butt against my wish	"	1525
B it was Edyrn, son of Nudd,	"	1629
b her, Tho' pale, yet happy	"	1727
B how the years which are not Time's	Aylmer's F.	601

behoof.

| break them more in their *b* | Princess, vi. | 45 |
| mask, tho' but in his own *b* | Maud, I. vi. | 48 |

being.

changes should control Our *b*	{ 'Love thou thy land,' etc.	42 }
current of my *b* sets to thee	Locksley H.	24
No Angel, but a dearer *b*	Princess, vii.	301
all the wheels of *B* slow	In Mem., xlix.	4
His *b* working in mine own	" lxxxiv.	43
strike his *b* into bounds	" Con.	124
b he loved best in all the world	Enid	952
peaceful *b* slowly passes by	Requiescat	7
spoils My bliss in *b*	Lucretius	219

Bel.

| Till the face of *B* he brighten'd | Boädicea | 16 |

belabour'd.

| so *b* him on rib and cheek | Princess, v. | 331 |

belaud.

| blush to *b* myself a moment | Hendecasyllabics | 18 |

belfry.

| white owl in the *b* sits (rep.) | The Owl | 7 |
| breezes fann'd the *b* bars | The Letters | 43 |

belied.

| liars *b* in the hubbub of lies | Maud, I. iv. | 51 |

belief.

| mine old *b* in womanhood | Elaine | 951 |
| quicker of *b* Than you believe me | " | 1198 |

believable.

| that he sinn'd, is not *b* | Vivien | 610 |

believe.

I *b* she wept	Talking O.	164
iron in the blood, And I *b* it	Princess, vi.	214
heard a voice, '*b* no more'	In Mem., cxxiii.	10
b him ashamed to be seen?	Maud, I. xiii.	25
b him Something far advanced	Ode on Well.	274
do *b* yourself against yourself	Enid	1592
will not *b* a man repents	"	1748
half *b* her true	Vivien	42
b that all about this world	"	391
b she tempted them and failed	"	668
I might *b* you then	"	771
I well *b*, the noblest	Elaine	360
could *b* the things you say	"	1091
may not well *b* that you	"	1190
quicker of belief Than you *b* me	"	1199
all as soon *b* that his	Guinevere	348
b, if you were fast my wife	En. Arden	411
Save Christ as we *b* him	Aylmer's F.	573
nor *b* me Too presumptuous	Hendecasyllabics	16
Gods there are, for all men so *b*	Lucretius	117

believed.

	POEM.	LINE.
often she *b* that I should die	Princess, vii.	85
I *b* that in the living world	"	142
The woman cannot be *b*	The Letters	32
Not less Geraint *b* it	Enid	28
I *b* myself Unconquerable	"	1683
Enid easily *b*	"	1722
and half *b* her true	Vivien	250, 742
b This filthy marriage-hindering	Aylmer's F.	373
when he came again, his flock *b*	"	600
saw, but scarce *b*	Sea Dreams	34

believing.

| *B* where we cannot prove | In Mem. Pro. | 4 |
| *B* 'lo! mine helpmate, one to feel | Guinevere | 481 |

bell.

dropping low their crimson *b's*	Arabian N's.	62
with white *b's* the clover-hill swells	Sea Fairies	14
bridle *b's* rang merrily	L. of Shalott, iii.	13
placed great *b's* that swung	Pal. of Art	129
those great *b's* Began to chime	"	157
midnight *b's* cease ringing suddenly	D. of F. Wom.	247
hundred *b's* began to peal	M. d'Arthur, Ep.	29
sound of funeral or of marriage *b's*	Gardener's D.	36
from them clashed The *b's*	"	216
when the *b's* were ringing, Allan call'd	Dora	39
do not hear the *b's* upon my cap	Ed. Morris	56
blow The sound of minster *b's*	Talking O.	272
foxglove cluster dappled *b's*	Two Voices	72
sweet church *b's* began to peal	"	408
shrill *b* rings, the censer swings	Sir Galahad	35
hark the *b* For dinner	Princess, ii.	410
the chapel *b's* Call'd us	"	446
half open'd *b* of the woods	" vi.	176
like a *b* Toll'd by an earthquake	"	311
'lights and rings the gateway *b*	In Mem. viii.	3
hear the *b* struck in the night	" x.	2
Christmas *b's* from hill to hill	" xxviii.	1
Before I heard those *b's* again	"	16
The merry merry *b's* of Yule	"	20
One set slow bell will seem to toll	" lvi.	10
A single peal of *b's* below	" ciii.	5
these are not the *b's* I know	" cv.	1
Ring out, wild *b's* (rep.)	"	6
Ring, happy *b's*, across the snow	" Con.	64
dead leaf trembles to the *b's*	Maud, I. vi.	62
Is cap and *b's* for a fool	" II. v.	24
Not a *b* was rung, not a prayer	The Letters	48
comes a sound of marriage *b's*	Ode on Well.	46
Let the *b* be toll'd	En. Arden 80,	507
were wed, and merrily rang the *b's*	"	616
the pealing of his parish *b's*	W. to Alexan.	18
Clash, ye *b's*, in the merry March air!		

Bellerophon.

| White Rose, *B*, the Jilt | The Brook | 161 |

bell-like.

| many a deep-hued *b-l* flower | Eleänore | 37 |

bell-mouth'd.

| whom the *b-m* glass had wrought | Princess, iv. | 137 |

bellowed.

| ever overhend *B* the tempest | Vivien | 806 |

bellowing.

| *B* victory, *b* doom | Ode on Well. | 66 |

belonging.

| things *b* to thy peace and ours! | Aylmer's F. | 740 |
| I knew it—Of and *b* to me | Lucretius | 44 |

beloved.

Revered, *b*—O you that hold	To the Queen	1
O this world's curse,—*b* but hated	Love and Duty	47
love reflects the thing *b*	In Mem. ii.	2
Maud the *b* of my mother	Maud, I. i.	72
the liquid note *b* of men	Enid	336

belt (s.)

Unclasp'd the wedded eagles of her *b*	Godiva	43
A gleaming crag with *b's* of pines	Two Voices	189
Half-lost in *b's* of hop	Princess, Con.	45
From *b* to *b* of crimson seas	In Mem. lxxxv.	13
summer *b's* of wheat and vine	" xcvii.	4

	POEM.	LINE.
a mighty purse, Hung at his *b*	*Enid*	872
seem a sword beneath a *b* of three	*Vivien*	360
faltering sideways downward to her *b*	"	699
glories of the broad *b* of the world	*En. Arden*	580
A *b*, it seem'd, of luminous vapour	*Sea Dreams*	202
ridge Of breaker issued from the *b*	"	205
same as that Living within the *b*	"	209
past into the *b* and swell'd again	"	213

belt (verb.)
woods that *b* the gray hill-side . *Ode to Mem.* 55

belted.
with puff'd cheek the *b* hunter blew *Pal. of Art* 63

bench.
Jack on his ale-house *b*. . *Maud*, I. iv. 9

bench'd.
stately theatres *B* crescent-wise . *Princess*, ii. 348

bencher.
wrinkled *B*'s often talk'd of him . *Aylmer's F.* 473

bend.
that I could not *b* One will	*D. of F. Wom.*	137
sweet are looks that ladies *b* .	*Sir Galahad*	13
fathers *b* Above more graves.	*In Mem.* xcvii.	15
On me she *b*'s her blissful eyes	" *Con.*	29
tyranny now should *b* or cease	*Maud*, III. vi.	20

bending.
erect, but *b* from his height . *Aylmer's F.* 119

Bengal.
in branding summers of *B* . . *The Brook* 16

bent.
lowly *b*, With melodious airs	*Adeline*	54
yon blue heavens above as *b*	*L. C. V. de Vere*	50
Nor *b*, nor broke, nor shunn'd	*Princess, Pro.*	38
Cupid *b* above a scroll .	" i.	238
B their broad faces toward us	" iv.	529
Her head a little *b*	" vi.	252
thrice as large as man he *b* .	*In Mem.* cii.	42
b he seem'd on going the third day	*Enid*	604
B as he seem'd on going	"	625
b the spirits of the hills	*Guinevere*	281
b or broke The little reluctant boughs	*En. Arden*	377
b as he was To make disproof	*Aylmer's F.*	445
King *b* low, with hand on brow	*The Victim*	57

bereave.
nothing can *b* him Of the force . *Ode on Well.* 272

berg.
like glittering *b*'s of ice . . *Princess*, iv. 53

Berkshire.
weed the white horse on the *B* hills *Enid* . 1784

berried.
about my feet The *b* briony fold . *Talking O.* 148

berry.
With bunch and *b* and flower . *Œnone* . 100

beseech.
do *b* you by the love you bear . *En. Arden* 306

beseem.
might well *b* His princess . *Enid* . 759

beseem'd.
true answer, as *b* Thy fealty . *M. d'Arthur* 74

besotted.
A drowning life, *b* in sweet self . *Princess*, vii. 295

besought.
the knight *b* him, 'Follow me .	*Enid*.	1655
B Lavaine to write as she devised	*Elaine*	1097
B me to be plain and blunt .	"	1293
B him, supplicating, if he cared .	*En. Arden*	163

Bess.
Black *B*, Tantivy, Tallyho, . . *The Brook* . 160

Bessy Marris.
B M's barn (rep.) . . *N. Farmer* . 14

best.

	POEM.	LINE.
Kind nature is the *b* . .	*Walk. to the M.*	56
b That ever came from pipe .	*Will Water.*	75
gave the people of his *b* '*You might have won*,' etc.		25
worst he kept, his *b* he gave	"	26
cancell'd nature's *b* . .	*In Mem.* lxxi.	20
as the stateliest and the *b* .	*Enid*	20
child is set forth at her *b* .	"	728
arms for guerdon : choose the *b*.'	"	1067
desired the humbling of their *b*	"	1486
women, worst and *b*, as Heaven and Hell	*Vivien*	664
do my *b* to win . .	*Elaine*	221
yet would I do my *b* . .	"	222
meats and vintage of their *b* .	"	266
for his children, ever at its *b* .	"	335
when they love their *b* Closest	"	865
She deem'd she look's her *b* .	"	903
having loved God's *b* And greatest	"	1087
free love is for the *b* .	"	1372
b, if not so pure a love . .	"	1374
You chose the *b* among us .	*En. Arden*	292
b and brightest, when they dwelt	*Aylmer's F.*	69
that second thoughts are *b*? .	*Sea Dreams*	65
did his holy oily *b* . .	"	191
could have wept with the *b* .	*Grandmother* 20,	100
b and stateliest of the land .	*Lucretius*	172

best-natured.
'Which was prettiest, *B-n*?' . *Princess*, i. 231

bestrode.
b my Grandsire, when he fell . *Princess*, ii. 224

bethink.
B thee, Lord, while thou and all . *St S. Stylites* 103

bethought.
b her of a faded silk . .	*Enid*	134
b her of her promise given .	"	602
b her how she used to watch .	"	647

betide.
All-armed I ride, whate'er *b* . *Sir Galahad* 83

betray.
b me for the precious hilt, .	*M. d'Arthur*	126
Break lock and seal; *b* the trust	'*You might have won*,' etc.	18
Simpler than any child, *b*'s itself .	*Guinevere*	369
I should *b* myself . .	*En. Arden*	790

betray'd
Thou hast *b* thy nature .	*M. d'Arthur*	73
B my secret penance . .	*St S. Stylites*	67
b her cause and mine .	*Princess*, v.	73
let them know themselves *b* .	*Aylmer's F.*	524

betraying.
statesman there, *b* His party-secret *Maud*, II. v. 34

betroth'd.
b To one, a neighbouring Princess	*Princess*, i.	31
of why we came, And my *b* .	"	119
B us over their wine, .	*Maud*, I. xix.	39
far-off cousin and *b* .	*The Brook*	75

betrothment.
how the strange *b* was to end . *Princess*, v. 463

betted.
they *b*; made a hundred friends *Princess, Pro.* 162

better (adj. and adv.)
b than to own A crown .	*Ode to Mem.*	120
'Twere *b* I should cease .	*To J. S.*	66
men *b* than sheep or goats .	*M. d'Arthur*	250
Something *b* than his dog, .	*Locksley H.*	50
B thou wert dead before me, .	"	56
B thou and I were lying .	"	57
held it *b* men should perish .	"	179
B fifty years of Europe .	"	184
b not to be? . .	*Two Voices*	3, 48
Is boundless *b*, boundless worse,	"	27
b not to breathe or speak .	"	94
A murmur, 'Be of *b* cheer, .	"	429
B to me the meanest weed .	*Amphion*	93
B not be at all Than not be noble .	*Princess*, ii.	79

	POEM.	LINE.
B to clear prime forests	Princess, iii.	111
he seems no *b* than a girl	" ii.	202
in the distance pealing news Of *b*.	" iv.	64
hold the woman is the *b* man	"	391
maids were *b* at their homes	" v.	418
b or worse Than the heart of the	Maud, I. i.	23
peace or war? *b*, war! loud war	"	47
b to be born To labour	" xviii.	33
as it seems, to the *b* mind	" III. vi.	56
b to fight for the good	"	57
b were I laid in the dark earth	Enid	97
B the king's waste hearth	Guinevere	520
griefs Like his have worse or *b*	En. Arden	742
himself has done much *b*	Spiteful Let.	4

***better* (s.)**
Go, therefore, thou I thy *b's* went	Will Water.	185
Thine elders and thy *b's*	"	192
striking at her *b*, miss'd	Vivien	349
Thy *b* born unhappily from thee	Aylmer's F.	675

***better* (verb.)**
| his work That practice *b's*? | Princess, iii. | 281 |
| cared to *b* his own kind | Sea Dreams | 196 |

bettering.
| who, *b* not with Time | Will | 10 |

bevy.
| a *b* of Eroses apple-cheek'd | The Islet | 11 |

bewail'd.
| with one mind *B* their lot | In Mem. cii. | 46 |

beware.
| *b* Lest, where you seek | Princess, vi. | 155 |

Bible.
| oft at *B* meetings, o'er the rest | Sea Dreams | 190 |

bicker.
b's into red and emerald	Princess, v.	253
To *b* down a valley	The Brook	26
b with the things they love	Enid	1174
points of lances *b* in it	"	1298

bid.
lest I should *b* thee live	Princess, vi.	372
b her abide by her word?	Maud, I. xvi.	25
b him bring Charger and palfrey	Enid	1249
arise and *b* me do it	"	1513
And *b* me cast it	"	1555
I *b* the stranger welcome	Vivien	119
b farewell to sweet Lavaine	Elaine	340
b call the ghostly man	"	1093
b to speak of such a one	Aylmer's F.	677
of him I was not *b* to speak	"	710

bidden.
| I knock'd and, *b*, enter'd | Princess iii. | 114 |

bidding.
| *b* him Disband himself | Enid | 1645 |

bide.
well, to *b* mine hour	Two Voices	76
why she should *B* by this issue	Princess, v.	316
lord of Astolat, '*B* with us	Elaine	629
if I *b*, to I this wild flower	"	641
B,' answer'd he: 'we needs must hear	"	752
into sanctuary And *b* my doom	Guinevere	121
b your year as I *b* mine?'	En. Arden	435
Philip answer'd 'I will *b* my year'	"	436

bided.
| *b* tryst at village stile | Vivien | 228 |

bier.
borne with *b* and pall	In Mem. lxxxiv.	1
him and the *b* in which he lay	Enid	1420
yonder man upon the *b* arise	"	1505

big.
| apt at arms and *b* of bone | Enid | 489 |
| Cried out with a *b* voice | " | 1390 |

bigger.
| enter'd in the *b* boy | Princess, ii. | 382 |
| No *b* than a glowworm | " iv. | 7 |

	POEM.	LINE.
spangle dances in *b* and bay	Sea Fairies	24

***bill* (beak.)**
| that gold dagger of thy *b* | The Blackbird | 11 |
| A golden *b* I the silver tongue | " | 13 |

***bill* (parliamentary measure.)**
| it was this *b* that past | Walk. to the M. | 59 |
| shall we pass the *b* | Day-Dm. | 159 |

bill of sale.
| A *b o s* gleamed thro' the drizzle | En. Arden | 689 |

billow.
| to the *b* the fountain calls | Sea Fairies | 9 |
| a *b*, blown against, Falls back | Two Voices | 316 |

billowing.
a *b* fountain in the midst	Princess, ii.	14
his river *b* ran	Maud, I. iv.	32
b in a hollow of it	Lucretius	31

bin.
| In musty *b's* and chambers | Will Water. | 102 |

bind.
cords that *b* and strain 'Clear-headed friend,' etc.		4
an athlete, strong to break or *b*.	Pal. of Art	153
that, working strongly, *b's* ' Love thou thy land,' etc.		34
woodbine wreaths that *b* her	Amphion	34
Faster *b's* a tyrant's power	Vision of Sin	128
my vow *B's* me to speak	Princess, ii.	185
wont to *b* my throbbing brow	"	232
b the scatterd scheme of seven	" Con.	8
may read that *b's* the sheaf	In Mem.xxxvi.	13
frame that *b's* him in	" xliv.	11
the thorns to *b* my brows	" lxviii.	7
b a book, may line a box	" lxxvi.	6
b The two together	Enid	790
what is worthy love Could *b* him	Elaine	1370
yet thee She fail'd to *b*	"	1376
That Love could *b* them closer	Aylmer's F.	41

bindweed-bell.
| fragile *b-b's* and briony rings | The Brook | 203 |

bine.
| When burr and *b* were gather'd | Aylmer's F. | 113 |

binn.
| a *b* reserved For banquets | Aylmer's F. | 405 |

bird.
the merry *b* chants	Poet's Mind	22
b would sing, nor lamb would bleat	Mariana in the S.	37
song of *b*, or sound of rill	D. of F. Wom.	66
clearer than the crested *b*	"	179
lusty *b* takes every hour	M. d'Arthur, Ep.	11
as tho' he were the *b* of day	Gardener's D.	95
These *b's* have joyful thoughts	"	98
Slides the *b* o'er lustrous woodland	Locksley H.	102
every *b* of Eden burst In carol	Day-Dm.	255
long-tail'd *b's* of Paradise	"	275
fly, like a *b*, from tree to tree	Ed. Gray	30
b that pipes his lone desire 'You might have won,' etc.		31
the *b*, the fish, the shell, the flower	Princess, ii.	361
As flies the shadow of a *b*	" iii.	80
b of passage flying south	"	194
pipe of half-awaken'd *b's*	" iv.	32
wild *b's* on the light Dash	"	474
b's that piped their Valentines	" v.	229
b That early woke to feed	" vii.	235
b's the charming serpent draws	In Mem. xxxiv.	14
Wild *b*, whose warble, liquid sweet	" lxxxvii.	1
the sea-blue *b* of March	" xc.	4
loud with voices of the *b's*	" xcviii.	2
low love-language of the *b*	" ci.	11
happy *b's*, that change their sky	" cxiv.	15
I hear a chirp of *b's*	" cxviii.	5
Beginning, and the wakeful *b*	" cxx.	11
B's in the high Hall-garden (rep.)	Maud, I. xii.	1
B's in our wood sang	"	9
the *b* of prey will hover	" xx.	28
silence fell with the waking *b*	" xxii.	17
My *b* with the shining head	" II. iv.	45
chatter'd more than brook or *b*	The Brook	51

	POEM.	LINE.
as the sweet voice of a *b*	*Enid*	329
think what kind of *b* it is	"	331
b's song you may learn the nest	"	359
the dancing shadows of the *b*'s	"	601
were *b*'s Of sunny plume	"	658
live like two *b*'s in one nest	"	1475
brush and blotted out the *b*	*Vivien*	328
foul *b* of rapine whose whole prey	"	578
a little helpless, innocent *b*	*Elaine*	890
Like the caged *b* escaping suddenly	*En. Arden*	268
flash of insect and of *b*	"	576
beacon-blaze allures The *b* of passage	"	730
The *b*'s were warm, (rep.)	*Aylmer's F.*	260
as the *b* returns, at night	*Sea Dreams*	43
and every *b* that sings	"	100
one *b* with a musical throat	*The Islet*	27
Make music, O *b*, in the	*W. to Alexan.*	11
b in air, and fishes turn'd	*The Victim*	19
b Makes his heart voice	*Lucretius*	100
b or fish, or opulent flower	"	245
B's love, and *b*'s song (rep.)	*The Window*	62
Arn't we *b*'s of a feather	"	75
we'll be *B*'s of a feather	"	83
Be merry all *b*'s to-day	"	144

birdie.
Sleep, little *b*, sleep, (rep.)	*Sea Dreams*	271

bird's-eye-view.
b-e-v of all the ungracious past	*Princess,* ii.	109

birk.
Shadows of the silver *b*	*A Dirge*	5

birth.
power of brain, or *b*	*To the Queen*	3
At the moment of thy *b*	*Eleänore*	15
God renew me from my *b*	*Miller's D.*	27
slew him with your noble *b*	*L. C. V. de Vere*	48
hadst not between death and *b*	*Two Voices*	169
that first nothing ere his *b*	"	332
Titanic forces taking *b*	*Day-Dm.*	229
does not love me for my *b*	*Lady Clare*	9
one act at once, The *b* of light	*Princess,* iii.	309
draws near the *b* of Christ	*In Mem.* xxviii. 1, ciii.	1
Beyond the second *b* of Death	" xliv.	16
breaks his *b*'s invidious bar	" lxiii.	5
Evil haunts The *b*, the bridal	" xcvii.	14
Memories of bridal, or of *b*	" xcviii.	15
Becoming, when the time has *b*	" cxii.	14
shaping an infant ripe for his *b*	*Maud,* I. iv.	34
mine by a right, from *b* till death	" xix.	42
By the home that gave me *b*	" II. iv.	7
voiceless thro' the fault of *b*	*Enid*	1115
mystery From all men, like his *b*	*Guinevere*	296
marriage, and the *b* Of Philip's child	*En. Arden*	709

birth-day.
Each month, a *b-d* coming on	*Will Water.*	93
night Before my Enid's *b-d*	*Enid*	458
on the night Before her *b-d*	"	633

Biscay.
The *B*, roughly ridging eastward	*En. Arden*	528

bit (s.)
Nobbut a *b* on it's left	*N. Farmer*	41
b's of roasting ox Moan	*Lucretius*	131

bit (verb.)
b his lips, And broke away	*Dora*	31
helmet thro', and *b* the bone	*Enid*	573
fingers till they *b* the palm	*Elaine*	608

bite (s.)
showing the aspick's *b*	*D. of F. Wom.*	160

bite (verb.)
B's it for true heart	*Princess, Pro.*	172
B, frost, *b* (rep.)	*The Window*	49
b far into the heart of the house	"	53

biting.
b laws to scarce the beasts of prey	*Princess,* v.	383

bitten.
	POEM.	LINE.
b the heel of the going year	*The Window*	48
b into the heart of the earth	"	60

bitter.
to give the *b* of the sweet	*D. of F. Wom.*	286
O sweet and *b* in a breath	*In Mem.* iii.	3
My own less *b*, rather more	" vi.	6
If I find the world so *b*	*Maud,* I. vi.	33
world were not so *b* (rep.)	"	38
and fail'd, She is so *b*	*Vivien*	669
b death must be: Love, thou art *b*;	*Elaine*	1004

bitterer.
Yet *b* from his readings	*Aylmer's F.*	553

bitterly.
B weeping I turn'd away	*Ed. Gray*	6, 33
B wept I over the stone	"	34
spake the Queen, and somewhat *b*	*Guinevere*	269
long and *b* meditating	*Boädicea*	35

bitterness.
fretted all to dust and *b*	*Princess,* vi.	247
wake the old *b* again	*In Mem.* lxxxiii.	47

blabbing.
physician, *b* The case of his patient	*Maud,* II. v.	36
curse me the *b* lip	"	57

black.
B the garden-bowers and grots	*Arabian N's.*	78
yew-wood *b* as night	*Oriana*	19
foreground *b* with stones and slags	*Pal. of Art*	81
More *b* than ashbuds	*Gardener's D.*	28
in its coarse *b*'s or whites	*Walk. to the M.*	97
streets were *b* with smoke	*In Mem.* lxviii.	3
b and brown on kindred brows	" lxxviii.	16
ready on the river, cloth'd in *b*	*Elaine*	1117
Wear *b* and white, and *b* a nun	*Guinevere*	669
You so fair! am I so *b*?	*The Window*	74

Black (Sea.)
the *B* and the Baltic deep,	*Maud,* III. vi.	51

black-beaded.
Glancing with *b-b* eyes	*Lilian*	15

black-bearded.
stern *b-b* kings with wolfish eyes	*D. of F. Wom.*	111

blackbird.
O *B*! sing me something well	*The Blackbird*	1
b on the pippin hung	*Audley Ct.*	37

black'd.
B with thy branding thunder,	*St S. Stylites*	75

blacken.
upon a throne, And *B*'s every blot	*Idylls, Ded.*	27
pierces the liver and *b*'s the blood	*The Islet*	35
bark and *b* innumerable,	*Boädicea*	13
B round the Roman carrion	"	14

blacken'd.
b all her world in secret	*Princess,* vii.	27
the walls *B* about us	" *Con.*	110

blackening.
b over heath and holt	*Locksley H.*	191
b, swallow'd all the land	*Guinevere*	82

blackest.
half a truth is ever the *b* of lies	*Grandmother*	30

black-heart.
unnetted *b-h* ripen dark	*The Blackbird*	7

black-hooded.
Black-stoled, *b-h*, like a dream	*M d' Arthur*	197

blackness.
With *b* as a solid wall	*Pal. of Art*	274
b round the tombing sod	*On a Mourner*	27

blacksmith-border.
The *b-b* marriage—one they knew	*Aylmer's F.*	263

black-stoled.
B-s, black-hooded like a dream	*M. d' Arthur*	197

	POEM.	LINE.
blackthorn.		
never see The blossom on the *b*	*May Queen*, ii.	8
blade (spire of grass.)		
varying year with *b* and sheaf	*Day-Dm.*	21
b, or bloom may find	"	206
life was yet in bud and *b*	*Princess*, i.	31
sun yet beat a dewy *b*	*Enid*	1295
voice clings to each *b* of grass	*Elaine*	108
blade (part of sword, etc.)		
good *b* carves the casques of men	*Sir Galahad*	1
struck out and shouted ; the *b* glanced	*Princess*, v.	529
Geraint's, who heaved his *b* aloft	*Enid*	572
with the *b* he prick'd his hand	*Aylmer's F.*	239
was engraven on the *b*	"	598
bore the *b* of Liberty	*The Voyage*	72
blade (shoulder-bone.)		
arms were shatter'd to the shoulder *b*	*Princess*, vi.	36
blame (s.)		
Joyful and free from *b*	*D. of F. Wom.*	80
smile away my maiden *b*	"	214
he is chill to praise or *b*	*Two Voices.*	258
crime of malice, and is equal *b*	*Vision of Sin*	216
such reverence for his *b*	*In Mem.* l.	6
has worn so pure of *b*	*Ode on Well.*	72
white blamelessness accounted *b*	*Vivien*	648
Nor yours the *b*—for who beside	*Aylmer's F.*	735
blame (verb.)		
in truth you must *b* Love	*Miller's D.*	192
I have been to *b*—to *b*	*Dora*	156
Am I to *b* for this	*St S. Stylites*	122
she had a will ; was he to *b*	*Princess*, i.	
b you not so much for fear	" iv.	485
I da—'sdeath ! you *b* the man	" vi.	204
B not thyself too much,' I said, 'nor *b*	" vii.	239
B not thou the winds	*In Mem.* xlviii.	10
b not thou thy plaintive song	" li.	5
Nor *b* I Death, because he bare	" lxxxi.	9
count me all to *b* if I	" Con.	85
did not wish to *b* him	*Maud* I. xx.	5
who should *b* me then ?'	*Vivien*	511
To *b*, my lord Sir Lancelot, much to *b*	*Elaine*	98
They are all to *b*, they are all to *b*	*Sailor Boy*	20
O Ringlet, I count you much to *b*	*The Ringlet*	46
blamed.		
love be *b* for want of faith ?	*In Mem.* l.	10
b herself for telling hearsay tales	*Vivien*	800
blameless.		
b is he, centred in the sphere	*Ulysses*	39
the white flower of a *b* life	*Idylls, Ded.*	24
mild face of the *b* king	*Enid*	1660
Yourself were first the *b* cause	"	1674
The *b* king went forth	"	1780
fighting for the *b* king	"	1818
should attempt the *b* King	*Vivien*	20
b King and stainless man ?'	"	628
blamelessness.		
thy white *b* accounted blame !'	*Vivien*	648
blanch.		
boom and *b* on the precipices	*Boädicea*	76
Blanche.		
Two widows, Lady Psyche, Lady *B*	*Princess*, i.	127
who were tutors. 'Lady *B*'	"	229
message here from Lady *B*	" ii.	298
saw The Lady *B*'s daughter	"	300
Lady *B* alone Of faded form	"	424
sent for *B* to accuse her face to face	" iv.	220
Lady *B* erect Stood up	"	271
but *B* At distance followed	" vi.	66
kisses, ere the days of Lady *B*	"	98
she had authority The Lady *B*	"	222
'Ay so?' said *B*, 'Amazed am I	"	304
B had gone, but left Her child	" vii.	41
Not tho' *B* had sworn	"	57
blanched.		
the *b* tablets of her heart	*Isabel*	17
a day *B* in our annals	*Princess*, vi.	47

	POEM.	LINE.
How *b* with darkness must I grow!	*In Mem.*, lx.	8
B with his mill, they found	*En. Arden*	364
blanching.		
scattered *b* on the grass	*Day-Dm.*	112
chanted on the *b* bones of men ?'	*Princess*, ii.	182
confluence of water-courses *B* and	*Lucretius*	31
bland.		
Shakespeare *b* and mild	*Pal. of Art*	134
small his voice, But *b* the smile	*Princess*, i.	114
bless thee, for thy lips are *b*	*In Mem.*, cxviii.	9
like the bountiful season, *b*	*Maud*, I. iv.	3
blandishment.		
an accent very low In *b*	*Isabel*	20
blank.		
made *b* of crimeful record,	*St S. Stylites*	156
As *b* as death in marble	*Princess*, i.	175
b And waste it seem'd	" vii.	27
breaks the *b* day	*In Mem.*, vii.	12
B, or at least with some device	*Elaine*	194
his shield is *b* enough	"	197
roll'd his eyes Yet *b* from sleep	"	816
blanket.		
When a *b* wraps the day	*Vision of Sin*	80
blankly.		
Had gazed upon her *b*	*Vivien*	17
blare (s.)		
b of bugle, clamour of men	*Ode on Well.*	115
blare (verb.)		
To *b* its own interpretation	*Elaine*	939
Warble, O bugle, and trumpet, *b*!	*W. to Alexan.*	14
blared.		
trumpet *b* At the barrier	*Princess*, v.	474
blaspheme.		
So they *b* the muse!	*Princess*, iv.	119
blasphemy.		
troops of devils, mad with *b*	*St S. Stylites*	4
blast (s.)		
burst thro' with heated *b*'s	*D. of F. Wom.*	29
The *b* was hard and harder	*The Goose*	50
b of sparkles up the flue	*M. d' Arthur, Ep.*	15
like fitful *b*'s of balm	*Gardener's D.*	67
Cramming all the *b* before it	*Locksley H.*	192
b of trumpets from the gate	*Princess, Pro.*	42
b and bray of the long horn	"	242
b's that blow the poplar white	*In Mem.*, lxxi.	3
Fiercely flies The *b* of North	" cvi.	7
shower and storm and *b*	*The Daisy*	70
To break the *b* of winter	*To F. D. Maurice*	22
like the *b* of doom, Would shatter	*En. Arden*	770
b's would rise and rave	*The Voyage*	85
blast (verb.)		
b The steep slate-quarry	*Golden Year*	74
blasted (adj.)		
a sunbeam by the *b* Pine	*Princess*, vii.	181
blasted (verb.)		
was *b* with a curse	*D. of F. Wom.*	103
are not Time's Had *b* him	*Aylmer's F.*	602
blasting.		
b the long quiet of my breast	*Lucretius*	162
blatant.		
strong man in a *b* land	*Maud*, I. x.	63
O *b* Magazines, regard me rather	*Hendecasyllabics*	17
blaze (s.)		
shadow on the *b* of kings	*In Mem.*, xcvii.	19
b upon the waters to the east 'rep.)	*En. Arden*	505
distant *b* of those dull banquets	*Aylmer's F.*	489
in the *b* of burning fire	*Spec. of Iliad*	70
voice amid the *b* of flowers	*Lucretius*	101
blaze (verb.)		
sun *b* on the turning scythe	*Enid*	1101
smouldering scandal break and *b*	*Guinevere*	91

	POEM.	LINE.
B by the rushing brook	Guinevere	397
B, making all the night a steam	"	593
B upon her window, sun	The Window	176

blazed.

thing was b about the court	Vivien	593
B the last diamond	Elaine	443
heart's sad secret b itself	"	832
many a fire before them b	Spec. of Iliad	10
b before the towers of Troy	"	18

blazon.

B your mottos of blessing	W. to Alexan.	12

blazoned (adj.)

From his b baldric slung	L. of Shalott, iii.	15
Sweat on his b chairs	Walk. to the M.	68
No b statesman he,	{ 'You might have won,' etc.	24
b lions o'er the imperial tent	Princess, v.	9
Bright let it be with its b deeds	Ode on Well.	56
giant windows' b fires	The Daisy	58

blazoned (part. and verb.)

b fair In diverse raiment	Pal. of Art	167
purple b with armorial gold	Godiva	52
b like Heaven and Earth	Princess, i.	220
monsters b what they were	" iv.	326
prophets b on the panes	In Mem., lxxxvi.	8
devices b on the shield	Elaine	9
be b on her tomb	"	1334

blazoning.

silken case with braided b's	Elaine	1143

bleached.

wizard brow b on the walls	Vivien	447
all their bones were b	Elaine	44

bleat.

b Of the thick-fleeced sheep	Ode to Mem.	65
bird would sing, nor lamb would b	Mariana in the S.	37

bleating.

I hear the b of the lamb	May Queen, iii.	2
a bitter b for its dam	Princess, iv.	373

bled.

B underneath his armour secretly	Enid	1351

bleed.

strain The heart until it b's 'Clear-headed friend,' etc.		5

bleedeth.

true breast B for both	To J. S.	63

blemish.

b in a name of note	Vivien	681

blench.

make thee somewhat b or fail	In Mem. lxi.	2

blent.

hatred of her weakness, b with	Princess, vii.	15

bless.

That God b thee, dear	Miller's D.	235
b him for the sake of him	Dora	68, 92
b me, mother, ere I go	Lady Clare	56
God b the narrow sea	Princess, Con. 51, 70
thy voice to soothe and b	In Mem. lv.	26
b thee, for thy lips are bland	" cxviii.	9
which we dare invoke to b	" cxxiii.	1
forty blest ones b him	Aylmer's F.	372

blessed (verb.) v. blest.

blessedness.

is there b like theirs?	In Mem. xxxii.	16

blessing (part.)

b those that look on them	Princess, iii.	239
B her, praying for her (rep.)	En. Arden	880
my son that I died b him	"	886

blessing (s.)

B's beyond hope or thought	Miller's D.	237
B's which no words can find	"	238
B's on his kindly voice (rep.)	May Queen, iii.	13
be tended by My b!	Love and Duty	85

	POEM.	LINE.
God's b on the day!	Lady Clare	8
b's on the falling out	Princess, i.	251
from Heaven, A b on her labours	" ii.	455
My b like a line of light	In Mem. xvii.	10
yield all b to the name	" xxxvi.	3
crown'd with b she doth rise	" xxxix.	5
prate of the b's of Peace?	Maud, I. i.	21
deaf To b or to cursing	Enid	1427
a b on his wife and babes	En. Arden	183
calling down a b on his head	"	324
your mottos of b and prayer!	W. to Alexan.	12

blest, blessed (part. and verb.)

A thousand times I b him	May Queen, iii.	16
soul laments, which hath been b	D. of F. Wom.	281
b herself, and cursed herself	The Goose	15
fruit of thine by Love is b	Talking O.	249
b them, and they wander'd on	Two Voices	424
As if the quiet bones were b	In Mem. xviii.	6
what may count itself as b	" xxvii.	9
b whose lives are faithful prayers	" xxxii.	13
more b than heart can tell	Maud, I. xviii.	82
B, but for some dark	"	83
As she looks among the b	" II. iv.	84
from a band of the b	" III. vi.	10
might as well have b her	Enid	1427
waving of the hands that b	Guinevere	578
b be the King, whom hath forgiven	"	627
to Philip that I b him too	En. Arden	887
forty b ones bless him	Aylmer's F.	372
made me for a moment b	Coquette, ii.	6
desires no isles of the b	Wages	8

blew.

breeze of a joyful dawn b free	Arabian N's.	1
B his own praises in his eyes	A Character	22
b His wreathed bugle-horn	Pal. of Art	63
Europa's mantle b unclasped	"	117
glass b in, the fire b out	The Goose	49
cap b off, her gown b up	"	51
full-fed with perfume, b Beyond us	Gardener's D.	112
hedge broke in, the banner b	Day-Dm.	141
b from the gates of the sun	Poet's Song	3
b the swoll'n cheek of a trumpeter,	Princess, ii.	343
bush-bearded Barons heaved and b	" v.	326
he b and b, but none appeared	In Mem. lxvii.	7
all the bugle breezes b	" xcv.	24
Altho' the trumpet b so loud	Ode on Well.	39
four-square to all the winds that b!	"	127
Last, the Prussian trumpet b	Elaine	453
anon The trumpets b	"	499
heralds b Proclaiming his the prize	Guinevere	525
a solitary trumpet b	Aylmer's F.	93
from the tiny pitted target b	"	427
the wind b; The rain of heaven		

blew (blossomed.)

A milky-bell'd amaryllis b	The Daisy	16
the first roses b	Enid	1612

blight (s.)

B and famine, plague and earthquake	Lotos-E's.	160
b Of ancient influence and scorn	Princess, ii.	152
like a b On my fresh hope	Maud, I. xix.	102
The b of low desires	Aylmer's F.	673
b and famine on all the lea	The Victim	48

blight (verb.)

Which would b the plants	Poet's Mind	18
Shall sharpest pathos b us	Love and Duty	82

blind (adj.)

All night long on darkness b	Adeline	44
parch'd and wither'd, deaf and b	Fatima	16
not b, who wait for day 'Love thou thy land,' etc.		15
almost b, And scarce can recognise	St S. Stylites	38
this dreamer, deaf and b	Two Voices	175
whose reason long was b	"	370
true eyes b for such a one	Princess, iv.	116
b with rage she miss'd the plank		159
shall I take a thing so b	In Mem., III.	13
would not make his judgment b	" xcv.	14
not b To the faults	Maud, I. xix.	67
were I stricken b That minute	Elaine	425

	POEM.	LINE.
he groped as *b*, and seemed	Aylmer's F.	821
cried myself well-nigh *b*	Grandmother	37
mate is *b* and captain lame	The Voyage	91
b or lame or sick or sound	"	93

blind (s.)

	POEM.	LINE.
your shadow cross'd the *b*	Miller's D.	124

blind (verb.)

	POEM.	LINE.
gems Should *b* my purpose	M. d'Arthur	153
To *b* the truth and me	Princess, iii.	96
shall not *b* his soul with clay	" vii.	312
good king means to *b* himself	Vivien	632
b's himself and all the Table Round	"	633
Ere yet they *b* the stars	Tithonus	39

blinded.

	POEM.	LINE.
whom passion hath not *b*	Ode to Mem.	117
blissful tears *b* my sight	Oriana	23
b With many a deep-hued	Eleänore	36
Droops *b* with his shining eye	Fatima	38
b with my tears, Still strove	D. of F. Wom.	108
Not with *b* eyesight poring	Locksley H.	172

blinder.

	POEM.	LINE.
Nature made them *b* motions	Locksley H.	150

blindfold.

	POEM.	LINE.
the *b* sense of wrong	In Mem., lxx.	7

blinding.

	POEM.	LINE.
Struck up against the *b* wall	Mariana in the S.	56
Dash'd together in *b* dew	Vision of Sin	42
raised the *b* bandage from his eyes	Princess, i.	240
b splendour from the sand	" vii.	24
fire is on my face, *B*	Lucretius	145

blindless.

	POEM.	LINE.
the *b* casement of the room	Enid	71

blindly.

	POEM.	LINE.
read his spirit *b* wise	Two Voices	287
while now she wonders *b*	L. of Burleigh	53
The stars,' she whispers, '*b* run	In Mem., iii.	5
staggers *b* ere she sink?	" xvi.	14
muffled motions *b* drown	" xlviii.	15
b rush'd on all the rout	Enid	1315

blindness.

	POEM.	LINE.
in this *b* of the frame	In Mem. xcii.	15

bliss.

	POEM.	LINE.
Then in madness and in *b*	Madeline	42
symbols of the settled *b*	Miller's D.	233
Above the thunder, with undying *b*	Œnone	130
Trust me, in *b* I shall abide	Pal. of Art	18
in we Me from my *b* of life	D. of F. Wom.	210
I rose up Full of his *b*	Gardener's D.	206
A man had given all other *b*	Sir L. and Q.G.	42
central warmth diffusing *b*	In Mem. lxxxiii.	6
triumph in conclusive *b*	" lxxxiv.	91
O *b*, when all in circle drawn	" lxxxviii.	21
gods in unconjectur'd *b*	" xcii.	10
A wither'd violet is her *b*	" xcvi.	26
fuller gain of after *b*	" cxvi.	4
have I felt so much of *b*	" Con.	5
Make answer, Maud my *b*	Maud, I. xviii.	57
My dream? do I dream of *b*?	" xix.	3
shall see him, My babe in *b*	En. Arden	899
spoils My *b* in being	Lucretius	219

blissful.

	POEM.	LINE.
here are the *b* downs	Sea Fairies	22
b tears blinded my sight	Oriana	23
sleep down from the *b* skies	Lotos-E's.	52
from some *b* neighbourhood	Two Voices	430
With *b* treble ringing clear	Sir L. and Q.G.	22
b palpitations in the blood	Princess, iv.	10
led him through the *b* climes	In Mem. lxxxiv.	25
she bends her *b* eyes	" Con.	20
B bride of a *b* heir	W. to Alexan.	27

blistering.

	POEM.	LINE.
her forehead to the *b* sun	Enid	1364

blithe.

	POEM.	LINE.
New Year *b* and bold	D. of the O. Year	35
B would her brother's acceptance be	Maud, I. x.	27

bloat.

	POEM.	LINE.
b himself, and ooze All over	Sea Dreams	150

bloated.

	POEM.	LINE.
merry *b* things Shoulder'd the spigot	Guinevere	265

block (s.)

	POEM.	LINE.
on black *b*'s A breadth of thunder	Princess, iii.	274
as a *b* Left in the quarry	" vii.	215

block (verb.)

	POEM.	LINE.
b and bar Your heart with system	Princess, iv.	442

block'd.

	POEM.	LINE.
knew mankind, And *b* them out	Princess, vi.	308

blockish.

	POEM.	LINE.
coarse and *b* God of acreage	Aylmer's F.	651

blonde.

	POEM.	LINE.
rosy *b*, and in a college gown	Princess, ii.	302

blood.

	POEM.	LINE.
leave as rulers of your *b*	To the Queen	21
no *b* upon her maiden robes	The Poet	41
feel the tears of *b* arise	Oriana	77
her *b* was frozen slowly	L. of Shallot, iv.	30
swift *b* that went and came	Fatima	16
my vigour, wedded to thy *b*	Œnone	158
mix'd her ancient *b* with shame	The Sisters	8
phantasms weeping tears of *b*	Pal. of Art	239
guilt of *b* is at your door	L.C.V. de Vere	43
simple faith than Norman *b*	"	56
ever-shifting currents of the *b*	D. of F. Wom.	133
Principles are rained in *b* 'Love thou thy land,' etc.		80
brow Striped with dark *b*	M. d'Arthur	212
morbid devil in his *b*	Walk. to the M.	13
slight she-slips of loyal *b*	Talking O.	57
It was the stirring of the *b*	Two Voices	159
knows a baseness in his *b*	"	301
prudent partner of his *b*	"	415
stays the *b* along the veins	Day-Dm.	24
bunches red as *b*	"	64
blessed vision! *b* of God!	Sir Galahad	45
Whig and Tory stir their *b*	Will Water.	53
make my *b* run quicker	"	110
said he 'the next in *b*	Lady Clare	84
We are men of ruin'd *b*	Vision of Sin	92
none of all our *b* should know	Princess, i.	3
enrich the *b* of the world	" ii.	164
b Was sprinkled on your kirtle	"	254
was fawn's *b*, not brother's	"	256
blissful palpitations in the *b*	" iv.	10
what mother's *b* You draw from	" v.	394
brethren of our *b* and cause	" vi.	55
dabbled with the *b* Of his own son	"	63
there is iron in the *b*	"	213
faith in womankind Beats with his *b*	" vii.	310
to fail from out my *b*	In Mem. ii.	15
crush her, like a vice of *b*	" iii.	15
in the chambers of the *b*	" xxiii.	20
sacred be the flesh and *b*	" xxxiii.	11
use may lie in *b* and breath	" xliv.	13
b creeps, and the nerves prick	" xlix.	2
Defects of doubt, and taints of *b*	" liii.	4
wilt thou rule my *b*	" lviii.	5
Delayest the sorrow in my *b*	" lxxxii.	14
branches of thy *b*; Thy *b*, my friend	" lxxxiii.	8
My *b* an even tenor kept	" lxxxiv.	17
false pride in place and *b*	" cv.	21
all the years of April *b*	" cviii.	12
lly *b* a king, at heart a clown	" cx.	4
all my *b*, a fuller wave	" cxxi.	11
the great Æon sinks in *b*	" cxxvi.	16
Remade the *b* and changed the frame	" Con.	11
drip with a silent horror of *b*	Maud, I. i.	3
sweeter *b* by the other side	" xiii.	34
so warmly ran my *b*	" xvii.	3
household Fury sprinkled with *b*	" xix.	32
true *b* spilt had in it a heat	"	44
soul of the rose went into my *b*	" xxii.	33
A cry for a brother's *b*	" II. i.	34
Am I guilty of *b*?	" ii.	73
are not roses, but *b*	" v.	78
man of long-enduring *b*	Ode on Well.	24

CONCORDANCE TO

	POEM.	LINE.
lash all Europe into *b*	To F. D. Maurice	34
Prince's *b* spirted upon the scarf	Enid	208
quiet night into her *b*	„	532
b Of their strong bodies	„	568
no; I do not mean *b*	„	1188
for his hurt and loss of *b*	„	1625
prideful sparkle in the *b*	„	1675
vicious quitch Of *b* and custom	„	1752
genial courses of his *b*	„	1775
As clean as *b* of babes	Vivien	194
my *b* Hath earnest in it	„	406
practice burns into the *b*	„	612
pale *b* of the wizard at her touch	„	798
rising sun with heathen *b*	Elaine	308
the *b* Sprang to her face	„	375
half his *b* burst forth	„	516
For twenty strokes of the *b*	„	716
far *b*, which dwelt at Camelot	„	799
b ran lustier in him again	„	877
as though you were my *b*	„	956
in the fantasy than the *b*	„	1126
what are they? flesh and *b*?	„	1249
reverencing king's *b* in a bad man	Guinevere	38
To save his *b* from scandal	„	510
down thro' all his *b* Drew in	En. Arden	660
is but one of all my *b*	„	893
kinship to the gracious *b*	Aylmer's F.	62
to flush his *b* with air	„	459
redden'd with no bandit's *b*	„	597
river of *b* to the sick sea	„	768
swept away The men of flesh and *b*	Sea Dreams	230
felt my *b* Glow with the glow	Tithonus	55
pierces the liver and blackens the *b*	The Islet	35
anger, not by *b* to be satiated	Boädicea	52
Burnt in each man's *b*	The Captain	16
scatter'd *B* and brains of men	„	48
In their *b*, as they lay dying	„	55
spill his *b* and heal the land	The Victim	46
the chemic labour of the *b*	Lucretius	20
all the *b* by Sylla shed	„	47
keep him from the lust of *b*	„	83
strikes through the thick *b* Of cattle	„	98
lust or lusty *b* or provender	„	195
b in sight of Collatine	„	235
Into my heart and my *b*!	The Window	193

bloodier.

hands of power Were *b*	Aylmer's F.	453

bloodily.

B flow'd the Tamesa rolling	Boädicea	27
B, *b* fall the battle-axe	„	56

bloodless.

b east began To quicken	Enid	534
now, the *b* point reversed	The Voyage	71

blood-red.

dabbled with *b-r* heath	Maud, I. i.	2
flames The *b-r* blossom of war	„ III. vi.	53
the *b-r* light of dawn	Elaine	1019

bloody.

shovell'd up into a *b* trench	Audley Ct.	41
raw mechanic's *b* thumbs	Walk. to the M.	67
Where the *b* conduit runs	Vision of Sin	144
b vengeance on you both	Princess, iv.	513

bloom.

inlay Of braided *B*'s unmown	Arabian N's	29
lovely freight Of overflowing *B*'s	Ode to Mem.	17
Whence that aery *b* of thine	Adeline	11
with stately *b*'s the breathing spring	The Poet	27
violet eyes, and all her Hebe *b*	Gardener's D.	136
in bud, or blade, or *b* may find	Day-Dm.	206
slope was rich in *b*	To E. L.	20
brake the wrathful *b*	Princess, iv.	364
not for the glow, the *b*	In Mem. ii.	9
every spirit's folded *b*	„ xlii.	2
sicken'd every living *b*	„ lxxi.	7
brake and *b* And meadow,	„ lxxxv.	3
passion pure in snowy *b*	„ cviii.	11
azure *b* of a crescent of sea	Maud, I. iv.	5

	POEM.	LINE.
in our sad world's best *b*	The Brook	218
each a nest in *b*	Aylmer's F.	150
bud ever breaks into *b* on the tree	The Islet	32
b profuse and cedar arches	Alcaics	11

bloom (verb.)

saw the water-lily *b*	L. of Shalott, iii.	39
b's below the barren peak	Lotos-E's.	145
b's the garden that I love	Gardener's D.	34
if it can it there may *b*	In Mem. viii.	23
from marge to marge shall *b*	„ xlv.	7
b to profit, otherwhere	„ lxxxi.	12
hearts are warm'd and faces *b*	„ Con.	82

bloomed.

low and *b* follage	Arabian N's.	13

blooming.

maid-of-honour *b* fair	Day-Dm.	48
Cupid-boys of *b* hue	„	278
her *b* mantle torn	Princess, vi.	129

blossom (s.)

Bursts into *b* in his sight	Fatima	35
prest the *b* of his lips to mine	Œnone	76
The *b* on the blackthorn	May Queen, ii.	8
we bear *b* of the dead 'Love thou thy land,' etc.	Walk. to the M.	94
b fades, and they that loved	Talking O.	79
maiden *b*'s of her teens	Will Water.	24
In full and kindly *b*	Princess, Pro.	163
the *b* of the flying terms	„	195
the pouted *b* of her lips	„ iv.	17
Fruit, *b*, viand, amber wine	„ v.	79
my babe, my *b*, ah my child	„ „	97
my little *b* at my feet	„ vi.	64
the *b* wavering fell	In Mem. c.	2
The tender *b* flutter down	Maud, III. vi.	53
flames The blood-red *b* of war	The Brook	56
With here a *b* sailing	The Daisy	32
rosy *b* in hot ravine	Enid	364
like a *b* vermeil-white	Elaine	966
will strike my *b* dead	Guinevere	387
look'd a paradise Of *b*	En. Arden	179
as Nature packs Her *b*	Aylmer's F.	142
Gather'd the *b* that rebloom'd	Sea Dreams	99
Into a land all sun and *b*	W. to Alexan.	9
Scatter the *b* under her feet!	The Window	152
tumble the *b*, the mad little tits!		

blossom (verb.)

A little garden *b*	Amphion	104
buds and *b*'s like the rest	In Mem. cxiv.	20
b in purple and red	Maud, I. xxii.	74
wilderness shall *b* as the rose	Aylmer's F.	649

blossom-ball.

Made *b-b* or daisy-chain	Aylmer's F.	87

blossom-belt.

garden's glowing *b-b*'s	Princess, v.	353

blossom'd (adj.)

white robe like a *b* branch	Princess, iv.	161
On the *b* gable-ends	Maud, I. vi.	9

blossom'd (verb.)

b up From out a common vein	Princess, ii.	292
wreath of March has *b*	To F. D. Maurice	43
branch'd And *b* in to the zenith	En. Arden	587

blossom-dust.

Foot-gilt with all the *b-d*	Vivien	131
like the working bee in *b-d*	En. Arden	363

blossom-fragrant.

b-f slipt the heavy dews	Princess, v.	233

blossoming.

the happy *b* shore	Sea Fairies	8

blot (s.)

'Tis the *b* upon the brain	Maud, II. iv.	60
a throne, And blackens every *b*	Idylls, Ded.	27
text that looks a little *b*	Vivien	521
Far off, a *b* upon the stream	Elaine	1383
A *b* in heaven, the Raven	Guinevere	132
With *b*'s of it about them	Aylmer's F.	620

TENNYSON'S WORKS. 33

	POEM.	LINE.
blot (verb.)		
B out the slope of sea	*Princess*, vii.	23
blotted.		
his brush, and *b* out the bird	*Vivien*	328
blow (s.)		
O cursed hand! O cursed *b!*	*Oriana*	82
iron to be shaped with *b's*	*Princess*, v.	200
clench'd his purpose like a *b!*	"	296
The large *b's* rain'd, as here	"	490
own *b's* they hurt themselves	" vi.	33
breasts the *b's* of circumstance	*In Mem*. lxiii.	7
in the present broke the *b*	" lxxxiv.	56
shocks of Chance—The *b's* of Death	" xciv.	43
must have life for a *b*	*Maud*, II. i.	27
red life spilt for a private *b*	" v.	93
Back to France with countless *b's*	*Ode on Well.*	111
mightful hand striking great *b's*	*Enid*	95
So often and with such *b's*	"	564
worse than a life of *b's!*	*Vivien*	719
slain his brother at a *b*	*Elaine*	42
hardly won with bruise and *b*	"	1159
like one that had received a *b*	*Sea Dreams*	157
Phantom sound of *b's* descending	*Boädicea*	25
knife uprising toward the *b*	*The Victim*	71
blow (to breathe, etc.)		
loud the Norland whirlwinds *b*	*Oriana*	6
April nights began to *b*	*Miller's D.*	106
as from deep gardens, *b*	*Fatima*	24
the wind *b's* the foam	*Œnone*	61
the summer airs *b* cool	*May Queen*, ii.	27
b's More softly round the open	*To J. S.*	1
Nor ever wind *b's* loudly	*M. d'Arthur*	261
light as any wind that *b's*	*Talking O.*	129
south-breeze around thee *b*	"	271
from all the compass shift and *b*	*Godiva*	33
B, flute, and stir the stiff-set sprigs	*Amphion*	63
Low, low, breathe and *b*	*Princess*, ii.	458
B him again to me	"	462
B, bugle, *b*, set the wild echoes (rep.)	" iii.	352
A moment, while the trumpets *b*	" iv.	558
make them pipes whereon to *b*	*In Mem*. xxi.	4
blasts that *b* the poplar white	" lxxi.	2
fan my brows and *b* The fever	" lxxxv.	8
A fresh association *b*	" cx.	18
all the breeze of Fancy *b's*	" cxxi.	17
mournful martial music *b*	*Ode on Well.*	17
gave order to let *b* His horns	*Enid*	152
hear the trumpet *b*; They summon me	*Guinevere*	565
b these sacrifices thro' the world	*Aylmer's F.*	758
And the wind did *b*	*The Captain*	34
Lady, let the trumpets *b* '*Lady, let the trumpets,*' etc.		5
Wet west wind how you *b*, you *b!*	*The Window*	119
B then, *b*, and when I am gone	"	122
blow (to blossom.)		
Round thee *b*, self-pleached deep	*A Dirge*	29
Gazing where the lilies *b*	*L. of Shalott*, i.	7
b the faint sweet cuckoo-flowers	*May Queen*, ii.	30
all the flowers that *b*	" iii.	7
b's by every winding creek	*Lotos-E's*	146
While the gold-lily *b's*	*Ed. Morris*	146
saw Your own Olivia *b*	*Talking O.*	76
all about the thorn will *b*	*Two Voices*	59
wildweed-flower that simply *b's*	*Day-Dm.*	202
b's upon its mountain	*Amphion*	94
violet of a legend *b*	*Will Water.*	147
the time when lilies *b*	*Lady Clare*	1
in due time the woodbine *b's*	*In Mem.* civ.	7
By ashen roots the violets *b*	" cxiv.	4
lilies, Myriads *b* together	*Maud*, I. xii.	8
lily and rose That *b* by night	" II. v.	75
blowing.		
deep myrrh-thickets *b* round	*Arabian N's*	104
winds were *b*, waters flowing	*Oriana*	14
Aloud the hollow bugle *b*	"	17
wind is *b* in turret and tree (rep.)	*The Sisters*	3
warm airs lull us, *b* lowly	*Lotos-E's*	134
a bark that, *b* forward, bore	*M. d'Arthur*,	8
wind *b* over meadowy holms	*Ed. Morris*	95
b havenward With silks	*Golden Year*	44

	POEM.	LINE.
B a noise of tongues and deeds	*Two Voices*	206
soften'd airs that *b* steal	"	406
Summer woods, about them *b*	*L. of Burleigh*	13
B the ringlet from the braid	*Sir L. and Q. G.*	55
b bosks of wilderness	*Princess*, 1.	110
horns of Elfland faintly *b!*	" iii.	357
No joy the *b* season gives	*In Mem.* xxxviii.	5
O'er the *b* ships, Over *b* seas	*Maud*, I. xvii.	12
south-west that *b* Bala lake	*Enid*	1777
Fear not, isle of *b* woodland	*Boädicea*	38
winds were roaring and *b*	1865–1866	3
Old Year roaring and *b* And New Year *b*	"	12
blown (adj.)		
petals from *b* roses	*Lotos-E's*	47
set His Briton in *b* seas	*Ode on Well.*	155
blown (part. and verb, breathed, etc.)		
b from his silver tongue	*The Poet*	13
yellow Lotos-dust is *b*	*Lotos-E's*	149
trumpets *b* for wars	*D. of F. Wom.*	20
Death is *b* in every wind	*To J. S.*	46
caught And *b* across the walk	*Gardener's D.*	124
billow, *b* against, Falls back	*Two Voices*	316
b about the foliage underneath	*Princess*, iii.	105
b to inmost north	" iv.	412
rooks are *b* about the skies	*In Mem.* xv.	4
b about the desert dust	" lv.	19
harp be touched, nor flute be *b*	" civ.	22
far-off sail is *b* by the breeze	*Maud*, I. iv.	4
musk of the roses *b*	" xxii.	6
b the lake beyond his limit	*The Daisy*	71
after trumpet *b*, Spake to the lady	*Enid*	551
hair *b* about the serious face	*Elaine*	391
a rumour wildly *b* about	*Guinevere*	151
dewy hair *b* back like flame	"	282
b by baffling winds	*En. Arden*	629
b across her ghostly wall	"	662
blown (blossom'd.)		
your branching limes have *b*	*L. C. V. de Vere*	27
blowzed.		
Huge women *b* with health	*Princess*, iv.	260
blue (adj.)		
less aërially *b*	*Margaret*	51
blue (s.)		
citron-shadows in the *b*	*Arabian N's*	15
glistening to the breezy *b*	*Miller's D.*	61
Shook in the stedfast *b*	*D. of F. Wom.*	56
yon sun prospers in the *b*	*Blackbird*	22
navies grappling in the central *b*	*Locksley II.*	124
breathed beneath the Syrian *b*	*In Mem.* li.	12
little speedwell's darling *b*	" lxxxii.	10
drown'd in yonder living *b*	" cxiv.	7
sweet the vapour-braided *b*	*The Letters*	42
like a shoaling sea the lovely *b*	*Enid*	1536
B's and reds They talk'd of: *b's* were	*Aylmer's F.*	251
star of morning in their *b*	"	692
bluebell.		
merry *b* rings To the mosses	*Adeline*	34
frail *b* peereth over	*A Dirge*	37
blue-eyed.		
A Prince I was, *b-e*	*Princess*, i.	1
bluff (adj.)		
B Harry broke into the spence	*Talking O.*	47
bluff (s.)		
round the hills from *b* to *b*	*Golden Year*	76
shadowing *b* that made the banks	*In Mem.* cii.	22
blunder'd.		
knew Some one had *b*	*Lt. Brigade*	12
blunt (adj.)		
So *b* in memory	*Gardener's D.*	52
b and stupid at the heart	*Enid*	1595
Besought me to be plain and *b*	*Elaine*	1293
blunt (verb.)		
discourtesy To *b* or break her passion	*Elaine*	969

C

CONCORDANCE TO

***blurr'd* (adj.)**   POEM.   LINE.
patched and *b* and lustreless . *Enid* . . 649

***blurr'd* (verb.)**
b the splendour of the sun . . *In Mem.* lxxi. 8
B by the creeping mist . . . *Guinevere* . 5

***blush* (s.)**
all Suffused with *B*'es . . . *Gardener's D.* 151
b is fixed upon her cheek . . *Day-Dm.* . 52
A flying charm of *b*'es . . . *Princess,* ii. 408
pardon, sweet Melissa, for a *b*? . " iii. 50
b and smile, a medicine in themselves " vii. 47
sick man forgot her simple *b* . *Elaine* . 860

***blush* (verb.)**
with shame she *b*'es . . . *L. of Burleigh* 63
Said Cyril: 'Pale one, *b* again . *Princess,* iii. 51
better *b* our lives away . . . " . 52
Pass and *b* the news . . . *Maud,* I. xvii. 11
B it thro' the West (rep.) . . " . 16
should have seen him *b* . . *Vivien* . 331
b to belaud myself a moment *Hendecasyllabics* 18

blush'd.
and how she *b* again . . . *Princess,* iii. 84
suddenly, sweetly, strangely *b* . *Maud,* I. viii. 6
Katie laugh'd, and laughing *b* . *The Brook* . 214
She neither *b* nor shook . . *Elaine* . 960
She *b* a rosy red . . . . *The Ringlet* 36

blushest.
Again thou *b* angerly . . . *Madeline* . 45

***blushing* (adj. and part.)**
On a *b* mission to me . . . *Maud,* I. xxi. 11
apple-blossom, *b* for a boon . *The Brook* . 90
chastely down, *B* upon them *b* . *Vivien* . 591

***blushing* (s.)**
how pretty Her *b* was . . . *Princess,* iii. 85

bluster.
B the winds and tides . . . *D. of F. Wom.* 38
'tis well that I should *b*! . . *Locksley H.* 63
b into stormy sobs . . . *Elaine* 1061

blustering.
b I know not what Of insolence . *Princess,* v. 386

Boädicea.
B, standing loftily charioted . *Boädicea* 3, 70

Boanerges.
Our *B* with his threats of doom . *Sea Dreams* 243

***board* (table.)**
This was cast upon the *b* . . *Œnone* . 77
cast the golden fruit upon the *b* . " . 222
pledge her silent at the *b* . . *Will Water.* 25
at a *b* with tome and paper . . *Princess,* ii. 18
subscribed, We enter'd on the *b*'s . " . 60
on the *b* the fluttering urn . . *In Mem.* xciv. 8
Arrange the *b* and brim the glass . " cvi. 16
boil'd the flesh, and spread the *b* . *Enid* . 391
knife's haft hard against the *b* . " . 1448
by main violence to the *b* . . " . 1502
silver on the burnish'd *b* . . *En. Arden* . 743

***board* (deck of ship.)**
I leap on *b*: no helmsman steers . *Sir Galahad* 39
like her? so they said on *b* . . *The Brook* . 223
a year On *b* a merchantman . . *En. Arden* . 53

***board* (for a game.)**
pushes us off from the *b* . . *Maud,* I. iv. 27

***board* (floor.)**
Pattering over the *b*'s . . . *Grandmother* 79

***boast* (s.)**
shame the *b* so often made '*Love thou thy land,*' etc. 71
bring her babe, and make her *b* . *In Mem.* xxxix. 26

***boast* (verb.)**
you know it—I will not *b* . . *Princess,* iv. 334
b, 'Behold the man that loved . *In Mem.* i. . 14
clipt palm of which they *b*; . . *The Daisy* . 8
b That they would slay you . . *Enid* . . 922

boastful.
ruled the hour, Tho' seeming *b* . *Aylmer's F.* 195

boat.   POEM.   LINE.
leaping lightly from the *b* . . *Arabian N's.* 92
Down she came and found a *b* . *L.of Shalott,* iv. 6
just alighted from the *b* . . *Audley Ct.* . 6
B, island, ruins of a castle . . *Ed. Morris* 6
sings in his *b* on the bay . '*Break, break,*' etc. 8
as when a *b* Tacks . . . *Princess,* ii. 168
b's and bridges for the use of men " vi. 31
b is drawn upon the shore . . *In Mem.* cxx. 6
market *b* is on the stream . . " . 13
There found a little *b* . . . *Vivien* . 47
the *b* Drave with a sudden wind . " . 49
two cities in a thousand *b*'s . . " . 411
great river in the boatman's *b* . *Elaine* 1032
rusty fluke, and *b*'s updrawn . *En. Arden* . 18
To purchase his own *b* . . . " . 47
purchased his own *b* . . . " . 58
sell the *b*—and yet he loved her . " . 134
horse he drove, the *b* he sold . " . 610
b that bears the hope of life . . " . 831

boated.
b over, ran My craft aground . *Ed. Morris* 108
They *b* and they cricketed . . *Princess,Pro.*159

boat-head.
turn away The *b-h* . . . *Arabian N's.* 25
as the *b-h* wound along . . *L. of Shalott,*iv. 24

boatman.
great river in a *b*'s hut . . . *Elaine,* 278, 1032
make the *boatmen* fishing-nets . *En. Arden* . 816

boatswain.
China-bound, And wanting yet a *b* *En. Arden* . 123

Boboli.
walks in *B*'s ducal bowers . . *The Daisy* . 44

bode.
there that night they *b* . . . *Elaine* . 411
And Lancelot *b* a little . . . " . 460
There *b* the night . . . . " . 842
b among them yet a little space . " . 917

bodied.
b forth the second whole '*Love thou thy land,*' etc. 66

bodily.
were she the prize of *b* force . *Enid* . . 541

body.
wrapt his *b* in the sheet . . *The Sisters* 34
A *b* slight and round . . . *Walk. to the M.* 45
strong and hale of *b* then . . *St S. Stylites* 28
touch my *b* and be heal'd . . " . 78
bodies and the bones of those . *Day-Dm.* . 109
lies the *b* of Ellen Adair . . *Ed. Gray* 27, 35
her *b*, drest In the dress . . *L. of Burleigh* 98
grovell'd on my *b* . . . . *Princess,* vi. 12
and to dance Its *b* . . . . " . 122
return To where the *b* sits . . *In Mem.* xii. 19
checks drop in; the *b* bows . . " xxxv. 3
Bare of the *b*, might it last . . " xlii. 6
long since a *b* was found . . *Maud,* I. i. 5
All this dead *b* of hate . . . " xix. 97
blood Of their strong *bodies,* flowing, *Enid* . 569
let the *bodies* lie, but bound . " . 945
being weak in *b* said no more . *Elaine* . 835
long-buried *b* of the king . . *Aylmer's F.* 3
adulteries That saturate soul with *b* " . 377
b half flung forward in pursuit . " . 587
thro' the fire *Bodies,* but souls . " . 672
There lay the sweet little *b* . . *Grandmother* 62
I look'd at the still little *b* . . " . 66
cast his *b*, and on we swept . . *The Voyage* 80
phantom *bodies* of horses and men *Boädicea* . 27
that break *B* toward death . . *Lucretius* . 154

boggle.
Theer wur a *b* in it . . . *N. Farmer* . 30

boil.
hell beneath Made me *b* over . *St S. Stylites* 168

boil'd.
burn'd in fire, or *b* in oil . . *St S. Stylites* 51
b the flesh, and spread the board . *Enid* . . 391

bold.	POEM.	LINE.		POEM.	LINE.
more pure and *b* and just	To J. S.	31	Echo round his *b*'s for evermore	Ode to Well.	12
wide in soul and *b* of tongue	Two Voices.	124	because his *b*'s are laid by thine	"	141
You are *b* indeed	Princess, iii.	233	apt at arms and big of *b*	Enid.	489
With what divine affections *b*	In Mem. xciii.	2	helmet thro', and bit the *b*	"	573
b to dwell On doubts	"	xciv. 29	good *b* Seems to be pluck'd at	"	1407
Among the wise and *b*	Ode on Well.	52	he fears To lose his *b*	"	1410
Am I so *b*, and could I so	Enid	102	all their *b*'s were bleach'd	Elaine	44
tho' keen and *b* and soldierly	Aylmer's F.	192	green Christmas crams with weary *b*'s	Coquette, iii.	14
bolder.			*b*'s long laid within the grave	Lucretius	252
me this knowledge *b* made	To J. S.	5	**bonnet.**		
no *b* than a beaten hound	Enid	910	Or the frock and gipsy *b*	Maud, I. xx.	19
boldest.			**Bonny Doon.**		
drawn of fairest Or *b* since	Ode to Mem.	90	a random bar of B D	The Brook	82
boldly.			**book.**		
for such a face had *b* died	D. of F. Wom.	98	this poor *b* of song	To the Queen	17
b ventured on the liberties	Princess, i.	202	his King Arthur, some twelve *b*'s	The Epic	28
I offer *b*: we will seat you	" iii.	143	twelve *b*'s of mine Were faint	"	38
If they rode and will	Lt. Brigade	23	old Sir Robert's pride, His *b*'s	Audley Ct.	58
morning of farewell Brightly and *b*	En. Arden	183	grow between me and my *b*	St S. Stylites	173
boldness.			poring over miserable *b*'s	Locksley H.	172
licensed *b* gather force	In Mem. cxii.	13	prose O'er *b*'s of travell'd seamen	Amphion	82
bole.			Nor yet the fear of little *b*'s	Will Water.	195
About my 'giant *b*'	Talking O.	136	the priest, above his *b* Leering	Vision of Sin	117
double in and out the *b*'s	Princess, iv.	243	miracle of women,' said the *b*	Princess, Pro.	35
rings of Spring In every *b*	" v.	228	kept the *b* and had my finger	"	43
bolt.			brought My *b* to mind	"	120
b's are hurled Far below them	Lotos-E's.	156	on lattice edges lay Or *b* or lute	" ii.	16
Appealing to the *b*'s of Heaven	Princess, iv.	353	can he not read—no *b*'s?	" iii.	198
out of heaven a *b*	Vivien	783	brooding turn The *b* of scorn	" v.	136
bond (adj.)			boys Brake on us at our *b*'s	"	385
dwarf'd or godlike, *b* or free	Princess, vii.	244	to and fro With *b*'s, with flowers	" vii.	11
bond restraint, etc.)			cramm'd with theorics out of *b*'s	Con.	35
force in *b*'s that might endure	Pal. of Art	154	bind a *b*, may line a box	In Mem. lxxvi.	6
obedience is the *b* of rule	M. d'Arthur	94	One lesson from one *b*	" lxxviii.	14
Unmanacled from *b*'s of sense	Two Voices	236	Discussed the *B*'s to love or hate	" lxxxviii.	34
his dearest *b* is this	Princess, vii.	261	With festal cheer, With *b*'s	cvi.	22
broke the *b* of dying use	In Mem. civ.	12	sits by her music and *b*'s	Maud, I. xiv.	13
some strong *b* which is to be	" cxv.	16	in the little *b* you lent me	The Daisy	99
our *b* Had best be loosed	Vivien	191	Read but one *b*, and ever reading	Vivien	472
howling forced them into *b*'s	"	594	his *b* came down to me	"	500
as you know, save by the *b*	Elaine	136	have the *b*: the charm is written	"	502
violating the *b* of like to like	"	241	You read the *b* (rep.)	"	517-526
daughter fled From *b*'s or death	"	277	bought them needful *b*'s	En. Arden	329
b, as not the *b* of man and wife	"	1185	desperately seized the holy *B*	"	491
b is not the *b* of man and wife	"	1200	closed the *B* and slept	"	495
b's that so defame me	"	1411	swear upon the *b* Not to reveal	"	839
Thou broke all *b*'s of courtesy	Aylmer's F.	323	on the *b*. And on the *b*, half-frighted	"	843
breaks all *b*'s but ours	"	425	After his *b*'s to flush his blood	Aylmer's F.	459
broke the *b* which they desired	"	778	Then to his *b*'s again	"	460
all her *b*'s Cracked	Lucretius	37	'Show me the *b*'s!'	Sea Dreams	144
bond (legal agreement.)			'The *b*'s! the *b*'s! but he, he could not	"	146
my will Seal'd not the *b*	Princess, v.	389	great *B*'s (see Daniel seven and ten)	"	148
dissolve the precious seal on a *b*	Maud, I. xix.	45	in the *B*, little Annie, the message	Grandmother	96
bondslave.			**bookless.**		
Your bride, your *b*!	Princess, iv.	521	flight from out your *b* wilds	Princess, ii.	42
bondsman.			**boom** (s.)		
My will is *b* to the dark	In Mem. iv.	2	Crashing went the *b*	The Captain	44
bone.			**boom** (verb.)		
mighty *b*'s of ancient men	M. d'Arthur	47	captain's-ear has heard them *b*	Ode on Well.	65
fragrant lamp before my *b*'s	St S. Stylites	193	*b* and blanch on the precipices	Boädicea	76
To feed thy *b*'s with lime	Two Voices	326	**boometh.**		
bodies and the *b*'s of those	Day-Dm.	109	At eve the beetle *b*	Claribel	9
You are *b*'s, and what of that?	Vision of Sin	175	**boon** (adj.)		
From the fashion of your *b*'s	"	182	all the *b* companions of the Earl	Enid	1327
the first *b*'s of Time	Princess, Pro.	15	**boon** (s.)		
on the blanching *b*'s of men	" ii.	182	*b* from me, From me, Heaven's Queen	Œnone	124
this epitaph above my *b*'s	"	190	At last she begg'd a *b*	Princess, i.	145
b's of some vast bulk	" iii.	277	apple-blossom, blushing for a *b*	The Brook	90
As these rude *b*'s to us	"	279	To what request for what strange *b*	Vivien	113
spilt our *b*'s in the flood	" iv.	511	*B*, yes there was a *b*	"	136
roots are wrapt about the *b*'s	In Mem. ii.	4	ask your *b*, for *b* I owe you	"	155
As if the quiet *b*'s were blest	" xviii.	6	take this *b* so strange	"	159
grins on a pile of children's *b*'s	Maud, I. i.	46	Whenever I have ask'd this very *b*	"	172
b's are shaken with pain	" II. v.	5	Yield my *b*, Till which I scarce	"	201
b's for his o'ergrown whelp to crack	"	55	never ask some other *b*?	"	225
			feels no heart to ask another *b*	"	232

	POEM.	LINE.
ever be too curious for a *b*	*Vivien*	336
Lo, there my *b*! What other?	"	344
snare her royal fancy with a *b*	*Elaine*	72
tale of diamonds for his destined *b*	"	92

boot.
Leisurely tapping a glossy *b*	*Maud*, I. xiii.	19

booth.
sport and song in *b* and tent.	*In Mem.* xcvii.	28

bootless.
proxy-wedded with a *b* calf	*Princess*, i.	33

booty.
chance of *b* from the morning's raid	*Enid*	1413

border (adj.)
A *b* fantasy of branch and flower	*Elaine*	11

border (s.)
broaden'd on the *b*'s of the dark	*D. of F. Wom.*	265
on the *b*'s of a territory	*Enid*	34
on the *b* of her couch they sat	*Guinevere*	100
From out the *b*'s of the morn	*On a Mourner*	24

border'd.
yellow down *B* with palm	*Lotos-E's*	22

bore (verb, to burrow.)
hedgehog underneath the plaintain *b*'s	*Aylmer's F.*	850

bore (pret. of bear.)
winds which *b* Them earthward	*The Poet*	17
broad stream *b* her far away	*L. of Shalott*, iv.	17
b a lady from a leaguer'd town	*D. of F. Wom.*	47
b him to a chapel nigh the field	*M. d'Arthur*	8
b him thro' the place of tombs	"	175
blowing forward, *b* King Arthur	" *Ep.*	21
in her bosom *b* the baby, Sleep	*Gardener's D.*	263
Dora *b* them meekly	*Dora*	34
b this better at the first	*St S. Stylites*	27
Not this alone I *b*	"	60
she Not less thro' all *b* up	*Godiva*	62
B and forbore, and did not tire	*Two Voices*	218
down by smoky Paul's they *b*	*Will Water.*	141
Three fair children first she *b* him	*L. of Burleigh*	87
B to earth her body, drest	"	98
A light-green tuft of plumes she *b*	*Sir L. and Q. G.*	26
b her back into the tent	*Princess*, iv.	175
b up in part from ancient love	"	284
b up in hope she would be known	"	301
b down a Prince, And Cyril, one.	" v.	353
me they *b* up the broad stairs	" vi.	353
b thee where I could not see	*In Mem.* xxii.	17
thus he *b* without abuse	" cx.	21
ghost of one who *b* your name	*The Brook*	229
b The means of goodly welcome	*Enid*	386
by her that *b* her understood	"	511
b Down by the length of lance	"	1311
b him to the naked hall of Doom	"	1418
b a knight of old repute to the earth	*Elaine*	491
b the prize and could not find	"	626
b her swooning to her tower	"	963
reverently they *b* her into hall	"	1259
B him another son, a sickly one	*En. Arden*	109
grieving held his will, and *b* it thro'	"	167
weight of the dead leaf *b* it down	"	679
Enoch *b* his weakness cheerfully	"	828
yet she *b* it: yet her cheek	*Aylmer's F.*	505
loneliness in grief *B* down in flood	"	633
her own people *b* along the nave	"	812
boundless deep *B* thro' the cave	*Sea Dreams*	90
motion of the great deep *b* me on	"	107
b the blade of Liberty	*The Voyage*	72
b but little game in hand	*The Victim*	44

boring.
B a little auger-hole in fear	*Godiva*	68

born.
in a golden clime was *b*	*The Poet*	1
in one hamlet *b* and bred	*Circumstance*	8
wert *b*, on a summer morn	*Eleänore*	7
features of her child Ere it is *b*	*Œnone*	249
never child be *b* of me	"	250

	POEM.	LINE.
was *b* Scorn of herself	*Pal. of Art*	230
call me before the day is *b*	*May Queen*, ii.	49
a thousand times I would be *b*	*D. of F. Wom.*	204
never *b* into the earth	*To J. S.*	32
B out of everything I heard	*Gardener's D.*	65
there was *b* a boy To William	*Dora*	46
conceived and *b* in sin	*St S. Stylites*	120
b In tea-cup times of hood	*Talking O..*	62
b too late: the fair new forms	*Golden Year*	15
Truth is *b* Beyond the polar gleam	*Two Voices*	181
thought and time be *b* again	*Day-Dm.*	70
serving-man As any, *b* of woman	*Will Water.*	152
I'm a beggar *b* (rep.)	*Lady Clare*	37
you are not the heiress *b* (rep.)	"	83
honour Unto which she was not *b*	*L. of Burleigh*	80
Every moment one is *b*	*Vision of Sin*, 98,	122
you were *b* for something great	*Princess*, iv.	288
Ere you were *b* to vex us?	" vi.	231
linnet *b* within the cage	*In Mem.* xxvii.	3
light that shone when Hope was *b*	" xxx.	32
brief lays, of Sorrow *b*	" xlvii.	1
dark house where she was *b*	" lix.	12
the day when he was *b*	" cvi.	1
b of love, the vague desire	" cix.	19
I was *b* to other things	" cxix.	12
Result in man, be *b* and think	" Con.	126
far better to be *b* To labour	*Maud*, I. xviii.	33
the day when Maud was *b*	" xix.	40
O Rivulet, *b* at the Hall	" xxi.	8
a juggle *b* of the brain?	" II. ii.	42
maggot *b* in an empty head	" v.	38
three dead wolves of woman *b*	*Enid*	943
creatures gently *b* But into bad hands	"	1040
anger *b* Of your misfaith	*Vivien*	381
but *b* of sickness, could not live	*Elaine*	876
B to the glory of thy name	"	1363
that no child is *b* of thee	*Guinevere*	421
children *b* of thee are sword	"	422
when her child was *b*	*En. Arden*	518
far-off seven happy years were *b*	"	587
B of a village girl, carpenter's son	*Aylmer's F.*	663
Thy better *b* unhappily from thee	"	675
A city clerk, but gently *b*	*Sea Dreams*	1
dead before he was *b* (rep.)	*Grandmother*	59
naw, naw, tha was not *b* then	*N. Farmer*	29
that dark world where I was *b*	*Tithonus*	33
fair child betwixt them *b*	*On a Mourner*	25

borne (carried.)
Adown the Tigris I was *b*	*Arabian N's.*	6
off her shoulder backward *b*	*Pal. of Art*	118
many a merry wind was *b*	*Day-Dm.*	178
on my goodly charger *b*	*Sir Galahad*	49
bear me with thee, smoothly *b*	'*Move eastward*,' etc.	9
ovation round Their statues, *b* aloft	*Princess*, vi.	51
B down by gladness so complete	*In Mem.* xxxii.	10
came *b* with bier and pall	" lxxxiv.	1
to glorious burial slowly *b*	*Ode on Well.*	193
wild Limours, *B* on a black horse	*Enid*	1307
Enoch lives: that is *b* in on me	*En. Arden*	318
b it with me all these years	"	896

borne (endured.)
I have *b* Rain, wind, frost	*St S. Stylites*	15
think that I have *b* as much	"	91
That a calamity hard to be *b*?	*Maud*, I. xiii.	3
shame The woman should have *b*.	*Aylmer's F.*	356

borough.
neighbouring *b* with their Institute	*Princess, Pro.*	5

borrow'd.
cap of Tyrol *b* from the hall	*Princess* iv.	578
B a glass, but all in vain	*En. Arden*	239

Bos.
thundering shores of Bude and *B*	*Guinevere*	289

bosk.
blowing *b*'s of wilderness	*Princess*, i.	110

boskage.
the sombre *b* of the wood	*D. of F. Wom.*	243

TENNYSON'S WORKS. 37

bosom.	POEM.	LINE.
b's prest To little harps of gold	Sea Fairies	3
From brow and *b* slowly down	Mariana in the S.	14
rising, from her *b* drew	"	61
Upon her balmy *b*	Miller's D.	183
From her warm brows and *b*	Œnone	173
from out the *b* of the lake	M. d' Arthur	30
in her *b* bore the baby, Sleep	Gardener's D.	263
about thy neck And on thy *b*	Love and Duty	42
b shaken with a sudden storm	Locksley H.	27
I will pluck it from my *b*	"	66
shut Within the *b* of the rose?	Day-Dm.	204
I will not vex my *b*	Amphion	102
of the year That in my *b* lies	St Agnes' Eve	12
New lifeblood warm the *b*	Will Water.	22
sun their milky *b*'s on the thatch	Princess, ii.	88
erring pearl Lost in her *b*	" iv.	45
lay me on her *b*	"	88
over brow And cheek and *b* brake	"	364
The sacred mother's *b*, panting	" vi.	132
hid her *b* with it	"	197
slips into the *b* of the lake	" vii.	172
slip Into my *b* and he lost	"	174
The *b* with long sighs labour'd	"	210
Slide from the *b* of the stars	In Mem. xvii.	16
Yniol's heart Danced in his *b*	Enid	505
beard Across her neck and *b*	Vivien	106
to her meek and modest *b* prest	Aylmer's F.	416
fondled on her lap, Warmed at her *b* !	"	687
b beating with a heart renew'd	Tithonus	36
bosom-friend.		
My *b-f* and half of life	In Mem. lviii.	3
boss.		
the silver *b* Of her own halo's	The Voyage	31
boss'd.		
b with lengths Of classic frieze	Princess, ii.	10
Botanic.		
They read *B* Treatises	Amphion	77
bottom (adj.)		
b agates seen to wave	Princess, ii.	306
bottom (s.)		
pierce Beyond the *b* of his eye	A Character	6
Tho' anchor'd to the *b*	Princess, iv.	238
made a plunge To the *b*	En. Arden	377
kill'd In such a *b*	Aylmer's F.	254
bough.		
beneath the dome Of hollow *b*'s	Arabian N's.	42
garlanding the gnarled *b*'s	Œnone	99
thick mysterious *b*'s	"	209
To rest beneath thy *b*'s	Talking O.	36-156
To sport beneath thy *b*'s	"	100
till thy *b*'s discern The front	"	247
grasping down the *b*'s I gain'd	Princess, iv.	171
while the holly *b*'s Entwine	In Mem. xxix.	9
found a wood with thorny *b*'s	" lxviii.	6
Saw the sky with flying *b*'s	" lxxi	24
the garden *b* shall sway	" c.	1
broke The lithe reluctant *b*'s	En. Arden	378
arm, which, like the pliant *b*	Sea Dreams	278
bought.		
have *b* A mansion incorruptible	Deserted H.	20
B ! what is it he cannot buy?	Maud, I. x.	32
b the farm we tenanted before	The Brook	222
sold and sold had *b* them bread	Enid	641
B Annie goods and stores	En. Arden	169
b them needful books	"	329
b Quaint monsters for the market	"	534
She that gave you's *b* and sold	The Ringlet	33
boulder.		
a glen, gray *b* and black tarn	Elaine	37
bound (adj.)		
B for the Hall I am sure	Maud, I. x.	25
B on a foray, rolling eyes of prey	Enid	1387
B on a matter he of life	Sea Dreams	147
'Was he so *b*, poor soul?'	"	165

bound (limit.)	POEM.	LINE.
make The *b*'s of freedom wider	To the Queen	32
utmost *b* of human thought	Ulysses	32
mete the *b*'s of hate and love	Two Voices	135
have dared to break our *b*	Princess, iv.	518
music in the *b*'s of law	In Mem. lxxxvi.	34
strike his being into *b*'s	" Con.	124
shun to break those *b*'s of courtesy	Elaine	1214
bound (spring.)		
but a single *b*, and with a sweep	Enid	1573
bound (pret and part of *bind.*)		
wild winds *b* within their cell	Mariana	54
Two lives fast *b* in one	Circumstance	5
In front they *b* the sheaves	Pal. of Art	78
earth is every way *B* by gold chains	M. d'Arthur	255
Art thou so *b* To men	Two Voices	109
only to one engine *b*	"	347
you think me *b* In some sort	Princess, i.	157
was he *b* to speak?	"	179
I *b* by precontract Your bride	" iv.	520
links that *b* Thy changes	In Mem. xl.	6
Had *b* us one to the other	Maud, I. xix.	38
b the suits Of armour on their horses	Enid	945
They *b* to vows of holy chastity!	Vivien	545
Her token on his helmet	Elaine	372
free love will not be *b*	"	1370
'Free love, so *b*, were fretest'	"	1371
I am *b*: you have my promise	En. Arden	434
I am always *b* to you	"	447
weeping answer'd 'I am *b*'	"	448
she knew that she was *b*	"	459
B in an immemorial intimacy	Aylmer's F.	39
nor by plight or broken ring *B*	"	136
beside his chariot *b* his own	Spec. of Iliad	3
b her in his rosy band	Coquette, i.	6
boundary.		
Close at the *b* of the liberties	Princess, i.	170
bounded.		
b in a shallower brain	Locksley H.	150
a spirit *b* and poor	Maud, I. iv.	38
bounteously.		
b made, And yet so finely	Aylmer's F.	74
bounty.		
God only thro' his *b*	St. S. Stylites	183
Here he lives in state and *b*	L. of Burleigh	57
Heav'n in lavish *b* moulded	Aylmer's F.	107
bourg.		
rustic cackle of your *b*	Enid	276
take the rustic murmur of their *b*	"	419
bourn.		
rang Beyond the *b* of sunset	Princess, Con.	100
bow (s.)		
great *b* shall waver in the sun	Pal. of Art	43
every dew-drop paints a *b*	In Mem. cxxi.	18
bow (part of a ship.)		
ripple feathering from her *b*	En. Arden	540
bow (verb.)		
B's down one thousand and two	St. S. Stylites	109
gay domestic *B*'s before him	L. of Burleigh	48
field of corn *B*'s all its ears	Princess, i.	234
She *b*'s, she bathes the Saviour's feet	In Mem. xxxii.	11
checks drop in; the body *b*'s	" xxxv.	3
bow-back'd.		
supporters on a shield, *B-b* with fear	Princess, vi.	339
bow'd.		
group of Houris *b* to see	Pal. of Art	102
power in his eye That *b* the will	M. d'Arthur	77
She *b* upon her hands (rep.)	Dora	101
knees are *b* in crypt and shrine	Sir Galahad	18
b her state to them	Princess, ii.	150
b as if to veil a noble tear	" iii.	272
handmaid on each side *B* toward her	" iv.	257
B on her palms and folded up	"	269
She *b*, she set the child	" vi.	104
Thy sailor—while thy head is *b*	In Mem. vi.	14

	POEM.	LINE.
When have I *b* to her father	Maud, I. iv.	13
not to her brother I *b*; I *b* to his	"	14
peaks of the wood are *b*	" vi.	4
redden'd her cheek When I *b*	" xix.	66
Low *b* the tributary Prince	Enid	174
back turn'd, and *b* above his work	"	267
lifted adoring eyes, *B* at her side	"	1154
b the all-amorous Earl	"	1209
low *b* the Prince, and felt	"	1768
b black knees Of homage	Vivien	427
b down upon her hands Silent	Guinevere	156
b her head nor spake	"	308
God-fearing man *B* himself down	En. Arden	186
Enoch was so brown, so *b*	"	704
'My God has *b* me down	"	857

bower.

sloping towards his western *b*	Mariana	80
Dwelling amid these yellowg. *b*'s { 'A spirit haunts,' etc.		2
Autumn in a *b* Grape-thicken'd	Eleänore	35
Then to the *b* they came	Œnone	92
to that smooth-swarded *b*	"	93
was left alone within the *b*	"	188
has wov'n its wavy *b*'s	May Queen, i.	29
promise of my bridal *b*	D. of F. Wom.	218
mellow brickwork on an isle of *b*'s	Ed. Morris	12
Pursue thy loves among the *b*'s	Talking O.	199
Droops the heavy-blossom'd *b*	Locksley H.	163
fled she to her inmost *b*	Godiva	42
even then she gained Her *b*	"	77
peacock in his laurel *b*	Day-Dm.	35
broader-grown the *b*'s Drew the	Princess, vii.	33
light Dies off at once from *b*	In Mem. viii.	6
sweeps with all its autumn *b*'s	" xi.	10
have clothed their branchy *b*'s	" lxxv.	13
With thy lost friend among the *b*'s	" ci.	15
moon Of Eden on its bridal *b*	" Con.	28
tends upon bed and *b*	Maud, I. xiv.	4
winding under woodbine *b*'s	The Brook	88
walks in Boboli's ducal *b*'s	The Daisy	44
b's of Camelot or of Usk	Guinevere	499
from a *b* of vine and honeysuckle	Aylmer's F.	156
havens hid in fairy *b*'s	The Voyage	54
music, O bird, in the new-budded *b*'s	W. to Alexan.	11
make her a *b* full of flowers	The Window	25
out of her *b* All of flowers	"	32

bower'd.

| *b* close With plaited alleys | Ode to Mem. | 105 |

bower-caves.

| A bow-shot from her *b-c* | L. of Shalott, iii. | 1 |
| Look out below your *b-c* | Margaret | 66 |

boweth.

| Earthward he *b* the heavy | 'A spirit haunts,' etc. | 7 |

bowing.

She spoke and *b* waved Dismissal	Princess, ii.	84
b at their own deserts	The Brook	128
b o'er the brook A tonsured head	"	199
b over him, Low to her own heart	Enid	84

bowl.

| farmer of his *b* of cream | Princess, v. | 214 |
| Nor *b* of wassail mantle warm | In Mem. civ. | 18 |

bowled.

| a herd of boys with clamour *b* | Princess, Pro. | 81 |

bow-shot.

| A *b-s* from her bower-eaves | L. of Shalott, iii. | 1 |

bow-string.

| His *b-s* slacken'd, languid Love | Eleänore | 117 |

box (case.)

| long green *b* of mignonette | Miller's D. | 83 |
| and the *b* of mignonette | May Queen, ii. | 48 |

box (a tree.)

| fading edges of *b* beneath | 'A spirit haunts,' etc. | 19 |

boy.

the long and listless *b*	Miller's D.	33
thought, What ails the *b*?	"	93
'No fair Hebrew *b* Shall smile	D. of F. Wom.	213

	POEM.	LINE.
there was born a *b* To William	Dora	46
look'd with tears upon her *b*	"	55
let me take the *b*	"	64
may see the *b*, And bless him	"	67
Well—for I will take the *b*	"	97
he took the *b*, that cried aloud	"	99
b's cry came to her from the field	"	102
saw the *b* Was not with Dora	"	109
My uncle took the *b*	"	112
he shall not have the *b*	"	117
will have my *b*, and bring him home	"	120
b set up betwixt his grandsire's knees	"	128
when the *b* beheld His mother	"	134
now, Sir, let me have my *b*	"	149
with his *b* Betwixt his knees	Walk. to the M.	32
was as a *b* Destructive	"	73
So seems she to the *b*	Talking O.	108
Eager-hearted as a *b*	Locksley H.	112
beat for ever like a *b*'s?	"	140
A merry *b* in sun and shade? (rep.)	Two Voices	321
A something-pottle-bodied *b*	Will Water.	131
O well for the fisherman's *b*	'Break, break,' etc.	5
a herd of *b*'s with clamour bowl'd	Princess, Pro.	81
embower the nest Some *b* would spy it	"	148
daughter and his housemaid were the *b*'s	" i.	188
Wretched *b*, How saw you not	" ii.	176
enter'd in the bigger *b*	"	382
'Poor *b*,' she said, 'can he not read	" iii.	198
when a *b*, you stooped to me	" iv.	109
more Than growing *b*'s their manhood	a	437
As *b*'s, that slink From ferule	" v.	36
idle *b*'s are cowards to their shame	"	299
'*B*'s!' shrieked the old king	"	318
rout of saucy *b*'s Brake on us	"	385
little *b*'s begin to shoot and stab	" Con.	61
Among six *b*'s, head under head	"	83
they controll'd me when a *b*	In Mem. xxviii.	18
A sober man, among his *b*'s	" lii.	2
When he was little more than *b*	" lxi.	6
b's of thine Had babbled 'Uncle'	" lxxxiii.	12
b's That crash'd the glass	" lxxxvi.	19
like an inconsiderate *b*	" cxxi.	14
the *b* Will have plenty (rep.)	Maud, I. vii.	7
Read with a *b*'s delight	"	10
take a wanton dissolute *b*	" x.	58
the primrose fancies of the *b*	The Brook	19
God-father, come and see your *b*	To F. D. Maurice	2
as free gift, then,' said the *b*	Enid	1071
b return'd And told them of a chamber	"	1109
pluck'd at by the village *b*'s	"	1408
two years after came a *b*	En. Arden	89
put the *b* and girl to school (rep.)	"	311
the youngest, hardly more than *b*	"	564
like her mother, and the *b*, my son	"	792
So much the *b* foreran	Aylmer's F.	80
b might get a notion into him	"	271
girl and *b*, Sir, know their differences	"	274
twenty *b*'s and girls should marry on it	"	371
O *b*, tho' thou art young and proud	Sailor Boy	7
Cut the Roman *b* to pieces	Boädicea	66
b began to leap and prance	'Home they brought,' etc.	7
Here is his dearest We take the *b*	The Victim	42

boyhood.

in the *b* of the year	Sir L. and Q. G.	19
Sweet love on pranks of saucy *b*	Princess, vii.	323
One whispers, here thy *b* sung	In Mem. ci.	9

box.

Old *b*'es, larded with the steam	Will Water.	223
call thee from the *b*	"	240
bind a book, may line a *b*	In Mem. lxxvi.	6

brace.

| *b* Of twins may weed her | Princess, v. | 454 |
| then against their *b* Of comrades | Enid | 936 |

bracelet.

| *b*'s of the diamond bright | Day-Dm. | 90 |

bracken.

| when the *b* rusted on their crags | Ed. Morris | 100 |
| Nowt at all but *b* an' fuzz | N. Farmer | 38 |

	POEM.	LINE.
braid.		
wound Her looser hair in *b*	*Gardener's D.*	155
fire-flies tangled in a silver *b*	*Locksley H.*	10
streaming from *a b* of pearl	*Day-Dm.*	82
Blowing the ringlet from the *b*	*Sir L. and Q. G.*	39
the *b* Slipt and uncoiled itself	*Vivien*	737
braided.		
b thereupon All the devices	*Elaine*	8
brain.		
arms, or power of *b*, or birth	*To the Queen*	3
Right to the heart and *b*	*Isabel*	22
b of the purple mountain	*Poet's Mind*	29
some odd corner of the *b*	*Miller's D.*	68
In my dry *b* my spirit soon	*Fatima*	26
Devil, large in heart and *b* To —.	*With Pal. of Art*	5
great thought strikes along the *b*	*D. of F. Wom.*	43
dawn's creeping beams, Stol'n to my *b*	"	262
burning *b* from the true heart	*Margaret*	39
from the spirit thro' the *b*	*To J. S.*	38
a blind life within the *b*	*M. d'Arthur*	251
whose *b* the sunshine bakes	*St S. Stylites*	161
the marrow *b*, the stony heart	*Love and Duty*	15
tear, that weigh'd Upon my *b*	"	44
that his *b* is over-wrought	*Locksley H.*	53
bounded in a shallower *b*	"	150
random arrow from the *b*	*Two Voices*	345
secrets of the *b*, the stars,	*Day-Dm.*	223
bars a seasoned *b* about	*Will Water.*	85
a his *b* Began to mellow	*Princess*, i.	177
Besides the *b* was like the hand	" ii.	134
dagg'd my *b's* for such a song	" iv.	136
Whose *b's* are in their hands	"	497
for the unquiet heart and *b*	*In Mem.* v.	5
narvel what possess'd my *b*	" xiv.	16
nake a picture in the *b*	" lxxix.	9
out the canker of the *b*	" xci.	3
Pallas from the *b* Of Demons?	" cxiii.	13
think we are not wholly *b*	" cxix.	2
life is darkened in the *b*	" cxx.	8
keep a temperate *b*	*Maud*, I. iv.	40
a lying trick of the *b?*	" II. i.	37
a juggle born of the *b?*	" ii.	42
'Tis the blot upon the *b*	" iv.	60
Beat into my scalp and my *b*	" v.	10
upon whose hand and heart and *b*	*Ode on Well.*	239
Perchance, to charm a vacant *b*	*The Daisy*	106
forethought roll'd about his *b*	*Vivien*	79
make My scheming *b* a cinder	"	782
Beating it in upon his weary *b*	*En. Arden*	797
dash the *b's* of the little one out	*Boädicea*	68
scatter'd Blood and *b's* of men	*The Captain*	48
the brute *b* within the man's	*Lucretius*	21
brain-feverous.		
B-*f* in his heat and agony	*Elaine*	850
brain-labour.		
prodigal of all *b-l* he	*Aylmer's F.*	447
brainless.		
Insolent, *b*, heartless!	*Aylmer's F.*	368
brainpan.		
if my *b* were an empty hall	*Princess*, ii.	376
brake (s.)		
Close-matted, bur and *b* and briar	*Day-Dm.*	66
over *b* and bloom And meadow	*In Mem.* lxxxv.	3
bristles all the *b's* and thorns	" cvi.	9
In every wavering *b* an ambuscade	*Enid*	900
brake (verb.)		
the crocus *b* like fire	*Œnone*	94
B with a blast of trumpets	*Princess*, Pro.	42
the involuntary sigh *B*	" iii.	176
and bosom *b* the wrathful bloom	" iv.	364
titter, out of which there *b*	" v.	15
saucy boys *B* on us at our books	"	385
b out my sire Lifting his grim head	" vi.	254
No spirit ever *b* the band	*In Mem.* xcii.	2
The fires of Hell *b* out	*Maud*, II. i.	9
thrice they *b* their spears	*Enid*	562
b short, and down his enemy roll'd	"	1009

	POEM.	LINE.
and the skull *B*, from the nape	*Elaine*	51
b a sudden-beaming tenderness	"	327
then out she *b*: ' Going?	"	922
next sun *b* from underground	"	1131
B from the vast oriel-embowering vine	"	1192
Stoopt, took, *b* seal, and read it	"	1264
maid, who brook'd No silence, *b* it	*Guinevere*	158
storm of anger *b* From Guinevere	"	359
there her voice *b* suddenly	"	601
on them *b* the sudden foe	*The Victim*	4
Suddenly from him *b* the wife	"	75
bramble-rose.		
B-*r's*, faint and pale	*A Dirge*	30
branch (s.)		
Like to some *b* of stars	*L. of Shalott*, iii.	11
B'es they bore of that enchanted	*Lotos-E's.*	28
With winds upon the *b*	"	72
b'es, fledged with clearest green,	*D. of F. Wom.*	59
dropt the *b* she held,	*Gardeners' D.*	154
topmost *b'es* can discern (rep. 95, 151)	*Talking O.*	31
From spray, and *b*, and stem,	"	190
white robe like a blossom'd *b*	*Princess*, iv.	161
b'es thereupon Spread out at top,	"	187
shook the *b'es* of the deer	*Con.*	98
makes the barren *b'es* loud ;	*In Mem.* xv.	13
all the *b'es* of thy blood ;	lxxxiii.	8
while these long *b'es* sway,	*Maud*, I. xviii.	29
and the rotten *b* Snapt	*Vivien*	806
border fantasy of *b* and flower	*Elaine*	11
Stagger'd and shook, holding the *b*,	*En. Arden.*	768
branch (verb.)		
b'es current yet in kindred veins.'	*Princess*, ii.	227
friths that *b* and spread	*In Mem., Con.*	115
branch'd.		
cloisters, *b* like mighty woods,	*Pal. of Art*	26
throve and *b* from clime to clime,	*In Mem.* cxvii.	13
dress All *b* and flower'd with gold,	*Enid*	631
b And blossom'd in the zenith,	*En. Arden.*	586
b itself, Fine as ice-ferns	*Aylmer's F.*	221
branch-work.		
Beneath *b-w* of costly sardonyx	*Pal. of Art*	95
brand (a mark.)		
had let appear the *b* of John—	*Aylmer's F.*	509
brand (a sword.)		
therefore take my *b* Excalibur,	*M. d'Arthur*	27
drew he forth the *b* Excalibur,	"	52
if indeed I cast the *b* away,	"	88
The great *b* Made lightnings	"	136
flash'd and fell the *b* Excalibur	"	142
The *b*, the buckler, and the spear—	*Two Voices*	129
hard *b's* shiver on the steel,	*Sir Galahad*	6
springs from *b* and mail ;	"	54
b, mace, and shaft, and shield,	*Princess*, v.	492
weapon, save a golden-hilted *b*,	*Enid*	166
Swung from his *b* a windy buffet	"	939
brand (verb.)		
b His nothingness into man	*Maud*, I. xviii.	39
b us, after, of whose fold	*Vivien*	614
brandish'd.		
by the hilt, and *b* him (rep. l. 160)	*M. d'Arthur*	145
brandishing.		
B in her hand a dart	*Boädicea*	71
brass.		
smooth as burnish'd *b*	*Pal. of Art*	5
dust, shut in an urn of *b!*	*Lotos-E's.*	113
A flying splendour out of *b*	*Princess*, vi.	345
knightly *b'es* of the graves,	*Vivien*	602
brave (adj.)		
Follow'd by the *b* of other lands,	*Ode on Well.*	194
left Not even Lancelot *b*,	*Vivien*	654
All *b*, and many generous,	"	667
B the Captain was :	*The Captain*	5

CONCORDANCE TO

brave (verb.) POEM. LINE.
never: here I *b* the worst;' . . Ed. Morris 117
However we *b* it out, . . . Maud, I. iv. 30

braved.
b a riotous heart in asking . . Elaine . 358

bravery.
Lancelot, the flower of *b*, . . Elaine . 114

brawl (s.)
wholly given to *b*'s and wine, . Enid . . 441

brawl (verb.)
what the sects may *b* . . . Pal. of Art 210
Cease to wail and *b!* . . Two Voices 199
drunken king To *b* at Shushan . Princess, iii. 214
b Their rights or wrongs like potherbs „ v. 448

brawler.
'What fear ye *b*'s? . . . Princess, iv. 477

brawling.
brook o'er a shingly bed *B*, . . Enid . . 249

bray.
loud rung out the bugle's *b*, . . Oriana . 48
blast and *b* of the long horn . . Princess, v. 242

brazen-headed.
O'erthwarted with the *b-h* spear . Œnone . 137

bread.
the truth, as I live by *b!* . . Lady Clare 26
sold to the poor for *b*, . . . Maud, I. i. 39
in her veil enfolded, manchet *b* . Enid . . 389
sold and sold had bought them *b*: „ . 641
Taking her *b* and theirs: . . En. Arden 111
b from out the houses brought, . Spec. of Iliad 6

breadth.
B's of tropic shade and palms . Locksley H. 160
on black blocks A *b* of thunder . Princess, iii. 275
need More *b* of culture . . „ v. 180
a *b* Of Autumn, dropping fruits . „ vi. 38
She mental *b*, nor fail in . . „ vii. 267
belts of hop, and *b*'s of wheat . Con. . 45
all thy *b* and height Of foliage . In Mem. lxxxviii. 3
narrow *b* to left and right . . En. Arden 675

break (s.) see *break of day.*
a *b* on the mist-wreathen isle . En. Arden 633

break (verb.)
About thee *b*'s and dances . . Madeline . 30
breaking heart that will not *b* . Oriana . 64
athlete, strong to *b* or bind . . Pal. of Art 153
'No voice *b*'s thro' the stillness „ . 259
thought to *b* a country heart . L. C. V. de Vere 3
b for your sweet sake . . „ . 13
loud when the day begins to *b* . May Queen, i. 10
lest a cry Should *b* his sleep . Walk. to the M. 66
old sore *b*'s out from age to age . „ . 71
Faltering, would *b* its syllables . Love and Duty 39
He *b*'s the hedge: he enters . Day-Dm. . 118
b it. In the name of wife . . „ . 265
B up the heavens, O Lord! . St Agnes' Eve 21
b In full and kindly blossom . Will Water. 23
B lock and seal: betray 'You might have won,' etc 18
B, *b*, *b*, On thy cold gray stones, 'Break, break,' etc. 1
b the council up.' . . . Princess, i. 88
wherefore *b* her troth? . . „ . 94
b my chain, to shake my mane . „ ii. 402
b us with ourselves— . . „ iii. 241
rough kex *b* The starr'd mosaic, . „ iv. 59
did I *b* Your precinct; . . „ . 401
On me, me, me, the storm first *b*'s „ . 478
have dared to *b* our bound . . „ . 518
she's yet a colt—Take, *b* her: . „ v. 446
b's, and cracks, and splits . . „ . 516
b them more in their behoof . „ vi. 45
Nemesis *B* from a darken'd future „ . 159
We *b* our laws with ease, . . „ . 303
your Highness *b*'s with ease. . „ . 305
b's the Pharos from his base . . „ . 319
in a pause I dared not *b*; . . „ vii. 233
B, thou deep vase of chilling tears In Mem. iv. 11

To evening, but some heart did *b* POEM. LINE.
                                    In Mem. vi. 8
bald street *b*'s the blank day. . „ vii. 12
B's hither over Indian seas, . . „ xxvi. 14
my hold on life would *b* . . „ xxviii. 15
b's about the dappled pools: . . „ xlviii. 4
b's his birth's invidious bar . . „ lxiii. 5
b The low beginnings of content . „ lxxxiii. 47
b the livelong summer day . . „ lxxxviii. 31
b's The rocket molten into flakes . „ xcvii. 31
into silver arrows *b* . . . „ c. 15
brine That *b*'s the coast . . „ cvi. 15
let his coltish nature *b* . . „ cx. 7
every thought *b*'s out a rose. . „ cxxi. 20
b from the ruby-budded lime . Maud, I. .v. 1
her word were it even for me? . xvi. 29
b the shore and evermore Make and *b*, Ode on Well 260
To *b* the blast of winter . . To F. D. Maurice 22
B not, O woman's-heart (rep.) . Idylls, Ded. 43
too vehemently to *b* upon it. . Enid . . 78
often they *b* covert at our feet. . „ . 183
fight him, and will *b* his pride . „ . 221
in April suddenly *B*'s from a coppice „ . 339
lightly *b*'s a faded flower-sheath „ . 365
b his pride, and have it of him. . „ . 416
b his pride, and learn his name, . „ . 424
I may *b* his pride . . . „ . 476
b perforce Upon a head so dear . „ . 161
upon his tongue May *b* it . . „ . 892
chance That *b*'s upon them perilously „ . 1203
blood *B* into furious flame . . „ . 1695
b her sports with graver fits . . Vivien . 5
in the slippery sand before it *b*'s? „ . 14
from Arthur's court To *b* the mood. „ . 141
wave about to *b* upon me . . „ . 151
gnat can *b* our dream When sweetest Elaine . 136
crying Christ and him, And *b* them; „ . 306
b faith with one I may not name? „ . 682
discourtesy To blunt or *b* her passion „ . 969
meant to *b* the passion in her) . „ . 1073
b those bounds of courtesy . . „ . 1214
To *b* her passion, some discourtesy „ . 1294
I needs must *b* These bonds. . „ . 1410
smouldering scandal *b* and blaze . Guinevere . 91
in a wind, ready to *b* and fly . „ . 363
b the heathen and uphold the Christ, „ . 467
no heart to *b* his purposes . . En. Arden . 155
your kindness *b*'s me down ; . „ . 317
not to *b* in upon her peace . . „ . 788
Which *b*'s all bonds but ours . Aylmer's F. 425
bond which they desired to *b*, . „ . 778
trifle makes a dream, a trifle *b*'s . Sea Dreams 140
ever *b*'s into bloom on the tree . The Islet . 32
B, happy land, into earlier flowers ! W. to Alexan. 10
b the works of the statuary, . . Boädicea . 64
heavens *B* open to their highest, . Spec. of Iliad 15
that *b* Body toward death . . Lucretius . 153
b's As I am breaking now ! . . „ . 238
Must I take you and *b* you, (rep.) The Window 136
take—*b*, *b*,—*B* you may *b* my heart, „ . 140
B, *b* and all's done . . . „ . 143

break (verb.)
beänt a-gooin' to *b* my rule . . N. Farmer 4
I weänt *b* rules for Doctor . . „ . 67

breaker (one who breaks.)
horn-handed *b*'s of the globe . Princess, ii. 143
b of the bitter news from home . Aylmer's F. 594

breaker (wave, etc.)
The mellow *b* murmur'd Ida . Princess, iv. 416
The *b* breaking on the beach . In Mem. lxx. 16
hoary Channel Tumbles a *b* . To F. D. Maurice 24
flying the white *b* . . . En. Arden . 21
hard upon the cry of '*b*'s' . . „ . 549
ridge Of *b* issued from the belt, . Sea Dreams 205
long swells of *b* sweep . . The Voyage 39
rolling *b*'s boom and blanch . . Boädicea . 76

breaker-beaten.
leagues along that *b-b* coast . . En. Arden . 51

breaking (part.)	POEM.	LINE.		POEM.	LINE.
heart is b, and my eyes are dim,	Œnone	31	massive square of his heroic b,	Enid	75
say his heart is b, mother.—	May Queen, i.	22	noble b and all-puissant arms,	"	86
thunders b at her feet:	'Of old sat Freedom,' etc.	2	tears upon his broad and naked b,	"	111
on all sides b loose	The Goose	53	thro' his manful b darted the pang	"	121
Just b over land and main?	Two Voices	84	sweet head upon her gentle b;	"	527
elms came b from the vine,	Amphion	45	and set foot upon his b,	"	574
b into song by fits,	In Mem. xxiii.	2	spear a cubit thro' his b	"	935
The breaker b on the beach.	" lxx.	16	Her arms upon her b across,	Vivien	759
b let the splendour fall	Con.	119	silent court of justice in his b,	Sea Dreams	170
cruelly meek, B a slumber	Maud, I. iii.	2	Chop the b's from off the mother,	Boädicea	68
B up my dream of delight.	" xix.	2	heart so near the beauteous b	Coquette, ii.	7
weeping, and b on my rest?	Ode on Well.	82	stood out the b's, The b's of Helen,	Lucretius	60
loud whisper b into storm,	Enid	27	blasting the long quiet of my b	"	162
b his command of silence	"	1239	Beat b, tore hair, cried out	"	273
Vivien b in upon him	Vivien	450	breast (verb.)		
lines of cliff b have left	En. Arden	1	b's the blows of circumstance,	In Mem. lxiii.	7
Nor let him be, but often b in,	"	702	breast-deep.		
a hope, a light b upon him.	Aylmer's F.	480	all night long b-d in corn,	Princess, ii.	365
b that, you made and broke	Sea Dreams	139	breath.		
breaks As I am b now l	Lucretius	238	b Of the fading edges of box	'A spirit haunts,' etc.	18
breaking (s.)			b Of the lilies at sunrise?	Adeline	36
Until the b of the light	'Clear-headed friend,' etc.	25	There is frost in your b.	Poet's Mind	17
ruin, and the b up of laws	Guinevere	423	I lose my colour, I lose my b,	Eleänore	137
but from the b of a glass,	Sea Dreams	240	fill'd the breast with purer b.	Miller's D.	92
break of day.			half-asleep his b he drew,	The Sisters	28
At b o d the College Portress came:	Princess, ii.	1	Long labour unto aged b,	Lotos-E's.	130
climbed the roofs at b o d;	The Daisy	61	first warbler, whose sweet b	D. of F. Wom.	5
breast (s.)			poison with her balmy b,	"	271
gleaned wealth into my open b,	Ode to Mem.	23	empty b And rumours of a doubt?	M. d'Arthur	99
Take the heart from out my b.	Adeline	8	King Arthur, drawing thicker b:	"	148
Fold thy palms across thy b,	A Dirge	2	Clothed with his b, and looking,	"	182
fill'd the b with purer breath.	Miller's D.	92	ears could hear Her lightest b's:	Ed. Morris	65
I crush'd them on my b,	Fatima	12	ever at a b She linger'd,	Godiva	44
snow-cold b and angry cheek	Œnone	140	life that breathes with human b	Two Voices	395
ruddy cheek upon my b,	The Sisters	20	b to heaven like vapour goes:	St Agnes' Eve	3
winters snow'd upon his b	Pal. of Art	139	Greet her with applausive b,	Vision of Sin	135
as I lie upon your b—	May Queen, iii.	59	While we keep a little b!	"	192
The polish'd argent of her b	D. of F. Wom.	158	rush'd Among us. out of b;	Princess, iv.	356
my true b Bleedeth for both;	To J. S.	62	b of life; O more than poor men	"	439
muscular he spread, so broad of b.	Gardener's D.	8	sweet and bitter in a b,	In Mem. iii.	3
such a b As pencil never drew.	"	138	scarce endure to draw the b,	" xx.	15
health and peace upon her b;	Audley Ct.	67	And so the Word had b,	" xxxvi.	9
An acorn in her b.	Talking O.	228	use may lie in blood and b,	" xliv.	13
comes upon the robin's b;	Locksley H.	17	spirit does but mean the b;	" lv.	7
press me from the mother's b.	"	90	Death's twin-brother, times my b;	" lxvii.	2
and he bears a laden b,	"	143	new life that feeds thy b	" lxxxv.	10
in his b a thunderbolt.	"	192	East and West, without a b,	" xciv.	62
Dominion in the head and b.'	Two Voices	21	where he breathed his latest b,	" xcvii.	5
palms are folded on his b:	"	247	wakenest with thy balmy b	" xcviii.	13
A vague suspicion of the b;	"	336	trust I have not wasted b,	" cxix.	1
Earl's daughter died at my b;	Lady Clare	25	quicken'd with a livelier b,	" cxxi.	13
arms across her b she laid;	Beggar Maid	1	Awe-stricken b's at a work divine,	Maud, I. x.	17
bear that heart within my b;	Princess, ii.	313	Prickle my skin and catch my b,	" xiv.	36
Rest, rest, on mother's b,	"	466	Catch not my b, O clamorous heart,	" xvi.	12
seem'd to stir within my b;	" iii.	28	live a life of truest b,	" xviii.	53
from my b the involuntary sigh	"	175	mine from her first sweet b.	" xix.	41
I smote him on the b;	" iv.	146	mix'd my b With a loyal people	" III. vi.	34
b, beaten with some great passion	"	368	low b Of tender air made tremble	The Brook	201
heart was molten in her b;	" vi.	103	ceased the kindly mother out of b;	Enid	732
if you loved The b that fed	"	165	fits of prayer, at every stroke a b.	"	1004
warmth about my barren b	"	185	never since I first drew b,	"	1467
something wild within her b,	" vii.	222	the b Of her sweet tendance.	"	1773
from a dewy b a cry for light:	"	237	b's of anger puff'd Her fairy nostril	Vivien	697
dead calm in that noble b	In Mem. xi.	19	At last he got his b and answer'd	Elaine	421
onward drags a labouring b,	" xv.	18	whereat she caught her b;	"	620
tenants of a single b,	" xvi.	3	King's b wander o'er her neck,	Guinevere	576
Against the circle of the b,	" xliv.	3	b of heaven came continually	En. Arden	531
faithful answer from the b,	" lxxxiv.	14	latest b Was spent in blessing	"	884
warms another living b.	"	116	on January panes Made by a b.	Aylmer's F.	223
haunt the silence of the b,	" xciii.	9	body that never had drawn a b.	Grandmother	62
woolly b's and beaded eyes;	" xciv.	12			
A single murmur in the b,	" ciii.	7	breathe.		
in my b Spring wakens too;	" cxiv.	17	odorous wind B's low	Eleänore	174
enter in at b and brow,	" cxxi.	11	should b a thought of pain	Miller's D.	26
warmth within the b would melt	" cxxiii.	13	b's low with mellower tone:	Lotos-E's.	147
jewel-thick Sunn'd itself on his b	Maud, I. xiii.	13	How hard he b's!	D. of the O. Year	37
pulse that is lord of her b,	" xvi.	13	to sit, to sleep, to wake, to b.'	Ed. Morris	40
ruddy shield on the Lion's b.	" III. vi.	14	not b, Not whisper, any murmur	St S. Stylites	21
shook her b with vague alarms—	The Letters	38	that, which b's within the leaf,	Talking O.	187

	POEM.	LINE.
As tho' to *b* were life.	*Ulysses*	24
better not to *b* or speak,	*Two Voices*	94
To *b* and loathe, to live and sigh,	"	104
life that *b*'s with human breath	"	395
yearn to *b* the airs of heaven	*Sir Galahad*	63
love-whispers may not *b*	*Princess*, ii.	203
Low, low, *b* and blow	"	458
b for one hour more in Heaven'	" iii.	53
your Highness *b*'s full East	"	215
Where shall I *b* ?	" v.	74
each May *b* himself, and quick!	"	306
b upon my brows;	" vii.	332
To let the people *b* ?	" Con.	104
b thee over lonely seas	*In Mem.* xvii.	4
b a thousand tender vows,	" xx.	2
slightest air of song shall *b*	" xlviii.	7
b's a novel world, the while	" lxi.	9
while we *b* beneath the sun,	" lxxiv.	14
b my loss is more than fame,	" lxxvi.	15
hourly-mellowing change May *b*,	" xc.	10
does not *b* Some gracious memory	" xcix.	3
landmark *b*'s of other days,	" ciii.	11
Thro' which the spirit *b*'s no more?	" civ.	20
tho' my lips may *b* adieu,	" cxxii.	11
b's in converse seasons.	*The Brook*	196
only *b* Short fits of prayer,	*Enid*	1003
b but accusation vast and vague,	*Vivien*	551
keener hunter after glory *b*'s.	*Elaine*	156
b's not one of you Will deem	"	539
could not *b* in that fine air	*Guinevere*	638
carefuller in peril, did not *b*	*En. Arden*	50
b it into earth and close it up	*Coquette*, iii.	12

breathed.

b in sleep a lower moan	*Mariana in the S.*	45
slowly to a music slowly *b*,	*Œnone*	40
B, like the covenant of a God,	*Gardener's D.*	204
b In some new planet :	*Ed. Morris*	114
I *b* upon her eyes	*Talking O.*	210
low wind hardly *b* for fear	*Godiva*	55
he had *b* the Proctor's dogs;	*Princess,Pro.*	113
look on Spirits *b* away	*In Mem.* xxxix.	2
b beneath the Syrian blue :	" li.	12
all things round me *b* of him.	" lxxxiv.	32
where he *b* his latest breath,	" xcvii.	5
b the spirit of the song ;	" cxxiv.	10
words of life *B* in his ear.	" Con.	53
while I *b* in sight of haven,	*The Brook*	157
twice they fought, and twice they *b*	*Enid*	567
Queen's fair name was *b* upon,	"	1709
rays, that lighten'd as he *b*;	*Elaine*	296
on him *b* Far purelier	*Aylmer's F.*	457

breather.

b's of an ampler day	*In Mem.* cxvii.	6

breathing (part.)

B Light against thy face	*Adeline*	56
Old letters, *b* of her worth,	*Mariana in the S.*	62
B like one that hath a weary dream	*Lotos-E's.*	6
spoke King Arthur, *b* heavily	*M. d'Arthur*	113
answer made King Arthur, *b* hard :	"	162
from the boat, And *b* of the sea.	*Audley Ct.*	7
Sleep, *b* health and peace	"	67
Sleep, *b* love and trust.	"	68
A hint, a whisper *b* low,	*Two Voices*	434
b down From over her arched brows,	*Princess*, ii.	24
B and sounding beauteous battle	" v.	154
Angel instincts, *b* Paradise,	" vii.	302
b thro' his lips impart	*In Mem.* xviii.	4
slowly *b* bare The round of space,	" lxxxv.	4
meadows *b* of the past,	" xcviii.	7
Bright English lily, *b* a prayer	*Maud*, I. xix.	55
bear him *b* low and equally.	*Enid*	1221
beast hard-ridden, *b* hard.	*Aylmer's F.*	291

breathing (s.)

b's are not heard In palace chambers	*Day-Dm.*	93
the heavy *b*'s of the house,	*Enid*	1251
the placid *b*'s of the King,	*Guinevere*	69
warm-blue *b*'s of a hidden hearth	*Aylmer's F.*	155

breathing-space.

	POEM.	LINE.
shall have scope and *b-s*;	*Locksley H.*	167
ballad or a song To give us *b-s*	*Princess,Pro.*	235

breathing-while.

when for a *b-w* at eve,	*Aylmer's F.*	449

bred.

in one hamlet born and *b*;	*Circumstance*	8
upon the board And *b* this change ;	*Œnone*	223
for his sake I *b* His daughter	*Dora*	17
her will *B* will in me	*Princess*, v.	341
out the doors where I was *b*,	*In Mem.* cii.	2
not being *b* To barter,	*En. Arden.*	248
clerk, but gently born and *b*.	*Sea Dreams*	1

brede.

in glowing gauze and golden *b*,	*Princess*, vi.	118

breed (s.)

b That with the napkin dally ;	*Will Water.*	117
we men are a little *b*.	*Maud*, I. iv.	30

breed (verb.)

graze and wallow, *b* and sleep ;	*Pal. of Art*	202
like *b*'s like, they say.	*Walk. to the M.*	55
Assurance only *b*'s resolve.'	*Two Voices*	315
much loth to *b* Dispute	*Princess*, i.	155
in thunderstorms, And *b* up warriors!	" v.	430
earth's embrace May *b* with him,	*In Mem.* lxxxi.	4
could he understand how money *b*'s	*The Brook*	6

breeze.

The *b*'s pause and die,	*Claribel*	2
b of a joyful dawn blew free	*Arabian N's.*	1
Little *b*'s dusk and shiver	*L. of Shalott*,i.	11
heard her native *b*'s pass,	*Mariana in the S.*	43
b's from our oaken glades,	*Eleänore*	10
Coming in the scented *b*,	"	24
b thro' all the garden swept,	*Day-Dm.*	138
Made noise with bees and *b*.	*Princess,Pro.*	68
long *b*'s rapt from inmost south	" iv.	411
music in the growing *b* of Time,	" vi.	40
such a *b* Compell'd thy canvas,	*In Mem.* xvii.	1
all the bugle *b*'s blew Reveillée	" lxvii.	7
round thee with the *b* of song	" lxxiv.	11
A *b* began to tremble o'er	" xciv.	54
all the *b* of Fancy blows,	" cxxi.	17
tells The joy to every wandering *b*	" Con.	62
blown by the *b* of a softer clime,	*Maud*, I. iv.	4
sighing for Lebanon In the long *b*	" xviii.	16
For a *b* of morning moves,	" xxii.	7
Low *b*'s fann'd the belfry bars,	*The Letters*	43
broke the *b* against the brow,	*The Voyage*	9

brethren.

all My *b* marvell'd greatly.	*St S. Stylites*	68
of her *b*, youths of puissance ;	*Princess*, i.	36
Arac, nor the twins Her *b*,	"	153
The *b* of our blood and cause,	" vi.	55
To where her wounded *b* lay ;	"	74
let me have him with my *b*	"	107
grieve Thy *b* with a fruitless tear?	*In Mem.* lvii.	10
till Doubt and Death, Ill *b*	" lxxxv.	10
his burnish'd *b* of the pool ;	*Enid*	650
My *b* have been all my fellowship,	*Elaine*	669
came her *b* saying, 'Peace to thee	"	990
two *b* slowly with bent brows	"	1132
two *b* from the chariot took	"	1140
friends in testimony, Her *b*	"	1292

Breton.

on the *B* strand ! *B*, not Briton ;	*Maud*, II. ii.	29
Back from the *B* coast,	"	43
touching *B* sands, they disembarked.	*Vivien*	51

brew'd.

found a witch Who *b* the philtre	*Lucretius*	16

brewer.

gloomy *b*'s soul Went by me,	*Talking O.*	55

bribe.

a costly *b* To guerdon silence,	*Princess*, i.	200
which for *b* had winked at wrong,	*Enid*	1787

bribed.

B with large promises the men	*Enid*	453

	POEM.	LINE.
brick.		
When we made *b*'s in Egypt.	Princess, iv.	110
brickwork.		
Tudor-chimnied bulk Of mellow *b*	Ed. Morris	12
bridal.		
Then reign the world's great *b*'s,	Princess, vii.	278
Evil haunts The birth, the *b*;	In Mem. xcvii.	14
Memories of *b*, or of birth,	" xcviii.	15
for her *b*'s like the sun.'	Enid	231, 836
bridal-gift.		
harsh groom for *b-g* a scourge,	Princess, v.	368
bride.		
like a *b* of old In triumph led,	Ode to Mem.	75
merry *b*'s are we : .	Sea Fairies	33
thy heart, my love, my *b*	Oriana	42
down I went to fetch my *b*:	Miller's D.	145
far-renowned *b*'s of ancient song	D. of F. Wom.	17
And gain her for my *b*.'	Talking O.	284
'Who is this? behold thy *b*,'	Love and Duty	49
Draw me, thy *b*, a glittering star	St Agnes' Eve	23
The Bridegroom with his *b* !	"	36
I myself, my *b* once seen,	Princess, i.	71
chafing me on fire to find my *b*)	"	164
prince to gain His rightful *b*	" iii.	145
I bound by precontract Your *b*,	" iv.	521
fight in tourney for my *b*,	" v.	343
the poor *b* Gives her harsh groom	"	367
My *b*, My wife, my life.	" vii.	338
cheer'd with tidings of the *b*,	In Mem. xxxix.	23
He sometimes lovely like a *b*,	" lviii.	10
Behold their *b*'s in other hands; .	" lxxxix.	14
I must give away the *b*;	Con.	42
O happy hour, behold the *b* .	"	69
drinking health to *b* and groom .	"	83
Bound for the Hall, and I think for a *b*.	Maud, I. x.	26
My *b* to be, my evermore delight,	" xviii.	73
dead man there to a spectral *b*,	" II. v.	80
ere you wed with any, bring your *b*,	Enid	228
mended fortunes and a Prince's *b*:	"	718
sweeter than the *b* of Cassivelaun,	"	744
promise, that whatever *b* I brought,	"	783
did her honour as the Prince's *b*,	"	835
own dear *b* propping his head,	"	1432
glowing on him, like a *b*'s	Vivien	466
never wrong'd his *b*. I know the tale.	"	579
Sees what his fair *b* is and does,	"	631
Blissful *b* of a blissful heir,	W. to Alexan.	27
B of the heir of the kings of the sea—	"	28
Hope and Memory, spouse and *b*,	On a Mourner	23
Passionless *b*, divine Tranquillity,	Lucretius	262
bridegroom.		
For me the Heavenly *B* waits,	St Agnes' Eve	31
The *B* with his bride !	"	36
learning this, the *b* will relent.	Guinevere	170
heard the *b* is so sweet .	"	175
bridge.		
Where from the frequent *b*,	Ode to Mem.	102
from the *b* I lean'd to hear	Miller's D.	49
Robin leaning on the *b*.	May Queen, i.	14
the brazen *b* of war	'Love thou thy land,' etc.	76
b Crown'd with the minster-towers.	Gardener's D.	43
half has fall'n and made a *b*;	Walk. to the M.	24
curves of mountain, *b*, float,	Ed. Morris	5
with grooms and porters on the *b*,	Godiva	2
By *b* and ford, by park and pale,	Sir Galahad	82
under arches of the marble *b*	Princess, ii.	434
o'er a *b* of pinewood crossing,	" iii.	317
knell to my desires, Clang'd on the *b*;	" iv.	157
boats and *b*'s for the use of men.	" vi.	31
cataract flashing from the *b*,	In Mem. lxx.	15
paced the shores, And many a *b*,	" lxxxvi.	12
half a hundred *b*'s.	The Brook	30
There is Darnley *b*, it has more ivy ;	"	36
old *b*, which half in ruins then,	"	79
b that spanned a dry ravine .	Enid	246, 294
Earl Yniol's, o'er the *b* Yonder.'	"	291
went her way across the *b*,	"	383
moving by me on the *b*,	"	429
tries the *b* he fears may fail,	"	1152

	POEM.	LINE.
naked marriages Flash from the *b*,	Aylmer's F.	766
all night upon the *b* of war .	Spec. of Iliad	9
bridle.		
gemmy *b* glitter'd free,	L. of Shalott, iii.	10
b bells rang merrily	"	13
bridle-rein.		
rings With jingling *b-r*'s.	Sir L. and Q. G.	36
tied the *b-r*'s of all the three	Enid . 947,	1032
sadly gazing on her *b-r*'s	"	1343
brief.		
days were *b* Whereof the poets talk	Talking O.	185
In endless time is scarce more *b*	Two Voices	113
b is life but love is long,	Princess, iv.	93
b the sun of summer in the North,	"	94
b the moon of beauty in the South.	"	95
fall'n leaf, isn't fame as *b*? (rep.)	Spiteful Let.	9
brier.		
bur and brake and *b*	Day-Dm.	66
little life of bank and *b*, 'You might have won,' etc.		30
drench'd with ooze, and torn with *b*'s,	Princess, v.	27
I have heard of thorns and *b*'s.	The Window	197
Over the thorns and *b*'s	"	198
Brigade.		
'Forward, the Light *B*!' (rep.)	Lt. Brigade	5
Honour the Light *B*,	"	54
bright.		
diamond-plots Of dark and *b*.	Arabian N's.	86
Clear and *b* it should be ever,	Poet's Mind	5
B as light, and clear as wind.	"	7
so full and *b*—Such eyes !	Miller's D.	86
made my dagger sharp and *b*.	The Sisters	26
but none so *b* as mine.	May Queen, i.	5
Remaining betwixt dark and *b*:	Margaret	28
shine, Make *b* our days 'Of old sat Freedom,' etc.		22
b and fierce and fickle is the South,	Princess, iv.	79
b As our pure love,	In Mem. ix.	10
Thy marble in dark appears,	" lxv.	5
voice was low, the look was *b*:	" lxviii.	15
flat lawn with dusk and *b*;	" lxxxviii.	2
b the friendship of thine eye ;	" cxviii.	10
To-day the grave is *b* for me,	" Con.	73
b and light as the crest Of a peacock,	Maud, I. xvi.	16
soft splendours that you look so *b*?	" xviii.	79
of Eden *b* over earth and sky	" II. i.	8
in a weary world my one thing *b*,	" III. vi.	9
B let it be with its blazon'd deeds	Ode on Well.	56
Geraint with eyes all *b* replied,	Enid	494
strange *b* and dreadful thing, a court,	"	616
she knew That all was *b*;	"	658
one so *b* in dark estate,	"	766
keep him *b* and clean as heretofore,	"	1785
face, *b* as for sin forgiven,	Elaine	1096
B was that afternoon, Sunny	En. Arden.	670
B with the sun upon the stream	Sea Dreams	95
brighten.		
brighten'd as the foam-bow *b*'s,	Œnone	60
seem to *b* as they pass ;	May Queen, i.	34
b like the star that shook	In Mem. Con.	31
eyes *b* slowly close to mine,	Tithonus	38
b's and darkens down on the plain,	The Window	2
b's and darkens and *b*'s like my hope	"	18
b's and darkens like my fear,	"	19
brightened.		
b as the foam-bow brightens	Œnone	60
pretty sports have *b* all again	Vivien	154
For so mine own was *b*:	Aylmer's F.	683
Till the face of Bel be *b*,	Boadicea	16
brightening.		
Like sheet lightning, Ever *b*	Poet's Mind	26
B the skirts of a long cloud,	M. d'Arthur	54
is *b* to his bridal morn.	Gardener's D.	72
Enid listen'd *b* as she lay :	Enid	733
brightest.		
b, when they dwelt on hers .	Aylmer's F.	60

brightly.
	POEM.	LINE.
faced this morning of farewell B	En. Arden.	183

brightness.
as babies for the moon, Vague *b*;	Princess, iv.	409
Of my contrasting *b*, overbore	Enid.	801

brilliance.
star The black earth with *b*	Ode to Mem.	20

brim (s.)
garden porches on the *b*,	Arabian N's.	16
froth'd his bumpers to the *b*;	D. of the O. Year	19
stars all night above the *b*	The Voyage	25

brim (verb.)
b with sorrow drowning song.	In Mem. xix.	12
Arrange the board and *b* the glass;	" cvi.	16

brimful.
heart, B of those wild tales	D. of F. Wom.	12

brimm'd.
B with delirious draughts	Eleänore	139
beaker *b* with noble wine.	Day-Dm.	56

brine.
gulf him fathom-deep in *b*;	In Mem. x.	18
darken on the rolling *b*	" cvi.	14
the low coast and quivering *b*	The Voyage	42

bring.
Music that *b*'s sweet sleep	Lotos-E's.	52
in its season *b* the law; 'Love thou thy land,' etc.		32
of knowledge *b* the sword,	"	87
nature *b*'s not back the Mastodon,	The Epic	36
lightly *b* me word	M d'Arthur 38, 44,	81
b the colour to my cheek	Gardener's D.	192
have my boy, and *b* him home;	Dora	120
b me offerings of fruit and flowers	St S. Stylites	126
Love himself will *b* The drooping	Love and Duty	23
hours that *b* us all things good,	"	56
hours that *b* us all things ill,	"	57
Nay, but Nature *b*'s thee solace;	Locksley H.	87
latest rival *b*'s thee rest.	"	89
B truth that sways the soul	Day-Dm.	72
b the fated fairy Prince.	"	76
'B the dress and put it on her,	L. of Burleigh	95
B me spices, *b* me wine;	Vision of Sin	76
And *b* her in a whirlwind;	Princess, i.	64
b's our friends up from the underworld,	" iv.	27
seasons *b* the flower again,	In Mem. ii.	5
b the firstling to the flock;	"	6
So *b* him: we have idle dreams;	" x.	9
not the burthen that they *b*.	" xiii.	20
one should *b* me this report,	" xiv.	1
all was good that Time could *b*,	" xxiii.	18
b me sorrow touch'd with joy,	" xxviii.	19
b's no more a welcome guest	" xxix.	5
b her babe, and make her boast,	" xxxxix.	26
often *b*'s but one to bear,	" liv.	12
I *b* to life, I *b* to death:	" lv.	6
b an opiate trebly strong,	" lxx.	6
verse that *b*'s myself relief,	" lxxiv.	2
B orchis, the foxglove spire,	" lxxxii.	9
Demanding, so to *b* relief	" lxxxiv.	6
take the imperfect gift I *b*,	"	117
every hour his couriers *b*.	" cxxv.	4
She may *b* me a curse.	Maud, I. i.	73
how God will *b* them about?	" iv.	44
wed with any, *b* your bride,	Enid	228
bid him *b* Charger and palfrey.'	"	1249
by Valence to *b* home the child.	Vivien	568
one dark hour which *b*'s remorse,	"	613
win, and *b* it in an hour	Elaine	204
let me *b* your colour back;	"	386
b as what he is and how he fares,	"	546
b fair weather yet to all of us.	En. Arden	191
that we shall *b* you round.'	"	842
arose Eager to *b* them down,	"	873
b Their own gray hairs with sorrow	Aylmer's F.	776
an' doesn *b* ma the yaäle?	N. Farmer.	65

bringer.
something more, A *b* of new things;	Ulysses	28

bringest.
	POEM.	LINE.
b the sailor to his wife,	In Mem. x.	5
Come quick, thou *b* all I love.	" xvii.	8

bringing.
b me down from the Hall	Maud, I. xxi.	2

bringing-up.
It is but *b-u*: no more	Princess, Pro.	129
give his child a better *b-u*	En. Arden	87
give his babes a better *b-u*	"	298

brink.
green *b* and the running foam,	Sea Fairies	2
with oar and sail Moved from the *b*,	M d'Arthur	266
Passion from the *b*'s of death;	Princess, vii.	141
voices hail it from the *b*;	In Mem. cxx.	14
man who stands upon the *b*.	Enid	1321
the woman walk'd upon the *b*:	Sea Dreams	108
now shake hands across the *b*	'My life is full,' etc.	6

briony.
about my feet The berried *b*	Talking O.	148
bindweed-bells and *b* rings;	The Brook	203

briony-vine.
b-v and ivy-wreath Ran forward	Amphion	29

bristle (verb.)
half stands up And *b*'s.	Walk. to the M.	24
b's all the brakes and thorns	In Mem. cvi.	9
hoar hair of the Baronet *b* up	Aylmer's F.	42

Britain.
name of B trebly great—	'You ask me why,' etc.	22
keeps our B, whole within herself,	Princess, Con.	52
B's one sole God be the millionaire	Maud, III. vi.	22
over many a windy wave To B,	Enid	338
Roman Cæsar first Invaded B,	"	746
dread Pendragon, B's king of kings,	Elaine	423
the golden dragon clung Of B,	Guinevere	589
Girt by half the tribes of B,	Boädicea	5
call us B's barbarous populaces,	"	7
Tear the noble heart of B,	"	12
Bark an answer, B's raven!	"	13
B light upon auguries happier?	"	45

British.
With a stony B stare.	Maud, I. xiii.	22
curse me the B vermin, the rat	" II. v.	58

Briton.
Breton, not B: here	Maud, II. ii.	30
set His B in blown seas	Ode on Well.	155
up my B's, on my chariot,	Boädicea.	69

Britoness.
haled the yellow-ringleted B—	Boädicea	55

broach.
Pull off, pull off, the *b* of gold,	Lady Clare	39
earn our prize, A golden *b*;	Princess, iii.	284

broad.
Grows green and *b*, and takes no care,	Lotos-E's	73
Make *b* thy shoulders to receive	M. d'Arthur	164
muscular he spread, so *b* of breast	Gardener's D.	8
Alas, I was so *b* of girth,	Talking O.	139
makes thee *b* and deep!	"	280
were a whole Atlantic *b*	Princess, Con.	71
those that saunter in the *b*	Aylmer's F.	744

broad-based.
B-*b* upon her people's will,	To the Queen	35
B-*b* flights of marble stairs	Arabian N's.	117

broad-blown.
b-b comeliness, red and white,	Maud, I. xiii.	9

broad-brimm'd.
b-b hawker of holy things,	Maud, I. x.	41

broadcast.
fiery grain Of freedom *b*	Princess, v.	412

broaden.
Freedom *b*'s slowly down	'You ask me why,' etc.	11
b into boundless day.	In Mem. xciv.	64

	POEM.	LINE.
broadened.		
Morn *b* on the borders of the dark,	*D. of F. Wom.*	265
broadening.		
b from her feet, And blackening,	*Guinevere*	81
broader.		
Sun grew *b* towards his death	*Princess,* iii.	346
broader-grown.		
b-g the bowers Drew the great	*Princess,* vii.	33
broad-faced.		
B.-f with under-fringe of russet	*Enid*	1386
broad-flung.		
in its *b-f* ship-wrecking roar,	*Maud,* I. iii.	11
broad-limbed.		
b-l Gods at random thrown	*To E. L.*	15
broad-shoulder'd		
great *b-s* genial Englishman,	*Princess,* Con.	85
brocade.		
an ancient dame in dim *b*;	*Enid*	363
stood from out a stiff *b*	*Aylmer's F.*	204
Broceliande.		
in the wild woods of *B,*	*Vivien*	2, 53
broidered.		
'red sleeve *B* with pearls,'	*Elaine*	372
b with great pearls,	"	602
broidery-frame.		
take the *b.-f*, and add A crimson	*Day-Dm.*	15
broidry.		
Rare *b* of the purple clover.	*A Dirge*	38
broke.		
thro' wavering lights and shadows *b,*	*Lotos-E's.*	12
love the gleams of good that *b*	{*Love thou thy land,*' etc.	89
b the stillness of that air	*Gardener's D.*	146
bit his lips, And *b* away.	*Dora*	32
She *b* out in praise To God,	"	110
b a close with force and arms:	*Ed. Morris*	131
Bluff Harry *b* into the spence	*Talking O.*	47
staff against the rocks And *b* it,—	*Golden Year*	61
What time the foeman's line is *b,*	*Two Voices*	155
out my sullen heart a power *B*	"	443
hedge *b* in, the banner blew,	*Day-Dm.*	141
The linden *b* her ranks,	*Amphion*	33
nor *b*, nor shunn'd a soldier's death,	*Princess,* Pro.	38
when the council *b,* I rose	" i.	89
b and buzz'd in knots of talk;	"	132
b out interpreting my thoughts:	" iii.	258
b the letter of it to keep the sense	" iv.	319
in the furrow *b* the ploughman's head	" v.	212
at our disguise *B* from their lips	"	262
b A genial warmth and light	" vi.	264
courts of twilight *b* them up:	" Con.	113
b our fair companionship,	*In Mem.* xxii.	13
idly *b* the peace Of hearts	" lvii.	5
in the present *b* the blow.	" lxxxiv.	56
strangely on the silence *b*	" xciv.	25
b the bond of dying use.	" civ.	12
the sunlight *b* from her lip?	*Maud,* I. vi.	86
horrible bellowing echoes *b*	" II. i.	24
long-winded tale, and *b* him short;	*The Brook*	109
if they *b* In thunder, silent;	*Ode on Well.*	176
Right thro' the line they *b*;	*Lt. Brigade*	33
b the sentence in his heart	*Enid*	800
b the bandit holds and cleansed	"	1792
storm *B* on the mountain	*Vivien*	353
but God *B* the strong lance,	*Elaine*	26
b into a little scornful laugh.	"	121
our good Arthur *b* The Pagan	"	270
next day *b* from underground,	"	412
heard mass, *b* fast, and rode away:	"	414
fairy-circle wheel'd and *b* (rep.)	*Guinevere*	255
after tempest, when the long wave *b*	"	288
wicked one, who *b* The vast design	"	661
my sorrow *b* me down;	*En. Arden.*	356
with jubilant cries *B* from their elders	"	375
b The lithe reluctant boughs	"	378

	POEM.	LINE.
tide of youth *B* with a phosphorescence	*Aylmer's F.*	116
B from a bower of vine	"	156
Then *b* all bonds of courtesy,	"	323
B into nature's music	"	694
b the bond which they desired	"	778
tumbled down and *b* The glass	*Sea Dreams*	138
you made and *b* your dream:	"	139
B, mixt with awful light,	" 208,	228
ever when it *b* The statues	"	216
His angel *b* his heart.	"	269
b the breeze against the brow,	*The Voyage*	9
Burnt and *b* the grove and altar	*Boädicea*	2
yearning never *b* her rest	*Coquette,* ii.	2
broken.		
my sleep was *b* thro'	*Miller's D.*	39
Let what is *b* so remain.	*Lotos-E's.*	125
all the man was *b* with remorse:	*Dora*	161
Oh, his. He was not *b*.	*Walk. to the M.*	12
Half shown, are *b* and withdrawn.	*Two Voices.*	306
clouds are *b* in the sky,	*Sir Galahad*	73
was *b,* When that cold vapour	*Vision of Sin*	57
horses that have *b* fence,	*Princess,* ii.	364
Your oath is *b*: we dismiss you:	" iv.	341
axe was *b* in their arms,	" vi.	35
iron will was *b* in her mind;	"	102
laws are *b*: let him enter	"	297
will never be *b* by Maud,	*Maud,* I. ii.	2
means were somewhat *b* into	*Enid*	455
My pride is *b*: men have seen	"	578
b down, for Enid sees my fall!'	"	590
had *b* on him A lance	"	937
From which old fires have *b,*	"	1070
There was I *b* down:	"	1699
have *b* up my melancholy.'	*Vivien*	116
false voice made way *b* with sobs.	"	706
cried 'They are *b,* they are *b*'	*Elaine*	310
It can be *b* easier.	"	1202
limb was *b* when they lifted him;	*En. Arden*	107
so foolish and so *b* down.	"	315
sunrise *b* into scarlet shafts	"	593
so brown, so bowed, So *b*—	"	705
grief and solitude have *b* me;	"	858
tented winter-field was *b* up	*Aylmer's F.*	110
creeper when the prop is *b,*	"	810
great Hall was wholly *b* down	"	846
Spars were splinter'd; decks were *b*	*The Captain*	49
bronzed.		
on the cheek, And bruised and *b,*	*Elaine*	259
brood (s.)		
many Lilies in the *b,*	*Princess,* Pro.	146
Swallow, that thy *b* is flown:	" iv.	90
sees his *b* about thy knee,	"	559
Because her *b* is stol'n away	*In Mem.* xxi.	28
sound to rout the *b* of cares	" lxxxviii.	17
Heathen, the *b* by Hengist left;	*Guinevere*	17
brood (verb.)		
and *b* and live again in memory.	*Lotos-E's.*	110
b's above the fallen sun,	*To J. S.*	51
About him *b*'s the twilight dim,	*Two Voices*	263
change their sky To build and *b*;	*In Mem.* cxiv.	16
nevermore to *b* On a horror	*Maud,* I. i.	55
brooded.		
air Which *b* round about her	*Gardener's D.*	147
b thus And grew half-guilty	*Guinevere*	404
brooding.		
where the sunbeam *b* warm	*In Mem.* xc.	14
broodeth (part.)		
rims of thunder *b* low,	*Pal. of Art*	75
b in the ruins of a life,	*Love and Duty*	12
Across my fancy, *b* warm,	*Day-Dm.*	10
b turn The book of scorn	*Princess,* v.	135
b on the dear one dead,	*In Mem.* xxxvii.	17
over all things *b* slept	" lxxvii.	7
tempest *b* round his heart,	*Enid*	860
brooding (s.)		
wordless *b*'s on the wasted cheek—	*Princess,* vii.	97

CONCORDANCE TO

brook (s.)

	POEM.	LINE.
Past Yabbok *b* the livelong night	*'Clear-headed friend,'* etc.	27
b that loves To purl o'er matted	*Ode to Mem.*	58
deep *b* groan'd beneath the mill;	*Miller's D.*	113
thirsted for the *b's*, the showers	*Fatima*	10
long *b* falling thro' the clov'n ravine	*Œnone*	8
O mountain *b's*, I am the daughter	"	36
torrent *b's* of hallow'd Israel	*D. of F. Wom.*	181
leap the rainbows of the *b's*	*Locksley H.*	171
drown'd within the whirling *b*:	*Princess, Pro.*	47
Spring that swells the narrow *b's*,	*In Mem.* lxxxiv.	70
The *b* alone far-off was heard,	" xciv.	7
swoll'n *b* that bubbles fast	" xcviii.	6
b shall babble down the plain,	" c.	10
Here by this *b* we parted;	*The Brook*	1
yet the *b* he loved,	"	15
'O *b*,' he says, 'O babbling *b*,'	"	20
the *b*, why not? replies.	"	22
Philip's farm where *b* and river meet.	"	38
chatter'd more than *b* or bird;	"	51
Beyond the *b*, waist-deep in	"	118
bowing o'er the *b* A tonsured head	"	199
slopes a wild *b* o'er a little stone,	*Enid*	77
broad *b* o'er a shingly bed	"	248
at the inrunning of a little *b*.	*Elaine*	1379
by the rushing *b* or silent well.	*Guinevere*	397
Little about it stirring save a *b* !	*Aylmer's F.*	32
b Vocal, with here and there a silence	"	145
Cataract *b's* to the ocean run,	*The Islet*	17
b's of Eden mazily murmuring,	*Milton*	10
O is it the *b*, or a pool,	*The Window*	4

brook. (verb.)

I would not *b* my fear	*D. of F. Wom.*	154
We *b* no farther insult	*Princess,* vi.	322
scarce could *b* the strain and stir	*In Mem.* xv.	12
shall I *b* to be supplicated?	*Boädicea*	9

brook'd.

She the appeal *B* not	*Princess,* vi.	124
little maid, who *b* No silence,	*Guinevere*	157
B not the expectant terror	*En. Arden.*	489
but she *b* no more:	*Aylmer's F.*	798
She *b* it not; but wrathful,	*Lucretius*	14

brooking.

b not the Tarquin in her veins,	*Lucretius*	234

broom.

walks were stript as bare as *b's*	*Princess, Pro.*	182

broth.

wicked *b* Confused the chemic labour	*Lucretius*	19

brother (v. brethren.)

vexed eddies of its wayward *b*	*Isabel*	33
Each to each is dearest *b*;	*Madeline*	21
Oh rest ye, *b* mariners,	*Lotos-E's.*	174
I knew your *b*: his mute dust	*To J. S.*	29
miss the *b* of your youth?	"	59
Thy *b's* and immortal souls. *'Love thou thy land,'* etc.		8
I and he, *B's* in Art;	*Gardener's D.*	4
She is my *b's* daughter;	*Dora*	15
Come, blessed *b*, come.	*St S. Stylites*	201
flies forward to his *b* Sun;	*Golden Year*	23
Men my *b's*, men the workers,	*Locksley H.*	117
b's of the weather stood Stock-still	*Will Water.*	135
Hob-and-nob with *b* Death!	*Vision of Sin*	194
no men, Not even her *b* Arac,	*Princess,* i.	152
'My *b* !' 'Well, my sister.'	" ii.	171
lies a *b* by a sister slain,	"	190
That was fawn's blood, not *b's*,	"	256
to save A prince, a *b*?	"	271
I give thee to the death My *b* !	"	288
one of those two *b's*, half aside	" v.	292
O *b*, you have known the pangs	"	364
B's, the woman's Angel guards you,	"	400
saved my life: my *b* slew him	" vi.	92
Help, father, *b*, help;	"	286
Your *b*, Lady,—Florian,—ask	"	293
the Prince Her *b* came	"	325
those twin *b's*, risen again	" vii.	74

	POEM.	LINE.
My friend, the *b* of my love :-	*In Mem.* ix.	16
More than my *b's* are to me. (rep. lxxviii. 1.)	"	20
'Where wert thou, *b*, those four days?'	" xxxi.	5
Roves from the living *b's* face,	" xxxii.	7
met her to-day with her *b*,	*Maud*, I. iv.	14
not to her *b* I bowed.	"	14
chuckle, and grin at a *b's* shame;	"	29
Her *b*, from whom I keep aloof	" vi.	46
Blithe would her *b's* acceptance be.	" x.	27
All, all upon the *b*.	" xiii.	43
b lingers late With a roystering	" xiv.	14
Her *b* is coming back to-night,	" xix.	1
only Maud and the *b* Hung	"	35
This *b* had laugh'd her down,	"	60
her *b* comes, like a blight	"	102
b ran in his rage to the gate	" II. i.	12
A cry for a *b's* blood:	"	34
My dearest *b*, Edmund, sleeps,	*The Brook*	187
b James is in the harvest-field:	"	227
two *b's*, one a king, had met	*Elaine*	40
each had slain his *b* at a blow,	"	42
yet unblazon'd shield, His *b's*;	"	379
rosy-kindled with her *b's* kiss—	"	392
Sir Modred's *b*, of a crafty house,	"	557
Came on her *b* with a happy face	"	787
should I quit your *b's* love,	"	940
b's heard, and thought With shuddering	"	1015
'Sweet *b's*, yesternight I seem'd	"	1028
'Fret not yourself, dear *b*,	"	1068
Leolin, his *b*, living oft	*Aylmer's F.*	57
his, a *b's* love, that hung	"	138
thro' the bright lawns to his *b's* ran	"	341
'*B*, for I have lov'd you more as son Than *b*,	"	351
b, where two fight The strongest	"	364
'O *b*, I am griev'd to learn	"	398
low his *b's* mood had fall'n,	"	407
Sent to the harrow'd *b*,	"	607
thy *b* man, the Lord from Heaven	"	667

brother-brute.

ever butted his rough *b-b*	*Lucretius*	194

brother-hands.

I, clasping *b-h*, aver	*In Mem.* lxxxiv.	102

brother-like.

kiss'd her with all pureness, *b-l*	*Enid*	1732

brother-oak.

honours that, Thy famous *b-o*,	*Talking O.*	296

brother-sister.

are you That *b-s* Psyche,	*Princess*, ii.	236

brought.

from the outward to the inward *b*.	*Eleänore*	14
the oriental fairy *b*,	"	14
my mother *b* To yield consent	*Miller's D.*	137
the loss that *b* us pain,	"	229
light-foot Iris *b* it yester-eve,	*Œnone*	81
I won his love, I *b* him home.	*The Sisters*	49
b Into the gulfs of sleep.	*D. of F. Wom.*	51
where'er I came I *b* calamity.	"	76
then at my request He *b* it;	*The Epic*	48
every morning *b* a noble chance,	*M d'Arthur*	230
every chance *b* out a noble knight	"	231
Autumn *b* an hour For Eustace,	*Gardener's D.*	202
B out a dusky leaf	*Audley Ct.*	21
bailiff *b* A Chartist pike.	*Walk. to the M.*	62
b the night In which we sat together	*Love and Duty*	58
all the mothers *b* Their children,	*Godiva*	14
how the mind was *b* To anchor	*Two Voices*	458
pint, you *b* me, was the best	*Will Water.*	75
Lord Ronald *b* a lily-white doe	*Lady Clare*	3
doe Lord Ronald had *b*	"	61
he *b*, and I Dived in a hoard,	*Princess, Pro.*	28
which *b* my book to mind:	"	119
these *b* back A present,	" i.	43
He *b* it, and himself, a sight	" ii.	197
She *b* us Academic silks,	"	2
b a message here from Lady	"	298
Queen's decease she *b* her up	" iii.	70
b her chain'd, a slave	" v.	133
Home they *b* her warrior dead:	"	532

	POEM.	LINE.
b but merchants' bales	*In Mem.* xiii.	19
precious relics *b* by thee;	" xvii.	18
he that *b* him back is there.	" xxxii.	4
b an eye for all he saw;	" lxxxviii.	9
b the harp and flung A ballad	"	27
b a summons from the sea:	" cii.	16
Large elements in order *b*,	" cxi.	13
b to understand A sad astrology,	*Maud,* I. xviii.	35
b sweet cakes to make them cheer	*Enid*	388
and he *b* me to a goodly house;	"	713
like a madman *b* her to the court,	"	725
promise, that whatever bride I *b*	"	783
b a mantle down and wrapt her	"	824
Prince had *b* his errant eyes Home	"	1094
b upon their forays out	"	1415
b in whole hogs and quarter beeves,	"	1450
miss'd, and *b* Her own claw back,	*Vivien*	349
scatter'd theirs and *b* her off,	"	414
He *b*, not found it therefore:	"	569
I by mere mischance have *b*,	*Elaine*	189
Broider'd with pearls,' and *b* it:	"	372
b the yet-unblazon'd shield,	"	378
b his horse to Lancelot	"	492
shield was *b*, and Gawain saw	"	659
have *b* thee, now a lonely man	"	1361
barge that *b* her moving down,	"	1382
Modred *b* His creatures	*Guinevere*	102
my tears have *b* me good:	"	200
with what she *b* Buy goods	*En. Arden.*	137
b the stinted commerce of those days;	"	818
letter which he *b*, and swore besides	*Aylmer's F.*	522
She *b* strange news.	*Sea Dreams*	258
bread from out the houses *b*.	*Spec. of Iliad*	6
b him home at even-fall:	*'Home they brought,' etc.*	2

brow.

laurel greener from the *b's*	*To the Queen*	7
Upon her bed, across her *b*..	*Mariana*	56
Falsehood shall bare her plaited *b*:	*'Clear-headed friend,' etc.*	11
Frowns perfect-sweet along the *b*	*Madeline*	15
o'er black *b's* drops down	"	34, 46
a *b* of pearl Tress'd with	*Arabian N's.*	137
as a maid, whose stately *b*	*Ode to Mem.*	13
With thy soften'd, shadow'd *b*,	*Adeline*	46
Her beautiful bold *b*	*The Poet*	38
broad clear *b* in sunlight glow'd;	*L. of Shalott.* iii.	28
From *b* and bosom slowly down	*Mariana in the S.*	19
blow Before him, striking on my *b*	*Fatima*	25
the charm of married *b's*.	*Œnone*	74
drew From her warm *b's* and bosom	"	173
our *b's* in slumber's holy balm;	*Lotos E's.*	66
the other with a downward *b*:	*D. of F. Wom.*	117
dead, my crown about my *b's*,	"	162
dropping bitter tears against his *b*	*M. d'Arthur*	211
the full day dwelt on her *b's*,	*Gardener's D.*	135
Love with knit *b's* went by,	"	240
whose bald *b's* in silent hours before	*St. S Stylites*	162
waited long; My *b's* are ready.	"	203
Look up the fold is on her *b*.	*Two Voices*	192
gain'd a laurel for your *b* 'You might have won,' etc.		3
Her sweet face from *b* to chin:	*L. of Burleigh*	62
sleepy light upon their *b's* and lips—	*Vision of Sin*	9
hue Of that cap upon her *b's*.	"	142
From over her arch'd *b's*,	*Princess,* ii.	25
and the Roman *b's* Of Agrippina.	"	70
gaunt old baron with his beetle *b*.	"	222
went to bind my throbbing *b*,	"	232
answering under crescent *b's*;	"	406
lilylike Melissa droop'd her *b's*;	" iv.	143
manlike, but his *b's* Had sprouted,	"	186
With hooded *b's* I crept into the hall,	"	206
single jewel on her *b* Burn	"	254
over *b* And cheek and bosom brake	"	364
cloak from *b's* as pale and smooth	" v.	70
veil'd her *b's*, and prone she sank,	"	104
laid A feeling finger on my *b's*,	" vi.	105
With *b* to *b* like night and evening	"	115
breathe upon my *b's*;	" vii.	332
crown'd The purple *b's* of Olivet.	*In Mem.* xxxi.	12
Urania speaks with darken'd *b*:	" xxxvii.	1

	POEM.	LINE.
took the thorns to bind my *b's*,	*In Mem.* lxviii.	7
Lift as thou may'st thy burthen'd *b's*	" lxxi.	21
dearest, now thy *b's* are cold,	" lxxiii.	5
black and brown on kindred *b's*.	" lxxviii.	16
fan my *b's* and blow The fever	" lxxxv.	8
large and lucid round thy *b*.	" xc.	8
enter in at breast and *b*,	" cxxi.	11
A band of pain across my *b*;	*The Letters*	6
seeing cloud upon the mother's *b*,	*Enid*	777
wizard *b* bleach'd on the walls:	*Vivien*	447
two brethren slowly with bent *b's*.	*Elaine*	1132
kiss'd her quiet *b's*, and saying	"	1144
Arthur who beheld his cloudy *b's*.	"	1344
Annie with her *b's* against the wall	*En. Arden*	313
o'er his bent *b's* linger'd Averill,	*Aylmer's F.*	625
placed upon the sick man's *b*	"	700
glimmer steals From thy pure *b's*,	*Tithonus*	35
broke the breeze against the *b*,	*The Voyage*	9
King bent low, with hand on *b*,	*The Victim*	57

browbeat.

clerk *B-B's* his desk below	*To J. M. K.*	12

brow-bound.

B-b with burning gold.	*D. of F. Wom.*	128

brown.

streaming curls of deepest *b*.	*Mariana in the S.*	16
beauties every shade of *b* and fair	*Princess,* ii.	414
all her autumn tresses falsely *b*	"	426
black and *b* on kindred brows.	*In Mem.* lxxviii.	16
under *b* Of lustier leaves	" xcvii.	2
that beech will gather *b*,	" c.	3
watch the twilight falling *b*	*To F. D. Maurice*	14
B, looking hardly human,	*En. Arden.*	639
Enoch was so *b*, so bow'd,	"	704

browsed.

b by deep-udder'd kine	*Gardener's D.*	45

bruise.

hardly won with *b* and blow,	*Elaine*	1159

bruised.

cursed and scorn'd, and *b* with stones:	*Two Voices*	222
that there Lie *b* and maimed,	*Princess,* vi.	56
b the herb, and crush'd the grape,	*In. Mem.* xxxv.	23
swordcut on the cheek, And *b*	*Elaine*	259

Brunelleschi.

Arno, and the dome Of *B*;	*The Brook*	190

brunette.

A quick *b*, well-moulded	*Princess,* ii.	91

brush (pencil.)

took his *b* and blotted out the bird,	*Vivien*	328

brush (tail of fox.)

'Peter had the *b*, My Peter,	*Aylmer's F.*	254

brush'd.

when, this gad-fly *b* aside	*Princess,* v.	404
b Thro' the dim meadow	*Aylmer's F.*	530

brushing.

b ankle-deep in flowers,	*In Mem.* lxxxviii.	49
brandish'd plume *B* his instep,	*Enid*	1209

brushwood.

lean Upon the dusky *b*	*D. of F. Wom.*	58

brute.

Take my *b*, and lead him in,	*Vision of Sin*	65
madest Life in man and *b*;	*In Mem. Pro.*	6
No longer half-akin to *b*,	" Con.	133
had not been a sultan of *b's*,	*Maud,* II. v.	81
b's of mountain back That carry kings	*Vivien*	426

Brutus.

The Lucius Junius *B* of my kind?	*Princess,* ii.	264

bubble (s.)

seem'd to watch the dancing *b*,	*Princess,* iii.	8

bubble (verb.)

swoll'n brook that *b's* fast	*In Mem.* xcviii.	6
And yet *b's* o'er like a city,	*Maud,* I. iv.	9
I *b* into eddying bays	*The Brook*	41

bubbled.
	POEM.	LINE.
at mine ear B the nightingale	Princess, iv.	247
milk that b in the pail,	In Mem. lxxxviii.	51

bucket.
rope that haled the B's	St S. Stylites	63

buckled.
B with golden clasps before;	Sir L. and Q. G.	25

buckler.
The brand, the b, and the spear—	Two Voices	129
Clash the darts and on the b beat	Boädicea	79

bud (s.)
chesnuts, when their b's Were glistening	Miller's D.	60
flowers, and b's and garlands gay,	May Queen, i.	11
leaf is woo'd from out the b	Lotos-E's.	71
Sweet as new b's in Spring.	D. of F. Wom.	272
all-too-full in b For puritanic stays:	Talking O.	59
While thou abodest in the b.	Two Voices.	158
In b or blade, or bloom, may find,	Day-Dm.	206
burst In carol, every b to flower	"	256
While life was yet in b and blade,	Princess, i.	31
Pretty b! Lily of the vale!	" vi.	176
longs to burst a frozen b,	In Mem. lxxxii.	15
when her life was yet in b,	" Con.	33
half-opening b's Of April,	Tithonus	59
b ever breaks into bloom	The Islet	32

bud (verb.)
when some new thought can b,	Golden Year	27
b's and blossoms like the rest.	In Mem. cxiv.	20
out of tyranny tyranny b's.	Boädicea	83

Bude.
thundering shores of B and Bos,	Guinevere	289

buffet (s.)
from his brand a windy b	Enid	939

buffet (verb.)
echo flap And b round the hills	Golden Year	76
Strove to b to land in vain.	Princess, iv.	167

bugle (adj.)
b breezes blew Reveillée	In Mem. lxvii.	8

bugle (s.)
Aloud the hollow b blowing,	Oriana	17
loud rung out the b's brays,	"	48
A mighty silver b hung,	L. of Shalott iii.	16
Blow, b, blow set the wild (rep.).	Princess, iii.	352
horn And serpent-throated b,	" v.	243
March with banner and b and fife	Maud, I. v.	10
blare of b, clamour of men,	Ode on Well.	115
Warble, O b, and trumpet, blare!	W. to Alexan.	14

bugle-horn.
blew His wreathed b-h.	Pal of Art	64
sound upon the b-h	Locksley H.	2
sounding on the b-h	"	145

build.
b up all My sorrow with my song,	Œnone	38
built When men knew how to b,	Ed. Morris	7
b Far off from men a college	Princess, Pro.	134
She had founded; they must b.	" ii.	129
lent my life to b up yours,	" iv.	332
b some plan Foursquare to opposition.	" v.	221
b's the house, or digs the grave,	In Mem. xxxvi.	14
change their sky To b and brood;	" cxiv.	16
Godlike men we b our trust.	Ode on Well.	266

builded.
house was b of the earth,	Deserted H.	15

built.
b up everywhere An under-roof	Dying Swan	3
b my soul a lordly pleasure-house,	Pal. of Art	1
Thereon I b it firm.	"	9
great mansion, that is b for me,	"	19
spacious mansion b for me	"	234
So lightly, beautifully b:	"	294
b When men knew how to build	Ed. Morris	6
b herself an everlasting name.	Godiva	79
B for pleasure and for state.	L. of Burleigh	32

	POEM.	LINE.
Rhodope, that b the pyramid,	Princess, ii.	68
crowned towers B to the Sun:	" iii.	327
plan was mine. I b the nest'	" iv.	346
conscious of what temper you are b,	" v.	381
Far off from men I b a fold	" v.	380
tho' he b upon the babe restored;	" vii.	60
towers fall'n as soon as b—.	In Mem. xxvi.	8
b him fanes of fruitless prayer,	" lv.	12
New as his title, b last year,	Maud, I. x.	19
B that new fort to overawe	Enid	460
Had b the King his havens,	Vivien	24
b their castles of dissolving sand	En. Arden	19
b, and thatch'd with leaves of palm,	"	560

bulbul.
Died round the b as he sung;	Arabian N's.	70
O B, any rose of Gulistan	Princess, iv.	104

bulge.
cheek B with the unswallow'd piece,	Enid	1479

bulk.
Tudor-chimnied b Of mellow brickwork	Ed. Morris	11
bones of some vast b that lived	Princess, iii.	277
those two b's at Arac's side,	" v.	488
grown a b Of spanless girth,	" vi.	19
Dark b's that tumble half alive	In Mem. lxix.	11

bulk'd.
an old-world mammoth b in ice,	Princess, v.	142

bull (s.)
The mild b's golden horn.	Pal. of Art	120
oil'd and curl'd Assyrian B.	Maud, I. vi.	44
shaking vassals call'd the B,	Enid	1288

Bull (Inn Sign.)
The B, the Fleece are cramm'd	Audley Ct.	1

Bull (surname.)
Edwin Morris and with Edward B	Ed. Morris	14
said the fat-faced curate Edward B	" 42,	90

bullet.
B's fell like rain;	The Captain	46

bulrush.
sword-grass and the b in the pool.	May Queen, ii.	28

bulrush-bed.
plunged Among the b-b's,	M. d'Arthur	135

bulwark.
When now they saw their b fallen,	Enid	1017

bummin'.
b awaäy loike a buzzard-clock	N. Farmer	18

bump'd.
b the ice into three several stars,	The Epic	12

bumper.
froth'd his B's to the brim;	D. of the O. Year	19

bunch.
With b and berry and flower	Œnone	100
grapes with b'es red as blood;	Day-Dm.	64

bundle.
now hastily caught His b	En. Arden	237

buoy.
left behind the painted b	The Voyage	1

buoyed.
vapour b the crescent-bark,	Day-Dm.	186
B upon floating tackle	En Arden	552

bur.
b and brake and briar,	Day-Dm.	66
like a wall of b's and thorns;	Sea Dreams	115

burden (v. burthen.)
people here, a beast of b	Pal. of Art	149
The daily b for the back.	In Mem. xxv.	4

burgeon.
space to b out of all Within her—	Princess, vii.	255
b's every maze of quick	In Mem. cxiv.	2

burgher.
Knight and b, lord and dame,	L. of Shalott, iv.	43

	POEM.	LINE.
burial (adj.)		
kills her babe for a *b* fee,	Maud, I. i.	45
burial (s.)		
hears his *b* talked of	Princess, vii.	137
to glorious *b* slowly borne,	Ode on Well.	193
Pray for my soul, and yield me *b*.	Elaine	1273
Fresh from the *b* of her little one,	En. Arden.	280
summer *b* deep in hollyhocks;	Aylmer's F.	164
buried.		
b her like my own sweet child,	Lady Clare	27
have they not *b* me deep enough?	Maud, II. v.	96
see that she be *b* worshipfully.	Elaine	1319
maiden *b*, not as one unknown,	"	1324
same week when Annie *b* it,	En. Arden.	270
when the *b* him the little port	"	915
b now seven decads deep	Aylmer's F.	442
b in some weightier argument,	Lucretius	9
Burleigh.		
Lord of B, fair and free,	L. of Burleigh	58
Deeply mourn'd the Lord of B,	"	91
Burleigh-house.		
B.-h by Stamford-town.	L. of Burleigh	92
burlesque.		
seem'd to wrestle with *b*,	Princess, Con.	16
burn.		
cricket chirps: the light *b*'s low:	D. of the O. Year	40
While the stars *b*, the moons	To J. S.	71
And *b* a fragrant lamp before	St S. Stylites	193
but my cheek Began to *b* and *b*,	Princess, iii.	30
b's Above the unrisen morrow:	" iv.	64
single jewel on her brow B	"	255
with the thought her colour *b*'s;	In Mem. vi	34
calm that let the tapers *b*	" xciv.	5
The maple *b* itself away;	" c.	4
Cold fires, yet with power to *b*	Maud, I. xviii.	39
cheek *b* and either eyelid fall,	Enid	775, 1283
sin that practice *b*'s into the blood,	Vivien.	612
Made my tears *b*—	Guinevere.	538
b the threshold of the night,	The Voyage	18
B, you glossy heretic, *b*, B, *b*.	The Ringlet	53
Wherefore in me *b*'s an anger,	Boädicea	52
Burst the gates, and *b* the palaces,	"	64
fires *b* clear, And frost is here,	The Window	46
burn'd.		
B like one burning flame together,	L. of Shalott, iii.	22
b The red anemone.	D. of F. Wom.	71
b in fire, or boil'd in oil.	St S. Stylites	51
that which in me *b*, The love.	Talking O.	10
eye, That *b* upon its object,	Love and Duty	62
Last night, when the sunset *b*	Maud, I. vi.	8
one low light betwixt them *b*	Guinevere	4
fire, That *b* as on an altar.	En. Arden.	72
At times the whole sea *b*,	The Voyage	51
still the foeman spoil'd and *b*	The Victim	17
burning.		
A love still *b* upward,	Isabel	18
Larger constellations *b*, mellow	Locksley H.	159
The tapers *b* fair	Sir Galahad	32
lifelong injuries *b* unavenged,	Enid	1544
burnish.		
to scream, to *b*, and to scour,	Princess, iv.	499
burnish'd.		
b without fear The brand	Two Voices	128
glitter *b* by the frosty dark;	Princess, v.	251
burnt.		
B like a fringe of fire	Pal. of Art	48
b His epic, his King Arthur	The Epic	27
chaff and draff, much better *b*,	"	40
good Sir Ralph had *b* them all—	Princess, Pro.	229
b Because he cast no shadow	" i.	6
Nor *b* the grange, nor buss'd	" v.	213
other thoughts than Peace B in us,	"	236
So *b* he was with passion,	Enid	560
wrong that *b* him all within,	"	956
and in it Far cities *b*	Guinevere	83
and *b*, Now chafing at his own	Aylmer's F.	536

	POEM.	LINE.
beaker.		
B and broke the grove and altar	Boädicea	2
B in each man's blood.	The Captain	16
burr.		
When *b* and bine were gather'd;	Aylmer's F.	113
burst (s.)		
Preluded those melodious *b*'s,	D. of F. Wom.	6
more than mortal in the *b* Of sunrise,	Princess, Pro.	40
given to starts and *b*'s Of revel;	" i.	53
B's of great heart and slips	" v.	191
storm, its *b* of passion spent.	Vivien.	810
Caught in a *b* of unexpected storm,	Aylmer's F.	285
burst (verb.)		
B's into blossom in his sight.	Fatima.	35
high shrine-doors *b* thro'	D. of F. Wom.	29
the old man *b* in sobs	Dora	155
with hoggish whine They *b* my prayer.	St S. Stylites	175
Or to *b* all links of habit—	Locksley H.	157
every bird of Eden *b* In carol	Day-Dm.	255
heaven *b*'s her starry floors,	St Agnes' Eve	27
great organ almost *b* his pipes,	Princess, ii.	450
rose of Gulistan Shall *b* her veil:	" iv.	105
b and flood the world with foam;	"	453
clad in iron *b* the ranks of war	"	483
in the saddle, then *b* out in words.	" v.	265
b the great bronze valves,	" vi.	59
b The laces toward her babe;	"	132
longs to *b* a frozen bud,	In Mem. lxxxii.	15
fiery-hot to *b* All barriers	" cxiii.	13
yearn'd to *b* the folded gloom,	" cxxi.	3
Ready to *b* in a colour'd flame;	Maud, I. vi.	19
b and drown with deluging storms	" II. i.	42
make your Enid *b* Sunlike	Enid.	788
pavement echoing, *b* Their drowze	"	1120
pearl-necklace of the Queen That *b*	Vivien.	302
half his blood *b* forth,	Elaine	508
b away To weep and wail in secret	"	1237
b away In search of stream	En. Arden.	635
B his own wyvern on the seal,	Aylmer's F.	516
high on waves that idly *b*	The Voyage	69
B the gates, and burn the palaces,	Boädicea	64
burthen (load.)		
Less *b*, by ten-hundred-fold,	St S. Stylites	24
to lift a *b* from thy heart	Love and Duty	93
With the *b* of an honour	L. of Burleigh	79
drew My *b* from mine arms,	Princess, iv.	174
not the *b* that they bring.	In Mem. xiii.	20
turns his *b* into gain.	" lxxix.	22
breathless *b* of low-folded heavens	Aylmer's F.	612
One *b* and she would not lighten it?	"	703
weep their *b* to the ground,	Tithonus	2
burthen (refrain.)		
they shriek'd the *b* 'Him!'	Ed. Morris	123
like a *b*, 'him or death.'	Elaine	899
As tho' it were the *b* of a song,	En. Arden.	798
bury.		
You'll *b* me, my mother,	May Queen, ii.	29
b me beside the gate,	Princess, ii.	189
I will *b* myself in myself,	Maud, I. i.	76
b All this dead body of hate,	" xix.	96
cannot even *b* a man;	" II. v.	22
come to *b* me, *b* me Deeper	"	103
b the Great Duke (rep.)	Ode on Well.	1
burying.		
Driving, hurrying, marrying, *b*,	Maud, II. v.	12
bush.		
all kiss'd Beneath the sacred *b*	The Epic	3
Hear how the *b*'es echo!	Gardener's D.	97
Holding the *l*, to fix it back,	"	126
underneath the barren *b*	In Mem. xc.	3
He dragg'd his eyebrow *b*'es down,	Vivien	656
in the *b* beside me chirrupt	Grandmother	40
What?—that the *b* were leafless?	Lucretius	203
bush-bearded.		
b-*b* Barons heaved and blew,	Princess, v.	20
business.		
in the tangled *b* of the world,	Princess, ii.	157
b often call'd her from it,	En. Arden.	263

buss.
	POEM.	LINE.
B me, thou rough sketch of man,	Vision of Sin	189

bussed.
nor b the milking-maid,	Princess, v.	213

bust.
show'd the house, Greek, set with B's:	Princess, Pro.	11
stood a b of Pallas for a sign,	" i.	219

busying.
B themselves about the flowerage	Aylmer's F.	203

butler.
sits the B with a flask	Day-Dm.	45
The b drank, the steward scrawl'd,	"	142

butt (s.)
like a b, and harsh as crabs.	Walk. to the M.	41
from b's of water on the slope,	Princess, Pro.	60
straddling on the b's While the wine	Guinevere	266

butt (verb.)
how you b against my wish,	Enid	1525

butted.
b his rough brother-brute	Lucretius	194

butter-bump.
Moäst like a b-b, for I 'eerd 'un	N. Farmer	31

butterfly.
Hast thou heard the butterflies	Adeline	28
round her lip Like a golden b;	Talking O.	220

buy.
Bought? what is it he cannot b?	Maud, I. x.	32
Go to the town and b us flesh	Enid	372
B goods and stores—set Annie forth	En. Arden	138
b strange shares in some Peruvian	Sea Dreams	15

buying.
less Than what she gave in b	En. Arden	255

buzz.
It b'es wildly round the point;	Vivien	282
vermin voices then May b so loud—	Elaine	140
shake off the bee that b'es at us;	"	781

buzzard-clock.
bummin' awaäy loike a b-c	N. Farmer	18

buzz'd.
palace bang'd and b, and clackt,	Day-Dm.	146
b in knots of talk	Princess, i.	132
b abroad About the maid of Astolat,	Elaine	718

buzzing.
b's of the honied hours,	In Mem. lxxxviii.	52

bygones.
trim our sails, and let old b be,	Princess, iv.	51

by-lane.
filthy b-l rings to the yell	Maud, I. i.	38

byre.
thorpe and b arose in fire,	The Victim	3

byway.
where this b joins The turnpike?	Walk. to the M.	4

byword.
fatal b of all years to come	Godiva	67

C

cabin.
Shaking their pretty c,	En. Arden	173

cabinet.
moving toward a cedarn c,	Enid	136

cabin-window.
I see the c-w bright;	In Mem. x.	3

cackle.
With c and with clatter.	The Goose	12
c of your bourg The murmur	Enid	276
c of the unborn about the grave,	Vivien	357

cackled.
It clack'd and c louder.	The Goose	24

cadence.
	POEM.	LINE.
a foot Lessening in perfect c,	Walk. to the M.	47
in mimic c answered James	Golden Year	53
when the preacher's c flow'd.	Aylmer's F.	729

Cadmean.
dragon warriors from C teeth,	Lucretius	50

Caerleon.
Held court at old C upon Usk.	Enid	146
When late I left C	"	781
all that week was old C gay.	"	837
at C the full-tided Usk,	"	965
With Arthur to C upon Usk.	"	1794
That at C; this at Camelot:	Elaine	23
at C had he help'd his lord,	"	297

Caerlyle.
this dealt him at C;	Elaine	22

Cæsar.
That dull cold-blooded C	D. of F. Wom.	139
for whose love the Roman C first.	Enid	745

cage (s.)
silent in the muffled c of life:	Princess, vii.	32
linnet born within the c,	In Mem. xxvii.	3

cage (verb.)
c a buxom captive here and there,	Vivien	392

cageling.
As the c newly flown returns,	Vivien	750

Cain.
lust of gain, in the spirit of C,	Maud, I. i.	23

cairn'd.
the c mountain was a shadow,	Vivien	488

caitiff (adj.)
bandit earls, and c knights,	Enid	35
tell him all their c talk	"	915

caitiff (s.)
striking great blows At c's	Enid	96
would track this c to his hold,	"	415
waiting for them, c's all;	"	907

cake.
sweet c's to make them cheer,	Enid	388

calamity.
Where'er I came I brought c.	D. of F. Wom.	96
That a c hard to be borne?	Maud, I. xiii.	3
all C's hugest waves confound,	Will	5
heart foreshadowing all c,	En. Arden	684

calculation.
Abhorrent of a c crost,	En. Arden	470

calendar'd.
register'd and c for saints.	St S. Stylites	130

calf (of the leg.)
proxy-wedded with a bootless c	Princess, i.	33

Caliphat.
great Pavilion of the C.	Arabian N's.	114

call (s.)
I saw a lady within c,	D. of F. Wom.	85
Whistle back the parrot's c,	Locksley H.	171
She answered to my c,	Will Water.	106
When they answer to his c,	L. of Burleigh	50
stable wench Came running at the c	Princess, i.	224
martial song like a trumpet's c!	Maud, I. v.	5
Hope at Beauty's c would perch	Coquette, i.	3

call (verb.)
thro' wild March the throstle c's,	To the Queen	14
to the billow the fountain c's:	Sea Fairies	9
saw me fight, she heard me c,	Oriana	32
c aloud in the dreamy dells,	The Merman	25
C to each other and whoop	"	26
if any came near I would c,	The Mermaid	38
will she answer if I c?	Miller's D.	118
must wake and c me early, (rep.)	May Queen, i, 1,	41
If you do not c me loud,	"	10
They c me cruel-hearted,	"	19
If you're waking c me early, (rep.)	" ii. 1,	52

	POEM.	LINE.
c me before the day is born,	*May Queen* ii.	49
I heard the angels *c*;	" iii.	25
I heard them *c* my soul,	"	28
that Rosamond, whom men *c* fair,	*D. of F. Wom.*	252
those who *c* them friend?	*M. d'Arthur*	253
a word with her he *c*'s his wife,	*Dora*	42
Father! — if you let me *c* you so—	"	137
'They *c* me what they will,'	*Golden Year*	14
as of old, the curlews *c*,	*Locksley H.*	3
Hark, my merry comrades *c* me,	"	145
c thee from the boxes,	*Will Water.*	240
when he *c*'s, and thou shalt cease,	"	241
would *c* them masterpieces:	*Princess,* i.	144
Brutus of my kind? Him you *c* great:	" ii.	265
Should I not *c* her wise,	"	374
c down from Heaven A blessing	"	454
She *c*'s her plagiarist,	" iii.	78
nebulous star we *c* the Sun,	" iv.	1
c her Ida, tho' I knew her not,	" vii.	81
c her sweet, as if in irony,	"	82
c her hard and cold	"	83
children *c*, and I Thy shepherd pipe,	"	202
c To what I feel is Lord	*In Mem.* liv.	18
clap their cheeks, to *c* them mine;	" lxxxiii.	18
c The spirits from their golden day,	" xciii.	5
To whom a thousand memories *c*,	" cx.	10
that those we *c* the dead	" cxvii.	5
you may *c* it a little too ripe,	*Maud,* I. ii.	9
Whatever they *c* him, what care I,	" x.	64
Who shall *c* me ungentle,	" xiii.	14
Scarcely, now, would I *c* him a cheat;	"	29
That heard me softly *c*,	" II. iv.	76
What do they *c* you?' 'Katie,'	*The Brook*	211
heard him *c* you fairest fair,	*Enid*	720
had heard C herself false:	"	963
C for the woman of the house,'	"	1112
bad the host C in what men	"	1135
I *c* mine own self wild,	"	1160
c it lovers' quarrels, yet I know	"	1173
C the host and bid him bring	"	1249
loved to *c* Enid the Fair,	"	1810
The people *c* you prophet:	*Vivien*	166
will *c* That three-days-long	"	168
c it, — well, I will not *c* it vice:	"	218
Envy *c*'s you Devil's son,	" 317,	347
Master, shall we *c* him overquick	"	574
c him were it not for womanhood)	"	635
Could *c* him the main cause	"	637
c you lily maid In earnest,	*Elaine*	385
'Me you *c* great:	"	445
'Father, you *c* me wilful,	"	746
Would *c* her friend and sister	"	861
follow death, who *c*'s for me	"	1011
C and I follow, I follow!	"	1012
I know not what you *c* the highest;	"	1074
bid *c* the ghostly man	"	1093
I *c* my friends in testimony,	"	1291
how dare I *c* him mine?	*Guinevere*	610
voice that *c*'s Doom upon kings,	*Aylmer's F.*	741
not *c* him, love, Before you prove	*Sea Dreams*	166
c us Britain's barbarous populaces,	*Boädicea*	7
From childly wont and ancient use I *c*—	*Lucretius*	206

call 'to visit.'
say the neighbours when they *c*,	*Amphion*	5

call'd.
Old voices *c* her from without,	*Mariana*	68
torrent *c* me from the cleft,	*Œnone*	53
c him by his name, complaining loud,	*M. d'Arthur*	210
C to me from the years to come,	*Gardener's D.*	176
day When Allan *c* his son,	*Dora*	9
c him Crichton, for he seem'd All-perfect	*Ed. Morris*	22
merry boy they *c* him then,	*Two Voices*	322
c mine host To council,	*Princess,* i.	171
riding in, we *c*;	" ii.	447
the chapel bells C us:	" iv.	209
Girl after girl was *c* to trial:	"	475
she *c* For Psyche's child to cast	"	564
c Across the tumult	"	
pique at what she *c* The raillery	"	

	POEM.	LINE.
C him worthy to be loved	*Princess,* v.	537
c them dear deliverers,	" vi.	76
or *c* On flying Time from all	" vii.	89
c me in the public squares	*In Mem.* lxviii.	11
c me fool, they *c* me child:	"	13
c old Philip out To show the farm;	*The Brook*	120
c her like that maiden in the tale,	*Enid*	742
c For Enid, and when Yniol,	"	755
hasty judger would have *c* her guilt	"	1282
whom his shaking vassals *c* the Bull,	"	1288
c for flesh and wine to feed his spears,	"	1449
They *c* him the great Prince,	"	1809
The people *c* him Wizard;	*Vivien*	29
c herself a gilded summer fly	"	107
Vivien *c* herself But rather seem'd	"	110
Who *c* her what he *c* her—	"	713
C her to shelter in the hollow oak	"	743
if I be what I am grossly *c*,	"	764
c him dear protector in her fright,	"	795
c him lord and liege, Her seer,	"	802
c his wound a little hurt	*Elaine*	848
Approaching thro' the darkness, *c*:	"	994
c her song 'The Song of Love and Death,'	"	999
c The father, and all three in hurry	"	1017
sometime *c* the maid of Astolat,	"	1266
c him the false son of Gerlois:	*Guinevere*	286
he, the King, C me polluted:	"	613
His hope he *c* it;	"	625
business often *c* her from it,	*En. Arden*	263
c him, Father Philip	"	351
Father Philip (as they *c* him)	"	362
'After the Lord has *c* me	"	811
c aloud for Miriam Lane,	"	837
C to the bar, but ever *c* away	*Aylmer's F.*	59
C all her vital spirits into each ear	"	201
the great Sicilian *c* Calliope.	*Lucretius*	93

callest.
C thou that thing a leg?	*Vision of Sin*	89

calling (part.)
hear the dewy echoes *c*	*Lotos-E's.*	139
C thyself a little lower Than angels.	*Two Voices*	198
Maud, they were crying and *c*,	*Maud,* I. xii.	1
Were crying and *c* to her,	"	26
chafing his pale hands, and *c* to him.	*Enid*	1430-3
Moaning and *c* out of other lands,	*Vivien*	811
pursued her, *c* 'Stay a little'!	*Elaine*	680
c down a blessing on his head	*En. Arden*	324
c, here and there, about the wood.	"	380

calling (s.)
came so loud a *c* of the sea,	*En. Arden*	909

Calliope.
called C to grace his golden verse—	*Lucretius*	94

calm (adj.)
lower down The bay was oily *c*:	*Audley Ct.*	85
world's great bridals, chaste and *c*:	*Princess,* vii.	278
C is the morn without a sound,	*In Mem.* xi.	1
C as to suit a calmer grief,	"	11
His eye was *c*, and suddenly she took	*Vivien*	703

calm (s.)
summer *c* of golden charity	*Isabel*	8
No tranced summer *c* is thine,	*Madeline*	2
shallop through the star-strown *c*,	*Arabian N's.*	36
'There is no joy but *c*!'	*Lotos-E's.*	68
some have striven Achieving *c*	*Two Voices*	209
Put on more *c* and added suppliantly;	*Princess,* vi.	198
if *c* at all, If any *c*, a calm despair;	*In Mem.* xi.	15
dead *c* in that noble breast	"	19
touch of change in *c* or storm;	" xvi.	6
c that let the tapers burn	" xciv.	5
tracts of *c* from tempest made,	" cxi.	14
moulded in colossal *c*,	" Con.	16
Long have I sigh'd for a *c*:	*Maud,* I. ii.	1
whom she answer'd with all *c*.	*Elaine*	991
follow'd *c*'s, and then winds variable,	*En. Arden*	541
mock'd him with returning *c*	*Lucretius*	25
center'd in eternal *c*,	"	79
Their sacred everlasting *c*!	"	110
so fine, nor so divine a *c*,	"	111

calming.

	POEM.	LINE.
C itself to the long-wish'd-for end,	Maud, I. xviii.	5

Calpe.

	POEM.	LINE.
From C unto Caucasus they sung,	The Poet	15

calumet.

	POEM.	LINE.
celts and c's, Claymore and snowshoe,	Princess, Pro.	18

calumny.

	POEM.	LINE.
Sweeter tones than c?	A Dirge	17

Cama.

	POEM.	LINE.
throne of Indian C slowly sail'd	Pal. of Art	115

came.

	POEM.	LINE.
the oxen's low C to her:	Mariana	29
whence that glory c Upon me,	Arabian N's.	94
c upon the great Pavilion	"	113
fall to the ground if you c in.	Poet's Mind	23
shrink to the earth if you c in.	"	37
if any c near I would call	The Mermaid	38
C two young lovers lately wed;	L. of Shalott, ii.	34
sun c dazzling through the leaves,	" iii.	3
Down she c and found a boat,	" iv.	6
Out upon the wharfs they c,	"	42
c a sound as of the sea:	Mariana in the S.	86
c and sat Below the chesnuts,	Miller's D.	59
went and c a thousand times.	"	72
off the wold I c, and lay	"	111
swift blood that went and c	Fatima	16
Hither c at noon Mournful Œnone	Œnone	14
C up from reedy Simois	"	51
to embrace him coming ere he c.	"	62
speech C down upon my heart.	"	68
to the bower they c, Naked they c	"	92
c, they cut away my tallest pines	"	204
panther's roar c muffled	"	210
The Abominable, that uninvited c	"	220
to care from whence I c.	L. C. V. de Vere	12
As I c up the valley	May Queen, i.	13
Till Charles's Wain c out	" ii.	12
To die before the snowdrop c,	" iii.	4
There came a sweeter token	"	22
c a swell of music on the wind.	" 32,	36
once again it c, and close beside	"	39
In the afternoon they c unto a	Lotos-E's.	3
melancholy Lotos-eaters c.	"	27
You c to us so readily,	D. of the O. Year	7
voice C rolling on the wind. 'Of old sat Freedom,' etc.		8
C on the shining levels	M. d'Arthur	51
to the barge they c.	"	205
c a bark that, blowing forward,	" Ep.	21
C, drew your pencil from you,	Gardener's D.	26
C voices of the well-contented doves.	"	88
some sweet answer, tho' no answer c,	"	156
More musical than ever c in one,	"	228
c Memory with sad eyes,	"	238
farewells—Of that which c between,	"	247
c a day When Allan call'd his son,	Dora	8
then distresses c on him;	"	47
evil c on William at the first	"	59
the farmer c into the field	"	72
when the morrow c, she rose and took	"	78
And the boy's cry c to her	"	102
the day when first she c,	"	104
they c in: but when the boy	"	134
never c a-begging for myself,	"	138
love c back a hundredfold	"	162
c again together on the king	Audley Ct.	35
C to the hammer here in March—	"	59
I went and c; Her voice fled	Ed. Morris	66
out they c Trustees and Aunts	"	120
those that c To touch my body	St S. Stylites	77
c To rest beneath thy boughs.—	Talking O. 35, 99,	155
with him Albert c on his.	"	105
here she c, and round me play'd,	"	133
c Like Death betwixt thy dear	Love and Duty	47
c a colour and a light,	Locksley H.	25
C out clear plates of sapphire	Two Voices	12
if thro' lower lives I c—	"	364
answer c there none:	"	425
C little copses climbing.	Amphion	32
C wet-shot alder from the wave	"	41
C yews, a dismal coterie;	Amphion	42
elms c breaking from the vine,	"	45
Cruelly c they back to-day	Ed. Gray	18
best That ever came from pipe.	Will Water.	76
since I c to live and learn,	"	81
I think he c like Ganymede,	"	119
C crowing over Thames.	"	140
went Long since, and c no more.	"	186
In there c old Alice the nurse,	Lady Clare	13
And he c to look upon her,	L. of Burleigh	93
C in a sun-lit fall of rain.	Sir L. and Q. G.	4
Bare-footed c the beggar maid	Beggar Maid	1
youth c riding toward a palace-gate.	Vision of Sin	2
from the palace c a child of sin,	"	5
C floating on for many a month	"	54
there c a further change:	"	207
satiated at length C to the ruins.	Princess, Pro.	91
C murmurs of her beauty	" i.	35
spake of why we c, And my betroth'd	"	118
stable wench C running at the call,	"	224
when we c where lies the child	"	255
the College Portress c:	" ii.	1
c to chivalry: When some respect	"	119
(what other way was left) I c.	"	199
arrow-wounded fawn C flying	"	252
as you c, to slip away, To-day,	"	276
so rapt, we gazing, c a voice,	"	297
Sheba c to ask of Solomon.'	"	325
if you c Among us, debtors	"	333
Will wonder why they c:	"	410
c Melissa hitting all we saw	"	443
C furrowing all the orient	" iii.	2
was agreed when first they c;	"	20
Then c these dreadful words out	"	41
your sister c she won the heart	"	71
Hither c Cyril, and yawning	"	107
who we were, And why we c?	"	120
c a message from the Head.	"	152
On a sudden my strange seizure c	"	167
c to where the river sloped	"	273
many weary moons before we c,	"	302
crossing, c On flowery levels	"	317
rosy heights c out above the lawns.	"	347
How c you here?' I told him:	" iv.	202
as we c, the crowd dividing clove	"	264
Then c, your new friend:	"	279
What student c but that you planed	"	296
Then c these wolves:	"	302
c to tell you: found that you	"	323
c a little stir About the doors,	"	354
C all in haste to hinder wrong,	"	382
C in long breezes rapt from	"	411
A man I c to see you:	"	421
that I c not all unauthorized	"	447
c On a sudden the weird seizure	"	538
went by As strangely as it c	"	546
touch of all mischance but c	"	550
washed with morning, as they c	" v.	254
batter'd at the doors; none c:	"	327
message and defiance went and c;	"	360
Then c a postscript dash'd across	"	414
like a flash the weird affection c:	"	466
c As comes a pillar of electric cloud,	"	512
Like summer tempest c her tears—	"	546
C Psyche, crowning for Aglaïa.	" vi.	13
enemies have fall'n, have fall'n: they c;	"	22-27
on they c, Their feet in flowers,	"	61
At distance follow'd: so they c:	"	67
When first she c, all flush'd you said	"	233
c to woo Your Highness—	"	308
the Prince Her brother c;	"	325
maidens c, they talked, They sang,	" vii.	7
down she c, And found fair peace	"	28
with her oft Melissa c;	"	41
When Cyril pleaded, Ida c behind	"	63
oft she sat: Then c a change	"	77
a touch C round my wrist,	"	123
when she c From barren deeps	"	148
There c a minute's pause	Con.	
looking back to whence I c,	In Mem. xxiii.	7
I murmur'd as I c along	" xxxvii.	21

	POEM.	LINE.
path we *c* by, thorn and flower,	*In Mem.* xlv.	2
c In whispers of the beauteous world,	" lxxviii.	11
truth *c* borne with bier and pall,	" lxxxiv.	1
if they *c* who past away,	" lxxxix.	13
c on that which is, and caught	" xciv.	39
c at length To find a stronger faith	" xcv.	16
out of darkness *c* the hands	" cxxiii.	23
went and *c*, Remade the blood	*Con.*	10
if an enemy's fleet *c* yonder	*Maud*, I. i.	49
when the morning *c* In a cloud,	" vi.	20
C out of her pitying womanhood,	"	64
She *c* to the village church,	" viii.	1
c one to the county town	" x.	37
However she *c* to be so allied	" xiii.	36
snow-limb'd Eve from whom she *c*.	" xviii.	28
no one ask me how it *c* to pass ;	"	49
at last, when each *c* home,	" xix.	61
He *c* with the babe-faced lord ;	" II. i.	13
ghost That never *c* from on high	" ii.	35
C glimmering thro' the laurels	" iv.	77
Everything *c* to be known :	" v.	51
he *c* not back From the wilderness	"	53
whether he *c* in the Hanover ship,	"	59
here I *c*, twenty years back—	*The Brook*	77
evermore her father *c* across	"	108
said Katie, 'we *c* back.'	"	221
how we *c* at last To Como ;	*The Daisy*	69
C thro' the jaws of Death	*Lt. Brigade*	46
Remembering when first he *c*	*Enid*	140, 842
Before him *c* a forester of Dean,	"	148
C quickly flashing through the shallow	"	167
thither *c* Geraint, and underneath	"	241
C forward with the helmet	"	285
c again with one, A youth	"	385
thither *c* the twain, and when Geraint	"	539
errant knights And ladies *c*,	"	546
c a clapping as of phantom hands.	"	566
c A stately queen whose name was	"	666
therewithal one *c* and seized on her,	"	673
C one with this and laid it in	"	699
c among you here so suddenly,	"	794
There *c* a fair-hair'd youth	"	1050
c near, lifted adoring eyes,	"	1153
but that your father *c* between	"	1163
Suddenly *c*, and at his side all pale	"	1359
her desolation *c* Upon her,	"	1367
C riding with a hundred lances	"	1388
ere he *c*, like one that hails	"	1389
out of her there *c* a power upon him ;	"	1461
Neigh'd with all gladness as they *c*,	"	1603
C purer pleasures unto mortal kind	"	1613
o'er her meek eyes *c* a happy mist	"	1617
you *c* But once you *c*,—	"	1693
thither *c* The King's own leech	"	1770
tyrants when they *c* to power)	*Vivien*	368
They said a light *c* from her	"	417
and his book *c* down to me.'	"	500
C to her old perch back,	"	752
neck glittering went and *c* ;	"	809
c the lily maid by that good shield	*Elaine*	28
when none knew from whence he *c*,	"	34
Arthur *c*, and labouring up the pass	"	48
c an old, dumb, myriad-wrinkled man,	"	170
c a cloud Of melancholy severe,	"	323
as she *c* from out the tower.	"	345
c on him a sort of sacred fear,	"	353
c the hermit out and bare him in,	"	518
C round their great Pendragon,	"	527
since the knight *C* not to us,	"	543
c at last, tho' late, to Astolat :	"	615
c The lord of Astolat out,	"	623
dame *C* suddenly on the Queen	"	726
C on her brother with a happy face	"	787
She *c* before Sir Lancelot,	"	904
c her father, saying in low tones	"	988
c her brethren, saying, 'Peace to thee	"	990
the King *C* girt with knights :	"	1254
Lancelot later *c* and mused at her,	"	1261
grim faces *c* and went Before her,	*Guinevere*	70
when she *c* to Almesbury she spake	"	137
rumour wildly blown about *C*,	"	152

	POEM.	LINE.
Her first thought when she *c*,	*Guinevere*	180
when at last he *c* to Camelot,	"	258
no man knew from whence he *c* ;	"	287
There *c* a day as still as heaven,	"	290
Lancelot *c*, Reputed the best knight	"	378
C to that point, when first she saw	"	400
then *c* silence, then a voice,	"	416
c they shameful sin with Lancelot ;	"	483
c the sin of Tristram and Isolt ;	"	484
c a kingdom's curse with thee—	"	546
two years after *c* a boy.	*En. Arden.*	89
c a change, as things human	"	101
hearing his mischance, *C*,	"	121
moving homeward *c* on Annie pale,	"	149
wife and babes Whatever *c* to him :	"	189
last of those last moments *c*,	"	217
day, that Enoch deem'd, *c*	"	238
Expectant of that news which never *c*	"	257
c to ask a favour of you.'	"	284
I *c* to speak to you of what he	"	290
the favour that I *c* to ask.	"	312
you *c* in my sorrow broke me	"	316
the woman when he *c* upon her,	"	342
no news of Enoch *c*.	"	358
know not when it first *c* there,	"	398
c the children laden with their spoil ;	"	442
new mother *c* about her heart,	"	520
breath of heaven *c* continually	"	531
upon the cry of 'breakers' *c* The crash	"	549
rainy seasons *c* and went	"	624
lonely doom *c* suddenly to an end.	"	628
None of these *c* from his county.	"	654
and he *c* upon the place.	"	682
and *c* out upon the waste.	"	778
languor *c* Upon him, gentle sickness,	"	824
c so loud a calling of the sea,	"	909
C from a grizzled cripple,	*Aylmer's F.*	8
half a score of swarthy faces *c*.	"	191
like a storm he *c*, And shook	"	215
The next day *c* a neighbour.	"	251
c Her sicklier iteration.	"	298
when *this* Aylmer *c* of age—	"	407
C at the moment Leolin's emissary,	"	518
passionately restless *c* and went,	"	546
c upon him half-arisen from sleep,	"	584
when he *c* again, his flock believ'd—	"	600
c a Lord in no wise like to Bäil.	"	647
when the second Christmas *c*, escaped	"	838
C, with a month's leave given	*Sea Dreams*	6
forth they *c* and paced the shore	"	32
when I *c* To know him more, I lost	"	71
'It *c*,' she said, 'by working	"	110
C men and women in dark clusters	"	219
c but from the breaking of a glass,	"	240
We *c* to warmer waves,	*The Voyage*	37
to colder climes we *c*,	"	71
Up there *c* a flower,	*The Flower*	3
great in story, Wheresoe'er he *c*.	*The Captain*	20
Joyful *c* his speech :	"	30
Fancy *c* and at her pillow sat,	*Coquette,*	i. 5
c the tenderness of tears,	" ii.	9
it seemed that an answer *c* :	*The Victim*	24
blood by Sylla shed *C* driving	*Lucretius*	48
camel.		
c's knelt Unbidden,	*Vivien*	425
Camelot.		
To many-tower'd *C* (rep.)	*L. of Shalott,*	i. 5
gardens and the halls Of *C*	*M. d'Arthur*	21
Shot thro' the lists at *C*,	"	224
eat in Arthur's hall at *C*	*Enid*	432
Adown the crystal dykes at *C*	"	1319
In Arthur's arras hall at *C* :	*Vivien*	99
That at Caerleon ; this at *C* :	*Elaine*	23
let proclaim a joust At *C*,	"	78
Shall I appear, O Queen, At *C*,	"	143
joust as one unknown At *C*	"	191
ride to *C* with this noble knight :	"	220
lived a knight Not far from *C*,	"	401
the lists By *C* in the meadow,	"	428

54 CONCORDANCE TO

	POEM.	LINE.
'What news from C, lord?.	Elaine	617
To C, and before the city-gates	"	786
far blood, which dwelt at C;	"	799
At C, ere the coming of the Queen.'	Guinevere	221
when at last he came to C,	"	258
in thy bowers of C or of Usk	"	499

earnest.

not as thou c of late,	Ode to Mem.	8
c with the morning mist	"	12, 21
c to thy goal So early, .	In Mem. cxiii.	23

camp.

the courts, the c's, the schools	Vision of Sin	104
at her head a follower of the c,	Princess, v.	57
a murmur ran Thro' all the c	"	107
Back rode we to my father's c,	"	321
be no traitors in your c:	"	415
c and college turn'd to hollow shows;	"	467
'Follow me, Prince, to the c,	Enid	1656
reached the c the King himself	"	1726

campanili.

slender c grew By bays,	The Daisy	13

Camulodune.

near the colony C,	Boädicea	5
lo their colony, C!	"	17, 31, 53
city and citadel, London, Verulam, C.	"	86

can.

'Tis but a steward of the c,	Will Water.	149
truth, that flies the flowing c,	"	171
Fill the cup, and fill the c: (rep.)	Vision of Sin	95
Fill the c, and fill the cup: (rep.)	"	131

canal.

boat-head down a broad c	Arabian N's.	25
c Is rounded to as clear a lake.	"	45

cancell'd.

c a sense misused;	Godiva	72
c in the world of sense?'	Two Voices	42
And c nature's best:	In Mem. lxxi.	20
At length my trance Was c,	" xciv.	44

cancer.

Cured lameness, palsies, c's.	St S. Stylites	81

candle-light.

with solemn rites by c-l—	Princess, v.	282

cane.

court-Galen poised his gilt-head c,	Princess, i.	19

canker (s.)

As but the c of the brain;	In Mem. xci.	3

canker (verb.)

No lapse of moons can c Love,	In Mem. xxvi.	3

Canning.

stow'd (when classic C died)	Will Water.	101

cannon.

wires and vials fired A c:	Princess, Pro.	66
woven across the c's throat;	Maud, III. vi.	27
volleying c thunder his loss;	Ode on Well.	62
Roll of c and clash of arms,	"	116
c's moulder on the seaward wall;..	"	173
C to right of them, C to left (rep.)	Lt. Brigade 18,	39

cannon-bullet.

c-b rust on a slothful shore,	Maud, III. vi.	26

Canopus.

lit Lamps which outburn'd C.	D. of F. Wom.	146

canopy.

in the costly c o'er him set,	Elaine	442

canvas.

glimmering lanes and walls of c,	Princess, v.	6
such a breeze Compell'd thy c,	In Mem. xvii.	2
In the north, her c flowing,	The Captain	27

canvass.

last night she fell to c you: .	Princess, iii.	24
our narrow world must c it:.	Aylmer's F.	774

canvassed.

	POEM.	LINE.
He c human mysteries,	A Character	20

canzonet.

A rogue of c's and serenades.	Princess, iv.	117

cap.

c blew off, her gown blew up,	The Goose	51
do not hear the bells upon my c,	Ed. Morris	56
hue Of that c upon her brows.	Vision of Sin	142
knightlike in his c instead of casque,	Princess, iv.	577
c and bells for a fool.	Maud, I. vi.	62

capability.

drained My capabilities of love :	In Mem. lxxxiv.	12

capable.

neither c of lies,	En. Arden	250

cape (headland.)

By grassy c's with fuller sound	Sir L. and Q. G.	14
lake and lawn, and isles and c's—	Vision of Sin	11
fold to fold, of mountain or of c ;	Princess, vi.	366
olive-hoary c in ocean;	The Daisy	31
c That has the poplar on it :	Elaine	1033
a long tumble about the C	En. Arden	528
past long lines of Northern c's	The Voyage	35
So they past by c's and islands	The Captain	21

cape (part of cloak.)

ermine c's And woolly breasts	In Mem. xciv.	11

caper.

Making a roan horse c	Elaine	788

captain.

hearts Of c's and of kings.	D. of F. Wom.	176
The c of my dreams Ruled	"	263
Communing with his c's of the war.	Princess, i.	66
young c's flash'd their glittering teeth	" v.	19
lightly pranced Three c's out ;	"	245
every c waits Hungry for honour,	"	303
a lord, a c, a padded shape,	Maud, I. x.	29
Foremost c of his time,	Ode on Well.	31
our dead c taught The tyrant,	"	69
for their c after fight,	Aylmer's F.	226
Without the c's knowledge :	"	717
mate is blind, and c lame,	The Voyage	91
Brave the C was :	The Captain	5
cruel Seem'd the C's mood.	"	14
the C's colour heighten'd,	"	29
beneath the water Crew and C lie ;	"	68

captain's-ear.

His c-e has heard them boom	Ode on Well.	65

captive.

'sdeath ! and he himself Your c,	Princess, v.	267
The c void of noble rage,	In Mem. xxvii.	2
cage a buxom c here and there,	Vivien	392

ear.

people behold The towering c,	Ode on Well.	55
Stood by their c's, waiting the	Spec. of Iliad 22, note.	

carcanet.

Make a c of rays,	Adeline	59

carcase.

make the c a skeleton,	Boädicea	14

card.

Insipid as the Queen upon a c ;	Aylmer's F.	28

care (s.)

the c That yokes with empire,	To the Queen	9
nor carketh c nor slander ;	A Dirge	8
little other c hath she,	L. of Shalott,ii.	8
green and broad, and takes no c,	Lotos-E's.	73
low voice, full of c, Murmur'd	D. of F. Wom.	249
took with c, and kneeling on one knee	M. d'Arthur	173
C and Pleasure, Hope and Pain,	Day-Dm.	75
Thy c is, under polish'd tins,	Will Water.	227
takes a lady's finger with all c,	Princess, Pro.	171
each by other drest with c	" iii.	3
had the c Of Lady Ida's youth	"	69
either she will die from want of c,	" v.	82
out of long frustration of her c,	" vii.	86
breadth, nor fail in childward c,	"	267

	POEM.	LINE.
once she foster'd up with c;	In Mem. viii.	16
this the end of all my c?	"	xii. 14
any c for what is here Survive	"	xxxviii. 9
c is not to part and prove;	"	xlvii. 5
falling with my weight of c's	"	liv. 14
sound to rout the brood of c's,	"	lxxxviii. 17
song that slights the coming c,	"	xcviii. 10
c's that petty shadows cast,	"	civ. 13
Ring out the want, the c,	"	cv. 17
if the song were full of c,	"	cxxiv. 9
take c of all that I think,	Maud, I. xv.	7
Come, when no graver c's employ	To F. D. Maurice	1
Forgetful of his princedom and its c's.	Enid	54
thought, 'In spite of all my c,	"	115
her fine c had saved his life.	Elaine	859
Cast all your c's on God;	En. Arden	222
cared for it With all a mother's c;	"	262
no c, No burthen, save my c for you	"	416
common c whom no one cared for,	Aylmer's F.	688
the shallow c's of fifty years;	"	814

care (verb.)

c not what the sects may brawl.	Pal. of Art	210
Too proud to care from whence	L.C.V. de Vere	12
I c not what they say,	May Queen, i.	19
I c not if I go to-day.	"	iii. 43
if you c indeed to listen, hear	Golden Year	20
be happy! wherefore should I c?	Locksley H.	97
choose your own you did not c;	Day-Dm.	242
that for which I c to live	"	268
What c I for any name?	Vision of Sin	85
c no longer, being all unblest: 'Come not when, etc.'		8
c not while we hear A trumpet	Princess, iv.	62
myself, what c I, war or no?	" v.	268
right or wrong, I c not;	"	280
c's to walk, With Death and Morning	" vii.	188
c's to fix itself to form.	In Mem. xxxiii.	4
I c for nothing, all shall go.	"	lv. 4
c not in these fading days	"	lxxiv. 9
Whatever they call him, what c I,	Maud, I. x.	64
now shine on, and what c I,	"	xviii. 41
C not thou to reply:	"	II. iii. 7
Him who c's not to be great,	Ode on Well.	199
c not for the cost; the cost is mine!'	Enid	1137
did I c or dare to speak with you,	"	1719
He c's not for me; only here	Ela	127
c's For triumph in our mimic wars,	"	311
she cried, 'I c not to be wife,	"	933
c not howsoever great he be,	"	1063
King should greatly c to live;	Guinevere	449
Not greatly c to lose; but rather	"	491
head is low, and no man c's for him.	En. Arden.	851
if my children c to see me dead,	"	889
c no more for Leolin's walking	Aylmer's F.	124
his answer 'Well—I c not for it	"	238
I c not for it either;	"	248
what do I care for Jane,	Grandmother	51
wealthy men who c not how they give.	Tithonus	17
shall we c to be pitiful?	Boädicea	32
c's to lisp in love's delicious creeds:	Coquette, i.	11
take the praise, and c no more.	" ii.	14
c to sit beside her where she sits—	" iii.	10
need he c Greatly for them,	Lucretius	150
'C not thou! What matters?'	"	276

cared.

you had hardly c to see.	L.C.V. de Vere	32
nor heard of her, nor c to hear.	Ed. Morris	138
Nor c for seed or scion!	Amphion	12
c not for the affection of the house;	Princess, i.	26
some they c not; till a clamour	" iv.	465
she nor c Nor knew it,	" vi.	133
little c for fades not yet.	In Mem. viii.	20
Nor c the serpent at thy side	" cix.	7
I thought that she c for me,	Maud, I. xiv.	25
c a broken egg-shell for her lord.	Enid	1213
c as much for as a summer shower:	"	1372
on the mountain and I c not for it.	Vivien	353
about the grave, I c not for it:	"	358
if he c For her or his dear children,	En. Arden	103
sicklier, tho' the mother c for it	"	261

	POEM.	LINE.
C not to look on any human face,	En. Arden.	281
aught of what he c to know.	"	655
head high, and c for no man,	"	849
prov'n or no, What c he?	Aylmer's F.	55
Me?—but I c not for it.	"	244
slowly lost Nor greatly c to lose,	"	568
common care whom no one c for,	"	688
ever c to better his own kind,	Sea Dreams	196

careful.

So c of the type she seems,	In Mem. liv.	7
'So c of the type?' but no.	" lv.	1
you, so c of the right	To F. D. Maurice	10
All in quantity, c of my motion,	Hendecasyllabics	5

carefuller.

A c in peril, did not breathe	En. Arden.	50

careless.

like Gods together, c of mankind,	Lotos-E's.	155
Rapt in her song, and c of the snare.	Princess, i.	218
So c of the single life;	In Mem. liv.	8
eats And uses, c of the rest;	Vivien	313
answer'd Merlin c of her words.	"	550
Merlin answer'd c of her charge,	"	604
Enoch's comrade, c of himself,	En. Arden.	569
c of the household faces near,	Aylmer's F.	575
that holds The Gods are c,	Lucretius	150
O ye Gods, I know you c,	"	205

careless-order'd.

All round a c-o garden.	To F.D. Maurice	15

caress (s.)

trance gave way To those c's,	Love and Duty	64
Or for chilling his c'es	Maud, I. xx.	12

caress (verb.)

may c The ringlets waving balm—	Talking O.	178
not wrathful with your maid; Cher;	Vivien	231

caressed.

C or chidden by the dainty hand,	Coquette, i.	1

carest.

c not How roughly men may woo	Lucretius	268

careworn.

contracting grew C and wan;	En. Arden.	484

Carian.

The C Artemesia strong in war,	Princess, ii.	67

caring.

c to embalm In dying songs	In Mem. Con.	13
not for his own self c but her,	En. Arden.	165

carketh.

Thee nor c care nor slander;	A Dirge	8

carnival.

Love in the sacred halls Held c	Princess, vii.	70

carol (s.)

forth on a c free and bold;	Dying Swan	30
Heard a c, mournful, holy,	L. of Shalott, iv.	28
as her c sadder grew,	Mariana in the S.	13
Losing her c I stood pensively,	D. of F. Wom.	245
fluting a wild c ere her death,	M. d'Arthur	267
bird of Eden burst In c,	Day-Dm.	256
hall with harp and c rang.	In Mem. cii.	9

Caroline.

and Mary, there's Kate and C:	May Queen, i.	6

carolling.

c as he went A true-love ballad,	Elaine	700

carouse.

'O Soul, make merry and c,	Pal. of Art	3
long and largely we c	Will Water.	91

carp.

Near that old home, a pool of golden c;	Enid	648

carpenter.

Cooper he was and c,	En. Arden.	815
Born of a village girl, c's son,	Aylmer's F.	668

carriage.

as I found when her c past,	Maud, I. ii.	3

CONCORDANCE TO

carried.
	POEM.	LINE.
see me c out from the threshold	May Queen, ii.	42

carrier-bird.
As light as c-b's in air ; .	In Mem. xxv.	6

carrion.
For whom the c vulture waits	{ 'You might have won,' etc.	35
c crows Hung like a cloud	Vivien	448
Blacken round the Roman c,	Boädicea	14

carry.
king of them all would c me,	The Mermaid	45
Warriors c the warrior's pall,	Ode on Well.	6
That c kings in castles,	Vivien	427

carve.
may c a shrine about my dust,	St S. Stylites	192
to c out Free space	Two Voices	136
good blade c's the casques of men,	Sir Galahad	1
males that c the living hound,	Princess, iii.	293
c's A portion from the solid present,	Vivien	311

carved.
Caucasian mind C out of nature	Pal. of Art	127
A million wrinkles c his skin ;	"	138
c my name Upon the cliffs	Audley Ct.	47
thou, whereon I c her name,	Talking O.	33, 97
name I c with many vows	"	154
Wept over her, c in stone ;	Maud, I. viii.	4
c himself a knightly shield of wood,	Vivien	323
our Lady's Head, C of one emerald,	Elaine	295
scarlet sleeve, Tho' c and cut,	"	803

carven.
shield of Lancelot at her feet Be c,	Elaine	1332

carven-work.
from the c-w behind him crept	Elaine	435

Caryatid.
great statues, Art And Science, C's	Princess, iv.	183

Casciné.
What drives about the fresh C,	The Daisy	43

case (covering.)
warm'd in crystal c's.	Amphion	88
fashion'd for it A c of silk,	Elaine	8
barr'd her door, Stript off the c,	"	16
Stript off the c, and gave the naked	"	973
shield was gone ; only the c	"	984
silken c with braided blazonings, .	"	1143

case (circumstance, etc.)
profits it to put An idle c?	In Mem. xxxv.	18
blabbing The c of his patient—	Maud, II. v.	37

casement.
at the c seen her stand ?	L. of Shalott, i.	25
all the c darken'd there.	Miller's D.	128
fires your narrow c glass,	"	243
from a c leans his head .	D. of F. Wom.	246
lodge, With all its c's bedded,	Audley Ct.	17
Many a night from yonder ivied c,	Locksley H.	7
arose, and I released The c,	Two Voices	404
Flew over roof and c:	Will Water.	134
c slowly grows a glimmering square ;	Princess, iv.	34
All night has the c jessamine stirr'd	Maud, I. xxii.	15
clamour'd from a c, 'run'	The Brook	85
through the blindless c of the room	Enid	71
Clear through the open c	"	328
In Arthur's c glimmer'd chastely	Vivien	590
Unclasping flung the c back,	Elaine	975
in her anguish found The c :	Guinevere	581

casement-curtain.
drew her c-c by,	Mariana	19

casement-edge.
That morning, on the c-e	Miller's D.	82

cask.
when their c's were filled they took	En. Arden	647

casque.
And loosed the shatter'd c.	M. d'Arthur	209
blade carves the c's of men,	Sir Galahad	1

cap.
	POEM.	LINE.
knightlike in his cap instead of c,	Princess, iv.	577
unlaced my c And grovelled	"	vi. 11
the c Fell, and he started up	Enid	1237
saw the c Of Lancelot on the wall :	Elaine	801

Cassandra.
Talk with the wild C,	Œnone	259

cassia.
turning round a c, full in view	Love and Death	4

Cassiopëia.
had you been Sphered up with C,	Princess, iv.	418

Cassivelaun.
sweeter than the bride of C, Flur,	Enid	744
hear it, Spirit of C !	Boädicea	20

cast (mould.)
Not only cunning c's in clay :	In Mem. cxix.	5
take the c Of those dead lineåments	Coquette, iii.	3

cast.
Lies the hawk's c,	Aylmer's F.	849

cast (verb.)
on her knees herself she c,	Mariana in the S.	27
c me down, nor thought of you,	Miller's D.	63
'This was c upon the board,	Œnone	77
c the golden fruit upon the board,	"	222
That are c in gentle mould.	To J. S.	4
Memory standing near C down her	"	54
if indeed I c the brand away,	M. d'Arthur	88
Dora c her eyes upon the ground,	Dora	87
c and balance at a desk,	Audley Ct.	43
since I first could c a shade,	Talking O.	85
'Let me not c in endless shade,	Two Voices	5
c upon its crusty side	Will Water.	103
burnt Because he c no shadow,	Princess, i.	7
entering here, to c and fling The tricks,	" ii.	48
suns, that wheeling c The planets :	"	103
Psyche's child to c it from the doors ;	iv.	219
c A liquid look on Ida,	"	349
c as rubbish to the void,	In Mem. liii.	7
if thou c thine eyes below,	lx.	5
if an eye that's downward c	lxi.	1
chances where our lots were c	xci.	5
cares that petty shadows c	civ.	13
I seem to c a careless eye	cxi.	1
moving, c the coverlet aside	Enid	73
she c her eyes upon her dress,	"	609
c it on the mixen that it die.'	"	672
c aside A splendour dear to women,	"	807
c about For that unnoticed failing	"	895
c him and the bier in which he lay	"	1420
c his lance aside, And doff'd his helm,	"	1443
poor gown I will not cast aside	"	1553
a living man, And bid me c it.	"	1555
and she c her arms About him,	"	1609
c his eyes On whom his father Uther	"	1780
Where children c their pins and nails,	Vivien	280
gentle wizard c a shielding arm.	"	757
if his own knight cast him down,	Elaine	313
c his eyes on fair Elaine :	"	637
Leaf after leaf, and tore, and c them off	"	1193
c him as a worm upon the way ;	Guinevere	36
C all your cares on God;	En. Arden.	222
C his strong arms about his drooping	"	227
'Enoch, poor man, was c away	"	714
muttering 'c away and lost ;'	"	716
c back upon him a piteous glance,	Aylmer's F.	283
that c her spirit into flesh,	"	481
c the curtains of their seat aside—	"	803
Shall Babylon be c into the sea ;	Sea Dreams	28
one stormy night H c his body,	The Voyage	80
I c to earth a seed.	The Flower	2
c her arms about the child	The Victim	33
mountain there has c his cloudy slough,	Lucretius	177

Castalies.
led you then to all the C	Princess, iv.	275

caste.
stamps the c of Vere de Vere	L. C. V. de Vere	40

castle (adj.)	POEM.	LINE.
stood upon the *c* wall,	*Oriana*	28
Atween me and the *c* wall,	"	35
splendour falls on *c* walls	*Princess*, iii.	348
rode Geraint into the *c* court,	*Enid*	311
while he waited in the *c* court,	"	326
Moving to meet him in the *c* court;	*Elaine*	175

castle (s.)		
c, built When men knew how	*Ed. Morris*	6
See the lordly *c*'s stand :	*L. of Burleigh*	18
lady of three *c*'s in that land :	*Princess*, i.	78
Well, Are *c*'s shadows?.	" ii.	392
three *c*'s patch my tatter'd coat?	"	394
dear are those three *c*'s to my wants,	"	395
Seeing his gewgaw *c* shine,	*Maud*, I. x.	18
that fair port below the *c*	*The Daisy*	79
on one side a *c* in decay,	*Enid*	245
keeps me in this ruinous *c* here,	"	462
That carry kings in *c*'s,	*Vivien*	427
Ran to the C of Astolat,	*Elaine*	167
and again By *c* Gurnion	"	293
fly to my strong *c* overseas :	*Guinevere*	112
strong *c* where he holds the Queen ;	"	192
built their *c*'s of dissolving sand	*En. Arden*	19

castle-well.		
pool or stream, The *c-w*, belike ;	*Elaine*	215

casualty.		
Howbeit ourself, foreseeing *c*,	*Princess*, iii.	300

cat.		
c's run home and light is come,	*The Owl*, i.	1
yelp'd the cur, and yawl'd the *c* ;	*The Goose*	33
like dove and dove were *c* and dog.	*Walk. to the M.*	50
gay-furr'd *c*'s a painted fantasy,	*Princess*, iii.	170
the two great *c*'s Close by her,	" vi.	337
Within the hearing of *c* or mouse,	*Maud*, II. v.	48

catacomb.		
water falls In vaults and *c*'s .	*In Mem.* lvii.	4

catalepsy.		
paw'd his beard, and mutter'd '*c*.'	*Princess*, i.	20

catapult.		
Your cities into shards with *c*'s	*Princess*, v.	132

cataract.		
In *c* after *c* to the sea,	*Œnone*	9
snowy peak and snow-white *c*	"	207
ocean-ridges roaring into *c*'s.	*Locksley H.*	6
Dashed downward in a *c*.	*Day-Dm.*	148
the river sloped To plunge in *c*,	*Princess*, iii.	274
the wild *c* leaps in glory.	"	351
c and the tumult and the kings	" iv.	542
Set in a *c* on an island-crag,	" v.	337
The *c* flashing from the bridge,	*In Mem.* lxx.	15
shock Of the *c* seas that snap	*Maud*, II. iv.	26
thro' the crash of the near *c* hears	*Enid*	1021
C brooks to the ocean run,	*The Islet*	17

catch.		
Whereof I *c* the issue,	*Œnone*	244
C me who can, and make the catcher	*Golden Year*	18
C the wild goat by the hair	*Locksley H.*	170
To *c* a dragon in a cherry net	*Princess*, v.	162
c Her hand in wild delirium,	" vii.	77
c The far off interest of tears	*In Mem.* i.	7
c at every mountain head	" Con.	114
Prickle my skin and *c* my breath,	*Maud*, I. xiv.	36
C not my breath, O clamorous heart,	" xvi.	31
c a friend of mine one stormy day ;	" II. v.	85
'Overquick are you To *c* a lothly plume	*Vivien*	577
C her, goatfoot ; nay, Hide .	*Lucretius*	200

catcher.		
and make the *c* crown'd—	*Golden Year*	18

catching.		
Seem'd *c* at a rootless thorn,	*Enid*	1227

caterpillar.		
Picks from the colewort a green *c*,	*Guinevere*	33

cat-footed.		
C. *f* thro' the town and half in dread	*Princess*, i.	103

Cathay.	POEM.	LINE.
than a cycle of C	*Locksley H.*	184

cathedral.		
laves The lawn by some *c*	*D. of F. Wom.*	190
c towers, Across a hazy glimmer	*Gardener's D.*	213
in the vast *c* leave him.	*Ode on Well.*	280
huge *c* fronts of every age,	*Sea Dreams*	211

Catieuchlanian.		
Hear Icenian, C, hear Coritanian (rep.)	*Boädicea*	10
Gods have answer'd, C, Trinobant	"	22
Shout Icenian, C, shout Coritanian,	"	57

Cato.		
A dwarf-like C cower'd.	*Princess*, vii.	111

catspaw.		
Him his *c* and the Cross his tool,	*Sea Dreams*	186

cattle.		
The *c* huddled on the lea ;	*In Mem.* xv.	6
c died, and deer in wood,	*The Victim*	18
strikes thro' the thick blood Of *c*	*Lucretius*	99

Catullus.		
All composed in a metre of C,	*Hendecasyllabics*	4
Thro' this metrification of C,	"	10

Caucasian.		
the supreme C mind Carved	*Pal. of Art*	126
our C's let themselves be sold.	*Aylmer's F.*	349

Caucasus.		
From Calpe unto C they sung,	*The Poet*	15

caught.		
eddying of her garments *c* from thee	*Ode to Mem.*	31
there a vision *c* my eye ;	*Miller's D.*	76
C in the frozen palms of Spring.	*The Blackbird*	24
c the white goose by the leg,	*The Goose*	9
dropt the goose, and *c* the pelf,	"	13
c him by the hilt, and brandish'd	*M. d' Arthur*	145, 160
the last night's gale had *c*,	*Gardener's D.*	123
c the younker tickling trout—	*Walk. to the M.*	25
c me up into thy rest	*St S. Stylites*	18
Abaddon and Asmodeus *c* at me.	"	169
C up the whole of love .	*Love and Duty*	80
truths of science waiting to be *c*	*Golden Year*	17
page has *c* her hand in his	*Day-Dm.*	49
C the sparkles, and in circles	*Vision of Sin*	30
C each other with wild grimaces,	"	35
c the blossom of the flying terms	*Princess*, Pro.	163
the flood drew : yet I *c* her ;	" iv.	164
on this we drove and *c* .	"	170
falling on my face was *c*	"	251
as if *c* at once from bed	"	266
Kneeling, I gave it, which she *c*,	"	449
things that being *c* feign death,	" v.	105
c within the record of her wrongs,	"	137
thro' the gates, and *c* his hair,	"	330
not less one glance he *c*	"	332
Fancy light from Fancy *c*,	*In Mem.* xxiii.	14
c once more the distant shout,	" lxxxvi.	9
c The deep pulsations of the world,	" xciv.	39
C and cuff'd by the gale :	*Maud*, I. vi.	5
By that you swore to withstand?	"	79
I *c* a glimpse of his face,	" xiii.	27
often I *c* her with eyes all wet	" xix.	23
His weary daylong chirping,	*The Brook*	52
C at the hilt, as to abolish him :	*Enid*	210
Yniol *c* His purple scarf,	"	376
men had *c* them la their flight,	"	642
Her by both hands he *c*,	"	778
C in a great old tyrant spider's web,	*Vivien*	108
one of Satan's shepherdesses *c*	"	608
c And set it on his head,	*Elaine*	54
heathen *c* and reft him of his tongue.	"	273
him they *c* and maimed	"	275
whereat she *c* her breath ;	"	620
now hastily *c* His bundle,	*En. Arden*	236
C at his hand and wrung it	"	325
C at and ever miss'd it,	"	753
pock-pitten fellow had been *c* ?	*Aylmer's F.*	250
C in a burst of unexpected storm,	"	285

	POEM.	LINE.
upon the prow C the shrill salt,	The Voyage	12
reach'd the ship and c the rope,	Sailor Boy	3
c her away with a sudden cry;	The Victim	74

cause.

	POEM.	LINE.
embattail and to wall about thy c	To J. M. K.	8
This woman was the c.	D. of F. Wom.	104
love were c enough for praise.'	Gardener's D.	104
Nor in a merely selfish c—	Two Voices	147
some good c, not in mine own,	"	148
well might harm The woman's c.	Princess, iii.	129
falling, protomartyr of our c,	" iv.	484
twice I sought to plead my c,	" v.	530
betrayed her c and mine—	" v.	73
storming in extremes Stood for her c,	"	169
the c's weigh'd, Fatherly fears—	"	206
in our noble sister's c?	"	302
Is not our c pure?	"	393
sole men to be mingled with our c,	"	401
vanquish'd and my c For ever lost,	" vi.	8
whose arms Champion'd our c	"	46
The brethren of our blood and c,	"	55
dream thy c embraced in mine,	"	183
not to judge their c from her	" vii.	220
know The woman's c is man's:	"	243
such compelling c to grieve	In Mem. xxix.	1
Ring out a slowly dying c,	" cv.	13
war be a c or a consequence?	Maud, I. x.	45
cleaved to a c that I felt to be pure	" III. vi.	31
have prov'd we have hearts in a c,	"	55
no c; James had no c: but when I prest the c,	The Brook	97
Am I the c, I the poor c	Enid	87
I am the c because I dare not	"	89
'Graver c than yours is mine	"	308
you that most had c To fear me	"	1672
Yourself were first the blameless c	"	1674
her good man jealous with good c.	Vivien	455
c had kept him sunder'd	"	565
him the main c of all their crime;	"	637
remains But little c for laughter:	Elaine	595
that I gave No c, not willingly,	"	1290
her c of flight, Sir Modred:	Guinevere	9
who most have c to sorrow for her—	Aylmer's F.	678
more c to weep have I:	Coquette, iii.	6

cauve (calve.)

Wi 'auf the cows to c	N. Farmer	52

cavalier.

A c from off his saddle-bow,	D. of F. Wom.	46

Cavall.

chiefly for the baying of C.	Enid	185

cave.

sweet is the colour of cove and c,	Sea Fairies	30
hear me O Hills, O C's	Œnone	35
within the c Behind yon whispering	"	85
rock-thwarted under bellowing c's,	Pal. of Art	71
dewy echoes calling From c to c	Lotos-E's.	140
Thro' every window c and alley lone	"	148
clash'd his harness in the icy c's	M d'Arthur	186
on a dull day in an Ocean c	Vivien	80
into some low c to crawl,	"	733
massive columns, like a shorecliff c,	Elaine	405
red fire and shadows thro' the c	"	413
across the poplar grove Led to the c's:	"	801
city to the fields, Thence to the c:	"	844
c ran in beneath the cliff:	En. Arden	23
a c Of touchwood,	Aylmer's F.	511
sand and cliff and deep-inrunning c,	Sea Dreams	17
in and out the long sea-framing c's,	"	33
c's that run beneath the cliffs.	"	88
boundless deep Bore thro' the c,	"	90
the landward exit of the c,	"	94
by rock and c and tree.	V. of Cauteretz	9
In c's about the dreary bay,	Sailor Boy	10

cavern.

under gloom Of c pillars;	To E. L.	18
creep Into some still c deep	Maud, II. iv.	96
Half hut, half native c.	En. Arden	561

cavern-shadowing.

	POEM.	LINE.
wilderness, And c-s laurels,	Lucretius	202

caw.

The building rook 'ill c.	May Queen, ii.	17

cease.

I shall c to be all alone,	Mariana in the S.	95
And the wicked c from troubling,	May Queen, iii.	60
fold our wings, And c from wanderings,	Lotos-E's.	65
ripen, fall and c:	"	97
midnight bells c ringing suddenly,	D. of F. Wom.	247
'Twere better I should c	To J. S.	66
the wise of heart would c 'Love thou thy land,' etc.	Gardener's D.	231
Shall I c here? Is this enough	"	
will not c to grasp the hope.	St S. Stylites	5
c I not to clamour and to cry,	"	41
wither'd palsy c to shake?'	Two Voices	57
C to wail and brawl I	"	199
make him sure that he shall c?	"	282
muse on joy that will not c	Sir Galahad	65
c To pace the gritted floor,	Will Water.	241
cannot c to follow you,	Princess, iv.	435
her father c to press my claim,	" vii.	72
c to move so near the Heavens,	"	160
c To glide a sunbeam	"	180
have their day and c to be:	In Mem. Pro.	18
jaws Of vacant darkness and to c.	" xxxiv.	16
cold crypts where they shall c.	" lvii.	8
the man I am may c to be!	Maud, I. x.	68
Pass and c to move about!	" II. iv.	59
tyranny now should bend or c,	" III. vi.	20
And c not from your quest,	Elaine	547
c, Sweet father, and bid call.	"	1092
Judge of us all when life shall c;	Grandmother	
blasts would rise and rave and c,	The Voyage	85
dream of life this hour may c.	Requiescat	6

ceased.

She c, and Paris held the costly fruit	Œnone	133
Here she c And Paris pondered,	"	164
all these things have c to be,	May Queen, iii.	48
She c in tears, fallen from hope	D. of F. Wom.	257
Before he c I turned	Gardener's D.	120
A little c, but recommenced	Two Voices	318
I c, and sat as one forlorn.	"	400
I c, and all the ladies, each at each,	Princess, iv.	99
Scarce had I c when from a tamarisk	"	239
She c: the Princess answer'd coldly	"	340
I c; he said 'Stubborn, but	" v.	428
C all on tremble: piteous was	" vi.	126
when we c There came a minute's	" Con.	3
We c: a gentler feeling crept	In Mem. xxx.	17
had c to share her heart,	Maud, I. xix.	30
c the kindly mother out of breath;	Enid	732
She c, and made her lithe arm	Vivien	464
Scarce had she c, when out of heaven	"	783
He spoke and c: the lily maid	Elaine	242
She c: her father promised;	"	1124
when he c, in one cold passive hand	"	1195
He c; and Miriam Lane Made such	En. Arden.	902
then the motion of the current c	Sea-Dreams	113
not one moment c to thunder,	"	121

ceasing.

C not, mingled, unrepress'd,	Arabian N's.	74
He c, came a message	Princess, iii.	152

Cecily.

Wound with white roses, slept St C;	Pal. of Art	99

cedar.

The stately c, tamarisks,	Arabian N's.	105
c spread his dark-green layers	Gardener's D.	115
thro' the thicken'd c in the dusk	"	162
in halls Of Lebanonian c:	Princess, ii.	331
A voice by the c tree,	Maud, I. v.	1
dance By his red c tree,	" xvii.	18
Sighing for Lebanon, Dark c,	" xviii.	18
bloom profuse and c arches	Milton	11

cedar-wood.

A mile beneath the c-w,	Eleánore	8

cede.

if Ida yet would c our claim,	Princess, v.	323

	POEM.	LINE.
celebrate.		
To *c* the golden prime . .	*Arabian N's.*	131
celebrated.		
thine the deeds to be *c*, .	*Boädicea*	41
Celidon.		
gloomy skirts Of *C* the forest ;	*Elaine*	292
cell.		
winds bound within their *c.* .	*Mariana*	54
the bee would range her *c's*, .	*Two Voices*	70
From *c's* of madness unconfined, .	"	371
weave their petty *c's* and die	*In Mem.* xlix.	12
track Suggestion to her inmost *c.*	" xciv.	32
The tiny *c* is forlorn, . .	*Maud,* II. ii.	13
Thro' *c's* of madness, haunts of horror	" III. i.	2
c's and chambers : all were fair	*Elaine*	406
gain'd the *c* in which he slept, .	"	807
havock among those tender *c's,* .	*Lucretius*	22
cellar.		
in the *c's* merry bloated things .	*Guinevere*	265
Celt.		
The blind hysterics of the *C* ; .	*In Mem.* cviii.	16
Teuton or *C,* or whatever we be, .	*IV. to Alexan.*	32
celt.		
c's and calumets, Claymore and .	*Princess, Pro.*	17
censer.		
incense free From one *c* . .	*Eleänore,*	59
bell rings, the *c* swings, . .	*Sir Galahad*	35
cent.		
mellow metres more than *c* for *c* ;	*The Brook* .	5
centre.		
toward the *c* set the starry tides,	*Princess,* ii.	102
thoughts that wait On you, their *c* ;	" iv.	424
in the *c* stood The common men .	" vi.	339
faith has *c* everywhere, . .	*In Mem.* xxxiii.	3
The *c* of a world's desire ; . .	" lxiii.	16
In the *c* stood A statue veil'd, .	" cii.	11
centre-bit.		
c-b's Grind on the wakeful ear .	*Maud,* I. i.	41
centred.		
music *c* In a doleful song . .	*Lotos-E's.*	162
c in the sphere Of common duties,	*Ulysses*	39
c in the sun Of silver rays, .	*Elaine*	295
century.		
When the *centuries* behind me .	*Locksley H.*	13
Had I lain for a *c* dead ; . .	*Maud,* I. xxii.	72
maiden of our *c,* yet most meek ;	*The Brook* .	68
thro' the *centuries* let a people's voice	*Ode on Well.*	142
years will roll into the *centuries* .	*Guinevere*	619
ceremony.		
Long summers back, a kind of *c—*	*Princess,* i.	123
Once fit for feasts of *c*) . .	*Enid* .	297
there be wedded with all *c* . .	"	608, 839
in the darkness, at the mystical *c*	*Boädicea*	36
certain.		
A prophet *c* of my prophecy, .	*Enid* .	814
not always *c* if they be alive .	*Grandmother*	84
chace.		
That stand within the *c.* . .	*Talking O.*	4
And overlook the *c* ; . .	"	94
Look further through the *c,* . .	"	246
crost the common into Darnley *c*	*The Brook* .	132
chafe.		
c's me that I could not bend .	*D. of F. Wom.*	137
to *c* as at a personal wrong. .	*En. Arden.*	471
chafed.		
his hands, And call'd him .	*M. d'Arthur*	209
chaff.		
c and draff, much better burnt.' .	*The Epic* .	40
will he *c* For every gust of chance,	*Princess,* iv.	336
vacant *c* well meant for grain. .	*In Mem.* vi.	4
c rope And gather dust and *c,* .	" liv.	18

	POEM.	LINE.
chafing.		
c me on fire to find my bride) .	*Princess,* i.	164
and the squire *C* his shoulder : .	*Enid* .	876
c his pale hands, and calling (rep.)	"	1430
c at his own great self defied, .	*Aylmer's F.*	537
chain (s.)		
loosed the *c,* and down she lay ;	*L. of Shalott,* iv.	16
by gold *c's* about the feet of God.	*M. d'Arthur*	255
such a *c* Of knitted purport, .	*Two Voices*	167
dallied with his golden *c,* .	*Day-Dm.* .	163
To break my *c,* to shake my mane :	*Princess,* ii.	402
Twofooted at the limit of his *c,*	*Aylmer's F.*	127
chain (verb.)		
c's regret to his decease, . .	*In Mem.* xxix.	3
chained.		
My right leg *c* into the crag, .	*St S. Stylites*	72
brought her *c,* a slave, . .	*Princess,* v.	133
chair.		
In yonder *c* I see him sit, . .	*Miller's D.*	9
the long shadow of the *c* . .	"	126
Two years his *c* is seen Empty .	*To J. S.*	22
vext packs up his beds and *c's* .	*Walk. to the M.*	31
Sweat on his blazon'd *c's* . .	"	68
in his *c* himself uprear'd, . .	*Day-Dm.* .	150
spirits sink To see the vacant *c*	*In Mem.* xx.	19
c's and thrones of civil power? .	" xxi.	16
plays with threads, he beats the *c*	" lxv.	13
sits he here in his father's *c* ? .	*Maud,* I. xiii.	23
pushing could move The *c* of Idris.	*Enid* .	543
in their *c's* set up a stronger race .	"	1788
to make Arms for his *c* . .	*Elaine* .	437
But kept the house, his *c* . .	*En. Arden* .	437
With nearing *c* and lower'd accent)	*Aylmer's F.*	267
cry to vacant *c's* and widow'd walls,	"	720
They come and sit by my *c,* .	*Grandmother*	83
chairman.		
A quarter-sessions *c,* abler none ;	*Princess, Con.*	90
chaise.		
Within the low-wheel'd *c,* . .	*Talking O.*	110
chalice.		
The *c* of the grapes of God ; .	*In Mem.* x.	16
chalk.		
all his joints Are full of *c* ? .	*Audley Ct.* .	46
c and alum and plaster are sold .	*Maud,* I. i.	39
Tumbles a breaker on *c* and sand ;	*To F. D. Maurice*	24
chalk'd.		
c her face, and wing'd Her transit	*Princess,* iv.	358
chalk-hill.		
On the *c-h* the bearded grass Is dry	*Miller's D.*	245
chalk-quarry.		
white *c-q* from the hill Gleam'd .	*Miller's D.*	115
chamber.		
thick as dust In vacant *c's,* . .	*To the Queen*	19
sunbeam lay Athwart the *c's,* .	*Mariana* .	79
secret bridal *c's* of the heart, .	*Gardener's D.*	244
In palace *c's* far apart, . .	*Day-Dm.* .	94
The quiet *c* far apart . .	"	128
In musty bins and *c's,* . .	*Will Water.*	102
one deep *c* shut from sound . .	*Princess,* vi.	355
all The *c's* emptied of delight : .	*In Mem.* viii.	8
The field, the street, . .	"	11
Moved in the *c's* of the blood ; .	" xxiii.	20
About its echoing *c's* wide, . .	*Maud,* l. vi.	74
In the *c* or the street, . .	" II. iv.	83
hire us some fair *c* for the night,	*Enid* .	1087
return'd And told them of a *c,* .	"	1110
Apart by all the *c's* width, . .	"	1114
High in her *c* up a tower . .	*Elaine* .	3
cells and *c's*: all were fair . .	"	406
the comrade of his *c* woke, .	*Aylmer's F.*	583
chamber-door.		
lightly as a sick man's *c-d,* . .	*En. Arden* .	777
champaign.		
river-sunder'd *c* cloth'd with corn	*Œnone* .	112

60   CONCORDANCE TO

	POEM.	LINE.
high Above the empurpled *c*,	*Princess*, iii.	104
shadowing down the *c* till it strikes	" v.	515

champing.
c golden grain, the horses stood	*Spec. of Iliad*	21

championed.
C our cause and won it	*Princess*, vi.	46

chance.
Many a *c* the years beget.	*Miller's D.*	206
that is not a common *c*	*To J. S.*	47
every morning brought a noble *c*,	*M. d'Arthur*	230
every *c* brought out a noble knight	"	231
'The years with *c* advance :	*Two Voices*	52
April hopes, the fools of *c*	*Vision of Sin*	164
Drink to Fortune, drink to C,	"	191
your *c* Almost at naked nothing.'	*Princess*, i.	159
open eyes, and we must take the *c*.	" iii.	127
wildness, and the *c's* of the dark.'	" iv.	225
chaff For every gust of *c*,	"	337
c Were caught within the record	" v.	136
she's comely : there's the fairer *c* :	"	450
was it *c*, She past my way.	" vi.	81
grasps the skirts of happy *c*,	*In Mem.* lxiii.	6
c's where our lots were cast	" xci.	5
steps of Time—the shocks of C—	" xciv.	42
leaps into the future *c*,	" cxiii.	7
sweeter *c* ever come to here ?	*Maud*, I. i.	62
had not been For a *c* of travel	" ii.	8
He gave them line : and how by *c*	*The Brook*	150
Dispute the claims, arrange the *c's*;	*To F. D. Maurice*	31
good *c* that we shall hear the hounds:	*Enid*	182
What *c* is this ? how is it I see	"	1158
common *c*—right well I know it—	"	1180
or guiltless, to stave off a *c*	"	1202
c of booty from the morning's raid ;	"	1413
endured Strange *c's* here alone ;	"	1658
Ready to spring, waiting a *c* :	*Guinevere*	13
c Will make the smouldering scandal	"	90
beyond all hope, against all *c*,	*En. Arden.*	400

chance-comer.
You set before *c-c's*	*Will Water.*	6

chanced.
mind all full of what had *c*,	*Enid.*	1626
King's own ear Speak what has *c* ;	"	1657
jewels, whereupon I *c* Divinely	*Elaine*	59

chance-gift.
eating not Except the spare *c-g*	*St. S. Stylites*	77

chancel.
A broken *c* with a broken cross,	*M. d'Arthur*	9
peer'd athwart the *c* pane.	*The Letters*	3

chancel-casement.
Upon the *c-c*, and upon that grave	*May Queen*, ii.	21

chancellor.
The *c*, sedate and vain,	*Day-Dm.*	161
C, or what is greatest would he be—	*Aylmer's F.*	397

chance-met.
cross-lightnings of four *c-m* eyes	*Aylmer's F.*	129

change·(s.)
without hope of *c*,	*Mariana*	29
airy forms of flitting *c*.	*Madeline*	7
upon the board, And bred this *c* ;	*Œnone*	223
mood And *c* of my still soul.	*Pal. of Art*	60
Full-welling fountain-heads of *c*,	"	166
but all hath suffer'd *c* ;	*Lotos-E's.*	116
'I govern'd men by *c*,	*D. of F. Wom.*	130
thro' all *c* Of liveliest utterance	"	167
Lie still, dry dust, secure of *c*.	*To J. S.*	76
c's should control Our being,	{'Love thou thy land,' etc.	41
let the *c* which comes be free	"	45
Of many *c's*, aptly join'd,	"	65
sick of home went overseas for *c*	*Walk. to the M.*	18
fear of *c* at home, that drove	"	60
all the varied *c's* of the dark,	*Ed. Morris*	36
shrivelling thro' me, and a cloudlike *c*,	*St S. Stylites*	196
down the ringing grooves of *c*.	*Locksley H.*	182

	POEM.	LINE.
'The years with *c* advance :	*Two Voices*	52
Then comes the check, the *c*,	"	163
rapt thro' many a rosy *c*,	*Day-Dm.*	187
The flower and quintessence of *c*	"	236
there came a further *c* :	*Vision of Sin*	207
dismal lyrics, prophesying *c*	*Princess*, i.	141
not as we, But suffers *c* of frame.	" v.	453
came a *c* : for sometimes I would catch	" vii.	77
notice of a *c* in the dark world	"	234
the *c*, This truthful *c* in thee	"	329
I perceived no touch of *c*,	*In Mem.* xiv.	17
touch of *c* in calm or storm ;	" xvi.	6
Each voice four *c's* on the wind	" xxviii.	9
links that bound Thy *c's*	" xl.	7
No more partaker of thy *c*.	"	8
men and minds, the dust of *c*,	" lxx.	10
cannot come a mellower *c*,	" lxxx.	3
c's wrought on form or face ;	" lxxxi.	2
Recalls, in *c* of light or gloom,	" lxxxiv.	74
touch'd the *c's* of the state	" lxxxviii.	11
summer's hourly-mellowing *c*	" xc.	9
abyss Of tenfold-complicated *c*	" xcii.	12
c of place, like growth of time,	" civ.	11
O earth, what *c's* hast thou seen !	" cxxii.	2
face with *c* of heart is changed.	*Enid*	1747
in *c* of glare and gloom.	*Vivien*	808
a *c*, as all things human change	*En. Arden.*	101
So much to look to—such a *c*—	"	458
the *c* and not the *c*,	*Aylmer's F.*	831
Changed with thy mystic *c*,	*Tithonus*	55
thro' every *c* of sharp and flat ;	*Coquette*, i.	4

change (verb.)
Not swift nor slow to *c*,	{'Love thou thy land,' etc.	31
c a word with her he calls his wife,	*Dora*	42
my uncle's mind will *c* !'	"	45
full music seem'd to move and *c*	*Ed. Morris.*	35
iris *c's* on the burnish'd dove ;	*Locksley H.*	19
She *c's* with that mood or this,	*Will Water.*	107
C, reverting to the years,	*Vision of Sin*	159
our old halls could *c* their sex,	*Princess, Pro.*	140
you began to *c*—I saw it	" iv.	279
at a dance to *c* The music—	"	566
When your skies *c* again ;	" vi.	261
Some patient force to *c* them	" Con.	56
Nor *c* to us, although they *c* ;	*In Mem.* xxx.	24
c my sweetness more and more,	" xxxv.	15
every winter *c* to spring.	" liii.	16
ransom'd reason *c* replies	" lx.	2
happy birds, that *c* their sky	" cxiv.	15
To *c* the bearing of a word,	" cxxvii.	16
the wine will *c* your will.'	*Enid*	1511
Must our true man *c* like a leaf	*Elaine*	683
together well might *c* the world.	*Guinevere*	299
a change, as all things human *c*,	*En. Arden.*	101
This cannot *c*, nor yet can I.'	*The Ringlet*	12
If this can *c*, why so can I.'	"	24, 42

changed.
all the crimson *c*, and past	*Mariana in the S.*	25
cruel heart,' she *c* her tone,	"	69
c a wholesome heart to gall.	*L. C. V. de Vere*	44
ere my flower to fruit C,	*D. of F. Wom.*	208
flute-notes are *c* to coarse,	*The Blackbird*	18
We are all *c* by still degrees,	{'Love thou thy land,' etc.	43
flower of knowledge *c* to fruit	*Love and Duty*	24
And her spirit *c* within.	*L. of Burleigh*	64
Moved with violence, *c* in hue,	*Vision of Sin*	34
thoughts that *c* from hue to hue	*Princess*, iv.	192
Our mind is *c* : we take it	"	343
her hue *c*, and she said :	" vi.	363
at their will, and everything was *c*.	"	363
one is sad ; her note is *c*,	*In Mem.* xxi.	27
'how *c* from where it ran	" xxiii.	9
then *c* to something else	" lxxvi.	16
can grief be *c* to less ?	" lxxvii.	16
place is *c* ; thou art the same.	" cxx.	20
Remade the blood and the frame	" Con.	11
gentle will has *c* my fate,	*Maud*, I. xviii.	23
mood is *c*, for it fell at a time	" III. vi.	4

	POEM.	LINE.
being young, he *c* himself,	Enid	593
fear no longer, I am *c*,	"	1673
kept myself aloof till I was *c*;	"	1720
fear not, cousin; I am *c* indeed.'	"	1721
have you seen how nobly *c*?	"	1745
face with change of heart is *c*	"	1747
c itself and echoed in her heart,	Elaine	778
I doubt not that however *c*,	"	1212
Denouncing judgment, but tho' *c*	Guinevere	418
that name has twice been *c*—	En. Arden	860
mind is *c*, for I shall see him,	"	898
C with thy mystic change,	Tithonus	55
C every moment as we flew	The Voyage	28

changeling.
| sorrow such a *c* be? | In Mem. xvi. | 4 |

changest.
| Who *c* not in any gale, | In Mem. ii. | 10 |

changeth.
| old order *c*, yielding place to new, | M. d'Arthur | 240 |

channel.
| Thro' every *c* of the State | 'You ask me why, etc.* | 23 |
| hoary C Tumbles a breaker | To F. D. Maurice | 23 |

chant.
of the garden the merry bird *c's*,	Poet's Mind	22
C me now some wicked stave,	Vision of Sin	151
c the history Of that great race	In Mem. cii.	34

chanted.
C loudly, *c* lowly,	L. of Shalott, iv.	29
c from an ill-used race of men	Lotos-E's.	165
c a melody loud and sweet,	Poet's Song	6
c on the blanching bones of men?'	Princess, ii.	486
whose hymns Are *c* in the minster,	Vivien	616
c snatches of mysterious song	Elaine	1397
c on the smoky mountain-tops,	Guinevere	280
So they *c*: how shall Britain light	Boädicea	45
So they *c* in the darkness,	"	46

chanting.
| mine own phantom *c* hymns? | In Mem. cvii. | 10 |

chapel.
bore him to a *c* nigh the field,	M. d'Arthur	8
the *c* bells Call'd us:	Princess, ii.	446
In the white rock a *c* and a hall	Elaine	404
To *c*: where a heated pulpiteer,	Sea Dreams	20

chapel-yard.
| in the precincts of the *c-y*, | Vivien | 601 |
| paced for coolness in the *c-y*; | " | 607 |

chap-fall'n.
| The *c-f* circle spreads: | Vision of Sin | 172 |

char.
| Nor ever lightning *c* thy grain, | Talking O. | 277 |

charactered.
| laws of marriage *c* in gold | Isabel | 16 |
| How dimly *c* and slight, | In Mem. lx. | 6 |

charade.
| C's and riddles as at Christmas | Princess, Pro. | 187 |

charge (imputation, etc.)
Redeem'd it from the *c* of nothingness—	M. d'Arthur, Ep.	7
left him gold, And in my *c*,	Enid	452
in *c* of whom? a girl:	"	974
whom his father Uther left in *c*	"	1781
Set up the *c* you know,	Vivien	553
Merlin answer'd careless of her *c*,	"	604
Modred whom he left in *c* of all	Guinevere	193
gave them *c* about the Queen,	"	585

charge (assault, etc.)
Surging *c's* foam'd themselves away	Ode on Well.	126
O the wild *c* they made!	Lt. Brigade	51
Honour the *c* they made!	"	53

charge (to enjoin, etc.)
| Come forth I *c* thee, arise, | Ode to Mem. | 46 |
| I *c* thee, quickly go again | M. d'Arthur | 79 |

	POEM.	LINE.
'I *c* you, ask not but obey.'	Enid	133
c the gardeners now To pick	"	670
I *c* you ride before,	"	863
I *c* you, on your duty as a wife	"	865
I *c* you, Enid, more especially,	"	1263
count it of small use To *c* you)	"	1266
I *c* you, follow me not.'	Elaine	506
c you that you get at once to horse.	"	538
that, I *c* thee, my last hope.	Guinevere	564
c you now, When you shall see her,	En. Arden	878

charge (to impute.)
| did that wrong you *c* him with, | Sea Dreams | 268 |

charge (to rush, etc.)
| 'C for the guns!' he said: | Lt. Brigade | 6 |
| beheld the King C at the head | Elaine | 304 |

charged (commissioned,)
| *c* by Valence to bring home the child. | Vivien | 568 |

charged (rush'd, etc.)
| *c* Before the eyes of ladies | M. d'Arthur | 224 |
| down we swept and *c* and overthrew | Ode on Well. | 130 |

charged (filled.)
| C both mine eyes with tears. | D. of F. Wom. | 13 |

charger.
on my goodly *c* borne	Sir Galahad	49
cried, 'My *c* and her palfrey,'	Enid	126
c trampling many a prickly star	"	313
Enid took his *c* to the stall;	"	382
bid him bring C and palfrey.'	"	1250
saw the *c's* of the two that fell	"	1330
great *c* stood, griev'd like a man.	"	1384
See ye take the *c* too,	"	1404
gentle *c* following him unled)	"	1419
fly, your *c* is without,	"	1597
Edyrn rein'd his *c* at her side,	"	1668
overbore Sir Lancelot and his *c*,	Elaine	486
a spear Down-glancing lamed the *c*,	"	487
from his *c* down he slid,	"	509
on my *c's*, trample them under us.'	Boädicea	69

charging.
| C an army, while All the world | Lt. Brigade | 30 |
| at the midmost *c*, Prince Geraint. | Enid | 934 |

charier.
| C of sleep, and wine, and exercise, | Aylmer's F. | 448 |

chariot.
a sound arose of hoof And *c*,	Princess, vi.	359
The double tides of *c's* flow	In Mem. xcvii.	23
two brethren from the *c* took	Elaine	1140
to the lychgate, where his *c* stood,	Aylmer's F.	824
Up my Britons, on my *c*,	Boädicea	69
all around the royal *c* agitated,	"	73
each beside his *c* bound his own;	Spec. of Iliad	3
horses stood Hard by their *c's*,	"	22

chariot-bier.
| let there be prepared a *c-b* | Elaine | 1115 |
| sad *c-b* Past like a shadow | " | 1133 |

charioted.
| Boädicea, standing loftily *c*, | Boädicea | 3, 70 |

Charioteer.
| the C And starry Gemini hang | Maud, III. vi. | 6 |

charitable.
| To save the offence of *c*, | En. Arden | 339 |

charity.
summer calm of golden *c*,	Isabel	8
thou of God in thy great *c*)	"	40
gentle satire, kin to *c*,	Princess, ii.	445
those fair *charities* Joined at her side.	" vii.	50
A patron of some thirty *charities*,	Con.	88
In reverence and in *c*,	In Mem. cxiii.	28
Valour and *c* more and more.	To F. D. Maurice	40

charlatan.
| Defamed by every *c*, | In Mem. cx. | 23 |

Charles.
| Wherein the younger C abode | Talking O. | 277 |

Charles's Wain.
	POEM.	LINE.
Till C W came out above the	May Queen, ii.	12

Charley, Charlie.
little King C snarling,	Maud, I. xii.	30
and C ploughing the hill.	Grandmother	80
Harry and C I hear them too—	"	81

charm (s.)
the c of married brows.'	Œnone	74
heart that doats on truer c's.	L. C. V. de Vere	14
all his life the c did talk	Day-Dm.	121
a kiss! the c was snapt.	"	133
c have power to make New lifeblood	Will Water.	21
loose A flying c of blushes	Princess, ii.	408
nameless c That none has else	" v.	67
Merlin once had told her of a c,	Vivien	54
see but him who wrought the c	"	61
Vivien ever sought to work the c	"	64
wish still more to learn this c	"	178
c so taught will charm us both	"	181
when I told you first of such a c.	"	209
as tho' you knew this cursed c,	"	285
vast c concluded in that star	"	362
power upon me thro' this c	"	364
this c on whom you say you love.'	"	375
fair c invented by yourself?	"	390
needed then no c to keep them	"	397
might teach the King Some c,	"	434
c Of nature in her overbore	"	445
they found—his foragers for c's—	"	469
save the King, who wrought the c,	"	493
the book : the c is written in it :	"	502
open, find and read the c:	"	510
every square of text an awful c,	"	523
in the comment did I find the c.	"	533
mutter'd in himself, 'tell her the c l	"	658
told her all the c, and slept.	"	815
in one moment, she put forth the c	"	816
Wrought as a c upon them	Guinevere	143
Each, its own c; and Edith's	Aylmer's F.	165

charm (verb.)
c Pallas and Juno sitting by:	A Character	14
to c from thence The wrath	Princess, v.	476
c's Her secret from the latest moon?	In Mem. xxi.	19
Perchance, to c a vacant brain,	The Daisy	106
so taught will c us both to rest.	Vivien	181
taught the King to c the Queen	"	491
bloom profuse and cedar arches C,	Milton	12

charmed.
c and tied To where he stands,—	D. of F. Wom.	193
her father c Her wounded soul	Princess, vi.	325
So much the gathering darkness c:	" Con.	107
C him through every labyrinth	Aylmer's F.	479

charnel
| Ev'n in c's of the dead | Two Voices | 215 |

charnel-cave.
| When Lazarus left his c-c, | In Mem. xxxi. | 1 |

chart (verb.)
| c's us all in its coarse blacks | Walk. to the M. | 97 |

Chartist.
| his bailiff brought A C pike. | Walk. to the M. | 63 |

chase (s.)
And in the c grew wild,	Talking O.	126
sleek and shining creatures of the c,	Princess, v.	148
being ever foremost in the c,	Enid	1807
Follow, follow the c l	The Window	11

chase (verb.)
rose To c the deer at five;	Talking O.	52
do I c The substance, or the	Princess, ii.	386
c a creature that was current	Vivien	258
'C,' he said : the ship flew forward	The Captain	33

chased (engraved.)
| hilt, How curiously and strangely c | M. d'Arthur | 86 |
| meadow gemlike c In the brown wild | Enid | 1047 |

chased (pursued.)
| shape c shape as swift | D.of F.Wom. | 37 |

	POEM.	LINE.
light wind c her on the wing,	Talking O.	125
c The wisp that flickers	Princess, iv.	338
c the flashes of his golden horns	Vivien	277
c away the still-recurring gnat	Coquette, i.	7

chasing.
| C itself at its own wild will, | Dying Swan | 17 |
| C each other merrily | The Merman | 20 |

chasm.
in the icy caves And barren c's,	M. d'Arthur	187
Heaven opens inward, c's yawn,	Two Voices	304
one wide c of time and frost	Princess, Pro.	93
every coppice-feather'd c and cleft,	" iv.	5
the little elves of c and cleft	Guinevere	246
lines of cliff breaking have left a c;	En. Arden.	1
in the c are foam and yellow sands ;	"	671
drawn thro' either c,	"	671
from the gaps and c's of ruin left	Sea Dreams	218

chaste.
| world's great bridals, c and calm ; | Princess, vii. | 278 |
| many generous, and some c. | Vivien | 666 |

chasten.
| love the Heaven that c's us. | Enid | 1637 |

chastisement.
| May not that earthly c suffice? | Aylmer's F. | 784 |

chastity.
clear-pointed flame of c,	Isabel	2
rode forth, clothed on with c:	Godiva	53
rode back, clothed on with c :	"	65
They bound to holy vows of c l	Vivien	545
To lead sweet lives in purest c,	Guinevere	470

Chatelet.
| The last wild thought of C, | Margaret | 37 |

chattel.
| Live c's, mincers of each other's fame, | Princess, iv. | 494 |

chatter.
Would c with the cold	St S. Stylites	70
crane,' I said, 'may c of the crane,	Princess, iii.	88
then to hear a dead man c	Maud, II. v.	19
I c over stony ways,	The Brook	39
I c, c, as I flow	"	47

chatter'd.
| They c trifles at the door : | In Mem. lxviii. | 4 |
| Philip c more than brook | The Brook. | 51 |

chattering.
| c stony names Of shale and | Princess, iii. | 343 |

Chaucer.
| Dan C, the first warbler, | D. of F. Wom. | 5 |

chaunt.
| I would mock thy c anew ; | The Owl, ii. | 8 |
| solemn c's resound between. | Sir Galahad | 36 |

chaunteth.
| C not the brooding bee | A Dirge | 16 |

cheat (s.)
| Yet, if she were not a c, | Maud, I. vi. 35, | 91 |
| Scarcely, now, would I call him a c | " xiii. | 29 |

cheat (verb.)
| love to c yourself with words ; | Princess, vii. | 314 |
| C and be cheated, and die : | Maud, I. i. | 32 |

cheated.
| Cheat and be c, and die ; | Maud, I. i. | 32 |

cheating.
| c the sick of a few last gasps | Maud, I. i. | 43 |

check (s.)
| Then comes the c, the change, | Two Voices | 163 |
| motions, c's, and counterchecks. | " | 300 |

check (verb.)
nuns would c her gadding tongue	Guinevere	311
c me too : Nor let me shame	"	315
pray you c me if I ask amiss—	"	322

	POEM.	LINE.
check'd.		
c His power to shape: . .	*Lucretius*	22
cheek.		
The baby-roses in her *c*'s; .	*Lilian*	17
then the tears run down my *c*,	*Oriana*	69
Leaning his *c* upon his hand,	*Eleänore*	118
c Flush'd like the coming of the day;	*Miller's D.*	131
Her *c* had lost the rose, . .	*Œnone*	17
c brighten'd as the foam-bow brightens	"	60
her snow-cold breast and angry *c*. .	"	140
His ruddy *c* upon my breast.	*The Sisters*	20
with puff'd *c* the belted hunter	*Pal. of Art*	63
From *c* and throat and chin. .	"	140
along the brain, And flushes all the *c*.	*D. of F. Wom.*	44
swarthy *c*'s and bold black eyes, .	"	127
dimples your transparent *c*, .	*Margaret*	15
Tie up the ringlets on your *c*: .	"	57
could bring the colour to my *c*;	*Gardener's D.*	192
clapt him on the hands and on the *c*'s,	*Dora*	130
laughter dimpled in his swarthy *c*;	*Ed. Morris*	61
pat The girls upon the *c*, .	*Talking O.*	1
flush'd her *c* with rosy light,	"	165
Then her *c* was pale and thinner	*Locksley H.*	21
On her pallid *c* and forehead .	"	25
barking cur Made her *c* flame;	*Godiva*	57
should smite him on the *c* .	*Two Voices*	251
dreaming on your damask *c*, .	*Day-Dm.*	3
blush is fix'd upon her *c*. .	"	52
The colour flies into his *c*'s; .	"	119
C by jowl, and knee by knee; .	*Vision of Sin*	84
On glassy water drove his *c* in lines;	*Princess*, i.	115
when the king Kiss'd her pale *c*,	" ii.	245
blew the swoll'n *c* of a trumpeter,	"	343
flying charm of blushes o'er this *c*	"	408
my *c* Began to burn and burn, .	" iii.	29
over brow And *c* and bosom brake	" iv.	364
my Sire, his rough *c* wet with tears,	" v.	22
so belabour'd him on rib and *c* .	"	331
wan was her *c* With hollow watch,	" vi.	128
love not hollow *c* or faded eye: .	"	370
wordless broodings on the wasted *c*—	" vii.	97
c's drop in; the body bows; .	*In Mem.* xxxv.	3
A touch of shame upon her *c*: .	" xxxvii.	10
let us go; your *c*'s are pale; .	" lvi.	5
clap their *c*'s, to call them mine, .	" lxxxiii.	18
blow The fever from my *c*, .	" lxxxv.	9
beam of an eyelash dead on the *c*,	*Maud*, I. iii.	3
Roses are her *c*'s . .	" xvii.	7, 27
Of my mother's faded *c* .	" xix.	19
was what had redden'd her *c*	"	65
with his whip, and cut his *c*.	*Enid*	207
first she kiss'd on either *c*, .	"	517
c burn and either eyelid fall, .	"	775, 1283
lived some colour in your *c*, .	"	1460
spearman let his *c* Bulge .	"	1478
However lightly, smote her on the *c*.	"	1566
White was her *c*; sharp breaths of	*Vivien*	697
with an ancient swordcut on the *c*	*Elaine*	258
Flamed in his *c*; and eager eyes, .	*Aylmer's F.*	66
Cooling her false *c* with a featherfan,	"	289
her *c* Kept colour: wondrous!	"	505
c begins to redden thro' the gloom,	*Tithonus*	37
thy tears are on my *c*, .	"	45
cheep.		
c and twitter twenty million loves	*Princess*, iv.	83
cheer (s.)		
would faint at your cruel *c*.	*Poet's Mind*	15
Died the sound of royal *c*; .	*L. of Shalott*, iv.	48
Naked I go, and void of *c*: .	*Two Voices*	239
A murmur, ' Be of better *c*.'	"	429
festal *c*, With books and music,	*In Mem.* cvi.	21
I make myself such evil *c*, .	*Maud*, I. xv.	2
sweet cakes to make them *c*, .	*Enid*	388
cried Geraint for wine and goodly *c*,	"	1132
maid had striven to make him *c*, .	*Elaine*	326
Welcome her, thundering *c* of the	*W. to Alexan.*	7
cheer (verb.)		
come, *c* up before I go.' .	*En. Arden*	200
my girl, *c* up, be comforted .	"	218

	POEM.	LINE.
cheer'd.		
he *c* her soul with love. .	*L. of Burleigh*	68
we with singing *c* the way, .	*In Mem.* xxii.	5
Be *c* with tidings of the bride .	" xxxix.	23
But he *c* me, my good man, .	*Grandmother*	69
cheerful.		
It wellnigh made her *c*; .	*Enid*	1292
grew so *c* that they deem'd .	*Elaine*	1125
cheerfully.		
Enoch bore his weakness *c*. .	*En. Arden*	828
cheerful-minded.		
Be *c-m*, talk and treat Of all things	*In Mem.* cvi.	19
cheering.		
phosphorescence *c* even My lady;	*Aylmer's F.*	116
chequer-work.		
A *c-w* of beam and shade .	*In Mem.* lxxi.	15
cherish.		
c that which bears but bitter fruit?	*Locksley H.*	65
love of all Thy daughters *c* Thee,	*Idylls, Ded.*	51
cherry.		
catch a dragon in a *c* net, .	*Princess*, v.	162
chesnut (tree.)		
those three *c*'s near, that hung	*Miller's D.*	55
came and sat Below the *c*'s .	"	60
those full *c*'s whisper by. .	"	168
in the *c* shade I found .	"	201
Parks with oak and *c* shady, .	*L. of Burleigh*	29
chesnut (fruit.)		
The *c* pattering to the ground; .	*In Mem.* xi.	4
c, when the shell Divides threefold	*The Brook*	72, 207
that islet in the *c-b* .	*Aylmer's F.*	65
chesnut-bloom.		
drooping *c-b*'s began To spread	*Sir L. and Q. G.*	16
chess.		
our wine and *c* beneath the planes,	*Princess*, vi.	229
chest (part of body.)		
like monstrous apes they crush'd my *c*:	*St. S. Stylites*	171
Live long, nor feel in head or *c* .	*Will Water.*	237
chest (box.)		
She took the little ivory *c*, .	*The Letters*	17
keep it like a puzzle *c* in *c*, .	*Vivien*	504
chew'd.		
c The thrice-turned cud of wrath,	*Princess*, i.	64
chid.		
be friends, like children being *c!*	*Princess*, vi.	271
C her, and forbid her to speak .	*Maud*, I. xix.	63
chidden.		
c by the dainty hand, .	*Coquette*, i.	1
chief (adj.)		
Lancelot, the *c* of knights. .	*Elaine*	141, 187
guess thee *c* of those, After the king,	"	183
chief (s.)		
heads of *c*'s and princes fell so fast,	*Aylmer's F.*	763
child (see *children.*)		
Fed thee, a *c*, lying alone, .	*Eleänore*	25
A glorious *c*, dreaming alone, .	"	27
features of her Ere it is born: her *c!*	*Œnone*	248
never *c* be born of me, Unblest, .	"	250
you have another *c*. .	*May Queen*, ii.	36
She'll be a better *c* to you .	"	44
dream of Father-land Of *c*, .	*Lotos-E's.*	40
Dora took the *c*, and went her way,	*Dora*	69
tell him Dora waited with the *c*; .	"	74
rose and took The *c* once more, .	"	79
Whose *c* is that? What are you doing	"	86
answer'd softly, 'This is William's *c!*'	"	88
take the *c* And bless him .	"	91
work for William's *c*, until he grows	"	124
for myself, Or William, or this *c*;	"	159
hours he sobb'd o'er William's *c*, .	"	163

CONCORDANCE TO

Entry	Poem	Line
cling About the darling c:	Talking O.	128
O, the c too clothes the father	Locksley H.	91
barbarian lower than the Christian c.	"	174
walk'd between his wife and c,	Two Voices	412
that c's heart within the man's	Will Water.	31
I speak the truth : you are my c..	Lady Clare	24
buried her like my own sweet c,	"	27
'Nay now, my c,' said Alice.	"	33, 41
Alas, my c, I sinn'd for thee.'	"	50
from the palace came a c of sin,	Vision of Sin	5
C, if it were thine error	'Come not, when,' etc.	7
His tenants, wife and c	Princess, Pro.	4
Half c half woman as she was,	"	101
lose the c, assume The woman :	" i.	136
odes About this losing of the c;	"	140
the c We lost in other years,	"	255
language proves you still the c.	" ii.	44
a c, In shining draperies,	"	93
slay this c, if good need were	"	267
turn'd to go, but Cyril took the c,	"	341
c Push'd her flat hand against	"	344
call'd For Psyche's c to cast it	" iv.	218
lay The lily-shining c;	"	268
lost lamb (she pointed to the c)	"	342
a hope The c of regal compact,	"	401
live, dear lady, for your c!	" v.	77
my babe, my blossom, ah my c,	"	79
when they say The c is hers (rep.)	"	84
my sweet Aglaïa, my one c:	"	98
Who gave me back my c?'	"	102
You have spoilt this c;	"	112
chiefest comfort is the little c	"	420
c shall grow To prize the authentic	"	422
training of a c Is woman's wisdom.'	"	455
Set his c upon her knee—	"	545
'Sweet my c, I live for thee.'	"	547
Knelt on one knee,—the c on one,—	" vi.	75
she set the c on the earth ;	"	104
not yours, but mine: give me the c.'	"	125
The mother, me, the c;	"	137
give her the c!	"	152, 163–7
mellowing, dwelt Full on the c;	"	175
Ida spoke not, rapt upon the c.	"	203
Blanche had gone, but left Her c.	" vii.	42
is but a c Yet in the go-cart.	Con.	77
Poor c, that waitest for thy love!	In Mem. vi.	28
call'd me fool, they call me c;	" lxvii.	13
find in c and wife An iron welcome	" lxxix.	7
Familiar to the stranger's c;	" c.	20
c would twine A trustful hand,	" cviii.	18
Half-grown as yet, a c, and vain—	" cxiii.	9
With wisdom, like the younger c:	"	20
like a c in doubt and fear:	" cxxiii.	17
Then was I as a c that cries,	"	19
I play'd with the girl when a c;	Maud, I. i.	68
O c, you wrong your beauty,	" iv.	17
have play'd with her when a c;	" vi.	87
then, perhaps, as a c of deceit,	" xii.	40
Made her only the c of her mother,	"	40
awoke in the heart of the c,	" xix.	48
darling Katie Willows, his one c!	The Brook	67
married Enid, Yniol's only c,	Enid	4
dear c hath often heard me praise	"	434
O noble host For this dear c,	"	497
'See here, my c, how fresh the colours	"	680
Look on it, c, and tell me if you	"	684
worn My faded suit, as you, my c	"	706
dear c is set forth at her best,	"	728
fair c shall wear your costly gift	"	819
wail you for him thus? you seem a c.	"	1396
neither eyes nor tongue—O stupid c!	Vivien	100
In you, that are no c,	"	216
a mere c Might use it	"	534
One c they had ; it lived with her:	"	566
by Valence to bring home the c.	"	568
is it clamour'd by the c,	"	621
bitter weeping like a beaten c	"	704
moral c without the craft to rule,	Elaine	146
true, my c. Well I will wear it :.	"	369
'Do me this grace, my c,	"	381
the diamond : wit you well, my c,	"	767
kiss the c That does the task assign'd	Elaine	824
Meeker than any c to a rough nurse,	"	853
Milder than any mother to a sick c	"	854
O my c, you seem Light-headed,	"	1056
seeing you desire your c to live,	"	1089
saying thou art fair, my c,	"	1399
c kill me with her innocent talk?'	Guinevere	212
c kill me with her foolish prate?'	"	223
found a naked c upon the sands	"	291
the simple, fearful c Meant nothing,	"	367
too-fearful guilt Simpler than any c,	"	369
so low, the c of one I honour'd	"	419
Well is it that no c is born of thee.	"	421
give his c a better bringing-up	En. Arden.	87
how should the c Remember this?'	"	232
the third c was sickly-born	"	260
common to her state Being with c:	"	518
when her c was born Then her new c	"	519
marriage, and the birth Of Philip's c	"	710
only c, his Edith, whom he loved	Aylmer's F.	23
Nursing a c, and turning to the warmth	"	185
—who could trust a c?	"	264
Their c.' 'Our c!' 'Our heiress!'	"	297
because I love their c They hate me:	"	423
read Writhing a letter from his c,	"	517
such a love as like a chidden c,	"	541
seldom crost his c without a sneer.	"	562
speak before the people of her c,	"	608
The poor c of shame, The common care	"	687
gentle attributes Of his lost c,	"	731
our own c on the narrow way,	"	743
childless mother went to seek her c;	"	829
in the narrow gloom By wife and c;	"	841
an unknown artist's orphan c—	Sea Dreams	234
Virgin Mother standing with her c	"	234
the c Clung to the mother,	"	236
mine but from the crying of a c.'	"	241
'C? No!' said he, 'but this tide's	"	242
flap, Good man, to please the c.	"	258
so loud) has roused the c again.	"	270
But I wept like a c that day,	Grandmother	64
like a c for the c that was dead	"	68
that fair c betwixt them born.	On a Mourner	25
King is happy In c and wife ;	The Victim	26
cast her arms about the c	"	33
c was only eight summers old,	"	34
taken the c To spill his blood	"	45

childhood.

Entry	Poem	Line
Ere c's flaxen ringlet turn'd	In Mem. lxxviii.	15
up from c shape His action	" cxix.	10
the dawn of rosy c past,	En. Arden.	37

childlike.

| lose the c in the larger mind ; | Princess, vii. | 268 |

children.

May c of our c say,	To the Queen	23
Two c in two neighbour villages	Circumstance	1
Two c in one hamlet born	"	8
been to blame. Kiss me, my c.'	Dora	159
our time, nor in our c's time,	Golden Year	55
mothers brought Their c, clamouring,	Godiva	15
Three fair c first she bore him,	L. of Burleigh	87
That love to keep us c!	Princess, Pro.	133
had but been, she thought, As c ;	" i.	136
baser courses, c of despair.'	" iii.	197
her due, Love, c, happiness ?'	"	229
c, would they grew Like field-flowers	"	234
But c die ; and let me tell you,	"	236
C—that men may pluck them	"	240
c—there is nothing upon earth	"	242
Whose name is yoked with c's,	" v.	408
be friends, like c being chid!	" vi.	271
c call, and I Thy shepherd pipe,	" vii.	202
by the hearth the c sit	In Mem. xx.	13
takes the c on his knee,	" lxv.	17
grins on a pile of c's bones,	Maud, I. i.	46
Late the little c clung :	Ode on Well.	237
c of the king in cloth of gold	Enid	664
all the c in their cloth of gold	"	668
cry of c, Enids and Geraints	"	1813

Entry	POEM	LINE
In *c* a great curiousness be well,	Vivien	214
Where *c* cast their pins and nails,	"	280
To one at least, who hath not *c*,	"	356
Lives for his *c*, ever at its best	Elaine	335
c born of thee are sword and fire,	Guinevere	422
either for his own or *c's* sake.	"	509
Three *c* of three houses,	En. Arden	11
c play'd at keeping house.	"	24
With *c*: first a daughter.	"	84
see his *c* leading evermore	"	115
When he was gone—the *c*—what to do?	"	132
cared For her or his dear *c*,	"	164
her *c*, let her plead in vain;	"	167
love you bear Him and his *c*	"	307
he sent Gifts by the *c*.	"	325
Philip was her *c's* all-in-all	"	345
prove A father to your *c*:	"	408
came the *c* laden with their spoil;	"	442
his own *c* tall and beautiful,	"	763
his rights and of his *c's* love,—	"	765
My *c* too! must I not speak	"	739
if my *c* care to see me dead,	"	889
A childly way with *c*.	Aylmer's F.	181
talk'd, Poor *c*, for their comfort:	"	427
Bodies, but souls—thy *c's*—	"	672
c's laughter in their hall	"	787
all my *c* have gone before me	Grandmother	18
c, Annie, they're all about me	"	76
Phantom wail of women and *c*,	Boädicea	26

chill.
he is *c* to praise or blame.	Two Voices	258
As wan, as *c*, as wild as now;	In Mem. lxxi.	17
dark the night and *c*!	Guinevere	166-172
fearing night and *c* for Annie	En. Arden	440
that afternoon Sunny but *c*;	"	671

chill'd.
| *c* the popular praises of the King | Guinevere | 14 |
| heavens Stilled and *c* at once: | Aylmer's F. | 613 |

chilling.
| *c* his caresses By the coldness | Maud, I. xx. | 12 |

chime (s.)
| for noise Of clocks and *c's*, | Princess, i. | 213 |

chime (verb.)
| those great bells Began to *c*. | Pal. of Art | 158 |
| sad will no less to *c* with his, | En. Arden | 247 |

chimera.
| *C's*, crotchets, Christmas solecisms, | Princess, Pro. | 199 |

chimney.
half the *c's* tumbled	The Goose	48
c's muffled in the leafy vine	Audley Ct.	13
now her father's *c* glows	In Mem. vi.	29

chimney-top.
| above the tall white *c-t's* | May Queen, ii. | 12 |

chin.
smooth'd his *c* and sleek'd his hair	A Character	11
His double *c*, his portly size	Miller's D.	2
From cheek and throat and *c*	Pal. of Art	140
Close up his eyes: tie up his *c*:	D. of the O. Year	48
sweet face from brow to *c*:	L. of Burleigh	62
reddening in the furrows of his *c*,	Princess, vi.	211
many-winter'd fleece of throat and *c*.	Vivien	690

China.
| laws Salique And little-footed *C*, | Princess, ii. | 118 |

China-bound.
| Reporting of his vessel *C-b*, | En. Arden | 122 |

chink (sound.)
| Even in dreams to the *c* of his pence, | Maud, I. x. | 43 |

chink (crevice.)
| walls Were full of *c's* and holes; | Godiva | 60 |

chirp (s.)
| I hear a *c* of birds: | In Mem. cxviii. | 5 |

chirp (verb.)
| The cricket *c's*: the light burns low: | D. of the O. Year | 40 |

chirping.
| caught His weary daylong *c*, | The Brook | 53 |

chirr'd.
| not a cricket *c*: | In Mem. xciv. | 6 |

chirrup.
| The sparrow's *c* on the roof, | Mariana | 73 |
| win her With his *c* at her ear. | Maud, I. xx. | 30 |

chirrupt.
| beside me *c* the nightingale | Grandmother | 40 |

chivalry.
| came to *c*: When some respect | Princess, ii. | 119 |

choice.
And told him of my *c*,	Talking O.	18
wherefore rather I made *c*.	Two Voices	460
have made the wiser *c*, 'You might have won,' etc.		5
weep the comrade of my *c*.	In Mem. xiii.	9
sweetness hardly leaves me a *c*	Maud, I. v.	24
glorious in his beauty and thy *c*	Tithonus	12
Teach that sick heart the stronger *c*,	On a Mourner	18

choke.
almost *c* with golden sand 'You ask me why,' etc.		24
'A quinsy *c* thy cursed note!'	The Goose	29
yellow vapours *c* The great city	Maud, II. iv.	63

choked.
I *c*. Again they shriek'd	Ed. Morris	123
Earth, and Time are *c*	St S. Stylites	102
Her voice *C*, and her forehead sank	Princess, vii.	231
are mine,' and saying that she *c*,	Elaine	604
His mercy *c* me.	Guinevere	609

choler.
| old, but full Of force and *c*, | Golden Year | 61 |

chooorch.
| voäted wi' Squoire an' *c* an' staäte, | N. Farmer | 15 |
| An' I allus coomed to 's *c* | " | 17 |

choose.
To *c* your own you did not care;	Day-Dm.	242
hardly worth my while to *c*	In Mem. xxxiv.	10
arms for guerdon; *c* the best.'	Enid	1067

chop (s.)
| His proper *c* to each. | Will Water. | 116 |
| Among the *c's* and steaks! | " | 148 |

chop (verb.)
| *C* the breasts from off the mother, | Boädicea | 68 |

chop-house.
| Head-waiter of the *c-h* here, | Will Water. | 209 |

chord.
clear twang of the golden *c's*	Sea Fairies	33
smote on all the *c's* with night.	Lockley H.	33
Consonant *c's* that shiver to one	Princess, iii.	74
deepest measure from the *c's*:	In Mem. xlvii.	12
flash along the *c's* and go.	" lxxxvii.	12
'Screw not the *c* too sharply	Aylmer's F.	469

chorus.
| Go' (shrill'd the cottonspinning *c*) | Ed. Morris | 122 |
| O you *c* of indolent reviewers, | Hendecasyllabics | 1, 12 |

chose.
smooth as burnish'd brass I *c*.	Pal. of Art.	6
sober-suited Freedom *c*, 'You ask me why,' etc.		6
your sake, the woman that he *c*,	Dora	61
ere the people *c* him for their king,	Elaine	35
C the green path that show'd	"	112
You *c* the best among us—	En. Arden	292

chosen.
c to wed I had been wedded earlier,	Elaine	930
Was *c* Abbess, there, an Abbess,	Guinevere	688
Who madest him thy *c*,	Tithonus	13
Gods, he said, 'would have *c* well;	The Victim	62

Christ.
C, the Virgin Mother, and the Saints;	St S. Stylites	110
So I clutch it. *C*! 'Tis gone;	"	704
time draws near the birth of *C*:	In Mem. xxviii.	1
Behold a man raised up by *C*!	" xxxi.	13

CONCORDANCE TO

	POEM.	LINE.
time draws near the birth of C :	In Mem. ciii.	1
Ring in the C that is to be.	„ cv.	32
Ah C, that it were possible .	Maud, II. iv.	13
churches have kill'd their C.	„ v.	29
God accept him, C receive him	Ode on Well.	281
saintly youth, the spotless lamb of C,	Vivien	599
all his legions crying C and him,	Elaine	305
everywhere about this land of C .	Guinevere	428
break the heathen and uphold the C,	„	467
lean on our fair father C,	„	558
Save C as we believe him—.	Aylmer's F.	573
as cried C ere His agony	„	793
preaching simple C to simple men,	Sea Dreams	21
C the bait to trap his dupe .	„	187

Christian.
barbarian lower than the C child.	Locksley H.	174
The graceful tact, the C art ;	In Mem. cix.	16
kept a tender C hope .	Sea Dreams	41

Christless.
C code, That must have life .	Maud, II. i.	26

Christmas.
old honour had from C gone,	The Epic	7
church-bells ring in the C morn.	M. d'Arthur, Ep.	31
cock crows ere the C morn, .	Sir Galahad	51
seven stay'd at C up to read ;	Princess, Pro.	176
Charades and riddles as at C here,	„	187
from mouth to mouth As here at C.'	„	190
Chimeras, crotchets, C solecisms,	„	199
C bells from hill to hill .	In Mem. xxviii.	3
holly round the C hearth ;	„ xxx.	2
Again at C did we weave	„	1
holly round the C hearth ;	„ lxxvii.	2
lastly there At C ;	Aylmer's F.	114
when the second C came, escaped	„	838
green C crams with weary bones.	Coquette, iii.	14

Christmas-eve.
At Francis Allen's on the C-e—	The Epic	1
How dare we keep our C-e ;	In Mem. xxix.	4
sadly fell our C-e.	„ xxx.	4
calmly fell our C-e ;	„ lxxvii.	4
strangely falls our C-e	„ civ.	4

chronicle.
keep a c With all about him'—	Princess, Pro.	27
So sang the gallant glorious c ;	„	49
The total c's of man .	„ ii.	359
ran thro' all the coltish c .	The Brook	159
dash'd Into the c of a deedful day,	Aylmer's F.	196

chrysalis.
dull c Cracks into shining wings	St S. Stylites	153
ruin'd c of one .	In Mem. lxxxi.	8

chuckle.
c, and grin at a brother's shame ; .	Maud, I. iv.	29

chuckled.
It clutter'd here, it c there, .	The Goose	25

church.
in the dark c like a ghost .	In Mem. lxvi.	15
A single c below the hill .	„ ciii.	3
She came to the village c, .	Maud, I. viii.	1
fragrant gloom Of foreign c'es—	„ xix.	54
kill their c, As the c'es have kill'd	„ II. v.	28
homeward by the c I drew.	The Letters	44
moulder'd c ; and higher Along street	Eu. Arden	4
c, —one night, except For greenish	Aylmer's F.	621
pious variers from the c,	Sea Dreams	19

church-commissioner.
Now harping on the c-c's, .	The Epic	15

church-bell.
Toll ye the c-b sad and slow,	D. of the O. Year	3
c-b's ring in the Christmas morn.	M. d'Arthur, Ep.	31
sweet c-b's began to peal. .	Two Voices	408

church-harpy.
church-harpies from the master's feast	To J. M. K.	3

churchmen.
c fain would kill their church,	Maud, II. v.	28
Should all our c foam in spite	ToF.D.Maurice	9

church-tower.
	POEM.	LINE.
grass-green beside a gray c-t,	Circumstance	6

churchwarden.
Until the grave c doff'd, .	The Goose	19

churl.
low c, compact of thankless earth .	Godiva	66
The c in spirit, up and down .	In Mem. cx.	1
The c in spirit, howe'er he veil	„	5
riding close behind an ancient c,	Enid	261
laugh'd the father saying, 'Fie, Sir C,	Elaine	200

cicala.
At eve a dry c sung, .	Marinua in the S.	85
the c sleeps. .	Œnone	27

cider.
flask of c from his father's vats,	Audley Ct.	26

cinder.
make My scheming brain a c,	Vivien	782

circle (s.)
round about the c's of the globes	The Poet	43
I watch'd the little c's die ;	Miller's D.	74
The greensward into greener c's	Gardener's D.	133
in the c of his arms Enwound us	„	211
his orbit, and the Moon Her c.	Love and Duty	23
all the c of the golden year ?'	Golden Year	51
In the same c we revolve.	Two Voices	314
music winding trembled, Wov'n in c's.	Vision of Sin	18
Caught the sparkles, and in c's,	„	30
The chap-fallen c spreads ; .	„	172
group of girls In c waited,	Princess, Pro.	69
c rounded under female hands	„ ii.	350
Thro' c's of the bounding sky,	In Mem. xxxi.	6
in a c hand-in-hand	„ xxx.	11
Against the c of the breast, .	„ xliv.	3
With all the c of the wise,	„ lx.	3
In c round the blessed gate .	„ lxxxiv.	23
all in c drawn About him,	„ lxxxviii.	21
From all the c of the hills.	„ c.	24
round me drove In narrowing c's.	Lucretius	57

circle (verb.)
knowledge c with the winds ; 'Love thou thy laud,' etc.		17
tho' I c in the grain, .	Talking O.	83
We c with the seasons. .	Will Water.	64
full voice which c's round the grave,	Princess, ii.	31
c moaning in the air : .	In Mem. xii.	15
It c's round, and fancy plays,	„ Con.	81

circled.
C thro' all experiences, pure law,	Œnone	163
I prosper, c with thy voice ; .	In Mem. cxxix.	15
settling c all the lists. .	Enid	547

circuit.
The c's of thine orbit round .	In Mem. lxii.	11

circumstance.
hollow orb of moving C .	Pal. of Art	255
breast the blows of c, .	In Mem. lxiii.	7

citadel.
Troas and Ilion's column'd c,	Œnone	13
beneath her shadowing c. .	„	116
A moulder'd c on the coast, .	The Daisy	28
Fell the colony, city, and c, .	Boädicea	86

citadel-crown'd.
Tempest-buffeted, c-c .	Will	9

citizen.
gravest c seems to lose his head,	Princess, Con.	59
heart of the c hissing in war .	Maud, I. i.	24

citron-shadow.
clove The c-s's in the blue : .	Arabian N's.	15

city.
Full of the c's stilly sound, .	Arabian N's.	103
a c glorious—A great and distant c—	Deserted H.	19
the open gates of the c afar,	Dying Swan	34
Below the c's eastern towers :	Fatima	9
in a clear-wall'd c on the sea,	Pal. of Art	97
I and Eustace from the c went	Gardener's D.	2
fable of the c where we dwelt.	„	6

	POEM.	LINE.		POEM.	LINE.
News from the humming c comes	Gardener's D.	35	spring to me, and c me thine,	Guinevere	561
O'er the mute c stole	"	182	with Edith, c A distant kinship	Aylmer's F.	62
the dust and drouth Of c life	Ed. Morris	4	*claiming.*		
Beyond the lodge the c lies,	Talking O.	5	c each This meed of fairest.	Œnone	85
cities of men And manners, climates,	Ulysses	13	before her face, C her promise.	En. Arden.	455
shaped The c's ancient legend	Godiva	4	*clamber'd.*		
rose a shriek as of a c sack'd;	Princess, iv.	147	c half way up The counter side;	Golden Year	6
dash'd Your cities into shards	" v.	132	c o'er at top with pain,	Princess, iv.	190
breathed his latest breath That C.	In Mem. xcvii.	6	street that c toward the mill.	En. Arden.	60
I come once more : the c sleeps;	" cxviii.	3	*clambering.*		
bubbles o'er like a c, with gossip,	Maud, I. iv.	8	c on a mast In harbour,	En. Arden.	105
For a tumult shakes the c,	" II. iv.	50	*clamour* (s.)		
choke The great c sounding wide;	"	64	fill'd the house with c.	The Goose	36
shines over city and river,	Ode on Well.	50	With peals of genial c sent	Will Water.	187
the long-illumined cities flame	"	228	herd of boys with c bowl'd	Princess, Pro.	81
c Of little Monaco, basking, glow'd.	The Daisy	8	hear my father's c at our backs	" i.	104
c glitter'd Thro' cypress avenues,	"	47	c thicken'd, mixt with inmost terms	" ii.	423
here to-night in this dark c,	"	95	c grew As of a new-world Babel,	" iv.	465
c sparkles like a grain of salt.	Will	20	trampling the flowers With c:	" v.	238
saw two cities in a thousand boats	Vivien	411	that blind c made me wise;	In Mem. cxxiii.	18
heads should moulder on the c gates.	"	444	the c of liars belied	Maud, I. iv.	51
arisen since With cities on their flanks.	"	526	C and rumble, and ringing	" II. v.	13
up the still rich c to his kin,	Elaine 798,	841	blare of bugle, c of men,	Ode on Well.	115
thro' the din rich c to the fields,	"	843	c of the rooks At distance	Enid	249
across the fields Far into the rich c,	"	887	all the windy c of the daws	"	1104
in it Far cities burnt,	Guinevere	83	fill'd the shores With c.	En. Arden.	637
King Ride toward her from the c,	"	401	*clamour* (verb.)		
made The harlot of the cities:	Aylmer's F.	375	to c, mourn, and sob,	St S. Stylites	6
A c clerk, but gently born,	Sea Dreams	1	cease I not to c and to cry,	"	41
Flash, ye cities, in rivers of fire!	W. to Alexan.	19	*clamour'd.*		
rioted in the c of Cunobeline	Boädicea	60	Lilia, then, for heroine,' c he,	Princess, Pro.	217
Fell the colony, c, and citadel,	"	86	Melissa c 'Flee the death ;'	" iv.	143
oxen from the c, and goodly sheep	Spec. of Iliad	4	he c from a casement, 'run'	The Brook	85
city-gate.			is it c by the child,	Vivien	621
before the c-g's Came on her brother	Elaine	786	'Dead' c the good woman	En. Arden.	841
city-gloom.			*clamouring.*		
Droopt in the giant-factoried c-g,	Sea Dreams	5	c, 'If we pay, we starve!'	Godiva	15
city-roar.			c etiquette to death,	Princess, v.	16
c-r that hails Premier or king!	Princess, Con.	101	c out 'Mine—mine—not yours,	" vi.	124
city-room.			c on, till Ida heard,	"	134
moss or musk, To grace my c-r's;	Gardener's D.	190	at the c of her enemy fainted	Boädicea	82
civility.			*clang* (s.)		
keep a touch of sweet c	Enid	1161	overhead Begins the clash and c.	In Mem. Con.	61
civilization.			*clang,* verb.)		
infant c be ruled with rod	Maud, I. iv.	47	among the stars Would c it,	Princess, iv.	415
clack'd.			the wood which grides and c's	In Mem. cvi.	11
It c and cackled louder.	The Goose	24	*clanged.*		
palace bang'd, and buzz'd and c,	Day-Dm.	146	bare black cliff c round him,	M. d'Arthur	188
clad.			knell to my desires C on the bridge;	Princess, iv.	157
long-hair'd page in crimson c,	L. of Shalott, ii.	22	*clanging.*		
She c herself in a russet gown,	Lady Clare	57	windy c of the minster clock	Gardener's D.	33
c her like an April daffodilly	Princess, ii.	303	*clap* (s.)		
Six hundred maidens c in purest white,	"	448	stammering cracks and c's That follow'd	Vivien	791
c in ir n hurst the ranks of war,	" iv.	483	Dead c's of thunder from within	Sea Dreams	55
looking hardly human, strangely c,	En. Arden	639	*clap,* verb.)		
Mixt with myrtle and c with vine,	The Islet	19	C's her tiny hands above me,	Lilian	4
claim (s.)			bird That c's his wings at dawn.	D. of F. Wom.	180
thousand c's to reverence closed	To the Queen	27	c their cheeks, to call them mine.	In Mem. lxxxiii.	18
Smile at the c's of long descent,	L. C. V. de Vere	52	*clapper.*		
she will not : waive your c:	Princess, v.	286	in a c clapping in a garth,	Princess, ii.	209
if Ida yet would cede our c,	"	323	*clapping.*		
t e combat for my c till death.	"	350	Laughing and c their hands,	The Merman	29
With c a c from right to right,	"	407	in a clapper c in a garth,	Princess, ii.	209
her father cease to press my c,	" vii.	72	noise Of songs, and c hands,	In Mem. lxxxvi.	19
ea h prefers his separate c,	In Mem. ci.	18	came a c as of phantom hands.	Enid	566
crush'd in the clash of jarring c's,	Maud, III. vi.	44	*clapt.*		
asserts his c In that dread sound	Ode on W'ell.	70	c her hands and cried, 'I marvel	Pal. of Art.	189
Atte t their great commander's c	"	148	c his hand On Everard's shoulder,	The Epic	21
Dispute t e c's, arrange the	To F. D. Maurice	11	c him on the hands, and on the cheeks	Dora	130
Lays c t) for the lady at his side,	Enid	487	c his hand in mine, and sang—	Audley Ct.	38
claim, verb.)			feet that ran, and doors that c,	Day-Dm.	135
sounder leaf than I can c ; 'You might have won,' etc.			c her hands and cried for war	Princess, iv.	567
much that Ida c's right	Princess, v.	104	c her hands and cried for war	Princess, iv.	567
Who but c's her as his due?	Maud, I. xx.	11	I mused a little, and then c her hands	Vivien	715
of us to c the prize,	Elaine	543			

Clara.
	POEM.	LINE.
Lady C Vere de Vere (rep.)	L.C.V.de Vere	1

Clare.
		POEM.	LINE.
To give his cousin, Lady C.		Lady Clare	4
you are not the Lady C		"	20
was no longer Lady C,		"	38
Lady C, you shame your worth!		"	66
you shall still be Lady C.'		"	88

Claribel.
Where C low-lieth (rep.)	Claribel	1

clash (s.)
overhead Begins the c and clang	In Mem. Con.	61
in the c of jarring claims	Maud, III.vi.	44
Roll of cannon and c of arms,	Ode on Well.	116
I heard the c so clearly.	Sea Dreams	132

clash (verb.)
O hard, when love and duty c!	Princess, ii.	273
you c them all in one,	" v.	172
C, ye bells, in the merry March air!	W. to Alexan.	18
C the darts and on the buckler	Boädicea	79
Fly on to c together again,	Lucretius	41

clash'd.
c his harness in the icy caves	M. d'Arthur	186
from them c The bells;	Gardener's D.	215
shameless noon Was c and hammer'd Godiva		75
one, that c in arms,	Princess, v.	5
horses yell'd: they c their arms;	"	240
c His iron palms together	"	343
save When armour c or jingled,	" vi.	343
As the music c in the hall;	Maud, I.xxii.	34
C with his fiery few and won;	Ode on Well.	100
thrice They c together	Enid	562
Touch'd, clink'd, and c, and vanish'd	Sea Dreams	131

clashing.
Enid heard the c of his fall	Enid	1358

clasp (embrace.)
glance and smile, and c and kiss,	In Mem. lxxxiii.	7

clasp (fastening.)
Buckled with golden c's before,	Sir L.and Q.G.	25

clasp (verb.)
I'd c it round so close and tight,	Miller's D.	180
c's the crag with hooked hands;	The Eagle	1
c it once again, And call her Ida,	Princess, vii.	80
Let Love c Grief	In Mem. i.	9
Some landing-place, to c and say	" xlvi.	15
Thy passion c's a secret joy:	" lxxxvii.	8
C thy little babes 'Lady, let the rolling,' etc.		6
c These idols to herself?	Lucretius	159
C her window, trail and twine,	The Window	22
Trail and twine, and c and kiss,	"	24

clasped.
Die, dying c in his embrace.	Fatima	42
her, who c in her last trance	D. of F.Wom.	266
Are c the moral of thy life,	Day-Dm.	267
But he c her like a lover,	L. of Burleigh	67
c the feet of a Mnemosyne,	Princess, iv.	250
hands so lately c with yours	" vi.	168
A hand that can be c no more—	In Mem. vii.	5
hands so often c in mine,	" x.	19
comfort c in truth reveal'd;	" xxxvii.	22
first he walk'd when c in clay?	" xcii.	4
He is c by a passion-flower.	Maud, I. xiv.	8
ivy-stems C the gray walls,	Enid	323
c and kiss'd her, and they rode away	"	825
turn'd and c me in his arms,	Grandmother	55
fell on him, C, kissed him,	Lucretius	276
C on her seal, my sweet!	The Window	135

clasping.
round me, c each in each,	Talking O.	143
I, c brother-hands, aver	In Mem.lxxxvii.	102

clatter.
With cackle and with c.	The Goose	12
rumble, and ringing, and c,	Maud, II. v.	13

clause.
	POEM.	LINE.
the little c 'take not his life:'	Princess, v.	459
in a train Of flowery c's	Lucretius	120

clave.
loved one only and who c to her'—	Idylls, Ded.	10
c Like its own mists	Elaine	38
his kith and kin C to him,	Guinevere	437
c To Modred, and a remnant stays	"	439

claw.
red in tooth and c With ravine	In Mem. lv.	15
miss'd, and brought Her own c back,	Vivien	350

clay.
should have trod me into c,	Oriana	62
c ta'en from the common To——.	(With Pal. of Art)	17
coarse to sympathize with c	Locksley H.	46
Doing dishonour to my c.'	Two Voices	102
shall not blind his soul with c.'	Princess, vii.	312
Half-conscious of their dying c,	In Mem.lvii.	7
first he walk'd when claspt in c?	" xcii.	4
Not only cunning casts in c:	" cxix.	5
judge all nature from her feet of c,	Vivien	684
seems to make us loveless c,	Elaine	1008
Rose from the c it work'd in	Aylmer's F.	170

claymore.
C and snowshoe, toys in lava,	Princess, Pro.	18

clean.
As c and white as privet	Walk. to the M.	48
whole, and c, and meet for Heaven.	St S. Stylites	210
make all c, and plant himself afresh,	Enid	1753
keep him bright and c as heretofore,	"	1785
will never make oneself c.	Grandmother	36

cleanse.
c this common sewer of all his	Enid	39, 1743

cleansed.
bandit holds and c the land.	Enid	1792

clear (adj.)
C, without heat, undying,	Isabel	3
C and bright it should be ever,	Poet's Mind	5
healthy, sound, and c and whole,	Miller's D.	15
O hark, O hear! how thin and c,	Princess, iii.	354
I feel so free and so c	Maud, I. xix.	98

clear (verb.)
Better to c prime forests,	Princess, iii.	111
c away the parasitic forms	" vii.	253

clear-cut.
But a cold and c-c face,	Maud, I. ii.	7
Cold and c-c face, why come you	" iii.	1

clear'd.
a whirlwind c the larder,	The Goose	52
everywhere C the dark places	Enid	1701
flash of semi-jealousy c it	Aylmer's F.	189

clearer.
The fires are all the c,	The Window	58

clearest.
c of ambitious crime,	Ode on Well.	28

clear-faced.
Until they found the c-f King,	Elaine	431

clear-featured.
that c-f face Was lovely,	Elaine	1153

clear-headed.
C-h friend, whose joyful 'Clear-headed friend,' etc.		1

clearness.
like the rest, No certain c,	Two Voices	335
The starry c of the free?	In Mem. lxxxiv.	86
The critic c of an eye,	" cviii.	3

clear-pointed.
the c-p flame of chastity	Isabel	2

clear-stemm'd.
c-s platans guard The outlet,	Arabian N's.	23

clear-voiced.
The c-v mavis dwelleth,	Claribel	16

	POEM.	LINE.
clear-wall'd.		
in a c-w city on the sea,	Pal. of Art	97
cleave (to adhere.)		
love thee well and c to thee,	Œnone	157
man will c unto his right,'	Lady Clare	40
C to your contract:	Princess, iv.	390
if I fall, c to the better man."	Enid	1001
love one maiden only, c to her,	Guinevere	471
shadow of another c's to me,	"	611
cleave (to divide.)		
race of men that c the soil,	Lotos-E's.	165
c the rift of difference deeper,	Princess, v.	291
mighty Love would c in twain	In Mem. xxv.	10
he, Would c the mark.	" lxxxvi.	30
c a creed in sects and cries,	" cxxvii.	15
hard earth c to the Nadir hell	Vivien	199
cleaved.		
c to a cause that I felt	Maud, III. vi.	31
cleaving.		
The fruitful wit C, took root,	The Poet	21
cleft (s.)		
torrent call'd me from the c:	Œnone	53
thro' mountain c's the dale was seen	Lotos-E's.	20
coppice-feather'd chasm and c,	Princess, iv.	5
trickling dropwise from the c,	Vivien	123
little elves of chasm and c	Guinevere	246
cleft verb.)		
He c me thro' the stomacher;	Princess, ii.	385
stands apart C from the main,	" iv.	263
Has risen and c the soil	" vi.	19
Clelia.		
C, Cornelia, with the Palmyrene	Princess, ii.	69
clematis.		
O'erflour'd with the hoary c:	Golden Year	63
Rose, rose, and c.	The Window 23, 30	
clench.		
who c their nerves to rush	Love and Duty	75
clench'd.		
c his purpose like a blow!	Princess, v.	296
c her fingers till they bit	Elaine	608
Cleopatra-like.		
C/as of old To entangle me	Maud, I. vi.	27
clergyman.		
that good man, the c,	May Queen, iii.	12
clerk.		
worn-out c Brow-beats his desk	To J. M. K.	11
now w left The c behind us	Ed Morris.	97
was a God, and is a lawyer's c,	"	102
A city c, but gently born	Sea Dreams	1
cleverness.		
not for all Aspasia's c,	Princess, ii.	323
click.		
merry milkmaids c the latch,	The Owl, i.	8
cliff.		
upon the wall Of purple c's,	Ode to Mem.	54
to her seat from the upper c.	Œnone	8
Along the c to fall and pause,	Lotos-E's.	9
bare black c clang'd round him	M.d'Arthur	188
c's that guard my native land	Audley Ct.	48
girt the region with high c	Vision of Sin	47
wound About the c's, the copses,	Princess, iii.	342
sweet and far from c and scar	"	356
stroke of cruel sunshine on the c,	" iv.	503
leave the c's, and haste away	In Mem. xii.	8
searped c and quarried stone	" iv.	2
like a crag that tumbles from the c,	Enid	318
steep c and the coming wave;	Guinevere	278
a stream that spouting from a c	"	602
lines of c breaking have left	En. Arden.	1
cave ran in beneath the c:	"	23
c and deep-inrunning cave,	Sea Dreams	17
on and they walk'd, and now on c,	"	37
thunder from within the c's	"	55

	POEM.	LINE.
caves that run beneath the c's.	Sea Dreams	68
on those c's broke, mixt with	"	207
lines of c's were c's no more,	"	210
cliff-side.		
broken rocks On some c-s,	Elaine	1246
climate.		
manners, c's, councils, governments	Ulysses	14
climax.		
'The c of his age!	Princess, ii.	36
climb.		
seem'd to hear them c and fall	Pal. of Art	70
'will you c the top of Art.	Gardener's D.	165
day wanes: the slow moon c's:	Ulysses	55
Cry, faint not, c:	Two Voices	184
c Beyond her own material prime?	"	377
I c the height ;	Sir Galahad	57
but we Set forth to c:	Princess, iii.	336
as one that c's a peak to gaze	" vii.	90
near us when we c or fall ;	In Mem. l.	13
C thy thick noon, disastrous day;	" lxxi.	26
I c the hill: from end to end	" xcix.	1
felt the knot C in her throat,	Elaine	737
would not or I could not c—	Guinevere	637
street c's to one tall-tower'd mill ;	En. Arden.	5
c into the windy halls	Lucretius	136
climbed.		
he had c across the spikes,	Princess, Pro.	111
we c The slope to Vivian-place,	" Con.	39
thither I c at dawn	Maud, I. xiv.	5
I have c nearer out of lonely Hell.	" xviii.	80
c upon a fair and even ridge,	Enid	239
Guinevere had c The giant tower,	"	826
on his foot She set her own and c;	"	1608
c That eastern tower,	Elaine	14
Then to her tower she c,	"	356
C to the high top of the garden-wall	Guinevere	26
c the hill, just where the prone edge	En. Arden.	66
I c to the top of the garth,	Grandmother	38
c as quickly, for the rim	The Voyage	27
climbing part.)		
ever c up the c wave?	Lotos-E's.	95
And ever c higher;	D.of F. Wom.	32
c up into my airy home,	St S. Stylites	214
Came little coppes c.	Amphion	32
c Cyril kept With Psyche,	Princess, iii.	336
turn'd his face And kiss'd her c,	Enid	1609
A lily-avenue c to the doors ;	Aylmer's F.	162
c up the valley ; at whom he shot.	"	228
climbing (s.)		
Maud with her venturous c's	Maud, I. i.	69
clime.		
poet in a golden c was born,	The Poet	1
in that unblissful c,	D of F. Wom.	82
what to me were sun or c?	Locksley H.	177
In divers seasons, divers c's,	Day-Dm.	230
on the tables every c and age	Princess, Pro.	16
led him through the blissful c's,	In Mem. lxxxiv.	25
throve and branch'd from c to c	" cxvii.	13
the breeze of a softer c,	Maud, I. iv.	4
For many a time in many a c	Ode on Well.	64
O hundred shores Of happy c's,	The Voyage	49
Again to colder c's we came.	"	80
Put forth and feel a gladder c.'	On a Mourner	15
cling.		
close as might be would he c	Talking O.	127
c's To the turrets and the walls ;	Maud, II. iv.	33
a cloud c's to the hill,	Enid	1570
voice c's to each blade of grass,	Elaine	108
c together in the ghastly sack—	Aylmer's F.	764
'My mother c's about my neck,	Sailor Boy	17
clinging.		
Not c to some ancient saw ;'	Love thou thy land,'etc.	29
Unshaken, c to her purpose,	Princess, v.	334
clink (s.)		
the tinsel c of compliment.	Princess, ii.	41

CONCORDANCE TO

clink (verb).
	POEM.	LINE.
hears't the village hammer c,	In Mem. cxx.	15

clink'd.
Touched, c, and clash'd and vanish'd,	Sea Dreams	131

clinking.
c, chattering stony names	Princess, iii.	343

clip.
Tho' fortune c my wings,	Will Water.	50

clipt.
read in arbours c and cut,	Amphion	85
wing'd affections c with crime:	Princess, vii.	297
c A tiny curl, and gave it	En. Arden.	234
thousand days Were c by horror	Aylmer's F.	603
She c you from her head	The Ringlet	38

cloak (s.)
the red c's of market girls	L. of Shalott, ii.	17
Pitiful sight, wrapt in a soldier's c	Princess, v.	53
raised the c from brows as pale	"	70
Wrapt in a c, as I saw him,	Maud, I. i.	59

cloak (verb.)
c's the wounds of loss with lies;	Vivien	667

cloaked.
The Shadow c from head to foot,	In Mem. xxiii.	4

clock.
The slow c ticking,	Mariana	74
windy clanging of the minster c;	Gardener's D.	38
heavy c's knolling the drowsy hours.	"	180
rose a noise of striking c's	Day-Dm.	134
speak for noise Of c's and chimes,	Princess, i.	213
the dark, when c's Throbb'd thunder	" vii.	88
c Beats out the little lives of men.	In Mem. ii.	7
And hark the c within,	Maud, I. xviii.	64

clock-work.
little c-w steamer paddling plied	Princess, Pro.	71

clog (s.)
To lighten this great c of thanks,	Princess, vi.	110
A c of lead was round my feet,	The Letters	5

clog (verb.)
fulsome Pleasure c him, and drown	Maud, I. xvi.	4

cloister.
c's, branch'd like mighty woods,	Pal. of Art	26
while our c's echo'd frosty feet,	Princess, Pro.	181
Walk your dim c, and distribute dole	Guinevere	675

clomb.
Imprisoning sweets, which, as they c	Arabian N's.	40
C to the roofs, and gazed alone	Princess, vii.	17

close (an enclosure.)
I broke a c with force and arms,	Ed. Morris	131
in a roofless c of ragged stones;	St S. Stylites	73
Are wither'd in the thorny c,	Day-Dm.	111

close (an end.)
sweet c of his delicious toils—	Pal. of Art	185
The c 'Your Letty, only yours;'.	Ed. Morris	106
never found his earthly c,	Love and Duty	1
and the bitter c of all,	Princess, vi.	101
drove us, last, to quite a solemn c—	" Con.	17
they said, as earnest as the c?	"	21
Such a war had such a c.	Ode on Well.	118
such a stern and iron-clashing c,	Vivien	269
Death dawning on him, and the c of all	En. Arden.	833
At c of day; slept, woke,	Sea Dreams	18
Then comes the c.'	"	29
it is here—the c of the year,	Spiteful Let.	1
Here is the golden c of love,	The Window	180

close (verb.)
forgets to c His curtains,	Adeline	42
C the door, the shutters c,	Deserted H.	9
C up his eyes: tie up his chin:	D.of the O. Year	48
To c the interests of all. 'Love thou thy land,' etc.		36
this be true, till Time shall c	"	79
Death c's all;	Ulysses	51
c with Cyril's random wish:	Princess, iii.	85
so employ'd, should c in love,	" vii.	52

	POEM.	LINE.
and the daisy c Her crimson fringes	In Mem. lxxi.	11
Until we c with all we lov'd,	" cxxx.	11
before his journey c's, He shall find	Ode on Well.	205
To c with her lord's pleasure;	Enid	1063
c again, and nip me flat,	Vivien	200
c the hand Upon it;	Elaine	1108
heard the ponderous door C,	Aylmer's F.	338
breathe it into earth and c it up	Coquette, iii.	12
one wide will that c's thine.	On a Mourner	20

close-buttoned.
turn'd once more, c-b to the storm;	Ed. Morris	136

closed.
thousand claims to reverence c	To the Queen	27
c mine eyelids, lest the gems	M. d'Arthur	152
Summ'd up and c in little;	Gardener's D.	13
She turn'd, we c, we kiss'd,	Ed. Morris	114
hoped that ere this period c	St S. Stylites	17
for the promise that it c:	Locksley H.	14
C in a golden ring.	Sir L. and Q. G.	27
And thus our conference c.	Princess, ii.	346
until they c In conflict.	" v.	479
darkness c me; and I fell.	"	531
spirit c with Ida's at the lips;	" vii.	143
So c our tale, of which I give	" Con.	1
the gates were c At sunset,	"	36
such as a c Welcome, farewell,	"	94
warm hands have prest and c,	In Mem. xiii.	7
such as c Grave doubts.	" xlvii.	2
dying eyes Were c with wail,	" lxxxix.	6
pulses c their gates with a shock	Maud, I. i.	15
The gates of Heaven are c,	" xviii.	12
by this my love has c her sight	"	67
they c a bargain, hand in hand.	The Brook.	156
Dash'd on Geraint, who c with him	Enid	1311
seem'd to lie C in the four walls	Vivien	58, 393
and the thicket c Behind her,	"	822
And c the hand upon it,	Elaine	1129
c about by narrowing nunnery-walls,	Guinevere	340
she c the Book and slept:	En. Arden.	495
when she c ' Enoch, poor man,	"	713
open'd it, and c, As lightly	"	776
c her access to the wealthier farms,	Aylmer's F.	503
fain had she c them now	"	805
c by those who mourn a friend	Lucretius	142

close-latticed.
C-l to the brooding heat,	Mariana in the S.	3

closelier.
once mine, now thine, is c mine,	Vivien	296

close-matted.
a wall of green C-m,	Day-Dm.	66

close-set.
wore A c-s robe of jasmine	Aylmer's F.	158

closet.
not to myself in the c alone,	Maud, II. v.	49

closeted.
with that woman c for hours!'	Princess, iii.	40

closing (part.)
c like an individual life—	Love and Duty	77
c eaves of wearied eyes	In Mem. lxvi.	11

closing (s.)
at the c of the day	L. of Shalott, iv.	15

clot.
Is a c of warmer dust,	Vision of Sin	113

cloth of gold.
With inwrought flowers, a c o g	Arabian N's.	149
children of the king in c o g	Enid	664-8
all the coverlid was c o g	Elaine	1151

clothe.
c the wold and meet the sky:	L. of Shalott, i.	3
the child too c's the father	Locksley H.	91
C's and reclothes the happy plains;	Day-Dm.	22
to c her heart with love,	Princess, iv.	87
tender ash delays To c herself,	"	89
Will c her for her bridals	Enid	231

	POEM.	LINE.
c yourself in this, that better fits	Enid	717
c her like the sun in Heaven.	"	784
poor gown he bad me *c* myself,	"	1550
Io, I *c* myself with wisdom,' .	Vivien	104
often toil'd to *c* your little ones ;	Aylmer's F.	699

clothed.
river-sunder'd champaign *c* with	Œnone	112
C in white samite, mystic,	M. d'Arthur	31,144,159
from ridge to ridge, C with his breath,	"	182
rode forth, *c* on with chastity :	Godiva	53, 65
spaces *c* in living beams,	Sir Galahad	66
which I *c* in act,	Princess, i.	192
have *c* their branchy bowers	In Mem. lxxv.	13
see her now, C with my gift	Enid	753
c her for her bridals like the sun ;	"	836
c her in apparel like the day.	"	1796
ready on the river, *c* in black.	Elaine	1117
C in so pure a loveliness ?	"	1375
worst self hast thou *c* thy God.	Aylmer's F.	646

clothes.
wholesome food, And wear warm *c*,	St S. Stylites	107
Like coarsest *c* against the cold : .	In Mem. v.	10
fairer in new *c* than old.	Enid	722
c they gave him and free passage	Eu. Arden	651

clothing.
upbearing parasite, C the stem,	Isabel	35

clotted.
c into points and hanging loose	M. d'Arthur	219

cloud.
Like little *c*'s sun-fringed,	Madeline	17
And with the evening *c*,	Ode to Mem.	22
gushes from beneath a low-hung *c*	"	71
any *c* would cross the vault	Mariana in the S.	38
Slowly, as from a *c* of gold,	Eleänore	73
A *c* that gather'd shape :	Œnone	41
one silvery *c* Had lost his way	"	99
o'er him flow'd a golden *c*	"	103
she withdrew into the golden *c*	"	187
moon lit slips of silver *c*	"	214
death, thou ever-floating *c*,	"	234
c of incense of all odour .	Pal. of Art	39
All barr'd with long white *c* .	"	83
and the *c*s are lightly curl'd	Lotos-E's.	157
Hold swollen *c*'s from raining,	D. of F. Wom.	11
The light white *c* swam over us,	"	221
Brightening the skirts of a long *c*,	M. d'Arthur	54
one large *c* Drew downward ;	Gardener's D.	77
c smoulders on the summer crag.	Ed. Morris	147
betwixt the meadow and the *c*,	St S. Stylites	14
a summer moon Half-dipt in *c* :	Godiva	46
dense *c* from base to cope.	Two Voices	186
Embracing *c*, Ixion-like ;	"	195
every *c*, that spreads above .	"	446
c's are broken in the sky,	Sir Galahad	73
c's are highest up in air,	Lady Clare	2
made the wild-swan pause in her *c*,	Poet's Song	7
molten on the waste Becomes a *c*,	Princess, iv.	55
of some fire against a stormy *c*,	"	365
Settled a gentle *c* of melancholy ;	"	547
As comes a pillar of electric *c*.	"	v. 513
thro' the *c* that dimm'd her broke	"	vi. 264
The *c* may stoop from heaven	"	365
a great black *c* Drag inward	"	vii. 2
c's of nameless trouble cross	In Mem. iv.	13
dote and pore on yonder *c*	" xv.	16
A rainy *c* possess'd the earth,	" xxx.	3
c's that drench the morning star,	" lxxi.	22
'Can *c*'s of nature stain	" lxxxiv.	85
in the darkness and the *c*,	" xcv.	21
steer'd her toward a crimson *c*	" cii.	55
The flying *c*, the frosty light ;	" cv.	2
Like *c*'s they shape themselves	" cxxii.	8
high in heaven the streaming *c*	" Con.	107
head in a *c* of poisonous flies.	Maud, I. iv.	54
fold upon fold of hueless *c*,	" vi.	3
when the morning came In a *c*,	"	21
Betwixt the *c* and the moor,	" ix.	4

	POEM.	LINE.
thro' sunshine, storm, and *c* ;	Enid	348
wheel and thou are shadows in the *c* ;	"	357
by and by Slips into golden *c*,	"	736
seeing *c* upon the mother's brow,	"	777
your Enid burst Sunlike from *c*—	"	789
all night long a *c* clings	"	1539
like a *c* above the gateway towers.'	Vivien	449
the vast eyelid of an inky *c*,	"	484
across him came a *c* Of melancholy	Elaine	323
Dispersed his resolution like a *c*	"	880
they cannot weep behind a *c* :	Guinevere	205
c Cuts off the fiery highway .	Eu. Arden	129
Sailing along before a gloomy *c*	Sea Dreams	120
soft air fans the *c* apart ;	Tithonus	32
creeps a *c*, or moves a wind .	Lucretius	106
C's that are racing above,	The Window	6
Gone, and a *c* in my heart,	"	40
No is trouble and *c* and storm	"	113

clouded.
spake he, *c* with his own conceit,	M. d'Arthur	110
all my mind is *c* with a doubt)	"	258

cloudlet.
From little *c*'s on the grass,	In Mem. Con.	94

cloud-tower.
C-t's by ghostly masons wrought	In Mem. lxix.	5

cloudy.
look so *c* and so cold ;	Enid	897

clove (s.)
nutmeg rocks and isles of *c*.	The Voyage	40

clove (verb.)
c The citron-shadows in the blue :	Arabian N's.	14
c An advent to the throne ;	Princess, iv.	264

cloven.
Was *c* with the million stars	Ode to Mem.	35
not a worm is *c* in vain ;	In Mem. liii.	9

clover.
broidry of the purple *c*.	A Dirge	38

clover-hill.
with white bells the *c-h* swells	Sea Fairies	14

clown.
thou art mated with a *c*,	Locksley H.	47
knave or *c* Shall hold their 'You might have won,' etc.	"	11
Shakespeare's curse on *c* and knave	"	27
this is proper to the *c*,	Princess, iv.	227
furr'd and purpled, still the *c*,	"	228
turnspits for the *c*,	"	495
Glorifying *c* and satyr ;	" v.	179
By blood a king, at heart a *c*	In Mem. cx.	4
mismated with a yawning *c*,	Enid	1275

club.
talk'd At wine, in *c*'s, of art,	Princess, Pro.	160

clung.
should have *c* to Fulvia's waist	D. of F. Wom.	259
c about The old man's neck,	Dora	159
mist of morn C to the lake.	Ed. Morris	108
When I *c* to all the present	Locksley H.	14
a moment after, *c* About him,	Princess, ii.	291
c The shadow of his sister	" v.	247
Late the little children *c* ;	Ode on W'ell	237
lets the day Strike where it *c* :	Enid	1541
c to him, Fixt in her will,	Vivien	43
c about her lissome limbs	"	72
about his neck, C like a snake ;	"	91
C but to crate and basket,	"	475
c to him and hugg'd him close ;	"	794
to his crown the golden dragon *c*	Elaine	433
C to the dead earth	Guinevere	8
for crest the golden dragon *c*	"	588
evil fancies *c* Like serpent eggs	Eu. Arden	476
from the beetling crag to which he *c*	Aylmer's F.	229
still C to their fancies)	Sea Dreams	36
and the child C to the mother	"	237

cluster (s.)
Below the starry *c*'s bright,	L. of Shalott, iii.	25

	POEM.	LINE.
tropic shade and palms in *c*,	*Locksley H.*	160
about a narrow wharf In *c*;	*En. Arden*.	4
tear away Their tawny *c*'s,	"	379
men and women in dark *c*'s	*Sea Dreams*	219

cluster (verb.)

| The foxglove *c* dappled bells.' | *Two Voices* | 72 |

clustered.

| sunny hair *C* about his temples | *Œnone* | 59 |

clutch.

| So I *c* it. Christ! 'Tis gone: | *St S. Stylites* | 204 |
| lives to *c* the golden keys, | *In Mem.* lxiii. | 10 |

clutch'd.

c the sword, And strongly wheel'd	*M. d' Arthur*	135
stoop'd and *c* him, fair and good,	*Will Water.*	133
my mother *c* The truth at once,	*Princess*, iii.	44
He, standing still, was *c*;	" iv.	241

cluttered.

| It *c* here, it chuckled there | *The Goose* | 25 |

coal.

| On the *c*'s I lay, A vessel | *St S. Stylites* | 166 |
| left his *c* all turn'd into gold | *Maud*, I. x. | 11 |

coal-black.

| flow'd His *c-b* curls as on he rode, | *L. of Shalott*, iii. | 31 |

coarse.

sense of touch is something *c*	*Talking O.*	163
growing *c* to sympathise with clay.	*Locksley H.*	46
daughter of our meadows, yet not *c*;	*The Brook*	69
eat also, tho' the fare is *c*,	*Enid*	1057

coarseness.

| According to the *c* of their kind, | *Princess*, iv. | 327 |

coast.

an iron *c* and angry waves.	*Pal. of Art*	69
All round the *c* the languid air	*Lotos-E's.*	5
A lucid veil from *c* to *c*,	*In Mem.* lxvi.	14
rolling brine That breaks the *c*.	" cvi.	15
a *c* Of ancient sable and fear—	*Maud*, II. ii.	31
Back from the Breton *c*	"	43
bad you guard the sacred *c*'s.	*Ode on Well.*	172
A moulder'd citadel on the *c*,	*The Daisy*	28
province with a hundred miles of *c*	*Vivien*	438–97
about a stone On the bare *c*.	*Guinevere*	53
After the sunset, down the *c*,	"	236
down the lonely *c* of Lyonnesse,	"	238
leagues along that breaker-beaten *c*	*En. Arden*	51
moving up the *c* they landed him,	"	666
hound for health they gained a *c*	*Sea Dreams*	16
having dream'd Of that same *c*.	"	201
all in shade, Gloom'd the low *c*	*The Voyage*	42

coat.

| castles patch my tatter'd *c* ? | *Princess*, ii. | 394 |

coat-of-arms.

| worth a hundred *c's-o-a* | *L. C. V. de Vere* | 16 |

cobweb.

The petty *c-s* we have spun:	*In Mem.* cxxiii.	8
c woven across the cannon's throat	*Maud*, III. vi.	27
could wish a *c* for the gnat,	*Vivien*	220

cock.

c sung out an hour ere light:	*Mariana*	27
c hath sung beneath the thatch	*The Owl*, i.	10
At midnight the *c* was crowing,	*Oriana*	12
Before the *c* crows	*May Queen*, ii.	23
heard just now the crowing *c*.	*D. of the O. Year*	38
sitting, as I said, The *c* crew loud	*M. d' Arthur, Ep.*	10
barking dogs, and crowing *c*'s;	*Day-Dm.*	136
c crows ere the Christmas morn,	*Sir Galahad*	51
plump head-waiter at The *C*,	*Will Water.*	1
The *C* was of a larger egg	"	121
the red *c* shouting to the light,	*Enid*	1233

cockney.

| (Look at it) pricking a *c* ear. | *Maud*, I. x. | 22 |

coco.

| The slender *c*'s drooping crown | *En. Arden*. | 575 |

cocoon.

	POEM.	LINE.
Spins, toiling out his own *c*.	*Two Voices*	180
rich as moths from dusk *c*'s	*Princess*, ii.	5

code.

| Christless *c*, That must have life, | *Maud*, II. i. | 26 |

Cogoletto.

| stay'd the wheels at *C*, | *The Daisy* | 23 |

coil.

| Hard *c*'s of cordage | *En. Arden*. | 17 |

coiled.

| *c* around the stately stems | *En. Arden*. | 578 |

coin.

| Light *c*, the tinsel clink | *Princess*, ii. | 41 |
| Him that made them current *c*; | *In Mem.* xxxvi. | 4 |

coinage.

| strown With gold and scatter'd *c*, | *Enid* | 875 |
| like proven golden *c* true | *Aylmer's F.* | 182 |

cold.

dew is *c* upon the ground,	*The Owl*, i.	2
Ere the placid lips be *c* ?	*Adeline*	20
Quiet, dispassionate, and *c*,	*A Character*	28
not more *c* to you than I	*L. C. V. de Vere*	24
our household hearths are *c*:	*Lotos-E's.*	117
Night is starry and *c* my friend	*D. of the O. Year*	34
fear My wound hath taken *c*	*M. d' Arthur*	166
in thirsts, fevers and *c*,	*St S. Stylites*	12
Would chatter with the *c*,	"	30
Because my memory is so *c*,	*Two Voices*.	341
Shy she was, and I thought her *c*;	*Ed. Gray*	13
'You might have won,' etc.	"	15
loyal warmth of Florian is not *c*,	*Princess*, ii.	226
motionlessly pale, *C* ev'n to her,	" vi.	86
And call her hard and *c*	" vii.	83
In height and *c*, the splendour	"	179
coarsest clothes against the *c*;	*In Mem.* v.	10
C in that atmosphere of Death	" xx.	14
spectral doubt which makes me *c*,	" xl.	19
How dwarf'd a growth of *c*	" lx.	9
dearest, now thy brows are *c*	" lxxiii.	5
c to all that might have been.	" lxxiv.	16
looks so *c*: she thinks him kind.	" xcvi.	24
And smile as sunny as *c*,	*Maud*, I. vi.	24
kind Only because she was *c*.	" xiv.	27
Full *c* my greeting was and dry;	*The Letters*	13
loved that hall, tho' white and *c*,	*The Daisy*	37
ill and weary, alone and *c*,	"	96
glanced at him, thought him *c*,	*Guinevere*	402
you think I am hard and *c*;	*Grandmother*	17
c Are all thy lights, and *c* my	*Tithonus*	66
all the comets in heaven are *c*,	*The Ringlet*	9
found Her master *c*;	*Lucretius*	2

cold-blooded.

| That dull *c-b* Cæsar. | *D. of F. Wom.* | 139 |

coldness.

| The faithless *c* of the times; | *In Mem.* cv. | 18 |
| By the *c* of her manners, | *Maud*, I. xx. | 13 |

cold-white.

| white against the *c-w* sky | *Dying Swan* | 12 |

colewort.

| from the *c* a green caterpillar | *Guinevere*. | 33 |

collar.

| iron *c* grinds my neck; | *St S. Stylites* | 115 |

Collatine.

| made her blood in sight of *C* | *Lucretius*. | 235 |

college.

knew your gift that way At *c*	*The Epic*	25
remember'd Everard's *c* fame	"	46
at school—a *c* in the South:.	*Walk. to the M.*	75
dragg'd her to the *c* tower	"	81
My *c* friendships glimmer.	*Will Water.*	40
I was there From *c*,	*Princess, Pro.*	7
we, unworthier, told Of *c*:	"	111
Far off from men a *c*	"	135
swore he long'd at *c*, only long'd	"	157

	POEM.	LINE.
talk of *c* and of ladies' rights,	*Princess, Pro.*	226
c lights began to glitter	" i.	204
At break of day the *C* Portress.	" ii.	1
rosy blonde, and in a *c* gown,	"	302
c and her maidens, empty masks,	" iii.	171
camp and *c* turn'd to hollow shows,	" v.	467
their fair *c* turn'd to hospital;	" vii.	2
a garden!" said my *c* friend,	*In Mem.* lxxxvi.	49
heard once more in *c* fanes	*In Mem.* lxxxvi.	5

college-council.

| Should eighty-thousand *c-c's* | *To F. D. Maurice* | 7 |

college-time.

| save for *c-t's* Or Temple-eaten terms | *Aylmer's F.* | 104 |

colony.

near the *c* Camolodune,	*Boädicea*	5
their *c* half-defended! lo their *c*	"	17
Then a phantom *c* smoulder'd	"	28
Lo the *c*, there they rioted	"	60
So the silent *c* hearing	"	78
Fell the *c*, city, and citadel	"	86

colossal.

| Let his great example stand *C* | *Ode on Well.* | 221 |

colour.

sweet is the *c* of cove and cave,	*Sea Fairies*	30
A magic web with *c's* gay.	*L. of Shalott,* ii.	2
I lose my *c*, I lose my breath,	*Eleänore*	137
could bring the *c* to my cheek;	*Gardener's D.*	192
came a *c* and a light,	*Locksley H.*	25
c flies into his cheek	*Day-Dm.*	119
c flu hes Her sweet face	*L. of Burleigh*	61
had touch'd her face With *c*	*Princess, Pro.*	214
April daffodilly Her mother's *c*)	" ii.	304
c's gayer than the morning mist	"	415
shook the woods, And danced the *c*,	" iii.	276
'Sir Ralph has got your *c's*,	" iv.	571
Psyche's *c* round his helmet	" v.	523
such as gather'd *c* day by day	" vii.	103
with the thought her *c* burns;	*In Mem.* vi.	34
be all the *c* f the flower;	" xli.	8
The *c's* of the crescent prime?	" cxv.	4
misento me Saying in odour and *c, Maud,* I xxi.		12
She wore the *c's* I approved.	*The Letters*	16
But distant *c*, happy hamlet,	*The Daisy*	7
my child, how fresh the *c's* look	*Enid*	680
h I I like *c* s of a shell	"	681
And made it of two *c's*;	"	1141
lived some *c* in your cheek	"	1469
In *c* like the satin-shining palm	*Vivien*	73
c's f the heart that are not theirs	"	671
gayer 's, like an opal warm'd	"	792
he heu'd into *c* with the crags;	*Elaine*	45
The l w sun makes th' *c*;	"	135
shape an la of a mind	"	334
let me bring your *c* back;	"	366
Has Lit if In the heart's *c's*	"	833
did not love the *c*;	"	836
I want d warmth and *c*	*Guinevere*	640
rough piece Of early rigid *c*,	*Aylmer's F.*	281
yet her cheek Kept *c*;	"	506
Then the Captain's *c* heightened	*The Captain*	29

colourless.

| face was white And *c,* | *M. d' Arthur* | 213 |

colt.

ran he, gamesome as the *c,*	*Talking O.*	121
she's yet a *c* 'Take, break her;	*Princess,* v.	445
He pointed out a pasturing *c*,	*The Brook*	136
Some had seen the *c* at grass,	"	139
the *c* would fetch its price;	"	140
wild Like *c's* about the waste.	*En. Arden*	304

colt-like.

| *c-l* whinny, and with hoggish whine | *St S. Stylites* | 174 |

Columbus.

| How young *C* seem'd to rave | *The Daisy* | 17 |

column.

Six *c's*, three on either side,	*Arabian N's.*	144
like a shatter'd *c* lay the King;	*M. d'Arthur*	21

	POEM.	LINE.
people hum About the *c's* base,	*St S. Stylites*	38
watcher on the *c* till the end;	"	160
in we stream'd Among the *c's*,	*Princess,* ii.	412
left and right, of those tall *c's*	" vi.	334
the knotted *c* of his throat	*Enid*	74
massive *c's*, like a shorecliff cave,	*Elaine*	405

comb (verb) see *comb of pearl.*

| I would *c* my hair (rep.) | *The Mermaid* | 11 |

combat (s.),

when the tide of *c* stands,	*Sir Galahad*	10
To prick us on to *c*	*Princess,* v.	294
Not dare to watch the *c,*	*Enid*	1003
In *c* with the follower of Limours	"	1350

combat (verb.)

| *c* for my claim till death | *Princess,* v. | 350 |

combed.

as I *c* I would sing and say	*The Mermaid*	12
I curl'd and *c* his comely head	*The Sisters.*	31

combing.

C her hair Under the sea,	*The Mermaid*	4
c out her long black hair	*Princess,* iv.	257

comb of pearl.

With a *c o p.*	*The Mermaid*	7, 11
Made with her right a *c o p.*	*Vivien*	93

come (see *come and go.*)

cats run home and light is *c,*	*The Owl,* i.	1
C not as thou camest of late	*Ode to Mem.*	8
C forth I charge thee,	"	46
C from the woods that belt	"	55
Dark-brow'd sophist, *c* not a near	*Poet's Mind*	8
frozen sneer *C* not here	"	11
O hither, *c* hither, (rep.)	*Sea Fairies*	16
C away: no more of mirth.	*Deserted H.*	13
C away: for Life and Thought	"	17
How could I rise and *c* away,	*Oriana*	57
dare not die and *c* to thee,	*L. of Shalott,* ii.	56
knights *c* riding two and two:	*L. of Shalott,* ii.	25
'The curse is *c* upon me,'	" iii.	44
night *c's* on that knows not morn,	*Mariana in the S.*	94
C's out thy deep ambrosial smile	*Eleänore*	74
Here *c's* to-day, Pallas and Aphrodite,	*Œnone*	83
Should *c* most welcome	"	127
(power of herself Would *c* uncall'd	"	145
c from the inmost hills,	"	245
her child!—a shudder *c's* Across me:	"	249
shrill happy laughter *c* to me	"	254
ere the stars *c* forth Talk	"	258
I made a feast; I bad him *c*;	*The Sisters*	13
There *c's* no murmur of reply	*Pal. of Art*	266
'ill *c* from far away,	*May Queen,* i.	27
till the snowdrops *c* again:	" ii.	14
and the sun *c* out on high:	"	15
the swallow 'ill *c* back again	"	19
When the flowers *c* again, mother,	"	25
you'll *c* sometimes and see me	"	30
If I can I'll *c* again, mother,	"	37
Don't let Effie *c* to see me	"	43
violet, that *c's* beneath the skies	" iii.	5
if it *c's* three times, I thought	"	38
little while till you and Effie *c*—	"	18
c like ghosts to trouble joy	*Lotos-E's.*	55
'*C* here, That I may look on thee.'	*D. of F.Wom.*	123
echoes of laborious day *C* to you,	*Margaret*	30
C down, *c* down, and hear me speak:	"	56
C's up to take his own.	*D. of the O. Year*	36
gently *c's* the world to those	*To J. S.*	3
Nothing *c's* to thee new	"	74
let the change which *c's* be ('*Love thou thy land,' etc.*		45
keep a thing, its use will *c.*	*The Epic*	42
Merlin sware that I should *c* again	*M. d'Arthur*	23
land, where no one *c's*, Or hath *c,*	"	202
'Arthur is *c* again: he cannot die.'	*Ep.*	24
c again, and thrice As fair;	"	29
c With all good things	"	25
c's to it In sound of funeral	*Gardener's D.*	75
Nor heard use, nor from her tendance	"	141
time Is *c* to raise the veil	"	269

	POEM.	LINE.
for this orphan, I am *c* to you	Dora	62
he cried out to *c* to her:	"	135
now I *c* For Dora:	"	139
I *c* to-morrow morn.	Audley Ct.	69
when does this *c* by?	Walk. to the M.	5
here it *c's* With five at top:	"	102
For that the evil ones *c* here,	St S. Stylites	96
here *c* those that worship me?	"	123
not say But that a time may *c*—	"	187
C, blessed brother, *c*.	"	201
down the way you use to *c*	Talking O.	115
in station, but the end had *c*.	Love and Duty	74
c like one that looks content,	"	90
sure *c's* up the golden year.	Golden Year	31
crimson *c's* upon the robin's breast	Locksley H.	17
to such length of years should *c*	"	67
Slowly *c's* a hungry people,	"	135
Knowledge *c's*, but wisdom lingers, (rep.)	"	141
Never *c's* the trader, never floats	"	161
C's a vapour from the margin,	"	191
dragon-fly *C* from the wells	Two Voices	9
Then *c's* the check, the change	"	163
days that never *c* again.	"	324
murmurs from the meadows *c*,	Day-Dm.	26
C, Care and Pleasure, Hope and Pain,	"	75
c's, scarce knowing what he seeks:	"	117
Love may *c*, and love may go,	Ed. Gray	29
Till Ellen Adair *c* back to me.	"	32
c's and dips Her laurel in the wine,	Will Water.	17
C's out, a perfect round,	"	68
all *c's* round so just and fair;	Lady Clare	18
c you drest like a village maid,	"	67–9
When beneath his roof they *c*.	L. of Burleigh	40
Here is custom *c* your way;	Vision of Sin	64
Therefore *c's* it we are wise,	"	100
C not, when I am dead,	'Come not when,' etc.	1
Will never *c* back to me.	'Break, break,' etc.	16
'C out,' he said, 'To the Abbey:	Princess, Pro.	50
we all say whatever *c's*.	"	232
'what, if these weird seizures *c*	" i.	81
ye *c*, The first-fruits of the stranger	" ii.	29
C from the dying moon, and blow	"	461
Father will *c* to thee soon; (rep.).	"	467
c's the feebler heiress of your plan,	" iii.	221
Nor willing men should *c* among us,	"	301
Would rather we had never *c*!	" iv.	224
those to avenge us and they *c*:	"	480
face across his fancy *c's*,	"	556
Had *c* on Psyche weeping:	" v.	48
c's With the air of the trumpet	"	154
did but *c* as goblins in the night,	"	211
c's a pillar of electric cloud	"	513
'C hither, O Psyche,' she cried	" vi.	266
C to the hollow heart they slander	"	270
C down, O maid, from yonder	" vii.	177
c, for Love is of the valley,	"	183
c thou down And find him;	"	184
c; for all the vales Await thee;	"	200
When *c's* another such?	"	229
c's the statelier Eden backs to men:	"	277
trust in all things high *C's* easy	"	311
new day *c's*, the light Dearer	"	325
I love thee: *c*, Yield thyself up:	"	342
whiff! there *c's* a sudden heat,	Con.	58
yet we trust it *c's* from thee,	In Mem., Pro.	23
From out waste places *c's* a cry,	" iii.	7
here to-morrow will he *c*.	" vi.	24
A happy lover who has *c*	" viii.	1
'*C's* he thus, my friend?	" xii.	13
C Time, and teach me, many years	" xiii.	13
C stepping lightly down the plank,	" xiv.	7
c The man half-divine	"	9
C quick, thou bringest all I love.	" xvii.	1
C then, pure hands, and bear the head	" xviii.	9
c, whatever loves to weep,	"	11
The praise that *c's* to constancy	" xxi.	12
hopes and light regrets that *c*	" xxxix.	7
The wonders that have *c* to thee,	" xl.	22
Peace: *c* away: we do him wrong	" lvi.	5
There *c's* a glory on the walls:	" lxvi.	4
likeness, hardly seen before, *C's* out—	" lxxiii.	4

	POEM.	LINE.
cannot *c* a mellower change,	In Mem. lxxx.	3
Ah dear, but *c* thou back to me:	" lxxxix.	21
he, the Spirit himself, may *c*	" xcii.	6
The violet *c's*, but we are gone.	" civ.	8
I *c* once more; the city sleeps;	" cxviii.	3
Behind thee *c's* the greater light:	" cxx.	12
faith that *c's* of self-control,	" cxxx.	9
back we *c* at fall of dew.	Con.	100
sweeter chance ever *c* to me here?	Maud, I. i.	62
why *c* you so cruelly meek,	" iii.	1
C sliding out of her sacred glove,	" vi.	85
let *c* what *c* may	" xi. 5,	12
One is *c* to woo her.	" xii.	28
old man never *c's* to his place:	" xiii.	24
shook my heart to think she *c's*	" xviii.	16
her brother *c's*, like a blight	" xix.	102
then, oh then, *c* out to me	" xx.	44
C out to your own true lover	"	46
C into the garden, Maud,	" xxii. 1,	3
when, the dances are done,	"	54
c to her waking, find her asleep	" II. ii.	81
Get thee hence, nor *c* again.	" iv.	56
The day *c's*, a dull red ball	"	65
Has *c* to pass as foretold;	" v.	44
c's from another stiller world	"	70
c's to the second corpse in the pit?	"	88
kind heart will *c* To bury me	"	102
c to be grateful at last.	" III. vi.	3
'Whence *c* you?' and the brook	The Brook	22
c from haunts of coot and hern,	"	23
Men may *c* and men may go, (rep.)	"	33
loves to talk of, *c* with me.	"	226
you will be welcome—O, *c* in!'	"	226
c's a sound of marriage bells	The Letters	48
To thee the greatest soldier *c's*;	Ode on Well.	88
C, when no graver cares employ,	To F. D. Maurice	1
God-father, and see your boy:	"	2
(Take it and *c*) to the Isle of Wight;	"	12
C, Maurice, *c*: the lawn as yet	"	41
pay but one, but *c* for many,	"	47
c like you to see the hunt,	Enid	179
find, at some place I shall *c* at	"	219
C's flying over many a windy wave	"	337
but a better time has *c*;	"	716
meadow, till she saw them *c*;	"	832
'Look, Here *c's* a laggard	"	909
'yonder *c's* a knight.	"	975
want me, let him *c* to me.	"	1080
c with no attendance, page or maid	"	1171
c with morn, And snatch me	"	1205
C slipping o'er their shadows	"	1320
And now their hour has *c*;	"	1545
I *c* the mouthpiece of our King	"	1644
then will Arthur *c* to you	"	1663
you would *c* To these my lists	"	1687
c To cleanse this common sewer	"	1742
'C from the storm'	Vivien	744
my shield In keeping till I *c*,'	Elaine	382
c to all I am And overcome it;	"	447
who has *c* Despite the wound	"	564
This will he send or *c* for;	"	632
ghostly man had *c* and gone,	"	1095
c to take the King to fairy land?	"	1250
Traitor, *c* out, ye are trapt	Guinevere	105
then she, 'the end is *c*	"	109
if there ever *c* a grief to me	"	198
knowest thou now from whence I *c*	"	430
that I *c* to urge thy crimes,	"	528
did not *c* to curse thee, Guinevere,	"	529
hither shall I never *c* again,	"	573
from this, whatever *c's* to me	En. Arden.	118
that all evil would *c* out of it)	"	162
merry, when I *c* home again.	"	199
to the babes and till I *c* again	"	219
if he *c* again, vext will he be	"	300
if you will, when Enoch *c's* again	"	308
'Come with us Father Philip'	"	365
If Enoch *c's*—but Enoch will not *c*—	"	428
dead man *c* to life beheld	"	759
let them *c*, I am their father;	"	890
but she must not *c*	"	891

	POEM.	LINE.
Cries 'c up hither,'	Aylmer's F.	745
Then c's the close.	Sea Dreams	29
they c too late for use	"	67
then c's what c's Hereafter;	"	173
Jenny, my cousin, had c to the place,	Grandmother	25
Often they c to the door	"	82
They c and sit by my chair,	"	83
Parson a' c's and a' goos,	N. Farmer	25
summun 'ul c ater meä mayhap	"	61
Man c's and tills the field	Tithonus	3
c's A glimpse of that dark world	"	32
doubt will only c for a kiss,	The Ringlet	21
C to us, love us and make us	W. to Alexan.	30
I c to the test, a tiny poem	Hendecasyllabics	3
every height c's out, and jutting peak	Spec. of Iliad	13
dreams that c Just were the waking;	Lucretius	35
there before you are c and gone,	The Window	14
Can't we c together?	"	77
Take my love, for love will c,	"	125
Love will c but once a life.	"	126
Sun c's, moon c's,	"	162
Flash! I am coming, I c,	"	190

come and go.

Thought seems to c a g	Eleänore	96
night-winds c a g, mother,	May Queen, i.	33
The flashes c a g	St Agnes Eve	26
To c a g, and come again,	Will Water.	229
The foolish neighbours c a g	In Mem. lix.	13
With thousand shocks that c a g,	" cxii.	17
she c's a g's at her will,	Grandmother	79

comed.

hallus c to 's choorch	N. Farmer	17
afoor I c to the plaäce.	"	34
sin fust I c to the 'All;	"	55

comeliness.

| a broad-blown c, red and white, | Maud, I. xiii. | 9 |

comely.

'C too by all that's fair'	Princess, ii.	99
say she's c; there's the fairer chance	" v.	450
Yet, since the face is c—	Enid	1400

comest.

Thou c not with shows	Ode to Mem.	48
atween me and the skies,	Oriana	75
Thou c, much wept for;	In Mem. xvii.	1
'Whence c thou, my guest,	Elaine	181

comet.

| all the c's in heaven are cold, | The Ringlet | 9 |

cometh.

At midnight the moon c,	Claribel	13
He c not, she said	Mariana 10 et pass.	
I know He c quickly;	Fatima	23
c, like an honour'd guest,	Ode on Well.	80
there c a victory now.	Boädicea	46

comfort (s.)

The c, I have found in thee;	Miller's D.	234
No c anywhere;	Pal. of Art	268
Comfort thyself: what c is in me?	M. d'Arthur	243
Then follow'd counsel, c,	Love and Duty	67
Where is c f in division of the	Locksley H.	69
C t c scorned of devils!	"	75
what c! none for me!'	Princess, v.	75
Take c: live, dear lady,	"	77
chiefest c is the little c	"	420
Sole c of my dark hour,	" vi.	177
out of words a c win;	In Mem. xx.	10
c clasp'd in truth reveal'd;	" xxxvii.	22
find his c in thy face;	" cviii.	20
take again That c from their converse	Enid	1798
saying in low tones 'I have c,'	Elaine	989
May be some little c;'	En. Arden.	275
Why, that would be her c;'	"	810
voice Of c and an open hand	Aylmer's F.	174
talk'd, Poor children, for their c:	"	427

comfort (verb.)

Effie, you must c her	May Queen, iii.	44
c's me in this one thought to dwell	D. of F. Wom.	233

	POEM.	LINE.
C thyself: what comfort is in me?	M. d'Arthur	243
Reach out dead hands to c me	In Mem. lxxix.	16
C her, c her, all things good,	Maud, II. ii.	75
c her tho' I die.	"	83
love of all Thy people c Thee,	Idylls, Ded.	52
Because I saw you sad, to c you.	Vivien	291
C your sorrows; for they do not	Guinevere	186
give her this, for it may c her.	En. Arden.	900
said the kindly wife to c him,	Sea Dreams	136

comfortable.

| Nor wholly c, | Will Water. | 158 |

comforted.

look up: be c;	Princess, v.	63
'Be c,' Said Cyril, 'you shall have it;	"	102
my girl, cheer up, be c,	En. Arden.	218

comforting.

| An image c the mind, | In Mem. lxxxiv. | 51 |

comic.

| Too c for the solemn things. | Princess, Con. | 67 |

coming (part.) see *coming and going.*

C in the scented breeze,	Eleänore	24
to embrace him c ere he came.	Œnone	62
C thro' Heaven, like a light	"	106
the New-year's c up, mother,	May Queen, ii.	7
some one c thro' the lawn,	D. of F. Wom.	178
Each month, a birth-day c on,	Will Water.	93
like swallows c out of time	Princess, ii.	409
they are c back from abroad;	Maud, I. i.	65
I see my Oread c down,	" xvi.	8
brother is c back to-night	" xix.	1
She is c, my dove, my dear (rep.)	" xxii.	61
If James were c. 'C every day,'	The Brook	106
But c back he learns it	Enid	1347
c up close to her said	"	1518
c up quite close, and in his mood	"	1562
storm was c, but the winds:	Vivien	1
trumpet-blowings in it, c down	"	208
from the outer doors Rang c	Guinevere	411
guard thee in the wild hour c on,	"	443
Philip c somewhat closer spoke.	En. Arden.	395
I mind him c down the street	"	848
his lonely life, his c back,	"	863
Lenlin, c after he was gone,	Aylmer's F.	234
c fitfully Like broken music,	"	476
crippled lad, and c turn'd to fly,	"	519
she to be c and slandering me	Grandmother	27
Flash! I am c, I come,	The Window	190

coming (s.)

Flush'd like the c of the day;	Miller's D.	132
and their c to the court	Enid	144, 846
look'd on ere the c of Geraint	"	614
will abide the c of my lord,	"	980
And she abode his c,	"	968
Would listen for her c	Elaine	82
ere the c of the Queen.'	Guinevere	221
Narrow'd her goings out and c's in;	Aylmer's F.	501

coming and going.

C a g, and he lay as dead	Vivien	62, 494
Wanderers c a g,	1865-1866	7

command (s.)

under whose c Is Earth	In Mem. Con.	130
He, that ever following her c's,	Ode on Well.	211
gave c that all which once was	Enid	646
one c I laid upon you,	"	926
his c of silence given	"	1215-39
the king's c to sally forth	Elaine	559

command ('verb.)

Will he obey when one c's?	Two Voices	244
Man to c and woman to obey;	Princess, v.	440
I cannot all c the strings;	In Mem. lxxxvii.	10

commander.

| Attest their great c's claim | Ode on Well. | 148 |

commeasure.

| C perfect freedom. | Œnone | 164 |

CONCORDANCE TO

	POEM.	LINE.
commenced.		
However then *c* the dawn :	Princess, ii.	122
c A to-and-fro, so pacing	"	282
comment.		
in rubric thus 'For wholesale *c*.'	Princess, iii.	35
heard in thought Their lavish *c*	Vivien	8
crost, and cramm'd With *c*,	"	528
read the *c* but myself	"	532
in the *c* did I find the charm.	"	533
commerce.		
Saw the heavens fill with *c*	Locksley H.	121
two crowned twins, C and conquest,	Princess, v.	411
So hold I *c* with the dead,	In Mem.lxxxiv.93	
No more shall *c* be all in all,	Maud, III. vi.	23
that *c* with the Queen,	Vivien	620
the stinted *c* of those days ;	En. Arden.	818
commercing.		
c with himself, He lost the sense	Walk. to the M.	15
commingled.		
C with the gloom of imminent war,	Idylls, Ded.	12
commission.		
A bought *c*, a waxen face,	Maud, I. x.	30
common (adj.)		
'Loss is *c* to the race'—And *c*	In Mem. vi.	2
That loss is *c* would not make	"	5
first flash in youth, Most *c* :	Elaine	946
fears were *c* to her state,	En. Arden.	517
common (s.)		
crost the *c* into Darnley chase	The Brook.	132
commonplace.		
And barren *c's* break	Will Water.	23
common is the *c* And vacant chaff	In Mem. vi.	3
common-sense.		
Rich in saving *c-s*,	Ode on Well.	32
Commonwealth.		
from it sprang the C, which breaks	Lucretius	238
commune (s.)		
days of happy *c* dead ;	In Mem. cxv.	14
Held *c* with herself,	Enid	1217
commune (verb.)		
To *c* with that barren voice	Two Voices	461
communed.		
c only with the little maid,	Guinevere	148
communicate.		
We two *c* no more.'	In Mem.lxxxiv.	84
communing.		
C with herself : 'All these are mine	Pal. of Art	181
C with his captains of the war.	Princess, i.	66
communion.		
An hour's *c* with the dead.	In Mem. xciii.	4
Como.		
how we came at last To C ;	The Daisy	70
past From C when the light.	"	73
compact (adj.)		
churl, *c* of thankless earth,	Godiva	66
C with lucid marbles,	Princess, ii.	10
compact (s.)		
He said there was a *c* ;	Princess, i.	46
there did a *c* pass	"	122
Our formal *c*, yet, not less	"	163
hope The child of regal *c*.	" iv.	401
'that our *c* be fulfill'd :	" v.	111
she would not keep Her *c*.'	"	314
companion.		
past From all her old *c's*,	Princess, ii.	244
Too harsh to your *c* yestermorn ;	" iii.	183
wine and free *c's* kindled him,	Enid	1142
all the boon *c's* of the Earl,	"	1326
the new *c's* past away	Elaine	398
companionless.		
I, the last, go forth *c*,	M. d'Arthur	236

	POEM.	LINE.
companionship.		
Who broke our fair *c*,	In Mem. xxii.	13
company.		
sat a *c* with heated eyes,	Vision of Sin	7
yes !—but a *c* forges the wine.	Maud, I. i.	36
lingers late With a roystering *c*)	" xiv.	15
twos and threes, or fuller *c's*,	Enid	57
A glorious *c*, the flower of men,	Guinevere	461
little wife would weep for *c*,	En Arden	34
comparison.		
half asleep she made *c*	Enid	651
compass (s.)		
in the *c* of three little words,	Gardener's D.	227
winds from all the *c* shift	Godiva	33
Might lie within their *c*,	Aylmer's F.	485
his *c* is but of a single note,	The Islet	28
compass (verb.)		
c our dear sisters' liberties.'	Princess, iii.	271
c her with sweet observances,	Enid	838
compass'd.		
c by the inviolate sea.'	To the Queen	36
With what dull pain C,	D. of F. Wom.	278
All beauty *c* in a female form,	Princess, ii.	20
Sat *c* with professors :	"	421
c by two armies and the noise,	" v.	335
c by the fires of Hell ;	In Mem. cxxvi.	17
c round with turbulent sound,	Will	7
c her with sweet observances	Enid	48
c round by the blind wall of night	En. Arden.	488
compel.		
I *c* all creatures to my will	Enid 1477,	1521
compell'd.		
such a breeze C thy canvas,	In Mem. xvii.	2
compensated.		
often fineness *c* size :	Princess, ii.	133
compensating.		
nor *c* the want By shrewdness	En. Arden.	249
competence.		
happy years of health and *c*,	En. Arden.	82
complaining.		
broad stream in his banks *c*,	L. of Shalott, iv.	3
C, 'Mother give me grace	Mariana in the S.	29
call'd him by his name, *c* loud,	M. d'Arthur	210
complaint.		
Not whisper, any murmur of *c*	St S. Stylites	22
What end is here to my *c* ?	In Mem. lxxx.	6
completer.		
gipsy bonnet Be the neater and *c* ;	Maud, I. xx.	20
completion.		
awaits C in a painful ' Love thou thy land,' etc.		58
fulfill'd itself Merged in *c* ?	Gardener's D.	234
complexity.		
many-corridor'd *complexities*	Vivien	582
compliment.		
Light coin, the tinsel clink of *c*.	Princess, ii.	41
composed.		
All *c* in a metre of Catullus,	Hendecasyllabics	4
compound.		
'No *c* of this earthly ball	Two Voices	35
comprest.		
rais'd her head with lips *c*,	The Letters	19
comrade.		
C's, leave me here a little,	Locksley H.	1
Hark, my merry *c's* call me	"	145
weep the *c* of my choice,	In Mem. xiii.	9
c of the lesser faith	" cxxvii.	3
then against his brace Of *c's*.	Enid	937
craven pair Of *c's*, making slowlier	"	1016
To laughter and his *c's* to applause	"	1145
Enoch's *c*, careless of himself,	En. Arden.	569
c's having fought their last below,	Aylmer's F.	227
the *c* of his chambers woke	"	583

	POEM.	LINE.
conceal.		
she knows too, And she *c*'s it.'	*Princess*, iii.	44
half *c* the Soul within.	*In Mem.* v.	4
conceal'd.		
Better to leave Excalibur *c*	*M. d'Arthur*	62
concealment.		
maiden-meek I pray'd *C*	*Princess*, iii.	119
conceit.		
clouded with his own *c*,	*M. d'Arthur*	110
conceived.		
sinful man, *c* and born in sin:	*St. S. Stylites*	120
concluded.		
At last a solemn grace *C*,	*Princess*, ii.	429
some vast charm *c* in that star	*Vivien*	362
conclusion.		
To those *c*'s when we saw	*In Mem.* lxxxvi.	35
concourse.		
banquet, and *c* of knights and kings.	*Elaine*	561
concubine.		
Sent like the twelve-divided *c*	*Aylmer's F.*	759
condemned.		
prisoner at the bar, ever *c*:	*Sea Dreams*	172
condensation.		
cramm'd With comment, densest *c*,	*Vivien*	528
condition.		
with sound of trumpet, all The hard *c*;	*Godiva*	37
yet—Hear my *c*'s:	*Princess*, ii.	275
conditioning.		
ebb and flow *c* their march,	*Golden Year*	30
conduct (verb.)		
C by paths of growing powers,	*In Mem.* lxxxiii.	31
conduit.		
Where the bloody *c* runs:	*Vision of Sin*	144
cone.		
masses thick with milky *c*'s.	*Miller's D.*	56
confederacy.		
between her daughters, o'er a wild *c*.	*Boädicea*	6
conference.		
And thus our *c* closed.	*Princess*, ii.	346
confess.		
I *c* with right) you think me	*Princess*, i.	157
As I *c* it needs must be;	*In Mem.* lviii.	4
conflict.		
c with the clash of shivering points,	*Princess*, v.	480
confluence.		
A riotous *c* of watercourses	*Lucretius*	30
confound.		
did all *c* Her sense:	*Mariana*	76
all Calamity's hugest waves *c*	*Will*	5
the victor, to *c* them more,	*Enid*	1018
confounded.		
Shame and wrath his heart *c*,	*The Captain*	61
confuse.		
with shadow'd hint *c* A life	*In Mem.* xxxiii.	7
confused.		
Makes thy memory *c*:	*A Dirge*	45
Remaining utterly *c* with fears,	*Pal. of Art*	269
Arriving all *c* among the rest	*Princess*, v.	205
C me like the unhappy bark	*In Mem.* xvi.	12
all that crowd *c* and loud,	*Maud*, II. iv.	71
C by brainless mobs	*Ode on Well.*	153
Enid look'd, but all *c* at first,	*Enid*	685
Sweet moons *c* his fatherhood.'	*Vivien*	562
C the chemic labour of the blood,	*Lucretius*	20
confusion.		
The airy hand *c* wrought,	*Pal. of Art*	226
Is there *c* in the little isle?	*Lotos-E's*	124
There is *c* worse than death,	"	128
Unsubject to *c*,	*Will Water.*	86

	POEM.	LINE.
woman to obey; All else *c*	*Princess*, v.	441
At first with all *c*:	" vii.	3
C's of a wasted youth;..	*In Mem. Pro.*	42
make *C* worse than death,	" lxxxix.	12
for wrong-done you by *c*,	*Vivien*	156
wrought *c* in the Table Round	*Guinevere*	218
conjecture (s.)		
make *C* of the plumage	*Enid*	333
conjecture verb.'		
C's of the features of her child	*Œnone*	248
if I *C* of a stiller guest	*In Mem. Con.*	86
conjecturing.		
C when and where:	*Elaine*	21
conquer.		
From barren deeps to *c* all	*Princess*, vii.	147
rack'd with pangs that *c* trust	*In Mem.* xlix.	6
your great name, This *c*'s:	*Elaine*	151
conquer'd.		
A cry above the *c* years	*In Mem.* cxxx.	7
let herself be *c* by him	*Vivien*	749
his great name *C*:	*Elaine*	579
conquest.		
two crowned twins, Commerce and *c*,	*Princess*, v.	411
conscience.		
A little grain of *c* made him sour,	*Vision of Sin*	218
My *c* will not count me fleckless	*Princess*, ii.	274
To whom a *c* never wakes;	*In Mem.* xxvii.	8
Without a *c* or an aim.	" xxxiv.	8
The *c* as a sea at rest	" xciii.	12
reverenced his *c* as his king;	*Idylls, Ded.*	7
Their *c*, and their *c* as their King,	*Guinevere*	465
wast, as is the *c* of a saint	"	632
all his *c* and one eye askew	*Sea Dreams*	176-80
conscious.		
c of ourselves, Perused the matting;	*Princess*, ii.	53
partly *c* of my own deserts,	" iv.	286
c of what temper you are built,	"	381
nor *c* of a bar Between them,	*Aylmer's F.*	134
Slowly and *c* of the rageful eye	"	336
consecrate.		
I dedicate, I *c* with tears	*Idylls, Ded.*	4
consent.		
To yield *c* to my desire:	*Miller's D.*	138
Her slow *c*, and marriage,	*En. Arden.*	709
consequence.		
wisdom in the scorn of *c*.	*Œnone*	748
duty duty, clear of *c*'s.	*Princess*, iii.	126
war be a cause or a *c*?	*Maud*, i. x.	45
consider.		
C, William: take a month	*Dora*	27
'*C* well,' the voice replied,	*Two Voices*	241
considering.		
c everywhere Her secret meaning	*In Mem.* liv.	9
consistent.		
liberal-minded, great, *C*;	*In Mem. Con.*	37
consolable.		
A long, long weeping, not *c*.	*Vivien*	705
consolidate.		
became *C* in mind and frame—	*Two Voices*	366
consort.		
And a gentle *c* made he,	*L. of Burleigh*	73
constancy.		
The praise that comes to *c*.'	*In Mem.* xxi.	12
constellation.		
Larger *c*'s burning,	*Locksley H.*	159
With *c* and with continent,	*Princess*, i.	221
constrained.		
cruel need *C* us,	*Enid*	617
consume.		
cruel immortality *C*'s	*Tithonus*	6

consumed.
	POEM.	LINE.
utterly *c* with sharp distress,	*Lotos-E's.*	58

contemplate.
when I *c* all alone,	*In Mem.* lxxxiii.	1
C all this work of Time,	" cxvii.	1

contemplating.
no form of creed But *c* all.'	*Pal. of Art*	211
C her own unworthiness ;	*Enid*	533

contemplation.
And luxury of *c* :	*Eleänore*	107

contempt.
touch'd on Mahomet With much *c*	*Princess,* ii.	119

contend.
C for loving masterdom.	*In Mem.* ci.	8

content (adj.)
I had been *c* to perish,	*Locksley H.*	103
well *c* that all was well	*Enid*	1800
Nor rested thus *c*, but day by day	*Elaine*	13
Queen, she would not be *c*	"	1304
c' he answer'd 'to be loved	*En. Arden.*	425

content (s.)
meditative grunts of much *c,*	*Walk. to the M.*	79
come like one that looks *c,*	*Love and Duty*	90
The low beginnings of *c*	*In Mem.*lxxxiii.	48
more *c,* He told me, lives	" xcvii.	25
sun of sweet *c* Re-risen	*The Brook.*	168
had power to rob it of *c.*	*Coquette,* ii.	8

contented.
into my arms, C there to die l	*D. of F. Wom.*	152

continent.
With constellation and with *c,*	*Princess,* i.	221
The dust of *c's* to be ;	*In Mem.*xxxv.	12

contradiction.
to live A *c* on the tongue,	*In Mem.*cxxiv.	4

contract.
Cleave to your *c :*	*Princess,* iv.	390

contracting.
Philip's rosy face *c* grew	*En. Arden.*	483

contrivance.
With great *c's* of Power.	*'Love thou thy land,' etc.*	64

contrived.
two *c* their daughter's good,	*Aylmer's F.*	848

contriving.
c their dear daughter's good—	*Aylmer's F.*	781

control (s.)
O friendship, equal-poised *c,*	*In Mem.*lxxxiv.	33
ours, O God, from brute *c*	*Ode on Well.*	159

control.
changes should *c* Our	*'Love thou thy land,' etc.*	41

controll'd.
they *c* me when a boy ;	*In Mem.*xxviii.	18

controlleth.
C all the soul and sense	*Eleänore.*	115

convent.
while I lived In the white *c.*	*St S. Stylites*	61

convention.
but *c* beats them down :	*Princess,Pro.*	128
Dwell with these, and lose C,	" ii.	72
We hold a great *c :*	" iv.	490

convent-roof.
Deep on the *c-r* the snows	*St Agnes' Eve*	1

convent-tower.
The shadows of the *c-t's*	*St Agnes' Eve*	5

converse (s.)
hold *c* with all forms	*Ode to Mem.*	115
open *c* is there none,	*In Mem.* xx.	17
Thy *c* drew us with delight	" cix.	1
suspends his *c* with a friend,	*Enid*	340
told her all their *c* in the hall	"	520
whom he held In *c* for a little,	"	1730
comfort from their *c* which he took	"	1798

converse (verb.)
	POEM.	LINE.
Hears him lovingly *c,*	*L. of Burleigh*	26

convolution.
saturate, out and out, Thro' every *c.*	*Will Water.*	88

convolvulus.
The lustre of the long *c'es*	*En. Arden.*	577

cony.
Or *conies* from the down,	*En. Arden.*	337

cool'd.
c his spleen, Communing with his	*Princess,* i.	65
Are but dainties *c* again :	*The Window*	131

cool (adj.)
as we enter'd in the *c.*	*Gardener'sD.*	113
she wept, and I strove to be *c,*	*Maud,* II. i.	15

cool (verb.)
Drink to lofty hopes that *c*—	*Vision of Sin,*	147
and grieved—to slacken and to *c ;*	*Princess,* iv.	280

cool'd.
c within the glooming wave ;	*In Mem.* lxxxviii.	45
upon the sick man's brow C it,	*Aylmer's F.*	701

cooling.
C her false cheek with a featherfan,	*Aylmer's F.*	289

coolness.
paced for *c* in the chapel-yard ;	*Vivien*	607

cooper.
C he was and carpenter,	*En. Arden.*	815

coöperant.
Is toil *c* to an end.	*In Mem.* cxxvii.	24

coot.
come from haunts of *c* and hern,	*The Brook.*	23

cope.
c Of the half-attain'd futurity,	*Ode to Mem.*	32
dense cloud from base to *c.*	*Two Voices.*	186

Cophetua.
Before the king C.	*Beggar Maid*	4
C swore a royal oath :	"	15

coppice.
suddenly Breaks from a *c*	*Enid.*	339
scour'd into the *c's* and was lost,	"	1383

coppice-feather'd.
every *c-f* chasm and cleft,	*Princess,* iv.	5

copse.
may-pole and in the hazel *c,*	*May Queen,* ii.	11
shadowy pine above the woven *c..*	*Lotos-E's.*	18
did we hear the *c's* ring.	*Locksley H.*	35
Came little *c's* climbing.	*Amphion.*	32
move the trees, the *c's* nod,	*Sir Galahad*	77
in *c* And linden alley :	*Princess,* i.	206
wound About the cliffs, the *c's,*	" iii.	342
In *c* and fern Twinkled	*The Brook.*	133

coquette.
the slight *c,* she cannot love,	*Coquette,* ii.	12

coquette-like.
or half *c-l* Maiden,	*Hendecasyllabics*	20

coquetting.
C with young beeches ;	*Amphion.*	28

cord.
wounding *c's* that bind '*Clear-headed friend,' etc.*	4
softly with a threefold *c* of love	*D. of F. Wom.*	211

cordage.
coils of *c,* swarthy fishing-nets,	*En Arden.*	17

cordon.
draw The *c* close and closer	*Aylmer's F.*	500

core.
Else earth is darkness at the *c,*	*In Mem.* xxxiv.	3
make a solid *c* of heat ;	" cvi.	18

Corinna's.
wrought With fair C's triumph ;	*Princess,* iii.	331

	POEM.	LINE.
Coritanian.		
hear C, Trinobant! (rep.)	*Boädicea*	10
corkscrew.		
up the *c* stair With hand and rope	*Walk. to the M.*	82
corn.		
champaign cloth'd with *c*,	*Œnone*	112
when a field of *c* Bows all its ears.	*Princess,* i.	233
all night long breast-deep in *c*,	" ii.	365
sweating underneath a sack of *c*,	*Enid*	263
Take him to stall, and give him *c*,	"	371
flaws in Summer laying lusty *c*:	"	764
land of hops and poppy-mingled *c*,	*Aylmer's F.*	31
Ruth among the fields of *c*,	"	680
corn-bin.		
horse That hears the *c-b* open,	*The Epic*	45
Cornelia.		
Clelia, C, with the Palmyrene	*Princess,* ii.	69
corner.		
some odd *c* of the brain.	*Miller's D.*	68
in dark *c's* of her palace stood	*Pal. of Art*	237
Sometimes a little *c* shines,	*Two Voices*	187
tread The *c's* of thine eyes:	*Will Water.*	236
Ralph Who shines so in the *c*;	*Princess, Pro.*	145
my own sad name in *c's* cried,	*Maud,* I. vi.	72
Found Enid with the *c* of his eye	*Enid*	1130
damsel drooping in a *c* of it.	"	1459
Or whisper'd in the *c*?	*Vivien*	622
Full lowly by the *c's* of his bed,	*Elaine*	822
shelf and *c* for the goods	*En. Arden.*	171
From distant *c's* of the street	"	346
cornice.		
watching high on mountain *c*,	*The Daisy*	19
Cornish.		
dark Dundagil by the C sea;	*Guinevere*	292
corn-laws.		
struck upon the *c-l*	*Audley Ct.*	34
coronach.		
Prevailing in weakness, the *c* stole	*Dying Swan*	26
coronet.		
Kind hearts are more than *c's*	*L.C.V. de Vere*	55
corpse.		
On *c's* three-months-old	*Pal. of Art*	243
('s across the threshold:	*D. of F. Wom.*	25
Step from the *c*, and let him in	*D. of the O. Year*	49
to the second *c* in the pit?	*Maud,* II. v.	83
correspond.		
for three years to *c* with home;	*Princess,* ii.	56
corridor.		
Full of long-sounding *c's*	*Pal. of Art*	53
corrupt.		
Plenty *c's* the melody	*The Blackbird*	15
good custom should *c* the world.	*M. d'Arthur*	242
C's the strength of heaven-descended Will	"	11
corselet.		
thro' the bulky bandit's *c* home,	*Enid*	1008
Cossack.		
C and Russian Reel'd	*Lt. Brigade*	34
cost (s.)		
care not for the *c*; the *c* is mine.	*Enid*	1137
cost (verb.)		
c me many a tear.	*Grandmother*	22
c me a world of woe,	"	23
cost (ast.)		
But a *c* cop, thot a did,	*N. Farmer.*	14
costliest.		
Black velvet of the *c*—	*Aylmer's F.*	804
costly.		
work To both appear'd so *c*,	*Enid*	638
'Let her tomb Be *c*,	*Elaine*	1330
costly-broider'd.		
Laid from her limbs the *c-b* gift,	*Enid*	769

	POEM.	LINE.
costly-made.		
half-cut-down, a pasty *c-m*,	*Audley Ct.*	22
costrel.		
youth, that following with a *c*	*Enid*	386
cot.		
and kiss'd him in his *c*	*En. Arden.*	233
coterie.		
Came yews, a dismal *c*;	*Amphion*	42
cottage.		
even a lowly *c* whence we see	*Ode to Mem.*	100
'Make me a *c* in the vale,'	*Pal. of Art*	291
Love will make our *c* pleasant,	*L. of Burleigh*	15
gaze On that *c* growing nearer,	"	35
Fair is her *c* in its place,	*Requiescat*	1
cottager.		
She was the daughter of a *c*,	*Walk. to the M.*	51
cottage-walls.		
robed your *c-w* with flowers.	*Aylmer's F.*	698
cotton.		
ear is cramm'd with his *c*	*Maud,* I. x.	42
cottonspinning.		
Go' (shrill'd the *c* chorus)	*Ed. Morris*	122
couch.		
Kings have no such *c* as thine,	*A Dirge*	40
She lying on her *c* alone,	*Day-Dm.*	78
light of healing, glanced about the *c*	*Princess,* vii.	44
Enid woke and sat beside the *c*,	*Enid*	73
which she laid Flat on the *c*,	"	679
left her maiden *c*, and robed herself,	"	737
wearied out made for the *c*,	*Vivien*	586
Down on the great King's *c*	*Elaine*	607
Low on the border of her *c* they sat	*Guinevere*	100
flung her down upon a *c* of fire,	*Aylmer's F.*	574
Rolling on their purple *c'es*	*Boädicea*	62
couchant.		
c with his eyes upon the throne,	*Guinevere*	12
couch'd.		
leopards *c* beside her throne,	*Princess,* ii.	19
c behind a Judith,	" iv.	207
wine-flask lying *c* in moss,	*In Mem.* lxxxviii.	44
c at ease, The white kine	" xciv.	14, 50
c their spears and prick'd their steeds	*Elaine*	478
passing by Spied where he *c*,	*Guinevere*	32
cough.		
c's, aches, stitches, ulcerous throes	*St S. Stylites*	13
council.		
statesmen at her *c* met	*To the Queen*	29
manners, climates, *c's*, governments,	*Ulysses*	14
In iron gauntlets: break the *c* up.'	*Princess,* i.	68
when the *c* broke, I rose	"	89
call'd mine host To *c*,	"	172
'everywhere Two heads in *c*,	"	156
Great in *c* and great in war,	*Ode on Well.*	30
c's thinn'd And armies wan'd	*Vivien*	422
council-hall.		
voice is silent in your *c-h*	*Ode on Well.*	174
The basest, far into that *c-h*	*Lucretius*	171
counsel advice.		
silver flow Of subtle-paced *c*	*Isabel*	21
Then follow'd *c*, comfort,	*Love and Duty*	67
prized my *c*, liv'd upon my lips:	*Princess,* iv.	274
ill *c* had misled the girl	" vii.	226
take my *c*: let me know it	*Vivien*	503
turn'd Her *c* up and down	*Elaine*	368
Her art, her hand, her *c*	*Aylmer's F.*	151
dealing good *c* from a height	"	172
counsel (counsellor.)		
Like sleepy *c* pleading:	*Amphion*	74
man is likewise *c* for himself.	*Sea Dreams*	178
counsellor.		
He play'd at *c's* and kings,	*In Mem.* lxiii.	23
count title.		
c's and kings Who laid about them	*Princess, Pro.*	30
C, baron—whom he smote, he	*Elaine*	464

count (reckoning.)

	POEM.	LINE.
'Heaven heads the *c* of crimes	*D. of F. Wom.*	201

count (verb.)

	POEM.	LINE.
can but *c* thee perfect gain,	*Pal. of Art*	198
neither *c* on praise: '*Love thou thy laud,*' etc.		26
but *c* not me the herd!	*Golden Year*	13
c the gray barbarian lower	*Locksley II.*	174
conscience will not *c* me fleckless	*Princess*, ii.	274
what every woman *c*'s her due,	" iii.	228
what may *c* itself as blest,	*In Mem.* xxvii.	9
c new things as dear as old:	" xxxix.	28
c it crime To mourn for any	" lxxxiv.	61
c their memories half divine;	" lxxxix.	12
Thy likeness, I might *c* it vain	" xci.	2
To-day they *c* as kindred souls;	" xcviii.	19
Nor *c* me all to blame if I	" Con.	85
c it of small use To charge you)	*Enid*	1265
be he dead, I *c* you for a fool;	"	1397
c it of no more avail, Dame,	"	1563
C the more base idolater	*Aylmer's F.*	670
O Ringlet, I *c* you much to blame,	*The Ringlet*	46
Deep as Hell I *c* his error.	*The Captain*	3
C's nothing that she meets with base,	*On a Mourner*	4

counted.

died Earl Doorm by him he *c* dead.	*Enid*	1578
only Queens are to be *c* so,	*Elaine*	238

countenance.

With a glassy *c*	*L. of Shalott,* iv.	13
If I make dark my *c*,	*Two Voices*	53
her *c* all over Pale again	*L. of Burleigh*	65
She sets her forward *c*	*In Mem.* cxiii.	6
o'er his *c* No shadow past,	*En. Arden*	710
Else I withdraw favour and *c*	*Aylmer's F.*	307

counter.

rogue would leap from his *c*.	*Maud,* I. i.	51

counterchange

Witch-elms that *c* the floor	*In Mem.* lxxxviii.	1

counter-changed.

c The level lake	*Arabian N's.*	84
half-disfame, And *c* with darkness?	*Vivien*	316

countercharm

c of space and hollow sky,	*Maud,* I. xviii.	43

countercheck.

With motions, checks, and *c*'s.	*Two Voices*	300

counter-gale.

to and thro' the *c-g*?	*The Voyage*	88

countermarch

would fight and march and *c*,	*Audley Ct.*	39

counter-scoff.

fiery-short was Cyril's *c-s*,	*Princess,* v.	297

countest.

See thou, that *c* reason ripe	*In Mem.* xxxiii.	13

counting.

C the dewy pebbles,	*M. d'Arthur*	84

country.

His *c*'s war-song thrill his ears:	*Two Voices*	153
O Prince, I have no *c*;	*Princess,* ii.	200
If love of *c* move thee there	*Ode on Well.*	140
neither court nor *c*, tho' they sought	*Enid*	729

country dance.

men and maids Arrang'd a *c d*,	*Princess,* Pro.	84

countryman.

behold the Prince Your *c*,	*Princess,* ii.	197

country-side.

tree by tree, The *c-s* descended;	*Amphion*	52

countrywoman.

countrywomen! she did not envy	*Princess,* iii.	25
the manners of your countrywomen?	" iv.	133
A foreigner, and I your *c*,	"	298

county.

Not a lord in all the *c*	*L. of Burleigh*	59
None of these Came from his *c*,	*En. Arden*	654
that almighty man, The *c* God—	*Aylmer's F.*	14

County Member.

	POEM.	LINE.
not the C M's with the vane:	*Walk. to the M.*	8

county town.

Last week came one to the *c t*	*Maud,* I. x.	37

couple.

a *c*, fair As ever painter painted,	*Aylmer's F.*	105

courage.

A *c* to endure and to obey;	*Isabel*	25
'*C!*' he said, and pointed toward the	*Lotos E's.*	1
C, St Simeon! This dull chrysalis	*St S. Stylites*	153
Till thy drooping *c* rise,	*Vision of Sin*	152
C, poor heart of stone.	*Maud,* II. iii.	1, 5

courier.

Which every hour his *c*'s bring.	*In Mem.* cxxv.	4
By *c*'s gone before	*Guinevere*	393

course.

held your *c* without remorse,	*L. C. V. de Vere*	45
Their *c*, till thou wert also man:	*Two Voices*	327
baser *c*'s, children of despair.'	*Princess,* iii.	197
outran The hearer in its fiery *c*;	*In Mem.* cviii.	8
roll it in another *c*,	" cxii.	16
all the *c*'s of the suns	" cxvi.	12
move his *c*, and show That life	" cxvii.	19
sees the *c* of human things	" cxxvii.	4
all the genial *c*'s of his blood	*Enid*	1775
c of life that seem'd so flowery	*Vivien*	729
baffling, a long *c* of them;	*En. Arden*	542
Like the Good Fortune, from her destin'd *c*,	"	630

coursed.

c about The subject most at heart,	*Gardener's D.*	217
C one another more on open ground	*Enid*	522

court.

Her *c* was pure;	*To the Queen*	25
Four *c*'s I made, East, West	*Pal. of Art*	21
round the cool green *c*'s there ran	"	25
seek my father's *c* with me,	*Day-Dm.*	191
old-world trains, upheld at *c*	"	277
Till in a *c* he saw	*Will Water.*	130
Thro' the *c*'s, the camps, the schools,	*Vision of Sin*	104
have a sister at the foreign *c*,	*Princess,* i.	74
I stole from *c* With Cyril	"	101
masque or pageant at my father's *c*.	"	195
a *c* Compact with lucid marbles,	" ii.	10
'We of the *c*,' said Cyril. 'From the *c*'	"	34
crost the *c* To Lady Psyche's:	"	85
thro' the *c* A long melodious thunder	"	451
c's that lay three parts In shadow,	" iii.	4
So saying from the *c* we paced,	"	101
there rose A hubbub in the *c*	" iv.	455
down the steps, and thro' the *c*,	"	533
Deepening the *c*'s of twilight	" Con.	113
pleased him, fresh from brawling *c*'s	*In Mem.* lxxxviii.	11
keep Within his *c* on earth,	" cxxv.	7
after her own self, in all the *c*.	*Enid*	18
and their coming to the *c*,	"	144, 846
Held *c* at old Caerleon	"	146
with the morning all the *c* were gone.	"	156
rode Geraint into the castle *c*	"	312
good knight's horse stands in the *c*;	"	370
ride with him this morning to the *c*,	"	606
bright and dreadful thing, a *c*	"	616
her own faded self, And the gay *c*,	"	653
lords and ladies of the high *c* went	"	662
like a madman brought her to the *c*,	"	725
neither *c* nor country, tho' they sought	"	729
I can scarcely ride with you to *c*.	"	749
a sense might make her long for *c*	"	803
poor gown I rode with him to *c*	"	1548
but to rest awhile within her *c*;	"	1703
thing was blazed about the *c*,	*Vivien*	593
the *c*, the king, dark in your light,	"	724
his *c* Hard on the river	*Elaine*	75
to meet him in the castle *c*;	"	175
great knight, the darling of the *c*,	"	261
heard Sir Lancelot cry in the *c*,	"	343
graces of the *c*, and songs,	"	645
we two May meet at *c* hereafter:	"	695
Thence to the *c* he past;	"	702

	POEM.	LINE.
all the gentle *c* will welcome me,	Elaine	1054
go in state to *c*, to meet the Queen,	"	1118
Queen Guinevere had fled the *c*,	Guinevere	1
one morn when all the *c*, Green-suited,	"	22
lissome Vivien, of her *c* The wiliest	"	29
the crimes and frailties of the *c*,	"	135
silent *c* of justice in his breast,	Sea Dreams	170
often, in that silent *c* of yours—	"	179
in earth forget these empty *c's*	Tithonus	75

courted.
| a well-worn pathway *c* as | Gardener's D. | 108 |

courteous.
Sir, I was *c*, 'every phrase well-oil'd,	Princess, iii.	117
Gawain, surnamed The C,	Elaine	554
Too *c* truly! you shall go no more	"	712
mighty *c* in the main—	Aylmer's F.	121

courtesy.
To greet the sheriff, needless *c*!	Ed. Morris	133
With garrulous ease and oily *courtesies*	Princess, i.	162
amends For a *c* not return'd.	Maud, I. vi.	14
Geraint, from utter *c* forbore.	Enid	381
II st and Earl, I pray your *c*;	"	403
of your *c*, He being as he is,	"	1489
I see you scorn my *courtesies*	"	1519
such a grace Of tenderest *c*,	"	1709
wonted *c*, C with a touch of traitor	Elaine	635
learn the *courtesies* of the court	"	696
Deeming our *c* is the truest law,	"	708
Obedience is the *c* due to kings.'	"	714
Shun to break those bounds of *c*	"	1214
loved thy *courtesies* and thee	"	1354
trustful *courtesies* of household life,	Guinevere	86
of the two first-famed for *c*—	"	321
Had yet that grace of *c* in him	"	433
Then broke all bonds of *c*	Aylmer's F.	323

court-favour.
| willing she should keep C.f: | Princess, vii. | 43 |

court-Galen.
| *c*-G poised his gilt-head cane, | Princess, i. | 19 |

court-lady.
| should some great *c*-*l* say | Enid | 723 |

courtliness.
| moving up with pliant *c* | Enid | 1127 |
| thought, and amiable words, And *c*, | Guinevere | 478 |

courtly.
| her, who is neither *c* nor kind, | Maud, I. v. | 27 |
| looking at her, Full *c*, yet not falsely, | Elaine | 236 |

courtsey.
| made me a mocking *c* and went | Grandmother | 46 |

courtship.
| Discussing how their *c* grew, | In Mem. Con. | 97 |

cousin.
a silent *c* stole Upon us	Ed. Morris	115
tru't me, *c*, all the current	Locksley H.	24
Saying 'Dost thou love me, *c*?'	"	30
O my *c*, shallow-hearted!	"	39
To give his *c*, Lady Clare.	Lady Clare	4
'It was my *c*,' said Lady Clare,	"	15
had a *c* tumbled on the plain,	Princess, vi.	299
her far-off *c* and betroth'd,	The Brook	75
c, slay not him who gave you life.'	Enid	1631
Fair and dear *c*, you that had most	"	1622
poor *c*, with your meek blue eyes,	"	1689
My lady's *c*. Half-sickening.	Aylmer's F.	460
Jenny, my *c*, had come to the place,	Grandmother	25

cove.
dimple in the dark of rushy *c's*,	Ode to Mem.	60
swept the *c* hour of *c* and cave	Sea Fairies	30
shadow does on a sunny shore,	Eleänore	18
waves that up a quiet *c* Rolling	"	108
curl'd Thro' all his eddying *c's*;	In Mem. lxxviii.	10
sailing in on in creek and *c*;	"	c. 16
steering, now, from a purple *c*,	The Daisy	20
Sat by the river in a *c*, and watch'd	Elaine	1380

	POEM.	LINE.
covenant.		
Breathed, like the *c* of a God,	Gardener's D.	204
Coventry.		
I waited for the train at C;	Godiva	1
grim Earl, who ruled In C:	"	13
cover (s.)		
I slide by hazel *c's*;	The Brook	171
cover (verb.)		
mercy, mercy; *c* all my sin.	St S. Stylites	83
coverlet.		
Across the purpled *c*,	Day-Dm.	79
moving, cast the *c* aside,	Enid	73
coverlid.		
The silk star-broidered *c*	Day-Dm.	85
all the *c* was cloth of gold	Elaine	1151
covert.		
Rode thro' the *c's* of the deer,	Sir L.and Q.G.	21
often they break *c* at our feet.'	Enid	183
coverture.		
In closest *c* upsprung	Arabian N's.	68
cow.		
his ploughs, his *c's*, his hogs,	'. The Brook	125
theer warn't not feäd for a *c*:	N. Farmer	37
Wi 'auf the *c's* to cauve	"	52
coward.		
The fear of men, a *c* still.	Two Voices	108
Where idle boys are *c's*	Princess, v.	299
doubts that drive the *c* back.	In Mem. xciv.	30
were he not crown'd king, *c*, and fool.	Vivien	638
cowardice.		
full of *c* and guilty shame,	Princess, iv.	329
thro' his *c* allow'd Her station	Guinevere	512
cover'd.		
A dwarf-like Cato *c*.	Princess, vii.	111
cowl.		
And turn'd the *c's* adrift	Talking O.	48
cowl'd.		
Some *c*, and some bare-headed,	Princess, vi.	61
cowslip.		
Letters *c's* on the hill?	Adeline	62
c and the crowfoot are over all	May Queen, i.	38
As *c* unto oxlip is,	Talking O.	107
little dells of *c*, fairy palms,	Aylmer's F.	91
crab.		
like a butt, and harsh as *c's*	Walk. to the M.	41
crack (s.)		
deafen'd with the stammering *c's*	Vivien	791
crack (verb.)		
chrysalis C's into shining wings,	St S. Stylites	153
splinter'd spear-shafts *c* and fly	Sir Galahad	7
hearts that *c* within the fire	Princess, v.	369
breaks, and *c's*, and splits,	"	516
whelp to *c*; C them now for yourself	Maud, II. v.	55
in one day C's all to pieces	Lucretius	248
cracked.		
mirror *c* from side to side;	L. of Shalott, iii.	43
The forest *c*, the waters curl'd,	In Mem. xv.	5
And *c* the helmet thro',	Enid	573
all her bonds C;	Lucretius	38
crackle.		
tempest *c's* on the leads,	Sir Galahad	53
crackling.		
hair as it were *c* into flames,	Aylmer's F.	585
cradle.		
To deck thy *c*, Eleänore	Eleänore	21
on my *c* shone the Northern star.	Princess, i.	4
rock the snowy *c* till I died.	" iv.	86
Then lightly rocking baby's *c*	En. Arden	194
sway'd The *c*, while she sang	Sea Dreams	280
cradled.		
Their Margaret *c* near them,	Sea Dreams	57

F

82   CONCORDANCE TO

	POEM.	LINE.
cradle-head.		
half embraced the basket c-h	Sea Dreams	277
craft (art, etc.)		
before we came, This c of healing.	Princess, iii.	303
less from Indian c Than beelike	" iv.	180
with such c as women use,	Enid	1201
untold the c herself had used ;	"	1242
moral child without the c to rule,	Elaine	146
c of kindred and the Godless hosts	Guinevere	424
craft (vessel.)		
boated over, ran My c aground,	Ed. Morris	109
pushing his black c among them	Vivien	413
Become the master of a larger c,	En. Arden	144
At times a carven c would shoot	The Voyage	53
crag.		
the c that fronts the Even,	Eleänore	40
long white cloud the scornful c's,	Pal. of Art	83
splinter'd c's that wall the dell	D. of F. Wom.	187
water lapping on the c.'	M. d' Arthur 71,	116
His feet on juts of slippery c	"	189
when the bracken rusted on their c's,	Ed. Morris	100
cloud smoulders on the summer c.	"	147
right leg chain'd into the c,	St S. Stylites	72
still hearth, among these barren c's,	Ulysses	2
swings the trailer from the c ;	Locksley H.	162
gleaming c with belts of pines,	Two Voices	189
clasps the c with hooked hands ;	The Eagle	1
At the foot of thy c's, O Sea!	'Break, break,' etc.	14
flowery levels underneath the c,	Princess, iii.	318
like a jewel set In the dark c :	"	341
They tremble, the' sustaining c's ;	In Mem. cxxvi.	11
the toppling c's of Duty scaled	Ode on Well.	215
like a c that tumbles from the cliff,	Enid	318
like a c was gay with wilding flowers;	"	319
lichen'd into colour with the c's :	Elaine	45
beetling c to which he clung	Aylmer's F.	229
crag-platform.		
huge c-p, smooth as burnish'd brass	Pal. of Art	5
crake.		
flood the haunts of hern and c ;	In Mem. c.	14
cram.		
'Give, C us with all,'	Golden Year	13
c him with the fragments of the grave	Princess, iii.	294
should c our ears with wool	" iv.	47
green Christmas c's with weary bones.	Coquette, iii.	14
cramm'd.		
The Bull, the Fleece are c,	Audley Ct.	1
And c a plumper crop :	Will Water.	124
your Princess, c with erring pride	Princess, iii.	86
Titanic shapes, they c The forum	" vii.	109
c with theories out of books,	" Con.	35
Whose ear is c with his cotton,	Maud, I. x.	42
crost, and c With comment	Vivien	528
cramming.		
C all the blast before it.	Locksley H.	192
cramp (s.)		
stitches, ulcerous throes, and c's,	St S. Stylites	13
cramp (verb.)		
c its use, if I Should hook it	Day-Dm.	211
I will not c my heart,	Will Water.	51
To c the student at his desk,	In Mem. cxxvii.	18
cramp'd.		
women, up to this C	Princess, iii.	261
crane.		
c,' I said, 'may chatter of the c	Princess, iii.	88
cranny.		
In an ancient mansion's crannies	Maud, II. v.	61
crash (s.)		
with the c of shivering points,	Princess, v.	480
thro' the c of the near cataract	Enid	1021
c of ruin, and the loss of all	En. Arden.	550
at his right and with a sudden c,	The Islet	8
crash (verb.)		
The fortress c'es from on high,	In Mem. cxxvi.	14
crash'd.		
c the glass and beat the floor ;	In Mem. lxxxvi.	20
crashing.		
c with long echoes thro' the land,	Aylmer's F.	338
C went the boom,	The Captain	44
crate.		
Clung but to c and basket,	Vivien	475
crave.		
moaning, household shelter c	Two Voices	260
I c your pardon, O my friend ;	In Mem. lxxxiv.	100
C pardon for that insult	Enid	583
craved.		
c a fair permission to depart,	Enid	40
at the palace c Audience of Guinevere	Elaine	1156
craven.		
'A c : how he hangs his head.'	Enid	976
crawl.		
inch by inch to darkness c ?	Two Voices	200
wrinkled sea beneath him c's ;	The Eagle	4
into some low cave to c	Vivien	733
creaked.		
doors upon their hinges c ;	Mariana	62
cream.		
fruits and c Served in the weeping	Gardener's D.	190
robb'd the farmer of his bowl of c	Princess, v.	214
cream-white.		
Her c-w mule his pastern set :	Sir L. and Q. G.	31
crease (weapon.)		
cursed Malayan c, and battle-clubs	Princess, Pro.	21
create.		
Life eminent c's the shade of death ;	Love and Death	13
creation.		
could not all c pierce	A Character	5
all c is one act at once,	Princess, iii.	308
serene C minted in the golden moods	" v.	186
love C's final law—	In Mem. lv.	14
To which the whole c moves.	" Con.	144
creature.		
Did never c pass So slightly	Talking O.	86
not a c was in sight	"	167
c laid his muzzle on your lap,	Princess, ii.	253
Like some wild c newly-caged,	"	281
that same fair c at the door	"	308
sleek and shining c's of the chase,	" v.	148
lovely, lordly c floated on	" vi.	73
c's native unto gracious act,	" vii.	12
Thy c, whom I found so fair.	In Mem. Pro.	38
play As with the c of my love ;	" lviii.	12
O beautiful c, what am I	Maud, I. xvi.	10
A c wholly given to brawls	Enid	441
pick the faded c from the pool,	"	671
themselves, like c's gently born	"	1040
c's voiceless thro' the fault of birth	"	1115
I compel all c's to my will.' (rep. l. 1521)	"	1477
chase a c that was current then	Vivien	258
sat the lifelong c of the house,	Elaine	1137
His c's to the basement of the tower	Guinevere	103
his c's took and bare him off	"	108
but loved thy highest c here ?	"	649
God grants To any of his c's.	En. Arden.	414
hunters round a hunted c draw	Aylmer's F.	499
the gentle c shut from all	"	565
credible.		
almost think That idiot legend c.	Princess, v.	146
credit (s.)		
Hadst thou such c with the soul ?	In Mem. lxx.	5
His c thus shall set me free ;	" lxxix.	13
credit (verb.)		
world which c's what is done	In Mem. lxxiv.	15
creditor.		
They set an ancient c to work :	Ed. Morris	130
credulous.		
c Of what they long for,	Enid	1723

credulousness.	POEM.	LINE.
darken, as he cursed his *c*	Sea Dreams	13

creed.

knots that tangle human *c*'s,	{'Clear-headed friend,' etc.	3
other than his form of *c*,	A Character	29
as God holding no form of *c*	Pal. of Art	211
A dust of systems and of *c*'s.	Two Voices	207
Who keeps the keys of all the *c*'s,	In Mem. xxiii.	5
wrought With human hands the *c* of *c*'s	,, xxxvi.	10
shriek'd against his *c*—	,, lv.	16
Believe me, than in half the *c*'s.	,, xcv.	12
cleave a *c* in sects and cries,	,, cxxvii.	15
Against the scarlet woman and her *c*:	Sea Dreams	23
lisp in love's delicious *c*'s;	Coquette, i.	11

creek.

desolate *c*'s and pools among,	Dying Swan	41
Lotos blows by every winding *c*:	Lotos-E's	146
sailing moon in *c* and cove;	In Mem. c.	16

creep.

These in every shower *c*	A Dirge	33
languid fire *c*'s Thro' my veins	Eleänore	130
c's from pine to pine, And loiters	Œnone	4
thro' the moss the ivies *c*,	Lotos-E's	54
lost their edges, and did *c*	D. of F. Wom.	50
C's to the garden water-pipes	,,	206
c's on Barge-laden, to three arches	Gardener's D.	43
like a guilty thing I *c*	In Mem. vii.	7
the blood *c*'s, and the nerves prick	,, xlix.	2
Must *I* too *c* to the hollow	Maud, I. i.	54
Felt a horror over me *c*,	,, xiv.	35
Always I long to *c*	,, II. iv.	95
Some ship of battle slowly *c*,	To F. D. Maurice	26
slow tear *c* from her closed eyelid	Vivien	755
new disease, unknown to men, *C*'s	Guinevere	515
slow-worm *c*'s, and the thin weasel	Aylmer's F.	852
c's a cloud, or moves a wind,	Lucretius	106
dead flesh *c*, or bits of roasting ox	,,	131

creeper.

A *c* when the prop is broken,	Aylmer's F.	810

creeping.

c on from point to point;	Locksley H.	134
Still *c* with the *c* hours.	St Agnes' Eve	7

crept.

The cluster'd marish-mosses *c*.	Mariana	40
blooms unmown, which *c* Adown	Arabian N's.	29
out I stept, and up I *c*:	Ed. Morris	111
down my surface *c*.	Talking O.	162
With hooded brows I *c* into the hall,	Princess, iv.	206
a gentler feeling *c* Upon us:	In Mem. xxx.	17
till he *c* from a gutted mine.	Maud, I. x.	9
c so long on a broken wing.	,, III. vi.	1
As on The Lariano *c*	The Daisy	78
from the carven-work behind him *c*	Elaine	435
C to her father, while he mused	,,	744
in the pause she *c* an inch Nearer	Guinevere	523
C down into the hollows of the wood	En. Arden	76
hand *c* too across his trade	,,	110
He *c* into the shadow	,,	384
C to the gate, and open'd it.	,,	776

crescent (adj.)

many a youth Now *c*, who will come	Elaine	447

crescent (s.)

Hundreds of *c*'s on the roof.	Arabian N's.	129
April's *c* glimmer of cold,	Miller's D.	107
a moon, that, just In *c*.	Audley Ct.	80
When down the stormy *c* goes,	Sir Galahad	10
the sun, a *c* of eclipse,	Vision of Sin	10
To which thy *c* would have grown;	In Mem. lxxxiii.	4
yon hard *c*, as she hangs	,, cvi.	10
azure bloom of a *c* of sea,	Maud, I. iv.	5
downward *c* of her minion mouth	Aylmer's F.	533

crescent-bark.

range Of vapour buoy'd the *c-b*	Day-Dm.	186

crescent-curve.

Set in a gleaming river's *c-c*,	Princess, i.	169

crescent-lit.	POEM.	LINE.
while the balmy glooming, *c-l*,	Gardener's D.	258

crescent-wise.

thro' stately theatres Bench'd *c-w*.	Princess, ii.	348

cress.

To purl o'er matted *c*	Ode to Mem.	59
I loiter round my *c*es;	The Brook	181

crest.

watch'd my *c* among them all,	Oriana	30
lapwing gets himself another *c*;	Locksley II.	18
light as the *c* Of a peacock.	Maud, I. xvi.	16
giant tower, from whose high *c*,	Enid	827
c's that smoke against the skies,	Elaine	483
for *c* the golden dragon clung	Guinevere	588

Crete.

Had rest by stony hills of *C*.	On a Mourner	35

crevice.

from the *c* peer'd about.	Mariana	65
fretful as the wind Pent in a *c*:	Princess, iii.	65

crew.

sent a *c* that landing burst.	En. Arden	635
ever as he mingled with the *c*,	,,	644
half the *c* are sick or dead.	The Voyage	92
a *c* that is neither rude nor rash,	The Islet	10
the seamen Made a gallant *c*,	The Captain	6
beneath the water *C* and Captain lie;	,,	68

crew (pret. of crow.)

sitting, as I said, The cock *c*	M. d'Arthur, Ep.	10

Crichton.

I call'd him *C*, for he seem'd.	Ed. Morris	21

cricket.

c chirps: the light burns low:	D. of the O. Year	40
not a *c* chirr'd:	In Mem. xciv.	6
of the myriad *c* of the mead,	Elaine	107

cricketed.

They boated and they *c*;	Princess, Pro.	159

cried.

took the boy, that *c* aloud.	Dora	99
boy beheld His mother he *c* out	,,	135
clapt her hands and *c* for war,	Princess, iv.	567
thrice they *c*, I likewise.	,, Con.	104
my own sad name in corners *c*.	Maud, I. vi.	72
had you *c*, or knelt, or pray'd	Enid	1692
I *c* because you would not pass	Elaine	1036
Leolin *c* out the more upon them—	Aylmer's F.	367
I *c* myself well-nigh blind,	Grandmother	37

crime.

intellect to part Error from *c*;	Isabel	15
And all alone in *c*:	Pal. of Art	272
'Heaven heads the count of *c*'s	D. of F. Wom.	201
When single thought is civil *c*, 'You ask me why,' etc.		19
c Of sense aveng'd by sense.	Vision of Sin	213
of sense became The *c* of malice	,,	215
if it were thine error or thy *c* 'Come not when,' etc.		7
wing'd affections clipt with *c*:	Princess, vii.	297
Unfetter'd by the sense of *c*,	In Mem. xxvii.	7
mark'd as one hideous *c*,	,, lxxi.	18
count it *c* To mourn for any	,, lxxxiv.	61
from madness, perhaps from *c*,	Maud, I. xvi.	22
clearest of ambitious *c*,	Ode on Well.	28
ever weaker grows thro' acted *c*,	Will	12
main Cause of all their *c*;	Vivien	637
most impute a *c* Are pronest	,,	674
c's and frailties of the court,	Guinevere	135
that I come to urge thy *c*'s,	,,	528

crimson.

all the *c* changed, and past.	Mariana in the S.	25
In the Spring a fuller *c*	Locksley H.	17
add A *c* to the quaint Macaw.	Day-Dm.	16
molten into flakes Of *c*	In Mem. xcvii.	32
In *c*'s and in purples and in gems	Enid	10

crimson (verb.)

C's over an inland mere,	Eleänore	42

crimson-circled.

Before the *c-c* star.	In Mem. lxxxviii.	47

crimson'd.	POEM.	LINE.
slowly *c* all Thy presence	*Tithonus*	56
crimson-hued.		
c-h the stately palmwoods	*Milton*	15
crimson-rolling.		
when the *c-r* eye Glares ruin,	*Princess,* iv.	473
crimson-threaded.		
When from *c-t* lips	*Lilian*	23
cripple.		
Came from a grizzled *c*,	*Aylmer's F.*	8
crispeth.		
The babbling runnel *c*	*Claribel*	19
critic.		
No *c* I—would call them	*Princess,* i.	144
Musician, painter, sculptor, *c*,	" ii.	161
critic-pen.		
Unboding *c-p*,	*Will Water.*	42
croak.		
c thee sister, or the meadow-crake	*Princess,* iv.	106
a raven ever *c's*, at my side	*Maud,* vi.	57
croak'd.		
the Raven, flying high, *C*	*Guinevere*	133
crocodile.		
C's wept tears for thee:	*A Dirge*	22
crocus.		
the *c* brake like fire,	*Œnone*	94
From one hand droop'd a *c:*	*Pal. of Art*	119
C, anemone, violet,	*To F. D. Maurice*	44
crofts.		
Thro' *c's* and pastures wet with dew	*Two Voices*	14
crop (of a bird.)		
And cramm'd a plumper *c*;	*Will Water.*	124
crop (verb.)		
overquick To *c* his own sweet rose	*Vivien*	575
cross (s.)		
A broken chancel, with a broken *c*,	*M. d'Arthur*	9
I lift the *c*, And strive	*St S. Stylites*	116
I smote them with the *c*	"	170
happy with the mission of the *C*;	*Golden Year*	43
mark'd it with the red *c* to the fall	*Princess,* vi.	25
Under the *c* of gold	*Ode on Well.*	49
Thro' the dome of the golden *c*;	"	61
his catspaw and the *C* his tool,	*Sea Dreams*	186
cross (verb.)		
any cloud would *c* the vault	*Mariana in the S.*	38
wrong to *c* his father thus	*Dora*	145
Should my Shadow *c* thy thoughts	*Love and Duty*	85
Should it *c* thy dreams,	"	89
for three years to *c* the liberties	*Princess,* ii.	57
It *c'es* here, it *c'es* there	*Maud,* II. iv.	70
shadow of mistrust can *c*	*Enid*	815, 1097
leave, my lord, to *c* the room,	"	1147
He shall not *c* us more;	"	1191
forbear you thus; *c* me no more	"	1526
c our mighty Lancelot in his loves!	*Elaine*	683
And the lonely seabird *c'es*	*The Captain*	71
cross-bones.		
carved *c-b*, the types of Death,	*Will Water.*	245
crossed—crost.		
they *c* themselves for fear,	*L. of Shalott,* iv.	49
your shadow *c* the blind	*Miller's D.*	124
c the garden to the gardener's	*Audley Ct.*	16
then we *c* Between the lakes,	*Golden Year*	5
then we *c* To a livelier land;	*Princess,* i.	108
back again we *c* the court	" ii.	85
We *c* the street and gain'd	" iv.	535
shade by which my life was *c*,	*In Mem.* lxv.	5
c By that old bridge which,	*The Brook*	78
where the waters marry—*c*,	"	81
c the common into Darnley chase	"	132
when we *c* the Lombard plain	*The Daisy*	49
little thumb That *c* the trencher	*Enid*	396
C and came near, lifted adoring	"	1153

	POEM.	LINE.
c, and cramm'd With comment,	*Vivien*	527
And seldom *c* her threshold,	*En. Arden*	334
Abhorrent of a calculation *c*	"	470
seldom *c* his child without a sneer	*Aylmer's F.*	562
crossing (part.)		
past him, I was *c* his lands:	*Maud,* I. xiii.	6
Rivulet *c* my ground,	" xxi.	1
c, oft we saw the glisten	*The Daisy*	35
crossing (s.)		
Who sweep the *c's*, wet or dry,	*Will Water.*	47
cross-lightnings.		
c-l of four chance-met eyes	*Aylmer's F.*	129
cross-pipes.		
carved *c-p*, and, underneath	*Will Water.*	247
crotchet.		
Chimeras, *c's*, Christmas solecisms,	*Princess,* Pro.	190
crouched.		
C fawning in the weed.	*Œnone*	197
c on one that rose Twenty	*St S. Stylites*	87
crow (s.)		
like a *c* upon a three-legg'd stool	*Audley Ct.*	44
many-winter'd *c* that leads	*Lockslep H.*	68
ere the hateful *c* shall tread	*Will Water.*	235
carrion *c's* Hung like a cloud	*Vivien*	448
crow (verb.)		
she heard the night-fowl *c*	*Mariana*	26
Before the red cock *c's*	*May Queen,* ii.	23
cock *c's* ere the Christmas morn,	*Sir Galahad*	51
crowd.		
c's in column'd sanctuaries;	*D. of F. Wom.*	22
The *c's*, the temples, waver'd,	"	114
methought, who waited with a *c*,	*M. d'Arthur, Ep.*	20
c of hopes That sought to sow	*Gardener's D.*	63
his heart before the *c*! 'You might have won,' etc.		36
The park, the *c*, the house;	*Princess,* Pro.	94
An universal culture for the *c*,	"	109
as we came, the *c* dividing clove	" iv.	264
know Your faces there in the *c*	"	489
thereat the *c* Muttering, dissolved:	"	501
the *c* were swarming now,	" Con.	37
Civic manhood firm against the *c*	"	57
the genial day, the happy *c*,	"	75
c's that stream from yawning doors	*In Mem.* lxix.	9
He told me, lives in any *c*,	" xcvii.	26
To fool the *c* with glorious lies,	" cxxvii.	14
Thro' all that *c* confused and loud,	*Maud,* II. iv.	71
held their heads above the *c*,	*The Brook*	10
the sorrowing *c* about it grow,	*Ode on Well.*	16
Till *c's* at length be sane	"	169
The dark *c* moves,	"	268
thy wheel above the staring *c*;	*Enid*	356
blows, that all the *c* Wonder'd,	"	564
in this Are harlots like the *c*,	*Vivien*	680
c Will murmur, lo the shameless	*Elaine*	100
of the *c* you took no more account	"	106
the honest shoulders of the *c*	*Sea Dreams*	162
while none mark'd it, on the *c*	"	227
c's that in an hour Of civic tumult	*Lucretius*	168
crow'd.		
C lustier late and early,	*Will Water.*	126
maid, That ever *c* for kisses.	*Princess,* ii.	261
crow-foot.		
c are over over all the hill,	*May Queen,* i.	38
crowing.		
At midnight the cock was *c*,	*Oriana*	12
Came *c* over Thames.	*Will Water.*	140
crown (diadem, etc.)		
Revered Isabel, the *c* and head,	*Isabel*	10
better than to own A *c*, a sceptre,	*Ode to Mem.*	121
With a *c* of gold, On a throne?	*The Merman*	6
under my starry sea-bud *c*	*The Mermaid*	16
column'd citadel, The *c* of Troas	*Œnone*	14
from all neighbour *c's* Alliance	"	122
heads and *c's* of kings;	*Pal. of Art*	152

	POEM.	LINE.
Last May we made a c of flowers:	May Queen, ii.	9
the roof and c of things?	Lotos-E's.	69
my c about my brows,	D. of F. Wom.	162
King-like, wears the c: 'Of old sat Freedom,' etc.		16
Three Queens with c's of gold—	M. d'Arthur	198
moments when we met The c of all,	Ed. Morris	70
angel there That holds a c?	St S. Stylites	201
'tis here again; the c! the c!	"	205
That a sorrow's c of sorrow.	Locksley H.	76
from his cold c And crystal silence	Two Voices	85
mountain stirr'd its bushy c,	Amphion	25
those that wear the Poet's c:	{ 'You might have won,' etc.	10
In robe and c the King stept down	Beggar Maid	5
wears her error like a c	Princess, iii.	95
were pack'd to make your c,	" iv.	522
wore them like a civic c:	In Mem. lxviii.	8
f ol that wears a c of thorns:	"	12
look'd upon my c and smiled:	"	16
ill for him that wears a c,	" cxxvi.	9
sought but Duty's iron c	Ode on Well.	122
I e sane and c's be just.	"	169
wears a truer c Than any wreath.	"	276
leaves The C a lonely splendour.	Idylls, Ded.	48
had on a c Of diamonds,	Elaine	46
from the skull the c Roll'd	"	51
this c the golden dragon clung,	"	433
coco's drooping c of plumes,	En. Arden	575
It wore a c of light,	The Flower	10
you my wren with a c of gold,	The Window	80
king of the wrens with a c of fire.	"	159
crown ('five shillings.)		
and he gave the ringers a c.	Grandmother	58
crown 'verb.)		
high dial which my sorrow c's—	St S. Stylites	94
stars that c a happy day	Maud, I. xviii.	30
C thyself, worm, and worship	Aylmer's F.	650
crowned.		
C dying day with stars.	Pal. of Art	184
l ing robed and c,	D. of F. Wom.	163
I ws J Vea, c a saint.	St S. Stylites	151
i ur g, robed and c,	Godiva	77
simil senses c his head:	Two Voices	277
s all th ee son lent,	In Mem. xxii.	6
the purple brows of Olivet	" xxxi.	11
with blessing she doth rise.	" xxxiii.	5
see thee sitting c with good.	" lxxxiii.	5
c with attributes of woe.	" cxvii.	18
c A happy life with a fair death,	Enid	1815
c the state pavilion of the King,	Guinevere	396
two fortunes, Both c with stars	Sea Dreams	233
Like Heavenly hope she c the sea	The Voyage	70
C with a flower or two.	Lucretius	226
crowsfoot.		
crafty c round his eye;	Sea Dreams	183
crucified.		
either they were stoned or c,	St S. Stylites	50
crucifix.		
the maid-mother by a c,	Pal. of Art.	93
cruel.		
c as a schoolboy ere he grows	Walk. to the M.	99
C, c the words I said!	Ed. Gray	17
no tenderness Too hard, too c:	Princess, v.	505
Seem'd the Captain's mood.	The Captain	13
cruel-hearted.		
call me c-h, but I care not.	May Queen, i.	19
crueller.		
than was ever told in tale,	Vivien	707
C: as not passing thro'	Aylmer's F.	671
cruel.		
gentlemen, That trifle with the c.	Will Water.	232
crumbled.		
public wrong be c into dust,	Ode on Well.	167
crumpled.		
c than a poppy from the sheath	Princess, v.	28

	POEM.	LINE.
crupper.		
and arm beyond The c.	Enid	1313
crush (s.)		
great the c was, and each base,	Princess, vi.	333
crush (verb.)		
Like a rose-leaf I will c thee,	Lilian	29
c her pretty maiden fancies dead	Princess, i.	87
c her, like a vice of blood,	In Mem. iii.	15
crush'd.		
c them on my breast, my mouth:	Fatima	12
c My spirit flat before thee.	St S. Stylites	25
monstrous apes they c my chest:	"	171
Lady Psyche will be c;	Princess, iii.	47
she c The scrolls together,	" iv.	374
record of her wrongs And c to death	" v.	138
bruised the herb and c the grape,	In Mem. xxxv.	23
Mangled, and flatten'd, and c	Maud, I. i.	7
c with a tap Of my finger-nail	" II. ii.	21
c in the clash of jarring claims,	" III. vi.	44
found, tho' c to hard and dry,	The Daisy	97
feet unseen C the wild passion	Elaine	738
crushing.		
and c down his mate:	Princess, ii.	106
crust.		
one slough and c of sin,	St S. Stylites	2
woman thro' the c of iron moods	Princess, vii.	321
crusted.		
thickly c one and all:	Mariana	2
crutch.		
Truth a-leaning on her c, 'Clear-headed friend,' etc.		18
cry (s.)		
none hear my *cries*	Oriana	73
one deep c Of great wild beasts;	Pal. of Art	282
deep behind him, and a c Before.	M. d'Arthur	184
c that shiver'd to the tingling stars	"	199
boy's c came to her from the field	Dora	102
lest a c Should break his sleep	Walk. to the M.	65
blind c of passion and of pain,	Love and Duty	78
the scandal and the c 'You might have won,' etc.		16
The plaintive c jarr'd on her ire;	Princess, iv.	374
scared by the c they made,	" v.	91
rose a c As if to greet the king;	"	238
iron palms together with a c;	"	344
She nor swoon'd, nor utter'd c:	"	533
a great c, The Prince is slain.	" vi.	9
piteous was tho c:	"	126
out of languor leapt a c;	" vii.	140
from a dewy breast a c for light:	"	237
these wild and wandering *cries*	In Mem. Pro.	41
out waste places comes a c,	" iii.	7
with no language but a c.	" liii.	20
raise a c that lasts not long	" lxxiv.	10
love's dumb c defying change	" xciv.	2
roofs, that heard our earliest c,	" ci.	3
With overthrowings, and with *cries*,	" cxii.	10
cleave a creed in sects and *cries*,	" cxxvii.	15
A c above the conquer'd years	" cxxx.	7
wounded thing with a rancourouse	Maud, I. x.	34
there rises ever a passionate c	" II. i.	5
on a sudden a passionate c (rep. iv. 47)	"	33
loyal people shouting a battle c	" III. vi.	35
Whose crying is a c for gold:	The Daisy	94
a c That Edyrn's men were on them	Enid	638
a sudden sharp and bitter c,	"	1570
C of children, Enids and Geraints	"	1813
Uttered a little tender dolorous c.	Elaine	813
cities burnt, and with a c she woke.	Guinevere	83
I cry my c in silence,	"	199
on a sudden a c, 'The King.'	"	408
With his first babe's first c,	En. Arden	85
she started with a happy c,	"	151
younger ones with jubilant *cries*	"	374
hard upon the c of 'breakers'	"	540
send abroad a shrill and terrible c,	"	769
half-incredulous, half-hysterical c	"	854
wherefore he had made the c;	Aylmer's F.	589
to the mother, and sent out a c	Sea Dreams	237
music harmonizing our wild *cries*	"	247

CONCORDANCE TO

	POEM.	LINE.
caught her away with a sudden *c*;	The Victim	74
Greater than I—isn't that your *c*?	Spiteful Let.	17

cry (verb.)

Call to each other and whoop and *c*	The Merman	26
did so laugh and *c* with you,	D. of the O. Y'car	25
cease I not to clamour and to *c*,	St S. Stylites	41
for a tender voice will *c*	Locksley H.	87
C down the past, not only	Godiva	7
bade him *c*, with sound of trumpet,	"	36
c for strength, remaining weak,	Two Voices	95
C, faint not:	"	181-4
c For that which all deny	Will Water.	45
wind sweep and the plover *c*	'Come not when,' etc.	5
Earth Reels, and the herdsmen *c*;	Princess, v.	518
cries against my wish for thee.	In Mem. lxxxix.	24
C thro' the sense to hearten trust	" cxv.	7
was I as a child that *cries*,	" cxxiii.	19
I to *c* out on pride	Maud, I. xii.	17
c to the steps above my head	" II. v.	101
I *c* my cry in silence	Guinevere	199
c to these the last of theirs	Aylmer's F.	792
I cannot *c* for him, Annie:	Grandmother	15
c to thee To kiss thy Mavors,	Lucretius	81

crying (part.)

Some *c* there was an army	Princess, iv.	463
An infant *c* in the night (rep.)	In Mem. liii.	18
c, knows his father near	" cxxiii.	20
They were *c* and calling	Maud, I. xii.	4, 26
his legions *c* Christ and him,	Elaine	305
c that his prize is death.'	"	530
novice *c*, with clasp'd hands	Guinevere	309
c to each other And calling	En. Arden.	379
c upon the name of Leolin,	Aylmer's F.	576

crying (s.)

Whose *c* is a cry for gold:	The Daisy	94
mine but from the *c* of a child.'	Sea Dreams	241

crypt.

knees are bow'd in *c* and shrine:	Sir Galahad	18
fall'n into the dusty *c*	Will Water.	183
cold *c's* where they shall cease.	In Mem. lvii.	8

crystal.

down the streaming *c* dropt	Princess, vii.	150
Became a *c*, and he saw them	Vivien	480
In a shallop of *c* ivory-beak'd,	The Islet	12

cube.

hard-grained Muses of the *c*	Princess, Pro.	178

cubit.

upon a pillar, high Six *c's*,	St S. Stylites	86
numbers forty *c's* from the soil.	"	90
spear a *c* thro' his breast	Enid	935

cuckoo.

c told his name to all the hills;	Gardener's D.	92
nest,' she said, 'To hatch the *c*.	Princess, iv.	347
'*C* l *c* l' was ever a May so fine?:	The Window	153

cuckoo-flower.

blow the faint sweet *c-f's*;	May Queen, i.	30
As perfume of the *c-f*?	Margaret	8

cud.

chew'd The thrice-turn'd *c* of wrath,	Princess, i.	65

cuff'd.

Caught and *c* by the gale:	Maud, I. vi.	5

cuirass.

on his *c* worn our Lady's Head,	Elaine	294
spear Prick'd sharply his own *c*,	"	488

cuisses.

c dash'd with drops Of onset;	M. d'Arthur	215

cull'd.

honey in fairy gardens *c*—	Eleänore	26
words, tho' *c* with choicest art,	D. of F. Wom.	285
but one, by those fair fingers *c*,	Gardener's D	148
lady palms I *c* the spring	Vivien	122

culminate.

light up, and *c* in peace,	Princess, ii.	327

culmination.

	POEM.	LINE.
starry *c* drop Balm-dews	Talking O.	267

cultivation.

months of toil, And years of *c*,	Amphion	98

culture.

An universal *c* for the crowd,	Princess, Pro.	109
need More breadth of *c*:	" v.	180

cunning-simple.

So innocent-arch, so *c-s*,	Lilian	13

Cunobeline.

rioted in the city of *C* l	Boädicea	60

cup.

drink the *c* of a costly death,	Eleänore	138
fingers round the old silver *c*—	Miller's D.	10
steam'd From out a golden *c*.	Pal. of Art	40
last drop in the *c* of gall.	Walk. to the M.	61
My little oakling from the *c*,	Talking O.	231
Will haunt the vacant *c*:	Will Water.	172
Fill the *c*, and fill the can: (rep.)	Vision of Sin	95
crowning *c*, the three-times-three,	In Mem. Con.	104
indeed to drink: no *c* had we:	Vivien	121
pretty *c* of both my hands	"	124
c's and silver on the burnish'd board	En. Arden.	743
magic *c* that fill'd itself anew.	Aylmer's F.	143
There they drank in *c's* of emerald,	Boädicea	61
not in any cheerful *c*,	Coquette, iii.	9
such *c's* as left us friendly-warm,	Lucretius	212

Cupid.

rentroll *C* of our rainy isles.	Ed. Morris	103
The modest *C* of the day,	Talking O.	67
seal was *C* bent above a scroll,	Princess, i.	238

Cupid-boys.

By *C-b* of blooming hue—	Day-Dm.	278

cur.

yelp'd the *c*, and yawl'd the cat;	The Goose	33
barking *c* Made her cheek flame:	Godiva	57

curate.

and with Edward Bull The *c*;	Ed. Morris	15
said the fat-faced *c* Edward Bull,	"	42, 90

curb.

Wild natures need wise *c's*.	Princess, v.	165

curbed.

strongly groom'd and straitly *c*	Princess, v.	446

curdled.

wolf's-milk *c* in their veins,	Princess, vii.	115

cure (benefice.)

The curate; ho was fatter than his *c*.	Ed. Morris	15

cure (remedy.)

declined And trusted any *c*.	Pal. of Art	156

cured.

C lameness, palsies, cancers,	St S. Stylites	81
c some halt and maim'd;	"	138

curious.

Too *c*, Vivien, tho' you talk	Vivien	208
ever be too *c* for a boon	"	336
Hetairai, *c* in their art,	Lucretius	52

curiousness.

In children a great *c* be well,	Vivien	214

curl (s.)

In many a dark delicious *c*,	Arabian N's.	139
In a golden *c* With a comb	The Mermaid	6
flow'd His coal-black *c's*	L. of Shalott, iii.	31
streaming *c's* of deepest brown	Mariana in the S.	16
the light and lustrous *c's*—	M. d'Arthur	216
moves not on the rounded *c*	Day-Dm.	84
took him by the *c*, and led him in	Vision of Sin	6
play'd the patron with her *c's*	Princess, Pro.	138
Melissa shook her doubtful *c's*,	" ii.	59
From the flaxen *c* to the gray lock	" iv.	406
on their *c's* From the high tree	" vi.	63
down dead-heavy sank her *c's*	"	131
winds their *c's* about his hand:	In Mem. lxv.	12
little head, sunning over with *c's*,	Maud, I. xxii.	57

	POEM.	LINE.		POEM.	LINE.
clipt A tiny *c*, and gave it:	*En. Arden*	235	In *c*'s the yellowing river ran,	*Sir L. and Q.C.*	15
dim *c*'s kindle into sunny rings;	*Tithonus*	54	left and right thro' meadowy *c*'s	*In Mem.* xcix.	15
curl (verb.)			least little delicate aquiline *c*	*Maud*, I. ii.	10
c round my silver feet silently,	*The Mermaid*	50	With many a *c* my banks I fret	*The Brook*	43
serve to *c* a maiden's locks;	*In Mem.* lxxvi.	7	*curve.*		
curl'd.			out again I *c* and flow	*The Brook*	182
about His dusty forehead drily *c*	*Miller's D.*	6	*curved.*		
c and comb'd his comely head,	*The Sisters*	31	*c* an arm about his neck,	*Vivien*	90
her serpent pride had *c*.	*Pal. of Art*	257	*curvet.*		
the clouds are lightly *c*	*Lotos-E's*	157	a roan horse caper and *c*	*Elaine*	788
Faint shadows, vapours lightly *c*,	*Day-Dm.*	25	*curving.*		
All-graceful head, so richly *c*,	"	250	*c* a contumelious lip,	*Maud*, I. xiii.	20
The forest crack'd, the waters *c*,	*In Mem.* xv.	5	*cushion.*		
the same cold streamlet *c*	" lxxviii.	9	On silken *c*'s half reclined;	*Eleänore*	126
curlew.			*c*'s of whose touch may press	*Talking O.*	179
as of old, the *c*'s call,	*Locksley H.*	3	*custom* (habit.)		
current.			one good *c* should corrupt the world	*M. d'Arthur*	242
in its onward *c* it absorbs	*Isabel*	31	Appraised the Lycian *c*,	*Princess*, ii.	112
From those four jets four *c*'s	*Pal. of Art*	33	Disyoke their necks from *c*,	"	127
ever-shifting *c*'s of the blood	*D. of F. Wom.*	133	moved beyond his *c*, Gama said	" vi.	212
c of my being sets to thee.'	*Locksley H.*	24	reverencing the *c* of the house	*Enid*	380
runs The *c* of my days	*Will Water.*	36	by the power Of intermitted *c*;	"	811
crystal *c*'s of clear morning seas.	*Princess*, ii.	307	vicious quitch Of blood and *c*	"	1752
turn'd your warmer *c*'s all to her,	" iv.	282	*cut* (s.)		
c of his talk to graver things	*En. Arden*	203	this *c* is fresh; That ten years	*Elaine*	21
flow'd the *c* of her easy tears	"	866	*cut* (verb.)		
then the motion of the *c* ceased,	*Sea Dreams*	113	*c*'s atwain The knots	'Clear-headed friend,' etc.	2
curse (s.)			*c* away my tallest pines	*Œnone*	204
A curse is on her if she stay	*L. of Shalott*, ii.	4	*c* off from hope in that sad place,	*D. of F. Wom.*	105
knows not what the *c* may be,	"	6	C Prejudice against the grain:	{ 'Love thou thy laud,' etc.	22
'The *c* is come upon me,'	" iii.	44	where the hedge-row *c*'s the pathway,	*Gardener's D.*	85
was blasted with a *c*:	*D. of F. Wom.*	103	*c* this epitaph above my bones;	*Princess*, ii.	190
This is the *c* of time.	*To J. S.*	17	What is she, *c* from love and faith,	*In Mem.* cxiii.	11
this world's *c*,—beloved but hated—	*Love and Duty*	47	Jealousy, down! *c* off from the mind	*Maud*, I. x.	48
I said, ' I toil beneath the *c*,	*Two Voices*	229	with his whip, and *c* his cheek.	*Enid*	207
My Shakespeare's *c* on 'You might have won,' etc.		27	little cloud C's off the fiery highway	*En. Arden*	730
remember'd that burnt sorcerer's *c*	*Princess*, v.	464	C off the length of highway	"	674
when she turn'd, the *c* Had fallen	*In Mem.* vi.	37	she *c* it off and gave it,	"	895
we have made them a *c*.	*Maud*, I. i.	31	C the Roman boy to pieces	*Boädicea*	66
She may bring me a *c*.	"	73	*cutting.*		
the sparrow-hawk, My *c*, my	*Enid*	445	*c* eights that day upon the pond,	*The Epic*	10
'That is love's *c*; pass on,	*Elaine*	1343	*cycle* (s.)		
came a kingdom's *c* with thee—	*Guinevere*	546	With *c*'s of the human tale,	*Pal. of Art*	146
left their memories a world's *c*	*Aylmer's F.*	795	than a *c* of Cathay.	*Locksley H.*	184
A *c* in his God-bless-you	*Sea Dreams*	160	Young Nature thro' five *c*'s ran,	*Two Voices*	17
curse (verb.)			The closing *c* rich in good.	*In Mem.* civ.	28
I *c* not nature, no, nor death;	*In Mem.* lxxii.	7	at her will Thro' all her *c*'s—	*Lucretius*	244
c me the blabbing lip, And *c* me	*Maud*, II. v.	57	*cycle* (verb.)		
To *c* this hedgerow thief	*Enid*	309	Falls off, but *c*'s always round.	*Two Voices*	348
I did not come to *c* thee	*Guinevere*	529	*cygnet.*		
cursed.			Is tawnier than her *c*'s:	*Elaine*	1179
bless'd herself, and *c* herself	*The Goose*	15	*cymbal.*		
C be the social wants (rep.).	*Locksley H.*	59	With shawms, and with *c*'s,	*Dying Swan*	32
c and scorn'd, and bruised with	*Two Voices*	222	*cypress.*		
have *c* him even to lifeless things)	*Maud*, I. xix.	15	With *c* promenaded.	*Amphion*	38
darken, as he *c* his credulousness,	*Sea Dreams*	13	waves the *c* in the palace walk	*Princess*, vii.	162
C me and my flower.	*The Flower*	8	Made *c* of her orange flower,	*In Mem.* lxxxiii.	15
cursing (part.)			A *c* in the moonlight shake,	*The Daisy*	82
stood With Florian, *c* Cyril,	*Princess*, iv.	153	*Cyril.*		
I was *c* them and my doom,	*Maud*, I. xix.	51	With C and with Florian,	*Princess*, i. 51,162	
c their lost time, and the dead man,	*Enid*	1424	C took the child, And held her	" ii.	341
cursing (s.)			to close with Cyrian wish,	" iii.	85
she was deaf To blessing or to *c*	*Enid*	1426	Hither came C, and yawning	"	108
curtain.			climbing, C kept With Psyche,	"	336
In the white *c*, to and fro,	*Mariana*	51	C, with whom the bell-mouth'd glass	" iv.	137
forgets to close His *c*'s,	*Adeline*	43	stood With Florian, cursing C,	"	153
jolly ghost, that shook The *c*'s	*Walk. to the M.*	29	Psyche, C? both are fled:	"	222
The death-white *c* rep.)	*Maud*, I. xiv.	34	C, howe'er He deal in frolic,	"	230
By the *c*'s of my bed	" iv.	54	Go: C told us all.	" v.	38
cast the *c*'s of their sent aside—	*Aylmer's F.*	803	C met us, A little shy	"	42
curtseying.			To whom remorseful C.	"	76
c her obeisance, let us know	*Princess*, ii.	6	if C spake her true,	"	161
curve (s.)					
rainbow lives in the *c* of the sand;	*Sea Fairies*	27			
c's of mountain, bridge, boat,	*Ed. Morris*	5			

	POEM.	LINE.
fiery-short was *C's* counter-scoff	*Princess*, v.	297
bore down a Prince, And *C*, one.	″	508
C seeing it, pushed against	″	522
Beside us, *C*, batter'd as he was,	″ vi.	138
When *C* pleaded, Ida came behind	″ vii.	63

Cyrus.
what she did to *C* after fight . *Princess*, v. 356

Czar.
has as many lies as a *C*; . *Maud*, I. iv. 9

D

dabbled.
| *d* with the blood Of his own son, | *Princess*, vi. | 88 |
| are *d* with blood-red heath, | *Maud*, I. i. | 2 |

dabbling.
| *D* a shameless hand | *Princess*, iii. | 297 |
| *d* in the fount of fictive tears, | *The Brook* . | 93 |

daffodil.
The shining *d* dead,	*Maud*, I. iii.	14
On a bed of *d* sky,	″ xxii.	10
And the shining *d* dies,	″ III. vi.	6

daffodilly.
clad her like an April *d* . *Princess*, ii. 303

dagger.
made my *d* sharp and bright,	*The Sisters*	26
thrust The *d* thro' her side.	*D. of F. Wom.*	260
With that gold *d* of of thy bill	*The Blackbird*	11
Shot sidelong *d's* at us,	*Princess*, ii.	427
Makes *d's* at the sharpen'd eaves,	*In Mem.* cvi.	8
had she found a *d* there	*Vivien*	700
A *d*, in rich sheath with jewels	*Aylmer's F.*	220
rascal at his feet, This *d* with him,	″	231
alone he pluck'd her *d* forth,	″	470
d which himself Gave Edith,	″	596

daily.
D and hourly, more and more. . *Eleänore* . 71

daily-dwindling.
With *d-d* profits held the house . *En. Arden* . 697

dainty (s.)
Are but *dainties* cook'd again . *The Window* 131

dainty-woeful.
dew Of *d-w* sympathies. . *Margaret* . 53

dăis.
I hung The royal *d* round. . *Pal. of Art* 132

dăis-throne.
rising sun High from the *d-t—* . *M. d'Arthur* 218

daisy.
linger'd there Till every *d* slept,	*Gardener's D.*	161
Touch'd by his feet the *d* slept.	*Two Voices*	276
the *d* close Her crimson fringes	*In Mem.* lxxi.	11
And left the *daisies* rosy.	*Maud*, I. xii.	24
I pluck'd a *d*, I gave it you.	*The Daisy* .	88

daisy-blossomed.
Wash'd with still rains and *d-b*; . *Circumstance* 7

daisy-chain.
Made blossom-ball or *d-c*, . *Aylmer's F.* 87

dale.
the blissful downs and *d's*,	*Sea Fairies*	22
long purples of the *d*	*A Dirge*	31
rivulet in the flowery *d*.	*May Queen*, i.	39
thro' mountain clefts the *d* Was seen	*Lotos-E's.*	20
went by *d*, and she went by down	*Lady Clare*	59
Till over down and over *d*	*In Mem. Con.*	110
in loops and links among the *d's*	*Elaine*	166
at noon in some delicious *d*	*Guinevere*	390
was rising over the *d*,	*Grandmother*	39

dalliance.
O the *d* and the wit, . *D. of F. Wom.* 147

dallied.
d with his golden chain, . *Day-Dm.* . 163

dally.

	POEM.	LINE.
That with the napkin *d*;	*Will Water.*	118

dallying.
lieu of idly *d* with the truth, . *Elaine* . 588

dam (obstruction.)
| sleepy pool above the *d*, | *Miller's D.* | 99 |
| waits a river level with the *d* | *Princess*, iv. | 452 |

dam (mother.)
a bitter bleating for its *d* . *Princess*, iv. 373

damask-work.
d-w, and deep inlay Of braided . *Arabian N's.* 28

dame.
Knight and burgher, lord and *d*,	*L. of Shalott*, iv.	43
have a *d* indoors, that trims us	*Ed. Morris*	46
d That whisper'd 'Asses' ears'	*Princess*, ii.	97
Like that great *d* of Lapidoth	″ vi.	16
d's and heroines of the golden year	″	48
behind A train of *d's*	″ vii.	113
an ancient *d* in dim brocade ;	*Enid*	363
that old *d*, to whom full tenderly	″	508
no more avail, *D*, to be gentle	″	1564
neither *d* nor damsel then Wroth	*Vivien*	456
wedded with an outland *d*:	″	564
One old *d* Came suddenly	*Elaine*	725
in the reading, lords and *d's* Wept,	″	1276
the lords and *d's* And people,	″	1336

damp (adj.)
| The air is *d*, and hush'd, | 'A spirit haunts,' etc. | 13 |
| black hair *D* from the river ; | *Princess*, iv. | 258 |

damp (s.)
| hail, *d*, and sleet, and snow ; | *St S. Stylites* | 16 |
| Sucking the *d's* for drink | ″ | 76 |

damsel.
Sometimes a troop of *d's* glad,	*L. of Shalott*, ii.	19
and his *d* shall be ours.'	*Enid*	912
and your *d* should be theirs.'	″	924
let her eat ; the *d* is so faint.'	″	1055
While your good *d* rests,	″	1073
d there who sits apart,	″	1148
d drooping in a corner of it.	″	1459
neither dame nor *d* then Wroth	*Vivien*	456
in this *d's* golden hair	*Elaine*	205
d, in the light of your blue eyes :	″	657
d, for I deem you know	″	686
This will I do, dear *d*,	″	958
rose And pointed to the *d*,	″	1256
dreamt the *d* would have died,	″	1297
You loved me, *d*, surely	″	1385
prettiest little *d* in the port,	*En. Arden* .	12

Dan.
D Chaucer, the first warbler, . *D. of F. Wom.* 5

Danaë.
Earth all *D* to the stars, . *Princess*, vii. 167

Danaïd.
The *D* of a leaky vase, . *Princess*, ii. 319

dance (s.) see *country dance.*
with the choral starry *d* Joined not	*Pal. of Art*	253
Leaving the *d* and song,	*D. of F. Wom.*	208
d's broke and buzz'd in knots	*Princess*, i.	132
at a *d* to change The music—	″ iv.	566
In *d* and song and game	*In Mem.* xxix.	8
d and song and hoodman-blind.	″ lxxvii.	12
wheels the circled *d*, and breaks	″ xcvii.	30
No *d*, no motion, save alone	″ civ.	23
last the *d*;—till I retire :	*Con,*	105
A dinner and then a *d* .	*Maud*, I. xx.	34
She is weary of *d* and play.'	″ xxii.	22
Come hither, the *d's* are done,	″	54

dance (verb.)
About thee breaks and *d's*;	*Madeline*	30
spangle *d's* in bight and bay,	*Sea Fairies*	24
says His fire *d's* before her	*Œnone*	260
make her *d* attendance ;	*Amphion*	62
And the dead begin to dance.	*Vision of Sin*	166
to dress, to *d*, to thrum,	*Princess*, iv.	498

	POEM.	LINE.
d Its body, and reach its fatling	Princess, vi.	121
let the torrent *d* thee down	" vii.	194
To *d* with death, to beat the ground	In Mem. i.	12
d the lights on lawn and lea	" cxiv.	9
Till the red man *d*	Maud, I. xvii.	17
make the netted sunbeam *d*	The Brook	176
to *d* and sing, be gaily drest,	Coquette, ii.	3

danced.

we *d* about the may-pole	May Queen, ii.	11
all the tables *d* again,	The Goose	47
d The greensward into greener	Gardener's D.	132
D into light, and died	"	198
gilded ball *D* like a wisp:	Princess, Pro.	64
shook the woods, And *d* the colour	" iii.	276
I that *d* her on my knee,	In Mem. Con.	45
Yniol's heart *D* in his bosom,	Enid	505
madly *d* our hearts with joy,	The Voyage	3

dancer.

the *d*'s dancing in tune;	Maud, I. xxii.	16
the *d*'s leave her alone?	"	21
A wreath of airy *d*'s	Guinevere	259

dancing (part.)

in *d* after Letty Hill,	Ed. Morris	55
keeps A thousand pulses *d*	In Mem. cxxiv.	16
To the dancers *d* in tune;	Maud, I. xxii.	16
burst in *d*, and the pearls	Vivien	302

dancing.

Till the *d* will be over	Maud, I. xx.	43

dandle.

shall we *d* it amorously?	Boädicea	33

dandled.

nor petty babes To be *d*,	Princess, iv.	129
arm that *d* you,	" vi.	165

dandy-despot.

What if that *d-d*, he	Maud, I. vi.	42

Dane.

Saxon and Norman and *D* are we,	W. to A lexan.	3, 31
all of us *D*'s in our welcome	"	4
each all *D* in our welcome of thee,	"	33

danger.

life of shocks, *D*'s, and deeds	Œnone	161
Her household fled the *d*	The Goose	54
see the *d* which you cannot	Enid	1270
my part Of *d* on the roaring sea,	The Sailor	22

dangled.

when my father *d* the grapes,	Maud, I. i.	71
D a length of ribbon	En. Arden.	751

Daniel.

(see *D* seven and ten	Sea Dreams	148

Danish.

gray down With *D* barrows;	En. Arden.	7
from the *D* barrow overhead;	"	439

Dante.

world-worn *D* grasped his song	Pal. of Art	135

Danube.

The *D* to the Severn gave	In Mem. xix.	1
Let her great *D* rolling fair	" xcvii.	9

dare.

d to kiss Thy taper fingers	Madeline	43
I *d* not think of thee,	Oriana	93
d not die and come to thee	"	96
you *d* to answer thus I	Dora	24
men *D* tell him Dora waited	"	74
Then not to *d* to see!	Love and Duty	38
doubt would rest, I *d* not solve.	Two Voices	313
will speak out, for I *d* not lie.	Lady Clare	38
I must go: I *d* not tarry'	Princess, iii.	79
'*D* we dream of that,' I ask'd	"	280
I *d* All these male thunderbolts;	" iv.	478
does the thing they *d* not do,	" v.	153
What *d*'s not Ida do	"	166
d we keep our Christmas-eve	In Mem. xxix.	4
Nor *d* she trust a larger lay	" xlvii.	13
d we to this fancy give,	In Mem. lii.	5
By which we *d* to live or die.	" lxxxiv.	40
D I say No spirit ever brake	" xcii.	1
That which we *d* invoke to bless;	" cxxiii.	1
Who can rule and *d* not lie	Maud, I. x.	66
That I *d* to look her way;	" xvi.	11
D I bid her abide by her word?	"	25
d's foreshadow for an only son	Idylls, Ded.	28
the cause because I *d* not speak	Enid	89
d to tell him what I think,	"	105
d obey him to his harm?	"	985
Not *d* to watch the combat	"	1003
care or *d* to speak with you,	"	1719
d the full-fed liars say of me?	Vivien	542
no man there will *d* to mock	Elaine	1047
how *d* I call him mine?	Guinevere	610

dared.

when at last I *d* to speak,	Miller's D.	129
d to flow In these words	To J. S.	6
yet you *d* To slight it.	Dora	96
d not tarry' men will say,	Two Voices	101
d To leap the rotten pales	Princess, ii.	125
have *d* to break our bound,	" iv.	518
in a pause I *d* not break	" vii.	233
D not to glance at her good	Enid	766
d to waste a perilous pity	"	1374
thought,' he had not *d* to do it,	"	1568
Yet *d* not stir to do it,	Aylmer's F.	806

darest.

scarcely *d* to inquire	In Mem. iv.	7

daring.

now it were too *d*.	Guinevere	647

dark.

thickest *d* did trance the sky,	Mariana	18
Which upon the *d* afloat,	The Owl, ii.	3
diamond-plots Of *d* and bright.	Arabian N's.	86
to shame The hollow-vaulted *d*,	"	126
dimple in the *d* of rushy coves,	Ode to Mem.	60
thro' the wreaths of floating *d*	The Poet	35
All within is *d* as night;	Deserted H.	5
Ere the light on *d* was growing,	Oriana	10
into the *d* Arrows of lightnings,	To J. M. K.	14
the *d* was over all;	May Queen, iii.	19
broaden'd on the borders of the *d*,	D. of F. Wom.	265
Remaining betwixt *d* and bright	Margaret	28
Shot on the sudden into *d*.	To J. S.	28
sea and air are *d* 'Love thou thy land,' etc.		63
bright horizon rimm'd the *d*.	Gardener's D.	177
sun fell, and all the land was *d*.	Dora	77, 107
all the varied changes of the *d*,'	Ed. Morris	36
Till now the *d* was worn,	Love and Duty	49
in the *d* of hazel eyes —	Locksley H.	38
If I make *d* my countenance,	Two Voices	53
'If all be *d*, vague voice,'	"	265
tresses be so *d*, How of those	Day-Dm.	131
twilight died into the *d*	"	188
white robes are soil'd and *d*,	St Agnes' Eve	13
I float till all is *d*.	Sir Galahad	40
o'er the *d* a glory spreads,	"	55
d and true and tender is the North.	Princess, iv.	80
wildness, and the chances of the *d*,'	"	225
in the *d* invested you,	" v.	385
burnish'd by the frosty *d*;	" v.	251
Seed they laugh'd at in the *d*,	" vi.	18
mixt Their *d* and gray,	"	116
watches in the dead, the *d*,	" vii.	68
My will is bondsman to the *d*;	In Mem. iv.	2
all the place is *d*, and all	" viii.	7
all is *d* where thou art not	"	12
balmy drops in summer *d*	" xvii.	15
marble bright in *d* appears,	" lxvi.	7
Immantled in ambrosial *d*,	" lxxxviii.	14
shade falls on us like the *d*	" Con.	93
the drift of the Maker is *d*,	Maud, I. iv.	43
Tho' the livelong hours of the *d*	" vi.	17
Then returns the *d*	" ix.	15
D in its funeral fold,	Ode on Well.	57
tho' she lay *d* in the pool,	Enid	657

	POEM.	LINE.
D in the glass of some presageful	*Vivien*	144
the court, the king, *d* in your light,	"	724
Arthur to the banquet, *d* in mood,	*Elaine*	563
late! and *d* the night and chill!	*Guinevere*	166–72
With wakes of fire we tore the *d* .	*The Voyage*	52

dark-blue.
D-b the deep sphere overhead,	*Arabian N's.*	89
d-b sky, Vaulted o'er the *d-b* sea.	*Lotos-E's.*	84

dark-brow'd.
D-b sophist, come not anear .	*Poet's Mind*	8

dark-dawning.
d-d youth, Darken'd watching	*Maud*, I. xix.	7

darken.
And the days *d* round me, .	*M. d' Arthur*	237
never more *d* my doors again.'	*Dora*	30
d on the rolling brine .	*In Mem.* cvi.	14
Not close and *d* above me .	*Maud*, I. xi.	9
Tho' many a light shall *d*,	" III. vi.	43
just heaven, that *d's* o'er me,	*Vivien*	780
flash of youth, would *d* down .	*Elaine*	1308
d with the gathering wolf, .	*Aylmer's F.*	767
d, as he cursed his credulousness	*Sea Dreams*	13
brightens and *d's* down on the plain	*The Window*	2
d's and brightens like my hope,	"	18
d's and brightens and *d's* like my fear.	"	19

darkened.
her eyes were *d* wholly	*L. of Shalott*, iv.	31
all the casement *d* there.	*Miller's D.*	128
in your own light and *d* mine	*Princess*, iv.	295
d sanctities with song.'	*In Mem.* xxxvii.	24
life is *d* in the brain.	" cxx.	8
D watching a mother decline	*Maud*, I. xix.	8
He had *d* into a frown .	"	62
d from the high light in his eyes,	*Enid*	100
eye *d* and his helmet wagg'd :	"	1354
d all the northward of her Hall.	*Aylmer's F.*	416
all the sails were *d* in the west,	*Sea Dreams*	39

darkening.
swarms of men *D* her female field :	*Princess*, vii.	19
drew like eclipse, *D* the world.	*Idylls, Ded.*	14
d thine own To thine own likeness ;	*Aylmer's F.*	673

darker.
Your hair is *d*, and your eyes	*Margaret*	49
eyes *D* than darkest pansies	*Gardener's D.*	27
make men *d* than they are, .	*Vivien*	725
lonelier, *d*, earthlier for my loss.	*Aylmer's F.*	750

dark-green.
spread his *d-g* layers of shade .	*Gardener's D.*	115

darkness.
which possess'd The *d* of the world,	*Arabian N's.*	72
lashes like to rays Of *d*,	"	137
All night long on *d* blind,	*Adeline*	44
Howling in outer *d*. To ——	*With Pal. of Art*	16
Gross *d* of the inner sepulchre	*D. of F. Wom.*	67
Had wink'd and threaten'd *d*,	*M. d' Arthur, Ep.*	2
would I were The pilot of the *d*	*A udley Ct.*	71
shrivell'd into *d* in his head,	*Godiva*	70
inch by inch to *d* crawl ?	*Two Voices*	200
heads were touched Above the *d* .	*Princess*, iii.	6
d closed me ; and I fell.	" v.	531
So much the gathering *d* charm'd :	" *Con.*	107
A beam in *d* : let it grow	*In Mem. Pro.*	24
Let *d* keep her raven gloss :	" i.	10
Else earth is *d* at the core, .	" xxxiv.	3
jaws Of vacant *d* .	"	16
slope thro' *d* up to God,	" liv.	16
blanch'd with *d* must I grow !	" lx.	8
Death has made His *d* beautiful .	" lxxiii.	12
woke The *d* of our planet, .	" lxxv.	10
makes the *d* and the light, .	" xcv.	19
in the *d* and the cloud, .	"	21
A treble *d*, Evil haunts	" xcvii.	13
Ring out the *d* of the land, .	" cv.	31
The Power in *d* whom we guess ;	" cxxiii.	4
out of *d* came the hands	"	23
over whom thy *d* must have spread	*Maud*, I. xviii.	25

	POEM.	LINE.
d into the light shall leap,	*Maud*, III. vi.	46
And counterchanged with *d* ?	*Vivien*	316
Approaching thro' the *d*, call'd ;	*Elaine*	994
her face a *d* from the King :	*Guinevere*	414
in the *d* o'er her fallen head,	"	577
kiss'd each other In *d*, .	*Aylmer's F.*	431
their own *d* as the Highest ?	"	643
May Pharaoh's *d*, folds as dense .	"	771
heaved upon it In *d*:	*Sea Dreams*	91
the *d* from their loosen'd manes,	*Tithonus*	41
There I heard them in the *d*	*Boädicea*	36
So they chanted in the *d*,	"	46

dark-purple.
in *d-p* spheres of sea. .	*Locksley H.*	164

dark-splendid.
face before her lived, *D-s*, .	*Elaine*	337

darling.
The *d* of my manhood, .	*Gardener's D.*	272
Her feet, my *d*, on the dead ;	*In Mem. Con.*	50
the moon-faced *d* of all,— .	*Maud*, I. i.	72
You are not her *d*.	" xii.	32
All homage to his own *d*,	" xx.	49
shall it ? answer, *d*, answer, no.	*Vivien*	247
great knight, the *d* of the court,	*Elaine*	261
pale she had touch'd *D*, to-night !	*Aylmer's F.*	380
Seventy years ago, my *d*,	*Grandmother*	24–56
me, not him, my *d*, no !'	*The Victim*	73

Darnley.
There is *D* bridge, .	*The Brook*	36
crost the common into *D* chase	"	132

dart (s.)
Love tipt his keenest *d's* ;	*D. of F. Wom.*	173
Brandishing in her hand a *d* .	*Boädicea*	71
Madly dash'd the *d's* together, .	"	74
Clash the *d's* and on the buckler .	"	79

dart (verb.)
forward *d* again, and play .	*In Mem.* xii.	17

darted.
thro' his manful breast *d* the pang.	*Enid*	121

dash.
on the light *D* themselves dead.	*Princess*, iv.	475
d myself down and die. .	*Maud*, I. i.	54
Waves on a diamond shingle *d*,	*The Islet*	16
d the brains of the little one out,	*Boädicea*	68
D them anew together .	*Lucretius*	243

dash'd (rushed, etc.)
D downward in a cataract. .	*Day-Dm.*	148
d about the drunken leaves .	*Amphion*	55
D together in blinding dew : .	*Vision of Sin*	42
into rhythm have *d* The passion	*Princess*, iv.	121
d Unopen'd at her feet ; .	"	449
d Your cities into shards .	" v.	132
roll The torrents, *d* to the vale :	"	340
a postscript *d* across the rest. .	"	414
wildly *d* on tower and tree .	*In Mem.* xv.	7
D on every rocky square	*Ode on Well.*	125
uttering a dry shriek, *D* on Geraint	*Enid*	1311
d Into the chronicle of a deedful	*Aylmer's F.*	195
in flood, and *d* his angry heart	"	633
Again we *d* into the dawn !	*The Voyage*	24
a ground-swell *d* on the strand,	*W. to Alexan.*	23
Madly *d* the darts together, .	*Boädicea*	74

dash'd (bespatter'd, etc.)
d with drops Of onset ; .	*M. d' Arthur*	215
d with death He reddens what he .	*Princess*, v.	157
d with wandering isles of night	*In Mem.* xxiv.	14
life is *d* with flecks of sin. .	" li.	14
Deep tulips *d* with fiery dew, .	" lxxiii.	11
where it *d* the reddening meadow,	*Lucretius*	49

dashing.
d down on a tall wayside flower, .	*Guinevere*	251

date.
when his *d* Doubled her own, .	*Aylmer's F.*	80

daughter.	POEM.	LINE.
It is the miller's *d*,	*Miller's D.*	169
I am the *d* of a River-God,	*Œnone*	37
We were two *d*'s of one race	*The Sisters*	1
The *d* of a hundred Earls,	*L.C.V.deVere*	7
A *d* of the gods, divinely tall,	*D. of F. Wom.*	87
The *d* of the warrior Gilead ite	"	197
went To see the Gardener's *D*;	*Gardener's D.*	3
Go and see The Gardener's *d*:	"	30
not heard Of Rose, the Gardener's *d*?	"	51
The *d*'s of the year, One after one,	"	195
She is my brother's *d*:	*Dora*	15
for his sake I bred His *d* Dora;	"	18
A labourer's *d*, Mary Morrison.	"	38
d of a cottager, Out of her sphere,	*Walk. to the M.*	51
like the *d*'s of the horseleech,	*Golden Year*	12
preaching down a *d*'s heart,	*Locksley H.*	94
His little *d*, whose sweet face	*Two Voices*	253
old Earl's *d* died at my breast;	*Lady Clare*	25
knowledge, so my *d* held,	*Princess*, i.	134
d and his housemaid were the boys:	"	188
we saw The Lady Blanche's *d*	" ii.	300
d's of the plough, stronger than men,	" iv.	259
A Niobëan *d*, one arm out,	"	352
Fair *d*, when we sent the Prince	"	379
eight mighty *d*'s of the plough	"	528
I would he had our *d*	" v.	205
hen To her false *d*'s in the pool;	"	319
those eight *d*'s of the plough Came	"	329
loved A *d* of our house;	*In Mem. Con.*	7
d of our meadows, yet not coarse	*The Brook*	69
was the thing his *d* wish'd,	"	140
love of all Thy *d*'s cherish Thee	*Idylls, Ded.*	51
were she the *d* of a king,	*Enid*	229
The voice of Enid, Yniol's *d*,	"	327
Enid, all in faded silk, Her *d*.	"	367
turn'd her *d* round, and said	"	740
I my sons and little *d* fled	*Elaine*	276
With children; first a *d*,	*En. Arden*	84
evermore the *d* prest upon her	"	480
tell my *d* Annie, whom I saw	"	883
sons of men D's of God;	*Aylmer's F.*	45
walk So freely with his *d*?	"	270
Pale as the Jeptha's *d*,	"	280
never yet had set his *d* forth	"	347
contriving their dear *d*'s good—.	"	781
devising their own *d*'s death!	"	783
contrived their *d*'s good,	"	848
Sea kings' *d* from over the sea,	*W. to Alexan.*	1
sea-kings' *d* as happy as fair,	"	26
Yell'd and shriek'd between her *d*'s	*Boädicea*	6, 72

daw.		
haunted by the wrangling *d*;	*In Mem.* xcix.	12
all the windy clamour of the *d*'s	*Enid*	1104

Dawes.		
as with his tenant, Jocky *D*.	*Walk. to the M.*	21

dawn (s.)		
breeze of a joyful *d* blew free,	*Arabian N's.*	1
dewy *d* of memory.	*Ode to Mem.* 7, 45,	124
dew-impearled winds of *d*	"	14
Fronting the *d* he moved	*Œnone*	57
tearful glimmer of the languid *d*	*D. of F. Wom.*	74
That claps his wings at *d*.	"	180
the white *d*'s creeping beams,	"	261
He will not see the *d* of day	*D. of the O. Year*	11
bridal *d* of thunder-peals, '*Love thou thy land,'* etc.	*M. d'Arthur*	271
black dot against the verge of *d*	" *Ep.*	11
lusty bird takes every hour for *d*.	"	18
to *d*, when dreams begin to feel	"	18
flaring like a dreary *d*;	*Locksley H.*	114
Vast images in glimmering *d*	*Two Voices*	305
made himself an awful rose of *d*,	*Vision of Sin* 50,	224
gave the letter to be sent with *d*;	*Princess*, i.	241
However then commenced the *d*;	" ii.	122
strange as in dark summer *d*'s	" iv.	41
at eve and *d* With Ida, Ida	"	412
deep *d* behind the tomb,	*In Mem.* xlv.	6
Thy tablet glimmers to the *d*.	" lxvi.	16
Risest thou thus, dim *d*, 'xcviii. 1)	" lxxi.	2
said 'The *d*, the *d*,' and died away	" xciv.	61

	POEM.	LINE.
A light-blue lane of early *d*,	*In Mem.* cxviii.	7
thither I climb'd at *d*	*Maud*, I. xiv.	5
Now and then in the dim gray *d*;	"	32
They sigh'd for the *d* and thee.	" xxii.	52
d of Eden bright over earth and	" II. i.	8
In the shuddering *d*, behold,	" iv.	52
the rich *d* of an ampler day—	*Ded. of Idylls.*	35
gray *d* stole o'er the dewy world,	*Enid*	1234
with the *d* ascending lets the day	"	1540
passing one, at the high peep of *d*,	*Vivien*	410
high *d* piercing the royal rose	"	589
woke with *d*, and past Down	*Elaine*	842
lo! the bloodred light of *d*.	"	1019
the *d* of rosy childhood past,	*En. Arden*	37
as a figure seen in early *d*	"	354
the chill November *d*'s	"	611
the mate had seen at early *d*	"	632
Such dear familiarities of *d*?	*Aylmer's F.*	131
d Aroused the black republic	"	528
Again we dash'd into the *d*!	*The Voyage*	24
rose at *d* and, fired with hope,	*Sailor Boy*	1
by their chariots, waiting for the *d*.	*Spec. of Iliad*	22

dawn (verb.)		
let your blue eyes *d* Upon me	*Margaret*	67

dawned.		
twilight *d*: and morn by morn the	*Princess*, vii.	30
D sometime thro' the doorway?	*Aylmer's F.*	685

dawning (part.)		
All the spirit deeply *d*,	*Locksley H.*	28
he saw Death *d* on him,	*En. Arden*	833

dawning (s.)		
in a fiery *d* wild with wind	*Elaine*	1014
thro' that *d* gleam'd a kindlier hope	*En. Arden*	834

day.		
As noble till the latest *d*!	*To the Queen*	22
only said, 'The *d* is dreary,	*Mariana*	33
d Was sloping toward his western	"	79
gloom of yesternight On the white *d*;	*Ode to Mem.*	10
prime labour of thine early *d*'s:	"	94
Looking at the set of *d*	*Adeline*	17
It was the middle of the *d*,	*Dying Swan*	8
Now is done thy long *d*'s work;	*A Dirge*	1
could I look upon the *d*?	*Oriana*	59
at the closing of the *d*	*L. of Shalott*, iv.	15
d increased from heat to heat,	*Mariana in the S.*	39
sometimes in the falling *d*	"	73
From heat to heat the *d* decreased,	"	78
d to night, the night to morn (rep.)	"	81
we may die the self-same *d*.	*Miller's D.*	24
Flush'd like the coming of the *d*;	"	132
gave you, Alice, on the *d*	"	162
d, when in the chesnut shade	"	201
while *d* sank or mounted higher	*Pal. of Art*	46
Crown'd dying *d* with stars,	"	184
the maddest, merriest *d*,	*May Queen*, i.	3,43
loud when the *d* begins to break:	"	10
woo me any summer *d*,	"	23
we had a merry *d*;	" ii.	9
before the *d* I die	"	16
call me before the *d* is born	"	49
ere this *d* is done	" iii.	63
All its allotted length of *d*'s,	*Lotos-E's*,	80
Lull'd echoes of laborious *d*	*Margaret*	29
gave you on your natal *d*;	"	42
will not see the dawn of *d*	*D. of the O. Year*	11
Make bright our *d*'s '*Of old sat Freedom,' etc.*	{ '*Love thou thy land,'* etc.	22 15
those, not blind, who wait for *d*,		
freshest in the fashion of the *d*	*The Epic*	32
Of Camelot, as in the *d*'s that were.	*M. d' Arthur*	21
In those old *d*'s, one summer noon,	"	29
the *d*'s darken round me	"	237
feel the truth and stir of *d*,	" *Ep.*	19
morning is the morning of the *d*,	*Gardener's D.*	1
as we went To see her.	"	74
as tho' he were the bird of *d*.	"	95
full *d* dwelt on her brows,	"	135
chambers of the heart, Let in the *d*.'	"	245

	POEM.	LINE.
dwelt on by the common *d*.	*Gardener's D.*	266
d When Allan call'd his son,	*Dora*	8
d's went on, and there was born	,,	46
the *d* when first she came,	,,	104
either twilight and the *d* between;	*Ed. Morris*	37
her name alone. Thrice-happy *d*'s!	,,	68
a part of those fresh *d*'s to me;	,,	142
The modest Cupid of the *d*,	*Talking O.*	67
ah! my friend, the *d*'s were brief	,,	185
little more: the *d* was warm	,,	205
Some happy future *d*.	,,	252
eye glazed o'er with sapless *d*'s,	*Love and Duty*	16
A tongue-tied Poet in the feverous *d*'s,	*Golden Year*	10
Happy *d*'s Roll onward, leading up	,,	40
The long *d* wanes: the slow moon	*Ulysses*	55
in old *d*'s Moved earth and heaven;	,,	66
lighting upon *d*'s like these?	*Lockeley H.*	99
When I heard my *d*'s before me	,,	110
at the gateways of the *d*.	,,	158
sweep into the younger *d*:	,,	183
sweep the tracts of *d* and night.	*Two Voices*.	69
grows the *d* of human power?'	,,	78
hope that warm'd me in the *d*'s	,,	122
d's that never come again.	,,	324
troubles number with his *d*'s:	,,	330
Stillness with love, and *d* with light.	*Day-Dm.*	92
strove in other *d*'s to pass,	,,	110
deep into the dying *d*	,,	171
Beyond the night, across the *d*,	,,	195
In *d*'s of old Amphion,	*Amphion*	10
runs The current of my *d*'s:	*Will Water.*	36
down Into the common *d*?	,,	154
d's, that deal in ana,	,,	199
God's blessing on the *d*!	*Lady Clare*	8
they twain will spend their *d*'s	*L. of Burleigh*	36
'She is more beautiful than *d*.'	*Beggar Maid*	8
When a blanket wraps the *d*,	*Vision of Sin*	80
tender grace of a *d* that is dead	*Break, break*, etc.	15
Took this fair *d* for text,	*Princess, Pro.*	108
in the midst of men and *d*,	,, i.	15
d's drew nigh that I should wed,	,,	40
gentler *d*'s, your arrow-wounded fawn	,, ii.	251
then *d* droopt: the chapel bells	,,	446
Agreed to, this, the *d* fled on	,, iii.	160
mould The woman to the fuller *d*.'	,,	315
the *d*'s that are no more. (rep.)	,, iv.	25
not thus, O Princess, in old *d*'s:	,,	273
a *d* Blanch'd in our annals,	,, vi.	46
a *d* Rose from the distance	,,	95
the *d*, Descending, struck	,,	343
memories of her kindlier *d*'s	,, vii.	91
shares with man His nights, his *d*'s	,,	247
the new *d* comes, the light	,,	325
the genial *d*, the happy crowd,	*Con.*	75
little systems have their *d*:	*In Mem. Pro.*	17
bald street breaks the blank *d*.	,, vii.	12
roar from yonder dropping *d*:	,, xv.	2
Week after week: the *d*'s go by:	,, xvii.	7
d of my delight As pure	,, xxiv.	1
The very source and fount of *D*	,,	213
the *d* prepared The daily burden.	,, xxv.	3
Old sisters of a *d* gone by,	,, xxix.	13
the cheerful *d* from night:	,, xxx.	30
wert thou, brother, those four *d*'s?'	,, xxxi.	5
life that leads melodious *d*'s.	,, xxxiii.	8
d When first she wears,	,, xxxix.	3
he forgets her *d*'s before	,, xliii.	7
d's have vanished, tone and tint,	,,	5
D's order'd in a wealthy peace,	,, xlv.	11
The twilight of eternal *d*,	,, xlix.	16
She sighs amid her narrow *d*'s,	,, lix.	10
tease her till the *d* draws by:	,,	14
His inner *d* can never die,	,, lxv.	15
d's that grow to something strange,	,, lxx.	11
D, when my crown'd estate begun	,, lxxi.	5
D, mark'd as with some hideous crime,	,,	18
Climb thy thick noon, disastrous *d*;	,,	26
care not in these fading *d*'s	,, lxxiv.	9
Can trouble live with April *d*'s,	,, lxxxii.	7
now the *d* was drawing on,	,, lxxxiii.	10
sun by sun the happy *d*'s	,,	27

	POEM.	LINE.
Whatever way my *d*'s decline,	*In Mem.* lxxxiv.	41
break the livelong summer *d*	,, lxxxviii.	31
will not yield them for a *d*.	,, lxxxix.	16
cast Together in the *d*'s behind,	,, xci.	6
Spirits from their golden *d*,	,, xciii.	6
broaden into boundless *d*.	,, xciv.	64
The *d*'s she never can forget	,, xcvi.	14
D, when I lost the flower of men;	,, xcviii.	4
two have striven half the *d*,	,, cl.	17
landmark breathes of other *d*'s,	,, ciii.	11
It is the *d* when he was born,	,, cvi.	1
We keep the *d*. With festal cheer,	,,	21
d's of happy commune dead;	,, cxv.	14
O *d*'s and hours, your work is this,	,, cxvi.	1
breathers of an ampler *d*	,, cxvii.	6
think of early *d*'s and thee,	,, cxviii.	8
In that it is thy marriage *d*	*Con.*	3
Since that dark *d* a *d* like this;	,,	84
wish them store of happy *d*'s.	,,	84
But these are the *d*'s of advance,	*Maud*, I, i.	25
slurring the *d*'s gone by	,,	33
riding at set of *d*	,, ix.	5
I shall have had my *d*,	,, xi.	7, 14
this is the *d* when I must speak (rep.)	,, xvi.	7
Go not, happy *d*, (rep.)	,, xvii.	1
fair stars that crown a happy *d*	,, xviii.	30
the fragments of the golden *d*.	,,	70
On the *d* when Maud was born;	,, xix.	40
half to the rising *d*;	,, xxii.	24
The *d* comes, a dull red ball	,, II. iv.	65
tithes in the *d*'s that are gone,	,, v.	23
catch a friend of mine one stormy *d*;	,,	85
knew her in her English *d*'s,	*The Brook*.	224
d's That most she loves to talk of,	,,	225
Warring on a later *d*,	*Ode on Well.*	102
A *d* of onsets of despair!	,,	124
Peace, it is a *d* of pain	,,	235–7
In the rich dawn of an ampler *d*—	*Idylls, Ded.*	35
nephew fights In next *d*'s tourney	*Enid*	476
Danced in his bosom, seeing better *d*'s.	,,	505
third *d* from the hunting morn Made	,,	597
In former *d*'s you saw me favourably.	,,	1164
overtoil'd By that *d*'s grief and travel	,,	1220
lets the *d* Strike where it clung:	,,	1540
hardest tyrants in their *d* of power,	,,	1543
clothed her in apparel like the *d*.	,,	1796
on a dull *d* In an Ocean cave	*Vivien*	80
the *d*'s when I was all unknown	,,	351
Well, those were not our *d*'s:	,,	462
Dull *d*'s were those, till our good	*Elaine*	279
next *d* broke from underground,	,,	412
our knight thro' whom we won the *d*	,,	528
my good *d*'s are done'	,,	943
There came a *d* as still as heaven,	*Guinevere*	290
in the golden *d*'s before thy sin.	,,	496
The *d* will grow to weeks,	,,	617
sombre close of that voluptuous *d*,	,,	680
pass his *d*'s in peace among his own.	*En. Arden*.	147
passes here (He named the *d*)	,,	215
d, that Enoch mention'd, came,	,,	238
in *d*'s of difficulty And pressure,	,,	253
the dead flame of the fallen *d*	,,	438
November *d* Was growing duller,	,,	722
the chronicle of a deedful *d*,	*Aylmer's F.*	196
many thousand *d*'s Were clipt by horror	,,	602
Darkly that *d* rose:	,,	609
In her next peep of *d*? (rep.)	*Sea Dreams*	282
d that followed the *d* she was wed,	*The Islet*	4
autumn into seeming-leafless *d*'s.	*A Dedication*	10
My life is full of weary *d*'s,	'*My life is full*,' etc.	1
first beam of my latest *d*?	*Lucretius*	59
and the sun from the *d*!	*The Window*	39
for ever and ever, and one *d* more	,,	147
Love, fix a *d*.	,,	165
You shall fix a *d*.'	,,	173
In honour of the day.	,,	177

daylight.

Flood with full *d* glebe and town?	*Two Voices*.	87

daylong.

His weary *d* chirping	*The Brook*.	53

	POEM.	LINE.
dazed.		
sudden light *D* me half-blind :	*Princess*, v.	11
dazzled.		
That both his eyes were *d*,	*M. d'Arthur*	59
rhymes are *d* from their place	*Day-Dm.*	19
boyish dream involved and *d* down	*Princess*, iv.	430
Be *d* by the wildfire Love	" v.	431
d by the livid-flickering fork,	*Vivien*	790
dazzling.		
Sun came *d* thro' the leaves,	*L. of Shalott*, iii.	3
dead.		
I would that I were *d* ! (rep.)	*Mariana*	12
look'd so grand when he was *d*,	*The Sisters*	32
of the rising from the *d*,	*Pal. of Art*	206
I beheld young Laurence *d*.	*L. C. V. de Vere*	28
soldier found Me lying *d*,	*D. of F. Wom.*	162
And the old year is *d*.	"	248
he'll be *d* before.	*D. of the O. Year*	32
we bear blossoms of the *d*; '*Love thou thy land*,' etc.		94
true old times are *d*,	*M. d'Arthur*	229
who was *d*, Who married,	*Audley Ct.*	28
d, become Mere highway dust ?	*Love and Duty*	10
Better thou wert *d* before me,	*Locksley H.*	56
Can I think of her as *d*,	"	73
Ev'n in the charnels of the *d*,	*Two Voices.*	215
canst thou show the *d* are *d*,	"	267
We find no motion in the *d*.'	"	279
He gazes on the silent *d* :	*Day-Dm.*	113
thy kiss would wake the *d* !'	"	184
And the *d* begin to dance.	*Vision of Sin*	166
Come not, when I am *d*, '*Come not, when*,' etc.		1
grace of a day that is *d*,	'*Break, break*,' etc.	15
Peace be with her. She is *d*.	*Princess*, iv.	118
strikes him *d* for thine and thee.	"	561
watching like a watcher by the *d*.	v.	59
cold reverence worse than she were *d*.	"	89
old God of war himself were *d*,	"	139
Home they brought her warrior *d* :	"	532
he lives : he is not *d* :	vi.	106
he is *d*, Or all as *d* :	"	153
wat hes in the *d*, the dark,	vii.	88
lift thine eyes ; my doubts are *d*,	"	327
name the under-lying *d*,	*In Mem.* ii.	2
hear the ritual of the *d*	" xviii.	12
lies the master newly *d* ;	" xx.	4
he was *d*, and there he sits,	" xxxii.	3
brooding on the dear one *d*,	" xxxvii.	17
How fires it with the happy *d* ?	" xliii.	1
desire the *d* Should still be near	" l.	1
d sh ll look me thro' and thro',	"	12
Eternal greetings to the *d* ;	" lvi.	14
Nor in I dream of thee as *d* ;	" lxvii.	4
Shall I commerce with the *d* ;	" lxxxiv.	93
could the *d*, whose dying eyes	" lxxxix.	5
An hour's communion with the *d*.	" xciii.	4
The noble letters of the *d* ;	" xciv.	24
woodbine holy to the *d*,	" xcviii.	8
I dre m'd a vision of the *d*,	" cii.	3
trust that those we call the *d*,	" cxvii.	5
Should pile her barricades with *d*.	" cxxvi.	8
Resret is *d*, but love is more	*Con.*	17
Her feet, my darling, on the *d* ;	"	50
The shining daffodil *d*,	*Maud*, I. iii.	14
hear the *d* at midday moan,	" vi.	70
Had I lain for a century *d* ;	" xvii.	72
Strike *d* the whole weak race	" II. "	46
Who knows, if he be *d* ?	"	71
She is but *d*, and the time is at hand	" iii.	8
There is some one dying or *d*,	" iv.	48
D, long *d*, Long *d* !	" v.	1
I thought the *d* had peace,	"	15
world of the *d* ;	" 25, 40,	70
talk I as if her love were *d*,	*The Letters*	27
be he *d* I know not	*Enid*	442
to left him stunn'd or *d*,	"	1313
'What, is he *d* !' 'No, no, not *d* !'	"	1390
if he be not *d*, Why wail you	"	1395
Lay till, and feigned himself as *d*,	"	1436
were I *d* who is it would weep	"	1466
yonder man is surely *d* ;	"	1520

	POEM.	LINE.
surely knew my lord was *d*,'	*Enid*	1569
died Earl Doorm by him he counted *d*.	"	1578
Coming and going, and he lay as *d*	*Vivien*	62, 494
by the cold Hic Jacets of the *d* !'	"	603
in the hollow oak he lay as *d*,	"	818
that will strike my blossom *d*.	*Elaine*	966
good fortune, I will strike him *d*,	"	1065
a Steer'd by the dumb went upward	"	1147
not seem as *d* But fast asleep,	"	1154
may judge the living by the *d*,	"	1359
happy, *d* before thy shame?	*Guinevere*	420
strike him *d*, and meet myself Death	"	570
thinking '*d* or *d* to me !'	*En. Arden.*	690
could tell her you had seen him *d*,	"	809
reveal it, till you see me *d*.' '*D*'	"	840
my children care to see me *d*,	"	889
Were *d* to him already ; bent as	*Aylmer's F.*	445
Yes, as the *d* we weep for testify—	"	747
D for two years before his death	"	837
must forgive the *d*.' '*D* ! who is *d* ?'	*Sea Dreams*	261
d of heart-disease.' '*D* ? he ?' (rep.)	"	264
was *d* before he was born,	*Grandmother*	59, 68
if they be alive or *d*.	"	84
grassy barrows of the happier *d*.	*Tithonus*	71
half the crew are sick or *d*	*The Voyage*	92
was as the voice of the *d*,	*V. of Canteretz*	8
voice of the *d* was a living voice	"	10
deadly wounded Falling on the *d*.	*The Captain*	64
once at *d* of night did greet Troy's	*On a Mourner*	32
shine among the *d* Hereafter : tales !	*Lucretius*	129
when I am there and *d* am gone,	*The Window*	116

dead.
afoor moy Sally wur *d*,	*N. Farmer*	17
toner 'ed shot un as *d* as a nadil.	"	35

dead-blue.
a lack-lustre *d-b* eye,	*A Character*	17

deaden.
learns to deaden Love of self,	*Ode on Well.*	204

dead-heavy.
down *d-h* sank her curls,	*Princess*, vi.	131

Dead March.
the *D M* wails in the people's ears :	*Ode on Well.*	267

dead-pale.
D-p between the houses high,	*L. of Shalott*, iv.	40

deaf.
parch'd and wither'd, *d* and blind,	*Fatima*	6
end draws nigh ; half *d* I am,	*St. S. Stylites*	95
this dreamer, *d* and blind,	*Two Voices*	175
she was *d* To blessing or to cursing	*Enid*	1426

deafened.
d with the stammering cracks	*Vivien*	791

deal.
know so ill to *d* with time,	*L. C. V. de Vere*	63
Nor *d* in watch-words overmuch	{'*Love thou thy land*,' etc.	28}
Ere days, that *d* in ann,	*Will Water.*	169
'Leave me to *d* with that.'	*Princess*, iii.	133
d's in that Which men delight in,	"	199
d's with the other distance	" iv.	68
Cyril, howe'er He *d* in frolic,	"	231
learn With whom they *d*,	"	492
Shall we *d* with it as an infant ?	*Boädicea*	33

dealing (part.)
memory *d* but with time,	*Two Voices*	376
d goodly counsel from a height	*Aylmer's F.*	172

dealing (s.)
full of *d*'s with the world ?	*Miller's D.*	8

dealt.
deathful stabs were *d* apace.	*Oriana*	50
My nerves have *d* with stiffer,	*Will Water.*	73
hoard of tales that *d* with knights	*Princess, Pro.*	29
Wisdom *d* with mortal powers,	*In Mem.* xxxvi.	5
this *d* him at Caerlyle ;	*Elaine*	22
of Arthur's noblest *d* in scorn ;	*Guinevere*	41

CONCORDANCE TO

	Dean (forest.)	POEM.	LINE.
Before him came a forester of *D*,		*Enid* .	. 148

dean (dignitary.)
		POEM.	LINE.
prudes for proctors, dowagers for *d's*,	*Princess, Pro.* 141
they vext the souls of *d's*;	. . " . 161

dear.
she is grown so *d*, so *d*,	.	*Miller's D.* .	. 170
D is the memory of our wedded	.	*Lotos-E's.*	. 114
d the last embraces	.	"	. 115
As thou art lief and *d*,	.	*M. d' Arthur*	80
holds thee *d* For this good pint	*Will Water.*	211
wrong As a bitter jest is *d*.	.	*Vision of Sin*	198
ancient ties Would still be *d*	.	*Princess,* ii.	246
D as remember'd kisses	.	" iv.	36
no rose that's half so *d* .	.	" v.	152
D as the mother to the son,	.	*In Mem.* ix.	19
d to me as sacred wine.	.	" xxxvii.	19
count new things as *d* as old :	.	" xxxix.	28
Knowing the primrose yet is *d*,	.	" lxxxiv.	118
this hath made them trebly *d*.'	.	" ci.	16
If *I* be *d* to some one else, (rep.)	.	*Maud,* I. xv.	3
makes Love himself more *d*.'	.	" xviii.	61
D to the man that is *d* to God ;	*To F.D. Maurice*	36
those are few we hold as *d* ;	.	"	46
His Memory—since he held them *d*, *Ded. of Idylls*	1
d to Science, *d* to Art,	.	"	. 39
D to thy land and ours,	.	"	. 40
D, near and true—no truer Time	*A Dedication*	1
Yet both are near, and both are *d*,	*The Victim*	63
down to the window-pane of my *d*,	*The Window*	17
frost is here, And fuel is *d*	.	"	. 44

dearer.
a little *d* than his horse.	.	*Locksley H.*	50
All he shows her makes him *d* :	.	*L. of Burleigh*	33
Our wood, that is *d* than all ;	.	*Maud,* I. xxii.	38
therefore tenfold *d* by the power	.	*Enid* .	810
reverence, *D* to true young hearts,	*Elaine*	. 418
make you evermore *D* and nearer	*A Dedication*	3
The fuel is all the *d*,	.	*The Window*	57

dearest.
I, thy *d*, sat apart,	.	*In Mem.* cix.	13
our nearest, Were it our *d*, (rep.)	.	*The Victim*	14

dearness.
with a *d* not his due,	.	*Locksley H.*	91
A distant *d* in the hill,	.	*In Mem.* lxiii.	19

death.
gentler *d* shall Falsehood ' *Clear-headed friend,' etc.* 16
Life, anguish, *d*, immortal love,	*Arabian N's.*	73
ropose An hour before *d* ' *A Spirit haunts,' etc.*	15
He saw thro' life and *d*	.	*The Poet.*	5
In your eye there is *d* .	.	*Poet's Mind*	16
D, walking all alone	.	*Love and Death*	5
creates the shade of *d* ;	.	"	13
drink the cup of a costly *d*	.	*Eleänore,*	138
I should die an early *d* :	.	*Miller's D.* .	90
O *d, d, d*, thou ever floating cloud,	*Œnone* .	234
cold and starless road of *D*,	.	"	. 255
d and life she hated equally	.	*Pal. of Art*	265
sweeter far is *d* than life	.	*May Queen,* iii.	8
D is the end of life :	.	*Lotos-E's.* .	86
d, dark or dreamful ease.	.	"	. 98
There *is* confusion worse than *d*	.	"	. 128
The downward slope to *d*,	.	*D. of F. Wom.*	16
bright *d* quivered at the victim's	.	"	. 115
I was ripe for *d*,	.	"	. 208
knew that Love can vanquish *D*, .	"	. 269
thro' mine own doors *D* did pass ;	*To J. S.*	. 19
D is blown in every wind ;' .	.	"	. 46
fluting a wild carol ere her *d*,	*M. d' Arthur*	267
Dora lived unmarried till her *d*.	*Dora* .	9
had wither'd, nipt to *d* by him	*Ed. Morris*	101
all thy martyrs die one *d* ?	.	*St. S. Stylites*	49
whole years long, a life of *d*	.	"	. 53
hope ere *d* Spreads more and more	.	"	. 154
Like *D* betwixt my dear embrace	*Love and Duty*	48
Like bitter accusation ev'n to *d*	.	"	. 79
sweat her sixty minutes to the *d*,	*Golden Year*	68
D closes all ; but something	*Ulysses*	. 51
hadst not between *d* and birth	*Two Voices.*	169

	POEM.	LINE.
Know I not *D* ? the outward signs?	*Two Voices*	270
ever truly long'd for *d*.	"	. 396
life, not *d*, for which we pant ;	"	. 398
mellow *D*, like some late guest,	.	*Will Water.*	239
carved cross-bones, the types of *D*,	"	. 245
Pale again as *d* did prove :	.	*L. of Burleigh*	66
gap-tooth'd man as lean as *d*,	*Vision of Sin*	60
Let us hob-and-nob with *D*.	"	74, 194
D is king, and Vivat Rex ! .	"	. 179
nor shunn'd a soldier's *d*,	.	*Princess, Pro.*	38
make it *d* For any male thing	.	"	. 150
As blank as *d* in marble ; .	"	i.	175
MAN ENTER IN ON PAIN OF *D*	"	ii.	178
I give thee to the *d* My brother !'	"	. 287
give three gallant gentlemen to *d*.'	"	. 314
war to come and many *d's*,	"	iii.	134
you will shock him ev'n to *d*,	"	. 196
Of immolation, any phase of *d*,	"	. 268
Sun Grew broader toward his *d*.	"	. 346
remember'd kisses after *d*,	"	iv.	36
O *D* in Life, the days that are	"	. 40
Melissa clamour'd ' Flee the *d* ;' .	"	. 148
clamouring etiquette to *d*,	"	v.	16
mourn half-shrouded over *d* .	"	. 71
dash'd with *d* He reddens what	"	. 157
had not shunn'd the *d*,	"	. 170
to combat for my claim till *d*.	"	. 350
that there is no one hurt to *d*,	"	vi.	225
might mix his draught with *d*	"	. 260
well-nigh close to *d* For weakness :	"	vii.	104
fiery Passion from the brinks of *d* ;	"	. 141
cares to walk With *D* and Morning	"	. 169
in sad experience worse than *d*,	"	. 296
Thou madest *D*; and lo, thy foot	*In Mem. Pro.*	7
To dance with *d*, to beat the ground	"	i.	12
O Priestess in the vaults of *D*,	"	iii.	2
No hint of *d* in all his frame	"	xiv.	18
Cold in that atmosphere of *D*,	"	xx.	14
If *D* were seen At first as *D*,	"	xxxv.	18
that vague fear implied in *d* ;	"	xl.	14
If Sleep and *D* be truly one,	"	xlii.	1
(If *D* so taste Lethean springs)	"	xliii.	10
Beyond the second birth of *D*.	"	xliv.	16
must be wisdom with great *D* :	"	xlv.	11
I bring to life, I bring to *d* : .	"	lv.	6
Sleep *D's* twin-brother, times my .	"	lxvii.	2
Sleep, *D's* twin-brother, knows not *D*,	"	. 3
kinsman thou to *d* and trance	"	lxx.	1
curse not nature, no, nor *d* ;	"	lxxii.	7
D has made His darkness beautiful	"	lxxiii.	11
holy *D* ere Arthur died	"	lxxix.	2
D returns an answer sweet :	"	lxxx.	9
wage not any feud with *D*	"	lxxxi.	1
blame I *D*, because he bare .	"	"	9
For this alone on *D* I wreak	"	"	13
till Doubt and *D*, Ill brethren,	"	lxxxv.	11
make Confusion worse than *d*,	"	lxxxix.	19
shocks of Chance—The blows of *D*.	"	xciv.	43
dim lights, like life and *d*,	"	"	63
gleams On Lethe in the eyes of *D*.	"	xcvii.	6
unto myriads more, of *d*	"	xcviii.	16
one would sing the *d* of war,	"	cii.	33
dive below the wells of *D* ?	"	cvii.	8
on the depths of *d* there swims	"	cxiii.	11
cannot fight the fear of *d*.	"	cxiii.	10
Paul with beasts, I fought with *D* ;	"	cxix.	4
slip the thoughts of life and *d* ;	"	cxxi.	16
Unpalsied when he met with *D*,	"	cxxvii.	2
whatever is ask'd her, answers ' *D*.'	*Maud,* I. i.	4
To the *d*, to her native land.	"	v.	10
Singing of *D*, and of Honour	"	"	16
like a fool of the sleep of *d*.	"	xiv.	38
sullen-seeming *D* may give	"	xviii.	46
fair banquet with the dust of *d* ?	"	"	56
strand of *D* inwoven here	"	"	60
given false *d* her hand,	"	"	68
by a right. from birth till *d*,	"	xix.	42
battle, and seas of *d*.	"	III. vi.	37
All in the valley of *D*. (rep.)	*Lt. Brigade*	3
Into the jaws of *D*, (rep.)	"	. 24
pierced to *d* before mine eyes,	*Enid* .	. 104

	POEM.	LINE.
he would put me soon to d,	Enid	463
or hunger for my d,	"	930
I am weary to the d.'	"	1207
that he sickens nigh to d;	"	1348
himself nigh wounded to the d.'	"	1767
crown'd A happy life with a fair d,	"	1816
Fame that follows d is nothing	Vivien	314
the bare-grinning skeleton of d!	"	696
daughter fled From bonds or d,	Elaine	277
no prizes, for my prize is d!	"	505
crying that his prize is d.'	"	530
died the d In any knightly fashion	"	866
or d,' she mutter'd, 'd or him,' (rep.)	"	898
to the d, as tho' you were my blood,	"	956
D, like a friend's voice .	"	993
her song 'The Song of Love and D,'	"	999
d who puts an end to pain	"	1002
Sweet? then bitter d must be:	"	1004
bitter: sweet is d to me.	"	1005
if d be sweeter, let me die.	"	1006
Sweet d, that seems to make us	"	1008
I needs must follow d,	"	1011
ever shrieks before a d,	"	1017
I shall guard it even in d.	"	1109
d Was rather in the fantasy	"	1125
bruise and blow, With d's of others,	"	1160
my true love has been my d.	"	1270
for this most gentle maiden's d	"	1283
would have help'd her from her d.'	"	1302
after heaven, on our dull side of d,	"	1373
help it from the d that cannot die	Guinevere	66
thought 'he spies a field of d;'	"	133
many a mystic lay of life and d	"	279
thou shalt be guarded till my d.	"	445
doom of treason and the flaming d,	"	534
strike him dead, and meet myself D,	"	571
In those two d's he read God's	En. Arden	572
II's baby's d, her growing poverty,	"	706
saw D dawning on him,	"	833
peace which each had prick'd to d.	Aylmer's F.	52
no, nor d could alter her:	"	418
close and closer toward the d,	"	500
letter edged with d Beside him	"	505
went and gazed upon his d.	"	522
second d Scarce touch'd her	"	604
hapless loves And double d.	"	617
wounded to the d that cannot die;	"	662
devising their own daughter's d!	"	783
Stumbling across the market to his d,	"	820
Dea I for two years before his d	"	837
dark retinue reverencing d	"	842
on a matter he of life and d:	Sea Dreams	147
that ever I thought of d.	Grandmother	61
d is sure To those that stay	Sailor Boy	13
father raves of d and wreck,	"	19
Far worse than any d to me.'	"	24
With secret d for ever,	Coquette, iii.	13
The wages of sin is d;	Wages	6
that break body toward d,	Lucretius	154

deathbed.
| Kind? but the d desire | Maud, I. xix. | 77 |

death-blow.
| d-b struck the dateless doom | Lucretius | 233 |

deathful-grinning.
| d-g mouths of the fortress, | Maud, III. vi. | 52 |

death-hymn.
| wild swan's d h took the soul | Dying Swan | 21 |

death-in-life.
| ling ring out a three-years' d-i-l | En. Arden | 566 |
| paly, d-i-l, And wretched age— | Lucretius | 154 |

deathless.
| That Gods there are, and d. | Lucretius | 121 |

deathlike.
| Luminous, gemlike, ghostlike, d | Maud, I. iii. | 8 |

deathly-pale.
| d-p Stood grasping what was | Elaine | 960 |

	POEM.	LINE.
D-p, for lack of gentle maiden's aid.	Elaine	761

death-scaffold.
| hear Her own d-s raising, | En. Arden | 175 |

death's-head.
| not a d-h at the wine | Princess, iv. | 69 |

death-watch.
| dog howl, mother, or the d-w beat | MayQueen,iii. | 21 |

death-white.
| beheld The d-w curtain drawn | Maud, I. xiv. | 34 |
| d-w curtain meant but sleep, | " | 37 |

debate.
| Where once we held d, | In Mem. lxxxvi. | 21 |

debating.
| D his command of silence given, | Enid | 1215 |

debt.
Love the gift is Love the d	Miller's D.	207
Deep, indeed, Their debt of thanks	Princess, ii.	125
my d to him, This nightmare	" vi.	280
lawyers and harass'd with d:	Maud, I. xix.	22
I feel I shall owe you a d,	"	87
That I owe this d to you	"	90
voice, with which to pay the d	Ode on Well.	156
the whole dear d of all you are.	Enid	1168

debtors.
| d's for our lives to you. | Princess, ii. | 334 |

decad.
Thro' sunny d's new and strange,	Day-Dm.	234
Averill was a d and a half	Aylmer's F.	82
buried now seven d's deep	"	442

decay (s.)
| Upon the general d of faith | The Epic | 18 |
| on one side a castle in d, | Enid | 245 |

decay (verb.)
| The woods d, the woods d and fall, | Tithonus | 1 |
| And all her stars d.' | The Ringlet | 10 |

decay'd.
| old prowess were in aught d: | Elaine | 583 |

decease.
| from the Queen's d she brought | Princess, iii. | 70 |
| chains regret to his d, | In Mem. xxix. | 3 |

deceased.
| when our summers have d, | Maud, I. xviii. | 14 |

deceit.
| some coquettish d. | Maud, I. vi. | 26,90 |
| then, perhaps, as a child of d | " xiii. | 30 |

deceived.
| I never will be twice d. | The Letters | 30 |

December.
| The gloom of ten D's. | Will Water. | 104 |
| meeting, made D June, | In Mem. xcvi. | 11 |

decent.
| d not to fail In offices of | Ulysses | 40 |

decide.
'D not ere you pause.	Princess, iii.	140
D's it, 'sdeath I against my father's	" v.	288
'D it here: why not?	"	300

decided.
| beardless apple-arbiter D fairest, | Lucretius | 92 |

decision.
The intuitive d of a bright	Isabel	13
kept watch, waiting d,	Œnone	141
Since, what d! if we fail,	Princess, v.	312

deck (s.)
d's were dense with stately forms	M. d'Arthur	196
glimmer on the dewy d's.	In Mem. ix.	12
man we lov'd was there on d,	"	41
I stood on a giant d	Maud, III. vi.	24
And on the black d's laid her	Elaine	1141
while he stood on d Waving,	En. Arden	243

	POEM.	LINE.
d's were shatter'd, Bullets fell	The Captain	45
Over mast and d were scatter'd	"	47
Spars were splinter'd ; d's were broken :	"	49
On the d's as they were lying	"	53

deck (verb.)

To d thy cradle, Eleánore	Eleánore	21
flowers or leaves To d the banquet,	In Mem. cvi.	6
d it like the Queen's For richness,	Elaine	1112
to her pearls ; D her with these ;	"	1219

deck'd.

d her out For worship without end ;	Princess, vii.	153
A life that all the Muses d .	In Mem.lxxxiv.	45
d her, as the loveliest, .	Enid	17

declare.

D when last Olivia came	Talking O.	99
Such as no language may d.'	Two Voices	384

declared.

| d that ancient ties Would still | Princess, ii. | 245 |

decline (s.)

| Looks thro' in his sad d | Adeline | 13 |

decline (verb.)

d On a lower range of feelings	Locksley H.	43
Sap dries up ; the plant d's .	Two Voices	268
Whatever way my days d,	In Mem. lxxxiv.	41
Darken'd watching a mother d	Maud, I. xix.	8

declined.

like some sick man d,	Pal. of Art	155
thou, as one that once d,	In Mem. lxi.	5

decrease.

| now dilate, and now d, | In Mem. xxviii. | 10 |

decreased.

| From heat to heat the day d. | Mariana in the S. | 78 |

decree.

By shaping some august d	To the Queen	33
mould a mighty state's d's, .	In Mem. lxiii.	11

dedicate.

| I d, I d, I consecrate with tears | Ded. of Idylls, | 3 |

Dee.

| Bala lake Fills all the sacred D. | Enid | 1778 |

deed.

a life of shocks, Dangers and d's	Œnone	161
possession of man's mind and d.	Pal. of Art	209
great d's as half-forgotten things .	Lotos-E's.	123
serve his kind in d and word ' Love thou thy land,' etc.		86
souls with talk of knightly d, .	M. d'Arthur	19
the Powers, who wait On noble d's,	Godiva	72
Fruitful of further thought and d,	Two Voices	144
a noise of tongues and d's	"	206
perish'd in their daring d's.'	Day-Dm.	114
I am yours in word and in d.	Lady Clare	74
your great d's For issue, .	Princess, iii.	226
great d's cannot die ;	"	237
on the highest Foam of men's d's	" v.	310
In loveliness of perfect d's .	In Mem. xxxvi.	11
Her secret meaning in her d's,	" liv.	10
What fame is left for human d's	" lxxii.	11
On songs, and d's, and lives	" lxxvi.	11
true in word, and tried in d,	" lxxxiv.	5
Perplext in faith, but pure in d's	" xcv.	9
thro' our d's and make them pure,	" cxxx.	4
Feeling from her mate the D.	The Brook	95
Bright let it be with its blazon'd d's,	Ode on Well.	56
far-sounded among men For noble d's ?	Enid	428
grateful is the noise of noble d's .	"	437
knew my d's of noble .	"	1706
love of God and men And noble d's	Vivien	263
each incited each to noble d's	"	264
the great d's Of Lancelot, .	Elaine	82
almost overdo the d's Of Lancelot ;	"	468
here and there a d Of prowess	Guinevere	455
worship her by years of noble d's,	"	472
hear high talk of noble d's .	"	495
for her good d's and her pure life,	"	685

	POEM.	LINE.
Nor d's of gift, but gifts of grace .	Sea Dreams	180
d's yet live, the worst is yet	"	301
thine the d's to be celebrated	Boädicea	41

deem.

d this maid Might wear	Elaine	239
d this prize of ours is rashly .	"	540
for I d you know full well	"	666

deem'd.

d no mist of earth could dull	Ode to Mem.	38
the peace, that I d no peace,	Maud, III. vi.	50
wherein she d she look'd her best,	Elaine	903
d der death Was rather in the	"	1125
had d he felt the tale Less .	En. Arden	712
Things in an Aylmer d impossible	Aylmer's F.	305

deeming.

Vivien d Merlin overborne .	Vivien	649
D our courtesy is the truest law, .	Elaine	708

deep (adj.)

Tho' d not fathomless, .	Ode to Mem.	34
full and d In thy large eyes	Eleánore	85
So full, so d, so slow	"	95
then, because his wound was d, .	M. d'Arthur	5
rain That makes thee broad and d !	Talking O.	280
D as Hell I count his error. .	The Captain	3

deep (s.)

drove The fragrant, glistening d's	Arabian N's.	14
coiled sleeps in the central d's	The Mermaid	24
drives them to the d. .	Pal. of Art	204
The abysmal d's of Personality, .	"	223
roaring d's and fiery sands, .	Lotos-E's.	160
wrought it, sitting in the d's .	M. d'Arthur	105
He heard the d behind him, .	"	184
d Moans round with many voices.	Ulysses	55
Drag inward from the d's, .	Princess, vii.	22
From barren d's to conquer all	"	149
heaves but with the heaving d.	In Mem. xi.	20
stir the spirit's inner d's	" xli.	10
A higher height, a deeper d.	" lxii.	12
we to draw From d to d,	" cii.	39
landlike slept along the d.	" cxxii.	16
rolls the d where grew the tree	" cxxiii.	1
tumbled in the Godless d ; .	" cxxviii.	12
seek thee on the mystic d's .	" cxxiv.	14
of the height, and Powers of the d,	Maud, II. ii.	82
the Black and the Baltic d, .	" III. vi.	51
Glimmer away to the lonely d,	To F. D. Maurice	28
a sudden wind across the d's, .	Vivien	50
wild down above the windy d, .	"	508
either haven open'd on the d's, .	En. Arden	672
in perilous places o'er a d: .	Sea Dreams	11
from out the boundless outer d	"	86
the motion of the boundless d .	"	89
motion of the great d bore me on,	"	107
To the waste d's together. . .	"	231

deep-asleep.

| d-a he seem'd, yet all awake . | Lotos-E's. | 35 |

deep-blue.

| Floods all the d-b gloom . | D. of F. Wom. | 186 |

deep-chested.

| D-c music, and to this result. . | The Epic | 51 |

deep-desired.

| on thy bosom (d-d relief !) . | Love and Duty | 42 |

deep-domed.

| as the d-d empyrean Rings . | Milton | 7 |

deepen.

d's on and up ! the gates Roll back,	St Agnes' Eve	29
Ay me, the sorrow d's down, .	In Mem. xlviii.	14
old rut would d year by year .	Aylmer's F.	34

deepened.

| battle d in its place, . | Oriana | 51 |

deepening.

d thro' the silent spheres, .	Mariana in the S.	91
D the courts of twilight .	Princess, Con.	113
D thy voice with the d of the night,	V. of Cauteretz	2

	POEM.	LINE.
deep-hued.		
many a *d-h* bell-like flower	*Eleänore*	37
deep-inrunning.		
sand and cliff and *d-i* cave,	*Sea Dreams.*	17
deeply-wounded.		
mythic Uther's *d-w* son	*Pal. of Art*	105
deep-meadow'd.		
lies *D-m*, happy, fair	*M. d' Arthur*	262
deep-seated.		
D-s in our mystic frame,	*In Mem.* xxxvi.	2
deep-set.		
d-s windows, stain'd and traced	*Pal. of Art*	49
deep-ruddered.		
dewy-fresh, browsed by *d-u* kine,	*Gardener's D.*	45
deer.		
To chase the *d* at five;	*Talking O.*	52
thro' the coverts of the *d*,	*Sir L. and Q.G.*	21
monstrous horns of elk and *d*,	*Princess, Pro.*	23
shook the branches of the *d*,	" Con.	98
To show Sir Arthur's *d*.	*The Brook.*	133
flies that haunt a wound, or *d*	*Aylmer's F.*	571
cattle died, and *d* in wood,	*The Victim*	18
defacing.		
Defaming and *d*, till she left	*Vivien*	653
defame.		
These bonds that so *d* me:	*Elaine*	1411
defamed.		
D by every charlatan,	*In Mem.* cx.	23
defaming.		
D and defacing, till she left	*Vivien*	653
defeat.		
wish me victory or *d*,	*Enid*	920
not dwell on that *d* of fame	*Guinevere*	621
defect.		
each fulfils *D* in each,	*Princess,* vii.	286
D's of doubt, and taints of blood;	*In Mem.* liii.	4
an hour's *d* of the rose,	*Maud,* I. ii.	8
trust To make up that *d*:	*Elaine*	1187
was allow'd as part of his *d*,	*Guinevere*	44
defence.		
war would arise in *d* of the right,	*Maud,* III. vi.	19
defend.		
thou might'st *d* The thesis	*Two Voices*	337
And there *d* his marches;	*Enid*	41,1737
deferentially.		
(*d* With nearing chair	*Aylmer's F.*	266
defiance.		
flung *d*-down Gagelike to man,	*Princess,* v.	169
With message and *d*, went and came:	"	360
With one smile of still *d*	*The Captain*	59
defiant.		
Sullen, *d*, pitying, wroth	*Aylmer's F.*	492
deficiency.		
Who'll weep for thy *d*?	*Two Voices*	39
defied.		
chafing at his own great self *d*,	*Aylmer's F.*	537
define.		
Hold thou the good: *d* it well:	*In Mem.* liii.	13
defined.		
His isolation grows *d*.	*In Mem.* xliv.	12
deformed.		
Vext with unworthy manners, and *d. Aylmer's F.*		335
defying.		
We drink *d* trouble	*Will Water.*	94
love's dumb cry of change	*In Mem.* xciv.	27
degrade.		
And throned races may *d*;	*In Mem.* cxxvii.	7
degree.		
by *d's* to fullness wrought 'You ask me why,' etc.		14

	POEM.	LINE.
all are changed by still *d's*, 'Love thou thy land,' etc.		43
thro' soft *d's* Subdue them	*Ulysses*	37
What for order or *d*?	*Vision of Sin*	86
More than is of man's *d*	*Ode on Well.*	242
deity.		
Such is Rome, and this her *d*:	*Boädicea*	20
will outlast thy *D*? *D*? nay,	*Lucretius*	72
D false in human-amorous	"	90
Delay s.)		
Haste, half-sister to *D*. 'Love thou thy land,' etc.		96
easy grace, No doubt, for slight *d*, *Princess,* iv.		312
dull the voyage was with long *d's*, *En. Arden*.		656
Ah, the long *d*.	*The Window*	171
delay (verb.)		
now *d* not; take Excalibur	*M. d' Arthur*	36
tender ash *d's* To clothe herself,	*Princess,* iv.	88
Delaying long, *d* no more.	*In Mem.* lxxxii.	4
'*D* no longer, speak your wish	*Elaine*	920
delayest.		
D the sorrow in my blood,	*In Mem.* lxxxii.	14
delaying.		
D as the tender ash delays	*Princess,* iv.	88
new-year *d* long	*In Mem.* lxxxii. 2,13	
D long, delay no more.	"	4
delayingly.		
yet she held him on *d*	*En. Arden*.	465
delicacy.		
could not out of bashful *d*;	*Enid*.	66
delicate-handed.		
dilettante, *D-h* priest intone;	*Maud,* I. viii.	11
delicately.		
Most *d* hour by hour	*A Character*	19
Enid took a little *d*	*Enid*	1061
delicious.		
made the air Of Life *d*,	*Gardener's D.*	69
Were not his words *d*,	*Ed. Morris*	71
delicto.		
what's the Latin word?—*D*:	*Walk. to the M.*	27
delight (s.)		
So took echo with *d*, (rep.)	*The Owl,* ii.	4
d, Life, anguish, death	*Arabian N's.*	72
Falling into a still *d*,	*Eleänore*	106
I die with my *d*,	"	140
pierc'd thro' with fierce *d*,	*Fatima*	34
'I marvel if my still *d*	*Pal. of Art*	190
great *d* and shuddering took hold *May Queen,* iii.		35
I knew not for *d*	*D. of F. Wom.*	169
feedeth The senses with a still *d*	*Margaret*	17
Thy sole *d* is, sitting still,	*The Blackbird*	10
common mouth, So gross to express *d Gardener's D.*		55
drunk *d* of battle with my peers,	*Ulysses*	16
Some vague emotion of *d*	*Two Voices*	361
shape the song for your *d*	*Day-Dm.*	274
chambers emptied of *d*:	*In Mem.* viii.	8
was the day of my *d* As pure	" xxiv.	1
shower'd largess of *d*,	" xxix.	7
what *d's* can equal those	" xli.	9
Thy converse drew us with *d*,	" cix.	8
D a hundredfold accrue,	" cxvi.	8
Maud the *d* of the village,	*Maud,* I. i.	70
seems But an ashen-gray *d*.	" vi.	22
something Read with a boy's *d*,	" vii.	10
my *D* Had a sudden desire,	" xiv.	19
have spread With such *d*	" xviii.	26
My bride to be, my evermore *d*,	"	73
Breaking up my dream of *d*.	" xix.	2
The *d* of early skies	" II. iv.	25
The *d* of low replies.	"	30
yet it yielded a dear *d*	" III. vi.	15
reddening in extremity of *d*,	*Enid*	1068
themselves with some insane *d*,	*Vivien*	683
and fill'd her with *d*:	*Elaine*	376
delight (verb.)		
in her web she still *d's*,	*L. of Shalott,* ii.	28

G

	POEM.	LINE.		POEM.	LINE.
D our souls with talk of	. *M. d'Arthur*	19	*d* his heart his dearest wish,	. *En. Arden.*	333
deals in that Which men *d* in,	. *Princess,* iii.	200	with us Father Philip' he *d*;	. "	365

delighted.

| *D* with the freshness and the sound. | *Ed. Morris* | 99 |
| I am all as well *d*, | *Maud,* I. xx. | 40 |

delighteth.

| *d* to prolong Her low preamble | *Pal. of Art* | 173 |

delirium.

| catch Her hand in wild *d*, | *Princess,* vii. | 78 |

Delius.

| the Sun, Apollo, *D.* or of older | *Lucretius* | 125 |

deliver.

D not the tasks of might ' *Love thou thy land,*' etc.		13
D me the blessed sacrament ;	*St S. Stylites*	215
Thy tribute wave *d*,	*A Farewell*	2
Ignorance *D's* brawling judgments,	*Vivien*	515
take This diamond, and *d* it,	*Elaine*	545

deliverer.

| and call'd them dear *d's* | *Princess,* vi. | 76 |

delivering.

| *D,* that to me, by common voice | *Œnone* | 82 |
| *D* seal'd dispatches which the Head | *Princess,* iv. | 360 |

dell.

live-green heart of the *d's*	*Sea Fairies*	12
call aloud in the dreamy *d's,*	*The Merman*	25
diamond-ledges that jut from the *d's*	*The Mermaid*	40
in falling thro' the *d,*	*D. of F. Wom.*	183
splinter'd crags that wall the *d*	"	187
furzy prickle fire the *d's,*	*Two Voices*	71
How richly down the rocky *d*	*The Daisy*	9
snowy *d's* in a golden air.	"	68
little *d's* of cowslip, fairy palms,	*Aylmer's F.*	91

delver.

| careful robins eye the *d's* toil, | *Enid* | 774, 1280 |

demand (s.)

| make *d* of modern rhyme, | *To the Queen* | 11 |

demand (verb.)

king *d* An act unprofitable,	*M. d'Arthur*	95
sense of human will *d's*	*In Mem.* lxxxiv.	39
D not thou a marriage lay ;	" *Con.*	2
sent Her maiden to *d* it	*Enid.*	193
maiden to *d* the name,	"	411

demanded.

d who we were, And why we came ?	*Princess,* iii.	119
then, *d* if her mother knew,	" iv.	214
Was this *d*—if he yearn'd	*In Mem.* xxxi.	3
when the King *d* how she knew,	*Elaine*	574

demanding.

| then to me *d* why ? | *The Epic* | 29 |
| *D,* so to bring relief | *In Mem.* lxxxiv. | 6 |

demigod.

| Where paced the *D's* of old, | *Princess,* iii. | 325 |

democrat.

| what care I, Aristocrat, *d,* | *Maud,* I. x. | 65 |

demon.

| Pallas from the brain Of *D's* ? | *In Mem.* cxiii. | 13 |

demonstration.

| female hands With flawless *d:* | *Princess,* ii. | 351 |

demur.

| wroth and red, with fierce *d:* | *Princess,* v. | 348 |

den.

| lion roaring from his *d* | *D. of F. Wom.* | 222 |
| Trooping from their mouldy *d's* | *Vision of Sin* | 171 |

denial.

| by *d* flush her babbling wells | *Princess,* v. | 324 |

denied.

closer prest, *d* it not,	*Princess,* iv.	273
she affirm'd not, or *d*:	"	215
'you never yet *D* my fancies—	*Elaine*	1105

denouncing.

| like a Ghost's *D* judgment, | *Guinevere* | 418 |

dense.

| decks were *d* with stately forms | *M. d'Arthur* | 196 |
| *d* as those Which hid the Holiest | *Aylmer's F.* | 771 |

deny.

What ! *d* it now ? Nay, draw	*St S. Stylites*	203
For that which all *d* them—.	*Will Water.*	46
hold your own, *d* not hers to her,	*Princess,* vi.	162
father, tender and true, *D* me not,'	*Elaine*	1105
would if ask'd *d* it.	*En. Arden.*	44

denying.

| *D* not these weather-beaten limbs | *St S. Stylites* | 19 |

denyingly!

| How hard you look and how *d* ! | *Vivien* | 187 |

depart.

| craved a fair permission to *d,* | *Enid* | 40 |

departed.

cousin stole Upon us and *d*:	*Ed. Morris*	116
James *d* vext with him and her.'	*The Brook*	110
then *d,* hot in haste to join	*Enid*	1422
watch'd it, and *d* weeping for him;	*En. Arden.*	245

departest.

| before thine answer given *D,* | *Tithonus* | 45 |

departing.

| With frequent smile and nod *d* | *Enid* | 515 |

deplore.

Still mine, that cannot but *d,*	*In Mem.* lxxxiv.	109
lay the man whom we *d* ?	*Ode on Well.*	8
Such was he whom we *d.*	"	40

deploring.

| Matter enough for *d,* | *1865–1866* | 8 |

depress'd.

| lips *d* as he were meek, | *A Character* | 25 |

depth.

springs of life, the *d's* of awe,	*Two Voices*	140
of some divine despair	*Princess,* iv.	22
on the *d's* of death there swims	*In Mem.* cvii.	11

derive.

| *D's* it not from what we have | *In Mem.* liv. | 3 |

descend.

d, and proffer these The brethren	*Princess,* vi.	54
D below the golden hills,	*In Mem.* lxxxiii.	28
D, and touch, and enter ;	" xcii.	13
then my scorn might well *d*	" cxxvii.	21
Would the happy Spirit *d,*	*Maud,* II. iv.	81

descendant.

| On him their last *d,* | *Aylmer's F.* | 834 |

descended.

The country-side *d*;	*Amphion*	52
D to the courts that lay	*Princess,* iii.	4
As we *d* following Hope,	*In Mem.* xxii.	11
in her ancient suit again, And so *d.*	*Enid*	771
Then all *d* to the port,	*En. Arden.*	443

descending.

angels rising and *d* met,	*Pal. of Art*	143
d they were ware That all the decks	*M. d'Arthur*	195
Once she lean'd on me, *D*;	*Princess,* iv.	9
D, burst the great bronze valves,	" vi.	59
day, *D,* struck athwart the hall,	"	344
d met them at the gates,	*Enid*	833
Phantom sound of blows *d,*	*Boädicea*	25

descent.

| Smile at the claims of long *d.* | *L. C. V. de Vere* | 52 |
| might by a true *d* be untrue ; | *Maud,* I. xiii. | 31 |

descried.

| wall Of purple cliffs, aloof *d*: | *Ode to Mem.* | 54 |

descry.

| *d* The stern black-bearded kings | *D. of F. Wom.* | 110 |

desert (merit.)	POEM.	LINE.
To one of less *d* allows,	To the Queen	6
partly conscious of my own *d's*,	Princess, iv.	286
bowing at their own *d's*?	The Brook	128

desert (waste.)		
that long *d* to the south.	Fatima	14
makes a *d* in the mind,	In Mem. lxv.	6

deserve.		
d That we this night should pluck	Princess, iv.	394
might that man not *d* of me,	" v.	101

deserved.		
Since we *d* the name of friends,	In Mem. lxiv.	9

design.		
were wrought Two grand *d's*;	Princess, vii.	107
A miracle of *d*!	Maud, II. ii.	8
d's Of his labour'd rampart-lines	Ode on Well.	104
warn'd me of their fierce *d*	Elaine	274
d wherein they lost themselves,	"	440
vast *d* and purpose of the king.	Guinevere	662

design'd.		
Not less than truth *d*.	Pal. of Art	92
Not less than life, *d*.	"	128

desire (s.)		
Visit my low *d*!	Ode to Mem.	4
many dreams Of high *d*.	The Poet	32
yield consent to my *d*:	Miller's D.	138
skies stoop down in their *d*;	Fatima	32
d is but to pass to Him	May Queen, iii.	20
ceased to be, with my *d* of life.	"	48
came to me that equall'd my *d*.	D. of F. Wom.	230
d's, like fitful blasts of balm	Gardener's D.	67
my *d*, like all strongest hopes	"	232
this gray spirit yearning in *d*	Ulysses	30
Which did accomplish their *d*,	Two Voices	217
Bird that pipes his lone *d* ' You might have won,' etc.		31
lent my knee *d* to kneel,	Princess, iii.	177
fail so far In high *d*,	"	263
every hoof a knell to my *d's*	" iv.	156
thou should'st fail from thy *d*	In Mem. iv.	6
not a moth with vain *d*	" liii.	10
The centre of a world's *d*;	" lxiii.	16
If any vague *d* should rise,	" lxxix.	1
seem to meet their least *d*,	" lxxxii.	17
horn of love, the vague *d*	" cix.	19
Submitting all things to *d*.	" cxiii.	8
D of nearness doubly sweet;	" cxvi.	6
Dear friend, far off, my lost *d*,	" cxxviii.	1
my Delight Had a sudden *d*	Maud, I. xiv.	20
d that awoke in the heart of the	" xix.	48
but the deathbed *d* Spurn'd	"	77
of a people beat with one *d*;	" III. vi.	49
d To close with her lord's pleasure;	Enid	1062
low *d* Not to feel lowest	Vivien	676
flash'd on her a wild *d*,	Elaine	356
you work against your own *d*;	"	1090
courtliness, and the *d* of fame,	Guinevere	478
the smoke The blight of low *d's*	Aylmer's F.	673
thro' their own *d* accomplish'd	"	776
Melt into stars for the land's *d*!	W. to Alexan.	21
welcome her, welcome the land's *d*,	"	25
and throstle, and have your *d*!	The Window	157

desire (verb.)		
He ropen eyes *d* the truth.	'Of old sat Freedom,' etc.	17
And I *d* to rest	'Come not, when,' etc.	10
not of those that men *d*,	Princess, ii.	62
d you more Than growing boys	" iv.	437
woke *D* in me to infuse	" v.	230
Do we indeed *d* the dead	In Mem. l.	1
Not to *d* or admire, if a man	Maud, I. iv.	41
Rich in the grace all women *d*,	" x.	13
save yourself *d* it, We will not	Enid	310
seeing you *d* your child to live,	Elaine	1089
howsoever much they may *d* Silence,	Guinevere	204
man *d* in any way To vary, .	Tithonus	28
She *d's* no isles of the blest,	Wages	8

desired.		
You are not one to be *d*.	L. C. V. de Vere	8
d A certain miracle of symmetry,	Gardener's D.	10

	POEM.	LINE.
d his name, and sent Her maiden.	Enid	192
now *d* the humbling of their best,	"	1485
broke the bond which they *d* to break,	Aylmer's F.	778
Had what they *d*:	The Captain	38

desiring.		
D what is mingled with past years,	D. of F. Wom.	282

desk.		
clerk Brow-beats his *d* below.	To J. M. K.	12
cast and balance at a *d*,	Audley Ct.	43
Erect behind a *d* of satin-wood,	Princess, ii.	90
cramp the student at his *d*,	In Mem. cxxvii.	18

deskwork.		
a dozen years Of dust and *d*:	Sea Dreams	78

desolate.		
Your house is left unto you *d*!	Aylmer's F.	629 et pass.
'My house is left unto me *d*.'	"	721
his one word was '*d*;'.	"	836

desolation.		
her *d* came Upon her,	Enid	1367
Against the *d's* of the world,	Aylmer's F.	634
No *d* but by sword and fire?	"	748

despair.		
Plagued her with sore *d*	Pal. of Art	224
nothing saw, for her *d*,	"	266
lest I wither by *d*,	Locksley H.	98
Whisper'd 'Listen to my *d*:	Ed. Gray	22
shake The midriff of *d* with laughter,	Princess, i.	193
baser courses, children of *d*.'	" iii.	197
from the depth of some divine *d*	" iv.	22
becomes no man to nurse *d*,	"	444
If any calm, a calm *d*:	In Mem. xi.	16
Can calm *d* and wild unrest .	" xvi.	2
D of Hope, and earth of thee.	" lxxxiii.	16
ever wann'd with *d*,	Maud, I. i.	10
yet it lighten'd my *d*	" III. vi.	18
A day of onsets of *d*!	Ode on Well.	124

despaired.		
approach To save the life *d* of,	En. Arden	832

despise.		
my flesh, which I *d* and hate,	St S. Stylites	57
strong sons of the world *d*;	The Brook	3
his pride too much *d's* me:	Enid	464
I myself sometimes *d* myself;	"	465

despite.		
have done *d* and wrong To one	Elaine	1203

despondence.		
Listless in all *d*, —read;	Aylmer's F.	534

despot.		
fire Where smoulder their dead *d's*;	Princess, v.	370

destined.		
opposite Of all my heart had *d*	Guinevere	488

destiny.		
can be more wise than *d*.	D. of F. Wom.	94
heavy hands, The weight of *d*:	Princess, iv.	532

destroy'd.		
not one life shall be *d*,	In Mem. liii.	6
this *d* him; for the wicked broth	Lucretius	19

destructive.		
was as a boy *D*,	Walk. to the M.	74

detaching.		
d, fold by fold, From those still	Vision of Sin	51

detail.		
Another kind of beauty in *d*	Princess, iv.	428

detention.		
for the rest, Our own *d*, why,	Princess, v.	206

determined.		
Thus Enoch in his heart *d* all:	En. Arden	148

detestable.		
might not rank with those *d*	Princess, v.	447

100 CONCORDANCE TO

developed.
	POEM.	LINE.
Beyond all grades d?	Gardener's D.	236

development.
present The world with some d.	Two Voices	75

device.
our d: wrought to the life;	Princess, iii.	286
All the d's blazon'd on the shield	Elaine	9
at least with some d not mine.'	"	194

devil.
A glorious D, large in To——.	With Pal. of Art	5
some brainless d enters in,	Pal. of Art	203
Quoth she, 'The D take the goose,	The Goose	55
Vex'd with a morbid d in his blood	Walk. to the M.	13
his d goes with him,	"	20
scarce meet For troops of d's,	St S. Stylites	4
D's pluck'd my sleeve;	"	168
Comfort? comfort scorned of d's!	Locksley H.	75
and the D may pipe to his own.	Maud, I. i.	76
Envy calls you D's son	Vivien	317-47
stirs the pulse With d's leaps,	Guinevere	518
by his own stale d spurr'd,	Aylmer's F.	290
True D's with no ear,	Sea Dreams	252
in tune With nothing but the D!'	"	253
d in man, there is an angel too,	"	267
A d rises in my heart,	Sailor Boy	24

Devil-born.
You tell me, doubt is D-b.	In Mem. xcv.	4

devised.
Lavaine to write as she d	Elaine	1097
he wrote The letter she d;	"	1103
her lips, Who had d the letter,	"	1280

devising.
moist and dry, d long, 'Love thou thy land,' etc.		38
d their own daughter's death!	Aylmer's F.	783

devoir.
weary of my service and d,	Elaine	119

devolved.
D his rounded periods.	A Character	18

Devon.
A tributary prince of D,	Enid	2
I am Geraint Of D—	"	410
was it for him she wept In D?'	"	1247

devotion.
gaze upon him With such a fixt d,	Vivien	39

dew.
and there rain'd a ghastly d.	Locksley H.	123
crofts and pastures wet with d	Two Voices	14
Dash'd together in blinding d:	Vision of Sin	42
gracious d's Began to glisten	Princess, ii.	295
blossom-fragrant slipt the heavy d's	" v.	233
the d Dwelt in her eyes,	" vii.	120
on these d's that drench the furze	In Mem. xi.	6
all our path was fresh with d,	" lxvii.	6
tulips dash'd with fiery d,	" lxxxii.	11
sweep of scythe in morning d,	" lxxxviii.	18
back we come at fall of d	" Con.	100
The d of their great labour,	Enid	568
than the sward with drops of d,	"	1538

dewed.
d with showery drops,	Lotos-E's.	17

dewdrop.
when two d's on the petal shake	Princess, vii.	53

dew-fed.
in the moon Nightly d-f;	Lotos-E's.	75

dew-impearled.
d-i winds of dawn have kiss'd,	Ode to Mem.	14

dewless.
grass Is dry and d.	Miller's D.	246

dew-lit.
those d-l eyes of thine,	Adeline	47

dewy-dark.
lawn was d-d, And d-d aloft	Œnone	47

dewy-fresh.
	POEM.	LINE.
The fields between Are d-f,	Gardener's D.	45

dewy-glooming.
November dawns and d-g downs,	En. Arden.	611

dewy-tassell'd.
green gleam of d-t trees:	Princess, i.	93
Thro' all the d-t wood,	In Mem. lxxxv.	6

dewy-warm.
eyelids, growing d-w With kisses	Tithonus	58

dexter.
Eagle rising or, the Sun In d chief;	Vivien	326

diagonal.
I moved as in a strange d,	Princess, Con.	27

dial.
this high d, which my sorrow crowns	St S. Stylites	94

diamond.
fillip'd at the d in her ear;	Godiva	25
bracelets of the d bright:	Day-Dm.	90
For the great d in the d jousts	Elaine	31
since a d was the prize,	"	33
king, had on a crown Of d's,	"	47
Lancelot won the d of the year,	"	69
Now for the central d and the last	"	74
my love is more Than many d's,'.	"	89
make complete The tale of d's	"	92
unknown At Camelot for the d,	"	191
some one put this d in her hand,	"	212
And you shall win this d—	"	227
I hear, It is a fair large d,	"	228
'A fair large d,' added plain	"	230
the last d of the nameless king.	"	443
take your prize The d;	"	503
'd me No d's! for God's love,	"	503
take This d, and deliver it,	"	545
he took, And gave, the d:	"	550
with his d, wearied of the quest,	"	613
with you; the d also: here!.	"	688
love or not, A d is a d.	"	692
hand to which he gave, The d,	"	699
gave the d: she will render it;	"	709
with mine own hand give his d	"	756
'Ay, ay, the d: wit you well,	"	767
saying 'Your prize the d	"	817
tale Of King and Prince, the d sent	"	820
laid the d in his open hand.	"	823
The nine-years-fought-for d's:	"	1161
What are these? D's for me!	"	1206
add my d's to her pearls;	"	1218
Was richer than these d's	"	1223
flash'd, as it were, D's to meet them,	"	1230

diamond-drift.
showering wide Sleet of d-d.	Vision of Sin	22

diamond-ledge.
d-l's that jut from the dells;.	The Mermaid	40

diamond-plot.
d-p's Of dark and bright.	Arabian N's.	85

Dian.
set a wrathful D's moon on flame,	Princess, vi.	348

diaper'd.
Engarlanded and d With inwrought	Arabian N's.	148

Dictator.
The mulberry-faced D's orgies	Lucretius	54

die.
The breezes pause and d,	Claribel	2
death shall Falsehood d, 'Clear-headed friend,' etc.		16
dare not d and come to thee,	Oriana	96
D in their hearts for the love of me.	The Mermaid	30
Live forgotten and d forlorn.'	Mariana in the S.	60,72
I d with my delight,	Eleänore	140
My own sweet Alice, we must d	Miller's D.	18
may d the selfsame day.	"	24
I watch'd the little circles d;	"	74
I should d an early death:	"	90
I will possess him or will d.	Fatima	39

	POEM.	LINE.
Grow, live, d looking on his face,	Fatima	41
Dear mother Ida, harken ere I d	Œnone 23 et pass.	
shall be alone until I d .	"	190
shadow all my soul, that I may d	"	238
heavy on my eyelids: let me d.	"	240
I will not d alone .	"	242-53
have found A new land, but I d.'	Pal. of Art	284
save me lest I d?'	"	288
a flower so before the day I d.	May Queen, ii.	20
To d before the snowdrop came	" iii.	4
to Heaven and d among the stars.	"	40
Waiting to see me d.	D. of F. Wom.	112
my arms Contented there to d!	"	152
I would be born and d.	"	204
beautiful a thing it was to d.	"	231
Old year, you must not d	D. of the O. Year 6 et pass.	
half a mind to d with you,	"	26
Old year, if you must d	"	27
To see him d, across the waste	"	30
Shake hands, before you d.	"	42
Speak out before you d.	"	45
see before I d The palms	'You ask me why,' etc.	27
see here, or elsewhere, till I d,	M. d'Arthur	154
wound hath taken cold, and I shall d.'	"	166
fear it is too late, and I shall d.'	"	180
'Arthur is come again: he cannot d.'	" Ep.	24
grandchild on my knees before I d:	Dora	11
all thy martyrs d one death?	St S. Stylites	49
I d here, To-day, and whole years	"	52
strive and wrestle with thee till I d:	"	117
I prophesy that I shall d to-night,	"	217
Of all the western stars, until I d.	Ulysses	61
'But I would d,' said she.	Godiva	23
I wept, 'Tho' I should d, I know	Two Voices	58
once from dread of pain to d.	"	105
To flatter me that I may d!	"	204
Not simple as a thing that d's.	"	288
When will the hundred summers d,	Day-Dm.	69
The thick-set hazel d's;	Will Water.	234
now the Poet cannot d 'You might have won,' etc.		13
d's unheard within his tree,	"	32
Tho' I should d to-night.'	Lady Clare	48
Every moment d's a man,	Vision of Sin	97
Yet we will not d forlorn.'	"	206
gossip and spite And slander d.	Princess, ii.	79
'Let me d too,' said Cyril	" iii.	193
speak, and let the topic d.'	" iii.	189
like them well: but children d:	"	236
great deeds cannot d;	"	237
O love, they d in you rich sky	" iv.	360
follow up the worthiest till he d:	"	446
protomartyr of our cause, D:	"	485
lisping of the innumerous leaf and d's,	" v.	13
either she will d from want of care,	"	82
the question settled d.'	"	307
'She must weep or she will d.'	"	535
girls flit, Till the storm d I	" vi.	318
my friend, I will not have you d I	"	371
she believed that I should d;	" vii.	85
be perfect. I shall d to-night.	"	134
seem to kiss me ere I d.'	"	135
thinks he was not made to d;	In Mem. Pro.	11
all the magic light D's off	" viii.	6
dying, there at least may d.	"	24
life, that almost d's in me;	" xviii.	17
d's not, but endures with pain,	" xxix.	16
Before their time? they too will d.	" xxx.	22
do not d Nor lose their mortal	" xxxi.	7
telling what it is to d	" xxxiv.	5
use A little patience ere I d;	" xxxv.	4
Man d's: nor is there hope in dust:'	" xxxviii.	3
Half-dead to know that I shall d.'	" xlix.	9
purple from the distance d's .	" lvi.	9
weave their petty cells and d.	" lxi.	16
in these ears, till hearing d's,	" lxv.	15
His other passion wholly d's,	" lxvi.	10
His inner day can never d,	" lxxvii.	17
off my bed the moonlight d's;	" lxxxiv.	40
O last regret, regret can d!',	" xcvi.	12
By which we dare to live or d.		
Their every parting was to d.		

	POEM.	LINE.
I think once more he seems to d.	In Mem. xcix	20
Ring out, wild bells, and let him d.	" cv.	4
let the ape and tiger d.	" cxvii.	28
ready, thou, to d with him,	" cxx.	2
heavenly friend that canst not d,	" cxxviii.	7
I shall not lose thee tho' I d.	" cxxix.	16
Cheat and be cheated, and d:	Maud, I. i.	32
dash myself down and d	" v.	54
and of Honour that cannot d,	" v.	16
I must tell her, or d .	" xvi.	34
do accept my madness, and would d	" xviii.	44-6
Not d; but live a life of	"	53
so did I let my freshness d.	" xix.	11
To faint in his light, and to d.	" xxii.	12
my ears, till I d, till I d.	" II. i.	35
comfort her tho' I d.	" ii.	83
When thou shalt more than d.	" iii.	9
for yourself, and howl, and d.	" v.	56
And the shining daffodil d's,	" III. vi.	6
hysterical mock-disease should d.'	"	33
not to d a listener, I arose,	The Brook	163
'Their's but to do and d;	Lt. Brigade	15
shalt thou do, or thou shalt d.'	Enid	586
cast it on the mixen that it d.'	"	672
liever by his dear hand had I d,	"	917
if he d, why earth has earth enough	"	1403
not look at wine until I d.'	"	1515
if I draw it, you will d.'	Elaine	512
'I d already with it: draw—	"	513
in daily doubt Whether to live or d,	"	520
And ridd'n away to d?'	"	567
'Being so very wilful you must d.'	"	770
not love me: how then? must I d.'	"	889
half the night repeating, 'must I d?'	"	895
d for want of one bold word.'	"	923
I love you: let me d.'	"	926
if death be sweeter, let me d.	"	1006
I follow, I follow ! let me d,'	"	1012
she shrilling, 'Let me d!'	"	1020
I should but d the sooner;	"	1092
let me shrive me clean, and d,'	"	1094
letter in my hand A little ere I d,	"	1108
do hold our Arthur cannot d,	"	1251
knowing he should d a holy man.	"	1419
help it from the death that cannot d,	Guinevere	66
vast pity almost makes me d	"	530
let me hold my purpose till I d.	En. Arden	272
the living scandal that shall d—	Aylmer's F.	444
wounded to the death that cannot d;	"	662
what heart had he To d of?.	Sea Dreams	266
after many a summer d's the swan	Tithonus	4
happy men that have the power to d,	"	70
fairer she, but ah how soon to d !	Requiescat	5
tears that Love can d.	Coquette, iii.	8
wages of going on, and not to d.	Wages	10
soul flies out and d's in the air.'	Lucretius	279
I may d but the grass will grow.	The Window	109

died.

D round the bulbul he sung;	Arabian N's.	70
Singing in her song she d,	L. of Shalott, iv.	35
D the sound of royal cheer,	"	48
She d: she went to burning flame:	The Sisters	7
to Him that d for me.	May Queen, iii.	20
The dim red morn had d,	D. of F. Wom.	61
Many drew swords and d.	"	95
for such a face had boldly d,'	"	98
there to die ! And there he d:	"	153
I d a Queen. The Roman soldier	"	161
d To save her father's vow ;	"	195
the Egyptian: 'O, you tamely d !'	"	258
on the mere the wailing d away.	M. d'Arthur	272
into light, and d into the shade ;	Gardener's D.	198
hard words, and parted, and he d	Dora	16
and in harvest time he d.	"	53
when William d, he d at peace	"	141
like endless welcome, lived and d.	Love and Duty	66
face, that two hours since hath d;	Two Voices	242
twilight d into the dark.	Day-Dm.	188
stow'd (when classic Canning d)	Will Water.	101
old Earl's daughter d at my breast;	Lady Clare	25

	POEM.	LINE.
Then before her time she *d*,	*L. of Burleigh*	88
music touch'd the gates and *d*;	*Vision of Sin*	23
'When the years have *d* away.'	*Poet's Song*	16
laid about them at their wills and *d*;	*Princess, Pro.*	31
teaching him that *d* Of hemlock ;	" iii.	285
rock the snowy cradle till I *d*.	" iv.	86
Better have *d* and spilt our bones	"	511
My dream had never *d*.	" vi.	1
Ida has a heart'—just ere she *d*—	"	218
d Of fright in far apartments.	"	350
holy Death ere Arthur *d*	*In Mem.* lxxix.	2
He that *d* in Holy Land	" lxxxiii.	42
'The dawn, the dawn,' and *d* away ;	" xciv.	61
So many a summer since she *d*,	*Maud*, I. vi.	66
old grand-father has lately *d*,	" x.	5
past in bridal white, And *d* to live,	" xviii.	66
he *d* at Florence, quite worn out,	*The Brook*	35
but, overtaken, *d* the death	*Enid*	1026
So *d* Earl Doorm by him he	"	1578
and the spiteful whisper *d*:	"	1806
it lived with her : she *d*;	*Vivien*	566
his anger slowly *d* Within him,	"	740
better have *d* Thrice than have ask'd	"	767
the living smile *d* from his lips,	*Elaine*	323
d the death In any knightly fashion	"	866
the little bed on which I *d*	"	1111
closed the hand upon it, and she *d*.	"	1129
dreamt the damsel would have *d*	"	1297
this she would not, and she *d*.'	"	1315
and he *d* Kill'd in a tilt,	*Guinevere*	318
till in time their Abbess *d*.	"	684
that mysterious instinct wholly *d*.	*En. Arden*.	522
Surely the man had *d* of solitude.	"	622
that I *d* Blessing her,	"	879
my son that I *d* blessing him.	"	886
That dimpling *d* into each other,	*Aylmer's F.*	149
scandals that have lived and *d*,	"	443
her dear Lord who *d* for all,	*Sea Dreams*	47
thought I could have *d* to save it)	"	130
musical note Swell'd up and *d*;	"	204
he *d*, and I could not weep—	*Grandmother*	72
that I, too, then could have *d*:	"	73
when the zoning eve has *d*	*On a Mourner*	21
So think they of the people cried	*The Victim*	5
cattle *d*, and deer in wood,	"	18
first embrace had *d* Between them	*Lucretius*	3

diest.

shalt thou do or else thou *d*.	*Enid*	580

differ.

Or do my peptics *d*?	*Will Water.*	80
at most *d* as Heaven and Earth,	*Vivien*	663

difference.

Might I not tell Of *d*,	*Gardener's D.*	252
thy peculiar *d* Is cancell'd	*Two Voices*	41
They have as many *d*'s as we.	*Princess,* v.	173
cleave the rift of *d* deeper yet ;	"	291
Not like to like, but like in *d*.	" vii.	262
Ay me, the *d* I discern!	*In Mem.* xxxix.	21
girl and boy, Sir, know their *d*'s!'	*Aylmer's F.*	274
when some heat of *d* sparkled out,	"	705

difficulty.

With *d* in mild obedience	*Enid*	953
in days of *d* And pressure,	*En. Arden*.	253

diffused.

D the shock thro' all my life,	*In Mem.* lxxxiv.	55
Thy God is far *d* in noble groves	*Aylmer's F.*	653

diffusing.

A central warmth *d* bliss	*In Mem.* lxxxiii.	6

dig.

builds the house, or *d*'s the grave,	*In Mem.* xxxvi.	14
d, pick, open, find and read	*Vivien*	510

dilate.

That now *d* and now decrease,	*In Mem.* xxviii.	10
joyous to *d*, as toward the light.	*Aylmer's F.*	77

dilating.

wind of prophecy *D* on the future ;	*Princess,* ii.	155

dilation.

	POEM.	LINE.
her eye with slow *d* roll'd	*Princess,* vi.	172

dilettante.

snowy-banded, *d*, Delicate-handed	*Maud,* I. viii.	10

dim (adj.)

'heart is breaking, and my eyes are *d*,	*Œnone*	31
d with gazing on the pilot-stars.	*Lotos-E's.*	132
Till all the paths were *d*,	*Talking O.*	298
eyes are *d* with glorious tears,	*Two Voices.*	151
sung, tho' every eye was *d*,	*In Mem.* xxx.	14
Is *d*, or will be *d*, with weeds :	" lxxii.	10
I remain'd, whose hopes were *d*,	" lxxxiv.	29
all things ever *d* And dimmer,	" cxx.	3
Myself would work eye *d*,	*Enid*.	628
hall was *d* with steam of flesh :	"	1451
eye was *d*, hand tremulous ;	*En. Arden.*	241
He saw not far : his eyes were *d*:	*The Voyage*	75

dim (verb.)

in hues to *d* The Titianic Flora.	*Gardener's D.*	166

dim-gray.

Now and then in the *d-g* dawn ;	*Maud,* I. xiv.	32

diminutive.

babyisms, and dear *d*'s,	*Aylmer's F.*	539

dim-lit.

while he past the *d-l* woods,	*Guinevere*	249

dimm'd.

thro' the cloud that *d* her broke	*Princess,* vi.	264
trust in things above Be *d* of sorrow,	*In Mem.* lxxxiv.	10
the sorrow *d* her sight,	*Elaine*	885

dimmer.

all things ever dim And *d*,	*In Mem.* cxx.	4

dimple.

the lightning laughters *d*	*Lilian*	16
d in the dark of rushy coves,	*Ode to Mem.*	60
d's your transparent cheek,	*Margaret*	15

dimpled.

laughter *d* in his swarthy cheek ;	*Ed. Morris*	61

dimpling.

knolls That *d* died into each other,	*Aylmer's F.*	149

dim-yellow.

fair head in the *d-y* light,	*Enid*	600

din.

groves within The wild-bird's *d*.	*Poet's Mind*	21
The dust and *d* and steam of town :	*In Mem.* lxxxviii.	8
when the heart is full of *d*,	" xciii.	13

dine.

have no scandal while you *d*,	*To F. D. Maurice*	17
shall we fast, or *d*?	*Enid*	1339

dinner.

steam Of thirty thousand *d*'s.	*Will Water.*	224
the bell For *d*, let us go!'	*Princess,* ii.	411
A grand political *d*	*Maud,* I. xx. 25,	31
A *d*, and then a dance	"	34

dinnerless.

when I left your mowers *d*.	*Enid*	1083
lusty mowers labouring *d*	"	1100

dint.

Sharp-smitten with the *d* of armed	*M. d'Arthur*	190
every *d* a sword had beaten in it,	*Elaine*	19

dinted.

crush'd and *d* into the ground,	*Maud,* I. i.	7

Diotima.

beneath an emerald plane Sits *D*,	*Princess,* iii.	285

dip (s.)

The *d* of certain strata to the North.	*Princess,* iii.	154
the last *d* of the vanishing sail	*En. Arden*	244

dip (verb.)

prime swallow *d*'s his wing,	*Ed. Morris*	145
should not *d* His hand into the bag	*Golden Year*	70
d's Her laurel in the wine,	*Will Water.*	17

	POEM.	LINE.
D forward under starry light, 'Move eastward,' etc.		10
d Their wings in tears, and skim away.	In Mem. xlvii.	15
D down upon the northern shore,	" lxxxii.	1

dipt.

D down to sea and sands.	Pal. of Art	32
ere he d the surface, rose an arm	M. d'Arthur	143
d And mix'd with shadows	Gardener's D.	133
ever and anon D by itself	Audley Ct.	87
d and rose, And turn'd to look at her.	Talking O.	131
When I d into the future	Locksley H.	15, 119
d in all That treats of whatsoever	Princess, ii.	357
d Beneath the satin dome	" iv.	12
dearer being, all d In Angel instincts	" vii.	301
sleep till dusk is d in gray :	In Mem. lxvi.	12
d in baths of hissing tears,	" cxvii.	23
until they d below the downs.	Elaine	395
d Against the rush of the air	Aylmer's F.	85

direct.

Now over and now under, now d,	Lucretius	62

dirt.

these, tho' fed with careful d,	Amphion	89

disappear.

black earth yawns: the mortal d's	Ode on Well.	269

disappear'd.

up the rocky pathway d,	Enid	1092

disarmed.

The proud was half d of pride,	In Mem. cix.	6
let him into lodging and d.	Elaine	171

disarrayed.

found, Half d as to her rest,	Enid	516

disband.

bidding him D himself, and scatter	Enid	1646

discern.

d The roofs of Sumner-place! (rep.)	Talking O.	31
Till a gateway she d's	L. of Burleigh	42
Ay me, the difference I d!	In Mem. xxxix.	21
I wake, and I d the truth	" lxvii.	14

discerned.

into my inmost ring A pleasure I d,	Talking O.	174

discerning.

d to fulfil This labour,	Ulysses	36

disclaimed.

each D all knowledge of us:	Princess, iv.	210

disclosed.

D a fruit of pure Hesperian gold.	Œnone	65

discomfort.

this d he hath done the house.'	Elaine	1066

disconsolate.

the Robin piped D,	En. Arden.	678

discontent.

She look'd with d.	Talking O.	116
lent The pulse of hope to d.	Two Voices	450
muttering d Cursed me and my flower.	The Flower	7

discord.

soul Of D race the rising wind.	{ 'Love thou thy land,' etc.	68
A monster then, a dream A d.	In Mem. lv.	22
like The d's dear to the musician	Sea Dreams	250

discouraged.

I grew d, Sir; but since I knew	Princess, iii.	137

discourse.

In such d we gain'd the garden rails,	Princess, Con.	80

discourtesy.

I pray you, use some rough d	Elaine	968
the one d that he used.	"	982
some d Against my nature:	"	1294

discover'd.

All precious things, d late,	Day-Dm.	101

discovery.

the d And newness of thine art	Ode to Mem.	87

	POEM.	LINE.
discredit.		
heaven, how much I shall d him!	Enid	621
Far liefer than so much d him.	"	629

discuss.

We might d the Northern sin	To F. D. Maurice	29

discuss'd.

d the farm, The fourfield system,	Audley Ct.	32
D his tutor, rough to common men,	Princess, Pro.	114
D a doubt and tost it to and fro:	" ii.	422
D the books to love or hate,	In Mem. lxxxviii.	34

discussing.

D how their courtship grew,	In Mem. Con.	97

discussion.

That from D's lip may fall 'Love thou thy land,' etc.		33

disdain.

my d is my reply.	L. C. V. de Vere	22
with some d Answer'd the Princess	Princess, iv.	43
surprise and thrice as much d Turn'd	Enid	557
not with half d Hid under grace,	Elaine	263

disdained.

Tolerant of what he half d	Vivien	34
Perceiving that she was but half d,	"	35

disease.

sickening of a vague d,	L. C. V. de Vere	62
Ring out old shapes of foul d;	In Mem. cv.	25
A d, a hard mechanic ghost.	Maud, II. ii.	34
like a new d, unknown to men,	Guinevere	514
wretched age—and worst d of all,	Lucretius	155

diseased.

thought my heart too far d;	In Mem. lxv.	1
ours he swore were all d.	The Voyage	76
The land is sick, the people d,	The Victim	47

disedge.

served a little to d The sharpness.	Enid	1038

disembarked.

touching Breton sands, they d	Vivien	51

disgrace.

hidden from the heart's d,	Locksley H.	57
Alone might hint of my d;	Two Voices	360
Heap'd on her terms of d,	Maud, II. i.	14
why, the greater their d!	Aylmer's F.	384

disguise.

common light of smiles at our d	Princess, v.	261

disgust.

Sir Lancelot leant, in half d At love	Elaine	1231

dish.

thrust the d before her, crying,	Enid	1503
harpies miring every d	Lucretius	159

dishelmed.

saw me lying stark, D and mute,	Princess, vi.	85

dishonour.

Doing d to my clay.'	Two Voices	102
Becomes d to her race—	"	255
honour rooted in d stood,	Elaine	872

dishonourable.

Ungenerous, d, base,	Aylmer's F.	292

dishorsed.

each, d and drawing, lash'd at each	Enid	563

disjoint.

Nor wielded axe d,	Talking O.	262

disk.

studded wide With d's and tiars,	Arabian N's.	64
with flames her d of seed,	In Mem. c.	6

dislinked.

D with shrieks and laughter:	Princess, Pro.	70
she d herself at once and rose,	Vivien	738

dislodging.

D pinnacle and parapet	D. of F. Wom.	26

dismay'd.

Was there a man d?	Lt. Brigade	10

dismember.
May never saw *d* thee, . . *Talking O.* 261

dismiss.
D me, and I prophesy your plan . *Princess,* iv. 335
Your oath is broken : we *d* you : . " . 341

dismissal.
spoke, and bowing waved *D:* . *Princess,* ii. 85

dismissed.
d in shame to live No wiser . . *Princess,* iv. 492

dismounting.
d like a man That skins . . *Enid* . 941
d, pick'd the lance That pleased him, " . 1028
d on the sward They let the horses " . 1059
at his side all pale *D,* loosed . " . 1360

disobey.
Deep harm to *d,* . . . *M. d'Arthur* 93
needs must *d* him for his good ; . *Enid* . 984
not to *d* her lord's behest, . . " . 1299

disorderly.
D the women. Alone I stood . *Princess,* iv. 152
from the high door streaming, brake *D, Elaine* 1338

disparagement.
with some prelude of *d,* . . *The Epic* . 49
Flush'd slightly at the slight *d* . *Elaine* . 234
silent smiles of slow *d;* . . *Guinevere* . 15

dispassionate.
Quiet, *d,* and cold, . . *A Character* 28

dispatch.
Delivering sealed *d's* which the . *Princess,* iv. 360

dispell'd.
I loved, and love *d* the fear . . *Miller's D.* 89

dispenser.
drowsy hours, *d's* of all good, . *Gardener's D.* 181

dispensing.
D harvest, sowing the To-be, . *Princess,* vii. 273

dispersed.
D his resolution like a cloud. . *Elaine* . 880
a plunge To the bottom, and *d* . *En. Arden* . 377

displaced.
this false traitor have *d* his lord . *Guinevere* . 214

display'd.
D a splendid silk of foreign loom, *Enid* . 1535

dispraise.
hissing *d* Because their natures are *Maud,* I. iv. 52
In praise and in *d* the same, . . *Ode on Well.* 73

disprinced.
one rag, *d* from head to heel. . *Princess,* v. 29

disproof.
To make *d* of scorn, . . . *Aylmer's F.* 446

dispute (s.)
breed *D* betwixt myself and mine ; *Princess,* i. 156
she took no part In our *d:* . " *Con.* 30
deep *d,* and graceful jest ; . *In Mem. lxxxiii.* 24

dispute (verb.)
D the claims, arrange the . *To F. D. Maurice* 31

disquiet.
long *d* merged in rest. . . *Two Voices* 249

disrobed.
If gazing on divinity *d* . . *Œnone* . 154
D the glimmering statue . . *Princess, Con.* 117

disrooted.
Whate'er I was *D,* what I am . *Princess,* ii. 202

disruption.
To make *d* in the Table Round . *Guinevere* . 18

dissecting.
wayward modern mind *D* passion. *Ed. Morris* 88

dissipated.
For fear our solid aim be *d* . . *Princess,* iii. 249

dissoluble.
Gods Being atomic not be *d,* . *Lucretius* . 113

dissolution.
nerves to rush Upon their *d,* . *Love and Duty* 76

dissolve.
d the precious seal on a bond, . *Maud,* I. xix. 45

dissolved.
d the mystery Of folded sleep . *D. of F. Wom.* 262
now the whole ROUND TABLE is *d M. d'Arthur* 234
D the riddle of the earth. . . *Two Voices* 170
thereat the crowd Muttering, *d:* . *Princess,* iv. 502

dissolvingly.
to all my frame *D* and slowly : . *Eleänore* . 132

distance.
stands in the *d* yonder : . . *Poet's Mind* 30
blue peaks in the *d* rose, . . *Dying Swan* 11
such a *d* from his youth in grief, . *Gardener's D.* 53
in the *d* overlooks the sandy . *Locksley H.* 5
a song from out the *d* . . " . 84
Not in vain the *d* beacons. . . " . 181
shows At *d* like a little wood . *Day-Dm.* . 62
A trumpet in the *d* pealing news . *Princess,* iv. 63
other *d* and the hues Of promise ; " . 68
but Blanche At *d* follow'd : . " vi. 67
Rose from the *d* on her memory, . " . 96
made No purple in the *d,* . . " . 179
see the sails at *d* rise, . . *In Mem.* xii. 11
The purple from the *d* dies, . . " xxxviii. 3
O, from the *d* of the abyss . . " xcii. 11
The *d* takes a lovelier hue, . . " cxiv. 6
out of *d* might ensue . . . " cxvi. 5
like a clamour of the rooks At *d* . *Enid* . 250
thunder of the huger fall At *d* . " . 1023

distant.
in her throat Her voice seem'd *d* . *To J. S.* . 55
from the field, More and more *d* . *Dora* . . 103

distill'd.
D from some worm-canker'd homily *To J. M. K.* 6

distilling.
D odours on me as they went . *Gardener's D.* 183

distinct.
D with vivid stars inlaid, . . *Arabian N's.* 90
D in individualities . . . *Princess,* vii. 275

distress.
flow Of subtle-paced counsel in *d* . *Isabel* . . 21
Small thought was there of life's *d* ; *Ode to Mem.* 37
utterly consumed with sharp *d,* . *Lotos-E's.* . 58
then *d'es* came on him ; . . *Dora* . . 47
Who show'd a token of *d* ? . *In Mem.* lxxvii. 13
No limit to his *d* ; . . . *Maud,* II. v. 31

distribute.
Walk your dim cloister, and *d* dole *Guinevere* . 675

disturb.
Woman, *d* me not now at the last, *En. Arden* . 875

disturbed.
D me with the doubt 'if this were *Princess,* iv. 198

disyoke.
D their necks from custom, . . *Princess,* ii. 127

dive.
they shall *d,* and they shall run, . *Locksley H.* 169
d below the wells of Death ?. . *In Mem.* cvii. 8
d's In yonder greening gleam, . " cxiv. 13

dived.
I *D* in a hoard of tales . . *Princess, Pro.* 29

diverse.
not undeveloped man, But *d* : . *Princess,* vii. 260

divide.
d the night with flying flame, . *D. of F. Wom.* 225
these two parties still *d* the world—*Walk. to the Jl.* 69
Eternal form shall still *d* . . *In Mem.* xlvi. 6
D us not, be with me now, . . " cxxi. 10
of a mother *d* the shuddering night *Maud,* I. i. . 16
She seem'd to *d* in a dream . . " III. vi. 10

	POEM.	LINE.
D's threefold to show the fruit	The Brook	73, 208
scarce d it from her foolish dream :	Enid	686

divided.

d quite The kingdom of her thought.	Pal. of Art	227
D in a graceful quiet	Gardener's D.	153
Of shingle, and a walk d it	En. Arden	738

dividing.

d the swift mind In act to throw	M. d'Arthur	60
the crowd d clove An advent	Princess, iv.	264

Divil.

blessed feälds wi' the D's oän teäm.	N. Farmer.	62

divine (adj.)

Scarce of earth nor all d,	Adeline	3
You are not less d,	Margaret	46
That my youth was half d,	Vision of Sin	78
Thou seemest human and d.	In Mem. Pro.	13
known and unknown : human, d;	" cxxviii.	5
the Teacher whom he held d.	Lucretius	13

divine (verb.)

A deeper tale my heart d's.	Two Voices	269
Nor the meaning can d,	L. of Burleigh	54
She is not of us, as I d.	Maud, II. v.	69

divinely.

D thro' all hindrance finds the man	Elaine	332

divinity.

Saw no d in grass.	A Character	8
If gazing on d disrobed	Œnone	154
lift the woman's fall'n d.	Princess, iii.	207

division.

in d of the records of the mind ?	Locksley H.	69
'betwixt these two D smoulders	Princess, iii.	62

divorce.

D the Feeling from her mate the.	The Brook	95

divorced.

your plan, D from my experience,	Princess, iv.	336

doat.

sisters That d upon each	To ——. With Pal. of Art	11
heart that d's on truer charms	L. C. V. de Vere	14

dock'd.

For which his gains were d,	Sea Dreams	7

doctor.

lilted out By violet-hooded D's,	Princess, ii.	354
then the D's ! O to hear The D s !	"	399
leg for a babe of a week !' says d;	Grandmother	11
whoy, D's abeän an' agoïn ;	N. Farmer.	2
Il's, they knaws nowt,	"	5
D's a 'tottler, lass,	"	66
I weänt break rules for D,	"	67

doctrine.

if we held the d sound	In Mem. lii.	9

dodged.

d me with a long and loose account.	Sea Dreams	145

doe.

Lord Ronald brought a lily-white d,	Lady Clare	3
lily-white d Lord Ronald had brought	"	61
follow'd up by a hundred airy d's	Princess, vi.	71

doff'd.

Until the grave churchwarden d	The Goose	19
his lance aside, And d his helm 1	Enid	1441

dog.

did not hear the d howl, mother,	May Queen, iii.	21
tho' d's of Faction bay, 'Love thou thy land,' etc.		85
like dove and dove were cat and d.	Walk. to the M.	50
Something better than his d,	Locksley H.	50
Like a d, he hunts in dreams,	"	79
stro le About the hall, among his d's	Godiva	31
with great strides among his d's.	"	31
barking d's, and crowing cocks,	Day-Dm.	136
he had breath'd the Proctor's d's ;	Princess, Pro.	113
swine were sows, and all the d's	" i.	191
p oughs, his cows, his hogs, his d's	The Brook	125

	POEM.	LINE.
advanced, Each growling like a d	Enid	1407
lash you from them like a d;	Aylmer's F.	325
d With inward yelp, and restless	Lucretius	44

doing.

See here, my d :	Ed. Morris.	5
their own d; this is none of mine	St S. Stylites	121
With all its d's had and had not	Princess, iv.	544

dole (lamentation.)

that day there was d in Astolat	Elaine	1130

dole (pittance.)

distribute d To poor sick people	Guinevere	675

dole (verb.)

I mete and d Unequal laws.	Ulysses	3

dome.

beneath the d Of hollow boughs.	Arabian N's.	41
Upon the mooned d's aloof	"	127
dipt Beneath the satin d	Princess, iv.	13
Arno, and the d Of Brunelleschi ;	The Brook	189
Thro' the d of the golden cross ;	Ode on Well.	61

domestic.

Many a gallant gay d	L. of Burleigh	47

dominion.

D in the head and breast.'	Two Voices	21
Think I may hold d sweet	Maud, I. xvi.	12

doom (s.)

Hard is my d and thine :	Love and Duty	53
miss'd the irreverent d 'You might have won,' etc.	"	9
lies and dreads his d.	Princess, vii.	139
souls, the lesser lords of d.	In Mem. cxi.	8
batter'd with the shocks of d.	" cxvii.	24
While I rose up against my d,	" cxxi.	2
I was cursing them and my d,	Maud, I. xix.	51
purpose of God, and the d assign'd.	" III. vi.	59
Bellowing victory, bellowing d :	Ode on Well.	66
own false d, That shadow of mistrust	Enid	1096
with that love which was her d.	Elaine	260
into sanctuary, And bide my d.'	Guinevere	121
that he scape the d of fire,	"	345
weep for her, who drew him to his d.'	"	346
that I march to meet my d.	"	447
d of treason and the flaming death,	"	534
that my d is, I love thee still.	"	555
I know not what mysterious d.	"	571
moving ghostlike to his d.	"	599
in their eyes and faces reads his d;	En. Arden.	73
lonely d Came suddenly to an end.	"	627
like the blast of d, Would shatter	"	770
voice that calls D upon kings,	Aylmer's F.	742
Announced the coming d,	Sea Dreams	22
Boanerges with his threats of d,	"	243
thunder Roaring out their d;	The Captain	42
struck the dateless d of kings,	Lucretius	233

doom (verb.)

O Ringlet, I d you to the flame.	The Ringlet	50

doomed.

D them to the lash.	The Captain	12

doomsday.

as grand as d and as grave : .	Princess, i.	185

Doon (see Bonny Doon.)

door.

d's upon their hinges creak'd	Mariana	62
faces glimmer'd thro' the d's,	"	66
costly d's flung open wide.	Arabian N's.	17
Right to the carven cedarn d's	"	115
stand beside my father's d,	Ode to Mem.	57
Leaving d and windows wide :	Deserted H.	3
no murmur at the d,	"	9
Close the d, the shutters close,	Mariana in the S.	65, 74
image seem'd to pass the d,	Miller's D.	103
The very air about the d	"	158
near this d you sat apart,	L. C. V. de Vere	43
guilt of blood is at your d :	May Queen, ii.	42
from the threshold of the d ;	D. of F. Wom.	190
thro' the d Hearing the holy organ		

	POEM.	LINE.
alone, And waiteth at the *d* .	*D. of the O. Year*	51
a new face at the *d* (rep.)	"	53
thro' mine own *d*'s Death did pass ;	*To J. S.*	19
There strode a stranger to the *d*,	*The Goose*	3, 39
d's, that bar The secret bridal	*Gardener's D.*	243
never more darken my *d*'s again.'	*Dora*	30
The *d* was off the latch : they peep'd	"	127
whined in lobbies, tapt at *d*'s,	*Walk. to the M.*	29
I say, that time is at the *d*'s	*St S. Stylites*	189
same grand year is ever at the *d*'s.	*Golden Year*	73
Every *d* is barr'd with gold,	*Locksley H.*	100
all Should keep within, *d* shut,	*Godiva*	41
feet that ran, and *d*'s that clapt,	*Day-Dm.*	135
lifts me to the golden *d*'s ;	*St Agnes' Eve*	25
stalls are void, the *d*'s are wide,	*Sir Galahad*	31
One fix'd for ever at the *d*,	*Will Water.*	143
Bows before him at the *d*.	*L. of Burleigh*	48
that same fair creature at the *d*.	*Princess,* ii.	308
Psyche's child to cast it from the *d*'s ;	" iv.	219
came a little stir About the *d*'s,	"	355
I will go and sit beside the *d*'s,	" v.	93
He batter'd at the *d*'s ; none came ;	"	327
glance he caught Thro' open *d*'s of Ida	"	333
'Fling our *d*'s wide ! all, all,	" vi.	314
bare Straight to the *d*'s : to them the *d*'s	"	329
long-laid galleries past a hundred *d*'s	"	354
roll the torrent out of dusky *d*'s : .	" vii.	193
D's, where my heart was (rep. cxviii. 1)	*In Mem.* vii.	3
creep At earliest morning to the *d*	"	8
as if a *d* Were shut between me and	" xxviii.	7
enter in at lowly *d*'s.	" xxxvi.	8
They chatter'd trifles at the *d* :	" lxviii.	4
crowd that stream from yawning *d*'s,	" lxix.	9
Another name was on the *d* :	" lxxxvi.	17
out the *d*'s where I was bred,	" cii.	2
Thou listenest to the closing *d*,	" cxx.	7
touch with shade the bridal *d*'s,	*Con.*	117
Look, a horse at the *d*,	*Maud,* I. xii.	29
even then I heard her close the *d*,	" xviii.	11
Did he stand at the diamond *d*	" II. ii.	16
when they follow'd us from Philip's *d*,	*The Brook*	167
Thro' open *d*'s and hospitality :	*Enid*	. 456
Glanced at the *d*'s or gambol'd down	"	665
d, Push'd from without, drave	"	1121
heard the wild Earl at the *d*,	"	1230
found a *d* And darkling felt .	*Vivien*	. 583
entering barr'd her *d*,	*Elaine*	15
guide me to that palace, to the *d*'s.'	"	1123
two stood arm'd, and kept the *d* ;	"	1240
pointed to the damsel, and the *d*'s.	"	1256
people, from the high *d* streaming,	"	1337
some doubtful noise of creaking *d*'s,	*Guinevere*	. 72
rode an armed warrior to the *d*'s.	"	406
long gallery from the outer *d*'s	"	410
waiting by the *d*'s the warhorse neigh'd	"	526
lo, he sat on horseback at the *d* !	"	583
Paus'd for a moment at an inner *d*,	*En. Arden*	277
there At Annie's *d* he paus'd	"	444
A lily-avenue climbing to the *d*'s ;	*Aylmer's F.*	162
Withdrawing by the counter *d*	"	282
Should I find you by my *d*'s again	"	324
heard the ponderous *d* Close,	"	337
the noise about their *d*'s,	"	488
oaken finials till he touch'd the *d*.	"	823
Often they come to the *d*	*Grandmother*	82
jam the *d*'s, and bear The keepers	*Lucretius*	169

Doorm.

D, whom his shaking vassals call'd,	*Enid*	. 1288
may meet the horsemen of Earl *D*,	"	. 1341
took him for a victim of Earl *D*,	"	. 1373
flying from the wrath of *D*	"	. 1379
at the point of noon the huge Earl *D*,	"	. 1385
bore him to the naked hall of *D*,	"	. 1418
The huge Earl *D* with plunder .	"	. 1440
Earl *D* Struck with a knife's haft	"	. 1447
when Earl *D* had eaten all he would,	"	. 1457
died Earl *D* by him he counted dead.	"	. 1578
took you for a bandit knight of *D* ;	"	. 1634
mouthpiece of our King to *D*	"	. 1644
lo the powers of *D* Are scatter'd'.	"	. 1649

doorway.

	POEM.	LINE.
God shut the *d*'s of his head.	*In Mem.* xliii.	4
Dawn'd sometime thro' the *d* ?	*Aylmer's F.*	685

Dora.

at the farm abode William and *D Dora*	.	. 2
D felt her uncle's will in all .	"	. 5
Thought not of *D* .	"	. 8
Now therefore look to *D*	"	. 13
for his sake I bred His daughter *D*:	"	. 18
'I cannot marry *D*; (rep.)	"	. 21
ways were harsh ; But *D* bore them	"	. 34
D promised, being meek,	"	. 44
D stored what little she could save,	"	. 50
Then *D* went to Mary.	"	. 54, 108
Hard things of *D. D* came	"	. 56
D took the child, and went .	"	. 69
Dare tell him *D* waited	"	. 74
D would have risen and gone to him	"	. 75
D cast her eyes upon the ground .	"	. 87
wreath of flowers fell At *D*'s feet .	"	. 101
saw the boy Was not with *D*.	"	. 110
now I come For *D*: take her back ;	"	. 140
take *D* back And let all this be .	"	. 151
D hid her face By Mary.	"	. 153
D lived unmarried till her death. .	"	. 167

dormouse.

blue woodlouse, and the plump *d*,	*The Window*	51

dot.

one black *d* against the verge	*M. d'Arthur*	271

dote.

d and pore on yonder cloud .	*In Mem.* xv.	16

double.

And then we drank it *d* ;	*Will Water.*	95

double (verb.)

d in and out the boles .	*Princess,* iv.	243

doubled.

d his own warmth against her lips,	*Gardener's D.*	137
Was wroth, and *d* up his hands,	*Dora*	. 23
when his date *D* her own,	*Aylmer's F.*	81

doubling.

d all his master's vice of pride,	*Enid*	. 195

doubt (s.)

Roof'd the world with *d* and fear.	*Eleänore*	. 99
d my mother would not see ;	*Miller's D.*	. 154
In *d* and great perplexity,	*Pal. of Art*	278
empty breath And rumours of a *d* !	*M. d' Arthur*	100
all my mind is clouded with a *d*) .	"	. 253
Free space for every human *d*,	*Two Voices*	137
are wrapt in *d* and dread,	"	. 266
There must be answer to his *d*.	"	. 309
d would rest, I dare not solve.	"	. 313
Discuss'd a *d* and tost it to and fro	*Princess,* ii.	422
the *d* 'if this were she'	" iv.	198
the weird seizure and the *d* :	"	. 538
spite of *d*'s And sudden ghostly	"	. 548
Deeper than those weird *d*'s	" vii.	. 316
have heard Of your strange *d*'s : .	"	. 316
my *d*'s are dead, My haunting sense	"	. 327
spectral *d* which makes me cold,	*In Mem.* xl.	19
turn their round resolve the *d* ;	" xliii.	14
Such as closed Grave *d*'s,	" xlvii.	3
slender shade of *d* may flit,	" liii.	7
Defects of *d*, and taints of blood ;	" lxvii.	12
can my dream resolve the *d* :	" lxvii.	12
D and Death, Ill brethren,	" lxxxv.	11
d beside the portal waits,	" xciii.	14
d's that drive the coward back,	" xciv.	30
Was cancell'd, stricken thro' with *d*.	"	. 44
You tell me, *d* is Devil-born.	" xcv.	4
lives more faith in honest *d*.	"	. 11
fought his *d*'s and gather'd strength	"	. 13
seize and throw the *d*'s of man ;	" cviii.	6
Our dearest faith : our ghastliest *d* ;	" cxxiii.	2
like a child in *d* and fear :	"	. 17
Mix not memory with *d*,	*Maud,* II. iv.	57
in daily *d* Whether to live or die .	*Elaine*	. 519
lying thus inactive, *d* and gloom.	*En. Arden.*	113

	POEM.	LINE.
Such *d*'s and fears were common	*En. Arden*.	517
One spiritual *d* she did not soothe?	*Aylmer's F.*	704
d's and fears were all amiss,	*The Ringlet*	19

doubt (verb.)

	POEM.	LINE.
I *d* not thro' the ages	*Locksley H.*	137
By which he *d*'s against the sense?	*Two Voices*	285
'True,' she said, 'We *d* not that.'	*Princess*, Pro.	167
'*D* my word again!' he said	"	174
can I *d*, who knew thee keen	*In Mem.* cxii.	5
I *d* not what thou wouldst have been:	"	8
we *d* not that for one so true	*Ode on Well.*	255
I do not *d* To find, at some place	*Enid*	218
Henceforward I will rather die than *d*.	"	1586
nor did he *d* her more	"	1814
I *d* not that however changed	*Elaine*	1212
To *d* her fairness were to want	"	1367
To *d* her pureness were to want	"	1368
D ye not the Gods have answered,	*Boädicea*	2

doubted.

	POEM.	LINE.
I *d* whether filial tenderness	*Enid*.	797

doubtful.

	POEM.	LINE.
I answer'd nothing, *d* in myself	*Princess*, iii.	255
old man Tho' *d*, felt the flattery	*Vivien*	40

dove.

	POEM.	LINE.
oft I heard the tender *d*	*Miller's D.*	41
voices of the well-contented *d*'s.	*Gardener's D.*	88
Like *d*'s about a dovecote	"	219
loved At first like *d* and *d*	*Walk. to the M.*	50
changes on the burnish'd *d*;	*Locksley II.*	19
morning *d*'s That sun their milky	*Princess*, ii.	87
The *d* may murmur of the *d*,	" iii.	89
troop of snowy *d*'s athwart the dusk,	" iv.	150
moan of *d*'s in immemorial elms.	" vii.	206
somewhere, meek unconscious *d*,	*In Mem.* vi.	25
as a *d* when up she springs	" xii.	1
flew in a *d* And brought a summons	" cii.	15
She is coming, my *d*, my dear,	*Maud*, I. xxii.	61
My own *d* with the tender eye?	" II. iv.	46
I would not one of thine own *d*'s,	*Lucretius*.	68
O merry, the linnet and *d*	*The Window*	156

dovecote.

	POEM.	LINE.
Like doves about a *d*,	*Gardener's D.*	219

dovecote-doors.

	POEM.	LINE.
some one batters at the *d-d*'s,	*Princess*, iv.	151

dowager.

	POEM.	LINE.
prudes for proctors, *d*'s for deans,	*Princess*,Pro.	141

dower.

	POEM.	LINE.
your mortal *d* Of pensive thought	*Margaret*	5

dowered.

	POEM.	LINE.
D with the hate of hate,	*The Poet*.	3

down (hill.)

	POEM.	LINE.
the blissful *d*'s and dales,	*Sea Fairies*	22
the yellow *d* Bordered with palm,	*Lotos-E's.*	21
Round and round the spicy *d*'s	"	149
She went by dale, and she went by *d*,	*Lady Clare*	59
on the *d*'s a rising fire:	*In Mem. Con.*	108
rise, O moon, from yonder *d*,	"	109
Till over *d* and over dale	"	110
night is fair on the dewy *d*'s,	*Maud*, III. vi.	5
Close to the ridge of a noble *d*.	*ToF.D.Maurice*	16
Some wild *d* above the windy deep.	*Vivien*	508
there among the solitary *d*'s,	*Elaine*	163
waste *d*'s whereon I lost myself,	"	225
until they dipt below the *d*'s.	"	395
long backs of the bushless *d*'s,	"	399,785
a cray *d* With Danish barrows;	*En. Arden*.	6
in a cuplike hollow of the *d*.	"	9
in the leafy lanes behind the *d*,	"	97
conies from the *d*,	"	337
after scaling half the weary *d*,	"	369
November dawns and dewy-glooming *d*'s,	"	611

down (feathers.)

	POEM.	LINE.
silk-soft folds, upon yielding *d*,	*Eleänore*	28
Half-buried in the Eagle's *d*,	*Pal. of Art*	122
Stood with the *d* on his beak,	*Poet's Song.*	11

	POEM.	LINE.
in broider'd *d* we sank Our elbows:	*Princess*, iv.	14
When in the *d* I sink my head,	*In Mem.* lxvii.	1

downcast.

	POEM.	LINE.
her eyes were *d*, not to be seen)	*Maud*, I. ii.	5

down-deepening.

	POEM.	LINE.
D-d from swoon to swoon,	*Fatima*	27

down-drooped.

	POEM.	LINE.
D-d, in many a floating fold,	*Arabian N's*	147

down-dropt.

	POEM.	LINE.
Eyes not *d-d* nor overbright,	*Isabel*.	1
With *d-d* eyes I sat alone,	*Œnone*	55

downfall.

	POEM.	LINE.
'tween the spring and *d* of the light,	*St S. Stylites*	108

down-glancing.

	POEM.	LINE.
a spear *D-g* lamed the charger,	*Elaine*.	487

down-lapsing.

	POEM.	LINE.
by *d-l* thought Stream'd onward,	*D. of F. Wom.*	49

down-streaming.

	POEM.	LINE.
dread sweep of the *d-s* seas:	*En. Arden*.	55

dowry.

	POEM.	LINE.
Large dowries doth the raptur'd	*Ode to Mem.*	72

doy (die.)

	POEM.	LINE.
gin I mun *d* I mun *d*	*N. Farmer*	64-8

doze.

	POEM.	LINE.
Fell in a *d*; and half-awake I heard	*The Epic*.	13
half in *d* I seemed To float about.	*Princess*, i.	242
Did I hear it half in a *d*	*Maud*, I. vii.	1
In a wakeful *d* I sorrow	" II. iv.	26

dozed.

	POEM.	LINE.
the pimpernel *d* on the lea;	*Maud*,I.xxii.	48
d awhile herself, but overtoil'd	*Enid*	1225
Miriam watch'd and *d* at intervals,	*En. Arden*.	908

dozing.

	POEM.	LINE.
Lay, *d* in the vale of Avalon,	*Pal. of Art*	107

draff.

	POEM.	LINE.
chaff and *d*, much better burnt.'	*The Epic*.	40

drag.

	POEM.	LINE.
will have weight to *d* thee down.	*Locksley H.*	43
poor Psyche whom she *d*'s in tow.'	*Princess*, iii.	87
d you down, and some great Nemesis	" vi.	158
d's me down From my fixt height	"	288
black cloud *D* inward from the deeps	" vii.	22
seem to keep her up but *d* her down—	"	254
onward *d*'s a labouring breast,	*In Mem.* xv.	18
And that *d*'s down his life:	*Sea Dreams*	173

dragged.

	POEM.	LINE.
d her to the college tower	*Walk.to the M.*	81
d my brains for such a song,	*Princess*, iv.	136
madden'd beach *d* down by the	*Maud*, I. iii.	12
by force they *d* him to the King.	*Vivien*	490
He *d* his eyebrow bushes down,	"	656
What Roman would be *d* in triumph	*Lucretius*	231

dragging.

	POEM.	LINE.
Grimy nakedness *d* his trucks	*Maud*, I. x.	7
a dream Of *d* down his enemy	*Elaine*.	810

dragon.

	POEM.	LINE.
golden gorge of *d*'s spouted forth.	*Pal. of Art*	23
catch a *d* in a cherry net,	*Princess*, v.	162
D's of the prime That tare	*In Mem.* lv.	22
to his crown the golden *d* clung,	*Elaine*	433
the *d* writhed in gold	"	434
behind him crept Two *d*'s gilded	"	436
The *D* of the great Pendragonship,	*Guinevere*	395,592
the golden *d* clung Of Britain;	"	589
A gilded *d*, also, for the babes.	*En. Arden*.	536

Dragon (Inn Sign.)

	POEM.	LINE.
At the *D* on the heath!	*Vision of Sin*	72

dragon-fly.

	POEM.	LINE.
'To-day I saw the *d-f*.	*Two Voices*	8
glancing like a *d-f* In summer suit	*Enid*.	172

108 CONCORDANCE TO

drain (s.)

	POEM.	LINE.
sucking up the *d's*,	*Princess*, v.	514

drain (verb.)

	POEM.	LINE.
a lip to *d* thy trouble dry.	*Locksley H.*	88
d's The chalice of the grapes of God ;	*In Mem.* x.	15

drained.

	POEM.	LINE.
Ida stood nor spoke, *d* of her force	*Princess*, vi.	249
d My capabilities of love ;	*In Mem.* lxxxiv.	11
scheme that had left us flaccid and *d*.	*Maud*, I. i.	20
flowing, *d* their force.	*Enid*	569
hurt that *d* her dear lord's life.	"	1365

drank.

	POEM.	LINE.
d the Libyan Sun to sleep,	*D.of F.Wom.*	145
The butler *d*, the steward scrawl'd,	*Day-Dm.*	142
d the gale That blown about the	*Princess*, iii.	104
Nor ever *d* the inviolate spring	*In Mem.* lxxxix.	2
d, and loyally *d* to him.	*The Daisy*	24
D till he jested with all ease,	*Enid*	1139
then you *d* And knew no more,	*Vivien*	125
d The magic cup that fill'd itself.	*Aylmer's F.*	142
d and past it ; till at length the	"	408
D the large air, and saw,	*Sea Dreams*	34
Sat at his table ; *d* his costly wines ;	"	74
d himself into his grave.	*Grandmother*	6
There they *d* in cups of emerald,	*Boädicea*	61

draped.

	POEM.	LINE.
sweet sculpture *d* from head to foot,	*Princess*, v.	54

drapery.

	POEM.	LINE.
a child, In shining *draperies*	*Princess*, ii.	94

draught.

	POEM.	LINE.
delirious *d's* of warmest life.	*Eleänore*	139
Some *d* of Lethe might await	*Two Voices*	350
From *d's* of balmy air.	*Sir L.and Q.G.*	9
mix the foaming *d* Of fever,	*Princess*, ii.	233
you might mix his *d* with death,	" vi.	260
ere half thy *d* be done,	*In Mem.* vi.	11

drave.

	POEM.	LINE.
I *d* Among the thickest	*Princess*, v.	506
D the long spear a cubit thro'	*Enid*	935
door, Push'd from without, *d*	"	1122
the boat *D* with a sudden wind	*Vivien*	50
d his kith and kin And all the Table	*Elaine*	497
d her ere her time across the fields	"	886

draw.

	POEM.	LINE.
mountain *d's* it from heaven above	*Poet's Mind*	32
d itself to what it was before ;	*Eleänore*	94
seas *d* backward from the land	*Pal. of Art*	251
her stately stature *d's* ;	*D. of F. Wom.*	102
what main-currents *d* the 'Love thou thy land,' etc.	21
'My end *d's* nigh ; 'tis time that	*M. d'Arthur*	163
d's The greater to the lesser,	*Gardener's D.*	9
end *d's* nigh ; I hope my end *d's*.	*St S. Stylites*	35
deny it now? Nay, *d*, *d*, *d* nigh.	"	204
D's different threads, and late and	*Two Voices*	179
d's the veil from hidden worth.	*Day-Dm.*	104
D me, thy bride, a glittering star,	*St Agnes' Eve*	23
d's me down into the common day?	*Will Water.*	153
what mother's blood You *d* from,	*Princess*, v.	395
the moon may *d* the sea ;	" vi.	364
d The sting from pain ;	" vii.	48
d him home to those that mourn	*In Mem.* ix.	5
scarce endure to *d* the breath,	" xx.	15
d's near the birth of Christ ; (ciii. 1)	" xxviii.	1
D forth the cheerful day from night ;	" xxx.	30
birds the charming serpent *d's*,	" xxxiv.	14
D down Æonian hills,	" xxxv.	11
d The deepest measure from the	" xlvii.	11
tease her till the day *d's* by ;	" lix.	7
virtue such as *d's* A faithful answer	" lxxxiv.	13
we to *d* From deep to deep,	" cii.	38
To *d*, to sheathe a useless sword,	" cxxvii.	13
they must go, the time *d's* on,	*Con.*	89
A soul shall *d* from out the vast	"	123
undercurrent woe That seems to *d*—	*Maud*, I. xviii.	84
d them all along, and flow	*The Brook*	63
fail'd to *d* The quiet night	*Enid*	531
as the worm *d's* in the wither'd leaf	"	1481
to Sir Lavaine, '*d* the lance-head : '	*Elaine*	510

drawing.

	POEM.	LINE.
'I dread me, if I *d* it, you will die.'	*Elaine*	512
'I die already with it, *d—D*'	"	513
I will *d* me into sanctuary,	*Guinevere*	120
but held off to *d* him on ;	*En. Arden*	473
hunters round a hunted creature *d*	*Aylmer's F.*	499
D toward the long frost	*A Dedication*	11
yet he *d's* Nearer and nearer,	*Lucretius*	191

drawing.

	POEM.	LINE.
D into his narrow earthen urn,	*Ode to Mem.*	61
D nigh Half-whisper'd in his ear	*Œnone*	181
bright river *d* slowly His waters	*Lotos-E's.*	137
o'er him, *d* it, the winter moon,	*M. d'Arthur*	53
spoke King Arthur, *d* thicker breath ;	"	148
newer knowledge, *d* nigh,	*Day-Dm.*	71
slowly *d* near, A vapour heavy,	*Vision of Sin*	52
now the day was *d* on,	*In Mem.* lxxxii.	10
each, dishorsed and *d*, lashed at each	*Enid*	563
d foul ensample from fair names,	*Guinevere*	486

drawn.

	POEM.	LINE.
thro' the garden I was *d*—	*Arabian N's.*	100
hast *d* of fairest Or boldest since	*Ode to Mem.*	89
all night it is ever *d*	*Poet's Mind*	28
D from each other mellow-deep ;	*Eleänore*	67
from pine to pine, And loiters, slowly *d*.	*Œnone*	5
dew, *D* from the spirit.	*To J. S.*	38
dusky highway near and nearer *d*,	*Locksley H.*	113
all my heart is *d* above,	*Sir Galahad*	17
reasons *d* from age and state,	*Princess*, v.	347
foreheads *d* in Roman scowls,	" vii.	114
then I know the mist is *d*	*In Mem.* lxvi.	13
might have *d* from after-heat.'	" lxxx.	12
O bliss, when all in circle *d*	" lxxxviii.	21
silvery haze of summer *d* ;	" xciv.	4
boat is *d* upon the shore ;	" cxx.	6
beheld The death-white curtain *d* ;	*Maud*, I. xiv.	34
souls the old serpent long had *d*	*Enid*	1480
cloth of gold *D* to her waist,	*Elaine*	1152
till *d* thro' either chasm,	*En. Arden*	671
body that never had *d* a breath.	*Grandmother*	62
twilight slowly downward *d*,	*The Voyage*	22

dread (s.)

	POEM.	LINE.
Deep *d* and loathing of her solitude	*Pal. of Art*	229
once from *d* of pain to die.	*Two Voices*	105
things are wrapt in doubt and *d*,	"	266
in *d* To hear my father's clamour	*Princess*, i.	103
am I sick of a jealous *d*?	*Maud*, I. x.	1
dream of her beauty with tender *d*,	" xvi.	14

dread (verb.)

	POEM.	LINE.
might I *d* that you, With only Fame	*Princess*, iii.	225
I *d* his wildness, and the chances	" iv.	224
lies and *d's* his doom.	" vii.	139
No inner vileness that we *d*?	*In Mem.* l.	4
rather *d* the loss of use than fame ;	*Vivien*	369
'I *d* me, if I draw it, you will die.'	*Elaine*	512

dreaded.

	POEM.	LINE.
he, she *d* most, bare down upon him,	*Enid*	1005

dream (s.)

	POEM.	LINE.
sweet *d's* softer than unbroken rest	*Ode to Mem.*	29
flow'd upon the soul in many *d's*.	*The Poet*	31
shake All evil *d's* of power—	"	47
Dreaming, she knew it was a *d* :	*Mariana in the S.*	49
Before I dream'd that pleasant *d*—	*Miller's D.*	46
like one that hath a weary *d*.	*Lotos-E's.*	6
thick with sighs As in a *d*.	*D. of F. Wom.*	110
The captain of my *d's* Ruled	"	263
Into that wondrous track of *d's*	"	279
But no two *d's* are alike.	"	280
bright our days and light our *d's*,	{ 'Of old sat Freedom,' etc.	22
Black-stoled, black-hooded, like a *d*—	*M. d'Arthur*	197
when *d's* Begin to feel the truth	*Ep.*	18
sweeter than the *d* Dream'd by a	*Gardener's D.*	70
The pilot of the darkness and the *d*	*Audley Ct.*	71
give to light on such a *d*?'	*Ed. Morris*	58
Should it cross thy *d's*,	*Love and Duty*	89
Like a dog, he hunts in *d's*,	*Locksley H.*	79
Fool, again the *d*, the fancy !	"	173

	POEM.	LINE.
said the voice, 'thy *d* was good,	Two Voices	157
did not dream it was a *d*;	"	213
men Forget the *d* that happens then	"	353
Like glimpses of forgotten *d's*—	"	381
'I talk,' said he, 'Not with thy *d's*.	"	386
whose odours haunt my *d's*;	Sir Galahad	68
But, as in *d's*, I could not.	Vision of Sin	57
like shadows in a *d*—	Princess, Pro.	222
truly, waking *d's* were, more or less,	i.	12
feel myself the shadow of a *d*.	"	18
read My sickness down to happy *d's*?	ii.	235
her, who rapt in glorious *d's*,	"	419
I myself the shadow of a *d*,	iii.	172
We had our *d's*: perhaps he mixt	"	204
I found My boyish *d* involved	iv.	430
To dream myself the shadow of a *d*:	v.	470
seem'd a *d*, I dream'd Of fighting.	"	481
and in my *d* I glanced aside,	"	496
make my *d* All that I would.	"	508
d and truth Flow'd from me;	"	530
My *d* had never died	vi.	1
lonely listenings to my mutter'd *d*,	vii.	95
what I think you, some sweet *d*,	"	130
if a *d*, Sweet *d*, be perfect.	"	133
A *d* That once was mine!	"	290
with as wise a *d* As some of theirs—	Con.	69
wildest *d's* Are but the needful	"	73
So bring him: we have idle *d's*:	In Mem. x.	9
I do not suffer in a *d*;	xiii.	14
vaster *d* can hit the mood Of Love	xlvi.	11
So runs my *d*: but what am I?	liii.	17
Nature lends such evil *d's*?	liv.	6
A monster then, a *d*, A discord.	lv.	21
feels, as in a pensive *d*,	lxiii.	17
can my *d* resolve the doubt:	lxvii.	12
threaded some Socratic *d*;	lxxxviii.	36
dream my *d*, and hold it true;	cxxii.	10
Behold, I dream a *d* of good,	cxxxviii.	11
What is she now? My *d's* are bad.	Maud, I. i.	73
warm in the heart of my *d's*,	vi.	18
Even in *d's* to the chink of his pence,	x.	43
Breaking up my *d* of delight.	xix.	2
My *d*! do I dream of bliss?	"	3
Half in *d's* I sorrow after	II. iv.	24
And I wake, my *d* is fled;	"	51
in a *d* from a band of the blest,	III. vi.	10
was but a *d* yet it yielded a dear	"	15
tho' but in a *d*, upon eyes so fair,	"	16
but a *d*, yet it lighten'd my despair	"	18
a glimmering strangeness in his *d*.	The Brook	216
all men else their nobler *d's* forget,	Ode on Well.	152
heated the strong warrior in his *d's*;	Enid	72
late into the morn, Lost in sweet *d's*,	"	158
All overshadow'd by the foolish *d*,	"	675
scarce divide it from her foolish *d*;	"	686
ears to hear you even in his *d's*.'	"	1278
in the jumbled rubbish of a *d*,	Vivien	197
tiny-trumpeting gnat can break our *d*	Elaine	138
I behold him in my *d's* Gaunt	"	759
a *d* Of dragging down his enemy.	"	809
if she slept, she dream'd An awful *d*;	Guinevere	76
Uncertain as a vision or a *d*,	En. Arden	353
teeth that ground As in a dreadful *d*,	Aylmer's F.	329
After an angry *d* this kindlier glow	"	411
oft from out a despot *d* The father	"	527
Had you ill *d's*?'	Sea Dreams	84
'That was then your *d*,' she said,	"	102
Now I see My *d* was Life;	"	133
you made and broke your *d*:	"	139
A trifle makes a *d*, a trifle breaks.'	"	140
I ask'd the woman in my *d*.	"	143
But will you hear my *d*,	"	198
she grieved In her strange *d*,	"	223
d awed me: well but what are *d's*?	"	239
Went both to make your *d*;	"	246
in a pleasant kind of a *d*,	Grandmother	82
white-hair'd shadow roaming like a *d*	Tithonus	8
quiet *d* of life this hour may cease.	Requiescat	6
what *d's*, ye holy Gods, what *d's*!	Lucretius	33
thrice I waken'd after *d's*.	"	34
d's that come Just ere the waking:	"	35

	POEM.	LINE.
that was mine, my *d*, I knew it—	Lucretius	43
thought my *d* would show to me,	"	51
dream (verb.)		
sweet it was to *d* of Father-land,	Lotos-E's.	39
To *d* and *d*, like yonder amber light	"	102
by prayer Than this world *d's* of.	M. d'Arthur	248
Ellen Aubrey, sleep, and *d* of me:	Audley Ct.	61
haply of her arm is mine.	"	63
Ellen Aubrey, love, and *d* of me.'	"	72
as much as this—Or else I *d*—	St S. Stylites	92
She sleeps, nor *d's*, but ever dwells	Day-Dm.	99
D's over lake and lawn, and isles.	Vision of Sin	11
Indeed, We *d* not of him;	Princess, ii.	45
'Dare we *d* of that,' I ask'd,	iii.	280
but to *d* our maids should ape	"	292
To *d* myself the shadow of a dream:	v.	470
To *d* thy cause embraced in mine,	vi.	183
made me *d* I rank'd with him.	In Mem. xli.	4
Nor can I *d* of thee as dead:	lxvii.	4
rather *d* that there, A treble darkness,	xcvii.	12
d of human love and truth,	cxvii.	3
d my dream, and hold it true;	cxxii.	10
Behold, I *d* a dream of good,	cxxxviii.	11
Did I *d* it an hour ago,	Maud, I. vi.	3
of her beauty with tender dread,	xvi.	14
My dream? do I *d* of bliss?.	xix.	3
Perchance, to *d* you still beside me.	The Daisy	107
d she could be guilty of foul act,	Enid	120
full oft shall *d* I see my princess,.	"	751
'Man *d's* of Fame while woman.	Vivien	310
because you *d* they babble of you.'	"	540
wholly true to *d* of untruth in thee,.	Guinevere	537
Let no man *d* but that I love	"	556
Let no man *d* but that he loves	"	666
to *d* That Love could bind them.	Aylmer's F.	40
D in the sliding tides.	Requiescat	4
dreamed.		
Before I *d* that pleasant dream—	Miller's D.	46
the dream *D* by a happy man,	Gardener's D.	71
In midst of knowledge, *d* not yet.	Two Voices	90
I too *d*, until at last	Day-Dm.	7
it seem'd a dream, I *d* Of fighting.	Princess, v.	481
I *d* there would be Spring no more,	In Mem. lxviii.	1
I *d* a vision of the dead	cii.	3
her smile were all that I *d*,	Maud, I. vi.	37,93
maiden *d* That some one put this.	Elaine	211
had not *d* she was so beautiful.	"	352
d my knight the greatest knight	"	664
'And if I *d*,' said Gawain,	"	665
if she slept, she *d* An awful dream;	Guinevere	75
such a feast As never man had *d*;	"	262
and as yet no sin was *d*,)	"	385
'I *d* Of such a tide swelling.	Sea Dreams	84
I *d* that still The motion	"	106
having *d* Of that same coast.	"	200
such as that you *d* about,	"	248
dreamer.		
—we forward: *d's* both;	Golden Year	66
Much less this *d*, deaf and blind,	Two Voices	175
in the Northern *d's* heavens,	Aylmer's F.	161
dreaming.		
D, she knew it was a dream;	Mariana in the S.	49
A glorious child, *d* alone,	Eleänore	27
d on your damask cheek,	Day-Dm.	3
To see you *d*—and, behind	"	7
For pastime, *d* of the sky;	In Mem. lxv.	14
how should England *d* of his sons	Ded. of Idylls	30
d of her love For Lancelot.	Enid	158
wrathful, petulant, *D* some rival,	Lucretius	15
dreamt.		
d herself was such a faded form	Enid	654
d Of some vast charm concluded.	Vivien	361
d the damsel would have died,	Elaine	1297
dreary.		
She only said, 'My life is *d*, rep.)	Mariana	9
dregs.		
D of life, and lees of man:	Vision of Sin	205

CONCORDANCE TO

drench.
	POEM.	LINE.
stoop'd To d his dark locks	Princess, iv.	169
on these dews that d the furze,	In Mem. xi.	6
clouds that d the morning star,	" lxxi.	22

drench'd.
dark wood-walks d in dew,	D. of F. Wom.	75
For I was d with ooze,	Princess, v.	27
So d it is with tempest,	" vii.	127

dress (s.)
This d and that by turns you tried,	Miller's D.	147
'Bring the d and put it on her,	L. of Burleigh	95
In the d that she was wed in,	"	99
'What do you here? and in this d?	Princess, ii.	172
look well too in your woman's d:	" iv.	508
Nay, the plainness of her d's?	Maud, I. xx.	14
your worst and meanest d	Enid	130, 848
came on her Drest in that d,	"	141, 843
all her foolish fears about the d,	"	142, 844
(His d a suit of fray'd magnificence	"	296
she cast her eyes upon her d,	"	609
d that now she look'd on to the d.	"	613
Enid fell in longing for a d	"	630
your wretched d, A wretched insult	"	1176

dress (verb.)
d the victim to the offering up,	Princess, iv	112
to flaunt, to d, to dance, to thrum,	"	498
d her beautifully and keep her true	Enid	899

dressing.
D their hair with the white sea-flower,	The Merman	13
flout and scorn By d it in rags?	Enid	1524

dressed—drest.
come you d like a village maid	Lady Clare	67-9
her body, d In the dress	L. of Burleigh	98
each by other d with care	Princess, iii.	3
'What, if you d it up poetically!'	" Con.	6
came on her, D in that dress,	Enid	141, 843
A tribe of women, d in many hues,	"	1446
to dance and sing, be gaily d,	Coquette, ii.	3

drew.
she d her casement-curtain by	Mariana	19
Thro' rosy taper fingers d	Mariana in the S.	15
from her bosom d Old letters,	"	61
once he d With one long kiss	Fatima	19
rosy slender fingers backward d	Œnone	172
half-asleep his breath he d,	The Sisters	28
morn from Memnon, d Rivers of	Pal. of Art	171
Many d swords and died.	D. of F. Wom.	95
they d into two burning rings	"	174
D forth the poison with her balmy	"	271
d he forth the brand Excalibur,	M. d' Arthur	52
d him under in the mere.	"	146, 161
d the languid hands	"	174
Came, d your pencil from you,	Gardener's D.	26
one large cloud D downward:	"	78
such a breast As never pencil d.	"	139
Light pretexts d me:	"	188
d My little oakling from the cup,	Talking O.	230
rear'd a font of stone And d	Princess, Pro.	60
days d nigh that I should wed,	" i.	40
I d near; I gazed.	" iii.	166
the flood d; yet I caught her;	" iv.	164
d My burthen from mine arms;	"	173
on the earth and rose again and d:	" v.	486
D from my neck the painting	" vi.	94
d Her robe to meet his lips.	"	139
Whence d you this steel temper?	"	215
D the great night into themselves,	" vii.	34
Thy converse d us with delight	In Mem. cix.	1
D in the expression of an eye,	" cx.	19
from which their omens all men d,	Ode on Well.	36
Round affrighted Lisbon d.	"	103
up the snowy Splugen d,	The Daisy	86
shadow of His loss d like eclipse,	Ded. of Idylls	13
d from those dead wolves	Enid	1029
never since I first d breath,	"	1467
d The vast and shaggy mantle	Vivien	104
magnet-like she d The rustiest iron	"	423
d back, and let her eyes Speak	"	465
D the vast eyelid of an inky cloud,	"	484

	POEM.	LINE.
when the time d nigh Spake	Elaine	78
she d Nearer and stood.	"	348
draw—Draw,'—and Lavaine d,	"	514
D near, and sigh'd in passing	"	1340
when she d No answer, and by	Guinevere	159
weep for her, who d him to his	"	346
d The knighthood-errant of this	"	457
as their faces d together, groan'd,	En. Arden	74
thro' all his blood D in the dewy	"	661
amulet d her down to that old oak	Aylmer's F.	507
the great ridge d, Lessening	Sea Dreams	213

dried.
tears fell ere the dews were d;	Mariana	14
all his juice is d, and all his joints	Audley Ct.	45
d his wings; like gauze they grew:	Two Voices	13

drift.
city lies Beneath its d of smoke;	Talking O.	6
Thro' scudding d's the rainy	Ulysses	10
in the d's that pass To darken	In Mem. cvi.	13
For the d of the Maker is dark,	Maud, I. iv.	43
Wrapt in d's of lurid smoke	" II. iv.	66

drifted.
These d, stranding on an isle	En. Arden	553

drifting.
d up the stream In fancy,	Sea Dreams	104

drill.
d the raw world for the march	Ode on Well.	168

drink (s.)
sometimes Sucking the damps for d,	St S. Stylites	76
Yea ev'n of wretched meat and d,	Maud, I. xv.	8
pinch a murderous dust into her d,	Vivien	460
at times, she mingled with his d,	Lucretius	18

drink (verb.)
d the cup of a costly death,	Eleänore	138
I will d Life to the lees;	Ulysses	6
We d defying trouble,	Will Water.	94
I am old, but let me d;	Vision of Sin	75
D, and let the parties rave;	"	123
D to lofty hopes that cool—	"	147
D we, last, the public fool,	"	149
D to Fortune, d to Chance,	"	191
D to heavy Ignorance!	"	193
D deep, until the habits of the slave,	Princess, ii.	77
To d the cooler air, and mark	In Mem. lxxxviii.	15
d to him, whate'er he be,	" cvi.	23
'D, then,' he answer'd. 'Here!'	Enid	1506
D therefore and the wine will change	"	1511
I will not d Till my dear lord	"	1572
bid me do it, And d with me:	"	1524
Not eat nor d? And wherefore wail	"	1522
open'd lip, Except indeed to d:	Vivien	121
Forgot to d to Lancelot and the Queen,	Elaine	733

drinketh.
as sunlight d dew.	Fatima	21

drinking.
d health to bride and groom	In Mem. Con.	83
Men were d together,	Maud, I, vii.	5

drinking-song.
why should Love, like men in d-s's,	Maud, I. xviii.	55

drip.
woodbine and eglatere D sweeter dews	A Dirge	24
When the rotten woodland d's,	Vision of Sin	81
d with a silent horror of blood,	Maud I. i.	3

dripping.
D with Sabæan spice	Adeline	53

drive (s.)
What d's about the fresh Cascine,	The Daisy	43

drive (verb.)
d's them to the deep.'	Pal. of Art	204
Nature's evil star D men 'Love thou thy land,' etc.		
shoals of pucker'd faces d;	In Mem. lxix.	10
doubts that d the coward back,	" xciv.	2
Is enough to d one mad.	Maud, II. v.	20
'D them on Before you;'	Enid	948, 1037
d The Heathen, who, some say,	Elaine	65

driven.   POEM.   LINE.
morning *d* her plow of pearl   *Love and Duty* 96
plumes *d* backward by the wind . *Elaine*   . 479
driveth.
Let us alone. Time *d* onward fast, *Lotos-E's.*   . 88
driving.
D, hurrying, marrying, burying, . *Maud,* II. v. 12
in mild obedience D them on : . *Enid*   . 954
blood by Sylla shed Came *d* rainlike *Lucretius* . 48
drizzle.
Thicker the *d* grew,   .   .   *En. Arden* . 680
bill of sale gleam'd thro' the *d*) . . " . 689
droop.
Fair-fronted Truth shall *d* '*Clear-headed friend*,' etc. 12
I cannot veil, or *d* my sight,   . *Eleänore* . 87
D's both his wings, regarding thee, " . 119
D's blinded with his shining eye : *Fatima* . 38
The purple flowers *d*   .   . *Œnone* . 28
I 's the heavy-blossom'd bower . *Locksley H.* 163
Here *d's* the banner on the tower, *Day-Dm.* . 33
from the golden pegs D sleepily ; " . 40
Where on the double rosebud *d's*   " . 239
d's the milkwhite peacock like a *Princess*, vii. 165
D from his mighty shoulder, *Vivien* . 92
his own head began to *d*, to fall ; . *Aylmer's F.* 835

drooped—droopt.
leopard-skin D from his shoulder, *Œnone* . 58
From one hand *d* a crocus : . *Pal. of Art* 119
So she *d* and *d* before him, . *L. of Burleigh* 85
then *d'y d*; The chapel bells Called *Princess*, ii. 446
lily'like Melissa *d* her brows ; " iv. 143
above her *d* a lamp   . . " . 253
how my life had *d* 'd late,   . *In Mem.* xiv. 14
glance At Enid, where she *d* : . *Enid* . 1096
t ast her clear germander eye D . *Sea Dreams* 5

drooping.
A damsel *d* in a corner of it.   . *Enid* . 1459
her meek head yet D,   .   .   " . 1489

drop (s.)
There will not be a *d* of rain . *May Queen* i. 35
d w'd with h wery *d's*   . *Lotos-E's*. . 17
came a *d* sh'd with *d's* Of onset ; *M. d'Arthur* 215
the la t *d* in the cup of gall. *Walk. to the M. Ct*
The glittering *d's* on her sad friend. *Princess*, vi. 266
lorn *d'* in summer dark   . *In Mem.* xvii. 15
A *d* by *d* the water falls   .   " lvii. 3
than the sword with *d's* of dew *Enid* . 1538

drop (verb.)
o'er black brows *d's* down   . *Madeline* 34, 46
D's in a ent autumn night.   . *Lotos-E's.* . 79
Till all my limbs *d* piecemeal . *St S. Stylites* 43
All starry culmination *d* Balm-dews *Talking O.* 267
larger or g Than modern poultry *d Will Water.* 122
d's at Ct ry's temple-gates,
              ('You might have won,' etc.) . 34
d thy f—l—h tears upon my 'Come not, when,' etc. 2
the lark *d* down at his feet. . *Poet's Song* 8
on *d* ead from the signs. . *Princess*, vii. 230
d's in his vast and wandering grave. *In Mem.* vi. 16
d head forem st in the jaws   .   " xxxiv. 15
'The tanks *d* in ; the body bows' " xxxv. 1
d me a flower, D me a flower. *The Window* 26, 31

dropped—dropt.
d of re my eyelids *d* their shade, *D. of F. Wom.* 1
tear D n the letters as I wrote. *To J. S.* . 56
d the goose, and caught the pelf, *The Goose* . 13
d the branch she held, and turning *Gardener's D.* 154
to th, which now are *d* away, *St S. Stylites* 29
eyelid *d* their silken eaves. . *Talking O.* 209
D down upon her golden head, . " . 227
darkness in his head, And *d* before him. *Godiva* 71
D her head in the maiden's hand, *Lady Clare* 63
d a fairy parachute and past : . *Princess, Pro.* 76
Like thread *d* spiders, one by one, we *d*, " i. 107
d with evening on a rustic town . " . 186
Two plummets *d* for one   .   . " ii. 159
D thro' the ambrosial gloom . " iv. 6

                                                POEM.   LINE.
at top with pain, D on the sward, *Princess*, iv. 191
down the streaming crystal *d* ; " vii. 150
find him *d* upon the firths of ice, . " . 191
d the dust on tearless eyes ; . *In Mem.* lxxix. 4
D off gorged from a scheme . *Maud*, I. i. 20
suddenly *d* dead of heart-disease.' *Sea Dreams* 264
Nor anchor *d* at eve or morn ; . *The Voyage* 82
Down they *d*—no word was spoken— *The Captain* 51
a flower, a flower, D, a flower. *The Window* 34

dropping.
d low their crimson bells   . *Arabian N's.* 62
slowly *d* fragrant dew,   . *Œnone* . 104
d bitter tears against his brow . *M. d'Arthur* 211
d down with costly bales ;   . *Locksley H.* 122
Autumn, *d* fruits of power ; . *Princess*, vi. 39
D the too rough H in Hell   . *Sea Dreams* 192

dropping-wells.
Laburnums, *d-w* of fire.   . *In Mem.* lxxxii. 12

dropwise.
gather'd trickling *d* from the cleft, *Vivien* . 123

dross.
scurf of salt, and scum of *d* . *Vision of Sin* 211

drought.
stony *d* and steaming salt ; . *Mariana in the S.* 40

drouth.
I look'd athwart the burning *d*. *Fatima* . 13
Oasis in the dust and *d* Of city life I *Ed. Morris* .
dust and *d* of London Life . " . 143

drove (s.)
watch the darkening *d's* of swine *Pal. of Art* 199
of all the *d* should touch me : swine !' *Vivien* 549

drove (verb.)
d The fragrant, glistening deeps. *Arabian N's* 13
His own thought *d* him like a goad. *M. d'Arthur* 185
d his heel into the smoulder'd log,   " *Ep.* 14
change at home, that *d* him hence. *Walk. to the M.* 60
d her foes with slaughter   . *Princess, Pro.* 123
d his cheek in lines ;   .   .   " i. 115
Right on this we *d* and caught,   " iv. 170
d us, last, to quite a solemn close— " *Con.* 17
of the ruin'd woodlands *d* thro' the air. *Maud*, I. i. 12
and she *d* them thro' the waste. *Enid* . 949
and she *d* them thro' the wood.   " . 1034
d the dust against her veilless eyes : " . 1378
d him into wastes and solitudes . *Elaine* . 252
d her under moonless heavens   . *En. Arden* . 543
The horse he *d*, the boat he sold,   " . 610
harass'd him, and *d* him forth, . " . 721
d The footstool from before him, *Aylmer's F.* 326
D in upon the student once or twice, " . 462
Across the boundless east we *d*, *The Voyage* 38
whence were those that *d* the sail " . 86
goodly sheep In haste they *d* . *Spec. of Iliad* 5
d the knife into his side :   . *Lucretius* . 271

drown.
muffled motions blindly *d*   . *In Mem.* xlviii. 15
d His heart in the gross mud-honey *Maud*, I. xvi. 4
burst and *d* with deluging storms . " II. i. 42
Might *d* all life in the eye,— . " ii. 61

drowned.
I *d* the whoopings of the owl . *St S. Stylites* 32
d within the whirling brook : . *Princess, Pro.* 47
glens are *d* in azure gloom   . " iv. 504
d In silken fluctuation .   . " vi. 334
Love clasp Grief lest both be *d*, *In Mem.* i. 9
d in passing thro' the ford,   . " vi. 39
d in yonder living blue   .   " cxiv. 7
all spleenful folly was *d*,   . *Maud*, I. iii. 2
Would she had *d* me in it,   . *Elaine* 1402

drowning.
I brim with sorrow *d* song.   . *In Mem.* xix. 12

drowse.
Let not your prudence, dearest, *d Princess*, ii. 318

drowze.
burst Their *d*; and either started. *Enid* . 1121

CONCORDANCE TO

drug (s.)   POEM.   LINE.
'What *d* can make A wither'd palsy *Two Voices* 56

drug (verb.)
D thy memories, lest thou learn it, *Locksley H.* 77
D down the blindfold sense . . *In Mem.* lxx. 7

Druid.
Each was like a *D* rock ; . . *Princess*, iv. 261
altar of the *D* and Druidess, . *Boädicea* . 2

Druidess.
altar of the Druid and *D*, . . *Boädicea* . 2

drum.
murmurs of the *d* and fife . . *Talking O.* 215
voice is heard thro' rolling *d's*, . *Princess*, iv. 554
clash'd their arms ; the *d* Beat ; . " v. 240
Now, to the roll of muffled *d's*, . *Ode on Well.* 87
Lady, let the rolling *d's* ' *Lady, let the,*' etc. 1

drunk.
d delight of battle with my peers, *Ulysses* . 16
sweeter to be *d* with loss, . . *In Mem.* i. . 11
D even when he woo'd ; . . *Enid* . . 442

drunkard.
d's football, laughing-stocks of Time,*Princess*, iv. 496
Shaking a little like a *d's* hand, . *En. Arden* . 462

drunken.
Before I well have *d*, scarce can eat : *Enid* 1510

dry (adj.)
bearded grass Is *d* and dewless . *Miller's D.* 246
tongue Cold February loved, is *d The Blackbird* 14
Keep *d* their light from tears { ' *Of old sat Free-*
                      dom,' etc. 20
moist and *d*, devising ' *Love thou thy land*,' etc. 38
sweeping thro' me left me *d*, . *Locksley H.* 131
near me when my faith is *d*, . *In Mem.* xlix. 9
with long use her tears are *d*. . " lxxvii. 20
underfoot the herb was *d* . . " xciv. 2
Full cold my greeting was and *d The Letters* 13
I found, tho' crush'd to hard and *d*, *The Daisy* . 97
chambers ; all were fair and *d* ; . *Elaine* . 406
pious talk, when most his heart was *d*. *Sea Dreams*182

dry (verb.)
The sap *dries* up : the plant declines *Two Voices* 268

Dryad-like.
D-*l*, shall wear Alternate leaf . *Talking O.* . 286

dry-tongued.
d-t laurels' pattering talk . . *Maud*,i.xviii. 8

Dubric.
the hands of *D*, the high saint, . *Enid* . . 838
talk'd with *D*, the high saint, . " 1713

duct.
Before the little *d's* began . . *Two Voices* 325

due (adj.)
question unto whom 'twere *d* : . *Œnone* . 80
Up in one night and *d* to sudden , *Princess*, iv. 293
d To languid limbs and sickness : " vi. 355

due (s.)
little *d's* of wheat, and wine and oil; *Lotos-E's*. . 167
with a dearness not his *d*. . . *Locksley H.* 91
So many years from his *d*.' . . *Lady Clare* . 32
what every woman counts her *d*, . *Princess*, iii. 228
as frankly theirs As *d's* of Nature. " v. 196
miss their yearly *d* Before their time? *In Mem.* xxix. 15
render human love his *d's* ; . " xxxvii. 16
else were fruitless of their *d*, . " xliv. 14
Who but claims her as his *d* ? . *Maud*, I. xx. 11
give the Fiend himself his *d*, *To F. D. Maurice* 11

dug.
iron *d* from central gloom, . . *In Mem.*cxvii. 21
falling prone he *d* His fingers . *En. Arden* . 780

Duglas.
wild battles by the shore Of *D* ; . *Elaine* . 290

duke.
Bury the Great *D*. . . . *Ode on Well.* 1-3
Truth-lover was our English *D*; . " . 189
King, *d*, earl, Count, baron— . *Elaine* . 463

dull (adj.)   POEM.   LINE.
the *d* Saw no divinity in grass, . *A Character* 7
your ears are so *d* ; . . . *Poet's Mind* 35
How *d* it is to pause, . . . *Ulysses* . 22
d and self-involved, Tall and erect, *Aylmer's F.* . 118

dull (verb.)
d Those spirit-thrilling eyes . . *Ode to Mem.* 38
weeping *d*'s the inward pain.' . *To J. S.* . 40

dull'd.
d the murmur on thy lip, . . *In Mem.*xxii. 16

duller.
something *d* than at first, . . *Will Water.* 157

dumb.
far-off stream is *d*, . . . *The Owl*, i. . 3
in a little while our lips are *d*. . *Lotos-E's*. . 89
The streets are of silver with snow. *Sir Galahad* 52
lands where not a leaf was *d* ; . *In Mem.*xxiii. 10
lo, thy deepest lays are *d* . . " lxxv. 7
D is that tower which spake . . " Con. 106
Then I cannot be wholly *d* ; . . *Maud*, II. v. 100
and the dead Steer'd by the *d* . *Elaine* . 1148
Winds are loud and you are *d* : . *The Window* 124

dungeon.
Of battle, bold adventure, *d*, . *Aylmer's F.* 98

duomo.
Of tower or *d*, sunny-sweet, . . *The Daisy* . 46

Dundagil.
dark *D* by the Cornish sea ; . . *Guinevere* . 292

dunghill.
Upon an ampler *d* trod, . . *Will Water.* 125

dupe.
Christ the bait to trap his *d* . . *Sea Dreams* 187

dusk (s.)
thro' the thicken'd cedar in the *d*. *Gardener'sD.*162
troop of snowy doves athwart the *d Princess*, iv. 150
in the *d* of thee, the clock . . *In Mem.* ii. 7
I sleep till *d* is dipt in gray : . " lxvi. 12
flat lawn with *d* and bright ; . . " lxxxviii. 2
haunt the *d*, with ermine capes, . " xciv. 11
doubtful *d* revealed The knolls . " . 50

dusk (verb.)
Little breezes *d* and shiver . . *L.of Shalott*,I.11

dusky-rafter'd.
The *d-r* many-cobweb'd Hall, . *Enid* . . 362

dust.
thick as *d* In vacant chambers, . *To the Queen* 18
Two handfuls of white *d*, . . *Lotos-E's*. . 113
his mute *d* I honour . . . *To J. S.* . 29
Lie still, dry *d*, secure of change. . " 76
parch'd with *d* ; Or, clotted into . *M. d' Arthur* 218
pillar'd *d* of sounding sycamores, . *Audley Ct.* . 15
the *d* and drouth Of city life ! . *Ed. Morris* . 3
the *d* and drouth of London life . " 143
carve a shrine about my *d*, . . *St S.Stylites* 192
With anthers and with *d* : . . *Talking O.* 184
dead, become Mere highway *d* ? . *Love and Duty*11
right ear, that is fill'd with *d*, . *Two Voices* 116
soil'd with noble *d*, he hears . . " 152
A *d* of systems and of creeds. . " 207
Is a clot of warmer *d*, . . . *Vision of Sin* 113
Are but *d* that rises up, . . " 133, 169
And vex the unhappy *d* ' *Come not, when*,' etc. 4
fretted all to *d* and bitterness.' . *Princess*, vi. 247
will not leave us in the *d* : . . *In Mem.* Pro. 9
Ye never knew the sacred *d* : . " xxi. 22
d and ashes all that is ; . . " xxxiv. 4
nor is there hope in *d* :' . . " xxxv. 4
The *d* of continents to be ; . . " . 12
Time, a maniac scattering *d*, . . " xlix. 7
grope, And gather *d* and chaff, . " liv. 18
He blown about the desert *d*, . " lv. 19
men and minds, the *d* of change, . " lxx. 10
To stir a little *d* of praise. . . " lxxix. 12
dropt the *d* on tearless eyes ; . " lxxix. 4
d and din and steam of town : . " lxxxviii. 8

	POEM.	LINE.
Our father's *d* is left alone	In Mem. civ.	5
The life re-orient out of *d*,	" cxv.	6
we may lift from out of *d*	" cxxx.	5
who knows? we are ashes and *d*.	Maud, I. i.	32
fair banquet with the *d* of death?	" xviii.	56
My *d* would hear her and beat,	" xxii.	71
sting each other here in the *d*;	" II. i.	47
my heart is a handful of *d*,	" v.	3
public wrong be crumbled into *d*,	Ode on Well.	167
Ashes to ashes, *d* to *d*;	"	270
turning round she saw *d*.	Enid.	1298
finger up, and pointed to the *d*.	"	1302
d against her veilless eyes:	"	1378
pinch a murderous *d* into her drink	Vivien	460
in the *d* of half-forgotten kings,	Elaine	1338
knew the Prince tho' marr'd with *d*,	Guinevere	37
D are our frames; and, gilded *d*,	Aylmer's F.	1
a dozen years Of *d* and deskwork:	Sea Dreams	78
if the wages of Virtue be *d*,	Wages	6

dusty-dry.
| Where all but yester-eve was *d-d*. | Lucretius | 32 |

dusty-white.
| The river-bed was *d-w*; | Mariana in the S. | 54 |

Dutch.
| sometimes a *D* love For tulips; | Gardener's D. | 188 |

duty.
a man may fail in *d* twice,	M. d'Arthur	129
taught my *d*, and by you I	Dora	95
and *D* loved of Love—	Love and Duty	46
in the sphere Of common *duties*	Ulysses	40
To all *duties* of her rank:	L. of Burleigh	72
O hard, when love and *d* clash!	Princess, ii.	273
My brother! it was *d* spoke,	"	288
replied, her *d* was to speak,	" iii.	135
d d, clear of consequences.	"	136
thro' all Its range of *duties*	"	161
love their voices more than *d*,	" iv.	491
Some sense of *d*, something of a	" Con.	54
As it were a *d* done to the tomb,	Maud, I. xix.	49
sought but *D*'s iron crown	Ode on Well.	122
path of *d* was the way to glory	"	202-10
the toppling crags of *D* scaled	"	215
path of *d* be the way to glory?	"	224
charge you, on your *d* as a wife,	Enid	865
was my *d* to have loved the highest	Guinevere	650
one who does his *d* by his own,	En. Arden	330
Swerve from her *d* to herself and us	Aylmer's F.	304
I done my *d* by un	N. Farmer	12, 24
I done my *d* by Squoire	"	64
As having fail'd in *d* to him,	Lucretius	274

dwarf (s.)
D's of gynæceum.	Princess, iii.	262
after seen The *d*'s of presage;	" iv.	427
a knight, lady, and *d*;	Enid	187
Where *d* the *d* lagg'd latest,	"	188
maiden to demand it of the *d*;	"	193
Made sharply to the *d*, and ask'd it	"	204
His *d*, a vicious under-shapen thing,	"	412
thou thyself, thy lady, and thy *d*,	"	581

dwarf (verb.)
| *d*'s the petty love of one to one. | Vivien | 342 |

dwarf'd.
| rise or sink Together, *d* or godlike, | Princess, vii. | 244 |
| How *d* a growth of cold and night, | In Mem. lx. | 7 |

dwarf-like.
| among the rest A *d-l* Cato cower'd. | Princess, vii. | 111 |

dwell.
Life and Thought Here no longer *d*;	Deserted H.	18
light upon the letter *d*'s,	Miller's D.	189
those kind eyes for ever *d* I	"	220
Wherein at ease the aye to *d*.	Pal. of Art	"
My Gods, with whom I *d*!	"	196
others in Elysian valleys *d*,	Lotos-E's	169
thou may'st warble, eat and *d*.	The Blackbird	4
d's in heaven half the night.	To J. S.	52
would *d* One earnest, earnest	Love and Duty	36

	POEM.	LINE.
d's A perfect form in perfect rest.	Day-Dm.	99
Where the wealthy nobles *d*.'	L. of Burleigh	24
D with these, and lose Convention	Princess, ii.	71
more of reverence in us *d*;	In Mem. Pro.	26
the vigour, bold to *d* On doubts	" xciv.	29
d's not in the light alone,	" xcv.	20
d's on him with faithful eyes,	" xcvi.	35
in my spirit will I *d*,	" cxxii.	9
dark a mind within me *d*'s,	Maud, I. xv.	1
wastes where footless fancies *d*	" xviii.	69
in me there *d*'s No greatness,	Elaine	448
when we *d* upon a word we know	"	1021
not *d* on that defeat of fame.	Guinevere	621
d with you; Wear black and white,	"	668
d in presence of immortal youth,	Tithonus	21
there—there—they *d* no more.	Boädicea	63

dwelleth.
| The clear-voiced mavis *d*, | Claribel | 16 |

dwelling (part.)
D amid these yellowing	'A Spirit haunts,' etc.	2
d on his boundless love,	Enid	63
Her fancy *d* in this dusky hall:	"	802

dwelling (s.)
Unto the *d* she must sway.	Ode to Mem.	79
How mend the *d*'s, of the poor:	To F. D. Maurice	38
Philip's *d* fronted on the street,	En. Arden	732

dwelt.
the full day *d* on her brows,	Gardener's D.	135
from that Eden where she *d*.	"	187
not be *d* on by the common day.	"	266
when I *d* upon your old affiance,	Princess, iii.	123
d an iron nature in the grain:	" vi.	34
mellowing, *d* Full on the child;	"	174
doubtful smile *d* like a clouded moon	"	253
the dew *D* in her eyes,	" vii.	121
see the rooms in which he *d*.	In Mem. lxxxvi.	16
they *d* with eye on eye,	" xcvi.	9
Methought I *d* within a hall,	" cii.	5
they *d* languidly On Lancelot,	Elaine	85
d among the woods By the great river	"	277
far blood, which *d* at Camelot	"	799
larger thro' his leanness, *d* upon her,	"	831
So *d* the father on her face	"	1024
when we *d* among the woods,	"	1030
D with them, till in time their	Guinevere	684
d a moment on his kindly face,	En. Arden	323
as she *d* upon his latest words,	"	451
hand *d* lingeringly on the latch,	"	515
D with eternal summer, ill-content.	"	563
brightest, when they *d* on hers,	Aylmer's F.	69
There they *d* and there they rioted;	Boädicea	63

dwindle.
| Thou shalt wax and he shall *d*, | Boädicea | 40 |

dwindled.
| *d* down to some odd games | The Epic | 8 |

dyeing.
| spirted upon the scarf, *D* it; | Enid | 209 |

dyke.
| Adown the crystal *d*'s at Camelot | Enid | 1319 |

dying.
I would be evermore,	Eleänore	143
Die, *d* clasped in his embrace	Fatima	42
say he's *d* all for love	May Queen, i.	21
Then *d* of a mortal stroke,	Two Voices	154
Ellen Adair was *d* for me,	Ed. Gray	16
foretold, *D*. that none of all our	Princess, i.	8
He, *d* lately, left her, as I hear	" iii.	77
answer, echoes, *d*, *d*, *d*. (rep.)	" iii.	353
d, there at least may die.	In Mem. viii.	24
The aye is *d* in the night;	" cv.	3
D abroad and it seems apart	Maud, I. xix.	29
When he lay *d* there,	" II. ii.	67
There is some one *d* or dead,	" iv.	48
laughter *d* down as the great knight	Elaine	179
as they lay *d*, Did they smile on him.	The Captain	55

E

eager
	POEM.	LINE.
arose *E* to bring them down,	*En. Arden.*	873

eager-hearted.
E-h as a boy when first he	*Locksley H.*	112

Eagle.
Half-buried in the *E's* down,	*Pal. of Art*	122
Shall *e's* not be *e's*? wrens be wrens!	*Golden Year*	37
wonder of the *e* were the less,	"	39
he not less the *e.*	"	40
Unclasp'd the wedded *e's* of her belt,	*Godiva*	
An *e* clang an *e* to the sphere.	*Princess*, iii.	43
and Hope, a poising *e*, burns	" iv.	90
by axe and *e* sat, With all their	" vii.	64
wild Lean-headed *E's* yelp alone.	"	113
e's wing, or insect's eye;	*InMem.*cxxiii.	196
Till o'er the hills her *e's* flew	*Ode on Well.*	6
Again their ravening *e* rose	"	112
an *E* rising or, the Sun In dexter	*Vivien*	119
ever-ravening *e's* beak and talon	*Boädicea*	325
Tho' the Roman *e* shadow thee	"	11
		39

eaglet.
Foster'd the callow *e*—.	*Œnone*	208

ear.
round mine *e's* the livelong bleat	*Ode to Mem.*	65
your *e's* are so dull;	*Poet's Mind*	35
at first to the *e* The warble	*Dying Swan*	23
With dinning sound my *e's* are rife,	*Eleänore*	135
jewel That trembles at her *e;*	*Miller's D..*	172
Half-whisper'd in his *e,*	*Œnone*	182
Rings ever in her *e's* of armed men.	"	261
hollowing one hand against his *e,*	*Pal. of Art*	109
Herod, when the shout was in his *e's,*	"	219
music in his *e's* his beating heart	*Lotos-E's.*	36
under-tone Thrill'd thro' mine *e's .*	*D.of F.Wom.*	82
corn-bin open, prick'd my *e's;*	*The Epic*	45
murmuring at his *e* 'Quick, Quick!	*M. d'Arthur*	179
Rings in mine *e's.* The steer forgot	*Gardener'sD.*	84
e's could hear Her lightest breaths;	*Ed. Morris*	
(And hear me with thine *e's,*)	*Talking O..*	82
sense is hard To alien *e's,*	*Love and Duty*51	
in the ringing of thine *e's;*	*Locksley H.*	84
fillip'd at the diamond in her *e;*	*Godiva*	
right *e,* that is fill'd with dust,	*Two Voices*	116
country's war-song thrill his *e's;*	"	153
	"	427
A second voice was at mine *e,*		
whisper'd voices at his *e.*	*Day-Dm.*	124
In her *e* he whispers. gaily,	*L.of Burleigh*	1
twinn'd as horse's *e* and eye.	*Princess*, i.	56
very *e's* were hot To hear them:	"	133
dame That whisper'd 'Asses' *e's'*.	" ii.	98
To dying *e's,* when unto dying eyes	" iv.	33
we Should cram our *e's* with wool	"	47
at mine *e* Bubbled the nightingale	"	247
Each hissing in his neighbour's *e;*	" v.	14
tale of love In the old king's *e's*	"	231
each *e* was prick'd to attend,	" vi.	263
should turn mine *e's* and hear	*InMem.*xxxv.	8
Not all ungrateful to thine *e.*	" xxxviii.	12
in these *e's,* till hearing dies,	" lvi.	9
on mine *e* this message falls,	" lxxxiv.	18
A willing *e* We lent him.	" lxxxvi.	30
heart and *e* were fed To hear him,	" lxxxviii.	22
words of life Breath'd in her *e.*	" Con.	53
centre-bits Grind on the wakeful *e*	*Maud,* I. i.	42
(Look at it) pricking a cockney *e.*	" x.	2
Whose *e* is cramm'd with his cotton	"	42
the evil tongue and the evil *e,*	"	51
win her With my chirrup at her *e.*	" xx.	30
in my heart and my *e's* till I die	" II. i.	35
An old song vexes my *e;*	" ii.	47
Twinkled the innumerable *e*	*The Brook.*	134
March wails in the people's *e's:*	*Ode on Well.*	267
sow'd a slander in the common *e,*	*Enid*	450
could speak whom his own *e* had,	"	962
prick'd their light *e's,* and felt	"	1042
e's to hear you even in his dreams.'	"	1298
heavily-galloping hoof Smote on her *e,*	"	1297

	POEM.	LINE.
hiss'd each at other's *e* What	*Enid*	1482
mine own *e's* heard you yester-morn—	"	1588
in the King's own *e* Speak	"	1656
glorious roundel echoing in our *e's,*	*Vivien*	276
All *e's* were prick'd at once,	*Elaine*	720
father's latest word humm'd in her *e,*	"	776
till the *e* Wearies to hear it,	"	893
the world, All *e* and eye,	"	937
stupid heart To interpret *e* and eye,	"	938
still in green, and *e* and eye,	*Guinevere*	25
vex an *e* too sad to listen to me	"	313
Worried his passive *e* with petty	*En. Arden.*	349
whisper in her *e* She knew not what	"	511
likewise, in the ringing of his *e's,*	"	614
all her vital spirits into each *e*	*Aylmer's F.*	201
foam'd away her heart at Averill's *e:*	"	342
His message ringing in thine *e's,*	"	666
mysterious way Thro' the seal'd *e*	"	696
True Devils with no *e,*	*Sea Dreams*	252
lend an *e* to Plato where he says,	*Lucretius*	147

ear (of corn.)
all its *e's* before the roaring East;	*Princess,* i.	234
pluck'd the ripen'd *e's,*	"	247
now is love mature in *e.*'	*In Mem.* lxxx.	4

Earl.
O the *E* was fair to see! (rep.)	*The Sisters*	6
The daughter of a hundred *E's*	*L.C.V. de Vere*	7
grim *E,* who ruled In Coventry:	*Godiva*	12
eagles of her belt, The grim *E's* gift;	"	44
old *E's* daughter died at my breast	*Lady Clare*	25
bandit *e's,* and caitiff knights,	*Enid*	35
musing sat the hoary-headed *E,*	"	295
sigh'd and smiled the hoary-headed *E,*	"	307
none spake word except the hoary *E:*	"	369
Prince and *E* Yet spoke together,	"	384
suddenly addrest the hoary *E:*	"	402
Fair Host and *E,* I pray your	"	403
So spake the kindly-hearted *E,*	"	514
E, entreat her by my love,	"	760
victual for these mowers of our *E;*	"	1074
into no *E's* palace will I go	"	1084
bow'd the all-amorous *E*	"	1209
heard the wild *E* at the door,	"	1230
the waste earldom of another *E,*	"	1287
all the boon companions of the *E,*	"	1326
on a mission to the bandit *E;*	"	1376
their own *E,* and their own souls,	"	1425
huge *E* cried out upon her talk,	"	1499
strode the brute *E* up and down	"	1560
knew this *E,* when I myself	"	1642
huge *E* lay slain within his hall	"	1654
King, duke, *e,* Count, baron—	*Elaine*	463

earldom.
From mine own *e* foully ousted me;	*Enid*	459
give back their *e* to thy kin.	"	585
prince who now our *e* back,	"	619
have our *e* back again.	"	701
To the waste *e* of another earl,	"	1287
share my *e* with me, girl,	"	1474

earlier.
'Alone' I said 'from *e* than I know,	*Princess,* vii.	292

earliest.
they are the *e* of the year.)	*Ode to Mem.*	27

early-silvering.
over Enoch's *e-s* head	*En. Arden.*	623

earn.
E well the thrifty months, '*Love thou thy land,'etc.*		95
lease Of life, shalt *e* no more;	*Will Water.*	244
metaphysics! read and *e* our prize,	*Princess,* iii.	283
popular name such manhood *e's,*	*Vivien*	636

earned.
e himself the name of sparrow-hawk.	*Enid*	492
e a scanty living for himself:	*En. Arden.*	819

earnest.
words were half in *e,* half in jest),	*Gardner's D.*	23
take it—*e* wed with sport,	*Day-Dm.*	279

	POEM.	LINE.
jest and *e* working side by side,	*Princess*, iv.	541
all, they said, as *e* as the close?	" *Con.*	21

earnest (pledge.)

e of the things that they shall do:	*Locksley H.*	118
e that he loves her yet,	*In Mem.* xcvi.	15
e in it of far springs to be.	*Vivien*	407

earning.

save all *e*'s to the uttermost,	*En. Arden*	86

earth.

star The black *e* with brilliance	*Ode to Mem.*	20
deem'd no mist of *e* could dull	"	38
Over the dark dewy *e* forlorn,	"	69
Scarce of *e* nor all divine,	*Adeline*	3
said the *e* was beautiful.	*A Character*	12
Making *e* wonder,	*The Poet*	52
shrink to the *e* if you came in.	*Poet's Mind*	37
house was builded of the *e*,	*Deserted H.*	15
choicest wealth of all the *e*,	*Eleänore*	19
Have I not found a happy *e* ?	*Miller's D.*	25
Hear me O *E*,	*Œnone*	35, 253
O happy *e*, how canst thou bear	"	233
enough unhappy on this *e*,	"	235
E and air seem only burning fire.	"	264
clay ta'en from the common *e*,	*To—WithPal.ofArt*	17
Lord of the visible *e*,	*Pal. of Art*	179
the riddle of the painful *e*	"	213
with the dull *e*'s mouldering sod,	"	261
never born into the *e*.	*To J. S.*	32
lost for ever from the *e*,	*M. d'Arthur*	90
round *e* is every way Bound	"	254
Felt *e* as air beneath me,	*Gardener's D.*	207
Unfit for *e*, unfit for heaven,	*St S. Stylites*	3
Heaven, and *E*, and Time are choked.	"	102
dark *E* follows wheel'd in her ellipse;	*Golden Year*	24
in old days Moved *e* and heaven;	*Ulysses*	67
the kindly *e* shall slumber,	*Locksley H.*	130
that the *e* should stand at gaze	"	180
churl, compact of thankless *e*,	*Godiva*	66
Dissolved the riddle of the *e*.	*Two Voices*	170
that last nothing under *e* !'	"	333
we are Ancients of the *e*,	*Day-Dm.*	231
e is rich in man and maid ;	*Will Water.*	65
whole wide *e* of light and shade	"	67
That are the flower of the *e t*'	*Lady Clare*	15
Bore to *e* her body, drest	*L.of Burleigh*	98
Move eastward, happy *e*, and '*Move eastward*,'*etc*. 1
lamps blazon'd like Heaven and *E Princess*, i.	220
upon the Sun Than our man's *e* ;	" ii.	23
broad and bounteous *E* Should bear	"	162
nothing upon *e* More miserable	" iii.	242
from the dewy shoulders of the *E*,	" v.	41
sweet influences Of *e* and heaven?	"	184
the roots of *e* and base of all ;	"	436
Part roll'd on the *e* and rose again	"	466
such a roar that *E* Reels,	"	518
lies the *E* all Danaë to the stars,	" vii.	167
Where he in English *e* is laid,	*In Mem.* xviii.	2
This *e* had been the Paradise	" xxiv.	6
A rainy cloud possess'd the *e*,	" xxx.	3
Else *e* is darkness at the core,	" xxxiv.	3
The baby new to *e* and sky,	" xliv.	1
The silent snow possess'd the *e*,	" lxxvii.	3
life that *e*'s embrace May breed	" lxxxi.	3
bare The use of virtue out of *e* :	"	10
To wander on a darken'd *e*,	" lxxxix.	31
To myriads on the genial *e*,	" xcviii.	14
A lever to uplift the *e*	" cxii.	15
As dying Nature's *e* and lime ;	" cxvii.	4
say, The solid *e* whereon we trend	"	8
O *e*, what changes hast thou seen !	" cxxii.	2
The brute *e* lightens to the sky,	" cxxvi.	15
under whose command Is *E* and *E*'s,	" cxxxi.	14
of old the Lord and Master of *E*,	*Maud*, I. iv.	31
the passions that make a Hell I	" x.	46
lamp of *e* has left his estate	" xvi.	1
whole *e* gone nearer to the glow	" xviii.	78
Were it *e* in an earthy bed ;	" xxii.	70
dawn of Eden bright over *e* and sky,	" II. i.	8
'Cold altar, Heaven and *e* shall meet	*The Letters*	7

	POEM.	LINE.
e yawns: the mortal disappears ;	*Ode on Well.*	269
gloom that saddens Heaven and *E*,	*The Daisy*	102
better were I laid in the dark *e*,	*Enid*	97
track this vermin to their *e*'s:	"	217
'I have track'd him to his *e*.'	"	253
why *e* has *e* enough To hide him.	"	1403
in the wither'd leaf And makes it *e*,	"	1482
O Merlin, may this *e*, if ever I	*Vivien*	195
hard *e* cleave to the Nadir hell	"	199
men at most differ as Heaven and *e*,	"	663
splinters of the wood The dark *e*.	"	787
loves me must have a touch of *e* ;	*Elaine*	134
hard *e* shake, and a low thunder	"	450
Cling to the dead *e*, and the land	*Guinevere*	8
heavens upbreaking thro' the *e*,	"	388
dug His fingers into the wet *e*,	*En. Arden*	781
this, a milky-way on *e*,	*Aylmer's F.*	160
since our bad *e* became one sea	"	635
e Lightens from her own central Hell	"	760
All over earthy, like a piece of *e*,	*Sea Dreams*	97
In days far-off, on that dark *e*,	*Tithonus*	48
I *e* in *e* forget these empty courts,	"	75
I cast to *e* a seed.	*The Flower*	2
To a sweet little Eden on *e*	*The Islet*	14
breathe it into *e* and close it up	*Coquette*, iii.	12
bitten into the heart of the *e* .	*The Window*	60

earthlier.

lonelier, darker, *e* for my loss.	*Aylmer's F.*	750

earthly.

For she is *e* of the mind,	*In Mem.*cxiii.	21

earthquake.

Blight and famine, plague and *e*,	*Lotos-E's.*	160
like a bell Toll'd by an *e*	*Princess*, vi.	312
flood, fire, *e*, thunder, wrought	*Aylmer's F.*	639
out of sight, and sink Past *e*—	*Lucretius*	154
Shatter'd into one *e* in one day	"	247

earthy.

All over *e*, like a piece of earth,	*Sea Dreams*	97

ease.

bound fast in one with golden *e* ;	*Circumstance*	5
Alice, you were ill at *e* ;	*Miller's D.*	146
Wherein at *e* for aye to dwell.	*Pal. of Art*	2
dark death, or dreamful *e*.	*Lotos-E's.*	98
You ask me, why, tho' ill at *e*, '*You ask me why*,' *etc.* 1
lest we rust in *e*.	'*Love thou thy land*,' *etc.*	42
if man rot in dreamless *e*,	*Two Voices*	280
garrulous *e* and oily courtesies	*Princess*, i.	162
We break our laws with *e*,	" vi.	303
your Highness breaks with *e* The law	"	305
I would set their pains at *e*.	*In Mem.*lxi.	8
Drank till he jested with all *e*,	*Enid*	1139
let his wisdom go For *e* of heart,	*Vivien*	742
surely I can silence with all *e*.	*Elaine*	110
they lost themselves Yet with all *e*,	"	441
found no *e* in turning or in rest ;	"	897
with how great *e* Nature can smile,	*Lucretius*	174

east.

slowly rounded to the *e*	*Mariana in the S.*	79
courts I made, *E*, West and South	*Pal. of Art*	21
fresh beam of the springing *e* ;	*M.a'Arthur*	214
dark *E*, Unseen, is brightening	*Gardener's D.*	71
greet their fairer sisters of the *E*.	"	184
freshness in the dawning *e*,	*Two Voices*	405
all its ears before the roaring *E* ;	*Princess*, i.	234
Nor stunted squaws of West or *E* ;	" ii.	64
the darkness from their native *E*.	" iii.	6
'Alas your Highness breathes full *E*'	"	215
beam Of the *E*, that play'd.	" v.	240
O Father, touch the *e*, and light	*In Mem.*xxx.	31
windless flame Up the deep *E*,	" lxxi.	14
E and West, without a breath	" xciv.	62
What lightens in the lucid *e* .	" civ.	24
Fiercely flies The blast of North and *E*,	" cvi.	7
Blush from West to *E*, (rep.)	*Maud*, I. xvii.	21
that streams to thy delicious *E*,	" xviii.	16
I to the *E* And he for Italy—	*The Brook*	1
The bitter *e*, the misty summer,	*The Daisy*	103

	POEM.	LINE.
pale and bloodless *e* began To quicken *Enid*	.	534
lived a king in the most Eastern E,	*Vivien*	. 405
her chamber up a tower to the *e*	. *Elaine*	3
blaze upon the waters to the *e*;	. *En. Arden*.	595
in the west, And rosed in the *e*:	. *Sea Dreams*	40
ever silent spaces of the E,	. *Tithonus*	9
hold me not for ever in thine *E*:	"	64
Across the boundless *e* we drove,	. *The Voyage*	38
Far in the E Boädicea, standing	. *Boädicea*	3
King of the E altho' he seem,	. *Lucretius*	. 133
Flown to the *e* or the west,	. *The Window*	41

east-wind.

In the stormy *e-w* straining,	. *L. of Shalott*,iv.1

easy.

Of my long life have made it *e* to me. *Vivien*	. 530
For it's *e* to find a rhyme.	. *The Window* 149-55

eat.

princes over-bold Have *e* our substance, *Lotos-E's*.121		
thou may'st warble, *e* and dwell:	. *The Blackbird*	4
sat and *e* And talk'd old matters	. *Audley Ct*.	. 27
e wholesome food, And wear warm *St S. Stylites* 106		
I will not *e* my heart alone,	. *In Mem*. cvii.	3
thousand pips *e* up your sparrow-hawk! *Enid*	. 274	
I will enter, I will *e*	"	. 305
e in Arthur's hall at Camelot.	"	. 432
let her *e*; the damsel is so faint.' .	"	1055
e also, tho' the fare is coarse,	"	1057
on the sudden he said, 'E!'	"	1462
mad to see you weep. E!.	"	1465
E and be glad, for I account you mine."	"	1495
thrust the dish before her, crying, 'E.'	"	1503
no,' said Enid, vext, 'I will not *e*,	"	1504
upon the bier arise, And *e* with me."	"	1506
well have drunken, scarce can *e* :	"	1510
Not *e* nor drink? And wherefore	"	1522
meant to *e* her up in that wild wood *Vivien*	. 109	
e's And uses, careless of the rest:	"	. 312
After the king, who *e* in Arthur's halls. *Elaine*	. 184	

eaten.

after all had *e*, then Geraint,	. *Enid*	. 397
' Boy,' said he, 'I have *e* all,	"	. 1066
Earl Doorm had *e* all he would,	"	. 1457

eating.

E the Lotos day by day,	. *Lotos-E's*.	105
ulcer, *e* thro' my skin,	. *St S. Stylites*	66
e not, Except the spare chance-gift	"	. 76
boys Who love to vex him *e*,	. *Enid*	. 1409
e hoary grain and pulse	. *Spec. of Iliad* 22, ii.	

eavedrops.

Then I rise, the *e* fall,	. *Maud*, II. iv. 62

eaves.

eyelids dropp'd their silken *e*.	. *Talking O*.	. 209
fall upon her gilded *e*	. *Princess*, iv.	76
closing *e* of wearied eyes	. *In Mem*. lxvi.	11
murmurest in the foliaged *e*	. " xcviii.	5
Makes daggers at the sharpen'd *e*,	" cvi.	8
almost to the martin-haunted *e*	. *Aylmer's F*.	163

ebb (s.)

left the dying *e* that faintly lipp'd	. *Audley Ct*.	. 11
e and flow conditioning their march, *Golden Year*	. 118	
could rest, a rock in *e*'s and flows,	*Enid*	. 812

ebb (verb.)

According to my humour *e* and flow *D. of F. Wom*.134		
When the tide *e*'s in sunshine,	. *Princess*, vi.	146

ebb'd.

the wassail-bowl Then half-way *e* :	*The Epic*	. 6
mine have *e* away for evermore,	. *Vivien*	. 289
He flow'd and *e* uncertain,	. *Aylmer's F*.	218

ebbing.

felt them slowly *e*, name and fame.' *Vivien*	. 287

ebony.

Tress'd with redolent *e*,	. *Arabian N's*.138
there at tables of *e* lay,	. *Boädicea*	. 61

echo (s.)

	POEM.	LINE.
So took *e* with delight, :	. *The Owl*, ii.	4
An *e* from a measur'd strain,	. *Miller's D*.	. 66
To hear the dewy *e*'s calling	. *Lotos-E's*.	. 139
Lull'd *e*'s of laborious day.	. *Margaret*	. 29
faint Homeric *e*'s, nothing-worth,	*The Epic*	. 39
the great *e* flap And buffet	. *Golden Year*	75
Like hints and *e*'s of the world	. *Day-Dm*.	. 27
E answer'd in her sleep	. *Princess,Pro*. 66	
An *e* like a ghostly woodpecker,	. "	. 211
set the wild *e*'s flying, (rep.).	. "	iii. 352
Blow, bugle; answer, *e*'s, (rep.).	"	. 353
A step Of lightest *e*,	, "	iv. 196
a wild horn in a land Of *e*'s,	. "	v. 476
now and then an *e* started up,	. "	vi. 349
A hollow *e* of my own,—	. *In Mem*. lii.	11
Like *e*'s in sepulchral halls,	. "	lvii. 2
e's out of weaker times,	. "	Con. 22
E there, whatever is asked her,	. *Maud*, I. i.	6
Is at an *e* of something Read	. "	vii. 9
million horrible bellowing *e*'s broke	. " II. i.	24
And the woodland *e* rings;	. "	iv. 38
proof and echo of all human fame, *Ode on Well*. 145		
Queen, In words whose *e* lasts,	. *Enid*	. 782
Like *e*'s from beyond a hollow,	. *Aylmer's F*. 298	
crashing with long *e*'s thro' the land	"	. 338
hears E's in his empty '*Home they brought him,*'*etc*.4		

echo (verb.)

Hear a song that *e*'s cheerly	. *L. of Shalott*,i. 30
With sounds that *e* still.	. *D. of F. Wom*. 8
'Hear how the bushes *e*!	. *Gardener's D*. 97
The haunts of memory *e* not.	. *Two Voices* 369
The last wheel *e*'s away.	. *Maud*, I. xxii. 26
E round his bones for evermore.	. *Ode on Well*. 12
wave that *e*'s round the world;	. *Enid*	. 420
made his pleasure *e*, hand to hand, *Aylmer's F*. 257	

echoed.

further inland voices *e*—' come *M. d' Arthur, Ep*. 27	
while our cloisters *e* frosty feet, *Princess,Pro*. 181	
and the forest *e* 'fool.'	. *Vivien*	. 823
chang'd itself and *e* in her heart,	. *Elaine*	. 778

echoing.

E all night to that sonorous flow *Pc'l. of Art*	27
Illyrian woodlands, *e* falls Of water *To E. L*.	1
heel against the pavement *e*,	. *Enid*	. 1120
glorious roundel *e* in our ears,	. *Vivien*	. 276
the Father answer'd, *e* 'highest ?'	*Elaine*	1072
ghostly footfall *e* on the stair.	. *Guinevere*	. 503
e me you cry 'Our house is left	. *Aylmer's F*.	736

echo-like.

Then *e-l* our voices rang;	. *In Mem*. xxx.	13

eclipse.

Gaiety without *e* Wearieth me	. *Lilian*.	. 20
the sun, a crescent of *e*,	. *Vision of Sin*	10
shadow of His loss drew like *e*,	. *Ded. of Idylls*	13

ecliptic.

Sear'd by the close *e*,	. *Aylmer's F*. 193

eddied.

e into suns, that wheeling cast	. *Princess*, ii. 103

eddy (s.)

eddies of its wayward brother;	. *Isabel*.	. 33
There the river *e* whirls,	. *L.of Shalott*,ii. 15	
In crystal *eddies* glance and poise, *Miller's D*.	. 52	
I cannot keep My heart an *e*	. *Princess*, vi.	302
fancy's tenderest *e* wreathe,	. *In Mem*.xlviii.	6
No doubt vast *eddies* in the flood	" cxxvii.	5

eddy (verb.)

those that *e* round and round?	. *In Mem*. lii.	12

eddying.

e of her garments caught from thee *Ode to Mem*. 31

Eden.

that E where she dwelt.	. *Gardener'sD*.187
Summer isles of E lying	. *Locksley H*. 164
Saw distant gates of E gleam,	. *Two Voices* 212
every bird of E burst In carol,	. *Day-Dm*. . 255
comes the statelier E back to men: *Princess*, vii. 277	

	POEM.	LINE.
Rings *E* thro' the budded quicks,	*In Mem.*	lxxxvii. 2
moon Of *E* on its bridal bower : .	" Con.	28
dawn of *E* bright over earth and sky,	*Maud*, II. i.	8
kept the heart of *E* green . .	*Enid*	1618
Set in this *E* of all plenteousness,	*En. Arden*	562
sweet little *E* on earth that I know,	*The Islet*	14
brooks of *E* mazily murmuring,	*Milton*	10

edge.
fading *e's* of box beneath,	'*A spirit haunts*,' etc.	19
Stream'd onward, lost their *e's*,	*D. of F. Wom.*	50
three times slipping from the outer *e*,	*The Epic*	11
here and there on lattice *e's* lay	*Princess*, ii.	15
That axelike *e* unturnable,	"	186
growing longest by the meadow's *e*,	*Enid*	1106
prone *e* of the wood began	*En. Arden*	67, 370

edged.
E with sharp laughter, '*Clear-headed friend*,' etc.		2
a letter *e* with death Beside him,	*Aylmer's F.*	595

edge-tools.
ill jesting with *e-t* !	*Princess*, ii.	184

Edith.
his *E*, whom he loved As heiress	*Aylmer's F.*	23
in his walks with *E*, claim	"	61
shook the heart of *E* hearing him.	"	63
E, whose pensive beauty, perfect	"	70
roll'd His hoop to pleasure *E*,	"	85
make-believes For *E* and himself :	"	96
labourers' homes A frequent haunt of *E*,	"	148
its own charm ; and *E's* everywhere ;	"	165
E ever visitant with him,	"	166
He but less loved than *E*,	"	167
E's eager fancy hurried with him .	"	208
gifts on everyone And most on *E* :	"	215
E whom his pleasure was to please,	"	232
was *E* that same night : Pale	"	279
its worth Was being *E's*.	"	379
would go, Labour for his own *E*,	"	420
remembering His former talks with *E*,	"	457
shriek 'yes love, yes *E*, yes,'	"	582
dagger which himself Gave *E*,	"	597
'From *E*' was engraven on the blade.	"	598
known *E* among the hamlets round,	"	615

educated.
all his pretty young ones *e*,	*En. Arden*	146

Edmund.
brook,' says *E* in his rhyme,	*The Brook*	21
week Before I parted with poor *E* ;	"	78
My dearest brother, *E*, sleeps,	"	187

Edward (see Bull, Head, Gray.)

Edwin (see Morris.)
Friend *E*, do not think yourself	*Ed. Morris*	77
I and *E* laugh'd	"	93
So left the place, left *E*,	"	137

Edyrn.
answer, groaning, '*E*, son of Nudd !	*Enid*	576
'Then, *E*, son of Nudd,' replied .	"	579
when *E* sack'd their house,	"	634
a cry That *E's* men were on them	"	639
E's men had caught them	"	642
Beholding it was *E* son of Nudd	"	1629
one from *E*. Every now and then,	"	1667
When *E* rein'd his charger .	"	1668
went apart with *E*, whom he held	"	1729
E and with others : have you look'd At *E* ?	"	1744
E has done it, weeding all his heart	"	1754
work of *E* wrought upon himself	"	1760

'eer'd 'heard.'
'e un a bummin' awaäy loike	*N. Farmer*	18
I often *'e* un mysen ;	"	30
I *'e* un aboot an' aboot,	"	31

effect (s.)
thine *e* so lives in me	*In Mem.*, lxiv.	10

effect (verb.)
tho' she herself *e* But little ;	*Princess*, iii.	247

effeminacy.
	POEM.	LINE.
his force Is melted into mere *e* ?	*Enid*	107
purple couches in their tender *e*	*Boädicea*	62

effeminate.
'*E* as I am, I will not fight my way	*Enid*	869

Effie.
Little *E* shall go with me	*May Queen*, i.	25
Don't let *E* come to see me .	" ii.	43
And *E* on the other side	" iii.	24
I thought of you and *E* dear ;	"	29
But, *E*, you must comfort her	"	44
little while till you and *E* come— .	"	58

eft.
A monstrous *e* was of old the Lord	*Maud*, I. iv.	31

egalities.
That cursed France with her *e* !	*Aylmer's F.*	265

Egbert.
doing nothing Since *E*—why,	*Aylmer's F.*	384

egg.
The goose let fall a golden *e*	*The Goose*	11
stole his fruit, His hens, his *e's* ;	*Walk. to the M.*	77
Roof-haunting martins warm their *e's* :	*Day-Dm.*	37
The Cock was of a larger *e*	*Will Water.*	121
lay their *e's*, and sting and sing,	*In Mem.* xlix.	11
evil fancies clung Like serpent *e's*	*En. Arden*	477
in the plain *e's* of the nightingale	*Aylmer's F.*	103

egg-shell.
Nor cared a broken *e-s* for her lord.	*Enid*	1213

eglantine.
Vine, vine and *e*, (rep.)	*The Window*	21

eglatere.
woodbine and *e* Drip sweeter dews	*A Dirge*	23

Egypt.
O my life In *E* !	*D. of F. Wom.*	147
time When we made bricks in *E*.	*Princess*, iv.	110

Egyptian.
To whom the *E* : 'O, you tamely	*D. of F. Wom.*	258

Egypt-plague.
our arms fail'd—this *E-p* of men	*Princess*, v.	417

eight.
cutting *e's* that day upon the pond,	*The Epic*	10
E that were left to make a purer world	*Aylmer's F.*	638

Elaine.
E the fair, *E* the loveable, *E*, the lily	*Elaine*	1
behind them stept the lily maid *E*,	"	177
E, and heard her name so tost	"	233
E, Won by the mellow voice	"	242
parted with his own to fair *E* ;	"	380
cast his eyes on fair *E* :	"	637
'Torre and *E* ! why here ?	"	792
rose *E* and glided thro' the fields,	"	839
call her friend and sister, sweet *E*.	"	861
had been wedded earlier, sweet *E* :	"	931
on her face and thought 'Is this *E* ?'	"	1025

elbow.
In every *e* and turn,	*Ode to Mem.*	62
in broider'd down we sank our *e's* :	*Princess*, iv.	15

elbow-chair.
She shifted in her *e-c*,	*The Goose*	27

elbow-deep.
e-d in sawdust, slept	*Will Water.*	92

Elder.
led The holy *E's* with the gift	*M. d'Arthur*	233
Thine *e's* and thy betters.	*Will Water.*	192
passion of youth Toward greatness in its *e*,	*Elaine*	283
with jubilant cries Broke from their *e's*,	*En. Arden*	375

elder-thicket.
white-flower'd *e-t* from the field,	*Godiva*	63

eldest-born.
Whatever *e-b* of rank or wealth	*Aylmer's F.*	484
And Willy, my *e-b*, is gone,	*Grandmother*	1
Willy, my beauty, my *e-b* .	"	9, 101
Willy, my *e-b*, at nigh threescore	"	87

Eleanor.

	POEM.	LINE.
Those dragon eyes of anger'd E	D. of F. Wom.	255

Eleänore.

To deck thy cradle, E.	Eleänore	21
Serene, imperial E	"	81, 121
In thy large eyes, imperial E.	"	97

elected.

by common voice, E umpire,	Œnone	83

elegy.

elegies And quoted odes,	Princess, ii.	354

element.

The e's were kindlier mix'd.'	Two Voices	228
in their own clear e, they moved.	Princess, vii.	13
Large e's in order brought,	In Mem. cxi.	13
One God, one law, one e,	" Con.	142
I am not made of so slight e's.	Guinevere	506
soul to soul Strike thro' a finer e	Aylmer's F.	579

elf.

the little elves of chasm and cleft	Guinevere	246

elf-god.

'I saw the little e-g eyeless once	Vivien	98

Elfland.

The horns of E faintly blowing!	Princess, iii.	357

Elizabeth.

The spacious times of great E	D.of F. Wom.	7
there is Aunt E And sister Lilia	Princess, Pro.	51
here we lit on Aunt E,	"	96
in arts of government E and others;	" ii.	146

elk.

the monstrous horns of e and deer,	Princess, Pro.	23

Ellen (see Aubrey.)

Sleep, E, folded in thy sister's arm,(rep.)	Audley Ct.	62

Ellen Adair.

E A she loved me well,	Ed. Gray	9
E A was dying for me.	"	16
Here lies the body of E A;	"	27
Till E A come back to me.	"	32

Elle vous suit.

sent a note, the seal an E vs,	Ed. Morris	105

ellipse.

Earth follows wheel'd in her e;	Golden Year	24

elm.

The seven e's, the poplars four	Ode to Mem.	56
The mellow ouzel fluted in the e;	Gardener's D.	93
fruits and cream Served in the weeping e;	"	191
Old e's came breaking from the vine,	Amphion	45
friends, none closer, e and vine:	Princess, ii.	316
from the lily as far As oak from e:	" v.	175
moan of doves in immemorial e's,	" vii.	206
approaching rookery swerve From the e's,	" Con.	97
Rock'd the full-foliaged e's,	In Mem.xciv.	58
Aroused the black republic on his e's,	Aylmer's F.	529

elm-tree.

'ill caw from the windy tall e-t,	May Queen,ii.	17
The topmost e-t gather'd green	Sir L.and Q.G.	8

elmtree-bole.

Enormous e-b's did stoop and lean	D.of F. Wom.	57

eloquence.

A full-cell'd honeycomb of e	Ed. Morris	26
golden e And amorous adulation	Elaine	646

eloquent.

the form alone is e!	Coquette, ii.	1

Elysian.

others in E valleys dwell,	Lotos-E's.	169
lovelier not the E lawns,	Princess, iii.	324

emancipation.

on whom The secular e turns	Princess, ii.	269

embalm.

e In dying songs a dead regret,	In Mem. Con.	13

embassy.

touches are but embassies of love,	Gardener's D.	18

embattail.

	POEM.	LINE.
To e and to wall about thy cause	To J. M. K.	8

embellish.

revenue Wherewith to e state,	Œnone	111

emblem.

Graven with e's of the time,	Arabian N's.	108
Like e's of infinity,	Ode to Mem.	103
Caryatids, lifted up A weight of e,	Princess, iv.	184

emblematic.

Amazon As e of a nobler age;	Princess, ii.	111

embodied.

truth e in a tale	In Mem.xxxvi.	7

emboss'd.

bronze valves, e with Tomyris	Princess, v.	355

embower.

However deep you might e the nest,	Princess,Pro.	147

embrace (s.)

Die, dying clasp'd in his e.	Fatima	42
the last e's of our wives	Lotos-E's.	115
betwixt thy dear e and mine,	Love and Duty	48
silent in a last e.	Locksley H.	58
face He kiss'd, taking his last e,	Two Voices	254
slipt away from my e's	Will Water.	182
Twisted hard in fierce e's,	Vision of Sin	40
parting with a long e	In Mem. xxxix.	11
life that earth's e May breed	" lxxxi.	3
yet remembers his e	" lxxxiv.	111
A little while from his e,	" cxvi.	3
We stood tranced in long e's	Maud, II. iv.	8
first e had died Between them,	Lucretius	3

embrace (verb.)

heart Went forth to e him	Œnone	62
E our aims; work out your freedom.	Princess, ii.	75
e me, come, Quick while I melt;	" vi.	267
we e you yet once more	"	276
By faith, and faith alone, e	In Mem. Pro.	3
E her as my natural good	" iii.	14
I e the purpose of God,	Maud,III.vi.	59
will e me in the world-to-be:	En. Arden.	894

embraced.

I could not be e.	Talking O.	140
E his Eve in happy hour,	Day-Dm.	254
dream thy cause e in mine	Princess, vi.	183
E her with all welcome as a friend,	Enid	834
Queen once more e her friend	"	1795
half e the basket cradle-head	Sea Dreams	277

embracing.

while we stood like fools E,	Ed. Morris	119
E cloud, Ixion-like;	Two Voices	195
when he saw the Queen, e ask'd,	Elaine	569

emerald.

lights, rose, amber, e, blue,	Pal. of Art	169
beneath an e plane Sits Diotima,	Princess, iii.	284
bickers round and e,	" v.	253
flakes Of crimson or in e rain.	In Mem.xcvii.	32
A million e's break from the	Maud, I. iv.	1
A livelier e twinkles in the grass,	" xviii.	51
our Lady's Head, Carved of one e,	Elaine	295
There they drank in cups of e,	Boädicea	61

emerald-colour'd.

watch the e-c water falling	Lotos-E's.	141

emerged.

E, I came upon the great Pavilion	Arabian N's.	113

Emilia.

Sleep, Ellen, folded in E's arm;	Audley Ct.	64

emissary.

Came at the moment Leolin's e,	Aylmer's F.	518

Emma (see Moreland.)

emotion.

Hide me from my deep e,	Locksley H.	108
Some vague e of delight	Two Voices	361
play The Spartan Mother with e,	Princess, ii.	263

	POEM.	LINE.
empanoplied.		
E and plumed We enter'd in,	Princess, v.	472
emperor.		
E, Ottoman, which shall win:	To F. D. Maurice	32
emperor-idiot.		
liars worship a gluttonous e-i.	Boädicea	19
emperor-moth.		
But move as rich as E-m's,	Princess, Pro.	144
empire.		
the care That yokes with e,	To the Queen	10
ere he found E for life?	Gardener's D.	20
to law, System and e?	Love and Duty	8
'Three ladies of the Northern e	Princess, i.	235
Persian, Grecian, Roman lines Of e,	" ii.	115
With an e's lamentation,	Ode on Well.	2
like a household god Promising e;	On a Mourner	31
employ.		
fierce extremes e Thy spirits	In Mem. lxxxvii.	5
Come, when no graver cares e,	To F. D. Maurice	1
employed.		
So gentle, so e, should close in love,	Princess, vii.	52
emptied.		
e of all joy, Leaving the dance	D. of F. Wom.	215
all The chambers e of delight:	In Mem. viii.	8
affluent Fortune e all her horn.	Ode on Well.	197
emptiness.		
From e and the waste wide	Two Voices	119
The sins of e, gossip and spite	Princess, ii.	78
empty.		
Two years his chair is seen E	To J. S.	23
feels Her place is e	In Mem. xiii.	4
when he found all e, was amazed	Enid	1065
empyrean.		
deep-domed e Rings to the roar	Milton	7
encarnalize.		
with shameful jest, E their spirits:	Princess, iii.	298
enchanted.		
' He is e, cannot speak—and she,	Elaine	1247
enchanter.		
Upon the great E of the Time,	Vivien	65
enchantress.		
A great e you may be;	L. C. V. de Vere	30
encircle.		
E's all the heart, and feedeth	Margaret	16
enclosing.		
hollow shades e hearts of flame,	Pal. of Art	241
every marge e in the midst	Vivien	520
encompass.		
The love of all Thy sons e Thee,	Ded. of Idylls	50
encompassed.		
sleep E by his faithful guard,	In Mem. cxxv.	8
encounter.		
A little in the late e strain'd,	Enid	1007
end (s.)		
cruel lowe, whose e is scorn	Mariana in the S.	70
Is this the e to be left alone,	"	71
in all action is the e of all	Œnone	120
Death is the e of life; ah, why	Lotos-E's.	86
all thine own, Until the e of time.'	D. of F. Wom.	84
Sleep till the e, true soul	To J. S.	73
endures not sordid e's	''Love thou thy land,' etc.	6
'My e draws nigh: 'tis time that I	M. d'Arthur	163
Here, then, my words have e.	Gardener's D.	245
my e draws nigh: I hope my e draws	St S. Stylites	35
watcher on the column till the e;	"	160
The e! the e! Surely the e	"	198
set gray life, and apathetic e.	Love and Duty	18
shapes it to some perfect e.	"	26
in station, but the e had come	"	74
dull it is to pause, to make an e,	Ulysses	22
something ere the e, Some work	"	51

	POEM.	LINE.
A labour working to an e.	Two Voices	297
e and the beginning vex His reason;	"	298
'I see the e, and know the good'.	"	432
hook it to some useful e.	Day-Dm.	212
Enough if at the e of all	Amphion	103
For them I battle till the e	Sir Galahad	15
moves to gracious e's 'You might have won,' etc.		6
bees and breeze from e to e.	Princess, Pro.	88
from e to e With beauties every	" ii.	413
if our e were less achievable	" iii.	266
iron laws, in the e Found golden	" iv.	57
great is song Used to great e's:	"	120
grand fight to kill and make an e:	"	568
you failing, I abide What e soever:	" v.	396
at the further e Was Ida by the throne	" vi.	336
For worship without e; nor e of mine,	" vii.	154
Yoked in all exercise of noble e,	"	340
O what to her shall be the e?	In Mem. vi.	41
'Is this the e? Is this the e?	" xii.	16
move thee on to noble e's.	" lxiv.	12
Are sharpen'd to a needle's e;	" lxxv.	4
What e is here to my complaint?	" lxxx.	6
Now looking to some settled e,	" lxxxiv.	97
I climb the hill: from e to e.	" xcix.	1
ampler day For ever nobler e's	" cxvii.	7
toil coöperant to an e.	" cxxvii.	24
itself to the long-wish'd-for e	Maud, I. xviii.	5
never an e to the stream of passing	" II. v.	11
at either e whereof There swung an	Enid	169
O to what e, except a jealous one,	Vivien	388
and to this e Had made the pretext	Elaine	580
sweet is death who puts an e to pain:	"	1002
An e to this! A strange one	"	1216
Serving his traitorous e;	Guinevere	20
'the e is come And I am shamed	"	109
Down at the far e of an avenue	En. Arden	355
lonely doom Came suddenly to an e.	"	628
rioted his life out, and made an e.	Aylmer's F.	391
every labyrinth till he saw An e,	"	480
wanted at his e The dark retinue.	"	841
a flower or two, and there an e—	Lucretius	226
Gone till the e of the year,	The Window	36
Over the world to the e of it.	"	200
end (verb.)		
to begin implies to e;	Two Voices	339
the strange betrothment was to e:	Princess, v.	463
will I hide thee, till my life shall e,	Guinevere	113
could not e me, left me maim'd	Tithonus	20
Whether I mean this day to e myself,	Lucretius	146
manlike e myself?—our privilege—	"	229
endear.		
falling out That all the more e's	Princess, i.	252
ended.		
Here e Hall, and our last light,	M. d'Arthur, Ep.	1
Thus far he flow'd, and e;	Golden Year	52
When, ere his song was e,	Amphion	50
She e here, and beckon'd us:	Princess, ii.	165
e with such passion that the tear,	" iv.	41
when the jousts were e yesterday,	Enid	692
e with apology so sweet	"	1243
this was e, and his careful hand—	En. Arden	176
E he had not, but she brook'd	Aylmer's F.	798
when the wordy storm Had e,	Sea Dreams	32
ending.		
She, e, waved her hands:	Princess, iv.	501
e in a ruin—nothing left,	Vivien	732
endow.		
E you with broad land and territory	Elaine	953
endurance.		
until e grow Sinew'd with action,	Œnone	161
endure.		
A courage to e and to obey;	Isabel	25
All force in bonds that might e,	Pal. of Art	154
e's not sordid ends,	'Love thou thy land,' etc.	6
dies not, but e's with pain.	In Mem. xviii.	17
scarce e to draw the breath,	" xx.	15
Whose loves in higher love e;	" xxxii.	14

CONCORDANCE TO

	POEM.	LINE.
O living will that shalt *e*	*In Mem.* cxxx.	1
Let the sweet heavens *e*,	*Maud*, I. xi.	8
As long as my life *e's*	" xix.	86
while the races of mankind *e*,	*Ode on Well.*	219
not, O woman's-heart, but still *e*;	*Ded. of Idylls*	43
Break not, for thou art Royal, but *e*,	"	44
E's not that her guest should serve	*Enid* .	379
can *e* it all most patiently.'	"	473
thought to do while he might yet *e*,	*Elaine*	494
I will nevermore *e* To sit	*Sailor Boy* .	15
heart to *e* for the life of the worm.	*Wages*	7

endured.

Have all in all *e* as much,	*St S. Stylites*	128
yet *e* to meet her opening eyes,	*Princess*, iv.	177
they knew her: they *e*,	"	302
surely have *e* Strange chances	*Enid* .	1657

'enemies (anemones.)

| Doon i' the woild '*e* | *N. Farmer* . | 34 |

enemy.

enemies have fall'n, have fall'n: (rep.)	*Princess*, vi.	17
if an *e's* fleet came yonder	*Maud*, I. i.	49
arms, arms, arms to fight my *e*?	*Enid* .	282
down his *e* roll'd, And there lay still;	"	1009
roll'd his *e* down, And saved him:	*Elaine*	26
knights Are half of them our *enemies*,	"	100
a dream Of dragging down his *e*	"	810
said, 'mine *enemies* Pursue me,	*Guinevere*	138
Ev'n in the presence of an *e's* fleet,	"	277
moan of an *e* massacred,	*Boädicea*	25
tho' the gathering *e* narrow thee,	"	39
pulses at the clamouring of her *e*,	"	82

energy.

spurr'd at heart with fieriest *e*	*To J. M. K.*	7
By its own *e* fulfill'd itself	*Gardener's D.*	233
full-grown *energies* of heaven.	*In Mem.* xxxix.	20
With agonies, with *energies*,	" cxii.	18

enfold.

large grief which these *e*	*In Mem.* v.	11
So dear a life your arms *e*	*The Daisy* .	93

enfolded.

Two mutually *e*; Love, the third,	*Gardener's D.*	210
in her veil *e*, manchet bread.	*Enid* .	389

engarlanded.

| *E* and diaper'd With inwrought | *Arabian N's.* | 148 |

engine.

| Which only to one *e* bound | *Two Voices* | 347 |

engirt.

| *E* with many a florid maiden-cheek, | *Princess*, iii. | 332 |

England.

more than *E* honours that,	*Talking O.*	295
From *E* to Van Diemen.	*Amphion*	84
freedom in her regal seat Of *E*;	*In Mem.* cviii.	15
thanks to the Giver, *E*, for thy son.	*Ode on Well.*	45
For this is *E's* greatest son,	"	95
E pouring on her foes.	"	117
keep our noble *E* whole,	"	161
Truth-teller was our *E's* Alfred	"	168
It told of *E* then to me,	*The Daisy* .	89
how should *E* dreaming of *his* sons	*Ded. of Idylls*	30
dewy meadowy morning-breath Of *E*,	*En. Arden*	662
God-gifted organ-voice of *E*,	*Milton*	3

English.

first reveal'd themselves to *E* air,	*Eleänore*	2
one, an *E* home—gray twilight	*Pal. of Art*	85
E natures, freemen, friends, '*Love thou thy land,' etc.*	7
sweet as *E* air could make her,	*Princess*, *Pro.*	154
Where he in *E* earth is laid,	*In Mem.* xviii.	2
like sunny gems on an *E* green,	*Maud*, I. v.	14
I see her there, Bright *E* lily,	" xix.	55
if you knew her in *E* days	*The Brook* .	224
Nor ever lost an *E* gun;	*Ode on Well.*	97
Truth-lover was our *E* Duke;	"	189
Gallant sons of *E* freemen,	*The Captain*	7

Englishman.

| A great broad-shoulder'd genial *E*, | *Princess, Con.* | 85 |
| The last great *E* is low. | *Ode on Well.* | 18 |

engrailed.

	POEM.	LINE.
hills with peaky tops *e*,	*Pal. of Art*	113

engrained.

| with vary-colour'd shells Wander'd *e*. | *Arabian N's.* | 58 |

engraven.

| 'From Edith' was *e* on the blade | *Aylmer's F.* | 598 |

Enid.

E, Yniol's only child,	.	. *Enid*	.	4
E, but to please her husband's eye	"	.	11
E loved the Queen, and with true	"	.	19
Allowing it, the Prince and *E* rode,	"	.	43
Told *E*, and they sadden'd her	"	.	64
E woke and sat beside the couch,	"	.	79
'If *E* errs, let *E* learn her fault.'	"	.	132
The voice of *E*, Yniol's daughter,	"	.	327
sweet voice of *E* moved Geraint,	"	.	334
song that *E* sang was one Of Fortune	"	.	345
Moved the fair *E*, all in faded silk	"	.	366
the Prince, as *E* past him, fain To	"	.	375
E took his charger to the stall;	"	.	382
E brought sweet cakes	"	.	368
E at her lowly handmaid-work,	"	.	400
the night before my *E's* birthday,	"	.	458
looking round he saw not *E* there,	"	.	506
Across the face of *E* hearing her;	"	.	524
broken down, for *E* sees my fall!'	"	.	590
E, for she lay With her fair head	"	.	599
E fell in longing for a dress .	"	.	630
E started waking, with her heart	"	.	674
E look'd, but all confused at first	"	.	685
E listen'd brightening as she lay;	"	.	733
good mother making *E* gay .	"	.	757
E all abash'd she knew not why,	"	.	765
make your *E* burst Sunlike from	"	.	768
how should *E* find A nobler friend?	"	.	792
E ever kept the faded silk,	"	.	841
not a word!' and *E* was aghast;	"	.	867
last sight that *E* had of home	"	.	873
E leading down the tracks	"	.	877
E was aware of three tall knights	"	.	905
Then *E* ponder'd in her heart,	"	.	913-79
E waited pale and sorrowful,	"	.	932
E, keeping watch, behold In the first	"	.	967
E stood aside to wait the event,	"	.	1002
Had ruth again on *E* looking pale;	"	.	1052
E took a little delicately,	"	.	1061
glance At *E*, where she droopt:	"	.	1096
Found *E* with the corner of his eye,	"	.	1130
E, the pilot star of my lone life,	"	.	1155
E my early and my only love,	"	.	1156
E the loss of whom has turn'd me	"	.	1157
E, you and he, I see it with joy—	"	.	1169
E fear'd his eyes, Moist as they were,	"	.	1199
E never loved a man but him,	"	.	1212
E left alone with Prince Geraint .	"	.	1214
E had no heart To wake him,	"	.	1218
Went *E* with her sullen follower on	"	.	1289
E heard the clashing of his fall,	"	.	1358
for long hours sat *E* by her lord,	"	.	1428
E shrank far back into herself	"	.	1455
E answer'd, harder to be moved .	"	.	1542
E, in her utter helplessness,	"	.	1567
'The voice of *E*,' said the knight:	"	.	1628
fear not, *E*, I should fall upon him	"	.	1635
E in their going had two fears,	"	.	1665
E easily believed, Like simple noble	"	.	1722
past to *E's* tent: and thither came	"	.	1770
E tended on him there:	"	.	1772
E, whom her ladies loved to call *E* the	"	.	1810
grateful people named *E* the Good,	"	.	1812
cry of children, *E's* and Geraints	"	.	1813
betwixt her best *E*, and lissome Vivien, *Guinevere*	29

enjoy.

| saints *E* themselves in heaven, | *St S. Stylites* | 104 |

enjoyed.

| all times I have *e* Greatly, | *Ulysses* | 7 |

enjoying.

| *E* each the other's good; | *In Mem.* xlvi. | 10 |

	POEM.	LINE.
enjoyment.		
There methinks would be *e*	*Locksley H.*	165
enlighten.		
Strengthen me, *e* me!	*Ode to Mem.* 5, 43,	122
Enna.		
Like Proserpine in *E*, gathering	*Ed. Morris.*	112
Enoch (see Arden.)		
E was host one day,	*En. Arden.*	25
E would hold possession for a week;	"	27
E stronger-made Was master:	"	30
E spoke his love, But Philip	"	40
E set A purpose evermore before his	"	44
Than *E*. Likewise had he served	"	52
E and Annie, sitting hand-in-hand,	"	69
E was abroad on wrathful seas,	"	91
E's white horse, and *E's* ocean-spoil	"	93
Friday fare was *E's* ministering	"	100
thither used *E* at times to go	"	104
master of that ship *E* had served in	"	120
Would *E* have the place?	"	125
E all at once assented to it,	"	126
E lay long-pondering on his plans;	"	133
E in his heart determined all	"	148
E took, and handled all his limbs	"	153
first since *E's* golden ring had girt	"	157
E parted with his old sea-friend,	"	168
all day long till *E's* last at home,	"	172
E faced this morning of farewell	"	182
E as a brave God-fearing man	"	185
O *E*, you are wise; And yet	"	210
E rose, Cast his strong arms	"	226
when the day, that *E* mentioned, came	"	238
foreboding 'What would *E* say?	"	252
Since *E* left he had not look'd	"	272
of what he wish'd, *E*, your husband;	"	291
if you will, when *E* comes again	"	308
E lives; that is borne in on me:	"	318
Philip gained As *E* lost: for *E* seem'd	"	352
E left his hearth and native land,	"	357
no news of *E* came.	"	358
be ever loved As *E* was?	"	424
'to be loved A little after *E*.'	"	426
If *E* comes—but *E* will not come—	"	428
for a sign 'my *E* is he gone?'	"	487
E sitting on a height, Under a palmtree,	"	496
where was *E*? prosperously sail'd	"	523
E traded for himself, and bought	"	534
loss of all But *E* and two others,	"	551
E's comrade, careless of himself,	"	569
over *E's* early-silvering head	"	623
E spoke no word to anyone,	"	668
There *E* rested silent many days.	"	700
E was so brown, so bow'd, So broken—	"	704
'*E*, poor man, was cast away and lost'	"	714
E yearn'd to see her face again;	"	718
E shunn'd the middle walk	"	739
have worse or better, *E* saw.	"	742
E set himself, Scorning an alms,	"	812
meet the day When *E* had return'd,	"	824
E bore his weakness cheerfully	"	828
E thinking 'after I am gone	"	835
E rolling his gray eyes upon her,	"	845
E hung A moment on her words	"	873
E slumber'd motionless and pale,	"	907
enrich.		
E the markets of the golden year.	*Golden Year*	46
thoughts *e* the blood of the world.'	*Princess,* ii.	164
e the threshold of the night	*In Mem.* xxix.	6
enringed.		
E a billowing fountain	*Princess,* ii.	14
enroll.		
Highness would *e* them with your own,	*Princess,* i.	236
In many a figured leaf *e's*	*In Mem.* xliii.	11
ensample.		
drawing foul *e* from fair names,	*Guinevere*	486
ensign.		
drowsy folds of our great *e* shake,	*Princess,* v.	8

	POEM.	LINE.
ensue.		
might *e* With this old soul	*Two Voices*	392
out of distance might *e* Desire	*In Mem.* cxvi.	6
ensued.		
then *e* A Martin's summer	*Aylmer's F.*	560
entangle.		
To *e* me when we met,	*Maud,* I. vi.	23
entangled.		
girl might be *e* ere she knew.	*Aylmer's F.*	272
entanglest.		
All my bounding heart *e*	*Madeline*	40
enter.		
some brainless devil *e's* in,	*Pal. of Art*	203
e not the toil of life.	*Margaret*	24
He breaks the hedge: he *e's* there:	*Day-Dm.*	118
NO MAN *E* IN ON PAIN OF DEATH?	*Princess,* ii.	178
laws are broken: let him *e* too.'	" vi.	297
friend or foe, Shall *e*, if he will.	"	317
in a tale Shall *e* in at lowly doors.	*In Mem.* xxxvi.	8
She *e's* other realms of love;	" xxxix.	12
Descend, and touch, and *e*;	" xcii.	13
'*E* likewise ye And go with us:'	" cii.	51
e in at breast and brow,	" cxxi.	11
She *e's*, glowing like the moon	" *Con.*	27
Then Yniol, '*E* therefore and partake	*Enid*	300
I will *e*, I will eat With all	"	305
Said Yniol: '*E* quickly.'	"	360
There will I *e* in among them all,	*Elaine*	1046
late! but we can *e* still.	*Guinevere*	167
too late! ye cannot *e* now. (rep.)	"	168
on the latch, Fearing to *e*:	*En. Arden*	516
entered.		
another night in night I *e*,	*Arabian N's.*	38
as we *e* in the cool.	*Gardener's D.*	113
Each *e* like a welcome guest	*Two Voices*	411
e an old hostel, call'd mine host	*Princess,* i.	171
subscribed, We *e* on the boards:	" ii.	60
as we *e* in, There sat along the forms,	"	86
With me, Sir, *e* in the bigger boy,	" iii.	382
I knock'd and, bidden, *e*;	" iv.	114
Beneath the satin dome and *e* in,	"	13
e in, and there Among piled arms	" v.	51
Empanoplied and plumed We *e* in.	"	472
go with us:' they *e* in.	*In Mem.* cii.	32
e, and were lost behind the walls.	*Enid.*	252
E, the wild lord of the place, Limours.	"	1126
and, no one opening, *E*;	*En. Arden.*	279
What ail'd her then, that ere she *e*,	"	514
e one Of those dark caves	*Sea Dreams*	87
entering.		
do well, Ladies, in *e* here,	*Princess,* ii.	48
E, the sudden light Dazed me half-blind:	" v.	11
E then, Right o'er a mount	*Enid.*	360
e barr'd her door, Stript off the case,	*Elaine*	15
e fill'd the house with sudden light.	*Aylmer's F.*	682
for on *e* He had cast the curtains	"	802
entertained.		
talk and minstrel melody *e*.	*Elaine*	267
entertainment.		
slender *e* of a house Once rich,	*Enid.*	301
entranced.		
E with that place and time,	*Arabian N's.*	97
entreat.		
'Earl, *e* her by my love,	*Enid.*	760
entreaty.		
manifold entreaties, many a tear,	*En. Arden.*	160
entry.		
Above an *e*: riding in, we call'd:	*Princess,* i.	222
A column'd *e* shone and marble	" v.	354
in the Vestal *e* shriek'd The virgin	" vi.	330
entry-gates.		
from his walls and wing'd his *e-g's*	*Aylmer's F.*	18
entwine.		
Round my true heart thine armse;	*Miller's D.*	216
E the cold baptismal font,	*In Mem.* xxix.	10

envy (s.)

	POEM	LINE.
that E calls you Devil's son,	Vivien	317-47
far aloof From e, hate and pity,	Lucretius	77
No lewdness, narrowing e,	"	208

envy (verb).

Her countrywomen! she did not e	Princess, iii.	25
I e not in any moods	In Mem. xxvii.	1
I e not the beast that takes	"	5

envying.

e all that meet him there.	In Mem. lix.	8
Leolin, I almost sin in e you;	Aylmer's F.	360

enwind.

Danube rolling fair E her isles,	In Mem. xcvii.	10

enwound.

circle of his arms E us both;	Gardener's D.	212
E him fold by fold, and made	Guinevere	597

epic.

'he burnt His e, his King Arthur,	The Epic	28
Princess, six feet high, Grand, e,	Princess, Pro.	219
scraps of thundrous E lilted out	" ii.	353

epicurean.

like a stoic, or like A wiser e,	Maud, I. iv.	21
majesties Of settled, sweet, E life.	Lucretius	215

epitaph.

cut this e above my bones;	Princess, ii.	190

epithet.

your fine e Is accurate too,	Vivien	382
pelted with outrageous e's,	Aylmer's F.	286

equal.

woman were an e to the man.	Princess, i.	130
this proud watchword rest Of e;	" vii.	283
in true marriage lies Nor e, nor	"	285

equal (verb.)

what delights can e those	In Mem. xli.	9

equal-blowing.

Beneath a broad and e-b wind,	Gardener's D.	76

equalled.

came to me that e my desire.	D. of F. Wom.	230

equal-poised.

O friendship, e-p control,	In Mem. lxxxiv.	33

equinox.

in head or chest Our changeful e'es,	Will Water.	238

erect.

E behind a desk of satin-wood,	Princess, ii.	90
E and silent, striking with her	" vi.	136
e, but bending from his height	Aylmer's F.	119
from sorrow, soldierlike, E;	"	729
e, but in the middle aisle Reel'd,	"	818
from the porch, tall, and e again.	"	825

Eros.

a bevy of E'es, apple-cheek'd,	The Islet	11

err.

e from honest Nature's rule!	Locksley H.	61
O my princess! true she e's,	Princess, iii.	91
has a son And sees him e.	"	244
nothing is that e's from law.	In Mem. lxxii.	8
'If Enid e's, let Enid learn	Enid	132

err'd.

Aim'd at the helm, his lance e:	Enid	1006
if ancient prophecies Have e not,	Guinevere	447

error.

intellect to part E from crime;	Isabel	15
Shall E in the round of time	Love and Duty	4
if it were thine e or thy crime	'Come not when,' etc	7
some gross e lies In this report,	Princess, i.	68
wears her e like a crown	" iii.	95
Deep as Hell I count his e.	The Captain	3
Dismal e! fearful slaughter!	"	65

Esau.

a heart as rough as E's hand,	Godiva	28

escape.

	POEM.	LINE.
and tumbles and childish e's,	Maud, I. i.	69
From which was no e for evermore;	Vivien	59, 394

escaped.

From which I e heart-free,	Maud, ii.	11
second Christmas came, e His keepers	Aylmer's F.	838

escaping.

Like the caged bird e suddenly,	En. Arden.	268

espalier.

The e's and the standards all	The Blackbird	5

essay.

dearly love thy first e,	Ode to Mem.	83

essayed.

e, by tenderest-touching terms	Vivien	747

essence.

floated free, As naked e,	Two Voices	374
O sacred e, other form,	In Mem. lxxxiv.	35
his e's turn'd the live air sick,	Maud, I. xiii.	11

estate (condition.)

Whose life in low e began	In Mem. lxiii.	3
my crown'd e begun To pine	" lxxi.	5
one so bright in dark e,	Enid	786

estate (property.)

now lord of the broad e	Maud, I. i.	19
lump of earth has left his e	" xvi.	1

estate (verb.)

E them with large land	Elaine.	1312

esteem.

talk kindlier: we e you for it—	Princess, v.	203

esteem'd.

you e us not Too harsh	Princess, iii.	182

Esther.

those of old That lighted on Queen E,	Enid	731

estuary.

smoulder'd on the refluent e;	Boädicea	28

eternal.

masters Time indeed, and is E,	In Mem. lxxxiv.	66

eternity.

in the light of great e	Love and Death	12
dreadful time, dreadful e,	Pal. of Art	267
He names the name E.	Two Voices	291
The sabbaths of E,	St Agnes' Eve	33
Music's golden sea Setting toward e,	Ode on Well.	253
O skill'd to sing of Time or E,	Milton	2

etiquette.

clamouring e to death,	Princess, v.	16

Europa.

sweet E's mantle blew unclasp'd,	Pal. of Art	117

Europe.

Better fifty years of E	Locksley H.	184
guard the eye, the soul Of E,	Ode on Well.	161
the weight and fate of E hung.	"	240
lash all E into blood;	To F. D Maurice	34

European.

never floats an E flag,	Locksley H.	161

Europe-shadowing.

wheel'd on E-s wings.	Ode on Well.	120

Eustace.

I and E from the city went	Gardener's D.	2
E might have sat for Hercules:	"	7
E painted her, And said to me	"	20
E turn'd, and smiling said	"	96
'E,' I said, 'This wonder keeps	"	118
solemn dignity did E banter me.	"	164
Autumn brought an hour For E,	"	203

evangelist.

seal'd The lips of that E.	In Mem. xxxi.	16

eve.

At e the beetle boometh	Claribel	9
At e a dry cicala sung,	Mariana in the S.	85

	POEM.	LINE.
From fringes of the faded *e*, 'Move eastward,' etc.		3
thro' the land at *e* we went,	Princess,	i. 246
at *e* and dawn With Ida, Ida, Ida,	"	iv. 412
strangely falls our Christmas *e*,	In Mem. civ.	4
No later than last *e* to Prince	Enid.	603
her bard, her silver star of *e*,	Vivien	803
on the winding waters, *e* and morn	Elaine	1398
for a breathing-while at *e*,	Aylmer's F.	449
at home in my father's farm at *e*;	Grandmother	90
Nor anchor dropt at *e* or morn;	The Voyage	82
when the zoning *e* has died	On a Mourner	21

Eve.

Adam first Embraced his *E*.	Day-Dm.	254
Shadowing the snow-limb'd *E*	Maud, I. xviii.	28

even.

tears fell with the dews at *e*;	Mariana	13
the crag that fronts the *E*,	Eleänore	40
Whisper in odorous heights of *e*.	Milton	16

evenfall.

thro' the laurels At the quiet *e*,	Maud, II. iv.	78
brought him home at *e*; 'Home they brought,' etc.		2

evening.

in stillest *e's* With what voice	Adeline	30
Many an *e* by the waters	Locksley H.	37
dropt with *e* on a rustic town	Princess, i.	168
brow to brow like night and *e* mixt	"	vi. 115
it was *e*: silent light Slept	"	vii. 105
Never morning wore To *e*	In Mem.	8
from the gorgeous gloom Of *e*	"	lxxxv. 3
It leads me forth at *e*,	Maud, II. iv.	17
the sallow-rifted glooms Of *e*,	Elaine	997
At *e* when the dull November day	En. Arden.	722
all of an *e* late I climb'd to the top	Grandmother	37

evening-lighted.

From the *e-l* wood,	Margaret	10

event.

such refraction of *e's* As often rises	In Mem. xci.	15
one far-off divine *e*,	"	Con. 143
Enid stood aside to wait the *e*,	Enid	1002
remaining here wilt learn the *e*;	Guinevere	572

eventide.

Either at morn or *e*.	Mariana	16
at *e*, listening earnestly.	'A spirit haunts,' etc.	4
on a golden autumn *e*,	En. Arden.	61

Everard (see Hall.)

clapt his hand On *E's* shoulder,	The Epic	22
I remember'd *E's* college fame	"	46

ever-breaking.

heard an *e-b* shore That tumbled	In Mem. cxxiii.	11

ever-echoing.

e-e avenues of song.	Ode on Well.	79

ever-fancied.

Before an *e-f* arrow,	Enid	1380

ever-floating.

death, death, thou *e-f* cloud,	Œnone	234

evergreen.

in it throve an ancient *e*,	En. Arden.	736
my heart, my heart is an *e*:	Spiteful Let.	23

ever-loyal.

Their *e-l* iron leader's fame,	Ode on Well.	229

ever-murdered.

e-m France, By shores that darken	Aylmer's F.	766

ever-ravening.

e-r eagle's beak and talon	Boädicea	11

ever-shifting.

e-s currents of the blood	D of F. Wom.	133

ever-tremulous.

falling showers, And *e-t* aspen-trees,	Elaine	523

evidence.

That heat of inward *e*,	Two Voices	284

evil.	POEM.	LINE.
can we have To war with *e*?	Lotos-E's.	94
e came on William the first.	Dora	59
For that the *e* ones come here,	St S. Stylites	96
all good things from *e*,	Love and Duty	58
E haunts The birth, the bridal;	In Mem. xcvii.	13
whatsoever *e* happen to me,	Enid.	471
they do not flow From *e* done;	Guinevere	187
(Sure that all *e* would come out of it)	En. Arden.	162
let us too, let all *e*, sleep.	Sea Dreams	297
Out of *e e* flourishes,	Boädicea	83

evil-hearted.

Beautiful Paris, *e-h* Paris,	Œnone	49

evil-starred.

fell my father *e-s*;—	Locksley II.	155

ewe.

snowy shoulders, thick as herded *e's*,	Princess,	iv. 458

example.

make me an *e* to mankind,	St S. Stylites	185
let them take *E*, pattern;	"	220
your *e* pilot, told her all.	Princess, iii.	121
Unused *e* from the grave	In Mem. lxxix.	15
Let his great *e* stand	Ode on Well.	220

Excalibur.

Thou therefore take my brand *E*.	M. d'Arthur	27
take *E*, And fling him far	"	36
drew he forth the brand *E*,	"	52
Better to leave *E* conceal'd	"	62
'King Arthur's sword, *E*,	"	103
hid *E* the second time,	"	111
if thou spare to fling *E*,	"	131
flash'd and fell the brand *E*:	"	142

exceed.

one whose rank *e's* her own.	In Mem. lix.	4

excess.

like one that sees his own *e*,	Aylmer's F.	400

excuse.

for my *e* What looks so little graceful:	Princess, iii.	36
Made such *e's* as he might,	Guinevere	39
With many a scarce-believable *e*,	En. Arden.	466

execration.

with a sudden *e* drove The footstool	Aylmer's F.	326

exempt.

she herself was not *e*—.	Locksley II.	95

exercise.

men delight in, martial *e*?	Princess, iii.	200
Yoked in all *e* of noble end,	"	vii. 340
The sad mechanic *e*,	In Mem. v.	7
Charier of sleep, and wine, and *e*,	Aylmer's F.	448

exiled.

e from eternal God,	Pal. of Art	263

existence.

deep heart of *e* beat for ever	Locksley II.	140

exit.

the landward *e* of the cave,	Sea Dreams	94

expanse.

down the river's dim *e*—	L. of Shalott, iv.	10
going O'er the lone *e*,	The Captain	26

expect.

king *e's*—was there no precontract?	Princess, iii.	191

expectant.

E of that news which never came,	En. Arden.	257

expectation.

eyes Of shining *e* fixt on mine.	Princess, iv.	135
glows In *e* of a guest;	In Mem. vi.	30

expecting.

E when a fountain should arise:	Vision of Sin	8
E still his advent home;	In Mem. vi.	21

experience.

full-grown will, Circled thro' all *e's*,	Œnone	163
worth The *e* of the wise.	Ed. Morris	66

	POEM.	LINE.
all *e* is an arch	Ulysses	19
a laden breast, Full of sad *e*,	Locksley H.	144
tho' all *e* past became Consolidate	Two Voices	365
what Our own *e* preaches.	Will Water.	176
strange *e's* Unmeet for ladies.	Princess, iv.	140
your plan, Divorced from my *e*,	"	336
pines in sad *e* worse than death,	" vii.	296
A lord of large *e*,	In Mem. xli.	7

experiment.
| setting round thy first *e* | Ode to Mem. | 81 |
| yonder, shrieks and strange *e's* | Princess, Pro. | 228 |

expert.
| howsoe'er In fitting aptest words | In Mem. lxxiv. | 5 |

explain.
| answer'd 'ever longing to *e*, | The Brook | 107 |

explained.
| shame that cannot be *e* for shame | Vivien | 548 |

exploring.
| Science enough and *e*, | 1865-1866 | 6 |

expound.
| not of those that can *e* themselves. | Vivien | 167 |

expounder.
| Take Vivien for *e*; | Vivien | 168 |

express.
How may full-sail'd verse *e*,	Eleänore	44
Who may *e* thee, Eleänore?	"	68
common mouth, So gross to *e* delight,	Gardener's D.	55
e All-comprehensive tenderness,	In Mem. lxxxiv.	46

express'd—exprest.
yearnings that can never be *e*	D. of F. Wom.	283
no other thing *e* But long disquiet	Two Voices	248
Thro' light reproaches, half *e*,	In Mem. lxxxiv.	15
more *e* Than hid her,	Vivien	71

expression.
| But beyond *e* fair. | Adeline | 5 |
| Drew in the *e* of an eye, | In Mem. cx. | 19 |

expunge.
| tarn by tarn *E* the world! | Princess, vii. | 26 |

exquisite.
| kisses press'd On lips less *e* than | Gardener's D. | 150 |

extending.
| innocently *e* her white arms, | Elaine | 928 |

extremes.
The falsehood of *e*! 'Of old sat Freedom,' etc.		24
such *e*, I told her, Well might harm	Princess, iii.	128
storming in *e* Stood for her cause,	" v.	168
fierce *e* employ Thy spirits	In Mem. lxxxvii.	1
save it even in *e*,	Guinevere	67

extremity.
| reddening in *e* of delight, | Enid | 1068 |

exult.
| Fade wholly, while the soul *e's*, | In Mem. lxxii. | 14 |

exulted.
| The Priest *e*, And cried with joy, | The Victim | 38 |

eye.
Glancing with black-beaded *e's*	Lilian	15
E's not down-dropt nor over bright,	Isabel	1
Light-glooming over *e's* divine,	Madeline	16
Serene with argent-lidded *e's*	Arabian N's.	135
his deep *e* laughter-stirr'd	"	150
spirit-thrilling *e's* so keen and	Ode to Mem.	39
of the many tongues, the myriad *e's!*	"	47
Unto mine inner *e*, Divinest Memory!	"	49
Large dowries doth the raptured *e*	"	72
Thy rose-lips and full blue *e's*	Adeline	7
those dew-lit *e's* of thine,	"	11
Beyond the bottom of his *e*.	A Character	6
a lack-lustre dead-blue *e*,	"	17
Blew his own praises in his *e's*,	"	22
rites and forms before his burning *e's*	The Poet	39
globes Of her keen *e's*.	"	44
In your *e* there is death,	Poet's Mind	16

	POEM.	LINE.
listen, listen, your *e's* shall glisten	Sea Fairies	35
about him roll'd his lustrous *e's*;	Love and Death	3
Up from my heart unto my eyes	Oriana	78
large cake *e's* for the love of me.	The Mermaid	27
her *e's* were darken'd wholly,	L. of Shalott, iv.	31
Her melancholy *e's* divine,	Mariana in the S.	19
To look into her *e's* and say,	"	75
Thy dark *e's* open'd not,	Eleänore	1
The languors of thy love-deep *e's*.	"	76
full and deep In thy large *e's*,	"	86
seems to come and go In thy large *e's*	"	97
busy wrinkles round his *e's?*	Miller's D.	4
see his gray *e's* twinkle yet (rep.)	"	11
ere I saw your *e's*, my love,	"	43
there a vision caught my *e*;	"	76
when I raised my *e's*, above	"	85
Such *e's!* I swear to you,	"	87
E's with idle tears are wet.	"	211
Look thro' mine *e's* with thine.	"	215
those kind *e's* for ever dwell!	"	220
not shed a many tears, Dear *e's*	"	222
Droops blinded with his shining *e*:	Fatima	38
My *e's* are full of tears,	Œnone	30
heart is breaking, and my *e's* are dim,	"	31
With down-dropt *e's* I sat alone;	"	55
above, her full and earnest *e*	"	139
mortal *e's* are frail to judge of fair,	"	155
subtle smile in her mild *e's*,	"	180
beheld great Here's angry *e's*,	"	186
to vex me with his father's *e's!*	"	251
My palace with unblinded *e's*,	Pal. of Art	42
e's That said, We wait for thee.	"	103
Flush'd in her temples and her *e's*,	"	170
fair to sate my various *e's!*	"	193
your sweet *e's*, your low replies:	L. C. V. de Vere	29
languid light of your proud *e's*	"	59
many a black black *e*, they say,	May Queen, i.	5
tir'd eyelids upon thy dead *e's*;	Lotos-E's.	51
With half-shut *e's* ever to seem	"	100
e's grown dim with gazing on the,	"	132
Charged both mine *e's* with tears.	D. of F. Wom.	13
star-like sorrows of immortal *e's*,	"	91
black-bearded kings with wolfish *e's*	"	111
with swarthy cheeks and bold black *e's*,	"	127
tame and tutor with mine *e*	"	138
dragon *e's* of anger'd Eleanor	"	255
lit your *e's* with tearful power,	Margaret	3
e's Touch'd with a somewhat darker	"	49
let your blue *e's* dawn Upon me	"	67
tho' his *e's* are waking dim,	D. of the O. Year	21
Close up his *e's*: tie up his chin:	"	48
tho' mine own *e's* fill with dew,	To J. S.	37
standing near Cast down her *e's*,	"	54
open *e's* desire the truth. 'Of old sat Freedom,' etc.		17
nor veil his *e's*: 'Love thou thy land,' etc.		90
long That both his *e's* were dazzled,	M. d'Arthur	59
pleased the *e's* of many men.	"	91
widow'd of the power in his *e*	"	122
the giddy pleasure of the *e's*.	"	128
see I by thine *e's* that this is done.	"	149
wide blue *e's* As in a picture.	"	169
the *e's* of ladies and of kings.	"	225
hide my forehead and my *e's?*	"	228
e's Darker than darkest pansies,	Gardener's D.	26
Her violet *e's*, and all her Hebe bloom,	"	136
fill my *e's* with happy dew;	"	193
following her dark *e's* Felt earth	"	206
came Memory with sad *e's*,	"	238
whole hour your *e's* have been Intent	"	264
Make thine heart ready with thine *e's*:	"	268
I will set him in my uncle's *e*	Dora	65
make him pleasing in her uncle's *e*.	"	82
Dora cast her *e's* upon the ground,	"	87
like a pearl In growing, modest *e's*	Walk. to the M.	46
e's Should see the raw mechanic's	"	66
made thick These heavy horny *e's*.	St S. Stylites	198
ah! with what delighted *e's* I turn	Talking O.	7
I breathed upon her *e's*.	"	210
To light her shaded *e*;	"	228
Streaming *e's* and breaking hearts?	Love and Duty	2
staring *e* glazed o'er with sapless	"	16

	POEM.	LINE.		POEM.	LINE.
e's, love-languid thro' half-tears,	Love and Duty	36	See with clear *e* some hidden shame	Princess, l.	7
utterance by the yearning of an *e*,	"	61	With larger other *e*'s than ours,	"	15
quiet *e*'s unfaithful to the truth,	"	91	Such splendid purpose in his *e*'s,	" lv.	10
far as human *e* could see;	Locksley H. 15,119		ever look'd with human *e*'s.	" lvi.	12
her *e*'s on all my motions	"	22	if thou cast thine *e*'s below,	" lx.	5
dawning in the dark of hazel *e*'s—	"	28	if an *e* that's downward cast	" lxi.	1
What is this? his *e*'s are heavy:	"	51	in the light of deeper *e*'s	'	11
e shall vex thee, looking ancient	"	85	closing eaves of wearied *e*'s.	" lxvi.	11
left me with the jaundiced *e*;	"	132	I find a trouble in thine *e*,	" lxvii.	10
E, to which all order festers,	"	133	turns a musing *e* On songs,	" lxxii.	2
No *e* look down, she passing;	Godiva	40	dropt the dust on tearless *e*'s;	" lxxix.	4
spout Had cunning *e*'s to see:	"	57	And over those ethereal *e*'s	" lxxxvi.	39
his *e*'s, before they had their will,	"	69	brought an *e* for all he saw;	" lxxxviii.	9
e's are dim with glorious tears,	Two Voices	131	dying *e*'s Were closed with wail,	" lxxxix.	5
He owns the fatal gift of *e*'s,	"	286	woolly breasts and beaded *e*'s;	" xciv.	12
Nor look with that too-earnest *e*—	Day-Dm.	18	whose light-blue *e*'s Are tender	" xcv.	2
A fairy Prince, with joyful *e*'s,	"	107	These two—they dwelt with *e* on *e*.	" xcvi.	9
dark those hidden *e*'s must be!',	"	132	gleams On Lethe in the *e*'s of Death.	" xcvii.	8
'O *e*'s long laid in happy sleep!',	"	181	each has pleased a kindred *e*,	" xcix.	17
So much your *e*'s my fancy take—	"	238	The critic clearness of an *e*,	" cviii.	3
might kiss those *e*'s awake!	"	240	Drew in the expression of an *e*,	" cx.	19
e's like thine, have waken'd hopes?	"	257	I, who gaze with temperate *e*'s	" cxi.	2
this heart and *e*'s, Are touch'd	Sir Galahad	71	I seem to cast a careless *e*	"	7
tread The corners of thine *e*'s:	Will Water.	236	bright the friendship of thine *e*;	" cxviii.	10
look'd into Lord Ronald's *e*'s,	Lady Clare	79	eagle's wing, or insect's *e*;	" cxxiii.	6
One praised her ancles, one her *e*'s,	Beggar Maid	11	did but look thro' dimmer *e*'s;	" cxxiv.	6
sat a company with heated *e*'s,	Vision of Sin	7	Sweet human hand and lips and *e*	" cxxviii.	6
Hair, and *e*'s. and limbs, and faces,	"	39	On me she bends her blissful *e*'s	" Con.	29
Glimmer in thy rheumy *e*'s.	"	154	village *e*'s as yet unborn;	"	59
cannot praise the fire In your *e*—	"	184	*e* to *e*, shall look On knowledge;	"	129
glass herself in dewy *e*'s	'Move eastward,' etc.	7	*e*'s were downcast, not to be seen)	Maud, I. ii.	5
her arm lifted, *e*'s on fire—	Princess, Pro.	41	An *e* well-practised in nature,	" iv.	38
thro' gilt wires a crafty loving *e*,	"	170	What if tho' her *e* seem'd full	" vi.	40
twinn'd as horse's ear and *e*.	" i.	56	a moist mirage in desert *e*'s,	"	53
the blinding bandage from his *e*'s:	"	240	once, but once, she lifted her *e*'s,	" viii.	5
such *e*'s were in her head,	" ii.	23	tongue be a thrall to my *e*,	" xvi.	32
all her thoughts as fair within her *e*'s,	"	305	Innumerable, pitiless, passionless *e*'s,	" xviii.	38
Abase those *e*'s that ever loved	"	405	often I caught her with *e*'s all wet,	" xix.	23
from his wits Pierced thro' with *e*'s;	"	418	every *e* but mine will glance	" xx.	36
glowing round her dewy *e*'s	" iii.	10	In violets blue as your *e*'s.	" xxii.	42
her lynx *e* To fix and make me hotter,	"	30	he lay there with a fading *e*?	" II. i.	29
in her *e*'s The green malignant light	"	115	only moves with the moving *e*,	" ii.	37
had limed ourselves With open *e*'s,	"	127	Might drown all life in the *e*,—	"	61
smote me with the light of *e*'s	"	176	For the hand, the lips, the *e*'s,	" iv.	27
She spake With kindled *e*'s:	"	316	My own dove with the tender *e*?	"	46
Rise in the heart, and gather to the *e*'s,	" iv.	23	but in a dream, upon *e*'s so fair,	" III. vi.	16
unto dying *e*'s The casement slowly	"	33	O passionate heart and morbid *e*,	"	32
Stared with great *e*'s, and laugh'd	"	101	Her *e*'s a bashful azure,	The Brook 72,	206
her true *e*'s blind for such a one	"	116	snatch'd her *e*'s at once from mine,	"	101
e's Of shining expectation	"	134	sweet content Re-risen in Katie's *e*'s,	"	169
yet endured to meet her opening *e*'s,	"	177	I saw with half-unconscious *e*	The Letters	15
an *e* like mine, A lidless watcher	"	305	guard the *e*, the soul Of Europe	Ode on Well.	160
Fear Stared in her *e*'s,	"	358	Enid, but to please her husband's *e*,	Enid	11
gems and gemlike *e*'s, And gold	"	459	she gather'd from the people's *e*'s:	"	61
crimson-rolling *e* Glares ruin,	"	473	darken'd from the high light in his *e*'s,	"	100
ferule and the trespass-chiding *e*,	" v.	36	pierced to death before mine *e*'s,	"	104
fluttering scarfs and ladies' *e*'s,	"	498	with fixt *e* following the three.	"	237
loved me closer than his own right *e*,	"	520	Let his *e* rove in following,	"	399
old lion, glaring with his whelpless *e*,	" vi.	83	Geraint with *e*'s all bright replied,	"	494
grief and mother's hunger in her *e*.	"	130	lift an *e* nor speak a word,	"	528
her *e* with slow dilation roll'd	"	172	she cast her *e*'s upon her dress,	"	609
with an *e* that swum in thanks:	"	193	Myself would work *e* dim,	"	628
turn'd askance a wintry *e*:	"	310	by the mother's careful hand and *e*	"	738
The common men with rolling *e*'s;	"	340	Prince had brought his errant *e*'s	"	1094
love not hollow cheek or faded *e*:	"	370	Found Enid with the corner of his *e*,	"	1130
Nor knew what *e* was on me,	" vii.	38	came near, lifted adoring *e*'s,	"	1153
the dew Dwelt in her *e*'s,	"	121	not make them laughable in all *e*'s,	"	1175
I on her Fixt my faint *e*'s,	"	120	his *e* moist; but Enid fear'd his *e*'s,	"	1199
with shut *e*'s I lay Listening;	"	208	*e*'s to find you out however far,	"	1277
yearlong poring on thy pictur'd *e*'s,	"	319	*e* darken'd and his helmet wagg'd;	"	1354
lift thine *e*'s; my doubts are dead,	"	327	drove the dust against her veillesse *e*'s:	"	1378
All night below the darken'd *e*'s:	In Mem. iv.	14	on a foray, rolling *e*'s of prey,	"	1387
since it pleased a vanish'd *e*.	" viii.	21	half-frighted, with dilated *e*'s;	"	1445
e's have leisure for their tears;	" xiii.	16	He roll'd his *e*'s about the hall,	"	1458
Paradise It never look'd to human *e*'s	" xxiv.	1	o'er her meek *e*'s came a happy mist,	"	1617
if that *e* which watches guilt	" xxvi.	5	with your meek blue *e*'s, The truest *e*'s	"	1689
Oh, if indeed that *e* foresee	"	9	with your own true *e*'s Beheld the	"	1694
We sung, tho' every *e* was dim,	" xxx.	14	having look'd too much thro' alien *e*'s	"	1740
Her *e*'s are homes of silent prayer,	" xxxii.	1	King went forth and cast his *e*'s	"	1780
those wild *e*'s that watch the wave	" xxxvi.	15	With reverent *e*'s mock-loyal,	Vivien	13
Make April of her tender *e*'s;	" xxxix.	8	neither *e*'s nor tongue—O stupid child!	"	100

CONCORDANCE TO

	POEM.	LINE.
gleam'd her *e*'s behind her tears	Enid	232
those isle-nurtured *e*'s Waged	"	420
unwilling war With those fine *e*'s;	"	454
to flirt a venom at her *e*'s,	"	459
let her *e*'s Speak for her, glowing	"	465
So lean his *e*'s were monstrous;	"	474
often o'er the sun's bright *e* Drew	"	483
condensation, hard To mind and *e*;	"	529
snowy penthouse for his hollow *e*'s,	"	657
Without the will to lift their *e*'s,	"	685
His *e* was calm, and suddenly she took	"	703
He raised his *e*'s and saw The tree	"	787
e's and neck glittering went and came;	"	809
Lifted her *e*'s, and they dwelt	Elaine	85
gleam'd a vague suspicion in his *e*'s:	"	128
held her *e*'s upon the ground,	"	232
Lifted her *e*'s, and read his lineaments.	"	244
noblest, when she lifted up her *e*'s.	"	256
lifted up her *e*'s And loved him,	"	259
e's Run thro' the peopled gallery.	"	428
cast his *e*'s on fair Elaine;	"	637
damsel, in the light of your blue *e*'s:	"	657
roll'd his *e*'s Yet blank from sleep,	"	815
His *e*'s glisten'd: she fancied	"	818
his large black *e*'s, Yet larger thro'	"	830
the world, All ear and *e*,	"	937
stupid heart To interpret ear and *e*,	"	938
a still good-morrow with her *e*'s.	"	1027
old servitor on deck, Winking his *e*'s,	"	1139
saw with a sidelong *e* The shadow	"	1167
underneath his *e*'s, and right across	"	1233
e's that ask'd 'What is it?'	"	1242
men Shape to their fancy's *e*	"	1245
From the half-face to the full *e*,	"	1255
their *e*'s met and hers fell,	"	1303
answer'd with his *e*'s upon the ground,	"	1342
doubt her fairness were to want an *e*,	"	1367
lifted up his *e*'s And saw the barge	"	1381
couchant with his *e*'s upon the	Guinevere	12
Modred still in green, all ear and *e*,	"	25
smile, and gray persistent *e*:	"	64
hands in hands, and *e* to *e*,	"	99
Makes wicked lightnings of her *e*s,	"	516
hand Grasp'd, made her vail her *e*'s:	"	655
richer in his *e*'s Who ransom'd us,	"	676
Philip, his blue *e*'s All flooded	En. Arden	31
A purpose evermore before his *e*'s,	"	45
gray *e*'s and weather-beaten face	"	70
In their *e*'s and faces read his doom;	"	73
not fix the glass to suit her *e*;	"	240
Perhaps her *e* was dim,	"	241
fixt her swimming *e*'s upon him,	"	322
e's Full of that lifelong hunger,	"	460
His *e*'s upon the stones, he reach'd	"	685
Enoch rolling his gray *e*'s upon her,	"	843
once again he roll'd his *e*'s upon her	"	904
e's from under a pyramidal head	Aylmer's F.	20
eager *e*'s, that still Took joyful note	"	66
cross-lightnings of four chance-met *e*'s	"	129
Leolin ever watchful of her *e*	"	210
conscious of the rageful *e* That watch'd	"	336
With a weird bright, *e*, sweating and	"	585
innocent *e*'s Had such a star of	"	691
hid the Holiest from the people's *e*'s	"	772
Then their *e*'s vext her;	"	802
those fixt *e*'s of painted ancestors.	"	832
that her clear germander *e* Droopt	Sea Dreams	4
the night-light flickering in my *e*'s	"	101
my *e*'s Pursued him down the street,	"	160
all his conscience and one *e* askew—	"	176-180
the crafty crowsfoot round his *e*;	"	183
florid, stern, as far as *e* could see,	"	212
e's Glaring, and passionate looks,	"	228
wistful *e*'s on two fair images,	"	232
dead?' 'The man your *e* pursued.	"	262
turn'd, and I saw his *e*'s all wet	Grandmother	49
thank God that I keep my *e*'s	"	106
Shines in those tremulous *e*'s	Tithonus	26
e's brighten slowly close to mine,	"	38
with what other *e*'s I used to watch—	"	51
He saw not far; his *e*'s were dim:	The Voyage	75

	POEM.	LINE.
lighten'd In the *e*'s of each.	The Captain	32
win all *e*'s with all accomplishment:	Coquette, ii.	4
here he glances on an *e* new-born,	Lucretius	137
a jewel dear to a lover's *e*!	The Window	3
Fine little heart and merry blue *e*.	"	89
Tell my wish to her merry blue *e*,	"	101
lighten into my *e*'s and my heart,	"	192

eye (verb.)
careful robins *e* the delver's toil,	Enid	774, 1280

eyebrow.
makes a hoary *e* for the gleam	The Brook	80
He dragg'd his *e* bushes down,	Vivien	656

eyed.
pard, E like the evening star	Œnone	196

eyelash.
The lifting of whose *e* is my lord,	Princess, v.	134
golden beam of an *e* dead on the	Maud, I. iii.	3

eyeless.
'I saw the little elf-god *e* once	Vivien	98

eyelid.
Ray-fringed *e*'s of the	'Clear-headed friend,' etc.	6
Her *e* quiver'd as she spake.	Miller's D.	144
Weigh heavy on my *e*'s:	Œnone	240
I kiss'd his *e*'s into rest:	The Sisters	2
tir'd *e*'s upon tir'd eyes;	Lotos-E's.	51
With half-dropt *e*'s still,	"	135
before my *e*'s dropt their shade,	D. of F. Wom.	1
I closed mine *e*'s, lest the gems	M. d'Arthur	252
Her *e*'s dropp'd their silken eaves.	Talking O.	209
Pacing with downward *e*'s pure.	Two Voices	420
Beat balm upon our *e*'s,	Princess, iii.	107
on my heavy *e*'s My anguish hangs	Maud, II. iv.	73
A little flutter'd, with her *e*'s down,	The Brook	89
cheek burn and either *e* fall,	Enid	775, 1283
answer, either *e* wet with tears.	Vivien	229
the vast *e* of an inky cloud,	"	484
slow tear creep from her closed *e*.	Tithonus	755
forehead, *e*'s growing dewy-warm	Tithonus	58
here upon a yellow *e* fall'n	Lucretius	141

eyesight.
Not with blinded *e* poring	Locksley H.	172

eye-witness.
would'st against thine own *e-w* fain	Vivien	642

F

faäce.
fun un theer a-laäid on 'is *f*.	N. Farmer	33

fable (s.)
we grew The *f* of the city	Gardener's D.	6
coast Of ancient *f* and fear—	Maud, II. ii.	32
Read my little *f*:	The Flower	17

fable (verb.)
aught they *f* of the quiet Gods.	Lucretius	55

fabled.
why we came? If nothing fair,	Princess, iii.	120

face.
Old *f*'s glimmer'd thro' the doors,	Mariana	66
Breathing Light against thy *f*,	Adeline	56
Sweet *f*'s, rounded arms, and bosoms	Sea Fairies	3
I was down upon my *f*,	Oriana	53
O pale, pale *f* so sweet and meek,	"	66
He said, 'She has a lovely *f*;	L. of Shalott, iv.	52
The clear perfection of her *f*.	Mariana in the S.	32
slowly grow To a full *f*,	Eleänore	91
While I muse upon thy *f*;	"	129
turning look'd upon your *f*,	Miller's D.	157
Grow, live, die looking on his *f*,	Fatima	41
tell her to her *f* how much I hate	Œnone	224
Heaven, how canst thou see my *f*?	"	232
She was the fairest in the *f*:	The Sisters	2
Two godlike *f*'s gazed below;	Pal. of Art	162
silent *f*'s of the Great and Wise.	"	195
f's pale, Dark *f*'s pale against that	Lotos E's.	25
With those old *f*'s of our infancy.	"	111

	POEM.	LINE.		POEM.	LINE.
turning on my *f* The star-like	D. of F. Wom.	90	His *f*, as I grant, in spite of spite,	Maud, xiii.	8
for such a *f* had boldly died,"	"	98	Last year, I caught a glimpse of his *f*,	"	27
father held his hand upon his *f*;	"	107	struck me, madman, over the *f*,	" II. i.	18
her *f* Glow'd, as I look'd at her.	"	239	And the *f*'s that one meets,	" iv.	93
His *f* is growing sharp and thin.	D. of the O. Year	46	*f* of night is fair on the dewy downs,	" III. vi.	5
a new *f* at the door, my friend,	"	53	sweet *f* of her Whom he loves most,	Enid	122
The fullness of her *f*— ' Of old sat Freedom,'etc.		12	visor up, and shew'd a youthful *f*,	"	189
all his *f* was white And colourless,	M. d'Arthur	212	Guinevere, not mindful of the *f*	"	191
new men, strange *f*'s, other minds.'	"	238	kept her off and gazed upon her *f*,	"	519
If thou should'st never see my *f* again,	"	246	Across the *f* of Enid hearing her;	"	524
Then he turn'd His *f* and pass'd—	Dora	148	all his *f* Glow'd like the heart	"	558
Dora hid her *f* By Mary.	"	153	glance at her good mother's *f*,	"	766
on the king With heated *f*'s;	Audley Ct.	36	rested with her sweet *f* satisfied;	"	776
hid his *f* From all men,	Walk. to the M.	14	to her own bright *f* Accuse her	"	959
A pretty *f* is well, and this is well,	Ed. Morris	45	Greeted Geraint full *f*, but stealthily,	"	1128
f's grow between me and my book;	St S. Stylites.	173	sweet *f*'s make good fellows fools	"	1248
I know thy glittering *f*,	"	202	mar a comely *f* with idiot tears.	"	1399
Once more before my *f* I see	Talking O.	2	Yet, since the *f* is comely— .	"	1400
seen some score of those Fresh *f*'s,	"	50	warm tears falling on his *f*;	"	1434
God's glory smote him on the *f*.'	Two Voices	225	turn'd his *f* And kiss'd her climbing;	"	1608
His *f*, that two hours since hath died;	"	242	mild *f* of the blameless King,	"	1660
daughter, whose sweet *f* He kiss'd,	"	253	*f* with change of heart is changed.	"	1747
Whose wrinkles gather'd on his *f*,	"	329	lifted up A *f* of sad appeal,	Vivien	83
Turn your *f*, Nor look with that	Day-Dm.	17	still I find Your *f* is practised,	"	217
Grave *f*'s gather'd in a ring.	"	58	So tender was her voice, so fair her *f*	"	251
yawn'd, and rubb'd his *f*, and spoke,	"	151	For, look upon his *f*!—	"	611
There I put my *f* in the grass—	Ed. Gray	21	harlots paint their talk as well as *f*	"	670
crypt Of darken'd forms and *f*'s.	Will Water.	184	shoulder, and the *f* Hand-hidden	"	745
flushes Her sweet *f* from brow to	L. of Burleigh	62	with what *f*, after my pretext made,	Elaine	142
So sweet a *f*, such angel grace,	Beggar Maid	13	Had marr'd his *f*, and mark'd it .	"	247
panted hand in hand with *f*'s pale	Vision of Sin	19	all night long his *f* before her	"	330
Hair, and eyes, and limbs, and *f*'s,	"	39	a painter, poring on a *f*, Divinely	"	331
Every *f*, however full, I'added	"	176	and so paints him that his *f*,	"	333
town With happy *f*'s and with	Princess, Pro.	56	so the *f* before her lived,	"	336
sense of wrong had touch'd her *f*.	"	213	Rapt on his *f* as if it were a God's.	"	355
Prince I was, blue-eyed, and fair in *f*,	" i.	1	the blood Sprang to her *f*	"	376
saw my father's *f* Grew long	"	57	bright hair blown about the serious *f*	"	391
keep your hoods about the *f*,	" ii.	337	with smiling *f* arose, With smiling *f*—	"	551
Push'd her flat hand against his *f*,	"	345	sharply turn'd about to hide her *f*,	"	605
sent for Blanche to accuse her *f* to *f*;	" iv.	220	Where could he found *f* daintier?	"	638
falling on my *f* was caught .	"	251	lifted her fair *f* and moved away:	"	679
Half-drooping from her, turn'd her *f*,	"	349	Some read the King's *f*,	"	723
Stared in her eyes, and chalk'd her *f*.	"	358	Sat on his knee, stroked his gray *f*	"	745
I know Your *f*'s there in the crowd—	"	489	Came on her brother with a happy *f*	"	787
Bent their broad *f*'s toward us .	"	529	Her *f* was near, and as we kiss .	"	824
so from her *f* They push'd us,	"	532	task assign'd, he kiss'd her *f*.	"	825
Thy *f* across his fancy comes,	"	556	heart's colours on her simple *f*;	"	833
every *f* she look'd on justify it)	" v.	128	often the sweet image of one *f*,	"	878
therefore I set my *f* Against all men,	"	378	like a ghost she lifted up her *f*,	"	914
Took the face-cloth from the *f*.	" vi.	87	' Not to be with you, not to see your *f*—	"	942
haggard father's face and reverend	"	87	bloodred light of dawn Flared on her *f*,	"	1020
once more she look'd at my pale *f*:	"	99	So dwelt the father on her *f*	"	1024
And turn'd each *f* her way: .	"	128	*f*, bright as for sin forgiven,	"	1096
when she learnt his *f*, Remembering.	"	142	Winking his eyes, and twisted all his *f*.	"	1139
thro' the parted silks the tender *f* peep'd,	" vii.	45	her *f*, and that clear-featured *f* Was	"	1153
at which her *f* A little flush'd,	"	65	that oarsman's haggard *f*,	"	1243
Hortensia, pleading; angry was her *f*.	"	117	*f* that men Shape to their fancy's eye	"	1244
ran Mine down my *f*, .	"	125	looking often from his *f* who read	"	1277
Pale was the perfect *f*,	"	209	By God for thee alone, and from her *f*,	"	1358
we, that have not seen thy *f*,	In Mem. Pro.	2	like a face-cloth to the *f*,	Guinevere	7
Roves from the living brother's *f*,	" xxxii.	7	Modred's narrow foxy *f*,	"	63
tears are on the mother's *f*,	" xxxix.	10	grim *f*'s came and went Before her,	"	70
strive to paint The *f* I knew;	" lxix.	3	clear *f* of the guileless King,	"	85
Looks thy fair *f* and makes it still.	"	16	Fired all the pale *f* of the Queen, .	"	355
As sometimes in a dead man's *f*,	" lxxiii.	1	grovell'd with her *f* against the floor;	"	412
in a moment set thy *f* .	" lxxv.	2	made her *f* a darkness from the King;	"	414
changes wrought on form and *f*;	" lxxxi.	2	might see his *f*, and not be seen.'	"	582
I see their unborn *f*'s shine .	" lxxxiii.	19	so she did not see the *f*,	"	589
The God within him light his *f*.	" lxxxvi.	36	gray eyes and weather-beaten *f* .	En. Arden.	70
swims The reflex of a human *f*.	" cvii.	12	in their eyes and *f*'s read his doom;	"	73
find his comfort in thy *f*;	" cviii.	20	as their *f*'s drew together, groan'd,	"	74
Not all regret; the *f* will shine .	" cxv.	9	his *f*, Rough-redden'd with a thousand	"	94
Many a merry *f* Salutes them—	Con.	66	shall look upon your *f* no more.'	"	212
hearts are warm'd and *f*'s bloom,	"	82	Spy out my *f*, and laugh at all .	"	216
set my *f* as a flint, .	Maud, I. i.	31	Cared not to look on any human *f*,	"	281
a cold and clear-cut (rep. iii. 1).	" ii.	3	' I cannot look you in the *f*;	"	314
Passionless, pale, cold *f*, star-sweet	" iii.	4	dwelt a moment on his kindly *f*,	"	323
ride flash'd over her beautiful *f*,	" iv.	16	her *f* had fall'n upon her hands; .	"	388
Maud with her exquisite *f*,	" v.	19	before her *f*, Claiming her promise.	"	454
A *f* of tenderness might be feign'd,	" vi.	52	Philip's rosy *f* contracting grew	"	483
A bought commission, a waxen *f*,	" x.	30	could not see, the kindly human *f*,	"	582

	POEM.	LINE.
Enoch yearn'd to see her ƒ again	En. Arden	718
might look on her sweet ƒ again	"	719
dead ƒ would vex her after-life.	"	802
With half a score of swarthy ƒ's	Aylmer's F.	191
a hoary ƒ Meet for the reverence	"	332
her sweet ƒ and faith Held him	"	392
mixt Upon their ƒ's, as they kiss'd	"	430
ƒ to With twenty months of silence,	"	566
careless of the household ƒ's near,	"	575
His ƒ magnetic to the hand	"	626
the wife, who watch'd his ƒ, Paled	"	731
he veil'd His ƒ with the other,	"	809
pendent hands, and narrow meagre ƒ	"	813
rabbit fondles his own harmless ƒ,	"	851
sitting all alone, his ƒ Would darken,	Sea Dreams	12
His dear little ƒ was troubled,	Grandmother	65
Her ƒ was evermore unseen,	The Voyage	61
Till the ƒ of Del be brighten'd,	Boädicea	16
hide their ƒ's, miserable in ignominy !	"	51
Were their ƒ's grim.	The Captain	54
Imitates God, and turns her ƒ	On a Mourner	2
His ƒ was ruddy, his hair was gold,	The Victim	36
altho' his fire is on my ƒ	Lucretius	144
flying over her sweet little ƒ ?	The Window	13
Ah my lady, if ask'd to her ƒ,	"	96

face-cloth.
| Took the ƒ-c from the face | Princess, v. | 542 |
| like a ƒ-c to the face, Clung | Guinevere | 7 |

faced.
| He ƒ the spectres of the mind | In Mem. xcv. | 15 |
| ƒ this morning of farewell Brightly | En. Arden | 182 |

face-flatterer.
| F-ƒ's and backbiters are the same. | Vivien | 673 |

facet.
| sparkle like a gem Of fifty ƒ's ; | Enid | 1144 |
| ƒ's of the glorious mountain flash. | The Islet | 22 |

fact.
Thought hath wedded F. 'Love thou thy land,'etc.	59
that plain ƒ, as taught by these,	Two Voices	281
Taught them with ƒ's.	Princess, Pro.	59
A ƒ within the coming year ;	In Mem. xci.	10

faction.
Where ƒ seldom gathers head, 'You ask me why,' etc.	13
Not less, tho' dogs of F bay, 'Love thou thy land,etc.	85
Not swaying to this ƒ or to that ;	Ded. of Idylls,	20

faculty.
| all my *faculties* are lamed. | Lucretius | 123 |

fade.
then as slowly ƒ again,	Eleänore	93
Ripens and ƒ's, and falls,	Lotos-E's.	82
Ay, ay, the blossom ƒ's,	Walk. to the M.	49
margin ƒ's For ever and for ever	Ulysses	20
little cared for ƒ's not yet.	In Mem. viii.	20
Before the spirits ƒ away,	" xlvi.	14
Be near me when I ƒ away,	" xlix.	13
F wholly, while the soul exults,	" lxxii.	14
year by year our memory ƒ's	" c.	23
ƒ's the last long streak of snow,	" cxiv.	19
flame or ƒ, and the war roll down.	Maud, III. vi.	54
When can their glory ƒ ?	Lt. Brigade	50
love, that seems not made to ƒ	Elaine	1007
since the nobler pleasure seems to ƒ,	Lucretius	227

faded.
the heart Faints, ƒ by its heat.	D. of F. Wom.	288
by Nature's law, Have ƒ long ago ;	Talking O.	74
ƒ, and seems But an ashen-gray	Maud, I. vi.	21
this kindlier glow F with morning,	Aylmer's F.	412

fading.
| F slowly from his side ; | L. of Burleigh | 86 |
| Growing and ƒ and growing upon | Maud, I. iii. | 7-9 |

faggot.
| we will make it ƒ's for the hearth, | Princess, vi. | 29 |

fail.
thy hand F from the sceptre-staff.	Œnone	124
So wrought, they will not ƒ.	Pal. of Art	143
Lest she should ƒ and perish utterly,	"	221

	POEM.	LINE.
for a man may ƒ in duty twice,	M. d'Arthur	129
ƒ to match his masterpiece.'	Gardener's D.	31
cannot ƒ but work in hues to dim	"	106
made a saint, if I ƒ here ?	St S. Stylites	47
Thy leaf shall never ƒ, nor yet	Talking O.	239
not to ƒ In offices of tenderness,	Ulysses	40
I shall not ƒ to find her now.	Two Voices	191
'The many ƒ: the one succeeds.'	Day-Dm.	116
Her heart within her did not ƒ:	Lady Clare	73
Rose again from where it seem'd to ƒ,	Vision of Sin	24
perchance your life may ƒ ;	Princess, iii.	220
ƒ so far In high desire,	"	262
If we ƒ, we ƒ, And if we win, we ƒ :	" v.	312
What end soever : ƒ you will not	"	396
breadth, nor ƒ in childward care,	" vii.	267
Forgive them where they ƒ in truth,	In Mem. Pro.	43
seem to ƒ from out thy blood	" ii.	15
thou should'st ƒ from thy desire,	" iv.	6
Swell out and ƒ, as if a door	" xxviii.	7
ƒ not in a world of sin,	" xxxiii.	15
truth in closest words shall ƒ,	" xxxvi.	6
life should ƒ in looking back.	" xlv.	4
No life may ƒ beyond the grave,	" liv.	2
I shall pass ; my work will ƒ.	" lvi.	8
make thee somewhat blench or ƒ.	" lxi.	2
spirit should ƒ from off the globe ;	" lxxxiii.	36
A thousand pulses dancing, ƒ.	" cxxiv.	16
shall I shriek if a Hungary ƒ ?	Maud, I. iv.	46
solid ground Not ƒ beneath my feet	" xi.	2
tries the bridge he fears may ƒ,	Enid	1152
fine plots may ƒ, Tho' harlots paint	Vivien	669
spouting from a cliff F's in mid air,	Guinevere	603
ƒ's at last And perishes as I must ;	Lucretius	260
ƒ to find thee, being as thou art	"	264

failed.
sweet incense rose and never ƒ,	Pal. of Art	45
heart ƒ her ; and the reapers reap'd,	Dora	76
the year in which our olives ƒ,	Princess, i.	124
none to trust Since our arms ƒ—	" v.	417
Old studies ƒ: seldom she spoke :	" vii.	16
had ƒ In sweet humility ; had ƒ in all :	"	213
for a vast speculation had ƒ.	Maud, I. i.	9
ever ƒ to draw The quiet night	Enid	531
on all those who tried and ƒ,	Vivien	440
many tried and ƒ, because the charm	"	445
believe she tempted them and ƒ,	"	668
ƒ to find him tho' I rode	Elaine	705
yet thee She ƒ to bind,	"	1376
She ƒ and sadden'd knowing it ;	En. Arden	256
all her force F her ;	"	372
thought and nature ƒ a little,	"	793
As having ƒ in duty to him,	Lucretius	274

failing (part.)
F to give the bitter of the sweet,	D. of F. Wom.	286
utterance ƒ her, She whirl'd them	Princess, iv.	376
you ƒ, I abide What end soever :	" v.	395

failing (s.)
| that unnoticed ƒ in herself, | Enid | 896 |

fain.
| how ƒ was I To dream thy cause | Princess, vi. | 182 |
| ƒ Have all men true and leal | Vivien | 642 |

faint (adj.)
F she grew, and ever fainter,	L. of Burleigh	81
The voice grew ƒ: there came a	Vision of Sin	207
hues are ƒ And mix with hollow	In Mem. lxix.	
haunting whisper makes me ƒ	" lxxx.	7
let her eat ; the damsel is so ƒ.'	Enid	1055
And I was ƒ to swooning,	Vivien	130
too ƒ and sick am I For anger :	Elaine	1080
F as a figure seen in early dawn	En. Arden	354

faint (verb.)
I ƒ in this obscurity,	Ode to Mem. 6,44,123
My very heart ƒ's	'A spirit haunts,' etc.	16
flowers would ƒ at your cruel cheer,	Poet's Mind	15
F's like a dazzled morning moon.	Fatima	28
the heart F's, faded by its heat.	D. of F. Wom.	288
Cry, ƒ not	Two Voices	81, 184
They ƒ on hill or field or river :	Princess, iii.	361
to ƒ in the light that she loves (rep.)	Maud, I. xxii.	9

	POEM.	LINE.
faint-blue.		
A *f-b* ridge upon the right,	*Mariana in the S.*	5
fainted.		
at the clamouring of her enemy *f*	*Boädicea*	82
fainter.		
Faint she grew and ever *f,*	*L. of Burleigh*	81
faintlier.		
Then laugh'd again, but *f,*	*Guinevere*	58
faintly.		
ho' *f,* merrily—far and far away—	*En. Arden*	615
faintly-flushed.		
w *f-f,* how phantom-fair,	*The Daisy*	65
faintly-shadow'd.		
- traced a *f-s* track,	*Elaine*	165
faintly-venomed.		
smiles, and *f-v* points Of slander.	*Vivien*	28
fair.		
But beyond expression *f*	*Adeline*	5
rind ingrav'n ' For the most *f,*'	*Œnone*	71
mortal eyes are frail to judge of *f,*	"	155
why fairest wife? am I not *f*?	"	192
Methinks I must be *f,* for yesterday,	"	194
O the Earl was *f* to see! (rep.)	*The Sisters*	6
divinely tall, And most divinely *f.*	*D. of F. Wom.*	88
that Rosamond, whom men call *f,*	"	251
'come again, and thrice as *f;*	*M. d'Arthur, Ep.*	26
maid of spouse, As *f* as my Olivia,	*Talking O.*	35
oak on lea Shall grow so *f* as this,'	"	244
What moral is in being *f.*	*Day-Dm.*	200
' What wonder, if he thinks me *f*?'	"	272
Tomohrit, Athos, all things *f,*	*To E. L.*	5
Sees whatever *f* and splendid	*L. of Burleigh*	27
She was more *f* than words can say	*Beggar Maid*	2
' Comely too by all that's *f,*	*Princess,* ii.	99
thoughts as *f* within her eyes,	"	305
beauties every shade of brown and *f*	"	414
' O *f* and strong and terrible!	" vi.	147
she not *f,* began To gather light	" vii.	8
Thy creature, whom I found so *f.*	*In Mem. Pro.*	38
glad to find thyself so *f,*	" vi.	27
all we met was *f* and good,	" xxiii.	17
If all was good and *f* we met,	" xxiv.	5
Man, her last work, who seem'd so *f,*	" lv.	9
that which made the world so *f.*	" cxv.	8
grews For ever, and as *f* as good.	" Con.	36
she promised then to be *f.*	*Maud,* I. i.	68
I had fancied it would be *f.*	" vi.	6
f without, faithful within.	" xiii.	37
face of night is *f* on the dewy downs, " III. vi.		5
' Too happy, fresh, and *f,* rep.	*The Brook*	217
can see elsewhere, anything so *f.*	*Enid*	499
' Advance and take as fairest of the *f,*	"	553
you won the prize of fairest *f,* rep.)	"	719
however *f,* She is not fairer in new	"	721
never yet had seen her half so *f;*	"	741
femininely *f* and dissolutely pale,	"	1124
It'd her meek honour as the fairest *f,*	"	1681
ladies I ved to call Enid the F,	"	1811
tender was her voice, so *f* her face,	*Vivien*	251
as noble, as their Queen was *f*	"	458
Flame the *f,* Elaine the loveable	*Elaine*	1
' If what is *f* be but for what is *f,*	"	237
chemisers: all were *f* and dry;	"	406
a faith once *f* Was richer than these	"	1222
Delicately pure and marvellously *f,*	"	1360
' *F* she was, my King. Pure	"	1365
She kiss'd me saying thou art *f,*	"	1399
frequent interchange of foul and *f,*	*En. Arden*	529
Sear'd by the close ecliptic, was not *f;*	*Aylmer's F.*	193
a by miracle, grow straight and *f—*	"	676
f as the Angel that said ' hail'	"	681
a fearful night '' ' Not fearful; *f,*	*Sea Dreams*	81
if every star in heaven Can make it *f;*	"	83
f is her cottage in its place,	*Requiescat*	5
sea king's daughter as happy as *f,*	*W. to Alexan.*	26
you so small and you so *f,* (rep.)	"	31
if I am I so black?	*The Window*	72
You so *f* I am I so black?	"	74

	POEM.	LINE.
(fair 's.)		
the *f* Was holden at the town;	*Talking O.*	101
fairer.		
guerdon could not alter me To *f.*	*Œnone*	151
Emilia, *f* than all else but thou,	*Audley Ct.*	65
thou art *f* than all else that is.	"	66
Stiller, not *f* than mine.	*Maud,* II. v.	71
F than aught in the world beside,	"	73
f in new clothes than old.	*Enid*	722
as much *f—*as a faith once fair	*Elaine*	1222
F his talk, a tongue that ruled the	*Aylmer's F.*	194
F than Rachel by the palmy well,	"	679
F than Ruth among the fields of corn,	"	680
f she, but ah how soon to die!	*Requiescat*	5
fairest.		
all which thou hast drawn of *f*	*Ode to Mem.*	89
claiming each This meed of *f.*	*Œnone*	85
So shalt thou find me *f.*	"	153
F—why *f* wife? am I not fair?	"	192
She was the *f* in the face:	*The Sisters*	2
the tallest of them all And *f,*	*M. d'Arthur*	208
prize of beauty for the *f* there,	*Enid*	485
' Advance and take as *f* of the fair,	"	553
beardless apple-arbiter Decided *f*	*Lucretius*	92
fairest-spoken.		
Thou art the *f-s* tree	*Talking O.*	263
fair-fronted.		
F-f Truth shall droop not 'Clear-headed friend,' etc.		12
fair-haired.		
F-h and redder than a windy morn;	*Princess, Con.*	91
a *f-h* youth, that in his hand Bare	*Enid*	1030
when the *f-h* youth came by him	"	1038
a loftier Annie Lee, *F-h* and tall,	*En. Arden.*	750
fairily.		
Made so *f* well With delicate spire	*Maud,* II. ii.	5
fairily-delicate.		
F-d palaces shine	*The Islet*	10
fairness.		
To doubt her *f* were to want an eye,	*Elaine*	1367
fairplay.		
but space and *f* for her scheme;	*Princess,* v.	272
fairy.		
The oriental *f* brought,	*Eleänore*	14
As to *fairies,* that will flit	*Talking O.*	89
fairy-circle.		
The flickering *f-c* wheel'd and broke	*Guinevere*	235
Fairy Queen.		
Look how she sleeps—the *F Q,* so fair!	*Elaine*	1243
fairy-tale.		
told her *f-t's,* Show'd her the fairy	*Aylmer's F.*	89
faith.		
simple *f* than Norman blood.	*L. C. V. deVere*	56
' Upon the general decay of *f*	*The Epic*	13
run My *f* beyond my practice	*Ed. Morris*	54
we closed, we kiss'd, swore *f,*	"	114
with a larger *f* appeal'd	*Talking O.*	15
Wait: my *f* is large in Time,	*Love and Duty*	6
keep I fair thro' faith and prayer.	*Sir Galahad*	23
If there be any *f* in man.'	*Lady Clare*	44
' Nay now, what *f* t' said Alice	"	45
why kept ye not your *f*?	*Princess,* v.	74
their sinless *f,* A maiden moon	"	177
f in womankind Beats with his blood,	" vii.	307
Some sense of duty, something of a *f,*	" Con.	54
sport half-science, fill me with a *f*	"	76
By *f,* and *f* alone, embrace,	*In Mem. Pro.*	3
We have but *f:* we cannot know;	"	21
Whose *f* has centre everywhere,	" xxxiii.	3
Her *f* thro' form is pure as thine,	" xxxiii.	9
This *f* has many a purer priest,	" xxxvii.	9
f as vague as all unsweet:	" xlvi.	3
Be near me when my *f* is dry,	" xlix.	9
love be blamed for want of *f*	" l.	10
stretch lame hands of *f,* and grope	" liv.	17

	POEM.	LINE.
breed with him, can fright my *f*.	*In Mem.* lxxxi.	4
The *f*, the vigour, bold to dwell	" xciv.	29
Perplext in *f*, but pure in deeds,	" xcv.	9
lives more *f* in honest doubt,	"	11
To find a stronger *f* his own ;	"	17
to him she sings Of early *f*.	" xcvi.	30
Her *f* is fixt and cannot move,	"	33
What profit lies in barren *f*,	" cvii.	5
What is she, cut from love and *f*,	" cxiii.	11
Our dearest *f*; our ghastliest doubt ;	" cxxiii.	2
all is well, tho' *f* and form Be sunder'd	" cxxv.	1
comrade of the lesser *f*.	" cxxvii.	3
f that comes of self-control,	" cxxx.	9
have *f* in a tradesman's ware or his word?	*Maud*, I. i.	26
a rock in ebbs and flows, Fixt on her *f*.	*Enid*	813
F and unfaith can ne'er be equal powers :	*Vivien*	238
Unfaith in nught is want of *f* in all.	"	239
break *f* with one I may not name?	*Elaine*	682
f unfaithful kept him falsely true.	"	873
f once fair Was richer than these	"	1222
His resolve Upbore him, and firm *f*,	*En. Arden*.	801
sweet face and *f* Held him from that :	*Aylmer's F.*	392
Have *f*, have *f*! We live by *f*,' said he;	*Sea Dreams*	153
Has given all my *f* a turn? .	*The Ringlet*	52
honouring your sweet *f* in him,	*A Dedication*	1
F from tracts no feet have trod,	*On a Mourner*	29

faithful.

Lean'd on him, *f*, gentle, good	*Two Voices*	416
fair without, *f* within,	*Maud.* I. xiii.	37
for all my pains, She is not *f* to me	*Enid*	117

faithless.

Lest I be found as *f* in the quest	*Elaine*	757

falcon.

If all the world were *f*'s, what of	*Golden Year*	38
Forgetful of the *f* and the hunt,	*Enid*	51
No surer than our *f* yesterday,	*Elaine*	653

falcon-eyed.

A quick brunette, well-moulded, *f-e*,	*Princess*, ii.	91

fall (s.)

many a *f* Of diamond rillets	*Arabian N's*.	47
comes the check, the change, the *f*,	*Two Voices*	163
woodlands, echoing *f*'s Of water,	*To E. L.*	5
Came in a sun-lit *f* of rain.	*Sir L. and Q. G.*	4
the river made a *f* Out yonder :	*Princess*, iii.	156
Rapt to the horrible *f*;	" iv.	162
mark'd it with the red cross to the *f*,	" vi.	25
huddling slant in furrow-cloven *f*'s	" vii.	192
leaves that redden to the *f*;	*In Mem.* xi.	14
back we came at *f* of dew.	" Con.	100
Here at the head of a tinkling *f*,	*Maud*, I. xxi.	6
pride is broken : men have seen my *f*.'	*Enid*	578
broken down, for Enid sees my *f*!'	"	590
drumming thunder of the huger *f*	"	1022
Enid heard the clashing of his *f*,	"	1358
never woman yet, since man's first *f*,	*Elaine*	855
to think of Modred's dusty *f*,	*Guinevere*	55
meän'd to 'a stubb'd it at *f*,	*N. Farmer*.	41
rapid of life Shoots to the *f*—	*A Dedication*	4
like the flakes In a *f* of snow,	*Lucretius*	167

fall (verb.)

Letting the rose-leaves *f*:	*Claribel*	3
Place it, where sweetest sunlight *f*'s	*Ode to Mem.*	85
f to the ground if you came in.	*Poet's Mind*	23
shall *f* again to ground.	*Deserted H.*	16
passeth when the tree shall *f*,	*Love and Death*	14
my ringlets would *f* Low adown,	*The Mermaid*	14
all day long to *f* and rise	*Miller's D.*	182
seem'd to hear them climb and *f*,	*Pal. of Art*	70
dully sound Of human footsteps *f*.	"	276
to *f* and pause and *f* did seem.	*Lotos-E's*.	9
sweet music here that softer *f*'s	"	46
*F*s, and floats adown the air.	"	76
fades, and *f*'s, and hath no toil,	"	82
In silence : ripen, *f* and cease :	"	97
thunder-drops/on a sleeping sea	*D. of F. Wom.*	122
f down and glance From tone to tone,	"	166
F into shadow, soonest lost :	*To J. S.*	11
that on which it throve *F*'s off,	"	16

	POEM.	LINE.
from Discussion's lip may *f* '*Love thou thy land,*' etc.		33
The goose let *f* a golden egg	*The Goose*	11
f's not hail, or rain, or any snow,	*M. d'Arthur*	260
'*F* down, O Simeon : thou hast	*St S. Stylites*	97
oft I *f*, Maybe for months,	"	100
Once more the gate behind me *f*'s;	*Talking O.*	1
when my marriage morn may *f*,	"	285
not leap forth and *f* about thy neck,	*Love and Duty*	41
and the shadows rise and *f*.	*Locksley H.*	80
now for the roof-tree *f*.	"	190
Let it *f* on Locksley Hall,	"	193
Then did my response clearer *f* :	*Two Voices*	34
billow, blown against, *F*'s back,	"	317
to one engine bound *F*'s off,	"	343
Until they *f* in trance again.	"	354
I'll take the showers as they *f*,	*Amphion*	102
Perfume and flowers *f* in showers,	*Sir Galahad*	11
On whom their favours *f*!	"	14
Swells up, and shakes and *f*'s.	"	76
like a thunderbolt he *f*'s	*The Eagle*	6
with shadows and to *f*. (rep. v. 465)	*Princess*, i.	10
but prepare : I speak ; it *f*'s.'	" ii.	206
gracious dews Began to glisten and to *f* :	"	296
The splendour *f*'s on castle walls.	" iii.	348
Bred will in me to overcome it or *f*.	" v.	341
Yea, let her see me *f*!	"	506
tho' he trip and *f* He shall not blind	" vii.	311
Her place is empty, *f* like these ;	*In Mem.* xiii.	4
fill'd with tears that cannot *f*,	" xix.	15
My deeper anguish also *f*'s,	"	15
If such a dreamy touch should *f*,	" xliii.	13
f Remerging in the general Soul,	" xlvi.	3
Be near us when we climb or *f* :	" l.	13
can but trust that good shall *f*	" liii.	14
drop by drop the water *f*'s	" lvii.	3
on my bed the moonlight *f*'s,	" lxvi.	1
on mine ear this message *f*'s,	" lxxxiv.	18
lightly does the whisper *f*,	"	89
strangely *f*'s our Christmas eve.	" civ.	7
A shade *f*'s on us like the dark	" Con.	93
breaking let the splendour *f*.	"	119
Shall I weep if a Poland *f*?	*Maud*, I. iv.	46
f before Her feet on the meadow	" v.	25
For I heard your rivulet *f*	" xxii.	36
heavens *f* in a gentle rain,	" II. i.	41
dewy splendour *f*'s on the little	" iv.	32
Then I rise, the eavedrops *f*,	"	62
Mourning when their leaders *f*,	*Ode on Well.*	5
if I *f* her name will yet remain	*Enid*	500
slowly falling as a scale that *f*'s,	"	525
cheek burn and either eyelid *f*,	"	775, 1283
Before he turn to *f* seaward again,	"	966
when he passes *f* upon him.'	"	970
they will *f* upon him unawares.	"	903
will *f* upon you while you pass.'	"	994
if I *f*, cleave to the better man.'	"	1001
a dreadful loss *F*'s in a far land	"	1346
made as if to *f* upon him.	"	1624
fear not, Enid, I should *f* upon him,	"	1635
for three days seen, ready to *f*.	*Vivien*	145
charge you know, to stand or *f*!	"	553
the victim's flowers before he *f*.'	*Elaine*	906
footstep seem'd to *f* beside her	*En. Arden*.	510
F back upon a name! rest, rot in	*Aylmer's F.*	385
heads of chiefs and princes *f* so fast,	"	763
as *f*'s A creeper when the prop is	"	809
seem'd Always about to *f*,	"	822
his own head Began to droop, to *f* ;	"	835
'Set them up ! they shall not *f*!'.	*Sea Dreams*	220
woods decay, the woods decay and *f*.	*Tithonus*	1
F from his Ocean-lane of fire,	*The Voyage*	19
Bloodily, bloodily *f* the battle-axe,	*Boädicea*	56
she felt the heart within her *f*	"	81
f unawares before the people	*Hendecasyllabics*	7
f's the least white star of snow,	*Lucretius*	107
She heard him raging, heard him *f*;	"	272

fallen.

stem, which else had *f* quite,	*Isabel*.	35
F silver-chiming, seem'd to shake	*Arabian N's*.	51
dews, that would have *f* in tears,	*Miller's D.*	151

	POEM.	LINE.
She ceased in tears, ƒ from hope	D. of F. Wom.	257
ƒ in Lyonness about their Lord,	M. d'Arthur	4
half has ƒ and made a bridge ;	Walk. to the M.	24
ƒ into the dusty crypt	Will Water.	183
The rain had ƒ, the Poet arose,	Poet's Song.	1
When ƒ in darker ways.'	Princess, v.	65
Our enemies have ƒ, have ƒ: rep.)	" vi.	17
when she turn'd, the curse Had ƒ,	In Mem. vi.	38
words are these have ƒ from me ?	" xvi.	1
towers ƒ as soon as built —	" xxvi.	8
Had ƒ into her father's grave,	" lxxxviii.	48
There has ƒ a splendid tear	Maud, l. xxii.	59
ƒ at length that tower of strength	Ode on Well.	38
not ƒ so low as some would wish,	Enid	129
So that I be not ƒ in fight.	"	223
here had ƒ a great part of a tower,	"	317
When now they saw their bulwark ƒ,	"	1017
gently born But into bad hands ƒ,	"	1041
catch a lothly plume ƒ from the wing	Vivien	577
Lay like a rainbow ƒ upon the grass,	Elaine	430
Where these had ƒ, slowly past	"	1234
what has ƒ upon the realm?	Guinevere	273
reel'd, and would have ƒ,	"	302
her face had ƒ upon her hands ;	En. Arden.	388
thunders of the house Had ƒ first.	Aylmer's F.	279
How low his brother's mood had ƒ,	"	404
'Let them lie, for they have ƒ.'	Sea Dreams	221
here upon a yellow eyelid ƒ.	Lucretius	141

falling.

alleys ƒ down to twilight grots,	Ode to Mem.	107
leaves upon her ƒ light—	L. of Shalott, iv.	21
F into a still delight, And luxury.	Eleänore	106
Lo, ƒ from my constant mind,	Fatima	5
brook ƒ thro' the clov'n ravine	Œnone	8
watch the emerald-colour'd water ƒ	Lotos-E's.	141
all night long, in ƒ thro' the dell,	D. of F. Wom.	183
perish, ƒ on the foeman's ground,	Locksley II.	103
Rising, ƒ, like a wave	Vision of Sin	125
ƒ on them like a thunderbolt,	Princess, Pro.	43
silver hammers ƒ On silver anvils,	" i.	213
slanted forward, ƒ in a land Of promise ;	" ii.	123
ƒ on my face was caught and known.	" iv.	251
ƒ, protomartyr of our cause, Die ;	"	484
kill'd in ƒ from his horse.	In Mem. vi.	40
I, ƒ on his faithful heart,	" xviii.	14
I wander, often ƒ flame,	" xxiii.	6
ƒ with my weight of cares	" liv.	14
ƒ, idly broke the peace Of hearts	" lxvii.	5
When twilight was ƒ,	Maud, l. xii.	2
I watch the twilight ƒ brown	To F. D. Maurice	14
slowly ƒ as a scale that falls,	Enid	525
felt the warm tears ƒ on his face ;	"	1434
ƒ prone he dug His fingers	En. Arden.	780
F had let appear the brand of John—	Aylmer's F.	509
deadly wounded F on the dead.	The Captain	64

falling out.

blessings on the ƒ o	Princess, i.	251

fall out.

When we ƒ o with those we love	Princess, i.	253

fallow.

thousand hearts lie ƒ in these halls,	Princess, ii.	378
By many a field and ƒ,	The Brook	44

false.

seem'd A touch of something ƒ,	Ed. Morris	74
Hears little of the ƒ or just.'	Two Voices	117
what, I would not aught of ƒ—	Princess, v.	392
true to thee as ƒ, ƒ, ƒ to me I	" vi.	187
Ah ƒ but dear, Dear traitor,	"	274
flashes into ƒ and true,	In Mem. xvi.	19
Ring out the ƒ, ring in the true.	" cv.	8
taking true for ƒ, or ƒ for true ;	Enid	853
own ear had heard Call herself ƒ ;	"	963
ƒ and foul As the poach'd filth	Vivien	646
lets the wife Whom he knows ƒ, abide	Guinevere	511
So ƒ, he partly took himself for true ;	Sea Dreams	181
Her Deity ƒ in human-amorous tears ;	Lucretius	90

falsehood.

	POEM.	LINE.
F shall bare her plaited 'Clear-headed friend,' etc.		11
A gentler death shall F die,	"	16
The ƒ of extremes ! 'Of old sat Freedom.' etc.		24
To war with ƒ to the knife,	Two Voices	131
Your ƒ and yourself are hateful to us :	Princess, iv.	524

falsely.

'F, ƒ have ye done, O mother,'	Lady Clare	29
might play me ƒ, having power,	Vivien	365
looking at her, Full courtly, yet not ƒ,	Elaine	236

falser.

F than all fancy fathoms, ƒ than ,	Locksley II.	41

falsest.

Whose spirits ƒ in the mist, 'You ask me why,' etc.		3
He to lips, that fondly ƒ,	L. of Burleigh	9
progress ƒ to the woman's goal.'	Princess, vi.	111
I ƒ where I firmly trod,	In Mem. liv.	13
happy Yes F's from her lips,	Maud, I. xvii.	10
Nor let her true hand ƒ,	Enid	1361
wirer of their innocent hare F before	Aylmer's F.	491

faltered.

in the middle of his song He ƒ,	Guinevere	301

faltereth.

My tremulous tongue ƒ,	Eleänore	136

faltering.

Made me most happy, ƒ 'I am thine.'	Gardener's D.	230
F, would break its syllables,	Love and Duty	39
voice F and fluttering in her throat,	Princess, ii.	170
ƒ sideways downward to her belt,	Vivien	699

falteringly.

Philip standing up said ƒ	En. Arden.	283

fame.

threaded The secretest walks of ƒ :	The Poet	10
with a worm I balk'd his ƒ,	D. of F. Wom.	155
remember'd Everard's college ƒ.	The Epic	45
much honour and much ƒ were lost.'	M. d'Arthur	103
among us lived Her ƒ from lip to lip.	Gardener's D.	50
my ƒ is loud amongst mankind,	St. S. Stylites	80
Name and ƒ! to fly sublime	Vision of Sin	103
grief to find her less than ƒ,	Princess, i.	72
With only F for spouse	" iii.	226
nor would we work for ƒ;	"	244
mincers of each other's ƒ,	" iv.	494
The ƒ is quench'd that I foresaw,	In Mem. lxxii.	5
What ƒ is left for human deeds	"	13
O hollow wraith of dying ƒ;	" lxxiv.	17
here shall silence guard thy ƒ;	" lxxvi.	15
To breathe my loss is more than ƒ,	Maud, l. i.	18
his honest ƒ should at least by me	Ode on Well.	78
Preserve a broad approach of ƒ,	"	145
proof and echo of all human ƒ,	"	229
Their ever-loyal iron lender's ƒ	Vivien	63
use and name and ƒ. (153, 190, 224, 819)	"	267
such fire for ƒ, Such trumpet-blowings	"	287
felt them slowly ebbing, name and ƒ.	"	294
touching ƒ, howe'er you scorn my song,	"	297
For ƒ, could ƒ be mine, that ƒ were thine,	"	310
Man dreams of F while woman wakes	"	313
F, The F that follows death is nothing	"	315
what is F in life but half-disfame,	"	326
the scroll ' I follow ƒ.'	"	320
for motto, 'Rather use than ƒ.'	"	338
F with men Being but ampler means	"	343
Use gave me F at first, and F again	"	354
well know I that F is half-disfame,	"	355
ƒ, To one at least, who hath not children	"	363
in that star 'To make ƒ nothing :	"	369
rather dread the loss of use than ƒ ;	Elaine	1363
Born to the glory of thy name and ƒ,	"	1391
your crescent fear for name and ƒ,	Guinevere	478
courtliness, and the desire of ƒ,	"	621
must not dwell on that defeat of ƒ,	Aylmer's F.	439
beat a pathway out to wealth and ƒ,	Spiteful Let.	3
ƒ in song hath done him much wrong,	"	9, 13
This fallen leaf, isn't ƒ as brief?		

familiar.

the Royal mind, ƒ with her,	Princess, iv.	216
grow F to the stranger's child ;	In Mem. c.	20

132   CONCORDANCE TO

familiarity.
	POEM.	LINE.
Such dear *familiarities* of dawn?	Aylmer's F.	131

famine.
Blight and *f*, plague and earthquake,	Lotos-E's.	160
A *f* after laid them low,	The Victim	2
'Help us from *f* And plague	"	9
blight and *f* on all the lea:	"	48

famous.
made thee *f* once, when young:	The Blackbird	16

fan (s.)
To spread into the perfect *f*,	Sir L. and Q. G.	17
toys in lava, *f's* Of sandal, amber,	Princess, Pro.	18

fan (verb.)
f my brows and blow The fever	In Mem. lxxxv.	8
A soft air *f's* the cloud apart;	Tithonus	32

fancied.
I had *f* it would be fair,	Maud, I. vi.	6
she *f* 'Is it for me?'	Elaine	818

fancy (s.)
With youthful *f* reinspired,	Ode to Mem.	114
scarce my life with *f* play'd	Miller's D.	45
thought that it was *f*, and I listen'd	May Queen,iii.	33
sharp *fancies*, by down-lapsing	D. of F. Wom.	49
if I said that F, led by Love,	Gardener's D.	58
In the Spring a young man's *f*	Locksley H.	20
Falser than all *f* fathoms,	"	41
Soothe him with thy finer *fancies*,	"	54
I have but an angry *f*:	"	102
Fool, again the dream, the *f*!	"	173
well thro' all my *f* yet.	"	188
Across my *f*, brooding warm,	Day-Dm.	10
So much your eyes my *f* take—	"	238
My *f*, ranging thro' and thro',	"	246
But whither would my *f* go?	Will Water.	145
Set thy hoary *fancies* free;	Vision of Sin	156
maiden *fancies*; loved to live alone	Princess, i.	48
crush her pretty maiden *fancies* dead	"	87
What were those *fancies*?	"	94
fair philosophies That lift the *f*;	" iii.	323
sweet as those by hopeless *f* feign'd	" iv.	37
fancies hatch'd In silken-folded	"	48
melted Florian's *f* as she hung,	"	351
Thy face across his *f* comes,	"	556
understanding all the foolish work Of F, " vi.		101
fancies like the vermin in a nut	"	246
flatters thus Our home-bred *fancies*:	In Mem. x.	11
My *fancies* time to rise on wing	" xiii.	17
but for *fancies*, which aver	" xv.	9
Whose *f* uses old and new,	" xvi.	28
And F light from F caught,	" xxiii.	14
I vex my heart with *fancies* dim:	" xli.	1
f's tenderest eddy wreathe,	" xlviii.	6
dare we to this *f* give,	" lii.	5
I lull a *f* trouble-tost	" lxiv.	1
You wonder when my *fancies* play	" lxv.	2
Take wings of *f*, and ascend,	" lxxv.	1
Then *f* shapes, as *f* can, The grief	" lxxix.	5
Ah, backward *f*, wherefore wake	" lxxxiii.	46
Ill brethren, let the *f* fly.	" lxxxv.	12
villain *f* fleeting by,	" cx.	18
all the breeze of F blows,	" cxxi.	17
It circles round, and *f* plays,	Con.	81
The *f* flatter'd my mind,	Maud, I.xiv.	23
wastes where footless *fancies* dwell	" xviii.	69
the primrose *fancies* of the boy,	The Brook	3
Lay your earthly *fancies* down,	Ode on Well.	279
My *f* fled to the South again.	The Daisy	108
let her *f* flit across the past,	Enid	645
Her *f* dwelling in this dusky hall;	"	802
sweet self-pity, or the *f* of it,	"	1198
which lately gloom'd Your *f*	Vivien	175
fixt her *f* on him : let him be.	"	626
once to me Mere matter of the *f*.		773
snare her royal *f* with a boon	Elaine	72
Rapt in this *f* of his Table Round,	"	130
Full often lost in *f*, lost his way;	"	164
ghostly grace Beam'd on his *f*,	"	882
her *fancies* with the sallow-rifted	"	996
you never yet Denied my *fancies*—	"	1106

	POEM.	LINE.
For her I for your new *f*.	Elaine	1210
men Shape to their *f's* eye	"	1245
evil *fancies* clung Like serpent eggs	En. Arden.	476
His *f* fled before the lazy wind	"	653
Edith's eager *f* hurried with him	Aylmer's F.	208
still Clung to their *fancies*)	Sea Dreams	36
drifting up the stream In *f*,	"	105
Like F made of golden air,	The Voyage	66
F came and at her pillow sat,	Coquette, I.	5
F watches in the wilderness,	"	12
Poor F sadder than a single star,	"	13
f made me for a moment blest	" ii.	6

fancy (verb.)
I *f* her sweetness only due	Maud, I. xiii.	33
may hear, or see, Or *f*	Enid	1205

fancy-borne.
f-b perhaps upon the rise And long	Lucretius	10

fancy-fed.
And pining life be *f-f*.	InMem.lxxxiv.	96

fancy-flies.
love the mud, Rising to no *f-f*.	Vision of Sin	107

fancying.
f that her glory would be great	Vivien	66

fane.
translucent *f* Of her still spirit;	Isabel	4
built him *f's* of fruitless prayer,	In Mem. lv.	12
heard once more in college *f's*	" lxxxvi.	5
As befits a solemn *f*:	Ode on Well.	250
hopes and hates, his homes and *f's*,	Lucretius.	251

fang.
f's Shall move the stony bases	Princess, vi.	41

fann'd.
flame, By veering passion *f*,	Madeline	29
bounteous forehead was not *f*	Eleänore	9
A summer *f* with spice.	Pal. of Art	116
Low breezes *f* the belfry bars,	The Letters	43
f the gardens of that rival rose	Aylmer's F.	455

fantastical.
Albeit I know my knights *f*,	Elaine	592
So *f* is the dainty metre.	Hendecasyllabics	14

fantasy.
Her gay-furr'd cats a painted *f*,	Princess, iii.	170
A border *f* of branch and flower,	Elaine	11
so she lived in *f*.	" 27,	397
rather in the *f* than the blood.	"	1126

far-blazing.
F-b from the rear of Philip's house,	En. Arden.	728

far-brought.
love f-b From out the storied 'Love thou thy land,' etc.		1

farce.
made myself a Queen of *f*!	Princess, vii.	228

fare (s.)
store of rich apparel, sumptuous *f*,	Enid	709
My lord, eat also, tho' the *f* is coarse,	"	1057
costlier than with mowers' *f*.'	"	1080
said Geraint, 'I wish no better *f*:	"	1081
Friday *f* was Enoch's ministering.	En. Arden.	100

fare (verb.)
So *f's* it since the years began,	Will Water.	169
O heart, how *f's* it with thee now	In Mem. iv.	5
How *f's* it with the happy dead?	" xliii.	1
bring us what he is and how he *f's*,	Elaine	546
F you well A thousand times !—	"	692
How *f's* my lord Sir Lancelot?'	"	1198
F's richly, in fine linen, not a hair	Aylmer's F.	659
All is over : F thee well !'	Lucretius	277

fared.
so *f* she gazing there ;	Princess, vii.	26
Whereon with equal feet we *f*;	InMem.xxv.	2
So *f* it with Geraint, (rep. 857, 1349)	Enid	343

farewell.
might I tell of meetings, of *f's*—	Gardener's D.	246
F, like endless welcome, lived and	Love and Duty	66

	POEM.	LINE.
a long farewell to Locksley Hall!	Locksley H.	189
reach'd White hands of ƒ to my sire	Princess, v.	223
pithy, such as closed Welcome, ƒ.	" Con.	95
In those sad words I took ƒ:	In Mem. lvii.	1
I cannot think the thing ƒ.	" cxxii.	12
needs must bid ƒ to sweet Lavaine,	Elaine	340
a thousand times ƒ!	"	693
Nor bad ƒ, but sadly rode away	"	981
bad a thousand ƒ's to me	"	1030
for you left me taking no ƒ,	"	1267
to take my last ƒ of you.	"	1268
I left her and I bad her no ƒ.	"	1236
their last hour, A madness of ƒ's.	Guinevere	102
for we have taken our ƒ's.	"	116
Ƒ ? I should have answer'd his ƒ.	"	608
faced this morning of ƒ Brightly	En. Arden	182

far-fleeted.

F-ƒ by the purple island-sides,	Princess, vii.	151

far-folded.

F-ƒ mists, and gleaming halls of morn.	Tithonus	10

far-heard.

F-h beneath the moon.	D. of F. Wom.	1

farm.

crows from the ƒ upon the hill,	May Queen, ii.	23
With farmer Allan at the ƒ abode.	Dora	1
set out, and reach'd the ƒ	"	126
discuss'd the ƒ, The fourfield system	Audley Ct.	32
crowded ƒ's and lessening towers,	In Mem. xi.	11
To leave the pleasant fields and ƒ's	" ci.	22
Till last by Philip's ƒ I flow	The Brook	31
Philip's ƒ where brook and river meet	"	38
call'd old Philip out To show the ƒ:	"	121
how he sent the bailiff to the ƒ	"	141
found the bailiff riding by the ƒ,	"	153
'Are you from the ƒ?'	"	209
bought the ƒ we tenanted before	"	222
closed her access to the wealthier ƒ's,	Aylmer's F.	503
princely halls, and ƒ's, and flowing	"	634
broad woodland, parcell'd into ƒ's;	"	847
Willy had not been down to the ƒ	Grandmother	33
past by the gate of the ƒ, Willy,	"	41
at home in my father's ƒ at eve:	"	90

farmer.

With ƒ Allan at the farm abode.	Dora	1
Far off the ƒ came into the field	"	72
when the ƒ pass'd into the field	"	83
Francis Hale, The ƒ's son,	Audley Ct.	74
The ƒ vext packs up his beds	Walk. to the M.	31
robb'd the ƒ of his bowl of cream:	Princess, v.	214

farmstead.

he, by ƒ, thorpe and spire,	Will Water.	137

far-off.

And the f-o stream is dumb,	The Owl, i.	3
dimly see My f-o doubtful purpose,	Œnone	247
sorcerer, whom a f-o grandsire burnt	Princess, i.	6
The f-o interest of tears?	In Mem. i.	8
one f-o divine event,	" Con.	143
f-o sail is blown by the breeze	Maud, I. iv.	4
her f-o cousin and betrothed,	The Brook	75
some f-o touch Of greatness to know	Elaine	449
In those f-o seven happy years	En. Arden	687

far-renowned.

f-r brides of ancient song	D. of F. Wom.	17

far-shadowing.

half in light, and half F-'s from the	Princess, Con.	42

far-sighted.

F-s summoner of War and Waste.	Ded. of Idylls.	36

far-sounded.

Geraint, a name f-s among men	Enid	427

fashion s.)

After the ƒ of the time.	Arabian N's.	119
Looks freshest in the ƒ of the day:	The Epic	32
From the ƒ of your bones.	Vision of Sin	182
want in forms for ƒ's sake,	In Mem. cx.	6

	POEM.	LINE.
No more in soldier ƒ will he greet	Ode on Well.	21
sumptuously According to his ƒ,	Enid	1134
In any knightly ƒ for her sake.	Elaine	667
In sailor ƒ roughly sermonizing	En. Arden	204
Fire-hollowing this in Indian ƒ,	"	570

fashion verb.)

skill To strive, to ƒ, to fulfil—	In Mem. cxii.	7

fashioned.

ƒ for it A case of silk, and braided	Elaine	7
all the passion of a twelve hours' ƒ.'	Enid	306
heard mass, broke ƒ, and rode away:	Elaine	414
Fast with your ƒ's, not feasting	Guinevere	670

fast verb.)

If it may be, ƒ Whole Lents, and	St S. Stylites	178
bear his armour? shall we ƒ, or dine?	Enid	1329
F with your fasts, not feasting	Guinevere	670

fast (s.)

if she be ƒ to this fool lord,	Maud, I. xvi.	24

fastening.

loosed the ƒ's of his arms,	Enid	1560

fast-rooted.

F-r in the fruitful soil	Lotos-E's.	83

fat.

Old Summers, when the monk was ƒ,	Talking O.	71
grew On Lusitanian summers.	Will Water.	7
Padded round with flesh and ƒ,	Vision of Sin	177

fatal.

sweet a voice and vague, ƒ to men,	Princess, iv.	45

fate.

right of full-accomplish'd F;	Pal. of Art	207
hearts, Made weak by time and ƒ,	Ulysses	69
love in sequel works with ƒ,	Day-Dm.	103
The sphere thy ƒ allots;	Will Water.	218
we three Sat muffled like the Fs;	Princess, ii.	443
thy ƒ and mine are seal'd;	" vi.	374
The limit of his narrower ƒ,	In Mem. lxiii.	21
link'd with thine in love and ƒ,	" lxxxiii.	38
whose gentle will has changed my ƒ,	Maud, I. xviii.	23
She is coming, my life, my ƒ;	" xxii.	62
the weight and ƒ of Europe hung.	Ode on Well.	240
man is man and master of his ƒ.	Enid	355
me some slight power upon your ƒ,	Vivien	182
My ƒ or fault, omitting gayer youth	"	776

fat-faced.

said the f-f curate Edward Bull,	Ed. Morris	42, 90

father (s.)

stand beside my ƒ's door,	Ode to Mem.	57
to vex me with his ƒ's eyes!	Œnone	251
there the Ionian ƒ of the rest;	Pal. of Art	137
ƒ held his hand upon his face;	D. of F. Wom.	107
died To save her ƒ's vow;	"	196
My God, my land, my ƒ—these did	"	209
subdued me to my ƒ's will;	"	234
in her last trance Her murder'd ƒ's head,	"	267
in my time a ƒ's word was law	Dora	25
left his ƒ's house, And hired himself	"	35
ƒ's gate, Heart-broken, and his ƒ help'd	"	48
O F!—if you let me call you so—	"	137
was wrong to cross his ƒ thus:	"	145
learn to slight His ƒ's memory;	"	151
flask of cider from his ƒ's vats,	Audley Ct.	46
Her ƒ left his good arm-chair,	Talking O.	103
Puppet to a ƒ's threat,	Locksley H.	42
O, the child too clothes the ƒ	"	91
first he leaves his ƒ's field,	"	112
fell my ƒ evil-starr'd ƒ:—	"	155
'Where wert thou when thy ƒ play'd	Two Voices	319
'O seek my ƒ's court with me,	Day-Dm.	191
My ƒ left a park to me,	Amphion	1
Against her ƒ's and mother's will;	Ed. Gray	10
And they leave her ƒ's roof.	L. of Burleigh	12
my good ƒ thought a king a king;	Princess, i.	25
My ƒ sent ambassadors with furs	"	41

	POEM.	LINE.
broken means (His *f*'s fault) . *Princess*,	i.	53
my *f*'s face Grew long and troubled	,,	57
'My *f*, let me go. It cannot be .	,,	67
hear my *f*'s clamour at our backs	,,	104
Hard by your *f*'s frontier : .	,,	147
masque or pageant at my *f*'s court.	,,	195
hangs his portrait in my *f*'s hall .	ii.	221
F will come to thee soon ;	,,	465
F will come to his babe in the nest,	,,	468
I never knew my *f*, but she says .	iii.	66
Into his *f*'s hands, who has this night,	iv.	383
The second was my *f*'s running thus :	,,	387
Behold your *f*'s letter.'	,,	448
since our *f*—Wasps in our good hive,	,,	514
'then we fell Into your *f*'s hand,	v.	49
And roughly spake My *f*,	,,	144
Your captive, yet my *f* wills not war :	,,	267
'sdeath ! against my *f*'s will.'	,,	288
Back rode we to my *f*'s camp,	,,	321
My *f* heard and ran In on the lists,	vi.	10
haggard *f*'s face and reverend beard	,,	87
My *f* stoop'd, re-father'd o'er my .	,,	113
Not one word ; No ! tho' your *f* sues :	,,	223
Help, *f*, brother, help ; speak to the	,,	286
king her *f* charm'd Her wounded soul	,,	325
her *f* cease to press my claim,	vii.	72
sidelong glances at my *f*'s grief,	,,	92
O *f*, wheresoe'er thou be, . *In Mem.*	vi.	9
f's chimney glows In expectation	,,	29
O *F*, touch the east, and light .	xxx.	31
doubtful joys the *f* move, .	,, xxxix.	9
How many a *f* have I seen, . .	lii.	1
Had fall'n into her *f*'s grave	,, lxxxviii.	48
f's bend Above more graves, .	xcvii.	15
Our *f*'s dust is left alone .	,, civ.	5
crying, knows his *f* near ; .	,, cxxiii.	20
O *f*! O God ! was it well ?— . *Maud*, I.	i.	6
as my *f* raged in his mood ?	,,	53
purse-mouth when my *f* dangled .	,,	71
When have I how'd to her *f*,	iv.	13
Your *f* has wealth well-gotten,	,,	18
Your *f* is ever in London, .	,,	59
Why sits he here in his *f*'s chair ?	xiii.	23
Not touch on her *f*'s sin ; .	xix.	17
Maud's dark *f* and mine .	,,	37
Mine, mine—our *f*'s have sworn .	,,	43
evermore her *f* came across . *The Brook* .		108
would I take her *f* for one hour, .	,,	114
As looks a *f* on the things . *The Letters*		23
Thou noble *F* of her Kings to be, *Ded. of Idylls*		33
Affirming that his *f* left him gold, *Enid*		451
thought, but that your *f* came .	,,	1163
loved me serving in my *f*'s hall :	,,	1547
slain your *f*, seized yourself. .	,,	1686
whom his *f* Uther left in charge .	,,	1781
Leaving her household and good *f Elaine*		14
Here laugh'd the *f* saying 'Fie, .	,,	200
Nay, *f*, nay, good *f*, shame me not	,,	207
But *f* give me leave, an if he will .	,,	219
Crept to her *f*, while he mused alone,	,,	744
Then her *f* nodding said, 'Ay, ay,	,,	766
Her *f*'s latest word humm'd in her	,,	776
brother's love, And your good *f*'s	,,	941
came her *f*, saying in low tones	,,	988
call'd The *f*, and all three in hurry	,,	1018
So dwelt the *f* on her face .	,,	1024
sweet *f*, tender and true, Deny me	,,	1104
She ceased : her *f* promised ; .	,,	1124
Her *f* laid the letter in her hand,	,,	1128
testimony, Her brethren, and her *f*,	,,	1292
said my *f*, and himself was knight *Guinevere*		232
So said my *f*—yea, and furthermore,	,,	248
Not even thy wise *f* with his signs	,,	272
one, a bard : of whom my *f* said,	,,	275
So said my *f*—and that night the bard	,,	283
tales Which my good *f* told, .	,,	315
Nor let me shame my *f*'s memory,	,,	316
so thou lean on our fair *f* Christ,	,,	558
(His *f* lying sick and needing him) *En. Arden*		65
would prove A *f* to your children :	,,	408
think They love me as a *f* : .	,,	409
	POEM.	LINE.
o'er her second *f* stoopt a girl, . *En. Arden*		748
Hers, yet not his, upon the *f*'s knee,	,,	761
Uphold me, *F*, in my loneliness .	,,	785
Never : no *f*'s kiss for me— .	,,	791
let them come, I am their *f* ; .	,,	891
lean'd not on his *f*'s but himself. . *Aylmer's F.*		56
was his, had been his *f*'s friend :	,,	344
out a despot dream The *f* panting	,,	528
f suddenly cried, ' A wreck, . *Sea Dreams*		50
her *f* was not the man to save, . *Grandmother*		5
remember a quarrel I had with your *f*,	,,	21
at sixty, your *f* at sixty-five : .	,,	66
at home in my *f*'s farm at eve :	,,	90
My *f* raves of death and wreck, .	,,	19
warrior *f* meets the foe, ' *Lady, let the rolling,' etc.*		2
upon his *f*'s lance, ' *Home they brought him,' etc.*		8
Beat upon his *f*'s shield— ,, ,,		9

father (verb.)

in the round of time Still *f* Truth ? *Love and Duty*		5

father-fool.

Thwarted by one of these old *f-f*'s, *Aylmer's F.*		300

fatherhood.

twelve sweet moons confused his *f*. *Vivien*		502

father-grape.

f-g grew fat On Lusitanian summers. *Will Water.*		7

Father-land.

sweet it was to dream of *F-l*, . *Lotos-E's.*		30

fatherlike.

Appraised his weight and fondled *f*, *En. Arden* .		154

fathom.

Falser than all fancy *f*'s. . *Locksley H.*		41
'Tis hard for thee to *f* this ; . *In Mem.* lxxxiv.		90
Philip did not *f* Annie's mind : . *En. Arden* .		341

fathom-deep.

gulf him *f d* in brine ; . . *In Mem.*	x.	18

fathomless.

half-attain'd futurity, Tho' deep not *f*, *Ode to Mem.*		33

fatten.

many streams to *f* lower lands, . *Golden Year*		34

fatter.

he was *f* than his cure. . . *Ed. Morris*		15

fault.

tho' the *f*'s were thick as dust . *To the Queen*		18
f's he would not show : ' *You might have won,' etc.*		17
broken means (His father's *f*) . *Princess*, i.		53
'My *f* she wept ' my *f* ! and yet	,, iii.	14
child is hers—for every little *f*, .	,, v.	84
The *f* one *f* The tenderness, not yours,	,, vi.	169
dearer thou for *f*'s Lived over ; .	,, vii.	326
let it be granted her : where is the *f* ? *Maud*, I. ii.		4
the *f*'s of his heart and mind, .	,, xix.	68
'The *f* was mine, the *f* was mine'—	II. i.	1
'The *f* was mine, he whisper'd, 'fly !'	,,	30
seeming-genial venial *f*, . . *Will*		13
' If Enid errs, let Enid learn her *f*.' *Enid*		132
voiceless thro' the *f* of birth .	,,	1115
My fate or *f*, omitting gayer youth *Vivien*		776
for her one *f* she wept Of petulancy ;	,,	801
He is all *f* who hath no *f* at all : *Elaine*		133
call me wilful, and the *f* Is yours .	,,	746
it is no more Sir Lancelot's *f* .	,,	1069
Nor mine the *f*, if losing both of . *Aylmer's F.*		719

faultless.

Faultily *f*, icily regular, . . *Maud*, I. ii.		6

Fawn.

| Arise and fly The reeling *F*, . *In Mem.* cxvii. | | 26 |
| quickens into Nymph and *F*; . *Lucretius* . | | 107 |

Faunus.

in the garden snared Picus and *F*, *Lucretius* .		102

favour.

On whom their *f*'s fall ! . . *Sir Galahad*		14
the *f*, and assumed the Prince. . *Princess*, iv.		577
Who have won her *f* ! . . *Maud*, I. xii.		13

	POEM.	LINE.
seek a second *f* at his hands.	Enid	626
love or fear, or seeking *f* of us,	"	700
should wear her *f* at the tilt.	Elaine	357
wear My *f* at this tourney?'	"	361
worn *F* of any lady in the lists.	"	363, 473
came to ask a *f* of you.'	En. Arden	284
'*F* from one so sad	"	286
the *f* that I came to ask.	"	312
Else I withdraw *f* and countenance	Aylmer's F.	307

favouritism.

'So puddled as it is with *f*.'	Princess, iii.	130

fawn (s.)

your arrow-wounded *f* Came flying	Princess, ii.	251
That was *f*'s blood not brother's,	"	256

fawn (verb.)

And *f* at a victor's feet.	Maud, I. vi.	30

fawning.

Crouch'd *f* in the weed.	Œnone	197

feāld.

an' now theer's lots o' *f*,	N. Farmer	39

feāld.

Mezzin' an' maāizin' the blessed *f*'s	N. Farmer	62

fealty.

true answer, as beseem'd Thy *f*,	M. d'Arthur	75
doubt her more But rested in her *f*,	Enid	1815
Forgetful of their truth and *f*,	Guinevere	439
saps The *f* of our friends,	"	517

fear (s.)

What hope or *f* or joy is thine?	Adeline	23
Whispering to each other half in *f*,	Sea Fairies	5
they cross'd themselves for *f*,	L. of Shalott, iv.	49
Roof'd the world with doubt and *f*,	Eleānore	99
love dispell'd the *f* That I should die	Miller's D.	89
loved you better for your *f*'s,	"	149
Acting the law we live by without *f*;	Œnone	146
I shut my sight for *f*:	"	184
Remaining utterly confused with *f*'s,	Pal. of Art	269
would not brook my *f* Of the other;	D. of F. Wom.	154
f of change at home, that drove	Walk. to the M.	60
low wind hardly breathed for *f*.	Godiva	55
Boring a little augur-hole in *f*,	"	68
this mould of hopes and *f*'s	Two Voices	28
heaping up the *f* of ill The *f* of men	"	107
burnish'd without *f* The brand,	"	128
Such hope, I know not *f*;	Sir Galahad	62
Nor yet the *f* of little books	Will Water.	195
Hush'd all the groves from *f* of Sir L. and Q. G.		13
for *f* This whole foundation ruin,	Princess, ii.	319
f our solid aim is dissipated	" iii.	249
F Stared in her eyes,	" iv.	357
I blame you not so much for *f*;	"	485
Six thousand years of *f* have made	"	486
Fatherly *f*'s you used at courteously	" v.	207
Bow-back'd with *f*:	" vi.	339
but for *f* it is not so, The wild unrest	In Mem. xv.	14
All subtle thought, all curious *f*'s,	" xxxii.	9
that vague *f* implied in death;	" xl.	14
Beneath all fancied hopes and *f*'s	" xlviii.	13
wrong the grave with *f*'s untrue:	" l.	9
For *f* divine Philosophy	" lii.	14
is Eternal, separate from *f*'s:	" lxxxiv.	66
The feeble soul, a haunt of *f*'s,	" cix.	3
cannot fight the *f* of death.	" cxiii.	10
heated hot with burning *f*'s,	" cxviii.	22
like a child in doubt and *f*:	" cxxiii.	17
sunder'd in the night of *f*:	" cxxvi.	2
Wild Hours that fly with Hope and *F*,	" cxxvii.	9
the place and the pit and the *f*	Maud, I. i.	64
bitter springs of anger and *f*;	" iv.	49
Sick once, with a *f* of worse,	" xix.	73
should grow light-headed, I *f*,	"	100
coast Of ancient fable and *f*—	" II. ii.	32
Sick of a nameless *f*,	"	44
haunts of horror and *f*,	" III. vi.	2
all her foolish *f*'s about the dress,	Enid	142, 844
Rapt in the *f* and in the wonder of it;	"	529

	POEM.	LINE.
For love or *f*, or seeking favour	Enid	700
way smoke beneath him in his *f*;	"	1181
Enid in their going had two *f*'s,	"	1665
She shook from *f*, and for her fault	Vivien	801
First as in *f*, step after step, she stole	Elaine	341
came on him a sort of sacred *f*,	"	353
f our people call you lily maid	"	385
So fine a *f* in our large Lancelot	"	593
in hurry and *F* Ran to her,	"	1018
your crescent *f* for name and fame	"	1391
or a vague spiritual *f*—	Guinevere	71
All his Annie's *f*'s, Save, as his	En. Arden	183
and laugh at all your *f*'s.	"	216
f's were common to her state,	"	517
no *f* that her first husband lives?'	"	807
poor soul,' said Miriam, '*f* enow!	"	808
doubts and *f*'s were all amiss,	The Ringlet	19
And a *f* to be kiss'd away.'	"	22
The King was shaken with holy *f*;	The Victim	61
hollow as the hopes and *f*'s of men.	Lucretius	180
brightens and darkens like my *f*,	The Window	19

fear (verb.)

to name my spirit loathes and *f*'s:	D. of F. Wom.	106
I *f* My wound hath taken cold,	M. d'Arthur	165
I *f* it is too late, and I shall die.'	"	180
f That we shall miss the mail:	Walk. to the M.	101
I *f* to slide from bad to worse.	Two Voices	231
What is it that I may not *f*'	"	240
F not thou to loose thy tongue;	Vision of Sin	155
I *f*, If there were many Lilias	Princess Pro.	145
Let them not *f*: some said their heads	" ii.	131
I *f* My conscience will not count me	"	273
dearest Lady, pray you *f* me not,	"	312
'Ah, *f* me not' Replied Melissa	"	321
'What *f* ye brawlers?	" iv.	477
what is it ye *f*? Peace!	"	479
'We *f*, indeed, you spent a stormy	" v.	113
f we not To break them more	" vi.	44
Sighing she spoke 'I *f* They will not.'	" vii.	260
Approach and *f* not; breathe upon my	"	332
mock thee when we do not *f*:	In Mem. Pro.	30
She *f*'s not, or with thee beside	Con.	43
me behind her, will not *f*:	"	44
I *f*, the new strong wine of love,	Maud, I. vi.	82
some one else may have much to *f*;	" v.	4
Should I *f* to greet my friend	" II. iv.	85
f they are not roses, but blood;	" v.	78
I *f* that I am no true wife.'	Enid	108
tries the bridge he *f*'s may fail,	"	1152
f me not: I call mine own self wild,	"	1150
and he *f*'s To lose his bone,	"	1409
f not, Enid, I should fall upon him,	"	1035
men may *f* Fresh fire and ruin.	"	1670
had cause To *f* me, *f* no longer	"	1673
f not, cousin; I am changed indeed.'	"	1721
f still more you are not mine,	Vivien	176
Wherefore, if I *f*, Giving you power	"	363
for I *f* My fate or fault,	"	775
a flash, I *f* me, that will strike	Elaine	966
F not: thou shalt be guarded	Guinevere	445
f no more for me; or if you *f*	En. Arden	221
if you'll listen to tales, be jealous	Grandmother	54
F not, isle of blowing woodland,	Boādicea	38

feared.

f To meet a cold 'We thank you,	Princess, iv.	308
f To incense the Head once more;	" vii.	62
she *f* that I should lose my mind,	"	84
There sat the Shadow *f* of man;	In Mem. xxii.	12
that she *f* she was not a true wife.	Enid	114
f In every wavering brake an	"	899
Enid *f* his eyes, Moist as they were,	"	1199
ever *f* you were not wholly mine;	Vivien	164
ridd'n away to die?' So *f* the King,	Elaine	567
f To send abroad a shrill	En. Arden	768
I *f* Lest the gay navy there	Sea Dreams	126

fearful.

Too *f* that you should not please,	Miller's D.	148
Half *f* that, with self at strife	Will Water.	101

fearing.

	POEM.	LINE
hid my feelings, *f* they should do	Locksley H.	29
F to lose, and all for a dead man,	Enid	1412
f for his hurt and loss of blood,	,,	1625
F the mild face of the blameless	,,	1660
f heaven had heard her oath,	Vivien	789
f rust or soilure fashion'd for it	Elaine	7
Still hoping, *f* 'is it yet too late?'	Guinevere	683
F the lazy gossip of the port,	En. Arden.	332
f night and chill for Annie	,,	440
lingeringly on the latch, *F* to enter;	,,	516
f waved my arm to warn them off;	Sea Dreams	128

feast (s.)

church-harpies from the master's *f*;	To J. M. K.	3
I made a *f*; I bade him come;	The Sisters	13
Rise from the *f* of sorrow, lady,	Margaret	62
while Audley *f* Humm'd like a hive	Audley Ct.	3
near his tomb a *f* Shone, silver-set;	Princess, Pro.	105
Nymph, or Goddess, at high tide of *f*,	,, i.	194
Blanch'd in our annals, and perpetual *f*,	,, vi.	47
we shall sit at endless *f*,	In Mem. xlvi.	9
neither song, nor game, nor *f*;	,, civ.	21
The reeling Faun, the sensual *f*;	,, cxvii.	26
stay to share the morning *f*,	,, Con.	75
Again the *f*, the speech, the glee,	,,	101
Once fit for *f*'s of ceremony)	Enid	297
wine-heated from the *f*;	,,	1200
our knights at *f* Have pledged us	Elaine	115
such a *f* As never man had dream'd;	Guinevere	261
not feasting with your *f*'s;	,,	670
No larger *f* than under plane	Lucretius	210

feast (verb.)

f with these in honour of their earl;	Enid.	1136

feasted.

three days he *f* us,	Princess, i.	117
F the woman wisest then,	,, ii.	330

feasting.

not *f* with your feasts;	Guinevere	670

feat.

often heard me praise Your *f*'s of arms,	Enid	435

feather.

All grass of silky *f* grow—	Talking O.	269
I did but shear a *f*,	Princess, v.	530
whether The habit, hat, and *f*,	Maud, I. xx.	18
Arn't we birds of a *f*?	The Window	75
We'll be birds of a *f*.	,,	83

feather (verb.)

all 'bout the large lime *f*'s low,	Gardener's D.	46
wood began To *f* toward him,	En. Arden 68,	371

featherfan.

Cooling her false cheek with a *f*	Aylmer's F.	289

feathering.

the ripple *f* from her bows:	En. Arden.	540

feature.

chisell'd *f*'s clear and sleek.	A Character	30
Conjectures of the *f*'s of her child	Œnone	248
Reading her perfect *f*'s in the	Gardener's D.	171
I cannot see the *f*'s right,	In Mem. lxix.	1

February.

silver tongue, Cold *F* loved is dry;	The Blackbird	14

fed.

f With the clear-pointed flame	Isabel.	1
f the time With odour	Arabian N's.	64
F thee, a child, lying alone,	Eleänore	25
these, tho' *f* with careful dirt,	Amphion	89
By dancing rivulets *f* his flocks,	To E. L.	22
f her theories, in and out of place	Princess, i.	128
f you with the milk of every Muse;	,, iv.	276
breast that *f* or arm that dandled you,	,, vi.	165
heart and ear were *f* To hear him,	In Mem. lxxxviii.	22
hidden summits *f* with rills,	,, cii.	7
You have but *f* on the roses,	Maud, I. iv.	60
f With honey'd rain and delicate air,	,, xviii.	20

federation.

the *F* of the world.	Locksley H.	128
The *F*'s and the Powers:	Day-Dm.	228

fee.

	POEM.	LINE.
To hold the costliest love in *f*.	In Mem. lxxviii.	4
kills her babe for a burial *f*.	Maud, I. i.	45

feeble.

Now am I *f* grown;	St S. Stylites	35
f, all unconscious of itself,	Princess, vii.	102
knees Were *f*, so that falling prone	En. Arden.	780

feed.

kingly intellect shall *f*, 'Clear-headed friend,' etc.		20
Some honey-converse *f*'s thy mind,	Adeline	40
Upon himself himself did *f*:	A Character	27
f with crude imaginings 'Love thou thy land,' etc.		10
The fat earth *f* thy branchy root,	Talking O.	273
race, That hoard, and sleep, and *f*,	Ulysses	5
little ducts began To *f* thy bones	Two Voices	326
early woke to *f* her little ones,	Princess, vii	236
full new life that *f*'s thy breath	In Mem. lxxxv.	10
f the mothers of the flock;	,, xcix.	16
rose-carnation *f* With summer spice	,, c.	7
f with sighs a passing wind :	,, cvii.	4
goodly cheer To *f* the sudden guest,	Enid	1133
flesh and wine to *f* his spears.	,,	1449
like horses when you hear them *f*;	,,	1454

feedeth.

f The senses with a still delight	Margaret	16

feeding.

water-pipes beneath, *F* the flower	D. of F. Wom.	207
f high, and living soft,	The Goose	17
F like horses when you hear them	Enid	1454

feel.

I feel the tears of blood arise	Oriana	77
f their immortality Die	The Mermaid	29
Joying to *f* herself alive,	Pal. of Art	178
one that *f*'s a nightmare on his bed	M. d'Arthur	177
to *f* the truth and stir of day,	,, Ep.	19
man *f* strong in speaking truth	,,	68
my heart so slow To *f* it.	Love and Duty	35
f about my feet The berried briony	Talking O.	147
him who works, and *f*'s he works.	Golden Year	72
guinea helps the hurt that Honour *f*'s,	Locksley H.	105
Make me *f* the wild pulsation	,,	109
To *f* altho' no tongue can prove	Two Voices	445
master-chord of all I felt and *f*.	Will Water.	28
Live long, nor *f* in head or chest	,,	237
f myself the shadow of a dream.	Princess, i.	18
put in words the grief I *f*;	In Mem. v.	2
f's Her place is empty,	,, xiii.	3
I should not *f* it to be strange	,, xiv.	20
her arms To *f* from world to world,	,, xxi.	19
I *f* it, when I sorrow most;	,, xxvii.	14
call To what I *f* is Lord of all,	,, liv.	19
Yet *f*'s, as in a pensive dream	,, lxiii.	17
I felt and *f*, tho' left alone,	,, lxxxiv.	42
Canst thou *f* for me Some painless	,,	87
My Ghost may *f* that thine is near.	,, xcii.	16
darkly *f*'s him great and wise,	,, xcvi.	34
To *f* once more, in placid awe,	,, cxxi.	5
f There is a lower and a higher;	,, cxxviii.	3
f thee some diffusive power,	,, cxxix.	7
I *f* with thee the drowsy spell.	Maud, I. xviii.	72
I *f* I shall owe you a debt,	,, xix.	87
I *f* so free and so clear.	,,	98
f's a glimmering strangeness in his	The Brook	216
let her *f* herself forgiven	Vivien	231
f's no heart to ask another boon.	,,	232
Might *f* some sudden turn of anger	,,	381
low desire Not to *f* lowest	,,	677
helpmate, one to *f* My purpose	Guinevere	481
voices make me *f* so solitary.'	En. Arden.	394
living nerves to *f* the rent ;	Aylmer's F.	536
who *f*'s the immeasurable world,	A Dedication	7
Put forth and *f* a gladder clime.	On a Mourner	15

feeling (part.)

often *f* of the helpless hands,	Princess, vii.	96
blind way *f* round his long sea-hall	Vivien	81
f that you felt me worthy trust,	,,	183
downward to her belt, And *f*;	,,	700
f all along the garden-wall,	En. Arden.	774

	POEM.	LINE.		POEM.	LINE.
feeling (s.)			hurl'd him headlong, and he *f*	*Guinevere*	107
of love, To tamper with the *f's,*	*Gardener's D.*	19	his hand *f* from the harp,	"	301
Saying 'I have hid my *f's,*	*Locksley H.*	29	prone from oft her seat she *f,*	"	411
On a range of lower *f's*	"	44	by mischance he slipt and *f:*	*En. Arden*	106
were dangerous guides the *f's*—	"	95	on him *f,* Altho' a grave and staid	"	111
speak their *f* as it is,	*In Mem.* xx.	5	these things *f* on her Sharp as reproach.	"	484
a gentler *f* crept Upon us:	" xxx.	7	*f* Sun-stricken, and that other lived	"	570
Divorce the *F* from her mate the	*The Brook.*	95	so *f* back and spoke no more.	"	913
feign.			Tho' Leolin flamed and *f* again,	*Aylmer's F.*	409
things that being caught *f* death,	*Princess,* v.	105	*f* The woman shrieking at his feet,	"	810
feigned.			*f* In vast sea-cataracts—	*Sea Dreams*	53
those by hopeless fancy *f*	*Princess,* iv.	37	statues, king or saint, or founder *f;*	"	217
A face of tenderness might be *f,*	*Maud,* I. vi.	52	down their statue of Victory *f,*	*Boädicea*	30
lay still, and *f* himself as dead,	*Enid*	1436	*F* the colony, city, and citadel,	"	86
f a sleep until he slept.	*Elaine*	838	Bullets *f* like rain;	*The Captain*	46
feigning.			A plague upon the people *f,*	*The Victim*	1
f pique at what she call'd The raillery,	*Princess,*iv.	564	*f* on him, Clasp'd, kiss'd him,	*Lucretius*	275
fell (covering.)			*fell out.*		
Half-suffocated in the hoary *f*	*Vivien*	688	We *f o,* my wife and I,	*Princess,* i.	248
fell (mountain.)			we *f o* I know not why,	"	249
ye meanwhile far over moor and *f*	*Maud,*I.xviii.	76	*fell to work.*		
fell (verb.)			He spoke and *f t w* again.	*Enid*	292
rusted nails *f* from the knots.	*Mariana*	3	*fell'd.*		
tears *f* with the dews at even;	"	13	*f* him, and set foot upon his breast,	*Enid*	574
shadow of the poplar *f*	"	55	*fellow.*		
forth anew Where'er they *f,*	*The Poet*	22	if his *f* spake, His voice was thin,	*Lotos-E's.*	33
babble of the stream *F,*	*Mariana in theS.*	52	lowing to his *f's.*	*Gardener's D.*	67
kiss'd away before they *f,*	*Miller's D.*	152	'This *f* would make weakness weak,	*In Mem.* xxi.	7
They were together, and she *f;*	*The Sisters*	4	he, Poor *f,* could he help it?	*The Brook.*	158
folds, that floating as they *f,*	*Pal. of Art*	35	a hart Taller than all his *f's,*	*Enid*	150
on the fourth she *f.* Like Herod,	"	218	heard one crying to his *f,* 'Look	"	908
loathing of her solitude *F* on her,	"	230	sweet faces make good *f's* fools	"	1248
kiss he gave me, ere I *f,*	*D.of F.Wom.*	235	look On this proud *f* again,	*Elaine*	1059
f in a doze; and half-awake	*The Epic*	13	pock-pitten *f* had been caught?	*Aylmer's F.*	256
flash'd and *f* the brand Excalibur	*M. d'Arthur*	142	let that handsome *f* Averill walk	"	269
threaten d darkness, flared and *f:*	*Ep.*	2	*fellow-citizen.*		
sun *f,* and all the land was dark.	*Dora*	77, 107	Welcome, *f-c's,* Hollow hearts	*Vision of Sin*	173
wreath of flowers *f* At Dora's feet.	"	100	*fellowship.*		
in wild Mahratta-battle *f* my father	*Locksley H.*	155	goodliest *f* of famous knights	*M. d'Arthur*	15
silver lily heaved and *f;*	*To F. L.*	19	O sorrow, cruel *f,*	*In Mem.* iii.	1
bestrode my Grandsire, when he *f,*	*Princess,* ii.	224	Mere *f* of sluggish moods,	" xxxv.	21
Grew wonder toward his death and *f,*	" iii.	346	give him the grasp of *f;*	*Maud,* I. xiii.	16
a sudden transport rose and *f.*	" iv.	11	your *f* O'er these waste downs	*Elaine*	224
the tear She sang of, shook and fell,	"	42	My brethren have been all my *f,*	"	669
transit to the throne, whereby she *f*	"	359	*fellow-worker.*		
f Into his father's hands,	"	382	In which I might your *f-w* be,	*Princess,* iv.	289
Across the tumult and the tumult *f.*	"	476	*felt.*		
'then we *f* Into your father's hand	" v.	48	*f* he was and was not there.	*Mariana in the S.*	50
darkness closed me; and I *f.*	"	531	pray'd for both, and so I *f* resign'd	*May Queen,* iii.31
high tree the blossom wavering *f,*	" vi.	64	She *f* her heart grow prouder:	*The Goose*	22
sadness on the soul of Ida *f,*	" vii.	14	*F* earth as air beneath me,	*Gardener's D.*207
Star after star, arose and *f;*	"	35	Dora *f* her uncle's will in all,	*Dora*	5
back I *f,* and from mine arms	"	144	I *f* a pang within	*TalkingO.*	234
moved, and at her feet the volume *f.*	"	238	pulsation that I *f* before the strife,	*Locksley H.*	109
Thro' four sweet years arose and *f,*	*In Mem.* xxii.	3	search thro' all I *f* or saw,	*Two Voices*	139
sadly *f* our Christmas-eve.	" xxx.	4	something *f,* like something here;	"	382
In vaults and catacombs, they *f;*	" lvii.	4	round her waist she *f* it fold	*Day-Dm.*	166
calmly *f* our Christmas-eve;	" lxxvii.	4	I never *f* the kiss of love,	*Sir Galahad*	19
f in silence on his neck:	" cii.	44	master-chord Of all I *f* and feel.	*Will Water.*	28
f with him when he *f.*	*Maud,* I. i.	8	I read and *f* that I was there:	*To E. L.*	8
silence *f* with the waking bird,	" xxii.	17	*f* My heart beat thick with passion	*Princess,* iii.	173
white lake-blossom *f* into the lake	"	47	*f* the blind wildbeast of force,	" vi.	256
ch. nged, for it *f* at a time of the year	" III. vi.	4	you have known the pangs we *f,*	"	364
The torrent vineyard streaming *f*	*The Daisy*	10	tender orphan hands *F* at my heart	"	426
While horse and hero *f,*	*Lt. Brigade*	44	*f* my veins Stretch with fierce heat;	"	526
there fell A horror on him,	*Enid*	28	'Thy helpless warmth about my	" vi.	184
f at last In the great battle	"	595	*f* it sound and whole from head to foot,	"	194
f Like flaws in summer	"	763	perhaps they *f* their power,	*Con.*	13
Jangling, the casque *F,*	"	1238	I *f* it, when I sorrow'd most,	*In Mem.*lxxxiv.	2
the chargers of the two that *f.*	"	1330	I *f* and feel, tho' left alone,	"	42
with out a word, from his horse *f.*	"	1357	*f* The same, but not the same;	" lxxxvi.	13
fair death, and *f* Against the heathen	"	1816	I *f* the thews of Anakim,	" cii.	31
f upon him a great melancholy;	*Vivien*	45	A love of freedom merely *f,*	" cviii.	13
f and made the glen abhorr'd:	*Elaine*	43	*f* thy triumph was as mine;	" cix.	14
f into some pool or stream,	"	214	Stood up and answer'd 'I have *f:*	" cxxii.	16
Treroit, Where many a heathen *f;*	"	302	Because he *f* so fix'd in truth:	" cxxiv.	8
Of all this will I nothing:' and so *f,*	"	962	Nor have I *f* so much of bliss	*Con.*	5
lock the maiden *f.* Then gave a	"	1025			
their eyes met and hers *f,*	"	1303			

	POEM.	LINE.
f himself in his force to be Nature's	*Maud*, I. iv.	33
F a horror over me creep,	„ xiv.	35
I *f* she was slowly dying	„ xix.	21
Strange, that I *f* so gay,	„ xx.	1
cause that I *f* to be pure	„ III. vi.	31
I have *f* with my native land,	„	58
His love, unseen but *f*, o'ershadow	*Ded. of Idylls*	49
F you were somewhat, yea	*Enid*	430
f, were she the prize of bodily force,	„	541
I *f* That I could rest, a rock	„	811
f that tempest brooding round his	„	860
f Her low firm voice	„	1042
f the warm tears falling on his face	„	1434
so blunt and stupid at the heart:	„	1595
f him hers again:	„	1616
f His work was neither great	„	1768
old man, Tho' doubtful, *f* the flattery,	*Vivien*	40
feeling that you *f* me worthy trust,	„	183
f as tho' you knew this cursed charm,	„	285
lay And *f* them slowly ebbing,	„	287
darkling *f* the sculptur'd ornament	„	584
own side she *f* the sharp lance go:	*Elaine*	621
f the knot Climb in her throat,	„	736
the King's breath wander o'er her neck,	*Guinevere*	576
life's ascending sun Was *f* by either,	*En. Arden*	39
well had deem'd he *f* the tale Less	„	712
when he *f* the silence of his house	*Aylmer's F.*	830
keepers, and the silence which he *f*	„	839
f my blood Glow with the glow	*Tithonus*	55
f the good ship shake and reel,	*The Voyage*	15
f the heart within her fall	*Boädicea*	81

female.

| then a loftier form Than *f*, | *Princess*, iv. | 197 |

fen.

| From the dark *f* of the oxen's low | *Mariana* | 28 |
| o'er waste *f*'s and windy fields, | *Sir Galahad* | 60 |

fence.

| three horses that have broken *f*, | *Princess*, ii. | 364 |
| Robins—a niver mended a *f*: | *N. Farmer* | 50 |

fenced (fought.)

| voice with which I *f* A little ceased | *Two Voices* | 317 |

fenced (hedged.)

| I *f* it round with gallant institutes, | *Princess*, v. | 382 |

fern.

learned names of agaric, moss, and *f*,	*Ed. Morris*	17
Hail hidden to the knees in *f*,	*Talking O.*	29
hide thy knotted knees in *f*, (201, 245)	„	93, 149
From slope to slope thro' distant *f*'s,	*Princess, Con.*	99
Sparkle out among the *f*,	*The Brook*	25
In copse and *f* Twinkled the innumerable	„	133
shatter'd archway plumed with *f*;	*Enid*	316
palms and *f*'s and precipices;	*En. Arden*	594

ferule.

| As boys that slink From *f*, | *Princess*, v. | 36 |

fescue.

| Sweeping the frothfly from the *f* | *Aylmer's F.* | 530 |

fester.

| Eye, to which all order *f*'s, | *Locksley H.* | 133 |

festival.

| Two strangers meeting at a *f*; | *Circumstance* | 3 |

festoon.

| in many a wild *f* Ran riot, | *Œnone* | 98 |

festooning.

| humid arms *f* tree to tree, | *D. of F. Wom.* | 70 |

fetch.

Go *f* your Alice here,'	*Miller's D.*	143
down I went to *f* my bride:	„	145
Go *f* a pint of port:	*Will Water.*	4
with furs And jewels, gifts, to *f* her	*Princess*, i.	42
f the wine, Arrange the board	*In Mem.* cvi.	15
the colt would *f* its price;	*The Brook*	149
f Fresh victual for these mowers	*Enid*	1073
I will *f* you forage from all fields,	„	1476
went ambassador, at first, To *f* her,	*Vivien*	625

	POEM.	LINE.
Well, I will wear it: *f* it out to me:	*Elaine*	370
'Eh, let me *f* 'em, Arden,'	*En. Arden*	872

fetched.

| *f* His richest beeswing. | *Aylmer's F.* | 404 |

feud.

Rose *f*, with question unto whom	*Œnone*	80
New and Old, disastrous *f*, 'Love thou thy land.'	77
this *f* betwixt the right and left.'	*Princess*, iii.	61
rose a little *f* betwixt the two,	*Con.*	23
I wage not any *f* with Death	*In Mem.* lxxxi.	1
Ring out the *f* of rich and poor,	„ cv.	11
ever mourning over the *f*,	*Maud*, I. xix.	31
and to splinter it into *f*'s.	*Guinevere*	19
mar this little by their *f*'s.	*Sea Dreams*	49

fever.

at last a *f* seized On William,	*Dora*	52
hungers and in thirsts, *f*'s and cold,	*St S. Stylites*	12
mix the foaming draught Of *f*,	*Princess*, ii.	234
blow The *f* from my cheek,	*In Mem.* lxxxv.	9
some low *f* ranging round to spy	*Aylmer's F.*	569

few.

| Clash'd with his fiery *f* and won; | *Ode on Well.* | 100 |
| that honest *f* Who give the Fiend | *To F. D. Maurice* | 5 |

fiat.

| This *f* somewhat sooth'd himself. | *Aylmer's F.* | 26 |

fibre.

| Thy *f*'s net the dreamless head, | *In Mem.* ii. | 3 |

fickle.

'You're too slight and *f*,' I said,	*Ed. Gray*	19
fierce and *f* is the South,	*Princess*, iv.	79
Rapt from the *f* and the frail	*In Mem.* xxx.	25

fiddle.

| And ta'en my *f* to the gate, (rep.) | *Amphion* | 11 |
| Twang out my *f*! shake the twigs! | „ | 61 |

fiddled.

| And *f* in the timber! | *Amphion* | 16 |

field.

high *f* on the bushless Pike,	*Ode to Mem.*	96
Whither away from the high green *f*,	*Sea Fairies*	8
Long *f*'s of barley and of rye,	*L. of Shalott*, i.	2
thro' the *f* the road runs by	„	4
willowy hills and *f*'s among,	iv.	25
in the long gray *f*'s at night;	*May Queen*, ii.	26
in the *f*'s all round I hear	„ iii.	2
He shines upon a hundred *f*'s,	„	50
the wandering *f*'s of barren foam.	*Lotos-E's.*	42
in fair *f* Myself for such a face	*D. of F. Wom.*	97
she down thro' town and *f* 'Of old sat Freedom,'etc.	9
bore him to a chapel nigh the *f*,	*M. d'Arthur*	8
The *f*'s between Are dewy-fresh,	*Gardener's D.*	44
his horns into the neighbour *f*,	„	86
hired himself to work within the *f*'s;	*Dora*	36
the farmer came into the *f*,	„	72
when the farmer pass'd into the *f*	„	83
boy's cry came to her from the *f*	„	102
can recognise the *f*'s I know;	*St S. Stylites*	39
To yonder oak within the *f*.	*Talking O.*	13
Beyond the fair green *f*	*Love and Duty*	98
first he leaves his father's *f*,	*Locksley H.*	112
white-flower'd elder-thicket from the *f*	*Godiva*	63
thy father play'd In his free *f*,	*Two Voices*	320
forth into the *f*'s I went	„	448
o'er waste fens and windy *f*'s.	*Sir Galahad*	60
in her sleep From hollow *f*'s:	*Princess, Pro.*	67
when a *f* of corn Bows all its ears	„ i.	233
First in the *f*: some ages had been	„ ii.	137
for indeed these *f*'s Are lovely,	„ iii.	323
faint on hill or *f* or river:	„	361
your claim: If not, the foughten *f*,	„ v.	287
ran the *f* Flat to the garden-wall:	„	351
Man for the *f* and woman for	„	437
Thro' open *f* into the lists	„ vi.	68
men Darkening her female *f*:	„ vii.	19
after that dark night among the *f*'s,	„	58
The *f*, the chamber and the street,	*In Mem.* viii.	11

	POEM.	LINE.
takes His license in the *f* of time	*In Mem.* xxvii.	6
loiter'd in the master's *f*,	" xxxvii.	23
My paths are in the *f*'s I know	" xxxix.	31
howlings from forgotten *f*'s ;	" xl.	16
those five years its richest *f*.	" xlv.	12
A bounded *f*, nor extended far ;	" "	14
hill and wood and *f* did print	" lxxviii.	7
their dark arms about the *f*.	" xciv. 16,	52
leave the pleasant *f*'s and farms ;	" ci.	22
Its lips in the *f* above are dabbled	*Maud,* l. i.	2
not, happy day, From the shining *f*'s,	" xvii.	2
By many a *f* and fallow,	*The Brook*	44
all about the *f*'s you caught	"	52
knight soever be in *f* Lays claim	*Enid*	486
Beheld her first in *f*, awaiting him	"	540
these are his, and all the *f* is his,	"	1075
fetch you forage from all *f*'s,	"	1476
scatter'd,' and he pointed to the *f*	"	1650
the bandit scatter'd in the *f*,	"	1666
in the *f* were Lancelot's kith	*Elaine*	465
vanish'd suddenly from the *f*	"	507
went sore wounded from the *f* :	"	598
crown'd with gold, Ramp in the *f*,	"	661
For pleasure all about a *f* of flowers :	"	789
rose Elaine and glided thro' the *f*'s,	"	839
thro' the dim rich city to the *f*'s,	"	843
drave her ere her time across the *f*'s	"	886
like a friend's voice from a distant *f*	"	993
Past like a shadow thro' the *f*	"	1134
she thought 'he spies a *f* of death ;	*Guinevere*	133
pace the sacred old familiar *f*'s,	*En. Arden.*	626
Sunning himself in a waste *f* alone—	*Aylmer's F.*	9
became in other *f*'s A mockery	"	496
Ruth among the *f*'s of corn,	"	680
all neglected places of the *f*	"	693
Follows the mouse, and all is open *f*.	"	853
tills the *f* and lies beneath,	*Tithonus*	3
Floats up from those dim *f*'s	"	69
houseless ocean's heaving *f*,	*The Voyage*	30
peep'd in from open *f*, '*Home they brought him,*' etc.		6
Return from pacings in the *f*,	*Lucretius*	6
glory fly along the Italian *f*,	"	71

field-flower.
Like arrow seeds of the *f-f*,	*The Poet*	19
grew Like *f-f*'s everywhere !	*Princess,* iii.	235

fiend.
f best knows whether woman or man	*Maud,* l. i.	75
give the F himself his due, a *f*,	*To F. D. Maurice*	6
His mood was often like a *f*,	*Elaine*	251

fierce.
bright and *f* and fickle is the South,	*Princess,* iv.	79
I that knew him *f* and turbulent	*Enid*	447

fiery-hot.
f-h to burst All barriers	*In Mem.* cxiii.	13

fiery-new.
yet unkept Had relish *f-n*	*Will Water.*	98

fiery-short.
f-s was Cyril's counter-scoff,	*Princess,* v.	297

fife.
The murmurs of the drum and *f*	*Talking O.*	215
merrily-blowing shrill'd the martial *f* ;	*Princess,* i.	241
March with banner and bugle and *f*	*Maud,* l, v.	10

fifty.
More, more, some *f* on a side,	*Princess,* v.	305
waited, *f* there Opposed to *f*,	"	473
Ah, what shall I be at *f*	*Maud,* l. vi.	31
Sat *f* in the blaze of burning fire ;	*Spec. of Iliad*	20

fight (s.)
Ere I rode into the *f*,	*Oriana*	21
Clanging *f*'s, and flaming towns,	*Lotos-E's.*	161
Laid by the tumult of the *f*.	*Margaret*	26
Sun-shaded in the heat of dusty *f*'s	*Princess,* iii.	223
some grand *f* to kill and make an end :	" iv.	568
what she did to Cyrus after *f*,	" v.	356
something real, A gallant *f*, a noble	*Con.*	19

	POEM.	LINE.
He that gain'd a hundred *f*'s,	*Ode on Well.*	96
So that I be not fall'n in *f*.	*Enid*	223
My lord is weary with the *f* before,	"	982
find him yet unwounded after *f*,	"	1220
I, myself, when flush'd with *f*,	"	1518
stretch his limbs in lawful *f*,	"	1602
having been With Arthur in the *f*	*Elaine*	287
got it ; for their captain after *f*,	*Aylmer's F.*	226

fight (verb.)
She saw me *f*, she heard me call,	*Oriana*	32
f and march and countermarch,	*Audley Ct.*	32
f with shadows and to fall. (rep.v.465)	*Princess,* i.	15
Nor would I *f* with iron laws,	" iv.	57
prove Your knight, and *f* your battle,	"	572
make yourself a man to *f* with men.	" v.	34
f in tourney for my bride	"	343
what mother's blood You draw from, *f* ;	"	395
F and *f* well ; strike and strike home.	"	399
sees me *f*, Yea let her see me fall l	"	505
sooner *f* thrice o'er than see it.'	" v.	209
king is scared, the soldier will not *f*,	*Con.*	60
cannot *f* the fear of death.	*In Mem.* cxiii.	10
true life to *f* with mortal wrongs—	*Maud,* I.xviii.	54
better to *f* for the good, than to rail	" III. vi.	57
f him, and will break his pride,	*Enid*	221, 416
arms, arms, to *f* my enemy ?	"	282
nephew *f*'s In next day's tourney	"	475
you, that have no lady, cannot *f*.	"	493
not *f* my way with gilded arms,	"	870
where two *f* The strongest wins,	*Aylmer's F.*	364
is a harder matter to *f*.	*Grandmother*	32
Glory of Virtue, to *f*, to struggle	*Wages*	3

fighter.
rustiest iron of old *f*'s hearts ;	*Vivien*	424

fighting.
'No *f* shadows here !	*Princess,* iii.	109
seem'd a dream, I dream'd Of *f*.	" v.	482
In the great battle *f* for the king.	*Enid*	596
In battle, *f* for the blameless King.	"	1818
All *f* for a woman on the sea.	*Vivien*	412

figtree.
wild *f* split Their monstrous idols,	*Princess,* iv.	61

figure.
Tall as a *f* lengthen'd on the sand	*Princess,* vi.	145
Some *f* like a wizard's pentagram.	*The Brook*	103
Faint as a *f* seen in early dawn	*En. Arden.*	354

figure-head.
full-busted *f-h* Stared o'er the ripple	*En. Arden*	539

file.
in the foremost *f*'s of time—	*Locksley H.*	178

filed.
grated down and *f* away with thought,	*Vivien*	473

fill.
f the sea-halls with a voice of power ;	*The Merman*	10
f my glass : give me one kiss ;	*Miller's D.*	17
f The spacious times of great Elizabeth	*D.of E.Wom.*	6
tho' mine own eyes *f* with dew,	*To J. S.*	37
f my eyes with happy dew ;	*Gardener's D.*	193
Saw the heavens *f* with commerce,	*Locksley H.*	121
Heard the heavens *f* with shouting,	"	123
F the cup, and *f* the can : (rep.)	*Vision of Sin*	95
from all the provinces, And *f* the hive.'	*Princess,* ii.	84
sport half-science, *f* me with a faith.	*Con.*	76
twice a day the Severn *f*'s ;	*In Mem.* xix.	5
prosperous labour *f*'s The lips of men	" lxxxiii.	25
Hala lake F's all the sacred Dee.	*Enid*	1778
the fire of God F's him :	*Elaine*	316
on him that used to *f* it for her,	*En. Arden*	208
tremulous eyes that *f* with tears	*Tithonus*	26
F's out the homely quickset-screens.	*On a Mourner*	6

filled.
f the breast with purer breath.	*Miller's D.*	92
f with light The interval of sound.	*D. of E. Wom.*	171
f the house with clamour.	*The Goose*	36
right ear, that is *f* with dust,	*Two Voices*	110
woods were *f* so full with song,	"	455

	POEM.	LINE.
F I was with folly and spite,	Ed. Gray	15
They are ƒ with idle spleen;	Vision of Sin	124
F thro' and thro' with Love,	Princess, vii.	157
ƒ with tears that cannot fall,	In Mem. xix.	11
streets were ƒ with joyful sound,	„ xxxi.	10
ƒ a horn with wine and held it	Enid	1507
F all the genial courses of his blood	„	1775
Sprang to her face and ƒ her with	Elaine	376
and the ways Were ƒ with rapine,	Guinevere	455
ƒ the shores With clamour.	En. Arden	636
when their casks were ƒ they took	„	647
magic cup that ƒ itself anew.	Aylmer's F.	143
ƒ the house with sudden light,	„	682

fillest.

| ƒ all the room Of all my love, | In Mem. cxi. | 5 |

filling.

| F with light And vagrant melodies | The Poet | 16 |

fillip'd,

| ƒ at the diamond in her ear; | Godiva | 25 |

film.

| with a grosser ƒ made thick | St S. Stylites | 197 |

filth.

| poach'd ƒ that floods the middle | Vivien | 647 |

fin.

| gold ƒ in the porphyry font; | Princess, vii. | 163 |
| is not left the twinkle of a ƒ. | Enid | 1323 |

find.

blessings which no words can ƒ.	Miller's D.	238
So shalt thou ƒ me fairest	Œnone	153
meeker pupil you must ƒ	L. C. V. de Vere	18
ƒ my garden-tools upon the	May Queen, ii.	45
can't be long before I ƒ release;	„ iii.	11
But they smile, they ƒ a music	Lotos-E's.	162a
to seek, to ƒ, and not to yield.	Ulysses	70
ƒ no statelier than his peers	Two Voices	29
seem to ƒ, but still to seek.	„	96
to seem to ƒ Asks what thou lackest,	„	97
man, may hope some truth to ƒ,	„	176
I shall not fail to ƒ her now.	„	191
undo One riddle, and to ƒ the true,	„	233
Wilt thou ƒ passion, pain, or pride?	„	243
'We ƒ no motion in the dead.'	„	279
In Nature can he nowhere ƒ.	„	293
Could his dark wisdom ƒ it out,	„	308
As here we ƒ in trances,	„	352
ƒ The quiet chamber far apart.	Day-Dm.	127
if you ƒ no moral there,	„	198
In bud or blade, or bloom, may ƒ;	„	206
Nor ƒ's a closer truth than this	„	249
if you ƒ a meaning there	„	270
I ƒ a magic bark;	Sir Galahad	38
Until I ƒ the holy Grail.	„	84
grief to ƒ her less than fame,	Princess, i.	72
chafing me on fire to ƒ my bride)	„	164
As yet we ƒ in barbarous isles,	„ ii.	107
'But you will ƒ it otherwise'	„	183
Less welcome ƒ among us, if you	„	333
ƒ you here but in the second place,	„ iii.	141
should ƒ the land Worth seeing;	„	155
come thou down And ƒ him;	„ vii.	185
ƒ him dropt upon the firths of ice,	„	191
dance thee down To ƒ him in the.	„	195
there I ƒ him worthier to be loved.	In Mem. Pro.	40
ƒ in loss a gain to match?	„ i.	6
glad to ƒ thyself so fair,	„ vi.	27
So ƒ I every pleasant spot	„ viii.	9
ƒ A flower beat with rain	„	14
Treasuring the look it cannot ƒ,	„ xviii.	19
ƒ Another service such as this.'	„ xx.	7
Then might I ƒ, ere yet the morn	„ xxvi.	13
ƒ's 'I am not what I see,	„ xliv.	7
ƒ's the baseness of her lot,	„ lix.	6
To ƒ me gay among the gay	„ lxv.	3
I ƒ a trouble in thine eye,	„ lxvii.	10
A man upon a stall may ƒ,	„ lxxvi.	9
ƒ An image comforting the mind,	„ lxxxiv.	50
would but ƒ in wife and child	„ lxxxix.	7

	POEM.	LINE.
I ƒ not yet one lonely thought	In Mem. lxxxix.	23
To ƒ a stronger faith his own;	„ xcv.	17
ƒ's on misty mountain-ground	„ xcvi.	2
I ƒ no place that does not breathe	„ xcix.	3
What ƒ I in the highest place,	„ cvii.	9
ƒ his comfort in thy face;	„ cviii.	20
God grant I may ƒ it at last!	Maud, I. ii.	1
If I ƒ the world so bitter	„ vi.	33
To ƒ they were met by my own;	„ viii.	7
ƒ what he went to seek,	„ xvi.	3
I ƒ whenever she touch'd on me	„ xix.	59
come to her waking, ƒ her asleep,	„ II. ii.	81
To ƒ the arms of my true love	„ iv.	3
shall ƒ the stubborn thistle bursting	Ode on Well.	206
ƒ, at some place I shall come at,	Enid	219
thought to ƒ Arms in your town,	„	417
how should Enid ƒ A nobler friend?	„	792
ƒ him yet unwounded after fight,	„	1220
eyes to ƒ you out however far,	„	1277
ƒ that it had been the wolf's indeed:	„	1712
none could ƒ that man for evermore,	Vivien	60
still I ƒ Your face is practised,	„	216
hide it, hide it; I shall ƒ it out;	„	376
ƒ a wizard who might teach the King	„	433
but did they ƒ A wizard?	„	462
open, ƒ and read the charm:	„	510
in the comment did I ƒ the charm.	„	533
if they ƒ Some stain or blemish	„	680
vile term of yours, I ƒ with grief!	„	771
listen to me If I must ƒ you wit:	Elaine	143
thro' all hindrance ƒ's the man	„	332
ride forth and ƒ the knight.	„	535
cease not from your quest, until you ƒ.'	„	547
the prize and could not ƒ the victor,	„	625
fail'd to ƒ him tho' I rode all round	„	705
'and ƒ out our dear Lavaine.	„	750
needs must hence And ƒ that other,	„	755
Until I ƒ the palace of the King.	„	1045
that we may ƒ the light!	Guinevere	173
And weighing ƒ them less;	„	190
could he ƒ A woman in her womanhood	„	296
sigh'd to ƒ Her journey done,	„	401
ƒ the precious morning hours were	En. Arden	301
Suddenly set it wide to ƒ a sign,	„	492
you ƒ That you meant nothing—.	Aylmer's F.	312
should I ƒ you by my doors again,	„	324
being used to ƒ her pastor texts,	„	605
ƒ a deeper in the narrow gloom	„	840
ƒ A sort of absolution in the sound	Sea Dreams	60
I should ƒ he meant me well;	„	149
to ƒ Their wildest wailings never out	„	223
I ƒ myself often laughing at things	Grandmother	92
blest To ƒ my heart so near	Coquette, ii.	7
beastlike as I ƒ myself, Not manlike	Lucretius	264
fail to ƒ thee, being as thou art	„	264
For it's easy to ƒ a rhyme. (rep.)	The Window	149

finding.

ƒ that of fifty seeds	In Mem. liv.	11
there unconsciously Some image	Ded. of Idylls	2
ƒ neither light nor murmur there	En. Arden	638

fine.

| What is ƒ within thee growing coarse | Locksley H. | 46 |
| cuckoo!' was ever a May so ƒ? | The Window | 153 |

fineness.

| often ƒ compensated size; | Princess, ii. | 133 |
| some pretext of ƒ in the meal | En. Arden | 338 |

finest.

| because he was The ƒ on the tree. | Talking O. | 238 |

finger.

weary with a ƒ's touch 'Clear-headed friend,' etc.		22
kiss Thy taper ƒ's amorously,	Madeline	44
Thro' rosy taper ƒ's drew	Mariana in the S.	15
Three ƒ's round the old silver cup	Miller's D.	10
With rosy slender ƒ's backward	Œnone	173
one, by those fair ƒ's cull'd,	Gardener's D.	148
with a flying ƒ swept my lips	„	241
save her little ƒ from a scratch	Ed. Morris	63
Baby ƒ's, waxen touches,	Locksley H.	90

Entry	POEM	LINE
little ƒ ache For such as *these ?'*	Godiva	22
Her gradual ƒ's steal	Will Water.	26
kept the book and had my ƒ in it	Princess, Pro.	53
takes a lady's ƒ with all care,	"	171
now a pointed ƒ, told them all;	" v.	260
laid A feeling ƒ on my brows,	" vi.	105
innocent arms And lazy lingering ƒ's.	"	123
With trembling ƒ's did we weave.	In Mem. xxx.	1
God's ƒ touch'd him, and he slept.	" lxxxiv.	20
A fiery ƒ on the leaves ;	" xcviii.	12
would work eye dim, and ƒ lame,	Enid	628
He sits unarm'd ; I hold a ƒ up,		1186
moving back she held Her ƒ up,	"	1302
clench'd her ƒ's till they bit.	Elaine	608
Enoch's golden ring had girt Her ƒ,	En. Arden.	158
Suddenly put her ƒ on the text,	"	493
dug His ƒ's into the wet earth,	"	781
My lady with her ƒ's interlock'd	Aylmer's F.	199
And on thy heart a ƒ lays,	On a Mourner	11

fingering.

ƒ at the hair about his lip,	Princess, v.	293

finger nail.

seem'd All-perfect, finished to the ƒ n.	Ed. Morris	22
tap Of my ƒ-n on the sand,	Maud, II. ii.	22

finger-tips.

sway'd The rein with dainty ƒ-t,	Sir L. and Q.G.	41

finials.

grasping the pews And oaken ƒ's	Aylmer's F.	823

finished.

when four years were wholly ƒ,	Pal. of Art	289
All-perfect, ƒ to the finger nail.	Ed. Morris	22

fire (s.)

Thou who stealest ƒ,	Ode to Mem.	1
Tho' one did fling the ƒ.	The Poet	30
Losing his ƒ and active might	Eleänore	104
a languid ƒ creeps Thro' my veins	"	130
O Love, O ƒ! once he drew.	Fatima	19
from beyond the noon a ƒ Is pour'd	"	30
at their feet the crocus brake like ƒ,	Œnone	94
she says A ƒ dances before her,	"	260
earth and air seem only burning ƒ.	"	264
Burnt like a fringe of ƒ.	Pal. of Art	48
Would seem slow-flaming crimson ƒ's	"	50
And highest, snow and ƒ.	"	84
She howl'd aloud, ' I am on ƒ within	"	285
wild marsh-marigold shines like ƒ	May Queen, i.	31
before the fluttering tongues of ƒ;	D. of F. Wom.	30
with their ƒ's Love tipt his keenest	"	173
The glass blew in, ƒ blew out,	The Goose	49
Allan's watch, and sparkled by the ƒ	Dora	133
Or burn'd in ƒ, or boil'd in oil,	St S. Stylites	51
Sit with their wives by ƒ's,	"	106
Have scrambled past those pits of ƒ,	"	181
winks behind a slowly-dying ƒ.	Locksley H.	136
with rain or hail, or ƒ or snow ;	"	193
Like Stephen, an unquenched ƒ.	Two Voices	219
On the hall-hearths the festal ƒ's	Day-Dm.	34
The ƒ shot up, the martin flew,	"	143
No, I cannot praise the ƒ.	Vision of Sin	183
her arm lifted, eyes on ƒ—	Princess, Pro.	41
finest Gothic, lighter than a ƒ,	"	92
kill Time by the ƒ in winter.'	"	201
chafing me on ƒ to find my bride)	" i.	164
like the mystic ƒ on a mast-head	" iv.	255
some ƒ against a stormy cloud	"	365
like ƒ he meets the foe,	"	560
red-faced war has rods of steel and ƒ;	" v.	114
living hearts that crack within the ƒ,	"	369
ƒ's of Hell Mix with his hearth :	"	444
out of stricken helmets sprang the ƒ,	"	484
from a darken'd future, crown'd with ƒ,	" vi.	159
A looming bastion fringed with ƒ.	In Mem. xv.	20
Is shrivel'd in a fruitless ƒ,	" liii.	11
Laburnums, dropping-wells of ƒ..	" lxxxii.	11
shine Beside the never-lighted ƒ	" lxxxiii.	20
on her forehead sits a ƒ:	" cxiii.	5
compass'd by the ƒ's of Hell ;	" cxxvi.	17

Entry	POEM	LINE
ƒ of a foolish pride flash'd over	Maud, I. iv.	16
Cold ƒ's, yet with power to burn.	" xviii.	39
ƒ's of Hell brake out of thy rising	" II. i.	9
ƒ's of Hell and of Hate ;	"	10
blossom of war with a heart of ƒ.	" III. vi.	53
in my words were seeds of ƒ.	The Letters	28
The giant windows' blazon'd ƒ's.	The Daisy	58
like the heart of a great ƒ at Yule,	Enid	559
night of ƒ, when Edyrn sack'd	"	634
loosed in words of sudden ƒ the	"	955
land, From which old ƒ's have	"	1670
men may fear Fresh ƒ and ruin.	"	1671
into such a song, such ƒ for fame,	Vivien	267
like a ƒ among the noblest names,	"	651
godlike head crown'd with spiritual ƒ,	"	686
the ƒ of God Fills him ;	Elaine	315
shot red ƒ and shadows thro' the cave,	"	413
ran the tale like ƒ about the court,	"	730
F in dry stubble a nine days' wonder	"	731
that he scape the doom of ƒ,	Guinevere	345
children born of thee are sword and ƒ,	"	422
making all the night a steam of ƒ.	"	593
All-kindled by a still and sacred ƒ,	En. Arden.	71
clean hearth and a clear ƒ for me,	"	192
flung her down upon a couch of ƒ,	Aylmer's F.	574
flood, ƒ, earthquake, thunder, wrought	"	639
not passing thro' the ƒ Bodies, but	"	671
No desolation but by sword and ƒ?	"	748
tongue is a ƒ as you know, my dear,	Grandmother	23
The moon like a rick on ƒ	"	39
beat the twilight into flakes of ƒ.	Tithonus	42
Fall from his Ocean-lane of ƒ,	The Voyage	19
With wakes of ƒ we tore the dark ;	"	52
Flash, ye cities, in rivers of ƒ!	W. to Alexan.	19
Thunder, a flying ƒ in heaven.	Boädicea	24
many a ƒ before them blazed :	Spec. of Iliad	10
many a ƒ between the ships and	"	17
Sat fifty in the blaze of burning ƒ :	"	20
thorpe and byre arose in ƒ,	The Victim	3
a ƒ, The ƒ that left a roofless Ilion,	Lucretius	64
altho' his ƒ is on my face	"	144
ƒ's burn clear, And frost is here,	The Window	46
ƒ's are all the clearer,	"	58
king of the wrens with a crown of ƒ.	"	159

fire (verb.)

ƒ's your narrow casement glass,	Miller's D.	243
furzy prickle ƒ the dells,	Two Voices	71

fire-balloon.

a ƒ-b Rose gem-like	Princess, Pro.	74

firebrand.

this ƒ—gentleness To such as her !	Princess, v.	160

fire-crown'd.

ƒ-c king of the wrens from out of	The Window	151

fired.

wires and vials ƒ A cannon :	Princess, Pro.	65
ƒ an angry Pallas on the helm,	" vi.	347
saw F from the west, far on a hill,	Elaine	168
F all the pale face of the Queen,	Guinevere	355
rose at dawn and, ƒ with hope,	Sailor Boy	1
Not a gun was ƒ.	The Captain	40

fire-fly.

Glitter like a swarm of fire-flies	Locksley H.	10
ƒ-ƒ wakens : waken thou with me.	Princess, vii.	164

firefly-like.

glitter ƒ-l in copse And linden alley:	Princess, i.	205

fire-hollowing.

F-h this in Indian fashion, fell	En. Arden.	570

fireside.

her old ƒ Be cheer'd with tidings.	In Mem. xxxix.	22
at your own ƒ, With the evil tongue	Maud, I. x.	50

firewood.

heap'd Their ƒ, and the winds	Spec. of Iliad	7

firm (adj.)

nor slow to change, but ƒ: 'Love thou thy land,' etc.		31
ƒ upon his feet, And like an oaken	Golden Year	61

142   CONCORDANCE TO

	POEM.	LINE.
f Tho' compass'd by two armies	*Princess*, v.	334
he stood *f*; and so the matter hung;	*The Brook*	144-8
the soldier *f*, the statesman pure :	*Ode on Well.*	222
Met his full frown timidly *f*,	*Enid*	. 920

firm (s.)
Head of all the golden-shafted *f*, . *Princess*, ii. 383

firmness.
said to him With timid *f*, . . *Enid* . . 989

first-born.
love thou bearest The *f-b* of thy genius. *Ode to Mem.* 92
Love at first sight, *f-b*, and heir . *Gardener's D.* 185
meal she makes On the *f-b* of her sons. *Vision of Sin* 146

first-famed.
of the two *f-f* for courtesy— . *Guinevere* . 321

first-fruits.
The *f-f* of the stranger : . . *Princess*, ii. 30

firstling.
bring the *f* to the flock ; . . *In Mem.* ii. 6

firth.
find him dropt upon the *f*'s of ice, *Princess*, vii. 191

fish.
F are we that love the mud, . *Vision of Sin* 101
The star, the bird, the *f*, the shell, *Princess*, ii. 361
'if we have *f* at all Let them be gold ; *Enid* . 669
panic-stricken, like a shoal Of darting *f*, „ 1318
bird in air, and *f*'es turn'd . *The Victim* 19
beast or bird or *f*, or opulent flower— *Lucretius* 245

fisherman.
O well for the *f*'s boy, . . '*Break, break,*' etc. 5
A luckier or a bolder *f*, . . *En. Arden* . 49

fishing-nets.
coils of cordage, swarthy *f-n*, . *En. Arden* . 17
wrought To make the boatmen *f-n*, „ 816

fit (s.)
Gleam'd to the flying moon by *f*'s. *Miller's D.* 116
in a *f* of frolic mirth . . *Talking O.* . 137
breaking into song by *f*'s, . *In Mem.* xxiii. 2
only breathe Short *f*'s of prayer, *Enid* . 1004
break her sports with graver *f*'s, *Vivien* . 36

fit (verb.)
f us like a nature second-hand : *Walk. to the M.* 57
slow As *f*'s an universal woe, . *Ode on Well.* 14
better *f*'s Our mended fortunes . *Enid* . 717
f their little streetward sitting-room *En. Arden* . 170

fitly.
flower of life To one more *f* yours, *Elaine* . 949

fitted.
Power *f* to the season ; . . *Œnone* . 121
pure white, that *f* to the shape— *Gardener's D.* 125
now 'tis *f* on and grows to me, . *St S. Stylites* 206
f to thy pretty part, . . *Locksley H.* 93
As his unlikeness *f* mine. . *In Mem.* lxxviii. 20

fitting.
expert In *f* aptest words to things, *In Mem.* lxxiv. 6

five-acre.
While Harry is in the *f-a* . *Grandmother* 80

five-headed.
The tender pink *f-b* baby-soles, . *Aylmer's F.* 186

five-words-long.
quoted odes, and jewels *f-w-l* . *Princess*, ii. 355

fix.
Holding the bush, to *f* it back. *Gardener's D.* 126
all as one to *f* our hopes on Heaven *Golden Year* 57
lynx eye To *f* and make me hotter, *Princess*, iii. 31
Nor cares to *f* itself to form, . *In Mem.* xxxiii. 4
f my thoughts on all the glow . „ lxxxiii. 3
Who shall *f* Her pillars ? . . „ cxiii. 3
could not *f* the glass to suit her eye ; *En. Arden* 240
Sun sets, moon sets, Love, *f* a day. *The Window* 165
wait a little, *You* shall *f* a day' . „ 173

	fixed—fixt. POEM.	LINE.
there like a sun remain *F*— .	*Eleänore*	93
last, you *f* a vacant stare, .	*L. C. V. de Vere*	47
the dewy pebbles, *f* in thought ; .	*M. d'Arthur*	84
that the grounds of hope were *f*, .	*Two Voices*	227
Be *f* and froz'n to permanence : .	„	237
The blush is *f* upon her cheek. .	*Day-Dm.*	52
One *f* for ever at the door, .	*Will Water.*	143
eyes Of shining expectation *f* on	*Princess*, iv.	135
F lik- a beacon-tower above the waves	„	472
this is *f* As are the roots of earth .	„ v.	435
F in yourself, never in your own arms	„ vi.	161
I on her *F* my faint eyes, . .	„ vii.	129
f A showery glance upon her aunt,	„ *Con.*	32
Her faith is *f* and cannot move, .	*In Mem.* xcvi.	33
Because he felt so *f* in truth : .	„ cxxiv.	8
a morbid eating lichen *f* . .	*Maud*, I. vi.	77
forks are *f* into the meadow ground,	*Enid* . 482,	548
in ebbs and flows, *F* on her faith .	„	813
clung to him, *F* in her will, .	*Vivien* .	44
So *f* her fancy on him ; . .	„	626
you *f* Your limit, oft returning .	*Elaine*	1034
either *f* his heart On that one girl ;	*En. Arden* .	39
where he *f* his heart he set his hand	„	293
f her swimming eyes upon him, .	„	322
f the Sabbath. Darkly that day .	*Aylmer's F.*	609
f My wistful eyes on two fair images,	*Sea Dreams*	231
f upon the far sea-line ; . .	*The Voyage*	62

flaccid.
scheme that had left us *f* and drain'd. *Maud*, I. i. 20

flag.
never floats an European *f*, . *Locksley H.* 161
F's, flutter out upon turrets . *W. to Alexan.* 15

flag-flower.
tall *f-f*'s when they sprung . *Miller's D.* . 53

flagrant.
in *f*—what's the Latin word ?— *Walk. to the M.* 26

flail.
From Arac's arm, as from a giant's *f*, *Princess*, v. 489

flake.
sang Shrill, chill, with *f*'s of foam. *M. d'Arthur* 49
Before me shower'd the rose in *f*'s ; *Princess*, iv. 245
f of rainbow flying on the highest . „ v. 309
rocket molten into *f*'s Of crimson *In Mem.* xcvii. 31
here and there a foamy *f* . . *The Brook* . 59
beat the twilight into *f*'s of fire. . *Tithonus* . 42
thicker, like the *f*'s In a fall of snow, *Lucretius* . 169

flame (s.)
the clear-pointed *f* of chastity, . *Isabel* . 2
A subtle, sudden *f*, . . *Madeline* . 28
As with the quintessence of *f*, . *Arabian N.'s.* 123
headed And wing'd with *f*, . *The Poet* . 12
was traced in *f* WISDOM, . „ . 45
Burn'd like one burning *f* together,, *L. of Shalott*, iii. 22
A thousand little shafts of *f* . *Fatima* . 17
She died : she went to burning *f* : *The Sisters* . 30
thro' the topmost Oriels' coloured *f Pal. of Art* 161
hollow shades enclosing hearts of *f*, „ . 241
Dark faces pale against that rosy *f*, *Lotos-E's.* . 26
God divide the night with flying *f*, *D. of F. Wom.* 225
in the midst A fragrant *f* rose, . *Princess*, iv. 16
with slow dilation roll'd Dry *f*, . „ vi. 173
set a wrathful Dian's moon on *f*, . „ . 348
Pierces the keen seraphic *f* . . *In Mem.* xxvii. 27
This round of green, this orb of *f*, „ xxxiv. 5
Life, a Fury slinging flame. . . „ xlix. 8
As slowly steals a silver *f* . . „ lxvi. 6
might'st have heaved a windless *f* „ lxxi. 13
Ray round with *f*'s her disk of seed, „ c. 6
Ready to burst in a colour'd *f* ; . *Maud*, I. vi. 19
blood Break into furious *f* ; . *Enid* . 1676
To rise hereafter in a stiller *f*. . *Elaine* 1309
hair as it were crackling into *f*'s, *Guinevere* . 282
the dead *f* of the fallen day . *En. Arden* . 438
hair as it were crackling into *f*'s, *Aylmer's F.* . 586
I doom you to the *f*. . . *The Ringlet* . 50
F's, on the windy headland flare ! *W. to Alexan.* 16
down in a furrow scathed with *f* : . *The Victim* . 22
girt With song and *f* and fragrance, *Lucretius* . 134

	POEM.	LINE.
flame (verb.)		
barking cur Made her cheek *f*:	*Godiva*	58
peasant rights himself, the rick *F*'s,	*Princess*, iv.	307
f or him did his high sun *f*,	*Maud*, I. iv.	32
f's The blood-red blossom of war	" III. vi.	52
Let it *f* or fade,	"	54
when the long-illumined cities *f*,	*Ode on Well.*	228
headland after headland *f*	*Guinevere*	241
f and sparkle and stream as of old,	*The Ringlet*	8
flamed.		
f upon the brazen greaves	*L. of Shalott*, iii.	4
F in his cheek ; and eager eyes,	*Aylmer's F.*	66
Tho' Leolin *f* and fell again,	"	409
By peaks that *f*, or, all in shade,	*The Voyage*	41
flaming.		
f downward over all	*Mariana in the S.*	77
flank.		
arisen since With cities on their *f*'s—	*Vivien*	526
flap.		
great echo *f* And buffet	*Golden Year*	75
b at Tacks, and the slacken'd sail *f*'s,	*Princess*, ii.	169
dimpled flounce of the sea-furbelow *f*,	*Sea Dreams*	257
flapped.		
They *f* my light out as I read :	*St S. Stylites*	172
flare.		
Flames, on the windy headland *f* !	*W. to Alexan.*	16
flared.		
threaten'd darkness, *f* and fell :	*M. d'Arthur, Ep.*	2
in dry stubble a nine days' wonder *f*:	*Elaine*	731
bloodred light of dawn *F* on her face,	"	1020
a great mist-blotted light *F* on him,	*En. Arden.*	682
flaring.		
A million tapers *f* bright	*Arabian N's.*	124
in heaven the light of London *f*	*Locksley H.*	114
flash (s.)		
without speaking, like a *f* of light.	*May Queen*, i.	18
a shape, a shade, A *f* of light.	*St S. Stylites*	200
A living *f* of light he flew.'	*Two Voices*	15
The *f*'es come and go :	*St Agnes' Eve*	26
I learnt more from her in a *f*,	*Princess*, ii.	375
These *f*'es on the surface are not he.	" iv.	234
like a *f* the weird affection came :.	" v.	466
A little *f*, a mystic hint ;	*In Mem.* xliii.	8
As in the former *f* of joy,	" cxxi.	15
at the *f* and motion of the man	*Enid*	1316
chased the *f*'es of his golden horns	*Vivien*	277
send One *f*, that, missing all things else	"	781
free *f*'es from a height Above her,	*Elaine*	644
love's first *f* in youth, Most common :	"	945
' Ay, ay, I fear me, that will strike	"	965
her love Was but the *f* of youth,	"	1308
lightning *f* of insect and of bird,	*En. Arden.*	576
A *f* of semi-jealousy clear'd it to her.	*Aylmer's F.*	189
once the *f* of a thunderbolt--	*Lucretius*	27
Down in the South is a *f* and a groan :	*The Window*	42
You send a *f* to the sun	"	179
I ! I am coming, I come,	"	190
flash (verb.)		
F in the pools of whirling Simois	*Œnone*	202
f the lightnings, weigh the Sun—.	*Locksley H.*	186
This proverb *f*'es thro' his head,	*Day-Dm.*	115
f es into false and true,	*In Mem.* xvi.	19
f at once, my friend, to thee :	" xl.	12
Will *f* along the chords and go.	" lxxxvii.	12
Re-makes itself, and *f*'es down the vale	*Guinevere*	604
F into fiery life from nothing,	*Aylmer's F.*	130
naked marriages *F* from the bridge,	"	766
facets of the glorious mountain *f*.	*The Islet*	22
F, ye cities, in rivers of fire !	*W. to Alexan.*	19
You *f* and lighten afar :	*The Window*	187
F for a million miles,	"	201
flashed.		
He *f* into the crystal mirror,	*L. of Shalott*, iii.	34
F thro' her as she sat alone,	*Pal. of Art*	214
f and fell the brand Excalibur :	*M. d'Arthur*	142

	POEM.	LINE.
The distant battle *f* and rung.	*Two Voices*	126
He *f* his random speeches :	*Will Water.*	198
f a saucy message to and fro	*Princess, Pro.*	78
thought *f* thro' me which I clothed	" i.	192
young captains *f* their glittering teeth,	" v.	19
His living soul was *f* on mine,	*In Mem.* xciv.	36
pride *f* over her beautiful face.	*Maud*, I. iv.	16
Something *f* in the sun,	" ix.	10
Heaven *f* a sudden jubilant ray,	*Ode on Well.*	129
F all their sabres bare, *F* as they	*Lt. Brigade*	27
Geraint *f* into sudden spleen :	*Enid*	273
out he *f* And into such a song,	*Vivien*	246
F the bare-grinning skeleton of death !	"	696
Suddenly *f* on her a wild desire,	*Elaine*	356
f into wild tears, and rose again,	"	610
down they *f*, and smote the stream.	"	1228
f, as it were, Diamonds to meet them,	"	1229
autumn into autumn *f* again,	*En. Arden.*	453
jests, that *f* about the pleader's room,	*Aylmer's F.*	440
flashest.		
along the valley, stream that *f* white,	*V. of Cauteretz*	1
flashing.		
She, *f* forth a haughty smile,	*D. of F. Wom.*	129
f round and round, and whirl'd	*M. d'Arthur*	138
The cataract *f* from the bridge,	*In Mem.* lxx.	15
quickly thro' the shallow ford	*Enid*	167
Was all the marble threshold *f*,	"	874
flask.		
A *f* of cider from his father's vats,	*Audley Ct.*	26
Here sits the Butler with a *f*	*Day-Dm.*	45
I leave an empty *f*:	*Will Water.*	164
flat (a level.)		
glanced athwart the glooming *f*'s.	*Mariana*	20
here upon the *f* All that long morn	*Princess*, v.	357
all about The same gray *f*'s again,	*In Mem.* lxxxvi.	13
By sands and steaming *f*'s,	*The Voyage*	45
flat (note in music.)		
thro' every change of sharp and *f*;	*Coquette*, i.	4
flattened.		
Mangled, and *f*, and crush'd,	*Maud*, I. i.	7
flatter.		
sue me, and woo me, and *f* me,	*The Mermaid*	43
To *f* me that I may die ?	*Two Voices*	204
F myself that always everywhere	*Princess*, ii.	390
This look of quiet *f*'s thus	*In Mem.* x.	10
f his own wish in age for love,	*Vivien*	41
flattered.		
thought of power *F* his spirit ;	*Œnone*	135
He *f* to the height.	*Pal. of Art*	192
snares them by the score *F* and	*Princess*, v.	157
The fancy *f* my mind,	*Maud*, I. xiv.	23
flattering.		
f the golden prime	*Arabian N's.*	76
f thy childish thought	*Eleänore*	13
O, I, that *f* my true passion, saw	*Vivien*	723
splendid presence *f* the poor roofs	*Aylmer's F.*	175
flattery.		
the wit, The *f* and the strife,	*D. of F. Wom.*	148
Nor speak I now from foolish *f*;	*Enid*	433
old man, Tho' doubtful, felt the *f*,	*Vivien*	40
flaunt.		
f With prides for proctors,	*Princess, Pro.*	140
to *f*, to dress, to dance, to thrum,	" iv.	408
a time for these to *f* their pride ?	*Aylmer's F.*	770
flaw.		
Like *f*'s in summer laying lusty	*Enid*	764
flay-flint.		
There lived a *f* near ; we stole	*Walk. to the M.*	76
flaying.		
F the roofs and sucking up the	*Princess*, v.	514
flea.		
text no larger than the limbs of *f*'s	*Vivien*	522

	POEM.	LINE.
fleck.		
slid, a sunny *f*, From head to ancle	*Talking O.*	223
life is dash'd with *f*'s of sin.	*In Mem.* li.	14
fleckless.		
conscience will not count me *f*;	*Princess*, ii.	274
fled.		
Her household *f* the danger,	*The Goose*	54
voice *f* always thro' the summer	*Ed. Morris*	67
I read, and *f* by night, and flying	"	134
Then *f* she to her inmost bower,	*Godiva*	42
'O happy sleep, that lightly *f*!'	*Day-Dm.*	182
Thought her proud, and *f* over the	*Ed. Gray*	14
f fast thro' sun and shade.	*Sir L. and Q. G.*	37
For maidens, on the spur she *f*;	*Princess*, i.	150
when he fell, And all else *f*:	" ii.	225
They *f*, who might have shamed us:	"	279
As flies the shadow of a bird, she *f*.	" iii.	80
day *f* on thro' all Its range of duties	"	160
f, as flies A troop of snowy doves.	" iv.	149
Amazed he *f* away Thro' the dark	" v.	46
shuddering *f* from room to room,	" vi.	350
Less yearning for the friendship *f*,	*In Mem.* cxv.	15
wise if I *f* from the place	*Maud*, I. i.	64
Whether I need have *f*?	" II. ii.	72
And I wake, my dream is *f*;	" iv.	51
My fancy *f* to the South again.	*The Daisy*	108
f With little save the jewels	*Enid*	639
f all the boon companions of the	"	1326
f Yelling as from a spectre,	"	1580
staring and aghast, While some yet *f*;	"	1653
f from Arthur's court To break the	*Vivien*	146
f like a glittering rivulet to the	*Elaine*	53
I my sons and little daughter *f*	"	276
f ever thro' the woodwork,	"	439
that day when Lancelot *f* the lists,	"	524
Queen Guinevere had *f* the court,	*Guinevere*	1
hither had she *f*, her cause of flight	"	9
f all night long by glimmering waste	"	127
Moan as she *f*, or thought she heard	"	129
had added 'get thee hence' *F* frighted	"	365
F forward, and no news of Enoch	*En. Arden.*	358
His fancy *f* before the lazy wind.	"	658
For one fair Vision ever *f*.	*The Voyage*	57
fledged.		
branches, *f* with clearest green,	*D. of F. Wom.*	59
lightlier move The minutes *f* with	*Princess*, iv.	19
F as it were with Mercury's ankle-wing,	*Lucretius*	198
flee.		
Melissa clamour'd '*F* the death;'	*Princess*, iv.	148
What time mine own might also *f*,	*In Mem.* lxxxiii.	37
f from the cruel madness of love,	*Maud*, I. iv.	55
if I *f* to these Can I go from Him?	*En. Arden.*	224
fleece.		
heavens between their fairy *f*'s pale	*Gardener's D.*	256
many-wintered *f* of throat and chin.	*Vivien*	690
Fleece (Inn Sign.)		
The Bull, the *F* are cramm'd,	*Audley Ct.*	1
fleet (adj.)		
f I was of foot: Before me shower'd	*Princess*, iv.	244
fleet (s.)		
I trust if an enemy's *f* came yonder	*Maud*, I. i.	49
Ev'n in the presence of an enemy's *f*,	*Guinevere*	277
f of glass, That seem'd a *f* of jewels	*Sea Dreams*	118
An idle signal, for the brittle *f*	"	129
my poor venture but a *f* of glass.	"	134
Welcome her, thunders of fort and of *f*!	*IV. to Alexan.*	6
all the *f* Had rest by stony hills	*On a Mourner*	34
fleet (verb.)		
And the light and shadow *f*;	*Maud*, II. iv.	36
And the shadow flits and *f*'s	"	90
fleeted.		
As fast we *f* to the South:	*The Voyage*	4
fleeter.		
Whether smile or frown be *f*?	*Madeline*	12

	POEM.	LINE.
fleeting.		
Or that this anguish *f* hence,	*Two Voices*	235
Or villain fancy *f* by,	*In Mem.* cx.	18
f thro' the boundless universe,	*Lucretius*	161
flesh.		
my *f*, which I despise and hate,	*St S. Stylites*	57
Mortify Your *f*, like me,	"	177
far too spare of *f*.	*Talking O.*	92
Padded round with *f* and fat,	*Vision of Sin*	177
Oh, sacred be the *f* and blood	*In Mem.* xxxiii.	11
All knowledge that the sons of *f*	" lxxxiv.	27
O heart of stone, are you *f*,	*Maud*, I. vi.	79
Go to the town and buy us *f*	*Enid*	372
means of goodly welcome, *f* and wine.	"	387
boil'd the *f*, and spread the board.	"	391
call'd for *f* and wine to feed his spears.	"	1449
hall was dim with steam of *f*:	"	1451
touch'd fierce wine, nor tasted *f*,	*Vivien*	477
how pale! what are they? *f* and blood?	*Elaine*	1249
cannot take thy hand; that too is *f*,	*Guinevere*	549
in the *f* thou hast sinn'd; and mine own *f*,	"	550
My love thro' *f* hath wrought	"	554
they that cast her spirit into *f*,	*Aylmer's F.*	481
wilt not gash thy *f* for *him*;	"	658
swept away The men of *f* and blood,	*Sea Dreams*	230
never yet on earth Could dead *f* creep,	*Lucretius*	131
flew.		
Out *f* the web and floated wide;	*L. of Shalott*, iii.	42
loosely *f* to left and right—	" iv.	20
goose *f* this way and *f* that,	*The Goose*	35
A living flash of light he *f*.	*Two Voices*	17
The fire shot up, the martin *f*,	*Day-Dm.*	143
F over roof and casement:	*Will Water.*	134
till they *f*, Hair, and eyes, and limbs,	*Vision of Sin*	38
dance, and *f* thro' light And shadow,	*Princess*, Pro.	84
f kite, and raced the purple fly,	" ii.	230
gust that round the garden *f*,	*In Mem.* lxxxviii.	19
f in a dove And brought a summons	" cii.	15
o'er the hills her eagles *f*	*Ode on Well.*	112
f Before it, till it touch'd her,	*Guinevere*	79
Changed every moment as we *f*.	*The Voyage*	28
'Chase,' he said: the ship *f* forward,	*The Captain*	33
flexile.		
So youthful and so *f* then,	*Amphion*	59
flicker.		
The shadows *f* to and fro:	*D. of the O. Year*	29
Where the dying night-lamp *f*'s,	*Locksley H.*	80
wisp that *f*'s where no foot can tread.'	*Princess*, iv.	339
To *f* with his double tongue.	*In Mem.* cix.	8
flickered.		
high masts *f* as they lay afloat:	*D. of F. Wom.*	113
flickering.		
night-light *f* in my eyes Awoke me.'	*Sea Dreams*	101
flight (flying.)		
And of so fierce a *f*,	*The Poet*	14
spread his sheeny vans for *f*;	*Love and Death*	8
Rapt after heaven's starry *f*,	*Two Voices*	68
Beyond the furthest *f*'s of hope,	"	185
f from out your bookless wilds	*Princess*, ii.	42
Edyrn's men had caught them in their *f*,	*Enid*	642
her cause of *f* Sir Modred;	*Guinevere*	1
What look'd a *f* of fairy arrows	*Aylmer's F.*	94
F's, terrors, sudden rescues,	"	99
In hope to gain upon her *f*.	*The Voyage*	60
flight (of stairs.)		
Broad-based *f*'s of marble stairs	*Arabian N's.*	117
up a *f* of stairs into the hall.	*Princess*, ii.	17
fling (s.)		
Give me my *f*, and let me say my say.'	*Aylmer's F.*	399
fling (verb.)		
f The winged shafts of truth,	*The Poet*	25
Tho' one did *f* the fire.	"	30
f on each side my low-flowing locks,	*The Mermaid*	32
take Excalibur And *f* him far	*M. d'Arthur*	37
if thou spare to *f* Excalibur,	"	131
good luck Shall *f* her old shoe after.	*Will Water.*	216
f the diamond necklace by.'	*Lady Clare*	40

	POEM.	LINE.
ƒThe tricks, which make us toys!	Princess, ii.	48
all prophetic pity, ƒTheir pretty maids	" v.	371
'F'our doors wide I all, all, .	" vi.	314
ƒit like a viper off, and shriek	" vii.	79
ƒThis bitter seed among mankind	In Mem.lxxxix.	3
ƒ's Her shadow on the blaze of kings:	" xcvii.	18
Did heƒhimself down? Who knows?	Maud, I. i.	9
ƒme deep in that forgotten mere, .	Elaine	1416
Never a man couldƒ him: . .	Grandmother	10
notƒ this horror off me again, .	Lucretius	173
will sheƒherself, Shameless upon me?	"	199

flinging.

Fthe gloom of yesternight .	. Ode to Mem.	9

flint.

sparkling ƒ's beneath the prow, .	Arabian N's.	52
ƒ's batter'd with clanging hoofs: .	D. of F. Wom.	21
one part of sense not ƒ to prayer, .	Princess, vi.	166
out upon you, ƒ! You love nor her,	"	242
set my face as aƒ, . . .	Maud, I. i.	31
But then what a ƒis he I . .	" xix.	57
no stoning save withƒ and rock? .	Aylmer's F.	746

flippant.

Theƒ put himself to school . .	In Mem. cix.	10

flirt.

Not one toƒa venom at her eyes, .	Vivien	459

flit.

ƒTo make the greensward fresh, .	Talking O..	89
Let our girls ƒ, Till the storm die!	Princess, vi.	317
like to noiseless phantoms ƒ: .	In Mem. xx.	16
What slender shade of doubt may ƒ,	" xlvii.	7
F's by the sea-blue bird of March:	" xc.	4
A shadow ƒ's before me, . .	Maud, II. iv.	11
And the shadow ƒ's and fleets .	"	90
let her fancyƒ across the past, .	Enid	645
Look, look, how he ƒ's, . .	The Window	150
ƒlike the king of the wrens . .	"	159

flitted.

F across into the night, . .	Miller's D.	127
The little innocent soulƒaway .	En. Arden	269
unawares theyƒ off, . .	Aylmer's F.	202
Gone—ƒaway! . . .	The Window	38
ƒI know not where I . .	"	41

flitteth.

The shallopƒ silken-sail'd . .	L. of Shalott, i.	22

flitting (part.)

'What! You're ƒ!' 'Yes, we're ƒ,'	Walk. to the M.	35

flitting (s.)

After the ƒ of the bats, . .	Mariana	17
Plagued with a ƒ to and fro, .	Maud, II. ii.	33

float.

of thy love-deep eyes F on to me.	Eleänore	77
Floated her hair or seem'd toƒ .	Œnone	18
Falls, and ƒ's adown the air. .	Lotos-E's.	76
F by you on the verge of night. .	Margaret	31
ƒabout the threshold of an age, .	Golden Year	16
never ƒ's an European flag, . .	Locksley H.	161
ƒthro' Heaven, and cannot light?	Day-Dm.	276
ƒ till all is dark. . . .	Sir Galahad	40
seem'd Toƒabout a glimmering .	Princess, i.	243
bottom agates seen to wave and ƒ	" ii.	306
streams that ƒ us each and all .	" iv.	52
F's up from those dim fields .	Tithonus	69

floated.

Adown it ƒ a dying swan . .	Dying Swan	6
Out flew the web and ƒ wide; .	L. of Shalott, ii.	4
She ƒ down to Camelot . .	" iv.	23
A gleaming shape she ƒ hy, . .	"	30
F her hair or seem'd to float .	Œnone	18
F the glowing sunlights, as she .	"	178
if first Iƒ free, As naked essence,	Two Voices	373
she ƒ to us and said: 'You have .	Princess, iv.	505
The lovely, lordly creatureƒon .	" vi.	73

floating.

ƒabout the under-sky . .	Dying Swan	25
F thro' an evening atmosphere, .	Eleänore	100

	POEM.	LINE.
misty folds, that ƒ as they fell .	Pal. of Art.	35
Cameƒ on for many a month .	Vision of Sin	54

flock.

By dancing rivulets fed his ƒ's, .	To E. L. .	22
bring the firstling to the ƒ; .	In Mem. ii.	6
That feed the mothers of the ƒ; .	" xcix.	16
The ƒ's are whiter down the vale,	" cxiv.	10
he came again, his ƒ believed— .	Aylmer's F.	600
half amazed full frighted all his ƒ;	"	631
my eldest-born, the flower of the ƒ;	Grandmother	9

flocked.

thither ƒ at noon His tenants, .	Princess, Pro.	3

flood (s.)

They past into the level ƒ, .	Miller's D.	75
spouted forth A ƒ of fountain-foam.	Pal. of Art	24
From the westward-winding ƒ, .	Margaret	9
takes the ƒ With swarthy webs. .	M. d'Arthur	268
the ƒ drew; yet I caught her; .	Princess, iv.	164
died and spilt our bones in the ƒ—	"	511
Their pretty maids in the runningƒ,	" v.	372
Thro' prosperous ƒ's his holy urn	In Mem. ix.	8
Summer on the steaming ƒ's, .	" lxxxiv.	69
shadowing down the horned ƒ .	" lxxxv.	7
At anchor in the ƒ below, . .	" cii.	20
roll'd the ƒ's in grander space, .	" cxxvi.	26
molten up, and roar in ƒ; .	" cxxvi.	13
No doubt vast eddies in the ƒ .	" cxxvii.	5
used to take me with the ƒ .	Elaine	1031
far up the shining ƒ Until we found	"	1037
I was all alone upon the ƒ, .	"	1040
Beyond the poplar and far up the ƒ,	"	1044
the dumb went upward with the ƒ—	"	1148
his passions all inƒ And masters .	Aylmer's F.	339
Bore down in ƒ, and dash'd .	"	633
ƒ, fire, earthquake, thunder, .	"	639
sands and steaming flats, and ƒ's .	The Voyage	45
whiten'd all the rolling ƒ; .	The Victim	20

flood (verb.)

F's all the deep-blue gloom .	D. of F. Wom.	186
F with full daylight glebe and .	Two Voices	87
burst and ƒ the world with foam: .	Princess, iv.	453
ƒa fresher throat with song. .	In Mem. lxxxii.	16
ƒthe haunts of hern and crake; .	" c.	14
filth that ƒ's the middle street .	Vivien	647

flooded.

Wereƒ over with eddying song .	Dying Swan	42
before his time And ƒ at our nod.	D. of F. Wom.	144
beyond his limit, And all was ƒ; .	The Daisy	72
ƒ with the helpless wrath of tears,	En. Arden .	32

floor.

Old footsteps trod the upper ƒ's .	Mariana	67
Flung inward over spangled ƒ's, .	Arabian N's.	116
meal-sacks on the whiten'd ƒ, .	Miller's D.	101
garden-tables upon the granary ƒ:	May Queen, ii.	45
waves Of sound on roof and ƒ .	D. of F. Wom.	192
There's a new foot on the ƒ, .	D. of the O. Year	57
head and heels upon the ƒ .	The Goose	37
All heaven bursts her starry ƒ's .	St Agnes' Eve	27
cease To pace the gritted ƒ, .	Will Water.	242
plank and beam for roof and ƒ, .	Princess, vi.	30
Throbb'd thunder thro' the palace ƒ's,	" vii.	89
crash'd the glass and beat the ƒ: .	In Mem. lxxxvi.	20
Witch-elms that counterchange the ƒ	" lxxxviii.	1
let no footstep beat the ƒ, .	" civ.	17
russet-bearded head roll'd on the ƒ.	Enid	1517
wild passion out against the ƒ .	Elaine	738
she slipt like water to the ƒ. .	"	826
grovell'd with her face against the ƒ:	Guinevere	412

Flora.

hues to dim The Titanic F..	Gardener's D.	167
O, Lady F, let me speak: .	Day-Dm.	1
So, Lady F, take my lay, . .	"	197, 269

Florence.

Abroad, at F, at Rome, . .	Maud, I. xix.	58
'Poor lad, he died at F, . .	The Brook	35
At F too what golden hours, .	The Daisy	41

K

146   CONCORDANCE TO

	POEM.	LINE.
I stood With Cyril and with *F*,	*Princess*, i.	51
from court With Cyril and with *F*,	"	102
F, but no livelier than the dame,	" ii.	97
fifth in line from that old *F*,	"	220
loyal warmth of *F* is not cold	"	226
pacing till she paused By *F*;	"	283
sad and glad To see you, *F*.	"	288
What think you of it, *F* ?	"	386
murmur'd *F* gazing after her.	" iii.	81
Cyril kept With Psyche, with Melissa *F*,	"	337
F nodded at him, I frowning ;	" iv.	141
Alone I stood With *F*, cursing Cyril,	"	153
'if this were the' But it was *F*.	"	199
melted *F*'s fancy as she hung,	"	351
Then *F* knelt, and 'Come' he whisper'd	" v.	60
F, he That loved me closer	"	519
'Your brother, —*F*,—ask	" vi.	293
But Psyche tended *F* :.	" vii.	40

florid.

| *f*, stern, as far as eye could see, | *Sea Dreams* | 212 |

flounce.

| dimpled *f* of the sea-furbelow flap, | *Sea Dreams* | 257 |

flounder.

| to move, And *f* into hornpipes. | *Amphion* | 24 |
| *f* awhile without a tumble | *Hendecasyllabics* | 9 |

floundered.

| They *f* all together, | *The Goose* | 38 |

flour.

| *f* From his tall mill | *En. Arden* | 339 |

flourish (s.)

| In the mid might and *f* of his May, | *Elaine* | 553 |

flourish (verb.)

O *f* high, with leafy towers,	*Talking O.*	197
O *f*, hidden deep in fern,	"	201
life in him Could scarce be said to *f*,	*The Brook*	12
f'es Green in a cuplike hollow	*En. Arden*	8
Out of evil evil *f*'es,	*Boädicea*	83

flourish'd.

From all a closer interest *f* up,	*Princess*, vii.	98
f then or then ; but life in him	*The Brook*	11
F a little garden square	*En. Arden*	735

flout.

| put your beauty to this *f* and scorn *Enid* . | | 1523 |

flow (s.)

silver *f* Of subtle-paced counsel	*Isabel*	20
Down from the central fountain's *f*	*Arabian N's.*	50
sonorous *f* Of spouted fountain-floods.	*Pal. of Art*	27
f Of music left the lips of her	*D. of F. Woman*	194
ebb and *f* conditioning their march,	*Golden Year*	30
rock in ebbs and *f*'s Fixt on her faith.	*Enid*	812

flow (verb.)

All night the silence seems to *f*,	*Oriana*	86
now thy beauty *f*'s away,	*Mariana in the S.*	67
Motions *f* To one another	*Eleänore*	61
There's somewhat *f*'s to us in life,	*Miller's D.*	21
saw the gleaming river seaward *f*,	*Lotos-E's.*	14
According to my humour ebb and *f*.	*D. of F. Wom.*	134
dared to *f* In these words toward you,	*To J. S.*	5
such tears As *f* but once a life.	*Love and Duty*	63
F down, cold rivulet, to the sea,	*A Farewell*	1
F, softly *f*, by lawn and lea,	"	"
great name *f* on with broadening time	*Princess*, iii.	148
tide *f*'s down, The wave again is	*In Mem.* xix.	12
The double tides of chariots *f*	" xcvii.	23
The hills are shadows, and they *f*	" cxxii.	5
F thro' our deeds and make them pure,	" cxxx.	4
all we *f* from, soul in soul.	"	12
Till last by Philip's farm I *f*	*The Brook*	31
f To join the brimming river (rep. 63 182)	"	47
let the turbid streams of rumour *f*	*Ode on Well.*	181
they do not *f* From evil done ;	*Guinevere*	186
the valley, where thy waters *f*,	*V. of Cauteretz*	3

flowed.

tide of time *f* back with me,	*Arabian N's.*	3
f upon the soul in many dreams.	*The Poet*	31
Rare sunrise *f*.	"	36

	POEM.	LINE.
F forth on a carol free and bold ;	*Dying Swan*	30
From underneath his helmet *f*	*L. of Shalott*, iii.	30
o'er him *f* a golden cloud,	*Œnone*	103
Thus far he *f*, and ended ;	*Golden Year*	52
dream and truth *F* from me ;	*Princess*, v.	531
by and by the town *F* in	*Enid*	546
Fast *f* the current of her easy tears,	*En. Arden*	866
(possibly He *f* and ebb'd uncertain,	*Aylmer's F.*	218
mother *f* in shallower acrimonies;	"	563
when the preacher's cadence *f* Softening	"	729
Bloodily *f* the Tamesa rolling	*Boädicea*	27

flower (s.)

The stately *f* of female fortitude,	*Isabel*	11
In order, eastern *f*'s large,	*Arabian N's.*	61
diaper'd With inwrought *f*'s	"	149
peerless *f*'s which in the rudest wind	*Ode to Mem.*	24
sweet showers Of festal *f*'s,	"	78
stalks Of the mouldering *f*'s : 'A spirit haunts,' etc.		8
grew A *f* all gold,	*The Poet*	24
pour Into every spicy *f*	*Poet's Mind*	13
f's would faint at your cruel cheer.	"	15
Overlook a space of *f*'s,	*L. of Shalott*, i.	16
many a deep-hued bell-like *f*	*Eleänore*	37
you were gay With bridal *f*'s—	*Miller's D.*	165
I roll'd among the tender *f*'s :	*Fatima*	11
midway down Hang rich in *f*'s	*Œnone*	7
The purple *f*'s droop : the golden bee	"	28
and berry and *f* thro' and thro',	"	100
A simple maiden in her *f*	*L. C. V. de Vere*	15
I must gather knots of *f*'s	*May Queen*, i.	11
Last May we made a crown of *f*'s :	" ii.	9
There's not a *f* on all the hills :	"	13
I long to see a *f* so	"	16
When the *f*'s come again, mother,	"	25
land about, and all the *f*'s that blow,	" iii.	7
Wild *f*'s in the valley for other hands	"	52
enchanted stem, Laden with fruit and *f*,	*Lotos-E's.*	29
in the stream the long-leaved *f*'s weep,	"	55
The *f* ripens in its place,	"	81
I knew the *f*'s, I knew the leaves,	*D. of F. Wom.*	73
Feeding the *f* ; but ere my *f* to fruit	"	207
shadow of the *f*'s Stole all the golden	*Gardener's D.*	128
Each garlanded with her peculiar *f*	"	197
made a little wreath of all the *f*'s	*Dora*	80
wreath of *f*'s fell At Dora's feet.	"	100
of eloquence Stored from all *f*'s ?	*Ed. Morris*	27
The *f* of each, those moments when	"	69
Proserpine in Enna, gathering *f*'s :	"	112
bring me offerings of fruit and *f*'s :	*St S. Stylites*	126
The *f*, she touch'd on, dipt and rose,	*Talking O.*	131
f of knowledge changed to fruit	*Love and Duty*	24
Live happy ; tend thy *f*'s,	"	84
About the opening of *f*'s.	*Two Voices*	161
scarce could see the grass for *f*'s.	"	453
the *f* and quintessence of change.	*Day-Dm.*	236
burst In carol, every bud to *f*	"	256
Perfume and *f*'s fall in showers,	*Sir Galahad*	11
That are the *f* of the earth ?'	*Lady Clare*	68
What ! the *f* of life is past ;	*Vision of Sin*	69
F's of all heavens, and lovelier	*Princess, Pro.*	12
Laid it on *f*'s, and watch'd it	" i.	92
and with great urns of *f*'s.	" ii.	8
the bird, the fish, the shell, the *f*,	"	361
long hall glitter'd like a bed of *f*'s.	"	416
Fluctuated, as *f*'s in storm,	" iv.	461
Remembering her mother : O my *f* !	" v.	86
household *f* Torn from the lintel—	"	122
of the Prince, trampling the *f*'s	"	237
I take her for the *f* of womankind,	"	277
Their feet in *f*'s, their loveliest :	" vi.	62
With books, with *f*'s, with Angel	" vii.	126
like a *f* that cannot all unfold,	"	126
The seasons bring the *f* again,	*In Mem.* ii.	7
A *f* beat with rain and wind,	" viii.	15
This poor *f* of poesy	"	19
From *f* to *f*, from snow to snow :	" xxii.	4
Be all the colour of the *f*:	" xlii.	8
The path we came by, thorn and *f*,	" xlv.	2
The perfect *f* of human time ;	" lx.	4
Made cypress of her orange *f*,	" lxxxiii.	15

	POEM.	LINE.
brushing ankle-deep in *f*'s,	*In Mem.* lxxxviii.	49
Day, when I lost the *f* of men ;	„ xcviii.	4
The time admits not *f*'s or leaves	„ cvi.	5
f And native growth of noble mind ;	„ cx.	15
tho' I seem in star and *f*	„ cxxix.	6
But where is she, the bridal *f*,	*Con.*	25
weight Of learning lightly like a *f*.	„	40
pelt us in the porch with *f*'s.	„	68
seed Of what in them is *f* and fruit ;	„	136
Beauty fair in her *f*;	*Maud*, I. iv.	25
To the *f*'s, and be their sun.	„ xxii.	58
For a shell, or a *f*, little things	„ II. ii.	64
On the little *f* that clings	„ iv.	33
It is only *f*'s, they had no fruits,	„ v.	77
the white *f* of a blameless life,	*Ded. of Idylls*	24
like a crag was gay with wilding *f*'s: *Enid*		319
Gwydion made by glamour out of *f*'s, „		743
Betwixt the cressy islets white in *f*; „		1324
noble deeds, the *f* of all the world. *Vivien*		263
'to pluck the *f* in season ;'	„	572
A border fantasy of branch and *f*, *Elaine*		11
Lancelot, the *f* of bravery,	„	114
The *f* of all the west	„	249
So saying from the carven *f* above,	„	548
if I bide, lo! this wild *f* for me !'	„	641
For pleasure all about a field of *f*'s:	„	789
the victim's *f*'s before he fall.'	„	906
when you yield your *f* of life	„	948
dashing down on a tall wayside *f*, *Guinevere*		251
A glorious company, the *f* of men,	„	461
robed your cottage-walls with *f*'s *Aylmer's F.*		698
my eldest-born, the *f* of the flock : *Grandmother*		9
little Annie, *f* and thorn.	„	60
my beauty, my eldest-born, my *f*;	„	101
we nor paused for fruit nor *f*'s.	*The Voyage*	56
Up there came a *f*,	*The Flower*	
Cursed me and my *f*,	„	8
people cried 'Splendid is the *f*.'	„	16
Most can raise the *f*'s now,	„	19
Break, happy land, into earlier *f*'s. *W. to Alexan.*		10
in our winter woodland looks a *f*. *A Dedication*		13
heart voice amid the blaze of *f*'s: *Lucretius*		101
Crown'd with a *f* or two,	„	226
bird or fish, or opulent *f* —	„	245
All of *f*'s, and drop me a *f*, (rep.) . *The Window*		26
Cannot a *f*, a *f* be mine,	„	29
Drop me a *f*, a *f* to kiss	„	31
her bower, All of *f*'s, a *f*, a *f* Dropt a *f*. „		33

flower (verb.)

white as privet when it *f*'s.	*Walk. to the M.*	48
as poets' seasons when they *f*,	*Golden Year*	28

flowerage.

| Busying themselves about the *f* | *Aylmer's F.* | 203 |

flower-bells.

| cluster'd *f-b* and ambrosial orbs | *Isabel* | 36 |

flowered.

| All branch'd and *f* with gold, | *Enid* | 631 |

flowering.

| *f* high, the last night's gale had | *Gardener's D.* | 123 |

flower-pot.

| With blackest moss the *f-p*'s . | *Mariana* | 1 |

flower-sheath.

| lightly breaks a faded *f-s*, | *Enid* | 365 |

flowery.

| course of life that seem'd so *f* to me *Vivien* | | 729 |

floweth.

| From thy rose-red lips MY name *F*; *Eleänore* | | 134 |

flowing.

clear stream *f* with a muddy one, *Isabel*		30
f rapidly between Their interspaces, *Arabian N's.*		83
F beneath her rose-hued zone ;	„	140
music *f* from The illimitable years. *Ode to Mem.*		41
F like a crystal river ;	*Poet's Mind*	6
Winds were blowing, waters *f*, *Oriana*		14
F down to Camelot.	*L. of Shalott*, i.	14
The rapt oration *f* free,	*In Mem.* lxxxvi.	32

	POEM.	LINE.
blood Of their strong bodies, *f*,	*Enid*	569
canvas *f*, Rose a ship of France,	*The Captain*	27
My tears, no tears of love, are *f*	*Coquette*, iii.	7
Seas at my feet were *f*, .	*1865–1866*	10

flown.

as tho' it were The hour just *f*,	*Gardener's D.*	82
horse with wings, that would have *f*, *Vision of Sin*		3
tell her, Swallow, that thy brood is *f*: *Princess*, iv.		90
in the summers that are *f*,	*In Mem. Con.*	18
the black bat, night, has *f*,	*Maud*, I. xxii.	2
as the cageling newly *f* returns,	*Vivien*	750
Had tost his ball and *f* his kite,	*Aylmer's F.*	84
F to the east or the west,	*The Window*	41

floy (fly.)

| a knaws naw moor nor a *f*; | *N. Farmer* | 67 |

fluctuate.

| And *f* all the still perfume, | *In Mem.* xciv. | 56 |

fluctuated.

| *F*, as flowers in storm ; Some red, *Princess*, iv. | | 461 |

fluctuation.

| columns drown'd In silken *f* | *Princess*, vi. | 335 |
| world-wide *f* sway'd In vassal tides *In Mem.* cxi. | | 15 |

flue.

| a blast of sparkles up the *f*: . | *M. d'Arthur, Ep.* | 15 |

fluke.

| Anchors of rusty *f*, and boats updrawn *En. Arden* | | 18 |

flung.

costly doors *f* open wide,	*Arabian N's.*	17
F inward over spangled floors,	„	116
Backward the lattice-blind she *f*, *Mariana in the S.*		27
Then with both hands I *f* him,	*M. d'Arthur*	157
And *f* him in the dew.	*Talking O.*	232
F the torrent rainbow round :	*Vision of Sin*	32
F ball, flew kite, and raced the purple *Princess*, ii.		230
she *f* it. 'Fight' she said,	„ iv.	575
f defiance down Gagelike to man,	„ v.	170
She *f* it from her, thinking : .	„ *Con.*	32
f A ballad to the brightening moon: *In Mem.* lxxxviii.		27
f The lilies to and fro,	„ xciv.	59
he *f* n wrathful answer back :	*Enid*	995
f herself Down on the great King's *Elaine*		606
Unclasping the casement back,	„	975
F them, and down they flash'd,	„	1228
f One arm about his neck,	„	1345
f her down upon a couch of fire, . *Aylmer's F.*		574
His body half *f* forward in pursuit,	„	587

Flur.

| *F*, for whose love the Roman Cæsar *Enid* | | 745 |

flush (s.)

The *f* of anger'd shame.	*Madeline*	32
here a sudden *f* of wrathful heat	*Guinevere*	354
when the morning *f* Of passion	*Lucretius*	2

flush (verb.)

the brain And *f*'es all the cheek.	*D. of F. Wom.*	44
the colour *f*'es Her sweet face	*L. of Burleigh*	61
by denial *f* her babbling wells	*Princess*, v.	324
f'es up in the ruffian's head,	*Maud*, I. i.	37
his books, to *f* his blood with air,	*Aylmer's F.*	459

flushed.

Fall the leaves with rich gold-green, *Arabian N's.*		82
F like the coming of the day :	*Miller's D.*	132
F in her temples and her eyes,	*Pal. of Art*	170
Then *f* her cheek with rosy light,.	*Talking O.*	165
Psyche *f* and wann'd and shook :	*Princess*, iv.	142
first she came, all *f* you said to me	„ vi.	233
her face A little *f*, and she past on ;	„ vii.	66
Where oleanders *f* the bed	*The Daisy*	33
f with fight, or hot, God's truth,	*Enid*	1508
that other *f*, And hung his head,	„	1658
Upright and *f* before him :	*Vivien*	761
F slightly at the slight disparagement *Elaine*		234

flushing.

| rosy red *f* in the northern night. | *Locksley H.* | 26 |
| *f* the guiltless air, Spout | *Lucretius* | 236 |

CONCORDANCE TO

flustered. POEM. LINE.
them by the score Flatter'd and *f*, . *Princess*, v. 157
once in life was *f* with new wine, . *Vivien* . 606
him that *f* his poor parish wits . *Aylmer's F.* 521

flute (s.)
Blow, *f*, and stir the stiff-set sprigs, *Amphion* . 63
rang To many a *f* of Arcady. . *In Mem.* xxiii. 24
Nor harp be touch'd, nor *f* be blown ; " civ. 22
heard The *f*, violin, bassoon ; . *Maud*, I. xxii. 14
sound of dancing music and *f's*: . " II. v. 76

flute (verb.)
That lute and *f* fantastic tenderness, *Princess*, iv. 111

fluted.
mellow ouzel *f* in the elm ; . . *Gardener's D.* 93
f to the morning sea. . . . *To E. L.* . 24

flute-notes.
thy *f-n* are changed to coarse, . *The Blackbird* 18

fluting.
f a wild carol ere her death, . *M. d'Arthur* 267

flutter.
His spirit *f's* like a lark, . . *Day-Dm.* . 129
Wings *f*, voices hover clear: . *Sir Galahad* 78
There *f's* up a happy thought, . *In Mem.* lxiv. 7
The tender blossom *f* down, . " c. 2
Flags, *f* out upon turrets and towers ! *IV. to Alexan.* 15
heart within her fall and *f* tremulously, *Boädicea* 81

fluttered.
F about my senses and my soul, . *Gardener's D.* 66
A second *f* round her lip . . *Talking O.* , 219
melody *F* headlong from the sky. *Vision of Sin* 45
A little *f*, with her eyelids down, . *The Brook* . 89
there *f* in, Half-bold, half-frighted, *Enid* . 1444

fluttering (part.)
voice Faltering and *f* in her throat, *Princess*, ii. 170

fluttering (s.)
I watch'd the little *f's*, . . *Miller's D.* . 153

fly (s.)
The blue *f* sung in the pane: . *Mariana* . 63
flew kite, and raced the purple *f*, . *Princess*, ii 230
In lieu of many mortal *flies*, . " iii. 251
men the *flies* of latter spring *In Mem.* xlix. 10
tender over drowning *flies*, . . " xcv. 3
head in a cloud of poisonous *flies*. *Maud*, I. iv. 54
call'd herself a gilded summer *f* . *Vivien* . 107
since you name yourself the summer *f*, " . 219
Like *flies* that haunt a wound, . *Aylmer's F.* 571
the life of the worm and the *f*? . *Wages* . 7
bees are still'd and the *flies* are kill'd, *The Window* 52

fly (verb.)
Then away she *flies*. . . . *Lilian* . 18
whither away? *f* no more. . . *Sea-Fairies* 7, 42
rainbow forms and *flies* on the land " . 25
Reverence, *f* Before her ' *Love thou thy land*,' etc. 18
ingrowe itself with that, which *flies*, " . 46
Sun *flies* forward to his brother Sun : *Golden Year* 23
F, happy, happy sails and bear the Press : " . 42
F, happy with the mission of the Cross ; " . 43
Here sits he shaping wings to *f* : . *Two Voices* 289
order'd words asunder *f*. . . *Day-Dm.* . 20
The colour *flies* into his cheeks : . " . 119
splinter'd spear-shafts crack and *f*. *Sir Galahad* 7
F o'er waste fens and windy fields. " . 60
f, like a bird, from tree to tree : . *Ed. Gray* . 30
The truth, that *flies* the flowing can, *Will Water.* 171
to *f* sublime Thro' the courts, . *Vision of Sin* 103
F twanging headless arrows. . *Princess*, ii. 380
f' she cried, 'O *f*, while yet you may! " iii. 12
may yet be saved, and therefore *f*: " . 48
As *flies* the shadow of a bird, . " . 80
F to her, and fall upon her gilded eaves, " iv. 76
F to her, and pipe and woo her, . " . 97
as *flies* A troop of snowy doves . " . 149
some sense of shame, she *flies* ; . " . 330
She *flies* too high, she *flies* too high! " v. 271-6
As *flies* the lighter thro' the gross. *In Mem.* xl. 4
Ill brethren, let the fancy *f*, . " lxxxv. 12

Fiercely *flies* The blast of North *In Mem.* cvi. 6
f The happy birds, that change . " cxiv. 14
Arise and *f* The reeling Faun, . " cxvii. 25
Wild Hours that *f* with Hope and Fear, " cxxvii. 9
fault was mine,' he whisper'd, '*f*!' *Maud*, II. i. 30
saw the dreary phantom arise and *f* " III. vi. 36
wildly *f*, Mixt with the flyers. . *Enid* . 1331
'*F*, they will return And slay you ; " . 1596
f, your charger is without . . " . 1597
When did not rumours *f*? . . *Elaine* . 1188
f to my strong castle overseas: . *Guinevere* . 112
yet rise now, and let us *f*, . . " . 119
Stands in a wind, ready to break and *f*, " . 363
crippled lad, and coming turn'd to *f*, *Aylmer's F.* 519
Let me *f*, says little birdie, (rep.) *Sea Dreams* 283
We follow that which *flies* before : *The Voyage* 94
F on to clash together again, . *Lucretius* . 41
glory *f* along the Italian field, . " . 71
do they *f* Now thinner, and now thicker " . 165
soul *flies* out and dies in the air.' " . 270
The lights and shadows *f*! . . *The Window* 1
F little letter, apace, apace, . " . 98
to the light in the valley *f*, (rep.) " . 99

flyer.
all *f's* from the hand Of justice, . *Enid* . 36
wildly fly, Mixt with the *f's*. . " . 1331
arms stretch'd as to grasp a *f*: . *Aylmer's F.* 588

flying.
fled by night, and *f* turn'd ; . . *Ed. Morris* 134
Dreary gleams of moorland *f* . *Locksley H.* 4
in the *f* of a wheel Cry down the past, *Godiva* . 6
we dropt, And *f* reach'd the frontier : *Princess*, i. 108
your arrow-wounded fawn Came *f* " ii. 252
not see The bird of passage *f* south " iii. 194
blow, set the wild echoes *f*, . . " . 352-64
O Swallow, Swallow, *f*, *f* South, . " iv. 75
O Swallow, *f* from the golden woods, " . 96
f on the highest Foam of men's deeds— " v. 309
f struck With showers of random sweet " vii. 70
F along the land and the main—. *Maud*, II. ii. 38
Comes *f* over many a windy wave *Enid* . 337
white sails *f* on the yellow sea ; . " . 829
F, but, overtaken, died the death " . 1026
f from the wrath of Doorm . . " . 1379
f back and crying out, 'O Merlin, *Vivien* . 792
hear of rumours *f* thro' your court. *Elaine* . 1184
A blot in heaven, the Raven, *f* high, *Guinevere* 132
wheel'd and broke *F*, (rep.) . . " . 256
following up And *f* the white breaker, *En. Arden* 21
Or *f* shone, the silver boss . . *The Voyage* 31
Paid with a voice *f* by to be lost . *Wages* . 2
are you *f* over her sweet little face? *The Window* 13
and birds' song *F* here and there, " . 63

foam (s.)
the green brink and the running *f* *Sea-Fairies* 2
When the wind blows the *f*, . . *Œnone* . 61
Aphrodite beautiful Fresh as the *f*, . " . 171
Rolling a slumbrous sheet of *f* helow. *Lotos-E's.* 13
the wandering fields of barren *f*. . " . 42
the white cold heavy-plunging *f*, *D. of F. Wom.* 118
Shrill, chill, with flakes of *f*, . *M. d'Arthur* 49
burst and flood the world with *f*: *Princess*, iv. 453
on the highest *F* of men's deeds— " v. 310
from the three-decker out of the *f*, *Maud*, I. i. 50
tremulously as *f* upon the beach . *Guinevere* . 362
in the chasm are *f* and yellow sands ; *En. Arden* 2
scaled in sheets of wasteful *f*, . *Sea Dreams* 53

foam (verb.)
forward-creeping tides Began to *f*, *In Mem.* cii. 38
Should all our churchmen *f* in spite *To F. D. Maurice* 9

foam-bow.
cheek brighten'd as the *f-b* brightens *Œnone* . 60

foamed.
surging charges *f* themselves away ; *Ode on Well.* 126
f away his heart at Averill's ear ; . *Aylmer's F.* 342

foam-fountains.
monster spouted his *f-f* in the sea. *Lotos-E's.* . 152

	POEM.	LINE.		POEM.	LINE.
foam-flakes.			*foliage.*		
Crisp *f.-f* scud along the level sand,	*D. of F. Wom.*	39	rustling thro' The low and bloomed *f,*	*Arabian N.'s.*	13
foe.			blown about the *f* underneath	*Princess,* iii.	105
tho' his *f's* speak ill of him,	*D. of the O. Year*	22	all thy breadth and height Of *f,*	*In Mem.*lxxxviii.	4
where girt with friends or *f's* 'You ask me why,' etc.		7	*folk.*		
ever shock, like armed *f's,* 'Love thou thy land,' etc.		78	slay the *f,* and spoil the land.'	*Guinevere*	136
Had beat her *f's* with slaughter	*Princess,Pro.*	34,123	*f* that knew not their own minds	*En. Arden.*	475
The next, like fire he meets the *f,*	"	iv. 560	*follow.*		
The general *f.* More soluble is	"	v. 129	lightning to the thunder Which *f's* it,	*The Poet*	51
Truest friend and noblest *f;*	.	. 538	because right is right, to *f* right	*Œnone*	147
those two *f's* above my fallen life,	"	vi. 114	To *f* flying steps of Truth 'Love thou thy land,' etc.		75
friend or *f,* Shall enter, if he will.	.	316	good should *f* this, if this were done?	*M. d' Arthur*	92
Friend, to be struck by the public *f,*	*Maud,* II. v.	89	dark Earth *f's* wheel'd in her ellipse;	*Golden Year*	24
His *f's* were thine ; he kept us free ;	*Ode on Well.*	91	*f* knowledge like a sinking star,	*Ulysses*	31
England pouring on her *f's.*	"	117	The vine stream'd out to *f,*	*Amphion*	46
Who never spoke against a *f,*	.	185	May my soul *f* soon !	*StAgnes'Eve*	4
was your *f,* the sparrow-hawk,	*Enid*	. 444	The rest would *f,* each in turn ;	*Princess,*Pro.	197
they long for, good in friend or *f,*	"	1724	'Then *f* me, the Prince,' I answer'd,	"	220
no friend who never made a *f.*	*Elaine*	1083	Voice Went with it, '*F, f,* thou shalt win.'	i.	99
hold that man the worst of public *f's*	*Guinevere*	. 508	land Of promise ; fruit would *f,*	" ii.	124
divine to warn them of their *f's:*	*Sea Dreams*	69	If more and acted on, what *f's?*	"	211
Till she near'd the *f.*	*The Captain*	36	Whence *f's* many a vacant pang ;	"	381
warrior father meets the *f,* 'Lady, let the rolling,'		7	flying south but long'd To *f:*	" iii.	195
on them brake the sudden *f;*	*The Victim*	4	O Swallow, Swallow, if I could *f,*	" iv.	81
foeman.			tell her, tell her, that I *f* thee.	"	98
forth there stept a *f* tall,	*Oriana*	33	I cannot cease to *f* you,	"	435
perish, falling on the *f's* ground,	*Locksley H.*	103	To *f* up the worthiest till he die :	"	446
What time the *f's* line is broke,	*Two Voices*	155	*F* us : who knows? we four may build	" v.	221
foemen scared, like that false pair	*Enid*	. 1025	on the '*F, f,* thou shalt win.'	"	461
But they heard the *f's* thunder	*The Captain*	41	*f* : let the torrent dance thee down	" vii.	194
still the *f* spoil'd and burn'd,	*The Victim*	17	welcome for the year To *f:*	*Con.*	96
fold (doubling, etc.)			Nor *f,* tho' I walk in haste,	*In Mem.*xxii.	18
Down-droop'd, in many a floating *f,*	*Arabian N's.*	147	Prince, as Enid past him, fain To *f,*	*Enid*	376
In silk-soft *f's,* upon yielding down,	*Eleänore*	28	when the knight besought him, '*F* me,	"	1655
Winds all the vale in rosy *f's,*	*Miller's D.*	242	'Enough,' he said, '*I, f,*' and they went.	"	1664
misty *f's,* that floating as they fell	*Pal. of Art*	35	Fame that *f's* death is nothing	*Vivien*	314
Look up, the *f* is on her brow.	*Two Voices*	192	the scroll '*I f* fame.'	"	326
detaching, *f* by *f,* From those still	*Vision of Sin*	51	I charge you, *f* me not.'	*Elaine*	506
drowsy *f's* of our great ensign shake	*Princess,* v.	8	serve you, and to *f* you thro' the	"	935
With *f* to *f,* of mountain or of cape ;	" vi.	366	fain would *f* love, if that could be ;	"	1010
wrapt these formless in the *f,*	*In Mem.* xxii.	15	I needs must *f* death,	"	1011
f upon *f* of hueless cloud,	*Maud,* I. vi.	3	Call and *I f, I f !* let me die.'	"	1012
Dark in its funeral *f.*	*Ode on Well.*	57	might she *f* me thro' the world,	"	1306
sprigs of summer laid between the *f's,*	*Enid*	. 138	*f* Such dear familiarities	*Aylmer's F.*	130
knots and loops and *f's* innumerable	*Elaine*	438	One who cried 'leave all and *f* me.'	"	664
Enwound him *f* by *f,* and made him	*Guinevere*	. 597	thin weasel there *F's* the mouse,	"	853
f's as dense as those Which hid	*Aylmer's F.*	772	I *f* till I make thee mine.'	*The Voyage*	64
fold (enclosure.)			We *f* that which flies before :	"	94
thick-fleeced sheep from wattled *f's,*	*Ode to Mem.*	66	which all our greatest fain Would *f,*	*Lucretius*	79
that somewhere in the ruin'd *f's,*	*Œnone*	. 217	Not *f* the great law ?	"	116
who are these ? a wolf within the *f !*	*Princess,* ii.	173	A satyr, a satyr, see—*F's* ;	"	190
Far off from men I built a *f.*	" v.	380	*F, f,* the chase !	*The Window*	11
No gray old grange, or lonely *f,*	*In Mem.* xcix.	5	*F* them down the slope.	"	16
some black wether of St Satan's *f.*	*Vivien*	. 600	*f* them down to the window-pane.	"	17
brand us, after, of whose *f* we be :	"	614	*followed.*		
very whitest lamb in all my *f.*	*Aylmer's F.*	361	surer sign had *f,*	*M. d'Arthur,*	76
fold (verb.)			Then *f* counsel, comfort,	*Love and Duty*	67
F thy palms across thy breast,	*A Dirge*	2	The happy princess *f* him.	*Day-Dm.*	172
F thine arms, turn to thy rest.	"	3	Thro' all the world she *f* him.	"	196
the green that *f's* thy grave	" 6, *et pass.*		And *f* with acclaims,	*Will Water.*	138
f our wings, And cease from	*Lotos-E's.*	64	And *f* her all the way.	*Lady Clare*	64
sure this orbit of the memory *f's*	*Gardener's D.*	73	I began, And the rest *f:*	*Princess,*Pro.	236
The berried briony *f.*	*Talking O.*	148	We *f* up the river as we rode,	" i.	203
High up the vapours *f* and swim	*Two Voices*	262	*f* then A classic lecture,	" ii.	251
round her waist she felt it *f,*	*Day-Dm.*	166	resolder'd pence, whereon *F* his tale.	" v.	46
f's the lily all her sweetness up,	*Princess,*vii.	171	but Blanche At distance *f:*	" vi.	67
f thyself, my dearest, thou	"	173	*f* up by a hundred airy does.	"	71
folded.			tears *F;* the king replied not :	"	292
Thought *f* over thought, smiling.	*Eleänore*	. 84	silence *f,* and we wept.	*In Mem.*xxx.	20
Sleep, Ellen, *f* in thy sister's arm,	*Audley Ct.*	. 1	vassal tides that *f* thought.	" cxi.	16
sleep, Ellen, *f* in Emilia's arm,	"	64	when they *f* us from Philip's door,	*The Brook*	167
His palms are *f* on his breast ;	*Two Voices*	247	*F* up in valley and glen	*Ode on Well.*	114
To spirits *f* in the womb.	*Day-Dm.*	28	*F* by the brave of other lands,	"	194
on her palms and *f* up from wrong,	*Princess,* iv.	269	He *f* nearer ; ruth began to work	*Enid.*	950
Is pealing, *f* in the mist.	*In Mem.*ciii.	6	He *f* nearer still ; the pain she had	"	1035
to be *f* more in these dear arms,	*Enid*	. 99	overthrew the next that *f* him,	"	1314
Wherein she kept them *f* reverently	"	. 137	His lusty spearmen *f* him with noise :	"	1441
which being writ And *f*	*Elaine*	1104	Vivien *f,* but he mark'd her not.	*Vivien*	48
			then she *f* Merlin all the way	"	52
			Dear feet, that I have *f* thro' the world,	"	76

150 CONCORDANCE TO

	POEM.	LINE.
You *f* me unask'd ;	*Vivien*	147
stammering cracks and claps That *f*,	"	792
Then *f* calms, and then winds variable,	*En. Arden*	541
Aylmer *f* Aylmer at the Hall	*Aylmer's F.*	36
the fierce old man *F*,	"	331
Seconded, for my lady *f* suit,	"	558
f out Tall and erect,	"	817
I *f*: and at top She pointed seaward :	*Sea Dreams*	117
still we *f* where she led,	*The Voyage*	59, 90
day that *f* the day she was wed,	*The Islet*	4

follower.

at her head a *f* of the camp,	*Princess*, v.	57
my *f*'s ring him round :	*Enid*	1185
With all his rout of random *f*'s,	"	1231
Went Enid with her sullen *f* on.	"	1289
In combat with the *f* of Limours,	"	1350
tho' thou numberest with the *f*'s	*Aylmer's F.*	663

following.

f her dark eyes, Felt earth as air,	*Gardener's D.*	206
f thro' the porch that sang	*Princess*, ii.	8
in long retinue *f* up The river ;	" iii.	179
ever *f* those two crowned twins,	" v.	410
As we descended *f* Hope,	*In Mem.* xxii.	11
f with an upward mind.	" xl.	21
f our own shadows thrice as long.	*The Brook*	166
He, that ever *f* her commands,	*Ode on Well.*	211
with fixt eye *f* the three.	*Enid*	237
youth, that *f* with a costrel bore.	"	386
Let his eye rove in *f*,	"	399
gentle charger *f* him unled) ;	"	1419
I look'd, and saw you *f* still,	*Vivien*	148
fancy when you saw me *f* you,	"	175
f you to this wild wood,	"	290
f these my mightiest knights,	*Guinevere*	485
f up And flying the white breaker,	*En. Arden*	20

folly.

'Ah, *f* !' in mimic cadence answer'd	*Golden Year*	53
'Ah, *f* ! for it lies so far away,	"	54
Fill'd I was with *f* and spite,	*Ed. Gray*	15
others' *follies* teach us not,	*Will Water.*	173
brace Of twins may weed her of her *f*.	*Princess*, v.	454
Deep *f*; yet that this could be—	*In Mem.* xl.	9
in which all spleenful *f* was drown'd,	*Maud*, I. iii.	2
poet is whirl'd into *f* and vice.	" iv.	39
perplext her With his worldly talk and *f*;	" xx.	7
the *f* taking wings Slipt o'er	*Aylmer's F.*	494
I hate the spites and the *follies*.	*Spiteful Let.*	24

fond.

| But O too *f*, when have I answer'd | *Princess*, vi. | 367 |

fonder.

| man of science himself is *f* of glory, | *Maud*, I. iv. | 37 |

fondle.

| rabbit *f*'s his own harmless face, | *Aylmer's F.* | 851 |

fondled.

all this morning when I *f* you :	*Vivien*	135
Appraised his weight and *f* fatherlike,	*En. Arden*	154
Too ragged to be *f* on her lap,	*Aylmer's F.*	686

fondling.

| *f* all her hand in his | *Enid* | 509 |

font.

One rear'd a *f* of stone And drew,	*Princess, Pro.*	59
winks the gold fin in the porphyry *f*:	" vii.	163
Entwine the cold baptismal *f*,	*In Mem.* xxix.	10

food.

| eat wholesome food, And wear | *St S. Stylites* | 106 |
| And wine and food were brought, | *Enid* | 1138 |

fool (s.)

an absent *f*, I cast me down,	*Miller's D.*	62
should mimic this raw *f* the world,	*Walk. to the M.*	96
while we stood like *f*'s Embracing	*Ed. Morris*	118
happy season back,—The more *f*'s	*Golden Year*	66
gilds the straiten'd forehead of the *f*	*Locksley H.*	62
F, again the dream, the fancy !	"	173
Bandied by the hands of *f*'s.	*Vision of Sin*	106
Drink we, last, the public *f*,	"	149
April hopes, the *f*'s of chance ;	"	164

	POEM.	LINE.
(God help her) she was wedded to a *f*;	*Princess*, iii.	67
slaves at home and *f*'s abroad	" iv.	500
'Ah *f*, and made myself a Queen of farce!'	" vii.	228
We are *f*, and slight ;	*In Mem. Pro.*	29
'Thou shalt not be the *f* of loss.'	" iv.	16
O to us The *f*'s of habit,	" x.	12
The *f* that wears a crown of thorns :	" lxviii.	12
They call'd me *f*, they call'd me child :	"	13
and the brazen *f* Was soften'd,	" cix.	11
who but a *f* would have faith	*Maud*, I. i.	26
Is cap and bells for a *f*. .	"	62
F that I am to be vext with his pride !	" xiii.	5
thought like a *f* of the sleep of death.	" xiv.	38
if she be fasten'd to this *f* lord,	" xvi.	24
Struck me before the languid *f*,	" II. i.	19
His party-secret, *f*, to the press ;	" v.	35
sweet faces make good fellows *f*'s	*Enid*	1248
a wanton *f*, Or hasty judger.	"	1281
be he dead, I count you for a *f*;	"	1397
he not crown'd king, coward and *f*.'	*Vivien*	638
shrieking out 'O *f* !' the harlot leapt	"	821
and the forest echo'd '*f*.'	"	823
f's With such a vantage-ground	*Aylmer's F.*	386
Went further, *f* ! and trusted him	*Sea Dreams*	76
bait to trap his dupe and *f*;	"	187
Ah, there's no *f* like the old one—	*Grandmother*	44
but I be lint a *f*:	*N. Farmer.*	3
ship of *f*'s' he shriek'd in spite (rep.)	*The Voyage*	77
'*F*,' he answer'd, 'death is sure	*Sailor Boy*	1
And a *f* may say his say ;	*The Ringlet*	18

fool.

| To *f* the crowd with glorious lies, | *In Mem.* cxxvii. | 14 |

fool'd.

| Ah ! let me not be *f*, sweet saints | *St S. Stylites* | 209 |
| half *f* to let you tend our son, | *Princess*, vi. | 257 |

fooleries.

| these your pretty tricks and *f*, | *Vivien* | 114 |

fool-fury.

| The red *f-f* of the Seine | *In Mem.* cxxvi. | 7 |

foolish.

help thy *f* ones to bear ;	*In Mem. Pro.*	31
whether very wise Or very *f*;	*Enid*	470
I seem so *f* and so broken down.	*En. Arden*	315

foot.

O ! hither lead thy *feet* !	*Ode to Mem.*	64
with echoing *feet* he threaded	*The Poet*	9
curl round my silver *feet* silently,	*The Mermaid*	50
one black shadow at its *feet*,	*Mariana in the S.*	1
at their *feet* the crocus brake	*Œnone*	94
from the violets her light *f* Shone	"	175
laid him at his mother's *feet*.	*The Sisters*	1
With your *feet* above my head	*May Queen*, ii.	32
There's a new *f* on the floor,	*D. of the O. Year*	52
full of rest from head to *feet* :	*To J. S.*	75
breaking at her *feet* :	*'Of old sat Freedom,' etc*	2
feet on juts of slippery crag	*M. d'Arthur*	189
by gold chains about the *feet* of God	"	255
So light of *f*, so light of spirit—	*Gardener's D.*	14
a *f*, that might have danced	"	132
wreath of flowers fell At Dora's *feet*	*Dora*	101
a *f* Lessening in perfect cadence,	*Walk. to the M.*	46
But put your best *f* forward,	"	101
Or when I feel about my *feet*.	*Talking O.*	147
And at my *feet* she lay.	"	208
Balm-dews to bathe thy *feet* !	"	268
choler, and firm upon his *feet*,	*Golden Year*	61
till noon no *f* though we paced the street,	*Godiva*	39
Thy *feet*, millenniums hence, be set	*Two Voices*	89
Touch'd by his *feet* the daisy slept.	"	276
Year after year unto her *f*,	*Day-Dm.*	77
feet that ran, and doors that clapt,	"	135
pluck'd his one *f* from the grave,	*Amphion*	43
With folded *feet*, in stoles of white,	*Sir Galahad*	43
At the *f* of thy crags, O Sea !	*'Break, break,' etc.*	14
lark drop down at his *feet*.	*Poet's Song*	8
stared, with his *f* on the prey,	"	12
tapt her tiny silken-sandal'd *f*:	*Princess, Pro.*	149

	POEM.	LINE.
our cloisters echo'd frosty *feet*,	*Princess*, Pro.	181
started on his *feet*, Tore the king's	" i.	59
of her long hands, And to her *feet*	" ii.	27
if I might sit beside your *feet*,	"	240
her *f* on one Of those tame leopards.	" iii.	164
light *f* shone like a jewel set	"	340
But when we planted level *feet*,	" iv.	12
fleet I was of *f*;	"	244
clasp'd the *feet* of a Mnemosyne,	"	250
mask was patent, and my *f* Was to you;	"	307
flickers where no *f* can tread.'	"	339
the lost lamb at her *feet*	"	372
dash'd Unopen'd at her *feet*:	"	450
lay my little blossom at my *feet*,	" v.	97
iron-camp'd their women's *feet*;	"	366
plant a solid *f* into the Time,	"	405
Their *feet* in flowers, her loveliest;	" vi.	62
Steps with a tender *f*, light as ou air,	"	72
See, your *f* is on our necks,	"	150
on her *f* she hung A moment,	" vii.	64
at her *feet* the volume fell.	"	238
f Is on the skull which thou hast	*In Mem.* Pro.	7
Whereon with equal *feet* we fared;	" xxv.	2
she bathes the Saviour's feet	" xxxii.	11
On thy Parnassus set thy *feet*,	" xxxvii.	6
nothing walks with aimless *feet*;	" liii.	5
feet are guided thro' the land,	" lxv.	9
feet have stray'd in after hours	" ci.	14
feet are set To leave the pleasant	"	21
Her *feet*, my darling, on the dead;	Con.	50
feet like sunny gems on an	*Maud*, I. v.	14
before Her *feet* on the meadow grass,	"	26
solid ground Not fail beneath my *feet*	" xi.	2
her *feet* have touch'd the meadows	" xii.	23
delicate Arab arch of her *feet*	" xvi.	15
light *f* along the garden walk,	" xviii.	9
sets the jewel-print of your *feet*	" xxii.	41
start and tremble under her *feet*,	"	73
A shadow there at my *feet*,	" II. i.	39
Lying close to my *f*,	" ii.	3
A golden *f* or a fairy horn	"	19
rivulet at her *feet* Ripples on	" iv.	41
end to the stream of passing *feet*,	" v.	11
sketching with her slender pointed *f*	*The Brook*.	102
clog of lead was round my *feet*,	*The Letters*	5
feet of those he fought for,	*Ode on Well.*	11
Thro' cypress avenues, at our *feet*.	*The Daisy*.	48
break covert at our *feet*.'	*Enid*.	183
Word by the *feet* that now were silent,	"	321
fell'd him, and set *f* upon his breast,	"	574
rose Limours and looking at his *feet*,	"	1151
lays his *f* upon it, Gnawing and	"	1410
on his *f* She set her own and climb'd;	"	1607
set his *f* upon me, and give me life.	"	1698
At Merlin's *feet* the wily Vivien lay.	*Vivien*.	5
kiss'd his *feet*, As if in deepest reverence,	"	68
Dear *feet*, that I have follow'd	"	76
twined her hollow *feet* Together,	"	89
bathed your *feet* before her own?	"	133
by the noise upstarted at our *feet*,	"	272
feet unmortised from their ankle bones	"	402
judge all nature from her *feet* of clay,	"	684
green path that show'd the rarer *f*,	*Elaine*	162
From forehead down to *f* perfect—	"	639
From *f* to forehead exquisitely turn'd:	"	640
with her *feet* unseen Crush'd the wild	"	737
wellnigh kiss'd her *feet* For loyal awe,	"	1166
shield of Lancelot at her *feet*	"	1311
broadening from her *feet* And	*Guinevere*.	81
let us in, tho' late, to kiss his *feet*!	"	176
a wild sea-light about his *feet*,	"	240
armed *feet* Thro' the long gallery	"	409
heard his armed *feet* Pause by her;	"	415
laid her hands about his *feet*,	"	524
pride in happier summers, at my *feet*.	"	532
while she grovell'd at his *feet*,	"	575
Tumbled the tawny rascal at his *feet*,	*Aylmer's F.*	230
with His light about thy *feet*,	"	665
fell The woman shrieking at his *feet*,	"	811
her strong *feet* up the steep hill	*Sea Dreams*	116
cold my wrinkled *feet*	*Tithonus*	67

	POEM.	LINE.
Scatter the blossom under her *feet*!	*W. to Alexan.*	9
kiss'd her *feet* a thousand years,	*Coquette*, ii.	13
Faith from tracts no *feet* have trod,	*On a Mourner*	29
Seas at my *feet* were flowing,	1865-1866	10
woman heard his *f* Return from	*Lucretius*	5
golden *feet* on those empurpled	"	135
Fine little hands, fine little *feet*,	*The Window*	63
football.		
drunkard's *f*, laughing-stocks of	*Princess*, iv.	496
footcloth.		
tumbled on the purple *f*,	*Princess*, iv.	267
foot-fall.		
a *f-f*, ere he saw The wood-nymph,	*Pal. of Art*	112
palfrey's *f* shot Light horrors	*Godiva*	58
measured *f* of firm and mild,	*Two Voices*	413
ghostly *f* echoing on the stair.	*Guinevere*	503
footings.		
Show'd her the fairy *f* on the grass,	*Aylmer's F.*	90
foot-gilt.		
lay F-g with all the blossom-dust	*Vivien*	131
footprint.		
only make that *f* upon sand	*Princess*, iii.	223
sandy *f* harden into stone,'	"	254
little *f* daily wash'd away.	*En. Arden.*	22
footsore.		
as a *f* ox in crowded ways	*Aylmer's F.*	819
footstep.		
Old *f*'s trod the upper floors,	*Mariana*	67
Like *f*'s upon wool.	*Œnone*	246
dully sound Of human *f*'s fall.	*Pal. of Art*	276
f's smite the threshold stairs	*St S. Stylites*	188
More close and close his *f*'s wind:	*Day-Dm.*	125
While he treads with *f* firmer,	*L.of Burleigh*	51
The *f*'s of his life in mine;	*In Mem.* lxxxiv.	44
at his *f* leaps no more,	"	112
let no *f* beat the floor,	" civ.	17
guide Her *f*'s, moving side by side	" cxiii.	19
He seems as one whose *f*'s halt,	*Will*	15
I prest my *f*'s into his,	*Lucretius*	118
footstool.		
drove The *f* from before him,	*Aylmer's F.*	327
forage.		
will fetch you *f* from all fields,	*Enid*	1476
forager.		
they found—his *f*'s for charms—	*Vivien*	489
foray.		
Bound on a *f*, rolling eyes of prey,	*Enid*	1387
brought upon their *f*'s out	"	1415
forbad.		
F her first the house of Averill,	*Aylmer's F.*	502
forbear.		
'F' the Princess cried; 'F, Sir' I;	*Princess*, iv.	144
purple scarf, and held, and said 'F!	*Enid*	377
'F: there is a worthier,'	"	556
That I *f* you thus: cross me no	"	1526
forbearance.		
Arguing boundless *f*:	*Aylmer's F.*	317
forbid.		
'did I not F you, Dora?'	*Dora*	90
Chid her, and *f* her to speak	*Maud*, I. xix.	63
forlorn.		
Bore and *f*, and did not tire,	*Two Voices*	218
Gemint, from utter courtesy, *f*.	*Enid*	381
the meek maid Sweetly *f* him ever,	*Elaine*	852
F his own advantage, 'rep.]	*Guinevere*	329
awed and promise-bounden she *f*,	*En. Arden.*	870
force (s.)		
f to make me rhyme in youth,	*Miller's D.*	193
All *f* in bonds that might endure,	*Pal. of Art*	154
broke a close with *f* and arms:	*Ed. Morris.*	131
old, but full Of *f* and choler,	*Golden Year*	61
passion shall have spent its novel *f*,	*Locksley II.*	42

	POEM.	LINE.
Titanic *f*'s taking birth	*Day-Dm.*	229
freedom, *f* and growth Of spirit	*Princess*, iv.	123
felt the blind wildbeast of *f*,	" v.	256
stood nor spoke, drain'd of her *f*,	" vi.	249
patient *f* to change them when we	" *Con.*	56
makes by *f* his merit known	*In Mem.* lxiii.	9
f that would have forged a name..	" lxxii.	16
I know thee of what *f* thou art	" lxxviii.	3
Seraphic intellect and *f*	" cviii.	6
with *f* and skill To strive,	" cxii.	6
Should licensed boldness gather *f*,	"	13
this electric *f*, that keeps	" cxxiv.	15
in his *f* to be Nature's crowning race.	*Maud*, I.iv.	33
of *f* to withstand, Year after year,	" II. ii.	24
I spoke with heart, and heat and *f*,	*The Letters*	37
bereave him Of the *f* he made his own	*Ode on Well.*	273
saying all your *f* is gone ?	*Enid*	88
f Is melted into mere effeminacy ?	"	106
were she the prize of bodily *f*,	"	541
strong bodies, flowing, drain'd their *f*."	"	569
either's *f* was match'd till Yniol's cry,"	"	570
could I someway prove such *f* in her "	"	805
elemental secrets, powers And *f*'s ;	*Vivien*	483
by *f* they dragg'd him to the King.	"	490
I do not mean the *f* alone,	*Elaine*	470
what *f* is yours to go,	"	1057
toward the hollow, all her *f* Failed her ;	*En. Arden*	371
promised that no *f*, Persuasion, no,	*Aylmer's F.*	418

force (verb.)
F's on the freer hour.	*Vision of Sin*	130
this wild king to *f* her to his wish,	*Princess, Pro.*	37

forced.
If a way Thro' solid opposition	*Princess*, iii.	109
f Sweet love on pranks of saucy boyhood ;	" vii.	322
world howling *f* them into bonds,	*Vivien*	594
f my thoughts on that fierce law,	*Guinevere*	533

forcing.
f far apart Those blind beginnings	*Lucretius*	241

ford.
By bridge and *f*, by park and pale,	*Sir Galahad*	82
drown'd in passing thro' the *f*,	*In Mem.* vi.	39
quickly flashing thro' the shallow *f*	*Enid*	167

forded.
f Usk, and gain'd the wood ;	*Enid*	161

forebode.
His heart *f*'s a mystery :	*Two Voices*	290

foreboding.
f ' what would Enoch say ?'	*En. Arden*	252

forecast.
who shall so *f* the years	*In Mem.* i.	5

forefathers.
His own *f* arms and armour hung.	*Princess, Pro.*	24
great *F* of the thornless garden,	*Maud*, I. xviii.	27

forefinger.
on the stretched *f* of all Time Sparkle	*Princess*, ii.	356

forefoot.
With inward yelp and restless *f*	*Lucretius*	45

foregone.
could I, as in times *f*,	*Talking O.*	189

foreground.
a *f* black with stones and slags,	*Pal. of Art*	81

forehead.
Thy bounteous *f* was not fann'd	*Eleänore*	9
about His dusty *f* drily curl'd,	*Miller's D.*	6
with dim fretted *f*'s all,	*Pal. of Art*	242
made his *f* like a rising sun	*M. d'Arthur*	217
Where shall I hide my *f*	"	228
opposed Free hearts, free *f*'s—	*Ulysses*	49
On her pallid cheek and *f*	*Locksley H.*	25
the straiten'd *f* of the fool !	"	62
f, to herd with narrow *f*'s,	"	175
With that she kiss'd His *f*,	*Princess*, ii.	291
o'er her *f* past A shadow,	" vi.	90

	POEM.	LINE.
all their *f*'s drawn in Roman scowls,	*Princess*,vii.	114
her *f* sank upon her hands,	"	231
on her *f* sits a fire ;	*In Mem.* cxiii.	5
turn'd our *f*'s from the falling sun,	*The Brook*	165
bared her *f* to the blistering sun,	*Enid*	1364
From *f* down to foot perfect—	*Elaine*	639
From foot to *f* exquisitely turn'd ;	"	640
Annie from her baby's *f* clipt	*En. Arden*	234
at last he said Lifting his honest *f*	"	385
f, eyelids, growing dewy-warm	*Tithonus*	50

foreigner.
A *f*, and I your countrywoman,	*Princess*, iv.	290

foreland.
many a fairy *f* set With willow-weed	*The Brook*	45

forelock.
Are taken by the *f*. Let it be.	*Golden Year*	17

foremost.
f in thy various gallery Place it,	*Ode to Mem.*	84
being ever *f* in the chase,	*Enid*	1007

foreran.
So much the boy *f*;	*Aylmer's F.*	60

forerun.
F thy peers, thy time	*Two Voices*	88
in the cold wind that *f*'s the morn	*Guinevere*	131

foresaw.
The flame is quench'd that I *f*,	*In Mem.*lxxii.	5
what doubt that he *f* This evil work	*Guinevere*	304

foresee.
Oh, if indeed that eye *f*,	*In Mem.*xxvi.	9
none of them *f*, Not even thy wise	*Guinevere*	271

foreseeing.
Howbeit ourself, *f* casualty,	*Princess*, iii.	300

foreshadow.
Who dares *f* for an only son.	*Ded. of Idylls*	28

foreshadowing.
Immersed in rich *f*'s of the world,	*Princess*, vii.	29
His heart *f* all calamity,	*En. Arden*	684

foresight.
Whose *f* preaches peace,	*Love and Duty*	34
Take wings of *f*; lighten thro'	*In Mem.*lxxv.	5

foreshortened.
lie *F* in the tract of time ?	*In Mem.*lxxvi.	4

forest.
so deadly still As that wide *f*.	*D. of F. Wom.*	69
Between dark stems the *f* glows,	*Sir Galahad*	27
Better to clear prime *f*'s,	*Princess*, iii.	111
The *f* crack'd, the waters curl'd,	*In Mem.* xv.	5
the harlot leapt Adown the *f*,	*Vivien*	822
and the *f* echo'd 'fool.'	"	823
gloomy skirts Of Celidon the *f*;	*Elaine*	292
The petty marestail *f*, fairy pines,	*Aylmer's F.*	92
While I roved about the *f*,	*Boädicea*	35

forest-deeps.
far, in *f*-d unseen,	*Sir L. and Q.G.*	7

forester.
Before him came a *f* of Dean,	*Enid*	148

forethought.
So dark a *f* roll'd about his brain,	*Vivien*	79

foretold.
f, Dying, that none of all our blood	*Princess*, i.	7
He too *f* the perfect rose.	*In Mem.Con.*	34
Has come to pass as *f*;	*Maud*, II. v.	44

forfeits.
game of *f* done—the girls all kiss'd	*The Epic*	2
magic music, *f*, all the rest.	*Princess,Pro.*	192

forgave.
there the Queen *f* him easily.	*Enid*	592
he *f* me, and I could not speak.	*Guinevere*	607

forge.
a company *f*'s the wine.	*Maud*, I. i.	36
f a life-long trouble for ourselves,	*Enid*	852

forged.
	POEM.	LINE.
∫ a thousand theories of the rocks,	Ed. Morris	18
Who ∫ that other influence,	Two Voices	283
We ∫ a sevenfold story.	Princess, Pro.	198
∫ at last A night-long Present	In Mem. lxx.	2
force that would have ∫ a name.	" lxxii.	16
∫, But that was later, boyish histories	Aylmer's F.	96
gifts of grace he ∫,	Sea Dreams	188

forget.
∫'s to close His curtains	Adeline	42
who that knew him could ∫ .	Miller's D.	3
Can he pass, and we ∫ ?	"	204
What is love ? for we ∫ :	"	213
I shall not ∫ you, mother,	May Queen, ii.	31
God ∫ the stranger !'	The Goose	56
Authority ∫'s a dying king,	M. d'Arthur	121
men F the dream that happens	Two Voices	353
I might ∫ my weaker lot ;	"	397
Swear by St something—I ∫ her	Princess, v.	283
Could we ∫ the widow'd hour	In Mem. xxxix.	1
But he ∫'s the days before	" xliii.	3
Nor can it suit me to ∫.	" lxxxiv.	59
The days she never can ∫	" xcvi.	14
should ∫ That I owe this debt	Maud, I. xix.	89
all men else their nobler dreams ∫,	Ode on Well.	152
∫ Obedience is the courtesy due	Elaine	713
Perplext her, made her half ∫ herself,	Aylmer's F.	303
ten years back, or more, if I don't ∫.	Grandmother	75
earth in earth ∫ these empty courts,	Tithonus	75

forgetful.
F of Maud and me,	Maud, I. xxi.	4
F of the falcon and the hunt (rep.)	Enid	51, 159
F of their troth and fealty,	Guinevere	439
F how my rich procœmion makes	Lucretius	70

forgetfulness.
this ∫ was hateful to her.	Enid	55

forget-me-not.
I found the blue F-m-n.	Miller's D.	202
∫-m-n's That grow for happy lovers.	The Brook	172

forgetteth.
The place he knew ∫ him.'	Two Voices	264

forgive.
wayward, but you'll ∫ me now: (rep.)	May Queen, ii.	33
May God ∫ me !—I have been to	Dora	158
F me, I waste my heart in signs:	Princess, iv.	337
F what seem'd my sin in me	In Mem. Pro.	33
F my grief for one removed,	"	37
F these wild and wandering cries,	"	41
little hearts that know not how to ∫:	Maud, II. i.	44
Or to say ∫ the wrong,'	" iv.	86
F me ; mine was jealousy in love.'	Elaine	1341
∫ thee, as Eternal God F's:	Guinevere	540
easily ∫ s it as his own,	Aylmer's F.	401
' Love, ∫ him :' but he did not	Sea Dreams	45
' F ! How many will say, ∫,'	"	60
neither God nor man can well ∫,	"	63
prove him, rogue, and proved, ∫.	"	167
We must ∫ the dead.'	"	261
∫ him, dear, And I shall sleep	"	299
I do ∫ him !' ' Thanks, my love,'	"	303

forgiven.
not easily ∫ Are those, who setting	Gardener's D.	242
one soft word and let me part ∫.'	Princess, vi.	202
let her feel herself ∫	Vivien	231
a face, bright as for sin ∫,	Elaine	1096
pass on, my Queen, ∫.',	"	1343
blessed be the King, who hath ∫,	Guinevere	627
' Yea, little maid, for am I not ∫ ?'	"	657

forgiveness.
I seem no more : I want ∫ too :	Princess, vi.	272
you yet once more With all ∫,	"	277

forgiving.
set my heart on your ∫ him	Sea Dreams	260

forgot.
having seen, ∫ ? The common mouth	Gardener's D.	54
The steer ∫ to graze	"	84

	POEM.	LINE.
For is not our first year ∫ ?	Two Voices	368
F his weakness in thy sight.	In Mem. cix.	4
May or April, he ∫,	The Brook	151
I ∫ the clouded Forth,	The Daisy	101
Nor yet ∫ her practice in her fright,	Vivien	796
F to drink to Lancelot and the	Elaine	733
sick man ∫ her simple blush,	"	860
sitting at her side ∕ Her presence	En. Arden	381
Sir Aylmer half ∫ his lazy smile	Aylmer's F.	197

forgotten.
live ∫, and love forlorn.'	Mariana in the S.	12, et pass.
not to be ∫—not at once—Not all ∫.	Love and Duty	88
F, rusting on his iron hills,	Princess, v.	140
meant ? I have ∫ what I meant :	Lucretius	122

fork.
grasps the triple ∫'s,	'Of old sat Freedom,' etc.	15
Ruin'd trunks on wither'd ∫'s,	Vision of Sin	93
double hill ran up his furrowy ∫'s	Princess, iii.	158
∫'s are fixt into the meadow ground,	Enid	482
they fixt the ∫'s into the ground,	"	548
dazzled by the livid-flickering ∫,	Vivien	790
I never saw so fierce a ∫—	Lucretius	28

forked.
things that are ∫, and horned, and	The Mermaid	53
∫ Of the near storm, and aiming	Aylmer's F.	726

forlorn.
In sleep she seem'd to walk ∫,	Mariana	30
live forgotten, and love ∫.'	Mariana in the S.	12
(Enone, wandering ∫ Of Paris,	Œnone	15
I ceased, and sat as one ∫,	Two Voices	400
Yet we will not die ∫.'	Vision of Sin	206
The little village looks ∫;	In Mem. lix.	9
I walk as ere I walk'd ∫,	" lxvii.	5
Who am no more so all ∫,	Maud, I. xviii.	32
once scarce less ∫, Dying abroad	" xix.	28
The tiny cell is ∫,	" II. ii.	13
A tonsured head in middle age ∫,	The Brook	200
' Favour from one so sad and so ∫	En. Arden	286

form (shape, etc.)
her fairest ∫'s are types of thee	Isabel	39
airy ∫'s of flitting change.	Madeline	7
all ∫'s Of the many-sided mind	Ode to Mem.	115
other than his ∫ of creed,	A Character	29
rites and ∫'s before his burning eyes	The Poet	39
Fretteth thine enshrouded ∫.	A Dirge	10
'Is this the ∫,' she made her moan,	Mariana in the S.	33
The reflex of a beauteous ∫,	Miller's D.	77
her rounded ∫ Between the shadows	Œnone	176
as God holding no ∫ of creed,	Pal. of Art	211
∫'s that pass'd at windows	D. of F. Wom.	23
fair ∫ may stand and shine	'Of old sat Freedom,' etc.	21
Matures the individual ∫.	' Love thou thy land,' etc.	40
Phantoms of other ∫'s of rule,	"	59
decks were dense with stately ∫'s	M. d'Arthur	196
play with flying ∫'s and images,	Gardener's D.	59
fair new ∫'s That float about	Golden Year	15
Cursed be the sickly ∫'s	Locksley H.	61
loosely settled into ∫.	Day-Dm.	12
either side her tranced ∫	"	81
A perfect ∫ in perfect rest.	"	100
blessed ∫'s in whistling storms	Sir Galahad	59
crypt Of darken'd ∫'s and faces.	Will Water.	184
slowly quickening into lower ∫'s	Vision of Sin	210
All beauty compass'd in a female ∫,	Princess, ii.	20
to look on noble ∫'s Makes noble	"	72
Of faded and haughtiest lineaments,	"	425
a loftier ∫ Than female,	" iv.	196
I saw the ∫'s : I knew not where.	" vii.	118
clear away the parasitic ∫'s	"	253
A hollow ∫ with empty hands.'	In Mem. iii.	12
A late-lost ∫ that sleep reveals,	" xiii.	2
knows no more of transient ∫	" xvi.	7
Nor cares to fix itself to ∫,	" xxxiii.	4
faith thro' ∫ is pure as thine	"	9
Eternal ∫ shall still divide	" xlvi.	6
thy first ∫ was made a man : .	" lx.	10
same sweet ∫'s in either mind.	" lxxviii.	8
changes wrought on ∫ and face ;	" lxxxi.	2

	POEM.	LINE.
O sacred essence, other *f*,	*In Mem.*lxxxiv.	35
seem to lift the *f*, and glow	" lxxxvi.	37
merge' he said 'in *f* and gloss	" lxxxviii.	41
wear the *f* by which I know .	" xc.	5
beauteous in thine after *f*,	"	15
matter-moulded *f*'s of speech,	" xciv.	46
who would keep an ancient *f*	" civ.	19
ancient *f*'s of party strife ;	" cv.	14
want in *f*'s for fashion's sake,	" cx.	6
grew to seeming-random *f*'s,	" cxvii.	10
flow From *f* to *f*, and nothing stands ;	" cxxii.	6
tho' faith and *f* Be sunder'd .	" cxxvi.	1
other *f*'s of life than ours,	*Ode on Well*.	264
Conjecture of the plumage and the *f*; *Enid*	.	333
dreamt herself was such a faded *f*	"	654
O imperial-moulded *f*, .	. *Guinevere*	544
The *f*, the *f* alone is eloquent !	*Coquette*, ii.	1
form (bench.)
sat along the *f*'s, like morning doves	*Princess*, ii.	87
form (verb.)
rainbow *f*'s and flies on the land	. *Sea-Fairies*	25
Slowly *f*'s the firmer mind,	. *In Mem.*xviii.	18
formal.
O, I see thee old and *f*.	. *Locksley H.*	93
formed.
his picture *f* And grew between	*Elaine*	986
forming.
The lucid outline *f* round thee ;	. *Tithonus*	53
formless.
wrapt thee *f* in the fold .	. *In Mem.* xxii.	15
forsake.
Ah yet, tho' all the world *f*, .	. *Will Water.*	49
fort.
that new *f* to overawe my friends,	*Enid* .	460
Welcome her, thunders of *f* and	. *W. to Alexan.*	6
Forth.
And I forgot the clouded *F*, .	. *The Daisy*	101
fortitude.
stately flower of female *f*, .	. *Isabel* .	11
fortress.
The *f*, and the mountain ridge,	. *In Mem.* lxx.	14
The *f* crashes from on high .	. " cxxvi.	14
deathful-grinning mouths of the *f*,	*Maud*,III.vi.	52
White from the mason's hand, a *f* rose ; *Enid*	.	244
onward to the *f* rode the three,	. "	251
into that new *f* by your town,	. "	407
fortune.
rode sublime On *F*'s neck ; .	. *D.of F.Wom.*	142
Tho' *f* clip my wings, .	. *Will Water.*	50
I am but as my *f*'s are :	. *Lady Clare*	70
Drink to *F*, drink to Chance,	. *Vision of Sin*	191
ally Your *f*'s, justlier balanced,	. *Princess*, ii.	52
Becomes on *F*'s crowning slope	. *In Mem.* lxiii.	14
affluent *F* emptied all her horn.	. *Ode on Well.*	197
loved her in a state Of broken *f*'s,	*Enid* .	13
was one Of *F* and her wheel,	. "	346
Turn, *F*, turn thy wheel (rep.)	. "	347
since our *f* slipt from sun to shade	"	714
better his Our mended *f*'s .	. "	718
good *f*, I will strike him dead,	. *Elaine*	1065
mark me! for your *f*'s are to make. *Aylmer's F.*		300
Naine, *f* too ; the world should ring	"	395
a few, by wit or *f* led, .	. "	438
besides Their slender household *f*'s	*Sea Dreams*	9
forum.
Titanic shapes, they cramm'd The *f*,	*Princess*,vii.	110
forward-creeping.
f-c tides Began to foam, .	. *In Mem.* cii.	37
forward-flowing.
The *f-f* tide of time ; .	. *Arabian N.'s.*	4
fossil.
lark and leveret lay, Like *f*'s of the rock, *Audley Ct.*		24

	POEM.	LINE.
foster.
guard and *f* her for evermore.	. *Guinevere*	586
fostered.
F the callow eaglet— .	. *Œnone*	208
once she *f* up with care ;	. *In Mem.* viii.	16
that was Arthur ; and they *f* him	*Guinevere*	293
fought.
the Palmyrene That *f* Aurelian,	. *Princess*, ii.	70
nursed by those for whom you *f*	. " vi.	79
I and mine have *f* Your battle :	. "	207
f his doubts and gather'd strength,	*In Mem.* xcv.	13
Like Paul with beasts, I *f* with Death ;	" cxix.	4
the feet of those he *f* for,	. . *Ode on Well.*	11
great men who *f*, and kept it ours.	"	158
Than when he *f* at Waterloo,	. "	257
They that had *f* so well	. *Lt. Brigade*	45
twice they *f*, and twice they breathed, *Enid*	.	567
one a king, had met And *f* together ; *Elaine*	.	41
if I went and if I *f*, .	. "	216
' you have *f*. O tell us— .	. "	283
half-miracle To those he *f* with—	"	497
greatest knight ? I *f* for it,	. "	1404
Annie *f* against his will :	. *En. Arden*	158
comrades having *f* their last below, *Aylmer's F.*		227
F with what seem'd my own	. *Sea Dreams*	73
may be met and *f* with outright,	. *Grandmother*	31
the babe had *f* for his life. .	. "	64
foul.
where you are : you are *f* with sin ;	*Poet's Mind*	36
as false and *f* As the poach'd filth	*Vivien*	646
frequent interchange of *f* and fair,	*En. Arden* .	529
foully.
phantom husks of something *f* done	*Lucretius* .	160
foulness.
of the horrid *f* that he wrought,	. *Vivien*	598
To all the *f* that they work.	. "	634
found (pret. and part. of *find*.)
Down she came and *f* a boat	. *L.of Shalott*,iv.	6
Have I not *f* a happy earth ?	. *Miller's D.*	25
I *f* the blue Forget-me-not. .	. "	202
The comfort, I have *f* in thee :	. "	234
' I have *f* A new land, but I die.'	*Pal. of Art*	283
The Roman soldier *f* Me lying dead, *D. of F. Wom.*		161
woke, and *f* him settled down	. *The Epic* .	17
would have spoken, but he *f* not words, *M. d' Arthur*		172
ere he *f* Empire for life? .	. *Gardener's D.*	19
I *f* it in a volume, all of songs,	. *Audley Ct.*	56
They *f* you out ? *James*. Not they. *Walk.to the M.*		93
witness, if I could have *f* a way	. *St S. Stylites*	54
I *f* him garrulously given,	. *Talking O.* .	23
f, and kiss'd the name she *f*	. "	159
She had not *f* me so remiss ;	. "	193
love that never *f* his earthly close,	*Love and Duty*	1
Sin itself be *f* The cloudy porch	. "	8
f him in Llanberris : .	. *Golden Year*	5
f him, where he strode About the	*Godiva*	16
there she *f* her palfrey trapt	. "	51
f him when my years were few ;	. *Two Voices*	271
It may be that no life is *f*,	. "	346
f My spirits in the golden age.	. *To E. L.*	11
F a still place, and pluck'd her	. *Princess*, i.	91
in the imperial palace the king.	. "	112
f her there At point to move,	. " iii.	114
not *f* among them all One anatomic.'	"	289
iron laws, in the end *F* golden :	. " iv.	58
Nor *f* my friends ; but push'd	. "	178
f at length The garden portals.	. "	181
f that you had gone Ridd'n to the	"	323
in you I *f* My boyish dream involved	"	429
F the gray kings at parle :	. " v.	110
f He thrice had sent a herald	. "	321
f fair peace once more among the	. " vii.	175
she *f* a small Sweet Idyl,	. *In Mem. Pro.*	38
Thy creature, whom I *f* so fair.	. " xiv.	4
f thee lying in the port ; .	. "	19
f him all in all the same,	. " lxviii.	6
I *f* a wood with thorny boughs :	. "	14
I *f* an angel of the night ;	. " lxxxviii.	6
My Arthur *f* your shadows fair,	.	

	POEM.	LINE.
I ƒ Him not in world or sun,	In Mem. cxxiii.	5
pit long since a body was ƒ,	Maud, I. i.	5
as I ƒ when her carriage past,	" ii.	3
ƒ The shining daffodil dead,	" iii.	13
What, has he ƒ my jewel out?	" x.	23
life has ƒ What some have ƒ so	" xi.	3
in this stormy gulf have ƒ a pearl	" xviii.	42
This garden-rose that I ƒ,	" xxi.	3
ƒ the bailiff riding by the farm,	The Brook	153
ƒ the sun of sweet content Re-risen	"	168
I ƒ, tho' crush'd to hard and dry,	The Daisy	97
ƒ and loved her in a state	Enid	12
being ƒ, Then will I fight him,	"	220
F every hostel full,	"	255
ƒ an ancient dame in dim brocade.	"	363
ƒ Half disarray'd as to her rest,	"	515
ƒ no rest, and ever fail'd to draw	"	531
Prince had ƒ her in her ancient home;	"	644
ƒ the sack and plunder of our house	"	694
ƒ And took it, and array'd herself.	"	848
when he ƒ all empty, was amazed;	"	1065
F Enid with the corner of his eye,	"	1130
issuing arm'd he ƒ the host	"	1256
ƒ his own dear bride propping his	"	1432
ƒ A damsel drooping in a corner	"	1458
my dear lord ƒ me first,	"	1546
moving out they ƒ the stately horse,	"	1600
ƒ, Instead of scornful pity	"	1706
He look'd and ƒ them wanting;	"	1783
ƒ a little boat, and stept into it;	Vivien	47
my Master, have you ƒ your voice?	"	118
ƒ a fair young squire who sat alone,	"	322
being ƒ take heed of Vivien.	"	379
they ƒ—his foragers for charms—	"	469
on returning ƒ Not two but three:	"	558
He brought, not ƒ it therefore;	"	569
ƒ a door And darkling felt	"	583
had she ƒ a dagger there	"	700
Should have ƒ in him a greater heart.	"	722
ƒ a glen, gray boulder and black	Elaine	37
issuing ƒ the Lord of Astolat	"	173
ƒ it true, and answer'd, 'true, my	"	369
Until they ƒ The new design	"	439
Where could be ƒ face daintier?	"	638
I be ƒ as faithless in the quest	"	757
ƒ no ease in turning or in rest:	"	897
ƒ her in among the garden yews	"	919
Until we ƒ the palace of the king.	"	1038
Would track her guilt until he ƒ,	Guinevere	60
ƒ a naked child upon the sands	"	291
in her anguish ƒ The casement:	"	580
warmth and colour which I ƒ In Lancelot	"	640
Blanch'd with his mill, they ƒ;	En. Arden	364
The two remaining ƒ a fallen stem;	"	568
swoon and tumble and be ƒ,	"	775
Flying with his urns and ornaments	Aylmer's F.	6
Slipt into ashes and was ƒ no more.	"	6
written as she ƒ Or made occasion,	"	477
F for himself a bitter treasure-trove;	"	515
ƒ the girl And flung her down	"	573
F a dead man, a letter edged with	"	595
in moving on I ƒ Only the landward	Sea Dreams	93
ƒ a hard friend in his loose accounts,	"	158
ƒ for it was close beside)	"	276
They ƒ the mother sitting still;	The Victim	32
wedded to Lucretius, ƒ Her master cold;	Lucretius	1
ƒ a witch Who brew'd the philtre.	"	15
found ('to establish.)		
All wild to ƒ an University	Princess, i.	149
foundation.		
for fear This whole ƒ ruin,	Princess, ii.	320
foundation-stone.		
Whereof the strong ƒ-s's were laid	Pal. of Art	235
founded.		
She had ƒ; they must build.	Princess, ii.	129
Which good King Arthur ƒ,	Guinevere	219
founder.		
statues, king or saint, or ƒ fell;	Sea Dreams	217

	POEM.	LINE.
founding.		
About the ƒ of a Table Round,	Vivien	261
the great Table—at the ƒ of it;	Guinevere	233
foundress.		
The ƒ of the Babylonian wall,	Princess, ii.	66
the third—the authentic ƒ you.	" iii.	142
fount.		
Ancient ƒ's of inspiration well	Locksley H.	188
There while we stood beside the ƒ,	Princess, iii.	7
The very source and ƒ of Day	In Mem. xxiv.	3
dabbling in the ƒ of fictive tears,	The Brook	93
burst away In search of stream or ƒ,	En. Arden	636
the living ƒ of pity in Heaven,	Aylmer's F.	752
fountain.		
Down from the central ƒ's flow	Arabian N's.	50
fire, From the ƒ's of the past,	Ode to Mem.	2
In the middle leaps a ƒ	Poet's Mind	24
to the billow the ƒ calls:	Sea-Fairies.	9
I should look like a ƒ of gold	The Mermaid	18
Rise like a ƒ for me night and day	M. d' Arthur	249
The ƒ to his place returns	Day-Dm.	31
sixty feet the ƒ leapt.	"	140
Beside its native ƒ.	Amphion	96
Against its ƒ upward runs	Will Water.	35
Expecting when a ƒ should arise:	Vision of Sin	8
the ƒ spouted, showering wide	"	21
The ƒ of the moment, playing now	Princess, Pro.	61
splash and stir Of ƒ's spouted up	" i.	215
E nring'd a billowing ƒ in the midst;	" ii.	14
Knowledge is now no more a ƒ seal'd:	"	75
and race By all the ƒ's;	" iv.	244
tears that at their ƒ freeze:	In Mem. xx.	12
show'd him in the ƒ fresh	" lxxxiv.	26
household ƒ's never dry;	" cviii.	2
ƒ's of sweet water in the sea,	En. Arden	604
Spout from the maiden ƒ in her heart.	Lucretius	227
fountain-flood.		
sonorous flow Of spouted ƒ-ƒ's.	Pal. of Art	20
fountain-foam.		
dragons spouted forth A flood of ƒ-ƒ.	Pal. of Art	24
fountain-head.		
Full-welling ƒ-h's of change,	Pal. of Art	165
The murmur of the ƒ-h—	Two Voices.	213
fountain-jets.		
others tost a ball Above the ƒ-j,	Princess, ii.	431
fountain-urns.		
Gods at random thrown By ƒ-u;	To E. L.	16
fourfield.		
The ƒ system, and the price of grain;	Audley Ct.	33
four-in-hand.		
as quaint a ƒ-i-h As you shall see—	Walk. to the M.	103
foursquare.		
build some plan F to opposition.'.	Princess, v.	222
ƒ to all the winds that blew!	Ode on Well.	39
four-year-old.		
'That was the ƒ-y-o I sold the Squire.'	The Brook	137
fowl.		
To scare the ƒ from fruit:	Princess, ii.	210
fox.		
whole hill-side was redder than a ƒ,	Walk. to the M.	3
And lighter-footed than the ƒ.	Day-Dm.	108
Then of the latest ƒ—where started—	Aylmer's F.	253
foxglove.		
The ƒ cluster dappled bells.'.	Two Voices	72
Bring orchis, bring the ƒ spire,	In Mem. lxxxii.	9
foxlike.		
Or ƒ in the vine,	Princess, vii.	188
fraction.		
Some niggard ƒ of an hour,	Aylmer's F.	450
fragment.		
leaning on a ƒ twined with vine,	Œnone	10
the ƒ's tumbled from the glens,	"	213
ƒ's of her mighty voice	'Of old sat Freedom,' etc.	7

	POEM.	LINE.
silver *f*'s of a broken voice, . .	*Gardener's D.*	229
cram him with the *f*'s of the grave,	*Princess,* iii.	294
Among the *f*'s of the golden day.	*Maud,* I. xviii.	70
heard but *f*'s of her later words,	*Enid*	. 113
Among the tumbled *f*'s of the hills.'	*Elaine*	1417

fragrance.
With song and flame and *f*, . . *Lucretius* . 134

fragrant.
gardens of that rival rose Yet *f* . *Aylmer's F.* 456

frail.
mortal eyes are *f* to judge of fair	. *Œnone*	. 155
f at first And feeble, all unconscious	*Princess,* vii.	101
Rapt from the fickle and the *f*	. *In Mem.* xxx.	25
O life a futile, then, as *f*!	. " lv.	25
F, but a work divine, . .	. *Maud,* II. ii.	4
F, but of force to withstand,	. " .	24

frailty.
| Nor human *f* do me wrong. . . | . *In Mem.* li. | 8 |
| the crimes and *frailties* of the court, | *Guinevere* | 135 |

frame (s.)
Thro' all my veins to all my *f*,	. *Eleänore*	. 131
Shiver'd in my narrow *f*.	. *Fatima*	. 18
into my empty soul and *f* . .	*D. of F. Wom.*	78
'A healthy *f*, a quiet mind.' .	. *Two Voices*	99
Consolidate in mind and *f*—	. "	366
The morals, something of the *f*,	*Princess,* ii.	360
not as we, But suffers change of *f*.	" v.	453
No hint of death in all his *f*,	. *In Mem.* xiv.	18
Deep-seated in our mystic *f*,	. " xxxvi.	2
thro' the *f* that binds him in .	. " xliv.	11
near me when the sensuous *f*	. " xlix.	5
mixt with all this mystic *f* . .	. " lxxvii.	18
feeds thy breath Throughout my *f*,	" lxxxv.	11
in this blindness of the *f*. .	. " xcii.	15
Remade the blood and changed the *f*,	" *Con.*	11
I steal, a wasted *f*, . .	. *Maud,* II. iv.	69
A man of well-attemper'd *f* .	. *Ode on Well.*	74
Dust are our *f*'s ; and, gilded dust,	*Aylmer's F.*	1
Another and another *f* of things	. *Lucretius*	. 42

frame (verb.)
Vague words! but ah, how hard to *f In Mem.*xciv.45

framed.
Neither modell'd, glazed, or *f*: . *Vision of Sin* 188

frame-work.
With royal *f-w* of wrought gold ;.	*Ode to Mem.*	82
with such a *f* scarce could be.	. *Princess, Con.*	22
all the *f* of the land ; . .	*In Mem.* lxxxvi.	24

France.
A light of ancient *F*: . .	. *D. of F. Wom.*	268
more than seen, the skirts of *F*.	. *Princess, Con.*	48
In which we went thro' summer *F*.	*In Mem.* lxx.	4
foaming grape of eastern *F*. .	" *Con.*	80
Back to *F* her hundred swarms,	. *Ode on Well.*	110
Back to *F* with countless blows,	. "	111
That cursed *F* with her egalities!	*Aylmer's F.*	265
golden hopes for *F* and all mankind,	"	464
ever-murder'd *F*, By shores that darken	"	766
Rose a ship of *F*. . .	. *The Captain*	28

Francis (see Allen, Hale.)
F, laughing, clapt his hand . .	. *The Epic*	. 21
F, muttering like a man ill-used,	*M. d'Arthur, Ep.*	12
F, with a basket on his arm,	. *Audley Ct.*	. 5
F, just alighted from the boat,	. "	. 6
F laid A damask napkin . .	. "	. 19

frankincense.
sweet I spikenard, and balm, and *f*. *St S. Stylites* 208

frankly.
as *f* theirs As dues of Nature. . *Princess,* v. 195

fraught.
when *f* With a passion so intense . *Maud,* II. ii. 58

free.
| to have been Joyful and *f* from blame. | *D. of F. Wom.* | 80 |
| change which comes be *f* | '*Love thou thy land,*' etc. | 45 |

	POEM.	LINE.
'King, you are *f*! We did but keep	*Princess,* v.	23
Knowledge in our own land make her *f*,	"	409
dwarf'd or godlike, bond or *f*:	. " vii.	244
jest among his friends is *f*, .	. *In Mem.* lxv.	10
The starry clearness of the *f*!	. " lxxxiv.	86
I feel so *f* and so clear . .	. *Maud,* I. xix.	98
His foes were thine ; he kept us *f*,	*Ode on Well.*	91
all too *f* For such a wise humility	"	. 248
f to stretch his limbs in lawful fight,	*Enid*	1602
'Let love be *f*; *f* love is for the best:	*Elaine*	1372
always bound to you, but you are *f*.'	*En. Arden.*	447
—*f* of alms her hand—. .	. *Aylmer's F.*	697
peace, so it be *f* from pain, .	. *Grandmother*	97

freedom.
make The bounds of *f* wider yet	. *To the Queen*	32
F rear'd in that august sunrise	. *The Poet*	37
pure law, Commeasure perfect *f*.	*Œnone*	. 164
sober-suited *F* chose, .	'*You ask me why,*' etc.	6
F broadens slowly down .	. "	11
individual *f* mute : . .	. "	. 20
Of old sat *F* on the heights, '*Of old sat Freedom,*' etc.1
shout For some blind glimpse of *f*	*Love and Duty*	6
F, gaily doth she tread ; .	. *Vision of Sin*	136
Embrace our aims; work out your *f*.	*Princess,* ii.	75
song Is duer unto *f*, . .	. " iv.	123
shower the fiery grain Of *f* broadcast	" v.	412
the yoke, I wish it Gentle as *f*—	" vi.	188
A love of *f* rarely felt, . .	. *In Mem.*cviii.	13
save the one true seed of *f* sown	. *Ode on Well.*	162
sober *f* out of which there springs	. "	164

freemen.
It is the land that *f* till, .	'*You ask me why,*' etc.	5
English natures. *f*, friends, '*Love thou thy land,*' etc.		7
Gallant sons of English *f*, .	. *The Captain*	7

freer.
| leave thee *f*, till thou wake . | . *Love and Duty* | 94 |
| noble thought be *f* under the sun, | *Maud,*III.vi. | 48 |

freest.
' Free love, so bound, were *f*,' . *Elaine* 1371

freeze.
| tears that at their fountain *f*; | . *In Mem.* xx. | 11 |
| eighty winters *f* with one rebuke | . *Ode on Well.* | 168 |

freight.
| lovely *f* Of overflowing blooms, | . *Ode to Mem.* | 16 |
| thy dark *f*, a vanish'd life. . | . *In Mem.* x. . | 8 |

frequence.
Not in this *f* can I lend full tongue, *Princess,* iv. 422

frequent.
So *f* on its hinge before. . . *Deserted H.* 8

fresh.
Aphrodite beautiful *F* as the foam,	*Œnone*	. 171
All the valley, mother, 'ill be *f*	. *May Queen,* I.	37
How *f* the meadows look .	. *Walk. to the M.*	1
flit To make the greensward *f*,	. *Talking O.*	. 90
Oh, nature first was *f* to men,	. *Amphion*	. 57
F as the first beam glittering	. *Princess,* iv.	26
so *f*, the days that are no more.	. "	30
all our path was *f* with dew,	. *In Mem.*lxvii.	6
If not so *f*, with love as true,	. " lxxxiv.	101
pleased him, *f* from brawling courts	" lxxxviii.	11
'Too happy, *f* and fair, Too *f*.	*The Brook*	. 217
So *f* they rose in shadow'd swells ;	*The Letters*	46
how *f* the colours look, .	. *Enid*	. 680
this cut is *f*; That ten years back :	*Elaine*	. 21
F from the burial of her little one,	*En. Arden.*	280
How *f* was every sight and sound.	*The Voyage*	5

freshen.
They *f* the silvery-crimson shells, . *Sea-Fairies* 13

fresher.
Bright Phosphor, *f* for the night, . *In Mem.* cxx. 9

freshest.
Looks *f* in the fashion of the day : *The Epic* . 32

freshly-flowered.
lay Upon the *f-f* slope. . . *Miller's D.* . 112

	POEM.	LINE.
Freshmen.		
Everard's college fame When we were *F*:	*The Epic*	47
freshness.		
Delighted with the *f* and the sound.	*Ed. Morris*	99
increased With *f* in the dawning east.	*Two Voices*	405
so did I let my *f* die.	*Maud*, I. xix.	11
fresh-washed.		
f-w in coolest dew,	*D. of F. Wom.*	54
fret (s.)		
Love is hurt with jar and *f*.	*Miller's D.*	209
(all) *f*'s But chafing me on fire	*Princess*, i.	163
fret (verb.)		
should not *f* for me, mother,	*May Queen*, ii.	36
kind word, and tell him not to *f*;	" iii.	45
To *f* the summer jenneting.	*The Blackbird*	12
We *f*, we fume, would shift our skins,	*Will Water.*	225
'So *f* not, like an idle girl,'	*In Mem.* li.	13
that a matter to make me *f*?	*Maud*, I. xiii.	2
With many a curve my banks I *f*.	*The Brook*	43
'*F* not yourself, dear brother,	*Elaine*.	1068
fretful.		
f as the wind Pent in a crevice:	*Princess*, iii.	64
fretted.		
f all to dust and bitterness.'	*Princess*, vi.	247
fretteth.		
f thine enshrouded form.	*A Dirge*	10
fretwork.		
holds a stately *f* to the Sun,	*Princess*, vi.	70
Friday.		
Whose *F* fare was Enoch's ministering.	*En. Arden*	100
friend.		
Clear-headed *f*, whose 'Clear-headed friend,' etc.		1
My *f*, with you to live alone,	*Ode to Mem.*	119
f's to man, Living . To——. With Pal. of Art		11
Prythee, *f*, Where is Mark Antony? *D. of F. Wom.*		139
gave me a *f*, and a true true-love, *D. of the O. Year*		13
He was a *f* to me.	"	23
Alack, our *f* is gone.	"	47
he too was a *f* to me: Both are my *f*'s, *To J. S.*		61
land, where girt with *f*'s or foes 'You ask me why,'		7
natures, freemen, *f*s, 'Love thou thy land,' etc.		7
and those who call them *f*	*M. d'Arthur*	253
who lived across the bay, My *f*; *Audley Ct.*		75
Sets out, and meets a *f* who hails *Walk. to the M.*		34
ah! my *f*, the days were brief	*Talking O.*	185
Come, my *f*'s, 'Tis not too late	*Ulysses*	56
seems to hear a Heavenly F,	*Two Voices*	295
In Art like Nature, dearest *f*;	*Day-Dm.*	210
To fall asleep with all one's *f*'s;	"	216
troops of unrecording *f*'s, 'You might have won,' etc.		7
lady *f*'s From neighbour seats:	*Princess*, Pro.	97
they betted; made a hundred *f*'s,	"	162
Cyril and with Florian, my two *f*'s:	" i.	51
Went forth again with both my *f*'s.	"	165
always *f*'s, none closer, elm and vine:	" ii.	316
brings our *f*'s up from the underworld,	" iv.	295
Nor found my *f*'s; but push'd alone	"	178
Then came your new *f*:	"	279
I your old *f* and tried. she new in all?	"	299
'my *f* Parted from her—	" v.	72
—and ours shall see us *f*'s.	"	219
Truest *f* and noblest foe;	" vi.	538
a world Of traitorous *f* and broken	"	199
'We two were *f*'s: I go to mine own	"	234
had got a *f* of your own age,	"	266
glittering drops on her sad *f*.	"	271
le *f*'s, like children, being chid!	"	316
Whatever man lies wounded, *f* or foe,	"	371
O my *f*, I will not have thee die!	" vii.	137
hears his burial talk'd of by his *f*'s,	*Con.*	49
a garden I' said my college *f*,		
One writes, that 'Other *f*'s remain, *In Mem.* vi.		1
unto me no second *f*.	" ix.	44
My *f*, the brother of my love;	" xii.	16
Saying: 'Comes he thus, my *f*?	" xl.	13
flash at once, my *f*, to thee:.	" lvi.	12
Methinks my *f* is richly shrined;		7

	POEM.	LINE.
'Does my old *f* remember me?'	*In Mem.* lxiii.	28
Since we deserved the name of *f*'s,	" lxiv.	9
Whose jest among his *f*'s is free,	" lxv.	10
Thy blood, my *f*, and partly mine;	" lxxxiii.	9
other *f*'s that once I met;	" lxxxiv.	58
I crave your pardon, O my *f*;	"	100
held debate, a band Of youthful *f*'s,	" lxxxvi.	22
f from *f* Is oftener parted,	" xcvii.	14
Some gracious memory of my *f*;	" xcix.	4
thy lost *f* among the bowers,	" ci.	15
O, *f*, who camest to thy goal	" cxiii.	23
To hear the tidings of my *f*,	" cxxv.	3
Dear *f*, far off, my lost desire,	" cxxviii.	1
Dear heavenly *f* that canst not die,	"	7
Strange *f*, past, present, and to be;	"	9
That *f* of mine who lives in God,	" Con.	140
led her home, my love, my only *f*. *Maud*, I. xviii.		1
To be *f*'s for her sake, to be.	" xix.	50-6
To me, her *f* of the years before;	"	64
Should I fear to greet my *f*.	" II. iv.	85
To catch a *f* of mine one stormy day; "	v.	85
F, to be struck by the public foe,	"	89
those, his *f*'s, for whom they were; *The Brook*		131
She told me all her *f*'s had said; *The Letters*		25
O *f*'s, our chief state-oracle is mute: *Ode on Well.*		23
Thunder 'Anathema,' *f*, at you; *To F. D. Maurice*		8
'O *f*, I seek a harbourage for the *Enid*		299
'Thanks, venerable *f*,' replied	"	303
suspends his converse with a *f*,	"	340
that new fort to overawe my *f*'s,	"	460
how should Enid find A nobler *f*?	"	793
Embraced her with all welcome as a *f*, "		834
Call in what men soever were his *f*'s,	"	1135
of one mind and all right-honest *f*'s I "		1333
what they long for, good in *f* or foe,	"	1724
great Queen once more embraced her *f* "		1795
the Table Round, my *f*'s of old; *Vivien*		665
were I glad of you as guide and *f*; *Elaine*		226
his kin and most familiar *f*.	"	590
Marr'd her *f*'s point with pale	"	729
call her *f* and sister, sweet Elaine,	"	861
like a *f*'s voice from a distant field	"	993
makes no *f* who never made a foe.	"	1083
To this I call my *f*'s in testimony,	"	1291
Nay, *f*, for we have taken our *Guinevere*		116
most disloyal *f* in all the world.'	"	338
saps The fealty of our *f*'s,	"	517
warhorse neigh'd As at a *f*'s voice,	"	527
his, had been his father's, *f*: *Aylmer's F.*		344
his nearer *f* would say 'Screw not	"	468
F's, I was bid to speak of such a one	"	677
their guest, their host, their ancient *f*,	"	790
'My dearest *f*, Have faith, have. *Sea Dreams*		152
a hard *f* in his loose accounts,	"	158
he that wrongs his *f* Wrongs himself	"	168
painting some dead *f* from memory.' *Coquette*, iii.		4
by those who mourn a *f* in vain, *Lucretius*		142
friendly-warm.		
Only such cups as left us *f-w*,	*Lucretius*	212
friendship.		
a *f* so complete Portion'd in halves *Gardener's D.*		4
My college *f*'s glimmer.	*Will Water.*	40
F *f*—to be two in one—	*Vision of Sin*	107
O *f*, equal-poised control,	*In Mem.* lxxxiv.	33
such *f* as had master'd Time;	"	64
A *f* for the years to come.	"	80
First love, first *f*, equal powers,	"	107
Less yearning for the *f* fled,	" cvv.	15
bright the *f* of thine eye;	" cxviii.	10
So vanish *f*'s only made in wine. *Enid*		1328
frieze.		
boss'd with lengths Of classic *f*, *Princess*, ii.		11
fright (s.)		
died Of *f* in far apartments. *Princess*, vi.		351
dead weight trail'd, by a whisper'd *f*, *Maud*, I. i.		14
call'd him dear protector in her *f*, *Vivien*		795
Nor yet forgot her practice in her *f*, "		796
fright (verb.)		
breed with him, can *f* my faith, . *In Mem.* lxxxi.		4

CONCORDANCE TO

		POEM.	LINE.
frighted.			
had added 'get thee hence' Fled *f*.	*Guinevere*		365
half amazed half *f* all his flock : .	*Aylmer's F.*		631
frill.			
door Of his house in a rainbow *f* ?	*Maud,* II. ii.		17
fringe.			
Burnt like a *f* of fire. . . .	*Pal. of Art*		48
Torn from the *f* of spray. . .	*D. of F. Wom.*		40
tagg'd with icy *f*'s in the moon,	*St S. Stylites*		31
From *f*'s of the faded eve, 'Move eastward,' etc.			3
the skirt and *f* of our fair land, .	*Princess,* v.		210
close Her crimson *f*'s to the shower ;	*In Mem.* lxxi.		12
fringed.			
knightly growth that *f* his lips. .	*M. d' Arthur*		220
A looming bastion *f* with fire. .	*In Mem.* xv.		20
frith.			
o'er the *f*'s that branch and spread	*In Mem. Con.*		115
frock.			
Or the *f* and gipsy bonnet . .	*Maud,* I. xx.		19
frolic (s.)			
Cyril, howe'er He deal in *f*, .	*Princess,* iv.		231
frolic (verb.)			
come hither and *f* and play ; .	*Sea-Fairies*		18
front.			
ashbuds in the *f* of March.'. .	*Gardener's D.*		28
discern The *f* of Sumner-place. .	*Talking O.*		248
some inscription ran along the *f* .	*Princess,* i.		209
terrace ranged along the Northern *f*,	" iii.		102
And riders *f* to *f*, until they closed	" v.		479
Betwixt the black *f*'s long-withdrawn	*In Mem.* cxviii.		6
f to *f* in an hour we stood, .	*Maud,* II. i.		23
thicker down the *f* With jewels .	*Enid*		1537
white star upon his noble *f*, .	"		1605
A *f* of timber-crost antiquity, .	*En. Arden.*		693
huge cathedral *f*'s of every age	*Sea Dreams*		211
front (verb.)			
the crag that *f*'s the Even, . .	*Eleänore*		40
rarely could she *f* in Hall, . .	*Guinevere*		62
fronted.			
daily *f* him In some fresh splendour ;	*Enid*		13
Philip's dwelling *f* on the street, .	*En. Arden.*		732
when first I *f* him, Said 'trust him not ;'	*Sea Dreams*		170
frontier.			
flying reach'd the *f*: . . .	*Princess,* i.		108
Hard by your father's *f*: . .	"		147
fronting.			
F the dawn he moved ; . .	*Œnone*		57
frost.			
There is *f* in your breath . .	*Poet's Mind*		17
the *f* is on the pane : . . .	*May Queen,* ii.		13
sparkled keen with *f* against the hilt :	*M. d' Arthur*		55
Rain, wind *f*, heat, hail, . .	*St S. Stylites*		16
stiff with crackling *f*. . . .	"		113
one wide chasm of time and *f* .	*Princess, Pro.*		93
grief hath shaken into *f*! . .	*In Mem.* iv.		12
streets were black with smoke and *f*,	" lxviii.		5
yule-log sparkled keen with *f*, .	" lxxvii.		5
'My sudden *f* was sudden gain, .	" lxxx.		10
toward the long *f* and longest night,	*A Dedication*		11
f is here, And fuel is dear, (rep.) .	*The Window*		43
Bite, *f*, bite !	"		49, 55
frost-like.			
tipt with *f-l* spires. . . .	*Pal. of Art*		52
froth.			
Upon the topmost *f* of thought. .	*In Mem.* li.		4
frothed.			
He *f* his bumpers to the brim ;	*D. of the O. Year*		19
is your spleen *f* out, or have ye more ?	*Vivien*		617
frothly.			
Sweeping the *f* from the fescue	*Aylmer's F.*		530
frown (s.)			
Whether smile or *f* be fleeter ? (rep.)	*Madeline*		12
F's perfect-sweet along the brow .	"		15
smile and *f* are not aloof . .	"		19
drops down A sudden-curved *f* (rep.)	"		35

		POEM.	LINE.
He had darken'd into a *f* . .	*Maud,* I. xix.		62
turn thy wheel with smile or *f*; .	*Enid*		350
Met his full *f* timidly firm, . .	"		920
other *f*'s than those That knit .	*Aylmer's F.*		723
frown (verb.)			
F and we smile, the lords of our .	*Enid*		354
frowned.			
The seldom-frowning King *f*, .	*Elaine*		711
frowning.			
Smiling, *f*, evermore, (rep.) . .	*Madeline*		8
Florian nodded at him, I *f*; . .	*Princess,* iv.		142
Vivien, *f* in true anger, said : .	*Vivien*		541
Vivien answer'd *f* wrathfully. .	"	554,	618
froze.			
with surprise *F* my swift speech : .	*D. of F. Wom.*		90
To me you *f*: this was my meed .	*Princess,* iv.		223
frozen.			
Till her blood was *f* slowly, .	*L. of Shalott,* iv.		70
Be fix'd and *f* to permanence : .	*Two Voices*		237
stood Stiff as a viper *f*; . .	*Vivien*		694
fruit.			
giving safe pledge of *f*'s, . .	*Ode to Mem.*		13
a *f* of pure Hesperian gold, . .	*Œnone*		65
Behold this *f*, whose gleaming rind	"		70
Paris held the costly *f* Out at .	"		133
cast the golden *f* upon the board .	"		222
stem, Laden with flower and *f* .	*Lotos-E's.*		29
ere my flower to *f* Changed, .	*D. of F. Wom.*		207
f's and cream Served in the .	*Gardener's D.*		190
we stole his *f*, His hens, his eggs ;	*Walk. to the M.*		76
bring me offerings of *f* and flowers :	*St S. Stylites*		126
This *f* of thine by Love is blest, .	*Talking O.*		249
fairer *f* of Love may rest . .	"		251
flower of knowledge changed to *f*	*Love and Duty*		24
and *f*'s, and spices, clear of toll, .	*Golden Year*		45
that which hears but bitter *f* ? .	*Locksley H.*		65
babies roll'd about Like tumbled *f*	*Princess, Pro.*		83
land Of promise : *f* would follow.	" ii.		124
To scare the fowl from *f*: . .	"		210
F, blossom, vine, amber wine, .	" iv.		17
breadth Of Autumn, dropping *f*'s	" vi.		39
A life that bears immortal *f* .	*In Mem.* xxxix.		18
I'll rather take what *f* may be .	" cvii.		13
Of what in them is flower and *f*; .	" Con.		136
It is only flowers, they had no *f*'s,	*Maud,* II. v.		77
threefold to show the *f* within. .	*The Brook* 73,		208
little pitted speck in garner'd *f*, .	*Vivien*		244
sure I think this *f* is hung too high	*Elaine*		770
not idle, but the *f* Of loyal nature,	*Guinevere*		333
be manners such fair *f* ? . .	"		335
by the children, garden-herbs and *f*,	*En. Arden.*		335
The red *f* of an old idolatry— .	*Aylmer's F.*		762
With naked limbs and flowers and *f*,	*The Voyage*		55
we nor paused for *f* nor flowers. .	"		56
his wisdom lightly, like the *f* .	*A Dedication*		12
fruitage.			
f golden-rinded On golden salvers,	*Eleänore*		33
Soft *f*, mighty nuts, and nourishing	*En. Arden.*		556
fruit-bunches.			
rich *f-b* leaning on each other—	*Isabel*		37
fruitful.			
F of further thought and deed, .	*Two Voices*		144
fruitless.			
Which else were *f* of their due, .	*In Mem.* xliv.		14
frustration.			
out of long *f* of her care, . .	*Princess,* vii.		86
fuel.			
Secret wrath like smother'd *f* Burnt	*The Captain*		15
frost is here, And *f* is dear, . .	*The Window*		44
The *f* is all the dearer, . .	"		57
fulfil.			
God *f*'s himself in many ways, .	*M. d' Arthur*		241
discerning *f* This labour, . .	*Ulysses*		43
would but ask you to *f* yourself : .	*Princess,* vii.		131
each *f*'s Defect in each, . .	"		285
To strive, to fashion, to *f*— . .	*In Mem.* cxii.		7

fulfilled.
By its own energy *f* itself, . . *Gardener's D.* 233
For daily hope *f*, to rise again . *Ed. Morris*. 38
My father 'that our compact be *f*: *Princess*, v. 111
    fulfilment.
to rise again Revolving toward *f*, *Ed. Morris*. 39
    full-accomplished.
hers by right of *f-a* Fate; . . *Pal. of Art* 207
    full-blown.
sail'd, *F-b*, before us into rooms . *Princess*, i. . 226
    full-breasted.
f-b swan That, fluting a wild carol *M. d'Arthur* 266
    full-busted.
f-b figure-head Stared o'er the ripple *En. Arden* . 539
    full-celled.
A *f-c* honeycomb of eloquence . *Ed. Morris* 26
    fullest.
his children, ever at its best And *f*; *Elaine* . 336
    full-faced.
all the *f-f* presence of the Gods . *Œnone* . 78
f-f above the valley stood the moon; *Lotos-E's*. . 7
glowing *f-f* welcome, she Began . *Princess*, ii. 166
    full-fed.
a *f-f* river winding slow . . *Pal. of Art* 73
one warm gust, *f-f* with perfume, . *Gardener's D.* 112
What dare the *f-f* liars say of me? *Vivien* . 542
    full-flowing.
f-f harmony Of thy swan-like . *Eleänore* . 46
the *f-f* river of speech Came down *Œnone* . 67
    full-foliaged.
Rock'd the *f-f* elms, and swung . *In Mem.* xciv. 58
    full-grown.
f-g will, Circled thro' all experiences, *Œnone* . 162
suit The *f-g* energies of heaven. . *In Mem.* xxxix. 20
    full-juiced.
The *f-j* apple, waxing over-mellow, *Lotos-E's*. . 78
    full-limbed.
those whom God has made *f-l* and tall, *Guinevere* 43
    fullness.
by degrees to *f* wrought, 'You ask me why,' etc. 14
reveal'd The *f* of her face— 'Of old sat Freedom,' etc. 12
my pulses with the *f* of the Spring. *Locksley H.* 36
The *f* of the pensive mind; . . *Day-Dm.* . 260
Lest of the *f* of my life I leave *Will Water*. 163
weep the *f* from the mind: . . *In Mem.* xx. 6
note Had reach'd a thunderous *f*, . *Sea Dreams* 207
    full-sailed.
How may *f-s* verse express, . . *Eleänore* . 44
    full-summed.
side by side, *f-s* in all their powers, *Princess*, vii. 272
    full-summer.
thro' the field, that shone *F-s*, . *Elaine* . 1135
    full-tided.
at Caerleon the *f-t* Usk, . . *Enid* . . 965
    full-toned.
High over the *f-t* sea: . . . *Sea-Fairies* 15
    full-tuned.
its syllables, to keep My own *f-t*— *Love and Duty* 40
    full-welling.
Few fountain-heads of change, . *Pal. of Art* 166
    fulminated.
f Against the scarlet woman . . *Sea Dreams* 22
    fulmined.
f out her scorn of laws Salique . *Princess*, ii. 117
    Fulvia.
Y' u should have clung to *F's* waist, *D. of F. Wom.* 259
    fume (s.)
in every is the *f* of little hearts. *Guinevere* . 626

fume (verb.)
We fret, we *f*, would shift our skins, *Will Water*. 225
    fun (found.)
f un theer a-laäid on 'is faäce . *N. Farmer* 33
    function.
plies His *f* of the woodland: . . *Lucretius* . 46
    funeral.
A *f*, with plumes and lights, . *L. of Shalott*, ii. 31
Had seldom seen a costlier *f*. . *En. Arden*. 915
    fur.
My father sent ambassadors with *f's Princess*, i. 41
    furiously.
f Down thro' the bright lawns . *Aylmer's F.* 310
    furl.
come hither and *f* your sails, . *Sea-Fairies* 16, 21
    furled.
battle-flags were *f* in the Parliament *Locksley H.* 127
And never sail of ours was *f*. . *The Voyage* 81
    furlough.
To yield us farther *f*: . . *Princess*, iii. 53
    furnace.
all the *f* of the light Struck up *Mariana in the S.* 55
    furnished.
bravely *f* all abroad to fling . . *The Poet* . 25
    furred.
Tho' smock'd, or *f* and purpled, . *Princess*, iv. 228
    furrow.
smite The sounding *f's*; . . *Ulysses* . 59
in the *f* broke the ploughman's head, *Princess*, v. 212
reddening in the *f's* of his chin, .   " vi. 211
meteor on, and leaves A shining *f*, .   " vii. 170
Or in the *f* musing stands; . . *In Mem.* lxiii. 27
down in a *f* scathed with flame: . *The Victim* 22
    furrow-cloven.
huddling slant in *f-c* falls . . *Princess*, vii. 192
    furrowing.
f into light the mounded rack, *Love and Duty* 97
f all the orient into gold. . . *Princess*, iii. 2
struck, *F* a giant oak, . . . *Vivien* . 785
    fury.
such warbling *f* thro' the words *Princess*, iv. 563
'How then? who then?' a *f* seized, *Elaine* . 475
    Fury (a deity.)
Like to *Furies*, like to Graces, . *Vision of Sin* 41
And Life, a *F* slinging flame. . *In Mem.* xlix. 8
household *F* sprinkled with blood *Maud*, I. xix. 32
numbs the *F's* ringlet-snake, . *Lucretius* . 258
    furze.
on these dews that drench the *f*, . *In Mem.* xi. 6
    fuse.
Whose fancy *f's* old and new, . *In Mem.* xvi. 18
    fused.
manhood *f* with female grace . *In Mem.* cviii. 17
    fusing.
f all The skirts of self again, . *In Mem.* xlvi. 2
    futile.
O life as *f*, then, as frail! . . *In Mem.* lv. 25
    future.
When I dipt into the *f*. . . *Locksley H.* 15, 119
wind of prophecy Dilating on the *f*; *Princess*, ii. 155
Nemesis break from a darken'd *f*,   " vi. 150
this he kept Thro' all his *f*; . . *En. Arden*. 236
    futurity.
cope Of the half-attain'd *f*. . . *Ode to Mem.* 33
    fuzz.
Nowt at all but bracken an' *f*, . *N. Farmer*. 38

G

gabble.   POEM.   LINE.
Nothing but idiot g! . . . Maud, II. v. 41

gable.
half A score of g's. . . Walk. to the M. 10
overhead Fantastic g's, crowding, Godiva . 61

gable-ends.
burn'd On the blossom'd g-e. . Maud, I. vi. 9

Gabriel.
Whose Titan angels, G, Abdiel, . Milton . 5

gad-fly.
sung to, when, this g-f brush'd aside, Princess, v. 404

Gaffer.
Ran G, stumbled Gammer. . . The Goose . 34

gagelike.
flung defiance down G to man, . Princess, v. 170

gaiety.
G without eclipse Weareth me, . Lilian . 20

gain (s.)
I can but count thee perfect g, . Pal. of Art 198
gentle words are always g: 'Love thou thy land,' etc. 23
foreheads, vacant of our glorious g's, Locksley H. 175
find in loss a g to match? . . In Mem. i. . 6
Or but subserves another's g,   "   liii. 12
turns his burthen into g.   "   lxxix. 12
'My sudden frost was sudden g, .   "   lxxx. 10
fuller g of after bliss; . .   "   cxvi. 4
lust of g, in the spirit of Cain, . Maud, I. i. . 23
Ours the pain, be his the g! . Ode on Well. 241
g Of glory, and has added wound Elaine . 565
my pretext, as for g Of purer glory.'   "   . 585
his g's were dock'd, however small: Sea Dreams 7
Small were his g's, and hard his work,   "   . 8
His g is loss; for he that wrongs .   "   . 168
never naming God except for g, .   "   . 184

gain (verb.)
And g her for my bride. . . Talking O. . 284
seas, that daily g upon the shore, . Golden Year 29
help my prince to g His rightful bride, Princess,iii. 144
play the slave to g the tyranny; .   "   iv. 114
g in sweetness and in moral height,   "   vii. 265
g The praise that comes to constancy.' In Mem. xxi. 11
How g in life, as life advances, To F. D. Maurice 39
could I g her, our kind Queen, . Enid . . 787
to g Him, the most famous man . Vivien . 21
In hope to g upon her flight. . The Voyage 60
man may g Letting his own life go. Lucretius . 112

gained.
even then she g Her bower; . Godiva . 76
hast not g a real height, . . Two Voices . 91
g a laurel for your brow 'You might have won,' etc. 3
g the mother-city thick with towers, Princess, i. 111
g A little street half garden . .   "   . 210
we paced, and g The terrace .   "   iii. 101
thus much, nor more I g.' . .   "   . 151
grasping down the boughs I g the shore. " iv. 171
cross'd the street and g a petty mound " . 535
on they moved and g the hall, .   "   vi. 332
In such discourse we g the garden rails," Con. 80
A wretched vote may be g. . Maud, I. vi. 56
He that g a hundred fights, . Ode on Well. 96
forded Usk, and g the wood; . Enid . . 161
Of honour, where no honour can be g:" . 1552
leaving Arthur's court he g the beach; Vivien . 46
g the cell in which he slept, . Elaine . 807
G for her own scanty sustenance, En. Arden . 258
Philip g As Enoch lost; . .   "   . 351
seaward-bound for health they g a coast, Sea Dreams 16

Galahad.
Not even Lancelot brave, nor G clean. Vivien . 654
pure Sir G to uplift the maid; . Elaine . 1258

Galaxy.
Hung in the golden G. . L. of Shalott,iii.12

gale.   POEM.   LINE.
merrily, merrily carol the g's . Sea-Fairies . 23
Sweet g's, as from deep gardens, blow Fatima . 24
strong g's Hold swollen clouds from D. of F. Wom.10
the last night's g had caught, . Gardener's D.123
Storm'd in orbs of song, a growing g; Vision of Sin 25
drank the g That blown about the Princess, iii. 104
Who changest not in any g, . In Mem. ii. 10
Caught and cuff'd by the g: . Maud, I. vi. 5
with a thousand winter g's . . En. Arden . 95
Caught the shrill salt, and sheer'd the g. The Voyage 12

Galilee.
still'd the rolling wave of G! . Aylmer's F. 709

galingale.
meadow, set with slender g; . Lotos-E's . 23

gall (bile, etc.)
changed a wholesome heart to g. L.C.V.de Vere 44
the last drop in the cup of g. . Walk. to the M. 61
Unto me my maudlin g . Vision of Sin 201

gall (oak-apple.)
insects prick Each leaf into a g) . Talking O. . 70

gallery.
in thy various g Place it, . . Ode to Mem. 84
By garden-wall and g, . . L. of Shalott,iv.38
round the roofs a gilded g . . Pal. of Art 29
light aërial g, golden-rail'd, .   "   . 47
long-laid galleries past a hundred Princess, vi. 354
golden hours, In those long galleries The Daisy 42
let his eyes Run thro' the peopled g Elaine . 429
armed feet Thro' the long g . . Guinevere . 410

gallopaded.
willows two and two By rivers g. . Amphion . 40

galloped.
and so g up the knoll. . . Enid . . 168
as he g up To join them, . . " . . 171

galloping.
g hoofs bare on the ridge of spears Princess, v. 478

Gama.
His name was G; crack'd and small Princess, i. 113
Then G turn'd to me: 'We fear, indeed, " v. 115
This G swamp'd in lazy tolerance. " . 433
can this be he From G's dwarfish loins? " . 495

gambol.
For these your dainty g's: . Vivien . 158
mother he had never known In g's; Aylmer's F. 691

gambolled.
when she g on the greens . . Talking O. . 77
We g, making vain pretence Of In Mem. xxx. 6
Glanced at the doors or g down . Enid . . 665

game (animals.)
touch'd upon the g, how scarce it was Audley Ct. 31
Man is the hunter; woman is his g; Princess, v. 147
No, there is fatter g on the moor; Maud, I. i. 74
He bore but little g in hand; . The Victim . 44

game (pastime.)
The g of forfeits done— . The Epic . 2
some odd g's In some odd nooks . " . 8
She remember'd that: A pleasant g Princess,Pro.191
Quoit, tennis, ball—no g's? . " iii. 199
dance and song and g and jest. In Mem. xxix. 8
Again our ancient g's had place, . " lxxvii. 10
Poor rivals in a losing g, . . " ci. 19
Be neither song, nor g, nor feast; " civ. 21
moved by an unseen hand at a g. Maud, I. iv. 26
play the g of the despot kings, . " x. 39
At civic revel and pomp and g, Ode on Well. 147,227

gamesome.
Then ran she, g as a colt, . . Talking O. 121

Gammer.
Ran Gaffer, stumbled G. . . The Goose . 34

gamut.
their shrieks Ran highest up the g, Sea Dreams 226

Ganymede.	POEM.	LINE.
flush'd G, his rosy thigh Half-buried	Pal. of Art	121
I think he came like G,	Will Water.	119
'they mounted, G's, To tumble, Vulcans	Princess, iii.	55

gap.

from the *g*'s and chasms of ruin left *Sea Dreams* 218

gape.

| A gulf that ever shuts and *g*'s, | In Mem. lxix. | 6 |
| any mouth to *g* for save a Queen's— | Elaine | 771 |

gaped.

| Lavaine *g* upon him . | Elaine | 451 |
| tier over tier, Were added mouths that *g*, | " | 1242 |

gaping.

| The passive oxen *g*, | Amphion | 72 |
| fool, Who was *g* and grinning by ; | Maud, II. i. | 20 |

gap-tooth'd.

A grey and *g-t* man as lean as death, *Vision of Sin* 60

garden.

High-wall'd *g*'s green and old ;	Arabian N's.	8
Thence thro' the *g* I was drawn—	"	100
rooted in the *g* of the mind, .	Ode to Mem.	26
g bower'd close With plaited alleys	"	105
the world Like one great *g* show'd,	The Poet	34
In the heart of the *g* the merry bird	Poet's Mind	22
whitest honey in fairy *g*'s cull'd—	Eleänore	26
sweet gales, as from deep *g*'s, blow	Fatima	24
g full of flowering weeds To——	With Pal. of Art	4
the *g*'s and the halls Of Camelot,	M. d'Arthur	20
blooms the *g* that I love.	Gardener's D.	34
between it and the *g* lies A league	"	39
The *g* stretches southward.	"	114
One after one, thro' that still *g* pass'd :	"	196
cross'd the *g* to the gardener's lodge,	Audley Ct.	16
A breeze thro' all the *g* swept,	Day-Dm.	138
A *g* too with scarce a tree,	Amphion	3
at the end of all A little *g* blossom.	"	104
Parks and order'd *g*'s great,	L. of Burleigh	30
A little street half *g* and half house ;	Princess,	1. 211
grace Concluded, and we sought the *g*'s :	"	ii. 429
Above the *g*'s glowing blossom-belts,	"	v. 353
'Look there, a *g !*' said my college	Con.	49
Since Adam left his *g* yet.	In Mem. xxiv.	8
So that still *g* of the souls	"	xlii. 10
gust that round the *g* flew,	"	lxxxviii. 19
Till from the *g* and the wild .	"	c. 17
like the sultan of old in a *g* of spice.	Maud, I. iv.	42
Maud has a *g* of roses .	"	xiv. 1
great Forefathers of the thornless *g*,	"	xviii. 27
Come into the *g*, Maud, (rep.)	"	xxii. 1
Queen rose of the rosebud *g* of girls,	"	53
g by the turrets Of the old manorial	"	II. iv. 79
I know where a *g* grows,	"	v. 72
All round a careless-order'd *g*	To F. D. Maurice	15
this was in the *g* of a king ;	Enid	656
Flourished a little *g* square and	En. Arden	735
arranged Her *g*, sow'd her name.	Aylmer's F.	68
fann'd the *g*'s of that rival rose	"	455
Kept to the *g* now, and grove of	"	550
in the *g* snared Picus and Faunus,	Lucretius	181

garden (verb.)

I shall never *g* more : . . . *May Queen*, ii. 46

garden-bower.

| Black the *g-b*'s and grots | Arabian N's | 78 |
| To and fro they went Thro' my *g-b*, | The Flower | 6 |

gardener.

The grand old *g* and his wife	L. C. V. de Vere	51
went To see the *G*'s Daughter ;	Gardener's D.	3
'Go and see The *G*'s daughter ;	"	30
not heard Of Rose, the *G*'s daughter ?	"	51
cross'd the garden to the *g*'s lodge,	Audley Ct.	16
charge the *g*'s now To pick the	Enid	670
made a *G* putting in a graff,	Vivien	329
g's hand Picks from the colewort	Guinevere	32

garden-gate.

And stood by her *g-g* ; .	Maud, I. xiv.	6
looks Upon Maud's own *g-g* ;	"	16
push'd at Philip's *g-g*.	The Brook	83

garden-glass.	POEM.	LINE.
The *g-g*'es shone, and momently	Gardener's D.	116

garden-herbs.

Gifts by the children, *g-h* and fruit, *En. Arden* . 335

gardening.

Botanic Treatises, And Works on *G Amphion* . 78

garden-isles.

meadowy holms, And alders, *g-i* ; *Ed. Morris* 96

garden-rose.

| This *g-r* that I found. | Maud, I. xxi. | 3 |
| outredden All voluptuous *g-r*'s. | Ode on Well. | 208 |

garden-square.

And in the sultry *g-s*'s, . . . *The Blackbird* 17

garden-squirt.

Half-conscious of the *g-s*, . . . *Amphion* . 91

garden-tools.

my *g-t* upon the granary floor : . *May Queen*, ii. 45

garden-wall.

That held the pear to the *g-w*	Mariana	4
By *g-w* and gallery,	L. of Shalott, iv.	38
ran the field Flat to the *g-w* :	Princess, v.	352
Climb'd to the high top of the *g-w*	Guinevere	26
feeling all along the *g-w*,	En. Arden	774

garden-walks.

As down the *g-w* I muve, . . *In Mem.* ci. 6

Gargarus.

topmost G Stands up and takes . *Œnone* . 10

garland.

Do make a *g* for the heart :	Miller's D.	198
knots of flowers, and buds and *g*'s	May Queen, i.	11
spears That soon should wear the *g* ;	Aylmer's F.	112

garlanded.

Each *g* with her peculiar flower . *Gardener's D.* 297

garlanding.

g the gnarled boughs With bunch *Œnone* . 97

garment.

| eddying of her *g*'s caught from thee | Ode to Mem. | 32 |
| woman's *g* hid the woman's heart.' | Princess, v. | 293 |

garner.

wrath that *g*'s in my heart ; . . *In Mem.* lxxxi. 14

garnet.

Each like a *g* or a turkis in it ; . *Enid* . 662

garrulity.

Shame on her own *g* garrulously, *Guinevere* . 310

garrulous.

| *G* under a roof of pine ; . | To F. D. Maurice | 20 |
| Miriam Lane was good and *g*, | En. Arden | 701 |

garrulously.

To whom the little novice *g*. . *Guinevere* 229-74

garth.

in a clapper clapping in a *g*,	Princess, ii.	209
past into the little *g* beyond.	En. Arden	326
I climb'd to the top of the *g*,	Grandmother	38

gash.

| 'G thyself, priest, and honour | Aylmer's F. | 644 |
| wilt not *g* thy flesh for him ; | " | 658 |

gas-light.

The *g-l* wavers dimmer ; . . *Will Water.* 38

gasp.

cheating the sick of a few last *g*'s, *Maud*, I. i. . 43

gasping.

G to Sir Lavaine, 'draw . . . *Elaine* . 510

gate.

Thro' the open *g*'s of the city afar,	Dying Swan	34
look in at the *g* With his large calm	The Mermaid	26
The lion on your old stone *g*'s	L. C. V. de Vere	23
Are there no beggars at your *g*,	"	67
along From Mizpeh's tower'd *g*,	D. of F. Wom.	199
pass'd his father's *g*, Heart-broken,	Dora	48

L

	POEM.	LINE.
we reach'd The griffin-guarded g's,	Audley Ct.	14
Battering the g's of heaven with	St S. Stylites	7
Once more the g behind me falls;	Talking O.	1
Her mother trundled to the g,	"	111
Every g is throng'd with suitors	Locksley H.	101
Saw distant g's of Eden gleam,	Two Voices	212
ta'en my fiddle to the g, (rep.)	Amphion	11
the g's Roll back, and far within	St Agnes' Eve	29
And beneath the g she turns;	L. of Burleigh	44
music touch'd and died;	Vision of Sin	23
cold vapour touch'd the palace g,	"	58
wind blew from the g's of the sun,	Poet's Song	3
thro' the g, Had beat her foes	Princess, Pro.	33
with a blast of trumpets from the g,	"	42
saw you not the inscription on the g,	" ii.	177
bury me beside the g,	"	189
urged the fierce inscription on the g,	" iii.	125
paint the g's of Hell with Paradise,	" iv.	113
at top, and grimly spiked the g's.	"	188
Here, push them out at g's.'	"	527
with grim laughter thrust us out at g's.	"	534
thrice had sent a herald to the g's,	" v.	322
Came sallying thro' the g's, and caught	"	330
thro' those dark g's across the wild	" vii.	341
the g's were closed At sunset,	Con.	36
In circle round the blessed g,	In Mem. lxxxiv.	23
They can but listen at the g's,	" xciii.	15
My pulses closed their g's	Maud, I. i.	15
g's of Heaven are closed, and she is	" xviii.	12
I am here at the g alone	" xxii.	4
From the passion-flower at the g.	"	60
her brother ran in his rage to the g,	" II. i.	12
The g, Half-parted from a weak	The Brook	83
descending met them at the g's,	Enid	833
should moulder on the city g's.	Vivien	444
Then made a sudden step to the g,	Elaine	390
and under the strong-statued g,	"	796
beneath the wildly-sculptured g's	"	840
small g that open'd on the waste,	En. Arden	734
Crept to the g, and open'd it, and.	"	776
Stands at thy g for thee to grovel	Aylmer's F.	652
nevermore did either pass the g	"	826
stood by the road at the g.	Grandmother	38
there past by the g of the farm,	"	41
Burst the g's, and burn the palaces,	Boädicea	64

gateway.
at the g's of the day.	Locksley H.	158
until she reach'd The g;	Godiva	51
Or in the g's of of the morn.	Two Voices	183
Till a g she discerns	L. of Burleigh	42
Right in the g of the bandit hold,	Enid	1622
in the g, standing by the shield	Elaine	393

gather.
words did g thunder as they ran	The Poet	49
I must g knots of flowers,	May Queen, i.	11
To g and tell o'er Each little sound	D. of F. Wom.	276
Where faction seldom g's head 'You ask me why,' etc.		13
Rise in the heart, and g to the eyes,	Princess, iv.	23
she not fair, began To g light,	" vii.	9
as he grows his g's much,	In Mem. xliv.	5
g dust and chaff, and call	" liv.	18
Shall g in the cycled times.	" lxxxiv.	28
Unloved, that beech will g brown,	" c.	3
Should licensed boldness g force,	" cxii.	13
'I sit and g honey;	Vivien	451
Sigh'd, and began to g heart again,	Guinevere	366

gathered.
A cloud that g shape!	Œnone	41
When I am g to the glorious saints.	St S. Stylites	194
Have suck'd and g into one The life	Talking O.	191
Whose wrinkles g on his face,	Two Voices	329
Grave faces g in a ring.	Day-Dm.	58
Till they be g up;	Will Water.	170
The topmost elmtrees g green	Sir L. and Q. G.	8
Easily g either guilt.	Princess, iv.	217
of half the maids G together:	"	456
the heavy dews G by night and	" v.	234
such as g colour day by day.	" vii.	103

	POEM.	LINE.
Abide: thy wealth is g in,	In Mem. li.	15
fought his doubts and g strength,	" xcv.	13
The maidens g strength and grace	" cii.	27
g the bones for his o'ergrown	Maud, II. v.	55
this she g from the people's eyes:	Enid	61
g trickling dropwise from the cleft,	Vivien	123
again When burr and bine were g;	Aylmer's F.	113
G the blossom that rebloom'd,	"	142

gathering (part.)
the mighty moon was g light	Love and Death	1
Proserpine in Enna, g flowers:	Ed. Morris	112
G up from all the lower ground;	Vision of Sin	15
And g freshlier overhead,	In Mem. xciv.	57
G woodland lilies, Myriads blow	Maud, I. xii.	7
Vivien g somewhat of his mood,	Vivien	691
g at the base Re-makes itself,	Guinevere	603

gathering (s.)
| A g of the Tory, | Maud, I. xx. | 33 |

gaudy-day.
| Amends hereafter by some g-d, | Enid | 610 |

gaunt.
| G as it were the skeleton of himself, | Elaine | 762, 012 |

gauntlet.
| maiden fancies dead In iron g's: | Princess, i. | 60 |

gauze.
dried his wings: like g they grew:	Two Voices	13
Purple g's, golden hazes, liquid	Vision of Sin	31
Half-lapt in glowing g and golden	Princess, vi.	113

gave.
God g her peace; her land	To the Queen	26
the foolish song I g you, Alice,	Miller's D.	15
look, mother, I g him yesterday—	May Queen, i.	15
and fruit, whereof they g To each	Lotos-E's.	29
my bliss of life, that Nature g,	D. of F. Wom.	210
the kiss he g me, ere I fell,	"	235
g you on your natal day.	Margaret	42
g me a friend, and a true	D. of the O. Year	13
perform'd my mission which I g?	M. d' Arthur	67
yielding, g into a grassy walk	Gardener's D.	110
Kissing the rose she g me o'er and	"	172
G utterance by the yearning of an	Love and Duty	61
g him mind, the lordliest	Two Voices	19
g the people of their best 'You might have won,'		25
worst he kept, his best he g.	"	26
G his broad lawns until the set of	Princess, Pro.	2
they g The park, the crowd, the	"	93
said no, Yet being an easy man, g it:	" i.	148
g a costly bribe To guerdon silence,	"	200
rooms which g Upon a pillar'd porch,	"	226
g the letter to be sent with dawn;	"	241
a glance I g, No more;	" iv.	162
On one knee Kneeling, I g it,	"	449
Who g me back my child?'	" v.	102
Let out so much as g us leave to go.	"	225
Was it for this we g our palace up,	" vi.	227
Refuse her proffer, lastly g his hand.	"	327
the men, the women: I g assent;	Con.	7
The Danube to the Severn g	In Mem. xix.	11
g all ripeness to the grain	" lxxxiv.	11
Received and g him welcome there;	" lxxxiv.	24
him to whom her hand I g.	" Con.	70
He fiercely g me the lie,	Maud, II. i.	16
By the home that g me birth,	" iv.	7
the matter hung: He g them line	The Brook	145, 150
g my letters back to me.	The Letters	20
And g the trinkets and the rings,	"	21
I pluck'd a daisy, I g it you.	The Daisy	88
good king g order to let blow	Enid	152
g command that all which once was	"	696
he but g a wrathful groan,	"	1247
cousin, slay not him who g you life.'	"	1631
all-shamed, hating the life He g me,	"	1701
knew no more, nor g me one poor	Vivien	126
Use g me Fame at first,	"	343
Fame again Increasing g me use.	"	344
brother's; which he g to Lancelot,	Elaine	379
g A marvellous great shriek.	"	514

	POEM.	LINE.
he took, And g, the diamond:	Elaine	550
g, And slightly kiss'd the hand to which he g,	"	697
I g the diamond: she will render it;	"	709
off the case, and g the naked shield;	"	973
Then g a languid hand to each,	"	1026
that I g No cause, not willingly,	"	1289
and he g them charge about the Queen,	Guinevere	585
clipt A tiny curl, and g it:	En. Arden	235
less Than what she g in buying	"	255
he paused and g his hand,	"	444
clothes they g him and free passage	"	651
Pitying the lonely man, and g him it.	"	665
the woman g A half-incredulous	"	853
she cut it off and g it,	"	895
scared with threats of jail and halter g	Aylmer's F.	520
dagger which himself G Edith,	"	597
g the verse 'Behold Your house	"	628
and he g the ringers a crown.	Grandmother	58
She that g you's bought and sold,	The Ringlet	33
g you me, and said, 'Come, kiss it,	"	40

gave way.

trance g w To those caresses,	Love and Duty	63
everything G w before him:	Princess, v.	519
to them the doors g w Groaning,	" vi.	329

Gawain.

G, rise, My nephew, and ride forth,	Elaine	535
G, surnamed The Courteous, fair and	"	554
G the while thro' all the region round	"	612
G saw Sir Lancelot's azure lions,	"	659
there the fine G will wonder at me,	"	1048
G, who bad a thousand farewells	"	1050
came the fine G and wonder'd at her,	"	1260

gay.

you were g With bridal flowers—	Miller's D.	164
g, or grave, or sweet, or stern,	Pal. of Art	91
never a one so g,	Poet's Song	14
propt against the wall As g as any.	Princess, Pro.	100
one is glad; her note is g,	In Mem. xxi.	25
To find me g among the g,	" lxv.	2
all is g with lamps, and loud	" xcvii.	27
Like things of the season g,	Maud, i. iv.	3
if I cannot be g let a passionless peace	"	50
Strange, that I felt so g,	" xx.	1
With whom she has heart to be g.	" xxii.	20
seeing one so g in purple silks,	Enid	284
like a crag was g with wilding flowers:	"	319
with my gift, and g among the g.'	"	753
that good mother, old Enid g	"	757
a'l that week was old Caerleon g,	"	837
How g, how suited to the house of	"	1531

gay-furred.

| Her g-f cats a painted fantasy, | Princess, iii. | 170 |

gaze (s.)

| Than that the earth should stand at g | Locksley H. | 180 |
| her ardent g Roves from the living | In Mem. xxxii. | 6 |

gaze (verb.)

Ever retiring thou dost g	Ode to Mem.	93
ev'n while we g on it,	Eleänore	90
g upon My palace with unblinded eyes,	Pal. of Art	41
He g's on the silent dead:	Day-Dm.	113
Evermore she seems to g	L. of Burleigh	34
climbs a peak to g O'er land and main,	Princess, vii.	20
I, who g with temperate eyes	In Mem. cxi.	2
Sigh fully, or all-silent g upon him	Vivien	38
who can g upon the Sun in heaven?	Elaine	124
fain would g upon him to the last;	Lucretius	140

gazed.

G on the Persian girl alone,	Arabian N's.	134
Two godlike faces g below;	Pal. of Art	162
g so long That both his eyes were	M. d'Arthur	58
long we g, but satiated at length	Princess, Pro.	100
I drew near; I g.	" iii.	167
She g awhile and said, 'As these rude	"	278
while We g upon her came a little stir	" iv.	354
to the roofs, and g alone for hours	" vii.	17
Where first we g upon the sky;	In Mem. ci.	2

	POEM.	LINE.
kept her off and g upon her face,	Enid	519
g upon her blankly and gone by:	Vivien	17
never g upon it but I dreamt	"	361
G at the heaving shoulder,	"	745
while he g wonderingly at her, came	Elaine	623
Averill went and g upon his death.	Aylmer's F.	599

gazer.

| With lifted hand the g in the street. | Ode on Well. | 22 |

gazest.

| When thou g at the skies? | Adeline | 50 |

gazing.

G where the lilies blow	L. of Shalott, i.	7
G on thee for evermore,	Eleänore	80
with most intensity G, I seem to see	"	83
sense Of Passion g upon thee.	"	116
If g on divinity disrobed	Œnone	154
dim with g on the pilot-stars.	Lotos-E's.	132
From her isle-altar g down,	'Of old sat Freedom', etc.	14
In g up an Alpine height,	Two Voices	362
stood, so rapt, we g, came a voice,	Princess, ii.	297
murmur'd Florian g after her,	" iii.	81
All open-mouth'd, all g to the light,	" iv.	462
Ida spoke not, g on the ground,	" vi.	210
so fared she g there;	" vii.	26
g on thee, sullen tree,	In Mem. ii.	13
sadly g on her bridle-reins,	Enid	1343
There he sat down g on all below;	En. Arden	724
His g in on Annie, his resolve	"	864

gear.

| sent mine host to purchase female g; | Princess, i. | 196 |

gem.

In hollow'd moons of g's.	Pal. of Art	188
lest the g's Should blind my purpose,	M. d'Arthur	152
Airing a snowy hand and signet g,	Princess, i.	120
rainbow robes, and g's and gemlike eyes,	" iv.	459
like sunny g's on an English green.	Maud, I. v.	14
How like a g, beneath, the city	The Daisy	7
In crimsons and in purples and in g's.	Enid	10
wont to glance and sparkle like a g	"	1143
so thickly shone the g's.	"	1541
had the g's Pluck'd from the crown,	Elaine	57
Received at once and laid aside the g's	"	1196

Gemini.

| starry G hang like glorious crowns. | Maud, III. vi. | 7 |

gem-like.

a fire-balloon Rose g-l up	Princess, Pro.	75
rainbow robes, and gems and g eyes,	" iv.	459
Luminous, g, ghostlike, deathlike,	Maud, I. iii.	8
a meadow g chased In the brown wild,	Enid	1047

gemmi'd.

| a coppice g with green and red, | Enid | 339 |

generation.

| mould a g strong to move | Princess, v. | 406 |
| knit The g's each with each; | In Mem. xxxix. | 16 |

generous.

| All brave, and many g, and some chaste. | Vivien | 666 |

genial.

| and shone; so g was the hearth: | En. Arden | 744 |

genins.

| thou hearest The first-born of thy g. | Ode to Mem. | 92 |
| A fairy shield your G made. | Margaret | 41 |

Genovese.

| The grave, severe G of old. | The Daisy | 40 |

gentle.

Lean'd on him, faithful, g, good,	Two Voices	416
the yoke, I wish it G as freedom'—	Princess, vi.	38
So g, so employ'd, should close in love,	" vii.	52
As g; liberal-minded, great,	In Mem. Con.	38
My mother, who was so g and good?	Maud, I. vi.	67
Was it g to reprove her	" xx.	8
much too g, have not used my power;	Enid	467
Pray you be g, pray you let me be;	"	1556
to be g than ungentle with you;	"	1564

CONCORDANCE TO

	POEM.	LINE.
thought that he was *g*, being great :	*Vivien*	720
Unbound as yet, and *g*, as I know'	*Elaine*	1377

gentle-hearted.
The *g-h* wife Sat shuddering	*Sea Dreams*	29

gentleman.
King Arthur, like a modern *g*	*M. d'Arthur, Ep.*	22
watch'd by silent *gentlemen*,	*Will Water.*	231
a *g* of broken means	*Princess,* i.	52
three gallant *gentlemen* to death.'	" ii.	314
'You have done well and like a *g*,	" iv.	506-9
The grand old name of *g*,	*In Mem.* cx.	22
O selfless man and stainless *g*,	*Vivien*	641

gentleness.
Winning its way with extreme *g*	*Isabel*	23
More soluble is this knot, By *g*	*Princess,* v.	130
this firebrand—*g* To such as her!.	"	160
The *g* he seem'd to be,	*In Mem.* cx.	12
Yea, God, I pray you of your *g*,	*Enid*	1358
Subdued me somewhat to that *g*	"	1715

gentler-born.
The *g-b* the maiden, the more bound	*Elaine*	762

gentlewoman.
hammer at this reverend *g*.	*Princess,* iii.	113
not one among my *gentlewomen*	*Enid*	1470
see you not my *gentlewomen* here	"	1530
one among his *gentlewomen* .	"	1534
stood A virtuous *g* deeply wrong'd,	*Vivien*	760

gentlier.
Music that *g* on the spirit lies,	*Lotos-E's.*	50

geology.
Now hawking at G and schism ;	*The Epic*	16

Geraint.
The brave G, a knight of Arthur's	*Enid*	1
loved G To make her beauty vary	"	8
Grateful to Prince G for service	"	15
in their common love rejoiced G..	"	23
Not less G believed it ;..	"	28
day by day she thought to tell G,	"	65
Prince G, Late also, wearing	"	164
G Exclaiming, ' Surely I will learn	"	202
Prince G, now thinking that he heard	"	232
thither came G, and underneath .	"	241
G flash'd into sudden spleen	"	273
rode G, a little spleenful yet,	"	293
rode G into the castle court,	"	312
the sweet voice of Enid moved G ;	"	334
So fared it with G, who	" 343,	857, 1349
thought G, ' Here by God's rood .	"	367
G, from utter courtesy, forbore..	"	381
G had longing in him evermore	"	394
after all had eaten, then G,	"	397
—I am G Of Devon—.	"	409
G, a name far-sounded among men	"	427
G with eyes all bright replied,	"	494
waited there for Yniol and G.	"	538
when G Beheld her first in field,	"	539
Increased G's, who heaved his blade	"	572
No later than last eve to Prince G—	"	603
She look'd on ere the coming of G.	"	614
G Woke where he slept in the high	"	754
G to greet her thus attired ;.	"	772
at the midmost charging, Prince G	"	934
lance err'd ; but G's, A little	"	1006
G, dismounting, pick'd the lance	"	1028
G had ruth again on Enid	"	1051
G Ate all the mowers' victual	"	1063
Her suitor in old years before G,	"	1125
Greeted G full face, but stealthily,	"	1128
cried G for wine and goodly cheer	"	1132
Enid left alone with Prince G,	"	1214
G look'd and was not satisfied	"	1284
G Waving an angry hand	"	1292
uttering a dry shriek, Dash'd on G,	"	1311
like a stormy sunlight smiled G,	"	1329
heard G, and grasping at his sword,	"	1573
then G upon the horse Mounted,	"	1606
' My lord G, I greet you with all	"	1633

	POEM.	LINE.
while G lay healing of his hurt,	*Enid*	1779
when G was whole again, they past	"	1793
tho' G could never take again	"	1797
Enids and G's Of times to be ;.	"	1813
after Lancelot, Tristram, and G	*Elaine*	555

germ.
in it is the *g* of all That grows	*Amphion*	7

germander.
that her clear *g* eye Droopt .	*Sea Dreams*	

gewgaw.
Seeing his *g* castle shine	*Maud,* I. x.	13

ghastly.
g thro' the drizzling rain	*In Mem.* vii.	11

ghost.
He thought I was a *g*, mother	*May Queen,* I.	17
come like *g*'s to trouble joy.	*Lotos-E's.*	110
Was haunted with a jolly *g*	*Walk. to the M.*	28
'Yes, we're flitting,' says the *g*	"	35
Old wishes, *g*'s of broken plans,	*Will Water.*	29
move among a world of *g*'s, (iv. 539)	*Princess,* i.	17
doing battle with forgotten *g*'s,	" v.	469
droops the milkwhite peacock like a *g*,	" vii.	165
like a *g* she glimmers on to me.	"	166
in the dark church like a *g*	*In Mem.* lxvi.	15
O solemn *g*, O crowned soul !	" lxxxiv.	36
Spirit to Spirit, G to G.	"	xcii. 8
My G may feel that thine is near.	"	16
desire, like a glorious *g* to glide,	*Maud,* I. xiv.	20
A disease, a hard mechanic *g*—	" II. ii.	34
the *g* of one who bore your name.	*The Brook*	219
sunders *g*'s and shadow-casting men	*Vivien*	479
like a *g* she lifted up her face,	*Elaine*	914
like a *g* without the power to speak.	"	915
Monotonous and hollow like a G's	*Guinevere*	417
A *g* of passion that no smiles restore	*Coquette,* ii.	11

ghost-like.
Luminous, gemlike, *g*, deathlike,	*Maud,* I. iii.	8
In either twilight *g-l* to and fro	*Elaine*	845
moving *g* to his doom..	*Guinevere*	599

giant.
that you made About my ' *g* bole ;'	*Talking O.*	136
g's living, each, a thousand years	*Princess,* iii.	252
those three stars of the airy G's zone,	" v.	250
The genial *g*, Arac, roll'd himself,	"	264
From Arac's arm, as from a *g*'s flail,	"	489
The *g* labouring in his youth ;	*In Mem.* cxvii.	2
tho' the G Ages heave the hill	*Ode on Well.*	259
g answer'd merrily, 'Yea, but one ?	*Enid*	977
seem'd the phantom of a G in it,	*Guinevere*	596

giant-factoried.
Droopt in the *g-f* city-gloom,	*Sea Dreams*	5

gibe.
solemn *g* did Eustace banter me.	*Gardener's D.*	164

gied (gave.)
toithe were due, an' I *g* it in hond ;	*N. Farmer.*	11

gift.
God's great *g* of speech abused	*A Dirge*	44
Love the *g* is Love the debt.	*Miller's D.*	207
' I woo thee not with *g*'s.	*Œnone*	150
soul possess'd of many *g*'s, To—	*With Pal. of Art*	3
met With interchange of *g*.	*Pal. of Art*	144
knew your *g* that way At College ;	*The Epic*	24
holy Elders with the *g* of myrrh.	*M. d'Arthur*	233
Requiring at her hand the greatest *g*,	*Gardener's D.*	224
And yet it was a graceful *g*—	*Talking O.*	233
eaglesof her belt, The grim Earl's *g*;	*Godiva*	44
He owns the fatal *g* of eyes,	*Two Voices*	286
jewels, *g*'s, to fetch her:	*Princess,* i.	42
g's of grace, that might express	*In Mem.* lxxxiv.	46
take the imperfect *g* I bring,	"	117
She keeps the *g* of years before,	"	xcvi. 25
g's, when *g*'s of mine could please ;	*The Letters*	22
flower'd with gold, a costly *g*.	*Enid*	621
'Yea, I know it ; your good *g*,	"	688
Your own good *g*.' 'Yea, surely,'	"	690

	POEM.	LINE.
Clothed with my *g*, and gay	Enid	753
from her limbs the costly-broider'd *g*,	"	769
fair child shall wear your costly *g*	"	819
Who knows? another *g* of the high God,	"	821
take it as free *g*, then,' said the boy,	"	1071
months' babe had been a truer *g*.	Vivien	561
pearls, Some gentle maiden's *g*.	Elaine	603
should ask some goodly *g* of him.	"	908
price of half a realm, his costly *g*,	"	1158
thrice their worth Being your *g*,	"	1207
value of all *g*'s Must vary as the	"	1208
I guard as God's high *g*	Guinevere	490
G's by the children, garden-herbs,	En. Arden	335
His oriental *g*'s on everyone	Aylmer's F.	214
Among the *g*'s he left her	"	217
'A gracious *g* to give a lady, this!'	"	240
' Were I to give this *g* of his to one	"	242
'Take it,' she added sweetly, 'tho' his *g*;	"	246
Nor deeds of *g*, but *g*'s of grace he.	Sea Dreams	188
Let me go: take back thy *g*:	Tithonus	27
Gods themselves cannot recall their *g*'s.'	"	49

gifted.

As some divinely *g* man,	In Mem. lxiii.	2

gigantesque.

The sort of mock-heroic *g*,	Princess, Con.	11

gild.

g's the straiten'd forehead of the fool!	Locksley H.	62

gilded.

nature *g* by the gracious gleam	Ded. of Idylls	38

Gileadite.

The daughter of the warrior G,	D. of F. Wom.	197

gillyflowers.

a rosy sea of *g* About it:	Aylmer's F.	159

gilt.

g by the touch of a millionaire ;	Maud, I. i.	66

gilt-head.

court-Galen poised his *g-h* cane,	Princess, i.	19

gipsy.

Or the frock and *g* bonnet	Maud, I. xx.	19

gird.

minds did *g* their orbs with beams,	The Poet	29
Uncared for, *g* the windy grove,	In Mem. c.	13
liever had I *g* his harness on him,	Enid	93

girdle.

And I would be the *g*	Miller's D.	175
twist his *g* tight, and pat The girls	Talking O.	43

girdled.

g with the gleaming world ;	Lotos-E's.	158
And *g* her with music.	Princess, vii.	308

girl.

Gazed on the Persian *g* alone,	Arabian N's.	134
the red cloaks of market *g*'s,	L. of Shalott, ii.	17
g's all kiss'd beneath the sacred bush	The Epic	2
like a *g* Valuing the giddy pleasure	M. d'Arthur	127
'My *g*, I love you well ;	Dora	40
'Go ! G, get you in !'	Ed. Morris.	125
pat The *g*'s upon the cheek,	Talking O.	44
This *g*, for whom your heart is sick,	"	11
a group of *g*'s In circle waited,	Princess, Pro.	68
like as many *g*'s—Sick for the hollies	"	184
lengths of yellow ringlets, like a *g*,	"	i. 3
'G, Knowledge is now no more	"	ii. 75
G's more like men !'	"	iii. 27
Men! *g*'s, like men! why, if they	"	33
nurse a blind ideal like a *g*,	"	201
he seems no better than a *g*;	"	202
As *g*'s were once, as we ourself	"	203
children die ; and let me tell you, *g*,	"	236
G after *g* was call'd to trial ;	"	iv. 209
like enough, O *g*'s, To unfurl the maiden	"	481
and they will beat my *g*	"	v. 85
stormy time With our strange *g* ;	"	117
'Tut, you know them not, the *g*'s.	"	144
Let our *g*'s flit, Till the storm die !	"	vi. 317

	POEM.	LINE.
ill counsel had misled the *g*	Princess, vii.	226
yet was she but a *g*—	"	227
'So fret not, like an idle *g*,	In Mem. li.	13
Like some poor *g* whose heart is set	"	lix. 3
I play'd with the *g* when a child ;	Maud, I. i.	68
'Well if it prove a *g*, the boy	"	vii. 7, 15
soften as if to a *g*,	"	x. 16
from some slight shame one simple *g*	"	xviii. 45
Queen rose of the rosebud garden of *g*'s,	"	xxii. 53
disarray'd as to her rest, the *g* ;	Enid	516
all in charge of whom ? a *g* :	"	974
shall share my earldom with me, *g*,	"	1474
'G, for I see you scorn my courtesies,	"	1513
fixt her heart On that one *g* ;	En. Arden	40
the *g* Seem'd kinder unto Philip	"	41
be back, my *g*, before you know it.'	"	193
as the village *g* Who sets her pitcher	"	206
'Annie, my *g*, cheer up,	"	213
let me put the boy and *g* to school :	"	211-28
o'er her second father stoopt a *g*,	"	748
the *g* So like her mother,	"	791
once with Leolin at her side the *g*,	Aylmer's F.	184
be more gracious,' asked the *g*	"	241
g might be entangled ere she knew.	"	272
g and boy, Sir, know their differences!'	"	274
twenty boys and *g*'s should marry on it,	"	371
found the *g* And flung her down	"	573
Born of a village *g*, carpenter's son,	"	668
a lad may wink, and a *g* may hint,	The Ringlet	17
g's, Hetairai, curious in their art,	Lucretius	52

girl-graduates.

sweet *g-g* in their golden hair.	Princess, Pro.	142

girt.

g round With blackness as a solid wall,	Pal. of Art	273
where *g* with friends or foes, ' You ask me why,'etc.	"	7
g with doubtful light ' Love thou thy land,' etc.	"	16
g the region with high cliff	Vision of Sin	47
the King Came *g* with knights :	Elaine	1254
Enoch's golden ring had *g* Her finger,	En. Arden	157
G by half the tribes of Britain,	Boadicea	5
With song and flame and fragrance,	Lucretius	133

girth.

Alas, I was so broad of *g*,	Talking O.	139
grown a bulk Of spanless *g*,	Princess, vi.	20

give.

Could *g* the warrior kings of old,	To the Queen	4
Complaining, 'Mother, *g* me grace	Mariana in the S.	29
fill my glass : *g* me one kiss :	Miller's D.	17
O would she *g* me vow for vow,	"	119
'O Paris, G it to Pallas !'	Œnone	166
G us long rest or death,	Lotos-E's.	98
Failing to *g* the bitter of the sweet,	D. of F. Wom.	216
God *g*'s us love.	To J. S.	13
g to light on such a dream ?'	Ed. Morris	58
'G ? G all thou art'	"	59
the daughters of the horseleech, 'G,	Golden Year	12
in the rights that name may *g*,	Day-Dm.	266
To *g* his cousin, Lady Clare,	Lady Clare	4
g one kiss to your mother dear !	"	47
Little can I *g* my wife.	L. of Burleigh	14
or a song To *g* us breathing-space.'	Princess, Pro.	235
here I *g* the story and the songs.	"	239
I can *g* you letters to her ;	"	i. 158
'We *g* you welcome : not without	"	ii. 28
I *g* thee to the death My brother !	"	287
g three gallant gentlemen to death.'	"	314
we *g* you, being strange, A license :	"	iii. 188
g them surer, quicker proof—	"	265
g's the manners of your countrywomen ?'	"	iv. 133
g him your hand : Cleave to your	"	380
g's the battle to his hands.	"	557
G us, then, your mind at large :	"	v. 118
G's her harsh groom for bridal-gift	"	368
not yours, but mine ; *g* me the child.'	"	vi. 125
g her the child !	"	152, 163-7
G me it ; I will *g* it her.'	"	171
what answer should I *g*?	"	301
make herself her own To *g* or keep,	"	vii. 257

	POEM.	LINE.
g you all The random scheme	Princess, Con.	1
required that I should g throughout	"	10
yet to g the story as it rose,	"	26
G it time To learn its limbs:	"	78
these great Sirs G up their parks .	"	103
To Sleep I g my powers away:	In Mem. iv.	1
No joy the blowing season g's,	" xxxviii.	5
the hoarding sense G's out at times	" xliii.	7
dare we to this fancy g,	" liii.	5
Hath power to g thee as thou wert?	" lxxiv.	8
meets the year, and g's and takes	" cxv.	3
bitter notes my harp would g,	" cxxiv.	2
I must g away the bride;	" Con.	42
To g him the grasp of fellowship;	Maud, I, xiii.	16
sullen-seeming Death may g More life	" xviii.	46
g A grand political dinner	" xx.	24
Could g it a clumsy name	II. ii.	10
O g him welcome, this is he .	Ode on Well.	92
Who g the Fiend himself his due,	To F. D. Maurice	6
one lay-hearth would g you welcome	"	11
Take him to stall, and g him corn,	Enid	371
g back their earldom to thy kin.	"	585
Albeit I g no reason but my wish,	"	761
not to g you warning, that seems	"	1271
to g him warning, for he rode	"	1300
I will not yield to g you power	Vivien	223
wish'd to g them greater minds: .	"	346
father g me leave, an if he will,	Elaine	219
if you love, it will be sweet to g it;	"	689
with mine own hand g his diamond	"	756
yea, and you must g it—	"	769
G me good fortune, I will strike	"	1065
g at last The price of half a realm,	"	1157
g his child a better bringing-up	En. Arden 87,	298
—a month—G her a month—	"	459
g me strength Not to tell her,	"	786
g her this, for it may comfort her:	"	900
'A gracious gift to g a lady, this!'	Aylmer's F.	240
'Were I to g this gift of his to one	"	242
G me my fling, and let me say my say,'	"	399
G me your prayers, for he is past .	"	751
a weänt niver g it to Joänes,	N. Farmer.	59
I ask'd thee, 'Give me immortality.'	Tithonus	15
wealthy men who care not how they g.	"	17
If you will g me one, but one,	The Ringlet	3
'We g you his life.'	The Victim	16
Take you his dearest, G us a life.	"	29
'O, Father Odin, We g you a life.	"	80
We g them the wife!'	"	84
G her the glory of going on,	Wages	5, 10

given.

difference, reconciliation, pledges g,	Gardener's D.	252
I found him garrulously g,	Talking O.	23
Achieving calm, to whom was g .	Two Voices	209
to me is g Such hope, I know not	Sir Galahad	61
A man had g all other bliss,	Sir L. and Q. G.	42
g to starts and bursts Of revel :	Princess, i.	7
king,' he said, 'Had g us letters,	"	179
with mutual pardon asked and g .	" v.	44
G back to life, to life indeed,	" vii.	324
Is g in outline and no more.	In Mem. v.	12
shock, so harshly g, Confused me	" xvi.	11
is g A life that bears immortal fruit	" xxxix.	17
His who had g me life—	Maud, I. i.	6
g her word to a thing so low?	" xvi.	27
false death her hand,	" xviii.	68
For the prophecy g of old	" II. v.	42
wholly g to brawls and wine,	Enid	441
bethought her of her promise g	"	602
not leave her, till her promise g—	"	605
g her on the night Before her	"	632
gladly g again this happy morn.	"	691
(No reason g her) she could cast aside	"	807
his command of silence g,	"	1215-39
thanks than might a goat have g.	Vivien	127
promised more than ever king has g,	"	436
deem this prize of ours is rashly g:	Elaine	540
Sweet is true love tho' g in vain,	"	1001
if I do not there is penance g—	Guinevere	185
with a month's leave g them,	Sea Dreams	6

	POEM.	LINE.
before thine answer g Departest,	Tithonus	44
Has g all my faith a turn?	The Ringlet	52

giver.

| Render thanks to the G, (rep.) | Ode on Well. | 44 |
| of all gifts Must vary as the g's. | Elaine | 1209 |

giving.

g light To read those laws;	Isabel	18
g safe pledge of fruits .	Ode to Mem.	18
of the glance That graced the g—	Gardener's D.	174
part it, g half to him.	In Mem. xxv.	12
G you power upon me thro' this	Vivien	364

glacier.

| with tears By some cold morning g; | Princess, vii. | 101 |

glad.

So full of summer warmth, so g,	Miller's D.	14
heart is g Of the full harvest	Dora	66
and we were g at heart.	Audley Ct.	87
I'm g I walk'd. How fresh	Walk. to the M.	1
I am sad and g To see you, Florian.	Princess, ii.	286
g to find thyself so fair. .	In Mem. vi.	27
one is g; her note is gay,	" xxi.	25
g at heart from May to May:	" xxii.	8
Be g, because his bones are laid	Ode on Well.	141
Eat and be g, for I account you	Enid	1495
'How should I be g Henceforth .	"	1496
star upon his noble front, G also;	"	1606
g of you as guide and friend;	Elaine	225
so g were spirits and men .	Guinevere	267
'Were they so g? ill prophets	"	270
I was g at first To think	Sea Dreams	124
light is large and lambs are g	Lucretius	99

gladden.

| and the Shepherd g's in his heart: | Spec. of Iliad | 16 |

glade.

With breezes from our oaken g's,	Eleänore	10
His wonted glebe, or lops the g's;	In Mem. c.	22
thro' many a grassy g And valley,	Enid	236
winding g's high up like ways	En. Arden.	574

gladlier.

| For sure no g does the stranded wreck | En. Arden. | 829 |

gladness.

I grew in g till I found .	To E. L.	11
Makes former g loom so great?	In Mem. xxiv.	10
making vain pretence Of g,	" xxx.	7
A solemn g even crown'd	" xxxi.	11
Borne down by g so complete,	" xxxii.	10
Neigh'd with all g as they came,	Enid	1603
cloudy g lighten'd In the eyes	The Captain	31

glamour.

| Gwydion made by g out of flowers, | Enid . | 743 |

glance.

not a g so keen as thine: 'Clear-headed friend,' etc.		7
Sudden g's, sweet and strange	Madeline	5
O'erflows thy calmer g's,	"	33
Every turn and g of thine,	Eleänore	52
shaping faithful record of the g	Gardener's D.	173
a g I gave, No more;	Princess, iv.	162
one g he caught Thro' open doors	" v.	332
striking with her g The mother,	" vi.	136
sidelong g's at my father's grief,	" vii.	92
fixt A showery g upon her aunt,	" Con.	33
g and smile, and clasp and kiss.	In Mem. lxxxiii.	7
upon him A piteous g, and vanish'd	Aylmer's F.	284
and rolling g's lioness-like,	Bondicea	71

glance (verb.)

In crystal eddies g and poise,	Miller's D.	52
'ill merrily g and play,	May Queen, i.	39
fall down and g From tone to tone,	D. of F. Wom.	166
made them g Like those three stars	Princess, v.	249
g about the approaching sails,	In Mem. xiii.	18
Let random influences g	" xlviii.	2
And every eye but mine will g	Maud, I. xx.	36
I slip, I slide, I gloom, I g. .	The Brook	174
not to g at her good mother's face,	Enid .	766
sideways he let them g At Enid,	"	1095

	POEM.	LINE.
stare at open space, nor *g* The one	*Enid*	1117
wont to *g* and sparkle like a gem .	"	1143
pure heart, nor seem to *g* at thee?	*Guinevere*	498
here he *g*'s on an eye new-born,	*Lucretius*	137

glanced.

g athwart the glooming flats,	*Mariana*	20
The damned arrow *g* aside,	*Oriana*	41
She *g* across the plain ; .	*Talking O.*	166
We sat : the Lady *g* : .	*Princess,* ii.	96
G at the legendary Amazon .	"	110
G like a touch of sunshine	" iii.	339
g aside, and saw the palace-front .	" v.	497
struck out and shouted ; the blade *g*;	"	529
light of healing, *g* about the couch,	" vii.	44
glided forth, Nor *g* behind her,	"	156
we *g* from theme to theme,	*In Mem.* lxxxviii.	33
G at the doors or gambol'd down .	*Enid*	665
the King G first at him, then her .	*Elaine*	96
Lancelot, when they *g* at Guinevere,	"	270
maid G at, and cried 'What news	"	617
g not up, nor waved his hand,	"	980
g at him, thought him cold .	*Guinevere*	402

glancing.

G with black-beaded eyes,	*Lilian*	15
g thence, discussed the farm,	*Audley Ct.*	32
g like a dragon-fly In summer suit	*Enid*	172
g all at once as keenly at her,	"	773
g round the waste she fear'd	"	899
g for a minute, till he saw her Pass	"	1734
slander, *g* here and grazing there ;	*Vivien*	29
g up beheld the holy nuns .	*Guinevere*	658
Philip *g* up Beheld the dead flame	*En. Arden*	437
mother *g* often toward her babe,	"	755

glare (s.)

steady *g* Shrank one sick willow	*Mariana in the S.*	52
No sun, but a wannish *g* .	*Maud,* I. vi.	2
in change of *g* and gloom Her eyes	*Vivien*	808

glare (verb.)

G's at one that nods and winks .	*Locksley II.*	136
the crimson-rolling eye G's ruin,	*Princess,* iv.	474
But the broad light *g*'s and beats,	*Maud,* II. iv.	89

glared.

amazed They *g* upon the women,	*Princess,* vi.	341

glaring.

old lion, *g* with his whelpless eye,	*Princess,* vi.	83
g, by his own stale devil spurr'd,	*Aylmer's F.*	290
their eyes G, and passionate looks,	*Sea Dreams*	229

glass (substance.)

fires your narrow casement *g*,	*Miller's D.*	243
The *g* blew in, the fire blew out, .	*The Goose*	49
falls Of water, sheets of summer *g*,	*To E. L.*	2
Athwart a plane of molten *g*, .	*In Mem.* xv.	11
fleet of *g*, That seem'd a fleet	*Sea Dreams*	118
my poor venture but a fleet of *g* .	"	134

glass (mirror.)

looking as 'twere in a *g*, .	*A Character*	10
Go, look in any *g* and say, .	*Day-Dm.*	199
O whisper to your *g*, and say,	"	271
having left the *g*, she turns .	*In Mem.* vi.	35
in the *g* of some presageful mood	*Vivien*	144

glass (drinking-vessel.)

fill my *g*: give me one kiss :	*Miller's D.*	17
Make prisms in every carven *g*,	*Day-Dm.*	55
I sit my empty *g* reversed, .	*Will Water.*	159
It is but yonder empty *g* .	"	207
whom the bell-mouth'd *g* had wrought	*Princess,* iv.	137
crash'd the *g* and beat the floor;	*In Mem.* lxxxvi.	20
Arrange the board and brim the *g*;	" cvi.	16
g with little Margaret's medicine	*Sea Dreams*	138
came but from the breaking of a *g*,	"	240

glass (telescope.)

get you a seaman's *g*, Spy out	*En. Arden*	215
Borrow'd a *g*, but all in vain :	"	239
not fix the *g* to suit her eye :	"	240

glass (verb.)

	POEM.	LINE.
To *g* herself in dewy eyes	*'Move eastward,'* etc.	7

glass'd.

coming wave G in the slippery sand	*Vivien*	142

glasses.

Get me my *g*, Annie : .	*Grandmother*	106

glassy-headed.

A little *g*-h hairless man, .	*Vivien*	470

glazed.

staring eye *g* o'er with sapless days,	*Love and Duty*	16
think not they are *g* with wine.	*Locksley II.*	51
Neither modell'd, *g*, or framed :	*Vision of Sin*	188
A full sea *g* with muffled moonlight	*Princess,* i.	244

gleam (s.)

g's of mellow light Float by you .	*Margaret*	30
Would love the *g*'s of good *'Love thou thy land,'* etc.		89
Dreary *g*'s about the moorland .	*Locksley II.*	
Beyond the polar *g* forlorn, .	*Two Voices*	182
touches me with mystic *g*'s, .	"	380
Thou battenest by the greasy *g* .	*Will Water.*	221
green *g* of the dewy-tassell'd trees :	*Princess,* i.	93
A doubtful *g* of solace lives. .	*In Mem.* xxxviii.	8
dives In yonder greening *g*, .	" cxiv.	14
makes a hoary eyebrow for the *g*.	*The Brook*	80
gilded by the gracious *g* Of letters,	*Ded. of Idylls*	38
sallows in the windy *g*'s of March :	*Vivien*	74
strike it, and awake her with the *g*;	*Elaine*	6

gleam (verb.)

wherethro' G's that untravell'd world.	*Ulysses*	20
G thro' the Gothic archways .	*Godiva*	64
Saw distant gates of Eden *g*, .	*Two Voices*	212
Fair *g*'s the snowy altar-cloth, .	*Sir Galahad*	33
g's On Lethe in the eyes of Death.	*In Mem.* xcvii.	7

gleamed.

G to the flying moon by fits. .	*Miller's D.*	116
We parted : sweetly *g* the stars. .	*The Letters*	41
sweetly *g* her eyes behind her tears	*Vivien*	252
g a vague suspicion in his eyes : .	*Elaine*	128
(A bill of sale *g* thro' the drizzle) .	*En. Arden*	689
g a kindlier hope On Enoch .	"	834
now we lost her, now she *g* .	*The Voyage*	65

glean.

And *g* your scatter'd sapience.' .	*Princess,* ii.	241

glebe.

Flood with full daylight *g* and town?	*Two Voices*	87
horn-handed breakers of the *g*, .	*Princess,* ii.	143
the labourer tills His wonted *g*, .	*In Mem.* c.	22
Sons of the *g*, with other frowns .	*Aylmer's F.*	723

glee (mirth.)

the tyrant's cruel *g* Forces on the	*Vision of Sin*	129

glee (part-music.)

Again the feast, the speech, the *g*,	*In Mem. Con.*	101

Glem.

the white mouth of the violent G;	*Elaine*	288

glen.

runlets babbling down the *g*. .	*Mariana in the S.*	44
vapour slopes athwart the *g*, .	*Œnone*	3
the piney sides Of this long *g*. .	"	92
the fragments tumbled from the *g*'s,	"	218
from the darken'd *g*, Saw God divide	*D. of F. Wom.*	224
watch me from the *g* below. *'Move eastward,'* etc.		8
And snared the squirrel of the *g*? .	*Princess,* ii.	231
let us hear the purple *g*'s replying :	" iii.	358
g's are drown'd in azure gloom .	" iv.	504
Follow'd up in valley and *g* .	*Ode on Well.*	114
a *g*, gray boulder and black tarn. .	*Elaine*	37
they fell and made the *g* abhorr'd :	"	43

glide

g a sunbeam by the blasted Pine, .	*Princess,* vii.	181
g, Like a beam of the seventh Heaven,	*Maud,* I. xiv.	20
shadow still would *g* from room to room,	*Guinevere*	500
would she *g* between your wraths,	*Aylmer's F.*	706
broad water sweetly slowly *g*'s. .	*Requiescat*	2

glided.

g thro' all change Of liveliest .	*D. of F. Wom.*	167
but mute she *g* forth, .	*Princess,* vii.	155

CONCORDANCE TO

	POEM.	LINE.
We *g* under winding ranks Of iris,	*In Mem.* cii.	23
Then *g* out of the joyous wood	*Maud,* II. i.	31
g out Among the heavy breathings	*Enid*	1250
rose Elaine and *g* thro' the fields,	*Elaine*	839

gliding.

ghost-like to and fro *G,*	*Elaine*	846

glimmer (s.)

tearful *g* of the languid dawn	*D. of F. Wom.*	74
Across a hazy *g* of the west	*Gardener's D.*	214
in a wintry wind by a ghastly *g,*	*Maud,* I. iii.	13
gloss of satin and *g* of pearls,	" xxii.	34
the old mysterious *g* steals	*Tithonus*	55

glimmer (verb.)

A third would *g* on her neck	*Talking O.*	221
My college friendships *g.*	*Will Water.*	40
G in thy rheumy eyes.	*Vision of Sin*	154
like a ghost she *g's* on to me.	*Princess,* vii.	166
Shall *g* on the dewy decks.	*In Mem.* ix.	12
Thy tablet *g's* to the dawn.	" lxvi.	16
by a red rock, *g's* the Hall;	*Maud,* I. iv.	10
G away to the lonely deep	*To F. D. Maurice*	28

glimmered.

Old faces *g* thro' the doors,	*Mariana*	66
April's crescent *g* cold,	*Miller's D.*	107
Her taper *g* in the lake below:	*Ed. Morris.*	135
The white kine *g,* and the trees	*In Mem.* xciv. 15,	51
g on his armour in the room.	*Enid*	1235
In Arthur's casement *g* chastely down,	*Vivien.*	590

glimmering (part.)

Came *g* thro' the laurels	*Maud,* II. iv.	77

glimmering (s.)

greenish *g's* thro' the lancets,—	*Aylmer's F.*	622

glimpse (s.)

For some blind *g* of freedom	*Love and Duty*	6
Like *g's* of forgotten dreams—	*Two Voices,*	381
Yet *g's* of the true.	*Will Water.*	60
The shimmering *g's* of a stream;	*Princess, Con.*	46
Last year, I caught a *g* of his face,	*Maud,* I. 13	27
never had a *g* of mine untruth,	*Elaine*	126
g of that dark world where I was	*Tithonus*	33
never a *g* of her window-pane!	*The Window*	108

glimpse (verb.)

lift the hidden ore That *g's,*	*D. of F. Wom.*	275

glimpsing.

g over these, just seen,	*Day-Dm.*	67

glisten (s.)

oft we saw the *g* Of ice,	*The Daisy*	35

glisten (verb.)

O listen, listen, your eyes shall *g*	*Sea-Fairies*	35
dews Began to *g* and to fall:	*Princess,* ii.	296

glistened.

torrent ever pour'd And *g*—.	*To E. L.*	14
His eyes *g;* she fancied 'is it for	*Elaine*	818

glistening.

Were *g* to the breezy blue;	*Miller's D.*	61

glitter.

G like a swarm of fire-flies	*Locksley H.*	10
His mantle *g's* on the rocks—	*Day-Dm.*	106
Began to *g* firefly-like in copse	*Princess,* i.	205
g burnish'd by the frosty dark;	"	251

glittered.

The gemmy bridle *g* free,	*L. of Shalott,* iii.	10
Large Hesper *g* on her tears,	*Mariana in the S.*	50
long hall *g* like a bed of flowers.	*Princess,* ii.	416
city *g* Thro' cypress avenues,	*The Daisy*	47

glittering.

Gold *g* thro' lamplight dim,	*Arabian N's.*	18
the first beam *g* on a sail,	*Princess,* iv.	26
eyes and neck *g* went and came;	*Vivien*	809
Whom *g* in enamell'd arms the maid	*Elaine*	616

globe.

circles of the *g's* Of her keen eyes	*The Poet*	43
Thro' the shadow of the *g* we sweep	*Locksley H.*	183

	POEM.	LINE.
spirit should fail from off the *g;*	*In Mem.* lxxxiii.	36
As thro' the slumber of the *g*	*The Voyage*	23

globed.

stars that *g* themselves in Heaven,	*En. Arden.*	593

gloom (s.)

Flinging the *g* of yesternight	*Ode to Mem.*	9
over-vaulted grateful *g,*	*Pal. of Art*	54
Floods all the deep-blue *g*	*D. of F. Wom.*	186
motion toiling in the *g*—	*'Love thou thy land,' etc.*	54
her perfect features in the *g,*	*Gardener's D.*	171
The *g* of ten Decembers.	*Will Water.*	104
shoulder under *g* Of cavern pillars;	*To E. L.*	17
Dropt thro' the ambrosial *g*	*Princess,* iv.	6
Out I sprang from glow to *g:*	"	160
moving thro' the uncertain *g,*	"	197
all the glens are drown'd in azure *g*	"	504
touch thy thousand years of *g:*	*In Mem.* ii.	12
Thro' all its intervital *g*	" xliii.	3
When on the *g* I strive to paint	" lxix.	2
Recalls, in change of light or *g,*	" lxxxiv.	74
rollest from the gorgeous *g*	" lxxxv.	2
suck'd from out the distant *g,*	" xciv.	53
touch'd with no ascetic *g;*	" cviii.	10
iron dug from central *g,*	" cxvii.	21
yearn'd to burst the folded *g,*	" cxxi.	
With tender *g* the roof, the wall;	" *Con.*	118
star-sweet on a *g* profound	*Maud,* I. iii.	4
laying his trams in a poison'd *g*	" x.	8
Set in the heart of the carven *g,*	" xiv.	11
in the fragrant *g* Of foreign churches—	" xix.	53
The height, the space, the *g,*	*The Daisy*	59
The *g* that saddens Heaven and Earth,	"	102
Commingled with the *g* of imminent	*Ded. o' Idylls,*	12
a *g* of stubborn-shafted oaks,	*Enid*	969
thro' the green *g* of the wood	"	1044
That three-days-long presageful *g*	*Vivien*	169
shone white-listed thro' the *g.*	"	788
in change of glare and *g* Her eyes	"	808
sallow-rifted *g's* Of evening	*Elaine*	996
lying thus inactive, doubt and *g.*	*En. Arden.*	113
the drizzle grew, deeper the *g;*	"	680
To find a deeper in the narrow *g,*	*Aylmer's F.*	840
cheek begins to redden thro' the *g,*	*Tithonus*	37
from utter *g* stood out the breasts,	*Lucretius*	60

gloom (verb.)

There *g* the dark broad seas.	*Ulysses*	45
I slip, I slide, I *g,* I glance,	*The Brook*	174

gloomed.

twilight *g;* and broader-grown the	*Princess,* vii.	33
black yew *g* the stagnant air,	*The Letters*	2
that, which lately *g* Your fancy	*Vivien.*	174
G the low coast and quivering brine	*The Voyage*	42

glooming.

while the balmy *g,* crescent-lit,	*Gardener's D.*	258

glorify.

fountains of the past, To *g* the present;	*Ode to Mem.*	3

glorifying.

sparkles on a sty, *G* clown and satyr;	*Princess,* v.	179

glorious.

So *g* in his beauty and thy choice,	*Tithonus*	12

glory.

In marvel whence that *g* came	*Arabian N's.*	94
'*G* to God,' she sang, and past afar,	*D. of F. Wom.*	242
long *glories* of the winter moon.	*M. d'Arthur*	192
God's *g* smote him on the face.'	*Two Voices*	225
down dark tides the *g* slides,	*Sir Galahad*	47
o'er the dark a *g* spreads,	"	55
as they are, But thro' a kind of *g.*	*Will Water.*	72
drops at *G's* temple-side '*You might have won,'* etc.		34
redound Of use and *g* to yourselves	*Princess,* ii.	29
wild cataract leaps in *g.*	" iii.	351
Like a Saint's *g* up in heaven;	" v.	503
win A *g* from its being far;	*In Mem.* xxiv.	14
There comes a *g* on the walls;	" lxvi.	9
The mystic *g* swims away;	"	9
He reach'd the *g* of a hand,	" lxviii.	17

	POEM.	LINE.
The *g* of the sum of things	*In Mem.* lxxxvii.	11
attributes of woe Like *glories*	" cxvii.	19
dim And dimmer, and a *g* done:	" cxx.	4
man of science himself is funder of *g*,	*Maud*, I. iv.	37
A *g* I shall not find	" v.	22
glance At Maud in all her *g*.	" xx.	37
true lover may see Your *g* also,	" "	46
g of manhood stand on his ancient	" III. vi.	21
path of duty was the way to *g*:	*Ode on Well.*	202-10-24
height, the space, the gloom, the *g*!	*The Daisy*	59
When can their *g* fade?	*Lt. Brigade*	50
g was, redressing human wrong;	*Ded. of Idylls*	8
Forgetful of his *g* and his name,	*Enid*	53
court And all its dangerous *glories*:	"	804
f.neying that her *g* would be great	*Vivien*	66
crying 'I have made his *g* mine,'	"	820
pretext, O my knight, As all for *g*:	*Elaine*	154
No keener hunter after *g* breathes.	"	156
need to speak Of Lancelot in his *g*:	"	463
Lancelot, and a *g* one with theirs.	"	477
spake of, all for gain Of *g*,	"	566
pretext, as for gain Of purer *g*.'	"	586
my *g* to have loved One peerless.	"	1084
Born to the *g* of thy name	"	1363
glows And *glories* of the broad belt	*En. Arden*	580
between the less And greater *g*	*Aylmer's F.*	73
loved the *glories* of the world,	*The Voyage*	83
Thine the liberty, thine the *g*,	*Boädicea*	41
Yet he hoped to purchase *g*,	*The Captain*	17
G of warrior, *g* of orator, *g* of song,	*Wages*	1
G of Virtue, to fight, to struggle,	"	3
aim'd not at *g*, no lover of *g* she:	"	4
Give her the *g* of going on,	"	5
Thy *g* fly along the Italian field,	*Lucretius*	71

glory-crown'd.

His own vast shadow *g-c*;	*In Mem.* xcvi.	3

glorying.

upon the bridge of war Sat *g*;	*Spec. of Iliad*	10

gloss.

of the flowers Stole all the golden *g*	*Gardener's D.*	129
darkness keep her raven *g*:	*In Mem.* i.	10
merge' he said 'in form and *g*	" lxxxviii.	41
g of satin and glimmer of pearls,	*Maud*, I. xxii.	53
hair In *g* and hue the chestnut,	*The Brook*	72, 207

glove.

her empty *g* upon the tomb	*Princess*, iv.	573
Come sliding out of her sacred *g*,	*Maud*, I. vi.	85
fit to wear your slipper for a *g*	*Enid*	1471
blots of it about them, ribbon, *g*	*Aylmer's F.*	620

glow (s.)

sunset *g* That stays upon thee?	*Eleänore*	55
the heavens are in a *g*:	*May Queen*, iii.	49
Had yet their native *g*:	*Will Water.*	194
Out I sprang from *g* to gloom;	*Princess*, iv.	160
not for thee the *g*, the bloom,	*In Mem.* ii.	9
reach the *g* of southern skies,	" xii.	10
fix my thoughts on all the *g*,	" lxxxiii.	3
the *g* Of your soft splendours	*Maud*, I. xviii.	78
g's And glories of the broad belt	*En. Arden*	579
kindlier *g* Faded with morning	*Aylmer's F.*	411
with the *g* that slowly crimson'd	*Tithonus*	56
With a satin sail of a ruby *g*,	*The Islet*	13

glow (verb.)

vines that *g* Beneath the battled	*D. of F. Wom.*	219
G's firth each softly-shadow'd arm	*Day-Dm.*	89
Between dark stems the forest *g*'s,	*Sir Galahad*	27
g Thy silver sister-world, 'Move eastward,' etc.		5
from his ivied nook G like a	*Princess*, Pro.	105
now her father's chimney *g*'s	*In Mem.* vi.	29
g In azure orbits heavenly-wise;	" lxxxvi.	37
The wizard lightnings deeply *g*,	" cxxi.	19
felt in my blood G with the glow	*Tithonus*	56

glow'd.

broad clear brow in sunlight *g*;	*L. of Shalott*, iii.	28
on the liquid mirror *g*,	*Mariana in the S.*	31
her face G, as I look'd at her.	*D. of F. Wom.*	240
before us *g* Fruit, blossom,	*Princess*, iv.	16

	POEM.	LINE.
g like a ruddy shield	*Maud*, III. vi.	14
city Of little Monaco, basking, *g*.	*The Daisy*	8
face G like the heart of a great fire	*Enid*	552
G for a moment as we past.	*The Voyage*	48

glowing.

g full-faced welcome, she Began	*Princess*, ii.	166
g round her dewy eyes	" iii.	10
rose G all over noble shame;	" vii.	145
g like the moon Of Eden	*In Mem. Con.*	27
g on him, like a bride's	*Vivien*	466

glow-worm.

the *g-w* of the grave Glimmer	*Vision of Sin*	153
No bigger than a *g-w* shone the	*Princess*, iv.	7
Now poring on the *g*, now the	"	103
lapt in wreaths of *g* light	"	425

glutted.

g all night long breast-deep in corn	*Princess*, ii.	225

gnarr.

thousand wants G at the heels	*In Mem.* xcvii.	17

gnat.

Not even of a *g* that sings.	*Day-Dm.*	41
well could wish a cobweb for the *g*,	*Vivien*	250
tiny-trumpeting *g* can break	*Elaine*	138
chased away the still-recurring *g*,	*Coquette*, i.	7

gnawed.

g his under, now his upper lip,	*Enid*	1527

gnawing.

lays his foot upon it, G	*Enid*	1412

go (see **come and go**.)

the whirring sail *goes* round, (rep.)	*The Owl*, i.	4
A weary, weary way I *g*,	*Oriana*	80
up and down the people *g*,	*L. of Shalott*, i.	6
Goes by to tower'd Camelot;	" ii.	23
dry and dewless. Let us *g*.	*Miller's D.*	246
will rise and *g* Down into Troy,	*Œnone*	257
let the foolish yeoman *g*.	*L. C. V. de Vere*	72
Little Effie shall *g* with me	*May Queen*, i.	25
forgive me ere I *g*;	" ii.	34
than life to me that long to *g*.	" iii.	0
seem'd to *g* right up to Heaven	"	40
way my soul will have to *g*.	"	42
care not if I *g* to-day.	"	43
veils of thinnest lawn, did *g*:	*Lotos-E's.*	11
Old year, you must not *g*; (rep.)	*D. of the O. Year*	15
I charge thee, quickly *g* again	*M. d'Arthur*	79
my lord Arthur, whither shall I *g*?	"	227
I, the last, *g* forth companionless	"	236
these thou see'st—if indeed I *g*—	"	257
g you hence, and never see me	*Dora*	93
will *g*, And I will have my boy,	"	119
I *g* to-night: I come to-morrow	*Audley Ct.*	69
I *g*, but I return: I would I were	"	70
let him *g*; his devil *goes* with him,	*Walk. to the M.*	20
G? (shrilled the cottonspinning chorus)	*Ed. Morris*	122
'G!—Girl, get you in!'	"	124
Power *goes* forth from me.	*St S. Stylites*	143
G to him: it is thy duty:	*Locksley H.*	52
roaring seaward, and I *g*.	"	194
G, vexed Spirit, sleep in trust;	*Two Voices*	115
I will *g* forward, sayest thou,	"	190
I *g*, weak from suffering here;	"	238
Naked I *g*, and void of cheer:	"	239
breath to heaven like vapour *goes*:	*St Agnes' Eve*	3
down the stormy crescent *goes*,	*Sir Galahad*	15
Thro' dreaming towns I *g*,	"	50
Love may come, and love may *g*,	*Ed. Gray*	29
And all the world *g* by them.	*Will Water.*	48
But whither would my fancy *g*?	"	145
'Tis gone, and let it *g*.	"	180
G, therefore, thou I thy betters went	"	185
G down among the pots;	"	270
bless me, mother, ere I *g*.'	*Lady Clare*	56
So she *goes* by him attended,	*L. of Burleigh*	25
Let her *g*! her thirst she slakes	*Vision of Sin*	143
But thou, *g* by I	'Come not, when', etc. 6, 12
O, happy planet, eastward *g*;	'Move eastward', etc.	4

170   CONCORDANCE TO

	POEM.	LINE.
And the stately ships *g* on	'*Break, break,*' etc.	9
I spoke. 'My father, let me *g*.	*Princess*, i.	67
against all rules For any man to *g*:	"	177
I shudder at the sequel, but I *g*.	" ii.	218
'Thanks,' she answered '*g*: we have	"	336
turn'd to *g*, but Cyril took the child	"	341
the bell For dinner, let us *g*!'	"	411
Over the rolling waters *g*,	"	460
goes to inform The Princess:	" iii.	46
heal me with your pardon ere you *g*.'	"	49
I must *g*: I dare not tarry'	"	79
Would we *g* with her? we should find	"	155
goes, like glittering bergs of ice,	" iv.	53
oath is broken; we dismiss you: *g*.	"	341
'Stand, who *goes*?' 'Two from the palace'	" v.	3
G: Cyril told us all.'	"	35
will take her up and *g* my way,	"	99
smoke *g* up thro' which I loom to her	"	124
so much as gave us leave to *g*,	"	225
'All good *g* with thee I take it Sir'	" vi.	190
I *g* to mine own land For ever:	"	199
I *g* to plant it on his tomb,	*In Mem.* viii.	22
Like him I *g*; I cannot stay;	" xii.	5
Week after week; the days *g* by:	" xvii.	7
path by which we twain did *g*,	" xxii.	1
Yet *g*, and while the holly boughs	" xxix.	9
G down beside thy native rill,	"xxxvii.	5
look thy look, and *g* thy way,	" xlviii.	9
I care for nothing, all shall *g*.	" lv.	4
let us *g*. Come; let us *g*:	" lvi.	4
Will flash along the chords and *g*.	"lxxxvii.	12
g By summer belts of wheat and vine	" xcvii.	4
We *g*, but ere we *g* from home,	" ci.	3
I turn to *g*: my feet are set	"	21
when they learnt that I must *g*	" cli.	17
'Enter likewise ye And *g* with us;'	"	52
The year is going, let him *g*;	" cv.	7
clouds they shape themselves and *g*.	" cxxii.	8
they must *g*, the time draws on,	" *Con.*	89
nine months *g* to the shaping an infant	*Maud*, I.iv.	34
G not, happy day,	" xvii.	1–3
G in and out as if at merry play,	" xviii.	31
It is but for a little space I *g*:	"	75
brief night *goes* In babble and revel	" xxii.	27
me and my passionate love *g* by,	" II. ii.	77
me and my harmful love *g* by;	"	80
And the wheels *g* over my head,	" v.	4
Let it *g* or stay, so I wake	" III.vi.	38
such a time as *goes* before the leaf,	*The Brook*	13
men may come and men may *g*,	" 33, *et pass.*	
But I *g* on for ever,	" 34 *et pass.*	
Let the long long procession *g*,	*Ode on Well.*	15
in, *g* in; for save yourself desire it,	*Enid*	310
wheel we *g* not up or down;	"	351
G to the town and buy us flesh	"	372
G thou to rest, but ere thou *g* to rest	"	512
Yniol *goes*, and I full oft shall dream	"	751
'I will *g* back a little to my lord,	"	914
into no Earl's palace will I *g*.	"	1084
love that beauty should *g* beautifully	"	1529-32
'Yea,' said Enid, 'let us *g*.'	"	1599
'If you will not *g* To Arthur, then	"	1662
I will weed this land before I *g*.	"	1755
not worth the keeping; let it *g*:	*Vivien*	246
let his wisdom *g* For ease of heart,	"	741
reckon worth the taking? I will *g*.	"	766
Why *g* you not to these fair jousts?	*Elaine*	99
hear my words: *g* to the jousts:	"	137
g down before your spear at a touch	"	149
hide it therefore; *g* unknown:	"	151
since I *g* to joust as one unknown	"	190
so sullen, vext he could not *g*:	"	210
own side she felt the sharp lance *g*;	"	621
shall *g* no more On quest of mine,	"	712
Being so very wilful you must *g*.	"	773-7
your wish, Seeing I must *g* to-day:'	"	921
what force is yours to *g*, So far,	"	1057
I *g* in state to court, to meet the	"	1118
dumb old man alone *G* with me,	"	1122
let the younger and unskill'd *g* by	"	1352
Now—ere he *goes* to the great Battle?	*Guinevere*	645

	POEM.	LINE.
used Enoch at times to *g* by land	*En. Arden*.	104
yet a boatswain. Would he *g*?	"	123
g This voyage more than once?	"	141
her or his dear children, not to *g*.	"	164
come, cheer up before I *g*.'	"	200
everything shipshape, for I must *g*.	"	220
Can I *g* from Him?	"	225
wherefore did he *g* this weary way,	"	295
Annie's children long'd To *g* with others	"	360
Annie would *g* with them;	"	361
children pluck'd at him to *g*,	"	366
'See your bairns before you *g*!'	"	871
would *g*, Labour for his own Edith,	*Aylmer's F.*	419
'Let not the sun *g* down upon	*Sea Dreams*	44
Patter she *goes*, my own little Annie,	*Grandmother*	78
I, too, shall *g* in a minute,	"	104
Let me *g*: take back thy gift:	*Tithonus*	27
O whither love shall we *g*,	*The Islet*	1, 5
O thither, love, let us *g*.	"	24
mock me not! love, let us *g*.'	"	30
that deep grave to which I *g*:	'*My life is full*' etc.	7
if I *g* my work is left Unfinish'd—		
if I *g*.	*Lucretius*	103
man may gain Letting his own life *g*.	"	113
Shall I write to her? shall I *g*?	*The Window*	90
west wind and the world will *g* on.	" 111,-17-23	
	goad.	
prick'd with *g's* and stings;	*Pal. of Art*	150
His own thought drove him like a *g*.	*M. d'Arthur*	183
	goal.	
Making for one sure *g*.	*Pal. of Art*	248
progress falter to the woman's *g*.'	*Princess*, vi.	111
moves with him to one *g*,	" vii.	247
good Will be the final *g* of ill,	*In Mem.* liii.	2
Touch thy dull *g* of joyless gray,	" lxxi.	27
Arrive at last the blessed *g*.	" lxxxiii.	41
earnest to thy *g* So early,	" cxiii.	23
pass beyond the *g* of ordinance,	*Tithonus*	30
	goat.	
Leading a jet-black *g* white-horn'd,	*Œnone*	50
men better than sheep or *g's*	*M. d'Arthur*	250
Catch the wild *g* by the hair	*Locksley H.*	170
beard-blown *g* Hang on the shaft,	*Princess*, iv.	60
no more thanks than might a *g*	*Vivien*	127
	goatfoot.	
Catch her, *g*: nay, Hide, hide them,	*Lucretius*	200
	goatskin.	
wear an undress'd *g* on my back;	*St S. Stylites*	114
	go-between.	
To play their *g-b* as heretofore	*Aylmer's F.*	523
	goblin.	
did but come as *g's* in the night,	*Princess*, v.	211
	go-cart.	
is but a child Yet in the *g-c*.	*Princess, Con.*	78
	God.	
G gave her peace; her land reposed;	*To the Queen*	26
thou of G in thy great charity)	*Isabel*	40
not the *g's* More purely,	*A Character*	13
G's great gift of speech abused	*A Dirge*	44
Half G's good sabbath,	*To J. M. K.*	11
G in his mercy lend her grace,	*L. of Shalott*,iv.53	
Would G renew me from my birth	*Miller's D.*	27
But that G bless thee, dear—	"	235
about his temples like a G's;	*Œnone*	59
all the full-faced presence of the Gs	"	78
see thy Paris judge of G's.'	"	88
the G's Rise up for reverence.	"	107
likest *g's*, who have attained Rest.	"	128
strike within thy pulses, like a G's,	"	159
presence, hated both of G's and men.	"	225
Moulded by G, and To——With	*Pal. of Art*	18
My G's, with whom I dwell!	*Pal. of Art*	
as G holding no form of creed,	"	211
G, before whom ever lie bare	"	222
exiled from eternal G,	"	263

	POEM.	LINE.		POEM.	LINE.
To lie within the light of G,	MayQueen,	iii. 59	G's just wrath shall be wreak'd	Maud,	III. vi. 45
The G's are hard to reconcile :	Lotos-E's.	. 126	I embrace the purpose of G,	"	. 59
On the hills like G's together,	"	. 155	ours, O G, from brute control ;	Ode on Well.	159
A daughter of the g's, divinely tall,	D. of F. Wom.	87	palter'd with Eternal G for power ;	"	. 180
we sat as G by G:	"	. 142	our G himself is moon and sun,	"	. 217
My G, my land, my father—	"	. 209	On G and Godlike men we build .	"	. 266
Saw G divide the night	"	. 225	G accept him, Christ receive him.	"	. 281
to die For G and for my sire !	"	. 232	Dear to the man that is dear to G ;	To F. D. Maurice	36
'Glory to G,' she sang, and past afar,	"	. 242	G's love set Thee at his side again !	Ded. of Idylls,	53
G gives us love.	To J. S.	. 13	by G's grace, is the one voice for me.'	Enid	. 344
not say 'G's ordinance Of Death	"	. 45	by G's rood is the one maid for me,'	"	. 368
G forget the stranger !'.	The Goose	. 56	Who knows? another gift of the high G,	"	. 821
G knows: he has a mint of reasons;	The Epic	. 33	I know, G knows, too much of palaces !	"	. 1085
G fulfils himself in many ways,	M. d'Arthur	241	G's curse, it makes me mad .	"	. 1464
knowing G, they lift not hands of	"	. 252	hot, G's curse, with anger—	"	. 1500
by gold chains about the feet of G.	"	. 255	Yea, G, I pray you of your gentleness,	"	. 1558
Breath'd, like the covenant of a G,	Gardener's D.	204	by G's rood, I trusted you too much.'	Vivien	. 226
broke out in praise To G,	Dora	. 111	love of G and men And noble deeds,	"	. 262
'G bless him !' he said, 'and may he	"	. 146	Her G, her Merlin, the one passionate	"	. 804
May G forgive me !—I have been	"	. 158	G's mercy what a stroke was there !	Elaine	. 24
G made the woman for the man,	Ed. Morris	43, 50, 91	G Broke the strong lance,	"	. 25
was a G, and is a lawyer's clerk,	"	. 102	the land Hereafter, which G hinder.'	"	. 67
just, dreadful, mighty G,	St S. Stylites	9	his own word, As if it were his G's?'	"	. 145
had not stinted practice, O my G.	"	. 58	G wot, his shield is blank enough.	"	. 197
in your looking you may kneel to G.	"	. 139	the fire of G Fills him ;	"	. 315
G reaps a harvest in me (rep.)	"	. 146	Rapt on his face as if it were a G's.	"	. 355
G hath now Sponged and made blank	"	. 155	for G's love, a little air !	"	. 504
G only thro' his bounty hath thought	"	. 183	'Yea, by G's death,' said he, ' you love	"	. 676
a priest, a man of G, Among you .	"	. 211	having loved G's best And greatest,	"	. 1087
for a man is not as G,	Love and Duty	30	would to G, For the wild people say	"	. 1355
G love us, as if the seedsman, rapt	Golden Year	69	may G, I pray him, send a sudden	"	. 1413
I meet adoration to my household g's,	Ulysses	. 42	those whom G had made full-limbed	Guinevere	. 43
unbecoming men that strove with G's.	"	. 53	Would G, that thou could'st hide	"	. 117
Would to G—for I had loved thee	Locksley H.	. 64	I guard as G's high gift .	"	. 490
G's glory smote him on the face.	Two Voices	225	Lo ! I forgive thee, as Eternal G	"	. 540
On to G's house the people prest;	"	. 409	We two may meet before high G,	"	. 560
Ah, blessed vision ! blood of G !	Sir Galahad	. 45	in the heavens Before high G.	"	. 631
just and faithful knight of G !	"	. 79	my G, What might I not have made	"	. 647
Sipt wine from silver, praising G,	Will Water.	127	this voyage by the grace of G	En. Arden	. 190
broad-limb'd G's at random thrown	To E. L.	. 15	G bless him, he shall sit upon my	"	. 197
G's blessing on the day !	Lady Clare	8	Cast all your cares on G ;	"	. 222
G be thank'd !' said Alice the nurse,	"	. 17	might be still as happy as G grants	"	. 413
'As G's above,' said Alice the nurse,	"	. 23	have heen as G's good angel	"	. 400
G made himself an awful rose of	Vision of Sin	50-224	G bless you for it, G reward you .	"	. 421
Lo ! G's likeness—the ground-plan—	"	. 187	for G's sake,' he answer'd, ' both our	"	. 505
(G help her) she was wedded to a fool;	Princess,	iii. 67	he read G's warning 'wait.' .	"	. 572
tho' your Prince's love were like a G's,	"	. 231	O G Almighty, blessed Saviour,	"	. 783
old G of war himself were dead,	"	v. 139	' My G has bow'd me down .	"	. 857
Interpreter between the G's and men	"	vii. 303	that almighty man, The county G—	Aylmer's F.	. 14
G bless the narrow sea .	"	Con. 51, 70	sons of men Daughters of G ;	"	. 45
Strong Son of G, immortal Love,	In Mem. Pro.	1	'Bless, G bless 'em : marriages are made	"	. 168
O mother, praying G will save .	"	vi. 13	all but those who knew the living G—	"	. 637
The chalice of the grapes of G ;	"	x. 16	coarse and blockish G of acreage .	"	. 651
What then were G to such as I ?	"	xxxiv. 9	Thy G is far diffused in noble groves	"	. 653
G shut the doorways of his head.	"	xliii. 4	shape dost thou behold thy G.	"	. 657
Ye watch, like G, the rolling hours	"	l. 14	Prince of Peace, the Mighty G,	"	. 669
When G hath made the pile complete;	"	liii. 8	' O pray G that he hold up'	"	. 733
The likest G within the soul ?	"	liv. 4	rushing tempest of the wrath of G	"	. 757
Are G and Nature then at strife,	"	. 5	made Their own traditions G,	"	. 795
slope thro' darkness up to G,	"	. 16	neither G nor man can well forgive	Sea-Dreams	63
Who trusted G was love indeed	"	lv. 8	never naming G except for gain,	"	. 184
In endless age? It rests with G .	"	lxxii. 12	I wish'd it had been G's will .	Grandmother	73
stay'd in peace with G and man : .	"	lxxix. 8	G, not man, is the Judge of us	"	. 95
G's finger touch'd him, and he slept.	"	lxxxiv. 20	thank G that I keep my eyes.	"	. 106
G within him light his face,	"	lxxxiv. 36	great heart none other than a G !	Tithonus	. 14
With g's in unconjectur'd bliss,	"	xcii. 10	G's themselves cannot recall their	"	. 49
Israel made their g's of gold,	"	xcv. 23	G help me ! save I take my part .	Sailor Boy	. 21
Where G and Nature met in light :	"	cx. 20	Hear it, G's ! the G's have heard it,	Boädicea	. 21
mix'd with G and Nature thou,	"	cxxix. 11	Doubt not ye the G's have .	"	. 22
That friend of mine who lives in G,	Con.	140	thine the battle-thunder of G.'	"	. 44
That G, which ever lives and loves,	"	. 141	Imitates G, and turns her face	On a Mourner	2
One G, one law, one element,	"	. 142	Virtue, like a household g.	"	. 30
O father ! O G ! was it well ?—	Maud, I. i.	6	G's are moved against the land.'	The Victim	6
ah G, as he used to rave.	"	. 60	holy G's, they must be appeased,	"	. 49
G grant I may find it at last !	"	ii. 1	G's, he said, ' would have chosen	"	. 62
how G will bring them about ?	"	iv. 44	The G's have answered :	"	. 83
Ah G, for a man with heart,	"	x. 60	ye holy G's, what dreams !	Lucretius	. 33
May G make me more wretched .	"	xix. 94	aught they fable of the quiet G's.	"	. 55
Arise, my G, and strike,	"	II. i. 49	Rather, O ye G's, Poet-like	"	. 92
as long, O G, as she Have a grain	"	ii. 52	appear the work of mighty G's.	"	. 102
Britain's one sole G be the millionaire ;	"	III. vi. 22	The G's ! and if I go *my* work	"	. 103

CONCORDANCE TO

	POEM.	LINE.
The G's, who haunt The lucid	Lucretius	104
The G's, the G's! If all be atoms, how then should the G's Being atomic	"	113
My master held That G's there are,	"	117
G's there are, and deathless.	"	121
another of our G's, the Sun,	"	124
quit the post Allotted by the G's:	"	149
he that holds The G's are careless,	"	150
Picus and Faunus, rustic G's?	"	182
O ye G's, I know you careless,	"	204

godamoighty.

g an' parson 'ud nobbut let ma	N. Farmer	43
Do g knaw what a's doing	"	45
g a moost taäke meä	"	51

God-bless-you.

Sneeze out a full G-b-y right and	Ed. Morris	80
Gript my hand hard, and with G-b-y	Sea Dreams	156
A curse in his G-b-y;	"	160

goddess.

presented Maid Or Nymph, or G,	Princess, i.	194
if thou can'st, O G, like ourselves	Lucretius	80

God-father.

G-f, come and see your boy;	To F. D. Maurice	2

God-fearing.

Altho' a grave and staid G-f man	En. Arden	112
Enoch as a brave G-f man	"	185

God-gifted.

G-g organ-voice of England,	Milton	3

God-in-man.

G-i-m is one with man-in-God,	En. Arden	187

Godiva.

G, wife to that grim Earl,	Godiva	12

Godless.

tumbled in the G deep;	In Mem. cxxiii.	12
craft of kindred and the G hosts	Guinevere	424

Godlike.

then most G being most a man.	Love and Duty	31
Together, dwarf'd or g, bond or	Princess, vii.	244

goest.

whither g thou, tell me where?'	Day-Dm.	190

going (part.) see coming and going.

heard the steeds to hattle g,	Oriana	15
I am g a long way With these	M. d' Arthur	256
They by parks and lodges g	L. of Burleigh	17
thinner, clearer, farther g	Princess, iii.	355
The year is g, let him go;	In Mem. cv.	7
g to the king, He made this.	Enid	32
bent he seem'd on g the third day,	"	604-25
Enid in their g had two fears,	"	1665
'G? and we shall never see you	Elaine	922
of an avenue, G we knew not	En. Arden	356
On a day when they were g	The Captain	25
G before to some far shrine,	On a Mourner	17
Give her the glory of g on,	Wages	5
Give her the wages of g on,	"	10

going out.

Narrow'd her g's o and comings in;	Aylmer's F.	501

gold (see cloth of gold.)

laws of marriage character'd in g	Isabel	16
Bagdat's shrines of fretted g,	Arabian N's.	7
G glittering thro' lamplight dim,	"	18
royal frame-work of wrought g;	Ode to Mem.	82
grew A flower all g,	The Poet	24
bosoms prest To little harps of g;	Sea-Fairies	4
with cymbals, and harps of g,	Dying Swan	32
With a crown of g On a throne?	The Merman	6
I should look like a fountain of g	The Mermaid	18
Slowly, as from a cloud of g,	Eleänore	73
a fruit of pure Hesperian g,	Œnone	65
Brow-bound with burning g.	D. of F. Wom.	128
from lust of g, or like a girl	M. d' Arthur	127
Three Queens with crowns of g—	"	198
Cursed be the g that gilds the	Locksley H.	62
Every door is barred with g,	"	100

	POEM.	LINE.
purple blazon'd with armorial g.	Godiva	52
Pull off, pull off, the broach of g,	Lady Clare	39
silken hood to each, And zoned with g;	Princess, ii.	4
furrowing all the orient into g.	" iii.	2
viand, amber wine, and g.	" iv.	17
gemlike eyes, And g and golden heads;	"	460
all the g That veins the world	"	521
single band of g about her hair	" v.	502
twinkle into green and g:	In Mem.' xi.	8
Israel made their gods of g,	" xcv.	23
Ring out the narrowing lust of g;	" cv.	26
flying g of the ruin'd woodlands	Maud, I. i.	12
left his coal all turn'd into g.	" x.	11
lost for a little her lust of g,	" III. vi.	39
Under the cross of g	Ode on Well	49
Whose crying is a cry for g:	The Daisy	94
swung an apple of the purest g.	Enid	170
Affirming that his father left him g,	"	451
All branch'd and flower'd with g,	"	631
fish at all Let them be g;	"	670
strown With g and scatter'd coinage,	"	875
A twist of g was round her hair;	Vivien	70
The snake of g slid from her hair,	"	737
down his robe the dragon writhed in g,	Elaine	434
azure lions, crown'd with g,	"	660
a manelike mass of rolling g,	Aylmer's F.	68
g that branch'd itself Fine as ice-ferns	"	221
the baits Of g and beauty,	"	487
heaps of living g that daily grow,	"	655
Not by the temple but the g,	"	794
a gulf of ruin, swallowing g,	Sea Dreams	79
long reef of g, Or what seem'd g:	"	123
Still so much g was left;	"	126
Wreck'd on a reef of visionary g.'	"	135
then shall I know it is all true g	The Ringlet	7
I that took you for true g,	"	32
face was ruddy, his hair was g,	The Victim	36
And you with g for hair.	The Window	65
you my wren with a crown of g,	"	80

golden.

Grow g all about the sky;	Eleänore	101
g round her lucid throat	Œnone	174
iron laws, in the end Found g:	Princess, iv.	58

Golden Fleece.

met the bailiff at the G F,	The Brook	146

golden-gay.

your ringlets, That look so g-g,	The Ringlet	2, 14
O Ringlet, You still are g-g,	"	28

golden-hilted.

Nor weapon, save a g-h brand,	Enid	106

golden-netted.

heart entanglest In a g-n smile;	Madeline	41

golden-railed.

The light aërial gallery, g-r,	Pal. of Art	47

golden-rinded.

with fruitage g-r On golden salvers,	Eleänore	33

golden-shafted.

The Head of all the g-s firm,	Princess, ii.	383

gold-eyed.

The g-e kingcups fine;	A Dirge	36

gold-fringed.

upswells The g-f pillow lightly prest,	Day-Dm.	98

gold-green.

Flush'd all the leaves with rich g-g,	Arabian N's.	82

gold-lily.

While the g-l blows,	Ed. Morris.	146

gold-mine.

from the deep G-m's of thought	D. of F. Wom.	274

gone.

Life and Thought have g away	Deserted H.	1
now those vivid hours are g,	Miller's D.	195
when I'm g, to train the rose-bush	May Queen, ii.	47
Alack! our friend is g.	D. of the O. Year	47
honour had from Christmas G, Or g,	The Epic	7

	POEM.	LINE.		POEM.	LINE.
'tis time that I were g.	M. d'Arthur	163	G and the light g with her	The Window	37
for the sake of him that's g,	Dora	60-8, 92	G—flitted away,	"	38
would have risen and g to him,	"	75	G, and a cloud in my heart	"	40
The troubles I have g thro'!'	"	147	grass will grow when I am g,	"	110
penances I cannot have g thro',	St S. Stylites	99	when I am there and dead and g,	"	116
Christ! 'Tis g: 'tis here again;	"	205	Blow, then, blow, and when I am g,	"	122
to my household gods, When I am g.	Ulysses	43			
spirit leaps within him to be g	Locksley H.	115	*goo* (go.)		
I said, 'When I am g away,	Two Voices	100	Parson a comes an' a g's	N. Farmer.	25
The dull and bitter voice was g.	"	426			
my pleasant hour. 'tis g, 'Tis g,	Will Water.	179	*good.*		
'Tis g: a thousand such have slipt	"	181	wrought her people lasting g;	To the Queen	24
Well I know, when I am g,	Vision of Sin	109	thro' life and death, thro' g and ill,	The Poet	5
you had g to her, She told, perforce;	Princess, iv.	310	if G, G only for its beauty	To—. With Pal. of Art	8
found that you had g, Ridd'n to the	"	323	Beauty, G, and Knowledge are	"	10
many a pleasant hour with her that's g,	vi.	230	'Tis only noble to be g.	L. C. V. de Vere	54
brook no further insult but are g.'	"	322	love the gleams of g	'Love thou thy land,' etc.	89
Blanche had g, but left Her child	vii.	41	What g should follow this,	M. d'Arthur	92
learns her g and far from home;	In Mem. viii.	4	waked with silence, grunted 'G!'	Ep.	4
'How good I how kind I and he is g.'	xx.	20	drowsy hours, dispensers of all g,	Gardener's D.	181
Old sisters of a day g by,	xxix.	13	the g and increase of the world.	Ed. Morris 44.	51,92
My prospect and horizon g.	xxxviii.	4	then why not ill for g?	Love and Duty	27
'a thousand types are g:	lv.	3	all men's g Be each man's rule,	Golden Year	47
Quite in the love of what is g,	lxxiv.	114	them to the useful and the g.	Ulysses	38
The violet comes, but we are g.	civ.	8	not to lose the g of life—	Two Voices	132
Farewell, we kiss, and they are g.	Con.	92	said the voice, 'thy dream was g,	"	157
and slurring the days g by,	Maud, I. i.	33	Lean'd on him, faithful, gentle, g,	"	416
many a million of ages have g	iv.	35	'I see the end, and know the g.'	"	432
In a moment they were g':	ix.	12	But for some true result of g	Will Water.	55
lately died, G to a blacker pit,	x.	6	I hold it g, g things should pass :	"	203
some of the simple great ones g	"	61	Wine is g for shrivell'd lips,	Vision of Sin	79
stay for a year who has g for a week:	xvi.	6	Virtue I—to be g and just—	"	111
of Heaven are closed, and she is g.	xviii.	12	for the common g of womankind	Princess, ii.	192
whole earth g nearer to the glow	"	78	'G: Your oath is broken;	iv.	340
half to the setting moon are g,	xxii.	23	all we would be, great and g.'	"	576
Is it g? my pulses beat—	II. i.	36	ourselves but half as g, as kind,	v.	193
It is g: and the heavens fall in a	"	41	'All g go with thee! take it Sir'	vi.	190
our tithes in the days that are g,	v.	23	Embrace her as my natural g;	In Mem. iii.	14
and these are g, All g.	The Brook	186	what to me remains of g?	vi.	42
in converse seasons. All are g.	"	196	'How g! how kind! and he is gone	xx.	20
He is g who seem'd so great.—G;	Ode on Well.	271	all we met was fair and g,	xxiii.	17
We have lost him: he is g:	Ded. of Idylls	14	If all was g and fair we met,	xxiv.	5
a prince whose manhood was all g,	Enid	59	Her hands are quicker into g:	xxxiii.	10
saying all your force is g?	"	88	Enjoying each the other's g:	xlvi.	10
the morning all the court were g.	"	156	Hold thou the g: define it well :	lii.	12
fourth part of the day was g,	"	904	g Will be the final goal of ill,	liii.	14
man's love once g never returns.	"	1182	can but trust that g shall fall	"	12
gazed upon her blankly and g by:	Vivien	17	If thou wilt have me wise and g,	lviii.	6
such a beard as youth g out.	"	94	see thee sitting crown'd with g,	lxxxiii.	5
in a language that has long g by.	"	524	sang of what is wise and g	cii.	10
Was one year g, and on returning	"	558	The closing cycle rich in g.	civ.	20
No sooner g than suddenly she	Elaine	97	Ring in the common love of g.	cv.	24
now the trustful king is g!'	"	102	High nature amorous of the g.	cviii.	6
g sore wounded, and hath left his	"	529	Yet O ye mysteries of g,	cxxvii.	8
mean nothing: so then, get you g,	"	772	Behold, I dream a dream of g,	cxxviii.	11
helm, from which her sleeve had g.	"	976	grows For ever, and as fair as g,	Con.	35
His very shield was g;	"	984	mother, who was so gentle and g?	Maud, I. vi.	72
the ghostly man had come and g,	"	1095	close on the promised g.	xviii.	6
heat is g from out my heart,	"	1110	any man think for the public g	II. v.	45
g he is To wage grim war	Guinevere	190	blow by night, when the season is g,	"	73
by couriers g before ; and on again.	"	393	It is better to fight for the g,	III. vi.	57
listening till those armed steps were g,	"	579	Whole in himself, a common g.	Ode on Well.	26
'G!' my lord! G thro' my sin	"	605	needs must disobey him for his g.	Enid	984
G, my lord the King, My own true	"	609	what they long for, g in friend or foe,	"	1774
When he was g—the children—	En. Arden.	132	This g is in it, whatso'er of ill,	Elaine	1001
keep the house while he was g.	"	140	Right heavy am I: for g she was	"	1514
a sign 'my Enoch is he g!'	"	487	my tears have brought me g:	Guinevere	200
'He is g' she thought 'he is happy,	"	498	Miriam Lane was g and garrulous,	En. Arden.	701
After he was g, The two remaining	"	567	never meant us anything but g.	"	888
thought it must have g: but he was g	"	695	'G! my lady's kinsman! g!'	Aylmer's F.	198
'after I am g, Then may she learn	"	835	sell her, these g parents, for her g.	"	483
when I am g, Take, give her this,	"	899	contriving their dear daughter's g—	"	781-843
Leolin, coming after he was g,	Aylmer's F.	234	work together for the g Of those—	Sea Dreams	154
Willy, my eldest-born, is g,	Grandmother 1, 8,	101			
I ought to have g before him :	"	14	*Good Fortune.*		
all my children have g before me .	"	18	prosperously sail'd The ship 'G F,'	En. Arden.	524
at things that have long g by.	"	92	by baffling winds, Like the G F.	"	630
he has but g for an hour ;	"	102			
G for a minute, my son,	"	102	*goodman.*		
there before you are come and g,	The Window	14	her small g Shrinks in his arm-chair	Princess, v.	443
G! G till the end of the year	"	35	*good-morrow.*		
			Speaking a still g-m with her eyes.	Elaine	1027

174 CONCORDANCE TO

goodness. POEM. LINE.
eye which watches guilt And g, . *In Mem.* xxvi. 6

goodnight.
G, g, when I have said g for evermore *May Queen*, ii. 41
G, sweet mother: call me . . " . 49
stout Prince bade him a loud g. . *Enid* . 1210

goods.
with what she brought Buy g . *En. Arden.* 138
Bought Annie g and stores, . . " . 169
shelf and corner for the g and stores " . 171

goodwill.
and g, g and peace, Peace and g, *In Mem.* xxviii. 11

goose.
g upon his arm, . . . *The Goose* 5, 41
take the g, and keep you warm, . " . 7
caught the white g by the leg, A g— " . 9
g let fall a golden egg . . . " . 11
dropt the g, and caught the pelf, . " . 13
ah! the more the white g laid . " . 23
take the g, and wring her throat, " . 31
g flew this way and flew that, . " . 35
Quoth she, 'The Devil take the g, " . 55
From the long-neck'd g geese of the world *Maud*, I. iv. 52
his hens, his geese, his guinea-hens *The Brook* . 126

gorge.
The g's opening wide apart, reveal *Œnone* . 12
High over the blue g, . . " . 206
golden g of dragons spouted forth *Pal. of Art* . 23
Thro' the long g to the far light . *Ode on Well.* 213
Sat often in the seaward-gazing g, *En. Arden.* 590
Downward from his mountain g . " . 637

gorged.
We issued g with knowledge, . *Princess*, ii. 366
Dropt off g from scheme that . *Maud*, I. i. 20
snakelike slimed his victim ere he g; *Sea-Dreams* 189

gorgonised.
G me from head to foot . . *Maud*, I. xiii. 21

Gorlois.
call'd him the false son of G: . *Guinevere* . 286

gossamer.
To trip a tigress with a g, . . *Princess*, v. 163
all the silvery g's That twinkle . *In Mem.* xi. 7

gossip (s.)
sins of emptiness, g and spite . *Princess*, ii. 78
like a city, with g, scandal, and spite; *Maud*, I. iv. 8
Fearing the lazy g of the port, . *En. Arden.* 332
By this the lazy g of the port " . 469

gossip (verb.)
only hear the magpie g . . *To F. D. Maurice* 19
neighbours come and laugh and g, *Grandmother* 91

got.
G up betwixt you and the woman there. *Dora* . 94
'Sir Ralph has g your colours: . *Princess*, iv. 571
g a friend of your own age, . . " vi. 234
At last he g his breath and answer'd *Elaine* . 421
up the side, sweating with agony, g, " . 493
So Lancelot g her horse, . . *Guinevere* . 121
storming a hill-fort of thieves He g it; *Aylmer's F.* 226
all have g the seed. . . *The Flower* 20

Gothic.
Gleam thro' the G archways in the wall. *Godiva* 64
finest G lighter than a fire, . *Princess*, Pro. 92
A G ruin and a Grecian house, . " . 225

gotten.
you have g the wings of love, . *The Window* 158

gourd.
By heaps of g's, and skins of wine, *Vision of Sin* 13
In us true growth, in her a Jonah's g, *Princess*, iv. 292

gout.
g and stone, that break Body toward *Lucretius* 153

govern.
have no men to g in this wood: . *D. of F. Wom.* 135

governed.
'I g men by change, and so I sway'd *D. of F. Wom.* 130

government. POEM. LINE.
A land of settled g, 'You ask me why,' etc. 9
manners, climates, councils, g's, . *Ulysses* . 14
in arts of g Elizabeth and others; *Princess*, ii. 143
low firm voice and tender g. . *Enid* . 1043

gown.
Her cap blew off, her g blew up, . *The Goose* . 51
She clad herself in a russet g, . *Lady Clare* 57
A g of grass-green silk she wore, *Sir L. and Q. G.* 24
should not wear our rusty g's, . *Princess*, Pro. 143
A rosy blonde, and in a college g, " ii. 302
In which of old I wore the g; . *In Mem.* lxxxvi. 2
Without a mirror, in the gorgeous g; *Enid* . 739
put off to please me this poor g, " . 1527
'Do me this poor g my dear lord " . 1546
In this poor g I rode with him to court, " . 1548
In this poor g he bade me clothe myself " . 1550
this poor g I will not cast aside . " . 1553
I wore a lilac g; . . *Grandmother* 57

gowned.
One arm aloft—G in pure white, . *Gardener's D.* 125

grace (s.)
Victoria,—since your royal g . *To the Queen* 5
God in his mercy lend her g, . *L. of Shalott*, iv. 53
Complaining, 'Mother give me g *Mariana in the S.* 29
I watch thy g; and in its place . *Eleänore* . 127
with a silent g Approaching, . *Miller's D.* 159
loveliest in all g Of movement, . *Œnone* . 73
you have won A tearful g . . *Margaret* . 12
all g Summ'd up and closed in little; *Gardener's D.* 12
shelter'd here Whatever maiden g *Talking O.* . 38
looking upward, full of g, . *Two Voices* . 223
So sweet a face, such angel g, . *Beggar Maid* 13
tender g of a day that is dead *Break, break,* etc. 15
so much g and power, breathing down *Princess*, ii. 24
arts of g Sappho and others . . " . 147
At last a solemn g Concluded, . " . 428
easy g, No doubt, for slight delay, " iv. 311
Come, a g to me! I am your warrior: " vi. 206
mimic picture's breathing g, *In Mem.* lxxvii. 11
With gifts of g, that might express " lxxxvi. 46
with power and g And music . " lxxxvi. 33
maidens gather'd strength and g . " cii. 27
manhood fused with female g . " cviii. 17
light of her youth and her g, *Maud*, I. v. 15
Rich in the g all women desire, . " x. 13
Some peculiar mystic g . . " xiii. 39
g that, bright and light as the crest " xvi. 16
nothing there her maiden g affright! " xviii. 71
(Claspt hands and that petitionary g *The Brook* 112
all g Of womanhood and queenhood, *Enid* . 173
by God's g, is the one voice for me.' " . 344
were but little g in any of us, . " . 624
might amend it by the g of heaven, " . 902
such g Of tenderest courtesy, . " . 1709
g and will to pick the vicious quitch " . 1751
into that rude hall Stept with all g *Elaine* . 263
half disdain Hid under g, . . " . 264
'Do me this g, my child. . . " . 381
'A g to me,' She answer'd, . . " . 382
The g and versatility of the man— " . 471
g's of the court, and songs, Sighs,— " . 645
'Stay a little! One golden minute's g: " . 681
ghostly g Beam'd on his fancy, . " . 881
at least have done her so much g, " . 1301
beauty, g and power, Wrought as a *Guinevere* . 142
see your tender g and stateliness. " . 188
Had yet that g of courtesy in him " . 433
this voyage by the g of God . *En. Arden.* 190
deeds of gift, but gifts of g he forged, *Sea-Dreams* 183
and there is G to be had; . *Grandmother* 94

Grace (deity.)
Like to Furies, like to G's, . *Vision of Sin* 41
Muses and the G's, group'd in threes, *Princess*, ii. 13
meet her G's, where they deck'd her " vii. 153

grace (verb.)
moss or musk, To g my city-rooms: *Gardener's D.* 190
'So you will g me,' answer'd Lancelot *Elaine* . 223
Calliope to g his golden verse— . *Lucretius* . 94

	POEM.	LINE.
graced.		
the glance That *g* the giving—	Gardener's D.	174
graceful.		
What looks so little *g*: 'men'	Princess, iii.	37
what is wise and good And *g*.	In Mem. cii.	11
keep So much of what is *g*:	Elaine	1213
gracefulness.		
symmetry Of thy floating *g*,	Eleänore	50
gracious.		
So *g* was her tact and tenderness:	Princess, i.	24
the Lord be *g* to me!	" ii.	174
Maud could be *g* too, no doubt,	Maud, I. x.	28
Was *g* to all ladies,	Guinevere	327
would it be more *g*' ask'd the girl	Aylmer's F.	241
'G! No' said the 'Me?'—	"	243
gradation.		
Regard *g*, lest the soul Of *'Love thou thy land,'* etc. 67		
grade.		
g's Beyond all *g*'s develop'd?	Gardener's D.	235
scaling slow from *g* to *g*;	Two Voices	174
leap the *g*'s of life and light,	In Mem. xl.	11
gradually.		
g the powers of the night,	Princess, Con.	111
graff.		
made a Gardener putting in a *g*,	Vivien	329
grafted.		
Disrooted, what I am is *g* here.	Princess, ii.	202
Grail.		
Three angels bear the holy G:	Sir Galahad	42
Until I find the holy G.	"	84
grain (corn.)		
fourfield system, and the price of *g*;	Audley Ct.	33
the fiery *g* Of freedom broadcast.	Princess, v.	411
pamphleteer on guano and on *g*,	" Con.	89
vacant chaff well meant for *g*	In Mem. vi.	4
grown The *g* by which a man may live?	" lii.	8
gave all ripeness to the *g*,	" lxxx.	11
champing golden *g*, the horses stood	Spec. of Iliad	21
eating hoary *g* and pulse the steeds	"	Note
grain (fibre.)		
Cut Prejudice against the *g*	*'Love thou thy land,'*	22
tho' I circle in the *g*	Talking O.	83
Nor ever lightning char thy *g*,	"	277
the Master, as a rogue in *g*	Princess, Pro.	116
the stem Less *g* than touchwood,	" iv.	314
twists the *g* with such a roar	" v.	517
dwelt an iron nature in the *g*:	" vi.	34
prurient for a proof against the *g*.	Vivien	337
grain (particle.)		
g of conscience made him sour.'	Vision of Sin	218
A little *g* shall not be spilt.'	In Mem. lxiv.	4
every *g* of sand that runs,	" cxvi.	9
Have a *g* of love for me,	Maud, II. ii.	53
city sparkles like a *g* of salt.	Will	20
weight is added only *g* by *g*,	Enid	526
granary.		
garden-tools upon the *g* floor:	May Queen, ii.	45
grand.		
look'd so *g* when he was dead.	The Sisters	32
six feet high, G, epic, homicidal;	Princess, Pro.	219
She look'd as *g* as doomsday	" i.	185
grandchild.		
wish to see My *g* on my knees	Dora	11
grandfather.		
Whose old *g-f* has lately died,	Maud, I. x.	5
I mean your *g*, Annie:	Grandmother	23
grandsire.		
boy set up betwixt his *g*'s knees,	Dora	128
sorcerer, whom a far-off *g* burnt	Princess, i.	6
he bestrode my G, when he fell,	" ii.	224
grandson.		
To a *g*, first of his noble line,	Maud, I. x.	12

	POEM.	LINE.
grange.		
Upon the lonely moated *g*.	Mariana	8, 33
So pass I hostel, hall, and *g*;	Sir Galahad	81
so by tilth and *g*, And vines,	Princess, i.	109
nail me like a weasel on a *g*.	" ii.	188
burnt the *g*, nor buss'd the milking-maid, "	v.	213
ripple round the lonely *g*;	In Mem. xc.	12
No gray old *g*, or lonely fold,	" xcix.	5
granite.		
shadowy *g*, in a gleaming pass;	Lotos-Es.	49
faintly lipp'd The flat red *g*;	Audley Ct.	12
grant.		
'Good soul! suppose I *g* it thee,	Two Voices	38
But if I *g*, thou might'st defend	"	337
You *g* me license; might I use it?	Princess, iii.	219
I *g* in her some sense of shame,	" iv.	330
G me your son, to nurse,	" vi.	279
g my prayer. Help, father, brother,	"	285
God *g* I may find it at last!	Maud, I. ii.	1
His face, as I *g*, in spite of spite,	" xiii.	8
G me pardon for my thoughts:	Enid	816
g me some slight power upon your	Vivien	182
g my re-reiterated wish,	"	203
O *g* my worship of Words, as we		
g grief tears	Elaine	1181
Only this G me, I pray you:	"	1211
if I *g* the jealousy as of love,	"	1390
be still as happy as God *g*'s.	En. Arden	413
(Altho' I *g* but little music there).	Sea Dreams	245
g mine asking with a smile,	Tithonus	16
granted.		
Nor yet refused the rose, but *g* it,	Gardener's D.	157
Perfectly beautiful: let it be *g* her:	Maud, I. ii.	4
be *g* which your own gross heart	Vivien	765
grape.		
g's with bunches red as blood;	Day-Dm.	64
Let there he thistles, there are *g*'s;	Will Water.	57
skins of wine, and piles of *g*'s.	Vision of Sin	13
The chalice of the *g*'s of God;	In Mem. x.	16
bruised the herb and crush'd the *g*,	" xxxv.	23
The foaming *g* of eastern France.	" Con.	80
when my father dangled the *g*'s,	Maud, I. i.	71
grape-loaded.		
The valleys of *g-l* vines that glow	D. of F. Wom.	219
grape-thicken'd.		
in a bower G-*t* from the light,	Eleänore	36
grapple.		
And *g*'s with his evil star;	In Mem. lxiii.	8
grappling.		
airy navies *g* in the central blue;.	Locksley H.	124
grasp (s.)		
To give him the *g* of fellowship;.	Maud, I. xiii.	16
A *g* Having the warmth and muscle	Aylmer's F.	179
grasp (verb.)		
God-like, *g*'s the tiple	*'Of old sat Freedom.'* etc.	15
not cease to *g* the hope I hold	St S. Stylites	5
g's the skirts of happy chance,	In Mem. lxiii.	6
To him who *g*'s a golden ball.	" cx.	3
long arms stretch'd as to *g* a flyer:	Aylmer's F.	588
grasped.		
g The mild bull's golden horn.	Pal. of Art	119
world-worn Dante *g* his song,	"	135
hand G, made her vail her eyes:	Guinevere	655
graspest.		
Old Yew, which *g* at the stones	In Mem. ii.	1
grasping.		
g down the boughs I gain'd the	Princess, iv.	171
lo! it was her mother *g* her .	Enid	676
heard Geraint, and *g* at his sword,	"	1573
deathly-pale Stood *g* what was	Elaine	961
g the pews And oaken finials	Aylmer's F.	822
grass.		
the dull Saw no divinity in *g*,	A Character	8
seem'd knee-deep in mountain *g*,	Mariana in the S.	42
the bearded *g* is dry and dewless,	Miller's D.	245

	POEM.	LINE.
grasshopper is silent in the *g*:	*Œnone*	25
level meadow-bases of deep *g*	*Pal. of Art*	7
in the long and pleasant *g*.	*MayQueen*,ii.	32
petals from blown roses on the *g*,	*Lotos-E's.*	47
Heap'd over with a mound of *g*,	"	112
thro' lush green *g'es* burn'd	*D.of F. Wom.*	71
A league of *g*, wash'd by a slow	*Gardener's D.*	40
So light upon the *g*,	*Talking O.*	88
He lies beside thee on the *g*.	"	239
All *g* of silky feather grow—	"	269
Make thy *g* hoar with early rime.	*Two Voices*	66
scarce could see the *g* for flowers.	"	453
scatter'd blanching on the *g*.	*Day-Dm.*	112
There I put my face in the *g*—	*Ed. Gray*	21
roll'd about Like tumbled fruit in *g*;	*Princess,Pro.*	83
Grate her harsh kindred in the *g*:	" iv.	107
like a new-fall'n meteor on the *g*,	" vi.	119
she sat, she pluck'd the *g*,	" *Con.*	31
since the *g'es* round me wave,	*In Mem.* xxi.	7
I take the *g'es* of the grave,	"	3
tuft with *g* a feudal tower ;	" cxxvii.	20
From little cloudlets on the *g*,	" *Con.*	94
fall before Her feet on the meadow *g*.*Maud*, I. v.		26
A livelier emerald twinkles in the *g*,	" xviii.	51
grigs that leap in summer *g*.	*The Brook*	54
Squire had seen the colt at *g*,	"	139
pluck'd the *g* There growing longest *Enid*		1105
happily down on a bank of *g*,	"	1356
lived alone in a great wild on *g* ;	*Vivien*	471
back to his old wild, and lived on *g*,	"	499
own voice clings to each blade of *g*,	*Elaine*	108
like a rainbow fall'n upon the *g*,	"	430
and the flowering grove Of *g'es*	*Guinevere*	8
Show'd her the fairy footings on the *g*,	*Aylmer'sF.*	90
With neighbours laid along the *g*,	*Lucretius*	211
I may die but the *g* will grow, (rep.)	*TheWindow*	109
Spring is here with leaf and *g*:	"	128

grass-green.

graves *g-g* beside a gray church-tower,	*Circumstance*	6
A gown of *g-g* silk she wore,	*Sir L. and Q. G.*	24

grasshopper.

| The *g* is silent in the grass ; | *Œnone* | 25 |

grassy.

| The plain was *g*, wild and bare, | *Dying Swan* | 1 |

grate (s.)

| glimmering vaults with iron *g's*, | *D.of F.Wom.* | 35 |

grate (verb.)

I *g* on rusty hinges here :'	*Princess,* i.	85
G her harsh kindred in the grass ;	" iv.	107
harsh shingle should *g* underfoot	*En. Arden*	773

grated.

| *g* down and filed away with thought | *Vivien* | 473 |

grateful.

g at last for a little thing :	*Maud*, III. vi.	3
G to Prince Geraint for service done,	*Enid*	15
So *g* is the noise of noble deeds	"	437

gratify.

| would do much to *g* your Prince— | *Princess,* v. | 208 |

gratitude.

| This nightmare weight of *g*, | *Princess,* vi. | 281 |
| Out of full heart and boundless *g* | *En. Arden* | 343 |

gratulation.

| and was moving on In *g*, | *Princess,* ii. | 168 |

grave (adj.)

Or gay, or *g*, or sweet, or stern,	*Pal. of Art*	91
a hero lies beneath, *G*, solemn l'	*Princess,Pro.*	208
as grand as doomsday and as *g* :	" i.	185
G, florid, stern, as far as eye	*Sea Dreams*	212

grave (s.)

Over its *g* i' the earth (rep.)	'*A spirit haunts*,' etc.	10
the green that folds thy *g*. (rep.)	*A Dirge*	6
Two *g's* grass-green beside a gray	*Circumstance*	6
mother, within the mouldering *g*.	*MayQueen,* ii.	20
and upon that *g* of mine,	"	21
See me till my *g* be growing green :	"	43

	POEM.	LINE.
cord of love Down to a silent *g*.	*D.of F.Wom.*	212
winter rains that beat his *g*.	*Two Voices*	261
A shadow on the *g's* I knew,	"	272
From *g* to *g* the shadow crept :	"	274
Each pluck'd his one foot from the *g*,	*Amphion*	43
By Ellen's *g*, on the windy hill.	*Ed. Gray*	12
the glow-worm of the *g* Glimmer	*Vision of Sin*	153
Till the *g's* begin to move,	"	165
foolish tears upon my *g*, '*Come not, when, etc.*		2
There above the little *g*, (rep.)	*Princess,* i.	257
full voice which circles round the *g*,	" ii.	31
cram him with the fragments of the *g*	" iii.	294
Drops in his vast and wandering *g*.	*In Mem.* vi.	16
I take the grasses of the *g*,	" xxi.	3
hear her weeping by his *g* ?	" xxxi.	4
builds the house, or digs the *g*,	" xxxvi.	14
I wrong the *g* with fears untrue : .	" l.	9
No life may fail beyond the *g*,	" liv.	2
Unused example from the *g*	" lxxix.	15
my prime passion in the *g* :	" lxxxv.	76
Had fall'n into her father's *g*,	" lxxxviii.	48
fathers bend Above more *g's*,	" xcvii.	16
with me, and the *g* Divide us not,	" cxxi.	9
That has to-day its sunny side..	" *Con.*	71
To-day the *g* is bright for me,	"	73
that had made false haste to the *g*—	*Maud,* I. i.	58
and Orion low in his *g*.	" iii.	14
Your mother is mute in her *g*	" iv.	58
Perhaps from a selfish *g*.	" xvi.	23
into a shallow *g* they are thrust,	" II. v.	6
no peace in the *g*, is that not sad ?	"	16
kind to have made me a *g* so rough	"	97
Orion's *g* down in the west,	" III.vi.	8
The very *g's* appear'd to smile,	*The Letters*	45
cackle of the unborn about the *g*,	*Vivien*	357
the knightly brasses of the *g's*,	"	602
some one steps across my *g* :'	*Guinevere*	57
that his *g* should be a mystery	"	295
mourn'd his absence as his *g*,	*En. Arden*	246
would vex him even in his *g*,	"	302
thought to bear it with me to my *g* ;	"	897
these mouldy Aylmers in their *g's* :	*Aylmer's F.*	396
with his hopes in either *g*.	"	624
gray hairs with sorrow to the *g*—.	"	777
Pity, the violet on the tyrant's *g*,	"	845
drank himself into his *g*.	*Grandmother*	6
seest all things, thou wilt see my *g* :	*Tithonus*	73
that deep *g* to which I go : '*My life is full,* etc.		7
bones long laid within the *g*,	*Lucretius*	252
sides of the *g* itself shall pass,	"	253

gravel.

| waterbreak Above the golden *g*, | *The Brook* | 62 |
| wizard's pentagram On garden *g*, | " | 104 |

gravel-spread.

| bed Of silent torrents, *g-s* ; | *The Daisy* | 34 |

graven.

| *G* with emblems of the time, | *Arabian N's.* | 103 |
| A pint-pot, neatly *g*. | *Will Water.* | 248 |

graver.

| No *g* than a schoolboy's barring out ; | *Princess,Con.* | 66 |
| No *g* than as when some little cloud | *En. Arden* | 129 |

gray.

The level waste, the rounding *g*.	*Mariana*	44
An under-roof of doleful *g*.	*Dying Swan*	4
my hair Is *g* before I know it.	*Will Water.*	168
mixt Their dark and *g*,	*Princess,* vi.	116
I sleep till dusk is dipt in *g* :	*In Mem.* lxvi.	12
Touch thy dull goal of joyless *g*,	" lxxi.	27
From Como, when the light was *g*,	*The Daisy*	73
made him *g* And grayer,	*Guinevere*	597
whelm'd the world in *g* ;	*En.Arden*	673
a year hence.' ' We shall both be *g*.'	*The Window*	167

Gray (surname.)

| are you married yet, Edward *G* ? | *Ed. Gray* | 4 |
| Can touch the heart of Edward *G*. (rep.) | " | 8 |

grayer.

| made him gray And *g*, | *Guinevere* | 598 |

TENNYSON'S WORKS.

	POEM.	LINE.
grays.		
Behind the dappled *g.*	*Talking O.*	112
gray-eyed.		
cold winds woke the *g-e* morn	*Mariana*	31
grayling.		
And here and there a *g,*	*The Brook*	58
graze.		
They *g* and wallow, breed and sleep;	*Pal. of Art*	202
The steer forgot to *g,*	*Gardener's D.*	84
let the horses *g,* and ate themselves	*Enid*	1060
grazing.		
slander, glancing here and *g* there;	*Vivien*	29
great.		
O silent faces of the G and Wise,	*Pal. of Art*	195
name of Britain trebly *g*—'*You ask me why,*' *etc.*		22
are indeed the manners of the *g.*	*Walk. to the M.*	58
g with pig, wallowing in sun	"	80
O had I lived when song was *g*	*Amphion*	9, 13
Brutus of my kind? Him you call *g*:	*Princess,* ii.	265
might reap the applause of G,	" iii.	245
g is song Used to *g* ends:	" iv.	119
all we would be, *g* and good.'	"	576
g the crush was, and each base,	" vi.	333
Makes former gladness loom so *g?*	*In Mem.* xxiv.	10
Thy kindred with the *g* of old.	" lxxiii.	8
darkly feels him *g* and wise	" xcvi.	34
liberal-minded, *g,* Consistent;	*Con.*	38
Like some of the simple *g* ones gone	*Maud,* I. x.	61
G in council and *g* in war,	*Ode on Well.*	30
Was *g* by land as thou by sea;	"	84, 90
And ever *g* and greater grew,	"	108
Him who cares not to be *g,*	"	199
He is gone who seem'd so *g.*—	"	271
heard is little, but our hearts are *g.*	*Enid*	352-74
This work of his is *g* and wonderful.	"	1746
thousand-fold more *g* and wonderful	"	1762
work was neither *g* nor wonderful,	"	1769
fancying that her glory would be *g*	*Vivien*	66
therefore be as *g* as you are named,	"	185
thought that he was gentle, being *g*:	"	720
'Me you call *g*: mine is the firmer	*Elaine*	445
to know well I am not *g*:	"	430
I care not howsoever *g* he be	"	1063
sin seem less, the sinner seeming *g.*'	"	1408
needs be thrice as *g* as any of ours.	*Guinevere*	196
I thank the saints, I am not *g.*	"	197
As *g* as those of *g* ones,	"	202
added to the griefs the *g* must bear,	"	203
A woman in her womanhood as *g*	"	297
g and small, Went nutting to the	*En. Arden*	63
name Of his vessel *g* in story,	*The Captain*	19
bliss in being; and it was not *g*;	*Lucretius*	219
Heart, are you *g* enough (rep.)	*The Window*	194
greater.		
draws The *g* to the lesser,	*Gardener's D.*	10
more thro' love, and *g* than thy	*Love and Duty*	21
g than all knowledge, bent her	*Princess,* vii.	223
My shame is *g* who remain,	*In Mem.* cviii.	23
ever great and *g* grew,	*Ode on Well.*	108
What know we *g* than the soul?	"	265
why, the *g* their disgrace!	*Aylmer's F.*	384
to than I—isn't that your cry?	*Spiteful Let.*	17
greatest.		
Our *g* yet with least pretence,	*Ode on Well.*	29
as the *g* only are, In his simplicity	"	31
grieving that their *g* are so small.	*Vivien*	682
knight were whole, Being our *g*;	*Elaine*	769
having loved God's best And *g,*	"	1088
Chancellor, or what is *g* would he be—	*Aylmer's F.*	397
all our *g* fain Would follow,	*Lucretius*	78
greatness.		
should your *g,* and the care	*To the Queen*	9
I leave thy *g* to be guess'd;	*In Mem.* lxxiv.	4
She knows not what his *g* is;	" xcvi.	27
Remembering all his *g* in the Past.	*Ode on Well.*	20
According to his *g* whom she	*Vivien*	67
passion of youth Toward *g* in its	*Elaine*	283
g, save it be some far-off touch Of *g*	"	449

	POEM.	LINE.
greaves.		
flamed upon the brazen *g*	*L. of Shalott,* iii.	4
g and cuisses dash'd with drops	*M. d'Arthur*	215
Grecian.		
A Gothic ruin and a G house,	*Princess, Pro.*	225
Ran down the Persian, G, Roman	" ii.	114
Greece.		
fairest and most loving wife in G,'	*Œnone*	183
Greek.		
my ancient love With the G woman.	*Œnone*	257
show'd the house, G, set with busts:	*Princess, Pro.*	11
green (adj. and s.)		
earliest shoots Of orient *g,*	*Ode to Mem.*	18
Shot over with purple, and *g,*	*Dying Swan*	20
the *g* that folds thy grave.	*A Dirge* 6, *et pass.*	
Under the hollow-hung ocean *g!*	*The Merman*	38
some fair space of sloping *g's*	*Pal. of Art*	106
go with me to-morrow to the *g,*	*May Queen,* i.	25
'll be fresh and *g* and still,	"	37
Beneath the hawthorn on the *g*	" ii.	10
till my grave be growing *g*:	"	43
branches, fledged with clearest *g,*	*D. of F. Wom.*	59
smell of violets, hidden in the *g,*	"	77
like a purple beech among the *g's*	*Ed. Morris*	84
when she gamboll'd on the *g's*	*Talking O.*	77
All creeping plants, a wall of *g*	*Pay-Dm.*	65
Are neither *g* nor sappy:	*Amphion*	90
The topmost elmtree gather'd *g*	*Sir L. and Q. G.*	8
herself, when all the woods are *g*?	*Princess,* iv.	89
lines of *g* that streak the white	" v.	188
twinkle into *g* and gold:	*In Mem.* xi.	8
Within the *g* the moulder'd tree,	" xxvi.	7
This round of *g,* this orb of flame,	" xxxiv.	5
on a simple village *g*;	" lxiii.	4
Thy leaf has perish'd in the *g,*	" lxxiv.	13
fall'n leaves which kept their *g,*	" xciv.	23
like sunny gems on an English *g,*	*Maud,* I. v.	14
the wood stands in a mist of *g,*	*The Brook*	14
coppice gemm'd with *g* and red,	*Enid*	339
the lovely hue Play'd into *g,*	"	1537
kept the heart of Eden *g,*	"	1618
the place whereon she stood was *g*;	*Elaine*	1194
Modred still in *g,* all ear and eye,	*Guinevere*	25
sow'd her name and kept it *g*	*Aylmer's F.*	88
green (verb.)		
g's The swamp where hums the	*On a Mourner*	8
green-glimmering.		
G-*g* toward the summit.	*Elaine*	482
green-suited.		
G-*s,* but with plumes that mock'd.	*Guinevere*	23
greensward.		
danced The *g* into greener circles	*Gardener's D.*	133
greenwood.		
liest beneath the *g* tree,	*Oriana*	95
greet.		
g their fairer sisters of the East.	*Gardener's D.*	184
To *g* the sheriff, needless courtesy!	*Ed. Morris*	133
To meet and *g* her on her way:	*Beggar Maid*	6
G her with applausive breath,	*Vision of Sin*	135
a cry As if to *g* the king,	*Princess,* v.	350
large as man he bent To *g* us.	*In Mem.* cii.	43
To meet and *g* a whiter sun;	" Con.	78
Should I fear to *g* my friend	*Maud,* II. iv.	85
in soldier fashion will he *g*	*Ode on Well.*	21
lord Geraint, I *g* you with all love;	*Enid*	1633
King himself, Advanced to *g* them,	"	1727
g his hearty welcome heartily;	*En. Arden*	347
g her, wasting his forgotten heart,	*Aylmer's F.*	689
did *g* Troy's wandering prince,	*On a Mourner*	32
ran To *g* him with a kiss,	*Lucretius*	7
greeted.		
G Geraint full face,	*Enid*	1128
Vivien, being *g* fair, Would fain	*Vivien*	11
silent, tho' he *g* her, she stood	*Elaine*	354
'Have comfort,' whom she *g* quietly.	"	98
Passion-pale they met And *g*:	*Guinevere*	99
Maiden, not to be *g* unbenignly.	*Hendecasyllabics*	21

M

CONCORDANCE TO

	POEM.	LINE.
greeting.		
Eternal *g*'s to the dead ;	*In Mem.* lvi.	14
Full cold my *g* was and dry ;	*The Letters*	13
gets for *g* but a wail of pain ;	*Lucretius*	138
grew.		
G darker from that under-flame :	*Arabian N's.*	91
g A flower all gold,	*The Poet*	23
as her carol sadder *g*,	*Mariana in the S.*	13
Single I *g*, like some green plant,	*D. of F. Wom.*	205
G plump and able-bodied ;	*The Goose*	18
we *g* The fable of the city	*Gardener's D.*	5
hoarded in herself, G, seldom seen:	"	49
in praise of her G oratory.	"	56
up the porch there *g* an Eastern rose,	"	122
Her beauty *g*; till Autumn brought	"	202
unsown, where many poppies *g*.	*Dora*	71
wreath of all the flowers That *g*	"	81
different ages, like twin-sisters *g*	*Ed. Morris*	32
g Twice ten long weary weary years	*St S. Stylites*	88
And in the chase *g* wild,	*Talking O.*	126
dried his wings : like gauze they *g*:	*Two Voices*	13
To look as if they *g* there.	*Amphion*	80
such whose father-grape *g* fat	*Will Water.*	7
g in gladness till I found My spirits	*To E. L.*	11
That she *g* a noble lady,	*L. of Burleigh*	75
Faint she *g*, and ever fainter,	"	81
that madman ere it *g* too late :	*Vision of Sin*	56
The voice *g* faint :.	"	207
than their names, G side by side ;	*Princess,Pro.*	13
like the hand, and G With using :.	" ii.	134
'How *g* this feud betwixt the right	" iii.	61
they were still together, *g*	"	72
I *g* discouraged, Sir ;	"	137
g Like field-flowers everywhere ! .	" iii.	234
Sun G broader toward his death .	"	346
all men *g* to rate us at our worth,	" iv.	127
a noble scheme G up from seed	"	291
g Another kind of beauty in detail	"	427
clamour *g* As of a new-world Babel,	"	465
all things *g* more tragic	" vi.	7
o'er him *g* Tall as a figure lengthen'd	"	144
still as vaster *g* the shore, .	*In Mem.* cii.	25
would the great world *g* like thee,	" cxiii.	25
g to seeming-random forms, .	" cxvii.	10
rolls the deep where *g* the tree.	" cxxii.	1
For thee she *g*, for thee she grows	*Con.*	35
Discussing how their courtship *g*,	"	97
When it slowly *g* so thin,	*Maud*, i. xix.	20
ran on and rumour of battle *g*,	" III. vi.	29
ever great and greater *g*,	*Ode on Well.*	108
What slender campanili *g*	*The Daisy*	13
g Forgetful of his promise to the king,	*Enid*	49
g To hate the sin that seem'd so like	"	593
look'd, and still the terror *g* .	"	615
lie still, and yet the sapling *g*:	"	1014
g Tolerant of what he half disdained	*Vivien*	33
g So grated down and filed away .	"	472
dark wood *g* darker toward the storm	"	739
g between her and the pictured wall.	*Elaine*	987
g so cheerful that they deem'd her death	"	1125
all this trouble did not pass but *g*;	*Guinevere*	84
g half-guilty in her thoughts again,	"	405
sickly-born and *g* Yet sicklier,	*En. Arden.*	260
contracting *g* Careworn and wan ;	"	483
Thicker the drizzle *g*, deeper the gloom ;	"	680
Heaven in lavish bounty moulded, *g*.	*Aylmer's F.*	107
still G with the growing note,	*Sea Dreams*	206
g so tall It wore a crown of light,	*The Flower*	9
g Tired of so much within our little life,	*Lucretius*	222
grewest.		
Who *g* not alone in power .	*In Mem.* cxiii.	26
gride.		
g's and clangs Its leafless ribs	*In Mem.* cvi.	11
grief.		
nor let your *g* be wild, .	*May Queen* ii.	35
g became A solemn scorn of ills.	*D. of F. Wom.*	227
In *g* I am not all unlearn'd ;	*To J. S.*	18
Let G be her own mistress still.	"	41
weaker than your *g* would make G more.	"	65

	POEM.	LINE.
such a distance from his youth in *g*,	*Gardener's D.*	53
g to find her less than fame,	*Princess*, i.	72
wan from lack of sleep, Or *g*,	" iii.	10
Red *g* and mother's hunger in her eye,	" vi.	130
answer'd full of *g* and scorn.	"	313
Forgive my *g* for one removed,	*In Mem.Pro.*	37
Let Love clasp G lest both be drown'd,	" i.	9
g hath shaken into frost !	" iv.	12
To put in words the *g* I feel ;	" v.	2
that large *g* which these enfold	"	11
Calm as to suit a calmer *g*,	" xi.	2
hush'd my deepest *g* of all,	" xix.	10
The lesser *g*'s that may be said,	" xx.	1
is it that the haze of *g* .	" xxiv.	9
voice was not the voice of *g*,	" xxviii.	19
by the measure of my *g*	" lxxiv.	3
A *g*, then changed to something else,	" lxxvi.	11
O *g*, can *g* be changed to less ?	" lxxviii.	16
g my loss in him had wrought,	" lxxix.	6
A *g* as deep as life or thought,	"	7
To this which is our common *g*,	" lxxxiv.	7
in my *g* a strength reserved,	"	52
Or so shall *g* with symbols play,	"	95
in the midmost heart of *g*	" lxxxvii.	7
No more shall wayward *g* abuse	" civ.	9
Ring out the *g* that saps the mind,	" cv.	9
possible After long *g* and pain	*Maud*, II. iv.	2
overtoil'd By that day's *g* and travel,	*Enid*	1226
I have *g*'s enough : Pray you be gentle,	"	1555
Hand-hidden, as for utmost *g* or shame ;	*Vivien*	746
I find with *g* ! I might believe you	"	771
Words, as we grant *g* tears.	*Elaine*	1182
nor sought, Wrapt in her *g*, for housel	*Guinevere*	147
the King's *g* For his own self,	"	194
if there ever come a *g* to me	"	198
even were the *g*'s of little ones	"	201
g Is added to the *g*'s the great must bear,	"	202
common *g* of all the realm ?'	"	215
all woman's *g*, That *she* is woman,	"	216
Grieve with your *g*'s, not grieving	"	671
Annie, seated with her *g*.	*En. Arden.*	279
if *g*'s Like his have worse or better,	"	741
My *g* and solitude have broken me ;	"	858
I am grieved to learn your *g*—	*Aylmer's F.*	398
from his height and loneliness of *g*	"	632
grieve.		
faints and my whole soul *g*'s 'A spirit haunts,' etc.		16
With such compelling cause to *g*.	*In Mem.xxix.*	1
g Thy brethren with a fruitless tear ?	" lvii.	9
G with the common grief of all the .	*Guinevere*	215
G with your griefs, not grieving at your joys,	"	671
I *g* to see you poor and wanting help ;	*En. Arden*	403
it is not often I *g*;	*Grandmother*	89
grieved.		
began to change—I saw it and *g*—	*Princess*, iv.	280
be not wroth or *g* At your own son,	*Enid*	779
great charger stood, *g* like a man.	"	1384
I am *g* to learn your grief—	*Aylmer's F.*	398
she *g* In her strange dream .	*Sea Dreams*	222
grieving.		
g that their greatest are so small.	*Vivien*	682
not *g* at your joys,	*Guinevere*	671
g held his will, and bore it thro'.	*En. Arden.*	167
griffin-guarded.		
we reached The *g-g* gates.	*Audley Ct.*	14
grig.		
like the dry High-elbow'd *g*'s	*The Brook*	54
grim.		
Were their faces *g*.	*The Captain*	54
grimace.		
Caught each other with wild *g*'s,	*Vision of Sin*	35
grin.		
g's on a pile of children's bones,	*Maud*, I. i.	46
chuckle and *g* at a brother's shame ;	" iv.	29
grind.		
A grazing iron collar *g*'s my neck ;	*St S. Stylites*	115
centre-bits G on the wakeful ear	*Maud*, I. i.	42

	POEM.	LINE.
grinning.		
Who was gaping and *g* by : .	*Maud*, II. i.	20
grip.		
in the hard *g* of his hand, .	*Sea Dreams*	159
gripe.		
hand in wild delirium, *g* it hard,	*Princess*, vii.	78
gript.		
last *G* my hand hard, . .	*Sea Dreams*	156
groan.		
exprest By sighs or *g's* or tears ; .	*D. of F. Wom.*	284
he but gave a wrathful *g*, .	*Enid*	1247
marvellous great shriek and ghastly *g*,	*Elaine*	515
Down in the S is a flash and a *g* ;	*The Window*	42
groaned.		
deep brook *g* beneath the mill ;	*Miller's D.*	113
g Sir Lancelot in remorseful pain,	*Elaine*	1418
as their faces drew together, *g*,	*En. Arden*	74
'No trifle,' *g* the husband ; .	*Sea Dreams*	141
groaning.		
almost burst his pipes, *G* for power,	*Princess*, ii.	451
to them the doors gave way *G*,	" vi.	330
the fallen man Made answer, *g*,	*Enid*	576
turn'd, and *g* said, 'Forgive !	*Sea Dreams*	59
groom (a servant.)		
hung with *g's* and porters on the bridge,	*Godiva*	2
groom (married man.)		
Gives her harsh *g* for bridal-gift	*Princess*, v.	368
drinking health to bride and *g*	*In Mem. Con.*	83
groom'd.		
strongly *g* and straitly curb'd	*Princess*, v.	446
now so long By bandits *g*, .	*Enid*	1042
groove.		
down the ringing *g's* of change.	*Locksley H.*	182
grope.		
g, And gather dust and chaff,	*In Mem.* liv.	17
groped.		
g as blind, and seem'd Always about	*Aylmer's F.*	821
groping.		
feeble twilight of this world *G*,	*Enid*	855
gross.		
month So *g* to express delight	*Gardener's D.*	55
a sphere Too *g* to tread, .	*Princess*, vii.	306
flies the lighter thro' the *g*.	*In Mem.* xl.	4
grossest.		
Love, tho' Love were of the *g*,	*Vivien*	311
grossness.		
the *g* of his nature will have weight	*Locksley H.*	48
grot.		
The hollow *g* replieth . .	*Claribel*	20
Black the garden-bowers and *g's* .	*Arabian N's.*	78
alleys falling down to twilight *g's*,	*Ode to Mem.*	107
shadow'd *g's* of arches interlaced .	*Pal. of Art*	51
grotesque.		
raillery, or *g*, or false sublime—	*Princess*, iv.	565
ground (earth, etc.)		
dew is cold upon the *g*, . .	*The Owl*, i.	2
All the place is holy *g* ; . .	*Poet's Mind*	9
fall to the *g* if you came in. .	"	23
And shall fall again to *g*. . .	*Deserted H.*	16
from the *g* She raised her piercing	*D. of F. Wom.*	170
keep smooth plats of fruitful *g*, .	*The Blackbird*	3
near'd His happy home, the *g*. .	*Gardener's D.*	91
with shadows of the common *g* !	"	134
Dora cast her eyes upon the *g*, .	*Dora*	87
falling on the foeman's *g* ! .	*Locksley H.*	103
O Lord ! 'tis in my neighbour's *g*,	*Amphion*	75
To yonder shining *g*, . .	*St Agnes' Eve*	14
track'd you still on classic *g*, .	*To E. L.*	10
Above the teeming *g*. . .	*Sir L. and Q. G.*	18
Gathering up from all the lower *g*;	*Vision of Sin*	15
fair length upon the *g* she lay ; .	*Princess*, v.	56
Ida spoke not, gazing on the *g*, .	" vi.	210

	POEM.	LINE.
To dance with death, to beat the *g*,	*In Mem.* i.	12
chesnut pattering to the *g* : .	" xi.	4
here upon the *g*, No more partaker	" xi.	7
hide thy shame beneath the *g*. .	" lxxi.	28
all is new unhallow'd *g*. . .	" ciii.	12
crush'd, and dinted into the *g* :	*Maud*, I. i.	7
myself in my own dark garden *g*,	" iii.	10
O let the solid *g* Not fail .	" xi.	1
Rivulet crossing my *g*, . .	" xxi.	1
forks are fixt into the meadow *g*,	*Enid*	482
Coursed one another more on open *g*	"	522
they fixt the forks into the *g*	"	548
moving downward to the meadow *g*,	"	1053
held her eyes upon the *g*, .	*Elaine*	232
answer'd with his eyes upon the *g*.	"	1342
weep their burthen to the *g*, .	*Tithonus*	2
restore me to the *g* ; . .	"	72
ground (primary reason.)		
'Not that the *g's* of hope were fix'd,	*Two Voices*	227
ground (verb.)		
'*g* in yonder social mill . .	*In Mem.* lxxxviii.	39
teeth that *g* As in a dreadful dream,	*Aylmer's F.*	328
ground-plan.		
Lo ! God's likeness—the *g-p*— .	*Vision of Sin*	187
ground-swell.		
a full tide Rose with *g-s*, .	*Sea Dreams*	51
Roll as a *g-s* dash'd on the strand,	*W. to Alexan.*	23
group.		
A *g* of Houris bow'd to see .	*Pal. of Art*	102
shadow'd many a *g* Of beauties.	*Talking O.*	61
a *g* of girls in circle waited, .	*Princess*, *Pro.*	68
in *g's* they stream'd away .	" *Con.*	105
grouped.		
Muses and the Graces, *g* in threes,	*Princess*, ii.	13
stood her maidens glimmeringly *g*	" iv.	172
grove.		
From the *g's* within The wild-bird's	*Poet's Mind*	20
I, rooted here among the *g's*, .	*Talking O.*	181
Wherever in a lonely *g*. . .	*Amphion*	21
Hush'd all the *g's* from fear of	*Sir L. and Q. G.*	1
gem-like up before the dusky *g's*,	*Princess*, *Pro.*	75
in a poplar *g* when a light wind	" v.	12
halls alone among their massive *g's* ;	" *Con.*	43
Uncared for, gird the windy *g*, .	*In Mem.* c.	13
In the little *g* where I sit— .	*Maud*, I. iv.	2
Yet present in his natal *g*, .	*The Daisy*	18
g's of pine on either hand, .	*To F. D. Maurice*	21
knot, beneath, of snakes, aloft, a *g*.	*Enid*	325
young Lavaine into the poplar *g*.	*Elaine*	508
wide world's rumour by the *g* .	"	521
all points, except the poplar *g*, .	"	614
Lavaine across the poplar *g* Led .	"	800
high wall and the flowering *g* Of .	*Guinevere*	34
under *g's* that look'd a paradise .	"	386
to the garden now, and *g* of pines,	*Aylmer's F.*	550
Thy God is far diffused in noble *g's*	"	653
Burnt and broke the *g* and altar .	*Boadicea*	2
To rest in a golden *g*, . .	*Wages*	9
grovel.		
Stands at thy gate for thee to *g* to—	*Aylmer's F.*	652
grovelike.		
Once *g*, each huge arm a tree, .	*Aylmer's F.*	510
grovelled.		
unlaced my casque And *g* on my .	*Princess*, vi.	12
g with her face against the floor ; .	*Guinevere*	412
while she *g* at his feet, . .	"	575
grow.		
in the rudest wind Never *g* sere, .	*Ode to Mem.*	25
g so full and deep In thy large .	*Eleänore*	85
slowly *g* To a full face, . .	"	91
G golden all about the sky ; . .	"	101
g round him in his place, *G*, live .	*Fatima*	40
a light that *g's* Larger and clearer,	*Œnone*	106
endurance *g* Sinew'd with action,	"	161
G's green and broad, and takes no	*Lotos-E's.*	73

	POEM.	LINE.
g's to guerdon after-days:	'Love thou thy land,' etc.	27
felt her heart g prouder:	The Goose	22
until he g's Of age to help us.'	Dora	124
schoolboy ere he g's To Pity—'	Walk. to the M.	99
that my soul might g to thee,	St S. Stylites	70
faces g between me and my book	''	173
'tis fitted on and g's to me,	''	206
shall g so fair as this.'	Talking O.	244
All grass of silky feather g—	''	269
But we g old. Ah! when shall	Golden Year	47
g's the day of human power?'	Two Voices	78
sons g up that bear his name,	''	256
Some g to honour, some to shame—	''	237
The vast Republics that may g	Dav-Dm.	227
That g's within the woodland	Amphion	4
g's From England to Van Diemen.	''	83
To g my own plantation	''	100
I g in worth, and wit, and sense,	Will Water.	41
my father's face G long and troubled	Princess, i.	58
might g To use and power	'' ii.	130
And g for ever and for ever.	'' iii.	363
slowly g's a glimmering square,	'' iv.	34
g To prize the authentic mother	'' v.	422
this shall g A night of Summer	'' vi.	37
miserable, How shall men g?	'' vii.	250
in the long years liker must they g;	''	263
in purpose, will in will, they g,	''	287
A beam in darkness: let it g.	In Mem. Pro.	24
knowledge g from more to more,	''	25
g incorporate into thee.	'' ii.	16
as he g's he gathers much,	'' xliv.	5
His isolation g's defined.	'' lii.	12
blanch'd with darkness must I g!	'' lx.	8
days that g to something strange,	'' lxx.	11
year by year the landscape g	'' c.	19
For thee she grew, for thee she g's	'' Con.	35
I should g light-headed, I fear	Maud, I. xix.	100
ever afresh they seem'd to g.	'' II. i.	28
I know where a garden g's,	'' v.	72
That g for happy lovers.	The Brook	173
let the sorrowing crowd about it g,	Ode on Well.	16
weaker g's thro' acted crime,	Will	12
ourselves shall g In use of arms	Elaine	64
days will g to weeks, the weeks	Guinevere	617
your growth, I seem'd again to g,	Aylmer's F.	359
heaps of living gold that daily g,	''	655
as by miracle, g straight and fair—	''	676
I may die but the grass will g, (rep.)	The Window	109

growest.

| ever thus thou g beautiful | Tithonus | 43 |

growing.

ere the light on dark was g,	Oriana	10
till my grave be g green:	May Queen, ii.	43
His face is g sharp and thin.	D. of the O. Year	46
like a pear In g,	Walk. to the M.	46
g coarse to sympathise with clay.	Locksley H.	46
On that cottage g nearer,	L. of Burleigh	35
G and fading and g upon me (rep.)	Maud, I. iii.	7
had a sapling g on it,	Enid	1012
g longest by the meadow's edge,	''	1106
November day Was g duller twilight,	En. Arden	723
g dewy-warm With kisses balmier	Tithonus	58

growled.

| farewell to my sire who g An answer | Princess, v. | 223 |
| so the ruffians g, Fearing to lose, | Enid | 1411 |

growling.

g like a dog, when his good bone	Enid	1407
lays his foot upon it, Gnawing and g;	''	1411
g as before, And cursing	''	1423

grown.

That her voice untuneful g,	The Owl, ii.	6
she is g so dear, so dear,	Miller's D.	170
eyes g dim with gazing on the	Lotos-E's.	132
when love is g To ripeness,	To J. S.	14
am I feeble g; my end draws nigh	St S. Stylites	35
matin-chirp hath g Full quire,	Love and Duty	95
maiden's jet-black hair has g,	Day-Dm.	80
My beard has g into my lap.'	''	154
wake on science g to more,	''	222

	POEM.	LINE.
tho' you have g You scarce have	Princess, ii.	285
g a bulk Of spanless girth,	'' vi.	19
left barren, scarce had g The grain	In Mem. lii.	7
thy crescent would have g;	'' lxxxiii.	4
I myself with these have g,	'' Con.	19
morbid hate and horror have g	Maud, I. vi.	75
now has g The vast necessity	Vivien	773
g a part of me; but what use in it?	Elaine	1406
mean Vileness, we are g so proud—	Aylmer's F.	756

growth.

G's of jasmine turn'd Their humid	D. of F. Wom.	69
seed of men and g of minds.	'Love thou thy land,'	20
knightly g that fringed his lips.	M. d'Arthur	220
Or that Thessalian g,	Talking O.	292
bear a double g of those rare souls,	Princess, ii.	163
freedom, force and g Of spirit	'' iv.	123
no song, the true g of your soil,	''	132
In us true g, in her a Jonah's gourd	''	292
train To riper g the mind,	In Mem. xli.	8
dwarf'd a g of cold and night,	'' lx.	7
change of place, like g of time,	'' civ.	11
native g of noble mind;	'' cx.	16
Watching your g, I seem'd again to	Aylmer's F.	359

grunt.

| meditative g's of much content, | Walk. to the M. | 79 |

grunted.

| waked with silence, g 'Good!' | M. d'Arthur, Ep. | 4 |

grunter.

| tends her bristled g's in the sludge;' | Princess, v. | 26 |

guano.

| A pamphleteer on g and on grain, | Princess, Con. | 89 |

guard (s.)

| Encompass'd by his faithful g, | In Mem. cxxv. | 8 |

guard (verb.)

clear-stemm'd platans g The outlet	Arabian N's.	23
cliffs that g my native land,	Audley Ct.	48
Brothers, the woman's Angel g's you,	Princess, v.	400
like a beacon g's thee home.	In Mem. xvii.	12
g the portals of the house;	'' xxix.	12
here shall silence g thy fame;	'' lxxiv.	17
myself from myself I g,	Maud, I. vi.	60
g us, g the eye, the soul Of Europe,	Ode on Well.	160
bad you g the sacred coasts.	''	172
arms to g his head and yours,	Enid	1276
to g the justice of the King:	''	1782
I shall g it even in death.	Elaine	1109
g thee in the wild hour coming on,	Guinevere	443
I g as God's high gift	''	490
g and foster her for evermore.	''	586
enough, Sir! I can g my own.'	Aylmer's F.	276

guarded.

| G the sacred shield of Lancelot; | Elaine | 4 |
| thou shalt be g till my death. | Guinevere | 445 |

guarding.

| G kings and realms from shame; | Ode on Well. | 68 |

guerdon (s.)

Sequel of g could not alter me	Œnone	151
take A horse and arms for g;	Enid	1067
free gift, then,' said the boy, 'Not g;	''	1072
legend as in g for your rhyme?	Vivien	404

guerdon (verb.)

| grows to g after-days: | 'Love thou thy land,' etc. | 27 |
| a costly bribe To g silence, | Princess, i. | 201 |

guess.

cannot g How much their welfare	Princess, iii.	263
Power in darkness whom we g;	In Mem. cxxiii.	4
What art thou then? I cannot g;	'' cxxix.	5
To his own great self, as I g,	Maud, II. v.	33
I might g thee chief of those,	Elaine	183

guess'd.

I leave thy greatness to be g;	In Mem. lxxiv.	4
might have g you one of those	Enid	431
g a hidden meaning in his arms,	Elaine	17

guest.	POEM.	LINE.
Each enter'd like a welcome *g*.	*Two Voices*	411
honour'd by the *g* Half-mused,	*Will Water.*	73
mellow Death, like some late *g*,	"	237
silver-set; about it lay the *g's*,	*Princess,Pro.*	106
You, likewise, our late *g's*,	" v.	220
glows In expectation of a *g*;	*In Mem.* vi.	30
brings no more a welcome *g*.	" xxix.	5
I see myself an honour'd *g*,	" lxxxiii.	21
A *g*. or happy sister, sung,	" lxxxviii.	26
Conjecture of a stiller *g*,	" Con.	86
that cometh, like an honour'd *g*,	*Ode on Well.*	80
that her *g* should serve himself.'	*Enid*	379
goodly cheer To feed the sudden *g*,	"	1133
'Whence comest thou, my *g*,	*Elaine*	181
g, their host, their ancient friend,	*Aylmer's F.*	790

guide (s.)
were dangerous *g's* the feelings—	*Locksley H.*	95
each by turns was *g* to each,	*In Mem.*xxiii.	13
With you for *g* and master,	*Vivien*	730
were I glad of you as *g* and friend;	*Elaine*	226
with good Sir Torre for *g*	"	784
the silver star, thy *g*, Shines	*Tithonus*	25

guide (verb.)
there is a hand that *g's*.	*Princess,Con.*	79
g Her footsteps, moving side by side	*In Mem.*cxiii.	18
and He that made it will *g*.	*Maud*, I iv.	48
he Will *g* me to that palace,	*Elaine*	1123

guided.
| Whose feet are *g* thro' the land, | *In Mem.*lxv. | 9 |
| not alone had *g* me, | " cxii. | 3 |

guile.
| pure as he from taint of craven *g*, | *Ode on Well.* | 135 |

guilt.
When I have purged my *g*.'	*Pal. of Art*	296
g of blood is at your door	*L.C.V.de Vere*	43
hope thro' shame and *g*, 'Love thou thy land,' etc.	82
Easily gather'd either *g*.	*Princess* iv.	217
eye which watches *g* And goodness,	*In Mem.*xxvi.	5
judger would have call'd her *g*,	*Enid*	1282
subtle beast, Would track her *g*	*Guinevere*	60
too-fearful *g* Simpler than any child	"	368
wreck itself without the pilot's *g*,	*Aylmer's F.*	716

guiltless.
| Guilty or *g*, to stave off a chance . *Enid* | 1202 |

guilty.
Am I *g* of blood?	*Maud*, II. ii.	73
dream she could be *g* of foul act,	*Enid*	120
G or guiltless, to stave off a chance	"	1202
rooted out the slothful officer Or *g*,	"	1787

guinea.
| jingling of the *g* helps the hurt | *Locksley H.* | 105 |

guinea-hens.
| praised his hens, his geese, his *g-h*; *The Brook* | 126 |

Guinevere.
Sir Launcelot and Queen *G* Rode	*Sir L. and Q. G.*	20
Thro' that great tenderness for *G*, *Enid*	30
G, lay late into the morn,	"	157
G, not mindful of his face	"	191
stately queen whose name was *G*,	"	667
thrice that morning *G* had climb'd	"	826
Spake 'for she had been sick') to *G Elaine*	79
G, The pearl of beauty:	"	114
Lancelot, when they glanced at *G*	"	270
at the palace craved Audience of *G*,	"	1157
And therefore to our lady *G*,	"	1271
Queen *G* had fled the court,	*Guinevere*	1
storm of anger brake From *G*,	"	360
did not come to curse thee, *G*,	"	529
yet no less, O *G*, For I was ever virgin	"	552

gulf s.)
brought Into the *g's* of sleep.	*D. of F. Wom.*	52
Sow'd all their mystic *g's*	*Gardener's D.*	257
that the *g's* will wash us down ;	*Ulysses*	62
down the fiery *g* as talk of it,	*Princess*, iii.	270
Nor shudders at the *g's* beneath	*In Mem.* xl.	15
A *g* that ever shuts and gapes,	" lxix.	6

	POEM.	LINE.
in this stormy *g* have found a pearl *Maud*, I. xviii.	42
a *g* of ruin, Swallowing gold,	*Sea Dreams*	79

gulf (verb.)
| Should *g* him fathom-deep in brine ; *In Mem.* x. | 18 |

Gulistan.
| any rose of *G* Shall burst her veil : *Princess*, iv. | 104 |

gulled.
| break our bound, and *g* Our servants, *Princess*, iv. | 518 |

gun.
Nor ever lost an English *g* ;	*Ode on Well.*	97
'Charge for the *g's* !' he said :	*Lt. Brigade*	6
Not a *g* was fired.	*The Captain*	40
Each beside his *g*.	"	52

gunner.
| Sabring the *g's* there | *Lt. Brigade* | 29 |

gurgle.
| All throats that *g* sweet! | *Talking O.* | 266 |

Gurnion.
| By castle *G* where the glorious King *Elaine* | 293 |

gush.
| *g'es* from beneath a low-hung cloud. *Ode to Mem.* | 71 |

gushing.
| *g* of the wave Far far away did seem *Lotos-E's* | 31 |

gust.
one warm *g*, full-fed with perfume, *Gardener's D.*	112
chaff for every *g* of chance,	*Princess*, iv.	337
g that round the garden flew,	*In Mem.*lxxxviii.	19
An angry *g* of wind Puff'd out	*Vivien*	580

Gwydion.
| *G* made by glamour out of flowers, *Enid* | 743 |

gynæceum.
| Dwarfs of the *g*, fail so far | *Princess*, iii. | 262 |

gyre.
| Shot up and shrill'd in flickering *g's*, *Princess*, vii. | 31 |

H

H.
| too rough *H* in Hell and Heaven, *Sea Dreams* | 192 |

haäcre.
| Warnt worth nowt a *h*, | *N. Farmer* | 39 |
| wi haäte oonderd *h* o' Squoire's, | " | 44 |

habit (custom.)
Idle *h* links us yet.	*Miller's D.*	212
Or to burst all links of *h*—	*Locksley H.*	157
Drink deep, until the *h's* of the slave, *Princess*, ii.	77
to us, The fools of *h*, sweeter seems *In Mem.* x.	12
memory from old *h* of the mind	*Guinevere*	376

habit (riding dress.)
| whether The *h*, hat, and feather, . *Maud*, I. xx. | 18 |

Hades.
| or the enthroned Persephone in *H, Princess*, iv. | 419 |

haft.
| *h* twinkled with diamond sparks, | *M. d'Arthur* | 56 |
| knife's *h* hard against the board, | *Enid* | 1448 |

haggard.
| arm to which the Queen's Is *h* | *Elaine* | 1221 |

hail (s.)
Where falls not *h*, or rain,	*M. d'Arthur*	260
Rain, wind, frost, heat, *h*, damp,	*St S. Stylites*	16
with rain or *h*, or fire or snow ;	*Locksley H.*	193
And gilds the driving *h*.	*Sir Galahad*	56
Sleet of diamond-drift and pearly *h; Vision of Sin*	22

hail (verb.)
meets a friend who *h's* him,	*Walk. to the M.*	34
H, hidden to the knees in fern,	*Talking O.*	29
city-roar that *h's* Premier or king ! *Princess*, Con.	101
voices *h* it from the brink ;	*In Mem.* cxx.	14
h once more to the banner of battle *Maud*, III. vi.	42

	POEM.	LINE.
ere he came, like one that *h*'s a ship,	*Enid*	1389
Fair as the Angel that said '*h*'	*Aylmer's F.*	681

hailed.

| Walter, *h* a score of names upon her, | *Princess, Pro.* | 155 |

hair.

With thy floating flaxen *h*;	*Adeline*	6
smooth'd his chin and sleck'd his *h*,	*A Character*	11
Dressing their *h* with the white	*The Merman*	13
Combing her *h* Under the sea,	*The Mermaid*	4
I would comb my *h* (rep.)	"	11
round her neck floated her *h*	*Œnone*	18
sunny *h* Cluster'd about his temples	"	58
her deep *h* Ambrosial, golden	"	173
her *h* Wound with white roses,	*Pal. of Art*	98
kindly voice and on his silver *h* !	*May Queen,* iii.	13
Your *h* is darker, and your eyes	*Margaret*	49
that *h* More black than ashbuds	*Gardener's D.*	27
single stream of all her soft brown *h*	"	127
wound Her looser *h* in braid,	"	155
In wreath about her *h*.	*Talking O.*	288
Catch the wild goat by the *h*,	*Locksley H.*	170
and his *h* A yard behind.	*Godiva*	18
maiden's jet-black *h* has grown,	*Day-Dm.*	80
my *h* Is gray before I know it.	*Will Water.*	167
With a single rose in her *h*.	*Lady Clare.*	60
One her dark *h* and lovesome mien.	*Beggar Maid*	12
H, and eyes, and limbs, and faces,	*Vision of Sin*	39
girl-graduates in their golden *h*.	*Princess,Pro.*	142
long black *h* Damp from the river,	" iv.	257
touch not a *h* of his head:	"	388
in the long night of her deep *h*,	"	470
fingering at the *h* about his lip,	" v.	293
caught his *h*, And so' belabour'd him	"	330
single band of gold about her *h*,	"	502
sittest ranging golden *h* ;	*In Mem.* vi.	26
youth and babe and hoary *h's*:	" lxviii.	10
To reverence and the silver *h* ;	" lxxxiii.	32
the roots of my *h* were stirred	*Maud,* I. i.	13
What if with her sunny *h*,	" vi.	23
thought It is his mother's *h*.	" II. ii.	70
h In gloss and hue, the chesnut,	*The Brook* 71,	206
A twist of gold was round her *h*;	*Vivien*	70
snake of gold slid from her *h*,	"	737
Set it in this damsel's golden *h*,	*Elaine*	205
bright *h* blown about the serious face	"	391
shook his *h*, strode off, and buzz'd	"	718
all her bright *h* streaming down—	"	1150
seize me by the *h* and bear me far,—	"	1415
dewy *h* blown back like flame :	*Guinevere*	282
milkwhite arms and shadowy *h*	"	413
a *h* of this low head be harm'd.	"	444
golden *h*, with which I used to play	"	543
This *h* is his; she cut it off .	*En. Arden.*	895
hoar *h* of the Baronet bristle up	*Aylmer's F.*	42
h as it were crackling into flames.	"	586
not a *h* Ruffled upon the scarfskin,	"	659
gray *h's* with sorrow to the grave—	"	777
face was ruddy, his *h* was gold,	*The Victim*	36
Beat breast, tore *h*, cried out	*Lucretius.*	273
And you with gold for *h*,	*The Window*	65

hairy-fibred.

| Claspt the gray walls with *h-f* arms, | *Enid* | 323 |

hale (adj.)

| was strong and *h* of body then ; | *St S. Stylites* | 28 |
| wears his manhood *h* and green : | *In Mem.* lii. | 4 |

Hale (surname.)

| Francis *H*, The farmer's son, | *Audley Ct.* | 73 |

haled.

we *h* the groaning sow,	*Walk. to the M.*	83
They *h* us to the Princess	*Princess,* iv.	252
h him out into the world,	*Aylmer's F.*	467
h the yellow-ringleted Britoness—	*Boädicea*	55

haler.

| and *h* too than I : | *Guinevere* | 677 |

half.

| Portioned in *halves* between us, | *Gardener's D.* | 5 |
| *h* stands up And bristles ; *h* has fall'n | *Walk.to the M.* | 23 |

H is thine and *h* is his :	*Locksley H.*	92
h Without you ; with you, whole ;	*Princess,* iv.	440
of those *halves* You worthiest	"	441
either sex alone Is *h* itself,	" vii.	284
part it, giving *h* to him .	*InMem.*xxv.	12
My bosom friend and *h* of life ;	" lviii.	3
divided *h* of such A friendship	" lxxxiv.	63
h to the setting moon are gone,	*Maud,* I. xxii.	23
h to the rising day ;	"	24

half-aghast.

| Leolin still Retreated *h-a*, | *Aylmer's F.* | 330 |

half-akin.

| No longer *h-a* to brute, | *In Mem. Con.* | 133 |

half-allowing.

| *h-a* smiles for all the world, | *Aylmer's F.* | 120 |

half-amazed.

| Whereat he stared, replying, *h-a*. | *Godiva* | 21 |
| dispatches which the Head Took *h-a*, | *Princess,* iv. | 361 |

half-angered.

| *H-a* with my happy lot, | *Miller's D.* | 200 |

half-arisen.

| came upon him *h-a* from sleep, | *Aylmer's F.* | 584 |

half-attained.

| cope Of the *h-a* futurity, | *Ode to Mem.* | 33 |

half-asleep.

| As *h-a* his breath he drew, | *The Sisters* | 28 |

half-awake.

| *h-a* I heard The parson taking wide | *The Epic* | 13 |

half-awakened.

| The earliest pipe of *h-a* birds | *Princess,* iv. | 32 |

half-blind.

| sudden light Dazed me *h-b* : | *Princess,* v. | 11 |

half-bold.

| *H-b*, half-frighted, with dilated eyes, | *Enid* | 1445 |

half-buried.

| *H-b* in the Eagle's down, | *Pal. of Art* | 122 |

half-canonized.

| *H-c* by all that look'd on her, | *Princess,* i. | 23 |

half-cheated.

| rathe she rose, *h-c* in the thought. | *Elaine* | 339 |

half-clench'd.

| hand *h-c* Went faltering sideways | *Vivien* | 698 |

half-closed.

| dropping low their crimson bells *H-c*, | *Arabian N's.* | 62 |

half-conscious,

| *H-c* of the garden-squirt, | *Amphion* | 91 |
| *H-c* of their dying clay, | *In Mem.*lvii. | 7 |

half-consent.

| Assumed from thence a *h-c*. | *Princess,* vii. | 67 |

half-crown.

| Is it the weight of that *h-c*, | *Will Water.* | 155 |

half-crushed.

| *h-c* among the rest A dwarf-like Cato | *Princess,* vii. | 110 |

half-cut-down.

| *h-c-d*, a pasty costly-made, | *Audley Ct.* | 22 |

half-dead.

H-d to know that I shall die.'	*InMem.*xxxv.	16
Maybe still I am but *h-d* ;	*Maud,* II. v.	99
And all things look'd *h-d*,	*Grandmother*	34

half-defended.

| Lo their colony *h-d* ! | *Boädicea* | 17 |

half-despised.

| not look up, or *h-d* the height | *Guinevere* | 636 |

half-dipt.

| a summer moon *H-d* in cloud : | *Godiva* | 46 |

half-disdain.

| *h-d* Perch'd on the pouted blossom | *Princess,Pro.* | 194 |

TENNYSON'S WORKS. 183

	half-disfame.	POEM.	LINE.
what is Fame in life but *h-d*,		*Vivien*	315
well know I that Fame is *h-d*,		"	354

half-disrooted.
A tree was *h-d* from his place . *Princess*, iv. 168

half-divine.
The man I held as *h-d* ; . . *In Mem.* xiv. 10

half-drain'd.
a flask Between his knees, *h-d*; *Day-Dm.* . 46

half-dream.
Falling asleep in a *h-d* ! . . *Lotos-E's.* . 101

half-drooping.
half on her mother propt, *H-d* from *Princess*, iv. 349

half-dropt.
With *h-d* eyelids still, . . . *Lotos-E's.* . 135

half-English.
the sweet *h-E* Neilgherry air . *The Brook* . 17

half-envious.
H-e of the flattering hand, . . *Elaine* . 348

half-face.
From the *h-f* to the full eye, . *Elaine* 1255

half-fallen.
H-f across the threshold of the sun *D. of F. Wom.* 63

half-falling.
h-f from his knees, Half-nestled . *Vivien* . 753

half-foresaw.
h-f that he, the subtle beast, . *Guinevere* . 59

half-forgotten.
our great deeds, as *h-f* things. . *Lotos-E's.* . 123
random rhymes, Ere they be *h-f*; *Will Water.* 14
Low in the dust of *h-f* kings, . *Elaine* 1328

half-frightened.
Look'd down, half-pleased, *h-f*, . *Amphion* . 54

half-frighted.
Half-bold, *h-f* with dilated eyes, . *Enid* . 1445
on the book, *h-f*, Miriam swore. . *En. Arden* . 844

half-glance.
With a *h-g* upon the sky . . *A Character* 1

half-grown.
H-g as yet, a child, and vain— . *In Mem.* cxiii. 9

half-guilty.
grew *h-g* in her thoughts again, . *Guinevere* . 405

half-hid.
Here *h-h* in the gleaming wood, . *Maud*, I. vi. 69

half-historic.
dealt with knights Half-legend, *h-h*, *Princess, Pro.* 30

half-hour.
For one *h-h* and let him talk to me !' *The Brook* . 115

half-hysterical.
A half-incredulous, *h-h* cry. . . *En. Arden* . 854

half-incredulous.
A *h-i*, half-hysterical cry. . . *En. Arden* . 854

half-invisible.
H-i to the view, Wheeling . . *Vision of Sin* 36

half-lapt.
H-l in glowing gauze . . . *Princess*, vi. 118

half-legend.
dealt with knights *H-l*, half-historic *Princess, Pro.* 30

half-lost.
H-l in belts of hop . . . *Princess, Con.* 45
H-l in the liquid azure bloom . *Maud*, I. iv. 5
Owe you me nothing for a life *h-l*? *Enid* . 1167

half-miracle.
seem'd *h-m* To those he fought with— *Elaine* . 496

half-muffled.
answer which, *h-m* in his beard, . *Princess*, v. 224

half-mused.
the guest *H-m*, or reeling ripe, . *Will Water.* 74

	half-naked.	POEM.	LINE.
H-n as if caught at once from bed		*Princess*, iv. 266

half-nestled.
half-falling from his knees, *H-n* at his heart, *Vivien* 754

half-oblivious.
(For I was *h-o* of my mask) . . *Princess*, iii. 320

half-open.
Thro' *h-o* lattices . . . . *Eleänore* . 23

half-opened.
h-o bell of the woods ! . . . *Princess*, vi. 176

half-opening.
balmier than *h-o* buds Of April, . *Tithonus* . 59

half-parted.
H-p from a weak and scolding hinge, *The Brook* 64

half-pleased.
Look'd down, *h-p*, half-frighten'd *Amphion* . 54

half-possessed.
So Lilia sang : We thought her *h-p*, *Princess*, iv. 562

half-right.
I thought her *h-r* talking of her wrongs: *Princess*, v. 275

half-sardonically.
I ask'd him *h-s*. . . . . *Ed. Morris* . 59

half-science.
The sport *h-s*, fill me with a faith. *Princess, Con.* 76

half-self.
my other heart, And almost my *h-s*, *Princess*, i. 55

half-shrouded.
h-s over death In deathless marble. *Princess*, v. 71

half-shut.
With *h-s* eyes ever to seem Falling *Lotos-E's.* . 100

half-shy.
And so it was—half-sly, *h-s*, . *Miller's D.* . 133

half-sick.
h-s at heart, return'd. . . *Princess*, iv. 204

half-sickening.
H-s of his pension'd afternoon, . *Aylmer's F.* 461

half-sister.
Raw Haste, *h-s* to Delay. '*Love thou thy land*,'etc. 96

half-sly.
And so it was—*h-s*, half-shy, . *Miller's D.* . 133

half-suffocated.
H-s in the hoary fell . . . *Vivien* . 689
till I yell'd again *H-s*, . . . *Lucretius* . 58

half-tears.
Eyes, love-languid thro' *h-t*, . *Love and Duty* 36

half-thinking.
h-t that her lips Who had devised *Elaine* 1279

half-turned.
lichen fixt On a heart *h-t* to stone. *Maud*, I. vi. 78

half-unconscious.
I saw with *h-u* eye . . . *The Letters* 15

half-uncut.
She left the novel *h-u* . . . *Talking O.* . 117

half-views.
nor take *H-v* of men and things. . *Will Water.* 52

half-whispered.
drawing nigh *H-w* in his ear, . *Œnone* . 182

half-within.
Seem'd *h-w* and half-without, . *Miller's D.* . 7

half-without.
Seem'd half-within and *h-w*, . *Miller's D.* . 7

half-world.
yonder morning on the blind *h-w*; *Princess*, vii. 331

hall.
the throne In the midst of the *h*: *The Mermaid* 22
Round the *h* where I sate, . . " . 26

	POEM.	LINE.
Gods Ranged in the *h*'s of Peleus;	Œnone	79
she shriek'd in that lone *h*,	Pal. of Art	258
stands a spectre in your *h*:	L.C.V.de Vere	42
pine among your *h*'s and towers	"	58
about the gardens and the *h*'s	M.d'Arthur	20
who would rent the *h*:	Audley Ct.	30
strode About the *h*, among his dogs	Godiva	17
A sudden hubbub shook the *h*,	Day-Dm.	139
So pass I hostel, *h*, and grange;	Sir Galahad	81
Leading on from *h* to *h*.	L. of Burleigh	52
from vases in the *h* Flowers	Princess, Pro.	11
If our old *h*'s could change their sex	"	140
up a flight of stairs into the *h*.	" ii.	17
thought in our own *h* to hear	"	39
Look, our *h*! Our statues!—	"	61
his portrait in my father's *h* .	"	221
in *h*'s Of Lebanonian cedar:	"	330
hearts lie fallow in these *h*'s .	"	378
round these *h*'s a thousand baby	"	379
h glitter'd like a bed of flowers.	"	416
hooded brows I crept into the *h*,	" iv.	206
where she sat High in the *h*:	"	253
from the illumined *h* Long lanes	"	456
cap of Tyrol borrow'd from the *h*,	"	578
on they moved and gain'd the *h*,	" vi.	332
Descending, struck athwart the *h*,	"	344
Love in the sacred *h*'s Held carnival	" vii.	69
Gray *h*'s alone among their massive	Con.	43
Dies off at once from bower and *h*,	In Mem. viii.	6
our old pastimes in the *h*	" xxx.	5
echoes in sepulchral *h*'s	" lvii.	2
saw the tumult of the *h*'s;	" lxxxvi.	4
Imperial *h*'s, or open plain;	" xcvii.	29
Methought I dwelt within a *h*,	" cii.	5
The *h* with harp and carol rung.	"	9
white-faced *h*'s, the glancing rills,	Con.	113
lord of the broad estate and the *H*,	Maud, I. i.	19
I am sick of the *H* and the hill	"	61
Workmen up at the *H*!—	"	65
by a red rock glimmers the *H*;	" iv.	10
In the meadow under the *H*!	" v.	2
Bound for the *H*, (rep.)	" x.	25
On my fresh hope, to the *H* to-night	" xix.	103
bringing me down from the *H*	" xxi.	2
O Rivulet, born at the *H*,	"	8
As the music clash'd in the *h*;	" xxii.	34
Of the old manorial *h*.	" II. iv.	80
Sorrow darkens hamlet and *h*.	Ode on Well.	7
loved that *h*, tho' white and cold,	The Daisy	37
some gay knight in Arthur's *h*.'	Enid	118
on a day, he sitting high in *h*,	"	147
mindful of his face In the king's *h*,	"	192
thro' the open casement of the *H*,	"	328
dusky-rafter'd many-cobweb'd *H*,	"	362
because their *h* must also serve	"	390
here, now there, about the dusky *h*;	"	401
eat in Arthur's *h* at Camelot.	"	432
all their converse in the *h*,	"	520
Woke where he slept in the high *h*,	"	755
fancy dwelling in this dusky *h*;	"	802
remembering her old ruin'd *h*,	"	1103
take him up, and bear him to our *h*:	"	1401
to the naked of Doorm,	"	1418
on an oaken settle in the *h*,	"	1421
in the naked *h*, propping his head,	"	1429
Earl Doorm with plunder to the *h*.	"	1440
all the *h* was dim with steam of flesh:	"	1451
ate with tumult in the naked *h*,	"	1453
He roll'd his eyes about the *h*,	"	1458
turn'd all red and paced his *h*,	"	1516
loved me serving in my father's *h*:	"	1547
the brute Earl up and down his *h*,	"	1560
all the men and women in the *h*	"	1579
huge Earl lay slain within his *h*.	"	1654
in their *h*'s arose The cry of children,	"	1812
the King his havens, ships, and *h*'s,	Vivien	24
Arthur's arras *h* at Camelot	"	99
After the king, who eat in Arthur's *h*'s.	Elaine	184
'Known am I, and of Arthur's *h*,	"	188
ever among ladies ate in *H*,	"	255
into that rude *h* Stept with all grace,	"	262

	POEM.	LINE.
a chapel and a *h* On massive columns	Elaine	404
reverently they bore her into *h*.	"	1259
rarely could she frout in *H*,	Guinevere	62
the lighted lantern of the *h*;	"	260
in the *h* itself was such a feast	"	261
sit once more within his lonely *h*,	"	493
peacock-yewtree of the lonely *H*,	En. Arden 99,	609
county God—in whose capacious *h*,	Aylmer's F.	14
Aylmer follow'd Aylmer at the *H*	"	36
so that Rectory and *H*, Bound	"	38
ever welcome at the *H*,	"	114
darken'd all the northward of her *H*.	"	415
groves And princely *h*'s, and farms,	"	654
children's laughter in their *h*	"	787
great *H* was wholly broken down,	"	846
gleaming *h*'s of morn.	Tithonus	10
Echoes in his empty *h* 'Home they brought him, etc.		
climb into the windy *h*'s of heaven:	Lucretius	136

Hall (surname.)

the poet Everard *H*,	The Epic	4
Here ended *H*, and our last light,	M. d'Arthur,Ep.	1

hall-ceiling.

the fair *h-c* stately-set	Pal. of Art	141

hall-garden.

up in the high *H-g* I see her pass	Maud, I. iv.	11
birds in the high *H-g*	" xii. 1,	25

hall-hearths.

On the *h-h* the festal fires,	Day-Dm.	34

halloo.

With a lengthen'd loud *h*,	The Owl, ii.	13
in the *h* Will topple to the trumpet	Princess, ii.	213

hallowed.

Your very armour *h*,	Princess, v.	403

halo.

hence this *h* lives about	Will Water.	113
her own *h*'s dusky shield;	The Voyage	32

halt (adj.)

cured some *h* and maim'd;	St S. Stylites	135
is there any of you *h* or maim'd?	"	140
if a man were *h* or hunch'd,	Guinevere	42

halt (s.)

they made a *h*; The horses yell'd;	Princess, v.	239

halt (verb.)

He seems as one whose footsteps *h*,	Will	15
cry '*H*,' and to her own brigand face	Enid	959

halted.

hung his head, and *h* in reply,	Enid	1659
when we *h* at that other well,	Vivien	129

halter.

scared with threats of jail and *h*	Aylmer's F.	520

hamlet.

Two children in one *h* born	Circumstance	8
massive groves: Trim *h*'s;	Princess,Con.	44
where the kneeling *h* drains	In Mem. x.	15
Four voices of four *h*'s round,	" xxviii.	5
sorrow darkens *h* and hall.	Ode on Well.	7
distant colour, happy *h*,	The Daisy	27
known Edith among the *h*'s round,	Aylmer'sF.	615

hammer (s.)

Came to the *h* here in March—	Audley Ct.	59
silver *h*'s falling On silver anvils,	Princess, i.	213
iron-clanging anvil bang'd With *h*'s;	" v.	494
hear'st the village *h* clink,	In Mem. cxx.	15
everywhere Was *h* laid to hoof,	Enid	256
h and axe, Auger and saw,	En. Arden.	173

hammer (verb.)

h at this reverend gentlewoman,	Princess, iii.	113

hammered.

h from a hundred towers,	Godiva	75
long morn the lists were *h* up,	Princess, v.	358

hammering.

H and clinking, chattering stony	Princess, iii.	343

	POEM.	LINE.
hammock-shroud.		
His heavy-shotted h-s	In Mem. vi.	15
hand.		
to take Occasion by the h,	To the Queen	31
Claps her tiny h's above me,	Lilian	4
When I would kiss thy h,	Madeline	31
leddest by the h thine infant Hope.	Ode to Mem.	30
O cursed h! O cursed blow!	Oriana	82
Laughing and clapping their h's.	The Merman	29
who hath seen her wave her h?	L. of Shalott,	i. 24
Leaning his cheek upon his h,	Eleänore	118
till thy h Fail from the sceptre-staff.	Œnone	123
on this h, and sitting on this stone?	"	229
h's and eyes That said, We wait.	Pal. of Art	103
hollowing one h against his ear,	"	109
From one h droop'd a crocus:	"	119
clapt her h's and cried, "I marvel	"	189
The airy h confusion wrought,	"	226
If Time be heavy on your h's,	L. C. V. de Vere	66
put your h in mine,	May Queen, iii.	23
for other h's than mine.	"	52
Sinking ships, and praying h's.	Lotos-E's.	161
Beauty and anguish walking h in h	D. of F. Wom.	15
father held his h upon his face;	"	107
Shake h's, before you die.	D. of the O. Year	42
with his h against the hilt, 'Love thou thy land,' etc.	"	83
clapt his h On Everard's shoulder,	The Epic	21
'either h, Or voice, or else a motion	M. d'Arthur	76
arise and slay thee with my h's.'	"	132
Then with both h's I flung him,	"	157
drew the languid h's,	"	174
three Queens Put forth their h's,	"	206
chafed his h's, And call'd him	"	209
knowing God, they lift not h's of prayer,	"	252
at her h the greatest gift,	Gardener's D.	224
Was wroth, and doubled up his h's,	Dora	23
She bow'd upon her h's,	"	101
clapt him on the h's and on the cheeks,	"	130
clapt his h in mine and sang—	Audley Ct.	38
modest eyes, a h, a foot	Walk. to the M.	46
With h and rope we haled	"	83
with h's of wild rejection 'Go!—	Ed. Morris	124
She might have lock'd her h's.	Talking O.	144
kingdoms overset, Or lapse from h to h,	"	258
not dip His h into the bag:	Golden Year	71
turn'd it in his glowing h's;	Locksley H.	31
kiss him: take his h in thine.	"	52
tho' I slew thee with my h!	"	56
Then a h shall pass before thee,	"	167
a heart as rough as Esau's h,	Godiva	28
answer should one press his h's?	Two Voices.	245
The page has caught her h in his:	Day-Dm.	49
lightly rain from ladies' h's.	Sir Galahad	12
Nor maiden's h in mine.	"	20
stricken by an angel's h,	"	69
hold their h's to all, and cry.	Will Water.	45
halo lives about The waiter's h's,	"	114
lay your h upon my head.	Lady Clare	55
Dropt her head in the maiden's h,	"	63
Painted h in h with faces pale,	Vision of Sin	19
Bandied by the h's of fools.	"	106
And the warmth of h in h.	"	162
clasps the crag with hooked h's;	The Eagle	1
the touch of a vanish'd h,	'Break, break,' etc.	11
sport Went h in h with Science;	Princess, Pro.	80
h that play'd the patron with her curls.	"	138
long arms and h's Reach'd out,	"	i. 3
Airing a snowy h and signet gem,	"	120
to the tips of her long h's,	"	ii. 26
set our h To this great work,	"	45
Besides the brain was like the h,	"	134
Took both h's, and smiling faintly	"	284
Melissa, with her h upon the lock,	"	301
Push'd her flat h against his face.	"	345
circle rounded under female h's	"	350
one In this h held a volume	"	431
Lady Psyche was the right h now,	"	iii. 21
hush'd amaze of h and eye.	"	122
shameless h with shameful jest,	"	297
Many a little h Glanced	"	338
once or twice she lent her h,	"	iv. 9

	POEM.	LINE.
Palpitated, her h shook,	Princess, iv.	370
fell In to his father's h's,	"	383
up unscathed: give him your h:.	"	389
Whose brains are in their h's	"	497
She, ending, waved her h's:	"	501
on my shoulder flung their heavy h's,	"	531
gives the battle to his h's:	"	557
clapt her h's and cried for war,	"	567
Lay by her like a model of her h.	"	574
fell Into your father's h,	v.	49
push'd by rude h's from its pedestal,	"	55
White h's of farewell to my sire,	"	223
now a wandering h And now a pointed	"	259
tender orphan h's Felt at my heart,	"	425
king's right h in thunder-storms,	"	429
a moment h to h, And sword to sword,	"	527
female h's and hospitality.'	vi. 57,	80
prest Their h's, and call'd them dear	"	76
h's so lately claspt with yours,	"	168
soft babe in his hard-mailed h's	"	191
take her h, she weeps: 'Sdeath!	"	208
the rougher h Is safer:	"	261
Refuse her proffer, lastly gave his h.	"	327
Low voices with the ministering h	vii.	6
nor the h That nursed me,	"	38
catch Her h in wild delirium,	"	78
often feeling of the helpless h's,	"	96
and tears upon my h:	"	123
h in h with Plenty in the maize,	"	186
the voice trembled and the h.	"	212
her forehead sank upon her h's,	"	231
all the fair young planet in her h's—	"	248
Lay thy sweet h's in mine	"	345
there is a h that guides.'	Con.	79
Now shaking h's with him, now him,	"	92
reach a h thro' time to catch	In Mem. i.	7
A hollow form with empty h's.'	iii.	12
waiting for a h, A h that can be	vii.	4
letters unto trembling h's	x.	7
h's so often clasp'd in mine,	"	19
where warm h's have prest and clos'd,	xiii	
strike a sudden h in mine,	xiv	11
Come then, pure h's, and bear the	xviii.	9
Her h's are quicker into good:	xxxiii.	10
With human h's the creed of creeds	xxxvi.	10
thou and I have shaken h's,	xxxix.	29
I stretch lame h's of faith,	liv.	17
reaps the labour of his h's,	lxiii.	26
winds their curls about his h:	lxv.	12
He reach'd the glory of a h,	lxviii.	17
A h that points, and palled shapes	lxix.	7
dark h struck down thro' time,	lxxi.	19
Whate'er thy h's are set to do	lxxiv.	19
Reach out dead h's to comfort me.	lxxix.	16
reach us out the shining h,	lxxxiii.	43
How much of act at human h's	lxxxiv.	38
noise Of songs, and clapping h's,	lxxxvi.	19
Behold their brides in other h's;	lxxxix.	14
The larger heart, the kindlier h;	cv.	30
child would twine A trustful h,	cviii.	19
A higher h must make her mild,	cxiii.	17
I take the pressure of thine h.	cxviii.	12
out of darkness came the h's	cxxii.	23
Sweet human h and lips and eye;	cxxviii.	6
him to whom her h I gave.	Con.	70
in their h Is Nature like an open book:	"	131
Pickpockets, each h lusting for all	Maud, I. i.	2
moved by an unseen h at a game,	iv.	26
Ready in heart and ready in h,	v.	9
touch'd my h with a smile so sweet	vi.	12
the treasured splendour, her h,	"	84
She waved to me with her h.	ix.	8
God, for a man with heart, head, h,	x.	60
I kiss'd her slender h,	xii.	13
Sunn'd itself on his breast and his h's.	xiii.	13
if a h, as white As ocean-foam	xiv.	17
labour and the mattock-harden'd h,	xviii.	34
given false death her h,	"	60
It is this guilty h!—	II. i.	4
sorrow For the h, the lips, the eyes,	iv.	27
(Claspt h's and that petitionary grace	The Brook	112

186   CONCORDANCE TO

	POEM.	LINE.
greet With lifted *h* the gazer	*Ode on Well.*	22
both her open *h's* Lavish Honour	"	195
toil of heart and knees and *h's*,	"	212
upon whose *h* and heart and brain	"	239
with her own white *h's* Array'd	*Enid*	16
flyers from the *h* Of Justice,	"	36
mightful *h* striking great blows	"	95
instinctive *h* Caught at the hilt,	"	209
White from the mason's *h*,	"	244, 408
forward with the helmet yet in *h*	"	285
Or it may be the labour of his *h's*,	"	341
the lords of our own *h's*;	"	354
fondling all her *h* in his	"	509
On either shining shoulder laid a *h*,	"	518
came a clapping as of phantom *h's*.	"	566
seek a second favour at his *h's*.	"	626
in her *h* A suit of bright apparel,	"	678
with this and laid it in my *h*,	"	699
Help'd by the mother's careful *h*	"	738
Her by both *h's* he caught,	"	778
our kind Queen, No *h* but hers,	"	788
by the *h's* of Dubric, the high saint,	"	838
liever by his dear *h* had I die,	"	917
gently born But into bad *h's* fall'n,	"	1041
in his *h* Bare victual for the mowers:	"	1050
mid-warmth of welcome and graspt *h*,	"	1129
Geraint Waving an angry *h* .	"	1293
lift a shining *h* against the sun,	"	1322
Nor let her true *h* falter,	"	1361
after all was done that *h* could do,	"	1366
chafing his pale *h's*, and calling	"	1430-3
unknightly with flat *h*	"	1565
reach'd a *h*, and on his foot	"	1607
h to *h* beneath her husband's heart,	"	1615
wrought too long with delegated *h's*,	"	1741
a stronger race With hearts and *h's*,	"	1789
left *h* Droop from his mighty	*Vivien*	91
made a pretty cup of both my *h's*.	"	124
Merlin lock'd his *h* in hers	"	139, 320
woven paces and of waving *h's*,	"	179, 817
Merlin loosed his *h* from hers	"	206
lives dispersedly in many *h's*	"	307
The wrist is parted from the *h*	"	401
ringing with their serpent *h's*,	"	428
her *h* half-clench'd Went faltering	"	698
clapt her *h's* Together with a wailing	"	715
Some one put this diamond in her *h*	*Elaine*	212
Half-envious of the flattering *h*,	"	348
kiss'd her, and Sir Lancelot his own *h*,	"	388
smote her *h*: well-nigh she swoon'd:	"	622
sweet to have it From your own *h*;	"	691
slightly kiss'd the *h* to which he gave	"	698
with mine own *h* give his diamond	"	756
battle-writhen arms and mighty *h's*	"	808
laid the diamond in his open *h*.	"	823
glanced not up, nor waved his *h*,	"	980
Then gave a languid *h* to each,	"	1026
lay the letter in my *h*	"	1107-28
close the *h* Upon it;	"	1108-29
Set in her *h* a lily,	"	1142-49
in one cold passive *h* Received at once	"	1195
Arthur spied the letter in her *h*,	"	1263
Be carven, and her lily in her *h*.	"	1332
gardener's *h* Picks from the colewort	*Guinevere*	32
h's in *h's*, and eye to eye,	"	99
bow'd down upon her *h's* Silent,	"	156
passionately, Her head upon her *h's*,	"	179
meat he long'd for served By *h's* unseen;	"	264
his *h* fell from the harp,	"	301
the novice crying, with clasp'd *h's*,	"	309
spared to lift his *h* against the King	"	434
lay their *h's* in mine and swear	"	464
laid her *h's* about his feet,	"	524
I cannot take thy *h*;	"	549
waving of the *h's* that blest.	"	578
her *h* Grasp'd, made her vail her eyes:	"	654
Another *h* crept too across his trade	*En. Arden*	110
set his *h* To fit their little streetward	"	169
his careful *h*—The space was narrow	"	176
waved his *h*, and went his way.	"	237
eye was dim, *h* tremulous;	"	241

	POEM.	LINE.
fixt his heart he set his *h*	*En. Arden*	293
Caught at his *h*, and wrung it	"	325
her face had fall'n upon her *h's*;	"	388
door he paused and gave his *h*,	"	444
Shaking a little like a drunkard's *h*,	"	462
h dwelt lingeringly on the latch,	"	515
from her lifted *h* Dangled a length	"	730
to all things could he turn his *h*.	"	814
Her art, her *h*, her counsel	*Aylmer's F.*	151
Queenly responsive when the loyal *h*	"	169
and an open *h* of help,	"	174
with the blade he prick'd his *h*,	"	239
stood Storming with lifted *h's*,	"	332
whiter even than her pretty *h*:	"	363
and the *h's* of power Were bloodier	"	452
His face magnetic to the *h*	"	626
free of alms her *h*—The *h* that robed	"	697
Wifelike, her *h* in one of his,	"	808
bore along the nave Her pendent *h's*,	"	813
A pickaxe in her *h*:	*Sea Dreams*	151
last Gript my *h* hard,	"	156
loose one in the hard grip of his *h*,	"	159
Left him one *h*, and reaching thro'	"	275
Strong of his *h's*, and strong on his legs	*Grandmother*	13
sit with empty *h's* at home.	*Sailor Boy*	16
Brandishing in her *h* a dart	*Boädicea*	71
beat with rapid unanimous *h*,	"	79
now shake *h's* across the brink	'*My life is full*,' etc.	6
Shake *h's* once more: I cannot sink	"	8
Caress'd or chidden by the dainty *h*,	*Coquette*, i.	1
To Thor and Odin lifted a *h*.	*The Victim*	8
King bent low, with *h* on brow,	"	57
h's they mixt, and yell'd	*Lucretius*	56
vast and filthy *h's* upon my will,	"	217
Fine little *h's*, fine little feet,	*The Window*	88
Two little *h's* that meet,	"	134-7
And loving *h's* must part,—	"	139

hand (hand-writing.)

such a *h* as when a field of corn	*Princess*, i.	233
Last, Ida's answer, in a royal *h*,	" v.	361

hand (verb.)

Hebes are they to *h* ambrosia,	*Princess*, iii.	97

handful.

Two *h's* of white dust,	*Lotos-E's.*	113
And my heart is a *h* of dust,	*Maud*, II. v.	3

hand-hidden.

face *H-h*, as for utmost grief	*Vivien*	746

hand-in-hand.

in a circle *h-i-h* Sat silent,	*In Mem.* xxx.	11
A wreath of airy dancers *h-i-h*	*Guinevere*	259
Enoch and Annie, sitting *h-i-h*,	*En. Arden*	69

handle.

the sense that *h's* daily life—	*Walk. to the M.*	16
loved to *h* spiritual strife,	*In Mem.* lxxxiv.	54

handled.

Enoch took, and *h* all his limbs	*En. Arden*	153

handmaid.

a *h* on each side Bow'd toward her,	*Princess*, iv.	256

handmaid-work.

On Enid, at her lowly *h-w*,	*Enid*	400

hand-to-mouth.

Low miserable lives of *h-t-m*	*En. Arden*	116

hang.

h's the broad sunflower (rep.)	'*A spirit haunts*,' etc.	9
rainbow *h's* on the poising wave,	*Sea-Fairies*.	29
h's before her all the year,	*L. of Shalott*, ii.	11
midway down *H* rich in flowers,	*Œnone*	7
statue seem'd To *h* on tiptoe,	*Pal. of Art*.	38
the poppy *h's* in sleep.	*Lotos-E's.*	56
h's the heavy-fruited tree—	*Locksley H.*	163
the thunderbolt *H's* silent;	*Princess*, ii.	206
h's his portrait in my father's hall	"	221
is knowledge, and this matter *h's*:	" iii.	299
beard-blown goat *H* on the shaft,	" iv.	61
Can *h* no weight upon my heart	*In Mem.* lxii.	3
yon hard crescent, as she *h's*	" cvi.	10

	POEM.	LINE.
My anguish *h's* like shame.	*Maud,* II. iv.	74
starry Gemini *h* like glorious crowns	" III. vi.	7
'A craven: how he *h's* his head.'.	*Enid* .	976
As the wind-hover *h's* in balance,	*Aylmer's F.*	321
For it *h's* one moment later.	*Spiteful Let.*	16

hanging.

clotted into points and *h* loose,	*M. d'Arthur*	219
Was Monte Rosa, *h* there	*The Daisy* .	66
a laggard *h* down his head.	*Enid* .	909

Hanover.

whether he came in the *H* ship,	*Maud,* II. v.	59

happen.

Forget the dream that *h's* then,	*Two Voices* .	353
Whatever *h* to me!	*Maud,* II. ii.	79
whatsoever evil *h* to me,	*Enid* .	471
Whatever *h's*, not to speak to me,	" .	866

happier.

Make me a little *h*:	*Enid* .	1166
with something *h* than myself.	*En. Arden* .	422

happiness.

her due, Love, children, *h!*	*Princess,* iii.	229
all the warmth, the peace, the *h,*	*En. Arden* .	762
shatter all the *h* of the hearth.	" .	771

happy.

O *h* thou that liest low,	*Oriana* .	84
She wish'd me *h*, but she thought	*Miller's D.*	139
would make him *h* yet.	*May Queen,* iii.	46
but it lies Deep-meadow'd, *h*, fair.	*M. d'Arthur*	262
Made me most *h*, faltering	*Gardener's D.*	230
Might have been *h*; but what lot	*Walk. to the M.*	89
yourself alone Of all men *h*.	*Ed. Morris.*	78
Live *h*; tend thy flowers;	*Love and Duty*	84
h with the mission of the Cross;	*Golden Year*	43
Is it well to wish thee *h*?	*Locksley H.*	43
Overlive it—lower yet—be *h!*	"	97
H he With such a mother!	*Princess,* vii.	308
It seems that I am *h*,	*Maud,* I. xviii.	50
'Too *h*, fresh and fair, Too fresh	*The Brook* .	217
beholding her Tho' pale, yet *h*,	*Enid* .	1728
as it chanced they are *h*, being pure.'	*Vivien*	595
She was *h* enough, and shook it off,	*Elaine* .	780
So that would make you *h*:	"	955
h as when we dwelt among the woods,	"	1030
make me *h*, making them An armlet	"	1176
h, dead before thy shame?	*Guinevere* .	420
might be still as *h* as God grants	*En. Arden* .	413
'he is *h*, he is singing Hosanna	" .	498
face again And know that she is *h*.'	" .	720
you are *h*: let her parents be.'	*Aylmer's F.*	366
we two shall be *h* still.	*Grandmother*	52
And *h* has been my life;	"	98
sea-kings' daughter as *h* as fair,	*W. to Alexan.*	26
King is *h* In child and wife:	*The Victim*	25
Priest was *h*, His victim won.	"	65, 78

harangue.

Lady Psyche will *h* The fresh	*Princess,* ii.	81

harassed.

Vext with lawyers and *h* with debt:	*Maud,* I. xix.	22
the thought Haunted *h* him,	*En. Arden* .	721

harbour.

clambering on a mast In *h*,	*En. Arden* .	106
that *h* whence he sail'd before.	" .	667

harbourage.

get me *h* for the night?.	*Enid* .	281
If ! truth, good truth, I have not,	" .	290
I seek a *h* for the night.'	" .	299

harbour-bar.

Shot o'er the seething *h-b*	*Sailor Boy* .	2

harbour-buoy.

the *h-b* With one green sparkle	*Audley Ct.* .	85

harbour-mouth.

waft me from the *h-m*,	'You ask me why,' etc.	25
buoy That tosses at the *h-m*;	*The Voyage*	2
Many a *h-m*,	*The Captain*	22

hard.

	POEM.	LINE.
It seem'd so *h* at first, mother,	*May Queen,* iii.	9
now it seems as *h* to stay,	" .	10
The Gods are *h* to reconcile:	*Lotos-E's.* .	126
'Tis *h* to settle order once again.	" .	127
How *h* he breathes!	*D. of the O. Year*	37
saying, *h* to shape in act; '*Love thou thy land,*' etc.		49
vague in vapour, *h* to mark;	" .	62
The blast was *h* and harder.	*The Goose* .	50
you Will make him *h*,	*Dora* .	150
h it seem'd to me, When eyes,	*Love and Duty*	35
If the sense is *h* To alien ears,	" .	50
H is my doom and thine:	" .	53
'Your riddle is *h* to read.'	*Lady Clare*	76
O *h*, when love and duty clash!	*Princess,* ii.	273
rock so *h* but that a little wave	" iii.	138
will take her, they will make her *h*,	" v.	87
no tenderness—Too *h*, too cruel:.	" .	505
These men are *h* upon us	" vi.	181
woman is so *h* Upon the woman.	" .	205
And call her *h* and cold	" vii.	83
'It will be *h*' they say 'to find	*In Mem.* xx.	7
words were *h* to understand.	" lxvii.	20
"'Tis *h* for thee to fathom this	" lxxxiv.	90
h to frame In matter-moulded forms	" xciv.	45
I found, tho' crush'd to *h* and dry	*The Daisy* .	97
to give you warning, that seems *h*;	*Enid* .	1271
How *h* you look and how denyingly!	*Vivien* .	187
h and still as is the face that men.	*Elaine*	1244
h to take The helpless life	*En. Arden* .	557
'Too *h* to bear! why did they take	" .	782
Small were his gains, and *h* his work;	*Sea Dreams*	8
think I am *h* and cold;	*Grandmother*	17
be jealous and *h* and unkind.'	" .	54
H, *h*, *h* is it only not to tumble,	*Hendecasyllabics*	13
O foolish bard, is your lot so *h*,	*Spiteful Let.*	5

harden.

sandy footprint *h* into stone.'	*Princess,* iii.	254

harder.

The blast was hard and *h*.	*The Goose* .	50
Enid answer'd, *h* to be moved	*Enid* .	1542
then indeed *H* the times were,	*Aylmer's F.*	452
hearts of men Seem'd *h* too;	" .	454

hard-grained.

h-g Muses of the cube and square	*Princess, Pro.*	170

hardihood.

Sick for thy stubborn *h*,	*In Mem.* ii.	14

hard-mailed.

Laid the soft babe in his *h-m* hands,	*Princess,* vi.	191

hardness.

For he will teach him *h*,	*Dora* .	118

hard-ridden.

like a beast *h-r*, breathing hard.	*Aylmer's F.*	291

hard-set.

smile a *h-s* smile, like a stoic,	*Maud,* I. iv.	20

hard-won.

h-w and hardly won with bruise	*Elaine*	1159

hare.

nightly wirer of their innocent *h*	*Aylmer's F.*	490

harebell.

Like an Alpine *h* hung with tears	*Princess,* vii.	100

hark.

hating to *h* The humming	*To J. M. K.*	9
h the bell For dinner,	*Princess,* ii.	410
h the clock within, the silver knell	*Maud,* I. xviii.	64
'*H* the Phantom of the house	*Elaine*	1016

harken.

mother Ida, *h* ere I die.	*Œnone* 21, *et pass.*	
I shall *h* what you say,	*May Queen,* ii.	30
h what the inner spirit sings.	*Lotos-E's.* .	67

harlot.

h's paint their talk as well as face	*Vivien* .	670
in this Are *h's* like the crowd,	" .	680
hearing '*h*' mutter'd twice or thrice,	" .	692
the *h* leapt Adown the forest,	" .	821
Mammon made The *h* of the cities:	*Aylmer's F.*	375

harm (s.)

	POEM.	LINE.
What *h*, undone? deep *h* to disobey,	*M. d'Arthur*	93
bites it for true heart and not for *h*,	*Princess,Pro.*	172
shielded all her life from *h* .	*In Mem. Con.*	47
a *h* no preacher can heal ; .	*Maud*, I. iv.	22
dare obey him to his *h* ? .	*Enid* .	985
use it to the *h* of any one, .	*Vivien*	535

harm (verb.)

little thing may *h* a wounded man,	*M. d'Arthur*	42
well might *h* The woman's cause.	*Princess*, iii.	128
To *h* the thing that trusts him,	,, iv.	229
not *h*'s distinctive womanhood. .	,, vii.	258

harmed.

satire, kin to charity, That *h* not :	*Princess*, ii.	446
h where she would heal ; .	*Guinevere*	353
a hair of this low head be *h*.	,,	444

harmonizing.

A music *h* our wild cries, ,	*Sea Dreams*	247

harmony.

adore The full-flowing *h* .	*Eleänore*	46
mighty-mouthed inventor of *harmonies*, *Milton*		1

harness.

clash'd his *h* in the icy caves	*M. d'Arthur*	186
and the golden scale Of *h*, .	*Princess*, v.	40
liever had I gird his *h* on him,	*Enid* .	93

Haroun Alraschid.

Of good H A. . .	*Arabian N's.* 11, *et pass.*	

harp (s.)

bosoms prest To little *h*'s of gold ;	*Sea-Fairies*	4
with cymbals, and *h*'s of gold,	*Dying Swan*	32
Love took up the *h* of Life, .	*Locksley H.*	33
Like an Æolian *h* that wakes	*Two Voices*	436
smote her *h*, and sang. .	*Princess*, iv.	20
To one clear *h* in divers tones,	*In Mem.* i.	2
I—my *h* would prelude woe—	,, lxxxvii.	9
brought the *h* and flung A ballad	,, lxxxviii.	27
The hall with *h* and carol rang. .	,, cii.	9
Nor *h* be touch'd, nor flute be blown ;	,, civ.	22
bitter notes my *h* would give, .	,, cxxiv.	2
his hand fell from the *h*, .	*Guinevere* .	301

harp (verb.)

to *h* on such a moulder'd string? .	*Locksley H.*	147

harped.

equal to the man. They *h* on this ;	*Princess*, i.	131

harping.

Now *h* on the church-commissioners,	*The Epic*	15

harpy.

harpies miring every dish, .	*Lucretius* .	159

harry.

h me, pretty spy And traitress,'	*Guinevere* .	358

Harry.

Bluff H broke into the spence	*Talking O.*	47
While H is in the five-acre .	*Grandmother*	80
H and Charlie, I hear them too—	,,	81
For H went at sixty, . .	,,	86

harsh.

his ways were *h*; But Dora bore them	*Dora* .	33
like a butt, and *h* as crabs. .	*Walk. to the M.*	41
not Too *h* to your companion	*Princess*, iii.	183
Day by day more *h* and cruel	*The Captain*	13
To make a truth less *h*, .	*Lucretius* .	222

harshness.

My needful seeming *h*, pardon it.	*Princess*, ii.	289
parents' *h* and the hapless loves .	*Aylmer's F.*	616

hart.

a *h* Taller than all his fellows,	*Enid* .	149
heard The noble *h* at bay, .	,,	233
the *h* with golden horns. .	*Vivien* .	259

harvest.

reap the *h* with enduring toil,	*Lotos-E's.*	166
for these five years So full a *h*	*Dora* .	64
heart is glad Of the full *h*, .	,, .	67
God reaps a *h* in me (rep.) .	*St S. Stylites*	146

	POEM.	LINE.
rapt Upon the teeming *h*, .	*Golden Year*	70
reaps not *h* of his youthful joys,	*Locksley H.*	139
Dispensing *h*, sowing the To-be,	*Princess*, vii.	273
And watch her *h* ripen, .	*Maud*, III. vi.	25

harvest-field.

brother James is in the *h-f*: .	*The Brook* .	227

harvest time.

and in *h t* he died. .	*Dora* .	53

hasp.

were laid On the *h* of the window,	*Maud*, I. xiv.	19

haste (s.)

H, half-sister to Delay, '*Love thou thy land,' etc.*		96
all miscounted as malignant *h*, .	*Princess*, iv.	315
made false *h* to the grave— .	*Maud*, I. i.	58
not dead !' she answer'd in all *h*. .	*Enid* .	1391

haste (verb.)

oh, *h*, Visit my low desire ! .	*Ode to Mem.*	3
h away O'er ocean-mirrors .	*In Mem.* xii.	8

hat.

grew about, and tied it round his *h*	*Dora* .	81
slavish *h* from the villager's head?	*Maud*, I. x.	4
whether The habit, *h*, and feather,	,, xx.	18

hatch.

the nest,' she said, 'To *h* the cuckoo.	*Princess*, iv.	347

hatched.

fancies *h* In silken-folded idleness ;	*Princess*, iv.	48

hate (s.)

A *h* of gossip parlance, .	*Isabel* .	26
the *h* of *h*, the scorn of scorn, .	*The Poet*	2
hated him with the *h* of hell, .	*The Sisters*	22
mete the bounds of *h* and love— .	*Two Voices*	135
Frantic love and frantic *h*. .	*Vision of Sin*	150
common *h* with the revolving wheel	*Princess*, vi.	157
morbid *h* and horror have grown .	*Maud*, I. vi.	75
All this dead body of *h*, .	,, xix.	97
fires of Hell and of H; .	,, II. i.	10
in a wink the false love turns to *h*)	*Vivien* .	701
sharpen'd by strong *h* for Lancelot.	*Guinevere* .	21
'With what a *h* the people and the	,,	155
Hated him with a momentary *h*. .	*Aylmer's F.*	211
shriek of *h* would jar all the hymns	*Sea Dreams*	251
aloof From envy, *h*, and pity, .	*Lucretius* .	77
his hopes and *h*'s, his homes and .	,,	251

hate (verb.)

how much I *h* Her presence, .	*Œnone* .	225
my flesh, which I despise and *h*, .	*St S. Stylites*	57
men have done it ; how I *h* you all !	*Princess,Pro.*	130
(tho' you should *h* me for it) .	,, iv.	322
h to hear me like a wind .	,, v.	95
mars her plan, but then would *h*, .	,,	126
Discuss'd the books to love or *h*,	*InMem.*lxxxviii.	34
I *h* the dreadful hollow .	*Maud*, I. i.	1
Well, he may live to *h* me yet. .	,, xiii.	1
h that he should linger here ; .	*Enid* .	91
wheel and we neither love nor *h*. .	,,	349–58
h the sin that seem'd so like his own	,,	594
people and the King Must *h* me,' .	*Guinevere* .	156
Shriek out, 'I *h* you, Enoch,' .	*En. Arden.*	33
height That makes the lowest *h* it,	*Aylmer's F.*	173
because I love their child They *h* me :	,,	424
To *h* a little longer ! .	*Sea Dreams*	62
h me not, but abide your lot : .	*Spiteful Let.*	11
yellow leaf *h*'s the greener leaf .	,,	15
I *h* the spites and the follies. .	,,	24
I *h*, abhor, spit, sicken at him ; .	*Lucretius* .	196

hated.

presence, *h* both of Gods and men.	*Œnone* .	225
h him with the hate of hell, .	*The Sisters* .	22
death and sin she *h* equally, .	*Pal. of Art.*	265
madness, *h* by the wise, .	*Love and Duty*	7
this world's curse,—beloved but *h*	,,	47
Men *h* learned women : .	*Princess*, ii.	442
h banter, wish'd for something real,	,, Con.	18
h her, who took no thought of them,	*Enid*	1487
She *h* all the knights, .	*Vivien* .	7

	POEM.	LINE.
and she *h* all who pledged, .	Elaine	740
H him with a momentary hate, .	Aylmer's F.	211
But they *h* his oppression .	The Captain	9
they look'd at him they *h*, .	"	37

hateful.

H is the dark-blue sky, .	Lotos-E's. .	84
falsehood and yourself are *h* to us:	Princess, iv.	524
h, monstrous, not to be told ; .	Maud, III. vi.	41
this forgetfulness was *h* to her.	Enid .	55

hater.

| What room is here for a *h* ? . | Spiteful Let. | 14 |

hating.

| *h* to hark The humming . | To J. M. K. | 9 |

hatred.

| *h* of her weakness, blent with shame | Princess, vii. | 15 |

haunch.

| On his *h*'es rose the steed, . | Princess, v. | 482 |

haunt (s.)

A *h* of ancient Peace. . .	Pal. of Art.	88
The *h*'s of memory echo not. .	Two Voices.	369
In *h*'s of hungry sinners, .	Will Water.	222
flood the *h*'s of hern and crake : .	In Mem. c.	14
The feeble soul, a *h* of fears, .	" cix.	3
h's of horror and fear, . .	Maud, III. vi.	2
I come from *h*'s of coot and hern,.	The Brook .	23
A *h* of brawling seamen once, .	En. Arden .	698
A frequent *h* of Edith, . .	Aylmer's F.	148

haunt (verb.)

h's the year's last hours ' A spirit haunts,' etc. .		1
whatever Oread *h* The knolls of Ida, Œnone .		72
Whose odours *h* my dreams ; .	Sir Galahad	68
Will *h* the vacant cup : .	Will Water.	172
h About the moulder'd lodges .	Princess, iv.	44
They *h* the silence of the breast, .	In Mem. xciii.	9
the filmy shapes That *h* the dusk,	" xciv.	11
Evil *h*'s The birth, the bridal : .	" xcvii.	13
Like flies that *h* a wound, .	Aylmer's F.	571
Gods, who *h* The lucid interspace	Lucretius .	104

haunted.

It *h* me, the morning long, .	Miller's D..	69
Was *h* with a jolly ghost, .	Walk. to the M.	28
h by the wrangling daw ; .	In Mem. xcix.	12
h by the starry head . .	Maud, I. xviii.	22
By autumn nutters *h*, .	En. Arden .	8
the thought *H* and harass'd him, .	"	721

haunting (part.)

phantoms moved Before him *h* him, En. Arden .		604
he himself Moved *h* people, .	"	605
Christian hope *H* a holy text, .	Sea Dreams	42

haunting (s.)

| No ghostly *h*'s like his Highness. . | Princess, ii. | 389 |
| out of *h*'s of my spoken love, . | " vii. | 94 |

haven.

inland town and *h* large, .	Œnone .	115
To their *h* under the hill ; .	'Break, break,' etc.	10
Had built the King his *h*'s, .	Vivien	24
Open'd a larger *h* : . .	En. Arden .	103
Till silent in her oriental *h*. .	"	533
either *h* opened on the deeps, .	"	672
rush abroad all round the little *h*, .	"	868
all the houses in the *h* rang. .	"	910
h's hid in fairy bowers, .	The Voyage	54

havock.

| wrought Such waste and *h* . . | Aylmer's F. | 640 |
| Made *h* among those tender cells . | Lucretius . | 22 |

haw.

| hoary knoll of ash and *h* . | In Mem. xcix. | 9 |

hawk (s.)

wild *h* stood with the down .	Poet's Song.	11
pastime both of *H* and hound, .	Enid .	711
Lies the *h*'s cast, . .	Aylmer's F.	849

hawk (verb.)

| when a hawker *h*'s his wares, . | The Blackbird | 20 |

hawker,	POEM.	LINE.
when a *h* hawks his wares. .	The Blackbird	20
This broad-brimm'd *h* of holy things, Maud, I. x.		41

hawking.

| Now *h* at Geology and schism ; . | The Epic . | 16 |

hawk-mad.

| if you be not like the rest, *h-m*, . | Enid . | 280 |

hawthorn.

| Beneath the *h* on the green . | May Queen, ii. | 10 |
| just beneath the *h* shade . | " | 29 |

hay.

| rarely smells the new-mown *h*, . | The Owl, i. | 9 |
| Stuff his ribs with mouldy *h*. . | Vision of Sin | 66 |

haze.

light *h* along the river-shores, .	Gardener's D.	259
Purple gauzes, golden *h*'s, .	Vision of Sin	31
world was once a fluid *h* of light, .	Princess, ii.	101
is it that the *h* of grief . .	In Mem. xxiv.	9
silvery *h* of summer drawn ; .	" xciv.	4
thro' the dripping *h* The dead weight En. Arden.		678

hazel.

may-pole and in the *h* copse, .	May Queen, ii.	11
in the dark of *h* eyes— . .	Locksley H.	28
The thick-set *h* dies ; . .	Will Water.	232
In native *h*'s tassel-hung. .	In Mem. ci.	12
as lissome as a *h* wand ; .	The Brook .	70
I slide by *h* covers ; . .	"	171
Went nutting to the *h*'s. .	En. Arden .	64
Down thro' the whitening *h*'s .	"	376

hazel-tree.

| on the bridge beneath the *h-t* ? . | May Queen, i. | 14 |

hazelwood.

| a *h* By autumn nutters haunted, . | En. Arden . | 7 |

head.

Madonna-wise on either side her *h* ;	Isabel .	6
Revered Isabel, the crown and *h*, .	"	10
Thou wilt never raise thine *h* .	A Dirge .	19
Beat time to nothing in my *h*. .	Miller's D. .	67
Upon my lap he laid his *h* : .	The Sisters	17
curl'd and comb'd his comely *h*, .	"	31
The *h*'s and crowns of kings ; .	Pal. of Art	152
put strange memories in my *h*, .	L. C. V. de Vere	26
With your feet above my *h* .	May Queen, ii.	32
kindly heart and on his silver *h* ! .	" iii.	15
from a casement leans his *h*, .	D. of F. Wom.	246
Her murder'd father's *h*, .	"	267
full of rest from *h* to feet : .	To J. S.	75
faction seldom gathers *h*, 'You ask me why,' etc		13
heap their ashes on the *h* ; 'Love thou thy land,' etc.		70
h and heels upon the floor .	The Goose .	37
laid his *h* upon her lap, .	M. d'Arthur	208
May with me from *h* to heel. .	Gardener's D.	80
She bow'd down her *h*, . .	Dora .	103
turn the horses' *h*'s and home again.	Walk. to the M.	38
stiff spine can hold my weary *h*, .	St S. Stylites	42
She sank her *h* upon her arm .	Talking O.	207
From *h* to ancle fine. . .	"	224
Dropt dews upon her golden *h*, .	"	227
shook her *h*, And shower'd the .	Godiva .	46
wide-mouth'd *h*'s upon the spout .	"	56
shrivell'd into darkness in his *h*, .	"	70
from *h* to tail Came out clear .	Two Voices	11
Dominion in the *h* and breast.' .	"	21
simple senses crown'd his *h* ; .	Day-Dm.	277
proverb flashes thro' his *h*, .	"	115
You shake your *h*. A random string	"	213
All-graceful *h*, so richly curl'd, .	"	250
This wheel within my *h*, .	Will Water.	84
Live long, ere from thy topmost *h*	"	233
Live long, nor feel in *h* or chest .	"	237
lay your hand upon my *h*, .	Lady Clare	55
Dropt her *h* in the maiden's hand	"	63
I saw within my *h* A grey .	Vision of Sin	50
In her left a human *h*. .	"	138
Hollow hearts and empty *h*'s ! .	"	174
trample round my fallen *h*, 'Come not when,' etc.		3
one that arm'd Her own fair *h* .	Princess, Pro.	33

	POEM.	LINE.
the multitude, a thousand *h's*:	Princes, Pro.	57
above their *h's* I saw The feudal	″	118
Ask'd Walter, patting Lilia's *h*	″	125
o'er his *h* Uranian Venus hung,	″ i.	239
such eyes were in her *h*,	″ ii.	23
some said their *h's* were less:	″	131
'everywhere Two *h's* in council,	″	156
axelike edge unturnable, our *H*,	″	186
by the bright *h* of my little niece,	″	257
H of all the golden-shafted firm,	″	383
the Muses' *h's* were touch'd	″ iii.	5
Princess should have been the *H*,	″	18
h and heart of all our fair she-world,	″	147
came a message from the *H*.	″	152
Among her maidens, higher by the *h*,	″	163
turn'd her sumptuous *h* with eyes	″ iv.	134
'The *H*, the *H*, the Princess, O the *H*!'	″	158
underneath The *h* of Holofernes	″	208
partly that you were my civil *h*,	″	287
seal'd dispatches which the *H* Took	″	360
touch not a hair of his *h*:	″	388
after-beauty makes Such *h*	″	432
gemlike eyes, And gold and golden *h's*;	″	460
Not peace she look'd, the *H*:	″	469
fear ye brawlers? am not I your *H*?	″	477
one rag, disprinced from *h* to heel	″ v.	29
sweet sculpture draped from *h* to foot,	″	54
at her *h* a follower of the camp,	″	57
'Lift up your *h*, sweet sister:	″	61
in the furrow broke the ploughman's *h*,	″	212
each light air On our mail'd *h's*:	″	235
Man with the *h* and woman with the	″	439
sound and whole from *h* to foot	″ vi.	194
Her *h* a little bent;	″	252
Lifting his grim *h* from my wounds.	″	255
ask for him Of your great *h*—	″	294
o'er the statues leapt from *h* to *h*,	″	346
small bright *h*, A light of healing,	″ vii.	43
fear'd To incense the *H* once more;	″	62
gravest citizen seems to lose his *h*,	Con.	59
Among six boys, *h* under *h*,	″	83
fibres net the dreamless *h*,	In Mem. ii.	3
cave Thy sailor—while thy *h* is bow'd,	″ vi.	14
Come then, pure hands, and bear the *h*	xviii.	9
The Shadow cloak'd from *h* to foot,	″ xxiii.	4
God shut the doorways of his *h*.	″ xliii.	4
When in the down I sink my *h*,	″ lxvii.	1
h hath miss'd an earthly wreath:	″ lxxii.	6
pure at heart and sound in *h*,	″ xciii.	1
Their pensive tablets round her *h*,	Con.	51
catch at every mountain *h*,	″	114
flushes up in the ruffian's *h*,	Maud, I. i.	37
her father, the wrinkled *h* of the race?	″ iv.	13
h in a cloud of poisonous flies.	″	54
At the *h* of the village street	″ vi.	10
slavish hat from the villager's *h*?	″ x.	4
for a man with heart, *h*, hand,	″	60
Gorgonised me from *h* to foot	″ xiii.	21
sits on her shining *h*,	″ xvi.	17
haunted by the starry *h*	″ xviii.	22
Shaking her *h* at her son and sighing	″ xix.	24
Here at the *h* of a tinkling fall,	″ xxi.	6
little *h*, sunning over with curls	″ xxii.	57
My bird with the shining *h*,	″ II. iv.	45
the wheels go over my *h*,	″ v.	5
maggot born in an empty *h*,	″	38
she is standing here at my *h*;	″	65
cry to the steps above my *h*,	″	101
held their *h's* above the crowd	The Brook.	10
holds her *h* to other stars	″	195
A tonsured *h* in middle age forlorn,	″	200
raised her *h* with lips comprest,	The Letters	19
good gray *h* which all men knew,	Ode on Well.	35
ice, far up on a mountain *h*,	The Daisy.	36
the women who attired her *h*,	Enid.	62
sweet *h* upon her gentle breast;	″	527
fair *h* in the dim-yellow light,	″	600
Upon a *h* so dear in thunder,	″	862
laggard hanging down his *h*,	″	909
'A craven; how he hangs his *h*.'	″	976
h high, and thought himself a knight,	″	1091

	POEM.	LINE.
arms to guard his *h* and yours,	Enid.	1276
in the naked hall, propping his *h*,	″	1429-32
russet-bearded *h* roll'd on the floor.	″	1577
hung his *h*, and halted in reply,	″	1659
h's should moulder on the city gates.	Vivien.	444
godlike *h* crown'd with spiritual fire,	″	686
she turn'd away, she hung her *h*,	″	736
caught And set it on his *h*,	Elaine.	55
on his cuirass worn our Lady's *H*,	″	294
at the *h* of all his Table Round,	″	304
the *h* Pierced thro' his side,	″	488
'Nay, by mine *h*,' said he,	″	655
by mine *h* she knows his hiding-place.'	″	710
He raised his *h*, their eyes met	″	1303
mine, as *h* of all our Table Round,	″	1318
knights had laid her comely *h*	″	1327
passionately, Her *h* upon her hands,	Guinevere	179
Each with a beacon-star upon his *h*,	″	239
bow'd her *h* nor spake.	″	308
hair of this low *h* be harm'd.	″	444
realms together under me, their *H*,	″	459
laying there thy golden *h*,	″	531
in the darkness o'er her fallen *h*.	″	577
calling down a blessing on his *h*.	En. Arden.	324
over Enoch's early-silvering *h*	″	623
shaking his gray *h* pathetically	″	715
Held his *h* high, and cared for no man,	″	849
h is low, and no man cares for him	″	851
when she laid her *h* beside my own.	″	882
eyes from under a pyramidal *h*	Aylmer's F.	20
heart, I think, help'd *h*:	″	475
made Still paler the pale *h* of him,	″	623
near storm, and aiming at his *h*,	″	727
h's of chiefs and princes fall so fast,	″	763
his own *h* Began to droop, to fall;	″	834
not a word; she shook her *h*.	Sea Dreams	112
Like her, he shook his *h*.	″	144
Hadn't a *h* to manage,	Grandmother	6
singer shaking his curly *h*	The Islet	6
She clipt you from her *h*,	The Ringlet	33
hoary Roman *h* and shatter it	Boädicea.	65

Head (surname.)

Sir Edward *H's*; But he 's abroad: *Walk. to the M.* 10

head (verb.)

h's the count of crimes With that wild *D. of F. Wom.* 201

headed.

h And wing'd with flame, . The Poet . 11
In shining draperies, *h* like a star, Princess, ii. 54

headland.

saw them—*h* after *h* flame . Guinevere . 241
Flames, on the windy *h* flare! W. to Alexan. 16

headstone.

About the moss'd *h*: . . Claribel . 12

head-waiter.

O plump *h-w* at The Cock, . Will Water. 1
H-w, honour'd by the guest . ″ 73
And one became *h-w*. . . ″ 144
H-w of the chop-house here, . ″ 209

heal.

will *h* me of my grievous wound.'. *M. d'Arthur* 264
I can *h* him. Power goes forth . St S. Stylites 143
h me with your pardon ere you go.' Princess, iii. 49
a harm no preacher can *h*; . Maud, I. iv. 40
harm'd where she would *h*; . Guinevere . 353
loathsome hurts and *h* mine own; . ″ 678
To spill his blood and *h* the land: The Victim. 46

healed.

To touch my body and be *h*, . St S. Stylites 78
They say that they are *h*. . ″ 144

healing.

before we came, This craft of *h*. Princess, iii. 303
light of *h*, glanced about the couch ″ vii. 44
Geraint lay *h* of his hurt, . Enid . 1779

health.

In glowing *h* with boundless wealth *L. C. V. de Vere* 61
breathing *h* and peace upon her breast: *Audley Ct.* 67

	POEM.	LINE.
Huge women blowzed with *h*,	*Princess*, iv.	260
wasted here *h*, wealth, and time,	"	333
poor men wealth, Than sick men *h*—	"	440
drinking *h* to bride and groom	*In Mem. Con.*	83
the double *h*, 'The crowning cup,	"	103
happy years of *h* and competence.	*En. Arden.*	82
Now seaward-bound for *h*	*Sea Dreams*	16

healthy.
| So *h*, sound, and clear and whole, | *Miller's D.* | 15 |

heap (s.)
no more shall rest in mounded *h*'s,	*Golden Year*	32
h's of gourds, and skins of wine,	*Vision of Sin*	13
Each hurling down a *h* of things	*Enid.*	1442
stand High on a *h* of slain,	*Elaine*	307
h's of living gold that daily grow,	*Aylmer's F.*	655

heap (vb.)
| *h* their ashes on the head ; '*Love thou thy land,' etc.* | 70 |

heaped.
H over with a mound of grass,	*Lotos-E's.*	112
Pain *h* ten-hundred-fold to this,	*St S. Stylites*	23
h the whole inherited sin	*Maud*, I. xiii.	41
H on her terms of disgrace,	"	II, i. 14
h The pieces of his armour	*Enid*	1222
h Their firewood, and the winds	*Spec. of Iliad*	6

heaping.
| Still *h* on the fear of ill | *Two Voices* | 107 |

hear.
you may *h* him sob and sigh	'*A spirit haunts,' etc.*	5
cannot *h* From the groves within	*Poet's Mind*	19
never would *h* it : your ears are so	"	35
I cry aloud : none *h* my cries,	*Oriana*	73
I *h* the roaring of the sea,	"	98
H a song that echoes cheerly	*L. of Shalott*, i.	30
I *h* what I would *h* from thee	*Eleánore*	141
from the bridge I lean'd to *h*	*Miller's D.*	49
H me O Earth, *H* me O Hills,	*Œnone*	35
H me, for I will speak,	"	38
unheard *H* all, and see thy Paris.	"	88
heard me not, Or hearing would not *h*	"	167
h me yet before I die	"	203
as I *h* Dead sounds at night.	"	244
H me, O Earth. I will not die	"	253
seem'd to *h* them climb and fall	*Pal. of Art*	70
to *h* Of wisdom and of law.	"	111
my soul to *h* her echo'd song	"	175
h's all night The plunging seas	"	250
h the dully sound Of human footsteps	"	275
h's the low Moan of an unknown sea ;	"	279
I shall *h* you when you pass,	*MayQueen*, ii.	31
I *h* the bleating of the lamb.	" iii.	2
I did not *h* the dog howl,	"	21
To *h* each other's whisper'd speech ;	*Lotos-E's.*	104
To *h* the dewy echoes calling	"	139
h and see the far-off sparkling brine,	"	143
To *h* the murmur of the strife,	*Margaret*	23
come down, and *h* me speak :	"	56
I *h* thee not at all, or hoarse	*The Blackbird*	19
we *h* with inward strife	'*Love thou thy land,' etc.*	53
horse That *h*'s the corn-bin open,	*The Epic*	45
h The windy clanging of the minster	*Gardener's D.*	37
'*H* how the bushes echo!'	"	97
for the pleasure that I took to *h*	"	223
on the pippin hung To *h* him,	*Audley Ct.*	38
do not *h* the bells upon my cap,	*Ed. Morris.*	44
I scarce *h* other music	"	57
my ears could *h* Her lightest breaths :	"	64
About the windings of the marge to *h*	"	94
nor heard of her, nor cared to *h* (rep.)	"	138
scarce can *h* the people hum	*St S. Stylites*	37
(And *h* me with thine ears,)	*Talking O.*	82
h me swear a solemn oath,	"	281
paused Among her stars to *h* us ;	*Love and Duty*	72
h These measured words, my work	*Golden Year*	20
did we *h* the copses ring,	*Locksley H.*	35
Thou shalt *h* the 'Never, never,'	"	—
H's little of the false or just.'	*Two Voices*	117
h's His country's war-song thrill	"	152
will not *h* the north-wind rave,	*Two Voices*	257
seems to *h* a Heavenly Friend,	"	295
'O wake for ever, love,' she *h*'s,	*Day-Dm.*	175
lets thee neither *h* nor see :	"	264
what is that I *h*? a sound	*Amphion*	73
I *h* a noise of hymns :	*Sir Galahad*	28
I *h* a voice, but none are there ;	"	30
H's him lovingly converse,	*L. of Burleigh*	26
He, dying lately, left her, as I *h*,	*Princess*, i.	77
h my father's clamour at our backs	"	104
very ears were hot To *h* them :	"	134
h each other speak for noise Of clocks	"	212
thought in our own hall to *h*	" ii.	39
there was one to *h* And help them :	"	248
H my conditions : promise	"	275
the Doctors! O to *h* the Doctors!	"	399
mine in part. O *h* me, pardon me	" iii.	15
O hark, O *h* ! how thin and clear,	"	354
let us *h* the purple glens replying	"	358
h A trumpet in the distance	" iv.	62
what they were, and she to *h* ;	"	304
h of it From Lady Psyche :'	"	309
For thus I *h* ; and known at last	"	328
h You hold the woman is the better	"	390
h me, for I bear, Tho' man, yet human	"	404
seem'd to *h* As in a poplar grove	" v.	11
hate to *h* me like a wind	"	95
when I *h* you prate I almost think	"	145
'Amazed am I to *h* Your Highness ;	" vi.	304
h's his burial talk'd of by his friends,	" vii.	137
I *h* the noise about thy keel ;	*In Mem.* x.	1
I *h* the bell struck in the night ;	"	2
h the ritual of the dead.	" xviii.	12
traveller *h*'s me now and then,	" xxi.	5
h her weeping by his grave ?	" xxxi.	4
h The moanings of the homeless sea,	" xxxv.	8
h thy laurel whisper sweet	" xxxvii.	7
I *h* it now, and o'er and o'er,	" lvi.	13
I *h* a wizard music roll,	" lxix.	14
I *h* the sentence that he speaks ;	" lxxix.	10
We cannot *h* each other speak.	" lxxxi.	16
hung to *h* The rapt oration	" lxxxvi.	31
heart and ear were fed To *h* him,	" lxxxviii.	23
h a wind Of memory murmuring	" xci.	7
h The wish too strong for words	" xcii.	13
h the household jar within.	" xciii.	16
h's the latest linnet trill,	" xcix.	10
sing the songs he loved to *h*.	" cvi.	24
I *h* a chirp of birds ;	" cxviii.	5
h the tidings of my friend,	" cxxv.	3
h at times a sentinel	"	9
h A deeper voice across the storm,	" cxxvi.	3
I *h* thee where the waters run ;	" cxxix.	2
A voice as unto them that *h*'s,	" cxxx.	6
Still! I will *h* you no more,	*Maud*, I. v.	23
h the dead at midday moan,	" vi.	70
Did I *h* it half in a doze	" vii.	1
Strange, that *h* a two men,	"	13
h again The chivalrous battle-song	" x.	53
The larkspur listens, 'I *h*, I *h*;'	" xxii.	65
My heart would *h* her and beat,	"	69-71
Do I *h* her sing as of old,	" II. iv.	44
then to *h* a dead man chatter	" v.	10
Before you *h* my marriage vow.'	*The Letters*	8
h The tides of Music's golden sea.	*Ode on W'ell.*	251
only *h* the magpie gossip	*To F. D. Maurice*	19
stay'd Waiting to *h* the hounds ;	*Enid.*	163
chance that we shall *h* the hounds	"	182
They would not *h* me speak :	"	421
ask'd again, and ever loved to *h* ;	"	436
thro' the crash of the near cataract *h*'s	"	1021
soldiers wont to *h* His voice in battle	"	1023
h him breathing low and equally.	"	1221
What thing sneyer you may *h*,	"	1264
h the violent threats you do not *h*,	"	1269
ears to *h* you even in his dreams.'	"	1278
horses when you *h* them feed :	"	1454
h's the judgment of the King of Kings.',	"	1648
By Heaven that *h*'s I tell you	*Vivien*	193
will you *h* The legend as in guerdon	"	403
h my words : go to the jousts ;	*Elaine*	137

	POEM.	LINE.
h it said That men go down before	*Elaine*	148
as I *h* It is a fair large diamond—.	"	227
'*h*. but hold my name Hidden,	"	415
we shall *h* anon, Needs must we *h*.'	"	633, 752
till the ear Wearies to *h* it,	"	894
that I live to *h*,' he said, 'is yours.'	"	924
h of rumours flying thro' your court.	"	1184
liege Arthur, and all ye that *h*,	"	1282
h high talk of noble deeds.	*Guinevere*	495
Thro' the thick night I *h* the trumpet	"	565
seem'd to *h* Her own death-scaffold	*En. Arden*.	174
H's and not *h*'s, and lets it overflow.	"	209
Nor ever *h* a kindly voice,	"	583
clamour'd the good woman, '*h* him	"	841
plain-faced tabernacle To *h* him;	*Aylmer's F.*	619
you do but *h* the tide.	*Sea Dreams*	83
But will you *h* my dream,	"	198
Eh!—but he wouldn't *h* me—	*Grandmother*	8
eyes that fill with tears To *h* me?.	*Tithonus*	27
and could *h* the lips that kiss'd	"	60
That it makes one weary to *h*.'	*The Islet*	29
Did they *h* me, would they listen,	*Boddicea*	8
H Iceniau, Catieuchlanian,	"	10, 34, 47
h it, Spirit of Cassivelaun!	"	20
H it, Gods! the Gods have heard it,	"	21
Till the victim *h* within and yearn	"	58
Let him *h* my song.	*The Captain*	4
h's Echoes in his empty '*Home they brought him,*' etc.		3
I *h* the roll of the ages.	*Spiteful Let.*	8

heard.

	POEM.	LINE.
she *h* the night-fowl crow;	*Mariana*	26
Hast thou *h* the butterflies	*Adeline*	28
We *h* the steeds to battle going,	*Oriana*	15
She saw me fight, she *h* me call,	"	32
She has *h* a whisper say,	*L. of Shalott*, ii.	3
h her singing her last song,	" iv.	26
H a carol, mournful, holy,	"	28
h her native breezes pass,	*Mariana in the S.*	43
oft I *h* the tender dove	*Miller's D.*	41
Sometimes I *h* you sing within;	"	123
Then first I *h* the voice of her,	*Œnone*	105
Give it to Pallas!' but he *h* me not,	"	166
Indeed I *h* one bitter word	*L. C. V. de Vere*	37
I *h* the angels call;	*May Queen*, iii.	25
I *h* them call my soul.	"	28
made His music *h* below;	*D. of F. Wom.*	4
h sounds of insult, shame, and wrong,	"	19
Sudden I *h* a voice that cried,	"	123
h my name Sigh'd forth with life	"	153
A noise of some one coming	"	177
h the lion roaring from his den;	"	222
I *h* Him, for He spake,	"	227
h just now the crowing cock.	*D. of the O. Year*	38
She *h* the torrents meet.	'*Of old sat Freedom,*' etc.	4
half-awake I *h* The parson	*The Epic*	13
hast seen? or what hast *h*?	*M. d'Arthur* 68,	114
h the ripple washing in the reeds,	"	70
h the water lapping on the crag,	"	116
what is it thou hast *h*, or seen?	"	150
He *h* the deep behind him,	"	184
h indeed The clear church-bells	*Ep.*	20
h Of Rose, the Gardener's daughter?	*Gardener's D.*	30
when I *h* her name My heart was	"	61
out of everything I *h* and saw,	"	65
Nor *h* us come, nor from her tendance	"	143
h the watchman peal The sliding season;	"	178
h The heavy clocks knolling	"	179
when I *h* his deep 'I will,'	"	203
h it was this bill that past,	*Walk. to the M.*	59
h with beating heart The Sweet-Gale	*Ed. Morris*	109
nor *h* of her, nor cared to hear.	"	138
since I *h* him make reply	*Talking O.*	25
That oft hast *h* my vows,	"	65
When I *h* my days before me,	*Locksley H.*	110
H the heavens fill with shouting,	"	129
h, by secret transport led,	*Two Voices*	214
her breathings are not *h*	*Day-Dm.*	93
methought I *h* a mellow sound,	*Vision of Sin*	14
they that *h* it sigh'd,	"	18
I *h* a voice upon the slope	"	219

	POEM.	LINE.
he *h* her speak; She scared him;	*Princess*, i.	183
seen And *h* the Lady Psyche.'	" ii.	194
'Ah—Melissa—you! You *h* us?'	"	310
I *h*, I could not help it,	"	311
we *h* The grave Professor.	"	348
like parting hopes I *h* them passing	" iv.	155
behind I *h* the puff'd pursuer	"	246
we *h* In the dead hush the papers	"	370
h of, after seen The dwarfs of presage:	"	426
h The voices murmuring.	"	536
voice is *h* thro' rolling drums,	"	554
h The drowsy folds of our great ensign	" v.	7
She *h*, she moved, She moan'd,	"	68
when first I *h* War-music,	"	255
h Of those that iron-cramp'd	"	365
Seeing I saw not, hearing not I *h*:	" vi.	3
My father *h* and ran In on the lists	"	10
A noise of songs they would not	"	23
clamouring on, till Ida *h*,	"	134
h that there is iron in the blood,	"	213
had a heart—I *h* her say it—	"	217
hung A moment, and she *h*,	" vii.	65
I *h* her turn the page;	"	175
I have *h* Of your strange doubts:	"	315
words that are not *h* again.	*In Mem.* xviii.	20
Before I *h* those bells again?	" xxviii.	16
h them sweep the winter land;	" xxx.	10
h once more in college fanes.	" lxxxvi.	5
h behind the woodbine veil	" lxxxviii.	50
brook alone far-off was *h*,	" xciv.	7
yet myself have *h* him say,	" xcvii.	20
roofs, that *h* our earliest cry,	" ci.	3
h The low love-language of the bird	"	10
put himself to school And *h* thee,	" cix.	11
great world's work is *h* Beginning,	" cxx.	10
I *h* a voice 'believe no more'	" cxxiii.	10
h an ever-breaking shore	"	11
h The shrill-edged shriek of a mother	*Maud*, I. i.	15
I have *h*, I know not whence,	"	67
h no longer The snowy-banded,	" viii.	9
I *h* no sound where I stood	" xiv.	28
even then I *h* her close the door,	" xviii.	11
All night have the roses *h*.	" xxii.	13
I *h* your rivulet fall	"	36
That *h* me softly call,	" II. iv.	76
h it shouted at once from the top	" v.	50
'Have you not *h*?' said Katie,	*The Brook*	221
His captain's-ear has *h* them boom	*Ode on Well.*	65
was *h* The world's loud whisper.	*Enid*	26
h but fragments of her later words,	"	113
h instead A sudden sound of hoofs,	"	163
thinking that he *h* The noble hart	"	232
H by the lander in a lonely isle,	"	330
dear child hath often *h* me praise.	"	434
tho' I *h* him call you fairest fair	"	720
h one crying to his fellow,	"	908
h them boast That they would slay	"	922
own ear had *h* Call herself false;	"	962
h the wild Earl at the door,	"	1230
for he rode As if he *h* not,	"	1301
Enid *h* the clashing of his fall,	"	1358
so low he hardly *h* her speak,	"	1491
This *h* Geraint, and grasping	"	1573
Not, tho' mine own ears *h* you	"	1588
h you say, that you were no true wife:	"	1590
h in thought Their lavish comment	*Vivien*	7
h the great Sir Lancelot sing it	"	235
was the song that once I *h*.	"	255
h their voices talk behind the wall,	"	481
in words part *h*, in whispers part,	"	688
fearing heaven had *h* her oath,	"	789
in his heart *H* murmurs 'lo, thou	*Elaine*	56
h her name So tost about,	"	233
H from the Baron that, ten years.	"	272
h Sir Lancelot cry in the court	"	343
h mass, broke fast, and rode away:	"	414
that had *h* the noise of it before,	"	727
when she *h* his horse upon the stones,	"	974
still he *h* him, still his picture form'd	"	986
brothers *h*, and thought With	"	1015
song *H* on the winding waters	"	1398

	POEM.	LINE.
h by the watcher in a haunted	Guinevere	73
h the Spirits of the waste and weald	"	128
or thought she *h* them moan :	"	129
when she *h*, the Queen look'd up,	"	162
h the bridegroom is so sweet?	"	175
down the coast, he *h* Strange music,	"	236
in the darkness *h* his armed feet .	"	415
running on thus hopefully she *h*,	En. Arden	201
she *h*, *h* and not *h* him	"	205
h The myriad shriek of wheeling	"	583
h the pealing of his parish bells :	"	616
h them talking, his long-bounden	"	645
things seen are mightier than things *h*,	"	767
As the woman *h*, Fast flow'd	"	865
worse than had he *h* his priest	Aylmer's F.	43
h the good mother softly whisper	"	187
loved nor liked the thing he *h*.	"	250
had Sir Aylmer *h*—Nay, but he must—	"	261
h the ponderous door Close,	"	337
h thro' the living roar.	Sea Dreams	56
I *h* the clash so clearly	"	132
strange song I *h* Apollo sing,	Tithonus	62
He *h* a fierce mermaiden cry,	Sailor Boy	6
Mad and maddening all that *h* her	Boädicea	4
Hear it, Gods I the Gods have *h* it,	"	21
a murmur *h* aërially,	"	24
There I *h* them in the darkness,	"	36
they *h* the foeman's thunder	The Captain	41
often when the woman *h* his foot .	Lucretius	5
thrice I *h* the rain Rushing	"	26
She *h* him raging, *h* him fall :	"	272
I have *h* of thorns and briers.	The Window	197

hearer.

	POEM.	LINE.
outran The *h* in its fiery course :	In Mem. cviii.	8
While thus he spoke, his *h*'s wept ;	Aylmer's F.	722

hear'st.

	POEM.	LINE.
h the village hammer clink,	In Mem. cxx.	15

hearing (part.)

	POEM.	LINE.
Or *h* would not hear me,	Œnone	167
h the downward stream,	Lotos-E's.	99
h the holy organ rolling waves	D. of F. Wom.	191
Seeing I saw not, *h* not I heard :	Princess, vi.	3
h any more his noble voice,	Enid	98
h her own name had slipt away)	"	507
Across the face of Enid, *h* her ;	"	524
h 'harlot' mutter'd twice or thrice,	Vivien	692
h his mischance, Came,	En. Arden	120
shook the heart of Edith *h* him.	Aylmer's F.	63
h her tumultuous adversaries	Boädicea	78

hearing (s.)

	POEM.	LINE.
And in the *h* of the wave.	In Mem. xix.	4
in these ears, till *h* dies,	" lvi.	9
Within the *h* of cat or mouse,	Maud, II. v.	48

hearsay.

	POEM.	LINE.
blamed herself for telling *h* tales :	Vivien	800

heart.

	POEM.	LINE.
Thro' my very *h* it thrilleth	Lilian	22
the blanched tablets of her *h* ;	Isabel	17
Right to the *h* and brain,	"	22
strain the *h* until it bleeds. 'Clear-headed friend,' etc.		5
All my bounding *h* entanglest	Madeline	40
h faints and my whole soul 'A spirit haunts,' etc.		
Take the *h* from out my breast.	Adeline	8
beating *h*'s of salient springs	"	26
woos to his *h* the silver dews?	"	32
In the *h* of the garden the merry bird	Poet's Mind	22
Out of the live-green *h* of the dells	Sea-Fairies	12
My *h* is wasted with my woe,	Oriana	1
pierced thy *h*, my love, my bride (rep.)	"	42
breaking *h* that will not break,	"	64
Up from my *h* unto my eyes,	"	78
Within thy *h* my arrow lies,	"	80
Die in their *h*'s for the love of me.	The Mermaid	30
My hope and *h* is with thee—	To J. M. K.	1
spurr'd at *h* with fieriest energy	"	7
'O cruel *h*,' she changed her tone,	Mariana in the S.	69
And the *h*'s of purple hills	Eléanore	17
My *h* a charmed slumber keeps,	"	128

	POEM.	LINE.
full at *h* of trembling hope	Miller's D.	110
Approaching, press'd you *h* to *h*	"	160
her *h* would beat against me,	"	177
Do make a garland for the *h* :	"	198
Round my true *h* thine arms entwine ;	"	216
The still affection of the *h*	"	225
My *h*, pierced thro' with fierce delight,	Fatima	34
eyes are full of tears, my *h* of love,	Œnone	30
h is breaking, and my eyes are dim,	"	31
h may wander from its deeper woe.	"	43
all my *h* Went forth to embrace him	"	61
river of speech Came down upon my *h*.	"	68
weighest heavy on the *h* within,	"	239
Devil, large in *h* and brain, To——.	With Pal. of Art	5
hollow shades enclosing *h*'s of flame,	Pal. of Art	241
thought to break a country *h*	L. C. V. de Vere	3
h that doats on truer charms.	"	14
changed a wholesome *h* to gall.	"	44
Kind *h*'s are more than coronets,	"	55
Pray Heaven for a human *h*,	"	71
They say his *h* is breaking, mother,	May Queen, i.	22
O blessings on his kindly *h*	" iii.	15
in his ears his beating *h* did make.	Lotos-E's.	36
To lend our *h*'s and spirits wholly.	"	108
h's worn out by many wars .	"	131
h Brimful of those wild tales,	D. of F. Wom.	1
mighty *h*'s Of captains and of kings.	"	175
h Faints, faded by its heat.	"	287
Encircles all the *h*, and feedeth	Margaret	16
burning brain from the true *h*,	"	39
live alone In all our *h*'s,	To J. S.	50
Sleep sweetly, tender *h*, in peace :	"	69
wild *h*'s and feeble wings, 'Love thou thy land,' etc.		11
Not yet the wise of *h* would cease	"	81
She felt her *h* grow prouder :	The Goose	22
Summer pilot of an empty *h*	Gardener's D.	16
So blunt in memory, so old at *h*,	"	52
h was like a prophet to my *h*,	"	62
coursed about The subject most at *h*,	"	218
A woman's *h*, the *h* of her I loved ;	"	225
secret bridal chambers of the *h*,	"	244
h on one wild leap Hung tranced .	"	254
Make thine *h* ready with thine eyes :	"	268
beheld her ere she knew my *h*,	"	270
have set my *h* upon a match.	Dora	12
h is glad Of the full harvest,	"	66
gone to him, But her *h* failed her ;	"	76
'With all my *h*,' said Francis.	Audley Ct.	7
all my *h* turn'd from her,	"	53
Dipt by itself, and we were glad at *h*.	"	87
hid her needle in my *h*,	Ed. Morris	62
heard with beating *h* The Sweet-Gale	"	109
Until he plagiarised a *h*,	Talking O.	19
girl, for whom your *h* is sick,	"	71
When last with throbbing *h* I came	"	155
Streaming eyes and breaking *h*'s ?	Love and Duty	2
the narrow brain, the stony *h*,	"	15
peace, my *h* so slow To feel it I	"	34
the want, that hollow'd all the *h*,	"	60
to lift a burthen from thy *h*	"	93
always roaming with a hungry *h*.	Ulysses	12
and opposed Free *h*'s, free foreheads—	"	49
One equal temper of heroic *h*'s	"	68
and a narrower *h* than mine !	Locksley H.	44
hidden from the *h*'s disgrace,	"	57
tho' my *h* be at the root.	"	66
lest thy *h* be put to proof,	"	77
preaching down a daughter's *h*.	"	94
Left me with the palsied *h*,	"	132
deep *h* of existence beat for ever .	"	140
h as rough as Esau's hand .	Godiva	28
my full *h*, that work'd below,	Two Voices	44
Nor sold his *h* to idle moans,	"	221
A deeper tale my *h* divines.	"	269
His *h* forbodes a mystery :	"	290
My frozen *h* began to beat,	"	422
From out my sullen *h* a power	"	443
lie upon her charmed *h*.	Day-Dm.	96
The Magic Music in his *h*	"	126
Because my *h* is pure.	Sir Galahad	4
all my *h* is drawn above	"	17

CONCORDANCE TO

	POEM.	LINE.
A virgin h in work and will. .	Sir Galahad	24
This weight and size, this h and eyes.	"	71
'And have you lost your h?'	Ed. Gray	3
the h of Edward Gray. . .	"	8, et pass.
that child's h within the man's	Will Water.	31
I will not cramp my h, . .	"	51
all his vast h sherris-warm'd .	"	197
tear his h before the crowd ' You might have won.'		36
her h within her did not fail ;	Lady Clare	78
' If my h by signs can tell,	L. of Burleigh	2
Thus her h rejoices greatly, .	"	41
Shaped her h with woman's meekness	"	71
did win my h from me !'	"	84
waste his whole h in one kiss	Sir L. and O. G.	44
Every h, when sifted well,	Vision of Sin	112
Hollow h's and empty heads !	"	174
Pass on, weak h, and leave 'Come not, when,' etc.		11
'O noble h who, being strait-besieged	Princess, Pro.	36
bites it for true h and not for harm	"	172
still I wore her picture by my h, .	" i.	37
my other h, And almost my half-self.	"	54
with all my h, With my full h : .	"	125
think I bear that h within my breast,	" ii.	313
h's lie fallow in these halls, .	"	378
twanging headless arrows at the h's,	"	380
dear is sister Psyche to my h, .	"	396
sister came she won the h Of Ida ;	" iii.	71
I tried the mother's h. . .	"	131
h of all our fair she-world, .	"	147
My h beat thick with passion	"	174
men may pluck them from our h's.	"	240
in the dark dissolving human h, .	"	295
Rise in the h, and gather to the eyes,	" iv.	23
her h Would rock the snowy cradle	"	85
cursing Cyril, vext at h, .	"	153
half-sick at h, return'd. .	"	204
Beaten with some great passion at her h,	"	369
block and bar Your h with system	"	443
Bursts of great h and slips .	" v.	191
woman's garment hid the woman's h.'	"	295
from the dark h of the long hills .	"	339
living h's that crack within the fire	"	369
h Made for all noble motion : .	"	373
tender orphan hands Felt at my h,	"	426
Man with the head and woman with the h:	"	439
noble h was molten in her breast ;	" vi.	103
Win you the h's of women ; .	"	155
She said You had a h— .	"	217
'Our Ida has a h— . .	"	218
will not ? well—no h have you,	"	245
to the hollow h they slander so ! .	"	270
I cannot keep My h an eddy	"	302
stranger seem'd that h's So gentle,	" vii.	51
at the happy lovers h in h—	"	93
all thy h lies open unto me. .	"	168
misled the girl To vex true h's	"	227
great h thro' all the faultful Past	"	232
The two-cell'd h beating, .	"	289
I waste my h in signs ; let be. .	"	338
with my h I muse and say : .	In Mem. iv.	4
O h, how fares it with thee .	" v.	5
for the unquiet h and brain, .	"	5
but some h did break. . .	" vi.	8
my h was used to beat (rep. cxviii. 1)	" vii.	3
O my forsaken h, with thee .	" viii.	18
in my h, if calm at all . .	" xi.	15
void where h on h reposed ; .	" xiii.	6
I, falling on his faithful h, .	" xviii.	14
darken'd h that beat no more ; .	" xix.	2
melt the waxen h's of men.' .	" xxi.	8
glad at h from May to May : .	" xxii.	8
Nor could I weary, h or limb, .	" xxv.	9
The h that never plighted troth .	" xxvii.	8
lull with song an aching h, .	" xxxvii.	15
vex my h with fancies dim ; .	" xli.	1
the h is sick, And all the wheels .	" xlix.	3
h's that beat from day to day, .	" lvii.	6
Like some poor girl whose h is set	" lix.	3
On some unworthy h with joy, .	" lxi.	7
hang no weight upon my h .	" lxii.	3
thought my h too far diseased: .	" lxv.	1

	POEM.	LINE.
Let not this vex thee, noble h!	In Mem. lxxviii.	2
wrath that garners in my h ; .	" lxxxi.	14
O h, with kindliest motion warm,	" lxxxiv.	34
marry with the virgin h. . .	"	108
My h, tho' widow'd, may not rest	"	113
in the midmost h of grief .	" lxxxvii.	7
h and ear were fed To hear him, .	" lxxxviii.	22
pure at h and sound in head .	" xciii.	1
when the h is full of din, .	"	13
A hunger seized my h ; . .	" xciv.	21
h's of old have beat in tune, .	" xcvi.	10
seems to slight her simple h. .	"	20
The pulses of a Titan's h ; .	" cii.	32
The larger h, the kindlier hand ; .	" cv.	30
I will not eat my h alone, .	" cvii.	3
By blood a king, at h a clown .	" cx.	4
the h Stood up and answer'd .	" cxxii.	15
h's are warm'd and faces bloom, .	" Con.	82
closed their gates with a shock on my h Maud, I.i.		15
h of the citizen hissing in war .	"	24
May make my h as a millstone, .	"	31
passionate h of the poet is whirl'd	" iv.	39
Ready in h and ready in hand, .	" v.	9
warm in the h of my dreams, .	" vi.	18
On a h half-turn'd to stone. .	"	78
O h of stone, are you flesh, .	"	79
suddenly, sweetly, my h beat stronger	" viii.	8
Sick, sick to the h of life, am I. .	" x.	36
Ah God, for a man with h, head, .	"	60
Set in the h of the carven gloom, .	" xiv.	11
drown His h in the gross mud-honey	" xvi.	5
Catch not my breath, O clamorous h,	"	31
shook my h to think she comes .	" xviii.	10
Dear h, I feel with thee the drowsy	"	70
My own h's h and ownest own farewell ;	"	74
my h more blest than h can tell, .	"	82
that dead man at her h and mine :	" xix.	9
who had ceased to share her h, .	"	30
awoke in the h of the child, .	"	48
faults of his h and mind, .	"	68
one With whom she has h to be gay.	" xxii.	20
My h would hear her and beat, .	"	63
It will ring in my h and my ears, .	" II. i.	35
h's that know not how to forgive ;	"	44
Shall I nurse in my dark h, .	" ii.	55
Courage, poor h of stone ! .	" iii.	1, 5
H's with no love for me ; .	" iv.	94
my h is a handful of dust, .	" v.	3
surely, some kind h will come .	"	10
it is time, O passionate h,' said I .	" III.vi.	30
h of a people beat with one desire :	"	49
blossom of war with a h of fire .	"	53
proved we have h's in a cause, .	"	55
of one name and h with her. .	The Brook	76
mellow'd all his h with ale, .	"	155
mock'd the wholesome human h, .	The Letters	10
spoke with h, and heat and force, .	"	37
deeper knell in the h be knoll'd .	Ode on Well.	59
What long-enduring h's could do .	"	132
toil of h and knees and hands, .	"	212
upon whose hand and h and brain .	"	239
Uplifted high in h and hope are we,	"	254
inheritance Of such a life, a h, .	Ded. of Idylls	32
with true h Adored her, as the stateliest Enid		19
to her own h piteously she said : .	"	85
hoard is little, but our h's are great.	"	352-74
noise of noble deeds To noble h's .	"	438
seem to suffer nothing h or limb, .	"	472
' Well said, true h,' replied Geraint,	"	474
Yniol's h Danced in his bosom .	"	505
prove her h toward the Prince.' .	"	513
converse in the hall, Proving her h :	"	521
like the h of a great fire at Yule, .	"	559
softly to her own sweet h .	"	618
h All overshadow'd by the foolish .	"	674
tempest brooding round his h, .	"	860
broke the sentence in his h .	"	890
plover's human whistle amazed Her h,	"	899
Enid ponder'd in her h, .	"	913-79
sharpness of that pain about her h :	"	1039
in the h of waste and wilderness. .	"	1102

	POEM.	LINE.		POEM.	LINE.
Enid had no *h* To wake him,	*Enid*	1218	*h*, I think, help'd head :	*Aylmer's F.*	475
sadden'd all her *h* again.	"	1294	Hating his own lean *h*	"	525
h enough To bear his armour?	"	1338	bad him with good *h* sustain himself—	"	544
to his own *h*, 'she weeps for me:'	"	1435-9	in flood, and dash'd his angry *h* ;	"	633
all but empty *h* and weariness	"	1500	To greet her, wasting his forgotten *h*,	"	649
blunt and stupid at the *h*	"	1595	her *h* had beat remorselessly,	"	792
kept the *h* of Eden green	"	1618	from tender *h*'s, And those who sorrow'd	"	843
one main purpose ever at my *h*	"	1679	pious talk, when most his *h* was dry,	*Sea Dreams*	162
face with change of *h* is changed.	"	1747	loathe it ; he had never kindly *h*,	"	193
Edyrn has done it, weeding all his *h*	"	1754	set my *h* on your forgiving him,	"	260
a stronger race With *h*'s and hands,	"	1789	what *h* had he To die of?	"	265
mildly, that all *h*'s Applauded	"	1805	His angel broke his *h*.	"	269
Without the full *h* back may merit	*Vivien*	384	To his great *h* none other than a God!	*Tithonus*	14
fall *h* of yours Whereof you prattle,	"	398	bosom beating with a *h* renew'd.	"	36
rustiest iron of old fighters' *h*'s ;	"	424	ay me! with what another *h*	"	50
Merlin to his own *h*, loathing,	"	639	madly danced our *h*'s with joy,	*The Voyage*	3
colours of the *h* that are not theirs.	"	671	Across the whirlwind's *h* of peace,	"	87
through the *h*'s affections to the *h*!	"	717	in thy *h* the scrawl shall play.'	*Sailor Boy*	12
have found in him a greater *h*.	"	722	A devil rises in my *h*,	"	23
let his wisdom go For ease of *h*,	"	742	Tear the noble *h* of Britain	*Boädicea*	12
Half-nestled at his *h*,	"	754	*h* within her fall and flutter	"	81
h Would reckon worth the taking?	"	765	and the Shepherd gladdens in his *h*	*Spec. of Iliad*	16
vast necessity of *h* and life.	"	774	Shame and wrath his *h* confounded,	*The Captain*	61
in his *h* Heard murmurs 'lo, thou	*Elaine*	55	my *h* so near the beauteous breast.	*Coquette*, ii.	7
a *h* Love-loyal to the least wish	"	89	on thy *h* a finger lays,	*On a Mourner*	11
Low to her own *h* said the lily maid	"	318	Teach that sick *h* the stronger,	"	18
braved a riotous *h* in asking .	"	358	my *h*, my *h* is an evergreen :	*Spiteful Let.*	23
reverence Dearer to true young *h*'s	"	418	*h* to endure for the life of the worm	*Wages*	7
To which it made a restless *h*,	"	549	bird Makes his *h* voice .	*Lucretius*	101
With smiling face and frowning *h*,	"	552	What beast has *h* to do it?	"	230
Lancelot is no more a lonely *h*.	"	600	from the maiden fountain in her *h*.	"	237
one-day-seen Sir Lancelot in her *h*,	"	743	my *h* is there before you are come	*The Window*	14
changed itself and echoed in her *h*,	"	778	Gone, and a cloud in my *h*,	"	40
in her *h* she answer'd it .	"	782	bite far into the *h* of the house,	"	55
in her *h* she laugh'd,	"	804	bitten into the *h* of the earth,	"	60
h's sad secret blazed itself In the *h*'s colours .	"	832	Fine little *h* and merry blue eye.	"	69
a treacherous quiet in his *h*,	"	879	Break, you may break my *h*.	"	141
wish most near to your true *h*;	"	910	Faint *h* never won—	"	142
stupid *h* To interpret ear and eye,	"	937	O merry my *h*, you have gotten	"	158
heat is gone from out my *h*,	"	1110	lighten Into my eyes and my *h*	"	192
parted, laughing in his courtly *h*.	"	1170	Into my *h* and my blood	"	193
in my *h* of *h*'s I did acknowledge nobler	"	1204	*H*, are you great enough	"	194-6
To loyal *h*'s the value of all gifts	"	1208	*heart-affluence.*		
all true *h*'s be blazon'd on her tomb	"	1334	*H-a* in discursive talk .	*In Mem.* cviii	1
doubt her pureness were to want a *h*—	"	1368	*heart-broken.*		
'Ah simple *h* and sweet,	"	1384	he pass'd his father's gate, *H-b* .	*Dora*	49
a man Not after Arthur's *h*!	"	1410	*heart-disease.*		
Rankled in him and ruffled all his *h*,	*Guinevere*	50	suddenly dropt dead of *h-d*.' .	*Sea Dreams*	261
unbind my *h* that I may weep.'	"	164	of *h-d*? what heart had he To die of?	"	265
to her own sad *h* mutter'd the Queen,	"	211	*hearten.*		
into the rich *h* of the west	"	242	Cry thro' the sense to *h* trust	*In Mem.* cxv.	7
began to gather *h* again,	"	366	*heart-free.*		
opposite Of all my *h* had destined	"	488	escaped *h-f* with the least little	*Maud,* I. ii.	11
could speak Of the pure *h*, nor seem	"	498	*hearth.*		
King's waste hearth and aching *h*	"	520	now our household *h*'s are cold ;	*Lotos-E's.*	117
while I weigh'd thy *h* with one .	"	536	'pick'd the eleventh from this *h*.	*The Epic*	41
mockery is the fume of little *h*'s.	"	626	an idle king, By this still *h*,	*Ulysses*	2
in mine own *h* I can live down sin	"	629	Two heads in council, two beside the *h*,	*Princess,* ii.	156
her *h* was loosed Within her,	"	659	household talk, and phrases of the *h*,	"	294
either fixt his *h* On that one girl :.	*En. Arden*	39	Man for the field and woman for the *h*:	"	v. 437
bearing a lifelong hunger in his *h*.	"	70	fires of Hell Mix with his *h*;	"	445
Enoch in his *h* determined all ;	"	148	will make it faggots for the *h*,	"	vi. 29
had I no *h* to break his purposes	"	155	Till happier times each to her proper *h*:	"	284
Philip's true *h*, which hunger'd	"	271	azure pillars of the *h* Arise to these ;	"	vii. 201
fixt his *h* he set his hand .	"	293	by the *h* the children sit .	*In Mem.* xx.	13
oft denied his *h* his dearest wish,	"	333	holly round the Christmas *h*; lxxvii. a)	" xxx.	2
full *h* and boundless gratitude	"	343	prey By each cold *h*,	" xcvii.	18
the expectant terror of her *h*,	"	485	whose *h*'s he saved from shame	*Ode on Well*	225
never merrily beat Annie's *h*.	"	501	Beside your own warm *h*,	*Enid*	820
new mother came about her *h*,	"	520	King's waste *h* and aching heart	*Guinevere*	520
had not his poor *h* Spoken with That,	"	619	clean *h* and a clear fire for me,	*En. Arden*	192
h foreshadowing all calamity,	"	684	left his *h* and native land	"	357
in her *h* she yearn'd incessantly	"	867	so genial was the *h*:	"	744
shook the *h* of Edith hearing him.	*Aylmer's F.*	63	on the right hand of the *h* he saw	"	745, 754
young *h*'s not knowing that they loved,	"	133	shatter all the happiness of the *h*,	"	771
the warmth and muscle of the *h*,	"	180	warm-blue breathings of a hidden *h*	*Aylmer's F.*	115
foam'd away his *h* at Averill's ear;	"	342	On either side the *h*, indignant ;	"	188
according *h*'s of men Seem'd harder too;	"	453	Meet for the reverence of the *h*,	"	333
fragrant in a *h* remembering .	"	436			
his worthless *h* had kept it warm,	"	471			

	POEM.	LINE.
beside your *h's* Can take her place	*Aylmer's F.*	735
strangers at my *h* Not welcome,	*Lucretius*	158

hearth-flower.

	POEM.	LINE.
The little *h-f* Lilia.	*Princess, Pro.*	165

heart-hiding.

	POEM.	LINE.
H-*h* smile, and gray persistent eye:	*Guinevere*	64

hearthstone.

	POEM.	LINE.
hissing in war or his own *h*?	*Maud*, I. i.	24

heartless.

	POEM.	LINE.
Insolent, brainless, *h*!	*Aylmer's F.*	368

heat.

	POEM.	LINE.
Clear, without *h*, undying,	*Isabel*	3
Close-latticed to the brooding *h*,	*Mariana in the S.*	3
day increased from *h* to *h*,	"	39
From *h* to *h* the day decreased	"	78
Throbbing thro' all thy *h* and light,	*Fatima*	4
the heart Faints, faded by its *h*.	*D. of F. Wom.*	288
Rain, wind, frost, *h*, hail, damp,	*St S. Stylites*	16
That *h* of inward evidence,	*Two Voices*	284
Remembering its ancient *h*.	"	423
in the *h* of dusty fights'	*Princess*, ii.	223
Hung, shadow'd from the *h*:	"	435
my honest *h* Were all miscounted	"	iv. 314
What *h's* of indignation	"	v. 365
my veins Stretch with fierce *h*;	"	527
A night of Summer from the *h*,	"	vi. 38
Where we withdrew from summer *h's*	"	228
whiff! there comes a sudden *h*,	" *Con.*	58
life outliving *h's* of youth,	*In Mem.* lii.	10
The landscape winking thro' the *h*:	" lxxxviii.	16
To make a solid core of *h*;	" cvi.	18
the schoolboy *h*, The blind hysterics	" cviii.	15
In tracts of fluent *h* began,	" cxvii.	9
true blood spilt had in it a *h*	*Maud*, I. xix.	14
I spoke with heart, and *h* and force,	*The Letters*	37
after nodded sleepily in the *h*.	*Enid*	1102
with mild *h* of holy oratory,	"	1714
Brain-feverous in his *h* and agony,	*Elaine*	850
h is gone from out my heart,	"	1110
the casement standing wide for *h*,	"	1227
a sudden flush of wrathful *h*	*Guinevere*	354
some *h* of difference sparkled out	*Aylmer's F.*	705
all-generating powers and genial *h*	*Lucretius*	97
animal *h* and dire insanity.	"	163

heated.

	POEM.	LINE.
h thro' and thro' with wrath and love.	*Princess*, iv.	145
h hot with burning fears,	*In Mem.* cxvii.	22
h the strong warrior in his dreams;	*Enid*	72

heath (over-grown place.)

	POEM.	LINE.
blackening over *h* and holt,	*Locksley H.*	191
slowly rode across a wither'd *h*,	*Vision of Sin*	61
At the dragon on the *h*!	"	72
Priest went out by *h* and hill;	*The Victim*	30

heath (heather.)

	POEM.	LINE.
are dabbled with blood-red *h*,	*Maud*, I. i.	2

heathen.

	POEM.	LINE.
the *h* of the Northern Sea (*Guinevere* 134)	*Enid*	1817
till we drive The *H*, who, some say,	*Elaine*	66
h caught and reft him of his tongue	"	273
Trath Treroit, Where many a *h* fell;	"	302
Red as the rising sun with *h* blood	"	308
in this *h* war the fire of God	"	315
H, the brood by Hengist left;	*Guinevere*	17
And leagued with the *h* hosts	"	153
and the Godless hosts Of *h*	"	425
break the *h* and uphold the Christ,	"	467

heave.

	POEM.	LINE.
h and thump A league of street	*Princess*, iii.	111
h's but with the heaving deep.	*In Mem.* xi.	20
tho' the Giant Ages *h* the hill	*Ode on Well.*	259
rough Torre began to *h* and move,	*Elaine*	1060

heaved.

	POEM.	LINE.
silver lily *h* and fell;	*To E. L.*	19
bush-bearded Barons *h* and blew,	*Princess*, v.	20
might'st have *h* a windless flame.	*In Mem.* lxxi.	13

	POEM.	LINE.
only *h* with a summer swell.	*The Daisy*	12
h his blade aloft, And crack'd the helmet	*Enid*	572
I was *h* upon it In darkness:	*Sea Dreams*	90

heaven.

	POEM.	LINE.
could not look on the sweet *h*,	*Mariana*	15
h's mazed signs stood still '*Clear-headed friend*' etc.	28
Sure she was nigher to *h's* spheres,	*Ode to Mem.*	40
H flow'd upon the soul in many dreams	*The Poet*	31
mountain draws it from *H* above,	*Poet's Mind*	32
from a throne Mounted in *h*	*To J. M. K.*	13
H over *H* rose the night.	*Mariana in the S.*	92
Sleepeth over all the *h*,	*Eleänore*	39
As tho' a star, in inmost *h* set,	"	89
Coming thro' *H* like a light	*Œnone*	106
From me, *H's* Queen, Paris, to thee	"	125
O happy *H*, how canst thou see my face?	"	232
hollow'd moons of gems, To mimic *h*,	*Pal. of Art*	189
From yon blue *h's* above us bent	*L. C. V. de Vere*	50
Pray *H* for a human heart,	"	71
seem'd to go right up to *H*	*May Queen*, iii.	40
the *h's* are in a glow;	"	49
Beneath a *h* dark and holy,	*Lotos-E's.*	136
'*H* heads the count of crimes	*D. of F. Wom.*	201
with you thro' a little arc Of *h*,	*To J. S.*	27
dwells in *h* half the night.	"	52
else of *H* was pure Up to the Sun,	*Gardener's D.*	78
praise the *h's* for what they have?'	"	101
to praise the *h's* but only love	"	103
h's between their fairy fleeces pale	"	256
—*H* knows—as much within:	*Ed. Morris*	82
Unfit for earth, unfit for *h*,	*St S. Stylites*	3
Battering the gates of *h*	"	7
H, and Earth, and Time are choked.	"	102
saints Enjoy themselves in *h*	"	104
know I have some power with *H*	"	141
whole, and clean, and meet for *H*.	"	210
under *H* None else could understand;	*Talking O.*	21
all as one to fix our hopes on *H*	*Golden Year*	57
in old days Moved earth and *h*;	*Ulysses*	67
Sees in *h* the light of London	*Locksley H.*	1
Saw the *h's* fill with commerce,	"	121
Heard the *h's* fill with shouting	"	123
Rapt after *h's* starry flight	*Two Voices*	68
joy that mixes man with *H*:	"	210
H opens inward, chasms yawn,	"	304
float thro' *H*, and cannot light?	*Day-Dm.*	276
My breath to *h* like vapour goes	*St Agnes' Eve*	3
Break up the *h's*, O Lord!	"	21
All *h* bursts her starry floors,	"	27
I yearn to breathe the airs of *h*	*Sir Galahad*	63
set in *H's* third story,	*Will Water.*	70
Shall show these past to *H*:	"	246
With tears and smiles from *h* again	*Sir L. and Q. G.*	2
Blue isles of *h* laugh'd between	"	"
vases in the hall Flowers of all *h's*,	*Princess, Pro.*	12
weird seizures, *H* knows what:	" i.	14
lamps blazon'd like *H* and Earth	"	220
to call down from *H* A blessing	" ii.	454
breathe for one hour more in *H*'	" iii.	53
Appealing to the bolts of *H*;	" iv.	353
his anger reddens in the *h's*	"	367
sweet influences Of earth and *h*?	" v.	184
Like a Saint's glory up in *h*;	"	503
And right ascension, *H* knows what;	" vi.	240
The cloud may stoop from *h*	"	365
H, Star after star, arose and fell;	" vii.	34
cease to move so near the *H's*,	"	180
Beyond all thought into the *H* of *H's*.	*Con.*	115
Sleep, gentle *h's*, before the prow;	*In Mem.* ix.	14
bear thro' *H* a tale of woe,	" xii.	10
Hung in the shadow of a *h*?	" xvi.	10
Her early *H*, her happy views;	" xxxiii.	6
The full-grown energies of *h*.	" xxxix.	20
In its assumptions up to *h*;	" lxii.	4
all the starry *h's* of space	" lxx.	2
the inviolate spring Where nighest *h*,	" lxxxix.	3
scale the *h's* highest height,	" cvii.	7
To bare the eternal *H's* again,	" cxxi.	4
high in *h* the streaming cloud	*Con.*	107
Let the sweet *h's* endure,	*Maud*, I. xi.	8

	POEM.	LINE.
O Maud were sure of *H*	*Maud*, I. xii.	19
glide Like a beam of the seventh *H*,	" xiv.	21
The gates of *H* are closed	" xviii.	12
up into *H* the Christless code,	" II. i.	26
and the *h's* fall in a gentle rain,	"	41
'Cold altar, *H* and earth shall meet	*The Letters*	7
H flash'd a sudden jubilant ray,	*Ode on Well.*	129
gloom that saddens *H* and Earth,	*The Daisy*	102
as he loved the light of *H*.	*Enid*	5
as the light of *H* varies,	"	6
aid me *H* when at mine uttermost,	"	502
on open ground Beneath a troubled *h*,	"	523
Sweet *h*, how much I shall discredit	"	621
clothe her like the sun in *H*.	"	784
was ever praying the sweet *h's*	"	893
might amend it by the grace of *h*,	"	902
issuing under open *h's* beheld	"	1045
'by *H*, I will not drink,	"	1512
love the *H* that chastens us.	"	1637
truest eyes that ever answer'd *h*,	"	1690
Bard, and knew the starry *h's*;	*Vivien*	25
By *H* that hears I tell you	"	193
men at most differ as *H* and earth	"	663
women, worst and best, as *H* and Hell.	"	664
yon just *h*, that darkens o'er me,	"	780
she ceased, when out of *h* a bolt	"	783
fearing *h* had heard her oath,	"	789
who can gaze upon the Sun in *h*?.	*Elaine*	124
'*H* hinder,' said the King	"	531
lose it, as we lose the lark in *h*,	"	656
after *h*, on our dull side of death,	"	1373
A blot in *h*, the Raven	*Guinevere*	132
There came a day as still as *h*,	"	290
help me, *h*, for surely I repent.	"	370
the *h's* upbreaking thro' the earth	"	388
no more subtle master under *h*	"	474
be his mate hereafter in the *h's*	"	630
high in *h* behind it a gray down	*En. Arden*	6
On providence and trust in *H*,	"	205
The breath of *h* came continually	"	531
such as drove her under moonless *h's*	"	543
glades high up like ways to *H*,	"	574
stars that globed themselves in *H*,	"	598
a touch of light, an air of *h*,	*Aylmer's F.*	5
H in lavish bounty moulded,	"	107
in the Northern dreamer's *h's*,	"	161
marriages are made in *H*.'	"	188
rain of *h*, and their own bitter tears,	"	428
Tears, and the careless rain of *h*,	"	429
breathless burthen of low-folded *h's*	"	612
Shot up their shadows to the *H* of *H's*,	"	642
thy brother man, the Lord from *H*,	"	667
roof so lowly but that beam of *H*	"	684
the living fount of pity in *H*.	"	752
if every star in *h* Can make it fair:	*Sea Dreams*	82
trees As high as *h*,	"	100
the too rough H in Hell and *H*,	"	192
would jar all the hymns of *h*:	"	251
Till all the comets in *h* are cold,	*The Ringlet*	9
Thunder, a flying fire in *h*,	*Boädicea*	24
rich vapour far into the *h*.	*Spec. of Iliad*	8
when in *h* the stars about the moon	"	11
immeasurable *h's* Break open	"	14
Slide from that quiet *h* of hers,	*Lucretius*	87
climb into the windy halls of *h*:	"	136
Be merry in *h*, O larks, and far away	*The Window*	146
heaven-descended.		
Corrupts the strength of *h-d* Will,	*Will*	11
heavenly.		
But Wisdom *h* of the soul.	*In Mem.*cxiii.	22
heavenly-toned.		
So *h-t*, that in that hour	*Two Voices*	442
heavenly-wise.		
glow In azure orbits *h-w*;	*In Mem.*lxxxvi.	38
heavier.		
tougher, *h*, stronger, he that smote.	*Princess*, v.	525
heavily-galloping.		
The sound of many a *h-g* hoof	*Enid*	1296

	POEM.	LINE.
heaviness.		
Why are we weighed upon with *h*,	*Lotos-E's.*	57
heavy.		
If Time be *h* on your hands,	*L. C. V. de l'ere*	66
What is this? his eyes are *h*:	*Lockstey H.*	51
gentle maiden's death Right *h* am I;	*Elaine*	1284
heavy-blossom'd.		
Droops the *h-b* bower,	*Lockstey H.*	163
heavy-folded.		
swung The *h-f* rose,	*In Mem.*xciv.	59
heavy-fruited.		
hangs the *h-f* tree—	*Lockstey H.*	163
heavy-plunging.		
would the white cold *h-p* foam,	*D. of F. Wom.*	118
heavy-shotted.		
His *h-s* hammock-shroud	*In Mem.* vi.	15
Hebe.		
violet eyes, and all her *H* bloom,	*Gardener's D.*	136
H's are they to hand ambrosia,	*Princess*, iii.	97
Hebrew.		
'No fair *H* boy Shall smile away.	*D. of F. Wom.*	213
blame among The *H* mothers'	"	215
Hector.		
So *H* said, and sea-like roar'd his host;	*Spec. of Iliad*	1
hedge (s.)		
one green wicket in a privet *h*;	*Gardener's D.*	109
All round a *h* upshoots,	*Day-Dm.*	61
He breaks the *h*; he enters there;	"	118
The *h* broke in, the banner blew,	"	141
The very sparrows in the *h*	*Amphion*	67
seated on a style In the long *h*,	*The Brook*	198
air made tremble in the *h*	"	202
tho' she were a beggar from the *h*,	*Enid*	230
pick'd a ragged-robin from the *h*	"	724
hedge (verb.)		
laurel-shrubs that *h* it around.	*Poet's Mind*	14
hedgehog.		
h underneath the plantain bores	*Aylmer's F.*	850
hedge-row.		
where the *h-r* cuts the pathway,	*Gardener's D.*	85
heed (see *take heed.*)		
whether he *h* it or not,	*Maud*, I. iv.	53
Shall I *h* them in their anguish?	*Boädicea*	9
heeded.		
He *h* not reviling tones,	*Two Voices*	220
Bubbled the nightingale and *h* not,	*Princess*, iv.	137
All would be well—the lover *h* not,	*Aylmer's F.*	545
heedlessness.		
pleased her with a babbling *h*	*Guinevere*	149
heehaw.		
A jackass *h's* from the rick,	*Amphion*	71
heel (for head to heel, etc., see *head*.)		
with the dint of armed *h's*—	*M. d'Arthur*	150
drove his *h* into the smoulder'd log,	*Fp.*	14
snarling at each other's *h's*.	*Lockstey H.*	106
trampled some beneath her horses' *h's*,	*Princess*, Pro.	44
brains are in their hands and in their *h's*,	" iv.	497
virgin marble under iron *h's*:	" vi.	331
Gnarr at the *h's* of men,	*In Mem.*xcvii.	17
h against the pavement echoing,	*Enid*	1120
her palfrey whinnying lifted *h*,	"	1382
lissome Vivien, holding by his *h*,	*Vivien*	67
Lancelot pluck'd him by the *h*,	*Guinevere*	35
precipitate *h*, Fledged as it were	*Lucretius*	167
bitten the *h* of the going year.	*The Window*	48
height.		
from thy noonday *h* Shudderest	*Fatima*	2
Beyond, a line of *h's*, and higher	*Pal. of Art*	82
Be flatter'd to the *h*.	"	192
not leave the myrrh-bush on the *h*;	*Lotos-E's.*	103
To her full *h* her stately stature	*D. of F. Wom.*	102
sat Freedom on the *h's*, 'Of old sat Freedom,' etc.		1

	POEM.	LINE.
hast not gain'd a real *h*,	*Two Voices*	91
In gazing up an Alpine *h*,	"	362
leave the plain, I climb the *h*;	*Sir Galahad*	57
fold by fold, From those still *h's*	*Vision of Sin*	52
She rose her *h*, and said:	*Princess*, ii.	27
rosy *h's* came out above the lawns.	" iii.	347
When storm is on the *h's*,	" v.	338
arose Once more thro' all her *h*,	" vi.	144
drags me down From my fixt *h*	"	289
O maid, from yonder mountain *h*:	" vii.	177
What pleasure lies in *h*	"	178
In *h* and cold, the splendour	"	179
gain in sweetness and in moral *h*,	"	265
On Argive's *h's* divinely sang	*In Mem.* xxiii.	22
Upon the last and sharpest *h*,	" xlvi.	13
A higher *h*, a deeper deep.	" lxii.	12
all thy breadth and *h* Of foliage	" lxxxviii.	3
About empyreal *h's* of thought,	" xciv.	38
To scale the heaven's highest *h*,	" cvii.	7
Powers of the *h*, Powers of the deep,	*Maud*, II. ii.	82
manhood stand on his ancient *h*,	" III. vi.	21
The *h*, the space, the gloom, the glory!	*The Daisy*	59
Another sinning on such *h's* .	*Elaine*	248
free flashes from a *h* Above her,	"	644
not look up, or half-despised the *h*	*Guinevere*	636
lo! her Enoch sitting on a *h*,	*En. Arden*	496
hending from his *h* With half-allowing	*Aylmer's F.*	119
dealing goodly counsel from a *h*	"	172
from his *h* and loneliness of grief.	"	632
Whisper in odorous *h's* of even.	*Milton*	16
every *h* comes out, and jutting	*Spec. of Iliad*	13

heightened.
Then the Captain's colour *h*,	*The Captain*	29

heir.
His son and *h* doth ride post haste,	*D. of the O. Year*	31
first-born, and *h* to all,	*Gardener's D.*	185
I the *h* of all the ages,	*Locksley H.*	178
Lord Ronald is *h* of all your lands,	*Lady Clare*	19
And I,' said he, 'the lawful *h*,	"	86
hard *h* strides about their lands,	*In Mem.* lxxxix.	15
Spurn'd by this *h* of the liar—	*Maud*, I. xix.	78
dead love's harsh *h*, jealous pride?	*Elaine*	1389
heiress and not *h* regretfully?	*Aylmer's F.*	24
Blissful bride of a blissful *h*,	*W. to Alexan*	27
Bride of the *h* of the kings of the sea—	"	28

heiress.
'If you are not the *h* born,	*Lady Clare*	83-5
comes the feebler *h* of your plan,	*Princess*, iii.	221
As *h* and not heir regretfully?	*Aylmer's F.*	24
Their child.' 'Our child!' 'Our *h*!'	"	297
h, wealth, Their wealth, their *h*!.	"	368

heirless.
now a lonely man Wifeless and *h*,	*Elaine*	1362

held.
h the pear to the garden-wall.	*Mariana*	4
Paris *h* the costly fruit Out .	*Œnone*	133
h she her solemn mirth,	*Pal. of Art*	215
h your course without remorse,	*L. C. V. de l'ève*	45
h me above the subject,	*D. of F. Wom.*	10
father *h* his hand upon his face;	"	107
Her rags scarce *h* together;	*The Goose*	2
He *h* a goose upon his arm .	"	
h a talk, How all the old honour	*The Epic*	6
so we *h* it then) What came of that?	"	
dropt the hranch she *h*, and turning	*Gardener's D.*	154
h it better men should perish	*Locksley H.*	179
She *h* it out; and as a parrot	*Princess, Pro.*	169
h his sceptre like a pedant's wand	" i.	27
so my daughter *h*, Was all in all:	"	134
h her round the knees	" ii.	342
In this hand *h* a volume as to read,	"	431
the papers that she *h* Rustle:	" iv.	371
some pretext Of baby troth	" v.	387
pored upon her letter which I *h*,	"	438
painting and the tress And *h* them up:	" vi.	95
Love in sacred halls *H* carnival	" vii.	70
h A volume of the Poets of her land;	"	158
h it truth, with him who sings	*In Mem.* i.	1

	POEM.	LINE.
man I *h* as half-divine;	*In Mem.* xiv.	10
if we *h* the doctrine sound	" lii.	9
Where once we *h* debate,	" lxxxvi.	21
h that sorrow makes us wise, (cxii. 1)	" cvii.	15
h their heads above the crowd,	*The Brook*	10
His Memory—since he *h* them dear,	*Ded. of Idylls*	1
H court at old Caerleon upon Usk.	*Enid*	146
caught His purple scarf, and *h*,	"	377
meadow where the jousts were *h*,	"	537
H his head high, and thought himself	"	1091
H commune with herself,	"	1217
moving back she *h* Her finger up,	"	1301
with a horn with wine and *h* it to her,)	"	1507
whom he *h* In converse for a little,	"	1730
was too slippery to be *h*,	*Vivien*	18
she, who *h* her eyes upon the ground	*Elaine*	213
h her from her sleep.	"	232
and they that *h* the lists,	"	338
the Table Round that *h* the lists,	"	454
h her tenderly, And loved her	"	466-98
H her awake: or if she slept,	*Guinevere*	863
grieving *h* his will, and bore it thro'.	*En. Arden*	75
yet she *h* him on delayingly.	"	167
that she but *h* off to draw him on;	"	465
daily-dwindling profits *h* the house;	"	473
H his head high, and cared for no man,	"	697
face and faith *H* him from that:	*Aylmer's F.*	393
Faded with morning, but his purpose *h*.	"	412
as if he *h* The Apocalyptic millstone,	*Sea Dreams*	25
My master *h* that Gods there are,	*Lucretius*	116

Helen.
the breasts, The breasts of *H*,	*Lucretius*	61

Heliconian.
H honey in living words,	*Lucretius*	221

hell.
hated him with the hate of *h*,	*The Sisters*	22
Struck thro' with pangs of *h*.	*Pal. of Art*	220
down in *h* Suffer endless anguish,	*Lotos-E's.*	160
all *h* beneath Made me boil over.	*St S. Stylites*	167
Mix'd with cunning sparks of *h*.	*Vision of Sin*	114
paint the gates of *H* with Paradise,	*Princess*, iii.	113
fires of *H* Mix with his hearth;	" v.	444
Procuress to the Lords of *H*.	*In Mem.* lii.	15
compass'd by the fires of *H*;	" cxxvi.	17
passions that make earth *H*!	*Maud*, I. x.	25
I have climbed nearer out of lonely *H*.	" xviii.	60
fires of *H* brake out of thy rising .	" II. i.	9
fires of *H* and of Hate;	"	10
slander, meanest spawn of *H*	*The Letters*	33
Into the mouth of *H*	*Lt. Brigade*	25-47
halfway down the slope to *H*,	*Enid*	1639
hard earth cleave to the Nadir *h*, .	*Vivien*	199
worst and best, as Heaven and *H*.	"	664
Lightens from her own central *H*—	*Aylmer's F.*	761
too rough H in *H* and Heaven,	*Sea Dreams*	192
Deep as *H* I count his error.	*The Captain*	3
mortal soul from out immortal *h*,	*Lucretius*	259

helm (helmet.)
so deeply smitten thro' the *h*	*M. d'Arthur*	25, 41
scarf of orange round the stony *h*,	*Princess*, Pro.	102
fired an angry Pallas on the *h*,	" vi.	347
Aim'd at the *h*, his lance err'd;	*Enid*	1006
his lance aside, And doff'd his *h*:	"	1444
upon his *h* A sleeve of scarlet,	*Elaine*	601
he had not loosed it from his *h*,	"	805
look'd Down on his *h*, from which	"	976
spake to these his *h* was lower'd,	*Guinevere*	507

helm (of a boat.)
She took the *h* and he the sail;	*Vivien*	49

helm (verb.)
the bark, And him that *h's* it,	*Elaine*	435

helmet.
The *h* and the helmet-feather	*L. of Shalott*, iii.	21
From underneath his *h* flow'd	"	30
She saw the *h* and the plume,	"	40
out of stricken *h's* sprang the fire.	*Princess*, v.	494
Psyche's colour round his *h*,	"	523

				POEM.	LINE.
riveting a *h* on his knee,	.	*Enid*	.	.	268
forward with the *h* yet in hand	.	"	.	.	285
crack'd the *h* thro', and bit the bone,	"	.	.	.	573
eye darken'd, and his *h* wagg'd ;	.	"	.	.	1354
bound Her token on his *h*,	.	*Elaine*	.	.	373

helmet-feather.
The helmet and the *h.f* Burned *L. of Shalott*, iii. 21

helmsman.
I leap on board: no *h* steers : . *Sir Galahad* 32

help (s.)
without *h* I cannot last till morn. . *M. d'Arthur* 26
promised *h*, and oozed All o'er . *Princess*, v. 231
Because it needed *h* of Love : *In Mem.* xxv. 8
shall I kill myself? What *h* in that? *Guinevere* . 614
to see you poor and wanting *h*: . *En. Arden* . 403
comfort and an open hand of *h*, . *Aylmer's F.* 174

help (verb.)
grace To *h* me of my weary load.' *Mariana in the S.* 29
until he grows Of age to *h* us.' . *Dora* . . 125
h's the hurt that Honour feels, . *Locksley II.* 105
h me as when life begun : . " . . 185
there was one to hear And *h* them : *Princess*, ii. 249
I heard, I could not *h* it, . . " . . 311
oh, Sirs, could I *h* it, but my cheek " iii. 29
(God *h* her) she was wedded to a . " . . 67
h my prince to gain His rightful . " . . 144
H, father, brother, *h* ; . . . " vi. 286
scorn'd to *h* their equal rights . " vii. 218
h thy foolish ones to bear ; . *In Mem. Pro.* 31
H thy vain worlds to bear thy light " . 32
How could I *h* her? . . *The Brook* . 111
Poor fellow, could he *h* it ? . " . 158
saving that, ye *h* to save mankind *Ode on Well.* 166
How best to *h* the slender store, *To F. D. Maurice* 37
name Slip from my lips if I can *h* it— *Enid* . 446
weak beast seeking to *h* herself . *Vivien* . 348
so I *h* him back to life ?' . *Elaine* . 783
h it from the death that cannot die, *Guinevere* . 66
h me, heaven, for surely I repent. . " . 370
cannot *h* you as I wish to do . *En. Arden* . 404
H me not to break in upon her peace. . " . 788
God *h* me I save I take my part . *Sailor Boy* . 21
H us from famine And plague . *The Victim* . 9

helped.
and his father *h* him not. . . *Dora* . . 49
God, that *h* her in her widowhood. . " . 111
running at the call, and *h* us down. *Princess*, i. 224
H by the mother's careful hand . *Enid* . . 738
Yea, would have *h* him to it : . " . . 1486
at Caerleon had he *h* his lord, . *Elaine* . 297
And *h* her from herself. . . " . 1299
would have *h* her from her death.' . " . 1302
h At lading and unlading . . *En. Arden* . 816
For heart, I think, *h* head . . *Aylmer's F.* 475

helper.
Henceforth thou hast a *h*, me, . *Princess*, vii. 242

helping.
mother silent too, nor *h* her, . *Enid* . . 768

helplessness.
Enid, in her utter *h*, . . *Enid* . . 1567

helpmate.
'Io mine *h*, one to feel My purpose . *Guinevere* . 481

hem.
in her raiment's *h* was traced in flame *The Poet* . 45

hemlock.
Diotima, teaching him that died Of *h*; *Princess*,iii. 286

hen.
we stole his fruit, His *h*'s, his eggs; *Walk. to the M.* 77
h To her false daughters in the pool ; *Princess*, v. 318
praised his *h*'s,his geese,his guinea-hens *The Brook* 126

Hengist.
Heathen, the brood by *H* left : . *Guinevere* . 17

herald.
The *h* of her triumph, . . *Œnone* . 181
her *h*, Reverence, fly ' *Love thou thy hand,*' etc. 18

				POEM.	LINE.
sent a *h* forth, And bade him cry,	*Godiva*	.	35
had sent a *h* to the gates.	.	*Princess*, v.	322
all that morn the *h*'s to and fro,	.	"	. 359
The *H* of a higher race,	.	*In Mem.* cxvii.14
h's blew Proclaiming his the prize,	*Elaine*	.	499

heraldry.
title scrolls and gorgeous *heraldries*. *Aylmer's F.* 656

herb.
Step deeper yet in *h* and fern, . *Talking O.* . 245
The vilest *h* that runs to seed . *Amphion* . 95
bruised the *h* and crush'd the grape, *In Mem.*xxxv. 23
underfoot the *h* was dry ; . . " xciv. 2

Hercules.
My *H*, my Roman Antony, . *D. of F. Wom.*150
My Eustace might have sat for *H* ; *Gardener's D.* 7

herd (s.)
h's upon an endless plain, . . *Pal. of Art.* 74
The *h*, wild hearts and ' *Love thou thy land,*' etc. 11
count not me the *h* ! . . *Golden Year* 13
a *h* of boys with clamour bowl'd . *Princess*, Pro. 81
and as the leader of the *h* . " vi. 69
So thick with lowings of the *h*'s, . *In Mem.* xcviii. 3
her harvest ripen, her *h* increase, . *Maud*, III. vi. 25

herd (verb.)
I, to *h* with narrow foreheads, . *Locksley II.* 175

herdsman.
Earth Reels, and the *herdsmen* cry : *Princess*, v. 518

Here.
H comes to-day, Pallas and Aphrodite, *Œnone.* 83
beheld great *H*'s angry eyes, . . " . 186
Samian *H* rises and she speaks . *Princess*, iii. 99

heresy.
woman is the better man; A rampant *h*, *Princess*,iv.392

heretic.
Burn, you glossy *h*, burn, . . *The Ringlet* 53

heritage.
Will not another take their *h* ? . *Aylmer's F.* 786

hermit.
now for forty years A *h*, . . *Elaine* . 402
came the *h* out and bare him in, . " . 518
h, skill'd in all The simples . . " . 857

hern.
floods the haunts of *h* and crake ; *In Mem.* c. 14
I come from haunts of Coot and *h*, *The Brook* . 23
and pools, waste places of the *h*, . *Enid* . 880
lost the *h* we slipt him at, . . *Elaine* . 654

hero.
H's tall Dislodging pinnacle . *D. of F. Wom.* 25
Heroic, for a *h* lies beneath, . *Princess*, Pro. 207
be yourself your *h* if you will.' . " . 216
each be *h* in his turn ! . . " . 221
While horse and *h* fell, . . *Lt. Brigade* 44

Herod.
H, when the shout was in his ears, *Pal. of Art* 219

heroic.
H, for a hero lies beneath, . *Princess*, Pro. 207
H if you will, or what you will " . 215
H seems our Princess as required— " . 223
mock *h*'s stranger than our own ; . " *Con.* 64

heroine.
'Take Lilia, then, for *h*' . . *Princess*,Pro.217
dames and *h*'s of the golden year . " vi. 48

hesitating.
Down the long tower-stairs, *h* : . *Elaine* . 342

Hesper.
Large *H* glitter'd on her tears, *Mariana in the S.* 90
Sad *H* o'er the buried sun . . *In Mem.* cxx. 1

Hesperian.
Disclosed a fruit of pure *H* gold, . *Œnone* . 65

Hesper-Phosphor.
Sweet *H-P*, double name . . *In Mem.* cxx. 17

	POEM.	LINE.
hest.		
I thy *h* will all perform at full,	*M. d' Arthur*	43
Hetairai.		
girls, *H,* curious in their art,	*Lucretius*	52
hew.		
lifted to *h* down A cavalier	*D. of F. Wom.*	45
hewed.		
my race *H* Ammon, hip and thigh,	*D. of F. Wom.*	238
hewn.		
With rugged maxims *h* from life;	*Ode on Well.*	184
hexameter.		
rise And long roll of the *H*—	*Lucretius*	11
Hic Jacets.		
by the cold *H J* of the dead!'	*Vivien*	603
hid.		
h in ringlets day and night,	*Miller's D.*	173
h Excalibur the second time,	*M. d' Arthur*	111
Dora *h* her face By Mary.	*Dora*	153
h his face From all men,	*Walk. to the M.*	14
have *h* her needle in my heart,	*Ed. Morris*	62
Saying, 'I have *h* my feelings,	*Locksley H.*	29
ghostly woodpecker, *H* in the ruins;	*Princess, Pro*	212
some *h* and sought In the orange thickets;	" ii.	435
woman's garment *h* the woman's heart.'	" v.	295
mumbled it, And *h* her bosom with it;	" vi.	197
moon is *h*; the night is still; (ciii. 2)	*In Mem.* xxviii.	2
an Isis *h* by the veil	*Maud,* I. iv.	43
more exprest Than *h* her,	*Vivien*	72
half disdain *h* under grace,	*Elaine*	264
H from the wide world's rumour	"	521
h the Holiest from the people's eyes	*Aylmer's F.*	772
havens *h* in fairy bowers,	*The Voyage*	54
Woods where we *h* from the wet	*The Window*	183
hidden.		
joy *H* in sorrow: .	*Dying Swan*	23
violets, *h* in the green,	*D. of F. Wom.*	77
Hail, *h* to the knees in fern,	*Talking O.* 29,	201
h from the heart's disgrace,	*Locksley H.*	57
these two Division smoulders *h*;'	*Princess,* iii.	63
'hear, but hold my name *H,*	*Elaine*	416
Where your great knight is *h,*	"	687
(When first I learnt thee *h* here)	*Guinevere*	535
h as the music of the moon	*Aylmer's F.*	102
hide.		
run to and fro, and *h* and seek,	*The Mermaid*	35
neither *h* the ray From '*Love thou thy land,*' etc.		14
h my forehead and my eyes?	*M. d' Arthur*	228
h thy knotted knees in fern,	*Talking O.*	93
H me from my deep emotion,	*Locksley H.*	108
cannot *h* that some have striven,	*Two Voices*	208
Is there no baseness we would *h*?	*In Mem.* l.	1
h thy shame beneath the ground.	" lxxi.	28
earth has earth enough To *h* him.	*Enid*	1404
Well, *h* it, *h* it; I shall find it out;	*Vivien*	378
h it therefore; go unknown:	*Elaine*	151
therefore would he *h* his name	"	579
sharply turned about to *h* her face,	"	605
There will I *h* thee, till my life	*Guinevere*	113
thou could'st *h* me from myself!	"	117
See they sit, they *h* their faces,	*Boädicea*	51
H, h them, million-myrtled wilderness,	*Lucretius*	201
cavern-shadowing laurels, *h*!	"	202
hiding-place.		
by mine head she knows his *h-p.*	*Elaine*	710
high.		
Did ever rise from *h* to higher;	*In Mem.* xl.	2
moving up from *h* to higher,	" lxiii.	13
either babbling world of *h* or low;	*Ode on Well.*	182
If this be *h,* what is it to be low?'.	*Elaine*	1078
H, self-contain'd, and passionless,	*Guinevere*	403
high-arched.		
H-a and ivy-claspt, Of finest Gothic	*Princess, Pro*	91
high-built.		
storm their *h-b* organs make,	*In Mem.* lxxxvi.	6

	POEM.	LINE.
high-elbowed.		
H-e grigs that leap in summer grass.	*The Brook*	54
higher.		
might have look'd a little *h*;	*Miller's D.*	140
never saw woman *h* in this world—	*Walk. to the M.*	88
sensuous organism That which is *h.*	*Princess,* ii.	74
Among her maidens, *h* by the head,	" iii.	163
Did ever rise from high to *h*;	*In Mem.* xl.	2
moving up from high to *h,*	" lxiii.	13
feel There is a lower and a *h*;	" cxxviii.	4
highest.		
The *h* is the measure of the man,	*Princess,* ii.	141
midmost and the *h* Was Arac:	" v.	246
of all men who seems to me the *h.*'	*Elaine*	1071
'*H*?' the Father answer'd, echoing '*h*?'	"	1072
know not what you call the *h*;	"	1074
Thou art the *h* and most human too,	*Guinevere*	642
my duty to have loved the *h*;	"	650
We needs must love the *h*	"	653
Singing Hosanna in the *h*;	*En. Arden*	499-502
their own darkness as the *H*?	*Aylmer's F.*	643
heavens Break open to their *h,*	*Spec. of Iliad*	15
highest-mounted.		
'The *h-m* mind,' he said,	*Two Voices*	79
highlands.		
Sailing under palmy *h*	*The Captain*	23
Highness.		
Your *H* would enroll them with your	*Princess,* i.	236
One rose in all the world, your *H*	" ii.	37
No ghostly hauntings like his *H.*	" iii.	186
Your *H* might have seem'd the thing	" iii.	186
if your *H* keep Your purport,	"	195
'Alas your *H* breathes full East,'	"	215
'pass on; His *H* wakes:'	" v.	5
'Amazed am I to hear Your *H*:	" vi.	305
your *H* breaks with ease The law		
your *H* did not make	"	306
these men came to woo Your *H*—	"	309
high-walled.		
H-w gardens green and old;	*Arabian N's.*	8
highway.		
There she sees the *h* near	*L. of Shalott,* ii.	13
at night along the dusky *h*	*Locksley H.*	113
Cuts off the fiery *h* of the sun,	*En. Arden*	130
Cut off the length of *h* on before,	"	674
hill.		
heaped *h's* that mound the sea,	*Ode to Mem.*	98
Spring Letters cowslips on the *h*?.	*Adeline*	62
The willowy *h's* and fields among,	*L. of Shalott,* iv.	25
And the hearts of purple *h's,*	*Eleänore*	17
white chalk-quarry from the *h*	*Miller's D.*	115
Before he mounts the *h,* I know	*Fatima*	22
a fire Is poured upon the *h's,*	"	31
all the valleys of Ionian *h's*	*Œnone*	2
Paris, once her playmate on the *h's.*	"	16
noonday quiet holds the *h*;	"	24
Hear me O Earth, hear me O *H's,*	"	35
waited underneath the dawning *h's,*	"	46
In this green valley, under this green *h,*	"	228
at night come from the inmost *h's,*	"	245
over *h's* with peaky tops engrail'd,	*Pal. of Art*	113
and the crowfoot are over all the *h,*	*May Queen,* i.	38
There's not a flower on all the *h's*:	" ii.	13
crows from the farm upon the *h*	"	23
His waters from the purple *h*—	*Lotos-E's.*	138
On the *h's* like Gods together,	"	155
thunder on the everlasting *h's.*	*D. of F. Wom.*	226
Upon the hidden bases of the *h's.*	*M. d' Arthur*	106
than human on the frozen *h's.*	"	183
stood upon the *h's* behind	*Ep.*	5
cuckoo told his name to all the *h's*;	*Gardener's D.*	92
till we reach'd The limit of the *h's*;	*Audley Ct.*	82
round the *h's* from bluff to bluff.	*Golden Year*	76
Rift the *h's,* and roll the waters,	*Locksley H.*	186
far across the *h's* they went	*Day-Dm.*	167
across the *h's* and far away	" 169,	193
Ellen's grave, on the windy *h.*	*Ed. Gray*	12

	POEM.	LINE.
To their haven under the *h*;	'Break, break,' etc.	10
From *h's*, that look'd across a land	*Princess*, i.	167
sang about the morning *h's*,	" ii.	229
still be dear beyond the southern *h's*;	"	246
double *h* ran up his furrowy forks	" iii.	158
river as it narrow'd to the *h's*.	"	180
They faint on *h* or field or river:	"	361
you had gone, Ridd'n to the *h's*,	" iv.	324
night to him that sitting on a *h*	"	551
hit the Northern *h's*.	" v.	42
Forgotten, rusting on his iron *h's*,	"	140
from the dark heart of the long *h's*	"	339
and cold, the splendour of the *h's*?	" vii.	179
makes a silence in the *h's*.	*In Mem.* xix.	8
all the lavish *h's* would hum.	" xxiii.	11
Christmas bells from *h* to *h*.	" xxviii.	3
Draw down Æonian *h's*,	" xxxv.	11
About the ledges of the *h*.	" xxxvii.	8
seal'd within the iron *h's*?	" lv.	20
A distant dearness in the *h*.	" lxiii.	19
beam and shade Along the *h's*,	" lxxi.	16
h and wood and field did print	" lxxviii.	7
Descend below the golden *h's*	" lxxxiii.	28
Beyond the bounding *h* to stray,	" lxxxviii.	30
those fair *h's* I sail'd below,	" xcvii.	2
I climb the *h*: from end to end	" xcix.	1
quarry trench'd along the *h*,	"	11
From all the circle of the *h's*.	"	c. 24
distant *h's* From hidden summits.	"	cii. 6
A single church below the *h*.	"	ciii. 3
The *h's* are shadows, and they flow	"	cxxii. 5
sleeping silver thro' the *h's*;	*Con.*	116
fleet came yonder round by the *h*,	*Maud*, I. i.	49
I am sick of the Hall and the *h*,	"	61
Down by the *h* I saw them ride,	" ix.	11
harmless wild-flower on the *h*?—.	" II. i.	3
By thirty *h's* I hurry down,	*The Brook*	27
o'er the *h's* her eagles flew	*Ode on Well.*	112
tho' the Giant Ages heave the *h*	"	259
in a wrinkle of the monstrous *h*.	*Will*	19
Men saw the goodly *h'r* of Somerset,	*Enid*	828
not to goodly *h* or yellow sea	"	830
all night long a cloud clings to the *h*,	"	1539
the white horse on the Berkshire *h's*	"	1784
Fired from the west, far on a *h*,	*Elaine*	168
yet once more on Badon *h*.'	"	280
the tumbled fragments of the *h's*.	"	1417
bent the spirits of the *h's*	*Guinevere*	281
from *h* to *h*, and every day beheld	"	389
as he climb'd the *h*,	*En. Arden.*	66
silent water slipping from the *h's*,	"	634
to the *h*. There he sat down	"	723
up the steep *h* Trod out a path:	*Sea Dreams*	116
and Charlie ploughing the *h*.	*Grandmother*	80
High towns on *h's* were dimly seen,	*The Voyage*	34
h's and scarlet-mingled woods	"	47
Steps from her airy *h*, and greens	*On a Mourner*	8
Had rest by stony *h's* of Crete.	"	35
Priest went out by heath and *h*;	*The Victim*	30
I stand on the slope of the *h*,	*The Window*	9

Hill (surname.)

| millionaires, Here lived the *H*'s— | *Ed. Morris* | 11 |
| in dancing after Letty *H*, | " | 55 |

hill-convent.

| Or tower, or high *h-c*, seen. | *The Daisy* | 29 |

hill-fort.

| Storming a *h.-f* of thieves He got it; | *Aylmer's F.* | 225 |

hillock.

| Peace Pipe on her pastoral *h* | *Maud*, III. vi. | 24 |

hill-side.

| woods that belt the gray *h-s*, | *Ode to Mem.* | 55 |
| whole *h-s* was redder than a fox. | *Walk. to the M.* | 3 |

hilt.

his hand against the *h*, 'Love thou thy land,' etc.		83
keen with frost against the *h*:	*M. d'Arthur*	17
when he saw the wonder of the *h*,	"	85
betray me for the precious *h*;	"	126
caught him by the *h*, and brandish'd	"	145, 160

	POEM.	LINE.
So great a miracle as yonder *h*.	*M. d'Arthur*	156
Caught at the *h*, as to abolish him:	*Enid*	210

hinder.

Came all in haste to *h* wrong,	*Princess*, iv.	382
What *h's* me To take such bloody	"	512
rule the land Hereafter, which God *h*.'	*Elaine*	67
'Heaven *h*,' said the King.	"	531

hindrance.

| Divinely thro' all *h* finds the man | *Elaine* | 332 |

hinge.

doors upon their *h's* creak'd;	*Mariana*	62
So frequent on its *h* before.	*Deserted H.*	8
I grate on rusty *h's* here;'	*Princess*, i.	85
Half-parted from a weak and scolding *h*,	*The Brook*	84

hint (s.)

A little *h* to solace woe, A *h*,	*Two Voices*	433
h's and echoes of the world.	*Day-Dm.*	27
No *h* of death in all his frame	*In Mem.* xiv.	18
with shadow'd *h* confuse A life	" xxxiii.	7
A little flash, a mystic *h*;	" xliii.	8
dark sweet *h's* of some who prized	*Vivien*	15

hint (verb.)

Alone might *h* of my disgrace:	*Two Voices*	360
We whisper, and *h*, and chuckle,	*Maud*, I. iv.	29
laughingly Would *h* at worse in either.	*En. Arden*	478
lad may wink, and a girl may *h*,	*The Ringlet*	17
h it not in human tones,	*Coquette*, iii.	11

hip and thigh.

| my race Hew'd Ammon, *h* a *t*, | *D. of F. Wom.* | 238 |

hire.

| *h* us some fair chamber for the night, | *Enid* | 1087 |

hired.

| *h* himself to work within the fields; | *Dora* | 36 |

hiss.

| the hot *h* And bustling whistle | *Enid* | 256 |

hiss'd.

| *h* each at other's ear | *Enid* | 1482 |

hissing.

Each *h* in his neighbour's ear;	*Princess*, v.	14
h in war on his own hearthstone?	*Maud*, I. i.	24
geese of the world that are ever *h* disprmise	" iv.	52

history.

chant the *h* Of that great race	*In Mem.* cii.	34
made a pretty *h* to herself	*Elaine*	18
boyish *histories* Of battle,	*Aylmer's F.*	97

hit (s.)

| With twisted quirks and happy *h's*, | *Will Water.* | 189 |

hit (verb.)

He scarcely *h* my humour.	*Ed. Morris*	76
h the Northern hills.	*Princess*, v.	42
h the mood Of Love on earth?	*In Mem.* xlvi.	11

hitting.

| *h* all we saw with shafts Of gentle satire, | *Princess*, ii. | 444 |
| aim'd All at one mark, all *h*: | *Aylmer's F.* | 95 |

hive.

Audley feast Humm'd like a *h*	*Audley Ct.*	4
from all the provinces, And fill the *h*.'	*Princess*, ii.	84
—Wasps in our good *h*	" iv.	514
There the *h* of Roman liars worship	*Boädicea*	19

hoar.

become Unnaturally *h* with rime,	*St. S. Stylites*	163
Make thy grass *h* with early rime.	*Two Voices*	66
lawn as yet Is *h* with rime,	*To F. D. Maurice*	42

hoard (s.)

With a *h* of little maxims.	*Locksley H.*	94
a *h* of tales that dealt with knights	*Princess*, Pro.	29
Our *h* is little, but our hearts are great.	*Enid*	352-74

hoard (verb.)

h it as a sugar-plum for Holmes.'.	*The Epic*	43
That *h*, and sleep, and feed,	*Ulysses*	5
three suns to store and *h* myself.	"	29
h all savings to the uttermost,	*En. Arden*	46

202 CONCORDANCE TO

hoarded.
	POEM.	LINE.
h in herself, Grew, seldom seen:	Gardener's D.	48

hoarse.
	POEM.	LINE.
I hear thee not at all, or h	The Blackbird	19

hoary.
	POEM.	LINE.
prodigal in oil, And h to the wind.	Pal. of Art	80

hoary-headed.
| There musing sat the h-h Earl, | Enid | 295 |
| sigh'd and smiled the h-h Earl, | " | 307 |

hob-and-nob.
| Let us h-a-n with Death. | Vision of Sin | 74 |
| H-a-n with brother Death! | " | 194 |

hog.
| his ploughs, his cows, his h's, his dogs; | The Brook | 125 |
| brought in whole h's and quarter beeves, | Enid | 1450 |

hold (grasp, etc.)
shuddering took h of all my mind,	May Queen, iii.	35
sweet As woodbine's fragile h,	Talking O.	146
that my h on life would break	In Mem. xxviii.	15
sweep me from my h upon the world,	Vivien	152
their law Relax'd its h upon us	Guinevere	454
cared to lose, her h on life.	Aylmer's F.	568

hold (fastness.)
new-comers in an ancient h,	Ed. Morris	9
to Memory's darkest h,	Love and Duty	87
would track this caitiff to his h,	Enid	415
when I reach'd this ruin'd h,	"	785
by bandit-haunted h's,	"	879
in the gateway of the bandit h,	"	1622
And broke the bandit h's	"	1792

hold (verb.)
h A nobler office upon earth	To the Queen	1
We may h converse with all forms	Ode to Mem.	115
noonday quiet h's the hill:	Œnone	24
H swollen clouds from raining,	D. of F. Wom.	11
h his hope thro' shame 'Love thou thy land,' etc.	82
no anchor, none, To h by,'	The Epic	21
Everard's shoulder, with 'I h by him.'	"	22
Whereof this word h's record	Al. d'Arthur	16
by some law that h's in love,	Gardener's D.	9
h From thence thro' all the worlds:	"	204
what it h's May not be dwelt on	"	265
not cease to grasp the hope I h	St S. Stylites	5
spine can h my weary head,	"	42
angel there That h's a crown?	"	201
I h them exquisitely knit	Talking O.	91
h passion in a leash,	Love and Duty	40
purpose h's To sail beyond the sunset,	Ulysses	59
h thee, when his passion shall have	Locksley H.	49
h a fretful realm in awe,	"	129
how should I for certain h,	Two Voices.	340
h their hands to all, and cry	Will Water.	45
h it good, good things should pass;	"	205
h thee dear For this good pint	"	211
h their orgies at your tomb 'You might have won,'	12
h Your promise: all, I trust, may yet	Princess, ii.	339
substance or the shadow? will it h?	"	387
such, my friend, We h them slight:	" iv.	109
h These flashes on the surface	s	233
h the woman is the better man:	"	391
h That it becomes no man to nurse	"	443
We h a great convention:	"	490
I h her, king, True woman:	" v.	171
h's a stately fretwork to the Sun,	" vi.	70
in your own arms To h your own,	"	162
I sometimes h it half a sin	In Mem. v.	1
h's the shadow of a lark	" xvi.	9
I h it true, whate'er befall;	" xxvii.	13
h's it sin and shame to draw.	" xlvii.	11
H thou the good: define it well.	" liii.	13
h the costliest love in fee.	" lxxviii.	4
h I commerce with the dead;	" lxxxiv.	93
they that h apart The promise	"	105
h An hour's communion with the dead.	" xciii.	3
h it solemn to the past.	" civ.	16
High wisdom h's my wisdom less,	" cxi.	1
h me from my proper place,	" cxvi.	2
dream my dream, and h it true:	" cxxii.	10

	POEM.	LINE.
h by the law that I made,	Maud, I. i.	55
h Awe-stricken breaths at a work.	" x.	16
Think I may h dominion sweet,	" xvi.	12
strike, for we h Thee just,	" II. i.	45
Whatever the Quaker h's,	" v.	92
h's her head to other stars,	The Brook	195
those are few we h as dear:	To F. D. Maurice	46
h a tourney here to-morrow morn,	Enid	287
h like colours of a shell.	"	681
I h a finger up; They understand:	"	1186
'hear, but h my name Hidden,	Elaine	415
if he love, and his love h,	"	694
some do h our Arthur cannot die,	"	1251
my years, however it h in youth.	"	1288
h thee with my life against the	Guinevere	114
'Lancelot, wilt thou h me so?	"	115
strong castle where he h's the Queen;	"	192
h that man the worst of public foes	"	508
Enoch would h possession for a week:	En. Arden	27
cares on God; that anchor h's.	"	222
let me h my purpose till I die.	"	876
'O pray God that he h up'.	Aylmer's F.	733
h me not for ever in thine East:	Tithonus	64
shatter it, it abominable,	Boädicea	65
he that h's The Gods are careless,	Lucretius	149

holden.
| the fair Was h at the town; | Talking O. | 102 |

holding.
h them back by their flowing locks	The Merman	14
sit as God h no form of creed,	Pal. of Art	211
mystic, wonderful, H the sword—	M. d'Arthur	32
H the bush, to fix it back,	Gardener's D.	126
H the folded annals of my youth;	"	239
h out her lily arms	Princess, ii.	283
reason ripe In h by the law within,	In Mem. xxxiii.	11
lissome Vivien, h by his heel,	Vivien	87
h then his court Hard on the river	Elaine	75
Stagger'd and shook, h the branch,	En. Arden	763

hole.
| walls Were full of chinks and h's; | Godiva | 60 |
| Would he have that h in his side? | Maud, II. v. | 82 |

holiday.
With happy faces and with h.	Princess, Pro.	56
In summer suits and silks of h.	Enid	173
younger people making h,	En. Arden	62

Holiest.
| hid the H from the people's eyes. | Aylmer's F. | 772 |

hollow (adj.)
Before an oak, so h huge and old.	Vivien	3
Monotonous and h like a Ghost's	Guinevere	417
h as the hopes and fears of men.	Lucretius	160

hollow (s.)
like fire in swamps and h's gray,	May Queen, i.	31
From craggy h's pouring,	D. of F. Wom.	182
bowery h's crown'd with summer	M. d'Arthur	263
the river-shores, And in the h's;	Gardener's D.	260
thrust him in the h's of his arm,	Dora	129
From many a cloudy h.	Amphion	48
strip a hundred h's bare of Spring,	Princess, vi.	49
I hate the dreadful h	Maud, I. i.	1
creep to the h and dash myself down	"	54
the woody h's in which we meet	" xxii.	43
the red-ribb'd h behind the wood,	" II. i.	25
All in the h of his shield,	Enid	1417
in a cuplike h of the down.	En. Arden	9
began To feather toward the h,	" 68,	371
Crept down into the h's of the wood;	"	76
Like echoes from beyond a h,	Aylmer's F.	298
Blanching and billowing in a h of it,	Lucretius	31

hollow'd.
| the want, that h all the heart, | Love and Duty | 60 |

hollower-bellowing.
| h-b ocean, and again The scarlet | En. Arden | 599 |

hollowing.
| h one hand against his car, | Pal. of Art | 109 |

	POEM.	LINE.		POEM.	LINE.
hollow-hung.			dim fields about the *h*'s Of happy men	*Tithonus* .	69
Under the *h-h* ocean green !	*The Merman*	38	his hopes and hates, his *h*'s and fanes,	*Lucretius*	251
hollow-vaulted.			one way to the *h* of my love,	*The Window*	8
look'd to shame The *h-v* dark,	*Arabian N's.*	126	*home-bred.*		
holly.			flatters thus Our *h-b* fancies :	*In Mem* x. .	11
Sick for the *hollies* and the yews .	*Princess, Pro*	185	*home-circle.*		
while the *h* boughs Entwine ,	*In Mem.* xxix.	9	from her own *h-c* of the poor	*Aylmer's F.*	503
A round the Christmas hearth (lxxvii. 2)	" xxx.	2	*Homer.*		
leave This laurel, let this *h* stand ;	" civ.	2	*H,* Plato, Verulam ; . . .	*Princess,* ii.	144
this is the time of *hollies.*	*Spiteful Letter*	22	*Homeric.*		
hollyhock.			faint *H* echoes, nothing-worth,	*The Epic* .	30
Heavily hangs the *h,* rep.) *'A spirit haunts,' etc.*		11	*homestead.*		
A Summer burial deep in *h's* ;	*Aylmer's F.*	164	the trampled year, The smouldering *h,*	*Princess,* v.	122
holly-oak.			*home-voyage.*		
Before a tower of crimson *h-o's,*	*Princess, Con.*	82	Less lucky her *h-v* ; . . .	*En. Arden* .	537
holm.			*homicidal.*		
soft wind blowing over meadowy *h*'s	*Ed. Morris.*	95	six feet high. Grand. epic, *h* ;	*Princess, Pro.*	219
an' Thornaby *h*'s to plow ! .	*N. Farmer*	52	*homily.*		
Holmes.			Distill'd from some worm-canker'd *h* ;	*To J. M. K.*	6
parson *H,* the poet Everard Hall,	*The Epic* .	4	*honest.*		
hoard it as a sugar-plum for *H.'*	" .	43	Suddenly *h,* answer'd in amaze,	*Enid*	1259
Holofernes.			I methinks till now Was *h*—	" .	1335
underneath The head of *H* peep'd	*Princess,* iv.	208	do you, being right *h,* pray ,	" .	1340
holp.			I too would still be *h.'* . .	" .	1342
h To lace us up, . . .	*Princess,* i.	108	*honey.*		
Sir Lancelot *h* To raise the Prince,	*Guinevere* .	46	whitest *h* in fairy gardens cull'd—	*Eleänore* .	26
holpen.			madness of love, The *h* of poison-flowers	*Maud,* I. iv.	56
being lustily *h* by the rest, .	*Elaine*	495	*'*I sit and gather *h* ; . .	*Vivien* .	431
holt.			Heliconian *h* in living words,	*Lucretius* .	221
sent her voice thro' all the *h* .	*Talking O.* .	173	*honeycomb.*		
blackening over heath and *h,*	*Locksley H.*	101	A full-cell'd *h* of eloquence .	*Ed. Morris.*	26
wither'd *h* or tilth or pasturage—	*En. Arden* .	676	*honey-converse.*		
Holy Ghost.			Some *h-c* feeds thy mind, .	*Adeline* .	40
the warning of the *H G* I prophesy	*St S. Stylites*	216	*honey-hearted.*		
Holy Land.			*h-h* wine And bread from out the .	*Spec. of Iliad*	5
He that died in *H L* . .	*In Mem.* lxxxiii.	42	*honeying.*		
homage.			*h* at the whisper of a lord : .	*Princess, Pro.*	115
'Honour,' she said, 'and *h,* tax	*Œnone* .	114	*honeymoon.*		
render All *h* to his own darling, .	*Maud,* I. xx.	49	thirty moons, one *h* to that, .	*Ed. Morris.*	27
bow'd black knees Of *h,* . .	*Vivien* .	428	*honeysuckle.*		
home.			The *h* round the porch has wov'n,	*MayQueen,* i.	29
The *h* of woe without a tear	*Mariana in the S.*	20	Broke from a bower of vine and *h* :	*Aylmer's F.*	156
an English *h*—gray twilight	*Pal. of Art*	85	*honour* (s.)		
for ever, all in a blessed *h*—	*May Queen,* iii.	57	In *h* of the golden prime .	*Arabian N's.*	109
'Our island *h* Is far beyond the	*Lotos-E's* .	44	*H,*' she said, 'and homage, tax	*Œnone* .	114
Then when I left my *h.'*	*D. of F. Wom.*	120	old *H* had from Christmas gone,	*The Epic* .	7
a summer *h* of murmurous wings	*Gardener's D.*	47	much *h* and much fame were lost.'	*M. d'Arthur*	109
near'd His happy *h,* the ground.	" .	91	Old age hath yet his *h* . .	*Ulysses* .	50
My *h* is none of yours. .	*Dora* .	43	helps the hurt that *H* feels, .	*Locksley H.* .	105
a dusky loaf that smelt of *h,*	*Audley Ct.* .	21	Some grow to *h,* some to shame—	*Two Voices* .	257
sick of *h* A went overseas for change.	*Walk. to the M.*	18	an *h* Unto which she was not born.	*L. of Burleigh*	79
subdue this *h* Of sin, my flesh,	*St S. Stylites*	56	hand and signet gem, 'All *h.*	*Princess,* i.	121
climbing up into my airy *h,*	" .	214	I lose My *h,* these their lives.'	" ii.	321
Lay betwixt his *h* and hers ;	*L. of Burleigh*	28	for *h* : every captain waits Hungry for *h,*	" v.	303
Ancient *h*'s of lord and lady,	" .	31	this *h,* if ye will. It needs must be for *h*	" .	310
He shall have a cheerful *h* ; .	" .	38	you think me touch'd In *h*—	" .	392
for the hollies and the yews of *h*—	*Princess, Pro.*	185	of Death, and of *H* that cannot die,	*Maud,* I. v.	10
three years to correspond with *h* ; .	" i.	56	*h, h, h, h,* to him, Eternal *h* to his	*Ode on W'ell.*	149, 230
h is in the sinews of a man, .	" v.	257	Lavish *H* shower'd all her stars, .	" .	196
maids were better at their *h*'s, .	" .	418	did her *h* as the Prince's bride,	*Enid* .	835
learns her gone and far from *h* ; .	*In Mem.* viii.	4	feast with these in *h* of their earl ;	" .	1130
ask a thousand things of *h* ; . .	" xiv.	12	upon this fatal quest Of *h,* .	" .	1552
Her eyes are *h*'s of silent prayer, .	" xxxiii.	1	will do him No customary *h* ;	*Elaine* .	542
take her latest leave of *h,* . .	" xxxix.	6	His *h* rooted in dishonour stood, .	" .	672
We go, but ere we go from *h,*	" ci.	5	win his *h* and to make his name, .	" .	1353
By the *h* that gave me birth, .	*Maud,* II. iv.	7	her window, sun, In *h* of the day.	*The Window*	177
Prince had found her in her ancient *h.*	*Enid* .	644	*honour* (verb.)		
Near that old *h,* a pool of golden carp :	" .	648	his mute dust I *h* . . .	*To J. S.* .	30
last sight that Enid had of *h* .	" .	873	more than England *h*'s that, .	*Talking O.* .	295
make a *h* For Annie ; . .	*En Arden*	47, 58	*H* the charge they made !' *H* the Light	*Lt. Brigade*	53
hom ward—*h* what *h* I had he a *h* !	" .	669	a king who *h*'s his own word, .	*Elaine* .	144
reach'd the *h* Where Annie lived .	" .	635	*h* thy brute Baäl, . . .	*Aylmer's F.*	644
Back toward his solitary *h* again, .	" .	795			
arose the labourers' *h*'s, . .	*Aylmer's F.*	147			
breaker of the bitter news from *h,*	" .	514			

honour'd.

	POEM.	LINE.
bard has *h* beech or lime,	Talking O.	291
not least, but *h* of them all ; .	Ulysses	15
To perish, wept for, *h*, known,	Two Voices	149
Head-waiter, *h* by the guest	Will Water.	73
the child of one I *h*,	Guinevere	420

honouring.

h your sweet faith in him,	A Dedication	5

hood.

teacup-times of *h* and hoop,	Talking O.	63
in hue The lilac, with a silken *h*	Princess, ii.	3
keep your *h*'s about the face :	"	337

hoodman-blind.

dance and song and *h-b*.	In Mem. lxxvii.	12

hoof.

On burnish'd *hooves* his war-horse	L. of Shalott, iii.	29
flints batter'd with clanging *h's* :	D of F. Wom.	21
h by *h* And every *h* a knell	Princess, iv.	155
galloping *h's* bare on the ridge	" v.	478
a sound arose of *h* And chariot,	" vi.	358
the *h's* of the horses beat, (rep.)	Maud, II. v.	8
heard instead A sudden sound of *h's*,	Enid	164
everywhere Was hammer laid to *h*,	"	256
sound of many a heavily-galloping *h*	"	1296
Not a *h* left ; and I methinks	"	1334

hook.

h it to some useful end.	Day-Dm.	212

hooked.

At last I *h* my ankle in a vine,	Princess, iv.	249

hoop.

teacup-times of hood and *h*,	Talking O.	63
roll'd His *h* to pleasure Edith,	Aylmer's F.	85

hop.

belts of *h* and breadths of wheat ;	Princess, Con.	45
land of *h's* and poppy-mingled corn,	Aylmer's F.	31

hope (s.)

without *h* of change,	Mariana	29
leddest by thy thine infant *H*.	Ode to Mem.	30
What *h* or fear or joy is thine ?	Adeline	23
breathing spring of *H* and Youth.	The Poet	28
My *h* and heart is with thee—	To J. M. K.	1
full at heart of trembling *h*	Miller's D.	110
blessings beyond *h* or thought,	"	237
cut off from *h* in that sad place,	D.of F. Wom.	105
in tears, fallen from *h* and trust :	"	82
his *h* thro' shame and guilt, 'Love thou thy land,' etc.		
A crowd of *h's* That sought to sow	Gardener's D.	63
my desire, like all strongest *h's*,	"	232
daily It fulfill'd, to rise again	Ed. Morris	38
not cease to grasp the *h* I hold	St S. Stylites	1
h ere death Spreads more and more	"	154
all as one to fix our *H's* on Hoavon	Golden Year	57
this mould of *h's* and fears	Two Voices	28
One *h* that warm'd me in the days	"	122
Beyond the furthest flights of *h*,	"	185
that the grounds of *h* were fix'd,	"	227
'A hidden *h*,' the voice replied :	"	441
lent The pulse of *h* to discontent.	"	450
Care and Pleasure, *H* and Pain,	Day-Dm.	75
eyes, like thine, have waken'd *h's* ?	"	257
Such *h*, I know not fear ;	Sir Galahad	1
phantom *h's* assemble ;	Will Water.	30
I had *h*, by something rare,	"	165
Drink to lofty *h's* that cool—	Vision of Sin	147
April *h's*, the fools of chance ;	"	164
Youthful *h's*, by scores, to all,	"	199
to the summit, 'Is there any *h* ?'.	"	220
look'd across a land of *h*,	Princess, i.	167
H, a poising eagle, burns	" iv.	64
like parting *h's* I heard them passing	"	154
all the *h's* of half the world,	"	166
bore up in *h* she would be known ;	"	301
a *h* The child of regal compact,	"	400
my *h's* and thine are one ;	" vii.	343
As we descended following *H*,	In Mem. xxii.	11
light that shone when *H* was born.	" xxx.	32
Man dies ; nor is there *h* in dust :'	" xxxv.	4
h's and light regrets that come	In Mem. xxxix.	7
Beneath all fancied *h's* and fears	" xlviii.	13
faintly trust the larger *h*.	" liv.	20
What *h* of answer, or redress ?	" lv.	27
so much *h* for years to come,	" lviii.	14
The pillar of a people's *h*,	" lxiii.	15
What *h* is here for modern rhyme	" lxxvi.	1
Love, then, had *h* of richer store :	" lxxx.	5
Despair of *H*, and earth of thee.	" lxxxiii.	16
I remain'd, whose *h's* were dim,	" lxxxiv.	29
mighty It's that make us men.	"	60
The *h* of unaccomplish'd years	" xc.	7
h could never hope too much,	" cxi.	11
H had never lost her youth ;	" cxxiv.	5
Hours that fly with *H* and Fear	" cxxvii.	9
I have neither *h* nor trust ;	Maud, I. i.	30
With no more *h* of light.	" ix.	16
comes, like a blight On my fresh *h*,	" xix.	103
a *h* for the world in the coming wars	" III. vi.	11
in that *h*, dear soul, let trouble	"	12
Uplifted high in heart and *h* are we,	Ode on Well.	254
lived in *h* that sometime you would	Enid	1687
'Yea, lord,' she said, 'Your *h's* are mine,'	Elaine	599
goodly *h's* are mine That Lancelot	"	604
me that, I charge thee, my last *h*	Guinevere	564
what *h* ? I think there was a *h*,	"	623
mock'd me when he spake of *h* ;	"	624
His *h* he call'd it ;	"	625
left me *H* That in mine own heart.	"	628
beyond all *h*, against all chance,	En. Arden.	400
His *h's* to see his own,	"	625
labour for himself, Work without *h*,	"	821
boat that bears the *h* of life	"	831
gleam'd a kindlier *h* On Enoch	"	834
strong in *h's*, And prodigal of all	Aylmer's F.	446
golden *h's* for France and all mankind,	"	464
a *h*, a light breaking upon him.	"	480
Seem'd *h's* returning rose :	"	559
with his *h's* in either grave.	"	624
who kept a tender Christian *h*	Sea Dreams	41
In *h* to gain upon her flight	The Voyage	60
Like Heavenly *H* she crown'd the sea.	"	70
rose at dawn and, fired with *h*,	Sailor Boy	1
Light *H* at Beauty's call would perch	Coquette, 1.	3
H is other *H* and wanders far.	"	10
Come *H* and Memory, spouse and	On a Mourner	23
hollow as the *h's* and fears of men.	Lucretius	180
his *h's* and hates, his homes and fanes,	"	251
darkens and brightens like my *h*,	The Window	18

hope (verb.)

I *h* my end draws nigh :	St S. Stylites	36
Could *h* itself return'd ;	Talking O.	12
man, may *h* some truth to find,	Two Voices	176
To that I *h* to be.	St Agnes' Eve	20
hope could never *h* too much,	In Mem. cxi.	11
That I never can *h* to pay ;	Maud, I.xix.	88
And the uttmost *h* to win her	" xx.	29
H more for these than some	Ded. of Idylls	31
h with me. Whose shame is that,	Aylmer's F.	717

hoped.

h that ere this period closed	St S. Stylites	17
partly that I *h* to win you back,	Princess, iv.	285
loved and did, And *h* and suffer'd,	In.Mem.Con.	135
heard, And almost *h* herself ;	En. Arden.	202
Yet he *h* to purchase glory,	The Captain	17
H to make the name Of his vessel	"	18

hopefuller.

He, passionately *h*, would go,	Aylmer's F.	419

hopeless.

hush'd itself at last *H* of answer ;	Aylmer's F.	543

hoping.

h, fearing 'is it yet too late ?'	Guinevere	683

horde.

There the *h* of Roman robbers	Boâdicea	18

horizon.

length of bright *h* rimm'd the dark.	Gardener's D.	177
By making all the *h* dark.	Two Voices	390

	POEM.	LINE.
With fair *h's* bound;	Will Water.	66
My prospect and *h* gone.	In Mem. xxxviii.	4
Ev'n to its last *h*,	Aylmer's F.	816

horn.

	POEM.	LINE.
wave-worn *h's* of the echoing bank	Dying Swan	39
grasp'd The mild bull's gold *h*.	Pal. of Art	120
his *h's* into the neighbour field,	Gardener's D.	86
bay runs up its latest *h*.	Audley Ct.	10
sound upon the bugle *h*.	Locksley H.	7
monstrous *h's* of elk and deer,	Princess, Pro.	23
The *h's* of Elfland faintly blowing!	" iii.	357
little space was left between the *h's*,	" iv.	189
blast and bray of the long *h*	" v.	242
a wild *h* in a land Of echoes,	"	475
leafless ribs and iron *h's* Together	In Mem.cvi.	12
A golden foot or a fairy *h*	Maud, II. ii.	19
affluent Fortune emptied all her *h*.	Ode on Well.	197
let blow his *h's* for hunting	Enid	153
noble hart at bay, now the far *h*	"	233
fill'd a *h* with wine and held it	"	1507
the hart with golden *h's*.	Vivien	259
chased the flashes of his golden *h's*	"	277
sent His *h's* of proclamation out	"	431
sit with knife in meat and wine in *h*.	"	544
made and wound the gateway *h*.	Elaine	169
answer, sounding like a distant *h*.	Guinevere	247

hornblende.

	POEM.	LINE.
chattering stony names Of shale and *h*,	Princess, iii.	344

horned.

	POEM.	LINE.
things that are forked, and *h*, and	The Mermaid	53

horn-handed.

	POEM.	LINE.
those *h-h* breakers of the glebe,	Princess, ii.	143

hornpipes.

	POEM.	LINE.
move, And flounder into *h*.	Amphion	24

horrible.

	POEM.	LINE.
H, hateful, monstrous, not to be told;	Maud, III. vi.	41

horror.

	POEM.	LINE.
shot Light *h's* thro' her pulses;	Godiva	59
h of the shame among them all:	Princess, v.	92
drip with a silent *h* of blood,	Maud, I. i.	3
brood On a *h* of shatter'd limbs	"	56
morbid hate and *h* have grown	" vi.	75
Felt a *h* over me creep,	" xiv.	35
cells of madness, haunts of *h* and fear,	" III. vi.	2
h on him, lest his gentle wife,	Enid	29
A *h* lived about the tarn,	Elaine	38
of the Baronet bristle up With *h*,	Aylmer's F.	43
clipt by *h* from his term of life,	"	603
Priest in *h* about his altar	The Victim	7
fling this *h* off me again,	Lucretius	173

horror-stricken.

	POEM.	LINE.
And Leolin's *h-s* answer, 'I.	Aylmer's F.	318

horse.

	POEM.	LINE.
barges trail'd By slow *h's*;	L. of Shalott, i.	21
h That hears the corn-bin open,	The Epic	44
napkin wrought with *h* and hound,	Audley Ct.	20
turn the *h's* heads and home again	Walk. to the M.	38
a little dearer than his *h*.	Locksley H.	50
The *h* and rider reel;	Sir Galahad	8
h with wings, that would have flown,	Vision of Sin	3
men and *h's* pierced with worms.	"	209
trampled some beneath her *h's* heels,	Princess, Pro.	44
twinn'd as *h's* ear and eye.	" i.	56
wing'd *h's* dark against the stars;	"	208
three *h's* that have broken fence,	" ii.	364
shook My pulses, till to *h* we got,	" iii.	178
'To *h*!' said Ida; 'home! to *h*!'	" iv.	148
her *h* was lost I left mine)	" v.	179
they yell'd; they clash'd their arms;	"	240
stumbled mixt with floundering *h's*.	"	487
stroke on stroke the *h* and horseman.	"	512
sword to sword, and *h* to *h* we huug,	"	528
kill'd in falling from his *h*.	In Mem. vi.	40
Yet pity for a *h* o'er-driven,	" lxii.	1
those white-favour'd *h's* wait;	Con.	90
Look, a *h* at the door,	Maud, I xii.	29
left his wine and *h's* and play	" xix.	74
the hoofs of the *h's* beat, beat (rep.)	" II. v.	8
praised his land, his *h's*, his machines:	The Brook	124
While *h* and hero fell,	Lt. Brigade	44
Took *h*, and forded Usk,	Enid	161
put her *h* toward the knight,	"	200-6
good knight's *h* stands in the court;	"	370
when they both had got to *h*,	"	858
will slay him and will have his *h*.	"	911
suits Of armour on their *h's*,	"	946
Three *h's* and three goodly suits of	"	973
bound them on their *h's*, each on each,	"	1031
let the *h's* graze, and ate themselves	"	1060
take A *h* and arms for guerdon;	"	1067
And stalling for the *h's*,	"	1068
disappear'd, Leading the *h*,	"	1093
'Take Five *h's* and their armours;'	"	1258
wild Limours, Borne on a black *h*,	"	1307
'*H* and man,' he said, 'All of one	"	1332
paid with *h's* and with arms;	"	1335
without a word, from his *h* fell.	"	1357
Feeding like *h's* when you hear them	"	1454
moving out they found the stately *h*,	"	1600
then Geraint upon the *h* Mounted,	"	1606
gravely smiling, lifted her from *h*,	"	1731
weed the white *h* on the Berkshire	"	1784
got Sir Lancelot suddenly to *h*,	Elaine	159
strong neighings of the wild white *H*	"	298
There to his proud *h* Lancelot turn'd,	"	346
brought his *h* to Lancelot where he lay,	"	492
charge you that you get at once to *h*.	"	538
all in wrath he got to *h* and went;	"	562
wearied of the quest Leapt on his *h*,	"	700
Making a roan *h* caper and curvet	"	788
heard his *h* upon the stones,	"	974
tamper'd with the Lords of the White *H*,	Guinevere	16
So Lancelot got her *h*, Set her thereon,	"	121
still at evenings on before his *h*	"	254
Leagued with the Lords of the White *H*	"	569
Enoch's white *h*, and Enoch's ocean-spoil	En. Arden	93
knew her, as a horseman knows his *h*—	"	136
The *h* he drove, the boat he sold.	"	610
rolling phantom bodies of *h's* and men;	Boädicea	27
loosed their sweating *h's* from the yoke	Spec. of Iliad	2
h's stood Hard by their chariots,	"	21

horseback.

	POEM.	LINE.
aware of three tall knights On *h*,	Enid	906
lo, he sat on *h* at the door!	Guinevere	583

horseleech.

	POEM.	LINE.
like the daughters of the *h*, 'Give,	Golden Year	12

horseman.

	POEM.	LINE.
With stroke on stroke the horse and *h*,	Princess, v.	512
Three other *horsemen* waiting,	Enid	970
meet the *horsemen* of Earl Doorm,	"	1341
knew her, as a *h* knows his horse—	En. Arden	136

Hortensia.

	POEM.	LINE.
H spoke against the tax;	Princess, vii.	112
before them paused *H*, pleading;	"	117

Hosanna.

	POEM.	LINE.
singing *H* in the highest;	En. Arden	497, 502

hospitable.

	POEM.	LINE.
all men rate as kind and *h*:	Princess, i.	70

hospital.

	POEM.	LINE.
their fair college turn'd to *h*;	Princess, vii.	2

hospitality.

	POEM.	LINE.
female hands and *h*.	Princess, vi.	57-80
broken into Thro' open doors and *h*;	Enid	456

host (landlord, etc.)

	POEM.	LINE.
h, and I sat round the wassail-bowl,	The Epic	5
enter'd an old hostel, call'd mine *h*	Princess, i.	171
sent mine *h* to purchase female gear	"	196
'Fair *H* and Earl, I pray your courtesy:	Enid	403
lay lance in rest, O noble *h*,	"	496
bad the *h* Call in what men,	"	1134

	POEM.	LINE.
Call the *h* and bid him bring .	*Enid*	1249
issuing arm'd he found the *h*	"	1256
the *h*, Suddenly honest, answer'd	"	1258
Enoch was *h* one day, Philip the next,	*En. Arden*	25
their guest, their *h*, their ancient .	*Aylmer's F.*	790

host (army.)

two *h's* that lay beside the walls, .	*Princess,* vi.	362
Remember him who led your *h's* ;	*Ode on Well.*	171
craft of kindred and the Godless *h's Guinevere* .		424
summon me their King to lead mine *h's*	"	566
Hector said, and sea-like roar'd his *h* ;	*Spec. of Iliad*	1

hostage.

| here he keeps me *h* for his son.' . | *Princess,* iv. | 386 |

hostel.

So pass I *h*. hall, and grange ; .	*Sir Galahad*	81
enter'd an old *h*, call'd mine host .	*Princess,* i.	171
riding wearily, Found every *h* full,	*Enid* .	255

hostess.

| There stept a buxom *h* forth, . | *Princess,* i. | 225 |

hot.

my very ears were *h* To hear them ;	*Princess,* i.	133
heated *h* with burning fears, .	*In Mem.* cxvii.	22
h in haste to join Their luckier mates,	*Enid* .	1422
h, God's curse, with anger—	"	1508

hot-and-hot.

| To serve the *h-a-h* ; . . | *Will Water.* | 228 |

Hottentot.

| Not the Kaffir, *H*, Malay, . | *Princess,* ii. | 142 |

hotter.

| her lynx eye To fix and make me *h*, | *Princess,* iii. | 31 |

hound.

napkin wrought with horse and *h*,	*Audley Ct.*	20
males that carve the living *h*, .	*Princess,* iii.	293
love in which my *h* has part, .	*In Mem.* lxii.	2
stay'd Waiting to hear the *h's* ; .	*Enid* .	163
good chance that we shall hear the *h's*: "		182
Cavall, King Arthur's *h* of deepest	"	186
pastime both of hawk and *h*, .	"	711
seems no bolder than a beaten *h* ; .	"	910

hour.

but most she loathed the *h* .	*Mariana*	77
haunts the year's last *h's* ;	*'A spirit haunts,' etc.*	1
ere he parted said, 'This *h* is thine :	*Love and Death*	9
Alice, what an *h* was that, .	*Miller's D.* .	57
now those vivid *h's* are gone, .	"	195
Last night I wasted hateful *h's* .	*Fatima*	2
Is wearied of the rolling *h's*. .	*L. C. V. de Vere*	60
warders of the growing *h*, 'Love thou thy land,' etc.		61
bird takes every *h* for dawn ; .	*M. d'Arthur, Ep.*	11
as tho' it were The *h* just flown, .	*Gardener's D.*	82
ere an *h* had pass'd, We reach'd .	"	106
heavy clocks knolling the drowsy *h's*.	"	180
Autumn brought an *h* For Eustace,	"	202
we met ; one *h* I had, no more : .	*Ed. Morris*	104
bald brows in silent *h's* become .	*St S. Stylites*	162
make reply Is many a weary *h* ; .	*Talking O.* .	26
An *h* had past—and, sitting straight	"	109
h's that bring us all things good,	*Love and Duty*	56
sad *h's* that bring us all things ill .	"	57
every *h* Must sweat her sixty minutes	*Golden Year*	67
every *h* is saved From that eternal	*Ulysses* .	26
Were this not well, to bide mine *h*	*Two Voices* ,	76
Who is it that could live an *h* ? .	"	162
So heavenly-toned, that in that *h*. .	"	442
I wonder'd at the bounteous *h's*, .	"	451
A pleasant *h* has past away .	*Day-Dm.* .	2
The Poet-forms of stronger *h's*, .	"	226
Embraced his Eve in happy *h*, .	"	254
Still creeping with the creeping *h's*	*St Agnes' Eve*	7
Thro' many an *h* of summer suns	*Will Water.*	33
But for my pleasant *h*, 'tis gone, .	"	179
H's, when the Poet's words and looks	"	193
Let us have a quiet *h*, . .	*Vision of Sin*	73
cruel glee Forces on the freer *h*, .	"	130

	POEM.	LINE.
range of duties to the appointed *h*.	*Princess,* iii.	161
Such head from act to act, from *h* to *h*	" iv.	432
Sole comfort of my dark *h*, .	" vi.	177
many a pleasant *h* with her that's gone,	"	230
My heart an eddy from the brawling *h* : "		302
wile the length from languorous *h's*,	" vii.	48
Melts mist-like into this bright *h*, .	"	334
that the victor *H's* should scorn .	*In Mem.* i.	13
wrought At that last *h* to please him	" vi.	18
That I have been an *h* away. .	" xii.	20
an *h* For private sorrow's barren song,	" xxi.	13
But for one *h*, O Love, I strive .	" xxxv.	6
Could we forget the widow'd *h* .	" xxxix.	1
Unconscious of the sliding *h*, .	" xlii.	5
Is shadow'd by the growing *h*, .	" xlv.	3
The fruitful *h's* of still increase ; .	"	10
watch, like God, the rolling *h's* .	" l.	14
usherest in the dolorous *h* . .	" lxxi.	2
that remorseless iron *h* , . .	" lxxxiii.	14
all the train of bounteous *h's* .	"	30
The promise of the golden *h's* ? .	" lxxxiv.	106
buzzings of the honied *h's*, . .	" lxxxviii.	52
An *h's* communion with the dead ;	" xcii.	4
Thy feet have stray'd in after *h's* .	" ci.	1
wakens at this *h* of rest . .	" ciii.	6
wayward grief abuse The genial *h*	" civ.	10
Each office of the social *h* . .	" cx.	14
In watching thee from *h* to *h*, .	" cxi.	12
O days and *h's*, your work is this,	" cxvi.	1
Wild *H's* that fly with Hope and Fear,	" cxxvii.	9
O happy, and happier *h's* Await them.	*Con.*	65
O happy *h*, behold the bride .	"	69
Thro' the livelong *h's* of the dark	*Maud,* I. vi.	17
twelve sweet *h's* that past in bridal white,	" xviii.	65
For one short *h* to see . .	" II. iv.	14
sold the truth to serve the *h*, .	*Ode on Well.*	179
O Love, what *h's* were thine and mine,	*The Daisy*	1
At Florence too what golden *h's*, .	"	41
How many among us at this very *h*	*Enid* .	851
pardon me ! the madness of that *h*	"	1195
And now their *h* has come ; .	"	1545
in that perilous *h* Put hand to hand	"	1614
Was half a bandit in my lawless *h*	"	1643
crop his own sweet rose before the *h* ?'	*Vivien*	575
the one dark *h* which brings remorse,	"	613
their last *h*, A madness of farewells.	*Guinevere*	101
so late ! What *h*, I wonder, now ?'	"	159
guard thee in the wild *h* coming on,	"	443
Had his dark *h* unseen, . .	*En. Arden*	78
precious morning *h's* were lost. .	"	301
one dark *h* Here in this wood, .	"	382
That was your *h* of weakness. .	"	446
He wasted *h's* with Averill ; .	*Aylmer's F.*	109
a tongue that ruled the *h*, . .	"	194
Lightning of the *h*, the pun, .	"	441
Some niggard fraction of an *h*, .	"	450
weary and yet ever wearier *h's*, .	"	828
strong *H's* indignant work'd their wills,	*Tithonus*	18
Once in a golden *h* I cast to earth	*The Flower*	1
in an *h* Of civic tumult jam the doors,	*Lucretius*	168
that *h* perhaps Is not so far . .	"	248
till that *h*, My golden work .	"	255

Houri.

| A group of *H's* bow'd to see . | *Pal. of Art* | 102 |

hourly.

| Daily and *h*, more and more. . | *Eleänore* | 11 |

hourly-mellowing.

| Summer's *h-m* change May breathe, | *In Mem.* xc. | 9 |

house (s.)

All day within the dreamy *h*, .	*Mariana*	61
vacancy Of the dark deserted *h*. .	*Deserted H.*	12
The *h* was builded of the earth, .	"	15
The first *h* by the water-side, .	*L. of Shalott,* iv.	34
Dead-pale between the *h's* high, .	"	40
h, thro' all the level shines, .	*Mariana in the S.*	2
move about the *h* with joy, .	*Miller's D.* .	95
In this great *h* so royal-rich, .	*Pal. of Art*	101
I saw you sitting in the *h*, . .	*May Queen,* iii.	30

	POEM.	LINE.
curl'd Round their golden *h*'s,	Lotos-E's.	138
fill'd the *h* with clamour.	The Goose	36
When all the *h* is mute.	M. d'Arthur	178
'This wonder keeps the *h*.'	Gardener's D.	118
So rapt, we near'd the *h*;	"	141
been always with her in the *h*,	Dora	7
he left his father's *h*,	"	35
Then Dora went to Mary's *h*,	"	108
thou and I will live within one *h*,	"	123
abode Within one *h* together	"	165
Whose *h* is that I see?	Walk. to the M.	7
h, for so they say, Was haunted	"	27
On to God's *h* the people prest:	Two Voices	409
So in mine earthly *h* I am,	St Agnes' Eve	19
For I am of a numerous *h*,	Will Water.	89
'Let us see these handsome *h*'s	L. of Burleigh	23
She is of an ancient *h*:	Vision of Sin	140
show'd the *h*, Greek, set with busts:	Princess, Pro.	10
gave The park, the crowd, the *h*;	"	94
A Gothic ruin and a Grecian *h*,	"	225
lived an ancient legend in our *h*.	" i.	5
old and strange affection of the *h*.	"	13
cared not for the affection of the *h*;	"	26
street half garden and half *h*;	"	211
wish'd to marry; they could rule a *h*;	" ii.	441
the weird vision of our *h*:	" iii.	168
Dark *h*, by which once more I stand	In Mem. vii.	1
Are but as servants in a *h*	" xx.	3
guard the portals of the *h*;	" xxix.	12
home to Mary's *h* return'd,	" xxxi.	2
From every *h* the neighbours met,	"	9
murmur from the narrow *h*,	" xxxv.	12
builds the *h*, or digs the grave.	" xxxvi.	14
that dark *h* where she was burn.	" lix.	12
with one Of mine own *h*,	" lxxxiii.	12
in the *h* light after light Went out,	" xciv.	19
She knows but matters of the *h*,	" xcvi.	31
loved A daughter of our *h*;	" Con.	7
Living alone in an empty *h*,	Maud, I. vi.	68
all round the *h* I beheld	" xiv.	33
By which our *h*'s are torn:	" xix.	33
for his *h* an irredeemable woe;	" II. i.	22
door Of his *h* in a rainbow frill?	" ii.	17
shouted at once from the top of the *h*;	" v.	50
entertainment of a *h* Once rich,	Enid	301
Rest! the good *h*, tho' ruin'd,	"	378
reverencing the custom of the *h*	"	380
my Enid's birthday, sack'd my *h*;	"	458
when Edyrn sack'd their *h*,	"	634
found the sack and plunder of our *h*	"	694
scatter'd thro' the *h*'s of the town;	"	695
he took me from a goodly *h*,	"	708
and he brought me to a goodly *h*;	"	713
Call for the woman of the *h*,'	"	1112
the heavy breathings of the *h*,	"	1251
how suited to the *h* of one,	"	1531
moth r of the *h* There was not:	Elaine	177
their fierce design Against my *h*,	"	275
Sir M lred's brother, of a crafty *h*,	"	557
'Hark the Phantom of the *h*	"	1016
this discomfort he hath done the *h*.'	"	1066
the lifelong creature of the *h*,	"	1137
saw One of her *h*, and sent him	"	1162
in the holy *h* at Almesbury.	Guinevere	2
by the watcher in a haunted *h*,	"	73
knows false, abide and rule the *h*:	"	511
eat blow (fice of your holy *h*;	"	674
Three (ho' Iron of three *h*'s.	En Arden	11
children play'd at keeping *h*.	"	24
my *h* and this my little wife.'	"	28
keep the *h* while he was gone.	"	140
Lord is of his *h* and of his mill	"	348
as God's good angel in our *h*.	"	420
their humble, Annie, the small *h*,	"	607
daily-dwindling profits held the *h*;	"	607
all the story of his *h*.	"	705
Far gazing from the rear of Philip's *h*,	"	728
The latest *h* to landward.	"	733
kept the *h*, his chair, and last his bed.	"	827
all the *h*'s in the haven rang.	"	910
a storm he came, And shook the *h*,	Aylmer's F.	216

	POEM.	LINE.
thunders of the *h* Had fallen first,	Aylmer's F.	278
beheld the Powers of the *H*	"	267
last remaining pillar of their *h*,	"	295
Forbad her first the *h* of Averill,	"	502
weakness of a people or a *h*,	"	570
h is left unto you desolate!'	(721-37-97) "	629
deathless ruler of thy dying *h*,	"	661
when he felt the silence of his *h*	"	830
bread from out the *h*'s brought,	Spec. of Iliad	6

house (verb.)

That *h* the cold crown'd snake	Œnone	36
H in the shade of comfortable roofs,	St S. Stylites	105

household.

Her *h* fled the danger,	The Goose	54
Leaving her *h* and good father	Elaine	14
lift the *h* out of poverty;	En. Arden	482

housel.

nor sought, Wrapt in her grief, for *h*	Guinevere	147

housemaid.

daughter and his *h* were the boys.	Princess, i.	163

hove.

how there *h* a dusky barge,	M. d'Arthur	193

hovell'd.

the poor are *h* and hustled together	Maud, I. i.	34

hover.

talk About his path, and *h* near	Day-Dm.	122
Wings flutter, voices *h* clear:	Sir Galahad	78
And the bird of prey will *h*,	Maud, I. xx.	2
they *h* about my bed— .	Grandmother	83

hovering.

h o'er the dolorous strait	In Mem. lxxxiii.	19
sweet tendance *h* over him,	Enid	1774
Whenever in her *h* to and fro	Elaine	325

hoveringly.

h a sword Now over and now under,	Lucretius	61

how.

setting the *how much* before the *h*,	Golden Year	11

howd (hold.)

who's to *h* the land ater meä	N. Farmer	58

howl.

I did not hear the dog *h*, mother,	May Queen, iii.	21
Crack them now for yourself, and *h*,	Maud, II. v.	56
h in tune With nothing but the	Sea Dreams	252

howled.

She *h* aloud, 'I am on fire	Pal. of Art	285

howlest.

h, issuing out of night,	In Mem. lxxi.	2

howling.

The wind is *h* in turret and tree.	The Sisters	9
lie *H* in outer darkness. To —,	With Pal. of Art	16
The *h*'s from forgotten fields	In Mem. xi.	16
world *h* forced them into bonds,	Vivien	594

how much.

setting the *h m* before the *how*	Golden Year	11

hubbub.

A sudden *h* shook the hall.	Day-Dm.	139
A *h* in the court of half the maids	Princess, iv.	455
for those That stir this *h*—	"	488
liars belied in the *h* of lies;	Maud, I. iv.	51
Thro' the *h* of the market I steal,	" II. v.	68
once more what meant the *h* here?	Enid	264

huckster.

This *h* put down war!	Maud, I. x.	44

huddled.

The cattle *h* on the lea;	In Mem. xv.	6
h here and there on mound and	Enid	1651

huddling.

h slant in furrow-cloven falls	Princess, vii.	192

hue.

H's of the silken sheeny woof	Madeline	52
shapes and *h*'s that please me well!	Pal. of Art	14

	POEM.	LINE.
Touch'd with a somewhat darker *h*, | *Margaret* | . 50
in *h's* to dim The Titianic Flora. | *Gardener's D.* | 166
By Cupid-boys of blooming *h*— | . *Day-Dm.* | 278
Moved with violence, changed in *h*, | *Vision of Sin* | 34
h Of that cap upon her brows. | " | 141
Academic silks, in *h* The lilac, | *Princess,* ii. | 2
the other distance and the *h's* Of promise; | " iv. | 68
thoughts that changed from *h* to *h*, | " v. | 192
as the fiery Sirius alters *h*, | " v. | 252
past A shadow, and her *h* changed, | " vi. | 91
h's are faint And mix with hollow | *In Mem.* lxix. | 3
The distance takes a lovelier *h*, | " cxiv. | 6
hair In gloss and *h* the chesnut, | *The Brook* 72, | 207
bays, The peacock's neck in *h*; | *The Daisy* | 14
tribe of woman, dress'd in many *h's, Enid.* | | 1446
a but less vivid *h* Than of that islet | *Aylmer's F.* | 64

huge.

Before an oak, so hollow *h* and old | *Vivien* | . 3

hugest.

place which now Is this world's *h*, | *Elaine* | . 77

hugged.

h and never *h* it close enough, | . *Princess,* vi. | 195
clung to him and *h* him close; | . *Vivien* | 794-7

Hugh.

'this' he said 'was *H*'s at Agincourt;' | *Princess, Pro.* | 25

hull.

till the *h* Look'd one black dot | . *M. d' Arthur* | 270
if my brainpan were an empty *h*, | . *Princess,* ii. | 376

hum (s.)

With the *h* of swarming bees | . *Eleänore* | 29

hum (verb.)

people *h* About the column's base, | *St S. Stylites* | 37
here by thee will *h* the bee, | . *A Farewell.* | 11
h The murmur of a happy Pan: | *In Mem.* xxiii. | 11
by and by began to *h* An air | . *Guinevere* | 160
swamp, where *h's* the droppingsnipe, | *On a Mourner* | 9

human.

not less divine, But more *h* in your moods, | *Margaret* | 47
Larger than *h* on the frozen hills. | *M. d' Arthur* | 183
for I bear, Tho' man, yet *h*, | . *Princess,* iv. | 405
Thou seemest *h* and divine, | . *In Mem. Pro.* | 13
Known and unknown: *h*, divine; | " cxxviii. | 5
Thou art the highest and most *h* too, | *Guinevere* | 642
looking hardly *h*, strangely clad, | . *En. Arden* | 639

human-amorous.

Her Deity false in *h-a* tears; | . *Lucretius* | . 90

human-hearted.

The *h-h* man I loved, | . *In Mem.* xiii. | 11

humankind.

springs the crowning race of *h* | . *Princess,* vii. | 279

humbling.

now desired the *h* of their best, | . *Enid* | . 1485

humiliated.

The woman should have borne, *h*, | . *Aylmer's F.* | 356
me they lash'd and *h*, | . *Boädicea* | 49-67

humility.

she had fail'd In sweet *h*; | . *Princess,* vii. | 214
all too free For such a wise *h* | . *Ode on Well.* | 249

hummed.

Audley feast *H* like a hive | . *Audley Ct.* | 4
Roundhead rode, And *h* a surly hymn. | *Talking O.* | 300
I turn'd and *h* a bitter song | . *The Letters* | 9
father's latest word *h* in her ear, | . *Elaine* | . 776

hummeth.

At noon the wild bee *h*. | . *Claribel* | 11

humming.

h of the drowsy pulpit-drone | . *To J. M. K.* | 10
while I past he was *h* an air, | . *Maud,* I. xiii. | 17
smooth'd The glossy shoulder, *h* to himself. | *Elaine* | 347

humour.

h of the golden prime | . *Arabian N's.* | 120
According to my *h* ebb and flow. | . *D. of F. Wom.* | 134

	POEM.	LINE.
He scarcely hit my *h*, | . *Ed. Morris.* | 76
According as his *h's* lead, | . *Day-Dm.* | 207

humpbacked.

There by the *h* willow; | . *Walk. to the M.* | 23

hunched.

if a man were halt or *h*, | . *Guinevere* | . 42

hundred-throated.

As 'twere a *h-t* nightingale, | . *Vision of Sin* | 27

hung.

H in the golden Galaxy. | *L. of Shalott,* iii. | 12
A mighty silver bugle *h* | " | 16
thunder-clouds that, *h* on high | . *Eleänore* | 98
h In masses thick with milky cones. | *Miller's D.* | 55
h with arms green and blue, | . *Pal. of Art* | 61
choice paintings of wise men I *h* | . " | 131
H tranced from all pulsation, | . *Gardener's D.* | 255
seal, that *h* From Allan's watch, | . *Dora* | . 132
blackbird on the pippin *h* | . *Audley Ct.* | 37
stars that *h* Love-charm'd to listen: | *Love and Duty* | 72
with a mute observance *h*. | . *Locksley H.* | 22
h with grooms and porters on the bridge, | *Godiva* | 2
forefathers' arms and armour *h*. | . *Princess, Pro.* | 24
wild woods that *h* about the town; | " i. | 90
o'er his head Uranian Venus *h*, | " | . 239
H, shadow'd from the heat: | " ii. | 435
melted Florian's fancy as she *h*, | " iv. | 351
on my shoulder *h* their heavy hands, | " | . 531
horse to horse we *h*, | " v. | 528
H round the sick: the maidens came, | " vii. | 7
on her foot she *h* A moment, | . " | . 64
an Alpine harebell *h* with tears | . " | . 100
H in the shadow of a heaven? | *In Mem.* xvi. | 10
h to hear The rapt oration | " lxxxvi. | 31
On thee the loyal-hearted *h*, | " cix. | 5
H over her dying bed— | . *Maud,* I. xix. | 36
h and so the matter *h*; | . *The Brook* | 144-8
weight and fate of Europe *h*. | . *Ode on Well.* | 240
loosed a mighty purse, *H* at his belt, | *Enid* | . 872
no heart To wake him, but *h* o'er him | " | . 1219
h his head, and halted in reply, | " | . 1659
carrion crows *H* like a cloud | . *Vivien* | . 449
she turn'd away, she *h* her head, | . " | . 736
think this fruit is *h* too high | . *Elaine* | . 770
o'er her *H* The silken case | . " | . 1142
h upon him, play'd with him | . *En. Arden* | . 350
Enoch *h* A moment on her words, | " | . 873
hall, *H* with a hundred shields, | . *Aylmer's F.* | 15
h With wings of brooding shelter | " | . 138
and Jenny *h* on his arm. | . *Grandmother* | 42

Hungary.

shall I shriek if a *H* fail? | . *Maud,* I. iv. | 46

hunger (s.)

In *h's* and in thirsts, fevers and cold | *St S. Stylites* | 12
grief and mother's *h* in her eye. | . *Princess,* vi. | 130
in her *h* mouth'd and mumbled it, | " | . 196
A *h* seized my heart; | . *In Mem.* xciv. | 21
Bearing a lifelong *h* in his heart. | . *En. Arden* | . 79
eyes Full of that lifelong *h*, | . " | . 461

hunger (verb.)

Long for my life, or *h* for my death, | *Enid* | . 930

hunger'd.

true heart, which *h* for her peace | . *En. Arden* | . 271

hungry.

Every captain waits *H* for honour, | *Princess,* v. | 304

hunt (s.)

Forgetful of the falcon and the *h*, | *Enid* | . 51
for his leave To see the *h*, | . " | . 155
For Lancelot, and forgetful of the *h*; | " | . 159
but come like you to see the *h*, | . " | . 179
while they listen'd for the distant *h*, | " | . 184
A little vext at losing of the *h*, | . " | . 234

hunt (verb.)

Do *h* me, day and night.' | . *D. of F. Wom.* | 256
Like a dog, he *h's* in dreams, | . *Locksley H.* | 79
'They *h* old trails' said Cyril | . *Princess,* ii. | 368
h them for the beauty of their skins; | " | . 149

	POEM.	LINE.
hunted.		
swallow stopt as he the *h* the bee,	Poet's Song	9
hunter (man.)		
with puff'd cheek the belted *h* blew	Pal. of Art	63
the *h* rued His rash intrusion,	Princess, iv.	185
Man is the *h*; woman is his game :	" v.	147
No keener *h* after glory breathes.	Elaine	156
h's round a hunted creature draw	Aylmer's F.	429
her that o'er her wounded *h* wept	Lucretius	89
hunter (horse.)		
And rode his *h* down.	Talking O.	104
hunting.		
order to let blow His horns for *h* .	Enid	153
The King was *h* in the wild ;	The Victim	31
hunting-dress.		
wearing neither *h*-*d* Nor weapon,	Enid	165
hunting-morn.		
the third day from the *h*-*m* .	Enid	597
hurl.		
h their lances in the sun ;	Locksley H.	170
he stopt we long'd to *h* together,	Vivien	270
hurl'd.		
bolts are *h* Far below them .	Lotos-E's.	156
And *h* the pan and kettle.	The Goose	28
h his huge limbs out of bed,	Enid	124
h it toward the squire.	"	872
h into it Against the stronger :	Elaine	461
Leapt on him, and *h* him headlong,	Guinevere	107
hurling.		
Each *h* down a heap of things	Enid	1442
hurricane.		
like the smoke in a *h* whirl'd	Boädicea	59
hurried.		
Edith's eager fancy *h* with him	Aylmer's F.	208
hurry (s.)		
all three in *h* and fear Ran to her,	Elaine	1018
hurry (verb.)		
By thirty hills I *h* down,	The Brook	27
yearn to *h* precipitously	Boädicea	58
hurrying.		
Myriads of rivulets *h* thro' the lawn,	Princess, vii.	205
Driving, *h*, marrying, burying,	Maud, II. v.	12
Another *h* past, a man-at-arms,	Enid	1375
hurt (adj.)		
almost all that is, hurting the *h*—	Aylmer's F.	572
hurt (s.)		
helps the *h* that Honour feels,	Locksley H.	105
h that drain'd her dear lord's life.	Enid	1365
fearing for his *h* and loss of blood,	"	1625
King's own leech to look into his *h* ;	"	1771
Geraint lay healing of his *h*,	"	1779
tho' he call'd his wound a little *h* .	Elaine	848
when Sir Lancelot's deadly *h* was	"	900
And treat their loathsome *h*'s	Guinevere	678
hurt (verb.)		
Love is *h* with jar and fret.	Miller's D.	209
their own blows they *h* themselves,	Princess, vi.	33
trust that there is no one *h* to death,	"	225
H in his first tilt was my son,	Elaine	196
parted from the jousts *H* in the side,'	"	620
h Whom she would soothe,	Guinevere	352
H in that night of sudden ruin	En. Arden	565
by a keeper shot at, slightly *h*,	Aylmer's F.	548
hurting.		
almost all that is, *h* the hurt—	Aylmer's F.	572
husband.		
As the *h* is, the wife is :	Locksley H.	47
Enid, but to please her *h*'s eye,	Enid	11
hand to hand beneath her *h*'s heart,	"	1615
I am thine *h* not a smaller soul,	Guinevere	562
of what he wish'd, Enoch, your *h*:	En. Arden	201
no fear that her first *h* lives ?	"	807

	POEM.	LINE.
near'd Her *h* inch by inch,	Aylmer's F.	807
'No trifle,' groan'd the *h* ;	Sea Dreams	141
husbandry.		
with equal *h* The woman were an .	Princess, i.	129
hush (s.)		
heard In the dead *h* the papers	Princess, iv.	371
in the *h* of the moonless nights,	Maud, I. i.	42
a *h* with the setting moon.	" xxii.	18
hush (verb.)		
If prayers will not *h* thee.	Lilian	27
h'es half the babbling Wye,	In Mem. xix.	7
H, the Dead March wails	Ode on Well.	267
hush'd.		
air is damp, and *h*, and close, 'A spirit haunts,' etc.		13
The town was *h* beneath us :	Audley Ct.	13
H all the groves from fear of	Sir L. and Q. G.	13
The Wye is *h* nor moved along,	In Mem. xix.	9
h my deepest grief of all,	"	10
h itself at last Hopeless of answer :	Aylmer's F.	542
husk.		
rent the veil Of his old *h*:	Two Voices	11
phantom *h*'s of something foully done,	Lucretius	160
hustings.		
so, when the rotten *h* shake	Maud, I. vi.	54
hustled.		
h together, each sex, like swine,	Maud, I. i.	34
hut.		
the great river in a boatman's *h*.	Elaine	278
a *h*, Half *h*, half native cavern.	En. Arden	560
h's At random scatter'd,	Aylmer's F.	149
huzzin'.		
H an' maäzin' the blessed feälds .	N. Farmer	62
hyacinth.		
sheets of *h* That seem'd the heavens	Guinevere	387
Hyades.		
Thro' scudding drifts the rainy *H*	Ulysses	10
hymn.		
sound Of pious *h*'s and psalms,	St S. Stylites	33
And humm'd a surly *h*.	Talking O.	300
I hear a noise of *h*'s ;	Sir Galahad	28
bearded Victor of ten-thousand *h*'s,	Princess, iii.	334
ourself have often tried Valkyrian *h*'s,	" iv.	121
mine own phantom chanting *h*'s ?	In Mem. cvii.	10
whose *h*'s Are chanted in the	Vivien	615
would jar all the *h*'s of heaven :	Sea Dreams	251
Hyperion.		
or of older use All-seeing *H*—	Lucretius	126
hypocrisy.		
H, I saw it in him at once.	Sea Dreams	64
hypothesis.		
If that *h* of theirs be sound' .	Princess, iv.	2
hysterics.		
The blind *h* of the Celt ;	In Mem. cviii.	16

I

I.
learns the use of '*I*' and 'me,'	In Mem. xliv.	6

ice.
bump'd the *i* into three several stars,	The Epic	12
goes, like glittering bergs of *i*,	Princess, iv.	53
old-world mammoth bulk'd in *i*,	" v.	142
find him dropt upon the firths of *i*,	" vii.	191
i Makes daggers at the sharpen'd	In Mem. cvii.	7
spires of *i* are toppled down,	" cxxvi.	12
oft we saw the glisten Of *i* .	The Daisy	36
skater on *i* that hardly bears him,	Hendecasyllabics	6

ice-ferns.
Fine as *i*-*f* on January panes	Aylmer's F.	222

Icenian.
Hear *I*, Catieuchlanian,	Boädicea, 10, 34,	47
Gods have heard it, O *I*,	"	21
Shout *I*, Catieuchlanian,	"	57

CONCORDANCE TO

iciele.
	POEM.	LINE.
lance that splinter'd like an i,	Enid	938

Ida (mountain of Phrygia.)
There lies a vale in I,	Œnone	1
O mother I, many-fountain'd I,	"	22
Dear mother I, (rep.)	"	
whatever Oread haunt The knolls of I,	"	73
all the pines of I shook to see	Lucretius	86

Ida (heroine of 'The Princess.')
let us know The Princess I waited:	Princess, ii.	7
affianced years ago To the Lady I:	"	198
silver litanies, The work of I,	"	454
had the care of Lady I's youth,	iii.	69
she won the heart Of I:	"	72
Princess I seem'd a hollow show,	"	169
cast A liquid look on I,	iv.	350
at eve and dawn With I, I, I,	"	413
The mellow breaker murmur'd I.	"	416
lend full tongue, O noble I,	"	423
now will cruel I keep her back;	v.	81
What dares not I do	"	166
is not I right? They worth it?	"	180
much that I claims as right	"	194
You talk almost like I: she can talk;	"	201
Arac's word is thrice As ours with I:	"	218
if I yet would cede our claim,	"	323
glance he caught Thro' open doors of I	"	333
I's answer, in a royal hand,	"	361
With Psyche's babe, was I watching us,	"	501
high upon the palace I stood	vi.	14
clamouring on, till I heard,	"	134
I spoke not, rapt upon the child.	"	203
'I—'sdeath! you blame the man;	"	204
I spoke not, gazing on the ground,	"	210
heard her say it—' Our I has a heart'—	"	218
But I stood nor spoke,	"	249
'Ay so' said I with a bitter smile,	"	296
I with a voice, that like a bell	"	311
Was I by the throne,	"	337
Then the voice of I sounded,	"	352
sadness on the soul Of I fell	vii.	14
When Cyril pleaded, I came behind	"	63
shriek 'You are not I;'	"	80
call her I, tho' I knew her not,	"	81
hollow shows: nor more Sweet I:	"	120
if you be that I whom I knew,	"	132
spirit closed with I's at the lips;	"	143
'But I,' Said I tremulously,	"	313

Idalian.
I Aphrodite beautiful	Œnone	170

ideal.
He worships your i.'	Princess, ii.	38
nurse a blind I like a girl,	" iii.	201
true To that i which he bears?	In Mem. li.	10

idioted.
being much befooled and i	Aylmer's F.	590

idiotlike.
mumbling, i it seem'd,	En. Arden	640

idle.
manners are not i, but the fruit	Guinevere	333

idleness.
hatch'd in silken-folded i;	Princess, iv.	49

idol.
the i of my youth,	Gardener's D.	271
wild figtree split Their monstrous i's,	Princess, iv.	62
The rosy i of her solitudes,	En. Arden	90
clasp These i's to herself?	Lucretius	165

idolater.
Count the more base i of the two;	Aylmer's F.	670

idolatry.
waste and havock as the idolatries,	Aylmer's F.	640
The red fruit of an old i—	"	762

idol-fires.
wind to puff your i-f,	'Love thou thy land,' etc.	69

Idris.
pushing could move The chair of I.	Enid	543

Idyll.
	POEM.	LINE.
she found a small Sweet I,	Princess, vii.	176
I consecrate with tears--These I's.	Ded. of Idylls	5

ignominy.
hide their faces, miserable in i!	Boädicea	51

ignorance.
more from i than will.	Walk, to the M.	100
Drink to heavy I!	Vision of Sin	193
that where blind and naked I	Vivien	514

ignorant.
I, devising their own daughter's death!	Aylmer's F.	783

Ilion.
Troas and I's column'd citadel,	Œnone	13
I like a mist rose into towers.	Tithonus	63
The fire that left a roofless I,	Lucretius	65

ill.
thro' life and death, thro' good and i,	The Poet	5
grief became A solemn scorn of i's.	D. of F. Wom.	228
then why not i for good?	Love and Duty	27
Still heaping on the fear of i.	Two Voices	107
Will be the final goal of i,	In Mem. liii.	2
Who loved, who suffer'd countless i's,	" lv.	17
and all the measureless i.	Maud, I. iv.	56
For years, a measureless i,	" II. ii.	49
than to rail at the i;	" III. vi.	57
i and weary, alone and cold,	The Daisy	96
i for him, who bettering not.	Will	10
who most have done them i.	Enid	1725
This good is in it, whatsoe'er of i,	Elaine	1201

ill-content.
Dwelt with eternal summer, i-c.	En. Arden	563

ill-fated.
If that I am, what lot is mine	Love and Duty	33

illiterate.
not i; nor of those Who dabbling	The Brook	92

ill-omen'd.
Remembering his i-o song,	Princess, vi.	143

illumined.
A fuller light i all,	Day-Dm.	137

illumineth.
I saw, wherever light i,	D. of F. Wom.	14

ill-usage.
Or sicken with i-u,	Princess, v.	83

ill-used.
Chanted from an i-u race of men.	Lotos-E's.	165
Francis, muttering, like a man i-u,	M. d'Arthur, Ep.	12

Illyrian.
I woodlands, echoing falls Of water	To E. L.	1

image.
An i seem'd to pass the door,	Mariana in the S.	65, 74
was an i of the mighty world;	M. d'Arthur	235
play with flying forms and i's,	Gardener's D.	59
Vast i's in glimmering dawn,	Two Voices	305
An i comforting the mind,	In Mem. lxxxiv.	51
To one pure i of regret.	" ci.	24
as her i in marble above;	Maud, I. iv.	58
unconsciously Some i of himself—	Ded. of Idylls	3
Full often the sweet i of one face,	Elaine	878
tomb Be costly, and her i thereupon.	"	1330
My wistful eyes on two fair i's,	Sea Dreams	232

imagination.
Poet-princess with her grand I's.	Princess, iii.	257
I's calm and fair,	In Mem. xciii.	10
strong i roll A sphere of stars	" cxxi.	6

imagined.
I more than seen, the skirts of France.	Princess, Con.	48

imagining.
feed with crude i's	'Love thou thy land,' etc.	10

imbecile.
the man became I;	Aylmer's F.	836

imbedded.
with golden yolks I and injellied;	Audley Ct.	25

	imbibing.	POEM.	LINE.		*incompetent.*	POEM.	LINE.
O to watch the thirsty plants *I*		*Princess*, ii.	401	must I be *I* of memory :		*Two Voices*	375
	imbower				*incorporate.*		
silent isle *i's* The Lady of Shalott,		*L. of Shalott*, i.	17	grow *i* into thee.		*In Mem.* ii.	16
	imbowered.				*increase* (s.)		
I vaults of pillar'd palm,		*Arabian N's.*	39	for the good and *i* of the world		*Ed. Morris*	44,51,92
	imitate.			The fruitful hours of still *i*;		*In Mem.* xlv.	10
I's God, and turns her face		*On a Mourner*	2		*increase* (verb.)		
	immantled.			While the stars burn, the moons *i*,		*To J. S.*	71
I in ambrosial dark,		*In Mem.* lxxxviii.	14	watch her harvest ripen, her herd *i*,		*Maud*, III. vi.	25
	immersed.				*increased.*		
I in rich foreshadowings of the world,		*Princess*, vii.	293	day *i* from heat to heat,		*Mariana in t::e S.*	39
the Queen *i* in such a trance,		*Guinevere*	398	and with each The year *i*.		*Gardener's D.*	195
	immodesty.			the light *i* With freshness		*Two Voices*	404
Accuse her of the least *i*:		*Enid*	960	Thy latter days *i* with peace		*Will Water.*	219
	immolation.			For them the light of life *i*,		*In. Mem. Con.*	74
than by single act Of *i*,		*Princess*, iii.	268	*i*, Upon a pastoral slope as fair,		*Maud*, I. xviii.	18
	immortality.			*I* Geraint's, who heaved his blade		*Enid*	572
feel their *i* Die in their hearts		*The Mermaid*	29	His beauty still with his years *i*,		*The Victim.*	35
Me only cruel *i* Consumes : .		*Tithonus*	5		*increasing.*		
I ask'd thee, 'Give me *i*.'		"	15	Fame again *I* gave me use.		*Vivien*	344
	impaled.				*India.*		
The King *i* him for his piracy :		*Vivien*	419	Where some refulgent sunset of *I*		*Milton*	13
	impart.				*Indian.*		
i The life that almost dies in me ;		*In Mem.* xviii.	15	*I* reeds blown from his silver tongue,		*The Poet*	13
	imperial-moulded.			The throne of *I* Cama slowly sail'd		*Pal. of Art*	115
O *i-m* form, And beauty		*Guinevere*	544	less from *I* craft Than beelike		*Princess*, iv.	180
	imperious.			Fire-hollowing this in *I* fashion,		*En. Arden*	570
I, and of haughtiest lineaments.		*Enid*	190	My lady's *I* kinsman unannounced		*Aylmer's F.*	190
	implied.			My lady's *I* kinsman rushing in,		"	593
that vague fear *i* in death ;		*In Mem.* xl.	14		*indifference.*		
	imply.			And Love the *i* to be,		*In. Mem.* xxvi.	12
to begin *implies* to end :		*Two Voices*	339	Attain the wise *i* of the wise ;		*A Dedication*	8
	impossible.				*indignant.*		
Things in an Aylmer deem'd *i*,		*Aylmer's F.*	305	she returned *I* to the Queen ;		*Enid*	202,414
Such a match as this ! *I*, prodigious !'		"	315	That makes me most *i*;		*Vivien*	191
but him I proved *i*;		*Lucretius*	190	On either side the hearth, *i*;		*Aylmer's F.*	288
	impotence.				*indignantly.*		
In *i* of fancied power.		*A Character*	24	And yet he answer'd half *i*.		*Vivien*	254
	impressions.				*indignation.*		
took Full easily all *i* from below,		*Guinevere*	635	What heats of *i* when we heard		*Princess*, v.	365
	imprisoning.			white neck Was rosed with *i*;		" vi.	324
pillar'd palm *I* sweets,		*Arabian N's.*	40		*individual.*		
	impulse.			And the *i* withers,		*Locksley H.*	142
An inner *i* rent the veil		*Two Voices*	10		*individuality.*		
	impute.			Distinct in *individualities*,		*Princess*, vii.	275
i a crime Are pronest to it, and *i*		*Vivien*	674		*induce.*		
	imputing.			persecute Opinion and *i* a time		*'You ask me why,'*	13
Polluting, and *i* her whole self,		*Vivien*	652		*inexorable.*		
	inactive.			No saint—*i*—no tenderness—		*Princess*, v.	504
lying thus *i*, doubt and gloom,		*En. Arden*	113	fall the battle-axe, unexhausted, *i*.		*Boädicea*	56
	inane.				*infancy.*		
Ruining along the illimitable *i*,		*Lucretius*	40	In the silken sail of *i*,		*Arabian N's.*	2
	incense (s.)			O'er the deep mind of dauntless *i*.		*Ode to Mem.*	36
Like two streams of *i* free		*Eleänore*	58	With those old faces of our *i*		*Lotos-E's.*	111
A cloud of *i* of all odour		*Pal. of Art*	39	To ailing wife or wailing *i*		*Aylmer's F.*	177
An I that sweet *i* rise ?'		"	44		*infant.*		
sweet *i* rose and never fail'd,		"	45	leddest by the hand thine *i* Hope.		*Ode to Mem.*	30
	incense (verb.)			more than *I's* in their sleep.		*Princess*, vii.	37
fear'd To *i* the Head once more ;		*Princess*, vii.	62	An *i* crying in the night : (rep.)		*In Mem.* liii.	13
	inch.			shaping an *i* ripe for his birth,		*Maud*, I. iv.	34
Why *i* by *i* to darkness crawl ?		*Two Voices*	200	laid the feeble *i* in his arms ;		*En. Arden*	152
in the pause she crept an *i* Nearer,		*Guinevere*	523	Shall we deal with it as an *i* ?		*Boädicea*	33
only near'd Her husband *i* by *i*,		*Aylmer's F.*	807		*infinite.*		
	incited.			Because the scale is *i*.		*Two Voices*	93
each *i* each to noble deeds.		*Vivien*	264		*infinity.*		
	incline.			Like emblems of *i*, The trenched		*Ode to Mem.*	103
over rainy mist *i's* A gleaming crag		*Two Voices*	188		*inflame.*		
Till all thy life one way *i*		*On a Mourner*	19	twelve-divided concubine 'To *i* the		*Aylmer's F.*	760
					inflamed.		
				like a rising moon, *I* with wrath :		*Princess*, i.	59

212 CONCORDANCE TO

	inflate.	POEM.	LINE.
I themselves with some insane		*Vivien*	683

influence.

self-same *i* Controlleth all the soul	*Eleänore*		114
i of mild-minded melancholy;	*Lotos-E's.*		109
Who forged that other *i,*	*Two Voices*		283
use Her *i* on the mind,	*Will Water.*		12
blight Of ancient *i* and scorn.	*Princess,* ii.		153
Twice as magnetic to sweet *i*'s	" v.		183
By many a varying *i*	" vi.		250
A kindlier *i* reigned ;	" vii.		5
in their silent *i* as they sat	" *Con.*		15
Let random *i*'s glance	*In Mem.* xlviii.		2
Mourn for the man of amplest *i,*	*Ode on Well.*		27

influence-rich.

i-r to soothe and save	*In Mem.* lxxix.		14

inform.

beauty doth *i* Stillness with love,	*Day-Dm.*		91
she goes to *i* The Princess :	*Princess,* iii.		46

infuse.

Desire in me to *i* my tale of love.	*Princess,* v.		230

ingraven.

rind *i* 'For the most fair,'	*Œnone*		70

ingress.

for your *i* here Upon the skirt	*Princess,* v.		209

ingroove.

be free To *i* itself	'*Love thou thy land,*' etc.		46

inhabitant.

liker to the *i* Of some clear planet	*Princess,* ii.		21

inherit.

Our sons *i* us : our looks are strange !	*Lotos-E's.*		118

inheritance.

some *i* Of such a life,	*Ded. of Idylls*		31

inherited.

he that next *i* the tale	*Princess,* lv.		569

injellied.

golden yolks Imbedded and *i*;	*Audley Ct.*		25

injuries.

life-long *i* burning unavenged,	*Enid*		1544

inlaid.

Distinct with vivid stars *i,*	*Arabian N's.*		90

inlay.

deep *i* Of braided blooms	*Arabian N's.*		28

inlet.

glaring sand and *i*'s bright,	*Mariana in the S.*		8

inn.

lighted at a ruin'd *i,*	*Vision of Sin*		62

innocent.

had wrought on many an *i.*	*Enid*		1027

innocent-arch.

So *i-a,* so cunning-simple,	*Lilian*		13

innumerable.

bark and blacken *i,*	*Boädicea*		13

inosculated.

(For so they said themselves) *i* ;	*Princess,* iii.		73

inquire.

Who scarcely darest to *i,*	*In Mem.* iv.		7

inrunning.

at the *i* of a little brook	*Elaine*		1379

insanity.

animal heat and dire *i.*	*Lucretius*		163

inscription.

some *i* ran along the front,	*Princess,* i.		209
saw you not the *i* on the gate,	" ii.		177
'for that *i* there, I think	" ii.		207
I urged the fierce *i* on the gate,	" iii.		125

insect.

i's prick Each leaf into a gall)	*Talking O.*		69
eagle's wing, or *i*'s eye ;	*In Mem.* cxxiii.		6
lightning flash of *i* and of bird.	*En. Arden*		576

	insipid.	POEM.	LINE.
I as the Queen upon a card ;		*Aylmer's F.*	28

insolence.

blustering I know not what Of *i*	*Princess,* v.		387
Smelling of musk and of *i,*	*Maud,* I. vi.		45

insolent.

I, brainless, heartless !	*Aylmer's F.*		368

inspiration.

Ancient founts of *i* well.	*Locksley H.*		188

instance.

deeming Merlin overborne By *i,*	*Vivien*		650
That wilderness of single *i*'s,	*Aylmer's F.*		437

instep.

brandish'd plume Brushing his *i,*	*Enid*		1209

instinct.

of the moral *i* would she prate	*Pal. of Art*		205
less from Indian craft Than beelike *i*	*Princess,* iv.		181
being, all dipt In Angel *i*'s,	" vii.		302
that mysterious *i* wholly died.	*En. Arden*		522

institute.

their *I* Of which he was the patron.	*Princess, Pro.*		5
patient leaders of their *I*	"		58
fenced it round with gallant *i*'s,	" v.		382

insufficiencies.

temperate eyes On glorious *i,*	*In Mem.* cxi.		3

insult.

sounds of *i,* shame, and wrong,	*D. of F. Wom.*		19
brook no further *i* but are gone.'	*Princess,* vi.		322
avenge this *i,* noble Queen,	*Enid*		215
this great *i* done the Queen.'	" 425,		571
Crave pardon for that *i*	"		583
wretched dress, A wretched *i* on you,"			1177

inwrathed.

I sometimes in wandering mist,	*St S. Stylites*		74

intellect.

i to part Error from crime ;	*Isabel*		14
kingly *i* shall feed,	'*Clear-headed friend,*' etc.		20
All-subtilising *i*:	*In Mem.* lxxxiv.		48
Or ev'n for *i* to reach	" xciv.		47
Seraphic *i* and force	" cviii.		5
who knew thee keen In *i.*	" cxii.		6

intelligence.

The great *I*'s fair	*In Mem.* lxxxiv.		21

intelligible.

From over-fineness not *i.*	*Vivien*		645

intend.

The thesis which thy words *i*—	*Two Voices*		338

intense.

will one beam be less *i,*	*Two Voices*		40
fraught With a passion so *i.*	*Maud,* II. ii.		59

intensity.

Sometimes, with most *i* Gazing,	*Eleänore*		82

intent (adj.)

have been *i* On that veil'd picture—	*Gardener's D.*		264
kept mine own *I* on her	*Princess,* ii.		419

intent (s.)

almost ere I knew mine own *i,*	*Gardener's D.*		145
eye seem'd full Of a kind *i* to me	*Maud,* I. vi.		41

interchange.

met With *i* of gift.	*Pal. of Art*		144
frequent *i* of foul and fair	*En. Arden*		529

interest.

To close the *i*'s of all.	'*Love thou thy land,*' etc.		36
a closer *i* flourish'd up,	*Princess,* vii.		98
catch The far-off interest of tears	*In Mem.* i.		8

interlaced.

shadow'd grots of arches *i,*	*Pal. of Art*		51

interlocked.

My lady with her fingers *i,*	*Aylmer's F.*		199

interpret.

True love *i*'s—right alone.	*Miller's D.*		188
stupid heart To *i* ear and eye,	*Elaine*		938

interpretation.	POEM.	LINE.
tongue To blare its own *i*— . . .	*Elaine*	. 939

interpreter.
| *I* between the Gods and men, | *Princess,* vii. | 303 |
| in the mouths of base *i*'s, | *Vivien* | . 644 |

interpreting.
| broke out *i* my thoughts! . . . | *Princess,* iii. | 258 |

interspace.
| flowing rapidly between Their *i*'s | *Arabian N's.* | 84 |
| The lucid *i* of world and world, | *Lucretius* | . 105 |

interval.
| fill'd with light The *i* of sound. . | *D. of F. Wom.* | 172 |
| Miriam watch'd and dozed at *i*'s, | *Eu. Arden* | . 908 |

intimacy.
| Bound in an immemorial *i*, . . | *Aylmer's F.* 39, | 136 |

intonation.
| Such happy *i*, ... | *Amphion* | . 18 |

intone.
| Delicate-handed priest *i* ; . . . | *Maud,* I. viii. | 11 |

intrusion.
| hunter rued His rash *i*, manlike, . | *Princess,* iv. | 186 |

invade.
| *I* Even with a verse your holy woe. | *To J. S.* | . 7 |

invaded.
'Our land *i*, 'sdeath !	*Princess,* v.	266
Roman Cæsar first *I* Britain, . .	*Enid* .	. 746
As this great prince *i* us, . . .	" .	. 747

invalid.
| *i*, since my will Seal'd not the bond— | *Princess,* v. | 388 |

invective.
| a tide of fierce *I* seem'd to wait . | *Princess,* iv. | 451 |

invent.
| the years *i* Each month is various | *Two Voices* | 73 |
| when did woman ever yet *i*?' . | *Princess,* ii. | 369 |

invented.
| Was this fair charm *i* by yourself? | *Vivien* | . 370 |

inventor.
| O mighty-mouth'd *i* of harmonies | *Milton* | 1 |

invested.
| Slipt round in the dark and *i* you, | *Princess,* iv. | 385 |

invited.
| For I am not *i*, ... | *Maud,* I. xx. | 38 |

invoke.
| That which we dare *i* to bless ; . | *InMem.*cxxxiii. | 1 |

involve.
| My love *i*'s the love before ; . . | *InMem.*cxxix. | 9 |

involved.
in you I found My boyish dream *i*	*Princess,* iv.	430
a half-consent *i* In stillness, . .	" vii.	67
To the other shore, *i* in thee, .	*InMem.*lxxxiii.	40
My mind *i* yourself the nearest thing	*Vivien*	. 149

inwoven.
| dusky strand of Death *i* here . | *Maud,* I. xviii. | 60 |

inwrapt.
| *I* tenfold in slothful shame, . . | *Pal. of Art* | 262 |

inwrought.
| diaper'd With *i* flowers. . . . | *ArabiauN's.* | 149 |

Ionian.
| all the valleys of *I* hills. . . . | *Œnone* | . 2 |
| there the *I* father of the rest ; . | *Pal. of Art* | 137 |

ire.
| The plaintive cry jarr'd on her *i*; | *Princess,* iv. | 374 |

iris (rainbow-hue.)
| *i* changes on the burnish'd dove ; . | *Locksley II.* | 19 |
| circled *I* of a night of tears ; . | *Princess,* iii. | 11 |

iris (flag-flower.)
| glided winding under ranks If *I*, . | *In Mem.* cii. | 24 |

Iris (messenger of the Gods.)
| light-foot *I* brought it yester-eve, | *Œnone* | . 81 |

iron.	POEM.	LINE.
clad in *i* burst the ranks of war, .	*Princess,* iv.	483
red-hot *i* to be shaped with blows,	" v.	200
heard that there is *i* in the blood,	" vi.	213
i dug from central gloom, . .	*InMem.*cxvii.	21
with gilded arms, All shall be *i*;'	*Enid* .	. 871
laughs at *i*—as our warriors did—	*Vivien*	. 279
rustiest *i* of old fighters' hearts ; .	" .	. 424

iron-clanging.
| an *i-c* anvil bang'd With hammers; | *Princess,* v. | 493 |

iron-clashing.
| such a stern and *i-c* close, . . | *Vivien* | . 269 |

iron-cramped.
| those that *i-c* their women's feet ; . | *Princess,* v. | 366 |

iron-jointed.
| *I-j*, supple-sinew'd, they shall dive, | *Locksley II.* | 169 |

iron-worded.
| wall about thy cause With *i-w* proof, | *To J. M. K.* | 9 |

irony.
| call her sweet, as if in *i*, . . | *Princess,* vii. | 82 |

irritable.
| being vicious, old and *i*, . . | *Enid* . | . 194 |

is.
| was, and *i*, and will be, are but *i*; | *Princess,* iii. | 307 |

Isabel.
| Revered *I*, the crown and head, . | *Isabel* . | . 10 |
| Crown'd *I*, thro' all her placid life | " . | . 27 |

Iscariot.
| Pontius and *I* by my side . . | *St S. Stylites* | 165 |

Isis.
| an *I* hid by the veil. . . . | *Maud,* I. iv. | 43 |

Islamite.
| Houris bow'd to see The dying *I*, | *Pal. of Art* | 103 |

island.
Over the *i*'s free ;	*Sea-Fairies*	26
Round an *i* there below . .	*L. of Shalott,* i.	8
The *i* of Shalott	"	9
By the *i* in the river . . .	"	13
Our *i* home Is far beyond the wave ;	*Lotos-E's.*	44
else the *i* princes over-bold . .	"	120
Boat, *i*, ruins of a castle, . .	*Ed. Morris*	6
On from *i* unto *i*	*Locksley II.*	158
Thine *i* loves thee well, . .	*Ode on Well.*	85
The blaze upon his *i* overhead ; .	*Eu. Arden* .	596
So they past by capes and *i*'s, .	*The Captain*	21

island-crag.
| Set in a cataract on an *i-c*. . . | *Princess,* v. | 337 |

island-sides.
| Far-fleeted by the purple *i-s* . | *Princess,* vii. | 151 |

island-story.
| Not once or twice in our rough *i-s*, | *Ode on Well.*201-9 |

island-valley.
| To the *i-v* of Avilion ; . . | *M. d' Arthur* 259 |

isle.
the silent *i* imbowers The Lady .	*L. of Shalott,*i. 17
Is there confusion in the little *i* ? .	*Lotos-E's.*	. 124
where the moving *i*'s of winter shock	*M. d' Arthur* 140
mellow brickwork on an *i* of bowers.	*Ed. Morris*	12
renroll Cupid of our rainy *i*'s, .	" .	103
I leave the sceptre and the *i*— .	*Ulysses*	. 34
may be we shall touch the Happy *I*'s,	" .	63
Summer *i*'s of Eden lying . .	*Locksley II.*	164
Blue *i*'s of heaven laugh'd between	*Sir L. and O. G.* 6
over lake and lawn, and *i*'s and capes—	*Vision of Sin* 11
battle-clubs From the *i*'s of palm ;	*Princess, Pro.*	22
As yet we find in barbarous *i*'s, .	" ii.	107
tremulous *i*'s of light Slided. .	" vi.	65
dash'd with wandering *i*'s of night.	*In Mem.* xxiv.	4
Danube rolling fair Enwind her *i*'s,	" xcvii.	10
O saviour of the silver-coasted *i*, .	*Ode on Well.*	136
over all whose realms to their last *i*,	*Ded. o Idylls,*11
the lander in a lonely *i*, . .	*Enid* .	. 330
had plunder'd twenty nameless *i*'s ;	*Vivien*	. 409

CONCORDANCE TO

	POEM.	LINE.
kings of desolate *i*'s, . . . *Elaine*	. 526
sent her sweetly by the golden *i*'s, *En. Arden*	. 532
stranding on an *i* at morn . . "	. 553
in a darker *i* beyond the line ; . "	. 606
beauteous hateful *i* Return'd upon him, "	. 618
Stay'd by this *i*, not knowing . "	. 631
a break on the mist-wreathen *i* . "	. 633
did'st uphold me on my lonely *i*, . "	. 784
Nutmeg rocks and *i*'s of clove . *The Voyage*	40
in all that exquisite *i*, my dear, . *The Islet*	. 26
'Fear not, *i* of blowing woodland, *Boädicea*	. 38
Streams o'er a rich ambrosial ocean *i*, *Milton*	. 14
She desires no *i*'s of the blest, . *Wages*	8

isle (verb.)
i's a light in the offing : . . *En. Arden* . 131

isle-altar.
From her *i-a* gazing down, '*Of old sat Freedom,*'etc.14

isled. .
i in sudden seas of light, . . *Fatima* . 33
Thank Him who *i* us here, . . *Ode on Well.* 154

isle-nurtured.
i-n eyes Waged such unwilling . *Vivien* . 420

Isle of Wight.
(Take it and come) to the *I o W* ; *To F.D.Maurice* 12

islet.
cressy *i*'s white in flower ; . . *Enid* . 1324
that *i* in the chesnut-bloom . . *Aylmer's F*. 65
The peaky *i* shifted shapes, . . *The Voyage* 33
A mountain *i* pointed and peak'd ; *The Islet* . 15

isolation.
O God-like *i* which art mine, . *Pal. of Art* . 197
remain Orb'd in your *i* : . . *Princess,* vi. 153
His *i* grows defined. . . *In Mem.* xliv. 12
shook His *i* from him. . . *En. Arden* . 653

Isolt.
Then came the sin of Tristram and *I*; *Guinevere* 484

Israel.
Wrestled with wandering *I*, '*Clear-headed friend*' 26
torrent brooks of hallow'd *I* . . *D. of F. Wom*.181
balmy moon of blessed *I* . . " . 185
I made their gods of gold, . . *In Mem.* xcv. 23

issue (s.)
Whereof I catch the *i*, . . *Œnone* . 244
your great deeds For *i*, . . *Princess*, iii. 227
float us each and all To the *i*, . " iv. 53
why she should Bide by this *i* : . " v. 316
had *i* other than she will'd. . *Vivien* . 655
noble *i*, sons Born to the glory . *Elaine*. 1362

issue (verb.)
To those that seek them *i* forth ; . *Day-Dm.* . 102

issued.
i in a court Compact with lucid . *Princess,* ii. 9
We *i* gorged with knowledge, . " . 366
i in the sun, that now Leapt . . " v. 40
Whence he *i* forth anew, . . *Ode on Well.* 107
i from the world of wood, . . *Enid* . 238
ridge Of breaker *i* from the belt, . *Sea Dreams* 205

issuing.
i shorn and sleek, . . . *Talking O.* . 42
lightly *i* thro', I would have paid . " . 194
voice Of Ida sounded, *i* ordinance : *Princess,* vi. 352
howlest, *i* out of night, . . *In Mem.* lxxi. 2
Geraint, who *i* forth That morning, *Enid* . 857
i under open heavens beheld . . " . 1045
i arm'd he found the host . . " . 1256
i found the Lord of Astolat . . *Elaine* . 173

Italian.
Fair ship, that from the *I* shore . *In Mem.* ix. 1
glory fly along the *I* field, . . *Lucretius* . 71

Italy.
I to the East And he for *I*— . *The Brook* . 2
And now it tells of *I.* . . *The Daisy* . 90

iteration.
came Her sicklier *i*. . . *Aylmer's F*. 299

	POEM.	LINE.
Ithacensian.
Like the *I* suitors in old time, . *Princess,* iv. 100
ivory.
Laborious orient *i* sphere in sphere, *Princess,* Pro. 20
ivory-beaked.
In a shallop of crystal *i-b,* . . *The Islet* . 12
ivy.
overhead the wandering *i* and vine, *Œnone* . 97
thro' the moss the *ivies* creep, . *Lotos-Es*. . 54
Thorns, *ivies*, woodbine, mistletoes, *Day-Dm*. . 63
There is Darnley bridge, It has more *i*; *The Brook* 37
wings Moved in her *i*, . . *Enid* . 599
ivy-clad.
In Autumn, parcel *i-c* ; . . *Aylmer's F*. 154
ivy-clasped.
High-arch'd and *i-c*, Of finest Gothic *Princess,Pro*.91
ivy-net.
Now on some twisted *i-n,* . *Sir L. and Q. G.* 28
ivy-stems.
monstrous *i-s* Claspt the gray walls *Enid* . . 322
'*ivy-wreath.*
briony-vine and *i-w* Ran forward. *Amphion* . 29
Ixionian.
stays the rolling *I* wheel, . . *Lucretius* . 257
Ixion-like.
Embracing cloud, *I-l*; . . *Two Voices*. 195
'*I will.*'
I heard his deep '*I w*,' Breath'd . *Gardener's D*.203
Her sweet '*I w*' has made ye one. *In Mem. Con.* 52

J

jacinth-work.
j-w Of subtlest jewellery. . . *M. d'Arthur* 57

Jack.
J, turn the horses' heads . *Walk. to the M.* 38
J on his ale-house bench . . *Maud,* I. iv. 9

jackass.
A *j* heehaws from the rick, . . *Amphion* . 71

Jael.
a cymbal'd Miriam and a *J*, . *Princess,* v. 500

jail.
scared with threats of *j* and halter *Aylmer's F*. 520

jam.
j the doors, and bear The keepers *Lucretius* . 169

James (see Willows.)
Old *J* was with me : . . *Golden Year* 3
in mimic cadence answer'd *J*— . " . 53
J,—you know him,—old, but full " . 60
She and *J* had quarrell'd. . . *The Brook* . 96
no cause ; *J* had no cause : . . " . 98
J had flickering jealousies . . " . 99
Who anger'd *J* ? I said. . . " . 100
till I ask'd If *J* were coming. . " . 106
J departed vext with him and her.' " . 110
I saw where *J* Made toward us, . " . 116
brother *J* is in the harvest field : . " . 227

Jane.
And what do I care for *J*, . . *Grandmother* 51

jangling.
j, the casque Fell, and he started up *Enid* . 1237

January.
Fine as ice-ferns on *J* panes . *Aylmer's F*. 222
woodlands, when they shiver in *J*, *Boädicea* . 75

jar (s.)
Love is hurt with *j* and fret. . *Miller's D*. . 209
hear the household *j* within. . *In Mem*.xciii. 16

jar (verb.)
j all the hymns of heaven : . . *Sea Dreams* 251
mortal motion *j*'s The blackness . *On a Mourner* 26

jarred.	POEM.	LINE.
something *j*: Whether he spoke	*Ed. Morris.*	72
The plaintive cry *j* on her ire;	*Princess,* iv.	374

jasmine.
Growths of *j* turn'd Their humid . *D. of F. Wom.* 69
meshes of the *j* and the rose: . *Princess,* i. 216
robe of *j* sown with stars: . . *Aylmer's F.* 158

jasmine-leaves.
dawn Upon me thro' the *j.-l.* . *Margaret* . 68

jasper.
In the branching *j*'s under the sea: *The Mermaid* 47

jaundice.
veil'd the world with *j,* . . *Walk. to the M.* 14

javelining.
j With darted spikes and splinters *Vivien* . 785

jaw.
in the *j*'s Of vacant darkness . *In Mem.* xxxiv. 15
Into the *j*'s of Death, . . *Lt. Brigade* 24
Came thro' the *j*'s of Death . " . 46

jealous.
Too *j,* often fretful as the wind . *Princess,* iii. 64
Half *j* of she knows not what, . *In Mem.* lix. 7
O to what end, except a *j* one, . *Vivien* . 388
one to make me *j* if I love, . " . 389
What wonder, being *j,* that he sent " . 430
made her good man *j* with good cause. " . 455
be *j* and hard and unkind.' . *Grandmother* 54
Never *j*—not he: . . . " . 71

jealousy.
avarice, pride, *J,* down ! . *Maud,* I. x. 48
James had flickering *jealousies* . *The Brook* . 99
all narrow *jealousies* Are silent . *Ded. of Idylls* 15
A sudden spurt of woman's *j,*— . *Vivien* . 374
as to woman's *j,* O why not ? . " . 387
mine was *j* in love.' . . *Elaine* . 1341
'*J* in love ?' Not rather dead love's " . 1388
Queen, if I grant the *j* as of love, " . 1390

jeer.
scoff and *j* and babble of him . *Enid* . . 58

Jehovah.
Starr'd from *J's* gorgeous armouries, *Milton* . 6

jenneting.
To fret the summer *j.* . . *The Blackbird* 12

Jenny.
J, my cousin, had come to the place *Grandmother* 25
J had tript in her time: . . " . 26
J, to slander me, who knew what *J* had " . 35
J hung on his arm. . . " . 42
J, the viper, made me a mocking courtsey " . 46

Jeptha.
Pale as the *J's* daughter, . . *Aylmer's F.* 280

jessamine.
All night has the casement *j* stirr'd *Maud,* xxii. 15

jest ('s.)
eyes twinkle yet At his own *j*— . *Miller's D.* 12
He was full of joke and *j,* . *D. of the O. Year* 28
half in earnest, half in *j,* . *Gardener's D.* 23
as wrong As a bitter *j* is dear. . *Vision of Sin* 198
shameless hand with shameful *j,* . *Princess,* iii. 297
j a I earnest working side by side, " iv. 541
beneath his vaulted palm A whisper'd *j* " v. 31
are the windy *j* I had labour'd down " . 262
dance and song and game and *j.* *In Mem.* xxix. 8
J among his friends is free, . " lxv. 10
deep dispute, and graceful *j*; . " lxxxiii. 24
will not touch upon him ev'n in *j.* *Enid* . 311
some light *j* among them rove . *Elaine* . 178
vext he could not go: A *j,* no more: " . 211
all was *j* and joke among ourselves) " . 217
keep it safelier All was *j.* . " . 218
j's that flash'd about the pleader's *Aylmer's F.* 440

jest (verb.)
'You *j*: ill jesting with edge-tools l *Princess,* ii. 184

jested.	POEM.	LINE.
while he *j* thus, A thought flash'd	*Princess,* i.	191
Drank till he *j* with all ease,	*Enid* .	1133

jesting.
ill *j* with edge-tools ! . . *Princess,* ii. 184

Jesus.
O *J,* if thou wilt not save my soul, *St S. Stylites* 45

jet.
From those four *j*'s four currents *Pal. of Art* 33

jet-black.
Leading a *j-b* goat white-horn'd, . *Œnone* . 50
The maiden's *j-b* hair has grown, . *Day-Dm.* . 80

jetted.
A dozen angry models *j* steam : . *Princess, Pro.* 73

jewel.
J or shell, or starry ore, . . *Eleänore* . 20
the *j* That trembles at her ear : . *Miller's D.* 171
furs And *j*'s, gifts, to fetch her : . *Princess,* i. 42
quoted odes, and *j*'s five-words-long " ii. 355
like a *j* set In the dark crag : . " iii. 340
single *j* on her brow Burn . . " iv. 254
What, has he found my *j* out ? . *Maud,* I. x. 23
And Maud will wear her *j*'s, . " xx. 27
little save the *j*'s they had on, . *Enid* . 640
thicker down the front With *j*'s . " . 1533
j's, whereupon I chanced Divinely *Elaine* . 50
wear as fair a *j* as is on earth, . " . 240
not won except for you, These *j*'s, " . 1176
in rich sheath with *j*'s on it . . *Aylmer's F.* 220
seem'd a fleet of *j*'s under me, . *Sea Dreams* 119
A *j,* a *j* dear to a lover's eye ! . *The Window* 3

jewellery.
jacinth-work Of subtlest *j.* . . *M. d'Arthur* 58

jewel-print.
sets the *j-p* of your feet In violets *Maud,* I. xxii. 41

jewel-thick.
barbarous opulence *j-t* . . *Maud,* I. xiii. 12

Jill.
White Rose, Bellerophon, the *J,* . *The Brook* . 161

jilted.
their pretty saying ? *j,* is it ? *J* I was : *Aylmer's F.* 353

jingled.
When armour clash'd or *j,* . . *Princess,* vi. 343

jingling.
j of the guinea helps the hurt . *Locksley H.* 105

Joan.
J of Arc, A light of ancient France : *D. of F. Wom.* 267
arts of war The peasant *J* and others ; *Princess,* ii. 147

Joänes.
J, as 'ant a 'aäpoth o' sense, . *N. Farmer* 49
a weänt niver give it to *J,* . . " . 50

Jocky (see Dawes.)

John.
had let appear the brand of *J*— . *Aylmer's F.* 509

join.
this byway *j*'s The turnpike ? . *Walk. to the M.* 4
truths in manhood darkly *j,* . . *In Mem.* xxxvi. 1
as he gallop'd up To *j* them, . *The Brook* . 32
to see the hunt, Not *j* it . . *Enid* . 172
in haste to *j* Their luckier mates, " . 1422

joined.
with the choral starry dance *J* not *Pal. of Art* 254
many changes, aptly *j,* 'Love thou thy land,' etc. 65
lips, like thine, so sweetly *j*! . *Day-Dm.* 258
lay the guests, And there we *j* them: *Princess, Pro.* 107
fair charities *J* at her side: . " vii. 51
j Each office of the social hour . *In Mem.* ex. 14

joining.
suck'd the *j* of the stones, . . *Enid* . . 324

joint.

	POEM.	LINE.
work, a *j* of state,	'Love thou thy land,' etc.	47
all his *j*'s Are full of chalk?	. Audley Ct.	45
all things here are out of *j*:	. Locksley H.	133
My *j*'s are somewhat stiff or so.	. Day-Dm.	158
J's of cunning workmanship.	. Vision of Sin	186

joke.

He was full of *j* and jest,	D. of the O. Year	28
all was jest and *j* among ourselves)	Elaine .	217

Jonah.

in her a *J*'s gourd,	. Princess, iv.	292

Joshua.

like *J*'s moon in Ajalon !	. Locksley H.	180

journey.

morn had died, her *j* done,	. D. of F. Wom.	61
before his *j* closes, He shall find	. Ode on Well.	205
And all his *j* to her,	" 143,	845
'Be prosperous in this *j*, as in all ;	"	225
sigh'd to find Her *j* done,	. Guinevere	402

journeying.

Or often *j* landward ;	. En. Arden .	92

joust (s.)

might show it at a *j* of arms,	. M. d' Arthur	102
meadow where the *j*'s were held,	. Enid	537
when the *j*'s were ended yesterday,	"	692
haughty *j*'s, and took a paramour ;	"	1680
for my main purpose in these *j*'s,	"	1685
diamond *j*'s, Which Arthur had	. Elaine	31
a *j* for one of these :	"	62
eight years past, eight *j*'s had been,	"	68
let proclaim a *j* At Camelot,	"	77
cannot move To these fair *j*'s ?'	"	81
Why go you not to these fair *j*'s ?	"	99
hear my words : go to the *j*'s :	"	137
triumph in our mimic wars, the *j*'s—	"	312
parted from the *j*'s Hurt in the side,'	"	619

joust (verb.)

I go to *j* as one unknown	. Elaine	190
he will ride, *J* for it, and win,	"	204
That he might *j* unknown of all,	"	582

jowl.

Cheek by *j*, and knee by knee :	. Vision of Sin	84

joy.

What hope or fear or *j* is thine ?	. Adeline	23
with *j* Hidden in sorrow :	. Dying Swan	22
move about the house with *j*,	. Miller's D.	95
'There is no *j* but calm !'	. Lotos-E's.	68
come like ghosts to trouble *j*.	"	119
emptied of all *j*, Leaving the dance	D. of F. Wom.	215
sit between *J* and woe,	. Margaret	64
Such *j* as you have seen with us,	D. of the O. Year	17
scarce get out his notes for *j*,	. Gardener's D.	89
but could not sleep for *j*,	"	170
perfect *J*, perplex'd for utterance,	"	250
I look'd at him with *j*:	. Talking O.	106
reaps not harvest of his youthful *j*'s,	Locksley H.	139
j that mixes man with Heaven :	. Two Voices	210
muse on *j* that will not cease,	. Sir Galahad	65
A private life was all his *j*,	. Will Water.	129
souls that balance *j* and pain,	. Sir L. and Q.G.	1
bring m sorrow touch'd with *j*,	. In Mem. xxviii.	19
doubtful *j* the father move,	" xxxix.	9
On som r worthy heart with *j*,	" lxi.	7
Thy passion clasps a secret *j*:	" lxxxvii.	8
O *j* to him in this retreat,	" lxxxviii.	13
As in the former flash of *j*,	" cxxi.	15
tells The *j* To every wandering breeze	Con.	62
tho' in silence, wishing *j*,	"	88
the ringing *j* of the Hall,	. Maud, I. i.	70
a *j* in which I cannot rejoice,	" v.	21
she warbled alone in her *j*,	" x.	53
Making the little one leap for *j*	To F. D. Maurice	4
but welcomed him with *j*,	. Enid .	748
I see it with *j*—You sit apart,	"	1169
my liege, in whom I have my *j*,	. Elaine	1174
I pray you : have your *j*'s apart.	"	1211
beheld three spirits mad with *j*	. Guinevere	250
and rejoicing in my *j*.	"	482
not grieving at your *j*'s, But not rejoicing ;	"	671
madly danced our hearts with *j*,	. The l'oyage	3
O *j* to the people and *j* to the throne.	IV. to Alexan.	29
'O hush, my *j*, my sorrow.''	Home they brought him	10
The Priest exulted, And cried with *j*,	The Victim	39

joyance.

To keep them in all *j* :	. Elaine .	1314

joyful.

J and free from blame.	. D. of F. Wom.	80
More *j* than the city-roar	. Princess, Con.	101
Took *j* note of all things *j*,	. Aylmer's F.	67
J came his speech :	. The Captain	30

joying.

J to feel herself alive,	. Pal. of Art.	178

joyous.

A *j* to dilate, as toward the light.	. Aylmer's F.	77

jubilee.

With pleasure and love and *j* :	. Sea-Fairies .	36
Utter your *j*, steeple and spire !	IV. to Alexan.	17

judge (s.)

Himself the *j* and jury,	. Sea Dreams	171
God, not man, is the *J* of us all	. Grandmother	95

judge (verb.)

see thy Paris *j* of Gods.	. Œnone .	88
J thou me by what I am,	"	152
mortal eyes are frail to *j* of fair,	"	155
' Let the Princess *J* Of that'	. Princess, ii.	216
not to *j* their cause from her	" vii.	220
j all nature from her feet of clay,	. Vivien.	684
may *j* the living by the dead,	. Elaine .	1359

judged.

now the Priest has *j* for me.'	. The Victim	60

judger.

hasty *j* would have call'd her guilt,	Enid .	1282

judgment.

pick'd offenders from the mass For *j*.	Princess, I.	30
You shame your mother's *j* too.	"	vi. 244
would not make his *j* blind,	. In Mem. xcv.	14
Shalt abide her *j* on it ;	. Enid .	584
hear the *j* of the King,'	"	1647
hears the *j* of the King of Kings,'	"	1648
naked Ignorance Delivers brawling *j*'s	Vivien .	515
Rash were my *j* then,	. Elaine .	239
hollow like a Ghost's Denouncing *j*,	Guinevere .	418

Judith.

couch'd behind a *J*,	. Princess, iv.	207

juggle.

a *j* born of the brain ?	. Maud, II. ii.	42

juice.

Till all his *j* is dried,	. Audley Ct.	45

Juliet.

J, she So light of foot,	. Gardener's D.	13
J, answer'd laughing, 'Go and see	"	29
Will you match My *J* ?	"	168

jumbled.

every clime and age *J* together ;	. Princess, Pro.	17

June.

Their meetings made December *J*,	In Mem. xcvi.	11

Junius (see Brutus.)

junketing.

growth Of spirit than to *j* and love.	Princess, iv.	124

Juno.

charm Pallas and *J* sitting by :	. A Character	15

jury.

Himself the judge and *j*,	. Sea Dreams	171

just.

A man more pure and bold and *j*	. To J. S.	31
Hears little of the false or *j*.	. Two Voices	117
'tis but *j* The many-headed '	You might have won,'	19

	POEM.	LINE.
all comes round so *j* and fair;	Lady Clare	18
Virtue!—to be good and *j*—.	Vision of Sin	111
woman's state in each, How far from *j*;	Princess, ii.	116
thou hast made him; thou art *j*,	In Mem. Pro.	12
battled for the True, the *J*, .	"	iv. 18
strike, for we hold Thee *j*, .	Maud, II. i.	45
be sane and crowns be *j*.	Ode on Well.	169
no quiet seats of the *j*, .	Wages	8

justice.
social truth shall spread And *j*,	In Mem. cxxvi	6
all flyers from the hand Of *J*,	Enid	37
to guard the *j* of the King; .	"	1762
there he kept the *j* of the King	"	1804
A silent court of *j* in his breast,	Sea Dreams	170

justified.
seem'd So *j* by that necessity,	Enid	1245

justify.
every face she look'd on *j* it)	Princess, v.	128

justly.
How *j*, after that vile term of yours,	Vivien	770

jut (s.)
zig-zag paths, and *j*'s of pointed rock,	M.d'Arthur	50
based His feet on *j*'s of slippery crag	"	189

jut (verb.)
diamond-ledges that *j* from the dells;	The Mermaid	40

K

Kaffir.
not the K', Hottentot, Malay,	Princess, ii.	142

Kate.
there's K' and Caroline; .	May Queen, i.	6

Katie (see Willows.)
Sweet K', once I did her a good turn,	The Brook	74
K' somewhere in the walks below.	"	86
'Run K'!' K' never ran; she moved	"	87
less of sentiment than sense Had K';	"	92
K' snatch'd her eyes at once from mine,	"	101
O K', what I suffer'd for your sake!	"	119
sweet content Re-risen in K''s eyes,	"	169
K' walks By the long wash .	"	193
What do they call you?' 'K'.	"	211
K' laugh'd, and laughing blush'd .	"	214

keeper.
K''s it wur; fo' they fun un theer	N. Farmer	33

keel.
round about the *k* with faces pale,	Lotos-E's.	25
rustle round the shelving *k*; .	Ed. Morris	110
no rider air perplex Thy sliding *k*,	In Mem. ix.	10
hear a noise about thy *k*; .	"	x. 1
broad seas swell'd to meet the *k*,	The Voyage	13

keen.
k thro' wordy snares to track	In Mem. xciv.	31
can I doubt, who knew thee *k*	"	cxii. 5
tho' *k* and bold and soldierly,	Aylmer's F.	192

keenly.
glancing all at once as *k* at her,	Enid	773, 179

keep (s.)
there is the *k*; He shall not cross us	Enid	1190

keep (verb.)
K' measure with thine own?.	Adeline	27
So *k* where you are; .	Poet's Mind	36
heart a charmed slumber *k*'s,	Eleänore	128
Let us swear an oath, and *k* it	Lotos-E's.	153
K''s real sorrow far away, .	Margaret	44
k smooth plats of fruitful ground,	The Blackbird	3
K' dry their light from 'Of old sat Freedom,' etc.	The Goose	20
take the goose, and *k* you warm,	The Goose	7
k y m cold, or *k* you warm, .	"	43
K' a thing, its use will come.	The Epic	42
'This wonder *k*'s the house.'	Gardener'sD.	118
k me from that Eden where she dwelt.	"	187
k's us all in order more or less—	Walk. to the M.	17

	POEM.	LINE.
trims us up, And *k*'s us tight;	Ed. Morris	47
try If yet he *k*'s the power, .	Talking O.	23
to *k* My own full-tuned—	Love and Duty	31
all Should *k* within, door shut,	Godiva	41
Nor any train of reason *k*: .	Two Voices .	50
His state the king reposing *k*'s,	Day-Dm.	5
k I fair thro' faith and prayer	Sir Galahad	23
K' nothing sacred: 'You might have won,' etc.	"	19
k the best man under the sun	Lady Clare	31
k the secret for your life, .	"	34–42
While we *k* a little breath! .	Vision of Sin	192
k a chronicle With all about him	Princess, P'ro.	27
love to *k* us children! .	"	133
k your hoods about the face;	"	ii. 337
if your Highness *k* Your purport,	"	iii. 15
broke the letter of it to *k* the sense	"	iv. 319
k's me hostage for his son.' .	"	336
but *k* you surety for our son,	"	v. 24
will cruel Ida *k* her back; .	"	81
she would not *k* Her compact.'	"	313
O if, I say, you *k* One pulse	"	vi. 173
cannot *k* her mind an hour;	"	260
What use to *k* them here now?	"	285
I cannot *k* My heart an eddy	"	301
willing she should *k* Court-favour;	"	vii. 42
seem to *k* her up but drag her down—	"	254
herself her own To give or *k*,	"	257
k's his wing'd affections clipt	"	297
the narrow sea which *k*'s her off,	Con.	51
k's our Britain, whole within herself,	"	52
Let darkness *k* her raven gloss;	In Mem. i.	10
k's the keys of all the creeds,	" xxiii.	5
How dare we *k* our Christmas-eve;	" xxix.	4
k so sweet a thing alive;' .	" xxxv.	7
'What *k*'s a spirit wholly true .	" li.	9
She *k*'s the gift of years before, .	" xcvi.	25
who would *k* an ancient form	" civ.	19
We *k* the day. With festal cheer,	" cvi.	21
k's A thousand pulses dancing	" cxxiv.	15
tho' as yet I *k* Within his court	" cxxv.	6
I *k* but a man and a maid, .	Maud, I. iv.	19
but *k* a temperate brain; .	"	40
Should Nature *k* me alive, .	" vi.	32
Her brother, from whom I *k* aloof,	"	46
K' watch and ward, *k* watch and	"	58
k it ours, O God, from brute	Ode on Well.	159
k our noble England whole, .	"	161
k the soldier firm, the statesman	"	222
k's me in this ruinous castle here,	Enid	462
k's the wear and polish of the wave.	"	682
dress her beautifully and *k* her	"	889
not to speak to me, And thus you *k*	"	928
k them in the wild ways of the wood,	"	1036
k a touch of sweet civility .	"	1161
if it were so do not *k* it back: .	"	1165
k him bright and clean as heretofore,	"	1785
We could not *k* him silent, .	Vivien	266
To *k* me ali to your own self, .	"	373
no charm to *k* them mine But youth	"	397
Might *k* her all his own; .	"	435
k it like a puzzle chest in chest,	"	504
But *k* that oath you swore, .	"	538
Then must she *k* it safelier, .	Elaine	218
you *k* So much of what is graceful;	"	1212
To *k* them in all joyance; .	"	1314
k's the rust of murder on the walls	Guinevere	74
Not only to *k* down the base in man,	"	476
k the house while he was gone.	En. Arden	140
K' a clean hearth and a clear fire .	"	192
K' everything shipshape .	"	220
Not *k* it noble, make it nobler?	Aylmer's F.	386
thank God that I *k* my eyes.	Grandmother	106
k him from the lust of blood .	Lucretius	83

keeper.
the *k* was one, so full of pride,	Maud, II. v.	70
by a *k* shot at, slightly hurt, .	Aylmer's F.	548
escaped His *k*'s, and the silence	"	833
jam the doors, and bear The *k*'s	Lucretius	170

keeping.
did Enid, *k* watch behold .	Enid	967

POEM. LINE.

It is not worth the *k:* let it go: . *Vivien* . 346
have my shield In *k* till I come.' . *Elaine* . 382
children play'd at *k* house . . *En. Arden* . 24

Kent.

lands in *K* and messuages in York, *Ed. Morris* 127

kep (kept.)

'Siver, I *k* un, I *k* un, my lass, . *N. Farmer*. 23

kept.

k her throne unshaken still. . . *To the Queen* 34
K watch, waiting decision, . . *Œnone* . 141
this *k*, Stored in some treasure-house *M. d'Arthur* 100
we *k* her till she pigg'd. *Walk. to the M.* 84
His worst he *k*, . *'You might have won,' etc.* 26
his heavy rider *k* him down. . *Vision of Sin* 4
k the book and had my finger in it) *Princess, Pro.* 53
k mine own Intent on her, . . " ii. 418
k her state, and left the drunken king " iii. 213
Cyril *k* With Psyche, . . . " . 336
they *k* apart, no mischief done; . " iv. 321
why *k* ye not your faith? . . " v. 74
part reel'd but *k* their seats: . " . 485
My blood an even tenor *k*, . . *In Mem.* lxxxiv. 17
fall'n leaves which *k* their green, . " xciv. 23
K itself warm in the heart of my . *Maud*, I. vi. 18
His foes were thine; he *k* us free: *Ode on Well.* 91
great men who fought, and *k* it ours. " . 158
Like ballad-burthen music, *k* . *The Daisy* . 77
k them folded reverently . . *Enid* . . 137
k her off and gazed upon her face " . . 519
k it for a sweet surprise at morn. . " . 703
Enid ever *k* the faded silk, . . " . 841
Because she *k* the letter of his word " . 1304
k the heart of Eden green . . " . 1618
k myself aloof till I was changed; " . 1720
he *k* the justice of the King. . " . 1804
some stolen, some as relics *k*, . *Vivien* . 303
k his mind on one sole aim . . " . 476
k him sunder'd from his wife: . " . 565
took the shield There *k* it, . . *Elaine* . 397
Might well have *k* his secret. . " . 591
k The one-day-seen Sir Lancelot . " . 742
faith unfaithful *k* him falsely true. " . 873
two stood arm'd, and *k* the door; " . 1240
this he *k* Thro' all his future; . *En. Arden* . 235
as having *k* aloof so long. . . " . 273
he was gone Who *k* it; . . . " . 696
little ones to school, And *k* them in it, " . 708
K him a living soul. . . . " . 805
k the house, his chair, . . . " . 827
his resolve, And how he *k* it. . " . 865
sow'd her name and *k* it green . *Aylmer's F.* 68
worldless heart had *k* it warm, . " . 471
yet her cheek *K* colour: wondrous! " . 506
K to the garden now, and grove of pines, " . 550
she, who *k* a tender Christian hope, *Sea Dreams* 41
good things have not *k* aloof, *'My life is full'* 2

kerchief.

about them, ribbon, glove, Or *k*; *Aylmer's F.* 621

kernel.

trash' he said 'but with a *k* in it. *Princess*, ii. 373

kestrel.

Kite and *k*, wolf and wolfkin, . *Boädicea* . 15

kettle.

hurl'd the pan and *k*. . . . *The Goose* . 28

kex.

tho' the rough *k* break The starr'd *Princess*, iv. 59

key.

opens but to golden *k's*. . . *Locksley H.* 100
Keeps the *k's* of all the creeds, . *In Mem.* xxiii. 5
That Shadow waiting with the *k's*, " xxvi. 15
lives to clutch the golden *k's*, . " lxiii. 10
With half a sigh she turn'd the *k*, *The Letters* 18

keys (of a piano.)

Turn'd as he sat, and struck the *k's* *The Islet* . 7

kick.

all women *k* against their Lords . *Princess*, iv. 393

POEM. LINE.

kid.

like the *k* in its own mother's milk! *Vivien* . 718

kill.

k Time by the fire in winter.' . *Princess, Pro.* 200
'*K* him now, The tyrant! *k* him. " . 201
K us with pity, break us with ourselves " iii. 241
grand fight to *k* and make an end: " iv. 568
tenderness, not yours, that could not *k*, " vi. 170
that Which *k's* me with myself, . " . 288
k's her babe for a burial fee, . *Maud*, I. i. 45
churchmen fain would *k* their church " II. v. 28
speak, and tho' he *k* me for it, . *Enid* . 986
child *k* me with her innocent talk?' *Guinevere* . 212
child *k* me with her foolish prate?' " . 223
shall I *k* myself? What help in that: " . 613
I cannot *k* my sin If soul be soul; " . 614
nor can I *k* my shame; . . " . 615
why should you *k* yourself . . *En. Arden* . 391

kill'd.

I have *k* my son. I have *k* him— *Dora* . . 156
k with some luxurious agony, . *Vision of Sin* 43
truthful change in thee has *k* it. . *Princess*, vii. 329
k in falling from his horse. . *In Mem.* vi. 40
I should not less have *k* him. . *Enid* . 1693
K with a word worse than a life of blows! *Vivien* 719
K with unutterable unkindliness.' " . 735
here a thrust that might have *k* . *Elaine* . 25
K in a tilt, come next, five summers *Guinevere* 319
k In such a bottom: . . . *Aylmer's F.* 253
bees are still'd, and the flies are *k*, *The Window* 52

killest.

O thou that *k*, had'st thou known, *Aylmer's F.* 738

kin (see *kith and kin.*)

lift His axe to slay my *k*. . . *Talking O.* 236
gentle satire, *k* to charity, . . *Princess*, ii. 445
give back their earldom to thy *k*. *Enid* . . 585
little cause for laughter: his own *k*—*Elaine* . 595
up the still rich city to his *k*, . " 798, 841
I am well-to-do—no *k*, no care, . *En. Arden* . 415

kind (adj.)

a nature never *k*! . . . *Walk. to the M.* 54
Her kisses were so close and *k*, . *Talking O.* 169
love her, as I knew her, *k*? . . *Locksley H.* 70
But may she still be *k*, . . *Will Water.* 10
all men rate as *k* and hospitable: *Princess*, i. 70
ourselves but half as good, as *k* . " v. 193
Is it *k*? Speak to her I say: . " vi. 231
'How good! how *k*! and he is gone.' *In Mem.* xx. 20
looks so cold: she thinks him *k*. . " xcvi. 24
we cannot be *k* to each other here *Maud*, I. iv. 28
who is neither courtly nor *k*, . " v. 27
says he is rough but *k*, . . " xix. 70
K? but the deathbed desire . " . 77
Rough but *k*? yet I know . . " . 79
K to Maud? that were not amiss. " . 82
rough but *k*; why let it be so: . " . 83
Not beautiful now, not even *k*; . " II. v. 66
k to have made me a grave so rough, " . 97
Manners so *k*, yet stately, . . *Enid* . 1709
silence is more wise than *k*.' . *Vivien* . 138
K, like a man, was he; . . *Grandmother* 70
Stiles where we stay'd to be *k*, . *The Window* 184

kind (s.)

She had the passions of her *k*, *L. C. V. de Vere* 35
serve his *k* in deed and *'Love thou thy land,' etc.* 66
all *k's* of thought, That verged upon *Gardener's D.* 69
Yet is there plenty of the *k*? . *Two Voices* 33
Lucius Junius Brutus of my *k*. . *Princess*, ii. 264
According to the coarseness of their *k*, " iv. 327
Another *k* of beauty in detail . " . 428
made me kindly with my *k* . . *In Mem.* lxv. 7
thou and I are one in *k*, . . " lxxviii. 5
What *k* of life is that I lead; . " lxxxiv. 8
I will not shut me from my *k*, . " cvii. 1
of a *k* The viler, as underhand, . *Maud*, I. i. 27
I am one with my *k*, . . . " III. vi. 58
think what *k* of bird it is . . *Enid* . 331
purer pleasures unto mortal *k* . " . 1613

		POEM.	LINE.
kindly man moving among his *k*:	Elaine		265
mirthful he but in a stately *k*—	"		321
ever cared to better his own *k*,	Sea Dreams		196
in a pleasant *k* of a dream.	Grandmother		82
Beastlier than any phantom of his *k*	Lucretius		193

kinder.

the girl Seem'd *k* unto Philip	En. Arden	42

kindle.

dim curls *k* into sunny rings;	Tithonus	54

kindled.

voice in battle, and be *k* by it,	Enid	1024
wine and free companions *k* him,	"	1142

kindlier.

since man's first fall Did *k* unto man,	Elaine	856
k than themselves To ailing wife	Aylmer's F.	176

kindly.

Proudly turns he round and *k*,	L. of Burleigh	55
made me *k* with my kind,	In Mem. lxv.	7
modest, *k*, all-accomplish'd,	Ded. of Idylls	17

kindly-hearted.

So spake the *k-h* Earl,	Enid	514

kindness.

I could trust Your *k*.	To the Queen	20
looking ancient *k* on thy pain.	Locksley H.	85
more in *k* than in love,	Vivien	756
brother's love And your good father's *k*.'	Elaine	941
think your *k* breaks me down	En. Arden	317
money can be repaid; Not *k*	"	320
Soul-stricken at their *k* to him,	Aylmer's F.	525
faded love, Or ordeal by *k*;	"	561

kindred.

Grate her harsh *k* in the grass:	Princess, iv.	107
Thy *k* with the great of old	In Mem. lxxiii.	8
craft of *k* and the Godless hosts	Guinevere	424

kine.

browsed by deep-udder'd *k*,	Gardener's D.	45
couch'd at ease, The white *k*.	In Mem. xciv.	15-51

king.

give the warrior *k*'s of old.	To the Queen	20
K's have no such couch as thine,	A Dirge	40
k of them all would carry me,	The Mermaid	45
Reign thou apart, a quiet *k*,	Pal. of Art.	14
stay'd the Ausonian *k* to hear	"	111
The heads and crowns of *k*'s;	"	152
black-bearded *k*'s with wolfish eyes,	D. of F. Wom.	111
hearts Of captains and of *k*'s.	"	176
with one arm about her *k*.	"	270
took it, and have worn it, like a *k*:	M. d'Arthur	33
not meet, Sir *K*, to leave thee thus,	"	40
back slow to the wounded *K*.	"	65-112
if a *k* demand An act unprofitable	"	95
K is sick, and knows not what he does,	"	97
Some treasure-house of mighty *k*'s,	"	101
Authority forgets a dying *k*,	"	121
lightly went the other to the *K*.	"	147
sigh'd the *K*, Muttering and murmuring	"	178
Put forth their hands, and took the *K*,	"	206
like a shatter'd column lay the *K*;	"	221
the eyes of ladies and of *k*'s.	"	225
came again together on the *k*	Audley Ct.	35
came a mystic token from the *k*	Ed. Morris.	132
It little profits that an idle *k*.	Ulysses	1
those old portraits of old *k*'s,	Day-Dm.	43
His state the *k* reposing keeps.	"	59
He must have been a jovial *k*.	"	60
lost with these the *k* awoke,	"	149
statesman he, nor *k*. ' You might have won,' etc.	"	24
In robe and crown the *k* stept down,	Beggar Maid	5
Death is *k*, and Vivat Rex!	Vision of Sin	179
counts and *k*'s Who laid about them	Princess, Pro.	30
strait-besieged By this wild *k*	"	17
my good father thought a *k* a *k*;	" i.	25
they saw the *k*; he took the gifts;	"	45
'Fore the *k*'s letter, snow'd it down,	"	60
In this report, this answer of a *k*,	"	69
'No!' Roar'd the rough *k*,	"	86

		POEM.	LINE.
in the imperial palace found the *k*.	Princess,	i.	112
without a star, Not like a *k*.		"	117
show'd the late-writ letters of the *k*.		"	173
' If the *k*,' he said, ' Had given us letters,		"	178
The *k* would bear him out;'		"	180
when the *k* Kiss'd her pale cheek		ii.	244
'Our *k* expects—was there no precontract?		iii.	191
kept her state, and left the drunken *k*		"	213
tumult and the *k*'s Were shadows:		iv.	542
old *k*'s Began to wag their baldness		v.	17
' *K*, you are free!		"	23
(thus the *K* Roar'd)		"	33
Found the gray *k*'s at parle:		"	110
' Not war, if possible, O *k*,'		"	120
I hold her, *k*, True woman:		"	171
with the old *k* across the lawns		"	226
tale of love In the old *k*'s ears,		"	231
a cry As if to greet the *k*;		"	239
then took the *k* His three broad sons;		"	258
Hungry for honour, angry for his *k*.		"	304
' Boys!' shriek'd the old *k*,		"	318
told the *k* that I was pledged		"	342
Upon a *k*'s right hand in thunder-storms		"	429
the spindling *k*, This Gama		"	432
Thus the hard old *k*		"	456
thought on all the wrathful *k* had		"	462
K, camp and college turned to		"	467
k in bitter scorn Drew from my neck		vi.	93
small *k* moved beyond his wont.		"	248
Before these *k*'s we embrace you		"	276
brother, help; speak to the *k*;		"	286
tears Follow'd; the *k* replied not;		"	292
k her father charm'd Her wounded		"	325
k is scared, the soldier will not fight,		Con.	60
city-roar that hails Premier or *k*		"	102
play'd at counsellors and *k*'s,	In Mem. lxiii.		23
shadow on the blaze of *k*'s:		xcvii.	19
By blood a *k*, at heart a clown;		cx.	4
Love is and was my Lord and *K*,		cxxv.	1-5
play the game of the despot *k*'s,	Maud,	I. x.	39
Guarding realms and *k*'s from shame	Ode on Well.		63
barking for the thrones of *k*'s;		"	121
loyal passion for our temperate *k*'s;		"	165
reverenced his conscience as his *k*;	Ded. of Idylls		7
going to the *k*, He made this	Enid		32
k himself should please To cleanse		"	38
k Mused for a little on his plea,		"	41
Forgetful of his promise to the *k*.		"	50
these things he told the *k*.		"	151
good *k* gave order to let blow		"	152
not mindful of his face In the *k*'s.		"	192
were she the daughter of a *k*,		"	229
In the great battle fighting for the *k*.		"	396
this was in the garden of a *k*;		"	656
children of the *k* in cloth of gold		"	664
mouthpiece of our *K* to Doorm		"	1644
(The *K* is close behind me)		"	1645
hear the judgment of the *K*.'		"	1647
hears the judgment of the *K* of *K*'s'		"	1648
in the *K*'s own ear Speak what has		"	1656
mild face of the blameless *K*,		"	1660
K himself Advanced to greet them		"	1726
So spake the *K*; low bow'd the Prince,		"	1768
K's own leech to look into his hurt;		"	1771
K went forth and cast his eyes		"	1780
to guard the justice of the *K*;		"	1782, 1804
fighting for the blameless *K*.		"	1818
K Had gazed upon her blankly	Vivien		16
Vivien should attempt the blameless *K*		"	20
Had built the *K* his havens		"	24
sons of *k*'s loving in pupillage		"	367
lived a *k* in the most Eastern East,		"	405
K impaled him for his piracy;		"	410
That carry *k*'s in castles,		"	427
a wizard who might teach the *K*		"	413
promised more than ever *k* has given,		"	436
K Pronounced a dismal sentence,		"	440
like a *k*, not to be trifled with		"	441
by force they dragg'd him to the *K*.		"	470
taught the *K* to charm the Queen		"	491
save the *K*, who wrought the charm,		"	493

220   CONCORDANCE TO

	POEM.	LINE.
K Made proffer of the league	Vivien	495
holy k, whose hymns Are chanted	"	615
she took him for the K;	"	625
blameless K and stainless man?'	"	628
good k means to blind himself,	"	632
were he not crown'd k, coward and fool.'	"	638
true and tender! O my liege and k!	"	640
the court, the k, dark in your light,	"	724
ere the people chose him for their k,	Elaine	35
two brothers, one a k, had met	"	40
he, that once was k, had on a crown	"	46
'lo, thou likewise shalt be k.'	"	56
when a k, he had the gems Pluck'd	"	57
are the kingdom's not the k's—	"	60
Lancelot, where he stood beside the K.	"	86
Sir K, mine ancient wound is hardly	"	94
K Glanced first at him, then her,	"	95
pastime now the trustful k is gone!'	"	102
the k Would listen smiling ..	"	116
a k who honours his own word	"	144
our true k Will then allow your	"	152
chief of those After the k,	"	184
castle Gurnion where the glorious K	"	293
beheld the K Charge at the head	"	303
the K, However mild he seems at home,	"	310
The dread Pendragon, Britain's k of k's,	"	423
Until they found the clear-faced K,	"	431
the last diamond of the nameless k.	"	443
K, duke, earl, Count, baron—	"	463
k's of desolate isles,	"	526
knights and k's, there breathes not one	"	539
Wroth at the k's command to sally forth	"	559
banquet,and concourse of knights and k's.	"	561
ridd'n away to die?' So fear'd the K,	"	567
when the K demanded how she knew,	"	574
hide his name From all men, ev'n the k,	"	580
Surely his k and most familiar friend	"	590
Down on the great K's couch,	"	607
O loyal nephew of our noble K,	"	649
Why slight your K, And lose the quest	"	651
'Right was the K! our Lancelot!	"	662
there told the K What the K knew	"	702
The seldom-frowning K frown'd	"	711
Obedience is the courtesy due to k's.'	"	714
Some read the K''s face, some the Queen's	"	723
the diamond sent you by the K:'	"	817
all the tale Of K and Prince,	"	820
Until we found the palace of the k.	"	1038–45
the K will know me and my love,	"	1052
come to take the K to fairy land?	"	1250
babbled of the K, the K Came	"	1253
Low in the dust of half-forgotten k's,	"	1328
'Fair she was, my K,	"	1365
Why did the K dwell on my name	"	1393
fair, my child, As a k's son	"	1400
nearest to the King, His nephew,	Guinevere	10
chill'd the popular praises of the K	"	14
reverencing k's blood in a bad inn,	"	38
he was answer'd softly by the K.	"	45
Beside the placid breathings of the K,	"	69
the clear face of the guileless K,	"	85
Before the people and our Lord the K.'	"	92
(When the good K should not be there)	"	97
K Was waging war on Lancelot	"	153
people and the K Must hate me	"	155
your sorrows with our lord the K's,	"	189
the K's grief For his own self,	"	194
the good K and his wicked Queen	"	207
were I such a K with such a Queen,	"	208
were I such a K it could not be.'	"	210
What canst thou know of K's	"	226
K As well-nigh more than man,	"	284
by miracle was approven k:	"	294
Lancelot or our Lord the K?'	"	324
the K In open battle or the tilting-field	"	329
Sir Lancelot's, were as noble as the k's,	"	349
crown'd the state pavilion of the K,	"	396
first she saw the K Ride toward her	"	400
on a sudden a cry, 'the K.'	"	408
her face a darkness from the K;	"	414
but tho' changed the K's.	"	418

	POEM.	LINE.
spared to lift his hand against the K.	Guinevere	434
that I the K should greatly care to live;	"	449
I was first of all the k's who drew	"	457
swear To reverence the K	"	465
and their conscience as their K,	"	466
K's waste hearth and aching heart	"	520
nay, they never were the K's.	"	548
They summon me their K to lead	"	566
K's breath wander o'er her neck,	"	576
moony vapour rolling round the K,	"	595
Gone, my lord the K,	"	609
he, the K, Call'd me polluted:	"	612
blessed be the K, who hath forgiven	"	627
none Will tell the K I love him	"	644
vast design and purpose of the K.	"	662
wrought the ruin of my lord the K.'	"	681
that long-buried body of the k,	Aylmer's F.	3
from the midriff of a prostrate k—	"	16
voice that calls Doom upon k's,	"	742
statues, k or saint, or founder fell.	Sea Dreams	217
Bride of the heir of the k's of the sea	W. to Alexan.	28
The K is happy In child and wife;	The Victim.	25
The K was hunting in the wild	"	31
The K return'd from out the wild	"	43
The K bent low, with hand on brow,	"	57
The K was shaken with holy fear;	"	61
K of the East altho' he seem,	Lucretius	133
struck the dateless doom of k's	"	233
I'll be the K of the Queen of the wrens	The Window	84
The fire-crown'd k of the wrens	"	151
flit like the k of the wrens	"	159

king-born.

	POEM.	LINE.
k-b, A shepherd all thy life but yet k-b,	Œnone	125

kingcup.

	POEM.	LINE.
The gold-eyed k's fine	A Dirge	36

kingdom.

	POEM.	LINE.
divided quite The k of her thought	Pal. of Art	228
But thou, while k's overset,	Talking O..	257
A k topples over with a shriek	Princess, Con.	62
are the k's not the king's—	Elaine	60
Until it came a k's curse with thee—	Guinevere	546

King-like.

	POEM.	LINE.
K-l, wears the crown: 'Of old sat Freedom,' etc.		16

kinship.

	POEM.	LINE.
A distant k to the gracious blood.	Aylmer's F.	62

kinsman.

	POEM.	LINE.
With many kinsmen gay,	Will Water.	90
k thou to death and trance	In Mem. lxx.	1
k left him watcher o'er his wife	Vivien	556
His k travelling on his own affair	"	567
My lady's Indian k unannounced.	Aylmer's F.	190
'Good! my lady's k! good!'	"	198
Once with this k, ah so long ago,	"	206
My lady's Indian k rushing in,	"	593

kirtle.

	POEM.	LINE.
blood Was sprinkled on your k	Princess, ii.	255

kiss (s.)

	POEM.	LINE.
kiss sweet k'es, and speak sweet words:	Sea-Fairies	34
fill my glass: give me one k:	Miller's D.	17
The k, The woven arms,	"	231
once he drew With one long k	Fatima	20
quick-falling dew Of fruitful k'es,	Œnone	201
Seal'd it with k'es?	"	230
wild k, when fresh from war's alarms,	D. of F. Wom.	149
k he gave me, ere I fell,	"	235
worth a hundred k'es press'd on lips	Gardener's D.	149
k'es, where the heart on one wild leap	"	254
Her k'es were so close and kind,	Talking O.	169
I would have paid her k for k,	"	195
that last k, which never was the last,	Love and Duty	65
His own are pouted to a k:	Day-Dm.	51
A touch, a k! the charm was snapt.	"	133
O love, for such another k;	"	174
'O happy k, that woke thy sleep!'	"	183
'O love, thy k would wake the dead!'	"	184
And evermore a costly k	"	251
A sleep by k'es undissolved,	"	263

	POEM.	LINE.
I never felt the *k* of love	Sir Galahad	19
Yet give one *k* to your mother dear	Lady Clare	49
here's a *k* for my mother dear,	"	53
waste his whole heart in one *k*	Sir L. and Q. G.	44
little maid That ever crow'd for *k*'es.'	Princess, ii.	261
Dear as remember'd *k*'es after death,	" iv.	36
her mother shore the tress With *k*'es,	" vi.	98
glance and smile, and clasp and *k*,	In Mem. lxxxiii.	7
every *k* of toothed wheels,	" cxvi.	11
She took the *k* sedately	Maud, I. xii.	14
my Maud by that long lover's *k*,	" xviii.	58
Mixt with *k*'es sweeter sweeter	" II. iv.	9
I am silent then And ask no *k*;'	Vivien	103
Win! by this *k* you will :	Elaine	152
rosy-kindled with her brother's *k*—	"	392
sad *k* by day by night renew'd	En. Arden	161
Never; no father's *k* for me—	"	791
that one *k* Was Leolin's one strong rival	Aylmer's F.	556
k'es balmier than half-opening buds	Tithonus	59
a doubt will only come for a *k*,	The Ringlet	21
ran To greet him with a *k*	Lucretius	7

kiss (verb.)

When I would *k* thy hand,	Madeline	31
If my lips should dare to *k*	"	43
k sweet kisses, and speak sweet words :	Sea-Fairies	34
would *k* them often under the sea,	The Merman	15-34
k them again till they kiss'd me	"	16-35
You'll *k* me, my own mother,	May Queen, ii.	34
have been to blame. *K*' me, my children.'	Dora	159
O *k* him once for me.	Talking O.	240
k him twice and thrice for me,	"	241
That have no lips to *k*,	"	242
I *k* it twice, I *k* it thrice,	"	253
Go to him : it is thy duty : *k* him :	Locksley H.	52
He stoops—to *k* her—on his knee.	Day-Dm.	130
That I might *k* those eyes awake !	"	240
I *k* the lips I once have kiss'd ;	Will Water.	37
And *k* again with tears !	Princess, i.	254
He reddens what he *k*'es :	" v.	158
k her : take her hand, she weeps :	" vi.	208
K' and be friends, like children	"	271
seem to *k* me ere I die .	" vii.	135
Farewell, we *k*, and they are gone.	In Mem. Con.	92
k the tender little thumb,	Enid	395
tread me down And I will *k* you for it ;'	Vivien	78
down the silken thread to *k* each other	"	305
k the child That does the task	Elaine	824
let us in, tho' late, to *k* his feet !	Guinevere	176
but one, To *k* it night and day	The Ringlet	4
'Then *k* it, love, and put it by :	"	23, 41
cry to thee To *k* thy Mavors,	Lucretius	82
Trail and twine and clasp and *k*, *K*, *k*,	The Window	24
a flower, a flower to *k*, *K*, *k*,	"	31

kissed.

winds of dawn have *k*,	Ode to Mem.	14
kiss them again till they *k* me	The Merman	35
not be *k* by all who would list,	The Mermaid	41
I *k* away before they fell.	Miller's D.	152
I *k* his eyelids into rest:	The Sisters.	19
girls all *k* beneath the sacred bush	The Epic	2
So the women *k* Each other,	Dora	125
old man's neck, and *k* him many times.	"	160
we closed, we *k*, swore faith,	Ed. Morris.	114
found, and *k* the name she found,	Talking O.	159
She *k* me once again.	"	168
daughter, whose sweet face He *k*,	Two Voices.	254
I kiss the lips I once have *k*;	Will Water.	37
turn'd and *k* her where she stood :	Lady Clare	82
And *k* again with tears.	Princess, i.	250-9
wh'n the king *K*' her pale cheek	" ii.	245
With that she *k* His forehead	"	290
I *k* it and I read.	" v.	364
here she *k* it : then—' All good	" vi.	189
k her slender hand,	Maud, I. xii.	13
Wh'n first she *k* on either cheek,	Enid	517
c' spit and *k* her, and they rode away,	"	825
K' the white star upon his noble front	"	1605
turn'd his face And *k* her climbing	"	1669
k her with all pureness, brother-like,	"	1732

	POEM.	LINE.
all her length and *k* his feet,	Vivien	68
k them, crying, 'Trample me,	"	75
k her, and Sir Lancelot his own hand,	Elaine	368
k the hand to which he gave,	"	698
task assign'd, he *k* her face,	"	825
And *k* her quiet brows,	"	1144
wellnigh *k* her feet For loyal awe	"	1166
k me saying thou art fair	"	1399
There *k*, and parted weeping :	Guinevere	124
k his wonder-stricken little ones ;	En. Arden	228
k him in his cot.	"	233
as they *k* each other In darkness,	Aylmer's F.	430
look'd so sweet, the *k* her tenderly,	"	555
could hear the lips that *k* Whispering	Tithonus	60
And a fear to be *k* away.'	The Ringlet	22
O Ringlet, I *k* you night and day	"	26
if you *k* her feet a thousand years,	Coquette, ii.	13
Clasp'd, *k* him, wailed :	Lucretius	276

kissing.

K the rose she gave me o'er and o'er,	Gardener's D.	172
satisfy my soul with *k* her :	Princess, v.	100
K' his vows upon it like a knight.	Aylmer's F.	472

kitchen.

hall must also serve For *k*,	Enid	391

kite (bird.)

K' and kestrel, wolf and wolf kin,	Boädicea	15

kite (toy.)

Flung ball, flew *k*, and raced the purple	Princess, ii.	230
Had tost his ball and flown his *k*,	Aylmer's F.	84

kith and kin.

in the field were Lancelot's *k* a *k*,	Elaine	465
drave his *k* a *k* And all the Table Round	"	497
k a *k*, not knowing, set upon him ;	"	597
all his *k* a *k* Clave to him,	Guinevere	436

kitten.

laugh As those that watch a *k*;	Vivien	33

kittenlike.

K' he roll'd And paw'd about her sandal.	Princess, iii.	165

kittle.

ater meä mayhap wi' 'is *k* o' steäm	N. Farmer.	61

knave.

neither *k* nor clown Shall hold 'You might have won'	"	11
Shakespeare's curse on clown and *k*	"	27
K's are men That lute and flute	Princess, iv.	110

knaw (know.)

Doctors, they *k*'s nowt,	N. Farmer.	5
Thof a *k*'s I hallus voäited wi' Squoire	"	15
tha *k*'s she laäid it to meä.	"	21
Do godamoighty *k* what a's doing	"	45
k's what I beän to Squoire	"	55
a *k*'s naw moor nor a floy ;	"	67

knaw'd (knew.)

An' I niver *k* what a meän'd	N. Farmer.	19

knee.

Low on her *k*'s herself she cast,	Mariana in the S.	27
took with care, and kneeling on one *k*,	M. d'Arthur	173
see My grandchild on my *k*'s	Dora	11
set up betwixt his grandsire's *k*'s,	"	128
with his boy betwixt his *k*'s,	Walk. to the M.	33
Hail, hidden to the *k*'s in fern,	Talking O.	29
lude thy knotted *k*'s in fern,	"	93
muffle round thy *k*'s with fern	"	142
round These knotted *k*'s of mine,	"	158
shower'd the rippled ringlets to her *k*;	Godiva	47
He sat upon the *k*'s of men	Two Voices	323
flask Between his *k*'s, half-drained ;	Day-Dm.	46
He stoops—to kiss her—on his *k*.	"	130
k's are bow'd in crypt and shrine ;	Sir Galahad	18
Cheek by jowl, and *k* by *k* :	Vision of Sin	84
held her round the *k*'s against his waist,	Princess, ii.	342
lent my *k* desire to kneel,	" iii.	278
On one *k* Kneeling, I gave it,	" iv.	448
sees his brood about thy *k*;	"	559
Set his child upon her *k*—	" v.	545
Knelt on one *k*—the child on one—	" vi.	75
Trail'd himself up on one *k* ;	"	139

CONCORDANCE TO

	POEM.	LINE.
takes the children on his *k*, .	*In Mem.* lxv.	11
At one dear *k* we proffer'd vows, .	„ lxxviii.	13
Had babbled ' Uncle ' on my *k*;	„ lxxxiii.	13
I that danced her on my *k*, .	„ *Con.*	45
toil of heart and *k*'s and hands, .	*Ode on Well.*	212
one about whose patriarchal *k*	„	236
riveting a helmet on his *k*, .	*Enid*	268
on her *k*'s, Who knows? another gift	„	820
slided up his *k* and sat, .	*Vivien*	88
Across her neck and bosom to her *k*,	„	106
bow'd black *k*'s Of homage, .	„	427
half-falling from his *k*'s, Half-nestled	„	753
Sat on his *k*, stroked his gray face	*Elaine*	745
Full sharply smote his *k*'s, and smiled	*Guinevere*	46
God bless him, he shall sit upon my *k*'s	*En. Arden*	197
rosy, with his babe across his *k*'s;	„	747
Hers, yet not his upon the father's *k*,	„	761
knelt, but that his *k*'s Were feeble,	„	779
rotatory thumbs on silken *k*'s, .	*Aylmer's F.*	200
scoundrel in the supple-sliding *k*.'	*Sea Dreams*	164
little babes about thy *k*: '*Lady, let the rolling,*' etc.		6
He stay'd his arms upon his *k*, .	*The Victim*	58

knee-deep.
seem'd *k-d* in mountain grass,	*Mariana in the S.*	42
Full *k-d* lies the winter snow, .	*D. of the O. Year*	1

kneel.
you do ill to *k* to me. .	*St S. Stylites*	131
in your looking you may *k* to God.	„	139
lent my knee desire to *k*, .	*Princess,* iii.	177

kneeled.
A red-cross knight for ever *k*	*L. of Shallot,* iii.	6

kneeler.
I loved you like this *k*, .	*Princess,* iv.	277

kneeling.
k, with one arm about her king,	*D. of F. Wom.*	270
took with care, and *k* on one knee,	*M. d'Arthur*	173
On one knee *K*, I gave it, .	*Princess,* iv.	449
And offer'd you it *k*: . .	*Vivien*	125
Lancelot *k* utter'd, ' Queen,	*Elaine*	1173

knell.
every hoof a *k* to my desires, .	*Princess,* iv.	156
the silver *k* Of twelve sweet hours	*Maud,* I. xviii.	64
a deeper *k* in the heart he knoll'd;	*Ode on Well.*	59

knelt.
as he *k* beside my bed, . .	*May Queen.* iii.	16
shaken with her sobs Melissa *k*; .	*Princess,* iv.	271
Florian *k*, and ' Come ' he whisper'd	„ v.	60
K on one knee—the child on one—	„ vi.	73
cried, or *k*, or pray'd to me, .	*Enid*	1692
camels *k* Unbidden, . .	*Vivien*	425
k Full lowly by the corners of his bed,	*Elaine*	822
have *k*, but that his knees Were feeble	*En. Arden*	779

knew.
k the seasons when to take Occasion	*To the Queen*	30
Dreaming, she *k* it was a dream;	*Mariana in the S.*	49
who that *k* him could forget	*Miller's D.*	3
I *k* your taper far away, .	„	109
k you could not look but well; .	„	150
Dear eyes, since first I *k* them well.	„	222
I *k* the flowers, I *k* the leaves, I *k*	*D. of F. Wom.*	73
Touch'd; and I *k* no more.' .	„	116
When she made pause I *k* not	„	169
k that Love can vanquish Death, .	„	269
I *k* your brother; his mute dust .	*To J. S.*	29
I *k* an old wife lean and poor, .	*The Goose*	1
k your gift that way At college: .	*The Epic*	24
almost ere I *k* mine own intent, .	*Gardener's D.*	145
tho' I knew it was mine own, .	„	222
beheld her ere she *k* my heart, .	„	270
You *k* my word was law, .	*Dora*	96
from his father's vats, Prime, which I *k*;	*Audley Ct.*	27
set the words and added names I *k*.	„	60
built When men *k* how to build, .	*Ed. Morris.*	7
k the names, Long learned names	„	16
since I *k* the right And did it; .	*Love and Duty*	29
the great Achilles, whom we *k*.	*Ulysses*	64

	POEM.	LINE.
love her, as I *k* her, kind? .	*Locksley H.*	70
Mother-Age (for mine I *k* not)	„	185
And she, that *k* not, pass'd: .	*Godiva*	73
place he *k* forgetteth him.' .	*Two Voices,*	264
A shadow on the graves I *k*,	„	272
' I *k* you at the first: . .	*Princess,* ii.	285
I never *k* my father, but she says .	„ iii.	66
knowing, saying not she *k*: .	„	132
since I *k* No rock so hard .	„	137
stammer'd that I *k* him—could have wish'd	„	190
alien lips, And *k* not what they meant;	„ iv.	102
She, question'd if she *k* us men, .	„	212
then, demanded if her mother *k*,	„	214
came these wolves; they *k* her; .	„	302
We *k* not your ungracious laws, .	„	380
nor *k* There dwelt an iron nature .	„ vi.	33
nor cared Nor *k* it, clamouring on,	„	134
had been wedded wife, I *k* mankind,	„	307
Nor *k* what eye was on me, .	„ vii.	38
call her Ida tho' I *k* her not, .	„	81
I *k* not where I was: . .	„	118
if you be that Ida whom I *k*, .	„	132
she *k* it, she had fail'd .	„	213
never *k* the sacred dust: .	*In Mem.* xxi.	22
never *k* the summer woods; .	„ xxvii.	4
I know not: one indeed I *k* .	„ xcv.	5
soften'd, and he *k* not why; .	„ cix.	12
can I doubt, who *k* thee keen .	„ cxii.	5
k that the death-white curtain meant	*Maud,* I. xiv.	37
O, if she *k* it, To know her beauty	„ xvi.	18
He *k* the man: the colt would fetch	*The Brook*	149
if you *k* her in her English days, .	„	224
good gray head which all men *k*, .	*Ode on Well.*	35
He *k* their voices of old .	„	63
Nor *k* we well what pleased us most,	*The Daisy,*	25
k Some one had blunder'd. .	*Lt. Brigade*	11
k him fierce and turbulent .	*Enid*	447
the goodly places that she *k*; .	„	646
she *k* That all was bright: .	„	657
suddenly she *k* it and rejoiced, .	„	687
Enid all abash'd she *k* not why, .	„	765
k her sitting sad and solitary. .	„	1131
surely *k* my lord was dead,' .	„	1569
k this Earl, when I myself Was half	„	1642
Because I *k* my deeds were known,	„	1706
k the range of all their arts, .	*Vivien*	23
Bard, and *k* the starry heavens; .	„	25
then you drank And *k* no more, .	„	126
as tho' you *k* this cursed charm,	„	285
either slept, nor *k* of other there; .	„	588
she that *k* not ev'n his name? .	*Elaine*	29
when none *k* from whence he came,	„	34
Sir Lancelot *k* there lived a knight	„	400
sally forth In quest of whom he *k* not,	„	560
King demanded how she *k*, .	„	574
' He won.' ' I *k* it,' she said. .	„	619
talk'd, Meseem'd, of what they *k* not;	„	672
k you what all others know, .	„	677
told the King What the King *k*.	„	703
k right well What the rough sickness	„	883
what this meant She *k* not, .	„	885
Lancelot *k* the little clinking sound	„	977
k that she was looking at him. .	„	979
k the Prince tho' marr'd with dust,	*Guinevere*	37
no man *k* from whence he came; .	„	287
indeed I *k* Of no more subtle matter	„	473
loved Enoch; tho' she *k* it not, .	*En. Arden*	43
he *k* the man and valued him, .	„	121
k her, as a horseman knows his horse—	„	136
had loved her longer than she *k*, .	„	452
she *k* that she would soon— .	„	459
folk that *k* not their own minds .	„	475
beside her path, She *k* not whence;	„	511
whisper on her ear, She *k* not what;	„	512
Philip thought he *k*; . .	„	516
tho' he *k* not wherefore, started up	„	617
making signs They *k* not what: .	„	642
a tavern which of old he *k*, .	„	692
' Know him?' she said ' I *k* him far away.	„	847
dead, Who hardly *k* me living .	„	890
one they *k*—Raw from the nursery—	*Aylmer's F.*	253

	POEM.	LINE.
might be entangled ere she *k*.	Aylmer's F.	272
but he had powers, he *k* it ;	"	393
Nor *k* he wherefore he had made the cry ;	"	589
all but those who *k* the living God—	"	637
always with her, whom you also *k*.	"	711
Poor souls, and *k* not what they did,	"	782
I lost it, *k* him less ;	Sea Dreams	72
In her strange dream, she *k* not why,	"	223
on your forgiving him Before you *k*.	"	261
k right well That Jenny had tript	Grandmother	25
I *k* but I would not tell.	"	26
who *k* what Jenny had been]	"	35
started, and spoke I scarce *k* how ;	"	43
I *k* them all as babies,	"	88
We *k* the merry world was round,	The Voyage	7
that was mine, my dream, I *k* it—	Lucretius	43

knife.

	POEM.	LINE.
To war with falsehood the *k*,	Two Voices	131
with a *k*'s haft hard against the board,	Enid	1448
with *k* in meat and wine in horn.	Vivien	544
The *k* uprising toward the blow,	The Victim	71
I am his dearest !' rushed on the *k*.	"	77
drove the *k* into his side	Lucretius	271

knight.

	POEM.	LINE.
The *k*'s come riding two and two :	L. of Shalott, ii.	25
She hath no loyal *k* and true,	"	26
A red-cross *k* for ever kneel'd	" iii.	6
K and burgher, lord and dame,	" iv.	43
All the *k*'s at Camelot :	"	50
Sir Bedivere, the last of all his *k*'s,	M. d'Arthur	7
goodliest fellowship of famous *k*'s,	"	15
bones of ancient men, Old *k*'s,	"	48
nor like a noble *k*:	"	75
the latest-left of all my *k*'s,	"	124
chance brought out a noble *k*.	"	231
A maiden *k*—to me is given .	Sir Galahad	61
just and faithful *k* of God !	"	79
A good *k* he ! we keep a chronicle .	Princess, Pro.	27
hoard of tales that dealt with *k*'s .	"	29
feudal *k* in silken masquerade,	"	227
prove Your *k*, and fight your battle	" iv.	572
many a bold *k* started up	" v.	349
and all the good *k*'s maim'd.	" vi.	224
other than my own ideal *k*,	Ded. of Idylls	6
Geraint, a *k* of Arthur's court,	Enid	1
bandit earls, and caitiff *k*'s	"	35
fifty *k*'s rode with them,	"	44, 1802
some gay *k* in Arthur's hall.'	"	118
a *k*, lady, and dwarf ;	"	187
the *k* Had visor up, and show'd	"	188
put her horse toward the *k*,	"	200–6
'Pardon me, O stranger *k*;	"	286
good *k*'s horse stands in the court ;	"	370
be the *k* whom late I saw	"	406
what *k* soever be in field	"	486
errant *k*'s And ladies came,	"	545
the *k* With some surprise, and thrice	"	556
Enid was aware of three tall *k*'s	"	905
said the second, 'yonder comes a *k*	"	975
head in th, and thought himself a *k*,	"	1091
k of Arthur's court, who laid his lance	"	1623
'The voice of Enid,' said the *k*;	"	1628
take you for a bandit *k* of Doorm	"	1634
made a *k* of Arthur's Table Round,	"	1641
k besought him, 'Follow me,	"	1655
same *k* of mine, risking his life	"	1763
She hated all the *k*'s,	Vivien	7
afterward He made a stalwart *k* .	"	333
The *k*'s, the court, the king, dark	"	724
and show'd them to his *k*'s, .	Elaine	58
k's Are half of them our enemies,	"	97
As to *k*'s Them surely I can silence	"	105
our *k*'s at feast Have pledged us .	"	115
answer'd Lancelot, the chief of *k*'s	"	141–87
ret xt, O my *k*, As all for glory :	"	153
loves it in his *k*'s more than himself :	"	157
dying down in the great *k* Approached	"	179
an answer for a noble *k*?	"	201
shame me not Before this noble *k*'	"	208
for, *k*, the maiden dream'd,	"	211
ride to Camelot with this noble *k*:	Elaine	220
disparagement Before the stranger *k*,	"	235
the great *k*, the darling of the court,	"	261
if his own *k* cast him down,	"	313
his *k*'s are better men than he—	"	314
lived a *k* Not far from Camelot,	"	400
wrathful that a stranger *k* Should do	"	467
bore a *k* of old repute to the earth	"	491
all the *k*'s His party, cried 'Advance	"	501
k's of utmost North and West,	"	525
our *k* thro' whom we won the day	"	528
So great a *k* as we have seen to-day—	"	532
ride forth and find the *k*.	"	536
k's and kings, there breathes not one	"	539
since the *k* Came not to us,	"	542
good *k*, but therewithal Sir Modred's	"	556
banquet, and concourse of *k*'s and kings	"	561
Albeit I know my *k*'s fantastical,	"	592
What of the *k* with the red sleeve?	"	613
Here was the *k*, and here he left	"	631
dream'd my *k* the greatest *k* of all.	"	664
that you love This greatest *k*	"	666
Where your great *k* is hidden,	"	687
King knew 'Sir Lancelot is the *k*.'	"	703
k's at banquet twice or thrice	"	732
serviceable To noble *k*'s in sickness	"	764
fain were I to learn this *k* were whole,	"	768
Woke the sick *k*,	"	815
the great *k* in his mid-sickness	"	874
should your good *k* be poor .	"	952
In all quarrels will I be your *k*	"	957
the King Came girt with *k*'s :	"	1254
As thou art a *k* peerless,'	"	1275
will be to your worship, as my *k*,	"	1317
k's had laid her comely head	"	1327
the lusty and long-practised *k*,	"	1351
My *k*, the great Sir Lancelot of the	"	1364
Pure, as you ever wish your *k*'s to be.	"	1366
profits me my name Of greatest *k*?	"	1404
Alas for Arthur's greatest *k*,	"	1409
k of Arthur's noblest dealt in scorn ;	Guinevere	41
said my father, and himself was *k*	"	232
every *k* Had whatsoever meat	"	262
'Sir Lancelot, as became a noble *k*,	"	326
If ever Lancelot, that most noble *k*,	"	343
Reputed the best *k* and goodliest man,	"	379
my right arm, The mightiest of my *k*'s	"	427
against the King Who made him *k*:	"	435
but many a *k* was slain ;	"	435
following these my mightiest *k*'s .	"	485
miss the wonted number of my *k*'s,	"	494
White Horse and *k*'s Once mine,	"	569
Among his warring senses, to thy *k*'s	"	633
Kissing his vows upon it like a *k*.	Aylmer's F.	472

knighthood.

	POEM.	LINE.
I swear by truth and *k* that I gave	Elaine	1289

knighthood-errant.

	POEM.	LINE.
drew The *k-e* of this realm	Guinevere	458

knightlike.

	POEM.	LINE.
k in his cap instead of casque,	Princess, iv.	577

knightly.

	POEM.	LINE.
Full *k* without scorn ;	Guinevere	40

knit.

	POEM.	LINE.
I hold them exquisitely *k*,	Talking O.	91
K land to land, and blowing havenward	Golden Year	44
I *k* a hundred others new ;	Two Voices	7
Some dolorous message *k* below .	In Mem. xii.	3
k The generations each with each ;	" xxxix.	15
k themselves for summer shadow,	Aylmer's F.	724

knob.

	POEM.	LINE.
A man with *k*'s and wires and vials	Princess, Pro.	65

knock'd.

	POEM.	LINE.
volume, all of songs, K down to me,	Audley Ct.	57
I *k* and, bidden, enter'd ;	Princess, iii.	114

knoll.

	POEM.	LINE.
Oread haunt The *k*'s of Ida .	Œnone	73
about the *k*'s A dozen angry models	Princess, Pro.	74

CONCORDANCE TO

	POEM.	LINE.
From *k* to *k*, where, couch'd at ease,	*In Mem.* xciv.	14
dusk revealed The *k*'s once more .	"	50
Nor hoary *k* of ash and haw .	" xcix.	9
on a little *k* beside it, stay'd .	*Enid* .	162
and so gallop'd up the *k*. .	"	168
on this little *k*, if anywhere, .	"	181
huddled here and there on mound and *k*,	"	1651
k's That dimpling died into each other	*Aylmer's F.*	148

knolled.
a deeper knell in the heart be *k* ;	*Ode on Well.*	59

knolling.
heavy clocks *k* the drowsy hours. .	*Gardener's D.*	180

knot (s.)
rusted nails fell from the *k*'s .	*Mariana* .	3
k's that tangle human creeds, ' *Clear-headed friend* '		3
I must gather *k*'s of flowers, .	*May Queen,* i.	11
palms in cluster, *k*'s of Paradise. .	*Locksley H.*	160
broke and buzz'd in *k*'s of talk ; .	*Princess,* i.	132
More solulile is this *k*, By gentleness	" v.	129
look'd A *k*, beneath, of snakes, .	*Enid* .	325
k's and loops and folds innumerable	*Elaine* .	438
felt the *k* Climb in her throat, .	"	736

knot (verb.)
as tight as I could *k* the noose ; .	*St S. Stylites*	64

knout.
he ruled with rod or with *k* ? .	*Maud,* I. iv.	47

know.
who may *k* Whether smile or frown	*Madeline*	11
k's not what the curse may be, .	*L. of Shalott,* ii.	6
night comes on that *k*'s not morn,	*Mariana in the S.*	94
I should *k* if it beat right, .	*Miller's D.*	179
I *k* He cometh quickly : .	*Fatima*	22
this may be I *k* not, but I *k* .	*Œnone*	262
The first of those who *k*. .	*Pal. of Art.*	164
k's not if it be thunder .	"	281
I *k* you, Clara Vere de Vere,	*L. C. V. de Vere*	57
You *k* so ill to deal with time .	"	63
I *k* not what was said ; .	*May Queen,* iii.	34
I *k* The blessed music went that way	"	41
fields, and all of them I *k*. .	"	50
k not how, All those sharp fancies,	*D. of F. Wom.*	48
I wrote I *k* not what. .	*To J. S.*	57
God *k*'s : he has a mint of reasons :	*The Epic*	33
sick, and *k*'s not what he does. .	*M. d'Arthur*	97
I *k* not : but we sitting .	*Ep.*	9
K you not Such touches are but .	*Gardener's D.*	17
nor did they *k* Who sent it ; .	*Dora* .	51
k there has not been for these five years	"	63
never *k* The troubles I have gone thro'!'	"	146
bloody trench Where no one *k*'s ? .	*Audley Ct.*	42
Nay, who *k*'s ? he's here and there.	*Walk. to the M.*	19
What *k* we of the secret of a man ? .	"	94
Heaven *k*'s—as much within ; .	*Ed. Morris.*	82
recognise the fields I *k*; .	*St S. Stylites*	39
k not well, For that the evil ones .	"	95
k I have some power with Heaven .	"	141
I *k* thy glittering face. .	"	202
James,—you *k* him,—old, but full .	*Golden Year*	60
I *k* That unto him who works, .	"	71
sleep, and feed, and *k* not me. .	*Ulysses*	5
but I *k* my words are wild, .	*Locksley H.*	173
would have said, 'Thou canst not *k*,'	*Two Voices*	43
K I not Death ? the outward signs ? .	"	270
He *k*'s a baseness in his blood .	"	301
something done, I *k* not where ; .	"	383
' I see the end, and *k* the good.' .	"	432
may not speak of what I *k*. .	"	435
Such hope, I *k* not fear ; .	*Sir Galahad*	62
hair Is gray before I *k* it. .	*Will Water.*	168
We *k* not what we *k*. .	"	178
many-headed beast should *k*.'	*You might have won,*	20
will *K* If there be any faith in man.'	*Lady Clare*	43
Well I *k*, when I am gone, .	*Vision of Sin*	109
For they *k* not what they mean. .	"	126
k the hue Of that cap .	"	141
Madam—if I *k* your sex, .	"	181
k The shadow from the substance,	*Princess,* i.	8

	POEM.	LINE.
weird seizures, Heaven *k*'s what : .	*Princess,* i.	14
they that *k* such things—I sought but	"	143
and mere We *k* not,—only this : .	"	151
O we fell out I *k* not why, .	"	249
let us *k* The Princess Ida waited : .	" ii.	6
answer'd, 'Then ye *k* the Prince ?'	"	35
I *k* the substance when I see it. .	"	391
fly, while yet you may ! My mother *k*'s :	" iii.	13
I shudder'd : ' and you *k* it.' .	"	42
she *k*'s too, And she conceals it.' .	"	43
calls her plagiarist ; I *k* not what :	"	78
At no man's beck, but *k* ourself .	"	211
I *k* the Prince, I prize his truth : .	"	216
so far In high desire, they *k* not .	"	263
yet we *k* Knowledge is knowledge,	"	298
Idle tears, I *k* not what they mean,	" iv.	21
' *K* you no song of your own land,'	"	66
K you no song, the true growth .	"	132
I—you *k* it—I will not boast ; .	"	334
We did not *k* the real light, .	"	338
k Your faces there in the crowd— .	"	488
'Tut, you *k* them not, the girls .	" v.	144
something may be done—I *k* not what—	"	219
who *k*'s ? we four may build some plan	"	221
What *k* I of these things ? .	"	274
blustering I *k* not what Of insolence	"	386
whereas I *k* Your prowess, Arac, .	"	393
name is yoked with children's, *k* herself.	"	408
right ascension, Heaven *k*'s what ; .	" vi.	240
weight of gratitude, I *k* it ; .	"	281
k The woman's cause is man's : .	" vii.	242
'from earlier than I *k*, Immersed .	"	292
across the wild That no man *k*'s. .	"	342
madest man, he *k*'s not why : .	*In Mem. Pro.*	10
Our wills are ours, we *k* not how ; .	"	15
We have but faith : we cannot *k* ; .	"	21
k no more than I who wrought .	" vi.	17
beckoning unto those they *k* ; .	" xiv.	8
k's no more of transient form .	" xvi.	7
I *k* that this was Life,— .	" xxv.	1
Half-dead to *k* that I shall die.' .	" xxxv.	16
My paths are in the fields I *k* .	" xxxix.	31
one that loves but *k*'s not, .	" xli.	11
truth from one that loves and *k*'s ? .	"	12
(he *k*'s not whence) A little flash, .	" xliii.	7
I shall *k* him when we meet : .	" xlvi.	8
Behold, we *k* not anything ; .	" liii.	13
mean the breath : I *k* no more.' .	" lv.	8
howsoe'er I *k* thee, some .	" lviii.	15
Half jealous of she *k*'s not what, .	" lix.	7
I *k* that in thy place of rest .	" lxvi.	2
then I *k* the mist is drawn .	"	13
Death's twin-brother, *k*'s not Death,	" lxvii.	3
makes me sad I *k* not why, .	"	11
strive to paint The face I *k* ; .	" lxix.	3
How *k* I what had need of thee, .	" lxxii.	3
k Thy likeness to the wise below, .	" lxxiii.	7
k thee of what force thou art .	" lxxviii.	3
I *k* transplanted human worth .	" lxxxi.	11
none could better *k* than I, .	" lxxxiv.	37
form by which I *k* Thy spirit .	" xc.	5
tell me, doubt is Devil-born. I *k* not :	" xcv.	5
She *k*'s not what his greatness is ; .	" xcvi.	27
She *k*'s but matters of the house, .	"	31
he, he *k*'s a thousand things. .	"	32
They *k* me not, but mourn with me.	" xcviii.	20
these are not the bells I *k*. .	" ciii.	8
Let her *k* her place ; .	" cxiii.	15
crying, *k*'s his father near ; .	" cxxii.	20
fling himself down ? who *k*'s ? .	*Maud,* I. i.	9
who *k*'s ? we are ashes and dust .	"	32
I have heard, I *k* not whence, .	"	67
the fiend best *k*'s whether woman .	"	75
I *k* it, and smile a hard-set smile, .	" iv.	20
Who *k*'s the ways of the world, .	"	44
doze Long since, I *k* not where ? .	" vii.	2
I *k* the way she went .	" xii.	21
To *k* her beauty might half undo it .	" xvi.	19
I *k* it the one bright thing to save .	"	20
I *k* He has plotted against me .	" xix.	79
Now I *k* her but in two, .	" xx.	15

	POEM.	LINE.		POEM.	LINE.
I *k* her own rose-garden,	Maud, I. xx.	41	be back, my girl, before you *k* it.'	En. Arden	193
ghastly Wraith of one that I *k*;	" II. i.	32	for all your wisdom well *k* I.	"	211
hearts that *k* not how to forgive:	"	44	*k* his babes were running wild	"	303
k Is a juggle born of the brain?	" ii.	41	of an avenue, Going we *k* not where:	"	356
Who *k*'s if he be dead?	"	71	I *k* not why—Their voices make me	"	393
k not whether he came in the Hanover	" v.	59	*k* not when it first came there,	"	398
I *k* that he lies and listens mute	"	60	I *k* that it will out at last.	"	399
I *k* where a garden grows;	"	72	Perhaps you *k* what I would have you *k*—	"	406
What *k* we greater than the soul?	Ode on Well.	265	loved you longer than you *k*.	"	418
he is gone: We *k* him now:	Ded. of Idylls	15	aught of what he cared to *k*.	"	655
answer sharply that she should not *k*.	Enid	196	face again And *k* that she is happy.'	"	720
Arms? truth! I *k* not:	"	289	Not to tell her, never to let her *k*.	"	787-9
Harbourage? truth, good truth, I *k* not,	"	270	not speak to these? They *k* me not.	"	790
k Where I can light on arms,	"	421	Lord has call'd me she shall *k*,	"	811
be he dead I *k* not,	"	443	*k* Enoch Arden of this town?'	"	846
Nor *k* I whether I be very base	"	468	'A' him?' she said 'I knew him	"	847
this I *k* That whatsoever evil	"	470	*k* you that I am he Who married—	"	829
tell me if you *k* it.'	"	684	to and fro, We *k* not wherefore:	Aylmer's F.	74
'Yea, I *k* it; your good gift,	"	688	I *k* not, for he spoke not,	"	213
k, When my dear child is set forth	"	727	I *k* not whence at first,	"	223
Who *k*'s? another gift of the high God,	"	821	did Sir Aylmer *k* That great pock-pitten	"	255
loves to *k* When men of mark	"	1077	girl and boy, Sir, *k* their differences!'	"	274
I *k*, God *k*'s, too much of palaces!	"	1085	I *k* her: the worst thought she has	"	362
victual for these men, and let us *k*.	"	1089	let them *k* themselves betrayed	"	524
a little happier: let me *k* it:	"	1166	came To *k* him more, I lost it,	Sea Dreams	72
I *k* Tho' men may bicker	"	1173	*k* for a truth, There's none of them	Grandmother	85
well I *k* it—pall'd—For I *k* men:	"	1180	We *k* the merry world is round,	The Voyage	95
'Yea, my lord, I *k* Your wish	"	1267	sweet little Eden on earth that I *k*	The Islet	14
in a far land and he *k*'s it not,	"	1346	then shall I *k* it is all true gold	The Ringlet	7
hardly *k* the tender rhyme	Vivien	233	far down, but I shall *k* Thy voice,	My life is full	9
k well that Envy calls you	"	317	if it be so, so it is, you *k*;	Spiteful Let.	17
k I that Fame is half-disfame	"	354	Nor *k*'s he what he sees;	Lucretius	132
take my counsel: let me *k* it at once:	"	503	O ye Gods, I *k* you careless,	"	205
If you *k*, Set up the charge you *k*,	"	552	I *k* thou surely must be mine	"	260
answer'd Merlin 'Nay, I *k* the tale,	"	563	flitted I *k* not where!	The Window	41
never wrong'd his bride, I *k* the tale.	"	580	somebody *k*'s that she'll say ay.'	"	93
whisper'd in the corner? do you *k* it?'	"	622			
answer'd sadly, 'Yea I *k* it.	"	623	*knowest.*		
man at all, who *k*'s and winks?'	"	630	*k* I bore this better at the first	St S. Stylites	27
I *k* the Table Round, my friends of old;	"	665	whereof, O God, thou *k* all.	"	69
I will not let her *k*:	"	672	Thou, O God, *k* alone.	"	82
believe you then, Who *k*'s? once more.	"	772	thou *k* what a man I am;	"	117
'Yea, lord,' she said, 'you *k* it.'	Elaine	81	my doom and thine: thou *k* it all.	Love and Duty	53
yours, Not Arthur's, as you *k*,	"	136	or if oblique Thou *k* not,	Two Voices	194
k right well, how meek soe'er he seem,	"	155	'What is it thou *k*, sweet voice?'	"	440
Hereafter you shall *k* me—	"	192	tell her Swallow, thou that *k* each,	Princess, iv.	78
you *k* Of Arthur's glorious wars.'	"	284	What *k* thou of the world,	Guinevere	341
'Fair lord, whose name I *k* not—	"	359	*k* thou now from whence I come—	"	430
my wont, as those, who *k* me, *k*.'	"	364			
That those who *k* should *k* you.'	"	367	*knowing.*		
to *k* well I am not great;	"	450	*k* God, they lift not hands of prayer,	M. d'Arthur	252
his wont, as we, that *k* him, *k*.'	"	474	spoke I *k* not the things that were	Ed. Morris	89
Albeit I *k* my knights fantastical	"	522	*k* all Life needs for life.	Love and Duty	82
your pardon! lo, you *k* it I.	"	666	*k* not the universe,	Two Voices	230
I *k* not if I *k* what true love is,			comes, scarce *k* what he seeks;	Day-Dm.	117
But if I *k*,	"	673	Shame might befall Melissa, *k*,	Princess, iii.	132
knew you what all others *k*.	"	677	Made them worth *k*;	" iv.	429
k full well Where your greatest knight	"	686	*k* Death has made His darkness	In Mem. lxxiii.	11
We two shall *k* each other,'	"	697	*k* the primrose yet is dear	" lxxxiv.	118
by mine head she *k*'s his hiding-place.'	"	710	smilest, *k* all is well.	" cxxvi.	20
How *k* you my lord's name is Lancelot?'	"	723	*k* your promise to me;	Maud, I. xxii.	50
yea I *k* it of mine own self:	"	946	I tarry for thee,'	" III. vi.	13
I *k* not which is sweeter, no, not I.	"	1003-5	what ail'd him, hardly *k* it himself,	Enid	1353
when we dwell upon a word we *k*	"	1021	let you rest, *k* you mine,	Vivien	184
till the word we *k* so well	"	1022	at a touch But *k* you are Lancelot	Elaine	150, 571
Becomes a wonder and we *k* not why,	"	1023	kith and kin, not *k*, set upon him.	"	597
the King will *k* me and my love,	"	1052	Not *k* he should die a holy man.	"	1410
this I *k*, for all the people *k* it,	"	1075	Who *k* nothing knows but to obey,	Guinevere	184
I *k* What thou hast been in battle.	"	1348	with which I used to play Not *k* I	"	544
Unbound as yet, and gentle, as I *k*.'	"	1377	She fail'd and sadden'd *k* it;	En. Arden.	230
if she will'd it! nay, Who *k*'s?	"	1413	this isle, not *k* where she lay;	"	631
knowing nothing *k*'s but to obey,	Guinevere	184	annals of the port, Not *k*—	"	704
None *k*'s it, and my tears have brought	"	200	young hearts not *k* that they loved,	Aylmer's F.	113
What can'st thou *k* of Kings	"	226	Not *k* what possess'd him:	"	550
'Yea, but I *k*: the land was full	"	230	aught that is worth the *k* I.	1865-1866	5-3
Howbeit I *k*, if ancient prophecies	"	446			
the wife Whom he *k*'s false, abide	"	511	*knowledge.*		
and *k* I am thine husband—	"	561	*k* of their own supremacy.	Œnone	151
I *k* not what mysterious doom.	"	571	*K* for its beauty;	To——, With Pal. of Art	3
Ye *k* me then, that wicked one,	"	663	Beauty, Good, and *K*, are three sisters	"	10
as a horseman *k*'s his horse—	En. Arden.	136	the *k* of his art Held me	D. of F. Wom.	9
			me this *k* bolder made,	To J. S.	5

P

	POEM.	LINE.
k circle with the winds: '*Love thou thy land*,' etc.		17
Certain, if *k* bring the sword,	"	87
k takes the sword away—	"	88
flower of *k* changed to fruit	*Love and Duty*	24
yearning in desire To follow *k*	*Ulysses*	31
K comes, but wisdom lingers,	*Locksley H.*	141-3
In midst of *k*, dream'd not yet.	*Two Voices*	90
men with *k* merely play'd,	"	172
newer *k*, drawing nigh.	*Day-Dm.*	71
k, so my daughter held, Was all in all,	*Princess*, i.	134
arguing love of *k* and of power;	" ii.	43
K is now no more a fountain seal'd :	"	76
We issued gorged with *k*,	"	366
yet we know *K* is *k*,	" iii.	299
each Disclaim'd all *k* of us: .	" iv.	210
K in our own land make her free,	" v.	409
less for truth than power In *k* :	" vii.	222
greater than all *k* beat her down.	"	223
k is of things we see;	*In Mem. Pro.*	22
Let *k* grow from more to more	"	25
all my *k* of myself;	" xvi.	16
all *k* that the sons of flesh Shall gather	" lxxxiv.	27
Who loves not *K*?	" cxiii.	1
not alone in power And *k*,	"	27
eye to eye, shall look On *k*; .	" Con.	130
Without *k*, without pity,	*Maud*, II. iv.	53
Without the captain's *k*: hope with me.	*Aylmer's F.*	717
Like Virtue firm, like *K* fair	*The Voyage*	68

known.

is she *k* in all the land,	*L. of Shalott*, i.	26
In aftertime, this also shall be *k*:	*M, d'Arthur*	35
one that never can be wholly *k*,	*Gardener's D.*	201
Much have I seen and *k*;	*Ulysses*	13
having *k* me—to decline	*Locksley H.*	43
To perish, wept for, honour'd, *k*,	*Two Voices*.	149
whatsoever can be taught and *k*;	*Princess*, ii.	363
falling on my face was caught and *k*.	" iv.	251
bore up in hope she would be *k*:	"	301
public use required she should be *k*;	"	317
and *k* at last (my work)	"	328
when *k*, there grew Another kind.	"	427
you have *k* the pangs we felt,	" v.	364
makes by force his merit *k*	*In Mem.* lxiii.	9
which, tho' veil'd, was *k* to me,	" cii.	13
that dear voice, I once have *k*	" cxv.	11
K and unknown; human, divine;	" cxxviii.	5
singing an air that is *k* to me,	*Maud*, I. v.	3
Everything came to be *k*:	" II. v.	51
'No more of love; your sex is *k*:	*The Letters*	29
be made *k* to the stately Queen,	*Enid*	607
Because I knew my deeds were *k*,	"	1706
not willing to be *k* He left the	*Elaine*	160
K as they are, to me they are unknown.'	"	186
K am I, and of Arthur's hall, and *k*,	"	188
in red samite, easily to be *k*,	"	432
women, whomsoever I have *k*	"	1286
men worse by making my sin *k*?	"	1407
surely was my profit had I *k*:	*Guinevere*	651
Not only to the market-cross were *k*,	*En. Arden*	96
k each other all our lives?	"	305, 417
k Far in a darker isle	"	605
He must have *k*, himself had *k*:	*Aylmer's F.*	346
had *k* a man, a quintessence of man,	"	388
a language *k* but smatteringly	"	433
had *k* Edith among the hamlets	"	614
As with the mother he had never *k*,	"	690
thou that killest, hadst thou *k*,	"	738

knuckled.

boy That *k* at the taw: .	*Will Water.*	132

Kypris.

Ay, and this *K* also—	*Lucretius*	95

L

ladid.

tha knaws she *l* it to meä.	*N. Farmer.*	21

laborious.

L for her people and her poor—	*Ded. of Idylls*	34

labour (s.)	POEM.	LINE.
prime *l* of thine early days; .	*Ode to Mem.*	94
why Should life all *l* be?	*Lotos-E's.*	87
Long *l* unto aged breath,	"	130
l in the deep mid-ocean	"	172
And rested from her *l's*.	*The Goose*	16
discerning to fulfil This *l*,	*Ulysses*	36
So were thy *l* little-worth.	*Two Voices*	171
A *l* working to an end.	"	297
A present, a great *l* of the loom,	*Princess*, i.	43
blessing on her *l's* for the world.	" ii.	455
health, and wind, and rain, And *l*.	" iv.	261
all her *l* was but as a block	" vii.	215
reaps the *l* of his hands	*In Mem.* lxiii.	26
prosperous *l* fills The lips of men	" lxxxiii.	25
on mind and art, And *l*,	" lxxxvi.	23
l and the mattock-harden'd hand .	*Maud*, I. xviii.	34
Or it may be the *l* of his hands,	*Enid*	341
The dew of their great *l*,	"	568
Her own poor work, her empty *l*,	*Elaine*	985
Confused the chemic *l* of the blood	*Lucretius*	20

labour (verb.)

No memory *l's* longer	*D. of F. Wom.*	273
he that *l's* for the sparrow-hawk	*Enid*	271
since he did but *l* for himself,	*En. Arden.*	820
would go *L* for his own Edith,	*Aylmer's F.*	420

labour'd.

l down within his ample lungs,	*Princess*, v.	263
The bosom with long sighs *l*;	" vii.	210
hermit, who had pray'd, *l* and	*Elaine*	402
l thro' His brief prayer-prelude	*Aylmer's F.*	628

labourer.

woo'd and wed A *l's* daughter,	*Dora*	38
the *l* tills His wonted glebe	*In Mem.* c.	21
sallowy rims, arose the *l's* homes	*Aylmer's F.*	147

labouring.

The giant *l* in his youth;	*In Mem.* cxvii.	2
lusty mowers *l* dinnerless	*Enid*	1100
Arthur came, and *l* up the pass	*Elaine*	48
ever *l* had scooped himself	"	403

laburnum.

L's, dropping-wells of fire.	*In Mem.* lxxxii.	12

labyrinth.

He thrids the *l* of the mind,	*In Mem.* xcvi.	21
Charm'd him thro' every *l*	*Aylmer's F.*	479

lace (net-work.)

shadow of a piece of pointed *l*,	*Elaine*	1168

lace (a string.)

burst The *l's* toward her babe;	*Princess*, vi.	133

lace (verb.)

holp To *l* us up,	*Princess*, i.	199

lack (s.)

tinged with wan from *l* of sleep,	*Princess*, iii.	9
for *l* of gentle maiden's aid	*Elaine*	761

lack (verb.)

We *l* not rhymes and reasons,	*Will Water.*	62

lackest.

what thou *l*, thought resign'd,	*Two Voices*	98

lack-lustre.

a *l-l* dead-blue eye,	*A Character*	17

lad.

many a bolder *l* 'ill woo me	*May Queen*, i.	23
shepherd *l's* on every side 'ill come	"	27
the *l* stretch'd out And babbled	*Dora*	131
O well for the sailor *l*,	'*Break, break,*' etc.	7
long-limb'd *l* that had a Psyche too;	*Princess*, ii.	384
would tilt it out among the *l's*:	" v.	345
Poor *l*, he died at Florence,	*The Brook*	35
Enoch Arden, a rough sailor's *l*	*En. Arden*.	14
Leolin's emissary, A crippled *l*,	*Aylmer's F.*	519
a *l* may wink, and a girl may hint,	*The Ringlet*	17

ladder.

lean a *l* on the shaft,	*St S. Stylites*	213

	POEM.	LINE.
laden.		
enchanted stem *L* with flower and fruit	*Lotos-E's.*	29
Two sets of three *l* with jingling arms,	*Enid*	1037
came the children *l* with their spoil;	*En. Arden*	442
lading.		
The *l* of a single pain,	*In Mem.* xxv.	11
l and unlading the tall barks,	*Eu. Arden*	817
lady.		
The sweetest *l* of the time,	*Arabian N's.*	141
The *L* of Shalott.	*L. of Shalott,* i. 9, *et pass.*	
kneel'd To a *l* in his shield	"	7
Before Our *L* murmur'd she;	*Mariana in the S.*	28
bore a *l* from a leaguer'd town;	*D. of F. Wom.*	47
I saw a *l* within call,	"	85
No marvel, sovereign *l*: in fair field	"	97
Rise from the feast of sorrow, *l*,	*Margaret.*	62
eyes of *ladies* and of kings.	*M. d'Arthur*	225
I met my *l* once: .	*Walk. to the M.*	40
lightly rain from *ladies'* hands,	*Sir Galahad*	12
sweet are looks that *ladies* bend	"	13
he shall have it,' the *l* replied,	*Lady Clare*	47
Ancient homes of lord and *l*,	*L. of Burleigh*	31
That she grew a noble *l*,	"	75
with these, a *l*, one that arm'd	*Princess, Pro.*	32
takes a *l's* finger with all care	"	172
talk of college and of *ladies'* rights	"	226
let the *ladies* sing us, if they will	"	233
l of three castles in that land:	" i.	78
'Three *ladies* of the Northern empire	"	235
ladies of your land so tall?'.	" ii.	33
do well, *Ladies*, in entering here	"	48
We sat: the *L* glanced:	"	96
dearest *L*, pray you fear me not,	"	312
all the *ladies*, each at each,	" iv.	99
strange experiences Unmeet for *ladies*	"	141
the *L* stretch'd a vulture throat,	"	344
live, dear *l*, for your child!	" v.	77
fluttering scarfs and *ladies'* eyes,	"	498
'Your brother, *L*—Florian,—ask	" vi.	293
slowly by a knight, *l*, and dwarf	*Enid*	187
the *l* he loves best be there.	"	481
claim to for the *l* at his side,	"	487
ever won it for the *l* with him,	"	490
you, that have no *l*, cannot fight.'	"	493
errant knights And *ladies* came	"	546
Spake to the *l* with him and proclaim'd	"	552
thyself, thy *l*, and thy dwarf,	"	581
lords and *ladies* of the high court	"	662
Sweet *l*, never since I first drew	"	1467
ladies I used to call Enid the Fair	"	1810
one verse more the *l* speaks it—	*Vivien*	295
The *l* never made *unwilling* war	"	453
ever among *ladies*, ate in Hall,	*Elaine*	255
on his cuirass worn our *L's* Head,	"	294
Favour of any *l* in the lists.	"	363, 473
L, my liege, in whom I have my joy,	"	1174
to all other *ladies* I make moan.	"	1272
whom the *L* of the Lake Stole	"	1305
needs *l*, weep no more;	*Guinevere*	182
Ah sweet *l*, the King's grief	"	194
sweet *l*, if I seem To vex an ear	"	312
We gracious to all *ladies*,	"	327
could think, sweet *l*, yours would be	"	350
the phrase cheering even My *l*;	*Aylmer's F.*	117
My *l's* Indian kinsman, unannounced	"	190
'Go I' my *l's* kinsman! good!'	"	198
My *l* with her fingers interlock'd,	"	199
'A gracious gift to give a *l*, this I'	"	240
gift of his to one That is no *l*'	"	243
My *l's* cousin, Half-sickening	"	461
Seized it, took home, and to my *l*,—	"	532
for my *l* so bow'd out,	"	558
My *l's* Indian kinsman rushing in,	"	593
l, let the rolling drums '	*Lady, let the rolling,'etc.*	1
l, let the trumpets blow	"	5
my *l*, if a k'd to her face,	*The Window*	96
never a line from my *l* yet,	"	120
lady-clad.		
The feudal warrior *l-c*;	*Princess, Pro.*	119

	POEM.	LINE.
Lady's-Head.		
The *L-H* upon the prow	*The Voyage*	11
lady-sister.		
I bow'd to his *l-s*	*Maud*, I. iv.	15
lag.		
To *l* behind, scared by the cry	*Princess*, v.	91
laggard.		
a *l* hanging down his head,	*Enid*	909
lagged.		
I *l* in answer loth to render up	*Princess*, v.	289
Whereof the dwarf *l* latest,	*Enid*	188
laid.		
Upon my lap he *l* his head:	*The Sisters*	17
l him at his mother's feet.	"	35
strong foundation-stones were *l*	*Pal. of Art*	235
see me where I am lowly *l*.	*May Queen*, ii.	30
breast to sight *L* bare.	*D. of F. Wom.*	159
L by the tumult of the fight.	*Margaret*	26
the more the white goose *l*	*The Goose*	23
L widow'd of the power in his eye	*M. d'Arthur*	122
l his head upon her lap,	"	208
Francis *l* A damask napkin:	*Audley Ct.*	19
and the winds are *l* with sound.	*Locksley H.*	104
l a tax Upon his town	*Godiva*	13
eyes long *l* in happy sleep!',	*Day-Dm.*	181
arms across her breast she *l*;	*Beggar Maid*	1
And is lightly *l* again.	*Vision of Sin*	134, 179
l about them at their wills and died;	*Princess, Pro.*	31
her likeness out; *L* it on flowers,	" i.	92
creature *l* his muzzle on your lap,	" ii.	253
were *l* up like winter bats,	" iv.	126
l A feeling finger on my brows,	" vi.	104
L the soft babe in his hard-mailed	"	191
And others otherwhere they *l*;	"	357
Where he in English earth is *l*,	*In Mem.* xviii.	2
They *l* him by the pleasant shore,	" xix	3
L their dark arms about the field.	" xciv. 16, 52
spectres of the mind And *l* them:	" xcv.	16
l On the hasp of the window	*Maud*, I. xiv.	18
He *l* a cruel snare in a pit	" II. v.	84
And worthy to be *l* by thee;	*Ode on Well.*	94
because his bones are *l* by thine.	"	141
where you tenderly *l* it by:	*The Daisy*	100
better were I *l* in the dark earth,	*Enid*	97
sprigs of summer *l* between the folds,	"	138
everywhere Was hammer *l* to hoof,	"	256
crost the trencher as she *l* it down;	"	396
over these is *l* a silver wand,	"	483
On either shining shoulder *l* a hand,	"	518
apparel, which she *l* Flat on the couch,	"	678
with this and *l* it in my hand,	"	699
L from her limbs the costly-broider'd	"	769
command I *l* upon you, not to speak	"	927
raised and *l* him on a litter-bier,	"	1414
l him on it All in the hollow of his	"	1416
l his lance In rest, and made as if.	"	1623
penance the Queen *l* upon me.	"	1702
l the diamond in his open hand.	*Elaine*	823
Her father *l* the letter in her hand,	"	1128
on the black decks *l* her	"	1141
Received at once and *l* aside the gems	"	1196
knights had *l* her comely head	"	1327
l her hands about his feet.	*Guinevere*	524
l the feeble infant in his arms;	*En. Arden*	152
when she *l* her head beside my own	"	882
yet had *l* No bar between them:	*Aylmer's F.*	117
l his feverous pillow smooth!	"	701
l, Wifelike, her hand in one of his,	"	807
beautiful, when all the winds are *l*.	*Spec of Iliad*	12
A famine after *l* them low,	*The Victim.*	2
With neighbours *l* along the grass,	*Lucretius*	211
bones long *l* within the grave,	"	252
lain.		
and *l* in the lilies of life.	*Maud*, I. iv.	60
Had I *l* for a century dead;	" xxii.	72
lake.		
See '*Lancelot of the Lake*' under '*Lancelot.*'		
canal Is rounded to as clear a *l*.	*Arabian N's.*	46
counterchanged The level *l*.	"	85

CONCORDANCE TO

	POEM.	LINE.
from out the bosom of the *l*,	*M. d'Arthur*	30
on the shining levels of the *l*.	"	51
Wrought by the lonely maiden of the *L*.	"	104
on a sudden, lo ! the level *l*,	"	191
my pleasant rambles by the *l*,	*Ed. Morris* 1,	13
ripply shallows of the lisping *l*,	"	98
mist of morn Clung to the *l*.	"	108
taper glimmer'd in the *l* below;	"	135
moves among my visions of the *l*,	"	144
then we crost Between the *l's*,	*Golden Year*	6
Deep in the garden *l* withdrawn.	*Day-Dm.*	32
Dreams over *l* and lawn,	*Vision of Sin*	11
the *l* A little clock-work steamer	*Princess, Pro.*	70
long light shakes across the *l's*	" iii.	350
quenching *l* by *l* and tarn by tarn	" vii.	25
slips into the bosom of the *l*:	"	172
dead *l* That holds the shadow	*In Mem.* xvi.	8
long by the garden *l* I stood,	*Maud*, I. xxii.	35
From the *l* to the meadow, and on	"	37
white lake-blossom fell into the *l*.	"	47
blown the *l* beyond his limit,	*The Daisy*	71
One tall Agavè above the *l*.	"	84
Bala *l* Fills all the sacred Dee.	*Enid*	1777
l whiten'd and the pinewood roar'd	*Vivien*	487
whom the Lady of the *L* Stole	*Elaine*	1395

lake-blossom.

| The while *l-b* fell into the lake | *Maud*, I. xxii. | 47 |

lamb.

bird would sing, nor *l* would bleat,	*Mariana in the S.*	37
I hear the bleating of the *l*,	*May Queen*, iii.	2
sweeter is the young *l's* voice	"	6
this lost *l* (she pointed to the child)	*Princess*, iv.	342
at once the lost *l* at her feet .	"	372
youth, the spotless *l* of Christ,	*Vivien*	599
whitest *l* in all my fold Loves you :	*Aylmer's F.*	361
light is large and *l's* are glad	*Lucretius*	99

Lamb (Christ.)

| So shows my soul before the *L*, | *St Agnes' Eve* | 17 |

lame.

abidest *l* and poor,	*Two Voices*	197
I wander, often falling *l*,	*In Mem.* xxiii.	6
would work eye dim, and finger *l*,	*Enid*	628
mate is blind and captain *l*,	*The Voyage*	91
But blind or *l* or sick or sound	"	93

Lamech.

| But that of *L* is mine. | *Maud*, II. ii. | 48 |

lamed.

| spear Down-glancing *l* the charger, | *Elaine* | 487 |
| all my faculties are *l*. | *Lucretius* | 123 |

lameness.

| Cured *l*, palsies, cancers. | *St S. Stylites* | 81 |

lament.

| And loudly did *l*. | *Dying Swan* | 7 |
| soul *l's*, which hath been blest, | *D. of F. Wom.* | 281 |

lamentation.

l and an ancient tale of wrong,	*Lotos-E's.*	163
as it were one voice, in agony Of *l*,	*M. d'Arthur*	201
Great Duke With an empire's *l*,	*Ode on Well.*	2

Lamorack.

| Lancelot, Tristram, and Geraint, And *L* Elaine | | 556 |

lamp.

'by that *l*,' I thought, 'she sits!'	*Miller's D.*	114
tho' my *l* was lighted late,	*May Queen*, iii.	18
lit *L's* which outburn'd Canopus.	*D. of F. Wom.*	146
burn a fragrant *l* before my bones,	*St S. Stylites*	193
yearning toward the *l's* of night.	*Two Voices*	363
l's blazon'd like Heaven and Earth	*Princess*, i.	220
above her droop'd a *l*,	" iv.	253
When all is gay with *l's*,	*In Mem.* xcvii.	27

lamplight.

| Gold glittering thro' *l* dim, | *Arabian N's.* | 18 |

lamp-lit.

| shone the tent *L-l* from the inner. | *Princess*, iv. | 8 |

Lancaster.

| York's white rose as red as *L's*, | *Aylmer's F.* | 51 |

lance.

	POEM.	LINE.
L's in ambush set ;	*D. of F. Wom.*	28
that Arthur who, with *l* in rest,	*M. d'Arthur*	222
hurl their *l's* in the sun ;	*Locksley II.*	170
My tough *l* thrusteth sure,	*Sir Galahad*	2
push'd with *l's* from the rock,	*Princess, Pro.*	46
into fiery splinters leapt the *l*,	v.	483
Like light in many a shiver'd *l*	*In Mem.* xlviii.	3
Let *me* lay *l* in rest, O noble host,	*Enid*	496
A *l* that splinter'd like an icicle,	"	938
Aim'd at the helm, his *l* err'd ;	"	1006
pick'd the *l* That pleased him best,	"	1028
the points of *l's* bicker in it	"	1298
Down by the length of *l* and arm	"	1312
riding with a hundred *l's* up;	"	1388
cast his *l* aside And doff'd his helm :	"	1443
l In rest, and made as if to fall	"	1623
every scratch a *l* had made upon it,	*Elaine*	20
but God Broke the strong *l*.	"	26
the truer seat, The firmer *l*:	"	446
Set *l* in rest, strike spur,	"	455
she felt the sharp *l* go;	"	621

lance-head.

| Gasping to Sir Lavaine, 'draw the *l-h*' | *Elaine* | 510 |

Lancelot.

brazen greaves Of bold Sir *L*.	*L. of Shalott*,iii.	5
by the river Sang Sir *L*.	"	36
L mused a little space ;	" iv.	51
Sir *L* and Queen Guinevere Rode	*Sir L, and Q. G.*	20
Touching her guilty love for *L*,	*Enid*	25
dreaming of her love For *L*	"	159
heard the great Sir *L* sing it once,	*Vivien*	235
what say ye to Sir *L*, friend?	"	619
Sir *L* went ambassador, at first,	"	624
Not even *L* brave, nor Gahalad clean	"	654
Guarded the sacred shield of *L* ;	*Elaine*	4
maid by that good shield of *L*,	"	29
L won the diamond of the year,	"	69
great deeds Of *L*, and his prowess	"	83
they dwelt languidly On *L*,	"	86
To blame, my lord Sir *L*,	"	98
L vext at having lied in vain :	"	103
L, the flower of bravery,	"	114
L, the chief of knights,	"	141-87
at a touch But knowing you are *L* ;	"	150, 573
got Sir *L* suddenly to horse	"	159
L marvell'd at the wordless man ;	"	172
L, when they glanced at Guinevere,	"	270
L spoke And answered him at full,	"	285
heard Sir *L* cry in the court,	"	343
to his proud horse *L* turn'd .	"	346
His brother's ; which he gave to *L*,	"	379
kiss'd her, and Sir *L* his own hand,	"	383
Sir *L* knew there lived a knight .	"	400
you ride with *L* of the Lake	"	416
after muttering 'the great *L*'	"	420
L bode a little, till he saw	"	460
little need to speak Of *L* in his glory:	"	463
in the field were *L's* kith and kin,	"	465
almost overdo the deeds Of *L* ;	"	469
Is it not *L* !' 'When has *L* worn	"	472
family passion for the name Of *L*,	"	477
overbore Sir *L* and his charger,	"	486
brought his horse to *L* where he lay	"	492
day when *L* fled the lists	"	524
He seem'd to me another *L*—	"	533
twenty times I thought him *L*—	"	534
after *L*, Tristram, and Geraint	"	555
L who has come Despite the wound	"	564
'Nay, Lord,' she said. 'And where is *L*?'	"	571
L told me of a common talk	"	576
Far lovelier in our *L* had it been	"	587
So fine a fear in our large *L*	"	593
L is no more a lonely heart.	"	600
Gawain saw Sir *L's* azure lions,	"	660
'Right was the King! our *L* !	"	662
cross our mighty *L* in his loves ! .	"	685
What the King knew ' Sir *L* is the	"	703
'The maid of Astolat loves Sir *L*,	"	721
Sir *L* loves the maid of Astolat.' .	"	722
sorrowing *L* should have stoop'd so low,	"	728

	POEM.	LINE.
Forgot to drink to L and the Queen,	Elaine	733
pledging L and the lily maid	"	734
one-day-seen Sir L in her heart	"	743
How fares my lord Sir L?'	"	791
Sir L! How know you my lord's name is L?'	"	792
Saw the casque Of L on the wall ;	"	802
L look'd and was perplext in mind,	"	834
L Would tho' he call'd his wound	"	847
when Sir L's deadly hurt was whole,	"	900
came before Sir L, for she thought	"	904
L ever prest upon the maid	"	907
L saw that she withheld her wish,	"	916
Too courteous are you, fair Lord L.	"	967
L knew the little clinking sound ;	"	977
L knew that she was looking at him,	"	973
there the great Sir L muse at me :	"	1042
L, who coldly went nor bad me one :	"	1051
it is no more Sir L's fault	"	1069
'Is it for L, is it for my dear lord?'	"	1099
'For L and the Queen and all the world	"	1101
on which I died For L's love,	"	1112
Sir L. at the palace craved Audience	"	1156
L kneeling utter'd, 'Queen,	"	1173
Than you believe me, L of the Lake	"	1199
while Sir L leant, in half disgust	"	1231
L later came and mused at her,	"	1261
'Most noble lord, L of the Lake,	"	1265
Pray for my soul thou too, Sir L,	"	1274
freely spoke Sir L to them all ;	"	1281
L sad beyond his wont,	"	1323
shield of L at her feet lie carven,	"	1331
mark'd Sir L where he moved apart	"	1339
sigh'd in passing 'L, Forgive me :	"	1340
L, my L, thou in whom I have Most	"	1347
My knight, the great Sir L of the Lake	"	1364
L answer'd nothing, but he went	"	1378
L, whom the Lady of the Lake Stole	"	1395
groan'd Sir L in remorseful pain,	"	1418
sharpen'd by strong hate for L.	Guinevere	21
Sir L passing by Spied where	"	31
L pluck'd him by the heel,	"	35
So Sir L help To raise the Prince,	"	46
Sir L told The matter to the Queen,	"	53
'O L, get thee hence.	"	83, 95
L ever promised, but remain'd,	"	93
L, who rushing outward lionlike,	"	106
'L, wilt thou hold me so?'	"	115
So L got her hence,	"	121
King Was waging war on L ;	"	154
To wage grim war against Sir L .	"	191
'This evil work of L. and the Queen?'	"	305
would say Sir L had the noblest ;	"	318
L or our lord the King?'	"	324
'Sir L, as became a noble knight,	"	326
L's needs must be a thousand-fold	"	336
If ever L, that most noble knight,	"	343
Sir L's, were as noble as the King's,	"	349
L came, Reputed the best knight	"	378
not like him, 'Not like my L'—	"	404
while yet Sir L, my right arm,	"	426
came thy shameful sin with L ;	"	483
they are not mine, But L's :	"	548
not a smaller soul, Nor L, nor another.	"	563
c lour which I found In L—	"	641
most human too, Not L, nor another.	"	643-54
	laucets.	
greenish glimmerings thro' the l,	Aylmer's F.	622
	land.	
God gave her peace : her l reposed,	To the Queen	26
rainbow forms and flies on the l	Sea-Fairies	25
is she known in all the l,	L. of Shalott,	i. 26
nursed in some delicious l	Eleänore	11
Pressing up against the l.	"	112
lent broad verge to distant l's,	Pal. of Art	30
paced for ever in a glimmering l,	"	67
the times of every l So wrought,	"	147
seas draw backward from the l	"	251
in strange l's a traveller walking	"	277
have found A new l, but I die.'	"	284

	POEM.	LINE.
any poor about your l's?	L. C. V. de Vere	68
as little Alice in all the l they say,	May Queen, i.	7
sweet is all the l about .	" iii.	7
and pointed toward the l,	Lotos-E's.	1
In the afternoon they came unto a l,	"	3
A l of streams!	"	10
seaward flow From the inner l:	"	15
l where all things always seem'd	"	24
looking over wasted l's,	"	159
In every l I saw, wherever light	D. of F. Wom.	13
when to l Bluster the winds and tides	"	37
My God, my l, my father—	"	209
the l that freemen till ;	'You ask me why,' etc.	7
l, where girt with friends or foes .	"	9
A l of settled government,	"	10
A l of just and old renown,	"	21
Tho' l Power should make from l to l	"	21
Love thou thy l, with love 'Love thou thy land,' etc.		1
pace the troubled l, like Peace ;	"	84
on a dark strait of barren l.	M. d'Arthur	10
waste l, where no one comes,	"	202
All the l in flowery squares,	Gardener's D.	75
and he died In foreign l's ;	Dora	17
sun fell, and all the l was dark.	"	77, 107
cliffs that guard my native l,	Audley Ct.	48
voice fled always thro' the summer l ;	Ed. Morris	67
l's in Kent and messuages in York,	"	127
will leave my relics in your l,	St S. Stylites	191
A babbler in the l.	Talking O.	24
nor yet Thine acorn in the l.	"	260
streams to fatten lower l's,	Golden Year	34
Knit l to l, and blowing havenward	"	44
like a shaft of light across the l.	"	49
like a fruitful l reposed ;	Locksley H.	13
Just breaking over l and main	Two Voices	84
It is not bad but good l,	Amphion	6
Nor for my l's so broad and fair ;	Lady Clare	10
Lord Ronald is heir of all your l's,	"	19
Made a murmur in the l.	L. of Burleigh	20
In all that l had never been :	Beggar Maid	14
an answer peal'd from that high l,	Vision of Sin	221
Close to the sun in lonely l's,	The Eagle	2
lady of three castles in that l :	Princess, i.	78
seizures come Upon you in those l's :	"	82
then we crost To a livelier l :	"	109
hills, that look'd across a l of hope,	"	167
l, he understood, for miles about	"	189
thro' the l at eve we went,	"	246
are the ladies of your l so tall?'	" ii.	33
falling in a l Of promise ;	"	123
promise you Some palace in our l,	" iii.	146
we should find the l Worth seeing ;	"	155
no song of your own l	" iv.	66
swallow winging south From mine own l,	"	72
Strove to buffet to l in vain.	"	167
like a spire of l that stands apart .	"	262
crying there was an army in the l,	"	463
fled away Thro' the dark l,	" v.	47
skirt and fringe of our fair l,	"	210
'Our l invaded, 'sdeath!	"	266
Of l's in which at the altar	"	367
Knowledge in our own l make her free,	"	409
a wild horn in a l Of echoes .	"	475
I go to mine own l For ever ;	" vi.	199
a peak to gaze O'er l and main,	" vii.	21
volume of the Poets of her l:	"	150
a l of peace : Gray halls	Con.	
travell'd men from foreign l's	In Mem. x.	6
thou hadst touch'd the l to-day,	" xiv.	2
The violet of his native l.	" xviii.	4
l's where not a leaf was dumb ;	" xxiii.	10
heard them sweep the winter l ;	" xxx.	10
thine in undiscover'd lands.	" xxxix.	32
Whose feet are guided thro' the l,	" lxv.	9
all the framework of the l ;	" lxxxvi.	24
hard heir strides about their l's	" lxxxix.	15
stays him from the native l,	" xcii.	3
l's where not a memory strays,	" ciii.	10
We live within the stranger's l,	" civ.	3
Ring out the darkness of the l,	" cv.	31
live their lives From l to l ;	" cxiv.	17

CONCORDANCE TO

	POEM.	LINE.
melt like mist, the solid *l*'s,	In Mem. cxxii.	7
loud war by *l* and by sea,	Maud, I. i.	47
sapphire-spangled marriage ring of the *l*?	" iv.	6
To the death, for their native *l*.	" v.	11
Over the dark moor *l*.	" ix.	6
still strong man in a blatant *l*,	" x.	63
I past him, I was crossing his *l*'s;	" xiii.	6
underneath the in the darkening *l*— .	" II. i.	6
High over the shadowy *l*.	"	40
Flying along the *l* and the main—	" ii.	38
l that has lost for a little her lust .	" III. vi.	39
I have felt with my native *l*,	"	58
praised his *l*, his horses, his machines	The Brook .	124
Was great by *l* as thou by sea.	Ode on Well.	84, 90
Follow'd by the brave of other *l*'s,	"	194
stand Colossal seen of every *l*,	"	221
in all *l*'s and thro' all human story	"	223
l whose hearths he saved from shame	"	225
In *l*'s of palm and southern pine ; .	The Daisy .	2
In *l*'s of palm, of orange-blossom,	"	3
To *l*'s of summer across the sea ; .	"	92
o'er a weary sultry *l*,	Will .	17
Dear to thy *l* and ours,	Ded. of Idylls	40
and they past to their own *l* ;	Enid .	45, 1803
and we smile, the lords of many *l*'s,	"	353
I know not, but he past to the wild *l*.	"	443
dreadful loss Falls in a far *l*.	"	1346
hollow *l*, From which old fires	"	1669
my leave To move to your own *l*,	"	1737
I will weed this *l* before I go.	"	1755
the bandit holds and cleansed the *l*.	"	1792
slipt away Thro' the dim *l* ; .	Vivien .	274
all day long we rode Thro' the dim *l*	"	275
two fair babes, and went to distant *l*'s;	"	557
Moaning and calling out of other *l*'s,	"	811
who, some say, shall rule the *l* .	Elaine .	66
Lord am I In mine own *l*,	"	913
Endow you with broad *l* and territory	"	953
to take the King to fairy *l*? .	"	1250
that he passes into fairy *l*.'	"	1252
Estate then with large *l* and territory	"	1312
the dead earth, and the *l* was still.	Guinevere .	8
blackening, swallow'd all the *l*,	"	82
get thee hence to thine own *l*,	"	88
Back to his *l* ; but she to Almesbury	"	126
slay the folk, and spoil the *L*'	"	136
l was full of signs And wonders	"	230
sent a deep sea-voice thro' all the *l*,	"	243
for all the *l* was full of life	"	257
everywhere about this *l* of Christ .	"	428
abode in his own *l*.	"	437
Enoch at times to go by *l* or sea ;	En. Arden .	104
left his hearth and native *l*,	"	337
ran Ev'n to the limit of the *l*,	"	579
l of hops and poppy-mingled corn,	Aylmer's F.	31
sleepy *l* where under the same wheel	"	33
so sleepy was the *l*.	"	45
he must—the *l* was ringing of it—	"	262
succeeder to their wealth, their *l*'s,	"	294
crashing with long echoes thro' the *l*,	"	338
The *l* all shambles.	"	765
such a tide swelling toward the *l*,	Sea Dreams	85
a *l* all sun and blossom,	"	99
Break, happy *l*, into earlier flowers!	W. to Alexan.	10
Melt into stars for the *l*'s desire!	"	21
as the sea when he welcomes the *l*,	"	24
welcome her, welcome the *l*'s desire	"	25
Thine the *l*'s of lasting summer,	Boädicea	43
Ran the *l* with Roman slaughter,	"	84
woke her with a lay from fairy *l*.	Coquette, i.	8
at twilight in a *l* of reeds.	"	14
To every *l* beneath the skies,	On a Mourner	5
Gods are moved against the *l*.'	The Victim	3
To spill his blood and heal the *l*:	"	46
l is sick, the people diseased,	"	47
the best and stateliest of the *l*?	Lucretius .	172

landed.
moving up the coast they *l* him, . En. Arden . 666
lander.
Heard by the *l* in a lonely isle, . Enid . . 330

landing.	POEM.	LINE.
sent a crew that *l* burst away	En. Arden .	635

landing-place.
Some *l-p*, to clasp and say, 'Farewell!' In Mem. xlvi. 15

landlike.
cloud That *l* slept along the deep In Mem. cii. 56

landmark.
Nor *l* breathes of other days, . In Mem. ciii. 11

landscape.		
Nor these alone, but every *l* fair,	Pal. of Art	89
The eternal *l* of the past :	In Mem. xlv.	8
The *l* winking thro' the heat ?	" lxxxviii.	16
Of all the *l* underneath .	" xcix.	2
l grow Familiar to the stranger's child:	" c.	20
the Lord of all the *l* round	Aylmer's F.	815

landscape-painter.
| He is but a *l-p*, | L. of Burleigh | 7 |
| that he Were once more that *l-p*, | " | 83 |

landskip.
man and woman, town And *l*, . Princess, iv. 426

landslip.
Like some great *l*, tree by tree, . Amphion . 51

landward.
The latest house to *l*; . . En. Arden . 733

lane.		
l's, you know, were white with may,	Miller's D. .	130
a *l* of beams athwart the sea,	Golden Year	50
Long *l*'s of splendour slanted	Princess, iv.	457
glimmering *l*'s and walls of canvas,	" v.	6
light-blue *l* of early dawn,	In Mem. cxviii.	7
thro' the short sweet-smelling *l*'s	The Brook .	122
in the leafy *l*'s behind the down	En. Arden .	97
climbing street, the mill, the leafy *l*'s,	"	608

Lane (surname).
kept it ; and his widow Miriam *L*	En. Arden .	696
Miriam *L* was good and garrulous,	"	701
tho' Miriam *L* had told him all,	"	766
call'd aloud for Miriam *L*.	"	837
Miriam *L* Made such a voluble	"	902

language.		
l wherewith Spring Letters cowslips	Adeline	61
Such as no *l* may declare.'	Two Voices	384
Your *l* proves you still the child.	Princess, ii.	44
A use in measur'd *l* lies ;	In Mem. v.	6
with no *l* but a cry.	" liii.	20
I rife With rugged maxims .	Ode on Well.	183
in a *l* that has long gone by .	Vivien .	524
a *l* known but smatteringly .	Aylmer's F.	433

languid.
And myself so *l* and base . . Maud, I. v. 18

languish.
| And so would *l* evermore, | Eleänore . | 120 |
| *l* for the purple seas? . | 'You ask me why,' etc. | 4 |

languor.		
art not steep'd in golden *l*'s,	Madeline .	1
The *l*'s of thy love-deep eyes	Eleänore .	76
thro' her limbs a drooping *l* wept:	Princess, vi.	251
all for *l* and self-pity ran Mine	" vii.	124
out of *l* leapt a cry	"	140
a *l* came Upon him,	En. Arden .	824

lantern.
round the lighted *l* of the hall ; . Guinevere . 260

lap.		
Upon my *l* he laid his head ?	The Sisters	17
in whose *l*'s our limbs are nursed,	To J. S.	10
fairest, laid his head upon her *l*,	M. d'Arthur	208
My beard has grown into my *l*.'	Day-Dm.	154
creature laid his muzzle on your *l*,	Princess, ii.	253
Leapt from her session on his *l* ;	Vivien	693
Too ragged to be fondled on her *l*,	Aylmer's F.	686

Lapidoth.
Like that great dame of *L* . . Princess, vi. 16

lapping.
the wild water *l* on the crag. M. d'Arthur 71, 116

lapse (s.) — POEM. LINE.
No *l* of moons can canker Love, *In Mem.* xxvi. 3
lapse (verb.)
overset, Or *l* from hand to hand, . *Talking O..* 258
lapsed.
if I *l* from nobler place, . . *Two Voices* 358
l into so long a pause again . . *Aylmer's F.* 630
lapt.
slumber, *l* in universal law. . . *Locksley H.* 130
l In the arms of leisure . . . *Princess*, ii. 151
l in wreaths of glowworm light . " iv. 415
lapwing.
l gets himself another crest; . *Locksley H.* 18
Lar.
lay at wine with *L* and Lucumo ; *Princess*, ii. 113
larboard.
Roll'd to starboard, roll'd to *l*, . *Lotos-E's.* . 151
larch.
rosy plumelets tufts the *l*, . . *In Mem.* xc. 1
There amid perky *l'es* and pine, . *Maud*, I. x. 20
larded.
Old boxes, *l* with the steam . . *Will Water.* 223
larder.
And a whirlwind clear'd the *l*: . *The Goose* . 52
large.
Wait; my faith is *l* in Time, . *Love and Duty* 25
O Love, thy province were not *l*, *In Mem.* xlv. 13
l and lucid round thy brow. . " xc. 8
thrice as *l* as man he bent . . " cii. 42
light is *l* and lambs are glad. . *Lucretius* . 99
large-brow'd.
Plato the wise, and *l-b* Verulam, . *Pal. of Art* 163
large-moulded.
that *l-m* man, His visage all agrin *Princess*, v. 509
larger.
light that grows *L* and clearer, . *Œnone* . 107
L than human on the frozen hills. *M. d'Arthur* 183
one seem'd far *l* than her lord. . *Enid* . 971
black eyes, Yet *l* thro' his leanness, *Elaine* . 831
larger-limbed.
one Is *l-l* than you are, . . *Enid* . . 993
every man were *l-l* than I . . " . . 997
largess.
With shower'd *l* of delight, . . *In Mem.* xxix. 7
golden *l* of thy praise. . . '*My life is full*,' etc. 5
Lariano.
The *L* crept To that fair port . *The Daisy* . 78
Lari Maxume.
Virgilian rustic measure Of *L M*. *The Daisy* . 76
lark.
l could scarce get out his notes . *Gardener's D.* 89
quail and pigeon, *l* and leveret lay, *Audley Ct.* . 23
And livelier than a *l*, . . . *Talking O.* . 122
His spirit flutters like a *l* . . *Day-Dm.* . 129
And the *l* drop down at his feet. . *Poet's Song* 8
the *l* Shot up and shrill'd . . *Princess*, vii. 30
holds the shadow of a *l* . . *In Mem.* xvi. 9
ere the *l* hath left the lea. . . " lxvii. 13
l becomes a sightless song. . . " cxiv. 8
as we lose the *l* in heaven, . . *Elaine* . 656
merry in heaven, O *l's*, and far away *The Window* 146
larkspur.
The *l* listens, 'I hear, I hear ;' . *Maud*, I. xxii. 65
larn learn.)
I reckons I 'annot sa mooch to *l* . *N. Farmer* . 13
larn'd.
L a ma' beä. . . . . . *N. Farmer* . 13
lash (of the eye.)
l'es like to rays Of darkness, . *Arabian N's.* 136
lash (whip.)
Doom'd them to the *l* . . . *The Captain* 12

lash (verb.) — POEM. LINE.
like a pedant's wand To *l* offence, *Princess*, i. 23
l with storm the streaming pane? *In Mem.* lxxi. 4
war's avenging rod Shall *l* all *To F. D. Maurice* 34
l you from them like a dog ; . *Aylmer's F.* 325
L the maiden into swooning, . *Boädicea* . 67
lash'd.
dishorsed and drawing, *l* at each . *Enid* . 563
l it at the base with slanting storm ; *Vivien* . 485
me they *l* and humiliated, . . *Boädicea* 49, 67
lass.
'Siver, I kep un, I kep un, my *l*, . *N. Farmer* . 23
D'ya moind the waäste, my *l* ? . " . 29
Doctor's a 'tottler, *l*, . . . " . 66
last (adj.)
Bedivere, the *l* of all his knights, *M. d'Arthur* 7
I, the *l*, go forth companionless, . " . 236
l kiss, which never was the *l*, . *Love and Duty* 65
He now is first, but is he the *l*? . *Maud*, l. iv. 36
Mourn, for to us he seems the *l*, . *Ode on Well.* 19
all day long till Enoch's *l* at home, *En. Arden* . 172
when the *l* of those *l* moments came, " . 217
might have been together till the *l. Aylmer's F.* 714
made by these the *l* of all my race " . 791
cry to these the *l* of theirs . . " . 792
last (verb.)
What is it that will *l* ? . . . *Lotos-E's.* . 90
without help I cannot *l* till morn, . *M. d'Arthur* 26
should I prize thee, couldst thou *l*, *Will Water.* 203
Bare of the body, might it *l*, . *In Mem.* xliii. 6
love will *l* as pure and whole . " . 13
there no shade can *l* . . . " xlv. 5
raise a cry that *l's* not long, . " lxxiv. 10
woke The darkness of our planet, *l*, " lxxv. 10
In words whose echo *l's*, . . *Enid* . . 782
beyond his object Love can *l*: . *Coquette*, iii. 5
I *l* but a moment longer. . . *Spiteful Let.* 12
latch.
Unlifted was the clinking *l* ; . *Mariana* . 6
merry milkmaids click the *l*, . *The Owl*, i. 8
door was off the *l*: they peep'd . *Dora* . 127
hand dwelt lingeringly on the *l*, . *En. Arden.* 515
late.
I fear it is too *l*, and I shall die.' *M. d'Arthur* 180
'But I was born too *l*: . . *Golden Year* 15
not too *l* to seek a newer world. . *Ulysses* . 57
out no *l* is out of rules. . . *Princess*, iv. 200
They rise, but linger ; it is *l*; > *In Mem. Con.* 91
white rose weeps, 'She is *l*; . *Maud*, I. xxii. 64
he for Italy—too *l*—too *l*: . *The Brook* . 2
'*L*, *l*, Sir Prince,' she said . . *Enid* . . 177
so *l* That I but come like you . " . . 178
in herself she moaned 'too *l*, too *l*!*Guinevere* . 130
'*l*! so *l*! What hour I wonder . " . . 158
air the nuns had taught her ; '*l*, so *l*!' " . . 161
L, *l*, so *l*! and dark .rep.) . . " . . 166
Too *l*, too *l*! ye cannot enter now (rep.) " . 108
hoping, fearing 'is it yet too *l*?' . " . . 683
too *l*! they come too *l* for use. . *Sea Dreams* 67
late-left.
L-l an orphan of the squire, . *Miller's D.* . 34
late-lost.
A *l-l* form that sleep reveals, . *In Mem.* xiii. 2
later.
Sir Prince,' she said '*l* than we !' *Enid* . . 177
or else he forged But that was *l*, . *Aylmer's F.* 97
l by an hour Here than ourselves, *Sea Dreams* 254
latest-born.
Nursing the sickly babe, her *l-b.* . *En. Arden* . 130
latest-left.
thou, the *l-l* of all my knights, . *M. d'Arthur* 124
late-writ.
show'd the *l-w* letters of the king . *Princess*, i. 173
Latin.
in *flagrante*—what's the *L* word ? *Walk. to the M.* 26
in the *L* song I learnt at school . *Ed. Morris.* 79

lattice.

	POEM.	LINE.
Thro' half-open *l*'s . . .	Eleänore	23
As by the *l* you reclined, .	Day-Dm.	5
here and there on *l* edges lay .	Princess, ii.	15
follow, and light Upon her *l*,	" iv.	82
thro' a *l* on the soul Looks thy fair face	In Mem. lxix.	15

lattice-blind.

Backward the *l-b* she flung, .	Mariana in the S.	87

laugh (s.)

Thereto she pointed with a *l*,	D. of F. Wom.	159
He laugh'd a *l* of merry scorn: .	Lady Clare.	81
with a low and chuckling *l*; .	Vivien	629
broke into a little scornful *l*. .	Elaine	121
a *l* Ringing like proven golden coinage	Aylmer's F.	181

laugh (verb.)

We did so *l* and cry with you,	D. of the O. Year	25
Baby lips will *l* me down : .	Locksley H.	89
she *l*'s at you and man : .	Princess, v.	112
l As those who watch a kitten ; .	Vivien	32
the fairy well That *l*'s at iron— .	"	279
and cry, 'L, little well,' .	"	281
l's Saying his knights are better men	Elaine	313
and *l* at all your fears.' .	En. Arden.	216
the neighbours come and *l* and gossip	Grandmother	91
a tale To *l* at—more to *l* at in myself—	Lucretius.	183

laughable.

not make them *l* in all eyes .	Enid	1175

laugh'd.

She spoke and *l*: I shut my sight	Œnone	184
He *l*, and I, though sleepy .	The Epic	44
l, as one that read my thought, .	Gardener's D.	105
heated faces; till he *l* aloud; .	Audley Ct.	36
And I and Edwin *l*; . .	Ed. Morris	93
l, and swore by Peter and by Paul :	Godiva	24
The still voice *l*. 'I talk,' said he,	Two Voices	385
l a laugh of merry scorn : .	Lady Clare	81
Blue isles of heaven *l* between,	Sir L. and O. G.	6
she spoke, and at herself she *l*;	Princess, Pro.	152
something so mock-solemn, that I *l*	"	209
flat hand against his face and *l*; .	" ii.	345
make me hotter, till she *l*: .	" iii.	31
l with alien lips, . .	" iv.	101
little seed they *l* at in the dark, .	" vi.	18
This brother had *l* her down, .	Maud, I. xix.	60
Katie *l*, and laughing blush'd, till		
he L also. . . .	The Brook.	214
l the father saying 'Fie, Sir Churl	Elaine	200
and in her heart she *l*, . .	"	804
to the Queen, at first she *l* Lightly,	Guinevere	54
Then *l* again, but faintlier, . .	"	58
He *l*, and yielded readily .	En. Arden.	367
others *l* at her and Philip too, .	"	474
ever miss'd it, and they *l* : .	"	753
forgives it as his own, He *l*; .	Aylmer's F.	402

laughing.

L all she can ; . . .	Lilian	5
L and clapping their hands between,	The Merman	29
Francis, *l*, clapt his hand .	The Epic	21
Juliet answer'd, 'Go and see .	Gardener's D.	29
l' what, if these weird seizures .	Princess, i.	81
Katie laugh'd, and *l* blush'd, .	The Brook.	214
He answer'd *l*, 'Nay, not like to me	Vivien	468
Lavaine said, *l*, 'Lily maid, .	Elaine	384
parted, *l* in his courtly heart. .	"	1170
l at things that have long gone by.	Grandmother	92

laughing-stock.

drunkard's football, *l-s*'s of Time.	Princess, iv.	496

laughter.

Till the lightning *l*'s dimple .	Lilian	16
Silver-treble *l* trilleth : . .	"	24
scorn, Edged with sharp *l*, 'Clear-headed friend'		2
With her *l* or her sighs, . .	Miller's D.	184
their shrill happy *l* come to me,	Œnone	254
L at her self-scorn. . .	Pal. of Art	232
l dimpled in his swarthy cheek ; .	Ed. Morris	61
Marrow of mirth and *l*; . .	Will Water.	214
Dislink'd with shrieks and *l*: .	Princess, Pro.	70
shake The midriff of despair with *l*	" i.	198
and back again With *l*: .	Princess, ii.	438
secret *l* tickled all my soul. .	" iv.	248
with grim *l* thrust us out at gates.	"	534
slain with *l* roll'd the gilded Squire.	" v.	21
began A blind and babbling *l* .	" vi.	121
The delight of happy *l*, .	Maud, II. iv.	29
thus he moved the Prince To *l*	Enid	1145
It made the *l* of an afternoon .	Vivien	19
jest among them rose With *l* .	Elaine	179
Must needs have moved my *l*: .	"	594
now remains But little cause for *l*:	"	595
Save, as his Annie's, were a *l* .	En. Arden.	184
And *l* to their lords : .	Aylmer's F.	198
children's *l* in their hall .	"	787
Waking *l* in indolent reviewers.	Hendecasyllabics	8

laughter-stirred.

his deep eye *l-s* . .	Arabian N's.	150

Launcelot see Lancelot.

laurel.

This *l* greener from the brows .	To the Queen	7
twinkling *l* scatter'd silver lights. .	Gardener's D.	117
dips Her *l* in the wine, .	Will Water.	18
gain'd a *l* for your brow 'You might have won,' etc.		3
porch, the bases lost In *l*: .	Princess, i.	228
porch, that sang All round with *l*	" ii.	9
hear thy *l* whisper sweet .	In Mem. xxxvii.	7
ungather'd let us leave This *l* .	" civ.	2
dry-tongued *l*'s pattering talk .	Maud, I. xviii.	8
Came glimmering thro' the *l*'s .	" II. iv.	77
cavern-shadowing *l*'s, hide ! .	Lucretius.	202

laurel-shrubs.

the *l-s* that hedge it around. .	Poet's Mind	14

Laurence.

Since I beheld young L dead. .	L. C. V. de Vere	28

lava.

Claymore and snowshoe, toys in *l*,	Princess, Pro.	18

Lavaine.

two strong sons, Sir Torre and Sir L,	Elaine	174
L, my younger here, He is so full .	"	202
needs must bid farewell to sweet L.	"	340
L Past inward, as she came .	"	344
L Returning brought the yet-unblazon'd	"	377
L said, laughing, Lily maid .	"	384
Abash'd L, whose instant reverence	"	417
So spake L, and when they reach'd	"	427
Lancelot answer'd young L and said	"	444
And L gaped upon him .	"	451
Sir L did well and worshipfully ; .	"	490
With young L into the poplar grove	"	508
Gasping to Sir L 'draw .	"	510
L drew, and that other gave .	"	514
'and find out our dear L' .	"	750
will not lose your wits for dear L :	"	751
'L,' she cried 'L, How fares my lord	"	790
L across the poplar grove Led .	"	800
Besought L to write as she devised	"	1097

lave.

l's The lawn by some cathedral, .	D. of F. Wom.	189

lavender.

Purple-spiked *l*: . . .	Ode to Mem.	110

law.

l's of marriage character'd in gold	Isabel.	16
giving light To read those *l*'s ; .	"	19
live by *l* Acting the *l* we live by .	Œnone	145
Circled thro' all experiences, pure *l*,	"	163
to hear Of wisdom and of *l*. .	Pal. of Art.	212
Roll'd round by one fix'd *l*. .	"	256
in its season bring the *l* ; ' Love thou thy land,' etc.		32
by some *l* that holds in love, .	Gardener's D.	9
a father's word was *l*, .	Dora	25
home is none of yours. My will is *l*.'	"	43
You knew my word was *l*, .	"	96
but there was *l* for us ; .	Walk. to the M.	77
by Nature's *l*, Have faded long ago ;	Talking O.	73
to *l* System and empire ? .	Love and Duty	7
dole Unequal *l*'s unto a savage race,	Ulysses	4

	POEM.	LINE.
lapt in universal *l*.	*Locksley H.*	130
reach the *l* within the *l* :	*Two Voices.*	141
fulmined out her scorn of *l's* Salique	*Princess,* ii.	117
Electric, chemic *l s*, and all the rest,	"	362
Nor would I fight with iron *l's*	" iv.	57
We knew not your ungracious *l's*,	"	380
truer to the *l* within ?	" v.	181
biting *l's* to scare the beasts of prey,	"	383
sanctuary Is violate, our *l's* broken :	" vi.	44
l's are broken: let him enter too.'.	"	297
We break our *l's* with ease,	"	303
l your Highness did not make	"	306
order lived again with other *l s*	" vii.	4
storm'd At the Oppian *l*.	"	109
sons of men, and barbarous *l's*	" 219,	240
reverence for the *l's* ourselves have made	" Con.	55
In holding by the *l* within	*In Mem.* xxxiii.	14
better serves a wholesome *l*,	" xlvii.	10
love Creation's final *l*—	" lv.	14
nothing is that errs from *l*.	" lxxii.	8
loyal unto kindly *l's*.	" lxxxiv.	16
music in the bounds of *l*,	" lxxxvi.	34
dusty purlieus of the *l*.	" lxxxviii.	12
sweeter manners, purer *l's*	" cv.	16
In all her motion one with *l* .	" cxxi.	8
One God, one *l*, one element	" Con.	142
hold by the *l* that I made,	*Maud,* I. i.	55
whatever loathes a *l*:	*Enid.*	37
clear'd the dark places and let in the *l*,	"	1791
Deeming our courtesy is the truest *l*.	*Elaine.*	708
ruin and the breaking up of *l's*,	*Guinevere.*	423
their *l* relaxed its hold on us	"	453
forced my thoughts on that fierce *l*,	"	533
the lawless science of our *l*,	*Aylmer's F.*	435
l's of nature were our scorn ;	*The Voyage.*	84
Not follow the great *l* ?	*Lucretius.*	116

lawn (grassy level.)

many a shadow-chequer'd *l*	*Arabian N's.*	102
springs on a level of bowery *l*,	*Poet's Mind.*	31
l's and meadow-ledges midway down	*Œnone.*	6
the mountain *l* was dewy-dark,	"	47
In each a squared *l*,	*Pal. of Art.*	22
Leading from *l* to *l*.	*D. of F. Wom.*	76
noise of some one coming thro' the *l*,	"	178
laves The *l* by some cathedral,	"	190
Or only look across the *l*,	*Margaret.*	65
the range of *l* and park :	*The Blackbird.*	6
Flow, softly flow, by *l* and lea,	*A Farewell.*	5
Dreams over lake and *l*,	*Vision of Sin.*	11
girt the region with high cliff and *l*:	"	47
his broad *l's* until the set of sun	*Princess, Pro.*	2
sward was trim as any garden *l*:	"	95
others lay about the *l's*,	" ii.	438
lovelier not the Elysian *l's*,	" iii.	324
rosy heights came out above the *l's*,	"	347
with the old king across the *l's*	" v.	226
rivulets hurrying thro' the *l*	" vii.	205
the floor Of this flat *l*	*In Mem.* lxxxviii.	9
read The Tuscan poets on the *l*:	"	24
By night we lingered on the *l*,	" xciv.	1
Now dance the lights on *l* and lea,	" cxix.	9
And lilies fair on a *l*:	*Maud,* I. xiv.	2
But the rivulet on from the *l*	"	29
I steal by *l's* and grassy plots	*The Brook.*	170
the *l* as yet 1s hoar with rime	*To F. D. Maurice.*	41
l's And winding glades high up	*En. Arden.*	573
thro' the bright *l's* to his brother's	*Aylmer's F.*	341
halls, and farms, and flowing *l's*,	"	654

lawn (linen.)

Slow-dropping veils of thinnest *l*,	*Lotos-E's.*	11

Lawrence, see Aylmer.

lawyer.

was a God, and is a *l's* clerk,	*Ed. Morris.*	102
Vext with *l's* and harass'd with debt	*Maud,* I. xix.	22

lay (s.)

So, Lady Flora, take my *l*,	*Day-Dm.* 197,	269
these brief *l's*, of Sorrow born,	*In Mem.* xlvii.	1
Nor dare she trust a larger *l*,	"	13

	POEM.	LINE.
lo, thy deepest *l's* are dumb.	*In Mem.* lxxv.	7
Demand not thou a marriage *l*	" Con.	2
link'd our names together in his *l*,	*Elaine.*	113
many a mystic *l* of life and death.	*Guinevere.*	273
woke her with a *l* from fairy land	*Coquette,* i.	3
l's that will outlast thy Deity?	*Lucretius.*	72

lay (to place, etc.)

you may *l* me low i' the mould	*MayQueen,*ii.	4
none of mine ; *L* it not to me.	*StS. Stylites.*	122
l's it thrice upon my lips,	*Will Water.*	19
l your hand upon my head,	*Lady Clare.*	55
L out the viands.'.	*Princess,* iii.	320
And *l* me on her bosom	" iv.	85
l my little blossom at my feet,	" v.	97
l's on every side A thousand arms	" vi.	20
or if you scorn to *l* it, Yourself	"	167
L thy sweet hands in mine	" vii.	345
Till growing winters *l* me low	*InMem.*xxxix.	30
l their eggs, and sting and sing	" xlix.	11
Then to strike him and *l* him low,	*Maud,* II. v.	90
l the man whom we deplore?	*Ode on Well.*	8
L your earthly fancies down,	"	279
L's claim to for the lady at his side,	*Enid.*	487
l lance in rest, O noble host	"	496
lose his bone, and *l's* his foot upon it,	"	1410
here I *l* this penance on myself	"	1587
l the letter in my hand	*Elaine.*	1107
all I have of rich, and *l* me on it.	"	1114
l their hands in mine and swear	*Guinevere.*	464
on thy heart a finger *l's*	*On a Mourner.*	11
l's His vast and filthy hands	*Lucretius.*	216

lay (pret. of *lie*.)

the thick-moted sunbeam *l*	*Mariana.*	78
An open scroll Before him *l*:	*The Poet.*	7
should have stabb'd me where I *l*,	*Oriana.*	55
loosed the chain, and down she *l*;	*L. of Shalott,*iv.	10
Upon the freshly-flower'd slope.	*Miller's D.*	111
To win his love I *l* in wait :	*The Sisters.*	19
L, dozing in the vale of Avalon,	*Pal. of Art.*	107
L there exiled from eternal God,	"	263
masts flicker'd as they *l* afloat ;	*D. of F. Wom.*	113
On one side *l* the Ocean,	*M. d'Arthur.*	11
on one *L* a great water,	"	12
l the mighty bones of ancient men,	"	47
like a shatter'd column *l* the K ;	"	221
quail and pigeon, lark and leveret *l*,	*Audley Ct.*	23
L great with pig, wallowing in sun	*Walk. to the M.*	80
I Pent in a roofless close	*StS. Stylites.*	72
On the coals I *l*, A vessel full of sin :	"	166
at my feet she *l*.	*Talking O.*	203
but a moment *l* Where fairer fruit	"	250
The dewy sister-eyelids *l*.	*Day-Dm.*	4
On the mossy stone, as I *l*,	*Ed. Gray.*	26
Leapt up from where she *l*,	*Lady Clare.*	6
L betwixt his home and hers ;	*L. of Burleigh.*	28
on the pavement *l* Carved stones	*Princess, Pro.*	13
about it *l* the guests,	"	106
patting Lilia's head (she *l* Beside him)	"	125
on lattice edges *l* Or book	" ii.	15
l at wine with Lar and Lucumo ;	"	113
others *l* about the lawns	"	438
l three parts In shadow,	" iii.	4
l The lily-shining child ;	" iv.	267
glove upon the tomb *L* hy her	"	574
fair length upon the ground she *l*:	" v.	50
in some mystic middle state I *l*,	" vi.	6
To where her wounded brethren *l*;	"	74
L like a new-fall'n meteor	"	119
he that *l* Beside us, Cyril,	"	137
two hosts that *l* beside the walls	"	302
L silent in the muffled cage of life	" vii.	32
Quite sunder'd from the moving *l*	"	36
I *l* still, and oft with me she sat :	"	76
l like one in trance,	"	136
with shut eyes I *l* Listening ;	"	203
l and read The Tuscan poets	*In Mem.*lxxxviii.	23
where a little shallop *l* At anchor	" (it. 1.)	
Sick once, with a fear of worse.	*Maud,* I. xix.	72
Was it he *l* there with a fading eye?	" II. i.	29
When he *l* dying there,	" ii.	67

CONCORDANCE TO

	POEM.	LINE.
Sun-smitten Alps before me *l*	*The Daisy*	62
his princedom *l* Close on the borders	*Enid*	33
Guinevere *l* late into the morn	"	157
l Contemplating her own unworthiness ;	"	532
l With her fair head in the dim-yellow	"	599
tho' she *l* in the dark pool,	"	657
Enid listen'd brightening as she *l;*	"	733
his enemy roll'd, And there *l* still ;	"	1010
So *l* the man transfixt.	"	1015
cast him and the bier in which he *l*	"	1420
l still, and feign'd himself as dead,	"	1436
l beside him in the hollow shield)	"	1574
huge Earl *l* slain within his hall.	"	1654
Geraint *l* healing of his hurt,	"	1779
At Merlin's feet the wily Vivien *l*	*Vivien*	5
l as dead And lost to life	"	62, 818
l she all her length and kiss'd	"	68
l Foot-gilt with all the blossom-dust	"	130
l And felt them slowly ebbing.	"	286
l as dead And lost all use	"	495
there *l* the reckling, one But one hour	"	559
l till all their bones were bleach'd	*Elaine*	44
L like a rainbow fall'n upon the grass,	"	430
his horse to Lancelot where he *l,*	"	492
hands *L* naked on the wolfskin	"	809
l, Speaking a still good-morrow	"	1026
all its length in blackest samite, *l.*	"	1136
and *l* as tho' she smiled	"	1155
lily maid of Astolat *l* smiling	"	1235
To hers which *l* so silent	"	1278
like a subtle beast *L* couchant	*Guinevere*	12
while he *l* recovering there,	*En. Arden.*	108
Enoch *l* long-pondering on his plans ;	"	133
L lingering out a three-years'	"	566
this isle, not knowing where she *l:*	"	631
sail'd a little, And he *l* tranced ;	"	794
L hidden as the music of the moon	*Aylmer's F.*	102
L deeper than to wear it as his ring—	"	122
silenced by that silence *l* the wife,	*Sea Dreams*	46
I *l,*' said he, ' And mused upon it,	"	103
right across its track there *l,*	"	122
belt, it seem'd, of luminous vapour, *l,*	"	202
There *l* the sweet little body	*Grandmother*	62
I *l,* Mouth, forehead, eyelids	*Tithonus*	57
there at tables of ebony *l,*	*Boädicea*	61
In their blood, as they *l* dying,	*The Captain*	55
dead men *l* all over the way,	*The Victim*	21

layer.

spread his dark-green *l's* of shade.	*Gardener's D.*	115

lay-hearth.

one *l-h* would give you welcome	*To F.D.Maurice*	11

laying.

l down an unctuous lease Of life	*Will Water.*	243
Autumn *l* here and there A fiery	*In Mem.*xcviii.	11
l his trams in a poison'd gloom	*Maud,* I. x.	8
flaws in summer *l* lusty corn :	*Enid*	764
l there thy golden head,	*Guinevere*	531

lazar.

And him, the *l,* in his rags	*In Mem.*cxxvi.	10

Lazarus.

When *L* left his charnel-cave,	*In Mem.*xxxi.	1

lea.

From wandering over the *l;*	*Sea-Fairies*	11
mad pranks along the heathy *l's;*	*Circumstance*	2
pipe along the fallow *l,*	*May Queen,* ii.	18
And overlook the *l,*	*Talking O.*	198
never yet was oak on *l.*	"	243
him that on the mountain *l*	*To E. L.*	21
Flow, softly flow, by lawn and *l,*	*A Farewell*	5
cattle huddled on the *l;*	*In Mem.* xv.	6
ploughs with pain his native *l*	" lxiii.	25
ere the lark hath left the *l*	" lxvii.	13
dance the lights on lawn and *l,*	" cxiv.	9
the pimpernel dozed on the *l,*	*Maud,*I.lxxii.	48
blight and famine on all the *l:*	*The Victim.*	48

lead (s.)

on the *l's* we kept her	*Walk. to the M.*	84
tempest crackles on the *l's,*	*Sir Galahad*	53
clog of *l* was round my feet,	*The Letters*	5

lead (verb.)	POEM.	LINE.
O ! hither *l* thy feet !	*Ode to Mem.*	64
l life to sovereign power	*Œnone*	143
l them to thy light.	*St S. Stylites*	220
l's the clanging rookery home.	*Locksley H.*	68
According as his humours *l,*	*Bay-Dm.*	207
That *l* me to my Lord :	*St Agnes' Eve*	8
L's her to the village altar,	*L. of Burleigh*	11
Take my brute, and *l* him in,	*Vision of Sin*	65
still may *l* The new light up,	*Princess,* ii.	326
l Thro' prosperous floods	*In Mem.* ix.	7
on to where the pathway *l's;*	" xxiii.	8
life that *l's* melodious days.	" xxxiii.	8
What kind of life is that I *l;*	" lxxxiv.	8
l The closing cycle rich in good	" civ.	27
It *l's* me forth at evening	*Maud,*II. iv.	17
L out the pageant : sad and slow,	*Ode on Well.*	13
Thro' which he bade her *l* him	*Enid*	878
to *l* her to his lord Arthur,	*Guinevere*	380
l sweet lives in purest chastity,	"	470
their King to *l* mine hosts	"	566
With fuller profits *l* an easier life,	*En. Arden.*	145
The babe shall *l* the lion.	*Aylmer's F.*	648
l an errant passion home again.	*Lucretius*	17
meant Surely to *l* my Memnius	"	119

leaden-coloured.

the low moan of *l-c* seas.	*En. Arden.*	613

leader.

patient *l's* of their Institute	*Princess,*Pro.	58
l wildswan in among the stars	" iv.	414
as the *l* of a herd That holds	" vi.	69
For a man and *l* of men.	*Maud,* I. x.	59
Mourning when their *l's* fall,	*Ode on Well.*	5
the *l* in these glorious wars	"	192
ever-loyal iron *l's* fame .'	"	229
there lives No greater *L*'	*Elaine*	317

leading.

l a jet-black goat	*Œnone*	50
L from lawn to lawn.	*D. of F. Wom.*	76
l up the golden year.	*Golden Year* 26,	41
L on from hall to hall.	*L. of Burleigh*	52
Enid *l* down the tracks	*Enid*	877
disappear'd, *L* the horse,	"	1093
Arthur *l,* slowly went The marshall'd	*Elaine*	1321
l evermore Low miserable lives	*En. Arden.*	115

lead-like.

those *l-l* tons of sin,	*St S. Stylites*	25

leaf.

Flush'd all the *leaves*	*Arabian N's.*	82
rich smell of the rotting *leaves,*	*'A spirit haunts'*	17
came dazzling thro' the *leaves,*	*L. of Shalott,* iii.	3
leaves upon her falling light—	" iv.	21
like *leaves* in roaring wind.	*Fatima*	7
blackthorn, the *l* upon the tree.	*May Queen,* ii.	8
l is woo'd from out the bud	*Lotos-E's.*	71
I knew the *leaves,* I knew	*D. of F. Wom.*	73
for want, ere *leaves* are new,	*The Blackbird*	23
sitting muffled in dark *leaves,*	*Gardener's D.*	37
like the whispers of the *leaves*	"	248
rain'd about the *l* Twilights	*Audley Ct.*	80
prick Each *l* into a gall)	*Talking O.*	70
swear, by *l,* and wind, and rain,	"	81
that, which breathes within the *l,*	"	187
all the summer of my *leaves*	"	211
Thy *l* shall never fail, nor yet	"	259
Alternate *l* and acorn-ball	"	287
The memory of the wither'd *l*	*Two Voices.*	112
rests the sap within the *l,*	*Day-Dm.*	23
dash'd about the drunken *leaves*	*Amphion*	55
sounder *l* than I can claim. ' You might have won'	4
And the *l* is stamp'd in clay.	*Vision of Sin*	82
lisping of the innumerous *l.*	*Princess,* v.	13
first snowdrop's inner *leaves;*	"	189
leaves were wet with women's tears :	" vi.	23
only thro' the faded *l*	*In Mem.* xi.	3
leaves that redden to the fall ;	"	14
last red *l* is whirl'd away.	" xv.	3
lands where not a *l* was dumb ;	" xxiii.	10
In many a figured *l* enrolls ;	" xlii.	11

	POEM.	LINE.
seem'd to touch it into *l*:	*In Mem.*lxviii.	18
Thy *l* has perish'd in the green,	" lxxiv.	13
Thy spirits in the darkening *l*,	"lxxxvii.	6
fall'n *leaves* which kept their green,	" xciv.	23
large *leaves* of the sycamore,	"	55
under brown Of lustier *leaves*;	" xcvii.	25
A fiery finger on the *leaves*;	" xcviii.	12
admits not flowers or *leaves*	" cvi.	5
dead *l* trembles to the bells.	" Con.	64
shiver of dancing *leaves* is thrown	*Maud*, I. vi.	73
such a time as goes before the *l*,	*The Brook*.	13
as a *l* in mid-November is	*Enid*	611
worm draws in the wither'd *l*	"	1481
from his mighty shoulder, as a *l*,	*Vivien*	92
true man change like a *l*	*Elaine*	683
L after *l*, and tore, and cast them	"	1193
thatch'd with *leaves* of palm, a hut.	*En. Arden*	560
the smell of dying *leaves*,	"	612
the *l* in a roaring whirlwind	*Boädicea*	59
fallen *l*, isn't fame as brief? (rep.)	*Spiteful Let.*	9
yellow *l* hates the greener *l*,	"	15
Spring is here with *l* and grass:	*The Window*	98

leafless.
| wish—What? that the bush were *l*? | *Lucretius* | 203 |

league.
For *l*'s no other tree did mark	*Mariana*	43
A *l* of grass, wash'd by a slow	*Gardener's D.*	40
Many a long *l* back to the North	*Princess*, i.	166
heave and thump A *l* of street	" iii.	112
we rode a *l* beyond,	"	316
l's of odour streaming far,	*In Mem.*lxxxv.	14
At the shouts, the *l*'s of lights,	*Maud*, II. iv.	21
Half a *l*, half a *l*, (rep.)	*Lt. Brigade*	1
l of mountain full of golden mines	*Vivien*	437
proffer of the *l* of golden mines,	"	496
l's along that breaker-beaten coast	*En. Arden*	51

leagued.
| And *l* him with the heathen, | *Guinevere* | 153 |
| *L* with the lords of White Horse. | " | 569 |

league-long.
| *l*-*l* roller thundering on the reef | *En. Arden* | 585 |

leaguer.
| for hours On that disastrous *l*, | *Princess*, vii. | 18 |

leal.
| fain Have all men true and *l*, | *Vivien* | 643 |

lean (adj.)
gap-tooth'd man as *l* as death,	*Vision of Sin*	60
lists were swell'd and mine were *l*;	*Princess*, iv.	300
So *l* his eyes were monstrous;	*Vivien*	474
smile That makes the widow *l*.	*Sea Dreams*	152

lean (verb.)
And a rose-bush *l*'s upon,	*Adeline*	14
l out from the hollow sphere	*The Mermaid*	54
elmtree-boles did stoop and *l*	*D. of F. Wom.*	57
from a casement *l*'s his head,	"	246
those we *l* on most,	*To J. S.*	9
l a ladder on the shaft,	*St S. Stylites*	213
On that which *l*'s to you.	*Princess*, iii.	106
l on our fair father Christ,	*Guinevere*	558

lean'd.
l upon the balcony.	*Mariana in the S.*	88
from the bridge I *l* to hear	*Miller's D.*	49
a golden cloud, and *l* Upon him,	*Œnone*	103
partner of his blood *L* on him,	*Two Voices*	416
Once she *l* on me, Descending;	*Princess*, iv.	8
l not on his fathers but himself.	*Aylmer's F.*	56

lean-headed.
| *L*-*h* Eagles yelp alone. | *Princess*, vii. | 196 |

leaning.
fruit-bunches *l* on each other—	*Isabel*	37
L his cheek upon his hand,	*Eleänore*	118
you were *l* from the ledge?	*Miller's D.*	84
l on a fragment twined with vine,	*Œnone*	19
Upon her pearly shoulder *l* cold,	"	138
Robin *l* on the bridge	*May Queen*, i.	14
L his horns into the neighbour field,	*Gardener's D.*	86

	POEM.	LINE.
l there on those balusters	*Princess*, iii.	103
l deep in broider'd down	" iv.	14
replied, *L* a little toward him,	*Enid*	495
speaking not, but *l* over him,	*Vivien*	327

leanness.
| black eyes Yet larger thro' his *l*, | *Elaine* | 831 |

leant.
on her lover's arm she *l*,	*Dor-Dm.*	165
What reed was that on which I *l*?	*In Mem.*lxxxiii.	45
Sir Lancelot *l*, in half disgust	*Elaine*	1231

leap (s.)
| heart on one wild *l* Hung tranced | *Gardener's D.* | 254 |
| stirs the pulse With devil's *l*'s | *Guinevere* | 513 |

leap (verb.)
In the middle *l*'s a fountain	*Poet's Mind*	24
like a wave I would *l*.	*The Mermaid*	39
l forth and fall about thy neck,	*Love and Duty*	41
And his spirit *l*'s within him	*Locksley H.*	115
l the rainbows of the brooks,	"	171
still the first to *l* to light	*Day-Dm.*	239
I *l* on board: no helmsman steers:	*Sir Galahad*	39
l the rotten pales of prejudice,	*Princess*, ii.	126
wild cataract *l*'s in glory.	" iii.	351
l's in Among the women, snares them	" v.	155
l the grades of life and light,	*In Mem.* xl.	11
at his footstep *l*'s no more,	" lxxxiv.	112
l's into the future chance,	" cxiii.	7
l from his counter and till.	*Maud*, I. i.	51
red man's babe *L*, beyond the sea.	" xvii.	20
darkness into the light shall *l*,	" III. vi.	46
grigs that *l* in summer grass.	*The Brook*	54
Whatever record *l* to light.	*Ode on Well.*	190
Making the little one *l* for joy	*To F. D. Maurice*	4
boy began to *l* and prance,	*'Home they brought him'*	7

leaped.
| About me *l* and laugh'd | *Talking O.* | 66 |

leaping.
l lightly from the boat,	*Arabian N's.*	92
l out upon them unseen	*The Merman*	33
l down the ridges lightly,	*M. d'Arthur*	134

leapt.
Then *l* a trout. In lazy mood	*Miller's D.*	73
mailed Bacchus *l* into my arms,	*D. of F.Wom.*	92
words *l* forth: 'Heaven heads	"	201
sixty feet the fountain *l*.	*Day-Dm.*	140
L up from where she lay,	*Lady Clare*	62
Two Proctors *l* upon us,	*Princess*, iv.	240
L from the dewy shoulders of the earth,	" v.	41
into fiery splinters *l* the lance,	"	483
o'er the statues *l* from head to head,	" vi.	346
out of langour *l* a cry; *L* fiery Passion	" vii.	140
Thought *l* out to wed with Thought	*In Mem.* xxiii.	15
L from her session on his lap	*Vivien*	693
harlot *L* A down the forest,	"	821
L on his horse and carolling.	*Elaine*	700
L on him, and hurl'd him headlong,	*Guinevere*	107
no one cared for, *l* To greet her	*Aylmer's F.*	628

learn.
l at full How passion rose	*Gardener's D.*	234
l to slight His father's memory;	*Dora*	150
thousand thanks for what I *l*	*Talking O.*	203
Drug thy memories, lest thou *l* it.	*Locksley H.*	77
l new things when I am not.'	*Two Voices*	63
l the world, and sleep again;	*Day-Dm.*	999
since I came to live and *l*,	*Will Water.*	81
l whatever men were taught:	*Princess*, ii.	130
were too barbarous, would not *l*;	"	278
l's the one ΥΟΥ ΣΤΟ	" iii.	465
With whom they deal,	" iv.	491
l if Ida yet would cede our claim,	" v.	323
to live and *l* and be	" vii.	257
Give it time To *l* its limbs:	" Con.	79
l's her gone and far from home;	*In Mem.*viii.	7
l That I have been an hour away.	" xii.	19
l's the use of 'I' and 'me'	" xliv.	6
Had man to *l* himself anew	"	15

	POEM.	LINE.
or admire, if a man could *l* it,	Maud, I. iv.	41
bailiff to the farm To *l* the price,	The Brook	142
l's to deaden Love of self,	Ode on Well.	204
'If Enid errs let Enid *l* her fault.'	Enid	132
'Surely I will *l* the name,'	"	203
by the bird's song you may *l* the nest'	"	359
break his pride and *l* his name,	"	424
But coming back he *l*'s it,	"	1347
wish still more to *l* this charm	Vivien	176
l themselves and all the world,	"	215
must *l* Which is our mightiest,	Elaine	63
l If his old prowess were in aught	"	582
'our true Arthur, when he *l*'s,	"	584
Whence you might *l* his name?	"	651
l the courtesies of the court,	"	696
to *l* this knight were whole,	"	768
a little space Till he should *l* it;	"	918
remaining here wilt *l* the event;	Guinevere	572
l I loved her to the last.'	En. Arden	836
grieved to *l* your grief—	Aylmer's F.	398
task ourselves To *l* a language	"	433
l A man is likewise counsel	Sea Dreams	177
what is this which now I *l*,	The Ringlet	51

learned (adj.)
l, save in gracious household ways	Princess, vii.	299

learned (verb.)
One lesson from one book we *l*,	In Mem. lxxviii.	14
shall have *l* to lisp you thanks.	Enid	822

learning (part.)
l this, the bridegroom will relent.	Guinevere	170

learning (s.)
what was *l* unto them?	Princess, ii.	440
wearing all that weight Of *l* lightly	In Mem. Con.	40

learnt.
the Latin song I *l* at school,	Ed. Morris	79
l No more from Psyche's lecture,	Princess, ii.	370
l? I *l* more from her in a flash	"	375
since we *l* our meaning here,	" iii.	206
l, For many weary moons	"	301
your ungracious laws, which *l*	" iv.	380
self-involved; but when she *l* the face,	" vi.	142
Much had she *l* in little time	" vii.	225
when they *l* that I must go,	In Mem. cii.	17
l that James had flickering jealousies	The Brook	99
ere he *l* it, 'Take Five horses	Enid	1257
l their elemental secrets,	Vivien	482
'He *l* and wam'd me	Elaine	274
'Sire, my liege, so much I *l*;	"	704
(When first I *l* thee hidden here)	Guinevere	535
a saying *l* In days far-off,	Tithonus	47

lease.
laying down an unctuous *l*.	Will Water.	243

leash.
hold passion in a *l*,	Love and Duty	40

least.
Myself not *l*, but honour'd of them	Ulysses	15
not they the *l* of men;	Princess, ii.	132
pratest here where thou art *l*	In Mem. xxxvii.	2

leave (permission.)
so much as gave us *l* to go.	Princess, v.	225
I'll have *l* at times to play	In Mem. lviii.	11
petitioned for his *l* To see the hunt,	Enid	154
'Your *l*! let *me* lay lance	"	495
'Have I *l* to speak?'	"	989
'Your *l*, my lord, to cross the room,	"	1147
free *l*' he said; 'Get her to speak:	"	1149
l To move to your own land,	"	1736
father give me *l*, an if he will,	Elaine	219
left him *l* to stammer,' is it indeed?	"	429
with a month's *l* given them,	Sea Dreams	6

leave (farewell.)
took my *l*, for it was nearly noon:	Princess, v.	457
swarming now, To take their *l*,	Con.	38
take her latest *l* of home,	In Mem. xxxix.	6
thou shalt take a nobler *l*.'	" lvii.	12
take last *l* of all I loved?	Guinevere	542

leave (verb.)
	POEM.	LINE.
l us rulers of your blood	To the Queen	21
to *l* the blessed sun,	May Queen, iii.	9
l the myrrh-bush on the height;	Lotos-E's.	103
not meet, Sir King, to *l* thee thus,	M. d'Arthur	40
Better to *l* Excalibur conceal'd	"	62
'*L*' she cried 'O *l* me!' 'Never,	Ed. Morris	116
l my relics in your land,	St S. Stylites	191
thou mine to me.	Talking O.	200
l thee fröer, till thou wake refresh'd,	Love and Duty	94
l l the sceptre and the isle—	Ulysses	34
Comrades, *l* me here a little,	Locksley H.	1
L me here, and when you want me	"	112
first he *l*'s his father's field,	"	164
l l the plain, I climb the height;	Sir Galahad	57
l an empty flask;	Will Water.	164
l his music as of old 'You might have won,' etc.	14	
And they *l* her father's roof.	L. of Burleigh	12
l me where I lie: 'Come not, when,' etc.	11	
l Yon orange sunset waning 'Move eastward,' etc.	1	
L us: you may go;	Princess, ii.	80
'*L* me to deal with that.'	" iii.	133
Ill mother that I was to *l* her	" v.	90
meteor on, and *l*'s A shining furrow	" vii.	169
l The monstrous ledges there to slope	"	196
l her space to burgeon out of all	"	255
wilt not *l* us in the dust;	In Mem. Pro.	9
l this mortal ark behind.	" xii.	6
l the cliffs, and haste away	"	8
L thou thy sister when she prays,	" xxxiii.	5
half my life I *l* behind!	" lvi.	6
what I see I *l* unsaid,	" lxxii.	10
I *l* thy praises unexpress'd	" lxxiv.	1
I *l* thy greatness to be guess'd;	"	4
You *l* us: you will see the Rhine,	" xcvii.	1
We *l* the well-beloved place	" ci.	1
l the pleasant fields and farms;	"	22
wilt thou *l* us now behind?'	" cii.	48
ungather'd let us *l* This laurel	" civ.	1
l the porch, they pass the grave	Con.	71
sweetness hardly *l*'s me a choice	Maud, I. v.	24
When will the dancers *l* her alone?	" xxii.	21
in the vast cathedral *l* him.	Ode on Well.	280
l's The Crown a lonely splendour.	Ded. of Idylls	47
not *l* her, till her promise given—	Enid	605
L me to-night: I am weary.	"	1207
To *l* an equal baseness;	Vivien	679
ere I *l* you let me swear once more	"	778
made him *l* The banquet	Elaine	560
let me *l* My quest with you;	"	687
of this remnant will I *l* a part,	Guinevere	441
l thee, woman, to thy shame.	"	507
L me that, I charge thee, My last hope.	"	563
this weary way, And *l* you lonely?	En. Arden	296
death-in-life. They could not *l* him.	"	567
One who cried '*l* all and follow me'	Aylmer's F.	664
l it gorily quivering?	Boädicea	12

leaven (s.)
the old *l* leaven'd all;	Princess, v.	376

leaven (verb.)
now to *l* play with profit	Princess, iv.	131

leavened.
the old leaven *l* all;	Princess, v.	376

leave-taking.
Low at *l-t*, with his brandish'd plume	Enid	1208

leaving.
L door and windows wide:	Deserted H.	3
l my ancient love With the Greek	Œnone	256
L the dance and song,	D. of F. Wom.	216
L the olive-gardens far below,	"	218
L the promise of my bridal bower,	"	218
L great legacies of thought,	In Mem. lxxxiii.	35
And, *l* these, to pass away,	" xcix.	19
l night forlorn.	" cvi.	4
So early, *l* me behind,	" cxiii.	24
never *l* her, and grew Forgetful	Enid	49
l Arthur's court he gain'd the beach	Vivien	46
L her household and good father,	Elaine	14

	Lebanon.	POEM.	LINE.
O, art thou sighing for *L* ,rep.)	*Maud*, I. xviii.		15
	Lebanonian.		
In halls Of *L* cedar;	*Princess*, ii.		331
	lecture.		
A classic *l*, rich in sentiment,	*Princess*, ii.		352
learnt No more from Psyche's *l*,	"		371
	lecture slate.		
On the *l* s The circle rounded	*Princess*, ii.		349
	ted.		
a bride of old In triumph *l*,	*Ode to Mem.*		76
light that *l* The holy Elders .	*M. d'Arthur*		232
Fancy, *l* by Love Would dare	*Gardener's D.*		58
heard, by secret transport *l*,	*Two Voices*		214
took him by the curls, and *l* him in,	*Vision of Sin*		6
l you then to all the Castalies ;	*Princess*, iv.		275
But *l* by golden wishes,	"		400
l Threading the soldier-city,	" v.		6
l A hundred maids in train .	" vi.		59
l by tracts that pleased us well	*In Mem.* xxii.		2
l him thro' the blissful climes,	" lxxxiv.		25
wept and wail'd, he *l* the way.	" cii.		18
I have *l* her home, my love,	*Maud*, I. xviii.		1
l me thro' the short sweet-smelling	*The Brook*		122
Remember him who *l* your hosts ;	*Ode on Well.*		171
L from the territory of false .	*Enid*		1286
answering not one word, she *l* the way.	"		1344
across the poplar grove *L* to the caves:	*Elaine*		801
l her forth, and far ahead .	*Guinevere*		381
l the way To where the rivulets .	*En. Arden*		642
a few, by wit or fortune *l*,	*Aylmer's F.*		438
still we follow'd where she *l*,	*The Voyage*		59, 90
	leddest.		
l by the hand thine infant Hope.	*Ode to Mem.*		30
	ledge.		
you were leaning from the *l*:	*Miller's D.* .		84
pines, that plumed the craggy *l*	*Œnone*		205
Of *l* or shelf The rock rose clear,	*Pal. of Art*		9
from the craggy *l* the puppy hangs	*Lotos-E's.*		56
leave The monstrous *l*'s there to	*Princess*, vii.		197
About the *l*'s of the hill.'	*In Mem.* xxxvii.		8
The red-ribbed *l*'s drip .	*Maud*, I. i.		3
Athwart the *l*'s of rock .	" II. ii.		28
on the window *l*, Close underneath	*Elaine*		1232
	ledger.		
When only the *l* lives .	*Maud*, I. i.		35
	Lee.		
Annie *L*, The prettiest little damsel	*En. Arden*		11
Later but a loftier Annie *L* .	"		749
	leech (an aquatic worm.)		
swarm'd His literary *l*'s.	*Will Water.*		200
	leech (a physician.)		
King's own *l* to look into his hurt;	*Enid*		1771
	leering.		
L at his neighbour's wife. .	*Vision of Sin*		118
	lees.		
I will drink Life to the *l*:	*Ulysses*		7
Dregs of life, and *l* of man : .	*Vision of Sin*		205
	left (left hand.)		
In her *l* a human head.	*Vision of Sin*		138
she the *l*, or not, or seldom used ;	*Princess*, iii.		22
this feud betwixt the right and *l*.'	"		61
Oaring one arm, and bearing in my *l*	" iv.		165
	left (verb.)		
With silver anchor *l* afloat, .	*Arabian N's.*		93
She *l* the web, she *l* the loom,	*L. of Shalott*, iii.		37
Beneath a willow *l* afloat, .	" iv.		7
Is this the end to be *l* alone,	*Mariana in the S.*		71
day and night I am *l* alone .	"		83
l a want unknown before ; .	*Miller's D.*		228
was *l* alone within the bower ;	*Œnone*		188
l behind The good old year,	*May Queen*, iii.		5
Then when I *l* my home."	*D. of F. Wom.*		120
What else was *l* ' look here l'	"		156
flow Of music *l* the lips	"		195
she *l* me where I stood ;	"		241

	POEM.	LINE.
Falls off, and love is *l* alone.	*To J. S.*	16
'at home was little *l* And none abroad ;	*The Epic*	19
moved away, and *l* me, statue-like,	*Gardener's D.*	158
l his father's house, And hired himself	*Dora*	35
and he *l* his men at work,	"	84
l the dying ebb that faintly lipp'd	*Audley Ct.*	11
He *l* his wife behind ;	*Walk. to the M.*	37
He *l* her, yes. I met my lady once :	"	40
l alone Upon her tower, the Niobe	"	90
now we *l* The clerk behind us,	*Ed. Morris*	96
l the place, *l* Edwin, nor have seen	"	137
this way was *l*, And by this way .	*St S. Stylites*	175
Her father *l* his good arm-chair, .	*Talking O.*	103
She *l* the novel half-uncut .	"	117
She *l* the new piano shut ;	"	119
passion sweeping thro' me *l* me dry,	*Locksley H.*	131
L me with the palsied heart, and *l* me	"	132
I was *l* a trampled orphan, .	"	156
l alone, the passions of her mind,	*Godiva*	32
My father *l* a park to me, .	*Amphion*	1
He *l* a small plantation ;	"	20
dying lately, *l* her, as I hear,	*Princess*, i.	77
she who had *l* her place, .	" ii.	149
(what other way was *l*, I came."	"	190
bells call'd us: we *l* the walks ;	"	447
l the drunken king To brawl at Shushan	" iii.	213
her horse was lost I *l* her mine)	" iv.	179
many thousand matters *l* to do,	"	438
what was *l* of faded woman-slough	" v.	38
We *l* her by the woman .	"	109
she *l*: She shall not have it .	"	421
Pharos from his base Had *l* us rock	" vi.	320
languid limbs and sickness ; *l* me in it ;	"	356
some were *l* of those Held sagest,	"	360
Blanche had gone, but *l* her child	" vii.	41
l her woman, lovelier in her mood	"	147
but as a block *L* in the quarry ; .	"	216
having *l* the glass, she turns .	*In Mem.* vi.	35
Since Adam *l* his garden yet.	" xxiv.	8
When Lazarus *l* his charnel-cave,	" xxxi.	1
soil, *l* barren, scarce had grown .	" lii.	7
ere the lark hath *l* the lea	" lxvii.	13
What fame is *l* for human deeds	" lxxii.	11
As in the winters *l* behind, .	" lxxvii.	9
I felt, and feel tho' *l* alone, .	" lxxxiv.	42
l my after-morn content.	" cii.	4
Our father's dust is *l* alone .	" civ.	5
had *l* us flaccid and drain'd. .	*Maud*, I. i.	20
l his coal all turn'd into gold .	" x.	11
And *l* the daisies rosy. .	" xii.	24
lump of earth has *l* his estate .	" xvi.	1
who was *l* to watch her but I ? .	" xix.	10
if *l* uncancell'd, had been so sweet ;	"	46
l his wine and horses and play, .	"	74
meadow your walks have *l* so sweet	" xxii.	39
thou art *l* for ever alone : .	" II. ii.	2
Affirming that his father *l* him gold	*Enid*	451
l her maiden couch, and robed herself,	"	737
When late I *l* Caerleon, our great	"	761
when I *l* your mowers dinnerless.	"	1063
the horse, and they were *l* alone.	"	1093
Enid *l* alone with Prince Geraint	"	1214
Nor *l* untold the craft herself .	"	1242
so *l* him stunn'd or dead .	"	1313
is not *l* the twinkle of a fin .	"	1323
l him lying in the public way ;	"	1327
Not a hoof *l*'	"	1334
But *l* two brawny spearmen,	"	1406
and the two Were *l* alone together	"	1552
trouble which has *l* me thrice your	"	1585
his father Uther *l* in charge .	"	1781
youth gone out Had *l* in ashes!	*Vivien*	95
kinsman *l* him watcher o'er his wife	"	556
l Not even Lancelot brave, .	"	653
ending in a ruin—nothing *l*, .	"	732
Had *l* the ravaged woodland .	"	812
l it with her, when he rode to tilt .	*Elaine*	30
l the barren-beaten thoroughfare, .	"	161
But *l* her all the paler, .	"	377
l him leave to stammer 'is it .	"	413
any man that day were *l* afield,	"	453

	POEM.	LINE.
and hath *l* his prize Untaken,	*Elaine*	529
the knight, and here he *l* a shield;	"	631
ask you not to see the shield he *l*	"	650
Prince who *l* the quest to me.	"	758
being in his moods *L* them,	"	796
poor work, her empty labour, *l.*	"	985
when they *l* her to herself again	"	992
l me taking no farewell,	"	1267
l her and I bad her no farewell.	"	1296
the brood by Hengist *l;*	*Guinevere*	17
Modred whom he *l* in charge of all;	"	193
five summers back, And *l* me;	"	320
that other *l* alone Sigh'd,	"	365
grace of courtesy in him *l,*	"	433
when the Roman *l* us, and their law	"	453
us, who might be *l,* could speak	"	497
l me hope That in mine own heart	"	628
breaking have *l* a chasm;	*En. Arden*	1
daily *l* The little footprint	"	21
(Since Enoch *l* he had not look'd	"	272
ten years Since Enoch *l* his hearth	"	357
l you ten long years ago	"	401
nor loved she to be *l* Alone at home,	"	512
l but narrow breadth to left and right	"	675
Among the gifts he *l* her	*Aylmer's F.*	217
l the living scandal that shall die—	"	444
l alone he pluck'd her dagger	"	470
l Their own gray tower,	"	617
house is *l* unto you desolate!"	"	629
were *l* to make a purer world—	"	638
love and reverence *l* them bare?	"	785
or one stone *L* on another,	"	789
l their memories a world's curse—	"	796
Still so much gold was *l;*	*Sea Dreams*	126
the gaps and chasms of ruin *l*	"	218
L him one hand, and reaching thro'	"	275
my Annie, who *l* me at two,	*Grandmother*	77
there's none of them *l* alive;	"	85
There is but a trifle *l* you	"	107
Nobbut a bit on it's *l,*	*N. Farmer*	41
could not end me, *l* me maim'd	*Tithonus*	20
l behind the painted buoy	*The Voyage*	1
if *l* to pass His autumn	*A Dedication*	9
scrolls *L* by the teacher whom he	*Lucretius*	13
fire that *l* a roofless Ilion,	"	65
if I go *my* work is *l* Unfinish'd—	"	103
such cups as *l* us friendly-warm	"	212
and *l* me in shadow here!	*The Window*	37

leg.

caught the white goose by the *l,*	*The Goose*	9
My right *l* chain'd into the crag,	*St S. Stylites*	72
l and arm with love-knots gay,	*Talking O.*	65
l's of trees were limber,	*Amphion*	14
Stept forward on a firmer *l,*	*Will Water.*	123
Callest thou that thing a *l?*	*Vision of Sin*	89
and white and strong on his *l's*	*Grandmother*	2
'Here's a *l* for a babe of a week!'	"	11
Strong of his hand, and strong on his *l's,*	"	13

legacy.

Leaving great *legacies* of thought,	*In Mem.* lxxxiii.	35

legend.

Nor these alone: but every *l* fair.	*Pal. of Art*	125
shaped The city's ancient l into this:—	*Godiva*	4
Some *l* of a fallen race	*Two Voices*	359
The reflex of a *l* past,	*Day-Dm.*	11
The violet of a *l* blow	*Will Water.*	147
lived an ancient *l* in our house.	*Princess,* i.	5
almost think That idiot *l* credible.	" v.	146
fading *l* of the past,	*In Mem.* lxi.	4
l as in guerdon for your rhyme?	*Vivien*	404

'The Legend of Good Women.'

'The *L o G W,*' long ago Sung	*D. of F. Wom.*	2

legion.

all his *l's* crying Christ and him,	*Elaine*	305

legionary.

those Neronian *legionaries*	*Boädicea*	1
many a valorous *l.*	"	85

leisure.

	POEM.	LINE.
in the fallow *l* of my life	*Audley Ct.*	76
lapt In the arms of *l,*	*Princess,* ii.	152
eyes have *l* for their tears;	*In Mem.* xiii.	16

lemon-grove.

l-g In closest coverture upsprung,	*Arabian N's.*	67

lend.

God in his mercy lend her grace,	*L. of Shalott,* iv.	53
l our hearts and spirits wholly	*Lotos-E's.*	108
Something to love He *l's* us;	*To J. S.*	14
in this frequence can I *l* full tongue,	*Princess,* iv.	422
Nature *l's* such evil dreams?	*In Mem.* liv.	6
l me one, if such you have, Blank,	*Elaine*	193
l an ear to Plato where he says,	*Lucretius*	147

length.

All its allotted *l* of days,	*Lotos-E's.*	80
l of bright horizon rimm'd the dark.	*Gardener's D.*	177
to such *l* of years should come	*Locksley H.*	67
l's of yellow ringlets, like a girl,	*Princess,* i.	3
boss'd with *l's* Of classic frieze	" ii.	10
All her fair *l* upon the ground	" v.	56
To wile the *l* from languorous hours	" vii.	48
lazy *l's* on boundless shores;	*In Mem.* lxix.	12
Down by the *l* of lance and arm	*Enid*	1312
all her *l* and kiss'd his feet,	*Vivien*	68
all its *l* in blackest samite,	*Elaine*	1136
Cut off the *l* of highway on before,	*En. Arden*	674
Dangled a *l* of ribbon	"	751

lengthen'd.

Tall as a figure *l* on the sand	*Princess,* vi.	145

Lent (fast.)

If it may be, fast Whole *L's*	*St S. Stylites*	179

lent (verb.)

l broad verge to distant lands,	*Pal. of Art*	30
Who *l* you, love, your mortal dower	*Margaret.*	5
l The pulse of hope to discontent.	*Two Voices*	449
l my knee desire to kneel,	*Princess,* iii.	177
once or twice she *l* her hand,	" iv.	9
have *l* my life to build up yours,	"	332
crown'd with all the season *l,*	*In Mem.* xxii.	6
A willing ear We *l* him.	" lxxxvi.	31
in the little book you *l* me,	*The Daisy*	99

Leolin.

L, his brother, living oft With Averill,	*Aylmer's F.*	57
L's first nurse was five years after	"	79
care no more for *L's* walking with her	"	124
Might have been other, save for *L's*—	"	140
once with *L* at her side the girl,	"	184
L ever watchful of her eye	"	210
L, coming after he was gone,	"	234
L's horror-stricken answer,	"	318
L still Retreated half-aghast,	"	329
Went *L;* then, his passions all in flood	"	339
he thought, had slandered *L* to him.	"	350
L, I almost sin in envying you:	"	360
L cried out the more upon them—	"	367
Tho' *L* flamed and fell again	"	409
L went: and as we task ourselves	"	432
return'd *L's* rejected rivals	"	493
Came at the moment *L's* emissary	"	518
L's one strong rival upon earth;	"	557
crying upon the name of *L,*	"	576

Leonard.

shall have that song which *L* wrote:	*Golden Year*	1
and I wish'd for *L* there,	"	4

leopard.

two tame *l's* couch'd beside her	*Princess,* ii.	19
foot on one Of those tame *l's.*	" iii.	165
I tamed my *l's:* shall I not tame these?	" v.	390

leopard skin.

a *l s* Droop'd from his shoulder	*Œnone*	57

leper.

'Last of the train, a moral *l,* I,	*Princess,* iv.	203

less.

Some said their heads were *l:*	*Princess,* ii.	131
can grief be changed to *l?*	*In Mem.* lxxvii.	16

	POEM.	LINE.
Not being *l* but more than all	*In Mem.* cx.	11
yet is love not *l*, but more; .	" Con.	12

lessen.

Nor will it *l* from to-day ; .	*In Mem.*lviii.	10

lessened.

And I be *l* in his love? .	*In Mem.* l.	8

lessening.

a foot *L* in perfect cadence, .	*Walk. to the M.*	47
L to the *l* music, . . .	*Sea Dreams*	214

lesser.

draws The greater to the *l*, .	*Gardener's D.*	10

lesson.

One *l* from one book we learn'd	*In Mem.*lxxviii.	14
Shall we teach it a Roman *l*?	*Boädicea*	32

let.

And *l*'s me from the saddle ;'	*Elaine*	95

lethargy.

for months, in such blind *lethargies*, *St S. Stylites*		101

Lethe.

Some draught of *L* might await	*Two Voices*	350
she that out of *L* scales with man	*Princess,* vii.	245
gleams On *L* in the eyes of Death.	*In Mem.*xcvii.	8

Lethean.

(If Death so taste *L* springs)	*In Mem.*xliii.	10

letter (epistle.)

from her bosom drew Old *l's*,	*Mariana in the S.*	62
Tore the king's *l*, snow'd it down,	*Princess,* i. .	60
I can give you *l's* to her ; .	"	158
show'd the late-writ *l's* of the king.	"	173
king,' he said ' Had given us *l's*,	"	179
gave the *l* to be sent with dawn ; .	"	241
I read —two *l's*—one her sire's. .	" iv.	378
Behold your father's *l*.'	"	448
I pored upon her *l* which I held, .	" v.	458
l's unto trembling hands ; .	*In Mem.* x.	7
The noble *l's* of the dead ; .	" xciv.	24
gave my *l's* back to me. .	*The Letters*	20
as she devised A *l*, word for word;	*Elaine*	1098
wrote The *l* she devised ; .	"	1103
lay the *l* in my hand . .	"	1107
father laid the *l* in her hand,	"	1128
in her left The *l—* . .	"	1150
Arthur spied the *l* in her hand .	"	1263
her lips, Who had devised the *l* .	"	1280
her *l's* too, Tho' far between,	*Aylmer's F.*	475
read Writhing a *l* from his child, .	"	517
The *l* which he brought and swore	"	522
a *l* edged with death Beside him,	"	575
And with it a spiteful *l* . .	*Spiteful Let.*	2
Fly little *l* apace, apace, .	*The Window*	98

letter (character.)

a tear Dropt on the *l's* as I wrote.	*To J. S.*	56
Along the *l's* of thy name, .	*In Mem.*lxvi.	7
on her tomb In *l's* gold and azure	*Elaine*	1335
kept it green In living *l's*, .	*Aylmer's F.*	89

letter (literal meaning.)

His light upon the *l* dwells, .	*Miller's D.* .	189
broke the *l* of it to keep the sense	*Princess,* iv.	319
Because she kept the *l* of his word	*Enid*	1304

letter (verb.)

Spring *L*'s cowslips on the hill? .	*Adeline*	62

letters (literature.)

From misty men of *l's*; .	*Will Water.*	199
in the flowery walk Of *l's*	*In Mem.*lxxxiii.	23
gilded by the gracious gleam Of *l's*,	*Ded. of Idylls*	39

Letty (see *Hill.*)

The close ' Your *L*, only yours ;'	*Ed. Morris*	106
I have pardon'd little *L*; .	"	140

level (s.)

Ridged the smooth *l*, . .	*Arabian N's.*	35
springs on a *l* of bowery lawn,	*Poet's Mind*	31
house thro' all the *l* shines,	*Mariana in the S.*	2
on the shining *l's* of the lake,	*M. d'Arthur*	51

	POEM.	LINE.
thou shalt lower to his *l* .	*Locksley II.*	45
flowery *l's* underneath the crag,	*Princess,* iii.	318
starts and slides Upon the *l* .	" iv.	237

level (verb.)

Not to feel lowest makes them *l* all ;	*Vivien*	677

lever.

A *l* to uplift the earth . .	*In Mem.* cxii.	15

leveret.

quail and pigeon, lark and *l* lay	*Audley Ct.* .	23

levied.

L a kindly tax upon themselves, .	*En. Arden* .	664

lewdness.

l, narrowing envy, monkey-spite,	*Lucretius* .	208

liar.

Let the canting *l* pack ! .	*Vision of Sin*	108
And rave at the lie and the *l*,	*Maud,* I. i.	60
l's belied in the hubbub of lies ; .	" iv.	51
Spurn'd by this heir of the *l—*	" xix.	78
wrath shall be wreaked on a giant *l*;	" III. vi.	45
I raged against the public *l*;	*The Letters*	26
' What dare the full-fed *l's* say	*Vivien*	542
slandering me, the base little *l l*	*Grandmother*	27
There the hive of Roman *l's*	*Boädicea* .	19

libation.

No vain *l* to the Muse, .	*Will Water.*	9

liberal.

but come, We will be *l*, .	*Princess,* vi.	52

liberal-minded.

l-m, great, Consistent ; .	*In Mem. Con.*	38

liberty.

He that roars for *l* . .	*Vision of Sin*	127
at the boundary of the *liberties* ;	*Princess,* i.	15
ventured on the *liberties* .	"	202
for three years to cross the *liberties*	" ii.	57
compass our dear sisters' *liberties*.	" iii.	271
She bore the blade of *L*. .	*The Voyage*	72
Thine the *l*, thine the glory .	*Boädicea* .	41
me the lover of *l*, . .	"	48

Libyan.

We drank the *L* Sun to sleep .	*D. of F. Wom.*	145

license.

give you, being strange, A *l*:	*Princess,* iii.	189
You grant me *l*; might I use it? .	"	219
takes His *l* in the field of time, .	*In Mem.* xxvii.	6

lichen.

a morbid eating *l* fixt . .	*Maud,* I. vi.	77
I scraped the *l* from it ; .	*The Brook* .	193

lichen'd.

l into colour with the crags; .	*Elaine* .	45

lichen-gilded.

turrets *l-g* like a rock ; . .	*Ed. Morris*	8

lie (s.)

do away that ancient *l*; 'Clear-headed friend,'etc.		15
Perplexing me with *l's* ; .	*St S. Stylites*	100
Cursed be the social *l's* .	*Locksley H.*	60
' Wilt thou make everything a *l*,	*Two Voices*	203
Love but play'd with gracious *l's*	*In Mem.*cxxiv.	7
fool the crowd with glorious *l's*,	" cxxvii.	14
and a wretched swindler's *l* .	*Maud,* I. l.	3
And rave at the *l* and the liar,	"	60
has as many *l's* as a Czar ; .	" iv.	9
liars belied in the hubbub of *l's*;	"	51
In another month to his brazen *l's*,	" vi.	55
He fiercely gave me the *l*. .	" II. i.	15
cloaks the wounds of loss with *l's*;	*Vivien*	667
neither capable of *l's*, .	*En. Arden* .	50
a *l* which is half a truth is ever the blackest of *l's*		
a *l* which is all a *l* may be met	*Grandmother*	30
a *l* which is part a truth .	"	31
lie You golden *l*. . .	*The Ringlet*	32

lie (to rest, etc.)

	POEM.	LINE.
Within thy heart my arrow *l*'s,	Oriana	80
On either side the river *l*	L. of Shalott,	i. 1
to *l* Beside the mill-wheel	Miller's D.	166
I would *l* so light, so light,	"	185
There *l*'s a vale in Ida,	Œnone	1
on her threshold *l* Howling To—	With Pal. of Art	15
God, before whom ever *l* bare	Pal. of Art	222
But I shall *l* alone, mother,	May Queen,	ii. 20
All night I *l* awake,	"	50
To *l* within the light of God,	" iii.	59
as I *l* upon her breast	"	59
gentlier on the spirit *l*'s	Lotos-E's.	50
For they *l* beside their nectar,	"	156
knee-deep *l*'s the winter snow	D. of the O. Year	1
the old year *l*'s a-dying.	"	5
L still, dry dust, secure of change.	To J. S.	76
l's Deep-meadow'd, happy, fair	M. d'Arthur	261
between it and the garden *l*'s	Gardener's D.	39
Beyond the lodge the city *l*'s,	Talking O.	5
l's beside thee on the grass.	"	239
Peace *L* like a shaft of light .	Golden Year	49
'Ah folly! for it *l*'s so far away,	"	54
There *l*'s the port ; the vessel puffs	Ulysses	44
from the wells where he did *l*.	Two Voices	9
l upon her charmed heart.	Day-Dm.	96
liberal applications *l* In Art	"	209
That in my bosom *l*'s.	St Agnes' Eve	12
Here *l*'s the body of Ellen Adair ;	Ed. Gray	27, 35
leave me where I *l*:	'Come not when,' etc.	11
Heroic, for a hero *l*'s beneath,	Princess, Pro.	207
gross error *l*'s In this report,	" i.	68
when we came where *l*'s the child	"	255
Here *l*'s a brother by a sister slain,	" ii.	191
hearts *l* fallow in these halls,	"	378
there she *l*'s, But will not speak	" v.	49
sweet sister : *l* not thus.	"	61
l in the tents with coarse mankind,	" vi.	53
that there *L* bruised and maim'd,	"	56
'You shall not *l* in the tents	"	78
Whatever man *l*'s wounded, friend	"	316
But *l*'s and dreads his doom.	" vii.	139
l's the Earth all Danaë to the stars,	"	167
all thy heart *l*'s open unto me.	"	168
as far as in us We two will serve	"	251
in true marriage *l*'s Nor equal	"	284
A use in measured language *l*'s	In Mem. v.	6
Where *l*'s the master newly dead ;	" xx.	4
use may *l* in blood and breath,	" xliv.	13
l Foreshorten'd in the tract of time?	" lxxvi.	3
Bring in great logs and let them *l*,	" cvi.	17
What profit *l*'s in barren faith,	" cvii.	5
There yet *l*'s the rock that fell	Maud, I. i.	8
And Sleep must *l* down arm'd,	"	41
l while these long branches sway	" xviii.	29
full of wolves, where he used to *l* ;	" II. v.	54
I know that he *l*'s and listens mute	"	60
let the bodies *l*, but bound the suits	Enid	945
l still, and yet the sapling grew :	"	1014
to *l* Closed in the four walls .	Vivien	57
did you never *l* upon the shore,	"	114
Never *l* by thy side, see thee no	Guinevere	574
l before your shrines?,	"	673
Might *l* within their compass	Aylmer's F.	485
L's the hawk's cast,	"	849
'Let them *l* for they have fall'n.'	Sea Dreams	221
tills the field and *l*'s beneath,	Tithonus	3
See the place where thou wilt *l*	Sailor Boy	8
Crew and Captain *l* ;	The Captain	68
dead lineaments that near thee *l*?	Coquette, iii.	2
Nature, so far as in her *l*'s,	On a Mourner	1

lie (to utter falsehood.)

a shameful thing for men to *l*.	M. d'Arthur	78
will speak out for I dare not *l*.	Lady Clare	38
when only not all men *l*;	Maud, I. i.	35
Who can rule and dare not *L*	" x.	66
scheming brain a cinder, if I *l*.'	Vivien	782

lied.

wrong'd and *l* and thwarted us—	Princess, iv.	519
vext at having *l* in vain ;	Elaine	103

lief.

	POEM.	LINE.
go again As thou art *l* and dear,	M. d'Arthur	80

liege.

true and tender ! O my *l* and king !	Vivien	640
call'd him lord and *l*, Her seer	"	802
my *l*, in whom I have my joy,	Elaine	1174

liege-lady.

he, he reverenced his *l-l* there ;	Princess, i.	186

liest.

O happy thou that *l* low,	Oriana	84
l beneath the greenwood tree,	"	95
L thou here so low,	Guinevere	419

lieth.

He *l* still : he doth not move ;	D. of the O. Year	10

lieu.

In *l* of many mortal flies,	Princess, iii.	251
In *l* of idly dallying with the truth	Elaine	588

liever—liefer.

Far *l* had I gird his harness	Enid	93
Far *l* than so much discredit him.	"	629
Far *l* by his dear hand had I die,	"	917

life.

court was pure ; her *l* serene ;	To the Queen	25
Crown'd Isabel, thro' all her placid *l*,	Isabel	27
She only said 'My *l* is dreary, (rep.)	Mariana	9
L, anguish, death, immortal love,	Arabian N's.	73
thought was there of *l*'s distress ;	Ode to Mem.	37
Whither in after *l* retired	"	111
L in dead stones, or spirit in air ;	A Character	9
He saw thro' *l* and death,	The Poet	5
L and Thought have gone away	Deserted H.	1
L and Thought Here no longer dwell	"	17
Thou art the shadow of *l*,	Love and Death	10
L eminent creates the shade of death ;	"	13
my *l*, my love, my bride,	Oriana	44
Two *lives* fast bound in one .	Circumstance	5
So runs the round of *l*.	"	7
Oh ! what a happy *l* were mine	The Merman	37
delirious draughts of warmest *l*.	Eleänore	139
somewhat flows to us in *l*,	Miller's D.	21
I'd almost live my *l* again.	"	28
scarce my *l* with fancy play'd	"	45
Like mine own *l* to me thou art,	"	196
My other dearer *l* in *l*,	"	217
I am all aweary of my *l*.	Œnone	32
A shepherd all thy *l*	"	126
lead *l* to sovereign power ;	"	143
forward thro' a *l* of shocks,	"	160
pass before my light of *l*,	"	237
Not less than *l*, design'd.	Pal. of Art	128
death and *l* she hated equally	"	265
sweeter far is death than *l*	May Queen, iii.	8
blessings on his whole *l* long,	"	14
ceased to be, with my desire of *l*.	"	48
what is *l*, that we should moan ?	"	56
Death is the end of *l* ; ah, why Should *l* all labour be ?	Lotos-E's.	86
memory of our wedded *lives* .	"	114
O my *l* In Egypt !	D. of F. Wom.	146
my name Sigh'd forth with *l*	"	154
move Me from my bliss of *l*,	"	210
enter not the toil of *l*.	Margaret	8
He hath no other *l* above.	D. of the O. Year	12
Without whose *l* I had not been.	To J. S.	24
With *L*, that, working strongly 'Love thou thy land'	"	34
Yearning to mix himself with *L*.	"	56
live three *lives* of mortal men .	M. d'Arthur	155
I have lived my *l*, and that which	"	244
nourish a blind *l* within the brain,	"	251
ere he found Empire for *l*?	Gardener's D.	20
made the air Of *L* delicious,	"	69
old Mays had thrice the *l* of these,)	"	83
by my *l*, These birds have joyful	"	97
such a noise of *l* Swarm'd	"	174
Love trebled *l* within me	"	194
by my *l*, I will not marry Dora.'	Dora	21
let me live my *l*. (rep.)	Audley Ct.	42
in the fallow leisure of my *l*	"	76
the sense that handles daily *l*—	Walk. to the M.	16

	POEM.	LINE.		POEM.	LINE.
dust and drouth Of city *l!*	Ed. Morris	4, 143	thy dark freight, a vanish'd *l.*	In Mem. x.	8
once I ask'd him of his early *l,*	"	23	An awful thought, a *l* removed,	" xiii.	10
whole years long, a *l* of death	St S. Stylites	53	how my *l* had droop'd of late,	" xiv.	14
smite the threshold stairs Of *l*	"	189	The *l* that almost dies in me :	" xviii.	16
The *l* that spreads in them,	Talking O.	192	I know that this was *L,*—	" xxv.	1
I took the swarming sound of *l*—	"	213	In more of *l* true *l* no more	" xxvi.	11
To riper *l* may magnetise	"	255	that my hold on *l* would break	" xxviii.	15
brooding in the ruins of a *l,*	Love and Duty	12	rests upon the *L* indeed.	" xxxii.	8
set gray *l,* and apathetic end.	"	18	blest whose *lives* are faithful prayers,	"	13
such tears As flow but once a *l.*	"	63	*l* that leads melodious days	" xxxiii.	8
—closing like an individual *l*—	"	77	My own dim *l* should teach me this,	" xxxiv.	1
knowing All *l* needs for *l* is possible	"	83	That *l* shall live for evermore,	"	2
I will drink *L* to the lees:	Ulysses	7	A *l* that bears immortal fruit	" xxxix.	13
L piled on *l* Were all too little,	"	24	leap the grades of *l* and light	" xl.	11
Love took up the harp of *L,*	Locksley H.	33	But evermore a life behind.	"	24
'Tis a purer *l* than thine ;	"	88	The total world since *l* began ;	" xlii.	12
and the tumult of my *l;*	"	110	Lest *l* should fail in looking back.	" xlv.	4
where my *l* began to beat ;	"	154	drown The bases of my *l* in tears	" xlviii.	16
help me as when *l* begun :	"	185	*L,* a Fury slinging flame.	" xlix.	8
shut my *l* from happier chance	Two Voices	54	on the low dark verge of *l*	"	15
not to lose the good of *l*—	"	132	*l* is dash'd with flecks of sin.	" li.	14
The springs of *l.* the depths of awe,	"	140	For *l* outliving heats of youth,	" lii.	10
when *L* her light withdraws,	"	145	not one *l* shall be destroy'd	" liii.	6
A *l* of nothings, nothing worth,	"	331	No *l* may fail beyond the grave,	" liv.	2
It may be that no *l* is found	"	346	So careless of the single *l;*	"	8
Or if thro' lower *lives* I came—	"	364	I bring to *l,* I bring to death ;	" lv.	6
No *l* that breathes with human breath	"	395	O *l* as futile, then, as frail !	"	25
l, whereof our nerves are scant	"	397	half my *l* leave behind :	" lvi.	7
l, not death, for which we pant :	"	398	My bosom-friend and half of *l;*	" lviii.	3
More *l,* and fuller, that I want.'	"	399	Whose *l* in low estate began	" lxiii.	3
in those the *l* is stay'd.	Day-Dm.	38	shade by which my *l* was crost,	" lxv.	3
all his *l* the charm did talk	"	121	On songs, and deeds, and *lives*	" lxxvi.	3
all the long-pent stream of *l.*	"	147	grief as deep as *l* or thought,	" lxxix.	7
Are clasp'd the moral of thy *l,*	"	267	No lower *l* that earth's embrace	" lxxxi.	3
smote Her *l* into the liquor.	Will Water.	112	put our *lives* so far apart	"	15
A private *l* was all his joy,	"	129	The *l* that had been thine below,	" lxxxii.	2
Lest of the fullness of my *l*	"	163	should'st link thy *l* with one	"	11
an unctuous lease Of *l,*	"	244	What kind of *l* is that I lead ;	" lxxxiv.	8
l that moves to gracious ends '	You might have won	6	Whose *l,* whose thoughts were little	"	30
A deedful *l,* a silent voice :	"	8	The footsteps of his *l* in mine ;	"	44
No public *l* was his on earth,	"	23	A *l* that all the Muses deck'd	"	45
The little *l* of bank and brier,	"	30	Diffused the shock thro' all my *l,*	"	55
keep the secret for your *l,*	Lady Clare	34	pining *l* be fancy-fed	"	96
And I love thee more than *l.'*	L. of Burleigh	16	full new *l* that feeds thy breath	" lxxxv.	10
What ! the flower of *l* is past :	Vision of Sin	69	Were closed with wail, resume their *l,*	" lxxxvi.	6
Whited thought and cleanly *l*	"	116	their dim lights, like *l* and death,	" xciv.	63
Dregs of *l,* and lees of man :	"	205	Two partners of a married *l*—	" xcvi.	5
While *l* was yet in bud and blade,	Princess, i.	31	Her *l* is lone, he sits apart	"	17
ripen'd earlier, and her *l* Was longer ;	" ii.	138	By which our *lives* are chiefly proved,	" civ.	14
Two in the liberal offices of *l,*	"	158	Ring in the nobler modes of *l,*	" cv.	15
' Well then, Psyche, take my *l,*	"	187	A *l* of civic action warm	" cxii.	9
I lose My honour, these their *lives.'*	"	321	live their *lives* From land to land ;	" cxiv.	16
debtors for our *lives* to you,	"	334	The *l* re-orient out of dust,	" cxv.	6
better blush our *lives* away.	" iii.	52	*l* is not as idle ore,	" cxvii.	20
our three *lives.* True—we had limed	"	126	*l* is darken'd in the brain.	" cxx.	8
perchance your *l* may fail ;	"	220	I slip the thoughts of *l* and death ;	" cxxi.	16
our device : wrought to the *l;*	"	286	when her *l* was yet in bud,	Con.	33
O Death in *L,* the days that are no more.	" iv.	40	shielded all her *l* from harm	"	47
brief is *l* but love is long.	"	93	living words of *l* Breathed in her ear	"	52
Is it my *l* to build up yours,	"	332	For them the light of *l* increased,	"	74
a *l* Less mine than yours :	"	406	moved thro' *l* of lower phase	"	125
matters left to do, The breath of *l;*	"	439	His who had given me *l*—	Maud, I. i.	1
saved our *l:* we owe you bitter	"	510	works in the very means of *l,*	"	40
Severer in the logic of a *l?*	" v.	182	Be mine a philosopher's *l.*	" iv.	40
l and soul ! I thought her half-right	"	274	and lain in the lilies of *L.*	"	60
babbling wells With her own people's *l:*	"	325	Singing alone in the morning of *l,*	" v.	6
Still Take not his *l:*	"	397	happy morning of *l* and of May.	"	7
on the little clause ' take not his *l:'*	"	459	sick to the heart of *l,* am I.	" x.	36
saved my *l:* my brother slew him	" vi.	92	Before my *l* has found	" xi.	3
two foes above my fallen *l,*	"	114	To a *l* that has been so sad,	"	13
silent in the muffled cage of *l*	" vii.	32	My yet young *l* in the wilds of Time,	" xvi.	21
with what *l* I had, And like a flower	"	125	made my *l* a perfumed altar-flame	" xviii.	24
type them now In our own *lives,*	"	282	More *l* to Love than is	"	47
beating, with one full stroke, *L.'*	"	290	live a *l* of truest breath,	"	53
drowning *l,* besotted in sweet self,	"	295	true *l* to fight with mortal wrongs	"	54
Given back to *l,* to *l* indeed, thro' thee,	"	324	*L* of my *l,* wilt thou not answer	"	59
My bride, My wife, my *l.*	"	339	As long as my *l* endures	" xix.	86
madest *L* in man and brute.	In Mem. Pro.	6	She is coming, my *l,* my fate ;	" xxii.	6
Beats out the little *lives* of men	" ii.	8	must have *l* for a blow	" II. i.	27
still'd the *l* that beat from thee.	" vi.	12	Might drown all *l* in the eye,—	" ii.	61
noise of *l* begins again,	" vii.	10	red *l* spilt for a private blow	" v.	53

Q

	POEM.	LINE.
l has crept so long on a broken wing	*Maud*, III. vi.	1
l in him Could scarce be said	*The Brook*	11
Thro' you, my *l* will be accurst.'	*The Letters*	36
long self-sacrifice of *l* is o'er	*Ode on Well.*	41
Whose *l* was work	"	183
rugged maxims hewn from *l*;	"	184
other forms of *l* than ours,	"	264
So dear a *l* your arms enfold	*The Daisy*	93
How gain in *l*, as *l* advances,	*To F. D. Maurice*	39
white flower of a blameless *l*,	*Ded. of Idylls*	24
A lovelier *l*, a more unstain'd,	"	29
for my *l*, or hunger for my death,	*Enid*	930
save a *l* dearer to me than mine.'.	"	987
pilot star of my lone *l*	"	1155
Owe you me nothing for a *l* half-lost?	"	1167
hurt that drain'd her dear lord's *l*.	"	1365
slay not him who gave you *L*.'	"	1631
foot upon me, and give me *L*	"	1698
hating the *l* He gave me,	"	1700
glance behind me at my former *l*,	"	1711
upon himself After a *l* of violence,	"	1761
some knight of mine. risking his *l*,	"	1763
crown'd A happy *l* with a fair death,	"	1816
to *l* and use and name (rep. 224, 819)	*Vivien*	63
what is Fame in *l* but half-disfame	"	315
as dead, And lost all use of *l*:	"	495
sleepless nights Of my long *l*	"	530
once in *l* was fluster'd with new wine,	"	606
from the rosy lips of *l* and love,	"	695
word worse than a *l* of blows!	"	719
course of *l* that seem'd so flowery	"	729
If the wolf spare me, weep my *l* away,	"	734
vast necessity of heart and *l*.	"	774
passionate love Of her whole *l*;	"	805
colour of a mind and *l*,	*Elaine*	334
so I help him back to *l*?'	"	783
her fine care had saved his *l*.	"	859
when you yield your flower of *l*	"	948
half disgust At love, *l*, all things	"	1232
trustful courtesies of household *l*,	*Guinevere*	86
hide thee, till my *l* shall end,	"	113
hold thee with my *l* against the world.'	"	114
whose disloyal *l* Hath wrought confusion	"	227
all the land was full of *L*	"	257
many a mystic lay of *l* and death.	"	279
hast not made my *l* so sweet	"	448
spoilt the purpose of my *l*.	"	450
lead sweet *lives* in purest chastity,	"	470
so that this *l* of mine I guard	"	489
thro' flesh hath wrought into my *l*	"	554
must tell him in that purer *l*,	"	646
for her good deeds and her pure *l*,	"	685
new warmth of *l*'s ascending sun	*En. Arden.*	38
pluck'd a *l* From the dread sweep	"	54
like a wounded *l* Crept down	"	75, 383
miserable *lives* of hand-to-mouth	"	116
fuller profits lead an easier *l*,	"	145
lived a *l* of silent melancholy	"	259
known each other all our *lives*?	"	305-407
as I have waited all my *l*	"	432
l so wild that it was tame	"	558
and beats out his weary *l*.	"	731
the dead man come to *l* beheld	"	759
l in it Whereby the man could live;	"	821
boat that bears the hope of *l*.	"	831
approach To save the *l* despair'd of,	"	832
his lonely *l*, his coming back,	"	863
Flash into fiery *l* from nothing	*Aylmer's F.*	130
Thro' the perilous passes of his *l*:	"	209
for years a stunted sunless *l*;	"	357
quintessence of man, The *l* of all—	"	389
Had rioted his *l* out,	"	391
cared to lose, her hold of *l*.	"	568
clipt by horror from his term of *L*	"	603
faded woods Was all the *l* of it;	"	611
meanness in her unresisting *l*.	"	801
musing on the little *lives* of men,	*Sea Dreams*	48
Now I see My dream was *L*;	"	133
on a matter he of *l* and death;	"	147
And that drags down his *l*:	"	173
Shadow and shine is *l*,	*Grandmother*	60

	POEM.	LINE.
the babe had fought for his *l*.	*Grandmother*	64
Judge of us all when *l* shall cease;	"	95
And happy has been my *l*	"	98
dream of *l* this hour may cease.	*Requiescat*	6
rapid of *l* Shoots to the fall—	*A Dedication*	3
My *l* is full of weary days '*My life is full*,' etc.		1
all thy *l* one way incline	*On a Mourner*	19
would you have of us? Human *l*?	*The Victim*	12
'We give you his *l*.'	"	16
Take you his dearest, Give us a *L*.'	"	29
taken our son, They will have his *l*.	"	52
O, Father Odin, We give you a *l*.	"	80
O summer leaf, isn't *l* as brief?	*Spiteful Let.*	21
the *l* of the worm and the fly?	*Wages*	7
Live the great *l* which all our greatest	*Lucretius*	78
may gain Letting his own *l* go.	"	113
settled, sweet, Epicurean *l*.	"	215
of so much within our little *l*,	"	223
so little in our little *l*,	"	224
little *l* that toddles half an hour	"	225
Ay is *l* for a hundred years,	*The Window*	114
Love will come but once a *l* (rep.)	"	126

lifeblood.

New *l* warm the bosom,	*Will Water.*	22

life-long.

forge a *l*-*l* trouble for ourselves,	*Enid*	852
l-*l* injuries burning unavenged,	"	1544
sat the *l*-*l* creature of the house,	*Elaine*	1137

lifetime.

Ere half the *l* of an oak.	*In Mem.* lxxv.	12

lift.

Many an arch high up did *l*,	*Pal. of Art*	142
to *l* the hidden ore That glimpses,	*D. of F. Wom.*	274
knowing God, they *l* not hands of	*M. d'Arthur*	252
lean arms I *l* the cross,	*St S. Stylites*	116
l His axe to slay my kin.	*Talking O.*	235
to *l* a burthen from my heart	*Love and Duty*	93
l's me to the golden doors;	*St Agnes' Eve*	25
l your natures up: Embrace our aims:	*Princess*, ii. 74
l the woman's fall'n divinity	"	iii. 207
fair philosophies That *l* the fancy;	"	323
'*L* up your head, sweet sister:	"	v. 61
l thine eyes; my doubts are dead,	"	vii. 327
Last thou may'st thy burthen'd brows	*In Mem.* lxxi. 11
seem to the form, and glow	"	lxxxvi. 37
A great ship *l* her shining sides.	"	cii. 40
That we may *l* from out of dust	"	cxxx. 5
Nor did she *l* an eye nor speak	*Enid*	528
l a shining hand against the sun,	"	1322
Without the will to *l* their eyes,	*Vivien*	685
He spared to *l* his hand	*Guinevere*	434
the household out of poverty;	*En. Arden.*	482
slowly *l*'s His golden feet	*Lucretius*	134

lifted.

once my arm was *l* to hew down	*D. of F. Wom.*	45
her arm *l*, eyes on fire—	*Princess, Pro.*	41
l up A weight of emblem	"	iv. 183
l up her voice and cried	"	v. 98
Then us they *l* up, dead weights,	"	vi. 328
once, but once, she *l* her eyes,	*Maud*, I. viii.	5
came near, *l* adoring eyes,	*Enid*	1153
her palfrey whinnying *l* heel,	"	1382
gravely smiling, *l* her from horse,	"	1731
l up A face of sad appeal,	*Vivien*	82
when my name was *l* up,	"	352
And the Queen *L* her eyes.	*Elaine*	85
L her eyes, and read his lineaments.	"	244
noblest, when she *l* up her eyes.	"	256
l up her eyes And loved him,	"	259
l her fair face and moved away;	"	679
like a ghost she *l* up her face,	"	914
l up his eyes And saw the barge	"	1381
limb was broken when they *l* him;	*En. Arden.*	107
l up in spirit he moved away.	"	327
To Thor and Odin *l* a hand.	*The Victim*	8

lifting (part.)

L his grim head from my wounds.	*Princess*, vi.	255
L his honest forehead	*En. Arden.*	385

	POEM.	LINE.
lifting (s.)		
l of whose eyelash is my lord,	Princess, v.	134
liggin' (lying.)		
meü *l*'ere aloün?	N. Farmer	1
light (adj.)		
she So *l* of foot, so *l* of spirit	Gardener's D.	14
So *l* upon the grass;	Talking O.	88
l as any wind that blows	"	129
a tender foot, *l* as on air,	Princess, vi.	72
l as the crest Of a peacock	Maud, 1. xvi.	16
light (s.)		
giving *l* To read those laws;	Isabel	18
swifter movement and in purer *l*	"	32
cock sung out an hour ere *l*:	Mariana	27
Until the breaking of the *l* 'Clear-headed friend'		25
Thro' *l* and shadow thou dost range,	Madeline	4
cats run home and *l* is come,	The Owl, i.	1
I enter'd, from the clearer *l*,	Arabian N's.	38
soften'd *l* Of orient state.	Ode to Mem.	10
The *l* of thy great presence;	"	32
A pillar of white *l*	"	53
Breathing *L* against thy face	Adeline	56
In the windows is no *l*;	Deserted H.	6
L. and shadow ever wander	A Dirge	12
mighty moon was gathering *l*	Love and Death	1
in the *l* of great eternity	"	12
Ere the *l* on dark was growing,	Oriana	10
thunder and *l* in the magic night—	The Merman	23
A funeral, with plumes and *l*'s	L. of Shalott, ii.	31
Some bearded meteor, trailing *l*,	" iii.	26
all the furnace of the *l*	Mariana in the S.	55
lavish *l*'s, and floating shades:	Eleänore	12
Grape-thicken'd from the *l*,	"	36
am as nothing in its *l*:	"	88
these have never lost their *l*.	Miller's D.	88
I saw the village *l*'s below:	"	108
you rose and moved the *l*.	"	125
His *l* upon the letter dwells,	"	189
Throbbing thro' all thy heat and *l*,	Fatima	4
isled in sudden seas of *l*,	"	33
l that grows Larger and clearer,	Œnone	106
pass before my *l* of life,	"	237
Suddenly scaled the *l*.	Pal. of Art	8
the *l*'s, rose, amber, emerald, blue	"	169
Lit *l* in wreaths and anadems,	"	186
spot of dull stagnation, without *l*	"	245
languid *l* of your proud eyes	L.C. V. de Vere	59
without speaking, like a flash of *l*.	May Queen, i.	18
again, mother, beneath the waning *l*	" ii.	25
and there his *l* may shine—	" iii.	51
To lie within the *l* of God,	"	59
thro' wavering *l*'s and shadows broke,	Lotos-E's.	12
sweeten'd with the summer *l*,	"	77
dream, like yonder amber *l*,	"	102
I saw, wherever *l* illumineth,	D. of F. Wom.	14
fill'd with *l* The interval of sound	"	171
with welcome *l*, With timbrel	"	199
that I should ever see the *ll*	"	254
Joan of Arc, A *l* of ancient France;	"	268
gleams of mellow *l* Float by you	Margaret	30
faint, rainy *l*'s are seen,	"	60
cricket chirps: the *l* burns low:	D. of the O. Year	40
mournful *l* That broods above	To J. S.	50
Above her shook the starry *l*'s 'Of old sat Freedom'		3
Keep dry their *l* from tears;	"	20
girt with doubtful *l*. 'Love thou thy land,' etc.		16
Set in all *l*'s by many minds,	"	35
l that led The holy Elders	M. d'Arthur	232
our last *l*, that long Had wink'd	Ep.	7
twinkling laurel Scatter'd silver *l*'s.	Gardener's D.	117
Danced into *l*, and died into the shade;	"	198
a *l* Of laughter dimpled	Ed. Morris	60
measure time by yon slow *l*,	St S. Stylites	93
the spring and downfall of the *l*,	"	108
flapp'd my *l* out as I read;	"	172
a shape, a shade, A flash of *l*.	"	200
lead them to thy *l*.	"	220
flush'd her cheek with rosy *l*.	Talking O.	165
l's of sunset and of sunrise mix'd	Love and Duty	70
point thee forward to a distant *l*,	"	92

	POEM.	LINE.
furrowing into *l* the mounded rack,	Love and Duty	97
smit with freër *l* shall slowly melt	Golden Year	33
l shall spread, and man be liker man	"	35
like a shaft of *l* across the land.	"	49
l's begin to twinkle from the rocks:	Ulysses	54
came a colour and a *l*,	Locksley H.	25
Sees in heaven the *l* of London	"	114
Underneath the *l* he looks at,	"	116
A living flash of *l* he flew.'	Two Voices	15
swift souls that yearn for *l*,	"	67
Those lonely *l*'s that still remain,	"	83
Nor art thou nearer to the *l*,	"	92
when Life her *l* withdraws,	"	145
the *l* increased With freshness	"	424
slumbrous *l* is rich and warm,	Day-Dm.	83
Stillness with love, and day with *l*.	"	92
A fuller *l* illumined all,	"	137
Be still the first to leap to *l*	"	239
strows her *l*'s below	St Agnes' Eve	28
A *l* upon the shining sea—	"	35
A *l* before me swims,	Sir Galahad	26
A gentle sound, an awful *l*!	"	41
Ten thousand broken *l*'s and shapes,	Will Water.	59
wide earth of *l* and shade	"	67
A sleepy *l* upon their brows	Vision of Sin	9
Dip forward under starry *l*, 'Move eastward.' etc.		10
flew thro' *l* And shadow,	Princess, Pro.	84
college *l*'s began to glitter	" i.	204
world was once a fluid haze of *l*,	" ii.	101
still may lead The new *l* up,	"	327
two streams of *l* from wall to wall,	"	449
green maligunt *l* of coming storm.	" iii.	110
smote me with the *l* of eyes.	"	176
with the sun and moon renew their *l*	"	238
Let there be *l* and there was *l*	"	300
one act at once, The birth of *l*:	"	309
long *l* shakes across the lakes,	"	350
in your own *l* and darken'd mine.	" iv.	295
we did not know the real *l*,	"	338
lived in all fair *l*'s,	"	410
lapt in wreaths of glowworm *l*	"	415
open-mouth'd, all gazing to the *l*,	"	462
wild birds on the *l* Dash themselves	"	474
would-be quenchers of the *l* to be,	"	515
saw the *l*'s, and heard The voices	"	536
sudden *l* Dazed me half-blind	" v.	10
common *l* of smiles at our disguise	"	261
tremulous isles of *l* Slided,	" vi.	056
A genial warmth and *l* once more	"	265
she not fair, began To gather *l*,	" vii.	9
small bright head, A *l* of healing,	"	44
silent *l* Slept on the painted walls,	"	105
double *l* in air and wave,	"	152
from a dewy breast a cry for *l*:	"	237
the *l* Dearer for night,	"	325
happy valleys, half in *l*,	Con.	41
Thine are these orbs of *l* and shade	In Mem. Pro.	5
are but broken *l*'s of thee,	"	19
vain worlds to bear thy *l*.	"	32
magic *l* Dies off at once	" viii.	5
thro' early *l* Shall glimmer	" ix.	11
Sphere all your *l*'s around, above;	"	13
still *l* on yon great plain	" xi.	10
My blessing, like a line of *l*,	" xvii.	10
Fancy from Fancy caught,	" xxiii.	11
l that shone when Hope was born.	" xxx.	32
leap the grades of life and *l*,	" xl.	11
'Farewell! We lose ourselves in *l*.'	" xlvi.	16
Like *l* In many a shiver'd lance	" xlviii.	3
near me when my *l* is low,	" xlix.	1
An infant crying for the *l*:	" liii.	19
in the *l* of deeper eyes	" lxi.	11
Recalls, in change of *l* or gloom.	" lxxxiv.	74
like a flower in *l*.	" xc.	16
in the house *l* after I Went out,	" xciv.	19
dim *l*'s, like life and death.	"	63
makes the darkness and the *l*,	" xcv.	19
dwells not in the *l* alone,	"	20
The flying cloud, the frosty *l*:	" cv.	8
God and Nature met in *l*;	" cx.	20
dance the *l*'s on lawn and lea	" cxiv.	9

	POEM.	LINE
Behind thee comes the greater *l*:	*In Mem.* cxx.	12
For them the *l* of life increased	" Con.	74
poison behind his crimson *l*'s.	*Maud*, I. i.	44
I see her pass like a *l* .	" iv.	11
if ever that *l* be my leading-star! .	"	12
Maud in the *l* of her youth and her grace	" v.	15
spark Of glowing and growing *l* .	" vi.	16
With no more hope of *l*.	" ix.	16
faint in the *l* that she loves (rep.) .	" xxii.	9
to faint in his *l*, and to die. .	"	12
At the shouts, the leagues of *l*'s, .	" II. iv.	21
And the *l* and shadow fleet ;	"	36
Ripples on in *l* and shadow .	"	42
From the realms of *l* and song,	"	82
broad *l* glares and beats,	"	89
Tho' many a *l* shall darken, .	" III. vi.	43
darkness into the *l* shall leap	"	46
Whatever record leap to *l* .	*Ode on Well.*	190
Thro' the long gorge to the far *l* .	"	213
A *l* amid its olives green ; .	*The Daisy*	30
From Como, when the *l* was gray,	"	73
on thro' zones of *l* and shadow	*To F. D. Maurice*	27
fierce *l* which beats upon a throne,	*Ded. of Idylls*	26
that ye made One *l* together,	"	46
as he loved the *l* of Heaven.	*Enid*	5
as the *l* of Heaven varies .	"	6
darken'd from the high *l* in his eyes	"	100
never *l* and shade Coursed one another	"	521
fair head in the dim-yellow *l*.	"	600
the red cock shouting to the *l*,	"	1233
l came from her when she moved :	*Vivien*	417
the court, the king, dark in your *l*,	"	724
the crown Roll'd into *l*,	*Elaine*	52
maiden standing in the dewy *l*.	"	351
green *l* from the meadows underneath	"	407
in the *l* of your blue eyes : .	"	657
lo! the bloodred *l* of dawn .	"	1019
one low *l* betwixt them burn'd	*Guinevere*	4
No *l* had we : for that we do repent ;	"	169
No *l*: so late ! and dark .	"	172
let us in. that we may find the *l*!.	"	173
in the *l* the white mermaiden swam	"	243
the world and all its *l*'s And shadows,	"	341
thou reseated in thy place of *l*,	"	521
the sad nuns with each a *l* .	"	584
smitten by the *l*'s The Dragon	"	591
pure severity of perfect *l*— .	"	639
isles a *l* in the offing .	*En. Arden*	131
from bed, and struck herself a *l*,	"	490
a great mist-blotted *l* .	"	681
finding neither *l* nor murmur	"	688
ruddy square of comfortable *l*,	"	727
a touch of *l*, an air of heaven,	*Aylmer's F.*	5
to dilate, as toward the *l*. .	"	77
n hope, a *l* breaking upon him.	"	480
Star to star vibrates *l*: .	"	578
from the low *l* of mortality .	"	641
with His *l* about thy feet, .	"	665
fill'd the house with sudden *l*.	"	682
near the *l* a giant woman sat,	*Sea Dreams*	96
—But round the North, n *l*, .	"	201
Broke, mixt with awful *l* .	"	208-28
cold Are all thy *l*'s, .	*Tithonus*	67
sleep beneath his pillar'd *l*! .	*The Voyage*	20
It wore a crown of *l*, .	*The Flower*	10
l and shadow illimitable, .	*Boädicea*	47
l is large and lambs are glad	*Lucretius*	99
The *l*'s and shadows fly	*The Window*	1
l's and shadows that cannot be still	"	7
O *l*'s are you flying over her sweet	"	13
Gone and the *l* gone with her	"	37
roll up away from the *l*. .	"	50
Down to the *l* in the valley fly	"	99
Fly to the *l* in the valley below. .	"	100
L, so low upon earth, .	"	178

light (to settle, etc.)

Who can *l* on as happy a shore	*Sea-Fairies*	40
could not *l* upon a sweeter thing :	*Walk. to the M.*	44
give to *l* on such a dream ?' .	*Ed. Morris*	58
trusts to *l* on something fair ;	*Day-Dm.*	120

	POEM.	LINE
float thro' Heaven, and cannot *l*?	*Day-Dm.*	276
follow, and *l* Upon her lattice,	*Princess*, iv.	81
may you *l* on all things that you love,	*Enid*	226
know Where I can *l* on arms,	"	422
L on a broken word to thank him	*En. Arden*	344
Britain *l* upon auguries happier ?	*Boädicea*	45

light (to illumine, etc.)

sunbeam slip, To *l* her shaded eye ;	*Talking O.*	218
l The light that shone when Hope	*In Mem.* xxx.	31
God within him *l* his face. .	" lxxxvi.	36
L's with herself, when alone	*Maud*, I. xiv.	12

light.

l's and rings the gateway bell,	*In Mem.* viii.	3

light-blue.

Sweet-hearted, you, whose *l-b* eyes	*In Mem.* xcv.	2
A *l-b* lane of early dawn, .	" cxviii.	7

Light Brigade.

' Forward the L B ! .	*L. Brigade*	5-9
Honour the L B .	"	54

lighted (kindled.)

tho' my lamp was *l* late, .	*May Queen*, iii.	18

lighted (alighted.)

And *l* at a ruin'd inn, .	*Vision of Sin*	62

lighted on.

those of old That *l o* Queen Esther	*Enid*	731
till she had *l o* his wound, .	"	1362
l o the maid, Whose sleeve he wore ;	*Elaine*	706

lighten (to flash, etc.)

now she *l*'s scorn At him that mars	*Princess*, v.	125
l thro' The secular abyss to come,	*In Mem.* lxxv.	5
What *l*'s in the lucid east .	" cxxvi.	15
brute earth *l*'s to the sky, .	*Aylmer's F.*	761
L's from her own central Hell—	*The Window*	187
You flash and *l* afar .	"	192
O *l* into my eyes and my heart .	"	

lighten (to make lighter.)

To *l* this great clog of thanks,	*Princess*, vi.	110
One burthen and she would not *l* it ?	*Aylmer's F.*	703

lightened (flashed, etc.)

The random sunshine *l*!	*Amphion*	56
rays, that *l* as be breath'd ; .	*Elaine*	296
brim Of waters *l* into view .	*The Voyage*	26
l In the eyes of each. .	*The Captain*	31

lightened (made lighter.)

yet it *l* my despair .	*Maud*, III. vi.	18

lighter.

finest Gothic *l* than a fire, .	*Princess, Pro.*	92
As flies the *l* thro' the gross .	*In Mem.* xl.	4

lighter-footed.

l-f than the fox. .	*Day-Dm.*	108

light-foot.

l-f Iris brought it yester-eve	*Œnone*	81

light-glooming.

L-g over eyes divine, .	*Madeline*	16

light-green.

A *l-g* tuft of plumes she bore	*Sir L. and Q. G.*	26

light-headed.

I should grow *l-h*, I fear, .	*Maud*, I. xix.	100
O my child, you seem *L-h*, .	*Elaine*	1057

lighting.

l upon days like these ? .	*Locksley H.*	99

lightning.

as the *l* to the thunder .	*The Poet*	50
a fountain Like sheet *l*, .	*The Poet's Mind*	25
into the dark Arrows of *l*'s. .	*To J. M. K.*	14
summer *l*'s of a soul .	*Miller's D.*	13
l's in the splendour of the moon,	*M. d'Arthur*	137
Nor ever *l* char thy grain, .	*Talking O.*	277
flash the *l*'s, weigh the Sun—	*Locksley H.*	186
The wizard *l*'s deeply glow .	*In Mem.* cxxi.	19
like a silent *l* under the stars .	*Maud*, III. vi.	9

	POEM.	LINE.
'Makes wicked *l*'s of her eyes,	Guinevere	516
L of the hour, the pun,	Aylmer's F.	441

like (adj. and s.)

	POEM.	LINE.
l men, *l* manners. *L* breeds *l*,	Walk. to the M.	55
those two *l*'s might meet and touch	Two Voices	357
life! he never saw the *l*;	Princess, i.	184
'*L* to *l*! The woman's garment hid	" v.	294
Pass, and mingle with your *l*'s.	" vi.	321
Not *l* to *l*, but *l* in difference.	" vii.	262
Am I so *l* her? so they said	The Brook	223
Not violating the bond of *l* to *l*.'	Elaine	241
I never saw his *l*;	"	316
one *l* him.' 'Why that *l* was he.'	"	573
his *l* that year in twenty parishes	Grandmother	12

like (verb.)

	POEM.	LINE.
we *l* them well: But children die:	Princess, iii.	235
l l her none the less for rating at her!	" v.	451
How *l* you this old satire?	Sea Dreams	194

liked.

	POEM.	LINE.
more he look'd at her The less he *l* her;	Dora	33
l it more Than magic music,	Princess, Pro.	191
Nor tho' she *l* him, yielded she,	" vii.	61
loved nor *l* the thing he heard.	Aylmer's F.	250

likelihood.

	POEM.	LINE.
Need must be lesser *l*,	Elaine	366

likely.

	POEM.	LINE.
'O ay,' said Vivien, 'that were *l* too.	Vivien	596

likeness.

	POEM.	LINE.
Lo! God's *l*—the ground-plan—	Vision of Sin	187
pluck'd her *l* out;	Princess, i.	91
A *l*, hardly seen before Comes out	In Mem. lxxiii.	3
Thy *l* to the wise below,	"	7
any vision should reveal Thy *l*,	" xci.	1
darkening thine own To thine own *l*	Aylmer's F.	674

liker.

	POEM.	LINE.
light shall spread, and man be *l* man	Golden Year	35
in the long years *l* must they grow;	Princess, vii.	263

likest.

	POEM.	LINE.
men, in power Only are *l* gods	Œnone	128

lilac.

	POEM.	LINE.
Academic silks, in hue The *l*,	Princess, ii.	3
makes the purple *l* ripe	On a Mourner	7

lilac-ambush.

	POEM.	LINE.
Thro' crowded *l*-a trimly pruned;	Gardener's D.	111

Lilia.

	POEM.	LINE.
And sister *L* with the rest.'	Princess, Pro.	52, 97
L, wild with sport, Half child	"	100
Ask'd Walter, patting *L*'s head	"	125
Quick answer'd *L* 'There are thousands"	"	127
many *L*'s in the brood	"	146
The little hearth-flower *L*.	"	165
not for harm, So he with *L*'s	"	173
As many little trifling *L*'s	"	186
L woke with sudden-shrilling mirth	"	210
'Take *L*, then, for heroine'	"	217
So *L* sang: we thought her	" iv.	562
With which we banter'd little *L*.	Con.	12
l, pleased me, for she took no part	"	29
L, rising quietly, Disrobed	"	116

Lilian.

	POEM.	LINE.
Airy, fairy *L*. (rep.)	Lilian	1
I'rythee weep, May *L*!	"	19–25

lilted.

	POEM.	LINE.
scraps of thundrous Epic *l* out	Princess, ii.	353

lily.

	POEM.	LINE.
level plots Of crowned lilies,	Ode to Mem.	109
a *l* which the sun Looks thro'	Adeline	12
breath Of the lilies at sunrise?	"	37
Gazing where the lilies blow	L. of Shalott, i.	7
asphodel, Lotos and lilies;	Œnone	96
Waves all its lazy lilies,	Gardener's D.	42
Pure lilies of eternal peace,	Sir Galahad	67
The silver *l* heaved and fell;	To E. L.	19
the time when lilies blow,	Lady Clare	1
paddling plied And shook the lilies	Princess, Pro.	72
than wear Those lilies, better blush	" iii.	52
violet varies from the *l* as far	" v.	174
'Pretty bud! *L* of the vale!	" vi.	176
Now folds the *l* all her sweetness up,	" vii.	171
flung The lilies to and fro,	In Mem. xciv.	60
lain in the lilies of life.	Maud, I. iv.	60
Gathering woodland lilies,	" xii.	
here In among the lilies.	"	12
And lilies fair on a lawn;	" xiv.	2
Bright English *l*, breathing a prayer	" xix.	55
I said to the *l*, 'There is but one	" xxii.	19
lilies and roses were all awake	"	51
Queen *l* and rose in one;	"	56
the *l* whispers, 'I wait.'	"	66
All made up of the *l* and rose	" II. v.	74
Have I beheld a *l* like yourself.	Enid	1468
Set in her hand a *l*,	Elaine	1142
In her right hand the *l*,	"	1149
Be carven, and her *l* in her hand.	"	1332
now at last—Farewell, fair *l*.	"	1388

lily-avenue.

	POEM.	LINE.
A *l-a* climbing to the doors;	Aylmer's F.	162

lily-cradled.

	POEM.	LINE.
The golden bee Is *l-c*:	Œnone	29

lily-handed.

	POEM.	LINE.
No little *l-h* Baronet he,	Princess, Con.	84

lilylike.

	POEM.	LINE.
The *l* Melissa droop'd her brows.	Princess, iv.	143

lily maid.

	POEM.	LINE.
Elaine, the *l m* of Astolat,	Elaine	2
came the *l m* by that good shield	"	28
close behind them stept the *l m*.	"	176
l m Elaine Won by the mellow voice	"	242
to her own heart said the *l m*	"	318
l m had striven to make him cheer	"	326
'*L m*, For fear our people call you		
l m In earnest	"	385
pledging Lancelot and the *l m*	"	734
Then spake the *l m* of Astolat	"	1079
the *l m* of Astolat Lay smiling	"	1235

lily-shining.

	POEM.	LINE.
lay The *l-s* child;	Princess, iv.	268

lily-white.

	POEM.	LINE.
Lord Ronald brought a *l-w* doe	Lady Clare	3
l-w doe Lord Ronald had brought	"	61

limb.

	POEM.	LINE.
writhed *l*'s of lightning said; 'Clear-headed friend'		23
clear and bared *l*'s O'erthwarted	Œnone	136
Resting weary *l*'s at last	Lotos-E's.	170
in whose laps our *l*'s are nursed,	To J. S.	10
Denying not these weather-beaten *l*'s St S. Stylites		19
all my *l*'s drop piecemeal	"	43
Unto her *l*'s itself doth mould	Day-Dm.	86
Hair, and eyes, and *l*'s, and faces,	Vision of Sin	39
thro' her *l*'s a drooping languor wept;	Princess, vi.	251
due To languid *l*'s and sickness;	"	356
Give it time To learn its *l*'s:	Con.	79
Nor could I weary, heart or *l*,	In Mem. xxv.	9
watch'd them, wax'd in every *l*;	"	cii.
brood On a horror of shatter'd *l*'s.	Maud, I. i.	56
tho' thy *l*'s have here increased	" xviii.	18
hurl'd his huge *l*'s out of bed,	Enid	124
to suffer nothing heart or *l*,	"	472
from her *l*'s the costly-broider'd gift,	"	764
striking out her *l*'s awoke;	"	1229
stretch his *l*'s in lawful fight,	"	1602
clung about her lissome *l*'s,	Vivien	72
no larger than the *l*'s of fleas;	"	522
l was broken when they lifted him;	En. Arden	107
Enoch took, and handled all his *l*'s	"	153
Till the little *l*'s are stronger,	Sea Dreams	294
naked *l*'s and flowers and fruit,	The Voyage	55

limber.

	POEM.	LINE.
And legs of trees were *l*,	Amphion	14

246 CONCORDANCE TO

lime (tree).
	POEM.	LINE.
your branching *l*'s have blown	*L. C. V. de Vere*	27
arching *l*'s are tall and shady,	*Margaret*	59
the large *l* feathers low,	*Gardener's D.*	46
l a summer home of murmurous wings	"	47
many a range Of waning *l*	"	213
bard has honour'd beech or *l*,	*Talking O.*	291
ambrosial aisles of lofty *l*	*Princess, Pro.*	87
Up that long walk of *l*'s I past	*In Mem.* lxxxvi.	15
break from the ruby-budded *l*	*Maud,* I. iv,	1
beech and *l* Put forth and feel	*On a Mourner*	14

lime (earth.)
To feed thy bones with *l*,	*Two Voices*	326
dying Nature's earth and *l*;	*In Mem.* cxvii.	4

lime (verb.)
every sophister can *l*. 'Love thou thy land,' etc.		12

limed.
True—we had *l* ourselves	*Princess,* iii.	126

limit.
reach'd The *l* of the hills ;	*Audley Ct.*	82
on the glimmering *l* far withdrawn	*Vision of Sin*	223
not breathe Within this vestal *l*,	*Princess,* ii.	204
The *l* of his narrower fate,	*In Mem.* lxiii.	21
No *l* to his distress ;	*Maud,* II. v.	31
blown the lake beyond his *l*,	*The Daisy*	71
in what *l*'s, and how tenderly ;	*Ded. of Idylls*	19
there you fixt Your *l*, oft returning	*Elaine*	1035
ran Ev'n to the *l* of the land,	*En. Arden.*	579
Twofooted at the *l* of his chain	*Aylmer's F.*	127
Slipt o'er those lazy *l*'s .	"	495
at the quiet *l* of the world,	*Tithonus*	7

Limours.
suitors as this maiden ; first *L*	*Enid*	440
wild lord of the place, *L*	"	1126
Earl *L* Drank till he jested	"	1138
when the Prince was merry, ask'd *L*	"	1146
rose *L* and looking at his feet,	"	1151
told him all that Earl *L* had said,	"	1240
from the territory of false *L*,	"	1280
wild *L*, Borne on a black horse,	"	1306
In combat with the follower of *L*,	"	1356

limpit.
on thy ribs the *l* sticks,	*Sailor Boy*	11

linden.
The *l* broke her ranks and rent	*Amphion*	33
in copse And *l* alley ;	*Princess,* i.	206
on the sward, and up the *l* walks,	" iv.	191

line (s.)
Beyond, a *l* of heights, and higher	*Pal. of Art*	82
curving *l*'s of creamy spray ;	*Lotos-E's.*	107
What time the foeman's *l* is broke,	*Two Voices*	155
drove his cheek in *l*'s :	*Princess,* i.	115
Persian, Grecian, Roman *l*'s	" ii.	1
fifth in *l* from that old Florian	"	220
l's of green that streak the white	" v.	188
ride with us to our *l*'s ,	"	216
long *l* of the approaching rookery.	" Con.	97
My blessing, like a *l* of light,	*In Mem.* xvii.	10
So word by word, and *l* by *l*,	" xciv.	33
a grandson, first of his noble *l*,	*Maud,* I. x.	12
He gave them *l*;	*The Brook*	145
Right thro' the *l* they broke ;	*Lt. Brigade*	33
face is practised, when I spell the *l*'s,	*Vivien*	217
one true *l*, the pearl of pearls :	"	309
the second in a *l* of stars	"	359
High with the last *l* scaled	*Elaine*	1013
Long *l*'s of cliff breaking have left	*En. Arden.*	7
a darker isle beyond the *l*;	"	606
Love, let me quote these *l*'s	*Sea Dreams*	177
l's of cliffs were cliffs no more,	"	210
past long *l*'s of Northern cones	*The Voyage*	35
never a *l* from my lady yet *l*.	*The Window*	120

line (verb.)
May bind a book, may *l* a box,	*In Mem.* lxxvi.	6

lineament.
Every *l* divine,	*Eleänore*	53

linen.
	POEM.	LINE.
faded form and haughtiest *l*'s,	*Princess,* ii.	425
Imperious, and of haughtiest *l*'s	*Enid*	190
Lifted her eyes, and read his *l*'s.	*Elaine*	244
writhing barbarous *l*'s,	*Boädicea*	74
take the cast Of those dead *l*'s	*Coquette,* iii.	2

linen.
Fares richly, in fine *l*,	*Aylmer's F.*	639

linger.
Knowledge comes, but wisdom *l*'s,	*Locksley H.*	141-3
l here with one that loved us.'	*Princess,* iii.	321
l weeping on the marge,	*In Mem.* xii.	12
They rise, but *l* ; it is late ;	" Con.	91
l's late With a roystering company)	*Maud,* I. xiv.	14
rose-garden, And mean to *l* in it	" xx.	42
I *l* by my shingly bars ;	*The Brook*	180
I hate that he should *l* here ;	*Enid*	91

linger'd.
charmed sunset *l* low adown	*Lotos-E's.*	19
l there Till every daisy slept,	*Gardener's D.*	160
ever at a breath She *l*,	*Godiva*	45
I *l*; all within was noise	*In Mem.* lxxxvi.	18
By night we *l* on the lawn	" xciv.	1
L that other, staring after him ;	*Elaine*	717
o'er his bent brows *l* Averill,	*Aylmer's F.*	625

lingereth.
Why *l* she to clothe her heart	*Princess,* iv.	87

lingering.
After a *l*,—ere she was aware,—	*En. Arden.*	267
l out a three years' death-in-life ;	"	566
L about the thymy promontories,	*Sea Dreams*	38

link (s.)
Or to burst all *l*'s of habit—	*Locksley H.*	157
maids, That have no *l*'s with men.	*Princess,* vi.	274
A *l* among the days, to knit	*In Mem.* xxxix.	15
lost the *l*'s that bound Thy changes;	" xl.	6
l Betwixt us and the crowning race	" Con.	127
loops and *l*'s among the dales	*Elaine*	166

link (verb.)
Idle habit *l*'s us yet.	*Miller's D.*	212
To which she *l*'s a truth divine !	*In Mem.* xxxiii.	12
should'st *l* thy life with one	" lxxxiii.	11

linked—linkt.
L month to month with such a	*Two Voices*	167
l again. I saw within my head	*Vision of Sin*	59
l with thine in love and fate,	*In Mem.* lxxxii.	38
l a dead man there to a spectral	*Maud,* II. v.	80
force in her *L* with such love for me	*Enid*	806
l our names together in his lay,	*Elaine*	113
broke Flying, and *l* again ;	*Guinevere*	256
l their race with times to come	*Aylmer's F.*	779

linnet.
Sometimes the *l* piped his song :	*Sir L. and Q. G.*	10
Like *l*'s in the pauses of the wind :	*Princess, Pro.*	238
pipe but as the *l*'s sing :	*In Mem.* xxi.	24
The *l* born within the cage	" xxvii.	3
hears the latest *l* trill,	" xcix.	10
three gray *l*'s wrangle for the seed :	*Guinevere*	253
O merry, the *l* and dove,	*The Window*	156

lintel.
household flower Torn from the *l*—	*Princess,* v.	123
and under his own *l* stood	*Aylmer's F.*	331

lintwhite.
Her song the *l* swelleth	*Claribel*	15

lion.
The *l* on your old stone gates	*L. C. V. de Vere*	23
the *l* roaring from his den ;	*D. of F. Wom.*	222
comes a hungry people, as a *l*,	*Locksley H.*	135
in her *l*'s mood Tore open,	*Princess,* iv.	361
blazon'd *l*'s o'er the imperial tent	" v.	9
old *l*, glaring with his whelpless eye,	" vi.	83
your long locks play the *L*'s mane !	"	148
her *l* roll in a silken net	*Maud,* I. vi.	29
A *l* ramps at the top	" xiv.	7
ruddy shield on the *L*'s breast.	" III. vi.	14
Porch-pillars on the *l* resting,	*The Daisy*	55

	POEM.	LINE.
Sir Lancelot's azure *l*'s	Elaine	660
The babe shall lead the *l*.	Aylmer's F.	648

lioness.

	POEM.	LINE.
L That with your long locks play	Princess, vi.	147

lioness-like.

and rolling glances *l-l*	Boädicea	71

lion-heart.

The *l-h*, Plantagenet,	Margaret	34

lionlike.

rushing outward *l* Leapt on him,	Guinevere	106

lion-whelp.

Far as the portal-warding *l-w*,	En. Arden	98

lip.

When from crimson-threaded *l*'s	Lilian	23
l's whereon perpetually did reign	Isabel	7
If my *l*'s should dare to kiss.	Madeline	43
Ere the placid *l*'s be cold?	Adeline	20
l's depress'd as he were meek,	A Character	25
Your ripe *l*'s moved not,	Miller's D.	131
my whole soul thro' My *l*'s,	Fatima	21
prest the blossom of his *l*'s to mine	Œnone	76
my hot *l*'s prest Close, close	"	199
from her *l*'s, as morn from Memnon	Pal. of Art	171
in a little while our *l*'s are dumb.	Lotos-E's.	89
with dead *l*'s smiled at the twilight	D. of F. Wom.	62
music left the *l*'s of her that died.	"	195
She lock'd her *l*'s: she left me	"	241
to scorn with *l*'s divine 'Of old sat Freedom,' etc.	"	23
from Discussion's *l* may 'Love thou thy land,' etc.	"	33
knightly growth that fringed his *l*'s.	M. d'Arthur	220
lived Her fame from *l* to *l*.	Gardener's D.	50
his own warmth against her *l*'s	"	137
kisses prest on *l*'s Less exquisite	"	149
stirr'd her *l*'s For some sweet answer,	"	155
with a flying finger swept my *l*'s,	"	241
answer'd madly; bit his *l*'s,	Dora	31
breathing love and trust against her *l*:	Audley Ct.	68
A second flutter'd round her *l*	Talking O.	219
me That have no *l*'s to kiss,	"	242
at the touching of the *l*'s.	Locksley H.	38
a *l* to drain thy trouble dry.	"	88
Baby *l*'s will laugh me down:	"	89
Her *l*'s are sever'd as to speak:	Day-Dm.	50
What *l*'s, like thine, so sweetly join'd?	"	258
lays it thrice upon my *l*'s,	Will Water.	17
These favour'd *l*'s of mine:	"	20
I kiss the *l*'s I once have kiss'd;	"	37
He to *l*'s, that fondly falter,	L. of Burleigh	9
Upon her perfect *l*'s.	Sir L. and Q. G.	45
sleepy light upon their brows and *l*'s—	Vision of Sin	9
Wine is good for shrivell'd *l*'s	"	79
fire In your eye—nor yet your *l*:	"	184
the pointed blossom of her *l*'s:	Princess, Pro.	195
Proud look'd the *l*'s;	" i.	95
l's apart, And all her thoughts	" ii.	304
On *l*'s that are for others;	" iv.	38
laugh'd with alien *l*'s,	"	101
in grosser *l*'s Beyond all pardon	"	232
lived upon my *l*'s:	"	274
from crooked *l*'s a haggard smile.	"	345
dying *l*'s, With many thousand matters	"	437
seem'd to wait behind her *l*'s,	"	451
at our disguise broke from their *l*'s,	" v.	262
fingering at the hair about his *l*	"	293
drew Her robe to meet his *l*'s	" vi.	140
spirit closed with Ida's at the *l*'s	" vii.	143
meek Seem'd the full *l*'s,	"	211
whispers from thy lying *l*?	In Mem. iii.	4
breathing thro' his *l*'s impart	" xviii.	15
dull'd the murmur on thy *l*,	" xxii.	16
seal'd The *l*'s of that Evangelist.	" xxxi.	16
as sacred wine To dying *l*'s.	" xxxvii.	20
from the *l* Short swallow-flights	" xlvii.	14
fills The *l*'s of men with honest praise	" lxxxiii.	26
could not win An answer from my *l*'s	" cii.	50
bless thee, for thy *l*'s are bland	" cxviii.	9
tho' my *l*'s may breathe adieu,	" cxxii.	11
Sweet human hand and *l*'s and eye;	" cxxviii.	6
l's in the field above are dabbled	Maud, I. i.	2
sunlight broke from her *l l*	" vi.	86
curving a contumelious *l*,	" xiii.	20
happy Yes Falters from her *l*'s,	" xvii.	10
For the hand, the *l*'s, the eyes,	" II. iv.	27
Prophet, curse me the blabbing *l*,	" v.	57
raised her head with *l*'s comprest,	The Letters	13
sworn From his own *l*'s to have it—	Enid	409
Slip from my *l*'s if I can help it	"	446
gnaw'd his under, now his upper *l*,	"	1517
yesterday you never open'd *l*,	Vivien	120
from the rosy *l*'s of life and love,	"	695
by what name Livest between the *l*'s?	Elaine	182
living smile Died from his *l*'s,	"	323
sat With *l*'s severely placid	"	736
her *l*'s, Who had devised the letter,	"	1279
I cannot touch thy *l*'s,	Guinevere	547
and could hear the *l*'s that kiss'd	Tithonus	60

lipp'd.

faintly *l* The flat red granite;	Audley Ct.	11

liquor.

smote Her life into the *l*.	Will Water.	112

Lisbon.

Round affrighted L drew	Ode on Well.	103

lissome.

but as *l* as a hazel wand;	The Brook.	70

lisp.

lightest wave of thought shall *l*,	In Mem. xlviii.	5
shall have learn'd to *l* you thanks.	Enid	822
l in love's delicious creeds;	Coquette, i.	11

lispeth.

The callow throstle *l*,	Claribel	17

lisping.

A *l* of the innumerous *l*	Princess, v.	13

lispt.

Was *l* about the acacias,	Princess, vii.	235

list (register, etc.)

But still her *l*'s were swell'd	Princess, iv.	300
meaning by it To keep the *l* low	Vivien	442

list (border.)

l's of such a beard as would	Vivien	94

list 'to choose.)

not be kiss'd by all who would *l*,	The Mermaid	41
O maiden, if indeed you *l* to sing,	Guinevere	163

list (to listen.)

To *l* a foot-fall, ere he saw	Pal. of Art	110

listen.

O *l*, *l*, your eyes shall glisten	Sea Fairies	35-37
Whither away? *l* and stay.	"	42
stars that hung Love-charm'd to *l*:	Love and Duty	73
if you care indeed to *l*, hear	Golden Year	20
Whisper'd 'L to my despair:'	Ed. Gray	22
l l here is proof that you were miss'd	Princess, Pro.	175
They can but *l* at the gates,	In Mem. xciii.	15
The larkspur *l*'s, 'I hear, I hear;'	Maud, I. xxii.	65
I know that he lies and *l*'s mute	" II. v.	60
l's near a torrent mountain-brook,	Enid	1020
l to me, and by me be ruled,	"	1474
it shall answer for me. L to it.	Vivien	236
while the king Would *l* smiling.	Elaine	117
l to me, If I must find you wit:	"	147
Would *l* for her coming, and regret	"	862
vex an ear too sad to *l* to me,	Guinevere	311
speak no slander, no, nor *l* to it,	"	469
'L, Annie, How merry they are.	En. Arden	385
Sit, *l*.' Then he told her	Aylmer's F.	862
spirits into each ear To *l*:	"	702
I fear you'll *l* to tales,	Grandmother	54
Did they hear me, would they *l*,	Boädicea	8

listened.

I look'd And *l*. the full-flowing	Œnone	67
and I *l* in my bed,	May Queen, iii.	31
from them clash'd The bells; we *l*:	Gardener's D.	210
The deep air *l* around her	Godiva	54
While I *l*, came On a sudden	Princess, iv.	537

	POEM.	LINE.
spoke no slander, no, nor *l* to it	*Ded. of Idylls*	9
while they *l* for the distant hunt,	*Enid*	184
Enid *l* brightening as she lay;	"	733
melted all who *l* to it; .	*En. Arden.*	650

listener.

not to die a *l*, I arose,	*The Brook*	163
every roof Sent out a *l*:	*Aylmer's F.*	614

listenest.

Thou *l* to the closing door,	*In Mem.* cxx.	7

listening (part.)

L the lordly music	*Ode to Mem.*	41
at eventide, *l* earnestly,	'*A spirit haunts*,' etc.	4
L, whispers "'Tis the fairy	*L. of Shalott*, i.	35
roll'd Dry flame, she *l*;	*Princess*, vi.	173
with shut eyes I lay *L*;	" vii.	209
L now to the tide in its broad-flung	*Maud*, I. iii.	11
she sat Stiff-stricken, *l*;	*Guinevere*	409
l till those armed steps were gone,	"	579

listening (s.)

lonely *l*'s to my mutter'd dream,	*Princess*, vii.	95

listless.

L in all despondence—.	*Aylmer's F.*	534

lists.

Shot thro' the *l* at Camelot,	*M. d'Arthur*	224
they roll in clanging *l*	*Sir Galahad*	9
the *l* were hammer'd up,	*Princess*, v.	358
The *l*'s were ready. Empanoplied	"	472
lord of the ringing *l*,	"	491
father heard and ran In on the *l*	" vi.	11
into the *l* they wound Timorously;	"	68
settling circled all the *l*	*Enid*	547
her gentle presence at the *l*.	"	795
come To these my *l* with him	"	1688
Lancelot, and his prowess in the *l*,	*Elaine*	83
Favour of any lady in the *l*,	"	363, 473
when they reached the *l* By Camelot	"	427
assail'd, and they that held the *l*	"	454
'Table Round that held the *l*	"	466-98
day when Lancelot fled the *l*,	"	524

lit (settled, etc.)

bore Them earthward till they *l*;	*The Poet*	18
a crested peacock,	*Œnone*	102
here we *l* on Aunt Elizabeth .	*Princess, Pro.*	96
wheel'd or *l* the filmy shapes	*In Mem.* xciv.	10

lit (kindled, etc.)

gray eyes *l* up With summer lightnings	*Miller's D.*	12
L up a torrent-bow.	*Pal. of Art*	36
L with a low large moon.	"	68
L light in wreaths and anadems,	"	186
l Lamps which outburn'd Canopus.	*D. of F. Wom.*	145
l your eyes with tearful power,	*Margaret*	3
l the spark within my throat,	*Will Water.*	109

litany.

solemn psalms, and silver *litanies*,	*Princess*, ii.	453

litter-bier.

raised and laid him on a *l-b*,	*Enid*	1414

little.

You would, and would not, *l* one!	*Miller's D.*	134
'at home was *l* left, And none abroad;	*The Epic*	19
Summ'd up and closed in *l*;	*Gardener's D.*	13
stored what *l* she could save,	*Dora*	50
'Tis *l* more; the day was warm	*Talking O.*	205
Life piled on life Were all too *l*,	*Ulysses*	25
of one to me *L* remains;	"	26
owning but a *l* more Than beasts,	*Two Voices*	196
L can I give my wife.	*L. of Burleigh*	14
While my *l* one, while my pretty one	*Princess*, ii.	463
Sleep, my *l* one, sleep .	"	471
early woke to feed her *l* ones	" vii.	236
'Tis *l*; but it looks in truth .	*In Mem.* xviii.	5
now her *l* ones have ranged .	" xxi.	26
So *l* done, such things to be,	" lxxii.	2
Because their natures are *l* .	*Maud*, I. iv.	53
Making the *l* one leap for joy,	*To F. D. Maurice*	4
hoard is *l*, but our hearts are great	*Enid*	352-74
Enid took a *l* delicately,	"	1001

	POEM.	LINE.
even were the griefs of *l* ones	*Guinevere*	201
pretty, puny, weakly *l* one,—	*En. Arden*	195
kiss'd his wonder-stricken *l* ones;	"	228
from the burial of her *l* one,	"	280
Philip put her *l* ones to school	"	707
toil'd to clothe your little ones;	*Aylmer's F.*	699
mar this *l* by their feuds.	*Sea Dreams*	49
dash the brains of the *l* one out,	*Boädicea*	68
of so *l* in our *l* life,	*Lucretius*	224

little-footed.

laws Salique And *l-f* China,	*Princess*, ii.	118

littleness.

a thousand peering *l*'es	*Ded. of Idylls*	25

little-worth.

So were thy labour *l-w*.	*Two Voices*	171

live.

Thou wilt not live in vain.	'*Clear-headed friend*'	9
My friend, with you to *l* alone,	*Ode to Mem.*	119
rainbow *l*'s in the curve of the sand;	*Sea-Fairies*	27
l forgotten, and love forlorn.(rep.)	*Mariana in the S.*	12
melody, Which *l*'s about thee,	*Eleänore*	65
I'd almost *l* my life again.	*Miller's D.*	28
Grow, *l*, die looking on his face,	*Fatima*	41
l by law, Acting the law we *l* by	*Œnone*	145
the happy souls, that love to *l*:	"	236
My soul would *l* alone unto herself	*Pal. of Art*	11
l till the snowdrops come again;	*May Queen*, ii.	14
brood and *l* again in memory,	*Lotos-E's.*	110
In the hollow Lotos-land to *l*	"	154
His memory long will *l* alone	*To J. S.*	49
l three lives of mortal men	*M. d'Arthur*	155
let me *l* and work with you;	*Dora*	113
thou and I will *l* within one house	"	123
but let me *l* my life. (rep.)	*Audley Ct.*	42
touch my body and be heal'd, and *l*:	*St S. Stylites*	78
L—yet *l*—Shall sharpest pathos	*Love and Duty*	81
L happy; tend thy flowers;	"	84
like the second world to us that *l*:	*Golden Year*	56
L on, God love us, as if the seedsman	"	69
To breathe and loathe, to *l* and sigh,	*Two Voices*	104
Who is it that could *l* an hour?	"	162
that for which I care to *l*.	*Day-Dm.*	268
since I came to *l* and learn,	*Will Water.*	81
hence this halo *l*'s about	"	113
L long, ere from thy topmost head	"	233
L long, nor feel in head or chest	"	237
the truth, as I *l* by bread!	*Lady Clare*	26
Here he *l*'s in state and bounty,	*L. of Burleigh*	57
'*l*'s there such a woman now?'	*Princess, Pro.*	126
'loved to *l* alone Among her women	" i.	48
Who am not mine, say, *l*:	" ii.	205
yet may *l* in vain, and miss,	" iii.	227
l, perforce, from thought to thought,	"	311
they cried ' She *l*'s:	" iv.	174
to *l* No wiser than their mothers,	"	492
l, dear lady, for your child!	" v.	77
risk'd it for my own; His mother *l*'s;	"	398
gray mare Is ill to *l* with,	"	442
'Sweet my child, I *l* for thee.'	"	547
'he *l*'s: he is not dead;	" vi.	106
at the happy word 'he *l*'s'	"	112
no more, lest I should bid thee *l*;	"	372
What pleasure *l*'s in height .	" vii.	178
to *l* and learn and be	"	257
he, that doth not, *l*'s A drowning life	"	294
merit *l*'s from man to man	*In Mem. Pro.*	35
I trust he *l*'s in thee	"	39
wild unrest that *l*'s in woe	" xv.	15
l's no record of reply,	" xxxi.	6
life shall *l* for evermore,	" xxxiv.	2
doubtful gleam of solace *l*'s	" xxxviii.	8
grain by which a man may *l*?	" lii.	3
O Sorrow, wilt thou *l* with me	" lviii.	1
I *l*'s to wed an equal mind;	" lxi.	8
l's to clutch the golden keys,	" lxiii.	10
thine effect so *l*'s in me,	" lxiv.	10
A part of mine may *l* in thee	"	11
Can trouble *l* with April days,	" lxxxii.	7
By which we dare to *l* or die,	" lxxxiv.	40

	POEM.	LINE.
l's more faith in honest doubt,	In Mem. xcv.	11
He told me, *l* 's in any crowd,	" xcvii.	26
l within the stranger's land,	" civ.	3
l their lives From land to land	" cxiv.	16
Yet less of sorrow *l*'s in me	" cxv.	13
seem'd to *l* A contradiction	" cxxiv.	3
friend of mine who *l*'s in God,	" Con.	140
That God, which ever *l*'s and loves	"	141
When only the ledger *l*'s,	Maud, I. i.	35
he may *l* to hate me yet,	" xiii.	4
world, where yet 'tis sweet to *l*.	" xviii.	48
l a life of truest breath,	"	53
died to *l*, long as my pulses play ;	"	66
But to-morrow, if we *l*,	" xx.	23
We are not worthy to *l*.	" II. i.	48
l to wed with her whom first	Enid.	227
if I *l*, So aid me Heaven	"	501
if he *l*, we will have him of our band ;"		1402
l like two birds in one nest,	"	1475
l's dispersedly in many bands,	Vivien	307
So *l* uncharm'd.	"	400
O tell us—for we *l* apart—	Elaine	284
there *l*'s 'No greater leader.'	"	316
L's for his children, ever at its best	"	335
doubt Whether to *l* or die,	"	520
as but born of sickness, could not *l*:	"	876
that I *l* to hear,' he said, ' is yours.'	"	924
seeing you desire your child to *l*,	"	1089
who love me still, for whom I *l*,	Guinevere	442
I the King should greatly care to *l*;	"	449
sad it were for Arthur, should he *l*,	"	472
nor by living can I *l* it down.	"	616
own heart I can *l* down sin	"	629
Enoch *l*'s; that is borne in on me:	En. Arden.	318
fear that her first husband *l*'s *l*'	"	807
to work whereby to *l*.	"	813
life in it Whereby the man could *l*;	"	822
not three days more to *l*;	"	852
Surely *l*'s in man and beast	Sea Dreams	68
' What a world,' I thought, 'To *l* in !'	"	93
have faith ! We *l* by faith,	"	153
' His deeds yet *l*,	"	301
but I would not *l* it again.	Grandmother	98
they *l* with Beauty less and less	Coquette, i.	9
His object *l*'s: more cause to weep	" iii.	6
l's and loves in every place ;	On a Mourner	5
And I shall *l* to see it.	Spiteful Let.	18
L the great life which all our	Lucretius	78

lived.

l and loved alone so long,	Miller's D.	38
If I had *l*—I cannot tell—	May Queen, iii.	47
You *l* with us so steadily	D. of the O. Year	8
have *l* my life, and that which I	M. d' Arthur	244
Her fame from lip to lip.	Gardener's D.	49
Dora *l* unmarried till her death.	Dora	167
farmer's son, who *l* across the bay,	Audley Ct.	74
There *l* a flayflint near ;	Walk. to the M.	76
Here the Hills—	Ed. Morris	11
while I *l* In the white convent	St S. Stylites	60
l up there on yonder mountain	"	71
Three years I *l* upon a pillar,	"	85
like endless welcome, *l* and died.	Love and Duty	66
said he *l* shut up within himself,	Golden Year	9
had I *l* when song was great (rep.)	Amphion	9
l an ancient legend in our house.	Princess, i.	5
L thro' her to the tips of her long hands,	" ii.	26
vast bulk that *l* and roar'd	" iii.	277
prized my counsel, *l* upon my lips;	" iv.	274
l in all fair lights,	"	410
equal baseness *l* in sleeker times	" v.	375
and *l* but for mine own.	"	379
dream had never died or *l* again.	" vi.	1
order *l* again with other laws :	" vii.	4
dearer thou for faults *L* over:	"	327
O had he *l*! In our schoolbooks	The Brook.	3
Tho' yet there *l* no proof	Enid.	26
so there *l* some colour in your cheek	"	1469
l thro' her, who in that perilous hour	"	1614
l in hope that sometime you would	"	1687
l a king in the most Eastern East,	Vivien.	405

	POEM.	LINE.
l there neither dame nor damsel	Vivien	456
l alone in a great wild on grass ;	"	471
to his old wild, and *l* on grass,	"	479
it *l* with her ; she died:	"	956
so she *l* in fantasy.	Elaine 27,	397
A horror *l* about the tarn	"	38
his face before her *l*,	"	330
face before her *l*. Dark-splendid,	"	336
Sir Lancelot knew there *l* a knight	"	400
l along the milky roofs ;	"	463
an Abbess, *l* For three brief years,	Guinevere	668
l a life of silent melancholy.	En. Arden	259
and that other *l* alone.	"	571
Where Annie *l* and loved him,	"	686
l for years a stunted sunless life ;	Aylmer's F.	357
scandals that have *l* and died	"	443
the sooner, for he *l* far away.	Grandmother	61
thought I *l* securely as yourselves	Lucretius	207

live-green.

| Out of the *l-g* heart of the dells | Sea-Fairies | 12 |

livelier.

And *l* than a lark	Talking O.	122
no *l* than the dame That whisper'd	Princess, ii.	97
All her splendour seems No *l*	In Mem. xcvii.	7

liver.

| pierces the *l* and blackens the blood, | The Islet | 35 |

livest.

| by what name *L* between the lips? | Elaine | 182 |

livid.

| *L* he pluck'd it forth, | Aylmer's F. | 627 |

livid-flickering.

| dazzled by the *l-f* fork, | Vivien | 790 |

living (part.)

giants *l*, each, a thousand years	Princess, iii.	252
L alone in an empty house	Maud, I. vi.	68
so much For any maiden *l*,'	Elaine	375
may judge the *l* by the dead,	"	1359
by *l* can I live it down.	Guinevere	616
Should still be *l*, well then—	En. Arden	402
Who hardly knew me *l*,	"	890
his brother, *l* oft With Averill	Aylmer's F.	57
same as that *L* within the belt)	Sea Dreams	209

living (s.)

| earn'd a scanty *l* for himself : | En. Arden | 819 |

lizard.

| *l*, with his shadow on the stone | Œnone | 26 |
| golden *l* on him paused, | En. Arden | 602 |

Lizard-point.

| fairest-spoken tree From here to *L-p*. | Talking O. | 264 |

Llauberris.

| And found him in *L* : | Golden Year | 5 |

load.

| help me of my weary *l*.' | Mariana in the S. | 30 |

loaf.

| a dusky *l* that smelt of home, | Audley Ct. | 21 |

loan.

| arms On *l*, or else for pledge ; | Enid | 220 |

loathe.

to name my spirit *l*'s and fears ;	D. of F. Wom.	106
To breathe and *l*, to live and sigh,	Two Voices	104
And I *l* the squares and streets	Maud, II. iv.	91
and whatever *l*'s a law	Enid	37
on thine polluted, cries ' I *l* thee.'	Guinevere	552
l it ; he had never kindly heart,	Sea Dreams	195
and she *L*'s him as well ;	Lucretius	197

loathed.

but most she *l* the hour	Mariana	77
l to see them overtax'd ;	Godiva	9
power to shape ; he *l* himself ;	Lucretius	23

loathing.

| dread and *l* of her solitude | Pal. of Art | 229 |
| to his own heart, *l*, said ; | Vivien | 639 |

250 CONCORDANCE TO

	POEM.	LINE.
loathsome.		
What is *l* to the young . .	Vision of Sin	157
lobby.		
whined in *lobbies*, tapt at doors,	Walk. to the M.	29
lock (hair.)		
l's not wide-dispread, . .	Isabel	5
Stays on her floating *l*'s .	Ode to Mem.	16
While his *l*'s a-drooping twined .	Adeline	57
them back by their flowing *l*'s .	The Merman	14
on each side my low-flowing *l*'s .	The Mermaid	32
When the *l*'s are crisp and curl'd ;	Vision of Sin	200
dark *l*'s in the gurgling wave .	Princess, iv.	169
From the flaxen curl to the gray *l*	"	406
with your long *l*'s play the Lion's	" vi.	148
Serve to curl a maiden's *l*'s; .	In Mem. lxxvi.	2
lock (fastening.)		
Break *l* and seal : ' *You might have won, etc.*		18
Melissa, with her hand upon the *l*,	Princess, ii.	301
locked.		
pool, *l* in with bars of sand ;	Pal. of Art	249
She *l* her lips: she left me . .	D.of F. Wom.	241
She might have *l* her hands. .	Talking O.	144
Merlin *l* his hand in hers . .	Vivien 139,	320
chest in chest, With each chest *l* .	"	505
Locksley Hall.		
flying over L H ; L H that in the Locksley H.		4
a long farewell to L H! . .	"	189
let it fall on L H . . .	"	193
lodge.		
the garden to the gardener's *l*,	Audley Ct.	16
Beyond the *l* the city lies, .	Talking O.	5
They by parks and *l*'s going .	L. of Burleigh	17
the moulder'd *l*'s of the Past .	Princess, iv.	45
beyond her *l*'s where the brook Vocal	Aylmer's F.	145
lodging.		
let him into *l* and disarm'd. .	Elaine	171
Lodi.		
At L, rain, Piacenza, rain. .	The Daisy	52
log.		
his heel into the smoulder'd *l*,	M. d'Arthur, Ep.	14
Bring in great *l*'s and let them lie,	In Mem. cvi.	17
logic.		
Severer in the *l* of a life? .	Princess, v.	182
Impassion'd *l*, which outran .	In Mem. cviii.	7
loiar (liar.)		
I weänt saäy men be *l*'s .	N. Farmer	27
loife (life.)		
an' *l* they says is sweet, . .	N. Farmer	63
loins.		
many weeks about my *l* I wore	St S. Stylites	62
From Gama's dwarfish *l* ? .	Princess, v.	495
loiter.		
l's slowly drawn . . .	Œnone	5
With weary steps I *l* on, .	In Mem. xxxviii.	1
I *l* round my cresses . .	The Brook	181
loiter'd.		
l in the master's field . .	In Mem. xxxvii.	23
Lombard.		
But when we crost the L plain	The Daisy	49
look'd the L piles ; . .	"	54
lond (land.)		
as I 'a done by the *l*. . .	N. Farmer 12-	24
an' *l* o' my oän. . . .	"	44
to howd the *l* ater meä. . .	"	58
London.		
dust and drouth of L life .	Ed. Morris	143
Sees in heaven the light of L .	Locksley H.	114
Your father is ever in L, .	Maud, I. iv.	59
in streaming L's central roar .	Ode on Well.	9
L, Verulam, Camulodune. .	Boädicea	86
lone.		
Her life is *l*, he sits apart, .	In Mem. xcvi.	17

	POEM.	LINE.
lonelier.		
l, darker, earthlier for my loss. .	Aylmer's F.	750
loneliest.		
the *l* in a lonely sea. . .	En. Arden	554
loneliness.		
Uphold me, Father, in my L .	En. Arden	785
from his height and *l* of grief .	Aylmer's F.	632
Me rather all that bowery *l*, .	Milton	9
lonely.		
loves most, *l* and miserable.. .	Enid	123
who sits apart, And seems so *l* ?'.	"	1149
this weary way, And leave you *l* ?	En. Arden	296
long (adj.)		
Thou art mazed, the night is *l* .	Vision of Sin	195
l and troubled like a rising moon,	Princess, i.	58
brief is life but love is *l*, .	" iv.	93
long (verb.)		
I *l* to see a flower so . .	May Queen,ii.	16
to me that *l* to go. . .	" iii.	8
l to prove No lapse of moons .	InMem.xxvi.	2
l's to burst a frozen bud, .	" lxxxii.	15
Always I *l* to creep . .	Maud,II. iv.	95
sense might make her *l* for court .	Enid	803
L for my life, or hunger for my death,	"	930
credulous Of what they *l* for, .	"	1724
that's all, and *l* for rest ; .	Grandmother	99
long-bearded.		
Stept the long-hair'd *l-b* solitary, .	En. Arden	638
long-betrothed.		
Lovers *l-b* were they : . .	Lady Clare	6
long-bounden.		
his *l-b* tongue Was loosen'd .	En. Arden	645
long-buried.		
Like that *l-b* body of the king, .	Aylmer's F.	3
long-closeted.		
L-c with her the yestermorn, .	Princess, iv.	303
longed.		
Has ever truly *l* for death. .	Two Voices	396
swore he *l* at college, only *l*, .	Princess,Pro.	157
flying south but *l* To follow ; .	" iii.	194
I *l* so heartily then and there .	Maud,I. xiii.	15
when he stopt we *l* to hurl together	Vivien	270
Had whatsoever meat he *l* for .	Guinevere	263
Annie's children *l* To go with others,	En. Arden	359
long-enduring.		
Mourn for the man of *l-e* blood, .	Ode on Well.	24
What *l-e* hearts could do . .	"	132
longer.		
ripen'd earlier, and her life Was *l*;	Princess, ii.	139
longest.		
growing *l* by the meadow's edge, .	Enid	1106
long-forgotten.		
Sung by a *l-f* mind. . .	InMem.lxxvi.	12
long-haired.		
l-h page in crimson clad .	L. of Shalott,ii.	22
Stept the *l-h* long-bearded solitary	En. Arden	638
long-illumined.		
when the *l-i* cities flame, .	Ode on Well.	228
longing (part.)		
ever *l* to explain, . .	The Brook	107
longing (s.)		
Geraint had *l* in him evermore .	Enid	394
Enid fell in *l* for a dress .	"	630
long-laid.		
l-l galleries past a hundred doors .	Princess, vi.	354
long-leaved.		
in the stream the *l-l* flowers weep,	Lotos-E's.	55
long-limbed.		
The *l-l* lad that had a Psyche too ;	Princess, ii.	384
long-neck'd.		
From the *l-n* geese of the world .	Maud, I. iv.	52

	POEM.	LINE.
long-pent.		
all the *l-p* stream of life	Day-Dm.	147
long-pondering.		
Enoch lay *l-p* on his plans ;	En. Arden	133
long-practised.		
Strike down the lusty and *l-p* knight	Elaine	1351
long-sounding.		
Full of *l-s* corridors it was,	Pal. of Art	53
long-sufferance.		
Trying his truth and his *l-s*	En. Arden	467
long-suffering.		
I that thought myself *l-s*,	Aylmer's F.	753
long-tailed.		
Like *l-t* birds of Paradise,	Day-Dm.	275
long-tormented.		
Thro' the *l-t* air	Ode on Well.	128
long-winded.		
came across With some *l-w* tale	The Brook	109
there he told a long *l-w* tale	"	138
long-wished-for.		
Calming itself to the *l-w-f* end	Maud, I. xviii.	5
long-withdrawn.		
Betwixt the black fronts *l-w*	In Mem. cxviii.	6
loōk (look.)		
Dubbut *l* at the waäste :	N. Farmer	37
an' fuzz, an' *l* at it now—	"	38
L 'ow quoloty smoiles	"	53
look ('s.)		
Wherefore those dim *l's* of thine,	Adeline	9
Hence that *l* and smile of thine,	"	63
thought of that sharp *l*, mother,	May Queen, i.	15
sons inherit us : our *l's* are strange	Lotos-E's.	118
sick and scornful *l's* averse,	D. of F. Wom.	101
sweet are *l's* that ladies bend	Sir Galahad	13
when the Poet's words and *l's*	Will Water.	193
A liquid *l* on Ida, full of prayer,	Princess, iv.	350
This *l* of quiet flatters thus	In Mem. x.	10
Treasuring the *l* it cannot find,	" xviii.	19
look thy *l*, and go thy way,	" xlviii.	9
voice was low, the *l* was bright :	" lxviii.	15
they meet thy *l* And brighten	" Con.	30
eyes Glaring, and passionate *l's*,	Sea Dreams	229
look (verb.)		
could not *l* on the sweet heaven,	Mariana	15
the sun L's thro' in his sad decline,	Adeline	13
How could I *l* upon the day?	Oriana	59
l in at the gate With his large calm	The Mermaid	26
stay To *l* down to Camelot. iv. 14)	L. of Shalott, ii.	1
To *l* at her with slight, and say,	Mariana in the S.	66
To *l* into her eyes and say,	"	75
L's down upon the village spire :	Miller's D.	36
L thro' mine eyes with thine rep.)	"	215
l, the sunset, south and north,	"	241
I shall *l* upon your face ;	May Queen, ii.	38
'Come here, That I may *l* on thee.'	D. of F. Wom.	124
What else was left? *l* here !	"	136
'Turn and *l* on me ;	"	250
only *l* across the lawn,	Margaret	65
L out below your bower-eaves,	"	66
He cried, ' L ! l !' Before he ceased	Gardener's D.	100
therefore *l* to Dora : she is well To *l* to ;	Dora	13
L to it ; Consider, William :	"	46
may *l* on me, And in your looking	St S. Stylites	138
rose, And turn'd to *l* at her.	Talking O.	132
L further thro' the chace,	"	246
come like one that *l's* content,	Love and Duty	90
Did I *l* on great Orion	Locksley H.	9
whom to *l* at was to love.	"	72
Underneath the light he *l's* at,	"	116
No eye *l* down, she passing ;	Godiva	40
L up thro' night ; the world is wide.	Two Voices	24
L up, the fold is on her brow,	"	192
l with that too-earnest eye—	Day-Dm.	18
Go, *l* in any glass and say,	"	199
I *l* at all things as they are,	Will Water.	71

	POEM.	LINE.
And he came to *l* upon her,	L. of Burleigh	93
as well can *l* Whited thought	Vision of Sin	115
l upon her As on a kind of paragon	Princess, i.	153
L, our hall ! Our statues	" ii.	61
to *l* on noble forms Makes noble	"	72
l! for such are these and I.'	"	240
blessing those that *l* on them.	" iii.	229
l well too in your woman's dress :	" iv.	508
we will not *l* upon you more.	"	526
'L, He has been among his shadows.'	" v.	31
l up : be comforted :	"	63
L up, and let thy nature strike on	" vii.	330
'L there, a garden I' said my college	" Con.	49
To *l* on her that loves him well,	In Mem. viii.	2
l on Spirits breath'd away,	" xxxix.	2
l thy look, and go thy way,	" xlviii.	9
dead shall *l* me thro' and thro'	" l.	12
l back on what hath been,	" lxiii.	1
L's thy fair face and makes it still.	" lxix.	16
did but *l* thro' dimmer eyes ;	" cxxiv.	6
eye to eye, shall *l* On knowledge :	Con.	129
(L at it, pricking a cockney ear.	Maud, I. x.	22
l's Upon Maud's own garden-gate ;	" xiv.	15
That I dare to *l* her way,	" xvi.	11
As *l's* a father on the things	The Letters	23
L on it, child, and tell me if you	Enid	684
once again she rose to *l* at it,	"	1236
Eat ! L yourself.	"	1465
Until my lord arise and *l* upon me?'	"	1498
will not *l* at wine until I die."	"	1515
own leech to *l* into his hurt :	"	1771
l upon his face l—but if he sinn'd,	Vivien	611
A sight you love to *l* on.'	Elaine	84
l On this proud fellow again	"	1053
and she, L how she sleeps—	"	1248
not *l* up, or half-despised the	Guinevere	636
I shall *l* upon your face no more	En. Arden	212
said Enoch, ' I shall *l* on yours.	"	213
L to the babes, and till I come	"	219
not to *l* on any human face,	"	281
' I cannot *l* you in the face,	"	314
So much to *l* to—such a change—	"	458
might *l* on her sweet face again	"	719
Why do you look at me, Annie ?	Grandmother	17
looked.		
l upon the breath Of the lilies	Adeline	36
She *l* down to Camelot.	L. of Shalott, iii.	41
might have *l* a little higher ;	Miller's D.	140
turning *l* upon your face,	"	157
l athwart the burning drouth	Fatima	13
I *l* And listen'd, the full-flowing	Œnone	66
when I *l*, Paris had raised his arm,	"	185
slept St Cecily ; An angel *l* at her.	Pal. of Art	100
her face Glow'd, as I *l* at her.	D. of F. Wom.	240
have not *l* upon you nigh,	To J. S.	33
when I *l* again, behold an arm	M. d'Arthur	158
long before I *l* upon her,	Gardener's D.	61
She *l*; but all Suffused with blushes	"	150
often *l* at them And often thought	Dora	3
more he *l* at her The less he liked	"	32
l with tears upon her boy,	"	55
I *l* at him with joy ;	Talking O.	106
She *l* with disconient,	"	116
L down, half-pleased, half-frighten'd	Amphion	54
l into Lord Ronald's eyes,	Lady Clare	79
l up toward a mountain-tract,	Vision of Sin	46
Half-canonized by all that *l* on her,	Princess, i.	23
l across a land of hope,	"	167
every face she *l* on justify it)	" v.	128
once more she *l* at my pale face :	" vi.	90
L up, and rising slowly from me,	"	135
At the arm'd man sideways,	"	140
I lay Listening ; then *l*.	" vii.	207
l all native to her place,	"	304
ever *l* with human eyes.	In Mem. lvi.	12
He *l* upon my crown and smiled :	" lxviii.	16
I *l* on these and thought of thee	" xcvi.	6
and thee mine eyes Have *l* on :	" cviii.	22
The sun *l* out with a smile	Maud, I. ix.	3
I *l*, and round, all round the house	" xiv.	33

	POEM.	LINE.
l, tho' but in a dream, upon eyes	*Maud*, IV. vi.	16
he *l* up. There stood a maiden	*The Brook*	204
lie *l* so self-perplext,	"	213
things Of his dead son, I *l* on these.	*The Letters*	24
l and saw that all was ruinous.	*Enid*	315
dress that now she *l* on to the dress	"	613
l on ere the coming of Geraint.	"	614
still she *l*, and still the terror grew	"	615
Enid *l*, but all confused at first	"	685
or yellow sea *L* the fair Queen,	"	831
turn'd and *l* as keenly at her	"	1279
Geraint *l* and was not satisfied.	"	1284
Once she *l* back, and when she saw	"	1290
l too much thro' alien eyes,	"	1740
have you *l* At Edyrn?	"	1744
He *l* and found them wanting;	"	1783
when I *l*, and saw you following	*Vivien*	148
Merlin *l* and half believed her true,	"	250
by the mellow voice before she *l*,	*Elaine*	243
l, and more amazed Than if seven	"	349
Lancelot *l* and was perplext in mind	"	834
l Down on his helm,	"	975
when she heard, the Queen *l* up	*Guinevere*	162
pale Queen *l* up and answer'd her,	"	325
l and saw The novice, weeping,	"	655
men *l* upon him favourably;	*En. Arden*	56
Philip *l*, And in their eyes	"	72
Enoch left he had not *l* upon her)	"	272
silent, tho' he often *l* his wish;	"	479
And after *l* into yourself,	*Aylmer's F*.	312
I *l* at the still little body—	*Grandmother*	66
Then they *l* at him they hated	*The Captain*	37
looketh.		
and *l* down alone,	*Claribel*	14
looking (part.)		
l thro' and thro' me	*Lilian*	10
l fixedly the while,	*Madeline*	39
in a well, *L* at the set of day,	*Adeline*	17
l as 'twere in a glass,	*A Character*	10
All *l* up for the love of me.	*The Mermaid*	51-55
live, die *l* on his face,	*Fatima*	41
l over wasted lands,	*Lotos-E's.*	159
Sang *l* thro' his prison bars?.	*Margaret*	35
l wistfully with wide blue eyes	*M. d'Arthur*	169
in your *l* you may kneel to God.	*St S. Stylites*	139
l ancient kindness on thy pain.	*Locksley H.*	85
l upward, full of grace,	*Two Voices*	223
l on the happy Autumn-fields,	*Princess*, iv.	24
placid marble Muses, *l* peace.	"	468
l back to whence I came	*In Mem.* xxiii.	7
Sat silent, *l* each at each.	" xxx.	12
life should fail in *l* back.	" xlv.	4
Now *l* to some settled end,	" lxxxiv.	97
l to the South, and fed.	*Maud*, I. xviii.	20
L, thinking of all I have lost	" II. ii.	46
l at her; 'Too happy, fresh.	*The Brook*	217
Not turning round, nor *l* at him,	*Enid*	270
l round he saw not Enid there,	"	506
rose Limours and *l* at his feet,	"	1151
spoke and said, Not *l* at her,	*Vivien*	96
'I once was *l* for a magic weed,	"	321
l at her, Full courtly, yet not falsely,	*Elaine*	235
Lancelot knew that she was *l* at him.	"	979
l often from his face who read	"	1277
Here *l* down on thine polluted,	*Guinevere*	551
looking (s.)		
With father *l*'s on.	*Miller's D.*	231
loom (s.)		
She left the web, she left the	*L. of Shalott*, iii.	37
A present, a great labour of the *l*;	*Princess*, i.	43
rent The wonder of the *l*	"	61
a splendid silk of foreign *l*,	*Enid*	1535
loom (verb.)		
smoke go up thro' which I *l* to her	*Princess*, v.	124
Makes former gladness *l* so great?	*In Mem.* xxiv.	10
loop.		
l's and links among the dales	*Elaine*	166
l's and folds innumerable	"	438

	POEM.	LINE.
loose (adj.)		
A *l* one in the hard grip	*Sea Dreams*	159
loose (verb.)		
that she would *l* The people;	*Godiva*	37
Let me *l* thy tongue with wine;	*Vision of Sin*	88
Fear not thou to *l* thy tongue;	"	155
l A flying charm of blushes	*Princess*, ii.	407
ran To *l* him at the stables,	*Aylmer's F.*	126
loosed.		
She *l* the chain, and down she lay;	*L. of Shalott*, iv.	16
And *l* the shatter'd casque	*M. d'Arthur*	209
l a mighty purse, Hung at his belt,	*Enid*	871
l in words of sudden fire the wrath	"	955
l the fastenings of his arms,	"	1360
our bond Had best be *l* for ever:	*Vivien*	192
Merlin *l* his hand from hers	"	206
pricked at once, all tongues were *l*:	*Elaine*	720
had not *l* it from his helm,	"	805
and her heart was *l* Within her,	*Guinevere*	659
l their sweating horses from the yoke	*Spec. of Iliad*	2
loosen.		
l's from the lip Short swallow-flights	*In Mem.* xlvii.	14
loosened.		
The team is *l* from the wain,	*In Mem.* cxx.	5
Skirts are *l* by the breaking storm.	*Enid*	1308
his long-bounden tongue Was *l*,	*En. Arden*	646
lop.		
or *l*'s the glades;	*In Mem.* c.	22
Lord (see *Lord of Astolat.*)		
come hither, and be our *l*'s.	*Sea-Fairies*	32
Knight and burgher, *l* and dame.	*L. of Shalott*, iv.	43
L over Nature, *L* of the visible		
earth, *L* of the senses five;	*Pal. of Art*	179
fall'n in Lyonness about their *L*,	*M. d'Arthur*	4
record, or what relic of my *l*	"	98
Such a *l* is Love,	*Gardener's D.*	56
by the *L* that made me, you shall pack *Dora*		29
It may be my *l* is weary,	*Locksley H.*	53
sought her *l*, and found him, where he	*Godiva*	16
robed and crown'd, To meet her *l*,	"	78
'Omega! thou art *L*,' they said,	*Two Voices*	278
That lead me to my *L*:	*St Agnes' Eve*	8
Break up the heavens, O *L*!	"	21
Ancient homes of *l* and lady,	*L. of Burleigh*	31
Not a *l* in all the county Is so great a *l*	"	59
honeying at the whisper of a *l*;	*Princess*, Pro.	115
with those self-styled our *l*'s	" ii.	2
the *L* be gracious to me! A plot	"	174
all women kick against their *L*'s	" iv.	493
lifting of whose eyelash is my *l*,	" v.	134
overborne by all his bearded *l*'s	"	346
l of the ringing lists,	"	491
and the great *l*'s out and in,	" vi.	361
A *l* of fat prize-oxen	*Con.*	86
thou, O *L*, art more than they.	*In Mem.* Pro.	20
not from man, O *L*, to thee	"	36
her future *L* Was drown'd	" vi.	38
A *l* of large experience,	" x.i.	7
Procuress to the *L*'s of Hell.	" lii.	16
To what I feel is *L* of all,	" liv.	19
souls, the lesser *l*'s of doom.	" cxi.	8
Love is and was my *L* and King,	" cxxv.	1-5
now *l* of the broad estate	*Maud*, I. i.	19
of old the *L* and Master of Earth,	" iv.	31
new-made *l*, whose splendour plucks	" x.	3
a *l*, a captain, a padded shape,	"	29
Go back, my *l*, across the moor	" xii.	28
L of the pulse that is *l* of her breast,	" xvi.	13
be fasten'd to this fool *l*	"	40
He came with the babe-faced *l*;	" II. i.	13
another, a *l* of all things, praying	" v.	32
ever yet was wife True to her *l*,	*Enid*	47
cannot love my *l* and not his name	"	92
l thro' me should suffer shame.	"	101
see my dear *l* wounded in the strife,	"	103
we smile, the *l*'s of many lands;	"	353
we smile, the *l*'s of our own hands;	"	354
l's and ladies of the high court	"	662
save her dear *l* whole from any wound.	"	894

	POEM.	LINE.		POEM.	LINE.
I will go back a little to my *l*,	Enid	914	Nor *l* their mortal sympathy,	In Mem. xxx.	23
my *l* should suffer loss or shame.'	"	918	We *l* ourselves in light.'	" xlvi.	16
one seem'd far larger than her *l*,	"	971	I shall not *l* thee tho' I die.	" cxxix.	16
I will abide the coming of my *l*,	"	980	and he fears To *l* his bone,	Enid	1410
My *l* is weary with the fight before,	"	982	Fearing to *l*, and all for a dead man	"	1412
To close with her *l*'s pleasure:	"	1063	*l* your use and name and fame,	Vivien	170
'Yea, my kind *l*,' said the glad youth,	"	1090	And *l* the quest he sent you on,	Elaine	652
the wild *l* of the place, Limours.	"	1126	*l* it, as we *l* the lark in heaven,	"	656
tending her rough *l*, tho' all unask'd	"	1254	will you let me *l* my wits?'	"	748
not to disobey her *l*'s behest,	"	1299	not *l* your wits for dear Lavaine.'	"	751
Start from their fallen *l*'s,	"	1331	to have it, none: to *l* it, pain;	"	1405
hurt that drain'd her dear *l*'s life.	"	1365	Not greatly care to *l*;	Guinevere	491
for long hours sat Enid by her *l*,	"	1428	Nor greatly cared to *l*,	Aylmer's F.	568
my *l* arise and look upon me?'	"	1498	*losing.*		
dear *l* arise and bid me do it,	"	1513	*L* his fire and active might	Eleänore	104
poor gown my dear *l* found me first,	"	1546	*L* her carol I stood pensively,	D.of F.Wom.	245
surely knew my *l* was dead,'	"	1569	odes About this *l* of the child;	Princess, i.	140
like a bride's On her new *l*,	Vivien	467	A little vext at *l* of the hunt,	Enid	234
she call'd him *l* and liege,	"	802	mine the fault, if *l* both of these	Aylmer's F.	719
be truer to your faultless *l*?'	Elaine	120	*loss.*		
passionate perfection, my good *l*—	"	123	*l* that brought us pain, That *l*	Miller's D.	229
battle with the love he bare his *l*,	"	246	Your *l* is rarer;	To J. S.	25
at Caerleon had he help'd his *l*	"	297	daily *l* of one she loved,	Walk. to the M.	66
our liege *l*, The dread Pendragon,	"	422	find in *l* a gain to match?	In Mem. i.	6
L of waste marshes, kings	"	526	sweeter to be drunk with *l*,	" "	11
I am *l* In mine own land,	"	912	shalt not be the fool of *l*.'	" iv.	16
for Lancelot, is it for my dear *l*?	"	1099	'*L* is common to the race	" vi.	2
by the mother of our *L* himself,	"	1224	That *l* is common would not make	"	
in the reading, *l*'s and dames Wept,	"	1276	weep a *l* for ever new,	" xiii.	5
when now the *l*'s and dames And people,	"	1336	Thy spirit ere our fatal *l*	" xl.	1
tamper'd with the *L*'s of the White Guinevere		16	His night of *l* is always there.	" lxv.	16
false traitor have displaced his *l*	"	214	To breathe my *l* is more than fame,	" lxxvi.	15
to lead her to his *l* Arthur,	"	380	grief my *l* in him had wrought,	" lxxix.	6
tho' thou would'st not love thy *l*,	"	504	The lighter by the *l* of his weight;	Maud, I. xvi.	2
I hath wholly lost his love	"	505	By the *l* of that dead weight	" xix.	99
Leagued with the *l*'s of the White Horse	"	569	volleying cannon thunder his *l*;	Ode on Well.	62
'Gone—my *l*! Gone thro' my sin	"	605	shadow of His *l* drew like eclipse,	Ded.of Idylls	13
my *l* the King, My own true *l*!	"	610	my lord should suffer *l* or shame	Enid	918
Ah great and gentle *l* Who wast	"	631	*l* of whom has turn'd me wild—	"	1157
L's of his house and of his mill	En. Arden.	348	dreadful *l* Falls in a far land.	"	1345
reigning in his place, *L* of his rights	"	765	So pains him that he sickens	"	1347
After the *L* has call'd me	"	811	fearing for his hurt and *l* of blood,	"	1625
Were he *l* of this, Why twenty boys	Aylmer's F.	370	dread the *l* of use than fame;	Vivien	369
And laughter to their *l*'s	"	478	*l* of half his people arrow-slain;	"	415
manorial *l* too curiously Raking	"	513	damsel then Wroth at a lover's *l*?	"	457
a *l*. in no wise like to Bäal.	"	647	cloaks the wounds of *l* with lies:	"	607
thy brother man, the *L* from heaven,	"	667	*l* of all But Enoch and two others.	En. Arden	550
light yoke of the *L* of love,	"	708	darker, earthlier for my *l*.	Aylmer's F.	750
scowl'd At their great *l*.	"	725	His gain is *l*: for he that wrongs	Sea Dreams	168
own traditions God, and slew the *L*,	"	795	*lost.*		
the *L* of all the landscape round.	"	815	never *l* their light.	Miller's D.	83
her dear *L* who died for all,	Sea Dreams	47	Her cheek had *l* the rose	Œnone	17
lord (verb.)			one silvery cloud Had *l* his way	"	91
every spoken tongue should *l* you.	Princess, iv.	523	*L* to her place and name;	Pal. of Art	264
lordlier.			Stream'd onward, *l* their edges,	D.of F.Wom.	50
assert None *l* than themselves	Princess, ii.	128	Fall into shadow, soonest *l*:	To J. S.	11
presence, *l* than before;	In Mem. cii.	28	be *l* for ever from the earth,	M. d'Arthur	90
lord-lover.			much honour and much fame were *l*.'	"	109
O young *l-l*, what sighs are those,	Maud, I. xxii.	29	*l* the sense that handles daily life—	Walk.to the M.	16
Lord of Astolat.			have you *l* your heart?' she said;	Ed. Gray	3
issuing found the *L o A*	Elaine	173	now when all was *l* or seem'd as *l*—	Princess, Pro.	20
then the *L o A* 'Whence comest thou,	"	180	They *l* their weeks;	"	161
said the *L o A* 'Here is Torre's;	"	195	porch, the bases *l* In laurel;	" i.	227
came The *L o A* out, to whom the Prince	"	624	child We *l* in other years,	"	256
the *L o A* 'Bide with us,	"	629	some ages had been *l*;	" ii.	137
lore.			an erring pearl *L* in her bosom;	" iv.	43
wild as aught of fairy *l*:	Day-Dm.	224	Wiser to weep a true occasion *l*,	"	50
lose.			since her horse was *l* I left her mine)	"	173
I *l* my colour, I *l* my breath,	Eleänore	137	'Be comforted: have I not *l* her too,	" v.	66
not to *l* the good of life—	Two Voices	132	vanquish'd and my cause For ever *l*	" vi.	9
l whole years of darker mind.	"	372	Into my bosom and be *l* in me.'	" vii.	174
l the child, assume The woman;	Princess, i.	136	'Behold the man that loved and *l*,	In Mem. i.	15
Dwell with these, and *l* Convention	" ii.	136	Something it is which thou hast *l*,	" iv.	9
I *l* My honour, these their lives.'	"	320	better to have loved and *l* (lxxxiv. 3)	" xxvii.	16
not war: Lest I *l* all.'	" v.	107	*l* the links that bound Thy changes;	" xl.	6
fear'd that I should *l* my mind,	" vii.	84	then were nothing *l* to man;	" xlii.	2
Nor *l* the wrestling thews that throw	"	266	'Love's too precious to be *l*,	" lxiv.	3
l the childlike in the larger mind;	"	268	like to him whose sight is *l*:	" lxv.	8
gravest citizen seems to *l* his head,	Con.	59	Nature's ancient power was *l*:	" lxviii.	2

	POEM.	LINE.
The quiet sense of something *l.*	*In Mem.* lxxvii.	8
No visual shade of some one *l,*	,, xcii.	5
Day, when I *l* the flower of men ;	,, xcviii.	4
Hope had never *l* her youth ;	,, cxxiv.	5
l in trouble and moving round	*Maud,* I. xxi.	5
Looking, thinking of all I have *l*	,, II. ii.	46
l for a little her lust of gold	,, III. vi.	39
Nor ever *l* an English gun ; .	*Ode on Well.*	97
We have *l* him: he is gone :	*Ded. of Idylls*	14
L in sweet dreams, and dreaming	*Enid*	158
enter'd, and were *l* behind the walls.	,,	252
sadly *l* on that unhappy night ;	,,	689
shall see my vigour is not *l.*	,,	931
scour'd into the coppices and was *l,*	,,	1383
charger is without, My palfrey *l.'*	,,	1398
l to life and use and name	*Vivien*	63, 819
and there We *l* him :	,,	283
Some *l,* some stolen, some as relics	,,	303
as dead And *l* all use of life :	,,	495
but their names were *l.*	*Elaine*	41
Else had he not *l* me ;	,,	147
Full often *l* in fancy, *l* his way :	,,	164
waste downs whereon I *l* myself,	,,	225
design wherein they *l* themselves,	,,	440
l the hern we slipt him at,	,,	654
had you not *l* your own.	,,	1207
wholly *l* his love for thee.	*Guinevere*	505
precious morning hours were *l.*	*En. Arden*	301
Philip gain'd As Enoch *l* ;	,,	352
'The ship was *l* ' he said ' the ship was *l !*	,,	390
poor man, was cast away and *l.'*	,,	714
muttering 'cast away and *l* ;'	,,	716
in deeper inward whispers '*l !*'	,,	717
slowly *l* Nor greatly cared to lose	*Aylmer's F.*	567
came To know him more, I *l* it,	*Sea Dreams*	72
now we *l* her, now she gleam'd	*The Voyage*	65
flying by to be *l* on an endless sea—	*Wages*	2

lot.

Half-anger'd with my happy *l,*	*Miller's D.*	200
been happy : but what *l* is pure?	*Walk. to the M.*	89
Ill-fated as I am, what *l* is mine	*Love and Duty*	33
I might forget my weaker *l* ;	*Two Voices*	367
Would quarrel with our *l,*	*Will Water.*	226
She finds the baseness of her *l,*	*In Mem.* lix.	6
chances where our *l's* were cast	,, xci.	
maidens with one mind Bewail'd their *l* ;	,, cii.	46
let a passionless peace be my *l,*	*Maud,* I. iv.	50
I stubb'd 'un oop wi' the *l*	*N. Farmer*	32
foolish bard, is your *l* so hard,	*Spiteful Let.*	
hate me not, but abide your *l* :	,,	11

lotos.

asphodel, *L* and lilies	*Œnone*	96
Eating the *L* day by day,	*Lotos-E's.*	105
L blooms below the barren peak :	,,	145
L blows by every winding creek :	,,	146

Lotos-dust.

| the yellow *L-d* is blown. | *Lotos-E's.* | 149 |

Lotos-eaters.

| mild-eyed melancholy *L-e* came. | *Lotos-E's.* | 27 |

Lotos-land.

| In the hollow *L-l* to live | *Lotos-E's.* | 154 |

Lot's wife.

| see how you stand Stiff as *L w* | *Princess,* vi. | 224 |

loud.

my fame is *l* amongst mankind,	*St S. Stylites*	80
makes the barren branches *l* :	*In Mem.* xv.	13
l With sport and song,	,, xcvii.	27
So *l* with voices of the birds,	,, xcviii.	2
l in the world of the dead ;	*Maud,* II. v.	25
the rest were *l* in merrymaking,	*En. Arden*	77

louder.

| a *l* one Was all but silence | *Aylmer's F.* | 696 |

loud-lunged.

| *l-l* Antibabylonianisms. | *Sea Dreams* | 244 |

lour.

| whatever tempests *l* For ever silent ; | *Ode on Well.* | 175 |

love (s.)	POEM.	LINE.
A *l* still burning upward,	*Isabel*	18
Life, anguish, death, immortal *l,*	*Arabian N's.*	73
l thou bearest The first-born of thy	*Ode to Mem.*	91
In *l* with thee forgets to close	*Adeline*	42
The scorn of scorn, The *l* of *l.*	*The Poet*	4
sings a song of undying *l* ;	*Poet's Mind*	33
pleasure and *l* and jubilee :	*Sea-Fairies*	36
L paced the thymy plots of Paradise,	*Love and Death*	2
L wept and spread his sheeny vans	,,	8
pierced thy heart, my *l,*	*Oriana*	42
for the *l* of me. (rep.)	*The Mermaid*	27
'*L,*' they said, ' must needs be	*Mariana in the S.*	63
cruel *l,* whose end is scorn,	,,	70
languid *L,* Leaning his cheek	*Eleänore*	117
I loved, and *l* dispell'd the fear	*Miller's D.*	89
l possess'd the atmosphere,	,,	91
true *l* spells—True *l* interprets—	,,	187
in truth You must blame *L.*	,,	192
L that hath us in the net,	,,	203
L the gift is *L* the debt.	,,	207
L is hurt with jar and fret.	,,	209
L is made a vague regret.	,,	210
What is *l* ? for we forget ;	,,	213
O *L, L, L !* O withering might !	*Fatima*	1
O *L,* O fire ! once he drew	,,	19
eyes are full of tears, my heart of *l,*	*Œnone*	30
My *l* has told me so a thousand times.	,,	193
sworn his *l* a thousand times.	,,	227
my ancient *l* With the Greek woman.	,,	256
To win his *l* I lay in wait :	*The Sisters.*	11
I won his *L* I brought him home.	,,	14
that shuts *L* out, in turn shall be		
Shut out from *L,* To ——.	*With Pal. of Art*	14
say he's dying all for *l,*	*May Queen,* i.	21
L tipt his keenest darts ;	*D. of F. Wom.*	173
beams of *L,* melting the mighty hearts	,,	175
with a threefold cord of *l*	,,	211
knew that *L* can vanquish Death,	,,	269
God gives us *l.* Something to love	*To J. S.*	13
when *l* is grown To ripeness	,,	14
Falls off, and *l* is left alone.	,,	16
thy land with *l* far-brought ' *Love thou thy land,*' etc.		1
l turn'd round on fixed poles,	,,	5
L, that endures not sordid ends,	,,	6
by some law that holds in *l,*	*Gardener's D.*	9
touches are but embassies of *l,*	,,	18
not your work, but *L's. L,* unperceived,	,,	24
Such a lord is *L.*	,,	56
Fancy, led by *L,* Would play	,,	58
to praise the heavens but only *l*	,,	103
l were cause enough for praise	,,	104
L's white star Beam'd	,,	161
the Master, *L,* A more ideal Artist	,,	168
L at first sight, first-born,	,,	185
sometimes a Dutch *l* For tulips ;	,,	188
l trebled life within me,	,,	194
L, the third, Between us	,,	210
L with knit brows went by,	,,	240
My first, last *l* ; the idol of my youth	,,	271
half in *l,* half spite, he woo'd	*Dora*	37
all his *l* came back a hundredfold ;	,,	162
not a room For *l* or money.	*Audley Ct.*	2
breathing *l* and trust against her lip :	,,	68
l for Nature is as old as I ;	*Ed. Morris*	28
rich sennights more, my *l* for her.	,,	30
l for Nature and my *l* for her,	,,	31
L to me As in the Latin song	,,	78
l, that makes me thrice a man,	*Talking O.*	11
My vapid vegetable *l's*	,,	183
Pursue thy *l's* among the bowers.	,,	199
This fruit of thine by *L* is blest,	,,	249
fairer fruit of *L* may rest	,,	251
l that never found his earthly close,	*Love and Duty*	1
the nobler thro' thy *l ?*	,,	19
likewise thou Art more thro' *L,*	,,	21
Wait, and *L* himself will bring	,,	23
L himself took part against himself	,,	45
Duty loved of *L.*—O this world's curse,	,,	46
Could *L* part thus ?	,,	54
Caught up the whole of *l*	,,	80
lightly turns to thoughts of *l.*	*Locksley H.*	20

	POEM.	LINE.
L took up the glass of Time,	*Locksley H.*	31
L took up the harp of Life,	"	33
love her for the *l* she bore?	"	73
l is *l* for evermore.	"	74
niete the bounds of hate, and *l*—	*Two Voices*	135
in their double *l* secure,	"	418
spreads above And veileth *l*, itself is *l*.	"	447
doth inform Stillness with *l*.	*Day-Dm.*	92
l in sequel works with fate,	"	103
I never felt the kiss of *l*,	*Sir Galahad*	19
l no more Can touch the heart	*Ed. Gray*	7
L may come, and *l* may go,	"	29
L will make our cottage pleasant	*L. of Burleigh*	15
he cheer'd her soul with *l*.	"	68
Frantic *l* and frantic hate	*Vision of Sin*	150
Tell me tales of thy first *l*—	"	163
We remember *l* ourselves (v. 198)	*Princess,* i.	121
As arguing *l* of knowledge	" ii.	43
O hard, when *l* and duty clash!	"	273
a thousand baby *l*'s Fly	"	379
half the students, all the *l*.	" iii.	23
angled with them for her pupil's *l*:	"	77
her due, *L*, children, happiness?"	"	229
tho' your Prince's *l* were like a God's,	"	231
deep as *l*, Deep as first *l*,	" iv.	38
twitter twenty million *l*'s.	"	83
to clothe her heart with *l*,	"	87
brief is life but *l* is long,	"	93
to junketing and *l*. *L* is it?	"	124
heated thro' and thro' with wrath and *l*,	"	145
bore up in part from ancient *l*,	"	284
I want her *l*.	" v.	130
tale of *l* In the old king's ears,	"	230
I know not what Of insolence and *l*,	"	387
Be dazzled by the wildfire *L*	"	431
L and Nature, these are two more	" vi.	149
seek the common *l* of these,	"	156
Pledge of a *l* not to be mine,	"	180
faster welded in one *l*	"	236
so employ'd, should close in *l*,	" vii.	52
L in the sacred halls Held carnival	"	69
out of hauntings of my spoken *l*,	"	94
L, like an Alpine harebell	"	100
deeps to conquer all with *l*	"	149
Fill'd thro' and thro' with *L*,	"	157
come, for *L* is of the valley, (rep.)	"	183
as the man, Sweet *L* were slain:	"	261
Sweet *l* on pranks of saucy boyhood	"	323
Strong Son of God, immortal *L*,	*In Mem.* Pro.	1
Let *L* clasp Grief,	" i.	9
scorn The long result of *l*,	"	14
Poor child, that waitest for thy *l*!	" vi.	28
Phosphor, bright As our pure *l*,	" ix.	11
My friend, the brother of my *l*;	"	16
Because it needed help of *L*:	" xxv.	8
mighty *L* would cleave in twain	"	10
No lapse of moons can canker *L*,	" xxvi.	3
L the indifference to be	"	12
one deep *l* doth supersede	" xxxii.	5
l's in higher *l*endure;	"	12
for one hour, O *L*, I strive	" xxxv.	6
L would answer with a sigh,	"	13
first as Death, *L* had not been,	"	19
render human *l* his dues;	" xxxvii.	16
enters other realms of *l*;	" xxxix.	12
I will last as pure and whole	" xlii.	13
O *L*, thy provinces were not large,	" xlv.	13
Look also, *L*., a brooding star,	"	15
hit the mood Of *L* on earth?	" xlvi.	8
makes it vassal unto *l*;	" xlvii.	8
I be lessen'd in his *l*!	" l.	8
Shall *l* be blamed for want of faith?	"	10
l reflects the thing beloved;	" li.	2
The Spirit of true *l* replied;	"	6
Who trusted God was *l* indeed	" liv.	13
l Creation's final law—	" lvi.	13
As with the creature of my *l*:	" lviii.	12
Then be my *l* an idle tale,	" lxi.	3
l in which my hound has part,	" lxii.	8
'*L*'s too precious to be lost,	" lxiv.	3
To utter *l* more sweet than praise	" lxxvi.	16
	POEM.	LINE.
hold the costliest *l* in fee.	*In Mem.* lxxviii.	4
l shall now no further range;	" lxxx.	2
now is *l* mature in ear.'	"	4
L, then, had hope of richer store;	"	5
link'd with thine in *l* and fate,	" lxxxiii.	38
l for him have drain'd My capabilities of *l*;	" lxxxiv.	11
I woo your *l*: I count it crime	"	61
A meeting somewhere, *l* with *l*,	"	99
If not so fresh, with *l* as true,	"	101
First *l*, first friendship, equal powers,	"	107
Quite in the *l* of what is gone,	"	114
tasted *l* with half his mind,	" lxxxix.	1
l's dumb cry defying change	" xciv.	27
My *l* has talk'd with rocks and trees;	" xcvi.	1
Their *l* has never past away,	"	13
Two spirits of a diverse *l*	" ci.	5
Ring in the *l* of truth and right.	" cv.	23
Ring in the common *l* of good.	"	24
A *l* of freedom rarely felt,	" cviii.	13
mine the *l* that will not tire,	" cix.	18
And, born of *l*, the vague desire	"	19
all the room Of all my *l*,	" cxi.	6
What is she, cut from *l* and faith,	" cxiii.	11
dream of human *l* and truth,	" cxvii.	3
L but play'd with gracious lies,	" cxxiv.	7
L is and was my Lord and King,	" cxxv.	1-5
The *l* that rose on stronger wings,	" cxxvii.	1
My *l* involves the *l* before;	" cxxix.	9
My *l* is vaster passion now;	"	10
yet is *l* not less, but more;	Con.	12
Regret is dead, but *l* is more	"	17
there was *l* in the passionate shriek,	*Maud,* I. i.	57
L for the silent thing that had made	"	58
flee from the cruel madness of *l*	" iv.	55
the new strong wine of *l*	" vi.	82
led her home, my *l*,	" xviii.	1
Death may give More life to *L*	"	47
L, like men in drinking-songs,	"	55
With dear *L*'s tie, makes *L* himself	"	61
by this my *l* has closed her sight	"	67
planet of *L* is on high,	" xxii.	3
Have a grain of *l* for me,	II. ii.	53
me and my passionate *l* go by,	"	77
Me and my harmful *l* go by;	"	80
To find the arms of my true *l*	" iv.	3
Hearts with no *l* for me:	"	94
l of a peace that was full of wrongs	III. vi.	40
talk'd as if her *l* were dead	*The Letters*	27
'No more of *l*; your sex is known:	"	29
l of country move thee there at all,	*Ode on Well.*	140
debt Of boundless *l* and reverence	"	157
learns to deaden *l* of self,	"	205
May all *l*, His *l*, unseen but felt,	*Ded. of Idylls*	48
l of all Thy sons encompass Thee,	"	50
l of all Thy daughters cherish Thee,	"	51
l of all Thy people comfort Thee,	"	52
God's *l* set Thee at his side again!	"	53
in their common *l* rejoiced Geraint	*Enid*	23
her guilty *l* for Lancelot,	"	25
dwelling on his boundless *l*,	"	63
dreaming of her *l* For Lancelot,	"	158
l or fear, or seeking favour of us	"	700
for whose *l* the Roman Cæsar first	"	745
'Earl, entreat her by my *l*,	"	760
force in her Link'd with such *l*	"	806
Enid my early and my only *l*,	"	1156
man's *l* once gone never returns—	"	1182
I greet you with all *l*:	"	1633
love you, Prince, with something of the *l*	"	1636
deeper and with ever deeper *l*,	"	1776
his own wish in age for *l*,	*Vivien*	41
in deepest reverence and in *l*.	"	61
wise in *l* Love most, say least.'	"	96
The great proof of your *l*:	"	204
In *L*, if *L* be *L*, if *L* be ours,	"	237
l of God and men And noble deeds,	"	262
of Fame while woman wakes to *l*.'	"	310
L, tho' *L* were of the grossest, carves	"	311
rest: and *L* should have some rest	"	335
work as vassal to the larger *l*,	"	341

256   CONCORDANCE TO

	POEM.	LINE.
dwarfs the petty *l* of one to one.	*Vivien*	. 342
l of mine Without the full heart back	,,	. 383
many a *l* in loving youth was mine,	,,	. 396
keep them mine But youth and *l*;	,,	. 398
from the rosy lips of life and *l*,	,,	. 695
in a wink the false *l* turns to hate)	,,	. 701
O vainly lavish'd *l!*	,,	. 708
what shame it will, So *l* be true,	,,	. 710
more in kindness than in *l*,	,,	. 756
must be now no passages of *l*	,,	. 762
one passionate *l* Of her whole life,	,,	. 804
my *l* is more Than many diamonds,'	*Elaine*	. 88
guilty *l* he bare the Queen,	,,	. 245
that *l* which was her doom.	,,	. 260
when often they have talk'd of *l*,	,,	. 670
know not if I know what true *l* is,	,,	. 673
cross our mighty Lancelot in his *l's!*	,,	. 685
if he love, and his *l* hold,	,,	. 694
About the maid of Astolat, and her *l*	,,	. 719
woman's *l*, Save one, he not regarded,	,,	. 836
her deep *l* Upbore her;	,,	. 856
loved her with all *l* except the *l*	,,	. 864
shackles of an old *l* straiten'd him	,,	. 871
'Your *l*,' she said, ' your *l*—to be your wife'	,,	. 929
ill then should I 'quit your brother's *l*,	,,	. 940
This is not *l*: but *l's* first flash	,,	. 945
by tact of *l* was well aware	,,	. 978
'The Song of *L* and Death,'	,,	. 999
Sweet is true *l* tho' given in vain,	,,	. 1001
L, art thou sweet? then bitter death	,,	. 1004
L, thou art bitter; sweet is death	,,	. 1005
Sweet *l*, that seems not made to fade,	,,	. 1007
fain would follow *l*, if that could be,	,,	. 1010
King will know me and my *l*,	,,	. 1052
returns his *l* in open shame.	,,	. 1077
tho' my *l* had no return:	,,	. 1088
on which I died For Lancelot's *l*,	,,	. 1112
in half disgust At *l*, life,	,,	. 1232
loved you, and my *l* had no return	,,	. 1269
my true *l* has been my death	,,	. 1270
a *l* beyond all *l* In women,	,,	. 1285
No cause, not willingly, for such a *l*:	,,	. 1290
her *l* Was but the flash of youth,	,,	. 1308
mine was jealousy in *l*.'	,,	. 1341
'That is *l's* curse ; pass on,	,,	. 1343
I have Most *l* and most affiance,	,,	. 1348
if what is worthy *l* Could bind him	,,	. 1369
free *l* will not be bound.'	,,	. 1370
' Free *l*, so bound, were freest '	,,	. 1371
' Let *l* be free; free *l* is for the best :	,,	. 1372
best, if not so pure a *l*	,,	. 1374
l Far tenderer than my Queen's.	,,	. 1385
'Jealousy in *l!*' Not rather dead *l's* harsh heir	,,	. 1388
if I grant the jealousy as of *l*,	,,	. 1390
as it waxes, of a *l* that wanes?	,,	. 1392
sweet talk or lively, all on *l*.	*Guinevere*	. 383
desire of fame, And *l* of truth	,,	. 479
wholly lost his *l* for thee.	,,	. 505
My *l* thro' flesh hath wrought	,,	. 554
Enoch spoke his *l*,	*En. Arden*	. 40
Mutual *l* and honourable toil ;	,,	. 83
beseech you by the *l* you bear Him	,,	. 306
his rights and of his children's *l*,—	,,	. 765
dream That *L* could bind them	*Aylmer's F.*	. 41
true *l* Crown'd after trial ;	,,	. 99
how should *L* Whom the cross-lightnings	,,	. 128
his, a brother's *l*, that hung	,,	. 138
truth and *l* are strength,	,,	. 365
such a *l* as like a chidden child	,,	. 541
Martin's summer of his faded *l*	,,	. 560
the hapless *l's* And double death	,,	. 616
light yoke of that Lord of *l*,	,,	. 708
loved, for he was worthy *l*.	,,	. 712
l and reverence left them bare	,,	. 785
thy *l*, Thy beauty, make amends,	*Tithonus*	. 23
lisp in *l's* delicious creeds	*Coquette,* i.	. 11
beyond his object *L* can last	,, iii.	. 5
My tears, no tears of *l*,	,,	. 7
No tears of *l*. but tears that *L* can die	,,	. 8
one way to the home of my *l*,	*The Window*	. 8

	POEM.	LINE.
Bird's *l* and bird's song (rep.)	*The Window*	(2
And women's *l* and men's !	,,	. 79
Take my *l*, for *l* will come,	,,	. 125
L will come but once a life.	,,	. 126
you have gotten the wings of *l*	,,	. 158
Here is the golden close of *l*.	,,	. 180
this is the golden morning of *l*	,,	. 188
For a *l* that never tires.	,,	. 195
are you great enough for *l* ?	,,	. 196
love (verb.)		
When I ask her if she *l* me,	*Lilian*	. 3
She'll not tell me if she *l* me,	,,	. 6
l's To purl o'er matted cress.	*Ode to Mem.*	58
dearly I thy first essay,	,,	. 83
'Who is it *l's* me? who *l's* not me?'	*The Mermaid*	13
To live forgotten, and *l* forlorn.'	*Mariana in the S.*	12
must I *l* her for your sake ;	*Miller's D.*	. 142
loss but made us *l* the more,	,,	. 230
l thee well and cleave to thee,	*Œnone*	. 157
the happy souls, that *l* to live:	,,	. 236
did *l* Beauty only . To—.	*With Pal. of Art*	6
sought to prove how I could *l*,	*L. C. V. de Vere*	21
You *l*, remaining peacefully,	*Margaret*	. 22
Those we *l* first are taken first.	*To J. S.*	. 12
Something to *l* He lends us;	,,	. 13
L thou thy land . ' *Love thou thy land,' etc.*	1
Would *l* the gleams of good	,,	. 89
blooms the garden that I *l*.	*Gardener's D.*	34
And told me I should *l*.	,,	. 63
' My girl, I *l* you well ;	*Dora*	. 40
take her back; she *l's* you well.	,,	. 140
who would *l*? I woo'd a woman	*Audley Ct.*	. 51
Ellen Aubrey, *l*, and dream of me.'	,,	. 72
Old oak, I *l* thee well ;.	*Talking O.*	. 202
God *l* us, as if the seedsman,	*Golden Year*	69
Saying, 'Dost thou *l* me, cousin?'	*Locksley H.*	30
l her, as I knew her, kind?	,,	. 70
whom to look at was to *l*.	,,	. 72
l her for the love she bore?	,,	. 73
Do men *l* thee ?	*Two Voices*	109
I will *l* no more, no more,	*Ed. Gray*	. 31
does not *l* me for my birth,	*Lady Clare*	9
l's me for my own true worth	,,	. 51
'There is none I *l* like thee.'	*L. of Burleigh*	6
I *l* thee more than life.'	,,	. 16
Says to her that *l's* him well,	,,	. 22
O but she will *l* him truly !	,,	. 37
Fish are we that *l* the mud,	*Vision of Sin*	101
No, I *l* not what is new ;	,,	. 139
That *l* to keep us children!	*Princess, Pro.*	133
Her brethren, tho' they *l* her,	,, i.	153
fall out with those we *l*.	,,	. 253
so mask'd, Madam, I *l* the truth ;	,, ii.	195
If I could *l*, why this were she :	,, iii.	83
'you *l* The metaphysics !	,,	. 262
with all we *l* below the verge ;	,, iv.	29
shame That which he says he *l's*	,,	. 230
l their voices more than duty,	,,	. 491
they say that still You *l* her,	,, v.	19
with catapults, She would not *l*;	,,	. 133
Not ever would she *l*; but brooding	,,	. 135
l us for it, and we ride them down	,,	. 150
one *l's* the soldier, one The silken priest	,,	. 175
can be sweet to those she *l's*,	,,	. 279
You *l* nor her, nor me, nor any ;	,, vi.	243
trust, not *l*, you less.	,,	. 278
l not hollow cheek or faded eye :	,,	. 370
like each other ev'n as those who *l*.	,, vii.	276
l to cheat yourself with words ?	,,	. 314
Never, Prince ; you cannot *l* me.'	,,	. 318
to life indeed, thro' thee, Indeed I *l*:	,,	. 325
I *l* thee : come, Yield thyself up :	,,	. 342
look on her that *l's* him well,	*In Mem.* viii.	2
thou bringest all I *l*.	,, xvii.	8
come, whatever *l's* to weep,	,, xviii.	11
l's to make parade of pain,	,, xxi.	10
in the songs I *l* to sing.	,, xxxviii.	7
one that *l's* but knows not,	,, xli.	11
truth from one that *l's* and knows?	,,	. 12
I cannot *l* thee as I ought,	,, li.	1

	POEM.	LINE.
My spirit loved and *l*'s him yet,	*In Mem.* lix.	2
How should he *l* a thing so low?'	"	16
I loved thee, Spirit, and *l*	" lx.	11
soul of Shakspeare *l* thee more.	"	12
More years had made me *l* thee more	" lxxx.	8
the books to *l* or hate,	" lxxxviii.	34
earnest that he *l*'s her yet	" xcvi.	15
He *l*'s her yet, she will not weep.	"	18
For that, for all, she *l*'s him more.	"	28
'I cannot understand: I *l*.'	"	36
him I loved, and *l* For ever;	" cii.	14
Who *l*'s not Knowledge?	" cxiii.	1
I do not therefore *l* thee less	" cxxix.	8
I seem to *l* thee more and more	"	12
be born with children, And act and *l*,	*Con.*	127
That God, which ever lives and *l*'s,	"	141
sure That there is one to *l* me :	*Maud,* I. xi.	11
Should I *l* her so well if she (rep.)	" xvi.	26
I see she cannot but *l* him	" xix.	69
faint in the light that she *l*'s (rep.)	" xxii.	9
But she, she would *l* me still ;	" II. ii.	51
wheedle a world that *l*'s him not,	" v.	39
days That most she *l*'s to talk of,	*The Brook*	226
Thine island *l*'s thee well,	*Ode on Well.*	85
cannot *l* my lord and not his name.	*Enid*	92
sweet face of her Whom he *l*'s most	"	123
light on all things that you *l*,	"	226
wed with her whom first you *l*:	"	227
wheel and thee we neither *l* nor hate.	"	349-58
there are those who *l* me yet ;	"	461
the lady he *l*'s best be there.	"	481
wish the two To *l* each other:	"	792
l's to know When men of mark	"	1077
does he *l* you as of old?	"	1172
may bicker with the things they *l*,	"	1174
that this man *l*'s you no more.	"	1178
here is one who *l*'s you as of old ;	"	1183
if you *l* me as in former years,	"	1204
boys Who *l* to vex him eating,	"	1409
l that beauty should go beautifully:	"	1529
never loved, can never *l* but him:	"	1557
l you, Prince, with something of the	"	1636
l the Heaven that chastens us.	"	1637
'O Merlin, do you *l* me?' (rep.)	*Vivien*	84
'Great Master, do you *l* me?	"	86
wise in love L most, say least'	"	97
do you *l* my tender rhyme?'	"	249
methinks you think you *l* me well	"	333
For me, I *l* you somewhat ;	"	334
grain Of him you say you *l*:	"	338
However well you think you *l* me	"	366
charm on whom you say you *l*.'	"	375
daily wonder is, I *l* at all,	"	386
one to make me jealous if I *l*,	"	389
must be to *l* you still.	"	777
tho' you do not *l* me, stave,	"	793
A sight you *l* to look on.'	*Elaine*	84
who *l*'s me must have a touch of earth ;	"	134
l's it in his knights more than himself:	"	157
Ill news, my Queen, for all who *l* him,	"	596
'that you *l* This greatest knight,	"	665
if I know, then, if I *l* not him	"	674
there is none other I can *l*.'	"	675
by God's death,' said he, 'you *l* him	"	676
others know, And whom he *l*'s.	"	678
if you *l*, it will be sweet to give it ;	"	689
if he *l*, it will be sweet to have it.	"	690
l or not, A diamond is a diamond.	"	691
If he *l*, and his love hold,	"	694
Whose sleeve he wore ; she *l*'s him ;	"	707
maid of Astolat *l*'s Sir Lancelot,	"	721
Sir Lancelot *l*'s the maid of Astolat.'	"	722
But did not *l* the colour ;	"	836
l their best, Closest and sweetest,	"	865
He will not *l* me : how then?	"	889
'I have gone mad. I *l* you :	"	926
Sir Lancelot's fault Not to *l* me,	"	1070
mine to *l* Him of all men	"	1070
l's the Queen, and in an open shame !	"	1076
to be loved makes not to *l* again ;	"	1287
if thou *l* me get thee hence	*Guinevere*	95

	POEM.	LINE.
True men who *l* me still,	*Guinevere*	442
l one maiden only, cleave to her,	"	471
tho' thou would'st not *l* thy lord	"	504
my doom is, I *l* thee still.	"	555
no man dream but that I *l* thee	"	556
tell the King I *l* him tho' so late?	"	644
he *l*'s me still. (rep.)	"	665
I *l* him all the better for it—	*En. Arden.*	196
think They *l* me as a father :	"	409
l them as if they were my own	"	410
Can one *l* twice ?	"	423
and he said 'Why then I *l* it:'	*Aylmer's F.*	249
whitest lamb in all my fold L's you ;	"	362
because I *l* their child They hate me ;	"	423
cannot *l* me at all, if you *l* not	*Grandmother*	48
Sweetheart, I *l* you so well.	"	50
the wild team Which *l* thee .	*Tithonus*	40
l us and make us your own :	*W. to Alexan.*	30
the slight coquette, she cannot *l*,	*Coquette,* ii.	12
lives and *l*'s in every place ;	*On a Mourner*	5
To *l* once and for ever :	*The Window*	69
L me now you'll *l* me then :	"	132

loveable.

Elaine the fair, Elaine the *l*,	*Elaine*	1

love-charmed.

stars that hung L *c* to listen :	*Love and Duty*	73

loved.

	POEM.	LINE.
Have lived and *l* alone so long,	*Miller's D.*	38
I *l*, and love dispell'd the fear	"	89
l the brimming wave that swam	"	97
I *l* you better for your fears,	"	149
l his beauty passing well.	*The Sisters*	23
in her sight he *l* so well?	*Margaret*	40
tongue Cold February !	*The Blackbird*	14
a sleep They sleep—the men I *l*.	*M. d'Arthur*	17
l the man, and prized his work ;	*E.P.*	8
the heart of her I *l*;	*Gardener's D.*	225
on the cheeks, Like one that *l* him :	*Dora*	131
I have kill'd him—but I *l* him —	"	157
l At first like dove and dove	*Walk. to the M.*	49
daily loss of one she *l*	"	86
and Duty *l* of Love—	*Love and Duty*	46
with those That *l* me, and alone ;	*Ulysses*	9
weeping, 'I have *l* thee long.'	*Locksley H.*	30
l thee more than ever wife was *l*.	"	64
No—she never *l* me truly ;	"	74
to have *l* so slight a thing.	"	148
have *l* the people well,	*Godiva*	8
therefore, as they *l* her well,	"	38
Ellen Adair she *l* me well,	*Ed. Gray*	9
And the people *l* her much.	*L. of Burleigh*	48
l to live alone Among her women ;	*Princess,* i.	48
ever *l* to meet Star-sisters	" ii.	405
'To linger here with one that *l* us.'	" iii.	321
I *l* her. Peace be with her.	" iv.	118
I *l* you like this kneeler,	"	277
l me closer than his own right eye,	" v.	520
Call'd him worthy to be *l*,	"	537
if you *l* The breast that fed	" vi.	164
Dear traitor, too much *l*, why?—why?	"	275
I *l* the woman : he, that doth not,	" vii.	294
there was one thro' whom I *l* her,	"	298
Ere seen I *l*, and *l* thee seen,	"	320
I find him worthier to be *l*.	*In Mem.* Pro.	40
'Behold the man that *l* and lost,	"	15
The human-hearted man I *l*,	" xiii.	11
I *l* the weight I had to bear,	" xxv.	7
better to have *l* and lost lxxxiv. 3)	" xxvii.	15
Than never to have *l* at all. (lxxxiv. 4)	"	16
when he *l* me here in Time,	" xliii.	17
Who *l*, who suffer'd countless ills,	" lv.	17
My spirit *l* and loves him yet,	" lix.	2
I *l* thee, Spirit, and love	" lx.	11
l to handle spiritual strife,	" lxxxiv.	11
He *l* to rail against it still,	" lxxxviii.	38
The shape of him I *l*, and love	" cii.	8
The man we *l* was there on deck,	"	41
A little spare the night I *l*,	" civ.	15
sing the songs he *l* to hear.	" cvi.	24

R

CONCORDANCE TO

	POEM.	LINE.
l them more, that they were thine,	*In Mem.* cix.	15
O *l* the most, when most I feel	,, cxxviii.	3
L deeplier, darklier understood ;	,,	10
Until we close with all we *l*,	,, cxxx.	11
he *l* A daughter of our house ;	,, Con.	6
all we thought and *l* and did.	,,	134
To speak of the mother she *l*	*Maud*, I. xix.	27
short hour to see The souls we *l*	,, II. iv.	15
yet the brook he *l*, For which,	*The Brook*	5
fancies of the boy, To me that *l* him ;	,,	20
you, whom once I *l* so well,	*The Letters*	35
We *l* that hall, tho' white and cold	*The Daisy*	37
one only and who clave to her—'	*Ded. of Idylls*	10
l her, as he *l* the light of Heaven.	*Enid*	5
l Geraint To make her beauty vary	,,	8
l her in a state Of broken fortunes,	,,	12
L her, and often with her own white	,,	16
And Enid *l* the Queen,	,,	19
l and reverenced her too much	,,	119
that dress, and how he *l* her in it,	,,	141, 843
ask'd again, and ever *l* to hear ;	,,	436
served for proof that I was *l*,	,,	796
because he *l* her passionately,	,,	859
being he *l* best in all the world,	,,	952
Not while they *l* them ;	,,	1176
Enid never *l* a man but him,	,,	1212
the passage that he *l* her not ;	,,	1241
l me serving in my father's hall :	,,	1547
I never *l*, can never love but him :	,,	1557
my lists with him whom best you *l* ;	,,	1688
true eyes Beheld the man you *l*	,,	1695
ladies *l* to call Enid the Fair,	,,	1810
that I had *l* a smaller man !	*Vivien*	721
l to make men darker than they are	,,	725
that summer, when you *l* me first.	*Elaine*	105
lifted up her eyes And *l* him,	,,	260
darling of the court, L of the loveliest,	,,	262
l her with all love except the love	,,	864
'If I be *l*, these are my festal robes,	,,	905
'I never *l* him : an I meet with him,	,,	1062
my glory to have *l* One peerless	,,	1084
having *l* God's best And greatest .	,,	1087
l you, and my love had no return,	,,	1269
l me with a love beyond all love	,,	1285
to he *l* makes not to love again :	,,	1287
And *l* thy courtesies and thee,	,,	1354
a man Made to be *l* ;	,,	1355
Thou could'st have *l* this maiden,	,,	1357
to be *l*, if what is worthy love	,,	1369
l me, damsel, surely with a love	,,	1385
take leave of all I *l* ?	*Guinevere*	542
l thy highest creature here ?	,,	649
my duty to have *l* the highest ;	,,	650
We needs must *l* the highest	,,	653
Philip *l* in silence ;	*En. Arden*	41
l Enoch : tho' she knew it not	,,	43
And her, he *l*, a beggar !	,,	117
sell the boat—and yet he *l* her	,,	134
l you longer than you know.'	,,	418-52
you be ever *l* As Enoch was?	,,	423
to be *l* A little after Enoch.'	,,	425
nor *l* she to be left Alone	,,	512
Where Annie lived and *l* him,	,,	686
learn I *l* her to the last.'	,,	836
l As heiress and not heir	*Aylmer's F.*	23
hearts not knowing that they *l*,	,,	113
He but less *l* than Edith,	,,	167
He, *l* for her and for himself.	,,	179
l nor liked the thing he heard,	,,	250
l you more as son Than brother	,,	351
madly *l*—and he, Thwarted ,	,,	389
l me, and because I love their child	,,	423
you *l*, for he was worthy love.	,,	712
half turn'd round from him she *l*,	*Sea Dreams*	274
l the glories of the world,	*The Voyage*	83
I walked with one I *l*	*V. of Canteretz*	4
tho' he *l* her none the less,	*Lucretius*	4
the mind, except it *l* them, clasp	,,	164

love-deep.

languors of thy *l-d* eyes	*Eleänore*	76

	POEM.	LINE.
love-knots.		
leg and arm with *l-k* gay,	*Talking O.*	65
love-language.		
heard The low *l-l* of the bird	*In Mem.* ci.	11
love-languid.		
eyes, *l-l* thro' half-tears,	*Love and Duty*	36
lovelier.		
l Than all the valleys of Ionian	*Œnone*	1
l than whatever Oread haunt	,,	72
all heavens, and *l* than their names,	*Princess, Pro.*	12
l not the Elysian lawns,	,, iii.	324
left her woman, *l* in her mood	,, vii.	147
Far *l* in our Lancelot had it been,	*Elaine*	587
What '*l* of his own had he than her,	*Aylmer's F.*	22
loveliest.		
true To what is *l* upon earth.'	*Mariana in the S.*	64
l in all grace Of movement,	*Œnone*	73
Their feet in flowers, her *l*:	*Princess*, vi.	62
deck'd her as the *l*,	*Enid*	17
l of all women upon earth.	,,	21
darling of the court, Loved of the *l*,	*Elaine*	262
loveliness.		
Her *l* with shame and with surprise	*D. of F. Wom.*	89
A miniature of *l*,	*Gardener's D.*	12
In *l* of perfect deeds,	*In Mem.* xxxvi.	11
love Clothed in so pure a *l*?	*Elaine*	1375
love-lore.		
Thou art perfect in *l-l*,	*Madeline*	26
lovelorn.		
With melodious airs *l*,	*Adeline*	55
love-loyal.		
l-l to the least wish of the (*Guinevere* 125) *Elaine* 90		
lovely.		
She look'd so *l*, as she sway'd	*Sir L. and Q. G.*	40
indeed these fields Are *l*,	*Princess*, iii.	324
Be sometimes *l* like a bride,	*In Mem.* lviii.	6
that clear-featured face Was *l*,	*Elaine*	1154
love-poem.		
and this A mere *l-p* !	*Princess*, iv.	108
lover.		
Two *l*'s whispering by an orchard wall	*Circumstance*	4
Came two young *l*'s lately wed ;	*L. of Shalott*, ii.	34
my *l*, with Whom I rode sublime	*D. of F. Wom.*	141
on her *l*'s arm she leant,	*Day-Dm.*	165
L's long-betrothed were they ;	*Lady Clare*	6
But he clasp'd her like a *l*,	*L. of Burleigh*	67
at the happy *l*'s heart in heart—	*Princess*, vii.	93
A happy *l* who has come	*In Mem.* viii.	1
my Maud by that long *l*'s kiss,	*Maud*, I. xviii.	58
From a little lazy *l*	,, xx.	10
Come out to your own true *l*,	,,	46
That your true *l* may see	,,	47
That grow for happy *l*'s.	*The Brook*	134
call it *l*'s quarrels, yet I know	*Enid*	1173
one true *l* which you ever had,	,,	1193
Shall we strip him there Your *l*?	,,	1338
little rift within the *l*'s lute	*Vivien*	243
damsel then Wroth at a *l*'s loss?	,,	457
like a *l* down thro' all his blood	*En. Arden*	660
by night again the *l*'s met,	*Aylmer's F.*	413
l heeded not But passionately restless	,,	545
me the *l* of liberty,	*Boädicea*	48
no *l* of glory she :	*Wages*	4
a jewel dear to a *l*'s eye !	*The Window*	3
love-sighs.		
passion seeks Pleasance in *l-s*	*Lilian*	9
love-song.		
A *l-s* I had somewhere read,	*Miller's D.*	65
lovest.		
L thou the doleful wind	*Adeline*	49
I think thou *l* me well.'	*L. of Burleigh*	4
loveth.		
l her own anguish deep	*To J. S.*	42

	POEM.	LINE.
love-whispers.		
Affianced, Sir? *l-w* may not breathe	*Princess*, ii.	203
loving.		
Most *l* is she?	*Œnone*	197
Gray nurses, *l* nothing new;	*In Mem.* xxix.	14
praying for her, *l* her;	*En. Arden*	880
l her, As when she laid her head	"	881
so lowly-lovely and so *l,* —	*Aylmer's F.*	168
low (adj.)		
ever when the moon was *l,*	*Mariana*	49
to the ear The warble was *l,*	*Dying Swan*	24
Sweet and *l,* sweet and *l,*	*Princess*, ii.	456
L, *l,* breathe and blow,	"	453
near me when my light is *l*	*In Mem.* xlix.	1
The voice was *l,* the look was bright	" lxviii.	15
babbling world of high or *l;*	*Ode on Well.*	182
this be high, what is it to be *l?*	*Elaine*	1078
L was her voice, but woo	*Aylmer's F.*	695
low (s.)		
From the dark fen the oxen's *l*	*Mariana*	28
low-cowering.		
L-c shall the Sophist sit *'Clear-headed friend,'* etc.		10
low-drooping.		
L-d till he well-nigh kiss'd her feet	*Elaine*	1166
lower (adj.)		
thyself a little *l* Than angels.	*Two Voices*	198
feel There is a *l* and a higher;	*In Mem.* cxxviii.	4
lower (verb.)		
l to his level day by day,	*Locksley H.*	45
turn thy wheel and *l* the proud;	*Enid*	347
lowered.		
L softly with a threefold cord of love	*D. of F. Wom.*	211
spake to these his helm was *l,*	*Guinevere*	587
lowest.		
barbarous isles, and here Among the *l.'*	*Princess*, ii.	108
low desire Not to feel *l*	*Vivien*	677
height That makes the *l* hate it	*Aylmer's F.*	173
low-flowing.		
fling on each side my *l-f* locks,	*The Mermaid*	32
low-folded.		
breathless burthen of *l-f* heavens	*Aylmer's F.*	612
low-hung.		
from beneath a *l-h* cloud.	*Ode to Mem.*	71
lowing (part.)		
And *l* to his fellows.	*Gardener's D.*	87
lowing (s.)		
So thick with *l's* of the herds,	*In Mem.* xcviii.	3
low-lieth.		
Where Claribel *l-l*	*Claribel*	1, 8, 21
lowlihead.		
perfect wifehood and pure *l.*	*Isabel*	12
lowliness.		
sure of Heaven If *l* could save her.	*Maud*, I. xii.	20
lowly-lovely.		
she—so *l-l* and so loving	*Aylmer's F.*	168
lowness.		
The *l* of the present state,	*In Mem.* xxiv.	11
low-spoken.		
L-s, and of so few words,	*Enid*	1244
low-toned.		
So she *l-t;* while with shut eyes I lay	*Princess*, vii.	208
low-tongued.		
Doth the *l-t* Orient Wander	*Adeline*	51
low-wheel'd.		
Within the *l-w* chaise,	*Talking O.*	110
loyal.		
l unto kindly laws.	*In Mem.* lxxxiv.	16
Nor often *l* to his word,	*Elaine*	558
l., the dumb old servitor,	"	1138
loyal-hearted.		
On thee the *l-h* hung	*In Mem.* cix.	5

	POEM.	LINE.
lucid.		
Be large and *l* round thy brow.	*In Mem.* xc.	8
Lucilia.		
L, wedded to Lucretius, found	*Lucretius*	1
Lucretius.		
Lucilia, wedded to L, found	*Lucretius*	1
Lucius Junius Brutus.		
The *L J B* of my kind?	*Princess*, ii.	264
luck.		
good *l* Shall fling her old shoe	*Will Water.*	215
Good *l* had your good man,	*Enid*	1465
lucky.		
Less *l* her home-voyage:	*En. Arden*	537
Lucumo.		
lay at wine with Lar and *L*;	*Princess*, ii.	113
lull.		
(while warm airs *l* us, blowing lowly)	*Lotos-E's.*	134
l with song an aching heart,	*In Mem.* xxxvii.	15
I *l* a fancy trouble-tost	" lxiv.	2
Perchance to *l* the throbs of pain,	*The Daisy*	105
lullabies..		
These mortal *l* of pain	*In Mem.* lxxvi.	5
lulled.		
Thy toowhits are *l* I wot.	*The Owl*, ii.	1
Into dreamful slumber *l.*	*Eleänore*	30
And *l* them in my own.	*Talking O.*	216
lumber.		
the waste and *l* of the shore.	*En. Arden*	16
luminous.		
L, gemlike, ghostlike, deathlike	*Maud*, I. iii.	8
lump.		
This *l* of earth has left his estate	*Maud*, I. xvi.	1
lungs.		
labour'd down within his ample *l's,*	*Princess*, v.	263
Lunnon (London.)		
Squoire's in L, an' summun.	*N. Farmer.*	57
lured.		
L by the crimes and frailties of the	*Guinevere*	135
often *l* her from herself;	"	150
l Into their net made pleasant	*Aylmer's F.*	485
one unctuous mouth which *l* him,	*Sea Dreams*	14
lurk.		
no more of deadly *l's* therein,	*Princess*, ii.	208
such as *l's* In some wild Poet,	*In Mem.* xxxiv.	6
l three villains yonder in the wood,	*Enid*	991
Lusitanian.		
father-grape grew fat On *L* summers.	*Will Water.*	8
lust.		
from *l* of gold, or like a girl	*M. d'Arthur*	127
Ring out the narrowing *l* of gold;	*In Mem.* cv.	26
l of gain, in the spirit of Cain,	*Maud*, I. i.	23
vassals of wine and anger and *l,*	" II. i.	43
lost for a little her *l* of gold,	" III. vi.	39
and worship thine own *l's l*	*Aylmer's F.*	650
in his *l* and voluptuousness,	*Boädicea*	66
keep him from the *l* of blood	*Lucretius*	83
shapes of *l,* unspeakable	"	157
l or lusty blood or provender:	"	195
lustihood.		
He is so full of *l,* he will ride,	*Elaine*	803
lusting.		
l for all that is not its own;	*Maud*, I. i.	22
lustre.		
Soft *l* bathes the range of urns	*Day-Dm.*	27
l of the long convolvuluses	*En. Arden*	577
lustreless.		
one was patch'd and blurr'd and *l*	*Enid*	643
lute (s.)		
on lattice edges lay Or book or *l;*	*Princess*, ii.	16
the little rift within the *l* (rep.)	*Vivien*	240

260   CONCORDANCE TO

	lute (verb).	POEM.	LINE.		*madden'd.*	POEM.	LINE.
l and flute fantastic tenderness,		Princess, iv.	111	ever he mutter'd and *m*,		Maud, I. i.	10

Luther.
thou wilt be A latter *L* . . . . *To J. M. K.* 2

luxury.
And *l* of contemplation : . . *Eleänore* . 107

lychgate.
to the *l*, where his chariot stood . *Aylmer's F.* 824

Lycian.
Appraised the *L* custom, . . *Princess*, ii. 112

lying.
L, robed in snowy white . . *L. of Shalott*, iv. 19
Fed thee, a child, *l* alone . . *Eleänore* . 25
l still Shadow forth the banks . " . 109
l broad awake I thought of you . *MayQueen*, iii. 29
Roman soldier found Me *l* dead, *D. of F. Wom*. 162
l robed and crown'd, . . " . 163
l, hidden from the heart's disgrace, *Locksley H.* 57
Summer isles of Eden *l* . . " . 164
Will vex thee *l* underground ? . *Two Voices* 111
She *l* on her couch alone, . . *Day-Dm.* . 78
sitting, *l*, languid shapes, . . *Vision of Sin* 12
l bathed In the green gleam . . *Princess*, i. 92
You *l* close upon his territory . " iv. 384
when she saw me *l* stark, . . " vi. 84
And found thee *l* in the port ; . *In Mem.* xiv. 4
wine-flask *l* couch'd in moss . . " lxxxviii. 44
L close to my foot . . . *Maud*, II. ii. 3
left him *l* in the public way ; . *Enid* . 1327
saw him *l* unsleek, unshorn, . *Elaine* . 811
father *l* sick and needing him) . *En. Arden* . 65
l thus inactive doubt and gloom . " . 113
l with his urns and ornaments, . *Aylmer's F.* 4
On the decks as they were *l*, · *The Captain* 53

lynx.
her *l* eye To fix and make me hotter, *Princess*, iii. 30

Lyonnesse.
Had fall'n in *L* about their Lord, . *M. d'Arthur* 1
Roving the trackless realms of *L*, *Elaine* . 36
And rode thereto from *L*, . *Guinevere* . 234
All down the lonely coast of *L*. . " . 238

lyre.
voice, a *l* of widest range . . *D. of F. Wom*. 165
touch'd a jarring *l* at first, . . *In Mem.* xcv. 7

lyrics.
dismal *l*, prophesying change . *Princess*, i. . 141

M

maäzin'.
Huzzin' an' *m* the blessed feälds . *N. Farmer* . 62

Macaw.
add A crimson to the quaint *M*, . *Day-Dm.* . 16

mace.
brand, *m*, and shaft, shield— . *Princess*, v. 492

machine.
praised his land, his horses, his *m*'s ; *The Brook* . 124

mad.
devils, *m* with blasphemy, . . *St S. Stylites* 4
Am I *m*, that I should cherish . *Locksley H.* 65
What matter if I go *m*, . . *Maud*, I. xi. 6
Is enough to drive one *m*. . . " II. v. 20
bailiff swore that he was *m*, . *The Brook* . 143
your town, where all the men are *m* ; *Enid* . . 418
makes me *m* to see you weep. . " . 1464
for I was well-nigh *m* : . . " . 1684
'I have gone *m*. I love you : . *Elaine* . 926
beheld three spirits *m* with joy. . *Guinevere* . 250
Squoire 'ull be sa *m* an' all— . *N. Farmer* . 47
M and maddening all that heard . *Boädicea* . 4

Madam.
M—if I know your sex, . . *Vision of Sin* 181

madden.
Is this a time to *m* madness . *Aylmer's F.* 769

maddening.
Mad and *m* all that heard her . *Boädicea* . 4

made.
So slightly, musically *m*, . . *Talking O*. . 87
What is so wonderfully *m*.' . *Two Voices* 6
I told thee—hardly nigher *m*, . " . 173
remember'd one myself had *m*, . *Princess*, iv. 70
part *m* long since, and part Now . " . 72
M at me thro' the press, . . " v. 511
thou hast *m* him : thou art just. . *In Mem. Pro*. 12
Of onward time shall yet be *m*, . " cxxvii. 6
Her sweet 'I will' has *m* ye one. . " Con. 56
not *m* the world, and He that *m* it *Maud*, I. iv. 48
M so fairly well . . . " II. ii. 5
Was ever man so grandly *m* as he ? *Enid* . 81
M him like a man abroad at morn . " . 335
And *m* it of two colours ; . . " . 1141
m as if to fall upon him. . . " . 1624
seems not *m* to fade away, . *Elaine* 1007
from the sun there swiftly *m* at her *Guinevere* . 78
m them lay their hands in mine . " . 464
I am not *m* of so slight elements. . " . 506
The sea is His : He *m* it.' . *En. Arden* . 226
duty by his own, *M* himself theirs : " . 331
bounteously *m* And yet so finely, *Aylmer's F.* 74
wherefore he had *m* the cry ; . " . 589
m by these the last of all my race . " . 791

Madeline.
Ever varying *M*. (rep.) . . *Madeline* . 3

madest.
Thou *m* Life in man and brute ; . *In Mem. Pro*. 6
Thou *m* Death ; and lo, thy foot . " . 7
Thou *m* man, he knows not why ; . " . 10
Who *m* him thy chosen, . . *Tithonus* . 13

madman.
warn'd that *m* ere it grew too late; *Vision of Sin* 56
struck me, *m*, over the face, . *Maud*, II. i. 18
like a *m* brought her to the court, *Enid* . . 725

madness.
Then in *m* and in bliss, . . *Madeline* . 42
Thro' *m*, hated by the wise, . . *Love and Duty* 7
From cells of *m* unconfined, . . *Two Voices* 371
Mingle *m*, mingle scorn ! . *Vision of Sin* 204
accomplice of your *m* unforgiven, *Princess*, vi. 259
to death and trance And *m*, . *In Mem.* lxx. 2
the vitriol *m* flushes up . . *Maud*, I. i. 37
flee from the cruel *m* of love, . " iv. 55
Perhaps from *m*, perhaps from crime, " xvi. 22
do accept my *m*, and would die . " xviii. 44
cells of *m*, haunts of horror . . " III. vi. 2
pardon me ! the *m* of that hour . *Enid* . 1195
after *m* acted question ask'd ; . " . 1661
their last hour, A *m* of farewells. *Guinevere* . 102
Vext with unworthy *m*, . . *Aylmer's F.* 335
Is this a time to madden *m* . . " . 769
No *m* of ambition, avarice, none : *Lucretius* . 209

Madonna.
M, sad is night and morn . *Mariana in the S*. 22

Madonna-wise.
M-w on either side her head ; . *Isabel* . . 6

Magazine.
O blatant *M*'s regard me rather— *Hendecasyllabics* 17

maggot.
the *m* born in an empty head, . *Maud*, II. v. 38

magic.
Is there some *m* in the place ? . *Will Water*. 79

magic music.
The *M M* in his heart . . *Day-Dm*. . 126
liked it more Than *m m*, . *Princess*, Pro. 192

magnetic.
Twice as *m* to sweet influences . *Princess*, v. 183
His face *m* to the hand . . *Aylmer's F*. 626

	POEM.	LINE.
magnetise.		
may *in* The baby-oak within—	*Talking O.*	255
magnet-like.		
m-l she drew The rustiest iron	*Vivien*	423
magnificence.		
(His dress a suit of fray'd *m*,	*Enid* .	296
magpie.		
And only hear the *m* gossip.	*To F. D. Maurice*	19
Mahomet.		
touch'd on *M* With much contempt,	*Princess,* ii.	118
Mahratta-battle.		
in wild *M-b* fell my father	*Locksley H.*	155

maid (see Maid of Astolet, lily maid.)

Even as a *m*, whose stately brow	*Ode to Mem.*	13
sitting, served by man and *m*,	*The Goose*	21
If ever *m* or spouse, As fair	*Talking O.*	34
m and page renew'd their strife,	*Day-Dm.*	145
earth is rich in man and *m*;	*Will Water.*	65
come you drest like a village *m*,	*Lady Clare*	67–9
and *m's* Arranged a country dance,	*Princess, Pro.*	83
presented *M* Or Nymph, or Goddess	" i.	193
mother of the sweetest little *m*,	" ii.	260
m's should ape Those monstrous males	" iii.	292
turning to her *m's*, 'Pitch our pavilion	"	327
a *m* Of those beside her, smote	" iv.	19
marsh-divers, rather, *m*, Shall croak	"	105
hubbub in the court of half the *m's*	"	435
pretty *m's* in the running flood,	" v.	372
Mask'd like our *m's*, blustering	"	386
our *m's* were better at their homes,	"	418
O *m's*, behold our sanctuary Is violate	" vi.	43
led A hundred *m's* in train	"	60
had to do with none but *m's*,	"	273
we will scatter all our *m's*	"	283
random sweet on *m* and man.	" vii.	71
down, O *m*, from yonder mountain	"	177
I keep but a man and a *m*,	*Maud,* I. iv.	19
For the *m's* and marriage-makers,	" xx.	35
by God's rood is the one *m* for me.	*Enid*	368
And page, and *m*, and squire,	"	710
with no attendance, page *or m*,	"	1171
Vivien, like the tenderest-hearted *m*	*Vivien*	227
be not wrathful with your *m*;	"	230
A *m* so smooth, so white,	"	416
stainless man beside a stainless *m*;	"	587
for Queens and not for simple *m's*,	*Elaine*	231
this *m* Might wear as fair a jewel	"	239
in enamell'd arms the *m* Glanced at,	"	616
till the *m* Rebell'd against it	"	647
the *m* Whose sleeve he wore;	"	706
Had marvel what the *m* might be,	"	724
m in Astolat, Her guiltless rival,	"	741
m had told him all her tale,	"	794-819
meek *m* sweetly forbore him	"	851
simple *m* Went half the night repeating,	"	894
Lancelot ever prest upon the *m*	"	907
'Nay, noble *m*,' he answer'd,	"	944
full meekly rose the *m*,	"	972
seem'd a curious little *m* again	"	1029
pure Sir Galahad to uplift the *m*;	"	1258
none with her save a little *m*,	*Guinevere*	3
communed only with the little *m*,	"	148
little *m*, who brook'd No silence	"	157
full willingly sang the little *m*,	"	165
little *m*, shut in by nunnery walls,	"	225
Than is the maiden passion for a *m*,	"	475
'Yea, little *m*, for am I not forgiven?'	"	657
Perish'd many a *m* and matron,	*Boädicea*	85
After-loves of *m's* and men	*The Window*	130

maiden.

phantom two hours old Of a *m*	*Adeline*	19
A simple *m* in her flower	*L. C. V. de Vere*	15
of the warrior Gileadite, A *m* pure;	*D. of F. Wom.*	198
been some *m* coarse and poor!	"	253
wrought by the lonely *m* of the Lake.	*M. d'Arthur*	35
press The *m's* tender palm.	*Talking O.*	180
The little *m* walk'd demure,	*Two Voices*	419
m's jet-black hair has grown,	*Day-Dm.*	80

	POEM.	LINE.
Nor *m's* hand in mine.	*Sir Galahad*	20
Dropt her head in the *m's* hand,	*Lady Clare*	63
M, I have watch'd thee daily,	*L. of Burleigh*	3
And a village *m* she.	"	8
found an University For *m's*,	*Princess,* i.	150
Six hundred *m's* clad in purest white,	" ii.	448
O marvellously modest *m*, you !	" iii.	32
open-hearted *m*, true and pure.	"	82
Among her *m's*, higher by the head,	"	163
college and her *m's*, empty masks,	"	171
Stood her *m's* glimmeringly group'd	" iv.	172
All her *m's*, watching, said,	" v.	534
stole a *m* from her place,	"	540
many a *m* passing home	" vi.	359
m's came, they talk'd, They sang,	" vii.	7
As on a *m* in the day	*In Mem.* xxxix.	3
serve to curl a *m's* locks;	" lxxvi.	7
within a hall And *m's* with me :	" cii.	6
m's gather'd strength and grace	"	27
m's with one mind Bewail'd their lot ;	"	45
m's of the place, That pelt us	*Con.*	67
Go not, happy day, Till the *m* yields.	*Maud.,* I. xvii.	4
m of our century, yet most meek ;	*The Brook*	68
stood a *m* near Waiting to pass.	"	204
a single *m* with her, Took horse,	*Enid* .	160
sent Her *m* to demand it	"	193
in your *m's* person to yourself ;	"	216
her own *m* to demand the name,	"	411
pair Of suitors as this *m*;	"	440
a *m* is a tender thing,	"	510
Let never *m* think, however fair,	"	721
m rose, And left her *m* couch,	"	736
call'd her like that *m* in the tale,	"	742
m dream'd That some one put	*Elaine*	211
yield it to this *m*, if you will.'	"	229
m standing in the dewy light.	"	351
so much For any *m* living,' .	"	375
great pearls Some gentle *m's* gift.'	"	603
for lack of gentle *m's* aid.	"	761
gentler-born the *m*, the more bound,	"	762
the *m*, while that ghostly grace	"	881
in her tower alone the *m* sat ;	"	983
Elaine ? ' till back the *m* fell,	"	1025
for this most gentle *m's* death	"	1283
m buried, not as one unknown,	"	1324
Thou could'st have loved this *m*,	"	1357
'O *m*, if indeed you list to sing	*Guinevere*	163
as thou art be never *m* more.	"	356
aghast the *m* rose,	"	360
love one *m* only, cleave to her,	"	471
Meek *m's*, from the voices crying	"	664
more and more, the *m* woman grown,	*Aylmer's F.*	108
Lash the *m* into swooning,	*Boädicea*	67
or half coquette-like *M*,	*Hendecasyllabics*	20

maiden-cheek.

Engirt with many a florid *m-c*,	*Princess,* iii.	332

maidenhood.

To her, perpetual *m*,	*In Mem.* vi.	43

maidenlike.

m as far As I could ape their treble,	*Princess,* iv.	73

maiden-meek.

m-m I pray'd Concealment:	*Princess,* iii.	118

maid-mother.

Or the *m-m* by a crucifix,	*Pal. of Art*	93

maid of Astolat.

Elaine the lily *m o A*,	*Elaine*	2
About the *m o A* and her love	"	719
The *m o A* loves Sir Lancelot,	"	721
Sir Lancelot loves the *m o A*.'	"	722
Then spake the lily *m o A* ;	"	1079
lily *m o A* Lay smiling,	"	1236
I, sometime call'd the *m o A*,	"	1266

maid of honour.

The *m o h* blooming fair ;	*Day-Dm.*	48
Poor soul! I had a *m o h* once ;	*Princess,* iv.	115

mail (armour.)

clear plates of sapphire *m*.	*Two Voices*	12
ringing, springs from brand and *m*;	*Sir Galahad*	54

CONCORDANCE TO

mail (coach.)

	POEM.	LINE.
The *m*? At one o'clock.	Walk. to the M.	6
fear That we shall miss the *m*:	"	102

maimed.

cured some halt and *m*;	St S. Stylites	135
is there any of you halt or *m*?	"	140
that there Lie bruised and *m*,	Princess, vi.	56
and all the good knights *m*.	"	224
and him they caught and *m*.	Elaine	275
could not end me, left me *m*	Tithonus	20

main.

Just breaking over land and *m*?	Two Voices	84
stands apart Cleft from the *m*,	Princess, iv.	263
great river take me to the *m*;	" vi.	376
gaze O'er land and *m*:	" vii.	21
mingle with the bounding *m*:	In Mem. xi.	12
I am sick of the moor and the *m*.	Maud, I. i.	61
Flying along the land and the *m*—	" II. ii.	38
On open *m* or winding shore!	The Voyage	6

main-current.

what *m-c's* draw the years 'Love thou thy land,' etc.		21

maintained.

at least by me be *m*:	Maud, I. i.	18

maintaining.

M that with equal husbandry	Princess, i.	129

maintenance.

all That appertains to noble *m*.	Enid	712

maize.

hand in hand with Plenty in the *m*,	Princess, vii.	186
olive, aloe, and *m* and vine.	The Daisy	4

majesty.

Majesties of mighty states—	'Love thou thy land'	60
such and so unmoved a *m*	Elaine	1164
to mar the sober *majesties*	Lucretius	214

make.

why *m* we such ado?	MayQueen,iii.	56
love, that *m's* me thrice a man,	Talking O.	11
'wilt thou *m* everything a lie,	Two Voices	203
might *m* it worth his while	Princess, i.	182
woo her, and *m* her mine,	" iv.	97
m us all we would be,	"	576
The mother *m's* us most—	" v.	496
m my dream All that I would.	"	508
let her *m* herself her own	" vii.	256
wills are ours, to *m* them thine	InMem.Pro.	16
himself could *m* The thing that is	The Brook	7
To *m* them like himself:	Elaine	132
that I *m* My will of yours,	"	912
sweetly could she *m* and sing.	"	1000
love of truth, and all that *m's* a man.	Guinevere	479
Roaring to *m* a third:	Aylmer's F.	128
for your fortunes are to *m*.	"	300
shall not *m* them out of mine.	"	301
Went both to *m* your dream:	Sea Dreams	246
follow till I *m* thee mine.'	The Voyage	64
love us, and *m* us your own:	W. to Alexan.	30
m Another and another frame	Lucretius	41

make-believes.

m-b For Edith and himself.	Aylmer's F.	95

Maker.

For the drift of the *M* is dark,	Maud, I. iv.	43

makest.

'Thou *m* thine appeal to me:	In Mem. lv.	5

making (part.)

M earth wonder,	The Poet	52
In firry woodlands *m* moan;	Miller's D.	42
M sweet close of his delicious toils	Pal. of Art	185
M for one sure goal.	"	248
Thro' many agents *m* strong,	'Love thou thy land,'	39
m all the horizon dark.	Two Voices	390
m vain pretence Of gladness,	In Mem. xxx.	6
M the little one leap for joy.	To F. D. Maurice	4
m his high place the lawless perch	Ded. of Idylls	21
good mother *m* Enid gay	Enid	757
comrades, *m* slowlier at the Prince,		1016

	POEM.	LINE.
M a roan horse caper	Elaine	788
M a treacherous quiet	"	879
m them An armlet for the roundest	"	1176
men worse by *m* my sin known?	"	1407
m all the night a steam of fire.	Guinevere	593
younger people *m* holiday,	En. Arden	62
m signs They knew not what:	"	641
swallowing gold, Not *m*.	Sea Dreams	80

making (s.)

since the *m* of the world.	M. d'Arthur	203
have gone to the *m* of man:	Maud, I. iv.	35
the sudden *m* of splendid names,	" III. vi.	47

Malay.

not the Kaffir, Hottentot, *M*,	Princess, ii.	142

Malayan.

The cursed *M* crease	Princess, Pro.	21
Ran a *M* muck against the times,	Aylmer's F.	463

male.

any *m* thing but to peep at us:	Princess, Pro.	151
should ape Those monstrous *m's*	" iii.	293

malice.

of sense became The crime of *m*,	Vision of Sin	216
My *m* is no deeper than a moat,	Enid	1189

malison.

I have no sorcerer's *m* on me,	Princess, ii.	383

mallow.

set With willow-weed and *m*	The Brook	46

Mammon.

This filthy marriage-hindering *M*	Aylmer's F.	374

Mammonite.

When a *M* mother kills her babe.	Maud, I. i.	45

mammoth.

old-world *m* bulk'd in ice,	Princess, v.	142

man (see *man and wife*.)

sick *m's* room when he taketh 'A spirit haunts,' etc.		14
riving the spirit of *m*	The Poet	51
with the certain step of *m*.	Miller's D.	96
men, in power Only, are likest gods,	Œnone	127
hated both of Gods and *men*.	"	225
ever in her ears of armed *men*.	"	261
friends to *m*, Living To—	With Pal. of Art	11
to the perfect shape of *m*.	"	19
choice painting of wise *men*	Pal. of Art	131
like some sick *m* declined	"	155
possession of *m's* mind and deed	"	209
that good *m*, the clergyman,	MayQueen,iii.	12
from an ill-used race of *men*.	Lotos-E's.	165
squares of *men* in brazen plates,	D. of F. Wom.	33
'I govern'd *men* by change,	"	130
long since I have seen a *m*.	"	131
no *men* to govern in this wood:	"	135
The *m*, my lover, with whom I rode	"	141
that Rosamond, whom *men* call fair,	"	251
m more pure and bold and just	To J. S.	31
m may speak the thing he will; 'You ask me why,'		8
part by part to *men* reveal'd 'Of old sn't Freedom,'		11
Bear seed of *men* 'Love thou thy land,' etc.		20
Nature's evil star Drive *men*	"	74
sitting, served by *m* and maid,	The Goose	21
why should any *m* Remodel models?	The Epic	37
King Arthur's table, *m* by *m*,	M. d'Arthur	3
They sleep—the *men* I loved.	"	17
little thing may harm a wounded *m*.	"	42
mighty bones of ancient *men*,	"	47
shameful thing for *men* to lie.	"	78
pleased the eyes of many *men*.	"	91
old *m* speak in the aftertime	"	107
for a *m* may fail in duty twice,	"	129
live three lives of mortal *men*	"	155
Among new *men*, strange faces,	"	238
men better than sheep or goats	"	250
loved the *m*, and prized his work;	" Ep.	8
Francis, muttering, like a *m* ill-used,	"	12
dream Dream'd by a happy *m*,	Gardener's D.	71
sight to make an old *m* young	"	140

	POEM.	LINE.		POEM.	LINE.
Then the old *m* Was wroth,	*Dora*	22	kind of tales did *men* tell *men*	*Princess, Pro.*	193
none of all his *men* Dare tell him	"	73	Between the rougher voices of the *men*	"	237
and he left his *men* at work,	"	84	in the midst of *men* and day,	" i.	15
he died at peace With all *men*;	"	142	would send a hundred thousand *men*	"	63
the old *m* burst in sobs:—	"	155	Whom all *men* rate as kind	"	70
clung about The old *m's* neck,	"	160	little dry old *m*, without a star,	"	116
all the *m* was broken with remorse;	"	161	woman were an equal to the *m*.	"	130
hid his face From all *men*,	*Walk. to the M.*	15	being an easy *m*, gave it:	"	148
You saw the *m*—on Monday, was it?—	"	22	see no *men*, Not ev'n her brother	"	151
Like *men*, like manners:	"	55	against all rules For any *m* to go;	"	177
know we of the secret of a *m*?	"	94	close upon the Sun, Than our *m's* earth;	" ii.	23
When *men* knew how to build,	*Ed. Morris*	7	barren verbiage, current among *men*,	"	40
God made the woman for the *m*,	"	43, 90, 91	tricks, which make us toys of *men*,	"	49
M is made of solid stuff.	"	42	three years to speak with any *men*,	"	58
yourself alone Of all *men* happy.	"	78	not of those that *men* desire,	"	62
m hath suffer'd more than I.	*St S. Stylites*	48	then the monster, then the *m*	"	104
men on earth House in the shade	"	104	that which made Woman and *m*.	"	129
what a *m* I am; A sinful *m*,	"	119	learn whatever *men* were taught:	"	130
by surname, Stylites, among *men*;	"	159	Some *men's* were small: not they		
if there be a priest, a *m* of God,	"	212	the least of *men*;	"	132
love, that makes me thrice a *m*,	*Talking O.*	11	thence the *m's*, if more was more,	"	135
To that *m* My work shall answer,	*Love and Duty* 28		The highest is the measure of the *m*	"	141
for a *m* is not as God,	"	30	Sappho and others vied with any *m*:	"	148
most Godlike being most a *m*.	"	31	NO *M* ENTER IN ON PAIN OF DEATH?	"	178
m feel strong in speaking truth;	"	68	on the blanching bones of *men*!'.	"	182
light shall spread, and *m* be liker *m*	*Golden Year*	35	the wisest *m* Feasted the woman.	"	329
all *men's* good Be each *m's* rule,	"	47	The total chronicles of *m*,	"	359
cities of *men* And manners	*Ulysses*	13	Abate the stride, which speaks of *m*,	"	407
men that strove with Gods.	"	53	might a *m* not wander from his wits.	"	417
In the Spring a young *m's* fancy	*Locksley H.*	20	*Men* hated learned women:	"	442
in among the throngs of *men*;	"	116	Girls? more like *men*!'	" iii.	27-33
Men, my brothers, *men* the workers,	"	117	*men* for still My mother went revolving	"	37
In the Parliament of *m*,	"	128	so they are—very like *men* indeed—	"	39
And the thoughts of *men* are widen'd	"	138	'Why—these—are—*men*.'	"	42
Woman is the lesser *m*,	"	151	noble than three score of *men*,	"	93
held it better *men* should perish	"	179	phrase well-roll'd, As *m's* could be;	"	118
New *men*, that in the flying of a wheel	*Godiva*	6	deals in that Which *men* delight in,	"	200
in the sixth she moulded *m*.	*Two Voices*	18	an even pedestal with *m*.'	"	208
men, thro' novel spheres of thought	"	61	move, my friend, At no *m's* beck,	"	211
dared not tarry,' *men* will say,	"	101	assail this gray preëminence of *m*!	"	218
on the fear of ill The fear of *men*,	"	108	*men* may pluck them from our hearts,	"	240
Do *men* love thee?	"	109	lived and roar'd Before *m* was.	"	278
Art thou so bound To *men*,	"	110	willing *men* should come among us,	"	301
men with knowledge merely play'd	"	172	all the *men* mourn'd at his side:	"	335
dreamer, deaf and blind. Named *m*,	"	176	voice and vague, fatal to *men*,	" iv.	46
joy that mixes *m* with Heaven:	"	210	Knaves are *men*, That lute and flute	"	110
if *m* rot in dreamless ease,	"	280	*men* grew to rate us at our worth,	"	127
sat upon the knees of *men*	"	323	questioned if she knew us *men*,	"	212
till thou wert also *m*;	"	327	stronger than *men*, Huge women.	"	259
in trances, *men* Forget the dream	"	352	*men* will say We did not know	"	337
men, whose reason long was blind,	"	370	hold the woman is the better *m*;	"	390
truth that sways the souls of *men*!	*Day-Dm.*	72	I bear, Tho' *m*, yet human	"	405
any *m* that walks the mead,	"	205	A *m* I came to see you;	"	421
silence from the paths of *men*;	"	218	many a famous *m* and woman,	"	425
nature first was fresh to *men*,	*Amphion*	57	more than poor *men* wealth,	"	439
blade carves the casques of *men*,	*Sir Galahad*	1	becomes no *m* to nurse despair,	"	444
child's heart within the *m's*	*Will Water.*	31	that *men* were in the very walls,	"	464
Which vexes public *men*,	"	44	Then *men* had said—but now—	"	512
Half-views of *men* and things.	"	52	make yourself a *m* to fight with *men*,	" v.	34
earth is rich in *m* and maid;	"	65	might that *m* not deserve of me.	"	101
From misty *men* of letters;	"	190	she laughs at you and *m*;	"	112
You shadow forth to distant *men*,	*To E. L.*	7	*M* is the hunter; woman is his game:	"	147
keep the best *m* under the sun	*Lady Clare*	31	defiance down Gagelike to *m*,	"	170
If there be any faith in *m*.'	"	44	the piebald miscellany, *m*,	"	190
m will cleave unto his right.'	"	46	had I seen Such thews of *men*:	"	246
A *m* had given all other bliss,	*Sir L. and Q. G.*	42	home is in the sinews of a *m*,	"	257
gap-tooth'd *m* as lean as death,	*Vision of Sin*	60	talk'd down the fifty wisest *men*,	"	284
Every moment dies a *m*,	"	97, 121	highest Form of *men's* deeds—	"	310
We are *men* of ruin'd blood;	"	99	in sleeker times With smoother *men*:	"	315
All the windy ways of *men*	"	132, 168	set my face Against all *men*,	"	379
Buss me, thou rough sketch of *m*,	"	189	Far off from *men* I built a fold	"	380
Dregs of life, and lees of *m*:	"	205	sole *men* to be mingled with our cause	"	401
men and horses pierced with worms,	"	209	The sole *men* we shall prize	"	402
tongue no *m* could understand:	"	222	this Egypt-plague of *men*!	"	417
m with knobs and wires and vials	*Princess, Pro.* 65		When the *m* wants weight, the woman	"	434
men and maids Arranged a country	"	83	*M* for the field, and woman	"	437
tutor, rough to common *men*	"	114	*M* for the sword, and for the needle	"	438
men have done it: how I hate you	"	130	*M* with the head, and woman with the	"	439
Far off from *men* a college like a *m'r*,	"	135	*M* to command and woman to obey;	"	440
teach them all that *men* are taught;	"	136	large-moulded *m*, His visage all agrin	"	509
never *m*, I think, So moulder'd	"	179	bridges for the use of *men*.	" vi.	31

	POEM.	LINE.
look'd At the arm'd *m* sideways,	*Princess*, vi.	141
These *men* are hard upon us	"	181
Ida—'sdeath! you blame the *m*;	"	204
men see Two women faster welded	"	235
maids, That have no links with *men*,	"	274
men came to woo Your Highness.	"	308
Whatever *m* lies wounded	"	316
The common *men* with rolling eyes;	"	340
men Darkening her female field;	vii.	18
shining in upon the wounded *m*	"	46
random sweet on maid and *m*	"	71
sons of *men*, and barbarous laws	"	219-40
know The woman's cause is *m*'s;	"	243
out of Lethe scales with *m*	"	245
shares with *m* His nights, his days,	"	246
miserable, How shall *men* grow?	"	250
woman is not undevelopt *m*	"	259
as the *m* Sweet love were slain	"	260
m be more of woman, she of *m*;	"	264
at the last she set herself to *m*	"	269
the statelier Eden back to *men*:	"	277
Interpreter between the Gods and *men*:	"	303
mask'd thee from *men*'s reverence	"	322
across the wild That no *m* knows.	"	342
So pray'd the *men*, the women;	" Con.	7
men required that I should give	"	10
Perchance upon the future *m*:	"	109
madest Life in *m* and brute	*In Mem. Pro.*	6
madest *m*, he knows not why;	"	10
merit lives from *m* to *m*	"	35
not from *m*, O Lord, to thee.	"	36
men may rise on stepping-stones	" i.	3
'Behold the *m* who loved and lost,	"	15
Beats out the little lives of *men*,	" ii.	8
travell'd *men* from foreign lands;	" x.	6
human-hearted *m* I loved,	" xiii.	11
m I held as half-divine;	" xiv.	10
made me that delirious *m*	" xvi.	17
melt the waxen hearts of *men*.'	" xxi.	8
sat the Shadow fear'd of *m*;	" xxii.	7
Behold a *m* raised up by Christ!	" xxxi.	13
some voice that *m* could trust	" xxxv.	1
M dies; nor is there hope in dust?'	"	4
So then were nothing lost to *m*;	" xlii.	9
here the *m* is more and more	" xliii.	7
Had *m* to learn himself anew	" xliv.	15
were such as *men* might scorn;	" xlvii.	4
men the flies of latter spring,	" xlix.	10
A sober *m*, among his boys,	" lii.	2
grain by which a *m* may live?	"	8
M, her last work, who seem'd so fair,	" lv.	9
first form was made a *m*;	" lx.	10
As some divinely gifted *m*,	" lxiii.	2
men and minds, the dust of change,	" lxx.	10
path that each *m* trod Is dim,	" lxxii.	9
sometimes in a dead *m*'s face,	" lxxiii.	1
A *m* upon a stall may find,	" lxxvi.	9
stay'd in peace with God and *m*.	" lxxix.	8
labour fills The lips of *men*	" lxxxiii.	26
mighty hopes that make us *men*.	" lxxxv.	36
The picturesque of *m* and *m*.'	" lxxxviii.	42
the *m* whose thoughts would hold	" xciii.	3
dead *m* touch'd me from the past,	" xciv.	34
wants Gnarr at the heels of *men*,	" xcvii.	17
Day, when I lost the flower of *men*;	" xcviii.	4
m we loved was there on deck,	" cii.	41
thrice as large as *m* he bent.	"	42
Ring in the valiant *m* and free,	" cv.	29
seize and throw the doubts of *m*;	" cviii.	6
men of rathe and riper years;	" cix.	2
mix With *men* and prosper!	" cxiii.	3
at the last arose the *m*;	" cxvii.	12
What matters Science unto *men*,	" cxix.	7
wiser *m* who springs Hereafter	"	9
thro' the questions *men* may try,	" cxxiii.	7
like a *m* in wrath the heart	"	15
What is, and no *m* understands;	"	22
reach thro' nature, moulding *m*.	"	24
Result in *m*, be born and think,	" Con.	126
Whereof the *m*, that with me trod	"	137
old *m*, now lord of the broad estate	*Maud*, I. i.	19

	POEM.	LINE.
the works of the *men* of mind,	*Maud*, I. i.	25
only not all *men* lie;	"	35
whether woman or *m* be the worse.	"	75
I keep but a *m* and a maid,	" iv.	19
We are puppets, *M* in his pride,	"	25
we *men* are a little breed.	"	30
have gone to the making of *m*;	"	35
m of science himself is fonder	"	37
desire or admire, if a *m* could learn it,	"	41
Singing of *men* that in battle array,	" v.	8
often a *m*'s own angry pride	" vi.	61
Men were drinking together,	" vii.	5
Strange, that I hear two *men*,	"	13
power that all *men* adore,	" x.	14
For a *m* and leader of *men*.	"	59
Ah God, for a *m* with heart	"	60
still strong in *m* in a blatant land,	"	63
And ah for a *m* to arise in me,	"	67
the *m* I am may cease to be.	"	68
old *m* never comes to his place;	" xiii.	24
Till the red *m* dance	" xvii.	17
And the red *m*'s babe Leap.	"	61
brand His nothingness into *m*.	" xviii.	40
Love, like *men* in drinking-songs,	"	55
that dead *m* at her heart and mine;	" xix.	9
To the *men* of many acres,	" xx.	32
a learned *m* Could give it	" II. ii.	9
Like a shipwreck'd *m* on a coast	"	31
cannot even bury a *m*;	" v.	22
dead *m* there to a spectral bride;	"	80
what will the old *m* say?	"	83
men may come and *men* may go, (rep.)	*The Brook*	33
knew the *m*; the colt would fetch	"	149
Henceforth I trust the *m* alone,	*The Letters*	31
lay the *m* whom we deplore?	*Ode on Well.*	8
for the *m* of long-enduring blood,	"	24
for the *m* of amplest influence,	"	27
gray head which all *men* knew,	"	35
their omens all *men* drew,	"	36
A *m* of well-attemper'd frame.	"	74
loves thee well, thou famous *m*,	"	85
blare of bugle, clamour of *men*,	"	115
all *men* else their nobler dreams	"	152
great *men* who fought, and kept it ours	"	158
spoke among you, and the *M* who spoke	"	178
More than is of *m*'s degree	"	242
Godlike *men* we build our trust.	"	266
any wreath that *m* can weave him.	"	277
Dear to the *m* that is dear to God;	*To F.D. Maurice*	36
Was there a *m* dismay'd?	*Lt. Brigade*	10
Was ever *m* so grandly made	*Enid*	81
poor cause that *men* Reproach you	"	87
For all my pains, poor *m*,	"	116
makes a *m*, in the sweet face of her	"	122
m Not turning round, nor looking	"	269
like a *m* abroad at morn	"	335
liquid note beloved of *men*	"	336
m is *m* and master of his fate.	"	355
your town, where all the *men* are mad;	"	418
a name far-sounded among *men*,	"	427
since the proud *m* often is the mean,	"	449
men who served About my person,	"	453
have let *men* be, and have their way	"	466
in this tournament can no *m* tilt,	"	480
fallen *m* Made answer, groaning,	"	575
men have seen my fall.'	"	578
cry That Edyrn's *men* were on them,	"	639
Edyrn's *men* had caught them	"	642
Never *m* rejoiced More than Geraint	"	771
Men saw the goodly hills of Somerset,	"	828
purblind people of miserable *men*,	"	850
m upon his tongue May break it,	"	891
like a *m* That skins the wild beast	"	941
every *m* were larger-limbed than I,	"	997
if I fall, cleave to the better *m*.'	"	1001
So lay the *m* transfixt	"	1015
tell him How great a *m* you are	"	1077
loves to know When *men* of mark	"	1078
return With victual for these *men*	"	1087
wild *men* supporters of a shield	"	1116
what *men* soever were his friends,	"	1135

	POEM.	LINE.
men may bicker with the things,	Enid	1174
this *m* loves you no more.	"	1178
m's love once gone never returns.	"	1182
moving homeward babbled to his *men*,	"	1211
Enid never loved a *m* but him,	"	1212
Seeing that you are wedded to a *m*,	"	1274
at the flash and motion of the *m*.	"	1316
if a *m* who stands upon the brink	"	1321
Scared but at the motion of the *m*,	"	1325
'Horse and *m*,' he said, 'All of one	"	1332
m to whom a dreadful loss Falls.	"	1345
charger stood, grieved like a *m*.	"	1384
to lose, and all for a dead *m*,	"	1412
their lost time, and the dead *m*,	"	1424
men brought in whole hogs.	"	1450
Good luck had your good *m*,	"	1465
yonder *m* upon the bier arise,	"	1505
yonder *m* is surely dead:	"	1520
Until himself arise a living *m*,	"	1554
men and women in the hall Rose	"	1579
when they saw the dead *m* rise,	"	1580
used you worse than that dead *m*;	"	1583
men and women staring aghast,	"	1652
men may fear Fresh fire and ruin.	"	1671
true eyes Beheld the *m* you loved	"	1695
weds with manhood, makes a *m*..	"	1716
world will not believe a *m* repents:	"	1748
Full seldom does a *m* repent,	"	1750
as now *Men* weed the white horse	"	1784
a thousand men To till the wastes,	"	1789
the great Prince and *m* of men..	"	1809
most famous *m* of all those men,	*Vivien*.	22
old *m*, Tho' doubtful, felt the flattery,	"	39
m so wrought on ever seem'd to lie	"	57
none could find that *m* for evermore,	"	60
ruin'd *m* Thro' woman the first hour;	"	212
was to be, for love of God and *men*	"	262
Lo now, what hearts have men!	"	292
'*M* dreams of Fame while woman	"	310
Fame with men Being but ampler	"	338
for *men* sought to prove me vile,	"	345
good *m* jealous with good cause.	"	455
new lord, her own, the first of *men*.	"	467
little glassy-headed hairless *m*,	"	470
sunders ghosts and shadow-casting men	"	479
here was the *m*. And so by force	"	489
that no *m* could see her more,	"	492
old *m* Went back to his old wild	"	493
you are *m*, you well can understand	"	547
sweet Sir Sagramore, That ardent *m*?	"	572
whole prey Is *m*'s good name;	"	579
stainless *m* beside a stainless maid;	"	587
'A sober *m* is Percivale	"	605
Arthur, blameless King and stainless *m*?'	"	628
'Him? is he *m* at all,	"	630
selfless *m* and stainless gentleman,	"	641
fain Have all *men* true and leal,	"	643
men at most differ as Heaven	"	663
that I had loved a smaller *m*!	"	721
loved to make men darker.	"	725
worship is allowed Of all *men*:	*Elaine*.	112
swearing men to vows impossible,	"	131
men go down before your spear	"	147-577
old, dumb, myriad-wrinkled *m*,	"	170
Lancelot marvell'd at the wordless *m*;	"	172
he seem'd the goodliest *m*,	"	254
kindly *m* moving among his kind:	"	265
speaking of the wordless *m*	"	271
thro' all hindrance finds the *m*	"	332
if seven *men* had set upon him,	"	350
I am not great: There is the *m*.'	"	451
a *m* far-off might well perceive	"	457
any *m* that day were left afield,	"	458
Strong *men*, and wrathful that a stranger	"	467
grace and versatility of the *m*--	"	471
hide his name From all *men*	"	580
our Lancelot! that true *m*!'	"	662
true *m* change like a leaf at last?	"	683
since *m*'s first fall Did kindlier unto *m*,	"	855
sick *m* forgot her simple blush,	"	860
m and woman when they love their best	"	865

	POEM.	LINE.
Another world for the sick *m*;	*Elaine*	870
no *m* there will dare to mock	"	1047
mine to love Him of all *men*	"	1071
noble *m* but made ignoble talk.	"	1082
bid call the ghostly *m*	"	1093
ghostly *m* had come and gone,	"	1095
dumb old *m* alone Go with me,	"	1121
men Shape to their fancy's eye	"	1244
then turn'd the tongueless *m*	"	1254
a *m* Made to be loved;	"	1355
now a lonely *m* Wifeless and heirless,	"	1361
men worse by making my sin known?	"	1407
a *m* Not after Arthur's heart!	"	1409
Not knowing he should die a holy *m*	"	1419
king's blood in a bad *m*,	*Guinevere*.	38
if a *m* were halt or hunch'd,	"	42
feast As never *m* had dream'd:	"	202
so glad were spirits and *men*	"	267
prophets were they all, Spirits and *men*:	"	271
King, As well-nigh more than *m*,	"	285
no *m* knew from whence he came;	"	287
mystery From all *men*, like his birth;	"	296
most nobly-manner'd *men* of all;	"	332
the best knight and goodliest *m*,	"	379
True *men* who love me still,	"	442
glorious company, the flower of *men*	"	461
keep down the base in *m*	"	476
love of truth, and all that makes a *m*.	"	479
that *m* the worst of public foes	"	508
new disease, unknown to *men*,	"	514
worst were that *m* he that reigns!	"	519
no *m* dream but that I love thee.	"	556
men look'd upon him favourably:	*En. Arden*.	56
grave and staid God-fearing *m*,	"	112
he knew the *m* and valued him,	"	121-185
the best among us--a strong *m*:	"	292
wed the *m* so dear to all of them.	"	481
Surely the *m* had died of solitude.	"	622
men Levied a kindly tax	"	663
Pitying the lonely *m*,	"	665
yet a bed for wandering *men*.	"	699
dead *m* come to life beheld	"	759
lightly as a sick *m*'s chamber-door,	"	777
life in it Whereby the *m* could live:	"	822
gradually Weakening the *m*,	"	826
night high, and cared for no *m*, he.'	"	849
head is low, and no *m* cares for him	"	851
I am the *m*.'	"	853
Sir Aylmer Aylmer that almighty *m*	*Aylmer's F*.	13
sons of *men* Daughters of God;	"	44
men shall lash you from them	"	325
the fierce old man Follow'd	"	330
m was his, had been his father's	"	344
known a *m*, a quintessence of *m*,	"	388
allowance must be made for *men*.	"	410
hearts of *men* Seem'd harder too;	"	453
haunt a wound, or deer, or *men*,	"	571
a dead *m*, a letter edged with death	"	595
thy brother *m*, the Lord from Heaven,	"	667
often placed upon the sick *m*'s brow	"	700
the *m* became Imbecile;	"	835
(for the *m* Had risk'd his little)	*Sea Dreams*	9
simple Christ to simple *men*,	"	21
musing on the little lives of *men*,	"	48
neither God nor *m* can well forgive,	"	63
surely lives in *m* and beast.	"	68
m is likewise counsel for himself.	"	178
men and women in dark clusters.	"	219
men of flesh and blood, and *men* of stone	"	230
dead?' 'The *m* your eye pursued.	"	262
devil in *m*, there is an angel too,	"	267
strong on his legs, he looks like a *m*	*Grandmother*	2
father was not the *m* to save,	"	5
Never a *m* could fling him;	"	10
Willy stood up like a *m*,	"	45
he cheer'd me, my good *m*,	"	69
Kind, like a *m*, was he;	"	70
like a *m*, too, would have his way:	"	70
and now they're elderly *men*.	"	88
God, not *m*, is the Judge of us	"	95
I weäänt saäy *men* be loiars,	*N. Farmer*.	27

	POEM.	LINE.
M comes and tills the field	Tithonus	3
this gray shadow, once a *m*	"	11
wealthy *men* who care not how	"	17
Why should a *m* desire in any way	"	28
vary from the kindly race of *men*	"	29
happy *men* that have the power to die,	"	70
each *m* murmur'd 'O my Queen	The Voyage	63
phantom bodies of horses and *men*;	Boädicea	27
Burnt in each *m's* blood.	The Captain	16
Blood and brains of *men*.	"	48
dead *men* lay all over the way,	The Victim	21
If *men* neglect your pages?	Spiteful Let.	6
brute brain within the *m's*	Lucretius	21
m may gain Letting his own life go.	"	112
Gods there are, for all *men* so believe	"	117
wrath were wreak'd on wretched *m*,	"	128
men like soldiers may not quit	"	148
as the hopes and fears of *men*.	"	180
what *m*, What Roman would be dragg'd	"	230
beginnings that have made me *m*	"	242
into *m* once more, Or beast, or bird,	"	244
not so far when momentary *m*	"	249
How roughly *men* may woo thee.	"	269
Bird's love and *men's* love (rep.)	The Window	68
And women's love and *men's!*	"	79
After-loves of maids and *men*	"	130

manage.

| Hadn't a head to *m*, | Grandmother | 6 |

man and wife.

often thought, 'I'll make them *m a w*.'	Dora	4
Lord Ronald's, When you are *m a w*.'	Lady Clare	36
Our bond, as not the bond of *m a w*,	Elaine 1:185, 200

man-at-arms.

| Another hurrying past, a *m-a-a*, | Enid | 1375 |

man-breasted.

| strong *m-b* things stood from the sea, | Guinevere | 244 |

mane.

To break my chain, to shake my *m*:	Princess, ii.	402
long locks play the Lion's *m !*	" vi.	148
darkness from their loosen'd *m's*,	Tithonus	41

manful.

| very base Or very *m*, | Enid | 469 |

manfulness.

| he, from his exceeding *m* | Enid | 211 |

man-girdled.

| Than thus *m-g* here: | Princess, v. | 419 |

mangled.

| *M*, and flatten'd and crush'd, | Maud, I. i. | 7 |

manhood.

evil star Drive men in *m*,	'Love thou thy land,'	74
The darling of my *m*,	Gardener's D.	272
more Than growing boys their *m*;	Princess, iv.	437
Accomplish thou my *m* and thyself;	" vii.	344
civic *m* firm against the crowd—	Con.	57
The highest, holiest *m*, thou;	InMem.Pro.	14
truths in *m* darkly join,	" xxxvi.	1
wears his *m* hale and green:	" lii.	4
m fused with female grace	" cviii.	17
glory of *m* stand on his ancient	Maud,III.vi.	21
prince whose *m* was all gone,	Enid	59
when it weds with *m*, makes a man.	"	1716
popular name such *m* earns,	Vivien	636
grow In use of arms and *m*,	Elaine	65
as great As he was in his *m*,	Guinevere	298

maniac.

| Time, a *m* scattering dust, | In Mem. xlix. | 7 |

man-in-God.

| God-in-man is one with *m-i-G*, | En. Arden. | 187 |

mankind.

like Gods together, careless of *m*.	Lotos-E's.	155
Altho' I be the basest of *m*,	St S. Stylites	7
my fame is loud amongst *m*,	"	80
make me an example to *m*,	"	185
in the thoughts that shake *m*.	Locksley H.	160

	POEM.	LINE.
in the tents with coarse *m*,	Princess, vi.	53
had been wedded wife, I knew *m*,	"	307
Peace and goodwill, to all *m*.	In Mem. xxviii.	12
This bitter seed among *m*;	" lxxxix.	4
Ring in redress to all *m*.	" cv.	12
each is at war with *m*.	Maud, I. x.	52
saving that, ye help to save *m*	Ode on Well.	166
while the races of *m* endure,	"	219
ampler means to serve *m*,	Vivien	339
golden hopes for France and all *m*,	Aylmer's F.	464

manlike.

| rued His rash intrusion, *m*, | Princess, iv. | 186 |
| *m* end myself?—our privilege— | Lucretius | 229 |

man-minded.

| When his *m-m* offset rose | Talking O. | 51 |

manners.

Her *m* had not that repose	L. C. V. de Vere	39
Like men, like *m*:	Walk. to the M.	55
Kind nature is the best: those *m* next	"	56
are indeed the *m* of the great.	"	58
cities of men, And *m*, climates,	Ulysses	14
the *m* of your countrywomen?	Princess, iv.	133
sweeter *m*, purer laws.	In Mem. cv.	16
To noble *m*, as the flower	" cx.	15
By the coldness of her *m*	Maud, I. xx.	13
M so kind, yet stately,	Enid	1709
tenderness Of *m* and of nature:	Elaine	328
father's memory, one Of noblest *m*,	Guinevere	317
For *m* are not idle,	"	333
'be *m* such fair fruit?	"	335

mansion.

have bought A *m* incorruptible.	Deserted H.	21
this old *m* mounted high	Miller's D.	35
this great *m*, that is built for me,	Pal. of Art	19
My spacious *m* built for me,	"	234
Sees a *m* more majestic	L. of Burleigh	45
In an ancient *m's* crannies	Maud, II. v.	61

mantle (s.)

sweet Europa's *m* blew unclasp'd,	Pal. of Art	117
m's from the golden pegs Droop	Day-Dm.	39
His *m* glitters on the rocks—	"	106
her blooming *m* torn,	Princess, vi.	129
spread his *m* dark and cold,	In Mem. xxii.	14
A faded *m* and a faded veil,	Enid	135
brought a *m* down and wrapt her in it,	"	824
vast and shaggy *m* of his beard	Vivien	105

mantle (verb.)

| Nor bowl of wassail *m* warm; | In Mem. civ. | 18 |

many-blossoming.

| *m-b* Paradises, | Boädicea | 43 |

many-colour'd.

| The dusky-rafter'd *m-c* Hall, | Enid | 362 |

many-corridor'd.

| *m-c* complexities Of Arthur's palace: | Vivien | 582 |

many-fountain'd.

| *m-f* Ida. | OEnone 22, et pass. |

many-headed.

| The *m-h* beast should know. 'You might have won' | 20 |

many-knotted.

| There in the *m-h* waterflags, | M. d'Arthur | 63 |

many-shielded.

| Have also set his *m-s* tree? | Aylmer's F. | 48 |

many-sided.

| all forms Of the *m-s* mind, | Ode to Mem. | 116 |

many-tower'd.

| To *m-t* Camelot; | L. of Shalott, i. | 5 |

many-winter'd.

| As the *m-w* crow that leads | Locksley H. | 68 |
| *m-w* fleece of throat and chin. | Vivien | 690 |

maple.

| This *m* burn itself away; | In Mem. c. | 4 |

mar.	POEM.	LINE.
scorn At him that *m*'s her plan,	*Princess*, v.	126
whatever tempest *m*'s Mid-ocean,	*In Mem.* xvii.	13
m a comely face with idint tears	*Enid* .	1399
m this little by their feuds. .	*Sea Dreams*	49
m Their sacred everlasting calm,	*Lucretius* .	109
Nothing to *m* the sober majesties	" .	214

marble.

Stiller than chisell'd *m*,	*D. of F. Wom.*	86
As blank as death in *m*;	*Princess*, i.	175
Compact with lucid *m*'s,	" ii.	10
I will melt this *m* into wax	" iii.	57
half-shrouded over death In deathless *m.*"	v.	72
virgin *m* under iron heels:	" vi.	331
Thy *m* bright in dark appears,	*In Mem.* lxvi.	5
as her image in *m* above:	*Maud*, I. iv.	58
A mount of *m*, a hundred spires!	*The Daisy* .	60

march (s.)

ebb and flow conditioning their *m*,	*Golden Year*	30
enjoyment more than in this *m* of mind,	*Locksley II.*	165
raw world for the *m* of mind,	*Ode on Well.*	168

March (month.)

thro' wild *M* the throstle calls,	*To the Queen*	14
ashbuds in the front of *M*'.	*Gardener's D.*	28
Came to the hammer here in *M*—	*Audley Ct.*	59
Flits by the sea-blue bird of *M*;	*In Mem.* xc.	4
the wreath of *M* has blossom'd,	*To F. D. Maurice*	43
swallows in the windy gleams of *M*:	*Vivien* .	74
ye bells, in the merry *M* air!	*W. to Alexan.*	18

march (verb.)

fight and *m* and countermarch,	*Audley Ct.* .	39
M with banner and bugle and fife	*Maud*, I. v.	10
that I *m* to meet my doom. .	*Guinevere* .	447

marches.

And there defend his *m*;	*Enid* .	41, 1738
past The *m*, and by bandit-haunted	" .	879
Lords of waste *m*,	*Elaine* .	526

March-morning.

All in the wild *M-m* I heard . *May Queen*, iii. 25

March-wind.

whenever a *M-w* sighs . . *Maud*, I. xxii. 40

mare.

made a point to post with *m*'s;	*Princess*, i.	187
the gray *m* Is ill to live with,	" v.	441

Margaret.

There's *M* and Mary, there's Kate	*May Queen*, i.	6
O sweet pale *M*, O rare pale *M*,	*Margaret*	1, 54
What can it matter, *M*,	"	32
Exquisite *M*, who can tell .	"	36
One babe was theirs, a *M*, .	*Sea Dreams*	3
Their *M* cradled near them,	"	57
glass with little *M*'s medicine	"	138
cry Which mixt with little *M*'s,	"	238

marge.

round about the fragrant *m*.	*Arabian N's.*	59
stiff and dry about the *m*. .	*M. d'Arthur*	64
About the windings of the *m*	*Ed. Morris.*	94
linger weeping on the *m*,	*In Mem.* xii.	12
clear from *m* to *m* shall bloom	" xlv.	7
A rosy warmth from *m* to *m*.	"	16
every page having an ample *m*,	*Vivien* .	519
every *m* enclosing in the midst	" .	520

margin.

By the *m*, willow-veil'd,	*L. of Shalott*, i.	19
A id bear me to the *m*;	*M. d'Arthur*	165
world, whose *m* fades For ever	*Ulysses* .	20
Comes a vapour from the *m*,	*Locksley II.*	191
every *m* scribbled, crost, and cramm'd	*Vivien* .	527

mariner.

Slow sail'd the weary *m*'s .	*Sea-Fairies* .	1
M, *m*, furl your sails, .	" .	21
m, *m*, fly no more .	" .	42
Oh rest ye, brother *m*'s,	*Lotos-E's.* .	173
My *m*'s, Souls that have toil'd	*Ulysses* .	45

marish.

thro' the *m* green and still . *Dying Swan* 18

marish-flowers.	POEM.	LINE.
the silvery *m-f* that throng .	*Dying Swan*	40

marish-mosses.

The cluster'd *m-m* crept. . . *Mariana* . 40

marish-pipe.

moss and braided with *m-p* . . *On a Mourner* 10

mark (s.)

he thought himself A *m* for all,	*Walk. to the M.*	65
thou,' said I, 'hast miss'd thy *m*,	*Two Voices*	388
push beyond her *m*, and be Procuress	*In Mem.* lii.	15
No single tear, no *m* of pain:	" lxxvii.	14
master-bowman, he, Would cleave the *m*.	lxxxvi.	30
men of *m* are in his territory:	*Enid* .	1078
stamp him with her master's *m*;	*Vivien* .	609
aim'd All at one *m*, all hitting:	*Aylmer's F.*	95

mark (verb.)

no other tree did *m* The level waste,	*Mariana* .	43
I will stand and *m*. . .	*To J. M. K.*	14
vague in vapour, hard to *m*; 'Love thou thy land'		62
m The landscape winking .	*In Mem.* lxxxviii.	15
m me and understand, .	*En. Arden.*	877
m me! for your fortunes are to make	*Aylmer's F.*	300

marked.

m it with the red cross to the fall,	*Princess*, vi.	25
m as with some hideous crime,	*In Mem.* lxxi.	18
saw me not, or *m* not if you saw:	*Enid* .	1718
Vivien follow'd, but he *m* her not;	*Vivien* .	48
his face, and *m* it ere his time, .	*Elaine* .	247
m Sir Lancelot where he moved apart, "		1339
wave, Returning while none *m* it,	*Sea Dreams*	227

market.

Enrich the *m*'s of the golden year.	*Golden Year*	46
all the *m*'s overflow. . .	*Locksley II.*	101
Thro' the hubbub of the *m* I steal	*Maud*, II. iv.	63
Quaint monsters for the *m* .	*En. Arden* .	535
across the *m* to his death, .	*Aylmer's F.*	820

market-cross.

Not only to the *m-c* were known, *En. Arden* . 96

market-night.

'ed my quart ivry *m-n* . . *N. Farmer* . 8

marr'd.

what follows? war; Your own work *m*:	*Princess*, ii.	212
at our books, and *m* our peace,	" v.	385
Had *m* his face, and mark'd it .	*Elaine* .	247
M as he was, he seem'd the goodliest	" .	254
However *m*, of more than twice	" .	257
M her friend's point . .	" .	729
knew the Prince, tho' *m* with dust,	*Guinevere* .	37
beat me down, and *m* and wasted me,	*Tithonus* .	19

marriage.

laws of *m* character'd in gold	*Isabel* .	16
The queen of *m*, a most perfect wife	" .	28
I have wish'd this *m*, night and day,	*Dora* .	19
true *m* lies Nor equal, nor unequal:	*Princess*, vii.	284
Her slow consent and *m*, .	*En. Arden* .	700
was an Aylmer-Averill once .	*Aylmer's F.*	42
m's are made in Heaven.' .	" .	128
This blacksmith-border *m*—	" .	263
naked *m*'s Flash from the bridge,	" .	765

marriage day.

In that it is thy *m-d* . . *In Mem. Con.* 3

marriage-hindering.

filthy *m-h* Mammon made The harlot *Aylmer's F.* 374

marriage-maker.

For the maids and *m-m*'s, . *Maud*, I. xx. 35

marriage-morn.

move me to my *m-m*, . 'Move eastward, etc. 11

marriage-pillow.

To thy widow'd *m-p*'s, . *Locksley II.* 82

married.

I *m* late, but I would wish to see	*Dora* .	10
Who *m*, who was like to be, .	*Audley Ct.* .	29
are you *m* yet, Edward Gray?'	*Ed. Gray* .	4

	POEM.	LINE.
Had *m* Enid, Yniol's only child,	Enid	4
know you that I am he Who *m*—	En. Arden.	860
I *m* her who *m* Philip Ray..	"	861

marrow.

| *M* of mirth and laughter; | Will Water. | 214 |

marry.

Woo me, and win me, and *m* me,	The Mermaid	46
I cannot *m* Dora; (rep.)	Dora	21
learning unto them? They wish'd to *m*;	Princess, ii.	441
That *m* with the virgin heart.	In Mem. lxxxiv.	108
where the waters *m*—	The Brook	81
marries her *marries* her name.'	Aylmer's F.	25
twenty boys and girls should *m* on it,	"	371
But *m* me out of hand:	Grandmother	52
'*M* you, Willy!' said I,	"	53
Ask her to *m* me by and by?	The Window	91

marrying.

| could not ever rue his *m* me— | Dora | 143 |
| Driving, hurrying, *m*, burying, | Maud, II. v. | 12 |

Mars.

| pointed to *M* As he glow'd | Maud, III. vi. | 13 |

marsh.

| wild the waste enormous *m*, | Ode to Mem. | 101 |

marsh-diver.

| *m-d's*, rather, maid, Shall croak | Princess, iv. | 105 |

marsh-marigold.

| the wild *m-m* shines like fire | May Queen, i. | 31 |

mart.

| labour, and the changing *m*, | In Mem. lxxxvi. | 23 |

martin.

| Roof-haunting *m*'s warm their eggs: | Day-Dm. | 37 |
| The fire shot up, the *m* flew, | " | 143 |

martin-haunted.

| almost to the *m-h* eaves | Aylmer's F. | 163 |

Martin's summer.

| A *M s* of his faded love | Aylmer's F. | 560 |

martyr.

| all thy *m*'s die one death? | St S. Stylites | 49 |

martyr-flames.

| *m-f*, nor trenchant swords 'Clear-headed friend,' | 14 |

marvel (s.)

In *m* whence that glory came	Arabian N's.	94
The *m* of the everlasting will,	The Poet	7
No *m*, sovereign lady:	D. of F. Wom.	97
Had *m* what the maid might be,	Elaine	724

marvel (verb.)

'I *m* if my still delight	Pal. of Art	190
m what possess'd my brain:	In Mem. xiv.	16
I would not *m* at either,	Maud, I. iv.	40

marvell'd.

all My brethren *m* greatly.	St S. Stylites	68
I *m* how the mind was brought	Two Voices	458
Lancelot *m* at the wordless man:	Elaine	172

Mary (see *Morrison*.)

'Ave *M*,' made she moan, (rep.)	Mariana in the S.	9
There's Margaret and *M*, there's Kate	May Queen, i.	6
Dora went to *M*. *M* sat	Dora	54
M, for the sake of him that's gone,	"	60
Then Dora went to *M*'s house,	"	108
M saw the boy Was not with Dora.	"	109
M, let me live and work with you:	"	113
Dora hid her face By *M*.	"	154
M took another mate;	"	166
home to *M*'s house return'd,	In Mem. xxxi.	2

mask (s.)

college and her maidens, empty *m*'s,	Princess, iii.	171
I was half-oblivious of my *m*)	"	320
Last night, their *m* was patent,	" iv.	307
sleeps or wears the *m* of sleep,	In Mem. xviii.	10
mix with hollow *m*'s of night;	" lxix.	4
genial hour with *m* and mime;	" civ.	10

mask (verb.)

	POEM.	LINE.
m, tho' but in his own behoof,	Maud, I. vi.	48

mask'd.

'Albeit so *m*, Madam, I love the	Princess, ii.	195
M like our maids, blustering	" v.	386
m thee from men's reverence up,	" vii.	322

mason.

| Cloud-towers by ghostly *m*'s wrought | In Mem. lxix. | 5 |
| White from the *m*'s hand, | Enid | 244, 408 |

mason-work.

| It look'd a tower of ruin'd *m-w*, | Vivien | 4 |

masque.

| *m* or pageant at my father's court. | Princess, i. | 195 |

masquerade.

| A feudal knight in silken *m*, | Princess, Pro. | 227 |

mass (heap, etc.)

m'es thick with milky cones.	Miller's D..	56
pick'd offenders from the *m*	Princess, i.	29
That jewell'd *m* of millinery,	Maud, I. vi.	43
a manelike *m* of rolling gold,	Aylmer's F.	68

mass (the Eucharist.)

| heard *m*, broke fast, and rode away: | Elaine | 414 |
| gorgeous obsequies, And *m*, | " | 1326 |

massacre.

| whelm All of them in one *m*? | Lucretius | 204 |

massacred.

| moan of an enemy *m*, | Boädicea | 25 |

mast.

wind-scatter'd over sails and *m*'s,	D. of F. Wom.	31
high *m*'s flicker'd as they lay afloat;	"	113
Ruffle thy mirror'd *m*,	In Mem. ix.	7
clambering on a *m* In harbour,	En. Arden	105
Over *m* and deck were scatter'd	The Captain	47

master (s.)

church-harpies from the *m*'s feast;	To J. M. K.	3
you, not you,—the *M*, Love,	Gardener's D.	168
one the *M*, as a rogue in grain	Princess, Pro.	116
Where lies the *m* newly dead;	In Mem. xx.	4
loiter'd in the *m*'s field.	" xxxvii.	23
of old the Lord and *M* of Earth,	Maud, I. iv.	31
M of half a servile shire	" x.	10
doubling all his *m*'s vice of pride.	Enid	195
youth who scour'd His *m*'s armour;	"	258
man is man and *m* of his fate.	"	355
'Great *M*, do you love me?'	Vivien	86
O my *M*, have you found your voice?	"	118
'Nay, *m*, be not wrathful	"	230
O, *m*, do you love my tender rhyme?	"	249
you seem the *M* of all Art,	"	318
would make you *M* of all Vice.'.	"	319
the great *M* merrily answer'd	"	395
smiling as a *M* smiles at one	"	512
O *M*, shall we call him overquick	"	574
stamp him with her *m*'s mark;	"	609
With you for guide and *m*,	"	730
no more subtle *m* under heaven	Guinevere	474
Enoch stronger-made Was *m*:	En. Arden.	31
m of the ship Enoch had served in,	"	119
Become the *m* of a larger craft,	"	144
when he does, *M* of all.	Aylmer's F.	32
in flood And *m*'s of his motion,	"	340
to Lucretius, found Her *m* cold;	Lucretius	2
the *m* took Small notice,	"	7
My *m* held That Gods there are	"	116

master (verb.)

| *m*'s Time indeed, and is Eternal | In Mem. lxxxiv. | 65 |
| when his passion *m*'s him. | Enid | 892 |

master-bowman.

| the *m-b*, he, Would cleave the mark. | In Mem. lxxxvi. | 29 |

master-chord.

| the *m-c* Of all I felt and feel. | Will Water. | 27 |

masterdom.

| Contend for loving *m*.. | In Mem. ci. | 8 |

	POEM.	LINE.
master'd.		
m by some modern term; 'Love thou thy laud,' etc.		30
call them masterpieces: They *m* me.	*Princess,* i.	145
m by the sense of sport,	" iv.	138
involved and dazzled down And *m,*	"	431
such A friendship as had *m* Time;	*In Mem.*lxxxiv.	64
mastering.		
M the lawless science of our law,	*Aylmer's F.*	435
masterpiece.		
scarce can fail to match his *m.'*	*Gardener's D.*	31
No critic I—would call them *m's:*	*Princess,* i.	144
mast-head.		
like the mystic fire on a *m-h*	*Princess,* iv.	255
Mastodon.		
nature brings not back the *M,*	*The Epic*	36
mast-thronged.		
M-t beneath her shadowing citadel.	*Œnone*	116
match (an equal.)		
lighted on Queen Esther, has her *m.'*	*Enid*	731
match (marriage contract.)		
have set my heart upon a *m.*	*Dora*	12
Such a *m* as this! Impossible	*Aylmer's F.*	314
enough was theirs For twenty *m'es.*	"	370
match (verb.)		
fail to *m* his masterpiece.'	*Gardener's D.*	31
Will you *m* My Juliet?	"	167
May *m* his pains with mine;	*St S. Stylites*	137
find in loss a gain to *m!*	*In Mem.* i.	6
match'd.		
M with an aged wife,	*Ulysses*	3
all thy passions, *m* with mine,	*Locksley H.*	151
Were mellow music *m* with him.	*In Mem.* lv.	24
either's force was *m* till Yniol's cry,	*Enid*	570
mate (companion, etc.)		
Your pride is yet no *m* for mine,	*L. C. V. de Vere*	11
Mary took another *m;*	*Dora*	166
and crushing down his *m;*	*Princess,* ii.	106
That I shall be thy *m* no more,	*In Mem.* xl.	20
one that was his earliest *m;*	" lxiii.	24
Feeling from her on the Deed.	*The Brook*	95
weeping for her murder'd *m*	*Enid*	1371
in haste to join Their luckier *m's,*	"	1423
his *m* hereafter in the heavens	*Guinevere*	630
mate (officer.)		
m had seen at early dawn	*En. Arden.*	632
m is blind and captain lame,	*The Voyage*	91
mated.		
thou art *m* with a clown,	*Locksley H.*	47
M with a squalid savage—	"	177
matin-chirp.		
low *m-c* hath grown Full quire,	*Love and Duty*	95
matin-song.		
the first *m-s* hath waken'd loud	*Ode to Mem.*	68
By some wild skylark's *m-s.*	*Miller's D.*	40
matron.		
Perish'd many a maid and *m,*	*Boädicea*	85
matter ('s.)		
No *m* what the sketch might be;	*Ode to Mem.*	95
A goose—'twas no great *m.*	*The Goose.*	10
eat And talk'd old *m's* over;	*Audley Ct.*	28
I cannot make thy *m* plain,	*Two Voices*	343
dealing but with time, And he with *m,*	"	377
this *m* might be sifted clean.'	*Princess,* i.	79
is knowledge, and this *m* hangs:.	" iii.	299
many thousand *m's* left to do,	" iv.	438
m for a flying smile.	*In Mem.* lxi	12
rapt in *m's* dark and deep	" xcvi.	19
She knows but *m's* of the house,	"	31
What *m* if I go mad,	*Maud,* I xi.	6
that a *m* to make me fret?	" xiii.	2
and so the *m* hung:	*The Brook*	144-8
Till you should turn to dearer *m's*	*To F. D. Maurice*	35
once to me Mere *m* of the fancy,	*Vivien*	773
'what *m,* so I help him back	*Elaine*	763

	POEM.	LINE.
Lancelot told This *m* to the Queen,	*Guinevere*	54
on a *m* he of life and death:	*Sea Dreams*	147
is a harder *m* to fight.	*Grandmother*	32
M enough for deploring	*1865-1866*	8
matter (verb.)		
What can it *m,* Margaret,	*Margaret*	32
then What *m's* Science unto men,	*In Mem.* cxix.	7
'Care not thou! What *m's?*	*Lucretius*	277
matter-moulded.		
In *m-m* forms of speech,	*In Mem.* xciv.	46
matting.		
conscious of ourselves, Perused the *m:*	*Princess,* ii.	54
mattock-harden'd.		
labour and the *m-h* hand,	*Maud,* I. xviii.	34
mature (adj.)		
now is love *m* in ear.'	*In Mem.* lxxx.	4
mature (verb.)		
M's the individual form. 'Love thou thy land,' etc.		40
Maud.		
of the singular beauty of *M;*	*Maud,* I. i.	67
M with her venturous climbings	"	69
M the delight of the village,	"	70
M with her sweet purse-mouth	"	71
M the beloved of my mother	"	72
It will never be broken by *M,*	" ii.	2
Ah, *M,* you milkwhite fawn,	" iv.	57
M with her exquisite face,	" v.	12
M in the light of her youth	"	15
Whom but *M* should I meet 'rep.)	" vi.	7
If *M* were all that she seem'd,	"	36-92
M could be gracious too, no doubt	" x.	28
M, M, M, M, They were crying	" xii.	1
Where was *M!* in our wood;	"	5
M is here, here, here,	"	11
M is not seventeen,	"	15
O *M* were sure of heaven	"	19
Where is *M, M, M,*	"	27
M is as true as *M* is sweet:	" xiii.	32
M to him is nothing akin;	"	38
M has a garden of roses	" l. xiv.	1
M's own little oak-room	"	9
Which *M,* like a precious stone	"	10
looks Upon *M's* own garden-gate:	"	16
Make answer, *M,* my bliss,	" xviii.	57
M made my *M* by that long	"	58
talk To gentle *M* in our walk	" xix.	13
And *M* too, *M* was moved	"	26
only *M* and the brother Hung	"	35
M's dark father and mine	"	37
On the day when *M* was born;	"	40
M, altho' not blind	"	67
kind to *M!* that were not amiss.	"	82
For shall not *M* have her will?	"	84
For, *M,* so tender and true,	"	85
can be sweeter Than maiden *M*	" xx.	22
M will wear her jewels,	"	27
glance At *M* in all her glory	"	37
Queen *M* in all her splendour.	"	50
Forgetful of *M* and me,	" xxi.	9
My *M* has sent it by thee	"	9
Come into the garden, *M,* 'rep.)	" xxii.	1
Why should it look like *M?*	" II. ii.	39
maudlin-moral.		
empty glass That makes me *m-m.*	*Will Water.*	208
Maurice.		
Come, *M,* come: the lawn as yet	*To F. D. Maurice*	41
mavis.		
The clear-voiced *m* dwelleth	*Claribel*	16
Mavors.		
cry to thee To kiss thy *M.*	*Lucretius*	82
mawkin.		
or a draggled *m,* thou,	*Princess,* v.	25
maxim.		
With a little hoard of *m's*	*Locksley H.*	94
rugged *m's* hewn from life;	*Ode on Well.*	184

CONCORDANCE TO

may (hawthorn-bloom.) POEM. LINE.
lanes, you know, were white with *m*, *Miller's D.* 130
I'm to be Queen o' the *M*, *May Queen*, i. 4, *et pass.*
they made me Queen of *M*; " ii. 10
with plumes that mock'd the *m* . *Guinevere* . 23

May (month.)
Last *M* we made a crown of flowers: *May Queen*, ii. 9
M from verge to verge, . *Gardener's D.* 79
M with me from head to heel " 80
old *M's* had thrice the life of these) " 83
temper amorous, as the first of *M*, *Princess*, i. 2
murmur'd that their *M* Was passing: " ii. 439
glad at heart from *M* to *M* : . *InMem.*xxii. 8
branchy bowers With fifty *M's*, " lxxv. 14
happy morning of life and of *M*, *Maud*, I. v. 7
M or April he forgot, . . *The Brook* . 151
last of April or the first of *M*) " 152
mid might and flourish of his *M*, . *Elaine* . 553
touch'd his one-and-twentieth *M* . *En. Arden.* 57
tho' it was the middle of *M*. . . *Grandmother* 34
cuckoo, was ever a *M* so fine ? . *The Window* 153

Mayfly.
The *M* is torn by the swallow, . *Maud*, I. iv. 23

may-pole.
And we danced about the *m-p* . *May Queen*, ii. 11

maytime.
(for the time Was *m*, . . *Guinevere* . 385

maze (s.)
gauzes, golden hazes, liquid *m's*, . *Vision of Sin* 31
To thrid the musky-circled *m's*, . *Princess*, iv. 242
Now burgeons every *m* of quick . *InMem.*cxiv. 2

mazed.
Thou art *m*, the night is long, . *Vision of Sin* 195

me.
learns the use of ' I ' and ' *me* ' . *InMem.*xliv. 6

mead.
any man that walks the *m*, . . *Day-Dm.* . 205
far and near, on *m* and moor, . *InMem.*xxviii. 6
Or simple stile from *m* to *m*, " xcix. 7
on by many a level *m*, . . " cii. 21
the myriad cricket of the *m*, . *Elaine* . 107

meadow.
Thro' quiet *m's* round the mill, . *Miller's D.* . 98
m, set with slender galingale : . *Lotos-E's.* . 23
reach'd a *m* slanting to the North : *Gardener's D.*107
m smooth from aftermath . *Audley Ct.* 13
How fresh the *m's* look . . *Walk. to the M.* 1
A sign betwixt the *m* and the cloud, *St S. Stylites* 14
Faint murmurs from the *m's* come, *Day-Dm.* . 26
over brake and bloom And *m*, *InMem.* lxxxv. 4
By *m's* breathing of the past, " xcviii. 7
I smell the *m* in the street ; . . " cxviii. 4
In the *m* under the Hall! . *Maud*, I. v. 2
move to the *m* and fall before Her feet " 25
her feet have touch'd the *m's* " xii. 23
to the *m* and on to the wood " xxii. 37
m your walks have left so sweet " 37
She is walking in the *m*, . . " II. iv. 37
She is singing in the *m*, . . " 40
A daughter of our *m's*, . . *The Brook* . 69
bore your name About these *m's*. " 220
m where the jousts were held, . *Enid* . 537
up the vale of Usk By the flat *m*, " 832
m gemlike chased In the brown wild " 1047
growing longest by the *m*, . . " 1106
blossom-dust of those Deep *m's* *Vivien* . 131
green light from the *m's* underneath *Elaine* . 407
in the *m's* tremulous aspen-trees . " 411
the lists By Camelot in the *m*, . " 428
dim *m* toward his treasure-trove, *Aylmer's F.* 531
dewy Northern *m's* green. . . *The Voyage* 36
where it dash'd the reddening *m* . *Lucretius* . 49
O the woods and the *m's* . . *The Window* 182
M's in which we met . . . " 185
By *m* and stile and wood . . " 191
Over the *m's* and stiles, . . " 199

meadow-bases. POEM. LINE.
From level *m-b* of deep grass . *Pal. of Art* 7

meadow-crake.
the *m-c* Grate her harsh kindred . *Princess*, iv. 106

meadow-grass.
come and go, mother, upon the *m-g*, *May Queen*, i. 33

meadow-ledges.
m-l midway down Hang rich in flowers, *Œnone* 6

meadow-sweet.
waist-deep in *m-s.* . . . *The Brook* . 118

meadow-trenches.
by the *m-t* blow the faint sweet . *May Queen*, i. 30

meal (repast.)
sweetest *m* she makes On the first-born *Vision of Sin* 145

meal (flour.)
Made misty with the floating *m.* . *Miller's D.* 104
Some pretext of fineness in the *m.* *En. Arden* . 338

meal-sacks.
The *m-s* on the whiten'd floor, . *Miller's D.* 101

mealy-mouth'd.
nursed by *m-m* philanthropies, . *The Brook* . 94

mean (adj.)
weep for a time so sordid and *m*, *Maud*, I. v. 17
the proud man o'te i is the *m*, . *Enid* . . 449
never yet had look'd so *m*, . . " . 610

mean (verb.)
which you had, I *m* of verse . *The Epic* . 26
For they know not what they *m*. *Vision of Sin* 126
tears, I know not what they *m*. *Princess*, iv. 21
spirit does but *m* the breath : . *In Mem.* lv. 7
rose-garden And *m* to linger in it *Maud*, I. xx. 42
' What *m's* the tumult in the town?' *Enid* . 259
no ; I do not *m* blood : . . . " 1187
good king *m's* to blind himself, . *Vivien* . 632
I do not *m* the force alone, . . *Elaine* . 470
Nay, I *m* nothing : so then get you " 772
What might she *m* by that ? . . " 830
m Vileness, we are grown so proud— *Aylmer's F.* 755
I *m* your grandfather, Annie : . *Grandmother* 23
Whether I *m* this day to end myself, *Lucretius* 146

meän'd.
An' I niver knaw'd whot a *m* . *N. Farmer* 19
I *m* to a stubb'd it at fall, . . " . 41
Done it ta-year I *m*, . . . " . 42

meaning (part.)
life He gave me, *m* to be rid of it. *Enid* . 1701
m by it To keep the list low . *Vivien* . 441
m all at once To snare . . . *Elaine* . 71

meaning (s.)
So was their *m* to her words. . *The Poet* . 53
Like a tale of little *m* . . . *Lotos-E's.* . 164
O take the *m*, Lord : . . . *St S. Stylites* 21
A *m* suited to his mind. . . *Day-Dm.* . 208
To search a *m* for the song, . . " . 247
if you find a *m* there, . . . " . 270
Nor the *m* can divine, . . . *L. of Burleigh* 54
since we learnt our *m* here, . . *Princess*, iii. 206
there's a downright honest *m* in her ; " v. 270
Her secret *m* in her deeds . . *In Mem.* liv. 10
I will not ask your *m* in it : . . *Enid* . 1591
guess'd a hidden *m* in his arms, . *Elaine* . 17
thinking that he read her *m* there, " . 87
nothing to her : No *m* there, . *En. Arden.* 495

meanness.
sense Of *m* in her unresisting life. *Aylmer's F.* 801

means.
a gentleman of broken *m* . . *Princess*, i. 52
works in the very *m* of life . . *Maud*, I. i. 40
bore The *m* of goodly welcome, *Enid* . 387
m were somewhat broken into . " . 455
ampler *m* to serve mankind, . *Vivien* . 339
should strike upon a sudden *m* . " . 509
m to pay the voice who best . *En. Arden.* 265

meant. POEM. LINE.
alien lips, And knew not what they *m; Princess*, iv. 102
vacant chaff well *m* for grain. . *In Mem.* vi. 4
She *m* to weave me a snare . . *Maud*, l. vi. 25
death-white curtain *m* but sleep, . " xiv. 37
met, but only *m* to part, . . *The Letters* 12
what *m* the hubbub here? . . *Enid* . 264
m to eat her up in that wild wood . *Vivien* . 109
m to stamp him with her master's mark " . 609
m once more perchance to tourney in it *Elaine* . 806
rough sickness *m*, but what this *m* " . 884
(He *m* to break the passion in her) " 1073
' the simple, fearful child *M*'nothing, *Guinevere* . 368
never *m* us anything but good. . *En. Arden* . 888
you find That you *m* nothing— . *Aylmer's F.* 313
I should find he *m* me well :. . *Sea Dreams* 149
he *m*, he said me *m*, Perhaps he *m*,
  or partly *m* you well.' . . " . 174
but I *m* not thee ; I *m* not her, . *Lucretius* . 85
m Surely to lead my Memnius . . " . 118
M? I *m*? I have forgotten what I *m:* " . 121
That she but *m* to win him back, , " . 275

measure (s.)
hearts of salient springs Keep *m* . *Adeline* . 27
one that rose Twenty by *m;* . *St S. Stylites* 88
And wanton without *m;* . . *Amphion* . 58
Tread a *m* on the stones, . *Vision of Sin* 180
The highest is the *m* of the man. . *Princess*, ii. 141
draw The deepest *m* from the chords: *In Mem.* xlvii. 12
by the *m* of my grief . . . lxxiv. 3
The rich Virgilian rustic *m* . . *The Daisy* . 75
meted by his *m* of himself . . *Aylmer's F.* 316

measure (verb.)
m time by yon slow light, . *St S. Stylites* 93

measured.
three paces *m* from the mound, . *Princess*, v. 1

measuring.
Æonian music *m* out . . *In Mem.* xciv. 41

meat.
ev'n of wretched *m* and drink, . *Maud*, I. xv. 8
with knife in *m* and wine in horn. . *Vivien* . 544
with *m*'s and vintage of their best *Elaine* . 266
the *m*'s became As wormwood, . " . 739
Had whatsoever *m* he long'd for . *Guinevere* . 263

mechanic.
the raw *m*'s bloody thumbs . *Walk. to the M.* 67

medicine.
blush and smile, a *m* in themselves *Princess*, vii. 47
glass with little Margaret's *m* in it ; *Sea Dreams* 138

meditated.
while I *m* A wind arose . . *Princess*, i. 95

meditating.
long and bitterly *m*. . . . *Boädicea* . 35

meditation.
In a silent *m*, ... *Eleänore* . 105

medley.
This were a *m* ! we should have him *Princess, Pro.* 230

meed.
claiming each This *m* of fairest . *Œnone* . 85
The *m* of saints, the white robe . *St S. Stylites* 20
this was my *m* for all. . . *Princess*, iv. 283

meek.
lips depress'd as he were *m*, . *A Character* 25
And Dora promised, being *m*. . *Dora* . 44
His lips are very mild and *m:* . *Two Voices* 250
m Seem'd the full lips, . . *Princess*, vii. 210
why come you so cruelly *m*, . *Maud*, I. iii. 1
maiden of our century, yet most *m;* *The Brook* 68
how *m* soe'er he seem No keener hunter *Elaine* 155
thought myself long-suffering, *m* *Aylmer's F.* 753

meeker.
M than any child to a rough nurse, *Elaine* . 353

meekness.
Shaped her heart with woman's *m L. of Burleigh* 71

meet (adj.) POEM. LINE.
M is it changes should control 'Love thou thy land' 41
not *m*, Sir King, to leave thee thus, *M. d'Arthur* 40
scarce *m* For troops of devils, . *St S. Stylites* 3
whole, and clean, and *m* for Heaven. " . 210
surely rest is *m:* . . . *In Mem.* xxx. 18
Becoming as is *m* and fit . . " xxxix. 14
only *m* for mowers ;' . . . *Enid* . 1058
M for the reverence of the hearth, *Aylmer's F.* 333
should pause, as is most *m* for all? *Tithonus* . 31

meet (verb.)
clothe the wold and *m* the sky . *L. of Shalott*, i. 3
could *m* with her, The Abominable, *Œnone* . 279
until he *m* me there ! . . *MayQueen*, iii. 14
token when the night and morning *m:* " . 22
She heard the torrents *m. 'Of old sat Freedom,' etc.* 4
should *m* the offices of all, . *M. d'Arthur* 125
m's a friend who hails him, . *Walk. to the M.* 34
robed and crown'd, To *m* her lord, *Godiva* . 78
two likes might *m* and touch. . *Two Voices* 357
airs of heaven That often *m* me . *Sir Galahad* 63
Sometimes two would *m* in one, . *Will Water.* 95
To *m* and greet her on her way ; . *Beggar Maid* 6
loved to *m* Star-sisters. . . *Princess*, ii. 405
endured to *m* her opening eyes, . " iv. 177
fear'd To *m* a cold ' We thank you, " . 309
like fire he *m*'s the foe, . . . " . 560
to *m* us lightly pranced Three captains " v. 244
drew Her robe to *m* his lips, . . " vi. 140
Psyche as she sprang To *m* it, . " . 193
m her Graces, where they deck'd her " vii. 153
In which we two were wont to *m*, *In Mem.* viii. 8
I shall know him when we *m:* . " xlvi. 8
envying all that *m* him there. . " lix. 8
seem to *m* their least desire, . " lxxxiii. 17
O tell me where the passions *m*, . " lxxxvii. 4
m's the year, and gives and takes . " cxv. 3
And unto meeting when we *m*, . " cxvi. 7
they *m* they look And brighten . " Con. 30
To *m* and greet a whiter sun ; . " . 78
Whom but Maud should I *m* . *Maud*, I. vi. 7
She remembers it now we *m*. . " . 88
woody hollows in which we *m* . " xxii. 43
When I was wont to *m* her . . " II. iv. 5
In a moment we shall *m* . . " . 39
And the faces that one *m*'s, . . " . 93
farm where brook and river *m*. . *The Brook* . 38
never ran ; she moved To *m* me. . " . 83
' Cold altar, Heaven and earth shall *m The Letters* 7
To *m* the sun and sunny waters, . *The Daisy* . 11
m's the surging shock, . . *Will* . 8
may *m* the horsemen of Earl Doorm, *Enid* . 1341
Moving to *m* him in the castle court ; *Elaine* . 175
suddenly move, *M* in the midst . " . 456
we two May *m* at court hereafter ; . " . 695
never loved him : an I *m* with him, " . 1062
in state to court, to *m* the Queen. " . 1118
as it were, Diamonds to *m* them, . " . 1230
if thou tarry we shall *m* again, . *Guinevere* . 89
if we *m* again, some evil chance . " . 90
to *m* And part for ever. . . " . 97
that I march to *m* my doom. . . " . 447
We two may *m* before high God, . " . 560
m myself Death, or I know not what " . 570
round again to *m* the day . . *En. Arden* . 823
broad seas swell'd to *m* the keel, . *The Voyage* 13
nothing that she *m*'s with base, . *On a Mourner* 4
'O years, that *m* in tears, . . 1865-1866 . 4
Two little hands that *m*, . *The Window* 134-7

meeting (part.)
Two strangers *m* at a festival ; . *Circumstance* 3
stranger *m* them had surely thought *Enid* . 883

meeting (s.)
might I tell of *m*'s, of farewells— *Gardener's D.* 246
A *m* somewhere, love with love, *In Mem.* lxxxiv. 99
Their *m*'s made December June, . " xcvi. 11
unto *m* when we meet . . " cxvi. 7
For the *m* of the morrow, . *Maud*, II. iv. 78
perilous *m* under the tall pines *Aylmer's F.* 414
oft at Bible *m*'s, o'er the rest . *Sea Dreams* 19

CONCORDANCE TO

Meg.
	POEM.	LINE.
tavern-catch Of Moll and *M*,	Princess, iv.	140

melancholy.
the influence of mild-minded *m*;	Lotos-E's.	109
Your *m* sweet and frail.	Margaret,	7
Settled a gentle cloud of *m*;	Princess, iv.	547
To beguile her *m*;	Maud, I. xx.	3
fell upon him a great *m*;	Vivien	45
have broken up my *m*.'	"	116
came a cloud Of *m* severe,	Elaine	324
lived a life of silent *m*.	En. Arden	259

Melissa.
M, with her hand upon the lock,	Princess, ii.	301
'Ah—*M*—you! You heard us?'	"	309
M hitting all we saw	"	444
approach'd *M*, tinged with wan	" iii.	9
pardon, sweet *M*, for a blush?'	"	50
M shook her doubtful curls, .	"	59
Shame might befal *M*,	"	132
Cyril kept With Psyche, with *M* Florian	"	337
lilylike *M* droop'd her brows;	" iv.	143
last of all, *M*:	"	211
shaken with her sobs, *M* knelt;	"	271
stoop'd to updrag *M*:	"	348
with her oft, *M* came;	" vii.	41

mellay.
here and everywhere He rode the *m*,	Princess, v.	491

mellow.
as his brain Began to *m*,	Princess, i.	178

mellow-deep.
Drawn from each other *m-d*;	Eleänore	67

mellowed.
m all his heart with ale,	The Brook	155

mellowing.
into mournful twilight *m*,	Princess, vi.	174

mellowness.
Touch'd by thy spirit's *m*,	Eleänore	103

melody.
ancient *m* Of an inward agony,	Claribel	6
with light And vagrant *melodies*.	The Poet	17
modulated so T'o an unheard *m*,	Eleänore	64
drew Rivers of *melodies*.	Pal. of Art	172
Plenty corrupts the *m*	The Blackbird	15
with precipitate paces To the *m*,	Vision of Sin	38
The nerve-dissolving *m*	"	44
chanted a *m* loud and sweet,	Poet's Song.	6
herald *melodies* of spring	InMem.xxxviii.	6
And talk and minstrel *m*	Elaine	267

melon.
A raiser of huge *m*'s and of pine,	Princess,Con.	87

Melpomene.
my *M* replies,	InMem.xxxvii.	9

melt.
I wish the snow would *m*	MayQueen.ii.	15
from it *m* the dews of Paradise,	StS. Stylites	207
shall slowly *m* In many streams	Golden Year	33
I will *m* this marble into wax	Princess, iii.	57
embrace me, come, Quick while I *m*;	" vi.	268
M's mist-like into this bright hour	" vii.	334
m the waxen hearts of men.'	In Mem.xxi.	8
They *m* like mist, the solid lands	" cxxii.	7
warmth within the breast would *m*	" cxxiii.	13
A purer sapphire *m*'s into the sea.	Maud, I. xviii.	52
M into stars for the land's desire!	W. to Alexan.	21

melted.
before his burning eyes *M* like snow.	The Poet.	40
The twilight *m* into morn.	Day-Dm.	180
m Florian's fancy as she hung,	Princess, iv.	351
m into mere effeminacy?	Enid	107
Amazed and *m* all who listen'd	En. Arden	650

melting.
m the mighty hearts Of captains	D. of F. Wom.	175

member (M.P.)
The Tory *m*'s elder son	Princess, Con.	50

Memmius.
	POEM.	LINE.
Surely to lead my *M* in a train	Lucretius	119

Memnon.
from *M* drew Rivers of melodies.	Pal. of Art	171
M smitten with the morning Sun.'	Princess, iii.	100

memorial.
I stored it full of rich *m*:	Princess, v.	381

memory.
Thou dewy dawn of *m*. (rep.)	Ode to Mem.	7
Unto mine inner eye, Divinest *M*!	"	50
hast thou done, great Artist *M*,	"	60
Makes thy *m* confused;	A Dirge	45
His *m* scarce can make me sad.	Miller's D.	16
laid Since my first *m*?'	Pal. of Art	236
put strange *memories* in my head.	L. C. V. de Vere	26
brood and live again in *m*,	Lotos-E's.	110
Dear is the *m* of our wedded lives,	"	114
No *m* labours longer from the deep	D. of F. Wom.	273
His *m* long will live alone	To J. S.	49
M standing near Cast down her eyes,	"	53
Revolving many *memories*,	M. d'Arthur	270
So blunt in *m*, so old at heart,	Gardener's D.	52
this orbit of the *m* folds	"	73
came *M* with sad eyes,	"	238
the most blessed *m* of mine age.	"	273
learn to slight His father's *m*;	Dora	151
to *M*'s darkest hold,	Love and Duty	87
Drug thy *memories*, lest thou learn it,	Locksley H.	77
The *m* of the wither'd leaf	Two Voices	112
Because my *m* is so cold,	"	341
The haunts of *m* echo not,	"	369
Incompetent of *m*;	"	375
m dealing but with time,	"	376
From out a common vein of *m*	Princess, ii.	293
Rose from the distance on her *m*,	" vi.	96
memories of her kindlier days,	" vii.	91
whence clear *m* may begin,	In Mem. xliv.	10
count their *memories* half divine;	" lxxxix.	12
I hear a wind Of *m* murmuring	" xci.	8
The *m* like a cloudless air,	" xciii.	11
for intellect to reach Thro' *m*	" xciv.	48
Memories of bridal, or of birth,	" xcviii.	15
Some gracious *m* of my friend;	" xcix.	4
year by year our *m* fades	" c.	23
lands where not a *m* strays,	" ciii.	6
To whom a thousand *memories* call	" cx.	10
My drooping *m* will not shun	Con.	79
Mix not *m* with doubt,	Maud, II. iv.	57
brawling *memories* all too free	Ode on Well.	248
to His *M*—since he held them dear	Ded. of Idylls	1
Nor let me shame my father's *m*,	Guinevere	316
Her *m* from old habit of the mind	"	376
thousand *memories* roll upon him,	En. Arden	725
old, and a mine of *memories*	Aylmer's F.	10
left their *memories* a world's curse—	"	796
painting some dead friend from *m*?	Coquette, iii.	4
Hope and *M*, spouse and bride,	On a Mourner	23

mend.
How *m* the dwellings of the poor	To F. D. Maurice	38

mended.
Robins—a niver *m* a fence;	N. Farmer	50

Mene.
Wrote '*M*, *m*,' and divided quite	Pal. of Art	227

mentioned.
bill I *m* half an hour ago!'	Day-Dm.	160
day, that Enoch *m*, came	En. Arden	238

merchant.
As tho' they brought but *m*'s' bales,	In Mem. xiii.	19

merchantman.
served a year On board a *m*,	En. Arden	53

Mercury.
as it were with *M*'s ankle-wing	Lucretius	198

mercy.
God in his *m* lend her grace,	L. of Shalott, iv.	53
He taught me all the *m*,	MayQueen,iii.	17
Have *m*, Lord, and take away my	St S. Stylites	8
Have *m*, *m*; take away my sin.	"	44, 83, 118

	POEM.	LINE.
ah God's *m* what a stroke	Elaine	24
His *m* choked me.	Guinevere	609

mere.

Crimsons over an inland *m*	Eleänore	42
fling him far into the middle *m*	M. d'Arthur	37
voice, or else a motion of the *m*,	"	77
and paced beside the *m*,	"	83
drew him under in the *m*,	"	146, 161
on the *m* the wailing died away.	"	272
When *m*'s begin to uncongeal,	Two Voices	407
bare me, pacing on the dusky *m*.	Elaine	1401
fling me deep in that forgotten *m*,	"	1416

merge.

m ' he said ' in form and gloss	In Mem. lxxxviii.	41

merged.

fulfill'd itself *M* in completion.	Gardener's D.	234
long disquiet *m* in rest.	Two Voices	249

merit (s.)

m lives from man to man,	In Mem. Pro.	35
makes by force his *m* known	" lxiii.	9
That were a public *m*, far,	Maud, II. v.	91

merit (verb.)

is it I can have done to *m* this?	St S. Stylites	132
m well Your term of overstrain'd.	Vivien	385

Merlin.

M sware that I should come again	M. d'Arthur	23
At *M*'s feet the wily Vivien lay	Vivien	5
M, who knew the range of all	"	23
she follow'd *M* all the way,	"	52
M once had told her of a charm,	"	54
'O *M*, do you love me?' rep.	"	84
M lock'd his hand in hers	"	139-320
O, *M*, teach it me.	"	180
O, *M*, may this earth, if ever I,	"	195
M loosed his hand from hers	"	206
M look'd and half believed her	"	250
answer'd *M*, careless of her words.	"	550-604
M, to his own heart, loathing,	"	639
Vivien deeming *M* overborne	"	649
'O *M*, tho' you do not love me, save,	"	793
her *M*, the one passionate love	"	804
M, overtalk'd and overworn,	"	814

mermaid.

With the *m*'s in and out of the rocks,	The Merman	12
would be A *m* fair,	The Mermaid	29

mermaiden.

in the light the white *m* swam,	Guinevere	243
He heard a fierce *m* cry,	Sailor Boy	6

merman.

would be A *m* bold	The Merman	2, 8
all the *mermen* under the sea	The Mermaid	28
and play With the *mermen*	"	34
bold merry mermen under the sea;	"	42

merrily-blowing.

m-b shrill'd the martial fife;	Princess, v.	241

merriment.

With *m* of kingly pride,	Arabian N's.	151

merry.

'O Soul, make *m* and carouse,	Pal. of Art	3
Fantastically *m*,	Maud, I. xix.	101
we will make us *m* as we may.	Enid	373
when the Prince was *m*, ask'd Limours	"	1146
of foreign parts, And make him *m*	En. Arden	109
How *m* they are down yonder	"	386
Be *m* all birds to-day rep.)	The Window	144

merry-making.

mirth Is here or *m-m* sound,	Deserted H.	14
while the rest were loud in *m*,	En. Arden	77

Mersey.

New-comers from the *M*,	Ed. Morris	10

meshes.

m of the jasmine and the rose;	Princess, i.	216

	POEM.	LINE.
message.		
flash'd a saucy *m* to and fro	Princess, Pro.	78
a *m* here from Lady Blanche.'	" ii.	298
ceasing, came a *m* from the Head.	" iii.	152
With *m* and defiance, went and came;	" v.	360
Some dolorous *m* knit below	In Mem. xii.	3
Till on mine ear this *m* falls,	" lxxxiv.	18
Yniol with that hard *m* went;	Enid	763
with His *m* ringing in thine ears,	Aylmer's F.	616
the *m* is one of Peace.	Grandmother	96

messuages.

lands in Kent and *m* in York,	Ed Morris	127

met.

statesmen at her council *m*	To the Queen	29
talking to himself, first *m* his sight:	Love and Death	6
m with two so full and bright—	Miller's D.	86
angels rising and descending *m*	Pal. of Art	143
When thus he *m* his mother's view,	L. C. V. de Vere	34
or as once we *m* Unheedful,	Gardener's D.	21
I *m* my lady once ;	Walk. to the M.	40
those moments when we *m*.	Ed. Morris	69
crown of all, we *m* to part no more	"	70
we *m*; one hour I had,	"	104
um a part of all that I have *m*;	Ulysses	18
M me walking on yonder way,	Ed. Gray	2
Here Cyril *m* us, A little shy	Princess, v.	42
And ever *m* him on his way.	In Mem. vi.	22
all we *m* was fair and good (xxiv. 5)	" xxiii.	17
From every house the neighbours *m*,	" xxxi.	9
I *m* with scoffs, I *m* with scorns	" lxviii.	9
For other friends that once I *m*;	" lxxxiv.	58
God and Nature *m* in light;	" ex.	20
Unpalsied when he *m* with Death,	" cxxvii.	2
I *m* her to-day with her brother,	Maud, I. iv.	14
To entangle me when we *m*,	" vi.	28
To find they were *m* by my own;	" viii.	7
Alas for her that *m* me,	" II. iv.	75
m the bailiff at the Golden Fleece,	The Brook	146
then we *m* in wrath and wrong,	The Letters	11
We *m*, but only meant to part.	"	12
when they *m* In twos and threes,	Enid	56
descending *m* them at the gates,	"	813
M his full frown timidly firm,	"	930
m her, Vivien, being greeted fair.	Vivien	11
often when they *m* Sigh fully	"	37
here we *m*, some ten or twelve	"	257
one a king, had *m* And fought	Elaine	40
oft they *m* among the garden yews,	"	642
They *m*, and Lancelot kneeling utter'd	"	1173
their eyes *m* and hers fell,	"	1303
And still they *m* and *m*.	Guinevere	94
Passion-pale they *m* And greeted	"	98
once by night again the lovers *m*,	Aylmer's F.	413
m him suddenly in the street,	Sea Dreams	142
may be *m* and fought with outright,	Grandmother	31
New Year and Old Year we *m*,	1865-1866	2
Meadows in which we *m*.	The Window	185

metaphysics.

'How,' she cried 'you love The *m*!	Princess, iii.	283

mete.

I *m* and dole Unequal laws	Ulysses	3
m the bounds of hate and love—	Two Voices	135

meted.

As *m* by his measure of himself,	Aylmer's F.	316

meteor.

Some bearded *m*, trailing light,	L. of Shalott, iii.	26
like a new-fall'n *m* on the grass,	Princess, vi.	119
Now slides the silent *m* on,	" vii.	119
The *m* of a splendid season,	Aylmer's F.	205

method.

M's of transplanting trees,	Amphion	71

metre.

mellow *m*'s more than cent for cent;	The Brook	5
All composed in a *m* of Catullus,	Hendecasyllabics	4
So fantastical is the dainty *m*.	"	14

metrification.

Thro' this *m* of Catulus,	Hendecasyllabics	10

S

CONCORDANCE TO

	POEM.	LINE.
metropolis.		
gray *m* of the North. . . .	*The Daisy*	104
mettle.		
It stirr'd the old wife's *m*, . .	*The Goose*	26
mew.		
Here it is only the *m* that wails	*Sea-Fairies*	19
and wail'd about with *m's*. . .	*Princess*, iv.	263
Michael Angelo.		
The bar of *M A* . . .	*In Mem.* lxxxvi.	40
Michaelmas.		
for Squoire come *M* thirty year. .	*N. Farmer*	48
microcosm.		
holy secrets of this *m*, . .	*Princess*, iii.	296
mid-channel.		
in the gurgling wave *M-c* . .	*Princess*, iv.	170
midmost.		
the *m* and the highest Was Arac :	*Princess*, v.	246
at the *m* charging, Prince Geraint	*Enid*	934
midnight.		
rode till *m* when the college lights	*Princess*, i.	204
Sees the midsummer, *m*, . .	" iv.	552
midnoon.		
It was the deep *m* . . .	*Œnone*	90
mid-November.		
as a leaf in *m-N* is . . .	*Enid* .	611
mid-ocean.		
Than labour in the deep *m-o* .	*Lotos-E's.*	172
whatever tempest mars *M-o*, .	*In Mem.* xvii.	14
mid-October.		
To what it was in *m-O*, . .	*Enid* .	612
midriff.		
shake The *m* of despair with laughter	*Princess,* i.	198
from the *m* of a prostrate king— .	*Aylmer's F.*	16
mid-sickness.		
great knight in his *m-s* made .	*Elaine*	874
midsummer.		
Sees the *m*, midnight, . .	*Princess*, iv.	552
mid-warmth.		
In the *m-w* of welcome . .	*Enid* .	1129
mien.		
One her dark hair and lovesome *m*.	*Beggar Maid*	12
might.		
Losing his fire and active *m* .	*Eleänore*	104
O Love, Love, Love ! O withering *m* !	*Fatima*	1
tasks of *m* To weakness, ' *Love thou thy land*,' etc.		13
smote on all the chords with *m* ; .	*Locksley H.*	33
great year of equal *m's* and rights,	*Princess*, iv.	56
could wing my will with *m* .	*In Mem.* xl.	10
with *m* To scale the heaven's .	" cvii.	6
In the mid *m* and flourish of his May,	*Elaine*	553
mightier.		
things seen are *m* than things heard,	*En. Arden*	767
mightiest.		
must learn Which is our *m*, .	*Elaine*	64
my right arm, The *m* of my knights,	*Guinevere*	427
mighty.		
thou shalt be the *m* one yet ! .	*Boädicea*	40
mighty-mouthed.		
O *m-m* inventor of harmonies .	*Milton*	1
mignonette.		
A long green box of *m*, . .	*Miller's D.*	83
parlour-windows and the box of *m*.	*May Queen*, ii.	48
miss'd the *m* of Vivian-place, .	*Princess, Pro.*	164
Milan.		
O *M*, O the chanting quires .	*The Daisy*	57
mild.		
to make *m* A rugged people, .	*Ulysses* .	36
His lips are very *m* and meek : .	*Two Voices* .	250

	POEM.	LINE.
mother was as *m* as any saint, .	*Princess*, i.	22
m the luminous eyes, . . .	" vii.	211
stern were *m* when thou wert by,	*In Mem.* cix.	9
A higher hand must make her *m*,	" cxiii.	17
However *m* he seems at home, .	*Elaine* .	311
milder.		
M than any mother to a sick child,	*Elaine* .	854
mildew'd.		
Who had *m* in their thousands, .	*Aylmer's F.*	383
mild-eyed.		
The *m-e* melancholy Lotos-Eaters	*Lotos-E's.* .	27
mildly.		
m, that all hearts Applauded .	*Enid* .	1805
mild-minded.		
the influence of *m-m* melancholy,	*Lotos-E's.* .	109
mile.		
a *m*, More than a *m* from the shore,	*Maud*, I. ix.	1
milk.		
fed you with the *m* of every Muse ;	*Princess*, iv.	276
The *m* that bubbled in the pail,	*In Mem.* lxxxviii.	51
clean as blood of babes, as white as *m* :	*Vivien* .	194
like the kid in its own mother's *m* !	"	718
milk-bloom.		
One long *m-b* on the tree ; .	*Maud*, I. xxii	46
milkier.		
m every milky sail . . .	*In Mem.* exiv.	10
milking-maid.		
burnt the grange, nor buss'd the *m-m*	*Princess*,v.	213
milkmaid.		
When merry *m's* click the latch, .	*The Owl*, i.	8
milky-bell'd.		
A *m-b* amaryllis blew . .	*The Daisy* .	16
milky-way.		
this, a *m-w* on earth . .	*Aylmer's F.*	160
milky-white.		
Taller than all his fellows, *m-w*, .	*Enid* .	150
mill.		
quiet meadows round the *m*, .	*Miller's D.*	93
brook groan'd beneath the *m* ; .	"	113
yon old *m* across the wolds ; .	"	240
' ground in yonder social *m* .	*In Mem.* lxxxviii.	39
climbs to yon tall-tower'd *m* ; .	*En. Arden* .	5
street that clamber'd toward the *m*	"	60
flour From his tall *m* . .	"	340
Lords of his house and of his *m* .	"	343
Blanch'd with his *m*, they found .	"	364
street, the *m*, the leafy lanes, .	"	608
milldam.		
The *m* rushing down with noise, .	*Miller's D.*	50
millennium.		
let Thy feet, *m's* hence, be set .	*Two Voices*	89
miller.		
I see the wealthy *m* yet, . .	*Miller's D.*	1
It is the *m's* daughter, . .	"	169
Philip Ray the *m's* only son. .	*En. Arden* .	13
' This *m's* wife' He said to Miriam	"	805
millinery.		
That jewell'd mass of *m*, . .	*Maud*, I. vi.	43
millionaire.		
New-comers from the Mersey, *m's*,	*Ed. Morris*	10
be gilt by the touch of a *m* : .	*Maud*, I. i.	66
Britain's one sole God be the *m* :	" III. vi.	22
million-myrtled.		
hide them, *m-m* wilderness, .	*Lucretius* .	201
millstone.		
May make my heart as a *m*, .	*Maud*, I. i.	31
as if he held The Apocalyptic *m*,	*Sea Dreams*	26
mill-wheel.		
Beside the *m-w* in the stream, .	*Miller's D.*	167

	POEM.	LINE.		POEM.	LINE.
Milton.			Nor other thought her *m* admits	*In Mem.* xxxii.	2
M like a seraph strong,	*Pal. of Art*	133	Tho' following with an upward *m*	" xl.	24
M, a name to resound for ages;	*Milton*	4	train To riper growth the *m*	" xli.	8
mime.			So rounds he to a separate *m*,	" xliv.	9
genial hour with mask and *m*;	*In Mem.* civ.	10	lives to wed an equal *m*;	" lxi.	8
mimic.			makes a desert in the *m*,	" lxv.	6
But I cannot *m* it;	*The Owl*, ii.	9	men and *m*'s, the dust of change,	" lxx.	10
moons of gems To *m* heaven;	*Pal. of Art*	189	Sung by a long-forgotten *m*,	" lxxvi.	12
should *m* this raw fool the world,	*Walk. to the M.*	96	same sweet forms in either *m*,	" lxxviii.	8
mimicry.			An image comforting the *m*,	" lxxxiv.	51
Soul of mincing *m!*	*Princess*, ii.	403	on *m* and art, And labour	" lxxxvi.	22
mincer.			tasted love with half his *m*,	" lxxxix.	1
m's of each other's fame,	*Princess*, iv.	494	He faced the spectres of the *m*	" xcv.	15
mind (s.)			He thrids the labyrinth of the *m*,	" xcvi.	21
rooted in the garden of the *m*,	*Ode to Mem.*	26	with one *m* Bewail'd their lot;	" cii.	45
deep *m* of dauntless infancy.	"	36	Ring out the grief that saps the *m*,	" cv.	9
all forms Of the many-sided *m*,	"	116	native growth of noble *m*;	" cx.	16
Some honey-converse feeds thy *m*,	*Adeline*	40	she is earthly of the *m*,	" cxiii.	21
stood aloof from other *m*'s	*A Character*	23	the works of the men of *m*,	*Maud*, I. i.	25
many *m*'s did gird their orbs	*The Poet*	29	Be still, for you only trouble the *m*	" v.	10
Vex not thou the poet's *m* (rep.)	*Poet's Mind*	1	cut off from the *m* The bitter springs	" x.	48
Two spirits to one equal *m*—	*Miller's D.*	236	The fancy flatter'd my *m*,	" xiv.	23
falling from my constant *m*,	*Fatima*	5	So dark a *m* within me dwells,	" xv.	1
with one *m* the Gods Rise up	*Œnone*	223	To the faults of his heart and *m*,	" xix.	68
that I might speak my *m*,	"	223	*m*, when fraught With a passion	" II. ii.	58
varieties of mould and *m*) To —,	*With Pal. of Art*	7	for she never speaks her *m*	" v.	57
fit for every mood of *m*,	*Pal. of Art*	90	awaked, as it seems, to the better *m*;	" III. vi.	36
the supreme Caucasian *m*	"	126	rolling in his *m* Old waifs of rhyme	*The Brook*	198
I take possession of man's *m*	"	209	raw world for the march of *m*,	*Ode on Well.*	168
could not stoop to such a *m*.	*L. C. V. de Vere*	20	a life, a heart, a *m* as thine,	*Ded. of Idylls*	32
old time, and all my peace of *m*,	*May Queen*, ii.	6	Across her *m*, and bowing over him,	*Enid*	84
shuddering took hold on all my *m*,	" iii.	35	ever in her *m* she cast about	"	895
keep it with an equal *m*	*Lotos-E's.*	153	one *m* and all right-honest friends!	"	1333
I've half a *m* to die with you,	*D. of the O. Year*	26	*m* all full of what had chanced,	"	1026
takes away a noble *m*.	*To J. S.*	48	My *m* involved yourself the nearest	*Vivien*	149
Seed of men, and growth of *m*'s.	*'Love thou thy land'*	20	wish'd to give them greater *m*'s:	"	346
Set in all lights by many *m*'s,	"	35	kept his *m* on one sole aim,	"	476
dividing the swift *m* In act to throw:	*M. d'Arthur*	60	condensation, hard To *m* and eye;	"	529
new men, strange faces, other *m*'s.'	"	238	sleek her ruffled peace of *m*.	"	748
all my *m* is clouded with a doubt)	"	258	shape and colour of a *m* and life,	*Elaine*	334
my uncle's *m* will change!'	*Dora*	45	counsel up and down within his *m*,	"	368
something of a wayward modern *m*	*Ed. Morris*	87	look'd and was perplext in *m*,	"	834
division of the records of the *m*?	*Locksley H.*	69	So cannot speak my *m*.	"	1216
more than in this march of *m*,	"	165	loyal nature, and of noble *m*,'	*Guinevere*	334
left alone, the passions of her *m*,	*Godiva*	32	memory from old habit of the *m*,	"	376
gave him *m*, the lordliest Proportion	*Two Voices*	19	Philip did not fathom Annie's *m*:	*En. Arden*	341
truth within thy *m* rehearse,	"	25	there is a thing upon my *m*,	"	396
spake, moreover, in my *m*:	"	31	has been upon my *m* so long,	"	397
'The highest-mounted *m*,' he said,	"	79	folk that knew not their own *m*'s	"	475
A healthy frame, a quiet mind.'	"	99	*M* is changed, for I shall see him,	"	898
the whole *m* might orb about—	"	138	but I needs must speak my *m*,	*Grandmother*	53
bears relation to the *m*.	"	177	*m* Half-buried in some weightier	*Lucretius*	8
That type of Perfect in his *m*	"	292	my *m* Stumbles, and all my faculties	"	122
Consolidate in *m* and frame—	"	366	How should the *m*, except it loved them,	"	164
I see whole years of darker *m*.	"	372	*mind* (verb.)		
marvell'd how the *m* was brought	"	458	*m* us of the time When we made	*Princess*, iv.	109
A meaning suited to his *m*.	*Day-Dm.*	208	I *m* him coming down the street;	*En. Arden*	843
The fullness of the pensive *m*;	"	260	*mindful.*		
use Her influence on the *m*,	*Will Water.*	12	Guinevere, not *m* of his face,	*Enid*	191
'Are ye out of your *m*, my nurse,	*Lady Clare*	21	*mind-mist.*		
And her gentle *m* was such	*L. of Burleigh*	74	yourself the nearest thing In that *m-m*:	*Vivien*	150
which brought My book to *m*:	*Princess*, Pro.	120	*mine.*		
science, and the secrets of the *m*:	" ii.	160	labour'd *m*'s undrainable of ore	*Œnone*	113
the *m*, The morals, something of the frame,	"	359	till he crept from a gutted *m*	*Maud*, I. x.	9
One *m* in all things	" iii.	75	mountain full of golden *m*'s,	*Vivien*	437
the Royal *m*, familiar with her,	" iv.	216	proffer of the league of golden *m*'s,	"	10
Our *m* is changed: we take it	"	343	Old, and a *m* of memories—	*Aylmer's F.*	10
Give us, then, your *m* at large;	" v.	118	shares in some Peruvian *m*,	*Sea Dreams*	15
the authentic mother of her *m*;	"	423	there is no such *m* None;	"	78
iron will was broken in her *m*.	" vi.	102	she said, 'by working in the *m*'s:'	"	110
cannot keep her *m* an hour;	"	269	*mingle*		
fear'd that I should lose my *m*,	" vii.	84	Thought and motion *m*, *M* ever.	*Eleänore*	60
lose the childlike in the larger *m*;	"	268	To *m* with the human race, 'Of old sat Freedom,' etc.		10
all mine *m*'s perforce Sway'd to her	"	306	star-like *m*'s with the stars.	*Sir Galahad*	48
m and soul, according well,	*In Mem.* Pro.	27	*M* madness, *m* scorn!	*Vision of Sin*	204
Upon the threshold of the *m*?	" iii.	16	Pass, and *m* with your likes.	*Princess*, vi.	321
A weight of nerves without a *m*,	" xii.		To *m* with the bounding main;	*In Mem.* xi.	12
slowly forms the larger *m*,	" xviii.	18	*m*'s all without a plan?.	" xvi.	20
weep the fullness from the *m*;	" xx.	6			

CONCORDANCE TO

	POEM.	LINE.
m all the world with thee.	*In Mem.* cxxviii.	12
m with your rites ;	*Guinevere*	672

mingled.

Ceasing not, *m*, unrepress'd,	*Arabian N's.*	74
what is *m* with past years,	*D.of F.Wom.*	282
m with her fragrant toil,	*Gardener's D.*	142
rank you nobly, *m* up with us.	*Princess,* ii.	32
sole men to be *m* with our cause,	'' v.	401
And *m* with the spearmen :	*Enid*	1447
ever as he *m* with the crew,	*En. Arden*	644
at times, she *m* with his drink,	*Lucretius*	18

miniature.

A *m* of loveliness,	*Gardener's D.*	12

minister.

Who may *m* to thee? Summer herself should *m*	*Eleänore*	31

ministering.

Friday fare was Enoch's *m*.	*En. Arden*	100

ministration.

And for the power of *m* in her,	*Guinevere*	686

ministries.

tender *m* Of female hands	*Princess,* vi.	56

Minneth.

from Aroer On Arnon unto *M*.'	*D. of F.Wom.*	239

minnow.

see the *m's* everywhere	*Miller's D.*	51

minster.

windy clanging of the *m* clock ;	*Gardener's D.*	38
The sound of *m* bells.	*Talking O.*	272
whose hymns Are chanted in the *m*,	*Vivien*	616

minster-front.

on one of those dark *m-f's*—	*Sea Dreams*	235

minster-tower.

bridge Crown'd with the *m-t's*.	*Gardener's D.*	44

minstrel.

and the *m* sings Before them	*Lotos-E's.*	121
ring the fuller *m* in.	*In Mem.* cv.	20
every *m* sings it differently ;	*Vivien*	308

mint.

he has a *m* of reasons : ask.	*The Epic*	33
moulded like in nature's *m* ;	*In Mem.* lxxviii.	6

minted.

Creation *m* in the golden moods	*Princess,* v.	186

minuet.

thro' the stately *m* of those days	*Aylmer's F.*	207

minute (adj.)

How exquisitely *m*,	*Maud,* I. ii.	7

minute (s.)

sweat her sixty *m's* to the death,	*Golden Year*	68
The *m's* fledged with music ;	*Princess,* iv.	19
came a *m's* pause, and Walter said,	'' Con.	4
For a *m*, but for a *m*,	*Maud,* I. xx.	45
suffering thus he made *M's* an age:	*Enid*	964
'Stay a little! one golden *m's* grace :	*Elaine*	681

miracle.

So great a *m* as yonder hilt.	*M. d'Arthur*	156
A certain *m* of symmetry,	*Gardener's D.*	11
they say then that I work'd *m's*,	*St S. Stylites*	79
may be I have wrought some *m's*,	''	134
Can I work *m's* and not be saved ?	''	148
'O *m* of women,' said the book	*Princess, Pro.*	35
O *m* of noble womanhood !'.	''	48
A *m* of design !	*Maud,* II. ii.	8
With signs and *m's* and wonders,	*Guinevere*	220
simple *m's* of thy nunnery ?'	''	228
he by *m* was approven king :	''	204
as by *m*, grow straight and fair—	*Aylmer's F.*	676

miraculous.

gaped upon him As on a thing *m*,	*Elaine*	452

mirage.

a moist *m* in desert eyes,	*Maud,* I. vi.	53

mire.	POEM.	LINE.
great heart and slips in sensual *m*,	*Princess,* v.	191

Miriam (see *Lane.*)

Between a cymbal'd *M* and a Jael,	*Princess,* v.	500
'This miller's wife' he said to *M*.	*En. Arden*	606
half-frighted, *M* swore.	''	844
M watch'd and dozed at intervals,	''	908

miring.

harpies *m* every dish,	*Lucretius*	159

mirror.

moving thro' a *m* clear.	*L.of Shalott,* ii.	10
sometimes thro' the *m* blue	''	24
To weave the *m's* magic sights,	''	29
He flash'd into the crystal *m*,	'' iii.	34
The *m* crack'd from side to side ;	''	43
On the liquid *m* glow'd	*Mariana in the S.*	31
Without a *m*, in the gorgeous gown	*Enid*	739

mirth.

no more of *m* Is here	*Deserted H.*	13
murmuring in her feastful *m*,	*Pal. of Art*	177
not the less held she her solemn *m*,	''	215
in a fit of frolic *m*	*Talking O.*	137
Marrow of *m* and laughter ;	*Will Water.*	214
Lilia woke with sudden-shrilling *m*	*Princess, Pro.*	210
etiquette to death, Unmeasured *m*;	'' v.	17

mirthful.

m he but in a stately kind	*Elaine*	321

miscellany.

Not like the piebald *m*, man,	*Princess,* v.	190

mischance.

Seeing all his own *m*—.	*L.of Shalott,* iv.	12
touch of all *m* but came As night	*Princess,* iv.	550
by great *m* He heard but fragments	*Enid*	112
What I by mere *m* have brought,	*Elaine*	189
hearing his *m*, Came,	*En. Arden*	120
now that shadow of *m* appear'd	''	128

mischief.

they kept apart, no *m* done ;	*Princess,* iv.	321

miscounted.

Were all *m* as malignant haste	*Princess,* iv.	315

miserable.

'Ah, *m* and unkind, untrue,	*M. d'Arthur*	119
More *m* than she that has a son	*Princess,* iii.	243
If she be small, slight-natured, *m*,	'' vii.	249
loves most, lonely and *m*.	*Enid*	123
Hating his own lean heart and *m*.	*Aylmer's F.*	526
hide their faces, *m* in ignominy	*Boädicea*	51

misery.

'Thou art so full of *m*,	*Two Voices*	2
'Thou art so steep'd in *m*,	''	47

misfaith.

anger born Of your *m* ;	*Vivien*	382

misled.

ill counsel had *m* the girl	*Princess,* vii.	226

mismated.

Not quite *m* with a yawning clown	*Enid*	1275

Miss.

The wither'd *M'es*! how they prose	*Amphion*	81

miss (verb.)

m the brother of your youth ?	*To J. S.*	59
fear That we shall *m* the mail :	*Walk. to the M.*	102
live in vain, and *m*, Meanwhile,	*Princess,* iii.	227
Why should they *m* their yearly	*In Mem.* xxix.	15
m,' he answer'd, 'the great deeds	*Elaine*	82
m the wonted number of my knights,	*Guinevere*	494
m to hear high talk of noble deeds	''	495

miss'd.

thou,' said I, 'hast *m* thy mark,	*Two Voices*	388
have *m* the irreverent doom 'You might have won'		9
m the mignonette of Vivian-place,	*Princess, Pro.*	164
O yes, you *m* us much.	''	167
here is proof that you were *m* :	''	175
blind with rage she *m* the plank,	'' iv.	153

	POEM.	LINE.
even those that *m* her most,	*In Mem.* xxxix.	27
head hath *m* an earthly wreath;	" lxxii.	6
m, and brought Her own claw back,	*Vivien*	349
Caught at and ever *m* it,	*En. Arden.*	753

missing.

one flash, that, *m* all things else,	*Vivien*	781

missile.

whelm'd with *m*'s of the wall,	*Princess, Pro.*	45

mission.

perform'd my *m* which I gave?	*M. d'Arthur*	67
happy with the *m* of the Cross;	*Golden Year*	43
Her lavish *m* richly wrought,	*In Mem.* lxxxiii.	34
A soul on highest *m* sent,	" cxii.	10
If this were all your *m* here,	" cxxvii.	12
On a blushing *m* to me	*Maud*, I. xxi.	11
on a *m* to the bandit Earl;	*Enid*	1376

missive.

let our *m* thro',	*Princess*, v.	316

mist.

thou camest with the morning *m*,	*Ode to Mem.*	12,21
deem'd no *m* of earth could dull	"	38
Œnone see the morning *m*	*Œnone*	212
spirits falter in the *m*,	*'You ask me why,' etc.*	3
m of morn Clung to the lake.	*Ed. Morris*	107
Inswathed sometimes in wandering *m*,	*St S.Stylites*	74
Rain out the heavy *m* of tears,	*Love and Duty*	43
As over rainy *m* inclines	*Two Voices*	188
softly, thro' a vinous *m*,	*Will Water.*	39
colours gayer than the morning *m*,	*Princess*, ii.	415
Answer each other in the *m*.	*In Mem.* xxviii.	4
then I know the *m* is drawn	" lxvi.	13
Is pealing, folded in the *m*.	" ciii.	4
They melt like *m*, the solid lands,	" cxxii.	2
wood stands in a *m* of green,	*The Brook*	14
o'er her meek eyes came a happy *m*	*Enid*	1617
in the noon of *m* and driving rain,	*Vivien*	486
clave Like its own *m*'s.	*Elaine*	39
Blurr'd by the creeping *m*,	*Guinevere*	5
The white *m*, like a face-cloth	"	7
she saw, Wet with the *m*'s	"	591
himself became as *m* Before her,	"	598
Far-folded *m*'s, and gleaming halls	*Tithonus*	10
Ilion like a *m* rose into towers	"	63
years were a *m* that rolls away;	*V. of Canteretz*	6
The *m* and the rain, the *m* and the	*The Window*	106

mist-blotted.

a great *m-b* light Flared on him	*En. Arden.*	681

mistletoe.

Thorns, ivies, woodbine, *m*'s,	*Day-Dm.*	63

mist-like.

Melts *m-l* into this bright hour,	*Princess*, vii.	334

mistress.

Let Grief be her own *m* still	*To J. S.*	41
Beauty such a *m* of the world	*Gardener's D.*	57
No casual *m*, but a wife,	*In Mem.* lviii.	2
While Annie still was *m*;	*En. Arden.*	26

mistrust.

never shadow of *m* can cross	*Enid*	815, 1097

mist-wreathen

Across a break on the *m-w* isle	*En. Arden*	633

misty.

Made *m* with the floating meal.	*Miller's D.*	104
not so *m* were her meek blue eyes	*Enid*	1620

misused.

Cancell'd a sense *m*.	*Godiva*	72

mix.

to *m* himself with Life. '*Love thou thy land,' etc.*		56
I myself must *m* with action,	*Locksley H.*	98
joy that *m*'es man with Heaven;	*Two Voices*	210
So *m* for ever with the past,	*Will Water.*	201
m the foaming draught Of fever	*Princess*, ii.	233
m not with the rest;	"	339
hand ambrosia, *m* The nectar;	" iii.	97
fires of Hell *M* with his hearth;	" v.	445
might *m* his draught with death.	" vi.	260

	POEM.	LINE.
m with hollow masks of night;	*In Mem.* lxix.	4
O tell me where the senses *m*,	" lxxxvii.	3
They *m* in one another's arms	" ci.	23
May she *m* With men and prosper!	" cxii.	2
M not memory with doubt,	*Maud*, II. iv.	57
my nature longer *m* with thine?	*Tithonus*	15
The sands and yeasty surges *m*	*Sailor Boy*	9

mixed—mixt.

m her ancient blood with shame.	*The Sisters.*	8
M with the knightly growth	*M. d'Arthur*	220
m with shadows of the common	*Gardener's D.*	134
A welcome *m* with sighs.	*Talking O.*	212
lights of sunset and of sunrise *m*	*Love and Duty*	70
The elements were kindlier *m*.'	*Two Voices*	228
In mosses *m* with violet	*Sir L. and Q. G.*	30
M with cunning sparks of hell.	*Vision of Sin*	114
And *m* with these, a lady	*Princess, Pro.*	32
m with inmost terms Of art and science;	" ii.	423
m with those Six hundred maidens	"	447
our dreams; Perhaps he *m* with them;	" iii.	204
stumbled *m* with floundering horses.	" v.	487
like night and evening *m*	" vi.	115
m with all this mystic frame.	*In Mem.* lxxxvii.	18
He *m* in all our simple sports;	" lxxxviii.	10
M their dim lights, like life and death,	" xciv.	63
m with God and Nature thou,	" cxxix.	11
a world in which I have hardly *m*,	*Maud*, I. vi.	76
M with kisses sweeter sweeter	" II. iv.	9
m my breath With a loyal people	" III. vi.	34
wildly fly, *M* with the flyers	*Enid*	1332
m Her fancies with the sallow-rifted	*Elaine*	995
Nor with them *m*, nor told her name,	*Guinevere*	146
m Upon their faces as they kiss'd	*Aylmer's F.*	429
Broke, *m* with awful light.	*Sea Dreams*	208-28
cry Which *m* with little Margaret's,	"	238
M with myrtle and clad with vine,	*The Islet*	19
hands they *m*, and yell'd	*Lucretius*	56

mixen.

cast it on the *m* that it die.'	*Enid*	672

mixing.

He *m* with his proper sphere,	*In Mem.* lix.	5

Mizpeh.

From *M*'s tower'd gate	*D. of F. Wom.*	199

Mnemosyne.

claspt the feet of a *M*,	*Princess*, iv.	250

moan (s.)

'Ave Mary,' made she *m*,	*Mariana in the S.*	9-21
breath'd in sleep a lower *m*,	"	45
She whisper'd, with a stifled *m*,	"	57
In firry woodlands making *m*;	*Miller's D.*	42
the low *M* of an unknown sea;	*Pal. of Art*	280
And make perpetual *m*,	*Lotos-E's.*	62
Nor sold his heart to idle *m*'s,	*Two Voices*	221
m of doves in immemorial elms,	*Princess*, vii.	206
that enchanted *m* only the swell	*Maud*, I. xviii.	62
to all other ladies, I make *m*.	*Elaine*	1272
low *m* of leaden-colour'd seas.	*En. Arden.*	613
m of an enemy massacred,	*Boädicea*	25

moan (verb.)

what is life that we should *m*?	*May Queen*, iii.	52
the deep *M*'s round with many voices.	*Ulysses*	56
such as *m*'s about the retrospect,	*Princess*, iv.	67
hear the dead at midday *m*,	*Maud*, I. vi.	70
Spirits of the waste and weald *M*	*Guinevere*	129
or thought she heard them *m*:	"	130
lowest roll of thunder *m*'s,	*Lucretius*	108
bits of roasting ox *M* round the spit	"	132

moaned.

She heard, she moved, She *m*,	*Princess*, v.	69
in herself she *m* 'too late	*Guinevere*	130
the passion in her *m* reply	*En. Arden.*	285
ever and aye the Priesthood *m*	*The Victim*	23

moaning (part.)

Nor *m*, household shelter crave	*Two Voices*	260
And circle *m* in the air	*In Mem.* xii.	15
M and calling out of other lands,	*Vivien*	811

278 CONCORDANCE TO

moaning (s.)   POEM.   LINE.
The *m's* of the homeless sea,   *In Mem.* xxxv. 9
evening, and the *m's* of the wind.   *Elaine*   997
Yes, as your *m's* witness,   *Aylmer's F,* 749
moat.
malice is no deeper than a *m,*   *Enid*   1189
mob (s.)
Confused by brainless *m's*   *Ode on Well.* 153
mob (verb.)
From my fixt height to *m* me up   *Princess,* vi. 289
mock (s.)
the loud world's random *m*   *Will*   .   4
mock (verb.)
I would *m* thy chaunt anew;   *The Owl,* ii. 8
We *m* thee when we do not fear: *In Mem.* Pro. 30
there will dare to *m* at me; .   *Elaine*   1047
but he never *m's,* .   *Guinevere* . 625
'*M* me not! *m* me not I love let us go.' *The Islet* 30
m at a barbarous adversary.   *Boādicea*   18
mock-disease.
old hysterical *m-d* should die.'   *Maud,* III. vi. 33
mocked.
m the wholesome human heart   *The Letters* 10
smote his thigh, and *m;*   *Elaine* . 661
with plumes that *m* the may;   *Guinevere* . 23
m me when he spake of hope; .   "   624
m him with returning calm   *Lucretius* . 25
mocker.
Betwixt the *m's* and the realists: *Princess,* Con. 24
mockery.
my *mockeries* of the world. .   *Vision of Sin* 202
I seem A *m* to my own self.   *Princess,* vii. 317
not wholly brain, Magnetic *mockeries;* *In Mem.*cxix. 3
m of my people, and their bane.' *Guinevere* . 522
m is the fume of little hearts.   "   626
A *m* to the yeomen over ale   *Aylmer's F.* 497
mock-heroic.
The sort of *m-h* gigantesque   *Princess, Con.* 11
mock-honour.
Did her *m-h* as the fairest fair, . *Enid*   1681
mock-Hymen.
M-H were laid up like winter-bats, *Princess,* iv. 126
mock-love.
same *m-l,* and this Mock-Hymen *Princess,* iv. 125
mock-loyal.
With reverent eyes *m-l,*   *Vivien*   13
mock-solemn.
something so *m-s,* that I laugh'd *Princess, Pro.* 209
mode.
Odalisques, or oracles of *m,* .   *Princess,* ii. 63
Ring in the nobler *m's* of life,   *In Mem.* cv. 15
model.
why should any man Remodel *m's*? *The Epic* . 38
dozen angry *m's* jetted steam; . *Princess, Pro.* 73
Lay by her like *m* of her hand.   "   iv. 574
This mother is your *m.*   "   vii. 315
serve as *m* for the mighty world, *Guinevere* . 462
modell'd.
Is but *m* on a skull. .   *Vision of Sin* 178
Neither *m,* glazed, or fram'd: "   188
moderate.
statesman-warrior, *m,* resolute, . *Ode on Well.* 25
modest.
How *m,* kindly, all-accomplish'd, *Ded. of Idylls* 17
Modred.
like his own Of *M,* Arthur's nephew *Enid* . 595
Sir *M's* brother, of a crafty house, *Elaine* . 557
her cause of flight Sir *M;* .   *Guinevere* . 10
M still in green, all ear and eye, .   " . 25
to think of *M's* dusty fall, .   " . 55
M's narrow foxy face, .   " . 63
M brought His creatures to the basement" . 102

that Sir *M* had usurped the realm, *Guinevere*   152
M whom he left in charge of all, .   "   . 193
many more when *M* raised revolt,   "   . 438
clave To *M,* and a remnant stays   "   . 440
modulate.
M me, Soul of mincing mimicry! *Princess,* ii. 403
modulated.
m so To an unheard melody,   *Eleänore* . 63
moind.
D'ya *m* the waäiste, my lass?   *N. Farmer* 29
moist.
m and dry, devising long, '*Love thou thy land,*'etc. 38
fancy of it, Made his eye *m;*   *Enid* . 1199
fear'd his eyes *M* as they were,   " . 1200
moisten.
hand falter, nor blue eye *M,*   *Enid* . 1362
mole.
the *m* has made his run,   *Aylmer's F.* 849
Moll.
tavern-catch Of *M* and Meg,   *Princess,* iv. 140
molten.
m on the waste Becomes a cloud: *Princess,* iv. 54
noble heart was *m* in her breast;   " vi. 103
The rocket *m* into flakes   *In Mem.* xcvii. 31
And *m* up, and roar in flood;   " cxxvi. 13
m down in mere uxoriousness. *Enid* . 60
moly.
propt on beds of amaranth and *m,* *Lotos-E's.* . 133
moment.
At the *m* of thy birth,   *Eleänore* . 15
flower of each, those *m's* when we met, *Ed. Morris* 69
One earnest, earnest *m* upon mine, *Love and Duty* 37
Every *m,* lightly shaken, ran itself *Locksley M.* 32
The fountain of the *m,* .   *Princess, Pro.* 61
a *m,* and once more The trumpet,   " v. 476
the last of those last *m's* came . *En. Arden* . 217
the *m* and the vessel past.   " . 243
She spoke: and in one *m* as it were, " . 449
mon (man.)
'what a *m* a beä sewer-ly!'   *N. Farmer* 54
Mona.
While about the shore of *M* . *Boādicea* . 1
Monaco.
city Of little *M,* basking, glow'd. *The Daisy* . 8
managed.
And I 'a *m* for Squoire   *N. Farmer* 48
Monday.
Saw the man—on *M,* was it?— *Walk. to the M.* 22
money.
not a room For love or *m.* .   *Audley Ct.* . 2
understand how *m* breeds, .   *The Brook* . 6
m can be repaid; Not kindness . *En. Arden* . 319
monk.
Old Summers, when the *n* was fat, *Talking O.* . 41
monkey-spite.
No lewdness, narrowing envy, *m-s, Lucretius* . 208
monotonous.
M and hollow like a Ghost's   *Guinevere* . 417
monster.
wallowing *m* spouted his foam-fountains *Lotos-E's.*152
Seven-headed *m's* only made to kill *Princess, Pro.*200
we seem a kind of *m* to you; .   " iii. 259
These *m's* blazon'd what they were, " iv. 326
loom to her Three times a *m* .   " v. 125
A *m,* then, a dream, A discord. . *In Mem.* lv. 21
Quaint *m's* for the market . *En. Arden* . 535
m lays His vast and filthy hands . *Lucretius* . 210
monstrous.
hateful, *m,* not to be told; .   *Maud,* III. vi. 41
So lean his eyes were *m;* .   *Vivien* . . 474

	POEM.	LINE.		POEM.	LINE.
Monte Rosa.			Lit with a low large *m*.	*Pal. of Art*	68
how phantom-fair, Was *M R.*	*The Daisy*	66	In hollow'd *m*'s of gems,	"	188
mouth.			It was when the *m* was setting,	*May Queen,* iii.	26
weeks and *m*'s, and early and late,	*The Sisters*	10	above the valley stood the *m*;	*Lotos-E's.*	7
Earn well the thrifty *m*'s, 'Love thou thy land,' etc.		95	Between the sun and *m* upon the shore	"	38
take a *m* to think,	*Dora*	27	in the *m* Nightly dew-fed;	"	74
before The *m* was out he left	"	35	Once, like the *m*, I made	*D.of F. Wom.*	132
in one *m* They wedded her	*Ed. Morris*	125	Far-heard beneath the *m*.	"	184
oft I fall, Maybe for *m*'s	*St S. Stylites*	101	The balmy *m* of blessed Israel	"	185
Each *m* is various to present	*Two Voices*	74	next *m* was roll'd into the sky,	"	229
Link'd *m* to *m* with such a chain	"	167	Which the *m* about her spreadeth,	*Margaret*	20
I must work thro' *m*'s of toil,	*Amphion*	97	While the stars burn, the *m*'s increase,	*To J. S.*	71
Each *m*, a birth-day coming on,	*Will Water.*	93	a great water, and the *m* was full.	*M. d'Arthur*	12
floating on for many a *m* and year	*Vision of Sin*	54	in the *m* athwart the place of tombs,	"	46
ere the silver sickle of that *m*	*Princess,* i.	100	winter *m* Brightening the skirts	"	53
The all-assuming *m*'s and years	*In Mem.* lxxxiv.	67	lightnings in the splendour of the *m*,	"	137
tho' the *m*'s, revolving near,	" xci.	11	long glories of the winter *m*.	"	192
As nine *m*'s go to the shaping	*Maud,* I. iv.	34	colourless, and like the wither'd *m*	"	213
m's ran on and rumour of battle	" III. vi.	29	for some three careless *m*'s	*Gardener's D.*	15
weeks to *m*'s, The *m*'s will add	*Guinevere*	617	beneath a *m*, that, just In crescent,	*Audley Ct.*	79
a change - a *m* - Give her a *m* (rep.)	*En. Arden*	458	thirty *m*'s, one honeymoon to that	*Ed. Morris*	92
m by *m* the noise about their doors,	*Aylmer's F.*	488	tagg'd with icy fringes in the *m*,	*St S. Stylites*	31
With twenty *m*'s of silence,	"	567	his orbit, and the *M* Her circle.	*Love and Duty*	22
Came, with a *m*'s leave given	*Sea Dreams*	6	day wanes; the slow *m* climbs;	*Ulysses*	55
'A *m* hence, a *m* hence.'	*The Window*	168	mellow *m*'s and happy skies,	*Locksley H.*	159
mood.			like Joshua's *m* in Ajalon!	"	180
fixed shadows of thy fixed *m*.	*Isabel*	9	like a summer *m* Half-dipt in cloud	*Godiva*	45
In lazy *m* I watch'd the little circles	*Miller's D.*	73	every worm beneath the *m*	*Two Voices*	178
m And change of my still soul.	*Pal. of Art*	59	snows Are sparkling to the *m*:	*St Agnes' Eve*	2
fit for every *m* of mind,	"	90	A thousand *m*'s will quiver;	*A Farewell*	14
from which *m* was born Scorn	"	230	As shines the *m* in clouded skies,	*Beggar Maid*	9
from out that *m* Laughter	"	231	long and troubled like a rising *m*,	*Princess,* i.	58
by change, and so I sway'd All *m*'s.	*D.of F.Wom.*	131	Come from the dying *m*, and blow	" ii.	461
more human in your *m*'s,	*Margaret*	47	Under the silver *m*	"	470
but betwixt this *m* and that,	*Gardener's D.*	152	with the sun and *m* renew their light	" iii.	238
I went thro' many wayward *m*'s	*Day-Dm.*	6	many weary *m*'s before we came	"	302
She changes with that *m* or this,	*Will Water.*	107	brief the *m* of beauty in the South.	" iv.	95
in her hon's *m* 'Tore open,	*Princess,* iv.	361	babbled for you, as babies for the *m*,	"	408
golden *m*'s Of sovereign artists;	" v.	186	maiden *m* that sparkles on a sty,	" v.	178
left her woman, lovelier in her *m*	" vii.	147	like a clouded *m* In a still water:	" vi.	253
woman thro' the crust of iron *m*'s	"	321	set a wrathful Dian's *m* on flame,	"	348
My lighter *m*'s are like to these.	*In Mem.* xxi.	9	the *m* may draw the sea;	"	364
I envy not in any *m*'s	" xxvii.	1	Her secret from the latest *m*?'	*In Mem.* xxi.	20
Mere fellowship of sluggish *m*'s,	" xxxv.	21	No lapse of *m*'s can canker Love,	" xxvi.	3
hit the *m* Of Love on earth?	" xlvi.	11	*m* is hid; the night is still; (ciii. 2)	" xxviii.	2
takes, when harsher *m*'s remit,	" xlvi.	6	when a thousand *m*'s shall wane	" lxxvi.	8
on thy harsher *m*'s aside,	" lviii.	7	Or sadness in the summer *m*'s?	" lxxxii.	8
Nor less it pleased in livelier *m*'s	" lxxxviii.	29	A ballad to the brightening *m*;	" lxxxviii.	28
as my father raged in his *m*?	*Maud,* I. i.	53	The sailing *m* in creek and cove;	" c.	16
My *m* is changed, for it fell	" III. vi.	9	glowing like the *m* Of Eden	*Con.*	27
coming up quite close, and his *m*	*Enid*	1562	rise, O *m*, from yonder down,	"	109
have wrought upon his cloudy *m*.	*Vivien*	12	white As ocean-foam in the *m*	*Maud,* I. xiv.	18
yielding to his kindlier *m*'s,	"	30	a hush with the setting *m*,	"	18
in the glass of some presageful *m*,	"	144	half to the setting *m* are gone,	*The Brook*	23
from Arthur's court To break the *m*.	"	147	I murmur under *m* and stars	*The Brook*	178
strange as that dark *m* of yours,	"	163	our God Himself is *m* and sun.	*Ode on Well.*	217
the same mistrustful *m*	"	170	by night With *m* and trembling stars	*Enid*	8
m as that, which lately gloom'd	"	174	*m*'s confused his fatherhood.'	*Vivien*	562
high as woman in her selfless *m*,	"	293	a *m* unseen albeit at full,	*Guinevere*	6
or a *m* Of overstrain'd affection,	"	371	beneath a clouded *m* He like a lover	*En. Arden*	659
Vivien, gathering somewhat of his *m*,	"	691	music of the *m* Sleeps in the plain eggs	*Aylmer's F.*	102
wrought upon his *m* and hugg'd him	"	797	a pale and unimpassion'd *m*,	"	334
His *m* was often like a fiend,	*Elaine*	251	The *m* like a rick on fire	*Grandmother*	39
Arthur to the banquet, dark in *m*,	"	563	Far ran the naked *m* across	*The Voyage*	29
being in his *m*'s Left them,	"	795	when in heaven the stars about the *m*	*Spec of Iliad*	11
Subject to the season or the *m*,	*Aylmer's F.*	71	Sun comes, *m* comes,	*The Window*	162
How low his brother's *m* had fallen	"	404	Sun sets, *m* sets,	"	164
cruel Seem'd the Captain's *m*.	*The Captain*	14	*moon-faced.*		
moon.			the *m-f* darling of all—	*Maud,* I. i.	72
At midnight the *m* cometh,	*Clarabel*	13	*moon-led.*		
mellow'd reflex of a winter *m*;	*Isabel*	29	Their *m-l* waters white.	*Pal. of Art*	252
ever when the *m* was low	*Mariana*	49	*moonlight.*		
when the *m* was very low,	"	53	By star-shine and by *m*,	*Oriana*	24
mighty *m* was gathering light	*Love and Death*	1	Like *m* on a falling shower?	*Margaret*	4
would be neither *m* nor star;	*The Merman*	21	Are as *m* unto sunlight,	*Locksley H.*	152
by the *m* the reaper weary,	*L. of Shalott,* ii.	33	full sea glared with muffled *m*,	*Princess,* i.	244
Or when the *m* was overhead,	" ii.	33	When on my bed the *m* falls,	*In Mem.* lxvi.	1
between the sunset and the *m*;	*Eleanore*	124	From off my bed the *m* dies:	"	10
Gleam'd to the flying *m* by fits,	*Miller's D.*	116	A cypress in the *m* shake,	*The Daisy*	82
like a dazzled morning *m*.	*Fatima*	26	The *m* touching o'er a terrace	"	83

CONCORDANCE TO

moon-lit.
	POEM.	LINE.
The sloping of the m-l sward	Arabian N's.	27
narrow m-l slips of silver cloud.	Œnone	214

moon-rise.
little before m-r hears the low Moan	Pal. of Art	279

moonshine.
up the pass All in a misty m,	Elaine	49
eyes all wet, in the sweet m:	Grandmother	49

moor.
From far and near, on mead and m,	In Mem. xxviii.	6
oft when sundown skirts the m	" xl.	17
sick of the m and the main .	Maud, I. i.	61
there is fatter game on the m;	" iv.	74
as she rode by on the m;	" iv.	15
Betwixt the cloud and the m,	" ix.	4
over the sullen-purple m	" x.	21
Go back, my lord, across the m,	" xii.	31
meanwhile far over m and fell	" xviii.	76
When I bow'd to her on the m.	" xix.	66

moorland.
Dreary gleams about the m .	Locksley H.	4
Many a morning on the m	"	35
O the dreary, dreary m!	"	40
all the glimmering m rings .	Sir L. and Q.G.	35

mooted.
ne'er been m, but as frankly theirs	Princess, v.	195

moral.
if you find no m there,	Day-Dm.	198
What m is in being fair.	"	200
is there any m shut	"	203
You'd have my m from the song,	"	243
Are clasp'd the m of thy life,	"	267
The m's, something of the frame .	Princess, ii	360

morass.
low m and whispering reed,	In Mem. xcix.	6

Moreland.
Sweet Emma M of yonder town .	Ed. Gray	1
Sweet Emma M spoke to me :	"	5
Sweet Emma M, love no more	"	7

morion.
shone Their m's, wash'd with morning,	Princess, v.	254

morn.
Either at m or eventide.	Mariana	16
cold winds woke the gray-eyed m	"	31
Ray-fringed eyelids of the m 'Clear-headed friend'		6
the amber m Forth gushes	Ode to Mem.	70
Wander from the side of the m,	Adeline	52
More inward than at night or m,	Mariana in the S.	58
'The day to night, the night to m,	"	82
night comes on that knows not m,	"	94
Thou wert born, on a summer m,	Eleänore	7
Each m my sleep was broken thro'	Miller's D.	39
in the dark m The panther's roar	Œnone	209
from her lips, as m from Memnon,	Pal. of Art	171
but I fall asleep at m ;	May Queen, ii.	50
The dim red m had died,	D. of F. Wom.	61
M broaden'd on the borders of the dark,	"	265
without help I cannot last till m. .	M. d'Arthur	26
a streamer of the northern m,	"	139
church-bells ring in the Christmas m.	" Ep.	31
brightening to his bridal m. .	Gardener's D.	72
that m with all its sound	"	82
I come to-morrow m.	Audley Ct.	69
mist of m Clung to the lake.	Ed. Morris	107
when my marriage m may fall,	Talking O.	285
while as yet 'tis early m : .	Locksley H.	1
make that m, from his cold crown	Two Voices	85
Or in the gateways of the m.	"	183
'Behold, it is the Sabbath m.'	"	402
The twilight melted into m.	Day-Dm.	180
cock crows ere the Christmas m,	Sir Galahad	51
They two will wed the morrow m :	Lady Clare	7
We two will wed to-morrow m.	"	87
Have a rouse before the m:	Vision of Sin	96, 120
on her bridal m before she past .	Princess, ii.	243
M in the white wake of the morning star	" iii.	1
tumble, Vulcans, on the second m.'	"	56

	POEM	LINE.
the Northern and the Southern m.'	Princess, v.	413
m by m the lark Shot up	" vii.	30
and this Is m to more,	"	335
redder than a windy m;	" Con.	91
Calm is the m without a sound,	In Mem. xi.	1
ere yet the m Breaks hither .	" xxvi.	13
Rise, happy m, rise, holy m,	" xxx.	29
Reveilée to the breaking m..	" lxvii.	8
With promise of a m as fair :	" lxxxiii.	29
Mute symbols of a joyful m,	" Con.	58
it chanced that on a summer m	Enid .	69
Guinevere lay late into the m,	"	157
like a man abroad at m	"	335
gladly given again this happy m.	"	691
white and glittering star of m	"	734
darting fish, that on a summer m	"	1318
m by m, arraying her sweet self .	Elaine	902
eve and m She kiss'd me saying .	"	1398
cold wind that foreruns the m	Guinevere .	131
I shall see him another m : .	Grandmother	67
mists, and gleaming halls of m.	Tithonus	10
renew thy beauty m by m	"	74
waiting the throned m .	Spec. of Iliad, Note	
From out the borders of the m,	On a Mourner	1
m That mock'd him with returning calm	Lucretius	25

morning.
It haunted me, the m long,	Miller's D.	69
that m, on the casement-edge	"	82
Gargarus Stands up and takes the m :	Œnone	11
Far up the solitary m smote	"	54
In the early, early m	May Queen, ii.	22
rose the m of the year!	" iii.	3
when the night and m meet .	"	22
It is a stormy m.' .	The Goose	44
every m brought a noble chance,	M. d'Arthur	230
This m is the m of the day,	Gardener's D.	1
The northern m o'er thee shoot,	Talking O.	275
m driv'n her plow of pearl	Love and Duty	96
Many a m on the moorland	Locksley H.	35
sees the sacred m spread	Two Voices	80
In her still place the m wept ;	"	275
And in the m of the times.	Day-Dm.	232
I saw that every m, far withdrawn	Vision of Sin	48
shone Their morions, wash'd with m,	Princess, v.	254
mused on that wild m in the woods,	"	460
Death and M on the silver horns,	" vii.	189
on the blind half-world ;	"	331
With m wakes the will,	In Mem. iv.	15
m wore To evening but some heart	" vi.	7
At earliest m to the door.	" vii.	8
Singing alone in the m of life.	Maud, I. v.	6
happy m of life and of May,	" vi.	1
M arises stormy and pale .	" vi.	7
when the m came In a cloud	"	20
O when did a m shine So rich	" xix.	5
For a breeze of m moves,	" xxii.	7
'Tis a m pure and sweet	" II. iv.	31-5
with the m all the court were gone.	Enid .	156
booty from the m's raid :	"	1413
m's earliest ray Might strike it,	Elaine	5
o'er and o'er For all an April m.	"	893
ten slow m's past, and on the eleventh	"	1127
Enoch faced this m of farewell	En. Arden .	182
uttermost Parts of the m?	"	224
kindlier glow Faded with m,	Aylmer's F.	412
such a star of m in their blue,	"	692
the winds are up in the m! (rep.)	The Window	5
this is the golden m of love .	"	188

morning-breath.
dewy meadowy m-b Of England !.	En. Arden .	661

morning-star.
Sung by the m s of song,	D. of F. Wom	3
maiden splendours of the m-s	"	55
Toward the m-s.	"	244
whistled to the m s.	Sailor Boy .	4

Morris.
with Edwin M and with Edward Bull	Ed. Morris	14
Edwin M, he that knew the names	"	16

	POEM.	LINE.		POEM.	LINE.
Morrison.			I tried the *m's* heart.	*Princess,* iii.	131
A labourer's daughter, Mary *M.*	*Dora*	38	then, demanded if her *m* knew,	" iv.	214
morrow.			and you me Your second *m:*	"	278
when the *m* came, she rose and took	*Dora*	78	half on her *m* propt,	"	348
burns Above the unrisen *m:*	*Princess,* iv.	65	to live No wiser than their *m's,*	"	423
For the meeting of the *m,*	*Maud,* II. iv.	28	beat my girl Remembering her *m:*	" v.	86
mortal.			Ill *m* that I was to leave her	"	90
Her stature more than *m*	*Princess,* Pro.	40	won Your *m,* a good *m,* a good wife,	"	159
to choose Of things all *m,*	*In Mem.* xxxiv.	11	she of whom you speak, My *m,*	"	185
earth yawns: the *m* disappears;	*Ode on Well.*	269	*M's*—that all prophetic pity,	"	371
mortality.			what *m's* blood You draw from,	"	394
from the low light of *m*	*Aylmer's F.*	641	risk'd it for my own: His *m* lives:	"	398
mortify.			child Of one unworthy *m*;	"	421
M Your flesh, like me,	*St S. Stylites*	176	the authentic *m* of her mind.	"	423
mosaic.			The *m* makes us most—	"	496
was all *m* choicely plann'd	*Pal. of Art*	145	good Queen, her *m,* shore the tress	" vi.	97
rough kex break The starr'd *m,*	*Princess,* iv.	60	spied its *m* and began	"	120
moss.			stood the unhappy *m* open-mouth'd,	"	127
With blackest *m* the flower-plots.	*Mariana*	1	grief and *m's* hunger in her eye,	"	130
bluebell rings To the *m'es* underneath?	*Adeline*	35	The sacred *m's* bosom, panting,	"	132
creeping *m'es* and clambering weeds,	*Dying Swan*	36	The *m,* me, the child;	"	137
hueless *m'es* under the sea	*The Mermaid*	49	thy *m* prove As true to thee	"	186
those long *m'es* in the stream.	*Miller's D.*	46	from your *m* now a saint with saints	"	216
cool *m'es* deep And thro' the *m* the ivies	*Lotos-E's.*	54	You shame your *m's* judgment	"	244
then for roses, *m* or musk,	*Gardener's D.*	189	Not only he, but by my *m's* soul,	"	315
learned names of agaric, *m* and fern,	*Ed. Morris*	17	Happy he With such a *m!*	" vii.	309
In *m'es* mixt with violet	*Sir L. and Q. G.*	30	This *m* is your model.	"	315
refuse patch'd with *m,*	*Vision of Sin*	212	O *m,* praying God will save	*In Mem.* vi.	13
wine-flask lying eouch'd in *m,*	*In Mem.* lxxxviii.	44	Dear as the *m* to the son,	" ix.	19
m and braided marish-pipe:	*On a Mourner*	10	tears are on the *m's* face	" xxxix.	10
moss-bed.			That feed the *m's* of the flock;	" xcix.	16
Soft are the *m-b's* under the sea:	*The Merman*	39	The shrill-edged shriek of a *m.*	*Maud,* I. i.	16
moth.			a Mammonite *m* kills her babe	"	45
rich as *m's* from dusk cocoons,	*Princess,* ii.	5	Maud the beloved of my *m,*	"	72
not a *m* with vain desire	*In Mem.* hii.	10	Your *m* is mute in her grave	" iv.	58
mother.			My *m,* who was so gentle and good?	" vi.	67
In her as *M,* Wife, and Queen:	*To the Queen*	28	Her *m* has been a thing complete,	" xiii.	35
Complaining '*M,* give me grace *Mariana in the S.*		29	Made her only the child of her *m*	"	40
Sweet *M,* let me not here alone	"	59	Darken'd watching a *m* decline	" xix.	8
My *m* thought, What ails the boy?	*Miller's D.*	93	Of my *m's* faded cheek	"	19
slowly was my *m* brought	"	137	To speak of the *m* she loved	"	27
The doubt my *m* would not see;	"	154	thought It is his *m's* hair.	" II. ii.	70
O *m* Ida, many-fountain'd Ida, rep.	*Œnone* 22, *et pass.*		from the plaintive *m's* teat he took	*The Brook*	129
O *m,* hear me yet before I die (rep.)	"	203	My *m,* as it seems you did	"	225
a *m* Conjectures of the features	"	247	*M,* a maiden is a tender thing,	*Enid*	510
laid him at his *m's* feet.	*The Sisters*	35	arose, and raised Her *m* too,	"	536
When thus he met his *m's* view,	*L. C. V. de l'ere*	34	a costly gift Of her good *m,*	"	632
call me early, *m* dear;	*May Queen,* i. 1, *et pass.*		while the *m* show'd it, and the two	"	636
blame among The Hebrew *m's*	*D. of F. Wom.*	215	lo! it was her *m* grasping her	"	676
Grave *m* of majestic works, 'Of old sat Freedom'		13	ceased the kindly *m* out of breath;	"	732
hardness, and to slight His *m;*	*Dora*	119	Help'd by the *m's* careful hand	"	738
when the boy beheld His *m,*	"	135	that good *m* making Enid gay	"	757
Christ, the Virgin *M,* and the Saints;	*St S. Stylites*	110	glance at her good *m's* face,	"	766
Her *m* trundled to the gate.	*Talking O.*	111	*m* silent too, nor helping her,	"	768
press me from the *m's* breast.	*Locksley H.*	90	seeing cloud upon the *m's* brow,	"	777
m't brought Their children, clamouring,	*Godiva*	14	'O my new *m,* be not wroth	"	779
Against her father's and *m's* will:	*Ed. Gray*	10	the *m* smiled, but half in tears,	"	823
O *m,'* she said, 'if this be true,	*Lady Clare*	30	like the kid in its own *m's* milk!	*Vivien*	713
give one kiss to your *m* dear!	"	49-53	*m* of the house There was not:	*Elaine*	177
O *m, m, m,'* she said	"	51	Wish'd it had been my *m,*	"	671
My *m* dear, if this be so,	"	54	than any *m* to a sick child,	"	854
bless me, *m,* ere I go.'	"	56	by the *m* of our Lord himself,	"	1224
so, my *m* said, the story ran.	*Princess,* i.	11	Lady of the Lake Stole from his *m*	"	1396
m pitying made a thousand prayers;	"	21	*m* cared for it With all a *m's* eare:	*En. Arden*	261
My *m* was as mild as any saint,	"	22	new *m* came about her heart,	"	520
m of the sweetest little maid,	" ii.	260	*m* glancing often toward her babe,	"	755
play The Spartan *M* with emotion,	"	263	the girl So like her *m,*	"	792
Our *m,* is she well?	"	290	Annie, whom I saw So like her *m,*	"	884
April daffodilly Her *m's* colour	"	304	Heard the good *m* softly whisper	*Aylmer's F.*	187
your *m's* jealous temperament—	"	317	*m* of the foul adulteries	"	376
Rest, rest, on *m's* breast,	"	465	*m* flow'd in shallower acrimonies;	"	563
while yet you may! My *m* knows;'	" iii.	13	the sad *m,* for the second death	"	604
My *m, 'tis* her wont	"	16	with the *m* he had never known,	"	600
m went rest lying on the word)	"	38	childless *m* went to seek her child;	"	820
So my *m* clutch'd The truth	"	44	wail'd and woke The *m.*	*Sea Dreams*	58
'tis my *m.* Too jealous,	"	63	Virgin *M* standing with her child	"	234
my *m* still Affirms your Psyche	"	75	the child Clung to the *m,*	"	237
			M, let me fly away.	"	284
			My *m* clings about my neck,	*Sailor Boy*	17
			Chop the breasts from off the *m.*	*Boadicea*	18
			Every *m's* son—Down they dropt—	*The Captain*	50

	POEM.	LINE.
They found the *m* sitting still ;	*The Victim*	32
glad Nosing the *m's* udder, .	*Lucretius*	100

mother-age.

O thou wondrous *M-A !*	*Locksley H.*	108
M-A (for mine I knew not) .	"	185

mother-city.

gain'd the *m-c* thick with towers, .	*Princess,*	i. 111

motion.

A *m* from the river won	*Arabian N's.*	34
Thought and *m* mingle	*Eleänore*	60
M's flow To one another,	"	61
With *m's* of the outer sea ;	"	113
I had no *m* of my own.	*Miller's D.*	44
those names, that in their *m* were	*Pal. of Art*	165
onward-sloping *m's* infinite .	"	247
enough of action, and of *m* we,	*Lotos-E's.*	150
no *m* in the dumb dead air,	*D. of F. Wom.*	65
with sudden *m* from the ground	"	170
A *m* toiling in the gloom—	*'Love thou thy land'*	54
or else a *m* of the mere.	*M. d'Arthur*	77
those blind *m's* of the Spring,	*Talking O.*	175
her eyes on all my *m's*,	*Locksley H.*	22
Nature made them blinder *m's*	"	150
We find no *m* in the dead.' .	*Two Voices*	279
m's, checks, and counterchecks.	"	300
Nature's living *m* lent .	"	449
faces toward us and address'd their *m*:	*Princess,*	iv. 530
about his *m* clung The shadow	"	v. 247
heart Made for all noble *m*;	"	374
That all thy *m's* gently pass.	*In Mem.*	xv. 10
muffled *m's* blindly drown	"	xlviii. 15
As, unto vaster *m's* bound,	"	lxii. 10
O heart, with kindliest *m* warm,	"	lxxxiv. 34
No dance, no *m*, save alone .	"	civ. 23
In all her *m* one with law ;	"	cxxi. 8
O, having the nerves of *m*	*Maud,*	I. i. 63
horse in *m* toward the knight,	*Enid*	206
at the flash and *m* of the man	"	1316
scared but at the *m* of the man,	"	1325
Her constant *m* round him,	"	1773
No shadow past, nor *m*:	*En. Arden*	711
in flood And masters of his *m*,	*Aylmer's F.*	340
the *m* of the boundless deep	*Sea Dreams*	89
m of the great deep bore me on,	"	107
the *m* of the current ceased,	"	113
rascal in the *m's* of his back,	"	163
All in quantity, careful of my *m*,	*Hendecasyllabics*	5
no mortal *m* jars The blackness	*On a Mourner*	26

motto.

this for *m*, 'Rather use than fame.'	*Vivien*	330
Blazon your *m's* of blessing .	*W. to Alexan.*	12

mould (shape.)

all varieties of *m* and mind) To——	*With Pal. of Art*	7
That are cast in gentle *m*.	*To J. S.*	1
this *m* of hopes and fears	*Two Voices*	28
'That I was first in human *m*?	"	342
Than in her *m* that other,	*Princess,*	vii. 148
niched shapes of noble *m*,	*The Daisy*	38

mould (earth.)

you may lay me low i' the *m*	*May Queen,*	ii. 4
render him to the *m*.	*Ode on Well.*	48

mould (verb.)

Unto her limbs itself doth *m*	*Day-Dm.*	86
m The woman to the fuller day.'	*Princess,*	iii. 314
m a generation strong to move	"	v. 406
m a mighty state's decrees,	*In Mem.*	lxiii. 11

moulded.

M thy baby thought.	*Eleänore*	5
M by God, and temper'd To——	*With Pal. of Art*	8
m like in nature's mint ;	*In Mem.*	lxxviii. 6
And *m* in colossal calm.	*Con.*	16
m by your wishes for her weal ;	*Enid*	799
Heaven in lavish bounty *m*,	*Aylmer's F.*	107

moulder.

cannons *m* on the seaward wall ;	*Ode on Well.*	173
rotting inward slowly *m's* all.	*Vivien*	245
heads should *m* on the city gates	"	444

mouldered.

	POEM.	LINE.
man, I think, So *m* in a sinecure.	*Princess, Pro.*	180

mouldering.

Before the *m* of a yew .	*In Mem.*	lxxv. 8
ocean tosses O'er them *m*,	*The Captain*	70

moulding.

reach thro' nature, *m* men.	*In Mem.*	cxxiii. 24

mound (s.)

A realm of pleasance, many a *m*,	*Arabian N's.*	101
Heap'd over with a *m* of grass,	*Lotos-E's.*	112
sat we down upon a garden *m*,	*Gardener's D.*	209
sat upon a *m* That was unsown,	*Dora*	70
child once more, and sat upon the *m* ;	"	79
gain'd a petty *m* Beyond it,	*Princess,*	iv. 535
three paces measured from the *m*,	"	v. 1
here and there on *m* and knoll,	*Enid*	1651
whelm all this beneath as vast a *m*	*Vivien*	506

mound (verb.)

heaped hills that *m* the sea,	*Ode to Mem.*	98

mount (s.)

A *m* of marble, a hundred spires !	*The Daisy*	60
o'er a *m* of newly-fallen stones,	*Enid*	361
on the *m* Of Badon I myself	*Elaine*	302

mount (verb.)

Before he *m's* the hill, I know	*Fatima*	22
As *m's* the heavenward altar-fire,	*In Mem.*	xl. 3
never *m* As high as woman .	*Vivien*	292
the wanton say? 'Not *m* as high ;'	"	662
Nor sound of human sorrow *m's*.	*Lucretius*	109

mountain.

the brain of the purple *m*	*Poet's Mind*	29
m draws it from Heaven above,	"	32
Across the *m* stream'd below	*Pal. of Art*	34
The wind, that beats the *m*,	*To J. S.*	1
Among the *m's* by the winter sea ;	*M. d'Arthur*	2
curves of *m*, bridge, Boat,	*Ed. Morris*	5
The *m* stirr'd its bushy crown,	*Amphion*	25
weed That blows upon its *m*,	"	94
fold to fold, of *m* or of cape ;	*Princess,*	vi. 366
storm Broke on the *m* and I cared not	*Vivien*	353
league of *m* full of golden mines,	"	437
And the cairn'd *m* was a shadow,	"	488
So long, that *m's* have arisen since	"	525
would pare the *m* to the plain,	"	678
The *m* wooded to the peak	*En. Arden*	573
A *m*, like a wall of burs	*Sea Dreams*	115
facets of the glorious *m* flash	*The Islet*	22
m there has cast its cloudy slough,	*Lucretius*	177
in serenest air, A *m* o'er a *m*,	"	179
m quickens into Nymph and Faun ;	"	187

mountain-brook.

listen near a torrent *m-b*,	*Enid*	1020

mountain-eaves.

shepherds from the *m-e*	*Amphion*	53

mountain-gorge.

in a seaward-gazing *m-g*	*En. Arden*	559

mountain-ground.

He finds on misty *m-g*	*In Mem.*	xcvi. 2

mountain-mere.

Sometimes on lonely *m-m's* .	*Sir Galahad*	37

mountain-range.

uprose the mystic *m-r*:	*Vision of Sin*	208

mountain-shade.

the *m-s* Sloped downward	*Œnone*	20

mountain-side.

up there on yonder *m s*.	*St S. Stylites*	71
like its own mists to all the *m s*;	*Elaine*	39
Struck out the streaming *m-s*,	*Lucretius*	29

mountain-top.

three *m-t's*, Three silent pinnacles,	*Lotos-E's*	15
chanted on the smoky *m-t's*,	*Guinevere*	280

mountain-tract.

then I look'd up toward a *m-t*,	*Vision of Sin*	46

	POEM.	LINE.
mountain-wall.		
thro' the m-w's A rolling	Sir Galahad	74
He watches from his m-w's	The Eagle	5
mounted.		
from a throne M in heaven	To J. M. K.	13
this old mansion m high	Miller's D.	35
while day sank or m higher	Pal. of Art	46
m our good steeds	Princess, i.	201
m, Ganymedes, To tumble, Vulcans	" iii.	55
M, and reach'd a hand,	Enid	1607
Set her thereon, and m on his own,	Guinevere	122
what you will—Has m yonder	Lucretius	127
mourn.		
'Where I may m and pray.	Pal. of Art	292
to m and rave On alien shores.	Lotos-E's.	32
to clamour, m and sob,	St S. Stylites	6
m half-shrouded over death	Princess, v.	71
to those that m In vain ;	In Mem. ix.	5
To m for any overmuch ;	" lxxxiv.	62
They know me not, but m with me.	" xcviii.	20
M, for to us he seems the last	Ode on Well.	19
M for the man of long-enduring blood	"	24
M for the man of amplest influence,	"	27
those who m a friend in vain,	Lucretius	142
mourned.		
Deeply m the Lord of Burleigh,	L. of Burleigh	91
all the men m at his side :	Princess, iii.	335
m his absence as his grave,	En. Arden	246
mourning (part.)		
I went m, 'No fair Hebrew boy	D. of F. Wom.	213
ever m over the feud	Maud, I. xix.	31
M when their leaders fall,	Ode on Well.	5
mourning (s.)		
the m of a mighty nation,	Ode on Well.	4
in m these, and those With blots of it	Aylmer's F.	619
mouse.		
m Behind the mouldering wainscot	Mariana	63
shrieking rush of the wainscot m,	Maud, I. vi.	71
Within the hearing of cat or m,	" II. v.	48
thin weasel there Follows the m,	Aylmer's F.	853
mouth (s.)		
crush'd them on my breast, my m :	Fatima	12
common m So gross to express delight	Gardener's D.	54
smite him on the cheek, And on the m,	Two Voices	251
often told a tale from m to m	Princess, Pro.	189
Walter warped his m at this	"	208
twitch of pain Tortured her m,	" vi.	90
on her m A doubtful smile	"	252
A rabbit m that is ever agape—	Maud, I. x.	31
And a rose her m.	" xvii.	8-28
deathful-grinning m's of the fortress	" III. vi.	52
Into the m of Hell	Lt. Brigade	25
Back from the m of Hell	"	47
King Arthur's hound of deepest m,	Enid	186
in the m's of base interpreters,	Vivien	644
white m of the violent Glem ;	Elaine	288
any m to gape for save a Queen's—	"	771
Were added m's that gaped,	"	1242
downward crescent of her minion m,	Aylmer's F.	533
sudden twitch of his iron m ;	"	732
unctuous m which lured him,	Sea Dreams	14
M, forehead, eyelids, growing	Tithonus	58
flats, and floods Of mighty m,	The Voyage	46
mouth (verb.)		
How she m's behind my back	Vision of Sin	110
mouthed.		
in her hunger m and mumbled it,	Princess, vi.	196
mouthing.		
m out his hollow oes and aes,	The Epic	50
mouthpiece.		
I come the m of our King to Doorm	Enid	1644
move.		
M's over still Shalott.	L. of Shalott, iii.	27
sometimes they swell and m,	Eleänore	111
m about the house with joy,	Miller's D.	95
there I m no longer now,	May Queen, iii.	51

	POEM.	LINE.
did m Me from my bliss of life,	D. of F. Wom.	209
You m not in such solitudes,	Margaret	45
He lieth still : he doth not m :	D. of the O. Year	10
full music seem'd to m and change	Ed. Morris	35
m's among my visions of the lake,	"	144
wake and sleep, but all things m ;	Golden Year	22
M onward leading up the golden year	"	26
For ever and for ever when I m.	Ulysses	21
sweetly did she speak and m :	Locksley H.	71
Science m's, but slowly slowly,	"	134
Some hidden principle to m,	Two Voices	133
m's not on the rounded curl.	Day-Dm.	84
gouty oak began to m,	Amphion	23
I could not m a thistle ;	"	66
mightier transports m and thrill ;	Sir Galahad	22
m the trees, the copses nod,	"	77
Begins to m and tremble.	Will Water.	32
wheresoe'er thou m, good luck	"	215
thou wilt never m from hence,	"	217
life that m's to gracious ends. 'You might have won'		6
Till the graves begin to m,	Vision of Sin	165
M eastward, happy earth, 'Move eastward,' etc.		1
m me to my marriage-morn,	"	11
m as rich as Emperor-moths,	Princess, Pro.	144
m among a world of ghosts (iv. 539)	" i.	17
Who m's about the Princess ;	"	75
whene'er she m's The Samian Here rises	" iii.	98
found her there At point to m,	"	115
m, my friend, At no man's beck,	"	210
after-hands May m the world,	"	247
m 'The minutes fledged with music.'	" iv.	18
a generation strong to m	" v.	406
to m in old memorial tilts,	"	468
m the stony bases of the world.	" vi.	42
speak, nor m, nor make one sign,	" vii.	138
cease to m so near the Heavens,	"	180
m's to hold m to one goal,	"	247
m's his doubtful arms, and feels	In Mem. xiii.	3
For I in spirit saw thee m	" xvii.	5
this it was that made me m.	" xxv.	5
doubtful joys the father m,	" xxxix.	9
Should m his rounds, and fusing all	" xlvi.	2
canst not m me from thy side,	" li.	7
My centred passion cannot m,	" lviii.	9
m thee on to noble ends	" lxiv.	12
Her faith is fixt and cannot m,	" xcvi.	33
As down the garden-walks I m,	" ci.	6
m his course, and show That life	" cxvii.	19
M upward, working out the beast,	"	27
Who m's about from place to place,	" cxxv.	10
To which the whole creation m's.	" Con.	144
Do we m ourselves, or are moved	Maud, I. iv.	26
m to the meadow and fall before	" v.	35
For a breeze of morning m's.	" xxii.	7
only m's with the moving eye,	" II. ii.	37
Pass and cease to m about ! .	" iv.	59
I m the sweet forget-me-nots	The Brook	172
If love of country m thee there	Ode on Well.	140
dark crowd m's, and there are sobs	"	268
nor m's the loud world's random mock	Will	4
pushing could m The chair of Idris.	Enid	542
parted from you, m's me yet.'	"	1196
leave To m to your own land,	"	1737
cannot m To these fair jousts?'	Elaine	80
strike spur, suddenly m,	"	455
down his enemy made them m.	"	810
rough Torre began to moan and m,	"	1060
as Arthur's Queen I m and rule :	"	1215
moving m's the nest and nestling,	Sea Dreams	279
Phantom of a wish that once could m,	Coquette, ii.	10
creeps a cloud, or m's a wind,	Lucretius	106
moved.		
you rose and m the light,	Miller's D.	125
Your ripe lips m not	"	131
Fronting the dawn he m.	Œnone	57
Floated the glowing sunlights, as she m	"	178
bells that swung, M of themselves,	Pal. of Art	130
Its office, m with sympathy. 'Love thou thy land'		48
with oar and sail M from the brink	M. d'Arthur	216
m away, and left me, statue-like,	Gardener's D.	158

CONCORDANCE TO

	POEM.	LINE.
m, Like Proserpine in Enna,	Ed. Morris	111
in old days *M* earth and heaven;	Ulysses	67
You *m* her at your pleasure.	Amphion	60
M with violence, changed in hue,	Vision of Sin	34
There *m* the multitude,	Princess, Pro.	57
for still we *m* Together,	" i.	55
so To the open window *m*,	" iv.	471
Set into sunrise; then we *m* away.	"	553
She heard, she *m*, She moan'd	" v.	68
Yet she neither spoke nor *m*.	"	539
Yet she neither *m* nor wept.	"	543
m by this, or was it chance,	" vi.	81
m beyond his custom, Gama said:	"	212
the small king *m* beyond his wont.	"	248
on they *m* and gain'd the hall,	" vii.	332
own clear element, they *m*.	"	13
rounder seem'd: I *m*; I sigh'd:	"	122
m, and at her feet the volume fell.	"	238
from their orbits as they *m*,	"	307
I *m* as in a strange diagonal,	Con.	27
The Wye is hush'd nor *m* along,	In Mem. xix.	9
M in the chambers of the blood;	" xxiii.	20
We saw not, when we *m* therein?	" xxiv.	16
m Upon the topmost froth	" li.	3
Had *m* me kindly from thy side,	" lxxix.	3
m thro' life of lower phase,	Con.	125
m by an unseen hand at a game	Maud, I. iv.	26
m To speak of the mother she loved	" xix.	26
Katie never ran: she *m*	The Brook	87
She faintly smiled, she hardly *m*;	The Letters	14
and we see him as he *m*,	Ded. of Idylls	16
sweet voice of Enid *m* Geraint,	Enid	334
M the fair Enid, all in faded silk,	"	366
they *m* Down to the meadow	"	536
and wings *M* in her ivy,	"	599
m the Prince To laughter	"	1144
harder to be *m* Than hardest tyrants	"	1542
m so much the more, and shriek'd	"	1630
light came from her when she *m*:	Vivien	417
thus they *m* away; she stay'd	Elaine	389
Must needs have *m* my laughter:	"	594
M to her chamber, and there flung	"	606
m about her palace, proud and pale.	"	611
lifted her fair face and *m* away:	"	679
had devised the letter, *m* again,	"	1280
Sir Lancelot where he *m* apart,	"	1339
noblest, while you *m* Among them,	Guinevere	323
lifted up in spirit he *m* away	En. Arden	327
A phantom made of many phantoms *m*	"	603
or he himself *M* haunting people,	"	605
'The Gods are *m* against the land.'	The Victim	6

movement.
it absorbs With swifter *m*	Isabel	32
loveliest in all grace Of *m*	Œnone	74
without light Or power of *m*,	Pal. of Art.	246

moving.
m thro' a mirror clear	L. of Shalott, ii.	10
hidden ore That glimpses, *m* up,	D. of F. Wom.	275
M thro' a fleecy night,	Margaret	21
M in the leavy beech,	"	61
m toward the stillness of his rest.	Locksley H.	144
m after truth long sought,	Two Voices	62
and was *m* on In gratulation,	Princess, ii.	167
m thro' the uncertain gloom,	" iv.	197
Slided, they *m* under shade;	" vi.	66
M about the household ways,	In Mem. lix.	11
m up from high to higher,	" lxiii.	13
Eternal process *m* on,	" lxxxi.	5
m side by side With wisdom,	" cxiii.	19
And see'st the *m* of the team.	" cxx.	16
lost in trouble and *m* round	Maud, I. xxi.	5
m, cast the coverlet aside	Enid	73
m toward a cedarn cabinet,	"	136
saw you *m* by me on the bridge,	"	429
m without answer to her rest	"	530
m downward to the meadow ground,	"	1053
m up with pliant courtliness,	"	1127
m homeward babbled to his men,	"	1211
m back she held Her finger up,	"	1301
m out they found the stately horse,	"	1600

	POEM.	LINE.
Edyrn *m* frankly forward spake:	Enid	1632
m everywhere Clear'd the dark places	"	1790
M to meet him in the castle court;	Elaine	175
kindly man *m* among his kind:	"	265
by the wind they made In *m*,	"	480
barge that brought her *m* down,	"	1382
ahead Of his and her retinue *m*,	Guinevere	382
m thro' the past unconsciously,	"	399
m ghostlike to his doom.	"	599
m homeward came on Annie pale,	En. Arden	149
m up the coast they landed him,	"	666
in *m* on I found Only the landward	Sea Dreams	93
m moves the nest and nestling,	"	279

mower.
and *m's* mowing in it:	Enid	1048
Bare victual for the *m's*:	"	1051
coarse, And only meet for *m's*;'	"	1058
Ate all the *m's* victual unawares,	"	1064
Fresh victual for these *m's*	"	1074
costlier than with *m's* fare.'	"	1080
when I left your *m's* dinnerless,	"	1083
lusty *m's* labouring dinnerless,	"	1100

mowing.
| and mowers *m* in it: | Enid | 1048 |

much-beloved.
| And he the *m-b* again, | In Mem. xli. | 6 |

muck.
| Ran a Malayan *m* against the times | Aylmer's F. | 463 |

mud.
| with pig, wallowing in sun and *m*. | Walk. to the M. | 80 |
| Fish are we that love the *m*. | Vision of Sin | 101 |

muddle.
| loud ater meū thot *m's* ma quoit | N. Farmer | 58 |

muddy.
| clear stream flowing with a *m* one, | Isabel | 30 |

mud-honey.
| His heart in the gross *m-h* of town, | Maud, I. xvi. | 5 |

muffle.
| O *m* round thy knees with fern, | Talking O. | 149 |

muffled.
The panther's roar came *m*	Œnone	210
sitting *m* in dark leaves,	Gardener's D.	37
chimneys *m* in the leafy vine.	Audley Ct.	18
we three Sat *m* like the Fates:	Princess, ii.	443
standing, *m* round with woe,	In Mem. xiv.	5
m round with selfish reticence.	Vivien	186

mulberry-faced.
| made the *m-f* Dictator's orgies worse | Lucretius | 54 |

mule.
| Her cream-white *m* his pastern set: | Sir L. and Q. G. | 31 |

multiplied.
| Thus truth was *m* on truth, | The Poet | 33 |
| Thrice *m* by superhuman pangs, | St S. Stylites | 11 |

multitude.
| moved the *m*, a thousand heads: | Princess, Pro. | 57 |
| and so press in, perforce Of *m*, | Lucretius | 168 |

mumbled.
| in her hunger mouth'd and *m* it, | Princess, vi. | 196 |

mumbling.
| Muttering and *m*, idiotlike | En. Arden | 640 |

murder.
| And the spirit of *m* works | Maud, I. i. | 40 |
| the rust of *m* on the walls— | Guinevere | 74 |

murmur (s.).
Overblown with *m's* harsh,	Ode to Mem.	99
And no *m* at the door,	Deserted H.	7
There comes no *m* of reply.	Pal. of Art	286
To hear the *m* of the strife,	Margaret	23
m broke the stillness of that air	Gardener's D.	146
Not whisper, any *m* of complaint.	St S. Stylites	22
The *m's* of the drum and fife	Talking O.	215

	POEM.	LINE.
The *m* of the fountain-head—	Two Voices	216
A *m* 'be of better cheer.'	"	479
Faint *m*'s from the meadows come,	Day-Dm.	26
Made a *m* in the land.	L. of Burleigh	20
And they speak in gentle *m*,	"	49
m's of her beauty from the South.	Princess, i.	35
a *m* ran Thro' all the camp	" v.	106
m's from the dying sun;	In Mem. iii.	8
dull'd the *m* on thy lip,	" xxii.	16
The *m* of a happy Pan:	" xxiii.	12
A single *m* in the breast,	" ciii.	7
cackle of your bourg The *m* of the world!	Enid.	277
take the rustic *m* of their bourg	"	419
m's 'lo, thou likewise shalt be king.'	Elaine	56
neither light nor *m* there	En. Arden	688
a *m* heard aërially,	Boädicea	24
m's of a deeper voice	On a Mourner	16

murmur (verb.)

And the nations do but *m*	Locksley II.	106
dove n ay *m* of the dove,	Princess, iii.	89
Should *m* from the narrow house,	In Mem. xxxv.	2
I *m* under moon and stars,	The Brook	178
Will *m*, lo the shameless ones,	Elaine	101

murmur'd.

Before Our Lady *m* she	Mariana in the S.	28
low voice, full of care, M beside me	D. of F. Wom.	249
m Arthur, 'Place me in the barge	M. d'Arthur	204
And sweetly *m* thine.	Talking O.	160
And she *m*, 'Oh, that he	L. of Burleigh	82
all the sloping pasture *m*,	Princess, Pro.	55
m that their May Was passing:	" ii.	439
m Florian gazing after her.	" iii.	81
The mellow breaker *m* Ida.	" iv.	416
I *m*, as I came along,	In Mem. xxxvii.	21
m, 'vain, in vain; it cannot be.	Elaine	868
double death were widely *m*,	Aylmer's F.	617
each man *m* 'O my Queen,	The Voyage	63

murmurest.

Who *m* in the foliaged eaves	In Mem. xcviii.	9

murmuring.

m, as at night and morn,	Mariana in the S.	46
m in her feastful mirth,	Pal. of Art	177
Muttering and *m* at his ear 'Quick	M. d'Arthur	179
and heard The voices *m*.	Princess, iv.	537
m of innumerable bees.'	" vii.	207
wind Of memory *m* the past.	In Mem. xci.	8
The brooks of Eden mazily *m*,	Milton	10

muscle.

on which the standing *m* sloped	Enid	76
the warmth and *m* of the heart,	Aylmer's F.	180

muscular.

So *m* he spread, so broad of breast.	Gardener's D.	8

Muse (s.)

The modern M's reading.	Amphion	76
No vain libation to the M,	Will Water.	9
The M, the jolly M, it is!	"	105
hard-grained M's of the cube and	Princess, Pro.	178
M's and the Graces, group'd in	" ii.	13
every M tumbled a science in.	"	377
but the M's heads were touch'd	" iii.	5
So they blaspheme the *m*!	" iv.	19
fed you with the milk of every M;	"	276
placid marble M's, looking peace,	"	468
For I am but an earthly M,	In Mem. xxxvii.	13
The high M answer'd: 'Wherefore	" lvii.	9
A life that all the M's deck'd	" lxxx'v.	45
That saw thro' all the M's walk;	" cvii.	4
O civic *m*, to such a name,	Ode on Well.	75

muse (verb.)

I *m*, as in a trance,	Eleänore	75
While I *m* upon thy face;	"	110
m and brood, and live again in	Lotos-E's.	110
I *m* on joy that will not cease,	Sir Galahad	65
with my heart I *m* and say:	In Mem. iv.	4
shine Upon me, while I *m* alone;	" cxv.	10
The great Sir Lancelot *m* at me;	Elaine	1049

	mused. POEM.	LINE.
while they *m*, Whispering to each	Sea-Fairies	4
Lancelot *m* a little space,	L. of Shalott, iv.	51
while I *m* came Memory	Gardener's D.	238
while I *m*, Love with knit brows	"	240
m on that wild morning in the woods.	Princess, v.	460
m on all I had to tell,	In Mem. vi.	19
is it pride, and *m* and sigh'd	Maud, I. viii.	12
M, and was mute.	The Brook	201
M for a little on his plea,	Enid	42
m a little, and then clapt her hands	Vivien	715
to her father, while he *m* alone	Elaine	744
Lancelot later came and *m* at her;	"	1261
m upon it, drifting up the stream	Sea Dreams	104
m where broad sunshine laves	D. of F. Wom.	189

music.

while a sweeter *m* wakes,	To the Queen	13
m flowing from The illimitable years.	Ode to Mem.	41
led With *m* and sweet showers	"	77
m reach'd them on the middle sea.	Sea-Fairies	6
With a *m* strange and manifold,	Dying Swan	20
Rain makes *m* in the tree,	A Dirge	26
wave would make *m* above us	The Merman	22
with plumes, and lights, And *m*,	L. of Shalott, ii.	32
slowly to a *m* slowly breath'd,	Œnone	21
came a swell of *m* on the wind.	May Queen, iii.	32-6
The blessed *m* went that way	"	42
m in his ears his beating heart did	Lotos-E's.	36
sweet *m* here that softer falls	"	46
M that gentlier on the spirit lies,	"	50
M that brings sweet sleep	"	52
a *m* centred in a doleful song	"	162
who made His *m* heard below;	D. of F. Wom.	4
that flow Of *m* left the lips of her.	"	195
Deep-chested *m*, and to this result.	The Epic	51
To some full *m* rose and sank the sun,	Ed. Morris	34
I scarce hear other *m*:	"	57
The *m* from the town—	Talking O.	214
pass'd in *m* out of sight.	Locksley H.	34
overtakes Far thought with *m*	Two Voices	438
have his *m* as of old, 'You might have won,' etc.	"	14
voluptuous *m* winding trembled,	Vision of Sin	17
m touch'd the gates and died;	"	23
move The minutes, fledged with *m*;'	Princess, iv.	19
as they say, The seal does *m*;	"	436
at a dance to change The *m*—	"	567
m in the growing breeze of Time,	" vi.	40
Like perfect *m* unto noble words;	" vii.	270
And girdled her with *m*.	"	308
May make one *m* as before,	In Mem. Pro.	28
With all the *m* in her tone,	" iii.	10
mellow *m* match'd with him.	" iv.	24
I hear a wizard *m* roll,	" lxix.	14
Shall ring with *m* all the same;	" lxxvi.	14
m in the bounds of law,	" lxxxvi.	34
Æonian *m* measuring out	" xciv.	41
At last he beat his *m* out.	" xcv.	10
A *m* out of sheet and shroud	" cii.	54
With festal cheer, With books and *m*	" cvi.	23
Is *m* more than any song.	Con.	4
She sits by her *m* and books,	Maud, I. xiv.	11
the noiseless *m* of the night.	" xviii.	77
as the *m* clash'd in the hall;	" xxii.	34
sound of dancing *m* and flutes:	" II. v.	76
mournful martial *m* blow;	Ode on Well.	17
With banner and with *m*	"	81
tides of M's golden sea	"	252
Like ballad-burthen *m*, kept,	The Daisy	77
by and by will make the *m* mute,	Vivien	251
mass, and rolling *m*, like a Queen.	Elaine	1326
heard Strange *m*, and he paused	Guinevere	277
as the *m* of the moon Sleeps	Aylmer's F.	103
coming fitfully Like broken *m*,	"	477
Broke into nature's *m*	"	604
one That altogether went to *m*,	Sea Dreams	1
Lessening to the lessening *m*,	"	214
swell'd again Slowly to *m*:	"	216
I grant but little *m* there	"	245
A *m* harmonizing our wild cries	"	247
Make *m*, O bird, in the new-budded	W. toElexan	11

286 CONCORDANCE TO

musical.
More *m* than ever came in one, . *Gardener's D.* 228

musician.
M, painter, sculptor, critic, . . *Princess*, ii. 161
The discords dear to the *m*. . . *Sea Dreams* 250

musing.
Or in the furrow *m* stands ; . . *In Mem.* lxiii. 27
m sat the hoary-headed Earl, . *Enid* . 293
M on him that used to fill it . *En Arden* . 208
m on the little lives of men, . *Sea Dreams* 48

musk.
moss or *m*, To grace my city-rooms ; *Gardener's D.* 189
Smelling of *m* and of insolence, . *Maud*, I. vi. 45
And the *m* of the roses blown. . " xxii. 6

musky-circled.
began To thrid the *m-c* mazes, . *Princess*, iv. 242

Mussulman.
True *M* was I and sworn, . . *Arabian N's.* 9

mute.
When all the house is *m*. . . *M. d'Arthur* 178
answer us to-day, Meantime be *m* : *Princess*, iii. 151
lying stark, Dishelm'd and *m* : . " vi. 85
m she glided forth, . . . " vii. 155
Your mother is *m* in her grave . *Maud*, I. iv. 58
Mused, and was *m*. . . . *The Brook* . 201
Our chief state-oracle is *m* ; . *Ode on Well*. 23
statued pinnacles, *m* as they, . *The Daisy* . 64
m As creatures voiceless . . *Enid* . 1114
I will kiss you for it ; ' he was *m* : *Vivien* . 78
do you love me ? ' he was *m*. . " . 86
by and by will make the music *m*, " . 241
both were *m*, till Philip glancing up *En. Arden* 437
He laugh'd ; and then was *m* ; . *Aylmer's F.* 402
M with folded arms they waited. *The Captain* 39

mutter'd.
paw'd his beard and *m* ' catalepsy.' *Princess*, i. 20
And ever he *m* and madden'd . *Maud*, I. i. 10
m in himself ' tell *her* the charm ! *Vivien* . 658
hearing ' harlot ' *m* twice or thrice, " . 692
' him or death' she *m*, . . *Elaine* . 898
to her own sad heart *m* the Queen. *Guinevere* . 211

muttering.
M and murmuring at his ear' Quick, *M. d'Arthur* 179
Francis, *m*, like a man ill-used, . " *Ep.* 12
thereat the crowd *M*, dissolved : . *Princess*, iv. 502
after *m* ' the great Lancelot ' . *Elaine* . 420
M and mumbling, idiotlike . . *En. Arden* . 640
Repeated *m* ' cast away and lost ; ' " . 716
m discontent Cursed me . . *The Flower* 7

muzzle.
creature laid his *m* on your lap, . *Princess*, ii. 253

myriad.
of the many tongues, the *m* eyes ! *Ode to Mem.* 47
M's of topaz-lights, and . . *M. d'Arthur* 57
To *m's* on the genial earth, . . *In Mem.* xcviii.14
And unto *m's* more, of death. . " 16
woodland lilies, *M's* blow together *Maud*, I. xii. 8
Against the *m's* of Assaye . . *Ode on Well*. 99
world on world in *m m's* roll . " . 262
That codeless *m* of precedent, . *Aylmer's F.* 436

myriad-minded.
Subtle-thoughted, *m-m*. . . *Ode to Mem.* 118

myriad-rolling.
Thine the *m-r* ocean. . . . *Boädicea* . 42

myriad-room'd.
Puff'd out his torch among the *m-r Vivien* . 581

myriad-wrinkled.
an old, dumb, *m-w* man, . . *Elaine* . 170

myrrh.
holy Elders with the gift of *m*. . *M. d'Arthur* 233

myrrh-bush.
leave the *m-b* on the height ; . *Lotos-E's*. 103

myrrh-thicket.
deep *m-t's* blowing round . . *Arabian N's* 104

myrtle.
Mixt with *m* and clad with vine, . *The Islet* . 19

mystery.
All the *m* is thine ; . . . *Madeline* . 24
M of *mysteries*, Faintly smiling . *Adeline* . 1
canvass'd human *mysteries*, . . *A Character* 20
dissolved the *m* Of folded sleep. . *D. of F. Wom.* 262
His heart forebodes a *m* : . . *Two Voices* 290
No purple in the distance, *m*, . *Princess*, vi. 179
Of thy prevailing *mysteries* . . *In Mem.* xxxvii. 12
In vastness and in *m*, . . . " xcvi. 7
O ye *mysteries* of good, . . " cxxvii. 8
that his grave should be a *m* . *Guinevere* . 295
that *m* Where God-in-man is one . *En. Arden* . 186
O *m* ! What amulet drew her . *Aylmer's F.* 506

mystic.
in white samite, *m*, wonderful, *M. d'Arthur* 31, 144-59

mythology.
As old *mythologies* relate, . . *Two Voices* 349

N

Nadir.
hard earth cleave to the *N* hell . *Vivien* . 199

Naiad.
smilest still, As a *N* in a well, . *Adeline* . 16
N's oar'd A glimmering shoulder. *To E. L.* . 16

nail (s.)
children cast their pins and *n's*, . *Vivien* . 280

nail (verb.)
n me like a weasel on a grange . *Princess*, ii. 188

naked.
All *n* in a sultry sky, . . . *Fatima* . 37
N they came to that smooth-swarded Œnone . 93
' Ride you *n* thro' the town, . *Godiva* . 29
N I go, and void of cheer : . . *Two Voices* 239
Far too *n* to be shamed ! . . *Vision of Sin* 190
N, a double light in air and wave, *Princess*, vii. 152
hands Lay *n* on the wolfskin, . *Elaine* . 809

nakedness.
shall see The *n* and vacancy . *Deserted H.* 11
Grimy *n* dragging his trucks . *Maud*, I x. 7
prodigies of myriad *n'es*, . . *Lucretius* . 156

name (s.)
WISDOM, a *n* to shake All evil dreams
of power—a sacred *n*. . . *The Poet* . 46
round the prow they read her *n*, *L. of Shalott*, iv. 44
From thy rose-red lips MY *n* . *Eleänore* . 133
tell my *n* again to me, . . " . 142
when some one spoke his *n*, . *Fatima* . 15
those *n's*, that in their motion were *Pal. of Art* 165
Lost to her place and *n* ; . . " . 264
know you proud to bear your *n*, *L. C. V. de Vere* 10
ask thou not my *n* : . . . *D. of F. Wom.* 93
heard my *n* Sigh'd forth with life " . 153
crown about my brows, A *n* for ever ! . " . 163
n of Britain trebly great— ' *You ask me why*,' *etc*. 22
betray'd thy nature and thy *n*, . *M. d'Arthur* 73
call'd him by his *n*, complaining loud " . 210
when I heard her *n*, My heart . *Gardener's D.* 61
cuckoo told his *n* to all the hills ; . " . 92
carved my *n* Upon the cliffs, . *Audley Ct.* . 47
set the words, and added *n's* I knew. " . 60
knew the *n's*, Long learned *n's* . *Ed. Morris* 16
I spoke her *n* alone. . . . " . 68
n's Are register'd and calendar'd . *St S. Stylites* 129
Say thou, whereon I carved her *n*, *Talking O.* 33-97
tell me, did she read the *n* . . " . 153
found, and kiss'd the *n* she found . " . 159
I am become a *n* ; . . . *Ulysses* . 11
built herself an everlasting *n*. . *Godiva* . 79
how thy *n* may sound Will vex thee *Two Voices* 110
sons grow up that bear his *n*, . " . 256
He names the *n* Eternity. . . " . 291
n of wife And in the rights that *n*
may give . . . *Day-Dm.* . 265
have won the Poet's *n*, ' *You might have won*,' *etc*. 1

	POEM.	LINE.
What care I for any *n*?	Vision of Sin	85
N and fame I to fly sublime.	"	103
lovelier than their *n*'s,	Princess, Pro.	12
hail'd a score of *n*'s upon her,	"	155
His *n* was Gama:	i.	113
albeit their glorious *n*'s Were fewer,	ii.	139
great *n* flow on with broadening time	iii.	148
stony *n*'s Of shale and horneblende	"	343
Proctors leapt upon us, crying '*N*'s;	iv.	240
St something—I forget her *n*—	v.	283
Whose *n* is yoked with children's,	"	408
happy warriors, and immortal *n*'s,	vi.	77
must wed him for her own good *n*;	vii.	59
Among familiar *n*'s to rest	In Mem. xviii.	7
yield all blessing to the *n*	" xxxvi.	3
hardly tell what *n* were thine	" lviii.	16
Since we deserved the *n* of friends,	" lxiv.	9
Along the letters of thy *n*,	" lxvi.	7
force that would have forged a *n*.	" lxxii.	16
Another *n* was on the door:	" lxxxvi.	17
The grand old *n* of gentleman;	" cx.	22
Sweet Hesper-Phosphor, double *n*	" cxx.	17
sign your *n*'s, which shall be read,	Con.	57
the *n*'s are sign'd, and overhead	"	60
my own sad *n* in corners cried,	Maud, I. vi.	72
learned man Could give it a clumsy *n*.	" II. ii.	10
sudden making of splendid *n*'s,	" III. vi.	47
of one *n* and heart with her.	The Brook	76
'Willows.' 'No!' 'That is my *n*.'	"	212
ghost of one who bore your *n*	"	219
In that dread sound to the great *n*,	Ode on Well.	64
O civic muse, to such an *n* (rep.)	"	75
Eternal honour to his *n*.	"	150
household *n*, Hereafter, thro' all time	Ded. of Idylls	41
Forgetful of his glory and his *n*,	Enid	53
live my lord and not his *n*.	"	94
desired his *n*, and sent Her maiden	"	192
'Surely I will learn the *n*,'	"	203
His *n*? but no, good faith,	"	405
own maiden to demand the *n*,	"	411
a *n* far-sounded among men	"	427
let his *n* Slip from my lips	"	445
earn'd himself the *n* of sparrow-hawk.	"	492
n will yet remain Untarnish'd	"	500
bearing her own *n* had slipt away)	"	507
'Thy *n*!' To whom the fallen man	"	575
stately queen whose *n* was Guinevere,	"	667
Queen's fair *n* was breath'd upon,	"	1799
lavish comment when her *n* was named.	Vivien	8
lost to life and use and *n*	"	63,224,819
My use and *n* and fame.	"	153,190
slowly ebbing, *n* and fame.'	"	287
My *n*, once mine, now thine,	"	296
when my *n* was lifted up,	"	352
whole prey Is man's good *n*:	"	572
popular *n* such manhood earns,	"	636
like a fire among the noblest *n*'s,	"	651
stain or blemish in a *n* of note,	"	681
she that knew not ev'n his *n*?	Elaine	29
and by that *n* Had named them,	"	32
fought together; but their *n*'s were lost.	"	41
link'd our *n*'s together in his lay,	"	113
your great *n*, That conquers:	"	157,578
by what *n* Livest between the lips?	"	181
heard her *n* so tost about,	"	233
'Fair lord, whose *n* I know not—	"	359
hear, but hold my *n* Hidden,	"	415
family passion for the *n* Of Lancelot,	"	476
therefore would he hide his *n*	"	579
Whence you might learn his *n*?	"	651
know you my lord's *n* is Lancelot?'	"	773
win his honour and to make his *n*,	"	1353
glory of thy *n* and fame,	"	1303
crescent fear for *n* and fame,	"	1391
King dwell on my *n* to me?.	"	1393
Mine own *n* shames me	"	1394
profits me my *n* Of greatest knight?	"	1403
be for evermore a *n* of scorn.	Guinevere	61
sanctuary, nor ask Her *n*,	"	141
Nor with them mix'd, nor told her *n*	"	146
foul ensample from fair *n*'s,	"	486

	POEM.	LINE.
mine will ever be a *n* of scorn.	Guinevere	620
but that *n* has twice been changed—	En. Arden	860
'he that marries her marries the *n*'	Aylmer's F.	25
almost all the village had one *n*;	"	35
sow'd her *n* and kept it green	"	83
one transmitter of their ancient *n*,	"	296
N, too, *n*? Their ancient *n*!	"	377
Fall back upon a *n*! rest,	"	385
make a *n*, *N*, fortune too:	"	394
crying upon the *n* of Leolin,	"	576
that moment, when she named his *n*,	"	581
never took that useful *n* in vain;	Sea Dreams	185
if you love not my good *n*,'	Grandmother	48
so well that your good *n* is mine	"	50
Milton, a *n* to resound for ages;	Milton	4
make the *n* Of his vessel great	The Captain	18
reliance, For his noble *n*,	"	53
take That popular *n* of thine	Lucretius	96
one *n* with her Whose death-blow	"	232

name (verb.)

yet to *n* my spirit loathes	D. of F. Wom.	106
He *n*'s the name Eternity.	Two Voices	291
That *n* the under-lying dead.	In Mem. ii.	2
wish too strong for words to *n*	" xcii.	14
The Sultan, as we *n* him,—	Maud, I. xx.	4
Let him *n* it who can,	" II. ii.	11
Since you *n* yourself the summer fly	Vivien	219
break faith with one I may not *n*?	Elaine	682

named.

dreamer, deaf and blind, *N* man,	Two Voices	176
bawl for civil rights, No woman *n*:	Princess, v.	378
was our England's Alfred *n*,	Ode on Well.	183
grateful people *n* Enid the Good:	Enid	1811
lavish comment when her name was *n*.	Vivien	8
be as great as you are *n*,	"	185
n them, since a diamond was the prize.	Elaine	33
passes here; He *n* the day	En. Arden	215
moment when she *n* his name,	Aylmer's F.	581

nameless.

| and I am *n* and poor. | Maud, I. iv. | 18 |

naming.

| *n* each, And *n* those, his friends, | The Brook | 130 |
| never *n* God except for gain, | Sea Dreams | 184 |

nap.

| 'Twas but an after-dinner's *n*. | Day-Dm. | 156 |

nape.

| very *n* of her white neck Was rosed | Princess, vi. | 323 |
| and the skull Brake from the *n*, | Elaine | 51 |

napkin.

| *n* wrought with horse and hound, | Audley Ct. | 20 |
| That with the *n* dally; | Will Water. | 113 |

Naples.

| quite worn out, Travelling to *N*. | The Brook | 36 |

narcotics.

| Like dull *n*'s, numbing pain. | In Mem. v. | 8 |

narrow (adj.)

| Oh! *n*, *n* was the space, | Oriana | 46 |
| his careful hand,—The space was *n* | En. Arden | 177 |

narrow (verb.)

| tho' the gathering enemy *n* thee, | Boädicea | 39 |

narrow'd.

| river as it *n* to the hills. | Princess, iii. | 180 |
| *N* her goings out and comings in; | Aylmer's F. | 501 |

narrowing.

| *N* in to where they sat assembled | Vision of Sin | 16 |

narrowness.

| Nor ever *n* or spite, | In Mem. cx. | 17 |

nation.

And the *n*'s do but murmur,	Locksley H.	106
From the *n*'s' airy navies	"	124
An *n* yet, the rulers and the ruled	Princess, Con.	53
the mourning of a mighty *n*,	Ode on Well.	4
n weeping, and breaking on my rest?	"	63

native.

	POEM.	LINE.
Who look'd all *n* to her place,	*Princess.* vii.	304

nature.

	POEM.	LINE.
a perfect whole From living *N*,	*Pal. of Art*	58
Carved out of *N* for itself,	"	127
Lord over *N*, Lord of the visible earth,	"	179
bliss of life, that *N* gave,	*D. of F. Wom.*	210
Great *N* is more wise than I;	*To J. S.*	35
English *n*'s, freemen, friends,	'*Love thou thy land*'	7
N also, cold and warm,	"	37
if *N*'s evil star Drive men	"	73
n brings not back the Mastodon.	*The Epic*	36
betray'd thy *n* and thy name,	*M. d'Arthur*	73
To what she is; a *n* never kind!	*Walk. to the M.*	54
Kind *n* is the best:	"	56
fit us like a *n* second-hand;	"	57
love for *N* is as old as I;	*Ed. Morris*	28
love for *N* and my love for her,	"	31
those and theirs, by *N*'s law,	*Talking O.*	73
grossness of his *n* will have weight	*Locksley H.*	48
err from honest *N*'s rule!	"	61
Nay, but *N* brings thee solace;	"	87
I am shamed thro' all my *n*	"	148
N made them blinder motions	"	150
Here at least, where *n* sickens,	"	153
Young *N* thro' five cycles ran,	*Two Voices*	17
If *N* put not forth her power	"	160
In *N* can he nowhere find	"	293
N's living motion lent	"	449
applications lie In Art like *N*,	*Day-Dm.*	210
Oh, *n* first was fresh to men,	*Amphion*	57
lift your *n*'s up; Embrace our aims;	*Princess*, ii.	74
'Wild *n*'s need wise curbs;	" v.	165
as frankly theirs As dues of *N*.	"	196
dwelt an iron *n* in the grain;	" vi.	34
Love and *N*, these are two more terrible	"	149
Thaw this male *n* to some touch	"	287
with man The shining steps of *N*,	" vii.	246
let thy *n* strike on mine,	"	330
all the phantom, *N*, stands—	*In Mem.* iii.	9
words, like *N*, half reveal	" v.	3
tho' my *n* rarely yields	" xl.	13
From art, from *n*, from the schools	" xlviii.	1
pangs of *n*, sins of will,	" liii.	3
Are God and *N* then at strife,	" liv.	5
That *N* lends such evil dreams?	"	6
N, red in tooth and claw	" lv.	15
That *N*'s ancient power was lost:	" lxviii.	2
And cancell'd *N*'s best:	" lxxi.	20
I curse not *n*, no, nor death;	" lxxii.	7
moulded like in *n*'s mint;	" lxxviii.	6
doest expectant *n* wrong;	" lxxxii.	3
'Can clouds of *n* stain.	" lxxxiv.	85
High *n* amorous of the good,	" cviii.	9
Will let his coltish *n* break	" cx.	7
Where God and *N* met in light:	"	20
dying *N*'s earth and lime;	" cxvii.	4
reach thro' *n*, moulding men.	" cxxiii.	24
mix'd with God and *N* thou,	" cxxix.	11
Is *N* like an open book;	*Con.*	132
For *n* is one with rapine,	*Maud*, I. iv.	22
in his force to be *N*'s crowning race.	"	35
An eye well-practised in *n*	"	38
Because their *n*'s are little,	"	53
Should *N* keep me alive,	" vi.	32
Sweet *n* gilded by the gracious gleam	*Ded. of Idylls*	38
suffer any taint In *n*:	*Enid*	32
suspicious that her *n* had a taint	"	68
filial tenderness, Or easy *n*,	"	798
n's prideful sparkle in the blood	"	1675
Like simple noble *n*'s, credulous	"	1723
charm Of *n* in her overbore	*Vivien*	446
judge all *n* from her feet of clay,	"	684
tenderness Of manners and of *n*,	*Elaine*	328
all was *n*, all, perchance for her.	"	329
some discourtesy Against my *n*:	"	1295
not idle, but the fruit Of loyal *n*,	*Guinevere*	334
as *N* packs Her blossom	*En. Arden*	178
thought and *n* fail'd a little,	"	793
n crost Was mother of the foul	*Aylmer's F.*	375
broke into *n*'s music when they saw	"	694

my *n* longer mix with thine?	*Tithonus*	65
laws of *n* were our scorn;	*The Voyage*	84
N, so far as in her lies,	*On a Mourner*	1
seem'd A void was made in *N*;	*Lucretius*	37
powers and genial heat Of *N*,	"	98
with how great ease *N* could smile,	"	174
Twy-natured is no *n*:	"	191
womb and tomb of all, Great *N*,	"	241

nave.

bore along the *n* Her pendent hands,	*Aylmer's F.*	812

navy.

From the nations' airy navies	*Locksley H.*	124
gay *n* there should splinter on it,	*Sea Dreams*	127

near.

now I think my time is *n*.	*May Queen*, iii.	41
Ride on! the prize is *n*.'	*Sir Galahad*	80
He seems so *n* and yet so far,	*In Mem.* xcvi.	23
red rose cries, 'She is *n*, she is *n*;	*Maud*, I. xxii.	63
not weep—my own time seem'd so *n*.	*Grandmother*	72
Dear, and true—no truer Time	*A Dedication*	1
both are *n*, and both are dear,	*The Victim*	63

near'd.

n His happy home, the ground.	*Gardener's D.*	90
So rapt, we *n* the house;	"	141
only *n* Her husband inch by inch,	*Aylmer's F.*	806
n, Touch'd, clink'd and clash'd	*Sea Dreams*	130
Till she *n* the foe.	*The Captain*	36

nearer.

make you evermore Dearer and *n*,	*A Dedication*	3

nearest.

Were it our *n*, Were it our dearest (rep.)	*The Victim*	13

nearness.

Desire of *n* doubly sweet;	*In Mem.* cxvi.	6
thro' that *n* of the first,	*Aylmer's F.*	605

neat.

a home For Annie, *n* and nestlike,	*En. Arden.*	59

neater.

Be the *n* and completer;	*Maud*, I. xx.	20

neat-herds.

while his *n-h* were abroad;	*Lucretius*	83

necessity.

seem'd So justified by that *n*,	*Enid*	1245
The vast *n* of heart and life.	*Vivien*	774

neck.

Round thy *n* in subtle ring	*Adeline*	58
A glowing arm, a gleaming *n*,	*Miller's D.*	78
touch her *n* so warm and white.	"	174
round her *n* Floated her hair	*Œnone*	17
rode sublime On Fortune's *n*:	*D. of F. Wom.*	142
clung about The old man's *n*,	*Dora*	160
grazing iron collar grinds my *n*:	*St. S. Stylites*	115
A third would glimmer on her *n*	*Talking O.*	221
leap forth and fall about thy *n*,	*Love and Duty*	41
Disyoke their *n*'s from custom	*Princess*, ii.	127
Drew from my *n* the painting	" vi.	94
See, your foot is on our *n*'s,	"	150
nape of her white *n* Was rosed	"	323
fell in silence on his *n*:	*In Mem.* cii.	44
bays, the peacock's *n* in hue;	*The Daisy*	14
Shore thro' the swarthy *n*,	*Enid*	1576
curved an arm about his *n*,	*Vivien*	90
mantle of his beard Across her *n*	"	106
kiss each other On her white *n*—.	"	306
lithe arm round his *n* Tighten,	"	464
eyes and *n* glittering went and came:	"	809
n to which the swan's Is tawnier	*Elaine*	1178
necklace for a *n* O as much fairer	"	1221
flung One arm about his *n*	"	1346
King's breath wander o'er her *n*,	*Guinevere*	576
My mother clings about my *n*,	*Sailor Boy*	17

necklace.

And I would be the *n*,	*Miller's D.*	181
To make the *n* shine;	*Talking O.*	222

	POEM.	LINE.
fling the diamond n by.'	Lady Clare	40
n for a neck to which the swan's	Elaine	1178
n for a neck O as much fairer—	"	1221

nectar.

For they lie beside their n,	Lotos-E's.	156
hand ambrosia, mix The n;	Princess, iii.	98

need (s.)

wasted Truth in her utmost n,	'Clear-headed friend'	19
dusted velvets have much n of thee	To J. M. K.	4
if some dreadful n should rise	'Love thou thy land'	91
where there was never n of vows,	Gardener's D.	253
slay this child, if good n were,	Princess, ii.	267
How know I what had n of thee,	In Mem. lxxii.	3
cruel n Constrain'd us,	Enid	715
to be there against a sudden n;	"	1224

need (verb.)

all Life n's for life is possible	Love and Duty	83
'Wild natures n wise curbs.	Princess, v.	165
they n More breadth of culture :	"	180
Whether I n have fled?	Maud, II. ii.	72

needed.

Because it n help of Love;	In Mem. xxv.	8
n then no charm to keep them	Vivien	397
With all that seamen n.	En. Arden.	139
twice or thrice—As oft as n—	"	143
thro' the want of what it n most,	"	264
Lest could tell What most it n—	"	266

needing.

father lying sick and n him)	En. Arden.	65

needle.

have hid her n in my heart,	Ed. Morris	62
Man for the sword and for the n she ;	Princess, v.	438
Are sharpen'd to a n's end ;	In Mem. lxxv.	4

neglect.

If men n your pages?	Spiteful Let.	6

neglected.

thanks it seems till now n,	Vivien	157

neighbour.

all the n's shoot thee round,	The Blackbird	2
And ran to tell her n's ;	The Goose	14
Yet say the n's when they call,	Amphion	5
O Lord! 'tis in my n's ground,	"	75
Leering at his n's wife.	Vision of Sin	118
Each hissing in his n's ear ;	Princess, v.	14
From every house the n's met	In Mem. xxxi.	9
The foolish n's come and go,	" lix.	13
The next day came a n.	Aylmer's F.	251
The n's come and laugh and gossip,	Grandmother	91
With n's laid along the grass,	Lucretius	211

neighbourhood.

Far off from human n,	Eleänore	6
As from some blissful n,	Two Voices	430
by one low voice to one dear n,	Aylmer's F.	60

neigh'd.

N with all gladness as they came,	Enid	1603
warhorse n As at a friend's voice,	Guinevere	526

neighing.

Strong n's of the wild white Horse	Elaine	298

Nettcherry.

the sweet half-English N air	The Brook	17

Nemesis.

great N break from a darken'd future,	Princess,vi.	158

nephew.

sparrow-hawk, My curse, my n—	Enid	444
if, as I suppose, your n fights	"	475
It is with my good n thereupon,	"	458
Vinol's n, after trumpet blown,	"	551
like his own Of Mildred, Arthur's n,	Elaine	505
Gawain, rice, My n, and ride forth	Elaine	536
O loyal n of our noble King,	"	640
His n, ever like a subtle beast.	Guinevere	11

Neronian.

the N legionaries	Boädicea	1

	POEM.	LINE.
His n's were wrong. What ails us	Walk. to the M.	95
those, who clench their n's to rush	Love and Duty	75
life, whereof our n's are scant,	Two Voices	397
My n's have dealt with stiffer.	Will Water.	73
When thy n's could understand	Vision of Sin	160
A weight of n's without a mind,	In Mem. xii.	7
and the n's prick And tingle ;	" xlix.	2
and the n of sense is numb ;	" xcii.	7
O, having the n's of motion	Maud, 1. i.	63
O iron n to true occasion true	Ode on Well.	37
Were living n's to feel the rent ;	Aylmer's F.	530

nerve-dissolving.

The n-d melody	Vision of Sin	44

nest.

From my high n of penance	St S. Stylites	164
deep you might embower the n	Princess,Pro.	147
Father will come to his babe in the n,	" ii.	408
in the North long since my n is made.	" iv.	92
built the n,'she said,'To hatch the cuckoo.n	"	349
We seem a n of traitors—	" v.	416
the bird's song you may learn the n.'	Enid	359
live like two birds in one n,	"	1475
yellow-throated nestling in the n.	Elaine	12
each a n in bloom.	Aylmer's F.	150
moving moves the n and nestling,	Sea Dreams	273
In her n at peep of day?	"	282
And we'll have a n together.	The Window	85

nestlike.

a home For Annie, neat and n,	En Arden.	59

nestling.

yellow-throated n in the nest.	Elaine	12
Moving moves the nest and n,	Sea Dreams	279

net (s.)

Love that hath us in the n,	Miller's D.	203
catch a dragon in a cherry n,	Princess, v.	162
have her lion roll in a silken n	Maud, I. vi.	29
n made pleasant by the baits Of gold	Aylmer's F.	486

net (verb.)

fibres n the dreamless head.	In Mem. ii.	3

nettled.

tho' n that he seem'd to slur	Princess, i.	161

never.

Thou shalt hear the 'N, n'	Locksley H.	83

never-lighted.

Beside the n-l fire.	In Mem.lxxxiii.	20

new.

green, N from its silken sheath.	D.of F. Wom.	60
sing for want, ere leaves are n,	The Blackbird	23
Nothing comes to thee n or strange	To J. S.	74
N and Old, disastrous feud,	'Love thou thy land'	77
order changeth, yielding place to n,	M. d'Arthur	240
I knit a hundred others n ;	Two Voices	234
If old things, there are n ;	Will Water.	53
No, I have not what is n ;	Vision of Sin	159
old friend and tried, she n in all?	Princess, iv.	303
Whose fancy fuses old and n,	In Mem. xvi.	13
Ring out the old, ring in the n,	" cv.	5
old results that look like n ;	" cxxvii.	11
N as his title, built last year,	Maud, I. x.	11
splendour dear to women, n to her	Enid	83
if not so n, Yet therefore tenfold	"	80

new-bathed.

n-b in Paphian wells	Œnone	171

new-born.

here he glances on an eye n-b,	Lucretius	137

new-budded.

music, O bird, in the n-b bowers!	W. to Alexan.	11

new-caged.

first as sullen as a beast n-c,	Enid	147

new-comer.

n-c's in an ancient hold,	Ed. Morris	2
N-c's from the Mersey, millionaire	"	12

CONCORDANCE TO

new-fallen.
	POEM.	LINE.
like a *n-f* meteor on the grass,	*Princess*, vi.	119

Newfoundland.
| Than for his old *N's* . | *Aylmer's F.* | 125 |

newly-caged.
| Like some wild creature *n-c*, | *Princess*, ii. | 281 |

newly-fallen.
| o'er a mount of *n-f* stones, . | *Enid* . | 361 |

new-made.
| one of the two at her side This *n-m* lord | *Maud*, I.x. | 3 |

new-mown.
| rarely smells the *n-m* hay . | *The Owl*, i. | 9 |

newness.
| the discovery And *n* of thine art . | *Ode to Mem.* | 88 |

new-risen.
| on the roof Of night *n-r*, . | *Arabian N's.* | 130 |

news.
N from the humming city comes .	*Gardener's D.*	35
in the distance pealing *n* Of better	*Princess*, iv.	63
Pass and blush the *n* .	*Maud*, I.xvii.	11
Pass the happy *n* .	"	15
Ill *n*, my Queen, for all who love .	*Elaine*	596
Yet good *n* too ; for goodly hopes	"	599
'What *n* from Camelot, lord ?	"	617
on the Queen with the sharp *n*.	"	726
Expectant of that *n* which never .	*En. Arden*	257
and no *n* of Enoch came. .	"	358
breaker of the bitter *n* from home,	*Aylmer's F.*	594
She brought strange *n*.	*Sea Dreams*	258

new-world.
| clamour grew As of a *n-w* Babel, | *Princess*, iv. | 466 |

New-Year.
of all the glad *N-y*, (rep.) .	*MayQueen*,i.	2
sun rise upon the glad *N-y*.	" ii.	2
ast *N-y* that I shall ever see,	"	3
And the *N-y's* coming up, mother,	"	7
And the *N-y* will take' em away.	*D. of the O. Year*	14
And the *N-y* blithe and bold,	"	35
O Sweet *n-y* delaying long ;	*In Mem.* lxxxii.	2-13
N Y and Old Year met .	1865-1866	2
N-Y blowing and roaring. .	"	13

niece.
William was his son And she his *n*, *Dora* .		3
Allan call'd His *n* and said :	"	40
by the bright head of my little *n* .	*Princess*,, ii.	257

nigh.
| Far off thou art, but ever *n* . | *In Mem.* cxxix. | 13 |

nigh-naked.
| On the *n-n* tree the Robin piped . | *En. Arden.* | 677 |

night.
only said. 'The *n* is dreary, .	*Mariana*	21-57
Upon the middle of the *n* .	"	25
another *n* in *n* I enter'd .	*Arabian N's.*	37
The living airs of middle *n* .	"	69
on the roof Of *n* new-risen, .	"	130
Nor was the *n* thy shroud. .	*Ode to Mem.*	28
All within is dark as *n*: .	*Deserted H.*	5
In the yew-wood black as *n*, .	*Oriana*	19
thunder and light in the magic *n*—	*The Merman*	23
often thro' the silent *n's* .	*L. of Shalott*, ii.	30
often thro' the purple *n* .	" iii.	24
Thro' the noises of circle *n* .	" iv.	22
'Madonna, sad is *n* and morn ;'	*Mariana in the S.*	22
'The day to *n*,' she made her moan	"	81
Heaven over Heaven rose the *n*. .	"	92
n comes on that knows not morn,	"	94
When April *n's* began to blow, .	*Miller's D.*	106
Flitted across into the *n*, .	"	127
may seem, As in the *n's* of old, .	"	166
I rose up in the silent *n*: .	*The Sisters*	25
young *n* divine Crown'd dying day	*Pal. of Art*	183
token when the *n* and morning meet :	*MayQueen*, iii.22
Drops in a silent autumn *n*, .	*Lotos-E's.*	79
Saw God divide the *n* .	*D. of F. Wom.*	223

	POEM.	LINE.
Moving thro' a fleecy *n*. .	*Margaret* .	21
Float by you on the verge of *n*. .	"	31
the last *n's* gale had caught, .	*Gardener's D.*	123
heir to all, Made this *n* his, .	"	160
N slid down one long stream .	"	262
ere the *n* we rose And sauter'd home	*Audley C.*	78
in the *n*, after a little sleep, I wake ;	*St S. Stylites*	111
brought the *n* In which we sat	*Love and Duty*	58
and of sunrise mix'd In that brief *n*;	"	71
summer *n*, that paused Among her stars	"	71
Many a *n* from yonder ivied casement	*Locksley H.*	7
Many a *n* I saw the Pleiads, .	"	9
flushing in the northern *n*, ..	"	26
In the dead unhappy *n*, .	"	78
Look up thro' *n*: the world is wide.	*Two Voices*	24
yearning toward the lamps of *n*. .	"	363
Beyond the *n*, across the day, .	*Day-Dm.*	195
a vision when the *n* was late : .	*Vision of Sin*	1
Thou art mazed, the *n* is long, .	"	195
And the longer *n* is near; .	"	196
round again to happy *n*. 'Move eastward,' etc.		12
from some bay-window shake the *n*;	*Princess*, i.	105
To float about a glimmering *n*, .	"	243
circled Iris of a *n* of tears ; .	" iii.	11
My mother, 'tis her wont from *n* to *n*	"	16
in one *n* and due to sudden sun : .	" iv.	293
the long *n* ot of her deep hair, .	"	470
long fantastic *n* With all its doings .	"	543
As *n* to him that sitting on a hill .	"	551
later in the *n* Had come on Psyche .	" v.	47
Come as goblins in the *n* .	"	211
dews Gathered by *n* and peace, .	"	234
A *n* of Summer from the heat, .	" vi.	58
like *n* and evening mixt .	"	115
whole *n's* long, up in the tower, .	"	238
from the deeps, a wall of *n*, .	" vii.	22
Drew the great *n* into themselves, .	"	34
after that dark *n* among the fields, .	"	58
Deep in the *n* I woke : .	"	158
shares with man His *n's*, his days, .	"	247
the light I carer for *n*, .	"	326
gradually the powers of the *n*, .	*Con.*	111
I hear the bell struck in the *n*; .	*In Mem.* x.	2
dash'd with wandering isles of *n*. .	" xxiv.	4
The moon is hid ; the *n* is still ; (ciii. 2)	" xxviii.	2
To enrich the threshold of the *n* .	" xxix.	6
Draw forth the cheerful day from *n* :	" xxx.	30
An infant crying in the *n*; .	" liii.	18
How dwarf'd a growth of cold and *n*,	" lx.	7
His *n* of loss is always there. .	" lxv.	16
I found an angel of the *n*; .	" lxviii.	14
mix with hollow masks of *n*; .	" lxix.	4
howlest, issuing out of *n*, .	" lxxi.	2
not in watches of the *n*, .	" xc.	13
Withdraw themselves from me and *n*,	" xciv.	18
Power was with him in the *n*, .	" xcv.	18
On that last *n* before we went .	" cii.	1
A little spare the *n* I loved, .	" civ.	15
The year is dying in the *n*; .	" cv.	3
bank Of vapour, leaving *n* forlorn. .	" cvi.	4
Bright Phosphor, fresher for the *n*, .	" cxx.	9
In the deep *n*, that all is well. .	" cxxv.	12
Be sunder'd in the *n* of fear ; .	" cxxvi.	2
in the hush of the moonless *n's*, .	"	42
ghostlike, deathlike, half the *n* long .	" iii.	8
nodding together In some Arabian *n* ?	" vii.	12
spark struck vainly in the *n*, .	" ix.	14
Heat to the noiseless music of the *n* !	" xviii.	77
The black bat, *n*, has flown, .	" xxii.	2
The brief *n* goes In babble .	"	27
Half the *n* I waste in sighs, .	" II. iv.	23
face of *n* is fair on the dewy downs .	" III. vi.	5
by *n* With moon and trembling stars,	*Enid* .	7
ere they settle for the *n*. .	"	250
get me harbourage for the *n* ? .	"	281-99
n Before my Enid's birthday, .	"	437-632
draw The quiet *n* into her blood .	"	532
n of fire, when Edyrn sack'd .	"	634
sadly lost on that unhappy *n*; .	"	689
hire us some fair chamber for the *n*	"	1087

	POEM.	LINE.
sleepless *n's* Of my long life	Vivien	329
tended him, And likewise many a *n* :	Elaine	847
like a star in blackest *n*.	"	1236
In the dead *n*, grim faces came	Guinevere	70
then they were agreed upon a *n*	"	96
dark the *n* and chill ! (rep.)	"	166
Thro' the thick *n* I hear the trumpet	"	565
making all the *n* a steam of fire.	"	593
seem'd, as in a nightmare of the *n*,	En. Arden	114
After a *n* of feverous wakefulness	"	230
fearing *n* and chill for Annie	"	440
compass'd round by the blind wall of *n*	"	458
Hurt in that *n* of sudden ruin	"	565
third *n* after this, While Enoch slumber'd	"	906
was Edith that same *n* ;	Aylmer's F.	279
once again by *n* the lovers met,	"	413
one *n*, except For greenish glimmering	"	621
sea roars Ruin : a fearful *n* !	Sea Dreams	81
reaching thro' the *n* Her other,	"	275
sleep for this one *n* be sound :	"	302
burn the threshold of the *n*,	The Voyage	18
overboard one stormy *n*	"	79
thy voice with the deepening of the *n*	V. of Cauteretz	2
toward the long frost and longest *n*	A Dedication	11
once at dead of *n* did greet	On a Mourner	32
Taken the stars from the *n*,	The Window	39

night-dew.

n-d's on still waters	Lotos-E's.	48

night-fowl.

Waking she heard the *n-f* crow	Mariana	26

nightingale.

No *n* delighteth to prolong	Pal. of Art	173
n Sang loud, as tho' he were the bird	Gardener's D.	94
That tremble round a *n*—	"	249
As 'twere a hundred-throated *n*,	Vision of Sin	27
n thought, 'I have sung many songs,	Poet's Song	13
all about us peal'd the *n*,	Princess, i.	217
at mine ear Bubbled the *n*	" iv.	247
think or say, 'There is the *n*;	Enid	342
Sleeps in the plain eggs of the *n*.	Aylmer's F.	103
beside me chirrupt the *n*.	Grandmother	40

night-lamp.

Where the dying *n-l* flickers,	Locksley H.	80

night-light.

n-l flickering in my eyes Awoke me.'	Sea Dreams	101

night-long.

A *n-l* Present of the Past	In Mem. lxx.	3

nightmare.

And horrible *n's*, And hollow shades	Pal. of Art	240
feels a *n* on his bed	M. d'Arthur	177
N of youth, the spectre of himself?	Love and Duty	13
This *n* weight of gratitude,	Princess, vi.	231
seem'd, as in a *n* of the night,	En. Arden	114

night-wind.

The *n-w's* come and go, mother,	May Queen, i.	33

Nile.

O shaker of the Baltic and the *N*,	Ode on Well.	137

Nilus.

N would have risen before his time	D. of F. Wom.	143

nine-years-fought-for.

The *n-y-f-f* diamonds :	Elaine	1161

Niobe.

Upon her tower, the *N* of swine,	Walk. to the M.	91

Niobean.

A *N* daughter, one arm out,	Princess, iv.	352

nip.

close again, and *n* me flat,	Vivien	200

nipt.

n to death by him That was a God,	E.J. Morris	101

Noaks.

Nor Thimble by—toner'ed shot un	N. Farmer	35
N wur 'ang'd for it oop at 'suize—	"	36

nobility.

	POEM.	LINE.
pure *n* of temperament,	Enid	212

noble (adj.)

As *n* till the latest day !	To the Queen	22
'Tis only *n* to be good.	L. C. V. de V'ere	54
to look on *n* forms Makes *n* .	Princess, ii.	72
Better not be at all Than not be *n*.	"	80
more *n* than three score of men	" iii.	93
hearts in a cause, we are *n* still	Maud, III. vi.	55
take the charger too, A *n* one.'	Enid	1405
makes you seem less *n* than yourself,	Vivien	171
as *n*, as their Queen was fair ?	"	458
whose name I know not—*n* it is,	Elaine	359
must be a thousand-fold Less *n*,	Guinevere	337
for one hour less *n* than himself	"	344
Sir Lancelot's, were as *n* as the King's	"	349
Not *keep* it *n*, make it nobler ?	Aylmer's F.	386

noble (s.)

Where the wealthy *n's* dwell,	L. of Burleigh	24

nobleman.

wedded with a *n* from thence :	Princess, i.	76

nobleness.

And much I praised her *n*,	Princess, Pro.	124
That you trust me in your own *n*,	Elaine	116
With such a vantage-ground for *n*	Aylmer's F.	367

nobler.

am I not the *n* thro' thy love ?	Love and Duty	19
heart of hearts I did acknowledge *n*.	Elaine	1205
Not *keep* it noble, make it *n* !	Aylmer's F.	386
n from her bath of storm,	Lucretius	175

noblest.

One of our *n*, our most valorous	Enid	1758
n, when she lifted up her eyes.	Elaine	256
noble it is, I well believe, the *n*—	"	360
of Arthur's *n* dealt in scorn ;	Guinevere	41
would say Sir Lancelot had the *n* ;	"	318
which had *n*, while you moved	"	323

nobly-manner'd.

Were the most *n-m* men of all ;	Guinevere	332

nod (s.)

And flooded at our *n*.	D. of F. Wom.	144
With frequent smile and *n* departing	Enid	515

nod (verb.)

Glares at one that *n's* and winks	Locksley H.	136
move the trees, the copses *n*,	Sir Galahad	77

nodded.

The parson smirk'd and *n*.	The Goose	20
He *n*, but a moment afterwards	Gardener's D.	119
And Walter *n* at me ;	Princess, Pro.	196
Florian *n* at him, I frowning ;	" iv.	141
after *n* sleepily in the heat.	Enid	1102

nodding.

n, as in scorn, He parted,	Godiva	30
Viziers *n* together .	Maud, I. vii.	11
her father *n* said, 'Ay, ay, the	Elaine	766

noise.

Thro' the *n's* of the night	L. of Shalott, iv.	22
milldam rushing down with *n*,	Miller's D.	50
n of some one coming thro' the	D. of F. Wom.	178
all day long the *n* of battle roll'd	M. d'Arthur	1
with *n's* of the northern sea.	"	141
such a *n* of life Swarm'd	Gardener's D.	174
a *n* of tongues and deeds,	Two Voices	206
rose a *n* of striking clocks,	Day-Dm.	134
I hear a *n* of hymns :	Sir Galahad	28
Made *n* with bees and breeze	Princess, Pro.	83
n Of clocks and chimes,	" i.	214
two armies and the *n* Of arms ;	" v.	335
n of songs they would not understand :	" vi.	24
The *n* of life begins again,	In Mem. vii.	10
I hear the *n* about thy keel	" x.	1
youth was full of foolish *n*,	" lii.	3
Autumn, with a *n* of rooks,	" lxxxiv.	7
all within was *n* Of songs,	" lxxxvi.	18
n of the mourning of a mighty	Ode on Well.	

CONCORDANCE TO

	POEM.	LINE.
far from *n* and smoke of town,	To F.D.Maurice	13
out of town and valley came a *n*	Enid	247
grateful is the *n* of noble deeds	"	437
spearmen follow'd him with *n*:	"	1441
Scared by the *n* upstarted	Vivien	272
poplars made a *n* of falling showers.	Elaine	410, 522
that had heard the *n* of it before,	"	727
some doubtful *n* of creaking doors,	Guinevere	72
the *n* about their doors	Aylmer's F.	488
Made the *n* of frosty woodlands,	Boädicea	75

none.
There is *n* like her, *n*, (rep.)	Maud, I. xviii.	2

nook.
odd games In some odd *n*'s like	The Epic	9
old warrior from his ivied *n*	Princess, Pro.	104

noon.
from beyond the *n* a fire	Fatima	30
In those old days, one summer *n*,	M.d'Arthur	29
the shameless *n* Was clash'd and.	Godiva	74
took my leave, for it was nearly *n*:	Princess, v.	457
ere I woke it was the point of *n*,'.	"	471
tendance in the all-weary *n*'s,	" vii.	87
Climb thy thick *n*, disastrous day;	In Mem. lxxi.	26
stays thee from the clouded *n*'s	" lxxxii.	5
must be made a wife ere *n*?	" Con.	26
now set out: the *n* is near,	"	41
at the point of *n* the huge Earl	Enid	1385
in the *n* of mist and driving rain,	Vivien	486

noorse (nurse).
N? thoort nowt o' a *n*:	N. Farmer	2

noose.
as tight as I could knot the *n*;	St S. Stylites	64

Norland.
loud the *N* whirlwinds blow	Oriana	6
N winds pipe down the sea,	"	91

Norman.
simple faith than *N* blood.	L.C.V.deVere	56
Saxon and *N* and Dane are we,	W.to Alexan.	3, 31

north.
a long league back to the *N*.	Princess, i.	166
dark and true and tender is the *N*.	" iv.	80
in the *N* long since my nest is made.	"	92
brief the sun of summer in the *N*,	"	94
blown to innost *n*;	"	412
Fiercely flies The blast of *N*	In Mem. cvi.	7
Far into the *N*, and battle,	Maud, III. vi.	37
gray metropolis of the *N*	The Daisy	104
knights of utmost *N* and West	Elaine	525
round the *N*, a light, A belt,	Sea Dreams	201
Thine the *N* and thine the South	Boädicea	44

Northern Sea. (See Sea.)

Northern Star.
on my cradle shone the *N* s.	Princess, i.	4

North-sea.
as a wild wave in the wide *N-s*,	Elaine	481

northward.
darken'd all the *n* of her Hall.	Aylmer's F.	415

north-wind.
He will not hear the *n-w* rave,	Two Voices	259

Norway.
N sun Set into sunrise;	Princess, iv.	552

nose.
aquiline curve in a sensitive *n*,	Maud, I. ii.	10

nosing.
N the mother's udder,	Lucretius	100

nostril.
anger puff'd Her fairy *n* out;	Vivien	698

note (notice, etc.)
a precious thing, one worthy *n*,	M.d'Arthur	89
work of noble *n*, may yet be done,	Ulysses	52
Stain or blemish in a name of *n*,	Vivien	681

	POEM.	LINE.
took *n* that when his living smile.	Elaine	322
Took joyful *n* of all things joyful,	Aylmer's F.	67

note (of music.)
'A quinsy choke thy cursed *n*!'.	The Goose	29
scarce get out his *n*'s for joy,	Gardener's D.	89
chords that shiver to one *n*;	Princess, iii.	74
one is glad; her *n* is gay,	In Mem. xxi.	2
one is sad; her *n* is changed,	"	27
Some bitter *n*'s my harp would give,	" cxxiv.	2
on her pastoral hillock a languid *n*;	Maud, III. vi.	24
the liquid *n* beloved of men	Enid	336
but one plain passage of few *n*'s	Elaine	891
musical *n* Swell'd up and died;	Sea Dreams	203
n Had reach'd a thunderous fullness,	"	206
never out of tune With that sweet *n*;	"	225
his compass is but of a single *n*,	The Islet	28

note (billet.)
sent a *n*, the seal an *Elle vous suit*,	Ed. Morris	105

nothing.
him that utter'd *n* base;	To the Queen	8
n here, Which, from the outward	Eleänore	3
in thee Is *n* sudden, *n* single;	"	57
am as *n* in its light;	"	88
Beat time to *n* in my head	Miller's D.	67
N comes to thee new or strange.	To J. S.	74
He thought that *n* new was said,	The Epic	30
Something so said 'twas n—	"	31
'There now—that's *n*!	M. d'Arthur, Ep.	13
Unto the shores of *n*!	Gardener's D.	17
n else For which to praise the heavens	"	102
where nature sickens, *n*.	Locksley H.	153
A life of *n*'s, *n* worth,	Two Voices	331
From that first *n* ere his birth	"	332
To that last *n* under earth!'	"	333
N but this; my very ears were hot	Princess, i.	133
your chance Almost at naked *n*.	"	160
there is *n* upon earth More miserable	"	242
So then were *n* lost to man;	In Mem. xlii.	9
n walks with aimless feet	" liii.	5
I care for *n*, all shall go.	" lv.	4
n is that errs from law.	" lxxii.	8
From form to form, and *n* stands;	" cxxii.	6
n there her maiden grace affright!	Maud, I. xviii.	71
n can be sweeter Than maiden Maud	" xx.	21
N but idiot gabble!	" II. v.	41
mist of green, And *n* perfect:	The Brook	15
n can bereave him Of the force	Ode on Well.	272
wing'd *n*'s peck him dead!	Enid	275
pipe of *n* but of sparrow-hawks!	"	279
Owe you me *n* for a life half-lost?	"	1167
weariness And sickly *n*;	"	1501
Fame that follows death is *n*	Vivien	314
in that star To make fame *n*.	"	363
there was *n* wild or strange,	"	709
n Poor Vivien had not done	"	711
ending in a ruin—*n* left,	"	732
And every voice is *n*	Elaine	109
'Of all this will I *n*;' and so fell,	"	962
a palmtree.' That was *n* to her:	En. Arden	494
from his windows *n* save his own—	Aylmer's F.	21
Flash into fiery life from *n*	"	130
in tune With *n* but the Devil!'	Sea Dreams	253
O fie, you golden *n*, fie,	The Ringlet	43
n that she meets with base,	On a Mourner	4
N to mar the sober majesties	Lucretius	214

nothingness.
Teach me the *n* of things.'	A Character	4
Redeem'd from the charge of *n*—	M.d'Arthur,Ep.	7
brand His *n* into man.	Maud, I. xviii.	40

nothing-worth.
faint Homeric echoes, *n-w*,	The Epic	39
A life of nothings, *n-w*,	Two Voices	331

notice.
A *n* faintly understood,	Two Voices	431
n of a change in the dark world	Princess, vii.	234
n of a hart Taller than all his fellows	Enid	149
the master took Small *n*, or austerely,	Lucretius	8

	POEM.	LINE.
noticed.		
I *n* one of his many rings	*Maud*, II. ii.	68
notion.		
boy might get a *n* into him;	*Aylmer's F.*	271
nourish.		
n a blind life within the brain,	*M. d'Arthur*	251
nourishing.		
n a youth sublime	*Locksley H.*	11
novel.		
She left the *n* half-uncut	*Talking O.*	117
November.		
N' dawns and dewy-glooming downs,	*En. Arden*	611
N' day Was growing duller twilight,	"	722
novice.		
save a little maid, A *n* :	*Guinevere*	4
sang the *n*, while full passionately,	"	178
Said the little *n* prattling to her.	"	181
To whom the little *n* garrulously.	"	229-74
the *n*, crying with clasp'd hands,	"	309
saw The *n*, weeping, suppliant,	"	656
Nudd (see *Edyrn.*)		
null.		
icily regular, splendidly *n*,	*Maud*, I. ii.	6
numb (adj.)		
all the nerve of sense is *n*;	*In Mem.* xcii.	7
numb (verb.)		
n's the Fairy's ringlet-snake,	*Lucretius*	258
number (s.)		
o'er the *n* of thy years.	*In Mem.* lxvi.	8
miss the wonted *n* of my knights.	*Guinevere*	494
number verb.)		
n's forty cubits from the soil.	*StS. Stylites*	90
Could *n* live from ten.	*Talking O.*	80
Whose troubles *n* with his days:	*Two Voices*	330
numbered.		
n o'er Some thrice three years:	*In Mem. Con.*	9
numberest.		
tho' thou *n* with the followers	*Aylmer's F.*	663
numbing.		
Like dull narcotics, *n* pain.	*In Mem.* v.	8
nun.		
she spake There to the *n*'s,	*Guinevere*	138
many a week, unknown, among the *n*'s;	"	145
An air the *n*'s had taught her:	"	161
simple-seeming Abbess and her *n*'s,	"	307
good *n*'s would check her gadding tongue	"	311
sad *n*'s with each a light Stood,	"	585
glancing up beheld the holy *n*'s	"	658
Wear black and white, and be a *n*;	"	668
nunnery.		
simple miracles of thy *n* !'	*Guinevere*	228
whisper thro' the *n* ran,	"	407
nunnery-walls.		
little maid, shut in by *n-w*,	*Guinevere*	225
close I about by narrowing *n-w*	"	340
shut me round with narrowing *n w*	"	663
nurse s.)		
In there came old Alice the *n*,	*Lady Clare*	13
said Alice the *n*,	" 17, *et pass.*	
Are ye out of your mind, my *n*, my *n*,	"	21
told him all her *n*'s tale,	"	80
my *n* would tell me of you:	*Princess*, iv.	407
Rose a *n* of ninety years,	" v.	544
with coarse mankind, Ill *n*'s.	" vi.	54
Gray *n*'s, loving nothing new;	*In Mem.* xxix.	14
watch'd her on her *n*'s arm,	" *Con.*	46
And tended her like a *n*,	*Maud*, I. xix.	76
than any child to a rough *n*,	*Elaine*	853
first *n* was, five years after, hers:	*Aylmer's F.*	79
nurse verb.)		
To *n* a blind ideal like a girl	*Princess*, iii.	201
becomes no man to *n* despair,	" iv.	444
Grant me your son, to *n*,	" vi.	279
Shall I *n* in my dark heart,	*Maud*, II. ii.	55

	POEM.	LINE.
nursed.		
wert not *n* by the waterfall	*Ode to Mem.*	51
wert *n* in some delicious land	*Eleänore*	11
in whose laps our limbs are *n*,	*To J. S.*	10
wrath I *n* against the world :	*Princess*, v.	427
n by those for whom you fought,	" vi.	79
nor the hand That *n* me,	" vii.	33
n me there from week to week :	"	224
n at ease and brought to understand	*Maud*, I.xviii.	35
n by mealy-mouth'd philanthropies,	*The Brook*	94
nurseling.		
This *n* of another sky	*The Daisy*	93
nursery.		
In our young *n* still unknown,	*Princess*, iv.	313
one they knew—Raw from the *n*—	*Aylmer's F.*	264
nursing.		
Annie pale, N' the sickly babe,	*En. Arden*	150
N' a child, and turning to the warmth	*Aylmer's F.*	165
nut.		
fancies like the vermin in a *n*	*Princess*, vi.	246
if the *n*'s' he said 'be ripe again :	*En. Arden*	456
mighty *n*'s, and nourishing roots;	"	556
nutmeg.		
The *n* rocks and isles of clove.	*The Voyage*	40
nutter.		
hazelwood, By autumn *n*'s haunted,	*En. Arden*	8
nutting.		
Went *n* to the hazels.	*En. Arden*	64
go with others, *n* to the wood	"	360
Nymph.		
presented Maid Or N', or Goddess,	*Princess*, i.	193
mountain quickens into N' and Faun;	*Lucretius*	167

O

mouthing out his hollow *o*'es	*The Epic*	50
oak.		
I turn to yonder *o*.	*Talking O.*	8
To yonder *o* within the field	"	13
Broad O of Sumner-chace,	"	30
Old *o*, I love thee well ;	"	202
never yet was *o* on lea	"	243
The gouty *o* began to move,	*Amphion*	23
Parks with *o* and chesnut shady,	*L. of Burleigh*	29
from the lily as far As *o* from elm :	*Princess*, v.	175
Ere half the lifetime of an *o*.	*InMem.*lxxv.	12
a gloom of stubborn-shafted *o*'s,	*Enid*	96
an *o*. so hollow huge and old	*Vivien*	3
once I heard By this huge *o*,	"	256
Call'd her to shelter in the hollow *o*,	"	743
struck, Furrowing a giant *o*,	"	785
in the hollow *o* he lay as dead	"	818
amulet drew her down to that old *o*,	*Aylmer's F.*	507
when the winds of winter tear an *o*	*Boädicea*	77
oakling.		
drew My little *o* from the cup,	*Talking O.*	23
oak-room.		
Maud's own little *o-r*	*Maud*, I. xiv.	9
oak-tree.		
But the solemn *o-t* sigheth,	*Claribel*	4
oar.		
weary seem'd the sea, weary the *o*,	*Lotos-E's.*	41
wind and wave and *o* ;	"	178
barge with *o* and sail Moved	*M. d'Arthur*	265
stirr'd with languid pulses of the *o*,	*Gardener's D.*	41
The measured pulse of racing *o*'s	*InMem.*lxxxvi.10	
oar'd.		
Naiads *o* A glimmering shoulder	*To E. L.*	16
Some to a low song *o* a shallop	*Princess*, ii.	433
oaring.		
O one arm, and bearing in my left	*Princess*, iv.	165
oarsman.		
o's haggard face As hard and still	*Elaine*	1243

Oasis.

	POEM.	LINE.
My one *O* in the dust and drouth	*Ed Morris* .	3
grow To use and power on this *O*	*Princess*, ii.	151

oat.

had the wild *o* not been sown	. *In Mem.* lii.	6

oat-grass.

On the *o-g* and the sword-grass,	. *May Queen*, ii.	28

oath.

Let us swear an *o*, and keep it	. *Lotos-E's*.	153
count of crimes With that wild *o*.'	*D. of F. Wom.*	202
hear me swear a solemn *o*,	. *Talking O.*	281
Cophetua sware a royal *o* ;	. *Beggar Maid*	15
my *o* was ta'en for public use,	. *Princess*, iv.	318
Your *o* is broken : we dismiss you :	"	341
But keep that *o* you swore, .	. *Vivien*	538
fearing heaven had heard her *o*,	. "	789

obedience.

Seeing *o* is the bond of rule.	. *M. d'Arthur*	94
silently, in all *o*, .	. *Enid*	767
in mild *o* Driving them on : .	. "	953
O is the courtesy due to kings.'	*Elaine*	714

obedient.

most valorous, Sanest and most *o* ;	*Enid* .	1759

obeisance.

curtseying her *o*, let us know,	. *Princess*, ii.	6

obelisk.

o's Graven with emblems of the time	*Arabian N's.*	107

obey.

A courage to endure and to *o* ;	. *Isabel* .	25
well to *o* then, if a king demand	. *M. d'Arthur*	95
Will he *o* when one commands ?	. *Two Voices*	244
Man to command and woman to *o* ;	*Princess*, v.	440
' I charge you, ask not but *o*.'	. *Enid* .	133
dare *o* him to his harm ? .	. "	985
As you that not *o* me. .	. "	1000
that you speak not but *o*.'	. "	1266
I know Your wish and would *o* ;	. "	1268
Almost beyond me : yet I would *o*.'	"	1272
robe yourself in this ; *o*.'	. "	1533
knowing nothing knows but to *o*,	. *Guinevere*	184

obey'd.

I have *o* my uncle until now,	. *Dora* .	57

object.

burn'd upon its *o* thro' such tears	*Love and Duty*	62
beyond his *o* Love can last : His *o* lives :	*Coquette*, iii.	5

oblique.

If straight thy track or if *o*, .	. *Two Voices*	193

oblivion.

With all forgiveness, all *o*, .	. *Princess*, vi.	277

obscurity.

I faint in this *o*, .	. *Ode to Mem.*	6, 44, 123

obsequies.

Nor meanly, but with gorgeous *o*,	*Elaine*	1325

observance.

with a mute *o* hung. .	. *Lockstey H.*	22
compass'd her with sweet *o's*	. *Enid*	48, 888

obstinacy.

At which the warrior in his *o*,	. *Enid* .	1303

obtain.

my heart had destined did *o*,	. *Guinevere*	488

obtained.

second suit *o* At first with Psyche.	*Princess*, vii.	56

occasion.

when to take *O* by the hand,	. *To the Queen*	31
Wiser to weep a true *o* lost, .	. *Princess*, iv.	50
iron nerve to true *o* true .	. *Ode on Well.*	37
A little at the vile *o*, .	. *Enid* .	235
written as she found Or made *o*,	. *Aylmer's F.*	478

ocean.

Under the hollow-hung *o* green !	. *The Merman*	38
On one side lay the *O*, .	. *M. d'Arthur*	11
By which they rest, and *o* sounds,	*In Mem. Con.*	121

	POEM.	LINE.
pacing mute by *o's* rim .	. *The Daisy* .	21
Or olive-hoary cape in *o* ; .	. " .	31
In middle *o* meets the surging shock,	*Will* .	8
on a dull day in an *O* cave .	. *Vivien* .	80
The hollower-bellowing *o*, .	. *En. Arden* .	599
The houseless *o's* heaving field,	. *The Voyage*	30
Cataract brooks to the *o* run,	. *The Islet*	17
Thine the myriad-rolling *o*, .	. *Boädicea* .	42
Charm, as a wanderer out in *o*,	. *Milton* .	12
There the sunlit *o* tosses .	. *The Captain*	69

ocean-foam.

as white As *o-f* in the moon, .	. *Maud*, I. xiv.	18

ocean-fowl.

The myriad shriek of wheeling *o-f*	*En. Arden* .	584

Ocean-lane.

Fall from his *O-l* of fire ; .	. *The Voyage*	19

ocean-mirror.

O'er *o-m's* rounded large, .	. *In Mem.* xii.	9

ocean-plain.

Sailest the placid *o-p's* . .	. *In Mem.* ix.	2

ocean-ridge.

hollow *o-r's* roaring into cataracts.	*Locksley H.*	6

ocean-smelling.

ocean-spoil In *o-s* osier, .	. *En. Arden* .	94

ocean-spoil.

o-s In ocean-smelling osier, .	. *En. Arden* .	93

o'clock.

'Tis nearly twelve *o* .	. *D. of the O. Year*	41
The mail ? At one *o*.	. *Walk. to the M.*	6
How goes the time ? 'Tis five *o*.	. *Will Water.*	3

Odalisques.

Sleek *O's*, or oracles of mode,	. *Princess*, ii.	63

ode.

then, Sir, awful *o's* she wrote,	. *Princess*, i. .	137
o's About this losing of the child ;	" .	139
quoted *o's*, and jewels five-words-long	"	ii. 355

Odin.

To Thor and *O* lifted a hand.	. *The Victim*	8
' O, Father *O*, We give you a life.	. " .	79

odour.

fed the time With *o* .	. *Arabian N's.*	65
cloud of incense of all *o* steam'd	. *Pal. of Art*	39
Distilling *o's* on me as they went .	*Gardener's D.*	183
Whose *o's* haunt my dreams ;	. *Sir Galahad*	68
On leagues of *o* streaming far,	. *InMem.*lxxxv.	14
Saying in *o* and colour .	. *Maud*, I. xxi.	12

Œnone.

Mournful Œ wandering forlorn	. *Œnone* .	15
My own Œ, Beautiful-brow'd Œ.	" .	68
never more Shall lone Œ see	. " .	212

o'er-driven.

pity for a horse *o-d* .	. *In Mem.*lxii.	1

o'erflow.

O's thy calmer glances, .	. *Madeline* .	33

o'erthwarted.

O with the brazen-headed spear	. *Œnone* .	137

o'erflourish'd.

O with the hoary clematis : .	. *Golden Year*	63

o'erlook'st.

O the tumult from afar, .	. *InMem.*cxxvi.	19

o'ershadow.

His love, unseen but felt, *o* Thee,	*Ded. of Idylls*	49

offence.

like a pedant's wand To lash *o*,	. *Princess*, i. .	28
without *o*, Has link'd our names	. *Elaine*	112
To save the *o* of charitable .	. *En. Arden* .	339

offend.

Your finer female sense sh. .	. *Day-Dm.* .	214

offender.

pick'd *o's* from the mass For judgment	*Princess*, i.	2

offer (s.)	POEM.	LINE.
I trample on your *o's* and on you:	*Princess*, iv.	525

offer (verb.)

| I *o* boldly: we will seat you highest: | *Princess*, iii. | 143 |

offered.

then and there had *o* something more,	*The Brook*	147
And *o* you it kneeling: .	*Vivien*	125
Not ev'n a rose, were *o* to thee?	*Lucretius*	69

offering.

| bring me *o's* of fruit and flowers: . | *St S. Stylites* | 126 |
| dress the victim to the *o* up . | *Princess*, iv. | 112 |

office.

A nobler *o* upon earth . . .	*To the Queen*	2
joint of state, that plies Its *o*,	'*Love thou thy land*'	48
should meet the *o's* of all, .	*M. d'Arthur*	125
not to fail In *o's* of tenderness,	*Ulysses*	41
Two in the liberal *o's* of life, .	*Princess*, ii.	158
With books, with flowers, with Angelo's,	" vii.	11
So kind an *o* hath been done, .	*In Mem.* xvii.	17
Her *o* there to rear, to teach,	" xxxix.	13
such great *o's* as suit . .	"	19
joined Each *o* of the social hour	" cx.	14
If all your *o* had to do . .	" cxxvii.	10
touch of their *o* might have sufficed,	*Maud*, II. v.	27
each low *o* of your holy house; .	*Guinevere*	674

officer.

an *o* Rose up, and read the statutes,	*Princess*, ii.	54
He rooted out the slothful *o* .	*Enid*	1786
o's and men Levied a kindly tax	*En. Arden*	663

offing.

| isles a light in the *o*: . . | *En. Arden* | 131 |

offset.

| man-minded *o* rose To chase the . | *Talking O.* | 51 |

often-ransacked.

| To think that in our *o-r* world . | *Sea-Dreams* | 125 |

Ogress.

| 'petty O,' and 'ungrateful Puss,' | *Princess, Pro.* | 156 |

oil.

realms of upland, prodigal in *o*, .	*Pal. of Art*	77
pure quintessences of precious *o's*	"	187
dues of wheat, and wine and *o*; .	*Lotos-E's.*	167
burn'd in fire, or boil'd in *o*, .	*St S. Stylites*	51

old.

New and O, disastrous feud, '*Love thou thy land*'		77
So blunt in memory, so *o* at heart,	*Gardener's D.*	52
shame and pride, New things and *o*,	*Walk. to the M.*	53
love for Nature is as *o* as I; .	*Ed. Morris*	28
we grow *o*. Ah! when shall all men's	*Golden Year*	47
o, but full Of force and choler, .	"	60
you and I are *o*; O age hath yet .	*Ulysses*	49
O, I see thee *o* and formal, .	*Locksley H.*	93
that new world which is the *o*, .	*Day-Dm.*	168
I am *o*, but let me drink; .	*Vision of Sin*	75
fancy fuses *o* and new, . .	*In Mem.* xvi.	18
count new things as dear as *o*: .	" xxxix.	28
Ring out the *o*, ring in the new, .	" cv.	5
being vicious, *o* and irritable, .	*Enid*	194
'Arms, indeed, but *o* And rusty, (rep.)	"	477
fairer in new clothes than *o* . .	"	722
o am I, and rough the ways . .	"	750
an oak, so hollow huge and *o* .	*Vivien*	3
Less *o* than I, yet older . .	"	406
omitting gayer youth for one so *o*,	"	777
propt, worm eaten, ruinously *o*, .	*En. Arden*	634
O, and a mine of memories— .	*Aylmer's F.*	10
So *o*, that twenty years before, .	"	508
have gone before me, I am so *o*: .	*Grandmother*	18
Ah, there's no fool like the *o* one—	"	44

older.

| *o*, for my blood Hath earnest in it | *Vivien* | 406 |

old-recurring.

| *o-r* waves of prejudice Resmooth . | *Princess*, iii. | 224 |

old-world.

| *o-w* trains, upheld at court . | *Day-Dm.* | 277 |
| *o-w* mammoth bulk'd in ice, . | *Princess*, v. | 142 |

old year.	POEM.	LINE.
And the *o y* is dead . .	*D. of F. Wom.*	243
For the *o y* lies a-dying .	*D. of the O. Year*	5
O *y*, you must not die; .	" 6, *et pass.*	
New Year and O *Y* met, .	1865-1866	2
O *Y* roaring and blowing, .	"	12

oleander.

| Where *o's* flush'd the bed . | *The Daisy* | 33 |

olive.

the year in which our *o's* fail'd.	*Princess*, i.	124
Peace sitting under her *o*, .	*Maud*, I. i.	33
Of *o*, aloe, and maize and vine,	*The Daisy*	4
A light amid its *o's* green; .	"	30

Olive.

| Will I to O plight my troth, . | *Talking O.* | 283 |

olive-gardens.

| Leaving the *o-g* far below, . | *D. of F. Wom.* | 217 |

olive-hoary.

| Or *o-h* cape in ocean; . . | *The Daisy* | 31 |

Olivet.

| crown'd The purple brows of O. . | *In Mem.* xxxi. | 12 |

Olivia.

maid or spouse, As fair as my O, .	*Talking O.*	35
saw Your own O blow, . .	"	76
Declare when last O came .	"	99

Omega.

| 'O! thou art Lord,' they said, . | *Two Voices* | 278 |

omen.

| from which their *o's* all men drew, | *Ode on Well.* | 36 |

omitting.

| *o* gayer youth For one so old, . | *Vivien* | 776 |

one-day-seen.

| The *o-d-s* Sir Lancelot in her heart | *Elaine* | 743 |

one-sided.

| 'O dull, *o-s* voice,' said I, . | *Two Voices* | 202 |

onset.

dash'd with drops Of *o*; .	*M. d'Arthur*	216
A day of *o's* of despair! .	*Ode on Well.*	174
Rings to the roar of an angel *o*—	*Milton*	8

onslaught.

| make an *o* single on a realm . | *Enid* | 1765 |

onward-sloping.

| 'Mid *o-s* motions infinite . | *Pal. of Art* | 247 |

ooze (s.)

| For I was drench'd with *o*, . | *Princess*, v. | 27 |

ooze (verb.)

| bloat himself, and *o* All over. . | *Sea Dreams* | 150 |

oozed.

| *o* All o'er with honey'd answer . | *Princess*, v. | 231 |

opal.

| gayer colours, like an *o* warm'd. | *Vivien* | 799 |

open (adj.)

Wide, wild, and *o* to the air, .	*Dying Swan*	2
in her lion's mood Tore *o*, .	*Princess*, iv.	362
all thy heart lies *o* unto me. .	" vii.	168
Were *o* to each other; . .	*Aylmer's F.*	40
heavens Break *o* to their highest .	*Spec. of Iliad*	15

open (verb.)

horse That hears the corn bin *o*, .	*The Epic*	45
o's but to golden keys. . .	*Locksley H.*	100
Heaven *o's* inward, chasms yawn,	*Two Voices*	304
o to me, And lay my little blossom	*Princess*, v.	96
o, find and read the charm: .	*Vivien*	510

open-door'd.

| Once rich, now poor, but always *o-d*.' | *Enid* | 302 |

opened.

Thy dark eyes *o* not, . .	*Eleänore*	1
yesterday you never *o* lip, .	*Vivien*	170
O a larger haven: . . .	*En. Arden*	103
Where either haven *o* on the deeps,	"	672

	POEM.	LINE.
small gate that *o* on the waste,	*En. Arden*	734
Crept to the gate, and *o* it,	"	776
counter door to that Which Leolin *o*	*Aylmer's F.*	283
Books (see Daniel seven and ten)		
Were *o*,	*Sea Dreams*	149

open-hearted.

| An *o-h* maiden, true and pure. | *Princess*, iii. | 82 |

opening (part.)

o upon level plots Of crowned lilies,	*Ode to Mem.*	108
The gorges, *o* wide apart,	*Œnone*	12
o out his milk-white palm	"	64
cloudy porch oft *o* on the Sun?	*Love and Duty*	9
o this I read Of old Sir Ralph	*Princess, Pro.*	120
thrice, and, no one *o*, Enter'd;	*En. Arden*	278

opening (s.)

| About the *o* of the flower, | *Two Voices* | 161 |

open-mouth'd.

| All *o-m*, all gazing to the light, | *Princess*, iv. | 462 |
| stood the unhappy mother *o-m*, | " vi. | 127 |

openness.

| taken with her seeming *o* | *Princess*, iv. | 281 |

open-work.

| *o-w* in which the hunter rued | *Princess*, iv. | 185 |

opiate.

| bring an *o* trebly strong, | *In Mem.* lxx. | 6 |

opinion.

| banded unions persecute O, 'You ask me why,' etc. | | 18 |

Oppian.

| and storm'd At the O law. | *Princess*, vii. | 109 |

opposed.

| and *o* Free hearts, free foreheads— | *Ulysses* | 48 |
| fifty there O to fifty, | *Princess*, v. | 473 |

opposite.

| loathsome *o* Of all my heart | *Guinevere* | 487 |

opposition.

Thro' solid *o* crabb'd and gnarl'd	*Princess*, iii.	110
some plan Foursquare to *o*.'	" v.	222
Yet not with brawling *o* she,	*En. Arden*	159

oppression.

| But they hated his *o*, | *The Captain* | 9 |

opulence.

| barbarous *o* jewel-thick | *Maud*, I. xiii. | 12 |

or.

| arms, Azure, an Eagle rising *or*, | *Vivien* | 325 |

oracle.

| Sleek Odalisques, or *o*'s of mode, | *Princess*, ii. | 63 |

orange.

| past Into deep *o* o'er the sea, | *Mariana in the S.* | 26 |
| A scarf of *o* round the stony helm, | *Princess, Pro.* | 102 |

orange-blossom.

| In lands of palm, of *o-b*, | *The Daisy* | 3 |

orange-flower.

| when first she wears her *o-f*! | *In Mem.* xxxix. | 4 |
| Made cypress of her *o-f*, | " lxxxiii. | 15 |

orange-thicket.

| some hid and sought in the *o t's*: | *Princess*, ii. | 436 |

oration.

| hung to hear The rapt *o* | *In Mem.* lxxxvi. | 32 |

oration-like.

| rolling words *O-l.* | *Princess*, v. | 363 |

orator.

| Stood up and spake, an affluent *o*. | *Princess*, iv. | 272 |
| Glory of warrior, glory of *o*, | *Wages* | 1 |

oratory.

| in praise of her Grew *o* | *Gardener's D.* | 56 |
| with mild heat of holy *o*, | *Enid* | 1714 |

orb (s.)

| ambrosial *o*'s Of rich fruit-bunches | *Isabel* | 36 |
| did gird their *o*'s with beams, | *The Poet* | 29 |

	POEM.	LINE.
should slowly round his *o*,	*Eleänore*	91
hollow *o* of moving Circumstance	*Pal. of Art*	255
She raised her piercing *o*'s,	*D. of F. Wom.*	171
Storm'd in *o*'s of song,	*Vision of Sin*	25
Thine are these *o*'s of light and	*In Mem. Pro.*	5
From *o* to *o*, from veil to veil.'	" xxx.	28
This round of green, this *o* of flame,	" xxxiv.	5
here he stays upon a freezing *o*	*Lucretius*	139

orb (verb.)

the whole mind might *o* about	*Two Voices*	138
o's Between the Northern and the	*Princess*, v.	412
o into the perfect star	*In Mem.* xxiv.	15

orbed.

| remain O in your isolation: | *Princess*, vi. | 153 |

orbit.

this *o* of the memory folds	*Gardener's D.*	73
The Sun will run his *o*,	*Love and Duty*	22
Sway'd to her from their *o*'s,	*Princess*, vii.	307
circuits of thine *o* round	*In Mem.* lxii.	11
In azure *o*'s heavenly-wise!	" lxxxvi.	38

orchard.

| There, on a slope of *o*, Francis laid | *Audley Ct.* | 19 |

orchard-lawns.

| happy, fair with *o-l* | *M. d'Arthur* | 262 |

orchis.

| Bring *o*. bring the foxglove spire, | *In Mem.* lxxxii. | 9 |

ordained.

| diamond jousts, Which Arthur had *o*, | *Elaine* | 32 |

ordeal.

| faded love, Or *o* by kindness; | *Aylmer's F.* | 561 |

order (arrangement, etc.)

fluted vase, and brazen urn In *o*,	*Arabian N's*	60
all things in *o* stored,	*Pal. of Art*	87
'Tis hard to settle *o* once again.	*Lotos-E's.*	127
old *o* changeth, yielding place to	*M. d'Arthur*	240
keeps us all in *o* more or less—	*Walk. to the M.*	17
sitting well in *o* smite	*Ulysses*	58
Eye, to which all *o* festers,	*Locksley H.*	133
The poplars, in long *o* due,	*Amphion*	37
What for *o* or degree?	*Vision of Sin*	86
sweet *o* sheld again with other laws:	*Princess*, vii.	4
Large elements in *o* brought,	*In Mem.* cxi.	13
that great *o* of the Table Round,	*Enid*	3
marshall'd *o* of their Table Round,	*Elaine*	1322
that fair *o* of my Table Round,	*Guinevere*	460
till this cosmic *o* everywhere	*Lucretius*	246

order (command.)

| good king gave *o* to let blow | *Enid* | 152 |

order (verb.)

| She will *o* all things duly, | *L. of Burleigh* | 39 |

ordered.

As all were *o*, ages since.	*Day-Dm.*	74
Days *o* in a wealthy peace.	*In Mem.* xlv.	11
having *o* all Almost as neat and close	*En. Arden*	177

ordinance.

'God's *o* Of Death is blown.	*To J. S.*	45
voice Of Ida sounded, issuing *o*:	*Princess*, vi.	352
pass beyond the goal of *o*	*Tithonus*	30

ore.

a rich Throne of the massive *o*,	*Arabian N's.*	146
Jewel or shell, or starry *o*,	*Eleänore*	20
labour'd mines undrainable of *o*.	*Œnone*	113
to lift the hidden *o* That glimpses	*D. of F. Wom.*	274
life is not as idle *o*,	*In Mem.* cxvii.	20

Oread.

whatever O haunt The knolls of Ida	*Œnone*	72
I see my O coming down,	*Maud*, I. xvi.	8
here an O, and this way she runs	*Lucretius*	188

organ.

holy *o* rolling waves Of sound	*D. of F. Wom.*	192
With this old soul in *o*'s new?	*Two Voices*	393
great *o* almost burst his pipes	*Princess*, ii.	450
storm their high-built *o*'s make,	*In Mem.* lxxxvi.	6

	POEM.	LINE.
organ-harmony.		
A rolling *o-h* Swells up,	Sir Galahad	75
organism.		
Makes noble thro' the sensuous *o*	Princess, ii.	73
organ-pipes.		
Near gilded *o-p,*	Pal. of Art.	98
organ-voice.		
God-gifted *o-v* of England,	Milton	3
orgies.		
hold their *o* at your tomb. 'You might have won'		12
mulberry-faced Dictator's *o*	Lucretius	54
Oriana.		
heart is wasted with my woe, O.	Oriana 2, et pass.	
oriel.		
She sat betwixt the shining *O's,*	Pal. of Art	159
the topmost *O's* coloured flame.	"	161
beams, that thro' the *O* shine,	Day-Dm.	54
All in an *o* on the summer side,	Elaine	1171
oriel-embowering.		
Brake from the vast *o-e* vine	Elaine	1192
Orient.		
Doth the low-tongued *O* Wander	Adeline	51
Deep in yonder shining *O,*	Locksley II.	154
furrowing all the *o* into gold.	Princess, iii.	2
Orion.		
great *O* sloping slowly to the West	Locksley II.	8
and *O* low in his grave.	Maud, I. iii.	14
O's grave low down in the west.	" III. vi.	8
ornament.		
darkling felt the sculptured *o*	Vivien	584
In hanging robe or vacant *o,*	Guinevere	502
lying with his urns and *o's,*	Aylmer's F.	4
orphan.		
Late-left an *o* of the squire,	Miller's D.	34
for this *o,* I am come to you;	Dora	62
I was left a trampled *o,*	Locksley II.	156
Made *o* by a winter shipwreck	En. Arden.	15
kill yourself And make them *o's* quite?'	"	392
an unknown artist's *o* child—	Sea Dreams	2
orphan-boy.		
Oh! teach the *o-b* to read,	L. C. V. de Vere	69
orphan-girl.		
teach the *o-g* to sew	L. C. V. de Vere	70
osier.		
ocean-spoil In ocean-smelling *o,*	En. Arden.	94
ostler.		
Wrinkled *o,* grim and thin I.	Vision of Sin	63
ostleress.		
A plump-arm'd *O* and a stable wench	Princess, i.	223
Ottoman.		
Emperor, *O,* which shall win:	To F. D. Maurice	32
ought.		
Sweet is it to have done the thing one *o,*	Princess, v.	64
I cannot love thee as I *o,*	In Mem. li.	1
ousted.		
From mine own earldom foully *o* me;	Enid	459
outburned.		
lit Lamps which *o* Canopus.	D. of F. Wom.	146
outlast.		
lays that will *o* thy Deity?	Lucretius	72
outlet.		
clear-stemm'd platans guard The *o,*	Arabian N's.	24
outline.		
Is given in *o* and no more.	In Mem. v.	12
The lucid *o* forming round thee:	Tithonus	53
outliving.		
For life *o* heats of youth,	In Mem. lii.	10
outran.		
o The hearer in its fiery course;	In Mem. cviii.	7
outredden.		
o All voluptuous garden-roses.	Ode on Well.	208
outstript.		
He still *o* me in the race;	In Mem. xli.	2
outwelleth.		
The slumbrous wave *o,*	Claribel	18
outworks.		
Thro' all the *o* of suspicious pride;	Isabel	24
ouzel.		
mellow *o* fluted in the elm:	Gardener's D.	93
ovation.		
rain an April of *o*	Princess, vi.	50
overawe.		
that new fort to *o* my friends,	Enid	460
overawed.		
to be *o* By what I cannot but know	Maud, II. ii.	40
overbear.		
o's the bark And him that helms it,	Elaine	484
overblown.		
O with murmurs harsh,	Ode to Mem.	99
overboard.		
o one stormy night He cast his body	The Voyage	79
over-bold.		
the island princes *o-b*	Lotos-E's.	120
And again seem'd *o*	Maud, I. xiv.	24
overbore.		
contrasting brightness, *o* Her fancy	Enid	801
charm Of nature in her *o* their own;	Vivien	446
o Sir Lancelot and his charger,	Elaine	485
overborne.		
o by all his bearded lords	Princess, v.	346
deeming Merlin *o* By instance,	Vivien	649
over-bright.		
Eyes not downdropt nor *o-b*	Isabel	1
overcame.		
Did more, and underwent, and *o,*	Godiva	10
overcome.		
Bred will in me to *o* it or fall.	Princess, v.	341
come to all I am And *o* it;	Elaine	448
overdo.		
almost *o* the deeds Of Lancelot;	Elaine	468
over-fineness.		
From *o-f* not intelligible	Vivien	645
overflow (s.)		
Rain'd thro' my sight its *o.*	Two Voices.	45
overflow (verb.)		
all the markets *o.*	Locksley II.	101
Hears and not hears, and lets it *o.*	En. Arden.	209
overflowed.		
dissolving sand To watch them *o,*	En. Arden.	20
overlaid.		
o With narrow moonlit slips.	Œnone	213
overlook.		
O a space of flowers,	L. of Shalott, i.	16
And *o* the chace;	Talking O.	94
And *o* the lea,	"	198
o's the sandy tracts,	Locksley II.	5
overlive.		
O it—lower yet—be happy!	Locksley II.	97
over-mellow.		
The full-juiced apple, waxing *o-m,*	Lotos-E's.	78
overmuch.		
Nor asking *o* and taking less	En. Arden.	251
overpay.		
'My lord, you *o* me fifty-fold.'	Enid	1069
overpower'd.		
o quite, I cannot veil, or droop	Eleänore	87

overquick.
	POEM.	LINE.
o To crop his own sweet rose	*Vivien*	574
'O are you To catch a lothly plume	"	577

overseas.
| sick of home went *o* for change. | *Walk. to the M.* | 18 |
| fly to my strong castle *o*: | *Guinevere* | 112 |

overset.
| But thou, while kingdoms *o*, | *Talking O.* | 257 |

overshadowed.
| All *o* by the foolish dream, | *Enid* | 675 |

over-smoothness.
| some self-conceit, Or *o-s*: | *Ed. Morris* | 75 |

overstrained.
| or a mood Of *o* affection, | *Vivien* | 372 |
| merit will Your term of *o*. | " | 385 |

overstream'd.
| *o* and silvery-streak'd | *The Islet* | 20 |

overtake.
| *o*'s Far thought with music | *Two Voices* | 437 |

overtaken.
| Flying, but, *o*, died the death | *Enid* | 1026 |

overtalked.
| Merlin, *o* and overworn Had yielded, | *Vivien* | 814 |

overtaxed.
| loathed to see them *o*; | *Godiva* | 9 |

overthrew.
down we swept and charged and *o*.	*Ode on Well.*	130
o the next that follow'd him,	*Enid*	1314
whom he smote, he *o*.	*Elaine*	464

overthrow (s.)
| quick! by *o* Of these or those, | *Princess*, v. | 306 |

overthrow (verb.)
| *o* My proud self, and my purpose | *Enid* | 1696 |

overthrowing (part.)
| By *o* me you threw me higher. | *Enid* | 1640 |

overthrowing (s.)
| With *o*'s, and with cries, | *In Mem.* cxii. | 19 |

overthrown.
And like a warrior *o*;	*Two Voices*	150
I have never yet been *o*, But thou hast *o* me,	*Enid*	588
In twelve great battles ruining *o*.	*Guinevere*	429

overtoiled.
| *o* By that day's grief and travel | *Enid* | 1225 |

overtrue.
| 'O ay,' said Vivien, '*o* a tale. | *Vivien* | 570 |

overtrust.
| wink no more in slothful *o*. | *Ode on Well.* | 170 |

overturn.
| Behold me *o* and trample on him. | *Enid* | 1691 |

overturned.
| schemed and wrought Until I *o* him: | *Enid* | 1678 |

over-vaulted.
| *o-v* grateful gloom, | *Pal. of Art* | 54 |

overwhelm'd.
| shook And almost *o* her, | *En. Arden.* | 526 |

overwise.
| has written: she never was *o*, | *Grandmother* 3, | 105 |

overworn.
| But all he was is *o*.' | *In Mem.* i. | 16 |
| overtalk'd and *o* Had yielded, | *Vivien* | 814 |

overwrought.
| that his brain is *o*: | *Locksley H.* | 53 |
| by being so *o* Suddenly strike | *Maud*, II. ii. | 62 |

owe.
we owe you bitter thanks:	*Princess*, iv.	510
I feel I shall *o* you a debt	*Maud*, I. xix.	87
forget That I *o* this debt to you	"	99

owed.
O you me nothing for a life half-lost?	*Enid*	1167
boon I *o* you thrice,	*Vivien*	155
Whole in ourselves and *o* to none	*Princess*, iv.	130

owl.
The white *o* in the belfry sits.	*The Owl*, i.	7,14
drown'd the whoopings of the *o*	*St S. Stylites*	32
bats wheel'd, and *o*'s whoop'd,	*Princess,Con.*	110
the *o*'s Wailing had power upon her,	*Elaine*	99*

own.
better than to *o* A crown, a sceptre,	*Ode to Mem.*	120
He *o*'s the fatal gift of eyes,	*Two Voices*	286
o one part of sense not flint	*Princess*, vi.	166

owned.
| Yourself have *o* you did me wrong. | *Vivien* | 165 |
| tasted flesh, Nor *o* a sensual wish, | " | 478 |

ownest.
| My own heart's heart and *o* own | *Maud*,I.xviii. | 74 |

owning.
| *o* but a little more Than beasts | *Two Voices* | 196 |
| earthly Muse, And *o* but a little art | *InMem.*xxxvii.14 |

ox.
From the dark fen the *oxen*'s low	*Mariana*	28
The passive *oxen* gaping.	*Amphion*	72
as a footsore *o* in crowded ways	*Aylmer's F.*	819
oxen from the river, and goodly sheep *Spec. of Iliad*	4
roasting *o* Moan round the spit—	*Lucretius*	131

oxlip.
| As cowslip unto *o* is, | *Talking O.* | 107 |

P

pace (s.)
She made three *p*'s thro' the room,	*L. of Shalott*,iii.	38
Wheeling with precipitate *p*'s	*Vision of Sin*	37
three *p*'s measured from the mound	*Princess*, v.	1
forth they rode, but scarce three *p*'s	*Enid*	868
Round was their *p* at first	"	882
went back some *p*'s of return,	"	919
woven *p*'s and with waving arms,	*Vivien* 56,179,817

pace (verb.)
Would *p* the troubled land,	*Love thou thy land'*	84
till noon no foot should *p* the street,	*Godiva*	39
To *p* the gritted floor,	*Will Water.*	242
our ears with wool And so *p* by:	*Princess*, iv.	48
p the sacred old familiar fields,	*En. Arden*,	626

paced.
p the thymy plots of Paradise,	*Love and Death*	2
p for ever in a glimmering land,	*Pal. of Art*	67
p beside the mere,	*M. d'Arthur*	83
I wonder'd, while I *p* along:	*Two Voices*	454
out we *p*, I first,	*Princess*, ii.	7
So saying from the court we *p*,	" iii.	161
Where *p* the Demigods of old,	"	323
p the terrace, till the Bear had wheel'd	" iv.	194
p the shores And many a bridge,	*InMem.*lxxxvi.11
turn'd all red and *p* his hall,	*Enid*	1516
ankle-bones Who *p* it, ages back	*Vivien*	402
p for coolness in the chapel-yard;	"	607
p Back toward his solitary home	*En. Arden*.	794
forth they came and *p* the shore,	*Sea Dreams*	32

pacing (part.)
some one *p* there alone,	*Pal. of Art*	66
P with downward eyelids pure.	*Two Voices*	420
Walking up and *p* down,	*L. of Burleigh*	00
so *p* till she paused By Florian;	*Princess*, ii.	282
p staid and still By twos and threes,	"	412
Now *p* mute by ocean's rim	*The Daisy*	21
bare me, *p* on the dusky mere.	*Elaine*	1401

pacing (s.)
| long mechanic *p*'s to and fro, | *Love and Duty* | 17 |
| his foot Return from *p*'s in the field | *Lucretius* | 6 |

pack (s.)
| wolf within the fold! A *p* of wolves! | *Princess*, ii. | 174 |

pack (verb.)	POEM.	LINE.
by the Lord that made me, you shall *p*,	*Dora* .	29
p's up his beds and chairs, . .	*Walk. to the M.*	31
Let the canting liar *p*! . . .	*Vision of Sin*	108
close as Nature *p's* Her blossom .	*En. Arden* .	178

pack'd.

had *p* the thing among the beds,)	*Walk. to the M.*	36
were *p* to make your crown, . .	*Princess*, IV.	522

pad.

An abbot on an ambling *p*, . .	*L. of Shalott*, ii. 20

padded.

P round with flesh and fat, . .	*Vision of Sin*	177

paddling.

clockwork steamer *p* plied . .	*Princess, Pro.*	71

padlock'd.

each chest lock'd and *p* thirty-fold,	*Vivien*	. 505

Pæan.

I sung the joyful P clear, . .	*Two Voices*	127

Pagan.

our good Arthur broke The *P* .	*Elaine*	. 280

page (boy.)

long-haired *p* in crimson clad, .	*L. of Shalott*, ii. 22
The *p* has caught her hand in his;	*Day-Dm.* . 49
maid and *p* renew'd their strife, .	" . 145
And *p*, and maid, and squire, .	*Enid* . . 710
with no attendance, *p* or maid, .	" . 1171

page (of a book.)

I will turn that earlier *p*. . .	*Locksley H.* 107
trust me while I turn'd the *p*, .	*To E. L.* . 9
p or two that rang With tilt . .	*Princess, Pro.* 121
I heard her turn the *p*; . .	" vii. 175
passing, turn the *p* that tells A grief	*In Mem.* lxxvi. 10
O ay, it is but twenty *p*'s long, .	*Vivien* . 518
every *p* having an ample marge, .	" . 519
If men neglect your *p's* . .	*Spiteful Let.* 6

pageant.

masque or *p* at my father's court.	*Princess*, i. 195
Lead out the *p*: sad and slow .	*Ode on Well.* 13

paid.

law for *us*: We *p* in person. .	*Walk. to the M.* 78
I would have *p* her kiss for kiss,	*Talking O.* 195
respect, however slight, was *p* .	*Princess*, ii. 120
p our tithes in the days that are	*Maud*, II. v. 23
p with horses and with arms; .	*Enid* . 1335
P with a voice flying by . .	*Wages* . 2

pail.

The milk that bubbled in the *p*,	*In Mem.* lxxxviii. 51

pain.

should breathe a thought of *p*. .	*Miller's D.* . 76
the loss that brought us *p*, . .	" . 229
Trouble on trouble, *p* on *p*, . .	*Lotos-E's.* . 129
or seem'd to start in *p*, . .	*D. of F. Wom.* 41
With what dull *p* Compass'd, .	" . 277
weeping dulls the inward *p*.' .	*To J. S.* . 48
with *p*, reclining on his arm, .	*M. d'Arthur* 168
P heap'd ten-hundred-fold to this,	*St S. Stylites* 23
May match his *p's* with mine; .	" . 137
faint steps, and much exceeding *p*	" . 180
sting of shrewdest *p* Ran shrivelling	" . 195
the blind cry of passion and of *p*,	*Love and Duty* 73
looking ancient kindness on thy *p*.	*Locksley H.* . 85
woman's pleasure, woman's *p*—	" . 147
like a beast with lower *p's*! .	" . 176
once from dread of *p* to die. .	*Two Voices* 105
p rises up, of Pleasures pall . .	" . 164
Lodst thou, thro' enduring *p*, .	" . 166
wilt thou find passion, *p* or pride?	" . 243
Thy *p* is a reality.' . . .	" . 387
Care and Pleasure, Hope and P, .	*Day-Dm.* . 75
scales that balance joy and *p*, .	*Sir L. and Q. G.* . 1
MAN ENTER IN ONE OF DEATH?'	*Princess*, ii. 178
your *p's* May only make that .	" iii. 222
clamber'd o'er at top with *p*, .	" iv. 190
twitch of *p* Tortured her mouth, .	" vi. 89
and draw The sting from *p*; .	" vii. 49

	POEM.	LINE.
Like dull narcotics, numbing *p*. .	*In Mem.* v. 8
And I should tell him all my *p*, .	" xiv. 13
dies not, but endures with *p*, .	" xviii. 17
He loves to make parade of *p*, .	" xxi. 10
The lading of a single *p*, . .	" xxv. 11
I slept and woke with *p*, . .	" xxviii. 13
I would set their *p's* at ease. .	" lxii. 8
ploughs with *p* his native lea .	" lxiii. 25
These mortal lullabies of *p* . .	" lxxvi. 5
No single tear, no mark of *p*; .	" lxxvii. 14
Some painless sympathy with *p*?'	" lxxxiv. 88
of motion as well as the nerves of *p*,	*Maud*, l. i. 63
possible After long grief and *p* .	" II. iv. 2
Pass, thou deathlike type of *p* .	" v. 58
my bones are shaken with *p*, .	" v. 5
A band of *p* across my brow; .	*The Letters* 6
Peace, it is a day of *p* . .	*Ode on Well.* 235. 8
Ours the *p*, be his the gain! .	" . 241
to lull the throbs of *p*, . .	*The Daisy* . 105
all my *p's*, poor man, for all my *p's*,	*Enid* . 116
p she had To keep them in the .	" . 1035
sharpness of that *p* about her heart;	" . 1039
down he sank For the pure *p* .	*Elaine* . 517
death who puts an end to *p*: .	" . 1002
to have it, none; to lose it, *p*; .	" . 1405
groan'd Sir Lancelot in remorseful *p*	" . 1413
troubled, as if with anger or *p*: .	*Grandmother* 65
peace, so it be free from *p*, . .	" . 97
gets for greeting but a wail of *p* .	*Lucretius* . 138
one pleasure and without one *p*, .	" . 265

pain (verb.)

p's him that he sickens nigh to death;	*Enid* 1348

pained.

P. and, as bearing in myself the shame	*Aylmer's F.* 355
Her crampt-up sorrow *p* her .	" . 800

paint.

'When will *you* *p* like this?'	*Gardener's D.* 22
p the gates of Hell with Paradise,	*Princess*, iv. 113
strive to *p* The face I know, .	*In Mem.* lxix. 2
every dew-drop *p's* a bow, . .	" cxxi. 18
harlots *p* their talk as well as face	*Vivien* . 670
so *p's* him that his face . .	*Elaine* . 333

painted.

Eustace *p* her, And said to me, .	*Gardener's D.* 20
supporters of a shield, *P*, . .	*Enid* . 1117
fair As ever painter *p*. . .	*Aylmer's F.* 106

painter.

Musician, *p*, sculptor, critic, .	*Princess*, ii. 161
As when a *p*, poring on a face, .	*Elaine* . 331
fair As ever *p* painted, . .	*Aylmer's F.* 106
Sorrowest thou, pale *P*, for the past,	*Coquette*, iii. 3

painting (part.)

was *p* on it fancied arms, . .	*Vivien* . 324
p some dead friend from memory?	*Coquette*, iii. 4

painting (s.)

with choice *p's* of wise men I hung	*Pal. of Art* 131
Drew from my neck the *p*. .	*Princess*, vi. 94

pair.

we went along, A pensive *p*, .	*Miller's D.* 164
in one love Than *p's* of wedlock	*Princess*, vi. 237
His craven *p* Of comrades . .	*Enid* . 1015
false *p* who turn'd Flying, . .	" . 1025
With a low whinny toward the *p*;	" . 1604

palace.

in the lighted *p* near . .	*L. of Shalott*, iv. 47
unto herself In her high *p* there.	*Pal. of Art* 12
upon My *p* with unblinded eyes,	" . 42
of great rooms and small the *p* stood,	" . 237
in dark corners of her *p* stood	*D. of F. Wom.* 24
The *p* bang'd, and buzz'd and clackt,	*Day-Dm.* 146
from the *p* came a child of sin, .	*Vision of Sin* 5
in the imperial *p* found the king. .	*Princess*, 1. 112
promise you Some *p* in our land, .	" iii. 146
look this *p*; but even from the first	" iv. 294
this night should pluck your *p* down;	" . 395

	POEM.	LINE.
'Two from the *p*' I.	*Princess*, v.	3
on this side the *p* ran the field	"	351
high upon the *p* Ida stood	" vi.	14
with my brethren here In our own *p*:	"	108
for this we gave our *p* up	"	227
Or *p*, how the city glitter'd,	*The Daisy*	47
he will have you to his *p* here,	*Enid*	1079
into no Earl's *p* will I go.	"	1084
God knows, too much of *p*'s.	"	1085
miles of coast, A *p*, and a princess	*Vivien*	439-98
complexities Of Arthur's *p*:	"	583
moved about her *p*, proud and pale	*Elaine*	611
Until we found the *p* of the king.	"	1038-45
he Will guide me to that *p*,	"	1123
Sir Lancelot at the *p* craved Audience	"	1156
of Arthur's *p* toward the stream,	"	1172
rolling o'er the *p*'s of the proud	*Aylmer's F.*	636
Fairily-delicate *p*'s shine	*The Islet*	18
Lo the *p*'s and the temple,	*Boädicea*	53
Burst the gates, and burn the *p*'s,	"	64

palace-doorway.
| On to the *p-d* sliding, paused. | *Elaine* | 1239 |

palace-front.
| *p-f* Alive with fluttering scarfs | *Princess*, v. | 497 |

palace-gate.
| youth came riding toward a *p-g*. | *Vision of Sin* | 2 |
| that cold vapour touch'd the *p-g*, | " | 58 |

palace-spire.
| High up, the topmost *p-s*. | *Day-Dm* | 68 |

palace-walls.
| Where all about your *p-w* | *To the Queen* | 15 |

palate.
| Wither beneath the *p*, | *D. of F. Wom.* | 287 |

pale (adj.)
Then her cheek was *p* and thinner	*Locksley H.*	21
P again as death did prove:	*L. of Burleigh*	66
P one, blush again:	*Princess*, iii.	51
some red, some *p*, All open-mouth'd,	" iv.	461
raised the cloak from brows as *p*	" v.	70
Dishelm'd and mute, and motionlessly *p*,	" vi.	85
P was the perfect face,	" vii.	209
Come; let us go: your cheeks are *p*;	*In Mem.* lvi.	5
P with the golden beam of an eyelash	*Maud,* I. iii.	
ever as *p* as before	"	11
Morning arises stormy and *p*,	" vi.	1
red and *p* Across the face of Enid	*Enid*	523
rode so slowly and they look'd so *p*,	"	884
Femininely fair and dissolutely *p*,	"	1124
at his side all *p* Dismounting,	"	1360
never yet beheld a thing so *p*.	"	1463
beholding her Tho' *p*, yet happy,	"	1728
graver fits, Turn red or *p*,	*Vivien*	37
moved about her palace, proud and *p*,	*Elaine*	611
how *p*! what are they? flesh and blood?	"	1249
and *p* he turn'd, and reel'd,	*Guinevere*	302
Enoch slumber'd motionless and *p*	*En. Arden*	907
P, for on her the thunders	*Aylmer's F.*	278
P as the Jeptha's daughter,	"	280
how *p* she had look'd Darling, to-night	"	379
P he turn'd and red,	*The Captain*	62

pale (s.)
By bridge and ford, by park and *p*,	*Sir Galahad*	82
leap the rotten *p*'s of prejudice,	*Princess*, ii.	126
break At seasons thro' the gilded *p*:	*In Mem.* cx.	8

paled.
| *P* at a sudden twitch | *Aylmer's F.* | 732 |

pale-green.
| *p-g* sea-groves straight and high | *The Merman* | 19 |

paleness.
| *p*, an hour's defect of the rose, | *Maud,* I. ii. | 8 |

paler.
make her *p* with a poison'd rose?	*Vivien*	461
But left her all the *p*,	*Elaine*	377
made Still *p* the pale head of him,	*Aylmer's F.*	623

palfrey.
	POEM.	LINE.
there she found her *p* trapt	*Godiva*	51
her *p*'s footfall shot Light horrors.	"	58
cried ' My charger and her *p*,'	*Enid*	126
bid him bring Charger and *p*	"	1250
p heart enough To bear his armour?	"	1338
her *p* whinnying lifted heel,	"	1382
charger is without, My *p* lost.'	"	1598

pall (s.)
truth came borne with bier and *p*,	*In Mem.* lxxxiv.	1
Warriors carry the warrior's *p*,	*Ode on Well.*	6
pass the gate, Save under *p*	*Aylmer's F.*	827

pall (verb.)
| Pain rises up, old pleasures *p*. | *Two Voices* | 164 |

Pallas.
charm *P* and Juno sitting by:	*A Character*	15
Here comes to-day, *P* and Aphrodite,	*Œnone*	84
P where she stood, Somewhat apart,	"	135
'O Paris, Give it to *P*!'	"	166
stood a bust of *P* for a sign	*Princess*, i.	219
fired an angry *P* on the helm,	" vi.	347
wild *P* from the brain Of Demons?	*In Mem* cxiii.	12

pall'd (cloaked.)
| *P* all its length in blackest samite, | *Elaine* | 1136 |

palled (surfeited.)
| well I know it—*p*—For I know men: | *Enid* | 1180 |

palm (of the hand.)
Fold thy *p*'s across thy breast,	*A Dirge*	2
opening out his milk-white *p*	*Œnone*	64
Caught in the frozen *p*'s of Spring.	*The Blackbird*	24
smote His *p*'s together, and he cried	*M. d'Arthur*	87
press The maiden's tender *p*.	*Talking O.*	180
His *p*'s are folded on his breast:	*Two Voices*	247
Bow'd on her *p*'s and folded up	*Princess*, iv.	269
beneath his vaulted *p* A whisper'd	" v.	30
clash'd His iron *p*'s together.	"	344
nor more Sweet Ida: *p* to *p* she sat:	" vii.	120
In mine own lady *p*'s I cull'd	*Vivien*	122
clench'd her fingers till they bit the *p*,	*Elaine*	608
Between his *p*'s a moment up and	*Aylmer's F.*	259

palm (tree.)
Imbower'd vaults of pillar'd *p*.	*Arabian N's.*	39
the solemn *p*'s were ranged Above,	"	79
many a tract of *p* and rice,	*Pal. of Art*	114
the yellow down Border'd with *p*,	*Lotos-E's.*	2
The *p*'s and temples of the South.	*'You ask me why,'*	28
the white robe and the *p*.	*St S. Stylites*	20
Breadths of tropic shade and *p*'s	*Locksley H.*	60
battle-clubs From the isles of *p*:	*Princess, Pro.*	22
at Shusan underneath the *p*'s.	" iii.	214
Betwixt the *p*'s of paradise	*In Mem. Con.*	32
lands of *p* and southern pine; (rep.)	*The Daisy*	2
The clipt *p* of which they boast;	"	26
these be the *p*'s Whereof the happy	*En. Arden*	500
thatch'd with leaves of *p*, a hut,	"	560
the *p*'s and ferns and precipices;	"	594
dells of cowslip, fairy *p*'s,	*Aylmer's F.*	91
Above the valleys of *p* and pine.'	*The Islet*	23

palm (sallow-bloom.)
| In colour like the satin-shining *p*. | *Vivien* | 73 |

palmtree.
| 'Under a *p*.' That was nothing to | *En. Arden* | 494 |
| Under a *p*, over him the Sun: | " | 497 |

palmwood.
| Crimson-hued the stately *p*'s, | *Milton* | 15 |

Palmyrene.
| with the *P* That fought Aurelian, | *Princess*, ii. | 69 |

palpitated.
| tempestuous treble throbbed and *p*; | *Vision of Sin* | 28 |
| *P*, her hand shook, | *Princess*, iv. | 370 |

palpitations.
| blissful *p*'s in the blood | *Princess*, iv. | 10 |

palsy.
| Cured lameness, *palsies*, cancers. | *St S. Stylites* | 81 |
| A wither'd *p* cease to shake?' | *Two Voices* | 57 |

	POEM	LINE
infancy Or old bedridden *p*,—	*Aylmer's F.*	178
p, death-in-life, And wretched age—	*Lucretius*	154

palter'd.
Nor *p* with eternal God for power ; *Ode on Well.* 180

pamper.
p not a hasty time, 'Love thou thy land,' etc. 9

pamphleteer.
A *p* on guano and on grain, . . *Princess, Con.* 89

pau (a vessel.)
hurl'd the *p* and kettle. . . *The Goose* . 28

Pan.
The murmur of a happy *P*: . . *In Mem.* xxiii. 12

pane.
The blue fly sung in the *p* ; .	*Mariana*	63
the frost is on the *p*:	*May Queen,* ii.	13
lash with storm the streaming *p*?	*In Mem.* lxxi.	4
The prophets blazon'd on the *p*'s ;	" lxxxvi.	8
I peer'd athwart the chancel *p*	*The Letters*	3
ice-ferns on January *p*'s .	*Aylmer's F.*	222

pang.
Struck thro' with *p*'s of hell. .	*Pal. of Art* .	220
multiplied by superhuman *p*'s, .	*St S. Stylites*	11
I felt a *p* within . . .	*Talking O.* .	234
Whence follows many a vacant *p*;	*Princess,* ii.	381
brother, you have known the *p*'s we	" v.	364
rack'd with *p*'s that conquer trust;	*In Mem.* xlix.	6
p's of nature, sins of will, .	" liii.	3
thro' his manful breast darted the *p*	*Enid* .	121
The *p*— which while I weigh'd thy	*Guinevere* .	536

panic-stricken.
p-s, like a shoal Of darting fish . *Enid* . 1317

pansy.
eyes Darker than darkest *pansies, Gardener's D.* 27

pant.
Life, not death, for which we *p* ; . *Two Voices* 398

panted.
as he walk'd, King Arthur *p* hard,	*M. d'Arthur*	176
p hand in hand with faces pale, .	*Vision of Sin*	19
p from weary sides 'King you are	*Princess,* v.	23
half-English Neilgherry air I *p* .	*The Brook* .	16

panther.
The *p*'s roar came muffled . . *Œnone* . 210

panting.
p, burst The laces toward her babe ; *Princess,* vi. 132

paper.
| at a board by tome and *p* sat . | *Princess,* ii. | 18 |
| the *p*'s that she held Rustle ; . | " iv. | 371 |

Paphian.
new-bathed in *P* wells . . . *Œnone* . 171

papist.
Than *p* unto Saint. . . . *Talking O.* . 16

parachute.
dropt a fairy *p* and past : . . *Princess, Pro.* 76

parade.
He loves to make *p* of pain, . *In Mem.* xxi. 10

Paradise.
paced the thymy plots of *P*, .	*Love and Death*	2
thronging all one porch of *P* .	*Pal. of Art*	101
from it melt the dews of *P*, .	*St S. Stylites*	207
palms in cluster, knots of *P*, .	*Lockstey H.*	160
Like long-tail'd birds of *P*, .	*Day-Dm.* .	275
paint the sates of Hell with *P*, .	*Princess,* iv.	113
dipt In Angel instincts, breathing *P*,	" vii.	302
This earth had been the *P* . .	*In Mem.* xxiv.	6
P twixt the palms of *p*. .	" *Con.*	32
And the valleys of *P*. . .	*Maud,* I. xxii.	44
never yet, since hugh in *P* .	*Enid*	1611
groves that look'd a *p* Of blossom,	*Guinevere* .	386
many-blossoming *P*'s, . .	*Boadicea*	43

paragon
look upon her As on a kind of *p* ; *Princess,* i. 154

	POEM	LINE
paramour.		
haughty jousts, and took a *p*; .	*Enid* .	1680
parapet.		
Dislodging pinnacle and *p* . .	*D. of F. Wom.*	26
Set every gilded *p* shuddering ; .	*Elaine* .	293
isle of silvery *p*'s ! . . .	*Boadicea* .	36
parasite.		
A leaning and upbearing *p*, . .	*Isabel* .	34
parcel.		
Portions and *p*'s of the dreadful Past.	*Lotos-E's.*	92
parcel-bearded.		
p-b with the traveller's-joy In Autumn,	*Aylmer's F.*	153
parcelled.		
the broad woodland *p* into farms ;	*Aylmer's F.*	847
parch'd.		
p and wither'd, deaf and blind, .	*Fatima* .	6
p with dust ; Or, clotted into points	*M. d'Arthur*	218
parish.		
that year in twenty *p*'es round. .	*Grandmother*	12
pard.		
a wild and wanton *p*, . . .	*Œnone* .	195

pardon s.)
heal me with your *p* ere you go.'	*Princess,* iii.	49
p, sweet Melissa, for a blush?' .	"	50
in grosser lips beyond all *p*— .	" iv.	233
with mutual *p* ask'd and given .	" v.	44
I crave your *p*, O my friend ; .	*In Mem.* lxxxiv.	100
with the Sultan's *p*, I am all as well	*Maud,* I. xx.	33
Crave *p* for that insult . .	*Enid* .	583
Grant me *p* for my thoughts : .	"	816
Your *p*, child. . . .	*Vivien* .	153
your *p*, lo, you know it ! . .	*Elaine* .	660

pardon (verb.)
I (*P* me saying it) were much loth	*Princess,* i.	155
needful seeming harshness, *p* it.	" ii.	289
'O *p* me ! I heard, I could not help	"	310
mine in part. O hear me, *p* me. .	" iii.	15
P, I am shamed That I must needs	"	35
We *p* it ; and for your ingress .	" v.	209
'Pray stay a little : *p* me ; . .	*The Brook* .	210
'*P* me, O stranger knight . .	*Enid* .	280
O *p* me ! the madness of that hour,	"	1105
sin in words, Perchance, we both can *p* :	*Elaine*	1183
I cared not for it. O *p* me, .	*Aylmer's F.*	244

pardoned.
I have *p* little Letty ; . . . *Ed. Morris* 140

pare.
would *p* the mountain to the plain *Vivien* . 678

parent.
and their *p*'s underground . .	*Aylmer's F.*	83
after our good *p*'s past away .	"	355
you are happy : let her *p*'s be.' .	"	356
sell her, those good *p*'s, for her good	"	443
p's harshness and the hapless loves	"	646

Paris.
(Enone, wandering forlorn Of *P*, .	*Œnone* .	16
Beautiful *P*, evil-hearted *P*, .	"	42
see thy *P* judge of Gods.' . .	"	88
to *P* made Proffer of royal power, .	"	183
From me, Heaven's Queen, *P*, to thee	"	125
P held the costly fruit Out . .	"	143
P ponder'd, and I cried, 'O *P*, .	"	165
when I look'd, *P* had rais'd his arm,	"	185

park.
the range of lawn and *p*: . .	*The Blackbird*	6
wild wind rang from *p* and plain,	*The Goose* .	45
Before her, and the *P*, . .	*Talking O.* .	124
My father left a *p* to me, . .	*Amphion* .	1
By bridge and ford, by *p* and pale,	*Sir Galahad*	84
They by *p*'s and lodges going .	*L. of Burleigh*	17
P's with oak and chesnut shady, .	"	21
P's and order'd gardens great, .	"	30
stones of the Abbey-ruin in the *p*.	*Princess, Pro.*	14
Down thro' the *p*; strange was the sight	"	54

	POEM.	LINE.
gave The *p*, the crowd, the house;	Princess, Pro.	94
hundred maids in train across the P	" vi.	60
their *p*'s some dozen times a year	" Con.	103
chariots flow By *p* and suburb	In Mem. xcvii.	24
To range the woods, to roam the *p*,	" Con.	96

parlance.
A hate of gossip *p*, ... Isabel .	26

parliament.
In the P of man, ... Locksley H.	128
A potent voice of P, . . . In Mem. cxii.	11

parlour-window.
rose-bush that I set About the *p-w* MayQueen, ii.	48

Parma.
rain at Reggio, rain at P; . . The Daisy .	51

Parnassus.
On thy P set thy feet, . . In Mem. xxxvii.	6

parrot.
Whistle back the *p*'s call, . . Locksley H.	171
The *p* in his gilded wires . . Day-Dm.	36
The *p* scream'd, the peacock squall'd "	144
p turns Up thro' gilt wires . Princess, Pro.	169

parson.
The *p* smirked and nodded . . The Goose .	20
The *p* Holmes, the poet Everard Hall, The Epic	4
The *p* taking wide and wider sweeps, "	14
the P, sent to sleep with sound, M. d'Arthur, Ep.	3
'P' said I 'you pitch the pipe . Ed. Morris	52
the *p* made it his text that week . Grandmother	29
P's abclu loikewoise . . . N. Farmer	9
But P a comes an' a goos, . . "	25
p 'ud nobbut let ma aloän, . . "	43

part (s.)
they had their *p* Of sorrow: . Miller's D.	223
seems a *p* of those fresh days to me Ed. Morris	142
Love himself took *p* against himself Love and Duty	45
I am a *p* of all that I have met; . Ulysses	18
fitted to thy petty *p*, . . Locksley H.	93
She seem'd a *p* of joyous Spring: Sir L. and Q.G.	23
p were drown'd within the whirling Princess, Pro.	47
As *p*'s, can see but *p*'s, . . " iii.	310
p made long since, and *p* Now " iv.	72
P sat like rocks; *p* reel'd . . " v.	485
P roll'd on the earth and rose again "	486
P stumbled mixt with floundering horses. "	487
one *p* of sense not flint to prayer, " vi.	166
took no *p* In our dispute: . . Con.	29
love in which my hound has *p*, . In Mem. lxii.	2
A *p* of mine may live in thee " lxiv.	11
Can take no *p* away from this: " lxxxiv.	68
A *p* of stillness, yearns to speak: . "	78
The freezing reason's colder *p*, " cxxiii.	14
Now grown a *p* of me: . . Elaine	1406
of this remnant will I leave a *p*, . Guinevere	441
tell him tales of foreign *p*'s . En. Arden	198
those uttermost P's of the morning? "	224
been himself a *p* of what he told. Aylmer's F.	12
a *p* Falling had let appear . "	508
God help me! save I take my *p* . Sailor Boy	21

part (to divide.)
an intellect to *p* Error from crime; Isabel .	14
Just ere the falling axe did *p* . Margaret .	38
Can I *p* her from herself . . Locksley H.	70
To put together, *p* and prove, . Two Voices	134
p it, giving half to him. . . In Mem. xxv.	12
Her care is not to *p* and prove; " xlvii.	5
star of morn P's from a bank of . Enid	735
to *p* The lists of such a beard . Vivien	93
And loving hands must *p*,— . The Window	139

part (to bid farewell.)
The crown of all, we met to *p* no . Ed. Morris	70
Could Love *p* thus? . . . Love and Duty	54
I too must *p*: I hold thee dear . Will Water.	211
I trow they did not *p* in scorn: . Lady Clare	5
We too must *p*: and yet how fain Princess, vi.	182
one soft word and let me *p* forgiven, "	202

	POEM.	LINE.
At last must *p* with her to thee . In Mem. Con.	48
I must tell her before we *p*, . . Maud, I. xvi.	33
For years, for ever, to *p*— . . II. ii.	50
We met, but only meant to *p*. . The Letters	12
to meet And *p* for ever . . Guinevere .	98
'Let us *p*; in a hundred years . Grandmother	47

partake.
Then Yniol, 'Enter therefore and *p* Enid .	300

partaker.
No more *p* of thy change . . In Mem. xl.	8

parted (divided, etc.)
'my friend—P from her— . . Princess, v.	73
friend from friend Is oftener *p*, . In Mem. xcvii.	15
one at other, *p* by the shield. . Enid	1118
wrist is *p* from the hand that waved, Vivien	401

parted (departed, etc.)
ere he *p* said 'This hour is thine Love and Death	9
Had once hard words, and *p*, . Dora	16
p, with great strides among his dogs. Godiva	31
beckon'd us: the rest P . . Princess, ii.	166
'Here, by this brook, we *p*; . The Brook	1
week Before I *p* with poor Edmund "	78
we *p*: sweetly gleam'd the stars, . The Letters	41
hour, When first I *p* from you . Enid	1196
without a word and *p* from her; . Vivien	592
p with his own to fair Elaine; . Elaine	380
no sooner had you *p* from us, . "	575
p from the jousts Hurt in the side,' "	619
He spake and *p*. Wroth but all in awe, "	715
'Farewell, sweet sister,' *p* all in tears, "	1146
p, laughing in his courtly heart, . "	1170
There kiss'd, and *p* weeping: . Guinevere	124
Enoch *p* with his old sea-friend . En. Arden	168
They *p*, and Sir Aylmer Aylmer . Aylmer's F.	277
A little after you had *p* with him, Sea Dreams	263

parting (part.)
p with a long embrace . . In Mem. xxxix.	11

parting (s.)
Their every *p* was to die. . . In Mem. xcvi.	12

partner.
The prudent *p* of his blood . . Two Voices	415
Thy *p* in the flowery walk . In Mem. lxxxiii.	22
Two *p*'s of a married life . . " xcvi.	5

partridge-breeder.
These *p-b*'s of a thousand years, . Aylmer's F.	382

party.
two parties still divide the world— Walk. to the M.	69
All parties work together. . . Will Water.	56
Drink, and let the parties rave; . Vision of Sin	123
holpen by the rest His *p*,— . . Elaine	496
knights His *p* cried 'Advance, "	502
His *p*, knights of utmost North . "	525

party-secret.
betraying His *p-s*, fool, to the press; Maud, II. v.	35

pass (s.)
shadowy granite, in a gleaming *p*; Lotos-E's.	49
The long divine Penefan *p*, . . To E. L.	3
Arthur came, and labouring up the *p* Elaine	48
thro the perilous *p*'es of his life: . Aylmer's F.	209

pass (verb.)
P onward from Shalott. . . L. of Shalott, ii.	18
heard her native breezes *p*, . Mariana in the S.	43
An image seem'd to *p* the door, "	65-74
Can he *p*, and we forget? . Miller's D.	204
P by the happy souls, that love to live: Œnone	236
p before my flight of life, . . "	237
the livelong day my soul did *p*, . Pal. of Art	55
seem to brighten as they *p*: . May Queen, i.	34
I shall hear you when you *p* . " iii.	31
I thought to *p* away before, . " iii.	1
p to Him that died for me. . . "	20
'P freely thro'; the wood is all thine D. of F. Wom.	83
thro' mine own doors Death did *p* To J. S.	19
Did never creature *p* . . . Talking O.	86
Then a hand shall *p* before thee, . Locksley H.	81

	POEM.	LINE.
To *p*, when Life her light withdraws,	Two Voices	145
Till all the hundred summers *p*,	Day-Dm.	53
strove in other days to *p*	"	110
My lord, and shall we *p* the bill	"	159
To *p* with all our social ties	"	217
So I hostel, hall, and grange ;	Sir Galahad	81
I hold it good, good things should *p*:	Will Water.	205
P on, weak heart, and leave me 'Come not when,' etc.		11
a compact *p* Long summers back,	Princess, i.	122
p With all fair theories	" ii.	214
they wait,' he said, '*p* on ;	" v.	4
she will *p* me by in after-life	"	88
P, and mingle with your likes.	" vi.	321
all thy motions gently *p*	In Mem. xv.	10
The salt sea-water *p*'es by,	" xix.	6
I shall *p*; my work will fail	" lvi.	8
We *p*: the path that each man trod	" lxxii.	9
these things *p*, and I shall prove	" lxxxiv.	98
leaving these, to *p* away,	" xcix.	19
drifts that *p* To darken	" cvi.	13
leave the porch, they *p* the grave	" Con.	71
sweeps away as out we *p*	"	95
To *p* the silent-lighted town,	"	112
I see her *p* like a light	Maud, I. iv.	11
P and blush the news	" xvii.	11
P the happy news	"	15
trying to *p* to the sea ;	" xxi.	7
P, thou deathlike type of pain	" II. iv.	58
P and cease to move about	"	59
let my query *p* Unclaim'd,	The Brook	104
a maiden near Waiting to *p*.	"	205
until we *p* and reach That other	Enid	835
when he *p*'es fall upon him.'	"	978
fall upon you while you *p*.'	"	994
till he saw her *P* into it,	"	1735
He must not *p* uncared for.	Elaine	535
you would not *p* beyond the cape	"	1033
cried because you would not *p*	"	1090
that I may *p* at last Beyond the poplar	"	1043
so let me *p*, My father,	"	1085
But that he *p*'es into fairy land.'	"	1252
p on, my Queen, forgiven.'	"	1343
trouble did not *p* but grew ;	Guinevere	84
p his days in peace among his own.	En. Arden	147
the ship I sail in *p*'es here	"	214
P from the Danish barrow overhead	"	439
nevermore did either *p* the gate	Aylmer's F.	826
p beyond the goal of ordinance	Tithonus	30
peaceful being slowly *p*'es by	Requiescat	7
if left to *p* His autumn	A Dedication	9
sides of the grave itself shall *p*,	Lucretius	253
Winds are loud and winds will *p*	The Window	127

passage (or *bird of passage*, see bird.)

Except the *p* that he loved her not ;	Enid	1241
must be now no *p*'s of love	Vivien	762
has but one plain *p* of few words	Elaine	891
sing the simple *p* o'er and o'er	"	892
they gave him and free *p* home ;	En. Arden	651

passenger.

| Should see thy *p*'s in rank | In Mem. xiv. | 6 |

passeth.

| shadow *p* When the tree shall fall, | Love and Death | 14 |

passing (part.)

each in *p* touch'd with some new	Gardener's D.	199
In *p*, with a grosser film made thick	St S. Stylites	197
N , eye look d own, she *p*;	Godiva	40
P the place where each must rest.	Two Voices	410
murmur'd that their May Was *p*;	Princess, ii.	440
like parting hopes I heard them *p*	" iv.	155
many a maiden *p* home	" vi.	359
drown'd I in *p* thro' the ford,	In Mem. vi.	39
p turn the page that tells	" lxxvi.	10
p one, at the high peep of dawn	Vivien	410
sigh'd in *p* 'Lancelot, Forgive me;	Elaine	1340
saw not, for Sir Lancelot by	Guinevere	31
p thro' the summer world again	En. Arden	395
sowing hedgerow texts and *p* by,	Aylmer's F.	171
not *p* thro' the fire bodies,	"	671
P with the weather	The Window	67

passing (s.)	POEM.	LINE.
The *p* of the sweetest soul	In Mem. lvi.	11

passion.

When my *p* seeks Pleasance	Lilian	8
By veering *p* fann'd	Madeline	29
those whom *p* hath not blinded	Ode to Mem.	117
all *p* becomes passionless,	Eleänore	102
all the soul and sense Of *P*	"	116
She had the *p*'s of her kind,	L. C. V. de Vere	35
lyre of widest range Struck by all *p*,	D. of F. Wom.	166
p rose thro' circumstantial grades	Gardener's D.	235
of his early life, And his first *p*;	Ed. Morris	74
wayward modern mind Dissecting *p*.	"	88
For when my *p* first began,	Talking O.	9
hold *p* in a leash,	Love and Duty	40
one blind cry of *p* and of pain,	"	78
p shall have spent its novel force,	Locksley II.	49
triumph'd ere my *p* sweeping thro' me	"	131
my foolish *p* were a target	"	146
all thy *p*'s, match'd with mine,	"	151
There the *p*'s cramp'd no longer	"	167
alone, the *p*'s of her mind, As winds	Godiva	32
Wilt thou find *p*, pain, or pride?	Two Voices	243
My heart beat thick with *p*,	Princess, iii.	174
their welfare is a *p* to us.	"	264
ended with such *p* that the tear	" iv.	41
dash'd The *p* of the prophetess ;	"	122
with some great *p* at her heart	"	349
fiery *P* from the brinks of death :	" vii.	141
My centred *p* cannot move,	In Mem. lviii.	9
His other *p* wholly dies,	" lxi.	10
And so my *p* hath not swerved	" lxxxiv.	49
my prime *p* in the grave :	"	76
O tell me where the *p*'s meet,	" lxxxvii.	4
Thy *p* clasps a secret joy :	" cviii.	8
p pure in snowy bloom ,	" cviii.	11
My love is vaster *p* now ;	" cxxix.	10
the *p*'s that make earth Hell!	Maud, I. x.	46
when fraught With a *p* so intense	" II. ii.	59
loyal *p* for our temperate kings ;	Ode on Well.	165
strong *p* in her made her weep	Enid	110
all the *p* of a twelve hours' fast.'	"	306
So burnt he was with *p*,	"	560
break it, when his *p* masters him	"	892
more exceeding *p* than of old ;	"	1184
all in *p* uttering a dry shriek,	"	1310
I, that flattering my true *p*, saw	Vivien	723
storm, its burst of *p* spent,	"	810
sweet and sudden *p* of youth	Elaine	282
A fiery family *p* for the name	"	476
wild *p* out against the floor	"	738
To blunt or break her *p*.'	"	969
(He meant to break the *p* in her)	"	969
To break her *p*, some discourtesy	"	1204
the maiden *p* for a maid,	Guinevere	475
the *p* in her moan'd reply	En. Arden	285
where a *p* yet unborn perhaps	Aylmer's F.	101
his *p*'s all in flood And masters	"	339
As if the living *p* symboll'd there.	"	535
make our *p*'s far too like The discords	Sea Dreams	24
A ghost of *p* that no smiles restore	Coquette, ii.	11
flush Of *p* and the first embrace	Lucretius	3
lead an errant *p* home again,	"	17

passionately.

| Then suddenly and *p* she spoke ; | Elaine | 925 |
| full *p*, Her head upon her hands, | Guinevere | 178 |

passion-flower.

| He is clasp't by a *p-f*, | Maud, I. xiv. | 6 |
| splendid tear From the *p-f* at the gate | " xxii. | 60 |

passionless.

| all passion becomes *p*, | Eleänore | 102 |
| High, self-contained, and *p*, | Guinevere | 403 |

passion-pale.

| *P-p* they met And greeted : | Guinevere | 98 |

passport.

| no false *p* to that easy realm, | Aylmer's F. | 183 |

past (adj. and s.)

| fire From the fountains of the *p*, | Ode to Mem. | 2 |

	POEM.	LINE.
P and Present, wound in one,	*Miller's D.*	197
From out the storied *P*, '*Love thou thy land*,' etc.		2
all the *p* of Time reveals		50
in the flying of a wheel Cry down the *p*,	*Godiva*	7
So mix for ever with the *p*,	*Will Water.*	201
bird's-eye-view of all the ungracious *p*;	*Princess*, ii.	109
the moulder'd lodges of the *P*	" iv.	45
let the *p* be past	"	58
great heart thro' all the faultful *P*	" vii.	232
all the *p* Melts mist-like	"	333
sets the *p* in this relief?	*In Mem.* xxiv.	12
the *p* will always win A glory	"	13
And silent traces of the *p*	" xlii.	7
The eternal landscape of the *p*;	" xlv.	8
fading legend of the *p*;	" lxi.	4
A night-long Present of the *P*	" lxx.	3
wind Of memory murmuring the *p*.	" xci.	8
dead man touch'd me from the *p*,	" xciv.	34
meadows breathing of the *p*,	" xcviii.	7
hold it solemn to the *p*.	" civ.	16
Thou, like my present and my *p*,	" cxx.	19
Strange friend, *p*, present, and to be :	" cxxviii.	9
all his greatness in the *P*.	*Ode on Well.*	20
let her fancy flit across the *p*	*Enid*	645
made the *p* so pleasant to us:	*Guinevere*	373
moving thro' the *p* unconsciously		399
sorrowest thou, pale Painter, for the *p*,	*Coquette*, iii.	3

past (verb.)

Of a maiden *p* away,	*Adeline*	19
p Into deep orange o'er the sea,	*Mariana in the S.*	25
They *p* into the level flood,	*Miller's D.*	75
into stillness *p* again,	"	227
When I *p* by, a wild and wanton pard,	*Œnone*	195
comfort *her* when I am *p* away.	*May Queen*, iii.	44
'Glory to God,' she sang, and *p* afar,	*D. of F. Wom.*	242
Beneath the sacred bush and *p* away—	*The Epic*	3
an hour had *p*, We reach'd a meadow	*Gardener's D.*	106
thro' that still garden *p*:	"	196
he *p* his father's gate, Heart-broken,	*Dora*	48
when the farmer *p* into the field	"	83
Then he turn'd His face and *p*—	"	148
p thro' all The pillar'd dust	*Audley Ct.*	14
heard it was this bill that *p*,	*Walk. to the M.*	59
An hour had *p*—and, sitting straight	*Talking O.*	109
trembling, *p* in music out of sight.	*Locksley H.*	34
And she, that knew not, *p* :	*Godiva*	73
A pleasant hour has *p* away	*Day-Dm.*	2
The reflex of a legend *p*	"	11
Shall show thee *p* to Heaven:	*Will Water.*	246
What ! the flower of life is *p*:	*Vision of Sin*	69
He *p* by the town and out of the street	*Poet's Song*	2
dropt a fairy parachute and *p*:	*Princess*, Pro.	76
rose and *p* Thro' the wild woods	" i.	89
She once had *p* that way ;	"	183
p an arch, Whereon a woman-statue	"	206
hastily we *p*, And up a flight	" ii.	16
p From all her old companions,	"	243
was it chance She *p* my way	" vi.	82
o'er her forehead *p* A shadow,	"	90
face A little flush'd, and she *p* on :	" vii.	66
He *p*; a soul of nobler tone :	*In Mem.* lix.	1
I *p* beside the reverend walls	" lxxxvi.	1
Up that long walk of limes I *p*	"	15
if they came who *p* away,	" lxxxix.	13
their love has never *p* away;	" xcvi.	13
as I found when her carriage *p*	*Maud*, I. ii.	3
I *p* him, I was crossing his lands ;	" xiii.	6
while I *p* he was humming an air,	"	17
sweet hours that *p* in bridal white,	" xviii.	65
else would have been *p* by !	" II. ii.	65
p From Como, when the light was gray,	*The Daisy*	72
has *p* and leaves The Crown	*Ded. of Idylls*	47
and they *p* to their own land ;	*Enid*	45, 1803
like a shadow, *p* the people's talk	"	82
Prince, as Enid *p* him, fain To follow,	"	375
know not, but he *p* to the wild land	"	443
they *p* The marches,	"	878
green gloom of the wood they *p*,	"	1044
many *p*, but none regarded her,	"	1369
p away But left two brawny spearmen,	"	1405

	POEM.	LINE.
And *p* to Enid's tent ;	*Enid*	1770
So *p* the days.	"	1778
p With Arthur to Caerleon	"	1793
P inward, as she came from out the	*Elaine*	345
the new companions *p* away.	"	398
to the banquet, dark in mood, *P*,	"	564
Thence to the court he *p* ;	"	702
P up the still rich city to his kin	"	798
p beneath the wildly-sculptured gates	"	840
Down thro' the dim rich city	"	842
p In either twilight ghost-like	"	844
But ten slow mornings *p*,	"	1127
P like a shadow thro' the field,	"	1134
Diamonds to meet them, and they *p*	"	1230
p the the barge Whereon the lily maid	"	1234
p, Love-loyal to the least with	*Guinevere*	124
while he *p* the dim-lit woods.	"	249
all is *p*, the sin is sinn'd,	"	539
p To where beyond these voices	"	689
p Bearing a lifelong hunger.	*En. Arden.*	78
the moment and the vessel *p*.	"	243
P thro' the solitary room in front,	"	276
p into the little garth beyond	"	326
o'er his countenance No shadow *p*,	"	711
p the strong heroic soul away.	"	914
from the clay it work'd in as she *p*,	*Aylmer's F.*	170
Sir Aylmer *p* And neither loved	"	249
after our good parents *p* away	"	358
Then drank and *p* it	"	408
with her the race of Aylmer, *p*.	"	577
p In sunshine : right across its track	*Sea Dreams*	121
p into the belt and swell'd again	"	215
p by the gate of the farm, Willy,—	*Grandmother*	41
trifle left you, when I shall have *p* away	"	107
p long lines of Northern capes	*The Voyage*	35
Glow'd for a moment as we *p*.	"	48
So they *p* by capes and islands,	*The Captain*	21
he *p* To turn and ponder	*Lucretius*	11

pastern.

cream-white mule his *p* set :	*Sir L. and Q. G.*	31

pastime.

break a country heart For *p*,	*L. C. V. de Vere*	4
Why took ye not your *p* ?	*Love and Duty*	8
play'd In his free field, and *p* made,	*Two Voices*	320
At our old *p*'s in the hall	*In Mem.* xxx.	5
he beats his chair For *p*,	" lxv.	14
And *p* both of hawk and hound,	*Enid*	711
p now the trustful king is gone !'	*Elaine*	102

pastor.

being used to find her *p* texts,	*Aylmer's F.*	606

pasturage.

wither'd holt or tilth or *p*.	*En. Arden.*	676

pasture.

gray twilight pour'd On dewy *p*'s,	*Pal. of Art*	86
In tracts of *p* sunny-warm,	"	94
Thro' crofts and *p*'s wet with dew	*Two Voices*	14
all the sloping *p* murmur'd,	*Princess*, Pro.	55

pasty.

half-cut-down, a *p* costly made,	*Audley Ct.*	22

pat.

p The girls upon the cheek,	*Talking O.*	43

patch (s.)

Or while the *p* was worn ;	*Talking O.*	64
Upon my proper *p* of soil	*Amphion*	99

patch (verb.)

three castles *p* my tatter'd coat ?	*Princess*, ii.	394

patch'd.

refuse *p* with moss.	*Vision of Sin*	212
one was *p* and blurr'd and lustreless	*Enid*	649

patent.

Last night, their mask was *p*,	*Princess*, iv.	307

path.

stepping down By zig-zag *p*'s,	*M. d'Arthur*	50
Till all the *p*'s were dim,	*Talking O.*	298

	POEM.	LINE.
charm did talk About his *p*,	Day-Dm.	122
To silence from the *p*'s of men;	"	218
planed her *p* To Lady Psyche,	Princess, iv.	296
The *p* by which we twain did go,	In Mem. xxii.	1
where the *p* we walk'd began To slope	"	9
My *p*'s are in the fields I know	" xxxix.	31
The *p* we came by, thorn and flower,	" xlv.	2
all our *p* was fresh with dew,	" lxvii.	6
the *p* that each man trod Is dim,	" lxxii.	9
Conduct by *p*'s of growing powers,	" lxxxiii.	31
He stood on the *p* a little aside;	Maud, I. xiii.	7
p of duty was the way to glory;	Ode on Well.202-10-24	
has won His *p* upward, and prevail'd	"	214
wildernesses, perilous *p*'s,	Enid	881
not to see before them on the *p*,	"	1621
green *p* that show'd the rarer foot,	Elaine	162
footstep seem'd to fall beside her *p*,	En. Arden	510
up the steep hill Trod out a *p*:	Sea Dreams	117

pathos.
Shall sharpest *p* blight us, . . Love and Duty 82

pathway.
where the hedge-row cuts the *p*,	Gardener's D.	85
a well-worn *p* courted us	"	108
on to where the *p* leads;	In Mem. xxiii.	8
down a rocky *p* from the place	Enid	1049
up the rocky *p* disappear'd	"	1092
becomes the sea-cliff *p*	Vivien	731
beat a *p* out to wealth	Aylmer's F.	439

patience.
'Have *p*,' I replied, 'ourselves are full	Princess,Con.	72
I'll give it time To learn its limbs:	"	78
use A little *p* ere I die:	In Mem. xxxiv.	12

patient (adj.)
P on this tall pillar I have borne	St S. Stylites	15
howsoever *p*, Yniol's heart Danced	Enid	504
And howsoever *p*, Yniol his.	"	707

patient s.)
blabbing The case of his *p* . . Maud, II. v. 37

patron.
Institute Of which he was the *p*,	Princess, Pro.	6
I lay'd the *p* with her curls.	"	138
A *p* of some thirty charities	" Con.	88
like a mighty *p*, satisfied	Enid	1492
half forgot his lazy smile Of *p*	Aylmer's F.	198

patter.
P she goes, my own little Annie, . Grandmother 78

pattering.
The chesnut *p* to the ground:	In Mem. xi.	4
P over the boards.	Grandmother	77-9

pattern.
let them take Example, *p*: . . St S. Stylites 220

patting.
Ask'd Walter, *p* Lilia's head. . Princess, Pro. 125

Paul.
laugh'd, and swore by Peter and by *P*:	Godiva	24
down by sin ky *P*'s they bore	Will Water.	141
Like *P* with beasts, I fought with	In Mem. cxix.	4

pause (s.)
and a sweep Of richest *p*'s,	Eleänore	66
in the *p*'s of the wind,	Miller's D.	122
When she made *p* I knew not	D. of F. Wom.	163
lunets in the *p*'s of the wind	Princess, Pro.	238
in a *p* I dared not break:	" ii.	233
There came a minute's *p*	" Con.	4
in the *p* she crept an inch Nearer	Guinevere	523
lap'ed into a long *p* again	Aylmer's F.	630

pause verb.)
The breez s *p* and die,	Claribel	2
to fall and *p* and fall did seem.	Lotos-Es.	9
How dull it is to *p*,	Ulysses	22
might be the wild swan *p* in her cloud,	Poet's Song	7
'Yet *p*,' I said: 'for that inscription	Princess, ii.	207
'Decide not ere you *p*,	" iii.	140
to far seaward again, *P*'s,	Enid	907

	POEM.	LINE.
heard his armed feet *P* by her;	Guinevere	416
goal of ordinance Where all should *p*.	Tithonus	31

paused.
p, And dropt the branch	Gardener's D.	153
p About the windings of the marge	Ed. Morris	93
p Among her stars to hear us;	Love and Duty	71
Among the tents I *p* and sang,	Two Voices	125
pacing till she *p* By Florian;	Princess, ii.	282
before them *p* Hortensia, pleading:	" vii.	116
She turn'd; she *p*; She stoop'd:	"	131
We *p*: the winds were in the beech;	In Mem.xxx.	9
often when I *p* Hath ask'd again,	Enid	425
She *p*, she turn'd away,	Vivien	736
P in the gateway, standing	Elaine	393
to the palace-doorway sliding, *p*.	"	1259
heard Strange music, and he *p*	Guinevere	237
He *p*, and in the pause she crept.	"	523
P for a moment at an inner door,	En. Arden	777
At Annie's door he *p*	"	444
the golden lizard on him *p*.	"	602
p Sir Aylmer reddening from the	Aylmer's F.	321
we nor *p* for fruit nor flowers.	The Voyage	56

pausing.
He *p*, Arthur answer'd, 'O my knight Elaine 1316

pavement.
from the *p* he half rose,	M.d'Arthur	167
on the *p* lay Carved stones	Princess,Pro.	13
heel against the *p* echoing,	Enid	1120
things that rang Against the *p*,	"	1443

Pavilion.
great *P* of the Caliphat.	Arabian N's.	114
Pitch our *p* here upon the sward;	Princess, iii.	328
vext at heart In the *p*:	" iv.	154
The silk *p*'s of King Arthur	Guinevere	391
crown'd the state *p* of the King,	"	396

paw'd.
p his beard, and mutter'd 'catalepsy.'	Princess, i.	90
roll'd And *p* about her sandal.	" iii.	166

pay.
p Meet adoration to my household	Ulysses	41
clamouring, 'If we *p*, we starve!'	Godiva	15
'If they *p* this tax, they starve.'	"	20
half-crown, Which I shall have to *p*!	Will Water.	146
debt That I never can hope to *p*;	Maud,I.xix.	88
a voice, with which to *p* the debt,	Ode on Well.	156
Or later, *p* one visit here,	To F. D. Maurice	45
Nor *p* but one, but come for many,	"	47
and I will *p* you worship;	Vivien	77
p the voice who best could tell	En. Arden	265

pea.
'ere a beän an' yonder a *p*; . N. Farmer. 46

peace.
God gave her *p*;	To the Queen	26
A haunt of ancient *P*.	Pal. of Art	83
let the world have *p* or wars,	"	182
old time, and all my *p* of mind;	MayQueen,ii.	6
has told me words of *p*.	" iii.	12
Is there any *p* In ever climbing	Lotos-Es.	94
place of him that sleeps in *p*.	To J. S.	63
Sleep sweetly, tender heart, in *p*:	"	61
pace the troubled land, like *P*;	'Lovethou thyland'	84
he died at *p* With all men;	Dora	141
breathing health and *p* upon her breast;	Audley Ct.	67
Whose foresight preaches *p*,	Love and Duty	1
cross thy thoughts Too sadly for their *p*,	"	86
universal *P* Lie like a shaft	Golden Year	43
Pure lilies of eternal *p*,	Sir Galahad	67
I sought but *p*; No critic I	Princess, i.	143
p! and why should I not play The Spartan	" ii.	262
new light up, and culminate in *p*,	"	327
'*P*, you young savage	" iii.	210
P be with her. She is dead.	" iv.	118
marble Muses looking *p*. Not *p* she look'd,	"	468
P! there are those to avenge us	"	485
resolder'd *p*, whereon Follow'd his tale.	" v.	45
one The silken priest of *p*,	"	176

U

CONCORDANCE TO

	POEM.	LINE.
dews Gather'd by night and *p*,	Princess, v.	234
other thoughts than *P* Burnt in us,	"	235
I that prated *p*, when first I heard	"	255
at our books, and marr'd our *p*,	"	385
fair *p* once more among the sick.	" vii.	29
plighted troth, and were at *p*.	"	68
from the west, a land of *p*;	" Con.	42
Calm and deep *p* on this high wold	In Mem. xi.	5,13
P and goodwill, goodwill and *p*, (rep.)	" xxviii.	11
As daily vexes household *p*, .	" xxix.	2
'Twere best at once to sink to *p*,	" xxxiv.	13
Days order'd in a wealthy *p*,	" xlv.	11
P; come away: the song of woe (rep.)	" lvi.	1
idly broke the *p* Of hearts	" lvii.	5
stay'd in *p* with God and man.	" lxxix.	8
A hundred spirits whisper '*P*.'	" lxxxv.	16
The pillars of domestic *p*.	" lxxxix.	20
My spirit is at *p* with all.	" xciii.	8
Ring in the thousand years of *p*.	" cv.	28
Why do they prate of the blessings of *P*?	Maud, I. i.	21
Is it *p* or war? Civil war, as I think,	"	27
P sitting under her olive,	"	33
P in her vineyard—yes!—	"	36
Is it *p* or war? better war!	"	47
let a passionless *p* be my lot,	" iv.	50
P, angry spirit, and let him be!	" xiii.	44
I thought the dead had *p*,	" II. v.	15
To have no *p* in the grave	"	10
P Pipe on her pastoral hillock	" III. vi.	23
love of a *p* that was full of wrongs	"	40
the *p*, that I deem'd no *p*, is over	"	50
sleeps in *p*: and he, poor Philip	The Brook.	190
P, his triumph will be sung	Ode on Well.	232
P, it is a day of pain	"	235-8
fruitful strifes and rivalries of *p*—	Ded. of Idylls	37
watch'd, and had not held his *p*; .	Vivien.	18
sunn'd The world to *p* again:	"	489
To sleek her ruffled *p* of mind	"	748
if I schemed against your *p* in this,	"	779
ravaged wood land yet once more To *p*;	"	813
saying, '*P* to thee, Sweet sister,'.	Elaine	990
'*P*,' said her father, 'O my child,	"	1056
beyond these voices there is *p*.	Guinevere	690
pass his days in *p* among his own	En. Arden.	147
true heart, which hunger'd for her *p*	"	271
all the warmth, the *p*, the happiness	"	762
not to break in upon her *p*.	"	788
p which each had prick'd to death.	Aylmer's F.	52
wings of brooding shelter o'er her *p*,	"	139
Jilted I was: I say it for your *p*.	"	354
Prince of *p*, the Mighty God,	"	669
The things belonging to thy *p*	"	740
For mine is a time of *p*,	Grandmother	89-94
the message is one of *P*.	"	96
age is a time of *p*,	"	97
Across the whirlwind's heart of *p*,	The Voyage	87
To some more perfect *p*.	Requiescat.	8

peacock.

On the tree-tops a crested *p* lit,	Œnone	102
The *p* in his laurel bower,	Day-Dm.	35
The parrot scream'd, the *p* squall'd,	"	144
smooth'd a petted *p* down	Princess, ii.	432
droops the milkwhite *p* like a ghost,	" vii.	165
bright and light as the crest Of a *p*,	Maud, I. xvi.	17
bays, the *p's* neck in hue	The Daisy.	14

peacock-yewtree.

p-y and the lonely Hall,	En. Arden	99-609

peak.

Some blue *p's* in the distance rose,	Dying Swan	11
snowy *p* and snow-white cataract	Œnone	207
high on every *p* a statue ;	Pal. of Art.	37
Lotos blooms below the barren *p*:	Lotos-E's.	145
climbs a *p* to gaze O'er land and main	Princess, vii.	20
over Sinai's *p's* of old	In Mem. xcv.	22
the budded *p's* of the wood are bow'd	Maud, I. vi.	4
The mountain wooded to the *p*,	En. Arden.	573
By *p's* that flam'd, or, all in shade,	The Voyage	41
every height comes out, and jutting *p*,	Spec. of Iliad	13

peal (s.)

	POEM.	LINE.
With *p's* of genial clamour sent	Will Water.	187
A single *p* of bells below,	In Mem. ciii.	5

peal (verb.)

a hundred bells began to *p*,	M. d'Arthur Ep.	29
the watchman *p* The sliding season :	Gardener's D.	178
sweet church bells began to *p*.	Two Voices	408

peal'd.

an answer *p* from that high land,	Vision of Sin	221
all about us *p* the nightingale,	Princess, i.	217
old songs that *p* From knoll to knoll,	In Mem. xciv.	13

pealing.

in the distance *p* news Of better	Princess, iv.	63
church below the hill Is *p*,	In Mem. ciii.	4
wild voice *p* up to the sunny sky,	Maud, I. v.	13
heard the *p* of his parish bells	En. Arden.	616

pear.

held the *p* to the garden-wall.	Mariana	4
and like a *p* In growing,	Walk. to the M.	45
tumbled half the mellowing *p's*!	In Mem. lxxxviii.	20

pearl (see comb of pearl.)

a brow of *p* Tress'd with redolent.	Arabian N's.	137
morning driv'n her plow of *p*.	Love and Duty	96
Forth streaming from a braid of *p*:	Day-Dm.	82
now a rain of *p's*, Or steep-up spout	Princess, Pro.	62
an erring *p* Lost in her bosom:	" iv.	42
Time hath sunder'd shell from *p*.'	In Mem. li.	16
in this stormy gulf have found a *p*	Maud, I. xviii.	42
In gloss of satin and glimmer of *p's*	" xxii.	5
Small and pure as a *p*,	" II. ii.	2
burst in dancing, and the *p's* were spilt;	Vivien.	302
never more the same two sister *p's*;	"	304
one true line, the *p* of *p's*;	"	309
Guinevere, The *p* of beauty:	Elaine	115
'a red sleeve Broider'd with *p's*,'	"	372
wore the sleeve Of scarlet, and the *p's*;	"	501
sleeve of scarlet, broidered with great *p's*,	"	602
carved and cut, and half the *p's* away,	"	803
add my diamonds to her *p's*;	"	1218

pearl-necklace.

Is like the fair *p-n* of the Queen,	Vivien.	301

peasant.

orts of war The *p* Joan and others;	Princess, ii.	147
When the wild *p* rights himself	" iv.	366

pebble.

Counting the dewy *p's*,	M. d'Arthur	84
I babble on the *p's*.	The Brook.	42

peck.

all wing'd nothings *p* him dead!	Enid.	275

pedant.

held his sceptre like a *p's* wand	Princess, i.	27

pedestal.

Upon an even *p* with man.'	Princess, iii.	208
push'd by rude hands from its *p*,	" v.	55
seat you sole upon my *p* Of worship—	Vivien.	727

peep (s.)

passing one, at the high *p* of dawn.	Vivien	410
In her nest at *p* of day?	Sea Dreams	282-90

peep (verb.)

any male thing but to *p* at us.'	Princess, Pro.	151

peep'd.

p, and saw The boy set up	Dora.	127
P—but his eyes, before they had their will,	Godiva	69
underneath The head of Holofernes *p*	Princess, iv.	208
the tender face *P*, shining in	" vii.	46
Sun *p* in from open field, 'Home they brought him'		6

peer (s.)

Regard the weakness of thy *p's*: 'Love thou thy land'		24
drunk delight of battle with my *p's*,	Ulysses	16
Could find no statelier than his *p's*	Two Voices	29
Forerun thy *p's*, thy time,	"	88
Surprise thee ranging with thy *p's*	In Mem. xliii.	12
Thy spirit in time among thy *p's*;	" xc.	6
in sight of Collatine And all his *p's*,	Lucretius.	236

Word/Phrase	Poem	Line
peer (verb.)		
not to pry and *p* on your reserve	Princess, iv.	399
peer'd.		
from the crevice *p* about	Mariana	65
I *p* athwart the chancel pane	The Letters	3
of all Who *p* at him so keenly,	Aylmer's F.	817
peereth.		
The frail bluebell *p* over	A Dirge	37
peerless.		
my glory to have loved One *p,*	Elaine	1084
peg.		
The mantles from the golden *p's*	Day-Dm.	39
Let me screw thee up a *p:*	Vision of Sin	87
Pelean.		
Into the fair *P* banquet hall,	Œnone	221
Peleus.		
Gods Ranged in the halls of *P;*	Œnone	79
pelf.		
dropt the goose, and caught the *p,*	The Goose	13
pelt.		
p me with starry spangles and shells,	The Merman	28
p us in the porch with flowers.	In Mem. Con.	68
pelted.		
p with outrageous epithets	Aylmer's F.	286
pen		
With such a pencil, such a *p,*	To E. L.	6
penance.		
Betray'd my secret *p,*	St S. Stylites	67
p s I cannot have gone thro',	"	99
power with Heaven From my long *p:*	"	142
From my high nest of *p* here	"	164
here I lay this *p* on myself,	Enid	1587
all the *p* the Queen laid upon me.	"	1702
if I do not there is *p* given—	Guinevere	185
pence.		
that eternal want of *p,*	Will Water.	43
Thy latter days increased with *p*	"	219
Even in dreams to the chink of his *p,*	Maud, 1. x.	43
pencil.		
Came, drew your *p* from you	Gardener's D.	26
such a breast As never *p* drew.	"	139
Then I took a *p,* and wrote	Ed. Gray	25
With such a *p,* such a pen,	To E. L.	6
Pendragon.		
The dread *P,* Britain's king of kings	Elaine	423
Came round their great *P,*	"	527
Pendragonship.		
The Dragon of the great *P,*	Guinevere	395-592
Penelan.		
The long divine *P* pass,	To E. L.	3
pension.		
place, or touch Of *p,*	'Love thou thy land,' etc.	26
pent.		
I lay *P* in a roofness close	St S. Stylites	73
fretful as the wind *P* in a crevice	Princess, iii.	65
pentagram.		
Some figure like a wizard's *p*	The Brook	103
penthouse.		
A snowy *p* for his hollow eyes,	Vivien	657
Penuel.		
In the dim tract of *P.*	'Clear-headed friend,' etc.	29
people.		
wrought her *p* lasting good;	To the Queen	24
Broad-based upon her *p* s will,	"	35
when a mighty *p* rejoice	Dying Swan	31
up and down the *p* go,	L. of Shalott, i.	6
The *p* here, a beast of burden slow,	Pal. of Art	149
I perish by this *p* which I made,—	M. d'Arthur	22
speak in the aftertime To all the *p,*	"	108
all the *p* cried 'Arthur is come again:	Ep.	23
scarce can hear the *p* hum	St S. Stylites	37
silly *p* take me for a saint,	"	125
Good *p,* you do ill to kneel to me.	"	131
O Lord, Aid all this foolish *p;*	"	219
to make mild A rugged *p,*	Ulysses	37
With the standards of the *p's*	Locksley H.	128
Slowly comes a hungry *p,*	"	135
have loved the *p* well,	Godiva	8
but that she would loose The *p:*	"	38
On to God's house the *p* prest:	Two Voices	402
He gave the *p* of his best: 'You might have won'	L. of Burleigh	23
And the *p* loved her much.	L. of Burleigh	76
Then her *p,* softly treading,	"	97
until the set of sun Up to the *p:*	Princess, Pro.	3
were there any of our *p* there	" ii.	247
babbling wells With her own *p's* life:	" v.	325
All *p* said she had authority—	" vi.	221
To let the *p* breathe?	" Con.	104
more and more the *p* throng.	In Mem. xxi.	15
The pillar of a *p's* hope,	" lxiii.	15
Whate'er the faithless *p* say.	" xcvi.	16
loyal *p* shouting a battle cry	Maud, III. vi.	35
heart of a *p* beat with one desire;	"	49
And a reverent *p* behold	Ode on Well.	54
thro' the centuries let a *p's* voice	"	142
A *p's* voice, The proof and echo	"	144
A *p's* voice, when they rejoice	"	146
A *p's* voice! we are a *p* yet.	"	151
Betwixt a *p* and their ancient throne,	"	163
Dead March wails in the *p's* ears:	"	267
A princely *p's* awful princes,	The Daisy	39
Laborious for her *p* and her poor—	Ded. of Idylls	34
love of all Thy *p* comfort Thee,	"	52
by and by the *p,* when they met	Enid	56
gathered from the *p's* eyes	"	61
like a shadow, past the *p's* talk	"	82
some of your kind *p* take him up,	"	1392
a grateful *p* named Enid the Good;	"	1811
The *p* call'd him Wizard:	Vivien	26
The *p* call you prophet:	"	166
loss of half his *p* arrow-slain;	"	415
cre the *p* chose him for their king,	Elaine	35
For fear our *p* call you lily maid	"	385
Of whom the *p* talk mysteriously,	"	424
this I know, for all the *p* know it,	"	1075
when now the lords and dames And *p,*	"	1337
the wild *p* say wild things of thee,	"	1356
break and Blaze before the *p,*	Guinevere	92
With what a hate the *p* and the King	"	155
The mockery of my *p,* and their bane.	"	522
To poor sick *p,* richer in his eyes	"	676
The younger *p* making holiday,	En. Arden	62
happy *p* strowing cried 'Hosanna	"	501
he himself Moved haunting *p,*	"	605
p talk'd—that it was wholly wise	Aylmer's F.	208
p talk'd--The boy might get a notion	"	270
The weakness of a *p* or a house,	"	570
speak before the *p* of her child,	"	608
hid the Holiest from the *p's* eyes	"	772
her own *p* bore along the nave	"	812
The *p* said, a weed	The Flower	4, 24
all the *p* cried 'Splendid is the flower.'	"	16
joy to the *p* and joy to the throne,	W. to Alexan.	29
her *p* all around the royal chariot	Boädicea	73
Lest I fall unawares before the *p,*	Hendecasyllabics	7
A plague upon the *p* fell,	The Victim	1
So thick they died the *p* cried	"	5
The land is sick, the *p* diseased	"	47
peopled.		
P the hollow dark,	D. of F. Wom.	18
peptics.		
Or do my *p* differ	Will Water.	80
perceive.		
a man fat-off might well *p*	Elaine	457
perceived.		
And I *p* no touch of change	In Mem. xiv.	17
P the waving of the hands that blest	Guinevere	573

perceiving.

	POEM.	LINE.
He, *p*, said : 'Fair and dear cousin,	*Enid* .	1671
P that she was but half disdain'd,	*Vivien*	. 35

perch (s.)

| the lawless *p* Of wing'd ambitions, | *Ded. of Idylls* | 21 |
| Came to her old *p* back, and settled. | *Vivien* . | 752 |

perch (verb.)

| Light Hope at Beauty's call would *p* Coquette, i. | 3 |

perch'd.

P like a crow upon a three-legg'd stool *AudleyCt.*	44
p about the knolls A dozen angry *Princess, Pro.*	72
P on the pouted blossom of her lips : "	. 193

Percivale.

What say ye then to fair Sir *P*	. *Vivien*	. 597
A sober man is *P* and pure ;	. "	. 605
So Arthur bad the meek Sir *P*	. *Elaine*	1237

perfect.

Thou art *p* in love-lore.	. *Madeline*	9
That type of *P* in his mind	. *Two Voices*	292
if a dream, Sweet dream, be *p*.	. *Princess,* vii.	134
Not *p*, nay, but full of tender wants	"	300
As pure and *p* as I say ?	. *In Mem.* xxiv.	2
a mist of green And nothing *p* :	. *The Brook*	. 15
From forehead down to foot *p*—	. *Elaine*	639

perfection.

The clear *p* of her face.	. *Mariana in the S.*	32
Dead *p*, no more ; nothing more,	. *Maud,* l. ii.	7
That passionate *p*, my good lord— *Elaine*	. 123

perfectness.

| Set light by narrower *p*. | . *In Mem.* cxi. | 4 |

perfect-sweet.

| Frowns *p-s* along the brow | . *Madeline* | . 15 |

perform.

| I thy hest will all *p* at full, | . *M. d'Arthur* | 43 |

performed.

| 'Hast thou *p* my mission which I gave? *M. d'Arthur* | 67 |

perfume.

As *p* of the cuckoo-flower ?	. *Margaret*	8
one warm gust, full-fed with *p*,	. *Gardener's D.*	112
P and flowers fall in showers,	. *Sir Galahad*	11
fluctuate all the still *p*,	. *In Mem.* xciv.	56

peril.

| any of our people there In want or *p, Princess,* ii. | 248 |
| A carefuller in *p*, did not breathe . *En. Arden* . | 50 |

period.

| Devolved his rounded *p*'s. | . *A Character* | 18 |
| hoped that ere this *p* closed . | . *St S. Stylites* | 17 |

perish.

Lest she should fail and *p* utterly,	*Pal. of Art*	221
Till they *p* and they suffer—	. *Lotos-E's.*	. 168
I *p* by this people which I made .	*M. d'Arthur*	22
P in thy self-contempt !	. *Locksley H.*	96
I had been content to *p*,	. "	. 103
better men should *p* one by one.	. "	. 179
To *p*, wept for, honour'd, known,	. *Two Voices*	149
promise otherwise You *p*)	. *Princess,* ii.	276
fails at last, And *p*'es as I must ;	. *Lucretius*	. 261

perish'd.

I remember one that *p* :	. *Locksley H.*	71
'They *p* in their daring deeds.'	. *Day-Dm.*	. 114
Thy leaf has *p* in the green, .	*In Mem.* lxxiv.	13
Not yet *p*, when his lonely doom	. *En. Arden* .	627
P many a maid and matron,	. *Boädicea*	. 85

permanence.

| Be fix'd and froz'n to *p* : | . *Two Voices* | 237 |

permission.

| He craved a fair *p* to depart, | . *Enid* . | . 40 |

perplex.

| many things *p* With motions, | . *Two Voices* | 299 |
| no ruder air *p* Thy sliding keel | . *Princess,* ix. | 9 |

perplex'd.

perfect Joy, *p* for utterance, .	*Gardener's D.*	250
And *p* her, night and morn. .	*L. of Burleigh*	78
P in faith, but pure in deeds—	. *In Mem.* xcv.	9

	POEM.	LINE.
But he vext her and *p* her	. *Maud,* I. xx.	6
look'd and was *p* in mind,	. *Elaine*	. 834
P her, made her half forget herself *Aylmer's F.*	303

perplexing.

| *P* me with lies ; | . *St S. Stylites* | 100 |

perplexity.

| In doubt and great *p*, | . *Pal. of Art* | 278 |

persecute.

| banded unions *p* Opinion, 'You ask me why,' etc. | 17 |

Persephone.

| or the enthroned *P* in Hades, | . *Princess,* iv. | 419 |

Persian.

| Gazed on the *P* girl alone, | . *Arabian N's.* | 134 |
| the *P*, Grecian, Roman lines | . *Princess,* ii. | 114 |

person.

law for *us* ; We paid in *p*.	. *Walk. to the M.*	78
Done in your maiden's *p* to yourself : *Enid*	. 216
the men who served About my *p*,	"	. 454
rusted arms Were on his princely *p*,	"	. 544

personal.

| And therefore splenetic, *p*, base, | . *Maud,* I. x. | 33 |

Personality.

| The abysmal deeps of *P*, | . *Pal. of Art* | 223 |

persuade.

| I might *p* myself then, | . *Maud,* I. x. | 56 |

persuasion.

| *P*, no, nor death could alter her : . *Aylmer's F.* | 418 |

perused.

| conscious of ourselves, *P* the matting; *Princess,* ii. | 54 |

Peruvian.

| strange shares in some *P* mine | . *Sea Dreams* | 15 |

pestle.

| To *p* a poison'd poison . | . *Maud,* I. i. | 44 |

pet.

| in a *p* she started up, | . *Talking O.* | . 229 |

petal.

p's from blown roses on the grass, *Lotos-E's.*	. 47
two dewdrops on the *p* shake	. *Princess,* vii.	53
'Now sleeps the crimson *p*,	. "	. 161

Peter.

| laugh'd, and swore by *P* and by Paul *Godiva* | . 24 |
| '*P* had the brush, My *P*, first.' | . *Aylmer's F.* | 254 |

Peter's-pence.

| Ere yet, in scorn of *P-p*, | . *Talking O.* | 45 |

petition.

make a wild *p* night and day,	. *Princess,* v.	94
At your new son, for my *p* to her *Enid*	. 780
for my strange *p* I will make Anends "	. 817

petitioned.

| *P* too for him. | . *Princess,* vi. | 300 |
| *p* for his leave To see the hunt, | . *Enid* | . 154 |

petulance.

| the Seer Would watch her at her *p, Vivien* | . 31 |

petulancy.

| for her fault she wept Of *p* | . *Vivien* | . 802 |

petulant.

| wrathful, *p*, Dreaming some rival, *Lucretius* | . 14 |

pew.

| grasping the *p*'s And oaken finials *Aylmer's F.* | 822 |

pewit.

| Returning like the *p*, | . *Will Water.* | 230 |

phalanx.

| into that *p* of the summer spears *Aylmer's F.* | 111 |

phantasm.

| white-eyed *p*'s weeping tears of blood, *Pal. of Art* | 239 |

phantom.

| a *p* two hours old Of a a maiden | . *Adeline* | . 18 |
| The *p* of a silent song, | . *Miller's D.* | 71 |

	POEM.	LINE.
P's of other forms of rule, '*Love thou thy land,*'*etc.*		59
make One act a *p* of succession :	*Princess*, iii.	312
all the *p*, Nature, stands— .	*In Mem.* iii.	9
like to noiseless *p*'s flit :	" xx.	16
mine own *p* chanting hymns ?	" cvii.	10
That abiding *p* cold.	*Maud*, II. iv.	55
Till I saw the dreary *p* arise and fly	" III. vi.	36
'Hark the *P* of the house .	*Elaine*	1016
Who seem'd the *p* of a Giant in it,	*Guinevere*	596
A *p* made of many *p*'s moved	*En. Arden*	603
p of a wish that once could move,	*Coquette*, ii.	10
Beastlier than any *p* of his kind	*Lucretius*	193

phantom-fair.

How faintly-flushed, how *p-f,* . . *The Daisy* . 65

phantom-warning.

Should prove the *p-w* true . . *In Mem.* xci. . 12

Pharaoh.

May *P*'s darkness, folds as dense *Aylmer's F.* 771

Pharos.

breaks the *P* from his base . . *Princess*, vi. 319

phase.

immolation, any *p* of death,	*Princess*, iii.	263
out of painful *p*'s wrought .	*In Mem.* lxiv.	6
moved thro' life of lower *p*,	" Con.	125

pheasant-lord.

old *p-l*'s, These partridge-breeders *Aylmer's F.* 381

Phenomenon.

Arbaces, and *P*, and the rest . *The Brook* . 162

philanthropies.

And nursed by mealy-mouth'd *p* . *The Brook* . 94

Philip (see Ray.)

last by *P*'s farm I flow .	. *The Brook*	. 31
P's farm where brook and river meet.	"	38
P chatter'd more than brook or bird ; Old *P* ;	"	51
push'd at *P*'s garden gate .	"	83
In I went, and call'd old *P* out	"	120
And with me *P*, talking still ;	"	164
when they follow'd us from *P*'s door,	"	167
Poor *P*, of all his lavish waste	"	191
Enoch was host one day, *P* the next, *En. Arden*		25
P, his blue eyes All flooded	"	31
P loved in silence ;	"	41
girl Seem'd kinder unto *P* .	"	42
P stay'd His father lying sick	"	64
P look'd And in their eyes	"	72
P's true heart, which hunger'd for her	"	271
P standing up said falteringly	"	283
P ask'd ' Then you will let me Annie?'	"	321
P put the boy and girl to school,	"	328
P did not fathom Annie's mind ;	"	341
P was her children's all-in-all	"	345
call'd him father *P*. *P* gain'd As Enoch	"	351
begg'd For Father *P* (as they call'd him)	"	362
' Come with us Father *P*' he denied	"	365
So *P* rested with his well-content ;	"	373
P sitting at her side forgot Her presence	"	381
P coming somewhat closer spoke	"	395
God reward you for it, *P*, .	"	422
' dear *P*, wait a little :	"	427
P sadly said ' Annie as I have waited	"	431
P glancing up Beheld the dead flame	"	437
P with his eyes Full of that lifelong	"	460
P did but trifle with her ;	"	472
laugh'd at her and *P* too,	"	474
P's rosy face contracting grew	"	483
P thought he knew ;	"	516
her good *P* was her all-in-all,	"	521
How *P* put her little ones to school,	"	707
marriage, and the birth Of *P*'s child :	"	710
Tar-blazing from the rear of *P*'s house,	"	728
P's dwelling fronted on the street,	"	732
P, the slighted suitor of old times,	"	746
say to *P* that I blest him too ;	"	887

philosopher.

Be mine a *p*'s life . . . *Maud*, I. iv. 47

	philosophy. POEM.	LINE.
fair *philosophies* That hit the fancy ;	*Princess*, iii.	322
And many an old *p* .	*In Mem.* xxiii.	21
For fear divine *P* Should push	"	iii. 14
Affirming each his own *p*— .	*Lucretius*	213

philtre.

brew'd the *p* which had power, they said *Lucretius* 16

Phosphor.

till *P*, bright As our pure love,	*In Mem.* ix.	10
Bright *P*, fresher for the night,	" cxx.	9

phosphorescence.

a *p* cheering even My lady, . . *Aylmer's F.* 116

phrase.

household talk, and *p*'s of the hearth *Princess*, ii.		294
every *p* well-oil'd,	" iii.	117
In *p*'s here and there at random	*Aylmer's F.*	434

physician.

a vile *p*, blabbing The case of his patient *Maud*, II. v. 36

Piacenza.

At Lodi, rain, *P*, rain . . *The Daisy* . 52

piano.

She left the new *p* shut ; . . *Talking O.* 119

pick.

p the faded creature from the pool, *Enid*	. 671
p the vicious quitch Of blood and custom "	1751
To dig, pick, open, find and read . *Vivien*	510
P's from the colewort a green caterpillar, *Guinevere*	33

pickaxe.

A *p* in her hand : . . . *Sea Dreams* 98

pick'd.

'*p* the eleventh from this hearth	. *The Epic*	. 41
p offenders from the mass .	*Princess*, i.	26
p a ragged-robin from the hedge,	*Enid*	" 724
p the lance That pleased him best,	"	1028

pickpocket.

P's, each hand lusting for all . *Maud*, I. i. 22

picnic.

Let us *p* there At Audley Court.' *Audley Ct.* . 2

picture.

with wide blue eyes As in a *p*.	*M. d'Arthur*	170
intent On that veil'd *p*—	*Gardener's D.*	265
More like a *p* seemeth all	. *Day-Dm.*	42
I wore her *p* by my heart,	. *Princess*, i.	37
The mimic *p*'s breathing grace,	*In Mem.* lxxvii.	
I make a *p* in the brain ;	" lxxix.	9
still his *p* form'd And grew	. *Elaine*	986

picturesque.

The *p* of man and man.'	*In Mem.* lxxxviii.	42
To make old bareness *p*	" cxxvii.	19

Picus.

snared *P* and Faunus, rustic Gods.' *Lucretius* . 182

piece.

wrinkled *p* of womanhood,	. *Princess*, v.	58
all, as in some *p* of art,	*In Mem.* cxxvii.	23
high above a *p* of turret stair,	*Enid*	. 320
Saw once a great *p* of a promontory	"	1011
p's of his armour in one place	"	1223
cheek Bulge with the unswallow'd *p*,	"	1470
shadow of a *p* of pointed lace,	. *Elaine*	1118
a lovely *p* of workmanship !	*Aylmer's F.*	237
a rough *p* Of early rigid colour	"	260
All over earthy, like a *p* of earth,	. *Sea Dreams*	97
Cut the Roman boy to *p*'s .	. *Boädicea*	66
a *p* of inmost Horticultural art	*Hendecasyllabics*	19
in one day Cracks all to *p*'s .	*Lucretius*	. 248

pieced.

I slept again, and *p* The broken vision; *Sea Dreams* 105

piecemeal.

Till all my limbs drop *p* . . *St. S. Stylites* 43

pierce.

Yet could not all creation *p* .	. *A Character*	5
P's the keen seraphic flame .	. *In Mem.* xxx.	27
one would *p* an outer ring, .	" lxxxvi.	27

	POEM.	LINE.
p's the liver and blackens the blood,	*The Islet*	35
Pointed itself to *p*, but sank down	*Lucretius*	63

pierced.

p thy heart, my love, my bride	*Oriana*	42
p thro' with fierce delight	*Fatima*	34
men and horses *p* with worms,	*Vision of Sin*	209
wander from his wits *P* thro' with eyes,	*Princess*, ii.	418
may be *p* to death before my eyes	*Enid*	104
and the head *P* thro' his side,	*Elaine*	489
walls of yew Their talk had *p*,	"	965

piercing.

high dawn *p* the royal rose	*Vivien*	589

pig.

great with *p*, wallowing in sun	*Walk. to the M.*	80

pigeon.

quail and *p*, lark and leveret lay,	*Audley Ct.*	23
p's, who in session on their roofs	*The Brook*	127

pigged.

on the leads we kept her till she *p*.	*Walk. to the M.*	84

pike.

when his bailiff brought A Chartist *p*.	*Walk. to the M.*	63
as prompt to spring against the *p*'s,	*Princess*, iii.	269

Pike.

high field on the bushless *P*,	*Ode to Mem.*	96

pile (s.)

skins of wine, and *p*'s of grapes.	*Vision of Sin*	13
When God hath made the *p* complete	*In Mem.* liii.	8
grins on a *p* of children's bones,	*Maud*, I. i.	46
look'd the Lombard *p*'s ;	*The Daisy*	54

pile (verb.)

should *p* her barricades with dead.	*In Mem.* cxxvi.	8

piled.

Life *p* on life Were all too little,	*Ulysses*	24

piling.

P sheaves in uplands airy,	*L. of Shalott*, i.	34

pillar.

A *p* of white light upon the wall	*Ode to Mem.*	53
Patient on this tall *p* I have borne	*St S. Stylites*	15
Three years I lived upon a *p*,	"	85
I, Simeon of the *p*, by surname	"	158
slid From *p* unto *p*,	*Godiva*	50
under gloom Of cavern *p*'s ;	*To E. L.*	78
ample awnings gay Betwixt the *p*'s,	*Princess*, ii.	12
Her back against a *p*	" iii.	164
As comes a *p* of electric cloud	" v.	513
azure *p*'s of the hearth Arise to thee ;	" vii.	201
The *p* of a people's hope	*In Mem.* lxiii.	15
shake The *p*'s of domestic peace	" lxxxix.	20
A *p* stedfast in the storm,	" cxii.	12
Who shall fix Her *p*'s ?.	" cxiii.	4
And sat by a *p* alone ;	*Maud*, I. viii.	2
last remaining *p* of their house,	*Aylmer's F.*	295

pillar-punishment.

not alone this *p-p*	*St S. Stylites*	59

pillow.

Dripping with Sabæan spice On thy *p*,	*Adeline*	54
Turn thee, turn thee on thy *p*:	*Locksley H.*	86
The gold-fringed *p* lightly prest ;	*Day-Dm.*	98
smooth my *p*, mix the foaming draught	*Princess*, ii.	233
laid his feverous *p* smooth !	*Aylmer's F.*	701
Fancy came and at her *p* sat,	*Coquette*, i.	5

pilot.

The summer *p* of an empty heart.	*Gardener's D.*	16
p of the darkness and the dream.	*Audley Ct.*	71
P's of the purple twilight,	*Locksley H.*	122
your example *p*, told her all.	*Princess*, iii.	121
wreck itself without the *p*'s guilt	*Aylmer's F.*	716

pilot-star.

grown dim with gazing on the *p-s*.	*Lotos-E's.*	132
Enid, the *p-s* of my lone life,	*Enid*	1155

pimpernel.

the *p* dozed on the lea :.	*Maud*, I. xxii.	48

pin.

	POEM.	LINE.
Where children cast their *p*'s and nails	*Vivien*	280

pinch.

p a murderous dust into her drink,	*Vivien*	460

pine (tree.)

creeps from *p* to *p*,	*Œnone*	4
dewy-dark aloft the mountain *p*:	"	48
yon whispering tuft of oldest *p*.	"	86
away my tallest *p*'s. My tall dark *p*'s	"	204
Up-clomb the shadowy *p*	*Lotos-E's.*	18
sweet, stretch'd out beneath the *p*.	"	144
A gleaming crag with belts of *p*'s	*Two Voices*	189
sweating rosin, plump'd the *p*	*Amphion*	47
a stately *P* Set in a cataract	*Princess*, v.	336
glide a sunbeam by the blasted *P*	" vii.	181
There amid perky larches and *p*,	*Maud*, I. x.	20
Beyond the Pyrenean *p*'s,	*Ode on Well.*	113
In lands of palm and southern *p* ;	*The Daisy*	2
Garrulous under a roof of *p*:	*To F. D. Maurice*	20
For groves of *p* on either hand,	"	21
petty marestail forest, fairy *p*'s,	*Aylmer's F.*	92
A perilous meeting under the tall *p*'s	"	414
and above them roar'd the *p*.	"	431
to the garden now, and grove of *p*'s	"	550
Fantastic plume or sable *p*;	*The Voyage*	44
Above the valleys of palm and *p*.'	*The Islet*	23
all the *p*'s of Ida shook to see	*Lucretius*	86
No larger feast than under plane or *p*	"	210
king of the wrens from out of the *p*.'	*The Window*	151

pine (fruit.)

A raiser of huge melons and of *p*,	*Princess, Con.*	87

pine (verb.)

You *p* among your halls and towers	*L. C. V. de Vere*	58
p's in sad experience worse than death	*Princess*, vii.	296
To *p* in that reverse of doom	*In Mem.* lxxi.	6

pinewood.

o'er a bridge of *p* crossing,	*Princess*, iii.	317
lake whiten'd and the *p* roar'd	*Vivien*	487

pinnacle.

Three silent *p*'s of aged snow	*Lotos-E's.*	16
Dislodging *p* and parapet	*D. of F. Wom.*	26
statued *p*'s, mute as they.	*The Daisy*	64

pint.

Go fetch a *p* of port :	*Will Water.*	4
The *p*, you brought me, was the best	"	75
No *p* of white or red	"	82
To each his perfect *p* of stout,	"	115
For this good *p* of port.	"	212

pint-pot.

underneath, A *p-p*, neatly graven.	*Will Water.*	248

pip.

A thousand *p*'s eat up your	*Enid*	274

pipe (tube, etc.)

' you pitch the *p* too low :	*Ed. Morris*	52
He set up his forlorn *p*'s,	*Amphion*	22
great organ almost burst his *p*'s,	*Princess*, ii.	450
earliest *p* of half-awaken'd birds	" iv.	32
make them *p*'s whereon to blow.	*In Mem.* xxi.	4

pipe (cask.)

the best That ever came from *p*.	*Will Water.*	76

pipe (verb.)

Norland winds *p* down the sea,	*Oriana*	91
plover *p* along the fallow lea,	*May Queen*, ii.	18
bird that *p*'s his lone desire 'You might have won,'	"	31
p and trill, And cheep and twitter	*Princess*, iv.	82
Fly to her, and *p* and woo her	"	97
children call, and I Thy shepherd *p*	" vii.	203
p but as the linnets sing :	*In Mem.* xxi.	24
rarely *p*'s the mounted thrush ;	" xc.	2
Where now the seamew *p*'s,	" cxiv.	13
and the Devil may *p* to his own.	*Maud*, I. i.	76
Peace *P* on her pastoral hillock	" III. vi.	24
p of nothing but of sparrow-hawks !	*Enid*	279

piped.

Sometimes the linnet *p* his song :	*Sir L. and Q. G.*	10

	POEM.	LINE.
birds that *p* their Valentines,	*Princess*, v.	229
the Robin *p* Disconsolate,	*En. Arden*.	677

piping.
That with his *p* he may gain	*In Mem.* xxi.	11

pippin.
while the blackbird on the *p* hung	*Audley Ct.*	37

pique.
feigning *p* at what she call'd	*Princess*, iv.	564

piracy.
King impaled him for his *p*:	*Vivien*	419

pirate.
A tawny *p* anchor'd in his port	*Vivien*	408
since the *p* would not yield her up	"	418

pirouetted.
Young ashes *p* down	*Amphion*	27

pit.
scrambled past those *p*'s of fire,	*St S. Stylites*	181
there in the ghastly *p* long since	*Maud*, I. i.	5
from the place and the *p* and the fear?	"	64
lately died, Gone to a blacker *p*,	" x.	6
He laid a cruel snare in a *p*	" II. v.	84
comes to the second corpse in the *p*?	"	88
p's Which some green Christmas crams	*Coquette*,iii.	13

pitch.
you *p* the pipe too low:	*Ed. Morris*	52
Your pavilion here upon the sward:	*Princess*,iii.	328

pitcher.
sets her *p* underneath the spring,	*En Arden*.	207

piteous.
p was the cry:	*Princess*, vi.	126

pitied.
trust me, Sir, I *p* her.	*Princess*, iv.	211
last the Queen herself and *p* her:	*Elaine*	1262

pitiful.
shall we care to be *p*?	*Boädicea*	32

pity (s.)
His looks—the more the *p*.	*Audley Ct.*	58
schoolboy ere he grows To *P*—	*Walk. to the M.*	100
for an hour, Till *p* won.	*Godiva*	35
Kill us with *p*, break us with ourselves	*Princess*,iii.	241
all prophetic *p*, fling Their pretty maids	" v.	371
p for a horse o'er-driven	*In Mem.* lxii.	1
Without knowledge, without *p*,	*Maud*, II. iv.	53
waste a perilous *p* on him:	*Enid*	1374
Instead of scornful *p* or pure scorn,	"	1707
whose vast *p* almost makes me die	*Guinevere*	530
Annie could have wept for *p* of him,	*En. Arden*	464
save for *p* was it hard to take	"	557
the living fount of *p* in Heaven.	*Aylmer's F.*	752
I, the violet on the tyrant's grave.	"	845
wrote satire, with no *p* in it.	*Sea Dreams*	197
far aloof From envy, hate and *p*,	*Lucretius*	77

pity (verb.)
there the Queen herself will *p* me,	*Elaine*	1053
rather pray for those and *p* them,	*Aylmer's F.*	775
did they *p* me supplicating?	*Boädicea*	8

pitying.
mother *p* made a thousand prayers;	*Princess*, i.	21
look'd At the arm'd man sideways, *p*	" vi.	141
tax upon themselves, *I*'the lonely man,	*En. Arden*	665
Sullen, defiant, *p*, wroth,	*Aylmer's F.*	492

plaäce.
afoor I comed to the *p*.	*N. Farmer*	34

place (s.)
A goodly *p*, a goodly time,	*Arabian N's.*	53
Apart from *p*, withholding time,	"	75
Entranced with that *p* and time,	"	97
Sole star of all that *p* and time,	"	152
All the *p* is holy ground:	*Poet's Mind*	.
took the soul Of that waste *p*	*Dying Swan*	22
battle deepen'd in its *p*	*Oriana*	51

	POEM.	LINE.
in its *p* My heart a charmed slumber	*Eleänore*	127
grow round him in his *p*.	*Fatima*	40
have attain'd Rest in a happy *p*	*Œnone*	129
is not this my *p* of strength,'	*Pal. of Art.*	233
Lost to her *p* and name;	"	274
The flower ripens in its *p*,	*Lotos-E's.*	81
Spoke slowly in her place.	*D. of F. Wom.*	92
cut off from hope in that sad *p*	"	105
The *p* of him that sleeps in peace.	*To J. S.*	68
in her *p* she did rejoice, 'Of old sat Freedom,' etc.	"	5
title, *p*, or touch Of pension, '*Love thou thy land*'		25
in the moon athwart the *p* of tombs.	*M. d'Arthur*	46
bore him thro' the *p* of tombs.	"	175
old order changeth, yielding *p* to new,	"	240
In that still *p* she, hoarded in herself	*Gardener's D.*	48
in that time and *p* I spoke to her.	"	221-6
the *p* is to be sold.	*Walk. to the M.*	11
among the greens Looks out of *p*	*Ed. Morris*	85
So left the *p*, left Edwin,	"	137
'Tis the *p*, and all around it,	*Locksley H.*	3
He pray'd, and from a happy *p*	*Two Voices*	224
The *p* he knew forgetteth him.	"	264
In her still *p* the morning wept:	"	275
if I lapsed from nobler *p*,	"	358
Passing the *p* where each must rest,	"	410
rhymes are dazzled from their *p*	*Day-Dm.*	19
The fountain to his *p* returns	"	31
Here all things in their *p* remain,	"	73
And alleys, faded *p*'s,	*Amphion*	86
Is there some magic in the *p*?	*Will Water.*	79
How out of *p* she makes The legend	"	146
Then they started from their *p*'s.	*Vision of Sin*	33
he sat him down in a lonely *p*,	*Poet's Song*	5
something it should be to suit the *p*,	*Princess,Pro.*	206
made to suit with Time and *p*,	"	224
still *p*, and pluck'd her likeness out;	" i.	91
she who had left her *p*,	" ii.	149
find you here but in the second *p*,	" iii.	141
A tree Was half-disrooted from his *p*,	" iv.	168
To push my rival out of *p*	"	316
you stoop'd to me From all high *p*'s	"	410
Stole a maiden from her *p*,	" v.	540
work no more alone! Our *p* is much:	" vii.	250
look'd all native to her *p*	"	304
From out waste *p*'s comes a cry,	*In Mem.* iii.	7
And all the *p* is dark	" viii.	7
and feels Her *p* is empty,	" xiii.	4
And in the *p*'s of his youth.	" xviii.	8
It was but unity of *p*	" xli.	5
And so may *I* retain us still,	" xliii.	16
will speak out In that high *p*,	" lxvi.	1
I know that in thy *p* of rest.	" lxxvii.	10
Again our ancient games had *p*	" lxxxii.	2
Thy sweetness from its proper *p*?	" lxxxiv.	110
beats within a lonely *p*,	" xcix.	3
I find no *p* that does not breathe.	" ci.	1
We leave the well-beloved *p*.	" civ.	11
change of *p*, like growth of time,	" cv.	21
false pride in *p* and blood,	" cvii.	9
What find I in the highest *p*,	" cxiii.	15
Let her know her *p*;	" cxvi.	2
hold me from my proper *p*,	" cxvii.	15
And of himself in higher *p*,	" cxx.	20
Thy *p* is changed; thou art the same.	" cxxv.	10
Who moves about from *p* to *p*,	*Con.*	67
maidens of the *p* That pelt us	*Maud*, I. i.	64
if I bled from the *p* and the pit	"	66
dark old *p* will be gilt by the touch	" xiii.	24
old man never comes to his *p*:	*II. iv.*	6
In the silent woody *p*'s	*Ded. of Idylls*	21
making his high *p* the lawless perch	*Enid*	219
at some *p* I shall come at, arms	"	146
roam the goodly *p*'s that she knew;	"	860
waste *p*'s of the hern,	"	1049
down a rocky pathway from the *p*	"	1126
the wild lord of the *p*, Limours.	"	1223
pieces of his armour in one *p*,	"	1791
Clear'd the dark *p*'s and let in the law,	*Elaine*	70
the *p* which now Is this world's hugest	"	814
sound not wonted in that *p*.	"	1194
all the *p* whereon she stood was green;	"	

CONCORDANCE TO

	POEM.	LINE.
thou reseated in thy *p* of light,	Guinevere	521
Would Enoch have the *p*?	En. Arden	125
haunting people, things and *p*'s	"	605
Flared on him, and he came upon the *p*	"	682
that other, reigning in his *p*,	"	764
a bygone Rector of the *p*,	Aylmer's F.	11
rustling once at night about the *p*,	"	547
all neglected *p*'s of the field.	"	693
beside your hearths Can take her *p*	"	730
Trembled in perilous *p*'s o'er a deep	Sea Dreams	11
Jenny, my cousin, had come to the *p*	Grandmother	25
Fair is her cottage in its *p*,	Requiescat	1
I see the *p* where thou wilt lie	Sailor Boy	8
lives and loves in every *p*;	On a Mourner	5

place (verb.)

in thy various gallery P it,	Ode to Mem.	85
murmur'd Arthur, 'P me in the barge,'	M. d'Arthur	204

placed.

in the towers I *p* great bells.	Pal. of Art	129
over that is *p* the sparrow-hawk,	Enid	484
over these they *p* a silver wand	"	549
And *p* them in this ruin;	"	643
p where morning's earliest ray	Elaine	5
often *p* upon the sick man's brow.	Aylmer's F.	700

plagiarised.

Until he *p* a heart.	Talking O.	19

plagiarist.

calls her *p*; I know not what:	Princess, iii.	78

plague (s.)

Blight and famine, *p* and earthquake	Lotos-E's.	160
Remember what a *p* of rain;	The Daisy	50
A *p* upon the people fell,	The Victim	1
Help us from famine And *p*.	"	10

plague (verb.)

began To vex and *p* her.	Guinevere	68
set on to *p* And play upon	"	357

plagued.

P her with sore despair.	Pal. of Art	224
P with a flitting to and fro,	Maud, II. ii.	33
worldly-wise begetters, *p* themselves	Aylmer's F.	482

plain (adj.)

will thirty seasons render *p*	Two Voices	82
I cannot make this matter *p*,	"	343
Besought me to be *p* and blunt,	Elaine	1293

plain (s.)

The plain was grassy, wild and bare,	Dying Swan	1
herds upon an endless *p*,	Pal. of Art	74
swine That range on yonder *p*.	"	200
smiled at the twilight *p*,	D. of F. Wom.	62
wild wind rang from park and *p*,	The Goose	45
She glanced across the *p*;	Talking O.	166
on the ringing *p*'s of windy Troy.	Ulysses	17
Clothes and reclothes the happy *p*'s;	Day-Dm.	22
I leave the *p*, I climb the height;	Sir Galahad	57
The maiden Spring upon the *p*	Sir L. and Q. G.	3
fleeter now she skimm'd the *p*'s	"	32
lord of the ringing lists, And all the *p*,—	Princess, v.	492
had a cousin tumbled on the *p*,	" vi.	299
Calm and still light on yon great *p*,	In Mem. xi.	9
Imperial hal's, or open *p*;	" xcvii.	29
The brook shall babble down the *p*,	" c.	10
when we crost the Lombard *p*.	The Daisy	49
sunlight on the *p* behind a shower	Vivien	253
they would pare the mountain to the *p*	"	678
On some vast *p* before a setting sun	Guinevere	77
winds from off the *p* Roll'd the rich	Spec. of Iliad	7
A thousand on the *p*;	"	19
brightens and darkens down on the *p*	The Window	2

plain-faced.

gray tower, or *p*-*f* tabernacle	Aylmer's F.	618

plainness.

Nay the *p* of her dresses,	Maud, I. xx.	14

plan (s.)

Old wishes, ghosts of broken *p*'s,	Will Water.	29

	POEM.	LINE.
comes the feebler heiress of your *p*,	Princess, iii.	221
Dismiss me, and I prophesy your *p*,	" iv.	335
'The *p* was mine. I built the nest.'	"	346
scorn At him that mars her *p*,	" v.	126
build some *p* Foursquare to opposition.'	"	221
I scarce am fit for your great *p*'s:	" vi.	201
mingles all without a *p*?	In Mem. xvi.	20
boundless *p* That makes you tyrants	Maud, I. xviii.	36
Enoch lay long-pondering on his *p*'s;	En. Arden	133

plan (verb.)

while I *p* and *p*, my hair Is gray.	Will Water.	167

plane (level surface.)

Athwart a *p* of molten glass.	In Mem. xv.	11

plane (a tree.)

beneath an emerald *p* Sits Diotima,	Princess, iii.	284
wine and chess beneath the *p*'s	" vi.	229
under *p* or pine With neighbours.	Lucretius	210

planed.

you *p* her path To Lady Psyche,	Princess, iv.	296

planet.

I breathed In some new *p*:	Ed. Morris	113
O, happy *p*, eastward go; 'Move eastward,' etc.		4
some clear *p* close upon the Sun,	Princess, ii.	22
suns, that wheeling cast The *p*'s.	"	104
all the fair young *p* in her hands—	" vii.	248
that woke The darkness of our *p*,	In Mem. lxxv.	10
that with me trod This *p*,	Con.	138
Our *p* is one, the suns are many,	Maud, I. iv.	45
And the *p* of love is on high	" xxii.	8

plank.

blind with rage she miss'd the *p*,	Princess, iv.	159
p and beam for roof and floor,	" vi.	30
come stepping lightly down the *p*,	In Mem. xiv.	7

plann'd.

all mosaic choicely *p*	Pal. of Art	145

plant (s.)

Like to the mother *p* in semblance,	The Poet	23
Which would blight the *p*'s.	Poet's Mind	18
I grow, like some green *p*,	D. of F. Wom.	205
The sap dries up: the *p* declines.	Two Voices	268
All creeping *p*'s, a wall of green	Day-Dm.	65
to watch the thirsty *p*'s Imbibing!	Princess, ii.	400

plant (verb.)

p a solid foot into the Time,	Princess, v.	405
I go to *p* it on his tomb,	In Mem. viii.	22
make all clean, and *p* himself afresh.	Enid	1753

Plantagenet.

The lion-heart, P,	Margaret	34

plantain.

hedgehog underneath the *p* bores	Aylmer's F.	850

plantation.

Is yon *p* where this byway joins	Walk. to the M.	4
He left a small *p*;	Amphion	20
To grow my own *p*.	"	100

planted.

when we *p* level feet,	Princess, iv.	12

plash.

p of rains, and refuse patch'd with	Vision of Sin	212

plaster.

alum and *p* are sold to the poor.	Maud, I. i.	39

plat.

I keep smooth *p*'s of fruitful ground	The Blackbird	3

platan.

clear-stemm'd *p*'s guard The outlet	Arabian N's.	23
The thick-leaved *p*'s of the vale.	Princess, iii.	159

plate.

squares of men in brazen *p*'s,	D. of F. Wom.	33
Came out clear *p*'s of sapphire mail.	Two Voices	12

Plato.

P the wise, and large-brow'd Verulam	Pal. of Art	163
But Homer, P, Verulam;	Princess, ii.	144
Or lend an ear to P where he says	Lucretius	147

play (s.)	POEM.	LINE.
At last, tired out with *p*,	*Talking O.*	206
shouts with his sister at *p!*	*'Break, break,'* etc.	6
now to leaven *p* with profit	*Princess,* iv.	131
Go in and out as if at merry *p*,	*Maud,* I. xviii.	31
left his wine and horses and *p,*	" xix.	74
She is weary of dance and *p,*	" xxii.	22
watch her at her petulance, and *p, Vivien*		31

play (verb.)
I would roam abroad and *p* .	*The Merman*	11
lightly vault from the throne and *p*	*The Mermaid*	33
needs must *p* such pranks as these.	*L.C.V. de Vere*	64
'Ill merrily glance and *p,*	*May Queen,* i.	39
p with flying forms and images,	*Gardener's D.*	59
'*P* me no tricks,' said Lord Ronald,	*Lady Clare*	73-5
p The Spartan Mother with emotion	*Princess,*ii.	262
p the slave to gain the tyranny .	" iv.	114
with your long locks *p* the Lion's mane!	" vi.	148
and *p* About the prow,	*In Mem.* xii.	17
The tender-pencil'd shadow *p*	" xlviii.	12
I'll have leave at times to *p*	" lviii.	11
You wonder when my fancies *p*	" lxv.	2
He *p*'s with threads, he beats his chair	"	13
So shall grief with symbols *p,*	" lxxxiv.	95
For him she *p*'s, to him she sings	" xcvi.	29
It circles round, and fancy *p*'s,	" Con.	81
p the game of the despot kings,	*Maud,* I. x.	31
to live, long as my pulses *p* .	" xviii.	70
might *p* me falsely, having power,	*Vivien*	365
he set himself to *p* up on her .	*Elaine*	643
Abbess and her nuns To *p* upon me	*Guinevere*	308
plague And *p* upon, and harry me	"	358
golden hair, with which I used to *p*	"	543
To *p* their go-between as heretofore	*Aylmer's F.*	523
in thy heart the scrawl shall *p*.'	*Sailor Boy* .	12

played.
Scarce my life with fancy *p* .	*Miller's D.*	45
If re *p,* a tiger, rolling to and fro	*Pal. of Art*	151
with the time we *p;* .	*Gardener's D.*	216
here she came, and round me *p,*	*Talking O.*	133
men with knowledge merely *p.*	*Two Voices*	172
when thy father *p* In his free field	"	319
The happy winds upon her *p,*	*Sir L. and O. G.*	33
p the patron with her curls.	*Princess,Pro.*	138
beam Of the East that *p* upon them	" v.	249
He *p* at council's and kings,	*In Mem.* lxiii.	23
A chequer-work of beam and shade	" lxxi.	14
Love but *p* with gracious lies,	" cxxiv.	7
I *p* with the girl when a child :	*Maud,* I. i.	68
I have *p* with her when a child	" vi.	87
took the word and *p* upon it,	*Enid*	1140
the lovely blue *P* into green,	"	1537
p about with slight and sprightly .	*Vivien*	27
Surely I but *p* on Torre :	*Elaine*	209
p Among the waste and lumber	*En. Arden*	15
children *p* at keeping house .	"	24
p with him And call'd him Father	"	350

playing.
P mad pranks along the heathy	*Circumstance*	2
now A twisted snake .	*Princess, Pro.*	61
p with the blade he prick'd his hand	*Aylmer's F.*	232

playmate.
| Paris, once her *p* on the hills . | *Œnone* | 16 |
| Doubled her own, for want of *p's* | *Aylmer's F.* | 61 |

plea.
| Mused for a little on his *p,* . | *Enid* | 42 |

plead.
| twice I sought to *p* my cause, | *Princess,* iv. | 530 |
| let her *p* in vain . | *En. Arden* | 166 |

pleaded.
| Although I *p* tenderly, . | *Miller's D.* | 135 |
| on a day When Cyril *p* | *Princess,* vii. | 63 |

pleader.
| jests, that flash'd about the *p's* room, | *Aylmer's F.* | 440 |

pleading.
| a sound Like sleepy counsel *p;* . | *Amphion* | 74 |
| before them paused Hortensia, *p:* | *Princess,* vii. | 117 |

pleasance.
| my passion seeks *P* in love-sighs . | *Lilian* | 9 |
| A realm of *p* . | *Arabian N's.* | 101 |

pleasant.
Love will make our cottage *p,*	*L. of Burleigh*	15
made the past so *p* to us :	*Guinevere*	373
net made *p* by the baits Of gold	*Aylmer's F.*	406
'beat quicker, for the time Is *p,*	*On a Mourner*	13
the woods and ways Are *p,*	"	14

pleasantry.
| From talk of war to traits of *p—* | *Elaine* | 320 |

please.
fearful that you should not *p.*	*Miller's D.*	148
shapes and hues that *p* me well !	*Pal. of Art*	194
She could not *p* herself.	*Talking O.*	10
betwixt them both, to *p* them both,	*Princess,Con.*	25
At that last hour to *p* him well	*In Mem.* vi.	18
thinking 'this will *p* him best,'	"	21
when gifts of mine could *p,* .	*The Letters*	22
Enid, but to *p* her husband's eye,	*Enid*	11
king himself should *p* To cleanse	"	70
To *p* her, dwelling on his boundless	"	63
put off to *p* me this poor gown,	"	1527
Edith whom his pleasure was to *p*	*Aylmer's F.*	232
flap, Good man, to *p* the child .	*Sea Dreams*	258

pleased.
newness of thine art so *p* thee,	*Ode to Mem.*	89
It *p* me well enough. .	*The Epic*	24
might have *p* the eyes of many men.	*M. d'Arthur*	91
that *p* us from its worth : 'You might have won'	"	22
it *p* us not : in truth We shudder .	*Princess,* iii.	262
neither *p* myself nor them. .	" Con.	3
But Lilia *p* me, .	"	3
since it *p* a vanish'd eye, .	*In Mem.* viii.	2
led by tracks that *p* us well, .	" xxii.	2
Like one with any trifle *p,* .	" lxv.	4
They *p* him, fresh from brawling courts	" lxxxvii.	11
Nor less it *p* in livelier moods, .	"	29
each has *p* a kindred eye, .	" xcix.	17
Nor knew we well what *p* us most	*The Daisy* .	25
pick'd the lance That *p* him best, .	*Enid*	102
wholly *p* To find him yet unwounded	"	1219
in a manner *p,* and turning, stood	"	1305
p her with a babbling heedlessness	*Guinevere*	149
that which *p* him, for he smiled .	*En. Arden*.	7, 8
him We *p* not—he was seldom *p:* .	*The Voyage*	74

pleasing.
| To make him *p* in her uncle's eye | *Dora* . | 82 |

pleasure (s.)
With *p* and love and jubilee : .	*Sea-Fairies*	36
What *p* can we have To war with evil?	*Lotos-E's.*	93
own anguish deep More than much *p*	*To J. S.*	43
the giddy *p* of the eyes. .	*M. d'Arthur*	128
for the *p* that I took to hear,	*Gardener's D.*	223
into my inmost ring A *p* I discern'd,	*Talking O.*	174
woman's *p,* woman's pain— .	*Locksley H.*	143
Like a beast with lower *p's,*	"	176
Pain rises up, old *p's* pall.	*Two Voices*	164
Come, Care and *P,* Hope and Pain	*Day-Dm.*	75
I will take my *p* there : .	"	244
You moved her at your *p.* .	*Amphion*	60
Built for *p* and for state. .	*L. of Burleigh*	32
What *p* lives in height .	*Princess,* vii.	178
Some *p* from thine early years.	*In Mem.* iv.	10
That so my *p* may be whole, .	*Maud,*I. xvi.	4
fulsome *P*' clog him and drown,	*Maud,*I. xvi.	4
nor a vantage-ground For *p;* .	*Ded. of Idylls*	23
desire To close with her lord's *p;* .	*Enid*	1063
Came purer *p* unto mortal kind .	"	1613
have some rest and *p* in himself, .	*Vivien*	335
have small rest or *p* in herself .	"	340
she had her *p* in it .	"	454
Because of that high *p* which I had	"	726
For *p* all about a field of flowers :	*Elaine*	775
P to have it, none ; to lose it, pain :	"	1405
on love And sports and tilts and *p,*	*Guinevere*	54
would have been my *p* had I seen .	"	652
not to see the world—For *p!* .	*En. Arden*.	297
with petty wrongs Or *p's,* .	"	350

314　　　　　　　　　　CONCORDANCE TO

	POEM.	LINE.
Edith whom his *p* was to please,	Aylmer's F.	232
made his *p* echo, hand to hand,	"	257
since the nobler *p* seems to fade,	Lucretius	227
Without one *p* or without one pain	"	265

pleasure (verb.)
roll'd His hoop to *p* Edith, . . Aylmer's F. 85

pleasureable.
Ev'n such a wave, but not so *p*, . Vivien . 143

pleasure-house.
I built my soul a lordly *p-h*, . Pal. of Art 1

pledge (s.)
giving safe *p* of fruits, . . Ode to Mem. 18
reconcilement, *p's* given, . . Gardener's D. 252
P of a love not to be mine, . Princess, vi. 180
arms On loan, or else for *p*; . Enid . 220

pledge (verb.)
I *p* her, and she comes and dips . Will Water. 17
I *p* her silent at the board; . . " 25
p you all In wassail: . . Princess, Pro. 183
To *p* them with a kindly tear, . In Mem. lxxxix. 10
p her not in any cheerful cup, . Coquette, iii. 9

pledged.
p To fight in tourney for my bride, . Princess, v. 342
Have *p* us in this union . . Elaine . 116
and she hated all who *p*. . . " 740

pledgest.
Who *p* now thy gallant son; . In Mem. vi. 10

pledging.
p Lancelot and the lily maid . Elaine . 734

Pleiads.
Many a night I saw the *P's*, . Locksley H. 9

plenteousness.
Set in this Eden of all *p*, . . En. Arden . 562

plenty.
P corrupts the melody . . . The Blackbird 15
Yet is there *p* of the kind.' . . Two Voices 33
hand in hand with *P* in the maize, Princess, vii. 186
the boy Will have *p*; . . Maud, I. vii. 8-16

plied.
clock-work steamer paddling *p* . Princess, Pro. 71
p him with his richest wines, . " i. 172

plight (s.)
nor by *p* or broken ring Bound, . Aylmer's F. 135

plight (verb.)
I to thee my troth did *p*, . . Oriana . 26
Will I to Olive *p* my troth, . . Talking O. 283

plighted.
p troth. and were at peace. . . Princess, vii. 68
The heart that never *p* troth . In Mem. xxvii. 10

plot (plat.)
level *p's* Of crowned lilies . Ode to Mem. 108
paced the thymy *p's* of Paradise, Love and Death 2
I steal by lawns and grassy *p's*, . The Brook . 170
all the turf was rich in *p's* . Enid . 660

plot (conspiracy.)
A *p*. a *p*, a *p*, to ruin all!' 'No *p*, no *p*' Princess, ii. 175
for fine *p's* may fail, . . Vivien . 669

plot.
That he *p's* against me still. . Maud, I. xix. 81

plotted.
He has *p* against me in this, . Maud, I. xix. 80

plough—plow (s.)
morning driv'n her *p* of pearl . Love and Duty 96
Eight daughters of the *p*, (v. 329) Princess, iv. 259
those eight mighty daughters of the *p* " 528
He praised his *p's*, his cows, his hogs, The Brook 125
an' runn'd *p* thruff it an' all, . N. Farmer . 42

plough—plow (verb.)
p's with pain his native lea . . In Mem. lxiii. 25
an' Thornaby holms to *p*! . . N. Farmer . 52

ploughing.	POEM.	LINE.
and Charlie *p* the hill	. . Grandmother	80

ploughman.
in the furrow broke the *p's* head, Princess, v. 212

plover.
tufted *p* pipe along the fallow lea, May Queen, ii. 18
wind sweep and the *p* cry: 'Come not, when,' etc. 5
the great *p's* human whistle . Enid . 898

pluck.
I will *p* it from my bosom, . . Locksley H. 66
'Hard task, to *p* resolve,' I cried Two Voices 118
that men may *p* them from our hearts, Princess, iii. 240
this night should *p* your palace down; " iv. 395
splendour *p's* The slavish hat . Maud, I. x. 3
' to *p* the flower in season;' So says Vivien . 572
p's The mortal soul from out . Lucretius . 258

pluck'd.
Devils *p* my sleeve; . . . St S. Stylites 168
she started up, And *p* it out . Talking O. 230
p his one foot from the grave, . Amphion . 43
and *p* her likeness out; . . Princess, i. 91
And *p* the ripen'd ears, . . " 247
she *p* the grass, She flung it from her Con. 21
I *p* a daisy, I gave it you. . . The Daisy . 83
p the grass There growing longest Enid . 1103
seems to be *p* at by the village boys " 1408
he had the gems *P* from the crown, Elaine . 58
Lancelot *p* him by the heel, . Guinevere . 35
p a life From the dread sweep . En. Arden . 54
the children *p* at him to go, . " 366
left alone he *p* her dagger forth Aylmer's F. 470
from which Livid he *p* it forth, . " 627

plucking.
P the harmless wild-flower . . Maud, II. i. 3

plumage.
Conjecture of the *p* and the form; Enid . 333

plume.
A funeral, with *p's* and lights . L. of Shalott, ii. 31
She saw the helmet and the *p*, . " iii. 40
From spur to *p* a star of tournament, M. d'Arthur 223
Ruffles her pure cold *p*, . . " 268
A light-green tuft of *p's* she bore Sir L. and Q. G. 26
each, in maiden *p's* We rustled: . Princess, i. 199
all about were birds Of sunny *p*, . Enid . 639
brandish'd *p* Brushing his instep, " 1208
a lothly *p* fall'n from the wing . Vivien . 577
from spur to *p* Red as the rising sun Elaine . 307
p's driv'n backward by the wind . " 479
with *p's* that mock'd the may, . Guinevere . 23
coco's drooping crown of *p's* . En. Arden . 575
Fantastic *p* or sable pine; . . The Voyage . 44

plumed.
pines, that *p* the craggy ledge . Œnone . 205
Empanoplied and *p* We enter'd in, Princess, v. 472
a shatter'd archway *p* with fern; . Enid . 316

plumelet.
When rosy *p's* tuft the larch, . In Mem. xc. 1

plummet.
Two *p's* dropt for one . . . Princess, ii. 159

plump.
Grew *p* and able-bodied; . . The Goose . 18
One shade more *p* than common . Will Water. 150

plump-armed.
A *p-a* Ostleress and a stable wench Princess, i. 223

plump'd.
sweating rosin, *p* the pine . . Amphion . 47

plunder (s.)
is a world of *p* and prey . . Maud, I. iv. 24
the sack and *p* of our house . . Enid . . 694
Earl Doorm with *p* to the hall. . " . 1440

plunder (verb.)
I cannot steal or *p*, no nor beg; . Enid . 1336

plundered.
bark had *p* twenty nameless isles; Vivien . 409

	POEM.	LINE.
plunge (s.)		
thro' the whitening hazels made a *p*	En. Arden	376
plunge (verb.)		
river sloped To *p* in cataract	Princess, iii.	274
nor rather *p* at once, Being troubled	Lucretius	151
plunged.		
p Among the bulrush-beds, .	M. d'Arthur	134
P in the battery-smoke	Lt. Brigade	32
down the shingly scaur he *p*,	Elaine	54
ply.		
joint of state, that *plies* Its 'Love thou thy land'		47
plies His function of the woodland:	Lucretius	45
pock-pitten.		
That great *p-p* fellow	Aylmer's F.	256
poem.		
Look, I come to the test, a tiny *p. Hendecasyllabics*		3
poesy.		
this poor flower of *p*	In Mem. viii.	19
poet.		
The *p* in a golden clime was born	The Poet	1
one poor *p's* scroll	"	55
Vex not thou the *p's* mind (rep.) .	Poet's Mind	1
The parson Holmes, the *p* Everard Hall	The Epic	4
and the *p* little urged	"	48
sing Like *p's*, from the vanity of song?	Gardener's D.	99
days were brief Whereof the *p's* talk	Talking O.	186
A tongue-tied *P* in the feverous days	Golden Year	10
as *p's* seasons when they flower,	"	28
this is truth the *p* sings	Locksley H.	75
To prove myself a *p*:	Will Water.	166
when the *P's* words and looks	"	193
might have won the *P's* name, 'You might have won'	"	1
those that wear the *P's* crown	"	10
now the *P* cannot die	"	13
The rain had fallen, the *P* arose,	Poet's Song.	1
P's, whose thoughts enrich the blood	Princess, ii.	164
A volume of the *P's* of her land :	" vii.	159
such as lurks In some wild *P*,	In Mem. xxxiv.	7
read The Tuscan *p's* on the lawn :	" lxxxviii.	24
passionate heart of the *p* is whirl'd	Maud, l. iv.	39
As ever painter painted, *p* sang,	Aylmer's F.	106
poetess.		
I wish I were Some mighty *p*,	Princess, Pro.	132
poet-forms.		
The *P's* of stronger hours,	Day-Dm.	226
poet-like.		
P-l he spoke. .	Ed. Morris	27
Rather, O ye Gods, *P-l*,	Lucretius	93
poet-princess.		
P-p with her grand Imaginations	Princess, iii.	256
point.		
clotted into *p's* and hanging loose,	M. d' Arthur	219
under looming shores, *P* after *p*; .	Ep.	18
slowly, creeping on from *p* to *p*	Locksley H.	134
To our *p*: not war : Lest I lose all.'	Princess, v.	196
touch'd upon the *p* Where idle boys	"	298
conflict with the crash of shivering *p's*	"	480
oration flowing free From *p* to *p*	In Mem.lxxxvi.	33
talking from the *p*, he drew him in,	The Brook	154
and the *p's* of lances bicker in it	Enid	1248
faintly-venom'd *p's* Of slander,	Vivien	28
It buzzes wildly round the *p*;	"	282
all *p's*, except the poplar-grove,	Elaine	614
her friend's *p* with pale tranquillity	"	729
that *p*, when first she saw the King	Guinevere	400
And now, the bloodless *p* reversed,	The Voyage	71
point (pint.)		
I've 'd my *p* o' yaäle ivry noight .	N. Farmer.	7
point (verb.)		
p thee forward to a distant light .	Love and Duty	92
p yon out the shadow from the truth!	Princess, i.	83
p to it, and we say, 'The loyal warmth'	" ii.	225
p the term of human strife, .	In Mem.xlix.	14
A hand that *p's*, and palled shapes	" lxix.	7

	POEM.	LINE.
pointed.		
and *p* toward the land .	Lotos-E's.	1
Thereto she *p* with a laugh, .	D. of F. Wom.	159
p on to where A double hill .	Princess, iii.	157
this lost lamb (she *p* to the child) .	" iv.	342
I tarry for thee,' and she *p* to Mars	Maud,III.vi.	13
He *p* out a pasturing colt .	The Brook.	130
finger up, and *p* to the dust .	Enid	1302
Are scatter'd, and he *p* to the field,	"	1650
and rose And *p* to the damsel, .	Elaine	1236
and at top She *p* seaward .	Sea Dreams	118
P itself to pierce, but sank down .	Lucretius	63
pointing.		
p to his drunken sleep, .	Locksley H.	81
poise.		
In crystal eddies glance and *p*, .	Miller's D.	52
poised.		
court-Galen *p* his gilt-head cane,	Princess, i.	19
poison (s.)		
the *p* with her balmy breath, .	D. of F.Wom.	271
Full of weak *p*, turnspits for the clown	Princess, iv.	495
To pestle a poison'd *p* .	Maud, I. i.	44
poison (verb.)		
now we 4 our babes, poor souls! .	Maud, II. v.	63
and *p's* half the young. .	Guinevere	518
poison-flowers.		
The honey of *p-f*. .	Maud, I. iv.	56
Poland.		
Shall I weep of a *P* fall? .	Maud, I. iv	46
polar star.		
Is twisting round the *p s* ; .	In Mem. c.	12
pole.		
love turn'd round on fixed *p's*, 'Love thou thy land'		5
Betwixt the slumber of the *p's* .	In.Mem.xcviii.	15
polish.		
keeps the wear and *p* of the wave.	Enid .	682
politics.		
At wine, in clubs, of art, of *p* .	Princess,Pro.	160
The fading *p* of mortal Rome, .	" ii.	266
polluted.		
Here looking down on thine *p* .	Guinevere	551
he, the King, Call'd me *p*: .	"	613
pollution.		
And makes me one *p*: .	Guinevere	612
polluting.		
P, and imputing her whole self .	Vivien	632
pomp.		
At civic revel and *p* and game,	Ode on Well.	147,227
poud.		
cutting eights that day upon the *p*	The Epic	10
ponder.		
p those three hundred scrolls .	Lucretius	12
ponder'd.		
Paris *p*, and I cried 'O Paris' .	Œnone	165
Then Enid *p* in her heart .	Enid .	913-79
Pontius.		
P and Iscariot by my side .	St S. Stylites	195
poodle.		
a score of pugs And *p's* yell'd .	Ed. Morris	120
pool.		
desolate creeks and *p's* among, .	Dying Swan	41
angled in the higher *p*. .	Miller's D.	14
sleepy *p* above the dam, The *p* beneath it	"	93
Touching the sullen *p* below ; .	"	244
Flash in the *p's* of whirling Simois.	Œnone	202
Salt *p*, lock'd in with bars of sand;	Pal. of Art	247
and the bulrush in the *p*. .	May Queen, ii.	28
hen To her false daughters in the *p*;	Princess, iv.	503
breaks about the dappled *p's*: .	In Mem. xlviii.	6
Near that old home, a *p* of golden carp:	Enid .	648
his burnish'd brethren of the *p*; .	"	650

316   CONCORDANCE TO

	POEM.	LINE
her burnish'd sisters of the *p*;	Enid	635
tho' she lay in the dark *p*,	"	657
pick the faded creature from the *p*,	"	671
Gray swamps and *p's*, waste places	"	860
slipt and fell into some *p* or stream,	Elaine	214
A little bitter *p* about a stone	Guinevere	52
Down to the *p* and narrow wharf	En. Arden.	691
the brook, or a *p*, or her window-pane	The Window	4

poor.
Nor any *p* about your lands?	L. C. V. de Vere	68
abidest lame and *p*,	Two Voices	197
But he was rich where I was *p*,	In Mem. lxxviii.	13
Ring out the feud of rich and *p*,	" cv.	11
the *p* are hovell'd and hustled together,	Maud, I. i.	34
are sold to the *p* for bread	"	39
and I am nameless and *p*.	" iv.	18
How mend the dwellings, of the *p*;	To F. D. Maurice	38
Laborious for her people and her *p*—	Ded. of Idylls	34
now *p*, but ever open-door'd.'	Enid	302
specially should your good knight be *p*,	Elaine	952, 1311
I grieve to see you *p*,	En. Arden.	403
but less loved than Edith, of her *p*:	Aylmer's F.	167
from her own home-circle of the *p*	"	504
meek, Exceeding '*p* in spirit.'	"	754
And some are *p* indeed;	The Flower	22

poplar (see *poplar grove* under *grove*.)
Hard by a *p* shook alway	Mariana	41
shadow of the *p* fell	"	55
to the wooing wind aloof The *p* made	"	76
The seven elms, the *p's* four	Ode to Mem.	56
The *p's*, in long order due,	Amphion	37
blasts which blow the *p* white	In Mem. lxxi.	3
p's made a noise of falling showers	Elaine	410-522
the cape That has the *p* on it:	"	1034
Beyond the *p* and far up the flood,	"	1044

poppy.
the *p* hangs in sleep	Lotos-E's.	56
unsown, where many *poppies* grew,	Dora	71
more crumpled than a *p* from the sheath,	Princess, v.	28

poppy-mingled.
A land of hops and *p-m* corn	Aylmer's F.	31

populace.
call us Britain's barbarous *p's*	Boädicea	7

porch.
garden *p'es* on the brim,	Arabian N's.	16
thronging all one *p* of Paradise	Pal. of Art	101
The honeysuckle round the *p*	May Queen, i.	29
up the *p* there grew an Eastern rose,	Gardener's D.	122
cloudy *p* oft opening on the Sun?	Love and Duty	9
rooms which gave Upon a pillar'd *p*,	Princess, i.	227
p that sang All round with laurel,	" ii.	8
Then summon'd to the *p* we went	" iii.	162
pelt us in the *p* with flowers.	In Mem. Con.	68
They leave the *p*, they pass the grave	"	71
'Dark *p*,' I said, ' and silent aisle,	The Letters	47
Strode from the *p*, tall and erect.	Aylmer's F.	825

porch-pillars.
P-*p* on the lion resting	The Daisy	55

porc.
dote and *p* on yonder cloud.	In Mem. xv.	16

pored.
I *p* upon her letter which I held	Princess, v.	458

poring.
p over miserable books—	Locksley H.	172
Now *p* on the glowworm. now the star,	Princess, iv.	193
yearlong *p* on thy pictured eyes	" vii.	319
As when a painter, *p* on a face,	Elaine	331

port (harbour.)
There lies the *p*: the vessel puffs	Ulysses	44
found thee lying in the *p*;	In Mem. xiv.	12
To that fair *p* below the castle	The Daisy	79
tawny pirate anchor'd in his *p*,	Vivien	408
prettiest little damsel in the *p*,	En. Arden.	12
northward of the narrow *p*	"	102
Sail'd from this *p*.	"	125

	POEM.	LINE.
Fearing the lazy gossip of the *p*,	En. Arden	332
Then all descended to the *p*,	"	443
By this the lazy gossips of the *p*	"	469
Told him, with other annals of the *p*	"	703
when they buried him the little *p*.	"	915

port (demeanour.)
modern gentleman Of stateliest *p*;	M. d'Arthur, Ep.	23

port (wine.)
Go fetch a pint of *p*:	Will Water.	4
tho' the *p* surpasses praise,	"	77
dear For this good pint of *p*.	"	212

portal.
found at length The garden *p's*.	Princess, iv.	182
guard the *p's* of the house	In Mem. xxix.	12
doubt beside the *p* waits,	" xciii.	14
crimson'd all Thy presence and thy *p's*,	Tithonus	57

portal-warding.
Far as the *p-w* lion-whelp	En. Arden	98

porter.
with grooms and *p's* on the bridge	Godiva	2

portion.
P's and parcels of the dreadful Past.	Lotos-E's.	92
carves A *p* from the solid present,	Vivien	312

portioned.
P in halves between us,	Gardener's D.	5

portrait.
those old *p's* of old kings,	Day-Dm.	43
hangs his *p* in my father's hall	Princess, ii.	221

Fortress.
At break of day the College P came	Princess, ii.	1

possess.
I *will p* him or will die.	Fatima	39
What souls *p* themselves so pure,	In Mem. xxxii.	15
and *p* your horse And armour,	Enid	923

possessed.
p The darkness of the world,	Arabian N's.	71
For love *p* the atmosphere,	Miller's D.	91
soul *p* of many gifts To—	With Pal. of Art	3
marvel what *p* my brain:	In Mem. xiv.	16
A rainy cloud *p* the earth,	" xxx.	3
The silent snow *p* the earth,	" lxxvii.	3
Not knowing what *p* him:	Aylmer's F.	556

possession.
I take *p* of man's mind and deed.	Pal. of Art	209
Enoch would hold *p* for a week:	En. Arden.	27

possible.
all Life needs for life is *p* to will—	Love and Duty	83
O that 'twere *p* After long grief	Maud, II. iv.	1
Ah Christ, that it were *p*	"	13

post (s.)
thro' twenty *p's* of telegraph	Princess, Pro.	77
quit the *p* Allotted by the Gods:	Lucretius	148

post (verb.)
made a point to *p* with mares;	Princess, i.	187

postscript.
came a *p* dash'd across the rest	Princess, v.	414

posy.
Home with her maiden *p*	Maud, I. xii.	22

pot.
Go down among the *p's*:	Will Water.	220

potherbs.
wrongs like *p's* in the street	Princess, v.	449

pouring.
Waves on the shingle *p*,	1865-1866	11

POU STO.
P S whence afterhands May move	Princess, iii.	246

poultry.
a larger egg Than modern *p* drop,	Will Water.	122

pound.
wedded her to sixty thousand *p's*.	Ed. Morris	126

	pour.	POEM.	LINE.		POEM.	LINE.
p round mine ears the livelong bleat		*Ode to Mem.*	65	Strong in the *p* that all men adore,	*Maud*, I. x.	14
Holy water will I *p*	.	*Poet's Mind*	12	Cold fires, yet with *p* to burn	" xviii.	39
poured.				*P's* of the height, *P's* of the deep.	" II. ii.	82
a fire Is *p* upon the hills,	.	*Fatima*	31	brainless mobs and lawless *P's*	. *Ode on Well.*	153
gray twilight *p* On dewy pastures	*Pal. of Art*	85	palter'd with Eternal God for *p*;	"	170
P back into my empty soul.	.	*D. of F. Wom.*	73	Round us, each with different *p's*.	"	263
soft brown hair *P* on one side:	*Gardener's D.*	123	too gentle, have not used my *p*: . *Enid*	.	407
For me the torrent ever *p*	.	*To E. L.*	13	dearer by the *p* Of intermitted custom;	"	810
pouring.				are in my *p* at last, are in my *p*.	"	1159
From craggy hollows *p*,	.	*D. of F. Wom.*	182	I will make use of all the *p* I have.	"	1114
And England *p* on her foes.	.	*Ode on Well.*	117	out of her there came a *p* upon him;	"	1401
poussetting.				hardest tyrants in their day of *p*,	"	1543
P with a sloe-tree:	.	*Amphion*	44	Disband himself, and scatter all his *p's*,	"	1646
pouted.				lo the *p's* of Doorm Are scatter'd,	"	1647
His own are *p* to a kiss;	.	*Day-Dm.*	51	some slight *p* upon your fate . *Vivien*		182
poverty.				I will not yield to give you *p*	"	223
lift the household out of *p*;	.	*En. Arden*	482	Faith and unfaith can ne'er be equal *p's*:	"	238
His baby's death, her growing *p*	"	706	*p* upon me thro' this charm,	"	364
power.				might play me falsely, having *p*,	"	565
arms, or *p* of brain, or birth . *To the Queen*	3	to tyrants when they came to *p*.	"	518
In impotence of fancied *p*.	.	*A Character*	24	elemental secrets, *p's* And forces:	"	482
shake All evil dreams of *p*.	.	*The Poet*	47	like a ghost without the *p* to speak. *Elaine*		915
fill the sea-halls with a voice of *p*; *The Merman*	10	the owls Wailing had *p* upon her,	"	995
to Paris made Proffer of royal *p*, .	*Œnone*	109	the *P's* that tend the soul, . *Guinevere*		65
and still she spake of *p*,	.	"	119	grace and *p*, Wrought as a charm	"	142
P fitted to the season;	.	"	121	for the *p* of ministration in her,	"	686
in *p* Only, are likest gods,	.	"	127	understand, While I have *p* to speak *En Arden*	878
thought of *p* Flatter'd his spirit;	.	"	134	Turning beheld the *P's* of the House *Aylmer's F.*	787
alone lead life to sovereign *p*.	.	"	143	but he had *p's*, he knew it:	"	393
Yet not for *p*. *p* of herself Would come	"	144	and the hands of *p* Were bloodier,	"	452
without light Or *p* of movement,	*Pal. of Art*	246	happy men that have the *p* to die *Tithonus*		70
lit your eyes with tearful *p*,	.	*Margaret*	3	once had *p* to rob it of content. *Coquette*, ii.		8
P should make from land to land *'You ask me why'*	21	the philtre which had *p*, they said *Lucretius*		16
future time by *p* of thought. *'Love thou thy land'*	4	check'd His *p* to shape;	.	"	23
great contrivances of *P*.	.	"	64	all generating *p's* and genial heat	"	97
widow'd of the *p* in his eye	.	*M. d'Arthur*	122	*practice* (s.)		
know I have some *p* with Heaven *St S. Stylites*	141	run My faith beyond my *p*	. *Ed Morris*	.	54
P goes forth from me.	.	"	143	had not stinted *p*, O my God. . *St S. Stylites*		58
the *p's* and princes of this world,	"	164	and his work, 'That *p* betters?' . *Princess*, iii.		282
try If yet he keeps the *p*	.	*Talking O.*	28	What *p* howsoe'er expert . *In Mem.* lxxiv.		5
the *P's*, who wait On noble deeds, *Godiva*	71	sin that *p* burns into the blood, . *Vivien*		612
How grows the day of human *p* *Two Voices*	78	Nor yet forgot her *p* in her fright,	"	796
If Nature put not forth her *p*	.	"	160	*practise* (verb.)		
From out my sullen heart a *p* Broke,	.	"	443	And do not *p* on me,	. *Enid*	.	1205
The Federations and the *P's*	.	*Day-Dm.*	228	*practised.*		
Until the charm have *p* to make . *Will Water.*	21	still I find Your force is *p*,	. *Vivien*	.	217
half the *p* to turn This wheel	.	"	83	inasmuch as you have *p* on her, . *Aylmer's F.*		302
Faster binds a tyrant's *p*;	.	*Vision of Sin*	128	*praise* (s.)		
He had not wholly quench'd his *p*;	"	217	Blew his own *p's* in his eyes, . *A Character*		22
so much grace and *p*, breathing down *Princess*, ii.	24	won his *p's* night and morn?' *Mariana in the S.*		34
arguing love of knowledge and of *p*;	"	41	neither count on *p*: . *'Love thou thy land,' etc.*		26
grow To use and *p* on this Oasis,	"	151	in *p* of her Grew oratory. . *Gardener's D.*		55
burst his pipes Groaning for *p*,	"	451	love were cause enough for *p*.'	"	104
to push my rival out of place and *p*.	" iv.	316	She broke out in *p* To God, . *Dora*		110
Autumn, dropping fruits of *p*;	" vi.	32	But yield not me the *p*: . *St S. Stylites*		182
less for truth than *p* In knowledge:	" vii.	221	And others, passing *p*, . *Talking O.*		58
full-summ'd in all their *p's*,	"	272	While still I yearn'd for human *p*, *Two Voices*		258
and perhaps they felt their *p*.	" Con.	13	he is chill to *p* or blame.	"	258
gradually the *p's* of the night	"	111	tho' the port surpasses *p*, . *Will Water.*		77
To Sleep I give my *p's* away; . *In Mem.* iv.	1	The *p* that comes to constancy.' *In Mem.* xxi.		12
stunn'd me from my *p* to think	" xvi.	13	Had surely added *p* to *p*.	. " xxxi.	8
The chairs and thrones of civil *p*?	" xxi.	16	I leave thy *p's* unexprest	. " lxxiv.	1
hath *p* to see Within the green	" xxvi.	6	To stir a little dust of *p*.	. "	12
With gather'd *p*, yet the same	" xxx.	26	fill The lips of men with honest *p*, " lxxxiii.		26
Wisdom dealt with mortal *p's*,	" xxxvi.	5	In *p* and in dispraise the same, . *Ode on Well.*		73
When all his active *p's* are still,	" lxiii.	18	no one word of loyal *p* For Arthur, *Vivien*		617
That Nature's ancient *p* was lost:	" lxviii.	6	to true young hearts than their own *p*, *Elaine*		418
Hath *p* to give thee as thou wert?	" lxxiv.	8	chill'd the popular *p's* of the King *Guinevere*		14
Conduct by paths of growing *p's*	" lxxxiii.	31	spite of *p* and scorn . *A Dedication*		6
First love, first friendship, equal *p's*, " lxxxiv.	107	golden largess of thy *p*. *'My life is full,' etc.*		5
with *p* and grace And music	" lxxxvi.	33	would take the *p* and care no more. *Coquette*, ii.		14
P was with him in the night,	" xcv.	13	*praise* (verb.)		
some sweet *p* Sprang up for ever	" cxi.	9	*p* the heavens for what they have?' *Gardener's D.*		101
in her onward race For *p*.	" cxii.	15	nothing else For which to *p* the heavens	"	3
Who greatest not alone in *p*.	"	26	And *p* thee more in both . *Talking O.*		70
The *P* in darkness whom we guess; " cxxiii.	4	No, I cannot *p* the fire . *Vision of Sin*		183
To shift an arbitrary *p*,	" cxxvii.	17	often heard me *p* Your feats of arms *Enid*		434
To see I owe some diffusive *p*,	" cxxix.	7			
thou art worthy; full of *p*;	" Con.	37			

318   CONCORDANCE TO

praised.
	POEM.	LINE.
One *p* her ancles, one her eyes,	Beggar Maid	11
And much I *p* her nobleness,	Princess, Pro.	124
Then they *p* him, soft and low,	" v.	536
If I *p* the busy town,	In Mem. lxxxviii.	37
He *p* his land, his horses, (rep.)	The Brook	124
p the waning red, and told The vintage	Aylmer's F.	406

praising.
Sipt wine from silver, *p* God,	Will Water.	127

prance.
boy began to leap and *p* '*Home they brought him*'		7

pranced.
lightly *p* Three captains out ;	Princess, v.	244

prancer.
she whose elfin *p* springs	Sir L. and Q. G.	33

prank.
mad *p*'s along the heathy leas ;	Circumstance	2
must play such *p*'s as these.	L. C. V. de Vere	64
Sweet love on *p*'s of saucy boyhood :	Princess, vii.	323

Prasutagus.
Me the wife of rich P, .	Boädicea	48

prate (s.)
child kill me with her foolish *p*?'	Guinevere	223

prate (verb.)
of the moral instinct would she *p*	Pal. of Art	205
p Of penances I cannot have gone	St S. Stylites	98
we, that *p* Of rights and wrongs,	Godiva	7
when I hear you *p* I almost think	Princess, v.	145
Why do they *p* of the blessings of Peace?	Maud, I. i.	21

prated.
I that *p* peace, when first I heard	Princess, v.	255

pratest.
'Thou *p* here where thou art least,	In Mem. xxxvii.	2

prattle.
full heart of yours Whereof you *p*,	Vivien	399

prattling.
P the primrose fancies of the boy,	The Brook	19
said the little novice *p* to her.	Guinevere	181
Unmannerly, with *p* and the tales	"	314

pray.
P, Alice, *p*, my darling wife,	Miller's D.	23
I *p* thee, pass before my light of life	Œnone	237
Where I may mourn and *p* .	Pal. of Art	292
P Heaven for a human heart,	L. C. V. de Vere	71
P for my soul. More things are .	M. d'Arthur	247
fast Whole Lents, and *p*, .	St S. Stylites	179
p Your highness would enroll them	Princess, i.	235
Yet I *p* Take comfort : .	" v.	76
Leave thou thy sister when she *p*'s,	In Mem. xxxiii.	5
p That we may meet the horsemen	Enid	1340
I *p* you of your courtesy, He being	"	1489
P you be gentle, *p* you let me be :	"	1555
Yea, God, I *p* you of your gentleness,	"	1558
I *p* you lend me one, if such you have	Elaine	193
let me hence I *p* you,'	"	766
P for my soul, and yield me burial.	"	1273
P for my soul thou too, Sir Lancelot,	"	1274
P for thy soul? Ay that will I.	"	1386
I *p* him, send a sudden Angel .	"	1414
P for him that he scape the doom	Guinevere	345
said the little novice, 'I *p* for both ;	"	347
P and be pray'd for ;	"	673
p them not to quarrel for her sake	En. Arden.	35
O hard *p* for those and pity them	Aylmer's F.	775
take this and *p* that he, Who wrote it	A Dedication	4

prayed.
With all my strength I *p* for both,	May Queen, ii.	31
He *p*, and from a happy place .	Two Voices	224
maiden-meek I *p* Concealment : .	Princess, iii.	118
p me not to judge their cause	" vii.	220
So *p* the men, the women .	Con.	7
had you cried, or knelt, or *p* to me,	Enid	1692
when of late you *p* me for my leave	"	1736
A hermit, who had *p*, labour'd and *p*,	Elaine	402
Pray and be *p* for, .	Guinevere	673

	POEM.	LINE.
then he *p* 'Save them from this,	En. Arden.	117
while he *p*, the master of that ship	"	119
P for a blessing on his wife and babes	"	168
P for a sign 'my Enoch is he gone?'	"	467
fingers into the wet earth, and *p*.	"	781

prayer.
If *p*'s will not hush thee.	Lilian	27
More things are wrought by *p* .	M. d'Arthur	247
knowing God, they lift not hands of *p*	"	252
gates of heaven with storms of *p*,	St S. Stylites	7
with hoggish whine They burst my *p*,	"	175
So keep I fair thro' faith and *p* .	Sir Galahad	23
pitying made a thousand *p*'s ;	Princess, i.	21
A liquid look on Ida, full of *p*,	" iv.	350
one part of sense not flint to *p*,	" vi.	166
grant my *p*. Help, father, brother	"	285
my *p* Was as the whisper of an air	In Mem. xvii.	2
Her eyes are homes of silent *p* .	" xxxii.	1
blest whose lives are faithful *p*'s,	"	13
built him fanes of fruitless *p* .	" lv.	12
breathing a *p* To be friends,	Maud, I. xix.	55
Not a bell was rung, not a *p* was read	" II. v.	24
only breathe Short fits of *p*, .	"	1004
wear out in almsdeed and in *p* .	Guinevere	679
Rejoicing at that answer to his *p* .	En. Arden.	127
evermore P from a living source .	"	802
me your *p*'s, for he is past your *p*'s,	Aylmer's F.	751
Blazon your mottos of blessing and *p*!	IV. ta Alexan.	12

prayer-prelude.
labour'd thro' His brief *p-p*, .	Aylmer's F.	628

praying.
P all I can, If prayers .	Lilian	26
p God will save Thy sailor .	In Mem. vi.	13
another, a lord of all things, *p* .	Maud, II. v.	32
she was ever *p* the sweet heavens	Enid	893
Blessing her, *p* for her .	En. Arden	880-5
p him To speak before the people	Aylmer's F.	607

preach.
I will not even *p* to you .	To J. S.	39
Whose foresight *p*'s peace, .	Love and Duty	34
Our own experience *p*'es. .	Will Water.	176
who would *p* it as a truth .	In Mem. iii.	11
p our poor little army down, .	Maud, I. x.	38
priest P an inverted scripture, .	Aylmer's F.	44

preached.
p An universal culture for the crowd	Princess, Pro.	108

preacher.
A harm no *p* can heal ; .	Maud, I. iv.	22
when the *p*'s cadence flow'd Softening	Aylmer's F.	729
p says, our sins should make us sad:	Grandmother	93

preaching.
p down a daughter's heart. .	Locksley H.	94
Not *p* simple Christ to simple men,	Sea Dreams	21

preamble.
prolong Her low *p* all alone .	Pal. of Art	174
tricks and fooleries, O Vivien, the *p*!	Vivien	115

precaution.
Creeps no *p* used, among the crowd,	Guinevere	515

precedent.
slowly down From *p* to *p*: 'You ask me why,' etc.		12
That codeless myriad of *p*, .	Aylmer's F.	436

precinct.
did I break Your *p*; .	Princess, iv.	402
in the *p*'s of the chapel-yard, .	Vivien	601

precious.
Love's too *p* to be lost .	In Mem. lxiv.	3

precipices.
from the lean and wrinkled *p*'s,	Princess, iv.	4
Went slipping down horrible *p*'s.	Enid	1228
Among the palms and ferns and *p*'s;	En. Arden.	594
breakers boom and blanch on the *p*'s,	Boädicea	76

precontract.
'Our king expects—was there no *p*?	Princess, iii.	191
as to *p*'s, we move, my friend, .	"	210
I wed with thee ! I bound by *p* .	" iv.	520
loth to render up My *p*, .	" v.	290

predoomed.
	POEM.	LINE.
most P her as unworthy.	Elaine	725

preëminence.
To assail this gray p of man!	Princess, iii.	218

prefer.
each p's his separate claim	In Mem. ci.	18

prefigured.
ah, you seem All he p.	Princess, iii.	193

prejudice.
Cut P against the grain: 'Love thou thy land,' etc.		22
leap the rotten pales of p	Princess, ii.	126
old-recurring waves of p Resmooth	" iii.	224

prelude ('s.)
with some p of disparagement	The Epic	49
This p has prepared thee.	Gardener's D.	267
The p to some brighter world.	Day-Dm.	252
Are but the needful p's to the truth:	Princess, Con.	74

prelude.
And I—my harp would p woe—	In Mem. lxxxvii.	9

preluded.
sweet breath P those melodious	D. of F. Wom.	6

premier.
city roar that hails P or king!	Princess, Con.	102

prepare.
but p: I speak: it falls.	Princess, ii.	206

prepared.
This prelude has p thee.	Gardener's D.	267
p The daily burden for the back.	In Mem. xxv.	3
let there be p a chariot-bier.	Elaine	1115
The rites p, the victim bared	The Victim	70

presage.
after seen The dwarfs of p:	Princess, iv.	427
No p, but the same mistrustful mood	Vivien	170

presence.
The light of thy great p;	Ode to Mem.	32
full-faced p of the Gods.	Œnone	78
hate Her p, hated both of Gods and men.	"	225
gather'd strength and grace And p,	In Mem. cii.	28
in his p I attend	" cxxv.	2
Your p will be sun in winter,	To F. D. Maurice	3
yea and by your state And p	Enid	431
her gentle p at the lists	"	795
by thy state And p I might guess	Elaine	183
Ev'n in the p of an enemy's fleet.	Guinevere	277
sitting at her side forgot Her p.	En. Arden	382
A splendid p flattering the poor roofs	Aylmer's F.	175
To dwell in p of immortal youth,	Tithonus	21
crimson'd all Thy p and thy portals,	"	57

presence room.
That morning in the p r I stood	Princess, i.	50

present (adj.)
Strange friend, past, p, and to be:	In Mem. cxxviii.	9
Yet p in his natal grove,	The Daisy	18

present (gift.)
'I can make no marriage p	L. of Burleigh	13
A p, a great labour of the loom	Princess, i.	43
Tost over all her p's petulantly:	Aylmer's F.	235

present (time.)
To glorify the p;	Ode to Mem.	2
Past and P wound in one,	Miller's D.	197
used Within the P	'Love thou thy land,' etc	3
Swarm'd in the golden p,	Gardener's D.	175
When I clung to all the p	Locksley H.	14
A night-long P of the Past	In Mem. lxx.	3
in the p broke the blow.	" lxxxiv.	26
Thou, like my p and my past,	" cxx.	19
carves A portion from the solid p,	Vivien	312

present (verb.)
To the young spirit p	Ode to Mem.	73
Each month is various to p	Two Voices	74
purpose to p them to the Queen,	Elaine	70

presented.
p Maid Or Nymph, or Goddess,	Princess, i.	193

presentiment.
	POEM.	LINE.
But spiritual p's,	In Mem. xci.	14

preserve.
P a broad approach of fame,	Ode on Well.	78

press (crowd.)
slanted o'er a p Of snowy shoulders	Princess, iv.	457
Made at me thro' the p,	" v.	511

press ('printing.)
happy sails and bear the P;	Golden Year	42
His party-secret, fool, to the p	Maud, II. v.	35

press (verb.)
p The maiden's tender palm	Talking O.	179
p me from the mother's breast.	Locksley H.	90
answer should one p his hands?	Two Voices	245
P es his without reproof:	L. of Burleigh	10
they p in from all the provinces	Princess, ii.	83
her father cease to p my claim,	" vii.	72
so p in, perforce Of multitude	Lucretius	167

press'd—prest.
bosoms p To little harps of gold	Sea-Fairies	3
Approaching, p you heart to heart.	Miller's D.	160
p the blossom of his lips to mine.	Œnone	76
hot lips p Close, close to thine	"	199
p on lips Less exquisite than thine.'	Gardener's D.	149
On to God's house the people p:	Two Voices	409
The gold-fringed pillow lightly p:	Day-Dm.	98
closer p, denied it not:	Princess, iv.	213
She p and p it on me—	" v.	273
p Their hands, and call'd them	" vi.	75
where warm hands have p and clos'd	In Mem. xiii.	7
What time his tender palm is p	" xliv.	2
when I p the cause, I learnt that James	The Brook	98
Lancelot ever p upon the maid	Elaine	907
evermore the daughter p upon her	En. Arden	480
to her meek and modest bosom p	Aylmer's F.	416
I p my footsteps into his,	Lucretius	118

pressing.
P up against the land,	Eleänore	112

pressure.
Yet seem'd the p thrice as sweet	Talking O.	145
I take the p of thine hand.	In Mem. cxviii.	12
days of difficulty And p,	En. Arden	254

presumptuous.
dishonourable, base, P!	Aylmer's F.	293
nor believe me Too p	Hendecasyllabics	16

pretence.
making vain p Of gladness,	In Mem. xxx.	6
Our greatest yet with least p,	Ode on Well.	29

pretenders.
To keep the list low and p's back,	Vivien	442

pretext.
Light p's drew me	Gardener's D.	188
some p held Of baby troth	Princess, v.	387
going to the king, He made this p,	Enid	33
with what face, after my p made	Elaine	142
king Will then allow your p,	"	153
made the p of a hindering wound,	"	581
when he learns Will well allow my p	"	585
Some p of fineness in the meal	En. Arden	338

prettiest.
'which was p, Best-natured?'	Princess, i.	230

prettily.
How p for his own sweet sake	Maud, I. vi.	51

pretty.
'P were the sight If our old halls	Princess, Pro.	139
while my p one, sleeps.	" ii.	463-71
Have all his p young ones educated,	En. Arden	146
This p, puny, weakly little one,	"	195
P enough, very p! but I was against it	Grandmother	7
And some are p enough,	The Flower	21

prevail.
Let her work p.	In Mem. cxiii.	4

prevailed.
won His path upward, and p,	Ode on Well.	214

prevailing.
	POEM.	LINE.
P in weakness, the coronach stole	Dying Swan	26

prey (for *bird of p, beast of p*, see *bird, beast*, etc.)
	POEM.	LINE.
stared, with his foot on the *p*	Poet's Song	12
The seeming *p* of cyclic storms	In Mem. cxvii.	11
is a world of plunder and *p*.	Maud, I. iv.	24
on a foray, rolling eyes of *p*,	Enid	1387
whole *p* is man's good name:	Vivien	578

prey (verb.)
p By each cold hearth	In Mem. xcvii.	17

price.
fourfield system, and the *p* of grain	Audley Ct.	33
learn the *p*, and what the *p* he ask'd,	The Brook	142
the colt would fetch its *p*;	"	149
a robe Of samite without *p*,	Enid	71
to give at last The *p* of half a realm	Elaine	1158

prick.
p Each leaf into a gall)	Talking O.	69
To *p* us on to combat	Princess, v.	294
the blood creeps, and the nerves *p*	In Mem. xlix.	2

pricked.
p with goads and stings;	Pal. of Art	150
corn-bin open, *p* my ears;	The Epic	45
while each ear was *p* to attend	Princess, vi.	263
p their light ears, and felt	Enid	1042
Geraint, who being *p* In combat	"	1349
I was *p* with some reproof,	"	1738
couch'd their spears and *p* their steeds	Elaine	478
a spear *P* sharply his own cuirass,	"	488
All ears were *p* at once,	"	720
peace which each had *p* to death.	Aylmer's F.	52
playing with the blade he *p* his hand,	"	239

pricking.
(Look at it) *p* a cockney ear.	Maud, I. x.	22

prickle (s.)
The furzy *p* fire the dells,	Two Voices	71

prickle (verb.)
P my skin and catch my breath,	Maud, I. xiv.	36

pride.
all the outworks of suspicious *p*;	Isabel	24
merriment of kingly *p*,	Arabian N's.	151
on herself her serpent *p* had curl'd.	Pal. of Art	237
Your *p* is yet no mate for mine,	L. C. V. de Vere	11
my brand Excalibur, Which was my *p*	M. d'Arthur	28
old Sir Robert's *p*, His books—	Audley Ct.	57
shame and *p*, New things and old,	Walk. to the M.	52
Self-blinded are you hy your *p*?	Two Voices	23
that abyss, or scornful *p*!	"	120
Wilt thou find passion, pain or *p*?	"	243
your Princess cramm'd with erring *p*,	Princess, iii.	86
Ring out false *p* in place and blood,	In Mem. cv.	21
The proud was half disarm'd of *p*,	" cix.	6
The fire of a foolish *p* flash'd	Maud, I. iv.	16
We are puppets, Man in his *p*	"	25
often a man's own angry *p*	" vi.	61
thought, is it *p*, and mused	" viii.	12
surely, now it cannot be *p*.'	"	13
Down with ambition, avarice,—	" x.	47
I to cry out on *p*	" xii.	17
that I am to be vext with his *p*!	" xiii.	5
the keeper was one, so full of *p*,	" II. v.	79
doubling all his master's vice of *p*,	Enid	195
will I fight him, and will break his *p*	"	221
break his *p* and have it of him,	"	416
break his *p*, and learn his name,	"	424
Refused her to him, then his *p* awoke;	"	448
But that his *p* too much despises me:	"	464
next day's tourney I may break his *p*.'	"	476
My *p* is broken: men have seen my fall.'	"	578
my *p* Is broken down, for Enid sees	"	589
when I was up so high in *p*,	"	1138
So wax'd it, that I believed myself	"	1683
dead love's harsh heir, jealous *p*?	Elaine	1389
My *p* in happier summers	Guinevere	532
To whom my false voluptuous *p*,	"	634
our *p* Looks only for a moment	Aylmer's F.	1
p Lay deeper than to wear it	"	121

	POEM.	LINE.
taking *p* in her, She look'd so sweet	Aylmer's F.	554
a time for these to flaunt their *p*?	"	770

priest.
if there be a *p*, a man of God,	St S. Stylites	211
As the *p*, above his book	Vision of Sin	117
one The silken *p* of peace,	Princess, v.	176
This faith has many a purer *p*,	In Mem. xxxvii.	3
dilettante, Delicate-handed *p*	Maud, I. viii.	11
with music, with soldier and with *p*,	Ode on Well.	81
his *p* Preach an inverted scripture	Aylmer's F.	43
'Gash thyself, *p*, and honour	"	644
The *P* in horror about his altar	The Victim	7
The *P* went out by heath and hill;	"	30
seem'd a victim due to the *p*.	"	37
The *P* exulted	"	38
now the *P* has judged for me.'	"	60
the *P* was happy	"	65-73

priestess.
O *P* in the vaults of Death,	In Mem. iii.	2

priesthood.
ever and aye the *P* moan'd	The Victim	23

prime (adj.)
from his father's vats, *P* which I knew;	Audley Ct.	27

prime (s.)
p Of good Haroun Alraschid	Arabian N's.	10, et pass.
gray *p* Make thy grass hoar.	Two Voices	65
Beyond her own material *p*?	"	378
Raw from the *p*, and crushing down	Princess, ii.	106
about my barren breast In the dead *p*:	" vi.	166
And at the spiritual *p*.	In Mem. xlii.	15
Dragons of the *p*, That tare each other	" lv.	22
The colours of the crescent *p*?	" cxv.	4

primrose.
p yet is dear, The *p* of the later year,	In Mem. lxxxiv.	118

prince (see Arac, Geraint.)
else the island *p*'s over-bold.	Lotos-E's.	120
the powers and *p*'s of this world,	St S. Stylites	184
bring the fated fairy *P*.	Day-Dm.	76
A fairy *P*, with joyful eyes,	"	107
be you The *P* to win her!	Princess, Pro.	220
'Then follow me, the *P*,' I answer'd,	"	220
A *P* I was, blue-eyed, and fair	" i.	1
She answer'd, 'then ye know the *P*?'	" ii.	35
in me behold the *P*	"	196
'O Sir, O *P*, I have no country;	"	200
to save A *p*, a brother?.	"	271
help my *p* to gain His rightful bride,	" iii.	114
I know the *P*, I prize his truth:	"	215
tho' your *P*'s love were like a God's	"	231
when we sent the *P* your way	" iv.	379
like a gentleman, And like a *p*:	"	507
Arranged the favour, and assum'd the *P*	"	579
could not slay Me, nor your *p*;	" v.	63
seems a gracious and a gallant *P*,	"	204
do much to gratify your *P*—	"	208
let your *P* our royal word upon it,	"	215
embattled squares, And squadrons of the *P*,	"	237
bore down a *P*, And Cyril, one.	"	507
Cyril seeing it push'd against the *P*,	"	522
a great cry, The *P* is slain.	" vi.	10
on to the tents: take up the *P*.'	"	262
may tend upon him with the *p*.'	"	295
but the *P* Her brother came;	"	317
Never, *P*; you cannot love me.'	" vii.	317
A princely people's awful *p*'s	The Daisy	39
a *P* indeed, Beyond all titles,	Ded. of Idylls	40
A tributary *p* of Devon	Enid	2
Allowing it, the *P* and Enid rode,	"	43
a *p* whose manhood was all gone	"	50
Low bow'd the tributary *P*,	"	174
P Had put his horse in motion	"	205
P's blood spirted upon the scarf	"	203
P, as Enid past him, fain To follow	"	375
the *P* and Earl Yet spake together,	"	384
prove her heart toward the *P*.'	"	513
Loudly spake the *P*, 'Forbear:	"	555
noble *p* who won our earldom back,	"	619

	POEM.	LINE.
being so beholden to the *P*,	*Enid*	623
P had found her in her ancient home:	"	644
you were talking sweetly with your *P*	"	698
mended fortunes and a *P's* bride:	"	718
the *P* Hath pick'd a ragged-robin	"	723
and, worse, might shame the *P*	"	726
As this great *p* invaded us	"	747
did her honour as the *P's* bride,	"	835
comrades, making slowlier at the *P—*	"	1016
I had brought his errant eyes Home	"	1094
thus he moved the *P* To laughter	"	1144
when the *P* was merry, ask'd Limours	"	1146
stout *P* bad him a loud good night	"	1210
P, without a word, from his horse fell.	"	1357
saw her Pass into it, turn'd to the *P*,	"	1735
So spake the King: low bow'd the *P*,	"	1708
call'd him the great *P* and man of men	"	1809
a *P* In the mid-night and flourish	*Elaine*	552
the *P* Reported who he was,	"	624
ride no longer wildly, noble *P*!	"	630
proud *P* who left the quest to me.	"	758
all the tale Of King and *P*,	"	820
I' and Lord am I In mine own land,	"	912
knew the *P* tho' marr'd with dust,	*Guinevere*	37
Sir Lancelot holp To raise the *P*,	"	47
P of peace, the Mighty God,	*Aylmer's F.*	669
heads of chiefs and *p's* fall so fast,	"	763
did greet Troy's wandering *P*	*On a Mourner*	33

princedom.
| this pretext, that his *p* lay | *Enid* | 33 |
| Forgetful of his *p* and its cares. | " | 54 |

princelike.
| thro' these *P* his bearing shone; | *Enid* | 545 |

princess (see Ida.)
The happy *p* follow'd him.	*Day-Dm.*	172
I wish That I were some great *P*	*Princess,Pro.*	134
some great *P*, six feet high,	"	218
Heroic seems our *P* as required—	"	223
betroth'd To one, a neighbouring *P*:	" i.	32
Who moves about the *P*;	"	75
The *P*; liker to the inhabitant	" ii.	21
edge unturnable, our Head, The *P*.	"	187
'Let the *P* judge Of that'	"	216
P should have been the Head,	" iii.	18
goes to inform The *P*:	"	47
your *P* cramm'd with erring pride	"	86
My *p*, O my *p*! true she errs,	" v.	91
'that afternoon the *P* rode	"	153
with some disdain Answer'd the *P*	" iv.	44
the Head, the *P*, O the Head!'	"	158
They haled as to the *P*	"	252
The *P* with her monstrous woman-guard,	"	540
She was a *P* too: and so I swore.	" v.	285
A gallant fight, a noble *p—*	*Con.*	19
Like our wild *P* with as wise a dream	"	69
shall dream I see my *p*.	*Enid*	752
as might well beseem His *p*,	"	759
miles of coast, A palace and a *p*,	*Vivien*	439-98

principle.
| *P's* are rain'd in blood: *'Love thou thy land,'* etc. | 80 |
| Some hidden *p* to move, | *Two Voices* | 133 |

print (s.)
| take the *p* Of the golden age— | *Maud*, I. i. | 29 |

print (verb.)
| hill and wood and field did *p* | *InMem.*lxxviii. | 7 |

prism.
| Make *p's* in every carven glass | *Day-Dm.* | 55 |

prisoner.
| and himself the *p* at the bar, | *Sea Dreams* | 172 |

privet.
| white as *p* when it flowers. | *Walk.to the M.* | 48 |

privilege.
| manlike end myself?— our *p—* | *Lucretius* | 229 |

prize (s.)
| 'Ride on! the *p* is near,' | *Sir Galahad* | 80 |

	POEM.	LINE.
earn our *p*, A golden broach:	*Princess*, iii.	283
The *p* of beauty for the fairest there.	*Enid*	485
were she the *p* of bodily force,	"	541
won it for thee, The *p* of beauty.'	"	555
tho' you won the *p* of fairest fair,	"	719
shook her pulses, crying 'Look, a *p*!'	"	972
since a diamond was the *p*,	*Elaine*	33
his the *p*, who wore the sleeve	"	500
'Advance and take your *p* The diamond;'	"	502
me nn *p's*, for my *p* is death!	"	505
p Untaken, crying that his *p* is death.'	"	530
deem this *p* of ours is rashly given:	"	540
Came not to us, of us to claim the *p*,	"	543
won he not your *p*?	"	572
bore the *p* and could not find	"	626
'Your *p* the diamond sent you	"	617

prize (verb.)
should I *p* thee, couldst thou last,	*Will Water.*	203
I know the Prince, I *p* his truth:	*Princess*, iii.	217
that she should *p* The soldier?'	" v.	166
sole men we shall *p* in the after-time	"	402
p the authentic mother of her mind.	"	423
prized him more Than who should *p* him	*Vivien*	16

prized.
loved the man, and *p* his work;	*M. d'Arthur*,Ep.	8
p my counsel, lived upon my lips:	*Princess*, iv.	274
p him more Than who should prize him	*Vivien*	15

prize-oxen.
| A lord of fat *p-o* and of sheep, | *Princess,Con.* | 86 |

process.
| widen'd with the *p* of the suns. | *Locksley II.* | 138 |
| Eternal *p* moving on, | *InMem.*lxxxi. | 5 |

procession.
| Let the long long *p* go | *Ode on Well.* | 15 |

proclaim.
From my high nest of penance here *p*	*St S. Stylites*	164
P the faults he would not show: *'You might have won'*		17
For many and many an age *p*	*Ode on Well.*	226
let *p* a joust At Camelot,	*Elaine*	77

proclaimed.
| Spake to the lady with him and *p*, | *Enid* | 552 |

proclaiming.
P social truth shall spread,	*InMem.*cxxxvi.	5
P his the prize, who wore the sleeve	*Elaine*	500
P Enoch Arden and his woes:	*En. Arden*	869

proclamation.
| sent His horns of *p* out | *Vivien* | 431 |

Proctor.
he had breath'd the *P's* dogs,	*Princess,Pro.*	113
prudes for *p's*, dowagers for deans,	"	141
Two *P's* leapt upon us, crying 'Names!'	" iv.	240

Procuress.
| *P* to the Lords of Hell. | *In Mem.* liii. | 16 |

prodigal.
| realms of upland, *p* in oil, | *Pal. of Art.* | 72 |
| *p* of all brain-labour | *Aylmer's F.* | 447 |

prodigious.
| a match as this! Impossible, *p*!' | *Aylmer's F.* | 315 |

Professor.
| we heard The grave *P*. | *Princess*, ii. | 340 |
| Sat compass'd with *p's*: | " | 421 |

proffer (s.)
P of royal power, ample rule	*Œnone*	109
nor did mine own Refuse her *p*,	*Princess*, vi.	327
Made *p* of the league of golden	*Vivien*	496

proffer (verb.)
| *p* these The brethren of our blood | *Princess*, vi. | 54 |

proffer'd.
| At one dear knee we *p* vows, | *In Mem* lxxviii. | 13 |

profit (s.)
| now to leaven play with *p*, | *Princess*, iv. | 111 |
| The lady Blanche: much *p* | " ii. | 222 |

	POEM.	LINE.
Will bloom to *p*, otherwhere.	*In Mem.*lxxxi.	12
What *p* lies in barren faith	" cvii.	5
surely was my *p* had I known :	*Guinevere*	651
With fuller *p*'s lead an easier life,	*En. Arden* .	145
With daily-dwindling *p*'s held	"	697

profit (verb.)
It little *p*'s that an idle king,	*Ulysses*	1
What *p*'s it to put An idle case?	*In Mem.*xxxv.	17
what *p*'s me my name Of greatest	*Elaine*	1403

progress.
| Our *p* falter to the woman's goal | *Princess,* vi. | 111 |
| With statelier *p* to and fro | *In Mem.*xcvii. | 22 |

prolong.
| *p* Her low preamble all alone, | *Pal. of Art* | 173 |

promenaded.
| With cypress *p*, | *Amphion* | 38 |

promise (s.)
the *p* of my bridal bower,	*D. of F. Wom.*	218
for the *p* that it closed :	*Locksley H.*	14
the crescent *p* of my spirit	"	187
words of *p* in his walk	*Day-Dm.*	123
falling in a land Of *p*;	*Princess,* ii.	124
hold Your *p*: all, I trust, may yet	"	340
other distance and the hues Of *p*;	" iv.	69
With *p* of a morn as fair;	*In Mem.* lxxxiii.	29
The *p* of the golden hours ?	" lxxxiv.	106
Knowing your *p* to me;	*Maud,*I.xxii.	50
Forgetful of his *p* to the king,	*Enid*	50
Bribed with large *p*'s the men who	"	453
bethought her of her *p* given	"	602
not leave her, till her *p* given—	"	605
Made *p*, that whatever bride I	"	783
you have my *p*—in a year;	*En. Arden*	434
before her face, Claiming her *p*.	"	455

promise (verb.)
p thee The fairest and most loving	*Œnone*	182
p (otherwise You perish)	*Princess,* ii.	275
might have shamed us : *p*, all.'	"	279
I *p* you Some palace in our land,	" iii.	145

promise-bounden.
| awed and *p-b* she forbore | *En. Arden* | 870 |

promised.
And Dora *p*, being meek.	*Dora*	44
What could we else, we *p* each ;	*Princess,* ii.	280
p help, and oozed All o'er	" v.	231
she *p* then to be fair.	*Maud,* I. i.	68
p more than ever king has given,	*Vivien*	436
She ceased : her father *p*;	*Elaine*	1124
Lancelot ever *p*, but remain'd	*Guinevere*	93
and once again She *p*.	*En. Arden*	906
p that no force, Persuasion, no,	*Aylmer's F.*	417

promising.
| Made such a voluble answer *p* all, | *En. Arden* | 903 |
| like a household god *P* empire : | *On a Mourner* | 31 |

promontory.
Who seems a *p* of rock,	*Will*	6
Saw once a great piece of a *p*,	*Enid*	1011
about the thymy *promontories*	*Sea Dreams*	38
tear an oak on a *p*	*Boädicea*	77

prompt.
| as *p* to spring against the pikes, | *Princess,* iii. | 269 |

prone.
She veil'd her brows, and *p* she sank,	*Princess,*v.	104
p from off her seat she fell,	*Guinevere*	411
falling *p* he dug His fingers .	*En. Arden*	780

pronest.
| that most impute a crime Arc *p* to it, | *Vivien* | 675 |

pronounce.
| Nor can *p* upon it | *Maud,* I. xx. | 16 |

pronounced.
| the King *P* a dismal sentence | *Vivien* | 441 |

prooemion.
| my rich *p* makes Thy glory fly | *Lucretius* | 70 |

proof.
	POEM.	LINE.
wall about thy cause With iron-worded *p*,	*To J.M.K.*	9
lest thy heart be put to *p*,	*Locksley H.*	77
here is *p* that you were miss'd	*Princess, Pro.*	175
give them surer, quicker *p*—	" iii.	265
p and echo of all human fame,	*Ode on Well.*	145
Tho' as yet there lived no *p*,	*Enid*	26
served for *p* that I was loved,	"	796
As *p* of trust. O Merlin, teach it me.	*Vivien*	180
The great *p* of your love :	"	204
prurient for a *p* against the grain,	"	337
p of trust—so often ask'd in vain !	"	769
by nine years' *p* we needs must learn	*Elaine*	63
flowery causes onward to the *p*	*Lucretius*	120

proofless.
| Spleen-born, I think, and *p*. | *Vivien* | 552 |

prop.
| falls A creeper when the *p* is broken, | *Aylmer's F.* | 810 |

proper.
| this is *p* to the clown, | *Princess,* iv. | 227 |

prophecy.
If aught of *p* be mine 'Clear-headed friend,' etc.	"	8
She rose upon a wind of *p*	*Princess,* ii.	154
might not seem thy *prophecies*	*In Mem.* xci.	13
For the *p* given of old	*Maud,* II. v.	42
A prophet certain of my *p*	*Enid*	814
if ancient *prophecies* Have err'd not	*Guinevere*	446

prophesied.
| Approvingly, and *p* his rise | *Aylmer's F.* | 474 |

prophesy.
| I *p* that I shall die to-night, | *St S. Stylites* | 217 |
| Dismiss me, and I *p* your plan | *Princess,* iv. | 335 |

prophesying.
| *p* change Beyond all reasons : | *Princess,* i. | 141 |

prophet.
heart was like a *p* to my heart,	*Gardener's D.*	62
fire on a masthead, P of storm :	*Princess,* iv.	256
The *p*'s blazon'd on the panes ;	*In Mem.* lxxxvi.	8
P, curse me the babbling lip,	*Maud,* II. v.	57
A *p* certain of my prophecy.	*Enid*	814
The people call you *p* :	*Vivien*	166
ill *p*'s were they all,	*Guinevere*	270
no *p* but the voice that calls	*Aylmer's F.*	741
Cries 'come up hither,' as a *p* to us	"	745

prophetess.
| have dash'd The passion of the *p*, | *Princess,* iv. | 122 |
| sang the terrible *p*'es. | *Boädicea* | 37 |

prophet-mind.
| Self-gather'd in her *p-m*, 'Of old sat Freedom,' etc. | | 6 |

propitiated.
| Taranis be *p*. | *Boädicea* | 16 |

proportion.
| gave him mind, the lordliest *P* | *Two Voices* | 20 |

proposed.
| Grave doubts and answers here *p*, | *In Mem.* xlvii. | 3 |

propping.
| in the naked hall, *p* his head, | *Enid* | 1429 |
| own dear bride *p* his head, | " | 1432 |

proprietress.
| Is she The sweet *p* a shadow? | *Princess,* ii. | 393 |

propt.
p on beds of amaranth and moly,	*Lotos-E's.*	133
broken statue *p* against the wall	*Princess,Pro.*	99
half on her mother *p*,	" iv.	348
So *p*, worm-eaten, ruinously old,	*En. Arden.*	694

prose (s.)
| I will work in *p* and rhyme, | *Talking O.* | 289 |
| Let raffs be rife in *p* and rhyme | *Will Water.* | 61 |

prose (verb.)
| *p* O'er books of travell'd seamen, | *Amphion* | 81 |

Proserpine.
| Like *P* in Enna, gathering flowers | *Ed. Morris* | 112 |

prospect.	POEM.	LINE.
Large range of *p* had the mother sow,	*Walk to the M.*	85
My *p* and horizon gone.	*In Mem.* xxxviii.	4

prosper.

While yon sun *p*'s in the blue,	*The Blackbird*	22
And the third time may *p*,	*M. d'Arthur*	130
thought he scarce would *p*	*Princess*, iii.	60
May she mix With men and *p* !	*In Mem.* cxiii.	3
I *p*, circled with thy voice ; .	" cxxix.	15

prosper'd.

throve and *p*: so three years She *p*:	*Pal. of Art*	217
And *p*; till a rout of saucy boys	*Princess*, v.	384
and so *p* that at last A luckier	*En. Arden*.	48

prosperity.

| In such a sunlight of *p*. | *Aylmer's F.* | 421 |

prosperous.

| Be *p* in this journey, as in all ; | *Enid* . | 225 |

protector.

| call'd him dear *p* in her fright, | *Vivien* | 795 |

protomartyr.

| falling, *p* of our cause, . | *Princess*, iv. | 484 |

proud.

know you *p* to bear your name,	*L.C.V. de Vere*	10
Too *p* to care from whence I came.	"	12
Thought her *p*, and fled over the sea;	*Ed. Gray*	14
P look'd the lips : .	*Princess*, i.	95
The *p* was half disarm'd of pride .	*In Mem.* cix.	6
believe it, in being so *p*;	*Maud*, I. iv.	17
turn thy wheel and lower the *p*;	*Enid* .	347
about her palace, *p* and pale.	*Elaine*	611
Their ancient name! they *might* be *p*;	*Aylmer's F.*	378
rolling o'er the palaces of the *p*,	"	636
mean Vileness, we are grown so *p*—	"	756
' O boy, tho' thou art young and *p*,	*Sailor Boy* .	7

prove.

sought to *p* how I could love,	*L.C.V. de Vere*	21
p me what it is I would not do.'	*Godiva*	27
To put together, part and *p*,	*Two Voices*	134
To feel, altho' no tongue can *p*,	"	445
To *p* myself a poet :	*Will Water.*	106
Pale again as death did *p*;	*L. of Burleigh*	66
Your language *p*'s you still the child.	*Princess*, ii.	44
p The Danaid of a leaky vase,	"	318
p Your knight, and fight your battle	" iv.	571
may thy mother *p* As true to thee	" vi.	186
Believing where we cannot *p*;	*In Mem. Pro.*	4
I long to *p* No lapse of moons	" xxvi.	2
Her care is not to part and *p*;	" xlvii.	5
and I shall *p* A meeting somewhere,	" lxxxiv.	98
Should *p* the phantom-warning true,	" xci.	12
Let Science *p* we are, and then	" cxix.	6
Or thou wilt *p* their tool	*Maud*, I. vi.	59
Well, if it *p* a girl .	" vii.	7-15
p h r heart toward the Prince.'	*Enid* .	513
s me way *p* such force in her	"	825
That he might *p* her to the uttermost	"	1437
yearn still more to *p* you mine,	*Vivien*	177
That I should *p* it on you unawares,	"	189
for men sought to *p* me vile,.	"	345
tho' you should not *p* it upon me,	"	537
the wish to *p* him wholly hers.'	"	714
They *p* to him his work :	*Elaine*	158
p No suffer than our falcon	"	652
would *p* A father to your children:	*En. Arden*.	407
She must *p* true : .	*Aylmer's F.*	364
call him, love, Before you *p* him, rogue	*Sea Dreams*	167
no truer Time himself Can *p* you	*A Dedication*	2

proved.

Hadst thou less unworthy *p*—	*Locksley H.*	63
By which our lives are chiefly *p*,	*In Mem.* civ.	14
The truths that never can be *p*	" cxxx.	10
nor *p* Since that dark day, a day like	*Con.*	7
have *p* we have hearts in a cause	*Maud*, III. vi.	25
p him everyway One of our noblest	*Enid* .	1757
prove him, rogue, and *p*, forgive.	*Sea Dreams*	167
but him I *p* impossible ; .	*Lucretius*	190

proven.	POEM.	LINE.
'Not *p*' Averill said,	*Aylmer's F.*	53
p or no, What cared he?	"	54

provender.

| For lust or lusty blood or *p*; | *Lucretius* | 195 |

proverb.

| This *p* flashes thro' his head, | *Day-Dm.* | 115 |

providence.

| sermonizing On *p* and trust in Heaven, | *En. Arden* | 205 |

province.

they press in from all the *p*'s,	*Princess*, ii.	83
O Love, thy *p* were not large,	*In Mem.* xlv.	13
tho' they sought 'Thro' all the *p*'s	*Enid* .	730
A *p* with a hundred miles of coast,	*Vivien*	436-97

proving.

| converse in the hall, *P* her heart : | *Enid* . | 521 |
| this cursed charm, Were *p* it on me | *Vivien* | 208 |

prow.

Sparkling flints beneath the *p*	*Arabian N's.*	52
round about the *p* she wrote	*L. of Shalott*, iv.	8
round the *p* they read her name,	"	44
Sleep, gentle heavens, before the *p*;	*In Mem.* ix.	14
and play About the *p* .	" xii.	18
The Lady's-head upon the *p*	*The Voyage*	11
Now nearer to the *p* she seem'd	"	67

prowess.

whereas I know Your *p*, Arac,	*Princess*, v.	394
Lancelot, and his *p* in the lists,	*Elaine*	83
His *p* was too wondrous.	"	541
old *p* were in aught decay'd	"	583
here and there a deed Of *p* done .	*Guinevere*	456

proxy-wedded.

| *p-w* with a bootless calf . | *Princess*, i. | 33 |

prude.

| *p*'s for proctors, dowagers for deans, | *Princess, Pro.* | 141 |

prudence.

a *p* to withhold .	*Isabel* .	15
by slow *p* to make mild	*Ulysses*	36
Let not your *p*, dearest, drowse,	*Princess*, ii.	318

pruned.

| Thro' crowded lilac-ambush trimly *p*; | *Gardener's D.* | 111 |

prurient.

| *p* for a proof against the grain | *Vivien* | 337 |

Prussian.

| Last, the *P* trumpet blew ; . | *Ode on Well.* | 127 |

pry.

| not to *p* and peer on your reserve, | *Princess*, iv. | 399 |

psalm.

with sound Of pious hymns and *p*'s	*St S. Stylites*	33
solemn *p*'s, and silver litanies	*Princess*, ii.	453
roll'd the *p* to wintry skies .	*In Mem.* lv.	11

Psyche.

Two widows, Lady *P*, Lady Blanche	*Princess*, i.	127
' Lady Blanche' she said, 'And Lady *P*.'	"	230
prettiest, Best-natured ? ' Lady *P*.	"	231
with your own, As Lady *P*'s pupils.'	"	237
Lady *P* will harangue The fresh arrivals	" ii.	81
crost the court To Lady *P*:	"	86
' Well then, *P*, take my life .	"	187
seen And heard the Lady *P*.	"	194
'are you that Lady *P*' (rep.)	"	219
While *P* watch'd them, smiling	"	344
learnt No more from *P*'s lecture .	"	371
long-limb'd lad that had a *P* too ;	"	384
dear is sister *P* to my heart,	" iii.	376
rail at Lady *P* and her side.	"	17
Herself and Lady *P* the two arms ;	"	19
Lady *P* will be crush'd ; .	"	47
Affirms your *P* thieved her theories	"	76
poor *P*' whom she drags in tow.'	"	87
climbing, Cyril kept With *P*,	"	337
P flush'd and wann'd and shook ;	" iv.	142
if her mother knew, Or *P*,	"	215
sent For *P*, but she was not there ;	"	218

324 CONCORDANCE TO

	POEM.	LINE.
call'd For *P's* child to cast it	*Princess,* iv.	219
where are *P,* Cyril? both are fled:	"	222
you planed her path To Lady *P,*	"	297
hear of it From Lady *P:*'	"	310
Had come on *P* weeping:	" v.	48
With *P's* babe, was Ida watching	"	501
With *P's* colour round his helmet,	"	523
Came *P,* sorrowing for Aglaïa,	" vi.	13
Ida stood With *P's* babe in arm:	"	15
P ever stole A little nearer,	"	116
turn'd half-round to *P* as she sprang	"	192
'Come hither, O *P,*' she cried out,	"	267
But *P* tended Florian:	" vii.	40
suit obtained At first with *P.*	"	57

puddled.
'So *p* as it is with favouritism.'	*Princess,* iii.	130

puff (s.)
upon the level in little *p's* of wind,	*Princess,* iv.	237

puff.
to *p* your idol-fires, '*Love thou thy land,*' etc.		63
the vessel *p's* her sail:	*Ulysses*	44

puff'd.
gust of wind *P* out his torch.	*Vivien*	581
p Her fairy nostril out:	"	697

pug.
a score of *p's* And poodles yell'd	*Ed. Morris*	119

puissance.
of her brethren, youths of *p*;	*Princess,* i.	36

pull.
p not down my palace towers,	*Pal. of Art*	293
P off, *p* off, the broach of gold,	*Lady Clare*	32
that make the rose *P* sideways	*In Mem.*lxxi.	11

pulpit-drone.
humming of the drowsy *p-d.*	*To J. M. K.*	10

pulpiteer.
To chapel; where a heated *p;*	*Sea Dreams*	20

pulsation.
Hung tranced from all *p*	*Gardener's D.*	255
Make me feel the wild *p*	*Locksley H.*	109
The wild *p* of her wings;	*In Mem.* xii.	4
The deep *p's* of the world,	" xciv.	40

pulse (beating.)
strike within thy *p's,* like a God's	*Œnone*	159
stirr'd with languid *p's* of the oar	*Gardener's D.*	41
And her whisper throng'd my *p's.*	*Locksley H.*	36
shot Light horrors thro' her *p's:*	*Godiva*	59
lent The *p* of hope to discontent.	*Two Voices*	450
desire to kneel, and shook My *p's,*	*Princess,* iii.	178
keep One *p* that beats true woman,	" vi.	164
My *p's* therefore beat again	*InMem.*lxxxiv.	57
every *p* of wind and wave	"	73
The measur'd *p* of racing oars ',	" lxxxvi.	21
The *p's* of a Titan's heart;	" cii.	32
keeps A thousand *p's* dancing,	" cxxiv.	16
my *p's* closed their gates with a shock	*Maud,* I. i.	15
Lord of the *p* that is lord of her breast	" xvi.	13
to live, long as my *p's* play	" xviii.	66
Is it gone? my *p's* beat—	" II. i.	36
shook her *p's,* crying, 'Look a prize!	*Enid*	922
stir the *p* With devil's leaps,	*Guinevere*	517
p's at the clamouring of her enemy	*Boädicea*	82

pulse (seeds.)
eating hoary grain and *p* the steeds	*Spec. of Iliad, Note*	

pun.
the *p,* the scurrilous tale—	*Aylmer's F.*	441

puny.
This pretty, *p,* weakly little one,—	*En. Arden*	195

pupil.
Some meeker *p* you must find	*L.C.V. de Vere*	18
with your own, As Lady Psyche's *p's.*'	*Princess,* i.	237
A patient range of *p's*;	" ii.	89
angled with them for her *p's* love:	" iii.	77

pupillage.
	POEM.	LINE.
sons of kings loving in *p*	*Vivien*	367

puppet.
P to a father's threat	*Locksley H.*	42
We are *p's,* Man in his pride	*Maud,* I. iv.	25

puppy.
blind and shuddering *puppies,*	*The Brook*	130

purchase.
sent mine host to *p* female gear;	*Princess,* i.	196
To *p* his own boat, and make a home	*En. Arden*	47
Yet he hoped to *p* glory,	*The Captain*	17

purchased.
p his own boat, and made a home	*En. Arden*	58

pure.
Her court was *p:*	*To the Queen*	25
A man more *p* and bold and just	*To J. S.*	31
May He within himself make *p!*	*M. d'Arthur*	245
all else of Heaven was *p*	*Gardener's D.*	78
but what lot is *p?*	*Walk. to the M.*	89
Make Thou my spirit *p* and clear	*St Agnes' Eve*	9
To make me *p* of sin.	"	32
Because my heart is *p.*	*Sir Galahad*	4
is not our cause *p?*	*Princess,* v.	393
As *p* and perfect as I say?	*In Mem.*xxiv.	12
What souls possess themselves so *p,*	" xxxii.	15
Her faith thro' form is *p* as thine,	" xxxiii.	9
love will last as *p* and whole	" xlii.	13
How *p* at heart and sound in head,	" xciii.	1
Flow thro' our deeds and make them *p—*	" cxxx.	4
Small and *p* as a pearl,	*Maud,* II. ii.	2
to a cause that I felt to be *p.*	" III. vi.	31
Which he has worn so *p* of blame	*Ode on Well.*	72
p as he from taint of craven guile	"	135
it chanced they are happy, being *p.*'	*Vivien*	595
all men true and leal, all women *p*;	"	643
Delicately *p* and marvellously fair,	*Elaine*	1360
P, as you ever wish your knights	"	1366
taken everywhere for *p,*	*Guinevere*	513
in that world where all are *p*	"	559

pureness.
kiss'd her with all *p,* brother-like,	*Enid*	1732
To doubt her *p* were to want a heart	*Elaine*	1368

purged.
When I have *p* my guilt'	*Pal. of Art*	296

purify.
and so thou *p* of thy soul	*Guinevere*	557

purity.
such a finish'd chasten'd *p,*	*Isabel*	41
wove coarse webs to snare her *p,*	*Aylmer's F.*	760

purl.
To *p* o'er matted cress	*Ode to Mem.*	59

purlieu.
dusky *p's* of the law.	*In Mem.*lxxxviii.	12

purple.
Shot over with *p,* and green,	*Dying Swan*	20
long *p's* of the dale.	*A Dirge*	31
p blazon'd with armorial gold.	*Godiva*	52
made No *p* in the distance, mystery	*Princess,* vi.	179
red with spirted *p* of the vats	" vii.	187
The *p* from the distance dies,	*In Mem.*xxxviii.	3
And blossom in *p* and red	*Maud,* I.xxii.	74
thistle bursting Into glossy *p's,*	*Ode on Well.*	207
In crimsons and in *p's* and in gems	*Enid*	10

purpled.
furr'd and *p,* still the clown	*Princess,* iv.	228

purple-frosty.
Behind a *p-f* bank	*In Mem.* cvi.	3

purple-skirted.
the *p-s* robe Of twilight	*The Voyage*	21

purple-spiked.
standing near *P-s* lavender	*Ode to Mem.*	110

purport.
with such a chain Of knitted *p,*	*Two Voices*	168
if your Highness keep Your *p,*	*Princess,* iii.	196

purpose.	POEM.	LINE.
see My far-off doubtful *p.*	*Œnone*	247
lest the gems Should blind my *p,*	*M. d'Arthur*	153
my *p* holds To sail beyond the	*Ulysses*	59
He will answer to the *p,*	*Locksley II.*	55
one increasing *p* runs,	"	137
clench'd his *p* like a blow!	*Princess,* v.	296
Unshaken, clinging to her *p,*	"	334
like a broken *p* waste in air:	" vii.	199
P in *p,* will in will,	"	287
Such splendid *p* in his eyes,	*In Mem.* lv.	10
I embrace the *p* of God,	*Maud,* III. vi.	59
one main *p* ever at my heart)	*Enid*	1679
for my main *p* in these jousts,	"	1685
and my *p* three years old,	"	1697
With *p* to present them to the Queen. *Elaine*		70
hast spoilt the *p* of my life.	*Guinevere*	450
mine helpmate, one to feel My *p.*	"	482
vast design and *p* of the King	"	662
A *p* evermore before his eyes,	*En. Arden*	45
no heart to break his *p's* To Annie.	"	155
let me hold my *p* till I die	"	876
Faded with morning, but his *p* held *Aylmer's F.*		412
purposed.		
p with ourself Never to wed	*Princess,* ii.	46
purse.		
loosed a mighty *p,* Hung at his belt *Enid*		871
purse-month.		
Maud with her sweet *p-m*	*Maud,* I. i.	71
pursue.		
'mine enemies *P* me,	*Guinevere*	139
pursued.		
out of breath, as one *p.*	*Princess,* iv.	356
he *p* her calling 'Stay a little!	*Elaine*	680
my eyes *P* him down the street	*Sea Dreams*	161
who is dead?' 'The man your eye *p.* "		262
pursuer.		
I heard the puff'd *p.*	*Princess,* iv.	246
pursuit.		
body half flung forward in *p,*	*Aylmer's F.*	537
push.		
p thee forward thro' a life of shocks *Œnone*		160
P off, and sitting well in order smite *Ulysses*		58
To *p* my rival out of place	*Princess,* iv.	316
Here, *p* them out at gates.'	"	527
Should *p* beyond her mark	*In Mem.* liii.	15
that *p'es* us off from the board,	*Maud,* I. iv.	27
Did he *p,* when he was uncurl'd	" II. ii.	18
No will *p* me down to the worm,	*The Window*	115
push'd.		
behold thy bride,' She *p* me from *Love and Duty*		50
p the happy season back,—	*Golden Year*	65
p with lances from the rock	*Princess, Pro.*	46
P her flat hand against his face	" ii.	345
but *p* alone on foot	" iv.	178
from her face They *p* us,	"	533
p by rude hands from its pedestal	" v.	55
Cyril seeing it, *p* against the Prince,	"	522
And *p* at Philip's garden-gate.	*The Brook*	83
door, *P* from without, drave backward *Enid*		1122
pushing.		
p could move The chair of Idris	*Enid*	542
p his black craft among them all	*Vivien*	413
Puss.		
'petty Ogress,' and 'ungrateful *P,'* *Princess, Pro.*		156
put.		
T *p* together, part and prove	*Two Voices*	134
'Bring the dress and *p* it on her,	*L. of Burleigh*	95
after that *P* on more calm	*Princess,* vi.	198
He *p* our lives so far apart	*In Mem.* lxxxi.	15
This huckster *p* down war	*Maud,* I. x.	44
p on your worst and meanest dress *Enid*		130, 848
p off to please me this poor gown,	"	1527
in one moment, she *p* forth the charm *Vivien*		816

	POEM.	LINE.
But she—she *p* him off—	*En. Arden*	457
Suddenly *p* her finger on the text	"	493
Then take it, love, and *p* it by	*The Ringlet*	11
P forth and feel a gladder clime	*On a Mourner*	15
putting.		
made a Gardener *p* in a graff,	*Vivien*	329
puzzle.		
keep it like a *p* chest in chest	*Vivien*	504
P. W.		
Remains the lean *P. W.* on his tomb: *The Brook*		192
pyebald.		
three *p's* and a roan.	*Walk. to the M.*	104
pyramid.		
The Rhodope, that built the *p,*	*Princess,* ii.	63
Pyrenean.		
Beyond the *P* pines;	*Ode on Well.*	113

Q

quail.		
q and pigeon, lark and leveret lay, *Audley Ct.*		23
Quaker.		
Whatever the *Q* holds, from sin:	*Maud,* II. v.	92
quantity.		
All in *q,* careful of my motion, *Hendecasyllabics*		5
quarrel (s.)		
Why? What cause of *q?*	*The Brook*	97
call it lovers' *q's,* yet I know	*Enid*	1173
In all your *q's* will I be your knight. *Elaine*		957
remember a *q* I had with your father, *Grandmother*		21
quarrel (verb.)		
With time I will not *q:*	*Will Water.*	206
Would *q* with our lot;.	"	216
pray them not to *q* for her sake,	*En. Arden.*	35
quarrell'd.		
She and James had *q.*	*The Brook*	96
if they *q,* Enoch stronger-made	*En. Arden.*	30
quarry.		
but as a block Left in the *q;*	*Princess,* vii.	216
Nor *q* trench'd along the hill,	*In Mem.* xcix.	11
quart.		
I've 'ed my *q* ivry market-noight	*N. Farmer*	8
quarter-sessions.		
A *q-s* chairman, abler none;	*Princess, Con.*	90
quay.		
like a hive all round the narrow *q,* *Audley Ct.*		4
rock to rock upon the glooming *q,*	"	83
And I went down unto the *q,*	*In Mem.* xiv.	3
queen.		
In her as Mother, Wife, and *Q;*	*To the Queen*	28
q of marriage, a most perfect wife *Isabel*		28
From me, Heaven's *Q,* Paris, to thee *Œnone*		125
watch'd by weeping *q's.*	*Pal. of Art*	108
were you *q* of all that is,	*L. C. V. de Vere*	19
I'm to be *Q* o the May. mother, *May Queen,* i. 4, *et pass.*		
to see me made the *Q;*	"	26
on the green they made me *Q* of May: "		ii. 10
A *q'* with swarthy cheeks	*D. of F. Wom.*	127
I died a *Q,*	"	161
Three *Q'* with crowns of gold—	*M. d'Arthur*	193
those three *Q's* Put forth their hands,	"	205
beggar maid shall be my *q!'*	*Beggar Maid*	16
swarm as bees about their *q*	*Princess,* i.	30
from the *Q's* decease she brought her up	" iii	70
good *Q,* her mother, shore the tress	" vi.	97
and made myself a *Q* of farce!	" vii.	223
Oherself, Grateful to Prince Geraint *Enid*		14
And Enid loved the *Q,*	"	10
when a rumour rose about the *Q.*	"	24
Q petitioned for his leave	"	154

	POEM.	LINE.
she return'd Indignant to the Q;	Enid	203, 414
Q Sent her own maiden to demand	"	410
this great insult done the Q.'	"	425, 571
pardon for that insult done the Q,	"	583
there the Q forgave him easily.	"	592
there be made known to the statelyQ,	"	607
stately Q whose name was Guinevere,	"	667
His princess, or indeed the stately q,	"	739
great Q. In words whose echo lasts,	"	781
our kind Q, No hand but hers,	"	787
Look'd the fair Q, but up the vale	"	831
there the Q army'd me like the sun:	"	1549
penance the Q laid upon me	"	1702
you were often there about the Q,	"	1717
great Q once more embraced her friend	"	1795
Q's fair name was breath'd upon,	"	1799
a rumour rife about the Q,	Vivien	10
like the fair pearl-necklace of the Q,	"	301
made her Q: but those isle-nurtur'd	"	420
charm, which being wrought upon the Q	"	434
as noble, as their Q was fair?	"	458
taught the King to charm the Q	"	491
that commerce with the Q, I ask you,	"	620
purpose to present them to the Q,	Elaine	70
And the Q Lifted her eyes,	"	84
Love-loyal to the least wish of the Q	"	90
were not once so wise, My Q,	"	105
for Q's and not for simple maids.'	"	231
only Q's are to be counted so,	"	238
guilty love he bane the Q,	"	245
when he saw the Q, embracing ask'd,	"	569
the Q amazed ' Was he not with you?	"	571
Ill news, my Q, for all who love him,	"	596
Some read the King's face, some the Q's,	"	723
suddenly on the Q with the sharp news.	"	726
to drink to Lancelot and the Q,	"	733
Q who sat With lips severely placid	"	735
any mouth to gape for save a Q's—	"	771
there the Q herself will pity me,	"	1053
loves the Q, and in an open shame:	"	1076
Lancelot and the Q and all the world,	"	1101
deck it like the Q's For richness,		
and me also like the Q	"	1112
go in state to court, to meet the Q.	"	1118
sent him to the Q Bearing his wish,		
whereto the Q agreed	"	1162
piece of pointed lace, In the Q's shadow,	"	1169
Lancelot kneeling utter'd, 'Q, Lady	"	1173
but, my Q, I hear of rumours	"	1183
half turn'd away, the Q Brake	"	1190
as Arthur's q I move and rule:	"	1215
an arm to which the Q's Is haggard,	"	1220
the wild Q, who saw not, burst away	"	1237
she sleeps—the Fairy Q, so fair!	"	1248
last the Q herself and pitied her:	"	1262
Then said the Q (Sea was her wrath,	"	1299
'Q, she would not be content	"	1304
mass, and rolling music, like a Q.	"	1326
the Q, Who mark'd Sir Lancelot	"	1338
pass on, my Q, forgiven.'	"	1343
a love Far tenderer than my Q's.	"	1386
Q, if I grant the jealousy as of love,	"	1390
Q who sat betwixt her best Enid.	Guinevere	28
Sir Lancelot told This matter to the Q,	"	54
the stately Q abode For many a week,	"	144
when she heard, the Q look'd up,	"	162
first she came, wept the sad Q.	"	180
strong castle where he holds the Q;	"	192
For his own self, and his own Q,	"	195
the good King and his wicked Q.	"	207
were I such a King with such a Q,	"	208
to her own sad heart mutter'd the Q.	"	211
ere the coming of the Q.'	"	221-31
thought the Q within herself again;	"	222
Before the coming of the sinful Q,'	"	268
snake the Q and somewhat bitterly.	"	269
This evil work of Lancelot and the Q?	"	305
thought the Q 'lo! they have set her on	"	306
the pale Q look'd up and answer'd her.	"	325
a mournful answer made the Q,	"	339
Such as they are, were you the sinful Q.'	"	351

	POEM.	LINE.
Fired all the pale face of the Q,	Guinevere	355
stood before the Q As tremulously	"	361
Q had added 'get thee hence'	"	364
the Q immersed in such a trance,	"	398
Rose the pale Q, and in her anguish	"	580
he gave them charge about the Q,	"	585
Insipid as the Q upon a card;	Aylmer's F.	28
each man murmur'd 'O my Q,	The Voyage	63
You my Q of the wrens! (rep.)	The Window	81
I'll be the King of the Q of the wrens	"	84
queenhood.		
with all grace Of womanhood and q	Enid	176
quench'd.		
The fame is q that I foresaw,	In Mem.lxxii.	5
his greatness whom she q.	Vivien	67
quencher.		
You would-be q's of the light to be,	Princess, iv.	515
quenching.		
q lake by lake and tarn by tarn.	Princess, vii.	25
query.		
let my q pass Unclaim'd,	The Brook	104
He put the self-same q,	Enid	269
all *queries* touching those at home	Aylmer's F.	465
quest.		
upon this fatal q Of honour,	Enid	1551
cease not from your q, until you find.'	Elaine	547
sally forth In q of whom he knew not,	"	560
with his diamond, wearied of the q,	"	613
who he was, and on what q Sent,	"	625
lose the q he sent you on,	"	652
let me leave My q with you;	"	688
wearied of the Q Leapt on his horse,	"	699
go no more On q of mine,	"	713
Lest I be found as faithless in the q	"	757
proud Prince who left the q to me,	"	758
q Assign'd to her not worthy of it,	"	820
question (s.)		
q unto whom 'twere due;	Œnone	80
smiling, put the q by.	Day-Dm.	164
your q now, Which touches the	Princess, iii.	304
this q of your troth remains:	" v.	269
the q settled die.	"	307
In many a subtle q versed,	In Mem xcv.	6
Nor thro' the q's men may try,	" cxxiii.	7
after madness acted q ask'd;	Enid	1661
q rose About the founding.	Vivien	260
question (verb.)		
'Twere well to q him, and try	Talking O.	27
questioned.		
She, q if she knew us men,	Princess, iv.	212
or could answer him, If q,	En. Arden	655
questioner.		
little time for idle q's.'	Enid	272
quick (adj.)		
We are twice as q!'	Princess, Pro.	137
—they say that women are so q—	En. Arden	405
quick (flesh.)		
I myself A Tory to the q.	Walk. to the M.	73
quick (hawthorn.)		
Rings Eden thro' the budded q's,	In Mem.lxxxvii.	2
burgeons every maze of q	" cxiv.	2
quicken.		
bloodless east began To q to the sun,	Enid	535
Your wailing will not q him:	"	1398
mountain q's into Nymph and Faun	Lucretius	187
quickened.		
Be q with a livelier breath,	In Mem. cxxi.	13
quickening.		
slowly q into lower forms;	Vision of Sin	210
quicker.		
Her hands are q unto good:	In Mem.xxxiii.	10
It may be, I am q of belief	Elaine	1198

quick-falling.   POEM.   LINE.
q-f dew Of fruitful kisses, . . *Œnone* . 200
quickset-screens.
Fills out the homely *q-s* . . *On a Mourner* 6
quiet.
Q, dispassionate, and cold, . . *A Character* 28
the noonday *q* holds the hill ; . *Œnone* . 24
Divided in a graceful *q*— . . *Gardener's D.* 153
all was *q* ; from the bastion'd walls *Princess*, i. 106
This look of *q* flatters thus. . . *In Mem.* x. 10
there, is the village, and looks how *q Maud*, 1. iv. 7
Making a treacherous *q* in his heart, *Elaine* . 870
blasting the long *q* of my breast . *Lucretius* . 162
quinquenniad.
Or gay *q*'s would we reap . . *Day-Dm.* . 235
quinsy.
' A *q* choke thy cursed note !' . *The Goose* . 29
quintessence.
As with the *q* of flame, . . *Arabian N's.* 123
pure *q*'s of precious oils . . *Pal. of Art* 187
The flower and *q* of change . . *Day-Dm.* . 236
He had known a man, a *q* of man, *Aylmer's F.* 388
quip.
all his merry *q*'s are o'er. . . *D. of the O. Year* 29
quire.
low matin-chirp hath grown Full *q*, *Love and Duty* 96
O Milan, O the chanting *q*'s, . *The Daisy* . 57
quirk.
With twisted *q*'s and happy hits *Will Water.* 189
quit require.)
ill then should I *q* your brother's . *Elaine* . 940
quit (leave.)
q the post Allotted by the Gods ; *Lucretius* . 148
quitch.
the vicious *q* Of blood and custom *Enid* . 1751
quiver.
Willows whiten, aspens *q*, . . *L. of Shalott*, i. 10
A thousand moons will *q* ; . . *A Farewell* . 14
quiver'd.
Her eyelid *q* as she spake. . . *Miller's D.* . 144
death *q* at the victim's throat ; . *D. of F. Wom.* 115
quivering.
heart of Britain, leave it gorily *q* ? *Boädicea* . 12
Sets all the tops *q*— . . . *Lucretius* . 186
quoit.
Q. tennis, ball—no games? . . *Princess*, iii. 199
quoloty.
Looük 'ow *q* smoiles . . . *N. Farmer* . 53
quoie.
—it makes me sick to *q* him— . *Sea Dreams* 155
Love, let me *q* these lines, . . „ . 177
quoted.
q odes, and jewels five-words-long *Princess*, ii. 355

R

raäte.
I wur niver agin the *r.* . . . *N. Farmer* . 16
raäved.
an' *r* an' rembled un oot. . . *N. Farmer* . 32
rabbit.
The *r* fondles his own harmless face, *Aylmer's F.* 851
rabble.
soft and milky *r* of womankind, . *Princess*, vi. 290
race (lineage, etc.)
We were two daughters of one *r* . *The Sisters* . 1
Chanted from an ill-used *r* of men *Lotos-E's.* . 165
my *r* Hew'd Ammon, hip and thigh *D. of F. Wom.* 237
mingle with the human *r*, 'Of old sat Freedom,' etc. 10
Unequal laws unto a savage *r*, . *Ulysses* . 4

she shall rear my dusky *r.* . . *Locksley H.* 168
Becomes dishonour to her *r*— . *Two Voices* 255
Who took a wife, who rear'd his *r*, „ . 328
Some legend of a fallen *r* . . „ . 352
r Of giants living, each, . . *Princess*, iii. 251
springs the crowning *r* of humankind „ vii. 272
That ' Loss is common to the *r*', . *In Mem.* vi. 2
Comes out —to some one of his *r*; „ lxxiii. 4
Will shelter one of stranger *r*, . „ ci. 4
that great *r*, which is to be . . „ cii. 35
The herald of a higher *r*, . . „ cxvii. 14
throned *r*'s may degrade ; . . „ cxxvii. 7
Betwixt us and the crowning *r* . *Con.* 128
her father, the wrinkled head of the *r? Maud*, i. iv. 13
in his force to be Nature's crowning *r* „ . 33
At war with myself and a wretched *r*, „ x. 35
That huge scapegoat of the *r* . „ xiii. 42
whole weak *r* of venomous worms, „ 11. i. 46
while the *r*'s of mankind endure, *Ode on Well.* 219
O purblind *r* of miserable men . *Enid* . 850
in their chairs set up a stronger *r* „ . 1783
' Some other *r* of Averills' . . *Aylmer's F.* 54
Nor of what *r*, the work ; . . „ . 224
with her the *r* of Aylmer, past. . „ . 577
link'd their *r* with times to come— „ . 773
made by these the last of all my *r* „ . 791
those who sorrow'd o'er a vanish'd *r* „ . 844
vary from the kindly *r* of men, . *Tithonus* . 29
race (running, etc.)
Till all my widow'd *r* be run (xvii. 20) *In Mem.* ix. 18
He still outstripp'd me in the *r*; „ xli. 2
in her onward *r* For power. . „ cxiii. 14
race (verb.)
and *r* By all the fountains ; . *Princess*, iv. 243
raced.
flew kite, and *r* the purple fly, . *Princess*, ii. 230
inward *r* the scouts With rumour „ v. 107
races.
how The *r* went, . . . *Audley Ct.* . 30
Rachel.
Fairer than *R* by the palmy well, *Aylmer's F.* 679
racing.
Clouds that are *r* above, . . *The Window* 6
rack.
furrowing into light the mounded *r*, *Love and Duty* 97
rack'd.
r with pangs that conquer trust ; . *In Mem.* xlix. 6
radiate.
where the passions meet, Whence *r: In Mem.* lxxxvii. 5
raff.
Let *r*'s be rife in prose and rhyme *Will Water.* 61
rag (tatters.)
Her *r*'s scarce held together ; . *The Goose* . 2
one *r*, disprinced from head to heel *Princess*, v. 29
And him, the lazar, in his *r*'s ; . *In Mem.* cxxvi. 10
flout and scorn By dressing it in *r*'s ? *Enid* 1524
this poor gown, This silken *r*, . „ 1528
and throng, their *r*'s and they, . *Lucretius* . 170
rag (stone.)
horneblende, *r* and trap and tuff, . *Princess*, iii. 344
rage (s.)
His early *r* Had force . . . *Miller's D.* . 192
blind with *r* she miss'd the plank . *Princess*, iv. 189
I remain on whom to wreak your *r* „ . 331
The captive void of noble *r*, . *In Mem.* xxvii. 2
her brother ran in his *r* to the gate *Maud*, II. i. 12
With inarticulate *r*, and making signs *En. Arden* 641
rage (verb.)
R like a fire among the noblest names, *Vivien* 651
raged.
as my father *r* in his mood . . *Maud*, 1. i. 53
I *r* against the public liar ; . . *The Letters* 26
ragged.
Too *r* to be fondled on her lap, . *Aylmer's F.* 686

ragged-robin.	POEM.	LINE.
Hath pick'd a *r-r* from the hedge,	*Enid* .	. 724
raging.		
The wind is *r* in turret and tree. .	*The Sisters*	21
What! am I *r* alone . . .	*Maud*, I. i.	53
shot at, slightly hurt *R* return'd:	*Aylmer's F.*	549
She heard him *r*, heard him fall; .	*Lucretius* .	272
raid.		
booty from the morning's *r*;	*Enid* .	1413
rail (s.)		
take their leave, about the garden *r's*	*Princess, Con.*	38
In such discourse we gain'd the garden *r's*. "		80
rail (verb.)		
To *r* at Lady Psyche and her side	*Princess*, iii.	17
He loved to *r* against it still,	*In Mem.* lxxxviii.	38
Who shall *r* Against her beauty ? "	cxiii.	1
fight for the good, than to *r* at the ill ;	*Maud*, III. vi.	57
if she had it, would she *r* on me .	*Vivien* .	659
rail'd.		
still she *r* against the state of things.	*Princess*, iii.	68
raillery.		
feigning pique at what she call'd The *r*,	*Princess*, iv.	565
railway.		
In the steamship, in the *r*, .	*Locksley H.*	166
A petty *r* ran . . .	*Princess, Pro.*	74
raiment.		
in her *r's* hem was traced in flame	*The Poet*	45
In diverse *r* strange: . .	*Pal. of Art*	168
In *r* white and clean. . .	*St Agnes' Eve*	24
A woman-post in flying *r*, .	*Princess*, iv.	357
Loosely robed in flying *r*. .	*Boädicea*	37
rain (s.)		
R makes music in the tree .	*A Dirge*	26
Wash'd with still *r's* . .	*Circumstance*	7
Autumn *r's* Flash in the pools	*Œnone* .	201
With shadow-streaks of *r*, .	*Pal. of Art*	76
There will not be a drop of *r*. .	*May Queen*, ii.	35
falls not hail, or *r*, or any snow,	*M. d'Arthur*	260
tho' beneath a whispering *r*	*Gardener's D.*	261
R, wind, frost, heat, hail, damp,	*St S. Stylites*	18
I swear, by leaf, and wind, and *r*,	*Talking O.* .	81
Low thunders bring the mellow *r*,	"	279
when the *r* is on the roof .	*Locksley H.*	78
r or hail, or fire or snow ; .	"	193
winter *r's* that beat his grave. .	*Two Voices*	261
Came in a sun-lit fall of *r*. .	*Sir L. and Q. G.*	4
Old plash of *r's*, and refuse .	*Vision of Sin*	212
The *r* had fallen, the Poet arose	*Poet's Song*.	1
and now a *r* of pearls . .	*Princess, Pro.*	62
blowzed with health, and wind, and *r*,	" iv.	260
ghastly thro' the drizzling *r* .	*In Mem.* vii.	11
A flower beat with *r* and wind,	" viii.	15
takes the sunshine and the *r's*, .	" x.	14
flakes Of crimson or in emerald *r*, .	" xcvii.	35
and fed With honey'd *r* . .	*Maud*, I. xviii.	21
and the heavens fall in a gentle *r*,	" II. i.	41
Remember what a plague of *r*; .	*The Daisy* .	50
r at Reggio, *r* at Parma (rep.) .	"	51
before the useful trouble of the *r*:	*Enid* .	1619
in the noon of mist and driving *r*,	*Vivien* .	486
r of heaven, and their own bitter tears	*Aylmer's F.*	428
Tears, and the careless *r* of heaven,	"	429
With ashy *r's*, that spreading made	*The Voyage*	43
Bullets fell like *r*; . .	*The Captain*	46
thrice I heard the *r* Rushing : .	*Lucretius* .	26
The mist and the *r*, the mist and the *r*	*The Window*	106
rain (verb.)		
R out the heavy mist of tears, .	*Love and Duty*	43
lightly *r* from ladies' hands. .	*Sir Galahad*	12
To *r* an April of ovation . .	*Princess*, vi.	50
rainbow.		
The *r* forms and flies on the land	*Sea-Fairies*	25
The *r* lives in the curve of the sand	"	27
r hangs on the poising wave. .	"	29
Between the *r* and the sun. .	*Margaret* .	13
leap the *r's* of the brooks, . .	*Locksley H.*	171

	POEM.	LINE.
Broke, like the *r* from the shower,	*Two Voices*	444
Flung the torrent *r* round : .	*Vision of Sin*	32
This flake of *r* flying on the highest	*Princess*, v.	309
like a *r* fall'n upon the grass .	*Elaine* .	430
rain'd.		
Principles are *r* in blood ; *'Love thou thy land,' etc.*		80
dimly *r* about the leaf Twilights .	*Audley Ct.* .	80
and there *r* a ghastly dew .	*Locksley H.*	123
R thro' my sight its overflow .	*Two Voices*	45
a giant's flail, The large blows *r*, .	*Princess*, v.	490
raining.		
Heavily the low sky *r* . .	*L. of Shalott*, iv.	4
Hold swollen clouds from *r*, .	*D. of F. Wom.*	11
raise.		
Thou wilt never *r* thine head .	*A Dirge*	19
R thy soul; Make thine heart ready	*Gardener's D.*	267
the time Is come to *r* the veil. .	"	269
could *r* One hope that warm'd me	*Two Voices*	121
To *r* a cry that lasts not long, .	*In Mem.* lxxiv.	10
Sir Lancelot holp To *r* the Prince,	*Guinevere* .	47
Most can *r* the flowers now, . .	*The Flower*	19
raised.		
when I *r* my eyes, above . .	*Miller's D.*	85
Paris had *r* his arm . .	*Œnone* .	185
She *r* her piercing orbs, . .	*D. of F. Wom.*	171
r the blinding bandage from his eyes:	*Princess*, i.	240
At the word, they *r* A tent of satin,	" iii.	329
r the cloak from brows as pale .	" v.	70
Behold a man *r* up by Christ ! .	*In Mem.* xxxi.	13
r her head with lips comprest, .	*The Letters*	19
R my own town against me .	*Enid* .	457
arose, and *r* Her mother too .	"	535
r and laid him on a litter-bier .	"	1414
He *r* his eyes and saw The tree .	*Vivien* .	787
He *r* his head, their eyes met .	*Elaine*	1303
silk pavilions of King Arthur *r* .	*Guinevere* .	391
many more when Modred *r* revolt	"	438
when Annie would have *r* him .	*En. Arden*.	231
'You *r* your arm, you tumbled down	*Sea Dreams*	137
raiser.		
A *r* of huge melons and of pine, .	*Princess, Con.*	87
raising.		
hear Her own death-scaffold *r* .	*En. Arden* .	175
raked.		
And *r* in golden barley. . .	*Will Water.*	128
raking.		
R in that millennial touchwood-dust	*Aylmer's F.*	514
Ralph.		
that was old Sir *R's* at Ascalon .	*Princess, Pro.*	26
there was *R* himself, A broken statue	"	98
read Of old Sir *R* a page or two .	"	121
R Who shines so in the corner .	"	144
the good Sir *R* had burnt them all—	"	229
Sir *R* has got your colours : .	" iv.	571
Disrobed the glimmering statue of Sir *R*	*Con.*	117
ramble.		
O me, my pleasant *r's* by the lake,	*Ed. Morris*	1, 13
rambling.		
oft in *r's* on the wold, . .	*Miller's D.*	105
ramp.		
A lion *r's* at the top, . .	*Maud*, I. xiv.	7
lions, crown'd with gold, *R* in the	*Elaine* .	661
rampart.		
The ranged *r's* bright . .	*Pal. of Art* .	6
rampart-lines.		
designs Of his labour'd *r-l* . .	*Ode on Well.*	105
ran.		
R up with golden balustrade, .	*Arabian N's.*	118
did gather thunder as they *r*, .	*The Poet* .	49
With an inner voice the river *r*, .	*Dying Swan*	5
in many a wild festoon *R* riot .	*Œnone* .	99
there *r* a row Of cloisters, . .	*Pal. of Art* .	25
I *r* by him without speaking .	*May Queen*, i.	18

	POEM.	LINE.		POEM.	LINE.
And *r* to tell her neighbours:	The Goose	14	A patient *r* of pupils:	Princess, ii.	89
R Gaffer, stumbled Gammer.	"	34	day fled on thro' all Its *r* of duties	" iii.	161
quickly rose Sir Bedivere, and	M. d'Arthur	133	Our voices took a higher *r*;	In Mem. xxx.	21
boated over, *r* My craft aground	Ed. Morris	108	O, therefore from thy sightless *r*	" xcii.	9
shrewdest pain *R* shrivelling thro'	St S. Stylites	196	who knew the *r* of all their arts,	Vivien	23
Then *r* she, gamesome as the colt,	Talking O.	121	impute themselves, Wanting the mental *r*	"	670
r itself in golden sands.	Locksley H.	32	beneath his own low *r* of roofs	Aylmer's F.	47
Young Nature thro' five cycles *r*,	Two Voices	17	*range* (verb.)		
feet that *r*, and doors that clapt,	Day-Dm.	135	Thro' light and shadow thou dost *r*,	Madeline	4
R forward to his rhyming	Amphion	30	swine That *r* on yonder plain.	Pal. of Art	200
In curves the yellowing river *r*,	Sir L and Q. G.	15	Forward, forward let us *r*.	Locksley H.	181
R into its giddiest whirl of sound	Vision of Sin	29	Not less the bee would *r* her cells,	Two Voices	70
A petty railway *r*:	Princess, Pro.	74	*r* above the region of the wind,	Princess, Con.	112
so, my mother said, the story *r*.	" i.	11	My love shall now no further *r*;	In Mem. lxxx.	2
double hill *r* up its furrowy forks.	" iii.	158	*r* above our mortal state,	" lxxxiv.	22
a murmur *r* Thro' all the camp	" v.	106	To *r* the woods, to roam the park	" Con.	96
father heard and *r* In on the lists	" vi.	10	*ranged.*		
'how changed from where it *r*	In Mem. xxiii.	9	the solemn palms were *r* Above	Arabian N's.	79
We talk'd: the stream beneath us *r*,	" lxxxviii.	43	the Gods *R* in the halls of Peleus	Œnone	71
and his river billowing *r*,	Maud, I. iv.	32	I *r* too high; what draws me down	Will Water.	153
never yet so warmly *r* my blood	" xviii.	3	terrace *r* along the Northern front	Princess, iii.	102
her brother *r* in his rage to the gate,	" II. i.	12	now her little ones have *r*	In Mem. xxi.	26
months *r* on and rumour of battle	" III. vi.	29	*R* with the Table Round	Elaine	466
'Run, Katie!' Katie never *r*:	The Brook	87	As down the shore he *r*,	En. Arden	589
r thro' all the coltish chronicle,	"	159	*ranging.*		
in their cloth of gold *R* to her,	Enid	669	My fancy, *r* thro' and thro',	Day-Dm.	246
sister pearls *R* down the silken	Vivien	305	That sittest *r* golden hair	In Mem. vi.	26
r the tale like fire about the court.	Elaine	730	Surprise thee *r* with thy peers	" xliii.	12
when the blood *r* lustier in him again,	"	877	We *r* down this lower track,	" xlv.	1
in hurry and fear *R* to her,	"	1019	some low fever *r* round to spy	Aylmer's F.	519
on the butts While the wine *r*	Guinevere	267	*rank* (line, etc.)		
whisper thro' the nunnery *r*,	"	407	When the *r*'s are roll'd in vapour.	Locksley H.	104
cave *r* in beneath the cliff:	En. Arden	23	The linden broke her *r*'s	Amphion	33
merrily *r* the years, seven happy	"	81	clad in iron burst the *r*'s of war,	Princess, iv.	463
r To greet his hearty welcome	"	346	Should see thy passengers in *r*	In Mem. xiv.	6
r Ev'n to the limit of the land,	"	578	glided winding under *r*'s Of iris,	" cii.	23
where the rivulets of sweet water *r*;	"	643	*rank* (social position.)		
all round it *r* a walk Of shingle	"	737	To all duties of her *r*:	L. of Burleigh	72
r By sallowy rims,	Aylmer's F.	146	one whose *r* exceeds her own.	In Mem. lx.	4
when they *r* To loose him at the	"	125	up or down Along the scale of *r*'s,	" cx.	2
Wife-hunting, as the rumour *r*,	"	212	for the high *r* she had borne,	Guinevere	687
the bright lawns to his brother's *r*,	"	341	eldest-born of *r* or wealth	Aylmer's F.	484
he *r* Beside the river bank	"	450	*rank* (verb.)		
R in and out the long sea-framing	Sea Dreams	33	*r* you nobly, mingled up with me	Princess, ii.	32
shrieks *R* highest up the gamut,	"	226	might not *r* with those detestable	" v.	448
Far *r* the naked moon across	The Voyage	29	*ranked.*		
R the Land with Roman slaughter,	Boädicea	84	made me dream I *r* with him.	In Mem. xli.	4
and *r* to greet him with a kiss,	Lucretius	6	*rankled.*		
r in, Beat breast, tore hair,	"	272	*R* in him and ruffled all his heart.	Guinevere	50
rang.			*ransom'd.*		
The bridle bells *r* merrily	L. of Shalott, iii.	13	richer in his eyes Who *r* us.	Guinevere	677
wild wind *r* from park and plain,	The Goose	45	*rapid.*		
juts of slippery crag that *r*	M. d'Arthur	189	as the *r* of life Shoots to the fall—	A Dedication	3
page or two that *r* With tilt	Princess, Pro.	121	*rapine.*		
with this our banquets *r*:	" i.	131	nature is one with *r*.	Maud, I. iv.	22
for still my voice *R* false:	" iv.	103	wing Of that foul bird of *r*.	Vivien	578
With Ida, Ida, Ida, *r* the woods;	"	413	and the ways Were fill'd with *r*	Guinevere	455
R ruin, answer'd full of grief	" v.	313	*rapt.*		
r Beyond the bourn of sunset:	" Con.	100	So tranced, so *r* in ecstacies.	Eleänore	78
round us all the thicket *r*.	In Mem. xxiii.	23	grunted 'Good!' but we Sat *r*:	M. d'Arthur, Ep.	5
echo-like our voices *r*;	" xxx.	13	So *r*, we near'd the house;	Gardener's D.	141
The hall with harp and carol *r*,	" cii.	9	seedsman, *r* Upon the teeming harvest	Golden Year	9
there *r* on a sudden a passionate	Maud, II. i.	33	*R* after heaven's starry flight,	Two Voices	63
r Clear thro' the open casement	Enid	327	*r* thro' many a rosy change,	Day-Dm.	187
things that *r* Against the pavement,	"	1442	I all in this, 'Come out,' he said	Princess, Pro.	50
R by the white mouth of the violent	Elaine	288	peal'd the nightingale *R* in her song,	" i.	217
were wed, and merrily *r* the bells	En. Arden	80-307, 8	so *r*, we gazing, came a voice,	" ii.	297
shrill'd and *r*, Till this was ended	"	175	her, who *r* in glorious dreams,	"	419
all the houses in the haven *r*.	"	910	She *r* upon her subject, he on her:	" iii.	287
And the ringers *r* with a will	Grandmother	58	*R* to the horrible fall:	" iv.	162
range (s.)			long breezes *r* from inmost south	"	411
Below the *r* of stepping-stones,	Miller's D.	54	Ida spoke not, *r* upon the child,	" vi.	203
R's of glimmering vaults	D. of F. Wom.	35	*r* in nameless reverie	" Con.	103
voice, a lyre of widest *r*	"	105			
the *r* of lawn and park;	The Blackbird	5			
over many a *r* Of waning lime	Gardener's D.	212			
r of prospect had the mother sow,	Walk to the M.	85			
On a *r* of lower feelings	Locksley H.	44			
Soft lustre bathes the *r* of urns	Day-Dm.	29			
o'er them many a flowing *r*.	"	185			

CONCORDANCE TO

	POEM.	LINE.
R from the fickle and the frail	In Mem. xxx.	25
r below Thro' all the dewy-tassell'd	" lxxxv.	5
r in matters dark and deep	" xcvi.	19
So r I was, they could not win	" cii.	49
R in the fear and in the wonder of it;	" Enid	529
R in this fancy of his Table Round	Elaine	130
r By all the sweet and sudden passion	"	281
R on his face as if it were a God's	"	355
R in sweet talk or lively, . .	Guinevere	363

rarer.
Your loss is r; . . . . To J. S. . 25

rascal.
Tumbled the tawny r at his feet, Aylmer's F. 230
Read r in the motions of his back Sea Dreams 163

rash.
R were my judgment then, .	Elaine	239
a crew that is neither rude nor r .	The Islet	10
Stern he was and r; . . .	The Captain	10

rashness.
if I should do This r, . . . Two Voices 392

rat.
tapt at doors, And rummaged like a r; Walk. to the M. 30
curse me the British vermin, the r; Maud, II. v. 58

rate.
all men r as kind and hospitable:	Princess, i.	70
r your chance Almost at naked nothing '	"	159
all men grew to r us at our worth,	" iv.	29
did not r him then This red-hot iron	" v.	199

rated.
must have r her Beyond all tolerance Aylmer's F. 380

ratify.
every voice she talk'd with r it, . Princess, v. 127

rating.
like her none the less for r at her ! Princess, v. 451

ravage.
from her bath of storm, At random r? Lucretius 176

rave.
Let them r.	A Dirge 4, et pass.
mourn and r On alien shores.	Lotos-E's. . 32
will not hear the north-wind r, .	Two Voices 259
Drink, and let the parties r; .	Vision of Sin 123
And r at the lie and the liar .	Maud, I. i. 60
blasts would rise and r and cease	The Voyage 85
My father r's of death and wreck,	Sailor Boy . 19

raven.
For a r ever croaks at my side .	Maud, I. vi.	57
the R, flying high, Croak'd .	Guinevere	132
Dark an answer, Britain's r ! .	Boädicea	13

ravine (mountain-gorge.)
brook falling thro' the clov'n r .	Œnone	8
snare him in the white r, . .	Princess, vii.	190
rosy blossom in hot r, . .	The Daisy	32
bridge that spann'd a dry r . .	Enid .	246-94

ravine (rapine.)
red in tooth and claw With r, . In Mem. lv. 15

raving.
The wind is r in turret and tree. . The Sisters 27

raw.
R from the prime . . . . Princess, ii. 106
one they knew—R from the nursery—Aylmer's F.264

ray (s.)
lashes like to r's Of darkness, .	Arabian N's.	136
Make a carcanet of r's, . .	Adeline	59
neither hide the r ' Love thou thy land,' etc.		14
Heaven flash'd a sudden jubilant r Ode on Well.		129
morning's earliest r Might strike it Elaine		5
center'd in a sun Of silver r's, .	"	296

Ray (Surname.)
Philip R the miller's only son . En. Arden . 13
married her who married Philip R. " . 861

ray (verb.)
R round with flames her disk of seed In Mem. c. 6

ray-fringed. POEM. LINE.
R-f eyelids of the morn 'Clear-headed friend,' etc. 6

reach (s.)
Beside the river's wooded r, . In Mem. lxx. 13

reach (verb.)
example to mankind, Which few can r St S. Stylites	185
r the law within the law: . .	Two Voices	141
r To each his perfect pint . .	Will Water.	114
r its fatling innocent arms .	Princess, vi.	122
than those weird doubts could r me,	" vii.	36
r a hand thro' time to catch . .	In Mem. i.	7
r the glow of southern skies, .	" xii.	10
When Science r'es forth her arms	" xxi.	18
R out dead hands to comfort me.	" lxxix.	16
r us out the shining hand, .	" lxxxiii.	43
Thy spirit up to mine can r; .	" lxxxiv.	82
Or even for intellect to r . .	" xciv.	47
the hands That r thro' nature,	" cxxiii.	24
until we pass and r That other .	Enid .	855

reached.
music r them on the middle sea .	Sea-Fairies	6
ere she r upon the tide . .	L. of Shalott, iv.	33
r a meadow slanting to the North ;	Gardener's D.	107
till I r The wicket-gate . .	"	207
set out, and r the farm. . .	Dora .	126
we r The griffin-guarded gates,	Audley Ct. .	13
till we r The limit of the hills ; .	"	81
until she r The gateway ; . .	Godiva	50
long arms and hands R out, .	Princess, i.	29
we dropt, And flying r the frontier	"	108
would have r you, had you been .	" iv.	417
r White hands of farewell to my sire,	" v.	222
seem to have r a purer air, .	In Mem. xxxiii.	2
He r the glory of a hand, . .	" lxviii.	17
ere we r the highest summit .	The Daisy .	87
across the bridge And r the town,	Enid .	384
when I r this ruin'd hold, . .	"	785
r a hand, and on his foot . .	"	1607
when they r the camp the King .	"	1726
when they r the lists By Camelot	Elaine .	427
he r the home Where Annie lived	En. Arden .	685
r A mountain, like a wall of burrs	Sea Dreams	114
Had r a thunderous fullness .	"	207
r the ship and caught the rope, .	Sailor Boy .	3

reaching.
r forward drew My burthen . . Princess, iv. 173
r thro' the night Her other. . . Sea Dreams 275

read (pres.)
giving light To r those laws ; .	Isabel .	19
Oh! teach the orphan-boy to r,	L. C. V. de Vere	69
tell me, did she r the name . .	Talking O. .	153
That r his spirit blindly wise .	Two Voices	287
They r Botanic Treatises, . .	Amphion .	77
They r in arbours clipt and cut .	"	85
Your riddle is hard to r.' . .	Lady Clare	76
stay'd at Christmas up to r; .	Princess, Pro.	176
took one tutor as to r: . .	"	177
r My sickness down to happy dreams?	" ii.	235
held a volume as to r, . .	" iii.	431
'can he not r—no books? . .	" iii.	198
r and earn our prize, A golden broach	"	283
on to me, as who should say ' R '	" iv.	378
he may r that binds the sheaf, .	In Mem. xxxvi.	13
Her r's the secret of the star, .	" xcvi.	22
(If I r her sweet will right) . .	Maud, I. xxi.	10
open, find and r the charm .	Vivien .	510
You r the book, ...	"	517-26
none can r the text, not even I ; .	"	531
none can r the comment but myself;	"	532
R my little fable : He that runs may r.	The Flower	17

read (pret.)
round the prow they r her name,	L. of Shalott, iv.	44
A love-song I had somewhere r,	Miller's D.	65
I r, before my eyelids dropt their .	D. of F. Wom.	1
R, mouthing out his hollow oes .	The Epic .	50
it was the tone with which he r	M. d'Arthur, Ep.	5
laugh'd, as one that r my thought	Gardener's D.	105
r me rhymes elaborately good .	Ed. Morris	20
I r, and fled by night . . .	" .	134

	POEM.	LINE.
They flapp'd my light out as I r.	St S. Stylites	172
I r and felt that I was there;	To E. L.	8
r Of old Sir Ralph a page or two.	Princess, Pro.	120
an officer Rose up, and r the statues	" ii.	55
Regarding, while she r	" iv.	303
I r—two letters—one her sire's—	"	378
So far I r; And then stood up and spoke	"	397
I kiss'd it and I r.	" v.	363
they talk'd, They sang, they r;	" vii.	8
to herself, all in low tones, she r.	"	160
once more, as low, she r;	"	176
r The Tuscan poets on the lawn;	In Mem. lxxxviii.	23
I r Of that glad year	" xciv.	21
sign your names, which shall be r	" Con.	57
something R with a boy's delight,	Maud, I. vii.	10
Sat with her, r to her, night and day	" xix.	75
Not a bell was rung, not a prayer was r;	" II. v.	24
R but one book, and ever reading it	Vivien	472
and r the naked shield,	Elaine	16
thinking that he r her meaning there,	"	87
Lifted her eyes, and r his lineaments	"	244
r the King's face, some the Queen's	"	723
Stoopt, took, brake seal, and r it;	"	1264
Thus he r, And ever in the reading	"	1275
looking often from his face who r	"	1277
in their eyes and faces r his doom;	En. Arden	73
he r God's warning 'wait.'	"	572
r Writhing a letter from his child	Aylmer's F.	516
r; and tore As if the living passion	"	534
R rascal in the motions of his back	Sea Dreams	163

read.
| a r's wonn sarmin a weeak, | N. Farmer | 28 |

reading.
R her perfect features in the gloom,	Gardener's D.	171
The Modern Muses r,	Amphion	76
Read but one book, and ever r	Vivien	472
ever in the r, lords and dames	Elaine	1276
Yet bitterer from his r's;	Aylmer's F.	553

ready.
Make thine heart r with thine eyes:	Gardener's D.	268
I waited long; My brows are r.	St S. Stylites	203
The lists were r	Princess, v.	472
r, thou, to die with him,	In Mem. cxx.	2
R in heart and r in hand	Maud, I. v.	9
R to burst in a colour'd flame;	" vi.	19
for three days seen, r to fall.	Vivien	145
while she made her r for her ride,	Elaine	775
and a barge Be r on the river	"	1117
in a wind, r to break and fly,	Guinevere	363

real.
| hated banter, wish'd for something r, | Princess, Con. | 18 |

realist.
| Betwixt the mockers and the r's; | Princess, Con. | 24 |

reality.
| Thy pain is a r.' | Two Voices | 387 |

realm.
A r of pleasance,	Arabian N's.	101
r's of upland, prodigal in oil,	Pal. of Art	77
shall hold a fretful r in awe	Locksley H.	129
She enters other r's of love;	In Mem. xxxix.	12
From the r's of light and song,	Maud, II. iv.	82
Guarding r's and kings from shame;	Ode on Well.	63
all whose r's to their last isle,	Ded. of Idylls	11
this common sewer of all his r,	Enid	39, 1743
in that r of lawless turbulence,	"	1765
make an onslaught single on a r	"	1765
the trackless r's of Lyonnesse,	Elaine	36
a boon Worth half her r,	"	73
half my r beyond the seas,	"	954
The price of half a r	"	1158
mine own r beyond the narrow seas,	"	1313
shrine which then in all the r Was richest	"	1320
Sir Modred had usurped the r,	Guinevere	152
and his own Queen, and r	"	195
the common grief of all the r!	"	215
what has fall'n upon the r!	"	271
the knighthood-errant of this r	"	458

	POEM.	LINE.
all The r's together under me,	Guinevere	459
no false passport to that easy r,	Aylmer's F.	163

reap.
Sow the seed, and r the harvest	Lotos-E's.	166
To-morrow yet would r to-day 'Love thou thy land'		93
God r's a harvest in me.	St S. Stylites	146-7
r's not harvest of his youthful joys,	Locksley H.	139
r The flower and quintessence	Day-Dm.	235
perhaps might r the applause of	Princess, iii.	245
r's A truth from one that loves	In Mem. xli.	11
r's the labour of his hands	" lxiii.	26

reaped.
| the reapers r And the sun fell, | Dora | 76-106 |

reaper.
Only r's. reaping early	L. of Shalott, i.	23
by the moon the r weary,	"	33
the r's at their sultry toil.	Pal. of Art	77
the r's reaped And the sun fell,	Dora	76-106

reaping.
| Only reapers, r early | L. of Shalott, i. | 28 |
| men the workers, ever r something | Locksley H. | 117 |

rear (s.)
| from the r of Philip's house | En. Arden | 728 |

rear (verb.)
| She shall r my dusky race. | Locksley H. | 163 |
| Her office there to r, to teach, | In Mem. xxxix. | 13 |

rear'd.
Freedom r in that august sunrise	The Poet	37
Who took a wife, who r his race,	Two Voices	323
One r a font of stone And drew,	Princess, Pro.	59
your statues R, sung to,	" v.	404
the babe, who r his creasy arms	En. Arden	752

reason (s.)
He utter'd rhyme and r,	The Goose	6
God knows: he has a mint of r's;	The Epic	33
Nor any train of r keep;	Two Voices	50
and the beginning vex His r;	"	289
men, whose r long was blind	"	370
We lack not rhymes and r's	Will Water.	62
prophesying change Beyond all r;	Princess, i.	142
worthy r's why she should bide	" v.	315
r's drawn from age and state,	"	347
thou, that countest r ripe	In Mem. xxxiii.	13
Thy ransom'd r change replies	" lx.	2
r why I seem to cast	" cxi.	6
The freezing r's colder part	" cxxiii.	14
Albeit I give no r but my wish	Enid	761
No r given her' she could cast	"	807
no r why we should not wed.'	En. Arden	504
when shutting r's up in rhythm,	Lucretius	220

reason (verb.)
| Their's not to r why, | Lt. Brigade | 14 |

rebell'd.
| till the maid R against it, | Elaine | 648 |

rebloom'd.
| Gather'd the blossom that r, | Aylmer's F. | 142 |

rebuke.
| eighty winters freeze with one r | Ode on Well. | 136 |

recall.
| R's, in change of light or gloom | In Mem. lxxxiv. | 74 |
| gods themselves cannot r their gifts.' | Tithonus | 49 |

receive.
whoso did r of them	Lotos-E's.	39
thy shoulders to r my weight,	M. d'Arthur	146
I love the truth; R it;	Princess, ii.	16
God accept him, Christ r him.	Ode on Well.	11
R, and yield me sanctuary,	Guinevere	140

received.
R and gave him welcome there	In Mem. lxxxiv	24
R at once and laid aside the gems.	Elaine	1116
like one that had r a blow;	Sea Dreams	157

reciting.
| One walked r by herself | Princess, ii. | 430 |

reckling.
there lay the *r*, one, But one hour . *Vivien* . 559

reckon.
heart Would *r* worth the taking . *Vivien* . 766
I *r's* I 'annot sa mooch to larn . *N. Farmer* 13
summun I *r's* 'ull 'a to wroite, . " . 57

reckoning.
'Thy *r*, friend?' and ere he learnt it, *Enid* . 1257

reclined.
On silken cushions half *r*; . . *Eleänore* . 126
to live and lie *r* On the hills . *Lotos-E's.* . 154
As by the lattice you *r*. . . *Day-Dm.* . 5

reclining.
with pain, *r* on his arm, . . *M. d'Arthur* 168

reclothes.
Clothes and *r* the happy plains ; . *Day-Dm.* . 22

recognise.
scarce can *r* the fields I know ; . *St S. Stylites* 39

recollect.
We do but *r* the dreams that come *Lucretius* . 35

recommenced.
A little ceased, but *r*. . . *Two Voices* 318
Poor fellow, could he help it? *r*, . *The Brook* . 158
r, and let her tongue Rage . . *Vivien* . 650

reconcile.
The Gods are hard to *r* : . . *Lotos-E's.* . 126

reconciled.
Nor did mine own now *r* ; . . *Princess,* vii. 73
friends for her sake, to be *r*! *Maud,* I.xviii.50-56

reconcilement.
difference, *r*, pledges given, . *Gardener'sD.* 252
while I melt ; make *r* sure . . *Princess,* vi. 268

record.
Whereof this world holds *r*. . . *M. d'Arthur* 16
What *r*, or what relic of my lord . " . 98
shaping faithful *r* of the glance *Gardener'sD.* 173
Sponged and made blank of crimeful *r StS Stylites* 156
in division of the *r's* of the mind? *Locksley H.* 69
caught within the *r* of her wrongs, *Princess,* v. 137
There lives no *r* of reply, . *In Mem.* xxxi. 6
What *r*? not the sinless years . " li. 11
Whatever *r* leap to light . . *Ode on Well.* 190

recorded.
each at other's ear What shall not be *r Enid* 1483

recovering.
while he lay *r* there, . . *En. Arden.* 108

Rector.
Long since, a bygone *R* of the place, *Aylmer's F.* 11

Rectory.
Averill Averill at the *R* . . *Aylmer's F.* 37
so that *R* and Hall Bound . . " . 38

recurring.
R and suggesting still ! . . *Will* . 14

red.
all dark and *r*—a tract of sand, . *Pal. of Art* 65
As I have seen the rosy *r* flushing *Locksley H.* 26
No pint of white or *r* . . *Will Water.* 82
bickers into *r* and emerald . *Princess,* v. 253
perforce He yielded, wroth and *r*, " . 348
r with spirted purple of the vats, " vii. 167
Nature, *r* in tooth and claw . *In Mem.* lv. 15
tremblest thro' thy darkling *r* . xcviii. 5
And blossom in purple and *r*. *Maud,* I. xxii. 74
coppice gemm'd with green and *r*, *Enid* . 339
r and pale Across the face of Enid " . 523
turn'd all *r* and paced his hall, . " . 1516
with graver fits, Turn *r* or pale . *Vivien* . 37
R as the rising sun with heathen blood, *Elaine* 308
York's white rose as *r* as Lancaster's *Aylmer's F.*
Blues and *r's* They talk'd of ; . " . 251
praised the waning *r* and told The vintage " . 406
She blush'd a rosy *r*, . . *The Ringlet* 36
Pale he turn'd and *r*, . . *The Captain* 62

redcap.
The *r* whistled ; and the nightingale *Gardener'sD* 94

red-cross.
A *r-c* knight for ever kneel'd . *L. of Shalott,* iii. 6

redden.
Sad as the last which *r's* over one *Princess,* iv. 28
and his anger *r's* in the heavens ; " . 367
He *r's* what he kisses ; . . " v. 158
These leaves that *r* to the fall . *In Mem.* xi. 14
cheek begins to *r* thro' the gloom, *Tithonus* . 37

redden'd.
this was what had *r* her cheek . *Maud,* I. xix. 65
r with no bandit's blood ; . . *Aylmer's F.* 597

reddening.
r in the furrows of his chin . . *Princess,* vi. 211
r in extremity of delight . . *Enid* . 1068
Sir Aylmer *r* from the storm within, *Aylmer's F.* 322

redder.
whole hill-side was *r* than a fox. *Walk. to the M.* 3
r than a windy morn ; . . *Princess, Con.* 91
When the red rose was *r* than itself, *Aylmer's F.* 50

redeem.
that From which I would *r* you ; *Princess,* iv. 487

redeemed.
R it from the charge of nothingness *M. d'Arthur,Ep.* 7

red-faced.
r-f war has rods of steel . . *Princess,* v. 114

red-hot.
This *r-h* iron to be shaped with blows. *Princess,* v. 200

redound.
not without *r* Of use and glory . *Princess,* ii. 28

redress.
What hope of answer, or *r*? . . *In Mem.* lv. 27
Ring in *r* to all mankind . . " cv. 12

redress'd.
prowess done *r* a random wrong . *Guinevere* . 456

redressing.
glory was, *r* human wrong ; . *Ded. of Idylls* 8
ride abroad *r* human wrongs ! . *Vivien* . 543
ride abroad *r* human wrongs, . *Guinevere* . 468

red-ribbed.
The *r-r* ledges drip . . . *Maud,* I. i. 3
From the *r-r* hollow behind the wood " II. i. 25

reed.
r's blown from his silver tongue, . *The Poet* . 13
wavy swell of the soughing *r's*, . *Dying Swan* 38
heard the ripple washing in the *r's*, *M. d'Arthur* 70, 117
What *r* was that on which I leant ? *In Mem.* lxxxiii. 45
low morass and whispering *r*, . " xcix. 6
iris, and the golden *r* ; . . " cii. 24
and watch'd The high *r* wave . *Elaine* . 1381
at twilight in a land of *r's*. . . *Coquette,* i. 14

reed-tops.
And took the *r-t* as it went. . . *Dying Swan* 10

reef.
In roarings round the coral *r* . *In Mem.* xxxvi. 16
roller thundering on the *r*, . . *En. Arden.* 585
in the water, a long *r* of gold, . *Sea Dreams* 123
Wreck'd on a *r* of visionary gold.' " . 135

reel.
The horse and rider *r* . . . *Sir Galahad* 8
They *r*, they roll in clanging lists, . " 9
Earth *R's,* and the herdsmen cry ; *Princess,* v. 518
R's, as the golden Autumn woodland *r's* " vii. 336
When all my spirit *r's* . . *Maud,* II. iv. 20
We felt the good ship shake and *r The Voyage* 15

reel'd.
part *r* but kept their seats ; . *Princess,* v. 485
R from the sabre-stroke . . *Lt. Brigade* 35
And pale he turn'd, and *r*, . *Guinevere* . 302
in the middle aisle *R*, . . *Aylmer's F.* 819

	POEM.	LINE.
re-father'd.		
stoop'd, *r* o'er my wounds...	*Princess,* vi.	113
reflect.		
love *r's* the thing beloved ;...	*In Mem.* li.	2
each *r's* a kindlier day ; ...	" xcix.	18
reflex.		
The mellow'd *r* of a winter moon ;	*Isabel* .	29
The *r* of a beauteous form, .	*Miller's D.* .	77
The *r* of a legend past, .	*Day-Dm.* .	11
The *r* of a human face .	*In Mem.* evii.	12
Reform.		
R, White Rose, Bellerophon	*The Brook* .	161
refraction.		
Such *r* of events . . .	*In Mem.* xci.	15
refrain.		
We revere, and we *r* . .	*Ode on Well.*	246
refrained.		
r From ev'n a word, . .	*Enid* . .	213
refresh'd.		
leave thee freer, till thou wake *r*,	*Love and Duty*	94
rest.		
heathen caught and *r* him of his tongue	*Elaine*	273
refuse (s.)		
r patch'd with moss. . .	*Vision of Sin*	212
refuse (verb.)		
nor did mine own *R* her proffer	*Princess,* vi.	327
refused.		
Nor yet *r* the rose, but granted it	*Gardener's D.*	157
R her to him, then his pride awoke ;	*Enid* . .	448
regard.		
R the weakness of thy peers :	*'Love thou thy land,'*	24
R gradation, lest the soul Of Discord	"	67
O blatant Magazines, *r* me rather—	*Hendecasyllabics*	17
regarded.		
Remorsefully *r* thro' his tears,	*M. d'Arthur*	171
daughters in the pool : for none *R* ;	*Princess,* v.	320
many past, but none *r* her, .	*Enid* .	1369
woman's love, Save one, he not *r*,	*Elaine* .	837
regarding.		
Droops both his wings, *r* thee, .	*Eleänore* .	119
we with blind surmise *R* . .	*Princess,* iv.	363
anyone, *R*, well had deem'd	*En. Arden* .	712
Reggio.		
rain at *R*, rain at Parma ; .	*The Daisy* .	51
region.		
Within this *r* I subsist,	*'You ask me why,' etc.*	2
girt the *r* with high cliff .	*Vision of Sin*	47
range above the *r* of the wind	*Princess,* Con.	112
No wing of wind the *r* swept, .	*In Mem.* lxxvii.	6
To the *r's* of thy rest ?' .	*Maud,* II. iv.	88
the while thro' all the *r* round	*Elaine* .	612
I rode all round The *r*: .	" .	706
register'd.		
Are *r* and calendar'd for saints.	*St S. Stylites*	130
regret.		
Love is made a vague *r*. .	*Miller's D.* .	210
wild with all *r*; . . .	*Princess,* iv.	39
So seems it in my deep *r*, .	*In Mem.* viii.	17
chains *r* to his decease, .	" xxix.	3
hopes and light *r's* that come	" xxxix.	7
O last *r*, *r* can die ! . .	" lxxvii.	17
To one pure image of *r*. .	" ci.	24
my *r* becomes an April violet, .	" exiv.	18
Is it, then, *r* for buried time	" cxv.	1
Not all *r*: the face will shine	"	9
embalm In dying songs a dead *r*,	" Con.	14
R is dead, but love is more .	"	17
love and reverence and *r* .	*Ode on Well.*	157
regret (verb.)		
and *r* Her parting step .	*Elaine* .	862
regular.		
Faultily faultless, icily *r*, .	*Maud,* I. ii.	6

	POEM.	LINE.
rehearse.		
This truth within thy mind *r*,	*Two Voices*	25
reign		
lips whereon perpetually did *r*	*Isabel* .	7
I shall *r* for ever over all.' .	*Love and Death*	15
'*R* thou apart, a quiet king, .	*Pal. of Art*	14
you shall *r* The head and heart	*Princess,* iii.	146
Then *r* the world's great bridals,	" vii.	278
the worst were that man he that *r's*	*Guinevere*	519
reigned.		
A kinder influence *r*; . .	*Princess,* vii.	5
reigning.		
him, that other, *r* in his place,	*En. Arden* .	764
rein.		
sway'd The *r* with dainty finger-tips,	*Sir L. and Q. G.*	41
reined.		
Edyrn *r* his charger at her side,	*Enid* .	1668
reinspired.		
With youthful fancy *r*, . .	*Ode to Mem.*	114
reassuring.		
whence *r*, robed and crown'd	*Godiva*	77
rejected.		
He should not be *r*. . .	*Aylmer's F.*	422
rejection.		
with hands of wild *r* 'Go !'—	*Ed. Morris*	124
rejoice.		
As when a mighty people *r*, .	*Dying Swan*	31
in her place she did *r*,	*'Of old sat Freedom,' etc.*	5
Than him that said '*R ! r !*' .	*Two Voices*	462
Thus her heart *r's* greatly, .	*L. of Burleigh*	41
I have thee still, and I *r*; .	*In Mem.* xxxix.	14
a joy in which I cannot *r*, .	*Maud,* I. v	21
A people's voice, when they *r*	*Ode on Well.*	146
Roll and *r*, jubilant voice, .	*W. to Alexan.*	22
rejoiced.		
in their common love *r* Geraint	*Enid* . .	23
suddenly she knew it and *r*, .	" .	667
while the women thus *r* .	" .	754
Never man *r* More than Geraint .	" .	771
rejoicing.		
feel My purpose and *r* in my joy.'	*Guinevere* .	483
not grieving at your joys, But not *r*;	" .	672
R at that answer to his prayer.	*En. Arden* .	127
relate.		
As old mythologies *r*, . .	*Two Voices*	349
relation.		
That bears *r* to the mind. .	*Two Voices*	177
Her deep *r's* are the same, .	*In Mem.* lxxvii.	19
relaxed.		
their law *R* its hold upon us.	*Guinevere* .	454
release (s.)		
can't be long before I find *r*;	*May Queen,* iii.	11
release (verb.)		
R me, and restore me to the ground ;	*Tithonus*	72
released.		
I arose, and I *r* The casement,	*Two Voices*	403
relent.		
learning this, the bridegroom will *r*.	*Guinevere* .	170
reliance.		
Those, in whom he had *r* .	*The Captain*	57
relic.		
What record, or what *r* of my lord	*M. d'Arthur*	98
I will leave my *r's* in your land, .	*St S. Stylites*	191
Such precious *r's* brought by thee ;	*In Mem.* xvii.	13
some stolen, some as *r's* kept, .	*Vivien* .	303
relief.		
on thy bosom, (deep-desired *r*.)	*Love and Duty*	42
That sets the past in this *r* f	*In Mem.* xxiv.	12
In verse that brings myself *r*, .	" lxxv.	2
Demanding, so to bring *r* .	" lxxxiv.	6

334   CONCORDANCE TO

relish (s.)
	POEM.	LINE.
Had *r* fiery-new, . . .	*Will Water.*	98

re-listen.
seems, as I *r* to it, Prattling	*The Brook*	18

relive.
Can I but *r* in sadness? .	*Locksley H.*	107

remade.
R the blood and changed the frame	*InMem.Con.*	11

remain.
there like a sun *r* Fix'd— .	*Eleänore*	92
Let what is broken so *r*. .	*Lotos-E's.*	125
And what *r's* to tell. . .	*Talking O*	204
of one to me Little *r's*: . .	*Ulysses*	26
Those lonely lights that still *r*,	*Two Voices*	83
Here all things in their place *r*,	*Day-Dm.*	73
I *r* on whom to wreak your rage,	*Princess,* iv.	331
this question of your troth *r's*:	" v.	269
r Orb'd in your isolation ; .	" vi.	152
One writes, that 'Other friends *r*,'	*In Mem.* vi.	1
what to me *r's* of good? . .	"	42
what are they when these *r*, .	" lxxv.	15
My shame is greater who *r*, .	" cviii.	23
R's the lean P. W. on his tomb :	*The Brook*	192
her name will yet *r* Untarnish'd	*Enid*	500
now *r's* But little cause for laughter:	*Elaine*	594
but of others who *r*, . .	*Guinevere*	320
we must *r* Sacred to one another.'	*Aylmer's F.*	425

remained.
r among us In our young nursery	*Princess,* iv.	312
I *r*, whose hopes were dim, .	*InMem.lxxxiv.*29
r Apart by all the chamber's width,	*Enid*	1114
there snapt, and *r*. . .	*Elaine*	489
there that day *r*, and toward even	"	971
I woke, but still the wish *r*. .	"	1042
Lancelot ever promised, but *r*	*Guinevere*	93

remaining.
R utterly confused with fears,	*Pal. of Art*	269
You love, *r* peacefully, . .	*Margaret*	22
R betwixt dark and bright : .	"	28
cry for strength, *r* weak, .	*Two Voices*	95
r there Fixt like a beacon-tower	*Princess,* iv.	471
thou *r* here wilt learn the event ; .	*Guinevere*	572
The two *r* found a fallen stem ;	*En. Arden*	568

remains.
With my lost Arthur's loved *r*,	*In Mem.* ix.	3

remaineth.
The rest *r* unreveal'd : . .	*In Mem.* xxxi.	14

re-make.
gathering at the base *R's* itself,	*Guinevere*	604

remand.
r it thou For calmer hours .	*Love and Duty*	86

remark.
least *r* was worth The experience	*Ed. Morris.*	65

remarked.
r The lusty mowers labouring	*Enid*	1099

remble.
a niver *r's* the stoáns . .	*N. Farmer*	60

rembled.
an' raäved an' *r* un oot. . .	*N. Farmer*	32

remedy.
There is one *r* for all. . .	*Two Voices* 165, 201

remember.
For you *r*, you had set. . .	*Miller's D.*	81
How sadly, I *r*, rose the morning	*May Queen,* iii.	3
times when I *r* to have been Joyful	*D. of F. Wom.*	79
Oh yet but I *r*, ten years back .	*Walk.to the M.*	42
I *r* one that perish'd : . .	*Locksley H.*	71
Such a one do I *r*, . . .	"	72
As one before, *r* much, . .	*Two Voices*	356
I *r*, when I think That my youth	*Vision of Sin*	77
We *r* love ourselves (*r*, 198) .	*Princess,* i.	121
'Does my old friend *r* me?'.	*InMem.*lxiii.	28
That yet *r's* his embrace, .	" lxxxiv.	111
I *r* the time, for the roots of my	*Maud,* I. i.	13

	POEM.	LINE.
She *r's* it now we meet. . .	*Maud,* I. vi.	68
I *r*, I, When he lay dying there	" II. ii.	66
R him who led your hosts ; .	*Ode on Well.*	171
r all He spoke among you .	"	177
R what a plague of rain ; .	*The Daisy*	50
R how we came at last To Como ;	"	69
R that great insult done the Queen,'	*Enid*	571
how should the child *R* this?'	*En. Arden*	233
I *r* a quarrel I had with your father,	*Grandmother*	21

remembered.
I *r* Everard's college fame .	*The Epic*	46
She *r* that : A pleasant game,	*Princess,Pro.*	190
I *r* one myself had made, .	" iv.	70
I *r* that burnt sorcerer's curse	" v.	464
he *r* her, and how she wept .	*Enid*	1460
r one dark hour Here in this wood	*En. Arden.*	382

rememberest.
thou *r* how In those old days .	*M..d'Arthur*	28

remembering.
R the day when first she came,	*Dora*	104
crown of sorrow is *r* happier things.	*Locksley H.*	76
R its ancient heat. . .	*Two Voices*	423
R how we three presented Maid	*Princess,* i.	193
will beat my girl *R* her mother	" v.	86
R his ill-omen'd song ; . .	" vi.	143
R all his greatness in the Past	*Ode on Well.*	20
R all the beauty of that star .	*Ded. of Idylls*	45
R when first he came on her	*Enid*	140,842
r her old ruin'd hall, . .	"	1103
R Her thought when first she came,	*Guinevere*	177
r His former talks with Edith,	*Aylmer's F.*	456
R her dear lord who died for all,	*Sea Dreams*	47

remerging.
R in the general Soul . .	*In Mem.* xlvi.	4

remiss.
She had not found me so *r* ; .	*Talking O.*	193

remit.
She takes, when harsher moods *r*,	*In Mem.* xlvii.	6

remnant.
a *r* stays with me. And of this *r*	*Guinevere*	440

remodel.
why should any man *R* models?	*The Epic*	38

remorse.
You held your course without *r*,	*L. C. V. de Vere.*	45
all the man was broken with *r* ; .	*Dora*	161
without *r* to strike her dead .	*Enid*	958
the one dark hour which brings *r*,	*Vivien*	613

removed.
Forgive my grief for one *r*, .	*In Mem.* Pro.	37
An awful thought, a life *r*, .	" xiii.	10

render.
statue-like, In act to *r* thanks.	*Gardener's D.*	159
Will thirty seasons *r* plain .	*Two Voices*	82
R him up unscath'd . .	*Princess,* iv.	389
loth to *r* up My precontract .	" v.	289
r human love his dues ; . .	*InMem.*xxxvii.16
r All homage to his own darling	*Maud,* I. xx,	48
R thanks to the Giver, (rep.)	*Ode on Well.*	44
r him to the mould . . .	"	48
gave the diamond : she will *r* it	*Elaine*	709

render'd.
She *r* answer high : . .	*D.of F.Wom.*	202
Survive in spirits *r* free, .	*InMem.*xxxviii.	10
in my charge, which was not *r* to him:	*Enid*	452
Arthur's wars were *r* mystically,	*Elaine*	797

rendering.
Not *r* true answer, . .	*M. d'Arthur*	74

renew.
Would God *r* me from my birth	*Miller's D.*	27
with the sun and moon *r* their light	*Princess,* iii.	238
wilt *r* thy beauty morn by morn	*Tithonus*	74

renewed.
The maid and page *r* their strife,	*Day-Dm.*	145

	POEM.	LINE.
a wish *r*, When two years after	*En. Arden*	88
sad kiss by day by night *r*	"	161
her new child was as herself *r*,	"	519
bosom beating with a heart *r*.	*Tithonus*	36

renown.
Of me you shall not win *r*!	*L.C.V.deVere*	2
A land of just and old *r*, 'You ask me why,' etc.		10
Speak no more of his *r*,	*Ode on Well.*	278

rent (s.)
Were living nerves to feel the *r*;	*Aylmer's F.*	536

rent (verb.)
who would *r* the hall.	*Audley Ct.*	30

rent (pret. of rend.)
An inner impulse *r* the veil	*Two Voices*	10
r The woodbine wreaths that bind her,	*Amphion*	33
r The wonder of the loom	*Princess*, i.	60

rentroll.
The *r* Cupid of our rainy isles	*Ed Morris*	103

re-orient.
The life *r* out of dust	*In Mem.*cxv.	6

repaid.
money can be *r*; Not kindness	*En. Arden*	319

repast.
For brief *r* or afternoon repose	*Guinevere*	392

repay.
Why then he shall *r* me—	*En. Arden*	309
He will *r* you: money can be repaid	"	319

repeal.
naked thro' the town, And I *r* it'	*Godiva*	30

repeat.
I must needs *r* for my excuse	*Princess*, iii.	36

repeated.
R, muttering 'cast away and lost	*En. Arden*	716

repeating.
half the night *r*, 'must I die?'	*Elaine*	895
R, till the word we know so well	"	1022
eyes upon her *R* all his wish'd,	*En. Arden*	905

repent.
I *r* me of all I did	*Ed. Gray*	23
world will not believe a man *r's*:	*Enid*	1748
Full seldom *does* a man *r*,	"	1750
No light had we : for that we do *r*;	*Guinevere*	169
help me, heaven, for surely I *r*	"	370
or in the waste '*R*!'	*Aylmer's F.*	742

repentance.
what is true *r* but in thought	*Guinevere*	371

replied.
He sang his song, and I *r* with mine:	*Audley Ct.*	55
Swung themselves, and in low tones *r*:	*Vision of Sin*	20
she *r*, her duty was to speak,	*Princess*, iii.	135
tears Follow'd: the king *r* not:	" vi.	292

replieth.
The hollow grot *r*.	*Claribel*	20

reply (s.)
waiting decision, made *r*,	*Œnone*	141
There comes no murmur of *r*,	*Pal. of Art.*	286
my disdain is my *r*,	*L.C.V.deVere*	22
sweet eyes, your low *replies*:	"	29
since I heard him make *r*	*Talking O.*	25
In courteous words return'd *r*:	*Day-Dm.*	162
There lives no record of *r*,	*In Mem.* xxxi.	6
Thy ransom'd reason change *replies*	" ix.	2
The delight of low *replies.*	*Maud*, II. iv.	30
Their's not to make *r*,	*Lt. Brigade*	13
hung his head, and halted in *r*,	*Enid*	1659
having no *r* Gazed at the heaving shoulder	*Vivien*	744
the passion in her moan'd *r*.	*En. Arden*	285

reply (verb.)
my Melpomene *replies*	*In Mem.* xxxvii.	9
Care not thou to *r*;	*Maud*, II. iii.	7
the brook, why not? *replies*.	*The Brook*	22

replying.
	POEM	LINE.
let us hear the purple glens *r*:	*Princess*, iii.	358

report (s.)
In this *r*, this answer of a king	*Princess*, i.	69
If one should bring me this *r*,	*In Mem.* xiv.	1
Yniol made *r* Of that good mother	*Enid*	756

reported.
R who he was, and on what quest	*Elaine*	625

reporting.
R of his vessel China-bound,	*En. Arden*	122

repose (s.)
sick man's room when he taketh *r* '*A spirit haunts*'		14
Her manners had not that *r*	*L. C. V. de Vere*	39
brief repast or afternoon *r*	*Guinevere*	392

reposed.
God gave her peace; her land *r*;	*To the Queen*	26
like a fruitful land *r*;	*Locksley H.*	13
A void where heart on heart *r*;	*In Mem.* xiii.	6

reposing.
His state the king *r* keeps.	*Day-Dm.*	50

repression.
what sublime *r* of himself,	*Ded. of Idylls*	18

reproach (s.)
may worship me without *r*;	*St S. Stylites*	190
Thro' light *r's*, half exprest	*In Mem.* lxxxiv.	15
never spake word of *r* to me,	*Elaine*	125
name shames me, seeming a *r*,	"	1394
fell on her Sharp as *r*.	*En. Arden*	485

reproach (verb.)
the poor cause that men *R* you	*Enid*	88

reproof.
Presses his without *r*	*L. of Burleigh*	10
I was prick'd with some *r*,	*Enid*	1738
I have not lack'd thy mild *r*, '*My life is full,*' etc.		4

reprove.
Was it gentle to *r* her	*Maud*, I. xx.	8

republic.
The vast *R's* that may grow,	*Day-Dm.*	227
Revolts, *r's*, revolutions	*Princess, Con.*	65
the black *r* on his elms	*Aylmer's F.*	529

repulsed.
being *r* By Yniol and yourself,	*Enid*	1676

repute.
bore a knight of old *r* to the earth,	*Elaine*	491

reputed.
R the best knight and goodliest man,	*Guinevere*	379

request.
at my *r* He brought it;	*The Epic*	47
'To what *r* for what strange boon	*Vivien*	113

required.
Heroic seems our Princess as *r*	*Princess, Pro.*	223
public use *r* she should be known;	" iv.	317
men *r* that I should give throughout	" Con.	10

requiring.
R, tho' I knew it was my own	*Gardener's D.*	222
R at her hand the greatest gift,	"	214

re-reiterated.
grant my *r-r* wish,	*Vivien*	203

Re-risen.
content *R-r* In Katie's eyes	*The Brook*	169

rescue.
Flights, terrors, sudden *r's*,	*Aylmer's F.*	99

reseated.
thou *r* in thy place of light	*Guinevere*	521

resembles.
And so my wealth *r's* thine,	*In Mem.* lxxviii.	17

reserve.
not to pry and peer on your *r*	*Princess*, iv.	392
Such fine *r*, and noble reticence	*Enid*	1739

CONCORDANCE TO

reserved.
	POEM.	LINE.
in my grief a strength r.	In Mem.lxxxiv.	52

resigned.
pray'd for both, and so I felt r,	May Queen, iii.	31
Asks what thou lackest, thought r,	Two Voices	98

resmooth.
waves of prejudice R to nothing:	Princess, iii.	225

resolder'd.
r peace, whereon Follow'd his tale.	Princess, v.	45

resolution.
Dispersed his r like a cloud.	Elaine	880

resolve (s.)
'Hard task, to pluck r,' I cried,	Two Voices	118
Assurance only breeds r,'	"	315
many a holy vow and pure r.	Elaine	875
His r Upbore him, and firm faith,	En. Arden	800
His gazing (in on Annie, his r	"	864

resolve (verb.)
turn thee round, r the doubt;	In Mem. xliii.	14
Nor can my dream r the doubt:	" lxvii.	12

resolved.
start in pain R on noble things,	D. of F. Wom.	42
Here she woke, R, sent for him	En. Arden	503

resort.
The Cock, To which I most r,	Will Water.	2,210

resound.
solemn chaunts r between.	Sir Galahad	36
Milton, a name to r for ages;	Milton	4

respect.
some r, however slight, was paid	Princess, ii.	120

response.
Then did my r clearer fall	Two Voices	34

responsive.
Queenly r when the loyal hand	Aylmer's F.	169

rest (repose.)
dreams softer than unbroken r	Ode to Mem.	29
Nor unhappy, nor at r,	Adeline	4
Fold thine arms, turn to thy r.	A Dirge	3
There is no r for me below	Oriana	.
beat against me, In sorrow and in r;	Miller's D.	178
seem'd to float in r	Œnone	18
have attain'd R in a happy place.	"	129
and the weary are at r.	MayQueen,iii.	60
All things else have r (rep.).	Lotos-E's	59
Give us long r or death,	"	98
Sleep full of r from head to feet:	To J. S.	75
caught me up into thy r,	St S. Stylites	18
And shadow'd all her r—	Talking O.	226
get thee to thy r again.	Locksley H.	86
my latest rival brings thee r.	"	89
toward the stillness of his r.	"	144
long disquiet merged in r.	Two Voices	249
A perfect form in perfect r.	Day-Dm.	100
That her spirit might have r.	L. of Burleigh	100
Nor any want-begotten r.	In Mem. xxvii.	12
surely r is meet	" xxx.	18
I know that in thy place of r	" lxvi.	2
wakens at this hour of r	" ciii.	6
To the regions of thy r?'	Maud, II. iv.	88
dear soul, let trouble have r,	" III. vi.	12
nation weeping, and breaking on my r?	Ode on Well.	82
Go thou to thy r, but ere thou go to r	Enid	512
Half disarray'd as to her r,	"	516
without answer to her r She found no r,'	"	530
will charm us both to r	Vivien	181
Love Should have some r	"	335
small r or pleasure in herself,	"	340
R must you have.' 'No r for me,'	Elaine	828
near you, fair lord, I am at r,'	"	829
found no ease in turning or in r.'	"	897
that's all, and long for r	Grandmother	99
nobler yearning never broke her r	Coquette, ii.	2
Had r by stony hills of Crete	On a Mourner	35

rest (remainder.)
	POEM.	LINE.
'These words,' I said, 'are like the r,	Two Voices	334
'He began, The r would follow,	Princess, Pro.	197
So I began And the r followed	"	236
beckon'd us: the r Parted;	" ii.	165
mix not with the r;	"	339

rest (verb.)
on the stone, R's like a shadow,	Œnone	27
r thee sure That I shall love thee	"	156
Oh r ye, brother mariners,	Lotos-E's.	173
came To r beneath thy boughs.	Talking O.	36,156
fairer fruit of Love may r	"	251
no more shall r in mounded heaps,	Golden Year	32
I cannot r from travel:	Ulysses	6
The doubt would r, I dare not solve.	Two Voices	313
Passing the place where each must r,	"	410
Here r's the sap within the leaf,	Day-Dm.	23
will not let his ashes r! 'You might have won,' etc.		28
sleep and r, sleep and r,	Princess, ii.	464
R, r, on mother's breast	"	466
Said Ida: 'let us down and r;'	" iv.	3
this proud watchword r Of equal;	" vii.	282
To r beneath the clover sod.	In Mem. x.	13
Among familiar names to r.	" xviii.	7
I sing to him that r's below,	" xxi.	1
'They r,' we said, 'their sleep is.	" xxx.	19
r's upon the Life indeed.	" xxxii.	8
It r's with God.	" lxxii.	12
My heart, tho' widow'd, may not r	" lxxxiv.	113
Who r to-night beside the sea	Con.	76
the happy shores By which they r	"	121
There he shall r for ever	Ode on Well.	51
rove in following or r On Enid	Enid	399
I could r, a rock in ebbs and flows	"	812
therefore, I do r, A prophet.	"	813
to r awhile within her court,	"	1703
Should r and let you r.	Vivien	184
I love you somewhat; r:	"	334
after my long voyage I shall r!'	Elaine	1055
sighing 'let me r' she said:	En. Arden	372
a name! r, rot in that !	Aylmer's F.	385
Birdie, r a little longer (rep.)	Sea Dreams	285
To r in a golden grove,	Wages	9

rested.
And r from her labours.	The Goose	16
gain'd the hall, and there R:	Princess, vi.	776
r with her sweet face satisfied;	Enid	776
r, and her desolation came Upon	"	1367
r well content that all was well	"	1800
But r in her fealty	"	1815
Nor r thus content, but day by day	Elaine	13
Philip r with her well-content;	En. Arden	373
Enoch r silent many days.	"	700

resting.
R weary limbs at last.	Lotos-E's.	170
Porch-pillars on the lion r;	The Daisy	55

resting-place.
come again, mother, from out my r-p	May Queen,ii.	37

restless.
Passionately r came and went	Aylmer's F.	546

restore.
Release me, and r me to the ground	Tithonus	72
ghost of passion that no smiles r—	Coquette, ii.	11

restored
tho' he built upon the babe r;	Princess, vii.	60

restraint.
I spoke without r,	Talking O.	14

result (s.)
Deep-chested music, and to this r.	The Epic	51
age to age With much the same r.	Walk. to the M.	72
and the long r of Time;	Locksley H.	12
The slow r of winter showers.	Two Voices	452
But for some true r of good.	Will Water.	55
scorn The long r of love	In Mem. i.	14
self-infolds the large r's	" lxxii.	15
that serene r of all.'	" lxxxiv.	92
old r's that look like new:	" cxxvii.	11
O, the r's are simple:	Vivien	534

	POEM.	LINE.
result (verb.)		
R in man, be born and think,	In Mem. Con.	126
resume.		
r their life, They would but find	In Mem. lxxxix.	6
retain.		
And so may Place r us still .	In Mem. xli.	5
reticence.		
Such fine reserve and noble r,	Enid	1708
muffled round with selfish r	Vivien	186
retinue.		
and so Went forth in long r .	Princess, iii.	177
ahead Of his and her r .	Guinevere	362
The dark r reverencing death	Aylmer's F.	842
retire.		
last the dance : till I r :	In Mem. Con.	105
How oft we saw the Sun r, .	The Voyage	17
retired.		
in after life r From brawling storms,	Ode to Mem.	111
I saw the snare, I r :	L.C.V. de Vere	6
retiring.		
Ever r thou dost gaze .	Ode to Mem.	93
retreat.		
Ah, for some r Deep in youder	Locksley H.	153
O joy to him in this r, .	In Mem. lxxxviii.	13
retreated.		
Leolin still R half-aghast .	Aylmer's F.	329
retrospect.		
Not such as moans about the r,	Princess, iv.	67
return (s.)		
Then she went back some paces of r,	Enid	919
tho' my love had no r :	Elaine	1088
I loved you, and my love had no r	"	1269
return verb.)		
I may r with others there .	Pal. of Art	295
some one said, 'We will r no more,'	Lotos-E's.	43
I go, but I r : I would I were	Audley Ct.	70
The fountain to his place r's	Day-Dm.	31
back r To where the body sits,	In Mem. xii.	13
How often she herself r,	" xxxix.	24
Death r's an answer sweet : .	" lxxx.	9
r's the dark With no more hope	Maud, I. ix.	15
r, and fetch Fresh victual	Enid	1073-88
man's love once gone never r's	"	1182
'Fly, they will r And slay you ;	"	1596
the cageling newly flown r's,	Vivien	750
win and r.	Elaine	158
diamond, and deliver it, and r,	"	545
r's his love in open shame	"	1077
to r When others had been tested)	Aylmer's F.	218
r In such a sunlight of prosperity	"	420
as the bird r's, at night,	Sea Dreams	43
his foot R from pacings in the field	Lucretius	6
returned.		
One went, who never hath r.	To J. S.	20
so r unfarrow'd to her sty.	Walk. to the M.	92
Could hope itself r :	Talking O.	12
In courteous words r reply : .	Day-Dm.	162
half-sick at heart, r.	Princess, iv.	204
home to Mary's house r.	In Mem xxxi.	2
amends For a courtesy not r.	Maud, I. vi.	14
she r Indignant to the Queen	Enid	201,413
boy r And told them of a chamber	"	1109
w ke the sleepers, and r :	"	1253
r The huge Earl Doorm	"	1439
In converse for a little, and r	"	1733
after two days' tarriance there, r.	Elaine	568
their wont, a-maying and r,	Guinevere	24
beauteous hateful i le R upon him,	En. Arden	618
to meet the day When Enoch had r,	"	824
r Leolin's rejected rivals	Aylmer's F.	412
shot at, slightly hurt, Raging r ;	"	547
The King r from out the wild,	The Victim	43
returning.		
human things r on themselves	Golden Year	25
R like the pewit, .	Will Water.	230

	POEM.	LINE.
And last, r from afar,	In Mem. lxxxviii.	46
on r found Not two but three	Vivien	558
R brought the yet-unblazon'd shield	Elaine	378
To Astolat r rode the three .	"	901
oft r with the tide.	"	1035
As oft as needed—last, r rich	En. Arden	143
fled before the lazy wind R, .	"	659
still to that R, as the bird returns	Sea Dreams	43
great wave R, while none marked	"	227
thee r on thy silver wheels .	Tithonus	76
reveal.		
gorges, opening wide apart, r Troas	Œnone	12
all the past of Time r's Love thou thy land,' etc.		50
words, like Nature, half r .	In Mem. v.	3
A late-lost form that sleep r's,	"	xiii. 2
any vision should r thy likeness	"	xci. 1
Not to r it, till you see me dead.'	En. Arden	840
revealed.		
first r themselves to English air	Eleänore	2
part by part to men r 'Of old sat Freedom,' etc.		11
R their shining windows : .	Gardener's D.	215
comfort clasp'd in truth r ;	In Mem. xxxvii.	22
A lifelong tract of time r ;	" xlv.	9
dusk r The knolls once more	" xciv.	47
A whisper half r her to herself	Aylmer's F.	144
revealing.		
R's deep and clear are thine .	Madeline	10
reveillée.		
blew R to the breaking morn.	In Mem. lxvii.	8
revel.		
given to starts and bursts Of r ;	Princess, i.	54
In babble and r and wine .	Maud, I. xxii.	23
At civic r and pomp and game,	Ode on W'ell.	147,227
revenge.		
Therefore r became me well .	The Sisters	5
Womanlike, taking r too deep .	Maud, I. iii.	5
revenue.		
overflowing r Wherewith to embellish	Œnone	111
revere.		
Whom we see not we r .rep.)	Ode on Well.	245
revered.		
R, beloved,—O you that hold	To the Queen	1
the poor roofs R as theirs,	Aylmer's F.	176
reverence.		
A thousand claims to r closed	To the Queen	27
the Gods Rise up for r .	Œnone	108
let her herald, R, fly 'Love thou thy land,' etc.		18
To all the people, winning r.	M d'Arthur	167
some cold r worse than she were dead	Princess, v.	89
mask'd thee from men's r up,	" vii.	322
r for the laws ourselves have made	" Con.	55
more of r in us dwell ; .	In Mem. Pro.	26
I had such r for his blame,	"	i. 6
To r and the silver hair ;	" lxxxiii.	32
In r and in charity	" cxiii.	28
debt Of boundless love and r	Ode on W'ell.	157
As if in deepest r and in love.	Vivien	63
no more sign of r than a beard.	"	128
Abash'd Lavaine, whose instant r	Elaine	417
Meet for the r of the hearth	Aylmer's F.	333
our love and r left them bare ?	"	785
reverence (verb)		
r the King as if he were Their conscience	Guinevere	465
reverenced.		
he, he r his liege-lady there :	Princess, i.	186
r his conscience as his king ;	Ded. of Idylls	7
tho' he loved and r her too much	Enid	119
reverencing.		
Self-reverent each and r each,	Princess, vii.	274
r the custom of the house .	Enid	382
r king's blood in a bad man .	Guinevere	38
The dark retinue r death .	Aylmer's F.	842
reverie.		
rapt in nameless r, .	Princess, Con.	108

Y

CONCORDANCE TO

	POEM.	LINE.
reverse.		
To pine in that *r* of doom,	*In Mem.* lxxi.	6
reversed.		
I sit (my empty glass *r*),	*Will Water.*	159
And now, the bloodless point *r*,	*The Voyage*	71
revert.		
Perforce will still *r* to you;	*Day-Dm.*	248
reverting.		
Change, *r* to the years,	*Vision of Sin*	159
reviewer.		
O yon chorus of indolent *r's*,	*Hendecasyllabics*	1-12
Irresponsible, indolent *r's*	"	2
Waking laughter in indolent *r's*	"	8
Too presumptuous, indolent *r's*	"	16
revolt.		
arose The women up in wild *r*,	*Princess,* vii.	108
R's, republics, revolutions,	" *Con.*	65
many more when Modred raised *r. Guinevere*		438
revolution.		
Revolts, republics, *r's*,	*Princess, Con.*	65
revolve.		
In the same circle we *r.*	*Two Voices*	314
revolving.		
stood Sir Bedivere *R* many memories *M. d'Arthur*		270
to rise again *R* toward fulfilment	*Ed. Morris*	39
My mother went *r* on the word)	*Princess,* iii.	38
tho' the months, *r* near,	*In Mem.* xci.	11
rewaken.		
R with the dawning soul.	*In Mem.* xlii.	16
reward.		
God bless you for it, God *r* you	*En. Arden.*	421
Rhine.		
You leave us: you will see the *R*	*In Mem.* xcvii.	1
Rhodope.		
The *R,* that built the pyramid,	*Princess,* ii.	68
rhyme.		
To make demand of modern *r*	*To the Queen*	11
weary sameness in the *r's,*	*Miller's D.*	70
He utter'd *r* and reason,	*The Goose*	6
read me *r's* elaborately good,	*Ed. Morris*	20
I will work in prose and *r,*	*Talking O.*	289
The *r's* are dazzled from their place *Day-Dm.*		19
To make me write my random *r's Will Water.*		13
Let raffs be rife in prose and *r,*	"	61
We lack not *r's* and reasons,	"	62
and *r's* And dismal lyrics,	*Princess,* i.	140
What hope is here for modern *r*	*In Mem.* lxxvi.	1
Ring out, ring out my mournful *r's*	" cv.	19
half but idle brawling *r's*	" *Con.*	23
lucky *r's* to him were scrip and share *The Brook*		4
says Edmund in his *r,*	"	21
rolling in his mind Old waifs of *r,*	"	199
you hardly know the tender *r*	*Vivien*	233
do you love my tender *r*?'	"	249
when you sang me that sweet *r,*	"	284
this *r* Is like the fair pearl necklace	"	300
so is it with this *r:*	"	306
legend as in guerdon for your *r*?	"	404
My *r's* may have been the stronger *Spiteful Let.*		10
For it's easy to find a *r.*	*The Window*	149
rhyme.		
force to make me *r* in youth,	*Miller's D.*	193
rhyming.		
R forward to his *r,*	*Amphion*	30
rhythm.		
into *r* have dash'd The passion	*Princess,* iv.	121
shutting reasons up in *r,*	*Lucretius*	220
rib.		
sawn In twain beneath the *r's;*	*St S. Stylites*	52
Stuff his *r's* with mouldy hay.	*Vision of Sin*	66
some wild shore with *r's* of wreck	*Princess,* v.	141
belabour'd him on *r* and cheek	"	331
clangs Its leafless *r's* and iron horns *In Mem.* cvi.		12

	POEM.	LINE.
crate and basket, *r's* and spine,	*Vivien*	475
on thy *r's* the limpet sticks,	*Sailor Boy*	11
riband.		
She takes a *r* or a rose:	*In Mem.* vi.	32
ribbed.		
long dun wolds are *r* with snow,	*Oriana*	5
ribbon.		
Dangled a length of *r*.	*En. Arden.*	751
blots of it about them, *r,* glove	*Aylmer's F.*	620
rice.		
many a tract of palm and *r,*	*Pal. of Art*	114
rich.		
midway down Hang *r* in flowers.	*Œnone*	7
slumbrous light is *r* and warm,	*Day-Dm.*	83
This earth is *r* in man and maid;	*Will Water.*	65
many a slope was *r* in bloom	*To E. L.*	20
move as *r* as Emperor-moths,	*Princess, Pro.*	144
dark shore just seen that it was *r.*	" i.	245
r as moths from dusk cocoons,	" ii.	5
But he was *r* where I was poor, *In Mem.* lxxviii.		18
lead The closing cycle *r* in good.	" civ.	28
Ring out the feud of *r* and poor	" cv.	11
R in the grace all women desire,	*Maud,* I. x.	13
So *r* in atonement as this	" xix.	6
R in saving common-sense	*Ode on Well.*	32
a house Once *r,* now poor,	*Enid*	302
all the turf was *r* in plots	"	660
like the Queen In all I have of *r, Elaine*		1114
last, returning *r,* Become the master *En. Arden*		143
for I am *r* and well-to-do.	"	310
R, but the loneliest in a lonely sea.	"	554
richer.		
Was *r* than these diamonds	*Elaine*	1223
r in his eyes Who ransom'd us,	*Guinevere*	676
richest.		
shrine which then in all the realm Was *r, Elaine*		1321
richest-toned.		
voice the *r-t* that sings,	*In Mem.* lxxiv.	7
richness.		
deck it like the Queen's For *r*	*Elaine*	1113
rick.		
A jackass heehaws from the *r,*	*Amphion*	71
the *r* Flames and his anger reddens *Princess,* iv.		366
The moon like a *r* on fire was rising *Grandmother*		39
ridden.		
you had gone, *R* to the hills,	*Princess,* iv.	324
Half *r* off with by the thing he rode, *Enid*		1309
wound to wound, And *r* away to die? *Elaine*		567
had *r* wildly round To seek him,	"	627
riddle.		
the *r* of the painful earth	*Pal. of Art*	213
Dissolved the *r* of the earth.	*Two Voices*	170
in seeking to undo One *r,*	"	233
'Your *r* is hard to read.'	*Lady Clare*	76
Charades and *r's* as at Christmas *Princess, Pro.*		187
ride (s.)		
while she made her ready for her *r, Elaine*		775
'Alas,' he said, 'your *r* has wearied you. "		827
ride (verb.)		
His son and heir doth *r* post-haste, *D. of the O. Year*		31
'*R* you naked thro' the town	*Godiva*	29
Then by some secret shrine I *r;*	*Sir Galahad*	29
R on! the prize is near.'	"	80
All-arm'd I *r,* whate'er betide,	"	90
love us for it, and we *r* them down *Princess,* v.		130
r with us to our lines, And speak.	"	216
Down by the hill I saw them *r,*	*Maud,* I. ix.	11
r with him to battle and stand by, *Enid*		94
'I will *r* forth into the wilderness	"	127
meanest dress And *r* with me.'	"	131
tho' I *r* unarmed, I do not doubt	"	218
late I saw *R* into that new fortress	"	407
Shalt *r* to Arthur's court,	"	582
r with him this morning to the court,	"	606

POEM. LINE.

I can scarcely *r* with you to court, *Enid* . . 749
r with me in her faded silk.' . . " . . 762
I charge you *r* before . . . " . . 863
when she saw him *r* More near . " . . 1290
'Then, Enid, shall you *r* Behind me.' " . . 1598
r abroad redressing human wrongs! *Vivien* . 543
he will *r*, Joust for it, and win, . *Elaine* . 203
r to Camelot with this noble knight " . 220
you *r* with Lancelot of the Lake.' " . 416
rise, My nephew, and *r* forth . " . 536
r no longer wildly, noble Prince! " . 630
the King *R* toward her from the city *Guinevere* . 401
r abroad redressing human wrongs " . 468

rider.

The horse and *r* reel: . . . *Sir Galahad* 8
his heavy *r* kept him down. . . *Vision of Sin* 4
r's front to front, until they closed *Princess*, v. 479

ridge.

sand-built *r* Of heaped hills . . *Ode to Mem.* 97
A faint-blue *r* upon the right, *Mariana in the S.* 5
Across the *r*, and paced beside the *M. d'Arthur* 83
leaping down the *r's* lightly, . " . 134
swiftly strode from *r* to *r*, . . " . 181
hoofs bare on the *r* of spears . *Princess*, v. 478
The fortress, and the mountain *r*, *In Mem.* lxx. 14
Or slip between the *r's*, . . *The Brook* . 28
Close to the *r* of a noble down. *To F. D. Maurice* 16
climb'd upon a fair and even *r*, . *Enid* . . 239
a *r* Of breaker issued from the belt *Sea Dreams* 204
and then the great *r* drew, . . " . 213

ridged.

R the smooth level, . . . *Arabian N's.* 35

ridging.

The Biscay, roughly *r* eastward . *En. Arden* . 525

riding.

The knights come *r* two and two: *L. of Shalott*, ii. 25
came *r* toward a palace-gate. . *Vision of Sin* 2
r in, we call'd; . . . . *Princess*, i. 222
r at set of day . . . . *Maud*, I. ix. 5
Rapidly *r* far away, . . . " . 7
found the bailiff *r* by the farm . *The Brook* . 153
down the long street *r* wearily, . *Enid* . . 254
r close behind an ancient churl, . " . . 261
r further past an armourer's, . " . . 266
r first, I hear the violent threats . " . 1268
Came *r* with a hundred lances up; " . 1388

riding whip.

Stopt and then with a *r w* . . *Maud*, I. xiii. 18

rife.

With dinning sound my ears are *r*, *Eleänore* . 135
Let raffs be *r* in prose and rhyme *Will Water.* 61
language *r* With rugged maxims *Ode on Well.* 183

rift (verb.)

R the hills, and roll the waters, . *Locksley H.* 186

rift (s.)

cleave the *r* of difference deeper yet *Princess*, v. 291
It is the little *r* within the lute, . *Vivien* 240-3

right (adj.)

For, am I *r*, or am I wrong, . *Day-Dm.* 241-5
is not Ida *r*? They worth it? . *Princess*, v. 180
wise world of ours is mainly *r*. . *Enid* . 1749

right (s.)

because *r* is *r*, to follow *r* Were wisdom *Œnone* 147
hers by *r* of full-accomplish'd Fate: *Pal. of Art* 207
since I knew the *r* And did it: *Love and Duty* 29
we, that prate Of *r's* and wrongs, *Godiva* . 8
in the *r's* that name may give, . *Day-Dm.* . 266
The man will cleave unto his *r*.' . *Lady Clare* 46
A talk of college and of ladies' *r's*, *Princess, Pro.* 226
he swerved from *r* to save A prince, " ii. 270
great year of equal mights and *r's* " iv. 56
unfurl the maiden banner of our *r's*, " . 482
bawl for civil *r's*, No woman named: " v. 377
With claim on claim from *r* to *r*. " . 407
r's or wrongs like potherbs in the " . 449

liberal, since our *r's* are won. . *Princess*, vi. 52
scorn'd to help their equal *r's* . " vii. 218
Ring in the love of truth and *r* . *In Mem.* cv. 23
mine by a *r*, from birth till death, *Maud* I. xix. 42
a war would arise in defence of the *r* " III. vi. 19
self-seekers trampling on the *r*: . *Ode on Well.* 187
only thirsting For the *r* . . " . 204
At you, so careful of the *r*, . *To F. D. Maurice* 10
reigning in his place, Lord of his *r's* *En. Arden* 765

right (verb.)

When the wild peasant *r's* himself, *Princess*, iv. 366
to fight, to struggle, to *r* the wrong—*Wages* . 3

righteousness.

yonder shines The Sun of *R*, . *En. Arden* . 500

rill.

old well-heads of haunted *r's*, . *Eleänore* . 16
song of bird or sound of *r*; . . *D. of F. Wom.* 66
Go down beside thy native *r* *In Mem.* xxxvii. 5
From hidden summits fed with *r's* " cii. 7
The white-faced halls, the glancing *r's*, " *Con.* 113

rillets.

fall Of diamond *r's* musical, . *Arabian N's.* 48

rim.

ragged *r's* of thunder brooding low, *Pal. of Art* 75
Beyond their utmost purple *r*, . *Day-Dm.* 170-94
Now pacing mute by ocean's *r* . *The Daisy* . 21
Roll'd into light, and turning on its *r's* *Elaine* . 52
ran By sallowy *r's*, . . . *Aylmer's F.* 147
the *r* Changed every moment . *The Voyage* 27

rime.

Unnaturally hoar with *r* . . *St S. Stylites* 163
Make thy grass hoar with early *r*. *Two Voices* 66
lawn as yet Is hoar with *r*, . . *To F. D. Maurice* 42

rimm'd.

length of bright horizon *r* the dark. *Gardener's D.* 177

rind.

gleaming *r* ingrav'n 'For the most fair *Œnone* 70
Hard wood I am, and wrinkled *r*, *Talking O.* 171

ring (s.)

Round thy neck in subtle *r* . . *Adeline* . 58
Sleeps on his luminous *r*.' . . *Pal. of Art* 16
drew into two burning *r's* . . *D. of F. Wom.* 174
Five hundred *r's* of years— . . *Talking O.* . 84
And even into my inmost *r* . . " . 173
Grave faces gather'd in a *r*. . *Day-Dm.* . 58
Closed in a golden *r*. . . *Sir L. and Q. G* 27
I'll stake my ruby *r* upon it . *Princess, Pro.* 163
a thousand *r's* of Spring In every bole " v 227
one would pierce an outer *r*. . *In Mem* lxxxvi 27
The *r* is on, The 'wilt thou' answer'd, " *Con.* 53
sapphire-spangled marriage *r* of the *Maud*, I. iv. 6
I noticed one of his many *r's* . " II. ii. 68
bindweed-bells and briony *r's* . *The Brook* . 203
And gave the trinkets and the *r's* *The Letters* 21
now beneath her marriage *r*. . *Enid* . 1168
Enoch's golden *r* had girt Her finger, *En. Arden* 157
a length of ribbon and a *r*. . . " . 751
deeper than to wear it as his *r*— . *Aylmer's F.* 122
nor by plight or broken *r* Bound, " . 135
dim curls kindle into sunny *r's*; . *Tithonus* . 54

ring (to resound, etc.)

How the merry bluebell *r's* . . *Adeline* . 34
a sound *R's* ever in her ears. . *Œnone* . 261
-bells *r* in the Christmas morn. *M. d'Arthur, Ep.* 31
R's in mine ears. The steer forgot *Gardener's D.* 84
did we hear the copses *r*, . . *Locksley H.* 35
The shrill bell *r's*, the censer swings, *Sir Galahad* 35
all the glimmering moorland *r's* *Sir L. and Q. G.* 35
'lights and *r's* the gateway bell, . *In Mem* viii. 3
Shall *r* with music all the same; . " lxxvi. 14
R out wild bells to the wild sky, (rep.) " cv. 1
Now *r's* the woodland loud and long, " cxiv. 5
r's to the yell of the trampled wife, *Maud*, I i. 39
r's Even in dreams to the chink " x. 42
It will *r* in my heart and my ears, " II. i. 35
And the woodland echo *r's*; . " iv. 38

340   CONCORDANCE TO

	POEM.	LINE.
r's on a sudden a passionate cry,	Maud, II. iv.	47
the world should r of him	Aylmer's F.	395
R's to the roar of an angel onset	Milton	8

ring (to encircle.)
| my followers r him round : | Enid | 1185 |

ringdove.
| In which the swarthy r sat, | Talking O. | 293 |

ringed.
| R with the azure world, he stands. | The Eagle | 3 |

ringer.
the r's rang with a will, and he gave
| the r's a crown | Grandmother | 58 |

ringing.
midnight bells cease r suddenly.	D. of F. Wom.	247
when the bells were r, Allan call'd	Dora	39
in the r of thine ears ;	Locksley H.	84
r, springs from brand and mail ;	Sir Galahad	54
With blissful treble r clear.	Sir L. and Q. G.	22
R thro' the vallies,	Maud, I. xii.	10
Clamour and rumble, and r and clatter,	II. v.	13
r with their serpent hands	Vivien	428
Once likewise, in the r of his ears,	En. Arden.	614
R like proven golden coinage	Aylmer's F.	182
he must—the land was r of it—	"	262
His message r in thine ears,	"	666

ringlet.
comb my hair till my r's would fall	The Mermaid	14
hid in r's day and night	Miller's D.	173
Tie up the r's on your cheek :	Margaret	57
The r's waving balm—	Talking O.	178
showered the rippled r's to her knee;	Godiva	47
full black r's downward roll'd,	Day-Dm.	88
Blowing the r from the braid	Sir L. and Q. G.	39
lengths of yellow r's, like a girl,	Princess, i.	
Once more to set a r right ;	In Mem. vi.	36
Ere childhood's flaxen r turn'd	" lxxviii	15
Your r's, your r's, That look so		
golden gay	The Ringlet 1, et pass.	

ringlet-snake
| numbs the Fury's r-s, | Lucretius | 258 |

riot.
| in many a wild festoon, Ran r | Œnone | 99 |
| a noiseless r underneath | Lucretius | 185 |

rioted.
r his life out, and made an end.	Aylmer's F.	391
r in the city of Cunobeline !	Boädicea	60
There they dwelt and there they r;	"	63

ripe.
when time was r, The still affection	Miller's D.	224
I was r for death	D. of F. Wom.	208
Made r in Sumner-chace :	Talking O.	40
Till all be r and rotten.	Will Water.	16
Half-mused, or reeling r,	"	74
thou, that countest reason r.	In Mem. xxxiii.	13
Appearing ere the times were r,	Con.	139
you may call it a little too r	Maud, I. ii.	9
shaping an infant r for his birth	" iv.	34
if the nuts' he said 'be r again :	En. Arden.	456
Too r, too late ! they come too late	Sea Dreams	67
makes the purple lilac r,	On a Mourner	7

ripen.
flower r's in its place, R's and fades,	Lotos-E's.	81
r toward the grave In silence	"	96
r, fall, and cease : .	"	97
The unnetted black-hearts r dark.	The Blackbird	7
watch her harvest r, her herd	Maud, III. vi.	25

ripen'd.
| woman r earlier, and her life | Princess, ii. | 138 |

ripeness.
| but, when love is grown To r | To J. S. | 15 |
| gave all r to the grain, | In Mem. lxxx. | 11 |

riper.
| first, and third, which are a r first? | Sea Dreams | 66 |

ripple (s.)
	POEM.	LINE.
watch the crisping r's on the beach	Lotos-E's.	106
I heard the r washing in the reeds	M. d'Arthur	70, 117
The seeming-wanton r break	In Mem. xlviii.	11
down the horned flood In r's	" lxxxv.	8
the r feathering from her bows :	En. Arden.	540

ripple (verb.)
| That r round the lonely grange : | In Mem. xc. | 12 |
| the rivulet at her feet R's on | Maud, II. iv. | 41 |

rise (s.)
throned on a flowery r.	D. of F. Wom.	125
and prophesied his r :	Aylmer's F.	474
the r, and long roll of the Hexameter	Lucretius	10

rise (verb.)
How could I r and come away	Oriana	57
fall and r Upon her balmy bosom,	Miller's D.	182
the Gods R up for reverence	Œnone	108
I will r and go Down into Troy,	"	257
And that sweet incense r ?'	Pal. of Art	44
For I would see the sun r	May Queen, ii. 2, 51	
lamb's voice to me that cannot r,	" iii.	6
O look ! the sun begins to r,	"	49
threshold of the sun, Never to r	D. of F. Wom.	64
large white stars r one by one,	"	223
R from the feast of sorrow, lady,	Margaret	62
if some dreadful need should r 'Love thou thy land'		91
let thy voice R like a fountain for	M. d'Arthur	249
to r again Revolving toward	Ed. Morris	38
and the shadows r and fall.	Locksley H.	80
Pain r's up, old pleasures pall.	Two Voices	164
every hundred years to r	Day-Dm.	215
Are but dust that r's up,	Vision of Sin	133-69
Till thy drooping courage r,	"	152
r To glass herself in dewy eyes 'Move eastward'		6
The Samian Here r's and she speaks	Princess, iii.	99
R in the heart, and gather to the eyes	" iv.	23
R I' and stoop'd to updrag Melissa :	"	347
they r or sink Together.	"	vii. 243
men may r on stepping-stones	In Mem. i.	3
see the sails at distance r,	" xii.	11
To-night the winds begin to r	" xv.	1
r's upward always higher	"	17
R happy morn, r, holy morn	" xxx.	29
crown'd with blessings she doth r	" xxxix.	5
Did ever r from high to higher ;	" xl.	2
if any vague desire should r,	" lxxi.	1
An iron welcome when they r :	" lxxxix.	8
of events As often r's ere they r.	" xci.	16
served the seasons that may r ;	" cxii.	4
R in the spiritual rock .	" cxxx.	3
They r, but linger : it is late ;	Con.	91
And r, O moon, from yonder down,	"	109
and thought he would r and speak	Maud, I. i.	
there r's ever a passionate cry	" II. i.	
Then I r, the eavedrops fall,	" iv.	62
if he r no more, I will not look on wine	Enid	1514
R therefore ; robe yourself in this :	"	1533
Rose when they saw the dead man r,	"	1580
Gawain, r, My nephew, and ride forth	Elaine	535
To r hereafter in a stiller flame	"	1309
but r, And fly to my strong castle	Guinevere	111
yet r now, and let us fly,	"	119
Let me r and fly away.	Sea Dreams	292
blasts would r and rave and cease,	The Voyage	85
A devil r's in my heart,	Sailor Boy	23

risen.
Nilus would have r before his time	D. of F. Wom.	143
Dora would have r and come to him,	Dora	75
thus early r she goes to inform	Princess, iii.	46
Has r and cleft the soil,	"	vi. 19
those twin brothers, r again and whole;	"	vii. 74

risest.
| R thou thus, dim dawn, again (xcviii. 1.) | In Mem. lxxi. | 1 |

rising.
r, from her bosom drew	Mariana in the S.	61
angels r and descending met	Pal. of Art	143
And of the r from the dead,	"	206
r bore him thro' the place of tombs.	M. d'Arthur	175

		POEM.	LINE.
r thro' the mellow shade,		Locksley H.	9
R to no fancy-flies.		Vision of Sin	102
R, falling, like a wave,		"	125
r up Robed in the long night		Princess, iv.	469
Look'd up, and *r* slowly from me,		" vi.	135
Last little Lilia, *r* quietly,		" Con.	116
r up, he rode to Arthur's court,		Enid .	591
r on the sudden he said, 'Eat I		"	1467
the Prince, who *r* twice or thrice		Guinevere	47
The moon like a rick on fire was *r*		Grandmother	39

risk'd.

| he *r* it for my own | | Princess, v. | 397 |
| (for the man Had *r* his little) | | Sea Dreams | 10 |

risking.

| some knight of mine, *r* his life | | Enid . | 1763 |

rite.

r's and forms before his burning eyes		The Poet .	39
with solemn *r*'s by candle-light—		Princess, v.	282
Worthy of our gorgeous *r*'s .		Ode on Well.	93
mingle with your *r*'s; Pray		Guinevere .	672
The *r*'s prepared, the victim bared,		The Victim	70

ritual.

| And hear the ritual of the dead. | | In Mem. xviii. | 12 |

rivage.

| From the green *r* many a fall | | Arabian N's. | 47 |

rival.

my latest *r* brings thee rest.		Locksley H.	89
To push my *r* out of place		Princess, iv.	316
Poor *r*'s in a losing game,		In Mem. ci.	10
the maid in Astolat, Her guiltless *r*,		Elaine .	742
Leolin's rejected *r*'s from their suit		Aylmer's F.	493
Leolin's one strong *r* upon earth;		"	557
wrathful, petulant, Dreaming some *r*,		Lucretius	15

rivalries.

| fruitful strifes and *r* of peace— | | Ded. of Idylls | 37 |

river.

canal From the main *r* sluiced,		Arabian N's.	26
A motion from the *r* won		"	34
Flowing like a crystal *r*;		Poet's Mind	6
With an inner voice the *r* ran,		Dying Swan	5
One willow over the *r* wept,		"	14
On either side the *r* lie		L. of Shalott, i	"
By the island in the *r*		"	13
From the *r* winding clearly,		"	31
There the *r* eddy whirls,		" ii.	15
From the bank and from the *r*		" iii.	13
by the *r* Sang Sir Lancelot.		"	35
down the *r*'s dim expanse—		" iv.	10
the full-flowing *r* of speech		Œnone .	67
one, a full-fed *r* winding slow		Pal. of Art .	73
drew *R*'s of melodies.		"	172
saw the gleaming *r* seaward flow		Lotos-E's.	14
long bright *r* drawing slowly His waters		"	137
fresh the meadows look Above the *r*,		Walk. to the M.	2
By *r*'s gallopaded.		Amphion .	40
In curves the yellowing *r* ran		Sir L. and Q. G.	15
A rivulet then a *r*;		A Farewell	6
in a gleaming *r*'s crescent-curve		Princess, i.	169
We follow'd up the *r* as we rode		"	203
the *r* made a fall Out yonder:'		" iii.	156
r as it narrow'd to the hills		"	180
up we came to where the *r* sloped		"	273
They faint on hill or field or *r*;		"	361
miss'd the plank, and roll'd In the *r*.		" iv.	166
Black hair Damp from the river:		"	258
As waits a *r* level with the dam		"	452
Let the great *r* take me to the main:		" vi.	376
Beside the *r*'s wooded reach,		In Mem. lxx.	13
A *r* sliding by the wall		" cii.	8
and his *r* billowing ran,		Maud, I. iv.	32
To join the brimming *r*, (rep.)		The Brook .	2
there the *r*: and there Stands Philip's farm		"	37
where brook and *r* meet		"	38
shines over city and *r* .		Ode on Well.	50
O'er the four *r*'s the first roses blew,		Enid	1612

		POEM	LINE.
holding then his court Hard on the *r*		Elaine .	76
By the great *r* in a boatman's hut		"	278,1032
a chariot-bier To take me to the *r*,		"	1116
and a large Be ready on the *r*,		"	1117
in a *r* of blood to the sick sea		Aylmer's F	768
Flash, ye cities, in *r*'s of fire!		W. to Alexan.	19

river-bank.

| he ran Beside the *r-b*: | | Aylmer's F. | 451 |

river-bed.

| An empty *r-b* before, | | Mariana in the S. | 6 |
| The *r-b* was dusty-white; | | " | 54 |

river-breeze.

| the soft *r-b*, Which fann'd the gardens | | Aylmer's F. | 454 |

River-God.

| I am the daughter of a *R-G*. | | Œnone . | 37 |

river-rain.

| Snapt in the rushing of the *r-r* | | Vivien . | 807 |

river-shore.

| Spread the light haze along the *r-s* | | Gardener's D. | 259 |

river-sunder'd.

| *r-s* champaign cloth'd with corn | | Œnone . | 112 |

river-tide.

| On the misty *r-t* . | | Maud, II. iv. | 67 |

riveting.

| Sat *r* a helmet on his knee, | | Enid . | 203 |

riving.

| *r* the spirit of man, | | The Poet . | 51 |

rivulet.

the *r* in the flowery dale		May Queen,	1. 22
By dancing *r*'s fed his flocks,		To E. L.	22
Now by some tinkling *r*,		Sir L. and Q. G	90
Flow down, cold *r*, to the sea,		A Farewell	1
A *r* then a river:		"	6
Myriads of *r*'s hurrying thro' the lawn		Princess, vii	205
Nor pastoral *r* that swerves		In Mem. xcix.	14
But the *r* on from the lawn		Maud, I. xiv.	29
R crossing my ground,		" xxi.	7
O *R*, born at the hall		"	8
For I heard your *r* fall		" xxii.	36
the *r* at her feet Ripples on		" II. iv.	41
Fled like a glittering *r* to the tarn:		Elaine .	53
sweep Of some precipitous *r*,		En. Arden .	588
where the *r*'s of sweet waters ran;		"	643
many a *r* high against the Sun		The Islet .	21

road.

thro' the field the *r* runs by		L. of Shalott, i.	4
cold and starless *r* of Death.		Œnone .	253
In ruin, by the mountain *r*;		The Daisy .	6
at a sudden swerving of the *r*,		Enid .	1155
and stood by the *r* at the gate.		Grandmother	18
Out into the *r* I started, and spoke		"	41

roam.

at night I would *r* abroad and play		The Merman	11
r, with tresses unconfined		Eleänore .	122
we will no longer *r*.		Lotos-E's.	45
Henceforth, wherever thou may'st *r*,		In Mem. xvii.	9
All winds that *r* the twilight		" lxxviii.	14
To range the woods, to *r* the park,		" Con.	96
r the goodly places that she knew:		Enid .	646
those that stay and those that *r*,		Sailor Boy .	14

roaming.

| always *r* with a hungry heart | | Ulysses . | 12 |
| A white-hair'd shadow *r* like a dream | | Tithonus | 8 |

roan.

| three pyebalds and a *r*. | | Walk. to the M. | 104 |

roar (s.)

The panther's *r* came muffled		Œnone .	210
such a *r* that Earth Reels,		Princess, v.	517
r that breaks the Pharos from his base		" vi.	319
in its broad-flung ship-wrecking *r*,		Maud, I. iii.	11
in streaming London's central *r*.		Ode on Well.	9
Heard thro' the living *r*.		Sea Dreams	56
'but this tide's *r*, and his,		"	242
Rings to the *r* of an angel onset—		Milton .	8

342   CONCORDANCE TO

roar (verb.)
	POEM.	LINE.
below them r's The long brook	Œnone	7
r rock-thwarted under bellowing caves	Pal. of Art.	71
He that r's for liberty	Vision of Sin	127
once or twice I thought to r,	Princess, ii.	401
r from yonder dropping day ;	In Mem. xv.	2
There where the long street r's,	" cxxii.	3
Well r's the storm to those that hear	" cxxvi.	3
And molten up, and r in flood ;	"	13
the sea r's Ruin : a fearful night !	Sea Dreams	80
R as the sea when he welcomes	W. to Alexan.	24

roared.
'No!' R the rough king,	Princess, i.	86
some vast bulk that lived and r	" iii.	277
(thus the King R).	" v.	34
lake whiten'd and the pinewood r	Vivien	487
and above them r the pine	Aylmer's F.	431
R as when the rolling breakers	Boädicea	76
Hector said, and sea-like r his host;	Spec. of Iliad	1

roaring.
I hear the r of the sea,	Oriana	97
The wind is r in turret and tree.	The Sisters	15
heard the lion r from his den ;	D. of F. Wom.	222
ocean-ridges r into cataracts.	Locksley H.	6
mighty wind arises, r seaward,	"	194
In r's round the coral reef	In Mem. xxxvi.	16
And the r of the wheels	Maud, II. iv.	22
R to make a third ;	Aylmer's F.	128
R out their doom	The Captain	42
winds were r and blowing : (rep.)	1865-1866	3

rob.
once had power to r it of content	Coquette, ii.	8

robbed.
r the farmer of his bowl of cream:	Princess, v.	214

robber.
onslaught single on a realm Of r's	Enid	1766
There the horde of Roman r's	Boädicea	18

robe (s.)
no blood upon her maiden r's	The Poet	41
She threw her royal r's away.	Pal. of Art	290
With that she tore her r apart.	D. of F. Wom.	157
the white r and the palm.	St. S. Stylites	20
As these white r's are soil'd and dark,	St Agnes' Eve	13
In r and crown the king stept down,	Beggar Maid	5
white r like a blossom'd branch	Princess, iv.	161
r's, and gems and gemlike eyes,	"	459
drew Her r to meet his lips,	" vi.	140
falser self slipt from her like a r,	" vii.	146
Till slowly worn her earthly r,	In Mem. lxxxiii.	33
In a cold white r before me .	Maud, II. iv.	19
a r Of samite without price..	Vivien	70
down his r the dragon writhed	Elaine	434
'If I be loved, these are my festal r's,	"	905
In hanging r or vacant ornament,	Guinevere	502
A close-set r of jasmine	Aylmer's F.	158
How oft the purple-skirted r	The Voyage	21

robe (verb.)
Rise therefore ; r yourself in this :	Enid	1533

robed.
r in soften'd light Of orient state.	Ode to Mem.	10
Lying, r in snowy white	L. of Shalott, iv.	19
lying r and crown'd,	D. of F. Wom.	163
reissuing, r and crown'd, To meet	Godiva	77
r the shoulders in a rosy silk	Princess, Pro	103
R in the long night of her deep hair	" iv.	470
r herself, Help'd by the mother's.	Enid	737
r them in her ancient suit again	"	770
R in red samite, easily to be known	Elaine	432
r your cottage-walls with flowers.	Aylmer's F.	698
Loosely r in flying raiment,	Boädicea	37

Robert.
old Sir R's pride, His books—	Audley Ct.	57
slight Sir R with his watery smile	Ed. Morris	128

robin.
crimson comes upon the r's breast	Locksley H.	17
careful r's eye the delver's toil,	Enid	774, 1280
On the nigh-naked tree the R piped	En. Arden	677

Robin.
	POEM.	LINE.
R leaning on the bridge	May Queen, i.	14
And say to R a kind word,	" iii.	44

Robins.
Or a mowt 'a taaken R	N. Farmer.	50
Noither a mount to R	"	60

rock (s.)
the mermaids in and out of the r's	The Merman	12
the mermen in and out of the r's.	The Mermaid	34
Of ledge or shelf The r rose clear,	Pal. of Art	10
or a sound of r's thrown down,	"	282
zig-zag paths, and juts of pointed r,	M d'Arthur	50
and leveret lay, Like fossils of the r,	Audley Ct.	24
as we sank From r to r	"	83
upon a r With turrets lichen-gilded like a r;	Ed. Morris	7
forged a thousand theories of the r's,	"	18
struck his staff against the r's	Golden Year	59
lights begin to twinkle from the r's:	Ulysses	54
His mantle glitters on the r's—	Day-Dm.	100
To him who sat upon the r's,	To E. L.	23
push'd with lances from the r,	Princess, Pro.	46
something of the frame, the r	" ii.	360
No r so hard but that a little wave	" iii.	138
like a touch of sunshine on the r's,	"	339
Each was like a Druid r ;	" iv.	261
Part sat like r's :	" v.	485
Pharos from his base Had left us r.	" vi.	320
My love has talk'd with r's and trees;	In Mem xcvi	1
Nor runlet tinkling from the r ;	" xcix.	13
Rise in the spiritual r,	" cxxx.	3
There yet lies the r that fell with him	Maud, I. i.	8
by a red r, glimmers the Hall ;	" iv	10
Athwart the ledges of r	" II. ii.	28
seems a promontory of r,	Will.	6
r in ebbs and flows, Fixt on her faith.	Enid	812
wholly arm'd behind a r In shadow	"	906
I saw three bandits by the r	"	921
town with towers, upon a r,	"	1046
errant eyes home from the r,	"	1096
In the white r a chapel and a hall	Elaine	404
to their fancy's eye from broken r's	"	1245
no stoning save with flint and r?	Aylmer's F.	740
on the foremost r's Touching, upjetted	Sea Dreams	51
for Willy stood like a r.	Grandmother	10
nutmeg r's and isles of clove.	The Voyage	40
by r and cave and tree.	V. of Cauteretz	9

rock (verb.)
O r upon thy towery top	Talking O.	265
r the snowy cradle till I died.	Princess, iv.	86
The blind wall r's, and on the trees	InMem. Con	63

rocked.
R the full-foliaged elms,	In Mem. xciv.	56

rocket.
The r molten into flakes	InMem xcvii.	31
Rush to the roof, sudden r,	W. to Alexan.	20

rocking.
Then lightly r baby's cradle	En. Arden	194

rock-thwarted.
r-t under bellowing caves	Pal. of Art	71

rod.
red-faced war has r's of steel and fire;	Princess, v.	114
be ruled with r or with knout ?	Maud, I. iv.	47
war's avenging r Shall lash all Europe	To F. D. Maurice	33

rode.
Ere I r into the fight,	Oriana	21
He r between the barley-sheaves,	L. of Shalott, iii.	2
As he r down to Camelot : (rep.)	"	14
as he r his armour rung,	"	17
my lover, with whom I r sublime	D. of F. Wom.	141
And r his hunter down.	Talking O.	104
far below the Roundhead r,	"	299
she r forth, cloth'd on with chastity.	Godiva	53, 65
deep air listen'd round her as she r,	"	54
R thro' the coverts of the deer	Sir L. and Q. G.	21

Entry	POEM.	LINE.
r a horse with wings, that would	Vision of Sin	3
slowly *r* across a wither'd heath	"	61
They *r*; they betted; made a hundred	Princess, Pro.	162
We *r* many a long league back	" i.	165
follow'd up the river as we *r*, And *r* till midnight	"	203
'That afternoon the Princess *r*	" iii.	153
I *r* beside her and to me she said	"	181
we *r* a league beyond,	"	316
Then *r* we with the old king	" v.	226
with honey'd answer as we *r*	"	232
Back *r* we to my father's camp	"	321
everywhere He *r* the mellay,	"	491
but Arac *r* him down:	"	521
as she *r* by on the moor;	Maud, I. iv.	15
one of the two that *r* at her side	" x.	24
R the six-hundred (rep.)	Lt. Brigade	4
Boldly they *r* and well,	"	23
Then they *r* back, but not	"	37
r And fifty knights *r* with them,	Enid	43, 1801
there *r* Full slowly by a knight,	"	186
r, By ups and downs,	"	235
onward to the fortress *r* the three	"	251
r Geraint, a little spleenful yet,	"	293
r Geraint into the castle court,	"	312
all unarm'd I *r*, and thought to find	"	417
rising up, he *r* to Arthur's court,	"	591
kiss'd her, and they *r* away.	"	825
forth they *r*, but scarce three paces	"	868
r so slowly and they look'd so pale,	"	884
for he *r* As if he heard not	"	1300
ridden off with by the thing he *r*,	"	1309
so *r* on, nor told his gentle wife	"	1352
R on a mission to the bandit earl	"	1376
poor gown I *r* with him to court,	"	1548
r upon this fatal quest Of honour	"	1551
and at once they *r* away.	"	1610
Tho' thence I *r* all-shamed	"	1700
all day long we *r* Thro' the dim land	Vivien	274
left it with her, when he *r* to tilt	Elaine	30
heard mass, broke fast, and *r* away;	"	414
all the region round *R* with his diamonds	"	613
A true-love ballad, lightly *r* away.	"	701
tho' I *r* all round The region;	"	705
R o'er the long backs of the bushless	"	785
To Astolat returning *r* the three.	"	901
Nor had farewell, but sadly *r* away	"	981
then they *r* to the divided way,	Guinevere	123
And *r* thereto from Lyonnesse,	"	234
as he *r*, an hour or maybe twain	"	235
R under groves that look'd a paradise	"	386
There *r* an armed warrior to the doors.	"	496
R upon his father's shield—'Home they brought him'		8

rogue.

Entry	POEM.	LINE.
one the Master, as a *r* in grain	Princess, Pro.	116
A *r* of canzonets and serenades.	" iv.	117
the smooth-faced snubnosed *r*.	Maud, I. i.	51
some meddling *r* has tamper'd with him—	Elaine	129
unctuous mouth which lured him, *r*,	Sea Dreams	14
before you prove him, *r*,	"	167

roisterer.

| midmost of a rout of *r*'s | Enid | 1123 |

roll (s.)

Now, to the *r* of muffled drums	Ode on Well.	87
R of cannon and clash of arms,	"	116
I hear the *r* of the ages	Spiteful Let.	8
rise And long *r* of the Hexameter	Lucretius	11
ever lowest *r* of thunder moans	"	108

roll (verb.)

they *r* a prurient skin,	Pal. of Art	201
and the wind began to *r*,	May Queen, iii.	27
wave will *r* us shoreward soon.'	Lotos-E's.	2
And the great ages onward *r*,	To J. S.	72
R onward, leading up the golden year.	Golden Year	41
r the waters, flash the lightnings,	Locksley H.	186
the gates *R* back, and far within	St Agnes' Eve	30
They reel, they *r* in clanging lists,	Sir Galahad	9

Entry	POEM.	LINE.
Our echoes *r* from soul to soul,	Princess, iii.	362
r The torrents, dash'd to the vale;	" v.	339
r the torrent out of dusky doors:	" vii.	193
down *r*'s the world In mock heroics	" Con.	63
I hear a wizard music *r*,	In Mem. lxix.	14
And *r* it in another course,	" cxii.	10
The strong imagination *r*	" cxxi.	6
r's the deep where grew the tree.	" cxxii.	1
have her lion *r* in a silken net	Maud, I. vi.	27
long waves that *r* in yonder bay?	" xviii.	63
and the war *r* down like a wind	" III. vi.	54
world on world in myriad myriads *r*	Ode on Well.	262
years will *r* into the centuries	Guinevere	619
a thousand memories *r* upon him,	En. Arden	725
were a mist that *r*'s away;	V. of Canteretz	6
R and rejoice, jubilant voice,	W. to Alexan.	22
R as a ground-swell dash'd	"	23
r thy tender arms Round him	Lucretius	82
You *r* up away from the light	The Window	50

roll'd.

tumult of their acclaim is *r*.	Dying Swan	33
about him *r* his lustrous eyes;	Love and Death	3
I *r* among the tender flowers;	Fatima	11
R round by one fixed law.	Pal. of Art	256
R to starboard, *r* to larboard,	Lotos-E's.	151
R on each other, rounded, smooth'd,	D. of F. Wom.	51
had *r* me deep below,	"	117
next moon was *r* into the sky,	"	227
all day long the noise of battle *r*	M. d'Arthur	1
R in one another's arms,	Locksley H.	58
When the ranks are *r* in vapour,	"	104
all the war is *r* in smoke.'	Two Voices	156
full black ringlets downward *r*,	Day-Dm	83
babies *r* about Like tumbled fruit	Princess, Pro.	82
Kitten-like he *r* And paw'd	" iii.	165
miss'd the plank, and *r* In the river	" iv.	159
r the gilded Squire	" v.	21
r himself Thrice in the saddle,	"	264
Part *r* on the earth and rose again	"	486
r With music in the growing breeze	" vi.	40
her eye with slow dilation *r*	"	172
r the psalm to mighty skies,	In Mem. lv.	11
r the floods in grander space,	" cii.	26
And a sullen thunder is *r*	Maud, II. iv.	47
sound of the sorrowing anthem *r*	Ode on Well.	
down his enemy *r*, And there lay still;	Enid	1009
He *r* his eyes about the hall,	"	1458
russet-bearded head *r* on the floor.	"	1577
forethought *r* about his brain	Vivien	77
r his enemy down, And saved him	Elaine	26
from the skull the crown *R* into light	"	52
r his eyes Yet blank from sleep,	"	815
R a sea-haze and whelm'd the world	En. Arden	673
the year *R* itself round again	"	823
once again he *r* his eyes upon her	"	904
r His hoop to pleasure Edith,	Aylmer's F.	84
R the rich vapour far into the heaven	Spec. of Iliad	8

roller.

| league-long *r* thundering on the reef | En. Arden | 585 |

rollest.

| *r* from the gorgeous gloom | In Mem. lxxxv. | 2 |

rolling.

up a quiet cove *R* slide,	Eleänore	107
r to and fro The heads and crowns	Pal. of Art	151
R a slumbrous sheet of foam	Lotos-E's.	13
holy organ *r* waves Of sound	D. of F. Wom.	191
Came *r* on the wind. 'Of old sat Freedom,' etc.		
r as in sleep, Low thunders	Talking O.	278
r thro' the court A long melodious	Princess, iii.	451
thunder-music, *r*, shake	In Mem. lxxxvi.	7
Let her great Danube *r* fair	" xcvii.	9
star and system *r* past,	Con.	122
r in his mind Old waifs of rhyme	The Brook	3
Hound on a foray, *r* eyes of prey,	Enid	1387
moony vapour *r* round the King,	Guinevere	595
Enoch *r* his gray eyes upon her,	En. Arden	845
r as it were the substance of it	Aylmer's F.	258
r o'er the palaces of the proud,	"	636
R on their purple couches	Boädicea	62

344 CONCORDANCE TO

	Roman.	POEM.	LINE.
My Hercules, my R Antony,		D.of F.Wom.	150
The R soldier found Me lying dead,		"	161
Worthy a R spouse,'		"	164
and the R brows Of Agrippina	. Princess,	ii.	70
the Persian, Grecian, R lines		"	114
foreheads drawn in R scowls		" vii.	114
What R strength Turbia show'd	. The Daisy	.	5
for whose love the R Cæsar first	. Enid	.	745
when the R left us, and their law	. Guinevere	.	453
Blacken round the R carrion	. Boädicea	.	14
There the horde of R robbers	. "	.	18
There the hive of R liars	. "	.	19
Lo their precious R bantling,	. "	.	31
Shall we teach it a R lesson	. "	.	32
Tho' the R eagle shadow thee	. "	.	39
Take the hoary R head and shatter it	"		65
Cut the R boy to pieces	. "	.	66
Ran the land with R slaughter	. "	.	84
What R would be dragg'd in triumph	Lucretius	.	231

Rome.

The fading politics of mortal R,	. Princess,	ii.	266
Abroad, at Florence, at R,	. Maud, I. xix.		58
Such is R, and this her deity :	. Boädicea	.	20
a steaming slaughter-house of R,	Lucretius	.	84

Ronald.

Lord R brought a lily-white doe	. Lady Clare		3
Lord R is heir of all your lands,		"	19
all you have will be Lord R's,		"	35
lily-white doe Lord R had brought		"	61
Down stept Lord R from his tower		"	65
She look'd into Lord R's eyes,		"	79

rood.

'By holy r, a royal beard !	. Day-Dm.		152
by God's r is the one maid for me'	Enid	.	368
by God's r, I trusted you too much.'	Vivien	.	226

roof.

The sparrow's chirrup on the r,	. Mariana	.	73
Hundreds of crescents on the r	. Arabian N's.		129
together under the same r, To——	With Pal.of Art		12
round the r's a gilded gallery	. Pal. of Art	.	29
the r and crown of things.	. Lotos-E's.	.	69
and on r's Of marble palaces.	. D. of F. Wom.		23
waves Of sound on r and floor		"	192
House in the shade of comfortable r's	St S. Stylites		105
The r's of Sumner-place!	. Talking O.	32,95,	152
And on the r she went,	. "		114
when the rain is on the r	. Lockstey H.		78
Flew over r and casement:	. Will Water.		134
And they leave her father's r	. L.of Burleigh		11
When beneath his r they come.	. "	.	40
Flaying the r's and sucking up the	Princess,	v.	514
there on the r's Like that great dame	"	vi.	15
shape it plank and beam for r and floor	"		30
Clomb to the r's, and gazed alone	. "	vii.	17
The r's, that heard our earliest cry	In Mem.	ci.	3
With tender gloom the r, the wall ;	"	Con.	118
in session on their r's Approv'd him	The Brook	.	127
I climb'd the r at break of day ;	The Daisy	.	61
Garrulous under a r of pine :	To F. D. Maurice		20
lived along the milky r's ;	. Elaine	.	408
red r's about a narrow wharf	. En. Arden	.	3
beneath his own low range of r's,	Aylmer's F.	.	47
presence flattering the poor r's	. "	.	175
every r Sent out a listener : .	. "	.	613
The r so lowly but that mean of Heaven	"	.	684
Rush to the r, sudden rocket,	. W. to Alexan.		20

roof (verb.)

R not a glance so keen	'Clear-headed friend,' etc.	7

roof'd.

| R the world with doubt and fear | . Eleänore | . | 99 |

roof-haunting.

| R-h martins warm their eggs : | . Day-Dm. | . | 37 |

roof-tree.

| now for me the r-t fall. | . Lockstey H. | | 190 |

rook

| The building r 'ill caw . | . May Queen, | ii. | 17 |

	POEM.	LINE.
r's are blown about the skies	In Mem.	xv. 4
Autumn, with a noise of r's .	" lxxxiv.	17
a clamour of the r's At distance	. Enid	. 249

rookery.

leads the clanging r home.	. Lockstey H.	68
line of the approaching r swerve.	. Princess, Con.	97

room (apartment.)

close, As a sick man's r	'A spirit haunts,' etc.	14
She made three paces thro' the r,	L. of Shalott,	iii. 38
pass, Well-pleased, from r to r.	. Pal. of Art .	56
Full of great r's and small the palace	"	. 57
There was silence in the r .	. Dora	. 154
not a r For love or money.	. Audley Ct.	. 1
r's which gave Upon a pillar'd porch	Princess,	i. 226
shuddering fled from r to r,	" vi.	350
To see the r's in which he dwelt	In Mem. lxxxvi.	16
thro' the blindness casement of the r,	Enid	. 71
'Your leave, my lord, to cross the r,	" .	1147
glimmer'd on his armour in the r. .		1235
shadow still would glide from r to r,	Guinevere .	500
Past thro' the solitary r in front,	. En. Arden .	276
jests, that flash'd about the pleader's r, Aylmer's F.		440
from this r into the next ;	. Grandmother	103

room (space.)

seem'd no r for sense of wrong.	. Two Voices	456
fillest all the r Of all my love	. In Mem.	cxi. 5
What r is here for a hater ? .	. Spiteful Let.	14

root.

Cleaving, took r, and springing forth	The Poet	21
at the r thro' lush green grasses	D. of F. Wom.	71
r Creeps to the garden water-pipes	"	205
The fat earth feed thy branchy r,	Talking O.	273
tho' my heart be at the r.	. Lockstey H.	66
And schirrhous r's and tendons.	. Amphion	. 64
fixt As are the r's of earth	. Princess,	v. 436
Thy r's are wrapt about the bones.	In Mem. ii.	4
By ashen r's the violets blow.	" cxiv.	4
for the r's of my hair were stirr'd .	Maud, I. i.	13
mighty nuts, and nourishing r's ;	. En. Arden .	556

rooted.

When r in the garden of the mind,	Ode to Mem.	26
I, r here among the groves,	. Talking O.	181
He r out the slothful officer .	. Enid	1786
His honour r in dishonour stood,	. Elaine	872

rope.

With hand and r we haled the	Walk. to the M.	83
I wore The r that haled the buckets	St S. Stylites	63
reach'd the ship and caught the r,	Sailor Boy	. 3

Rosamond.

| that R, whom men call fair, | . D. of F. Wom. | 251 |

rosary (rose-garden.)

| rosaries of the scented thorn, | . Arabian N's. | 106 |

rosary (string of beads.)

| amber, ancient rosaries, | . Princess, Pro. | 19 |

rose (adj.)

| the lights, r, amber, emerald, blue, | Pal. of Art | 169 |

rose (s.)

plaited alleys of the trailing r	. Ode to Mem.	106
And the year's last r.	'A spirit haunts,' etc.	20
Some spirit of a crimson r	. Adeline	41
Her cheek had lost the r	. Œnone	17
her hair Wound with white r's,	. Pal. of Art	99
petals from blown r's on the grass	Lotos-E's.	47
up the porch there grew an Eastern r,	Gardener's D.	122
but she, a Rose In r's,	"	141
'Ah, one r, One r, but one .	. "	147
Nor yet refused the r, but granted it,	"	157
Kissing the r she gave me o'er and o'er,	"	172
then for r's, moss or musk,	. "	189
Wearing the r of womanhood.	. Two Voices	417
Within the bosom of the r?	. Day-Dm.	204
With a single r in her hair,	. Lady Clare	60
God made himself an awful r of	Vision of Sin 50,	224
meshes of the jasmine and the r;	Princess, i.	216
as tho' there were One r in all the world	" ii.	37

	POEM.	LINE.
sated with the innumerable r	Princess, iii.	106
any r of Gulistan Shall burst herveil;	" iv.	104
Before me shower'd the r in flakes	"	245
there's no r that's half so dear to them	" v.	152
She takes a riband or a r;	In Mem. vi.	32
make the r Pull sideways,	" lxxi.	10
May breathe, with many r's sweet,	" xc.	10
and swung The heavy-folded r,	" xciv.	59
every thought breaks out a r.	" cxxi.	20
He too foretold the perfect r.	" Con.	34
An hour's defect of the r	Maud, I. ii.	8
You have but fed on the r's	" iv.	60
Maud has a garden of r's	" xiv.	1
R's are her cheeks, And a r her mouth	" xvii.	7, 27
'Ah, be Among the r's to-night .	" xxi.	13
And the musk of the r's blown	" xxii.	6
All night have the r's heard	"	13
I said to the r ' The brief night goes	"	27
but mine,' so I sware to the r	"	31
soul of the r went into my blood	"	33
the r was awake all night for your sake	"	49
lilies and r's were all awake,	"	51
Queen r of the rosebud garden of girls,	"	53
Queen lily and r in one;	"	56
The red r cries ' She is near	"	63
The white r weeps, 'she is late	"	64
All made up of the lily and r	II. v.	74
fear they are not r's, but blood;	"	78
O'er the four rivers the first r's blew,	Enid	1612
make her paler with a poison'd r!	Vivien	461
To crop his own sweet r	"	575
high dawn piercing the royal r	"	589
The late and early r's from his wall	En. Arden	336
red r was redder than itself	Aylmer's F.	50
York's white r as red as Lancaster's,	"	51
fann'd the gardens of that rival r	"	455
Seem'd hope's returning r:	"	559
wilderness shall blossom as the r,	"	649
As some rare little r	Hendecasyllabics	19
Not even a r, were offer'd to thee!	Lucretius	69
R, r and clematis	The Window	23, 30

Rose.

	POEM.	LINE.
Of R, the Gardener's daughter?	Gardener's D.	51
but she, a R' In roses,	"	141

rose (pret. of rise.)

Some blue peaks in the distance r,	Dying Swan	11
Heaven over Heaven r the night.	Mariana in the S.	92
At last you r and moved the light	Miller's D.	125
r, and, with a silent grace	"	150
R slowly to a music slowly breath'd	Œnone	40
R loud, with question unto whom	"	80
I r up in the silent night;	The Sisters	25
Of ledge or shelf The rock r clear,	Pal. of Art	57
that sweet incense r and never fail'd	"	45
Here r, an athlete, strong to break	"	153
r the morning of the year !	May Queen, iii.	3
R with you thro' a little arc	To J. S.	26
R up from out the bosom of the lake,	M. d'Arthur	30
Then quickly r Sir Bedivere,	"	133
r an arm Cloth'd in white samite,	"	143
from the pavement he half r,	"	167
from them r A cry which shiver'd	"	198
she, that r the tallest of them all	"	207
up we r, and on the spur we went,	Gardener's D.	32
but I r up Full of his bliss,	"	205
passion r thro' circumstantial grades	"	235
she r and took The child once more,	Dora	78
ere the night we r And saunter'd home	Audley Ct.	78
To some full music r and sank	Ed. Morris	34
one that r Twenty by measure;	St S. Stylites	87
When his man-minded offset r	Talking O.	51
flower, she touch'd on, dipt and r,	"	131
we two r, There—closing	Love and Duty	76
r a noise of striking clocks,	Day-Dm.	134
R again from where it seem'd to fail.	Vision of Sin	24
a fire-balloon R' gem-like up	Princess, Pro.	78
I r and past Thro' the wild woods	" I.	89
a woman-statue r with wings	"	207
She r her height, and said;	" ii.	27
an officer R up, and read the statutes,	"	55

	POEM.	LINE.
She r upon a wind of prophecy	Princess, ii.	154
We r, and each by other drest	" iii.	3
a sudden transport r and fell	" iv.	11
in the midst A fragrant flame r,	"	16
r a shriek as of a city sack'd ;	"	147
there r A hubbub in the court	"	454
beheld her, when she r The yesternight	" v.	167
r a cry As if to greet the king ,	"	218
On his haunches r the steed,	"	482
roll'd on the earth and r again	"	486
R a nurse of ninety years,	"	544
a day R from the distance	" vi.	96
soon He r up whole,	" vii.	50
from mine arms she r Glowing	"	144
random scheme as wildly as it r :	" Con.	2
a little feud betwixt the two	"	23
yet to give the story as it r,	"	26
But that there r a shout ;	"	36
shout r again, and made The long line	"	96
While I r up against my doom,	In Mem. cxxi.	2
The love that r on stronger wings,	" cxxvii.	1
full willingly he r ;	The Brook	121
So fresh they r in shadow'd swells ;	The Letters	46
Again their ravening eagle r	Ode on Well.	119
when a rumour r about the Queen	Enid	24
r at last, a single maiden with her,	"	160
from the mason's hand, a fortress r ;	"	244
r a cry That Edyrn's men were on	"	638
the maiden r And left her maiden	"	736
r Limours and looking at his feet,	"	1151
Anon she r, and stepping lightly	"	1222
once again she r to look at it,	"	1236
R when they saw the dead man rise	"	1580
I r and fled from Arthur's court	Vivien	146
the time when first the question r	"	260
r without a word and parted from her ;	"	592
She dislink'd herself at once and r,	"	758
some light jest among them r,	Elaine	178
r And drove him into wastes	"	251
rathe she r, half-cheated in the thought	"	339
They r, heard mass, broke fast,	"	414
flash'd into wild tears, and r again,	"	610
r Elaine and glided thro' the fields,	"	839
full meekly r the maid,	"	972
Then r the dumb old servitor	"	1147
and r And pointed to the damsel,	"	1255
the maiden r, White as her veil,	Guinevere	360
R the pale Queen, and in her anguish	"	550
r and past Bearing a lifelong hunger	En. Arden	78
She r, and fixt her swimming eyes	"	324
He woke, he r, he spread his arms	"	911
R from the clay it work'd in	Aylmer's F.	170
Darkly that day r:	"	609
He r at dawn and, fired with hope,	Sailor Boy	1
so that he r With sacrifice	On a Mourner	33

rosebud.

Where on the double r droops	Day-Dm.	209
A r set with little wilful thorns,	Princess, Pro.	153
Queen rose of the r garden of girls	Maud, I. xxii.	53

rose-bush.

And a r-b leans upon,	Adeline	14
to train the r-b that I set	May Queen, ii.	47

rose-carnation.

And many a r-c feed	In Mem. c.	7

rosed.

white neck Was r with indignation	Princess, vi.	324
darken'd in the west, And r in the east ;	Sea Dreams	40

rose-garden.

For I know her own r-g	Maud, I. xx.	41

rose-hued.

Flowing beneath her r-h zone ;	Arabian N's.	140

rose-leaf.

Letting the rose-leaves fall ;	Claribel	7
Like a r-l I will crush thee,	Lilian	21

rose-lips.

Thy r-l and full blue eyes	Adeline	7

346   CONCORDANCE TO

	POEM.	LINE.
rose-red.		
From thy *r-r* lips MY name Floweth	*Eleänore*	133
rosetree.		
One look'd all *r*, and another wore	*Aylmer's F.*	157
rosin.		
sweating *r*, plump'd the pine	*Amphion*	47
rosy.		
And left the daisies *r*.	*Maud*, I. xii.	24
R is the West, *R* is the South,	„ xvii.	5, 25
r, with his babe across his knees ;	*En. Arden*.	747
rosy-bright.		
all in spaces *r-b*	*Mariana in the S.*	89
rosy-kindled.		
r-k with her brother's kiss—.	*Elaine*	392
rosy-tinted.		
In tufts of *r-t* snow ;	*Two Voices*	60
rosy-white.		
her light foot Shone *r-w*	*Œnone*	176
rot.		
if man *r* in dreamless ease,	*Two Voices*	280
upon a name ! rest, *r* in that !	*Aylmer's F.*	385
rotted.		
my thighs are *r* with the dew ;	*St S. Stylites*	40
rotten.		
Till all be ripe and *r*.	*Will Water.*	16
rotting.		
At least, not *r* like a weed,	*Two Voices*	142
R on some wild shore .	*Princess*, v.	141
r inward slowly moulders all.	*Vivien*	245
rough.		
says he is *r* but kind,	*Maud*, I. xix.	70-9, 83
and *r* the ways and wild ;	*Enid*	750
rough-reddened		
R-r with a thousand winter gales,	*En. Arden*.	95
round (adj.)		
o'er it many, *r* and small,	*Mariana*	39
knew the merry world was *r*.	*The Voyage*	7, 95
round (s.)		
runs the *r* of life from hour to hour.	*Circumstance*	9
The dark *r* of the dripping wheel,	*Miller's D.*	102
Like the tender amber *r*,	*Margaret*	19
in the *r* of Time Still father Truth?	*Love and Duty*	4
To yonder argent *r* .	*St Agnes' Eve*	16
Comes out, a perfect *r*.	*Will Water.*	68
This *r* of green, this orb of flame,	*In Mem.* xxxiv.	5
Should move his *r's*, and fusing all	„ xlvi.	2
slowly breathing bare The *r* of space, „	lxxxv.	5
round (verb.)		
Should slowly *r* his orb,	*Eleänore*	91
So *r's* he to a separate mind	*In Mem.* xliv.	9
r A higher height,	„ lxii.	11
rounded.		
canal Is *r* to as clear a lake.	*Arabian N's.*	46
slowly *r* to the east	*Mariana in the S.*	79
Roll'd on each other, *r*, smooth'd	*D. of F. Wom.*	51
r by the stillness of the beach	*Audley Ct.*	9
circle *r* under female hands .	*Princess*, ii.	350
O'er ocean-mirrors *r* large,	*In Mem.* xii.	9
roundel.		
glorious *r* echoing in our ears,	*Vivien*	276
roundelay.		
Twice or thrice his *r*,	*The Owl*, i.	11
rounder.		
softer all her shape And *r* seem'd ;	*Princess*, vii.	122
Roundhead.		
And far below the *R* rode,	*Talking O.*	299
rouse (s.)		
Have a *r* before the morn :	*Vision of Sin* 96,	120
rouse (verb.)		
From deep thought himself he *r's*,	*L. of Burleigh*	21

	POEM.	LINE.
roused.		
has *r* the child again.	*Sea Dreams*	270
rout (s.)		
a *r* of saucy boys Brake on us	*Princess*, v.	384
midmost of a *r* of roisterers,	*Enid*	1123
all his *r* of random followers,	„	1231
blindly rush'd on all the *r* behind.	„	1315
rout (verb.)		
O sound to *r* the brood of cares,	*In Mem.* lxxxviii.	17
rove.		
R's from the living brother's face,	*In Mem.* xxxii.	7
How young Columbus seem'd to *r*,	*The Daisy*.	17
Let his eye *r* in following	*Enid*	399
roved.		
I *r* at random thro' the town,	*In Mem.* lxxxvi.	3
While I *r* about the forest	*Boädicea*	35
roving.		
after *r* in the woods	*Miller's D*	58
R the trackless realms of Lyonnesse	*Elaine*	36
row (s.)		
there ran a *r* Of cloisters,	*Pal. of Art*	25
row (verb.)		
taught me how to skate, to *r*,	*Ed. Morris*	19
he can steer and *r*, and he Will guide me	*Elaine*	1122
rowed.		
and how I *r* across And took it,	*M. d Arthur*	32
rowing.		
Who, *r* hard against the stream	*Two Voices*	211
royal.		
Break not, for thou art *R*,	*Ded. of Idylls*	44
royal-rich.		
So *r-r* and wide.	*Pal. of Art* 20,	191
rub.		
We *r* each other's angles down,	*In Mem.* lxxxviii	40
rubbed.		
And yawn'd, and *r* his face,	*Day-Dm.*	151
rubbish.		
Or cast as *r* to the void,	*In Mem.* liii.	7
in the jumbled *r* of a dream	*Vivien*.	197
rubric.		
set your thoughts in *r* thus .	*Princess*, iii.	34
ruby-budded.		
break from the *r-b* lime.	*Maud*, I. iv.	7
ruddy.		
R and white and strong on his legs	*Grandmother*	2
His face was *r*, his hair was gold,	*The Victim*	36
rude.		
a crew that is neither *r* nor rash,	*The Islet*	10
rue.		
Old year, we'll dearly *r* for you :	*D. of the O. Year*	43
could not ever *r* his marrying me	*Dora*	143
May *r* the bargain made.'	*Princess*, i.	73
rued.		
the hunter *r* His rash intrusion	*Princess*, iv.	185
ruffian.		
flushes up in the *r's* head,	*Maud*, I. i.	37
so the *r's* growl'd, Fearing to lose,	*Enid*	1411
ruffle.		
R's her pure cold plume,	*M. d Arthur*	268
R thy mirror'd mast,	*In Mem.* ix.	7
I swear it would not *r* me so much	*Enid*	999
sharp wind that *r's* all day long	*Guinevere*.	51
ruffled.		
Rankled in him and *r* all his heart	*Guinevere*	50
not a hair *R* upon the scarfskin	*Aylmer's F.*	660
ruin.		
Boat, island, *r's* of a castle,	*Ed. Morris*	6
Sit brooding in the *r's* of a life,	*Love and Duty*	12
satiated at length Came to the *r's*.	*Princess, Pro.*	91

TENNYSON'S WORKS.   347

	POEM.	LINE.
ghostly woodpecker, Hid in the r's;	Princess, Pro.	212
A Gothic r and a Grecian house .	"	225
the crimson-rolling eye Glares r, .	" iv.	474
Rang r, answer'd full of grief and scorn "	vi.	313
old bridge which, half in r's then,	The Brook .	79
strength Turbia show'd In r	The Daisy .	6
And placed them in this r; .	Enid .	643
men may fear Fresh fire and r.	"	1671
ending in a r—nothing left .	Vivien .	732
Red r, and the breaking up of laws	Guinevere .	423
wrought the r of my lord the King.'	"	681
The crash of r and the loss of all .	En. Arden .	550
Hurt in that night of sudden r	"	565
shuddering at the r of a world ;	Sea Dreams	30
a gulf of r, swallowing gold,	"	79
the sea roars R : .	"	81
gaps and chasms of r left	"	218

ruin (verb.)

A plot, a plot, a plot, to r all !	Princess, ii.	175
fear This whole foundation r,	"	320
heiress of your plan, And takes and r's all;	iii.	222

ruined.

the good house, tho' r, O my Son,	Enid .	378
r man Thro' woman the first hour ;	Vivien .	213
R ! r ! the sea roars Ruin ; .	Sea Dreams	80

ruining.

In twelve great battles r overthrown	Guinevere	429
R along the illimitable inane .	Lucretius .	40

ruinous.

He look'd and saw that all was r.	Enid .	315

rule (s.)

royal power, ample r Unquestion'd	Œnone .	109
Phantoms of other forms of r, '	Love thou thy land	59
obedience is the bond of r. .	M. d'Arthur	94
all men's good He each man's r,	Golden Year	48
err from honest Nature's r !	Locksley H.	61
Averring it was clear against all r's	Princess, i.	176
out so late is out of r's. .	" iv.	200
I beant a-gooin' to breäk my r. .	N. Farmer .	4
I weänt break r's for Doctor,	"	67

rule (verb.)

May you r us long, .	To the Queen	20
come again To r once more—	M. d'Arthur	12
That taught the Sabine how to r,	Princess, ii.	65
wish'd to marry: they could r a house:	"	441
But they my troubled spirit r,	In Mem. xxviii.	17
O Sorrow, wilt thou r my blood .	" lviii.	5
Who can r and dare not lie .	Maud, I. x.	66
Heathen, who, some say, shall r the	Elaine .	66
A moral child without the craft to r	"	146
as Arthur's queen I move and r : .	"	1215
knows false, abide and r the house:	Guinevere .	511
He that only r's by terror .	The Captain	1

ruled.

R in the eastern sky. .	D. of F. Wom.	264
grim Earl, who r In Coventry : .	Godiva .	12
A nation yet, the rulers and the r—	Princess, Con.	53
be r with rod or with knout? .	Maud, I. iv.	47
listen to me, and by me be r,	Enid .	1472
a tongue that r the hour, .	Aylmer's F.	194
There they r, and thence they wasted	Boädicea .	54

ruler.

leave us r's of your blood .	To the Queen	21
A nation yet, the r's and the ruled	Princess, Con.	53
deathless r of thy dying house .	Aylmer's F.	661

rumble.

Clamour and r, and ringing and clatter,	Maud, II. v.	13

rumbled.

And round the attics r .	The Goose .	46

rummaged.

tapt at doors, And r like a rat :	Walk. to the M.	30

rumour.

empty breath And r's of a doubt .	M. d'Arthur	100
r of Prince Arac hard at hand .	Princess, v.	108
mouths ran on and r of battle grew	Maud, III. vi.	29

	POEM.	LINE.
let the turbid streams of r flow .	Ode on Well.	181
when a r rose about the Queen .	Enid .	24
Vext at a r rife about the Queen .	Vivien .	10
Hid from the wide world's r. .	Elaine .	521
I hear of r's flying thro' your court.	"	1184
let r's be : When did not r's fly ? .	"	1187
a r wildly blown about Came .	Guinevere .	151
Less noble, being, as all r runs, .	"	337
Wife-hunting, as the r ran, .	Aylmer's F.	212
down the wind With r .	"	496

run (s.)

the mole has made his r. .	Aylmer's F.	849
so quick the r We felt the good ship	The Voyage	14

run (verb.)

When cats r home .	The Owl, i.	1
trenched waters r from sky to sky,	Ode to Mem.	104
R's up the ridged sea .	Sea-Fairies	39
Thro' the wave that r's for ever .	L. of Shalott, i.	12
'while the world r's round and round'	Pal. of Art	13
r before the fluttering tongues of fire;	D. of F. Wom.	30
where the bay r's up its latest horn	Audley Ct. .	10
can r My faith beyond my practice	Ed. Morris	53
The Sun will r his orbit, .	Love and Duty	22
one increasing purpose r's, .	Locksley H.	137
they shall dive, and they shall r, .	"	169
The vilest herb that r's to seed .	Amphion .	95
Against its fountain upward r's .	Will Water.	35
To make my blood r quicker .	"	110
Where the bloody conduit r's : .	Vision of Sin	144
'The stars,' she whispers, ' blindly r;	In Mem. iii.	5
Till all my widow'd race be r (17-20)	" ix.	18
So r's my dream : but what am I ? .	" liii.	17
R out your measured arcs .	" civ.	27
every grain of sand that r's .	" cxvi.	9
I hear thee where the waters r : .	" cxxix.	2
clamour'd from a casement ' r' .	The Brook .	85
' R, Katie !' Katie never r : .	"	87
He that r's may read. .	The Flower	18
Cataract brooks to the ocean r, .	The Islet .	17
an Oread, and this way she r's .	Lucretius .	183

rung.

Loud, loud r out the bugle's brays,	Oriana .	48
as he rode his armour r, .	L. of Shalott, iii	17
The distant battle flash'd and r .	Two Voices	126
Not a bell was r, not a prayer was read;	Maud, II. v.	24

runlet.

r's babbling down the glen. .	Mariana in the S.	44
Nor r tinkling from the rock ; .	In Mem. xcix.	13

runnel.

The babbling r crispeth, .	Claribel .	19

running.

stable wench Came r at the call .	Princess, i.	224
second was my father's r thus ; .	" iv.	387
R down to my own dark wood ; .	Maud, I. xiv.	30
R too vehemently to break upon it	Enid .	78
r on thus hopefully she heard, .	En. Arden .	201
While you were r down the sands,	Sea Dreams	256
You are all r on one way, (rep.) .	The Window	8

rush (s.)

the shrieking r of the wainscot mouse,	Maud, I. vi.	71
r of the air in the prone swing .	Aylmer's F.	86

rush (verb.)

those, who clench their nerves to r	Love and Duty	75
A thousand arms and r's to the Sun.	Princess, vi.	21
r abroad all round the little haven	En. Arden .	868
R to the roof, sudden rocket, .	W. to Alexan.	20

rushed.

And our spirits r together .	Locksley H.	38
A wind arose and r upon the South.	Princess, i.	96
on a sudden r Among us, .	" iv.	355
We r into each other's arms. .	The Letters	40
blindly r on all the rout behind. .	Enid .	1315
I am his dearest !' r on the knife .	The Victim	77

rushing.

The milldam r down with noise, .	Miller's D.	50
whisper of the south-wind r warm,	Locksley H.	145

348 CONCORDANCE TO

	POEM.	LINE.
Snapt in the *r* of the river-rain	*Vivien*	807
r outward lionlike Leapt on him,	*Guinevere*	106
Far purelier in his *r*'s to and fro,	*Aylmer's F.*	458
My lady's Indian kinsman *r* in,	"	593
thrice I heard the rain *R* ;	*Lucretius*	27

russet-bearded.
The *r-b* head roll'd on the floor. . *Enid* . 1577

Russian.
Cossack and *R* Reel'd . . . *Lt. Brigade* 34

rust (s.)
fearing *r* or soilure fashioned for it *Elaine* . 7
keeps the *r* of murder on the walls—*Guinevere* 74

rust.
lest we *r* in ease. . 'Love thou thy land,' etc. 42
To *r* unburnish'd, not to shine in use! *Ulysses* . 23
cannon-bullet *r* on a slothful shore *Maud*, III.vi. 26

rusted.
when the braken *r* on their crags, *Ed. Morris* 100

rusting.
r on his iron hills, . . . *Princess*, v. 140

rustle.
Sweet-Gale *r* round the shelving keel; *Ed. Morris* 110
papers that she held *R* : . . *Princess*, iv. 372

rustled.
in maiden plumes We *r*: . . *Princess*, i. 200

rustling.
r thro' The low and bloomed foliage, *ArabianN's*.12
r once at night about the place, . *Aylmer's F.* 547

rusty.
'Arms indeed, but old And *r*, (rep.) *Enid* . 477

rut.
The same old *r* would deepen . *Aylmer's F.* 34

ruth.
r began to work Against his anger *Enid* . 950
Had *r* again on Enid looking pale " . 1052
with another humorous *r* remark'd " . 1099

Ruth.
R among the fields of corn, . . *Aylmer's F.* 680

ruthless.
As *r* as a baby with a worm, *Walk. to the M.* 98

rye.
Long fields of barley and of *r*, . *L. of Shalott,* i. 2

S

sady.
use to *s* the things that a do . *N. Farmer* 6
I thowt a 'ad summut to *s*, . . " . 19
I wekint *s* men be loiars . . " . 27

Sabbath.
Half God's good *s*, . . . *To J. M. K.* 11
'Behold, it is the *S* morn.' . . *Two Voices* 402
The *s*'s of Eternity, One *s* deep and *St Agnes' Eve* 33
On that loud *s* shook the spoiler . *Ode on Well.* 123
fixt the *S*. Darkly that day rose: . *Aylmer's F.* 609
woke, and went the next, The *S,* . *Sea Dreams* 19

sabbath-drawler.
no *s-d* of old saws, . . . *To J. M. K.* 5

Sabine.
taught the *S* how to rule, . . *Princess*, ii. 65

Sabæan.
Dripping with *S* spice . . . *Adeline* . 53

sabre.
Flash'd all their *s*'s bare, . . *Lt. Brigade* 27

sabre-stroke.
Reel'd from the *s-s* . . . *Lt. Brigade* 35

sabring.
S the gunners there, . . . *Lt. Brigade* 29

	POEM.	LINE.
sack (bag.)		
sweating underneath a *s* of coru,	*Enid*	263
With bag and *s* and basket, .	*En. Arden*	63
Cling together in the ghastly *s*—	*Aylmer's F.*	764

sack (pillage.)
the *s* and plunder of our house . *Enid* . 694

sack'd.
rose a shriek as of a city *s* . . *Princess*, iv. 147
my Enid's birthday, *s* my house ; . *Enid* . 458
night of fire, when Edyrn *s* their house, " . 634

sacrament.
Deliver me the blessed *s*; . . *St S. Stylites* 215

sacred.
And either *s* unto you. . . . *Day-Dm.* . 280
Keep nothing *s*: 'You might have won,' etc. 19
s from the blight Of ancient influence *Princess*, ii. 152
Oh, *s* be the flesh and blood . *In Mem.* xxxiii. 11
we must remain *S* to one another.' *Aylmer's F.* 426

sacrifice (s.)
Have we not made ourself the *s* ? *Princess*, iii. 232
To blow these *s*'s thro' the world— *Aylmer's F.* 758
so that he rose With *s*, . . *On a Mourner* 34

sacrifice (verb.)
to thy worst self *s* thyself, . . *Aylmer's F.* 645

sad.
The broken sheds look'd *s* and strange *Mariana* 5
Madonna, *s* is night and morn *Mariana in the S.* 22
His memory scarce can make me *s*. *Miller's D.* 16
I am *s* and glad To see you, Florian. *Princess,*ii. 286
made me sick, and almost *s* ?' . " . 372
S as the last which reddens over one " iv. 28
So *s*, so fresh, the days that are no more. " 30-5
s and strange as in dark summer . " . 31
one is *s* ; her note is changed, . *In Mem.*xxi. 27
makes me *s* I know not why, . " lxvii. 11
To a life that has been so *s*, . *Maud*, I. xi. 13
no peace in the grave, is that not *s* ? " II. v. 16
stern and *s* (so rare the smiles . *The Daisy* . 53
knew her sitting *s* and solitary. . *Enid* . 1131
Because I saw you *s*, to comfort you *Vivien* . 291
rather think How *s* it were for Arthur, *Guinevere* 492
Favour from one so *s* . . . *En. Arden* . 286
your dream,' she said, 'Not *s*, but. *Sea Dreams* 103
says, our sins should make us *s* : . *Grandmother* 93

sadden.
He *s*'s, all the magic light. . . *In Mem.* viii. 5
The gloom that *s*'s Heaven and Earth, *The Daisy*102
While he that watch'd her *s,* . *Enid* . 67

sadden'd.
Told Enid, and they *s* her the more : *Enid* . 64
s all her heart again . . . " . 1294
She fail'd and *s* knowing it ; . *En. Arden* 256

sadder.
as her carol *s* grew, . . *Mariana in the S.* 13

saddle.
Arac, roll'd himself Thrice in the *s*, *Princess*, v. 265
lets me from the *s* ;' . . . *Elaine* . 95

saddle-bow.
A cavalier from off his *s-b*, . . *D. of F. Wom.* 46

saddle-leather.
Thick jewell'd shone the *s-l,* . *L. of Shalott,* iii. 20

sadness.
Can I but relive in *s* ? . . *Locksley H.* 107
s on the soul of Ida fell, . . *Princess,* vii. 14
Or *s* in the summer moons ? . *InMem.*lxxxii. 8
s flings Her shadow on the blaze . " xcvii. 18
roll upon him, Unspeakable for *s*. *En. Arden* . 726

safe.
(royal word upon it, He comes back *s*) *Princess,* v. 216

safer.
the rougher hand Is *s* : . . *Princess,* vi. 262

sagest.
some were left of those Held *s,* . *Princess,* vi. 301

Sagramore.	POEM.	LINE.
What say ye then to sweet Sir S,	Vivien	571

Sahib.		
At once the costly S yielded to her.	Aylmer's F.	233

said.		
have s goodnight for evermore	MayQueen,ii.	41
I know not what was s;	"	iii 34
He thought that nothing new was s,	The Epic	30
Something so s 'twas nothing—	"	31
Cruel, cruel the words I s!	Ed. Gray	17
I s no, Yet being an easy man,	Princess, i.	147
on all the wrathful king had s,	" v.	462
so it seem'd, or so they s to me,	" vi.	6
She s you had a heart—	"	217
The lesser griefs that may be s	In Mem. xx.	1
all he s of things divine,	" xxxvii.	18
To dying lips is all he s	"	20
Whatever I have s or sung,	" cxxiv.	1
how she look'd, and what he s,	" Con.	99
How strange was what she s.	Maud,I. xix.	34
so like her? so they s on board.	The Brook	223
told me all her friends had s;	The Letters	25
all that Earl Limours had s,	Enid	1240
What s the happy sire?.	Vivien	560
we hear it s That men go down	Elaine	148
being weak in body s no more;	"	835
s my father, and himself was knight	Guinevere	232
for he seldom s me nay	Grandmother	69
I thowt a s whot a owt to a s	N. Farmer	20
thof summun s it in 'aaste:	"	27

sait (s.)		
And the whirring s goes round rep.;	The Owl, i.	4
In the silken s of infancy	Arabian N's.	2
come hither and furl your s's,	Sea-Fairies	10
Mariner, mariner, furl your s,	"	21
wind-scatter'd over s's and masts	D. of F. Wom.	31
the barge with oar and s Moved	M.d'Arthur	265
happy s's and bear the Press;	Golden Year	2
the vessel puffs her s;	Ulysses	44
argosies of magic s's.	Locksley H.	121
boat Tacks, and the slacken'd s flaps	Princess, ii.	169
Silver s's all out of the west	"	469
the first beam glittering on a s,	" iv.	26
trim our s's, and let old bygones be,	"	51
the seas: A red s, or a white;	" Con.	72
see the s's at distance rise	In Mem. xii.	11
glance about the approaching s's.	" xiii.	18
milkier every milky s	" cxiv.	11
far-off s is blown by the breeze	Maud, I. iv.	4
white s's flying on the yellow sea;	Enid	829
She took the helm and he the s;	Vivien	49
to the last dip of the vanishing s	En. Arden	244
waiting for a s: No s from day to day,	"	591
scarlet shafts of sunrise—but no s.	"	600
Crying with a loud voice 'a s! a s!	"	912
all the s's were darken'd in the west,	Sea Dreams	39
Dry sang the tackle, sang the s	The Voyage	10
never s of ours was furl'd,	"	81
whence were those that drove the s	"	86
With a satin s of a ruby glow,	The Islet	13

sail (verb.)		
s with Arthur under looming	M. d'Arthur, Ep.	17
purpose holds To s beyond the sunset	Ulysses	60
On sleeping wings they s	Sir Galahad	44
Abiding with me till I s	InMem.cxxiv.	13
All night the shining vapour s	" Con.	111
The ship I s in passes here	En. Arden	214
we might s for evermore.	The Voyage	8,96
We seem'd to s Into the Sun I	"	16

sail'd.		
Slow s the weary mariners	Sea-Fairies	1
throne of Indian Cama slowly s	Pal. of Art	115
s, Full-blown before us into rooms	Princess, i.	226
those fair hills I s below,	InMem.xcvii.	2
weeks before she s, S from this port	En. Arden	12
prosperously s The ship 'Good Fortune,'	"	523
that harbour whence he s before,	"	667

sailest.		
S the placid ocean-plains	In Mem. ix.	2

sailing.	POEM.	LINE.
With here a blossom s,	The Brook	56
S along before a gloomy cloud	Sea Dreams	120
S under palmy highlands	The Captain	23

sailor.		
praying God will save Thy s,—	In Mem. vi.	13
I see the s at the wheel	" x.	4
Thou bringest the s to his wife	"	5
greatest s since our world began	Ode on Well.	86
Enoch Arden, a rough s's lad	En Arden	14
and made himself Full s;	"	54
A shipwreck'd s, waiting for a sail;	"	591
S's bold and true.	The Captain	8

saint (s.)		
The meed of s's, the white robe	St S. Stylites	20
Who may be made a s, if I fail here?	"	47
thou and all the s's Enjoy themselves	"	103
the Virgin Mother, and the S's,	"	110
silly people take me for a s,	"	125
register'd and calendar'd for s's.	"	130
no one, even among the s	"	136
not told of any. They were s's.	"	149
Yea, crown'd a s. They shout,'Behold a s!'	"	151
gather'd to the glorious s's	"	194
Ah! let me not be fool'd, sweet s's;	"	209
Than Papist unto S.	Talking O.	16
mother was as mild as any s,	Princess, i.	22
Swear by St something—	" v.	283
Like a S's glory up in heaven.	"	503
but she No s—inexorable—	"	504
your mother now a s with s's,	" vi.	216
the hands of Dubric, the high s,	Enid	838
oft I talk'd with Dubric, the high s,	"	1713
I thank the s's, I am not great.	Guinevere	197
Who wast, as is the conscience of a s	"	632
king of s, or founder fell:	Sea Dreams	217

saint (verb.)		
lower voices s me from above.	St S. Stylites	152

saintdom.		
grasp the hope I hold Of s.	St S. Stylites	6

sake.		
Yet must I love her for your s;	Miller's D	142
Nor would I break for your sweet s	L.C.V.deVere	13
for the s of him that's gone,	Dora	60-8,92
for her own dear s but this,	Ed. Morris	141
How prettily for his own sweet s	Maud, I.	51
And for your sweet s to yours;	" xix.	91
for God's s,' he answer'd, 'both our s's	En. Arden	505

Saligne.		
fulmined out her scorn of laws S	Princess, ii.	117

sallow.		
satin-shining palm On s's	Vivien	74

sallow-rifted.		
the s-r glooms Of evening	Elaine	996

sally (s.)		
I make a sudden s	The Brook	24
all at once should s out upon me,	Enid	998

Sally.		
to 's choorch afoor my S wur deäd	N. Farmer	17

sally (verb.)		
the king's command to s forth	Elaine	559

sallying.		
s thro' the gate, Had beat her foes	Princess,Pro.	33
s thro' the gates, and caught his hair,	" v.	330

saloon.		
Or, in a shadowy s,	Eleänore	125

salt.		
stony drought and steaming s;	Mariana in the S.	40
By shards and scurf of s,	Vision of Sin	211
she has neither savour nor s	Maud, I. ii.	2
city sparkles like a grain of s.	Will	20
Caught the shrill s, and sheer'd the gale	The Voyage	12

salute (s.)		
Take my s,' unknightly with flat hand	Enid	1515

salute (verb.)

	POEM.	LINE.
Many a merry face S's them—	In Mem. Con.	67

salver.

fruitage golden-rinded On golden s's,	Eleänore	34

sameness.

With weary s in the rhymes,	Miller's D.	70
welcome at the Hall, On whose dull s	Aylmer's F.	115

Samian.

whene'er she moves The S Herd rises	Princess, iii.	99

samite.

Clothed in white s, mystic	M. d'Arthur	31, 144-59
a robe Of s without price	Vivien	71
King, who sat Robed in red s,	Elaine	431
Palled all its length in blackest s,	"	1136

sanctities.

darken'd s with song.'	In Mem. xxxvii.	24

sanctuary.

crowds in column'd sanctuaries	D. of F. Wom.	22
behold our s Is violate,	Princess, vi.	43
So was their s violated,	" vii.	1
I will draw me into s,	Guinevere	120
yield me s, nor ask Her name,	"	140

sand.

purl o'er matted cress and ribbed s	Ode to Mem.	59
rainbow lives in the curve of the s :	Sea-Fairies	27
In glaring s and inlets bright.	Mariana in the S.	8
Dipt down to sea and s's.	Pal. of Art	32
seem'd all dark and red—a tract of s,	"	65
salt pool, lock'd in with bars of s.	"	249
sat them down upon the yellow s,	Lotos-E's.	37
roaring deeps and fiery s's,	"	160
foam-flakes scud along the level s,	D. of F. Wom.	39
almost choke with golden s—'You ask me why,'etc.		24
might as well have traced it in the s's	Audley Ct.	49
ran itself in golden s's	Locksley H.	32
only make that footprint upon s	Princess, iii.	223
as a figure lengthen'd on the s	" vi.	145
suck the blinding splendour from the s,	" vii.	24
every grain of s that runs	In Mem. cxvi.	9
Low on the s and loud on the stone	Maud, I. xxii.	25
a tap Of my finger-nail on the s	" II. ii.	22
Tumbles a breaker on chalk and s;	To F. D. Maurice	24
Toiling in immeasurable s,	Will	16
slipping o'er their shadows on the s	Enid	1320
touching Breton s's, they disembark'd	Vivien	1
in the slippery s before it breaks?	"	142
a naked child upon the s's	Guinevere	291
in the chasm are foam and yellow s's;	En. Arden	2
built their castles of dissolving s.	"	19
All s and cliff and deep-in running cave	Sea Dreams	17
now on s they walk'd, and now on cliff	"	37
While you were running down the s's,	"	256
By s's and steaming flats, and floods	The Voyage	45
The s's and yeasty surges mix.	Sailor Boy	9

sandal (shoe.)

he roll'd And paw'd about her s	Princess, iii.	166

sandal (wood.)

toys in lava, fans Of s	Princess, Pro.	19

sand-built.

Or even a s-b ridge	Ode to Mem.	97

sand-shore.

The waste s-s's of Trath Treroit,	Elaine	301

sane.

I woke s, but well-nigh close to death	Princess, vii.	104
Till crowds at length be s	Ode on Well.	169

sanest.

valorous, S and most obedient	Enid	1759

sang.

by the river S Sir Lancelot	L. of Shalott, iii.	35
S to the stillness,	Œnone	20
S looking thro' his prison bars?	Margaret	35
over them the sea-wind s	M. d'Arthur	48
and the nightingale S loud,	Gardener's D.	95
He s his song, and I replied with mine :	Audley Ct.	55
So s we each to either	"	73

	POEM.	LINE.
angel stand and watch me, as I s	St S. Stylites	34
s to me the whole Of those three	Talking O.	134
s the gallant glorious chronicle;	Princess, Pro.	49
the women s Between the rougher voices	"	236
Beyond all reason: these the women s	" i.	142
porch that s All round with laurel,	" ii.	8
With whom I s about the morning hills	"	229
smote her harp, and s.	" iv.	20
the tear, She s of, shook and fell,	"	42
part Now while I s,	"	73
So Lila s: we thought her	"	562
Violet, she that s the mournful song	" vi.	298
maidens came, they talk'd, They s,	" vii.	8
lives in height (the shepherd s)	"	178
something in the ballads which they s,	" Con.	14
On Argive heights divinely s,	In Mem. xxiii.	22
A merry song we s with him	" xxx.	15
impetuously we s;	"	16
Once more we s: 'They do not die	"	22
While now we s old songs that peal'd	" xciv.	13
They s of what is wise and good	" cii.	10
A statue veil'd, to which they s	"	12
s from the three-decker out of the foam,	Maud, I, i.	50
Birds in our wood s,	" xii.	9
the song that Enid s was one	Enid	345
when you s me that sweet rhyme	Vivien	284
And s it: sweetly could she make	Elaine	1000
full willingly s the little maid	Guinevere	165
So s the novice, while full passionately	"	178
S Arthur's glorious wars, and s the King	"	284
then, he s, The twain together	"	298
ever painter painted, poet s,	Aylmer's F.	106
while she s this baby song.	Sea Dreams	280
Dry s the tackle, s the sail	The Voyage	10
So s the terrible prophetesses.	Boädicea	37

sanguine.

S he was: a but less vivid hue	Aylmer's F.	64

sank.

I s In cool soft turf	Arabian N's.	96
while day s or mounted higher	Pal. of Art	46
full words s thro' the silence drear,	D. of F. Wom.	121
as we s From rock to rock	Audley Ct.	82
full music rose and s the sun,	Ed. Morris	34
She s her head upon her arm	Talking O.	207
Tho' at times her spirit s:	L. of Burleigh	70
deep in broider'd down we s	Princess, iv.	14
veil'd her brows, and prone she s,	" v.	104
down dead-heavy s her curls,	" vi.	131
after s and s And, into mournful twilight	"	173
I s and slept, Fill'd thro' and thro'	" vii.	156
her forehead s upon her hands,	"	231
A bitter day that early s	In Mem. cvi.	2
show'd themselves against the sky, and s	Enid	240
S her sweet head upon her gentle breast;	"	527
down he s For the pure pain	Elaine	516
s As into sleep again.	Aylmer's F.	591
s down shamed At all that beauty	Lucretius	63

sap (s.)

But yet my s was stirr'd	Talking O.	172
The s dries up; the plant declines:	Two Voices	268
Here rests the s within the leaf	Day-Dm.	23

sap (verb.)

Ring out the grief that s's the mind,	In Mem. cv.	9
s's The fealty of our friends,	Guinevere	526

sapience.

And glean your scatter'd s.	Princess, ii.	241

sapling.

had a s growing on it,	Enid	1012
lie still, and yet the s grew:	"	1014

sapphire.

A purer s melts into the sea	Maud, I. xviii.	52

sapphire-spangled.

The silent s-s marriage ring	Maud, I. iv.	6

Sappho.

arts of grace S and others	Princess, ii.	143

	POEM.	LINE.
sappy.		
Are neither green nor s;	Amphion	90
sardonyx.		
Beneath branch-work of costly s.	Pal. of Art	95
sarmin.		
But a reäds wonn s a weeäk	N. Farmer	28
sat.		
I came and s Below the chesnuts,	Miller's D.	59
near this door you s apart,	"	158
With down-dropt eyes I s alone:	Œnone	56
while I s Low in the valley.	"	210
S smiling, babe in arm.	Pal. of Art	96
s betwixt the shining Oriels,	"	159
Flash'd thro' her as she s alone,	"	214
s them down upon the yellow sand,	Lotos-E's.	37
we s as God by God;	D. of F. Wom.	142
Of old s Freedom on the heights, 'Of old s at Freedom'		1
and I s round the wassail-bowl,	The Epic	5
grunted 'Good!' but we S rapt:	M. d'Arthur,Ep.	6
Eustace might have s for Hercules	Gardener's D.	7
s we down upon a garden mound,	"	209
Mary r And look'd with tears	Dora	54
s upon a mound That was unsown,	"	70
once more, and s upon the mound;	"	79
so we s and eat And talk'd old matters	AudleyCt.	27
In which the swarthy ringdove s,	Talking O.	293
night In which we s together	Love and Duty	59
He s upon the knees of men	Two Voices	323
I ceased, and s as one forlorn.	"	400
Wherever he s down and sung	Amphion	19
To-day I s for an hour and wept,	Ed. Gray	11
To him who s upon the rocks	To E. L.	23
s a company with heated eyes	Vision of Sin	7
Narrowing in to where they s assembled	"	16
s him down in a lonely place	Poet's Song	5
I s down and wrote, In such a hand	Princess, i.	232
at a board by tome and paper s,	" ii.	18
s along the forms, like morning doves	"	87
We s: the Lady glanced;	"	96
while you s beside the well?	"	252
In each we s, we heard The grave	"	348
S compass'd with professors:	"	421
we three S muffled like the fates.	"	443
haled us to the Princess where she s	" iv.	252
up she s, And raised the cloak	" v.	69
Part s like rocks: part reel'd	"	485
I lay still, and with me oft she s.	" vii.	76
by axe and eagle s, With all their	"	113
palm to palm she s;	"	120
in their silent influence as they s,	" Con.	15
and she s, she pluck'd the grass,	"	31
went back to the Abbey, and s on,	"	106
we s But spoke not, rapt	"	107
There s the Shadow fear'd of man;	In Mem. xxii.	12
who s apart And watch'd them,	" cii.	29
And s by a pillar alone;	Maud, I. viii.	2
S with her, read to her, night and day,	" xix.	75
Enid woke and s beside the couch,	Enid	79
S riveting a helmet on his knee,	"	268
musing s the hoary-headed Earl.	"	295
for long hours s Enid by her Lord,	"	1428
none spake word, but all s down at once	"	1452
slided up his knee and s,	Vivien	88
a fair young squire who s alone,	"	322
while she s, half-falling from his knees,	"	753
King, who s Robed in red samite.	Elaine	431
down he slid, and s,	"	509
from where he s At Arthur's right	"	550
Queen who s With lips severely placid	"	735
S on his knee, stroked his gray face	"	745
in her tower alone the maiden s:	"	983
S the lifelong creature of the house,	"	1137
S by the river in a cove	"	1380
s There in the holy house	Guinevere	1
the Queen who s betwixt her best	"	28
on the border of her couch they s	"	100
She s, Stiff-stricken, listening;	"	408
lo, he s on horseback at the door!	"	583
S often in the seaward-gazing gorge,	En. Arden	590
There he s down gazing on all below;	"	724

	POEM.	LINE.
S anger-charm'd from sorrow,	Aylmer's F.	728
S at his table; drank his costly wines;	Sea Dreams	74
near the light a giant woman s,	"	96
Turn'd as he s and struck the keys	The Islet	7
upon the bridge of war S glorying;	Spec. of Iliad	10
S fifty in the blaze of burning fire;	"	20
Fancy came and at her pillow s,	Coquette, i.	5
Satan.		
'S take The old women	Princess, v.	32
some black wether of St S's fold.	Vivien	600
one of S's shepherdesses caught.	"	603
sate (to satisfy.)		
things fair to s my various eyes!	Pal. of Art	193
sate (pret. of sat.)		
Round the hall where I s	The Mermaid	26
sated.		
s with the innumerable rose.	Princess, iii.	106
satiate.		
Nor Arac, s with his victory.	Princess, vii.	75
satiated.		
s at length Came to the ruins	Princess,Pro.	90
not by blood to be s.	Boädicea	52
satin.		
A tent of s, elaborately wrought	Princess, iii.	330
In gloss of s and glimmer of pearls,	Maud,I.xxii.	55
satin-shining.		
In colour like the s-s palm.	Vivien	73
satin-wood.		
Erect behind a desk of s-w,	Princess, ii.	90
satire.		
shafts Of gentle s, kin to charity,	Princess, ii.	445
How like you this old s?	Sea Dreams	194
first wrote s, with no pity in it,	"	197
satisfied.		
rested with her sweet face s;	Enid	776
Geraint look'd and was not s.	"	1284
s With what himself had done	"	1492
satisfy.		
And s my soul with kissing her;	Princess, v.	100
saturate.		
soak'd and s, out and out,	Will Water.	87
adulteries That s soul with body.	Aylmer's F.	377
Saturn.		
while S whirls, his stedfast shade.	Pal. of Art	15
satyr.		
Glorifying clown and s;	Princess, v.	179
As, a s, see—Follows;	Lucretius	189
Satyr-shape.		
Or in his coarsest S-s.	In Mem.xxxv.	22
saunter.		
to those that s in the broad.	Aylmer's F.	744
saunter'd.		
s home beneath a moon,	Audley Ct.	79
savage.		
Mated with a squalid s—	Locksley H.	177
you young s of the Northern wild!	Princess, iii.	230
save.		
And s me lest I die?'	Pal. of Art	288
died To s her father's vow;	D. of F.Wom.	196
stored what little she could s,	Dora	50
s her little finger from a scratch	Ed. Morris	63
if thou wilt not s my soul,	St S. Stylites	45
To s from shame and thrall:	Sir Galahad	16
dust thou wouldst not s 'Come not, when,' etc.		4
to s A prince, a brother?	Princess, ii.	270
praying God with s Thy sailor,—	In Mem. vi.	13
influence-rich to sooth and s,	lxxix.	14
If lowliness could s her.	Maud,I. xii.	20
to s My yet young life.	" xvi.	21
To s from some slight shame	" xviii.	45

	POEM.	LINE.
s the one true seed of freedom	Ode on Well.	162
saving that, ye help to s mankind	"	166
But as he s's or serves the state,	"	200
s her dear lord whole from any	Enid	894
s a life dearer to me than mine.'	"	987
Tho' you do not love me, s, Yet s me!	Vivien	793
And s it even in extremes,	Guinevere	67
To s his blood from scandal,	"	510
s all earnings to the uttermost	En. Arden	86
then he pray'd 'S them from this	"	118
To s the offence of charitable,	"	339
To s the life despair'd of,	"	832
I could have died to s it)	Sea Dreams	130
her father was not the man to s,	Grandmother	5

saved.

	POEM.	LINE.
Who may be s? who is it may be s?	St S. Stylites	46
work miracles and not be s?,	"	148
cannot be but that I shall be s?	"	150
is s From that eternal silence,	Ulysses	26
Thou shalt not be s by works:	Vision of Sin	91
you may yet be s, and therefore fly	Princess, iii.	48
You s our life: we owe you bitter thanks:	" iv.	510
'He s my life: my brother slew him	" vi.	92
whose hearths he s from shame	Ode on Well.	225
was I broken down: there was I s:	Enid	1699
roll'd his enemy down, And s him:	Elaine	27
her fine care had s his life.	"	859
a sail! a sail! I am s'	En. Arden.	913

saving.

	POEM.	LINE.
s that, ye help to save mankind	Ode on Well.	166

savings.

	POEM.	LINE.
hoard all s to the uttermost	En. Arden.	46

Saviour.

	POEM.	LINE.
She bows, she bathes the S's feet.	In Mem.xxxii.	11
O s of the silver-coasted isle,	Ode on Well.	136
O God Almighty, blessed S,	En. Arden.	783

savour (s.)

	POEM.	LINE.
she has neither s nor salt,	Maud, I. ii.	2

savour (verb.)

	POEM.	LINE.
S's well to thee and me.	Vision of Sin	158

saw (maxim.)

	POEM.	LINE.
sabbath-drawler of old s's,	To J. M. K.	5
clinging to some ancient s;	'Love thou thy land'	29

saw (tool.)

	POEM.	LINE.
May never s dismember thee,	Talking O.	261
hammer and axe, Auger and s,	En. Arden.	174

saw (verb.)

	POEM.	LINE.
I s him—in his golden prime	Arabian N's.	153
the dull S no divinity in grass	A Character	8
He s thro' life and death,	The Poet	5
He s thro' his own soul,	"	7
ere I s your eyes, my love,	Miller's D.	43
I s the village lights below;	"	108
Sometimes I s you sit and spin;	"	121
a foot-fall, ere he s The wood-nymph	Pal. of Art	110
nothing s, for her despair	"	266
I s the snare, and I retired:	L. C. V. de Vere	6
To-night I s the sun set:	May Queen,ii.	5
I s you sitting in the house,	" iii.	30
s the gleaming river seaward flow	Lotos-E's.	14
I s, wherever light illumineth,	D.of F.lVom.	14
s crowds in column'd sanctuaries;	"	22
At length I s a lady within call,	"	85
turning s, throned on a flowery rise,	"	125
s the large white stars rise one by one,	"	223
S God divide the night.	"	225
Ere I s Who clasp'd	"	266
when he s the wonder of the hilt	M.d'Arthur	85
never s, Nor shall see, here or elsewhere	"	153
out of everything I heard and s,	Gardener's D.	65
I, that whole day S her no more,	"	160
s the boy Was not with Dora.	Dora	109
You s the man—on Monday,	Walk. to the M.	22
I s Your own Olivia blow,	Talking O.	75
Many a night I s the Pleiads	Locksley H.	9
S the Vision of the world,	"	16, 120
S the heavens fill with commerce,	"	121

	POEM.	LINE.
To-day I s the dragon-fly	Two Voices	8
To search thro' all I felt and s,	"	139
And see the vision that I s,	Day-Dm.	14
Till in a court he s	Will Water.	130
Than all those she s before:	L. of Burleigh	46
I s that every morning, far withdrawn	Vision of Sin	48
I s within my head	"	59
s The feudal warrior lady-clad	Princess, Pro.	118
they s the king; he took the gifts;	" i.	45
I s my father's face Grow long	"	57
life! he never s the like;	"	184
s you not the inscription on the gate,	" ii.	177
we s The Lady Blanche's daughter	"	299
Melissa hitting all we s with shafts	"	444
'Who ever s such wild barbarians?	" iii.	26
s The soft white vapour streak	"	325
began to change— I s it and grieved—	" iv.	280
S that they kept apart,	"	321
s the lights and heard The voices.	"	536
when we s the embattled squares,	" v.	236
Seeing I s not, hearing not I heard:	" vi.	3
if I s not, yet they told me all	"	4
when she s me lying stark	"	84
when she s The haggard father's face	"	86
she s them, and a day Rose from the	"	95
I s the forms: I knew not where I was	" vii.	118
s Thee woman thro' the crust	"	320
turning s The happy valleys,	Con.	40
s Sir Walter where he stood,	"	81
I in spirit s thee move.	In Mem. xvii.	5
We s not, when we moved therein?	" xxiv.	16
And s the tumult of the halls;	" lxxxvi.	4
brought an eye for all he s;	" lxxxviii.	9
s thro' all the Muses' walk:	" cviii.	4
Wrapt in a cloak, as I s him,	Maud, I. i.	59
Down by the hill I s them ride,	" ix.	11
Yet I thought I s her stand,	" II. i.	38
I s where James Made toward us,	The Brook	116
s the altar cold and bare	The Letters	4
I s with half-unconscious eye	"	15
oft we s the glisten Of ice,	The Daisy	35
look'd and s that all was ruinous.	Enid	315
if he be the knight whom late I s	"	406
s you moving by me on the bridge,	"	429
this dear child, because I never s,	"	497
looking round he s not Enid there,	"	506
men s the goodly hills of Somerset,	"	828
the flat meadow till she s them come;	"	832
I s three bandits by the rock	"	921
now they s their bulwark fall'n,	"	1017
In former days you s me favourably	"	1164
when she s him ride More near	"	1290
turning round she s Dust,	"	1297
s the chargers of the two that fell	"	1330
Rose when they s the dead man rise,	"	1580
s me not, or mark'd not if you s;	"	1718
for a minute till he s her Pass into it;	"	1734
s the little elf-god eyeless once	Vivien	98
look'd, and s you following still,	"	148
fancy, when you s me following you,	"	175
Because I s you sad, to comfort you	"	291
s two cities in a thousand boats	"	411
a crystal, and he s them thro' it,	"	480
Nor s We save the King,	"	493
s The knights, the court, the king	"	723
since he s The slow tear creep	"	754
S the tree that shone white-listed	"	787
s Fired from the west, far on a hill,	Elaine	168
I s him, after, stand High on a heap	"	306
I never s his like:	"	316
The maiden standing	"	350
till he s Which were the weaker;	"	461
when he s the Queen, embracing ask'd	"	569
'Whom when she s, "Lavaine" she	"	790
there first she s the casque Of Lancelot	"	801
s him lying unsleek, unshorn,	"	811
Lancelot s that she withheld her wish	"	916
s One of her own house, and sent him	"	1161
wild Queen, who s not, burst away	"	1237
s the barge that brought her moving	"	1382
s the Queen who sat betwixt	Guinevere	28

	POEM.	LINE.
more than this He *s not, . . *Guinevere*	.	31
golden days In which she *s him first,	"	378
that point, when first she *s the King	"	400
but she *s Wet with the mists .	"	590
she look'd and *s The novice, weeping	"	655
*s the pair, Enoch and Annie, . *En. Arden.*		63
She *s him not: and while he stood	"	242
All these he *s: but what he fain .	"	581
have worse and better, Enoch *s, .	"	742
*s the babe Hers, yet not his,	"	760
than he *s Death dawning on him,	"	832
my daughter Annie, whom I *s	"	883
grizzled cripple, whom I *s . *Aylmer's F.*		8
S from his windows nothing save his	"	21
thro' every labyrinth till he *s An end,	"	479
into nature's music when they *s her	"	694
s No pale sheet-lightnings from afar,	"	725
I *s* it in him at once . . *Sea Dreams*		64
then I *s* one lovely star .	"	91
He *s* not far: his eyes were dim: *The Voyage*		75
never *s* so fierce a fork . . *Lucretius*		8
I *s* the flaring atom-streams .	"	38

saw (sow.)

s's ere a beän an' yonder a peä, . *N. Farmer*		16

sawdust.

Or, elbow-deep in *s*, slept, . . *Will Water.*		99

sawn.

s In twain beneath the ribs; . *St S. Stylites*		51

Saxon.

S and Norman and Dane are we, *IV. to Alexan.*	3,	31

say (s.)

Give me my fling and let me say my *s*' *Aylmer's F.*		399
And a fool may say his *s* . *The Ringlet*		13

say (verb.)

What they say betwixt their wings? *Adeline*		29
I care not what they *s* . . *May Queen,* i.		19
I shall hearken what you *s*, . " ii.		39
s to Robin a kind word, . . " iii.		45
something I did wish to *s!* . . *To J. S.*		60
Is this enough to *s* That my desire *Gardener's D.*		231
scarce hear other music: yet *s* on. *Ed. Morris.*		57
I do not *s* But that a time may come *St S. Stylites*		186
S thou, whereon I carved her name, *Talking O.*		33
How *s* you? we have slept, my lords. *Day-Dm.*		153
As who shall *s* me nay: . . *Will Water.*		92
more fair than words can *s:* . *Beggar Maid*		2
we will *s* whatever comes. . *Princess, Pro.*		232
I, Who am not mine, *s,* live: "	iii.	205
the second place, Some *s* the third "		142
might have seem'd the thing you *s*. "		186
S to her, I do but wanton . "	iv.	91
to shame That which he *s*'s he loves "		230
neither seem'd there more to *s:* . "	v.	320
S one soft word and let me part . "	vi.	202
said you had a heart — I heard her *s* it— . "		217
As pure and perfect as I *s!* . *In Mem.* xxiv.		2
Whatever fickle tongues may *s* . " xxvi.		4
So methinks the dead would *s;* . " lxxxiv.		9
Whate'er the faithless people *s*. " xcvi.		16
O then, what then shall I *s?* . *Maud,* I. xix.		92
But what will the old man *s?* . " II. v.		83-7
what I think and what they *s*. . *Enid*		90
look so scared at what I *s:* . . "		1188
what *s* you, shall we strip him . "		1337
I nid could not *s* one tender word, . "		1594
wise in love Love most, *s* least,' . *Vivien*		97
Yet you are wise who *s* it; . . "		101
S's she not well? and there is more— "		300
Of him *y u s* you love: . . "		338-75
dare the full-fed liars *s* of me? . "		542
I might *s* that I had seen.' . *Elaine*		426
could believe the things you *s* . "		1093
wild people *s* wild things of thee . "		1356
still foreboding 'what would Enoch *s?' En. Arden*		252
Him and his children not to *s* me nay— "		307
s to Philip that I blest him too ; . "		887
you shall *s* that having spoken with *Aylmer's F.*		311

	POEM.	LINE.
Jilted I was: I *s* it for your peace *Aylmer's F.*		354
my fling, and let me *s* my say "		399
How many will *s* 'forgive, . *Sea Dreams*		60
on a *s*'s it easy an' free . . *N. Farmer.*		25
And a fool may *s* his say ; . . *The Ringlet*		18

saying (part.)

and I (Pardon me *s* it) . . *Princess,* i.		155
knowing, *s* not she knew . . " iii.		132
Reproach you, *s* all your force . *Enid*		83
s all his force Is melted . . "		106
S which she seized, And thro' the casement *Elaine*		1226
ev'n in *s* this, Her memory . *Guinevere*		375
s that which pleased him, for he smiled *En. Arden*		758

saying (s.)

A *s,* hard to shape in act; '*Love thou thy land,*' etc.		49
What is their pretty *s?* Jilted, is it? *Aylmer's F.*		353
a *s* learnt, In days far-off . *Tithonus*		47

scabbard.

when she show'd the wealthy *s,* . *Aylmer's F.*		236

scaffold.

S's, still sheets of water, . *D. of F. Wom.*		34

scald.

That let the bantling *s* at home, . *Princess,* v.		448

scale (series.)

Because the *s* is infinite . . *Two Voices*		93
Along the *s* of ranks, . . *In Mem.* cx.		2

scale (dish, etc.)

fortunes, justlier balanced, *s* with *s.' Princess,* ii.		52
and the golden *s* Of harness . " v.		39
takes it up, And topples down the *s*'s ; "		435
slowly falling as a *s* that falls, . *Enid*		525

scale (verb.)

she that out of Lethe *s*'s with man *Princess,* vii.		245
To *s* the heaven's highest height, . *In Mem.* cvii.		7

scaled.

Suddenly *s* the light, . . *Pal. of Art*		8
the toppling crags of Duty *s*. *Ode on Well.*		215
High with the last line *s* her voice *Elaine*		1013
s in sheets of wasteful foam, . *Sea Dreams*		53

scaling.

s slow from grade to grade ; . *Two Voices*		174
after *s* half the weary down . *En. Arden.*		369

scalp.

From *s* to sole one slough and crust *St S. Stylites*		2
Beat into my *s* and my brain, . *Maud,* I. v.		10

scan.

I *s* him now Beastlier than any . *Lucretius*		192

scandal.

Begins the *s* and the cry; '*You might have won*'		16
like a city, with gossip, *s*, and spite: *Maud,* I. iv.		8
You'll have no *s* while you dine, *To F. D. Maurice*		17
spy some secret *s* if he might . *Guinevere*		27
make the smouldering *s* break . "		91
To save his blood from *s,* . . "		510
Old *s*'s buried now seven decads . *Aylmer's F.*		442
other *s*'s that have lived and died . "		443
left the living *s* that shall die— "		444

scant.

'Tis life, whereof our nerves are *s,* *Two Voices*		397

*s*rape.

that he *s* the doom of fire, . *Guinevere*		345

'scaped.

by this way I *'s* them. . . *St S. Stylites*		176

scapegoat.

On that huge *s* of the race . *Maud,* I. xiii.		42

scar.

O sweet and far from cliff and *s* . *Princess,* iii.		350

scarce.

upon the game, how *s* it was . *Audley Ct.*		31

scarce-believable.

many a *s-b* excuse, . . *En. Arden.*		466

Z

354   CONCORDANCE TO

	POEM.	LINE.
scarce-credited.		
S-e at first but more and more	En. Arden	649
scarce-rocking.		
S-r, her full-busted figure head	En. Arden	539
scare.		
s church-harpies from the master's feast	To J. M. K.	3
To s the fowl from fruit	Princess,	ii. 210
biting laws to s the beasts of prey	"	v. 383
wilt thou ever s me with thy tears,	Tithonus	46
scarecrow.		
Empty s's, I and you!	Vision of Sin	94
scared.		
he heard her speak : She s him;	Princess,	i. 184
s by the cry they made,	"	v. 91
The king is s, the soldier will not fight,	Con.	60
foemen s, like that false pair	Enid	1025
Nor need you look so s	"	1188
s but at the motion of the man,	"	1325
beauteous beast S by the noise	Vivien	272
'O' she cried S as it were	En. Arden	427
s with threats of jail and halter	Aylmer's F.	520
scarf.		
One sitting on a crimson s unroll'd;	D.of F. Wom.	126
Dark as a funeral s from stem	M. d'Arthur	194
A s of orange round the stony helm,	Princess, Pro.	102
fluttering s's and ladies' eyes	"	v. 498
A purple s, at either end whereof	Enid	169
Prince's blood spirted upon the s,	"	208
Yniol caught His purple s, and held,	"	377
scarfskin.		
not a hair Ruffled upon the s	Aylmer's F.	660
scarlet.		
who wore the sleeve Of s,	Elaine	501
upon his helm A sleeve of s,	"	602
scarlet-mingled.		
hills and s-m woods	The Voyage	47
scathe.		
a s God's high gift from s and wrong	Guinevere	490
scathed.		
down in a furrow s with flame;	The Victim	22
scatter.		
we will s all our maids	Princess,	vi. 283
Disband himself, and s all his powers.	Enid	1646
S the blossom under her feet!	IV. to Alexan.	9
scatter'd.		
twinkling laurel s silver lights,	Gardener's D.	117
'Tho' thou wert s to the wind,	Two Voices	32
Or s blanching on the grass.	Day-Dm.	112
s all they had to all the winds;	Enid	635
All s thro' the houses of the town ;	"	695
lo, the powers of Doorm Are s,'	"	1650
One from the bandit s in the field,	"	1666
s theirs and brought her off,	Vivien	414
huts At random s, each a nest	Aylmer's F.	130
S all over the vocabulary	"	540
were s Blood and brains of men.	The Captain	47
scattering.		
Time, a maniac s dust,	In Mem. xlix.	7
scaur.		
down the shingly s he plunged,	Elaine	54
sceptre.		
A crown, a s, and a throne !	Ode to Mem.	121
To whom I leave the s and the isle—	Ulysses	34
held his s like a pedant's wand	Princess,	i. 27
would I had his s for one hour !	"	iv. 517
sceptre-staff.		
till thy hand Fail from the s-s	Œnone	124
scheme.		
a noble s Grew up from seed	Princess,	iv. 290
space and fairplay for her s ;	"	v. 272
I give you all The random s	"	Con. 2
how to bind the scatter'd s of seven	"	8
s that had left us flaccid and drain'd.	Maud,	l. i. 20

	POEM.	LINE.
schemed.		
s and wrought Until I overturn'd him ;	Enid	1677
if I s against your peace in this,	Vivien	779
schism.		
hawking at Geology and s ;	The Epic	16
school.		
Completion in a painful s ; '*Love thou thy land,*' etc.		58
I was at s—a college in the South;	Walk. to the M.	75
in the Latin song I learnt at s,	Ed. Morris	79
Thro' the courts, the camps, the s's,	Vision of Sin	104
For there are s's for all.'	Princess,	iii. 288
From art, from nature, from the s's	In Mem. xlviii.	1
The flippant put himself to s.	"	cix. 10
smile at one That is not of his s	Vivien	513
put the boy and girl to s ;	En. Arden	311-28
Philip put her little ones to s,	"	707
schoolbooks.		
In our s we say	The Brook	9
schoolboy.		
a s ere he grows To Pity— ;	Walk. to the M.	99
No graver than a s's barring out,	Princess, Con.	66
science.		
truths of S waiting to be caught—	Golden Year	17
With the fairy-tales of s,	Locksley H.	12
S moves, but slowly slowly,	"	134
wake on s grown to more,	Day-Dm.	222
sport Went hand in hand with S ;	Princess, Pro.	80
to sound the abyss Of s,	"	ii. 160
every Muse tumbled a s in.	"	377
inmost terms Of art and s ;	"	424
Two great statues, Art And S,	"	iv. 183
When S reaches forth her arms	In Mem. xxi.	18
Let S prove we are, and then What matters S unto men,	"	cxix. 6
man of s himself is fonder of glory	Maud,	I. iv. 37
dear to S, dear to Art,	Ded. of Idylls	39
The simples and the s of that time	Elaine	858
Mastering the lawless s of our law	Aylmer's F.	425
S enough and exploring,	1865—1866	6
scion.		
Nor cared for seed or s !	Amphion	12
scoff (s.)		
I met with s's, I met with scorns	In Mem. lxviii.	9
scoff (verb.)		
to s and jeer and babble of him	Enid	58
scooped.		
ever labouring had s himself	Elaine	403
scope.		
shall have s and breathing-space ;	Locksley H.	157
scorched.		
Shot out of them, and s me	Lucretius	66
scorn (s.)		
friend, whose joyful s ' *Clear-headed friend,*' etc.		1
the hate of hate, the s of s	The Poet	3
cruel love, whose end is s,	Mariana in the S.	70
Were wisdom in the s of consequence	Œnone	148
from which mood was born S of herself	Pal. of Art	231
grief became A solemn s of ills	D. of F. Wom.	228
Turning to s with lips divine '*Of old sat Freedom*'		23
Ere yet, in s of Peter's Pence,	Talking O.	45
passion were a target for their s ;	Locksley H.	146
Shall it not be s to me	"	147
nodding, as in s, He parted,	Godiva	30
Then said the voice, in quiet s,	Two Voices	401
I trow they did not part in s ;	Lady Clare	5
He laugh'd a laugh of merry s ;	"	81
Mingle madness, mingle s!	Vision of Sin	204
fulmin'd out her s of laws Salique	Princess,	ii. 117
blight Of ancient influence and s.	"	153
classic Angel speak In s of us,	"	iii. 54
lighten s At him that mars her plan	"	v. 125
but brooding turn The book of s	"	136
king in bitter s Drew from my neck.	"	vi. 93
answer'd full of grief and s	"	313
shroud me from my proper s.	In Mem. xxvi.	16
I met with scoffs, I met with s's	"	lxviii. 9

	POEM.	LINE.
You say, but with no touch of *s*,	*In Mem.* xcv.	1
(then my *s* might well descend	" cxxvii.	21
With a glassy smile his brutal *s*—	*Maud*, I. vi.	49
put your beauty to this flout and *s*	*Enid*	1523
Instead of scornful pity or pure *s*	"	1707
Full knightly without *s*;	*Guinevere*	40
of Arthur's noblest dealt in *s*;	"	41
S was allow'd as part of his defect	"	44
be for evermore a name of *s*	"	61,620
To make disproof of *s*,	*Aylmer's F.*	446
striking on huge stumbling-blocks of *s*	"	538
laws of nature were our *s*;	*The Voyage*	84
spite of praise and *s*, As one who feels	*A Dedication*	6
hate and pity, and spite and *s*	*Lucretius*	77

scorn (verb.)

or if you *s* to lay it, Yourself,	*Princess*, vi.	167
s The long result of love,	*In Mem.* i.	13
these were such as men might *s*;	" xlvii.	4
to be scorn'd by one that I *s*,	*Maud*, I. xiii.	1
for I see you *s* my courtesies,	*Enid*	1519
touching fame, howe'er you *s* my song.	*Vivien*	294
we *s* them, but they sting.	*Elaine*	140
proud fellow again who *s*'s us all?	"	1059
I must not *s* myself:	*Guinevere*	605
They that *s* the tribes and call us.	*Boädicea*	7

scorn'd.

Comfort? comfort *s* of devils?	*Locksley H.*	75
cursed and *s*, and bruised with stones:	*Two Voices*	222
s to help their equal rights	*Princess*, vii.	218
S, to be *s* by one that I scorn	*Maud*. I. xiii.	1

scorner.

| Not a *s* of your sex But venerator. | *Princess*, iv. | 402 |

scorning.

| He utter'd words of *s*: | *The Goose* | 42 |
| set himself, *S* an alms, to work | *En. Arden.* | 813 |

scoundrel.

| stammering '*s*' out of teeth that | *Aylmer's F.* | 328 |
| *s* in the supple-sliding knee.' | *Sea Dreams* | 164 |

scour.

| to scream, to burnish, and to *s* | *Princess*, iv. | 477 |

scour'd.

| youth who *s* His master's armour | *Enid* | 257 |
| *s* into the coppices and was lost, | " | 1383 |

scourge.

| Mortify Your flesh, like me, with *s*'s | *St S. Stylites* | 177 |
| harsh groom for bridal-gift a *s*; | *Princess*, v. | 368 |

scouring.

| told him, *s* still 'The sparrow-hawk!' | *Enid* | 260 |

scout.

| inward raced the *s*'s With rumour | *Princess*, v. | 107 |

scowl.

| foreheads drawn in Roman *s*'s | *Princess*, vii. | 114 |

scowled.

| *s* At their great lord. | *Aylmer's F.* | 724 |

scrambled.

| Have *s* past those pits of fire, | *St S. Stylites* | 181 |

scrap.

| *s*'s of thundrous Epic lilted out | *Princess*, ii. | 353 |

scraped.

| I *s* the lichen from it; | *The Brook* | 193 |

scraping.

| With strumming and with *s*, | *Amphion* | 70 |
| All my poor *s*'s from a dozen years | *Sea Dreams* | 77 |

scratch.

| save her little finger from a *s* | *Ed. Morris* | 63 |
| every *s* a lance had made upon it, | *Elaine* | 20 |

scrawl.

| in thy heart the *s* shall play | *Sailor Boy* | 12 |

scrawled.

| The butler drank, the steward *s*, | *Day-Dm.* | 142 |

	POEM.	LINE.
scream s.)		
Now to the *s* of a madden'd beach	*Maud*, I. iii.	12

scream (verb.)

| To tramp, to *s*, to burnish | *Princess*, iv. | 477 |

screamed.

| The parrot *s*, the peacock squall'd | *Day-Dm.* | 144 |

screw.

| Let me *s* thee up a peg: | *Vision of Sin* | 87 |
| *S* not the chord too sharply. | *Aylmer's F.* | 450 |

scribbled.

| every margin *s*, crost, and cramm'd | *Vivien* | 527 |

scrip.

| lucky rhymes to him were *s* and share | *The Brook* | 4 |

scripture.

| Preach an inverted *s*, | *Aylmer's F.* | 44 |

scroll.

An open *s*, Before him lay:	*The Poet*	8
But one poor poet's *s*,	"	55
The seal was Cupid bent above a *s*,	*Princess*, i.	238
she crush'd The *s*'s together	" iv.	375
the *s* 'I follow thine.'	*Vivien*	326
ponder those three hundred *s*'s	*Lucretius*	12

scud.

| foam-flakes *s* along the level sand | *D. of F. Wom.* | 39 |

scudded.

| Of mighty mouth, we *s* fast. | *The Voyage* | 46 |

scullery.

| whinny shrills From tile to *s*, | *Princess*, v. | 443 |

sculptor.

| Musician, painter, *s*, critic | *Princess*, ii. | 161 |
| Wan *S* weepest thou to take the cast | *Coquette*, iii. | 1 |

sculpture.

| some sweet *s* draped from head to foot | *Princess*, v. | 54 |

scum.

| scurf of salt, and *s* of dross, | *Vision of Sin* | 211 |

scurf.

| *s* of salt, and scum of dross, | *Vision of Sin* | 211 |

scythe.

| The sweep of *s* in morning dew, | *In Mem.* lxxxviii. | 18 |
| the sun blaze on the turning *s*, | *Enid* | 1101 |

sea.

compass'd by the inviolate *s*.'	*To the Queen*	36
heaped hills that mound the *s*,	*Ode to Mem.*	98
music reach'd them on the middle *s*.	*Sea-Fairies*	6
High over the full-toned *s*;	"	15
Runs up the ridged *s*,	"	32
Norland winds pipe down the *s*,	*Oriana*	91
I hear the roaring of the *s*,	"	98
Singing alone Under the *s*,	*The Merman*	5
kiss them often under the *s*,	"	15
Soft are the moss-beds under the *s*;	"	34
Combing her hair Under the *s*,	*The Mermaid*	5
great sea-snake under the *s*	"	23
mermen under the *s*	"	28, 42
silvery spikes are nighest the *s*.	"	37
purple twilights under the *s*;	"	44
branching jaspers under the *s*;	"	47
hueless mosses under the *s*,	"	49
from the hollow sphere of the *s*,	"	54
past Into deep orange o'er the *s*,	*Mariana in the S.*	26
There came a sound as of the *s*;	"	80
With motions of the outer *s*:	*Eleänore*	113
In cataract after cataract to the *s*.	*Œnone*	9
the sky Dipt down to *s* and sands.	*Pal. of Art*	32
in ... clear-wall'd city on the *s*,	"	97
The plunging *s*'s draw backward.	"	251
the low Moan of an unknown *s*;	"	280
Most weary seem'd the *s*,	*Lotos-E's.*	41
Vaulted o'er the dark-blue *s*,	"	85
spouted his foam-fountains in the *s*.	"	152
thunder-drops fall on a sleeping *s*:	*D. of F. Wom.*	122
Your spirit is the calmed *s*,	*Margaret*	25
languish for the purple *s*'s! 'You ask me why,' etc.		4

	POEM.	LINE.
round them *s* and air are dark	'*Love thou thy land*'	63
the mountains by the winter *s*	*M. d'Arthur*	2
with noises of the northern *s*.	"	141
hollows crown'd with summer *s*,	"	263
from the boat, And breathing of the *s*.	*Audley Ct.*	7
The *s* wastes all: but let me live my life.	"	50
as a thorn Turns from the *s*;	"	54
the fair green field and eastern *s*.	*Love and Duty*	98
s's, that daily gain upon the shore,	*Golden Year*	29
like a lane of beams athwart the *s*,	"	50
lying in dark-purple spheres of *s*.	*Lockstey H.*	164
A light upon the shining *s*—	*St Agnes' Eve*	35
Thought her proud, and fled over the *s*;	*Ed. Gray*	14
And fluted to the morning *s*.	*To E. L.*	24
Flow down, cold rivulet, to the *s*,	*A Farewell*	1
The wrinkled *s* beneath him crawls	*The Eagle*	4
On thy cold gray stones, O *S* ! '*Break, break,*' etc.		2-14
A full *s* glazed with muffled moonlight,	*Princess,* i.	244
currents of clear morning *s*'s.	" ii.	307
Wind of the western *s* .	"	437
the moon may draw the *s*;	" vi.	364
the slope of *s* from verge to shore,	" vii.	23
the *s*'s; A red sail, or a white;	" Con.	46
God bless the narrow *s*.	"	51, 70
Calm on the *s*'s, and silver sleep,	*In Mem.* xi.	17
To breathe thee over lonely *s*'s.	" xvii.	7
Breaks hither over Indian *s*'s,	" xxvi.	14
The moanings of the homeless *s*,	" xxxv.	9
From belt to belt of crimson *s*'s	" lxxxv.	13
The conscience as a *s* at rest:	" xciii.	12
brought a summons from the *s*:	" cii.	16
On winding stream or distant *s*;	" cxiv.	12
The stillness of the central *s*.	" cxxii.	4
Who rest to-night beside the *s*.	Con.	76
loud war by land and by *s*,	*Maud,* I. i.	47
azure bloom of a crescent of *s*,	" iv.	5
Over blowing *s*'s, Over *s*'s at rest	" xvii.	13
Leap, beyond the *s*.	"	20
A purer sapphire melts into the *s*	" xviii.	52
trying to pass to the *s*;	" xxi.	7
shock Of the cataract *s*'s that snap	" II. ii.	25
While I am over the *s* !	"	76
North, and battle, and *s*'s of death.	" III vi.	37
the long wash of Australasian *s*'s .	*The Brook*	194
Was great by land as thou by *s*.	*Ode on Well.*	84-90
roughly set His Briton in blown *s*'s	"	155
The tides of Music's golden *s*	"	252
To lands of summer across the *s*;	*The Daisy*	92
white sails flying on the yellow *s*;	*Enid*	829
not to goodly hill or yellow *s*	"	830
like a shoaling *s* the lovely blue	"	1535
Against the heathen of the Northern *S*	"	1817
fighting for a woman on the *s*.	*Vivien*	412
half my realm beyond the *s*'s,	*Elaine*	954
(*S* was her wrath, yet working	"	1300
realm beyond the narrow *s*'s,	"	1313
now the Heathen of the Northern *S*,	*Guinevere*	134
man-breasted things stood from the *s*,	"	244
dark Dundagil by the Cornish *s*,	"	292
heathen swarming o'er the Northern *S*	"	425
dread sweep of the down-streaming *s*'s:	*En. Arden*	55
Enoch was abroad on wrathful *s*'s,	"	91
many a rough *s* had he weather'd in her!	"	135
the *s* is His, The *s* is His: He made it.'	"	225
the loneliest in a lonely *s*.	"	554
the low moan of laden-colour'd *s*'s.	"	613
fountains of sweet water in the *s*,	"	804
came so loud a calling of the *s*,	"	909
This had a rosy *s* of gillyflowers	*Aylmer's F.*	139
since our bad earth became one *s*,	"	635
in a river of blood to the sick *s*	"	768
month's leave given them, to the *s*:	*Sea Dreams*	6
Shall Babylon be cast into the *s*	"	98
that they saw, the *s*.	"	36
the *s* roars Ruin: a fearful night !'	"	80
broad *s*'s swell'd to meet the keel,	*The Voyage*	13
At times the whole *s* burn'd,	"	51
Like Heavenly Hope she crown'd the *s*	"	70
my part Of danger on the roaring *s*	*Sailor Boy*	22
Singing, 'and shall it be over the *s*'s	*The Islet*	9
storm never wakes on the lonely *s*	"	33

	POEM.	LINE.
Sea-kings' daughter from over the *s*	*W. to Alexan.*	1
as the *s* when he welcomes the land	"	24
Bride of the heir of the kings of the *s*	"	28
flying by to be lost on an endless *s*—	*Wages*	2
S's at my feet were flowing, .	1865-1866	10
seabird.		
And the lonely *s* crosses	*The Captain*	71
sea-blue.		
Flits by the *s-b* bird of March;	*In Mem.* xc.	4
sea-bud.		
under my starry *s-b* crown	*The Mermaid*	16
sea-cataract.		
And fell In vast *s-c*'s .	*Sea Dreams*	54
sea-circle.		
first indeed Thro' many a fair *s-c*,	*En. Arden*	538
seäd (seed.)		
an' some on it doon in *s*.	*N. Farmer*.	40
sea-flower.		
Dressing their hair with the white *s-f*;	*The Merman*	13
sea-framing.		
in and out the long *s-f* caves,	*Sea Dreams*	33
sea-friend.		
Enoch parted with his old *s-f*	*En. Arden*.	168
sea-furbelow.		
dimpled flounce of the *s-f* flap,	*Sea Dreams*	257
sea-groves.		
the pale-green *s-g* straight and high,	*The Merman*	19
sea-hall.		
fill the *s-h*'s with a voice of power;	*The Merman*	10
blind wave feeling round his long *s-h*	*Vivien*	81
sea-haze.		
Roll'd a *s-h* and whelm'd the world	*En. Arden*.	673
sea-king.		
S-k's' daughter from over the sea,	*W. to Alexan.*	1
S-k's' daughter as happy as fair,	"	26
seal (of a letter, etc.)		
s, that hung From Allan's watch.	*Dora*	132
the *s* an *Elle vous suit*,	*Ed. Morris*	105
Break lock and *s*; betray the '*You might have won*'		18
The *s* was Cupid bent above a scroll,	*Princess,* i.	238
To dissolve the precious *s* on a bond,	*Maud,* I.xix.	45
Stoopt, took, brake *s*, and read it;	*Elaine*	1264
Burst his own wyvern on the *s*,	*Aylmer's F.*	516
Claspt on her *s*, my sweet !	*The Window*	135
seal (animal.)		
as they say The *s* does music;	*Princess,* iv.	435
sealed.		
S it with kisses? .	*Œnone*	230
This I *s*: The seal was Cupid	*Princess,* i.	237
is now no more a fountain *s*:	" ii.	76
since my will *S* not the bond—	" v.	389
thy fate and mine are *s*:	" vi.	374
s The lips of that Evangelist.	*In Mem.* xxxi.	15
s within the iron hills? .	" lv.	20
S her mine from her first sweet breath	*Maud,* I.xix.	41
sea-like.		
Hector said, and *s-l* roar'd his host;	*Spec. of Iliad*	1
sea-line.		
Back to the dark *s-l* .	*Maud,* II.ii.	45
fixt upon the far *s-l*;	*The Voyage*	62
sea-light.		
with a wild *s-l* about his feet,	*Guinevere*	240
seaman.		
books of travell'd *seamen*,	*Amphion*	82
Mighty *S*, this is he	*Ode on Well.*	83
Mighty *S*, tender and true,	"	134
With all that *seamen* needed	*En. Arden*.	139
get you a *s*'s glass,	"	215
A haunt of brawling *seamen* once,	"	698
the *seamen* Made a gallant crew	*The Captain*	5
seamed.		
S with an ancient swordcut .	*Elaine*	258
S with the shallow cares	*Aylmer's F.*	814

	POEM.	LINE.
senmew.		
Where now the *s* pipes . .	*In.Mem.*cxiv.	13
sear.		
And woods are *s* . . .	*The Window*	45
search (s.)		
and was wearied of the *s.*	*Elaine*	628
burst away In *s* of stream or fount	*En. Arden.*	636
search (verb.)		
To *s* thro' all I felt or saw, .	*Two Voices*	139
To *s* a meaning for the song, .	*Day-Dm.*	247
seared.		
S by the close ecliptic, . .	*Aylmer's F.*	193
searer.		
The woods are all the *s* .	*The Window*	56
sea-smoke.		
upjetted in spirits of wild *s-s*	*Sea Dreams*	52
sea-snake.		
that great *s-s* under the sea .	*The Mermaid*	23
season.		
know the *s's* when to take .	*To the Queen*	30
Power fitted to the *s* . .	*Œnone*	121
in its *s* bring the law ; ' *Love thou thy laud*,' etc.		32
It is a stormy ' . .	*The Goose*	8
watchman peal The sliding *s:*	*Gardener'sD.*	179
the game, how scarce it was This *s*;	*Audley Ct.*	32
as poets' *s's* when they flower	*Golden Year*	28
all the *s* of the golden year. .	„	36
writers push'd the happy *s* back,—	„	65
Will thirty *s's* render plain .	*Two Voices*	82
In divers *s's*, divers climes ; .	*Day-Dm.*	230
We circle with the *s's.* . .	*Will Water.*	64
the cube and square Were out of *s*;	*Princess,Pro.*	179
The *s's* bring the flower again,	*In Mem.*	5
crown'd with all the *s* lent, .	„ xxii.	6
No joy the blowing *s* gives .	„ xxxviii.	5
break At *s's* thro' the gilded pale :	„ cx.	8
served the *s's* that may rise ; .	„ cxii.	4
Like things of the *s* gay, like the bountiful *s* bland, . .	*Maud,* I. iv.	3
blow by night, when the *s* is good	„ II. v.	75
breathes in converse *s's.* . .	*The Brook*	190
Fixt in her will, and so the *s's* went.	*Vivien*	44
' to pluck the flower in *s*;' .	„	572
The sunny and the rainy *s's* came	*En. Arden.*	624
subject to the *s* or the mood, .	*Aylmer's F.*	71
The meteor of a splendid *s*, .	„	205
yet out of *s* thus I woo thee	*Lucretius*	267
seat (s.)		
downward to her *s* from the upper cliff	*Œnone*	21
Rest in a happy place and quiet *s's*	„	129
lady friend, From neighbour *s's*	*Princess,Pro.*	98
part reel'd but kept their *s's*:	„ v.	485
freedom in her regal *s* Of England;	*InMem.*cviii.	14
nine is the firmer *s*, . .	*Elaine*	445
prone from off her *s* she fell, .	*Guinevere*	411
Had cast the curtains of their *s* aside	*Aylmer's F.*	803
no quiet *s's* of the just, . .	*Wages*	8
seat (verb.)		
we will *s* you highest . .	*Princess,* iii.	143
To *s* you sole upon my pedestal	*Vivien*	727
seated.		
s on a serpent-rooted beech, .	*The Brook*	135
s on a style In the long hedge, .	„	197
Annie, *s* with her grief, .	*En. Arden.*	279
sea-voice.		
sent a deep *s-v* thro' all the land, .	*Guinevere*	245
seaward-bound.		
s-b for health they gain'd a coast,	*Sea Dreams*	16
seaward-gazing.		
in a *s-g* mountain-gorge . .	*En. Arden.*	559
Sat often in the *s-g* gorge, . .	„	590
sea-water.		
The salt *s-w* passes by, . .	*In Mem.* xix.	6

	POEM.	LINE.
sea-wave.		
voice of the long *s-w* as it swell'd	*Maud,* I. xiv.	31
sea-wind.		
over them the *s-w* sang . .	*M.d'Arthur*	48
sea-wold.		
On the broad *s-w's* in the crimson	*The Mermaid*	36
sea-worthy.		
The vessel scarce *s-w*, . .	*En. Arden.*	657
second.		
She is the *s.* not the first. .	*In Mem.*cxiii.	16
second-hand.		
fit us like a nature *s-h*; .	*Walk. to the M.*	57
second-sight.		
The *s-s* of some Astræan age .	*Princess,* ii.	420
secret.		
What know we of the *s* of a man	*Walk. to the M.*	94
s's of the brain, the stars, .	*Day-Dm.*	223
But keep the *s* for your life, .	*Lady Clare*	34-42
science, and the *s's* of the mind : .	*Princess,* ii.	160
the snake, My *s*, seem'd to stir	„ iii.	28
holy *s's* of this microcosm, .	„	296
charms Her *s* from the latest moon?'	*In Mem.* xxi.	20
all the *s* of the Spring . .	„ xxiii.	19
He reads the *s* of the star, .	„ xcvi.	22
And learnt their elemental *s's*, .	*Vivien*	482
Might well have kept his *s* .	*Elaine*	591
her heart's sad *s* blazed itself .	„	833
'Woman, I have a *s*—only swear,	*En. Arden.*	838
sect.		
I care not what the *s's* may brawl.	*Pal. of Art*	210
To cleave a creed in *s's* and cries,	*In Mem.* cxxvii.	15
secure.		
Lie still, dry dust, *s* of change .	*To J. S.*	76
in their double love *s*, . .	*Two Voices*	413
sedge.		
whisper'd 'Asses' ears' among the *s*,	*Princess,* ii.	98
see.		
Hither, come hither and *s*; .	*Sea-Fairies*	28
thro' the windows we shall *s* .	*Deserted H.*	10
There she *s's* the highway near	*L. of Shalott,* ii.	13
I *s* thy beauty gradually unfold .	*Eleänore*	70
I seem to *s* Thought folded over thought	„	83
s thee roam, with tresses unconfined,	„	122
I *s* the wealthy miller yet, .	*Miller's D.*	1
And *s* the minnows everywhere .	„	51
The doubt my mother would not *s*;	„	154
Shall I one Œnone *s* the morning mist	*Œnone*	212
Heaven, how canst thou *s* my face ?	„	232
dimly *s* My far-off Joubtful purpose,	„	246
O the Earl was fair to *s* I (rep.)	*The Sisters*	6
you had hardly cared to *s.* .	*L. C. V. de Vere*	32
whom think ye should I *s* .	*May Queen,* i.	13
to *s* me made the Queen ; .	„	26
I would *s* the sun rise . .	„ ii. 2,	51
last New-Year that I shall ever *s*,	„	3
never *s* The blossom on the blackthorn,	„	7
I long to *s* a flower so . .	„	16
never *s* me more in the long gray fields	„	20
you 'll come sometimes and *s* me	„	32
Tho' you 'll not *s* me, mother .	„	38
s me carried out from the threshold	„	42
Don't let Effie come to *s* me .	„	43
Waiting to *s* me die, . .	*D. of F.Wom.*	112
that I should ever *s* the light ! .	„	254
He will not *s* the dawn of day.	*D. of the O. Year*	11
A jollier year we shall not *s*. .	„	20
To *s* him die, across the waste .	„	30
will *s* before I die The palms '*You ask me why*,'etc.		27
Watch what I *s*, and lightly bring	*M. d'Arthur*	44
I *s* thee what thou art, . .	„	123
s I by thine eyes that this is done.	„	140
shall *s*, here or elsewhere, till I die,	„	154
now I *s* the true old times are dead	„	229
shouldst never *s* my face again, .	„	246
in itself the day we went To *s* her.	*Gardener'sD.*	75

	POEM.	LINE.
wish to *s* My grandchild on my knees	*Dora*	10
he may *s* the boy, And bless him	"	67
Allan said, ' I *s* it is a trick	"	93
go you hence, and never *s* me more.'	"	98, 114
Whose house is that I *s*?	*Walk to the M.*	7
s the raw mechanic's bloody thumbs	"	67
I *s* the moulder'd Abbey-walls,	*Talking O.*	3
when I *s* the woodman lift His axe	"	235
Then not to dare to *s*!	*Love and Duty*	38
s the great Achilles, whom we knew.	*Ulysses*	64
far as human eye could *s*;	*Locksley H.*	15, 119
O, I *s* thee old and formal,	"	93
S's in heaven the light of London	"	114
O, I *s* the crescent promise	"	187
And loath'd to *s* them overtax'd : .	*Godiva*	9
Had cunning eyes to *s*:	"	57
Still *s*'s the sacred morning spread	*Two Voices*	80
' I *s* the end, and know the good.'	"	432
scarce could *s* the grass for flowers.	"	453
And *s* the vision that I saw,	*Day-Dm.*	14
lets thee neither hear nor *s*:	"	264
And wasn't it a sight to *s*,	*Amphion*	49
Let us *s* these handsome houses	*L. of Burleigh*	23
S's whatever fair and splendid	"	27
S's a mansion more majestic	"	45
S that sheets are on my bed;	*Vision of Sin*	68
s no men, Not even her brother	*Princess*, i.	151
I am sad and glad To *s* you, Florian.	ii.	287
I know the substance when I *s* it.	"	391
s's herself in every woman else,	iii.	94
could not *s* The bird of passage flying	"	193
she that has a son And *s*'s him err:	"	244
That we might *s* our own work out,	"	253
As parts can *s* but parts	"	310
A man I came to *s* you:	iv.	421
s's his brood about thy knee;	"	559
sweet child, whom I shall *s* no more!	v.	80
and ours shall *s* us friends.	"	219
s's me fight, Yea, let her *s* me fall,	"	505
Sooner fight thrice o'er than *s* it.'.	vi.	209
s that some one with authority	"	219
s how you stand Stiff as Lot's wife	"	235
now should men *s* Two women faster	vii.	21
s's a great black cloud Drag inward	"	33
knowledge is of things we *s*;	*In Mem. Pro.*	22
he will *s* them on to-night : .	vi.	33
My Arthur, whom I shall not *s*	ix.	17
I *s* the cabin-window bright .	x.	3
I *s* the sailor at the wheel.	"	4
s the sails at distance rise,	xii	11
widower, when he *s*'s A late-lost form	xiii.	1
Should *s* thy passengers in rank	xiv.	6
The dust of him I shall not *s*	xvii.	19
spirits sink To *s* the vacant chair .	xx.	19
bore thee where I could not *s*	xxii.	17
s Within the green the moulder'd .	xxvi.	6
Or *s* (in Him is no before)	"	10
And finds ' I am not what I *s*,	xliv.	7
S with clear eye some hidden shame	l.	7
I cannot *s* the features right,	lxix.	1
I *s* thee what thou art, and know.	lxxiii.	6
there is more than I can *s*,	"	9
I *s* thee sitting crown'd with good,	lxxxiii.	5
I *s* their unborn faces shine .	"	19
I *s* myself an honour'd guest	"	21
To *s* the rooms in which he dwelt.	lxxxvi.	16
I shall not *s* thee. Dare I say	xcii.	1
He *s*'s himself in all he *s*'s.	xcvi.	4
You leave us : you will *s* the Rhine,	xcvii.	1
I have not seen, I will not *s* Vienna;	"	11
those that here we *s* no more;	cv.	10
I *s* Betwixt the black fronts .	cxviii.	5
That *s*'s the course of human things.	cxxvii.	4
I *s* in part That all, as in some	"	22
I *s* her pass like a light .	*Maud*, I. iv.	11
I *s* my Dread coming down .	xvi.	8
I *s* her there, Bright English lily	xix.	54
true lover may *s* Your glory also	xx.	47
S what a lovely shell	II. ii.	1
For one short hour to *s* .	iv.	14
S, there is one of us sobbing,	v.	30

	POEM.	LINE.
in summers that we shall not *s*	*Ode on Well.*	234
Whom we *s* not we revere,	"	245
God-father, come and *s* your boy:	*To F. D. Maurice*	2
we *s* him as he moved, How modest	*Ded. of Idylls*	16
s my dear lord wounded in the strife	*Enid*	103
I *s* her Weeping for some gay knight	"	117
petition'd for his leave To *s* the hunt	"	155
but come like you to *s* the hunt	"	179
hearts who *s* but acts of wrong :	"	438
can *s* elsewhere, anything so fair,	"	409
for Enid *s*'s my fall!'	"	590
while she thought ' they will not *s* me,'	"	666
s my princess as I *s* her now,	"	752
That other, where we *s* as we are seen !	"	856
shall *s* my vigour is not lost.'	"	931
how is it I *s* you here ? .	"	1158
I *s* it with joy—You sit apart,	"	1169
you may hear, or *s*, Or fancy	"	1264
I *s* the danger which you cannot *s*;	"	1270
makes me mad to *s* you weep.	"	1464
for I *s* you scorn my courtesies,	"	1519
s you not my gentlewomen here	"	1530
s's the trapper coming thro' the wood.	"	1572
not to *s* before them on the path, .	"	1621
s but him who wrought the charm .	*Vivien*	61
s you not, dear love, That such a mood	"	173
that no man could *s* her more,	"	402
S's what his fair bride is and does,	"	631
s Her godlike head crown'd	"	685
Why ask you not to *s* the shield .	*Elaine*	650
an you will it let me *s* the shield.'	"	658
Going ? and we shall never *s* you more.	"	922
to *s* your face, To serve you, .	"	934
' Not to be with you, not to *s* your face—	"	942
s that she be buried worshipfully.'	"	1319
to *s* The maiden buried, not as one	"	1323
s your tender grace and stateliness	*Guinevere*	188
sworn never to *s* him more, (rep.) .	"	374
almost makes me die To *s* thee	"	531
Never lie by thy side, *s* thee no more	"	574
might *s* his face, and not be seen.'	"	582
So she did not *s* the face,	"	589
now I *s* thee what thou art,	"	641
must love the highest when we *s* it,	"	653
s his children leading evermore	*En. Arden*	115
said Philip, ' I may *s* her now,	"	274
not to *s* the world—For pleasure?	"	296
to *s* you poor and wanting help;	"	403
be ripe again: Come out and *s*.	"	457
what he fain had seen He could not *s*	"	582
His hopes to *s* his own,	"	625
Enoch yearn'd to *s* her face again;	"	718
S thro' the gray skirts of a lifting squall	"	830
reveal it, till you *s* me dead.'	"	840
S your bairns before you go !	"	871
charge you now, When you shall *s* her,	"	879
if my children care to see me dead,	"	889
I shall *s* him My babe in bliss ;	"	898
when you *s* her—but you shall not *s* her.	*Aylmer's F.*	309
like one that *s*'s his own excess,	"	400
florid, stern, as far as eye could *s*,	*Sea Dreams*	212
Perhaps I shall *s* him the sooner .	*Grandmother*	16
Willy—he didn't *s* me,	"	42
I shall *s* him another morn : .	"	67
when they *s*'s ma a passin' by,	*N. Farmer*	53
for I couldn't abear to *s* it	"	64
slights, thou wilt *s* my grave :	*Tithonus*	73
s's itself from thatch to base .	*Requiescat*	3
I *s* the place where thou wilt lie	*Sailor Boy*	8
S they sit, they hide their faces	*Boädicea*	51
And I shall live to *s* it.	*Spiteful Let.*	11
nor knows he what he *s*'s ; .	*Lucretius*	132
he *s*'s not, nor at all can tell .	"	145

seed.

	POEM.	LINE.
Sow the *s*, and reap the harvest .	*Lotos-E's.*	166
s of men and growth of minds. '	*Love thou thy land*	20
sow themselves like winged *s*'s	*Gardener's D.*	64
we, the latest *s* of Time,	*Godiva*	5
having sown some generous *s*,	*Two Voices*	143
Nor cared for *s* or scion !	*Amphion*	12

	POEM.	LINE.
The vilest herb that runs to *s*	Amphion	95
a noble scheme Grew up from *s*	Princess, iv.	291
the *s*, The little *s* they laugh'd at.	" vi.	17
finding that of fifty *s*'s .	In Mem. liv.	11
This bitter *s* among mankind ;	" lxxxix.	4
Ray round with flames her disk of *s*,	" c.	6
Long sleeps the summer in the *s* ;	" civ.	26
is but *s* Of what in them is flower	" Con.	135
in my words were *s*'s of fire.	The Letters	28
the one true *s* of freedom sown	Ode on Well.	162
gray linnets wrangle for the *s* :	Guinevere	251
I cast to earth a *s*	The Flower	2
Stole the *s* by night.	"	12
For all have got the *s*.	"	20

seedling.

as Nature packs Her blossom or her *s*,	En. Arden	179

seedsman.

s, rapt Upon the teeming harvest,	Golden Year	67

seeing.

S all his own mischance—	L. of Shalott, iv.	12
we should find the land Worth *s* ;	Princess, iii.	156
S I saw not, hearing not I heard ;	" vi.	3
S his gewgaw castle shine	Maud, I. x.	18
s them so tender and so close,	Enid	22
s one so gay in purple silks,	"	284
s her so sweet and serviceable.	"	323
Danced in his bosom, *s* better days.	"	505
s cloud upon the mother's brow,	"	777
s me, with a great voice he cried	Elaine	309
s How low his brother's mood	Aylmer's F.	403

seek.

When my passion *s*'s Pleasance	Lilian	8
What wantest thou ? whom dost thou *s*	Oriana	71
run to and fro, and hide and *s*,	The Mermaid	35
I *s* a warmer sky, 'You ask me why,' etc	"	26
Not too late to *s* a newer world.	Ulysses	57
to *s*, to find, and not to yield.	"	70
seem to find, but still to *s*.	Two Voices	96
To those that *s* them issue forth :	Day-Dm.	102
scarce knowing what he *s*'s :	"	117
'O *s* my father's court with me,	"	191
Hist,' he said 'They *s* us:	Princess, iv.	200
where you *s* the common love of these,	" vi.	156
He *s*'s at least Upon the last	In Mem. xlvi.	12
s A friendship for the years to come.	" lxxxiv.	77
s's to beat in time with one .	" cxxiv.	113
To *s* thee on the mystic deeps,	" cxxiv.	14
so that he find what he went to *s*,	Maud, I. xvi.	3
I *s* a harbourage for the night.'	Enid	299
To *s* a second favour at his hands	"	626
had ridden wildly round To *s* him,	Elaine	331
childless mother went to *s* her child	Aylmer's F.	829

seeking.

in *s* to undo One riddle,	Two Voices	232
love or fear, or *s* a favour of us,	Enid	700
weak beast *s* to help herself .	Vivien	348
S a tavern which of old he knew,	En. Arden	692

seem.

Howe'er it be, it *s*'s to me,	L. C. V. de Vere	53
So *s*'s she to the boy. .	Talking O.	108
Moreover, something is or *s*'s,	Two Voices	379
I would be that for ever which I *s*	Princess, ii.	239
I *s* no more : I want forgiveness too :	" vi.	272
indeed He *s*'s to me Scarce other	Ded. of Idylls	5
made it *s* his own ;	Vivien	585
My father, howsoe'er I *s* to you,	Elaine	1036

seem'd.

neither *s* there more to say .	Princess, v.	320
so it *s*, or so they said to me,	" vi.	6
If Maud were all that she *s*,	Maud, I. vi.	36, 92

seeming-genial.

Or *s-g* venial fault,	Will	13

seeming-injured.

The *s-i* simple-hearted thing	Vivien	751

seeming-leafless.

pass his autumn into *s-l* days—	A Dedication	10

	POEM.	LINE.
grew to *s-r* forms,	In Mem. cxvii.	10

seeming-wanton.

make The *s-w* ripple break,	In Mem. xlviii.	11

seen.

who hath *s* her wave her hand ?	L. of Shalott, i.	24
at the casement *s* her stand .	"	25
'Beauty *s* Is In all varieties To—	With Pal. of Art	6
the dale Was *s* far inland.	Lotos-E's.	21
long since I have *s* a man.	D. of F. Wom.	131
And faint, rainy lights are *s*	Margaret	60
Such joy as you have *s* with us	D. of the O. Year	17
Two years his chair is *s* Empty	To J. S.	22
What is it thou hast *s* ?	M d'Arthur	68, 114
what is *s*t thou hast heard or *s* ?	"	150
That, having *s*, forgot ?	Gardener's D.	54
You should have *s* him wince	Walk. to the M.	63
nor have *s* Him since, nor heard of her	Ed. Morris	137
I have *s* some score of those	Talking O.	4
Much have I *s* and known	Ulysses	13
As I have seen the rosy red .	Locksley H.	26
glimpsing over these, just *s*,	Day-Dm.	67
She in her poor attire was *s* :	Beggar Maid	10
I myself, my bride once *s*,	Princess, i.	71
some dark shore just *s* that it was rich.	"	245
'having *s* And heard the Lady Psyche.'	" ii.	193
bottom agates *s* to wave and float	"	306
after *s* The dwarfs of presage :	" iv.	245
ever had I *s* Such thews of men :	" v.	245
So often that I speak as having *s* .	" vi.	5
Ida came behind *S* but of Psyche.	" vii.	64
Ere *s* I loved, and loved thee *s*	"	320
Imagined more than *s*, the skirts of France—	Con.	48
we, that have not *s* thy face,	In Mem. Pro.	2
If Death were *s* At first as Death .	" xxxv.	17
How many a father have I *s*,	" lii.	1
A likeness, hardly *s* before,	" lxxxii.	7
I have not *s*, I will not see Vienna	" xcvii.	11
O earth, what changes hast thou *s* !	" cxxii.	2
her eyes were downcast, not to be *s*	Maud, I. ii.	5
shall I believe him ashamed to be *s* ?	" xiii.	23
Squire had *s* the colt at grass	The Brook	139
World-victor's victor will be *s* no more	Ode on Well.	44
Colossal, *s* of every land,	"	221
s A light amid its olives green ;	The Daisy	29
milky-white, First *s* that day :	Enid	150
having *s* all beauties of our time.	"	498
pride is broken : men have *s* my fall.'	"	578
never yet had *s* her half so far ;	"	741
where we see as we are *s* !	"	650
have you *s* how nobly changed ?	"	1745
for three days *s*, ready to fall.	Vivien	145
You should have *s* him blush ;	"	331
Him have I *s* : the rest, his Table	Elaine	185
'One, One have I *s*—that other,	"	422
I might say that I had *s*.'	"	426
So great a knight as we have *s*	"	532
peradventure had he *s* her first	"	668
might see his face, and not be *s*.	Guinevere	582
would have *s* my pleasure had I *s*.	"	652
as a figure *s* in early dawn	En. Arden	354
what he fain had *s* He could not see,	"	581
the mate had *s* at early dawn	"	632
things *s* are mightier than things heard,	"	767
tell her you had *s* him dead .	"	807
seldom *s* a costlier funeral .	"	916
must have *s*, himself had *s* it long :	Aylmer's F.	345
she herself Had *s* to that :	"	805
High towns on hills were dimly *s*,	The Voyage	34

seër.

Like some bold *s* in a trance,	L. of Shalott, iv.	11
the *S* Would watch her at her petulance,	Vivien	30
Her *s*, her bard, her silver star	"	803

seest.

Watch what thou *s*,	M. d'Arthur	38
a long way With these thou *s*—	"	257
And *s* the moving of the team.	In Mem. cxx.	16
s all things, thou wilt see my grave :	Tithonus	73

seethed.

S like the kid in its own mother's	Vivien	713

seething.	POEM.	LINE.	
when the surge was *s* free	. *Lotos-E's.*	. 151	
Seine.			
The red fool-fury of the S	. *In Mem.*cxxvi. 7		
seize.			
'*s* the strangers,' is the cry.	. *Princess,* iv.	201	
To *s* and throw the doubts of man	; *In Mem.*cviii.	6	
sorrow *s* me if ever that light	. *Maud,* I. iv.	12	
To *s* me by the hair and bear me	. *Elaine*	1415	
seized.			
at last a fever *s* On William,	. *Dora* .	. 52	
A hunger *s* my heart; .	. *In Mem.* xciv.	21	
therewithal came one and *s* on her,	*Enid* .	. 673	
suddenly *s* on her, And bare her	. "	1501	
slain your father, *s* yourself.	. "	1686	
who then?' a fury *s* on them,	. *Elaine*	. 475	
she *s,* And, thro' the casement	. "	1226	
desperately *s* the holy Book,	. *En. Arden*	. 491	
S it, took home, and to my lady,—	*Aylmer's F.*	532	
Me they *s* and me they tortured,	*Boädicea*	. 49	
seizure.			
myself too had weird *s's*	. *Princess,* i.	14	
'what, if these weird *s's* come	. "	81	
On a sudden my strange *s* came	. " iii.	167	
On a sudden the weird *s*	. " iv.	538	
seldom-frowning.			
The *s-f* King frown'd	. *Elaine*	. 711	
self.			
Smote the chord of S,	. *Locksley H.*	34	
Half-fearful that, with *s* at strife	. *Will Water.*	161	
We touch on our dead *s,*	. *Princess,* iii.	205	
Her falser *s* slipt from her	. " vii.	146	
drowning life, besotted in sweet *s,*	"	295	
stepping-stones Of their dead *selves*	*In Mem.* i.	4	
transient form In her deep *s*	. " xvi.	7	
fusing all The skirts of *s* again,	. " xlvi.	3	
praying, To his own great *s,*	. *Maud,* II. v.	33	
learns to deader Love of *s,*	. *Ode on Well.*	205	
that and these to her own faded *s*	*Enid* .	. 652	
overthrow My proud *s,*	. "	1697	
To keep me all to your own *s,*	. *Vivien*	. 373	
and imputing her whole *s,*	. "	. 652	
'Save your great *s,* fair lord ;'	. *Elaine*	. 310	
morn by morn, arraying her sweet *s*	"	. 902	
the King's grief for his own *s*	. *Guinevere*	. 195	
He not For his own *s* caring	. *En. Arden.*	. 195	
chafing at his own great *s* defied,	*Aylmer's F.*	537	
to thy worst *s* sacrifice thyself	. "	. 645	
thy worst *s* hast thou clothed thy God.	"	. 646	
self-applause.			
Not void of righteous *s-a,*	. *Two Voices*	146	
self-balanced.			
S-*b* on a lightsome wing ;	. *In Mem.* lxiv.	8	
self-blinded.			
'S-*b* are you by your pride ;	. *Two Voices*	23	
self-conceit.			
Some *s-c,* Or over smoothness ;	. *Ed. Morris*	74	
self-contained.			
High, *s-c,* and passionless,	. *Guinevere*	. 403	
self-contempt.			
Perish in thy *s-c !* .	. *Locksley H.*	96	
self-control.			
Self-reverence, self-knowledge, *s-c*	*Œnone*	. 142	
faith that comes of *s-c*	. *In Mem.* cxxx.	9	
self-distrust.			
It is my shyness, or my *s-d,*	. *Ed. Morris*	86	
self-gather'd.			
S-*g* in her prophet-mind, 'Of old sat Freedom,' etc.	6		
self-infold.			
s-i's the large results Of force	*In Mem.* lxxii.	15	
self-involved.			
Which all too dearly *s-i,*	. *Day-Dm.*	. 261	
pitying, as it seem'd, Or *s-i*	. *Princess,* vi.	142	
dull and *s-i,* Tall and erect, .	*Aylmer's F.*	118	

self-knowledge.	POEM.	LINE.	
Self-reverence, *s-k,* self-control	*Œnone*	. 142	
self-perplext.			
look'd so *s-p* That Katie laugh'd,	*The Brook*	. 213	
self-pity.			
for languor and *s-p* ran Mine	. *Princess,* vii.	124	
sweet *s-p,* or the fancy of it, .	. *Enid*	. 1198	
self-pleached.			
Round thee blow, *s-p* deep,	. *A Dirge*	. 29	
self-possess'd.			
neither *s-p* Nor startled,	. *Gardener's D.*	151	
self-profit.			
judge of fair Unbiass'd by *s-p*	. *Œnone*	. 156	
self-reverence.			
S-*r,* self-knowledge, self-control	. *Œnone*	. 142	
self-reverent.			
S.*r* each and reverencing each,	. *Princess,* vii.	274	
self-sacrifice.			
The long *s-s* of life is o'er.	. *Ode on Well.*	41	
self-scorn.			
Laughter at her *s.s.*	. *Pal. of Art*	232	
self-seeker.			
All great *s-s's* trampling on the right; *Ode on Well.*	187		
self-styled.			
those *s-s* our lords ally Your fortunes *Princess,* ii.	51		
sell.			
To *s* the boat—and yet he loved her	*En. Arden*	. 134	
yet to *s* her—then with what	. "	. 137	
s her, those good parents, for her good	*Aylmer's F.*	483	
semblance.			
Like to the mother plant in *s.*	. *The Poet*	. 23	
semi-jealousy.			
A flash of *s-j* clear'd it to her	. *Aylmer's F.*	189	
send.			
would *s* a hundred thousand men, *Princess,* i.	. 63		
unless you *s* us back Our son	. " iv.	396	
"Sdeath ! but we will *s* to her,'	. " v.	314	
s it slackly from the string ; .	. *In Mem.*lxxxvi.	26	
s One flash, that missing all things	*Vivien*	. 780	
Ourselves will *s* it after.	. *Elaine*	. 544	
This will he *s* or come for ;	. "	. 632	
I pray him, *s* a sudden Angel down	"	. 1414	
s abroad a shrill and terrible cry,	. *En. Arden.*	769	
You *s* a flash to the sun	. *The Window*	179	
seneschal.			
maid, and squire, and *s*	. *Enid*	. 710	
sennight.			
three rich *s's* more, my love for her.	*Ed. Morris*	30	
sense.			
did all confound Her *s;*	. *Mariana*	. 77	
Controlleth all the soul and *s*	. *Eleänore*	. 115	
Lord of the *s's* five ; .	. *Pal. of Art*	160	
Slowly my *s* undazzled.	. *D. of F. Wom.*	177	
feedeth The *s's* with a still delight	*Margaret*	. 17	
Flutter'd about my *s's* and my soul; *Gardener's D.*	66		
have they any *s* of why they sing ?	. "	. 100	
lost the *s* that handles daily life—	*Walk. to the M.*	16	
my brain, my *s's* and my soul !	. *Love and Duty*	44	
If the *s* is hard To alien ears,	. "	. 50	
the common *s* of most shall hold	. *Locksley H.*	129	
cancell'd a *s* misused ; .	. *Godiva*	. 72	
Is cancell'd in the world of *s* ?'	. *Two Voices*	42	
Unmannacled from bonds of *s,*	. "	. 236	
The simple *s's* crown'd his head :.	. "	. 277	
By which he doubts against the *s?*	. "	. 285	
seem'd no room for *s* of wrong.	. "	. 456	
Your finer female *s* offends.	. *Day-Dm.*	. 214	
I grow in worth, and wit, and *s,*	. *Will Water.*	41	
a crime Of *s* avenged by *s*	. *Vision of Sin*	214	
crime of *s* became The crime of malice	"	. 215	
s of wrong had touch'd her face	. *Princess, Pro.*	213	
Or master'd by the *s* of sport,	. " iv.	138	
broke the letter of it to keep the *s*	"	. 319	

	POEM.	LINE.
I grant in her some *s* of shame,	Princess, iv.	330
'Nay, nay, you spake but *s* Said Gama	,, v.	197
sloughs That swallow eommon *s*,	,,	432
one part of *s* not flint to prayer,	,, vi.	166
My haunting *s* of hollow shows	,, vii.	328
Some *s* of duty, something of a faith	,, Con.	54
Unfetter'd by the *s* of erime,	In Mem. xxvii.	7
an awful *s* Of one mute Shadow	,, xxx.	7
the hoarding *s* Gives out at times	,, xliii.	6
Drug down the blindfold *s* of wrong	,, lxx.	7
The quiet *s* of something lost	,, lxxvii.	8
The *s* of human will demands	,, lxxxvi.	39
O tell me where the *s*'s mix,	,, lxxxvii.	7
Where all the nerve of *s* is numb;	,, xcii.	7
Cry thro' the *s* to hearten trust	,, cxv.	7
Who wants the finer politie *s*	Maud, I. vi.	47
Suddenly strike on a sharper *s*	,, II. ii.	63
less of sentiment than *s* Had Katie;	The Brook.	91
whether some false *s* in her own self	Enid.	800
s might make her long for court	,,	803
with every *s* as false and foul	Vivien.	646
of a saint Among his warring *s*'s,	Guinevere.	633
s Of meanness in her unresisting life,	Aylmer's F.	800
such a *s*, when first I fronted him,	Sea Dreams	70
Jodnes, as 'ant a 'aäpoth o' *s*,	N. Farmer.	49

sent.

s it them by stealth, nor did they know Who *s* it;	Dora.	51
She *s* her voice thro' all the holt	Talking O.	123
s a herald forth, And bade him cry,	Godiva.	35
With peals of genial clamour *s*	Will Water.	187
gave the letter to be *s* with dawn;	Princess, i.	241
s for Psyche, but she was not there;	,, iv.	217
s for Blanche to accuse her	,,	220
S out a bitter bleating for its dam:	,,	373
when we *s* the Prince your way	,,	379
s beneath his vaulted palm	,, v.	30
thrice had *s* a herald to the gates,	,,	322
A soul on highest mission *s*,	In Mem. cxii.	10
s the bailiff to the farm To learn	The Brook.	143
s Her maiden to demand it	Enid.	193,411
S forth a sudden sharp and bitter cry	,,	1570
s a thousand inen To till the wastes,	,,	1729
s His horns of proclamation out	Vivien.	430
who he was, and on what quest S,	Elaine.	626
lose the quest he *s* you on,	,,	652
the diamond *s* you by the King:'	,,	817
tale of King and Prince, the diamond *s*,	,,	820
toward even S for his shield	,,	972
he saw One of her house, and *s* him	,,	1162
s a deep sea-voice thro' all the land,	Guinevere.	245
yet he *s* Gifts by the children	En. Arden.	334
s his voice beneath him thro' the wood	,,	441
s for him and said wildly to him	,,	503
s her sweetly by the golden isles,	,,	532
s a erew that landing burst away.	,,	635
S to the harrow'd brother, praying	Aylmer's F.	607
every roof S out a listener:.	,,	614
S like the twelve-divided coneubine	,,	759
s out a cry Which mixt with little	Sea Dreams	237

sentence.

And mystie *s* spoke.	Talking O.	294
I hear the *s* that he speaks;	In Mem. lxxix.	10
there he broke the *s* in his heart	Enid.	890
the king Pronounc'd a dismal *s*,	Vivien.	441

sentiment.

A elassic lecture, rich in *s*,	Princess, ii.	352
less of *s* than sense Had Katie;	The Brook.	91

sentinel.

And hear at times a *s*	In Mem cxxv.	9

separate.

Eternal, *s* from fears;	In Mem. lxxxiv.	66

sepulchre.

Gross darkness of the inner *s*	D. of F. Wom.	67

sequel.

S of guerdon could not alter me	Œnone.	151
The *s* of to-day unsolders all	M. d'Arthur.	14

	POEM.	LINE.
What *s* ? Streaming eyes	Love and Duty	2
love in *s* works with fate,	Day-Dm.	103
I shudder at the *s*, but I go.'	Princess, ii.	218
the *s* of the tale Had touch'd her;	,, Con.	30

seraglio.

iron grates, And hush'd *s*'s.	D. of F. Wom.	36

seraph.

Milton like a *s* strong,	Pal. of Art	133
by my side Show'd like fair *s*'s.	St S. Stylites	166

sere.

in the rudest wind Never grow *s*,	Ode to Mem.	25
Shrank one siek willow sand small	Mariana in the S.	53

serenade.

A rogue of canzonets and *s*'s.	Princess, iv.	117

sermonizing.

In sailor fashion roughly *s*	En. Arden.	204

serpent.

Like birds the charming *s* draws,	In Mem. xxxiv.	14
Nor cared the *s* at thy side	,, cix.	7
whose souls the old *s* long had drawn	Enid	1480

serpent-rooted.

seated on a *s-r* beech,	The Brook.	125

serpent-throated.

long horn And *s-t* bugle	Princess, v.	243

servant.

rummaged like a rat: no *s* stay'd:	Walk. to the M.	30
gull'd Our *s s*, wrong'd and lied	Princess, iv.	519
Are but as *s*'s in a house	In Mem. xx.	5

serve.

s his kind in deed and word	'Love thou thy land'	86
Who'd *s* the state? for if I earved	Audley Ct.	47
To *s* the hot-and-hot;	Will Water.	228
I'll *s* you better in a strait;	Princess, i.	84
all things *s* their time	,, iv.	55
fellow-worker be, When time should *s*	,,	290
We two will *s* them both	,, vii.	252
better *s*'s a wholesome law,	In Mem. xlvii.	10
May *s* to curl a maiden's locks;	,, lxxvi.	7
never sold the truth to *s* the hour,	Ode on Well.	179
But as he saves or *s*'s the state	,,	200
do not *s* me sparrow-hawks.	Enid.	304
that her guest should *s* himself.'	,,	379
hall must also *s* For kitchen,	,,	390
s you costlier than with mowers' fare	,,	1080
attendanee, page or maid, To *s* you —	,,	1172
but ampler means to *s* mankind.	Vivien.	339
to see your face, To *s* you	Elaine.	935
To *s* as model for the mighty world,	Guinevere.	462

served.

So sitting, *s* by man and maid,	The Goose.	21
and ereani S in the weeping elm;	Gardener's D.	191
and *s* With female hands	Princess, vi.	79
We *s* thee here' they said 'so long	In Mem. cii.	4
s the seasons that may rise;	,, cxii.	4
the men who *s* About my person,	Enid	453
s a little to disedge The sharpness	,,	1033
s By hands unseen;	Guinevere.	263
s a year On board a merchantman	En. Arden.	52
master of that ship Enoch had *s* in	,,	55
s, Long sinee, a bygone Rector.	Aylmer's F.	10

service.

to find Another *s* sueh as this.'	In Mem. xx.	8
Grateful to Prince Geraint for *s* done	Enid.	15
s done so graeiously would bind	,,	790
did him *s* as a squire;	,,	1255
as one Speaks of a *s* done him)	,,	1696
weary of my *s* and devour,	Elaine.	119
Sueh have you done me, that I make	,,	911

serviceable.

seeing her so sweet and *s*,	Enid.	703
to be sweet and *s* To noble knights	Elaine.	703

servile.

s to a shrewish tongue!	Locksley H.	42

CONCORDANCE TO

serving.
	POEM.	LINE.
loved me *s* in my father's hall ;	Enid	1547
feuds *S* his traitorous end ; .	Guinevere	20

serving-man.
As just and mere a *s-m* .	Will Water.	151

servitor.
Loyal, the dumb old *s*, .	Elaine	1138
Then rose the dumb old *s*, .	"	1147

session.
in *s* on their roofs Approved him,	The Brook	127
Leapt from her *s* on his lap .	Vivien	693

set (s.)
For '*set of sun*,' '*set of day*,' etc., see *sun*, *day*, etc.

with others of our *s*, Five others :	Princess, Pro.	8
O wretched *s* of sparrows, .	Enid	278
Two *s*'s of three laden with jingling	"	1037

set (verb.)
s, That morning, on the casement-edge	Miller's D.	81
Many suns arise and *s*.	"	205
To-night I saw the sun *s* .	May Queen, ii.	5
The sun is just about to *s*, .	Margaret	58
S in all lights by many minds 'Love thou thy land,'		35
I have *s* my heart upon a match .	Dora	12
I will *s* him in my uncle's eye .	"	65
women kiss'd Each other, and *s* out,	"	126
s up betwixt his grandsire's knees,	"	128
Allan *s* him down, and Mary said :	"	136
I *s* the words, and added names .	Audley Ct.	60
S's out, and meets a friend .	Walk. to the M.	34
Time will *s* me right. .	Ed. Morris	88
s an ancient creditor to work ;	"	130
current of being *s*'s to thee.'	Locksley H.	24
promise of my spirit hath not *s*.	"	187
be *s* In midst of knowledge,	Two Voices	89
Why not *s* forth, if I should do	"	391
He *s* up his forlorn pipes, .	Amphion	22
You *s* before chance-comers,	Will Water.	6
And, *s* in Heaven's third story,	"	70
S thy hoary fancies free ;	Vision of Sin	156
show'd the house, Greek, *s* with busts :	Princess, Pro.	11
s with little wilful thorns, .	"	153
S in a gleaming river's crescent-curve,	" i.	169
when we *s* our hand To this great work,	" ii.	45
toward the centre *s* the starry tides,	" iii.	102
need not *s* your thoughts in rubric	" iii.	34
but we *S* forth to climb ; .	"	336
like a jewel *s* In the dark crag :	"	340
s the wild echoes flying, .	"	352-64
Norway sun *S* into sunrise .	" iv.	553
S in a cataract on an island-crag, .	" v.	113
I *s* my face Against all men, .	"	378
S his child upon her knee— .	"	545
at the last she *s* herself to man,	" vii.	269
Once more *s* a ringlet right :	In Mem. vi.	36
s's the past in this relief ?	" xxiv.	12
On thy Parnassus *s* thy feet,	" xxxvii.	6
s thee forth, for thou art mine,	" lviii.	13
some poor girl whose heart is *s*	" lix.	3
I would *s* their pains at ease.	" lxii.	8
Whate'er thy hands are *s* to do	" lxxiv.	19
in a moment *s* thy face .	" lxxv.	2
His credit thus shall *s* me free ;	" lxxix.	13
my feet are *s* To leave the pleasant	" ci.	21
S light by narrower perfectness .	" cxi.	4
She *s*'s her forward countenance .	" cxiii.	6
He *s* his royal signet there .	" cxxiv.	12
now *s* out : the noon is near .	Con.	41
s my face as a flint .	Maud, I. i.	31
S in the heart of the carven gloom	" xiv.	11
He *s*'s the jewel-print of your feet	" xxii.	41
s With willow-weed and mallow.	The Brook	45
roughly *s* His Briton in blown seas	Ode on Well.	154
God's love *s* Thee at his side again !	Ded. of Idylls	53
and *s* foot upon his breast, .	Enid	574
dear child is *s* forth at her best, .	"	728
in charge of whom ? a girl ; *s* on.	"	974
then *s* down His basket, .	"	1058
on his foot She *s* her own and climb'd : "		1608

	POEM.	LINE.
s his foot upon me, and give me life.	Enid	1698
in their chairs *s* up a stronger race	"	1788
s herself to gain Him, .	Vivien	21
S up the charge you know, .	"	553
and caught, And *s* it on his head,	Elaine	55
s it in this damsel's golden hair .	"	205
S every gilded parapet shuddering ;	"	299
Than if seven men had *s* upon him,	"	350
in the costly canopy o'er him *s*,	"	442
kith and kin, not knowing, *s* upon him.	"	597
s himself to play upon her .	"	643
S in her hand a lily, .	"	1142
Lancelot got her horse, *S* her thereon	Guinevere	122
thought the Queen 'lo ! they have *s* her on,	"	306
s on to plague And play upon .	"	357
s himself beside her, saying to her :	En. Arden	289
where he fixt his heart he *s* his hand	"	293
Suddenly *s* it wide to find a sign.	"	492
s himself, Scorning an alms, to work	"	812
also *s* his many-shielded tree ?	Aylmer's F.	48
never yet had *s* his daughter forth	"	347
'*S* them up ! they shall not fall !'	Sea Dreams	220
had *s* my heart on your forgiving him	"	260

setting.
s round thy first experiment .	Ode to Mem.	81
It was when the moon was *s*,	May Queen, iii.	26
s wide the doors, that bar .	Gardener's D.	243
s the *how much* before the *how*,	Golden Year	11
And in the *s* thou art fair. .	In Mem. cxxix.	4
Music's golden sea *S* toward eternity	Ode on Well.	253
at *s* forth The Biscay, .	En. Arden	524

settle (s.)
on an oaken *s* in the hall, .	Enid	1421

settle (verb.)
'Tis hard to *s* order once again.	Lotos-E's.	127
ere they *s* for the night. .	Enid	250
s's, beaten back, and beaten back *S*'s,	Vivien	221

settled.
s down Upon the general decay .	The Epic	17
central wish, until we *s* there.	Gardener's D.	220
Loosely *s* into form. .	Day-Dm.	12
s in her eyes The green malignant .	Princess, iii.	115
S a gentle cloud of melancholy ;	" iv.	547
the question *s* die.' .	" v.	307
to her old perch back, and *s* there.	Vivien	752

settling.
s circled all the lists, .	Enid	547

seven-headed.
S-h monsters only made to kill Time	Princess, Pro.	200

seventeen.
Maud is not *s*. .	Maud, I. xii.	15
petitionary grace Of sweet *s* .	The Brook	113

sever'd.
Her lips are *s* as to speak .	Day-Dm.	50

severer.
S in the logic of a life .	Princess, v.	182

severity.
That pure *s* of perfect light— .	Guinevere	639

Severn.
The Danube to the *S* gave .	In Mem. xix.	1
There twice a day the *S* fills ;	"	5
rode with them, to the shores Of *S*,	Enid	45, 1803

sew.
Or teach the orphan girl to *s*	L. C. V. de Vere	70

sewer.
cleanse this common *s* of all his realm	Enid	39, 1743

sex.
Madam—if I know your *s*, .	Vision of Sin	181
If our old halls could change their *s*,	Princess, Pro.	140
not a scorner of your *s* .	" iv.	402
She wrongs herself, her *s*, and me	" v.	113
either *s* alone Is half itself, .	" vii.	283
hustled together, each *s*, like swine,	Maud, I. i.	34
No more of love ; your *s* is known :	The Letters	29

	shackle.	POEM.	LINE.		POEM.	LINE.
The *s*'s of an old love straiten'd him,		*Elaine*	871	along the front, But deep in *s*:	*Princess,* i.	210
	shade.			chase The substance or the *s*?	" ii.	387
the long alley's latticed *s*		*Arabian N's.*	112	Well, Are castles *s*'s?	"	392
Life eminent creates the *s* of death		*Love and Death*	13	The sweet propnetress a *s*?	" iii.	303
lavish lights and floating *s*'s:		*Eleänore*	12	courts that lay three parts In *s*,	" iii.	5
when in the chesnut *s* I found		*Miller's D.*	201	As flies the *s* of a bird, she fled.	"	80
Untouch'd with any *s* of years,		"	219	No fighting *s*'s here!	"	109
stedfast *s* Sleeps on his luminous ring.'		*Pal. of Art*	15	somehow shapes the *s*, Time ;	"	311
hollow *s*'s enclosing hearts of flame,		"	241	But in the *s* will we work.	"	314
just beneath the hawthorn *s*,		*May Queen,* ii.	29	tumult and the kings Were *s*'s	" iv.	543
before my eyelids dropt their *s*,		*D. of F. Wom.*	1	He has been among his *s*'s.'	" v.	32
Your sorrow, only sorrow's *s*,		*Margaret*	43	Satan take The old women and their *s*'s!	"	33
spread his dark-green layers of *s*.		*Gardener's D.*	115	clung The *s* of his sister	"	248
trembled on her waist—Ah, happy *s*		"	131	o'er her forehead past A *s*,	" vi.	91
Half light, half *s*, She stood,		"	139	*s* of a lark Hung in the *s* of a heaven?	*In Mem.* xvi.	9
into light, and died into the *s*;		"	178	There sat the *S* fear'd of man;	" xxii.	12
in the *s* of comfortable roofs,		*St S. Stylites*	105	The *S* sits and waits for me,	"	20
What's here ? a shape, a *s*,		"	199	The *S* cloak'd from head to foot,	" xxiii.	4
Yet, since I first could cast a *s*,		*Talking O.*	85	That *S* waiting with the keys,	" xxvi.	15
rising thro' the mellow *s*		*Locksley H.*	9	one mute *S* watching all.	" xxx.	8
Breadth of tropic *s* and palms		"	160	The tender-pencil'd *s* play.	" xlviii.	12
Let me not cast in endless *s*		*Two Voices*	5	My Arthur found your *s*'s fair	" lxxxviii.	6
A merry boy in sun and *s* ?		"	321	His own vast *s* glory-crown'd,	" xcvi.	3
whole wide earth of light and *s*		*Will Water.*	67	Her *s* on the blaze of kings:	" xcvii.	10
As she fled fast thro' sun and *s*,		*Sir L. and Q. G.*	37	Let cares that petty *s*'s cast,	" civ.	13
Slided, they moving under *s*:		*Princess,* vi.	66	The hills are *s*'s, and they flow	" cxxii.	5
Thine are these orbs of light and *s*		*In Mem. Pro.*	5	A *s* there at my feet	*Maud,* II. i.	39
So be it : there no *s* can last		" xlv.	5	A *s* flits before me,	" iv.	11
What slender *s* of doubt may flit,		" xlvii.	7	And the light and *s* fleet;	"	36
The *s* by which my life was crost,		" lxv.	5	Ripples on in light and *s*	"	42
A chequer-work of beam and *s*		" lxxi.	15	The *s* still the same ;	"	72
No visual *s* of some one lost,		" xcii.	1	And the *s* flits and fleets	"	90
every span of *s* that steals		" cxvi.	10	following our own *s*'s thrice as long	*The Brook*	166
The sport of random sun and *s*		*Con.*	24	on thro' zones of light and *s*	*To F. D. Maurice*	27
A *s* falls on us like the dark		"	93	*s* of His loss drew like eclipse	*Ded. of Idylls*	13
The *s* of passing thought		"	102	like a *s*, past the people's talk	*Enid*	82
touch with *s* bridal doors		"	117	wheel, and thou are *s*'s in the cloud,	"	357
light and *s* Coursed one another		*Enid*	521	the dancing *s*'s of the birds,	"	601
our fortune slipt from sun to *s*,		"	714	never *s* of mistrust can cross	"	815,1097
shallow *s* of a deep wood,		"	968	wholly arm'd, behind a rock In *s*,	"	957
peaks that flamed, or, all in *s*,		*The Voyage*	41	Come slipping o'er their *s*'s.	"	1320
	shadow.			like a silver *s* slipt away	*Vivien*	273
Were fixed *s*'s of thy fixed mood,		*Isabel*	9	And the cairn'd mountain was a *s*,	"	463
She saw the gusty *s* sway.		*Mariana*	52	shot red fire and *s*'s thro' the cave,	*Elaine*	411
The *s* of the poplar fell		"	55	Past like a *s* thro' the field,	"	1134
Thro' light and *s* thou dost range		*Madeline*	4	*s* of a piece of pointed lace, In the Queen's *s*,	"	1183
S's of the silver birk		*A Dirge*	5	A ghastly something, and its *s* flew	*Guinevere*	79
Light and *s* ever wander		"	12	the world, and all its lights And *s*'s	"	342
Thou art the *s* of life,		*Love and Death*	10	*s* still would glide from room to room	"	510
s passeth when the tree shall fall,		"	14	the *s* of another cleaves to me	"	611
S's of the world appear.		*L. of Shalott,* ii.	12	now that *s* of mischance appear'd	*En. Arden*	118
'I am half-sick of *s*'s,'		"	35	like a wounded life He crept into the *s*:	"	384
With one black *s* at its feet,		*Mariana in the S.*	1	o'er his countenance No *s* past,	"	711
The one black *s* from the wall.		"	80	his own *s* in a sickly sun.	*Aylmer's F.*	30
Sometimes your *s* cross'd the blind.		*Miller's D.*	124	their *s*'s to the Heaven of Heavens,	"	642
the long *s* of the chair .		"	126	knit themselves for summer *s*,	"	774
with his *s* on the stone, Rests like a *s*,		*Œnone*	26	*S* and shine is life, little Annie,	*Grandmother*	60
Between the *s*'s of the vine-bunches		"	177	white-haired *s* roaming like a dream	*Tithonus*	8
thro' wavering lights and *s*'s broke,		*Lotos-E's*	12	Alas! for this gray *s*,	"	11
The *s*'s flicker to and fro ;		*D. of the O Year*	39	Coldly thy rosy *s*'s bathe me,	"	66
Fall into *s*, soonest lost		*To J. S.*	11	light and *s* illimitable,	*Boädicea*	42
s of the flowers Stole all the golden		*Gardener's D.*	128	The lights and *s*'s fly !	*The Window*	5
with *s*'s of the common ground		"	134	and left me in *s* here !	"	37
Should my *S* cross thy thoughts		*Love and Duty*	85		shadow (verb.)	
and the *s*'s rise and fall.		*Locksley H.*	80	*S* forth thee :—the world hath not	*Isabel*	38
Thro' the *s* of the globe we sweep		"	183	in the sun and *s*'s all beneath,	*Love and Death*	11
S's thou dost strike, Embracing cloud,		*Two Voices*	194	*S* forth the banks at will ;	*Eleänore*	110
A *s* on the graves I knew,		"	272	*s* all my soul, that I may die	*Œnone*	218
From grave to grave the *s* crept		"	274	And *s* Summer-chace !	*Talking O.*	150
Faint *s*'s, vapours lightly curl'd		*Day-Dm.*	25	You *s* forth to distant men,	*To E. L.*	7
The *s*'s of the conven*t*-towers		*St Agnes' Eve*	5	Tho' the Roman eagle *s* thee,	*Boädicea*	39
waves of *s* went over the wheat,		*Poet's Song*	4	*s* forth The all-generating powers.	*Lucretius*	96
and flew thro' light And *s*,		*Princess, Pro.*	85		shadow-casting.	
like *s*'s in a dream,—		"	222	sunders ghosts and *s*-c men	*Vivien*	473
burnt Because he cast no *s*,		" i.	7		shadow'd.	
should know The *s* from the substance		"	9	I have *s* many a group	*Talking O.*	61
fight with *s*'s and to fall. v. 465,.		"	10	And *s* all her rest—	"	226
myself the *s* of a dream (iii. 172, v. 470)		"	18	Hung, *s* from the heat : .	*Princess,* ii.	435
point you out the *s* from the truth !		"	83	Is *s* by the growing hour,	*In Mem.* xlv.	3

364   CONCORDANCE TO

	POEM.	LINE.
shadow-chequer'd.		
And many a *s-c* lawn	*Arabian N's.*	102
shadowing (part and *s.*)		
doubts And sudden ghostly *s's*	*Princess*, iv.	549
s down the champaign	" v.	515
s down the horned flood	*In Mem.*lxxxv.	7
S the snow-limb'd Eve	*Maud*,I.xviii.	28
shadow-streaks.		
With *s's* of rain.	*Pal. of Art*	76
shadowy-pencill'd.		
A thousand *s-p* valleys	*The Daisy*	67
shaft.		
shrilling *s's* of subtle wit.	'*Clear-headed friend*'	13
The winged *s's* of truth,	*The Poet*	26
A thousand little *s's* of flame	*Fatima*	17
Betwixt the slender *s's* were blazon'd	*Pal. of Art*	167
lean a ladder on the *s*	*St S. Stylites*	213
And shrill'd his tinsel *s.*	*Talking O.*	68
like a *s* of light across the land.	*Golden Year*	49
s's Of gentle satire, kin to charity,	*Princess*, ii.	444
beard-blown goat Hang on the *s*	" iv.	61
brand, mace, and *s,* and shield—	" v.	492
sunrise broken into scarlet *s's*	*En. Arden*	593
scarlet *s's* of sunrise—but no sail.	"	600
shake (for *shake hands*, see *hand.*)		
The sun-lit almond-blossom *s's*—	*To the Queen*	16
seem'd to *s* The sparkling flints	*Arabian N's.*	51
s All evil dreams of power—	*The Poet*	46
in the thoughts that *s* mankind	*Locksley H.*	166
A wither'd palsy cease to *s?*	*Two Voices*	57
You *s* your head. A random string	*Day-Dm.*	213
Twang out, my fiddle! *s* the twigs!	*Amphion*	61
Swells up, and *s's* and falls.	*Sir Galahad*	76
Ho! from some bay-window *s* the night;	*Princess*,i.	105
a sight to *s* The midriff of despair.	"	197
To break my chain, to *s* my mane:	" ii.	402
long light *s's* across the lakes	" iii.	350
folds of our great ensign *s,*	" v.	8
two dewdrops on the petal *s.*	" vii.	53
s The prophets blazon'd on the panes:	*In Mem.*lxxxvi.	7
s The pillars of domestic peace.	" lxxxix.	19
so, when the rotten hustings *s*	*Maud*, I. vi.	54
The slender acacia would not *s*	" xxii.	45
For a tumult *s's* the city,	" II. iv.	50
s its threaded tears in the wind	" III. vi.	28
A cypress in the moonlight *s*	*The Daisy*	82
The hard earth *s,* and a low thunder	*Elaine*	459
s off the bee that buzzes at us,	"	761
shook beneath them, as the thistle *s's*	*Guinevere*	252
s the darkness from their loosen'd manes,	*Tithonus*	41
felt the good ship *s* and reel,	*The Voyage*	15
shaken (for *shaken hands*, see *hand.*)		
s with a sudden storm of sighs—	*Locksley H.*	27
Every moment, lightly *s,* ran itself	"	32
white shoulder *s* with her sobs,	*Princess*, iv.	270
in a royal hand, But *s* here and there	" v.	362
grief hath *s* into frost!	*In Mem.* iv.	12
And my bones are *s* with pain,	*Maud*, II. v.	1
The King was *s* with holy fear:	*The Victim*	61
shaker.		
O *s* of the Baltic and the Nile,	*Ode on Well.*	137
Shakespeare.		
Beside him *S* bland and mild:	*Pal. of Art*	134
My *S's* curse on clown and	'*You might have won*'	27
The soul of *S* love thee more.	*In Mem.* lx.	12
shaking (for *shaking hands*, see *hand.*)		
thousand battles, and *s* a hundred thrones.	*Maud* I.i.48	
S her head at her son and sighing	" xix.	24
S their pretty cabin	*En. Arden*	173
S a little like a drunkard's hand	"	462
s his gray head pathetically,	"	715
the singer *s* his curly head	*The Islet*	6
shale.		
stony names Of *s* and hornblende	*Princess*, iii.	344
shallop.		
Anight my *s,* rustling thro'	*Arabian N's.*	12
My *s* thro' the star-strown calm,	"	36

	POEM.	LINE.
The *s* flitteth silken-sail'd	*L. of Shalott*,i.	22
to a low song oar'd a *s* by,	*Princess*, ii.	433
To where a little *s* lay	*In Mem.* cii.	19
In a *s* of crystal ivory-beak'd	*The Islet*	12
shallow.		
And *s's* on a distant shore,	*Mariana in the S.*	7
ripply *s's* of the lisping lake,	*Ed. Morris*	98
Against my sandy *s's*	*The Brook*	177
shallow-hearted.		
O my cousin, *s-h!* O my Amy,	*Locksley H.*	39
Shalott.		
The island of *S.*	*L. of Shalott*, i. 9, *et pass.*
shambles.		
The land all *s*—	*Aylmer's F.*	765
shame (s.)		
The flush of anger'd *s*	*Madeline*	32
look'd to *s* The hollow-vaulted dark	*Arabian N's.*	125
mix'd her ancient blood with *s.*	*The Sisters.*	8
Inwrapt tenfold in slothful *s,*	*Pal. of Art*	262
sounds of insult, *s,* and wrong,	*D. of F. Wom.*	19
Her loveliness with *s* and with surprise	"	89
hold his hope thro' *s* and guilt, '*Love thou thy land*'		82
s and pride, New things and old,	*Walk. to the M.*	52
Some grow to honour, some to *s,*—	*Two Voices*	257
To save from *s* and thrall:	*Sir Galahad*	16
As it were with *s* she blushes,	*L. of Burleigh*	63
Sit thee down, and have no *s,*	*Vision of Sin*	83
S might befall Melissa,	*Princess*, iii.	131
a kind of *s* within me wrought	" iv.	176
full of cowardice and guilty *s*	"	329
I grant in her some sense of *s,*	"	330
dismiss'd in *s* to live No wiser	"	492
horror of the *s* among them all:	" v.	92
idle boys are cowards to their *s,*	"	269
hatred of her weakness, blent with *s.*	" vii.	15
Glowing all over noble *s,*	"	145
A touch of *s* upon her cheek	*In Mem.*xxxvii.	10
holds it sin and *s* to draw	" xlvii.	11
See with clear eye some hidden *s.*	" l.	7
hide thy *s* beneath the ground;	" lxxi.	28
My *s* is greater who remain,	" cviii.	23
chuckle, and grin at a brother's *s; Maud,* I. iv.		29
from some slight *s* one simple girl.	" xviii.	45
My anguish hangs like *s.*	" II. iv.	74
that was full of wrongs and *s's,*	" III. vi.	40
Guarding realms and kings from *s: Ode on Well.*		68
whose hearths he saved from *s*	"	225
my lord thro' me should suffer *s*	*Enid*	101
my lord should suffer loss or *s.*'	"	918
And *s,* could *s* be thine, that *s* were mine.	*Vivien*	298
The *s* that cannot be explained for *s.*	"	548
what *s* in love, So love be true	"	710
as for utmost grief or *s;*	"	746
loves the Queen, and in an open *s Elaine*		1076
she returns his love in open *s.*	"	1077
'*Mine* be the *s;* mine was the sin: *Guinevere*		111
Mine is the *s,* for I was wife,	"	118
S on her own garrulity	"	310
happy, dead before thy *s?*'	"	420
leave thee, woman, to thy *s,*	"	507
nor can I kill my *s;*	"	613
from the voices crying '*s.*'	"	664
the *s* The woman should have borne, *Aylmer's F.*		355
poor child of *s* The common care.	"	687
Whose *s* is that, if he went hence with *s?*"		718
You put me much to *s,*	*The Ringlet*	48
Sold him unto *s.*	*The Captain*	60
S and wrath his heart confounded	"	61
shame (verb.)		
s the boast so often made '*Love thou thy land*,'etc.		71
O Lady Clare, you *s* your worth! *Lady Clare*		66
mighty poetess, I would *s* you then *Princess, Pro.*		132
to *s* That which he says he loves:	" iv.	229
You *s* your mother's judgment too.	" vi.	244
and, worse, might *s* the Prince.	*Enid*	726
nay good father, *s* me not	*Elaine*	207
Mine own name *s's* me,		1394
Nor let me *s* my father's memory,	*Guinevere*	316

	POEM.	LINE.
To *s* these mouldy Aylmers	*Aylmer's F.*	396
surely I shall *s* myself and him.	"	734

shamed.
I am *s* thro' all my nature	*Locksley H.*	148
Far too naked to be *s!*	*Vision of Sin*	190
s That I must needs repeat	*Princess,* iii.	35
He never shall be *s.*	*Ode on Well.*	191
Then were you *s,* and, worse,	*Enid*	726
end is come And I am *s* for ever	*Guinevere*	110
sank down *s* At all that beauty	*Lucretius*	63

shameless.
Ah *s!* for he did but sing ' *You might have won* '	21	
lo the *s* ones, who take Their pastime *Elaine*	101	
will she fling herself *S,* upon me? *Lucretius*	200	

shameful.
nothing wild or strange, Or seeming *s, Vivien*	710	

shape (s.)
A gleaming *s* she floated by,	*L. of Shalott,*iv.	30
A cloud that gather'd *s:*	*Œnone*	41
the perfect *s* of man To — With *Pal. of Art*	19	
O *s* s and hues that please me well	*Pal. of Art*	29
of her palace stood Uncertain *s's;*	"	238
So *s* chased *s* as swift	*D. of F. Wom.*	37
pure white, that fitted to the *s*	*Gardener's D.*	125
What's here? a *s,* a shade,	*St S.Stylites*	199
Ten thousand broken lights and *s's, Will Water.*	59	
them, sitting, lying, languid *s's,*	*Vision of Sin*	12
stoop from heaven and take the *s. Princess,* vi.	365	
Titanic *s's,* they cramm'd The forum " vii.	109	
softer all her *s* And rounder seem'd:	"	121
palled *s's* In shadowy thoroughfares *In Mem.*lxix.	7	
wheel'd or lit the filmy *s's*	"	xciv. 10
The *s* of him I loved, and love	"	cii. 14
King out old *s's* of foul disease ;	"	cv. 25
with the shocks of doom To *s* and use "	cxvii.	25
a lord, a captain, a padded *s*	*Maud,*l.x.	29
Those niched *s's* of noble mould	*The Daisy*	38
The *s* and colour of a mind and life, *Elaine*	334	
face daintier? then her *s*	"	638
a story which in rougher *s*	*Aylmer's F.*	7
s dost thou behold thy God —	"	657
The peaky islet shifted *s's,*	*The Voyage*	33
twisted *s's* of lust, unspeakable,	*Lucretius*	157

shape verb.)
thoughts Do *s* themselves within me *Œnone*	243	
saying, hard to *s* in act ; ' *Love thou thy land,' etc.*	41	
that which *s's* it to some perfect end. *Love and Duty*	26	
To *s* the song for your delight	*Day-Dm.*	274
somehow it *s* the shadow, Time ;	*Princess,* iii.	313
s it plank and beam for roof .	" vi.	30
And *s* the whisper of the throne	*In Mem.*lxiii.	12
Then fancy *s's,* as fancy can,	"	lxxix. 5
s His action like the greater ape,	"	cxix. 10
Like clouds they *s* themselves and go, "	cxxii.	8
face that men *S* to their fancy's eye *Elaine*	1245	
and check'd His power to *s:*	*Lucretius*	23

shaped.
s. The city's ancient legend into this:— *Godiva*	3	
S her heart with woman's meekness *L. of Burleigh*	71	
red-hot iron to be *s* with blows.	*Princess,* v.	200
s, it seems, By God for thee alone, *Elaine*	1357	

shaping.
By *s* some august decree,	*To the Queen*	33
s faithful record of the glance	*Gardener's D.*	173
Here sits he *s* wings to fly:	*Two Voices*	289
And one the *s* of a star ;	*In Mem.* cii.	36
s an infant ripe for his birth,	*Maud,* l. iv.	34

shard.
By *s's* and scurf of salt,	*Vision of Sin*	211
dash'd Your cities into *s's*	*Princess,* v.	132

share (s.)
rhymes to him were scrip and *s,*	*The Brook*	4
s's in some Peruvian mine.	*Sea Dreams*	15
O then to ask her of my *s's,*	"	111

	POEM.	LINE.
share (verb.)		
Now could you *s* your thought ;	*Princess,* vi.	235
s's with man His nights, his days,	" vii.	246
Who stay to *s* the morning feast	*In Mem.Con.*	75
him who had ceased to *s* her heart,	*Maud,*I.xix.	30
shall *s* my earldom with me, girl,	*Enid*	1474

shared.
one sorrow and she *s* it not?.	*Aylmer's F.*	702

sharp (adj. and s.)
I made my dagger *s* and bright.	*The Sisters*	26
His face is growing *s* and thin	*D. of the O. Year*	46
In little *s's* and trebles,	*The Brook*	40
Thro' every change of *s* and flat ;	*Coquette,* i.	4

sharpened.
Are *s* to a needle's end ;	*In Mem.*lxxv.	4
s by strong hate for Lancelot.	*Guinevere*	21

sharper.
she was *s* than an eastern wind	*Audley Ct.*	52

sharpness.
s of that pain about her heart ;	*Enid*	1037

sharp-smitten.
S-s with the dint of armed heels—	*M. d'Arthur*	190

shatter.
s all the happiness of the hearth.	*En. Arden*	771
the hoary Roman head and *s* it,	*Boadicea*	65

shattered.
arms were *s* to the shoulder blade	*Princess,* vi.	36
from the sabre-stroke *S* and sunder'd	*Lt. Brigade*	36
Spars were splinter'd, decks were *s,*	*The Captain*	45
S into one earthquake in one day	*Lucretius*	747

shattering.
plunge in cataract, *s* on black blocks *Princess,* iii.	274	

shawm.
With *s's,* and with cymbals,	*Dying Swan*	32

sheaf.
Piling *sheaves* in uplands airy,	*L. of Shalott,*i.24	
In front they bound the *sheaves*	*Pal. of Art*	78
The varying year with blade and *s*	*Day-Dm.*	21
scheme of seven Together in one *s?*	*Princess,Con.*	9
he may read that binds the *s,*	*In Mem.*xxxvi.	13
whirl the ungarner'd *s* afar,	"	lxxi. 23

shear.
I did but *s* a feather,	*Princess,* v.	530

sheath.
New from its silken *s.*	*D of F. Wom.*	60
crumpled than a poppy from the *s, Princess,* v.	28	
in rich *s* with jewels on it	*Aylmer's F.*	220

sheathe.
To draw, to *s* a useless sword,	*In Mem.*cxxvii.13	

Sheba.
S came to ask of Solomon.'	*Princess,* ii.	325
Solomon may come to *S* yet	"	328

shed (s.)
The broken *s's*look'd sad and strange *Mariana*	5	

shed (verb.)
have not *s* a many tears, (rep.)	*Miller's D.*	221
that all the blood by Sylla *s,*	*Lucretius*	47

sheep.
livelong bleat Of the thick-fleeced *s*	*Ode to Mem.*	66
what are men better than *s* or goats *M. d'Arthur*	250	
lord of fat prize-oxen and of *s,*	*Princess,Con.*	86
oxen from the city, and goodly *s.*	*Spec. of Iliad*	4

sheepwalk.
Or *s* up the windy wold ;	*In Mem.*xcix.	8

sheer'd.
Caught the shrill salt, and *s* the gale *The Voyage*	12	

sheet.
I wrapt his body in the *s,*	*The Sisters*	34
Rolling a slumbrous *s* of foam	*Lotos-E's.*	11
Scaffolds, still *s's* of water,	*D. of F. Wom.*	34
s's of summer glass,	*To E. L.*	9

366   CONCORDANCE TO

	POEM.	LINE.
See that *s*'s are on my bed .	*Vision of Sin*	68
A music out of *s* and shroud,	*In Mem.* cii.	54
s's of hyacinth That seem'd the heavens	*Guinevere*	387
scaled in *s*'s of wasteful foam .	*Sea Dreams*	53

sheet-lightnings.

| No pale *s-l* from afar . . | *Aylmer's F.* | 726 |

shelf.

Of ledge or *s* The rock rose clear .	*Pal. of Art*	9
Upon the rosewood *s*; . .	*Talking O.*	118
strikes by night a craggy *s*, .	*In Mem.* xvi.	13
With *s* and corner for the goods .	*En. Arden*	171

shell.

A walk with vary-colour'd *s*'s .	*Arabian N's.*	57
freshen the silvery-crimson *s*'s	*Sea-Fairies*	13
pelt me with starry spangles and *s*'s,	*The Merman*	28
broad sea-wolds in the crimson *s*'s	*The Mermaid*	36
Jewel or *s*, or starry ore, .	*Eleänore*	20
the bird, the fish, the *s*, the flower,	*Princess*, ii.	361
should toss with tangle and with *s*'s	*In Mem.* x.	20
Time hath sunder'd *s* from pearl.'.	„ li.	16
The ruin'd *s*'s of hollow towers? .	„ lxxv.	16
See what a lovely *s*, . .	*Maud*, II. ii.	1
For a *s*, or a flower, little things .	„	64
when the *s* Divides threefold .	*The Brook* 72,	207
Storm'd at with shot and *s* .	*Lt. Brigade* 22,	43
hold like colours of a *s* . .	*Enid* .	681

shelter (s.)

Nor, moaning, household *s* crave	*Two Voices*	260
No branchy thicket *s* yields: .	*Sir Galahad*	58
wings of brooding *s* o'er her peace,	*Aylmer's F.*	139

shelter (verb.)

| Will *s* one of stranger race. . | *In Mem.* ci. | 4 |
| Call'd her to *s* in the hollow oak, . | *Vivien* . | 743 |

shelter'd.

| O Walter, I have *s* here . . | *Talking O.* | 37 |

shepherd.

the *s* who watcheth the evening star.	*Dying Swan*	35
A *s* all thy life but yet king-born .	*Œnone*	126
Ah me, my mountain *s*, . „		198
And *s*'s from the mountain-caves .	*Amphion*	53
lives in height (the *s* sang) .	*Princess*, vii.	178
the children call, and I Thy *s* pipe	„	203
the *S* gladdens in his heart : .	*Spec. of Iliad*	16

shepherdess

| one of Satan's *s*'es caught . . | *Vivien* . | 608 |

shepherd-lad.

| Sometimes a curly *s-l*, . . | *L. of Shalott*, ii. | 21 |

sheriff.

| token from the king To greet the *s*, | *Ed. Morris* | 133 |

sherris-warm'd.

| all his vast heart *s-w* . . | *Will Water.* | 197 |

she-slip.

| The slight *s-s*'s of loyal blood . | *Talking O.* | 57 |

she-society.

| long'd, All else was well, for *s-s.* | *Princess*, Pro. | 158 |

she-world.

| head and heart of all our fair *s-w* | *Princess*, iii. | 147 |

shield.

To a lady in his *s*, . .	*L. of Shalott*, iii.	7
A fairy *s* your Genius made .	*Margaret*	41
that month Became her golden *s*, .	*Princess*, i.	101
brand, mace, and shaft, and *s*— .	„ v.	492
Close by her, like supporters on a *s*	„ vi.	338
like a ruddy *s* on the Lion's breast	*Maud*, III. vi.	14
wild men supporters of a *s* .	*Enid*	1116
one at other, parted by the *s* .	„	1118
All in the hollow of his *s*, .	„	1417
lay beside him in the hollow *s*) .	„	1574
carved himself a knightly *s* of wood,	*Vivien*	323
Guarded the sacred *s* of Lancelot;	*Elaine*	4
and read the naked *s*, .	„	16
came the lily maid by that good *s* .	„	28
by mere mischance have brought, my *s*. „		189
—and the *s*—I pray you lend me one „		192

	POEM.	LINE.
God wot, his *s* is blank enough. .	*Elaine*	197
'This *s*, my friend, where is it?' .	„	344
brought the sword of *s*, .	„	378
have my *s* In keeping till I come.'	„	381
standing by the *s* In silence, .	„	393
she climb'd, and took the *s*, .	„	396
the knight, and here he left a *s*; .	„	631
ask you not to see the *s* he left, .	„	650
an you will it let me see the *s*.' .	„	658
when the *s* was brought, and Gawain	„	659
toward even Sent for his *s*; .	„	972
His very *s* was gone; . .	„	984
the *s* of Lancelot at her feet .	„	1331
hall, Hung with a hundred *s*'s .	*Aylmer's F.*	15
Of her own halo's dusky *s* .	*The Voyage*	32
Beat upon his father's *s*—'*Home they brought him*	„	9

shielded.

| *s* all her life from harm . . | *In Mem. Con.* | 47 |

shift.

As winds from all the compass *s* .	*Godiva*	33
We fret, we fume, would *s* our skins,	*Will Water.*	225
To *s* an arbitrary power, .	*In Mem.* cxxvii.	17

shifted.

| She *s* in her elbow-chair, . | *The Goose* | 27 |
| The peaky islet *s* shapes . | *The Voyage* | 33 |

shine (s.)

| With spires of silver *s*.'. . | *D. of F. Wom.* | 188 |
| Shadow and *s* is life, little Annie . | *Grandmother* | 60 |

shine (verb.)

waterfall Which ever sounds and *s*'s	*Ode to Mem.*	52
house thro' all the level *s*'s, .	*Mariana in the S.*	2
wild marsh-marigold *s*'s like fire .	*May Queen*, i.	31
the summer sun 'ill *s* .	„ ii.	22
He *s*'s upon a hundred fields .	„ iii.	50
and there his light may *s*— .	„	51
fair form may stand and *s*, '*Of old sat Freedom*,' *etc.*		21
To make the necklace *s*; .	*Talking O.*	222
rust unburnish'd, not to *s* in use! .	*Ulysses*	23
Sometimes a little corner *s*'s, .	*Two Voices*	187
beams, that thro' the Oriel *s*. .	*Day-Dm.*	54
As *s*'s the moon in clouded skies, .	*Beggar Maid*	9
Ralph Who *s*'s so in the corner ; .	*Princess*, Pro.	145
I see their unborn faces *s* .	*In Mem.* lxxxiii.	19
Not all regret : the face will *s* .	„ cxv.	9
Seeing his gewgaw castle *s* .	*Maud*, I. x.	18
But now *s* on, and what care I, .	„ xviii.	41
O when did a morning *s* .	„ xix.	5
S out, little head, sunning over .	„ xxii.	57
s in the sudden making of splendid names „	III. vi.	47
That *s*'s over city and river, .	*Ode on Well.*	50
tell her, the *s*'s me down : .	*Elaine*	1219
yonder *s*'s The Sun of Righteousness,	*En. Arden*	499
S's in those tremulous eyes .	*Tithonus*	26
Fairly-delicate palaces *s* .	*The Islet*	18
all the stars *S*, and the Shepherd	*Spec. of Iliad*	16
he would only *s* among the dead .	*Lucretius*	129

shingle.

round it ran a walk Of *s* .	*En. Arden* .	733
harsh *s* should grate underfoot .	„	773
Waves on a diamond *s* dash, .	*The Islet*	16
Waves on the *s* pouring, . .	*1865-1866*	11

shining.

| *s* in upon the wounded man . | *Princess*, vii. | 46 |
| Unloved, the sun-flower, *s* fair . | *In Mem.* c. | 5 |

ship.

sinking *s*'s, and praying hands .	*Lotos-E's.*	161
did we watch the stately *s*'s, .	*Locksley H.*	37
And the stately *s*'s go on '*Break, break,*' *etc.*		9
Fair *s*, that from the Italian shore	*In Mem.* ix.	1
great *s* lift her shining sides .	„ cii.	40
blush the news, O'er the blowing *s*'s.	*Maud*, I. xvii.	12
whether he came in the Hanover *s*,	„ II. v.	59
Some *s* of battle slowly creep .	*To F. D. Maurice*	26
ere he came, like one that hails a *s*,	*Enid*	1389
Had built the king his havens, *s*'s,	*Vivien*	24
master of that *s* Enoch had served in	*En. Arden*	119

	POEM.	LINE.
Annie, the *s* I sail in passes here .	En. Arden .	214
'The *s* was lost' he said (rep.)	"	390
prosperously sail'd The *s* 'Good Fortune'	"	524
Another *s* (She wanted water)	"	628
felt the good *s* shake and reel .	The Voyage	15
'A *s* of fools' he shriek'd in spite (rep.)	"	77
reach'd the *s* and caught the rope,	Sailor Boy .	3
many a fire between the *s*'s and stream	Spec. of Iliad	17
Rose a *s* of France .	The Captain	28
'Chase' he said : the *s* flew forward	"	33

shipwreck.

Made orphan by a winter *s* .	En. Arden .	15

shire.

A sign to many a staring *s* .	Will Water.	139
Master of half a servile *s*, .	Maud, I. x.	10

shiver.

Little breezes dusk and *s* .	L. of Shalott,	i. 12
The hard brands *s* on the steel, .	Sir Galahad	6
And here thine aspen *s*. .	A Farewell	10
chords that *s* to one note ; .	Princess, iii.	74
the *s* of dancing leaves is thrown .	Maud, I. vi.	73
woodlands, when they *s* in January,	Boädicea .	75

shiver'd.

Were *s* in my narrow frame. .	Fatima .	19
A cry that *s* to the tingling stars, .	M. d'Arthur	199

shoal.

And *s*'s of pucker'd faces drive ;	In Mem. lxix.	10
like a *s* Of darting fish, .	Enid .	1317

shock (s.)

push thee forward thro' a life of *s*'s,	Œnone .	160
With twelve great *s*'s of sound, .	Godiva .	74
whom the electric *s* Dislink'd .	Princess, Pro.	65
has the *s*, so harshly given, .	In Mem. xvi.	11
Diffused the *s* thro' all my life, .	" lxxxiv.	55
The steps of Time—the *s*'s of Chance—	"	xciv. 42
With thousand *s*'s that come and go,	"	cxii. 17
batter'd with the *s*'s of doom .	"	cxvii. 24
When all that seems shall suffer *s* .	"	cxxx. 2
pulses closed their gates with a *s* .	Maud, I. i.	15
s Of the cataract seas that snap .	"	II. ii. 25
In middle ocean meets the surging *s*,	Will .	8

shock (verb.)

Must ever *s*, like armed foes, 'Love than thy land'	The Blackbird	78
where the moving isles of winter *s*	M. d'Arthur	140
you will *s* him ev'n to death, .	Princess, iii.	196
and there so furiously *S*, .	Elaine .	457

shock'd.

S, like an iron-clanging anvil .	Princess, v.	493

shock-head.

The *s-h* willows two and two .	Amphion .	39

shoe.

Shall fling her old *s* after. .	Will Water.	216

shone.

S out their crowning snows, .	Dying Swan .	13
Thick-jewell'd *s* the saddle-leather	L. of Shalott,	iii. 20
her light foot *S* rosy-white .	Œnone .	176
The garden-glasses *s*, and momently	Gardener's D.	116
near his tomb a feast *S*, silver-set	Princess, Pro.	106
on my cradle *s* the Northern star. .	"	i. 4
light foot *s* like a jewel .	"	iii. 340
than a glow-worm *s* the tent .	"	iv. 7
s Their morions, wash'd with morning,	"	v. 253
A column'd entry *s* and marble stairs	"	" 354
s Thro' glittering drops .	"	vi. 265
light that *s* when Hope was born.	In Mem. xxx.	32
star Which *s* so close beside Thee,	Ded. of Idylls	46
thro' these Princelike his bearing *s*	Enid .	545
so thickly *s* the gems. .	"	1541
that *s* white-listed thro' the gloom.	Vivien .	788
the field, that *s* Full-summer, .	Elaine .	1134
on the burnish'd board Sparkled and *s*;	En Arden	744
S like a mystic star .	Aylmer's F.	72
flying *s*, the silver boss .	The Voyage	31

shook.

Hard by a poplar *s* alway .	Mariana .	41
with *his* word She *s* the world, .	The Poet .	56

	POEM.	LINE.
s the wave as the wind did sigh ; .	Dying Swan	15
S in the stedfast blue, .	D. of F. Wom.	6
Above her *s* the starry lights : 'Of old sat Freedom'		3
his song together as he near'd .	Gardener's D.	60
a jolly ghost, that *s* The curtains	Walk. to the M.	28
I s him down because he was .	Talking O. .	237
anon she *s* her head, And shower'd	Godiva .	46
A sudden hubbub *s* the hall, .	Day-Dm. .	135
paddling plied And *s* the lilies : .	Princess, Pro.	72
s aside The hand that play'd the patron	"	137
s the songs, the whispers, .	"	i. 97
Melissa *s* her doubtful curls .	"	iii. 59
desire to kneel, and *s* My pulses .	"	" 177
s the woods, And danced the colour	"	" 275
the tear, She sang of, *s* and fell, .	"	iv. 42
Psyche flush'd and wann'd and *s* ;	"	" 142
Palpitated, her hand *s* .	"	" 370
Not long : I *s* it off; .	"	" 543
and *s* the branches of the deer .	Con. .	58
s to all the liberal air .	In Mem. lxxxviii.	7
brighten like the star that *s* .	" Con.	31
s my heart to think she comes .	Maud, I. xviii.	10
I s her breast with vague alarms .	The Letters	38
On that loud sabbath *s* the spoiler	Ode on Well.	123
s his drowsy squire awake .	Enid .	125
s her pulses, crying. 'Look a prize ! .	"	972
She *s* from fear, and for her fault .	Vivien .	801
Then *s* his hair, strode off .	Elaine .	718
she was happy enough and *s* it off, .	"	780
She neither blush'd nor *s*, .	"	960
wild with wind That *s* her tower, .	"	1015
s beneath them, as the thistle shakes	Guinevere	252
s And almost overwhelm'd her .	En. Arden .	525
and *s* His isolation from him. .	"	652
Stagger'd and *s*, holding the branch, .	"	788
s the heart of Edith hearing him. .	Aylmer's F.	63
like a storm he came, And *s* the house	"	210
but not a word : she *s* her head. .	Sea Dreams	112
Like her, he *s* his head .	"	144
Whom all the pines of Ida *s* to see	Lucretius .	86

shoot (s.)

and earliest *s*'s Of orient green, .	Ode to Mem.	17

shoot (verb.)

s into the dark Arrows of lightnings.	To J. M. K.	13
While all the neighbours *s* the, .	The Blackbird	2
The northern morning o'er thee *s*,	Talking O.	275
I would *s*, howe'er in vain .	Two Voices	344
little boys begin to *s* and stab, .	Princess, Con.	61
At times a carven craft would *s* .	The Voyage	53
as the rapid of life *S*'s to the fall .	A Dedication	4

shore (s.)

the happy blossoming *s*. .	Sea-Fairies	8
Who can light on as happy a *s* .	"	40
shallows on a distant *s*, .	Mariana in the S.	7
shadow'd coves on a sunny *s*, .	Eleänore .	18
All along the shadowy *s* .	"	41
with bars of sand ; Left on the *s*;	Pal. of Art	250
mourn and rave On alien *s*'s .	Lotos-E s.	33
Between the sun and moon upon the *s*	"	38
the *s*, Than labour in mid-ocean .	"	171
the temples, waver'd, and the *s*; .	D. of F. Wom.	114
sail with Arthur under looming *s*'s,	M. d'Arthur, Ep.	17
unto the *s*'s of nothing ! .	Gardener's D.	17
seas, that daily gain upon the *s*, .	Golden Year	29
on *s*, and when 'Thro' scudding drifts	Ulysses .	9
O the barren, barren *s* ! .	Locksley H.	40
wisdom lingers, and I linger on the *s*	"	141
dark *s* just seen that it was rich, .	Princess, i.	245
grasping down the boughs I gain'd the *s*	"	iv. 171
Rotting on some wild *s* .	"	v. 141
the slope of sea from verge to *s*, .	"	vii. 23
Fair ship, that from the Italian *s* .	In Mem. ix.	1
laid him by the pleasant *s* .	"	xix. 3
The sound of that forgetful *s* .	"	xxxv. 14
Yet turn thee to the doubtful *s*, .	"	lx. 9
lazy lengths on boundless *s*'s ; .	"	lxix. 12
Dip down upon the northern *s*, .	"	lxxxii. 1
To the other *s*, involved in thee, .	"	lxxxiii. 40
I watch thee from the quiet *s* .	"	lxxxiv. 61
paced the *s*'s And many a bridge, .	"	lxxxvi. 11

368 CONCORDANCE TO

	POEM.	LINE.
still as vaster grew the s,	In Mem. cii.	25
The boat is drawn upon the s;	" cxx.	6
And heard an ever-breaking s	" cxxiii.	11
To spangle all the happy s's	" Con.	120
More than a mile from the s.	Maud, I. ix.	2
That made it stir on the s	" II. ii.	15
cannon bullet rust on a slothful s	" III. vi.	26
heave the hill And break the s,	Ode on Well.	260
rode with them, to the s's Of Severn	Enid. 44,	1802
did you never lie upon the s.	Vivien.	140
wild battles by the s Of Duglas:	Elaine	289
the thundering s's of Bude and Bos	Guinevere.	289
the waste and lumber of the s,	En. Arden.	16
As down the s he ranged,	"	589
and fill'd the s's With clamour	"	636
s's that darken with the gathering	Aylmer's F..	767
forth they came and paced the s,	Sea Dreams	32
Swept with it to the s,	"	67
spoke with me on the s;	"	255
On open main or winding s!.	The Voyage	6
O hundred s's of happy climes,	"	49
While about the s of Mona	Boädicea	1

shore (verb.)
good Queen, her mother, s the tress	Princess, vi.	97
S thro' the swarthy neck,	Enid.	1576

shore-cliff.
From the long s-c's windy walls	Enid	1013

shorn.
And, issuing s and sleek,	Talking O..	42

shot (s.)
A s, ere half thy draught be done,	In Mem. vi.	11
Storm'd at with s and shell.	Lt. Brigade	22, 44

shot (verb.)
S thro' and thro' with cunning 'Clear-headed friend'		17
Momently s into each other.	Madeline	23
S over with purple, and green,	Dying Swan	20
as a flying star s thro' the sky	Pal. of Art	123
S on the sudden into dark	To J. S.	28
S like a streamer of the northern	M. d'Arthur	139
S thro' the lists at Camelot,	"	224
Be s for sixpence in a battle-field,	Audley Ct..	40
palfrey's footfall s Light horrors	Godiva	58
The fire s up, the martin flew,	Day-Dm..	143
S sidelong daggers at us,	Princess, ii.	427
s from crooked lips a haggard smile	" iv.	345
s A flying splendour out of brass.	" vi.	344
S up and shrill'd in flickering gyres,	" vii.	31
s red fire and shadows thro' the cave,	Elaine	413
climbing up the valley; at whom he s:	Aylmer's F.	228
by a keeper s at, slightly hurt, .	"	548
S up their shadows to the Heaven	"	642
toner 'cd s un as dead as a nasil	N. Farmer.	35
S o'er the seething harbour-bar,	Sailor Boy.	2
S out of them, and scorch'd me	Lucretius	66

shoulder.
a leopard skin Droop'd from his s.	Œnone	58
Upon her pearly s leaning cold	"	138
golden round her lucid throat And s	"	175
off her s backward borne:	Pal. of Art	118
clapt his hand On Everard's s	The Epic	22
Make broad thy s's to receive my	M. d'Arthur,	164
O'er both his s's drew the languid hands	"	174
Naiads oar'd A glimmering s	To E. L.	17
Till over thy dark s glow 'Move eastward,' etc.		5
robed the s's in a rosy silk,	Princess, Pro.	103
white s shaken with her sobs,	" iv.	270
slanted o'er a press Of snowy s's.	"	458
on my s hung their heavy hands, .	"	531
from the dewy s's of the Earth	" v.	41
On either shining s laid a hand,	Enid.	518
and the squire Chafing his s;	"	876
Droop from his mighty s,	Vivien	92
Gazed at the heaving s,	"	745
turn'd, and smooth'd The glossy s,	Elaine	347
a heaved s and a saucy smile	Aylmer's F.	466
Among the honest s's of the crowd	Sea Dreams	162
pure brows, and from thy s's pure,	Tithonus	35

shoulder'd.
	POEM.	LINE.
Then we s thro' the swarm.	Audley Ct..	8
bloated things S the spigot, .	Guinevere.	266

shout (s.)
Herod, when the s was in his ears,	Pal. of Art	219
O shall the braggart s.	Love and Duty	5
But that there rose a s:	Princess, Con.	36
a s rose again, and made The long line	"	96
a s More joyful than the city roar	" Con.	100
caught once more the distant s,	In Mem. lxxxvi.	9
At the s's, the leagues of lights,	Maud, II. iv.	21

shout (verb.)
hark! they s 'St Simeon Stylites.'	St S. Stylites	144
They s, 'Behold a saint!'	"	151
he s's with his sister at play!	'Break, break,' etc.	6
S Icenian, Catieuchlanian (rep.)	Boädicea	57

shouted.
Till I struck out and s;	Princess, v.	529
But I heard it s at once	Maud, II. v.	50

shouting.
Heard the heavens fill with s	Locksley H.	123
a loyal people s a battle cry,	Maud, III. vi.	35
the red cock s to the light, .	Enid.	1233

shovell'd.
s up into a bloody trench	Audley Ct.	41

show (s.)
not with s's of flaunting vines	Ode to Mem.	48
Had made him talk for s; .	Will Water.	196
Princess Ida seem'd a hollow s,	Princess, iv.	219
camp and college turn'd to hollow s's;	" v.	467
They did but look like hollow s's)	" vii.	119
My haunting sense of hollow s's:	"	328

show (verb.)
might s it at a joust of arms,	M. d'Arthur	102
S me the man hath suffer'd more	St S. Stylites	48
That s the year is turn'd.	Talking O.	176
Nor canst thou s the dead are dead.	Two Voices	267
S's At distance like a little wood.	Day-Dm..	61
all that else the years will s,	"	225
s you slips of all that grows .	Amphion	83
So s's me but seen before the Lamb,	St Agnes' Eve	17
Shall s thee past to Heaven:	Will Water.	246
the faults he would not s: 'You might have won'		17
All he s's her makes hers dearer:	L. of Burleigh	33
s That life is not as idle ore,	In Mem. cxvii.	19
That will s itself without.	Maud, II. iv.	61
threefold to s the fruit within.	The Brook	73-208
call'd old Philip out To s the farm:	"	121
into Darnley chase To s Sir Arthur's deer."		133
for the last time while I s,	Guinevere.	451
'S me the books!'	Sea Dreams	144
these I thought my dream would s to me	Lucretius	51

showed.
the world Like one great garden s,	The Poet	34
One s an iron const	Pal. of Art	69
for he s me all the sin.	MayQueen, iii.	17
by my side S like fair seraphs.	St S. Stylites	166
s the house, Greek, set with busts:	Princess, Pro.	10
s the late-writ letters of the king.	" i.	173
He s a tent A stone-shot off:	" v.	50
Who s a token of distress?	In Mem. lxxvii.	13
s him in the fountain fresh	" lxxxiv.	26
What Roman strength Turbia s	The Daisy	5
visor up, and s a youthful face,	Enid.	189
s themselves against the sky, and sank."		240
For while the mother s it,	"	636
s an empty tent allotted her,	"	1733
the crown, and s them to his knights,	Elaine	58
green path that s the rarer foot,	"	162
S her the fairy footings	Aylmer's F.	90
when she s the wealthy scabbard,	"	236
s their eyes Glaring, and passionate	Sea Dreams	228
s A riotous confluence.	Lucretius	29

shower (s.)
sweet s's Of festal flowers,	Ode to Mem.	77
These in every s creep.	A Dirge	33
I thirsted for the brooks, the s's:	Fatima	10

	POEM.	LINE.
moonlight on a falling *s*?	*Margaret*	4
like the rainbow from the *s*,	*Two Voices*	444
The slow result of winter *s's*:	"	452
I'll take the *s's* as they fall,	*Amphion*	101
Perfume and flowers fall in *s's*	*Sir Galahad*	11
s s of random sweet	*Princess*, vii.	71
close Her crimson fringes to the *s*;	*In Mem.* lxxi.	12
Sweet after *s's*, ambrosial air,	" lxxxv.	1
in blown seas and storming *s's*	*Ode on Well.*	155
s and storm and blast Had blown	*The Daisy*	70
cared as much for as a summer *s*:	*Enid*	1372
sunlight on the plain behind a *s*:	*Vivien*	253
poplars made a noise of falling *s's*.	*Elaine*	410, 522
The gentle *s*, the smell of dying leaves,	*En. Arden*	612

shower (verb.)

Down *s* the gambolling waterfalls	*Sea-Fairies*	10
s the fiery grain Of freedom.	*Princess*, v.	411

showered.

s the rippled ringlets to her knee;	*Godiva*	47
Before me *s* the rose in flakes	*Princess*, iv.	245
Lavish honour *s* all her stars,	*Ode on Well.*	196
s His oriental gifts on every one	*Aylmer's F.*	213

showering.

S thy gleaned wealth	*Ode to Mem.*	23
s wide Sleet of diamond-drift	*Vision of Sin*	21
fountains spouted up and *s* down	*Princess*, i.	215

showing.

S n gaudy summer-morn,	*Pal. of Art*	62
S the aspick *s* bite)	*D. of F. Wom.*	160

shown.

Half *s*, are broken and withdrawn.	*Two Voices*	306

shrank.

S one sick willow sere and small	*Mariana in the S.*	53
Enid *s* far back into herself,	*Enid*	1455
charger at her side, She *s* a little	"	1669

shrewdness.

nor compensating the want By *s*	*En. Arden*	250

shriek (s.)

Dislink'd with *s's* and laughter	*Princess, Pro.*	70
yonder, *s's* and strange experiments	"	228
the songs, the whispers, and the *s's*	" i.	97
rose a *s* as of a city sack'd	" iv.	147
then another *s*, 'The Head, the Head	" Con.	62
kingdom topples over with a *s*	"	
The shrill-edged *s* of a mother	*Maud*, I. i.	16
there was love in the passionate *s*,	"	57
all in passion uttering a dry *s*,	*Enid*	1310
hands Together with a wailing *s*,	*Vivien*	716
gave A marvellous great *s*	*Elaine*	515
myriad *s* of wheeling ocean-fowl,	*En. Arden*	584
the keen *s* 'yes love, yes Edith, yes'	*Aylmer's F.*	582
as their *s* Ran highest up the gamut	*Sea Dreams*	225
One *s* of hate would jar all the hymns	"	251

shriek (verb.)

if any came near I would call, and *s*,	*The Mermaid*	38
and *s* 'You are not Ida:'	*Princess*, vii.	79
shall I *s* if a Hungary fail?	*Maud*, I. iv.	46
'That ever *s's* before a death,'	*Elaine*	1017
S out 'I hate you, Enoch.'	*En. Arden*	33

shrieked.

Behind the mouldering wainscot *s*,	*Mariana*	64
'No voice,' she *s* in that lone hall,	*Pal. of Art*	258
Again they *s* the burden 'Him!'.	*Ed. Morris*	123
Daintily she *s* And wrung it .	*Princess, Pro.*	173
'Boys!' *s* the old king,	"	318
s The virgin marble	" vi.	337
s against his creed—	*In Mem.* lv.	16
S to the stranger, 'Slay not a dead *Enid*		1627
moved so much the more, and *s* again,	"	1630
s out 'traitor' to the unhearing wall,	*Elaine*	609
he swung his arms, and *s*	*Sea Dreams*	
'A ship of fools' he *s* in spite,	*The Voyage*	77
Yell'd and *s* between her daughters	*Boädicea*	6, 72
s That she but meant to win him	*Lucretius*	274

	POEM.	LINE.
shrieking.		
s out 'O fool!' the harlot leapt	*Vivien*	821
fell The woman *s* at his feet,	*Aylmer's F.*	811
s 'I am his dearest, I—'	*The Victim*	76

shrift.

And number'd bead, and *s*,	*Talking O.*	45
in her grief, for housel or for *s*	*Guinevere*	147

shrike.

the sparrow spear'd by the *s*,	*Maud*, I. iv.	23

shrill.

s's All night in a waste land,	*M. d'Arthur*	201
her whinny *s's* From tile to scullery	*Princess*, v.	442

shrill-edged.

The *s-e* shriek of a mother	*Maud*, I. i.	16

shrill'd.

(*s* the cottonspinning chorus)	*Ed. Morris*	122
And *s* his tinsel shaft.	*Talking O.*	63
merrily-blowing *s* the martial fife	*Princess*, v.	241
Shot up and *s* in flickering gyres,	" vii.	31
s and rang, Till this was ended	*En. Arden*	175

shrilleth.

The shattering trumpet *s* high	*Sir Galahad*	5

shrilling.

she *s* 'Let me die!'	*Elaine*	1020

shrine.

By Bagdat's *s's* of fretted gold,	*Arabian N's.*	7
Still-lighted in a secret *s*,	*Mariana in the S.*	18
From one censer, in one *s*,	*Eleänore*	59
from the ruin'd *s* he stept	*M. d'Arthur*	45
may carve a *s* about my dust,	*St S. Stylites*	193
My knees are bow'd in crypt and *s*:	*Sir Galahad*	18
Then by some secret *s* I ride	"	29
The desecrated *s*, the trampled year,	*Princess*, v.	121
that *s* which then in all the realm	*Elaine*	1320
lie before your *s's*;	*Guinevere*	673
Going before to some far *s*,	*On a Mourner*	17

shrined.

Methinks my friend is richly *s*,	*In Mem.* lvi.	7

shrine-doors.

s-d burst thro' with heated blasts	*D. of F. Wom.*	29

shrink.

s to the earth if you came in.	*Poet's Mind*	37
Smite, *s* not, spare not.	*St S. Stylites*	178
nor *s* For fear our solid aim	*Princess*, iii.	208
her small goodman S's in his arm-chair	" v.	444

shrive.

let me *s* me clean, and die.'	*Elaine*	1094

shrivell'd.

Were *s* into darkness in his head	*Godiva*	70
Is *s* in a fruitless fire,	*In Mem.* liii.	11

shrivelling.

sting of shrewdest pain Ran *s* thro' me,	*St S. Stylites*	196

shroud (s.)

Nor was the night thy *s*.	*Ode to Mem.*	28
A music out of sheet and *s*,	*In Mem.* cii.	54

shroud (verb.)

To *s* me from my proper scorn	*In Mem.* xxvi.	15
s this great sin from all!	*Aylmer's F.*	773

shrub.

Tall orient *s's*, and obelisks .	*Arabian N's.*	107

shudder (s.)

her child I—a *s* comes Across me	*Œnone*	249

shudder (verb.)

I *s* at the sequel, but I go.	*Princess*, ii.	218
s but to dream our maids should ape	" iii.	292
Nor *s's* at the gulfs beneath,	*In Mem.* xl.	15
'I *s*, some one steps across	*Guinevere*	57
if you do not *s* at me	"	627

shudder'd.

s, lest a cry Should break his sleep	*Walk. to the M.*	65
'Why these are men!' I *s*:	*Princess*, iii.	42
blood Of his own son, *s*,	" vi.	83

2 A

	POEM.	LINE.
Yet I *s* and thought like a fool	*Maud*, I. xiv.	38
s, as the village wife who cries	*Guinevere* .	56

shudderest.

S when I strain my sight,	. *Fatima* .	3

shuddering.

delight and *s* took hold of all my mind	*MayQueen*, iii.	35
s fled from room to room	. *Princess*, vi.	350
Set every gilded parapet *s*;	. *Elaine* .	299
thought With *s* 'Hark the Phantom	"	1016
knew not wherefore, started up S,	*En. Arden* .	618
s at the ruin of a world ;	. *Sea Dreams*	30

shun.

on our dead self, nor *s* to do it,	. *Princess*, iii.	205
will not *s* The foaming grape	. *In Mem. Con.*	79
s the wild ways of the lawless tribe	*Enid* .	1456
do not *s* To speak the wish	. *Elaine* .	909
s to break those bounds of courtesy	"	1214
did not *s* to smite me in worse way,	*Guinevere*	432
Nor *s* to call me sister,	. "	668

shunn'd.

nor *s* a soldier's death, .	. *Princess*, Pro.	38
and had not *s* the death,	. " v.	170
Enoch *s* the middle walk	. *En. Arden* .	739
which he better might have *s*	. " .	741

Shushan.

brawl at S underneath the palms	*Princess*, iii.	214

shut.

I *s* my sight for fear	. *Œnone* .	184
he that *s*'s Love out, To ——	*With Pal. of Art*	14
shall be S out from love	. " .	15
S up as in a crumbling tomb,	. *Pal. of Art*	273
white dust, *s* in an urn of brass!	. *Lotos-E's.* .	113
She left the new piano *s*:	. *Talking O.* .	119
said he lived *s* up within himself	. *Golden Year*	9
door *s*, and window barr'd.	. *Godiva* .	41
I *s* my life from happier chance.	. *Two Voices*	54
any moral *s* Within the bosom	. *Day-Dm.* .	203
By squares of tropic summer *s*	. *Amphion* .	87
one deep chamber *s* from sound	. *Princess*, vi.	355
sometimes in my sorrow *s*,	. *In Mem.* xxiii.	1
Were *s* between me and the sound	" xxviii.	8
Or been in narrowest working *s*,	. " xxxv.	20
God *s* the doorways of his head.	. " xliii.	4
A gulf that ever *s*'s and gapes,	. " lxix.	6
I will not *s* me from my kind,	. " cvii.	1
little maid, *s* in by nunnery walls,	. *Guinevere* .	225
s me round with narrowing nunnery-walls,	"	663
s from all Her charitable use	. *Aylmer's F.*	565

shutter.

Close the door, the *s*'s close,	. *Deserted H,*	9

shutting.

s reasons up in rhythm	. *Lucretius* .	220

shy.

S she was, and I thought her cold ;	*Ed. Gray* .	13
A little *s* at first, but by and by	. *Princess*, v.	43
Might say no, for she is but *s*:	. *The Window*	97

shyness.

It is my *s*, or my self-distrust,	. *Ed. Morris* .	86

sibilation.

with a long low *s*, stared	. *Princess*, i.	174

Sicilian.

as the great S called Calliope	. *Lucretius* .	93

sick.

'I am half *s* of shadows,'	. *L. of Shalott*, ii.	35
King is *s*, and knows not what he	*M. d'Arthur*	97
s of home went overseas for change.	*Walk. to the M.*	18
girl, for whom your heart is *s*,	. *Talking O.* .	71
S art thou—a divided will	. *Two Voices*	106
but I am *s* of Time, 'Come not, when,' etc.		9
S for the hollies and the yews	*Princess*, Pro.	185
talk'd The trash that made me *s*	. " ii.	372
Were you *s*, ourself Would tend upon you	" iii.	303
Hung round the *s*: the maidens came	" vii.	7
fair peace once more among the *s*.	" .	29

	POEM.	LINE.
S for thy stubborn hardihood	. *In Mem.* ii.	14
heart is *s*, And all the wheels	. " xlix.	3
cheating the *s* of a few last gasps	. *Maud*, I. i.	43
I am *s* of the Hall and the hill (rep.)	. "	61
S, am I *s* of a jealous dread ?	. " x.	1
S, *s* to the heart of Sin, am I.	. " .	36
his essences turn'd the live air *s*,	. " xiii.	11
S once, with a fear of worse,	. " xix.	73
S of a nameless fear,	. " II. ii.	44
Spake (for she had been *s*) to Guinevere	*Elaine* .	79
'Are you so *s*, my Queen,	. "	80
'stay with me, I am *s*;	. "	88
'Love, are you yet so *s*?'	. "	570
to go, So far, being *s*?'	. "	1058
too faint and *s* am I For anger :	. "	1080
father lying *s* and needing him)	. *En. Arden* .	65
—it makes me *s* to quote him—	. *Sea Dreams*	155
half the crew are *s* or dead .	. *The Voyage*	92
blind or lame or *s* or sound	. "	93
The land is *s*, the people diseased,	*The Victim* .	47

sicken.

Here at least, where nature *s*'s,	. *Locksley H.*	151
Or *s* with ill-usage,	. *Princess*, v.	83
A time to *s* and to swoon	. *In Mem.* xxi.	17
pains him that he *s*'s nigh to death ;	*Enid* .	1348
I hate, abhor, spit, *s* at him,	. *Lucretius* .	196

sicken'd.

Which *s* every living bloom.	. *In Mem.* lxxi.	7
war On all the youth, they *s*;	. *Vivien* .	422

sickening.

s of a vague disease	. *L. C. V. de Vere*	62

sickle.

ere the silver *s* of that month	. *Princess*, i.	100

sicklier.

sickly-born and grew Yet *s*,	. *En. Arden* .	260

sickly.

Bore him another son, a *s* one:	. *En. Arden* .	107
the third, the *s* one, who slept	. "	229

sickly-born.

Now the third child was *s-b*	. *En. Arden* .	260

sickness.

Some turn this *s* yet might take,	. *Two Voices*	55
read My *s* down to happy dreams	*Princess*, ii.	235
due To languid limbs and *s*;	. " vi.	356
serviceable To noble knights in *s*,	*Elaine* .	764
as but born of *s*, could not live :	. "	876
What the rough *s* meant,	. "	884
a languor came Upon him, gentle *s*,	*En. Arden*	825

side.

the piney *s*'s Of this long glen	. *Œnone* .	91
and thrust The dagger thro' her *s*.'	*D. of F. Wom.*	260
clamber'd half way up The counter *s*	*Golden Year*	7
Had cast upon its crusty *s*	. *Will Water.*	103
Whichever *s* be Victor,	. *Princess*, ii.	213
To rail at Lady Psyche and her *s*.	" iii.	17
when our *s* was vanquish'd	. " vi.	8
A great ship lift her shining *s*'s	. *In Mem.* cii.	40
Up the *s* I went,	. "	43
That has to-day its sunny *s*.	. " Con.	72
There were two at her *s*,	. *Maud*, I. ix.	9
Was not one of the two at her *s*	. " x.	2
sweeter blood by the other *s*	. " xiii.	34
Would he have that hole in his *s*?	" II. v.	82
'Not at my *s*. I charge you ride before *Enid*.		863
the head Pierced thro' his *s*,	. *Elaine* .	489
up the *s*, sweating with agony,	. "	493
parted from the jousts Hurt in the *s*,'	"	620
Thro' her own *s* she felt the sharp lance	"	621
in an oriel on the summer *s*,	. "	1171
on our dull *s* of death,	. "	1373
Never lie by thy *s*, see thee no more	*Guinevere*	574
The very *s*'s of the grave itself	. *Lucretius* .	253
drove the knife into his *s*	. "	271

siding.

Wheedling and *s* with them !	. *Princess*, v.	151

	POEM.	LINE.		POEM.	LINE.
sifted.			as a viper frozen : loathsome *s*	*Vivien*	694
heedfully I *s* all my thoughts	*St S. Stylites*	55	A *s* you love to look on.'	*Elaine*	84
Every heart, when *s* well,	*Vision of Sin*	112	and the sorrow dimm'd her *s*,	"	885
this matter might be *s* clean.'	*Princess*, i.	79	How fresh was every *s* and sound	*The Voyage*	5
sigh (s.)			out of *s*, and sink Past earthquake	*Lucretius*	152
wasting odorous *s's* All night long	*Adeline*	43	in *s* of Collatine And all his peers,	"	235
With her laughter or her *s's*,	*Miller's D.*	184	**sign (s.)**		
my voice was thick with *s's* .	*D. of F. Wom.*	109	heaven's mazed *s's* stood still 'Clear-headed friend'		28
in *s's* Which perfect Joy, perplex'd	*Gardener's D.*	249	and I will tell the *s*.	*May Queen*, iii.	24
A welcome mix'd with *s's*.	*Talking O.*	212	I thought, I take it for a *s*.	"	38
shaken with a sudden storm of *s's*—	*Locksley H.*	27	By *s's* or groans or tears;	*D. of F. Wom.*	284
The bosom with long *s's* labour'd,	*Princess*, vii.	210	surer *s* had follow'd, either hand,	*M. d'Arthur*	76
Love would answer with a *s*,	*In Mem.* xxxv.	13	A *s* betwixt the meadow and the cloud,	*St S. Stylites*	14
Nor feed with *s's* a passing wind	"	cvii. 4	Know I not Death ? the outward *s's* ?	*Two Voices*	270
in my thoughts with scarce a *s*	"	cxviii. 11	A *s* to many a staring shire	*Will Water.*	139
Young lord-lover, what *s's* are those,	*Maud*, I. xxii.	29	If my heart by *s's* can tell,	*L. of Burleigh*	2
Half the night I waste in *s's*	"	II. iv. 23	stood a bust of Pallas for a *s*.	*Princess*, i.	219
With half a *s* she turn'd the key,	*The Letters*	18	cannot speak, nor move, nor make one *s*,	" vii.	138
songs, *S's*, slow smiles,	*Elaine*	646	Till the Sun drop dead from the *s's*.'	"	230
sigh (verb.)			no more *s* of reverence than a beard.	*Vivien*	128
you may hear him sob and *s* 'A spirit haunts,' etc.		5	With *s's* and miracles and wonders	*Guinevere*	220
shook the wave as the wind did *s*	*Dying Swan*	15	what of *s's* and wonders, but the *s's*	"	227
To breathe and loathe, to live and *s*,	*Two Voices*	104	thy wise father with his *s's*	"	272
here will *s* thine alder tree,	*A Farewell*	9	Pray'd for a *s* ' my Enoch is he gone ?'	*En. Arden*	487
She *s's* amid her narrow days,	*In Mem.* lix.	10	Suddenly set it wide to find a *s*,	"	492
and *s* The full new life .	" lxxxv.	9	making *s's* They knew not what : .	"	641
whenever a March-wind *s's*	*Maud*, I. xxii.	40	swang besides on many a windy *s*—	*Aylmer's F.*	19
often when they met *S* fully,	*Vivien*	38	**sign (verb.)**		
sigh'd.			Now *s* your names, which shall be read,	*In Mem. Con.*	57
my name *S* forth with life .	*D. of F. Wom.*	154	**signal.**		
So *s* the King, Muttering and	*M. d'Arthur*	178	An idle *s*, for the brittle fleet	*Sea Dreams*	129
they that heard it *s*,	*Vision of Sin*	18	**signed.**		
Cold ev'n to her, she *s*;	*Princess*, vi.	86	The names are *s*, and overhead	*In Mem. Con.*	60
I *s* : a touch Came round my wrist,	" vii.	122	**signet.**		
Long have I *s* for a calm .	*Maud*, I. ii.	1	He set his royal *s* there; .	*In Mem.* cxxiv.	12
thought, is it pride, and mused and *s*	" viii.	12	**silence.**		
They *s* for the dawn and thee.	" xxii.	52	All night the *s* seems to flow	*Oriana*	86
s and smiled the hoary-headed Earl,	*Enid*	307	One deep, deep *s* all !	*Pal. of Art*	260
came upon him, and he *s*;	"	1098	ripen toward the grave In *s*;	*Lotos-E's.*	97
S in passing 'Lancelot Forgive me ;	*Elaine*	1340	sank thro' the *s* drear,	*D. of F. Wom.*	121
S, and began to gather heart	*Guinevere*	366	only *s* suiteth best.	*To J. S.*	64
s to find Her journey done .	"	401	waked with *s*, grunted 'Good !'	*M. d'Arthur, Ep.*	8
sigheth.			There was *s* in the room ;	*Dora*	154
the solemn oak-tree, *s* .	*Claribel*	4	is saved From that eternal *s*,	*Ulysses*	27
sighing.			crystal *s* creeping down, .	*Two Voices*	86
winter winds are wearily *s* ; .	*D. of the O. Year*	2	To *s* from the paths of men :	*Day-Dm.*	218
by them went The enamour'd air *s*,	*Princess*, vi.	63	a costly bribe To guerdon *s*,	*Princess*, i.	201
S she spoke ' I fear They will not,'	" vii.	280	*S*, till I be silent too. .	*In Mem.* xiii.	8
O, art thou *s* for Lebanon rep.'	*Maud*, I. xviii.	15	And makes a *s* in the hills	" xix.	8
Shaking her head at her son and *s*	" xix.	24	And *s* follow'd, and we wept	" xxx.	20
turn'd *S*, and feign'd a sleep .	*Elaine*	838	here shall *s* guard thy fame ;	" lxxiv.	17
s 'let me rest' she said ; .	*En. Arden*	372	They haunt the *s* of the breast,	" xciii.	9
sight.			And strangely on the *s* broke	" xciv.	25
talking to himself, first met his *s* ;	*Love and Death*	6	And fell in *s* on his neck ; .	" cii.	8
blissful tears blinded my *s* .	*Oriana*	23	And, tho' in *s*, wishing joy. .	" Con.	88
To weave the mirror's magic *s's*	*L. of Shalott*, ii.	29	a *s* fell with the waking bird	*Maud*, 1. xxii.	17
I cannot veil, or droop my *s*,	*Eleänore*	87	pass Unclaim'd, in flushing *s*,	*The Brook*	105
Shudderest when I strain my *s*,	*Fatima*	3	wish Your warning or your *s* ?	*Enid*	926
Bursts into blossom in his *s*.	"	35	his command of *s* given,	"	1215-19
I shut my *s* for fear .	*(Enone*	184	In *s*, did him service as a squire ; .	"	1255
where'er she turn'd her *s* .	*Pal. of Art*	225	round his long sea-hall In *s*;	*Vivien*	82
polish'd argent of her breast to *s* .	*D. of F. Wom.*	158	let me think *S* is wisdom :	"	102
tell o'er Each little sound and *s*,	"	277	such a *s* is more wise than kind.'	"	138
Even in her *s* he loved so well?	*Margaret*	40	Dark-splendid, speaking in the *s*,	*Elaine*	337
a *s* to make an old man young.	*Gardener's D.*	140	standing by the shield In *s*,	"	394
Love at first *s*, first-born	"	185	little maid, who brook'd No *s*,	*Guinevere*	158
But not a creature was in *s* :	*Talking O.*	167	I cry my cry in *s*, .	"	199
trembling, pass'd in music out of *s*.	*Locksley H.*	34	howsoever much they may desire *S*,	"	205
Rain'd thro' my *s* its overflow.	*Two Voices*	55	then came *s*, then a voice,	"	416
And wasn't it a *s* to see .	*Amphion*	49	But Philip loved in *s* ; .	*En. Arden*	139
strange was the *s* .	*Princess, Pro.*	54, 89	Vocal, with here and there a *s*,	*Aylmer's F.*	146
Pretty were the *s* If our old halls .	"	139	With twenty months of *s*,	"	567
a *s* to shake The midriff of despair	" i.	197	a louder one Was all but *s*—	"	697
Pitiful *s*, wrapt in a soldier's cloak	" v.	53	felt the *s* of his house About him,	"	830
like to him whose *s* is lost ; .	*In Mem.* lxv.	8	escaped His keepers, and the *s*	"	839
Forgot his weakness in thy *s*.	" cix.	4	silenced by that *s* lay the wife,	*Sea Dreams*	46
by this my love has closed her *s*	*Maud*, I. xviii.	67	thou growest beautiful In *s*,	*Tithonus*	44
while I breath'd in *s* of haven,	*The Brook*	157	Thro' *s* and the trembling stars	*On a Mourner*	23
last *s* that Enid had of home	*Enid*	873			

silence (verb.)	POEM.	LINE.
ever widening slowly *s* all.	*Vivien*	242
surely can I *s* with all ease.	*Elaine*	110

silenced.
| *s* by that silence lay the wife, | *Sea Dreams* | 46 |

silent.
S into Camelot	*L. of Shalott,* iv.	41
s in its dusty vines:	*Mariana in the S.*	4
grasshopper is *s* in the grass:	*Œnone*	25
s in a last embrace.	*Locksley H.*	58
I pledge her *s* at the board:	*Will Water.*	25
knew us men, at first Was *s*,	*Princess,* iv.	213
s we with blind surmise	"	362
with his whelpless eye, *S;*	" vi.	84
Erect and *s*, striking with her glance	"	136
all *s*, save When armour clash'd	"	342
s in the muffled cage of life:	" vii.	32
Silence, till I he *s* too.	*In Mem.*xiii.	8
Sat *s*, looking each at each.	" xxx.	12
And *s* under other snows;	" civ.	6
is ever the one thing *s* here.	*Maud,* II. v.	68
voice is *s* in your council-hall	*Ode on Well.*	174
whatever tempests lour For ever *s*	"	176
even if they broke In thunder, *s;*	"	177
all narrow jealousies Are *s;*	*Ded. of Idylls*	16
Worn by the feet that now were *s,*	*Enid*	321
I am *s* then And ask no kiss;'	*Vivien*	102
We could not keep him *s,*	"	266
s, tho' he greeted her, she stood	*Elaine*	354
To hers which lay so *s,*	"	1278
bowed down upon her hands *S,*	*Guinevere*	157
Her own son Was *s,*	*En. Arden.*	479
s in her oriental haven.	"	533
Enoch rested *s* many days.	"	700
s when I spoke to-night?	*Sea Dreams*	259

silent-lighted.
| And pass the *s-l* town, | *In Mem.Con.*112 |

silently.
| *s*, in all obedience | *Enid* | 767 |

silent-speaking.
| on the silence broke The *s-s* words | *In Mem.*xciv. | 26 |

silk.
trod on *s*, as if the winds	*A Character*	21
s's, and fruits, and spices, clear of toll,	*Golden Year*	45
A gown of grass-green *s* she wore,	*Sir L. and Q. G.*	24
robed the shoulders in a rosy *s,*	*Princess, Pro.*	103
She brought us Academic *s's,*	" ii.	2
thro' the parted *s's* the tender face	" vii.	45
statue of Sir Kingdom From those rich *s's*	*Con.*	118
she bethought her of a faded *s.*	*Enid*	134
In summer suit and *s's* of holiday	"	173
seeing one so gay in purple *s's*	"	284
the fair Enid, all in faded *s,*	"	366
All staring at her in her faded *s :*	"	617
ride with me in her faded *s.*'	"	762
Enid ever kept the faded *s,*	"	841
tearing off her veil of faded *s*	"	1363
a splendid *s* of foreign loom,	"	1535
fashioned for it A case of *s,*	*Elaine*	8

silk-soft.
| *s-s* folds, upon yielding down | *Eleänore* | 28 |

silken-folded.
| fancies hatch'd In *s-f* idleness | *Princess,* iv. | 49 |

silken-sailed.
| The shallop flitteth *s-s* | *L. of Shalott,*i.22 |

silken-sandal'd.
| tapt her tiny *s-s* foot | *Princess, Pro.* 149 |

silver.
flaring bright From twisted *s's*	*Arabian N's.*	125
three on either side, Pure *s*	"	145
Twilights of airy *s,*	*Audley Ct.*	81
Sipt wine from *s*, praising God.	*Will Water.*	127
spread Their sleeping *s* thro' the hills;	*In Mem.Con.*116
cups and *s* on the burnish'd board	*En. Arden.*	743

silver-chiming.
| the central fountain's flow Fall'n *s-c* | *Arabian N's.* | 51 |

silver-clear.	POEM.	LINE.
A little whisper *s-c,*	*Two Voices*	428

silver-coasted.
| O saviour of the *s-c* isle, | *Ode on Well.* | 136 |

silver-gray.
| Will turn it *s-g;* | *The Ringlet* 6, | 16 |
| You should be *s-g;* | " | 30 |

silver-green.
| All *s-g* with gnarled bark; | *Mariana* | 42 |

silver-set.
| near his tomb a feast Shone, *s-s;* | *Princess,*Pro.106 |

silver-treble.
| *S-t* laughter trilleth: | *Lilian* | 24 |

silvery-crimson.
| They freshen the *s-c* shells | *Sea-Fairies* | 13 |

silvery-streak'd.
| And overstream'd and *s-s* | *The Islet* | 20 |

Simeon (see *Stylites*).
| 'Fall down, O *S*: thou hast suffer'd *St S. Stylites* 07 |
| Courage, St *S !* | " | 153 |
| I, *S* of the pillar, by surname Stylites(rep.)" | | 158 |

Simois.
| Came up from reedy *S* all alone | *Œnone* | 51 |
| Flash in the pools of whirling *S* | " | 202 |

simper.
| *s* and set their voices lower | *Maud,* I. x. | 15 |

simple (adj.)
Not *s* as a thing that dies	*Two Voices*	288
some of the *s* great ones gone	*Maud,* I. x.	61
Full *s* was her answer ' What know I?	*Elaine*	668

simple (s.)
| the hermit, skill'd in all The *s's* | *Elaine* | 858 |

simple-hearted.
| The seeming-injured *s-h* thing | *Vivien* | 751 |

simpler.
| guilt *S* than any child, | *Guinevere* | 369 |

simple-seeming.
| Our *s-s* Abbess and her nuns | *Guinevere* | 307 |

simplicity.
| In his *s* sublime | *Ode on Well.* | 34 |

sin (s.)
you are foul with *s;*	*Poet's Mind*	36
that will take away my *s,*	*Pal. of Art*	287
for he show'd me all the *s.*	*May Queen,*iii.17
one slough and crust of *s,*	*St S. Stylites*	2
mercy, Lord, and take away my *s.*	"	8,14
those lead-like tons of *s,*	"	25
subdue this home Of *s,* my flesh	"	57
mercy, mercy : cover all my *s.*	"	83
mercy, mercy ! wash away my *s.*	"	118
sinful man, conceiv'd and born in *s :*	"	120
On the coals I lay, A vessel full of *s :*	"	167
S itself be found The cloudy porch *Love and Duty* 8
To make me pure of *s,*	*St Agnes' Eve*	32
from the palace came a child of *s,*	*Vision of Sin*	5
s's of emptiness, gossip and spite	*Princess,* ii.	78
Forgive what seem'd my *s* in me	*In Mem. Pro.*	33
I sometimes hold it half a *s*	" v.	1
Thou fail not in a world *s,*	" xxxiii.	15
holds it *s* and shame to draw	" xlvii.	11
life is dash'd with flecks of *s.*	" li.	14
pangs of nature, *s's* of will,	" liii.	3
Ring out the want, the care, the *s*	" cv.	17
heap'd the whole inherited *s*	*Maud,*I.xiii.	41
Not touch on her father's *s*	" xix.	51
Whatever the Quaker holds, from *s;*	" II. v.	92
We might discuss the Northern *s*	*To F. D. Maurice*29
s that seem'd so like his own	*Enid*	594
s that practice burns into the blood,	*Vivien*	612
a face, bright as for *s* forgiven,	*Elaine*	1296
Such *s* in words, Perchance,	"	1182
men worse by making my *s* known?	"	1407
s seem less, the sinner seeming great?	"	1408

	POEM.	LINE.
Mine be the thame ; mine was the *s* ;	*Guinevere*	111
s's that made the past so pleasant	"	373
and as yet no *s* was dream'd	"	385
the *s* which thou hast sinn'd—	"	452
thy shameful *s* with Lancelot ;	"	483
came the *s* of Tristram and Isolt	"	484
in the golden days before thy *s*.	"	496
all is past, the *s* is sinn'd,	"	539
Gone thro' my *s* to slay and to be slain !	"	606
I cannot kill my *s*, If soul be soul ;	"	614
in mine own heart I can live down *s*	"	629
shroud this great *s* from all !	*Aylmer's F.*	773
the *s* That neither God nor man	*Sea Dreams*	62
says, our *s*'s should make us sad ;	*Grandmother*	93
An' a towd ma my *s*'s	*N. Farmer*	11
The wages of *s* is death,	*Wages*	6

sin (verb.)

s against the strength of youth !	*Locksley H.*	59
is your beauty, and I *s* In speaking	*Elaine*	1180
I almost *s* in envying you :	*Aylmer's F.*	360

Sinaï.

As over *S's* peaks of old	*In Mem.* xcv.	22

sine.

Of *s* and arc, spheroïd and azimuth,	*Princess*, vi.	239

sinecure.

So moulder'd in a *s* as he ;	*Princess*, Pro.	180

sinew.

home is in the *s*'s of a man,	*Princess*, v.	257

sinew-corded.

supple, *s-c*, apt at arms ;	*Princess*, v.	524

sinewed.

until endurance grow *S* with action	*Œnone*	162

sing.

S's a song of undying love ;	*Poet's Mind*	33
We will *s* to you all the day ;	*Sea-Fairies*	20
sit and *s* the whole of the day ;	*The Merman*	9
s to myself the whole of the day ;	*The Mermaid*	10
as I comb'd I would *s* and say,	"	12
bird would *s*, nor lamb would bleat, *Mariana in theS.*		37
Sometimes I heard you *s* within	*Miller's D.*	123
Ah, well—but *s* the foolish song	"	161
So *s* that other song I made,	"	199
To *s* her songs alone.	*Pal. of Art*	160
harken what the inner spirit *s*'s,	*Lotos-E's.*	67
and the minstrel *s*'s Before them	"	121
O Blackbird ! *s* me something well ;	*The Blackbird*	1
Take warning ! he that will not *s*	"	21
s for want, ere leaves are new,	"	23
Think you they *s* Like poets,	*Gardener's D.*	98
any sense of why they *s* ?	"	100
that still *S* in mine ears.	*St S. Stylites*	182
this is truth the poet *s*'s,	*Locksley H.*	75
Not even of a pant that *s*'s.	*Day-Dm.*	41
Ah shameless ! for he did but *s* '*You might have won*'		21
That he *s*'s in his boat on the bay I ' *Break, break* '		8
he *s*'s of what the world will be	*Poet's Song*	15
let the ladies *s* us, if they will,	*Princess,Pro.*	233
' Let some one *s* to us : lightlier move	" iv.	18
held it truth, with him who *s*'s	*In Mem.* i.	1
I *s* to him that rests below,	" xxi.	1
I do but *s* because I must,	"	23
pipe but as the linnets *s* ;	"	24
in the songs I love to *s*	" xxxviii.	7
Then are these songs I *s* of thee.	"	11
lay their eggs, and sting and *s*,	" xlix.	11
we do him wrong To *s* so wildly ;	" lvi.	4
And in that solace can I *s*,	" lxiv.	5
voice the richest-toned that *s*'s	" lxxiv.	7
For him she plays, to him she *s*'s	" xcvi.	29
one would *s* the death of war.	" cii.	33
And *s* the songs he loved to hear.	" cvi.	10
To the ballad that she *s*'s	*Maud*, II.iv.	43
Do I hear her *s* as of old,	"	44
That *s*'s so delicately clear,	*Enid*	332
heard the great Sir Lancelot *s* it	*Vivien*	235
every minstrel *s*'s it differently ;	"	308

	POEM.	LINE.
s the simple passage o'er and o'er	*Elaine*	852
sweetly could she make and *s*.	"	1060
if indeed you list to *s*, *S*,	*Guinevere*	163
and every bird that *s*'s ;	*Sea Dreams*	160
sleep, And I will *s* you ' birdie.'	"	273
I hear them too—they *s* to their team : *Grandmother* 81		
strange song I heard Apollo *s*	*Tithonus*	62
O skill'd to *s* of 'Time and Eternity, *Milton*		2
to dance and *s*, be gaily drest	*Coquette*, ii.	3

singer.

The sweet little wife of the *s* said,	*The Islet*	3
And the *s* shaking his curly head	"	6

singing.

S alone Under the sea,	*The Merman*	4
A mermaid fair, *S* alone,	*The Mermaid*	3
heard her *s* her last song,	*L. of Shalott*, iv.	26
S in her song she died,	"	35
S and murmuring in her feastful mirth, *Pal.of Art*177		
s clearer than the crested bird	*D. of F. Wom.*	179
And we with *s* cheer'd the way,	*In Mem.* xxii.	5
She is *s* an air that is known to me	*Maud*, I. v.	3
S alone in the morning of life	"	6
S of men that in battle array	"	8
S of Death and of Honour	"	16
She is *s* in the meadow,	" II. iv.	40
casement of the Hall, *S* ;	*Enid*	329
half *s* a coarse song,	"	1377
he is *s* Hosanna in the highest	*En. Arden*.	498
S ' and shall it be over the seas	*The Islet*	9
s airy trifles this or that,	*Coquette*, i.	2

single.

in thee Is nothing sudden, nothing *s* ;	*Eleänore*	57
S I grew, like some green plant, *D. of F. Wom.*		205
make an onslaught *s* on a realm	*Enid*	1765

sink.

And while he *s*'s or swells	*Talking O.*	270
s's the nebulous star we call the Sun, *Princess*, iv.		1
s's with all we love below the verge	"	29
they rise or *s* Together,	" vii.	243
staggers blindly ere she *s* ?	*In Mem.*xvi.	14
So much the vital spirits *s*	" xx.	18
'Twere best at once to *s* to peace,	" xxxiv.	13
When in the down I *s* my head,	" lxvii.	1
And the great Æon *s*'s in blood,	" cxxvi.	16
we scarce can *s* as low ;	*Vivien*	662
I cannot *s* So far—far down ' *My life is full,' etc.*		8
out of sight, and *s* Past earthquake *Lucretius*		152

sinned.

I have *s*, for it was all thro' me	*Dora*	58
Alas, my child, I *s* for thee.'	*Lady Clare*	50
s in grosser lips Beyond all pardon *Princess*, iv.		232
that he *s*, is not believable ;	*Vivien*	610
if he *s*, The sin that practice burns	"	611
the sin which thou hast *s*.	*Guinevere*	452
ensample from fair names, *S* also,	"	487
all is past, the sin is *s*,	"	539
in the flesh thou hast *s* ;	"	550

sinner.

I am a *s* viler than you all.	*St S. Stylites*	133
In haunts of hungry *s*'s,	*Will Water.*	222
Thou hast been a *s* too ;	*Vision of Sin*	92
sin seem less, the *s* seeming great ?	*Elaine*	1408

sinning.

Another *s* on such height, with one,	*Elaine*	248

sipt.

S wine from silver, praising God,	*Will Water.*	127

Sir.

these great *S*'s Give up their parks*Princess, Con.*102		

sire.

to die For God and for my *s* !	*D.of F. Wom.*	222
That we are wiser than our *s*'s. '*Love thou thy land*'72		
I read—two letters—one her *s*'s.	*Princess*, iv.	378
my *S*, his rough cheek wet with tears	" v.	102
White hands of farewell to my *s*,	"	223
' O *S*,' she said, ' he lives ;	" vi.	106
brake out my *s* Lifting his grim head	"	254

	POEM.	LINE.
yet-loved *s* would make Confusion	*In Mem.*lxxxix.	18
What said the happy *s*? . . *Vivien*	.	560

siren.

| O sister, *S's* tho' they be, were such *Princess*, ii. | 181 |

Sirius.

| as the fiery *S* alters hue . . *Princess*, v. | 252 |

sister.

	POEM.	LINE.
three *s's* That doat upon *To* ——. *With Pal. of Art*		10
greet their fairer *s's* of the East. . *Gardener's D.*		184
Stole from her *s* Sorrow. . . "	.	251
Sleep, Ellen, folded in thy *s's* arm, *Audley Ct.* .	.	62
shouts with his *s* at play ! 'Break, break,' etc.		6
I have a *s* at the foreign court, . *Princess*, i.		74
'My *s.*' 'Comely too . . . " ii.		99
'My brother !' 'Well, my *s.*' . . "		171
O *s*, Sirens tho' they be, were such "		181
Here lies a brother by a s *slain*, . . "		191
when your *s* came she won the heart "	iii.	71
compass our dear *s's* liberties.' . . "		271
Shall croak thee *s*, . . . "	iv.	106
Lift up your head, sweet *s*: . . "	v.	61
clung The shadow of his *s*, . . "	.	248
and in our noble *s's* cause ? . . "	.	302
Old *s's* of a day gone by, . *In Mem.*xxix.		13
Leave thou thy *s* when she prays "	xxxiii.	5
A guest, or happy *s*, sung . " lxxxviii.		26
Has not his *s* smiled on me ? . *Maud,* I.xii.		45
Among her burnish'd *s's* of the pool. *Enid*		655
Would call her friend and *s*, . *Elaine*		861
'Ah *s*,' answer'd Lancelot, . . "		927
'Peace to thee Sweet *s*,' . . "		991
To which the gentle *s* made reply, "		1067
'S, farewell for ever,' (rep.) . . "		1145
must strike against my *s's* son, . *Guinevere*		568
Nor shun to call me *s*, . . . "		668
My *s's* crying 'stay for shame ;' . *Sailor Boy*	.	18

sister-eyelids.

| The dewy *s-e* lay. . . . *Day-Dm.* | . | 4 |

sisterhood.

| O peaceful *S*, Receive | . *Guinevere* | . 139 |

sister-world.

| glow Thy silver *s-w,* . '*Move eastward,*' etc. | | 6 |

sit.

Low-cowering shall the sophist *s*; { 'Clear-headed *s friend,*'etc.		10
The white owl in the belfry *s's*. . *The Owl,* i. 7,		14
s and sing the whole of the day ; . *The Merman*		9
In yonder chair I see him *s*, . *Miller's D.*		9
'by that lamp,' I thought, 'she *s's* !' "		114
Sometimes I saw you *s* and spin ;. . "		121
I *s* as God holding no form of creed, *Pal. of Art*		211
But *s* beside my bed, mother . *May Queen*,iii.		23
you *s* between Joy and woe, . *Margaret*	.	63
to *s*, to sleep, to wake, to breathe.' *Ed. Morris*		40
S with their wives by fires, . . *St S. Stylites*		106
S brooding in the ruins of a life, *Love and Duty*		12
Here *s's* he shaping wings to fly :. *Two Voices*		289
Here *s's* the Butler with a flask . *Day-Dm.*	.	45
I *s* (my empty glass reversed), . *Will Water.*		159
S thee down, and have no shame, *Vision of Sin*		83
s beside your feet And glean . *Princess,* ii.		240
beneath an emerald plane *S's* Diotima " iii.		285
I will go and *s* beside the doors, . "	v.	93
may *s* Upon a king's right hand . "		428
To *s* a star upon the sparkling spire ; "	vii.	182
upon the skirts of Time, *S* side by side "		272
I *s* within a helmless bark . . *In Mem.* iv.		3
back return To where the body *s's*, "	xii.	19
By the hearth the children *s* . "	xx.	13
The Shadow *s's* and waits for me. "	xxii.	20
Alone, alone, to where he *s's*, . "	xxiii.	3
he was dead, and there he *s's*, . "	xxxii.	3
And we shall *s* at endless feast, . "	xlvi.	9
Her life is lone, he *s's* apart, . "	xcvi.	17
on her forehead *s's* a fire ; . "	cxiii.	5

	POEM.	LINE.
In the little grove where I *s* . *Maud,* I. iv, 2,		24
Why *s's* he here in his father's chair " xlii.		23
She *s's* by her music and books, . " xiv.		13
s's on her shining head . . " xvi.		17
your good damsel there who *s's* apart, *Enid*		1148
I see it with joy—You *s* apart, . "		1170
He *s's* unarmed ; I hold a finger up; "		1186
sung nearly where we *s*; . *Vivien*	.	256
I *s* and gather honey ; . . "	.	451
They *s* with knife in meat . . "	.	544
To *s* once more within his lonely hall, *Guinevere*		493
God bless him, he shall *s* upon my knees *En. Arden*		197
S, listen.' Then he told her . "	.	862
S down again ; mark me . . "	.	877
They come and *s* by my chair, . *Grandmother*		83
To *s* with empty hands at home. . *Sailor Boy*		16
See they *s*, they hide their faces, *Boädicea*	.	51
care to *s* beside her where she *s's*— *Coquette,* iii.		10
All alone she *s's* and hears '*Home they brought*'		3
s the best and stateliest of the land? *Lucretius*		172

sittest.

| That *s* ranging golden hair ; . *In Mem.* vi. | | 26 |

sittin'.

| an' a *s* 'ere o' my bed, . . *N. Farmer* | | 9 |

sitting.

charm Pallas and Juno *s* by ; . *A Character*		15
A merman bold, *S* alone, . *The Merman*		3
on this hand, and *s* on this stone ? *Œnone*		229
I saw you *s* in the house, . *May Queen,* iii.		30
s on a crimson scarf unroll'd ; . *D. of F. Wom.*		126
s girt with doubtful light. '*Love thou thy land*'		16
s, served by man and maid, . *The Goose*	.	21
s in the deeps Upon the hidden bases *M. d' Arthur*105		
we *s*, as I said, The cock crew " *Ep.*		9
she *s* with us then, . . *Gardener's D.*		21
s muffled in dark leaves, . . "	.	37
s straight Within the low-wheel'd chaise, *Talking O.*		101
Push off, and *s* well in order smite *Ulysses*		58
s, burnish'd without fear The brand, *Two Voices*		128
s, lying, languid shapes, . *Vision of Sin*		12
As night to him that *s* on a hill . *Princess,* iv.		551
I see thee *s* crown'd with good, . *In Mem.* lxxxii.		5
Peace *s* under her olive . . *Maud,* I. i.		33
she *s* so stunn'd and still . " II. i.		2
on a day, he *s* high in hall, . *Enid*	.	147
knew her *s* sad and solitary. . "		1131
Enoch and Annie, *s* hand in hand, *En. Arden.*		69
s at her side forgot Her presence, "		381
lo ! her Enoch *s* on a height . "		496
s all alone, his face Would darken, *Sea Dreams*		12
I am oftener *s* at home . . *Grandmother*		90
They found the mother *s* still ; . *The Victim*		32

sitting-room.

| To fit their little streetward *s-r* . *En. Arden.* | | 170 |

six hundred.

| Rode the *s h.* . . . *Lt. Brigade* 3, *et pass.* | | |

sixpence.

| Be shot for *s* in a battle-field, . *Audley Ct.* | . | 40 |

size.

His double chin, his portly *s*, . *Miller's D.*		2
This weight and *s*, this heart and eyes, *Sir Galahad*		71
often fineness compensated *s* . *Princess,* ii.		133

skate.

| taught me how to *s*, to row, . *Ed. Morris* | | 19 |

skater.

| the *s* on ice that hardly bears him, *Hendecasyllabics* | | 6 |

skeleton.

the bare-grinning *s* of death ! . *Vivien*	.	696
Had trodden that crown'd *s*, . *Elaine*	.	50
Gaunt as it were the *s* of himself, " 760-		812
make the carcase a *s*, . *Boädicea*	.	14

sketch.

No matter what the *s* might be ; . *Ode to Mem.*		95
Buss me, thou rough *s* of man, . *Vision of Sin*		189
s'es rude and faint, . . *Aylmer's F.*		100

	sketcher.	POEM. LINE
I was a *s* then: See here,	*Ed. Morris*	4
	sketching.	
s with her slender pointed foot	*The Brook.*	102
	skill.	
Nor mine the sweetness or the *s*,	*In Mem.* cix.	17
with force and *s* To strive	" cxii.	6
	skill'd	
the hermit, *s* in all The simples	*Elaine*	837
O *s* to sing of Time and Eternity,	*Milton*	2
	skim.	
wings in tears, and *s* away.	*In Mem* xlvii.	16
	skimm'd.	
fleeter now she *s* the plains	*Sir L. and Q.G.*	32
	skimming.	
S down to Camelot:	*L. of Shalott*, i.	23
	skin (s.)	
A million wrinkles carved his *s*;	*Pal. of Art*	138
they roll a prurient *s*,	"	201
a *s* As clean and white as privet	*Walk to the M.*	47
scratch No deeper than the *s*:	*Ed. Morris*	64
the ulcer, eating thro' my *s*,	*St. S. Stylites*	66
We fret, we fume, would shift our *s's*,	*Will Water.*	225
s of wine, and piles of grapes.	*Vision of Sin*	13
or wooded, winter-clad in *s's*	*Princess*, ii	105
hunt them for the beauty of their *s's*	" v.	149
Prickle my *s* and catch my breath	*Maud*, I xiv.	36
the *s* Clung but to crate and basket	*Vivien*	474
	skin (verb.)	
s's the wild beast after slaying him	*Enid*	942
	skirt (s.)	
Brightening the *s's* of a long cloud	*M. d'Arthur*	54
thro' warp and woof From *s* to *s*;	*Princess*, i.	62
the *s* and fringe of our fair land,	" v.	210
upon the *s's* of Time, Sit side by side	" vii.	271
more than seen, the *s's* of France.	" Con.	43
fusing all The *s's* of self again,	*In Mem.* xlvi.	3
grasps the *s's* of happy chance,	" lxiii.	6
s are loosen'd by the breaking storm	*Enid.*	1308
gloomy *s's* Of Celidon the forest:	*Elaine*	291
thro' the gray *s's* of a lifting squall	*En. Arden.*	830
	skirt (verb.)	
oft when sundown *s's* the moor	*In Mem.* xl.	17
	skull.	
Is but modell'd on a *s*.	*Vision of Sin*	178
on the *s* which thou hast made	*In Mem. Pro.*	8
and the *s* Brake from the nape,	*Elaine*	50
from the *s* the crown Roll'd	"	52
	sky.	
thickest dark did trance the *s*,	*Mariana*	18
trenched waters run from *s* to *s*,	*Ode to Mem.*	104
When thou gazest at the *skies*?	*Adeline*	50
With a half-glance upon the *s*	*A Character*	5
Sunn'd by those orient *skies*.	*The Poet*	42
white against the cold-white *s*,	*Dying Swan*	12
comest atween me and the *skies*,	*Oriana*	75
clothe the wold and meet the *s*;	*L. of Shalott*, i.	3
Heavily the low *s* raining	" iv.	4
Grow golden all about the *s*,	*Eleänore*	101
skies stoop down in their desire;	*Fatima*	32
All naked in a sultry *s*,	"	37
s Dipt down to sea and sands.	*Pal. of Art*	32
as a flying star shot thro' the *s*	"	123
violet, that comes beneath the *skies*,	*May Queen*, iii.	5
sleep down from the blissful *skies*	*Lotos-E's.*	52
Hateful is the dark-blue *s*,	"	84
next moon was roll'd into the *s*,	*D. of F. Wom.*	229
Ruled in the eastern *s*.	"	264
I seek a warmer *s*,	*'You ask me why,' etc.*	26
whatever *s* Bear seed of men	*'Love thou thy land'*	19
mellow moons and happy *skies*,	*Locksley H.*	39
He travels far from other *skies*—	*Day-Dm.*	105
clear As are the frosty *skies*,	*St. Agnes' Eve*	10
The clouds are broken in the *s*,	*Sir Galahad*	73
shines the moon in clouded *skies*,	*Beggar Maid*	9
Flutter'd headlong from the *s*.	*Vision of Sin*	45

		POEM. LINE.
O love, they die in yon rich *s*,	*Princess*, iii.	360
When your *skies* change again:	" vi	261
A web is wov'n across the *s*;	*In Mem.* iii.	6
reach the glow of southern *skies*	" xii.	10
rooks are blown about the *skies*;	" xv.	4
circles of the bounding *s*,	" xvii.	6
The baby new to earth and *s*	" xliv.	1
roll'd the psalm to wintry *skies*	" lv.	11
For pastime, dreaming of the *s*;	" lxv.	14
sow the *s* with flying boughs,	" lxxi.	24
o'er the *s* The silvery haze	" xciv.	3
bats went round in fragrant *skies*,	"	9
Where first we gazed upon the *s*;	" ci.	2
Ring out wild bells to the wild *s*,	" cv.	1
Of sorrow under human *skies*:	" cvii.	14
change their *s* To build and brood;	" cxiv.	15
The brute earth lightens to the *s*,	" cxxvi.	15
wild voice pealing up to the sunny *s*	*Maud*, I. v.	13
makes you tyrants in your iron *skies*	" xviii.	37
countercharm of space and hollow *s*	"	43
On a bed of daffodils	" xxii	10
dawn of Eden bright over earth and *s*,	" II. i.	8
The delight of early *skies*;	" iv.	25
This nurseling of another *s*	*The Daisy*	08
show'd themselves against the *s*, and sank	*Enid*	240
crests that smoke against the *skies*,	*Elaine*	483
every land beneath the *skies*,	*On a Mourner*	3
or to bask in a summer *s*;	*Wages*	9
Such another beneath the *s*?	*The Window*	87
	skylark.	
some wild *s's* matin song	*Miller's D.*	40
	slacken.	
I saw it and grieved—to *s* and to cool;	*Princess*, iv.	280
	slacken'd.	
His bow-string *s*, languid Love	*Eleänore*	117
their pace at first, but *s* soon.	*Enid.*	842
	slag.	
foreground black with stones and *s's*,	*Pal. of Art*	81
	slain.	
With thine own weapon art thou *s*,	*Two Voices*	311
Here lies a brother by a sister's	*Princess*, ii.	101
s with laughter roll'd the gilded Squire	" v.	73
a great cry, The Prince is *s*.	" vi.	10
make her as the man, Sweet Love were *s*:	" vii.	261
huge Earl lay *s* within his hall.	*Enid.*	1654
I should have *s* your father,	"	1686
after furious battle turfs the *s*	*Vivien*	507
each had *s* his brother at a blow,	*Elaine*	42
High on a heap of *s*,	"	307
but many a knight was *s*;	*Guinevere*	435
thro' my sin to slay and to be *s*!	"	601
they brought him *s* with *'Home they brought him*	1
	slake.	
Let her go! her thirst she *s's*	*Vision of Sin*	143
	slander.	
Thee nor carketh care nor *s*:	*A Dirge*	8
emptiness, gossip and spite And *s*	*Princess*, ii.	70
The civic *s* and the spite	*In Mem* cv.	22
'Thro *s*, meanest spawn of Hell	*The Letters*	33
(And women's *s* is the worst)	"	34
spake no *s*, no, nor listen'd to it	*Ded. of Idylls*	0
sow'd a *s* in the common ear	*Enid.*	450
faintly-venom'd points Of *s*,	*Vivien*	21
these are *s's*: never yet Was noble man	*Elaine*	1081
speak no *s*, no, nor listen to it,	*Guinevere*	463
	slander (verb.)	
the hollow heart they *s* so!	*Princess*, vi.	270
ever ready to *s* and steal;	*Maud*, I. iv.	56
Jenny, to *s* me, who knew what Jenny	*Grandmother*	35
	slander'd.	
he thought, had *s* Leolin to him.	*Aylmer's F.*	350
	slandering.	
And she to be coming and *s* me,	*Grandmother*	27
	slant.	
S down the snowy sward,	*St. Agnes' Eve*	6

	POEM.	LINE.
huddling *s* in furrow-cloven falls	*Princess*, vii.	192
To *s* the fifth autumnal slope,	*In Mem.* xxii.	10

slanted.

	POEM.	LINE.
a beam Had *s* forward .	*Princess*, ii.	123
Long lanes of splendour *s* o'er a press	" iv.	457

slanting.

| reach'd a meadow *s* to the North . | *Gardener's D.* | 107 |

slate-quarry.

| I heard them blast The steep *s-q*, | *Golden Year* | 75 |

slaughter.

beat her foes with *s* from her walls	*Princess, Pro.*	34, 123
Ran the land with Roman *s*,	*Boädicea* .	84
Dismal error! fearful *s!* .	*The Captain*	65

slaughter-house.

| makes a steaming *s-h* of Rome. | *Lucretius* . | 84 |

slave.

Of child, and wife, and *s;* .	*Lotos-E's*.	40
Drink deep, until the habits of the *s*,	*Princess*, ii.	77
play the *s* to gain the tyranny.	" iv.	114
s's at home and fools abroad.'	" v.	500
or brought her chain'd, a *s*, .	" v.	133

slay.

arise and *s* thee with my hands.	*M. d'Arthur*	132
lift His axe to *s* my kin .	*Talking O.*	236
s this child, if good need were, .	*Princess*, ii.	267
that except you *s* me here .	" iv.	433
you could not *s* Me, nor your prince:	" v.	62
we will *s* him and will have his horse	*Enid* .	911
would *s* you, and possess your horse	"	923
'Fly, they will return And *s* you;	"	1597
'*S* not a dead man!' .	"	1627
s not him who gave you life.' .	"	1631
to *s* the folk, and spoil the land.' .	*Guinevere*	136
thro' my sin to *s* and to be slain !	"	606

slaying.

| be he wroth even to *s* me, . | *Enid* . | 916 |
| skins the wild beast after *s* him, . | " | 942 |

sleek (adj.)

| chisell'd features clear and *s*. | *A Character* | 30 |
| And, issuing shorn and *s*, . | *Talking O.* | 42 |

sleek (verb.)

| To *s* her ruffled peace of mind, . | *Vivien* . | 748 |

sleeked.

| smooth'd his chin and *s* his hair | *A Character* | 11 |

sleeker.

| Had been the *s* for it : . . | *Elaine* . | 250 |

sleep (s.)

In *s* she seem'd to walk forlorn	*Mariana*	30
in *s* I sank In cool soft turf .	*Arabian N's.*	95
coiled *s's* in the central deeps	*The Mermaid*	24
breathed in *s* a lower moan,	*Mariana in the S.*	45
Each morn my *s* was broken thro'	*Miller's D.*	39
Softer than *s*—all things in order	*Pal. of Art*	87
sweet *s* down from the blissful skies.	*Lotos-E's*.	52
the poppy hangs in *s*, .	"	56
brought Into the gulfs of *s*.	*D. of F. Wom.*	52
We drank the Libyan Sun to *s*,	"	145
dissolved the mystery Of folded *s*.	"	263
I from *s* To gather and tell o'er	"	275
Such a *s* They sleep . .	*M. d'Arthur*	16
yet in *s* I seem'd To sail .	" *Ep.*	16
in her bosom bore the baby, *S.*	*Gardener's D.*	263
a cry Should break his *s* by night	*Walk. to the M.*	66
after a little *s*, I wake : .	*St S. Stylites*	111
But, rolling as in *s*, . .	*Talking O.*	278
pointing to his drunken *s*, .	*Locksley H.*	81
'O eyes long laid in happy *s!*	*Day-Dm.*	181
'O happy *s*, that lightly fled !'	"	182
'O happy kiss, that woke thy *s!*'	"	183
So sleeping, so aroused from *s*	"	233
Yet sleeps a dreamless *s* to me ; .	"	262
As *s* by kisses undissolved, .	"	263
Echo answer'd in her *s* . .	*Princess, Pro.*	66
tinged with wan from lack of *s*,	" iii.	9
more than infants in their *s*.	*Princess*, vii.	39
thro' and thro' with Love, a happy *s*	"	157
To *S* I give my powers away ; .	*In Mem.* iv.	1
Calm on the seas, and silver *s*,	" xi.	17
A late-lost form that *s* reveals,	" xiii.	2
sleeps or wears the mask of *s* .	" xviii.	10
'They rest,' we said, 'their *s* is sweet,'	" xxx.	19
If *S* and death be truly one, .	" xlii.	1
S, Death's twin-brother (rep.) .	" lxvii.	2
foolish *s* transfers to thee .	"	16
S, kinsman thou to death and trance	" lxx.	1
And *S* must lie down arm'd .	*Maud*, I. i.	41
death-white curtain meant but *s*.	" xiv.	37
thought like a fool of the *s* of death.	"	38
and held her from her *s* . .	*Elaine* .	338
he roll'd his eyes Yet blank from *s*,	"	816
feign'd a *s* until he slept .	"	838
Chaner of *s*, and wine, and exercise,	*Aylmer's F.*	448
came upon him half arisen from *s*,	"	584
sank As into *s* again. . .	"	592
sleeps—another *s* than ours. .	*Sea Dreams*	208
let your *s* for this one night be sound :	"	302

sleep (verb.)

I *s* forgotten, I wake forlorn.'	*Mariana in the S.*	36
and the cicala *s's*. . .	*Œnone*	27
S's on his luminous ring.' .	*Pal. of Art*	16
graze and wallow, breed and *s;* .	"	202
I *s* so sound all night, mother,	*May Queen*, i.	9
The place of him that *s's* in peace	*To J. S.*	68
S sweetly, tender heart, in peace :	"	69
S, holy spirit, blessed soul, .	"	70
S till the end, true soul and sweet.	"	73
S full of rest from head to feet .	"	75
Such a sleep They *s*— .	*M. d'Arthur*	17
home I went, but could not *s* for joy,	*Gardener's D.*	170
S, Ellen Aubrey, *s*, and dream (rep.)	*Audley Ct.*	61
to sit, to *s*, to wake, to breathe.'	*Ed. Morris*	40
We *s* and wake and *s*, but all things	*Golden Year*	22
s and feed, and know not me.	*Ulysses*	5
Thine anguish will not let thee *s*,	*Two Voices*	49
Go, vexed Spirit, *s* in trust ; .	"	115
Each baron at the banquet *s's*,	*Day-Dm.*	57
She *s's:* her breathings are not heard	"	93
She *s's:* on either hand upswells	"	97
She *s's*, nor dreams, but ever dwells	"	99
I'd *s* another hundred years, .	"	173
And learn the world, and *s* again ;	"	220
To *s* thro' terms of mighty wars .	"	221
Yet *s's* a dreamless sleep to me ; .	"	262
while my pretty one, *s's*. (rep.) .	*Princess*, ii.	463
S and rest, *s* and rest, . .	"	464
Behold me, for I cannot *s*, .	*In Mem.* vii.	6
S, gentle heavens, before the prow ;	" ix.	14
S, gentle winds, as he *s's* now,	"	15
S's or wears the mask of sleep .	" xviii.	10
I *s* till dusk is dipt in gray . .	" lxvi.	12
Long *s's* the summer in the seed .	" civ.	26
Whatever wisdom *s* with thee .	" cvii.	16
how much wisdom *s's* with thee .	" cxii.	2
I come once more ; the city *s's;* .	" cxviii.	3
s Encompass'd by his faithful guard,	" cxxv.	7
My dearest brother, Edmund, *s's*,	*The Brook*	187
s's in peace : and he, Poor Philip	"	190
Look how she *s's*—the Fairy Queen,	*Elaine*	1248
'Wake him not ; let him *s;* .	*En. Arden*	232
it chanced That Annie could not *s*,	"	486
S's in the plain eggs of the nightingale	*Aylmer's F.*	103
S, little birdie, *s!* will she not *s* (rep.)	*Sea Dreams*	271
She *s's;* let us too, let all evil, *s*. .	"	297
He also *s's*—another sleep than ours.	"	298
And I shall *s* the sounder I' .	"	300
s beneath his pillar'd light ! .	*The Voyage*	20

sleeper.

watch the *s's* from the wall. .	*Day-Dm.*	44
Me, that was never a quiet *s?*	*Maud*, II. v.	98
Beat, till she woke the *s's*, .	*Enid* .	1253

sleepeth.

| *S* over all the heaven, . . | *Eleänore* . | 33 |

	POEM.	LINE
sleeping.		
you were *s;* and I said, 'It's not	*MayQueen*,iii.	37
s, haply dream her arm is mine.	*Audley Ct.*	63
So *s*, so aroused from sleep,	*Day-Dm.*	233
summer morn (They *s* by each other)	*Enid*	70
thought me *s*, but I heard you say,	"	1589
while the two were *s*, a full tide Rose	*Sea Dreams*	50
sleepy.		
I, though *s*, like a horse That hears	*The Epic*	44
so *s* was the land.	*Aylmer's F.*	45
sleet.		
hail, damp, and *s*, and snow;	*St.S. Stylites*	16
S of diamond-drift and pearly hail;	*Vision of Sin*	22
sleeve.		
Devils pluck'd my *s*;	*St.S. Stylites*	168
'a red *s* broider'd with pearls,'	*Elaine*	371
his the prize, who wore the *s* Of scarlet,	"	500
upon his helm A *s* of scarlet,	"	602
What of the knight with the red *s*?'	"	618
he wore your *s* : Would he break faith	"	681
on the maid, Whose *s* he wore;	"	707
her scarlet *s*, Tho' carved and cut,	"	802
helm, from which her *s* had gone.	"	976
slept.		
A sluice with blacken'd waters *s*,	*Mariana*	38
Adown to where the water *s*.	*Arabian N's.*	30
The tangled water-courses *s*,	*Dying Swan*	19
now at noon she *s* again,	*Mariana in the S.*	41
s St Cecily : An angel look'd at her.	*Pal. of Art*	99
linger'd there Till every daisy *s*	*Gardener's D.*	161
Touch'd by his feet the daisy *s*,	*Two Voices*	276
How say you? we have *s*, my lords.	*Day-Dm.*	153
elbow-deep in sawdust, *s*,	*Will Water.*	99
a double April old, Aglaïa *s*.	*Princess*, ii.	96
silent light *S* on the painted walls,	" vii.	106
I sank and *s*, Fill'd thro' and thro'	"	156
This year I *s* and woke with pain,	*In Mem.* xxviii.	13
over all things brooding *s*	" lxxvii.	7
God's finger touch'd him, and he *s*,	" lxxxiv.	20
landlike *s* along the deep.	" cii.	56
Of Queen Theodolind, where we *s*;	*The Daisy*	80
Or hardly *s*, but watch'd awake	"	81
Woke where he *s* in the high hall,	*Enid*	755
made for the couch and *s*,	*Vivien*	586
either *s*, nor knew of other there;	"	588
told her all the charm, and *s*.	"	815
gain'd the cell in which he *s*,	*Elaine*	807
feign'd a sleep until he *s*.	"	838
if she *s*, she dream'd An awful dream	*Guinevere*	75
Ascending tired, heavily *s* till morn	*En. Arden*	181
the third, the sickly one, who *s*	"	229
she closed the Book and *s*:	"	495
s, woke, and went the next,	*Sea Dreams*	18
up the stream In fancy, till I *s* again,	"	105
will be the sweeter,' and they *s*.	"	304
fain had *s* at his side.	*Grandmother*	74
slew.		
s him with your noble birth,	*L. C. V. de Vere*	48
tho' I *s* thee with my hand !	*Locksley H.*	56
S both his sons;	*Princess*, ii.	268
my brother *s* him for it.'	" vi.	92
stunn'd the twain Or *s* them,	*Enid*	941
tho' he *s* them one by one,	"	1766
own traditions God, and *s* the Lord,	*Aylmer's F.*	795
slid.		
Night *s* down one long stream	*Gardener's D.*	262
Another *s*, a sunny fleck,	*Talking O.*	223
s From pillar unto pillar,	*Godiva*	49
The sullen answer *s* betwixt:	*Two Voices*	226
The snake of gold *s* from her hair,	*Vivien*	717
There from his charger down he *s*,	*Elaine*	509
slide.		
S the heavy barges trail'd	*L. of Shalott*, i.	20
up a quiet cove Rolling *s*.	*Eleänore*	109
S's the bird o'er lustrous woodland,	*Locksley H.*	162
I fear to *s* from bad to worse.	*Two Voices*	231
down dark tides the glory *s's*,	*Sir Galahad*	47
as the waterlily starts and *s's*	*Princess*, iv.	236
Now *s's* the silent meteor on,	" vii.	169
S from the bosom of the stars.	*In Mem.* xvii.	16
I *s* by hazel covers ;	*The Brook*	171
I slip, I *s*, I gloom, I glance	"	174
S from that quiet heaven of hers,	*Lucretius*	67
slided.		
tremulous isles of light *S*,	*Princess*, vi.	66
s up his knee and sat,	*Vivien*	83
sliding.		
Come *s* out of her sacred glove,	*Maud*, I. vi.	85
On to the palace-doorway *s*.	*Elaine*	1239
slight (adj.)		
'You 're too *s* and fickle,' I said,	*Ed. Gray*	19
for such, my friend, We hold them *s* :	*Princess*, iv.	109
We are fools and *s*	*In Mem. l'ro.*	29
How dimly character'd and *s*	" lx.	6
S, to be crush'd with a tap.	*Maud*, II. ii	21
S was his answer 'Well—I care not	*Aylmer's F.*	238
slight (s.)		
To look at her with *s*, and say	*Mariana in the S.*	66
slight (verb.)		
yet you dared To *s* it.	*Dora*	97
hardness, and to *s* His mother;	"	118
will learn to *s* His father's memory;	"	150
He seems to *s* her simple heart.	*In Mem.* xcvi.	20
A song that *s's* the coming care,	" xcviii.	10
Why *s* your King And lose the quest	*Elaine*	652
Wherefore *s* me not wholly.	*Hendecasyllabics*	15
slight-natured.		
If she be small, *s-n*, miserable,	*Princess*, vii.	249
slime.		
tare each other in their *s*,	*In Mem.* lv.	23
slimed		
snakelike *s* his victim ere he gorged ;	*Sea Dreams*	183
slink.		
As boys that *s* From ferule.	*Princess*, v.	35
slip (s.)		
moon-lit *s's* of silver cloud	*Œnone*	214
show you *s's* of all that grows	*Amphion*	83
great heart, and *s's* in sensual mire,	*Princess*, v.	191
slip (verb.)		
Could *s* its bark and walk	*Talking O.*	188
Sometimes I let a sunbeam *s*,	"	217
to *s* away, To-day, to-morrow, soon ;	*Princess*, ii.	276
s at once all-fragrant into one.	" vii.	55
s's into the bosom of the lake :	"	172
and *s* Into my bosom	"	173
s the thoughts of life and death ;	*In Mem.* cxxi.	16
Or *s* between the ridges,	*The Brook*	28
I *s*, I slide, I gloom, I glance,	"	174
not let his name *S* from my lips	*Enid*	446
by and by *S's* into golden cloud,	"	736
s From the long shore-cliff's windy	"	1012
moon comes, 'Time *s's* away,	*The Window*	163
slipper		
fit to wear Your *s* for a glove.	*Enid*	1471
slippery.		
that it was too *s* to be held,	*Elaine*	213
slipping.		
three times *s* from the outer edge	*The Epic*	11
The *s* thro' from state to state.	*Two Voices*	351
Went *s* down horrible precipices,	*Enid*	1228
S o'ur their shadows on the sand,	"	1320
S back upon the golden days	*Guinevere*	377
The silent water *s* from the hills,	*En. Arden*	634
slipt.		
'Tis gone : a thousand such have *s*	*Will Water*	181
The snake *s* under a spray.	*Poet's Song*	10
I *s* out : but whither will you	*Princess*, iv.	221
S round and in the dark invested you,	"	385
blossom-fragrant *s* the heavy dews	" vii.	233
falser self *s* from her like a robe,	" vii.	146
hearing her own name had *s* away	*Enid*	507
our fortune *s* from sun to shade,	"	724

378 CONCORDANCE TO

	POEM.	LINE.
like a silver shadow *s* away	*Vivien*	273
the braid *s* and uncoil'd itself,	"	738
s and fell into some pool	*Elaine*	214
lost the hem we *s* him at,	"	654
her suit allow'd, she *s* away,	"	774
S like water to the floor	"	826
s aside, and like a wounded life	*En. Arden.*	75
by mischance he *s* and fell:	"	106
half-another year had *s* away.	"	468
s across the summer of the world,	"	527
S into ashes and was found no more.	*Aylmer's F.*	6
S o'er those lazy limits	"	495
out I *s* Into a land all sun	*Sea Dreams*	98

sloe-tree.
| Poussetting with a *s-t* : | *Amphion* | 44 |

slope (s.)
on the *s*, an absent fool	*Miller's D.*	62
Upon the freshly-flower'd *s*.	"	112
The downward *s* to death.	*D of F. Wom.*	16
on a *s* of orchard, Francis laid	*Audley Ct.*	19
many a *s* was rich in bloom .	*To E L.*	20
At last I heard a voice upon the *s*	*Vision of Sin*	219
from butts of water on the *s*,	*Princess, Pro.*	60
the *s* of sea from verge to shore	" vii.	23
we climb'd The *s* to Vivian-place	" Con.	40
From *s* to *s* thro' distant ferns	"	99
To slant the fifth autumnal *s*	*In Mem.* xxii.	10
Becomes on Fortune's crowning *s*	" lxiii.	14
Upon a pastoral *s* as fair,	*Maud,* I.xviii.	19
half way down the *s* to Hell,	*Enid*	1639
and I stand on the *s* of the hill	*The Window*	9
Follow them down the *s*!	"	16

slope (verb.)
swimming vapour *s*'*s* athwart the glen	*Œnone*	3
the summits *s* Beyond the furthest	*Two Voices*	184
The monstrous ledges there to *s*,	*Princess,* vii.	197
S thro' darkness up to God,	*In Mem.* liv.	16
As *s*'*s* a wild brook o'er a little stone	*Enid*	77

sloped.
the mountain-shade *S* downward.	*Œnone*	21
up we came to where the river *s*	*Princess,* iii.	273
arms on which the standing muscle *s*,	*Enid*	76

sloping.
Was *s* toward his western bower	*Mariana*	80
The *s* of the moon-lit sward	*Arabian N's.*	27
great Orion *s* slowly to the West.	*Locksley H.*	8
s down to make Arms for his chair	*Elaine*	436

sloth.
| stagnates in the weeds of *s*; | *In Mem.* xxvii. | 11 |

slough.
In filthy *s*'*s* they roll a prurient skin	*Pal. of Art*	201
one *s* and crust of sin,	*St S. Stylites*	2
s'*s* That swallow common sense,	*Princess,* v.	432
mountain there has cast his cloudy *s*,	*Lucretius*	177

slow.
So full, so deep, so *s*,	*Eleänore*	95
Not swift nor *s* to change, 'Love thou thy land,' etc.		31
my heart so *s* To feel it!	*Love and Duty*	34

slow-developed.
| A *s-d* strength awaits ' Love thou thy land,' etc. | | 57 |

slow-dropping.
| *S-d* veils of thinnest lawn | *Lotos-E's.* | 11 |

slow-flaming.
| Would seem *s-f* crimson fires | *Pal. of Art* | 50 |

slowly-dying.
| winks behind a *s-d* fire, | *Locksley H.* | 136 |
| Ring out a *s-d* cause, | *In Mem.* cv. | 13 |

slowly-painful.
| More *s-p* to subdue this home Of sin, | *St S. Stylites* | 56 |

slow-worn
| The *s-w* creeps, and the thin weasel | *Aylmer's F.* | 852 |

sludge.
| tends her bristle grunters in the *s*:' | *Princess,* v. | 26 |

sluice.
	POEM.	LINE.
A *s* with blacken'd waters slept,	*Mariana*	38

sluiced.
| canal From the main river *s*, | *Arabian N's.* | 26 |

slumber (s.)
Into dreamful *s* lull'd.	*Eleänore*	30
My heart a charmed *s* keeps,	"	128
steep our brows in *s*'*s* holy balm;	*Lotos-E's.*	66
s is more sweet than toil	"	171
Betwixt the *s* of the poles	*In Mem.* xcviii.	18
s in which all spleenful folly .	*Maud,* I. iii.	2
As thro' the *s* of the globe	*The Voyage*	23

slumber (verb.)
| And the kindly earth shall *s*, | *Locksley H.* | 130 |
| In some long trance should *s* on; | *In Mem.* xlii. | 4 |

slumber'd.
| the garden-bowers and grots *S*: | *Arabian N's.* | 79 |
| While Enoch *s* motionless and pale, | *En. Arden.* | 907 |

slung.
| from his blazon'd baldric *s* | *L. of Shalott,* iii. | 15 |

slur.
| seem'd to *s* With garrulous ease | *Princess,* i. | 161 |
| *s* him, saying all his force Is melted | *Enid* | 106 |

slurring.
| And *s* the days gone by, | *Maud,* I. i. | 33 |

smacking.
| and *s* of the time; | *Princess, Pro.* | 89 |

small.
o'er it many, round and *s*	*Mariana*	39
heads were less: Some men's were;	*Princess,* ii.	132
If she be *s*, slight-natured	" vii.	249
the village, and looks how quiet and *s*!	*Maud,* I.iv.	7
S, but a work divine	" II. ii.	23
grieving that their greatest are so *s*,	*Vivien*	682
my words, the words of one so *s*,	*Guinevere*	183
gains were dock'd, however *s*: *S*		
were his gains,	*Sea Dreams*	8
you so *s*, and you so fair (rep)	*The Window*	72

smell (s.)
moist rich *s* of the rotting leaves 'A spirit haunts'		17
The *s* of violets, hidden in the green	*D. of F. Wom*	77
the gentle shower, the *s* of dying leaves,	*En. Arden*	612

smell (verb.)
| rarely *s*'*s* the new mown hay, | *The Owl,* i. | 9 |
| I *s* the meadow in the street | *In Mem.* cxviii. | 4 |

smelling.
| *S* of musk and of insolence | *Maud,* I. vi. | 45 |

smelt.
Hesperian gold, That *s* ambrosially	*Œnone*	66
S of the coming summer,	*Gardener's D.*	77
a dusky loaf that *s* of home,	*Audley Ct,*	21

smile (s.)
wealthy *s*'*s*: but who may know Whether *s* or frown be fleeter (rep.)	*Madeline*	11
s and frown are not aloof	"	19
In a golden-netted *s*;	"	41
Wherefore those faint *s*'*s* of thine,	*Adeline*	21-38
Hence that look and *s* of thine	"	63
Hollow *s* and frozen sneer	*Poet's Mind*	10
Comes out thy deep ambrosial *s*	*Eleänore*	74
The slow wise *s* that, round about	*Miller's D.*	5
a subtle *s* in her mild eyes	*Œnone*	180
She, flashing forth a haughty *s*,	*D. of F. Wom.*	129
The very *s* before you speak,	*Margaret*	14
slight Sir Robert with his watery *s*	*Ed. Morris.*	128
With tears and *s*'*s* from heaven again	*Sir L and Q.G.*	2
s that like a wrinkling wind .	*Princess,* i.	114
paused, and added with a haughtier *s*	" iii.	209
from crooked lips a haggard *s*,	" iv.	345
s, that looked A stroke of cruel sunshine	"	503
common light of *s*'*s* at our disguise	" v.	261
doubtful *s* dwelt like a clouded moon	" vi.	253
' Ay so,' said Ida with a bitter *s*,	"	296
blush and *s*, a medicine in themselves	" vii.	47

Entry	POEM	LINE
Is matter for a flying s	In Mem. lxi.	12
In glance and s, and clasp and kiss	" lxxxiii.	7
I know it and smile a hard-set s	Maud, I. iv.	20
touch'd my hand with a s so sweet	" vi.	12
And s as sunny as cold	" "	24
And her s were all that I dream'd	" 37,	93
But a s could make it sweet.	" 39,	95
With a glassy s his brutal scorn—	"	49
Perhaps the s and tender tone	"	63
The sun look'd out with a s	" ix.	3
So rare the s's Of sunlight	The Daisy	53
turn thy wheel with s or frown;	Enid	350
With frequent s and nod departing	"	515
slight and sprightly talk, And vivid s's,	Vivien	28
when the living s Died from his lips,	Elaine	322
token on his helmet, with a s	"	373
slow s's, and golden eloquence	"	646
silent s's of slow disparagement:	Guinevere	15
Heart-hiding s, and gray persistent eye:	"	64
half-allowing s's for all the world,	Aylmer's F.	120
half forgot his lazy s Of patron	"	197
a heaved shoulder and a saucy s,	"	466
Never one kindly s, one kindly word:	"	564
with the fat affectionate s	Sea Dreams	151
grant mine asking with a s,	Tithonus	16
With one s of still defiance	The Captain	59
ghost of passion that no s's restore	Coquette, ii.	11

smile (verb.)

Entry	POEM	LINE
S at the claims of long descent	L. C. V. de Vere	52
s in secret, looking over wasted lands	Lotos-E's	159
But they s, they find a music	"	162
Shall s away my maiden blame	D. of F. Wom	214
He will not s—not speak to me	To J. S.	21
I know it, and s a hard-set smile	Maud, I. iv.	20
The very graves appear'd to s,	The Letters	45
S and we s, the lords of many lands:	Enid	353
Frown and we s, the lords of our own hands.	"	354
To make her s, her golden ankle-bells,	Vivien	429
smiling us a Master s's at one	"	512
you yourself will s at your own self.	Elaine	947
Did they s on him.	The Captain	56
with how great ease Nature can s,	Lucretius	174

smiled

Entry	POEM	LINE
He s, and opening out his milk-white palm	Œnone	64
And somewhat grimly s.	Pal. of Art	136
At me you s, but unbeguiled	L. C. V. de Vere	5
with dead lips s at the twilight plain,	D. of F. Wom.	62
And now and then he gravely s.	Two Voices	414
He look'd upon my crown and s:	In Mem. lxviii.	10
Has not his sister s on me?	Maud, I. xiii.	45
She faintly s, she hardly moved;	The Letters	14
sigh'd and s the hoary-headed Earl,	Enid	307
the mother s, but half in tears,	"	823
like a stormy sunlight s Geraint	"	1329
till he sadly s: 'To what request	Vivien	112
S at each other, while the Queen	Elaine	735
and lay as tho' she s	"	1155
Full sharply smote his knees, and s	Guinevere	48
that which pleased him, for he s.	En. Arden	758

smiler

Entry	POEM	LINE
Thou faint s, Adeline?	Adeline	48

smilest

Entry	POEM	LINE
Thou that faintly s still,	Adeline	15
Thou s, but thou dost not speak,	Oriana	68
And s, knowing all is well.	In Mem. cxxvi.	20

smiling.

Entry	POEM	LINE
S, never speaks:	Lilian	12
S, frowning, evermore.	Madeline	8
Thought folded over thought, s asleep,	Eleänore	84
Sat s, babe in arm.	Pal. of Art	96
Eustace turn'd, and s said to me.	Gardener's D.	96
And, s, put the question by.	Day-Dm	164
one said s 'Pretty were the sight	Princess, Pro.	139
Took both his hands, and s faintly	" ii.	284
While Psyche watch'd them, s,	"	344
but s 'Not for thee,' she said,	" iv.	103
gravely s, lifted her from horse,	Enid	1731

Entry	POEM	LINE
Vivien answer'd s saucily	Vivien	117, 501
Vivien answer'd s mournfully;	"	160, 288
Vivien answer'd s as in wrath.	"	376
s as a Master smiles at one	"	512
while the king Would listen s.	Elaine	117
lily maid of Astolat Lay s,	"	1236

smirk'd.

Entry	POEM	LINE
The parson s and nodded.	The Goose	22

smit.

Entry	POEM	LINE
s with freer light shall slowly melt	Golden Year	33

smite.

Entry	POEM	LINE
S, shrink not, spare not.	St S. Stylites	173
his footsteps s the threshold stairs	"	188
s The sounding furrows;	Ulysses	58
Tho' one should s him on the cheek	Two Voices	251
not shun to s me in worse way,	Guinevere	432

smitten.

Entry	POEM	LINE
I am so deeply s thro' the helm	M. d'Arthur	25, 41
s by the dusty sloping beam,	Enid	262
mists and s by the lights,	Guinevere	591

smock'd.

Entry	POEM	LINE
Tho' s, or furr'd and purpled,	Princess, iv.	228

smole.

Entry	POEM	LINE
Looäk 'ow quoloty s's.	N. Farmer	53

smoke (s.)

Entry	POEM	LINE
And like a downward s	Lotos-E's	8, 10
Beneath its drift of s;	Talking O.	6
And all the war is roll'd in s.'	Two Voices	156
A s go up thro' which I loom to her	Princess, v.	174
Athwart the s of burning weeds	" vii.	337
streets were black with s and frost,	In Mem. lxviii.	9
Wrapt in drifts of lurid s	Maud, II. iv.	66
far from noise and s of town,	To F. D. Maurice	13
thro' the s, The blight of low desires	Aylmer's F.	672
like the s in a hurricane whirl'd	Boädicea	51

smoke (verb.)

Entry	POEM	LINE
long way s beneath him in his fear;	Enid	1381
stormy crests that s against the skies,	Elaine	481

smoothe.

Entry	POEM	LINE
s my pillow, mix the foaming draught	Princess, ii.	233

smooth'd.

Entry	POEM	LINE
He s his chin and sleek'd his hair.	A Character	11
Roll'd on each other, rounded, s	D. of F. Wom.	51
s a petted peacock down	Princess, ii.	432
turn'd, and s The glossy shoulder,	Elaine	346

smooth-swarded.

Entry	POEM	LINE
Naked they came to that s-s bower	Œnone	93

smote.

Entry	POEM	LINE
morning s The streaks of virgin snow	Œnone	54
he s His palms together	M. d'Arthur	86
wither'd moon S by the fresh beam	"	214
I s them with the cross,	St S. Stylites	170
s on all the chords with might;	Locksley H.	33
S the chord of Self,	"	34
God's glory s him on the face.'	Two Voices	225
s Her life into the liquor.	Will Water.	111
as she s me with the light of eyes	Princess, iii.	176
s her harp, and sang.	" iv.	20
I s him on the breast;	"	146
tougher, heavier, stronger, he that s	v.	525
heavily-galloping hoof S on her ear,	Enid	1207
However lightly, s her on the cheek	"	1566
whom he s, he overthrew.	Elaine	464
Thereon she s her hand;	"	522
s his thigh and mock'd;	"	661
they flash'd, and s the stream.	"	1228
Full sharply s his knees, and smiled	Guinevere	48
S him, as having kept aloof.	En. Arden	273

smoulder.

Entry	POEM	LINE
light cloud s's on the summer crag	Ed Morris	147
betwixt these two Division s's	Princess, iii.	63
Where s their dead despots	" v.	370

smoulder'd.

Entry	POEM	LINE
s on the refluent estuary;	Boädicea	23

380 CONCORDANCE TO

	snake.	POEM.	LINE.
house the cold crown'd *s*!		Œnone	36
The *s* slipt under a spray,		Poet's Song	10
playing now A twisted *s*,		Princess, Pro.	62
at these words the, My secret		,, iii.	27
look'd A knot, beneath, of *s's*		Enid	325
about his neck, Clung like a *s*,		Vivien	91
The *s* of gold slid from her hair,		,,	737

snakelike.
s slimed his victim ere he gorged; *Sea Dreams* 189

snap.
S The three-decker's oaken . *Maud*, II. ii. 26
S The three-decker's oaken . *Maud*, II. ii. 26
chord too sharply lest it *s*' . *Aylmer's F.* 469

snapt.
A touch, a kiss! the charm was *s*. *Day-Dm.* 133
S in the rushing of the river-rain. *Vivien* 807
Pierced thro' his side, and there *s*, *Elaine* 489

snare (s.)
I saw the *s*, and I retired . *L. C. V. de Vere* 6
Rapt in her song, and careless of the *s*. *Princess*, i. 218
thro' wordy *s's* to track Suggestion *In Mem* xciv. 31
She meant to weave me a *s* . *Maud*, I. vi. 25
He laid a cruel *s* in a pit . ,, II. v. 84

snare (verb.)
s's them by the score . . *Princess*, v. 156
s him in the white ravine, . . ,, vii. 190
rail on me To *s* the next, . *Vivien* 660
s her royal fancy with a boon . *Elaine* 72
coarse webs to *s* her purity, . *Aylmer's F.* 780

snared.
And *s* the squirrel of the glen? *Princess*, ii. 231
in the garden *s* Picus and Faunus, *Lucretius* 181

snarling.
s at each other's heels. . *Locksley H.* 106
And little King Charley *s* . *Maud*, I. xii. 30

snatch (s.)
chanted *s'es* of mysterious song . *Elaine* 1397

snatch (verb.)
s me from him as by violence: . *Enid* . 1206

snatch'd.
s her eyes at once from mine . *The Brook* . 101
S thro' the perilous passes of his life *Aylmer's F.* 209

sneer.
Hollow smile and frozen *s* . *Poet's Mind* 10
crost his child without a *s*: . *Aylmer's F.* 562

sneer'd.
'A ship of fools' he *s* and wept . *The Voyage* 78

sneeze.
S out a full God-bless-you . *Ed. Morris* 80

snipe.
swamp, where hums the dropping *s*, *On a Mourner* 9

snow.
before his burning eyes Melted like *s. The Poet* 40
Shone out their crowning *s's*, . *Dying Swan* 13
dun wolds are ribb'd with *s*, . *Oriana* 5
smote The streaks of virgin *s* . *Œnone* 55
And highest, *s* and fire. . *Pal. of Art* 84
I wish the *s* would melt . *May Queen*, ii. 15
Three silent pinnacles of aged *s* . *Lotos-E's.* 16
knee-deep lies the winter *s*, *D. of the O. I'ear* 1
over the *s* I heard just now . ,, 37
falls not hail, or rain, or any *s*, . *M. d'Arthur* 260
heat, hail, damp, and sleet, and *s* *St S. Stylites* 16
with rain or hail, or fire or *s*; . *Locksley H.* 193
In tufts of rosy-tinted *s*; . *Two Voices* 60
Deep on the convent-roof the *s's* . *St Agnes' Eve* 1
The streets are dumb with *s* . *Sir Galahad* 52
From flower to flower, from *s* to *s In Mem.* xxii. 4
The silent *s* possess'd the earth . ,, lxxvii. 3
And silent under other *s's*: . ,, civ. 6
Ring, happy bells, across the *s*: . ,, cv. 6
fades the last long streak of *s*, . ,, cxiv. 1
star of morn Parts from a bank of *s, Enid* . 735
falls the least white star of *s*, . *Lucretius* 107
like the flakes In a fall of *s*, . ,, 167

	snow-cold.	POEM.	LINE.
Over her *s-c* breast and angry cheek *Œnone* . 140

Snowdon.
we that day had been Up *S*; . *Golden Year* 4

snowdrop.
to live till the *s's* come again; . *May Queen*, ii. 14
To die before the *s* came, . ,, iii. 4
Or this first *s* of the year . *St Agnes' Eve* 11
white Of the first *s's* inner leaves; *Princess*, v. 189

snowed.
A hundred winters *s* upon his breast, *Pal. of Art* 139
Tore the king's letter, *s* it down, . *Princess*, i. 60

snow-limbed.
the *s-l* Eve from whom she came. *Maud*, I. xviii. 28

snowshoe.
Claymore and *s*, toys in lava, . *Princess*, Pro. 18

snow-white.
The snowy peak and *s-w* cataract *Œnone* . 207

snowy-banded.
The *s-b*, dilettante, . . *Maud*, I. viii. 10

soak'd.
Tho' *s* and saturate, out and out, *Will Water.* 87

sob (s.)
all at once the old man burst in *s's: Dora* . 155
shaken with her *s's*, Melissa knelt; *Princess*, iv. 270
dark crowd moves, and there are *s's Ode on Well.* 268
false voice made way broken with *s's Vivien* . 706
And bluster into stormy *s's* . *Elaine* 1061

sob (verb.)
hear him *s* and sigh In the walks *A spirit haunts'* 5
to clamour, mourn and *s*, . *St S. Stylites* 6

sobbed.
for three hours he *s* o'er William's child *Dora* . 163
And *s*, and you *s* with it . *Princess*, ii. 254

sobbing.
See, there is one of us *s*, . *Maud*, II. v. 30

sober-suited.
s-s Freedom chose . 'You ask me why,' etc. 6

Socratic.
Or threaded some *S* dream; *In Mem.* lxxxviii. 36

sod.
with the dull earth's mouldering *s*, *Pal. of Art* 261
To rest beneath the clover *s*, . *In Mem.* x. 13
The blackness round the tombing *s On a Mourner* 27

sofa.
broider'd *s's* on each side: . *Arabian N's.* 19

soft.
S are the moss-beds under the sea *The Merman* 39
that are forked, and horned, and *s The Mermaid* 53

soften.
And *s* as if to a girl, . . *Maud*, I. x. 16

softened.
and the brazen fool Was *s* . *In Mem.* cix. 12

softening.
S thro' all the gentle attributes . *Aylmer's F.* 730

softer.
S than sleep—all things in order . *Pal. of Art* 87
s all her shape And rounder seem'd: *Princess*, vii. 121

softly-shadow'd.
Glows forth each *s-s* arm . *Day-Dm.* . 89

soil.
Fast-rooted in the fruitful *s.* . *Lotos-E's* 83
race of men that cleave the *s*, . ,, 165
numbers forty cubits from the *s*. . *St S. Stylites* 90
Upon my proper patch of *s* . *Amphion* 99
song, the true growth of your *s*, *Princess*, iv. 132
Has risen and cleft the *s*, . ,, vi. 19
The *s*, left barren, scarce had grown *In Mem.* lii. 7

soiled.
When, *s* with noble dust, he hears *Two Voices* 152

	POEM.	LINE.
As these white robes are s and dark	St Agnes' Eve	13
And s with all ignoble use .	In Mem. cx.	24
soiling.		
s another, Annie, will never make	Grandmother	36
soiture.		
fearing rust or s fashioned for it	Elaine	7
'soize.		
Noäks wur 'ang'd for it oop at 's—	N. Farmer	36
solace (s.)		
Vain s! Memory standing near	To J. S.	53
Nay, but Nature brings thee s;	Locksley H.	87
A doubtful gleam of s lives .	In Mem. xxxviii.	8
And in that s can I sing,	" lxiv.	5
solace (verb.)		
A little hint to s woe, .	Two Voices	433
solaced.		
Whom Averill s as he might .	Aylmer's F.	343
sold.		
Himself unto himself he s: .	A Character	26
he's abroad: the place is to be s	Walk. to the M.	11
Nor s his heart to idle moans,	Two Voices	221
are s to the poor for bread,	Maud, I. i.	39
the four-year-old I s the Squire."	The Brook	137
never s the truth to serve the hour	Ode on Well.	179
being s and s had bought them bread:	Enid	641
s her wares for less Than what she		
gave in buying what she s:	En. Arden	254
The horse he drove, the boat he s,	"	610
our Caucasians let themselves be s.	Aylmer's F.	349
She that gave you's bought and s	The Ringlet	33
S him unto shame.	The Captain	60
soldier.		
The Roman s found Me lying dead,	D. of F. Wom.	161
nor shunn'd a s's death .	Princess, Pro.	38
Pitiful sight, wrapp'd in a s's cloak	" v.	53
The s! No: What dares not I do		
do that she should prize The s?.	"	165
not shunn'd the death, No, not the s's	"	171
one loves the s, one The silken priest	"	175
king is scared, the s will not fight	Con.	60
with music, with s and with priest,	Ode on Well.	81
To thee the greatest s comes; .	"	88
So great a s taught us there .	"	131
keep the s firm, the statesman pure	"	222
Not tho' the s knew .	Lt. Brigade	11
s's wont to hear His voice in battle,	Enid	1023
like s's may not quit the post .	Lucretius	148
soldier-city.		
led Threading the s-c, .	Princess, v.	7
Soldier-laddie.		
violin Struck up with S-l, .	Princess, Pro.	86
soldierlike.		
anger-charm'd from sorrow, s,	Aylmer's F.	728
soldierly.		
His own, tho' keen and bold and s,	Aylmer's F.	192
soldier-priest.		
A latter Luther, and a s-p	To J. M. K.	2
sole.		
From scalp to s one slough and crust	St S. Stylites	2
solecism.		
Chimeras, crotchets, Christmas s's	Princess, Pro.	199
solemn.		
a hero lies beneath, Grave, s !"	Princess, Pro.	208
Too s for the comic touches in them	" Con.	69
And hold it s to the past.	In Mem. civ.	16
solemnity.		
watching here At this, our great s.	Ode on Well.	244
solid-set.		
But like a statue s-s. .	In Mem. Con.	15
solitary.		
knew her sitting sad and s, .	Enid	1131

	POEM.	LINE.
Their voices make me feel so s.'	En. Arden	394
the long-hair'd long-bearded s,	"	638
solitude.		
Deep dread and loathing of her s	Pal. of Art	229
You move not in such s's,	Margaret	45
drove him into wastes and s's	Elaine	252
The rosy idol of her s's,	En. Arden	90
Surely the man had died of s.	"	622
My grief and s have broken me : .	"	853
Solomon.		
That Sheba came to ask of S.'	Princess, ii.	325
S may come to Sheba yet .	"	323
solstice.		
A league of street in summer s down,	Princess, iii.	112
soluble.		
More s is this knot By gentleness	Princess, v.	129
solve.		
The doubt would rest, I dare not s.	Two Voices	313
somebody.		
s, surely, some kind heart will come	Maud, II. v.	102
S said that she'd say no, (rep.)	The Window	92
s knows that she'll say ay.	"	93
something.		
s which possess'd The darkness	Arabian N's	71
And then did s speak to me—	May Queen, iii.	34
O Blackbird ! sing me s well,	The Blackbird	1
S to love He lends us ; .	To J. S.	13
Yet s I did wish to say :	"	60
S so said 'twas nothing .	The Epic	41
Or this or s like to this he spoke.	Ed. Morris	41
s jarr'd ; Whether he spoke too	"	72
there seem'd A touch of s false,	"	74
s ere the end, Some work of noble	Ulysses	51
men the workers, ever reaping s	Locksley II.	117
such strange war with s good	Two Voices	302
Moreover, s is or seems,	"	379
Of s felt, like s here ; (rep.) .	"	382
He trusts to light on a fair , .	Day-Dm.	120
I had hope, by s rare, .	Will Water.	165
Ah, were I s great !	Princess, Pro.	131
chiefly you were born for s great,	" iv.	288
there is s in it as you say ; .	" v.	202
s may be done— I know not what	"	213
Swear by St s—I forget her name—	"	283
to think I might be s to thee,	" vi.	184
s wild within her breast, .	" vii.	222
S it is which thou hast lost, .	In Mem. iv.	9
'Tis well ; 'tis s; we may stand	" xviii.	1
thou art turn'd to s strange,	" xl.	5
grown To s greater than before : .	" Con.	20
none of us thought of a s beyond	Maud, I. xix.	47
S far advanced in State, .	Ode on Well.	275
swiftly made at her A ghastly s,	Guinevere	72
with s happier than myself. .	En. Arden	422
S divine to warn them of their foes :	Sea Dreams	69
phantom husks of s foully done,	Lucretius	160
seem no more a s to himself,	"	250
something-pottle-bodied.		
in a court He saw A s-p-b boy	Will Water.	131
somewhat.		
There's s in this world amiss	Miller's D.	17
There's s flows to us in life .	"	21
Ha! ha! They think that I am s.	St S. Stylites	124
Felt you were s, yea and by your	Enid	430
son.		
mythic Uther's deeply wounded s	Pal. of Art	105
Our s's inherit us : our looks are	Lotos-E's.	111
s and heir doth ride post-haste	D. of the O. Year	31
William was his s, And she his niece.	Dora	1
'My s, I married late .	"	9
speak with him that was my s,	"	41
I have kill'd my s. I have kill'd him	"	156
- but I loved him—my dear s	"	157
Francis Hale, 'The farmer's s	Audley Ct.	71
O my s's, my s's, I, Simeon of the pillar,	St S. Stylites	157
my s, mine own Telemachus,	Ulysses	33

CONCORDANCE TO

	POEM.	LINE.
His s's grow up that bear his name,	Two Voices	256
On the first-born of her s's.	Vision of Sin	146
visiting the s,—the s A Walter too,—	Princess, Pro.	7
Slew both his s's :	" ii.	268
that has a s And sees him err :	" iii.	243
here he keeps me hostage for his s.'	" iv.	386
'You have our s: touch not a hair	"	388
unless you send us back Our s,	"	397
did but keep you surety for our s,	" v.	24
took the king His three broad s's;	"	259
dabbled with the blood Of his own s,	" vi.	89
half fool'd to let you tend our s,	"	257
O Sire, Grant me your s, to nurse	"	279
s's of men, and barbarous laws	" vii	219-40
The Tory member's elder s .	Con.	50
Strong S of God, immortal love,	In Mem. Pro.	1
Who pledgest now thy gallant s,	" vi.	10
Dear as the mother to the s,	" ix.	19
All knowledge that the s's of flesh	" lxxxiv.	27
tho' their s's were none of these,	" lxxxix.	17
Shaking her head at her s and sighing	Maud, I. xix.	24
whom the strong s's of the world despise ;	The Brook	3
on the things Of his dead s	The Letters	24
thanks to the Giver, England, for thy s	Ode on Well.	45
this is England's greatest s,	"	95
dares foreshadow for an only s	Ded. of Idylls	28
England dreaming of his s's	"	30
love of all Thy s's encompass Thee,	"	50
'Whither, fair s !' to whom Geraint	Enid	298
good house, tho' ruin'd, O my S,	"	378
wroth or grieved At your new s,	"	780
' Envy calls you Devil's s,	Vivien	317-47
S's of kings loving in pupillage	"	367
two strong s's, Sir Torre and Sir Lavaine,	Elaine	174
Hurt in his first tilt was my s,	"	196
I my s's and little daughter fled	"	276
furthermore Our s is with him ;	"	633
s's born to the glory of thy name	"	1362
fair, my child, As a king's s.	"	1400
call'd him the false s of Girlois	Guinevere	286
I must strike against my sister's s.	"	568
Philip Ray the miller's only s	En. Arden.	13
Bore him another s, a sickly one	"	109
Her own s Was silent,	"	478
Her s, who stood beside her.	"	757
like her mother, and the boy, my s.'	"	792
tell my s that I died blessing him.	"	886
s's of men Daughters of God ;	Aylmer's F.	44
loved you more as s than brother,	"	351
Born of a village girl, carpenter's s,	"	668
some, S's of the glebe, with other frowns	"	723
Gone for a minute, my s,	Grandmother	103
Gallant s's of English freemen	The Captain	7
Every mother's s—Down they dropt—	"	50
They have taken our s,	The Victim	51
We have his dearest, His only s !'	"	69

song.

Take, Madam, this poor book of s ;	To the Queen	17
Her s the lintwhite swelleth	Claribel	15
sings a s of undying love ;	Poet's Mind	33
flooded over with eddying s ,	Dying Swan	42
Hear a s that echoes cheerly	L. of Shalott, i.	30
heard her singing her last s,	" iv.	26
Singing in her s she died,	"	35
some wild skylark's matin s.	Miller's D.	40
The phantom of a silent s,	"	71
Ah, well—but sing the foolish s	"	161
So sing that other s I made,	"	199
build up all My sorrow with my s	Œnone	39
the world-worn Dante grasped his s,	Pal. of Art	135
To sing her s's alone.	"	160
my soul to hear her echo'd s	"	175
a music centred in a doleful s	Lotos-E's.	162
Sung by the morning star of s,	D. of F. Wom.	3
far-renowned brides of ancient s	"	17
With timbrel and with s,	"	200
Leaving the dance and s,	"	216
What s's below the waning stars	Margaret	33
shook his s together as he near'd	Gardener's D.	90
Like poets, from the vanity of s ?	"	99

	POEM.	LINE.
He sang his s, and I replied with	Audley Ct.	55
found it in a volume, all of s's,	"	56
in the Latin s I learnt at school,	Ed. Morris	79
shall have that s which Leonard	Golden Year	1
that same s of his He told me ;	"	7
falser than all s's have sung,	Locksley H.	41
And a s from out the distance	"	84
The woods were fill'd so full with s,	Two Voices	455
You'd have my moral from the s,	Day-Dm.	243
To search a meaning for the s,	"	247
To shape the s for your delight	"	274
Had I lived when s was great	Amphion	9, 13
When, ere his s was ended	"	50
A s that pleased us from its 'You might have won'	"	22
Sometimes the linnet piped his s :	Sir L. and Q. G.	10
Storm'd in orbs of s,	Vision of Sin	25
nightingale thought 'I have sung many s's	Poet's Song	13
time to time some ballad or a s	Princess, Pro.	234
here I give the story and the s's.	"	239
shook the s's, the whispers,	" i.	97
the nightingale, Rapt in her s,	"	218
to a low s oar'd a shallop by,	" ii.	433
' Know you no s of your own land,'	" iv.	66
great is s Used to great ends :	"	119
for s Is duer unto freedom	"	122
s, the true growth of your soil	"	132
dragg'd my brains for such a s,	"	136
the s Might have been worse	"	231
pardon ask'd and given For stroke and s,	" v.	45
a s on every spray Of birds	"	228
noise of s's they would not understand :	" vi.	24
Remembering his ill-omen'd s,	"	143
she that sang the mournful s,	"	288
I brim with sorrow drowning s	In Mem xix.	12
For private sorrow's barren s,	" xxi.	14
Or breaking into s by fits	" xxiii.	2
In dance and s and game and jest	" xxix.	8
A merry s we sang with him	" xxx.	15
To lull with s an aching heart,	" xxxvii.	15
darken'd sanctities with s.'	"	24
in the s's I love to sing	" xxxviii.	11
Then are these s's I sing of thee	" xlvii.	15
Short swallow-flights of s,	" xlviii.	15
slightest air of s shall breathe	" l.	5
blame not thou thy plaintive s,'	" lvi.	7
s of woe Is after all an earthly s :	" lxxiv.	11
round thee with the breeze of s	" lxxv.	9
if the matin s's, that woke	"	14
With fifty Mays, thy s's are vain :	" lxxvi.	3
a musing eye On s's and deeds	" lxxvii.	12
dance and s and hoodman-blind	" lxxxii.	16
flood a fresher throat with s.	" lxxxvi.	19
noise Of s's, and clapping hands,	" xciv	13
now we sang old s's that peal'd	" xcvii.	28
With sport and s, in booth and tent	" xcviii.	10
A s that slights the coming care	" ci.	21
boyhood sung Long since its matin s	" civ.	24
Be neither s, nor game, nor feast ;	" cvi.	8
And sing the s's he loved to hear.	" cxiv.	9
The lark becomes a sightless s.	" cxv.	10
the s's, the stirring air, The life re-orient	" cxxiv.	4
if the s were full of care,	Con.	10
He breath'd the spirit of the s ;	Con.	4
Is music more than any s	"	14
In dying s's a dead regret,	"	21
makes appear the s's I made	Maud, I. v.	5
A martial s like a trumpet's call!	II. ii.	47
And old s vexes my ear ;	iv.	82
descend From the realms of light and s,	The Letters	9
I turn'd and humm'd a bitter s	Ode on Well.	79
And ever-echoing avenues of s	"	345
s that Enid sang was one Of Fortune	Enid	359
by the bird's s you may learn the nest'	"	1377
and half singing a coarse s,	Vivien	255
Far other was the s that once I	"	267
such a s, such fire for fame,	"	283
such a noble s was that.	"	294
howe'er you scorn my s,	"	573
says the s, ' I trow it is no treason.'	"	708
told in tale, Or sung in s !		

POEM.	LINE.
graces of the court, and *s*'s, . . *Elaine*	645
in those days she made a little *s* . . "	698
call'd her *s* 'The *S* of Love and Death,' "	499
chanted snatches of mysterious *s* . . "	1397
even in the middle of his *s* . . . *Guinevere*	300
As tho' it were the burthen of a *s*, . *En. Arden*	728
while she sang this baby *s* . . *Sea Dreams*	280
that strange *s* I heard Apollo sing *Tithonus*	62
Let him hear my *s* . . . . *The Captain*	4
My fame in *s* has done him much wrong *Spiteful Let*	3
glory of orator, glory of *s*, . . . *Wages*	1
girl With *s* and flame and fragrance *Lucretius* .	134
Bird's love and bird's *s* (rep) *The Window*	62
Ay is the *s* of the wedded spheres . "	112

sootflake
(The *s* of so many a summer still *Sea Dreams* 35

soothe.
How should I *s* you anyway, . . *To J. S.*	58
S him with thy finer fancies, . *Locksley H.*	54
O for thy voice to *s* and bless! *In Mem.* lv.	26
influence-rich to *s* and save . " lxxix.	14
hurt Whom she would *s*, . . *Guinevere* .	351
One spiritual doubt she did not *s*? *Aylmer's F.*	704

soothed
This fiat somewhat *s* himself . *Aylmer's F.* 26

sophist.
| Low-cowering shall the *S* sit: *Clear-headed friend* | 10 |
| Dark-brow'd *s*, come not anear; . *Poet's Mind* | 8 |

sophister
every *s* can lime. . *'Love thou thy land,'* etc. 12

sorcerer.
s whom a far-off grandsire burnt, *Princess,* i.	6
I have no *s*'s malison on me . . " ii.	388
I remember'd that burnt *s*'s curse . " v.	464

sore.
old *s* breaks out from age to age *Walk. to the M.* 71

sorrow (s.)
with joy Hidden in *s*; . . *Dying Swan*	23
beat against me In *s* and in rest; . *Miller's D.*	178
they had their part Of *s*; . . . "	224
build up all My *s* with my song . *Œnone*	32
Still from one *s* to another thrown; *Lotos-E's*	63
The star-like *s*'s of immortal eyes, *D. of F. Wom.*	91
dainty *s* without sound. . . *Margaret*	18
Your *s*, only *s*'s shade, Keeps real *s*	
far away. . . . . . "	43
Rise from the feast of *s*, lady, . . "	62
Stole from her sister *S*. . . *Gardener's D.*	251
high dial, which my *s* crowns— . *St S. Stylites*	94
a *s*'s crown of *s* is remembering . *Locksley H.*	76
Whatever crazy *s* saith, . . *Two Voices*	394
O *S*, cruel fellowship, . . *In Mem.* iii.	1
Or *s* such a changeling be? . . " xvi.	4
I brim with *s* drowning song . . " xix.	12
For private *s*'s barren song, ; . " xxi.	14
sometimes in my *s* shut, . . . " xxii.	1
They bring me *s* touch'd with joy, . " xxviii.	19
these brief lays, of *S* born . . " xlvii.	2
Ay me, the *s* deepens down, . . " xlviii.	6
O *S*, wilt thou live with me . . " lviii.	1
O *S*, wilt thou rule my blood, . . "	5
O *s*, then can *s* wane? . . . " lxxvii.	15
I delayest the *s* in my blood, . . " lxxxii.	14
trust in things above He dimm'd of *s*, " lxxxiv.	10
what fruit may be Of *s* . . . " cvii.	14
'Tis held that *s* makes us wise (extl 1) . "	15
Yet less of *s* lives in me . . . " cxv.	13
Would there be *s* for *me*? . . *Maud,* I. i.	57
s seize me if ever that light . . " iv.	12
s darkens hamlet and hall, . *Ode on Well.*	7
and the *s* dimm'd her sight, . . *Elaine*	885
Comfort your *s*'s; for they do not flow, *Guinevere*	186
weigh your *s*'s with our lord the King's, . "	189
my *s* broke me down; . . *En. Arden*	316
one *s* and she shared it not? . *Aylmer's F.*	702
Sat anger-charm'd from *s*, . . "	728
gray hairs with *s* to the grave— . "	777
Her cramp't-up *s* pain'd her, . . "	800

POEM.	LINE.
And makes it a *s* to be' . . *The Islet*	36
'O hush, my joy, my *s*,' *Home they brought him*	10
sound of human *s* mounts to mar . *Lucretius*	109

sorrow (verb.)
And he should *s* o'er my state . *In Mem.* xiv.	15
I feel it, when I *s* most; . . " xxviii.	14
s after The delight of early skies; *Maud,* II. iv.	24
In a wakeful doze I *s* . . . "	26
who most have cause to *s* for her— *Aylmer's F.*	678

sorrowed.
| I felt it, when I *s* most . . *In Mem.* lxxxiv. | 2 |
| those who *s* o'er a vanish'd race . *Aylmer's F.* | 844 |

sorrowest.
O *s* thou, pale Painter, for the past *Coquette,* iii. 3

sorrowing.
Came Psyche, *s* for Aglaia. . *Princess,* vi	13
s in a pause I dared not break . . " vii.	233
s Lancelot should have stoop'd so low, *Elaine*	726

sort.
older *s*, and murmur'd that their May *Princess,* ii. 432

sought.
You *s* to prove how I could love *L.C.V. de Vere*	21
s to strike Into that wondrous track *D. of F. Wom.*	273
s to sow themselves like winged seeds *Gardener's D.*	64
She *s* her lord, and found him, . *Godiva*	16
Still moving after truth long *s*, . *Two Voices*	62
I *s* but peace; No critic I—. . *Princess,* i.	143
grace Concluded, and we *s* the gardens; " ii.	429
some hid and *s* In the orange thickets; "	435
twice I *s* to plead my cause, . . " iv.	530
and I—I *s* for one—All people . " vi.	220
s far less for truth than power . . " vii.	221
s but Duty's iron crown . . *Ode on Well.*	122
though they *s* Thro' all the provinces *Enid* .	729
Vivien ever *s* to work the charm . *Vivien*	64
for men *s* to prove me vile, . . . "	345
s To make disruption in the Table *Guinevere*	17
nor *s*, Wrapt in her grief, for house! . "	146
s and found a witch Who brewed *Lucretius*	15

sought'st.
Who *s* to wreck my mortal ark, . *Two Voices* 389

soul.
and my whole *s* grieves *'A spirit haunts,'* etc.	16
He saw thro' his own *s*. . . *The Poet*	6
Heaven flow'd upon the *s* in many dreams "	31
took the *s* Of that waste place . *Dying Swan*	21
Controlleth all the *s* and sense . *Eleänore*	115
With summer lightnings of a *s* . *Miller's D.*	13
Look thro' my very *s* with thine!. . "	218
With one long kiss my whole *s*, . *Fatima*	20
My whole *s* waiting silently, . . "	36
Beautiful-brow'd Œnone, my own *s*, *Œnone*	63
the happy *s*'s, that love to live; . "	236
shadow all my *s*, that I may die. . "	238
s possess'd of many gifts, *To—With Pal. of Art*	3
built my *s* a lordly pleasure house, *Pal. of Art*	1
'*O S*, make merry and carouse, Dear *s*, "	3
My *s* would live alone unto herself . "	11
my *s* made answer readily; . . "	17
the livelong day my *s* did pass, . "	55
every mood And change of my still *s*. "	60
my *s* to heal her echo'd song . . "	175
power of movement, seem'd my *s*, . "	246
I heard them call my *s*. . *May Queen,* iii. 28
that way my *s* will have to go, . . "	42
with those just *s*'s and true— . . "	55
into my empty *s* and frame . *D. of F. Wom.*	78
s laments, which hath been blest, . "	281
Since that dear *s* hath fall'n asleep. *To J. S.*	34
Sleep, holy spirit, blessed *s*. . . "	70
Sleep till the end, true *s* and sweet. . "	71
Thy brothers and immortal *s*'s. *'Love thou thy land'*	8
All but the basis of the *s*. . . "	44
s Of Discord race the rising wind; . "	67
our *s*'s with talk of knightly deeds *M. d'Arthur*	19
see my face again, Pray for my *s*, . "	247
about my senses and my *s*; . *Gardener's D.*	66

384 CONCORDANCE TO

	POEM.	LINE.
Raise thy s; Make thine heart	Gardener's D	267
if thou wilt not save my s,	St S. Stylites	45
spake not of it to a single s,	"	65
that my s might grow to thee,	"	70
O my s, God reaps a harvest	"	146
In which the gloomy brewer's s	Talking O.	55
my brain, my senses and my s!	Love and Duty	44
S's that have toil'd, and wrought	Ulysses	36
'Good s I suppose I grant it thee,	Two Voices	38
Not less swift s's that yearn for light,	"	67
wide in s and bold of tongue,	"	124
With this old s in organs new?	"	393
truth that sways the s of men?	Day-Dm.	72
May my s follow soon!	St Agnes' Eve	4
So shows my s before the Lamb,	"	17
And he cheer'd her s with love.	L. of Burleigh	68
Like s's that balance joy and pain	Sir L. and Q.G.	1
they vext the s's of deans;	Princess, Pro.	161
a double growth of these rare s's,	" ii.	163
S' of mincing mimicry!	"	403
Our echoes roll from s to s,	" iii.	362
secret laughter tickled all my s.	" iv.	248
And satisfy my s with kissing her:	" v.	100
Not only he, but by my mother's s,	" vi.	315
charm'd Her wounded s with words:	"	326
sadness on the s of Ida fell	" vii.	14
shall not blind his s with clay.'	"	312
mind and s, according well,	In Mem. Pro.	27
half conceal the S within	" v.	4
What s's possess themselves so pure,	" xxxii.	15
So that still garden of the s's	" xliii.	16
Rewaken with the dawning s.	"	16
Remerging in the general S,	" xlvi.	4
shall still divide The eternal s	"	7
The likest God within the s?	" liv.	2
The passing of the sweetest s	" lvi.	1
He past : a s of nobler tone:	" lix.	1
The s of Shakspeare love thee more.	" lx.	12
Sweet s, do with me as thou wilt;	" lxiv.	5
thro' a lattice on the s,	" lxix.	15
Hadst thou such credit with the s?	" lxx.	5
Fade wholly, while the s exults,	" lxxii.	14
And take us as a single s,	" lxxxiii.	44
O solemn ghost, O crowned s!	" lxxxiv.	36
His living s was flash'd on mine,	" xcvi.	36
To-day they count as kindred s's	" xcviii.	19
The feeble s, a haunt of fears,	" cix.	3
On s's, the lesser lords of doom,	" cxi.	8
A s on highest mission sent	" cxii.	10
Wisdom heavenly of the s	" cxiii.	2
A sphere of stars about my s,	" cxxi.	7
all we flow from, s in s.	" cxxx.	12
A s shall draw from out the vast	" Con.	123
s of the rose went into my blood,	Maud, I. xxii	33
sweet s, had hardly spoken a word,	" II. i.	11
to see The s's we loved	" IV.	15
weep My whole s out to thee	"	98
guard the eye, the s Of Europe	Ode on Well.	160
What know we greater than the s?	"	265
own Earl, and their own s's, and her	Enid	1425
whose s's the old serpent long had drawn	"	1480
For agony, who was yet a living s.	Elaine	253
Pray for my s, and yield me burial (rep.)	"	1273
Pray for thy s? Ay, that will I.	"	1386
the Powers that tend the s,	Guinevere	65
do thou for thine own s the rest.	"	541
and so thou purify thy s,	"	557
not a smaller s, Nor Lancelot,	"	562
I cannot kill my sin If s be s;	"	615
little innocent s flitted away	En. Arden,	269
Kept him a living s,	"	805
'Ay, ay, poor s' said Miriam	"	808
So past the strong heroic s away	"	914
adulteries That saturates s with body.	Aylmer's F.	377
s to s Strike thro' a finer element	"	578
passing thro' the fire Bodies, but s's—	"	672
mortal s from out immortal hell	Lucretius	259
s flies out and dies in the air.'	"	270

soul-stricken.

	POEM.	LINE.
S-s at their kindness to him	Aylmer's F.	525

sound (adj.)

	POEM.	LINE.
healthy, s, and clear and whole,	Miller's D.	15
What ails us, who are s,	Walk. to the M.	95
that hypothesis of theirs be s	Princess, iv.	2
felt it s and whole from head to foot	" vi.	194
Oh, if we held the doctrine s	In Mem. lii.	9
How pure at heart and s in head	" xciii.	1
only for a moment whole and s;	Aylmer's F.	2
let your sleep for this one night be s:	Sea Dreams	302
blind or lame or sick or s	The Voyage	93

sound (s.)

	POEM.	LINE.
the s Which to the wooing wind	Mariana	74
Full of the city's stilly s,	Arabian N's.	103
mirth Is here or merry-making s.	Deserted H.	14
Springing alone With a shrill inner s	The Mermaid	20
Died the s of royal cheer;	L. of Shalott, iv.	48
There came a s as of the sea;	Mariana in the S.	86
With dinning s my ears are rife,	Eleänore	135
as I hear Dead s's at night	Œnone	245
a s Rings ever in her ears	"	260
Mov'd of themselves, with silver s;	Pal. of Art	130
the dully s Of human footsteps	"	275
or a s Of rocks thrown down,	"	281
With s's that echo still.	D. of F. Wom.	8
s's of insult, shame, and wrong,	"	19
song of bird or s of rill;	"	66
fill'd with light The interval of s.	"	172
organ rolling waves Of s	"	192
With that sharp s the white dawn's	"	261
tell o'er Each little s and sight.	"	277
Of dainty sorrow without s,	Margaret	18
sent to sleep with s,	M. d'Arthur, Ep.	3
That with the s I woke	"	30
s of funeral or of marriage bells;	Gardener's D.	36
that morn with all its s,	"	82
with the freshness and the s.	Ed. Morris	99
s Of pious hymns and psalms,	St S. Stylites	32
I took the swarming s of life—	Talking O.	213
The s of minster bells.	"	272
and the winds are laid with s.	Locksley H.	104
bade him cry, with s of trumpet,	Godiva	36
With twelve great shocks of s	"	74
no s is made, Not even of a gnat	Day-Dm.	40
a s Like sleepy counsel pleading;	Amphion	23
A gentle s, an awful light!	Sir Galahad	41
By grassy capes with fuller s	Sir L. and Q. G.	14
methought I heard a mellow s,	Vision of Sin	7
Ran into its giddiest whirl of s,	"	29
the s of a voice that is still!	'Break, break,' etc.	12
to the s Of solemn psalms	Princess, ii.	452
one door chamber shut from s	" vi.	355
a s arose of hoof And chariot	"	358
and sweet is every s, (rep)	" vii.	203
Calm is the morn without a s,	In Mem. xi.	1
shut between me and the s?	" xxviii.	8
streets were fill'd with joyful s,	" xxxi.	10
The s of streams that swift or slow	" xxxv.	10
'The s of that forgetful shore	"	14
up thy vault with roaring s	" lxxi.	25
O s to rout the brood of cares	" lxxxviii.	17
growing upon me without a s.	Maud, I iii.	7
I heard no s where I stood	" xiv.	28
To the s of dancing music and flutes;	" II. v.	76
There comes a s of marriage bells	The Letters	48
Let the s of those he wrought for,	Ode on Well.	10
s of the sorrowing anthem roll'd	"	60
In that dread s to the great name,	"	71
compass'd round with turbulent s,	Will	7
heard instead A sudden s of hoofs	Enid	164
the tender s of his own voice	"	1197
s of many a heavily-galloping hoof	"	1296
s not wonted in a place so still	Elaine	814
Lancelot knew the little clinking s;	"	977
A sort of absolution in the s	Sea Dreams	61
How fresh was every sight and s	The Voyage	5
Phantom s of blows descending	Boädicea	25
Nor s of human sorrow mounts	Lucretius	109

sound (to make a noise.)

	POEM.	LINE.
the waterfall Which ever s's	Ode to Mem.	52
The wind s's like a silver wire,	Fatima	29

	POEM.	LINE.
s all night long, in falling	*D. of F. Wom.*	183
s upon the bugle horn	*Locksley H.*	2
how thy name may *s* Will vex thee	*Two Voices*	110
Like strangers' voices here they *s*	*In Mem* ciii.	9
S on a dreadful trumpet, summoning her;	*Enid*	1232

sound (to sink a plummet.)
to *s* the abyss Of science,	*Princess,* ii.	159

sounded.
Then the voice Of Ida *s*,	*Princess,* vi.	352

sounding.
call me, *s* on the bugle-horn.	*Locksley H.*	145
Breathing and *s* beauteous battle.	*Princess,* v.	154
The great city *s* wide ;	*Maud,* II. iv.	64
Made answer, *s* like a distant horn.	*Guinevere*	247
empty hall, *S* on the morrow. 'Home they brought him' *s*		5

sour.
Slip-shod waiter, lank and *s*,	*Vision of Sin*	71
little grain of conscience made him *s*	"	218

source.
A teardrop trembled from its *s*,	*Talking O.*	161
The very *s* and fount of Day	*In Mem* xxiv.	3
Like torrents from a mountain *s*	*The Letters*	39
Prayer from a living *s* within the.	*En Arden.*	802

soured.
she *s* To what she is :	*Walk. to the M.*	53

south.
The palms and temples of the *S*.	*'You ask me why'*	28
at school—a college in the *S*:	*Walk. to the M.*	75
fierce and fickle is the *S*,	*Princess,* iv.	79
I do but wanton in the *S*	"	91
brief the moon of beauty in the *S*.	"	95
long breezes rapt from inmost *s*	"	411
Rosy is the West, Rosy is the *S*,	*Maud,* I xvii 6, 20
looking to the *S*, and fed	" xviii.	20
My fancy fled to the *S* again	*The Daisy*	108
As fast we fleeted to the *S*;	*The Voyage*	4
Thine the North and thine the *S*.	*Boädicea*	44
palmy highlands Far within the *S*.	*The Captain*	24
Down in the *S* is a flash and a groan	*The Window*	42

south-breeze.
The full *s-b* around thee blow	*Talking O.*	271

South-sea-isle.
under worse than *S-s-i* taboo,	*Princess,* iii.	261

south-west.
s-w that blowing Bala lake	*Enid*	1777

south-wind
whisper of the *s-w* rushing warm.	*Locksley H.*	125

sow (s.) see swine.
He had a *s*, sir.	*Walk. to the M.*	78
we haled the groaning *s*,	"	83
range of prospect had the mother *s*,	"	85
never *s* was higher in this world	"	88
all the swine were a *s*, And all the dogs—	*Princess,* i.	190

sow (verb.)
S the seed, and reap the harvest.	*Lotos-E's.*	166
to *s* themselves like winged seeds,	*Gardener's D.*	64
He *s* himself on every wind.	*Two Voices*	294
s The dust of continents to-be ;	*In Mem* xxxv.	11
s the sky with flying boughs,	" lxxi.	24

sowed
S all their mystic gulfs,	*Gardener's D*	257
He *s* a slander in the common ear,	*Enid.*	450
s her name and kept it green	*Aylmer's F.*	88
S it far and wide By every town.	*The Flower*	13

sowing
Dispensing harvest, *s* the To-be,	*Princess,* vii	273
s hedgerow texts and passing by,	*Aylmer's F.*	171

sown.
having *s* some generous seed,	*Two Voices*	143
murmur'd, *s* With happy faces	*Princess,* Pro.	55
seed we two long since had *s* ;	" iv.	291
had the wild oat not been *s*,	*In Mem.* lii.	6

	POEM.	LINE.
the one true seed of freedom *s*	*Ode on Well.*	162
S in a wrinkle of the monstrous hill,	*Will*	11
robe of jasmine *s* with stars:	*Aylmer's F.*	153

space.
Oh ! narrow, narrow was the *s*,	*Oriana*	46
Overlook a *s* of flowers,	*L. of Shalott,* i.	16
Lancelot mused a little *s* ;	" iv.	51
There all in *s s* rosy-bright	*Mariana in the S.*	83
In some fair *s* of sloping greens	*Pal. of Art*	106
time and *s* to work and spread.	*'You ask me why'*	16
Free *s* for every human doubt.	*Two Voices*	137
Pure *s*'s clothed in living beams,	*Sir Galahad*	66
little *s* was left between the horns,	*Princess,* iv.	189
ask'd but *s* and fairplay for her scheme	" v.	272
leave her *s* to burgeon out of all	" vii.	255
Thro' all the silent *s s* of the worlds	" *Con.*	114
all the starry heavens of *s*	*In Mem.* lxxv.	3
breathing bare The round of *s*	" lxxxv.	5
roll'd the floods in grander *s*,	" cii.	26
whispers to the worlds of *s*.	" cxxv.	11
countercharm of *s* and hollow sky	*Maud,* I.xviii.	43
It is but for a little *s* I go :	"	75
The height, the *s*, the gloom,	*The Daisy*	59
Painted, who stare at open *s*,	*Enid.*	1118
after tarrying for a *s* they rode,	"	1801
bode among them yet a little *s*	*Elaine*	917
The *s* was narrow,—having order'd	*En Arden.*	177
The ever silent *s*'s of the East,	*Tithonus*	9

spake.
He *s* of duty : that the dull	*A Character*	7
He *s* of virtue : not the gods	"	13
when she *s*, Her words did gather	*The Poet*	43
Her eyelid quiver'd as she *s*.	*Miller's D.*	144
Still she *s* on, and still she *s* of power	*Œnone*	112
She *s* some certain truths of you.	*L.C V. de Vere*	36
if his fellow *s*, His voice was thin.	*Lotos-E's.*	33
I heard Him, for He *s*,	*D. of F. Wom.*	227
s he, clouded with his own conceit	*M. d'Arthur*	112
s not of it to a single soul,	*St S. Stylites*	65
While I *s* then, a sting of shrewdest pain	"	195
A still small voice *s* unto me,	*Two Voices*	1
It *s*, moreover, in my mind :	"	31
Again the voice *s* unto me :	"	46
on the fourth *s* of why we came	*Princess,* i.	118
companion yestermorn ; Unwillingly we *s*.	" iii.	183
but to one of whom we *s*	"	185
She *s* With kindled eyes :	"	315
a moral leper, I, To whom none *s*,	" iv.	204
Stood up and *s*, an affluent orator	"	272
such as her ! if Cyril *s* her true,	" v.	161
'Nay, nay, you *s* but sense'	"	197
Yea, tho' it *s* and made appeal	*In Mem* xci.	4
Yea, tho' it *s* and bared to view	"	9
Dumb is that tower which *s* so loud	*Con.*	106
s no slander, no, nor listen'd to it ;	*Ded of Idylls*	9
none *s* word except the hoary Earl;	*Enid.*	369
S to the lady with him and proclaim'd	"	552
Loudly the Prince, ' Forbear :	"	555
none *s* word, but all sat down at once.	"	1452
s so low he hardly heard her speak,	"	1491
He never *s* word of reproach to me,	*Elaine*	125
has come Despite the wound he *s* of,	"	565
openly she *s* and said to her :	*Guinevere*	224
and bow'd her head nor *s*.	"	308
while he *s* to these his helm	"	557
mock'd me when he *s* of hope	"	624

span (s.)
every *s* of shade that steals,	*In Mem.* envi.	10

span (verb.)
She strove to *s* my waist :	*Talking O.*	137

spangle (s.)
the *s* dances in bight and bay	*Sea-Fairies*	24
pelt me with starry *s*'s and shells,	*The Merman*	28

spangle (verb.)
To *s* all the happy shores	*In Mem.Con.*	120

spann'd.
a bridge that *s* a dry ravine :	*Enid.*	246, 294

2 B

386   CONCORDANCE TO

spar.   POEM.   LINE.
upon floating tackle and broken *s*'s *En. Arden* . 552
S's were splinter'd, . . . *The Captain* 45-9

spare (adj)
But far too *s* of flesh.' . . . . *Talking O.* . 92

spare (verb.)
if thou *s* to fling Excalibur . . *M. d'Arthur* 131
Smite, shrink not, *s* not. . . *St S. Stylites* 178
kindly word, Not one to *s* her : . *Princess,* vi. 242
s thee, sacred bark ; . . . *In Mem.* xvii. 14
And yet I *s* them sympathy . .   "   lxii.   7
A little *s* the night I loved . .   "   civ.   15
If the wolf *s* me, weep my life away, *Vivien* . 734

spared.
tho' I *s* thee all the spring, . . *The Blackbird* 9
and they *s* To ask it, . . . *Guinevere* . 143
s to lift his hand against the King   "   . 434

sparhawk.
Sometimes the *s* wheel'd along *Sir L. and Q. G.* 12

spark.
the haft twinkled with diamond *s*'s, *M. d'Arthur* 56
As this pale taper's earthly *s,* . *St Agnes' Eve* 15
She lit the *s* within my throat, . *Will Water.* 109
Mix'd with cunning *s*'s of hell. . *Vision of Sin* 114
s Of glowing and growing light . *Maud,* I. vi. 15
Like a sudden *s* Struck vainly .   "   ix.   13
However weary, a *s* of will . .   "   II. ii.   56

sparkle (s)
sent a blast of *s*'s up the flue . *M. d'Arthur, Ep.* 15
With one green *s* ever and anon . *Audley Ct* . 86
Caught the *s*'s, and in circles, . *Vision of Sin* 30
nature's prideful *s* in the blood . *Enid*   1675

sparkle (verb.)
I wake : the chill stars *s* ; . . *St S. Stylites* 112
The silver vessels *s* clean, . . *Sir Galahad* 34
forefinger of all Time *S* for ever : *Princess,* ii. 357
maiden moon that *s*'s on a sty .   "   v. 178
And *s* out among the fern, . . *The Brook* . 25
city *s*'s like a grain of salt. . . *Will* . . 20
s like a gem Of fifty facets' . . *Enid* . 1143
watch'd their arms far-off *S,* . *Elaine* . 395
flame and *s* and stream as of old, . *The Ringlet* 2

sparkled.
shield That *s* on the yellow field *L. of Shalott,* iii. 8
s keen with frost against the hilt . *M. d'Arthur* 55
From Allan's watch, and *s* by the fire. *Dora* . 333
yule-log *s* keen with frost, . . *In Mem.* lxxvii. 5
on the burnish'd board *S* and shone : *En. Arden* 744
when some heat of difference *s* out, *Aylmer's F.* 705

sparkling.
the snows Are *s* to the moon : . *St Agnes' Eve* 2

sparrow.
The *s*'s chirrup on the roof, . . *Mariana* . 73
The very *s*'s in the hedge . . *Amphion* . 67
the *s* spear'd by the shrike, . . *Maud,* I. iv. 23
() wretched set of *s*'s, one and all, *Enid* . . 278
And swallow, and *s,* and throstle . *The Window* 157

sparrow-hawk.
told him, scouring still ' The *s-h* !' *Enid* . . 260
answer'd gruffly, ' Ugh ! the *s-h* !'   "   . 265
he that labours for the *s-h,* . .   "   . 271
thousand pips eat up your *s-h* ! .   "   . 274
pipe of nothing but of *s-h*'s ! . .   "   . 279
' So that you do not serve me *s-h*'s .   "   . 304
curse this hedgerow thief, the *s-h* :   "   . 309
This *s-h,* what is he, . . .   "   . 404
The second was your foe, the *s-h,* .   "   . 414
over that is placed the *s-h,* . .   "   . 484
earn'd himself the name of *s-h.* .   "   . 492
over that a golden *s-h.* . . .   "   . 550

Spartan.
play The *S* Mother with emotion *Princess,* ii. 263

spawn.
Thro' slander meanest *s* of Hell . *The Letters* 33

speak.   POEM.   LINE.
Smiling, never *s*'s . . . . *Lilian* . 12
kiss sweet kisses, and *s* sweet words: *Sea-Fairies* 34
Thou smilest, but thou dost not *s,* *Oriana* . 63
when at last I dared to *s* . . *Miller's D.* 129
Hear me, for I will *s,* and build up all *Œnone* . 38
it may be That, while I *s* of it, .   "   . 42
that I might *s* my mind And tell her   "   . 223
Tho' I cannot speak a word . *May Queen,* ii. 39
And then did something *s* to me—   "   iii. 34
on noble things, and strove to *s* . *D. of F. Wom* 42
Still strove to *s* : my voice was thick .   "   . 109
The very smile before you *s* . . *Margaret* . 14
come down, and hear me *s* : . .   "   . 56
And tread softly and *s* low, . *D. of the O Year* 4
tho' his foes *s* ill of him . .   "   . 22
S out before you die . . .   "   . 45
may speak the thing he will ; ' *You ask me, why* ' 8
some old man *s* in the aftertime . *M. d'Arthur* 107
S out : what is it thou hast heard .   "   . 130
if you *s* with him that was my son *Dora* . 41
S ! is there any of you halt . . *St S. Stylites* 7, 140
let him *s* his wish. . . .   "   . 142
S, if there be a priest . . .   "   . 211
To alien ears, I did not *s* to these *Love and Duty* 51
was it not well to *s,* To have spoken once " 54
s, and *s* the truth to me, . . *Locksley H.* 23
sweetly did she *s* and move : . .   "   . 71
'Twere better not to breathe or *s,* *Two Voices* . 94
on the mouth, he will not *s.* . .   "   . 252
' I may not *s* of what I know.' .   "   . 435
O, Lady Flora, let me *s* . . . *Day-Dm.* . 1
Her lips are sever'd as to *s* : . .   "   . 50
S a little, Ellen Adair !' . . *Ed. Gray* . 71
Said Lady Clare ' that ye *s* so wild ?' *Lady Clare* 22
I *s* the truth ; you are my child. .   "   . 24
I *s* the truth, as I live by bread .   "   . 26
I will *s* out, for I dare not lie. .   "   . 28
And they *s* in gentle murmur . *L. of Burleigh* 49
letters, was he bound to *s* ? . . *Princess,* i. 179
he heard her *s* ; She scared him ;   "   . 183
scarce could hear each other *s* .   "   . 212
for three years to *s* with any men,   "   ii. 58
my vow Binds me to *s,* . . .   "   . 185
but prepare : I *s* ; it falls.' . .   "   . 206
S little ; mix not with the rest ; .   "   . 339
Abate the stride, which *s*'s of man,   "   . 407
some classic Angel *s* In scorn of us,   "   iii. 68
she *s*'s A Memnon smitten . .   "   . 99
she replied, her duty was to *s,* .   "   . 135
s, and let the topic die.' . . .   "   . 189
surely she will *s* ; if not, then I *s* .   "   iv. 325
made a sudden turn As if to *s,* .   "   . 376
there she lies, But will not *s,* .   "   v. 50
she of whom you *s,* My mother, .   "   . 184
to our lines, And *s* with Arac : .   "   . 217
So often that I *s* as having seen. .   "   vi. 5
Or *s* to her, your dearest, . .   "   . 169
yet *s* to me, Say one soft word .   "   . 201
Is it kind ? *S* to her I say : . .   "   . 232
brother, help ; *s* to the king : . .   "   . 286
cannot *s,* nor move, nor make one sign, " vii. 138
And I can *s* a little then. . . *In Mem.* xix. 16
Who *s* their feeling not it is, . .   "   xx. 5
sometimes harshly will he *s* ; . .   "   xxi. 6
Behold ye *s* an idle thing . . .   "   . 21
Urania *s*'s with darken'd brow : .   "   xxxvii. 1
' I am not worthy ev'n to *s* . .   "   xliii. 15
My guardian angel will *s* out . .   "   lxxiii. 11
Nor *s* it, knowing Death has made   "   lxxix. 10
I hear the sentence that he *s*'s ; .   "   lxxxi. 16
We cannot hear each other *s.* . .   "   lxxxiv. 78
A part of stillness, yearns to *s* . .   "   cxv. 12
Still *s* to me of me and mine . *Maud,* I. i. 59
and thought he would rise and *s* .   "   xvi. 7
this is the day when I must *s* . .   "   xix. 18
I am sure I did but *s* . . .   "   . 27
To *s* of the mother she loved . .   "   . 63
Chid her, and forbid her to *s* . .   "   II ii. 78
s to her things holy and high, . .   "   v. 67
for she never *s*'s her mind . .   "   . 67
S no more of his renown, . . *Ode on Well.* 278

	POEM.	LINE.
the cause because I dare not *s*	*Enid*	89
art not worthy ev'n to *s* of him;'	"	199
S, if you be not like the rest, hawk-mad	"	280
They would not hear me *s*:	"	421
Nor *s* I now from foolish flattery;	"	413
lift an eye nor *s* a word,	"	528
Whatever happens, not to *s* to me	"	866
would only *s* and tell me of it.'	"	903
I laid upon you, not to *s* to me	"	927
That she could *s* whom his own ear	"	962
Needs must I *s*, and tho' he kill me	"	986
' Have I leave to *s*?'	"	989
and *s* To your good damsel there	"	1147
'Get her to *s*: she does not *s* to me.	"	1150
You sit apart, you do not *s* to him,	"	1170
dumbly *s's* Your story	"	1177
s the word: my followers ring him	"	1185
s but the word: Or *s* it not:	"	1191
that you *s* not but obey.'	"	1266
so low he hardly heard her *s*,	"	1491
King's own ear S what has chanced,	"	1657
(I *s* as one S's of a service done him)	"	1695
did I care or dare to *s* with you	"	1719
one verse more—the lady *s's* it—	*Vivien*	205
let her eyes S for her, glowing on him,	"	466
Urged him to *s* against the truth,	*Elaine*	93
to *s* him true, You know right well,	"	154
little need to *s* Of Lancelot in his glory	"	462
S therefore: shall I waste myself	"	667
s the wish most near to your true heart	"	910
like a ghost without the power to *s*.	"	915
'Delay no longer, *s* your wish,	"	920
'S: that I live to hear,' he said	"	924
surely I shall *s* for mine own self,	"	1119
none of you can *s* for me so well,	"	1120
So cannot *s* my mind. An end to this!	"	1216
'He is enchanted, cannot *s*—	"	1247
S, as it waxes, of a love that wanes?	"	1332
s no slander, no, nor listen to it,	*Guinevere*	409
could *s* Of the pure heart, nor seem	"	407
he forgave me, and I could not *s*.	"	607
came to *s* to you of what he wish'd	*En. Arden*	209
'Tired, Annie?' for she did not *s*	"	387
still be living: well then—let me *s*:	"	402
who *s's* with Him, seem all alone.	"	621
turning now and then to *s* with him,	"	756
must I not *s* to these?	"	780
understand, While I have power to *s*.	"	878
s before the people of her child,	*Aylmer's F.*	668
I was bid to *s* of such a one .	"	677
—of him I was not bid to *s*—	"	710
'Love, forgive him:' but he did not *s*;	*Sea Dreams*	45
let her *s* of you well or ill;	*Grandmother*	51
'but I needs must *s* my mind,	"	53
s to me not without a welcome,	*Hendecasyllabics*	11
My tongue Trips, or I *s* profanely.	*Lucretius*	74

speaking.
And I ran by him without *s*,	*May Queen*,i.	18
The voice, that now is *s*,	"	54
make a man feel strong in *s* truth;	*Love and Duty*	68
He said, 'You take it, *s*,'	*Enid*	990
s not, but leaning over him,	*Vivien*	327
Suddenly *s* of the wordless man,	*Elaine*	271
Dark-splendid, *s* in the silence,	"	317
S a still good-morrow with her eyes.	"	1027
is your beauty, and I sin In *s*,	"	1181

spear.
O'erthwarted with the brazen-headed *s*	*Œnone*	117
The brand, the buckler, and the *s* —	*Two Voices*	129
hoofs bare on the ridge of *s's*	*Princess*, v.	478
and thrice they break their *s's*.	*Enid*	562
the long *s* a cubit thro' his breast.	"	935
flesh and wine to feed his *s's*.	"	1449
down before your *s* at a touch.	*Elaine*	140
couch'd their *s's* and prick'd their steeds	"	478
a *s* Down-glancing lamed the charger,	"	486
a *s* Prick'd sharply his own cuirass,	"	487
went down before his *s* at a touch,	"	577
that phalanx of the summer *s's*	*Aylmer's F*	111
brought him slain with *s's*, *'Home they brought him'*		

	POEM.	LINE.
the sparrow *s* by the shrike.	*Maud*, I. iv.	23

spearman.
But left two brawny *spearmen*	*Enid*	1406
His lusty *spearmen* follow'd him	"	1441
And mingled with the *spearmen*	"	1447
the brawny *s* let his cheek bulge.	"	1478

spear-shaft.
The splinter'd *s-s's* crack and fly	*Sir Galahad*	7

speck.
little pitted *s* in garner'd fruit	*Vivien*	244

spectre.
There stands a *s* in your hall:	*L. C. V. de Vere*	42
Nightmare of youth, the *s* of himself:	*Love and Duty*	13
He faced the *s's* of the mind	*In Mem.* xcv.	15
fled Yelling as from a *s*,	*Enid*	1581

speculation.
for a vast *s* had failed.	*Maud*, I. i.	9

speech.
God's great gift of *s* abused.	*A Dirge*	44
full-flowing river of *s*.	*Œnone*	47
hear each other's whisper'd *s*;	*Lotos-Es.*	104
with surprise Froze my swift *s*:	*D. of F. Wom.*	40
He flash'd his random *s'es*;	*Will Water.*	108
address'd to *s*, Who spoke few words	*Princess,Con.*	93
Ere Thought could wed itself to S;	*In Mem.* xxiii.	16
But in dear words of human *s*	" lxxxiv.	83
In matter-moulded forms of *s*,	" xciv.	40
Again the feast, the *s*, the glee	" Con.	101
There *s* and thought and nature failed	*En. Arden*	793
Joyful came his *s*:	*The Captain*	30

speed.
writhed limbs of lightning *s*; '*Clear-headed friend*		25
a favourable *s* Ruffle thy mirror'd	*In Mem.* ix.	6

speedwell.
The little *s's* darling blue	*In Mem.* lxxxii.	10

spell ('s.)
I feel with thee the drowsy *s*.	*Maud*, I. xviii.	72

spell (verb.)
A trifle, sweet! which true love *s's*	*Miller's D.*	187
face is practised, when I *s* the lines,	*Vivien*	217

spence.
Bluff Harry broke into the *s*	*Talking O.*	47

spend.
Where they twain will *s* their days.	*L. of Burleigh*	36

spent.
passion shall have *s* its novel force	*Locksley H.*	10
fear, indeed, you *s* a stormy time	*Princess*, v.	116
I scarce have *s* the worth of one!'	*Enid*	1260
the storm, its burst of passion *s*,	*Vivien*	810
latest breath Was *s* in blessing her	*En. Arden*	885

sphere ('s.)
Dark-blue the deep *s* overhead.	*Arabian N's.*	8
Sure she was nigher to heaven's *s's*,	*Ode to Mem.*	40
from the hollow *s* of the sea,	*The Mermaid*	54
Deepening thro' the silent *s's*,	*Mariana in the S*	91
daughter of a cottager, Out of her *s*.	*Walk. to the M.*	52
centred in *s* Of common duties,	*Ulysses*	39
in dark purple *s's* of sea.	*Locksley H.*	104
In yonder hundred million *s's*'	*Two Voices*	30
men, thro' novel *s's* of thought	"	61
The *s* thy fate allots;	*Will Water.*	218
orient ivory *s* in *s*,	*Princess, Pro*	20
An eagle clang an eagle to the *s*.	" iii.	90
to touch upon a *s* Too gross to tread,	" vii.	305
He mixing with his proper *s*,	*In Mem* lix.	5
A *s* of stars about my soul	" cxxi.	7
Ay is the song of the wedded *s*:	*The Window*	112

sphere (verb.)
S all your lights around, above;	*In Mem.* ix.	13

sphered.
and *s* Whole in ourselves	*Princess*, iv	179
had you been S up with Cassiopëia,	"	414

CONCORDANCE TO

sphere-music.
	POEM.	LINE.
S-m such as that you dream'd about	Sea Dreams	248

spherold.
Of sine and arc, s and azimuth	Princess, vi.	239

spice (s.)
Dripping with Sabæan s	Adeline	53
A summer fann'd with s.	Pal. of Art	116
silks, and fruits, and s's, clear of toll.	Golden Year	45
Bring me s's bring me wine ;	Vision of Sin	76
With summer s the humming air	In Mem. c.	8
like the sultan of old in a garden of s Maud, I iv.		42

spice (verb.)
S his fair banquet with the dust of Maud, I. xviii.		56

spider.
the bastion'd walls Like threaded s's, Princess, i.		107
in a great old tyrant s's web,	Vivien	108

spied.
came into the field and s her not :	Dora	73
s her, and he left his men at work,	"	84
Uncared for, s its mother	Princess, vi.	120
Arthur s the letter in her hand,	Elaine	1263
passing by S where he couch'd,	Guinevere	32

spigot.
merry bloated things Shoulder'd the s, Guinevere		266

spike.
silvery s's are nighest the sea.	The Mermaid	37
High up, in silver s's !	Talking O.	276
he had climb'd across the s's,	Princess, Pro.	111
darted s's and splinters of the wood Vivien		786

spiked.
and grimly s the gates .	Princess, iv.	388

spikenard.
Sweet ! sweet ! s, and balm,	St S. Stylites	208
With costly s and with tears.	In Mem. xxxii	12

spill.
slope, and s Their thousand wreaths Princess, vii.		197
To s his blood and heal the land.	The Victim	46

spilt.
have died and s our bones in the flood— Princess, iv.		511
A little grain shall not be s.'	In Mem. lxiv.	12
the true blood s had in it a heat	Maud, I. xix.	4
the red life s for a private blow	" II. v.	93
burst in dancing, and the pearls were s;	Vivien	302

spin.
Sometimes I saw you sit and s ;	Miller's D.	121
Let the great world s for ever	Locksley H.	182
S's, toiling out his own cocoon.	Two Voices	180

spindling.
The s's look unhappy.	Amphion	92

spine.
stiff s can hold my weary head,	St S. Stylites	42
The three-decker's oaken s	Maud, II. ii.	27
to crate and basket, ribs and s.	Vivien	473

spire.
Looks down upon the village s :	Miller's D.	76
And tipt with frost-like s's.	Pal. of Art	52
With s's of silver shine.'	D. of F. Wom.	188
To watch the three tall s's ;	Godiva	3
he, by farmstead, thorpe and s,	Will Water.	137
like a s of land that stands apart	Princess, vii.	182
a star upon the sparkling s ;	" vii.	182
Bring orchis, bring the foxglove s	In Mem lxxxii.	9
The s's of ice are toppled down,	" cxxvi.	12
With delicate s and whorl,	Maud, II. ii.	6
the well known stream and rustic s,	The Brook	188
A mount of marble, a hundred s's !	The Daisy	60
blazing wyvern weathercock'd the s, Aylmer's F.		17
Utter your jubilee steeple and s !	W. to Alexan.	17

spirit
translucent fane Of her still s ;	Isabel	5
To the young s present	Ode to Mem.	73
A s haunts the year's last hours 'A spirit haunts,' etc.		1
Some s of a crimson rose	Adeline	41

	POEM.	LINE.
Life in dead stones, or s in air ;	A Character	8
riving the s of man,	The Poet	51
She thought, 'My s is here alone, Mariana in the S		47
'Touch'd by thy s's mellowness,	Eleanore	103
all the s is his own.	Miller's D	190
wrought To s to one equal mind—	"	236
In my dry brain my s soon,	Fatima	26
thought of power Flatter'd his s,	Œnone	135
Music that genther on the s lies,	Lotos-E's.	90
harken what the inner s sings,	"	67
lend our hearts and s's wholly	"	108
to name my s loathes and fears ;	D. of F. Wom.	106
Sweetens the s still	"	236
Your s is the calmed sea	Margaret	25
from the s thro' the brain,	To J. S.	38
Sleep, holy s, blessed soul,	"	70
Whose s's falter in the mist 'You ask me why,' etc.		3
The S of the years to come 'Love thou thy land,' etc.		55
so light of foot, so light of s—	Gardener's D.	14
crush'd My s flat before thee.	St S. Stylites	26
this gray s yearning in desire	Ulysses	30
All the s deeply dawning	Locksley H.	28
And our s s rush'd together .	"	38
And his s leaps within him	"	115
promise of my s hath not set.	"	187
Go, vexed S, sleep in trust ; .	Two Voices	115
That read his s blindly wise.	"	287
To s's folded in the womb.	Day-Dm.	28
His s flutters like a lark,	"	129
Make Thou my s pure and clear .	St Agnes' Eve	9
My s before Thee ;	"	18
My s beats her mortal bars	Sir Galahad	46
found My s's in the golden age.	To E. L.	12
And her s changed within.	L. of Burleigh	64
Tho' at times her s sank :	"	70
That her s might have rest.	"	100
Encarnalize their s's :	Princess, iii.	298
freedom, force and growth Of s	" iv.	124
on my s's Settled a gentle cloud	"	546
My s closed with Ida's at the lips ;	" vii.	143
A S. not a breathing voice.	In Mem. xiii.	12
For I in s saw thee move	" xvii.	5
So much the vital s's sink	" xx.	18
But they my troubled s rule .	" xxviii.	17
Survive in s's render'd free,	" xxxvii.	10
look on S's breath'd away,	" xxxix.	2
Thy s ere our fatal loss.	" xl.	1
That stir the s's inner deeps,	" xli.	10
And every s's folded bloom	" xlii.	2
Before the s's fade away,	" xlvi.	14
The S of true love replied ; .	" li.	6
'What keeps a s wholly true	"	6
The s does but mean the breath	" lv.	7
My s loved and loves him yet,	" lix.	2
I loved thee, S, and love	" lx.	11
From state to state the s walks : .	" lxxxi.	6
Thy s should fail from off the globe ;	" lxxxiii.	36
Thy s up to mine can reach ;	" lxxxiv.	82
A hundred s's whisper ' Peace.'	" lxxxv.	16
fierce extremes employ Thy s's	" lxxxvii.	6
Thy s in time among thy peers ;	" xc.	6
No s ever brake the band	" xcii.	2
he, the S him-self, may come	"	8
S to S, Ghost to Ghost.	"	8
call The S from their golden day,	" xciii.	6
My s is at peace with all.	" xcvi.	8
And of my s as of a wife.	"	8
Two s's of a diverse love	" ci.	7
Thro' which the s breathes no more ?	" civ.	20
The churl in s, up or down .	" cx.	5
The churl in s, howe'er he veil	"	5
But in my s will I dwell,	" cxxii.	9
He breathed the s of the song ;	" cxxiv.	10
While thou, dear s, happy star,	" cxxvi.	18
Let all my genial s's advance.	Con.	77
lust of gain, in the s of Cain,	Maud, I. i.	23
And the s of murder works	"	40
a s bounded and poor ; .	" iv.	38
Peace, angry s, and let him be !	" xiii.	44
When all my s reels	II. iv.	20
Would the happy s descend ?	"	81

	POEM.	LINE.
Touch a *s* among things divine,	Ode on Well.	139
like a household *S* at the walls,	Enid	1252
heard the *S*'s of the waste and weald	Guinevere	128
beheld three *s*'s mad with joy	"	250
so glad were *s*'s and men	"	267
ill prophets were they all, *S*'s and men:	"	271
round him bent the *s*'s of the hills	"	281
lifted up in *s* he moved away.	En. Arden.	327
all her vital *s*'s into each ear,	Aylmer's F.	201
they that cast her *s* into flesh,	"	481
meek, Exceeding 'poor in *s*'—	"	754
hear it, *S* of Cassivelaun!	Boädicea	20

spirit-thrilling.
Those *s-t* eyes so keen and beautiful Ode to Mem. 39

spirit.
upjetted in *s*'s of wild sea-smoke . Sea Dreams 52

spirited.
Prince's blood *s* upon the scarf, . Enid . 208

spit (s.)
bits of roasting ox Moan round the *s* Lucretius . 132

spit (verb.)
I hate, abhor, *s*, sicken at him; . Lucretius . 196

spite.
Delicious *s*'s and darling angers	Madeline	6
half in love, half *s*, he woo'd and wed	Dora	37
Fill'd I was with folly and *s*,	E.l. Gray	15
sins of emptiness, gossip and *s*	Princess, ii.	78
The civic slander and the *s*:	In Mem. cv.	22
Nor ever narrowness or *s*,	"	cx. 17
a city, with gossip, scandal and *s*;	Maud, I. iv.	8
His face, as I grant, in *s* of *s*,	"	xiii. 8
all our churchmen foam in *s*:	To F. D. Maurice	9
'A ship of fools' he shriek'd in *s*.	The Voyage	77
I hate the *s*'s and the follies.	Spiteful Let.	21
hate and pity, and *s* and scorn	Lucretius	77

splash.
and the *s* and stir Of fountains . Princess, i. 214

spleen.
They are fill'd with idle *s*;	Vision of Sin	124
cook'd his *s*, Communing with his.	Princess, i.	65
with the least little touch of *s*.	Maud, I. ii.	11
Geraint flash'd into sudden *s*:	Enid	273
is your *s* froth'd out, or have ye more?'	Vivien	617

spleen-born.
S-b, I think, and proofless . . Vivien . 552

spleenful.
rode Geraint, a little *s* yet, . . Enid . 293

splendid.
Sees whatever fair and *s*	L. of Burleigh	27
So *s* in his acts and his attire,	Enid	620
people cried '*S* is the flower.'	The Flower	16

splendour.
A sudden *s* from behind	Arabian N*'s.	81
The maiden *s*'s of the morning star	D. of F. Wom.	55
Made lightnings in the *s* of the moon	M.d'Arthur	137
The *s* falls on castle walls	Princess, iii.	348
long lines of *s* slanted o'er a press	"	iv. 457
sheathing *s*'s and the golden scale	"	v. 39
A flying *s* out of brass and steel,	"	vi. 345
suck a blinding *s* from the sand,	"	vii. 24
height and cold, and the *s* of the hills?	"	179
burn'd the *s* of the sun :	In Mem. lxxi.	8
All her *s* seems No livelier	"	xcvii. 6
And breaking let the *s* fall	"	Con. 119
I saw the treasured *s*, her hand,	Maud, I. vi.	84
whose *s* plucks The slavish hat	"	x. 3
nearer to the glow Of your soft *s*'s	"	xviii. 79
Queen Maud in all her *s*.	"	xix. 50
And a dewy *s* falls	"	II iv. 32
leaves The Crown a lonely *s*.	Ded. of Idylls	48
daily fronted him In some fresh *s*;	Enid	14
Made a low *s* in the world,	"	598
cast aside A *s* dear to women	"	608

splenetic.
And therefore *s*, personal, base, . Maud, I x. 33

	POEM.	LINE.
into fiery *s*'s leapt the lance	Princess, v.	483
darted spikes and *s*'s of the wood.	Vivien	726

splinter (verb.)
| and to *s* it into feuds | Guinevere | 17 |
| gay navy there should *s* on it, | Sea Dreams | 127 |

splinter'd.
| A lance that *s* like an icicle | Enid | 938 |
| Spars were *s*, | The Captain | 45, 49 |

split.
upon the corn-laws, where we *s*,	Audley Ct.	34
wild figtree *s* Their monstrous idols	Princess, iv.	61
takes, and breaks, and cracks, and *s*'s,	"	v. 516

Splugen.
And up the snowy *S* drew, . The Daisy . 86

spoil (s.)
the children laden with their *s*: . En. Arden . 442

spoil (verb.)
| to slay the folk, and *s* the land. | Guinevere | 136 |
| and *s*'s My bliss in being; | Lucretius | 218 |

spoil'd.
still the foeman *s* and burn'd . The Victim 17

spoiler.
loud sabbath shook the *s* down; . Ode on Well. 123

spoilt.
| You have *s* this child; | Princess, v. | 112 |
| thou hast *s* the purpose of my life | Guinevere | 450 |

spoke.
She *s* at large of many things	Miller's D.	155
at the last she *s* of me	"	156
Last night, when some one *s* his name,	Fatima	1
She *s* and laugh'd: I shut my sight	Œnone	184
S slowly in her place.	D. of F. Wom	92
We *s* of other things; we coursed	Gardener's D.	217
in that time and place, I *s* to her,	"	221
I *s*, while Audley feast Humm'd.	Audley Ct.	3
Poet-like he *s*	E.L. Morris	27
this or something like to this he *s*.	"	41
I *s* her name alone.	"	68
Whether he *s* too largely :	"	71
So I *s* knowing not the things that were.	"	89
I *s* without restraint,	Talking O.	1
And mystic sentence *s*;	"	294
I *s*, but answer came there none :	Two Voices	425
Sweet Emma Moreland *s* to me :	Ed. Gray	5
Petulant she *s*, and at herself	Princess, Pro.	152
s of those That lay at wine	"	ii. 112
it was duty *s*, not I.	"	268
s of war to come and many deaths	"	iii. 134
I *s* not then at first, but watch'd.	"	iv. 320
then stood up, and *s* impetuously	"	358
being caught, feign death, *S* not.	"	v. 106
Yet she neither *s* nor moved	"	530
Ida *s* not, rapt upon the child	"	vi. 203
Ida *s* not, gazing on the ground,	"	213
Old studies failed; seldom she *s*;	"	vii. 16
Hortensia *s* against the tax;	"	112
Who *s* few words and pithy,	Con.	94
But *s* not, rapt in nameless reverie	"	108
I with as fierce an anger *s*.	Maud, II. i.	17
And *s* of a hope for the world	" III. vi.	11
sweet seventeen subdued me ere she *s*	The Brook	113
while she *s*, I saw where James	"	116
I *s* with heart, and heat and force	The Letters	37
He *s* among you, and the Man who *s*;	Ode on Well.	178
Who never *s* against a foe	"	185
Half-inwardly, half audibly she *s*	Enid	101
He *s* and fell to work again.	"	202
Prince and Earl Yet *s* together,	"	385
if he *s* at all, would break perforce	"	671
He *s* in words part heard,	Vivien	683
Lancelot *s* And answer'd him at full,	Elaine	285
s, he answer'd not, Or short and coldly	"	802
While he *s* She neither blush'd	"	959
and Enoch *s* his love,	En. Arden.	40
till the morrow, when he *s*	"	116
Philip coming somewhat closer *s*.	"	359

	POEM.	LINE.
answer'd Annie; tenderly she s:	En. Arden	419
gently 'Annie, when I s to you,	"	414
Enoch s no word to anyone,	"	668
so fell back and s no more,	"	913
I know not, for he s not	Aylmer's F.	213
While thus he s, his hearers wept	"	722
s with me on the shore;	Sea Dreams	255
were you silent when I s to-night?	"	259
your rough voice (You s so loud)	"	270
I started, and s I scarce knew how:	Grandmother	43

spoken.

would have s, but he found not words	M. d'Arthur	172
well to speak, To have s once?	Love and Duty	55
would have s, And warn'd that madman	Vision of Sin	55
so she would have s, but there rose	Princess, iv.	454
sweet soul, had hardly s a word,	Maud, II. i.	11
s to her, And loosed in words	Enid	954
half her realm, had never s word.	Elaine	73
Has Arthur s aught?	"	118
had not his poor heart S with That,	En Arden	620
you shall say that having s with me	Aylmer's F	311
Down they dropt—no word was s—	The Captain	51

sponged.

S and made blank of crimeful record . . *St S Stylites* 156

spongy-wet

Is hoar with rime, or s-w; . . *To F. D. Maurice* 42

sport (s.)

But take it—earnest wed with s,	Day-Dm	279
s Went hand in hand with Science;	Princess, Pro.	79
otherwhere Pure s:	"	81
Lilia, wild with s,	"	100
Or master'd by the sense of s,	" iv.	138
—the striplings!—for their s!—	" v.	389
The s half-science, fill me with a faith	" Con.	76
He mixt in all our simple s s;	In Mem. lxxxviii.	10
and loud With s and song.	" xcvii.	28
The s of random sun and shade.	Con.	24
to break her s's with graver fits	Vivien	36
pretty s's have brighten'd all again	"	754
on love And s and tilts and pleasure,	Guinevere	384
Me the s of ribald Veterans,	Boädicea	50

sport (verb).

To s beneath thy boughs	Talking O.	100
hence, indeed, she s's with words,	In Mem. xlvii.	9

spot.

A s of dull stagnation	Pal. of Art	245
So find I every pleasant s	In Mem. viii.	9

spouse.

'Worthy a Roman s.'	D. of F. Wom.	164
If ever maid or s,	Talking O.	74
With only Fame for s,	Princess, iii.	226
Hope and Memory, s and bride.	On a Mourner	23

spout (s.)

little wide-mouth'd heads upon the s	Godiva	56
s whereon the gilded ball Danced	Princess, Pro.	63

spout (verb)

S from the maiden fountain in her . . *Lucretius* . 237

spouted.

golden gorge of dragons s forth	Pal. of Art	23
s his foam-fountains in the sea	Lotos-E's.	152
the fountain s, showering wide	Vision of Sin	21
fountains s up and showering down	Princess, i.	215

spouting.

as a stream that s from a cliff . . *Guinevere* . 602

sprang.

Out I s from glow to gloom;	Princess, iv.	160
out of stricken helmets s the fire.	" v.	484
Psyche as she s To meet it,	" vi.	392
S up for ever at a touch,	In Mem. cxi.	10
and the blood S to her face	Elaine	376
S from the midriff of a prostrate king	Aylmer's F.	16
To the altar-stone she s alone,	The Victim	72
s No dragon warriors from Cadmean	Lucretius	49
yell'd again Half-suffocated, and s up	"	58
And from it s the Commonwealth,	"	238

spray (foam.)	POEM.	LINE.
tender curving lines of creamy s;	Lotos-E's.	107
Torn from the fringe of s.	D. of F. Wom.	40

spray (twig.)

From s, and branch, and stem,	Talking O.	190
The snake slipt under a s,	Poet's Song	10
a song on every s Of birds	Princess, v.	228
touchwood, with a single flourishing s	Aylmer's F.	512

spread.

s his sheeny vans for flight;	Love and Death	8
time and space to work and s. 'You ask me why, 'etc.		16
So muscular he s,	Gardener's D.	8
A cedar s his dark-green layers	"	115
S the light haze along the river-shores	"	259
hope ere death S's more and more	St S Stylites	155
The life that s s in them,	Talking O.	192
close and dark my arms I s,	"	225
S upward till thy boughs discern	"	247
light shall s, and man be liker man	Golden Year	35
sees the sacred morning s	Two Voices	80
every cloud, that s's above	"	446
o'er the dark a glory s's,	Sir Galahad	55
To s into the perfect fan,	Sir L. and Q. G.	17
The chap-fallen circle s's:	Vision of Sin	172
branches thereupon S out at top	Princess, iv.	188
A rampant heresy, such as if it s	"	392
S thy full wings, and waft him o'er.	In Mem. ix.	4
S his mantle dark and cold,	" xxii.	14
Proclaiming social truth shall s	" cxxvi.	5
o'er the friths that branch and s	Con.	115
over whom thy darkness must have s	Maud, I. xviii.	10
boil'd the flesh, and s the board,	Enid	391
he rose, he s his arms abroad	En Arden	911
s the Word by which himself had	Sea Dreams	193

spreadeth.

Which the moon about her s . . *Margaret* . 20

spreading.

s made Fantastic plume . . *The Voyage* . 43

sprig.

s's of summer laid between the folds, *Enid* . 130

spring (fountain, etc.)

Do beating hearts of salient s's	Adeline	26
The s's of life, the depths of awe,	Two Voices	140
(If Death so taste Lethean s's)	In Mem. xliii.	10
While yet beside its vocal s's	" lxiii.	22
Nor ever drank the inviolate s	" lxxxix.	2
The bitter s's of anger and fear;	Maud, I. x.	49
In mine own lady palms I cull'd the s	Vivien	122
sets her pitcher underneath the s,	En. Arden	207

Spring (season.)

S Letters cowslips on the hill?	Adeline	61
the breathings Of Hope and Youth.	The Poet	27
Sweet as new buds in S.	D. of F. Wom.	272
tho' I spared thee all the s,	The Blackbird	9
Caught in the frozen palms of S.	"	24
'tween the sand and downfall of the light	St S. Stylites	108
in these latter s's I saw	Talking O.	75
Like those blind motions of the S,	"	175
In the S a fuller crimson comes (rep.)	Locksley H.	17
my pulses with the fullness of the S.	"	36
The maiden S upon the plain	Sir L. and Q. G.	3
She seem'd a part of joyous S;	"	23
a thousand rings of S In every bole,	Princess, v.	227
strip a hundred hollows bare of S	" vi.	49
And all the secret of the S.	In Mem. xxiii.	19
The herald melodies of s,	" xxxviii.	6
And men the flies of latter s.	" xlix.	10
And every winter change to s	" lii.	16
I dream'd there would be S no more,	" lxviii.	1
S that swells the narrow brooks	" lxxxiv.	10
As not unlike to that of S.	"	120
in my breast S wakens too;	" cxiv.	18
earnest in it of far s's to be.	Vivien	407
My s is all the nearer,	The Window	59
S is here with leaf and grass?	"	128

spring (verb.)

s's on a level of bowery lawn,	Poet's Mind	31
ringing, s's from brand and mail;	Sir Galahad	54

	POEM.	LINE.
she whose elfin prancer *s*'s	Sir L. and Q. C.	33
a tiger-cat In act to *s*.	Princess, ii.	427
as prompt to *s* against the pikes	"	269
s's the clowning race of humankind	" vii.	279
as a dove when up she *s*'s	In Mem xii.	1
the wiser man who *s*'s Hereafter,	" cxix.	7
sober freedom out of which there *s*'s	Ode on Well	164
Ready to *s*, waiting a chance:	Guinevere	13
Wilt *s* to me, and claim me thine,	"	561

springing.
| took root, and *s* forth anew | The Poet | 21 |
| *S* alone With a shrill inner sound, | The Mermaid | 19 |

sprinkled.
and the blood Was *s* on your kirtle.	Princess, ii.	255
household Fury *s* with blood	Maud, I. xix.	32
jewels on it *S* about in gold	Aylmer's F.	221

sprouted.
| manlike, but his brows Had *s*, | Princess, iv. | 187 |

sprung.
| tall flag-flowers when they *s*. | Miller's D. | 53 |

spun.
| wheels of Time *S* round in station, | Love and Duty | 74 |
| The petty cobwebs we have *s*: | In Mem cxxii. | 8 |

spur (s.)
From *s* to plume a star of tournament	M. d'Arthur	222
up we rose, and on the *s* we went.	Gardener's D.	32
on the *s* she fled; and more We know not	Princess,i	150
it seems my *s*'s are yet to win.	Enid	128
from *s* to plume Red as the rising sun	Elaine	307
Set lance in rest, strike *s*,	"	455

spur (verb.)
| desire That *s*'s an imitative will | In Mem. cix. | 20 |

spurn'd.
| *S* by this heir of the har— | Maud, I. xix. | 78 |

spurr'd.
s at heart with fieriest energy	To J. M. K.	7
last I *s*; I felt my veins Stretch	Princess, v.	526
S with his terrible war-cry;	Enid	1019
by his own stale devil *s*,	Aylmer's F.	790

spurt.
| A sudden *r* of woman's jealousy— | Vivien | 374 |

spy's.
| harry me, petty *s* And traitress.' | Guinevere | 358 |

spy (verb.)
embower the nest, Some boy would *s*	Princess,Pro.	148
To *s* some secret scandal if he might	Guinevere	27
she thought ' he *spies* a field of death.	"	113
a seaman's glass, *S* out my face	En. Arden	216
to *s* The weakness of a people	Aylmer's F.	569

squadron
| *S*'s and squares of men in brazen | D. of F. Wom. | 33 |
| embattled squares, And *s*'s of the Prince | Princess,v. | 237 |

squall
| *s* nor storm Could keep me from | Gardener's D. | 186 |
| thro' the gray skirts of a lifting *s*. | En. Arden | 830 |

squall'd.
| The parrot scream'd, the peacock *s*, | Day-Dm. | 144 |

square.
s's of men in brazen plates,	D. of F. Wom.	33
All the land In flowery *s*'s,	Gardener's D.	75
s s of tropic summer shut	Amphion	87
Muses of the cube and *s*	Princess,Pro.	178
casement slowly grows a glimmering *s*.	" iv.	34
embattled *s*'s And squadrons of the	" v.	236
They call'd me in the public *s*'s.	In Mem lxviii	11
maze of quick About the flowering *s*,	" cxiv.	3
And I loathe the *s*'s and streets	Maud,II iv.	52
Dash'd on every rocky *s*	Ode on Well.	174
massive *s* of his heroic breast,	Enid	75
A *s* of text that looks a little blot,	Vivien	521
every *r* of text an awful charm,	"	523
The ruddy *s* of comfortable light,	En. Arden	727

	POEM.	LINE.
stunted *s*'s of West or East:	Princess, ii.	64

squeezed.
| he had *s* himself betwixt the bars | Princess, Pro. | 112 |

squire.
Late-left an orphan of the *s*,	Miller's D.	35
slain with laughter roll'd the gilded *S*.	Princess,v.	35
Our ponderous *s* will give	Maud. I. xx.	74
the four-year-old I sold the *S*.'	The Brook	137
the *S* had seen the colt at grass	"	110
shook his drowsy *s* awake	Enid	125
page, and maid, and *s*, and seneschal	"	710
and hurl'd it toward the *s*	"	872
and the *s* Chafing his shoulder:	"	875
In silence, did him service as a *s*;	"	1255
a fair young *s* who sat alone.	Vivien	522
twice to-day. I am your *S*.'	Elaine	383

squireling.
| dinner To half the *s*'s near; | Maud, I. xx. | 26 |

squirrel.
| And snared the *s* of the glen? | Princess, ii. | 251 |

squoir.
Tho' a knaws I hallus voäted wi' *S* .*N*	Farmer	15
wi' haäte oonderd haäcre o' *S*'s	"	41
An' *S* 'ull be sa mad an' all	"	47
I 'a monaged for *S* coom Michaelmas	"	43
they knaws what I beän to *S*	"	55
I done my duty by *S*	"	56
S's in Lunnon, an' summun I reckons	"	57

staäte.
| voäted wi' Squoire an' choorch an' *s* | N. Farmer | 15 |

stab (s.)
| deathful *s*'s were dealt apace, | Oriana | 52 |

stab (verb.)
| little boys begin to shoot and *s* | Princess,Con. | 61 |

stabbed.
should have *s* me where I lay	Oriana	55
Three times I *s* him thro' and thro'	The Sisters.	29
She would have *s* him:	Vivien	702
S thro' the heart's affections	"	717

stable.
| ran To loose him at the *s s*. | Aylmer's F. | 126 |

stable-wench.
| A plump-arm'd Ostleress and a *s-w* | Princess, i. | 223 |

staff.
| struck his *s* against the rocks | Golden Year | 53 |

stagger.
| I *s* in the stream: | Princess, vi. | 301 |
| And as blindly ere she sink? | In Mem. xvi. | 14 |

stagger'd.
| *S* and shook, holding the branch. | En. Arden | 768 |

staggering.
| and *s* back With stroke on stroke. | Princess, v. | 512 |

stagnate.
| *s*'s in the weeds of sloth, | In Mem.xxvii. | 11 |
| let foul wrong *s* and be, | Enid | 173 |

stagnation.
| A spot of dull *s*, without light | Pal. of Art | 245 |

stain (s.)
| Some *s* or blemish in a name of note, | Vivien | 681 |
| to have loved One peerless, without *s*; | Elaine | 1035 |

stain (verb.)
| And I, 'Can clouds of nature *s* | In Mem.lxxxiv.85 |

stair.
Broad-based flights of angels *s*'s.	Arabian N's.	117
The rock rose clear, or winding *s*.	Pal. of Art	12
up the corkscrew *s* With hand and	Walk. to the M.82
his footsteps smite the threshold *s*'s	St S. Stylites	183
adown the *s* Stole on:	Godiva	43
up a flight of *s*'s into the hall.	Princess, ii.	17
A column'd entry shone and marble *s*'s	" v.	351
me they bore up the broad *s*'s,	" vi.	353

	POEM.	LINE.
high above a piece of turret s,	Enid	320
All up the marble s, tier over tier,	Elaine	1241
ghostly footfall echoing on the s.	Guinevere	503
golden feet on these empurpled s's	Lucretius	135

stake
I'll s my ruby ring upon it . . Princess, Pro. 168

stalk.
he boweth the heavy s's ' A spirit haunts,' etc 7
these are but the shatter'd s s . InMem lxxxi. 7

stall.
and even beasts have s's, .	St S. Stylites	107
The s's are void, the doors are wide	Sir Galahad	31
A man upon a s may find, .	InMem, lxxvi.	9
Take him to s and give him corn.	Enid	371
Enoch took his charger to the s,	"	382

stalling.
chamber for the night, And s for the horses Enid 1088

Stamford-town.
Burleigh house by S-t . . . L of Burleigh 92

stammer
| made my tongue so s and trip | Maud, I. vi. | 83 |
| left him leave to s, 'is it indeed?' | Elaine | 419 |

stammer'd.
I s that I knew him— . . Princess, iii. 190

stammering.
| they sat S and staring; . | Guinevere | 101 |
| s ' scoundrel' out of teeth that ground | Aylmer's F. | 328 |

stamp.
| s's the caste of Vere de Vere | L C V. de Vere | 40 |
| to s him with her master's mark :. | Vivien | 609 |

stamped.
And the leaf is s in clay. . . Vision of Sin 82

staunched.
bare him in, There s his wound, . Elaine 519

staud.
s beside my father's door, .	' Ode to Mem.	57
Where you s you cannot hear	Poet's Mind	19
s's in the distance yonder : .	"	30
S's in the sun and shadows all	Love and Death	11
I will s and mark. . .	To J. M. K.	14
at the casement seen her s? .	L. of Shalott, i.	25
I s before thee, Eleanore ; . .	Eleanore	69
To s apart, and to adore, . .	"	79
Gargarus S's up and takes the morning Œnone		11
s's a spectre in your hall . .	L. C. V. de Vere	42
charm'd and tied To where he s's,—	D. of F. Wom.	194
her fair form may s and shine, 'Of old sat	Freedom'	21
half s's up And bristles; . .	Walk. to the M.	23
saw An angel s and watch me, .	St. S. Stylites	34
That s within the chace. . .	Talking O.	4
That here beside me s's, . .	"	142
Than that earth should s at gaze .	Lockstey H.	180
when the tide of combat s's, .	Sir Galahad	10
See the lordly castles s : . .	L. of Burleigh	18
Ring'd with the azure world he s's.	The Eagle	3
like a spire of land that s's apart .	Princess, IV.	262
beat to battle where he s's ; . .	"	555
'S, who goes?' Two from the palace	"	v. 3
this is all, I s upon her side ; .	"	281
see how you s Stiff as Lot's wife .	"	vi. 223
all the phantom, Nature, s's— .	InMem. iii.	9
Dark house, by which once more I s	"	vii. 1
we may s Where he in English .	"	xvii.
in the furrow musing s's ; . .	"	lxiii. 21
let this holly s ; . . .	"	civ. 6
From form to form. and nothing s's ; .	"	cxxii. 6
Six feet two, as I think. he s's, .	Maud, I xiii.	10
Yet I thought I saw her s . .	" II. i.	36
Did he s at the diamond door .	" III. i.	16
glory of manhood s on his ancient	" III. vi.	21
all the wood s s in a mist of green	The Brook	14
and there S's Philip's farm . .	"	38
Let his great example s Colossal .	Ode on Well	220
To break the blast of winter. s ;	To F. D Maurice	22

	POEM.	LINE.
ride with him to battle and s by, .	Enid	94
so bold, and could I so s by .	"	102
good knight's horse s's in the court	"	370
S aside, And if I fall . .	"	1000
if a man who s's upon the brink .	"	1321
Set up the charge you know, to s or fall!	Vivien	553
s High on a heap of slain, . .	Elaine	306
seem'd to s On some vast plain .	Guinevere	76
S's in a wind, ready to break and fly,	"	367
S's at thy gate for thee to grovel to—	Aylmer's F.	632
at Beauty's gate call would perch and s	Coquette, i.	3
Shall s : ay surely ; then it fails .	Lucretius	260
and I s on the slope of the hill .	The Window	9

standard (ensign.)
With the s's of the peoples . . Locksley H. 126

standard (tree.)
espaliers and the s's all Are thine ; The Blackbird 5

standest.
Thou s in the rising sun, . . In Mem. cxxix. 3

standeth.
That s there alone, . . D. of the O. Year 50

standing.
lilies, s near Purple-spiked lavender :	Ode to Mem	109
Joined not, but stood, and s saw .	Pal. of Art	254
Stiller than chisell'd marble, s there ;	D. of F. Wom.	86
Memory s near Cast down her eyes,	To J. S.	53
wicket-gate and found her s there	Gardener'sD.	208
He, s still, was clutch'd ; . .	Princess, iv.	241
s like a stately Pine . . .	" v.	336
And s, muffled round with woe, .	In Mem xiv.	5
she is s here at my head ; . .	Maud, II. v.	65
The maiden s in the dewy light. .	Elaine	351
s by the shield In silence, . .	"	393
thro' the casement s wide for heat .	"	1227
Philip s up said falteringly . .	En. Arden.	283
The Virgin Mother s with her child	Sea Dreams	214
s loftily charioted, . . .	Boädicea	3. 70

stannin'.
What atta s theer for, . . . N Farmer 65

stanza.
those three s's that you made . Talking O 135

star.
Distinct with vivid s's inlaid. .	Arabian N's.	90
Sole s of all that place and time, .	"	152
Was cloven with the million s's .	Ode to Mem.	55
With golden s's above . .	The Poet	7
shepherd who watcheth the evening s,	Dying Swan	35
There would be neither moon nor s.	The Merman	21
Like to some branch of s's we see	L. of Shalott,	iii 11
a s, in inmost heaven set . .	Eleanore	89
white-breasted like a s . . .	Œnone	56
wanton pard Eyed like the evening s	"	196
the loud stream and the trembling s's	"	215
into Troy, and ere the s's come forth	"	258
Sole as a flying s shot thro' the sky	Pal. of Art	123
Crown'd dying day with s's, .	"	184
A s that with the choral starry dance	"	252
happy s's above them seem to brighten	MayQueen, i.	34
up to Heaven and die among the s's	" iii.	40
the hollow dark, like burning s's, .	D. of F. Wom.	18
large white s's rise one by one .	"	223
You are the evening s, alway .	Margaret	27
What songs belcw the waning s's.	"	33
this s Rose with you thro a little arc	To J. S.	25
While the s's burn, the moons increase	"	71
if Nature's evil s Drive men ' Love thou thy land'		73
bump'd the ice into three several s's	The Epic	12
cry that shiver'd to the tingling s's	M. d'Arthur	190
From spur to plume a s of tournament	"	223
ere a s can wink, beheld her there.	Gardener'sD	121
and Love's white s Beam'd . .	"	161
all their mystic gulfs with fleeting s's,	"	257
I wake ' the still s's sparkle : .	St S. Stylites	112
paused Among her s's to hear us;	Love and Duty	72
s's that hung Love-charm'd to listen ;	"	72
follow knowledge like a sinking s,	Ulysses	31
the baths Of all the western s's, .	"	61

	POEM.	LINE.
o'er them many a sliding s.	Day-Dm.	177
On secrets of the brain, the s's,	"	223
Draw me, thy bride, a glittering s,	St Agnes' Eve	23
star-like mingles with the s	Sir Galahad	48
on my cradle shone the Northern s	Princess, i.	4
without a s, Not like a king:	"	116
wing'd horses dark against the s's	"	208
In shining draperies, headed like a s,	" ii	94
glorious names Were fewer, scatter'd s's,	"	140
The s, the bird, the fish, the shell	"	361
in the white wake of the morning s	iii.	1
the nebulous s we call the Sun,	iv.	1
Now poring on the glowworm, now the s,	"	193
leader wildswan in among the s's,	"	414
those three s's of the airy Giant's zone,	v.	250
The tops shall strike from s to s,	xi	41
S after s, arose and fell;	vii.	35
lies the Earth, all Danaë to the s's	"	167
sit a s upon the sparkling spire,	"	182
'The s's,' she whispers, 'blindly run;	In Mem iii.	5
Slide from the bosom of the s's,	" xvii.	16
orb into the perfect s	" xxiv.	15
Look also, Love, a brooding s,	" xlv.	15
grapples with his evil s;	" lxii.	8
clouds that drench the morning s	" lxxi.	22
To where in yonder orient s	" lxxxv.	15
Before the crimson-circled s	" lxxxviii.	47
He reads the secret of the s,	" xcvi.	22
And one the shaping of a s,	" cii.	36
A sphere of s's about my soul,	" cxxi.	7
While thou, dear spirit, happy s,	" cxxvi.	18
But tho' I seem in s and flower	" cxxix.	6
brighten like the s that shook	" Con.	31
s and system rolling past	"	122
if ever that light be my leading s	Maud, I. iv.	12
you fair s's that crown a happy day	" xviii.	30
Beat, happy s's, timing with things	"	81
like a silent lightning under the s's	III. vi.	9
I murmur under moon and s's	The Brook	178
holds her head to other s's,	"	145
sweetly gleam'd the s's.	The Letters	41
Lavish Honour shower'd all her s's	Ode on Well.	196
Remembering all the beauty of that s	Ded. of Idylls	45
With moon and trembling s's	Enid	8
chargers trampling many a prickly s	"	313
as the white and glittering s of morn	"	734
Kiss'd the white s upon his noble front,	"	1605
rather seem'd a lovely baleful s	Vivien	111
misty s, Which is the second in a line of s's	"	358
her bald, her silver s of eve,	"	803
like a s in blackest night.	Elaine	1236
the great s s that globed themselves	En Arden	598
Shone like a mystic s	Aylmer's F.	72
robe of jasmine sown with s's:	"	158
S to s vibrates light;	"	578
such a s of morning in their blue,	"	692
every s in heaven Can make it fair;	Sea Dreams	82
I saw one lovely s Larger and larger.	"	91
crown'd with s and high among the s's,	"	233
Close over us, the silver s	Tithonus	25
Ere yet they blind the s's	"	39
New s's all night above the brim	The Voyage	25
And all her s's decay	The Ringlet	10
Melt into s's for the land's desire	Wel. to Alexan	21
the s's about the moon Look beautiful,	Spec. of Iliad	1
all the s's Shine, and the Shepherd gladdens	"	15
Fancy sadder than a single s	Coquette,	1
Tho' silence and the trembling s s	On a Mourner	26
falls the least white s of snow,	Lucretius	107
Taken the s's from the night	The Window	39
And you are his morning s	"	189

star (verb.)

| s The black earth with brilliance | Ode to Mem. | 19 |

starboard

| Roll'd to s, roll'd to larboard | Lotos-E's | 151 |

star-broider'd.

| The silk s-b coverlid | Day-Dm. | 85 |

	POEM	LINE.
stare (s.)		
last, you fix'd a vacant r,	L. C. V. de Vere	47
With a stony British s.	Maud, I. xiii.	22
stare (verb)		
Painted, who s at open space,	Enid	1117
stared.		
Whereat he s, replying, half-amazed,	Godiva	21
Fantastic gables, crowding, s	"	61
And s, with his foot on the prey.	Poet's Song.	12
s As blank as death in marble;	Princess, i.	174
S with great eyes, and laugh'd	" iv.	101
Fear S in her eyes,	"	358
aghast The women s at these	" vi.	342
S on eyes a bashful azure,	The Brook	205
he started up and s at her.	Enid	1238
unswallow'd piece, and turning s;	"	1429
full-busted figure-head So'er the ripple	En Arden	65
as I s, a fire, The fire that left	Lucretius	64
staring.		
and thou art s at the wall,	Locksley H.	79
All s at her in her faded silk:	Enid	611
men and women s and aghast,	"	2652
Linger'd that other, s after him;	Elaine	717
they sat Stammering and s:	Guinevere	101
S for ever from their gilded walls	Aylmer's F.	833
stark.		
but when she saw me lying s	Princess, vi.	81
starlight.		
Thro' all yon s keen,	St Agnes' Eve	22
star-like.		
The s-l sorrows of immortal eyes,	D of F. Wom	91
And s-l mingles with the stars.	Sir Galahad	43
starred.		
S from Jehovah's gorgeous armouries	Milton	6
starry.		
The night is s and cold, my friend	D. of the O. Year	31
star-shine.		
By s-s and by moonlight	Oriana	24
star-sisters.		
S-s answering under crescent brows	Princess, ii.	406
star-strown.		
My shallop thro' the s-s calm,	Arabian N's.	76
star-sweet.		
s-s on a gloom profound	Maud, I. iii.	4
start (s.)		
given to s's and bursts Of revel	Princess, v.	53
start (vero.)		
I started once, or seem'd to s in pain.	D. of F Wom.	41
Would s and tremble under her feet,	Maud, I. xxii.	71
s from their fallen lords,	Enid	1311
started.		
I s once, or seem'd to start in pain,	D. of F Wom	41
But in a pet she s up.	Talking O.	229
Then they s from their place,	Vision of Sin	33
s on his feet, Tore the king's letter	Princess, i.	59
Back s she, and turning round we saw	" ii.	291
smote him on the breast; he s up,	" iv.	140
many a bold knight s up in heat	" v.	349
Up s from my side The old lion,	" vi.	82
now and then an echo s up,	"	349
seized on her, And kind s waking,	Enid	674
and either s while the door,	"	1121
he s up and stared at her	"	1238
Yet blank from sleep, she s to him	Elaine	816
Forward she s with a happy cry,	En. Arden	151
S from bed, and struck herself a light	"	452
knew not wherefore, s up Shuddering,	"	617
of the latest fox—where s—	Aylmer's F.	253
Out into the road I s,	Grandmother	41
startled.		
neither self-possess'd Nor s,	Gardener's D.	152

	starve.	POEM.	LINE.
clamouring. 'If we pay, we *s*!'		*Godiva*	15
'If they pay this tax, they *s*,'		"	20

state (condition, etc.)

		POEM.	LINE.
soften'd light Of orient *s*.		*Ode to Mem.*	11
revenue Wherewith to embellish *s*		*Œnone*	111
The slipping thro' from *s* to *s*.		*Two Voices*	351
if our *s* were such As one before,		"	355
His *s* the king reposing keeps.		*Day-Dm.*	59
Built for pleasure and for *s*.		*L. of Burleigh*	32
Here he lives, in *s* and bounty,		"	57
and the woman *s* in each,		*Princess,* ii.	115
And bow'd her *s* to them,		"	150
still she rail'd against the *s* of things		" iii.	68
Summon'd out She kept her *s*,		"	213
reasons drawn from age and *s*,		" v.	347
in some mystic middle *s* I lay.		" vi.	2
withdrew from summer heats and *s*,		"	228
And he should sorrow o'er my *s*		*In Mem.*xiv.	15
The lowness of the present *s*		" xxiv.	11
If, in thy second *s* sublime		" lx.	1
From *s* to *s* the spirit walks:		" lxxxi.	6
range above our mortal *s*,		" lxxxiv.	22
There she walks in her *s*,		*Maud,*I.xiv.	3
Something far advanced in *S*,		*Ode on Well.*	275
loved her in a *s* Of broken fortunes,		*Enid*	12
yea by your *s* And presence		"	430
In silver tissue talking things of *s*;		"	663
by your *s* And presence I might		*Elaine*	182
go in *s* to court, to meet the Queen.		"	1118
doubts and fears were common to her *s*,		*En. Arden*	517

state (commonwealth.)

Tho' every channel of the *S* 'You ask me why,' etc.			23
And work, a joint of *s*, 'Love thou thy land,' etc			47
New Majesties of mighty *S's*—		"	60
Who'd serve the *s*? for if I carved		*Audley Ct*	47
Visions of a perfect *S*:		*Vision of Sin*	148
the *s*, The total chronicles of man		*Princess,* ii.	358
mould a mighty *s's* decrees		*InMem.*lxiii.	11
Or touch'd the changes of the *s*,		" lxxxviii.	35
the *s* has done it and thrice as well:		*Maud,* I. x.	40
But as he saves or serves the *s*.		*Ode on Well.*	200

statelier.

Could find no *s* than his peers		*Two Voices*	29

stateliest.

nor end of mine *S*, for thee!		*Princess,* vii.	155
Adored her, as the *s* and the best		*Enid*	20
sit the best and *s* of the land?		*Lucretius*	172

stateliness.

harmony Of thy swan-like *s*,		*Eleänore*	47
Who see your tender grace and *s*.		*Guinevere*	188

stately.

But she is tall and *s*.		*Maud,* I. xii	16

stately-set.

the fair hall-ceiling *s-s*		*Pal. of Art*	141

state-oracle.

O friends, our chief *s-o* is mute:		*Ode on Well.*	23

statesman.

statesmen at her council met		*To the Queen*	29
No blazon'd *s* he, nor king. 'You might have won'			24
a *s* there, betraying His party-secret,		*Maud,*II. v.	35
O Statesmen, guard us, guard the eye*Ode on Well*			160
keep the soldier firm, the *s* pure:		"	222

statesman-warrior.

The *s-w*, moderate, resolute,		*Ode on Well.*	25

station.

wheels of Time Spun round in *s*,		*Love and Duty*	74
to and fro Between the minic *s's*;		*Princess, Pro.*	79
thro' his cowardice allow'd Her *s*,		*Guinevere*	513

stationed.

Ida *s* there Unshaken		*Princess,* v.	333

statuary.

break the works of the *s*,		*Boädicea*	64

statue.

high on every peak a *s*.		*Pal. of Art*	37

	POEM.	LINE.
broken *s* propt against the wall	*Princess, Pro.*	99
Look, our hall! Our *s's*!	" ii.	62
two great *s's* Art And Science	" iv	182
Half turning to the broken *s*	"	570
your *s's* Rear'd, sung to,	" v.	403
highest, among the *s's*, statue-like	"	499
April of ovation round Their *s's*	" vi.	51
o'er the *s's* leapt from head to head,	"	346
Disrobed the glimmering *s* of Sir Ralph	*Con.*	117
In the centre stood A *s* veil'd,	*In Mem* cii.	12
But like a *s* solid-set,	*Con.*	15
I stood among the silent *s's*,	*The Daisy*	63
She might have seem'd her *s*,	*Elaine*	1165
s's, king or saint, or founder fell;	*Sea Dreams*	217
down their *s* of Victory fell.	*Boädicea*	30

statue-like.

s-l, In act to render thanks,	*Gardener's D.*	158
highest, among the statues, *s*	*Princess,* v.	499

stature.

her full height her stately *s* draws;	*D. of F. Wom.*	102
Her *s* more than mortal	*Princess, Pro.*	40

statute

an officer Rose up, and read the *s's*,	*Princess,* ii.	55

statute-book.

According to your bitter *s-b*,	*Princess,* iv.	434

stave (s.)

Chant me now some wicked *s*,	*Vision of Sin*	151

stave (verb)

s off a chance That breaks upon them	*Enid*	1202

stay.

Thou, willing me to *s*	*Madeline*	37
S's on her floating locks the lovely	*Ode to Mem.*	16
Whither away? listen and *s*:	*Sea-Fairies*	42
A curse is on her if she *s*	*L. of Shalott*, ii.	4
sunset glow, That *s's* upon thee?	*Eleänore*	56
And now it seems as hard to *s*	*MayQueen,*iii.	10
Here *s's* the blood along the veins.	*Day-Dm.*	24
S's all the fair young planet	*Princess,* vii.	248
Like her I go; I cannot *s*;	*In Mem.* xii.	5
s's thee from the clouded noons	" lxxxii.	5
s's him from the native land,	" xcii.	5
At least to me? I would not *s*.	" cxix.	8
who *s* to share the morning feast	*Con.*	75
Why should I *s*? can a sweeter chance *Maud*, I. i.		62
may *s* for a year, who has gone for a week »	xvi.	6
Let it go or *s*, so I wake	" III. vi.	38
'Pray *s* a little: pardon me:	*The Brook*	210
could make me *s*—That proof of trust	*Vivien*	768
'*S* with me, I am sick;	*Elaine*	88
he pursued her calling '*S* a little!	"	680
and a remnant *s's* with me.	*Guinevere*	440
I have not long to *s*;	*Grandmother*	15,108
To those that *s* and those that roam	*Sailor Boy*	14
My sisters crying '*s* for shame;	"	18
here he *s's* upon a freezing orb	*Lucretius*	139
s's the rolling Ixionian wheel,	"	257

stay'd.

s beneath the dome Of hollow boughs.	*Arabian N's.*	41
Would they could have *s* with us!	*Deserted H.*	22
s the Ausonian king to hear	*Pal. of Art*	111
I had not *s* so long to tell you all	*Gardener's D.*	237
rummaged like a rat: no servant *s*:	*Walk.to the M.*	30
But, as for her, she *s* at home,	*Talking O.*	113
In these, in those the life is *s*.	*Day-Dm.*	38
seven *s* at Christmas up to read;	*Princess,Pro.*	176
there *s*; Knelt on one knee,—	" vi.	74
But *s* in peace with God and man	*InMem.*lxxix.	8
I *s* the wheels at Cogoletto	*The Daisy*	23
on a little knoll beside it, *s*	*Enid*	162
s; and cast his eyes on fair Elaine	*Elaine*	389
have fall'n But that they *s* him up:	*Guinevere*	303
Philip *s* (His father lying sick	*En. Arden*	637
S by this isle, not knowing where she lay »		631
He *s* his arms upon his knee:	*The Victim*	50
Stiles where we *s* to be kind,	*The Window*	184

	POEM.	LINE.
stays		
all-too-full in bud For puritanic s;	*Talking O.*	60
steak.		
Among the chops and s's!	*Will Water.*	148
steal.		
Like soften'd airs that blowing s .	*Two Voices*	406
Her gradual fingers s .	*Will Water.*	26
As slowly s's a silver flame	*In Mem.*lxvi.	6
every span of shade that s's,	" cxvi.	10
ever ready to slander and s;	*Maud,* I. iv.	19
It lightly winds and s's .	" II. iv.	18
I s, a wasted frame,	"	69
I s by lawns and grassy plots,	*The Brook.*	170
I cannot s or plunder, no nor beg:	*Enid*	1336
And s you from each other!	*Aylmer's F.*	707
the old mysterious glimmer s's	*Tithonus*	34
stealest.		
s fire From the fountains of the past,	*Ode to Mem.*	1
stealing.		
to reprove her For s out of view .	*Maud,* I. xx.	9
stealth.		
And sent it them by s .	*Dora*	51
stealthily.		
s In the midwarmth of welcome	*Enid*	1128
steam.		
Old boxes, larded with the s	*Will Water.*	223
dozen angry models jetted s :	*Princess,Pro.*	73
The dust and din and s of town:	*In Mem.*lxxxviii.	8
all the hall was dim with s of flesh :	*Enid*	1451
making all the night a s of fire	*Guinevere*	593
s Floats up from those dim fields .	*Tithonus*	68
steam.		
ater in ea mayhap wi' 'is kittle o' s	*N. Farmer.*	61
steamer.		
clock-work s paddling plied .	*Princess, Pro.*	71
steamed.		
s From out a golden cup .	*Pal. of Art*	40
steaming.		
centred in a doleful song S up,	*Lotos-E's.*	163
steamship.		
In the s, in the railway,	*Locksley II.*	166
steed.		
heard the s's to battle going,	*Oriana*	15
mounted our good s's, And boldly .	*Princess,* i.	201
On his haunches rose the s,	"	v. 482
The towering car, the sable s's:	*Ode on Well.*	55
couch'd their spears and prick'd their s's	*Elaine*	478
steel.		
The hard brands shiver on the s, .	*Sir Galahad*	6
red-faced war has rods of s .	*Princess,* v.	111
A flying splendour out of brass and s,	" vi.	345
steep (s.)		
adown the s like a wave I would leap	*The Mermaid*	39
below the milky s Some ship	*To F. D. Maurice*	25
steep (verb.)		
s our brows in slumber's holy balm ;	*Lotos-E's.*	69
steeped.		
art not s in golden languors,	*Madeline*	1
Thou art so s in misery,	*Two Voices*	47
steeple.		
Utter your jubilee, s and spire !	*Wel. to Alexan.*	17
steer (s.)		
The s forgot to graze, .	*Gardener's D.*	84
steer (verb.)		
I leap on board : no helmsman's :	*Sir Galahad*	39
alone Go with me, he can s and row	*Elaine*	1124
steer'd.		
We s her toward a crimson cloud .	*In Mem.* cii.	85
and the dead S by the dumb	*Elaine*	1145
steering.		
s, now, from a purple cove .	*The Daisy*	20

	POEM.	LINE.
stem.		
upbearing parasite, Clothing the s	*Isabel*	35
Branches they bore of that enchanted s,	*Lotos-E's*	28
as a funeral scarf from s to stern .	*M. d'Arthur*	194
From spray, and branch, and s,	*Talking O.*	192
Between dark s's the forest glows	*Sir Galahad*	27
the s Less grain than touchwood .	*Princess,* iv.	313
The two remaining found a fallen s;	*En. Arden*	568
That coil'd around the stately s,	"	578
step (s.)		
And with the certain s of man. .	*Miller's D.*	96
To follow flying s's of Truth '*Love thou thy land*'	75
with slow s's, With slow, faint s's,	*St S. Stylites*	179
No more by thee my s's shall be, (rep.) *A Farewell*	3
A s Of lightest echo, .	*Princess,* iv.	195
down the s's, and thro' the court .	"	533
scales with man The shining s of Nature	" vii.	246
With weary s's I loiter on, .	*In Mem.* xxxviii.	1
measuring out The s's of Time—	" xciv.	42
By a shuffled s, by a dead weight	*Maud,* I. i.	14
There were but a s to be made. .	" xiv.	22
I will cry to the s's above my head,	" II. v.	101
First as in fear, s after s, she stole	*Elaine*	341
made a sudden s to the gate, .	"	390
and regret Her parting s, .	"	863
listening till those armed s's were gone	*Guinevere*	579
step (verb.)		
S from the corpse, and let him in,	*D. of the O. Year*	49
S deeper yet in herb and fern .	*Talking O.*	245
S's with a tender foot, light as on air	*Princess,*vi.	72
some one s's across my grave ; .	*Guinevere*	57
S's from her airy hill, .	*On a Mourner*	8
Stephen.		
Like S, an unquenched fire. .	*Two Voices*	219
stepping.		
He, s down By zig-zag paths .	*M. d'Arthur*	49
Come s lightly down the plank,	*In Mem.* xiv.	7
s lightly, heap'd The pieces .	*Enid*	1222
stepping-stones.		
Below the range of s-s, .	*Miller's D.*	54
That men may rise on s-s .	*In Mem.* i.	3
stept.		
forth there s a foeman tall, .	*Oriana*	33
s she down thro' town and field '*Of old sat Freedom*'	9
from the ruin'd shrine he s .	*M. d'Arthur*	45
And out I s, and up I crept :	*Ed. Morris*	111
S forward on a firmer leg, .	*Will Water.*	123
Down s Lord Ronald from his tower :	*Lady Clare*	65
In robe and crown the king s down,	*Beggar Maid*	5
Then s a buxom hostess forth .	*Princess,* i.	225
Lightly to the warrior s, .	"	v. 541
found a little boat, and s into it .	*Vivien*	47
close behind them s the lily maid .	*Elaine*	176
into that rude hall S with all grace,	"	263
S the long-haired long-bearded solitary,	*En. Arden*	638
S thro' the stately minuet .	*Aylmer's F.*	207
stern (adj.)		
Or gay, or grave, or sweet, or s, .	*Pal. of Art*	91
The s were mild when thou wert by,	*In Mem.* cix.	9
s and sad (so rare the smiles .	*The Daisy*	53
Grave, florid, s, as far as eye could see	*Sea Dreams*	21
S he was and rash ; .	*The Captain*	10
stern (s.)		
as a funeral scarf from stem to s .	*M. d'Arthur*	194
steward.		
The wrinkled s at his task .	*Day-Dm.*	47
The butler drank, the s scrawled,	"	149
'Tis but a s of the can, .	*Will Water.*	153
stick.		
on thy ribs the limpet s's .	*Sailor Boy*	10
stiff.		
or s with crackling frost, .	*St S. Stylites*	173
My joints are somewhat s or so. .	*Day-Dm.*	196
stood S as a viper frozen .	*Vivien*	634
stiffen.		
last I s into stone, .	*In Mem.* cvii.	2

	POEM.	LINE.
stiffening.		
Sir Aylmer Aylmer slowly *s* spoke ;	*Aylmer's F.*	273
stiffer.		
My nerves have dealt with *s.*	*Will Water.*	78
stiff-stricken.		
She sat *S-s*, listening ;	*Guinevere*	409
stifled.		
low-folded heavens *S* and chill'd at	*Aylmer's F.*	613
stile.		
Or simple *s* from mead to mead	*In Mem.* xcix.	7
So Lawrence Aylmer, seated on a *s*	*The Brook*	197
ever bided tryst at village *s*,	*Vivien*	228
S's where we stay'd to be kind,	*The Window*	184
By meadow and *s* and wood.	"	191
Over the meadows and *s's*	"	199
still.		
The pool beneath it never *s*,	*Miller's D.*	100
'ill be fresh and green and *s,*	*May Queen,* i.	37
and all the world is *s*	" ii.	24
not so deadly *s* As that wide forest.	*D. of F. Wom.*	68
the sound of a voice that is *s* !	*'Break, break,'* etc.	12
The moon is hid; the night is *s* (ciii. 2)	*InMem.*xxviii.	2
When all his active powers are *s,*	" lxiii.	18
Looks thy fair face and makes it *s.*	" lxix.	16
sitting here so stunn'd and *s,*	*Maud,*II. i.	2
storm was coming, but the winds were *s*	*Vivien*	1
hard and *s* as is the face that men	*Elaine*	1244
to the dead earth, and the land was *s.*	*Guinevere*	8
took and bare him off And all was *s*:	"	109
There came a day as *s* as heaven,	"	290
strong on his legs, but *s* of his tongue	*Grandmother*	13
still'd.		
Hath *s* the life that beat from thee	*In Mem.* vi.	12
Who *s* the rolling wave of Galilee !	*Aylmer's F.*	709
bees are *s* and the flies are kill'd	*The Window*	52
stiller.		
S than chisell'd marble,	*D. of F. Wom.*	86
s world of the dead, *S*, not fairer	*Maud,* II. v.	70
but now *S*, with yet a bed	*En. Arden*	699
still-lighted.		
S-l in a secret shrine,	*Mariana in the S.*	18
stillness.		
That into *s* past again,	*Miller's D.*	227
Sang to the *s*, till the mountain-shade	*Œnone*	20
breaks thro' the *s* of this world :	*Pal. of Art*	259
murmur broke the *s* of that air	*Gardener'sD.*146
rounded by the *s* of the beach	*Audley Ct.*	9
moving toward the *s* of his rest.	*Locksley H.*	144
beauty doth inform *S* with love,	*Day-Dm.*	92
a half-consent involved In *s* .	*Princess,* vii.	67
A part of *s,* yearns to speak.	*InMem.*lxxxiv.	78
The *s* of the central sea.	" cxxii.	4
still-recurring.		
chased away the *s-r* gnat,	*Coquette,* i.	7
sting (s.)		
prick'd with goads and *s's* ;	*Pal. of Art*	150
a *s* of shrewdest pain Ran shrivelling	*StS Stylites*	195
and draw the *s* from pain ;	*Princess,* vii.	49
sting (verb.)		
She fain would *s* us too,	*Princess,* vi.	320
lay their eggs, and *s* and sing	*InMem.*xlix.	11
s each other here in the dust ;	*Maud,* II. i.	47
we scorn them, but they *s.'*	*Elaine*	140
stinted.		
I had not *s* practice, O my God.	*StS.Stylites*	58
stir (s.)		
to feel the truth and *s* of day,	*M. d'Arthur,*Ep.19
and the splash and *s* Of fountains.	*Princess,* i.	214
came a little *s* About the doors	" iv.	354
I scarce could brook the strain and *s*	*In Mem.* xv.	12
stir (verb.)		
So fleetly did she *s,*	*Talking O.*	130
Blow, flute, and *s* the stiff-set sprigs	*Amphion*	63
Let Whig and Tory *s* their blood .	*Will Water.*	53

	POEM.	LINE.
secret, seem'd to *s* within my breast ;	*Princess,* iii.	28
for those That *s* this hubbub—	" iv.	488
But will not speak, nor *s.'*	" v.	50
S in me as to strike ;	"	258
That *s* the spirit's inner deeps	*In Mem.* xli.	10
To *s* a little dust of praise.	" lxxiv.	12
That made it *s* on the shore.	*Maud,* II ii.	15
s's the pulse With devil's leaps	*Guinevere*	517
Yet dared not *s* to do it,	*Aylmer's F.*	896
stirr'd.		
It *s* the old wife's mettle :	*The Goose*	26
s with languid pulses of the oar,	*Gardener'sD.*	41
s her lips For some sweet answer,	"	155
But yet my sap was *s:*	*Talking O.*	172
The fragrant tresses are not *s*	*Day-Dm.*	95
The mountain *s* its bushy crown,	*Amphion*	25
for the roots of my hair were *s*	*Maud,* I. i	13
has the casement jessamine *s*	" xxii.	15
s this vice in you which ruin'd man	*Vivien*	212
stirring.		
It was the *s* of the blood.	*Two Voices*	159
S a sudden transport	*Princess,* iv.	11
Little about it *s* save a brook !	*Aylmer's F.*	32
stitches.		
In coughs, aches, *s*, ulcerous throes	*StS.Stylites* 13
stoan.		
a niver rembles the *s's,*	*N. Farmer*	60
stock.		
like an oaken *s* in winter woods	*Golden Year*	62
stock-still.		
stood *S-s* for sheer amazement.	*Will Water.*	136
stoic.		
like a *s*, or like A wiser epicurean	*Maud,* I. iv.	20
stole (s.)		
With folded feet, in *s's* of white,	*Sir Galahad*	43
stole (verb.)		
Then *s* I up and trancedly Gazed	*Arabian N's.*133
Prevailing in weakness, the coronach *s*	*DyingSwan*26
S all the golden gloss	*Gardener'sD.*	129
O'er the mute city *s* with folded wings	"	182
S from her sister Sorrow.	"	251
we *s* his fruit, His hens, his eggs ;	*Walk.totheM.* 76
a silent cousin *s* Upon us	*Ed. Morris*	115
adown the stair *S* on ;	*Godiva*	49
s from court With Cyril and with Florian,	*Princess,*i.101
Away we *s*, and transient in a trice	" v.	37
S a maiden from her place	"	540
Psyche ever *s* A little nearer,	" vi.	116
gray dawn *s* o'er the dewy world	*Enid*	1234
wily Vivien *s* from Arthur's court :	*Vivien*	6
First as in fear, step after step, she *s*	*Elaine*	341
Lady of the Lake, *S* from his mother	"	1396
s Up by the wall, behind the yew ;	*En. Arden*	740
S the seed by night.	*The Flower*	12
stolen.		
dawn's creeping beams, *S* to my brain	*D.ofF.Wom.*262
Because her brood is *s* away	*In Mem.*xxi.	28
s away To dreamful wastes	*Maud,* I. xviii.	68
some *s*, some as relics kept.	*Vivien*	303
down the long street having slowly *s,*	*En. Arden*683
stomach.		
Less having *s* for it than desire	*Enid*	1062
stomacher.		
He cleft me thro' the *s,*	*Princess,* ii.	385
stone (mineral substance)		
Life in dead *s's*, or spirit in air ;	*A Character*	9
lizard, with his shadow on the *s*	*Œnone*	26
on this hand and sitting on this *s?*	"	229
foreground black with *s's* and slags,	*Pal. of Art*	81
Throb thro' the ribbed *s*;	"	176
A rolling *s* of here and everywhere,	*Audley Ct.*	77
all my limbs drop piecemeal from the *s*	*StS.Stylites*	43
in a roofless close of ragged *s's* ;	"	73
cursed and scorn'd,and bruised with *s's*;	*TwoVoices*222

	POEM.	LINE.
On the mossy s, as I lay,	Ed. Gray	26
Bitterly wept I over the s;	"	33
'I read a measure on the s's,	Vision of Sin	180
On thy cold gray s's, O Sea!	'Break, Break,' etc.	2
Carved s's of the Abbey-ruin	Princess, Pro.	14
One rear'd a font of s And drew	"	59
sandy footprint harden into s.	" iii.	254
Old Yew, which graspest at the s's	In Mem. ii.	1
From scarped cliff and quarried s	" lv.	2
lest I stiffen into s,	" cvii.	2
On a heart half-turn'd to s	Maud, I. vi.	78
O heart of s, are you flesh	"	79
Wept over her, carved in s;	" viii.	4
Maud, like a precious s	" xiv.	10
Low on the sand and loud on the s	" xxii.	25
Courage poor heart of s! (rep.)	" II. iii.	1
slopes a wild brook o'er a little s,	Enid	77
sprouted thistle on the broken s's.	"	314
suck'd the joining of the s's,	"	324
o'er a mount of newly-fall'n s's,	"	361
when she heard his horse upon the s's,	Elaine	974
A little bitter pool about a s	Guinevere	52
eyes upon the s's, he reach'd the home	En. Arden	685
or one s Left on another	Aylmer's F.	788
men of flesh and blood, and men of s	Sea Dreams	230

stone (disease.)

Past earthquake—ay, and gout and s,	Lucretius	153

stone-cast.

About a s-c from the wall	Mariana	37

stoned.

either they were s, or crucified,	St S. Stylites	50

stone-shot.

He show'd a tent A s-s off	Princess, v.	51

stonest.

O thou that s, had'st thou understood	Aylmer's F.	749

stoning.

no s save with flint and rock?	Aylmer's F.	746

stood.

heaven's mazed signs s still,	'Clear-headed friend'	28
s aloof from other minds	A Character	23
She s upon the castle wall,	Oriana	28
Pallas where she s Somewhat apart	Œnone	135
of great rooms and small the palace s,	Pal. of Art	57
in dark corners of her palace s	"	237
That s against the wall	"	244
Join'd not, but s, and standing saw	"	254
above the valley s the moon	Lotos-E's.	7
pinnacles of aged snow S' sunset-flush'd	"	17
I appeal'd To one that s beside	D. of F. Wom.	100
so s I, when that flow Of music	"	104
she left me where I s:	"	241
Losing her carol I s pensively,	"	245
s Between the rainbow and the sun	Margaret	12
s on a dark strait of barren land.	M. d'Arthur	10
his eyes were dazzled, as he s,	"	59
Long s Sir Bedivere Revolving	"	269
those that s upon the hills behind	E.p.	25
s, Leaning his horns into the	Gardener's D.	85
Holding the bush, to fix it back, she s	"	126
Half light, half shade, She s,	"	140
to Mary's house, and s Upon the threshold.	Dora	108
while we s like fools Embracing	Ed. Morris	118
brothers of the weather s Stock-still	Will Water.	135
turn'd and kiss'd her where she s:	Lady Clare	82
wild hawk s with the down on his beak	Poet's Song	11
in the presence room I s With Cyril	Princess, i.	50
s a bust of Pallas for a sign,	"	219
while They s, not so rapt, we gazing.	" ii.	297
Lady Blanche's daughter where she s,	"	300
s that same fair creature at the door	"	308
There while we s beside the fount	" iii.	7
She s Among her maidens, higher	"	162
Alone I s With Florian	" iv.	152
s her maidens glimmeringly group'd	"	172
Lady Blanche erect S up and spake,	"	272
s in your own light and darken'd mine.	"	295
then s up and spoke impetuously	"	398

	POEM.	LINE.
s The placid marble Muses	Princess, iv.	467
I s and seem'd to hear, As in a poplargrove	" v.	11
storming in extremes S for her cause	"	169
high upon the palace Ida s	" vi.	14
S the unhappy mother open-mouth'd	"	127
slowly from me, s Erect and silent;	"	135
had you s by us, The roar that breaks	"	318
in the centre s The common men.	"	339
we saw Sir Walter where he s,	Con.	81
of those That s the nearest—	"	93
In the centre s A statue veil'd	In Mem. cii.	11
S up and answer'd 'I have felt.'	" cxxiii.	16
He s on the path a little aside;	Maud, I. xiii.	7
And s by her garden gate;	" xiv.	6
S behind, and waited on the three.	Enid	392
Enid s aside to wait the event,	"	1002
now they saw their bulwark fallen, s;	"	1017
in a manner pleased, and turning, s.	"	1305
great charger s, grieved like a man.	"	1384
s Still as a viper frozen;	Vivien	693
and s A virtuous gentlewoman	"	759
Lancelot, where he s beside the King.	Elaine	86
she drew Nearer and s.	"	349
silent, tho' he greeted her, she s	"	354
His honour rooted in dishonour s,	"	872
S grasping what was nearest	"	961
all the place whereon she s was green;	"	1194
There two s armed, and kept the door;	"	1240
man-breasted things s from the sea,	Guinevere	244
s before the Queen As tremulously	"	361
sad nuns with each a light S,	"	585
while he s on deck Waving,	En. Arden	242
he s once more before her face,	"	454
Her son, who s beside her	"	757
S from his walls and wing'd	Aylmer's F.	18
s from out a stiff brocade	"	204
under his own lintel s Storming	"	331
to the lychgate, where his chariot s,	"	824
I s like one that had received a blow:	Sea Dreams	157
for Willy s like a rock	Grandmother	10
and s by the road at the gate,	"	38
Willy s up like a man,	"	45
champing golden grain, the horse s	Spec. of Iliad	21
I s on a tower in the wet	1865-1866	1
s out the breasts, The breasts of Helen	Lucretius	60

stool.

like a crow upon a three-legg'd s.	Audley Ct.	44

stoop.

The skies s down in their desire:	Fatima	32
I could not s to such a mind.	L.C.V. de Vere	20
elmtree-boles did s and lean.	D. of F. Wom.	57
He s's—to kiss her—on his knee.	Day-Dm.	130
The cloud may s from heaven	Princess, vi.	365
S down and seem to kiss me	" vii.	135
s and kiss the tender little thumb.	Enid	395

stooped.

He s and clutch'd him, fair and good,	Will Water	113
s To drench his dark locks	Princess, iv.	118
s to updrag Melissa:	"	347
you s to me From all high places,	"	409
My father s, refather'd o'er my wounds	" vi.	113
She turn'd; she paused; She s;	" vii.	140
s With a low whinny toward the pair:	Enid	1603
Lancelot should have s so low,	Elaine	728
S, took, break seal, and read it;	"	1264
o'er her second father s a girl,	En. Arden	748

stopt.

The swallow s as he hunted the bee,	Poet's Song	9
S, and then with a riding whip	Maud, I. xiii.	18
when he s we had to hurl together,	Vivien	270
All of a sudden he s:	Grandmother	41

store.

Love, then, had hope of richer s	In Mem. lxxx.	5
We wish them s of happy days	Con.	84
How best to help the slender s,	To F D Maurice	37
s of rich apparel, sumptuous fare,	Enid	709
what she brought Buy goods and s's—	En. Arden	138
Bought Annie goods and s's,	"	160
shelf and corner for the goods and s's.	"	171

	POEM.	LINE.
store (verb.)		
to *s* and hoard myself,	*Ulysses*	29
stored.		
all things in order *s*,	*Pal. of Art*	87
S in some treasure-house of mighty	*M. d'Arthur*	101
Dora *s* what little she could save,	*Dora*	50
eloquence *S* from all flowers?	*Ed. Morris*	27
I *s* it full of rich memorial:	*Princess*, v.	381
storing.		
S yearly little dues of wheat	*Lotos-E's.*	167
stork.		
Went by me, like a *s*:	*Talking O.*	56
storm.		
retired From brawling *s's*,	*Ode to Mem.*	112
Henceforward neither squall nor *s*	*Gardener's D.*	186
once more, close-button'd to the *s*;	*Ed. Morris*	136
gates of heaven with *s's* of prayer,	*St S. Stylites*	7
shaken with a sudden *s* of sighs—	*Lockley H.*	27
blessed forms in whistling *s's*	*Sir Galahad*	59
green malignant light of coming *s*.	*Princess*, iii.	116
fire on a mast-head Prophet of *s*:	" iv.	256
Fluctuated, as flowers in *s*,	"	461
On me, me, me, the *s* first breaks:	"	478
When *s* is on the heights	" v.	338
at which the *s* Of galloping hoofs.	"	477
let our girls flit Till the *s* die!	" vi.	318
The touch of change in calm or *s*.	*In Mem.* xvi.	6
O thou that after toil and *s*	" xxxiii.	12
lash with *s* the streaming pane?	" lxxi.	4
s their high-built organs make,	" lxxxvi.	6
A pillar stedfast in the *s*,	" cxii.	12
The seeming prey of cyclic *s's*,	" cxvii.	11
Well roars the *s* to those that hear	" cxxvi.	3
A deeper voice across the *s*,	"	4
burst and drown with deluging *s's*	*Maud*, II. i.	42
s and blast Had blown the lake	*The Daisy*	70
world's loud whisper breaking into *s*	*Enid*	27
wheel thro' sunshine, *s*, and cloud	"	348
skirts are loosen'd by the breaking *s*	"	1308
A *s* was coming, but the winds were still	*Vivien*	1
s Broke on the mountain and I cared not	"	352
lash'd it at the base with slanting *s*;	"	485
dark wood grew darker toward the *s*	"	739
'Come from the *s*' and having no reply,	"	744
now the *s* was close above them)	"	784
now the *s*, its burst of passion spent	"	610
(Sea was her wrath, yet working after *s*)	*Elaine*	1300
s of anger Brake from Guinevere	*Guinevere*	359
S, such as drove her under moonless	*En. Arden*	543
like a *s* he came, And shook the house, and like a *s* he went	*Aylmer's F.*	215
Caught in a burst of unexpected *s*	"	285
reddening from the *s* within,	"	322
but presently Wept like a *s*:	"	493
but fork'd Of the near *s*,	"	727
when the wordy *s* Had ended,	*Sea Dreams*	31
s never wakes on the lonely sea	*The Islet*	33
S in the night! for thrice I heard	*Lucretius*	20
S, and what dreams, ye holy Gods	"	33
nobler from her bath of *s*,	"	175
cloud in my heart, and a *s* in the air!	*The Window*	40
No is trouble and cloud and *s*	"	113
stormed.		
S in orbs of song, a growing gale;	*Vision of Sin*	
and *s* At the Oppian law	*Princess*, vii.	108
S at with shot and shell,	*Lt. Brigade*	22,43
storming.		
s in extremes Stood for her cause	*Princess*, v.	168
s a hill-fort of thieves He got it,	*Aylmer's F.*	225
stood *S* with lifted hands,	"	332
stormy.		
Morning arises *s* and pale,	*Maud*, I. vi.	1
story (narrative, etc.)		
We forged a sevenfold *s*	*Princess, Pro.*	198
here I give the *s* and the songs	"	239
so, my mother said, the *s* ran	" i.	11
And snowy summits old in *s*:	" iii.	349
yet to give the *s* as it rose,	" Con.	26

	POEM.	LINE.
in all lands and thro' all human *s*.	*One on Well.*	223
dumbly speaks Your *s*,	*Enid*	1178
let the *s* of her dolorous voyage	*Elaine*	1333
Stole from her mother—as the *s* runs—	"	1356
—all the *s* of his house.	*En. Arden*	705
Here is a *s* which in rougher shape	*Aylmer's F.*	7
but as he told The *s*,	"	225
All for a slanderous *s*,	*Grandmother*	22
name Of his vessel great in *s*,	*The Captain*	19
story (floor)		
And, set in Heaven's third *s*,	*Will Water.*	70
stout (adj.)		
S, rosy, with his babe across his knees,	*En. Arden*	747
stout (s.)		
To each his perfect pint of *s*,	*Will Water.*	115
stowed.		
Or *s* (when classic Canning died)	*Will Water.*	101
straddling.		
s on the butts While the wine ran;	*Guinevere*	266
straight.		
If *s* thy track, or if oblique,	*Two Voices*	193
S, but as lissome as a hazel wand;	*The Brook*	70
as by miracle, grow *s* and fair—	*Aylmer's F.*	676
strain (s.)		
An echo from a measured *s*,	*Miller's D.*	66
scarce could brook the *s* and stir	*In Mem.* xv.	12
strain (verb.)		
cords that bind and *s* The heart	*'Clear-headed friend'*	4
Shudderest when I *s* my sight,	*Fatima*	3
strained.		
a little in the late encounter *s*,	*Enid*	1007
straining.		
In the stormy east-wind *s*,	*L. of Shalott*, iv.	1
strait.		
on a dark *s* of barren land	*M. d'Arthur*	10
I'll serve you better in a *s*;	*Princess*, i.	84
hovering o'er the dolorous *s*	*In Mem.* lxxxiii.	39
strait-besieged.		
being *s-b* By this wild king	*Princess, Pro.*	36
straiten'd.		
The shackles of an old love *s* him,	*Elaine*	871
strait-laced.		
S-l, but all-too-full in bud	*Talking O.*	59
strand (shore.)		
Here on the Breton *s*!	*Maud*, II. ii.	29
as a ground-swell dash'd on the *s*	*W. to Alexan.*	23
strand (twist of a rope.)		
'The dusky *s* of Death in woven here	*Maud*, I. xviii.	60
stranding.		
s on an isle at morn	*En. Arden*	553
strange.		
The broken sheds look'd sad and *s*	*Mariana*	5
O sweet and *s* it seems to me	*May Queen*,iii.	53
sons inherit us: our looks are *s*:	*Lotos-E's.*	118
'Tis *s* that those we lean on most,	*To J. S.*	9
Nothing comes to thee new or *s*.	"	74
So *s* it seems to me.	*Lady Clare*	52
s was the sight	*Princess, Pro.*	54, 89
we give you, being *s*, A license:	" iii.	188
s as in dark summer dawns	" iv.	31
so *s*, the days that are no more.	" vi.	35
things grew more tragic and more *s*;	" vii.	7
s that soon He rose up whole	" vii.	49
so *s* do these things seem,	*In Mem.* xiii.	15
I should not feel it to be *s*.	" xiv.	20
and *s* Was love's dumb cry	" xciv.	26
S, that I hear two men,	*Maud*, I. vii.	13
How *s* was what she said,	" xix.	34
S; that I felt so gay, *S*, that I tried	" xx.	1
S, that the mind, when fraught	" II. ii.	58
'That were *s*. What surname?'	*The Brook*	211

	POEM.	LINE.
there was a boon, one not so s—	Vivien	136
this boon so s and not so s.'	"	159
not so s as my long asking it	"	161
so s as you yourself are s	"	162
so s as that dark mood of yours.	"	163
nothing wild or s, Or seeming shameful	"	709
—this, however s, My latest;	Elaine	1106
An end to this! A s one!	"	1217

strangeness.
feels a glimmering s in his dream	The Brook	216

stranger (adj.)
nor s seem'd that hearts So gentle,	Princess, vii.	51

stranger (s.)
Two s's meeting at a festival;	Circumstance	3
There strode a s to the door	The Goose	2, 39
God forget me s!'	"	56
The first-fruits of the s:	Princess, ii.	30
'seize the s's' is the cry.	" iv.	201
grow Familiar to the s's child	In Mem. c	20
Like s's' voices here they sound,	" ciii.	9
We live within the s's land	" civ.	3
A s meeting them had surely thought	Enid	883
Shriek'd to the s, 'Slay not a dead man!'	"	1627
I bid the s welcome.	Vivien	119
s's at my hearth Not welcome	Lucretius	158

strange-statued.
under the s-s gate, Where Arthur's wars	Elaine	796

strata.
dip of certain s to the North	Princess, iii.	154

stray.
Beyond the bounding hill to s,	In Mem.lxxxviii.	30
lands where not a memory s's,	" ciii.	10

stray'd.
Thy feet have s in after hours	In Mem ci.	14

streak (s.)
smote The s's of virgin snow	Œnone	53
fades the last long s of snow	In Mem.cxiv.	1

streak (verb.)
white vapour s the crowned towers	Princess, iii.	326
lines of green that s the white	" v.	188

stream (s.)
And the far-off s is dumb,	The Owl, i.	3
broad s in his banks complaining	L. of Shalott,iv.	3
broad s bore her far away,	"	17
the babble of the s Fell,	Mariana in the S.	51
Like two s's of incense free	Eleänore	58
Like those long mosses in the s.	Miller's D.	48
Beside the mill-wheel in the s,	"	167
loud s and the trembling stars	Œnone	215
like a downward smoke, the slender s	Lotos-E's.	8
A land of s's!	"	10
in the s the long-leaved flowers weep	"	55
sweet it were, hearing the downward s,	"	99
wash'd by a slow broad s,	Gardener's D.	40
single s of all her soft brown hair	"	127
Night slid down one long s	"	262
In many s's to fatten lower lands,	Golden Year	34
Who rowing hard against the s,	Two Voices	211
And all the long-pent s of life	Day-Dm.	147
two s's of light from wall to wall;	Princess, ii.	449
S's that float us each and all	" iv.	52
I stagger in the s;	" vi.	301
strove against the s and all in vain	"	375
The shimmering glimpses of a s;	Con.	46
The sound of s's that swift or slow	InMem.xxxv.	10
A secret sweetness in the s,	" lxiii.	20
the s beneath us ran,	" lxxxviii.	43
On winding s or distant sea;	" cxiv.	12
The market boat is on the s,	" cxx.	13
never an end to the s of passing feet,	Maud, II. v.	11
by the well-known s and rustic spire,	The Brook	188
let the turbid s's of rumour flow	Ode on Well.	181
slipt and fell into some pool or s,	Elaine	214
to that s whereon the barge,	"	1135
of Arthur's palace toward the s,	"	1172
down they flash'd, and smote the s.	"	1228

	POEM.	LINE.
Far-off, a blot upon the s	Elaine	1383
as a s that spouting from a cliff	Guinevere	602
burst away In search of s or fount	En. Arden	636
with the sun upon the s beyond	Sea Dreams	95
drifting up the s In fancy,	"	104
s that flashest white,	V. of Canteretz	1
many a fire between the ships and s	Spec. of Iliad	17

stream (verb.)
A thousand suns will s on thee,	A Farewell	13
crowds that s from yawning doors	InMem.lxix.	9
breeze that s's to thy delicious East,	Maud,I.xviii.	16
flame and sparkle and s as of old,	The Ringlet	8
S's o'er a rich ambrosial ocean isle,	Milton	14

streamed.
s Upon the mooned domes aloof	Arabian N's.	126
Across the mountain s below	Pal. of Art	34
S onward, lost their edges,	D of F.Wom.	50
s thro' many a golden bar,	Day-Dm.	173
The vine s out to follow,	Amphion	40
in we s Among the columns,	Princess, ii.	411
and in groups they s away	Con.	105
half the pearls away, S from it still;	Elaine	804
How swiftly s ye by the bark!	The Voyage	50

streamer.
Shot like a s of the northern morn	M. d'Arthur	139

streaming.
On leagues of odour s far,	InMem.lxxxv.	14
The torrent vineyard s fell	The Daisy	10
—all her bright hair s down—	Elaine	1150
people, from the high door s,	"	1337

streamlet.
For us the same cold s curl'd	InMem.lxxviii.	9

street.
till noon no foot should pace the s,	Godiva	39
The s's are dumb with snow.	Sir Galahad	52
Till, where the s grows straiter,	Will Water,	142
pass'd by the town and out of the s	Poet's Song.	2
A little s half garden and half house;	Princess, i.	211
heave and thump A league of s	" iii.	112
cross'd the s and gain'd a petty mound	" iv.	535
rights or wrongs like potherbs in the s	" v.	443
Here in the long unlovely s,	In Mem vii.	2
On the bald s breaks the blank day,	"	12
The field, the chamber and the s	" viii.	11
The s's were fill'd with joyful sound,	" xxxi.	10
s's were black with smoke and frost,	" lxviii.	3
I smell the meadow in the s;	" cxviii.	4
There where the long s roars,	" cxxii.	3
At the head of the village s,	Maud, I. vi.	10
only once, in the village s	" xiii.	26
In the chamber or the s	" II. iv.	6
I loathe the squares and s's,	"	92
Only a yard beneath the s	" v.	7
With lifted hand the gazer in the s.	Ode on Well.	22
Till, in a narrow s and dim,	The Daisy	22
Behold the long s of a little town	Enid	242
down the long s riding wearily,	"	254
many a voice along the s,	"	1319
poach'd filth that floods the middle s,	Vivien	647
long s climbs to one tall-tower'd mill	En Arden	5
narrow s that clamber'd toward the mill.	"	60
From distant corners of the s they ran	"	346
The climbing s, the mill, the leafy lanes	"	608
down the long s having slowly stolen,	"	683
Philip's dwelling fronted on the s,	"	732
down the long and narrow s he went	"	796
I mind him coming down the s;	"	843
'yesterday I met him suddenly in the s,	SeaDreams	142
my eyes Pursued him down the s,	"	171
thundering cheer of the s!	W. to Alexan.	7

strength.
is not this my place of s,	Pal. of Art	233
With all my s I pray'd for both	May Queen, iii.	31
S came to me that equall'd my desire	D.of F.Wom.	230
s of some diffusive thought	'You ask me why,' etc.	15
A slow-develop'd s awaits	'Love thou thy land,' etc.	17
not now that s which in old days	Ulysses	65

	POEM.	LINE.
sin against the *s* of youth!	Locksley H.	59
cry for *s*, remaining weak,	Two Voices	95
My *s* is as the *s* of ten,	Sir Galahad	3
He took advantage of his *s*	Princess, ii.	136
in my grief a *s* reserved	In Mem lxxxiv.	52
fought his doubts and gather'd *s*	" xcv.	13
The maidens gather'd *s* and grace	" cii.	27
fall'n at length that tower of *s*	Ode on Well.	38
What Roman *s* Turbia show'd	The Daisy	5
the *s* of heaven-descended Will,	Will	11
aid me, give me *s* Not to tell her	En Arden.	786
and truth and love are *s*,	Aylmer's F.	365
wonder'd at her *s*, and ask'd her	Sea Dreams	109

strengthen
S me, enlighten me!	Ode to Mem.	5, 43, 122

stretch.
The garden *s*'es southward.	Gardener's D.	114
I felt my veins *S* with fierce heat;	Princess. v.	527
I *s* lame hands of faith.	In Mem. liv.	17
free to *s* his limbs in lawful fight,	Enid.	1602

stretched
S wide and wild the waste enormous	Ode to Mem.	101
s out beneath the pine.	Lotos-E's.	144
s out And babbled for the golden seal,	Dora	131
the Lady *s* a vulture throat.	Princess, iv.	344
s her arms and call'd Across the tumult	"	475
s out her arms and cried aloud	Guinevere	600
long arms *s* as to grasp a flyer:	Aylmer's F.	588

stretching.
A bounded field, nor *s* far;	In Mem xlv.	14

stricken.
s by an angel's hand,	Sir Galahad	69
Was cancell'd, *s* thro' with doubt.	In Mem. xciv.	44
then were I *s* blind That minute,	Elaine	425

stride (s)
parted, with great *s*'s among his dogs.	Godiva.	31
Abate the *s*, which speaks of man,	Princess, ii.	407
fain To follow, strode a *s*	Enid.	376

stride (verb)
hard heir *s*'s about their lands	In Mem. lxxxix.	15

strife.
The flattery and the *s*;	D. of F. Wom.	148
To hear the murmur of the *s*	Margaret	23
we hear with inward *s*	'Love thou thy land,' etc.	
pulsation that I felt before the *s*,	Locksley H.	109
Waiting to strive a happy *s*,	Two Voices	130
maid and page renewed their *s*,	Day-Dm.	145
Half fearful that, with self at *s*	Will Water,	161
To point the term of human *s*,	In Mem. xlix.	15
Are God and Nature then at *s*,	" liv.	5
loved to handle spiritual *s*,	" lxxxv.	54
ancient forms of party *s*;	" cv.	14
fruitful *s*'s and rivalries of peace—	Ded. of Idylls	37
see my dear lord wounded in the *s*,	Enid.	103
from famine And plague and *s*!	The Victim	10

strike.
s within thy pulses, like a God's.	Œnone	159
great thought *s*'s along the brain,	D. of F. Wom.	43
s Into that wondrous track of dreams	"	278
s, and firmly, and one stroke:	'Love thou thy land'	92
That under deeply *s*'s!	Talking O.	274
Shadows thou dost *s*, Embracing.	Two Voices	194
s's him dead for thine and thee.	Princess, iv.	561
Stir in me as to *s*:	" v.	258
Fight and fight well : *s* and *s* home.	"	399
shadowing down the champaign till it *s*'s	"	515
The tops shall *s* front star to star,	" vi.	41
let thy nature *s* on mine	" vii.	330
Should *s* a sudden hand in mine,	In Mem. xiv.	11
The sunbeam *s*'s along the world;	" xv.	8
s's by night a craggy shelf.	" xvi.	13
s his being into bounds.	Con.	174
s, if he could, were it but with his	Maud, I. i.	52
my God, and *s*, for we hold Thee just	II. i.	45
S dead the whole weak race.	"	46
Suddenly *s* on a sharper sense	" ii.	63
Then to *s* him and lay him low,	" v.	90

	POEM.	LINE.
without remorse to *s* her dead,	Enid.	958
lets the day *S* where it clung:	"	1341
yet should *s* upon a sudden means	Vivien	509
morning's earliest ray Might *s* it.	Elaine	6
Set lance in rest, *s* spur,	"	455
that will *s* my blossom dead.	"	966
will I *s* at him and *s* him down	"	1064
good fortune, I will *s* him dead,	"	1065
S down the lusty and long-practised	"	1351
must *s* against my sister's son,	Guinevere	568
s him dead, and meet myself	"	570
till he madly *s*'s Against it,	En. Arden.	730
S thro' a finer element of her own?	Aylmer's F.	579
s's thro' the thick blood Of cattle.	Lucretius	98
riot underneath *S*'s thro the wood,	"	186

striking.
blow Before him, *s* on my brow	Fatima	25
s with her glance, The mother, me	Princess, vi.	136
his mightful hand *s* great blows.	Enid.	93
strongly *s* out her limbs awoke;	"	1229
help herself By *s* at her better,	Vivien	349
s on huge stumbling-blocks of scorn	Aylmer's F.	518

string.
to harp on such a moulder'd *s*?	Locksley H.	147
send it slackly from the *s*;	In Mem lxxxvi.	26
I cannot all command the *s*'s;	" lxxxvii.	10

strip.
s a hundred hollows bare of Spring	Princess, vi.	49
shall we *s* him there Your lover?	Enid.	1337

striped.
his brow *S* with dark blood:	M. d'Arthur	212

stripling.
the *s*'s!—for their sport!—	Princess, v.	389

stript.
walks were *s* as bare as brooms,	Princess, Pro	182
S from the three dead wolves	Enid.	943
barr'd her door, *S* off the case,	Elaine	16
rose the maid, *S* off the case,	"	973

strive.
s and wrestle with thee till I die:	St S. Stylites	117
strong in will To *s*, to seek, to find	Ulysses	70
Waiting to *s* a happy strife,	Two Voices	130
But for one hour, O Love, I *s*	In Mem xxxv.	6
When on the gloom I *s* to paint	" lxix.	2
To *s*, to fashion, to fulfil	" cxii.	7

striven.
I cannot hide that some have *s*,	Two Voices	208
These two have *s* half the day,	In Mem. ci.	17
lily maid had *s* to make him cheer,	Elaine	326

strode.
There *s* a stranger to the door,	The Goose	3, 39
s he back slow to the wounded	M. d'Arthur 65,	112
swiftly *s* from ridge to ridge.	"	181
About the hall, among his dogs,	Godiva.	16
fain To follow, *s* a stride,	Enid.	376
s the brute Earl up and down his hall,	"	1560
shook his hair, *s* off, and buzz'd abroad	Elaine	718
S from the porch, tall and erect	Aylmer's F.	825

stroke.
strike, and firmly, and one *s*:	'Love thou thy land'	92
Then dying of a mortal *s*,	Two Voices	154
A *s* of cruel sunshine on the cliff.	Princess, iv.	503
pardon ask'd and given For *s* and song	" v.	45
With *s* on *s* the horse and horseman	"	512
beating, with one full *s*, Life.'	" vii.	289
Struck for himself an evil *s*;	Mand, II. i.	21
fits of prayer, at every *s* a breath.	Enid.	1004
God's mercy what a *s* was there!	Elaine	21
For twenty *s*'s of the blood,	"	716

stroked.
Sat on his knee, *s* his gray face	Elaine	745

stroll.
all that from the town would *s*,	Talking O.	53

stroll'd.
then we *s* For half the day.	Princess. ii.	346

TENNYSON'S WORKS. 401

strong.
	POEM.	LINE.
tale of little meaning tho' the wnrdsare s;	Lotos-E's.	164
Thro' many agents making s, ' Love thou thy land'		39
I was s and hale of body then;	St S. Stylites	28
make a man feel s in speaking truth	Love and Duty	68
s in will To strive, to seek	Ulysses	69
S, supple, sinew-corded	Princess, v.	524
O fair and s and terrible!	" vi.	147
More s than all poetic thought;	In Mem. xxxvi.	12
thou wert s as thou wert true?	" lxxii.	4
The wish too s for words to name;	" xcii.	14
if the words were sweet and s	" cxxiv.	11
S in the power that all men adore	Maud, I. x.	14
well for him whose will is s!	Will	.
stood beside her tall and s,	En. Arden	757
disproof of senrn, and s in hopes.	Aylmer's F.	446
Ruddy and white, and s on his legs	Grandmother	2
S of his hands, and s on his legs	"	13

stronger.
daughters of the plough, s than men,	Princess,iv.	259
heavier, s, he that smote.	" v.	525
these are two more terrible And s.	" vi.	149
No s than a wail:	Enid	1190
hurl'd into it Against the s:	Elaine	462
Till the little wings are s.	Sea Dreams	286-94
My rhymes may have been the s.	Spiteful Let.	10

stronger-made.
Enoch s-m Was master:	En. Arden	30

strongest.
where two fight The s wins,	Aylmer's F.	365

strove.
Resolved on noble things, and s to	D.of F. Wom.	42
blinded with my tears, Still s to speak;	"	109
She s to span my waist:	Talking O..	138
unbecoming men that s with Gods	Ulysses	53
That s in other days to pass,	Day-Dm.	110
So she s against her weakness,	L. of Burleigh	69
s to buffet to land in vain	Princess, iv.	167
I s against the stream and all in vain:	vi.	375
Shall he for whose applause I s,	In Mem.	5
But ever s to make it true:	" xcv.	8
she wept, and I s to be cool,	Maud, II. i	15
And still they s and wrangled	Sea Dreams	222

strow.
And s's her lights below,	St Agnes' Eve	28

strowing.
the happy people s cried 'Hosanna	En. Arden.	501

strown.
would have s it, and are fall'n	Princess, vi.	26
s With gold and scatter'd coinage	Enid	874

struck.
S up against the blinding wall	Mariana in the S.	56
S thro' with pangs of hell.	Pal. of Art	220
I vreof widest range, S by all passion,	D. of F. Wom.	166
And s upon the corn-laws	Audley Ct.	34
he s his staff against the rocks	Golden Year	59
violin S up with Soldier-laddie,	Princess, Pro.	86
wrong him more than I That s him:	iv.	227
s such warbling fury thro' the words;	"	563
Till I s out and shouted	" v.	529
enemies have fall'n, have fall'n: they s;	" vi.	32
day, Descending, s athwart the hall	"	344
s With showers of random sweet	" vii.	70
I hear the bell s in the night;	In Mem. x.	2
the dark hand s down thro' time,	" lxxi.	19
spark S vainly in the night,	Maud, I. ix.	14
s me, madman, over the face,	" II. i.	18
S me, before the languid fool	"	19
S for himself an evil stroke;	"	21
Friend, to be s by the public foe,	" v.	89
S at her with his whip,	Enid	207-7, 413
S thro' the bulky bandit's corselet	"	1008
S with a knife's haft hard	"	1418
s Furrowing a giant oak,	Vivien	784
S up and lived along the milky roofs	Elaine	408
s it thrice, and, no one opening.	En. Arden.	273
Started from bed, and s herself a light	"	470

	POEM.	LINE.
s the keys There at his right	The Islet	7
S out the steaming mountain-side,	Lucretius	2
s the dateless doom of kings,	"	233

struggle.
Glory of Virtue, to fight, to s	Wages	3

struggled.
boy, that cried aloud And s hard.	Dora	103

strumming.
With s and with scraping,	Amphion	73

stubb'd.
an' I 'a s Thornaby waäste	N. Farmer	28
But I s un oop wi' the lot,	"	32
an' I meänd to 'a s it at fall,	"	41

stubble.
Fire in dry s a nine days' wonder	Elaine	731

stubborn.
'S, but she may sit Upon a king's	Princess, v.	423

stubborn-shafted.
Before a gloom of s-s oaks,	Enid	969

stuck.
s out The bones of some vast bulk	Princess, iii.	276
S and he clamour'd from a casement	The Brook	85

studded.
s wide With disks and tiars.	Arabian N's.	63

student.
half the s's, all the love.	Princess, iii.	23
What s came but that you planed	" iv.	275
To cramp the s at his desk	In Mem. cxxvii.	13
Drove in upon the s once or twice,	Aylmer's F.	462

study.
Old studies failed;	Princess, vii.	16
Back would he to his studies,	Aylmer's F.	394

stuff (s.)
and chairs, And all his household s;	Walk. to the M.	32
Man is made of solid s.	Ed. Morris	49
What s is this! Old writers push'd	Golden Year	64
household s, Live chattels,	Princess, iv.	493

stuff (verb.)
S his ribs with mouldy hay,	Vision of Sin	66

stumble.
my mind S's, and all my faculties	Lucretius	123

stumbled.
Ran Gaffer, s Gammer.	The Goose	34
We s on a stationary voice	Princess, v.	2
Part s mixt with floundering horses.	"	487

stumbling.
S across the market to his death,	Aylmer's F.	820

stumbling-block.
Striking on huge s-b's of scorn	Aylmer's F.	538

stumped.
with clamour bowled And s the wicket	Princess, Pro	82

stunned.
s me from my power to think	In Mem. xvi.	15
Sitting here so s and still,	Maud, II. i.	2
and s the twain Or slew them,	Enid	940
and so left him s or dead,	"	1313
hurl'd him headlong, and he fell S,	Guinevere	108

stupid.
felt so blunt and s at the heart	Enid	1595

sty.
so return'd unfarrow'd to her s.	Walk. to the M.	93
maiden moon that sparkles on a s,	Princess, v.	178

style.
the s of those heroic times?	The Epic	35
What s could suit?	Princess, Con.	9

Stylites.
hark! they shout 'St Simeon S.'	St S. Stylites	145
by surname, S, among men;	"	159

2 C

subdue.

	POEM.	LINE.
to *s* this home Of sin, my flesh,	*St S. Stylites*	56
S them to the useful and the good,	*Ulysses*	38

subdued.

I *s* me to my father's will ; .	*D. of F. Wom.*	234
grace Of sweet seventeen *s* me	*The Brook*	113
S me somewhat to that gentleness,	*Enid*	1715

subject (adj.)

| *s* to the season or the mood . | *Aylmer's F.* | 71 |

subject (s.)

Held me above the *s*, . .	*D.of F.Wom.*	10
coursed about The *s* most at heart	*Gardener's D.*	218
She rapt upon her *s*, he on her ;	*Princess*, iii.	287
My *s* with my *s*'s under him, .	*Enid*	1764

sublime.

my lover, with whom I rode *s*	*D.of F Wom.*	141
Name and fame! to fly *s*	*Vision of Sin*	103
raillery, or grotesque, or false *s*	*Princess*, iv.	565
In his simplicity *s*. . .	*Ode on Well.*	34

submit.

| *S*, and hear the judgment of the King.' | *Enid* | 1647 |

submitting.

| *S* all things to desire. . . . | *In Mem.* cxiii. | 8 |

subscribed.

| which hastily *s*, We enter'd . | *Princess*, ii. | 59 |

subserve.

| Or but *s*'s another's gain . | *In Mem.* liii. | 12 |

subsist.

| Within this region I *s*. 'You ask me, why,' etc. | | 2 |

substance.

island princes over-bold Have eat our *s*,	*Lotos-E's.*	121
know The shadow from the *s*	*Princess*, i.	9
do I chase The *s* or the shadow ? .	" ii.	387
I know the *s* when I see it. .	"	391
rolling as it were the *s* of it .	*Aylmer's F.*	258

subtle-paced.

| silver flow Of *s-p* counsel . | *Isabel* | 21 |

subtle-thoughted.

| *S-t*, myriad-minded. . . | *Ode to Mem.* | 118 |

suburb.

| By park and *s* under brown . | *In Mem.* xcvii. | 24 |

succeed.

I know that age to age *s*'s, .	*Two Voices*	205
'The many fail ; the one *s*'s,'	*Day-Dm.*	116
from the board and others ever *s* ?	*Maud*, I. iv.	27

succeeder.

| The sole *s* to their wealth . | *Aylmer's F.* | 294 |

succession.

| make One act a phantom of *s* : . | *Princess*, iii. | 312 |

successor.

| be dissipated By frail *s*'s. . | *Princess*, iii. | 250 |

such.

| from all things *s* Marrow of mirth | *Will Water.* | 213 |
| *s* the blinding splendour from the sand | *Princess*,vii. | 24 |

sucked.

Have *s* and gather'd into one .	*Talking O.*	191
S from the dark heart of the long hills	*Princess*,v.	339
s from out the distant gloom .	*In Mem.*xciv.	53
s the joining of the stones .	*Enid*	324

sucking.

| *S* the damps for drink, . . | *St S. Stylites* | 76 |
| Flaying the roofs and *s* up the drains | *Princess*, v. | 514 |

sudden.

| in thee Is nothing *s*, nothing single ; | *Eleänore* | 57 |

sudden-beaming.

| a *s-b* tenderness Of manners . | *Elaine* | 327 |

sudden-curved.

| drops down A *s-c* frown ; . | *Madeline* | 35 |

suddenly.

| I came among you here so *s*, | *Enid* | 794 |

sudden-shrilling.

	POEM.	LINE.
woke with *s-s* mirth An echo .	*Princess,Pro.*	210

sue.

| *s* me, and woo me, and flatter me, | *The Mermaid* | 43 |
| Not one word ; No! tho' your father's *s*: | *Princess*,vi. | 223 |

suffer.

they *s*—some, 'tis whisper'd—down in hell *S* endless anguish .	*Lotos-E's.*	168
not as we, But *s*'s change of frame.	*Princess*, v.	453
I do not *s* in a dream ; . .	*In Mem.*xiii.	14
When all that seems shall *s* shock,	" cxxx.	2
He *s*'s, but he will not *s* long ; .	*Will*	2
He *s*'s, but he cannot *s* wrong ; .	"	3
Had suffer'd, or should *s* any taint	*Enid*	31
my lord thro' me should *s* shame.	"	101
I seem to *s* nothing heart or limb,	"	472
my lord should *s* loss or shame.'	"	918

suffer'd.

but all hath *s* change ; . .	*Lotos-E's.*	116
the man hath *s* more than I ? .	*St S. Stylites*	48
thou hast *s* long For ages and for ages !'	"	97
I have enjoy'd Greatly, have *s* greatly,	*Ulysses*	8
Truly, she herself had *s*'— .	*Locksley H.*	96
Who loved, who *s* countless ills, .	*In Mem.* lv.	17
loved and did, And hoped and *s*,	" *Con.*	133
O Katie, what I *s* for your sake !.	*The Brook*	119
Had *s*, or should suffer any taint .	*Enid*	31
each had *s* some exceeding wrong	"	885

suffering.

| I go, weak from *s* here, . . | *Two Voices* | 238 |
| *s* thus he made Minutes an age ; . | *Enid* | 963 |

suffice.

| *S* it thee Thy pain is a reality. . | *Two Voices* | 386 |
| May not that earthly chastisement *s* ? | *Aylmer's F.* | 784 |

sufficed.

| touch of their office might have *s*, | *Maud*, II. v. | 27 |

suffused.

| She look'd : but all *S* with blushes— | *Gardener's D.* | 151 |
| *S* them, sitting, lying, languid shapes | *Vision of Sin* | 12 |

sugar-plum.

| I hoard it as a *s-p* for Holmes.' | *The Epic* | 43 |

suggesting.

| Recurring and *s* still ! . . | *Will* | 14 |

suggestion.

| track *S* to her inmost cell . | *In Mem.*xciv. | 32 |

suit (clothes, etc.)

In summer *s* and silks of holiday.	*Enid*	173
(His dress a *s* of fray'd magnificence,	"	296
in her hand A *s* of bright apparel .	"	678
unwillingly have worn My faded *s*,	"	706
robed them in her ancient *s* again	"	770
The three gay *s* of armour .	"	944, 1030
bound the *s*'s Of armour on their horses	"	945
and three goodly *s*'s of arms, .	"	973

suit (petition, etc.)

My *s* had wither'd, nipt to death .	*Ed. Morris*	101
second *s* obtain'd At first with Psyche	*Princess*,vii.	56
Lightly, her *s* allow'd, she slipt away,	*Elaine*	774
Leolin's rejected rivals from their *s*	*Aylmer's F.*	493

suit (verb.)

something it should be to *s* the place,	*Princess,Pro.*	206
made to *s* with Time and place, .	"	224
What style could *s* ? . .	" *Con.*	9
Calm as to *s* a calmer grief, .	*In Mem.* xi.	2
s The full-grown energies of heaven,	" xxxix.	19
Nor can it *s* me to forget .	" lxxxiv.	59
Could not fix the glass to *s* her eye ;	*En. Arden.*	240

suited.

| A meaning *s* to his mind . | *Day-Dm.* | 208 |
| How gay, how *s* to the house of one, | *Enid* | 1531 |

suiteth.

| only silence *s* best. . . | *To J. S.* | 64 |

suitor.

| Every gate is throng'd with *s*'s, . | *Locksley H.* | 101 |

	POEM.	LINE.
Like the Ithacensian *s*'s in old time,	Princess, iv.	100
a pair Of *s*'s as this maiden;	Enid .	440
Her *s* in old years before Geraint	"	1125
Philip, the slighted *s* of old times .	En. Arden .	746

sullen.

first as *s* as a beast new-caged,	Enid .	1704
seem'd so *s*, vext he could not go :	Elaine .	210
S, defiant, pitying, wroth.	Aylmer's F.	492

sullen-purple.

| And over the *s-p* moor . | Maud, I. x. | 21 |

sullen-seeming.

| for *s-s* Death may give . | Maud, I. xviii. | 46 |

sullen.

like the *s* of old in a garden of spice	Maud, I. iv.	42
The *S*, as we name him,—	" xx.	4
with the *S*'s pardon I am all as well	"	39
if he had not been a *S* of brutes,	" II. v.	81

sum.

| The glory of the *s* of things . | In Mem. lxxxvii. | 11 |

summ'd.

| all grace *S* up and closed in little ; | Gardener's D. | 13 |

summer.

S herself should minister .	Eleänore .	32
A *s* fann'd with spice .	Pal. of Art	116
come back again with *s* o'er the wave	May Queen, ii.	19
Smelt of the coming *s* .	Gardener's D.	77
The good old *S*'s, year by year	Talking O. .	39
Old *S*'s, when the monk was fat,	"	41
Thro' all the *s* of my leaves .	"	211
It was last *s* on a tour in Wales	Golden Year	2
s's to such length of years should come	Locksley H.	67
The woman of a thousand *s*'s back,	Godiva .	11
A *s* crisp with shining woods	Day-Dm. .	8
Till all the hundred *s*'s pass,	"	53
When will the hundred *s*'s die,	"	69
A hundred *s*'s ! can it be ? .	"	189
By squares of tropic *s* shut .	Amphion .	67
grew fat On Lusitanian *s*'s. .	Will Water.	8
all a *s*'s day Gave his broad lawns	Princess, Pro.	1
kill him in the *s* too,' .	"	202
'Why not a *s*'s as a winter's tale ?	"	204
did a compact pass Long *s*'s back	" i.	123
The *s* of the vine in all his veins—	"	181
hither side, or so she look'd, Of twenty *s*'s	" ii.	93
made to gild A stormless *s*,'	"	216
brief the sun of *s* in the North,	" iv.	94
grow A night of *S* from the heat .	" vi.	38
But *S* on the steaming floods	In Mem. lxxxiv	
s's hourly-mellowing change .	" xc.	9
o'er the sky The silvery haze of *s*	" xciv.	4
Long sleeps the *s* in the seed .	" civ.	26
Than in the *s*'s that are flown .	Con.	18
So many a *s* since she died .	Maud, I. vi.	66
Nor will be when our *s*'s have deceased.	" xviii.	14
in branding *s*'s of Bengal,	The Brook .	16
in *s*'s that we shall not see : .	Ode on Well.	234
To lands of *s* across the sea ;	The Daisy .	92
The bitter east, the misty *s* .	"	103
sprigs of *s* laid between the folds.	Enid .	138
now the wine made *s* in his veins	"	398
flaws in *s* laying lusty corn ;	"	764
that *s*, when you loved me first.	Elaine .	105
in a tilt, come next, five *s*'s back,	Guinevere .	319
My pride in happier *s*'s,	"	532
slipt across the *s* of the world .	En. Arden .	527
The soofflake of so many a *s* still	Sea Dreams	35
after many a *s* dies the swan.	Tithonus .	4
For a score of sweet little *s*'s or so.'	The Islet .	2
Thine the lands of lasting *s*,	Boädicea .	43
The child was only eight *s*'s old	The Victim .	34

summer-blanched.

| here was one that, *s-b*, . | Aylmer's F. | 152 |

summer-morn.

| many a sheeny *s-m*, . | Arabian N's. | 5 |
| Chowing a gaudy *s-m*, . | Pal. of Art . | 62 |

	POEM.	LINE.
a boon, A certain *s-p* .	Princess, i.	146

summit.

The silent *s* overhead. .	Two Voices	81
faint not, climb : the *s*'s slope	"	184
Cry to the *s*, ' Is there any hope ?'	Vision of Sin	220
And snowy *s*'s old in story : .	Princess, iii.	349
From hidden *s*'s fed with rills	In Mem. cii.	7
ere we reach'd the highest *s*	The Daisy .	87
Green-glimmering toward the *s*,	Elaine .	482

summon.

| *s* me their King to lead mine hosts | Guinevere . | 566 |

summon'd.

| Then *s* to the porch we went. | Princess, iii. | 162 |
| *S* out She kept her state, . | " | 212 |

summoner.

| Far-sighted *s* of War and Waste . | Ded. of Idylls | 36 |

summoning.

| on a dreadful trumpet, *s* her, . | Enid . | 1232 |

summons.

| And brought a *s* from the sea : . | In Mem cii. | 16 |

Summer-chace.

Broad oak of *S-c*, .	Talking O. .	20
Made ripe in *S-c* : .	"	40
And shadow *S-c* ! .	"	150

Summer-place.

| The roofs of *S-p* (rep. 96, 152) | Talking O. . | 32 |
| The front of *S-p*. . | " | 243 |

sumptuously.

| and *s* According to his fashion | Enid . | 1133 |

sun (s.)

a lily which the *s* Looks thro'	Adeline .	12
in the *s* and shadows all beneath	Love and Death	11
The *s* came dazzling thro' the leaves,	L. of Shalott, iii.	3
there like a *s* remain Fix'd .	Eleänore .	92
Many *s*'s arise and set. .	Miller's D. .	205
O *s*, that from thy noonday height	Fatima .	2
great bow will waver in the *s*, .	Pal. of Art	43
I would see the *s* rise . .	May Queen, ii. 2,	51
To-night I saw the *s* set : .	"	5
and the *s* come out on high : .	"	15
the summer's 'ill shine, .	"	58
at first, mother, to leave the blessed *s*,	" iii.	9
O look ! the *s* begins to rise, .	"	49
may be beyond the *s*—, .	"	54
Between the *s* and moon upon the shore	Lotos-E's.	38
across the threshold of the *s*, .	D. of F. Wom.	83
We drank the Lybian *S* to sleep, .	"	145
Between the rainbow and the *s*. .	Margaret .	13
The *s* is just about to set, .	"	58
While yon *s* prospers in the blue, .	The Blackbird	22
That broods above the fallen *s* .	To J. S. .	51
made his forehead like a rising *s* .	M. d'Arthur	217
of Heaven pure Up to the *S*, .	Gardener's D.	70
s fell, and all the land was dark. .	Dora .	77, 107
great with pig, wallowing in *s* .	Walk. to the M	80
full music rose and sank the *s*, .	Ed. Morris .	34
cloudy porch oft opening on the *S* ?	Love and Duty	9
The *S* will run his orbit, .	"	22
The *S* flies forward to his brother *S* ;	Golden Year	23
For some three *s*'s to store and hoard	Ulysses .	29
widen'd with the process of the *s*'s.	Locksley H. .	138
hurl their lances in the *s* ; .	"	170
what to me were *s* or clime ? .	"	177
flash the lightnings, weigh the *S*— .	"	186
A merry boy In *s* and shade ? .	Two Voices .	321
Thro' many an hour of summer *s*'s	Will Water.	33
To keep the best man under the *s*	Lady Clare .	31
As she fled fast thro' *s* and shade,	Sir L. and Q. G.	37
A thousand *s*'s will stream on thee,	A Farewell .	13
As when the *s*, a crescent of eclipse,	Vision of Sin	10
Close to the *s* in lonely lands, .	The Eagle .	2
blew from the gates of the *s*, .	Poet's Song	3
until the set of *s* Up to the people.	Princess, Pro.	8
some clear planet close upon the *S*	" ii.	22
set the starry tides, And eddied into *s*'s	"	163
Memnon smitten with the morning *S*.'	" iii.	100

	POEM.	LINE
with the *s* and moon renew their light	Princess, iii.	238
till the *S* Grew broader toward his death	"	345
the nebulous star we call the *S*	" iv.	1
brief the *s* of summer in the North	"	94
Thro' a great arc his seven slow *s*'s	"	195
in one night and due to sudden *s* :	"	293
Norway *s* Set into sunrise ; .	"	552
issued in the *s*, that now Leapt	" v.	40
thousand arms and rushes to the *S*.	" vi.	21
holds a stately fretwork to the *s*,	"	70
drench'd it is with tempest, to the *s*	" vii	127
Till the *S* drop dead from the signs.'	"	230
Nor branding summer *s*'s avail	In Mem. ii.	11
murmurs from the dying *s* : .	" iii.	8
blurr'd the splendour of the *s* ;	" lxxi.	8
while we breathe beneath the *s*,	" lxxiv.	14
s by *s* the happy days Descend	" lxxxiii.	27
Be *s* in the happy days Descend	" lxxxiii.	27
And all the courses of the *s*'s	" cxvi.	12
Sad Hesper o'er the buried *s*	" cxx.	1
I found Him not in world or *s*,	" cxxiii.	5
Thou standest in the rising *s*	" cxxix.	3
The sport of random *s* and shade .	" Con.	24
To meet and greet a whiter *s*	"	78
For him did his high *s* flame	Maud, I. iv.	32
Our planet is one, the *s*'s are many	"	45
No *s*, but a wannish glare .	" vi.	2
The *s* look'd out with a smile	" ix.	3
Something flash'd in the *s*,	"	10
in the light of the *s* that she loves	" xxii.	11
To the flowers, and be their *s*.	"	58
fires of Hell brake out of thy rising *s*,	" II. i.	9
noble thought be freër under the *s*	" III. vi.	48
turn'd our foreheads from the falling *s*	The Brook	165
s of sweet content Re-risen	"	168
And underneath another *s*,	Odeon Well.	101
our God Himself is moon and *s*.	"	217
To meet the *s* and sunny waters,	The Daisy	11
Your presence will be *s* in winter,	ToF.D Maurice	3
new *s* leat thro' the blindless casement	Enid	70
clothe her for her bridals like the *s*.'	"	231, 836
wound Bare to the *s*,	"	322
east began To quicken to the *s*	"	535
our fortune slipt from *s* to shade	"	714
would clothe her like the *s* in Heaven.	"	784
the *s* blaze on the turning scythe,	"	1101
while the *s* yet beat a dewy blade	"	1295
lift a shining hand against the *s*	"	1322
bared her forehead to the blistering *s*,	"	1364
bear him hence out of this cruel *s* :	"	1393
there the Queen array'd me like the *s* ;	"	1549
the *s* In dexter chief ; .	Vivien	325
often o'er the *s*'s bright eye	"	483
who can gaze upon the *S* in heaven?	Elaine	124
The low *s* makes the colour ;	"	135
center'd in a *s* Of silver rays,	"	295
Red as the rising *s* with heathen blood	"	308
when the next *s* brake from underground,'	"	1131
On some vast plain before a setting *s*	Guinevere	77
from the *s* there swiftly made at her,	"	78
once more ere set of *s* they saw	"	394
new warmth of life's ascending *s*	En. Arden	38
Cuts off the fiery highway of the *s*,	"	130
Under a palmtree, over him the *S* :	"	497
yonder shines The *S* of Righteousness	"	500
his own shadow in a sickly *s*	Aylmer's F.	30
the *s* go down upon your wrath,'	Sea Dreams	44
Bright with the *s* upon the stream	"	95
Into a land all *s* and blossom	"	92
We seem'd to sail into the *S* !	The Voyage	16
How oft we saw the *S* retire	"	17
many a rivulet high against the *S*	The Islet	21
The *S* peep'd in from open field	'Home they brought'	6
another of our Gods, the *S*, Apollo	Lucretius	124
stars from the night and the *s* from the	The Window	39
S sets, moon sets , .	"	164
Blaze, upon her window, *s*, .	"	176
You send a flash to the *s*.	"	179

sun (verb.)

s their milky bosoms on the thatch	Princess, ii.	89

sunbeam.

	POEM.	LINE.
When the thick-moted *s* lay .	Mariana	78
As when a *s* wavers warm .	Miller's D.	79
Sometimes I let a *s* slip, .	Talking O.	217
like a creeping *s*, slid .	Godiva	47
from his ivied nook Glow like a *s*	Princess, Pro.	105
To glide a *s* by the blasted Pine,	" vii.	181
The *s* strikes along the world :	In Mem. xv.	8
where the *s* broodeth warm,	" xc.	14
I make the netted *s* dance .	The Brook	176

sunder.

s's ghosts and shadow-casting men	Vivien	470

sunder'd.

never can be *s* without tears	To —— With P.of Art	13
Quite *s* from the moving Universe,	Princess, vii.	37
Time hath *s* shell from pearl'	In Mem. li	29
from the sabre-stroke Shatter'd and *s*	Lt. Brigade	36
cause had kept him *s* from his wife :	Vivien	565

sundown.

oft when *s* skirts the moor .	In Mem. xl.	17

sunflower.

Heavily hangs the broad *s* 'A spirit haunts,' etc.	9,	21
Unloved, the *s-f*, shining fair,	In Mem. c.	5

sun-fringed.

little clouds *s-f*, are thine, .	Madeline	17

sung.

cock *s* out an hour ere light ;	Mariana	27
The blue fly *s* in the pane ; .	"	63
the cock hath *s* beneath the thatch	The Owl, i.	10
Died round the bulbul as he *s* ;	Arabian N's.	70
From Calpe unto Caucasus they *s*,	The Poet	15
At eve a dry cicala *s*, .	Mariana in the S.	85
S by the morning star of song .	D. of F. Wom.	3
anthem *s*, is charmed and tied	"	193
wheresoever I am *s* or told .	M. d' Arthur	34
falser than all songs have *s*, .	Locksley H.	41
Among the tents I paused and *s*,	Two Voices	125
I *s* the joyful Pæan clear, .	"	127
Wherever he sat down and *s*	Amphion	19
nightingale thought, 'I have *s* many	Poet's Song	13
s to, when, this gad-fly brush'd aside,	Princess, v.	404
We *s*, tho' every eye was dim	In Mem xxx.	14
S by a long-forgotten mind.	" lxxvi.	12
A guest, or happy sister, *s*,	" lxxxviii.	26
One whispers, here thy boyhood *s*	" ci.	9
Whatever I have said or *s*, .	" cxxiv.	1
Peace, his triumph will be *s* .	Ode on Well.	232
s nearly where we sit .	Vivien	255
told in tale, Or *s* in song ! .	"	703
many a noble war-song had he *s*,	Guinevere	276

sunlight.

Place it, where sweetest *s* falls .	Ode to Mem.	85
clear brow in *s* glow'd ; .	L. of Shalott, iii.	28
as *s* drinketh dew. .	Fatima	21
Floated the glowing *s*'s as she moved.	Œnone	178
Are as moonlight unto *s*, .	Locksley H.	152
And the *s* broke from her lip .	Maud, I. vi.	86
'so rare the smiles Of *s*) .	The Daisy	54
like a stormy *s* smiled Geraint,	Enid	1329
s on the plain behind a shower ;	Vivien	253
return In such a *s* of prosperity	Aylmer's F.	421

sunlike.

make your Enid burst *S* from cloud	Enid	789

sunn'd.

S by those orient skies ; .	The Poet	42
and *s* Her violet eyes, .	Gardener's D.	135
S itself on his breast and hands.	Maud, I. xiii.	13
s The world to peace again :	Vivien	460

sunning.

little head, *s* over with curls, .	Maud, I. xxii.	57
S himself in a waste field alone	Aylmer's F.	9

sunny.

Bright was that afternoon, *S* but chill ;	En. Arden	671

sunny-sweet.

tower or duomo, *s-s*, .	The Daisy	46

	POEM.	LINE.
sunny-warm,		
tracts of pasture *s-w*	Pal. of Art	94
sunrise.		
the breath Of the lilies at *s?*	Adeline	37
Rare *s* flow'd.	The Poet	36
Freedom rear'd in that august *s*	"	37
lights of sunset and of *s* mix'd	Love and Duty	70
in the burst Of *s,*	Princess, Pro.	41
Norway sun Set into *s.*	" iv.	552
varies, now At *s,* now at sunset,	Enid	7
The *s* broken into scarlet shafts	En. Arden	593
The scarlet shafts of *s*—but no sail.	"	600
sunset.		
between the *s* and the moon;	Eleänore	124
the *s,* south and north, Winds all the	Miller's D.	241
charmed *s* linger'd low adown	Lotos-E's.	19
lights of *s* and of sunrise mix'd	Love and Duty	70
purpose holds To sail beyond the *s,*	Ulysses	60
Yon orange *s* waning slow; 'Move eastward,' etc.		2
the gates were closed At *s,*	Princess, Con.	37
rang Beyond the bourn of *s;*	"	100
Last night, when the *s* burn'd	Maud, I. vi.	8
varies, now At sunrise, now at *s,*	Enid	7
hour or maybe twain After the *s,*	Guinevere	236
some refulgent *s* of India.	Milton	13
sunset-flush'd.		
pinnacles of aged snow, Stood *s-f;*	Lotos-E's.	17
sun-shaded.		
S-s In the heat of dusty fights	Princess, ii.	223
sunshine.		
where broad *s* laves The lawn	D. of F. Wom.	189
Simeon, whose brain the *s* bakes	St S. Stylites	161
took The thunder and the *s,*	Ulysses	48
The random *s* lighten'd !	Amphion	56
like a touch of *s* on the rocks,	Princess, iii.	339
A stroke of cruel *s* on the cliff,	" iv.	503
When the tide ebbs in *s,*	" vi.	140
takes the *s* and the rains,	In Mem. x.	14
Turn thy wild wheel thro' *s,*	Enid	348
Autumn's mock *s* of the faded woods	Aylmer's F.	610
past In *s;* right across its track	Sea Dreams	122
sun-smitten,		
S-s Alps before me lay	The Daisy	62
sun-steep'd.		
S-s at noon, and in the moon	Lotos-E's.	74
sun-stricken.		
fell S-s, and that other lived alone	En. Arden	571
supersede.		
one deep love doth *s* All other,	In Mem. xxxii.	5
superstition.		
paid To woman, *s* all awry; .	Princess, ii.	121
supper.		
And after *s,* on a bed,	The Sisters	16
serve me sparrow-hawks For *s,*	Enid	305
supple.		
s, sinew-corded, apt at arms;	Princess, v.	524
supple-sinew'd.		
Iron-jointed, *s-s,* they shall dive	Locksley H.	169
supple-sliding.		
scoundrel in the *s-s* knee.'	Sea Dreams	164
suppliant.		
look'd and saw The novice, weeping, *s,*	Guinevere	656
supplicated.		
shall I brook to be *s?*	Boädicea	9
supplicating.		
Besought him, *s,* if he cared	En Arden	163
did they pity me *s?*	Boädicea	8
supplied.		
And he *s* my want the more	In Mem. lxxviii.	19
supporter.		
The *s's* on a shield, Bow-back'd	Princess, vi.	338
two wild men *s's* of a shield,	Enid	1116

	POEM.	LINE.
suppose.		
Good soul! *s* I grant it thee	Two Voices	53
if, as I *s,* your nephew fights	Enid	475
supremacy.		
In knowledge of their own *s.*	Œnone	131
sure.		
rest thee *s* That I shall love thee	Œnone	156
make him *s* that he shall cease?	Two Voices	282
Before I am quite quite *s*	Maud, I. xi.	10
O Maud were *s* of Heaven	" xii.	19
s am I, quite *s.* he is not dead,'	Enid	1394
evil done; right *s* am I of that,	Guinevere	187
'Fool,' he answer'd, 'death is *s*	Sailor Boy	13
surely.		
did but keep your *s* for our son	Princess, v.	24
surf.		
White *s* wind-scatter'd over sails	D of F. Wom.	21
like a wader in the *s,*	The Brook	117
surface.		
ere he dipt the *s,* rose an arm	M. d'Arthur	143
And down my *s* crept.	Talking O.	162
These flashes on the *s* are not he.	Princess, iv.	234
To make the sullen *s* crisp.	In Mem. xlviii.	3
Then from the smitten *s* flash'd,	Elaine	1229
surge.		
when the *s* was seething free,	Lotos-E's.	151
The sands and yeasty *s's* mix	Sailor Boy	9
surmise.		
silent we with blind *s*	Princess, iv.	362
surname.		
Simeon of the pillar, by *s* Stylites	St S. Stylites	158
'Katie.' 'That were strange. What *s*	The Brook	212
surpass.		
But tho' the port *s*'es praise	Will Water.	77
surprise (s.)		
with *s* Froze my swift speech;	D. of F Wom.	89
some *s* and thrice as much disdain	Enid	557
kept it for a sweet *s* at morn,	"	703
truly is it not a sweet *s?*	"	704
surprise (verb.)		
S thee ranging with thy peers	In Mem. xliii.	12
survive.		
S in spirits render'd free,	In Mem. xxxviii.	10
suspend.		
he *s's* his converse with a friend,	Enid	340
suspicion.		
A vague *s* of the breast;	Two Voices	336
gleam'd a vague *s* in his eyes:	Elaine	128
suspicious.		
S that her nature had a taint	Enid	68
sustain.		
bad him with good heart *s* himself	Aylmer's F.	544
sustained.		
Be dimm'd of sorrow, or *s;*	In Mem. lxxxiv.	10
sustenance.		
Gained for her own *s* scanty *s,*	En. Arden	258
No want was there of human *s,*	"	555
swallow (s.)		
Above in the wind was the *s,*	Dying Swan	16
And the *s* 'ill come back again	May Queen, ii.	17
While the prime *s* dips his wing,	Ed. Morris.	145
The *s* stopt as he hunted the bee.	Poet's Song	9
like *s's* coming out of time	Princess, ii.	460
watch'd the *s* winging south	" iv.	71
O S, S, flying, flying South (rep.).	"	75
The Mayfly is torn by the *s,*	Maud, I. iv.	23
Among my skimming *s's;*	The Brook	175
s and sparrow and throstle	The Window	157
swallow (verb.)		
to sloughs That *s* common sense	Princess, v.	432
swallow'd.		
And blackening, *s* all the land,	Guinevere	82

swallow-flight.

	POEM.	LINE.
loosens from the lip Short s-f's of	In Mem. xlvii.	15

swallowing
a gulf of ruin, s gold, Not making	Sea Dreams	79

swam.
I loved the brimming wave that s	Miller's D.	97
The light white cloud s over us.	D of F. Wom.	221
in the light the white mermaiden s,	Guinevere	243

swamp.
like fire in s's and hollows gray	May Queen, i.	31
Gray s's and pools, waste places	Enid	880
The s, where hums the dropping	On a Mourner	9

swamp'd.
This Gama s in lazy tolerance	Princess, v.	433

swan.
Adown it floated a dying s,	Dying Swan	6
The wild s's death-hymn took the soul	"	21
Far as the wild s wings	Pal. of Art.	31
the brink, like some full-breasted s	M. d'Arthur	266
a neck to which the s's Is tawnier	Elaine	1178
after many a summer dies the s.	Tithonus	4

swang.
s besides on many a windy sign—	Aylmer's F.	19

sward.
The sloping of the moon-lit s	Arabian N's.	27
Slant down the snowy s,	St Agnes' Eve	6
s was trim as any garden lawn:	Princess, Pro.	95
At this upon the s She tapt.	"	148
'Pitch our pavilion here upon the s;	"	iii. 328
on the s, and up the linden walks,	"	iv. 191
dismounting on the s They let the horses	Enid	1059
than the s with drops of dew,	"	1538

sware.
Merlin s that I should come again	M. d'Arthur	23
Cophetua s a royal oath:	Beggar Maid	15
at the last he s That he would send	Princess, i.	62
S to combat for my claim till death	" v.	330
but mine,' so I s to the rose,	Maud, I. xxii.	31
since he never s Except his wrath	Lucretius	127

swarm (s.)
Then we shoulder'd thro' the s,	Audley Ct.	8
Glitter like a s of fire-flies	Locksley H.	10
and the s Of female whisperers:	Princess, vi.	335
s's of men Darkening with female field,	" vii.	18
Back to France her banded s's,	Ode on Well.	110

swarm (verb.)
s as bees about their queen	Princess, i.	39

swarmed.
noise of life S in the golden present,	Gardener's D.	175
with the cross; they s again.	St S. Stylites	170
s His literary leeches,	Will Water.	199

swarming.
and the crowd were s now	Princess, Con.	37
heathen s o'er the Northern Sea.	Guinevere	425

swathed.
s the hurt that drain'd her dear lord's	Enid	1365

sway (s.)
A hate of gossip parlance, and of s,	Isabel	26

sway (verb.)
She saw the gusty shadow s.	Mariana	52
Unto the dwelling she must s.	Ode to Mem.	79
truth that s's the soul of men?	Day-Dm.	72
waves that s themselves in rest,	In Mem. xi.	18
Unwatch'd, the garden bough shall s,	" c.	1
while these long branches s,	Maud, I. xviii.	29

sway'd.
Still hither thither idly s	Miller's D.	47
and so I s All moods.	D. of F. Wom.	131
s The rein with dainty finger-tips,	Sir L. and Q. G.	40
S to her from their orbits	Princess, vii.	307
And world-wide fluctuation s	In Mem. cxi.	24
S round about him, as he gallop'd up	Enid	171
hundred under-kingdoms that he s	Vivien	432
s The cradle, while she sang	Sea Dreams	279

swaying.
Not s to this faction or to that;	Ded. of Idylls	20

swear.
Such eyes! I s to you, my love,	Miller's D.	87
Let us s an oath, and keep it	Lotos-E's.	153
I s (and else may insects prick	Talking O.	69
I s, by leaf, and wind, and rain,	"	81
And hear me s a solemn oath,	"	281
she made me s it—'Sdeath	Princess, v.	281
S by St something—	"	283
I s to you lawful and lawless war	Maud, II. v.	94
I s it would not ruffle me so much	Enid	999
I s I will not ask your meaning	"	1591
ere I leave you let me s once more	Vivien	778
I s by truth and knighthood that I gave	Elaine	1280
s To reverence the King,	Guinevere	464
a secret—only s Before I tell you	En. Arden.	838
s upon the book Not to reveal it,	"	839
'S' added Enoch sternly 'on the book	"	843
I s you shall not make them out of	Aylmer's F.	301
I s henceforth by this and this,	The Ringlet	20

swearing.
s men to vows impossible,	Elaine	131

sweat.
bloody thumbs S on his blazon'd	Walk. to the M.	68
s her sixty minutes to the death	Golden Year	68

sweating.
s rosin, plump'd the pine	Amphion	47
s underneath a sack of corn,	Enid	263
up the side, s with agony, got,	Elaine	493
a weird bright eye, s and trembling,	Aylmer's F.	585

sweep (s.)
and a s Of richest pauses,	Eleänore	65
parson taking wide and wider s's,	The Epic	14
by many a s Of meadow smooth	Audley Ct.	12
The s of scythe in morning dew,	In Mem. lxxxviii.	18
a single bound, and with a s of it.	Enid	1575
dread s of the down-streaming seas:	En. Arden	55
or the s Of some precipitous rivulet	"	587

sweep (verb.)
S the green that folds thy grave.	A Dirge	6
see the morning mist S thro' them	Œnone	213
we s into the younger day	Locksley H.	183
s the tracts of day and night.	Two Voices	69
s the crossings, wet or dry,	Will Water.	47
let the wind s and the plover cry;'Come not, when,' etc.		5
s s with all its autumn bowers	In Mem. xi.	10
heard them s the winter land;	" xxx.	10
the wind began to s A music	" cii.	53
s's away as out we pass.	" Con.	95
s me from my hold upon the world,	Vivien.	152
those long swells of breaker s	The Voyage	39

sweeping.
And with a s of the arm,	A Character	16
s thro' me left me dry,	Locksley H.	131
S the frothfly from the fescue	Aylmer's F.	530

sweet.
pillar'd palm, Imprisoning s's,	Arabian N's.	40
S is the colour of cove and cave	Sea-Fairies	30
s shall your welcome be	"	29
So s it seems with thee to walk	Miller's D.	29
A trifle, s! which true love spells	"	187
Or gay, or grave, or s, or stern,	Pal. of Art	91
O s is the new violet,	May Queen, iii.	5
And s is all the land about	"	7
O s and strange it seems to me,	"	53
s it was to dream of Father-land	Lotos-E's.	39
How s it were, hearing the downward	"	92
How s (while warm airs lull us,	"	134
Only to hear were s,	"	144
surely, slumber is more s than toil	"	171
S as new buds in Spring	D. of F. Wom.	272
Failing to give the bitter of the s,	"	287
which came between, more s than	Gardener's D.	247
made it s To walk, to sit	Ed. Morris	39
S! s! spikenard, and balm,	St S. Stylites	208
Yet seem'd the pressure thrice as s	Talking O.	145

	POEM.	LINE.		POEM.	LINE.
These three made unity so *s*,	Two Voices	421	your *s* hardly leaves me a choice	Maud, I v.	24
How *s* are looks that ladies bend	Sir Galahad	13	Tho' I fancy her *s* only due	" xiii.	33
made it seem more *s* to be	You might have won	20	*sweet smelling.*		
As *s* as English air could make her	Princess,Pro.	154	led me thro' the short *s-s* lanes	The Brook	122
S and low, *s* and low,	" ii.	456	*swell* (s.)		
O : and far, from cliff and scar	" iii.	356	the wavy *s* of the soughing reeds	Dying Swan	38
s as those by hopeless fancy feign'd	" iv.	37	four currents in one *s*	Pal. of Art	33
S is it to have done the thing one ought,	" v.	64	a *s* of music on the wind	May Queen, iii.	32
she can oe *s* to those she loves,	" .	279	on the *s* The silver lily heaved	To E L.	18
showers of random *s* on maid and man	" vii.	71	only the *s* Of the long waves	Maud, I xviii.	62
call her *s*, as if in irony,	" .	82	So fresh they rose in shadow'd *s's*	The Letters	46
and *s* is every sound (rep)	" .	203	only heaved with a summer *s*	The Daisy	12
O *S* and bitter in a breath	In Mem iii.	3	those long *s's* of breaker sweep	The Voyage	30
'They rest,' we said, 'their sleep is *s*,'	" xxx.	10	*swell* (verb.)		
To utter love more *s* than praise	" lxxvi.	16	with white bells the clover-hill *s's*	Sea-Fairies	14
S after showers, ambrosial air,	" lxxxv.	1	sometimes they *s* and move,	Eleänore	111
Desire of nearness doubly *s*:	" cxvi	6	And while he sinks or *s's*	Talking O.	270
if the words were *s* and strong	" cxxiv.	11	*S's* up, and shakes and falls.	Sir Galahad	76
But a smile could make it *s*	Maud, I. vi. 39,	95	*s* On some dark shore	Princess, i.	244
What some have found so *s*:	" xi.	4	*s* Out and fail, as if a door	InMem xxviii.	7
Maud is as true as Maud is *s*:	" xiii.	32	Spring that *s's* the narrow brooks	" lxxxiv.	70
low world, where yet 'tis *s* to live :	" xviii	48	*swell'd.*		
if left uncancell'd, had been so *s*:	" xix.	46	But still her lists were *s*	Princess, iv.	300
meadow your walks have left so *s*	" xxii.	39	voice of the long sea-wave as it *s*	Maud, I. xiv.	31
She is coming, my own, my *s*;	" .	67	low musical note *S* up and died :	Sea Dreams	204
seeing her so *s* and serviceable.	Enid	373	as it *s*, a ridge Of breaker issued	" .	204
words whose echo lasts, they were so *s*,	" .	782	and *s* again slowly to music	" .	215
S were the days when I was all unknown.	Vivien	351	The broad seas *s* to meet the keel,	The Voyage	13
if you love, it will be *s* to give it :	Elaine	689	*swelleth.*		
if he love, it will be *s* to have it	" .	690	Her song the lintwhite *s*,	Claribel	15
s and serviceable To noble knights	" .	763	*swelling.*		
then will I, for true you are and *s*	" .	950	Of such a tide *s* toward the land,	Sea Dreams	85
S is true love tho' given in vain,	" .	1001	*swept.*		
s is death who puts an end to pain:	" .	1002	with a flying finger *s* my lips,	Gardener'sD.	241
Love, art thou *s*? then bitter death	" .	1004	A breeze thro' all the garden *s*	Day-Dm	133
Love, thou art bitter : *s* is death	" .	1005	No wing of wind the region *s*,	InMem. lxxvii.	6
heard the bridegroom is so *s*!	Guinevere	173	Down we *s* and charged and overthrew	Ode on Well.	130
hast not made my life so *s* to me	" .	448	*S* with it to the shore	Sea Dreams	67
taking pride in her, She look'd so *s*,	Aylmer's F.	555	*s* away The men of flesh and blood,	" .	230
your dream, she said. 'Not sad, but *s*'	Sea Dreams	104	swell'd to meet the keel, And *s* behind	The Voyage	14
'So *s*, I lay' said he 'And mused	" .	103	He cast his body, and on we *s*	" .	80
an loile they says is *s*,	N. Farmer	63			
I knew not what of wild and *s*,	Tithonus	61	*swerve.*		
Where is another *s* as my *s*!	The Window	86	approaching rookery *s* From the elms	Princess,Con	97
Claspt on her seal, my *s*!	" .	135	Nor pastoral rivulet that *s's*	In Mem.xcix	14
sweeten.			*S* from her duty to herself and us—	Aylmer's F.	304
S's the spirit still.	D.ofF.Wom.	236	*swerved.*		
sweeten'd			be *s* from right to save A Prince	Princess, ii.	270
Lo! *s* with the summer light,	Lotos-E's.	77	And so my passion hath not *s*	In Mem. lxxxiv.	49
sweeter.			*swerving.*		
Whether smile or frown be *s*,	Madeline	13	at a sudden *s* of the road,	Enid	1355
s is the young lamb's voice	May Queen, iii	6	*swift.*		
s far is death than life	" .	8	Not *s* nor slow to change 'Love thou thy land,' etc.		31
s than the dream Dream'd by a happy	Gardener'sD	70	*swim.*		
S thy voice, but every sound is sweet:	Princess,vii	204	how to skate, to row, to *s*	Ed. Morris	19
s seems To rest beneath the clover sod	InMem. x	12	High up the vapours fold and *s*:	Two Voices	202
nothing can be *s* Than maiden Maud	Maud,I.xx	21	A light before me *s's*,	Sir Galahad	20
s than the bride of Cassivelaun,	Enid	744	The mystic glory *s s* away;	In Mem. lxvi.	9
I know not which is *s*, no, not I.	Elaine	100,1.9	on the depths of death there *s's*	" cvii.	11
if death be *s*, let me die.	" .	1006	*swindler.*		
'Your own will be the *s*,'	Sea Dreams	304	and a wretched *s's* lie?.	Maud, I. i.	56
sweetest.			*swine.*		
can break our dream When *s s*;	Elaine	139	watch the darkening droves of *s*	Pal. of Art	199
love their best Closest and *s*,	" .	866	Upon her tower, the Niobe of *s*,	Walk to the M.	91
Sweet-Gale.			all the *s* were sows, And all the dogs' —	Princess,I.i	71
S-G rustle round the shelving keel	Ed Morris	110	hustled together, each sex, like *s*,	Maud, I. i.	34
sweetheart.			of all the drove should touch me : *s*!	Vivien	547
S, I love you so well	Grandmother	50	*swing* (s.)		
sweet-hearted.			the rush of the air in the prone *s*	Aylmer's F.	86
S-h, you, whose light blue eyes	In Mem. xcv.	2	*swing* (verb.)		
sweetness.			*s's* the trailer from the crag ;	Locksley H.	163
folds the lily all her *s* up,	Princess, vii.	171	shrill bell rings, the censer *s's*,	Sir Galahad	35
He gain in *s* and in moral height	" .	265	*swoon* (s.)		
change my *s* more and more,	In Mem.xxxv.	15	as in a *s*, With dinning sound	Eleänore	131
A secret *s* in the stream,	" lxiii.	20			
Thy *s* from its proper place?	" lxxxi.	6			
Nor name the *s* on the skull	" cix.	17			

	POEM.	LINE.
Down-deepening from s to s	Fatima	27
at the last he waken'd from his s.	Enid	1431

swoon (verb)

the languid air did s.	Lotos-E's.	5
A time to sicken and to s,	In Mem. xxi.	17
Lest he should s and tumble	En. Arden.	775

swoon'd

She nor s, nor utter'd cry:	Princess, v.	513
the pure pain, and wholly s away.	Elaine	517
smote her hand: well-nigh she s:	"	622
woman shrieking at his feet, and s.	Aylmer's F.	811

swooning.

And I was faint to s,	Vivien	730
thus they bore her s to her tower.	Elaine	963
Lash the maiden into s,	Boadicea	67

swoops.

and s's The vulture, beak and talon,	Princess, v.	372

sword.

flames, nor trenchant s's 'Clear-headed friend,'etc		14
No s Of wrath her right arm whirl'd	The Poet	53
Many drew s's and died.	D of F. Wom.	95
if knowledge bring the s, That know-		
ledge takes the s away— 'Love thou thy land'		87
mystic, wonderful. Holding the s.	M. d Arthur	32
King Arthur's s, Excalibur	"	103
clutch'd the s And strongly wheel'd	"	135
Man for the s and for the needle she	Princess, v.	438
s to s, and horse to horse we hung	"	528
To draw, to sheathe a useless s,	In Mem cxxvii	13
not openly bearing the s.	Maud, I. i.	28
heard Geraint, and grasping at his s	Enid	1573
touch it with a s, It buzzes wildly	Vivien	281
seem a s beneath a belt of three,	"	360
every dint a s had beaten in it.	Elaine	19
children born of thee are s and fire	Guinevere	422
No desolation but by s and fire?	Aylmer's F.	748
hoveringly a s Now over	Lucretius	61

swordcut

Seam'd with an ancient s on the cheek	Elaine	258

sword-grass.

On the oat-grass and the s-g	MayQueen, ii.	28

swore.

we closed, we kiss'd, s faith.	Ed. Morris	114
s They said he lived shut up	Golden Year	8
laugh'd, and s by Peter and by Paul:	Godiva	24
The barons w, with many words,	Day-Dm.	155
s he long'd at college, only long	Princess, Pro.	157
She was a princess too; and so I s	" v.	285
caught By that you s to withstand?	Maud, I. vi.	80
bailiff s that he was mad,	The Brook	143
s That I would track this caitiff	Enid	414
But keep that oath you s,	Vivien	538
on the book, half-frighted. Miriam s.	En. Arden	844
s besides To play their go-between	Aylmer's F.	522
to those that s Not by the temple	"	793
ours he s were all diseased	The Voyage	76

sworn.

True Mussulman was I and s	Arabian N's.	9
s his love a thousand times	Œnone	227
Not tho' Blanche had s	Princess, vii.	
Mine, mine—our fathers have s.	Maud, I. xix.	43
s From his own lips to have it—	Enid	409
s That I will break his pride	"	423
'Have I not s? I am not trusted	Vivien	377
I have s never to see him more,	Guinevere	374

swum,

with an eye that s in thanks;	Princess, vi.	193

swung.

bells that s, Mov'd of themselves,	Pal. of Art	129
S themselves, and in low tones	Vision of Sin	20
and s The heavy-folded rose,	In Mem. xciv.	58
s an apple of the purest gold,	Enid	170
S from his brand a windy buffet	"	939
S round the lighted lantern	Guinevere	260
sideways up he s his arms,	Sea Dreams	24

	POEM.	LINE.
sycamore.		
The pillar'd dust of sounding s's,	Audley Ct.	15
height Of foliage, towering s;	InMem.lxxxviii	4
The large leaves of the s.	" xciv.	55

Sylla.

all the blood by S shed Came driving	Lucretius	4

syllable.

Faltering, would break its s s	Love and Duty	39

symbol.

Weak s's of the settled bliss,	Miller's D.	233
so shall grief with s's play,	InMem lxxxiv	93
Mute s's of a joyful morn,	" Con.	58

symbol'd.

As if the living passion s there	Aylmer's F.	535

symmetry.

s Of thy floating gracefulness	Eleänore	49
A certain miracle of s,	Gardener's D.	11

sympathise

growing coarse to s with clay.	Locksley H.	46

sympathy.

dainty-woeful sympathies.	Margaret	53
plies its office, moved with s. 'Love thou thy land'		48
Nor lose their mortal s.	In Mem.xxx.	23
And yet I spare them s	" lxii.	7
Some painless s with pain?'	" lxxxiv.	83

Syrian.

breath'd beneath the S blue:	In Mem. h.	12

system.

fourfield s, and the price of grain;	Audley Ct.	33
to law S and empire?	Love and Duty	8
A dust of s's and of creeds.	Two Voices	207
block and bar Your heart with s	Princess, iv.	443
world Of traitorous friend and broken s	" vi.	178
Our little s's have their day;	In Mem. Pro.	17
star and s rolling past,	" Con.	122

T

taäke.

But godamoighty a moost t meä.	N. Farmer.	51

taäken.

A mowt 'a t Joänes	N. Farmer.	49
Or a mowt 'a t Robins	"	50

taäkin'.

'The amoighty's a t o' you to issën	N. Farmer	10-26

taäle.

an a's hallus i' the owd t;	N. Farmer.	66

tabernacle.

gray tower, or plain-faced t.	Aylmer's F.	618

table (see Table Round.)

all the t's danced again,	The Goose	47
King Arthur's t, man by man,	M. d'Arthur	3
now the whole ROUND T is dissolved	"	234
And thrumming on the t;	Will Water.	160
on the t's every clime and age	Princess, Pro.	16
laid aside the gems There on a t.	Elaine	1197
softly by the King And all his T	Guinevere	46
himself was knight Of the great T—	"	233
Sat at his t; drank his costly wines	Sea Dreams	74
there at t's of ebony lay	Boädicea	61

table-land

Are close upon the shining t-l's	Ode on Well.	216

Table Round.

that great order of the T R	Enid	3
made a knight of Arthur's T R,	"	1641
I, therefore, made him of our T R	"	1736
About the founding of a T R,	Vivien	261
Assay it on some one of the T R.	"	539
blinds himself and all the T R	"	613
I know the T R, my friends of old;	"	665
Rapt in this fancy of his T R,	Elaine	130
the rest, his T R, Known as they are,	"	166
much they ask'd of court and T R,	"	268

	POEM.	LINE.
charge at the head of all his *T R*,	Elaine	304
with the *T R* that held the lists,	,,	466-98
mine, as head of all our *T R*,	,,	1318
The marshall'd order of their *T R*	,,	1322
To make disruption in the *T R*	Guinevere	18
Hath wrought confusion in the *T R*	,,	218
canst thou know of Kings and *T's R*	,,	226
In that fair order of my *T R*,	,,	460

tablet.
Thy *t* glimmers to the dawn	*In Mem*.lxvi.	16
Their pensive *t*'s round her head,	Con.	51

table-talk.
genial *t-t*, Or deep dispute,	*In Mem*.lxxxiii.	23

taboo.
worse than South-sea-isle *t*.	*Princess*, iii	261

tack.
till as when a boat *T*'s,	*Princess*, ii	169

tackle
Buoy'd upon floating *t*	*En. Arden*	532
Dry sang the *t*, sang the sail	*The Voyage*	10

tact
So gracious was her *t* and tenderness:	*Princess*,i.	24
The graceful *t*, the Christian art :	*In Mem*.cix.	16
she by *t* of love was well aware	*Elaine*	978

ta'en.
clay *t* from the common earth, To —	*With P.of Art*	17
And *t* my fiddle to the gate,	*Amphion*	11,15
oath was *t* for public use	*Princess*, iv.	318

tagged.
t with icy fringes in the moon	*St S. Stylites*	31

tail.
with playful *t* Crouch'd fawning	Œnone	196
from head to *t* Came out clear plates	*Two Voices*	11
the innumerable ear and *t*:	*The Brook*	134

taint.
Defects of doubt, and *t*'s of blood :	*In Mem* lii	4
pure as he from *t* of craven guile,	*Ode on Welt*	135
should suffer any *t* In nature :	*Enid*	31
Suspicious that her nature had a *t*.	,,	64

take.
T, Madam, this poor book of song :	*To the Queen*	17
when to *t* Occasion by the hand,	,,	30
T the heart from out my breast,	*Adeline*	8
Gargarus Stands up and *t*'s the morning	Œnone	11
that will *t* away my sin	*Pal. of Art*	287
Let her *t* 'em : they are hers:	*May Queen*,ii.	46
I thought, I *t* it for a sign.	,, iii.	38
Grows green and broad, and *t*'s no care	*Lotos-E's*.	73
T warning ! he that will not sing	*The Blackbird*	21
the New-year will *t* 'em away.	*D. of the O. Year*	14
Comes up to *t* his own.	,,	36
That *t*'s away a noble mind.	*To J. S.*	48
t The place of him that sleeps	,,	67
knowledge *t*'s the sword away —	'*Love thou thy land*	68
t the goose, and keep you warm,	*The Goose*	7
t the goose, and wring her throat,	,,	31
'The Devil *t* the goose,	,,	55
t the style of those heroic times?	*The Epic*	35
therefore *t* my brand Excalibur,	*M. d'Arthur*	27,36
t's the flood With swarthy webs	,,	268
lusty bird *t*'s every hour for dawn.	*Ep*.	11
t her for your wife.	*Dora*	18
t a month to think,	,,	27
let me *t* the boy,	,,	64
but *t* the child,	,,	91,97
thou shouldst *t* my trouble on thyself	,,	116
will beg of him to *t* thee back : [rep.]	,,	121
t her back : she loves you well.	,,	140-52
a beast To *t* them as I did ?	*Ed. Morris*	72
mercy, Lord, and *t* away my sin.	*St S. Stylites*	8,44
O *t* the meaning, Lord:	,,	21
silly people *t* me for a saint	,,	125
let them *t* Example, pattern ;	,,	219
kiss him : *t* his hand in thine.	*Locksley H*.	52
I will *t* some savage woman.	,,	168

	POEM.	LINE.
turn this sickness yet might *t*	*Two Voices*	55
t the broidery frame, and add	*Day-Dm*.	15
So, Lady Flora, *t* my lay	,,	177,249
So much your eyes my fancy *t* —		218
t it — earnest wed with sport,	,,	279
I'll *t* the showers as they fall	*Amphion*	101
t Half-views of men and things.	*Will Water*.	50
I *t* myself to task ;	,,	102
T my brute, and lead him in,	*Vision of Sin*	65
t's a lady's finger with all care,	*Princess,Pro*	171
'*T* Lilia, then, for heroine'.	,,	217
Cyril whisper'd : '*T* me with you too.'	i.	80
T me : I'll serve you better in a strait	,,	84
'Well then, Psyche, *t* my life	ii.	187
open eyes, and we must *t* the chance	iii.	127
t The dip of certain strata	,,	153
And *t*'s and ruins all ;	,,	222
were I thou that she might *t* me in,	iv.	84
mind is changed : we *t* it to ourself.'	,,	343
t such bloody vengeance on you both ?	,,	513
Satan *t* The old women	v.	32
'Yet I pray, *T* comfort:	,,	77
they will *t* her, they will make her hard,	,,	87
will *t* her up and go my way,	,,	99
t them all-in-all Were we ourselves	,,	192
I *t* her for the flower of womankind,	,,	277
Still *T* not his life	,,	397
man wants weight, the woman *t*'s it up	,,	434
she's yet a colt — *T*, break her :	,,	446
on the little clause ' *t* not his life :'	,,	452
t s, and breaks, and cracks, and splits,	,,	516
All good go with thee ' *T* it, Sir'	vi.	190
t her hand, she weeps: 'Sdeath !	,,	208
on to the tents : *t* up the Prince	,,	262
stoop from heaven and *t* the shape	,,	365
great river *t* me to the main :	,,	376
swarming now, To *t* their leave	Con.	38
shall I *t* a thing so blind,	*In Mem*. iii.	13
She *t*'s a riband or a rose	vi.	32
t's the sunshine and the rains,	x.	14
seem to *t* The touch of change	xvi.	5
I *t* the grasses of the grave	xxi.	3
t's His license in the field of time,	xxvii.	5
To *t* her latest leave of home,	xxxix.	6
She *t*'s, when harsher moods remit	xlvii.	6
thou shalt *t* a nobler leave.'.	lvii.	12
Who *t*'s the children on his knee,	lxv.	11
T wings of fancy, and ascend	lxxv.	1
T wings of foresight ; lighten thro'	,,	5
And *t* us as a single soul.	lxxxiii.	44
Can *t* no part away from this :	lxxxiv.	68
Ah, *t* the imperfect gift I bring,	,,	117
I'll rather take what fruit may be	cvii.	13
the distance *t*'s a lovelier hue,	cxiv.	6
t's The colours of the crescent prime ?	cxv.	3
I *t* the pressure of thine hand.	cxvii.	12
t the print Of the golden age	*Maud*, I. i.	29
To *t* a wanton dissolute boy	x.	58
Shall I not *t* care of all that I think.	xv.	7
Or to ask, *T* me, sweet,	II. iv.	87
He may *t* her now: for she never	v.	67
would I *t* her father for one hour	*The Brook*	114
T it and come to the Isle of	*To F. D. Maurice*	12
T him to stall, and give him corn.	*Enid*.	371
t the rustic murmur of their bourg	,,	411
and *t* as fairest of the fair,	,,	553
He said, 'You *t* it, speaking'	,,	902
t A horse and arms for guerdon;	,,	1016
'I *t* it as free gift, then,'	,,	1071
'*T* Five horses and their armours :'	,,	1257
some of your kind people *t* him up,	,,	1302
t him up, and bear him to our hall,	,,	1401
See ye *t* the charger too,	,,	1404
T warning : yonder man is surely dead:	,,	1520
T my salute,' unknightly	,,	1565
Geraint could never *t* again	,,	1797
t this boon so strange and not so strange.	*Vivien*	152
T Vivien for expounder	,,	168
T one verse more — the lady speaks it	,,	295
t my counsel : let me know it at once	,,	501
found it therefore : *t* the truth.	,,	350

410   CONCORDANCE TO

	POEM.	LINE.
shameless ones, who *t* Their pastime	*Elaine*	101
Advance, and *t* your prize The diamond,'	"	502
Wherefore *t* This diamond, and deliver it,	"	544
you used to *t* me with the flood	"	1031
t the little bed on which I died	"	1111
a chariot-bier To *t* me to the river,	"	1116
T, what I had not won except for you	"	1175
yet I *t* it with Amen.	"	1217
come to *t* the King to fairy land?	"	1250
to *t* my last farewell of you	"	1268
to *t* last leave of all I loved?	*Guinevere*	542
I cannot *t* thy hand;	"	549
T your own time, Annie (rep.)	*En. Arden*	463
was it hard to *t* The helpless life	"	557
why did they *t* me thence?	"	782
T, give her this, for it may comfort her	"	900
'*T* it,' she added sweetly	*Aylmer's F.*	246
who beside your hearths Can *t* her place	"	735
Will not another *t* their heritage?	"	786
he wouldn't *t* my advice.	*Grandmother*	4
Let me go: *t* back thy gift:	*Tithonus*	27
God help me! save I *t* my part	*Sailor Boy*	21
t it, love, and put it by;	*The Ringlet*	11
t this and pray that he Who wrote it	*A Dedication*	4
T the hoary Roman head	*Boädicea*	65
would *t* the praise and care no more	*Coquette,* ii.	14
weepest thou to *t* the east	"	111. 1
T you his nearest, *T* you his dearest	*The Victim*	27
Here is his dearest, We *t* the boy.	"	42
did I *t* That popular name of thine	*Lucretius*	95
t Only such cups as left us	"	213
Great Nature, *t*, and forcing far apart	"	241
T my love, for love will come	*The Window*	125
T my love, and be my wife	*i.*	129
Must I *t* you and break you	"	136-8
T, *t*,—break, break,—	"	140

take heed.
being found *t h* of Vivien	*Vivien*	379

taken.
more is *t* quite away.	*Miller's D.*	22
All things are *t* from us,	*Lotos-E's.*	91
Those we love first are *t* first	*To J. S.*	12
I fear My wound hath *t* cold,	*M. d'Arthur*	166
Are *t* by the forelock,	*Golden Year*	19
Tho' much is *t*. much abides;	*Ulysses*	65
t with her seeming openness	*Princess,* iv.	281
t to be such as closed Grave doubts	*In Mem.* xlvii.	2
As of a wild thing *t* in the trap	*Enid*	1575
for we have *t* our farewells.	*Guinevere*	116
t everywhere for pure,	"	513
mother said 'They have *t* the child.	*The Victim*	45
They have *t* our son	"	51
T the stars from the night	*The Window*	39

taketh
sick man's room when he *t* repose	*'A spirit haunts'*	14

taking
parson *t* wide and wider sweeps	*The Epic*	14
He kiss'd, *t* his last embrace,	*Two Voices*	254
Titanic forces *t* birth	*Day-Dm.*	229
Womanlike *t* revenge too deep	*Maud,* I. iii.	5
t true for false, or false for true;	*Enid*	853
grossheart Would reckon worth the *t*?	*Vivien*	766
for you left me *t* no farewell,	*Elaine*	1267
T her bread and theirs;	*En. Arden*	111
asking overmuch and *t* less,	"	251
So often, that the folly *t* wings	"	494
t pride in her, She look'd so sweet	*Aylmer's F.*	554

tale (story, etc)
With cycles of the human *t*.	*Pal. of Art*	146
an ancient *t* of wrong, Like a *t* of little meaning	*Lotos-E's.*	163
Brimful of those wild *t's*,	*D. of F. Wom.*	12
With the fairy *t's* of science	*Locksley H.*	12
A deeper *t* my heart divines.	*Two Voices*	269
And told him all her nurse's *t.*	*Lady Clare*	80
Tell me *t's* of thy first love—	*Vision of Sin*	163
a hoard of *t's* that dealt with knights,	*Princess,*Pro.	29
the *t* of her That drove their foes	"	122

	POEM.	LINE.
told a *t* from mouth to mouth	*Princess,*Pro	189
what kind of *t's* did men tell men	"	191
Why not a summer's as a winter's *t*?	"	204
A *t* for summer as befits the time	"	205
tell me pleasant *t's*, and read My sickness	ii.	234
he that next inherited the *t*	iv.	569
whereon Follow'd his *t*.	v.	46
my *t* of love In the old king's ears,	"	230
So closed our *t*, of which I give you all	*Con.*	1
the sequel of the *t* Had touched her;	"	30
To bear thro' Heaven a *t* of woe,	*In Mem.* xli.	2
When truth embodied in a *t*.	" xxxvi.	7
Then be my love an idle *t*,	" lxi.	3
across With some long-winded *t*	*The Brook*	109
there he told a long long-winded *t*,	"	138
call'd her like that maiden in the *t*,	*Enid*	742
lay still; as he that tells the *t*	"	1010
jested with all ease, and told Free *t's*,	"	1140
Were I not woman, I could tell a *t*,	*Vivien*	546
answer'd Merlin 'Nay, I know the *t*.	"	563
'O ay,' said Vivien, 'overtrue a *t*.	"	570
Crueller than was ever told in *t*,	"	707
blamed herself for telling hearsay *t's*	"	800
ran the *t* like fire about the court	*Elaine*	712
maid had told him all her *t*	"	794, 810
will tell him *t's* of foreign parts	*Guinevere*	314
there the *t* he utter'd brokenly,	*En. Arden*	198
felt the *t* Less than the teller:	"	648
the pun, the scurrilous *t*,—	"	712
And I fear you'll listen to *t's*	*Aylmer's F.*	441
t's for never yet on earth	*Grandmother*	54
rustic Gods! a *t* To laugh at—	*Lucretius*	130
	"	182

tale (number).
The *t* of diamonds for his destined boon	*Elaine*	92

talent.
health, wealth, and time, And *t's*	*Princess,* iv.	333

talk (s)
It seems in after-dinner *t*	*Miller's D.*	31
held a *t*, How all the old honour	*The Epic*	6
our soul with *t* of knightly deeds	*M. d'Arthur*	19
A *t* of college and of ladies' rights	*Princess,*Pro.	206
broke and buzzed in knots of *t*;	i.	132
household *t*, and phrases of the hearth,	ii.	294
Heart-affluence in discursive *t*	*In Mem.* cviii.	1
dry-tongued laurels' pattering *t*	*Maud,*I.xviii.	8
perplext her With his worldly *t*	xx.	7
From *t* of battles loud and vain,	*Ode on Well.*	247
honest *t* and wholesome wine,	*To F. D. Maurice*	18
like a shadow, past the people's *t*	*Enid*	82
I will tell him all their caitiff *t*;	"	915
his *t*, When wine and free companions	"	1141
huge Earl cried out upon her *t*	"	1499
play'd about with slight and sprightly *t*	*Vivien*	27
harlots paint their *t* as well as face	"	670
t and minstrel melody entertain'd	*Elaine*	267
From *t* of war to traits of pleasantry	"	320
Lancelot told me of a common *t*.	"	576
walls of yew Their *t* had pierced	"	965
noble man but made ignoble *t*	"	1082
child kill me with her innocent *t*!'	*Guinevere*	212
in sweet *t* or lively, all on love	"	383
miss to hear high *t* of noble deeds	"	495
current of his *t* to graver things	*En. Arden*	203
Fairer his *t*, a tongue that ruled.	*Aylmer's F.*	194
remembering His former *t's* with Edith	"	457
more and more allowance for his *t*	*Sea Dreams*	75
pious *t*, when most his heart was dry	"	182

talk (verb.)
To himself he *t's*.	*'A spirit haunts,'* etc.	3
And ye *t* together still	*Adeline*	60
makes me *t* too much in age.	*Miller's D.*	194
T with the wild Cassandra	*Œnone*	259
you can *t*? yours is a kindly vein	*Ed. Morris*	81
days were brief Whereof the poets *t*,	*Talking O.*	185
'O ay, ay, ay, you *t*!'	*Godiva*	26
'I *t*,' said he. 'Not with thy dreams.'	*Two Voices*	383
All his life the charm did *t*.	*Day-Dm.*	121

	POEM.	LINE.
Had made him *t* for show ; .	*Will Water.*	196
We did but *t* you over, pledge you	*Princess,Pro.*183	
down the fiery gulf as *t* of it,	" iii.	270
You *t* almost like Ida : *she* can *t* ;	" v.	201
you *t* kindlier : we esteem you for it	"	203
While now we *t* as once we talked	*In Mem.* lxx.	9
To *t* them o'er, to wish them here,	" lxxxix.	11
Be cheerful-minded, *t* and treat .	" cvi.	19
And *t* of others that are wed,	" Con.	98
I trust that I did not *t*, .	*Maud,*I. xix, 12-16	
one half-hour, and let him *t* to me !'	*The Brook*	115
days That most she loves to *t* of .	"	226
tho' you *t* of trust, .	*Vivien*	208
heard their voices *t* behind the wall	"	481
Of whom the people *t* mysteriously	*Elaine*	424
As even here they *t* at Almesbury	*Guinevere*	206
clamour'd the good woman 'hear him *t* !	*En. Arden*841	

talked
sat and eat And *t* old matters over	*Audley Ct.*	28
For oft I *t* with him apart, .	*Talking O.*	17
while they *t*, above their heads I saw	*Princess,Pro.*118	
they *t* At wine, in clubs, of art .	"	159
while I walk'd and *t* as heretofore	" i.	16
t The trash that made me sick .	" ii.	371
answer'd sharply that I *t* astray. .	" iii.	124
we are not *t* to thus : .	"	233
every voice she *t* with ratify it, .	" v.	127
t down the fifty wisest men ; .	"	284
she you walk'd with, she You *t* with	" vi.	238
maidens came, they *t*. They sang,	" vii.	7
hears his burial *t* of by his friends	"	137
While now we talk as once we *t* .	*In Mem.* lxx	9
We *t* : the stream beneath us ran,	" lxxxviii.	43
My love has *t* with rocks and trees	" xcvi.	1
She *t* as if her love were dead, .	*The Letters*	27
t with Dubric, the high saint, .	*Enid*	1713
when often they have *t* of love, .	*Elaine*	670
t, Meseem'd, of what they knew not ; "		671
Blues and reds They *t* of : .	*Aylmer's F.*	252
people *t*—that it was wholly wise	"	268
people *t*—The boy might get .	"	270
So they *t*, Poor children, for their comfort:	"	426
wrinkled benchers often *t* of him .	"	473

talketh
Who *t* with thee, Adeline ? .	*Adeline*	24

talking.
beneath a yew And *t* to himself	*Love and Death*	6
thought her half-right *t* of her wrongs	*Princess,* v.	275
Drinking and *t* of me ; . .	*Maud,* I. vii. 6,14	
t from the point, he drew him in .	*The Brook*	154
And with me Philip, *t* still ; .	"	164
In silver tissue *t* things of state .	*Enid*	663
you were *t* sweetly with your Prince	"	698
heard them *t*, his long-bounden tongue	*En. Arden*645	

tall.
divinely *t*, And most divinely fair.	*D.ofF.Wom.*	87
arching limes are *t* and shady .	*Margaret*	59
are the ladies of your land so *t* ?'	*Princess,* ii.	33
T as a figure lengthen'd on the sand	" vi.	145
But she is *t* and stately. .	*Maud,* I.xii	16
whom God had made full-limb'd and *t*,	*Guinevere*	43
loftier Annie Lee, Fair-hair'd and *t*,	*En. Arden.*	750
who stood beside her *t* and strong	"	757
his own children *t* and beautiful, .	"	763
dull and self-involved, *T* and erect,	*Aylmer's F.*	119
follow'd out *T* and erect, .	"	818
from the porch, *t* and erect again .	"	825
it grew so *t* It wore a crown .	*The Flower*	9
You so small ! am I so *t* ? .	*The Window*	76

taller.
a hart *T* than all his fellows, .	*Enid*	150

tallest.
she, that rose the *t* of them all .	*M. d'Arthur*	207

tall-tower'd.
long street climbs to one *t-t* mill .	*En. Arden.*	5

Tallyho.
Black Bess, Tantivy, *T*, .	*The Brook*	160

	talon.	POEM.	LINE.
	swoops The vulture, beak and *t*,	*Princess,* v.	373
	ever-ravening eagle's beak and *t*	*Boädicea*	11

tamarisk.
The stately cedar, *t*'s, .	*Arabian N's.*	105
from a *t* near Two Proctors .	*Princess,* iv.	233

tame (adj.)
were all as *t*, I mean as noble .	*Vivien*	457
helpless life so wild that it was *t* .	*En. Arden*	558

tame (verb.)
nor *t* and tutor with mine eye .	*D of F Wom.*138	
tamed my leopards : shall I not *t* these?	*Princess,*v	390

tamed.
I *t* my leopards : .	*Princess,* v.	370

Tamesa.
Bloodily flow'd the *T* . .	*Boädicea*	27

tamper
embassies of love, To *t* with the feelings	*Gardener's D*	19

tamper'd.
Some meddling rogue has *t* with him	*Elaine*	129
t with the Lords of the White Horse,	*Guinevere*	10

tangle (s.)
Should toss with *t* and with shells	*In Mem.* x.	20

tangle (verb.)
knots that *t* human creeds, *'Clear-headed friend,'* etc.3		

Tantivy.
Black Bess, *T*, Tallyho, .	*The Brook*	160

tap.
crush'd with a *t* Of my finger-nail.	*Maud,* II. ii.	21

taper.
A million *t*'s flaring bright .	*Arabian N's.*	124
I knew your *t* far away, .	*Miller's D.*	109
Her *t* glimmer'd in the lake below ;	*Ed. Morris*	135
As this pale *t*'s earthly spark, .	*St Agnes' Eve*	15
The *t*'s burning fair. .	*Sir Galahad*	32
calm that let the *t*'s burn .	*In Mem.* xciv.	5

tapping.
Leisurely *t* a glossy boot .	*Maud,* I. xiii.	13

tapt.
whined in lobbies, *t* at doors	*Walk.to the M.*	27
t her tiny silken-sandall'd foot .	*Princess,* Pro	143

Taranis.
T be propitiated. . .	*Boädicea*	16

tare.
That *t* each other in their slime, .	*In Mem.* lv.	23

target.
passion were a *t* for their scorn :	*Locksley H.*	146
from the tiny pitted *t* blew .	*Aylmer's F.*	93

tarn.
quenching lake by lake and *t* by *t*	*Princess,* vii.	25
a glen, gray boulder and black *t* .	*Elaine*	37
A horror lived about the *t* .	"	38
like a glittering rivulet to the *t* : .	"	51

Tarquin.
brooking not the *T* in her veins, .	*Lucretius*	234

tarriance.
after two days' *t* there return'd, .	*Elaine*	503

tarry.
'He dared not *t*,' men will say, .	*Two Voices*	101
I must go : I dare not *t* ' .	*Princess,* iii.	79
Knowing I *t* for thee,' .	*Maud,*III.vi.	13
Would he could *t* with us here	*Enid*	622
if he could but *t* a day or two, .	"	627
if thou *t* we shall meet again, .	*Guinevere*	89

tarrying.
after *t* for a space they rode .	*Enid*	1801

task (s.)
Sore *t* to hearts worn out .	*Lotos-E's.*	131
the *t*'s of might To weakness	*'Love thou thy land,'*	13
'Hard *t*, to pluck resolve,' I cried,	*Two Voices*	113

	POEM.	LINE.
The wrinkled steward at his *t*,	*Day-Dm.*	47
I take myself to *t* ;	*Will Water.*	162
and yawning 'O hard *t*,' he cried;	*Princess,* iii.	108
kiss the child That does the *t* assigned	*Elaine*	825

task (verb.)

as we *t* ourselves To learn a language	*Aylmer's F.*	432

tassel-hung.

In native hazels *t-h.* . . .	*In Mem.* ci.	12

taste.

whoso did receive of them And *t* .	*Lotos-E's.*	31
(If Death so *t* Lethean springs	*In Mem.* xliii.	10

tasted.

He *t* love with half his mind	*In Mem.* lxxxix.	1
touch'd fierce wine, nor *t* flesh,	*Vivien*	477

tatoo'd.

then the man : *T* or woaded,	*Princess,* ii.	105

taught.

He *t* me all the mercy . .	*MayQueen,* iii.	17
I must be *t* my duty, and by you	*Dora*	95
t me how to skate, to row,	*Ed. Morris*	19
that plain fact, as *t* by these,	*Two Voices*	281
T them with facts.	*Princess, Pro.*	59
teach them all that men are *t* ;	"	136
she That *t* the Sabine how to rule	" ii.	65
learn whatever men were *t* : .	"	130
whatsoever can be *t* and known ; .	"	363
what woman *t* you this?' .	" vii.	291
deep voices our dead captain *t*	*Ode on Well.*	69
So great a soldier *t* us there,	"	131
So *t* will charm us both to rest	*Vivien*	181
he *t* the King to charm the Queen	"	491
An air the nuns had *t* her ; .	*Guinevere*	161

taunt (s.)

A *t* that clench'd his purpose	*Princess,* v.	296

taunt (verb.)

T me no more : . . .	*Princess,* vi.	282

tavern.

Seeking a *t* which of old he knew	*En. Arden.*	692

tavern-catch.

To troll a careless, careless *t-c*	*Princess,* iv.	139

tavern-door.

From many a *t-d,* . .	*Will Water.*	188

tavern-hours.

The *t-h* of mighty wits— .	*Will Water.*	191

taw.

That knuckled at the *t*; .	*Will Water.*	132

tawnier.

the swan's Is *t* than her cygnet's :	*Elaine*	1179

tax.

'Honour,' she said, 'and homage, *t* and toll	*Œnone*	114
when he laid a *t* Upon his town,	*Godiva*	13
' If they pay this *t*, they starve,' .	"	20
she took the *t* away, . . .	"	78
Hortensia spoke against the *t* ; .	*Princess,* vii.	112
Levied a kindly *t* upon themselves	*En. Arden.*	664

teach.

T me the nothingness of things .	*A Character*	4
Oh ! *t* the orphan boy to read,	*L. C. V. de Vere*	69
And, as tradition *t'es,* . .	*Amphion*	26
others' follies *t* us not, . .	*Will Water.*	173
Nor much their wisdom *t's* ; .	"	174
t them all that men are taught ; .	*Princess, Pro.*	136
Come Time, and *t* me, many years,	*In Mem.* xiii.	13
My own dim life should *t* me this,	" xxxiv.	1
Her office there to rear, to *t*,	" xxxix.	13
t true life to fight with mortal wrongs	*Maud,* I. xviii.	54
As proof of trust O Merlin, *t* it me	*Vivien*	180
find a wizard who might *t* the King	"	433
t high thought, and amiable words	*Guinevere*	477
Shall we *t* it a Roman lesson? .	*Boädicea*	32
T that sick heart the stronger choice	*On a Mourner*	8

Teacher.

Left by the *T* whom he held divine.	*Lucretius*	13

	teaching.	POEM.	LINE.
t him that died Of hemlock .	.	*Princess,* iii.	285

team.

The *t* is loosen'd from the wain,	*In Mem.* cxx.	5
And see'st the moving of the *t*. .	"	16
I hear them too—they sing to their *t*	*Grandmother*	81
blessed fellds wi' the Divil's oan	*team N Farmer*	62
and the wild *t* Which love thee, .	*Tithonus*	39

teacup-times.

In *t-t* of hood and hoop, .	*Talking O.*	63

tear.

Her *t's* fell with the dews at even	*Mariana*	13
Crocodiles wept *t's* for thee .	*A Dirge*	22
sweeter dews than traitor's *t*	"	24
blissful *t's* blinded my sight	*Oriana*	23
the *t's* run down my cheek, .	"	69
I feel the *t's* of blood arise .	"	77
The home of woe without a *t*.	*Mariana in the S.*	20
Large Hesper glitter'd on her *t's*	"	90
dews, that would have fall'n in *t's*,	*Miller's D.*	151
Eyes with idle *t's* are wet. .	"	211
They have not shed a many *t's*, .	"	221
Yet *t's* they shed : . .	"	223
My eyes are full of *t's*, my heart of love	*Œnone*	30
water'd it with *t's* ? O happy *t's* .	"	230
be sunder'd without *t's* To ——.	*With Pal. of Art*	13
temper'd with the *t's* Of angels	"	18
phantasms weeping *t's* of blood .	*Pal. of Art*	239
ever unrelieved by dismal *t's*, .	"	271
embraces of our wives And their warm	*t's Lotos-E's.*	116
Charged both mine eyes with *t's*.	*D. of F. Wom.*	13
I, blinded with my *t's*, . .	"	108
She ceased in *t's*, fallen from hope	"	257
By sighs or groans or *t's* ; .	"	284
a *t* Dropt on the letters as I wrote.	*To J. S.*	55
keep dry their light from *t's* ;	*'Of old sat Freedom'*	20
Remorsefully regarded thro' his *t's*,	*M. d'Arthur*	171
dropping bitter *t's* against his brow	"	211
look'd with *t's* upon her boy, .	*Dora*	55
Rain out the heavy mist of *t's*,	*Love and Duty*	43
such *t's* As flow but once a life.	"	62
to the *t's* that thou wilt weep.	*Locksley H.*	82
She told him of their *t's*, .	*Godiva*	19
eyes are dim with glorious *t's*, .	*Two Voices*	151
t's and smiles from heaven again	*Sir L. and Q. G.*	2
What there is in loving *t's*, .	*Vision of Sin*	161
foolish *t's* upon my grave, ' *Come not, when,' etc.*	2
And kiss'd again with *t's* (rep.)	*Princess,* i.	250
circled Iris of a night of *t's* ;	" iii.	11
bow'd as if to veil a noble *t* ;	"	272
T's, idle *t's*, I know not what they mean	" iv.	21
T's from the depth of some divine despair	"	22
the *t* She sang of, shook and fell,	"	41
my Sire, his rough cheek wet with *t's*	" v.	22
Like summer tempest came her *t's*	"	546
leaves were wet with women's *t's* :	" vi.	23
Passionate *t's* Followed : .	"	291
like an Alpine harebell hung with *t's*	" vii.	100
round my wrist, and *t's* upon my hand :	"	123
The far-off interest of *t's* ?	*In Mem.* i.	8
thou deep vase of chilling *t's*	" iv.	11
T's of the widower when he sees	" xiii.	1
Mine eyes have leisure for their *t's*	"	16
fill'd with *t's* that cannot fall, .	" xix.	11
t's that at their fountain freeze	" xx.	12
With costly spikenard and with *t's* .	" xxxii.	12
t's are on the mother's face, .	" xxxix.	10
dip Their wings in *t's* and skim away	" xlvii.	6
drown The bases of my life in *t's*.	" xlviii.	16
grieve Thy brethren with a fruitless *t* ?	" lvii.	10
thy quick *t's* that make the rose .	" lxxi.	10
No single *t*, no mark of pain : .	" lxxvii.	14
with long use her *t's* are dry. .	"	20
To pledge them with a kindly *t*, .	" lxxxix.	10
dipt in baths of hissing *t's*, .	" cxvii.	23
There has fallen a splendid *t*	*Maud,* I. xxi.	59
shake its threaded *t's* in the wind. .	" III. vi.	28
dabbling in the fount of fictive *t's*.	*The Brook*	93
moves, and there are sobs and *t's* :	*Ode on Well.*	268
I consecrate with *t's*—These Idylls.	*Ded. of Idylls*	4

	POEM.	LINE.		POEM.	LINE.
t's upon his broad and naked breast	*Enid*	111	my nurse would *t* me of you:	*Princess*, iv.	407
the mother smiled, but half in *t's*,	"	823	'You—*t* us what we are'	*Con.*	34
mar a comely face with idiot *t's*	"	1399	mused on all I had to *t*,	*In Mem.* vi	19
felt the warm *t's* falling on his face	"	1434	And I should *t* him all my pain,	" xiv.	13
either eyelid wet with *t's*	*Vivien*	229	*t* them all they would have told,	" xxxix.	25
gleam'd her eyes behind her *t's*	"	252	In that high place, and *t* thee all.	" xliii.	16
slow *t* creep from her closed eyelid	"	755	Could hardly *t* what name were thine	" lviii.	16
Then flash'd into wild *t's*,	*Elaine*	610	turn the page that *t's* A grief,	" lxxvi.	10
'Farewell, sweet sister,' parted all in *t's*.	"	1145	O *t* me where the senses mix	" lxxxvii.	3
Words, as we grant grief *t's*	"	1182	O *t* me where the passions meet,	"	4
and my *t's* have brought me good:	*Guinevere*	200	You *t* me, doubt is Devil-born.	" xcv.	5
Made my *t's* burn—is also past,	"	538	clash and clang that *t's* The joy	" *Con.*	61
flooded with the helpless wrath of *t's*,	*En. Arden*	32	can he *t* Whether war be a cause.	*Maud*, I x.	44
manifold entreaties, many a *t*,	"	160	I must *t* her before we part (rep.)	" xvi.	33
flow'd the easy current of her *t's*.	"	806	more blest than heart can *t*	" xviii.	82
their own bitter *t's*, *T's*, and the careless	*Aylmer's F.*	428	*t's* me, when she lay Sick once	" xix.	72
story, that cost me many a *t*	*Grandmother*	28	*t* us What and where they be.	" II. iv.	15
those tremulous eyes that fill with *t's*	*Tithonus*	26	*T* him now: she is standing here	" v.	65
and thy *t's* are on my cheek.	"	45	And now it *t's* of Italy	*The Daisy*	90
thou ever scare me with thy *t's*	"	46	day by day she thought to *t* Geraint,	*Enid*	65
A moment came the tenderness of *t's*	*Coquette*, ii.	9	*t* him what I think and what they say	"	90
My *t's*, no *t's* of Love, are flowing fast	" iii.	7	not dare to *t* him what I think,	"	105
No *t's* of love, but *t's* that Love can die	"	8	sparrow-hawk, what is he, *t* me of him.	"	404
And I said, 'O years, that meet in *t's*	1865-1866	4	*t* me, seeing I have sworn	"	423
Deity false in human-amorous *t's*;	*Lucretius*	90	*T* her, and *t* rove her heart	"	513
			Ashamed am I that I should *t* it thee.	"	577
tear (verb.)			child, and *t* me if you know it.'	"	684
t his heart before the crowd! 'You might have won'	36	to *t* away Their tawny clusters,	*En. Arden*	378	yester-eve I would not *t* you of it,	"	702
T the noble heart of Britain.	*Boädicea*	12	would only speak and *t* me of it.'	"	903
winds of winter *t* an oak	"	77	I will *t* him all their caitiff talk;	"	915
			I will *t* him all their villany,	"	981
tear-drop.			lay still; as he that *t's* the tale	"	1010
A *t-d* trembled from its source	*Talking O.*	16	I will *t* him How great a man	"	1076
			for shall I *t* you truth? You seem'd	*Vivien*	150
tearing.			Heaven that hears I *t* you the clean	"	193
t off her veil of faded silk	*Enid*	1363	if you talk of trust I *t* you this	"	210
			T me, was he like to thee?'	"	463
tease.			Were I not woman, I could *t* a tale	"	546
t her till the day draws by:	*In Mem.* lix.	14	mutter'd in himself, '*t* her the charm!	"	653
			O *t* us—we live apart	*Elaine*	264
teat.			*t* her, she shines me down	"	1219
from the plaintive mother's *t* he took	*The Brook*	129	till her time To *t* you;'	*Guinevere*	141
			nor would he *t* His vision;	"	303
teens.			*t* the King I love him tho' so late?	"	644
The maiden blossom of her *t*	*Talking O.*	79	must *t* him in that purer life,	"	646
			will *t* him tales of foreign parts	*En. Arden*	193
telegraph.			who hest could *t* What most it needed	"	265
there thro' twenty posts of *t*,	*Princess, Pro.*	77	Not to *t* her, never to let her know.	"	787–9
			t her you had seen him dead	"	809
Telemachus.			a secret—only swear Before I *t* you	"	839
This is my son, mine own *T*,	*Ulysses*	33	*t* her that I died Blessing her	"	879
			t my daughter Annie, whom I saw	"	883
telescope.			*t* my son that I died blessing him	"	886
here were *t's* For azure views;	*Princess, Pro.*	67	let me *t* you: I myself—	*Aylmer's F.*	352
			I knew, but I would not *t*.	*Grandmother*	26
tell.			I pray you *t* the truth to me.	*The Victim*	50
She'll not *t* me if she love me,	*Lilian*	6	which the dearest I cannot *t!*	"	64
Yet *t* my name again to me,	*Eleänore*	142	nor at all can *t* Whether I mean	*Lucretius*	145
t her to her face how much I hate	*Œnone*	224	*T* my wish to her merry blue eye,	*The Window*	101
t her, when I'm gone, to train	*MayQueen*, ii.	47			
and I will *t* the sign	" iii.	24	*teller.*		
kind word, and *t* him not to fret	"	45	felt the tale Less than the *t*:	*En. Arden*	713
If I had lived—I cannot *t*—	"	47			
t o'er Each little sound and sight.	*D. of F. Wom.*	276	*telling.*		
Exquisite Margaret, who can *t*	*Margaret*	36	Which *t* what it is to die	*In Mem.* xxxi.	7
I will not *t* you not to weep	*To J. S.*	36	blamed herself for *t* hearsay tales:	*Vivien*	800
And ran to *t* her neighbours;	*The Goose*	14			
not staid so long to *t* you all,	*Gardener's D.*	237	*temper.*		
might I *t* of meetings, of farewells	"	246	One equal *t* of heroic hearts,	*Ulysses*	68
Might I not *t* Of difference,	"	251	Of *t* amorous, as the first of May,	*Princess,* i.	2
t him Dora waited with the child;	*Dora*	74	conscious of what *t* you are built,	" iv. 381
t me, did she read the name	*Talking O.*	153	Whence drew you this steel *t?*	" vi. 215
And what remains to *t*.	"	204			
And I will *t* it. Turn your face	*Day-Dm.*	17	*temperament.*		
whither goest thou, *t* me where?'	"	190	But yet your mother's jealous *t*—	*Princess,* ii.	317
If my heart by signs can *t*,	*L. of Burleigh*	2	He has a solid base of *t*:	" iv.	203
T me tales of thy first love—	*Vision of Sin*	163	And pure nobility of *t*	*Enid*	212
t me pleasant tales, and read.	*Princess,* ii.	234			
'no—I would not *t*. No,	"	322	*tempered.*		
'*T us*,' Florian ask'd, 'How grew this	" iii.	6	*t* with the tears Of angels *To* —.	*With Pal. of Art*	8
children die; and let me *t* you, girl,	"	236			
t her, *t* her, what I *t* to thee (rep.)	" iv.	77	*tempest.*		
t her, Swallow, thou that knowest each	"	78	The *t* crackles on the leads,	*Sir Galahad*	52
To *t* her what they were,	"	304	beacon-tower above the waves Of *t*,	*Princess,* iv.	473
I came to *t* you; found that you had gone	"	323			

	POEM	LINE
Like summer *t* came her tears—	*Princess*, v.	546
each ear was prick'd to attend A *t*,	" vi	264
So drench'd it is with *t*,	" vii.	127
whatever *t* mars Mid-ocean,	*InMem* xvii.	13
tracts of calm from *t* made,	" cxi	14
whatever *t*'s lour For ever silent;	*Ode on Well.*	175
that *t* brooding round his heart	*Enid*	860
ever overhead Bellow'd the *t*	*Vivien*	806
after *t*, when the long wave broke	*Guinevere*	288
A rushing *t* of the wrath of God	*Aylmer's F.*	757
After a *t* woke upon a morn	*Lucretius*	24

tempest-buffeted
| T-*b*, citadel-crown'd | . *Will* | . 9 |

temple (sanctuary)
The crowds, the *t s*, waver'd,	*D. of F Wom*	114
The palms and *t*'s of the South	'*You ask me, why*'	28
swore Not by the *t* but the gold	*Aylmer's F.*	794
Lo the palaces and the *t*	*Boädicea*	53

temple (side of the head)
| Cluster'd about his *t*'s like a God's | *Œnone* | 59 |
| Flush'd in her *t*'s and her eyes, | *Pal. of Art* | 170 |

Temple-bar
| High over roaring T-*b*, | . *Will Water.* | 69 |

Temple-eaten.
| college-times Or T-*e* terms, | . *Aylmer's F.* | 105 |

temple-gates.
| drops at Glory's *t-g*, '*You might have won,*' etc. | 34 |

tempt.
| and a ring To *t* the babe | . *En. Arden* | 752 |
| *t* The Trojan while his neat-herds | *Lucretius* | 87 |

tempted
| I do believe she *t* them and fail'd, | *Vivien* | 668 |

tenant.
Careless *t*'s they!	. *Deserted H.*	4
as with his *t*, Jocky Dawes.	*Walk. to the M.*	21
thither flock'd at noon His *t*'s	*Princess, Pro.*	4
Be *t s* of a single breast	*In Mem.* xvi.	3

tenanted.
| bought the farm we *t* before. | . *The Brook.* | 222 |

tend.
Live happy · *t* thy flowers;	. *Love and Duty*	84
ourself Would *t* upon you	. *Princess*, iii.	304
t's her bristled grunters in the sludge;'	" v.	26
we will *t* on him Like one of these,	" vi.	108
half fool'd to let you *t* our son,	"	257
may *t* upon him with the prince.'	"	295
And *t*'s upon bed and bower,	*Maud*, I. xiv.	4
I that wasted time to *t* upon her,	*Enid*	887
the Powers that *t* the soul,	*Guinevere*	65

tendance.
nor from her *t* turn'd	. *Gardener'sD.*	143
pensive *t* in the all-weary noons,	*Princess*, vii.	87
her sweet *t* hovering over him,	*Enid*	1774

tended.
t by Pure vestal thoughts	. *Isabel*	3
be *t* by My blessing	. *Love and Duty*	84
But Psyche *t* Florian;	. *Princess*, vii.	40
And *t* her like a nurse.	. *Maud*,I. xix.	76
And Enid *t* on him there;	. *Enid*	1772
and every day she *t* him,	. *Elaine*	846

tender.
dark and true and *t* is the North.	*Princess*, iv.	80
t over drowning flies,	. *In Mem.* xcv.	3
For, Maud, so *t* and true,	. *Maud*, I. xix.	85
seeing them so *t* and so close	. *Enid*	22
So *t* was her voice, so fair her face,	*Vivien*	251
O true and *t*! O my liege and king!	"	640
with all ease, so *t* was the work	. *Elaine*	441

tenderer.
| a love Far *t* than my Queen's. | . *Elaine* | 1386 |

tenderest-hearted.
| Vivien, like the *t-h* maid | . *Vivien* | 227 |

tenderest-touching. POEM. LINE.
| by *t-t* terms To sleek her ruffled peace | *Vivien* | 747 |

tenderly.
| in what limits, and how *t*; | . *Ded. of Idylls* | 19 |

tenderness.
decent not to fail In offices of *t*,	. *Ulysses*	41
So gracious was her tact and *t*:	. *Princess*, i.	24
lute and flute fantastic *t*,	" iv.	111
No saint—inexorable—no *t*—	" v.	504
The *t*, not yours, that could not kill	" vi.	170
T touch by touch, and last	" vii.	99
All-comprehensive *t*,	. *InMem* lxxxiv	47
A face of *t* might be feign'd,	. *Maud*, I vi.	52
Thro' that great *t* for Guinevere,	. *Enid*	30
whether filial *t*, Or easy nature,	"	797
a sudden-beaming *t* Of manners	. *Elaine*	327
His bashfulness and *t* at war,	. *En. Arden*	288
A moment came the *t* of tears	. *Coquette*, ii	9

tender-pencill'd.
| The *t-p* shadow play | . *InMem.* xlviii | 12 |

tending.
| *t* her rough lord, tho' all unask'd, | *Enid* | 1254 |

tendon.
| And scirrhous roots and *t s*. | . *Amphion* | 64 |

tenfold-complicated.
| abyss Of *t-c* change | . *In Mem.* xcii. | 12 |

tennis.
| Quoits, *t*, ball—no games? | . *Princess*, iii | 199 |

tenor.
| My blood an even *t* kept, | . *InMem* lxxxiv. | 17 |

tent.
Among the *t*'s I paused and sung.	*Two Voices*	125
A *t* of satin, elaborately wrought.	*Princess*, iii.	350
No bigger than a glowworm shone the *t*	" iv.	7
They bore her back into the *t*	"	175
blazon'd lions o'er the imperial *t*	" v.	9
He show'd a *t* A stone-shot off:	"	50
in the *t*'s with coarse mankind,	" vi.	53
shall not lie in the *t*'s but here,	"	78
on to the *t*'s: take up the Prince.'	"	262
sport and song, in booth and *t*,	*InMem.*xcvii.	28
show'd an empty *t* allotted her,	*Enid*	1733
And past to Enid's *t*;	. "	1770

term (expression, etc.)
Not master'd by some modern *t*; '*Love thou thy land*'	30
inmost *t*'s Of art and science:	. *Princess*, ii.	423
Heap'd on her *t*'s of disgrace,	*Maud*, II. i.	14
ment well Your *t* of overstrain'd.	*Vivien*	385
essay'd, by tenderest-touching *t*'s	"	747
after that vile *t* of yours	. "	770

term (period of time, etc.)
To sleep thro' *t*'s of mighty war,	*Day-Dm.*	221
caught the blossom of the flying *t*'s,	*Princess,Pro.*	163
To point the *t* of human strife	. *In Mem.* xlix.	14
college-times Or Temple-eaten *t*'s, *Aylmer's F.*	105
clipt by horror from his *t* of life.	. "	603

terrace
t ranged along the Northern front,	*Princess*, iii	102
I paced the *t*, till the Bear had wheel'd	" iv.	194
The moonlight touching o'er a *t*	. *The Daisy*	83

terrace-lawn.
| On every slanting *t-l*. | . *Day-Dm.* | 30 |

terrible.
O fair and strong and *t*!	. *Princess*, vi.	147
are two more ' And stronger	. "	147
t! for it seem'd A void was made	*Lucretius*	36

territory.
You lying close upon his *t*,	. *Princess*, iv.	384
Close on the borders of a *t*,	. *Enid*	34
When men of mark are in his *t*,	"	1073
Led from the *t* of false Limours	"	1286
Endow you with broad land and *t*	*Elaine* 953.	1312
they wasted all the flourishing *t*,	. *Boädicea*	54

terror.	POEM.	LINE.
Still she look'd, and still the *t* grew	Enid	615
the expectant *t* of her heart	En Arden	489
Flights, *t's*, sudden rescues,	Aylmer's F.	99
He that only rules by *t*	The Captain	1

test is.)
I come to the *t*, a tiny poem — Hendecasyllabics 3

test (verb.)
defying change To *t* his worth . In Mem. xciv. 28

tested.
to return When others had been *t*) Aylmer's F. 219

testify.
as the dead we weep for *t—.* . Aylmer's F. 747

testimony.
| To this I call my friends in *t*, | Elaine | 1291 |
| to the basement of the tower For *t*; | Guinevere | 104 |

Teuton.
T or Celt, or whatever we be, W. to Alexan. 32

text.
Took this fan day for *t*,	Princess, Pro	108
A square of *t* that looks a little blot,	Vivien	521
t no larger than the limbs of fleas:	"	522
every square of *t* an awful charm,	"	523
none can read the *t*, not even I;	"	531
Suddenly put her finger on the *t*,	En. Arden	493
sowing hedgerow *t's* and passing by,	Aylmer's F.	171
being used to find her pastor *t's*.	"	606
Christian hope Haunting a holy *t*,	Sea Dreams	42
And the parson made it his *t*	Grandmother	29

Thames.
Came crowing over *T.* . Will Water. 140

thank.
feared To meet a cold 'We *t* you	Princess, iv.	309
T Him who isled us here	Ode on Well	154
I *t* the saints, I am not great.	Guinevere	197
on a broken word to *t* him with	En. Arden	344
t God that I keep my eyes	Grandmother	100

thanked.
| God be *t!*' said Alice the nurse, | Lady Clare | 17 |
| Assumed that she had *t* him, | Enid | 1424 |

thankful
Not *t* that his troubles are no more Lucretius 143

thanks.
statue-like, In act to render *t.*	Gardener's D.	159
A thousand *t* for what I learn	Talking O.	203
Their debt of *t* to her who first	Princess, ii.	125
But '*T*,' she answer'd 'go;'	"	336
you have our *t* for all: .	"	iv. 507
we owe you bitter *t*: .	"	510
To lighten this great clog of *t*,	"	vi. 110
with an eye that swum in *t*;	"	193
T, for the fiend best knows	Maud, I. i.	75
Render *t* to the Giver,	Ode on Well.	44·7
'*T,* venerable friend,' replied Geraint	Enid	303
shall have learn'd to lisp you *t.*	"	822
to which She answer'd, '*T,* my lord'	"	1113
yet my *t* For these have broken	Vivien	115
the stranger welcome. *T* at last!	"	119
no more *t* than might a goat	"	127
your feet before her own? And yet no *t.* «	"	130
t it seems till now neglected,	"	153
T, but you work against your own	Elaine	1094
I do forgive him!' '*T,* my love,'.	Sea Dreams	307

thatch.
Weeded and worn the ancient *t*	Mariana	7
the cock hath sung beneath the *t*	The Owl, 1.	10
sun their milky bosoms on the *t*,	Princess, ii.	68
It sees itself from *t* to base .	Requiescat	3

thatched.
They built and *t* with leaves of palm, En. Arden 560

thaw.
T this male nature to some touch Princess, vi. 287

theatre.
stately *t's* Bench'd crescent-wise . Princess, ii. 347

theme.	POEM	LINE.
Seem but the *t* of writers,	Ed Morris	43
Ah, let the rusty *t* alone!	Will Water.	1·7
warming with her *t*, she fulmined out	Princess, ii.	115
Whereat we glanced from *t* to *t*	In Mem lxxxviii.	33

Theodolind
castle Of Queen *T,* where we slept. The Daisy . 82

theory.
forged a thousand *theories* of the rocks,	Ed Morris	18
Veneer'd with sanctimonious *t*	Princess, Pro.	117
fed her *theories,* in and out of place	"	i. 123
fair *theories* only made to gild	"	ii. 215
your Psyche thieved her *theories.*	"	iii. 75
cramm'd with *theories* out of books,	" Con.	35

Thessalian.
Or that *T* growth . . Talking O. . 292

thesis.
The *t* which thy words intend— . Two Voices 330

thew.
ever had I seen Such *t's* of men'.	Princess, v	246
the wrestling *t's* that throw the world;	" vii.	266
I felt the *t's* of Anakim,	In Mem. cii.	31

thick.
t as dust In vacant chambers,	To the Queen	13
t with white bells the clover-hill	Sea-Fairies	14
masses *t* with milky cones.	Miller's D.	56
t as Autumn rains Flash in the pools	Œnone	201
My voice was *t* with sighs.	D. of F. Wom	102
with a grosser film made *t*	St S. Stylites	167
the mother-city *t* with towers,	Princess, i	111
shoulders, *t* as herded ewes,	" iv	453
So *t* with lowings of the herds,	In Mem xcviii.	3

thicken'd
A clamour *t*, mixt with inmost terms Princess, ii 423

thicker
t down the front With jewels	Enid	1537
T the drizzle grew, deeper the gloom	En. Arden	600
Now thinner and now *t* like the flakes	Lucretius	166

thickest.
Among the *t* and bore down a prince Princess, v. 507

thicket.
Athwart the *t* lone:	Claribel	10
the dry *t's,* I could meet with her,	Œnone	219
No branchy *t* shelter yields .	Sir Galahad	53
hid and sought In the orange *t's*:	Princess, ii.	436
And round us all the *t* rang	In Mem. xxiii.	22
and the *t* closed Behind her,	Vivien	822

thick-leaved.
the *t-l* platans of the vale. . Princess, iii. 159

thick-moted
When the *t-m* sunbeam lay . . Mariana . 78

thick-leaved.
T-l, ambrosial, . . Claribel . 5

thick-fleeced.
livelong bleat Of the *t-f* sheep . Ode to Mem. 66

thick-jewell'd.
T-j shone the saddle-leather L. of Shalott, iii. 20

thick-twined.
thro' the *t-t* vine— . . Lotos-E's. . 140

thief
this hedgerow *t*, the sparrow-hawk;	Enid	307
now no more a vassal to the *t,*	"	16. 1
therefore turning softly like a *t,*	En. Arden	772
storming a hill-fort of *thieves*	Aylmer's F.	2.5
But *thieves* from o'er the wall.	The Flower	11

thieved
Affirms your Psyche *t* her theories, Princess, iii. 76

thigh.
| flush'd Ganymede, his rosy *t* | Pal. of Art | 121 |
| both my *t's* are rotted with the dew | St S. Stylites | 40 |
| he smote his *t*, and mock'd. . Elaine . 611 |

416 **CONCORDANCE TO**

	Thimbleby. POEM. LINE.
Moths or T—toner 'ed shot un	. N. Farmer . 35

thin (adj.)

if his fellow spake, His voice was t	Lotos-E's . 34
His face is growing sharp and t	D. of the O Year 46
O hark, O hear how t and clear,	Princess, iii. 354
When it slowly grew so t,	Maud, I. xix. 20

thin (verb.)

| or would seem to t her in a day | . Aylmer's F. 76 |

thing.

Teach me the nothingness of t's.'	A Character 4
all the dry pied t's that be	. The Mermaid 48
All t's that are forked and horned	" 53
She spoke at large of many t's	. Miller's D. 155
all t's in order stored,	. Pal. of Art 87
all t's fair to sate my various eyes!	" 193
But all these t's have ceased to be	May Queen, iii. 48
whereall t's always seem'd the same	Lotos-E's. 24
all t's else have rest from weariness? (rep.)	" 59
We only toil, who are the first of t's,	" 60
the roof and crown of t's?	" 69
All t's are taken from us	" 91
All t's have rest, and ripen	" 96
our great deeds, as half-forgotten t's.	" 123
to start in pain, Resolved on noble t's,	D. of F. Wom. 42
How beautiful a t it was to die	" 231
From all t's outward you have won	Margaret 11
A man may speak the t he will; 'You ask me, why, etc.	8
Keep a t, its use will come.	. The Epic 47
A little t may harm a wounded man	M. d' Arthur 42
is a shameful t for men to lie.	" 78
and do the t I bad thee,	" 80
a precious t, one worthy note,	" 89
More t's are wrought by prayer	" 247
'come With all good t's,	" Ep. 28
We spoke of other t's; we coursed	Gardener's D. 217
and thought Hard t's of Dora	. Dora 59
And all the t's that had been,	" 105
had pack'd the t among the beds,	Walk. to the M. 36
could not light upon a sweeter t:	" 44
shame and pride, New t's and old,	" 53
wince As from a venomous t:	" 64
spoke I knowing not the t's that were	Ed Morris 89
sweet hours that bring us all t's	Love and Duty 56-7
And all good t's from evil	" 58
wake and sleep, but all t's move:	Golden Year 22
something more, A bringer of new t's;	Ulysses 28
easy t's to understand—	. Locksley H. 55
crown of sorrow is remembering happier t's	" 76
earnest of the t's that they shall do	" 118
all t's here are out of joint	" 133
to have loved so slight a t.	" 148
Howsoever these t's be, a long farewell	" 189
learn new t's when I am not,'	Two Voices 63
There is no other t express'd	" 248
These t's are wrapt in doubt	" 266
Not simple as a t that dies.	" 288
vex His reason: many t's perplex,	" 299
He may not do the t he would	" 303
So variously seem'd all t's wrought,	" 457
Here all t's in their place remain	. Day-Dm. 73
All precious t's, discovered late,	" 101
Well—were it not a pleasant t	" 215
Half-views of men and t's.	. Will Water. 52
If old t's, there are new;	" 58
I look at all t's as they are,	" 71
Like all good t's on earth!	" 202
I hold it good, good t's should pass:	" 205
For this, thou shalt from all t's suck	" 213
Tomohrit, Athos, all t's fair	. To E. L. 5
She will order all t's duly,	. L. of Burleigh 39
Callest thou that t a leg?	. Vision of Sin 89
culture for the crowd, And all t's	Princess, Pro. 110
For any male t but to peep at us.'	" 151
And they that know such t's—	i. 143
to answer, Madam, all those hard t's	ii. 324
two dear t's are one of double worth,	" 397
still she rail'd against the state of t's,	iii. 68
One mind in all t's:	" 75
all t's were and were not (iv. 545)	" 173

	POEM. LINE.
might have seem'd the t you say.	Princess, iii. 185
for all t's serve their time	" iv. 55
To harm the t that trusts him,	" . 229
to have done the t one ought,	" v. 64
tender t's that being caught feign	" . 105
does the t they dare not do,	" . 153
I myself, What know I of these t's?	" . 274
all t's grew more tragic	" vi. 7
May these t's be!' Sighing she spoke	" vii. 280
trust in all t's high Comes easy	" . 310
Too comic for the solemn t's they are	" Con. 67
Of their dead selves to higher t's.	In Mem. i. 4
shall I take a t so blind	" iii. 13
Like a guilty t I creep	" vii. 7
now so strange do these t's seem	" xiii. 15
And ask a thousand t's of home;	" xiv. 12
Behold, ye speak an idle t	" xxi. 21
to choose Of t's all mortal,	" xxxiv. 11
To keep so sweet a t alive:'	" xxxv. 7
And all he said of t's divine,	" xxxvii. 18
Shall count new t's as dear as old:	" xxxix. 28
May some dim touch of earthly t's,	" xliii. 11
other than the t's I touch.'	" xliv. 8
love reflects the t beloved;	" li. 2
How should he love a t so low?'	" lix. 16
So little done, such t's to be.	" lxxii. 7
In fitting aptest words to t's,	" lxxiv. 6
Over all t's brooding slept	" lxxvii. 7
whether trust in t's above	" lxxxiv. 9
all t's round me breathed of him.	" 32
these t's pass, and I shall prove	" 93
The glory of the sum of t's	" lxxxvii. 11
And he, who knows a thousand t's.	" xcvi. 32
treat Of all t's ev'n as he were by.	" cvi. 20
Hast seem'd the t he was, and join'd	" cx. 13
Submitting all t's to desire.	" cxiii. 8
But I was born to other t's.	" cxix. 12
Thou watchest all t's ever dim	" cxx. 3
I cannot think the t farewell	" cxxii. 12
sees the course of human t's.	" cxxvii. 4
Love for the silent t that had made	Maud, I. i. 58
Like t's of the season gay	" iv. 3
A wounded t with a rancourous cry,	" x. 34
broad-brimm'd hawker of holy t's,	" 41
Her mother has been a t complete,	" xiii. 35
I know it the one bright t to save	" xvi. 20
given her word to a t so low?	" 27
happy stars, timing with t's below,	" xviii. 81
cursed him even to lifeless t's	" xix. 15
For a shell, or a flower, little t's	II. ii. 64
Comfort her, comfort her, all t's good.	" 75
speak to her all t's holy and high	" 78
sweeter Than any t on earth.	" iv. 10
another, a lord of all t's, praying	" v. 68
is ever the one t silent here	" III. vi. 3
grateful at last for a little t	" 17
in a weary world my one t bright;	" 17
money breeds, Thought is a dead t;	The Brook
how it was the t his daughter wish'd	" 140
in Katie's eyes, and all t's well.	" 169
a father on the t's Of his dead son	The Letters 23
If aught of t's that here befall	Ode on Well. 138
Touch a spirit among t's divine,	" 139
Yea, let all good t's await	" 198
these t's he told the king.	. Enid . 151
light on all t's that you love	" . 226
His dwarf, a vicious under-shapen t	" . 412
Mother, a maiden is a tender t	" . 510
These two t's shalt thou do,	" . 580-6
Edyrn answer'd, 'These t's will I do	" . 587
talking t's of state	" . 663
evermore it seem'd an easier t	" . 957
men may bicker with the t's they love,	" . 1174
What t soever you may hear, or see	" . 1264
ridden off with by the t he rode	" . 1309
Each hurling down a heap of t's	" . 1442
never yet beheld a t so pale	" . 1463
I will do the t I have not done	" . 1473
or what had been those gracious t's	" . 1565
As of a wild t taken in the trap,	" . 1571
involved yourself the nearest t	. Vivien . 149

	POEM.	LINE.		POEM.	LINE.
unashamed, On all *t*'s all day long	*Vivien*	516	And *t* of early days and thee,	*In Mem.*cxviii.	8
the *t* was blazed about the court,	"	593	I *t* we are not wholly brain,	" cxix.	2
t's with every sense as false and foul	"	646	I cannot *t* the thing farewell	" cxxii.	12
seeming-injured simple-hearted *t*.	"	751	Result in man, be born and *t*	*Con.*	176
but one *t* now—better have died.	"	767	Bound for the Hall, and I *t* for a bride	*Maud,* I. x.	26
One flash that missing all *t*'s else,	"	781	six feet two, as I *t*, he stands;	" xiii.	10
speaking in the silence, full Of noble *t*'s,	*Elaine*	338	Shall I not take care of all that I *t*,	" xv.	7
gaped upon him As on a *t* miraculous	"	452	T I may hold dominion sweet,	" xvi	12
if I could believe the *t*'s you say	"	1091	shook my heart to *t* she comes	" xviii.	10
in half disgust At love, life, all *t*'s	"	1232	*t* that it well Might drown all life	" II. ii.	60
the wild people say wild *t*'s of thee	"	1356	Not let any man *t* for the public good,	" v.	45
strong man-breasted *t*'s stood	*Guinevere*	244	I could even weep to *t* of it :	"	86
in the cellars merry bloated *t*'s	"	265	tell him what I *t* and what they say	*Enid*	90
a change, as all *t*'s human change	*En. Arden*	101	not dare to tell him what I *t*	"	105
current of his talk to grutter *t*'s	"	203	*t* the rustic cackle of your bourg.	"	276
set his hand To do the *t* he will'd	"	294	to *t* what kind of bird it is	"	331
there is a *t* upon my mind	"	396	*t* or say, 'There is the nightingale;'	"	342
t's fell on her Sharp as reproach	"	484	Let never maiden *t*, however fair	"	721
haunting people, *t*'s and places,	"	605	let me *t* Silence is wisdom :	*Vivien*	101
t's seen are mightier than *t*'s heard,	"	767	if you *t* this wickedness in me,	"	188
to all *t*'s could he turn his hand.	"	814	but *t* or not, By Heaven that hears	"	192
Took joyful note of all *t*'s joyful	*Aylmer's F.*	67	because I *t*, However wise, you hardly	"	204
loved nor liked the *t* he heard	"	250	I *t* you hardly know the tender rhyme	"	233
T's in an Aylmer deem'd impossible	"	305	methinks you *t* you love me well ;	"	333
The *t*'s belonging to thy peace	"	740	However well you *t* you love me now	"	366
is it a light *t* That I their guest,	"	789	I *t* she cloaks the wounds of loss	"	667
all *t*'s work together for the good	*Sea Dreams*	154	*t* kindly of me, for I fear	"	775
And all *t*'s look'd half-dead	*Grandmother*	34	I *t* this fruit is hung too high	*Elaine*	770
and look'd the *t* that he meant :	"	45	to *t* of Modred's dusty fall,	*Guinevere*	55
laughing at *t*'s that have long gone by	"	92	could *t*, sweet lady, yours would be	"	350
o' use to say the *t*'s that a do	*N. Farmer*	6	in inmost thought to *t* again.	"	372
sei'st all *t*'s thou wilt see my grave;	*Tithonus*	73	but rather *t* How sad it were	"	491
Welcome her, all *t*'s youthful and sweet,	*W. to Alexan.*	8	*t* not, tho' thou would'st not love.	"	501
good *t*'s have not kept aloof, '*My life is full,*' etc.		2	*t* not that I come to urge thy crimes,	"	528
Another and another frame of *t*'s.	*Lucretius*	42	what hope ? I *t* there was a hope,	"	623
t's appear the work of mighty Gods	"	102	I *t* your kindness breaks me down	*En. Arden*	317
think.			I do *t* They love me as a father	"	408
I walk, I dare not *t* of thee,	*Oriana*	93	T upon it : For I am well-to-do	"	414
When she would *t*, where'er she turn'd	*Pal. of Art*	225	I *t* I have not three days more to live ;	"	852
whom *t* ye should I see,	*May Queen,* i.	4	*t*—For people talk'd—that it was wholly	*Aylmer's F.*267
low i' the mould and *t* no more of me.	"	13	*t* that in our often-ransack'd world	*Sea Dreams* 125
when you *t* I'm far away	"	40	you *t* I am hard and cold	*Grandmother* 17
I *t* it can't be long before I find	" iii.	11	I *t* not much of yours or of mine	*Spiteful Let.*	7
So now I *t* my time is near,	"	41	*thinketh.*		
I *t* that we Shall never more	*M. d'Arthur*	17	*t*, 'I have found A new land,	*Pal. of Art*	283
T you they sing Like poets	*Gardener's D.*	98	*thinking.*		
Consider, William: take a month to *t*,	*Dora*	27	sobb'd o'er William's child T of William	*Dora*	164
now I *t*, he shall not have the boy,	"	117	*t* of the days that are no more.	*Princess,* iv.	25
t yourself alone Of all men happy	*Ed. Morris*	77	She flung it from her, *t* :	" *Con.*	32
I have, I *t*,—Heaven knows—as much	"	82	*t*, here to-day, Or here to-morrow	*In Mem.* vi.	2
I *t* that I have borne as much	*St. S. Stylites*	91	*t* ' this will please him best,'	"	31
let me *t* 'tis well for thee and me—	*Love and Duty* 32	Looking, *t* of all I have lost ;	*Maud,* II. ii.	46
t not they are glazed with wine.	*Locksley H.*	51	*t*, that if ever yet was wife	*Enid*	46
Can I *t* of her as dead.	"	73	*t* that he heard The noble hart	"	232
T you this mould of hopes and fears	*Two Voices*	28	*t* that he read her meaning there,	*Elaine*	87
canst not *t*, but thou wilt weep,'	"	51	*t* ' is it Lancelot, who has come	"	564
What wonder, if he *t*'s me fair ?'	*Day-Dm.*	272	*t* ' dead or dead to me !'	*En. Arden*	630
I *t* he came like Ganymede,	*Will Water.*	119	Enoch *t* ' after I am gone,	"	835
And I *t* thou lov'st me well.	*L. of Burleigh*	4	*t* that her clear germander eye Droopt	*Sea Dreams*	4
I remember, when I *t*,	*Vision of Sin*	77	*thinned.*		
And I *t* we know the hue	"	141	councils *t*, And armies waned,	*Vivien*	422
I confess with right you *t* me bound	*Princess,* i.	157	T, or would seem to thin her	*Aylmer's F.*	76
who could *t* The softer Adams	" ii.	179	*thinner.*		
I *t* no more of deadly lurks therein,	"	208	Then her cheek was pale and *t*	*Locksley H.*	21
t I bear that heart within my breast	"	315	*t*, clearer, farther going ?	*Princess,* iii.	365
What *t* you of it, Florian ?	"	386	Now *t*, and now thicker, like the flakes	*Lucretius*	106
grant me license: might I use it ? *t* ;	" iii.	219	*thinnest.*		
almost *t* That idiot legend credible :	" v.	146	Which is *t t* thine or mine ?	*Vision of Sin*	50
since you *t* me touch'd In honour,	"	391	*thirst*		
indeed I *t* Our chiefest comfort	"	419	In hungers and in *t*'s, fevers and cold,	*St. S. Stylites*	12
to *t* I might be something to thee	" vi.	163	Let her go ! her *t* she slakes	*Vision of Sin*	143
t that you might mix his draught.	"	260	*thirsted.*		
verily I *t* to win.'	"	309	I *t* for the brooks, the showers ;	*Fatima*	10
what I *t* you, some sweet dream	" vii.	139	*thirsting.*		
He *t*'s he was not made to die ;	*In Mem.* Pro.		only *t* For the right,	*Ode on Well.*	203
stunn'd me from my power to *t*	" xvi.	15	*thistle.*		
and *t* ' How good ! how kind !	" xx.	19	I could not move a *t*,	*Amphion*	66
And *t*, that somewhere in the waste	" xxii.	13			
He looks so cold; she *t*'s him kind	" xcvi.	24			
I *t* once more he seems to die	" xcix.	20			

2 D

	POEM.	LINE.
Let there be *t*'s, there are grapes;	*Will Water.*	57
t, bursting into glossy purples	*Ode on Well*	206
many a prickly star Of sprouted *t*	*Enid .*	314
shook beneath them, as the *t* shakes	*Guinevere .*	252

Thor.

To *T* and Odin lifted a hand	. *The Victim*	8

thorn.

Thick rosaries of scented *t*, .	*Arabian N's.*	106
as a *t* Turns from the sea ; .	*Audley Ct.*	53
like me, with scourges and with *t*'s ;	*St S. Stylites*	177
That all about the *t* will blow	*Two Voices*	59
T's, ivies, woodbine, mistletoes, .	*Day-Dm.*	63
A rosebud set with little wilful *t*'s	*Princess, Pro.*	153
The path we came by, *t* and flower,	*InMem.* xlv.	2
I took the *t*'s to bind my brows .	" lxviii.	7
The fool that wears a crown of *t*'s :	"	12
bristles all the breaks and *t*'s	" cvi.	9
Seem'd catching at a rootless *t*	*Enid .*	1227
mountain, like a wall of burs and *t*'s ;	*Sea Dreams*	115
life, little Annie, flower and *t*.	*Grandmother*	60
I have heard of *t*'s and briers,	*The Window*	197
Over the *t*'s and briers, .	"	198

Thornaby.

an' I 'a stubbed *T* waäste .	. *N. Farmer*	28
an' *T* holms to plow ! .	"	52

thorough-edged.

t-e intellect to part Error from crime ;	*Isabel .*	14

thoroughfare.

In shadowy *t*'s of thought : .	*In Mem.* lxix.	8
He left the barren-beaten *t*, .	*Elaine .*	161

thorpe.

he, by farmstead, *t* and spire, .	*Will Water.*	137
By twenty *t*'s, a little town, .	*The Brook .*	29
Then *t* and byre arose in fire, .	*The Victim*	3

thought (s.)

tended by Pure vestal *t*'s .	*Isabel .*	4
Small *t* of distress of life's distress	*Ode to Mem.*	37
The viewless arrows of his *t*'s .	*The Poet .*	11
Life and *T* have gone away .	*Deserted H.*	1
Life and *T* Here no longer dwell ;	"	17
Moulded thy baby *t*. .	*Eleänore .*	5
flattering thy childish *t* .	"	13
T and motion mingle, Mingle ever	"	60
T folded over *t*, smiling asleep .	"	84
T seems to come and go .	"	96
I least should breathe a *t* of pain	*Miller's D.*	26
blessings beyond hope or *t*, .	"	237
the *t* of power Flatter'd his spirit	*Œnone .*	134
fiery *t*'s Do shape themselves within	"	242
divided quite The kingdom of her *t*	*Pal. of Art*	228
great *t* strikes along the brain .	*D. of F. Wom.*	43
by down-lapsing *t* Stream'd onward	"	49
comforts me in this one *t* to dwell,	"	233
from the deep Gold-mines of *t* .	"	274
pensive *t* and aspect pale, .	*Margaret .*	6
The last wild *t* of Chatelet .	"	37
strength of some diffusive *t* ' You ask me why,' etc.		15
single *t* is civil crime, .	"	19
'Thro' future time by power of *t* 'Love thou thy land'		4
Wherever *T* hath wedded Fact. .	"	52
counting the dewy pebbles, fix'd in *t*	*M. d' Arthur*	84
His own *t* drove him like a goad .	"	185
kinds of *t*, That verged upon them,	*Gardener's D.*	69
These birds have joyful *t*'s .	"	98
he laugh'd, as one that read my *t*,	"	105
A *t* would fill my eyes with happy .	"	193
or should have, but for a *t* or two.	*Ed. Morris*	83
heedfully I sifted all my *t*) .	*St S. Stylites*	55
Should my Shadow cross thy *t*'s	*Love and Duty*	85
the times, when some new *t* can bud,	*Golden Year*	27
the utmost bound of human *t*.	*Ulysses .*	32
lightly turns to *t*'s of love. .	*Locksley H.*	20
touch him with thy lighter *t*. .	"	54
And the *t*'s of men are widen'd .	"	138
in the *t*'s that shake mankind .	"	166
men, thro' novel spheres of *t* .	*Two Voices*	61
what thou lackest, *t* resign'd, .	"	98

	POEM.	LINE.
Fruitful of further *t* and deed, .	*Two Voices .*	344
overtakes Far *t* with music .	"	438
To anchor by one gloomy *t* : .	"	459
would you have the *t* I had .	*Day-Dm.*	13
t and time be born again, .	"	70
From deep *t* himself he rouses, .	*L. of Burleigh*	21
Whited *t* and cleanly life .	*Vision of Sin*	116
The *t*'s that arise in me .	'*Break, break,*' etc.	4
Sweet *t*'s would swarm as bees	*Princess,* i.	39
A *t* flash'd thro' me which I cloth'd	"	192
t's enrich the blood of the world.'	" ii.	164
t's as fair within her eyes .	"	305
set your *t* in rubric thus .	" iii.	34
broke out interpreting my *t*'s :	"	258
live, perforce, from *t* to *t* .	"	311
tost on *t*'s that changed from hue to hue,	" iv.	192
those *t*'s that wait On you, their centre :	"	423
not a *t*, a touch, But pure as lines	" v.	187
other *t*'s than Peace Burnt in us .	"	235
Now could you share your *t* ; .	" vi.	235
shining furrow, as thy *t*'s in me. .	" vii.	170
always *t* in *t*, Purpose in purpose,	"	286
Beyond all *t* into the Heaven of Heavens	*Con.*	115
with the *t* her colour burns : .	*In Mem.* vi.	34
An awful *t*, a life removed. .	" xiii.	10
And *T* leapt out to wed with *T*	" xxiii.	15
Nor other *t* her mind admits .	" xxxii.	2
All subtle *t*, all curious fears, .	"	9
More strong than all poetic *t* ; .	" xxxvi.	12
The lightest wave of *t* shall lisp .	" xlviii.	5
Upon the topmost froth of *t* .	" li.	4
There flutters up a happy *t*, .	" lxiv.	7
In shadowy thoroughfares of *t* ; .	" lxix.	8
A grief as deep as life or *t*, . .	" lxxix.	7
fix my *t*'s on all the glow .	" lxxxiii.	3
Leaving great legacies of *t* .	"	35
Whose life, whose *t*'s were little worth,	" lxxxiv.	30
I find not yet one lonely *t* .	" lxxxix.	23
the man whose *t* would hold .	" xciii.	3
About empyreal heights of *t* .	" xciv.	8
In vassal tides that follow'd *t*. .	" cxi.	16
in my *t*'s with scarce a sigh .	" cxviii.	11
I slip the *t*'s of life and death : .	" cxxi.	16
And every *t* breaks out a rose .	"	20
The shade of passing *t* .	*Con.*	102
wrong Done but in *t* to your beauty	*Maud*, I iii.	6
letting a dangerous *t* run wild .	" xix.	52
noble *t* be freer under the sun, .	" III. vi.	48
Another *t* I had ; . .	*Enid .*	793
Grant me pardon for my *t*'s ; .	"	816
hated her, who took no *t* of them,	"	1487
heard in *t* Their lavish comment .	*Vivien .*	7
grated down and filed away with *t*	"	473
rathe she rose, half-cheated in the *t*	*Elaine .*	339
Her *t* when first she came .	*Guinevere .*	180
in *t*—Not ev'n in inmost *t* .	"	371
grew half-guilty in her *t*'s again, .	"	405
teach high *t*, and amiable words .	"	477
forced my *t*'s on that fierce law, .	"	533
the *t* Haunted and harass'd him .	*En. Arden.*	720
t and nature fail'd a little, .	"	793
Her all of *t* and bearing hardly more	*Aylmer's F.*	29
the worst *t* she has Is whiter .	"	362
true that second *t*'s are best ? .	*Sea Dreams*	65
my *t*'s are as quick and as quick .	*The Window*	12

thought (verb.)

She *t*, 'My spirit is here alone	*Mariann in the S.*	47
I cast me down, nor *t* of you .	*Miller's D. .*	63
My mother *t*, What ails the boy ? .	"	93
'by that lamp,' I *t*, 'she sits !' .	"	114
t I might have looked a little higher	"	139
she *t*, 'And who shall gaze .	*Pal. of Art .*	41
You *t* to break a country heart .	*L.C.V. de Vere*	3
He *t* of that sharp look, mother,	*May Queen*, i.	15
He *t* I was a ghost, mother, .	"	17
I *t* to pass away before .	" iii.	1
I *t* of you and Effie dear ; .	"	29
I *t* that it was fancy .	"	33
I *t*, I take it for a sign. .	"	38
He *t* that nothing new was said .	*The Epic .*	30

	POEM.	LINE.
often *t* 'I'll make them man and wife	*Dora*	4
with her in the house *T* not of Dora	"	8
She *t*, ' It cannot be : my uncle's mind	"	44
and *t* Hard things of Dora	"	55
he *t* himself A mark for all,	*Walk. to the M.*	64
thro' his bounty hath *t* fit,	"	22
toil'd, and wrought, and *t* with me —	*Ulysses*	46
Shy she was, and I *t* her cold ;	*Ed. Gray*	13
T her proud, and fled over the sea	"	14
and I *t* I would have spoken.	*Vision of Sin*	55
nightingale *t*, ' I have sung many songs,	*Poet's Song*	13
A pleasant game she *t*:	*Princess, Pro.*	191
my good father *t* a king a king :	"	1. 25
scarcely *t* in our own hall to hear	"	ii. 39
once or twice I *t* to roar,	"	401
t He scarce would prosper.	"	iii. 59
one anatomic.' 'Nay, we *t* of that,'	"	290
foot Was to you : but I *t* again :	"	iv. 308
I *t*, That surely she will speak ;	"	324
we *t* her half-possess'd	"	562
I *t* her half-right talking of her wrongs;	"	v. 275
t on all the wrathful King had said,	"	467
I *t*, can this be he From Gama's	"	493
whom we *t* woman even now	"	vi. 256
something written, something *t*;	*In Mem.*	vi. 20
Has never *t* that 'this is I:'.	"	xliv. 4
You *t* my heart too far diseased ;.	"	lxv. 1
I look'd on these and *t* of thee	"	xcvi. 6
all we *t* and loved and did	"	Con. 134
and *t* he would rise and speak	*Maud*, I. i. 59
t, is it pride, and mused and sigh'd	"	viii. 12
I *t* as I stood, if a hand, as white.	"	xiv. 17
Now I *t* that she cared for me,	"	25
t like a fool of the sleep of death.	"	38
none of us *t* of a something beyond,	"	xix. 47
Yet I *t* I saw her stand	"	II. i. 38
and *t* It is his mother's hair.	"	ii. 69
For I *t* the dead had peace,	"	v. 15
When I *t* that a war would arise	"	III. vi. 19
how money breeds, *T* it a dead thing;	*The Brook*	7
day by day she *t* to tell Geraint	*Enid*	65
t within herself, Was ever man	"	80
he *t*, ' In spite of all my care,	"	115
fared it with, Geraint who *t* and said,	"	343
In a moment *t* Geraint,	"	367
t to find Arms in your town,	"	417
t it never yet had look'd so mean.	"	610
while she *t* ' they will not see me'	"	667
t perhaps, That service done so	"	789
t That could I someway prove	"	804
A stranger meeting them had surely *t*,	"	883
t again, ' if there be such in me,	"	901
head high and *t* himself a knight,	"	1091
I *t*, but that your father came	"	1163
t she heard the wild Earl	"	1230
he *t* ' was it for him she wept	"	1246
since she *t*, ' he had not dared to do it	"	1568
You *t* me sleeping, but I heard you	"	1580
I *t* that he was gentle, being great.	*Vivien*	720
and she *t* That all was nature,	*Elaine*	328
t to do while he might yet endure,	"	494
twenty times I *t* him Lancelot	"	534
for she *t* ' If I be loved,	"	904
brothers heard, and *t* With shuddering	"	1015
on her face and *t* ' Is this Elaine?'	"	1024
or *t* she heard them moan ;	*Guinevere*	129
she *t* ' he spies a field of death ;	"	133
then she *t*, 'With what a hate	"	154
t the Queen within herself again ;	"	222
t the Queen, 'lo I they have set her on	"	306
glanced at him, *t* him cold	"	402
t I could not breathe in that fine air	"	638
I *t* not of it: but I know not why	*En. Arden*	393
t that Philip did but trifle	"	472
' He is gone ' she *t* ' he is happy',	"	498
Philip *t* he knew :.	"	516
He *t* it must have gone ;	"	695
he *t* ' After the Lord has call'd	"	810
t to bear it with me to my grave	"	897
blues were sure of it, he *t*;	*Aylmer's F.*	252
he *t*. had slander'd Leolin to him.	"	250

	POEM.	LINE.
pray God that he hold up ' she *t*	*Aylmer's F.*	733
t myself long-suffering, meek	"	753
t the motion of the boundless deep	*Sea Dreams*	89
' What a world,' I *t*, ' to live in	"	92
ask her of my shares, I *t*;	"	111
(I *t* I could have died to save it)	"	130
first time, too, that ever I *t* of death	*Grandmother*	61
t on all her evil tyrannies,	*Boadicea*	80
t that all the blood by Sylla shed.	*Lucretius*	47
these I *t* my dream would show to me	"	51
I *t* I lived securely as yourselves.	"	207
thousand.		
'There are *t*'s now Such women,	*Princess, Pro.*	127
Who had mildew'd in their *t*'s,	*Aylmer's F.*	383
thowl.		
I *t* a 'ad summut to saáy,	*N. Farmer*	19
I *t* a said whot a owt to a said	"	20
thrall		
To save from shame and *t*:	*Sir Galahad*	16
Let not my tongue be a *t* to my eye	*Maud*, I. xvi. 32
thread (s.)		
Draws different *t*'s, and late and soon	*Two Voices*	179
He plays with *t*'s, he beats his chair	*In Mem.* lxv. 13
threadbare		
theme of writers, and indeed Worn *t*.	*Ed. Morris*	49
threaded.		
he *t* The secretest walks of fame.	*The Poet*	9
Or *t* some Socratic dream ;	*In Mem.* lxxxviii. 30
threading.		
led *T* the soldier-city	*Princess*, v.	7
threat.		
Puppet to a father's *t*	*Locksley H.*	42
I hear the violent *t*'s you do not hear,	*Enid*	1269
scared with *t*'s of jail and halter	*Aylmer's F.*	520
Boanerges with his *t*'s of doom	*Sea Dreams*	243
threatened.		
Had wink'd and *t* darkness	*M. d'Arthur, Ep.* 2
three-days-long.		
That *t-d-l* presageful gloom of yours	*Vivien*	169
three-decker		
rushing battle-bolt sang from the *t-d*	*Maud*, I. i. 50
snap The *t-d*'s oaken spine	"	II ii. 27
three-months-old.		
On corpses *t-m-o* at noon she came	*Pal. of Art*	243
three-parts-sick.		
t-p-s With strumming and with scraping,	*Amphion*	69
three-times-three.		
The crowning cup, the *t-t-t*,	*In Mem. Con.* 104
threshold.		
on her *t* he Howling To —	*With Pal. of Art* 15
carried out from the *t* of the door;	*May Queen*, ii. 42
Corpses across the *t*;	*D. of F. Wom.* 25
Half-fall'n across the *t* of the sun,	"	63
and stood Upon the *t*.	*Dora*	109
footsteps smite the *t* stairs Of life	*St S. Stylites*	188
float about the *t* of an age	*Golden Year*	16
find him : by the happy *t*, he,	*Princess*, vii. 185
Upon the *t* of the mind?	*In Mem.* iii. 16
To enrich the *t* of the night	"	xxix. 6
all the marble *t* flashing	*Enid*	874
And seldom crost her *t*	*En. Arden*	334
reverencing death At golden *t*'s	*Aylmer's F.*	843
wrinkled feet Upon thy glimmering *t*'s	*Tithonus*	68
And burn the *t* of the night.	*The Voyage*	18
threw.		
She *t* her royal robes away.	*Pal. of Art*	290
And strongly wheel'd and *t* it.	*M. d'Arthur*	196
stronger he that smote And *t* him	*Princess*, v.	526
By overthrowing me you *t* me higher	*Enid*	1040
thrice-happy.		
T-h days I The flower of each	*Ed. Morris*	68
T-h he that may caress	*Talking O.*	177

420   CONCORDANCE TO

thrice-turned. POEM. LINE.
chew'd The *t-t* cud of wrath, . *Princess*, i. 65
thrid.
To *t* the musky-circled mazes . *Princess*, iv. 242
He *t's* the labyrinth of the mind . *In Mem.* xcvi. 21
thridding.
T the sombre boskage of the wood *D. of F. Wom.* 243
thrift.
like the little *t*, Trembled in perilous *Sea Dreams* 10
thrifty.
t too beyond her age. . . . *Dora* . . 14
thrill.
His country's war-song *t* his ears *Two Voices* 153
Me mightier transports move and *t Sir Galahad* 22
thrill'd.
a clear under-tone *T* thro' mine ears *D. of F. Wom.* 82
thrilleth.
Thro' my very heart it *t* . . *Lilian* . 22
thrive.
those Fresh faces, that would *t* . *Talking O.* 50
thriven.
Word by which himself had *t.*' . *Sea Dreams* 193
throat.
golden round her lucid *t* And shoulder *Œnone* . 174
From cheek and *t* and chin. . . *Pal. of Art* 140
there was that across his *t* . *L. C. V de Vere* 31
bright death quiver'd at the victim's *t D. of F. Wom.* 115
in her *t* Her voice seem'd distant, *To J. S.* . 54
take the goose, and wring her *t* . *The Goose* . 31
All *t's* that gurgle sweet ! . . *Talking O.* . 266
She lit the spark within my *t*, . *Will Water.* 109
Faltering and fluttering in her *t*, . *Princess*, ii. 170
treble of that bassoon, my *t*; . . " . 404
the Lady stretch'd a vulture *t*, . " iv. 344
t's would bawl for civil rights, . " v. 377
flood a fresher *t* with song. . *In Mem.* lxxxii. 16
cobweb woven across the cannon's *t Maud,* III. vi. 27
the knotted column of his *t*, . . *Enid* . 74
many-winter'd fleece of *t* and chin. *Vivien* . 690
felt the knot Climb in her *t*, . . *Elaine* . 737
but one bird with a musical *t*, . *The Islet* . 27
throb (s.)
Perchance, to lull the *t's* of pain, . *The Daisy* . 105
throb (verb.)
T thro' the ribbed stone ; . . *Pal. of Art* 176
throbbed.
Till the war-drum *t* no longer . *Locksley H.* 127
tempestuous treble *t* and palpitated *Vision of Sin* 28
T thunder thro' the palace floors, *Princess*, vii. 89
throbbing.
T thro' all thy heat and light, . *Fatima* . 4
throe.
coughs, aches, stitches, ulcerous *t's St S. Stylites* 13
throne.
kept her *t* unshaken still, . . *To the Queen* 34
a rich *T* of the massive ore, . *Arabian N's.* 146
to own A crown, a sceptre, and a *t* ! *Ode to Mem.* 121
With a crown of gold, On a *t* ? . *The Merman* 7
With a comb of pearl, On a *t* ? . *The Mermaid* 7
Over the *t* In the midst of the hall ; " . 21
lightly vault from the *t* and play . " . 33
Thou from a *t* Mounted in heaven *To J. M. K.* 12
The *t* of Indian Cama slowly sail'd *Pal. of Art* vi. 37
bells Began to chime She took her *t* : " . 158
solemn mirth, And intellectual *t*. . " . 216
tame leopards couch'd beside her *t Princess*, ii. 19
glittering bergs of ice, *T* after *t* . . " iv. 54
clove An advent to the *t* : . . " . 265
winged Her transit to the *t*, . . " . 359
at the farther end Was Ida by the *t* . " vi. 337
The chairs and *t's* of civil power . *In Mem.* xxi. 16
shape the whisper of the *t* ; . . " lxiii. 12
thousand battles, and shaking a hundred *t's Maud,* I. i. 48

barking for the *t's* of kings ; POEM. LINE.
. *Ode on Well.* 121
Betwixt a people and their ancient *t*, " . 163
fierce light which beats upon a *t*, *Ded. of Idylls* 26
couchant with his eyes upon the *t*, *Guinevere* . 12
joy to the people and joy to the *t Wel. to Alexan.* 29
throned.
wisdom-bred And *t* of wisdom . *Œnone* . 122
turning saw, *t* on a flowery rise, . *D. of F. Wom.* 125
throng (s.)
in among the *t's* of men ; . . *Locksley H.* 116
throng (verb.)
To *t* with stately blooms . . *The Poet* . 27
marish-flowers that *t* The desolate *Dying Swan* 40
the people *t* The chairs and thrones *In Mem.* xxi. 15
and *t*, their rags and they . . *Lucretius* . 170
thronged.
And her whisper *t* my pulses . *Locksley H.* . 36
Every gate is *t* with suitors, . " . 101
thronging.
t all one porch of Paradise . . *Pal. of Art* 101
t in and in, to where they waited . *Vision of Sin* 26
throstle.
thro' wild March the *t* calls . . *To the Queen.* 14
The callow *t* lispeth, . . . *Claribel* . 17
Sometimes the *t* whistled strong : *Sir L. and Q G.* 11
And swallow and sparrow and *t*, . *The Window* 157
throve.
And so she *t* and prosper'd : . *Pal. of Art* 217
that on which it *t* Falls off, . . *To J. S.* . 15
t and branch'd from clime to clime *In Mem.* cxvii. 13
all this *t* until I wedded thee ! . *Guinevere* . 480
t not in her trade, not being bred . *En. Arden.* 248
in it *t* an ancient evergreen, . . " . 736
throw.
I would *t* to them back in mine . *The Merman* 31
dividing the swift mind, In act to *t M. d'Arthur* 61
wrestling thews that *t* the world . . *Princess*, vii. 266
To seize and *t* the doubts of man ; *In Mem.* cviii. 6
thrown.
thunder or a sound Of rocks *t* down, *Pal. of Art* 281
from one sorrow to another *t* : . *Lotos-E's.* . 63
broad-limb'd Gods at random *t* . *To E. L.* . 15
shiver of dancing leaves is *t* . . *Maud,* I. vi. 73
thrum.
to flaunt, to dress, to dance, to *t*, . *Princess,* iv. 498
thrumming.
And *t* on the table : . . . *Will Water.* 160
thrush.
rarely pipes the mounted *t* ; . . *In Mem.* xc. 2
thrust (s.)
here a *t* that might have kill'd, . *Elaine* . 25
thrust (verb.)
and *t* The dagger thro' her side.' . *D. of F. Wom.* 259
t him in the hollows of his arm, . *Dora* . . 129
with grim laughter *t* us out at gates. *Princess,* iv. 534
T in between, but Arac rode him down " v. 521
into a shallow grave they are *t*, . *Maud,* II. v. 6
t the dish before her, crying ' Eat,' *Enid* . 1503
thrusteth.
My tough lance *t* sure . . . *Sir Galahad* 2
thumb.
the raw mechanic's bloody *t's* . *Walk. to the M.* 67
stoop and kiss the tender little *t*, . *Enid* . . 395
rotatory *t's* on silken knees, . . *Aylmer's F.* 200
thump.
heave and *t* A league of street . *Princess,* iii. 111
thunder (s.)
did gather *t* as they ran, . . *The Poet* . 49
as the lightning to the *t* . . " . 52
With a low melodious *t* ; . . *Poet's Mind* 27
t and light in the magic night— . *The Merman* 23
quiet seats Above the *t*, . . *Œnone* . 130

	POEM	LINE
ragged rims of *t* brooding low,	*Pal. of Art*	75
t or a sound Of rocks thrown down	"	261
t on the everlasting hills.	*D. of F. Wom.*	226
The *t's* breaking at her feet: 'Of old sat Freedom'		2
Black'd with thy branding *t*.	*St S. Stylites*	75
Low *t's* bring the mellow rain,	*Talking O.*	279
took The *t* and the sunshine.	*Ulysses*	48
A long melodious *t*	*Princess*, ii.	452
on black blocks A breadth of *t*.	" iii.	275
crash of shivering points, And *t*	" v.	481
Throbb'd *t* thro' the palace floors,	" vii.	69
And a sullen *t* is roll'd:	*Maud*, II. iv.	49
even if they broke In *t*, silent;	*Ode on Well.*	177
Upon a head so dear in *t*,	*Enid*	862
The drumming *t* of the huger fall	"	1022
earth shake, and a low *t* of arms.	*Elaine*	459
on her the *t's* of the house	*Aylmer's F.*	278
flood, fire, earthquake, *t*, wrought	"	639
claps of *t* from within the cliffs	*Sea Dreams*	55
And there was rolling *t*;	"	114
Welcome her, *t's* of fort and of fleet!	*IV. to Alexan.*	6
T, a flying fire in heaven,	*Boädicea*	24
But they heard the foeman's *t*	*The Captain*	41
Nor ever lowest roll of *t* moans,	*Lucretius*	108

thunder (verb.)

And the volleying cannon *t* his loss;	*Ode on Well*	62
T 'Anathema,' friend, at you:	*To F. D. Maurice*	8
That not one moment ceased to *t*	*Sea Dreams*	121

thunderbolt.

in its breast a *t*.	*Locksley H.*	192
And like a *t* he falls.	*The Eagle*	6
falling on them like a *t*,	*Princess, Pro.*	43
the *t* Hangs silent, but prepare;	" ii.	203
I dare All these male *t's*;	" iv.	479
and once the flash of a *t*—	*Lucretius*	27

thunder-cloud.

As *t-c's* that, hung on high,	*Eleänore*	68
like a *t-c* Whose skirts are loosen'd	*Enid*	1307

thunder-drops.

| As *t-d* fall on a sleeping sea; | *D. of F. Wom.* | 122 |

thundered.

t up into Heaven the Christless code	*Maud*, II. i.	26
Volleyed and *t*;	*Lt. Brigade*	21,42
t in and out the gloomy skirts	*Elaine*	291

thundering.

| The league-long roller *t* on the reef, | *En. Arden* | 585 |

thunder-music.

| *t-m*, rolling, shake The prophets | *In Mem.* lxxxvi. | 7 |

thunder-peals.

| A bridal dawn of *t-p*, 'Love thou thy land,' etc. | | 51 |

thunder-shower.

| are drown'd in gloom Of *t-s*. | *Princess*, iv. | 505 |

thunder-storm.

the peoples plunging thro' the *t-s*;	*Locksley H.*	126
Upon a king's right hand in *t-s's*,	*Princess*, v.	429

thwarted.

wrong'd and lied and *t* us—.	*Princess*, iv	519
T by one of these old father-fools,	*Aylmer's F.*	390

tiar

| studded wide With disks and *t's*, | *Arabian N's* | 64 |

ticking.

| The slow clock *t*, | *Mariana* | 74 |

tickle.

| *t* the maggot born in an empty head. | *Maud*, II. v | 38 |

tickled.

| secret laughter *t* all my soul. | *Princess*, iv. | 248 |

tickling.

caught the younker *t* trout	*Walk. to the M.*	25
t the brute brain within the man's	*Lucretius*	21

tide

The *t* of time flow'd back with me,	*Arabian N's.*	3
ere she reach'd upon the *t*	*L. of Shalott*, iv.	32

	POEM.	LINE.
Bluster the winds and *t's*	*D. of F. Wom.*	38
And when the *t* of combat stands,	*Sir Galahad*	10
down dark *t's* the glory slides,	"	47
at high *t* of feast, in masque	*Princess*, i.	194
toward the centre set the starry *t*,	" ii.	102
a *t* of fierce Invective seem'd to wait	" iv.	450
When the *t* ebbs in sunshine,	" vi.	146
The *t* flows down, the wave again	*In Mem.* x x.	13
The double *t's* of chariots flow	" xcvii.	23
forward-creeping *t's* Began to foam,	" cii.	37
In vassal *t's* that follow'd thought.	" cxi.	16
t in its broad-flung ship-wrecking roar,	*Maud*,I iii.	11
The *t's* of Music's golden sea	*Ode on Well.*	252
Your limit, oft returning with the *t*.	*Elaine*	1035
his full *t* of youth Broke	*Aylmer's F.*	115
a full *t* Rose with a ground-swell	*Sea Dreams*	50
you do but hear the *t*.	"	83
Of such a *t* swelling toward the land	"	85
No!' said he, 'but this *t's* roar	"	242
Dream in the sliding *t's*.	*Requiescat*.	4

tidings.

Be cheer'd with *t* of the bride,	*In Mem.* xxxix.	23
To hear the *t* of my friend,	" cxxv.	3

tie (s.)

To pass with all our social *t's*	*Day-Dm.*	217
ancient *t's* Would still be dear	*Princess*, ii.	245
inwoven here With dear Love's *t*	*Maud*, l.xviii.	61

tie (verb.)

T up the ringlets on your cheek:	*Margaret*.	57
Close up his eyes: *t* up his chin:	*D.of the O. Year*	48

tied.

chann'd and *t* To where he stands	*D. of F. Wom.*	193
t it round his hat To make him pleasing	*Dora*.	61
t the bridle-reins of all the three.	*Enid*	947,1032

tier.

| up the marble stair, *t* over *t*. | *Elaine* | 1241 |

tiger

Here play'd, a *t*, rolling to and fro	*Pal. of Art*	151
And let the ape and *t* die.	*In Mem.* cxviii.	28

tiger-cat.

| a *t-c* In act to spring: | *Princess*, ii. | 427 |

tiger-lily.

| Heavily hangs the *t-l*. 'A spirit haunts,' etc. | | 12,24 |

tighten.

| made her lithe arm round his neck *T*, *Vivien*. | | 464 |

tigress.

| To trip a *t* with a gossamer. | *Princess*, v. | 163 |

Tigris.

| Adown the *T* I was borne, | *Arabian N's.* | 6 |

tile.

| her whinny shrills From *t* to scullery | *Princess*, v. | 443 |

till (s.)

| rogue would leap from his counter and *t*, | *Maud*,I. i. | 51 |

till (verb.)

It is the land that freemen *t*, 'You ask me why,' etc.		5
the labourer *t's* His wonted glebe	*In Mem.* c.	21
sent a thousand men To *t* the wastes,	*Enid*.	1790
t's the field and lies beneath,	*Tithonus*.	3

till'd.

| for miles about Was *t* by women; | *Princess*, i. | 190 |

tilt game of arms.)

that rang With *t* and tourney,	*Princess, Pro.*	122
to move in old memorial *t s*,	" v.	468
Forgetful of the *t* and tournament	*Enid*.	52
victor at the *t* and tournament	"	1808
Hurt in his first *t* was my son,	*Elaine*	196
should wear her favour at the *t*	"	357
many a time have watch'd thee at the *t*	"	1350
Killed in a *t* come next, five summers	*Guinevere*.	319
on love And sports and *t's* and pleasure	"	384

tilt (of a cart.)

| his wife upon the *t*, | *Walk. to the M.* | 33 |

422 CONCORDANCE TO

	POEM.	LINE.
tilt (verb.)		
would *t* it out among the lads;	Princess,	v. 345
in this tournament can no man *t*,	Enid	. 480
t's with my good nephew thereupon,	"	. 488
left it with her when he rode to *t*	Elaine	. 30
tilth.		
and so by *t* and grange, And vines,	Princess,	i. 109
wither'd holt or *t* or pasturage.	En. Arden.	676
tilting-field.		
In open battle or the *t.-f*	Guinevere	328-30
timber.		
And fiddled in the *t!*	Amphion	. 16
timber-crost.		
A front of *t-c* antiquity,	En. Arden.	693
timbrel.		
With *t* and with song.	D.of F.Wom.	200
time (s.)		
yield you *t* To make demand	To the Queen	10
tide of *t* flow'd back with me,	Arabian N's.	3
The forward-flowing tide of *t*;	"	. 4
In sooth it was a goodly *t*, (rep)	"	. 20
fed the *t* With odour	"	. 64
Apart from place, withholding *t*,	"	. 75
Entranced with that place and *t*,	"	. 97
Graven with emblems of the *t*	"	. 108
After the fashion of the *t*,	"	. 119
night new-risen, that marvellous *t*	"	. 130
The sweetest lady of the *t*,	"	. 141
Sole star of all that place and *t*	"	. 152
What *t* the amber morn Forth gushes	Ode to Mem	70
t the mighty moon was gathering	Love and Death	1
Beat *t* to nothing in my head	Miller's D.	67
when *t* was ripe The still affection	"	. 224
From that *t* to this I am alone	Œnone	. 189
the *t*'s of every land So wrought	Pal. of Art	147
dreadful *t*, dreadful eternity,	"	. 267
ever worse with growing *t*,	"	. 270
You know so ill to deal with *t*,	L. C. V. de Vere	63
If *T* be heavy on your hands	"	. 66
happiest *t* of all the glad New-year;	MayQueen,	I.2,41
The good old year, the dear old *t*	"	ii. 6
So now I think my *t* is near.	"	iii. 41
T driveth onward fast	Lotos-E's.	88
The spacious *t*'s of great Elizabeth	D.of F.Wom.	7
The *t*'s when I remember to have been	"	. 79
thine own Until the end of *t*,'	"	. 84
Nilus would have risen before his *t*.	"	. 143
This is the curse of *t*.	To J. S.	17
t and space to work and spread 'You ask me, why'	16	
induce a *t* When single thought	"	. 18
transfused Thro' future *t* 'Love thou thy land,' etc.		4
pamper not a hasty *t*,	"	. 9
all the past of *T* reveals	"	. 50
this be true, till *T* shall close	"	. 79
the style of those heroic *t*'s?	The Epic	. 35
the Mastodon, Nor we those *t*'s;	"	. 37
never more, at any future *t*,	M. d'Arthur	18
'tis *t* that I were gone	"	. 163
I see the true old *t*'s are dead	"	. 229
Such *t*'s have not been since the light	"	. 232
cock crew loud; as at that *t* of year	Ep.	10
we listen'd : with the *t* we play'd :	Gardener's D.	216
in that *t* and place, I spoke to her,	"	221-6
the *t* Is come to raise the veil.	"	. 268
in my I a father's word was law	Dora	. 25
T will set me right.	Ed. Morris	88
for so long a *t*, If I may measure *t*.	St S. Stylites	92
and Earth, and *T* are choked.	"	. 102
one thousand and two hundred *t*'s	To Christ	. 109
do not say But that a *t* may come	"	. 187
I say, that *t* is at the doors	"	. 189
But could I, as in *t*'s foregone,	Talking O.	. 189
Shall Error in the round of *t*	Love and Duty	4
Wait ; my faith is large in *T*,	"	. 25
wheels of *T* Spun round in station,	"	. 73
the *t*'s, when some new thought can	Golden Year	27
in our *t*, nor in our children's *t*,	"	. 55
all *t*'s I have enjoy'd Greatly,	Ulysses	. 7
Made weak by *t* and fate,	"	" 60

	POEM	LINE.
and the long result of *T*;	Locksley H.	12
Love took up the glass of *T*,	"	. 31
in the foremost files of *t*	"	. 178
we, the latest seed of *T*,	Godiva	. 5
Forerun thy peers, thy *t*	Two Voices	88
memory of the wither'd leaf In endless *t*	"	. 113
What *t* the foeman's line is broke	"	. 155
memory dealing but with *t*,	"	. 376
thought and *t* be born again,	Day-Dm.	. 70
And in the morning of the *t*'s.	"	. 232
Forsince the *t* when Adam first	"	. 253
How goes the *t*? 'Tis five o'clock	Will Water.	3
on this whirligig of *T* We circle	"	. 63
With *t* I will not quarrel	"	. 206
It was the *t* when lilies blow,	Lady Clare	1
Then before her *t* she died	L. of Burleigh	88
Is to be the ball of *T*	Vision of Sin	105
avenged by sense that wore with *t*	"	. 214
thou wilt, but I am sick of *T*, 'Come not, when,' etc.		9
the sight and smacking of the *t*;	Princess, Pro.	15
one wide chasm of *t* and frost	"	. 80
to kill *T* by the fire in Winter	"	. 93
A tale for summer as befits the *t*,	"	. 201
something made to suit with *T* and place	"	. 205
Some future *t*, if so indeed you will	"	. 224
on the stretch'd forefinger of all *T*	"	ii. 50
like swallows coming out of *t*	"	. 356
great name flow on with broadening *t*	"	. 409
somehow shapes the shadow, *T*;	"	iii. 148
for all things serve their *t*	"	. 313
What *t* I watch'd the swallow	"	iv. 55
the Ithacensian suitors in old *t*,	"	. 71
t When we made bricks in Egypt.	"	. 100
those were gracious *t*'s.	"	. 109
fellow-worker be, When *t* should serve:	"	. 278
wasted here health, wealth, and *t*,	"	. 200
drunkard's football, laughing-stocks of *T*.	"	. 333
spent a stormy *t* With our strange girl ;	"	. 496
equal baseness lived in sleeker *t*'s	"	v. 116
plant a solid foot into the *T*,	"	. 375
music in the growing breeze of *T*	"	. 405
scatter all our maids Till happier *t*'s	"	vi. 40
passing home Till happier *t*'s;	"	. 284
call'd On flying *T* from all their silver	"	. 360
Much had she learnt in little *t*	"	vii. 90
these twain, upon the skirts of *T*,	"	. 225
Give it *t* To learn its limbs ;	"	. 271
reach a hand thro' *t* to catch	In Mem.	i. 78
Come *T*, and teach me, many years,	"	xiii. 13
My fancies *t* to rise on wing,	"	. 17
A *t* to sicken and to swoon.	"	xxi. 17
all was good that *T* could bring,	"	xxiii. 18
His license in the field of *t*,	"	xxvii. 6
t draws near the birth of Christ (ciii.1.)	"	xxviii. 1
miss their yearly due Before their *t*	"	xxix. 16
As when he loved me here in *T*,	"	xlii. 13
What *t* his tender palm is prest	"	xliv. 2
A lifelong tract of *t* revealed	"	xlv. 9
And *T*, a maniac scattering dust,	"	xlix. 7
When *T* hath sunder'd shell from pearl.'	"	li. 16
The perfect flower of human *t*;	"	lx. 4
the dark hand struck down thro' *t*,	"	lxxi. 19
Foreshorten'd in the tract of *t*?	"	lxxvi. 4
What *t* mine own might also flee,	"	lxxxiii. 37
Shall gather in the cycled *t*'s	"	lxxxiv. 28
such A friendship as had master'd *T*;	"	. 64
masters *T* indeed, and is Eternal,	"	. 65
Thy spirit in *t* among thy peers	"	xc. 6
measuring out The steps of *T*-	"	xciv. 42
There in due *t* the woodbine blows	"	civ. 7
change of place, like growth of *t*,	"	. 12
The *t*ithless coldness of the *t*'s	"	cv. 18
The admits not flowers or leaves	"	cvi. 9
Becoming, when the *t* has birth,	"	cxii. 14
Is it, then, regret for buried *t*	"	cxv. 1
Contemplate all this work of *T*,	"	cxvii. 1
If so he type this work of *t*	"	. 16
eddies in the flood Of onward *t*	"	cxxvii. 6
echoes out of weaker *t*'s	"	Con. 22
they must go, the *t* draws on	"	. 89

	POEM.	LINE.
Appearing ere the *t*'s were ripe,	*Princess*, Con.	139
I remember the *t*, for the roots	*Maud*, I. i.	13
weep for a *t* so sordid and mean	"	v. 17
My yet young life in the wilds of *T*.	"	xvi. 21
She is but dead, and the *t* is at hand	" II. iii	8
Wretchedest age, since *T* began	"	v. 21
is changed, for it fell at a *t* of year	" III. vi.	4
' It is *t*. it is *t*, O passionate heart,'	"	30
such a *t* as goes before the leaf,	*The Brook*	13
Foremost captain of his *t*	*Ode on Well.*	31
For many a *t* in many a clime	"	64
him, who bettering not with *t*	*Will*	10
Hereafter, thro' all *t*'s, Albert the Good	*Ded. of Idylls*	42
little *t* for idle questioners.	*Enid*	272
scantly *t* for half the work—	"	268
having seen all beauties of our *t*.	"	498
Constrain'd us, but a better *t* has come:	"	716
I that wasted *t* to tend upon her	"	807
in scarce longer *t* Than at Caerleon	"	964
And cursing their lost *t*.	"	1424
Enids and Geraints Of *t*'s to be ;	"	1814
most famous man of all those *t*'s	*Vivien*	22
Upon the great Enchanter of the *T*.	"	65
when the *t* drew nigh Spake	*Elaine*	78
marr'd his face and marked it ere his *t*.	"	247
Hid under grace, as in a smaller *t*	"	264
simples and the science of that *t*.	"	858
drave her ere her *t* across the fields	"	886
till her *t* To tell you :'	*Guinevere*	141
for the *t* Was maytime, and as yet	"	384
Bear with me for the last *t* while I show	"	451
be the fair beginning of a *t*.	"	463
till in *t* their Abbess died.	"	684
Take your own *t*, Annie rep.)	*En. Arden.*	463
monsters for the market of those *t*s.	"	535
slighted suitor of old *t*'s,	"	746
she shall know, I want His *t*.'	"	812
then indeed Harder the *t*s were,	*Aylmer's F.*	457
a Malayan muck against the *t*s	"	463
years which are not *T*'s had blasted him	"	601
Is this a *t* to madden madness	"	760
a *t* for these to flaunt their pride ?	"	770
link'd their race with *t*'s to come—	"	779
That Jenny had tript in her *t*	*Grandmother*	26
first *t*, too, that ever I thought	"	61
not weep—my own *t* seem'd so near.	"	72
For mine is a *t* of peace,	"	89
And age is a *t* of peace,	"	94
What *t* have I to be vext?	"	97
Then never chilling touch of *T*	*The Ringlet*	5, 15
no truer *T* himself Can prove you	*A Dedication*	1
O skill'd to sing of *T* or Eternity	*Milton*	2
beat quicker, for the *t* Is pleasant,	*On a Mourner*	17
But this is the *t* of hollies.	*Spiteful Let.*	27
noon comes, *T* slips away	*The Window*	163

time verb)
Death's twin-brother, *t*'s my breath, *In Mem.* lxvii 2

timing.
happy stars, *t* with things below, *Maud*, I xviii 81

Timour-Mammon.
T-M grins on a pile of children's bones, *Maud*, I. i 46

tin.
polish'd *t*'s, To serve the hot-and-hot *Will Water*, 227

tinct.
blazon'd on the shield In their own *t*, *Elaine* 10

tinged.
t with wan from lack of sleep, *Princess*, iii. 9

tingle.
and the nerves prick And *t*. *In Mem.* xlix. 3

tinkling.
Nor runlet *t* from the rock ; *In Mem.*xcix. 13

tint.
days have vanish'd, tone and *t*, *In Mem.* xliii. 5

tiny-trumpeting.
The *t-t* gnat can break our dream *Elaine* 138

	POEM.	LINE.
thro' her to the *t*'s of her long hands,	*Princess*, ii.	76

tipt.
t with frost-like spires. *Pal. of Art* 52
Love *t* his keenest darts ; *D. of F. Wom.* 173

tire.
Bore and forbore, and did not *t*, *Two Voices* 218
mine the love that will not *t*, *In Mem.* cix 18
For a love that never *t*s ! *The Window* 195

tired.
t out With cutting eights *The Epic* 9
At last, *t* out with play *Talking O* 76
Ascending *t*, heavily slept till morn *En. Arden* 181
'*T*, Annie?' for she did not speak (rep) 387
I began to be *t* a little, *Grandmother* 74-75
T of so much within our little life. *Lucretius* 223

' *Tirra lirra.*'
'*T l*,' by the river Sang Sir Lancelot *L. of Shalott*, iii 35

tissue.
In silver *t* talking things of state. *Enid* 663

tit.
T's, wrens, and all wing'd nothings *Enid* 775
tumble the blossom the mad little *t*'s *The Window* 152

Titan.
The pulses of a *T*'s heart *In Mem.* cii. 32
Whose *T* angels, Gabriel, Abdiel, *Milton* 5

Titanic.
T forces taking birth *Day-Dm.* 229
T shapes, they cramm'd The forum *Princess*, vii. 109

tithe.
paid our *t*s in the days that are gone *Maud*, II v. 23

Titianic.
in hues to dim The *T* Flora. *Gardener's D.* 167

title.
Nor toil for *t*, place. ' Love thou thy land,' etc 25
New as his *t*, built last year, *Maud*, I. x. 19
a Prince indeed. Beyond all *t*'s, *Ded. of Idylls* 41

title-scroll.
t-s's and gorgeous heraldries *Aylmer's F.* 656

titmouse.
And the *t* hope to win her *Maud*, I. xx. 20

titter.
and then A strangled *t* *Princess*, v. 15

to-and-fro.
commenced A *t-a-f*, so pacing *Princess*, ii. 205

to-be.
Dispensing harvest, sowing the *T-b*, *Princess*, vii. 274
Thro' all the secular *t-b*, *In Mem.* xl. 23

to-come.
and all the rich *t-c* Reels *Princess*, vii. 335

to-day.
To-morrow yet would reap *t-d*, ' Love thou thy land' 93
The sequel of *t-d* unsolders all *M. d'Arthur* 14

toddle.
Poor little life that *t*s half an hour *Lucretius* 225

toil s.)
the reapers at their sultry *t*. *Pal. of Art* 77
sweet close of his delicious *t*'s— " 185
fades, and falls, and hath no *t*, *Lotos-E's.* 82
reap the harvest with enduring *t*, " 160
surely, slumber is more sweet than *t* " 171
But enter not the *t* of life, *Margaret* 24
mingled with her fragrant *t*. *Gardener's D.* 142
age hath yet his honour and his *t*; *Ulysses* 50
I must work thro' months of *t* *Amphion* 97
O thou that after *t* and storm *In Mem.* xxxiii. 1
Is *t* cooperant to an end. " cxxvii. 24
t of heart and knees and hands, *Ode on Well.* 212
careful robins eye the delver's *t*. *Enid* 774,1280
mutual love and honourable *t*; *En. Arden* 83

CONCORDANCE TO

toil (verb.)
	POEM.	LINE.
Why should we *t* alone, We only *t* Lotos-E's.		60
Nor *t* for title, place 'Love thou thy land,'	etc.	25
I said, 'I *t* beneath the curse,	Two Voices	229

toiled.
T onward, prick'd with goads	Pal. of Art	150
Souls that have *t*, and wrought,	Ulysses	46
t Mastering the lawless science	Aylmer's F.	434
often *t* to clothe your little ones; .	"	699

toiling.
A motion *t* in the gloom — 'Love thou thy land,' etc.		54
Spins, *t* out his own cocoon.	Two Voices	180
T in unmeasurable sand	Will	16

toime.
i' the woost o' *t*'s I wur niver	N. Farmer	16

toithe.
an's *t* were due, an' I gied it in hond N. Farmer		11

token.
There came a sweeter *t*	May Queen,	iii. 22
came a mystic *t* from the king	Ed. Morris	132
Who show'd a *t* of distress?	In Mem. lxxvii.	13
then he bound Her *t* on his helmet	Elaine	373
When these have worn their *t*'s:	"	765
be a *t* to her, That I am he.'	En. Arden	901

told.
Sweet Alice, if I *t* her all?'	Miller's D.	120
My love hath *t* me so a thousand times	Œnone	193
has *t* me words of peace.	May Queen, iii.	12
wheresoever I am sung or *t*	M. d'Arthur	34
And *t* me I should love.	Gardener's D.	63
cuckoo *t* his name to all the hills	"	92
This is not *t* of any. They were saints	St S. Stylites	149
And *t* him of my choice,	Talking O.	78
that same song of his He *t* me;	Golden Year	8
She *t* him of their tears	Godiva	19
t him all her nurse's tale.	Lady Clare	80
we, unworthier, *t* Of college:	Princess, Pro.	110
t a tale from mouth to mouth	"	189
have him back Who *t* the 'Winter's Tale'	"	231
your example pilot, *t* her all.	iii.	121
such extremes, I *t* her, well might harm	"	128
t me she would answer us to-day	"	150
How came you here?' I *t* him:	iv.	202
me none *t*: not less to an eye	"	305
you had gone to her, She *t*, perforce;	"	311
Go: Cyril *t* us all.'	v.	35
now a pointed finger, *t* them all:	"	260
so I often *t* her, right or wrong,	"	278
t the king that I was pledged	"	342
if I saw not, yet they *t* me all	vi.	4
might have *t* For she was cramm'd	Con.	34
He *t* it not; or something seal'd	In Mem. xxxi.	15
tell them all they would have *t*,	" xxxix.	25
He *t* me, lives in any crowd,	" xcvii.	26
first he *t* me that he loved	Con.	6
What if he had *t* her yestermorn.	Maud, I. v.	50
Who *t* him we were there?	" II. v.	52
hateful, monstrous, not to be *t*:	" III. vi.	41
She *t* me. She and James had	The Brook	96
a long long-winded tale	"	138
She *t* me all her friends had said	The Letters	25
It *t* of England then to me,	The Daisy	89
T Enid, and they sadden'd her	Enid	64
journey to her, as himself Had *t* her,	"	144, 846
these things he *t* the king.	"	151
t him scouring still 'The sparrow-hawk!'	"	260
t her all their converse in the hall	"	520
return'd And *t* them of a chamber	"	1110
t Free tales, and took the word	"	1139
t him all that Earl Limours had said,	"	1240
nor *t* his gentle wife What ail'd him,	"	1352
plainlier *t* How the huge Earl	"	1653
Merlin once had *t* her of a charm,	Vivien	54
t you first of such a charm	"	209
I trusted, when I *t* you that,	"	211
crueller than was ever *t* in tale	"	707
t her all the charm, and slept.	"	815

	POEM.	LINE.
and she *t* him, 'a red sleeve	Elaine	371
Lancelot *t* me of a common talk	"	576
there *t* the King What the King knew	"	702
the maid had *t* him all her tale,	"	794, 819
T him that her fine care had saved	"	859
I *t* her that her love Was but the flash	"	1307
Sir Lancelot *t* This matter to the Queen, Guinevere		53
Nor with them mix'd, nor *t* her name,	"	146
the tales Which my good father *t*.	"	315
T him, with other annals of the port, En. Arden		703
tho' Miriam Lane had *t* him all,	"	766
He said to Miriam, 'that you *t* me of	"	806
Then he *t* her of his voyage,	"	862
been himself a part of what he *t*.	Aylmer's F.	12
t her fairy-tales,	"	89
as he *t* The story, storming a hill-fort	"	224
praised the waning red, and *t* The vintage	"	406
Then she *t* it, having dream'd	Sea Dreams	200
what is this which now I'm *t*	The Ringlet	31
These have *t* us all their anger	Boädicea	23
There was one who watch'd and *t* me	"	30
golden work in which I *t* a truth	Lucretius	256

tolerance.
Gama swamped in lazy *t*.	Princess, v.	433
must have rated her Beyond all *t*.	Aylmer's F.	381

tolerant.
T of what he half-disdain'd,	Vivien	34

toll (s.)
'Honour,' she said 'and homage, tax and *t*	Œnone	114
fruits and spices, clear of *t*,	Golden Year	45

toll (verb.)
T ye the church-bell sad and slow	D. of the O. Year	3
One set slow bell will seem to *t*	In Mem. lvi.	10

toll'd.
like a bell *T* by an earthquake	Princess, vi.	312
Let the bell be *t*: (rep.)	Ode on Well.	46

tomb.
Shut up as in a crumbling *t*,	Pal. of Art	273
in the moon athwart the place of *t*'s M. d'Arthur		46
hore him thro' the place of *t*'s	"	175
hold their orgies at your *t*. 'You might have won'		12
near his *t* a feast Shone,	Princess, Pro.	105
her empty glove upon the *t*.	" vi.	573
I go to plant it on his *t*,	In Mem. viii.	22
In that deep dawn behind the *t*,	" xlv.	6
My old affection of the *t*,	" lxxxiv.	75·7
As it were a duty done to the *t*,	Maud, I. xix.	49
Remains the lean P. W. on his *t*:	The Brook	192
'Let her *t* Be costly,	Elaine	1329
be blazoned on her *t*	"	1334
her, that is the womb and *t* of all,	Lucretius	240

tome.
at a board by *t* and paper sat	Princess, ii.	18

Tomohrit.
T, Athos, all things fair	To E. L.	5

to-morrow.
T 'ill be the happiest time	May Queen, i. 2,	42
T yet would reap to-day, 'Love thou thy land,' etc.		93

Tomyris.
bronze valves, emboss'd with *T*	Princess, v.	355

ton.
Than were those lead-like *t*'s of sin, St S. Stylites		25

tone.
Wears all day a fainter *t*.	The Owl, ii.	7
Sweeter *t*'s than calumny	A Dirge	11
'O cruel heart,' she changed her *t*, Mariana in the S.		69
wind breathes low with mellower *t*: Lotos-E's.		147
fall down and glance From *t* to *t*. D. of F. Wom.		167
it was the *t* with which he read	M d'Arthur, Ep.	5
He heeded not reviling *t*'s,	Two Voices	220
Swung themselves, and in low *t*'s. Vision of Sin		20
to herself, all in low *t*'s, she read. Princess, vii.		160
To one clear harp in divers *t*'s	In Mem. i.	2
With all the music in her *t*,	" iii.	10
days have vanish'd, *t* and tint,	" xliii.	5

	POEM.	LINE.
He past ; a soul of nobler *t* :	In Mem. lix.	1
Perhaps the smile and tender *t*	Maud, I. vi.	63
came her father, saying in low *t*'s .	Elaine	988
hint it not in human *t*'s . .	Coquette, iii.	11

tongue.

of the many *t*'s, the myriad eyes .	Ode to Mem.	47
Indian reeds blown from his silver *t*,	The Poet	13
My tremulous *t* faltereth . .	Eleänore	136
run before the fluttering *t*'s of fire	D. of F. Wom.	30
silver *t*, Cold February loved	The Blackbird	13
servile to a shrewish *t* ! . .	Locksley H.	42
wide in soul and bold of *t*, . .	Two Voices	124
Blowing a noise of *t*'s and deeds, .	"	206
To feel, altho' no *t* can prove, .	"	445
'Tis said he had a tuneful *t* . .	Amphion	17
Let me loose thy *t* with wine ; .	Vision of Sin	88
Fear not thou to loose thy *t*, . .	"	135
in a *t* no man could understand .	"	222
I would that my *t* could utter 'Break, break,' etc.		3
in this frequence can I lend full *t*	Princess, iv.	422
every spoken *t* should lord you. .	"	523
On flying Time from all their silver *t*'s	" vii.	90
Whatever fickle *t*'s may say. .	In Mem. xxvi.	4
To flicker with his double *t*. .	" cix.	8
A contradiction on the *t*, . .	" cxxiv.	4
made my *t* so stammer and trip .	Maud, I. vi.	83
With the evil *t* and the evil ear .	" x	51
Let not my *t* be a thrall to my eye	" xvi.	32
By some yet unmoulded *t* . .	Ode on Well.	213
as a man upon his *t* May break it.	Enid	891
neither eyes nor *t*—O stupid child !	Vivien	100
Your *t* has tript a little ; . .	"	452
let her *t* Rage like a fire . .	"	630
heathen caught and reft him of his *t*.	Elaine	273
prick'd at once, all *t*'s were loosed :	"	720
such a *t* To blare its own . .	"	918
good nuns would check her gadding *t*	Guinevere	311
his long-bounden *t* Was loos'd, .	En. Arden	645
a *t* that ruled the hour . .	Aylmer's F.	194
strong on his legs, but still of his *t* !	Grandmother	13
the *t* is a fire as you know, my dear rep...	"	78
My *t* Trips, or I speak profanely	Lucretius	73

tongue-tied.

A *t-t* Poet in the feverous days .	Golden Year	10
thus *t-t*, it made him wroth the more	Enid	961

too-earnest.

Nor look with that *t-e* eye . .	Day-Dm.	18

too-fearful.

t-f guilt Simpler than any child .	Guinevere	368

took.

So *t* echo with delight, (rep.) .	The Owl, ii.	4
Cleaving, *t* root, and springing forth	The Poet .	21
t the reed-tops as it went. .	Dying Swan	10
t the soul Of that waste place with joy	"	21
bells Began to chime. She *t* her throne :	Pal of Art	158
shuddering *t* hold of all my mind	May Queen, iii.	35
He *t* the goose upon his arm, .	The Goose	41
how I row'd across And *t* it .	M. d'Arthur	33
t with care, and kneeling on one knee,	"	173
Put forth their hands, and *t* the King,	"	206
for the pleasure that I *t* to hear .	Gardener's D.	223
Dora *t* the child, and went her way	Dora .	69
she rose and *t* The child once more,	"	78
he *t* the boy, that cried aloud .	"	99
Dora said, ' My uncle *t* the boy ; .	"	112
Mary *t* another mate . .	"	176
As one by one we *t* them— .	Walk. to the M.	87
We *t* them all, till she was left alone	"	90
I *t* the swarming sound of life .	Talking O.	213
Why *t* ye not your pastime ? .	Love and Duty	28
Love himself *t* part against himself .	"	45
with a frolic welcome *t* The thunder	Ulysses .	47
Love *t* up the glass of Time, .	Locksley H.	31
Love *t* up the harp of Life . .	"	33
she *t* the tax away, . .	Godiva .	78
Who *t* a wife, who reared his race,	Two Voices	228
Then I *t* a pencil, and wrote .	Ed. Gray .	25
t him by the curls, and led him in	Vision of Sin	6

	POEM.	LINE.
T this fair day for text, . .	Princess, Pro.	108
there we *t* one tutor as to read : .	"	177
they saw the King ; he *t* the gifts .	" i.	45
she *t* A bird's-eye view . .	" ii.	108
He *t* advantage of his strength .	"	136
T both his hands, and smiling faintly	"	284
turn'd to go, but Cyril *t* the child. .	"	341
We *t* this palace : but even from the first	" iv.	294
dispatches which the Head Thalf-amazed	"	361
She *t* it and she flung it. . .	"	575
then *t* the king His three broad sons,	" v.	258
t it for an hour in mine own bed .	"	424
t my leave, for it was nearly noon .	"	457
T the face-cloth from the face .	"	542
she *t* it : Pretty bud ! Lily of the vale !	" vi.	175
for she *t* no part In our dispute .	" Con.	29
Our voices *t* a higher range . .	In Mem. xxx.	21
In those sad words I *t* farewell : .	" lvii.	1
I *t* the thorns to bind my brows .	"	7
She *t* the kiss sedately . .	Maud, I. xii.	14
t Her blind and shuddering puppies,	The Brook	129
She *t* the little ivory chest, . .	The Letters	17
What more ? We *t* our last adieu.	The Daisy .	85
t them, and arrayed herself therein,	Enid .	139, 849
Enid *t* his charger to the stall .	"	382
he *t* me from a goodly house : .	"	708
Enid *t* a little delicately . .	"	1061
t the word and play'd upon it .	"	1140
t him for a victim of Earl Doorm, .	"	1373
hated her, who *t* no thought of them,	"	1487
t his russet beard between his teeth	"	1561
t you for a bandit knight of Doorm :	"	1634
haughty jousts and *t* a paramour ; .	"	1680
he *t* Before the Queen's fair name .	"	1798
She *t* the helm and he the sail ; .	Vivien	49
t his brush and blotted out the bird,	"	328
and she *t* him to the King : .	"	695
suddenly she *t* To bitter weeping .	"	703
at her touch T gayer colours, .	"	799
of the crowd you *t* no more account	Elaine .	106
t note that when the living smile .	"	322
and *t* the shield, There kept it, .	"	396
he *t*, And gave, the diamond : .	"	549
those two brethren from the chariot *t*	"	1140
Stoopt, *t*, brake seal, and read it ; .	"	1264
his creatures *t* and bare him off .	Guinevere .	168
t Full easily all impressions . .	"	634
they *t* her to themselves : . .	"	682
Enoch *t*, and handled all his limbs	En. Arden .	153
when their casks were fill'd they *t* aboard	"	647
T joyful note of all things joyful .	Aylmer's F.	67
innocent hare Falter before he *t* it .	"	491
Seized it, *t* home, and to my lady.—	"	537
he partly *t* himself for true . .	Sea Dreams	181
never *t* that useful name in vain ; .	"	185
I that *t* you for true gold . .	The Ringlet	31
the master *t* Small notice, or austerely	Lucretius	7

tool.

Or thou wilt prove their *t*. .	Maud, I. vi.	59
thou their *t*, set on to plague .	Guinevere .	357
Him his catspaw and the Cross his *t*,	Sea Dreams	186

tooth

my *teeth*, which now are dropt away	St S. Stylites	29
in the *teeth* of clench'd antagonism	Princess, iv.	445
captains flash'd their glittering *teeth*,	" v.	19
red in *t* and claw With ravine .	In Mem. lv.	15
russet beard between his *teeth* ; .	Enid .	1561
'scoundrel' out of *teeth* that ground	Aylmer's F.	328
dragon warriors from Cadmean *teeth*	Lucretius	50

top

hills with peaky *t*'s engrail'd, .	Pal. of Art	113
'will you climb the *t* of Art. .	Gardener's D.	165
here it comes With five at *t* : .	Walk. to the M.	103
O rock upon thy towery *t* . .	Talking O.	265
The *t*'s shall strike from star to star	Princess, vi.	41
shouted at once from the *t* of the house	Maud, II. v.	10
to the high *t* of the garden-wall .	Guinevere .	26
I climb'd to the *t* of the garth .	Grandmother	28
sets all the *t*'s quivering – . .	Lucretius .	186

CONCORDANCE TO

topaz-lights.   POEM.   LINE
Myriads of t-l and jacinth work . *M. d'Arthur* 57

topic.
speak, and let the *t* die ' . . *Princess,* iii. 189

topple.
Will *t* to the trumpet down . *Princess,* ii. 214
And *t's* down the scales ; . . " v. 438
A kingdom *t's* over with a shriek . *Con.* 67
And *t's* round the dreary west . *In Mem* xv. 19

toppled.
The spires of ice are *t* down, . *In Mem.* cxxvi. 12

toppling.
t over all antagonism . . *Enid* . 491,1682

torch
gust of wind Puff'd out his *t* . *Vivien* . 581

tore
With that she *t* her robe apart . *D. of F. Wom.*157
T the king's letter, snow'd it down, *Princess,* i. 60
in her lion's mood T open . . " iv. 362
Leaf after leaf, and *t,* and cast them off, *Elaine* 1193
t, As if the living passion . *Aylmer's F.* 534
With wakes of fire we *t* the dark *The Voyage* 52
ran in, Heat breast, *t* hair . *Lucretius* . 273

torn.
T from the fringe of spray . . *D of F Wom* 40
drench'd with ooze, and *t* with briers, *Princess,* v. 27
the household flower T from the lintel " 123
her blooming mantle *t,* . . " vi. 122
The Mayfly is torn by the swallow, *Maud,* I iv. 23
By which our houses are *t*? . . " xix. 33
All the air was *t* in sunder, . . *The Captain* 43

Torre.
two strong sons Sir *T* and Sir Lavaine *Elaine* . 174
' Here is *T's*; Hurt in his first tilt
    was my son, Sir *T* . . . " . 195
added plain Sir *T,* . . . " 198. 230
Surely I but play'd on *T*: . . " 429
far away with good Sir *T* for guide " . 784
T and Elaine! why here? . . " . 702
turn'd Sir *T,* and being in his moods " . 795
the rough *T* began to heave and move, " 1060

torrent.
the *t* called me from the cleft . *Œnone* . 51
She heard the *t's* meet 'Of old sat Freedom,' etc 4
For me the *t* ever pour'd . . *To E. L.* . 13
roll The *t's,* dash'd to the vale . *Princess,* v. 340
roll the *t* out of dusky doors ; . " vii. 193
let the *t* dance thee down . . " 291
Like *t's* from a mountain source . *The Letters* 18
flush'd the bed Of silent *t's,* . *The Daisy* . 34
t's of her myriad universe, . . *Lucretius* . 39

torrent-bow.
floating as they fell Lit up a *t-b.* . *Pal of Art* 36

tortoise.
Upon the *t* creeping to the wall . *D of F Wom.* 27

tortured.
a twitch of pain T her mouth, . *Princess,* vi. 96
Me they seized and me they *t* . *Boädicea* . 49

Tory.
I myself, A *T* to the quick . . *Walk to the M* 73
Let Whig and *T* stir their blood ; *Will Water,* 52
The *T* member's elder son . . *Princess,Con* 50
A gathering of the *T,* . . *Maud,* I. xx. 33

toss.
Should *t* with tangle and with shells *In Mem* x. 20
That *t's* at the harbour-mouth ; . *The Voyage* , 2
There the sunlit ocean *t's* . . *The Captain* 69

tossing.
t up A cloud of incense . . *Pal of Art* 38

tost
Discuss'd a doubt and *t* it to and fro ; *Princess,*ii. 422
t a ball Above the fountain-jets . " . 436
t on thoughts that changed from hue to hue " iv. 192
and heard her name so *t* about . *Elaine* . 233

Had *t* his ball and flown his kite . *Aylmer's F.* 84
T' over all her presents petulantly " . 235

totter.
Till she began to *t,* . . *Sea Dreams* 236
there? yon arbutus *T's;* . *Lucretius* . 185

tottering.
yester-even, suddenly giddily *t—* *Boädicea* . 29

tottler.
Doctor's a '*t,* lass, . . *N. Farmer* 66

touch (s.)
And weary with a finger's *t* ' *Clear-headed friend* 22
title, place, or *t* Of pension ' *Love thou thy land,'etc* 23
Perhaps some modern *t's* here and *M d'Arthur,Ep* 6
t's are but embassies of love . *Gardener's D.* 18
But I have sudden *t's* . . *Ed Morris.* 53
there seem'd A *t* of something false . " . 74
My sense of *t* is something coarse, *Talking O.* 163
The cushions of whose *t* may press " . 179
Baby fingers, waxen *t's,* . *Locksley H.* 90
A *t,* a kiss ! the charm was snapt. *Day-Dm.* . 133
O for the *t* of a vanish'd hand, *Break, break,'etc.* 11
like a *t* of sunshine on the rocks . *Princess,* iii 339
the *t* of all mischance but came . " iv. 550
not a thought, a *t,* But pure as lines " v. 187
some *t* of that Which kills me . " vi. 287
No more, dear love, for at a *t* I yield " . 377
Tenderness *t* by *t,* and last, to these " vii. 99
a *t* Came round my wrist . . " . 122
Too solemn for the comic *t's* in them, " *Con.* 68
And I perceived no *t* of change . *In Mem* xiv. 17
The *t* of change in calmer storm . " xvi. 6
A *t* of shame upon her cheek ; . " xxxvii. 10
some dim *t* of earthly things . " xliii. 11
If such a dreamy *t* should fall . " . 13
You say, but with no *t* of scorn, . " xcv. 7
Sprang up for ever at a *t* . . " cxi. 10
t with shade the bridal doors . . " *Con.* 11
gilt by the *t* of a millionaire ; *Maud,* I i. 66
heart-free, with the least little *t* of spleen. " . 71
A *t* of their office might have sufficed " II. v. 27
keep a *t* of sweet civility . *Enid* . 1161
pale blood of the wizard at her *t* . *Vivien* . 798
loves me must have a *t* of earth ; . *Elaine* . 134
go down before your spear at a *t* . " 149-577
save it be some far-off *t* Of greatness " . 449
Courtesy with a *t* of traitor in it . " . 636
at a *t* of light, an air of heaven, . *Aylmer's F.* 5
so finely, that a tremulous *t* Thinn'd, " . 71
never chilling *t* of lime . . *The Ringlet* 5, 15

touch (verb.)
I'd *t* her neck so warm and white. *Miller's D.* 174
with some new grace Or seem'n to *t Gardener's D.*200
t my body and be heal'd and live ; *St S. Stylites* 78
may be we shall *t* the Happy Isles, *Ulysses* . 63
t him with thy lighter thought . *Locksley H.* 54
those two likes might meet and *t.* *Two Voices* 357
t's me with mystic gleams, . . " . 380
Can *t* the heart of Edward Gray, . *Ed. Gray* . 8
And *t* upon the master-chord . *Will Water.* 27
We *t* on our dead self, . . *Princess,* iii. 205
t's on the workman and his work . " . 305
t not a hair of his head ; . . " iv. 388
t to *t* upon a sphere Too gross to tread " vii. 305
To *t* thy thousand years of gloom *In Mem* ii. 12
O Father, *t* the east, and light . " xxx. 31
other than the things I *t.*' . . " xliv. 8
seem'd to *t* it into leaf; . . " lxviii. 18
T thy dull goal of joyless gray. . " lxxi. 27
Descend, and *t,* and enter ; . . " xciii. 13
Not *t* on her father's sin ; . *Maud,* I xix. 17
T a spirit among things divine, . *Ode on Well.* 139
will not *t* upon him even in jest.' *Enid* . 311
t it with a sword, It buzzes wildly *Vivien* . 281
one of all the drove should *t* me : . " . 549
I cannot *t* thy lips, they are not mine *Guinevere* . 547
So, — from afar, — *t* as at once ? . *Aylmer's F.* 580
O Goddess, like ourselves *T,* and be *Lucretius* . 81

	POEM.	LINE.
T by thy spirit's mellowness,	*Eleänore*	103
T; and I knew no more.'	*D. of F.Wom.*	116
T with a somewhat darker hue	*Margaret*	50
t a foot, that might have danced	*Gardener's D.*	132
in passing *t* with some new grace .	"	199
t upon the game, how scarce it was	*Audley Ct.*	31
The flower, she *t* on, dipt and rose,	*Talking O.*	131
T by his feet the daisy slept.	*Two Voices*	276
Are *t*, are turn'd to finest air,	*Sir Galahad*	72
the music *t* the gates and died ;	*Vision of Sin*	23
that cold vapour *t* the palace gate,	"	58
sense of wrong had *t* her face	*Princess, Pro.*	213
t on Mahomet With much contempt	"	ii. 118
but the Muses' heads were *t*	"	iii. 5
t upon the point Where idle boys .	"	v. 298
since you think me *t* In honour —	"	391
the sequel of the tale Had *t* her ; .	"	Con. 31
thou hadst *t* the land to-day	*In Mem.* xiv.	2
God's finger *t* him, and he slept. .	"	lxxxiv. 20
t the changes of the state	"	lxxxviii. 35
The dead man *t* me from the past	"	xciv. 34
Who *t* a jarring lyre at first, .	"	xcv. 7
Nor harp be *t*, nor flute be blown ,	"	civ. 22
t with no ascetic gloom ;	"	cviii. 10
t my hand with a smile so sweet ,	*Maud,* I. vi.	12
For her feet have *t* the meadows .	"	xii. 2
I find whenever she *t* on me .	"	xix. 59
t On such a time as goes before .	*The Brook.*	12
rose to look at it, But *t* it unawares!	*Enid*	1237
Nor ever *t* fierce wine, .	*Vivien*	477
T at all points, except the poplar grove	*Elaine*	614
at times, So *t* were they, .	"	1279
shadow flew Before it, till it *t* her,	*Guinevere*	80
ere he *t* his one-and-twentieth May	*En Arden.*	57
the second death Scarce *t* her	*Aylmer's F.*	605
oaken finials till he *t* the door ;	"	823
T, clink'd, and clash'd, and vanish'd	*Sea Dreams*	131
like ourselves Touch, and be *t*	*Lucretius*	81

touching.

The sullen pool below : .	*Miller's D.*	244
at the *t* of the lips.	*Locksley H.*	38
The moonlight *t* o'er a terrace	*The Daisy*	83
T her guilty love for Lancelot,	*Enid*	25
t Breton sands, they disembark'd	*Vivien*	51
t fame, howe'er you scorn my song,	"	204
spiritual fire, And *t* other worlds.	"	687
all queries *t* those at home	*Aylmer's F.*	463
on the foremost rocks *T*, upjetted	*Sea Dreams*	52

touchwood.

the stem Less grain than *t*,	*Princess,* iv.	314
a cave Of *t*, .	*Aylmer's F.*	512

touchwood-dust.

| Raking in that millennial *t-d* | *Aylmer's F.* | 514 |

tough.

| *t*, Strong, supple, sinew-corded | *Princess,* v. | 523 |

tougher

| *t*, heavier, stronger he that smote | *Princess,* v. | 525 |

tour

| last summer on a *t* in Wales; | *Golden Year* | 2 |

tournament.

From spur to plume a star of *t*,	*M. d'Arthur*	223
Forgetful of the tilt and *t*, .	*Enid*	52
in this *t* can no man tilt,	"	480
victor at the tilt and *t*, .	"	1508

tourney s.}

that rang With tilt and *t*;	*Princess, Pro.*	122
To fight in *t* for my bride, .	"	v. 143
hold a *t* here to-morrow morn,	*Enid*	287
nephew fights In next day's *t*	"	476
wear My favour at this *t*! .	*Elaine*	361

tourney (verb.)

| once more perchance to *t* in it. | *Elaine* | 806 |

tow'd.

| An' a *t* ma my sins, . | *N. Farmer* | 11 |

tower s.}

Four gray walls, and four gray *t*'s	*L. of Shalott,* i.	15
Under *t* and balcony .	"	iv. 37

	POEM.	LINE.
Below the city's eastern *t*'s :	*Fatima*	9
In glassy bays among her tallest *t*'s	*Œnone*	117
in the *t*'s I placed great bells .	*Pal. of Art*	177
Yet pull not down my palace *t*'s ,	"	293
You pine among your halls and *t*'s :	*L. C. V. de Vere*	63
glow Beneath the battled *t*. .	*D. of F. Wom.*	219
waning lime the gray cathedral *t*'s,	*Gardener's D.*	213
we dragg'd her to the college *t*	*Walk. to the M.*	81
Upon her *t*, the Niobe of swine,	"	91
O flourish high, with leafy *t*'s,	*Talking O.*	197
clash'd and hammer'd from a hundred *t*'s,	*Godiva*	75
Tho' watching from a ruin'd *t*	*Two Voices*	77
Here droops the banner on the *t*,	*Day-Dm.*	33
stept Lord Ronald from his *t* :	*Lady Clare*	65
the mother-city thick with *t*'s	*Princess,* i.	111
white vapour streak the crowned *t*'s	"	iii. 326
whole nights long, up in the *t*,	"	vi. 238
Toll'd by an earthquake in a trembling *t*	"	312
here and there a rustic *t* .	"	Con. 44
Before a *t* of crimson holly-oaks,	"	"
crowded farms and lessening *t*'s,	*In Mem.* xi.	11
wildly dash'd in of and tree .	"	xv. 7
And *t*'s fall'n as soon as built —	"	xxvi. 8
The ruin'd shells of hollow *t*'s ?	"	lxxv. 16
And tuft with grass a feudal *t* :	"	cxxvii. 20
Dumb is that *t* which spake so loud,	"	Con. 106
Still on the *t* stood the vane,	*The Letters*	1
fall'n at length that *t* of strength	*Ode on Well.*	38
Or *t*, or high hill-convent,	*The Daisy*	29
Of *t* or duomo, sunny-sweet,	"	46
had fall'n a great part of a *t*,	*Enid*	317
Guinevere had climb'd The giant *t*,	"	827
beheld A little town with *t*'s,	"	1040
look'd a *t* of ruin'd masonwork	*Vivien*	4
in the four walls of a hollow *t*,	"	58, 393
like a cloud above the gateway *t*'s.'	"	449
in her chamber up a *t* to the east .	*Elaine*	3
climb'd That eastern *t*, and entering	"	15
from the west, far on a hill, the *t*'s.	"	168
as she came from out the *t*. .	"	345
Then to her *t* she climb'd,	"	396
bore her swooning to her *t* .	"	963
in her *t* alone the maiden sat : .	"	983
wild with wind That shook her *t*,	"	1015
creatures to the basement of the *t*	*Guinevere*	103
The broken base of a black *t* .	*Aylmer's F.*	511
own gray *t*, or plain-faced tabernacle	"	618
Ilion like a mist rose into *t*'s	*Tithonus*	63
By every town and *t*, .	*The Flower*	14
flutter out upon turret and *t*'s	*W. to Alexan.*	15
blazed before the *t*'s of Troy,	*Spec. of Iliad*	18
I stood on a *t* in the wet. .	*1865-1866*	1

tower verb.}

| *T*, as the deep-domed empyrean . | *Milton* | 7 |

tower'd.

| the pale head of him, who *t* Above | *Aylmer's F.* | 623 |

towering

| *t* o'er him in serenest air . | *Lucretius* | 178 |

tower-stairs.

| she stole Down the long *t-s* . | *Elaine* | 342 |

town.

many an inland *t* and haven large.	*Œnone*	115
thro' the sky Above the pillar'd *t*.	*Pal. of Art*	124
For pastime, ere you went to *t*.	*L. C. V. de Vere*	4
Clanging fights, and flaming *t*'s,	*Lotos-E's.*	161
bore a lady from a leaguer'd *t*.	*D. of F. Wom.*	47
stept she down thro' *t* and field	*'Of old sat Freedom'*	9
The *t* was hush'd beneath us	*Audley Ct.*	84
all that from the *t* would stroll,	*Talking O.*	53
fair Was hidden at the *t*; .	"	102
The music from the *t* — .	"	214
when he laid a tax Upon his *t*,	*Godiva*	14
'Ride you naked thro' the *t*	"	29
Flood with full daylight glebe and *t*	*Two Voices*	87
Thro' dreaming *t* I go, .	*Sir Galahad*	50
Sweet Emma Moreland of yonder *t*	*Ed. Gray.*	1
He pass'd by the *t* and out of the street,	*Poet's Song*	3

	POEM.	LINE.
wild woods that hung about the *t*;	*Princess*,	i. 90
Cat-footed thro' the *t* .	"	103
dropt with evening on a rustic *t* .	"	168
man and woman, *t* And landskip .	"	iv. 425
I wander'd from the noisy *t*,	*In Mem.*lxviii.	5
I roved at random thro' the *t* .	" lxxxvi.	3
The dust and din and steam of *t*:	" lxxxviii.	8
if I praised the busy *t*	"	37
That not in any mother *t* .	"	xcvii. 21
And pass the silent-lighted *t*,	*Con.*	112
heart in the gross mud-honey of *t*,	*Maud*,	I.xvi. 5
By twenty thorps, a little *t* .	*The Brook* .	29
far from noise and smoke of *t*,	*To F. D. Maurice*	13
Beheld the long street of a little *t*	*Enid*	. 242
out of *t* and valley came a noise .	"	. 247
'What means the tumult in the *t*?'	"	. 259
Go to the *t* and buy us flesh .	"	. 372
across the bridge, And reach'd the *t*,	"	. 384
into that new fortress by your *t*,	"	. 407
thought to find Arms in your *t*,	"	. 418
Raised my own *t* against me .	"	. 457
by and by the *t* Flow'd in .	"	. 546
Went Yniol thro' the *t*,	"	. 693
Scatter'd thro' the houses of the *t*;	"	. 695
beheld A little *t* with towers .	"	. 1046
Did you know Enoch Arden of this *t*?'	*En. Arden*	846
one of our *t*, but later by an hour .	*Sea Dreams*	254
High *t*'s on hills were dimly seen .	*The Voyage*	34
By every *t* and tower, .	*The Flower*	11

toy.

| *t*'s in lava, fans Of sandal, . | *Princess, Pro.* | 18 |
| The tricks, which make us *t*'s of men | " | ii. 49 |

trace.

| And silent *t*'s of the past . | *In Mem.* xlii. | 7 |

traced.

in her raiment's hem was *t* in flame	*The Poet*	45
deep-set windows, stained and *t*, .	*Pal. of Art* .	49
might as well have *t* it in the sands ;	*Audley Ct.*	49
as he *t* a faintly-shadowed track, .	*Elaine*	165

trachyte.

| trap and tuff. Amygdaloid and *t*, . | *Princess*, iii. | 345 |

track (s.)

Into that wondrous *t* of dreams .	*D. of F. Wom.*	279
If straight thy *t*, or if oblique, .	*Two Voices*	193
the *t* Whereon we fared with equal feet	*In Mem.*xxv.	1
We ranging down this lower *t*, .	" xlv.	1
Enid leading down the *t*'s .	*Enid* .	877
as he traced a faintly-shadow'd *t*, .	*Elaine*	165
right across its *t* there lay, .	*Sea Dreams*	122

track (verb.)

t Suggestion to her inmost cell, .	*In Mem.*xciv.	31
I will *t* this vermin to their earths :	*Enid* .	217
t this caitiff to his hold, .	"	415
the subtle beast Would *t* her guilt	*Guinevere*	60
impossible, Far as we *t* ourselves .	*Aylmer's F.*	306

tracked.

| *t* you still on classic ground . | *To E. L.* | 10 |
| thought Geraint, 'I have *t* him to | *Enid* . | 253 |

tract.

In the dim *t* of Penuel. 'Clear-headed friend,' etc.		29
all dark and red—a *t* of sand, .	*Pal. of Art*	65
In *t*'s of pasture sunny-warm, .	"	94
many a *t* of palm and rice, .	"	114
overlooks the sandy *t*'s. .	*Locksley H.*	5
sweep the *t*'s of day and night .	*Two Voices*	69
led by *t*'s that pleased us well, .	*In Mem.*xxii.	2
A lifelong *t* of time reveal'd ; .	" xlv.	9
Foreshorten'd in the *t* of time? .	" lxxvi.	4
t's of calm from tempest made .	" cxi.	14
In *t*'s of fluent heat began, .	" cxvii.	9
but thro' all this *t* of years .	*Ded. of Idylls*	23
Faith from *t*'s no feet have trod, .	*On a Mourner*	29

trade (s.)

Another hand crept too across his *t*	*En. Arden* .	110
set Annie forth in *t* .	"	. 138
But throve not in her *t*, .	"	. 248

	POEM.	LINE.
Should he not *t* himself out yonder?	*En. Arden* .	141

traded.

| There Enoch *t* for himself . | *En. Arden* . | 534 |

trader.

| Never comes the *t*, never floats . | *Locksley H.* | 161 |

tradesman.

| faith in a *t*'s ware or his word? . | *Maud*, I. i. | 27 |

tradition.

| as *t* teaches, Young ashes . | *Amphion* . | 26 |
| and made Their own *t*'s God, . | *Aylmer's F.* | 795 |

tragic.

| all things grew more *t* . | *Princess*, vi. | 7 |

trail (s.)

| hunt old *t*'s said Cyril 'very well; | *Princess*, ii. | 368 |

trail (verb.)

slowly *t* himself sevenfold .	*The Mermaid*	25
Clasp her window, *t* and twine, .	*The Window*	22
T and twine, and clasp and kiss .	"	24

trail'd.

barges *t* By slow horses ; .	*L. of Shalott*, i.	20
T himself up on one knee ; .	*Princess*, vi.	139
By a shuffled step, by a dead weight *t*,	*Maud*, I. i.	14

trailer.

| bell-like flower Of fragrant *t*'s, . | *Eleänore* . | 38 |
| swings the *t* from the crag ; . | *Locksley H.* | 162 |

trailing.

| Some bearded meteor, *t* light, . | *L. of Shalott*, iii. | 26 |

train (succession, etc.)

Nor any *t* of reason keep : .	*Two Voices*	50
old-world *t*'s, upheld at court .	*Day-Dm.* .	277
Last of the *t*, a moral leper, I, .	*Princess*, iv.	203
A hundred maids in *t* across the Park	" vi.	60
behind, A *t* of dames : .	"	vii. 113
all the *t* of bounteous hours .	*In Mem.* lxxxiii.	30
Memnius in a *t* of flowery clauses	*Lucretius* .	119

train (railway carriages.)

| I waited for the *t* at Coventry ; . | *Godiva* . | 1 |

train (verb.)

| to *t* the rose-bush that I set . | *May Queen*, ii. | 47 |
| *t* To riper growth the mind . | *In Mem.* xli. | 7 |

training.

| The bearing and the *t* of a child . | *Princess*, v. | 455 |

trait.

| From talk of war to *t*'s of pleasantry | *Elaine* . | 320 |

traitor.

sweeter dews than *t*'s tear. .	*A Dirge* .	24
that there be no *t*'s in your camp :	*Princess*, v.	415
We seem a nest of *t*'s .	"	416
Dear *t*, too much loved, why ? .	" vi.	275
And all thro' that young *t*, .	*Enid* .	715
make good fellows fools And *t*'s. .	"	1249
Sir Lancelot, friend ? *T* or true ?	*Vivien* .	620
shriek'd out '*t*' to the unhearing wall,	*Elaine*	609
Courtesy with a touch of *t* in it .	"	636
'*T*, come out, ye are trapt at last,	*Guinevere* .	105
left in charge of all, The *t*—.	"	194
this false *t* have displaced his lord .	"	214
So foul a *t* to myself and her, .	*Aylmer's F.*	319

traitor-hearted.

| unkind, untrue, Unknightly, *t-h* ! | *M. d'Arthur* | 120 |

traitress.

| If I be such a *t*. . | *Vivien* . | 201 |
| to harry me, petty spy, And *t*. . | *Guinevere* . | 359 |

tram.

| laying his *t*'s in a poison'd gloom | *Maud*, I. x. | 8 |

tramp.

| To *t*, to scream, to burnish . | *Princess*, iv. | 499 |

trample.

To *t* round my fallen head, 'Come not, when,' etc.		3
I *t* on your offers and on you ; .	*Princess*, iv.	525
Behold me overturn and *t* on him.	*Enid* .	1691

	POEM.	LINE.
'*T*me, Dear feet, that I have follow'd	*Vivien*	75
on my chargers, *t* them under us.'	*Boädicea*	69
trampled.		
t some beneath her horses' heels,	*Princess,Pro.*	44
a spark of will Not to be *t* out.	*Maud*, II. ii.	57
trampling.		
t the flowers With clamour	*Princess,* v.	237
great self seekers *t* on the right:	*Ode on Well.*	187
charger *t* many a prickly star	*Enid*	313
trance (s.)		
Like some bold seër in a *t*,	*L. of Shalott,* iv.	11
I muse, as in a *t*,	*Eleänore*	72-5
her, who clasp'd in her last *t*	*D. of F. Wom*	266
The *t* gave way To those caresses,	*Love and Duty*	63
As here we find in *t*'s, men	*Two Voices*	352
Until they fall in *t* again.	"	354
but lay like one in *t*,	*Princess,* vii.	136
In some long *t* should slumber on	*In Mem* xlii.	4
kinsman thou to death and *t*	" lxx.	1
At length my *t* Was cancell'd,	" xciv.	43
the Queen immersed in such a *t*,	*Guinevere*	398
trance (verb.)		
thickest dark did *t* the sky	*Mariana*	18
tranced.		
So *t*, so rapt in ecstacies,	*Eleänore*	78
Hung *t* from all pulsation	*Gardener's D.*	255
We stood *t* in long embraces	*Maud,* II. iv.	8
nature fail'd a little And he lay *t*	*En. Arden*	794
tranquillity.		
Marr'd her friend's point with pale *t*.	*Elaine*	729
O Thou, Passionless bride, divine *T*,	*Lucretius*	262
transfer.		
foolish sleep *t*'s to thee.	*In Mem.* lxvii	16
t The whole I felt for him to you.	" lxxxiv.	103
transfixt.		
So lay the man *t*.	*Enid*	1015
transfused.		
but *t* Thro' future time 'Love thou thy land,' etc.		3
transgression.		
So for every light *t*	*The Captain*	11
transient.		
Away we stole, and *t* in a trice	*Princess,* v.	37
transit.		
wing'd Her *t* to the throne	*Princess,* iv.	359
transmitter.		
The one *t* of their ancient name,	*Aylmer's F.*	296
transplanting.		
And Methods of *t* trees,	*Amphion*	79
transport.		
But heard, by secret *t* led,	*Two Voices*	214
Me mightier *t*'s move and thrill;	*Sir Galahad*	22
stirring a sudden *t* rose and fell.	*Princess,* iv.	11
trap stone.)		
horneblende, rag and *t* and tuff,	*Princess,* iii.	344
trap (snare)		
As of a wild thing taken in the *t*,	*Enid*	1571
trap verb.)		
Christ the bait to *t* his dupe.	*Sea Dreams*	187
trapper		
sees the *t* coming thro' the wood.	*Enid*	1572
trapt adorned		
there she found her palfrey *t*	*Godiva*	51
trapt snared.)		
'Traitor, come out, ye are *t* at last,'	*Guinevere*	105
trash.		
talk'd The *t* that made me sick,	*Princess,* ii.	372
'O *t*,' he said ' but with a kernel in it'	"	373
Trath Treroit.		
the waste sand-shores of *T T*	*Elaine*	301

	POEM.	LINE.
travel (s.)		
I cannot rest from *t* :	*Ulysses*	6
if it had not been For a chance of *t Maud*, I. ii.		8
overtoil'd By that day's grief and *t*,	*Enid*	1226
travel (verb.)		
blasts of balm To one that *t*'s quickly	*Gardener's D.*	68
He *t*'s far from other skies—	*Day-Dm.*	105
foamy flake Upon me, as I *t*	*The Brook*	60
traveller.		
in strange lands a *t* walking slow,	*Pal. of Art*	277
The *t* hears me now and then,	*In Mem.* xxi.	5
traveller's-joy.		
Was parcel-bearded with the *t-j*	*Aylmer's F.*	153
travelling.		
quite worn out, *T* to Naples.	*The Brook*	35
His kinsman *t* on his own affair	*Vivien*	567
traversed.		
Deep meadows we had *t*	*Vivien*	132
treachery.		
tript on such conjectural *t*—.	*Vivien*	198
tread (s.)		
Were it ever so airy a *t*	*Maud.* I. xxii.	68
tread (verb.)		
t softly and speak low,	*D. of the O. Year*	4
ere the hateful crow shall *t*	*Will Water.*	235
While he *t*'s with footstep firmer,	*L. of Burleigh*	51
Freedom, gaily doth she *t* ;	*Vision of Sin*	136
T a measure on the stones,	"	180
flickers where no foot can *t*.'	*Princess,* iv.	339
And *t* you on for ever :	" vi.	160
touch upon a sphere Too gross to *t*,	" vii.	306
The solid earth whereon we *t*	*In Mem.* cxvii.	8
t me down And I will kiss you for it;'	*Vivien*	77
treading.		
Then her people, softly *t*,	*L. of Burleigh*	97
treason.		
says the song 'I trow it is no *t*'	*Vivien*	573
doom of *t* and the flaming death,	*Guinevere*	534
treasure-house.		
in some *t-h* of mighty kings,	*M. d'Arthur*	101
treasure-trove.		
Found for himself a bitter *t-t*;	*Aylmer's F.*	515
Thro' the dim meadows toward his *t-t*,	"	531
treasuring.		
T the look it cannot find	*In Mem.* xviii.	19
treat.		
all That *t*'s of whatsoever is,	*Princess,* ii.	358
t Of all things ev'n as he were by ;	*In Mem.* cvi.	19
t their loathsome hurts and heal	*Guinevere*	678
treated.		
Too awful, sure, for what they *t* of,	*Princess,* i.	138
waiting to be *t* like a wolf,	*Enid*	1705
treatise.		
They read botanic *T*'s,	*Amphion*	77
treble.		
With blissful *t* ringing clear.	*Sir L, and Q. G.*	22
tempestuous *t* throbb'd and palpitated	*Vision of Sin*	28
liquid *t* of that bassoon, my throat ;	*Princess,* ii.	404
as far As I could ape their *t*,	" iv.	74
In little sharps and *t*'s,	*The Brook*	40
trebled.		
Love *t* life within me,	*Gardener's D.*	194
tree for cedar tree see *cedar*		
no other *t* did mark The level waste	*Mariana*	43
Rain makes music in the *t*	*A Dirge*	26
as the *t* Stands in the sun	*Love and Death*	10
shadow passeth when the *t* shall fall,	"	14
Thou liest beneath the greenwood *t*	*Oriana*	95
wind is blowing in turret and *t* rep.	*The Sisters*	3
On dewy pastures, dewy *t*'s,	*Pal. of Art*	81
the leaf upon the *t*.	*May Queen*, ii	8
The *t*'s began to whisper,	" iii.	27

	POEM.	LINE.
Their humid arms festooning *t* to *t*,	*D. of F. Wom.*	70
because he was The finest on the *t*.	*Talking O.*	238
Thou art the fairest-spoken *t*	"	263
hangs the heavy-fruited *t*— .	*Locksley H.*	163
A garden too with scarce a *t*,	*Amphion*	3
And legs of *t*'s were limber, .	"	14
Like some great landslip, *t* by *t* .	"	51
And Methods of transplanting *t*'s,	"	79
Then move the *t*'s, the copses nod,	*Sir Galahad*	77
fly, like a bird, from *t* to *t*: .	*Ed. Gray*	30
dies unheard within his *t*, 'You might have won' etc.		32
green gleam of dewy-tassell'd *t*'s:	*Princess,* i.	93
A *t* Was half-disrooted from his place	" iv.	167
across the lawns Beneath huge *t*'s	" v.	227
lo the *t*! But we will make it faggots	" vi.	28
From the high *t* the blossom wavering	"	64
And gazing on thee, sullen *t*,	*In Mem.* ii.	13
wildly dash'd on tower and *t*	" xv.	7
Within the green the moulder'd *t*.	" xxvi.	7
t's Laid their dark arms .	" xciv.	15,51
My love has talk'd with rocks and *t*'s;	" xcvi.	1
rolls the deep where grew the *t*.	" cxxii.	1
on the *t*'s The dead leaf trembles	" *Con.*	63
One long milk-bloom on the *t*;	*Maud,* I. xxii.	46
t that shone white-listed thro' the gloom.	*Vivien*	788
The moving whisper of huge *t*'s .	*En. Arden*	586
On the nigh-naked *t* the Robin piped	"	677
the family *t* Sprang from the midriff	*Aylmer's F.*	15
also set his many-shielded *t*?	"	48
Once grovelike, each huge arm a *t*	"	510
t's As high as heaven, .	*Sea Dreams*	99
by rock and cave and *t*,	*V. of Cauteretz*	9
bud ever breaks into bloom on the *t*,	*The Islet*	32

tree-tops.
On the *t-t*'s a crested peacock lit	*Œnone*	102

trellis-work.
birds Of sunny plume in gilded *t-w* ;	*Enid*	650

tremble.
stars which *t* O'er the deep mind .	*Ode to Mem.*	35
the jewel That *t*'s at her ear .	*Miller's D.*	172
leaves That *t* round a nightingale—	*Gardener's D.*	249
Begins to weep and *t*. .	*Will Water.*	32
and *t* deeper down, And slip at once,	*Princess,* vii.	54
In that fine air I *t*, .	"	333
A breeze began to *t* o'er .	*In Mem.* xciv.	54
They *t*, the sustaining crags; .	" cxxvi.	11
The dead leaf *t*'s to the bells. .	" *Con.*	64
Would start and *t* under her feet,	*Maud,* I. xxii.	73
tender air made *t* in the hedge .	*The Brook*	202
make me *t* lest a saying learnt, .	*Tithonus*	47

trembled.
Lovingly lower, *t* on her waist .	*Gardener's D.*	130
A teardrop *t* from its source, .	*Talking O.*	161
voluptuous music winding *t*, .	*Vision of Sin*	17
And the voice *t* and the hand. .	*Princess,* vii.	212
T in perilous places o'er a deep : .	*Sea Dreams*	11

tremblest.
Who *t* thro' thy darkling red .	*In Mem.* xcviii.	5

trembling.
ever *t* thro' the dew .	*Margaret*	52
t, pass'd in music out of sight. .	*Locksley H.*	34
weird bright eye, sweating and *t*,	*Aylmer's F.*	585

trench.
shovell'd up into a bloody *t* .	*Audley Ct.*	41

trenched.
Nor quarry *t* along the hill, .	*In Mem.* xcix.	11

trencher.
tender little thumb That crost the *t*	*Enid* .	396

trespass-chiding.
slink From ferule and the *t-c* eye,	*Princess,* v.	36

tress.
see thee roam, with *t*'es unconfined,	*Eleänore*	122
The fragrant *t*'es are not stirr'd .	*Day-Dm.*	95
Love, if thy *t*'es be so dark, .	"	131

	POEM.	LINE.
picture by my heart, And one dark *t*;	*Princess,* i.	78
all her autumn *t*'es falsely brown,	" ii.	426
from my neck the painting and the *t*	" vi.	94
good Queen, her mother, shore the *t*	"	97

tressed.
T with redolent ebony .	*Arabian N's.*	138

trial.
Girl after girl was call'd to *t*:	*Princess,* iv.	209
and true love Crown'd after *t*; .	*Aylmer's F.*	100

tribe.
A *t* of women, dress'd in many hues	*Enid*	1446
Shun the wild ways of the lawless *t*	"	1456
twelve-divided concubine To inflame the *t*'s .	*Aylmer's F.*	752
Girt by half the *t*'s of Britain .	*Boädicea*	5
They that scorn the *t*'s and call us	"	7

tribute.
The filter'd *t* of the rough woodland	*Ode to Mem.*	63

trick.
'I see it is a *t* Got up betwixt you	*Dora*	93
'Play me no *t*'s, said Lord Ronald	*Lady Clare*	73-5
The *t*'s, which make us toys of men,	*Princess,* ii.	49
a lying *t* of the brain? .	*Maud,* II. i.	77
your pretty *t* s and fooleries, .	*Vivien*	114

trickling.
t dropwise from the cleft, .	*Vivien*	123

tried.
This dress and that by turns you *t*,	*Miller's D.*	247
I *t* the mother's heart. .	*Princess,* iii.	131
have often *t* Valkyrian hymns .	" iv.	120
I your old friend and *t*, she new .	"	299
O true in word, and *t* in deed,	*In Mem.* lxxxiv.	5
O true and *t*, so well and long, .	" *Con.*	1
Strange, that *I t* to-day .	*Maud,* I. xx.	2
On all those who *t* and fail'd .	*Vivien*	440
And many *t* and fail'd .	"	445
if I *t* it, who should blame me then?'	"	511
frail bark of ours, when sorely *t* .	*Aylmer's F.*	715

trifle (s.)
A *t*, sweet! which true love spells—	*Miller's D.*	187
Like one with any *t* pleased. .	*In Mem.* lxv.	4
They chatter *t*'s at the door: .	" lxviii.	4
A *t* makes a dream, a *t* breaks.'	*Sea Dreams*	140
'No *t*,' groan'd the husband .	"	141
There is but a *t* left you, .	*Grandmother*	107
singing airy *t*'s this or that, .	*Coquette,* :.	2

trifle (verb.)
gentlemen, That *t* with the cruet.	*Will Water.*	232
thought that Philip did but *t* with her;	*En. Arden*	472

trifled.
Or like a king not to be *t* with— .	*Vivien*	443

trill.
Upon her lattice, I would pipe and *t*,	*Princess,* iv.	82
That hears the latest linnet *t*, .	*In Mem.* xcix.	10

trilleth.
Silver-treble laughter *t*: .	*Lilian*	24

trim (adj.)
sward was *t* as any garden lawn :	*Princess, Pro.*	95

trim (verb.)
have a dame indoors, that *t*'s us up,	*Ed. Morris*	46
t our sails, and let old bygones be,	*Princess,* iv.	51

trinket.
And gave the *t*'s and the rings .	*The Letters*	21

Trinobant.
hear Coritanian, *T*! (rep.) .	*Boädicea*	10
have answer'd, Catieuchlanian, *T*.	"	22

trip.
To *t* a tigress with a gossamer, .	*Princess,* v.	163
tho' he *t* and fall He shall not blind	"	311
made my tongue so stammer and *t*	*Maud,* I. vi.	83
My tongue *T*'s or I speak profanely	*Lucretius*	74

tripod.
on a *t* in the midst A fragrant flame	*Princess,* iv.	15

tript.	POEM.	LINE
t on such conjectural treachery	*Vivien*	168
methinks, Your tongue has *t* a little ;	"	452
That Jenny had *t* in her time :	*Grandmother*	26

Tristram.
after Lancelot, *T.* and Geraint . . *Elaine* . 555
came the sin of *T* and Isolt . . *Guinevere* . 484

triumph (s.)
like a bride of old In *t* led . . . *Ode to Mem* 76
The herald of her *t* . . . . *Œnone* . 181
wrought With fair Corinna's *t*; . *Princess.* iii. 311
And felt thy *t* was as mine ; . . *In Mem* cix . 14
Peace, his *t* will be sung . . *Ode on Well.* 232
nor cares For *t* in our mimic wars *Elaine* . 312
What Roman would be dragg'd in *t Lucretius* . 231

triumph (verb.)
I *t* in conclusive bliss, . . *In Mem* lxxxiv 91

triumph'd.
So I *t* ere my passion sweeping . *Locksley H.* 131

triumvir.
The fierce *t's*; and before them paused *Princess,*vii 116

Troas
reveal *T.* and Ilion's column'd citadel
The crown of *T.* . . . . *Œnone* . 13

trod.
Old footsteps *t* the upper floors, . *Mariana* . 67
t on silk, as if the winds . . *A Character* . 21
They should have *t* me into clay. . *Oriana* . 62
over these she *t*: and those great bells *Pal of Art*137
Upon an ampler dunghill *t* . . *Will Water.* 125
I falter where I firmly *t*, . . *In Mem* liv . 13
the path that each man *t* Is dim, . " lxxii. 9
man that with me *t* This planet, . *Con.* . 137
up the steep hill *T* out a path : . *Sea Dreams* 117
Faith from tracts no feet have *t*, . *On a Mourner* 29

trodden.
Had *t* that crown'd skeleton, . *Elaine* . 50

trode
On burnish'd hooves his war-horse *t*; *L. of Shalott,*iii.29

Trojan
tempt The *T.* while his neat-herds *Lucretius* . 88

troil.
To *t* a careless, careless tavern-catch *Princess,*iv. 139

troop.
Sometimes a *t* of damsels glad . *L. of Shalott,*ii. 19
t's of devils, mad with blasphemy, *St.S.Stylites* . 4
Thro' *t's* of unrecording friends, *You might,has e won* 7
A *t* of snowy doves athwart the dusk *Princess,*iv. 150
many weeks a *t* of carrion crows . *Vivien* . 448

trooping.
T from their mouldy dens . . *Vision of Sin* 171

troth.
I to thee my *t* did plight, . . *Oriana* . 26
Will I to Olive plight my *t*, . . *Talking O.* 283
wherefore break her *t?* . . *Princess,* i. 94
then this question of your *t* remains : " 269
some pretext held Of baby *t*, . . " 388
plighted *t*, and were at peace. . " vii. 68
The heart that never plighted *t* . *In Mem* xxvii. 10
Forgetful of their *t* and fealty . *Guinevere* . 437

trouble.
T on *t*, pain on pain . . . *Lotos-Es.* . 129
shouldst take my *t* on thyself ; . *Dora* . 116
never know The *t's* I have gone thro' I " . 147
a lip to drain thy *t* dry . . *Locksley H.* 88
Whose *t's* number with his days : *Two Voices* 330
We drink defying *t*, . . . *Will Water.* . 94
But a *t* weigh'd upon her, . *L.of Burleigh* 77
clouds of nameless *t* cross . . *In Mem.* iv . 13
An inner *t* I behold, . . . " lxvii. 10
I find a *t* in thine eye . . . " . 15
It is the *t* of my youth . . . " . 15
Can *t* live with April days . . " lxxxii. 7

A world of *t* within !	POEM.	L.N.E.
	Maud, I. six	23
lost in *t* and moving round	" xxi	5
dear soul, let *t* have rest,	" III. vi.	12
forge a life-long *t* for ourselves,	*Enid*	852
t which has left me thrice your own:	"	1585
Before the useful *t* of the rain :	"	1619
all this *t* did not pass but grew ;	*Guinevere*	84
his *t* had all been in vain	*Grandmother*	26
thankful that his *t's* are no more	*Lucretius*	143
No is *t* and cloud and storm	*The Window*	113

trouble (verb.)
should come like ghosts to *t* joy. . *Lotos-Es.* . 119
To *t* the heart of Edward Gray. . *Ed. Gray* . 10
Be still, for you only *t* the mind . *Maud,* I. v. . 20

troubled
Grow long and *t* like a rising moon *Princess,* i. 58
His dear little face was *t*, . . *Grandmother* 65
Being *t*, wholly out of sight . *Lucretius* . 152

trouble-tost.
I lull a fancy *t-t* . . . . *In Mem.* lxiv. 2

troubling.
And the wicked cease from *t* . *MayQueen,*iii. 60

trout.
Then leapt a *t.* In lazy mood . *Miller's D.* 73
he caught the younker tickling *t—Walk. to the M.* 25
here and there a lusty *t*, . . *The Brook* . 57

Troy.
I will rise and go Down into *T.* . *Œnone* . 258
the ten years' war in *T*, . . *Lotos-Es.* . 122
on the ringing plains of windy *T.* . *Ulysses* . 17
blazed before the towers of *T*, . *Spec. of Iliad* 18
did greet *T's* wandering prince . *On a Mourner* 33

truck.
Grimy nakedness dragging his *t's Maud,* I. x. . 7

true
'Love,' they said, 'must needs be *t*,*Mariana in the S.*63
this be *t*, till Time shall close . *Love thou tayland* 79
Yet this is also *t*, that, long before *Gardener's D.* 60
''Tis *t*, we met : one hour I had, . *Ed. Morris* 104
undo One riddle and to find the *t*, *Two Voices* 233
Yet glimpses of the *t*. . . *Will Water.* 60
'O mother,' she said, 'if this be *t*, *Lady Clare* . 30
'*T*,' she said, 'We doubt not that *Princess,*Pro 166
there was a compact : that was *t*; " 1. 46
dark and *t* and tender is the North " iv. 80
To such as her ! if Cyril spake her *t*, " v. 161
As *t* to thee as false, false, false to me " vi. 187
flashes into false and *t*, . . *In Mem* xvi. 19
I hold it *t*, whate'er befall ; . " xxvii. 13
What keeps a spirit wholly *t* . " li. 9
Who battled for the *T*, the Just . " lv. 18
thou wert strong as thou wert *t ?* . " lxxii. 4
O *t* in word, and tried in deed, . " lxxxiv. 5
If not so fresh, with love as *t*, . " . 101
Should prove the phantom-warning *t*, " xci. 12
But ever strove to make it *t ?* . " xcv. 8
Ring out the false, ring in the *t*, . " cv. 8
dream my dream, and hold it *t* ; . " cxxii. 10
O *t* and tried so well and long, . *Con.* . 1
Maud is as *t* as Maud is sweet : . *Maud,* I. xii. 32
a cause that I felt to be pure and *t* " III. vi. 31
O iron nerve to *t* occasion *t.* . *Ode on Well.* . 37
we doubt not that for one so *t* . " . 255
if ever yet was wife *T* to her lord *Enid* . 47
taking *t* for false, and false for *t*, " . 853
dress her beautifully and keep her *t* " . 889
And half believe her *t*: . . *Vivien* 42, 250, 742
Lancelot, friend? Traitor or *t ?* . " . 620
O *t* and tender ! O my liege . . " . 640
Have all men *t* and leal, all women pure " . 643
what shame in love, So love be *t*, " . 711
faith unfaithful kept him falsely *t*. *Elaine* . 873
then will I, for *t* you are and sweet " . 950
for good she was and *t*, . . " . 1284
Too wholly *t* to dream untruth . *Guinevere* . 537
like proven golden coinage *t* . *Aylmer's F.* 182
She must prove *t* : . . . " . 364

	POEM.	LINE.
he partly took himself for *t*;	Sea Dreams	181
for a says what's nawways *t*;	N. Farmer.	5
far-off, on that dark earth, be *t*?	Tithonus	48
Dear, near, and *t*—no truer.	A Dedication	1

true-heroic.

why Not make her *t-h*—	Princess, Con.	20

true-love.

He gave me a friend, and a true *t-l*,	D. of the O. Year	13

truer.

t to the law within?	Princess, v.	181
be *t* to your faultless lord?'	Elaine	120
no *t* Time himself Can prove you,	A Dedication	1

truer-hearted.

There is no *t-h*—ah, you seem	Princess, iii.	192

true-sublime.

make her true-heroic—*t-s*?	Princess, Con.	20

trumpet.

And *t*'s blown for wars;	D. of F. Wom.	20
bade him cry, with sound of *t*,	Godiva	36
The shattering *t* shrilleth high	Sir Galahad	5
with a blast of *t*'s from the gate	Princess, Pro.	42
Will topple to the *t* down	" ii.	214
A *t* in the distance pealing news	" iv.	63
A moment, while the *t*'s blow	"	558
With the air of the *t* round him,	" v.	155
till the *t* blared At the barrier	"	474
once more The *t*, and again:	"	477
Altho' the *t* blew so loud	In Mem. xcv.	24
A martial song like a *t*'s call!	Maud, I. v.	5
Last the Prussian *t* blew;	Ode on Well.	127
Yniol's nephew, after *t* blown;	Enid	551
Sound on a dreadful *t*, summoning her;	"	1232
and anon The *t*'s blew;	Elaine	453
Far off a solitary *t* blew.	Guinevere	525
Thro' the thick night I hear the *t*	"	565
Warble, O bugle, and *t* blare!	W. to Alexan.	14
Lady, let the *t*'s blow 'Lady, let the rolling,' etc.		5

trumpet-blowings.

Such fire for fame, Such *t-b* in it.	Vivien	268

trumpeter.

blew the swoll'n cheek of a *t*,	Princess, ii.	343

trundled.

Her mother *t* to the gate	Talking O.,	111

trunk.

Ruin'd *t*'s on wither'd forks,	Vision of Sin	93

trust (s.)

fallen from hope and *t*:	D. of F. Wom.	257
breathing love and *t* against her lip;	Audley Ct.	68
Go, vexed Spirit, sleep in *t*;	Two Voices	115
lock and seal; betray the *t*: 'You might have won'		18
t in all things high Comes easy	Princess, vii.	310
rack'd with pangs that conquer *t*;	In Mem. xlix.	6
whether *t* in things above He dimm'd	" lxxxiv.	9
Cry thro' the sense to hearten *t*.	" cxv.	7
why not? I have neither hope nor *t*;	Maud, I. 1.	30
Godlike men we build our *t*.	Ode on Well.	266
As proof of *t*. O, Merlin, teach it me	Vivien	180
feeling that you felt me worthy *t*.	"	183
curious Vivien, tho' you talk of *t*.	"	208
if you talk of *t* I tell you this,	"	210
Vivien had not done to win his *t*.	"	712
That proof of *t*—so often ask'd in vain!	"	769
Should have in it an absoluter *t*.	Elaine	1186
On providence and *t* in Heaven,	En. Arden	205

trust (verb.)

I could *t* Your kindness.	To the Queen	19
'*T* me, in bliss I shall abide	Pal. of Art	18
T me, Clara Vere de Vere	L. C. V. de Vere	49
I think my time is near. I *t* it is	May Queen, iii.	41
I *t* That I am whole and clean,	St S. Stylites	209
t me on my word, Hard wood I am	Talking O.	170
T me, cousin, all the current	Lockslcy H.	24
He *t*'s to light on something fair;	Day-Dm.	120
t me while I turn'd the page,	To E. L.	9

	POEM.	LINE.
'I *t* you' said that other 'for we two	Princess, ii.	315
all, I *t*, may yet be well.'	"	340
t that you esteem'd us not Too harsh	"	iii. 182
To harm the thing that *t*'s him,	"	iv. 229
none to *t* Since our arms fail'd—	"	v. 416
I *t* that there is no one hurt to death	"	vi. 225
And *t*, not love, you less.	"	278
sweet hands in mine and *t* to me.	"	vii. 345
And yet we *t* it comes from thee	In Mem. Pro.	23
I *t* he lives in thee,	"	39
if some voice that man could *t*	" xxxv.	1
Nor dare she *t* a larger lay,	" xlvii.	13
we *t* that somehow good	" liii.	1
I can but *t* that good shall fall	"	14
And faintly *t* the larger hope.	" liv.	20
t that those we call the dead	" cxvii.	5
I *t* I have not wasted breath:	" cxix.	1
To one that with us works, and *t*,	" cxxx.	8
I *t* if an enemy's fleet came yonder	Maud, I. i.	49
I *t* that it is not so.	" xvi.	30
I *t* that I did not talk	" xix. 12,16
Henceforth I *t* the man alone	The Letters	31
'*t* me not at all or all in all'	Vivien 234-48-99
as I *t* That you *t* me.	Elaine	1188
from the nursery—who could *t* a child?	Aylmer's F.	264
first I fronted him Said '*t* him not;'	Sea Dreams	71
May *t* himself; and spite of praise	A Dedication	6

trusted.

declined, And *t* any cure:	Pal. of Art	156
Who *t* God was love indeed	In Mem. lv.	13
Too much I *t*, when I told you that,	Vivien	211
by God's rood, I *t* you too much.'	"	226
Have I not sworn? I am not *t*	"	377
A woman and not *t*,	"	380
To have *t* me as he has *t* you	Elaine	589
t as he was with her,	Aylmer's F.	293
fool! and *t* him with all,	Sea Dreams	76

trustee.

T's and Aunts and Uncles.	Ed. Morris	121

truth.

Fair-fronted *T* shall droop not 'Clear-headed friend'	12
Weak *T* a-leaning on her crutch	"	18
wasted *T* in her utmost need	"	19
The winged shafts of *t*,	The Poet	26
Thus *t* was multiplied on *t*,	"	33
Not less than *t* design'd.	Pal. of Art	92
She spake some certain *t*'s of you.	L. C. V. de Vere	36
Her open eyes desire the *t*.	'Of old sat Freedom'	1
follow flying steps of *T* 'Love thou thy land,' etc.	75
a *t* Looks freshest in the fashion.	The Epic	31
to feel the *t* and stir of day.	M. d'Arthur, Ep.	19
in the round of time Still father *T*?	Love and Duty	5
man feel strong in speaking *t*;	"	91
quiet eyes unfaithful to the *t*,	"	91
t's of Science waiting to be caught	Golden Year	17
speak, and speak the *t* to me,	Locksley H.	23
that warp as from the living *t*!	"	60
this is *t* the poet sings,	"	75
This *t* within thy mind rehearse	Two Voices	25
Still moving after *t* long sought	"	62
Named man, may hope some *t* to find	"	176
Cry, faint not: either *T* is born	"	181
t that sways the soul of men?	Day-Dm.	72
Nor finds a closer *t* than this	"	249
The *t*, that flies the flowing can,	I Will Water.	171
I speak the *t*: you are my child. (rep.)	Lady Clare	24
point you out the shadow from the *t*!	Princess, i.	83
to speak the *t*, I rate your chance	"	159
so mask'd, Madam, I love the *t*;	" ii.	195
So my mother clutch'd The *t* at once,	" iii.	45
To blind the *t* and me:	"	96
I know the Prince, I prize his *t*:	"	217
dream and *t* Flow'd from me;	" v.	530
call her hard and cold which seem'd a *t*:	" vii.	83
less for *t* than power In knowledge,	"	221
but the needful preludes of the *t*:	Con.	74
Forgive them where they fail in *t*,	In Mem. Pro.	43
I held it *t* with him who sings	" i.	1
To which she links a *t* divine!	" xxxiii.	12

	POEM	LINE
Tho' *t*'s in manhood darkly join,	*In Mem.* xxxvi.	1
t in closest words shall fail	"	6
comfort clasp'd in *t* reveal'd ;	" xxxvii.	22
reaps A *t* from one that loves	" xli.	12
who would preach it as a *t*	" lii.	11
I wake, and I discern the *t;*	" lxvii.	14
This *t* came borne with bier and pall,	" lxxxiv.	1
Ring in the love of *t* and right,	" cv.	23
Nor dream of human love and *t*,	" cxvii.	3
Because he felt so fix'd in *t*,	" cxxiv.	8
Proclaiming social *t* shall spread,	" cxxvi.	5
The *t*'s that never can be proved	" cxxx.	10
I have walk'd awake with *T*.	*Maud*, I. xix.	4
never sold the *t* to serve the hour,	*Ode on Well.*	179
for shall I tell you *t?* You seem'd	*Vivien*	150
I tell you the clean *t*,	"	193
not found it therefore : take the *t.*'	"	569
Urged him to speak against the *t*	*Elaine*	93
In lieu of idly dallying with the *t*	"	988
I swear by *t* and knighthood that I gave	"	1289
love of *t*, and all that makes a man.	*Guinevere*	479
Trying his *t* and his long-sufferance	*En. Arden*	467
t and love are strength,	*Aylmer's F.*	365
That a lie which is half a *t*	*Grandmother*	30-2
I know for a *t*, there's none of them	"	85
So I pray you tell the *t* to me.	*The Victim.*	50
To make a *t* less harsh,	*Lucretius*	222
golden work in which I told a *t*	"	256

truth-lover.
T-*l* was our English Duke ; . *Ode on Well.* 189

truthful.
half as good, as kind, As *t*, . *Princess*, v. 194

truth-teller.
T-*t* was our England's Alfred named; *Ode on Well.* 188

try.
Twere well to question him, and *t*	*Talking O.*	27
thro' the questions men may *t*,	*In Mem.* cxxiii.	7
tries the bridge he fears may fail,	*Enid*	1152
t this charm on whom you say you love.'	*Vivien*	375

trying.
| And *t* to pass to the sea ; | *Maud*, I xxi. | 7 |
| T his truth and his long-sufferance, | *En. Arden* | 467 |

tryst.
That ever bided *t* at village stile. *Vivien* . 228

Tudor-chimnied.
a T-*c* bulk Of mellow brickwork. *Ed. Morris.* 11

tuff.
hornblende, rag and trap and *t*, *Princess*, iii. 344

tuft (s.)
yon whispering *t* of oldest pine	*Œnone*	86
In *t*'s of rosy-tinted snow ;	*Two Voices*	60
A light-green *t* of plumes she bore	*Sir L. and Q. G*	26

tuft (verb.)
| When rosy plumelets *t* the larch, | *In Mem.* xc. | 1 |
| And *t* with grass a feudal tower ; | " cxxvii. | 20 |

tulip.
| sometimes a Dutch love For *t*'s | *Gardener's D.* | 189 |
| Deep *t*'s dash'd with fiery dew, | *In Mem.* lxxxii. | 11 |

tumble (s.)
with her venturous climbings and *t*'s	*Maud*, I. i.	67
after a long *t* about the Cape	*En. Arden*	528
Should I flounder awhile without a *t*	*Hendecasyllabics*	9

tumble (verb.)
mounted Ganymedes, To *t*, Vulcans,	*Princess*, iii.	56
Dark bulks that *t* half alive,	*In Mem.* lxix.	11
T's a breaker on chalk and sand ;	*To F. D. Maurice*	24
like a crag that *t*'s from the cliff,	*Enid*	318
Lest he should swoon and *t*	*En. Arden*	775
hard, hard is it only not to *t*.	*Hendecasyllabics*	13
how they *t* the blossom, the mad little	*The Window*	152

tumbled.
| the fragments *t* from the glens | *Œnone* | 218 |
| And half the chimneys *t*. | *The Goose* | 48 |

	POEM	LINE
every Muse *t* a science in.	*Princess*, ii.	377
t on the purple footcloth	" iv.	267
had a cousin *t* on the plain	" vi.	299
t half the mellowing pears !	*In Mem.* lxxxviii.	20
That *t* in the Godless deep ;.	" cxxiii.	12
T the tawny rascal at his feet,	*Aylmer's F.*	230
you *t* down and broke The glass	*Sea Dreams*	137

tumult.
t of their acclaim is roll'd	*Dying Swan*	33
Laid by the *t* of the fight.	*Margaret*	26
and the *t* of my life	*Locksley H.*	110
call'd Across the *t* and the *t* fell	*Princess*, iv.	476
The cataract and the *t* and the kings	"	542
Is wrought with *t* of acclaim.	*In Mem.* lxxiv.	20
And saw the *t* of the halls ;	" lxxxvi.	4
O'erlook'st the *t* from afar,	" cxxvi.	19
For a *t* shakes the city,	*Maud*, II. iv.	50
What means the *t* in the town ?'	*Enid*	259
ate with *t* in the naked hall,	"	1453
in an hour Of civic *t* jam the doors.	*Lucretius*	10

tumultuously.
t Down thro' the whitening hazels *En. Arden* . 375

tune.
Their hearts of old have beat in *t*,	*In Mem.* xcvi.	10
wildest wailings never out of *t*	*Sea Dreams*	224
howl in *t* With nothing but the Devil	"	252

Turbia.
What Roman strength T show'd . *The Daisy* . 5

turbulence.
in that realm of lawless *t*, . *Enid* . 1370

turbulent.
I that knew him fierce and *t* . *Enid* . 447

turf ('s.)
| In cool soft *t* upon the bank, | *Arabian N's.* | 96 |
| all the *t* was rich in plots | *Enid* | 660 |

turf 'verb.)
after furious battle *t*'s the slain . *Vivien* . 507

turkis.
| T and agate and almondine : | *The Merman* | 32 |
| Each like a garnet or a *t* in it ; | *Enid* | 661 |

turn (s.)
thro' many a bowery *t*	*Arabian N's.*	56
In every elbow and *t*	*Ode to Mem.*	62
Every *t* and glance of thine	*Eleanore*	52
Some *t* this sickness yet might take	*Two Voices*	55
with every *t* Lived thro' her.	*Princess*, ii.	25
made a sudden *t* As if to speak	" iv.	375
Katie, once I did her a good *t*,	*The Brook.*	74
As some wild *t* of anger,	*Vivien*	378
Might feel some sudden *t* of anger	"	381
'Mine too' said Philip '*t* and *t* about.'	*En. Arden*	29
Has given all my faith a *t t* .	*The Ringlet*	52

turn (verb.)
But when I *t* away	*Madeline*	36
did I *t* away The boat-head.	*Arabian N's.*	24
Fold thine arms, *t* to thy rest,	*A Dirge*	3
Thou wilt not *t* upon thy bed	"	15
'T and look on me :	*D. of F. Wom.*	250
as a thorn T's from the sea ;	*Audley Ct.*	54
t the horses' heads and home again	*Walk. to the M.*	38
I *t* to yonder oak	*Talking O.*	8
lightly *t*'s to thoughts of love.	*Locksley H.*	20
What is that which I should *t* to	"	99
I will *t* that earlier page.	"	107
I will tell it, T your face,	*Day-Dm.*	11
half the power to *t* This wheel	*Will Water.*	83
And beneath the gate she *t*'s;	*L. of Burleigh*	44
Proudly *t*'s he round and kindly,	"	55
as a parrot *t*'s Up thro' gilt wires.	*Princess, Pro.*	169
The secular emancipation *t*'s	" ii.	42
but brooding *t* The book of scorn	" v.	135
Yet, as it may, *t*'s toward him	" vii.	128
I heard her *t* the page :	"	175
t's Once more to set a ringlet right ;	*In Mem.* vi.	35
I should *t* mine ears and hear	" xxxv.	8

2 E

	POEM.	LINE.		POEM.	LINE.
O *t* thee round, resolve the doubt	*In Mem.*xliii.	14	even then he *t*; and more and more	*Guinevere*	594
Yet *t* thee to the doubtful shore, .	" lx.	9	when he *t* The current of his talk .	*En. Arden* .	202
I *t* about, I find a trouble . .	" lxvii.	9	*t* her own toward the wall and wept.	" .	282
t's a musing eye On songs . .	" lxxvi.	2	There she *t*, She rose, and fixt .	" .	327
t the page that tells A grief, . .	" .	10	crippled lad, and coming *t* to fly,	*Aylmer's F.*	519
t's his burthen into gain . .	" lxxix.	12	half *t* round from him she loved ; .	*Sea Dreams*	274
I *t* to go : my feet are set . .	" ci.	21	he *t*, and I saw his eyes all wet	*Grandmother*	49
Till you should *t* to dearer matters,	*To F. D. Maurice*35		But he *t* and claspt me in his arms,	" .	55
T, Fortune, *t* thy wheel (rep.) .	*Enid* .	347	*T* as he sat, and struck the keys .	*The Islet* .	7
t to fall seaward again . .	" .	966	Pale he *t* and red, . . .	*The Captain*	62
with graver fits, *T* red or pale, .	*Vivien* .	37	And bird in air, and fishes *t* .	*The Victim*	19
in a wink the false love *t*'s to hate)	" .	701			
to all things could he *t* his hand.	*En. Arden* .	814	*turning.*		
Will *t* it silver-gray . .	*The Ringlet* 6,16		*t* round a cassia, full in view .	*Love and Death* 4
Imitates God, and *t*'s her face .	*On a Mourner*	2	And *t* look'd upon your face .	*Miller's D.*	157
t and ponder those three hundred scrolls	*Lucretius*12		*t* yellow Falls, and floats . .	*Lotos-E's.*	75
			t on my face The star-like sorrows	*D. of F. Wom.*	90
turned.			*t* I appeal'd To one that stood .	" .	99
T to tower'd Camelot. . .	*L. of Shalott,* iv.	32	*t* saw, throned on a flowery rise, .	" .	125
where'er she *t* her sight . .	*Pal. of Art*	225	*T* to scorn with lips divine 'Of old sat Freedom,' etc.	23
Growths of jasmine *t* l'heir humid arms.*D. of F. Wom.*69			dropt the branch she held, and *t*, .	*Gardener's D.*154
True love *t* round on fixed poles,	*'Love thou thy land'* 5		*t* round we saw The Lady Blanche's	*Princess,* ii. 299
Eustace *t*, and smiling said to me,	*Gardener's D.*	96	to her maids, 'Pitch our pavilion	" iii. 327
look !' Before he ceased I *t*, .	" .	120	Half *t* to the broken statue, .	" iv. 570
nor from her tendance *t* . .	" .	143	*t* saw The happy valleys, . .	" *Con.* 40
Then he *t* His face and pass'd .	*Dora* .	147	Not *t* round, nor looking at him, .	*Enid* . 270
And all my heart *t* from her, .	*Audley Ct.*	53	the armourer *t* all amazed . .	" . 283
She *t*, we closed, we kiss'd . .	*Ed. Morris*	114	the two Were *t* and admiring it, .	" . 637
fled by night, and flying *t* : .	" .	134	*t* round she saw Dust, and the points	" 1297
I *t* once more, close-button'd .	" .	136	in a manner pleased, and *t*, stood.	" 1305
And *t* the cowls adrift . .	*Talking O.*	48	unswallow'd piece, and *t* stared ; .	" 1479
That show the year is *t* . .	" .	176	Roll'd into light, and *t* on its rims	*Elaine* . 52
And she *t*—her bosom shaken .	*Locksley H.*	27	found no ease in *t* or in rest ; .	" . 897
and *t* it in his glowing hands ; .	" .	31	Strange music, and he paused and *t*	*Guinevere* . 237
Are touch'd, are *t* to finest air. .	*Sir Galahad*	72	*t* now and then to speak with him	*En. Arden.* 756
Bitterly weeping I *t* away ; . .	*Ed. Gray*	6,34	He therefore *t* softly like a thief .	" . 772
trust me while I *t* the page, .	*To E. L.*	9	*t* to the warmth The tender pink .	*Aylmer's F.* 185
t and kiss'd her where she stood :	*Lady Clare*	82	*T* beheld the Powers of the House	" . 287
t to me with 'As you will ; .	*Princess, Pro.*214			
t to go, but Cyril took the child .	" ii.	341	*turnpike.*		
we *t*, we wound About the cliffs, .	" iii.	341	where this byway joins The *t* .	*Walk. to the M.* 5
She spoke, and *t* her sumptuous head	" iv.	134			
t Your warmer currents all to her,	" .	282	*turnspit.*		
Half-drooping from her, *t* her face,	" .	349	*t*'s for the clown, . . .	*Princess,* iv. 495
camp and college *t* to hollow shows ;	" v.	467			
And *t* each face her way ; . .	" vi.	128	*turret.*		
t half-round to Psyche as she sprang	" .	192	The wind is blowing in *t* and tree (rep.)	*The Sisters* 3
t askance a wintry eye ; . .	" .	310	*t*'s lichen-gilded like a rock . .	*Ed. Morris* 8
their fair college *t* to hospital ; .	" vii.	2	clings to the *t*'s and the walls ; .	*Maud,* II. iv. 34
She *t*; she paused ; She stoop'd ;	" .	139	In the garden by the *t*'s . .	" . 79
even when she *t*, the curse Had fall'n	*In Mem.*vi.	37	the daws About her hollow *t* .	*Enid* . 1105
But thou art *t* to something strange,	" xi.	5	Flags, flutter out upon *t* s and towers:	*W. to Alexan.* 15
childhood's flaxen ringlet *t* . .	" lxxviii.	15			
left his coal all *t* into gold . .	*Maud,* I. x.	11	*Tuscan.*		
his essences *t* the live air sick .	" xiii.	11	read The *T* poets on the lawn :	*In Mem.* lxxxviii.24
t our foreheads from the falling sun,	*The Brook*	165			
I *t* and hummed a bitter song .	*The Letters*	9	*tutor* (s.)		
With half a sigh she *t* the key, .	" .	18	his *t*, rough to common men, .	*Princess, Pro.*114
Flash d as they *t* in air . .	*Lt. Brigade*	28	there we took one *t* as to read : .	" . 177
back *t*, and bow'd above his work,	*Enid* .	267	of that and this, And who were *t*'s	" i. 229
T, and beheld the four . .	" .	558			
Who, after, *t* her daughter round	" .	740	*tutor* (verb.)		
like that false pair who *t* Flying .	" .	1025	nor tame and *t* with mine eye .	*D. of F. Wom.* 138
the loss of whom has *t* me wild—	" .	1157			
t and look'd as keenly at her .	" .	1279	*tuwhit.*		
t all red and paced his hall, . .	" .	1516	Thy *t*'s are lull'd I wot (rep.) .	*The Owl,* ii. 1
t his face And kiss'd her climbing,	" .	1608			
saw her Pass into it, *t* to the Prince	" .	1735	*tuwhoo.*		
t to tyrants when they came to power)	*Vivien* .	368	Thy *t*'s of yesternight (rep.) . .	*The Owl,* ii. 2
she *t* away, she hung her head,. .	" .	736			
to his proud horse Lancelot *t*, .	*Elaine* .	346	*twang* (s.)		
he *t* Her counsel up and down .	" .	367	sharp clear *t* of the golden chords	*Sea-Fairies* 38
sharply *t* about to hide her face, .	" .	605			
foot to forehead exquisitely *t* : .	" .	640	*twang* (verb.)		
t Sir Torre, and being in his moods	" .	795	*T* out, my fiddle ! shake the twigs !	*Amphion* . 61
t Sighing, and feign'd a sleep .	" .	837			
now to right she *t*, and now to left,	" .	896	*twanging.*		
half *t* away, the Queen Brake .	" .	1191	Fly *t* headless arrows at the hearts,	*Princess,* ii. 380
then *t* the tongueless man . .	" .	1254			
till it touch'd her, and she *t*— .	*Guinevere* .	80	*twelve-divided.*		
And pale he *t*, and reel'd, . .	" .	302	like the *t-d* concubine . .	*Aylmer's F.* 759
			twenty-five.		
			so bitter When I am but *t-f* ? .	*Maud,* I. vi. 34
			twig.		
			Twang out, my fiddle ! shake the *t*'s !	*Amphion* 61

twilight	POEM.	LINE.
In the purple *t's* under the sea,	The Mermaid	44
an English home—gray *t*	Pal. of Art	85
T's of airy silver	Audley Ct	81
either *t* and the day between	Ed. Morris	37
Pilots of the purple *t*,	Locksley H.	122
About him broods the *t* dim	Two Voices	263
The *t* melted into morn	Day-Dm.	180
The *t* died into the dark.	"	183
into mournful *t* mellowing.	Princess, vi.	174
And *t* dawn'd : and morn by morn	" vii.	30
And *t* gloom'd ; and broader-grown	"	33
Deepening the courts of *t*	" Con	113
The *t* of eternal day.	In Mem xlix.	16
All winds that roam the *t* came	" lxxviii.	11
When *t* was falling,	Maud, I. xii.	2
I watch the *t* falling brown	To F. D. Maurice	14
thro' the feeble *t* of this world	Enid	854
In either *t* ghost-like to and fro	Elaine	845
November day Was growing duller *t*,	En. Arden	723
beat the *t* into flakes of fire.	Tithonus	42
the purple-skirted robe Of *t*	The Voyage	22
sets at *t* in a land of reeds.	Coquette, i.	14

twin.
nor the *t's* Her brethren, tho' they love	Princess, i.	152
twocrowned *t's*, Commerce and conquest,	" v.	410
A lusty brace Of *t's* may weed her	"	454

twin-brother.
| Sleep, Death's *t-b*, (rep.) | In Mem. lxvii. | 2 |

twine (s.)
| reverend beard Of grisly *t* | Princess, vi. | 88 |

twine (verb.)
the child would *t* A trustful hand,	In Mem.cviii.	18
Clasp her window, trail and *t*,	The Window	22
Trail and *t* and clasp and kiss	"	24

twined.
a drooping *t* Round thy neck	Adeline	57
leaning on a fragment *t* with vine	Œnone	17
Behind his ancle *t* her hollow feet	Vivien	83

twinkle (s.)
| There is not left the *t* of a fin | Enid | 1323 |

twinkle (verb.)
I see his gray eyes *t* yet	Miller's D.	11
lights begin to *t* from the rocks	Ulysses	54
That *t* into green and gold	In Mem. xi.	8
A livelier emerald *t's* in the grass	Maud, I. xviii.51	

twinkled
| all the haft *t* with diamond sparks | M. d' Arthur | 56 |
| *T* the innumerable ear and tail. | The Brook | 134 |

twinn'd.
| *t* as horse's ear and eye, | Princess, i. | 56 |

twin-sister.
| Than your *t-s*, Adeline. | Margaret | 43 |
| like *t-s* grew, *T-s's* differently beautiful | Ed Morris | 32 |

twist (s.)
| A *t* of gold was round her hair ; | Vivien | 70 |

twist (verb.)
| Would *t* his girdle tight, and pat | Talking O. | 43 |
| *t's* the grain with such a roar | Princess, v. | 517 |

twisted.
T as tight as I could knot the noose	St S. Stylites	64
T hard in fierce embraces,	Vision of Sin	40
W'n'ing his eyes, and *t* all his face.	Elaine	1110
words Have *t* back upon themselves,	Aylmer's F	755

twisting.
| Is *t* round the polar star ; | In Mem. c. | 12 |

twitch.
| a *t* of pain Tortur'd her mouth | Princess, vi. | 80 |
| at a sudden *t* of his iron mouth ; | Aylmer's F. | 732 |

twitter.
| and *t* twenty million loves | Princess, iv. | 83 |

two-cell'd.
| The *t-c* heart beating with one full | Princess, vii. | 289 |

twofooted	POEM.	LINE.
T at the limit of his chain,	Aylmer's F.	1-7

twy-natured.
| *T-n* is no nature : | Lucretius | 151 |

type (s.)
her fairest forms are *t's* of thee,	Isabel	30
Became an outward breathing *t*,	Miller's D.	206
That *t* of Perfect in his mind	Two Voices	292
carved cross-bones, the *t's* of Death,	Will Water.	243
And ev'n for want of such a *t*.	In Mem.xxxiii.	16
So careful of the *t* (lv 1)	" liv.	7
She cries 'a thousand *t's* are gone :	" lv	3
trod this planet, was a noble *t*	" Con.	138
Pass, thou deathlike *t* of pain,	Maud, II. iv.	53

type (verb.)
| Dear, but let us *t* them now | Princess, vii. | 281 |
| If so he *t* this work of time | In Mem.cxvii. | 16 |

tyranny.
play the slave to gain the *t*.	Princess, iv.	114
iron *t* now should bend or cease.	Maud,III.vi.	20
Thought on all her evil *tyrannies*.	Boädicea	80
out of *t t* buds	"	83

tyrant.
Faster binds a *t's* power ;	Vision of Sin	123
And the *t's* cruel glee	"	129
' Kill him now, 'The *t!*	Princess, Pro.	202
makes you *t's* in your iron skies,	Maud,I. xviii.	37
our dead captain taught The *t*,	Ode on Well.	70
hardest *t's* in their day of power,	Enid	1543
turn'd to *t's* when they came to power	Vivien	368
Pity, the violet on the *t s* grave.	Aylmer's F.	845

Tyrol.
| A cap of *T* borrow'd from the hall, | Princess, iv. | 578 |

U

udder.
| Nosing the mother's *u* | Lucretius | 100 |

ulcer.
| the *u*, eating thro' my skin, | St S. Stylites | 66 |

umpire.
| by common voice, Elected *u*, | Œnone | 83 |

unarmed.
tho' I ride *u*, I do not doubt	Enid	218
all *u* I rode, and thought to find	"	417
He sits *u* ; I hold a finger up	"	1186

unashamed.
| Delivers brawling judgments, *u*, | Vivien | 513 |

unasked.
A trustful hand, *u*, in thine,	In Mem.cviii	19
tending her rough lord, tho' all *u*,	Enid	1254
You followed me *u* ;	Vivien	147

unauthorised.
| that I came not all *u* | Princess, iv. | 447 |

unavenged.
| life-long injuries burning *u*, | Enid | 1544 |

unbeheld.
| Mayst well behold them *u*, | Œnone | 87 |

unbecoming.
| Not *u* men that strove with Gods, | Ulysses | 51 |

unbeguiled.
| At me you smiled, but *u* | L, C. V. de l'Ere | 5 |

unbiassed.
| *U* by self-profit | Œnone | 150 |

unbind.
| *u* my heart that I may weep,' | Guinevere | 164 |

unblest.
| never child be born of me, *U*, | Œnone | 251 |
| care no longer, being all *u* : 'Come not, when,' *etc.* | | 8 |

unbodying.
| *U* critic-pen, | Will Water. | 42 |

	POEM.	LINE.
unborn.		
village eyes as yet *u*;	*In Mem. Con.*	59
cackle of the *u* about the grave,	*Vivien*	357
unbound.		
being, as I think, *U* as yet,	*Elaine*	1377
unburnish'd.		
To rust *u*, not to shine in use !	*Ulysses*	23
uncalled for.		
(power of herself Would come *u f*)	*Œnone*	145
uncancell'd.		
if left *u*, had been so sweet.	*Maud,* I. xix.	46
uncared for.		
U f, spied its mother and began	*Princess,* vi.	120
U f, gird the windy grove,	*In Mem.* c.	13
He must not pass *u f*.	*Elaine*	535
uncertain.		
U as a vision or a dream,	*En. Arden.*	353
uncharity.		
Fought with what seem'd my own *u*;	*Sea Dreams*	73
uncharmed.		
assure you mine: So live *u.*	*Vivien*	400
unclad.		
U herself in haste: adown the stair	*Godiva*	48
unclaimed.		
query pass *U*, in flushing silence,	*The Brook.*	105
unclasped.		
I scarce should be *u* at night.	*Miller's D.*	186
sweet Europa's mantle blew *u*,	*Pal. of Art*	117
U the wedded eagles of her belt	*Godiva*	43
unclasping.		
U flung the casement back,	*Elaine*	975
uncle.		
Dora felt her *u's* will in all,	*Dora*	5
my *u's* mind will change !'	"	45
have obey'd my *u* until now.	"	57
I will set him in my *u's* eye.	"	65
make him pleasing in her *u's* eye.	"	82
'My *u* took the boy;	"	112
Trustees and Aunts and *U's.*	*Ed. Morris*	121
and a selfish *u's* ward.	*Locksley H.*	156
Had babbled '*U*' on my knee;	*In Mem.* lxxxiii.	13
uncoiled.		
the braid Slipt and *u* itself,	*Vivien*	738
uncomforted.		
U, leaving my ancient love.	*Œnone*	256
unconfined.		
From cells of madness *u*,	*Two Voices*	371
uncongeal.		
When meres begin to *u*,	*Two Voices*	407
unconquerable.		
I believed myself *U*,	*Enid.*	1683
unconscious.		
feeble, all *u* of itself,	*Princess,* vii.	102
U of the sliding hour,	*In Mem.* xlii.	5
uncourteous.		
in his heat and agony, seem *U*,	*Elaine*	851
uncurled.		
Did he push, when he was *u*,	*Maud,* II. ii.	18
undazzled.		
Slowly my sense *u*.	*D.of F.Wom.*	177
undercurrent.		
but for some dark *u* woe.	*Maud,* I.xviii.	83
under-flame.		
Grew darker from that *u-f*:	*Arabian N's.*	91
under-fringe.		
Broad-faced with *u-f* of russet beard,	*Enid*	1386
undergone.		
both have *u* That trouble	*Enid.*	1584

	POEM.	LINE.
underground.		
Will vex thee lying *u* ?	*Two Voices*	111
when the next day broke from *u*,	*Elaine*	412
when the next sun brake from *u*,	"	1131
underhand.		
of a kind The viler, as *u*,	*Maud,* I. i.	28
under-kingdom.		
The hundred *u-k's* that he sway'd	*Vivien*	432
underlip.		
u, you may call it a little too ripe	*Maud,* I. ii.	9
underpropt.		
u a rich Throne of the massive ore,	*Arabian N's.*	145
under-roof.		
An *u-r* of doleful gray.	*Dying Swan*	4
underscored.		
only yours;' and this Thrice *u*.	*Ed. Morris*	107
under-shapen.		
His dwarf, a vicious *u-s* thing,	*Enid.*	412
under-sky.		
And floating about the *u-s*,	*Dying Swan*	25
understand.		
(For you will *u* it) To ——.	*With Pal. of Art*	2
None else could *u*;	*Talking O.*	22
easy things to *u*—	*Locksley H.*	55
He answers not, nor *u's.*	*Two Voices*	246
when thy nerves could *u*	*Vision of Sin*	160
tongue no man could *u*:	"	222
songs they would not *u*:	*Princess,* vi.	24
The words were hard to *u*.	*In Mem.*lxviii.	20
'I cannot *u*: I love.	" xcvi.	36
What is and no man *u's*	" cxxiii.	22
nursed at ease and brought to *u*	*Maud,* I.xviii.	35
Thou canst not *u*.	" II. iii.	3
could he *u* how money breeds	*The Brook.*	6
I hold a finger up; They *u*:	*Enid.*	1187
you are man, you well can *u*	*Vivien*	547
Was loosen'd, till he made them *u*;	*En. Arden.*	646
mark me and *u*, While I have power	"	877
understanding.		
u all the foolish work Of Fancy,	*Princess,* vi.	100
understood.		
kep un, my lass, tha mun *u*;	*N. Farmer.*	23
understood.		
A notice faintly *u*,	*Two Voices*	431
The land, he *u*, for miles about	*Princess,* i.	189
Loved deeplier, darklier *u*	*In Mem.* cxxviii.	10
prophecy given of old And then not *u*	*Maud,* II. v.	43
by her that bore her *u*,	*Enid.*	511
thou that stonest, had'st thou *u*	*Aylmer's F.*	739
under-tone.		
from within me a clear *u-t*	*D. of F. Wom.*	81
underwent.		
Did more, and *u*, and overcame,	*Godiva*	10
underworld.		
brings our friends up from the *u*,	*Princess,* iv.	27
undescried.		
tho' *u* Winning its way.	*Isabel.*	22
undissolved.		
A sleep by kisses *u*,	*Day-Dm.*	263
undo.		
Thoroughly to *u* me,	*Lilian*	11
in seeking to *u* One riddle,	*Two Voices*	232
To know her beauty might half *u* it.	*Maud,* I. xvi.	19
never could *u* it: ask no more:	*Vivien*	536
undone.		
What harm, *u*? deep harm to disobey	*M. d'Arthur*	93
undrainable.		
labour'd mines *u* of ore.	*Œnone*	113
undulated.		
u The banner: anon to meet us	*Princess,* v.	243
undulation.		
cries, And *u's* to and fro.	*In Mem.* cxii.	20

	POEM.	LINE.
undying.		
Clear, without heat, *u*,	*Isabel*	3
unequal		
in true marriage lies Nor equal, nor *u*;	*Princess,* vii.	285
unexhausted.		
bloodily fall the battle-axe, *u*,	*Boädicea*	56
unexpress'd.		
I leave thy praises *u*	*In Mem.* lxxiv.	1
unfair.		
Who shall call me ungentle, *u*.	*Maud,* I. xiii.	14
unfaith.		
Faith and *u* can ne'er be equal powers:	*Vivien*	238
U in aught is want of faith in all.	"	239
unfurrowed.		
so return'd *u* to her sty.	*Walk. to the M.*	92
unfetter'd.		
U by the sense of crime,	*In Mem.* xxvii.	7
unfinished.		
work is left *U—if* I go.	*Lucretius*	104
unfit.		
U for earth, *u* for heaven,	*St S. Stylites*	3
unfold.		
I see thy beauty gradually *u*,	*Eleänore*	70
a flower that cannot all *u*,	*Princess,* vii.	126
unfurl.		
u the maiden banner of our rights,	*Princess,* iv.	482
ungathered.		
To-night *u* let us leave,	*In Mem.* civ.	1
ungenerous.		
'*U*, dishonourable, base,	*Aylmer's F.*	292
ungentle.		
Who shall call me *u*, unfair,	*Maud,* I. xiii.	14
to be gentle than *u* with you;	*Enid*	1564
ungracious.		
'*U?* answer'd Florian 'have you learnt	*Princess,* ii.	370
I am more *u* ev'n than you,	*Aylmer's F.*	247
ungraciousness.		
I seem to be *u* itself.	*Aylmer's F.*	245
ungrateful.		
Not all *u* to thine ear.	*In Mem.* xxxviii.	12
unhail'd.		
u The shallop flitteth silken-sail'd	*L. of Shalott,* i.	21
unhappy.		
Nor *u*, nor at rest,	*Adeline*	4
There are enough *u* on this earth	*Œnone*	235
and pass'd—*u* that I am	*Dora*	143
The spindlings look *u*	*Amphion*	92
Not all *u*, having loved God's best,	*Elaine*	1087
He was not all *u*.	*En. Arden*	800
unheard.		
behold them unbeheld, *u* Hear all	*Œnone*	87
unheedful.		
or as once we met *U*,	*Gardener's D.*	261
uninvited.		
The Abominable, that *u* came	*Œnone*	220
union.		
banded *u's* persecute Opinion 'You ask me why,' etc.		17
Have pledged us in this *u*,	*Elaine*	116
unity		
These three made *u* so sweet,	*Two Voices*	421
It was but *u* of place	*In Mem.* xli.	3
universe.		
wanderings Of this most intricate *U A Character*		3
in a boundless *u* Is boundless better	*Two Voices*	26
knowing not the *u*, I fear to slide	"	230
Quite sunder'd from the moving *U Princess,* vii.		37
torrents of her myriad *u*,	*Lucretius*	39
fleeting thro' the boundless *u*,	"	161
university.		
to found an *U*' For maidens,	*Princess,* i.	149

	POEM.	LINE.
unkept.		
vintage, yet *u*, Had relish	*Will Water.*	97
unkind.		
Ah, miserable and *u*, untrue,	*M. d'Arthur*	119
be jealous, and hard, and *u?*	*Grandmother*	54
unkindliness.		
Kill'd with unutterable *u?*	*Vivien*	735
unknightly.		
U, traitor-hearted! Woe is me!	*M. d'Arthur*	120
u with flat hand, However lightly	*Enid*	1365
unknown.		
left a want *u* before;	*Miller's D.*	228
Known and *u* : human, divine,	*In Mem.* cxxxviii.	5
Sweet were the days when I was all *u Vivien*		351
hide it therefore ' go *u*;	*Elaine*	151
Known as they are, to me they are *u*.'	"	186
since I go to joust as one *u* l.	"	190
That he might joust *u* of all,	"	582
The maiden buried, not as one *u*,	"	1324
many a week, *u*, among the nuns;	*Guinevere*	145
unlaced.		
u my casque And grovell'd	*Princess,* vi.	11
unlading.		
At lading and *u* the tall barks;	*En. Arden.*	817
unlearn'd.		
In grief I am not all *u*;	*To J. S.*	18
unled.		
gentle charger following him *u*)	*Enid*	1419
unlifted.		
U was the clinking latch;	*Mariana*	6
unlike.		
O happy tears, and how *u* to these	*Œnone*	231
unlikeness.		
As his *u* fitted mine.	*In Mem.* lxxviii.	20
unloveable.		
Ev'n when they seem'd *u*	*Vivien*	32
unmanacled.		
U from bonds of sense,	*Two Voices*	236
unmann'd.		
but that my zone *U* me;	*Princess,* ii.	393
unmannerly.		
U, with prattling and the tales	*Guinevere*	314
unmark'd		
Enwind her isles, *u* of me;	*In Mem.* xcvii.	10
unmarried.		
Dora lived *u* till her death,	*Dora*	167
unmeet.		
you are all *u* for a wife.	*Maud,* I. iv.	57
unmortised.		
The feet *u* from their ankle-bones	*Vivien*	402
unopened.		
dash'd *U* at her feet;	*Princess,* iv.	450
unpalsied.		
U when he met with Death,	*In Mem.* cxxvii.	2
unperceived.		
Love, *u*, A more ideal Artist	*Gardener's D.*	24
With Cyril and with Florian, *u*,	*Princess,* i.	102
unpitied.		
U: for he groped as blind,	*Aylmer's F.*	821
unrelieved.		
ever *u* by dismal tears,	*Pal. of Art.*	271
unrepress'd.		
Ceasing not, mingled, *u*,	*Arabian N's.*	74
unrest.		
The wild *u* that lives in woe	*In Mem.* xv.	15
Can calm despair and wild *u*	" xvi.	2
unrevealed.		
The rest remaineth *u*;	*In Mem.* xxxi.	14

438   CONCORDANCE TO

	POEM.	LINE.
unriddled.		
Shall be *u* by and by. . . .	*Miller's D.*	20
unroll'd.		
sitting on a crimson scarf *u* . .	*D. of F. Wom.*	126
to the banner of battle *u !* .	*Maud*, III. vi.	42
unsaid.		
what I see I leave *u*, . . .	*In Mem.* lxxiii.	10
unscathed.		
Render him up *u ;* . . .	*Princess*, iv.	389
unseen.		
leaping out upon them *u* . .	*The Merman*	33
the dark East, *U*, is brightening .	*Gardener's D*	72
His love, *u* but felt, o'ershadow Thee, *Ded. of Idylls* 149		
with her feet *u* Crush'd the wild passion *Elaine* . 737		
Had his dark hour *u*, . . .	*En. Arden.*	78
Her face was evermore *u*, . .	*The Voyage*	61
Into the *u* for ever . . .	*Lucretius*	255
unshaken.		
kept her throne *u* still. . .	*To the Queen*	34
Ida stationed there *U*, . . .	*Princess*, v.	333
unshorn.		
saw him lying unsleek, *u*, . .	*Elaine*	811
unskill'd.		
let the younger and *u* go by . .	*Elaine*	1352
unsleek.		
saw him lying *u*, unshorn, . .	*Elaine*	811
unsolder.		
u's all The goodliest fellowship .	*M. d'Arthur*	14
unsown.		
sat upon a mound That was *u*, .	*Dora* . .	71
unspeakable.		
memories roll upon him, *U* for sadness *En. Arden* 726		
twisted shapes of lust, *u*, . .	*Lucretius* .	157
unstained.		
A lovelier life, a more *u*, than his ? *Ded. of Idylls* 29		
unsubject.		
U to confusion, ...	*Will Water.*	86
unsweet.		
faith as vague as all *u :* . .	*In Mem.* xlvi.	5
untaken.		
hath left his prize *U*, . . .	*Elaine*	530
untarnish'd.		
name will yet remain *U* as before ; *Enid* . . 501		
untold.		
Nor left *u* the craft herself had used: *Enid* 1242		
untouch'd.		
U with any shade of years, . .	*Miller's D.*	219
untrue.		
Ah, miserable and unkind, *u*, .	*M. d'Arthur*	119
might by a true descent be *u ;* .	*Maud*, I. xiii.	31
untruth.		
never had a glimpse of mine *u*, .	*Elaine* .	126
Too wholly true to dream *u* in thee, *Guinevere* . 537		
untuneful.		
That her voice *u* grown . .	*The Owl* ii.	6
unvext.		
u She slipt across the summer .	*En. Arden* .	526
unwedded.		
I was wife, and thou *U:* . .	*Guinevere* .	119
unwise.		
What wonder I was all *u*, . .	*Day-Dm.* .	273
unwoo'd.		
u of summer wind ; . . .	*Arabian N's.*	80
unworthier.		
we, *u*. told Of college ; . .	*Princess, Pro.*	110
unworthily.		
some *u ;* their sinless faith . .	*Princess,* v.	177
unworthiness.		
Contemplating her own *u ;* . .	*Enid* . .	533

	POEM.	LINE.
unworthy.		
O three times less *u !* . .	*Love and Duty*	20
Hadst thou less *u* proved—. .	*Locksley H.*	63
most Predoom'd her as *u*. . .	*L'aine* .	725
unwounded.		
To find him yet *u* after fight, .	*Enid* .	1220
unwove.		
Wove and *u* it, till the boy return'd *Enid* . 1109		
upbore.		
but her deep love *U* her ; . .	*Elaine* .	857
His resolve *U* him, and firm faith, *En. Arden* . 801		
upbreaking.		
the heavens *u* thro' the earth, .	*Guinevere* .	388
up-clomb.		
U the shadowy pine . . .	*Lotos-E's.* .	18
upcurled.		
wreaths of floating dark *u*, . .	*The Poet* .	35
updrag		
' Rise . ' and stoop'd to *u* Melissa : *Princess*, iv. 347		
uphold.		
break the heathen-and *u* the Christ, *Guinevere* . 467		
didst *u* mo on my lonely isle, *U* me, *En. Arden* . 784		
upjetted.		
u in spirits of wild sea-smoke, .	*Sea Dreams*	52
upland.		
Piling sheaves in *u*'s airy, . .	*L. of Shalott*, i.	34
realms of *u*, prodigal in oil, . .	*Pal. of Art*	79
uplift.		
A lever to *u* the earth . . .	*In Mem.* cxii.	15
pure Sir Galahad to *u* the maid ; .	*Elaine*	1258
uplifted.		
The bold Sir Bedivere *u* him .	*M. d'Arthur*	6
U high in heart and hope are we, *Ode on Well.* 254		
upreared.		
in his chair himself *u*, . . .	*Day-Dm.* .	150
upright.		
U and flush'd before him ; . .	*Vivien* .	761
uprising.		
The knife *u* toward the blow, .	*The Victim*	71
uprose.		
u the mystic mountain-range : .	*Vision of Sin*	208
upshoot.		
All round a hedge *u*'s, . . .	*Day-Dm.* .	61
upsprung.		
In closest coverture *u*, . . .	*Arabian N's.*	68
upstarted.		
Scared by the noise *u* at our feet, .	*Vivien* .	272
upswell.		
u's The gold-fringed pillow . .	*Day-Dm.* .	97
Urania.		
U speaks with darken'd brow : .	*In Mem.* xxxvii.	1
Uranian.		
o'er his head *U* Venus hung, .	*Princess*, i.	239
urge.		
'To which the voice did *u* reply , .	*Two Voices*	7
that I come to *u* thy crime . .	*Guinevere* .	528
urged.		
and the poet little *u* . . .	*The Epic* .	48
I *u* the fierce inscription . .	*Princess*, iii.	125
U him to speak against the truth, *Elaine* . 97		
urn.		
From fluted vase, and brazen *u* .	*Arabian N's.*	60
Drawing into his narrow earthen *u* *Ode to Mem.* 61		
white dust, shut in an *u* of brass !	*Lotos-E's.* .	113
Soft lustre bathes the range of *u*'s *Day-Dm.* . 29		
with great *u*'s of flowers. . .	*Princess*, ii.	12
Thro' prosperous floods his holy *u*.	*In Mem.* ix.	8
on the board the fluttering *u*. .	" xciv	8
An angel watching an *u* . .	*Maud*, I. viii.	3
lying with his *u*'s and ornaments, .	*Aylmer's F.*	4

TENNYSON'S WORKS. 439

use (s.)	POEM.	LINE.
keep a thing, its *u* will come	*The Epic*	42
God made the woman for the *u* of man	*Ed. Morris*	91
rust unburnish'd, not to shine in *u* !	*Ulysses*	23
Oh, to what *u*'s shall we put	*Day-Dm.*	201
'twere to cramp its *u*, if I	"	211
redound Of *u* and glory to yourselves	*Princess*, ii.	29
grow To *u* and power on this Oasis,	"	151
public *u* required she should be known;	" iv.	317
oath was ta'en for public *u*,	"	318
boats and bridges for the *u* of men.	" vi.	31
What *u* to keep them here now? .	"	285
void was her *u*;	" vii.	19
A *u* in measured language lies; .	*In Mem.*	6
one wreath more for *U* and Wont.	" xxix.	11
learns the *u* of 'I' and 'me,'	" xliv.	2
This *u* may lie in blood and breath,	"	13
with long *u* her tears are dry.	" lxxvii.	20
bare The *u* of virtue out of earth;	" lxxxi.	10
broke the bond of dying *u*	" civ.	12
And soil'd with all ignoble *u*.	" cx.	24
shocks of doom To shape and *u* .	" cxvii.	25
I will make *u* of all the power I have	*Enid*	1194
count it of small *u* To charge you,	"	1205
u and name and fame (153, 190, 224, 819)	*Vivien*	63
'Rather *u* than fame' .	"	330
U gave me Fame at first,	"	343
Fame again Increasing gave me *u*.	"	344
rather dread the loss of *u* than fame;	"	369
lay as dead, And lost all *u* of life :	"	475
kingdom's not the king's — For public *u*:	*Elaine*	61
shall grow In *u* of arms and manhood,	"	65
put my wits to some rough *u*,	"	1258
part of me : but what *u* in it?	"	1406
shut from all Her charitable *u*,	*Aylmer's F.*	566
too late ! they come too late for *u*.	*Sea Dreams*	67
Naw soort o' koind o' *u*	*N. Farmer*	6
'O wife, what *u* to answer now ? .	*The Victim*	59
of older *u* All-seeing Hyperion— .	*Lucretius*	125
From childly wont and ancient *u* .	"	206

use (verb.)

u Her influence on the mind,	*Will Water.*	11
grant me license ; might I *u* it?	*Princess*, iii.	217
to *u* A little patience ere I die;	*In Mem.* xxxiv.	11
with such craft as women *u* .	*Enid*	1201
u Both grace and will to pick	"	1750
eats And *u*'s, careless of the rest;	*Vivien*	313
Might *u* it to the harm of any one,	"	535
since I cannot *u* it, you may have it.'	*Elaine*	199
pray you, *u* some rough discourtesy	"	968
to be plain and blunt, and *u*,	"	1293

used.

and *u* Within the Present, '*Love thou thy land*,' etc.	2
U all her fiery will, and smote . *Will Water.*	111
the left, or not, or seldom *u*; . *Princess*, iii.	22
great is song *U* to great ends: . " iv.	120
—you *u* us courteously— . " v.	207
It is all *u* up for that. . *Maud*, II. v.	64
too gentle, have not *u* my power: *Enid*	467
the craft herself had *u*; . "	1242
you *u* worse than that dead man ; "	1583
delegated hands, Not *u* mine own: "	1712
So *u* as I, My daily wonder is, . *Vivien*	385
the one discourtesy that he *u* . *Elaine*	982

used (accustomed.)

We are *u* to that . . *Princess*, iii.	260

useful.

Subdue them to the *u* and the good. *Ulysses* .	38

usherest.

Who *u* in the dolorous hour . *In Mem.* lxxi.	9

using.

like the hand, and grew With *u*; . *Princess*, ii.	135

Usk.

Held court at old Caerleon upon *U Enid* .	146
Took horse, and forded *U*, . "	161
up the vale of *U*, By the flat meadow, "	831
the full-tided *U*, Before he turn . "	965
With Arthur to Caerleon upon *U* "	1704
in thy bowers of Camelot or of *U Guinevere*	493

usury.	POEM.	LINE.
kiss for kiss, With *u* thereto.'	*Talking O.*	145

Uther.

mythic *U*'s deeply-wounded son . *Pal. of Art*	105
whom his father *U* left in charge *Enid* .	1701

utter.

would that my tongue could *u* '*Break, break*,' etc.	3
To *u* love more sweet than praise. *In Mem.* lxxvi.	10
U your jubilee, steeple and spire ! *W. to Alexan.*	17

utterance.

thro' all change Of liveliest *u*. . *D. of F. Wom.*	108
perfect Joy, perplex'd for *u* . . *Gardener's D.*	250
Gave *u* by the yearning of an eye *Love and Duty*	61
As if to speak, but *u* failing her, . *Princess*, iv.	376
Went on in passionate *u*. . . *Guinevere* .	605
their anger in miraculous *u*'s . . *Boädicea* .	23

uttered.

brows Of him that *u* nothing base ; *To the Queen*	8
He *u* rhyme and reason, . . *The Goose* .	6
He *u* words of scorning ; . . "	42
whole of love and *u* it. . . *Love and Duty*	62
She nor swoon'd, nor *u* cry : . *Princess*, v.	533
faint eyes, and *u* whisperingly . " vii.	129
Bow'd at her side and *u* whisperingly *Enid*	1154
While he *u* this, Low to her own heart *Elaine* .	317
U a little tender dolorous cry. . "	613
kneeling *u* 'Queen, Lady, my liege, "	1173
there the tale he *u* brokenly, . *En. Arden* .	646

uttering.

all in passion *u* a dry shriek, . . *Enid* .	1310

uttermost.

aid me Heaven when at nine *u*, . *Enid* .	502
might prove her to the *u*, . . "	1457

uxoriousness.

molten down in mere *u*. . . *Enid* .	60
And accusation of *u*. . . "	83

V

vacancy.

we shall see The nakedness and *v Deserted H.*	11

vacant.

v of our glorious gains, . . *Locksley H.*	175

vague.

v in vapour, hard to mark ; '*Love thou thy land*,' etc.	62
faith as *v*, as all unsweet: . . *In Mem.* xlvi.	5
who hath not children, *v* . . *Vivien* .	356

vail.

hand Grasp'd, made her *v* her eyes *Guinevere* .	653

vain.

Of knitted purport, all were *v*. . *Two Voices*	108
The chancellor, sedate and *v*, . *Day-Dm.* .	101
waste it seem'd and *v* ; . . *Princess*, vii.	28
At night she weeps, 'How *v* am I ! *In Mem.* lix.	15
With fifty Mays, thy songs are *v*; " lxxv.	14
Thy likeness, I might count it *v*. . " xci.	2
Half-grown as yet, a child, and *v* " cxiii.	9
fonder of glory and *v*, . . *Maud*, I. iv.	37
From talk of battles loud and *v* . *Ode on Well.*	247
She murmured '*v*, in *v* : it cannot be. *Elaine* .	888

vainlier.

v than a hen To her false daughters, *Princess*, v.	318

vale.

Winds all the *v* in rosy folds, . *Miller's D.*	242
There lies a *v* in Ida . . *Œnone* .	1
many a *v* And river-sunder'd champaign "	111
Lay, dozing in the *v* of Avalon . *Pal. of Art*	107
'Make me a cottage in the *v*,' . "	291
many a winding *v* And meadow, . *Lotos-Es.* .	22
the thick-leaved platans of the *v*. . *Princess*, iii.	159
roll The torrents, dash'd to the *v*: . " v.	340
'Pretty bud ! Lily of the *v* ! . . " vi.	176
all the *v*'s Await thee ; . . " vii.	200
flocks are whiter down the *v*, . *In Mem.* cxiv.	10
up the *v* of Usk By the flat meadow *Enid* .	831

	POEM.	LINE.
Re-makes itself, and flashes down the	*v—Guinevere*	604
Light, so low in the *v*.	*The Window*	186

Valence.
O ay, what say ye to Sir *V*	*Vivien*	555
Sir *V* wedded with an outland dame,	"	564
charged by *V* to bring home the child	"	568

Valentine.
birds that piped their *V's*,	*Princess*, v.	229

Valkyrian.
ourself have often tried *V* hymns,	*Princess*, iv.	121

valley.
all the *v's* of Ionian hills	*Œnone*	2
Behind the *v* topmost Gargarus	"	10
while I sat Low in the *v*	"	211
In this green *v*, under this green hill	"	228
As I came up the *v*	*May Queen*, i.	13
All the *v*, mother, 'ill be fresh	"	37
up the *v* came a swell of music	" iii.	32-6
Wild flowers in the *v*	"	52
above the *v* stood the moon	*Lotos-E's.*	7
Far below them in the *v's*,	"	157
others in Elysian *v's* dwell,	"	169
The *v's* of grape-loaded vines	*D. of F. Wom.*	219
white convent down the *v* there	*StS. Stylites*	61
from the *v's* underneath	*Amphion*	31
From some delightful *v*,	*Will Water.*	120
come, for Love is of the *v* (rep.)	*Princess*, vii.	183
To find him in the *v*	"	195
saw The happy *v's*, half in light	*Con.*	41
Ringing thro' the *vallies*	*Maud*, I. xii.	10
And the *v's* of Paradise	" xxii.	44
To bicker down a *v*.	*The Brook*	26
Follow'd up in *v* and glen	*Ode on Well.*	114
A thousand shadowy-pencil'd *v's*	*The Daisy*	67
All in the *v* of Death (rep.)	*Lt. Brigade*	3
thro' many a grassy glade And *v*,	*Enid*	237
street of a little town In a long *v*.	"	243
out of town and *v* came a noise	"	247
Was climbing up the *v*;	*Aylmer's F.*	228
All along the *v* (rep.).	*V. of Cauteretz*	1
Above the *v's* of palm and pine.	*The Islet*	23
and jutting peak And *v*	*Spec. of Iliad*	14
yon dark *v's* wind forlorn,	*On a Mourner*	22
Fly to the light in the *v* below (rep.)	*The Window*	99

valour.
V and charity more and more.	*To F. D. Maurice*	40

valorous.
One of our noblest, our most *v*,	*Enid*	1758

value.
To loyal hearts the *v* of all gifts	*Elaine*	1208

valued.
he knew the man and *v* him.	*En. Arden.*	121

valuing.
V the giddy pleasure of the eyes	*M. d'Arthur*	128

valve.
betwixt were *v's* Of open-work	*Princess*, iv.	184
marble stairs, And great bronze *v's*	" v.	355
Descending, burst the great bronze *v's*	" vi.	59

van.
spread his sheeny *v's* for flight	*Love and Death*	8

Van Diemen.
From England to *V. D.*	*Amphion*	84

vane.
County Member's with the *v*;	*Walk. to the M.*	8
Still on the tower stood the *v*.	*The Letters*	1

vanish.
v friendships only made in wine.	*Enid*	1328

vanish'd.
The days have *v*, tone and tint	*In Mem.* xliii.	5
v panic-stricken, like a shoal	*Enid*	1317
Until they *v* by the fairy well	*Vivien*	278
v, and his book came down to me.'	"	500
v suddenly from the field	*Elaine*	507

	POEM.	LINE.
upon him A piteous glance, and *v*	*Aylmer's F.*	284
clink'd, and clash'd, and *v*,	*Sea Dreams*	131

vanishing.
grave itself shall pass, *V* atom and void	*Lucretius*	253

vanity.
Like poets, from the *v* of song?	*Gardener's D.*	99

vanquish.
knew that Love can *v* Death,	*D. of F. Wom.*	269

vanquished.
when our side was *v*	*Princess*, vi.	8
We *v*, you the Victor	"	151

vantage-ground.
nor a *v-g* For pleasure;	*Ded. of Idylls*	22
With such a *v-g* for nobleness	*Aylmer's F.*	387

vapour.
swimming *v* slopes athwart the glen	*Œnone*	3
vague in *v*, hard to mark, 'Love thou thy land,' etc.		62
When the ranks are roll'd in *v*,	*Locksley H.*	104
Comes a *v* from the margin	"	191
High up the *v's* fold and swim :	*Two Voices*	262
Faint shadows, *v's* lightly curl'd,	*Day-Dm.*	25
range Of *v* buoy'd the crescent bark	"	186
breath to heaven like *v* goes :	*St Agnes' Eve*	3
In crystal *v* everywhere	*Sir L. and Q. G.*	5
A *v* heavy, hueless, formless	*Vision of Sin*	53
cold *v* touch'd the palace gate	"	58
soft white *v* streak	*Princess*, iii.	326
a purple-frosty bank Of *v*,	*In Mem.* cvi.	4
All night the shining *v* sail	"	111
yellow *v's* choke The great city	*Maud*, II. iv.	64
baleful star Veil'd in gray *v*;	*Vivien*	112
moony *v* rolling round the King,	*Guinevere*	595
belt, it seem'd, of luminous *v*,	*Sea Dreams*	203
v's weep their burthen to the ground	*Tithonus*	2
Roll'd the rich *v* far into the heaven	*Spec. of Iliad*	8

vapour-braided.
sweet the *v-b* blue.	*The Letters*	42

varier.
pious *v's* from the church,	*Sea Dreams*	19

varieties.
all *v* of mould and mind) To——	*With Pal. of Art*	7

various.
All *v*, each a perfect whole	*Pal. of Art*	58
Each month is *v* to present	*Two Voices*	74

vary.
The violet *varies* from the lily as far	*Princess*, v.	174
As the light of Heaven *varies*	*Enid*	6
make her beauty *v* day by day,	"	"
value of all gifts Must *v* as the givers	*Elaine*	1208
v from the kindly race of men,	*Tithonus*	29

varying.
v to and fro, We know not wherefore.	*Aylmer's F.*	73

vary-coloured.
A walk with *v-c* shells	*Arabian N's.*	57

vase.
From fluted *v*, and brazen urn	*Arabian N's.*	60
from *v's* in the hall Flowers of all	*Princess, Pro.*	11
The Danaid of a leaky *v*,	" ii.	319
Break, thou deep *v* of chilling tears	*In Mem.* iv.	11

Vashti.
O *V*, noble *V!* Summoned out She	*Princess*, iii.	210

vassal.
Not *v's* to be beat,	*Princess*, iv.	128
makes it *v* unto love :	*In Mem.* xlvii.	8
v's of wine and anger and lust,	*Maud*, II. i.	43
whom his shaking *v's* call'd the Bull	*Enid*	1288
no more a *v* to the thief,	"	1301
work as *v* to the larger love,	*Vivien*	341

vast.
Thine own shall wither in the *v*,	*In Mem.* lxxv.	11
A soul shall draw from out the *v*.	*Con.*	123

TENNYSON'S WORKS. 441

	POEM.	LINE.
vaster.		
one music as before But *v.*	*In Mem.* Pro.	29
till as *v* grew the shore,	" cii.	23
vastness.		
In *v* and in mystery,	*In Mem* xcvi.	7
vat.		
flask of cider from his father's *v's,*	*Audley Ct* .	26
red with spirted purple of the *v's,*	*Princess,* vii.	187
vault (s.)		
Imbower'd *v's* of pillar'd palm,	*Arabian Ns.*	39
Nor any cloud would cross the *v, Mariana in the S.* 38		
glimmering *v's* with iron grates,	*D of F Wom.*	35
O Priestess in the *v's* of Death,	*In Mem.* iii,	2
In *v s* and catacombs, they fell,	" lvii.	4
up thy *v* with roaring sound	" lxxi.	25
Far beneath a blazing *v,*	*Will* .	18
vault (verb.)		
lightly *v* from the throne and play	*The Mermaid*	33
vaulted.		
V o'er the dark-blue sea.	*Lotos-E's.*	85
veil (s)		
Slow-dropping *v's* of thinnest lawn	*Lotos-E's.*	11
time Is come to raise the *v,*	*Gardener's D,*	269
Inner impulse rent the *v.*	*Two Voices*	10
thro' thick *v's* to apprehend	"	296
draws the *v* from hidden worth	*Day-Dm.*	104
rose of Gulistan Shall burst her *v*	*Princess,* iv.	103
From orb to orb, from *v* to *v.*'	*In Mem.* xxx.	28
Behind the *v,* behind the *v.*	" lv.	28
A lucid *v* from coast to coast,	" lxvi.	14
We heard behind the woodbine *v.*	" lxxxviii.	50
A faded mantle and a faded *v,*	*Enid* .	135
in her *v* enfolded, manchet bread,	"	389
tearing off her *v* of faded silk	"	1363
the maiden rose, White as her *v,*	*Guinevere*	361
veil (verb.)		
I cannot *v,* or droop my sight,	*Eleänore*	87
nor *v* his eyes:	'*Love thou thy land,'* etc. 90	
Low'd as if to *v* a noble tear,	*Princess,* iii.	272
v His want in forms for fashion's sake *In Mem.* cx.		5
might I wish to *v* her wickedness	*Guinevere* .	209
veil'd.		
a picture—*v,* for what it holds	*Gardener's D*	265
v the world with jaundice,	*Walk.to the M*	14
v her brows, and prone she sank.	*Princess,* v.	104
a statue *v,* to which they sang:	*In Mem.* cii.	12
which, tho' *v,* was known to me	"	13
baleful star *V* in gray vapour	*V'rwen*	112
he *v* His face with the other,	*Aylmer's F.*	808
veileth.		
spreads above And *v* love,	*Two Voices*	447
vein (s)		
a languid fire creeps Thro my *v's*	*Eleänore* .	130
can talk: yours is a kindly *v:*	*Ed. Morris*	81
stays the blood along the *v s.*	*Day-Dm.*	24
summer of the vine in all his *v's—*	*Princess,*	181
branches current yet in kindred *v's?*	" ii.	227
From out a common *v* of memory	"	293
felt my *v's* Stretch with fierce heat;	" v.	526
wolf's-milk curdled in their *v's,*	" vii.	115
now the wine made summer in his *v's Enid*		398
brooking not the Tarquin in her *v's, Lucretius .*		234
vein (verb.)		
all the gold That *v's* the world	*Princess,* iv.	522
velvet.		
dusted *v's* have much need of thee;	*To J. M. K.*	4
Black *v* of the costliest	*Aylmer's F.*	804
veneer'd.		
V with sanctimonious theory.	*Princess,Pro.*	117
venerator.		
not a scorner of your sex But *v,*	*Princess,* iv.	403
vengeance.		
take such bloody *v* on you both?	*Princess,* iv.	513
Is this thy *v,* holy Venus,	*Lucretius* .	67

	POEM.	LINE.
venom.		
Not one to flirt a *v* at her eyes,	*Vivien*	452
venture.		
my poor *v* but a fleet of glass	*Sea Dreams*	134
ventured.		
And boldly *v* on the liberties.	*Princess,* i.	202
Alone at home, nor *v* out alone	*En. Arden*	513
Venus.		
o'er his head Uranian *V* hung,	*Princess,* i.	230
Is this thy vengeance, holy *V,*	*Lucretius* .	67
verbiage.		
This barren *v,* current among men *Princess,* ii.		40
Vere de Vere.		
Lady Clara *V de V*	*L. C. V. de Vere* 1, *et pass.*	
stamps the caste of *V de V* .	"	40
verge.		
lent broad *v* to distant lands,	*Pal. of Art*	30
Float by you on the *v* of night.	*Margaret* .	31
black dot against the *v* of dawn	*M. d' Arthur*	271
May from *v* to *v,*	*Gardener's D.*	79
sinks with all we love below the *v; Princess,* iv.		29
the slope of sea from *v* to shore,	" vii.	23
on the low dark *v* of life	*In Mem.* xlix.	15
verged		
kinds of thought, That *v* upon them *Gardener's D.* 70		
termed-white.		
near her, like a blossom *v-w,*	*Enid* .	364
vermin.		
fancies like the *v* in a nut	*Princess,* vi.	246
curse me the British *v* the rat	*Maud,* II v.	58
I will track this *v* to their earths:	*Enid* .	217
versatility.		
The grace and *v* of the man—	*Elaine* .	472
verse		
How may full-sail'd *v* express	*Eleänore* .	44
invade Even with a *v* your holy woe. *To J S.*		8
another which you had, I mean of *v The Epic* .		26
In *v* that brings myself relief	*In Mem.* lxxiv	2
Take one *v* more—the lady speaks *Vivien*		295
gave the *v* ' Behold Your house	*Aylmer's F.*	638
Calliope to grace his golden *v—*	*Lucretius* .	44
versed.		
In many a subtle question *v,*	*In Mem.* xcv.	6
Verulam (Lord Bacon.)		
Plato the wise, and large-brow'd *V, Pal of Art*		163
Homer, Plato, *V;*	*Princess,* ii.	144
Verulam (Roman Colony.)		
London, *V,* Camulodune.	*Boädicea* .	86
vessel		
On the coals I lay A *v* full of sin	*St S. Stylites*	167
the *v* puffs her sail.	*Ulysses* .	44
The silver *v* e sparkle clean	*Sir Galahad*	34
Reporting of his *v* China-bound	*En. Arden* .	122
the moment and the *v* past.	" .	243
The *v* scarce sea-worthy;	" .	657
name Of his *v* great in story,	*The Captain*	19
veteran.		
Me the sport of ribald *V's,*	*Boädicea* .	50
vex		
V not thou the poet's mind (rep.)	*Poet's Mind*	1
to *v* me with his father's eyes!	*Œnone* .	251
And an eye shall *v* thee	*Locksley H.*	85
Will *v* thee lying underground ?	*Two Voices*	110
The end and the beginning *v*	" .	208
I will not *v* my bosom ;	*Amphion* .	12
want of pence. Which *v'es* public men *Will Water*		44
Ere you were born to *v* us ?	*Princess,* vi.	231
misled the girl To *v* true hearts;	" vii.	227
daily *v'es* household peace,	*In Mem.* xxix.	2
I *v* my heart with fancies dim;	" ali.	1
Let this not *v* thee, noble heart !	" lxxvii.	2
An old song *v'es* my ear .	*Maud,* II. ii.	47
Who love to *v* him eating, .	*Enid* .	1409

	POEM.	LINE
began To *v* and plague her.	Guinevere	68
t' an ear too sad to listen to me,	"	313
it would *v* him even in his grave,	En. Arden	802
my dead face would *v* her after-life	"	892

vexed—vext
V with a morbid devil in his blood	Walk.to the M.	73
The farmer *v* packs up his beds	"	31
rainy Hyades *V* the dim sea,	Ulysses	11
they *v* the souls of deans;	Princess,Pro	161
cursing Cyril, *v* at heart,	" IV	153
Fool that I am to be *v* with his pride	Maud, I xiii.	5
V with lawyers and harass'd with debt	" xix.	22
He *v* her and perplext her	" xx.	6
James departed *v* with him and her.	The Brook	110
A little *v* at losing of the hunt,	Enid	234
'No, no,' said Enid, *v*, 'I will not eat,	"	1504
V at a rumour rife about the Queen	Vivien	10
Lancelot *v* at having lied in vain:	Elaine	103
so sullen, *v* he could not go;	"	210
I should evermore be *v* with thee	Guinevere	501
if he come again, *v* will he be	En Arden	300
V with unworthy madness,	Aylmer's F.	335
Then their eyes *v* her;	"	802
What time have I to be *v*?	Grandmother	104

vial.
A man with knobs and wires and *v*'s	Princess,Pro.	65

viand.
Lay out the *v*'s	Princess, iii.	379
Fruit, blossom, *v*, amber wine,	" iv.	17

vibrate
the Queen's shadow, *v* on the walls,	Elaine	1169
Star to star *v*'s light.	Aylmer's F.	578

vice.
crush her, like a *v* in blood,	In Mem. iii.	15
whirl'd into folly and *v*.	Maud, I. iv.	19
doubling all his master's *v* of pride,	Enid	195
stirr'd this *v* in you which ruin'd man	Vivien	212
well, I will not call it *v*;	"	218
would make you Master of all *V*.	"	319

vicious.
Who being *v*, old and irritable,	Enid	194

victim.
death quiver'd at the *v*'s throat;	D of F Wom.	115
dress the *v* to the offering up,	Princess, iv.	112
took him for a *v* of E Doorm,	Enid	1373
the *v*'s flowers befor he fall.	Elaine	906
slimed his *v* ere he gorged;	Sea Dreams	180
Till the *v* hear within	Boädicea	58
seem'd a *v* due to the Priest.	The Victim	37
Priest was happy His *v* won	"	66
The rites prepared, the *v* bared,	"	70

victor
Whichever side be *V*, in the halloo	Princess, ii.	213
bearded *V* of ten-thousand hymns,	" iii.	334
We vanquish'd, you the *V* of your will	" vi.	151
fawn at a *v*'s feet.	Maud, I. vi.	66
The great World-victor's *v*	Ode on Well.	42
And *V* he must ever be	"	258
the *v*, to confound them more,	Enid	1018
v at the tilt and tournament,	"	1808
prize and could not find The *v*	Elaine	627

Victoria.
V,—since your Royal grace.	To the Queen	5

victory.
Arac, satiate with his *v*.	Princess, vii.	75
Bellowing *v*, bellowing doom:	Ode on Well.	66
Whether you wish me *v* or defeat,	Enid	929
down their statue of *V* fell.	Boädicea	30
and there cometh a *v* now.	"	46

victual.
Bare *v* for the mowers;	Enid	1051
Ate all the mowers' *v* unawares	"	1064
fetch Fresh *v* for these mowers	"	1074
return With *v* for these men,	"	1089

	POEM.	LINE.
vied.		
Sappho and others *v* with any man;	Princess, ii.	148

Vienna.
in *V*'s fatal walls	In Mem.lxxxiv.	19
I have not seen, I will not see *V*.	" xcvii.	12

view
full in *v* Death, walking all alone.	Love and Death	4
When thus he met his mother's *v*,	L. C V. de Vere	34
Half-invisible to the *v*,	Vision of Sin	36
telescopes For azure *v*'s;	Princess,Pro	68
Her early Heaven, her happy *v*'s;	In Mem. xxxiii	6
somewhere, out of human *v*,	" lxxiv.	18
tho' it spake and bared to *v*.	" xci.	9
to reprove her For stealing out of *v*	Maud, I. xx.	9

vignette.
In bright *v*'s, and each complete,	The Daisy	45

vigorously.
So *v* yet mildly, that all hearts	Enid	1805

vigour.
my *v*, wedded to thy blood	Œnone	158
The faith, the *v*, bold to dwell	In Mem. xciv.	29
shall see my *v* is not lost'	Enid	931

vile.
v it were For some three suns to store	Ulysses	28
'This is more *v*,' he made reply,	Two Voices	103
men sought to prove me *v*,	Vivien	345
Hired animalisms, *v* as those that made	Lucretius	53

vileness.
No inner *v* that we dread?	In Mem l.	4
mean *V*, we are grown so proud	Aylmer's F.	756

viler.
of a kind The *v*, as underhand,	Maud, I. i.	28

village.
Two children in two neighbour *v*'s	Circumstance	1
The little *v* looks forlorn;	In Mem. lix.	9
Maud the delight of the *v*,	Maud, I. i.	70
Below me, there, is the *v*,	" iv.	7
almost all the *v* had one name;	Aylmer's F.	35

village-churls.
And there the surly *v-c*	L. of Shalott, ii.	16

villager.
slavish hat from the *v*'s head?	Maud, I. x.	4

villain.
One says, we are *v*'s all.	Maud, I. i.	17
lurk three *v*'s yonder in the wood,	Enid	991

villainy.
V somewhere! whose? One says	Maud, I. i.	17
I will tell him all their *v*.	Enid	981

vine.
comest not with shows of flaunting *v*'s	Ode to Mem	48
silent in its dusty *v*'s	Mariana in the S.	4
leaning on a fragment twined with *v*	Œnone	19
overhead the wandering ivy and *v*	"	97
Fromcave to cave thro'the thick-twined *v*	Lotos-E's.	140
The valleys of grape-loaded *v*'s	D. of F Wom.	219
chimneys muffled in the leafy *v*	Audley Ct.	18
old elms came breaking from the *v*	Amphion	45
The *v* stream'd out to follow	"	9
by tilth and grange, And *v*'s,	Princess, i.	110
summer of the *v* in all his veins—	"	181
friends, none closer, elm and *v*	" ii.	316
I hook'd my ancle in a *v*,	" iv.	249
foxlike in the *v*;	" vii.	188
Summer belts of wheat and *v*	In Mem. xcvii.	4
Beating from the wasted *v*'s	Ode on Well.	109
olive, aloe, and maize and *v*.	The Daisy	15
from the vast oriel-embowering *v*	Elaine	1192
from a bower of *v* and honeysuckle,	Aylmer's F.	156
Mixt with myrtle and clad with *v*	The Islet	19
V, *v*, and eglantine,	The Window	21,28

vine-bunches.
Between the shadows of the *v-b*	Œnone	177

vine-clad.
an oriel on the summer-side, *V-c*,	Elaine	1172

	vineyard.	POEM.	LINE.
Peace in her v—yes!—		*Maud,* I. i.	36
The torrent v streaming fell		*The Daisy* .	10
	vintage.		
Whether the v, yet unkept .		*Will Water.*	97
with meats and v of their best		*Elaine* .	266
praised the waning red, and told The v *Aylmer's F.* 407			
	violate.		
behold our sanctuary is v, .		*Princess,* vi	44
that she now perforce must v it.		*Enid* .	1216
	violated		
So was their sanctuary v, .		*Princess,* vii.	1
	violating		
t the bond of like to like		*Elaine*	241
	violater		
mine of ruffian v; i	.	*Boadicea* .	50
	violence		
Moved with v changed in hue,		*Vision of Sin*	34
snatch me from him as by v;		*Enid* .	1206
bare her by main v to the board,		" .	1502
wrought upon himself After a life of v. "			1761
small v done Rankled in him.		*Guinevere* .	49
and shriek'd 'Thus, thus with v, (rep) *Sea Dreams* 25			
	violet.		
With what voice the v woos .		*Adeline* .	31
V, amaracus and asphodel .		*Œnone* .	95
from the v's her light foot Shone .		" .	175
and now the v's here. . .		*May Queen,* iii.	4
O sweet is the new v, . .		" .	5
The smell of v's, hidden in the green, *D. of F. Wom.* 77			
The v of a legend blow		*Will Water.*	147
In mosses mix'd with v		*Sir L. and Q. G.*	30
The v varies from the lily as far		*Princess,* v.	174
The v of his native land.		*In Mem.* xviii.	4
A wither'd v is her bliss ;		" xcvi.	26
The v comes, but we are gone,		" civ.	8
By ashen roots the v's blow		" cxiv.	4
Becomes an April v, . .		" .	19
In v's blue as your eyes .		*Maud,* I. xxii.	42
Crocus, anemone, v, .		*To F. D. Maurice*	44
Pity, the v on the tyrant's grave.		*Aylmer's F.*	845
	Violet.		
V, she that sang the mournful song, *Princess,* vi. 298			
	violet-hooded.		
Epics lilted out By v-h Doctors, .		*Princess,* ii.	354
	violin.		
twangling v Struck up with Soldier-laddie,	.	*Princess, Pro.*	85
heard The flute, v, bassoon .		*Maud,* I. xxii.	14
	viper.		
fling it like a v off, and shriek		*Princess,* vii.	79
stood stiff as a v frozen :		*Vivien* .	694
Jenny, the v, made me a mocking *Grandmother* 46			
	Virgilian.		
The rich V rustic measure .		*The Daisy* .	75
	virgin.		
Christ, the V Mother, and the Saints *St S. Stylites* 110			
I was ever v save for thee, .		*Guinevere* .	553
The V Mother standing with her child *Sea Dreams* 234			
	virtue.		
He spake of v; not the gods		*A Character*	17
V !—to be good and just— .		*Vision of Sin*	111
The use of v out of earth : .		*In Mem.* lxxxi.	10
words have v such as draws .		" lxxxiv.	13
Like V firm, like Knowledge fair		*The Voyage*	68
V, like a household god .		*On a Mourner*	30
Glory of V, to fight, to struggle,		*Wages* .	3
if the wages of V be dust, .		" .	6
	visage.		
His v all agrin as at a wake, .		*Princess,* v.	510
	vision.		
With dazed v unawares .		*Arabian N's.*	112
there a v caught my eye ; .		*Miller's D.*	76
moves among my v's of the lake		*Ed. Morris*	144

	POEM.	LINE
on this v of the golden year.'	*Golden Year*	58
Saw the V of the world .	*Locksley H.*	16, 120
see the v that I saw. .	*Day-Dm.*	14
Ah, blessed v ! blood of God !	*Sir Galahad*	45
had a v when the night was late :	*Vision of Sin*	1
V's of a perfect State : .	"	148
the weird v of our house : .	*Princess,* iii.	168
If any v should reveal .	*In Mem.* xci.	1
I dream'd a v of the dead,	" cii.	3
nor would he tell His v; .	*Guinevere* .	304
Uncertain as a v or a dream,	*En. Arden*.	351
v's in the Northern dreamer's heavens, *Aylmer's F.* 161		
sleptagain, and pieced The broken v *Sea Dreams* 106		
For one fair V ever fled .	*The Voyage*	57
visit (s.)		
later, pay one t here, .	*To F. D. Maurice*	45
visit (verb)		
oh, haste, V my low desire !	*Ode to Mem.*	4
visitant.		
Edith ever z with him, .	*Aylmer's F.*	166
visiting.		
there From college, v the son,— .	*Princess, Pro.*	7
visor.		
and the knight Had z up, .	*Enid* .	189
Vivat Rex.		
Death is king, and V R ! .	*Vision of Sin*	179
Vivian.		
Sir Walter V all a summer's day .	*Princess, Pro*	1
Vivian-place.		
we were seven at V-p .	*Princess, Pro.*	9
miss'd the mignonette of V-p .	"	164
climb'd The slope to V-p .	" *Con.*	40
Vivien.		
At Metlin's feet the wily V lay .	*Vivien*	5
The wily V stole from Arthur's court	"	6
V, being greeted fair, Would fain	"	11
V should attempt the blameless King	"	10
V follow'd, but he mark'd her not	"	48
V ever sought to work the charm	"	64
lissome V, holding by his heel .	"	87
So V call'd herself But rather seem'd	"	110
tricks and fooleries, O V, the preamble?	"	115
V bath'd your feet before her own ?	"	113
Take V for expounder ; .	"	168
Too curious V, tho' you talk of trust,	"	208
V, like the tenderest-hearted maid being found take heed of V. .	"	227
V breaking in upon him, said : .	"	379
'You read the book, my pretty V'!	"	430
V, frowning in true anger, .	"	517
V deeming Merlin overborne, .	"	541
V, gathering somewhat of his mood	"	649
V had not done to win his trust .	"	691
V, fearing heaven had heard .	"	712
lissome V, of her court The wiliest *Guinevere*		23
Vizier.		
V's nodding together .	*Maud,* I. vii.	11
voated.		
a knaws I hallus v wi' Squoire .	*N Farmer* .	15
vocabulary.		
Scatter'd all over the v .	*Aylmer's F.*	540
vocal.		
Is z. in its wooded walls ; .	*In Mem.* xix.	14
V, with here and there a silence, .	*Aylmer's F.*	149
voice.		
Old v's call'd her from without .	*Mariana* .	63
That her z untuneful grown .	*The Owl,* ii.	6
With what z the violet woos .	*Adeline* .	31
tho' its z be so clear and full .	*Poet's Mind*	34
With an inner v the river ran, .	*Dying Swan*	5
anon her awful jubilant v, .	"	29
fill the sea-halls with a z of power : *The Merman* 10		
by common v, Elected umpire .	*Œnone* .	82
Then first I heard the v of her .	"	105

	POEM.	LINE
'Now' she shriek'd in that lone hall	*Pal. of Art*	258
No *v* breaks thro' the stillness	"	259
And sweeter is the young lamb's *v*	*May Queen*,iii.	6
O blessings on his kindly *v*	"	13
The *v*, that now is speaking,	"	54
His *v* was thin, as *v's* from the grave	*Lotos-E's.*	34
my *v* was thick with sighs	*D. of F. Wom.*	109
I heard a *v* that cried 'Come here,	"	123
Her warbling *v*, a lyre of widest range	"	165
a low *v*, full of care, Murmur'd	"	249
in her throat Her *v* seem'd distant	*To J. S.*	55
fragments of her mighty *v* '*Of old sat Freedom,' etc.*		7
v, or else a motion of the mere.	*M. d'Arthur*	77
one *v*, an agony Of lamentation,	"	200
let thy *v* Rise like a fountain	"	248
further inland, *v's* echoed—' come	*Ep.*	27
v's of the well-contented doves	*Gardener's D.*	88
such a *v* Call'd to me from the years	"	175
silver fragments of a broken *v*	"	229
v fled always thro' the summer land	*Ed. Morris*	67
lower *v's* saint me from above	*St S. Stylites*	152
a heart, And answer'd with a *v*.	*Talking O.*	20
sent her *v* thro' all the holt	"	123
low *v*, Faltering, would break its	*Love and Duty*	38
the deep Moans round with many *v's*	*Ulysses*	56
for a tender *v* will cry	*Lockley H.*	87
A still small *v* spake unto me,	*Two Voices*	1
'O dull, one-sided *v*,' said I	"	202
'If all be dark, vague *v*'	"	265
v with which I fenced A little ceased,	"	317
The still *v* laughed.	"	385
The dull and bitter *v* was gone.	"	426
A second voice was at mine ear	"	427
What is it thou knowest, sweet *v*?'	"	440
commune with that barren *v*,	"	461
whisper'd *v's* at his ear.	*Day-Dm.*	124
I hear a *v*, but none are there;	*Sir Galahad*	30
Wings flutter, *v's* hover clear;	"	78
A deedful life, a silent *v*: '*You might have won,' etc.*		8
The *v* grew faint:	*Vision of Sin*	207
I heard a *v* upon the slope	"	219
Between the rougher *v's* of the men,	*Princess, Pro.*	237
a *V* Went with it, 'Follow,	i.	98
crack'd and small his *v*	"	113
Hers are we,' One *v*, we cried:	"	232
full *v* which circles round the grave,	ii.	31
all her *v* Faltering and fluttering	"	169
so rapt, we gazing, came a *v*,	"	297
sweet a *v* and vague, fatal to men	iv.	46
still my *v* Rang false	"	102
love their *v's* more than duty	"	491
and heard The *v's* murmuring	"	517
v is heard thro' rolling drums,	"	554
stumbled on a stationary *v*,	v.	2
She moan'd, a folded *v*.	"	69
she lifted up her *v* and cried	"	78
every *v* she talk'd with ratify it,	"	127
an awful *v* within had warn'd him	"	328
Ida with a *v*, that like a bell	vi.	311
Then the *v* Of Ida sounded.	"	352
Low *v's* with the ministering hand	vii.	6
Sweeter thy *v*, but every sound is sweet	"	204
the *v* trembled and the hand	"	212
v Choked, and her forehead sank	"	230
A Spirit, not a breathing *v*	*In Mem* xiii.	12
Four *v's* of four hamlets round	" xxviii.	5
Each *v* four changes on the wind,	"	9
echo-like our *v's* rang;	" xxx.	13
Our *v's* took a higher range :	"	21
if some *v* that man could trust	" xxxv.	1
many an abler *v* than thou	" xxxvii.	4
O for thy *v* to soothe and bless!	" lv.	26
The *v* was low, the look was bright :	" lxviii.	15
The *v* was not the *v* of grief.	"	19
v, the richest-toned that sings	" lxxiv.	7
So loud with *v's* of the birds,	" xcviii.	2
Like strangers' *v's* here they sound	" ciii.	9
A potent *v* of Parliament,	" cxii.	11
that dear *v*, I once have known	" cxv.	11
v's hail it from the brink ;	" cxx.	14
I heard a *v* 'believe no more.'	" cxxiii.	10
	POEM.	LINE.
A deeper *v* across the storm,	*In Mem.* cxxvi.	4
Thy *v* is on the rolling air ;	" cxxix.	1
I prosper, circled with thy *v*;	"	15
A *v* as unto him that hears,	" cxxx.	6
A *v* by the cedar-tree,	*Maud*, I. v.	1
v pealing up to the sunny sky,	"	13
Silence, beautiful *v!*	"	19
Not her, not her, but a *v*.	"	28
simper and set their *v s* lower	x.	15
the *v* of the long sea-wave as it swell'd	xiv.	31
v from which their omens all men	*Ode on Well.*	36
He knew their *v's* of old	"	63
with those deep *v's* wrought	"	67
With those deep *v's* our dead captain	"	69
thro' the centuries let a people's *v* (rep.)	"	142
A people's *v*, when they rejoice	"	146
A people's *v*, we are a people yet.	"	151
We have a *v*, with which to pay	"	156
His *v* is silent in your council-hall	"	174
V in the rich dawn of an ampler day	*Ded. of Idylls*	35
hearing any more his noble *v*,	*Enid*	98
The *v* of Enid, Yniol's daughter,	"	327
as the sweet *v* of a bird,	"	329
Sweet *v* of Enid moved Geraint	"	334
by God's grace, is the one *v* for me.'	"	344
soldiers wont to hear His *v* in battle,	"	1024
low firm *v* and tender government,	"	1043
many a *v* along the street,	"	1119
tender sound of his own *v*	"	1197
with a big *v* 'What, is he dead?'.	"	1390
answer'd in low *v*, her meek head	"	1488
'The *v* of Enid,' said the knight ;	"	1628
reverent eyes mock-royal, shaken *v; Vivien*		13
O my Master, have you found your *v?*	"	118
So tender was her *v*, so fair her face,	"	251
heard their *v's* talk behind the wall,	"	481
false *v* made way broken with sobs	"	706
v clings to each blade of grass	*Elaine*	108
And every *v* is nothing.	"	109
vermin *v's* here May buzz so loud—	"	139
Won by the mellow *v* before she look'd	"	243
Seeing me, with a great *v* he cried	"	309
like a friend's *v* from a distant field	"	993
High with the last line scaled her *v*,	"	1013
crying with full *v* 'Traitor, come out,	*Guinevere*	104
silence, then a *v* Monotonous	"	416
warhorse neigh'd As at a friend's *v*,	"	527
there her *v* brake suddenly,	"	601
from the *v's* crying 'shame' .	"	664
where beyond these *v's* there is peace	"	690
pay the *v* who best could tell	*En Arden*	265
their *v's* make me feel so solitary	"	394
v beneath him thro' the wood	"	441
and his *v* Shaking a little	"	461
Nor ever hear a kindly *v*,	"	583
Crying with a full *v* 'a sail !	"	912
ever call'd away By one low *v*	*Aylmer's F.*	60
a *v* Of comfort and an open hand.	"	173
Low was her *v*, but won mysterious	"	695
no prophet but the *v* that calls	"	741
I wish'd my *v* A rushing tempest	"	756
your rough *v* (You spoke so loud)	*Sea Dreams*	269
Deepening thy *v* with the deepening	*V. of Cauteretz*	2
living *v* to me was as the *v* of the dead	"	8
v of the dead was a living *v* to me	"	10
Roll and rejoice, jubilant *v*.	*W. to Alexan.*	22
I shall know Thy *v*, and answer '*My life is full,' etc.*		10
murmurs of a deeper *v*,	*On a Mourner*	16
Paid with a *v* flying by to be lost.	*Wages*	2
and the bird Makes his heart *v*	*Lucretius*	101
voiceless.		
creatures *v* thro' the fault of birth	*Enid*	1115
void.		
Not *v* of righteous self applause,	*Two Voices.*	146
Naked I go, and void of cheer :	"	239
The stalls are *v*, the doors are wide,	*Sir Galahad*	31
v was her use ;	*Princess,* vii.	19
A *v* where heart on heart reposed	*In Mem* xiii.	6
cast as rubbish to the *v*,	" liii.	7
V of the little living will	*Maud,* II. ii.	14

	POEM	LINE
A *v* was made in Nature	*Lucretius*	37
Vanishing, atom and *v*, atom and *v*,	"	254

volley'd.
| V and thunder'd | *Lt. Brigade* | 21,42 |

volubility.
| in her fierce *v*, | *Boädicea* | 4, 72 |

volume.
found it in a *v*, all of songs,	*Audley Ct.*	56
held a *v* as to read,	*Princess*, ii.	431
A *v* of the Poets of her land:	" vii.	159
at her feet the *v* fell.	"	238

voluptuousness.
| in his lust and *v*, | *Boädicea* | 66 |

vote.
| A wretched *v* may be gain'd. | *Maud*, I. vi. | 56 |

vow.
O would she give me *v* for *v*,	*Miller's D.*	119
died, To save her father's *v*;	*D. of F Wom.*	196
v's, where there was never need of *v*'s	*Gardener's D.*	253
That oft hast heard my *v s*	*Talking O.*	98
name I carved with many *v*'s	"	154
my *v* blinds me to speak,	*Princess*, ii.	184
breathe a thousand tender *v*'s	*In Mem.* xx.	2
At one dear knee we proffer'd *v*'s.	" lxxviii.	13
early faith and plighted *v*'s;	" xcvi.	30
Before you hear my marriage *v*	*The Letters.*	8
They bound to holy *v*'s of chastity!	*Vivien*	545
swearing men to *v*'s impossible,	*Elaine*	131
Full many a holy *v* and pure resolve	"	875
Kissing his *v*'s upon it like a knight.	*Aylmer's F.*	472

vow'd.
| *v* that could I gain her, our kind Queen | *Enid* | 787 |

voyage.
after my long *v* I shall rest!	*Elaine*	1055
the story of her dolorous *v*	"	1333
go This *v* more than once?	*En. Arden*	142
this *v* by the grace of God	"	190
dull the *v* was with long delays,	"	656
Then he told her of his *v*,	"	862

Vulcan.
| mounted, Ganymedes, To tumble, *V*'s, | *Princess*, iii | 56 |

vulture
| For whom the carrion *v* waits 'You might have won' | | 35 |
| swoops The *v*, beak and talon, | *Princess*, v. | 373 |

W

waäste.
an' I 'a stubb'd Thornaby *w*.	*N. Farmer*	28
D' ya moind the *w*, my lass?	"	29
Dubbut looak at the *w*:	"	37

wader.
| toward us, like a *w* in the surf, | *The Brook* | 117 |

waft (s.)
| With one *w* of the wing. | *The Captain* | 72 |

waft (verb.)
| Yet *w* me from the harbour-mouth 'You ask me, why' | | 25 |
| Spread thy full wings, and *w* him o'er | *In Mem.* ix. | 4 |

wafted.
| the woodbine spices are *w* abroad | *Maud*, I. xxii. | 5 |

wag.
| to *w* their baldness up and down. | *Princess*, v. | 18 |

wage.
| I *w* not any feud with Death | *In Mem* lxxxi. | 1 |
| To *w* grim war against Sir Lancelot | *Guinevere* | 191 |

waged.
| *W* such unwilling tho' successful war | *Vivien* | 421 |

wages.
| The *w* of sin is death: if the *w* of Virtue be dust | *Wages* | 6 |
| Give her the *w* of going on, | " | 10 |

	POEM.	LINE.
wagged.		
eye darken'd and his helmet *w*;	*Enid*	1354

waging
| while the King Was *w* war on Lancelot: | *Guinevere* | 154 |
| From *w* bitter war with him: | " | 431 |

waif
| rolling in his mind Old *w*'s of rhyme | *The Brook* | 199 |

wail (s.)
whose dying eyes Were closed with *w*	*In Mem* lxxxix	6
Phantom *w* of women and children,	*Boädicea*	26
gets for greeting but a *w* of pain;	*Lucretius*	138

wail (verb.)
Here it is only the mew that *w*'s	*Sea-Fairies*	19
Cease to *w* and brawl!	*Two Voices*	199
Dead March *w*'s in the people's ears	*Ode on Well.*	267
not dead, Why *w* you for him thus?	*Enid*	1396
wherefore *w* for one Who put your	"	1522
burst away To weep and *w* in secret;	*Elaine*	1238

wailed.
and *w* about with mews.	*Princess*, iv.	263
They wept and *w*, but led the way	*In Mem* cii.	18
wind like a broken worldling *w*,	*Maud*, I. i.	11
w and woke The mother,	*Sea Dreams*	57
Claspt, kiss'd him, *w*:	*Lucretius*	276

wailing.
on the mere the *w* died away.	*M d'Arthur*	272
hear me hke a wind *W* for ever,	*Princess*, v.	96
Your *w* will not quicken him:	*Enid*	1398
the owls *W* had power upon her	*Elaine*	995
After much *w*, hush'd itself at last	*Aylmer's F*	542
Their wildest *w*'s never out of tune	*Sea Dreams*	224

wain.
| or when the lesser *w* Is twisting | *In Mem.* c. | 11 |
| The team is loosen'd from the *w*. | " cxx. | 5 |

wainscot
| Behind the mouldering *w* shriek'd, | *Mariana* | 64 |

waist.
the girdle About her dainty dainty *w*	*Miller's D.*	176
You should have clung to Fulvia's *w*.	*D. of F. Wom.*	259
Lovingly lower, trembled on her *w*—	*Gardener's D*	130
She strove to span my *w*:	*Talking. O.*	138
round her *w* she felt it fold,	*Day-Dm.*	166
her round the knees against his *w*,	*Princess*, ii.	342
cloth of gold Drawn to her *w*,	*Elaine*	1152

waist-deep.
| *w-d* in meadow-sweet. | *The Brook* | 118 |

wait.
eyes That said, We *w* for thee	*Pal. of Art*	104
And there to *w* a liittle while	*May Queen*, iii.	58
those, not blind, who *w* for day 'Love thou thy land'		15
W, nor Love himself will bring	*Love and Duty*	23
W: my faith is large in Time	"	25
the Powers, who *w* On noble deeds,	*Godiva*	71
For me the Heavenly Bridegroom *w*'s	*St Agnes' Eve*	31
whom the carrion vulture *w*'s 'You might have won'		35
thoughts that *w* On you, their centre	*Princess*, iv.	423
Invective seem'd to *w* behind her lips,	"	451
As *w*'s a river level with the dam.	"	452
'The second two: they *w*' he said	" v.	4
every captain *w*'s Hungry for honour	"	303
w upon him, Like mine own brother.	" vi.	279
The Shadow sits and *w*'s for me.	*In Mem.* xxii	20
doubt beside the portal *w*'s,	" xciii.	14
those white-favour'd horses *w*;	" *Con.*	90
And the lily whispers, 'I *w*.'	*Maud*, I xxii.	66
'Therefore *w* with me,' she said	*Enid*	180
W here, and when he passes	"	978
Enid stood aside to *w* the event,	"	1002
'dear Philip, *w* a while:	*En. Arden*	427
w a year, a year is not so long:	"	429
wiser in a year: O *w* a little I'	"	431
I well may *w* a little.'	"	433
he read God's warning, '*w*.'	"	572
she shall know, I *w* His time.	"	612
but, he, could not *w*,	*Sea Dreams*	146
W a little, *w* a little, You shall name	*The Window*	172

CONCORDANCE TO

waited.

	POEM.	LINE
I w underneath the dawning hills	Œnone	46
To me, methought, who w with	M d'Arthur, Ep	20
tell him Dora w with the child ;	Dora	74
I w long ; My brows are ready.	St S. Stylites	202
I w for the train at Coventry ;	Godiva	1
thronging in and in. to where they w.	Vision of Sin	26
a group of girls In circle w,	Princess, Pro.	69
let us know The Princess Ida w:	" ii	7
and w, fifty there Opposed to fifty.	" v.	471
while he w in the castle court	Enid	326
stood behind, and w on the three	"	392
w there for Yniol and Geraint	"	538
Then Enid w pale and sorrowful,	"	932
while we w, one, the youngest of us,	Vivien	265
'Annie, as I have w all my life	En. Arden	432
Mute with folded arms they w—	The Captain	39

waiter.

| halo lives About the w's hands | Will Water | 114 |
| Slip-shod w, lank and sour. | Vision of Sin | 71 |

waitest.

| What aileth thee? whom w thou. | Adeline | 45 |
| Poor child, that w for thy love! | In Mem vi. | 28 |

waiteth.

| standeth there alone And w at the D. of the O Year | | 51 |

waiting.

My whole soul w silently,	Fatima	36
Kept watch, w decision,	Œnone	141
W to see me die.	D of F. Wom.	112
truths of Science w to be caught—	Golden Year	17
W to strive a happy strife,	Two Voices	130
So quickly, w for a hand,	In Mem. vii	4
That Shadow w with the keys	" xxvi.	15
Now w to be made a wife	" Con.	49
stood a maiden near, W to pass.	The Brook	205
stay'd W to hear the hounds.	Enid	163
In shadow, w for them, caitiffs all ;	"	907
by the rock W to fall on you,	"	922
Three other horsemen w, wholly	"	970
w to be treated like a wolf	"	1705
Ready to spring, w a chance :	Guinevere	13
w by the doors the warhorse neigh'd	"	326
A shipwreck'd sailor, w for a sail	En. Arden	591
by their chariots, w for the dawn,	Spec of Iliad	22

waive.

| she will not : w your claim | Princess, v. | 286 |

wake (festival.)

| visage all agrin as at a w, | Princess, v. | 510 |

wake (track)

| in the white w of the morning star | Princess, iii. | 1 |
| With w's of fire we tore the dark ; | The Voyage | 52 |

wake (verb.)

while a sweeter music w's,	To the Queen	13
I w alone, I sleep forgotten, I w forlorn.'	Mariana in the S	35
You must w and call me early,	May Queen, I i.	41
I shall never w If you do not call me loud	"	10
to sit, to sleep, to w, to breathe	Ed. Morris	40
I w: the chill stars sparkle	St S. Stylites	112
freër, till thou w refresh'd	Love and Duty	94
We sleep and w and sleep,	Golden Year	22
Æolian harp that w's No certain air	Two Voices	436
'O w for ever, love,' she hears,	Day-Dm.	175
thy kiss would w the dead !'	"	184
w on science grown to more,	"	222
pass on : His Highness w's.	Princess, v.	5
w's A lisping of the innumerous leaf	"	12
With morning w's the will, and cries	In Mem iv.	15
To whom a conscience never w's ;	" xxvii.	8
I almost wish'd no more to w,	" xxviii.	14
I w, and I discern the truth ;	" lxvii.	14
wherefore w The old bitterness again	" lxxxii.	8
And I w, my dream is fled	Maud, II iv.	51
Let it go or stay, so I w to the higher	III vi.	38
but as one before he w's	The Brook	215
Enid had no heart To w him,	Enid	1219
of Fame while woman w's to love.'	Vivien	310

	POEM	LINE
'W him not : let him sleep	En. Arden	232
a storm never w's on the lonely sea	The Islet	33

waked.

| to sleep with sound, And w with | M. d'Arthur, Ep. | 4 |

wakefulness.

| After a night of feverous w, | En. Arden | 230 |

waken.

The fire-fly w's : w thou with me.	Princess, vii.	164
w's at this hour of rest.	In Mem. ciii.	6
in my breast Spring w's too :	" cxiv.	18

waken'd.

the first matin-song hath w loud	Ode to Mem.	68
eyes, like thine, have w hopes ?	Day-Dm.	257
at the last he w from his swoon,	Enid	1431
thrice I w after dreams.	Lucretius	34

wakenest.

| Who w with thy balmy breath | In Mem.xcviii. | 13 |

waking

W she heard the night-fowl crow	Mariana	26
If you're w call me early,	May Queen,ii	1,32
come to her w, find her asleep,	Maud, II. ii.	81
And Enid started w,	Enid	674
W laughter in indolent reviewers	Hendecasyllabics	8
dreams that come just ere the w	Lucretius	36

Wales.

| last summer on a tour in W: | Golden Year | 2 |

walk (s.)

A w with vary-colour'd shells	Arabian N's.	57
sob and sigh In the w's ; 'A spirit haunts,' etc.		6
The secretest w's of fame :	The Poet	10
said Death, 'these w's are mine.'	Love and Death	7
yielding, gave into a grassy w	Gardener's D	103
caught And blown across the w.	"	124
With words of promise in his w,	Day-Dm.	123
w's were stript as bare as brooms	Princess,Pro	182
bells Call'd us ; we left the w's,	" ii.	447
on the sward, and up the linden w's,	" iv.	191
Nor waves the cypress in the palace w	" vii.	162
In those deserted w's, may find	In Mem. viii.	14
in the flowery w Of letters,	" lxxxiii.	22
Up that long w of limes I past	" lxxxvi.	15
saw thro' all the Muses' w ;	" cviii.	4
light foot along the garden w,	Maud, I. xviii.	9
'To gentle Maud in our w	" xix.	13
the meadow your w's have left so sweet	" xxii.	39
Katie somewhere in the w's below,	The Brook	80
w's in Boboli's ducal bowers.	The Daisy	44
or gamboll'd down the w's ;	Enid	663
ran a w Of shingle, and a w divided it	En. Arden	737
Enoch shunn'd the middle w	"	739
often, in his w's with Edith, claim	Aylmer's F.	61

walk (verb.)

In sleep she seem'd to w forlorn	Mariana	30
I w, I dare not think of thee,	Oriana	91
W's forgotten, and is forlorn.'	Mariana in the S.	48
So sweet it seems with thee to w,	Miller's D.	29
made it sweet To w, to sit, to sleep	Ed. Morris	40
slip its bark and w.	Talking O	168
any man that w's the mead,	Day-Dm.	265
cares to w With Death and Morning	Princess, vii.	188
O we will w this world Yoked	"	339
Nor follow, tho' I w in haste	In Mem. xxii.	18
nothing w's with aimless feet	" liii.	5
I w as ere I walk'd forlorn,	" lxvii.	5
From state to state the spirit w's ;	" lxxxi.	6
to w all day like the sultan of old.	Maud, I. iv.	42
w's with his head in a cloud of poisonous	"	54
There she w's in her state,	" xiv.	3
Katie w's By the long wash.	The Brook	193
He that w's it, only thirsting	Ode on Well.	203
W your dim cloister, and distribute	Guinevere	675
w So freely with his daughter	Aylmer's F.	269

walked.

| as he w, King Arthur panted hard | M. d'Arthur | 176 |
| I'm glad I w. How fresh | Walk. to the M. | 1 |

	POEM.	LINE.
One w between his wife and child	Two Voices	412
The little maiden w demure,	"	419
while I w and talked as heretofore	Princess, i.	16
One w reciting by herself	" ii.	430
she you w with, she You talk'd with	" vi.	237
IV at their will, and everything was	"	363
where the path we w began	In Mem. xxii.	9
I walk as ere I w forlorn,	" lxvi.	5
In walking as of old we w	" lxx.	12
first he w when claspt in clay?	" xcii.	4
out he w where the wind like a broken	Maud, I. i.	11
IV in a wintry wind	" iii.	13
I have w awake with Truth.	" xix.	6
had he a home? His home, he w.	En. Arden.	670
for she w Wearing the light yoke	Aylmer's F.	707
now on sand they w, and now on cliff	Sea Dreams	37
that the woman w upon the brink	"	108
I w with one I loved	V. of Canteretz	4

walking.

Death, w all alone beneath a yew	Love and Death	5
IV the cold and starless road of Death	Œnone	255
in strange lands a traveller w slow	Pal. of Art	277
Beauty and anguish w hand in hand	D. of F. Wom.	15
IV about the gardens and the halls	M. d'Arthur	20
Met me w on yonder way,	Ed. Gray	2
IV up and pacing down,	L. of Burleigh	90
In w as of old we walk'd	In Mem. lxx.	12
I was w a mile,	Maud, I. ix.	1
She is w in the meadow	" II. v.	37
once, when Arthur w all alone,	Vivien	9
care no more for Leolin's w with her	Aylmer's F.	124

wall s.)

About a stone-cast from the w	Mariana	37
A pillar of white light upon the w	Ode to Mem.	53
falls Upon the storied w's;	"	86
She stood upon the castle w,	Oriana	28
lovers whispering by an orchard w;	Circumstance	4
Four gray w's and four gray towers,	L. of Shalott, i.	15
Struck up against the blinding w.	Mariana in the S.	56
one black shadow from the w	"	80
yonder w's Rose slowly to a music	Œnone	39
bellowing caves. Beneath the windy w.	Pal. of Art	72
That stood against the w.	"	244
With blackness as a solid w,	"	274
between w's Of shadowy granite	Lotos-E's.	48
the tortoise creeping to the w;	D. of F. Wom.	27
All thine, against the garden w.	The Blackbird	8
its w's And chimneys muffled	Audley Ct.	17
thou art staring at the w	Locksley H.	79
blind w's Were full of chinks and holes;	Godiva	59
thro' the Gothic archways in the w,	"	64
That watch the sleepers from the w.	Day-Dm.	44
All creeping plants, a w of green;	"	65
He watches from his mountain w's	The Eagle	5
on the w's, Betwixt the monstrous	Princess, Pro.	5
beat her foes with slaughter from her w's	"	34,123
whelm'd with missiles of the w,	"	45
broken statue propt against the w,	"	99
from the bastion'd w's Like threaded	" i.	106
foundress of the Babylonian w,	" ii.	66
two streams of light from w to w.	"	449
The splendour falls on castle w's	" iii.	348
some that men were in the very w's	" iv.	464
By glimmering lanes and w's of canvas	" v.	6
two hosts that lay beside the w's	" vi.	362
inward from the deeps, a w of night,	" vii.	22
silent light Slept on the painted w's	"	106
the w's Blacken'd about us	Con.	109
Is vocal in its wooded w's	In Mem. xix.	14
There comes a glory on the w's	" lxvi.	5
That in Vienna's fatal w's	" lxxxiv.	19
I past beside the reverend w's	" lxxxvi.	1
A river sliding by the w.	" cii.	8
The blind w rocks, and on the trees	Con.	63
With tender gloom the roof, the w;	"	118
clings To the turrets and the w's;	Maud, II. iv.	34
cannons moulder on the seaward w	Ode on Well.	173
enter'd, and were lost behind the w's.	Enid	252
Ivy-stems Claspt the gray w's	"	323

	POEM.	LINE.
and now and then from distant w's	Enid	505
the long shore-cliffs windy w's	"	1013
drave backward to the w,	"	1122
stronger than a w: there is the keep	"	1190
like a household Spirit at the w's	"	1252
in the four w's of a hollow tower.	Vivien	58,393
wizard brow bleach'd on the w's;	"	447
to him the w That sunders ghosts	"	478
heard their voices talk behind the w,	"	481
'traitor' to the unhearing w,	Elaine	609
the casque Of Lancelot on the w;	"	802
to him thro' those black w's of yew	"	964
grew between her and the pictured w.	"	987
Queen's shadow, vibrate on the w's.	"	1169
from the high w and the flowering grove	Guinevere	34
keeps the rust of murder on the w's	"	74
turn'd her own toward the w and wept	En. Arden	252
Annie with her brows against the w	"	313
late and early roses from his w	"	36
compass'd round by the blind w of night	"	448
blown across her ghostly w:	"	602
Up by the w, behind the yew;	"	740
Stood from his w's and wing'd	Aylmer's F.	18
I cry to vacant chairs and widow'd w's	"	720
Staring for ever from their gilded w's	"	833
A mountain, like a w of bars	Sea Dreams	115
But thieves from o'er the w.	The Flower	11

wall verb.)

To embattail and to w about thy cause	To J. M. K.	8
splinter'd crags that w the dell	D. of F. Wom.	147

wall'd.

a little garden square and w.	En. Arden	735

wallow.

They graze and w, breed and sleep:	Pal. of Art.	202
from the wilderness, w in it,	Boädicea	15

wallowing.

great with pig, w in sun and mud.	Walk. to the M.	80

walnut.

Across the w's and the wine—	Miller's D.	32

Walter.

O IV, I have shelter'd here	Talking O.	37
the son A W tou,—	Princess, Pro.	1
that morning W show'd the house	"	10
Ask'd W, patting Lilia's head	"	125
W hail'd a score of names upon her	"	155
W nodded at me; He began	"	140
W warped his mouth at this	"	203
we saw Sir W where he stood	Con.	61

waltzing-circle.

Yet in the w-c as we went	Coquette, ii.	5

wan.

tinged with w from lack of sleep,	Princess, iii.	9
w was her cheek With hollow watch	" vi.	128
As w, as chill, as wild as now	In Mem. lxxi.	17
face contracting grew Careworn and w;	En. Arden	484

wand.

held his sceptre like a pedant's w	Princess, i.	97
but as lissome as a hazel w;	The Brook	70
over these is laid a silver w,	Enid	483, 542

wander.

W from the side of the morn,	Adeline	52
Light and shadow ever w	A Dirge	12
Wild words w here and there	"	43
Alone I w to and fro,	Oriana	8
then we would w away, away	The Merman	18
at night I would w away, away,	The Mermaid	31
My heart may w from its deeper woe	Œnone	43
brother mariners, we will not w more	Lotos-E's.	173
there to w far away	Locksley H.	157
might a man not w from his wits	Princess, iv.	417
I w, often falling lame	In Mem. xxiii.	6
To w on a darken'd earth,	" lxxxiv.	31
you w about at your will;	Maud, I. iv.	57
felt the King's breath w o'er her neck,	Guinevere	576
Hope is other Hope and w's far	Coquette, i.	10

wander'd

	POEM	LINE
A walk with varycolour'd shells w	Arabian N's.	58
had w far In an old wood:	D. of F Wom	51
nor having w far Shot on the sudden	To J. S.	27
O yes, she w round and round	Talking O.	137
Here about the bench I w,	Locksley H.	11
I blest them, and they w on:	Two Voices.	424
I w from the noisy town,	In Mem lxviii.	5
W at will, but oft accompanied	Aylmer's F.	137
Who knows? but so they w,	"	141
Years have w by	The Captain	66
Nor w into other ways:	'My life is full,' etc.	3

wanderer.

Charm, as a w out in ocean,	Milton	12
W's coming and going	1865-1866	7

wandering

'The w's Of this most intricate Universe	A Character	2
From w over the lea	Sea-Fairies.	11
Œnone, w forlorn Of Paris	Œnone	15
fold our wings, And cease from w's,	Lotos-E's	65
as that other, w there	In Mem. viii.	13
How often, hither w down,	" lxxxviii.	5
(For often in lonely w s	Maud, I. xix.	14

wane

The long day w's: the slow moon climbs:	Ulysses	55
when a thousand moons shall w	In Mem lxxvi.	8
O Sorrow, then can sorrow w?	" lxxvii.	15
as it waxes, of a love that w's?	Elaine	1392

waned

councils thinn'd, And armies w,	Vivien	423

waning.

The pale yellow woods were w,	L of Shalott, iv.	2
Bitter barmaid, w fast!	Vision of Sin	67
Yon orange sunset w slow:	'Move eastward,' etc.	2

wann'd.

Psyche flush'd and w and shook	Princess iv.	142
and ever w with despair	Maud, I. i.	10

want (s.)

left a w unknown before:	Miller's D.	228
Shall sing for w, ere leaves are new,	The Blackbird	23
'tis from no w in her:	Ed. Morris	85
the w, that hollow'd all the heart,	Love and Duty	60
Cursed be the social w's	Locksley H.	59
that eternal w of pence	Will Water.	43
any of our people there In w or peril,	Princess, ii.	248
dear are those three castles to my w's	"	395
either she will die from w of care,	" v.	82
nay, but full of tender w's,	" vii.	300
And ev'n for w of such a type.	In Mem xxxiii.	16
love be blamed for w of faith?	"	l. 10
And he supplied my w the more	" lxxviii.	19
a thousand w's Gnarr at the heels	" xcvii.	16
Ring out the w, the care, the sin,	"	cv. 17
veil His w in forms	"	cx. 6
Unfaith in aught is w of faith in all	Vivien	239
must die for w of one bold word	Elaine	923
nor compensating the w By shrewdness.	En. Arden	249
thro' the w of what it needed most,	"	264
No w was there of human sustenance	"	555
Doubled her own, for w of playmates,	Aylmer's F.	81

want (verb.)

those that w, and those that have	Walk to the M.	50
you w me, sound upon the bugle-horn	Locksley H.	2
More life, and fuller, that I w.'	Two Voices	399
I w her love.	Princess, v.	130
When the man w's weight, the woman	"	434
I w forgiveness too:	" vi.	272
if he w, me let him come to me.	Enid	1086
doubt her fairness were to w an eye	Elaine	1367
her pureness were to w a heart—	"	1368

wanted.

truth! I know not; all are w here.	Enid	289
I w warmth and colour	Guinevere	640
Another ship (She w water)	En. Arden	629
nor w at his end The dark retinue	Aylmer's F.	841

wantest.

What w thou? whom dost thou seek,	Oriana	71

want-begotten.

	POEM.	LINE.
Nor any w-b rest.	In Mem. xxvii.	12

wanting.

He look'd and found them w	Enid	1783
impute themselves, W the mental range:	Vivien	676
w yet a boatswain. Would he go?	En. Arden	123
grieve to see you poor and w help	"	403

wanton (adj. and s.)

fresh to men, And w without measure:	Amphion	58
What did the w say?	Vivien	661

wanton (verb.)

Say to her, I do but w in the South,	Princess, iv	91

war (s.)

let the world have peace or w's	Pal. of Art	182
of the ten years' w in Troy,	Lotos-E's.	122
hearts worn out by many w's	"	131
trumpets blown for w's,	D. of F. Wom.	20
fresh from w's alarms	"	149
the brazen bridge of w—' Love thou thy land,' etc.		76
all good things, and w shall be no	M. d' Arthur, Ep.	28
w. upon each other for an hour	Godiva	34
all the w is roll'd in smoke.'	Two Voices	156
At such strange w with something good	"	302
sleep thro' terms of mighty w's,	Day-Dm.	221
Communing with his captains of the w.	Princess, i.	66
Carian Artemesia strong in w	" ii.	67
arts of w The peasant Joan	"	146
more and acted on, what follows? w;	"	211
I spoke of w to come and many deaths	" iii.	134
clad in iron burst the ranks of w,	" iv.	483
clapt her hands and cried for w,	"	567
o'er the imperial tent Whispers of w.	" v.	10
red-faced w has rods of steel and fire; She yields, or w.'	"	114
say you, w or not?' 'Not w if possible	"	119
lest from the abuse of w	"	120
this knot By gentleness than w.	"	130
would the old God of w himself were dead	"	139
To our point: not w: Lest I lose all.'	"	196
yet my father wills not w:	"	267
'sdeath' myself, what care I, w or no?	"	268
loth by brainless w To cleave the rift	"	290
As one would sing the death of w,	In Mem. cii.	33
Ring out the thousand w's of old,	"	cv. 27
heart of the citizen hissing in w	Maud, I. i.	24
Is it peace or w? Civil w, as I think,	"	27
Is it peace or w? better w! loud w! rep.'	"	47
At w with myself and a wretched race,"	"	x. 35
This huckster put down w?.	"	44
w be a cause or a consequence?	"	45
each is at w with mankind	"	52
I swear to you, lawful and lawless w	" II. v.	94
a hope for the world in the coming w's	" III. vi.	11
w would arise in defence of the right,	"	19
The blood-red blossom of w	"	53
and the w roll down like a wind	"	54
Great in council and great in w,	Ode on Well.	30
Such a w had such a close	"	118
the leader in these glorious w's	"	192
Which made a selfish w begin:	To F. D. Maurice	30
whether w's avenging rod Shall lash	"	33
with the gloom of imminent w	Ded. of Idylls	12
Far-sighted summoner of W and Waste	"	36
Waged such unwilling tho' successful w	Vivien	420
The lady never made unwilling w	"	453
you know Of Arthur's glorious w's	Elaine	285
then the w That thunder'd in and out	"	290
cares For triumph in our mimic w's,	"	312
in this heathen w the fire of God.	"	315
From talk of w to traits of pleasantry	"	320
Arthur's w's were rendered mystically	"	797
King Was waging w on Lancelot	Guinevere	154
To wage grim w against Sir Lancelot	"	191
the bard Sang Arthur's glorious w's,	"	284
From waging bitter w with him:.	"	431
His bashfulness and tenderness at w,	En. Arden	268
They hate me: there is w between us.	Aylmer's F.	424
these all night upon the bridge of w	Spec. of Iliad	9

	POEM.	LINE.
war (verb.)		
pleasure can we have To *w* with evil?	*Lotos-E's.*	94
To *w* with falsehood to the knife,	*Two Voices.*	131
warble (s.)		
at first to the ear The *w* was low,	*Dying Swan*	24
Wild bird, whose *w*, liquid sweet	*In Mem.*lxxxvii.	1
warble (verb.)		
thou may'st *w*, eat and dwell.	*The Blackbird*	4
he that *w's* long and loud '*You might have won*'		
W, O bugle, and trumpet blare	*W. to Alexan.*	14
warbled.		
That she *w* alone in her joy!	*Maud,* I. x.	55
warbler.		
Dan Chaucer, the first *w*,	*D.of F.Wom.*	5
warbling.		
springs By night to eery *w's*	*Sir L. and Q. G.*	34
war-cry.		
Spurr'd with his terrible *w-c*	*Enid*	1019
ward (minor.)		
and a selfish uncle's *w*.	*Locksley H.*	156
ward (guard.)		
Keep watch and *w* (rep.)	*Maud,* I. vi.	58
warder.		
The *w's* of the growing hour '*Love thou thy laud*'		61
war-drum.		
Till the *w-d* throbb'd no longer	*Locksley II.*	127
ware (adj.)		
they were *w* That all the decks were	*M.d'Arthur*	195
ware (s.)		
As when a hawker hawks his *w's*	*The Blackbird*	20
faith in a tradesman's *w* or his word?	*Maud,* l. i.	26
sold her *w's* for less Than what she	*En. Arden*	254
war-horse.		
On burnished hooves his *w-h* trode	*L. of Shalott,* iii.	29
waiting by the doors the *w* neigh'd	*Guinevere*	526
warm (adj.)		
take the goose, and keep you *w*,	*The Goose*	7, 43
'Tis little more: the day was *w*	*Talking O.*	205
The slumbrous light is rich and *w*	*Day-Dm.*	83
O heart, with kindliest motion *w*,	*In Mem.* lxxxiv.	34
'Twas well indeed, when *w* with wine	" lxxxix.	9
where the sunbeam broodeth *w*,	" xc.	14
w in the heart of my dreams,	*Maud,* 1. vi.	18
The birds were *w*, the birds were *w*	*Aylmer's F.*	260
worldless heart had kept it *w*	"	471
warm (verb.)		
Roof-haunting martins *w* their eggs:	*Day-Dm.*	37
New life-blood *w* the bosom,	*Will Water.*	22
w's another living breast	*In Mem.* lxxxiv.	116
warm-asleep.		
When you are *w-a*, mother,	*May Queen,* ii.	24
warm-blue.		
The *w-b* breathings of a hidden hearth	*Aylmer's F.*	155
warmed.		
One hope that *w* me in the days	*Two Voices*	122
And *w* in crystal cases.	*Amphion*	88
hearts are *w* and faces bloom,	*In Mem. Con.*	82
gayer colours, like an opal *w*.	*Vivien*	799
W with his wines, or taking pride in	*Aylmer's F.*	554
fondled on her lap, *W* at her bosom?	"	687
warming.		
Alone and warming his five wits	*The Owl,* i.	6, 13
w with her theme She fulmined out	*Princess,* ii.	116
warmth.		
So full of summer *w*, so glad,	*Miller's D.*	14
doubled his own *w* against her lips,	*Gardener's D.*	137
The *w* it thence shall win	*Talking O.*	254
And the *w* of hand in hand	*Vision of Sin*	162
loyal *w* of Florian is not cold	*Princess,* ii.	226
helpless *w* about my barren breast	" vi.	185
Broke A genial *w* and light once more	"	265

	POEM.	LINE.
A rosy *w* from marge to marge	*In Mem.* xlv.	16
A central *w* diffusing bliss	" lxxxiii.	6
the herb was dry; And genial *w*;	" xciv.	3
A *w* within the breast would melt	" cxxiii.	13
I wanted *w* and colour.	*Guinevere*	640
new *w* of life's ascending sun	*En. Arden.*	38
all the *w*, the peace, the happiness,	"	762
the *w* and muscle of the heart,	*Aylmer's F.*	180
turning to the *w* The tender pink.	"	185
war-music.		
when first I heard *W-m*,	*Princess,* v.	256
warn.		
part against himself To *w* us off	*Love and Duty*	46
divine to *w* them of their foes:	*Sea Dreams*	69
waved my arm to *w* them off	"	128
warn'd.		
spoken, And *w* that madman	*Vision of Sin*	50
An awful voice within had *w* him	*Princess,* v.	328
w me of their fierce design	*Elaine*	274
warning.		
Take *w*! he that will not sing	*The Blackbird*	21
by the *w* of the Holy Ghost,	*St S. Stylites*	216
like a weasel on a grange For *w*;	*Princess,* ii.	189
Did I wish your *w* or your silence?	*Enid*	926
not to give you *w*, that seems hard;	"	1271
yet to give him *w*, for he rode	"	1300
Take *w*: yonder man is surely dead	"	1520
he read God's *w* 'wait.'	*En. Arden.*	572
warp (s.)		
wonder of the loom thro' *w* and woof	*Princess,* i.	61
warp (verb.)		
w us from the living truth!	*Locksley II.*	60
'Ye are green wood, see ye *w* not.	*Princess,* ii.	61
warped.		
Walter *w* his mouth at this	*Princess, Pro.*	208
warrant.		
I *w*, man, that we shall bring you round	*En. Arden*	842
warren.		
waster than a *w*:	*Amphion*	4
warring.		
W on a later day,	*Ode on Well.*	102
warrior.		
like a *w* overthrown;	*Two Voices*	150
made the old *w* from his ivied nook	*Princess, Pro.*	104
I saw The feudal *w* lady-clad	"	119
in thunder-storms, And breed of *w's*	" v.	470
Home they brought her *w* dead:	"	532
Lightly to the *w* stept,	"	541
happy *w's*, and immortal names	" vi.	77
a grace to me! I am your *w*:	"	207
W's carry the *w's* pall,	*Ode on Well.*	6
heated the strong *w* in his dreams	*Enid*	72
At which the *w* in his obstinacy	"	1301
laughs at it on—as nur *w's* did—	*Vivien*	279
rode an armed *w* to the doors.	*Guinevere*	406
to battle where thy *w* stands: '*Lady, let the rolling*'		2
Glory of *w*, glory of orator.	*Wages*	1
No dragon *w's* from Cadmean teeth	*Lucretius*	50
war-song.		
His country's *w-s* thrill his ears:	*Two Voices*	181
many a noble *w-s* had he sung,	*Guinevere*	270
was.		
w, and is, and will be, are but is;	*Princess,* iii.	307
wash (s.)		
long *w* of Australasian seas	*The Brook.*	194
wash (verb.)		
mercy! *w* away my sin,	*St S. Stylites*	118
that the gulfs will *w* us down:	*Ulysses*	62
wash'd.		
W with still rains and daisy-blossom'd	*Circumstance*	7
w by a slow broad stream,	*Gardener's D.*	40
shone Their morions, *w* with morning.	*Princess,* v.	254
little footprint daily *w* away.	*En. Arden.*	23

2 F

CONCORDANCE TO

washing
	POEM.	LINE.
heard the ripple w in the reeds,	M d'Arthur	70, 117

wasp.
| W's in our good hive, | Princess. iv. | 514 |

wassail.
| pledge you all In w; | Princess, Pro. | 184 |
| Nor bowl of w mantle warm? | In Mem. civ. | 18 |

wassail-bowl.
| host and I sat round the w-b, | The Epic | 5 |
| I ' quoth Everard, ' by the w-b ' | " | 23 |

waste (adj. and s.)
The level w, the rounding gray	Mariana	44
across the w His son and heir	D of the O. Year	30
molten on the w Becomes a cloud	Princess, iv.	54
And w it seem'd and vain ;	" vii.	28
think, that somewhere in the w	In Mem xxii.	19
w's where footless fancies dwell	Maud, I xviii	69
of all his lavish w of words	The Brook	191
Far-sighted summoner of War and	W Ded. of Idylls	36
glancing round the w she feared	Enid	899
and she drove them thro' the w	"	949
Here in the heart of w and wilderness "		1162
sent a thousand men To till the w's,	"	1790
drove him into w's and solitudes	Elaine	252
by glimmering w and weald	Guinevere	127
heard the Spirits of the w and weald	"	128
Among the w and lumber of the shore	En Arden	16
Like colts about the w,	"	304
tall mill that whistled on the w,	"	340
one small gate that open'd on the w,	"	734
wrought Such w and havock	Aylmer's F.	640
Doom upon kings, or in the w ' Repent?' "		742

waste (verb)
if I w words now, in truth	Miller's D.	191
sea w's all ; but let me live my life	Audley Ct.	50
To w his whole heart in one kiss	Sir L. and Q. G.	44
like a broken purpose w in air ;	Princess, vii.	199
So w not thou ; but come ;	"	200
I w my heart in signs ; let be.	"	338
Half the night I w in sighs	Maud, II. iv.	23
dared to w a perilous pity on him ;	Enid	1374
shall I w myself in vain?	Elaine	667

wasted.
My heart is w with my woe,	Oriana	1
Last night I w hateful hours	Fatima	8
have w here health, wealth, and time	Princess, iv.	333
I trust I have not w breath ;	In Mem. cxix	1
I that w time to tend upon her,	Enid	887
He w hours with Averill,	Aylmer's F.	109
beat me down and marr'd and w me	Tithonus	19
There they ruled, and thence they w	Boädicea	54

waster.
| w than a warren ; | Amphion | 4 |

wasting
| w odorous sighs All night long | Adeline | 43 |
| greet her, w his forgotten heart | Aylmer's F. | 689 |

watch (vigil, etc.)
Kept w, waiting decision	Œnone	141
wan was her cheek With hollow w	Princess, vi.	129
w'es in the dead, the dark	" vii.	68
Come ; not in w'es of the night	In Mem xc.	13
Keep w and ward, keep w and ward	Maud, I. vi.	58
did Enid, keeping w, behold	Enid	967

watch (time-piece.)
| seal, that hung From Allan's w, | Dora | 133 |

watch (verb.)
I w thy grace ; and it its place	Eleänore	127
I w the darkening droves of swine	Pal. of Art	199
w the crisping ripples on the beach	Lotos-E's.	106
To w the long bright river	"	137
To w the emerald-colour'd water	"	141
W what main-currents draw '	Love thou thy land'	21
W what thou seëst, and lightly	M d'Arthur	38, 81
saw An angel stand and w me,	St S. Stylites	34
did we w the stately ships,	Locksley H.	37
To w the three tall spires ;	Godiva	3

	POEM.	LINE.
That w the sleepers from the wall.	Day-Dm.	44
He w'es from his mountain walls,	The Eagle	5
w me from the glen below. ' More eastward', etc.		8
w A full sea glazed	Princess, i.	243
O to w the thirsty plants Imbibing '	" ii.	400
Or seem'd to w the dancing bubble,	" iii	8
w The sandy footprint harden	"	253
eye which w'es guilt And goodness	In Mem xxvi.	5
those wild eyes that w the wave	" xxxvi.	15
Ye w, like God, the rolling hours	" l.	14
So may st thou w me where I weep,	" lxii.	9
To those that w it more and more	" lxxiii.	2
I w thee from the quiet shore	" lxxxiv.	81
who was left to w her but I?	Maud, I xix.	10
w her harvest ripen, her herd increase	" III. vi.	25
I w the twilight falling brown	To F. D. Maurice	14
w his mightful hand striking	Enid	95
bethought her how she used to w,	"	647
Not dare to w the combat	"	1003
as who should say ' You w me,'	"	1294
the Seer Would w her at her petulance	Vivien	31
laugh As those that w a kitten	"	33
w the curl'd white of the coming wave	"	141
sand To w them overflow'd	En. Arden	20
often as he watch'd or seem'd to w.	"	601
' Good ' said his friend ' but w !'	Aylmer's F.	275
one was set to w The watcher	"	551
I used to w—if I be he that watch'd	Tithonus	52
Fancy w'es in the wilderness	Coquette, i.	12

watched.
She w my crest among them all.	Oriana	30
I w the little circles die	Miller's D.	74
I w the little flutterings,	"	153
And w by weeping queens	Pal. of Art	108
And w by silent gentlemen,	Will Water.	231
Maiden, I have w thee daily,	L. f Burleigh	3
w it lying bath'd in the green gleam	Princess, i.	93
While Psyche w them, smiling	" ii.	344
w Or seem'd to watch the dancing bubble	" iii.	7
w the swallow winging south	" iv.	11
w them well, Saw that they kept apart	"	320
who sat apart And w them,	In Mem. cii.	30
w her on her nurse's arm	" Con.	46
but w awake A cypress	The Daisy	81
While he that w her sadden,	Enid	67
w The being he loved best	"	951
w the sun blaze on the turning scythe,	"	1101
one had w, and had not held his peace	Vivien	18
w their arms far-off Sparkle,	Elaine	394
many a time have w thee at the tilt	"	1150
in a cove, and w The high reed wave	"	1380
last dip of the vanishing sail She w it,	En. Arden	601
often as he w or seem'd to watch,	"	601
Miriam w and dozed at intervals,	"	908
and Sir Aylmer Aylmer w.	Aylmer's F	277
conscious of the rageful eye That w him	"	337
made occasion, being strictly w	"	478
grove of pines, W even there	"	551
and Sir Aylmer w them all,	"	552
the wife, who w his face, Paled	"	731
I used to watch—if I be he that w—	Tithonus	52
There was one who w and told me	Boädicea	30

watcher.
w on the column till the end :	St S. Stylites	160
A lidless w of the public weal	Princess, iv.	306
watching like a w by the dead	" v.	59
kinsman left him w o'er his wife	Vivien	556
Heard by the w in a haunted house,	Guinevere	71
one was set to w The watcher	Aylmer's F.	552

watchest.
| Thou w all things ever dim. | In Mem. cxx. | 3 |

watcheth.
| shepherd who w the evening star, | Dying Swan | 35 |

watchful.
| Leolin ever w of her eye | Aylmer's F. | 210 |

watching.
| Tho' w from a ruin'd tower | Two Voices | 77 |
| Sat w like a watcher by the dead. | Princess, v. | 59 |

	POEM.	LINE.
With Psyche's babe, was Ida *w* us,	*Princess*, v.	501
All her maidens, *w*, said,	"	534
one mute Shadow *w* all.	*In Mem.* xxx.	8
In *w* thee from hour to hour,	" cxi.	12
An angel *w* an urn	*Maud*, I. viii.	3
Darken'd *w* a mother decline	" xix.	8
where At this, our great solemnity	*Ode on Well.*	243
Now *w* high, on mountain cornice	*The Daisy.*	19
W your growth, I seem'd again to grow	*Aylmer's F.*	359

watchman.

| *w* peal The sliding season : | *Gardener's D.* | 178 |

watch-word.

| Nor deal in *w-w*'s overmuch; 'Love thou thy land' | 28 |
| this proud *w* rest Of equal | *Princess*, vii. | 282 |

water.

A sluice with blacken'd *w*'s slept	*Mariana*	38
Adown to where the *w* slept	*Arabian N's.*	30
trenched *w*'s run from sky to sky,	*Ode to Mem.*	104
Holy *w* will I pour	*Poet's Mind*	12
Winds were blowing, *w*'s flowing	*Oriana*	14
Their moon-led *w*'s white	*Pal. of Art*	252
night-dews on still *w*'s	*Lotos-E's.*	48
His *w*'s from the purple hill—	"	138
watch the emerald colour'd *w* falling	"	141
Scaffolds, still sheets of *w*,	*D. of F. Wom.*	34
on one Lay a great *w*,	*M. d'Arthur*	12
the wild *w* lapping on the crag.'	"	71-116
Many an evening by the *w*'s	*Locksley H.*	37
and as *w* unto wine	"	152
Rift the hills, and roll the *w*'s,	"	166
woodlands, echoing falls Of *w*	*To E. L.*	2
from butts of *w* on the slope,	*Princess, Pro.*	60
like a wrinkling wind On glassy *w*	" i.	115
Over the rolling *w*'s go,	" ii.	460
like a clouded moon In a still *w*:	" vi.	254
The forest crack'd, the *w*'s curl'd,	*In Mem.* xv.	5
Is on the *w*'s day and night	" xvii.	11
As drop by drop the *w* falls	" lvii.	3
By that broad *w* of the west,	" lxvi.	3
I hear thee where the *w*'s run,	" cxxix.	2
Beyond it, where the *w*'s marry—	*The Brook*	81
To meet the sun and sunny *w*'s,	*The Daisy*	11
she slipt like *w* to the floor.	*Elaine*	826
Heard on the winding *w*'s, eve and morn	"	1398
The blaze upon the *w*'s .	*En. Arden*	595-7
Another ship (She wanted *w*)	"	629
silent *w* slipping from the hills	"	634
where the rivulets of sweet *w*'s ran:	"	645
Like fountains of sweet *w* in the sea,	"	804
in the *w*, a long reef of gold .	*Sea Dreams*	123
all night above the hrim Of *w*'s .	*The Voyage*	26
Down the waste *w*'s day and night,	"	58
along the valley, where thv *w*'s flow,	*V. of Canterets*	3
broad *w* sweetly slowly glides	*Requiescat*	2
Side by side beneath the *w* .	*The Captain*	67

waterbreak.

| With many a silvery *w* . | *The Brook* | 61 |

water-course.

| The tangled *w*'s slept . | *Dying Swan* | 19 |
| A riotous confluence of *w*'s | *Lucretius* | 30 |

watered.

| Seal'd it with kisses? *w* it with tears? | *Œnone* | 230 |

waterfall.

| Thou wert not nursed by the *w* . | *Ode to Mem.* | 51 |
| Down shower the gambolling *w*'s . | *Sea-Fairies* | 10 |

waterflag.

| There in the many-knotted *w's* | *M. d'Arthur* | 63 |

water-lily.

| She saw the *w-l* bloom . | *L. of Shalott*, iii. | 39 |
| as a *w* starts and slides | *Princess*, iv. | 236 |

Waterloo.

in sawdust slept, As old as *W*.	*Will Water.*	100
In that world's-earthquake, *W*!	*Ode on Well.*	133
Than when he fought at *W*,	"	257

water-pipes.

| Creeps to the garden *w-p* beneath | *D. of F. Wom.* | 705 |

water-side.

	POEM.	LINE.
The first house by the *w-s* .	*L. of Shalott*, iv.	31

water-smoke.

| thousand wreaths of dangling *w-s*, | *Princess*, vii. | 198 |

water-world.

| Thro' his dim *w-w*! | *Maud*, II. ii. | 70 |

wave (s.)

The slumbrous *w* outwelleth	*Claribel*	18
rainbow hangs on the poising *w*	*Sea-Fairies*	29
shook the *w* as the wind did sigh ;	*Dying Swan*	15
the *w* would make music above us	*The Merman*	22
adown the steep like a *w* I would	*The Mermaid*	39
Thro' the *w* that runs for ever	*L. of Shalott*, i.	12
w's that up a quiet cove Rolling slide	*Eleänore*	108
I loved the brimming *w* that swam	*Miller's D.*	97
an iron coast and angry *w*'s .	*Pal. of Art*	69
back again with summer o'er the *w*	*May Queen*, ii.	19
mounting *w* will roll us shoreward	*Lotos-E's.*	2
gushing of the *w* Far far away	"	31
island home Is far beyond the *w*;	"	45
ever climbing up the climbing *w*?	"	95
wind and *w* and oar ;	"	172
holy organ rolling *w*'s Of sound	*D. of F. Wom.*	191
the bounteous *w* of such a breast	*Gardener's D.*	133
Came wet-shot alder from the *w* .	*Amphion*	41
Thy tribute *w* deliver :	*A Farewell*	2
Rising, falling, like a *w*	*Vision of Sin*	125
w's of shadow went over the wheat,	*Poet's Song*	4
No rock so hard but that a little *w*	*Princess*, iii.	138
old-recurring *w*'s of prejudice	"	224
drench his dark locks in the gurgling *w*	iv.	169
like a beacon-tower above the *w*'s	"	472
a double light in air and *w*, .	" vii.	152
w's that sway themselves in rest,	*In Mem.* xi.	18
And in the hearing of the *w*	" xix.	2
the *w* again Is vocal	"	13
those wild eyes that watch the *w*	" xxxvi.	15
The lightest *w* of thought shall lisp,	" xlviii.	5
every pulse of wind and *w* .	" lxxxiv.	73
Or cool'd within the glooming *w*;	" lxxxviii.	45
Upon the thousand *w*'s of wheat,	" xc.	11
all my blood, a fuller *w*,	" cxxi.	12
beach dragg'd down by the *w*,	*Maud*, I. iii.	12
the long *w*'s that roll in yonder hay	" xviii.	63
all Calamity's hugest *w*'s confound	*Will*	5
flying over many a windy *w*	*Enid*	337
great *w* that echoes round the world ;	"	420
keeps the wear and polish of the *w*	"	682
blind *w* feeling round his long sea-hall	*Vivien*	81
watch the curl'd white of the coming *w*	"	141
such a *w*, but not so pleasurable,	"	143
You seem'd that *w* about to break	"	151
as a wild *w* in the wide North-sea,	*Elaine*	481
the steep cliff and the coming *w*;	*Guinevere*	278
after tempest, when the long *w* broke	*En. Arden*	258
some precipitous rivulet to the *w*,	*En. Arden*	538
Who still'd the rolling *w* of Galilee	*Aylmer's F.*	709
great *w* Returning, while none mark'd	*Sea Dreams*	26
We came to warmer *w*'s, and deep	*The Voyage*	1
Now high on *w*'s that idly burst	"	69
W's on a diamond shingle dash,	*The Islet*	16
W's on the shingle pouring	1865-1866	11

wave (verb.)

who hath seen her *w* her hand?	*L. of Shalott*, i.	24
W's all its lazy lilies,	*Gardener's D.*	42
bottom agates seen to *w* and float	*Princess*, ii.	306
Nor *w*'s the cypress in the palace walk ;	" vii.	162
since the grasses round me *w*,	*In Mem.* xxi.	2
in a cove, and watch'd The high reed *w*,	*Elaine*	1381

waved.

She spoke, and bowing to Dismissal:	*Princess*, ii.	84
She, ending, *w* her hands	" iv.	501
She *w* to me with her hand.	*Maud*, I. ix.	8
wrist is parted from the hand that *w*	*Vivien*	401
glanced not up, nor *w* his hand,	*Elaine*	980
w his hand, and went his way,	*En. Arden*	237
w my arm to warn them off ;	*Sea Dreams*	128

waver.

| when a sunbeam *w*'s warm . | *Miller's D.* | 77 |

	POEM.	LINE.
this great bow will *w* in the sun,	Pal. of Art	43
The gas-light *w's* dimmer ;	Will Water.	38

waver'd.

	POEM.	LINE.
The crowds, the temples, *w*.	D of F.Wom.	114
for thus at times He *w*;	Vivien	43

wavering.

w Lovingly lower .	Gardener's D.	129
happy shade—and still went *w* down,	''	131
From the high tree the blossom *w* fell	Princess, vi.	64

wave-worn.

the *w-w* horns of the echoing bank	Dying Swan	39

waving.

W an angry hand as who should say	Enid .	1293
Perceived the *w* of his hands that blest	Guinevere	578
while he stood on deck *W*.	En. Arden.	243

wax (s.)

will melt this marble into *w* .	Princess, iii.	57

wax (verb.)

Speak, as it *w'es*, of a love that wanes?	Elaine	1392
Thou shalt *w* and he shall dwindle	Boädicea .	40

waxed.

Then *w* her anger stronger.	The Goose	30
And watch'd them, *w* in every limb.	In Mem. cii.	30
So *w* in pride, that I believed myself	Enid .	1683

waxing.

The full-juiced apple, *w* over mellow	Lotos-E's.	78
tho' his eyes are *w* dim .	D of the O. Year	21

way.

Winning its *w* with extreme gentleness	Isabel	23
A weary, weary *w* I go .	Oriana	89
one silvery cloud Had lost his *w* .	Œnone	91
This *w* and that, in many a wild festoon	''	98
The blessed music went that *w*	May Queen, iii.	42
winds and tides the self-same *w*,	D. of F.Wom.	38
goose flew this *w* and flew that	The Goose .	35
God fulfils himself in many *w's*	M. d'Arthur	241
going a long *w* With those thou seëst	''	256
all the livelong *w* With solemn gibe	Gardener's D.	163
and his *w's* were harsh ;	Dora .	33
went her *w* Across the wheat	''	69
these unreal *w's* Seem but the theme	Ed. Morris	47
witness, if I could have found a *w*	St S. Stylites	54
this *w* was left, And by this *w* I 'scaped	''	175
down the *w* you use to come,—	Talking O.	115
Met me walking on yonder *w*,	Ed Gray .	2
summer suns By many pleasant *w's*,	Will Water.	34
To meet and greet her on her *w*;	Beggar Maid	6
All the windy *w's* of men .	Vision of Sin	132, 168
That's your light *w*; .	Princess, Pro.	150
She once had past that *w*;	'' i.	183
And thus (what other *w* was left) .	'' ii.	199
she errs, But in her own grand *w*:	'' iii.	92
I forced a *w* Thro' solid opposition	''	110
when we sent the Prince your *w* .	'' iv.	379
thing one ought When fall'n in darker *w's*.''	'' v.	65
I will take her up and go my *w* .	''	99
or was it chance, She past my *w*.	'' vi.	82
These were the rough *w's* of the world	'' vii.	241
save in gracious household *w's*,	''	299
And ever met him on his *w* .	In Mem. vi.	22
we with singing cheer'd the *w*,	'' xxii.	5
Still onward winds the dreary *w*;	'' xxvi.	1
look thy look, and go thy *w*,	'' xlviii.	9
Moving about the household *w's* .	'' lix.	11
darken'd *w's* Shall ring with music	'' lxxvi.	13
Whatever *w* my days decline,	'' lxxxiv.	41
will not yield each other *w*.	'' ci.	20
They wept and wailed, but led the *w*	'' cii.	18
and let the world have its *w*:	Maud, I. iv.	21
Who knows the *w's* of the world .	''	44
in the quiet woodland *w's* .	''	49
I know the *w* she went .	'' xii.	21
That I dare to look her *w*; .	'' xvi.	11
I chatter over stony *w's*,	The Brook .	39
path of duty was the *w* to glory (rep.)	Ode on Well.	202
Of Lari Maxume, all the *w*, .	The Daisy .	76

	POEM.	LINE.
after went her *w* across the bridge,	Enid .	383
have let men be, and have their *w*;	''	466
and rough the *w's* and wild :	''	750
Ever a good *w* on before , .	''	864
will not fight my *w* with gilded arms	''	870
keep them in the wild *w's* of the wood,	''	1036
forward by a *w* which, beaten broad	''	1285
left him lying in the public *w*;	''	1327
answering not one word, she led the *w*.	''	1344
and she wept beside the *w*.	''	1368
long *w* smoke beneath him in his fear;	''	1381
the wild *w's* of the lawless tribe .	''	1456
then she followed Merlin all the *w*	Vivien	52
Then her false voice made *w* .	''	706
first at him, then her, and went his *w*.	Elaine	96
often lost in fancy, lost his *w* ;	''	164
cast him as a worm upon the *w*; .	Guinevere	36
then they rode to the divided *w*, .	''	123
did not shun to smite me in worse *w*,	''	432
and the *w's* Were filled with rapine,	''	454
waved his hand, and went his *w*.	En. Arden	237
wherefore did he go this weary *w*,	''	295
yet she went about her household *w's*	''	450
glades high up like *w's* to Heaven,	''	574
but led the *w* To where the rivulets	''	642
A childly *w* with children, .	Aylmer's F.	181
won mysterious *w* Thro' the seal'd ear	''	695
our own child on the narrow *w*,	''	743
as a footsore ox in crowded *w's*.	''	819
like a man, too, would have his *w*:	Grandmother	70
Nor wander'd into other *w's*. 'My life is full,' etc.	''	3
and the woods and *w's* Are pleasant	On a Mourner	13
all thy life one *w* incline	''	19
dead men lay all over the *w*, .	The Victim	21

wayward.

I have been wild and *w*, .	May Queen, ii.	33

weak.

heroic hearts, Made *w* by time and fate,	Ulysses	69
cry for strength, remaining *w* .	Two Voices	95
I go, *w* from suffering here ; .	''	238
This fellow would make weakness *w*,	In Mem. xxi.	7
being *w* in body said no more ; .	Elaine .	835

weakening.

gentle sickness, gradually *W* the man,	En. Arden	826

weaker.

Words *w* than your grief .	To J. S.	65
ever *w* grows thro' acted crime	Will .	12
till he saw Which were the *w*;	Elaine .	461

weakling.

Poor *w* ev'n as they are .	Princess, vi.	291

weakly.

This pretty, puny, *w*, little one .	En. Arden .	195

weakness.

Prevailing in *w*, the coronach stole	Dying Swan	26
the tasks of might To *w* ' Love thou thy land,' etc.		14
Regard the *w* of thy peers; .	''	24
W to be wroth with *w*/ .	Locksley H.	149
So she strove against her *w*,	L. of Burleigh	69
Our *w* somehow shapes the shadow	Princess, iii.	313
hatred of her *w*, blent with shame.	'' vii.	15
close to death For *w*: .	''	105
This fellow would make *w* weak, .	In Mem. xxi.	7
hath not swerved To works of *w*, .	'' lxxxiv.	50
Forgot his *w* in thy sight .	'' cix.	7
That was your hour of *w* .	En. Arden .	446
Enoch hore his *w* cheerfully .	''	828
to spy The *w* of a people .	Aylmer's F.	570

weal.

he for the common *w*, The fading .	Princess, ii.	265
A lidless watcher of the public *w*,	'' iv.	306
So far, so near in woe and *w* .	In Mem.cxxviii.	2
moulded by your wishes for her *w*	Enid .	799

weald.

by glimmering waste and *w*, .	Guinevere .	127
heard the Spirits of the waste and *w*	''	120

wealth.	POEM.	LINE.
gleaned w into my open breast	Ode to Mem.	23
choicest w of all the earth,	Eleänore	19
In glowing health, with boundless w	L. C. V. de Vere	61
w no more shall rest in mounded heaps	Golden Year	32
have wasted here health, w, and time	Princess, iv.	333
O more than poor men w	"	439
Abide; thy w is gather'd in,	In Mem. li.	15
And so my w resembles thine	" lxxviii.	17
the w Of words and wit	" Con.	102
Your father has w well-gotten	Maud, I. iv.	18
all the w and all the woe?	Guinevere	342
The sole succeeder to their w,	Aylmer's F.	294
w, Their w, their heiress!	"	368
w enough was theirs For twenty matches	"	369
beat a pathway out to w and fame	"	439
Whatever eldest-born of rank or w	"	464

wealthier.		
'You will be all the w,' cried the	Enid	1070-1261
and himself Be wealthy still, ay w	Aylmer's F.	373

wealthy.		
and himself Be w still, ay wealthier	Aylmer's F.	373

weapon.		
With thine own w art thou slain,	Two Voices	311
wearing neither hunting-dress Nor w	Enid	166

wear (s.)		
keeps the w and polish of the wave	Enid	682

wear (verb.)		
W's all day a fainter tone.	The Owl, ii.	7
King-like, w's the crown: 'Of old sat Freedom,' etc.		16
wholesome food, And w warm clothes,	St S. Stylites	107
w an undress'd goatskin on my back;	"	114
w Alternate leaf and acorn-ball	Talking O.	286
This mortal armour that I w,	Sir Galahad	70
those that w the Poet's crown: 'You might have won'		10
should not w our rusty gownt,	Princess, Pro.	143
than w Those lilies, better blush	" iii.	51
so she w's her error like a crown	"	95
sleeps or w's the mask of sleep,	In Mem. xviii.	10
first she w's her orange-flower	" xxxix.	4
w's his manhood hale and green;	" lii.	4
The fool that w's a crown of thorns;	" lxviii.	12
Come, w the form by which I know	" xc.	5
But ill for him that w's a crown,	" cxxvi.	9
And Maud will w her jewels	Maud, I. xx.	27
And that he w's a truer crown	Ode on Well.	276
fair child shall w your costly gift	Enid	819
fit to w your slipper for a glove	"	1471
w as fair a jewel as is on earth,	Elaine	240
w her favour at the tilt.	"	357
w My favour at this tourney?'	"	360
Well, I will w it: fetch it out to me:	"	370
W black and white, and be a nun	Guinevere	669
w out in almsdeed and in prayer	"	679
spears That soon should w the garland:	Aylmer's F.	112
deeper than to w it as his ring—	"	122

wearied.		
Is w of the rolling hours.	L. C. V. de Vere	60
w out made for the couch and slept,	Vivien	586
Wounded and w needs must he be near.	Elaine	537
with his diamond, w of the quest,	"	613
seek him, and was w of the search,	"	628
w of the quest Leapt on his horse	"	699
he said 'your ride has w you	"	707

wearieth.		
Gaiety without eclipse W me	Lilian	20

weariness.		
all things else have rest from w	Lotos-E's.	59
all but empty heart and w	Enid	1500
Settles, till one could yield for w;	Vivien	222

wearing.		
W the rose of womanhood	Two Voices	417
w all that weight Of learning lightly	In Mem. Con.	39
W the white flower of a blameless life	Ded. of Idylls	2
w neither hunting-dress Nor weapon	Enid	165
in w mine Needs must be lesser.	Elaine	365
W the light yoke of that Lord of love	Aylmer's F.	708
W his wisdom lightly	A Dedication	12

weary (adj.)	POEM.	LINE.
and the w are at rest	May Queen, iii.	60
w seem'd the sea, w the oar, W the wandering fields	Lotos-E's.	41
it may be my lord is w,	Locksley H.	53
She is w of dance and play.	Maud, I. xxii.	22
However w, a spark of will	" II. ii.	56
When ill and w, alone and cold	The Daisy	96
My lord is w with the fight before,	Enid	982
to-night: I am w to the death.'	"	1207
I am w of her.'	Vivien	687
w of my service and devoir,	Elaine	119
That it makes one w to hear.'	The Islet	29

weary (verb.)		
w with a finger's touch 'Clear-headed friend,' etc.		22
Nor could I w heart or limb,	In Mem. xxv.	9
till the ear Wearies to hear it,	Elaine	894

weasel.		
nail me like a w on a grange	Princess, ii.	183
the thin w there Follows the mouse	Aylmer's F.	852

weather.		
All in the blue unclouded w	L. of Shalott, iii.	19
And it was windy w;	The Goose	4,40
There must be stormy w;	Will Water.	54
His brothers of the w stood Stock-still	"	135
bring fair w yet to all of us)	En. Arden.	191
Passing with the w	The Window	67

weather-beaten.		
Denying not these w-b limbs	St S. Stylites	19
large gray eyes and w-b face	En. Arden.	70

weathercock'd.		
Whose blazing wyvern w the spire,	Aylmer's F.	17

weather'd.		
many a rough sea had he w in her!	En. Arden.	135

weave.		
There she w's by night and day	L. of Shalott, ii.	1
To w the mirror's magic sights	"	29
With trembling fingers did we w	In Mem. xxx.	1
And w their petty cells and die.	" xlix.	12
Again at Christmas did we w	" lxxvii.	1
She meant to w me a snare.	Maud, I. vi.	25
any wreath that man can w him.	Ode on Well.	277

weaveth.		
And so she w steadily	L. of Shalott, ii.	7

web.		
A magic w with colours gay	L. of Shalott, ii.	2
in her w she still delights	"	28
She left the w, she left the loom	" iii.	8
Out flew the w and floated wide	"	42
takes the flood With swarthy w's.	M. d'Arthur	26
A w is wov'n across the sky	In Mem. iii.	6
in a great old tyrant spider's w,	Vivien	108
wove coarse w's to snare her purity,	Aylmer's F.	780

wed.		
young spirit present When first she is w;	Ode to Mem.	74
Came two young lovers lately w.	L. of Shalott, ii.	34
And I was young—too young to w;	Miller's D.	141
nor w Raw Haste. 'Love thou thy land,' etc.		95
he woo'd and w A labourer's daughter;	Dora	37
take it—earnest w with sport,	Day-Dm.	279
They two will w the morrow morn;	Lady Clare	7
To-morrow he w's with me:	"	16
We two will w to-morrow morn,	"	87
That she wore when she was w.'	L. of Burleigh	96
In the dress that she was w in,	"	99
It is long before you w.	Vision of Sin	70
W whom thou wilt, but I am sick 'Come not, when'		9
days drew nigh that I should w	Princess, i.	40
certain, would not w.	"	42
purposed with ourself Never to w	" ii.	47
I w with thee! I bound by precontract	" iv.	520
the woman w is not as we,	" v.	452
must w him for her own good name;	" vii.	52
Thought leapt out to w with Thought	In Mem. xxiii.	15
lives to w an equal mind:	" lxi.	7
And talk of others that are w.	" Con.	98

	POEM.	LINE.
live to *w* with her whom first you love :	*Enid*	227
ere you *w* with any, bring your bride	"	228
when it *w's* with manhood, makes a	"	1716
'Had I chos'n to *w*, I had been wedded	*Elaine*	930
these were *w*, and merrily rang the	*En. Arden* 80,	507
w the man so dear to all of them .	"	481
'There is no reason why we should not *w*.'	"	504
So you will *w* me, let it be at once.	"	506
day that follow'd the day she was *w*	*The Islet*	4

wedded.

my vigour, *w* to thy blood, .	*Œnone*	158
Wherever Thought hath *w* Fact	*'Love thou thy land'*	52
w her to sixty thousand pounds .	*Ed. Morris*	126
w with a nobleman from thence :	*Princess*, i.	76
(God help her) she was *w* to a fool ;	" iii.	67
there be *w* with all ceremony .	*Enid* . 608,	839
Seeing that you are *w* to a man .	"	1274
Sir Valence *w* with an outland dame	*Vivien*	564
chos'n to wed, I had been *w* earlier,	*Elaine*	931
not be content Save that I *w* her,	"	1305
specially were he, she *w*, poor	"	1311
all this throve until I *w* thee ! .	*Guinevere*	480
So Willy and I were *w* : .	*Grandmother*	57
Lucilia, *w* to Lucretius .	*Lucretius*	1

wedlock.

in one love Than pairs of *w* ; .	*Princess*, vi.	237

weed (s.)

creeping mosses and clambering *w's*	*Dying Swan*	36
Crouch'd fawning in the *w* .	*Œnone*	197
garden full of flowering *w's* To —— .	*With Pal. of Art*	4
At least, not rotting like a *w*,	*Two Voices*	142
Better to me the meanest *w* .	*Amphion*	93
Athwart the smoke of burning *w's*	*Princess*, vii.	337
In words, like *w's*, I'll wrap me o'er	*In Mem.* v.	9
stagnates in the *w's* of sloth ;	" xxvii.	11
Is dim, or will be dim, with *w's* .	" lxxii.	10
this beggar-woman's *w*: .	*Enid*	1528
once was looking for a magic *w*,	*Vivien*	321
The people said, a *w*. .	*The Flower*	4
the people Call it but a *w*. .	"	24

weed (verb.)

twins may *w* her of her folly .	*Princess*, v.	453
As I will *w* this land before I go. .	*Enid*	1755
w the white horse on the Berkshire hills "		1764

weeded.

W and worn the ancient thatch .	*Mariana*	7

weeding.

Edyrn has done it, *w* all his heart	*Enid*	1754

week.

w's and months, and early and late	*The Sisters*	10
They lost their *w's* ; .	*Princess, Pro.*	161
fresh arrivals of the *w* before .	" ii.	82
nursed me there from *w* to *w* : .	" vii.	224
W after *w* the days go by : .	*In Mem.* xvii.	7
He bears the burthen of the *w's* .	" lxxix.	11
stay for a year who has gone for a *w*:	*Maud*, I. xvi.	6
w Before I parted with poor Edmund ;	*The Brook*	77
to live or die, for many a *w* . .	*Elaine*	520
days will grow to *w's*, the *w's* to months	*Guinevere*	617
Enoch would hold possession for a *w*:	*En. Arden*	27
yet were many *w's* before she sail'd,	"	124
same *w* when Annie buried it, .	"	270
'A *w* hence, a *w* hence.' .	*The Window*	170

weep.

Prythee *w*, May Lilian ! (rep.) .	*Lilian*	19
Nay, nay, you must not *w* .	*May Queen*, ii.	35
the long-leaved flowers *w*, .	*Lotos-E's.*	55
I will not tell you not to *w* .	*To J. S.*	36
'*W*, weeping dulls the inward pain	"	40
her will lie done—to *w* or not to *w*.	"	44
to the tears that thou wilt *w*.	*Locksley H.*	82
Who'll *w* for thy deficiency ? .	*Two Voices*	39
canst not think, but thou wilt *w*.'	"	51
Wiser to *w* a true occasion lost .	*Princess*, iv.	50
'She must *w* or she will die' .	" v.	535
kiss her : take her hand, she *w's* :.	" vi.	208

	POEM.	LINE.
Which *w* a loss for ever new, .	*In Mem.* xiii	5
w the comrade of my choice .	"	9
come, whatever loves to *w*, .	" xviii.	11
w the fullness from the mind : .	" xx.	6
At night she *w's*, 'How vain am I !	" lix.	15
So may'st thou watch me where I *w*,	" lxii.	9
He loves her yet, she will not *w*, .	" xcvi.	18
not as one that *w's* I come .	" cxvii.	2
Shall I *w* if a Poland fall ? .	*Maud*, I. iv.	46
w for a time so sordid and mean .	" v.	17
the white rose *w's*, 'She is late ;'.	" xxii.	64
to *w* and *w* and *w* My whole soul	" II. iv.	97
now I could even *w* to think of it ;	" v.	66
light shall darken, and many shall *w*	" III. vi.	43
strong passion in her made her *w*.	*Enid* .	110
to his own heart, 'she *w's* for me'	"	1435-8
it makes me mad to see you *w*. .	"	1464
I dead who is it would *w* for me ?.	"	1466
she did not *w* But o'er her meek eyes	"	1616
If the wolf spare me *w* my life away	*Vivien*	734
burst away To *w* and wail in secret,	*Elaine*	1228
unbind my heart that I may *w*.' .	*Guinevere*	164
pray you, noble lady, *w* no more ; .	"	182
they cannot *w* behind a cloud : .	"	205
w for her, who drew him to his doom.'	"	346
little wife would *w* for company .	*En. Arden* .	7
Yes, as the dead we *w* for testify .	*Aylmer's F.*	747
cannot *w* for Willy, nor can I *w* for	*Grandmother* 9,	67
could not *w*—my own time seem'd so near	"	72
But how can I *w* for Willy, .	"	102
vapours *w* their burthen to the ground,	*Tithonus*	2
W on : beyond his object Love can last	*Coquette*, iii.	5
more cause to *w* have I .	"	6

weepest.

Wan sculptor *w* thou to take the cast	*Coquette*, iii.	1

weeping.

w then she made her moan .	*Mariana in the S.*	93
phantasms *w* tears of blood .	*Pal. of Art*	239
'Weep, *w* dulls the inward pain .	*To J. S.*	40
w, 'I have loved thee long.' .	*Locksley H.*	30
Bitterly *w* I turn'd away : .	*Ed. Gray*	6, 34
W, *w* late and early, .	*L. of Burleigh*	89
Had come on Psyche *w* : .	*Princess*, v.	48
And linger *w* on the marge, .	*In Mem.* xii.	12
To hear her *w* by his grave ? .	" xxxi.	4
a nation *w*, and breaking on my rest	*Ode on Well.*	82
W for some gay knight .	*Enid*	118
A woman *w* for her murder'd mate	"	1371
To bitter *w* like a beaten child .	*Vivien*	704
A long, long *w*, not consolable. .	"	705
in the holy house at Almesbury *W*,	*Guinevere*	3
There kiss'd, and parted *w* : .	"	124
look'd and saw The novice, *w*, .	"	656
the holy nuns All round her, *w* ; .	"	659
and departed *w* for him ; .	*En. Arden*	245
Annie *w* answer'd 'I am bound.' .	"	448

weigh.

lightly *w's* With thee unto the love	*Ode to Mem.*	90
W heavy on my eyelids : let me die	*Œnone*	240
flash the lightnings, *w* the Sun—	*Locksley H.*	186
w your sorrows with our lord the King's,	*Guinevere*	180

weigh'd.

Why are we *w* upon with heaviness,	*Lotos-E's.*	57
mist of tears, that *w* Upon my brain,	*Love and Duty*	43
But a trouble *w* upon her, .	*L. of Burleigh*	77
why, the causes *w*, Fatherly fears—	*Princess*, v.	206
while I *w* thy heart with one .	*Guinevere*	536

weighest.

Thou *w* heavy on the heart within	*Œnone*	239

weighing.

And *w* find them less ; .	*Guinevere*	190

weight.

O happy earth, how canst thou bear my *w*!	*Œnone*	233
broad thy shoulders to receive my *w*,	*M. d'Arthur*	164
will have *w* to drag thee down. .	*Locksley H.*	43
This *w* and size, this heart and eyes,	*Sir Galahad*	71
Is it the *w* of that half-crown .	*Will Water.*	155

POEM.	LINE.

w of all the hopes of half the world. *Princess*, iv. 166
Caryatids, lifted up A *w* of emblem " . 184
their heavy hands, The *w* of destiny " . 532
When the man wants *w*, The woman " v. 434
This nightmare *w* of gratitude, " vi. 281
Then us they lifted up, dead *w's* . " . 328
A *w* of nerves without a mind . *In Mem.* xii. 7
I loved the *w* I had to bear, . " xxv. 7
falling with my *w* of cares . " liv. 14
Can hang no *w* upon my heart . " lxii. 3
wearing all that *w* Of learning lightly " *Con.* 39
by a dead *w* trail'd . . . *Maud*, I. i. 14
The lighter by the loss of his *w*; . " xvi. 2
By the loss of that dead *w*, . " xix. 99
Once the *w* and fate of Europe hung,*Ode on Well.*240
w is added only grain by grain . *Enid* . 526
Appraised his *w* and fondled . *En Arden* . 154
dead *w* of the dead leaf bore it down " . 679

welcome (adj. and s.)

sweet shall your *w* be . . *Sea-Fairies* 31
Should come most *w*, seeing men *Œnone* . 127
A *w* mix'd with sighs . . *Talking O.* 212
Farewell, like endless *w*, lived . *Love and Duty*66
with a frolic *w* took The thunder. *Ulysses* . 47
We give you *w*: not without redound *Princess*,ii. 78
glowing full-faced *w*, . . " . 166
Less to find among us, if you came " . 333
W, farewell, and *w* for the year . " *Con.* 95
Received and gave him *w* there ; *In Mem.*lxxxix. 24
An iron *w* when they rise . . " lxxxix. 8
you will be *w*—O, come in !' . *The Brook* . 228
O give him *w*, this is he . . *Ode on Well.* 92
one lay-hearth would give you *w ToF.D.Maurice* 11
means of goodly *w*, flesh and wine *Enid* . 387
Embraced her with all *w* as a friend " . 834
In the mid-warmth of *w* and graspt " 1129
I bid the stranger *w*, . . *Vivien* . 119
To greet his hearty *w* heartily; . *En. Arden*. 347
ever *w* at the Hall, . . *Aylmer's F.* 114
all of us Danes in our *w* of thee . *W. to Alexan.* 4
should speak to me not without a *wellendecasyllabics*11
strangers at my hearth Not *w*, . *Lucretius* . 159

welcome (verb.)

all the gentle court will *w* me . *Elaine* 1051
W her, thunders of fort (rep.) . *W. to Alexan.* 6
as the sea when he *w's* the land, " . 24
w her, *w* the land's desire . " . 25

welcomed.

Not beat him back, but *w* him . *Enid* . 748

welded.

Two women faster *w* in one love . *Princess*, vi. 236

welfare.

How much their *w* is a passion to us *Princess*,iii.264

well (adj.)

Nor would I now be *w*, mother *May Queen*, iii. 19

well (s.)

As a Naiad in a *w*, Looking, . *Adeline* . 16
new-bathed in Paphian *w's* . . *Œnone* . 171
haled the buckets from the *w* . *St S. Stylites* . 63
Come from the *w's* where he did he *Two Voices* 9
flying while you sat beside the *w! Princess*, iv. 252
by denial flush her babbling *w's*, . " v. 324
Than if with thee the roaring *w's In Mem* x. 17
dive below the *w's* of Death? . " cvii. 8
when we halted at that other *w*, . *Vivien* . 129
Until they vanish'd by the fairy *w* " . 278
and cry 'Laugh, little *w*' . . " . 281
by the rushing brook or silent *w* . *Guinevere* . 2
Fairer than Rachel by the palmy *w Aylmer's F.* 679

well (verb.)

w thro' all my fancy yet . . *Locksley II.* 183

well-attemper'd.

A man of *w-a* frame . . *Ode on Well.* 74

well-beloved.

We leave the *w-b* place . *In Mem.* ci. 1

	POEM.	LINE.

well-content.
Philip rested with her *w-c*; . *En. Arden*. 373

well-contented.
Voices of the *w-c* doves. . *Gardener's D.* 83

well-heads.
old *w-h* of haunted rills . *Eleänore* . 16

well-loved.
W-l of me, discerning to fulfil . *Ulysses* . 35

well-moulded.
A quick brunette, *w-m*, falcon-eyed *Princess*, ii. 91

well-oiled.
I was courteous, every phrase *w-o*, *Princess*, iii. 117

well-pleased.
pass, *W-p*, from room to room. . *Pal. of Art* 56
and home *w-p* we went. . *Princess,Con* 118

well-practised.
An eye *w-p* in nature . . *Maud*, I. iv. 33

well-to-do.
Annie—for I am rich and *w-t-d* . *En. Arden* . 310
I am *w-t-d*—no kin, no care, . " . 415

well-worn.
a *w-w* pathway courted us . *Gardener's D*.108

wending.
thither *w* there that night they bode. *Elaine* . 411

went.
Ever the weary wind *w* on, . *Dying Swan* 9
took the reed-tops as it *w*, . " . 10
The bitter arrow *w* aside (rep.) . *Oriana* . 37
lights And music, *w* to Camelot *L. of Shalott*,ii. 32
That *w* and came a thousand times. *Miller's D.* 72
down I *w* to fetch my bride; . " . 145
When, arm in arm, we *w* along, . " . 163
my swift blood that *w* and came . *Fatima* . 16
all my heart *W* forth to embrace him *Œnone* . 62
She died: she *w* to burning flame *The Sisters* . 7
For pasture, ere you *w* to town. *L. C. V. de Vere* 4
w along From Mizpeh's tower'd gate *D.of F.Wom*.163
I *w* mourning, 'No fair Hebrew boy " . 213
One *w*, who never hath return'd. . *To J. S.* . 20
w Sir Bedivere the second time . *M. d'Arthur* 14
lightly *w* the other to the King . " . 147
I and Eustace from the city *w* . *Gardener's D.* 2
up we rose, and on the spur we *w* " . 32
Love with knit brows *w* by, . " . 240
days *w* on, and there was born a boy *Dora* . 46
Then Dora *w* to Mary. . . " . 54
Dora took the child, and *w* her way " . 63
Then Dora *w* to Mary's house, . " . 108
how The races *w*, . . *Audley Ct.* 20
sick of home *w* overseas for change *Walk. to the M.*18
I *w* and came ; Her voice fled . *Ed. Morris* . 66
She *w*—and in one month They wedded " . 125
brewer's soul *W* by me, like a stork; *Talking O* 56
on the roof she *w*, . . " . 114
ivied casement, ere I *w* to rest, . *Locksley H.* 7
forth into the fields I *w*, . . *Two Voices* 448
I *w* thro' many wayward moods . *Day-Dm.* . 6
far across the hills they *w* . . " . 167
down the middle buzz ! she *w* . *Amphion* . 35
Go, therefore, thnu I thy betters *w Will Water.* 165
'Who was this that *w* from thee ?' *Lady Clare* 14
She *w* by dale, and she *w* by down, " . 50
waves of shadow *w* over the wheat, *Poet's Song* 4
sport *W* hand in hand with Science; *Princess,Pro.* 80
a Voice *W* with it, ' Follow, follow " I. 90
thro' the land at eve we *w* . " . 246
mother *w* revolving on the word . " iii. 38
Up *w* the hush'd amaze of hand and eye " . 122
Then summon'd to the porch we *w*. " . 162
This *w* by As strangely as it came " iv. 545
three times he *w*! The first, he blew " v. 360
With message and defiance, *w* and came;" . 360
w up a great cry The Prince is slain. " vi. 9
w The enamour'd air sighing, . " . 62
W sorrowing in a pause I dared not " vii. 231
So I and some *w* out to these ; . " *Con.* 39

CONCORDANCE TO

	POEM.	LINE.
But we w back to the Abbey	Princess, Con.	106
and home well-pleased we w	"	118
And I w down unto the quay	In Mem xiv.	3
From April on to April w,	" xxii.	7
In which we w thro' summer France	" lxx.	4
bats w round in fragrant skies.	" xciv.	9
in the house light after light IV out,	"	20
On that last night before we w	"	cii. 1
Up the side I w, And fell in silence	"	43
they w and came, Remade the blood	Con.	10
I know the way she w .	Maud, I. xii.	21
so that he find what he w to seek .	" xvi.	3
the soul of the rose w into my blood	" v.	543
in I w, and call'd old Philip out	The Brook	120
wheat-suburb, babbling as he w.	"	123
after w her way across the bridge	Enid	383
lords and ladies of the high court w	"	662
Yniol with that hard message w;	"	763
she w back some paces of return	"	919
kind lord,' said the glad youth, and w,	"	1090
told them of a chamber, and they w;	"	1110
IV slipping down horrible precipices,	"	1228
IV Enid with her sullen follower on	"	1289
'Enough,' he said, 'I follow,' and they w	"	1664
w apart with Edyrn, whom he held	"	1729
King w forth and cast his eyes	"	1780
Fixt in her will, and so the seasons w	Vivien	44
IV back to his old wild .	"	499
two fair babes, and w to distant lands,	"	557
Sir Lancelot w ambassador, at first	"	624
W faltering sideways downward .	"	699
eyes and neck glittering w and came	"	809
at him, then her, and w his way. .	Elaine	96
if I w and if I fought and won it.	"	216
in wrath he got to horse and w; .	"	562
w down before his spear at a touch,	"	577
w sore wounded from the field	"	598
and w To all the winds?'	"	654
carolling as he w A true-love ballad	"	700
who coldly w nor bad me one	"	1051
Steer'd by the dumb w upward	"	1148
slowly w The marshall'd order .	"	1321
he w, And at the inrunning .	"	1378
smote his knees, and smiled, and w:	Guinevere	48
grim faces came and w Before her,	"	70
IV slipping back upon the golden days	"	377
IV on in passionate utterance	"	603
great and small, IV nutting to the	En Arden	64
waved his hand, and w his way.	"	237
therefore w, Past thro' the solitary room	"	275
was not Annie with them? and they w	"	368
yet she w about her household ways	"	450
sunny and rainy seasons came and w	"	624
to the pool and narrow wharf he w	"	671
down the long and narrow street he w	"	796
and like a storm he w .	Aylmer's F.	46
IV Leolin ; then, his passions all in flood	"	339
So Leolin w; and as we task ourselves	"	432
w Hating his own lean heart. .	"	525
passionately restless came and w .	"	546
Averill w and gazed upon his death.	"	599
if he w hence with shame? .	"	718
childless mother w to seek her child;	"	728
woke, and w the next, The Sabbath	Sea Dreams	18
W further, fool ! and trusted him	"	76
and with God-bless-you w. .	"	156
That altogether w to music ?	"	199
IV both to make your dream? .	"	246
I wonder he w so young.	Grandmother	14
made me a mocking courtesy and w	"	46
For Harry w at sixty, .	"	86
and fro they w Thro' my garden-bower	The Flower	5
stately, lightly, w she Norward .	The Captain	35
Crashing w the boom, .	"	44
in the waltzing-circle as we w,	Coquette, ii.	5
The Priest w out by heath and hill	The Victim	30

wept.

One willow over the river w,	Dying Swan	14
Crocodiles w tears for thee,	A Dirge	22
Love w and spread his sheeny vans	Love and Death	8

	POEM.	LINE.
and took the King, and w .	M. d'Arthur	206
She bow'd down And w in secret ;	Dora	106
I believe she w .	Talking O.	164
I w 'Tho' I should die, I know,	Two Voices	58
To perish, w for, honour'd, known,	"	149
In her still place the morning w .	"	275
To-day I sat for an hour and w	Ed. Gray	11
Bitterly w I over the stone :	"	33
you w. That was fawn's blood,		
not brother's, yet you w .	Princess, ii.	256
'My fault' she w 'my fault ! .	" iii.	14
w her true eyes blind for such a one,	" iv.	116
yet she neither moved nor w. .	" v.	543
thro' her limbs a drooping languor w:	" vi.	251
Thou comest, much w for :	In Mem. xvii.	1
silence follow'd, and we w.	" xxx.	20
They w and wail'd, but led the way	" cii.	18
W over her, carved in stone	Maud, I. viii.	4
while she w, and I strove to be cool	" II. i.	15
'was it for him she w In Devon?'	Enid	1246
and she w beside the way. .	"	1368
remember'd her, and how she w;	"	1460
and uncoil'd itself. she w afresh,	Vivien	738
for her fault she w Of petulancy	"	801
IV, looking often from his face	Elaine	1277
first she came, w the sad Queen.	Guinevere	180
heart was loos'd Within her, and she w	"	660
her own toward the wall and w.	En. Arden	282
Annie could have w for pity of him,	"	464
but presently IV like a storm :	Aylmer's F.	403
While thus he spoke, his hearers w ;	"	722
I could have w with the best	Grandmother	20-100
I had not w, little Anne, not since	"	63
But I w like a child that day .	"	64,68
'A ship of fools' he sneer'd and w	The Voyage	78
that o'er her wounded hunter w	Lucretius	89

west

Four courts I made, East, IV	Pal of Art	21
linger'd low adown In the red IV	Lotos-E's.	20
Across a hazy glimmer of the w	Gardener's D.	214
Orion sloping slowly to the IV	Locksley H.	8
stunted squaws of IV or East ;	Princess, ii.	64
silver sails all out of the w,	"	469
half Far-shadowing from the w,	" Con.	42
And topples round the dreary w,	In Mem xv.	19
By that broad water of the w,	" lxvi.	3
And East and IV, without a breath	" xciv.	62
Rosy is the IV, Rosy is the South,	Maud, I xvii.	5
Blush it thro' the W (rep) .	"	16
Orion's grave low down in the IV	" III. vi.	8
Fired from the w, far on a hill	Elaine	168
flower of all the w and all the world,	"	249
knights of utmost North and IV,	"	525
into the rich heart of the w :	Guinevere	242
down to that great battle in the w,	"	567
blaze upon the waters to the w ;	En. Arden	597
Here in the woman-markets of the w,	Aylmer's F.	348
all the sails were darken'd in the w,	Sea Dreams	39
Flown to the east or the w .	The Window	41

westward-winding.

From the w-w flood	Margaret	9

wet.

Eyes with idle tears are w .	Miller's D.	211
I am w With drenching dews	St S. Stylites	14
crofts and pastures w with dew	Two Voices	14
Who sweep the crossings, w or dry,	Will Water.	47
my Sire, his rough cheek w with tears	Princess, v.	22
The leaves were w with women's tears :	" vi.	23
often I caught her with eyes all w,	Maud, I. xix.	7
forester of Dean, IV from the woods	Enid	149
either eyelid w with tears.	Vivien	229
IF with the mists and smitten by the	Guinevere	591
Made w the crafty crowsfoot	Sea Dreams	183
eyes all w, in the sweet moonshine:	Grandmother	49
I stood on a tower in the w .	1865-1866	1
wind and the w, the wind and the w	The Window	118
Woods where we hid from the w,	"	183

wether.

some black w of St Satan's fold.	Vivien	600

wet-shot
Came w-s alder from the wave, . Amphion . 41

wharf.
Out upon the w's they came . L of Shalott,iv.42
red roofs about a narrow w . . En Arden . 3
Down to the pool and narrow w . " . 691

what's my thought
w m t and when and where and how Princess,Pro.188

wheat
little dues of w, and wine and oil . Lotos-E's. . 167
in my uncle's eye Among the w ; . Dora . 66
went her way Across the w . . " . 70
waves of shadow went over the w Poet's Song. 4
belts of hop and breadths of w ; . Princess,Con. 45
Upon the thousand waves of w, . In Mem. xc. 11
By summer belts of w and vine . " xcvii. 4

wheat-suburb.
sweet-smelling lanes Of his w-s . The Brook . 123

wheedle.
And w a world that loves him not Maud, II. v. 30

wheedling.
W and siding with them ! . . Princess, v. 151

wheel (s.)
The dark round of the dripping w Miller's D. 102
w's of Time Spun round in station, Love and Duty74
in the flying of a w Cry down . Godiva . 6
turn This w within my head, . Will Water. 84
common hate with the revolving w Princess, vi. 157
I see the sailor at the w. . . In Mem. x. 4
And all the w's of Being slow . " xlix. 4
And every kiss of toothed w's, . " cxvi. 11
The last w echoes away. . . Maud, I. xxii. 26
And the roaring of the w's . " II. iv. 22
And the w's go over my head, . " v. 4
I stay'd the w's at Cogoletto, . The Daisy . 23
was one Of Fortune and her w, . Enid . 346
Turn, Fortune, turn thy w (rep.) . " . 347
Thy w and thee we neither love nor " . 349-58
With that wild w we go not up . " . 351
Thy w and thou are shadows . " . 357
sleepy land where under the same w Aylmer's F. 33
thee returning on thy silver w's . Tithonus . 76
stays the rolling Ixionian w, . Lucretius . 257

wheel (verb.)
And w's the circled dance . . In Mem. xcvii. 30

wheel'd.
strongly w and threw it. . . M d'Arthur 136
Earth follows w in her ellipse . Golden Year 24
Sometimes the sparhawk, w along, Sir L. and Q. G. 12
w Thro' a great arc his seven slow Princess, iv. 195
bats w, and owls whoop'd . . " Con. 110
w or lit the filmy shapes . . In Mem. xciv. 10
w on Europe-shadowing wings, . Ode on Well. 120
w and broke Flying, (rep.) . . Guinevere . 255

wheeling.
with both hands I flung him, w him ; M d'Arthur 157
w round The central wish, . Gardener's D. 219
W with precipitate paces . . Vision of Sin 37
suns, that w cast The planets . Princess, ii. 103

whelm.
w all this beneath as vast a mound Vivien . 506
w All of them in one massacre . Lucretius . 203

whelm'd.
some were w with missiles of the wall,Princess,Pro.45
a sea haze and w the world in gray. En. Arden . 671

whelp.
bones for his o'ergrown w to crack Maud, II. v. 55

when and where and how.
what's my thought and w a w a h, Princess,Pro.188

wherewithal.
having w, And in the fallow leisure Audley Ct . 75
for the w To give his babes . . En. Arden . 207

Whig.
Let W and Tory stir their blood . Will Water. 53

while.
we might make it worth his w . Princess, i. 282
hardly worth my w to choose . In Mem. xxxiv. 15

whim.
hurt to death, For your wild w : . Princess, vi. 226

whine.
colt-like whinny and with hoggish w StS.Stylites 174

whined.
w in lobbies, tapt at doors, . . Walk to the M. 27

whinny.
colt-like w and with hoggish whine StS.Stylites 174
her w shrills From tile to scullery, Princess, v. 441
With a low w toward the pair . Enid . 1604

whinnying.
her palfrey w lifted heel, . . Enid . 1382

whip.
Struck at her with his w, . . Enid 201-7, 413

whirl (s.)
Ran into its giddiest w of sound, Vision of Sin 27

whirl (verb.)
There the river eddy w's, . . L. of Shalott,ii. 15
I w like leaves in roaring wind. . Fatima . 7
while Saturn w's, his stedfast shade Pal. of Art 5
w the ungarner'd sheaf afar, . In Mem lxxi. 23
W's her to me ; but will she fling herself Lucretius19)

whirl'd.
No sword Of wrath her right arm w The Poet . 54
heavy-plunging foam, W by the wind, D. of F.Wom.119
round and round, and w in an arch M d'Arthur 138
There w her white robe . . Princess, iv 1⁄1
She w them on to me . . . " . 377
The last red leaf is w away, . In Mem xv. 3
w About empyreal heights . . " xciv. 37
is w into folly and vice . . Maud, I. iv. 31
like the smoke in a hurricane w . Boädicea . 51

whirligig.
As on this w of Time We circle . Will Water. 63

whirlwind.
loud the Norland w's blow . . Oriana . 6
And a w clear'd the larder: . . The Goose . 52
And bring her in a w, . . . Princess, i. 64
Across the w's heart of peace, . The Voyage 87
Like the leaf in a roaring w . . Boädicea . 51

whisker.
his watery smile And educated w. Ed. Morris 127

whisper (s)
She has heard a w say, . . L. of Shalott,ii. 3
In w's, like the w's of the leaves . Gardener's D. 248
And her w's throng'd my pulses . Locksley H. 36
Far along the world-wide w . " . 125
A little w silver-clear, . . Two Voices 428
Such seem'd the w at my side : . " . 431
honeying at the w of a lord ; . Princess,Pro.115
the songs, the w's, and the shrieks, " i. 97
o'er the imperial tent W's of war " v. 10
What w's from thy lying lip? . In Mem. in. 4
Was as the w of an air . . " xvii. 3
And shape the w of the throne ; . " lxiii. 12
In w s of the beauteous world, . " lxxviii. 12
This haunting w makes me faint, . " lxxx. 7
lightly does the w fall . . " lxxxiv. 8)
world's wide w breaking into storm, Enid . 27
and the spiteful w died : . . " . 186-6
in words part heard, in w's part, . Vivien . 688
A murmuring w thro' the nunnery ran, Guinevere 407
a w on her ear. She knew not what ; En. Arden 511
The moving w of huge trees . " . 586
Again in deeper inward w's 'lost !' . " . 717
A w half reveal'd her to herself . Aylmer's F. 144

whisper (verb.)
Listening, w's "'Tis the fairy . L. of Shalott,i 35
those full chesnuts w by. . . Miller's D. 108
The trees began to w. . . . MayQueen,iii.27
between Joy and woe, and w each. Margaret . 64
Not w, any murmur of complaint StS. Stylites 24

	POEM.	LINE.
O w to your glass, and say	Day-Dm.	271
w lovely words, and use	Will Water.	11
In her ear he w's gaily,	L. of Burleigh	1
'The stars,' she w's, 'blindly run	In Mem. iii.	5
And hear thy laurel w sweet	" xxxvii.	7
A hundred spirits w 'Peace.'	" lxxxv.	16
One w's, here thy boyhood sung	" ci.	9
w's to the worlds of space	" cxxv.	11
We w, and hint, and chuckle	Maud, I. iv.	27
And the lily w's, 'I wait	" xxii.	66
Heard the good mother softly w	Aylmer's F.	187
W in odorous heights of even	Milton	16

whisper'd.
She w, with a stifled moan	Mariana in the S.	57
some, 'tis w—down in hell	Lotos-E's.	108
Tho' what he w, under Heaven	Talking O.	21
'Never, never,' w by the phantom years	Locksley II.	83
Cyril w: 'Take me with you too'	Princess,	i. 80
the dame That w 'Asses' ears'	"	ii. 98
'Come' he w to her 'Lift up your head,	"	v. 60
The fault was mine,' he w, 'fly!'	Maud, II. i.	30
I never w a private affair	"	v. 47
Or w in the corner? do you know it?	Vivien	622

whisperer.
| and the swarm Of female w's: | Princess, | vi. 336 |

whispering.
W to each other half in fear	Sea-Fairies	5
Two lovers w by an orchard wall	Circumstance	4
or, w, play'd A chequer-work	In Mem. lxxi.	14
W I knew not what of wild	Tithonus	61

whistle (s.)
Scarce answer to my w;	Amphion	68
bustling w of the youth	Enid	257
the great plover's human w.	"	898

whistle (verb.)
| W back the parrot's call, | Locksley H. | 171 |

whistled.
w stiff and dry about the marge.	M. d'Arthur	64
The redcap w; and the nightingale	Gardener's D.	94
low and sweet I w thrice;	Ed. Morris	113
Sometimes the throstle w strong;	Sir L. and Q. G.	11
tall mill that w on the waste	En. Arden	340
And w to the morning star.	Sailor Boy	4
while he w long and loud	"	5

whistling.
| W a random bar of Bonny Doon. | The Brook | 82 |
| Half w and half singing a coarse song, | Enid | 1377 |

whit.
| Not a w of thy tuwhoo, | The Owl, | ii. 10 |

white.
w against the cold-white sky,	Dying Swan	12
Lying, robed in snowy w	L. of Shalott,	iv. 19
The lanes, you know, were w with may	Miller's D.	130
a ghost, mother, for I was all in w,	May Queen,	i. 17
all his face was w And colourless.	M. d'Arthur	212
One arm aloft—Gown'd in pure w,	Gardener's D.	124
As clean and w as priest when it	Walk. to the M.	48
charts us all in its coarse blacks or w's,	"	97
With folded feet, in stoles of w	Sir Galahad	43
No pint of w or red	Will Water.	82
Six hundred maidens clad in purest w	Princess,	ii. 448
lines of green that streak the w	"	v. 188
sleeps the crimson petal, now the w	"	vii. 161
the seas; A red sail, or a w;	Con.	47
blasts that blow the poplar w,	In Mem. lxxi.	3
A broad-blown comeliness, and w	Maud, I. xiii.	9
as w As ocean-foam in the moon,	"	xiv. 17
sweets hours that past in bridal w,	"	xviii.	65
We loved that hall, tho' w and cold,	The Daisy	37
W from the mason's hand, a fortress	Enid	244, 408
the cressy islets w in flower:	"	1324
watch the curl'd w of the coming wave	Vivien	141
clean as blood of babes, as w as milk	"	194
A maid so smooth, so w, so wonderful	"	416
W was her cheek: sharp breaths	"	607
she herself in w All but her face,	Elaine	1152

	POEM.	LINE.
the maiden rose, W as her veil,	Guinevere	361
Wear black and w, and be a nun	"	669
Ruddy and w, and strong on his legs	Grandmother	2
stream that flashest w,	V. of Cauteretz	1

white-breasted.
| w-b like a star Fronting the dawn | Œnone | 56 |

white-eyed.
| w-e phantasms weeping tears of blood | Pal. of Art | 239 |

white-faced.
| The w-f halls, the glancing rills, | In Mem. Con. | 113 |

white-favour'd.
| those w-f horses wait | In Mem. Con. | 90 |

white-flower'd.
| saw The w-f elder-thicket from the field | Godiva | 63 |

white-haired.
| A w-h shadow roaming like a dream | Tithonus | 8 |

white-hooved.
| a jet-black goat, white-horned, w-h | Œnone | 50 |

white-horned.
| a jet-black goat w-h, white-hooved | Œnone | 50 |

white-listed.
| tree that shone w-l thro' the gloom. | Vivien | 788 |

whiten.
| Willows w, aspens quiver, | L. of Shalott, | i. 10 |

whiten'd.
| lake w and the pinewood roar'd, | Vivien | 487 |
| w all the rolling flood; | The Victim | 20 |

whiter.
| The flocks are w down the vale, | In Mem. cxiv. | 10 |
| w even than her pretty hand: | Aylmer's F. | 363 |

White Rose.
| W R, Bellerophon, the Jilt, | The Brook | 161 |

Whitsuntide.
| Arthur on the W before | Enid | 145 |
| this was on the last year's W. | " | 840 |

whole.
So healthy, sound, and clear and w,	Miller's D.	15
All various, each a perfect w	Pal. of Art	58
Is bodied forth the second w, 'Love thou thy land'		66
w, and clean, and meet for Heaven.	St S. Stylites	210
W in ourselves and owed to none.	Princess,	iv. 130
half Without you; with you, w;	"	v. 441
looks as w as some serene Creation	"	v. 185
slips in sensual mire, But w and one	"	192
sound and w from head to foot	"	vi. 194
that soon He rose up w,	"	vii. 50
twin brothers, risen again and w;	"	74
keeps our Britain, w within herself	Con.	52
And love will last as pure and w	In Mem. xliii.	13
That each, who seems a separate w,	"	xlvi. 1
The wish, that of the living w	"	liv. 1
That so my pleasure may be w;	"	lxx. 8
W in himself, a common good.	Ode on Well.	26
keep our noble England w	"	161
W, like a crag that tumbles.	Enid	318
Save her dear lord w from any wound.	"	894
when Geraint was w again	"	1793
mine ancient wound is hardly w,	Elaine	94
to learn this knight were w,	"	768
Whereof he should be quickly w,	"	849
Sir Lancelot's deadly hurt was w,	"	900
our pride Looks only for a moment w	Aylmer's F.	2

whoop.
| Call to each other and w and cry. | The Merman | 26 |

whooped.
| bats wheel'd, and owls w, | Princess, Con. | 110 |

whooping.
| I drown'd the w's of the owl with sound | St S. Stylites | 32 |

whorl.
| With delicate spire and w | Maud, II. ii. | 6 |

	POEM.	LINE.
wicked.		
And the *w* cease from troubling	*MayQueen*,iii.	60
Ye know me then, that *w* one	*Guinevere*	601
wickedness.		
if you think this *w* in me,	*Vivien*	183
If you—and not so much from *w*,	"	370
might I wish to veil her *w*,	*Guinevere*	209
who hath forgiven my *w* to him,	"	628
wicket (gate.)		
one green *w* in a privet hedge;	*Gardener's D.*	109
wicket (cricket stump.)		
clamour bowl'd And stump'd the *w*;	*Princess,Pro.*	82
wicket-gate.		
reach'd The *w-g*, and found her	*Gardener's D.*	208
wide.		
W, wild and open to the air	*Dying Swan*	2
So royal-rich and *w*.'	*Pal. of Art* 20,	191
Look up thro' night : the world is *w*	*Two Voices*	24
the waste *w* Of that abyss,	"	110
w in soul and bold of tongue,	"	124
stalls are void, the doors are *w*,	*Sir Galahad*	31
the suns are many, the world is *w*	*Maud*, i. iv.	45
wide-dispread.		
locks not *w-d*,	*Isabel*	5
wide-mouthed.		
The little *w-m* heads upon the spout	*Godiva*	56
widened.		
And the thoughts of men are *w*	*Locksley H.*	138
widening.		
ever *w* slowly silence all.	*Vivien*	242
wider.		
The bounds of freedom *w* yet	*To the Queen*	32
widow.		
but there were *w*'s there, Two *w*'s	*Princess*, i.	126
his *w*, Miriam Lane, With daily-dwindling profits	*En. Arden*	696
smile That makes the *w* lean	*Sea Dreams*	152
widowed.		
w of the power in his eye	*M.d'Arthur*	122
My heart, tho' *w*, may not rest	*In.Mem.*lxxxiv.	113
widower.		
Tears of the *w*, when he sees	*In Mem.* xiii.	1
widowhood.		
God, that help'd her in her *w*.	*Dora*	111
width.		
Apart by all the chamber's *w*,	*Enid*	1114
wife (see man and wife.)		
In her as Mother, W, and Queen ;	*To the Queen*	28
The queen of marriage, a most perfect *w*.	*Isabel*	23
Pray, Alice, pray, my darling *w*	*Miller's D.*	23
True *w*, Round my true heart	"	215
fairest and most loving *w* in Greece	*Œnone*	183
why fairest *w*? am I not fair?	"	192
The grand old gardener and his *w*	*L.C.V.de Vere*	51
cannot tell—I might have been his *w*;	*MayQueen.*iii.	47
dream of Father-land Of child and *w*	*Lotos-E's.*	40
the last embraces of our *wives*	"	115
I knew an old *w* lean and poor,	*The Goose*	1
It stirr'd the old *w*'s mettle ;	"	56
take her for your *w* ;	*Dora*	13
a word with her he calls his *w*	"	42
I had been a patient *w*;	"	144
his *w* upon the tilt,	*Walk. to the M.*	33
He left his *w* behind ;	"	32
Sit with their *wives* by fires,	*St S. Stylites*	106
Match'd with an aged *w*	*Ulysses*	3
As the husband is, the *w* is :	*Locksley H.*	47
more than ever *w* was loved	"	64
Godiva, *w* to that grim Earl,	*Godiva*	1
Who took a *w*, who rear'd his race,	*Two Voices*	328
One walk'd between the *w* and child,	"	412
break it. In the name of *w*,	*Day-Dm.*	265
Little can I give my *w*	*L.of Burleigh*	14
Leering at his neighbour's *w*	*Vision of Sin*	118

	POEM	LINE.
flock'd at noon His tenants,*w* and child,	*Princess*,Pro.	4
We fell out, my *w* and I,	"	i. 243
a good mother, a good *w*, Worth winning	"	v. 159
had been wedded to, I knew mankind,	"	vi. 357
My bride, My *w*, my life.	"	vii. 359
Thou bringest the sailor to his *w*,	*In Mem.* x.	5
No casual mistress, but a *w*	"	lvin. 2
They would but find in child and *w*	"	lxxxix. 7
And of my spirit as of a *w*.	"	xcvi. 8
must be made a *w* ere noon	"	Con. 26
Now waiting to be made a *w*	"	42
rings to the yell of the trampled *w*	*Maud*. I. i.	33
you are all unmeet for a *w*	"	iv. 57
A horror on him, lest his gentle *w*	*Enid*	2
if ever yet was *w* True to her lord,	"	46
I fear that I am no true *w*.'	"	108,114
will make her truly my true *w*.'	"	503
charge you, on your duty as a *w*,	"	865
nor told his gentle *w* What ail'd him	"	1352
say, that you were no true *w*.'	"	1390
kinsman left him watcher o'er his *w*	*Vivien*	556
had kept him sunder'd from his *w*:	"	565
she said, ' your love—to be your *w*	*Elaine*	920
there never will be *w* of mine.'	"	932
no,' she cried, ' I care not to be *w*	"	933
as the village *w* who cries ' I shudder,	*Guinevere*	50
Mine is the shame, for I was *w*,	"	118
lets the *w* Whom he knows false,	"	510
my house, and this my little *w*.'	*En. Arden*	28
little *w* would weep for company,	"	74
say she would be little *w* to both,	"	36
his *w* Bore him another son,	"	103
yet the *w*—When he was gone—	"	131
all that seamen needed or their *wives*	"	137
Pray'd for a blessing on his *w* and babes	"	168
Cast his strong arms about his drooping *w*	"	227
I wish you for my *w*.	"	407
I believe, if you were fast my *w*,	"	411
beheld His *w*, his *w* no more,	"	760
'This miller's *w*' He said to Miriam	"	805
fiat somewhat soothed himself and *w*	*Aylmer's F.*	26
His *w* a faded beauty of the Baths	"	27
To ailing *w* or wailing infancy	"	177
the *w*, who watched his face, Paled	"	731
in the narrow gloom By *w* and child ;	"	841
His *w*, an unknown artist's orphan	*Sea Dreams*	2
The gentle-hearted *w* Sat shuddering	"	29
silenced by that silence lay the *w*,	"	46
Not fearful : fair,' Said the good *w*	"	82
said the kindly *w* to comfort him,	"	136
And Willy's *w* has written :	*Grandmother*	3,105
Never the *w* for Willy.	"	4
not since I had been a *w* ;	"	61
The sweet little *w* of the singer said,	*The Islet.*	3
Me the *w* of rich Prasutagus	*Boadicea*	48
King is happy In child and *w*	*The Victim*	10
O answer; Or I, the *w*.	"	56
O *w*, what use to answer now ?	"	59
Suddenly from him brake the *w*.	"	75
We give them the *w*!'	"	84
Take my love and be my *w*.	*The Window*	129
wifehood.		
perfect *w* and pure lowlihead	*Isabel*	12
wife-hunting.		
W-h, as the rumour ran	*Aylmer's F.*	212
wifeless.		
now a lonely man W and heirless	*Elaine*	1362
wifelike.		
W, her hand in one of his	*Aylmer's F.*	808
wild ('adj.)		
wide and *w* the waste enormous marsh	*Ode to Mem.*	101
The plain was grassy, *w* and bare	*Dying Swan*	1
I have been *w* and wayward	*May Queen*,ii.	33
nor let your grief be *w*	"	35
And in the chase grew *w*	*Talking O.*	112
but I *know* my words are *w*	*Locksley H.*	173
As *w* as aught of fairy lore ;	*Day-Dm.*	204
But it is *w* and barren,	*Amphion*	3

460 CONCORDANCE TO

	POEM.	LINE.
Lilia, *w* with sport,	*Princess*, Pro.	100
All *w* to found an University	" i.	149
Deep as first love, and *w* with all regret	iv.	39
on rib and cheek They made him *w*	" v.	332
As wan, as chill, as *w* as now ;	*In Mem*. lxxi.	17
loss of whom has turn'd me *w*—	*Enid*	1157
I call mine own self *w*,	"	1160
There was nothing *w* or strange,	*Vivien*	709
in a fiery dawning *w* with wind	*Elaine*	1014
know his babes were running *w*	*En. Arden*	303
helpless life so *w* that it was tame.	"	558
Whispering I knew not what of *w*	*Tithonus*	61

wild (s.)

flight from out your bookless *w's*	*Princess*, ii.	42
you young savage of the Northern *w l*	" iii.	230
across the *w* That no man knows.	" vii.	341
Till from the garden and the *w*	*In Mem*. c.	17
My yet young life in the *w's* of Time *Maud*, I. xvi.		21
then he cried again, 'To the *w's*!' *Enid*		877
meadow gemlike chased In the brown *w*,"		1048
lived alone in a great *w* on grass,	*Vivien*	471
Went back to his old *w*,	"	499
The King was hunting in the *w*;.	*The Victim*	31
King returned from out the *w*	"	43

wildbeast.

felt the blind *w* of force . *Princess*, v. 256

wild-bird.

From the groves within The *w-b's* din. *Poet's Mind* 21

wilderness.

vines, and blowing bosks of *w*	*Princess*, i.	110
w, full of wolves, where he used to lie *Maud*, II. v.		54
In brambly *w'es*;	*The Brook*	179
I will ride forth into the *w* ; .	*Enid*	127
And *w'es*, perilous paths, they rode	"	881
Here in the heart of waste and *w*	"	1162
That *w* of single instances,	*Aylmer's F*.	437
The *w* shall blossom as the rose.	"	649
wolf and wolfkin, from the *w*	*Boädicea*	15
And Fancy watches in the *w*	*Coquette*, i.	12
hide them, million-myrtled *w*,	*Lucretius*	201

wildfire.

Be dazzled by the *w* Love . *Princess*, v. 431

wild-flower.

Plucking the harmless *w-f* on the hill? *Maud*, II. i. 3

wildly-sculptured.

past beneath the *w-s* gates . *Elaine* . 840

wildness.

His *w*, and the chances of the dark *Princess*, iv. 225

wild-swan.

made the *w-s* pause in her cloud,	*Poet's Song*.	7
The leader *w* in among the stars.	*Princess*, iv.	414

wildweed-flower.

The *w-f* that simply blows ? . *Day-Dm*. . 202

Wild Will.

W W, Black Bess, Tantivy, . *The Brook* . 160

wile.

w the length from languorous hours, *Princess*, vii. 48

wilful.

To make her thrice as *w* as before.' *Elaine*		206
you call me *w* and the fault Is yours	"	746
being so very *w* you must go.'	"	773-7
'being so very *w* you must die	"	779

wiliest

of her court The *w* and the worst; *Guinevere* . 30

will (s.)

Broad-based upon her people's *w*,	To the Queen	35
The marvel of the everlasting *w*,	*The Poet*	7
Chasing itself at its own wild *w*,	*Dying Swan*	17
full-grown *w*, Circled thro' all	*Œnone*	162
and yet His *w* be done !	*May Queen*, iii	10
that I could not bend One *w*	*D.of F.Wom*.	138
I subdued me to my father's *w*;	"	234
Let her *w* Be done—to weep	*To J. S.*	43

	POEM.	LINE.
power in his eye That bow'd the *w*	*M. d'Arthur*	123
Dora felt her uncle's *w* in all,	*Dora*	5
home is none of yours. My *w* is law.'	"	43
more from ignorance than *w*	*Walk.to the M*.	100
needs for life is possible to *w*—	*Love and Duty*	83
strong in *w* To strive, to seek,	*Ulysses*	69
his eyes, before they had their *w*,	*Godiva*	69
Sick art thou—a divided *w*	*Two Voices*	106
A virgin heart in work and *w*.	*Sir Galahad*	24
Against her father's and mother's *w*:	*Ed Gray*	10
Used all her fiery *w*, and smote	*Will Water*.	111
laid about them at their *w's* and died *Princess*,Pro.		31
But then she had a *w*; .	"	i. 47
O that iron *w*, That axelike edge	"	ii. 185
babes To be dandled, no, but living *w's*	"	iv. 129
'sdeath ! against my father's *w*'.	"	v. 288
her *w* Bred *w* in me to overcome it	"	340
since my *w* Seal'd not the bond—	"	368
Her iron *w* was broken in her mind ;	"	vi. 102
you the Victor of your *w*.	"	151
Purpose in purpose, *w* in *w* .	"	vii. 287
Our *w's* are ours 'rep.)	*In Mem*. Pro.	15
My *w* is bondsman to the dark ; .	"	iv. 2
With morning wakes the *w*, and cries,"		15
That I could wing my *w* with might "		xl. 10
To riper growth the mind and *w:*	"	xli. 8
pangs of nature, sins of *w*, .	"	liii. 3
Till all at once beyond the *w*	"	lxix. 12
The sense of human *w* demands .	"	lxxxiv. 39
desire That spurs an imitative *w* .	"	cix. 20
O living *w* that shalt endure	"	cxxx. 1
Whose gentle *w* has changed my fate *Maud*, I. xviii.		23
For shall not Allah have her *w* ?	"	xix. 84
(If I read her sweet *w* right)	"	xxi. 10
Void of the little living *w*	"	II. ii. 14
However weary, a spark of *w*	"	56
Make and break, and work their *w*; *Ode on Well*.		261
well for him whose *w* is strong ? . *Will*		1
the strength of heaven-descended *W*,"		11
I compel all creatures to my *w*.	*Enid*	1477, 1521
and the wine will change your *w*.		1511
grace and *w* to pick the vicious quitch"		1751
Fixt in her *w*, and so the seasons went *Vivien*		44
Without the *w* to lift their eyes .	"	685
fault Is yours who let me have my *w*, *Elaine*		747
that I make My *w* of yours,	"	912
I said 'Now shall I have my *w* :'	"	1041
mine now to work my *w*—	"	1225
Annie fought against his *w*: .	*En. Arden*.	158
grieving held his *w*, and bore it thro'	"	167
her sad *w* no less to chime with his,	"	247
from a living source within the *w*,	"	802
But I wish'd it had been God's *w*, *Grandmother*		73
strong Hours indignant work'd their *w's*, *Tithonus*		18
Thither at their *w* they haled	*Boädicea*	55
With one wide *w* that closes thine *On a Mourner*		20
vast and filthy hands upon my *w*,	*Lucretius*	217
Dash them anew together at her *w*	"	243

will (verb.)

A man may speak the thing he *u*; '*You ask me, why*'		8
yet my father *w's* not war ; .	*Princess*, v.	267
and what I *w* I can :' .	*Elaine*	913
not without She *w's* it : .	"	1412

will be.

was, and is, and *w b*, are but is ; . *Princess*, iii. 307

will'd.

words had issue other than she *w*.	*Vivien*	655
would I, if she *w* it ? nay, Who knows ? *Elaine*		1412
set his hand To do the thing he *w*, *En. Arden*.		294
might not Averill, had he *w* it so . *Aylmer's F*.		46

William.

W and Dora. *W* was his son .	*Dora*	2
yearn'd towards *W*; but the youth	"	6
But *W* answer'd short ; .	"	20
Consider, *W*: take a month .	"	27
W answer'd madly ; bit his lips, .	"	31
there was born a boy To *W*; .	"	47
at last a fever seized On *W*,	"	53

	POEM.	LINE.
evil came on *w* at the first..	*Dora*	52
answer'd softly 'This is *w*'s child!'	"	58
work for *w*'s child, until he grows	"	124
for myself, Or *w*, or this child: .	"	139
when *w* died, he died at peace ..	"	141
sobb'd o'er *w*'s child, Thinking of *w*	"	163

willing.

Thou, *w* me to stay, .	*Madeline*	37
Nor *w* men should come among us	*Princess*, iii.	301
w she should keep Court-favour,	" vii.	42
Wroth at himself; not *w* to be known,	*Elaine*	160

witingly.

| 'Yea, *w*,' replied the youth; | *Enid* | 1056 |

willow.

One *w* over the river wept .	*Dying Swan*	14
W's whiten, aspens quiver, .	*L. of Shalott*, i.	10
Beneath a *w* left afloat	" iv.	7
Shrank one sick *w* sere and small	*Mariana in the S.*	53
There by the humpback'd *w*;	*Walk. to the M.*	23
The shock-head *w*'s two and two	*Amphion*	30
racing oars Among the *w*'s:	*In Mem* lxxxvi.	11

willow-branches.

| the *w-b* hoar and dank . | *Dying Swan* | 37 |

Willows.

O darling Katie *W*, his one child !	*The Brook*	67
James *W*, of one name and heart with her	"	76
'What surname?' '*W*.' 'No!'.	"	212

willow-veiled.

| By the margin, *w-v*, . | *L. of Shalott*, i. | 19 |

willow-weed.

| set With *w-w* and mallow | *The Brook* | 46 |

Willy.

And *W*, my eldest-born, is gone	*Grandmother*,1,9,	87
And *W*'s wife has written: .	"	3, 105
Never the wife for *W*	"	4
and *W*, you say, is gone. .	"	8
for *W* stood like a rock; .	"	10
I cannot weep for *W*, .	"	19, 67
And *W* had not been down to the farm	"	33
W,—he didn't see me,— .	"	42
W stood up like a man, .	"	45
'Marry you, *W*!' said I .	"	53
So *W* and I were wedded: .	"	57
So *W* has gone, my beauty .	"	101
But how can I weep for *W* .	"	102

wilt thou.

| '*w t*' answer'd, and again The *w t* ask'd | *In Mem.Con.* | 58 |

wimple.

| From beneath her gather'd *w* | *Lilian* | 14 |

win.

Woo me, and *w* me, and marry me	*The Mermaid*	46
To *w* his love I lay in wait:.	*The Sisters*	11
Of me you shall not *w* renown !	*L. C. V. de Vere*	2
The warmth it thence shall *w*	*Talking O.*	254
Which did *w* my heart from me !'	*L. of Burleigh*	84
and be you The Prince to *w* her !	*Princess*, Pro.	220
'Follow, follow, thou shalt *w* (v. 461)	" i.	99
partly that I hoped to *w* you back	" iv.	285
w's, tho' dash'd with death .	" v.	157
we fail, And if we *w*, we fail: .	"	313
W you the hearts of women; .	" vi.	155
verily I think to *w*.' .	"	309
That out of words a comfort *w*;	*In Mem.* xx	10
past will always *w* A glory .	" xxiv.	13
could not *w* An answer from my lips	" cii.	47
And the titmouse hope to *w* her .	*Maud*, I. xx.	79
Emperor, Ottoman, which shall *w*:	*To F. D Maurice*	32
seems my spurs are yet to *w* .	*Enid*	128
nor will you *w* him back, .	"	1181
Vivien had not done to *w* his trust	*Vivien*	712
W I by this kiss you will ; .	*Elaine*	152
w and return.' .	"	158
Joust for it, and *w*, and bring it .	"	204
W shall I not, but do my best to *w*!	"	221
And you shall *w* this diamond .	"	227
to *w* his honour and to make his name,	"	1353

	POEM.	LINE.
where two fight The strongest *w*'s	*Aylmer's F.*	365
w all eyes with all accomplishment	*Coquette*, ii.	4
roughly men may woo thee, so they *w*	*Lucretius*	263
That she but meant to *w* him back	"	275

wince.

| You should have seen him *w* | *Walk. to the M.* | 63 |

wind (s.)

Cold *w*'s woke the gray-eyed morn	*Mariana*	31
the shrill *w*'s were up and away .	"	50
wild *w*'s bound within their cell, .	"	54
to the wooing *w* aloof .	"	75
unwoo'd of summer *w*: .	*Arabian N's.*	80
The dew-imperaled *w*'s of dawn	*Ode to Mem.*	14
in the rudest *w* Never grow sere .	"	24
From brawling storms, From weary *w*	"	113
Lovest thou the doleful *w* .	*Adeline*	49
w's blew his own praises in his eyes	*A Character*	21
the *w*'s which bore Them earthward	*The Poet*	17
Bright as light, and clear as *w*	*Poet's Mind*	7
Ever the weary *w* went on, .	*Dying Swan*	9
shook the wave as the *w* did sigh;	"	15
Above in the *w* was the swallow, .	"	16
W's were blowing, waters flowing,	*Oriana*	14
Norland *w*'s pipe down the sea, .	"	41
amorous, odorous *w* Breathes low	*Eleánore*	123
in the pauses of the *w*, .	*Miller's D.*	122
whirl like leaves in roaring *w*. .	*Fatima*	7
The *w* sounds like a silver wire, .	"	23
foam-bow brightens When the *w* blows	*Œnone*	61
a *w* arose And overhead .	"	90
The *w* is blowing in turret and tree.	*The Sisters*	3
And hoary to the *w* .	*Pal. of Art*	268
and the *w* began to roll .	*May Queen*,iii.	27
a swell of music on the *w* .	"	37.6
With *w*'s upon the branch, .	*Lotos-E's.*	72
w and wave and oar ; .	"	172
Fluster the *w*'s and tides .	*D. of F. Wom.*	28
Whirl'd by the *w*, had roll'd me deep	"	110
winter *w*'s are wearily sighing .	*D. of the O. Year*	2
The *w*, that beats the mountain, blows	*To J. S.*	1
Death is blown in every *w*;' .	"	45
from the harbour-mouth, Wild *w*!	'You ask me, why'	26
Came rolling on the *w*. 'Of old zat Freedom', etc.	3
knowledge circle with the *w*'s; 'Love thou thy land'	17
soul Of Discord race the rising *w*;	"	18
A *w* to puff your idol-fires, .	"	69
wild *w* rang from park and plain,	*The Goose*	45
like a *w*, that shrills All night	*M. d'Arthur*	201
Nor ever *w* blows loudly ; .	"	261
a broad and equal blowing *w*, .	*Gardener's D.*	76
one long stream of sighing *w*, .	"	261
she was sharper than an eastern *w*,	*Audley Ct.*	52
soft *w* blowing over meadowy holms	*Ed. Morris*	95
Rain, *w*, frost, heat, hail .	*St S. Stylites*	16
Till that wild *w* made work .	*Talking O.*	54
I swear, by leaf, and *w*, and rain,	"	81
A light *w* chased her on the wing	"	125
light as any *w* that blows .	"	129
and the *w*'s are laid with sound .	*Locksley H.*	104
For the mighty *w* arises, .	"	194
As *w*'s from all the compass shift	*Godiva*	33
low *w* hardly breath'd for fear .	"	55
Tho' thou wert scatter'd to the *w*,	*Two Voices*	32
He sows himself on every *w* .	"	294
many a merry *w* was borne .	*Day-Dm.*	178
The happy *w*'s upon her play'd,	*Sir L.and Q. G.*	38
There let the *w* sweep 'Come not, when', etc.	5
light *w* blew from the gates of the sun,	*Poet's Song*	3
Like linnets in the pauses of the *w*:	*Princess*, Pro.	238
An answer vague as *w*: .	" i.	44
A *w* arose and rush'd upon the South,	"	96
like a wrinkling *w* On glassy water	"	114
She rose upon a *w* of prophecy .	" ii.	154
W of the western sea, .	"	457
fretful as the *w* Pent in a crevice, .	" iii.	64
Upon the level in little puffs of *w*, .	" iv.	237
blowzed with health, and *w*, and rain,	"	360
when a light *w* wakes A lisping .	" v.	12
hate to hear me like a *w* .	"	65
range above the region of the *w*, .	" Con.	112

	POEM.	LINE.
A flower beat with rain and w,	In Mem. viii	15
Sleep, gentle w's, as he sleeps now	" ix.	15
To-night the w's begin to rise,	" xv.	1
Each voice four changes on the w,	" xxviii.	9
the w's were in the beech :	" xxx.	9
blame not thou the w's that make	" xlvii.	10
No wing of w the region swept,	" lxxvii.	6
All w's that roam the twilight came	" lxxvii.	11
every pulse of w and wave	" lxxxiv.	73
I hear a w Of memory murmuring	" xci.	7
the w began to sweep A music	" cii.	53
Nor feed with sighs a passing w :	" cvii.	4
the w like a broken worldling wail'd, *Maud*, I.i.		11
in a wintry w by a ghastly glimmer	" ii.	13
shake its threaded tears in the w	" III.vi.	28
and the war roll down like a w	"	54
four-square to all the w's that blew ! *Ode on Well.*		39
scatter'd all they had to all the w's · *Enid* .		635
A storm was coming, but the w's were still *Vivien*		1
Drave with a sudden w across the deeps	"	50
Thro' the dim land against a rushing w,	"	275
gust of w Puff'd out his torch	"	580
plumes driven backward by the w they *Elaine*		479
and went To all the w's ?	"	655
and the moanings of the w.	"	997
in a fiery dawning wild with w	"	1014
sharp w that ruffles all day long . *Guinevere*		51
in the cold w that foreruns the morn,	"	131
in a w, ready to break and fly	"	363
follow'd calms, and then w's variable *En Arden*		541
blown by baffling w's Like the Good Fortune,	"	629
fancy fled before the lazy w .	"	658
the w blew ; The raiu of heaven . *Aylmer's F.*		427
o'er those lazy limits down the w	"	435
Yell'd as when the w's of winter . *Boädicea*		77
the w's from off the plain Roll'd the rich *Spec of Iliad*		7
when all the w's are laid	"	12
And the w did blow :	*The Captain*	34
w's were roaring and blowing ;	1865-1866	3
creeps a cloud, or moves a w .	*Lucretius*	106
the w's are up in the morning (rep) *The Window*		5
w's and lights and shadows that cannot	"	7
wet west w and the world will go on (rep)		111
The w and the wet, the w and the wet !	"	118
Wet west w how you blow ! you blow !	"	110
W's are loud and you are dumb .	"	124
W's are loud and w's will pass !	"	127

wind (verb.)

W's all the vale in rosy folds .	*Miller's D.*	242
More close and close his footsteps w : *Day-Dm.*		125
w And double in and out the boles, *Princess*, iv.		242
Still onward w's the dreary way ;	*In Mem* xxvi.	1
w's their curls about his hand ;	" lxv.	12
It lightly w's and steals .	*Maud*, II. iv.	18
I w about. and in and out .	*The Brook*	55
Where yon dark valleys w forlorn	*On a Mourner*	22

wind-hover.

| as long As the w-h hangs in balance *Aylmer's F.* | | 321 |

winding.

From the river w clearly, .	*L. of Shalott*, i.	31
W down to Camelot	" ii.	14
a full-fed river w slow .	*Pal. of Art*	73
paused About the w's of the marge	*Ed Morris*	94
Low voluptuous music w trembled	*Vision of Sin*	17
glided w under ranks Of iris	*In Mem* cii.	23
w under woodbine bowers, .	*The Brook*	88

window.

The fourscore w's all alight .	*Arabian N's.*	122
Leaving doors and w's wide :	*Deserted H.*	3
In the w's is no light ; .	"	6
Or thro' the w's we shall see	"	10
the deep-set w's, stain'd and traced,	*Pal. of Art*	49
forms that pass'd at w's and on roofs *D of F. Wom.*		23
Reveal'd their shining w's :	*Gardener's D.*	215
door shut, and w barr'd.	*Godiva*	41
so To the open w moved	*Princess*, iv	471
were laid On the hasp of the w.	*Maud*, I. xiv.	19
The giant w's blazon'd fires	*The Daisy*	58
Saw from his w's nothing save his own *Aylmer's F.*		21

	POEM.	LINE.
Clasp her w, trail and twine, .	*The Window*	22
Blaze upon her w, sun, .	"	176

window-bars.

| it came, and close beside the w-b . | *May Queen*, iii. | 39 |

window-pane.

the brook, or a pool, or her w-p .	*The Window*	4
down to the w-p of my dear .	"	17
And never a glimpse of her w-p .	"	108

wind-scatter'd.

| w-s over sails and masts, . | *D. of F. Wom.* | 31 |

wine.

Across the walnuts and the w— .	*Miller's D.*	32
little bags of wheat, and w and oil ;	*Lotos-E's.*	167
think not they are glazed with w .	*Locksley H.*	51
and as water unto w— .	"	152
beaker brimm'd with noble w.	*Day-Dm*	56
dips Her laurel in the w .	*Will Water.*	18
Sipt w from silver, praising God .	"	127
By heaps of gourds, and skins of w, *Vision of Sin*		13
Bring me spices, bring me w ;	"	76
W is good for shrivell'd lips .	"	79
Let me loose thy tongue with w :	"	88
At w, in clubs, of art, of politics .	*Princess, Pro.*	160
plied him with his richest w's.	" i.	172
lay at w with Lar and Lucumo ; .	" ii.	113
Fruit, blossom, viand, amber w,	" iv.	17
not a death's-head at the w.'	"	69
had our w and chess beneath the planes	" vi.	229
dear to me as sacred w .	*In Mem.* lxxxvii.	15
well, indeed, when warm with w	" lxxxix.	9
fetch the w, Arrange the board .	" cvi.	15
yes !—but a company forges the w. *Maud*, I. i.		36
I fear, the new strong w of love .	" vi.	82
Betroth'd us over their w, .	" xix.	39
he left his w and horses and play	"	74
In babble and revel and w. .	" xxii.	28
vassals of w and anger and lust .	II. i.	43
But honest talk and wholesome w, *To F. D. Maurice*		18
to the town and buy us flesh and w ; *Enid*		372
means of goodly welcome flesh and w.	"	387
now the w made summer in his veins.	"	398
wholly given to brawls and w,	"	441
cried Geraint for w and goodly cheer	"	1132
And w and food were brought,	"	1138
w and free companions kindled him	"	1142
vanish friendships only made in w.	"	1328
for flesh and w to feed his spears .	"	1449
fill'd a horn with w and held it to her)	"	1507
and the w will change your will. .	"	1511
I will not look at w until I die. .	"	1515
touch'd fierce w, nor tasted flesh, .	*Vivien*	477
with knife in meat and w in horn	"	544
once in life was fluster'd with new w	"	606
straddling the butts While the w ran.	*Guinevere*	267
Charier of sleep, and w, and exercise *Aylmer's F.*		448
Warm with his w's or taking pride	"	554
Sat at his table : drank his costly w's ; *Sea Dreams*		74
and honey hearted w And bread .	*Spec. of Iliad*	5

wine-flask.

| The w-f lying couch'd in moss | *In Mem.* lxxxviii | 44 |

wine-heated.

| Moist as they were, w-h from the feast , | *Enid* | 1200 |

wing (s)

What they say betwixt their w's ?	*Adeline*	29
Droops both his w's, regarding thee,	*Eleänore.*	119
fold our w's, And cease from wanderings, *Lotos-E's*		64
That claps his w's at dawn .	*D. of F. Wom.*	16
wild hearts and feeble w's *'Love thou thy land,'* etc		11
a summer home of murmurous w's *Gardener's D.*		7
stole with folded w's, Distilling odours	"	182
While the prime swallow dips his w, *Ed Morris*		145
dull chrysalis Cracks into shining w's, *St. S. Stylites*		154
A light wind chased her on the w, *Talking O*		125
He dried his w's : like gauze they grew *Two Voices*		13
Here sits he shaping w's to fly, .	"	289
On sleeping w's they sail .	*Sir Galahad*	44
W's flutter, voices hover clear ;	"	78

	POEM.	LINE.
Tho' fortune clip my w's,	Will Water.	50
He rode a horse with w's,	Vision of Sin	3
a woman-statue rose with w's	Princess, i.	207
Spread thy full w's, and waft him o'er.	In Mem ix.	4
The wild pulsation of her w's;	" xii.	4
My fancies time to rise on w,	" xiii.	17
that dip Their w's in tears.	" xlvi.	16
Self-balanced on a lightsome w:	" lxiv.	8
Take w's of fancy, and ascend	" lxxv.	1
Take w's of foresight; lighten thro'	"	5
N) t, of wind the region swept,	" lxxvii.	6
Or eagle's w, or insect's eye	" cxxiii.	6
The love that rose on stronger w's	" cxxvii.	1
crept so long on a broken w.	Maud, III. vi.	1
wheel'd on Europe-shadowing w's	Ode on Well.	120
w's Moved in her ivy,	Enid .	598
a lothly plume fall'n from the w.	Vivien	577
w's of brooding shelter o'er her peace,	Aylmer's F.	132
So often, that the folly taking w's	"	424
Till the little w's are stronger	Sea Dreams	289
With one waft of the w.	The Captain	72
you have gotten the w's of love,	The Window	153

wing (verb.)
Far as the wild swan w's,	Pal. of Art	31
That I could w my will with might	In Mem. xl.	10

wing'd.
headed And w with flame	The Poet	12
w Her transit to the throne,	Princess, iv	358
from his walls and w his entry-gates	Aylmer's F.	18

winging.
What time I watch'd the swallow w	Princess, iv.	71

wink (s.)
in a w the false love turns to hate:	Vivien	701

wink (verb.)
ere a star can w, beheld her there	Gardener's D.	121
w's behind a slowly dying fire.	Locksley II.	136
W at our advent: help my prince	Princess, iii.	144
w's the gold fin in the porphyry font:	" vii.	163
w no more in slothful overtrust.	Ode on Well.	170
man at all, who knows and w's?	Vivien	630
fair bride is and does, and w's?	"	631
A lad may w, and a girl may hint,	The Ringlet	17

winked.
last light, that long Had w	M d'Arthur, Ep.	2
which for bribe had w at wrong,	Enid	1787

winking
The landscape w thro' the heat:	In Mem. lxxxviii.	16
W his eyes, and twisted all his face	Elaine	1130

winning.
W its way with extreme gentleness	Isabel	23
To all the people, w reverence.	M.d'Arthur	108
If such be worth the w now, 'You might have won'	2	
w easy grace, No doubt, for slight	Princess, iv.	311
a good wife, Worth w;	" v.	160

winter
A hundred w's snow'd upon his breast,	Pal. of Art	139
moving isles of w shock	M. d'Arthur	140
Three w's, that my soul might grow.	St.S. Stylites	70
kill Time by the fire in w.'	Princess, Pro.	201
Why not a summer's as a w's tale?	"	204
Those w's of aheyance all worn out,	" iv.	420
Till growing w's lay me low.	In Mem. xxxix.	30
And every w change to spring.	" liii	15
As in the w's left behind	" lxxvii.	9
eighty w's freeze with one rebuke	Ode on Well.	186
Your presence will be sun in w.	To F. D. Maurice	2
To break the blast of w, stand;	"	22
Yell'd as when the winds of w	Boädicea	77

winter-clad.
'Tattoo'd or woaded, w-c in skins,	Princess, ii.	105

winter-field.
The tented w-f was broken up	Aylmer's F	110

Winter's Tale
have him back Who told the 'W t	Princess, Pro.	231

wintertide.
	POEM.	LINE.
in w shall star The black earth	Ode to Mem.	17

wire.
The wind sounds like a silver w,	Fatima	27
The parrot in his gilded w's.	Day-Dm.	36
A man with knobs and w's and vials	Princess, Pro.	65
Up thro' gilt w's a crafty loving eye,	"	170

wirer.
The nightly w of their innocent hare	Aylmer's F.	470

wisdom
raiment's hem was traced in flame	W. The Poet	48
wisdom-bred And throned of w.	Œnone	1.2
Were w in the scorn of consequence	"	143
stay'd the Ausonian King to hear Of w	Pal. of Art	112
The w of a thousand years 'Of old sat Freedom'		18
knowledge changed to fruit Of w.	Love and Duty	25
Knowledge comes, but w lingers.	Locksley II.	141-3
could his dark w find it out.	Two Voices	308
Not much their w teaches;	Will Water.	174
with a gossamer, Were w to it	Princess, v.	164
training of a child Is woman's w.'	"	456
in thy w make me wise	In Mem. Pro.	44
W dealt with mortal powers,	" xxxvi.	5
There must be w with great Death:	" l.	11
Whatever w sleep with thee	" cvii.	16
Nor let thy w make me wise	" cviii.	24
High w holds my w less	" cxi.	2
how much w sleeps with thee	" cxii.	2
moving side by side With w	" cxiii.	20
W heavenly of the soul.	"	22
let me think Silence is w:	Vivien	102
lo, I clothe myself with w,'	"	104
let his w go For ease of heart	"	741
for all your w well know I.	En. Arden.	211
Wearing his w lightly,	A Dedication	12

wisdom-bred
w-b And throned of wisdom	Œnone	121

wise.
O silent faces of the Great and W,	Pal. of Art	195
No one can be more w than destiny.	D. of F. Wom.	94
Great Nature is more w than I:	To J. S.	35
Not yet the w of heart would 'Love thou thy land'		81
'Be w: not easily forgiven Are those	Gardener's D.	242
was worth The experience of the w.	Ed. Morris	66
Thro' madness, hated by the w,	Love and Duty	7
read his spirit blindly w,	Two Voices	287
Therefore comes it we are w.	Vision of Sin	100
call her w, who made me w!	Princess, ii.	374
Lady Psyche, younger, not so w,	" iv	297
in thy wisdom make me w.	In Mem. Pro.	44
If thou wilt have me w and good.	" lviii.	8
With all the circle of the w,	" lx.	3
Thy likeness to the w below,	" lxxii.	7
She darkly feels him great and w,	" xcvi.	34
They sang of what is w and good	" cii.	10
'Tis held that sorrow makes us w	" cxii. i.	15
Nor let thy wisdom make me w.	" cvii.	24
that blind clamour made me w;	" cxxii.	18
Were it not w if I fled from the place	Maud, I. i.	64
Among the w and the bold.	Ode on Well.	52
modest, kindly, all-accomplished, w,	Ded. of Idylls	17
whether very w Or very foolish;	Enid.	469
'do it: be not too w.	"	1773
are w in love Love most say least'	Vivien	96
Yet you are w who say it,	"	101
surely you are w, But such a silence is more w than kind.'	"	137
However w, you hardly know me yet,'	"	195
'I never was less w, however w,	"	207
you so w? you were not once so w,	Elaine	104
'O Enoch, you are w: And yet.	En. Arden	213
wholly w To let that handsome fellow	Aylmer's F.	268
Attain the w indifference of the w.	A Dedication	8
Yearn'd after by the wisest of the w,	Lucretius	261

wiser.
we are w than our sires. 'Love thou thy land,' et.		72
W to weep a true occasion lost.	Princess, iv.	50
to live No w than their mothers,	"	433
Surely I shall be w in a year;	En. Arden.	470

CONCORDANCE TO

wisest.

	POEM.	LINE.
Yearn'd after by the *w* of the wise	Lucretius	263

wish (s.)

	POEM.	LINE.
wheeling round The central *w*,	Gardener's D.	220
let me have an answer to my *w*;	Dora	28
let him speak his *w*.	St S. Stylites	142
Old *w's*, ghosts of broken plans,	Will Water.	29
wild king to force her to his *w*,	Princess, Pro.	37
to close with Cyril's random *w*	" iii.	85
led by golden *w'es*, and a hope	" iv.	400
met him on his way With *w'es*,	In Mem. vi.	23
The *w*, that of the living whole	" liv.	1
cries against my *w* for thee.	" lxxxix.	24
The *w* too strong for words to name;	" xcii.	14
Albeit I give no reason but my *w*,	Enid	761
moulded by your *w'es* for her weal	"	799
I know Your *w* and would obey	"	1268
Beholding how you butt against my *w*.	"	1525
Flatter his own *w* in age for love	Vivien	41
grant my re-reiterated *w*,	"	203
Nor own'd a sensual *w*,	"	478
The *w* to prove him wholly hers.'	"	714
Love-loyal to the least *w* of the Queen	Elaine	90
the *w* most near to your true heart;	"	910
Lancelot saw that she withheld her *w*,	"	916
'Delay no longer, speak your *w*,	"	920
there I woke, but still the *w* remain'd	"	1042
sent him to the Queen Bearing his *w*,	"	1163
Love-loyal to the least *w* of the Queen	Guinevere	125
the noble *w* To save all earnings	En. Arden.	85
a *w* renew'd, When two years after	"	88
his had been, or yours: that was his *w*.	"	299
denied his heart his dearest *w*,	"	333
laugh'd, and yielded readily to their *w*,	"	367
silent, tho' he often look'd his *w*;	"	479
phantom of a *w* that once could move	Coquette, ii.	10
Tell my *w* to her merry blue eye.	The Window	101

wish (verb.)

	POEM.	LINE.
they *w* to charm Pallas and Juno	A Character	14
w that somewhere in the ruin'd folds	Œnone	217
only *w* to live till the snowdrops come	May Queen, ii.	14
I *w* the snow would melt	"	15
Yet something I did *w* to say:	To J. S.	60
w to see My grandchild on my knees	Dora	10
Is it well to *w* thee happy?—	Locksley H.	43
I *w* I were Some mighty poetess,	Princess, Pro.	131
I *w* That I were some great Princess	"	133
I could not help it, did not *w*:	" ii.	311
w'es at a dance to change The music—	" iv.	566
I *w* it Gentle as freedom '—	" vi.	188
I *w* she had not yielded !'	Con.	5
w they were a whole Atlantic broad	"	71
To talk them o'er, to *w* them here	In Mem. lxxxix.	11
We *w* them store of happy days	Con	84
I *w* I could hear again.	Maud, I. x.	53
And *w'es* me to approve him	" xix.	71
She did not *w* to blame him—	" xx.	5
fall'n so low as some would *w*.	Enid	129
for I *w* the two To love each other	"	791
'Did I *w* Your warning or your silence?'	"	925
Whether you *w* me victory or defeat,	"	929
said Geraint, ' I *w* no better fare.	"	1081
w still more to learn this charm	Vivien	178
I well could *w* a cobweb for the gnat	"	220
Pure, as you ever *w* your knights to be	Elaine	1366
might I *w* to veil her wickedness,	Guinevere	209
I cannot help that as I *w* to do	En. Arden	404
I *w* you for my wife.	"	407
Jo I *w*—What?—that the bush	Lucretius	202

wish'd.

	POEM.	LINE.
She *w* me happy, but she thought	Miller's D.	139
I have *w* this marriage, night and day,	Dora	19
I *w* myself the fair young beech	Talking O.	141
I *w* for Leonard there,	Golden Year	4
They *w* to marry: they could rule	Princess, ii.	441
that I knew him—could have *w*—	" iii.	190
Because he might have *w* it—	" vi.	238
hated banter, *w* for something real,	Con.	18
I almost *w* no more to wake,	In Mem. xxviii.	14
how it was the thing his daughter *w*	The Brook	140

	POEM.	LINE.
w The Prince had found her in her	Enid	643
I *w* to give them greater minds:	Vivien	346
IV it had been my mother.	Elaine	671
to speak to you of what he *w*,	En. Arden.	290
eyes upon her Repeating all he *w*	"	905
I *w* my voice A rushing tempest	Aylmer's F.	756
But I *w* it had been God's will	Grandmother	73

wishing.

	POEM.	LINE.
And, tho' in silence, *w* joy,	In Mem. Con.	88

wisp.

	POEM.	LINE.
gilded ball Danced like a *w*:	Princess, Pro.	64
w that flickers where no foot can tread.	" iv.	339
the *w* that gleams on Lethe	In Mem. xcvii.	7

wit.

	POEM.	LINE.
shrilling shafts of subtle *w*. 'Clear-headed friend'	13
Alone and warming his five *w's*,	The Owl, i.	6-13
The fruitful *w* Cleaving, took root,	The Poet.	20
With thy shallow *w*:	Poet's Mind	2
O the dalliance and the *w*,	D. of F. Wom.	147
I grow in worth, and *w*, and sense,	Will Water.	41
The tavern-hours of mighty *w's*	"	191
might a man not wander from his *w's*	Princess, ii.	417
the wealth Of words and *w*,	In Mem. Con.	103
these unwitty wandering *w's* of mine	Vivien	196
added, of her *w*, A border fantasy	Elaine	10
listen to me, If I must find you *w*:	"	148
sallying *w*, free flashes from a height	"	644
will you let me lose my *w's ?*	"	748
not lose your *w's* for dear Lavaine:	"	751
put my *w's* to some rough use,	"	1298
Thro' which a few, by *w* or fortune led,	Aylmer's F.	438
him that fluster'd his poor parish *w's*	"	521

witch.

	POEM.	LINE.
sought and found a *w*.	Lucretius	15

witch-elm.

	POEM.	LINE.
W-e's that counterchange the floor	In Mem lxxxviii.	1

withdraw.

	POEM.	LINE.
To pass, when Life her light *w's*,	Two Voices	145
Else I *w* favour and countenance	Aylmer's F.	307

withdrawing.

	POEM.	LINE.
IV by the counter door to that	Aylmer's F.	282

withdrawn.

	POEM.	LINE.
Half shown, are broken and *w*.	Two Voices	306
Deep in the garden lake *w*	Day-Dm.	32
every morning, far *w*	Vision of Sin	48
on the glimmering limit far *w*	"	223

withdrew.

	POEM.	LINE.
she *w* into the golden cloud	Œnone	187
w from summer heats and state,	Princess, vi.	228
IV themselves from me and night,	In Mem. xciv.	18

wither.

	POEM.	LINE.
IV beneath the palate,	D. of F. Wom.	287
lest I *w* by despair	Locksley H.	98
And the individual *w's*,	"	142
Now for me the woods may *w*	"	190
Thine own shall *w* in the vast	In Mem. lxxv.	11
I *w* slowly in thine arms,	Tithonus	6

wither'd.

	POEM.	LINE.
parch'd and *w*, deaf and blind,	Fatima	6
My suit had *w*, nipt to death by him	Ed. Morris	101
Are *w* in the thorny close,	Day-Dm.	111

withheld.

	POEM.	LINE.
Lancelot saw that she *w* her wish,	Elaine	916

withhold.

	POEM.	LINE.
a prudence to *w*.	Isabel	15

withholding.

	POEM.	LINE.
Apart from place, *w* time	Arabian N's.	75

withstand.

	POEM.	LINE.
caught By that you swore to *w*!	Maud, I. vi.	80
Frail, but of force to *w*,	" II. ii.	24

witness (s.)

	POEM.	LINE.
Bear *w*, if I could have found a way	St S. Stylites	54
(thou wilt bear *w* here)	"	127

	POEM	LINE
witness (verb.)		
Yes, as your moanings w.	Aylmer's F.	749
wizard.		
Some figure like a w's pentagram	The Brook	103
The people call'd him W;	Vivien	26
find a w who might teach the King	"	433
but did they find A w?	"	463
The gentle w cast a shielding arm.	"	757
pale blood of the w at her touch .	"	798
woaded.		
Tattoo'd or w, winter-clad in skins	Princess, ii.	105
woe.		
My heart is wasted with my w	Oriana	1
flow Beside me in my utter w,	"	87
The home of w without a tear	Mariana in the S.	20
heart may wander from its deeper w	Œnone	43
hearing would not hear me, w is me!	"	167
still sheets of water, divers w's,	D. of F.Wom.	34
That makes my only w	"	136
you sit between Joy and w	Margaret	64
Even with a verse your holy w.	To J. S.	8
A little hint to solace w,	Two Voices	433
To bear thro' Heaven a tale of w,	In Mem. xii.	2
standing, muffled round with w,	" xiv.	5
The wild unrest that lives in w	" xv.	15
Peace ; come away : the song of w	" lvi.	1
Likewise the imaginative w,	" lxxxiv.	53
And I—my harp would prelude w—	" lxxxvii.	9
Or, crown'd with attributes of w.	" cxviii.	18
So far, so near in w and weal ;	" cxxviii.	1
for some dark undercurrent w	Maud, I. xviii.	83
for his house an irredeemable w;	" II. i.	22
As fits an universal w,	Ode on Well.	14
all the wealth and all the w?	Guinevere	342
Proclaiming Enoch Arden and his w's	En. Arden	869
it cost me a world of w	Grandmother	23
woke.		
cold winds w the gray-eyed morn	Mariana	31
She w: the babble of the stream	Mariana in the S.	51
w, and found him settled down	The Epic	17
with the sound I w and heard	M.d'Arthur, Ep.	30
'O happy kiss, that w thy sleep!'	Day-Dm.	183
Lilia with sudden-shrilling mirth	Princess, Pro.	219
w Desire in me to infuse my tale .	" v.	229
ere I w it was the point of noon,	"	471
Last I w sane, but well-nigh	" vii.	104
Deep in the night I w:	"	158
early w to feed her little ones,	"	236
This year I slept and w with pain,	InMem.xxviii.	13
songs that w The darkness of our planet	" lxxv.	9
Enid w and sat beside the couch .	Enid	79
W and bethought her of her promise .	"	602
W where he slept in the high hall	"	755
Beat, till she w the sleepers,	"	1253
W the sick knight, and while he roll'd	Elaine	815
but w with dawn, and past	"	842
there I w, but still the wish remain'd.	"	1042
Far cities burnt and with a cry she w	Guinevere	83
w, With his first babe's first cry,	En. Arden	84
Here she w, Resolved, sent for him	"	502
He w, he rose, he spread his arms	"	911
a despot dream The father panting w.	Aylmer's F.	528
till the comrade of his chambers w,	"	583
slept, w, and went the next .	Sea Dreams	18
wail'd and w The mother,	"	57
I w, I heard the clash so clearly .	"	131
mix'd with little Margaret's, and I w,	"	238
w her with a lay from fairy land .	Coquette, i.	8
After a tempest w upon a morn .	Lucretius	24
scorch'd me that I w.	"	66
wold.		
wattled folds, Upon the ridged w's	Ode to Mem.	67
long dun w's are ribb'd with snow,	Oriana	5
clothe the w and meet the sky ;	L. of Shalott, i.	3
oft in ramblings on the w,	Miller's D.	105
From off the w I came, and lay .	"	111
yon old mill across the w's .	"	240
from the dry dark w the summer airs	May Queen,ii.	27
More softly round the open w,	To J. S.	2

	POEM	LINE.
Calm and deep peace on this high w,	In Mem. xi.	5
Or sheepwalk up the windy w ;	" xcix.	8
wolf.		
a w within the fold ! A pack of wolves!	Princess,ii.	173
Then came these wolves:	" iv.	302
A gray old w and a lean.	Maud, I xiii.	23
Not that gray old w.	" II. v.	53
From the wilderness, full of wolves	"	54
three dead wolves of woman born	Enid	943
and drew from those dead wolves	"	1027
waiting to be treated like a w	"	1705
find that it had been the w's indeed:	"	1712
If the w spare me, weep my life away	Vivien	734
that darken with the gathering w,	Aylmer's F.	707
Kite and kestrel, w and wolfkin,	Boädicea	15
wolfkin.		
Kite and kestrel, wolf and w,	Boädicea	15
wolfskin.		
mighty hands Lay naked on the w,	Elaine	807
wolf's-milk.		
half the w-m curdled in their veins,	Princess, vii.	115
woman.		
my ancient love With the Greek w	Œnone	256
This w was the cause	D of F.Wom.	104
the greatest gift A w's heart,	Gardener's D.	225
your sake, the w that he chose	Dora	61
betwixt you and the w there.	"	94
who would love ? I woo'd a w once	Audley Ct.	51
A w like a butt, and harsh as crabs	Walk. to the M	41
God made the w for the man	Ed. Morris 43,	50, 91
w's pleasure, w's pain—	Locksley H.	149
W is the lesser man,	"	151
I will take some savage w,	"	168
The w of a thousand summers back,	Godiva	11
a serving-man As any, born of w,	Will Water.	152
Shaped her heart with w's meekness	L.of Burleigh	71
'O miracle of women'	Princess, Pro.	35
Half child half w as she was	"	101
'lives there such a w now!'	"	126
'There are thousands now Such women	"	128
the rest follow'd : and the women sang	"	236
to live alone Among her women;	" i.	49
w were an equal to the man.	"	130
lose the child, assume The w:	"	137
these the women sang	"	142
for miles about Was till'd by women;	"	190
w's state in each, How far from just	" ii.	115
respect, however slight, was paid To w	"	121
that which made W and man.	"	129
But w ripen'd earlier	"	138
Plato, Verulam : even so With w	"	145
be that for ever which I seem W.	"	240
These women were too barbarous,	"	278
Feasted the w wisest then,	"	330
when did w ever yet invent ?	"	369
Men hated learned women	"	442
with that w closeted for hours!'	" iii.	40
sees herself in every w else,	"	94
well might harm The w's cause	"	137
lift the w's fall'n divinity	"	207
what every w counts her due	"	228
women, up till this Cramp'd	"	260
mould The w to the fuller day.'	"	315
Disorderly the women.	" iv.	12
Huge women blowzed with health	"	260
hold the w is the better man ;	"	291
all women kick against their Lords	"	323
Many a famous man and w	"	425
look well too in your w's dress :	"	508
'Satan take The old women	" v.	13
We left her by the w,	"	19
Man is the hunter ; w is his game ;	"	147
and leaps in Among the women	"	156
yet I hold her, king. True w:	"	172
The w's garment hid the w's heart.'	"	205
iron-cramp'd their women's feet,	"	316
bawl for civil rights, No w named :	"	378
the w's Angel guards you	"	400

2 G

466 CONCORDANCE TO

	POEM.	LINE.
man wants weight, the w takes it up	Princess, v.	434
Man for the field and w for the hearth;	"	437
Man with the head and w with the heart:	"	439
Man to command and w to obey;	"	440
the w wed is not as we,	"	452
training of a child Is w's wisdom.'	"	456
leaves were wet with women's tears:	" vi.	23
progress falter to the w's goal	"	111
Win you the hearts of women	"	155
One pulse that beats true w,	"	164
the w is so hard Upon the w.	"	205
Two women faster welded in one love	"	236
W, whom we thought w even now,	"	256
They glared upon the women	"	341
aghast The women stared at these	"	342
arose The women up in wild revolt	" vii.	108
left her w. lovelier in her mood	"	147
that know The w's cause is man's:	"	243
w is not undevelopt man,	"	259
man be more of w, she of man;	"	264
what w taught you this?	"	291
I loved the w: he, that doth not,	"	294
w thro' the crust of iron moods :	"	321
So pray'd the men, the women :	" Con.	7
The women—and perhaps they felt	"	13
over with a shriek Like an old w,	"	63
knows whether w or man be the worse	Maud, I. i.	75
Rich in the grace all women desire	" x.	13
The w cannot be believed.	The Letters	32
(And women's slander is the worst)	"	34
loveliest of all women upon earth.	Enid .	21
the women who attired her head .	"	62
never yet had w such a pair.	"	439
while the women thus rejoiced	"	754
A splendour dear to women .	"	808
the three dead wolves of w born .	"	943
Call for the w of the house. .	"	1112
such craft as women use,	"	1201
A w weeping for her murder'd mate	"	1371
A tribe of women, dress'd in many hues	"	1446
women they, Women or what had been	"	1483
all the men and women in the hall	"	1579
men and women staring and aghast	"	1652
ruin'd man Thro' w the first hour, .	Vivien	213
As high as w is in her selfless mood	"	293
of Fame while w wakes to love .	"	310
A sudden spurt of w's jealousy,—	"	374
A w and not trusted . .	"	380
as to w's jealousy, O why not? .	"	387
All fighting for a w on the sea .	"	412
Were I not w, I could tell a tale. .	"	546
all men true and leal, all women pure :	"	643
women, worst and best, as Heaven and	"	664
w's love, Save one, he not regarded.	Elaine	836
never w yet, since man's first fall	"	855
man and w when they love their best	"	865
a love beyond all love In women	"	1286
'this is all w's grief That she is w	Guinevere	216
A w in her womanhood as great .	"	297
must I leave thee, w, to thy shame.	"	507
beauty such as never w wore .	"	545
could the w when he came upon her,	En. Arden	342
they say that women are so quick	"	405
' W, I have a secret—only swear.	"	838
'Dead, clamour'd the good w	"	841
At which the w gave A half-incredulous	"	853
As the w heard, Fast flow'd the current	"	865
W, disturb me not now at the last	"	875
the shame The w should have borne,	Aylmer's F.	356
fell The w shrieking at his feet,	"	811
Against the scarlet w and her creed :	Sea Dreams	23
near the light a giant w sat,	"	96
that the w walked upon the brink	"	108
the w honest Work ; .	"	133
That which I ask'd the w .	"	143
men and women in dark clusters .	"	217
The w half turn'd round from him	"	274
But stay with the old w now :	Grandmother	108
Phantom wail of women and children	Boädicea.	26
when the w heard his foot Return	Lucretius .	5
And women's love and men's	The Window	79

woman-built.	POEM.	LINE.
As of a new-world Babel, w-b, .	Princess, iv.	466

woman-conquered.		
w-c there The bearded Victor	. Princess, iii.	333

woman-conqueror.		
many a florid maiden-cheek, The w-c;	Princess, iii.	333

woman-grown.		
more and more, the maiden w-g, .	Aylmer's F.	108

woman-guard.		
Princess with her monstrous w-g, .	Princess, iv.	540

womanhood.		
Wearing the rose of w. .	. Two Voices	417
O miracle of noble w!'.	. Princess, Pro.	48
A charr'd and wrinkled piece of w,	" v.	58
All that not harms distinctive w .	" vii.	258
Came out of her pitying w .	Maud, I. vi.	64
with all grace Of w and queenhood	Enid .	176
Could call him (were it not for w)	Vivien	625
Beyond mine old belief in w,	Elaine	951
A woman in her w as great .	Guinevere .	297

womankind.		
All for the common good of w. .	Princess, ii.	192
I take her for the flower of w,	" v.	277
The soft and milky rabble of w,	" vi.	290
faith in w Beats with his blood,	" vii.	309

womanlike.		
W, taking revenge too deep. .	Maud, I. iii.	5

woman-markets.		
Here in the w-m of the west .	Aylmer's F.	348

woman-post.		
A w-p in flying raiment .	. Princess, iv.	357

woman's-heart.		
Break not, O w-h, but still endure :	Ded. of Idylls	43

woman-slough.		
what was left of faded w-s .	. Princess, v.	38

woman-statue.		
a w-s rose with wings .	. Princess, i.	207

woman-vested.		
w-v as I was Plunged ; .	. Princess, iv.	163

womb.		
To spirits folded in the w. .	Day-Dm. .	28
Let her, that is the w and tomb of all	Lucretius .	240

won.		
A motion from the river w .	. Arabian N's.	34
w his praises night and morn?'	Mariana in the S.	34
I w his love, I brought him home.	The Sisters	14
you have w A tearful grace, .	. Margaret	11
might have w the Poet's name, 'You might have won'		1
when your sister came she w the heart	Princess, iii.	71
Imaginations might at all be w. .	"	257
thus I w Your mother, a good mother	" v.	158
w it with a day Blanch'd in our annals	" vi.	46
be liberal, since our rights are w .	"	52
Who have w her favour ! .	Maud, I. xii.	100
Clashed with his fiery few and w ;	Ode on Well.	100
has w His path upward, and prevail'd,	"	213
ever w it for the lady with him .	Enid .	490
these two years have w it for thee,	"	554
noble prince who w our earldom back,	"	619
tho' you w the prize of fairest fair	"	719
Lancelot w the diamond of the year	Elaine	69
them to the Queen When all were w ;	"	71
if I went and if I fought and w it	"	216
W by the mellow voice .	"	243
our knight thro' whom we w the day.	"	528
with you? w he not your prize?'	"	572
knight with the red sleeve?' 'He w.'	"	618
hardly w with bruise and blow,	"	1159
what I had not w except for you .	"	1175
years of noble deeds, Until they w her	Guinevere	473
w mysterious way Thro' the seal'd ear	Aylmer's F.	695
Priest was happy His victim w .	The Victim	66
Faint heart never w—. .	. The Window	142

wonder (s.)	POEM.	LINE
when he saw the w of the hilt,	M. d'Arthur	85
'This w keeps the house.'	Gardener's D.	118
w, dead, become Mere highway	Love and Duty	10
The w of the eagle were the less,	Golden Year	39
all the w that would be—	Locksley H. 16,	120
there are greater w's there.'	Day-Dm.	192
'What w, if he thinks me fair?'	"	272
What w I was all unwise,	"	273
'It is no w,' said the lords,	Beggar Maid	7
and rent The w of the loom	Princess, i.	61
The w's that have come to thee,	In Mem. xl.	22
Rapt in the fear and in the w of it,	Enid	529
My daily w is, I love at all.	Vivien	386
What w, being jealous, that he sent	"	430
in dry stubble a nine days' w flared:	Elaine	731
Becomes a w and we know not why,	"	1023
With signs, and miracles and w's,	Guinevere	220
Or what of signs and w's,	"	227
w's ere the coming of the Queen	"	231
wise father with his signs And w's	"	273

wonder (verb)

riving the spirit of man, Making earth w,	The Poet	52
while now she w's blindly,	L. of Burleigh	53
Will w why they came:	Princess, ii.	410
You w when my fancies play	In Mem. lxv.	2
there the fine Gawain will w at me,	Elaine	1048
I w he went so young.	Grandmother	14

wonder'd.

I w at the bounteous hours,	Two Voices	451
I w, while I paced along	"	454
tales did men tell men, She w	Princess, Pro.	194
All the world w.	Lt Brigade	31,52
such blows, that all the crowd	IV, Enid	565
came the fine Gawain and w at her,	Elaine	1260
I w at her strength, and ask'd her	Sea Dreams	109

wonderful.

in white samite, mystic, w	M. d'Arthur	31, 144-59
work of his is great and w.	Enid	1746
A thousand-fold more great and w	"	1762
work was neither great nor w	"	1769
A maid so smooth, so white, so w,	Vivien	416
W, Prince of peace, the Mighty God,	Aylmer's F.	669

wondering.

w, ask'd her 'Are you from the farm	The Brook	209

wonder-stricken.

kiss'd his w-s little ones;	En. Arden	228

wondrous.

His prowess was too w.	Elaine	541
yet her cheek Kept colour: w!	Aylmer's F.	506

wont.

w to bind my throbbing brow,	Princess, ii.	232
'tis her w from night to night	" iii.	16
the small king moved beyond his w	" vi.	248
In which we two were w to meet	In Mem. viii.	10
one wreath more for Use and W,	" xxix.	11
When I was w to meet her	Maud, II. iv.	5
w to hear His voice in battle,	Enid	1023
w to glance and sparkle like a gem	"	1143
my w, as those, who know me, know.'	Elaine 364,	474
He wore, against his w, upon his helm	"	601
Lancelot sad beyond his w,	"	1323
Had been, their w, a-maying	Guinevere	24
From childly w and ancient use	Lucretius	206

wonted.

The sound not w in a place so still	Elaine	814

woo.

Thee to w to thy tuwhit (rep.)	The Owl, ii.	11
With what voice the violet w's	Adeline	31
sue me, and w me, and flatter me,	The Mermaid	43
W me, and win me, and marry me,	"	46
once again to w thee mine—	Miller's D.	30
I w thee not with gifts	Œnone	150
many a bolder lad 'll w me	May Queen, i	23
Fly to her, and pipe and w her,	Princess, iv.	97
these men came to w Your Highness—	" vi.	308
I w your love: I count it crime	In Mem. lxxxiv.	61

	POEM.	LINE.
One is come to w her.	Maud, I. xii.	23
gold and beauty, wooing him to w	Aylmer's F.	487
I w thee roughly	Lucretius	208
carest not How roughly men may w	"	269

wood (forest, etc.)

the w's that belt the gray hill-side	Ode to Mem.	55
The pale yellow w's were waning,	L. of Shalott, iv.	2
When after roving in the w's	Miller's D.	58
cloisters, branch'd like mighty w's	Pal. of Art	26
Lo! in the middle of the w,	Lotos-E's.	70
had wander'd far In an old w:	D. of F. Wom.	54
'Pass freely thro': the w is all thine own,	"	63
no men to govern in this w:	"	135
the sombre boskage of the w,	"	243
From the evening-lighted w,	Margaret	10
From the w's Came voices of the	Gardener's D.	87
Like an oaken stock in winter w's	Golden Year	12
Now for me the w's may wither	Locksley H.	190
The w's were fill'd so full with song,	Two Voices	455
A summer crisp with shining w's.	Day-Dm.	8
At distance like a little w;	"	62
Summer w's, about them blowing,	L. of Burleigh	19
rose and past Thro' the wild w's	Princess, i.	90
shrieks Of the wild w's together;	"	98
shook the w's, And danced the colour	" iii.	275
when all the w's are green?	" iv.	13
flying from the golden w's,	"	96
Across the w's, and less from Indian craft	"	180
With Ida, Ida, Ida, rang the w's;	"	413
mused on that wild morning in the w's,	" v.	460
strikes On a w, and takes, and breaks,	"	516
half-open'd bell of the w's!	" vi.	176
That never knew the summer w's:	In Mem. xxvii.	4
bask'd and batten'd in the w's	" xxxv.	24
I found a w with thorny boughs:	" lxviii.	6
hill and w and field did print	" lxxviii.	7
That gather in the waning w's,	" lxxxiv.	72
Thro' all the dewy-tassell'd w	" lxxxv.	6
With banquet in the distant w's;	" lxxxviii.	32
Of rising worlds by yonder w.	" civ.	25
the w which grides and clangs	" cvi.	11
To range the w's, to roam the park	Con.	96
hollow behind the little w,	Maud, I. i.	1
And the whole little w where I sit	" iv.	24
the budded peaks of the w are bow'd	" vi.	4
Here half-hid in the gleaming w,	"	69
Where was Maud? in our w;	" xii.	5
Birds in our w sang	"	
Running down to my own dark w;	" xiv.	30
to the meadow and on to the w, (rep.)	" xxii.	37
the red-ribb'd hollow behind the w	" II. i.	25
Then glided out of the joyous w.	"	31
all the w stands in a mist of green	The Brook	14
a forester of Dean, Wet from the w's,	Enid	149
forded Usk, and gain'd the w;	"	161
issued from the world of w,	"	238
first shallow shade of a deep w,	"	968
lurk three villains yonder in the w,	"	961
if there were an hundred in the w,	"	996
and she drove them thro' the w.	"	1034
keep them in the wild ways of the w	"	1036
thro' the green gloom of the w they pass'd	"	1044
sees the trapper coming thro' the w	"	1572
in the wild w's of Brocéliande,	Vivien	2, 53
meant to eat her up in that wild w	"	109
and all thro' this wild w	"	134
current then In these wild w's,	"	259
thro' following you to this wild w,	"	290
dark w grew darker toward the storm	"	739
dwelt among the w's By the great river	Elaine	977
happy as when we dwelt among the w's	"	1030
while he past the dim-lit w's,	Guinevere	249
where the prone edge of the w began	En. Arden 67,	370
into the hollows of the w;	"	76
To go with others, nutting to the w,	"	360
calling, here and there, about the w,	"	380
one dark hour Here in this w,	"	383
merry they are down yonder in the w.	"	366
his voice beneath him thro' the w	"	441
mock sunshine of the faded w's	Aylmer's F.	610

	POEM.	LINE.
The w's decay, the w's decay and fall,	Tithonus	1
hills and scarlet-mingled w's	The Voyage	47
a worm is there in the lonely w,	The Islet	34
and the w's and ways Are pleasant,	On a Mourner	13
And cattle died, and deer in w,	The Victim	18
And w's are sere	The Window	45
The w's are all the searer,	''	56
O the w's and the meadows	''	182
W's where we hid from the wet,	''	183

wood (substance.)

Hard w I am, and wrinkled mind,	Talking O.	171
'Ye are green w, see ye warp not.	Princess, ii.	61
carved himself a knightly shield of w	Vivien	323
darted spikes and splinters of the w	''	786
riot underneath Strikes thro' the w	Lucretius	186

woo'd.

leaf is w from out the bud	Lotos-E's.	71
he w and wed A labourer's daughter	Dora	37
who would love? I w a woman once,	Audley Ct	51
Drunk even when he w ;	Enid	442

woodbine.

w and eglatere Drip sweeter dews	A Dirge	23
as sweet As w s fragile hold,	Talking O	146
Thorns, ivies, w, mistletoes,	Day-Dm.	63
The w wreaths that bind her,	Amphion	34
There in due time the w blows,	In Mem. civ.	7

wooded.

The mountain w to the peak,	En. Arden	573

woodland.

The filter'd tribute of the rough w,	Ode to Mem.	63
In firry w's making moan;	Miller's D	42
Slides the bird o'er lustrous w,	Locksley H.	162
That grows within the w	Amphion	8
Illyrian w's, echoing falls Of water,	To E. L.	1
When the rotten w drips,	Vision of Sin	81
as the golden Autumn w reels	Princess, vii.	336
And w's holy to the dead ;	In Mem. xcviii.	8
Now rings the w loud and long,	'' cxiv.	5
the flying gold of the ruin'd w's	Maud, I. i.	12
left the ravaged w yet once more	Vivien	812
broad w parcell'd into farms,	Aylmer's F.	847
in our winter w looks a flower.	A Dedication	13
'Fear not isle of blowing w	Boädicea	38
Made the noise of frosty w's	''	75
His function of the w:	Lucretius	46

woodlouse.

The blue w and the plump dormouse	The Window	51

woodman.

see the w lift His axe to slay	Talking O..	235
came, The woodmen with their axes	Princess, vi.	28

wood-nymph.

a foot-fall, ere he saw The w-n,	Pal. of Art	111

woodpecker.

An echo like a ghostly w,	Princess, Pro.	211

wood-walk.

dark w-w's drench'd in dew,	D. of F. Wom.	75

woodwork.

Fled ever thro' the w,	Elaine	439

wooest.

W not, nor vainly wranglest ;	Madeline	38

woof.

Hues of the silken sheeny w	Madeline	22
thro' warp and w From skirt to skirt	Princess, i.	61

wooing.

his long w her, Her slow consent,	En. Arden.	708
gold and beauty, w him to woo.	Aylmer's F.	487
All my w is done	The Window	181

wool.

Like footsteps upon w	Œnone	246
needs it we should cram our ears with w	Princess, iv.	47

woost (worst).

And i' the w o' toimes	N. Farmer	16

word.	POEM.	LINE.
and thro' with cunning w's.	'Clear-headed friend'	17
Her w's did gather thunder	The Poet	49
So was their meaning to her w's	''	53
with his w She shook the world.	''	55
kiss sweet kisses, and speak sweet w's	Sea-Fairies	34
Wild w's wander here and there :	A Dirge	43
How may measur'd w's adore	Eleänore	45
if I waste w's now, in truth .	Miller's D.	191
blessings which no w's can find.	''	238
Indeed I heard one bitter w.	L.C.V de Vere	37
Tho' I cannot speak a w, I shall	May Queen, ii.	39
the clergyman, has told me w's of peace.	'' iii.	12
And say to Robin a kind w	''	45
little meaning tho' the w's are strong;	Lotos-E's.	164
Herslow full w's sank thro' the silence	D. of F.Wom.	121
My w's leapt forth: 'Heaven heads	''	201
all w's, tho' cull'd with choicest art	''	285
to flow In these w's toward you,	To J. S.	6
W's weaker than your grief would	''	65
gentle w's are always gain: 'Love thou thy land'		23
serve his kind in deed and w,	''	86
He utter'd w's of scorning .	The Goose	42
and lightly bring me w.' (rep.)	M. d'Arthur	38
would have spoken, but he found not w's	''	172
(My w's were half in earnest	Gardener's D.	23
w could bring the colour to my cheek ;	''	192
in the compass of three little w's,	''	227
Here, then, my w's have end.	''	245
Had once hard w's, and parted,	Dora	16
in my time a father's w was law,	''	25
a w with her he calls his wife,	''	42
You knew my w was law	''	96
set the w's, and added names I knew	Audley Ct	60
in flagrante—what's the Latin w?	Walk. to the M.	26
And well his w's became him :	Ed. Morris	25
Were not his w's delicious,	''	71
the w's That make a man feel strong	Love and Duty	67
measured w's, my work of yestermorn	Golden Year	21
but I know my w's are wild,	Locksley H.	173
'These w's,' I said, 'are like the rest	Two Voices	334
The thesis which thy w's intend	''	338
order'd w's asunder fly.	Day-Dm.	20
With w's of promise in his walk,	''	123
The barons swore, with many w's,	''	155
In courteous w's return'd reply:	''	162
Cruel, cruel the w's I said!	Ed. Gray	17
whisper lovely w's, and use	Will Water.	10
when the Poet's w's and looks	''	193
I am yours in w and in deed.	Lady Clare	19
She was more fair than w's can say :	Beggar Maid	2
'Doubt my w again!' he said	Princess, Pro.	15
At those high w's, we conscious of	'' ii.	53
at these w's the snake, My secret	'' iii.	27
mother went revolving on the w)	''	38
came these dreadful w's out one by one,	''	41
truth at once, but with no w from me ;	''	45
such warbling fury thro' the w's ;	'' iv.	563
(our royal w spoilt, He comes back safe)	'' v.	215
Arac's w is thrice As ours with Ida :	''	217
in the saddle, then burst out in w's.	''	265
shall have her answer by the w.'	''	317
and rolling w's Oration-like	''	362
at the happy word 'he lives'	'' vi.	112
one soft w and let me part forgiven.'	''	202
Not one w? Not one?	''	214
Not one w; No I tho' your father sues	''	222
A w, but one, one little kindly w,	''	241
charm'd Her wounded soul with w's :	''	326
Perfect music unto noble w's ;	'' vii.	270
love to cheat yourself with w's :	''	314
The w's are mostly mine ;	'' Con.	94
Who spoke few w's and pithy	''	94
To put in w's the grief I feel ,	In Mem. v.	2
w's, like Nature, half reveal	''	3
In w's, like weeds, I'll wrap me o'er,	''	9
What w's are these have fall'n from me?	'' xvi.	1
The w's that are not heard again.	'' xviii.	20
That out of w's a comfort win ;	'' xx.	10
truth in closest w's shall fail,	'' xxxvi.	6
And so the W had breath, and wrought	''	9
hence, indeed, she sports with w's,	'' xlvii.	9

	POEM.	LINE.
My w's are only w's, and moved	Princess, li.	3
In those sad w's I took farewell :	" lvii.	1
The w's were hard to understand	" lxviii.	20
In fitting aptest w's to things,	" lxxiv.	6
O true in w, and tried in deed,	" lxxxiv.	5
Your w's have virtue such as draws	"	13
in dear w's of human speech	"	83
The wish too strong for w's to name ;	" xcii.	14
broke The silent-speaking w's,	" xciv.	26
So w by w, and line by line,	"	33
Vague w's! but ah, how hard to frame	" cxxiv.	45
if the w's were sweet and strong	" cxxvii.	11
To change the bearing of a w,	" cxxvii.	16
the most living w's of life	" Con.	52
the wealth Of w's and wit	"	103
faith in a tradesman's ware or his w?	Maud, I. i.	26
Dare I bid her abide by her w ?	" xvi.	25
given her w to a thing so low?	"	27
break her w were it even for me ?	"	29
sweet soul, had hardly spoken a w,	" II. i.	11
of all his lavish waste of w's	The Brook.	191
in my w's were seeds of fire.	The Letters	28
but fragments of her later w's,	Enid	113
refrained From ev'n a w,	"	214
None spake w except the hoary Earl	"	369
lift an eye nor speak a w,	"	528
w's whose echo lasts, they were so	"	782
that at a w (No reason given her)	"	806
not to speak to me, No not a w!'	"	867
loosed in w's of sudden fire the wrath	"	955
took the w and play'd upon it,	"	1140
speak the w : my followers ring him	"	1185
speak but the w : Or speak it not ;	"	1191
Low-spoken, and of so few w's	"	1244
Because she kept the letter of his w	"	1304
answering not one w, she led the way	"	1344
without a w, from his horse fell	"	1357
none spake w, but all sat down at once,	"	1452
Enid could not say one tender w,	"	1594
pale, yet happy, ask'd her not a w,	"	1728
in that wild wood Without one w.	Vivien	110
nor gave me one poor w ;	"	126
answer'd Merlin careless of her w's.	"	550
rose without a w and parted from her ;	"	592
have you no one w of loyal praise	"	627
Her w's had issue other than she will'd	"	655
in w's part heard, in whispers part,	"	688
with a w worse than a life of blows !	"	719
half her realm, had never spoken w.	Elaine	73
never spake w of reproach to me,	"	125
hear my w's : go to the jousts	"	137
a king who honours his own w,	"	144
Not often loyal to his w,	"	558
without a w, Linger'd that other	"	716
father's latest w humm'd in her ear,	"	776
must die for want of one bold w.'	"	923
when we dwell upon a we know	"	1021
w we know so well Becomes a wonder	"	1022
as she devised A letter, w for w;	"	1098
these are w's : Your beauty is your	"	1179
grant my worship of it W's,	"	1182
such sin w's, Perchance, we both	"	1182
let my w's, the w's of one so small,	Guinevere	183
teach high thought, and amiable w's	"	477
on a broken w to honour him with	En. Arden.	344
for she did not speak a w.	"	387
Ev'n as she dwelt upon his latest w's	"	451
Enoch spoke no w to anyone,	"	668
Enoch hung A moment on her w's,	"	874
were w's As meted by his measure	Aylmer's F.	315
Never one kindly smile, one kindly w	"	561
how the w's Have twisted back	"	754
his one w was 'desolate :'	"	836
not a w ; she shook her head.	Sea Dreams	112
the W by which himself had thriven.	"	193
Down they dropt—no w was spoken—	TheCaptains	
Heliconian honey in living w's	Lucretius	221

wore.

many weeks about my loins I w	St S. Stylites	62
That she w when she was wed.'	L. of Burleigh	96

	POEM.	LINE.
A gown of grass-green silk she w,	SirL. audQ.G.	24
avenged by sense that w with time.'	Vision of Sin	214
still I w her picture by my heart,	Princess, i.	37
Never morning w To evening,	In Mem. vi.	7
I w them like a civic crown ;	" lxviii.	8
In which of old I w the gown,	" lxxxvi.	2
She w the colours I approved	The Letters	16
gay suits of armour which they w,	Enid	944
his the prize, who w the sleeve	Elaine	500
He w, against his wont, upon his helm	"	681
he w your sleeve : Would he break faith	"	681
on the maid, Whose sleeve he w ;	"	707
beauty such as never woman w,	Guinevere	545
w A close-set robe of jasmine	Aylmer's F.	157
I w a lilac gown ;	Grandmother	57
It w a crown of light	The Flower	10

work (labour, etc.)

At his w you may hear him sob 'A spirit hauuts,'etc.		5
Now is done thy long day's w ;	A Dirge	1
Grave mother of majestic w's,	'Ofold sat Freedom'	13
And w, a joint of state, 'Love thou thy land,' etc.		47
loved the man, and prized his w ;	M.d'Arthur,Ep.	8
'Tis not your w, but Love's	Gardener's D.	24
Till that wild wind made w.	Talking O.	54
To that man My w shall answer,	Love and Duty	29
measured words, my w of yestermorn.	Golden Year	21
He works his w, I mine.	Ulysses	43
Some w of noble note may yet be done,	"	52
A virgin heart in w and will.	Sir Galahad	24
Thou shalt not be saved by w's :	Vision of Sin	91
set our hand To this great w,	Princess, ii.	46
Your own w marr'd :	"	212
silver litanies, The w of Ida	"	454
how vast a w To assail this gray.	" iii.	217
That we might see our own w out,	"	253
workman and his w, That practice betters?	"	281
touches on the workman and his w.	"	305
and known at last 'my w)	" iv.	328
understanding all the foolish w Of Fancy	" vi.	100
Man, her last w, who seem'd so fair,	InMem. lv.	9
I shall pass ; my w will fail.	" lvi.	8
hath not swerved To w's of weakness,	" lxxxiv.	50
Let her w prevail.	" cxiii.	4
O days and hours, your w is this,	" cxvi.	1
Contemplate all this w Of Time,	" cxvii.	1
If so he type this w of time.	"	16
the world's great w is heard.	" cxx.	10
the w's of the men of mind,	Maud, I. i.	25
Awe-stricken breaths at a w divine	" x.	17
Frail, but a w divine	" II. ii. 4,	23
There is none that does his w, not one	" v.	26
The treble w's, the vast designs	Odeon Well.	104
Whose life was w, whose language rise	"	183
Such was he : his w is done,	"	218
There must be other nobler w to do	"	256
back turn'd, and bow'd above his w	Enid	267
scantly time for half the w.	"	288
the w To both appear'd so costly,	"	637
This w of his is great and wonderful	"	1746
w of Edyrn wrought upon himself	"	1760
w was neither great nor wonderful,	"	1763
Yet needs must work my w.	Vivien	355
They prove to him his w :	Elaine	158
with all ease, so tender was the w ;	"	441
Her own poor w, her empty labour,	"	985
This evil w of Lancelot and the Queen?	Guinevere	305
Nor of what race, the w ;	Aylmer's F.	224
Small were his gains, and hard his w ;	Sea Dreams	8
the woman honest W ;	"	133
break the w's of the statuary	Boâdicea	64
things appear the w of mighty Gods.	Lucretius	104
if I go my w is left Unfinish'd	"	103

work (literary production.)

Botanic Treatises, And W's on Gardening	Amphion	78
My golden w in which I told a truth	Lucretius	256

work (verb.)

time and space to w and spread.	You ask me, why	16
w in lines to thin The Titanic Flora,	Gardener's D.	166
hired himself to w within the fields	Dora	16

CONCORDANCE TO

	POEM.	LINE.
Mary, let me live and *w* with you ;	*Dora*	. 113
w for William's child, until he grows	"	. 124
Can I *w* miracles and not be saved ?	*St S. Stylites*	148
I will *w* in prose and rhyme,	*Talking O.*	. 289
w itself Thro' madness, hated by the	*Love and Duty*	6
unto him who *w*'s, and feels he *w*'s,	*Golden Year*	72
He *w*'s his work, I mine.	*Ulysses*	. 43
love in sequel *w*'s with fate,	*Day-Dm.*	. 103
I must *w* thro' months of toil,	*Amphion*	. 97
All parties *w* together.	*Will Water.*	. 56
Embrace our aims : *w* out your freedom	*Princess,* ii.	75
nor would we *w* for fame ;	" iii.	244
But in the shadow will we *w,*	"	. 314
but *w* no more alone !	" vii.	250
w's Without a conscience or an aim.	*In Mem.* xxxiv.	7
To one that with us *w*'s,	" cxxx.	8
w's in the very means of life.	*Maud,* I. i.	40
Make and break, and *w* their will ;	*Ode on Well.*	261
would *w* eye dim, and finger lame,	*Enid*	. 628
ruth began to *w* Against his anger	"	. 950
Vivien ever sought to *w* the charm	*Vivien*	. 64
w as vassal to the larger love,	"	. 341
Yet, needs must *w* my work	"	. 355
To all the foulness that they *w.*	"	. 634
but you *w* against your own desire	*Elaine*	1090
hers or mine, mine now to *w* my will	"	1225
needs would *w* for Annie to the last	*En. Arden*	180
Scorning an alms, to *w* whereby to live	"	813
labour for himself. *W* without hope,	"	821
all things *w* together for the good	*Sea Dreams*	154

worked.

they say then that I *w* miracles,	*St S. Stylites*	79
my full heart, that *w* below,	*Two Voices*	. 44
oft he *w* among the rest	*En. Arden*	. 652
Rose from the clay it *w* in	*Aylmer's F.*	170
Strong Hours indignant *w* their wills	*Tithonus*	18

worker.

| Men, my brothers, men the *w*'s, | *Locksley H.* | 117 |

working.

Life, that, *w* strongly, binds	*'Love thou thy land'*	34
A labour *w* to an end.	*Two Voices*	297
jest and earnest *w* side by side	*Princess,* iv.	541
Or been in narrowest *w* shut,	*In Mem.* xxxv.	20
His being *w* in mine own,	" lxxiv.	43
Move upward, *w* out the beast	" cxvii.	27
(Sea was her wrath, yet *w* after storm)	*Elaine*	1300
she said, ' by *w* in the mines :'	*Sea Dreams*	110

workman.

the *w* and his work	*Princess,* iii.	281-305
Workmen up at the Hall !	*Maud,* I. i.	65

workmanship.

admire Joints of cunning *w.*	*Vision of Sin*	186
Look what a lovely piece of *w !*	*Aylmer's F.*	237

world.

w hath not another (Tho' all her fairest	*Isabel*	38
which possess'd The darkness of the *w*	*Arabian N's.*	72
the *w* Like one great garden show'd	*The Poet*	. 33
with *his* word She shook the *w.*	"	. 56
All the *w* o'er, (rep.)	*Sea-Fairies*	41
Shadows of the *w* appear	*L. of Shalott,* ii.	12
Roof'd the *w* with doubt and fear,	*Eleönore*	. 99
full of dealings with the *w ?*	*Miller's D.*	8
There's somewhat in this *w* amiss	"	. 19
'while the *w* runs round and round,'	*Pal. of Art*	13
the human tale Of this wide *w*	"	. 147
et the *w* have peace or wars,	"	. 182
breaks thro' the stillness of this *w* ;	"	. 259
and all the *w* is still.	*May Queen,* ii.	24
girdled with the gleaming *w:*	*Lotos-E's.*	158
gently comes the *w* to those	*To J. S.*	3
decay of faith Right thro' the *w,*	*The Epic*	. 19
knights Whereof this *w* holds record	*M. d' Arthur*	16
hath come, since the making of the *w*	"	. 203
was an image of the mighty *w ;*	"	. 235
one good custom should corrupt the *w*	"	. 242
by prayer Than this *w* dreams of.	"	. 248
Not wholly in the busy *w,*	*Gardener's D.*	33
Beauty such a mistress of the *w.*	"	. 57

	POEM,	LINE.
from her tendance turn'd Into the *w*	*Gardener's D.*	144
hold From thence thro' all the *w*'s ;	"	. 205
That veil'd the *w* with jaundice	*Walk. to the M.*	14
these two parties still divide the *w*	"	. 69
never sow was higher in this *w—.*	"	. 88
mimic this raw fool the *w,*	"	. 96
for the good and increase of the *w*	*Ed. Morris* 44,	51,92
powers and princes of this *w,*	*St S. Stylites*	184
this *w*'s curse,—beloved but hated—	*Love and Duty*	47
I fall the *w* were falcons, what of that?	*Golden Year*	38
like the second *w* to us that live	"	. 56
arch where thro' Gleams that untravell'd *w*	*Ulysses*	20
not too late to seek a newer *w.*	"	. 57
Saw the Vision of the *w,*	*Locksley H.*	16, 120
the Federation of the *w.*	"	. 128
and the *w* is more and more.	"	. 142
Let the great *w* spin for ever	"	. 182
I said 'When first the *w* began.	*Two Voices*	16
Look up thro' night : the *w* is wide.	"	. 24
Is cancell'd in the *w* of sense?'	"	. 42
present The *w* with some development.	"	. 75
Like hints and echoes of the *w*	*Day-Dm.*	. 27
In that new *w* which is the old :	"	. 168
Thro' all the *w* she follow'd him.	"	. 196
learn the *w,* and sleep again ;	"	. 220
The prelude to some brighter *w*	"	. 252
And all the *w* go by them.	*Will Water.*	48
Ah yet, tho' all the *w* forsake,	"	. 49
And my mockeries of the *w.*	*Vision of Sin*	202
Ring'd with the azure *w,* he stands	*The Eagle*	. 3
he sings of what the *w* will be	*Poet's Song*	. 15
move among a *w* of ghosts (iv. 539)	*Princess,* i.	17
One rose in all the *w,* your Highness	" ii.	. 37
This *w* was once a fluid haze of light	"	. 101
Two in the tangled business of the *w,*	"	. 157
thoughts enrich the blood of the *w.'*	"	. 164
emancipation turns Of half this *w,*	"	. 270
A blessing on her labours for the *w.*	"	. 455
whence after-hands May move the *w,*	" iii.	247
all the hopes of half the *w,*	" iv.	166
against their Lords Thro' all the *w,*	"	. 394
burst and flood the *w* with foam :	"	. 453
all the gold That veins the *w*	"	. 522
The wrath I nursed against the *w*	" v.	427
move the stony bases of the *w.*	" vi.	42
whom a *w* Of traitorous friend	"	. 177
tarn by tarn Expunge the *w :*	" vii.	26
blacken'd all her *w* in secret,	"	. 27
I believed that in the living *w*	"	. 142
notice of a change in the dark *w*	"	. 234
These were the rough ways of the *w*	"	. 241
the wrestling thews that throw the *w;*	"	. 266
Then reign the *w*'s great bridals,	"	. 278
in rich foreshadowings of the *w,*	"	. 293
O we will walk this *w*	"	. 339
down rolls the *w* In mock heroics	" *Con.*	63
fine old *w* of ours is but a child	"	. 77
and all the silent spaces of the *w*'s,	"	. 114
help thy vain *w*'s to bear thy light	*In Mem. Pro.*	32
sunbeam strikes along the *w :*	" xv.	8
her arms To feel from *w* to *w*	" xxi.	19
Thou fail not in a *w* of sin	" xxxiii.	15
The total *w* since life began :	" xlii.	12
Upon the great *w*'s altar-stairs	" liv.	15
breathes a novel *w,* the while	" lxi.	9
The centre of a *w*'s desire	" lxiii.	16
So many *w*'s, so much to do,	" lxxii.	1
The *w* which credits what is done	" lxxiv.	15
In whispers of the beauteous *w.*	" lxxviii.	15
The deep pulsations of the *w,*	" xciv.	40
rising *w*'s by yonder wood	" civ.	25
I would the great *w* grew like thee,	" cxiii.	25
In that which made the *w* so fair	" cxv.	8
the *w*'s great work is heard Beginning,	" cxx.	10
I found Him not in *w* or sun,	" cxxiii.	5
whispers to the *w*'s of space,	" cxxvi.	12
And mingles all the *w* with thee.	" cxxviii.	12
and let the *w* have its way ;	*Maud,* I. iv.	21
is a *w* of plunder and prey.	"	. 24
Who knows the ways of the *w*	"	. 44
the suns are many, the *w* is wide	"	. 45

	POEM.	LINE.
I have not made the w,	Maud, I iv.	43
From the long-neck'd geese of the w	"	52
If I find the w so bitter	" vi.	33
then the w were not so bitter	"	38, 94
a w in which I have hardly mixt	"	76
than is ever was In our low w,	" xviii.	48
A w of trouble within!	" xix.	25
makes us loud in the w of the dead;	" II. v.	25
a w that loves him not, For it is		
but a w of the dead	"	39
another stiller w of the dead	"	70
Fairer than aught in the w beside,	"	73
a hope for the w in the coming wars	" III. vi.	11
in a weary w my one thing bright	"	17
whom the strong sons of the w despise;	The Brook	3
in our sad w's best bloom	"	218
greatest sailor since our w began	Ode on Well.	86
raw w for the march of mind	"	168
either babbling w of high or low;	"	182
Tho' w on w in myriad myriads roll	"	262
nor moves the loud w's random mock	Will	4
All the w wonder'd	Lt. Brigade 31.	52
like eclipse Darkening the w	Ded. of Idylls	14
w's loud whisper breaking into storm	Enid	27
At caitiffs and at wrongers of the w	"	96
they issued from the w of wood,	"	238
of your bourg The murmur of the w!	"	277
great wave that echoes round the w;	"	420
Made a low splendour in the w,	"	598
thro' the feeble twilight of this w.	"	854
being he loved best in all the w,	"	952
gray dawn stole o'er the dewy w,.	"	1234
Henceforth in all the w at anything,	"	1497
w will not believe a man repents	"	1748
wise w of ours is mainly right	"	1749
feet, that I have follow'd thro' the w	Vivien	76
sweep me from my hold upon the w	"	152
to learn themselves and all the w	"	215
noble deeds, the flower of all the w	"	263
I well believe that all about this w	"	391
sunn'd The w to peace again;	"	489
brute w howling forced them into bonds"	"	594
And touching other w's	"	687
which now is this w's hugest	Elaine	77
flower of all the west and all the w	"	249
Hid from the wide w's rumour	"	521
this and that other w Another w		
for the sick man;	"	869
and to follow you thro' the w.'	"	935
'Nay, the w, the w, All ear and eye,	"	936
Lancelot and the Queen and all the w,"	"	1101
might she follow me thro' the w,	"	1306
hold thee with my life against the w.'	Guinevere	114
together well might change the w.	"	299
most disloyal friend in all the w.'	"	338
What knowest thou of the w,	"	341
To serve as model for the mighty w,	"	462
in that w where all are pure	"	559
Let the w be; that is but of the w,	"	622
might I not have made of thy fair w,	"	648
not to see the w—For pleasure?	En. Arden.	26
slipt across the summer of the w,	"	527
passing thro' the summer w again	"	530
sea-haze and whelm'd the w in gray;	"	673
beating up thro' all the bitter w,	"	803
half-allowing smiles for all the w,	Aylmer's F.	120
the w should ring of him	"	395
fain had haled him out into the w.	"	467
Against the desolations of the w	"	614
that were left to make a purer w—	"	638
blow these sacrifices thro' the w—	"	758
our narrow w must canvass it:	"	774
left their memories a w's curse	"	796
shuddering at the ruin of a w;	Sea Dreams	30
'What a w,' I thought, 'To live in!'	"	92
think that in our often-ransack'd w	"	125
it cost me a w of woe,	Grandmother	23
Here at the quiet limit of the w	Tithonus	7
that dark w where I was born	"	33
We knew the merry w was round,	The Voyage	7, 95
We loved the glories of the w,	"	83

	POEM.	LINE.
one who feels the immeasurable w	A Dedication	7
The lucid interspace of w and w,	Lucretius	15
west wind and the w will go on rep.)	The Window	111
Over the w to the end of it	"	200

worldling.
| the wind like a broken w wail'd, | Maud, I. i. | 21 |

worldly-wise.
| w-w begetters, plagued themselves | Aylmer's F. | 482 |

world's-earthquake.
| In that w-e, Waterloo! | Ode on Well. | 173 |

world-to-be.
| Who will embrace me in the w-t-b? | En. Arden. | 8, 4 |

World-victor.
| The great W-v's victor, | Ode on Well. | 42 |

world-worn.
| the w-w Dante grasp'd his song | Pal. of Art | 125 |

worm.
Nothing but the small cold w	A Dirge	9
with a w I balk'd his fame,	D. of F. Wom.	155
As ruthless as a baby with a w,	Walk. to the M.	98
every w beneath the moon	Two Voices	173
men and horses pierced with w's	Vision of Sin	20
That not a w is cloven in vain;	In Mem. liii.	9
whole weak race of venomous w's	Maud, II. i.	46
many rings 'For he had many, poor w'	" ii.	69
Wroth to be wroth at such a w,	Enid	213
as the w draws in the wither'd leaf	"	1481
cast him as a w upon the way;	Guinevere	36
Crown thyself, w, and worship thine	Aylmer's F.	650
a w is there in the lonely wood	The Islet	34
for the life of the w or the fly?	Wages	7
No will push me down to the w,	The Window	115

worm-canker'd.
| Distill'd from some w-c homily; | To J. M. K. | 6 |

worm-eaten.
| So propt, w-e, ruinously old, | En. Arden. | 64 |

wormwood.
| where the meats became As w | Elaine | 740 |

worn.
Weeded and w the ancient thatch	Mariana	7
hearts w out by many wars	Lotos-Ex.	131
took it, and have w it, like a king;	M. d'Arthur	33
of writers, and indeed W threadbare	Ed. Morris	41
Or while the patch was w;	Talking O.	64
Till now the dark was w,	Love and Duty	67
winters of abeyance all w out,	Princess, iv.	422
Till slowly w her earthly robe,	In Mem. lxxxiii.	33
died at Florence, quite w out,	The Brook	35
Which he has w so pure of blame,	Ode on Well.	72
W by the feet that now were silent,	Enid	221
it never yet was w, I trow:	"	1483
unwillingly have w My faded suit	"	705
on his cuirass w our Lady's Head	Elaine	294
w Favour of any lady in the lists—	"	362, 472
When these have w their tokens;	"	765

worn-out.
| while the w-o clerk Brow-beats his desk | To J. M. K. | 11 |

worried.
| W his passive ear with petty wrongs | En. Arden | 343 |

worse.
ever w with growing time,	Pal. of Art	270
There is confusion w than death,	Lotos-Ex.	128
Is boundless better, boundless w	Two Voices	294
I fear to slide from bad to w.	"	211
the song Might have been w	Princess, iv.	212
cold reverence w than she were dead	" v.	89
in sad experience w than death,	" vii.	296
would make Confusion w than death	In Mem. lxxxix.	19
whether woman or man be the w,	Maud, I. i.	75
Sirk once, with a fear of w,	" xix.	73
make men w by making my sin known?	Elaine	1407
laughingly Would hint at w in either.	En. Arden	478
if griefs Like his have w or better,	"	742

worse-confounded.
| Babel, woman-built, And w-c; | Princess, iv. | 457 |

worship (s.) POEM. LINE.
deck'd her out For *w* without end ; *Princess,* vii. 154
with sweet observances And *w*, . *Enid* . . 49
And I will pay you *w* ; . . *Vivien* . 77
sole upon my pedestal Of *w*— . " . 728
my loyal *w* is allow'd Of all men : *Elaine* . 111
grant my *w* of it Words, . . " 1181
It will be to your *w*, as my knight, " 1317

worship (verb.)
here come those that *w* me ? . *St S. Stylites* 123
may *w* me without reproach ; . " . 190
He *w's* your ideal :' . . . *Princess,* ii. 38
And beasts themselves would *w* ; *Vivien* . 425
w her by years of noble deeds . *Guinevere* . 472
worm, and *w* thine own lusts !— . *Aylmer's F.* 650
w a gluttonous emperor-idiot. . *Boädicea* . 19

worshipfully.
Sir Lavaine did well and *w* ; . *Elaine* . 490

worshipper.
outlast thy Deity ? Deity ? nay, thy *w's Lucretius* 73

worshipt.
w their own darkness as the Highest ? *Aylmer's F.* 643

worst.
never : here I brave the *w* :' . *Ed. Morris* 118
His *w* he kept, his best he gave '*You might have won*' 26
women's slander is the *w*, . . *The Letters* 34
of her court The wiliest and the *w* ; *Guinevere* . 30
I hold that man the *w* of public foes " . 508
W of the *w* were that man he that reigns ! " . 519
deeds yet live, the *w* is yet to come. *Sea Dreams* 301

worth (adj. and s.)
If aught of ancient *w* be there . *To the Queen* 12
Old letters, breathing of her *w*, *Mariana in the S.* 62
Is *w* a hundred coats-of-arms. *L. C. V. de Vere* 16
To make him trust his modest *w*, " . 46
dust I honour and his living *w* : . *To J. S.* . 30
Is three times *w* them all ; . . *Talking O.* 72
draws the veil from hidden *w* . *Day-Dm.* . 104
I grow in *w*, and wit, and sense, . *Will Water.* 41
most, of sterling *w*, is what . . " . 175
At half thy real *w* ? . . " . 204
song that pleased us from its *w* ; '*You might have won*' 22
He loves me for my own true *w*, . *Lady Clare* 11
'O Lady Clare, you shame your *w* ! " . 66
And all his worldly *w* for this, *Sir L. and Q. G.* 43
we might make it *w* his while . *Princess,* i. 182
two dear things are one of double *w*, " ii. 397
we should find the land *W* seeing ; " iii. 156
all men grew to rate us at our *w*, " iv. 127
beauty in detail Made them *w* knowing ; " . 429
a good wife, *W* winning . . " v. 160
is not Ida right ? They *w* it ? . " . 181
What seem'd my *w* since I began *In Mem. Pro.* 34
w my while to choose Of things all mortal " xxxiv. 11
I know transplanted human *w* . " lxxxi. 11
Whose life, whose thoughts were little *w*, " lxxxiv. 30
defying change To test his *w* ; . " xciv. 28
scarce have spent the *w* of one !' . *Enid* . 1260
It is not *w* the keeping : let it go : *Vivien* . 246
gross heart Would reckon *w* the taking " . 766
a boon *W* half her realm, . . *Elaine* . 73
they had been thrice their *w* . " 1206
its *w* Was being Edith's. . . *Aylmer's F.* 378
Warnt *w* nowt a haäcre, . . *N. Farmer* 39
aught that is *w* the knowing ? . 1865-1866 . 5, 9

worthier.
many a *w* than I, would make him *May Queen,* iii. 46
I find him *w* to be loved. . . *In Mem. Pro.* 40
'Forbear : there is a *w*,' . . *Enid* . . 556

worthiest.
of those halves You *w* ; . . *Princess,* iv. 442
follow up the *w* till he die : . . " . 446

worthy.
w of the golden prime . . *Arabian N's.* 98, 142
W a Roman spouse . . . *D. of F. Wom.* 164
a precious thing, one *w* note . *M. d'Arthur* 89
it will be *w* of the two. . . *Locksley H.* 92

POEM. LINE.
Call'd him *w* to be loved . . *Princess,* v. 537
'I am not *w* ev'n to speak . *In Mem.* xxxvii. 11
And thou art *w* ; full of power ; . " *Con.* 37
We are not *w* to live. . . . *Maud,* II. i. 48
W of our gorgeous rites . . *Ode on Well.* 93
w to be laid by thee ; . . . " . 94
not *w* ev'n to speak of him ;' . *Enid* . . 199
feeling that you felt me *w* trust, . *Vivien* . 183
quest Assign'd to her not *w* of it, *Elaine* . 821
Toward one more *w* of her— . " 1310
if what is *w* love Could bind him, " 1369
you loved, for he was *w* love. . *Aylmer's F.* 712

wound (s.)
then, because his *w* was deep, . *M. d'Arthur* 5
I fear My *w* hath taken cold " . 166
I will heal me of my grievous *w* . " . 264
refather'd o'er my *w's*. . . . *Princess,* vi. 113
Lifting his grim head from my *w's* " . 255
save her dear lord whole from any *w*, *Enid* . 894
till she had lighted on his *w*, . " 1362
cloaks the *w's* of loss with lies ; . *Vivien* . 667
mine ancient *w* is hardly whole . *Elaine* . 94
There stanch'd his *w* : . . . " . 519
who has come Despite the *w* he spoke of, " . 565
added *w* to *w* And ridd'n away to die " . 566
made the pretext of a hindering *w* " . 581
tho' he call'd his *w* a little hurt . " . 848
Like flies that haunt a *w*, . . *Aylmer's F.* 571

wound (verb.)
as the boat-head *w* along . *L. of Shalott,* iv. 24
Past and Present, *w* in one, . *Miller's D.* 197
that my arms Were *w* about thee *Œnone* . 199
her hair *W* with white roses . *Pal. of Art* 99
w Her looser hair in braid, . . *Gardener's D.* 154
w A scarf of orange round . . *Princess, Pro.* 101
we *w* About the cliffs, the copses " iii. 341
into the lists they *w* Timorously ; " vi. 68
And mine in his was *w*, . *In Mem.* xciv. 37
w Bare to the sun, . . . *Enid* . . 321
and *w* the gateway horn . . *Elaine* . 169

wounded.
Of your great head—for he is *w* too—*Princess,* vi. 294
Whatever man lies *w*, friend or foe, " . 316
see my dear lord *w* in the strife, . *Enid* . . 103
For those that might be *w* ; . " . 1416
were himself nigh *w* to the death.' " . 1767
claw back, and *w* her own heart. . *Vivien* . 350
gone sore *w*, and hath left his prize *Elaine* . 529
W and wearied needs must he be near. " . 537
he went sore *w* from the field : . " . 598
w to the death that cannot die ; . *Aylmer's F.* 662
Till himself was deadly *w* . . *The Captain* 63

wove.
beneath her marriage ring, *W* and unwove it, *Enid* 1109
w coarse webs to snare her purity *Aylmer's F.* 780

woven.
has *w* its wavy bowers, . . . *May Queen,* i. 29
music winding trembled, *W* in circles : *Vision of Sin* 18
A web is *w* across the sky, . . *In Mem* iii. 6
cobweb *w* across the cannon's throat *Maud,* III. vi 27

wraith.
O hollow *w* of dying fame, . . *In Mem.* lxxii. 13
The ghastly *W* of one that I know ; *Maud,* II. i. 32

wrangle.
three gray linnets *w* for the seed : *Guinevere* . 253

wrangled.
And still they strove and *w* : . *Sea Dreams* 222

wranglest.
Wooest not, nor vainly *w* ; . . *Madeline* . 38

wrap.
When a blanket *w's* the day . *Vision of Sin* 80
In words, like weeds, I'll *w* me o'er *In Mem.* v. 9

wrapt.
I *w* his body in the sheet, . . *The Sisters* 34
W in dense cloud from base to cope. *Two Voices* 186
These things are *w* in doubt and dread, " . 265

	POEM.	LINE.
Pitiful sight, *w* in a soldier's cloak,	*Princess*, v.	53
Thy roots are *w* about the bones.	*In Mem.* ii.	4
w thee formless in the fold,	” xxii.	15
W in a cloak, as I saw him,	*Maud*, I. i.	59
W in drifts of lurid smoke	” II. iv.	66
brought a mantle down and *w* her in it	*Enid*	824
nor sought, *W* in her grief, for housel	*Guinevere*	147

wrath.

No sword Of *w* her right arm whirl'd	*The Poet*	54
replied King Arthur, much in *w*:	*M. d'Arthur*	118
like a rising moon, Inflamed with *w*	*Princess*, i.	59
chew'd The thrice-turn d cud of *w*	”	65
heated thro' and thro' with *w* and love,	” iv.	145
The *w* I nursed against the *w*:	” v.	427
The *w* that garners in my heart ;	*In Mem.* lxxxi.	14
like a man in *w* the heart	” cxxiii.	15
just *w* shall be wreak'd on a giant liar	*Maud*, III vi.	45
And then we met in *w* and wrong,	*The Letters*	11
loosed in words of sudden fire the *w*	*Enid*	955
Another, flying from the *w* of Doorm	”	1379
Vivien answer'd smiling as in *w*.	*Vivien*	376
Vivien answer'd frowning yet in *w*;	”	618
all in *w* he got to horse and went ;	*Elaine*	562
(Sea was her *w*, yet working after storm	”	1300
The *w* which forced my thoughts	*Guinevere*	533
flooded with the helpless *w* of tears,	*En. Arden*	37
would she glide between your *w's*,	*Aylmer's F.*	706
A rushing tempest of the *w* of God	”	757
sun go down upon your *w*,'	*Sea Dreams*	44
Secret *w* like smother'd fuel.	*The Captain*	15
Shame and *w* his heart confounded,	”	61
Except his *w* were wreaked on wretched	*Lucretius*	128

wrathful.

be not *w* with your maid ;	*Vivien*	230
w that a stranger knight Should do	*Elaine*	467
She brook'd it not ; but *w*, petulant	*Lucretius*	14

wreak.

I remain on whom to *w* your rage	*Princess*, iv.	331
I *w* The wrath that garners	*In Mem.* lxxxi.	13

wreak'd.

wrath shall be *w* on a giant liar ;	*Maud*, III. vi.	45
wrath were *w* on wretched man,	*Lucretius*	128

wreath.

thro' the *w's* of floating dark upcurl'd	*The Poet*	35
Lit light in *w's* and anadems	*Pal. of Art*	186
made a little *w* of all the flowers	*Dora*	80
The *w* of flowers fell At Dora's feet	”	100
In *w* about her hair	*Talking O*	288
The woodbine *w's* that bind her,	*Amphion*	34
In her right a civic *w*,	*Vision of Sin*	137
lapt in *w's* of glowworm light	*Princess*, iv.	415
'for this wild *w* of air	” v.	308
thousand *w's* of dangling water-smoke	” vii	198
one *w* more for Use and Wont,	*In Mem.* xxix.	11
head hath miss'd an earthly *w*:	” lxxii.	6
any *w* that man can weave him	*Ode on Well.*	277
when the *w* of March has blossom'd To	*F. D. Maurice*	43
A *w* of airy dancers hand-in-hand	*Guinevere*	259

wreathe.

The fancy's tenderest eddy *w*	*In Mem.* xlviii.	6

wreathen.

the sculptured ornament That *w* round it	*Vivien*.	585

wreck (s.)

on some wild shore with ribs of *w*	*Princess*, v.	141
in that night of sudden ruin and *w*	*En. Arden*.	505
no gladlier does the stranded *w*	”	829
his voyage, His *w*, his lonely life,	”	863
battle, bold adventure, dungeon, *w*,	*Aylmer's F.*	98
father suddenly cried, 'A *w*, a *w*!'	*Sea Dreams*	59
My father raves of death and *w*,	*Sailor Boy*	19

wreck (verb.)

sought'st to *w* my mortal ark	*Two Voices*	389
w itself without the pilot's guilt,	*Aylmer's F.*	716

wreck'd.

W on a reef of visionary gold.'	*Sea Dreams*	135

	POEM.	LINE.
eagles not be eagles? *w's* be *w's*?	*Golden Year*	37
Tits, *w's*, and all wing'd nothings.	*Enid*	275
you my *w* with a crown of gold,	*The Window*	80
You my Queen of the *w's*	”	81-2
I'll be the King of the Queen of the *w's*	”	84
The fire-crown'd King of the *w's*,	”	151
like the king of the *w's* with a crown	”	159

wrenching.

W it backward into his:	*Lucretius*	213

wrestle.

strive and *w* with thee till I die:	*St S. Stylites*	117
ever seem'd to *w* with burlesque	*Princess, Con.*	16

wrestled.

W with wandering Israel 'Clear-headed friend'		26

wretched.

May God make me more *w*	*Maud*, I. xix.	94

wring.

take the goose, and *w* her throat,	*The Goose*	31

wrinkle.

The busy *w's* round his eyes?	*Miller's D*	4
A million *w's* carved his skin ;	*Pal. of Art*	138
Whose *w's* gather'd on his face,	*Two Voices*	329
Sown in a *w* of the monstrous hill,	*Will*	19

wrist.

a touch Came round my *w*,	*Princess*, vii.	123
The *w* is parted from the hand that waved,	*Vivien*	401

writ.

W in a language that has long gone by.	*Vivien*	524
which being *w* And folded,	*Elaine*	1103

write.

To make me *w* my random rhymes.	*Will Water.*	13
One *w's*, that 'Other friends remain	*In Mem.* vi.	1
Besought Lavaine to *w* as she devised	*Elaine*	1097
you shall *w*, and not to her, but me ;	*Aylmer's F.*	310
'*W* to me I They loved me,	”	422
Shall I *w* to her? shall I go?	*The Window*	90

writer.

Seem but the theme of *w's*	*Ed. Morris*	43
Old *w's* push'd the happy season back	*Golden Year*	65

writhed.

W toward him, slided up his knee	*Vivien*	88
down his robe the dragon *w* in gold	*Elaine*	434
great King's couch, and *w* upon it,	”	607

writhing.

read *W* a letter from his child,	*Aylmer's F.*	517
w barbarous lineaments,	*Boädicea*	74

written.

w that my race Hew'd Ammon,	*D. of F. Wom.*	237
And something *w*, something thought	*In Mem.* vi.	20
'You have the book : the charm is *w* in it :	*Vivien*	502
w as she found Or made occasion	*Aylmer's F.*	477
And Willy's wife has *w*:	*Grandmother*	3,105

wrote.

Summun I reckons 'ull 'a to *w*	*N. Farmer*	57

wrong (adj. and s.)

lamentation and an ancient tale of *w*	*Lotos-E's.*	163
sounds of insult, shame, and *w*,	*D. of F. Wom.*	11
was *w* to cross his father thus:	*Dora*	145
His nerves were *w*.	*Walk. to the M*	95
fearing they should do me *w*;'	*Locksley H.*	2
we, that prate Of rights and *w's*,	*Godiva*	8
seem'd no room for sense of *w*.	*Two Voices*	456
For am I right, or am I *w*,	*Day-Dm.*	241-5
What I I am not all as *w*	*Vision of Sin*	197
little sense of *w* had touch'd her face	*Princess,Pro.*	213
on her palms and folded up from *w*,	” iv.	269
Came all in haste to hinder *w*	”	382
yet human, whatsoe'er your *w*,	”	405
from the lintel—all the common *w*	” v.	123
caught within the record of her *w's*	”	137
half-right talking of her *w's*;	”	275
rights or *w's* like potherbs in the street	”	447
ourselves are full Of social *w*;	” *Con.*	73

474　　　　　　　　　　CONCORDANCE TO

	POEM.	LINE.
Nor human frailty do me w	In Mem. li.	8
we do him w 'To sing so wildly:	,, lvi.	3
Drug down the blindfold sense of w	,, lxx.	7
Thou dost expectant nature w, .	,, lxxxii.	3
Bewail'd their lot : I did them w;	,, cii.	46
revenge too deep for a transient w	Maud, I iii.	5
would not do herself this great w,	,, x.	57
true life to fight with mortal w s. .	,, xviii.	54
Or to say ' forgive the w,' .	,, II. iv	86
peace that was full of w's and shames,	,, III. vi.	40
' Would I—was it w ?'. .	. The Brook .	111
then we met in wrath and w,	. The Letters	11
public w be crumbled into dust	. Ode on Well.	167
He suffers, but he cannot suffer w	Will	3
glory was, redressing human w;	. Ded. of Idylls	8
noble hearts who see but acts of w	Enid .	438
each had suffer'd some exceeding w.	,,	885
smoulder'd w that burnt him all within	,,	956
that dead man ; Done you more w :	,,	1584
let foul w stagnate and be, .	,,	1739
which for bribe had wink'd at w,	,,	1787
Once for w done you by confusion,	Vivien	136
yourself have own'd you did me w	,,	165
ride abroad redressing human w's !	,,	543
many a year have done despite and w	Elaine	1203
prowess done redress'd a random w	Guinevere .	456
ride abroad redressing human w's,	,,	468
I was w. I am always bound to you	En. Arden	446
to chafe as at a personal w, .	,,	471
if he did that w you charge him with	Sea Dream	268
He can do no more w: .	,,	299
Doeth grievous w. .	. The Captain	2
fame in song has done him much w	Spiteful Let.	3
to struggle, to right the w—	. Wages	3

wrong (verb.)

you w him more than I That struck	Princess, iv.	226
She w's herself, her sex, and me,	,, v.	113
You w yourselves—the woman is so hard	,, vi.	205
I w the grave with fears untrue .	In Mem. l.	
you w your beauty, believe it, .	Maud, I. iv.	17
he that w's his friend W's himself .	Sea Dreams	168

wrong'd

w and lied and thwarted us— .	Princess, iv.	519
judge their cause from her That w it	,, vii.	221
How had I w you ? surely you are wise	Vivien .	137
he never w his bride. .	,,	579
A virtuous gentlewoman deeply w,	,,	760

wronger.

At caitiffs and at w's of the world. Enid . . 96

wrote.

round about the prow she w .	L. of Shalott, iv.	8
W ' Mene, mene,' and divided quite	Pal. of Art	227
Dropt on the letters as I w .	To J. S.	56
I w I know not what. .	,,	57
have that song which Leonard w:	Golden Year	1
Then I took a pencil, and w .	Ed. Gray .	25
then, Sir, awful odes she wrote .	Princess, i.	137
sat down and w, In such a hand .	,,	232
Then he w The letter she devised ;	Elaine	1102
tho' Averill w And bad him .	Aylmer's F.	543
first w satire, with no pity in it .	Sea Dreams	197
take this and pray that he Who w it	A Dedication	5

wroth.

Then the old man Was w, .	. Dora .	23
Weakness to be w with weakness	Locksley H.	149
perforce He yielded, w and red, .	Princess, v.	348
A third is w, ' Is this an hour .	In Mem. xxi.	13
W to be w at such a worm .	. Enid .	213
my new mother, be not w or grieved	,,	779
be he w even to slaying me, .	,,	916
w the more That she could speak	,,	961
damsel then W at a lover's loss ?	Vivien .	457
W at himself : not willing to be known	Elaine .	160
W that the king's command to sally forth	,,	559
W but all in awe, For twenty strokes	,,	715
Fret not yourself, dear brother, nor be w,	,,	1068
Sullen, defiant, pitying, w, .	Aylmer's F.	492

wrought.

	POEM.	LINE.
She w her people lasting good .	To the Queen	24
w Two spirits to one equal mind .	Miller's D.	235
So w, they will not fail. .	Pal. of Art	148
The airy hand confusion w .	,,	226
by degrees to fullness w, ' You ash me, why,' etc.		14
W by the lonely maiden of the Lake,	M. d' Arthur	104
Nine years she w it .	,,	105
w by prayer Than this world dreams of	,,	247
napkin w with horse and hound, .	Audley Ct.	20
may be I have w some miracles .	St S. Stylites	134
toil'd, and w, and thought with me—	Ulysses .	46
So variously seem'd all things w, .	Two Voices	457
dream of that,' I ask'd ' Which w us	Princess, iii.	281
our device ; w to the life ; .	,,	286
A tent of satin, elaborately w .	,,	330
with whom the bell-mouth'd glass had w	,, iv.	137
kind of shame within me w .	,,	176
wherein were w Two grand designs :	,, vii.	106
know no more than I who w .	In Mem. vi.	17
w With human hands the creed .	,, xxxvi.	6
out of painful phases w .	,, lxiv.	6
Cloud-towers by ghostly masons w,	,, lxix.	5
Is w with tumult of acclaim .	,, lxxiv.	20
The grief my loss in him had w, .	,, lxxix.	6
changes w on form and face ; .	,, lxxxi.	2
Her lavish mission richly w, .	,, lxxxiii.	34
Whatever change the years have w .	,, x.	22
what was it else within me w .	Maud, I. vi.	81
W, till he crept from a gutted mine .	,, x.	9
W for his house an irredeemable woe	,, II. i.	22
Let the sound of those he w for .	Ode on Well.	10
he with those deep voices w, .	,,	67
Themselves had w on many an innocent	Enid	1027
schemed and w Until I overturn'd him	,,	1677
w too long with delegated hands, .	,,	1741
work of Edyrn w upon himself .	,,	1760
fain have w upon his cloudy mood	Vivien .	12
which if any w on any one .	,,	55
man so w on ever seem'd to lie .	,,	57
see but him who w the charm .	,,	61
those who w it first, The wrist is parted	,,	400
charm, which being w upon the Queen	,,	434
save the King, who w the charm, .	,,	493
of the horrid foulness that he w, .	,,	598
w upon his mood and hugg'd him .	,,	797
gold and azure !' which was w Thereafter	Elaine	1335
grace and power, W as a charm .	Guinevere .	143
Hath w confusion in the Table Round	,,	218
thro' flesh hath w into my life .	,,	554
w the ruin of my lord the King.' .	,,	681
w To make the boatmen fishing-nets	En. Arden.	815
her counsel all had w About them	Aylmer's F.	151
w Such waste and havock .	,,	639

wrung.

Daintly she shriek'd And w it. .	Princess, Pro.	174
at his hand, and w it passionately.	En. Arden .	325

Wye.

And hushes half the babbling W,	In Mem. xix.	7
The W is hush'd nor moved along	,,	9

wyvern

blazing w weathercock'd the spire,	Aylmer's F.	17
Burst his own w on the seal . .	,,	516

X

Xanthus.

between the ships and stream Of X Spec. of Iliad 18

Y

yadle.

Says that I moänt 'a naw moor y :	N. Farmer .	3
Git ma my y .	,,	4, 36, 68
I've 'ed my point o' y ivry noight.	,,	7
an' doesn' bring ma the y ? .	,,	65

Yabbok.

Past Y brook . . ' Clear-headed friend' 27

yard.

and his hair A y behind. .	. Godiva .	19
Only a y beneath the street .	Maud, II. v.	7

	POEM.	LINE.
yardwand.		
but with his cheating *y,* home.—	*Maud,* I. i.	52
yawled.		
yelp'd the cur, and *y* the cat;	*The Goose*	33
yawn.		
Heaven opens inward, chasms *y,*	*Two Voices*	304
The black earth *y's*	*Ode on Well.*	269
yawned.		
y, and rubb'd his face, and spoke,	*Day-Dm.*	151
yawning.		
Hither came Cyril, and *y,*	*Princess,* iii.	108
yead (head.)		
loike a buzzard-clock ower my *y,*	*N. Farmer*	18
year (see Old Year, New Year.)		
Because they are the earliest of the *y*	*Ode to Mem.*	27
flowing from The illimitable *y's*	"	42
haunts the *y's* last hours '*A spirit haunts,'* etc.		1
And the *y's* last rose	"	20
hangs before her all the *y,*	*L. of Shalott,* ii.	11
Many a chance the *y's* beget	*Miller's D.*	206
Untouch'd with any shade of *y's*	"	219
so three *y's* She prosper'd;	*Pal. of Art*	217
when four *y's* were wholly finished	"	289
of all the *y* the maddest merriest	*May Queen,* i.	43
The good old *y,* the dear old time	" ii.	6
I remember, rose the morning of the *y!*	" iii.	3
what is mingled with past *y's*	*D. of F. Wom.*	282
A jollier *y* we shall not see	*D. of the O. Year*	20
Two *y's* his chair is seen Empty	*To J. S.*	22
wisdom of a thousand *y's 'Of old sat Freedom,'* etc.		18
main-currents draw the *y's*: '*Love thou thy land*'		21
The Spirit of the *y's* to come	"	55
days darken round me, and the *y's, M. d' Arthur*		237
at that time of *y* The lusty bird	" *Ep.*	10
Call'd to me from the *y's* to come.	*Gardener's D.*	176
with each The *y* increased.	"	195
The daughters of the *y,* One after one,	"	195
for these five *y's* So full a harvest	*Dora*	63
as *y's* Went forward, Mary took	"	165
wild, fresh three quarters of a *y.*	*Ed. Morris*	2
That show the *y* is turn'd	*Talking O.*	176
thro' love, and greater than thy *y's Love and Duty*		21
onward, leading up the golden *y* (rep.) *Golden Year*		26
This same grand *y* is ever at the doors,	"	73
to such length of *y's* should come.	*Locksley H.*	67
never,' whisper'd by the phantom *y's,*	"	83
excitement that the coming *y's* would	"	111
Better fifty *y's* of Europe	"	184
fatal byword of all *y's* to come,	*Godiva*	67
I said: 'The *y's* with change advance; *Two Voices*		52
I said 'That all the *y's* invent;	"	73
I found him when my *y's* were few;	"	271
is not our first *y* forgot?	"	368
Oft lose whole *y's* of darker mind.	"	372
The varying *y* with blade and sheaf *Day-Dm.*		
all that else the *y's* will show	"	225
And *y's* of cultivation.	*Amphion*	98
Or this first snowdrop of the *y*	*St Agnes' Eve*	11
So fares it since the *y's* began,	*Will Water.*	169
Then, in the boyhood of the *y*	*Sir L. and Q. G.*	19
Change, reverting to the *y's.*	*Vision of Sin*	159
When the *y's* have died away.'	*Poet's Song*	16
with a bootless calf At eighty *y's* old; *Princess,*		i. 34
the *y* in which our olives fail'd	"	124
the child We lost in other *y's,*	"	256
May beat admission in a thousand *y's*	" iii.	139
giants living, each, a thousand *y's,*	"	252
great *y* of equal mights and rights	" iv.	56
Six thousand *y's* of fear have made you	"	486
desecrated shrine, the trampled *y,*	" v.	121
Rose a nurse of ninety *y's,*	"	544
Dames and heroines of the golden *y*	" vi.	48
in the long *y's* liker must they grow;	" vii.	263
welcome for the *y* To follow.	*Con.*	95
who shall so forecast the *y's.*	*In Mem.* i.	5
touch thy thousand *y's* of gloom:.	" ii.	12
Some pleasure from thine early *y's*	" iv.	10
Come, Time, and teach me, many *y's,*	" xiii.	13
Thro' four sweet *y's* arose and fell,	" xxii.	3

	POEM.	LINE.
And in the long harmonious *y's*	*In Mem.* xliii.	9
And those five *y's* its richest field.	" xlv.	12
What record? not the sinless *y's.*	" li.	11
so much hope for *y's* to come,	" lviii.	14
And o'er the number of thy *y's.*	" lxvi.	8
More *y's* had made me love thee more.'	" lxxx.	8
The all-assuming months and *y's.*	" lxxxiv.	67
A friendship for the *y's* to come.	"	80
The primrose of the later *y,*	"	119
Whatever change the *y's* have wrought	" lxxxix.	22
The hope of unaccomplish'd *y's*	" xc.	7
A fact within the coming *y;*	" xci.	10
that glad *y* which once had been,	" xciv.	22
She keeps the gift of *y's* before,	" xcvi.	25
The *y* is dying in the night;	" cv.	3
The *y* is going, let him go;	"	7
Ring in the thousand *y's* of peace.	"	28
Thro' all the *y's* of April blood;	" cviii.	12
The men of rathe and riper *y's.*	" cix.	2
meets the *y,* and gives and takes.	" cxv.	3
A cry above the conquer'd *y's*	" cxxx.	7
number'd o'er Some thrice three *y's*	" *Con.*	10
stay for a *y* who has gone for a week *Maud,* I. xvi.		6
To me, her friend of the *y's* before;	" xix.	64
For *y's,* a measureless ill, Fury's, for	" II. ii.	49
mood is chang'd, for it fell at a time of *y*	" III. vi.	4
Many and many a happy *y.*	*To F. D. Maurice*	48
Thro' all this tract of *y's* Wearing	*Ded. of Idylls*	23
I these two *y's* past have won it	*Enid*	554
three sad *y's* ago, That night of fire	"	633
Her suitor in old *y's* before Geraint,	"	1125
if you love me as in former *y's,*	"	1204
one *y* gone, and on returning found *Vivien*		558
this cut is fresh; That ten *y's* back *Elaine*		22
by nine *y's* proof we needs must learn	"	63
eight *y's* past, eight jousts had been,	"	68
Lancelot won the diamond of the *y,*	"	69
marr'd, of more than twice her *y's,*	"	257
This many a *y* have done despite.	"	1203
not to love again; Not at my *y's,*	"	1287
worship her by *y's* of noble deeds, *Guinevere*		472
months will add themselves and make the *y's,*	"	618
The *y's* will roll into the centuries	"	619
ran the *y's,* seven happy *y's* (rep.) *En. Arden.*		81
ten *y's,* Since Enoch left his hearth	"	356
after all these sad uncertain *y's,*	"	412
Wait a *y,* a *y* is not so long:	"	429
Surely I shall be wiser in a *y:*	"	430
Will you not bide your *y* (rep.)	"	435
'Is it a *y*!' she ask'd.	"	455
half-another *y* had slipt away.	"	468
In those far-off seven happy *y's*	"	487
as the *y* Roll'd itself round again.	"	622
have borne it with me all these *y's,*	"	896
partridge-breeders of a thousand *y's Aylmer's F.*		382
y's which are not Time's Had blasted him	"	601
the shallow cares of fifty *y's.*	"	814
a dozen *y's* Of dust and deskwork *Sea Dreams*		77
Seventy *y's* ago, my darling 'rep. *Grandmother*		24, 56
in a hundred *y's* it 'ill all be the same	"	47
we had many a happy *y*;	"	71
And that was ten *y's* back, or more	"	75
two and thirty *y's* were a mist	*V. of Cauteretz*	6
y's have wander'd by,	*The Captain*	60
His beauty still with his *y's* increased *The Victim*		75
Here, it is here—the close of the *y. Spiteful Let.*		1
I said 'O *y's* that meet in tears.	*1865-1866*	4
Gone till the end of the *y*	*The Window*	36
bitten the heel of the going *y.*	"	68
Ay is life for a hundred *y's*	"	114
A *y* hence, a *y* hence.'	"	10
yearn.		
swift souls that *y* for light,	*Two Voices*	67
y to breathe the airs of Heaven	*Sir Galahad*	63
A part of stillness, *y's* to speak: *In Mem.* lxxxiv.		78
y still more to prove you mine,	*Vivien*	177
and *y* to hurry precipitously.	*Boädicea*	58
yearn'd.		
y towards William; but the youth *Dora*		6
while still I *y* for human praise.	*Two Voices*	123

	POEM.	LINE.
y To hear her weeping by his grave?	*In Mem* xxxi.	3
y to burst the folded gloom,	"	cxxi. 3
y to make complete The tale of diamonds	*Elaine*	91
Enoch *y* to see her face again;	*En. Arden.*	718
in her heart she *y* incessantly	"	867
Y after by the wisest of the wise.	*Lucretius*	263

yearning.

y's that can never be exprest	*D. of F. Wom.*	283
Y to mix himself with Life. '*Love thou thy land*'		56
Gave utterance by the *y* of an eye,	*Love and Duty*	61
this gray spirit *y* in desire	*Ulysses*	30
Y for the large excitement	*Locksley H.*	111
Some *y* toward the lamps of night	*Two Voices*	363
barren faith, And vacant *y*	*In Mem.* cvii.	6
Less *y* for the friendship fled,	" cxv.	15
team Which love thee, *y* for thy yoke,	*Tithonus*	40
A nobler *y* never broke her rest	*Coquette,* ii.	2

yell.

rings to the *y* of the trampled wife	*Maud,* I. i.	38

yell'd.

score of pugs And poodles *y* within,	*Ed. Morris*	120
they made a halt; The horses *y;*	*Princess,* v.	240
Y and shriek'd between her daughters	*Boädicea*	6, 72
y as when the winds of winter	"	77
y and round me drove In narrowing circles till I *y* again	*Lucretius*	56

yelling.

fled *Y* as from a spectre,	*Enid*	1581

yellow.

Shot over with purple, and green, and *y.*	*Dying Swan*	20
turning *y* Falls, and floats adown the air	*Lotos-E's*	75

yellow-banded.

Or the *y-b* bees	*Eleänore*	22

yellow-ringleted.

haled the *y-r* Britoness—	*Boädicea*	55

yellow-throated.

And *y-t* nestling in the nest.	*Elaine*	12

yelp (s.)

With inward *y* and restless forefoot	*Lucretius*	45

yelp (verb.)

wild Lean-headed Eagles *y* alone,	*Princess,* vii.	196

yelp'd.

y the cur, and yawl'd the cat,	*The Goose*	33

yeoman.

let the foolish *y* go.	*L. C. V. de Vere*	72
mockery to the *yeomen* over ale,	*Aylmer's F.*	497

yes.

When the happy *Y* Falters from her	*Maud,* I. xvii.	9

yesterday.

And now, As tho' 'twere *y,*	*Gardener's D.*	81
'Where were you *y?* Whose child is that?	*Dora*	85

yesternight.

the gloom of *y* On the white day;	*Ode to Mem.*	9

yet-loved.

the *y-l* sire would make Confusion	*In Mem.* lxxxix.	18

yet-unblazon'd.

Returning brought the *y-u* shield,	*Elaine*	378

yew.

Death, walking all alone beneath a *y,*	*Love and Death*	5
darkness in the village *y.*	*Two Voices*	72
Came *y's,* a dismal coterie;	*Amphion*	42
Sick for the hollies and the *y's* of	*Princess, Pro.*	185
Old *Y,* which graspest at the stones	*In Mem.* ii.	1
Before the mouldering of a *y;*	" lxxv.	8
A black *y* gloom'd the stagnant air,	*The Letters*	2
oft they met among the garden *y's,*	*Elaine*	642
found her in among the garden *y's,*	"	919
to whom thro' those black walls of *y*	"	964
Up by the wall, behind the *y;*	*En. Arden.*	740

yewtree.

Up higher with the *y* by it,	*Walk. to the M.*	9
throve an ancient evergreen, A *y.*	*En. Arden.*	737

yew-wood.

	POEM.	LINE.
In the *y-w* black as night,	*Oriana*	19

yield.

y you time To make demand	*To the Queen*	10
To *y* consent to my desire;	*Miller's D.*	138
But *y* not me the praise;	*St S. Stylites*	182
to seek, to find, and not to *y.*	*Ulysses*	70
that the coming years would *y*	*Locksley H.*	111
No branchy thicket shelter *y's;*	*Sir Galahad*	58
A little will I *y.*	*Princess,* ii.	271
To *y* us farther furlough;'	" iii.	58
She *y's,* or war.'	" v.	115
No more, dear love, for at a touch I *y*	" vi.	377
still were loth to yield herself to one,	" vii.	217
I love thee: come, *Y* thyself up:	"	343
We *y* all blessing to the name	*In Mem.* xxxvi.	3
rarely *y's* To that vague fear	" xl.	13
And will not *y* them for a day.	" lxxxix.	16
that will not *y* each other way	" ci.	20
Go not, happy day, Till the maiden *y's.*	*Maud,* I. xvii.	4
Y my boon, Till which I scarce can *y* you all I am	*Vivien*	201
till one could *y* for weariness;	"	222
I will not *y* to give you power	"	223
since the pirate would not *y* her up,	"	418
y it to this maiden, if you will.'	*Elaine*	229
when you *y* your flower of life	"	948
Pray for my soul, and *y* me burial.	"	1273
y me sanctuary, nor ask Her name, to whom ye *y* it.	*Guinevere*	140

yielded.

perforce He *y,* wroth and red	*Princess,* v.	348
Nor tho' she liked him, *y* she,	" vi.	61
'I wish she had not *y!*	" Con.	5
but a dream, yet it *y* a dear delight	*Maud,* III. vi.	15
Had *y,* told her all the charm,	*Vivien*	815
y, and a heart, Love-loyal	*Elaine*	89
He laugh'd, and *y* readily	*En. Arden.*	367
At once the costly Sahib *y* to her.	*Aylmer's F.*	233

yielding.

old order changeth, *y* place to new	*M. d'Arthur*	240
This, *y,* gave into a grassy walk	*Gardener's D.*	110
y to his kindlier moods	*Vivien*	30

Yniol.

Had married Enid, *Y's* only child	*Enid*	4
save It may be, at Earl *Y's,*	"	291
The voice of Enid, *Y's* daughter,	"	327
Y caught His purple scarf, and held,	"	376
Y's heart Danced in his bosom,	"	504
waited there for *Y* and Geraint	"	538
Y's rusted arms Were on his princely	"	543
Y's nephew, after trumpet blown,	"	551
force was match'd till *Y's* cry	"	570
Went *Y* thro' the town	"	693
And howsoever patient, *Y* his,	"	707
Y goes, and I full oft shall dream	"	751
Y made report Of that good mother	"	756
Y with that hard message went	"	763
being repulsed By *Y* and yourself,	"	1677

yoke (s.)

if thou needs must bear the *y,*	*Princess,* vi.	188
the light *y* of that Lord of love;	*Aylmer's F.*	708
Which love thee, yearning for thy *y,*	*Tithonus*	40
loosed their sweating horses from the *y*	*Spec. of Iliad*	2

yoke (verb.)

and the care That *y's* with empire,	*To the Queen*	10

yoked.

Whose name is *y* with children's	*Princess,* v.	408
Y in all exercise of noble end,	" vii.	340

yolk.

golden *y's* Imbedded and injellied;	*Audley Ct.*	24

York.

lands in Kent and messuages in *Y,*	*Ed. Morris*	127
Y's white rose as red as Lancaster's	*Aylmer's F.*	51

young.

And I was *y*—too *y* to wed;	*Miller's D.*	141
made thee famous once, when *y;*	*The Blackbird*	16

	POEM.	LINE.		POEM.	LINE.
a sight to make an old man *y*.	*Gardener's D.*	140	to keep them mine But *y* and love ;	*Vivien*	398
than should be for one so *y*,	*Locksley H.*	21	omitting gayer *y* For one so old,	"	776
What is loathsome to the *y*.	*Vision of Sin*	157	the sweet and sudden passion of *y*	*Elaine*	282
being *y*, he changed himself.	*Enid*	593	not love : but love's first flash in *y*,	"	945
Y as I am, yet would I do my best.'	*Elaine*	222	at my years, however it hold in *y*.	"	1288
devil's leaps, and poisons half the *y*	*Guinevere*	518	her love Was but the flash of *y*,	"	1308
Have all his pretty *y* ones educated	*En. Arden.*	146	his full tide of *y* Broke	*Aylmer's F.*	115
I wonder he went so *y*.	*Grandmother*	14	dwell in presence of immortal *y*,	*Tithonus*	21
'O boy tho' thou art *y* and proud,	*Sailor Boy.*	7	Immortal age, beside immortal *y*,	"	22

younger.

youth (young man)

Lady Psyche, *y*, not so wise.	*Princess,* iv.	297	yearn'd towards William ; but the *y*,	*Dora*	6
Lavaine, my *y* here, He is so full	*Elaine*	202	A *y* came riding toward a palace-gate	*Vision of Sin*	2
let the *y* and unskill'd go by	"	1352	of her brethren *y's* of puissance	*Princess,* i.	36
all the *y* ones with jubilant cries	*En. Arden.*	374	*y* who scour'd His master's armour;	*Enid*	257

youngest.

			A *y*, that following with a costrel.	"	36
while we waited, one, the *y* of us.	*Vivien*	265	There came a fair-hair'd *y*,	"	1050
one, the *y*, hardly more than boy,	*En. Arden.*	564	when the fair-hair'd *y* came by him	"	1054
			'Yea, my kind lord,' said the glad *y*,	"	

younker.

			war On all the *y*, they sicken'd	*Vivien*	422
he caught the *y* tickling trout—	*Walk. to the M.*	25	The saintly *y*, the spotless lamb of Christ,"	"	599
			there is many a *y* Now crescent	*Elaine*	446

youth (period of life.)

youthful.

the breathing spring Of Hope and *Y*.	*The Poet*	28	So *y* and so flexile then,	*Amphion*	59
force to make me rhyme in *y*,	*Miller's D.*	193			

yow (ewe.)

'My *y*,' she said, 'was blasted with	*D. of F. Wom.*	103	Fourscore *y's* upon it	*N. Farmer*	40
Who miss the brother of your *y*?	*To J. S.*	50			

Yule.

May perpetual *y* Keep dry 'Of old sat Freedom'		19	The merry merry bells of *Y*.	*In Mem.* xxviii.	20
Drive men in manhood, as in *y*,	*'Love thou thy land'*	74	like the heart of a great fire at *Y*,	*Enid*	559
such a distance from his *y* in grief,	*Gardener's D.*	53			

yule-log.

the folded annals of my *y*,	"	239	The *y-l* sparkled keen with frost,	*In Mem.* lxxvii	5

| My first, last love ; the idol of my *y*, | " | 271 | | | |

Z

Nightmare of *y*, the spectre of	*Love and Duty*	13			
nourishing a *y* sublime.	*Locksley H.*	11			

zealous.

Sin against the strength of *y*!	"	59	*z* it should be All that it might be	*Princess,* iv.	403

zenith.

That my *y* was half divine,	*Vision of Sin*	78	that branch'd And blossom'd in the *z*	*En. Arden*	587
love ourselves In our sweet *y* : (v.199)	*Princess,*i.	122			

zig-zag.

had the care of Lady Ida's *y*,	" iii.	69	*z-z* paths, and juts of pointed rock,	*M. d'Arthur*	50
Confusions of a wasted *y*	*In Mem. Pro.*	42			

zone

And in the places of his *y*	" xviii.	8	Flowing beneath her rose-hued *z*;	*Arabian N's.*	140
Whose *y* was full of foolish noise,	" lii.	3	but that my *z* Unmann'd me :	*Princess,* ii.	398
life outliving heats of *y*,	"	10	three stars of the airy Giant's *z*	" v.	750
It is the trouble of my *y*	" lxvii.	15	on thro' *z's* of light and shadow	*To F. D Maurice*	27
From *y* and babe and hoary hairs :	" lxviii.	10			

zoned.

The giant labouring in his *y* ;	" cxvii.	2	a silken hood to each, And *z* with gold;	*Princess,* ii.	4
Hope had never lost her *y* ;	" cxxiv.	5			
Maud in the light of her *y*	*Maud,* I. v.	15			
For my dark-dawning *y*	" xix.	7			
y gone out Had left in ashes :	*Vivien*	94			
many a love in loving *y* was mine,	"	396			

THE END.

Sanson & Co., Printers, Edinburgh.

www.ingramcontent.com/pod-product-compliance
Lightning Source LLC
Chambersburg PA
CBHW021423300426
44114CB00010B/626